**RAND MCNALLY**

# GOODE'S
## WORLD ATLAS

**Howard Veregin, Ph.D., Editor**

**Editorial Advisory Board**

Byron Augustin, D.A., Texas State University-San Marcos
Joshua Comenetz, Ph.D., University of Florida
Francis Galgano, Ph.D., United States Military Academy
Sallie A. Marston, Ph.D., University of Arizona
Virginia Thompson, Ph.D., Towson University

**21ST Edition**

# CONTENTS

*Goode's World Atlas*

Copyright ©2005 by Rand McNally & Company

Copyright ©1922, 1923, 1932, 1933, 1937, 1939, 1943, 1946, 1949, 1954, 1957, 1960, 1964, 1970, 1974, 1978, 1982, 1986, 1990, 1995, 2000 by Rand McNally & Company. All rights reserved.

Formerly *Goode's School Atlas*

Made in U.S.A.

Library of Congress Catalog Card Number 99-38535

Cover Photo: Machu Picchu, Peru

**The 21st Edition of *Goode's World Atlas***

*Goode's World Atlas* was first published by Rand McNally in 1923 as *Goode's School Atlas*, under the editorship of J. Paul Goode, a distinguished Professor of Geography at the University of Chicago. The atlas was designed for use in schools and universities, with the choice of topics and materials reflecting Goode's thirty years of experience as a geographic educator.

Many of the features of that first atlas continue to be relevant today, including its basic organization and layout, an emphasis on map accuracy and legibility, and the admixture of maps of different types and scales to facilitate interpretation of geographic phenomena. One of the more significant innovations of the 1923 edition was the introduction of an "interrupted" map of the world, which featured large discontinuities in oceanic areas in order to reduce map distortion of continental landmasses. Goode developed this map to allow geographic phenomena to be portrayed more accurately. This map, and its descendants, have given *Goode's World Atlas* a distinctive look for more than eighty years.

The 21st Edition boasts a number of innovative features of its own:

- The world, continental, and regional population density maps have been re-created using LandScan, a digital population database developed using satellite and computer-mapping technology.
- A number of new world thematic maps have been added, including HIV Infection, Military Power, Women's Rights, and Food Aid.
- A global telecommunications map has been added, showing the submarine fiber-optic network, and worldwide internet and telephone usage.
- The world cartogram series has been redrafted to make the cartograms easier to interpret.
- The United States demographic map series has been expanded from sixteen to twenty-four maps to provide additional coverage of key census variables.
- New graphs have been added to many of the maps, showing important statistical information, trends over time, and relationships between variables.

Other maps and graphs have been updated using the most current available data in accordance with the high standards and quality that have always been a defining feature of this atlas. This edition also retains many of the "classic" maps with which longtime users of the atlas will be familiar, including Natural Vegetation (A. W. Küchler), Landforms (Richard E. Murphy), Physiography (Erwin Raisz), Climatic Regions (Glenn T. Trewartha), Agricultural Regions (Derwent Whittlesey), and Languages (Bogdan Zaborski).

Putting together a complex atlas requires the dedication of a large and diverse team. The contributions of the following individuals helped make this 21st Edition a success:

Robert Argersinger, Gregory Babiak, Julie Bastian, Karen Cuiskelly, John Davies, Dave Duncan, Marzee Eckhoff, Justin Griffin, Felix Lopez, Nina Lusterman, Chuck MacDonald, Rob Merrill, Angela Mrotek, Darren Raffel, Pat Riley, Amy Ruggles, David Simmons, Andrew Skinner, Raymond Tobiaski, Tom Vitacco, Yanyan Zhang.

The 21st Edition benefited greatly from the creative efforts of Susan Hudson, head of Rand McNally's geographical research unit.

Important contributions were also made by the members of the Editorial Advisory Board:

Byron Augustin, D.A., Texas State University-San Marcos; Joshua Comenetz, Ph.D., University of Florida; Francis Galgano, Ph.D., United States Military Academy; Sallie A. Marston, Ph.D., University of Arizona; and Virginia Thompson, Ph.D., Towson University.

With the 21st Edition, *Goode's World Atlas* is well into its ninth consecutive decade of publication. While the atlas has changed with the times, it continues to be the same accurate and reliable educational resource that J. Paul Goode originally intended. We at Rand McNally remain committed to providing the most trusted tools to help you discover, map, and navigate your world.

*Howard Veregin*

Howard Veregin, Ph.D., Editor
Skokie, Illinois

# Introduction

## Basic Earth Properties

The subject matter of **geography** includes people, landforms, climate, and all the other physical and human phenomena that make up the earth's environments and give unique character to different places. Geographers construct maps to visualize the **spatial distributions** of these phenomena: that is, how the phenomena vary over geographic space. Maps help geographers understand and explain phenomena and their interactions.

To better understand how maps portray geographic distributions, it is helpful to have an understanding of the basic properties of the earth.

The earth is essentially **spherical** in shape. Two basic reference points — the **North and South Poles** — mark the locations of the earth's axis of rotation. Equidistant between the two poles and encircling the earth is the **equator**. The equator divides the earth into two halves, called the **northern and southern hemispheres**. (See the figures to the right.)

**Latitude and longitude** are used to identify the locations of features on the earth's surface. They are measured in degrees, minutes and seconds. There are 60 minutes in a degree and 60 seconds in a minute. Latitude is the angle north or south of the equator. The symbols °, ', and " represent degrees, minutes and seconds, respectively. The N means north of the equator. For latitudes south of the equator, S is used. For example, the Rand McNally head office in Skokie, Illinois, is located at 42°1'51" N. The minimum latitude of 0° occurs at the equator. The maximum latitudes of 90° N and 90° S occur at the North and South Poles.

A **line of latitude** is a line connecting all points on the earth having the same latitude. Lines of latitude are also called **parallels**, as they run parallel to each other. Two parallels of special importance are the **Tropic of Cancer** and the **Tropic of Capricorn**, at approximately 23°30' N and S respectively. This angle coincides with the inclination of the earth's axis relative to its orbital plane around the sun. These tropics are the lines of latitude where the noon sun is directly overhead on the solstices. (See figure on page 66.) Two other important parallels are the **Arctic Circle** and the **Antarctic Circle**, at approximately 66°30' N and S respectively. These lines mark the most northerly and southerly points at which the sun can be seen on the solstices.

While latitude measures locations in a north-south direction, longitude measures them east-west. Longitude is the angle east or west of the **Prime Meridian**. A **meridian** is a line of longitude, a straight line extending from the North Pole to the South Pole. The Prime Meridian is the meridian passing through the Royal Observatory in Greenwich, England. For this reason the Prime Meridian is sometimes referred to as the **Greenwich Meridian**. This location for the Prime Meridian was adopted at the International Meridian Conference in Washington, D.C., in 1884.

Like latitude, longitude is measured in degrees, minutes, and seconds. For example, the Rand McNally head office is located at 87°43'6" W. The qualifiers E and W indicate whether a location is east or west of the Greenwich Meridian. Longitude ranges from 0° at Greenwich to 180° E or W. The meridian at 180° E is the same as the meridian at 180° W. This meridian, together with the Greenwich Meridian, divides the earth into **eastern and western hemispheres**.

Any circle that divides the earth into equal hemispheres is called a **great circle**. The equator is an example. The shortest distance between any two points on the earth is along a great circle. Other circles, including all other lines of latitude, are called **small circles**. Small circles divide the earth into two unequal pieces.

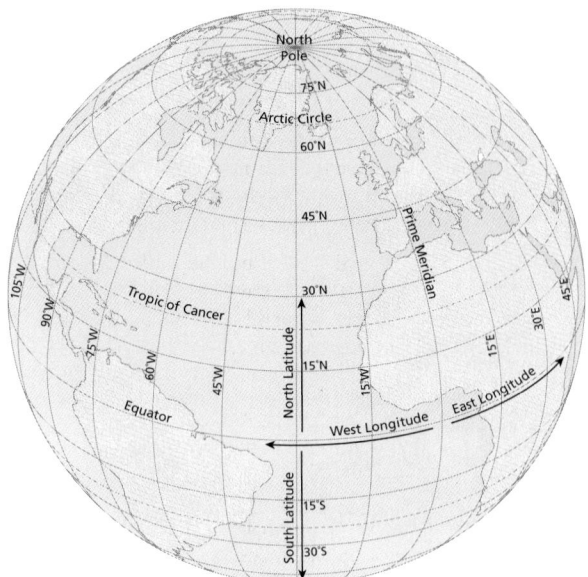

View of earth centered on 30° N, 30° W

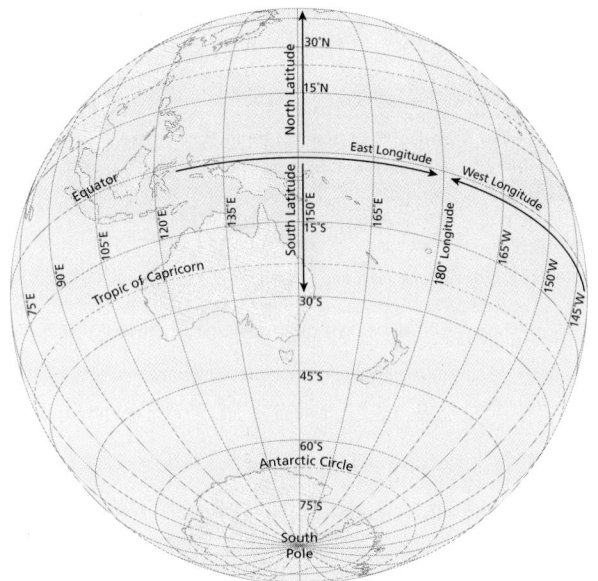

View of earth centered on 30° S, 150° E

### The Geographic Grid

The grid of lines of latitude and longitude is known as the **geographic grid**. The following are some important characteristics of the grid.

All lines of longitude are equal in length and meet at the North and South Poles. These lines are called meridians.

All lines of latitude are parallel and equally spaced along meridians. These lines are called parallels.

The length of parallels increases with distance from the poles. For example, the length of the parallel at 60° latitude is one-half the length of the equator.

Meridians get closer together with increasing distance from the equator, and finally converge at the poles.

Parallels and meridians meet at right angles.

# Map Scale

To use maps effectively it is important to have a basic understanding of map scale.

**Map scale** is defined as the ratio of distance on the map to distance on the earth's surface. For example, if a map shows two towns as separated by a distance of 1 inch, and these towns are actually 1 mile apart, then the scale of the map is 1 inch to 1 mile.

The statement "1 inch to 1 mile" is called a **verbal scale**. Verbal scales are simple and intuitive, but a drawback is that they are tied to the specific set of map and real-world units in the numerator and denominator of the ratio. This makes it difficult to compare the scales of different maps.

A more flexible way of expressing scale is as a **representative fraction**. In this case, both the numerator and denominator are converted to the same unit of measurement. For example, since there are 63,360 inches in a mile, the verbal scale "1 inch to 1 mile" can be expressed as the representative fraction 1:63,360. This means that 1 inch on the map represents 63,360 inches on the earth's surface. The advantage of the representative fraction is that it applies to any linear unit of measurement, including inches, feet, miles, meters, and kilometers.

Map scale can also be represented in graphical form. Many maps contain a **graphic scale** (or **bar scale**) showing real-world units such as miles or kilometers. The bar scale is usually subdivided to allow easy calculation of distance on the map.

Map scale has a significant effect on the amount of detail that can be portrayed on a map. This concept is illustrated here using a series of maps of the Washington, D.C., area. (See the figures to the right.) The scales of these maps range from 1:40,000,000 (top map) to 1:4,000,000 (center map) to 1:25,000 (bottom map). The top map has the **smallest scale** of the three maps, and the bottom map has the **largest scale**.

Note that as scale increases, the area of the earth's surface covered by the map decreases. The smallest-scale map covers thousands of square miles, while the largest-scale map covers only a few square miles within the city of Washington. This means that a given feature on the earth's surface will appear larger as map scale increases. On the smallest-scale map, Washington is represented by a small dot. As scale increases the dot becomes an orange shape representing the built-up area of Washington. At the largest scale Washington is so large that only a portion of it fits on the map.

Because small-scale maps cover such a large area, only the largest and most important features can be shown, such as large cities, major rivers and lakes, and international boundaries. In contrast, large-scale maps contain relatively small features, such as city streets, buildings, parks, and monuments.

Small-scale maps depict features in a more simplified manner than large-scale maps. As map scale decreases, the shapes of rivers and other features must be simplified to allow them to be depicted at a highly reduced size. This simplification process is known as **map generalization**.

Maps in *Goode's World Atlas* have a wide range of scales. The smallest scales are used for the world thematic map series, where scales range from approximately 1:200,000,000 to 1:75,000,000. Reference map scales range from a minimum of 1:100,000,000 for world maps to a maximum of 1:1,000,000 for city maps. Most reference maps are regional views with a scale of 1:4,000,000.

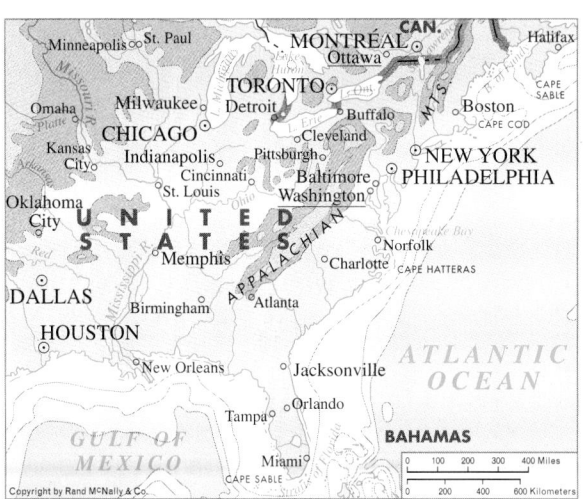

1:40,000,000 scale

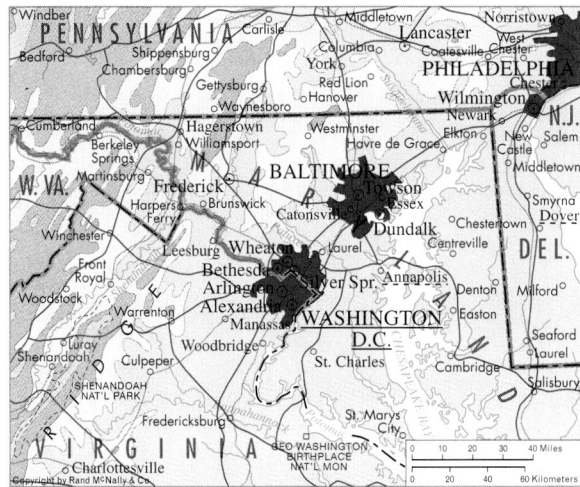

1:4,000,000 scale

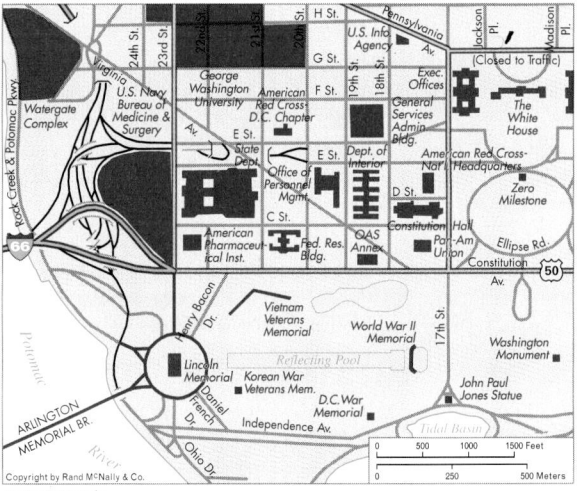

1:25,000 scale

## Map Projections

Map projections influence the appearance of features on the map and the ability to interpret geographic phenomena.

A **map projection** is a geometric representation of the earth's surface on a flat or plane surface. Since the earth's surface is curved, a map projection is needed to produce any flat map, whether a page in this atlas or a computer-generated map of driving directions on www.randmcnally.com. Hundreds of projections have been developed since the dawn of mapmaking. A limitation of all projections is that they distort some geometric properties of the earth, such as shape, area, distance, or direction. However, certain properties are preserved on some projections.

If shape is preserved, the projection is called **conformal**. On conformal projections the shapes of features agree with the shapes these features have on the earth. A limitation of conformal projections is that they necessarily distort area, sometimes severely.

**Equal-area** projections preserve area. On equal area projections the areas of features correspond to their areas on the earth. To achieve this effect, equal-area projections distort shape.

Some projections preserve neither shape nor area, but instead balance shape and area distortion to create an aesthetically-pleasing result. These are often referred to as **compromise** projections.

Distance is preserved on **equidistant** projections, but this can only be achieved selectively, such as along specific meridians or parallels. No projection correctly preserves distance in all directions at all locations. As a result, the stated scale of a map may be accurate for only a limited set of locations. This problem is especially acute for small-scale maps covering large areas.

The projection selected for a particular map depends on the relative importance of different types of distortion, which often depends on the purpose of the map. For example, world maps showing phenomena that vary with area, such as population density or the distribution of agricultural crops, often use an equal-area projection to give an accurate depiction of the importance of each region.

Map projections are created using mathematical procedures. To illustrate the general principles of projections without using mathematics, we can view a projection as the geometric transfer of information from a globe to a flat projection surface, such as a sheet of paper. If we allow the paper to be rolled in different ways, we can derive three basic types of map projections: **cylindrical, conic,** and **azimuthal**. (See the figures to the right.)

For cylindrical projections, the sheet of paper is rolled into a tube and wrapped around the globe so that it is **tangent** (touching) along the equator. Information from the globe is transferred to the tube, and the tube is then unrolled to produce the final flat map.

Conic projections use a cone rather than a cylinder. The figure shows the cone tangent to the earth along a line of latitude with the apex of the cone over the pole. The line of tangency is called the **standard parallel** of the projection.

Azimuthal projections use a flat projection surface that is tangent to the globe at a single point, such as one of the poles.

The figures show the **normal orientation** of each type of surface relative to the globe. The **transverse orientation** is produced when the surface is rotated 90 degrees from normal. For azimuthal projections this orientation is usually called **equatorial** rather than transverse. An **oblique orientation** is created if the projection surface is oriented at an angle between normal and transverse. In general, map distortion increases with distance away from the point or line of tangency. This is why the normal orientations of the cylindrical, conic, and azimuthal projections are often used for mapping equatorial, mid-latitude, and polar regions, respectively.

The projection surface model is a visual tool useful for illustrating how information from the globe can be projected to the map. However, each of the three projection surfaces actually represents scores of individual projections. There are, for example, many projections with the term "cylindrical" in the name, each of which has the same basic rectangular shape, but different spacings of parallels and meridians. The projection surface model does not account for the numerous mathematical details that differentiate one cylindrical, conic, or azimuthal projection from another.

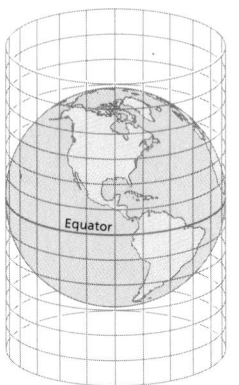
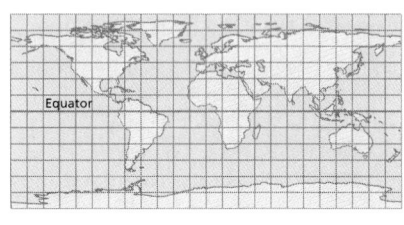

Cylindrical Projection

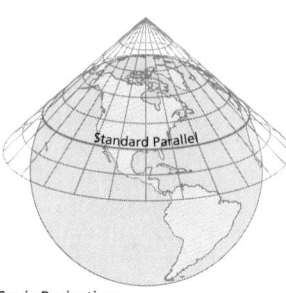
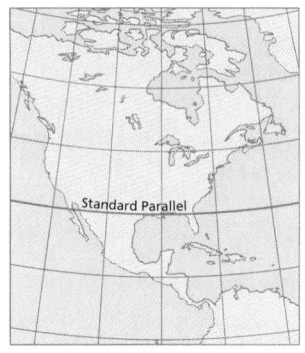

Conic Projection

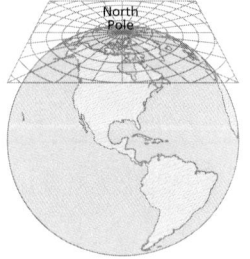

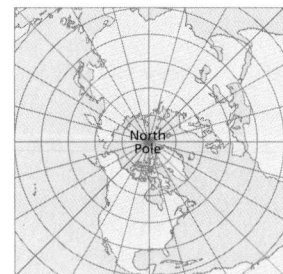

Azimuthal Projection

# Map Projections Used in *Goode's World Atlas*

Of the hundreds of projections that have been developed, only a fraction are in everyday use. The main projections used in *Goode's World Atlas* are described below.

## Simple Conic

**Type:** Conic     **Conformal:** No     **Equal-area:** No

**Notes:** Shape and area distortion on the Simple Conic projection are relatively low, even though the projection is neither conformal nor equal-area. The origins of the Simple Conic can be traced back nearly two thousand years, with the modern form of the projection dating to the 18th century.

**Uses in *Goode's World Atlas*:** Larger-scale reference maps of North America, Europe, Asia, and other regions.

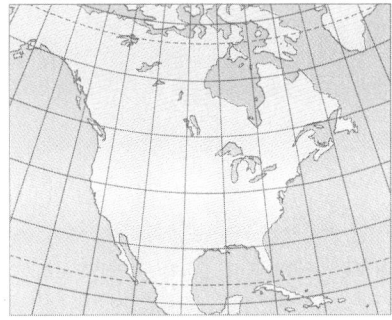

Simple Conic Projection

## Lambert Conformal Conic

**Type:** Conic     **Conformal:** Yes     **Equal-area:** No

**Notes:** On the Lambert Conformal Conic projection, spacing between parallels increases with distance away from the standard parallel, which allows the property of shape to be preserved. The projection is named after Johann Lambert, an 18th century mathematician who developed some of the most important projections in use today. It became widely used in the United States in the 20th century following its adoption for many statewide mapping programs.

**Uses in *Goode's World Atlas*:** Thematic maps of the United States and Canada, and reference maps of parts of Asia.

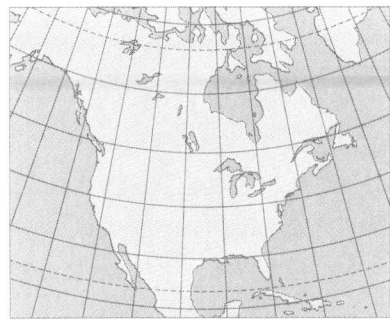

Lambert Conformal Conic Projection

## Albers Equal-Area Conic

**Type:** Conic     **Conformal:** No     **Equal-area:** Yes

**Notes:** On the Albers Equal-Area Conic projection, spacing between parallels decreases with distance away from the standard parallel, which allows the property of area to be preserved. The projection is named after Heinrich Albers, who developed it in 1805. It became widely used in the 20th century, when the United States Coast and Geodetic Survey made it a standard for equal area maps of the United States.

**Uses in *Goode's World Atlas*:** Thematic maps of North America and Asia.

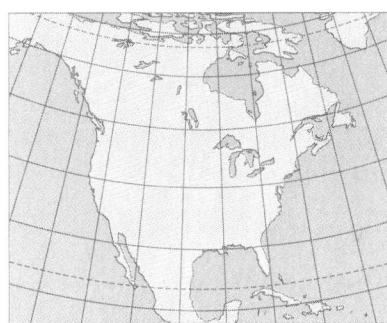

Albers Equal-Area Conic Projection

## Polyconic

**Type:** Conic     **Conformal:** No     **Equal-area:** No

**Notes:** The term polyconic — literally "many-cones" — refers to the fact that this projection is an assemblage of different cones, each tangent at a different line of latitude. In contrast to many other conic projections, parallels are not concentric, and meridians are curved rather than straight. The Polyconic was first proposed by Ferdinand Hassler, who became Head of the United States Survey of the Coast (later renamed the Coast and Geodetic Survey) in 1807. The United States Geological Survey used this projection exclusively for large-scale topographic maps until the mid-20th century.

**Uses in *Goode's World Atlas*:** Reference maps of North America and Asia.

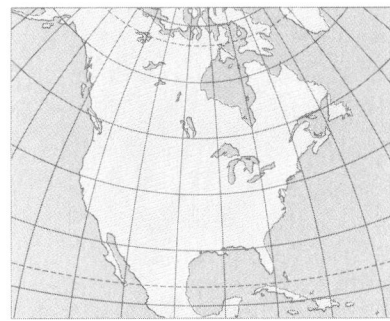

Polyconic Projection

## Lambert Azimuthal Equal-Area

**Type:** Azimuthal     **Conformal:** No     **Equal-area:** Yes

**Notes:** This projection (another named after Johann Lambert ) is useful for mapping large regions, as area is correctly preserved while shape distortion is relatively low. All orientations — polar, equatorial, and oblique — are common.

**Uses in *Goode's World Atlas*:** Thematic and reference maps of North and South America, Asia, Africa, Australia, and polar regions.

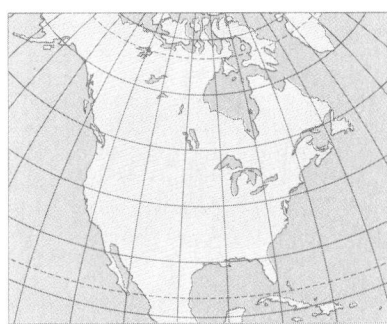

Lambert Azimuthal Equal-Area Projection

### Miller Cylindrical

**Type:** Cylindrical    **Conformal:** No    **Equal-area:** No

**Notes:** This projection is useful for showing the entire earth in a simple rectangular form. However, polar areas exhibit significant exaggeration of area, a problem common to many cylindrical projections. The projection is named after Osborn Miller, Director of the American Geographical Society, who developed it in 1942 as a compromise projection that is neither conformal nor equal-area.

**Uses in *Goode's World Atlas*:** World climate and time zone maps.

### Sinusoidal

**Type:** Pseudocylindrical    **Conformal:** No    **Equal-area:** Yes

**Notes:** The straight, evenly spaced parallels on this projection resemble the parallels on cylindrical projections. Unlike cylindrical projections, however, meridians are curved and converge at the poles. This causes significant shape distortion in polar regions. The Sinusoidal is the oldest-known pseudocylindrical projection, dating to the 16th century.

**Uses in *Goode's World Atlas*:** Reference maps of equatorial regions.

### Mollweide

**Type:** Pseudocylindrical    **Conformal:** No    **Equal-area:** Yes

**Notes:** The Mollweide (or Homolographic) projection resembles the Sinusoidal but has less shape distortion in polar areas due to its elliptical (or oval) form. One of several pseudocylindrical projections developed in the 19th century, it is named after Karl Mollweide, an astronomer and mathematician.

**Uses in *Goode's World Atlas*:** Oceanic reference maps.

### Goode's Interrupted Homolosine

**Type:** Pseudocylindrical    **Conformal:** No    **Equal-area:** Yes

**Notes:** This projection is a fusion of the Sinusoidal between 40º44'N and S, and the Mollweide between these parallels and the poles. The unique appearance of the projection is due to the introduction of discontinuities in oceanic regions, the goal of which is to reduce distortion for continental landmasses. A condensed version of the projection also exists in which the Atlantic Ocean is compressed in an east-west direction. This modification helps maximize the scale of the map on the page. The Interrupted Homolosine projection is named after J. Paul Goode of the University of Chicago, who developed it in 1923. Goode was an advocate of interrupted projections and, as editor of *Goode's School Atlas*, promoted their use in education.

**Uses in *Goode's World Atlas*:** Small-scale world thematic and reference maps. Both condensed and non-condensed forms are used. An uninterrupted example is used for the Pacific Ocean map.

### Robinson

**Type:** Pseudocylindrical    **Conformal:** No    **Equal-area:** No

**Notes:** This projection resembles the Mollweide except that polar regions are flattened and stretched out. While it is neither conformal nor equal-area, both shape and area distortion are relatively low. The projection was developed in 1963 by Arthur Robinson of the University of Wisconsin, at the request of Rand McNally.

**Uses in *Goode's World Atlas*:** World maps where the interrupted nature of Goode's Homolosine would be inappropriate, such as the World Oceanic Environments map.

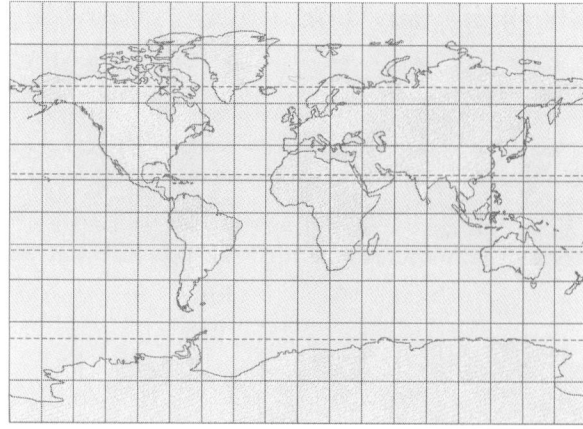

Miller Cylindrical Projection

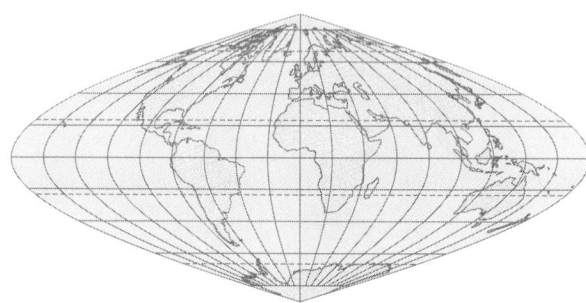

Sinusoidal Projection

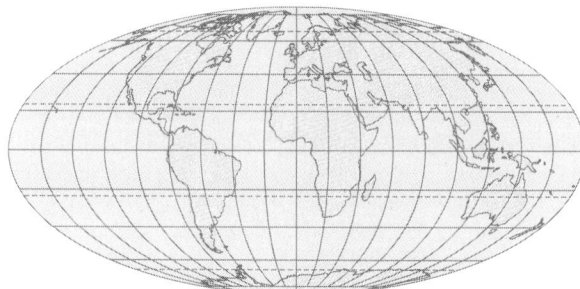

Mollweide Projection

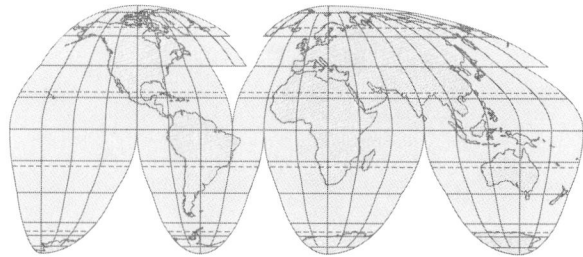

Goode's Interrupted Homolosine Projection

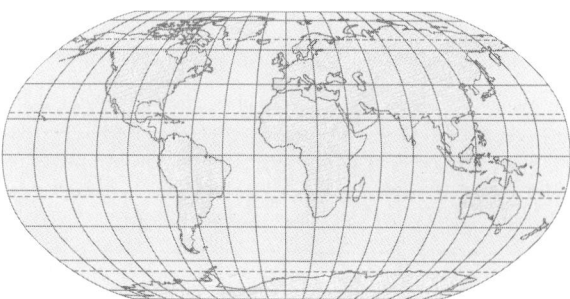

Robinson Projection

# Thematic Maps in *Goode's World Atlas*

Thematic maps depict a single "theme" such as population density, agricultural productivity, or annual precipitation. The selected theme is presented on a base of locational information, such as coastlines, country boundaries, and major drainage features. The primary purpose of a thematic map is to convey an impression of the overall geographic distribution of the theme. It is usually not the intent of the map to provide exact numerical values. To obtain such information, the graphs and tables accompanying the map should be used.

*Goode's World Atlas* contains many different types of thematic maps. The characteristics of each are summarized below.

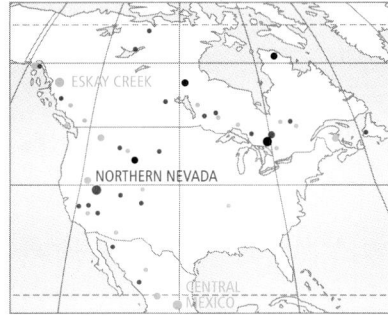
Point symbol map: Detail of Precious Metals (p. 55)

### Point Symbol Maps

Point symbol maps are perhaps the simplest type of thematic map. They show features that occur at discrete locations. Examples include earthquakes, nuclear power plants, and minerals-producing areas. The Precious Metals map (p. 55) is an example of a point symbol map showing the locations of areas producing gold, silver, and platinum. A different color is used for each type of metal, while symbol size indicates relative importance.

### Area Symbol Maps

Area symbol maps are useful for delineating regions of interest on the earth's surface. For example, the Tobacco and Fisheries map (p. 44) shows major tobacco-producing regions in one color and important fishing areas in another. On some area symbol maps, different shadings or colors are used to differentiate between major and minor areas.

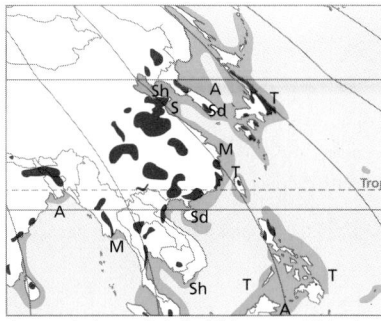
Area symbol map: Detail of Tobacco and Fisheries (p. 44)

### Dot Maps

Dot maps show a distribution using a pattern of dots, where each dot represents a certain quantity or amount. For example, on the Sugar map (p. 43), each dot represents 20,000 metric tons of sugar produced. Different dot colors are used to distinguish cane sugar from beet sugar. Dot maps are an effective way of representing the variable density of geographic phenomena over the earth's surface. This type of map is used extensively in *Goode's World Atlas* to show the distribution of agricultural commodities.

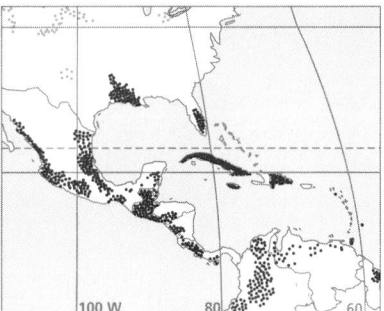
Dot map: Detail of Sugar (p. 43)

### Area Class Maps

On area class maps, the earth's surface is divided into areas based on different classes or categories of a particular geographic phenomenon. For example, the Ecoregions map (pp. 28-29) differentiates natural landscape categories, such as Tundra, Savanna, and Prairie. Other examples of area class maps in *Goode's World Atlas* include Landforms (pp. 6-7), Climatic Regions (pp. 14-15), Natural Vegetation (pp. 24-25), Soils (pp. 26-27), Agricultural Areas (p. 38-39), Languages (p. 35) and Religions (p. 35).

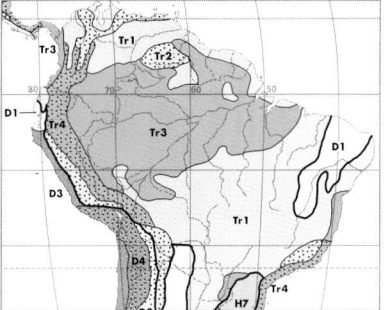
Area class map: Detail of Ecoregions (pp. 28-29)

### Isoline Maps

Isoline maps are used to portray quantities that vary smoothly over the surface of the earth. These maps are frequently used for climatic variables such as precipitation and temperature, but a variety of other quantities — from crop yield to population density — can also be treated in this way.

An isoline is a line on the map that joins locations with the same value. For example, the Summer (May to October) Precipitation map (p. 19) contains isolines at 5, 10, 20, and 40 inches. On this map, any 10-inch isoline separates areas that have less than 10 inches of precipitation from areas that have more than 10 inches. Note that the areas between isolines are given different colors to assist in map interpretation.

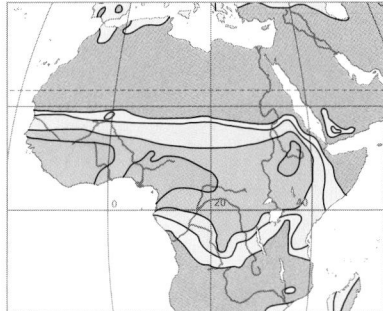
Isoline map: Detail of Precipitation (p. 19)

## Proportional Symbol Maps

Proportional symbol maps portray numerical quantities, such as the total population of each state, the total value of agricultural goods produced in different regions, or the amount of hydroelectricity generated in different countries. The symbols on these maps — usually circles —- are drawn such that the size of each is proportional to the value at that location. For example the Exports map (p. 60) shows the value of goods exported by each country in the world, in millions of U.S. dollars.

Proportional symbols are frequently subdivided based on the percentage of individual components making up the total. The Exports map uses wedges of different color to show the percentages of various types of exports, such as manufactured articles and raw materials.

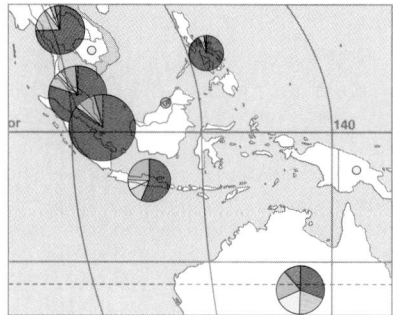

Proportional symbol map: Detail of Exports (p. 60)

## Flow Line Maps

Flow line maps show flows between locations. Usually, the thickness of the flow lines is proportional to flow volume. Flows may be physical commodities like petroleum, or less tangible quantities like information. The flow lines on the Mineral Fuels map (pp. 58-59) represent movement of petroleum measured in billions of U.S. dollars. Note that the locations of flow lines may not represent actual physical routes.

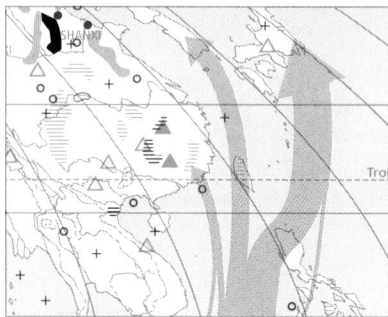

Flow line map: Detail of Mineral Fuels
(pp. 58-59)

## Choropleth Maps

Choropleth maps apply distinctive colors to predefined areas, such as counties or states, to represent different quantities in each area. The quantities shown are usually rates, percentages, or densities. For example, the Birth Rate map (p. 32) shows the annual number of births per one thousand people for each country.

## Digital Images

Some maps are actually digital images, analogous to the pictures captured by digital cameras. These maps are created from a very fine grid of cells called **pixels**, each of which is assigned a color that corresponds to a specific value or range of values. The population density maps in this atlas (e.g., pp. 30-31) are examples of this type. The effect is much like an isoline map, but the isolines themselves are not shown and the resulting geographic patterns are more subtle and variable. This approach is increasingly being used to map environmental phenomena observable from remote sensing systems.

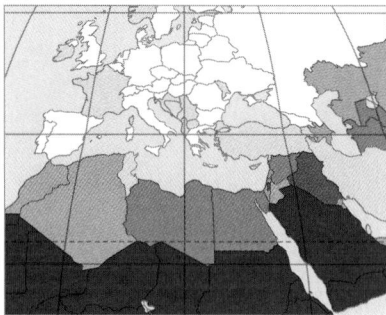

Choropleth map: Detail of Birth Rate (p. 32)

## Cartograms

Cartograms deliberately distort map shapes to achieve specific effects. On **area cartograms**, the size of each area, such as a country, is made proportional to its population. Countries with large populations are therefore drawn larger than countries with smaller populations, regardless of the actual size of these countries on the earth.

The world cartogram series in this atlas depicts each country as a rectangle. This is a departure from cartograms in earlier editions of the atlas, which attempted to preserve some of the salient shape characteristics for each country. The advantage of the rectangle method is that it is easier to compare the area of countries when their shapes are consistent.

The cartogram series incorporates choropleth shading on top of the rectangular cartogram base. In this way map readers can make inferences about the relationship between population and another thematic variable, such as HIV-infection rates (p. 37).

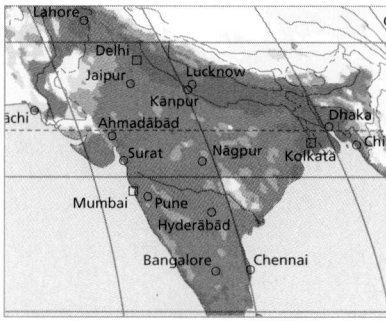

Digital image map: Detail of Population Density
(pp. 30-31)

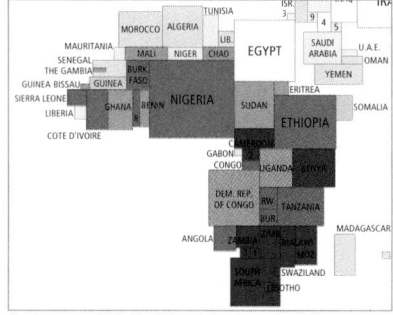

Cartogram: Detail of HIV Infection (p. 37)

# Map Legend

## Political Boundaries

| Political maps | Physical maps | |
|---|---|---|
| ----- | ▬▬▬ | International (Demarcated, Undemarcated, and Administrative) |
| --·-- | ▬ ·· | Disputed de facto |
| ········ | ▬▬ | Indefinite or Undefined |
| --·-- | ▬▬ | Secondary, State, Provincial, etc. |

| | |
|---|---|
| ▢ | Parks, Indian Reservations |
| 🖾 | City Limits |
| 🖤 | Urbanized Areas |

## Transportation

| Political maps | Physical maps | |
|---|---|---|
| ——— | ········ | Railroads |
| -------- | ········ | Railroad Ferries |
| ——— | | Major Roads |
| ——— | | Minor Roads |
| ·········· | | Caravan Routes |
| ✈ | | Airports |

## Cultural Features

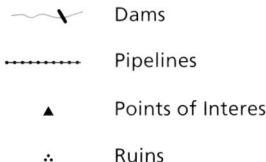

| | |
|---|---|
| ~∖ | Dams |
| ············ | Pipelines |
| ▲ | Points of Interest |
| ∴ | Ruins |

## Populated Places

| | |
|---|---|
| ⊙ | 1,000,000 and over |
| ◎ | 250,000 to 1,000,000 |
| ⊙ | 100,000 to 250,000 |
| • | 25,000 to 100,000 |
| ○ | Under 25,000 |
| ▫ | Neighborhoods, Sections of Cities |
| TŌKYŌ | National Capitals |
| Boise | Secondary Capitals |

Note: On maps at 1:20,000,000 and smaller, symbols do not follow the population classification shown above. Some other maps use a slightly different classification, which is shown in a separate legend in the map margin. On all maps, type size indicates the relative importance of the city.

## Land Features

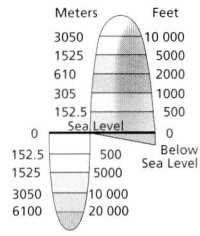

| | |
|---|---|
| △ | Peaks, Spot Heights |
| ≍ | Passes |
| ⣿ | Sand |
| ⬭ | Contours |

## Elevation

| Meters | | Feet |
|---|---|---|
| 3050 | | 10 000 |
| 1525 | | 5000 |
| 610 | | 2000 |
| 305 | | 1000 |
| 152.5 | | 500 |
| 0 | Sea Level | 0 |
| 152.5 | 500 | Below Sea Level |
| 1525 | 5000 | |
| 3050 | 10 000 | |
| 6100 | 20 000 | |

## Lakes and Reservoirs

| | |
|---|---|
| ⬭ | Fresh Water |
| ⬭ | Fresh Water: Intermittent |
| ⬭ | Salt Water |
| ⬭ | Salt Water: Intermittent |

## Other Water Features

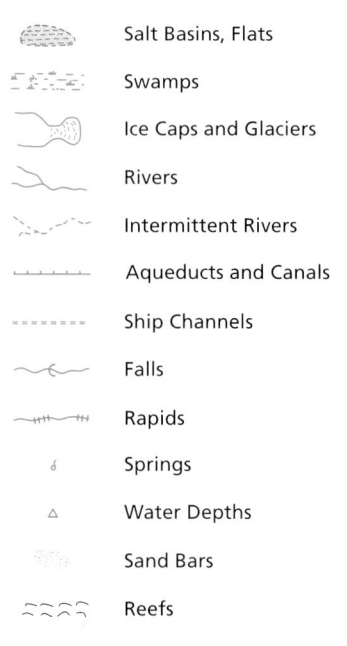

| | |
|---|---|
| ⬭ | Salt Basins, Flats |
| ⣿ | Swamps |
| ⬭ | Ice Caps and Glaciers |
| ~ | Rivers |
| ·~· | Intermittent Rivers |
| ⊢⊢⊢ | Aqueducts and Canals |
| -------- | Ship Channels |
| ~∈ | Falls |
| ~ⅢⅢ~ | Rapids |
| ∂ | Springs |
| △ | Water Depths |
| ⣿ | Sand Bars |
| ⌒⌒⌒ | Reefs |
| → | Warm Ocean Currents |
| → | Cold Ocean Currents |

The legend above shows the symbols used for the political and physical reference maps in *Goode's World Atlas*.

To portray relative areas correctly, uniform map scales have been used wherever possible:

> Continents – 1:40,000,000
> Countries and regions – between 1:4,000,000 and 1:20,000,000
> World, polar areas and oceans – between 1:50,000,000 and 1:100,000,000
> Urbanized areas – 1:1,000,000

Elevations on the maps are shown using a combination of shaded relief and hypsometric tints. Shaded relief (or hill-shading) gives a three-dimensional impression of the landscape, while hypsometric tints show elevation ranges in different colors.

The choice of names for mapped features is complicated by the fact that a variety of languages and alphabets are used throughout the world. A local-names policy is used in *Goode's World Atlas* for populated places and local physical features. For some major features, an English form of the name is used with the local name given below in parentheses. Examples include Moscow (Moskva), Vienna (Wien) and Naples (Napoli). In countries where more than one official language is used, names are given in the dominant local language. For large physical features spanning international borders, the conventional English form of the name is used. In cases where a non-Roman alphabet is used, names have been transliterated according to accepted practice.

Selected features are also listed in the Index (pp. 262-370), which includes a pronunciation guide. A list of foreign geographic terms is provided in the Glossary (p. 260).

Copyright by Rand McNally & Co.
Made in U.S.A.
N-GDS10000-P1- -1- -1

**POLITICAL**

ARCTIC OCEAN

GREENLAND (Den.)

RUS.
Nome
ALASKA (U.S.)
Anchorage
Juneau

Baffin Bay
Reykjavik
ICELAND

C A N A D A
Edmonton
Vancouver
Winnipeg
Seattle
Portland
HUDSON BAY
Québec
Montréal
Ottawa
St. John's
Chicago
Detroit
Toronto
Halifax
Boston
New York
Washington

U N I T E D   S T A T E S
San Francisco
St. Louis
Atlanta
Los Angeles
Phoenix
Dallas
Houston
New Orleans

BERMUDA (U.K.)

MEXICO
Guadalajara
Mexico City
GULF OF MEXICO
Miami
Havana
BAHAMAS
CUBA
HAITI
DOM. REP.
PUERTO RICO (U.S.)
JAMAICA
BELIZE
GUAT.
HOND.
EL SAL.
NIC.
COSTA RICA
PANAMA
GUADELOUPE (Fr.)
MARTINIQUE (Fr.)
BARBADOS
TRINIDAD AND TOBAGO
CARIBBEAN SEA

MIDWAY ISLANDS (U.S.)
HAWAII (U.S.)
Honolulu
JOHNSTON ATOLL (U.S.)

ATLANTIC OCEAN

PACIFIC OCEAN
Longitude West of Greenwich

HOWLAND ISLAND (U.S.)
BAKER ISLAND (U.S.)
JARVIS ISLAND (U.S.)
KIRIBATI

VENEZUELA
Caracas
GUYANA
Georgetown
SURINAME
FRENCH GUIANA (Fr.)
COLOMBIA
Bogotá
ECUADOR
Quito
Galapagos Is. (Ec.)
Manaus
Belém
Fortaleza
PERU
Lima
BRAZIL
Brasília
Recife
Salvador

TOKELAU (N.Z.)
SAMOA
AMERICAN SAMOA (U.S.)
COOK ISLANDS (N.Z.)
FRENCH POLYNESIA (Fr.)

BOLIVIA
La Paz
Sucre
Belo Horizonte
Rio de Janeiro
São Paulo
PARAGUAY
Asunción

TONGA
PITCAIRN ISLANDS (U.K.)

Antofagasta
Valparaíso
Santiago
ARGENTINA
Rosario
Porto Alegre
URUGUAY
Buenos Aires
Montevideo

SOUTHERN OCEAN
ROSS SEA

FALKLAND ISLANDS (U.K.)
SOUTH GEORGIA AND THE SOUTH SANDWICH ISLANDS (U.K.)

WEDDELL SEA

Antarctic Circle

GREENLAND
PORTUGAL
Lisbon
Azores (Port.)
MOROCCO
Casablanca
Madeira Is. (Port.)
Canary Is. (Sp.)
Tropic of Cancer
W. SAHARA
MAURITANIA
MALI
CAPE VERDE
Dakar
SENEGAL
THE GAMBIA
GUINEA-BISSAU
GUINEA
SIERRA LEONE
LIBERIA
CÔTE D'IVOIRE
GHANA
BURKINA FASO
NIGER
NIGERIA
Equator
ST. HELENA (U.K.)
Tropic of...

Scale 1 : 100 000 000 (approximate)
One inch to 1,600 miles
0   500   1000   1500   2000 miles
0   500   1000   1500   2000   2500 Kilometers

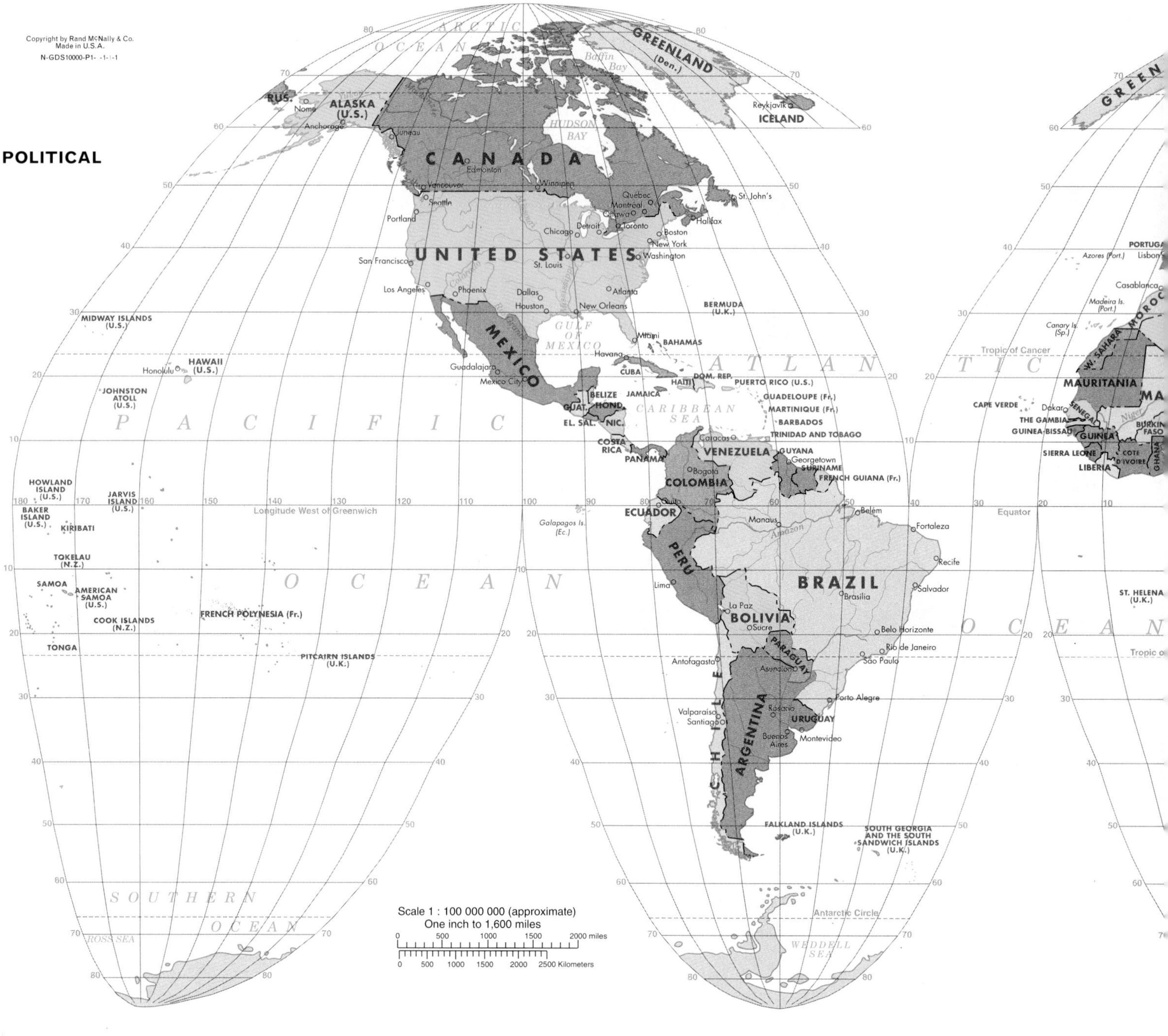

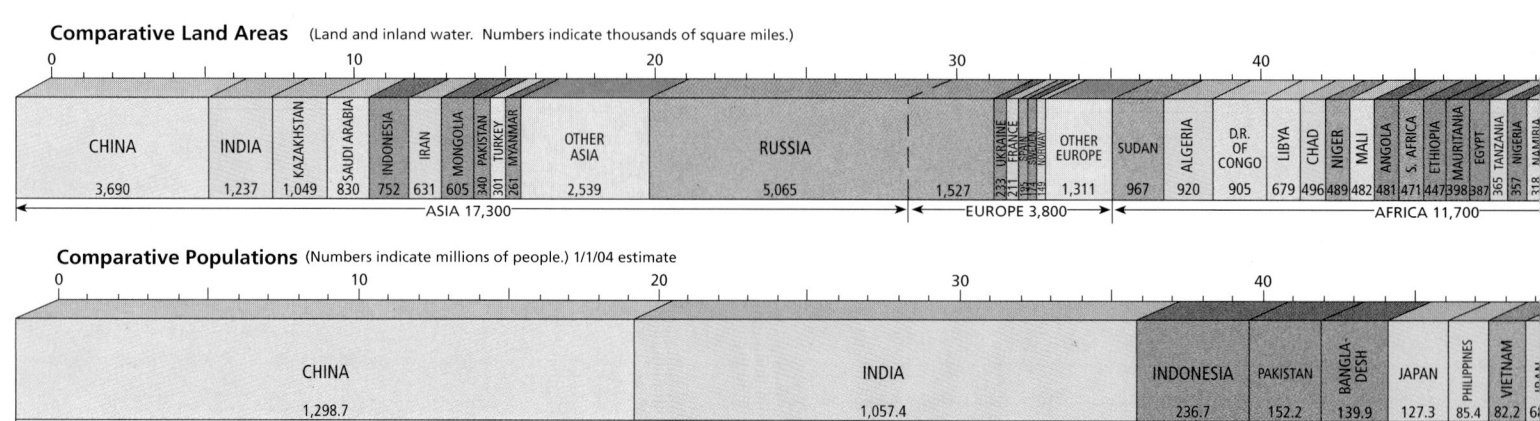

**Comparative Land Areas** (Land and inland water. Numbers indicate thousands of square miles.)

| 0 | 10 | 20 | 30 | 40 |
|---|----|----|----|----|

CHINA 3,690 | INDIA 1,237 | KAZAKHSTAN 1,049 | SAUDI ARABIA 830 | INDONESIA 752 | IRAN 631 | MONGOLIA 605 | PAKISTAN 340 | TURKEY 301 | MYANMAR 261 | OTHER ASIA 2,539 | RUSSIA 5,065 | 1,527 | UKRAINE 233 | FRANCE 211 | SPAIN 195 | SWEDEN 174 | OTHER EUROPE 1,311 | SUDAN 967 | ALGERIA 920 | D.R. OF CONGO 905 | LIBYA 679 | CHAD 496 | NIGER 489 | MALI 482 | ANGOLA 481 | S. AFRICA 471 | ETHIOPIA 447 | MAURITANIA 398 | EGYPT 387 | TANZANIA 365 | NIGERIA 357 | NAMIBIA 318

ASIA 17,300 — EUROPE 3,800 — AFRICA 11,700

**Comparative Populations** (Numbers indicate millions of people.) 1/1/04 estimate

| 0 | 10 | 20 | 30 | 40 |
|---|----|----|----|----|

CHINA 1,298.7 | INDIA 1,057.4 | INDONESIA 236.7 | PAKISTAN 152.2 | BANGLA-DESH 139.9 | JAPAN 127.3 | PHILIPPINES 85.4 | VIETNAM 82.2 | IRAN 68

ASIA 3,839.3

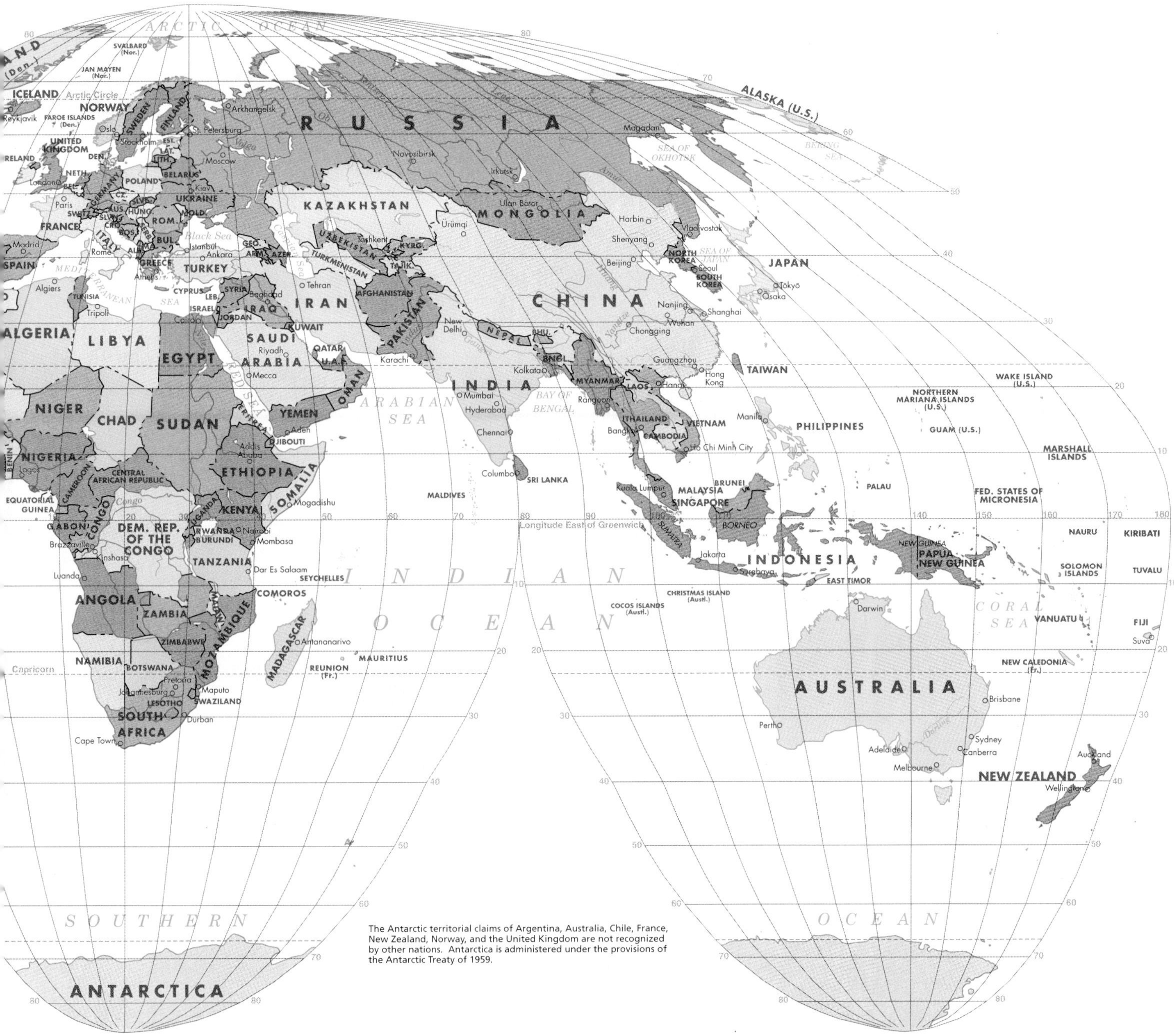

ARCTIC OCEAN

ICELAND
NORWAY
SWEDEN
FINLAND
UNITED KINGDOM
IRELAND
DENMARK
NETH.
GERMANY
POLAND
BELARUS
UKRAINE
FRANCE
SPAIN
ITALY
GREECE
TURKEY

R U S S I A

ALASKA (U.S.)

KAZAKHSTAN
MONGOLIA
UZBEKISTAN
TURKMENISTAN
AFGHANISTAN
IRAN
PAKISTAN
NEPAL
INDIA

C H I N A

NORTH KOREA
SOUTH KOREA
JAPAN

ALGERIA
LIBYA
EGYPT
SAUDI ARABIA
NIGER
CHAD
SUDAN
YEMEN
OMAN
U.A.E.
QATAR
KUWAIT
IRAQ
SYRIA
JORDAN
ISRAEL

NIGERIA
CAMEROON
CENTRAL AFRICAN REPUBLIC
ETHIOPIA
SOMALIA
KENYA
DEM. REP. OF THE CONGO
TANZANIA
ANGOLA
ZAMBIA
ZIMBABWE
MOZAMBIQUE
NAMIBIA
BOTSWANA
SOUTH AFRICA
MADAGASCAR

MYANMAR
THAILAND
LAOS
VIETNAM
CAMBODIA
PHILIPPINES
MALAYSIA
SINGAPORE
BRUNEI
INDONESIA
BORNEO
SUMATRA

TAIWAN
NORTHERN MARIANA ISLANDS (U.S.)
GUAM (U.S.)
MARSHALL ISLANDS
FED. STATES OF MICRONESIA
PALAU
NAURU
KIRIBATI
TUVALU
SOLOMON ISLANDS
PAPUA NEW GUINEA
EAST TIMOR
VANUATU
FIJI
NEW CALEDONIA (Fr.)

A U S T R A L I A

NEW ZEALAND

SRI LANKA
MALDIVES
SEYCHELLES
COMOROS
MAURITIUS
REUNION (Fr.)

I N D I A N   O C E A N
ARABIAN SEA
BAY OF BENGAL
CORAL SEA

SOUTHERN OCEAN

ANTARCTICA

The Antarctic territorial claims of Argentina, Australia, Chile, France, New Zealand, Norway, and the United Kingdom are not recognized by other nations. Antarctica is administered under the provisions of the Antarctic Treaty of 1959.

Goode's Homolosine Equal Area Projection

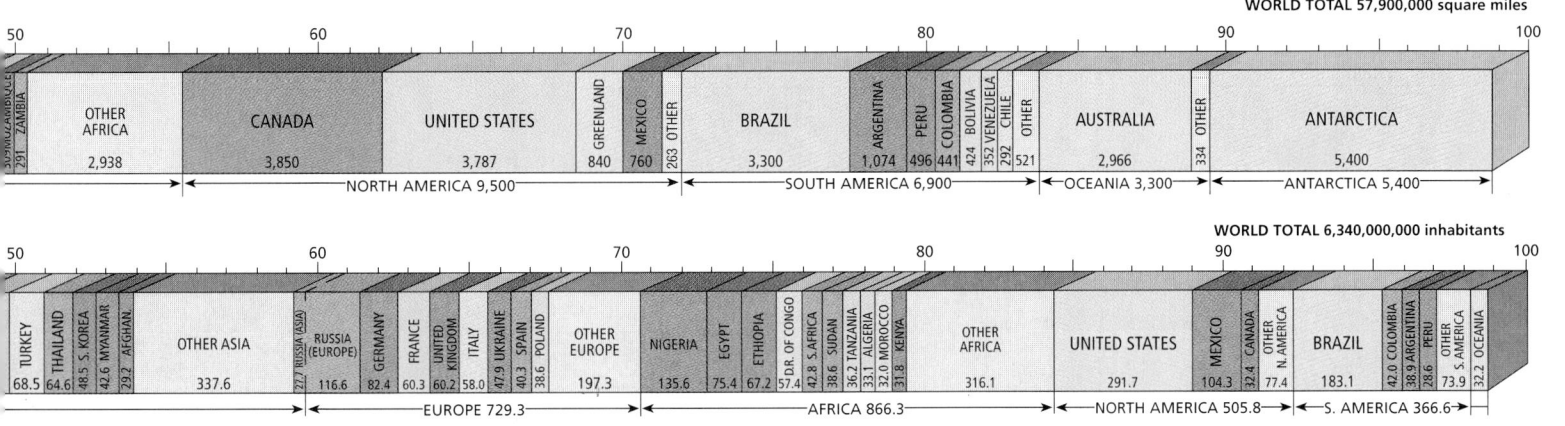

WORLD TOTAL 57,900,000 square miles

WORLD TOTAL 6,340,000,000 inhabitants

# PHYSICAL

ASIA · NORTH AMERICA · SOUTH AMERICA

ARCTIC OCEAN · North Pole · North Magnetic Pole · GREENLAND · ICELAND

PACIFIC OCEAN · ATLANTIC OCEAN · SOUTHERN OCEAN

Scale 1 : 100 000 000 (approximate)
One inch to 1,600 miles

0 500 1000 1500 2000 miles
0 500 1000 1500 2000 2500 Kilometers

| Meters | Feet | |
|---|---|---|
| 3 050 | 10 000 | |
| 1 525 | 5 000 | |
| 610 | 2 000 | |
| 305 | 1 000 | |
| 0 | SEA L. | |
| | | BELOW SEA LEVEL |
| 152.5 | 500 | |
| 3 050 | 10 000 | |
| 6 100 | 20 000 | |

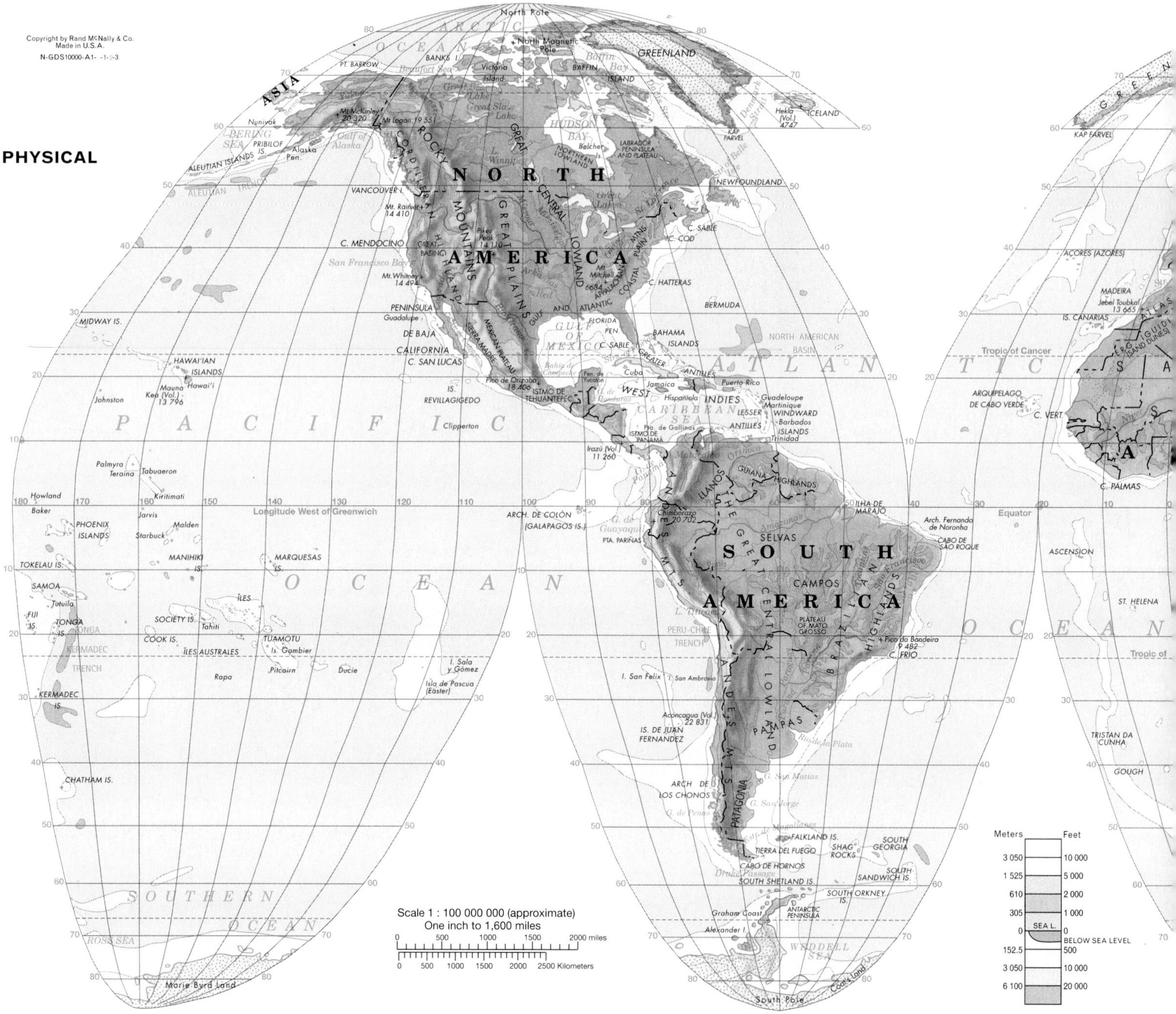

## Land Elevations in Profile

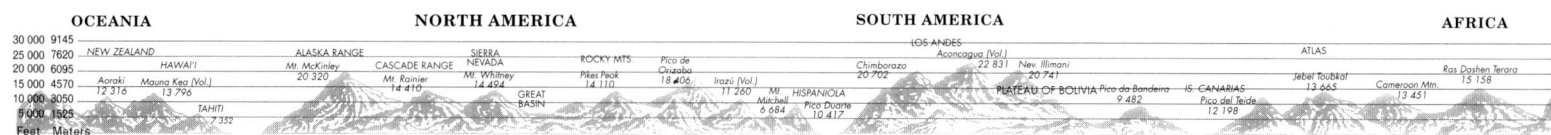

OCEANIA · NORTH AMERICA · SOUTH AMERICA · AFRICA

## Ocean Depths in Profile

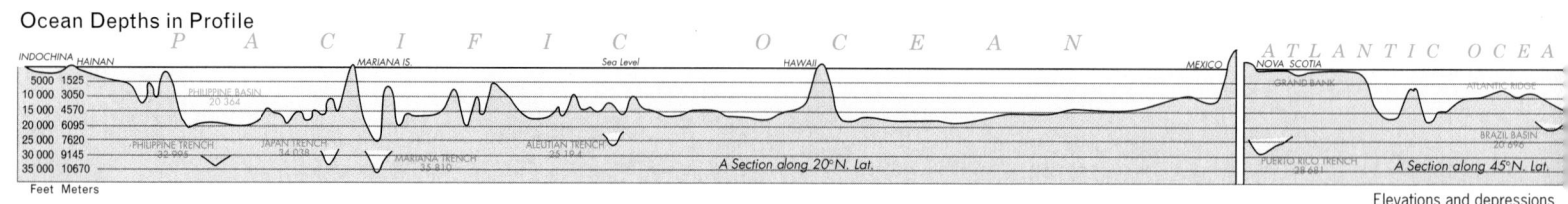

A Section along 20° N. Lat. · A Section along 45° N. Lat.

Elevations and depressions

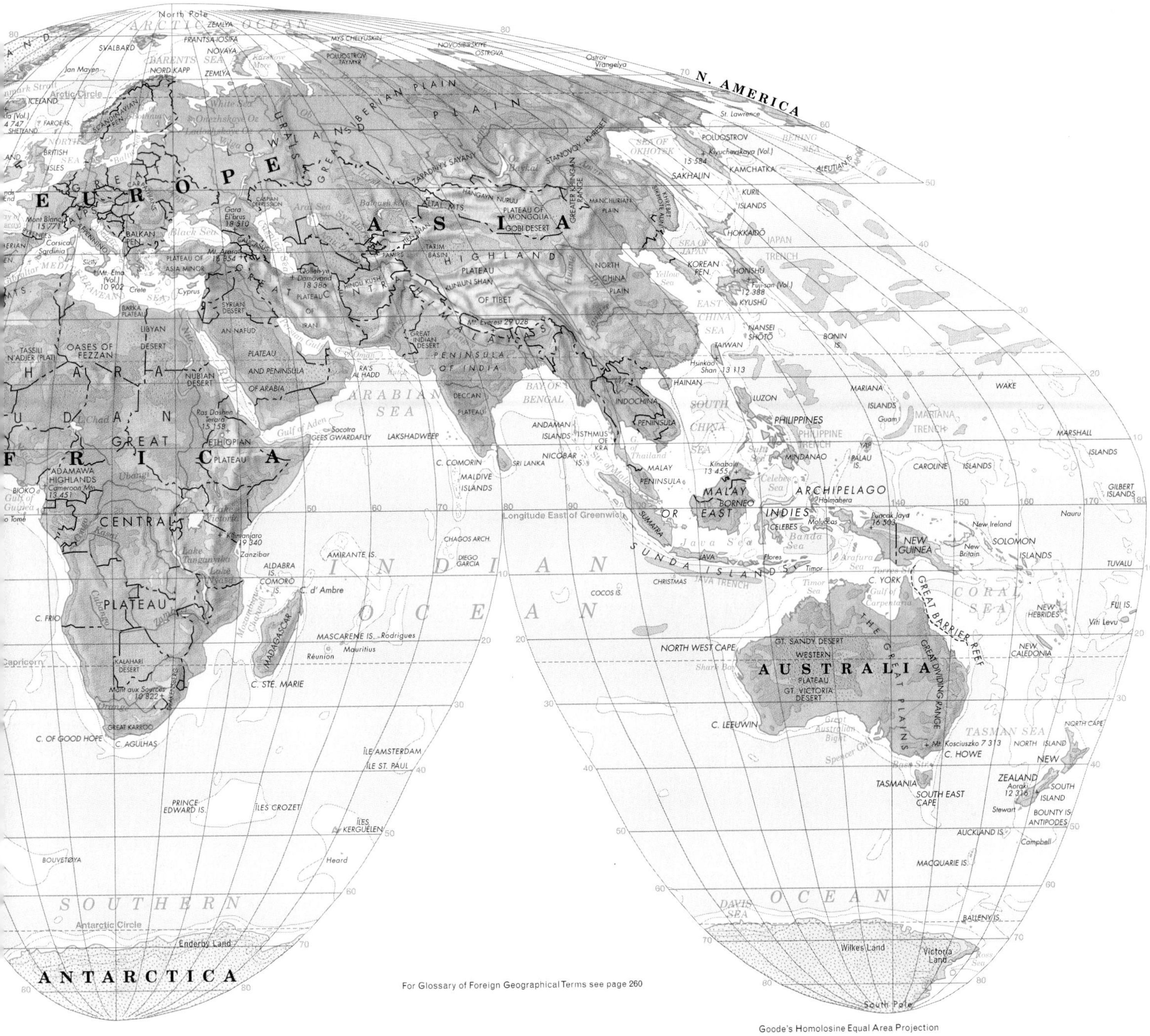

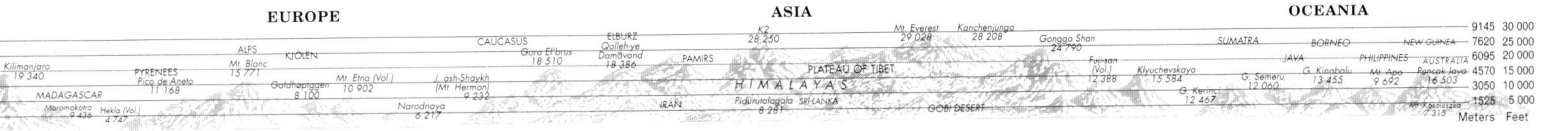

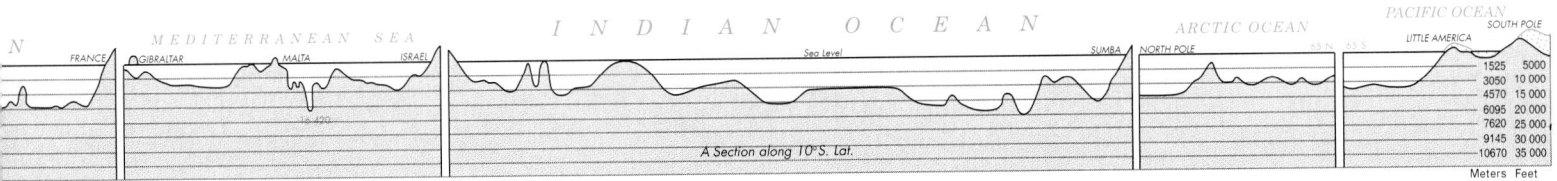

Goode's Homolosine Equal Area Projection

For Glossary of Foreign Geographical Terms see page 260

are given in feet

6

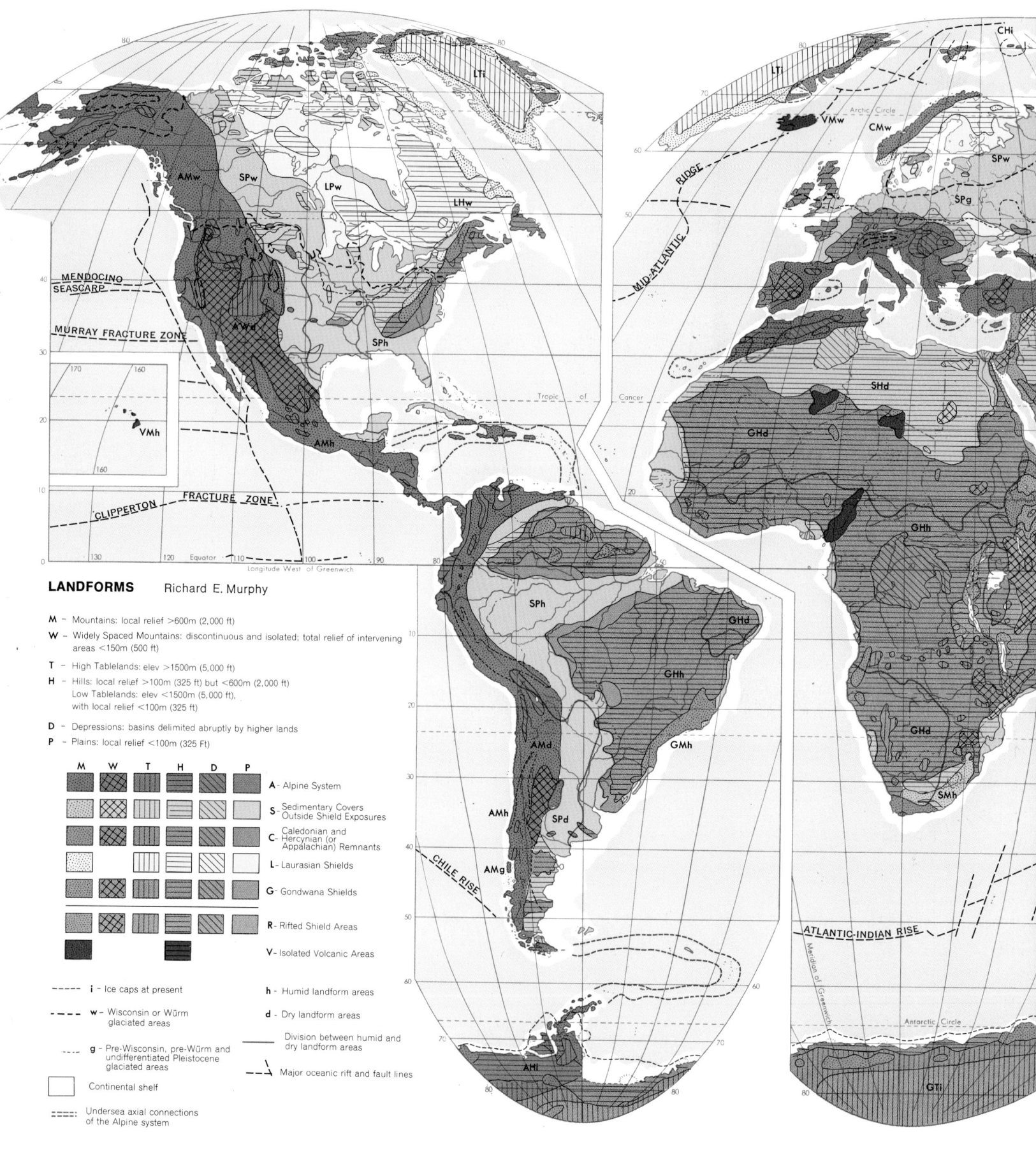

**LANDFORMS**    Richard E. Murphy

**M** – Mountains: local relief >600m (2,000 ft)

**W** – Widely Spaced Mountains: discontinuous and isolated; total relief of intervening areas <150m (500 ft)

**T** – High Tablelands: elev >1500m (5,000 ft)

**H** – Hills: local relief >100m (325 ft) but <600m (2,000 ft)
Low Tablelands: elev <1500m (5,000 ft), with local relief <100m (325 ft)

**D** – Depressions: basins delimited abruptly by higher lands

**P** – Plains: local relief <100m (325 Ft)

M    W    T    H    D    P

**A** – Alpine System

**S** – Sedimentary Covers Outside Shield Exposures

**C** – Caledonian and Hercynian (or Appalachian) Remnants

**L** – Laurasian Shields

**G** – Gondwana Shields

**R** – Rifted Shield Areas

**V** – Isolated Volcanic Areas

----- **i** – Ice caps at present

- - - **w** – Wisconsin or Würm glaciated areas

·- ·- **g** – Pre-Wisconsin, pre-Würm and undifferentiated Pleistocene glaciated areas

☐ Continental shelf

==== Undersea axial connections of the Alpine system

**h** – Humid landform areas

**d** – Dry landform areas

——— Division between humid and dry landform areas

- ·- Major oceanic rift and fault lines

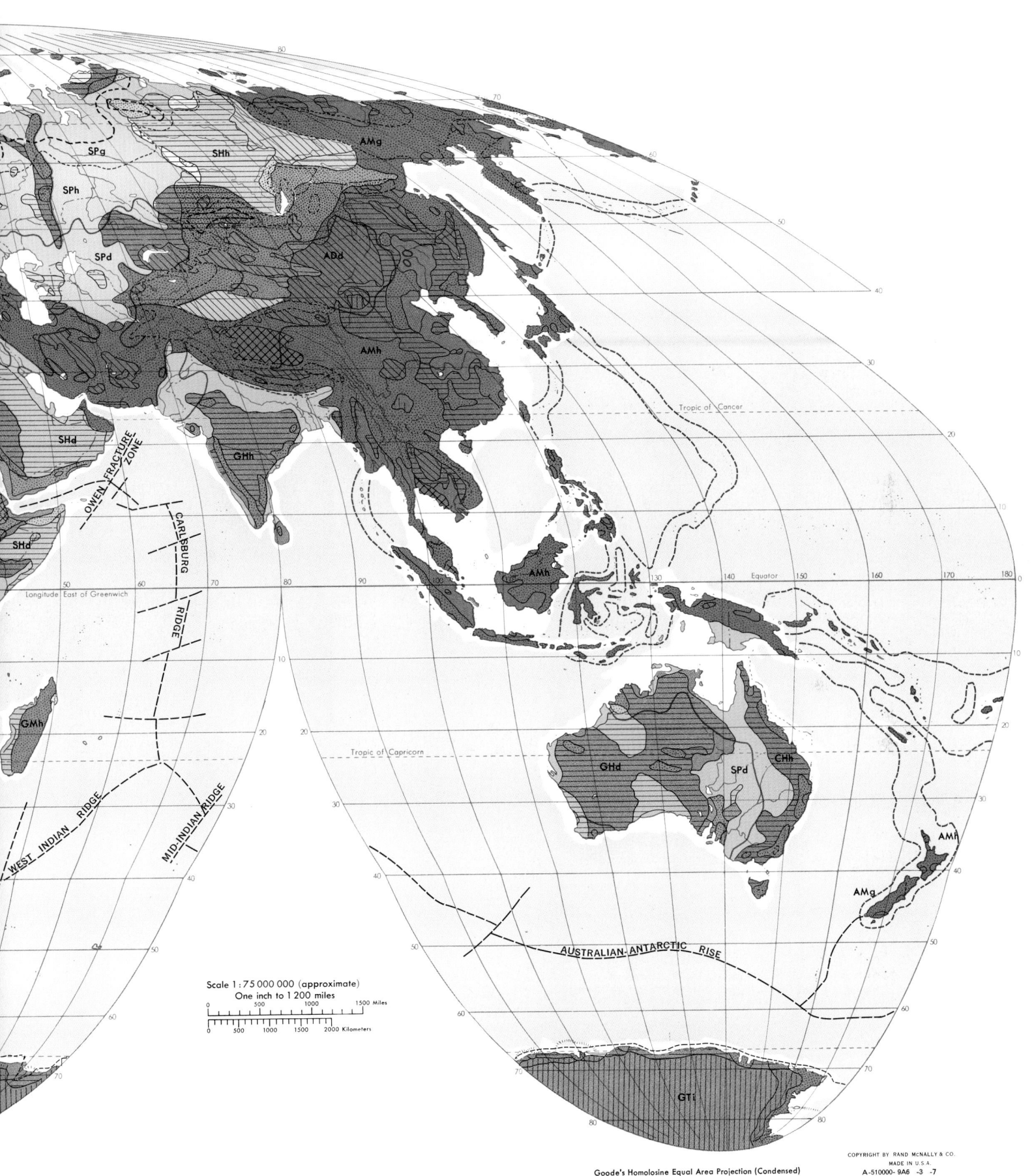

SPg
SPh
SHh
AMg
SPd
ADd
AMh

SHd

OWEN FRACTURE ZONE
CARLSBURG RIDGE
GHh

SHd

Tropic of Cancer

AMh

Longitude East of Greenwich

Equator

GMh

WEST INDIAN RIDGE
MID-INDIAN RIDGE

Tropic of Capricorn

AMh

GHd
SPd
CHh

AMg

AUSTRALIAN-ANTARCTIC RISE

GTi

Scale 1 : 75 000 000 (approximate)
One inch to 1 200 miles

0    500    1000    1500 Miles

0    500    1000    1500    2000 Kilometers

Goode's Homolosine Equal Area Projection (Condensed)

## CONTINENTAL DRIFT

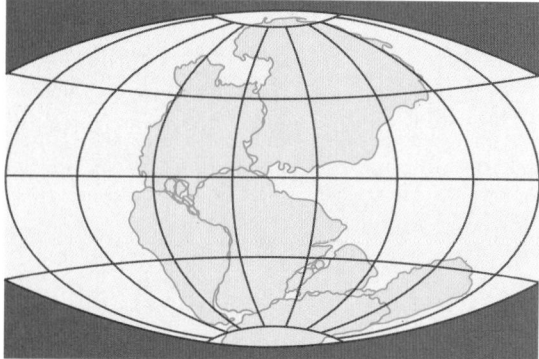

**225 million years ago** the supercontinent of Pangaea exists and Panthalassa forms the ancestral ocean. Tethys Sea separates Eurasia and Africa.

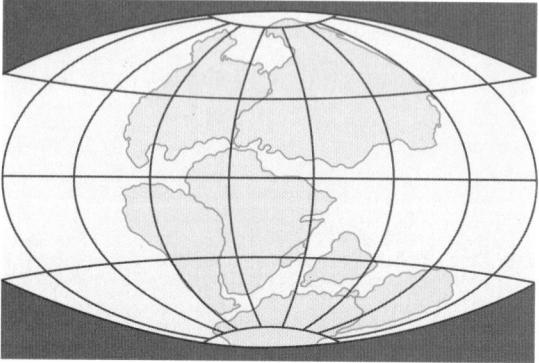

**180 million years ago** Pangaea splits, Laurasia drifts north. Gondwanaland breaks into South America/Africa, India, and Australia/Antarctica.

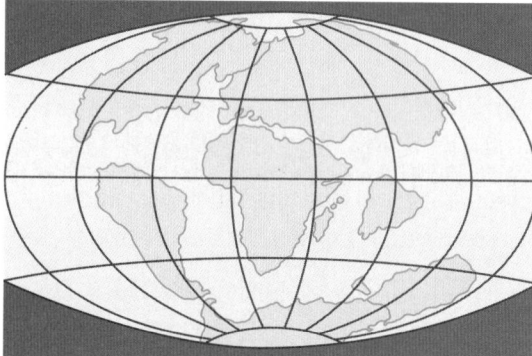

**65 million years ago** ocean basins take shape as South America and India move from Africa and the Tethys Sea closes to form the Mediterranean Sea.

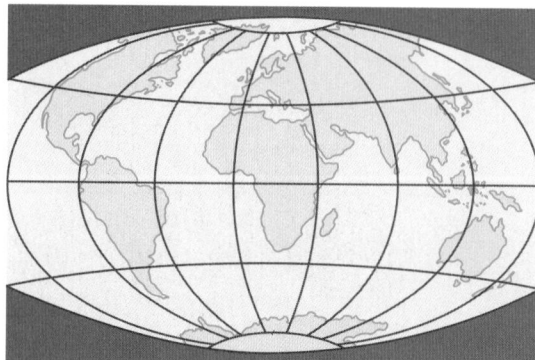

**The present day:** India has merged with Asia, Australia is free of Antarctica, and North America is free of Eurasia.

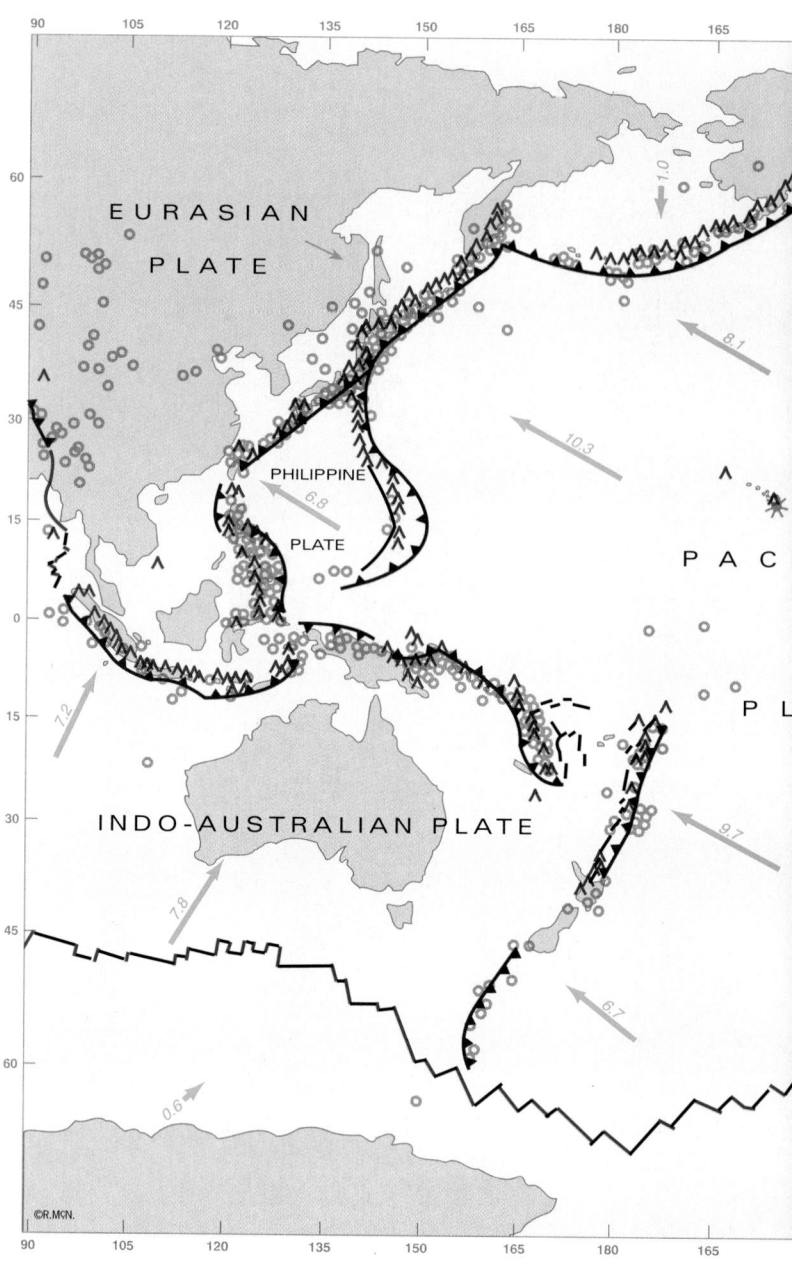

## PLATE TECTONICS

### Types of plate boundaries

**Divergent:** magma emerges from the earth's mantle at the mid-ocean ridges forming new crust and forcing the plates to spread apart at the ridges.

**Convergent:** plates collide at subduction zones where the denser plate is forced back into the earth's mantle forming deep ocean trenches.

**Transform:** plates slide past one another producing faults and fracture zones.

### Other map symbols

→ Direction of plate movement

6.7 → Length of arrow is proportional to the amount of plate movement (number indicates centimeters of movement per year)

○ Earthquake of magnitude 7.5 and above (from 10 A.D. to the present)

∧ Volcano (eruption since 1900)

✳ Selected hot spots

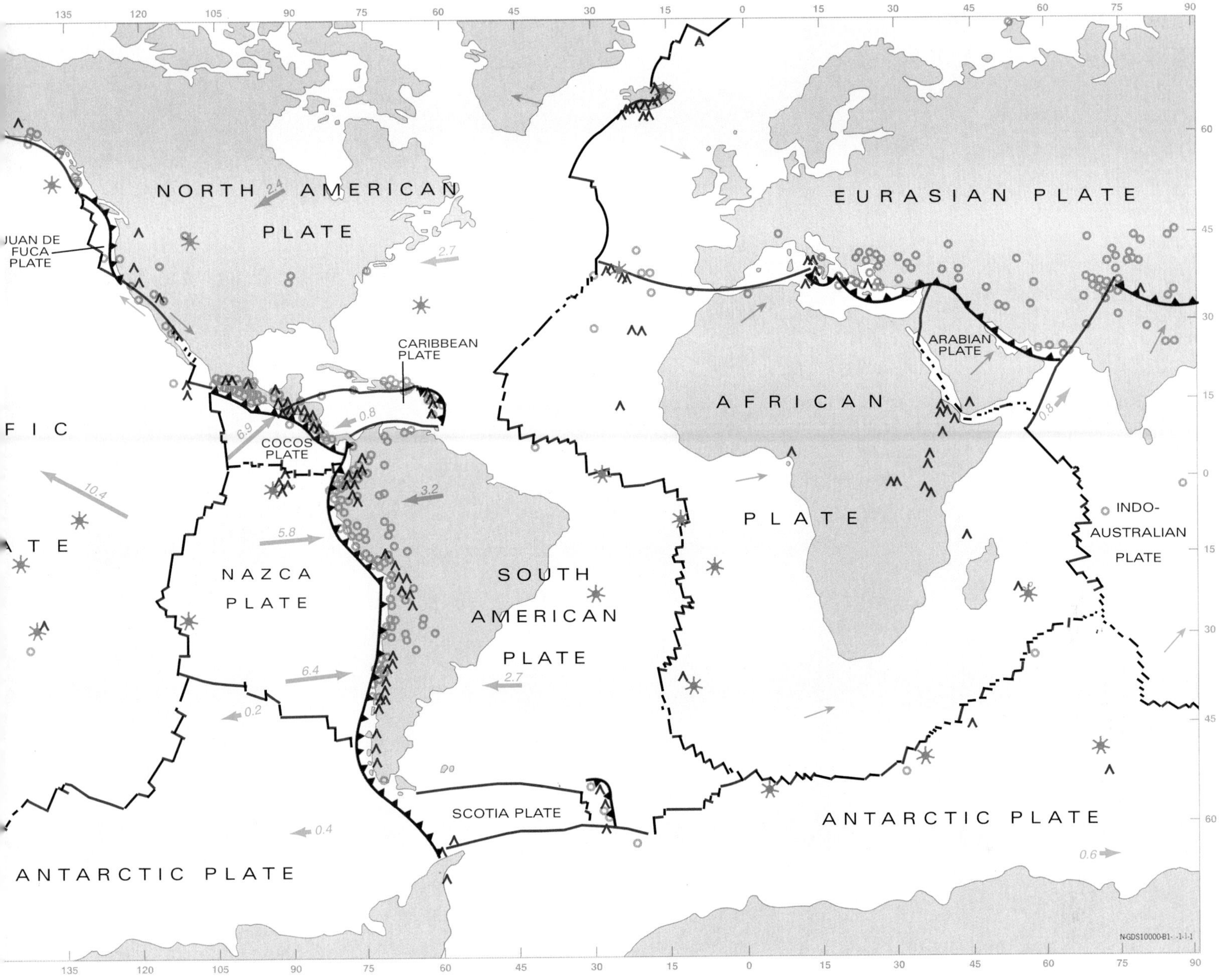

## Map labels

NORTH AMERICAN PLATE

JUAN DE FUCA PLATE

CARIBBEAN PLATE

COCOS PLATE

NAZCA PLATE

SOUTH AMERICAN PLATE

SCOTIA PLATE

ANTARCTIC PLATE

ANTARCTIC PLATE

EURASIAN PLATE

ARABIAN PLATE

AFRICAN PLATE

INDO-AUSTRALIAN PLATE

ANTARCTIC PLATE

N-GDS10000-B1- -1-1-1

The plate tectonic theory describes the movement of the earth's surface and subsurface and explains why surface features are where they are.

Stated concisely, the theory presumes the lithosphere - the outside crust and uppermost mantle of the earth - is divided into about a dozen major rigid plates and several smaller platelets that move relative to one another. The position and names of the plates are shown on the map above.

The motor that drives the plates is found deep in the mantle. The theory states that because of temperature differences in the mantle, slow convection currents circulate there. Where two molten currents converge and move upward, they separate, causing the crustal plates to bulge and move apart in mid-ocean regions. Transverse fractures disrupt these broad regions. Lava wells up at these points to cause volcanic activity and to form ridges. The plates grow larger by accretion along these mid-ocean ridges, cause vast regions of the crust to move apart, and force the plates to collide with one another. As the plates do so, they are destroyed at subduction zones, where the plates are consumed downward, back into the earth's mantle, forming deep ocean trenches. The diagrams to the right illustrate the processes.

Most of the earth's volcanic and seismic activities

occur where plates slide past each other at transform boundaries or collide along subduction zones. The friction and heat caused by the grinding motion of the subducted plates causes rock to liquify and rise to the surface as volcanoes and eventually form vast mountain ranges. Strong and deep earthquakes are common here.

Volcanoes and earthquakes also occur at random locations around the earth known as "hot spots". Hot rock from deep in the mantle rises to the surface creating some of the earth's tallest mountains. As the lithospheric plates move slowly over these stationary plumes of magma, island chains (such as the Hawaiian Islands) are formed.

The overall result of tectonic movement is that the crustal plates move slowly and inexorably as relatively rigid entitles, carrying the continents along with them. The history of this continental drifting is illustrated in the four maps to the left. It began with a single landmass called the supercontinent of Pangaea and the ancestral sea, the Panthalassa Ocean. Pangaea first split into a northern landmass called Laurasia and a southern block called Gondwanaland and subsequently into the continents we map today. The map of the future will be significantly different as the continents continue to drift.

Subduction Zone

Ocean Ridge Zone

Scale 1:72 000 000 at 40° latitude.

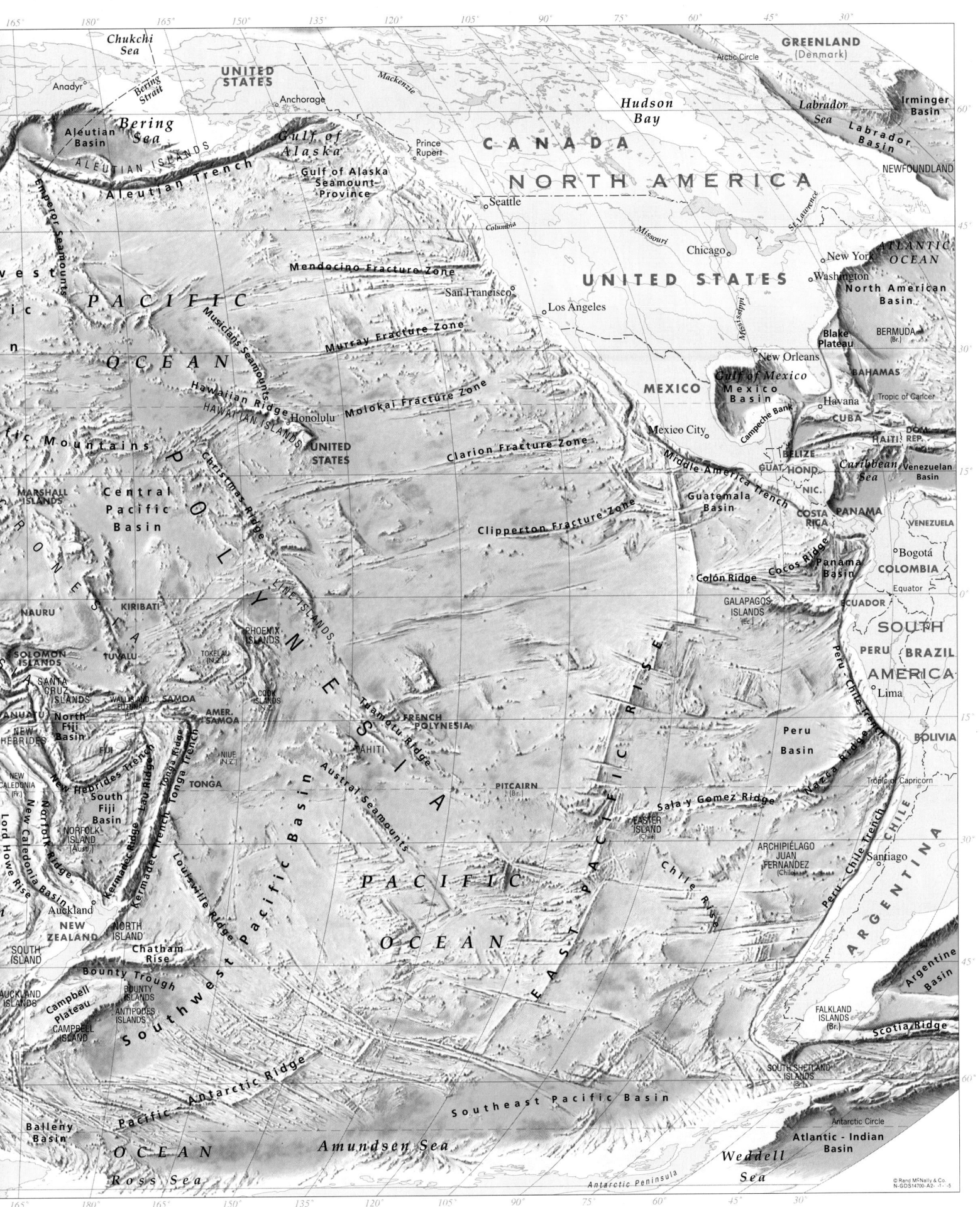

ROBINSON PROJECTION

Scale 1:72 000 000 at 40° latitude.  ROBINSON PROJECTION

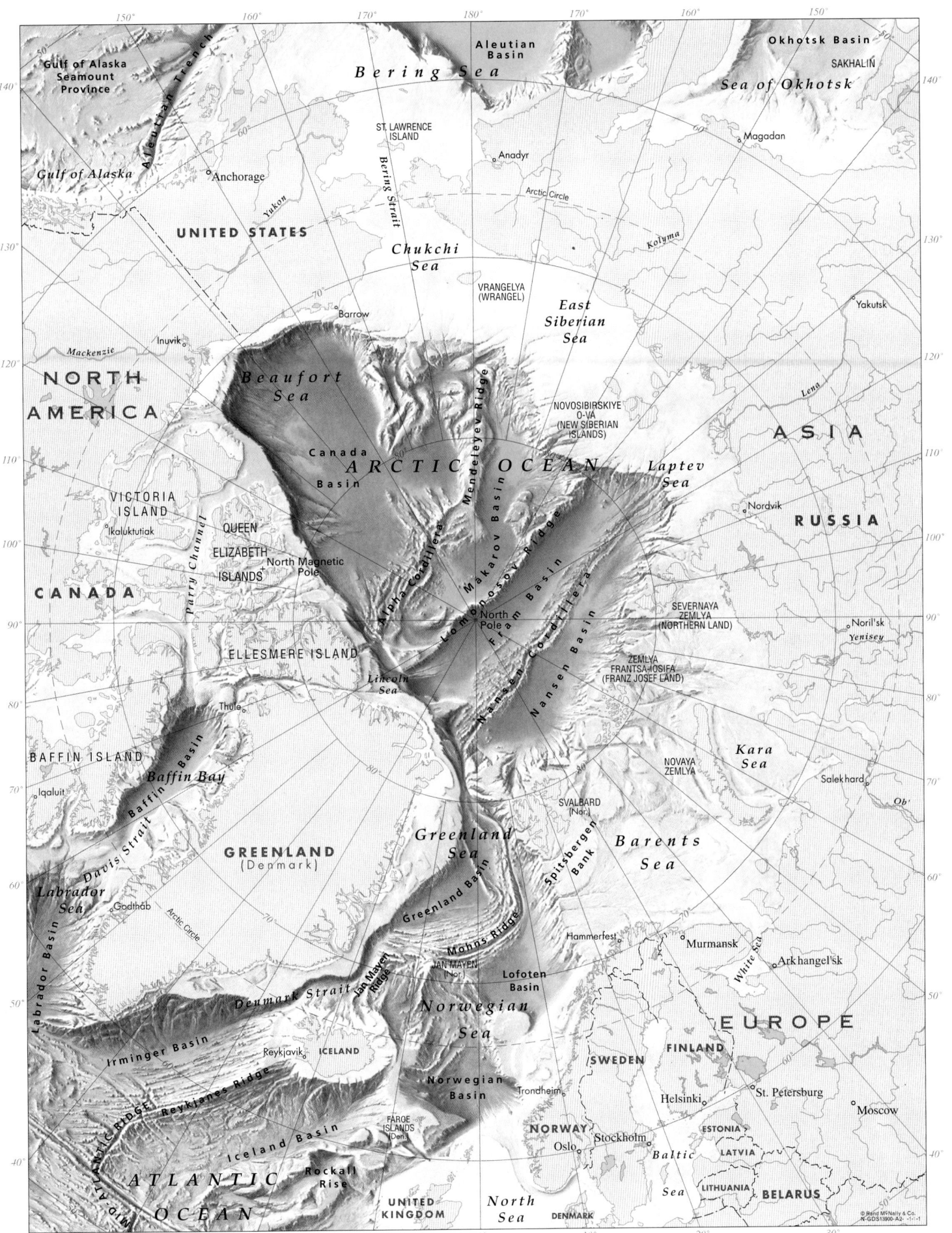

Scale 1:30 000 000.  LAMBERT AZIMUTHAL EQUAL AREA PROJECTION

14

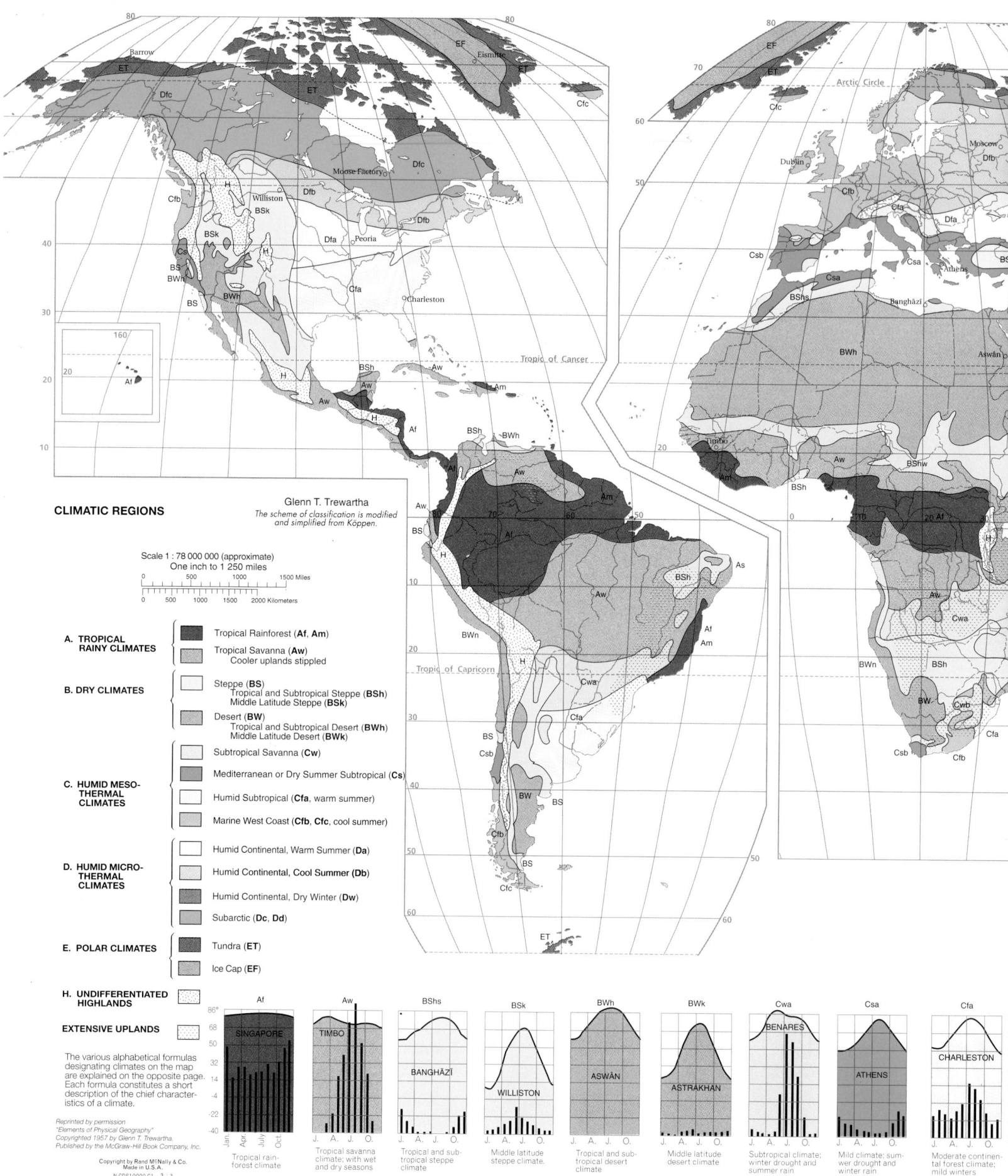

**CLIMATIC REGIONS**

Glenn T. Trewartha
*The scheme of classification is modified
and simplified from Köppen.*

Scale 1 : 78 000 000 (approximate)
One inch to 1 250 miles

0    500    1000    1500 Miles

0    500    1000    1500    2000 Kilometers

**A. TROPICAL RAINY CLIMATES**
- Tropical Rainforest (**Af, Am**)
- Tropical Savanna (**Aw**)
  Cooler uplands stippled

**B. DRY CLIMATES**
- Steppe (**BS**)
  Tropical and Subtropical Steppe (**BSh**)
  Middle Latitude Steppe (**BSk**)
- Desert (**BW**)
  Tropical and Subtropical Desert (**BWh**)
  Middle Latitude Desert (**BWk**)

**C. HUMID MESO-THERMAL CLIMATES**
- Subtropical Savanna (**Cw**)
- Mediterranean or Dry Summer Subtropical (**Cs**)
- Humid Subtropical (**Cfa**, warm summer)
- Marine West Coast (**Cfb, Cfc**, cool summer)

**D. HUMID MICRO-THERMAL CLIMATES**
- Humid Continental, Warm Summer (**Da**)
- Humid Continental, Cool Summer (**Db**)
- Humid Continental, Dry Winter (**Dw**)
- Subarctic (**Dc, Dd**)

**E. POLAR CLIMATES**
- Tundra (**ET**)
- Ice Cap (**EF**)

**H. UNDIFFERENTIATED HIGHLANDS**

**EXTENSIVE UPLANDS**

The various alphabetical formulas
designating climates on the map
are explained on the opposite page.
Each formula constitutes a short
description of the chief characteristics of a climate.

*Reprinted by permission
"Elements of Physical Geography"
Copyrighted 1957 by Glenn T. Trewartha.
Published by the McGraw-Hill Book Company, Inc.*

Copyright by Rand McNally & Co.
Made in U.S.A.
N-GDS10000-C1-  -2- -3

| Af SINGAPORE | Aw TIMBO | BShs BANGHĀZĪ | BSk WILLISTON | BWh ASWÂN | BWk ASTRAKHAN | Cwa BENARES | Csa ATHENS | Cfa CHARLESTON |

Tropical rain-
forest climate

Tropical savanna
climate; with wet
and dry seasons

Tropical and sub-
tropical steppe
climate

Middle latitude
steppe climate.

Tropical and sub-
tropical desert
climate

Middle latitude
desert climate

Subtropical climate;
winter drought and
summer rain

Mild climate; sum-
mer drought and
winter rain

Moderate continen-
tal forest climate;
mild winters

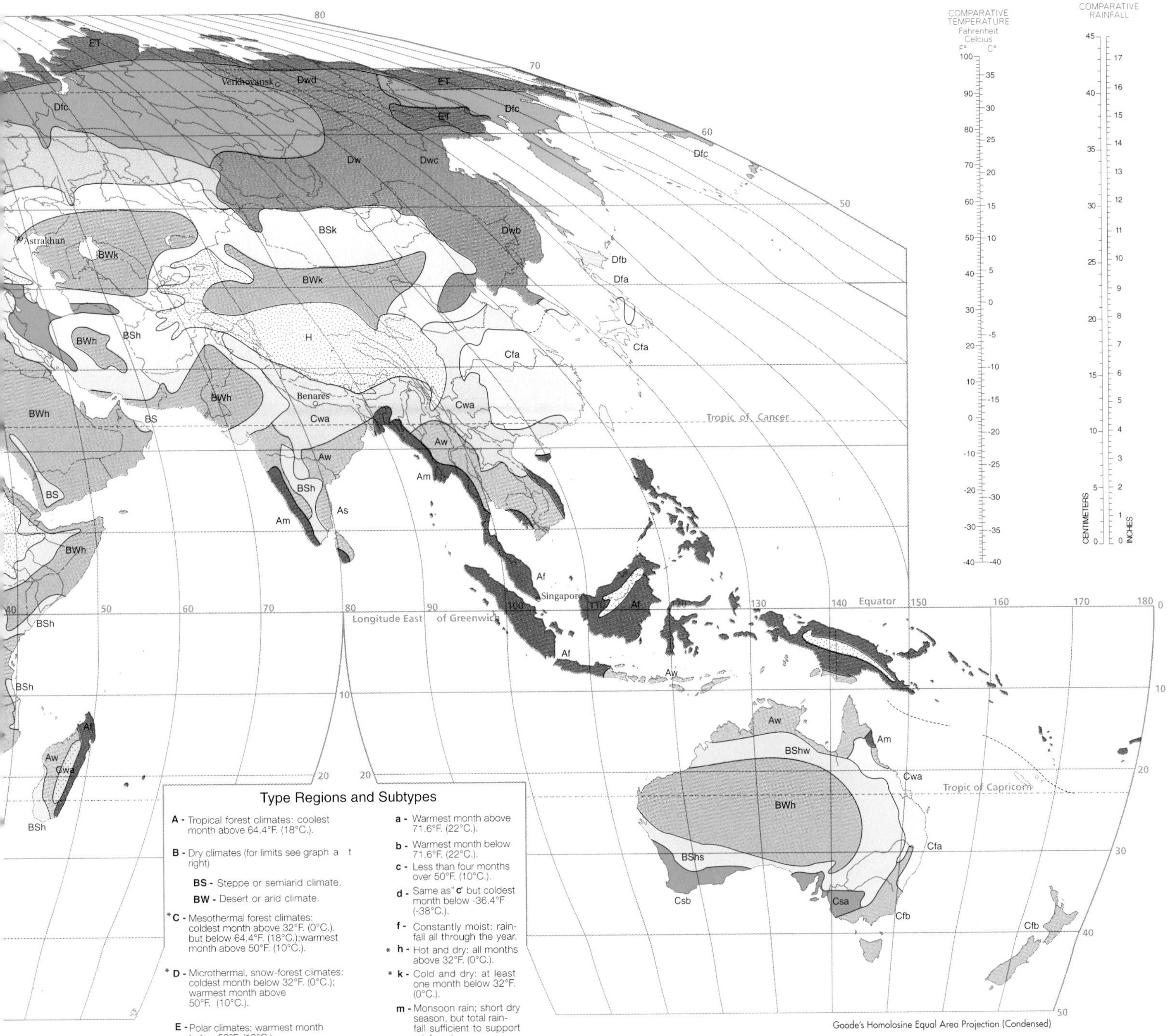

COMPARATIVE
TEMPERATURE
Fahrenheit
Celsius

COMPARATIVE
RAINFALL

*(Map labels, in reading order across the map)*

ET · Verkhoyansk · Dwd · ET · ET · Dfc · Dfc · Dfc · Dw · Dwc · Dwb · BSk · Astrakhan · BWk · BWk · Dfb · Dfa · H · BWh · BSh · BWh · BS · Cfa · Cfa · BWh · Benares · Cwa · Cwa · Tropic of Cancer · BS · Aw · Aw · Aw · BSh · Am · As · Am · Af · Singapore · Af · Af · BWh · Af · Af · Aw · BSh · BSh · Af · Aw · Cwa · BSh · Equator · Longitude East · of Greenwich · Aw · Aw · Am · BShw · Cwa · Tropic of Capricorn · BWh · Cfa · BShs · Csb · Csa · Cfb · Cfb

## Type Regions and Subtypes

**A** - Tropical forest climates: coolest month above 64.4°F. (18°C.).

**B** - Dry climates (for limits see graph a t right)

    **BS** - Steppe or semiarid climate.

    **BW** - Desert or arid climate.

\***C** - Mesothermal forest climates: coldest month above 32°F. (0°C.). but below 64.4°F. (18°C.);warmest month above 50°F. (10°C.).

\***D** - Microthermal, snow-forest climates: coldest month below 32°F. (0°C.); warmest month above 50°F. (10°C.).

**E** - Polar climates; warmest month below 50°F. (10°C.).

    **ET** - Tundra climate: warmest month below 50°F. (10°C.) but above 32°F. (0°C.).

    **EF** - Perpetual frost: all months below 32°F. (0°C.).

*\* Modification of Köppen definition*

**a** - Warmest month above 71.6°F. (22°C.).

**b** - Warmest month below 71.6°F. (22°C.).

**c** - Less than four months over 50°F. (10°C.).

**d** - Same as"**c**" but coldest month below -36.4°F (-38°C.).

**f** - Constantly moist: rainfall all through the year.

\* **h** - Hot and dry: all months above 32°F. (0°C.).

\* **k** - Cold and dry: at least one month below 32°F. (0°C.).

**m** - Monsoon rain; short dry season, but total rainfall sufficient to support rainforest.

**n** - Frequent fog.

**ń** - Infrequent fog, but high humidity and low rainfall.

**s** - Dry season in summer.

**w** - Dry season in winter.

Goode's Homolosine Equal Area Projection (Condensed)

CURVES SHOW FAHRENHEIT TEMPERATURE
VERTICAL BARS SHOW RAINFALL IN INCHES

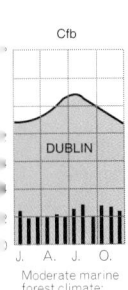

Cfb

DUBLIN

J. A. J. O.

Moderate marine forest climate; mild winters

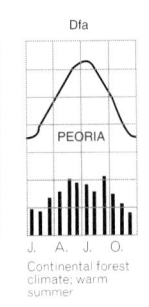

Dfa

PEORIA

J. A. J. O.

Continental forest climate; warm summer

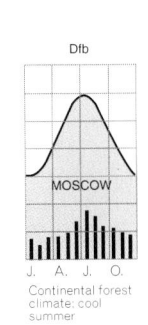

Dfb

MOSCOW

J. A. J. O.

Continental forest climate; cool summer

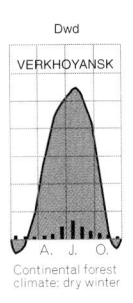

Dwd

VERKHOYANSK

A. J. O.

Continental forest climate; dry winter

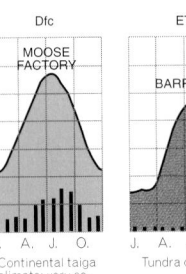

Dfc

MOOSE FACTORY

J. A. J. O.

Continental taiga climate; very severe winters

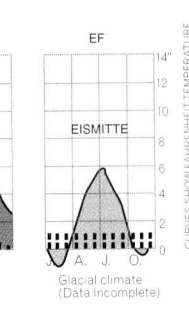

ET

BARROW

J. A. J. O.

Tundra climate

EF

EISMITTE

J. J.

Glacial climate (Data Incomplete)

## Limits of the Regions of Dry Climates

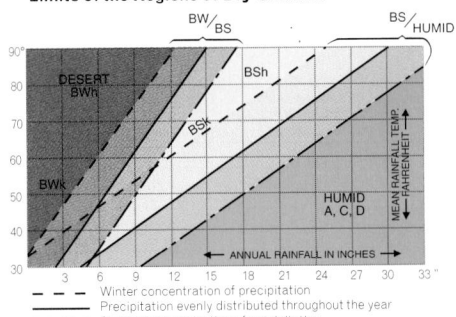

BW/BS · BS/HUMID · DESERT BWh · BSh · BSk · BWk · HUMID A, C, D · MEAN RAINFALL TEMP. FAHRENHEIT · ANNUAL RAINFALL IN INCHES

- - - Winter concentration of precipitation
—— Precipitation evenly distributed throughout the year
—·— Summer concentration of precipitation

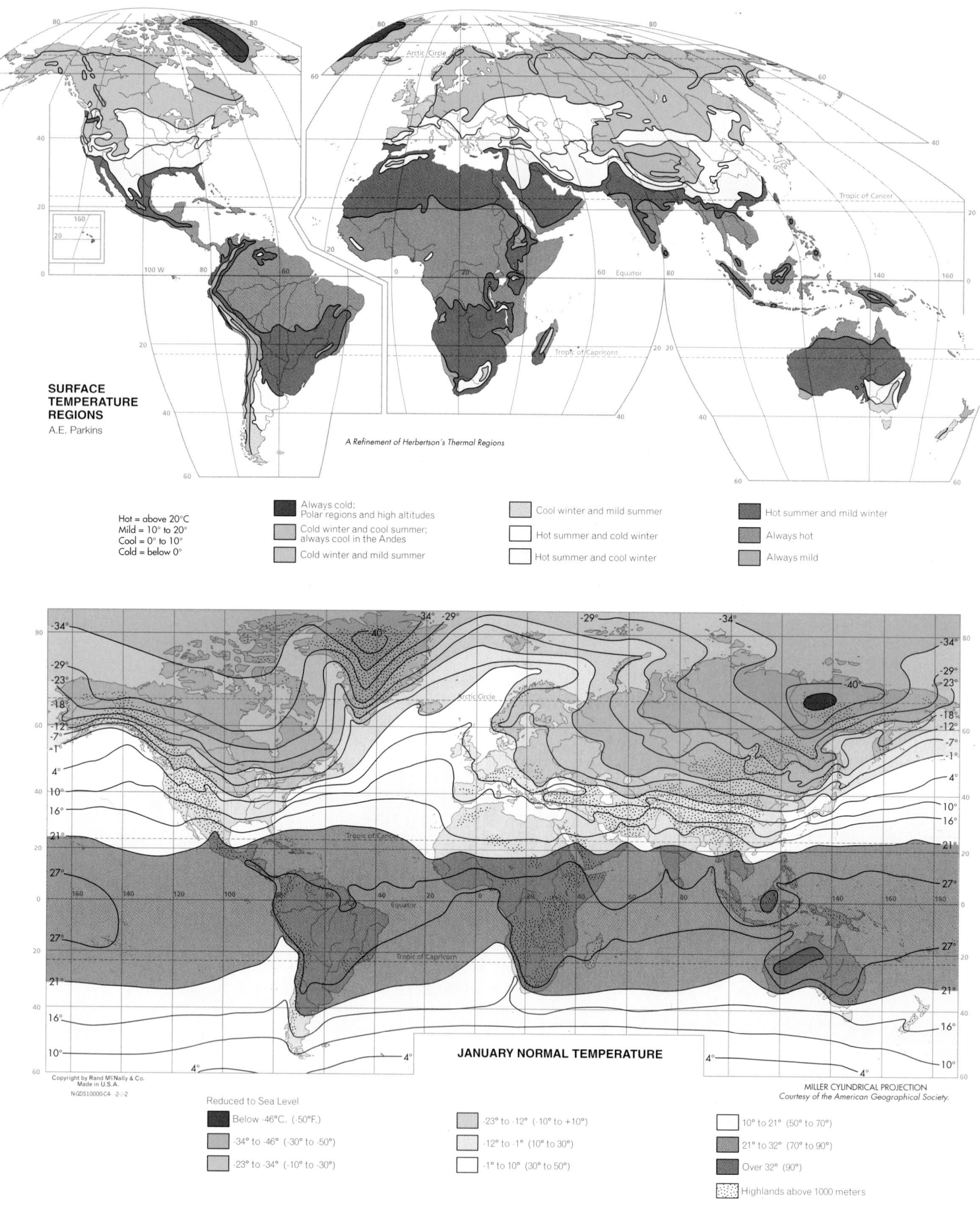

**SURFACE
TEMPERATURE
REGIONS**
A.E. Parkins

*A Refinement of Herbertson's Thermal Regions*

Hot = above 20°C
Mild = 10° to 20°
Cool = 0° to 10°
Cold = below 0°

- Always cold;
  Polar regions and high altitudes
- Cold winter and cool summer;
  always cool in the Andes
- Cold winter and mild summer

- Cool winter and mild summer
- Hot summer and cold winter
- Hot summer and cool winter

- Hot summer and mild winter
- Always hot
- Always mild

**JANUARY NORMAL TEMPERATURE**

MILLER CYLINDRICAL PROJECTION
*Courtesy of the American Geographical Society.*

Copyright by Rand McNally & Co.
Made in U.S.A.
NGDS10000-C4-·2-·-2

Reduced to Sea Level

- Below -46°C. (-50°F.)
- -34° to -46° (-30° to -50°)
- -23° to -34° (-10° to -30°)

- -23° to -12° (-10° to +10°)
- -12° to -1° (10° to 30°)
- -1° to 10° (30° to 50°)

- 10° to 21° (50° to 70°)
- 21° to 32° (70° to 90°)
- Over 32° (90°)
- Highlands above 1000 meters

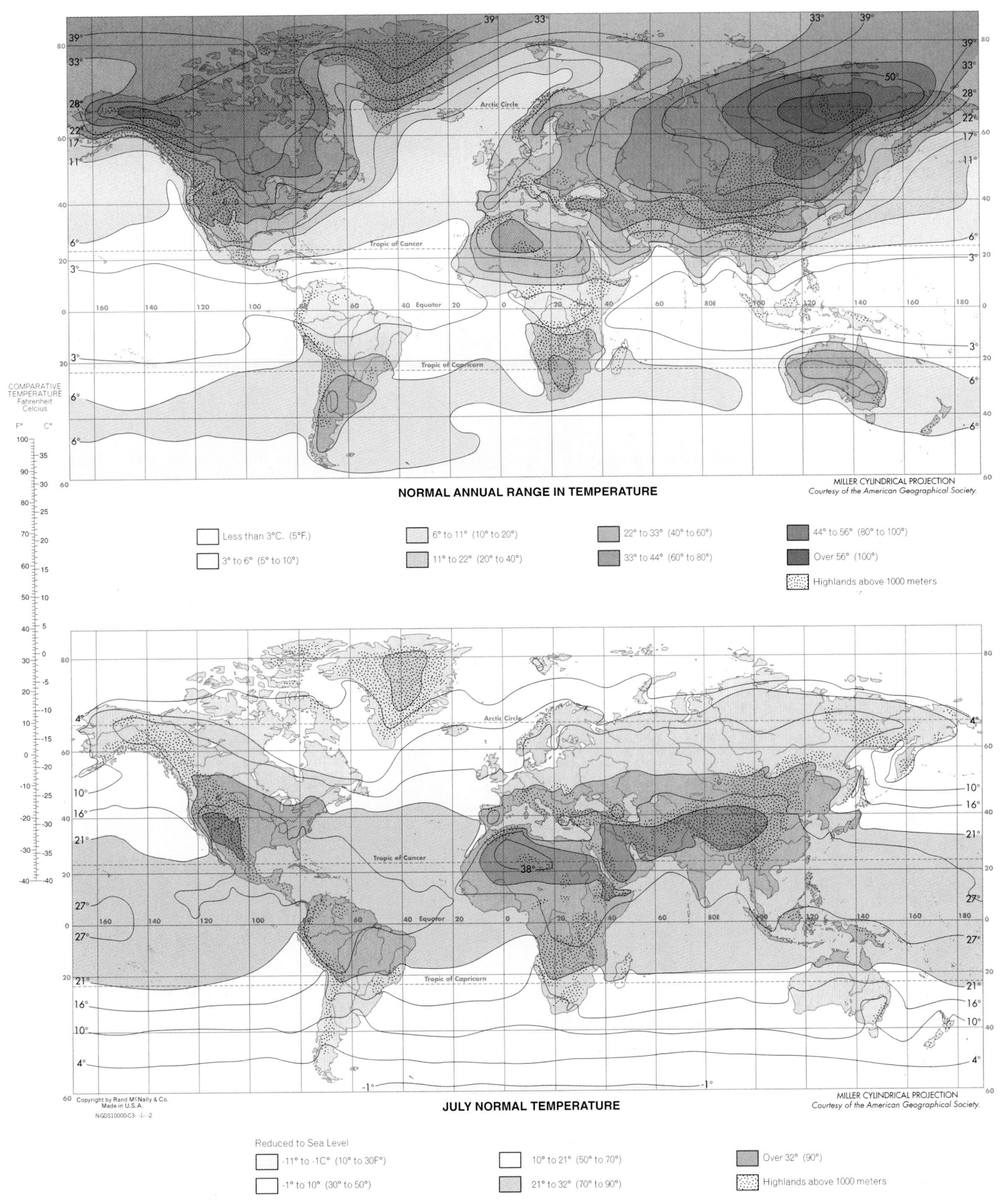

**NORMAL ANNUAL RANGE IN TEMPERATURE**

MILLER CYLINDRICAL PROJECTION
*Courtesy of the American Geographical Society.*

Less than 3°C. (5°F.)

3° to 6° (5° to 10°)

6° to 11° (10° to 20°)

11° to 22° (20° to 40°)

22° to 33° (40° to 60°)

33° to 44° (60° to 80°)

44° to 56° (80° to 100°)

Over 56° (100°)

Highlands above 1000 meters

COMPARATIVE
TEMPERATURE
Fahrenheit
Celcius

**JULY NORMAL TEMPERATURE**

MILLER CYLINDRICAL PROJECTION
*Courtesy of the American Geographical Society.*

Reduced to Sea Level

-11° to -1C° (10° to 30F°)

-1° to 10° (30° to 50°)

10° to 21° (50° to 70°)

21° to 32° (70° to 90°)

Over 32° (90°)

Highlands above 1000 meters

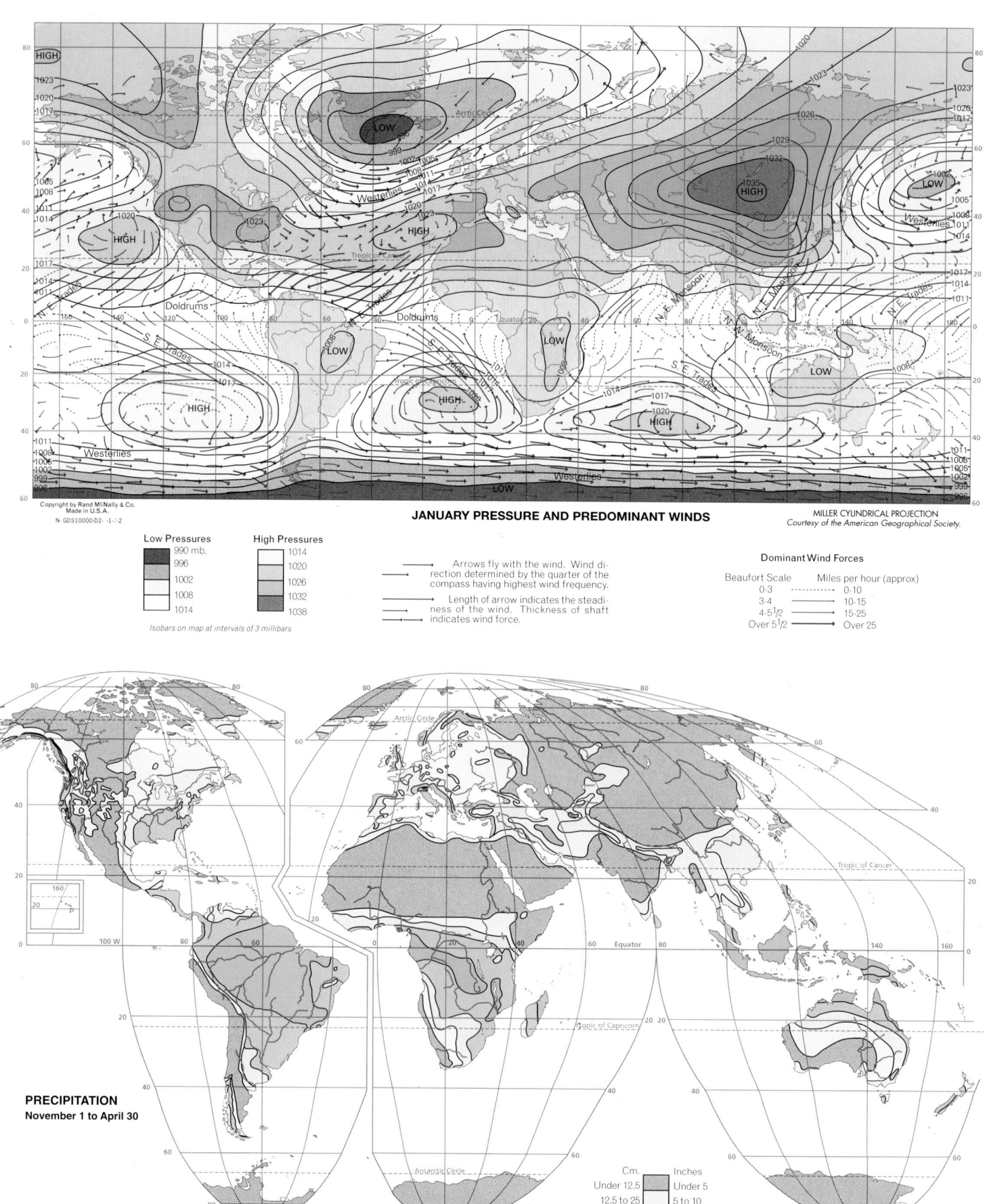

**JANUARY PRESSURE AND PREDOMINANT WINDS**

Copyright by Rand McNally & Co.
Made in U.S.A.
N- GDS10000-D2- -1-2-2

MILLER CYLINDRICAL PROJECTION
*Courtesy of the American Geographical Society.*

Low Pressures
990 mb.
996
1002
1008
1014

High Pressures
1014
1020
1026
1032
1038

*Isobars on map at intervals of 3 millibars*

Arrows fly with the wind. Wind direction determined by the quarter of the compass having highest wind frequency.

Length of arrow indicates the steadiness of the wind. Thickness of shaft indicates wind force.

Dominant Wind Forces

| Beaufort Scale | Miles per hour (approx) |
|---|---|
| 0-3 | 0-10 |
| 3-4 | 10-15 |
| 4-5½ | 15-25 |
| Over 5½ | Over 25 |

**PRECIPITATION**
**November 1 to April 30**

| Cm. | Inches |
|---|---|
| Under 12.5 | Under 5 |
| 12.5 to 25 | 5 to 10 |
| 25 to 50 | 10 to 20 |
| 50 to 100 | 20 to 40 |
| Over 100 | Over 40 |

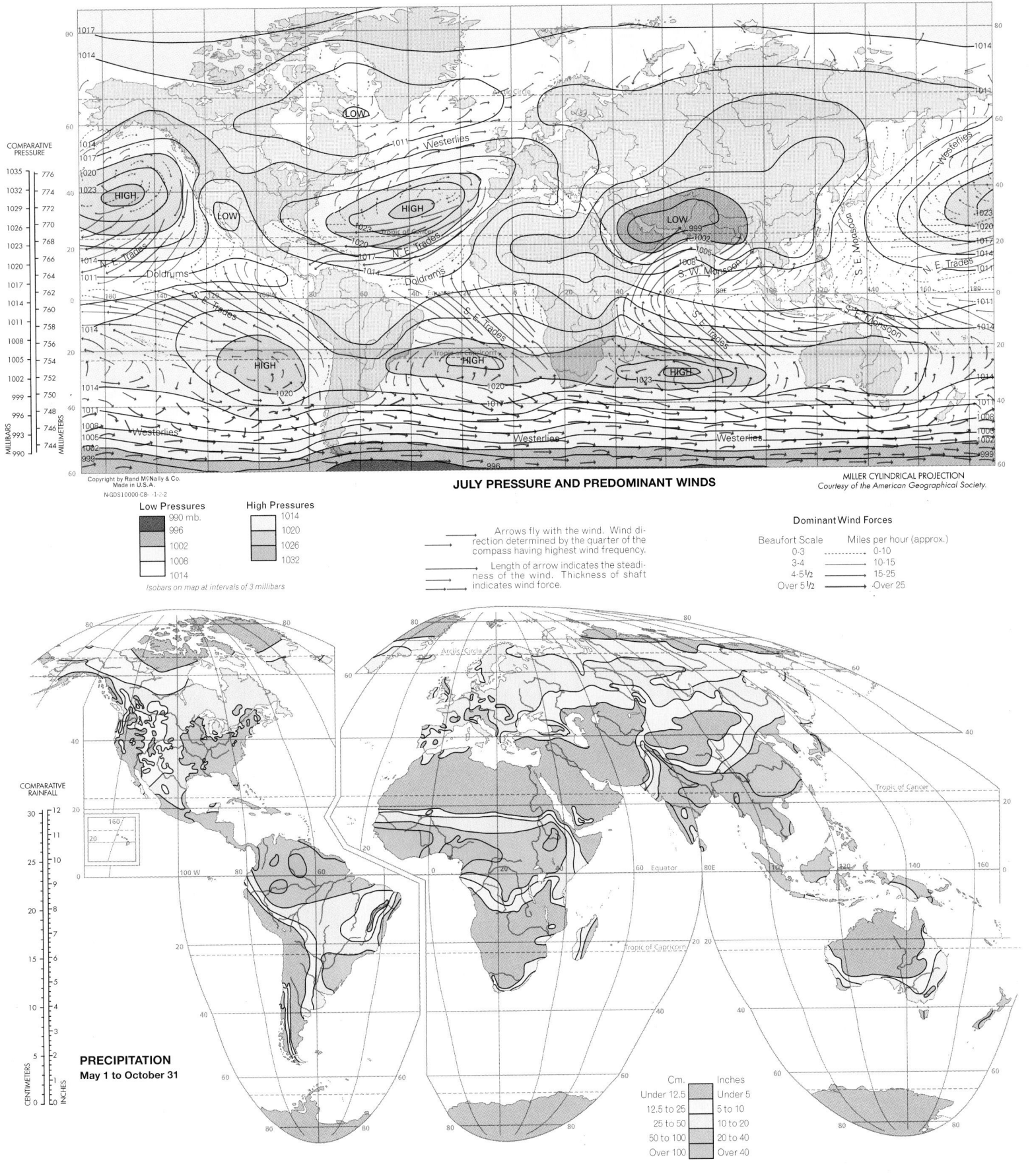

**COMPARATIVE PRESSURE**

| MILLIBARS | MILLIMETERS |
|---|---|
| 1035 | 776 |
| 1032 | 774 |
| 1029 | 772 |
| 1026 | 770 |
| 1023 | 768 |
| 1020 | 766 |
| 1017 | 764 |
| 1014 | 762 |
| 1011 | 760 |
| 1008 | 758 |
| 1005 | 756 |
| 1002 | 754 |
| 999 | 752 |
| 996 | 750 |
| 993 | 748 |
| 990 | 746 |
| | 744 |

Copyright by Rand McNally & Co.
Made in U.S.A.
N-GDS10000-C8- -1-2-2

**JULY PRESSURE AND PREDOMINANT WINDS**

MILLER CYLINDRICAL PROJECTION
*Courtesy of the American Geographical Society.*

**Low Pressures**
990 mb.
996
1002
1008
1014

**High Pressures**
1014
1020
1026
1032

*Isobars on map at intervals of 3 millibars*

Arrows fly with the wind. Wind direction determined by the quarter of the compass having highest wind frequency.

Length of arrow indicates the steadiness of the wind. Thickness of shaft indicates wind force.

**Dominant Wind Forces**

| Beaufort Scale | Miles per hour (approx.) |
|---|---|
| 0-3 | 0-10 |
| 3-4 | 10-15 |
| 4-5½ | 15-25 |
| Over 5½ | Over 25 |

**COMPARATIVE RAINFALL**

| CENTIMETERS | INCHES |
|---|---|
| 30 | 12 |
| | 11 |
| | 10 |
| 25 | |
| | 9 |
| | 8 |
| 20 | 7 |
| | 6 |
| 15 | 5 |
| | 4 |
| 10 | |
| | 3 |
| 5 | 2 |
| | 1 |
| 0 | 0 |

**PRECIPITATION**
May 1 to October 31

| Cm. | Inches |
|---|---|
| Under 12.5 | Under 5 |
| 12.5 to 25 | 5 to 10 |
| 25 to 50 | 10 to 20 |
| 50 to 100 | 20 to 40 |
| Over 100 | Over 40 |

**ANNUAL
PRECIPITATON
AND OCEAN
CURRENTS**

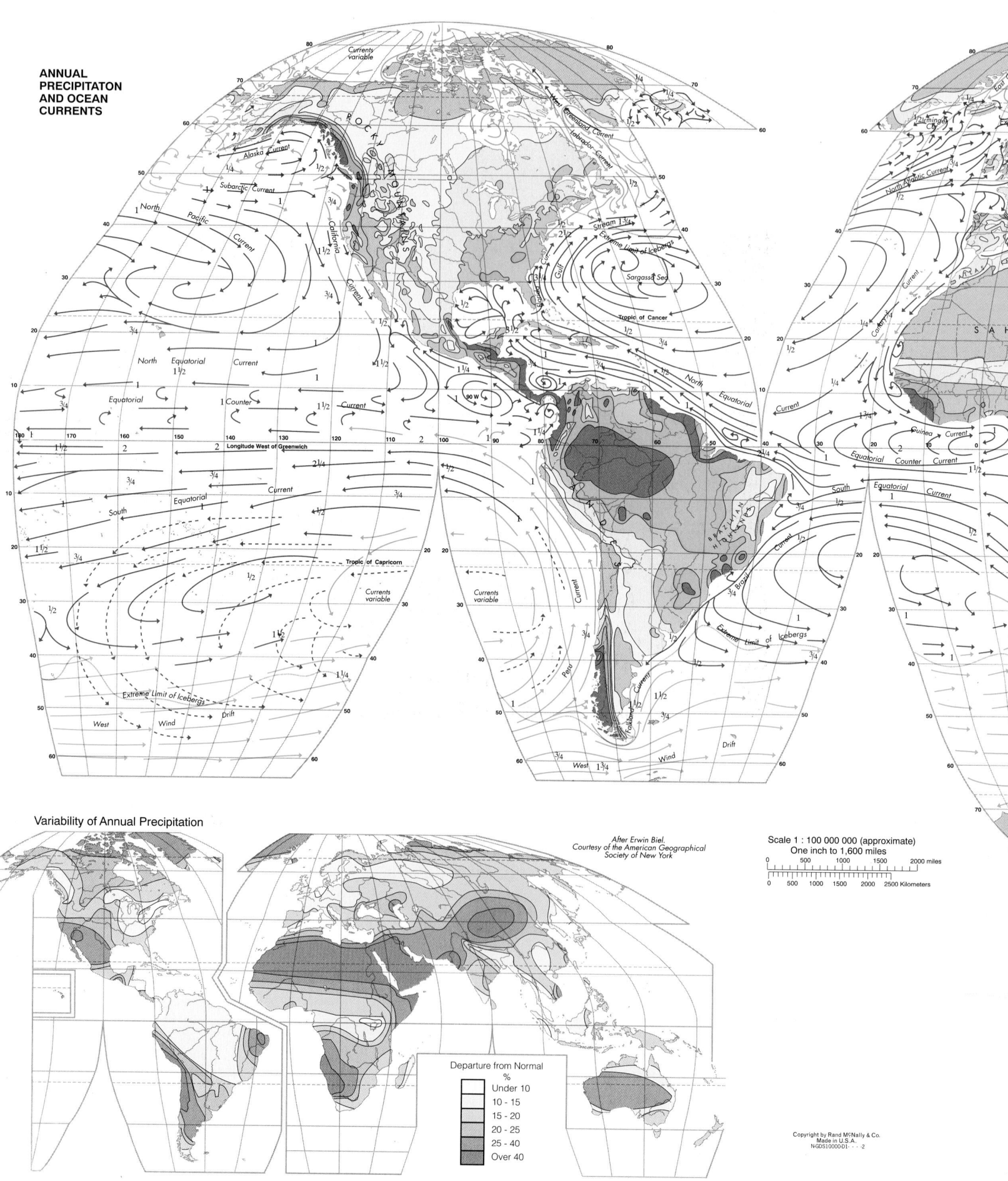

Variability of Annual Precipitation

*After Erwin Biel.
Courtesy of the American Geographical
Society of New York*

Scale 1 : 100 000 000 (approximate)
One inch to 1,600 miles

Departure from Normal
%
Under 10
10 - 15
15 - 20
20 - 25
25 - 40
Over 40

Copyright by Rand McNally & Co.
Made in U.S.A.
NGDS10000-D1- - - -2

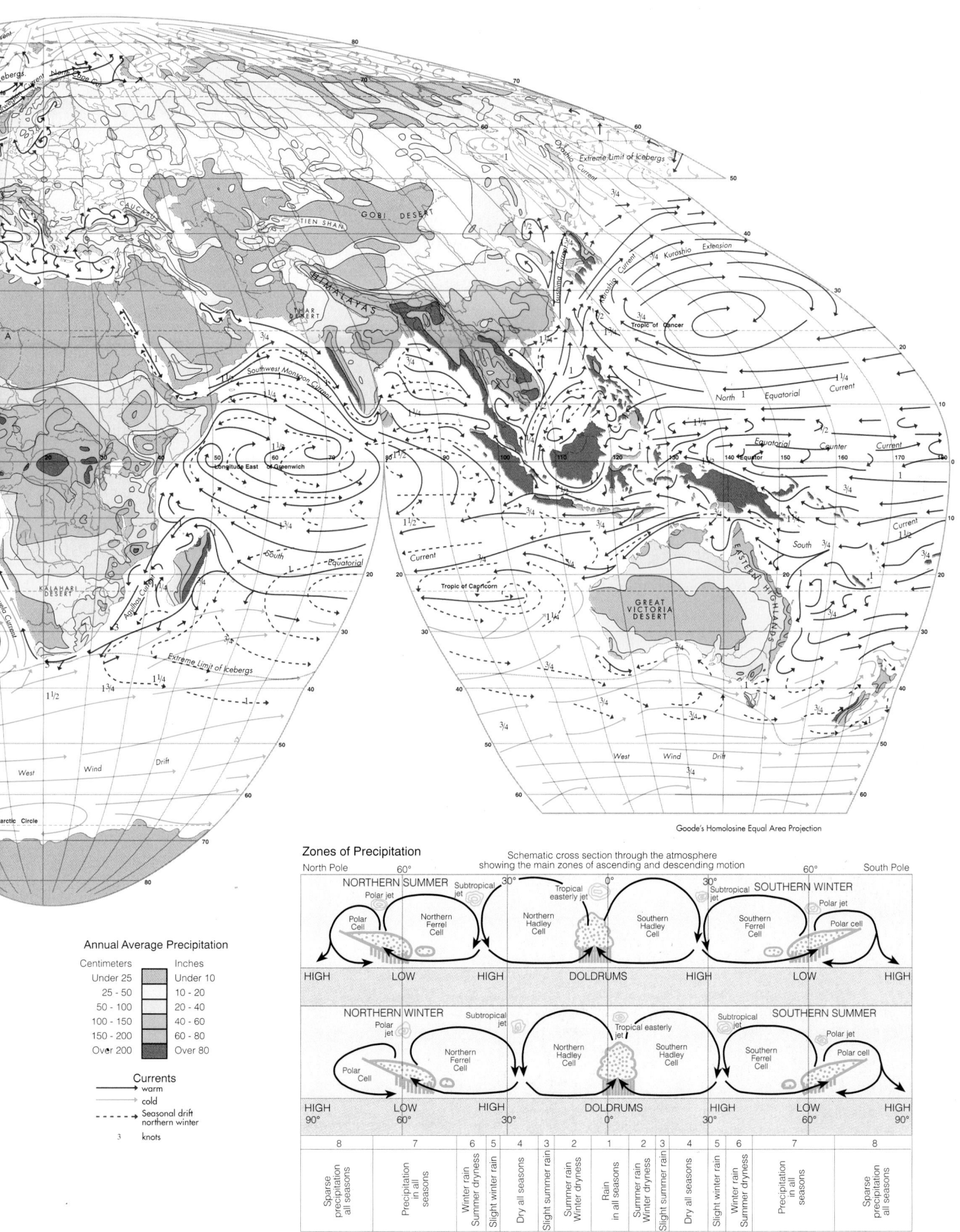

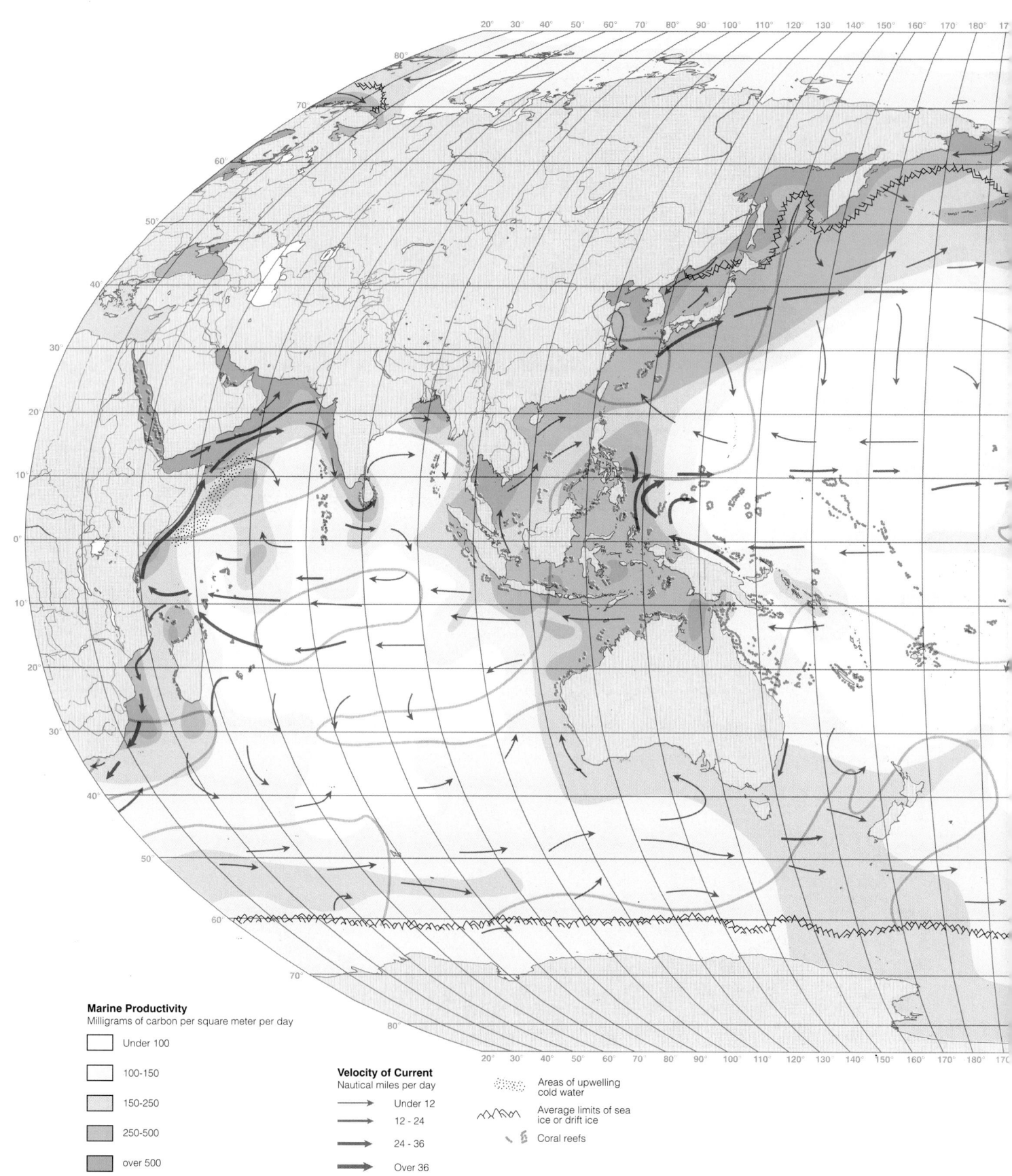

**Marine Productivity**
Milligrams of carbon per square meter per day

- Under 100
- 100-150
- 150-250
- 250-500
- over 500

**Velocity of Current**
Nautical miles per day

- → Under 12
- → 12 - 24
- → 24 - 36
- → Over 36

Areas of upwelling cold water

Average limits of sea ice or drift ice

Coral reefs

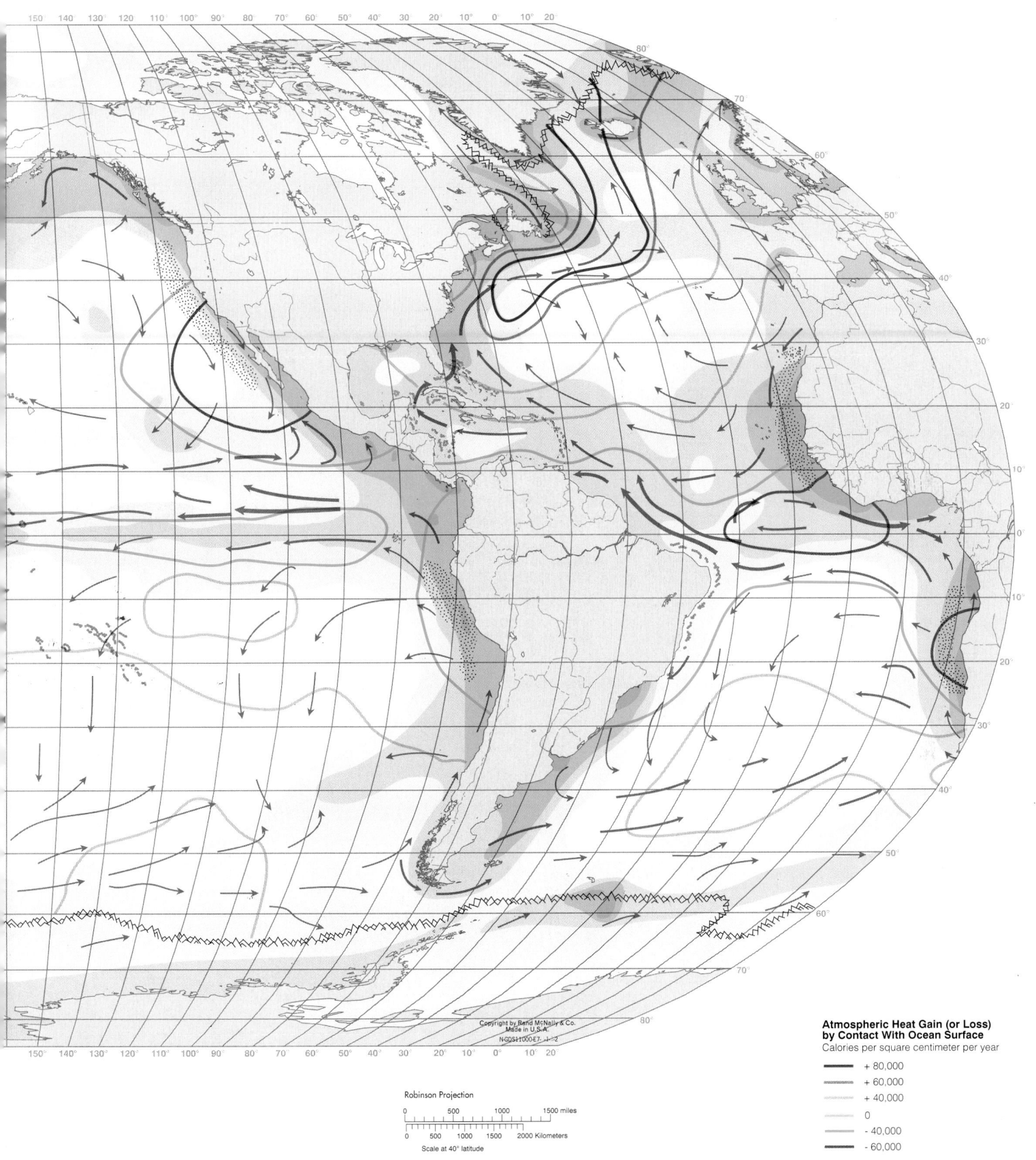

Copyright by Rand McNally & Co.
Made in U.S.A.
N GDS 1000-E7

Robinson Projection

0   500   1000   1500 miles

0   500   1000   1500   2000 Kilometers

Scale at 40° latitude

**Atmospheric Heat Gain (or Loss)
by Contact With Ocean Surface**
Calories per square centimeter per year

+ 80,000
+ 60,000
+ 40,000
0
- 40,000
- 60,000

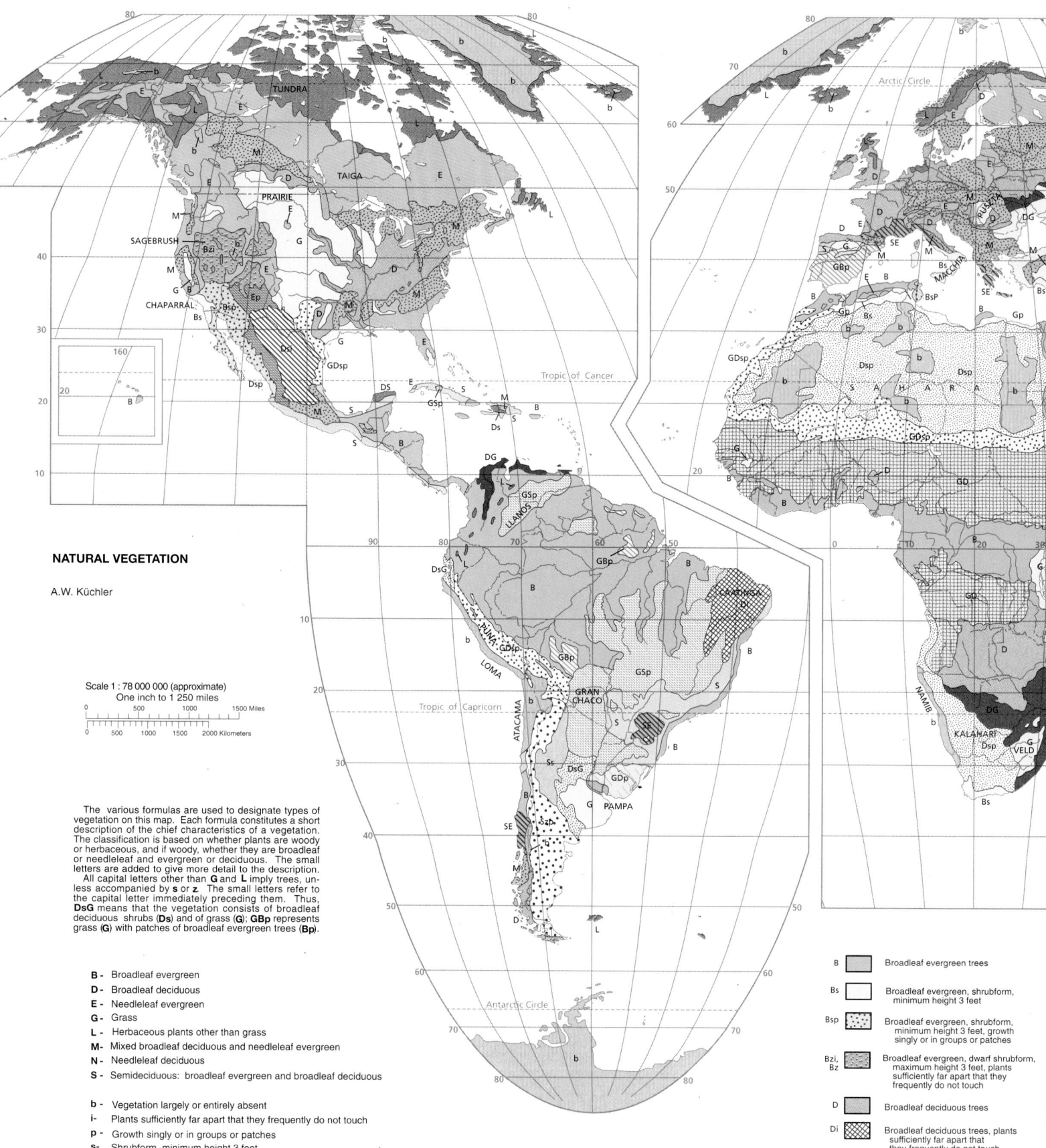

**NATURAL VEGETATION**

A.W. Küchler

Scale 1 : 78 000 000 (approximate)
One inch to 1 250 miles

0     500     1000          1500 Miles

0     500    1000    1500    2000 Kilometers

The various formulas are used to designate types of
vegetation on this map. Each formula constitutes a short
description of the chief characteristics of a vegetation.
The classification is based on whether plants are woody
or herbaceous, and if woody, whether they are broadleaf
or needleleaf and evergreen or deciduous. The small
letters are added to give more detail to the description.
All capital letters other than **G** and **L** imply trees, unless accompanied by **s** or **z**. The small letters refer to
the capital letter immediately preceding them. Thus,
**DsG** means that the vegetation consists of broadleaf
deciduous shrubs (**Ds**) and of grass (**G**); **GBp** represents
grass (**G**) with patches of broadleaf evergreen trees (**Bp**).

**B** - Broadleaf evergreen
**D** - Broadleaf deciduous
**E** - Needleleaf evergreen
**G** - Grass
**L** - Herbaceous plants other than grass
**M** - Mixed broadleaf deciduous and needleleaf evergreen
**N** - Needleleaf deciduous
**S** - Semideciduous: broadleaf evergreen and broadleaf deciduous

**b** - Vegetation largely or entirely absent
**i** - Plants sufficiently far apart that they frequently do not touch
**p** - Growth singly or in groups or patches
**s** - Shrubform, minimum height 3 feet
**z** - Dwarf shrubform, maximum height 3 feet

| | | |
|---|---|---|
| B | | Broadleaf evergreen trees |
| Bs | | Broadleaf evergreen, shrubform, minimum height 3 feet |
| Bsp | | Broadleaf evergreen, shrubform, minimum height 3 feet, growth singly or in groups or patches |
| Bzi, Bz | | Broadleaf evergreen, dwarf shrubform, maximum height 3 feet, plants sufficiently far apart that they frequently do not touch |
| D | | Broadleaf deciduous trees |
| Di | | Broadleaf deciduous trees, plants sufficiently far apart that they frequently do not touch |

Goode's Homolosine Equal Area Projection (Condensed)

| | | |
|---|---|---|
| Ds | | Broadleaf deciduous, shrubform, minimum height 3 feet |
| Dsi | | Broadleaf deciduous, shrubform, minimum height 3 feet, plants sufficiently far apart that they frequently do not touch |
| sp | | Broadleaf deciduous, shrubform, minimum height 3 feet, growth singly or in groups or patches |
| zp | | Broadleaf deciduous, dwarf shrubform, maximum height 3 feet, growth singly or in groups or patches |
| sG | | Broadleaf deciduous, shrubform, minimum height 3 feet Grass and other herbaceous plants |
| DG | | Broadleaf deciduous trees Grass and other herbaceous plants |
| Bs | | Broadleaf deciduous trees Broadleaf evergreen, shrubform, minimum height 3 feet |

| | | |
|---|---|---|
| E | | Needleleaf evergreen trees |
| Ep | | Needleleaf evergreen trees, growth singly or in groups or patches |
| G | | Grass and other herbaceous plants |
| Gp | | Grass and other herbaceous plants, growth singly or in groups or patches |
| GBp | | Grass and other herbaceous plants Broadleaf evergreen trees, growth singly or in groups or patches |
| GD | | Grass and other herbaceous plants Broadleaf deciduous trees |
| GDp | | Grass and other herbaceous plants Broadleaf deciduous trees, growth singly or in groups or patches |

| | | |
|---|---|---|
| GDsp | | Grass and other herbaceous plants Broadleaf deciduous, shrubform, minimum height 3 feet, growth singly or in groups or patches |
| GSp | | Grass and other herbaceous plants Semideciduous: broadleaf evergreen and broadleaf deciduous trees, growth singly or in groups or patches |
| ⊥ | | Herbaceous plants other than grass |
| M | | Mixed: broadleaf deciduous and needleleaf evergreen trees |
| N | | Needleleaf deciduous trees |
| ND | | Needleleaf deciduous trees Broadleaf deciduous trees |

| | | |
|---|---|---|
| S | | Semideciduous: broadleaf evergreen and broadleaf deciduous trees |
| Ss | | Semideciduous: broadleaf evergreen and broadleaf deciduous, shrubform, minimum height 3 feet |
| SsG | | Semideciduous: broadleaf evergreen and broadleaf deciduous, shrubform, minimum height 3 feet Grass and other herbaceous plants |
| Szp | | Semideciduous: broadleaf evergreen and broadleaf deciduous, dwarf shrubform, maxiumum height 3 feet, growth singly or in groups or patches |
| SE | | Semideciduous: broadleaf evergreen and broadleaf deciduous trees Needleleaf evergreen trees |
| b | | Vegetation largely or entirely absent |

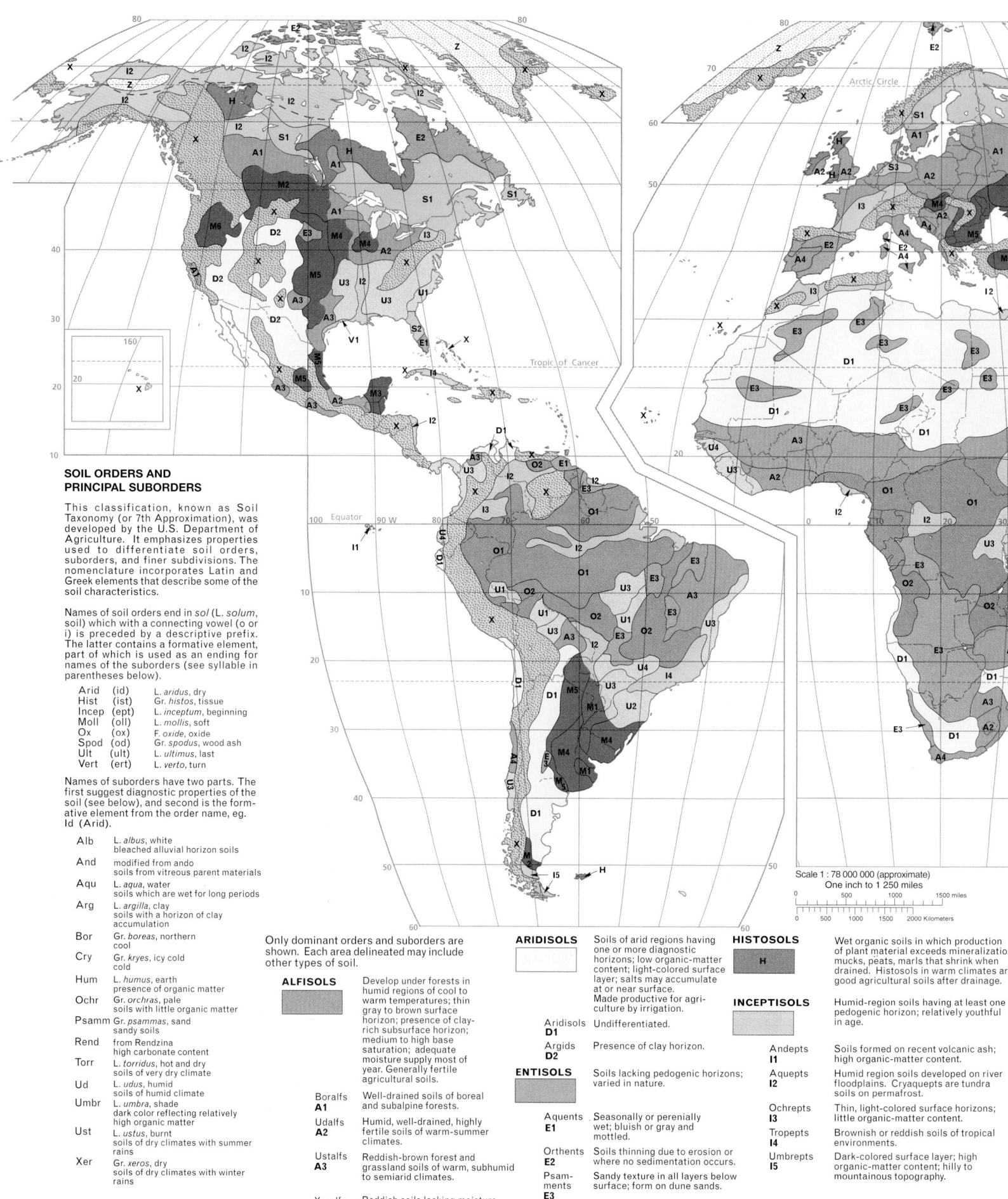

## SOIL ORDERS AND PRINCIPAL SUBORDERS

This classification, known as Soil Taxonomy (or 7th Approximation), was developed by the U.S. Department of Agriculture. It emphasizes properties used to differentiate soil orders, suborders, and finer subdivisions. The nomenclature incorporates Latin and Greek elements that describe some of the soil characteristics.

Names of soil orders end in *sol* (L. *solum*, soil) which with a connecting vowel (o or i) is preceded by a descriptive prefix. The latter contains a formative element, part of which is used as an ending for names of the suborders (see syllable in parentheses below).

| | | |
|---|---|---|
| Arid | (id) | L. *aridus*, dry |
| Hist | (ist) | Gr. *histos*, tissue |
| Incep | (ept) | L. *inceptum*, beginning |
| Moll | (oll) | L. *mollis*, soft |
| Ox | (ox) | F. *oxide*, oxide |
| Spod | (od) | Gr. *spodus*, wood ash |
| Ult | (ult) | L. *ultimus*, last |
| Vert | (ert) | L. *verto*, turn |

Names of suborders have two parts. The first suggest diagnostic properties of the soil (see below), and second is the formative element from the order name, eg. Id (Arid).

| | |
|---|---|
| Alb | L. *albus*, white; bleached alluvial horizon soils |
| And | modified from ando; soils from vitreous parent materials |
| Aqu | L. *aqua*, water; soils which are wet for long periods |
| Arg | L. *argilla*, clay; soils with a horizon of clay accumulation |
| Bor | Gr. *boreas*, northern; cool |
| Cry | Gr. *kryes*, icy cold; cold |
| Hum | L. *humus*, earth; presence of organic matter |
| Ochr | Gr. *orchras*, pale; soils with little organic matter |
| Psamm | Gr. *psammas*, sand; sandy soils |
| Rend | from Rendzina; high carbonate content |
| Torr | L. *torridus*, hot and dry; soils of very dry climate |
| Ud | L. *udus*, humid; soils of humid climate |
| Umbr | L. *umbra*, shade; dark color reflecting relatively high organic matter |
| Ust | L. *ustus*, burnt; soils of dry climates with summer rains |
| Xer | Gr. *xeros*, dry; soils of dry climates with winter rains |

Only dominant orders and suborders are shown. Each area delineated may include other types of soil.

### ALFISOLS

Develop under forests in humid regions of cool to warm temperatures; thin gray to brown surface horizon; presence of clay-rich subsurface horizon; medium to high base saturation; adequate moisture supply most of year. Generally fertile agricultural soils.

Boralfs **A1** — Well-drained soils of boreal and subalpine forests.

Udalfs **A2** — Humid, well-drained, highly fertile soils of warm-summer climates.

Ustalfs **A3** — Reddish-brown forest and grassland soils of warm, subhumid to semiarid climates.

Xeralfs **A4** — Reddish soils lacking moisture during summer in Mediterranean climate zones.

### ARIDISOLS

Soils of arid regions having one or more diagnostic horizons; low organic-matter content; light-colored surface layer; salts may accumulate at or near surface. Made productive for agriculture by irrigation.

Aridisols **D1** — Undifferentiated.

Argids **D2** — Presence of clay horizon.

### ENTISOLS

Soils lacking pedogenic horizons; varied in nature.

Aquents **E1** — Seasonally or perenially wet; bluish or gray and mottled.

Orthents **E2** — Soils thinning due to erosion or where no sedimentation occurs.

Psamments **E3** — Sandy texture in all layers below surface; form on dune sands.

### HISTOSOLS

Wet organic soils in which production of plant material exceeds mineralization; mucks, peats, marls that shrink when drained. Histosols in warm climates are good agricultural soils after drainage.

### INCEPTISOLS

Humid-region soils having at least one pedogenic horizon; relatively youthful in age.

Andepts **I1** — Soils formed on recent volcanic ash; high organic-matter content.

Aquepts **I2** — Humid region soils developed on river floodplains. Cryaquepts are tundra soils on permafrost.

Ochrepts **I3** — Thin, light-colored surface horizons; little organic-matter content.

Tropepts **I4** — Brownish or reddish soils of tropical environments.

Umbrepts **I5** — Dark-colored surface layer; high organic-matter content; hilly to mountainous topography.

Scale 1 : 78 000 000 (approximate)
One inch to 1 250 miles

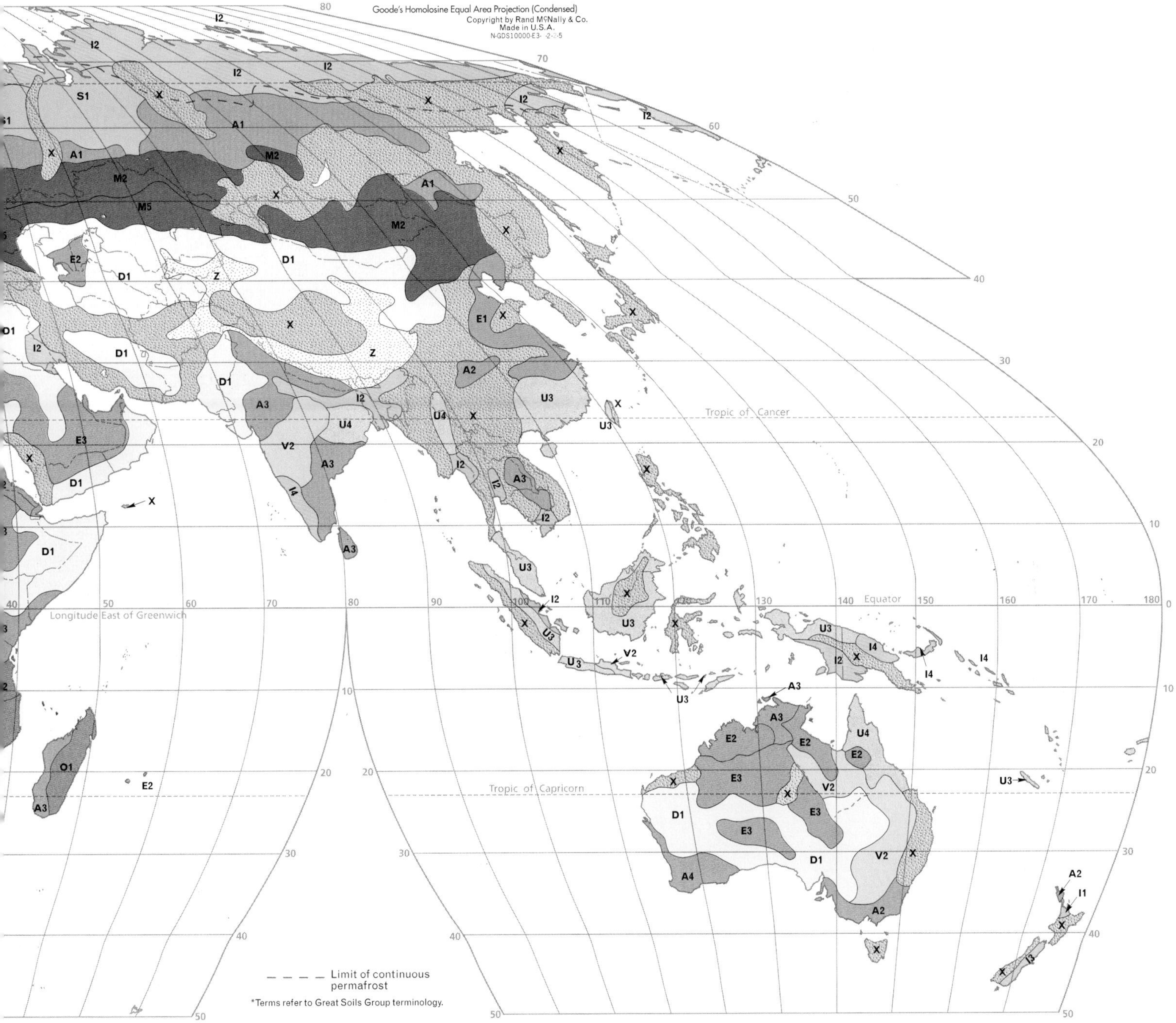

Goode's Homolosine Equal Area Projection (Condensed)
Copyright by Rand McNally & Co.
Made in U.S.A.
N-GDS10000-E3- -2- -5

Tropic of Cancer

Equator

Longitude East of Greenwich

Tropic of Capricorn

– – – – Limit of continuous permafrost

*Terms refer to Great Soils Group terminology.

| **MOLLISOLS** | Deep-profile soils with seasonal moisture deficit associated with grasslands; dark brown to black upper layer; may have subsurface horizon of calcium accumulation; high base saturation. Very productive for grain crops. |
|---|---|
| Albolls **M1** | Soils with a grayish subsurface horizon over clay layer and a fluctuating water table. |
| Borolls **M2** | Well-drained, fertile grassland soils of cool summers and cold winters. |
| Rendolls **M3** | Formed on calcareous limestones. |
| Udolls **M4** | Freely drained soils of humid regions with warm summers; excellent agricultural soils. |
| Ustolls **M5** | Fertile agricultural soils of subhumid climates. |
| Xerolls **M6** | Pronounced soil-moisture deficit during high-sun season; associated with Mediterranean climates. |

| **OXISOLS** | Deeply weathered tropical and subtropical soils of low natural fertility; low base saturation; limited ability to hold soil nutrients against leaching; presence of plinthite (laterite) layers. Generally unsuited to large-scale agricultural production. |
|---|---|
| Orthox **O1** | Hot and nearly always moist; associated with tropical rainforests. |
| Ustox **O2** | Hot to warm forest and savanna soils with a drier season of low soil-moisture availability. |

| **SPODOSOLS** | Soils of moist climates ranging from subtropical to cold conditions; include a spodic subsurface horizon incorporating active organic matter beneath a light-colored, leached, sandy horizon. Generally marginal for agriculture. |
|---|---|
| Spodosols **S1** | Undifferentiated, mostly in high latitudes. |
| Aquods **S2** | Seasonally wet developed on sandy parent material. |
| Humods **S3** | Considerable organic matter present in subsurface horizon. |
| Orthods **S4** | Subsurface accumulations of iron, aluminum, and organic matter. |

| **ULTISOLS** | Tropical and subtropical soils with a variety of soil moisture regimes; subsurface clay horizon; low base saturation; very old soils characterized by long weathering of clay minerals; low ability to hold nutrients against leaching. Often marginal for agriculture. |
|---|---|
| Aquults **U1** | Seasonally wet with mottled, gray subsurface horizon. |
| Humults **U2** | Dark soils with high organic-matter content, warm temperatures. |
| Udults **U3** | Low organic-matter content and temperate to hot conditions. |
| Ustults **U4** | Seasonally dry, warm to hot conditions. |

| **VERTISOLS** | Dark tropical and subtropical soils developed on heavy clays; deep shrinkage cracks appear during dry season which become filled with loose surface materials that absorb moisture and swell during wet season. Generally fertile and well suited to crop production. |
|---|---|
| Uderts **V1** | Generally moist with limited period for shrinkage cracks to develop. |
| Usterts **V2** | Over three months of shrinkage-crack formation. |

| **MOUNTAIN SOILS** | Soils with various moisture and temperature regimes; mainly high altitude soils forming on steep slopes; soils vary greatly within a short distance. |
|---|---|
| **X** | |
| **Z** | Areas with little or no soils. |

### APPROXIMATE CORRELATION WITH OTHER SOIL CLASSIFICATION SYSTEMS

| Soil Taxonomy | Great Soil Groups (former U.S. system) | Canadian system |
|---|---|---|
| Udalfs | Gray-brown Podzolic | Luvisolic Gray-Brown |
| Ustalfs | Reddish Chestnut; Red and Yellow Podzolic | |
| Aridisols | Desert and Reddish Desert Solonetz, Solonchak | |
| Entisols | Lithosols | Regosolic |
| Histosols | Bog | Organic |
| Inceptisol | | Brunisolic |
| Orthents | Lithosols | |
| Aquepts | Humic Gley | Gleysolic |
| Cryaquept | Tundra | Cryosolic |
| Boralfs | | Luvisolic Gray; Solonetzic |
| Borolls | Chernozem | Chernozemic, Solonetzic |
| | Chestnut Brown | |
| Rendolls | Rendzina | |
| Udolls | Prairie | |
| Ustolls | Brown | |
| Oxisols | Latosols | |
| Humod | | Humic Podzolic |
| Orthods | Podzols | Podzolic |
| Udults | Red and Yellow Podzolic Reddish Brown Lateritic | |
| Vertisols | Rendzina | |

28

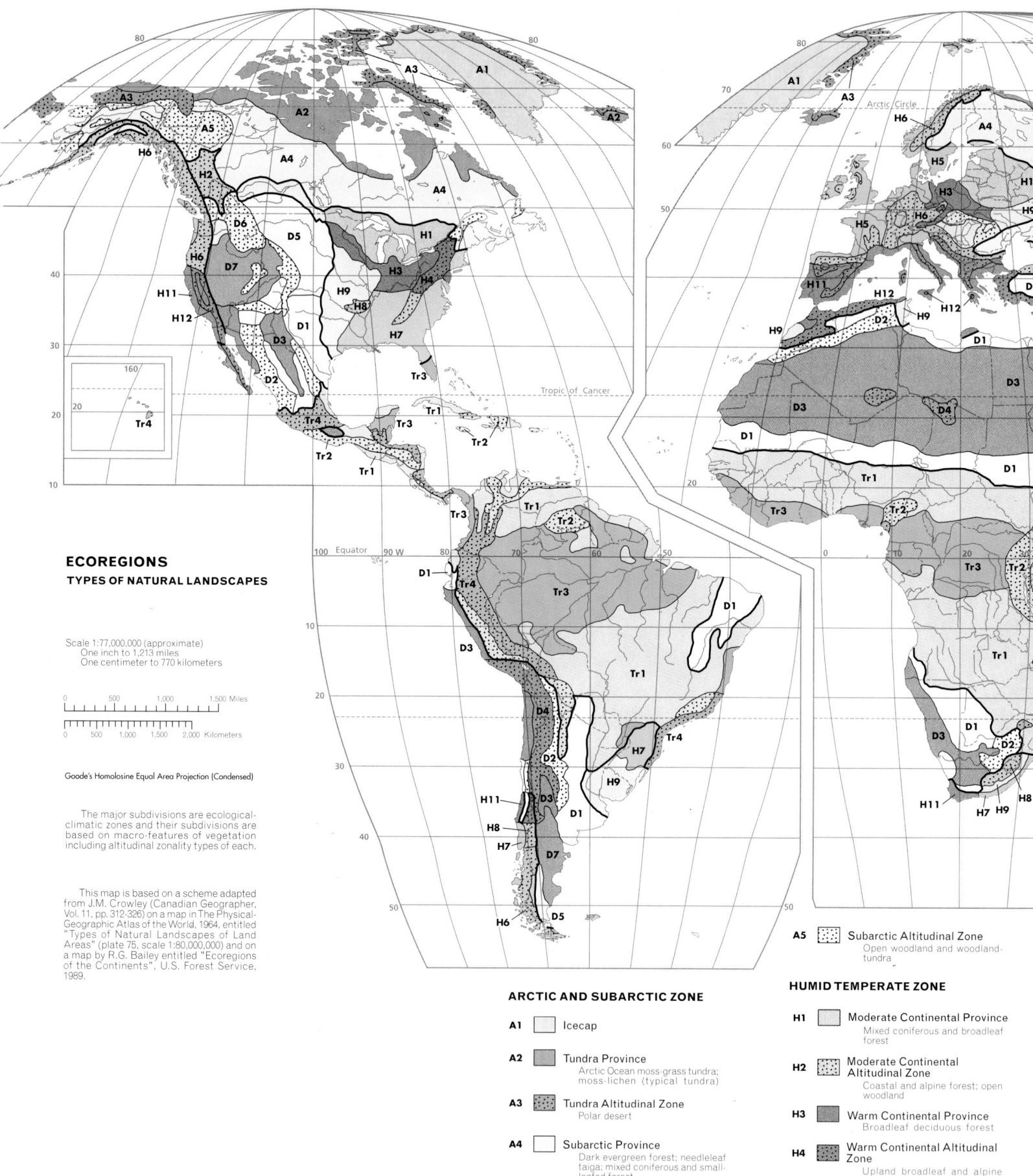

## ECOREGIONS

### TYPES OF NATURAL LANDSCAPES

Scale 1:77,000,000 (approximate)
One inch to 1,213 miles
One centimeter to 770 kilometers

```
0      500     1,000        1,500 Miles
0    500   1,000   1,500   2,000 Kilometers
```

Goode's Homolosine Equal Area Projection (Condensed)

The major subdivisions are ecological-
climatic zones and their subdivisions are
based on macro-features of vegetation
including altitudinal zonality types of each.

This map is based on a scheme adapted
from J.M. Crowley (Canadian Geographer,
Vol. 11, pp. 312-326) on a map in The Physical-
Geographic Atlas of the World, 1964, entitled
"Types of Natural Landscapes of Land
Areas" (plate 75, scale 1:80,000,000) and on
a map by R.G. Bailey entitled "Ecoregions
of the Continents", U.S. Forest Service,
1989.

**A5** ⬚ Subarctic Altitudinal Zone
Open woodland and woodland-
tundra

## ARCTIC AND SUBARCTIC ZONE

**A1** ☐ Icecap

**A2** ▨ Tundra Province
Arctic Ocean moss-grass tundra;
moss-lichen (typical tundra)

**A3** ▨ Tundra Altitudinal Zone
Polar desert

**A4** ☐ Subarctic Province
Dark evergreen forest; needleleaf
taiga; mixed coniferous and small-
leafed forest

## HUMID TEMPERATE ZONE

**H1** ▨ Moderate Continental Province
Mixed coniferous and broadleaf
forest

**H2** ⬚ Moderate Continental
Altitudinal Zone
Coastal and alpine forest; open
woodland

**H3** ▨ Warm Continental Province
Broadleaf deciduous forest

**H4** ▨ Warm Continental Altitudinal
Zone
Upland broadleaf and alpine
needleleaf forest

Copyright by Rand McNally & Co.
Made in U.S.A.
N-GDS10000-E5- -1- -5

**H5** Marine Province
Lowland, west-coastal humid forest

**H6** Marine Altitudinal Zone
Humid coastal and alpine coniferous forest

**H7** Humid Subtropical Province
Broadleaf evergreen and broadleaf deciduous forest

**H8** Humid Subtropical Altitudinal Zone
Upland, subtropical broadleaf forest

**H9** Prairie Province

**H10** Prairie Altitudinal Zone
Upland mixed prairie and woodland

**H11** Mediterranean Province
Sclerophyll woodland, shrub, and steppe

**H12** Mediterranean Altitudinal Zone
Upland shrub and steppe

**DRY AND DESERT ZONE**

**D1** Tropical/Subtropical Steppe Province
Dry steppe, desert shrub, semi-desert savanna

**D2** Tropical/Subtropical Steppe Altitudinal Zone
Upland steppe and desert shrub

**D3** Tropical/Subtropical Desert Province
Hot, lowland desert at subtropical and coastal locations

**D4** Tropical/Subtropical Desert Altitudinal Zone
Desert shrub

**D5** Temperate Steppe Province
Medium to short steppe grassland

**D6** Temperate Steppe Altitudinal Zone
Alpine meadow and coniferous woodland

**D7** Temperate Desert Province
Midlatitude rainshadow desert

**D8** Temperate Desert Altitudinal Zone
Extreme continental desert-steppe

**HUMID TROPICAL ZONE**

**Tr1** Savanna Province
Seasonally dry forest, open woodland, tall grass

**Tr2** Savanna Altitudinal Zone
Open woodland-steppe

**Tr3** Rainforest Province
Constantly humid, broadleaf evergreen forest

**Tr4** Rainforest Altitudinal Zone
Broadleaf evergreen and subtropical deciduous forest

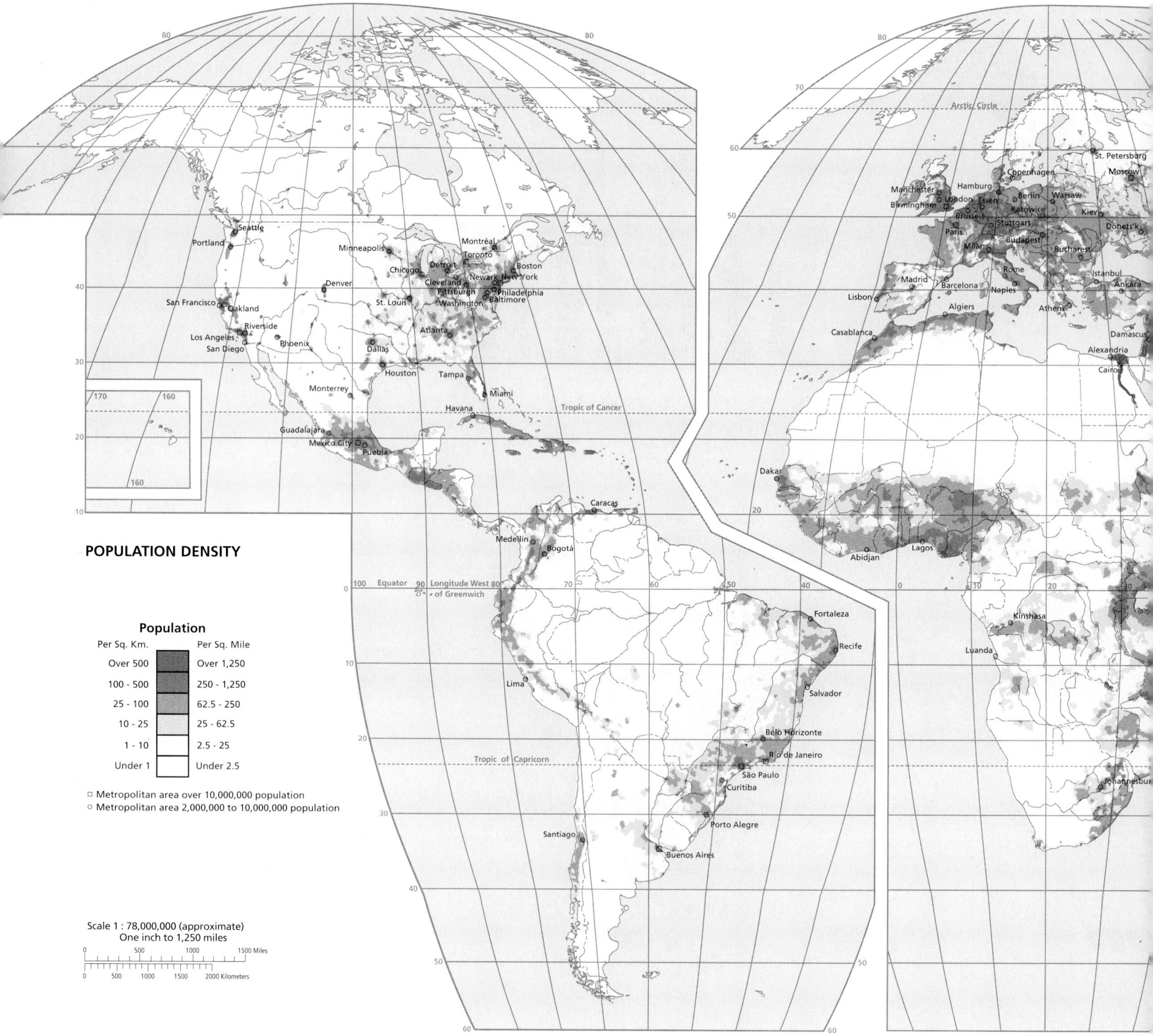

POPULATION DENSITY

**Population**

| Per Sq. Km. | Per Sq. Mile |
|---|---|
| Over 500 | Over 1,250 |
| 100 - 500 | 250 - 1,250 |
| 25 - 100 | 62.5 - 250 |
| 10 - 25 | 25 - 62.5 |
| 1 - 10 | 2.5 - 25 |
| Under 1 | Under 2.5 |

□ Metropolitan area over 10,000,000 population
○ Metropolitan area 2,000,000 to 10,000,000 population

Scale 1 : 78,000,000 (approximate)
One inch to 1,250 miles

0   500   1000   1500 Miles
0   500   1000   1500   2000 Kilometers

Largest Countries of the World 1950, 2000, 2050

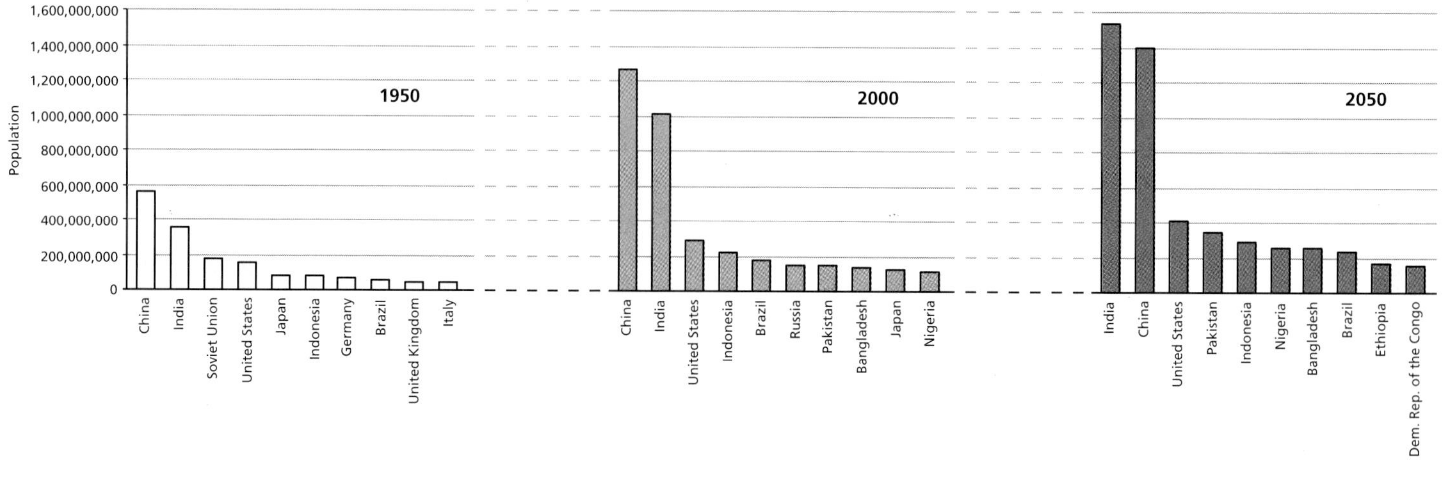

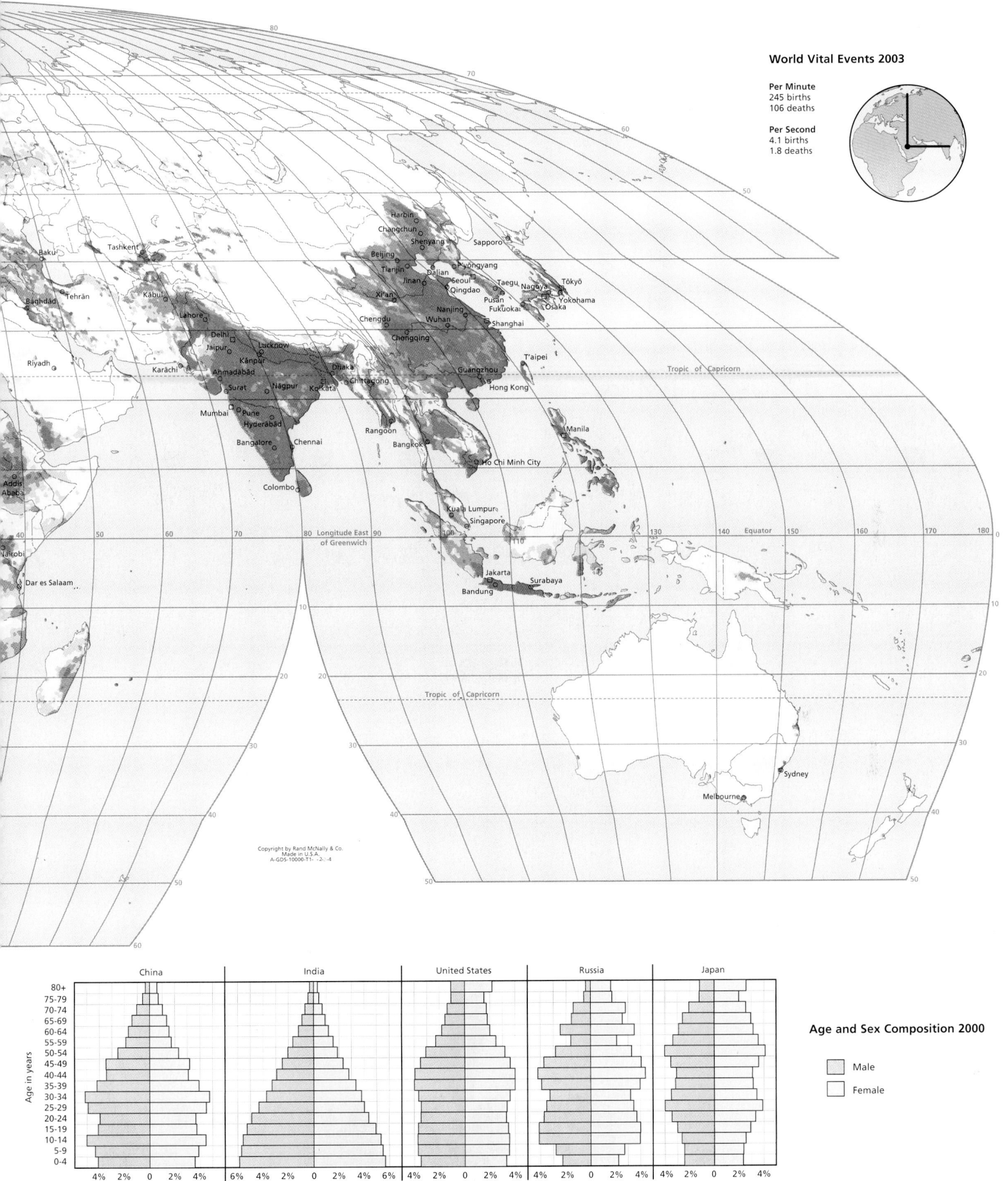

**World Vital Events 2003**

**Per Minute**
245 births
106 deaths

**Per Second**
4.1 births
1.8 deaths

**Age and Sex Composition 2000**

Male

Female

China

India

United States

Russia

Japan

Age in years

80+
75-79
70-74
65-69
60-64
55-59
50-54
45-49
40-44
35-39
30-34
25-29
20-24
15-19
10-14
5-9
0-4

Percent of total population

Copyright by Rand McNally & Co.
Made in U.S.A.
A-GDS-10000-T1- -2- -4

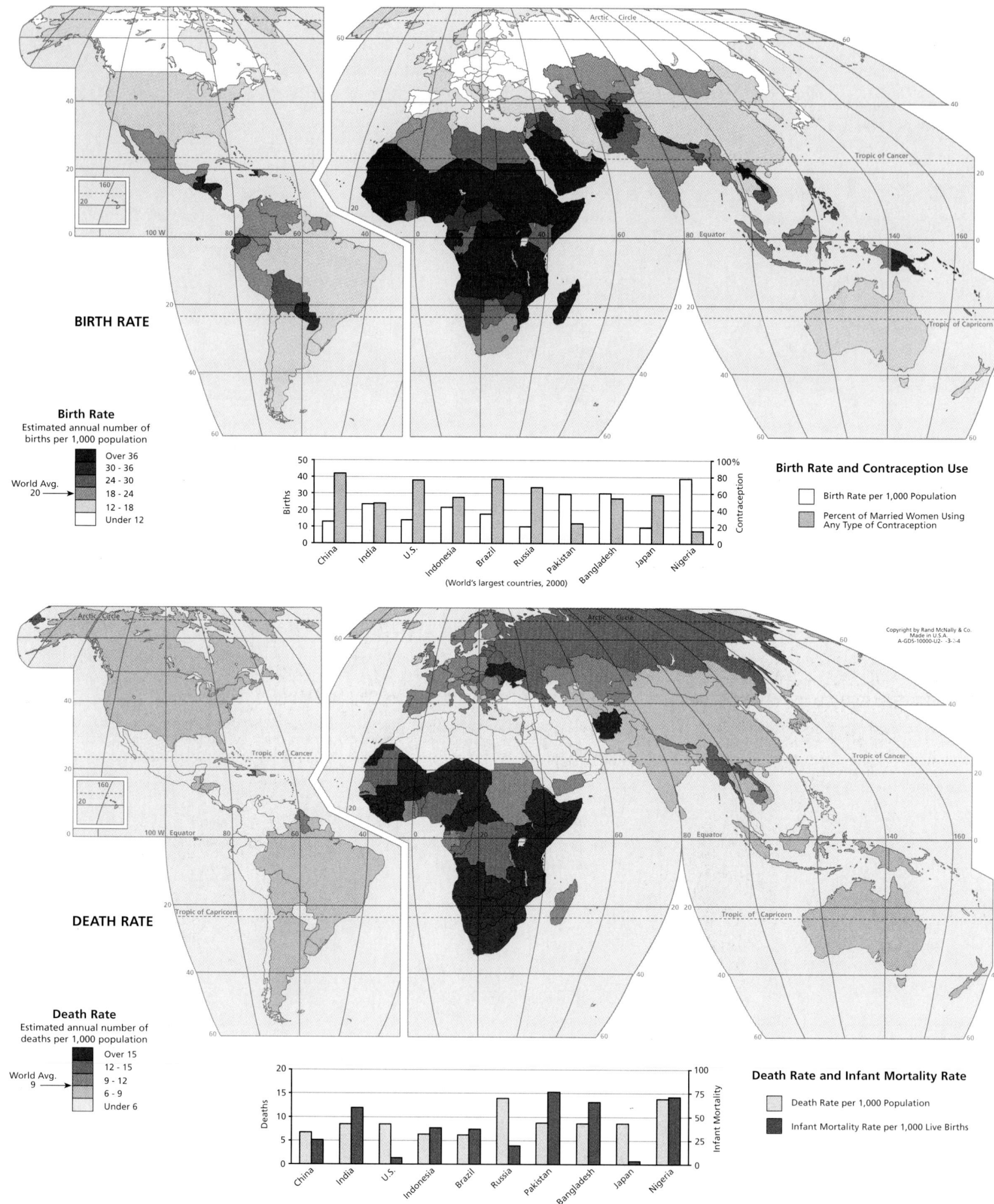

**BIRTH RATE**

**Birth Rate**
Estimated annual number of births per 1,000 population

| | |
|---|---|
| | Over 36 |
| | 30 – 36 |
| | 24 – 30 |
| | 18 – 24 |
| | 12 – 18 |
| | Under 12 |

World Avg.
20 →

**Birth Rate and Contraception Use**

☐ Birth Rate per 1,000 Population

☐ Percent of Married Women Using Any Type of Contraception

(World's largest countries, 2000)

**DEATH RATE**

**Death Rate**
Estimated annual number of deaths per 1,000 population

| | |
|---|---|
| | Over 15 |
| | 12 – 15 |
| | 9 – 12 |
| | 6 – 9 |
| | Under 6 |

World Avg.
9 →

**Death Rate and Infant Mortality Rate**

☐ Death Rate per 1,000 Population

☐ Infant Mortality Rate per 1,000 Live Births

(World's largest countries, 2000)

Copyright by Rand McNally & Co.
Made in U.S.A.
A-GDS-10000-U2- -3-:-4

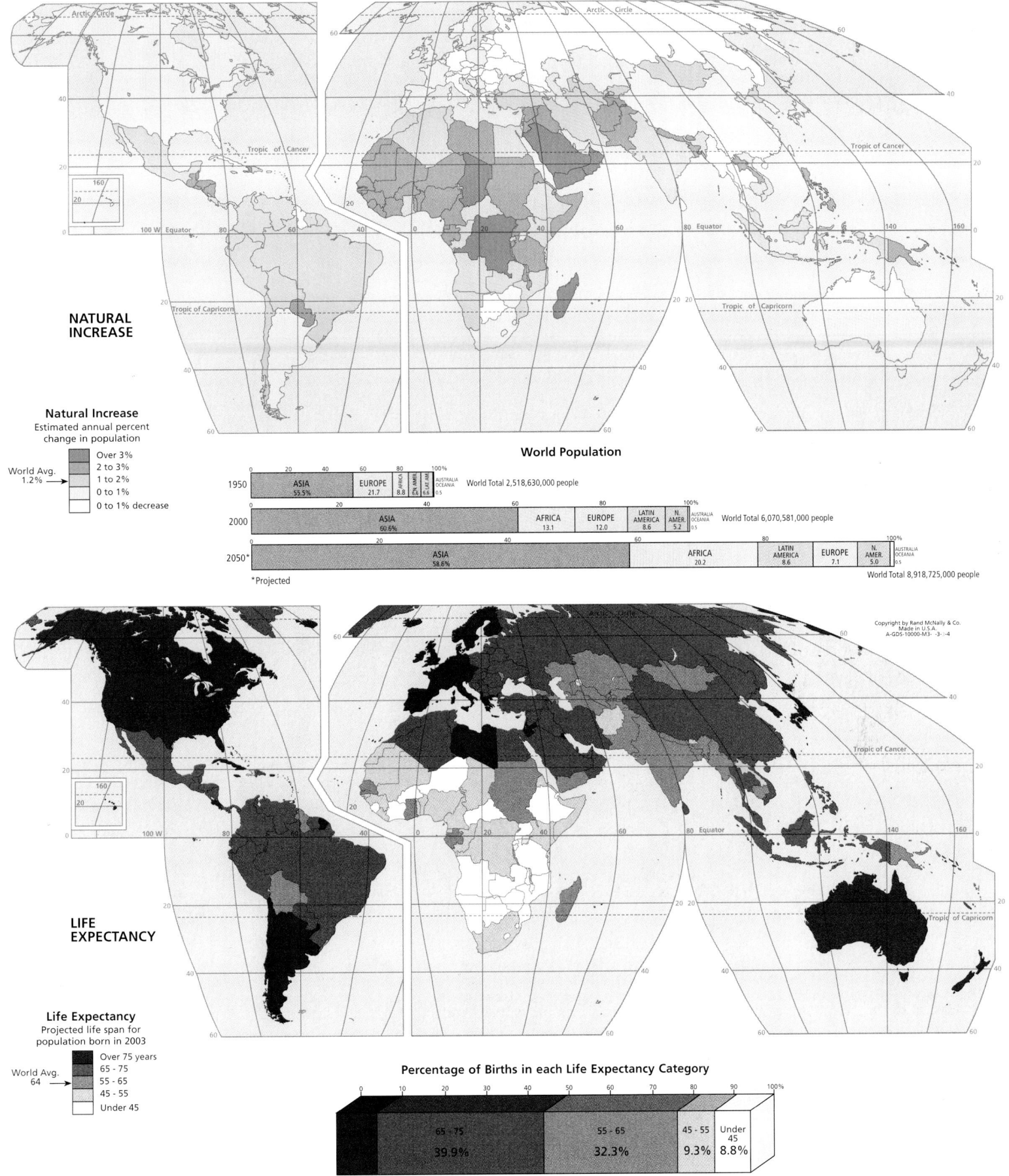

**NATURAL INCREASE**

**Natural Increase**
Estimated annual percent change in population

World Avg. 1.2% →
- Over 3%
- 2 to 3%
- 1 to 2%
- 0 to 1%
- 0 to 1% decrease

**World Population**

1950  ASIA 55.5% | EUROPE 21.7 | AFRICA 8.8 | N. AMER. 6.6 | LAT. AM. 6.6 | AUSTRALIA OCEANIA 0.5   World Total 2,518,630,000 people

2000  ASIA 60.6% | AFRICA 13.1 | EUROPE 12.0 | LATIN AMERICA 8.6 | N. AMER. 5.2 | AUSTRALIA OCEANIA 0.5   World Total 6,070,581,000 people

2050*  ASIA 58.6% | AFRICA 20.2 | LATIN AMERICA 8.6 | EUROPE 7.1 | N. AMER. 5.0 | AUSTRALIA OCEANIA 0.5   World Total 8,918,725,000 people

*Projected

Copyright by Rand McNally & Co.
Made in U.S.A.
A-GDS-10000-M3- -3- -4

**LIFE EXPECTANCY**

**Life Expectancy**
Projected life span for population born in 2003

World Avg. 64 →
- Over 75 years
- 65 - 75
- 55 - 65
- 45 - 55
- Under 45

**Percentage of Births in each Life Expectancy Category**

| | 65 - 75 39.9% | 55 - 65 32.3% | 45 - 55 9.3% | Under 45 8.8% |

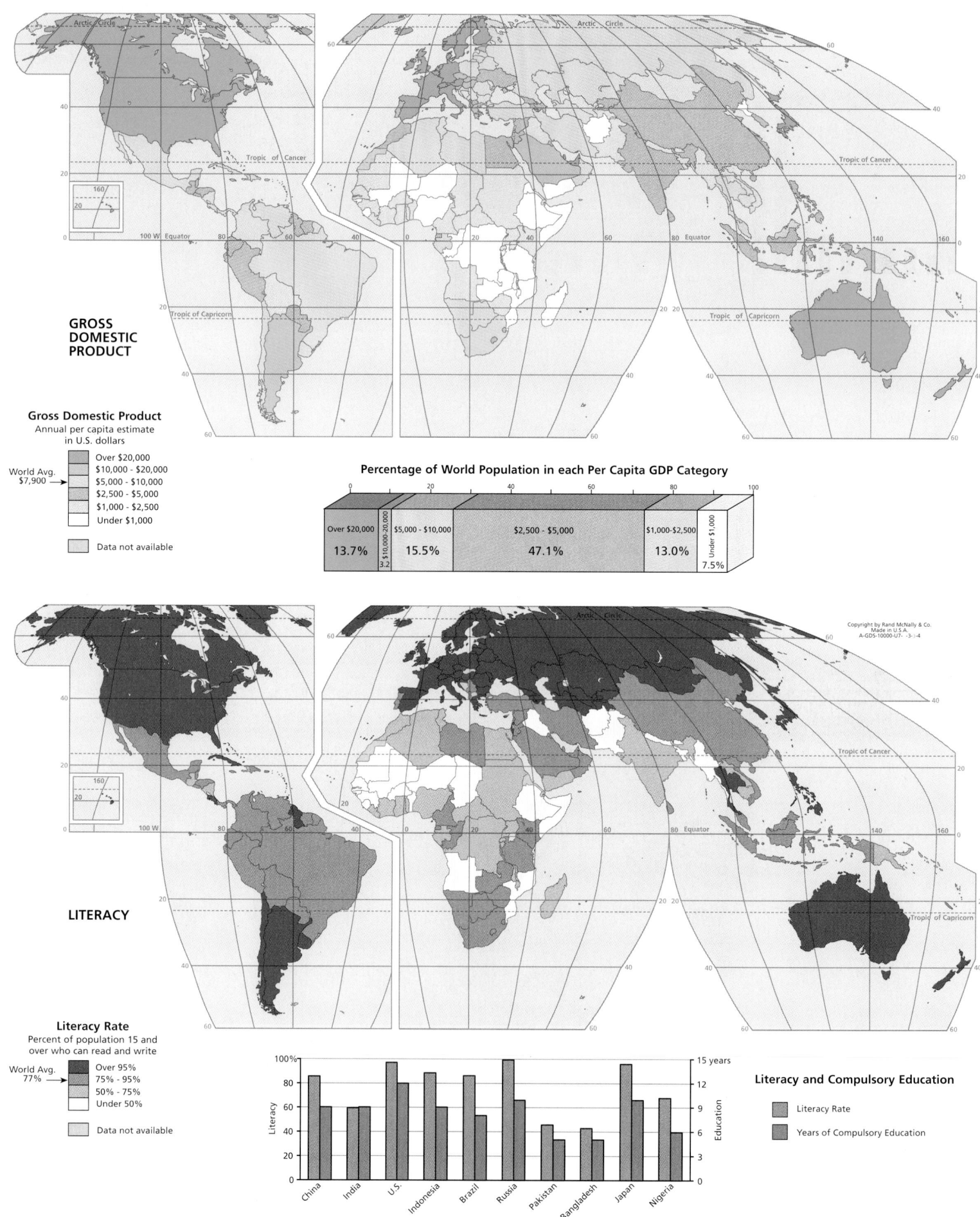

**GROSS
DOMESTIC
PRODUCT**

**Gross Domestic Product**
Annual per capita estimate
in U.S. dollars

World Avg.
$7,900

- Over $20,000
- $10,000 - $20,000
- $5,000 - $10,000
- $2,500 - $5,000
- $1,000 - $2,500
- Under $1,000

Data not available

**Percentage of World Population in each Per Capita GDP Category**

| Over $20,000 | $10,000-20,000 | $5,000 - $10,000 | $2,500 - $5,000 | $1,000-$2,500 | Under $1,000 |
|---|---|---|---|---|---|
| 13.7% | 3.2 | 15.5% | 47.1% | 13.0% | 7.5% |

Copyright by Rand McNally & Co.
Made in U.S.A.
A-GDS-10000-U7- -3-|-4

**LITERACY**

**Literacy Rate**
Percent of population 15 and
over who can read and write

World Avg.
77%

- Over 95%
- 75% - 95%
- 50% - 75%
- Under 50%

Data not available

**Literacy and Compulsory Education**

- Literacy Rate
- Years of Compulsory Education

(World's largest countries, 2000)

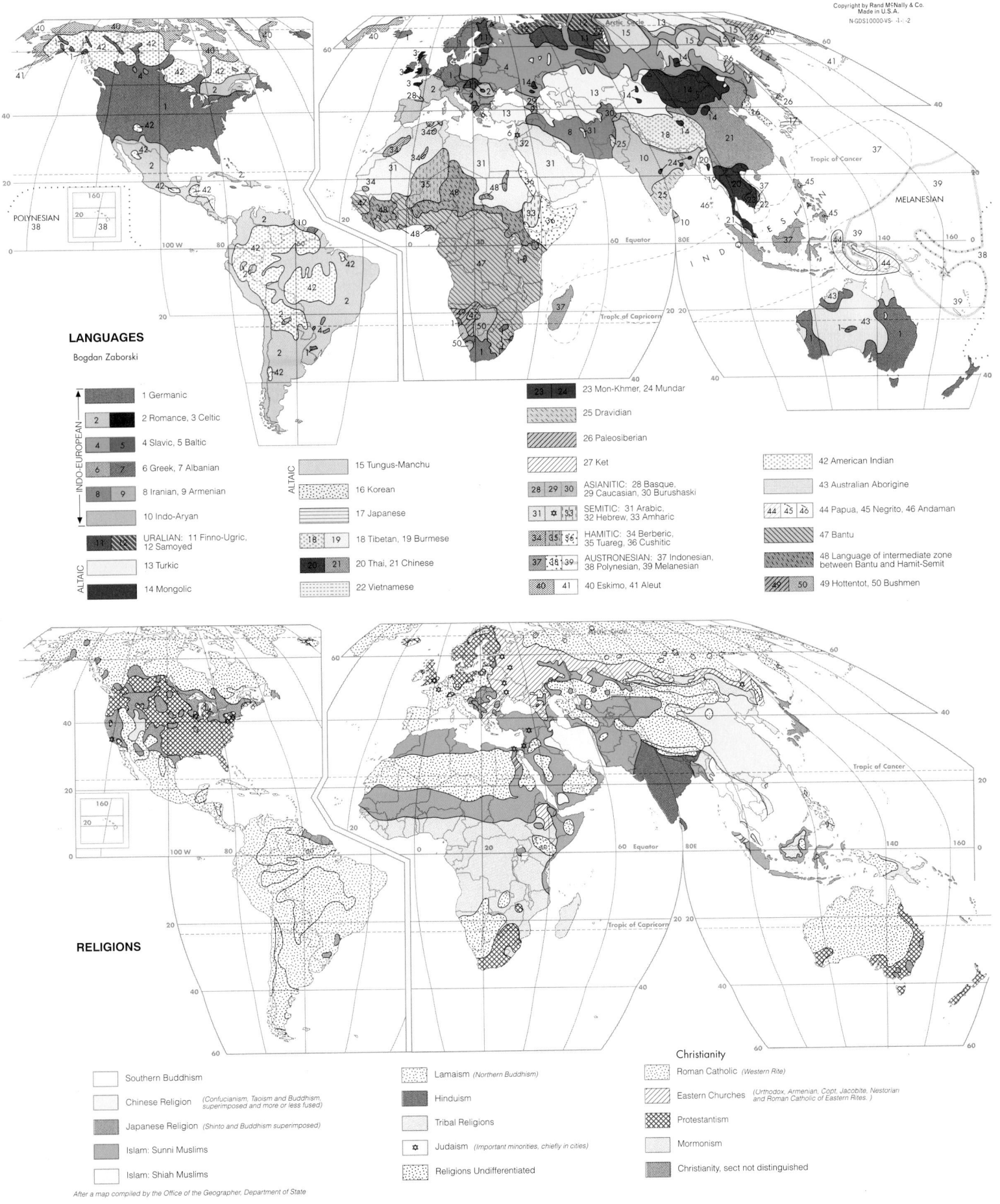

Copyright by Rand McNally & Co.
Made in U.S.A.
N-GDS10000-VS- -1- -2

**LANGUAGES**

Bogdan Zaborski

POLYNESIAN
38                38

MELANESIAN

**INDO-EUROPEAN**

1 Germanic
2 Romance, 3 Celtic
4 Slavic, 5 Baltic
6 Greek, 7 Albanian
8 Iranian, 9 Armenian
10 Indo-Aryan

URALIAN: 11 Finno-Ugric,
12 Samoyed

**ALTAIC**

13 Turkic
14 Mongolic
15 Tungus-Manchu
16 Korean
17 Japanese
18 Tibetan, 19 Burmese
20 Thai, 21 Chinese
22 Vietnamese

23 Mon-Khmer, 24 Mundar
25 Dravidian
26 Paleosiberian
27 Ket
ASIANITIC: 28 Basque,
29 Caucasian, 30 Burushaski
SEMITIC: 31 Arabic,
32 Hebrew, 33 Amharic
HAMITIC: 34 Berberic,
35 Tuareg, 36 Cushitic
AUSTRONESIAN: 37 Indonesian,
38 Polynesian, 39 Melanesian
40 Eskimo, 41 Aleut

42 American Indian
43 Australian Aborigine
44 Papua, 45 Negrito, 46 Andaman
47 Bantu
48 Language of intermediate zone
between Bantu and Hamit-Semit
49 Hottentot, 50 Bushmen

**RELIGIONS**

After a map compiled by the Office of the Geographer, Department of State

Southern Buddhism

Chinese Religion (Confucianism, Taoism and Buddhism,
superimposed and more or less fused)

Japanese Religion (Shinto and Buddhism superimposed)

Islam: Sunni Muslims

Islam: Shiah Muslims

Lamaism (Northern Buddhism)

Hinduism

Tribal Religions

Judaism (Important minorities, chiefly in cities)

Religions Undifferentiated

**Christianity**

Roman Catholic (Western Rite)

Eastern Churches (Orthodox, Armenian, Copt, Jacobite, Nestorian
and Roman Catholic of Eastern Rites.)

Protestantism

Mormonism

Christianity, sect not distinguished

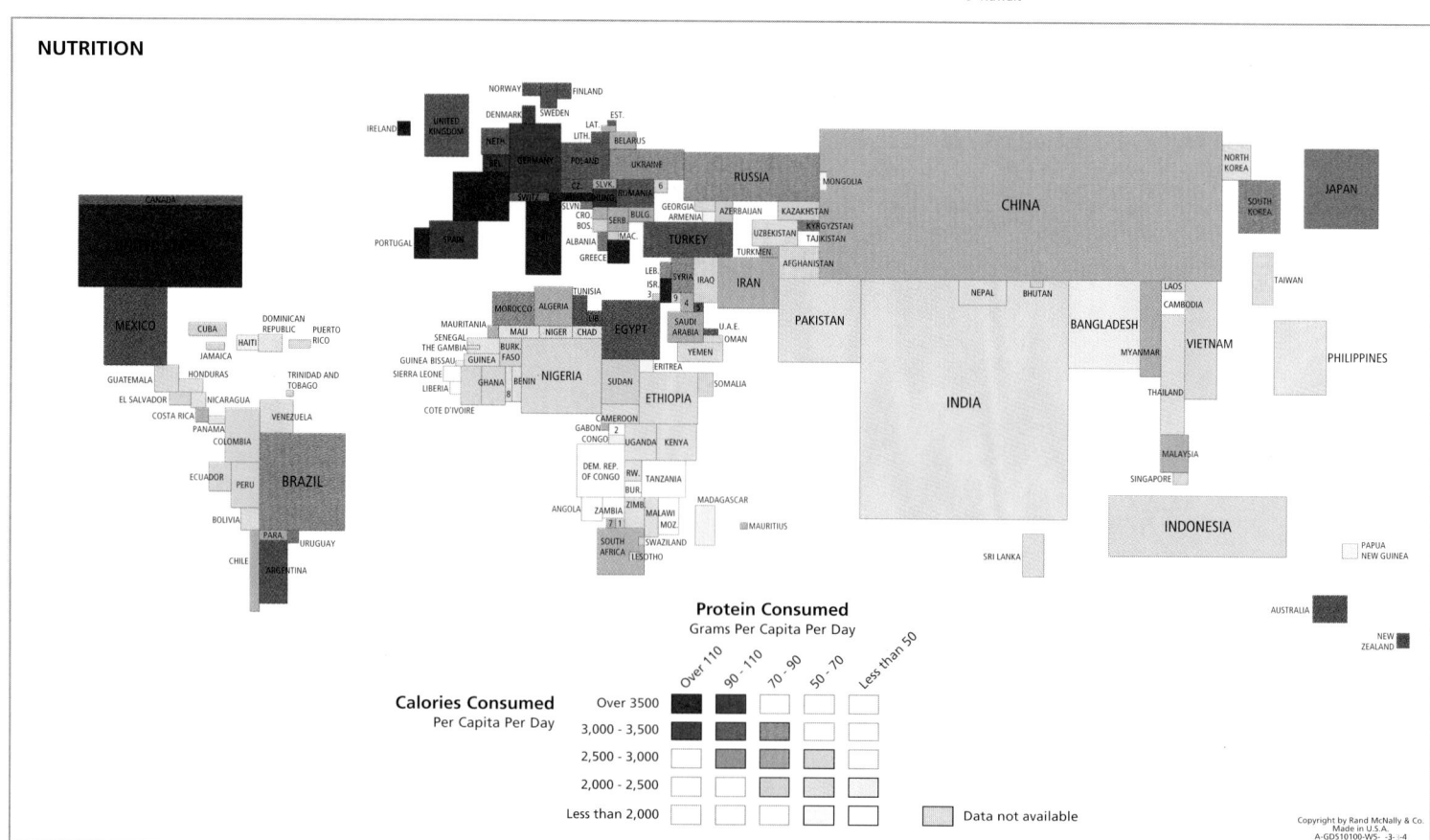

## URBANIZED POPULATION

**Percent of Population Living in Urban Areas - 2001**

- Over 80%
- 60 - 80%
- 40 - 60%
- 20 - 40%
- Under 20%

Copyright by Rand McNally & Co.
Made in U.S.A.

Size of each country is proportional to its population.

☐ = 25,000,000 people

Countries with populations under 1,000,000 are not shown.

1 Botswana
2 Central African Republic
3 Gaza Strip
4 Jordan
5 Kuwait
6 Moldova
7 Namibia
8 Togo
9 West Bank

## NUTRITION

**Protein Consumed**
Grams Per Capita Per Day

| Calories Consumed Per Capita Per Day | Over 110 | 90 - 110 | 70 - 90 | 50 - 70 | Less than 50 |
|---|---|---|---|---|---|
| Over 3500 | | | | | |
| 3,000 - 3,500 | | | | | |
| 2,500 - 3,000 | | | | | |
| 2,000 - 2,500 | | | | | |
| Less than 2,000 | | | | | |

☐ Data not available

Copyright by Rand McNally & Co.
Made in U.S.A.
A-GDS10100-W5- -3- -4

**PHYSICIANS**

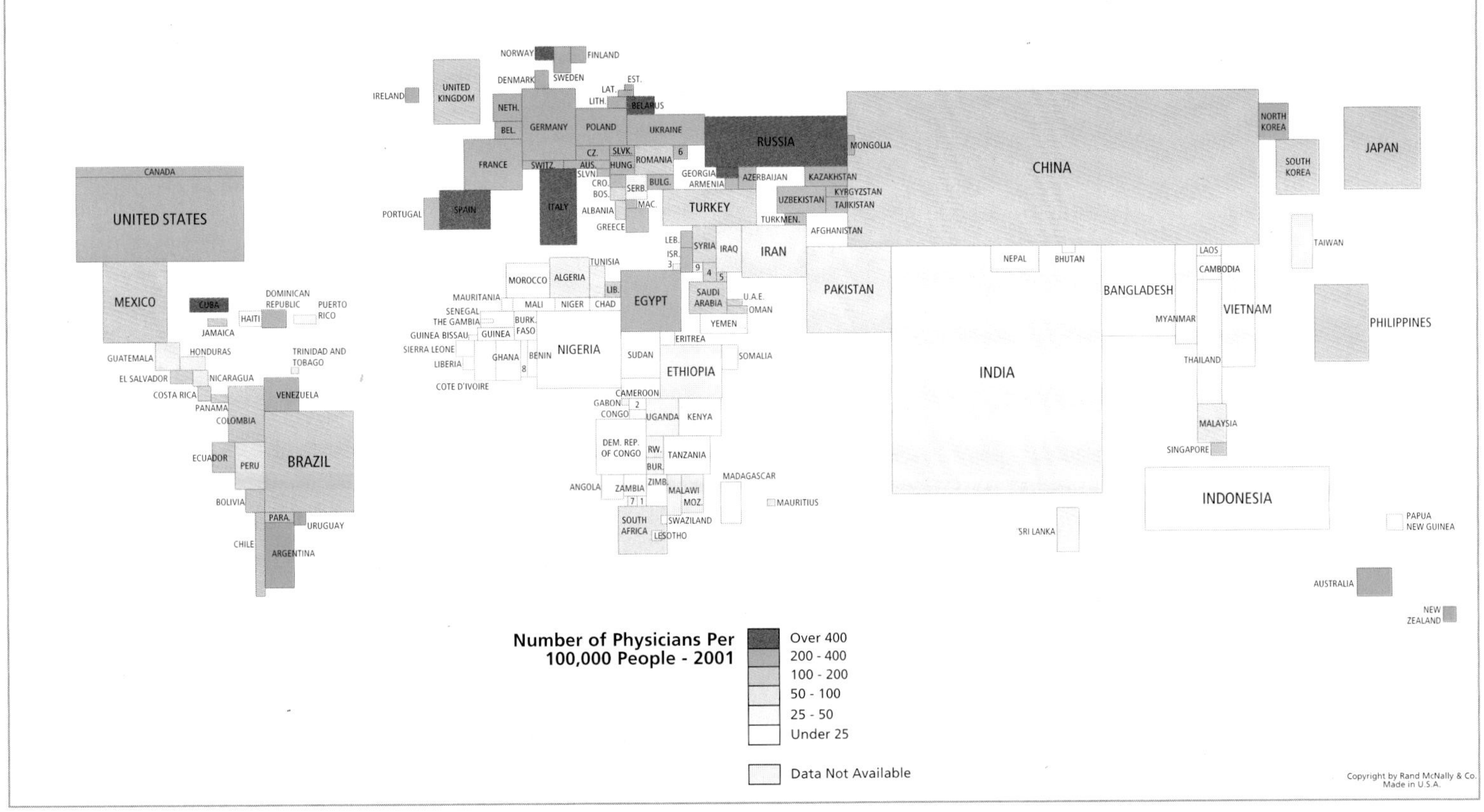

NORWAY FINLAND
IRELAND UNITED KINGDOM
DENMARK SWEDEN EST.
NETH. LAT.
BEL. LITH.
GERMANY POLAND BELARUS
CANADA FRANCE CZ. SLVK. UKRAINE RUSSIA MONGOLIA NORTH KOREA JAPAN
SWITZ. AUS. HUNG. ROMANIA 6
UNITED STATES SLVN. CRO. SERB. BULG. GEORGIA AZERBAIJAN KAZAKHSTAN CHINA SOUTH KOREA
PORTUGAL SPAIN ITALY BOS. MAC. ARMENIA KYRGYZSTAN
ALBANIA TURKEY TURKMEN. TAJIKISTAN TAIWAN
GREECE UZBEKISTAN
LEB. SYRIA IRAQ IRAN AFGHANISTAN LAOS
MEXICO CUBA DOMINICAN REPUBLIC PUERTO RICO MOROCCO TUNISIA ISR. 9 4 5 NEPAL BHUTAN CAMBODIA
HAITI ALGERIA SAUDI ARABIA U.A.E. PAKISTAN BANGLADESH VIETNAM
JAMAICA MAURITANIA MALI NIGER CHAD EGYPT OMAN MYANMAR PHILIPPINES
GUATEMALA HONDURAS TRINIDAD AND TOBAGO SENEGAL BURK. YEMEN THAILAND
EL SALVADOR NICARAGUA THE GAMBIA FASO ERITREA
COSTA RICA PANAMA VENEZUELA GUINEA BISSAU GUINEA NIGERIA SUDAN
COLOMBIA SIERRA LEONE GHANA BENIN SOMALIA INDIA
LIBERIA 8 ETHIOPIA
ECUADOR PERU BRAZIL COTE D'IVOIRE CAMEROON MALAYSIA
GABON UGANDA KENYA SINGAPORE
BOLIVIA CONGO 7 1 RW. BUR. TANZANIA INDONESIA
PARA. DEM. REP. OF CONGO ZIMB. MALAWI MAURITIUS PAPUA NEW GUINEA
URUGUAY ANGOLA ZAMBIA MOZ.
CHILE SOUTH AFRICA SWAZILAND MADAGASCAR
ARGENTINA LESOTHO AUSTRALIA
NEW ZEALAND

**Number of Physicians Per 100,000 People - 2001**

- Over 400
- 200 - 400
- 100 - 200
- 50 - 100
- 25 - 50
- Under 25

☐ Data Not Available

Copyright by Rand McNally & Co.
Made in U.S.A.

Size of each country is proportional to its population.

☐ = 25,000,000 people

Countries with populations under 1,000,000 are not shown.

| 1 Botswana | 6 Moldova |
| 2 Central African Republic | 7 Namibia |
| 3 Gaza Strip | 8 Togo |
| 4 Jordan | 9 West Bank |
| 5 Kuwait | |

**HIV INFECTION**

NORWAY FINLAND
IRELAND UNITED KINGDOM
DENMARK SWEDEN EST.
NETH. LAT.
BEL. LITH.
GERMANY POLAND BELARUS
CANADA FRANCE CZ. SLVK. UKRAINE RUSSIA MONGOLIA NORTH KOREA JAPAN
SWITZ. AUS. HUNG. ROMANIA 6
UNITED STATES SLVN. CRO. SERB. BULG. GEORGIA AZERBAIJAN KAZAKHSTAN CHINA SOUTH KOREA
PORTUGAL SPAIN ITALY BOS. MAC. ARMENIA KYRGYZSTAN
ALBANIA TURKEY TURKMEN. TAJIKISTAN TAIWAN
GREECE UZBEKISTAN
LEB. SYRIA IRAQ IRAN AFGHANISTAN LAOS
MEXICO CUBA DOMINICAN REPUBLIC PUERTO RICO MOROCCO TUNISIA ISR. 9 4 5 NEPAL BHUTAN CAMBODIA
HAITI ALGERIA SAUDI ARABIA U.A.E. PAKISTAN BANGLADESH VIETNAM
JAMAICA MAURITANIA MALI NIGER CHAD EGYPT OMAN MYANMAR PHILIPPINES
GUATEMALA HONDURAS TRINIDAD AND TOBAGO SENEGAL BURK. YEMEN THAILAND
EL SALVADOR NICARAGUA THE GAMBIA FASO ERITREA
COSTA RICA PANAMA VENEZUELA GUINEA BISSAU GUINEA NIGERIA SUDAN
COLOMBIA SIERRA LEONE GHANA BENIN SOMALIA INDIA
LIBERIA ETHIOPIA
ECUADOR PERU BRAZIL COTE D'IVOIRE CAMEROON MALAYSIA
GABON UGANDA SINGAPORE
BOLIVIA CONGO TANZANIA INDONESIA
PARA. DEM. REP. OF CONGO MAURITIUS PAPUA NEW GUINEA
URUGUAY ANGOLA
CHILE SWAZILAND MADAGASCAR
ARGENTINA LESOTHO SRI LANKA AUSTRALIA
NEW ZEALAND

**Percent of Adult Population Diagnosed HIV-Positive**

- Over 10%
- 5 - 10%
- 1 - 5%
- 0.5 - 1%
- 0.1 - 0.5%
- Under 0.1%

☐ Data Not Available

Copyright by Rand McNally & Co.
Made in U.S.A.
A-GDS10100-W3- -3- -4

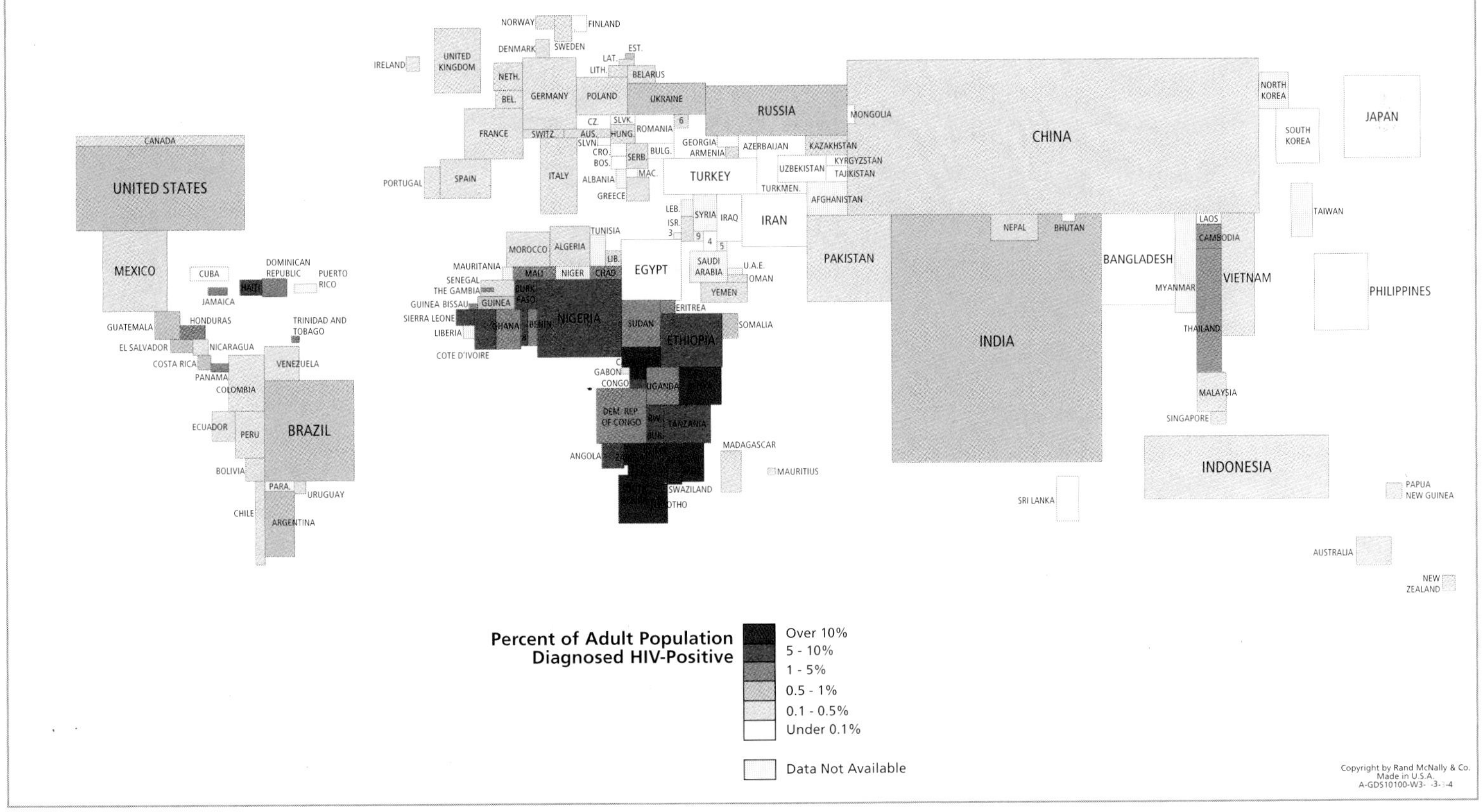

38

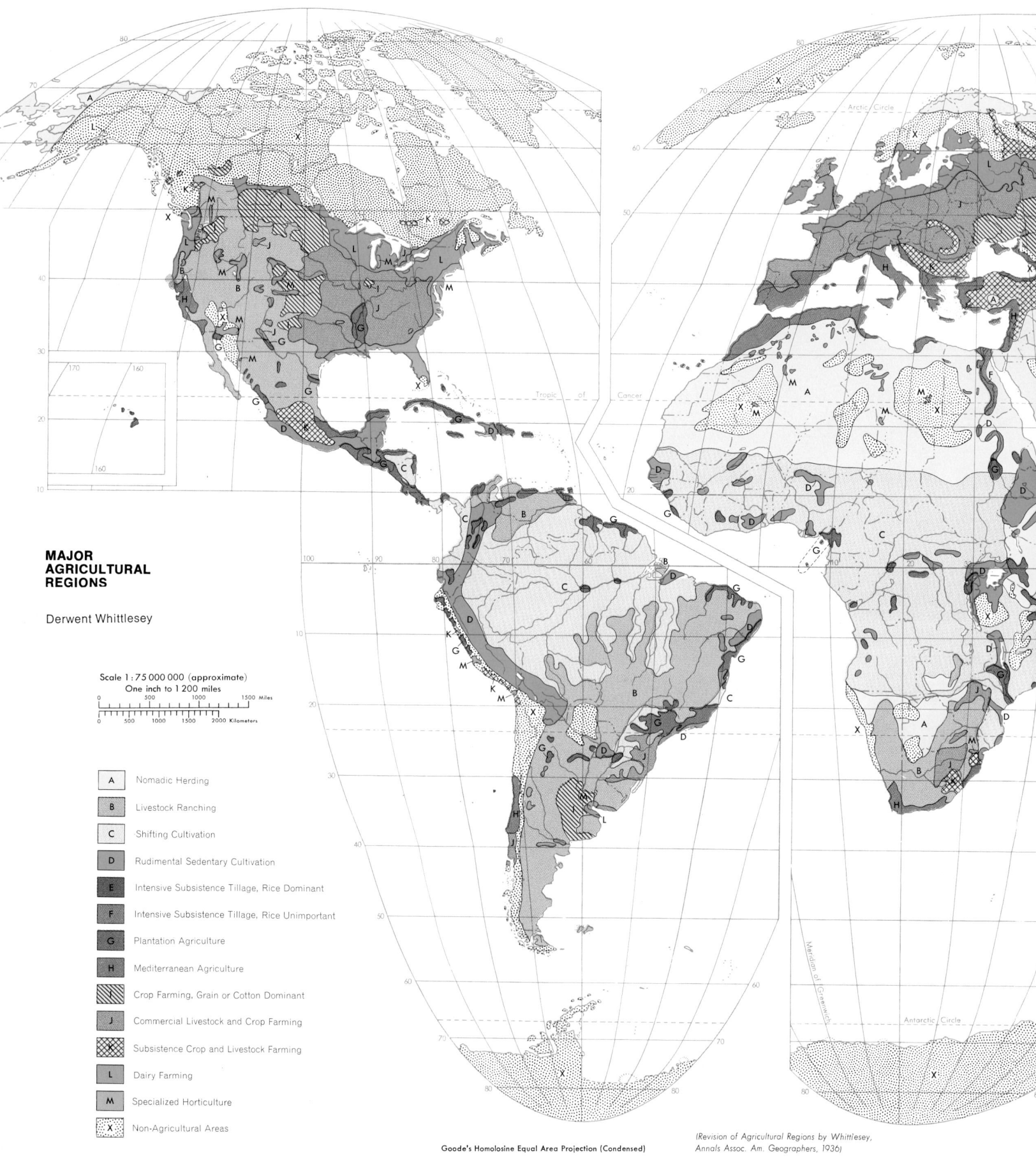

**MAJOR
AGRICULTURAL
REGIONS**

Derwent Whittlesey

Scale 1 : 75 000 000 (approximate)
One inch to 1 200 miles

| | |
|---|---|
| A | Nomadic Herding |
| B | Livestock Ranching |
| C | Shifting Cultivation |
| D | Rudimental Sedentary Cultivation |
| E | Intensive Subsistence Tillage, Rice Dominant |
| F | Intensive Subsistence Tillage, Rice Unimportant |
| G | Plantation Agriculture |
| H | Mediterranean Agriculture |
| I | Crop Farming, Grain or Cotton Dominant |
| J | Commercial Livestock and Crop Farming |
| K | Subsistence Crop and Livestock Farming |
| L | Dairy Farming |
| M | Specialized Horticulture |
| X | Non-Agricultural Areas |

Goode's Homolosine Equal Area Projection (Condensed)

(Revision of Agricultural Regions by Whittlesey,
Annals Assoc. Am. Geographers, 1936)

A-510000-56- -2 4- -7
Copyright by Rand McNally & Co.
Made in U.S.A.

Tropic of Cancer

Equator

Longitude East of Greenwich

Tropic of Capricorn

**Probable Origins of Cultivated Plants**

BEET
OLIVE
GRAPE
ONION GARLIC
LETTUCE

APPLE
ALMOND

SOYBEAN

BARLEY
DATE        BUCKWHEAT
FIG         APRICOT  PEACH
FLAX              GINGER  RICE
LENTIL      TEA
WHEAT   SUGAR  RICE   BAMBOO
            CANE           LIME
                    LEMON
                    ORANGE
                    GRAPEFRUIT

MILLET
COLA  RICE          SORGHUM
YAM   OKRA                COFFEE
      OIL       COTTON
      PALM                BANANA

AVOCADO
CACAO
COMMON BEANS    POTATO
COTTON          PEANUT         WATERMELON
MAIZE           TOMATO
PEPPER                          FORAGE
SQUASH                          GRASSES
SUNFLOWER
SWEET POTATO
TOBACCO         PEANUT
TOMATO          SQUASH
                SWEET
                POTATO

CLOVE
NUTMEG   SUGAR
         CANE      COCONUT

Hearth Areas

Based on Jack R. Harlan, Crops and Man
(Madison: American Society of Agronomy,
1975) and Erich Isaac, Geography of
Domestication (Prentice Hall, 1970)

Copyright by Rand McNally & Co.
Made in U.S.A.
DM-510000-5Z-GD1- -1- -2

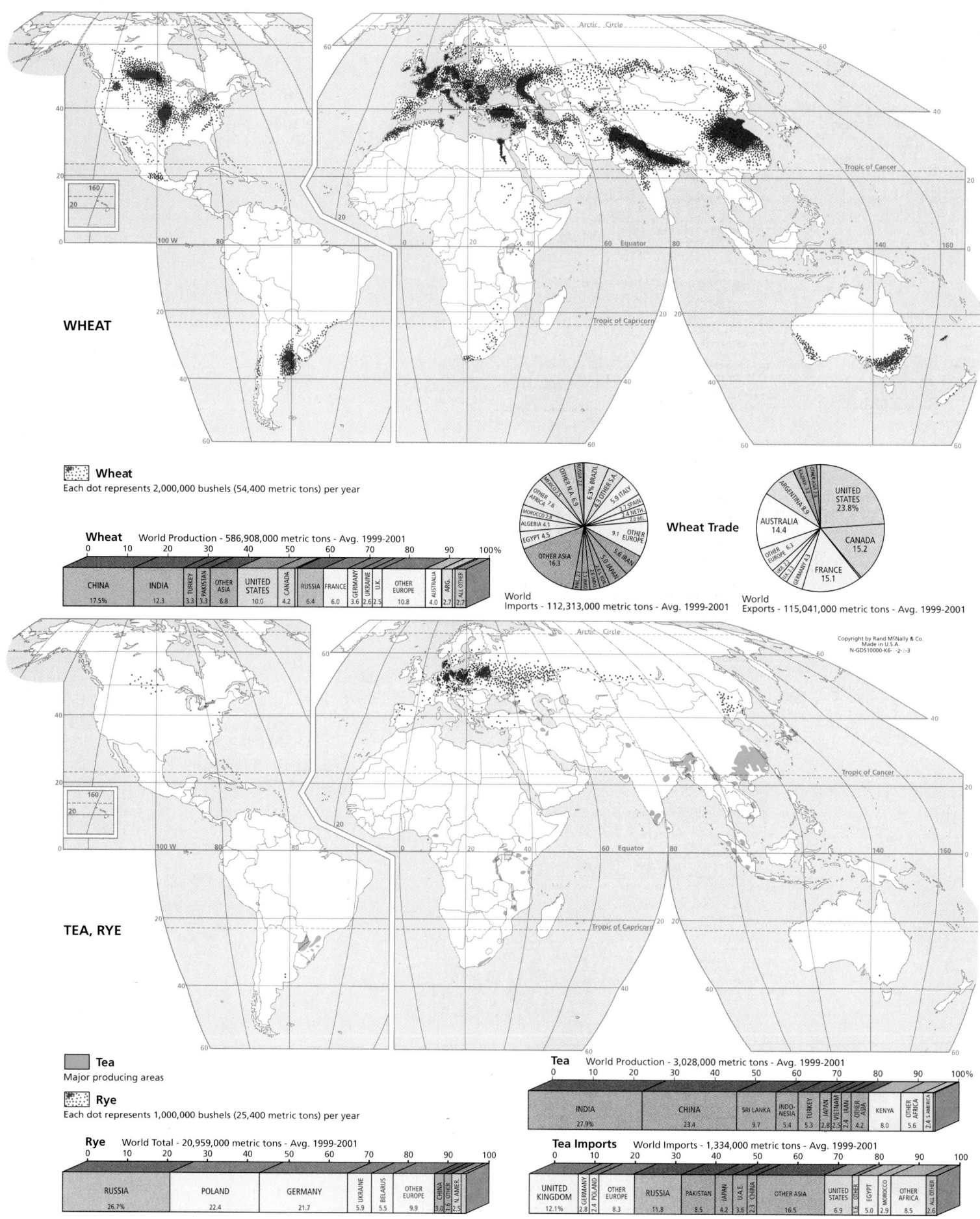

**WHEAT**

### Wheat
Each dot represents 2,000,000 bushels (54,400 metric tons) per year

**Wheat** World Production - 586,908,000 metric tons - Avg. 1999-2001

| 0 | 10 | 20 | 30 | 40 | 50 | 60 | 70 | 80 | 90 | 100% |
|---|---|---|---|---|---|---|---|---|---|---|

| CHINA | INDIA | TURKEY | PAKISTAN | OTHER ASIA | UNITED STATES | CANADA | RUSSIA | FRANCE | GERMANY | UKRAINE | U.K. | OTHER EUROPE | AUSTRALIA | ARG. | ALL OTHER |
|---|---|---|---|---|---|---|---|---|---|---|---|---|---|---|---|
| 17.5% | 12.3 | 3.3 | 3.3 | 6.8 | 10.0 | 4.2 | 6.4 | 6.0 | 3.6 | 2.6 | 2.5 | 10.8 | 4.0 | 2.7 | 2.7 |

**Wheat Trade**

World Imports - 112,313,000 metric tons - Avg. 1999-2001

Imports pie: OTHER N.A. 6.9, 6.3% BRAZIL, 4.3 OTHER S.A., 5.9 ITALY, 2.7 SPAIN, 2.4 NETH., 2.0 BEL., 9.1 OTHER EUROPE, 5.6 IRAN, 5.6 S.A. JAPAN, 2.6 S. KOR., 2.1 INDO., 1.9 PHIL., 16.3 OTHER ASIA, EGYPT 4.5, ALGERIA 4.1, MOROCCO 2.8, OTHER AFRICA 7.6

World Exports - 115,041,000 metric tons - Avg. 1999-2001

Exports pie: UNITED STATES 23.8%, CANADA 15.2, FRANCE 15.1, GERMANY 2.7, U.K. 2.3, OTHER EUROPE 6.3, ARGENTINA 8.9, AUSTRALIA 14.4, KAZAK. 4.7, INDIA 4.2

**TEA, RYE**

### Tea
Major producing areas

### Rye
Each dot represents 1,000,000 bushels (25,400 metric tons) per year

**Tea** World Production - 3,028,000 metric tons - Avg. 1999-2001

| 0 | 10 | 20 | 30 | 40 | 50 | 60 | 70 | 80 | 90 | 100% |
|---|---|---|---|---|---|---|---|---|---|---|

| INDIA | CHINA | SRI LANKA | INDO-NESIA | TURKEY | JAPAN | VIETNAM | IRAN | OTHER ASIA | KENYA | OTHER AFRICA | S. AMERICA |
|---|---|---|---|---|---|---|---|---|---|---|---|
| 27.9% | 23.4 | 9.7 | 5.4 | 5.3 | 2.8 | 2.9 | 2.4 | 4.2 | 8.0 | 5.6 | 2.4 |

**Rye** World Total - 20,959,000 metric tons - Avg. 1999-2001

| 0 | 10 | 20 | 30 | 40 | 50 | 60 | 70 | 80 | 90 | 100 |
|---|---|---|---|---|---|---|---|---|---|---|

| RUSSIA | POLAND | GERMANY | UKRAINE | BELARUS | OTHER EUROPE | CHINA | OTHER | N. AMER. |
|---|---|---|---|---|---|---|---|---|
| 26.7% | 22.4 | 21.7 | 5.9 | 5.5 | 9.9 | 3.0 | 1.6 | |

**Tea Imports** World Imports - 1,334,000 metric tons - Avg. 1999-2001

| 0 | 10 | 20 | 30 | 40 | 50 | 60 | 70 | 80 | 90 | 100 |
|---|---|---|---|---|---|---|---|---|---|---|

| UNITED KINGDOM | GERMANY | POLAND | OTHER EUROPE | RUSSIA | PAKISTAN | JAPAN | U.A.E. | CHINA | OTHER ASIA | UNITED STATES | EGYPT | MOROCCO | OTHER AFRICA | ALL OTHER |
|---|---|---|---|---|---|---|---|---|---|---|---|---|---|---|
| 12.1% | 2.4 | 2.4 | 8.3 | 11.8 | 8.5 | 4.2 | 3.5 | 2.3 | 16.5 | 6.9 | 1.6 | 5.0 | 2.9 | 8.5 | 2.6 |

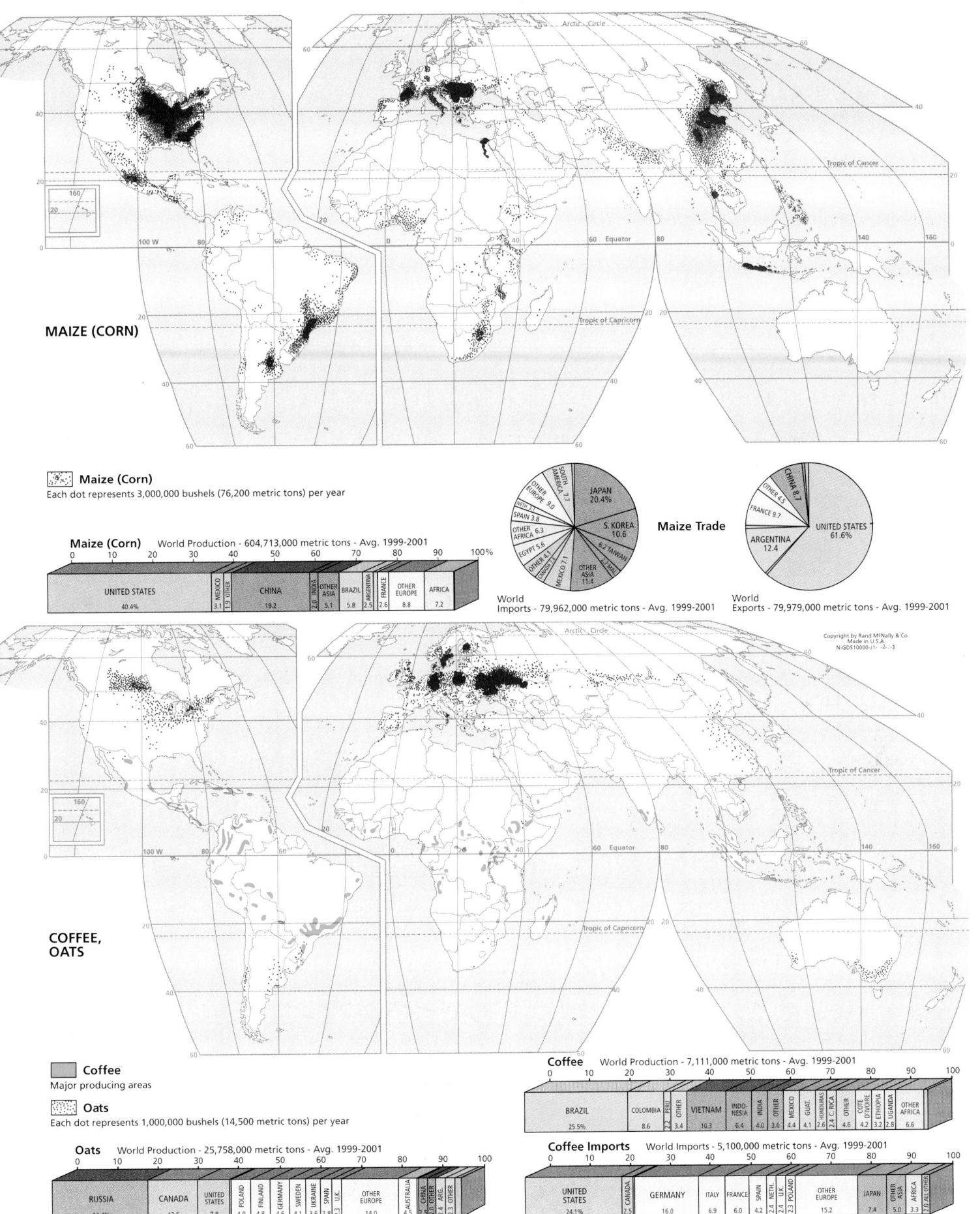

**MAIZE (CORN)**

### Maize (Corn)
Each dot represents 3,000,000 bushels (76,200 metric tons) per year

**Maize (Corn)** World Production - 604,713,000 metric tons - Avg. 1999-2001

| 0 | 10 | 20 | 30 | 40 | 50 | 60 | 70 | 80 | 90 | 100% |
|---|---|---|---|---|---|---|---|---|---|---|
| UNITED STATES 40.4% | | | | MEXICO 3.1 | OTHER 1.9 | CHINA 19.2 | | INDIA 2.0 | OTHER ASIA 5.1 | BRAZIL 5.8 | ARGENTINA 2.5 | FRANCE 2.6 | OTHER EUROPE 8.8 | AFRICA 7.2 |

**Maize Trade**

World Imports - 79,962,000 metric tons - Avg. 1999-2001

JAPAN 20.4%, S. KOREA 10.6, TAIWAN 6.2, ISRAEL 7.1, OTHER ASIA 11.4, MEXICO 7.1, CANADA 7.7, EGYPT 5.6, OTHER AFRICA 6.3, SPAIN 3.8, NETH. 2.1, OTHER EUROPE 9.0, SOUTH AMERICA 7.7

World Exports - 79,979,000 metric tons - Avg. 1999-2001

UNITED STATES 61.6%, ARGENTINA 12.4, FRANCE 9.7, OTHER 4.5, CHINA 8.7

Copyright by Rand McNally & Co.
Made in U.S.A.
N-GDS10000-J1- -2- -3

**COFFEE, OATS**

### Coffee
Major producing areas

### Oats
Each dot represents 1,000,000 bushels (14,500 metric tons) per year

**Coffee** World Production - 7,111,000 metric tons - Avg. 1999-2001

| 0 | 10 | 20 | 30 | 40 | 50 | 60 | 70 | 80 | 90 | 100 |
|---|---|---|---|---|---|---|---|---|---|---|
| BRAZIL 25.5% | | COLOMBIA 8.6 | PERU 2.2 | OTHER 3.4 | VIETNAM 10.3 | INDONESIA 6.4 | INDIA 4.0 | MEXICO 3.6 | GUAT. 4.4 | HONDURAS 4.1 | C. RICA 2.6 | COTE D'IVOIRE 4.2 | ETHIOPIA 3.2 | UGANDA 2.8 | OTHER AFRICA 6.6 |

**Oats** World Production - 25,758,000 metric tons - Avg. 1999-2001

| 0 | 10 | 20 | 30 | 40 | 50 | 60 | 70 | 80 | 90 | 100 |
|---|---|---|---|---|---|---|---|---|---|---|
| RUSSIA 23.4% | | CANADA 12.6 | UNITED STATES 7.8 | POLAND 4.9 | FINLAND 4.8 | GERMANY 4.6 | SWEDEN 4.1 | UKRAINE 3.6 | SPAIN 2.8 | U.K. 2.3 | OTHER EUROPE 14.0 | AUSTRALIA 4.5 | CHINA 2.0 | OTHER 2.0 | ARG. 2.3 | OTHER 2.3 |

**Coffee Imports** World Imports - 5,100,000 metric tons - Avg. 1999-2001

| 0 | 10 | 20 | 30 | 40 | 50 | 60 | 70 | 80 | 90 | 100 |
|---|---|---|---|---|---|---|---|---|---|---|
| UNITED STATES 24.1% | | CANADA 2.5 | GERMANY 16.0 | ITALY 6.9 | FRANCE 6.0 | SPAIN 4.2 | NETH. 2.4 | U.K. 2.4 | POLAND 2.3 | OTHER EUROPE 15.2 | JAPAN 7.4 | OTHER ASIA 5.0 | AFRICA 3.3 | ALL OTHER 2.0 |

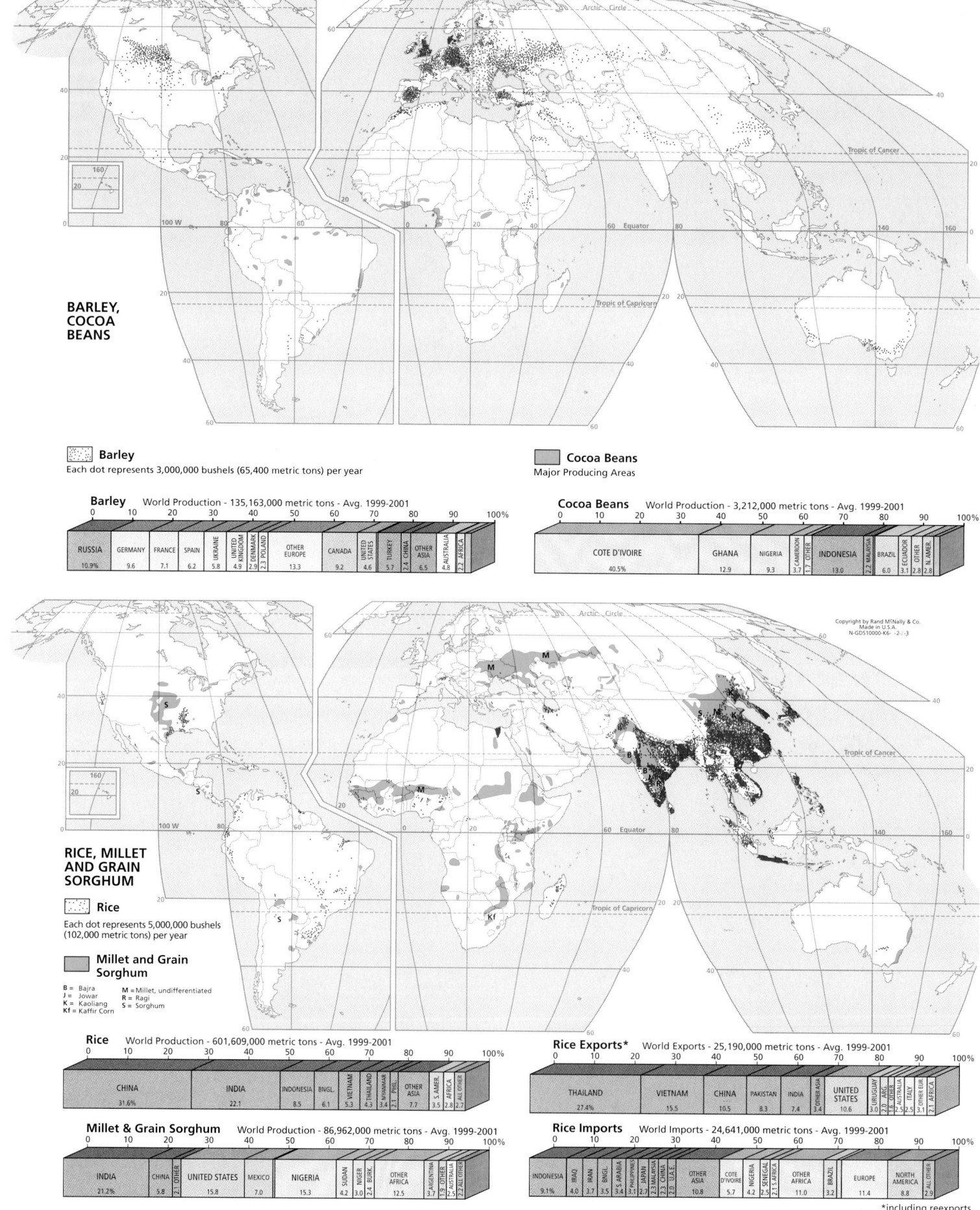

**BARLEY, COCOA BEANS**

**Barley**
Each dot represents 3,000,000 bushels (65,400 metric tons) per year

**Cocoa Beans**
Major Producing Areas

**Barley**  World Production - 135,163,000 metric tons - Avg. 1999-2001

| | | | | | | | | | | | | | | | |
|---|---|---|---|---|---|---|---|---|---|---|---|---|---|---|---|
| RUSSIA | GERMANY | FRANCE | SPAIN | UKRAINE | UNITED KINGDOM | DENMARK | POLAND | OTHER EUROPE | CANADA | UNITED STATES | TURKEY | CHINA | OTHER ASIA | AUSTRALIA | AFRICA |
| 10.9% | 9.6 | 7.1 | 6.2 | 5.8 | 4.9 | 2.9 | 2.3 | 13.3 | 9.2 | 4.6 | 5.7 | 2.4 | 6.5 | 4.8 | 2.2 |

**Cocoa Beans**  World Production - 3,212,000 metric tons - Avg. 1999-2001

| | | | | | | | | | |
|---|---|---|---|---|---|---|---|---|---|
| COTE D'IVOIRE | GHANA | NIGERIA | CAMEROON | OTHER | INDONESIA | MALAYSIA | BRAZIL | ECUADOR | OTHER | N. AMER. |
| 40.5% | 12.9 | 9.3 | 3.7 | 1.7 | 13.0 | 2.2 | 6.0 | 3.1 | 2.8 | 2.8 |

**RICE, MILLET AND GRAIN SORGHUM**

**Rice**
Each dot represents 5,000,000 bushels (102,000 metric tons) per year

**Millet and Grain Sorghum**

B = Bajra
J = Jowar
K = Kaoliang
Kf = Kaffir Corn
M = Millet, undifferentiated
R = Ragi
S = Sorghum

Copyright by Rand McNally & Co.
Made in U.S.A.
N-GDS10000-K6- -2-.-3

**Rice**  World Production - 601,609,000 metric tons - Avg. 1999-2001

| | | | | | | | | | | |
|---|---|---|---|---|---|---|---|---|---|---|
| CHINA | INDIA | INDONESIA | BNGL. | VIETNAM | THAILAND | MYANMAR | PHIL. | OTHER ASIA | S. AMER. | AFRICA | ALL OTHER |
| 31.6% | 22.1 | 8.5 | 6.1 | 5.3 | 4.3 | 3.4 | 2.1 | 7.7 | 3.5 | 2.8 | 2.7 |

**Rice Exports***  World Exports - 25,190,000 metric tons - Avg. 1999-2001

| | | | | | | | | | | | |
|---|---|---|---|---|---|---|---|---|---|---|---|
| THAILAND | VIETNAM | CHINA | PAKISTAN | INDIA | OTHER ASIA | UNITED STATES | URUGUAY | ARG. | OTHER | AUSTRALIA | OTHER EUR. | AFRICA |
| 27.4% | 15.5 | 10.5 | 8.3 | 7.4 | 3.4 | 10.6 | 3.0 | 2.0 | 1.6 | 2.5 | 3.1 | 2.1 |

**Millet & Grain Sorghum**  World Production - 86,962,000 metric tons - Avg. 1999-2001

| | | | | | | | | | | | |
|---|---|---|---|---|---|---|---|---|---|---|---|
| INDIA | CHINA | OTHER | UNITED STATES | MEXICO | NIGERIA | SUDAN | NIGER | BURK. | OTHER AFRICA | ARGENTINA | OTHER | ALL OTHER |
| 21.2% | 5.8 | 2.1 | 15.8 | 7.0 | 15.3 | 4.2 | 3.0 | 2.4 | 12.5 | 3.7 | 1.9 | 2.2 |

**Rice Imports**  World Imports - 24,641,000 metric tons - Avg. 1999-2001

| | | | | | | | | | | | | | | | | |
|---|---|---|---|---|---|---|---|---|---|---|---|---|---|---|---|---|
| INDONESIA | IRAQ | IRAN | BNGL. | S. ARABIA | PHILIPPINES | JAPAN | CHINA | U.A.E. | OTHER ASIA | COTE D'IVOIRE | NIGERIA | SENEGAL | S. AFRICA | OTHER AFRICA | BRAZIL | EUROPE | NORTH AMERICA | ALL OTHER |
| 9.1% | 4.0 | 3.7 | 3.5 | 3.4 | 3.1 | 2.7 | 2.3 | 2.0 | 10.8 | 5.7 | 4.2 | 2.5 | 2.1 | 11.0 | 3.2 | 11.4 | 8.8 | 2.9 |

*including reexports

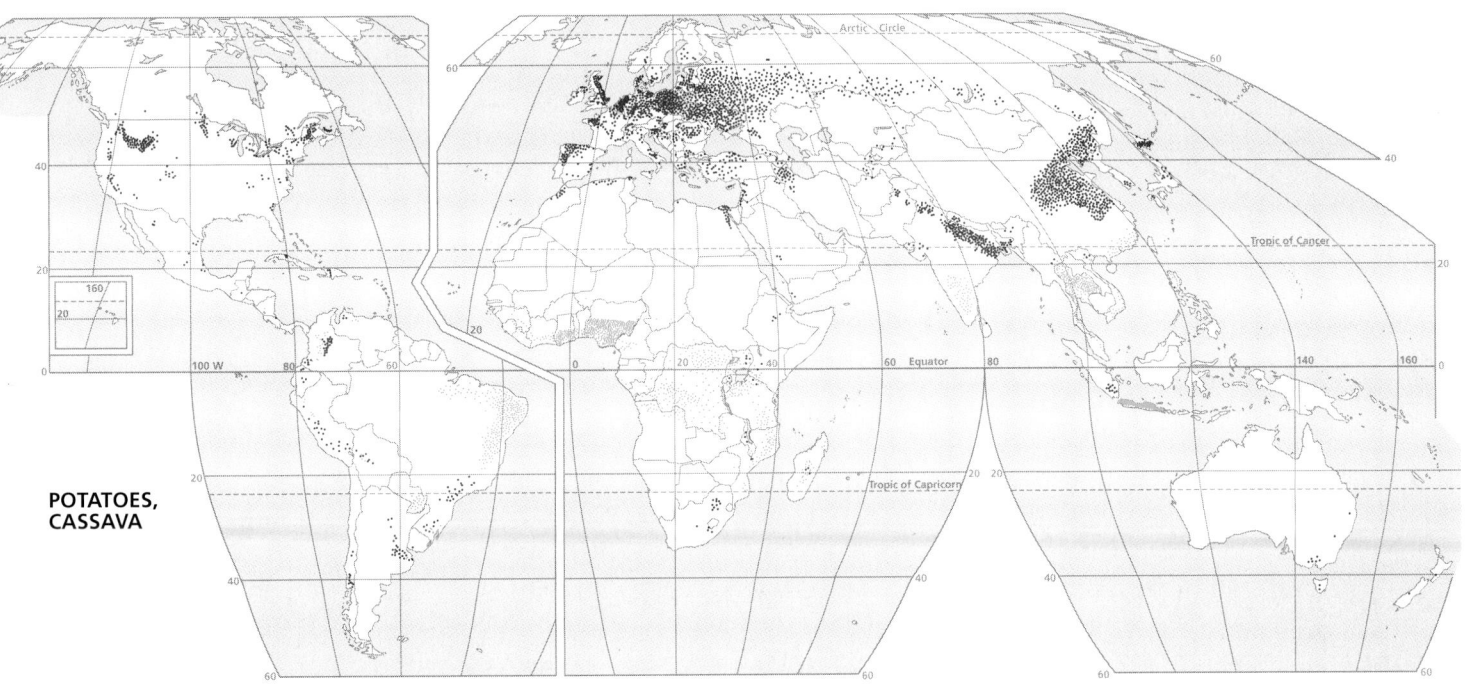

## POTATOES, CASSAVA

### Potatoes
Each dot represents 100,000 metric tons average annual production

### Cassava
Each dot represents 100,000 metric tons average annual production

**Potatoes**    World Total - 312,408,000 metric tons - Avg. 1999-2001

| 0 | 10 | 20 | 30 | 40 | 50 | 60 | 70 | 80 | 90 | 100% |

| CHINA 19.9% | INDIA 7.5 | OTHER ASIA 9.5 | RUSSIA 10.7 | UNITED STATES 6.9 | OTHER 2.1 | POLAND 6.8 | UKRAINE 5.3 | GERMANY 4.0 | BELARUS 2.6 | NETH. 2.5 | U.K. 2.2 | FRANCE 2.1 | OTHER EUROPE 8.9 | SOUTH AMERICA 4.4 | AFRICA 3.9 |

**Cassava**    World Production - 176,920,000 metric tons - Avg. 1999-2001

| 0 | 10 | 20 | 30 | 40 | 50 | 60 | 70 | 80 | 90 | 100% |

| NIGERIA 18.3% | DEM. REP. OF THE CONGO 9.0 | GHANA 4.7 | TANZANIA 3.5 | MOZ. 3.0 | UGANDA 2.9 | ANGOLA 2.5 | OTHER AFRICA 10.4 | BRAZIL 12.6 | OTHER 4.3 | THAILAND 10.2 | INDONESIA 9.2 | INDIA 3.9 | CHINA 2.2 | OTHER 2.6 |

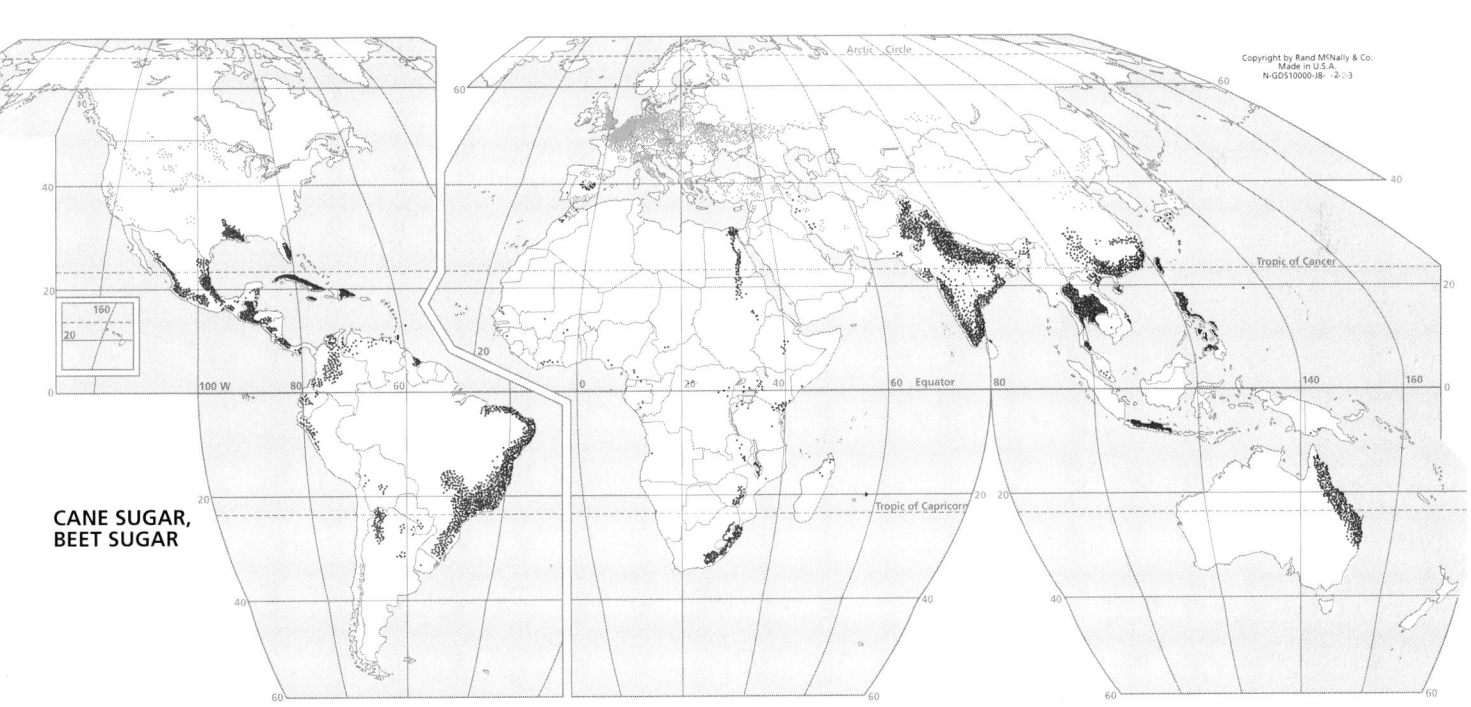

Copyright by Rand M°Nally & Co.
Made in U.S.A.
N-GDS10000-JB· ·2·2·3

## CANE SUGAR, BEET SUGAR

### Cane Sugar
Each dot represents 20,000 metric tons average annual production

### Beet Sugar
Each dot represents 20,000 metric tons average annual production

**Cane Sugar**    World Production - 98,587,000 metric tons - Avg. 1999-2001

| 0 | 10 | 20 | 30 | 40 | 50 | 60 | 70 | 80 | 90 | 100% |

| INDIA 20.3% | CHINA 7.0 | THAILAND 6.0 | PAKISTAN 2.9 | OTHER ASIA 5.8 | BRAZIL 19.5 | COL. 2.4 | OTHER S.A. 4.3 | MEXICO 5.2 | CUBA 3.9 | UNITED STATES 3.7 | OTHER N.A. 4.6 | AUSTRALIA 5.0 | S. AFRICA 2.5 | OTHER AFRICA 6.4 |

**Beet Sugar**    World Production - 35,732,000 metric tons - Avg. 1999-2001

| 0 | 10 | 20 | 30 | 40 | 50 | 60 | 70 | 80 | 90 | 100% |

| GERMANY 12.7% | FRANCE 12.6 | POLAND 5.4 | UKRAINE 4.9 | ITALY 4.6 | UNITED KINGDOM 4.2 | SPAIN 3.2 | NETH. 3.2 | BELGIUM 2.9 | OTHER EUROPE 12.7 | UNITED STATES 11.6 | TURKEY 6.3 | CHINA 2.6 | OTHER ASIA 4.4 | RUSSIA 4.8 | AFRICA 2.2 | OTHER |

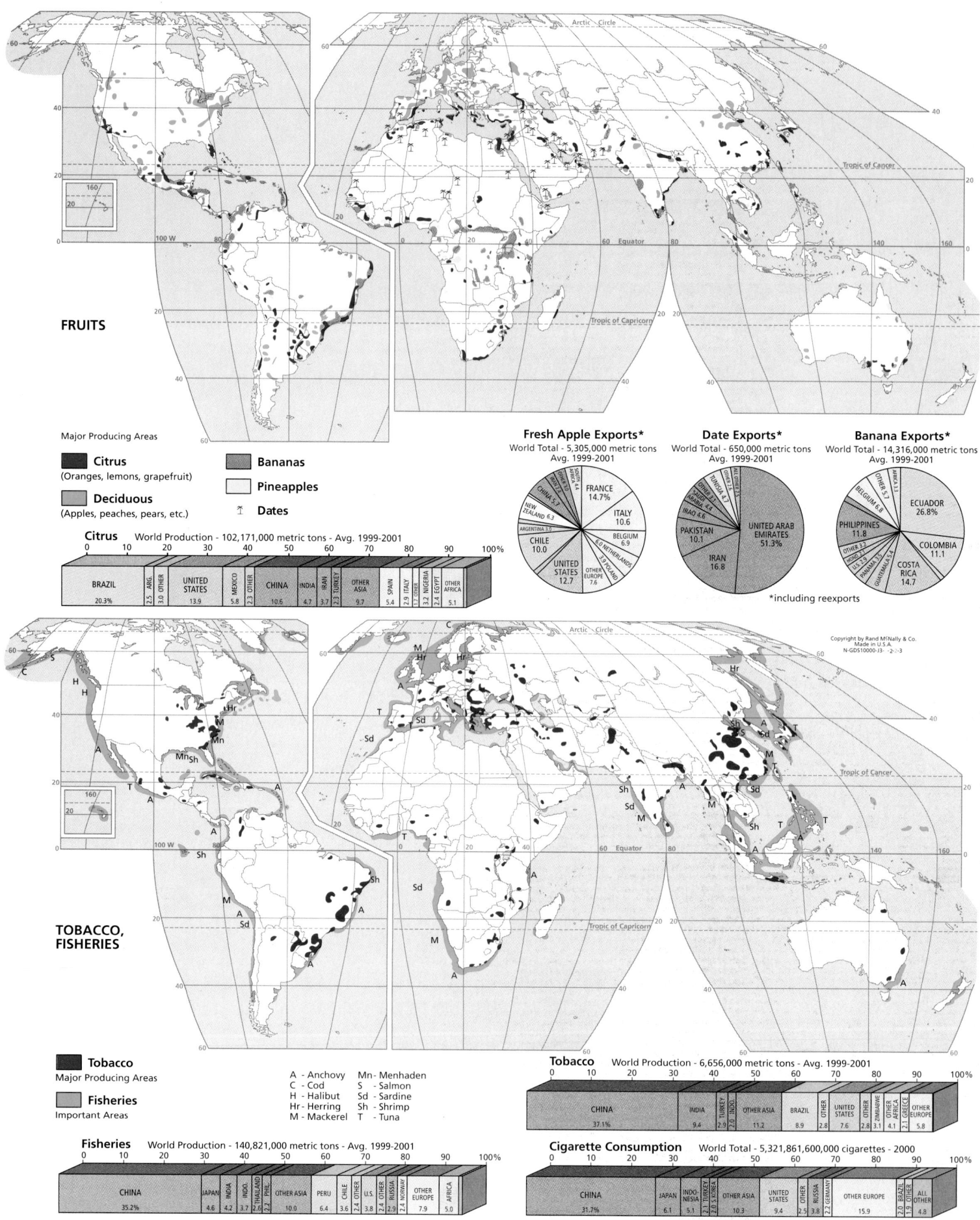

**FRUITS**

**Major Producing Areas**

■ **Citrus**
(Oranges, lemons, grapefruit)

■ **Deciduous**
(Apples, peaches, pears, etc.)

■ **Bananas**

□ **Pineapples**

⌘ **Dates**

**Citrus** World Production - 102,171,000 metric tons - Avg. 1999-2001

| BRAZIL 20.3% | ARG. 2.5 | OTHER 3.0 | UNITED STATES 13.9 | MEXICO 5.8 | OTHER 2.3 | CHINA 10.5 | INDIA 4.7 | IRAN 3.7 | TURKEY 2.3 | OTHER ASIA 9.7 | SPAIN 5.4 | ITALY 2.9 | OTHER 1.7 | NIGERIA 3.2 | EGYPT 2.4 | OTHER AFRICA 5.1 |
|---|---|---|---|---|---|---|---|---|---|---|---|---|---|---|---|---|

**Fresh Apple Exports***
World Total - 5,305,000 metric tons
Avg. 1999-2001

- FRANCE 14.7%
- ITALY 10.6
- BELGIUM 6.9
- NETHERLANDS 6.0
- POLAND 3.7
- OTHER EUROPE 7.6
- UNITED STATES 12.7
- CHILE 10.0
- ARGENTINA 3.0
- NEW ZEALAND 6.3
- CHINA 5.7
- SOUTH AFRICA 4.4
- OTHER 3.2

**Date Exports***
World Total - 650,000 metric tons
Avg. 1999-2001

- UNITED ARAB EMIRATES 51.3%
- IRAN 16.8
- PAKISTAN 10.1
- IRAQ 4.6
- SAUDI ARABIA 4.4
- TUNISIA 4.7
- OTHER 3.1
- ALL OTHER 4.5

**Banana Exports***
World Total - 14,316,000 metric tons
Avg. 1999-2001

- ECUADOR 26.8%
- COLOMBIA 11.1
- COSTA RICA 14.7
- GUATEMALA 5.4
- PANAMA 5.4
- HOND. 2.3
- U.S. 2.3
- OTHER 3.2
- PHILIPPINES 11.8
- BELGIUM 6.8
- OTHER 5.7
- AFRICA 4.4

*including reexports

**TOBACCO, FISHERIES**

■ **Tobacco**
Major Producing Areas

■ **Fisheries**
Important Areas

A - Anchovy    Mn- Menhaden
C - Cod        S - Salmon
H - Halibut    Sd - Sardine
Hr - Herring   Sh - Shrimp
M - Mackerel   T - Tuna

Copyright by Rand McNally & Co.
Made in U.S.A.
N-GDS10000-J3- -2--3

**Fisheries** World Production - 140,821,000 metric tons - Avg. 1999-2001

| CHINA 35.2% | JAPAN 4.6 | INDIA 4.2 | INDO. 3.7 | THAILAND 2.6 | PHIL. 2.2 | OTHER ASIA 10.0 | PERU 6.4 | CHILE 3.6 | U.S. 3.8 | RUSSIA 2.4 | NORWAY 2.4 | OTHER EUROPE 7.9 | AFRICA 5.0 |
|---|---|---|---|---|---|---|---|---|---|---|---|---|---|

**Tobacco** World Production - 6,656,000 metric tons - Avg. 1999-2001

| CHINA 37.1% | INDIA 9.4 | TURKEY 2.9 | INDO. 2.0 | OTHER ASIA 11.2 | BRAZIL 8.9 | OTHER 2.8 | UNITED STATES 7.6 | OTHER 2.8 | ZIMBABWE 3.1 | OTHER AFRICA 4.1 | GREECE 2.1 | OTHER EUROPE 5.8 |
|---|---|---|---|---|---|---|---|---|---|---|---|---|

**Cigarette Consumption** World Total - 5,321,861,600,000 cigarettes - 2000

| CHINA 31.7% | JAPAN 6.1 | INDONESIA 5.1 | TURKEY 2.1 | S. KOREA 2.0 | OTHER ASIA 10.3 | UNITED STATES 9.4 | OTHER 2.5 | RUSSIA 3.8 | GERMANY 2.2 | OTHER EUROPE 15.9 | BRAZIL 2.0 | OTHER 1.9 | ALL OTHER 4.8 |
|---|---|---|---|---|---|---|---|---|---|---|---|---|---|

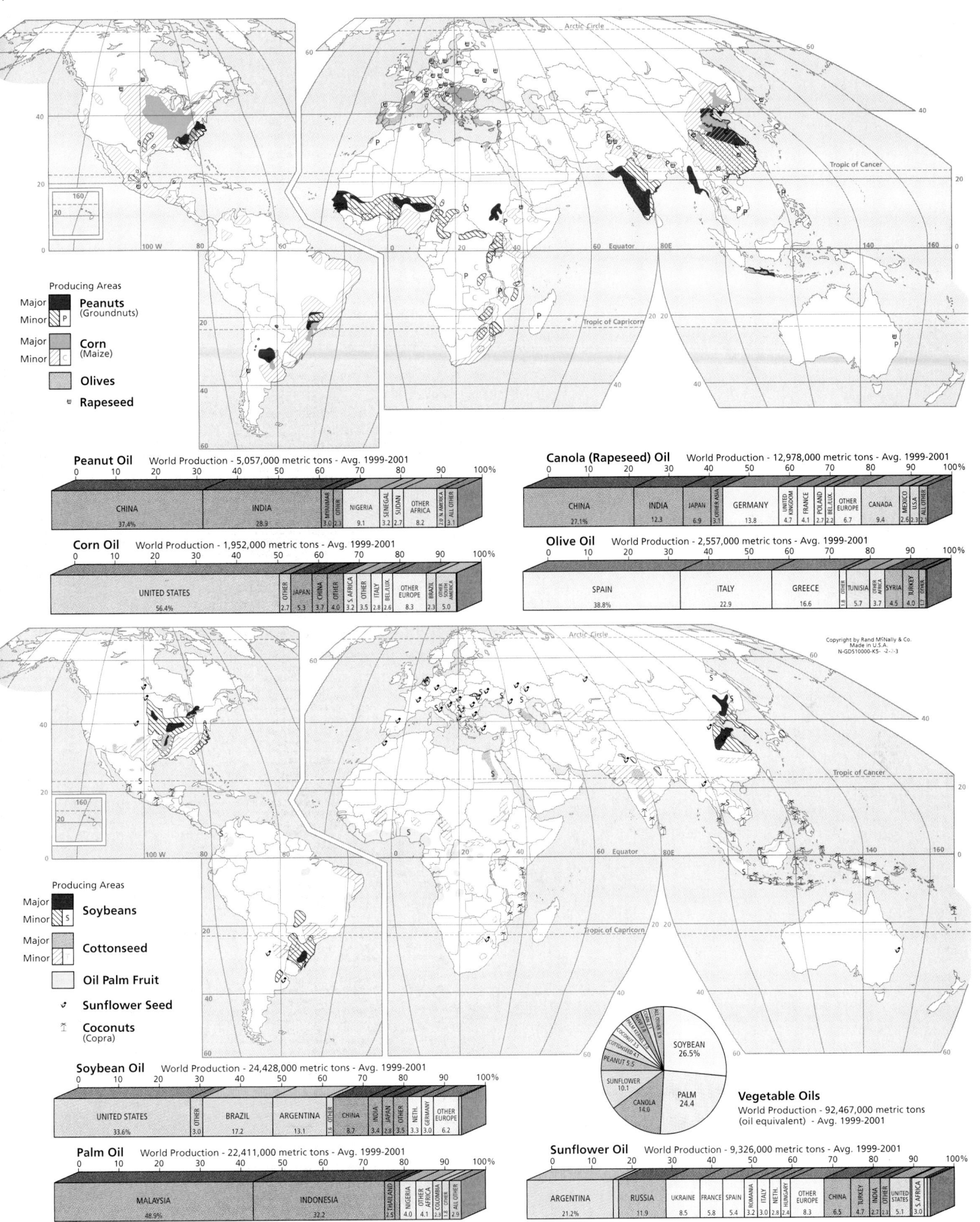

Producing Areas

Major | **Peanuts** (Groundnuts)
Minor | P

Major | **Corn** (Maize)
Minor | C

**Olives**

ш | **Rapeseed**

**Peanut Oil** World Production - 5,057,000 metric tons - Avg. 1999-2001

| CHINA 37.4% | INDIA 28.9 | MYANMAR 3.0 | OTHER 2.3 | NIGERIA 9.1 | SENEGAL 3.2 | SUDAN 2.7 | OTHER AFRICA 8.2 | N. AMERICA 2.0 | ALL OTHER 3.1 |

**Canola (Rapeseed) Oil** World Production - 12,978,000 metric tons - Avg. 1999-2001

| CHINA 27.1% | INDIA 12.3 | JAPAN 6.9 | OTHER ASIA 3.1 | GERMANY 13.8 | UNITED KINGDOM 4.7 | FRANCE 4.1 | POLAND 2.7 | BEL,LUX. 2.2 | OTHER EUROPE 6.7 | CANADA 9.4 | MEXICO 2.6 | U.S.A. 2.3 | ALL OTHER 2.1 |

**Corn Oil** World Production - 1,952,000 metric tons - Avg. 1999-2001

| UNITED STATES 56.4% | OTHER 2.7 | JAPAN 5.3 | CHINA 3.7 | OTHER 4.0 | S. AFRICA 3.2 | OTHER 3.5 | ITALY 2.8 | BEL,LUX. 2.6 | OTHER EUROPE 8.3 | BRAZIL 2.3 | OTHER SOUTH AMERICA 5.0 |

**Olive Oil** World Production - 2,557,000 metric tons - Avg. 1999-2001

| SPAIN 38.8% | ITALY 22.9 | GREECE 16.6 | OTHER 1.8 | TUNISIA 5.7 | OTHER AFRICA 3.7 | SYRIA 4.5 | TURKEY 4.0 | OTHER 1.7 |

Producing Areas

Major | **Soybeans**
Minor | S

Major | **Cottonseed**
Minor | I

**Oil Palm Fruit**

ʃ | **Sunflower Seed**

⊥ | **Coconuts** (Copra)

**Soybean Oil** World Production - 24,428,000 metric tons - Avg. 1999-2001

| UNITED STATES 33.6% | OTHER 3.0 | BRAZIL 17.2 | ARGENTINA 13.1 | OTHER 1.6 | CHINA 8.7 | INDIA 3.4 | JAPAN 2.8 | OTHER 3.5 | NETH. 3.3 | GERMANY 3.0 | OTHER EUROPE 6.2 |

**Palm Oil** World Production - 22,411,000 metric tons - Avg. 1999-2001

| MALAYSIA 48.9% | INDONESIA 32.2 | THAILAND 2.5 | NIGERIA 4.0 | OTHER AFRICA 4.1 | COLOMBIA 1.8 | ALL OTHER 2.9 |

**Vegetable Oils**
World Production - 92,467,000 metric tons
(oil equivalent) - Avg. 1999-2001

Pie chart: SOYBEAN 26.5%, PALM 24.4, CANOLA 14.0, SUNFLOWER 10.1, PEANUT 5.5, COTTONSEED 4.7, COCONUT 2.5, PALM KERNEL 2.7, CORN 2.1, OLIVE 2.8, ALL OTHER 2.2

**Sunflower Oil** World Production - 9,326,000 metric tons - Avg. 1999-2001

| ARGENTINA 21.2% | RUSSIA 11.9 | UKRAINE 8.5 | FRANCE 5.8 | SPAIN 5.4 | ROMANIA 3.2 | ITALY 3.0 | NETH. 2.8 | HUNGARY 2.4 | OTHER EUROPE 8.3 | CHINA 6.5 | TURKEY 4.7 | INDIA 2.7 | UNITED STATES 5.1 | S. AFRICA 3.0 |

Copyright by Rand McNally & Co.
Made in U.S.A.
N-GD510000-K5- -2-:-3

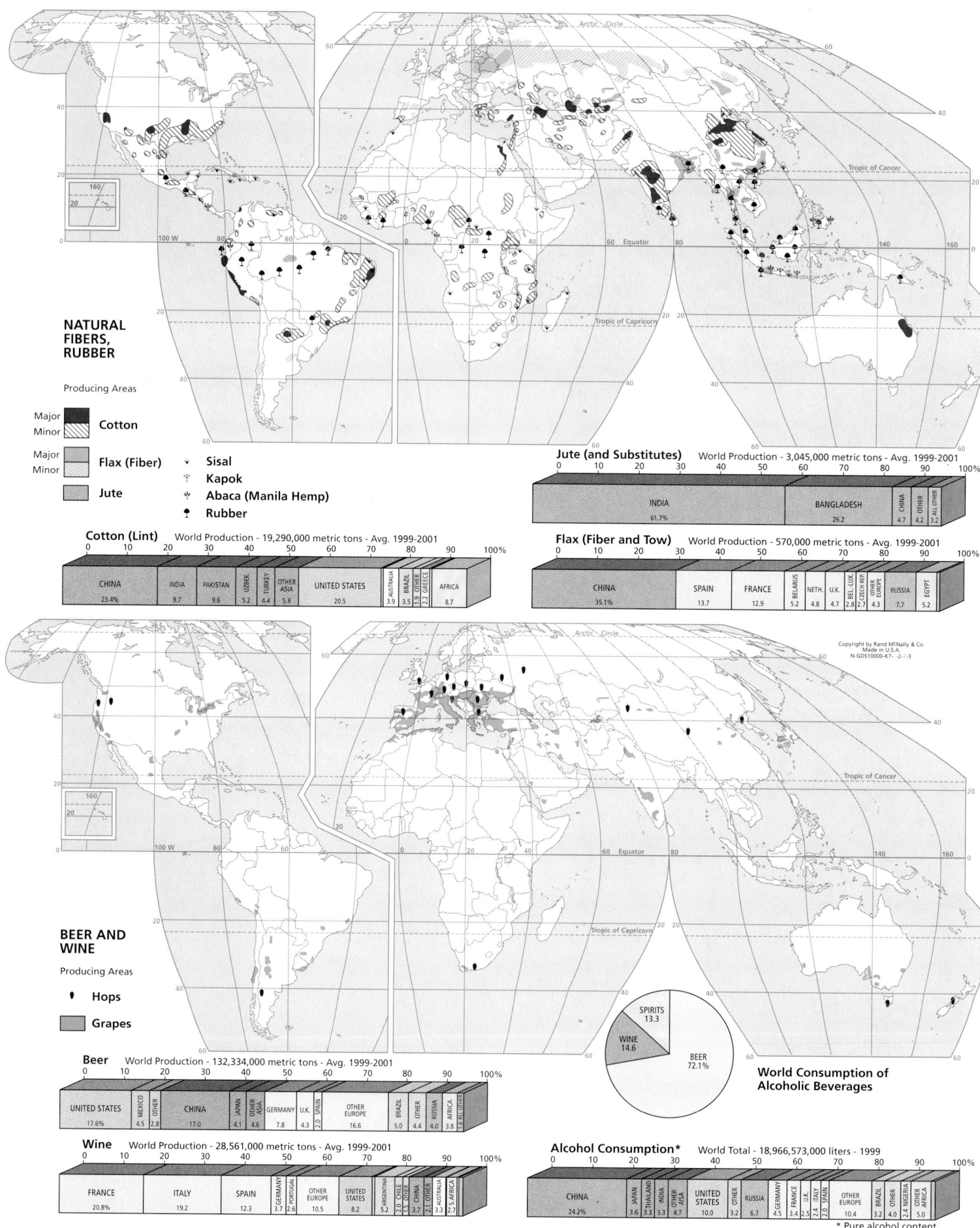

## NATURAL FIBERS, RUBBER

**Producing Areas**

| | |
|---|---|
| Major / Minor | **Cotton** |
| Major / Minor | **Flax (Fiber)** |
| | **Jute** |

- Sisal
- Kapok
- Abaca (Manila Hemp)
- Rubber

### Jute (and Substitutes)
World Production - 3,045,000 metric tons - Avg. 1999-2001

| INDIA 61.7% | BANGLADESH 26.2 | CHINA 4.7 | OTHER 4.2 | ALL OTHER 3.2 |
|---|---|---|---|---|

### Cotton (Lint)
World Production - 19,290,000 metric tons - Avg. 1999-2001

| CHINA 23.4% | INDIA 9.7 | PAKISTAN 9.6 | UZBEK. 5.2 | TURKEY 4.4 | OTHER ASIA 5.8 | UNITED STATES 20.5 | AUSTRALIA 3.9 | BRAZIL 3.5 | OTHER 1.9 | GREECE 2.2 | AFRICA 8.7 |
|---|---|---|---|---|---|---|---|---|---|---|---|

### Flax (Fiber and Tow)
World Production - 570,000 metric tons - Avg. 1999-2001

| CHINA 35.1% | SPAIN 13.7 | FRANCE 12.9 | BELARUS 5.2 | NETH. 4.8 | U.K. 4.7 | BEL.-LUX. 2.8 | CZECH REP. 2.7 | OTHER EUROPE 4.3 | RUSSIA 7.7 | EGYPT 5.2 |
|---|---|---|---|---|---|---|---|---|---|---|

## BEER AND WINE

**Producing Areas**

- Hops
- Grapes

### Beer
World Production - 132,334,000 metric tons - Avg. 1999-2001

| UNITED STATES 17.6% | MEXICO 4.5 | OTHER 2.8 | CHINA 17.0 | JAPAN 4.1 | OTHER ASIA 4.6 | GERMANY 7.8 | U.K. 4.3 | SPAIN 2.0 | OTHER EUROPE 16.6 | BRAZIL 5.0 | OTHER 4.4 | RUSSIA 4.0 | AFRICA 3.8 | ALL OTHER 1.6 |
|---|---|---|---|---|---|---|---|---|---|---|---|---|---|---|

### Wine
World Production - 28,561,000 metric tons - Avg. 1999-2001

| FRANCE 20.8% | ITALY 19.2 | SPAIN 12.3 | GERMANY 3.7 | PORTUGAL 2.6 | OTHER EUROPE 10.5 | UNITED STATES 8.2 | ARGENTINA 5.2 | CHILE 2.0 | OTHER 1.5 | CHINA 3.7 | OTHER 2.1 | AUSTRALIA 3.3 | S. AFRICA 2.7 |
|---|---|---|---|---|---|---|---|---|---|---|---|---|---|

### World Consumption of Alcoholic Beverages

- SPIRITS 13.3
- WINE 14.6
- BEER 72.1%

### Alcohol Consumption*
World Total - 18,966,573,000 liters - 1999

| CHINA 24.2% | JAPAN 3.6 | THAILAND 3.3 | INDIA 3.3 | OTHER ASIA 4.7 | UNITED STATES 10.0 | OTHER 3.2 | RUSSIA 6.7 | GERMANY 4.5 | FRANCE 3.4 | U.K. 2.5 | ITALY 2.4 | SPAIN 2.0 | OTHER EUROPE 10.4 | BRAZIL 3.2 | OTHER 4.0 | NIGERIA 2.4 | OTHER AFRICA 5.0 |
|---|---|---|---|---|---|---|---|---|---|---|---|---|---|---|---|---|---|

* Pure alcohol content

Copyright by Rand McNally & Co.
Made in U.S.A.
N-GDS10000-K7- -2-2-3

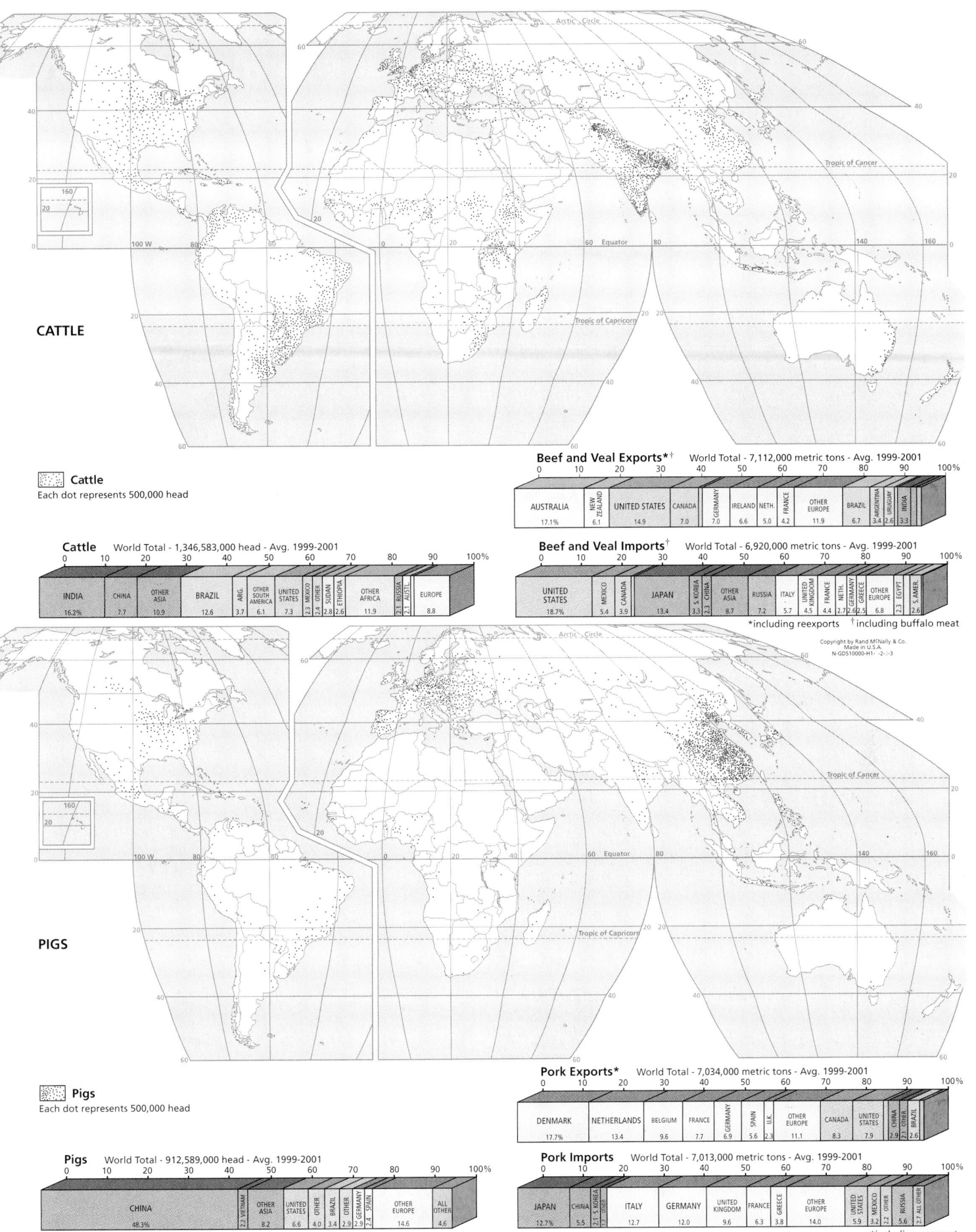

**CATTLE**

**Cattle**
Each dot represents 500,000 head

**Cattle** World Total - 1,346,583,000 head - Avg. 1999-2001

| | | | | | | | | | | | | |
|---|---|---|---|---|---|---|---|---|---|---|---|---|
| INDIA | CHINA | OTHER ASIA | BRAZIL | ARG. | OTHER SOUTH AMERICA | UNITED STATES | MEXICO | SUDAN | ETHIOPIA | OTHER AFRICA | RUSSIA | AUSTL. | EUROPE |
| 16.2% | 7.7 | 10.9 | 12.6 | 3.7 | 6.1 | 7.3 | 2.4 | 2.8 | 2.6 | 11.9 | 2.1 | 2.1 | 8.8 |

**Beef and Veal Exports\*†** World Total - 7,112,000 metric tons - Avg. 1999-2001

| | | | | | | | | | | | | | |
|---|---|---|---|---|---|---|---|---|---|---|---|---|---|
| AUSTRALIA | NEW ZEALAND | UNITED STATES | CANADA | GERMANY | IRELAND | NETH. | FRANCE | OTHER EUROPE | BRAZIL | ARGENTINA | URUGUAY | INDIA | |
| 17.1% | 6.1 | 14.9 | 7.0 | 7.0 | 6.6 | 5.0 | 4.2 | 11.9 | 6.7 | 3.4 | 2.6 | 3.3 | |

**Beef and Veal Imports†** World Total - 6,920,000 metric tons - Avg. 1999-2001

| | | | | | | | | | | | | | | | |
|---|---|---|---|---|---|---|---|---|---|---|---|---|---|---|---|
| UNITED STATES | MEXICO | CANADA | JAPAN | S. KOREA | CHINA | OTHER ASIA | RUSSIA | ITALY | UNITED KINGDOM | FRANCE | GERMANY | GREECE | OTHER EUROPE | EGYPT | S. AMER. |
| 18.7% | 5.4 | 3.9 | 13.4 | 3.3 | 2.3 | 8.7 | 7.2 | 5.7 | 4.5 | 4.4 | 2.7 | 2.6 | 6.8 | 2.3 | 2.6 |

\*including reexports  †including buffalo meat

Copyright by Rand McNally & Co.
Made in U.S.A.
N-GDS10000-H1- -2--3

**PIGS**

**Pigs**
Each dot represents 500,000 head

**Pigs** World Total - 912,589,000 head - Avg. 1999-2001

| | | | | | | | | | |
|---|---|---|---|---|---|---|---|---|---|
| CHINA | VIETNAM | OTHER ASIA | UNITED STATES | OTHER | BRAZIL | OTHER | GERMANY | SPAIN | OTHER EUROPE | ALL OTHER |
| 48.3% | 2.2 | 8.2 | 6.6 | 4.0 | 3.4 | 2.9 | 2.9 | 2.4 | 14.6 | 4.6 |

**Pork Exports\*** World Total - 7,034,000 metric tons - Avg. 1999-2001

| | | | | | | | | | | | | |
|---|---|---|---|---|---|---|---|---|---|---|---|---|
| DENMARK | NETHERLANDS | BELGIUM | FRANCE | GERMANY | SPAIN | U.K. | OTHER EUROPE | CANADA | UNITED STATES | CHINA | OTHER | BRAZIL |
| 17.7% | 13.4 | 9.6 | 7.7 | 6.9 | 5.6 | 2.3 | 11.1 | 8.3 | 7.9 | 2.9 | 2.1 | 2.6 |

**Pork Imports** World Total - 7,013,000 metric tons - Avg. 1999-2001

| | | | | | | | | | | | | |
|---|---|---|---|---|---|---|---|---|---|---|---|---|
| JAPAN | CHINA | S. KOREA | OTHER | ITALY | GERMANY | UNITED KINGDOM | FRANCE | GREECE | OTHER EUROPE | UNITED STATES | MEXICO | OTHER | RUSSIA | ALL OTHER |
| 12.7% | 5.5 | 2.1 | | 12.7 | 12.0 | 9.6 | 6.3 | 3.8 | 14.0 | 5.9 | 3.2 | 2.2 | 5.6 | 2.7 |

\*including reexports

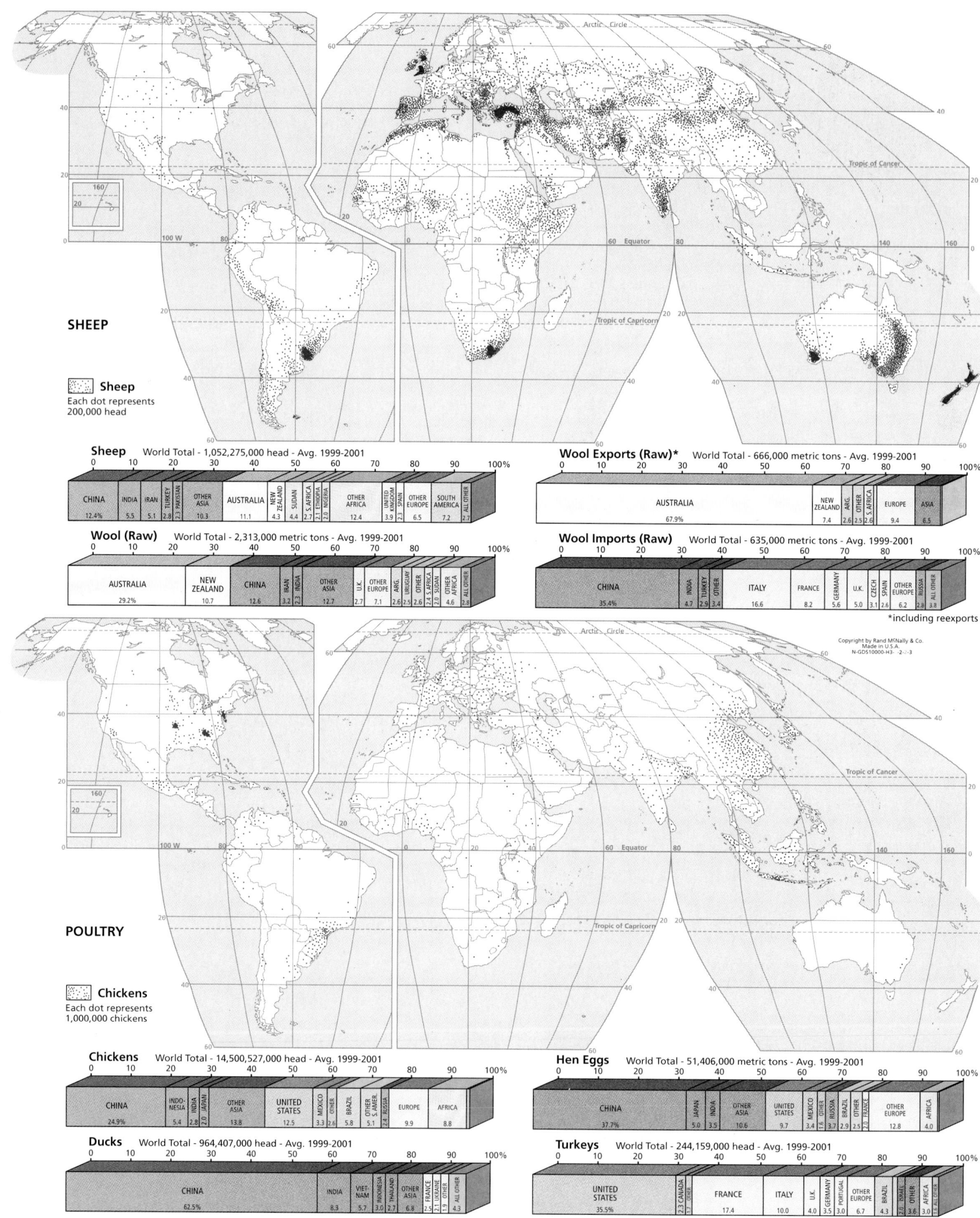

## SHEEP

**Sheep**
Each dot represents 200,000 head

**Sheep**   World Total - 1,052,275,000 head - Avg. 1999-2001

| CHINA 12.4% | INDIA 5.5 | IRAN 5.1 | TURKEY 2.3 | PAKISTAN 2.8 | OTHER ASIA 10.3 | AUSTRALIA 11.1 | NEW ZEALAND 4.3 | SUDAN 4.4 | S. AFRICA 2.7 | ETHIOPIA 2.1 | NIGERIA 2.0 | OTHER AFRICA 12.4 | UNITED KINGDOM 3.9 | SPAIN 2.3 | OTHER EUROPE 6.5 | SOUTH AMERICA 7.2 | ALL OTHER 2.7 |

**Wool (Raw)**   World Total - 2,313,000 metric tons - Avg. 1999-2001

| AUSTRALIA 29.2% | NEW ZEALAND 10.7 | CHINA 12.6 | IRAN 3.2 | INDIA 2.3 | OTHER ASIA 12.7 | U.K. 2.7 | OTHER EUROPE 7.1 | ARG. 2.6 | URUGUAY 2.5 | S. AFRICA 2.4 | SUDAN 2.0 | OTHER AFRICA 4.6 | ALL OTHER 2.8 |

**Wool Exports (Raw)***   World Total - 666,000 metric tons - Avg. 1999-2001

| AUSTRALIA 67.9% | NEW ZEALAND 7.4 | ARG. 2.6 | OTHER 2.5 | S. AFRICA 2.6 | EUROPE 9.4 | ASIA 6.5 |

**Wool Imports (Raw)**   World Total - 635,000 metric tons - Avg. 1999-2001

| CHINA 35.4% | INDIA 4.7 | TURKEY 2.9 | OTHER 3.4 | ITALY 16.6 | FRANCE 8.2 | GERMANY 5.6 | U.K. 5.0 | CZECH 3.1 | SPAIN 2.6 | OTHER EUROPE 6.2 | RUSSIA 2.8 | ALL OTHER 3.8 |

*including reexports

Copyright by Rand McNally & Co.
Made in U.S.A.
N-GDS10000-H3- -2-/- -3

## POULTRY

**Chickens**
Each dot represents 1,000,000 chickens

**Chickens**   World Total - 14,500,527,000 head - Avg. 1999-2001

| CHINA 24.9% | INDO-NESIA 5.4 | INDIA 2.8 | JAPAN 2.0 | OTHER ASIA 13.8 | UNITED STATES 12.5 | MEXICO 3.3 | OTHER 2.6 | BRAZIL 5.8 | OTHER S. AMER. 5.1 | RUSSIA 2.4 | EUROPE 9.9 | AFRICA 8.8 |

**Hen Eggs**   World Total - 51,406,000 metric tons - Avg. 1999-2001

| CHINA 37.7% | JAPAN 5.0 | INDIA 3.5 | OTHER ASIA 10.6 | UNITED STATES 9.7 | MEXICO 3.4 | OTHER 3.7 | RUSSIA 2.9 | BRAZIL 2.7 | FRANCE 2.1 | OTHER EUROPE 12.8 | AFRICA 4.0 |

**Ducks**   World Total - 964,407,000 head - Avg. 1999-2001

| CHINA 62.5% | INDIA 8.3 | VIET-NAM 5.7 | INDONESIA 3.0 | THAILAND 2.7 | OTHER ASIA 6.8 | FRANCE 2.5 | UKRAINE 2.1 | OTHER 1.9 | ALL OTHER 4.3 |

**Turkeys**   World Total - 244,159,000 head - Avg. 1999-2001

| UNITED STATES 35.5% | CANADA 2.3 | OTHER 1.7 | FRANCE 17.4 | ITALY 10.0 | U.K. 4.0 | GERMANY 3.7 | PORTUGAL 3.0 | OTHER EUROPE 6.7 | BRAZIL 4.3 | ISRAEL 2.3 | AFRICA 3.6 | ALL OTHER 3.0 |

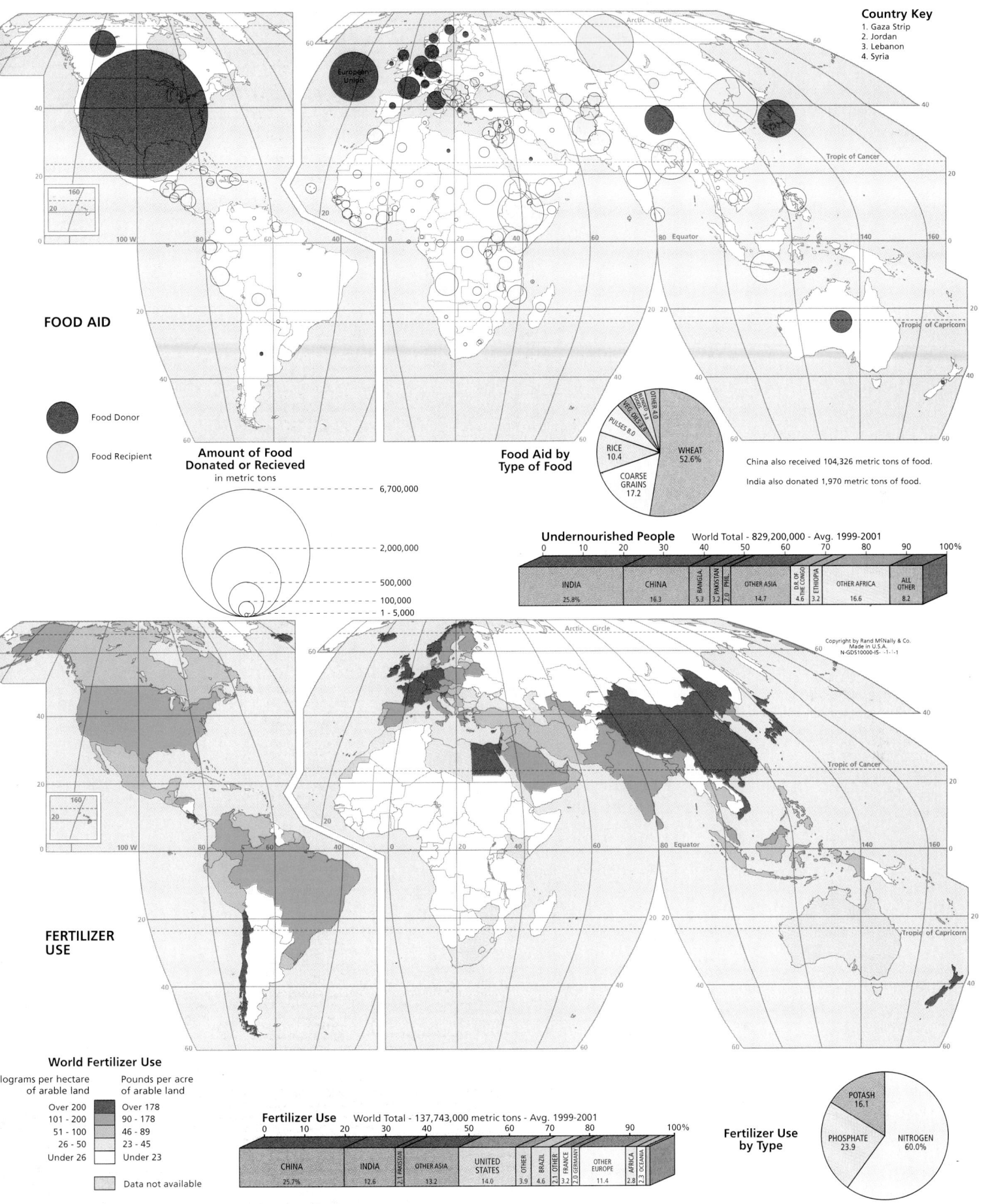

**Country Key**
1. Gaza Strip
2. Jordan
3. Lebanon
4. Syria

**FOOD AID**

Food Donor

Food Recipient

**Amount of Food Donated or Recieved**
in metric tons

6,700,000

2,000,000

500,000

100,000

1 - 5,000

**Food Aid by Type of Food**

OTHER 4.0
VEG. OILS 3.8
PULSES 8.0
RICE 10.4
COARSE GRAINS 17.2
WHEAT 52.6%

China also received 104,326 metric tons of food.

India also donated 1,970 metric tons of food.

**Undernourished People** World Total - 829,200,000 - Avg. 1999-2001

| | | | | | | | | | | |
|---|---|---|---|---|---|---|---|---|---|---|
| 0 | 10 | 20 | 30 | 40 | 50 | 60 | 70 | 80 | 90 | 100% |

| INDIA | CHINA | BANGLA. | PAKISTAN | PHIL. | OTHER ASIA | D.R. OF THE CONGO | ETHIOPIA | OTHER AFRICA | ALL OTHER |
|---|---|---|---|---|---|---|---|---|---|
| 25.8% | 16.3 | 5.3 | 3.2 | 2.0 | 14.7 | 4.6 | 3.2 | 16.6 | 8.2 |

Copyright by Rand McNally & Co.
Made in U.S.A.
N-GDS10000-15- -1-·-1

**FERTILIZER USE**

**World Fertilizer Use**

| Kilograms per hectare of arable land | Pounds per acre of arable land |
|---|---|
| Over 200 | Over 178 |
| 101 - 200 | 90 - 178 |
| 51 - 100 | 46 - 89 |
| 26 - 50 | 23 - 45 |
| Under 26 | Under 23 |

Data not available

**Fertilizer Use** World Total - 137,743,000 metric tons - Avg. 1999-2001

| | | | | | | | | | | |
|---|---|---|---|---|---|---|---|---|---|---|
| 0 | 10 | 20 | 30 | 40 | 50 | 60 | 70 | 80 | 90 | 100% |

| CHINA | INDIA | PAKISTAN | OTHER ASIA | UNITED STATES | OTHER | BRAZIL | OTHER | FRANCE | GERMANY | OTHER EUROPE | AFRICA | OCEANIA |
|---|---|---|---|---|---|---|---|---|---|---|---|---|
| 25.7% | 12.6 | 2.1 | 13.2 | 14.0 | 3.9 | 4.6 | 2.1 | 3.2 | 2.0 | 11.4 | 2.8 | 2.3 |

**Fertilizer Use by Type**

POTASH 16.1
PHOSPHATE 23.9
NITROGEN 60.0%

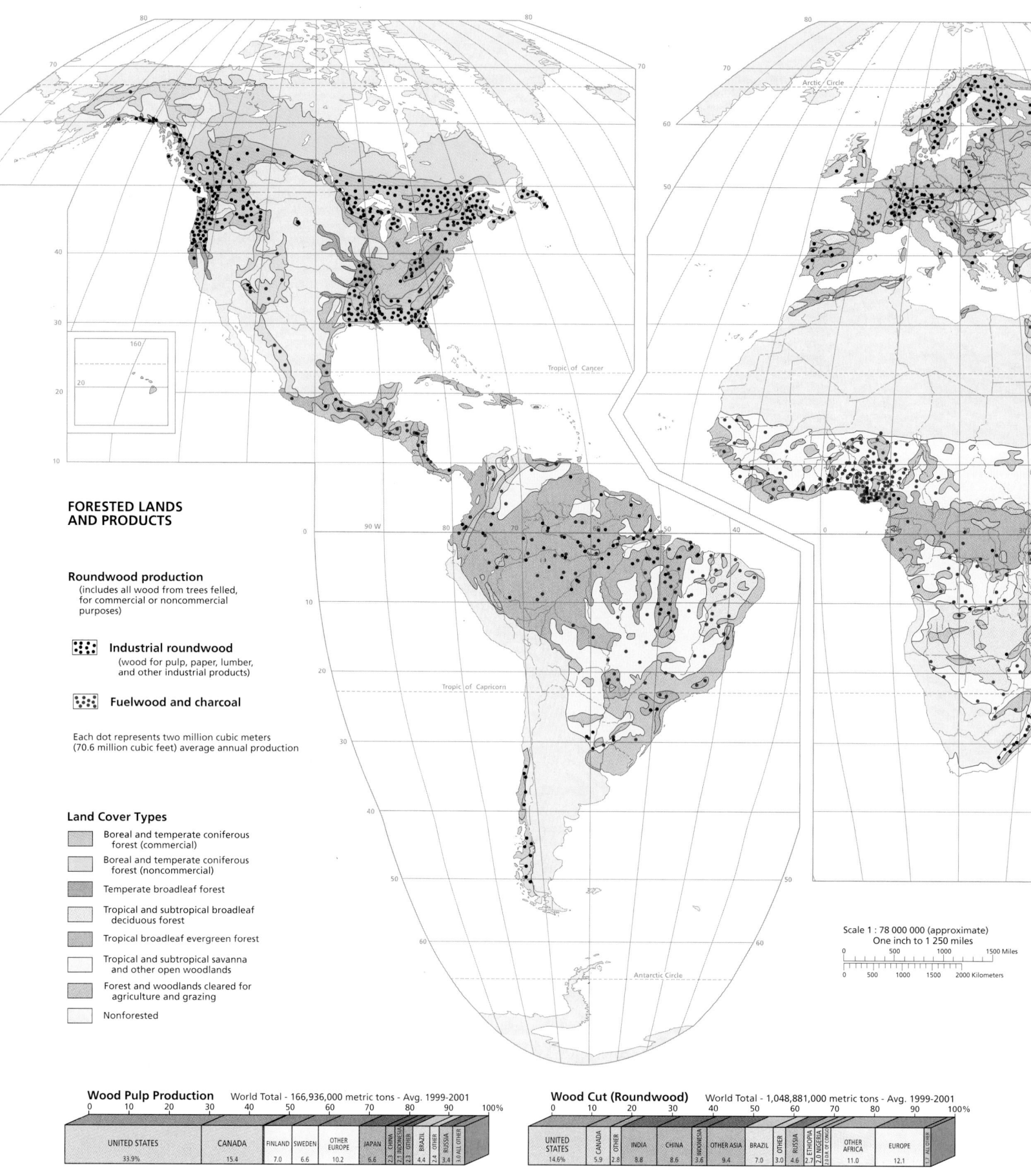

# FORESTED LANDS AND PRODUCTS

**Roundwood production**
(includes all wood from trees felled,
for commercial or noncommercial
purposes)

**Industrial roundwood**
(wood for pulp, paper, lumber,
and other industrial products)

**Fuelwood and charcoal**

Each dot represents two million cubic meters
(70.6 million cubic feet) average annual production

## Land Cover Types

Boreal and temperate coniferous
forest (commercial)

Boreal and temperate coniferous
forest (noncommercial)

Temperate broadleaf forest

Tropical and subtropical broadleaf
deciduous forest

Tropical broadleaf evergreen forest

Tropical and subtropical savanna
and other open woodlands

Forest and woodlands cleared for
agriculture and grazing

Nonforested

Scale 1 : 78 000 000 (approximate)
One inch to 1 250 miles

| 0 | 500 | 1000 | 1500 Miles |

| 0 | 500 | 1000 | 1500 | 2000 Kilometers |

**Wood Pulp Production** World Total - 166,936,000 metric tons - Avg. 1999-2001

| 0 | 10 | 20 | 30 | 40 | 50 | 60 | 70 | 80 | 90 | 100% |

| UNITED STATES 33.9% | CANADA 15.4 | FINLAND 7.0 | SWEDEN 6.6 | OTHER EUROPE 10.2 | JAPAN 6.6 | CHINA 2.3 | INDONESIA 2.1 | OTHER 2.3 | BRAZIL 4.4 | OTHER 2.4 | RUSSIA 3.4 | ALL OTHER 1.0 |

**Wood Cut (Roundwood)** World Total - 1,048,881,000 metric tons - Avg. 1999-2001

| 0 | 10 | 20 | 30 | 40 | 50 | 60 | 70 | 80 | 90 | 100% |

| UNITED STATES 14.6% | CANADA 5.9 | OTHER 2.8 | INDIA 8.8 | CHINA 8.6 | INDONESIA 3.6 | OTHER ASIA 9.4 | BRAZIL 7.0 | OTHER 3.0 | RUSSIA 4.6 | ETHIOPIA 2.7 | NIGERIA 2.0 | D.R. OF CONGO 1.0 | OTHER AFRICA 11.0 | EUROPE 12.1 | ALL OTHER 2.7 |

Tropic of Cancer

Equator

Longitude East of Greenwich

Tropic of Capricorn

Goode's Homolosine Equal Area Projection (Condensed)

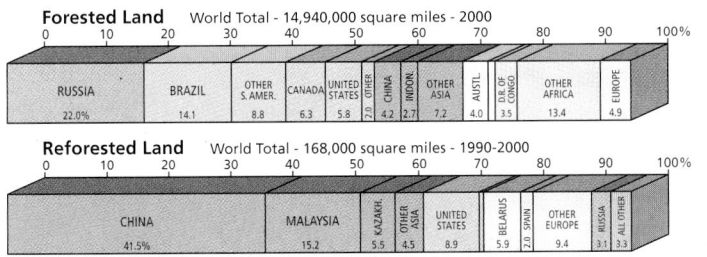

**Forested Land**  World Total - 14,940,000 square miles - 2000

| RUSSIA | BRAZIL | OTHER S. AMER. | CANADA | UNITED STATES | OTHER | CHINA | INDON. | OTHER ASIA | AUSTL. | D.R. OF CONGO | OTHER AFRICA | EUROPE |
|--------|--------|----------------|--------|---------------|-------|-------|--------|------------|--------|---------------|--------------|--------|
| 22.0% | 14.1 | 8.8 | 6.3 | 5.8 | 2.0 | 4.2 | 2.7 | 7.2 | 4.0 | 3.5 | 13.4 | 4.9 |

**Reforested Land**  World Total - 168,000 square miles - 1990-2000

| CHINA | MALAYSIA | KAZAKH. | OTHER ASIA | UNITED STATES | BELARUS | SPAIN | OTHER EUROPE | RUSSIA | ALL OTHER |
|-------|----------|---------|------------|---------------|---------|-------|--------------|--------|-----------|
| 41.5% | 15.2 | 5.5 | 4.5 | 8.9 | 5.9 | 2.0 | 9.4 | 3.1 | 3.3 |

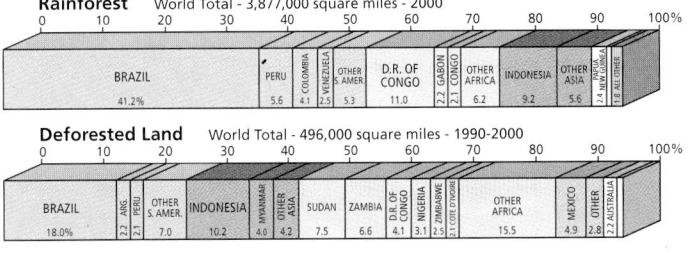

**Rainforest**  World Total - 3,877,000 square miles - 2000

| BRAZIL | PERU | COLOMBIA | VENEZUELA | OTHER S. AMER. | D.R. OF CONGO | GABON | CONGO | OTHER AFRICA | INDONESIA | OTHER ASIA | PAPUA NEW GUINEA | ALL OTHER |
|--------|------|----------|-----------|----------------|---------------|-------|-------|--------------|-----------|------------|------------------|-----------|
| 41.2% | 5.6 | 4.1 | 2.5 | 5.3 | 11.0 | 2.2 | 2.1 | 6.2 | 9.2 | 5.6 | 2.4 | 1.8 |

**Deforested Land**  World Total - 496,000 square miles - 1990-2000

| BRAZIL | ARG. | PERU | OTHER S. AMER. | INDONESIA | MYANMAR | OTHER ASIA | SUDAN | ZAMBIA | D.R. OF CONGO | NIGERIA | ZIMBABWE | CÔTE D'IVOIRE | OTHER AFRICA | MEXICO | OTHER | AUSTRALIA |
|--------|------|------|----------------|-----------|---------|------------|-------|--------|---------------|---------|----------|---------------|--------------|--------|-------|-----------|
| 18.0% | 2.2 | 2.1 | 7.0 | 10.2 | 4.0 | 4.2 | 7.5 | 6.6 | 4.1 | 3.1 | 2.5 | 1.1 | 15.5 | 4.9 | 2.8 | 2.2 |

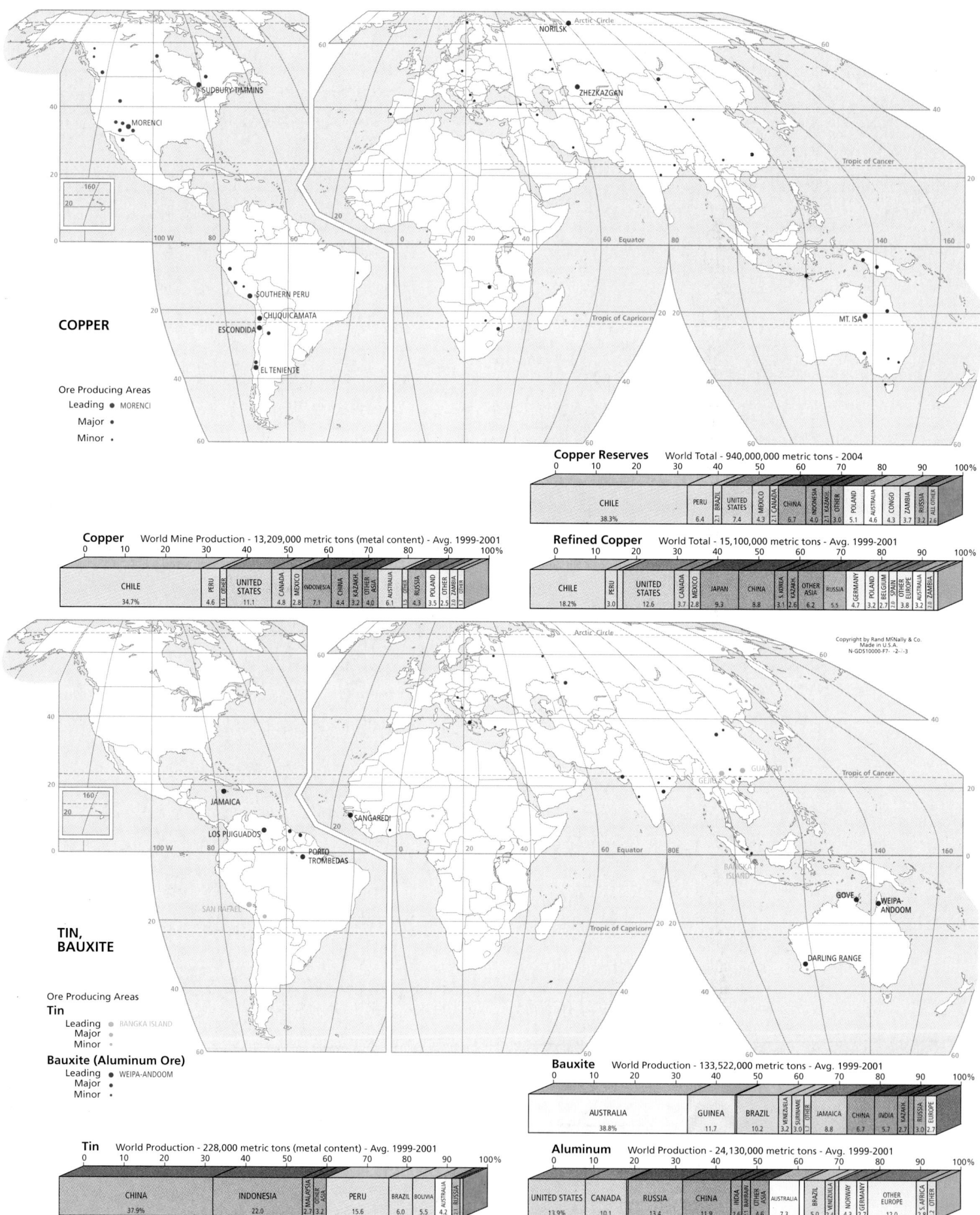

**COPPER**

NORILSK
SUDBURY-TIMMINS
MORENCI
ZHEZKAZGAN
SOUTHERN PERU
CHUQUICAMATA
ESCONDIDA
EL TENIENTE
MT. ISA

Ore Producing Areas
Leading ● MORENCI
Major ●
Minor ·

**TIN, BAUXITE**

JAMAICA
SANGAREDI
GUANGXI
GEJIU
LOS PIJIGUADOS
PORTO TROMBEDAS
BANGKA ISLAND
SAN RAFAEL
GOVE
WEIPA-ANDOOM
DARLING RANGE

Ore Producing Areas
**Tin**
Leading ● BANGKA ISLAND
Major ●
Minor ·

**Bauxite (Aluminum Ore)**
Leading ● WEIPA-ANDOOM
Major ●
Minor ·

Copyright by Rand McNally & Co.
Made in U.S.A.
N-GDS10000-F7- -2--3

**Copper Reserves** World Total - 940,000,000 metric tons - 2004

| 0 | 10 | 20 | 30 | 40 | 50 | 60 | 70 | 80 | 90 | 100% |

| CHILE 38.3% | PERU 6.4 | BRAZIL 2.1 | UNITED STATES 7.4 | MEXICO 4.3 | CANADA 2.1 | CHINA 6.7 | INDONESIA 4.0 | KAZAKH. 2.1 | OTHER 3.0 | POLAND 5.1 | AUSTRALIA 4.6 | CONGO 4.3 | ZAMBIA 3.7 | RUSSIA 3.2 | ALL OTHER 2.6 |

**Copper** World Mine Production - 13,209,000 metric tons (metal content) - Avg. 1999-2001

| 0 | 10 | 20 | 30 | 40 | 50 | 60 | 70 | 80 | 90 | 100% |

| CHILE 34.7% | PERU 4.6 | OTHER 1.6 | UNITED STATES 11.1 | CANADA 4.8 | MEXICO 2.8 | INDONESIA 7.1 | CHINA 4.4 | KAZAKH 3.2 | OTHER ASIA 4.0 | AUSTRALIA 6.1 | OTHER 1.5 | RUSSIA 4.3 | POLAND 3.5 | ZAMBIA 2.5 | OTHER 2.0 | OTHER 1.7 |

**Refined Copper** World Total - 15,100,000 metric tons - Avg. 1999-2001

| 0 | 10 | 20 | 30 | 40 | 50 | 60 | 70 | 80 | 90 | 100% |

| CHILE 18.2% | PERU 3.0 | UNITED STATES 12.6 | CANADA 3.7 | MEXICO 2.8 | JAPAN 9.3 | CHINA 8.8 | S. KOREA 3.1 | KAZAKH. 2.6 | OTHER ASIA 6.2 | RUSSIA 5.5 | GERMANY 4.7 | POLAND 3.2 | BELGIUM 2.7 | SPAIN 2.0 | OTHER EUROPE 3.8 | AUSTRALIA 3.2 | ZAMBIA 2.0 |

**Bauxite** World Production - 133,522,000 metric tons - Avg. 1999-2001

| 0 | 10 | 20 | 30 | 40 | 50 | 60 | 70 | 80 | 90 | 100% |

| AUSTRALIA 38.8% | GUINEA 11.7 | BRAZIL 10.2 | VENEZUELA 3.2 | SURINAME 3.0 | OTHER 1.7 | JAMAICA 8.8 | CHINA 6.7 | INDIA 5.7 | KAZAKH. 2.7 | RUSSIA 3.0 | EUROPE 2.7 |

**Tin** World Production - 228,000 metric tons (metal content) - Avg. 1999-2001

| 0 | 10 | 20 | 30 | 40 | 50 | 60 | 70 | 80 | 90 | 100% |

| CHINA 37.9% | INDONESIA 22.0 | MALAYSIA 2.7 | OTHER ASIA 3.2 | PERU 15.6 | BRAZIL 6.0 | BOLIVIA 5.5 | AUSTRALIA 4.2 | RUSSIA 2.1 |

**Aluminum** World Production - 24,130,000 metric tons - Avg. 1999-2001

| 0 | 10 | 20 | 30 | 40 | 50 | 60 | 70 | 80 | 90 | 100% |

| UNITED STATES 13.9% | CANADA 10.1 | RUSSIA 13.4 | CHINA 11.9 | INDIA 2.6 | BAHRAIN 2.1 | OTHER ASIA 4.6 | AUSTRALIA 7.3 | BRAZIL 5.0 | VENEZUELA 2.4 | NORWAY 4.3 | GERMANY 2.7 | OTHER EUROPE 12.0 | S. AFRICA 2.8 | OTHER 2.2 |

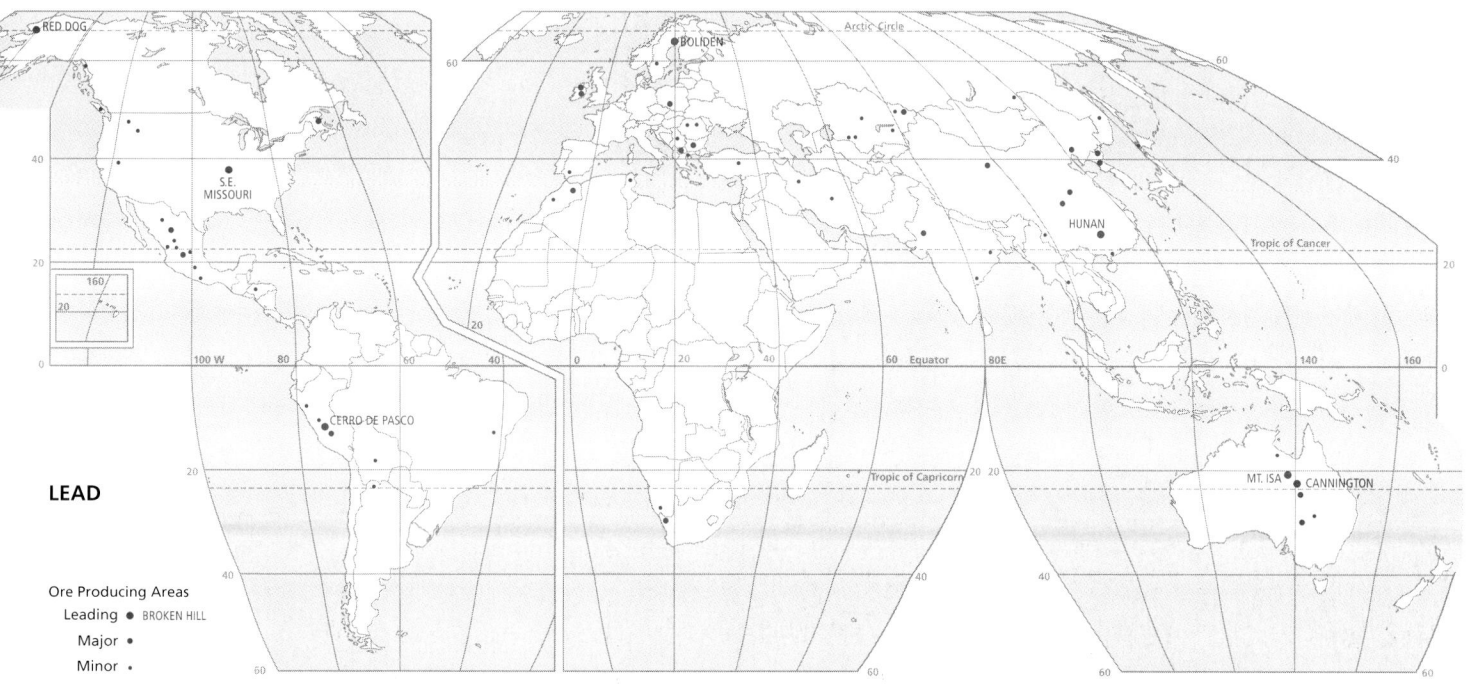

# LEAD

**Ore Producing Areas**

Leading ● BROKEN HILL

Major ●

Minor ·

The percentage of lead smelted by each country is not necessarily identical to its percentage of lead ore production. Some countries, such as Australia, export large amounts of ore to other countries for smelting.

**Lead**  World Mine Production - 3,124,000 metric tons (metal content) - Avg. 1999-2001

| 0 | 10 | 20 | 30 | 40 | 50 | 60 | 70 | 80 | 90 | 100% |

| AUSTRALIA 22.8% | CHINA 19.3 | N. KOREA 2.2 | OTHER ASIA 3.9 | UNITED STATES 15.5 | CANADA 5.0 | MEXICO 4.3 | PERU 8.7 | SWEDEN 3.4 | POLAND 2.8 | OTHER EUROPE 5.9 | MOROCCO 2.6 | S. AFRICA 2.2 |

**Lead Smelted***  World Production - 6,417,000 metric tons - Avg. 1999-2001

| 0 | 10 | 20 | 30 | 40 | 50 | 60 | 70 | 80 | 90 | 100% |

| UNITED STATES 22.4% | CANADA 4.3 | ARUBA 4.3 | MEXICO 2.2 | CHINA 16.6 | JAPAN 4.7 | S. KOREA 2.7 | KAZAKH. 2.6 | OTHER ASIA 6.0 | GERMANY 6.0 | U.K. 5.5 | FRANCE 4.0 | ITALY 3.6 | BELGIUM 1.6 | SPAIN 1.6 | OTHER EUROPE 1.8 | PERU 1.8 | ALL OTHER 4.0 |

*includes recycled materials

Copyright by Rand McNally & Co.
Made in U.S.A.
N-GDS10000-FB- -2- -3

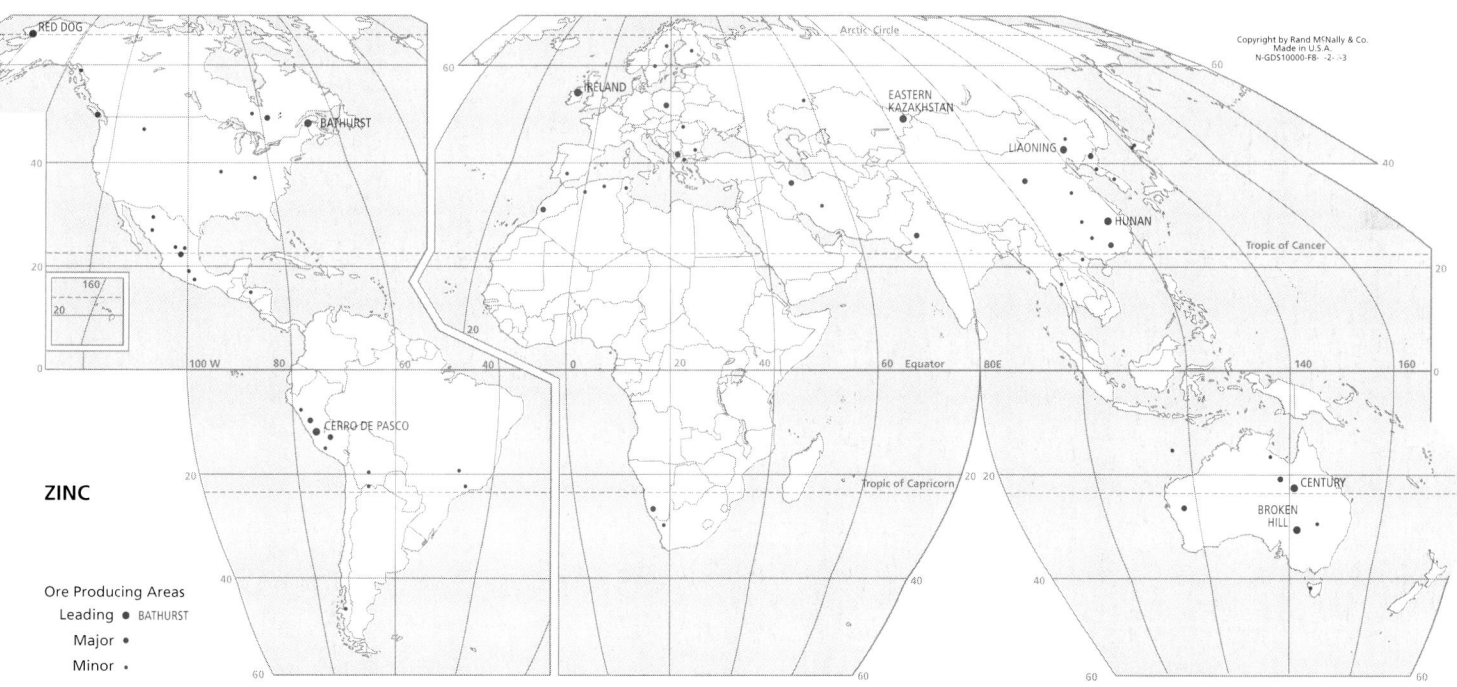

# ZINC

**Ore Producing Areas**

Leading ● BATHURST

Major ●

Minor ·

The percentage of zinc smelted by each country is not necessarily identical to its percentage of zinc ore production. Some countries, such as Australia, export large amounts of ore to other countries for smelting.

**Zinc**  World Mine Production - 8,559,000 metric tons (metal content) - Avg. 1999-2001

| 0 | 10 | 20 | 30 | 40 | 50 | 60 | 70 | 80 | 90 | 100% |

| CHINA 18.9% | KAZAKHSTAN 3.7 | N. KOREA 2.2 | OTHER ASIA 4.1 | AUSTRALIA 16.0 | CANADA 11.3 | UNITED STATES 9.9 | MEXICO 4.5 | PERU 11.2 | OTHER S. AMERICA 3.3 | IRELAND 2.8 | OTHER EUROPE 6.6 | ALL OTHER 5.1 |

**Zinc Smelted***  World Production - 9,011,000, metric tons - Avg. 1999-2001

| 0 | 10 | 20 | 30 | 40 | 50 | 60 | 70 | 80 | 90 | 100% |

| CHINA 21.2% | JAPAN 7.7 | SOUTH KOREA 5.1 | KAZAKHSTAN 2.9 | INDIA 2.3 | N. KOREA 2.1 | CANADA 8.7 | UNITED STATES 3.9 | MEXICO 2.6 | AUSTL. 5.2 | SPAIN 4.1 | GERMANY 3.9 | FRANCE 3.8 | BELGIUM 2.7 | FINLAND 2.6 | NETH. 2.4 | OTHER EUROPE 8.5 | RUSSIA 2.5 | PERU 2.2 | BRAZIL 2.2 | ALL OTHER 1.6 |

*includes recycled materials

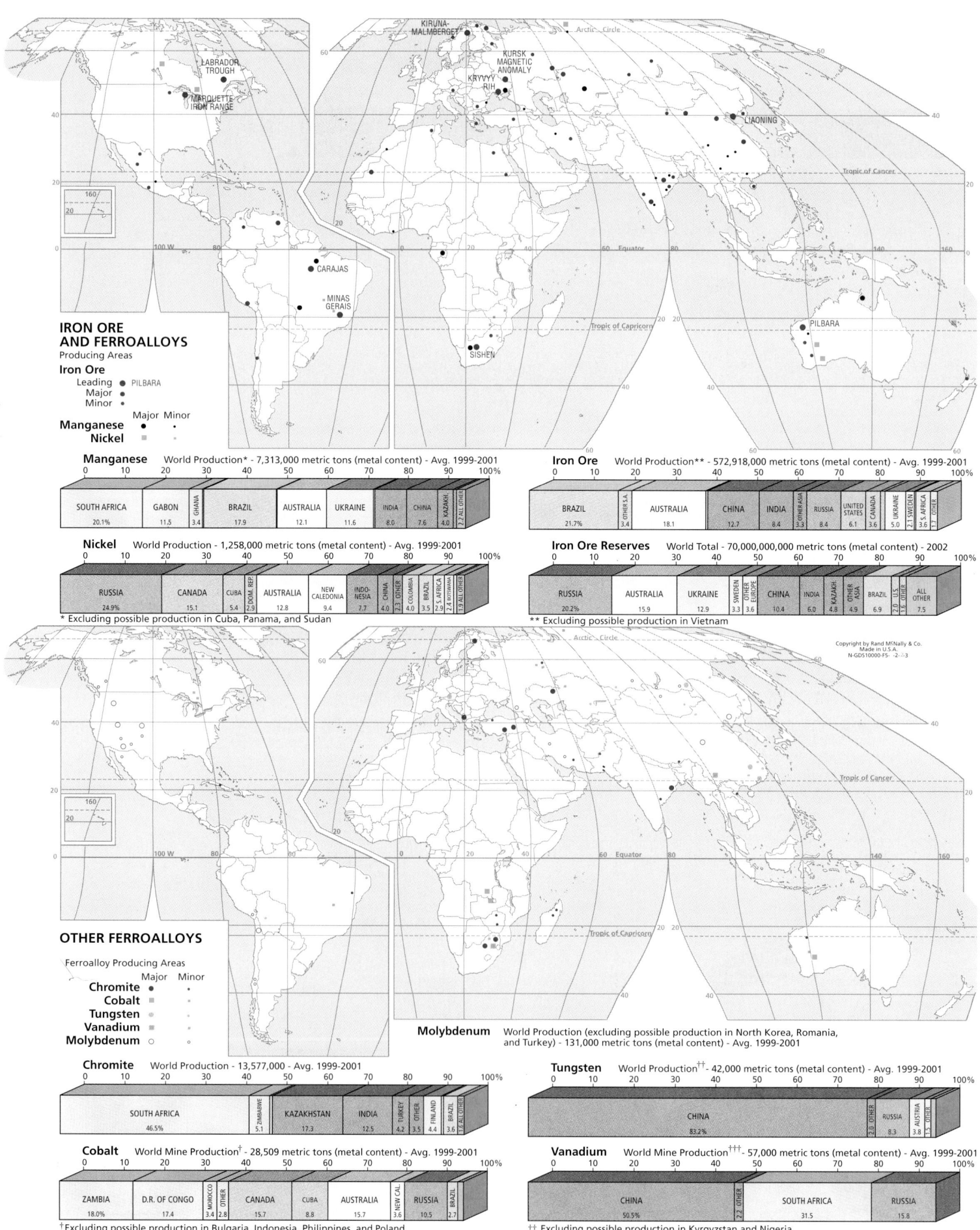

## IRON ORE AND FERROALLOYS
Producing Areas

**Iron Ore**
- Leading ● PILBARA
- Major ●
- Minor •

Major Minor
**Manganese** ■ ▪
**Nickel** ■ ▪

### Manganese
World Production* - 7,313,000 metric tons (metal content) - Avg. 1999-2001

| SOUTH AFRICA | GABON | GHANA | BRAZIL | AUSTRALIA | UKRAINE | INDIA | CHINA | KAZAKH. | ALL OTHER |
|---|---|---|---|---|---|---|---|---|---|
| 20.1% | 11.5 | 3.4 | 17.9 | 12.1 | 11.6 | 8.0 | 7.6 | 4.0 | 2.7 |

### Nickel
World Production - 1,258,000 metric tons (metal content) - Avg. 1999-2001

| RUSSIA | CANADA | CUBA | DOM. REP. | AUSTRALIA | NEW CALEDONIA | INDO-NESIA | CHINA | OTHER | COLOMBIA | BRAZIL | S. AFRICA | BOTSWANA | ALL OTHER |
|---|---|---|---|---|---|---|---|---|---|---|---|---|---|
| 24.9% | 15.1 | 5.4 | 2.9 | 12.8 | 9.4 | 7.7 | 4.0 | 2.3 | 4.0 | 3.5 | 2.9 | 2.4 | 1.9 |

\* Excluding possible production in Cuba, Panama, and Sudan

### Iron Ore
World Production** - 572,918,000 metric tons (metal content) - Avg. 1999-2001

| BRAZIL | OTHER S.A. | AUSTRALIA | CHINA | INDIA | RUSSIA | OTHER ASIA | UNITED STATES | CANADA | UKRAINE | SWEDEN | S. AFRICA | OTHER |
|---|---|---|---|---|---|---|---|---|---|---|---|---|
| 21.7% | 3.4 | 18.1 | 12.7 | 8.4 | 8.4 | 3.3 | 6.1 | 3.6 | 5.0 | 2.1 | 3.6 | 1.7 |

### Iron Ore Reserves
World Total - 70,000,000,000 metric tons (metal content) - 2002

| RUSSIA | AUSTRALIA | UKRAINE | SWEDEN | OTHER EUROPE | CHINA | INDIA | KAZAKH. | OTHER ASIA | BRAZIL | U.S. | ALL OTHER |
|---|---|---|---|---|---|---|---|---|---|---|---|
| 20.2% | 15.9 | 10.4 | 3.3 | 3.6 | 10.4 | 6.0 | 4.8 | 4.9 | 6.9 | 2.0 1.6 | 7.5 |

\*\* Excluding possible production in Vietnam

Copyright by Rand McNally & Co.
Made in U.S.A.
N-GDS10000-FS- -2->-3

## OTHER FERROALLOYS

Ferroalloy Producing Areas

Major Minor
- **Chromite** ● •
- **Cobalt** ■ ▪
- **Tungsten** ● •
- **Vanadium** ■ ▪
- **Molybdenum** ○ ∘

**Molybdenum** World Production (excluding possible production in North Korea, Romania, and Turkey) - 131,000 metric tons (metal content) - Avg. 1999-2001

### Chromite
World Production - 13,577,000 - Avg. 1999-2001

| SOUTH AFRICA | ZIMBABWE | KAZAKHSTAN | INDIA | TURKEY | OTHER | FINLAND | BRAZIL | ALL OTHER |
|---|---|---|---|---|---|---|---|---|
| 46.5% | 5.1 | 17.3 | 12.5 | 4.2 | 3.5 | 4.4 | 1.6 | 3.8 |

### Cobalt
World Mine Production† - 28,509 metric tons (metal content) - Avg. 1999-2001

| ZAMBIA | D.R. OF CONGO | MOROCCO | OTHER | CANADA | CUBA | AUSTRALIA | NEW CAL. | RUSSIA | BRAZIL |
|---|---|---|---|---|---|---|---|---|---|
| 18.0% | 17.4 | 3.4 | 2.8 | 15.7 | 8.8 | 15.7 | 3.6 | 10.5 | 2.7 |

†Excluding possible production in Bulgaria, Indonesia, Philippines, and Poland

### Tungsten
World Production†† - 42,000 metric tons (metal content) - Avg. 1999-2001

| CHINA | OTHER | RUSSIA | AUSTRIA | OTHER |
|---|---|---|---|---|
| 83.2% | 2.0 | 8.3 | 3.8 | 1.5 |

### Vanadium
World Mine Production††† - 57,000 metric tons (metal content) - Avg. 1999-2001

| CHINA | OTHER | SOUTH AFRICA | RUSSIA |
|---|---|---|---|
| 50.5% | 2.2 | 31.5 | 15.8 |

†† Excluding possible production in Kyrgyzstan and Nigeria

††† Excluding possible production in Australia, Germany, and the United States

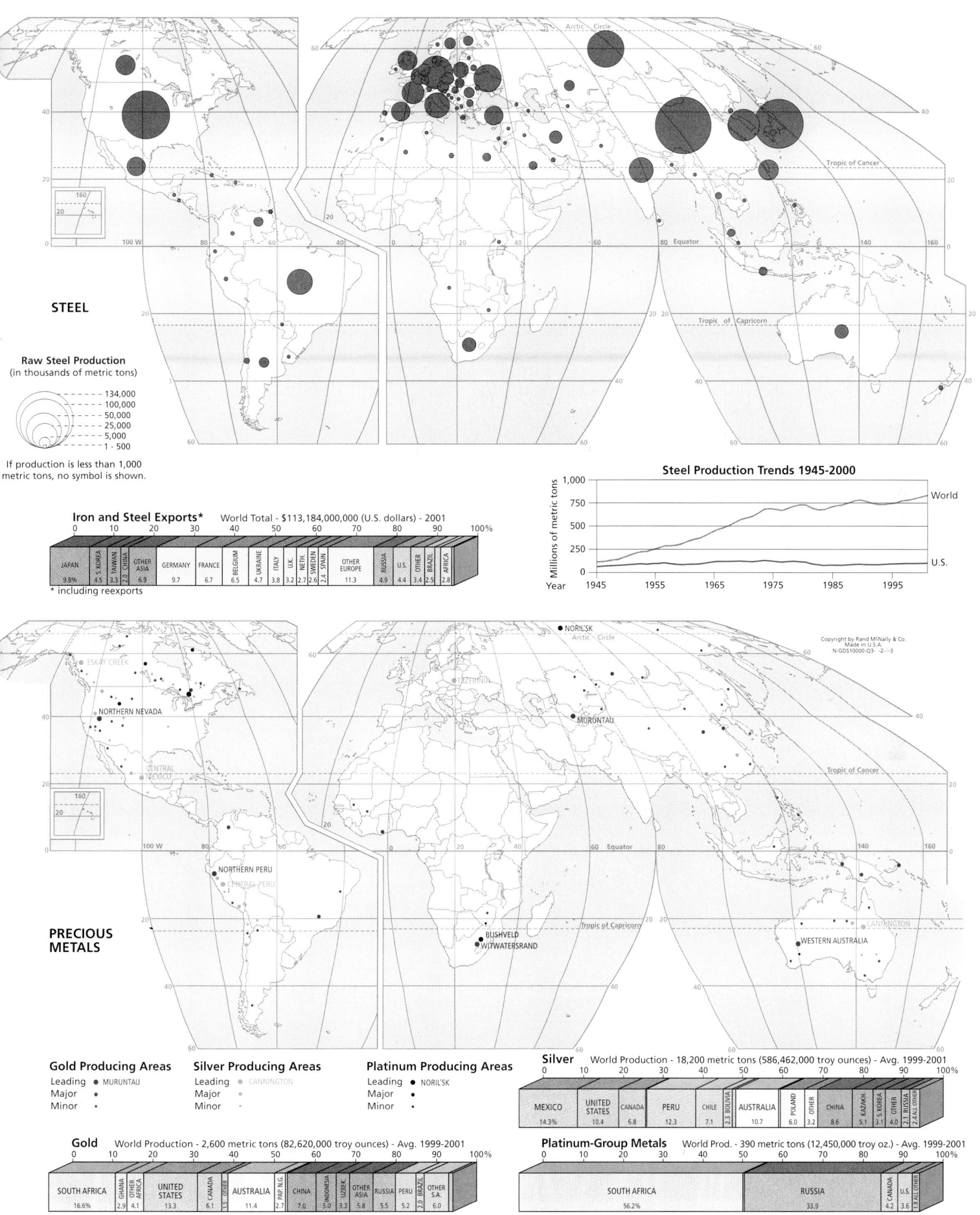

## STEEL

**Raw Steel Production**
(in thousands of metric tons)

- 134,000
- 100,000
- 50,000
- 25,000
- 5,000
- 1 - 500

If production is less than 1,000 metric tons, no symbol is shown.

### Iron and Steel Exports*
World Total - $113,184,000,000 (U.S. dollars) - 2001

| 0 | 10 | 20 | 30 | 40 | 50 | 60 | 70 | 80 | 90 | 100% |
|---|----|----|----|----|----|----|----|----|----|------|

| JAPAN 9.8% | S. KOREA 4.5 | TAIWAN 3.3 | CHINA 2.9 | OTHER ASIA 6.9 | GERMANY 9.7 | FRANCE 6.7 | BELGIUM 6.5 | UKRAINE 4.7 | ITALY 3.8 | U.K. 3.2 | NETH. 2.7 | SWEDEN 2.6 | SPAIN 2.4 | OTHER EUROPE 11.3 | RUSSIA 4.9 | U.S. 4.4 | OTHER 3.4 | BRAZIL 2.5 | AFRICA 2.8 |

\* including reexports

### Steel Production Trends 1945-2000

*World*

*U.S.*

Year: 1945, 1955, 1965, 1975, 1985, 1995

(Millions of metric tons: 250, 500, 750, 1,000)

Copyright by Rand McNally & Co.
Made in U.S.A.
N-GDS10000-Q3- -2- -3

## PRECIOUS METALS

### Gold Producing Areas
- Leading ● MURUNTAU
- Major •
- Minor ·

### Silver Producing Areas
- Leading ● CANNINGTON
- Major •
- Minor ·

### Platinum Producing Areas
- Leading ● NORIL'SK
- Major •
- Minor ·

### Silver
World Production - 18,200 metric tons (586,462,000 troy ounces) - Avg. 1999-2001

| 0 | 10 | 20 | 30 | 40 | 50 | 60 | 70 | 80 | 90 | 100% |
|---|----|----|----|----|----|----|----|----|----|------|

| MEXICO 14.3% | UNITED STATES 10.4 | CANADA 6.8 | PERU 12.3 | CHILE 7.1 | BOLIVIA 2.3 | AUSTRALIA 10.7 | POLAND 6.0 | OTHER 3.2 | CHINA 8.6 | KAZAKH. 5.1 | S. KOREA 3.1 | OTHER 4.0 | RUSSIA 2.1 | ALL OTHER 2.4 |

### Gold
World Production - 2,600 metric tons (82,620,000 troy ounces) - Avg. 1999-2001

| 0 | 10 | 20 | 30 | 40 | 50 | 60 | 70 | 80 | 90 | 100% |
|---|----|----|----|----|----|----|----|----|----|------|

| SOUTH AFRICA 16.6% | GHANA 2.9 | OTHER AFRICA 4.1 | UNITED STATES 13.3 | CANADA 6.1 | OTHER 1.5 | AUSTRALIA 11.4 | PAP. N.G. 2.7 | CHINA 7.0 | INDONESIA 5.0 | UZBK. 3.3 | OTHER ASIA 5.8 | RUSSIA 5.5 | PERU 5.2 | BRAZIL 2.0 | OTHER S.A. 6.0 |

### Platinum-Group Metals
World Prod. - 390 metric tons (12,450,000 troy oz.) - Avg. 1999-2001

| 0 | 10 | 20 | 30 | 40 | 50 | 60 | 70 | 80 | 90 | 100% |
|---|----|----|----|----|----|----|----|----|----|------|

| SOUTH AFRICA 56.2% | RUSSIA 33.9 | CANADA 4.2 | U.S. 1.8 | ALL OTHER 2.4 |

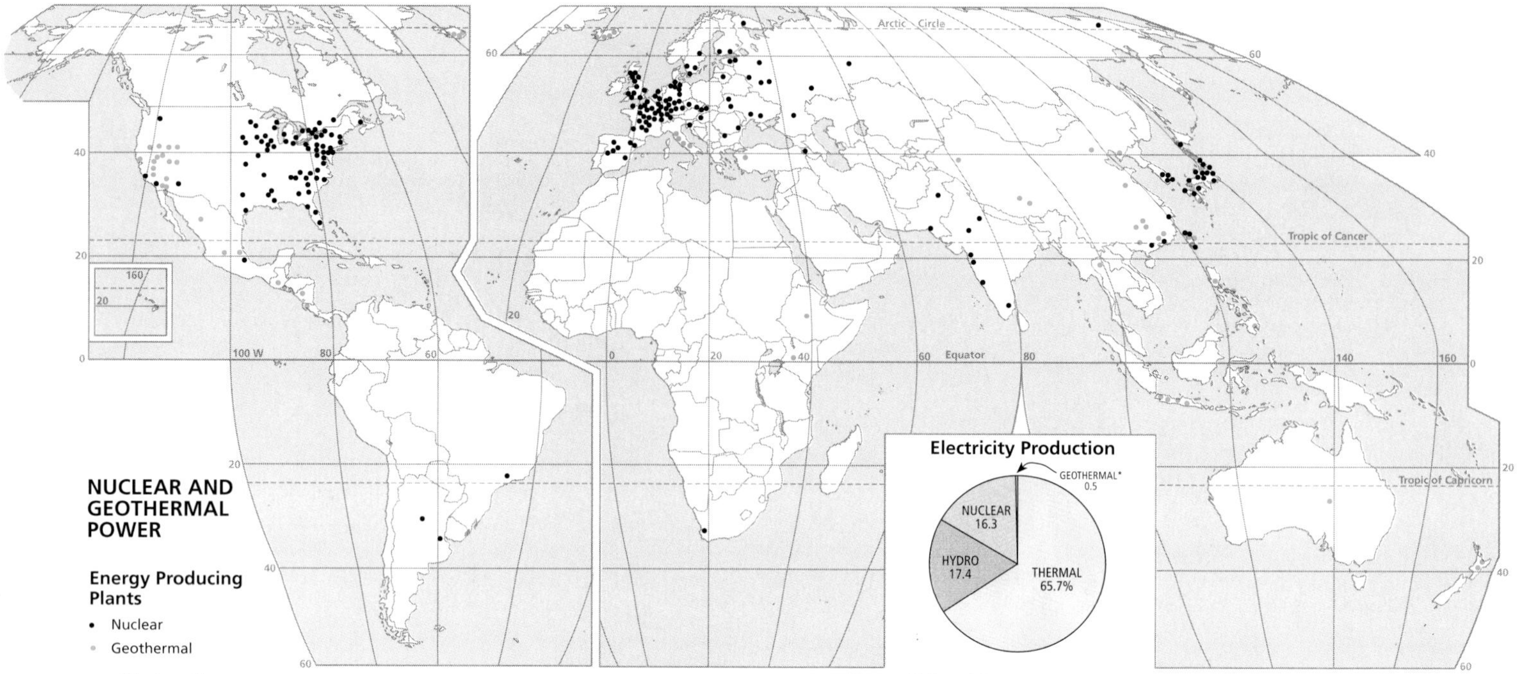

## NUCLEAR AND GEOTHERMAL POWER

**Energy Producing Plants**

- Nuclear
- Geothermal

### Electricity Production

GEOTHERMAL*
0.5

NUCLEAR
16.3

HYDRO
17.4

THERMAL
65.7%

### Nuclear Energy
World Production - 2,547,000 gigawatt hours - 2000

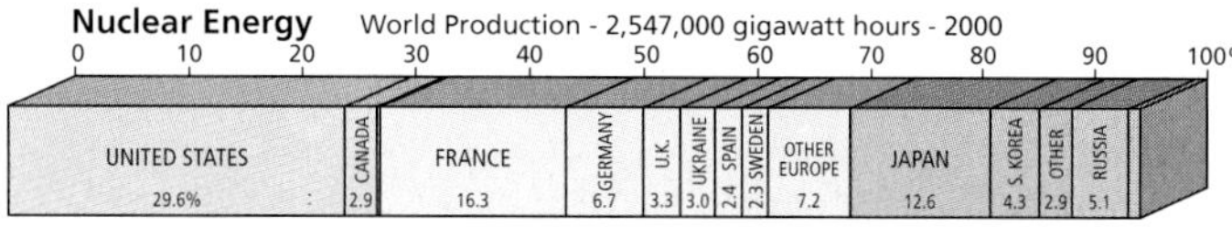

| | | | | | | | | | | | | |
|---|---|---|---|---|---|---|---|---|---|---|---|---|
| 0 | 10 | 20 | 30 | 40 | 50 | 60 | 70 | 80 | 90 | 100% |

| UNITED STATES 29.6% | CANADA 2.9 | FRANCE 16.3 | GERMANY 6.7 | U.K. 3.3 | UKRAINE 3.0 | SPAIN 2.4 | SWEDEN 2.3 | OTHER EUROPE 7.2 | JAPAN 12.6 | S. KOREA 4.3 | OTHER 2.9 | RUSSIA 5.1 |

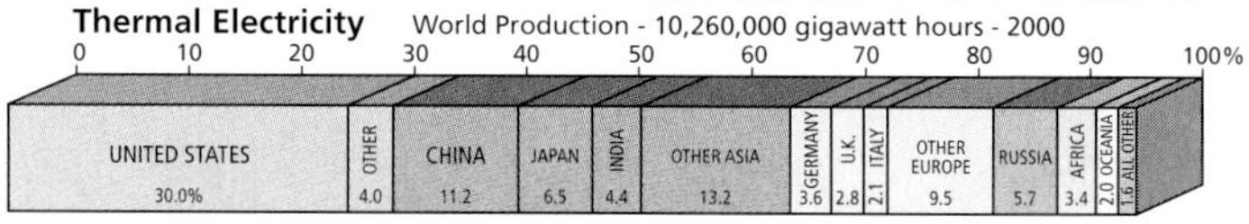

### Geothermal Electricity*
World Production - 85,000 gigawatt hours - 2000

| | | | | | | | | | | | |
|---|---|---|---|---|---|---|---|---|---|---|---|
| 0 | 10 | 20 | 30 | 40 | 50 | 60 | 70 | 80 | 90 | 100% |

| UNITED STATES 28.3% | MEXICO 6.9 | OTHER 3.2 | PHILIPPINES 13.6 | JAPAN 4.0 | INDO. 3.1 | OTHER 2.7 | GERMANY 11.3 | ITALY 6.2 | SPAIN | DENMARK 5.3 | OTHER EUROPE 5.9 | N.Z. 3.4 |

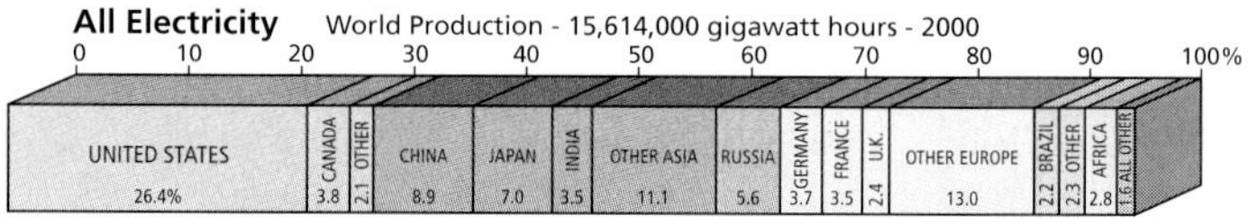

\* May include other sources of electricity, such as solar or wind energy.

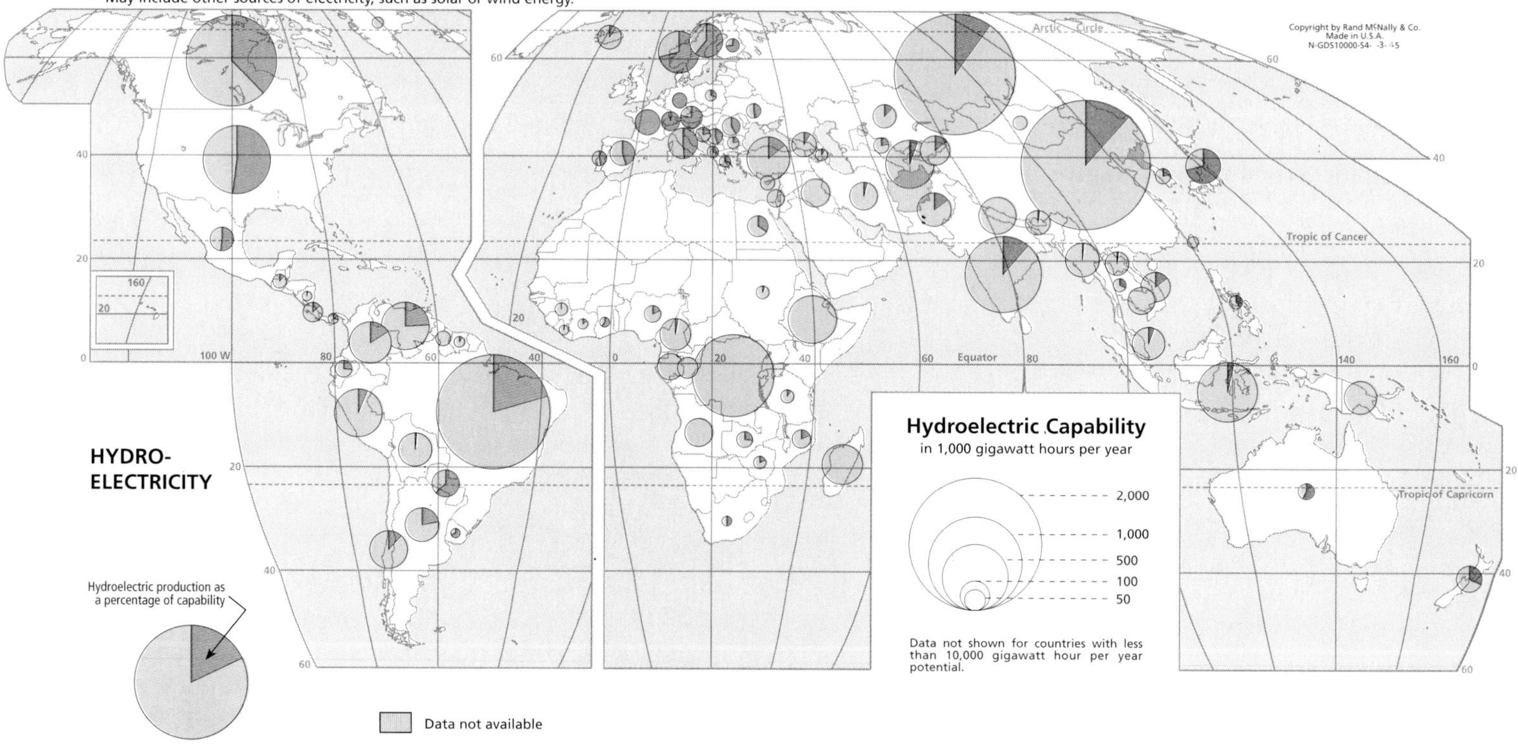

### Thermal Electricity
World Production - 10,260,000 gigawatt hours - 2000

| | | | | | | | | | | | |
|---|---|---|---|---|---|---|---|---|---|---|---|
| 0 | 10 | 20 | 30 | 40 | 50 | 60 | 70 | 80 | 90 | 100% |

| UNITED STATES 30.0% | OTHER 4.0 | CHINA 11.2 | JAPAN 6.5 | INDIA 4.4 | OTHER ASIA 13.2 | GERMANY 3.6 | U.K. 2.8 | ITALY 2.1 | OTHER EUROPE 9.5 | RUSSIA 5.7 | AFRICA 3.4 | OCEANIA 2.0 | ALL OTHER 1.6 |

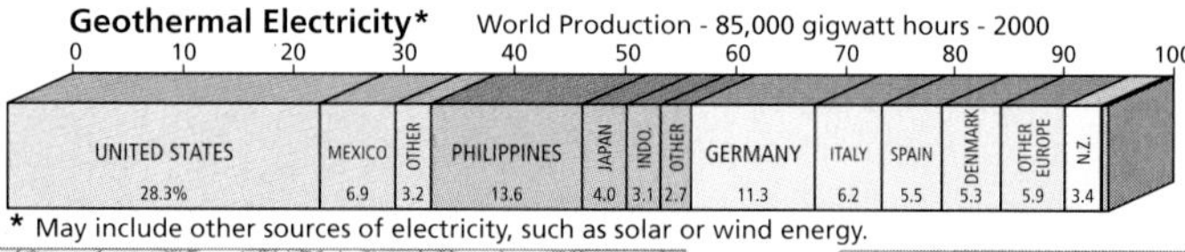

### All Electricity
World Production - 15,614,000 gigawatt hours - 2000

| | | | | | | | | | | | |
|---|---|---|---|---|---|---|---|---|---|---|---|
| 0 | 10 | 20 | 30 | 40 | 50 | 60 | 70 | 80 | 90 | 100% |

| UNITED STATES 26.4% | CANADA 3.8 | OTHER 2.1 | CHINA 8.9 | JAPAN 7.0 | INDIA 3.5 | OTHER ASIA 11.1 | RUSSIA 5.6 | GERMANY 3.7 | FRANCE 3.5 | U.K. 2.4 | OTHER EUROPE 13.0 | BRAZIL 2.2 | OTHER 2.3 | AFRICA 2.8 | ALL OTHER 1.6 |

Copyright by Rand McNally & Co.
Made in U.S.A.
N-GDS10000-54- -3- -45

## HYDRO-ELECTRICITY

### Hydroelectric Capability
in 1,000 gigawatt hours per year

2,000
1,000
500
100
50

Data not shown for countries with less than 10,000 gigawatt hour per year potential.

Hydroelectric production as a percentage of capability

Data not available

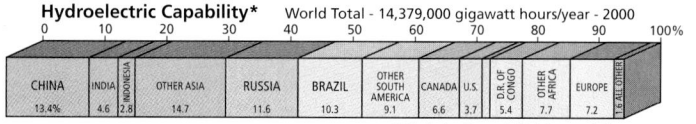

### Hydroelectric Capability*
World Total - 14,379,000 gigawatt hours/year - 2000

| | | | | | | | | | | | |
|---|---|---|---|---|---|---|---|---|---|---|---|
| 0 | 10 | 20 | 30 | 40 | 50 | 60 | 70 | 80 | 90 | 100% |

| CHINA 13.4% | INDIA 4.6 | INDONESIA 2.8 | OTHER ASIA 14.7 | RUSSIA 11.6 | BRAZIL 10.3 | OTHER SOUTH AMERICA 9.1 | CANADA 6.6 | U.S. 3.7 | D.R. OF CONGO 5.4 | OTHER AFRICA 7.7 | EUROPE 7.2 | ALL OTHER 1.6 |

\* Technically exploitable capability

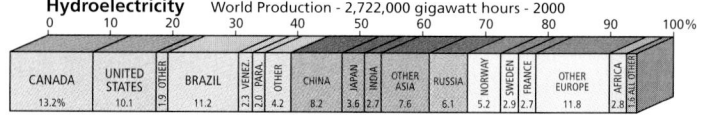

### Hydroelectricity
World Production - 2,722,000 gigawatt hours - 2000

| | | | | | | | | | | | |
|---|---|---|---|---|---|---|---|---|---|---|---|
| 0 | 10 | 20 | 30 | 40 | 50 | 60 | 70 | 80 | 90 | 100% |

| CANADA 13.2% | UNITED STATES 10.1 | OTHER 1.9 | BRAZIL 11.2 | VENEZ. 2.3 | PARA. 2.0 | OTHER 4.2 | CHINA 8.2 | JAPAN 3.6 | INDIA 2.7 | OTHER ASIA 7.6 | RUSSIA 6.1 | NORWAY 5.2 | SWEDEN 2.9 | FRANCE 2.7 | OTHER EUROPE 11.8 | AFRICA 2.8 | ALL OTHER 1.6 |

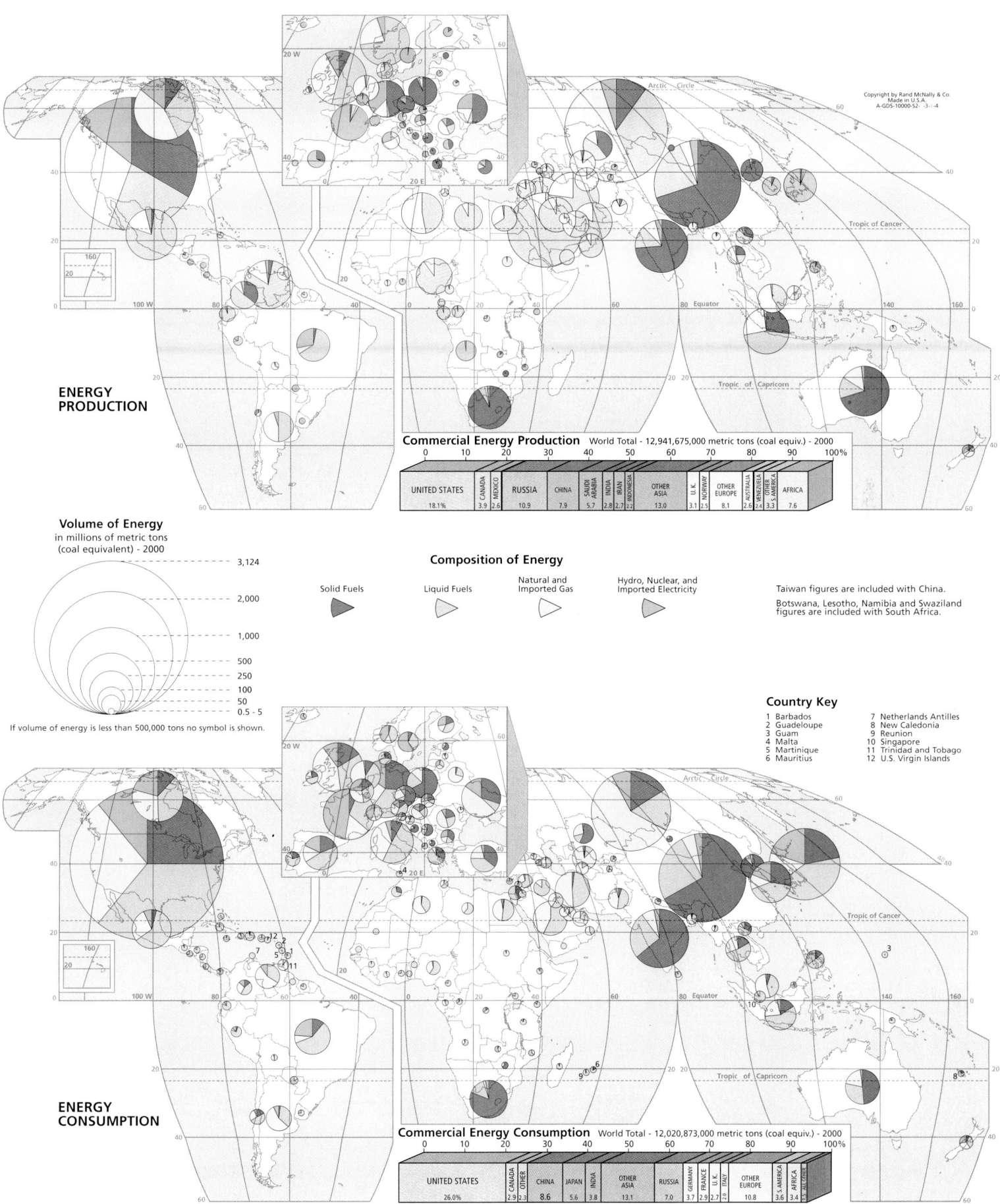

ENERGY
PRODUCTION

**Commercial Energy Production** World Total - 12,941,675,000 metric tons (coal equiv.) - 2000

| | | | | | | | | | | | | | | | |
|---|---|---|---|---|---|---|---|---|---|---|---|---|---|---|---|
| 0 | 10 | 20 | 30 | 40 | 50 | 60 | 70 | 80 | 90 | 100% | | | | | |

| UNITED STATES | CANADA | MEXICO | RUSSIA | CHINA | SAUDI ARABIA | INDIA | IRAN | INDONESIA | OTHER ASIA | U.K. | NORWAY | OTHER EUROPE | AUSTRALIA | VENEZUELA | OTHER S. AMERICA | AFRICA |
|---|---|---|---|---|---|---|---|---|---|---|---|---|---|---|---|---|
| 18.1% | 3.9 | 2.6 | 10.9 | 7.9 | 5.7 | 2.8 | 2.7 | 2.2 | 13.0 | 3.1 | 2.5 | 8.1 | 2.6 | 2.4 | 3.3 | 7.6 |

**Volume of Energy**
in millions of metric tons
(coal equivalent) - 2000

- 3,124
- 2,000
- 1,000
- 500
- 250
- 100
- 50
- 0.5 - 5

If volume of energy is less than 500,000 tons no symbol is shown.

**Composition of Energy**

Solid Fuels  Liquid Fuels  Natural and Imported Gas  Hydro, Nuclear, and Imported Electricity

Taiwan figures are included with China.

Botswana, Lesotho, Namibia and Swaziland figures are included with South Africa.

**Country Key**

| | | | |
|---|---|---|---|
| 1 | Barbados | 7 | Netherlands Antilles |
| 2 | Guadeloupe | 8 | New Caledonia |
| 3 | Guam | 9 | Reunion |
| 4 | Malta | 10 | Singapore |
| 5 | Martinique | 11 | Trinidad and Tobago |
| 6 | Mauritius | 12 | U.S. Virgin Islands |

ENERGY
CONSUMPTION

**Commercial Energy Consumption** World Total - 12,020,873,000 metric tons (coal equiv.) - 2000

| | | | | | | | | | | | |
|---|---|---|---|---|---|---|---|---|---|---|---|
| 0 | 10 | 20 | 30 | 40 | 50 | 60 | 70 | 80 | 90 | 100% | |

| UNITED STATES | CANADA | OTHER | CHINA | JAPAN | INDIA | OTHER ASIA | RUSSIA | GERMANY | FRANCE | U.K. | ITALY | OTHER EUROPE | S. AMERICA | AFRICA | ALL OTHER |
|---|---|---|---|---|---|---|---|---|---|---|---|---|---|---|---|
| 26.0% | 2.9 | 2.3 | 8.6 | 5.6 | 3.8 | 13.1 | 7.0 | 3.7 | 2.9 | 2.7 | 2.3 | 10.8 | 3.6 | 3.4 | 1.5 |

Copyright by Rand McNally & Co.
Made in U.S.A.
A-GDS-10000-52- -3-I- -4

58

MINERAL FUELS

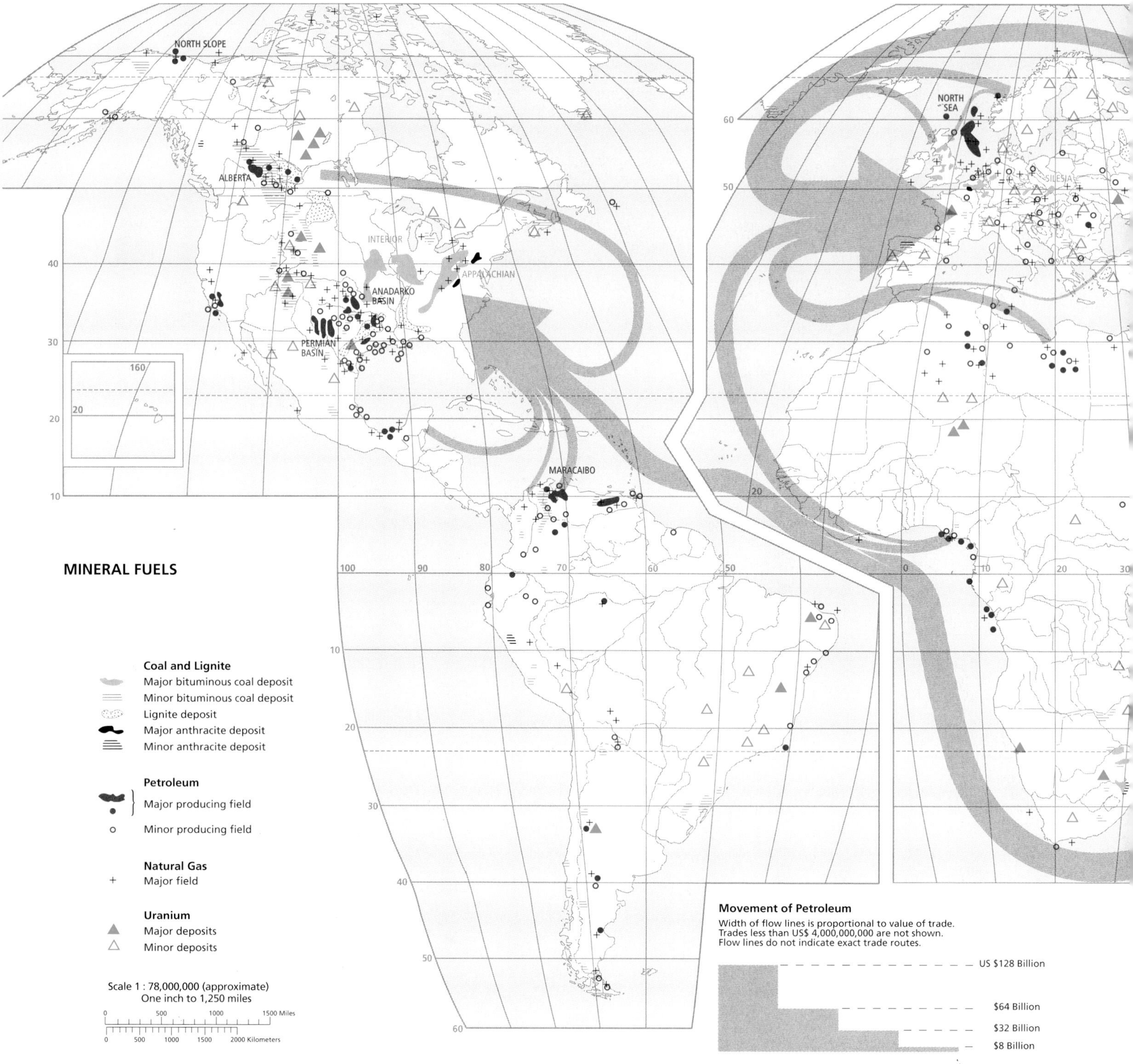

NORTH SLOPE

ALBERTA

INTERIOR

ANADARKO
BASIN

APPALACHIAN

PERMIAN
BASIN

MARACAIBO

NORTH
SEA

SILESIA

160

20

**Coal and Lignite**
▨ Major bituminous coal deposit
▤ Minor bituminous coal deposit
▨ Lignite deposit
◆ Major anthracite deposit
▤ Minor anthracite deposit

**Petroleum**
🔲 ● } Major producing field
○ Minor producing field

**Natural Gas**
+ Major field

**Uranium**
▲ Major deposits
△ Minor deposits

Scale 1 : 78,000,000 (approximate)
One inch to 1,250 miles

0   500   1000   1500 Miles

0   500   1000   1500   2000 Kilometers

**Movement of Petroleum**
Width of flow lines is proportional to value of trade.
Trades less than US$ 4,000,000,000 are not shown.
Flow lines do not indicate exact trade routes.

─ ─ US $128 Billion

─ ─ $64 Billion

─ ─ $32 Billion

─ $8 Billion

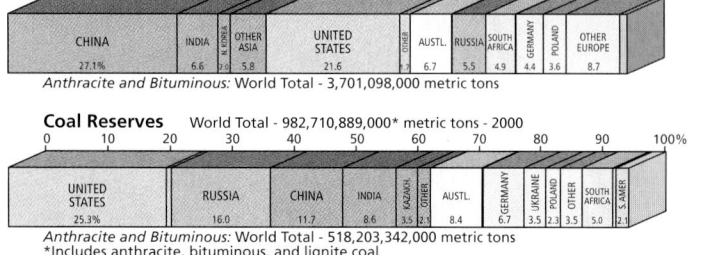

**Coal**   World Production - 4,183,295,000* metric tons - Avg. 1999-2001

| | 0 | 10 | 20 | 30 | 40 | 50 | 60 | 70 | 80 | 90 | 100% |
|---|---|---|---|---|---|---|---|---|---|---|---|

| CHINA | INDIA | N. KOREA | OTHER ASIA | UNITED STATES | OTHER | AUSTL. | RUSSIA | SOUTH AFRICA | GERMANY | POLAND | OTHER EUROPE |
|---|---|---|---|---|---|---|---|---|---|---|---|
| 27.1% | 6.6 | 2.6 | 5.8 | 21.6 | | 6.7 | 5.5 | 4.9 | 4.4 | 3.6 | 8.7 |

*Anthracite and Bituminous: World Total - 3,701,098,000 metric tons*

**Coal Reserves**   World Total - 982,710,889,000* metric tons - 2000

| | 0 | 10 | 20 | 30 | 40 | 50 | 60 | 70 | 80 | 90 | 100% |
|---|---|---|---|---|---|---|---|---|---|---|---|

| UNITED STATES | RUSSIA | CHINA | INDIA | KAZAKH. | OTHER | AUSTL. | GERMANY | UKRAINE | POLAND | OTHER | SOUTH AFRICA | S. AMER. |
|---|---|---|---|---|---|---|---|---|---|---|---|---|
| 25.3% | 16.0 | 11.7 | 8.6 | 3.5 | 2.1 | 8.4 | 6.7 | 3.5 | 2.3 | 5.0 | | 2.1 |

*Anthracite and Bituminous: World Total - 518,203,342,000 metric tons*
*Includes anthracite, bituminous, and lignite coal*

**Petroleum**   World Production - 3,346,515,000** metric tons (24,606,731,000 barrels) - Avg. 1999-2001

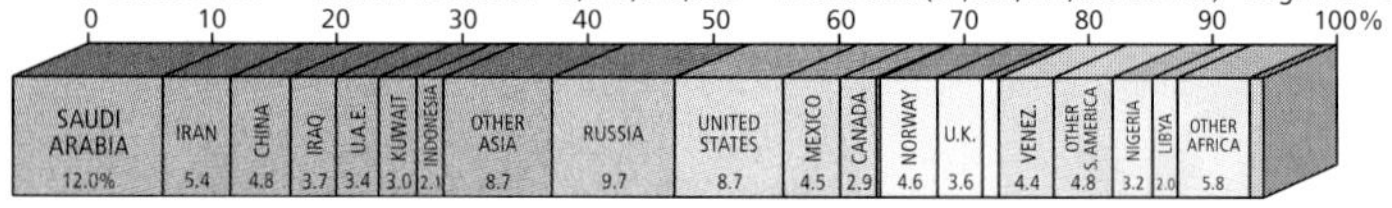

| | 0 | 10 | 20 | 30 | 40 | 50 | 60 | 70 | 80 | 90 | 100% |
|---|---|---|---|---|---|---|---|---|---|---|---|

| SAUDI ARABIA | IRAN | CHINA | IRAQ | U.A.E. | KUWAIT | INDONESIA | OTHER ASIA | RUSSIA | UNITED STATES | MEXICO | CANADA | NORWAY | U.K. | VENEZ. | OTHER S. AMERICA | NIGERIA | OTHER AFRICA |
|---|---|---|---|---|---|---|---|---|---|---|---|---|---|---|---|---|---|
| 12.0% | 5.4 | 4.8 | 3.7 | 3.4 | 3.0 | 2.1 | 8.7 | 9.7 | 8.7 | 4.5 | 2.9 | 4.6 | 3.6 | 4.4 | 4.8 | 3.2 | 5.8 |

**Petroleum Reserves**   World Total - 139,445,735,000** metric tons (1,025,336,289,000 barrels) - 2002

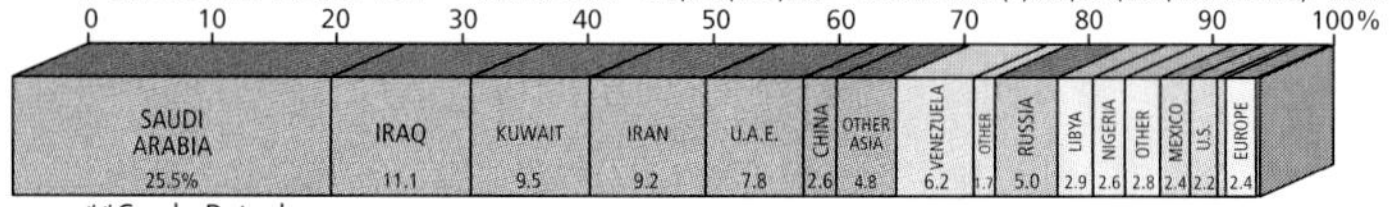

| | 0 | 10 | 20 | 30 | 40 | 50 | 60 | 70 | 80 | 90 | 100% |
|---|---|---|---|---|---|---|---|---|---|---|---|

| SAUDI ARABIA | IRAQ | KUWAIT | IRAN | U.A.E. | CHINA | OTHER ASIA | VENEZUELA | OTHER | RUSSIA | LIBYA | NIGERIA | OTHER | MEXICO | U.S. | EUROPE |
|---|---|---|---|---|---|---|---|---|---|---|---|---|---|---|---|
| 25.5% | 11.1 | 9.5 | 9.2 | 7.8 | 2.6 | 4.8 | 6.2 | | 5.0 | 2.9 | 2.6 | 2.8 | 2.4 | 2.2 | 2.4 |

**Crude Petroleum*

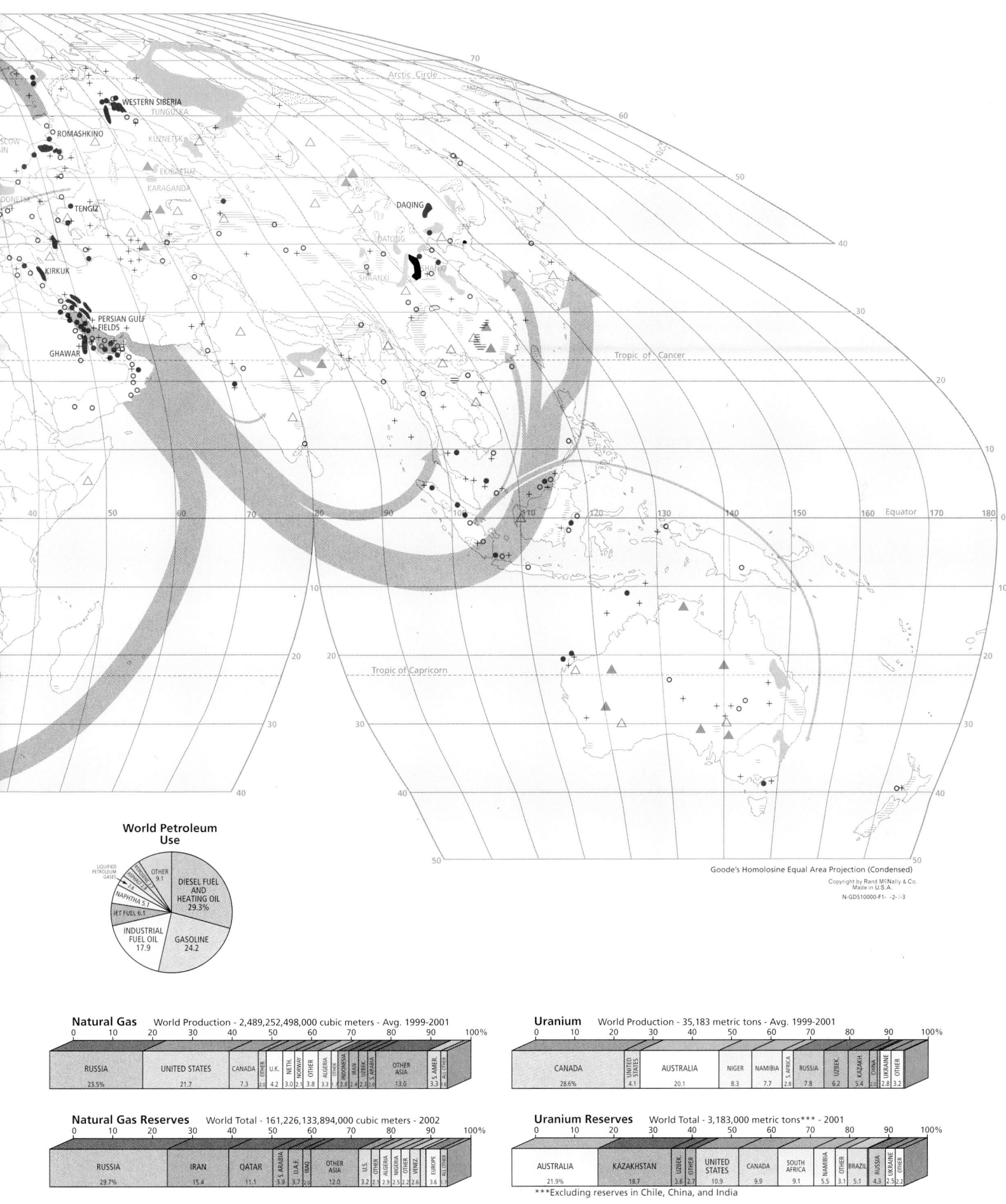

Arctic Circle

WESTERN SIBERIA
TUNGUSKA
ROMASHKINO
SCOW
IN
KUZNETSK
EKIBASTUZ
KARAGANDA
DONETSK
TENGIZ
DAQING
DATONG
KIRKUK
SHANXI
SHAANXI
PERSIAN GULF
FIELDS
GHAWAR

Tropic of Cancer

Equator

Tropic of Capricorn

Goode's Homolosine Equal Area Projection (Condensed)

Copyright by Rand McNally & Co.
Made in U.S.A.
N-GDS10000-F1- -2- -3

## World Petroleum Use

LIQUIFIED
PETROLEUM
GASES
LUBRICANTS
ASPHALT
OTHER 9.1
NAPHTHA 5.1
JET FUEL 6.1
DIESEL FUEL
AND
HEATING OIL
29.3%
INDUSTRIAL
FUEL OIL
17.9
GASOLINE
24.2

## Natural Gas — World Production - 2,489,252,498,000 cubic meters - Avg. 1999-2001

| RUSSIA | UNITED STATES | CANADA | U.K. | NETH. | NORWAY | OTHER | ALGERIA | OTHER | INDONESIA | IRAN | UZBEK. | S. ARABIA | OTHER ASIA | S. AMER. | ALL OTHER |
|---|---|---|---|---|---|---|---|---|---|---|---|---|---|---|---|
| 23.5% | 21.7 | 7.3 | 2.6 | 4.2 | 3.0 | 2.1 | 3.8 | 2.4 | 2.8 | 2.3 | 2.1 | 2.0 | 13.0 | 3.3 | 1.6 |

## Natural Gas Reserves — World Total - 161,226,133,894,000 cubic meters - 2002

| RUSSIA | IRAN | QATAR | S. ARABIA | U.A.E. | IRAQ | OTHER ASIA | U.S. | OTHER | ALGERIA | NIGERIA | VENEZ. | EUROPE | ALL OTHER |
|---|---|---|---|---|---|---|---|---|---|---|---|---|---|
| 29.7% | 15.4 | 11.1 | 3.9 | 3.7 | 2.0 | 12.0 | 3.2 | 2.1 | 2.9 | 2.5 | 2.2 | 2.6 | 3.6 |

## Uranium — World Production - 35,183 metric tons - Avg. 1999-2001

| CANADA | UNITED STATES | AUSTRALIA | NIGER | NAMIBIA | S. AFRICA | RUSSIA | UZBEK. | KAZAKH. | CHINA | UKRAINE | OTHER |
|---|---|---|---|---|---|---|---|---|---|---|---|
| 28.6% | 4.1 | 20.1 | 8.3 | 7.7 | 2.8 | 7.8 | 6.2 | 5.4 | 2.8 | 2.8 | 3.2 |

## Uranium Reserves — World Total - 3,183,000 metric tons*** - 2001

| AUSTRALIA | KAZAKHSTAN | UZBEK. | OTHER | UNITED STATES | CANADA | SOUTH AFRICA | NAMIBIA | OTHER | BRAZIL | RUSSIA | UKRAINE | OTHER |
|---|---|---|---|---|---|---|---|---|---|---|---|---|
| 21.9% | 18.7 | 3.6 | 2.7 | 10.9 | 9.9 | 9.1 | 5.5 | 3.1 | 5.1 | 4.3 | 2.5 | 2.2 |

***Excluding reserves in Chile, China, and India

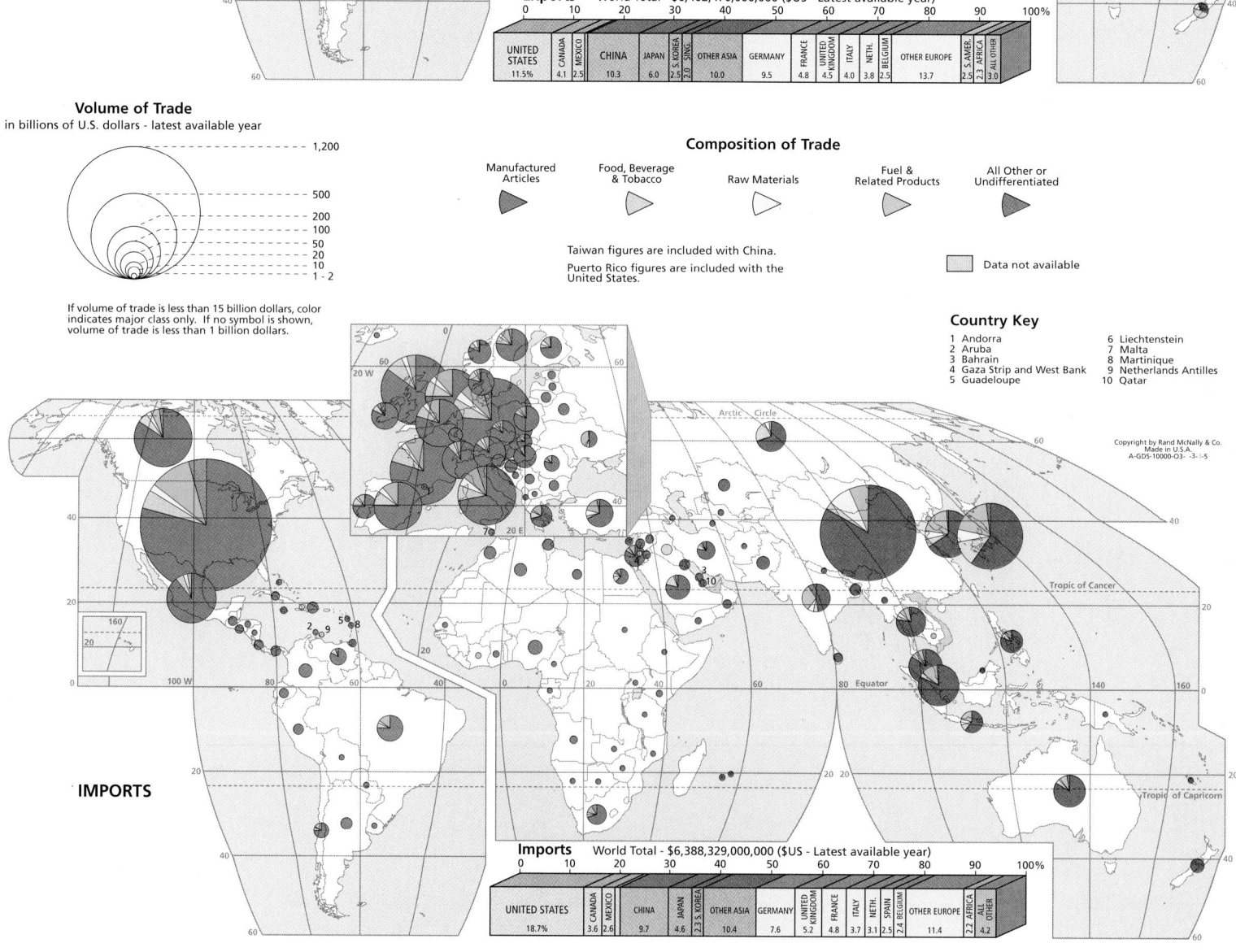

**EXPORTS**

**Exports**  World Total - $6,402,470,000,000 ($US - Latest available year)

| | 0 | 10 | 20 | 30 | 40 | 50 | 60 | 70 | 80 | 90 | 100% |
|---|---|---|---|---|---|---|---|---|---|---|---|

| UNITED STATES | CANADA | MEXICO | CHINA | JAPAN | S. KOREA | SING. | OTHER ASIA | GERMANY | FRANCE | UNITED KINGDOM | ITALY | NETH. | BELGIUM | OTHER EUROPE | S. AMER. | AFRICA | ALL OTHER |
|---|---|---|---|---|---|---|---|---|---|---|---|---|---|---|---|---|---|
| 11.5% | 4.1 | 2.5 | 10.3 | 6.0 | 2.5 | 2.0 | 10.0 | 9.5 | 4.8 | 4.5 | 4.0 | 3.8 | 2.5 | 13.7 | 2.5 | 2.3 | 3.0 |

**Volume of Trade**
in billions of U.S. dollars - latest available year

- 1,200
- 500
- 200
- 100
- 50
- 20
- 10
- 1 - 2

If volume of trade is less than 15 billion dollars, color indicates major class only.  If no symbol is shown, volume of trade is less than 1 billion dollars.

**Composition of Trade**

Manufactured Articles   Food, Beverage & Tobacco   Raw Materials   Fuel & Related Products   All Other or Undifferentiated

Taiwan figures are included with China.

Puerto Rico figures are included with the United States.

Data not available

**Country Key**

| 1 Andorra | 6 Liechtenstein |
|---|---|
| 2 Aruba | 7 Malta |
| 3 Bahrain | 8 Martinique |
| 4 Gaza Strip and West Bank | 9 Netherlands Antilles |
| 5 Guadeloupe | 10 Qatar |

Copyright by Rand McNally & Co.
Made in U.S.A.
A-GDS-10000-O3- -3- -:-5

**IMPORTS**

**Imports**  World Total - $6,388,329,000,000 ($US - Latest available year)

| | 0 | 10 | 20 | 30 | 40 | 50 | 60 | 70 | 80 | 90 | 100% |
|---|---|---|---|---|---|---|---|---|---|---|---|

| UNITED STATES | CANADA | MEXICO | CHINA | JAPAN | S. KOREA | OTHER ASIA | GERMANY | UNITED KINGDOM | FRANCE | ITALY | NETH. | SPAIN | BELGIUM | OTHER EUROPE | AFRICA | ALL OTHER |
|---|---|---|---|---|---|---|---|---|---|---|---|---|---|---|---|---|
| 18.7% | 3.6 | 2.6 | 9.7 | 4.6 | 2.3 | 10.4 | 7.6 | 5.2 | 4.8 | 3.7 | 3.1 | 2.5 | 2.4 | 11.4 | 2.2 | 4.2 |

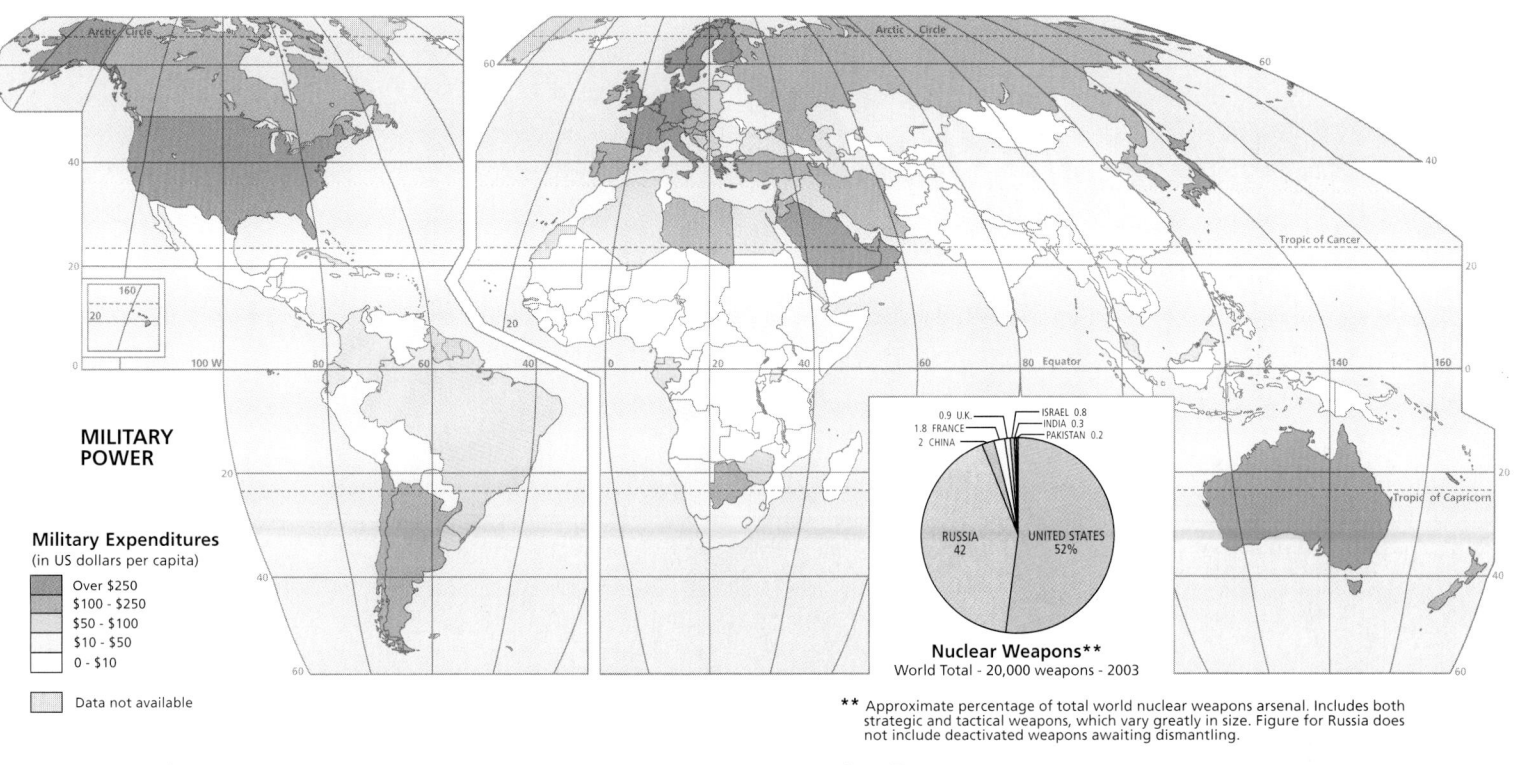

## MILITARY POWER

### Military Expenditures
(in US dollars per capita)

- Over $250
- $100 - $250
- $50 - $100
- $10 - $50
- 0 - $10

- Data not available

**Nuclear Weapons\*\***
World Total - 20,000 weapons - 2003

UNITED STATES 52%
RUSSIA 42
2 CHINA
1.8 FRANCE
0.9 U.K.
ISRAEL 0.8
INDIA 0.3
PAKISTAN 0.2

\*\* Approximate percentage of total world nuclear weapons arsenal. Includes both strategic and tactical weapons, which vary greatly in size. Figure for Russia does not include deactivated weapons awaiting dismantling.

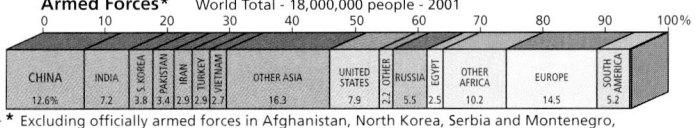

**Armed Forces\***  World Total - 18,000,000 people - 2001

| | | | | | | | | | | | | | |
|---|---|---|---|---|---|---|---|---|---|---|---|---|---|
| CHINA | INDIA | S. KOREA | PAKISTAN | IRAN | TURKEY | VIETNAM | OTHER ASIA | UNITED STATES | OTHER | RUSSIA | EGYPT | OTHER AFRICA | EUROPE | SOUTH AMERICA |
| 12.6% | 7.2 | 3.8 | 3.4 | 2.9 | 2.9 | 2.7 | 16.3 | 7.9 | 2.2 | 5.5 | 2.5 | 10.2 | 14.5 | 5.2 |

\* Excluding officially armed forces in Afghanistan, North Korea, Serbia and Montenegro, Somalia, and Taiwan.

**Arms Exports**  World Total - $31,470,000,000 (U.S.) - Avg. 1999-2001

| | | | | | | |
|---|---|---|---|---|---|---|
| UNITED STATES | UNITED KINGDOM | FRANCE | GERMANY | OTHER EUROPE | RUSSIA | CHINA | ALL OTHER |
| 45.2% | 16.1 | 7.3 | 3.8 | 8.8 | 11.2 | 1.8 | 5.9 |

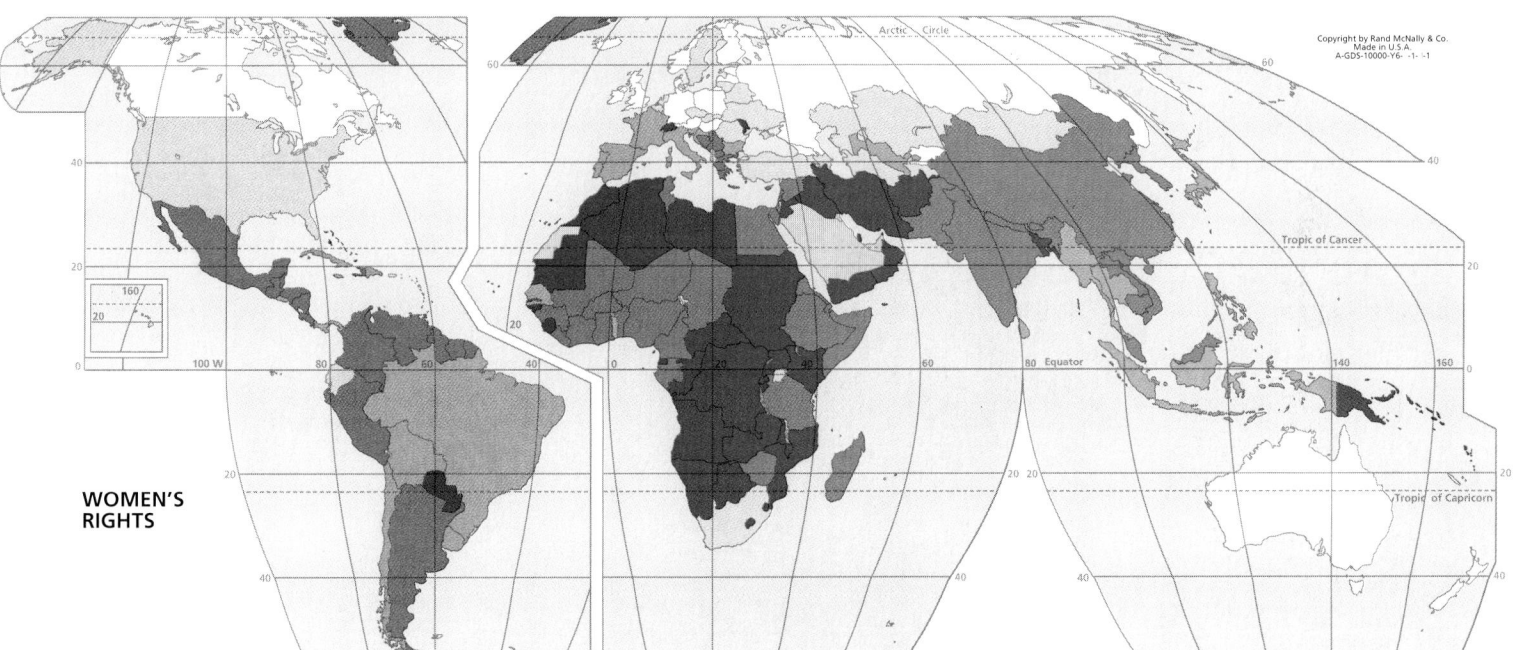

Copyright by Rand McNally & Co.
Made in U.S.A.
A-GDS-10000-Y6- -1- -1

## WOMEN'S RIGHTS

### Voting Rights
Year women received the right to vote

- After 1960
- 1946 - 1960
- 1931 - 1945
- 1919 - 1930
- Before 1919

- Not Applicable\*

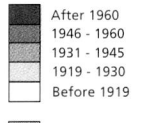

\*Women are not allowed to vote in Kuwait. Neither women nor men are allowed to vote in Brunei, Saudi Arabia, United Arab Emirates, or Western Sahara.

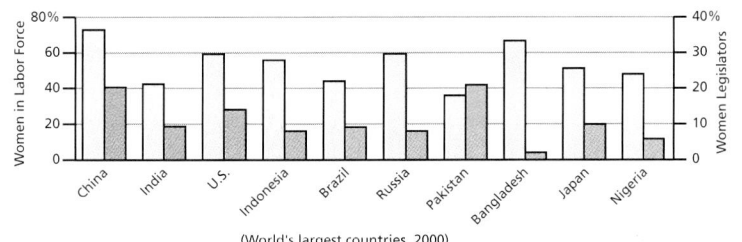

(World's largest countries, 2000)

### Women's Economic Activity and Legislative Participation Rates

- Percentage of women aged 15 and above in the economically active labor force
- Percentage of seats in national legislature held by women

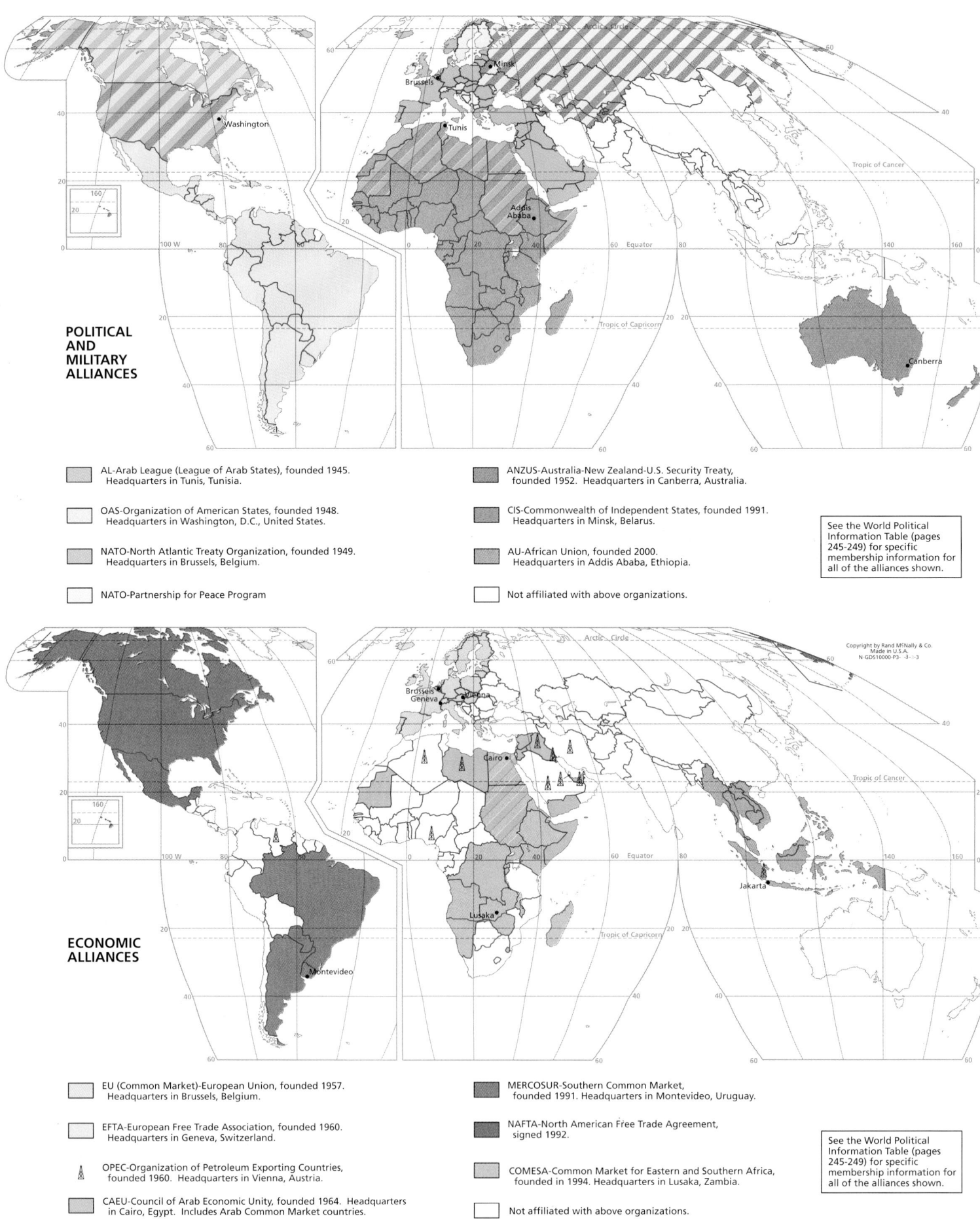

**POLITICAL AND MILITARY ALLIANCES**

AL-Arab League (League of Arab States), founded 1945. Headquarters in Tunis, Tunisia.

OAS-Organization of American States, founded 1948. Headquarters in Washington, D.C., United States.

NATO-North Atlantic Treaty Organization, founded 1949. Headquarters in Brussels, Belgium.

NATO-Partnership for Peace Program

ANZUS-Australia-New Zealand-U.S. Security Treaty, founded 1952. Headquarters in Canberra, Australia.

CIS-Commonwealth of Independent States, founded 1991. Headquarters in Minsk, Belarus.

AU-African Union, founded 2000. Headquarters in Addis Ababa, Ethiopia.

Not affiliated with above organizations.

See the World Political Information Table (pages 245-249) for specific membership information for all of the alliances shown.

**ECONOMIC ALLIANCES**

EU (Common Market)-European Union, founded 1957. Headquarters in Brussels, Belgium.

EFTA-European Free Trade Association, founded 1960. Headquarters in Geneva, Switzerland.

OPEC-Organization of Petroleum Exporting Countries, founded 1960. Headquarters in Vienna, Austria.

CAEU-Council of Arab Economic Unity, founded 1964. Headquarters in Cairo, Egypt. Includes Arab Common Market countries.

ASEAN-Association of Southeast Asian Nations, founded 1967. Headquarters in Jakarta, Indonesia.

MERCOSUR-Southern Common Market, founded 1991. Headquarters in Montevideo, Uruguay.

NAFTA-North American Free Trade Agreement, signed 1992.

COMESA-Common Market for Eastern and Southern Africa, founded in 1994. Headquarters in Lusaka, Zambia.

Not affiliated with above organizations.

See the World Political Information Table (pages 245-249) for specific membership information for all of the alliances shown.

Copyright by Rand McNally & Co.
Made in U.S.A.
N-GDS10000-P3- -3-I-3

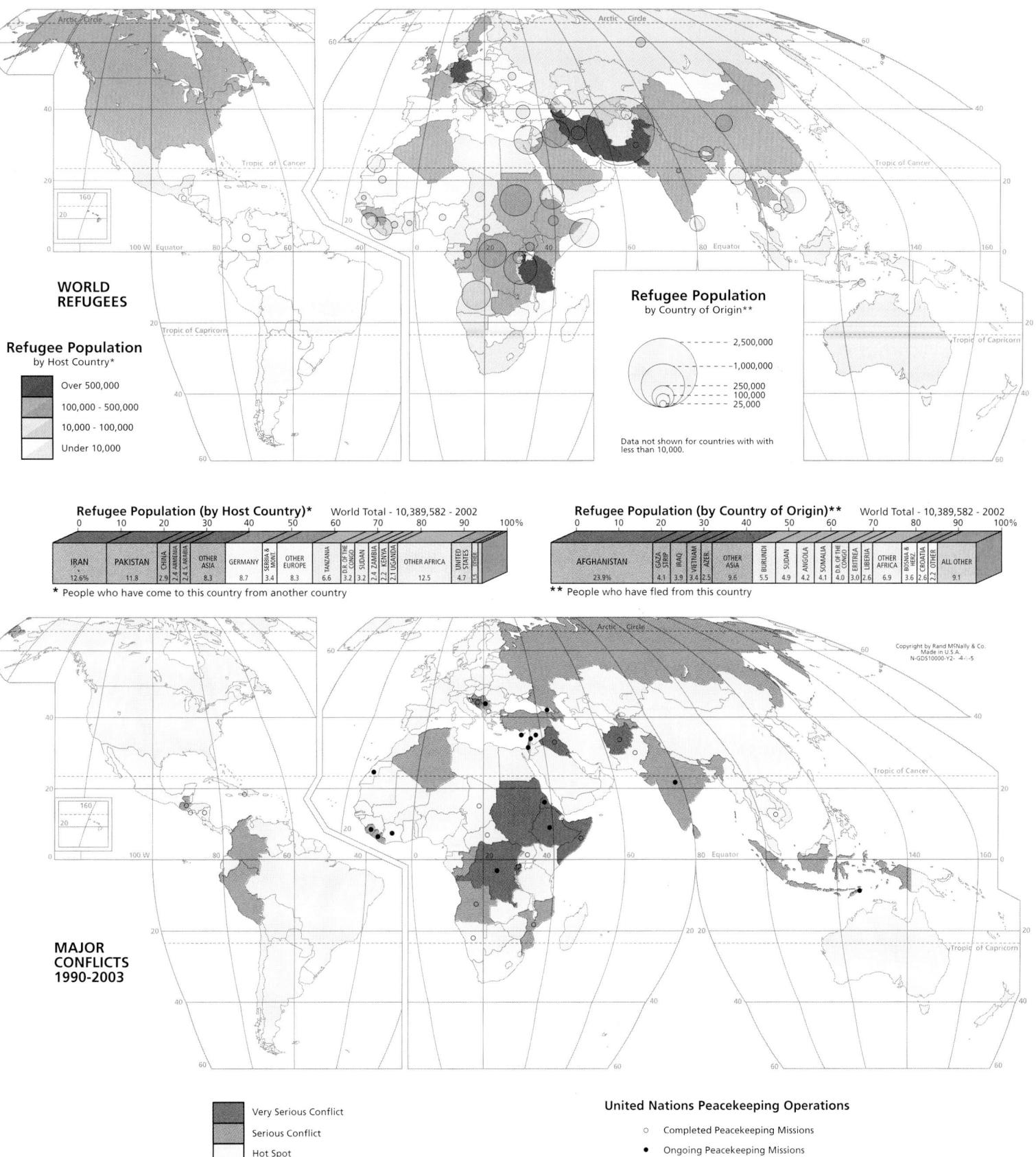

## WORLD REFUGEES

### Refugee Population
by Host Country*

- Over 500,000
- 100,000 - 500,000
- 10,000 - 100,000
- Under 10,000

### Refugee Population
by Country of Origin**

- 2,500,000
- 1,000,000
- 250,000
- 100,000
- 25,000

Data not shown for countries with with less than 10,000.

**Refugee Population (by Host Country)***    World Total - 10,389,582 - 2002

| 0 | 10 | 20 | 30 | 40 | 50 | 60 | 70 | 80 | 90 | 100% |
|---|---|---|---|---|---|---|---|---|---|---|

| IRAN | PAKISTAN | CHINA | ARMENIA | S. ARABIA | OTHER ASIA | GERMANY | SERBIA & MONT. | OTHER EUROPE | TANZANIA | D.R. OF THE CONGO | SUDAN | ZAMBIA | KENYA | UGANDA | OTHER AFRICA | UNITED STATES | OTHER |
|---|---|---|---|---|---|---|---|---|---|---|---|---|---|---|---|---|---|
| 12.6% | 11.8 | 2.9 | 2.4 | 2.4 | 8.3 | 8.7 | 3.4 | 8.3 | 6.6 | 3.2 | 3.2 | 2.4 | 2.2 | 2.1 | 12.5 | 4.7 | 1.5 |

\* People who have come to this country from another country

**Refugee Population (by Country of Origin)***    World Total - 10,389,582 - 2002

| 0 | 10 | 20 | 30 | 40 | 50 | 60 | 70 | 80 | 90 | 100% |
|---|---|---|---|---|---|---|---|---|---|---|

| AFGHANISTAN | GAZA STRIP | IRAQ | VIETNAM | AZER. | OTHER ASIA | BURUNDI | SUDAN | ANGOLA | SOMALIA | D.R. OF THE CONGO | ERITREA | LIBERIA | OTHER AFRICA | BOSNIA & HERZ. | CROATIA | OTHER | ALL OTHER |
|---|---|---|---|---|---|---|---|---|---|---|---|---|---|---|---|---|---|
| 23.9% | 4.1 | 3.9 | 3.4 | 2.5 | 9.6 | 5.5 | 4.9 | 4.2 | 4.1 | 4.0 | 3.0 | 2.6 | 6.9 | 3.6 | 2.6 | 2.2 | 9.1 |

\*\* People who have fled from this country

Copyright by Rand McNally & Co.
Made in U.S.A.
N-GDS10000-Y2- 4- -5

## MAJOR CONFLICTS 1990-2003

- Very Serious Conflict
- Serious Conflict
- Hot Spot

### United Nations Peacekeeping Operations

- ○ Completed Peacekeeping Missions
- ● Ongoing Peacekeeping Missions

## TELECOMMUNICATIONS

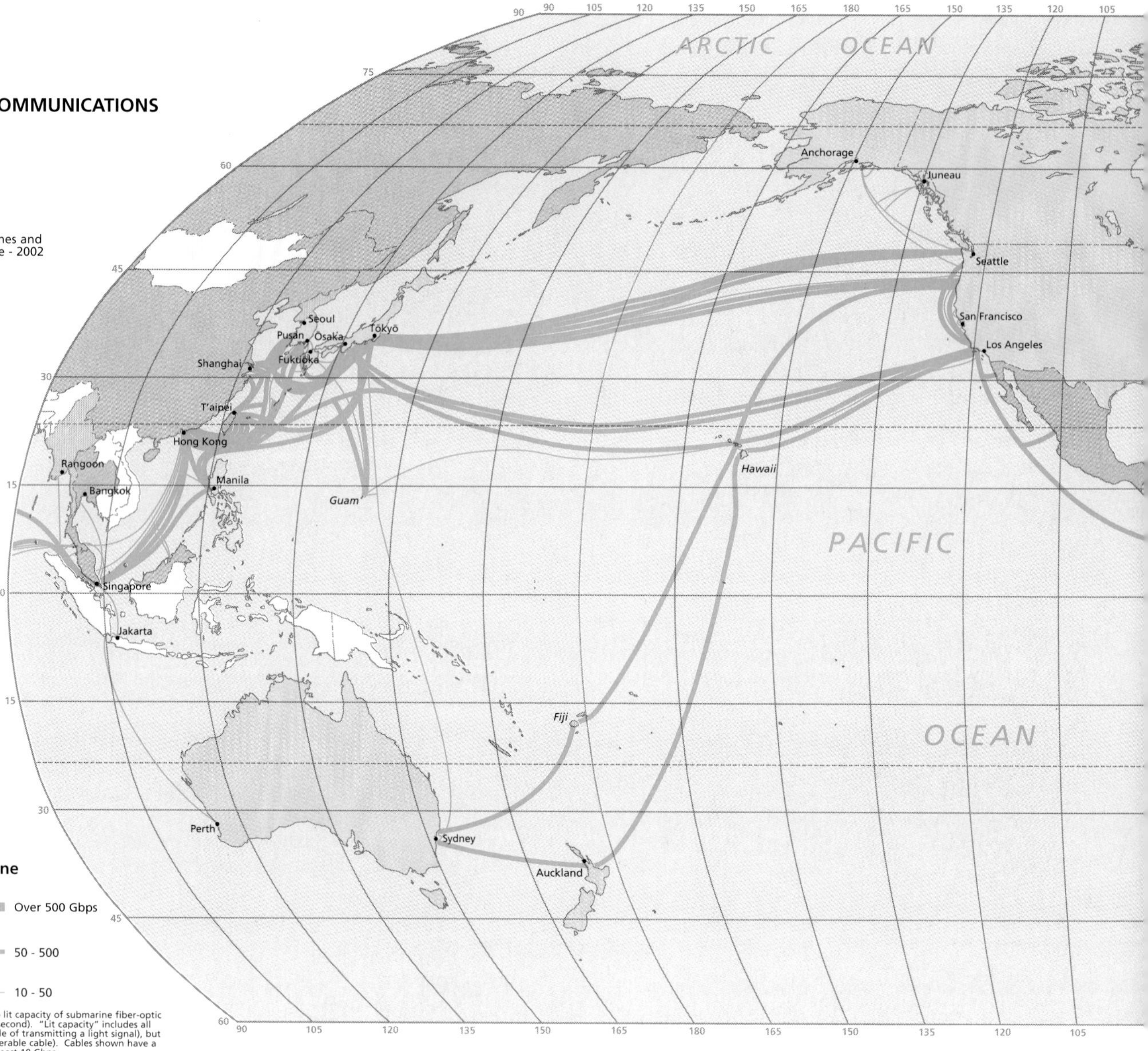

### Teledensity
Number of fixed telephone lines and
mobile phones per 100 people - 2002

- Over 120
- 60 - 120
- 30 - 60
- 15 - 30
- Under 15

No data available

### International Submarine
### Cable Capacity - 2004

- Over 500 Gbps
- 50 - 500
- 10 - 50

Note: Line thickness is proportional to lit capacity of submarine fiber-optic
cable measured in Gbps (Gigabits per second). "Lit capacity" includes all
cable that is "lit" (operable and capable of transmitting a light signal), but
excludes "dark fiber" (inactive or inoperable cable). Cables shown have a
maximum upgradeable capacity of at least 10 Gbps.

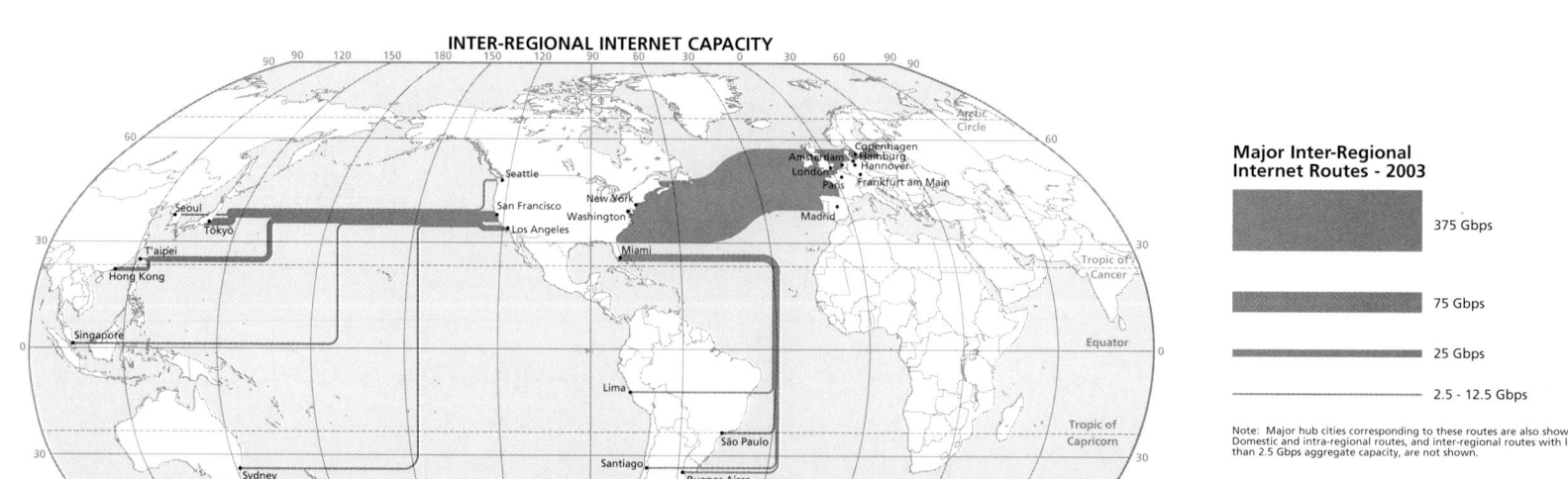

## INTER-REGIONAL INTERNET CAPACITY

### Major Inter-Regional
### Internet Routes - 2003

- 375 Gbps
- 75 Gbps
- 25 Gbps
- 2.5 - 12.5 Gbps

Note: Major hub cities corresponding to these routes are also shown.
Domestic and intra-regional routes, and inter-regional routes with less
than 2.5 Gbps aggregate capacity, are not shown.

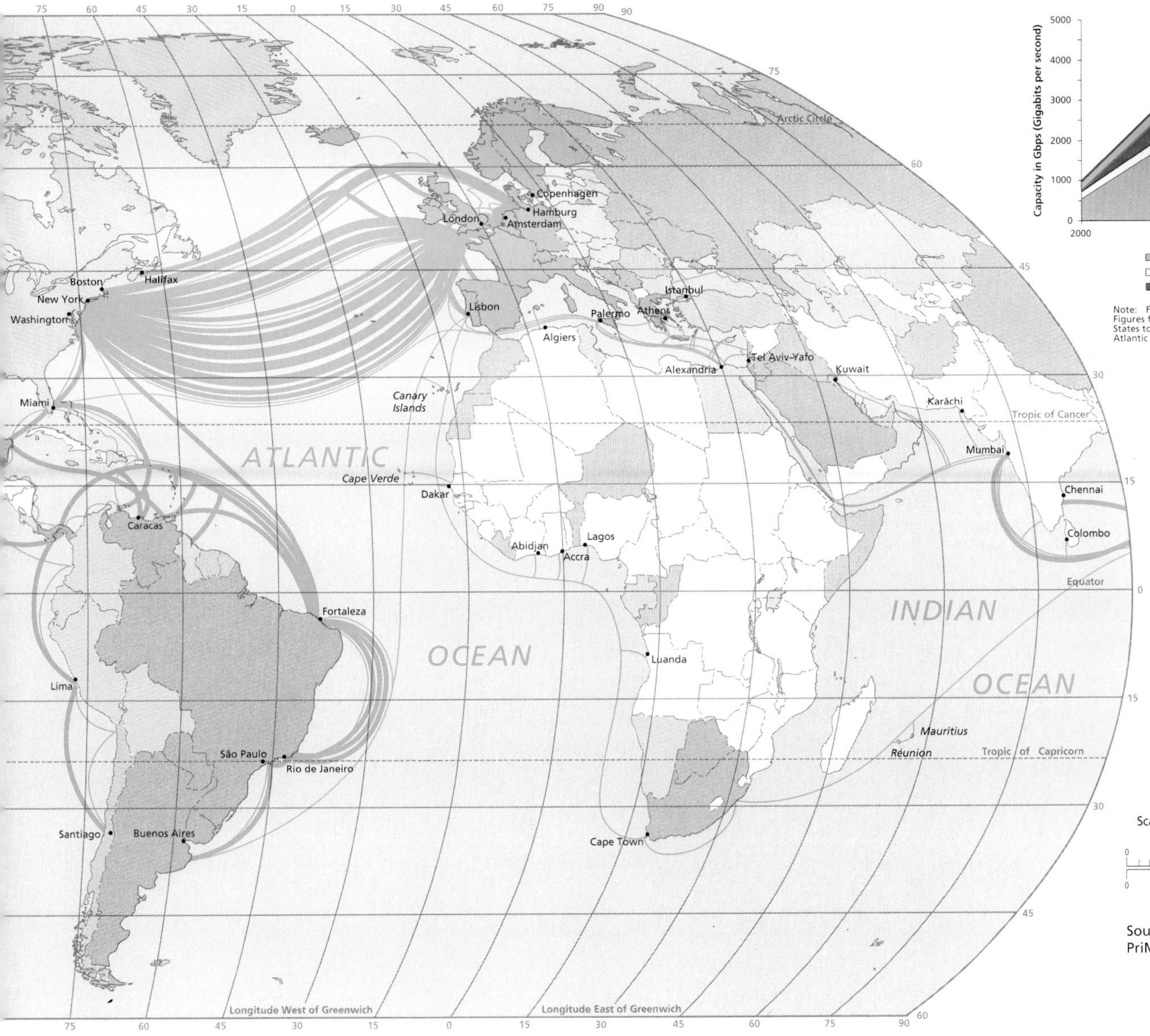

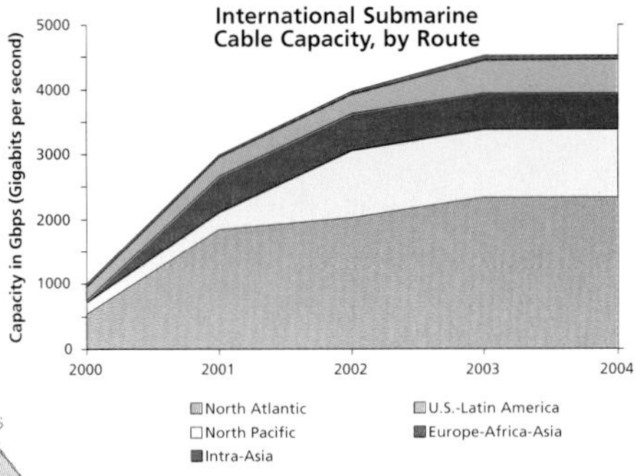

## International Submarine Cable Capacity, by Route

Capacity in Gbps (Gigabits per second)

- North Atlantic
- North Pacific
- Intra-Asia
- U.S.-Latin America
- Europe-Africa-Asia

Note: Figures denote lit capacity of submarine fiber-optic cable. Figures for the North Pacific exclude cables linking the United States to Australia and New Zealand. Figures for the North Atlantic exclude cables linking South America to Europe.

Robinson Projection
Scale 1 : 100,000,000 (approximate)
One inch to 1,600 miles

Source: TeleGeography research,
PriMetrica, Inc. (www.primetrica.com)

Copyright by Rand McNally & Co.
Made in U.S.A.
A-GDS-10000-T1- -2- -4

## INTER-REGIONAL INTERNET HUBS

**Fifty Largest Inter-Regional Internet Hubs - 2003**

Circle size is proportional to each metropolitan area's aggregate capacity connected across international borders.

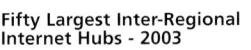
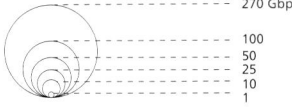

270 Gbps
100
50
25
10
1

Note: Hubs for domestic and intra-regional routes are not shown. Internet bandwidth for domestic and intra-regional routes is excluded.

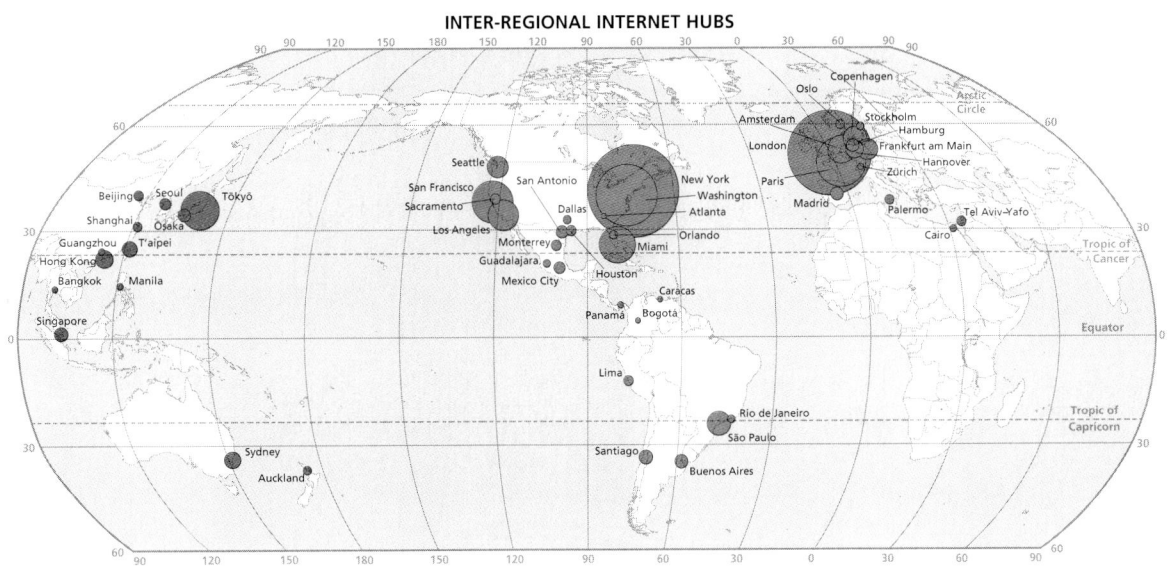

## THE SEASONS (NORTHERN HEMISPHERE)

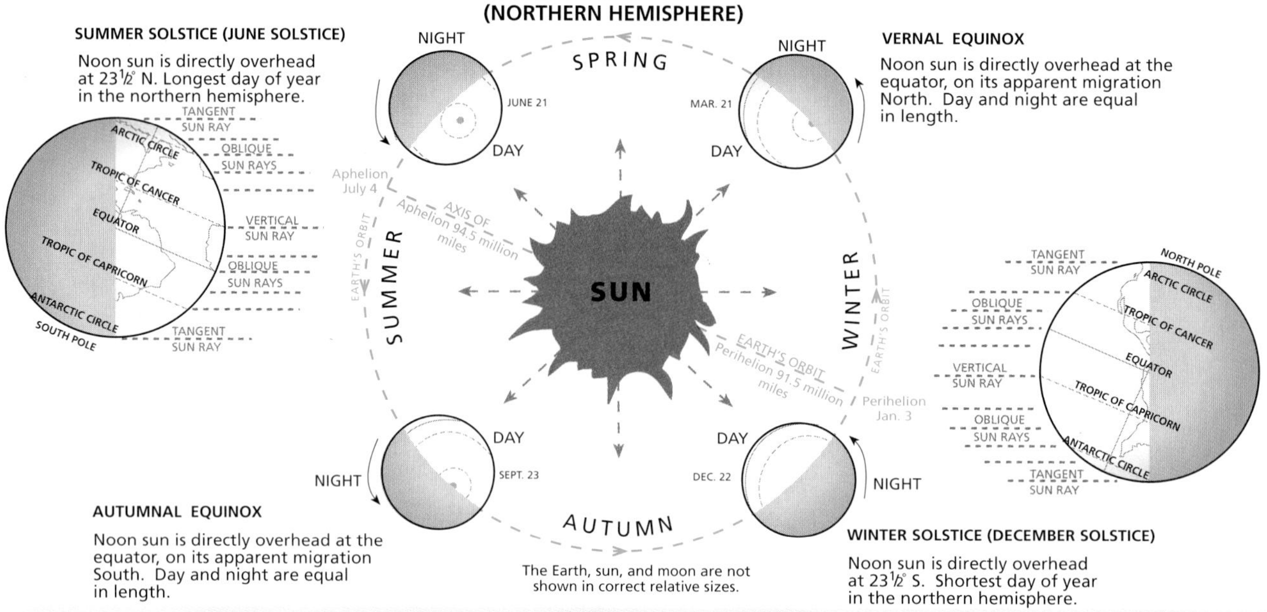

**SUMMER SOLSTICE (JUNE SOLSTICE)**
Noon sun is directly overhead at 23½° N. Longest day of year in the northern hemisphere.

**VERNAL EQUINOX**
Noon sun is directly overhead at the equator, on its apparent migration North. Day and night are equal in length.

**AUTUMNAL EQUINOX**
Noon sun is directly overhead at the equator, on its apparent migration South. Day and night are equal in length.

**WINTER SOLSTICE (DECEMBER SOLSTICE)**
Noon sun is directly overhead at 23½° S. Shortest day of year in the northern hemisphere.

The Earth, sun, and moon are not shown in correct relative sizes.

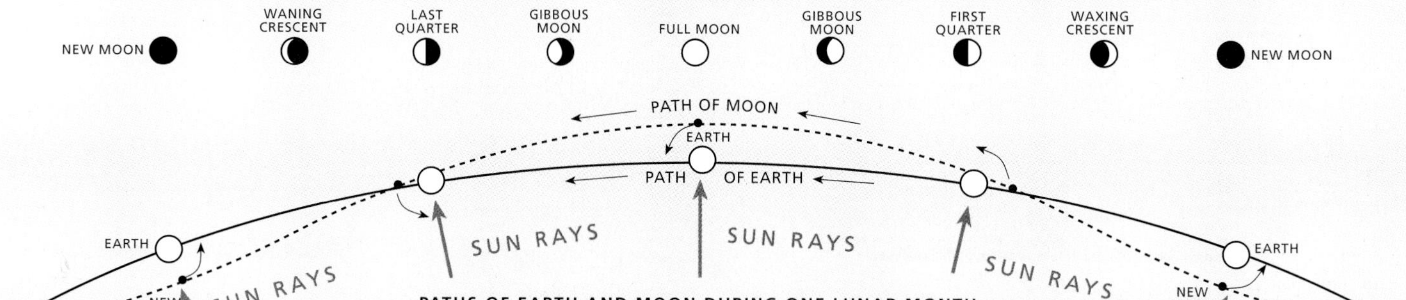

SPRING
SUMMER
WINTER
AUTUMN

NIGHT — JUNE 21 — DAY
NIGHT — MAR. 21 — DAY
DAY — SEPT. 23 — NIGHT
DAY — DEC. 22 — NIGHT

Aphelion July 4
AXIS OF Aphelion 94.5 million miles
EARTH'S ORBIT
Perihelion Jan. 3
EARTH'S ORBIT Perihelion 91.5 million miles

SUN

TANGENT SUN RAY
OBLIQUE SUN RAYS
VERTICAL SUN RAY
OBLIQUE SUN RAYS
TANGENT SUN RAY

ARCTIC CIRCLE
TROPIC OF CANCER
EQUATOR
TROPIC OF CAPRICORN
ANTARCTIC CIRCLE
SOUTH POLE

NORTH POLE
ARCTIC CIRCLE
TROPIC OF CANCER
EQUATOR
TROPIC OF CAPRICORN
ANTARCTIC CIRCLE

NEW MOON · WANING CRESCENT · LAST QUARTER · GIBBOUS MOON · FULL MOON · GIBBOUS MOON · FIRST QUARTER · WAXING CRESCENT · NEW MOON

PATH OF MOON
EARTH
PATH OF EARTH
SUN RAYS
EARTH
NEW MOON
NEW MOON

**PATHS OF EARTH AND MOON DURING ONE LUNAR MONTH**

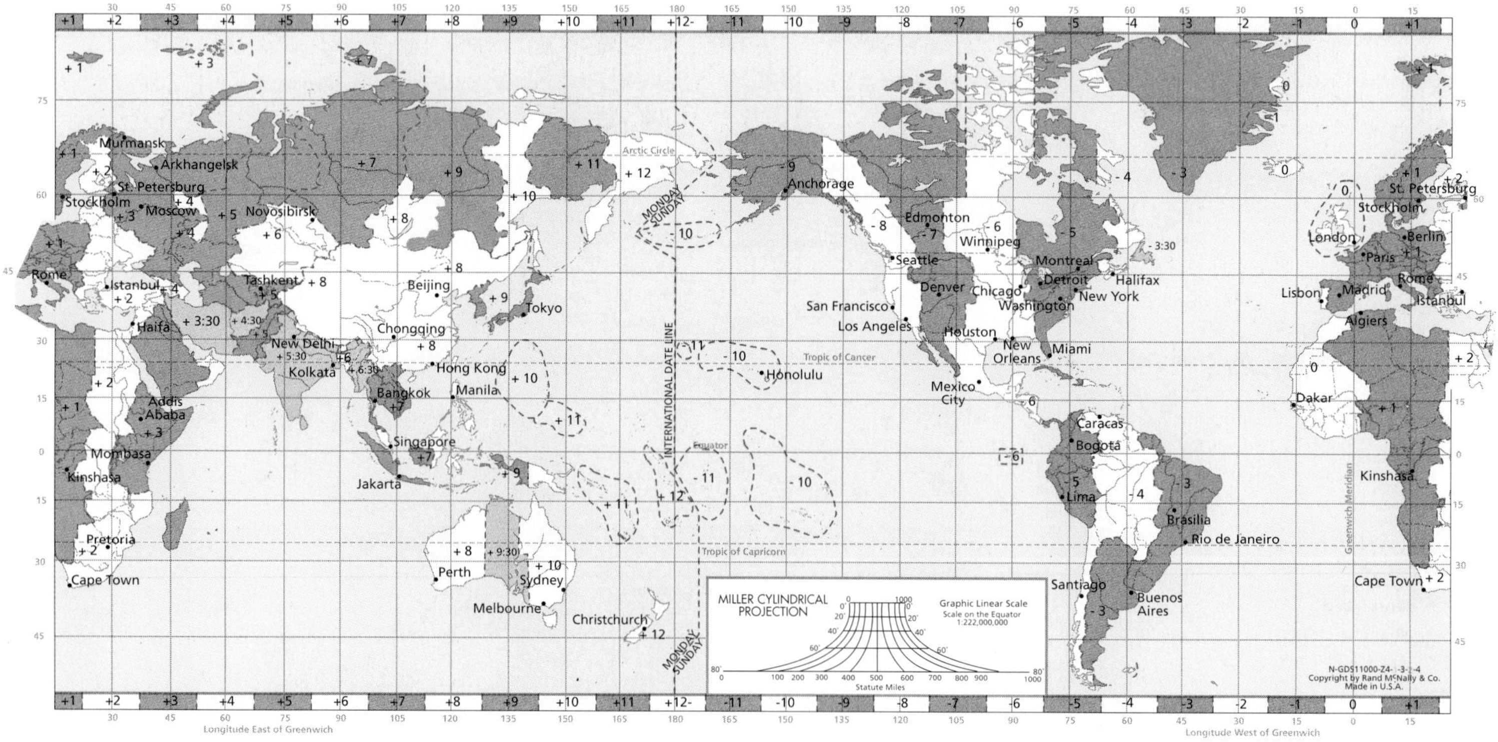

MILLER CYLINDRICAL PROJECTION
Graphic Linear Scale
Scale on the Equator
1:222,000,000
Statute Miles

N-GDS11000-Z4- -3- -4
Copyright by Rand McNally & Co.
Made in U.S.A.

## Time Zones

The surface of the earth is divided into 24 time zones. Each zone represents 15° of longitude or one hour of time. The time of the initial, or zero, zone is based on the Greenwich Meridian and extends eastward and westward for a distance of 7½° of longitude. Each of the zones is designated by a number representing the hours (+ or -) by which its standard time differs from Greenwich mean time. These standard time zones are indicated by bands of orange and yellow. Areas which have a fractional deviation from standard time are shown in an intermediate color. The irregularities in the zones and the fractional deviations are due to political and economic factors.

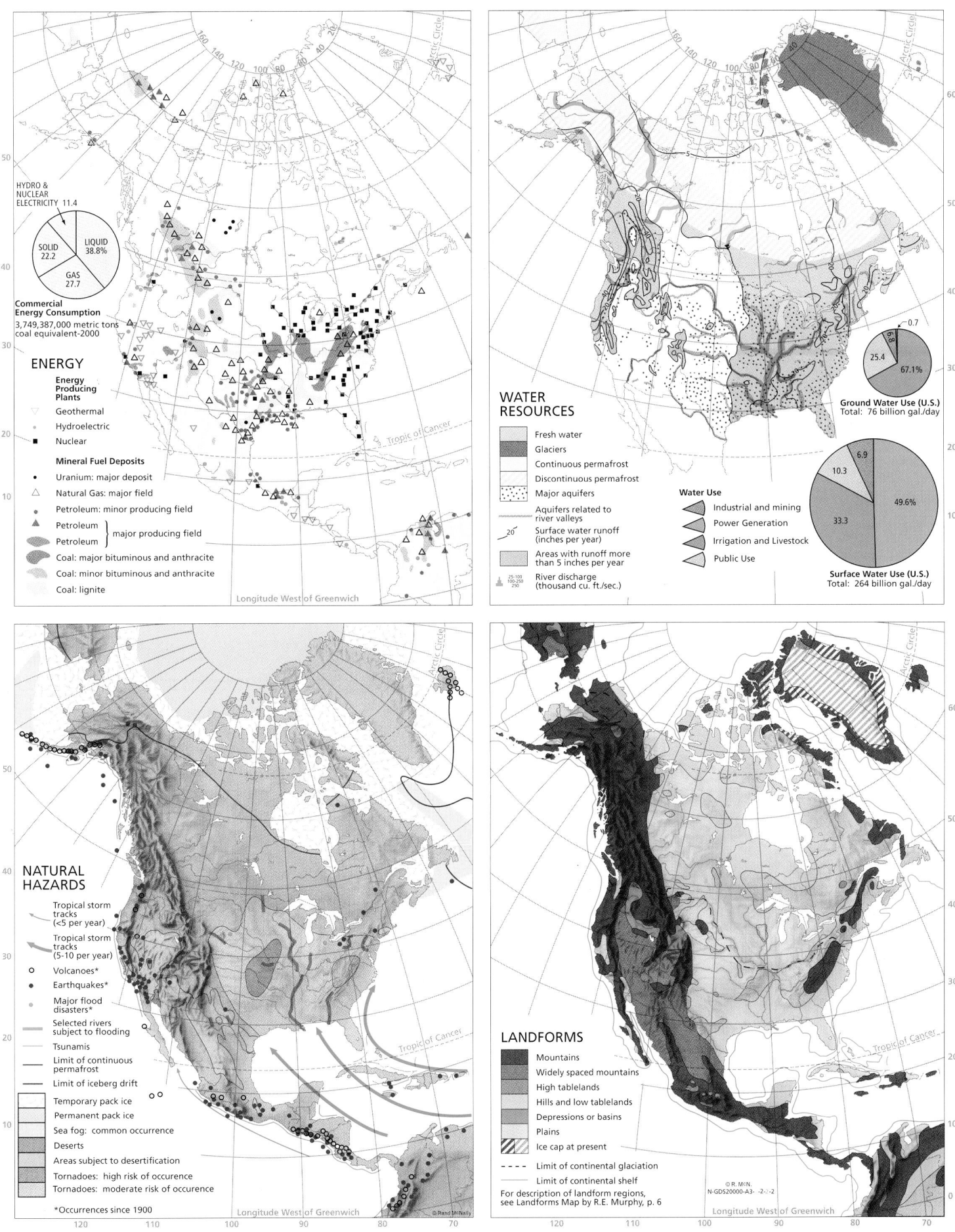

## ENERGY

HYDRO &
NUCLEAR
ELECTRICITY 11.4

SOLID 22.2

LIQUID 38.8%

GAS 27.7

**Commercial
Energy Consumption**
3,749,387,000 metric tons
coal equivalent-2000

**Energy
Producing
Plants**
▽ Geothermal
• Hydroelectric
■ Nuclear

**Mineral Fuel Deposits**
• Uranium: major deposit
△ Natural Gas: major field
• Petroleum: minor producing field
▲ Petroleum } major producing field
▰ Petroleum }
Coal: major bituminous and anthracite
Coal: minor bituminous and anthracite
Coal: lignite

Longitude West of Greenwich

## WATER RESOURCES

Fresh water
Glaciers
Continuous permafrost
Discontinuous permafrost
Major aquifers
Aquifers related to
river valleys
20 Surface water runoff
(inches per year)
Areas with runoff more
than 5 inches per year
River discharge
(thousand cu. ft./sec.)
25-100
100-250
250

**Water Use**
▷ Industrial and mining
▷ Power Generation
▷ Irrigation and Livestock
▷ Public Use

0.7

6.9

25.4

67.1%

**Ground Water Use (U.S.)**
Total: 76 billion gal./day

6.9

10.3

33.3

49.6%

**Surface Water Use (U.S.)**
Total: 264 billion gal./day

## NATURAL HAZARDS

Tropical storm
tracks
(<5 per year)
Tropical storm
tracks
(5-10 per year)
○ Volcanoes*
• Earthquakes*
• Major flood
disasters*
Selected rivers
subject to flooding
Tsunamis
Limit of continuous
permafrost
Limit of iceberg drift
Temporary pack ice
Permanent pack ice
Sea fog: common occurrence
Deserts
Areas subject to desertification
Tornadoes: high risk of occurence
Tornadoes: moderate risk of occurence

*Occurrences since 1900

Tropic of Cancer

Longitude West of Greenwich

## LANDFORMS

Mountains
Widely spaced mountains
High tablelands
Hills and low tablelands
Depressions or basins
Plains
Ice cap at present

--- Limit of continental glaciation
— Limit of continental shelf
For description of landform regions,
see Landforms Map by R.E. Murphy, p. 6

© R. McN.
N-GDS20000-A3- -2-.-2

Tropic of Cancer

Longitude West of Greenwich

© Rand McNally

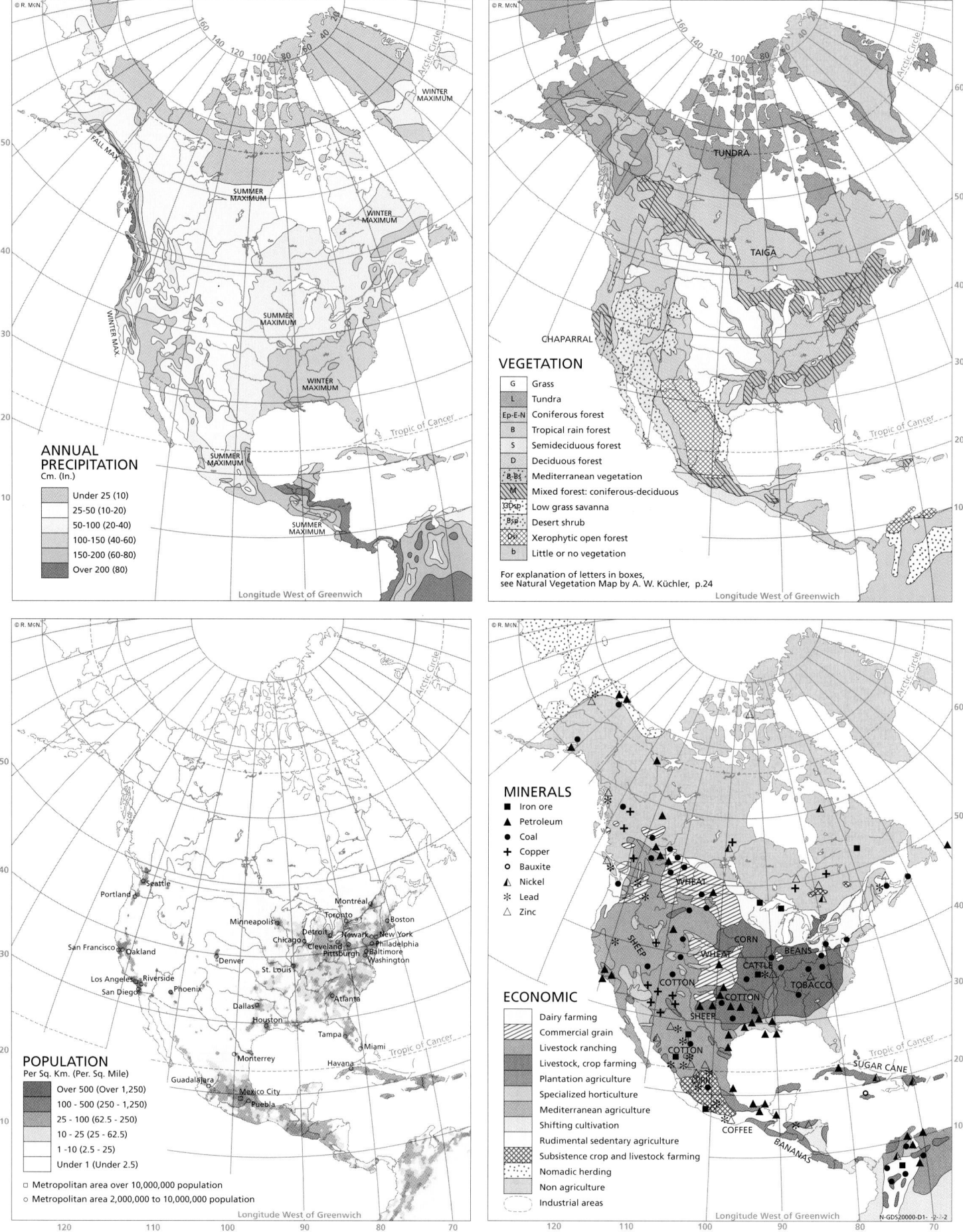

© R. McN.

**ANNUAL PRECIPITATION**
Cm. (In.)

- Under 25 (10)
- 25-50 (10-20)
- 50-100 (20-40)
- 100-150 (40-60)
- 150-200 (60-80)
- Over 200 (80)

Longitude West of Greenwich

**VEGETATION**

| G | Grass |
| L | Tundra |
| Ep-E-N | Coniferous forest |
| B | Tropical rain forest |
| S | Semideciduous forest |
| D | Deciduous forest |
| B-BS | Mediterranean vegetation |
| M | Mixed forest: coniferous-deciduous |
| GDsp | Low grass savanna |
| Bsp | Desert shrub |
| DU | Xerophytic open forest |
| b | Little or no vegetation |

For explanation of letters in boxes,
see Natural Vegetation Map by A. W. Küchler, p.24

Longitude West of Greenwich

**POPULATION**
Per Sq. Km. (Per. Sq. Mile)

- Over 500 (Over 1,250)
- 100 - 500 (250 - 1,250)
- 25 - 100 (62.5 - 250)
- 10 - 25 (25 - 62.5)
- 1 -10 (2.5 - 25)
- Under 1 (Under 2.5)

□ Metropolitan area over 10,000,000 population
○ Metropolitan area 2,000,000 to 10,000,000 population

Longitude West of Greenwich

**MINERALS**

- ■ Iron ore
- ▲ Petroleum
- ● Coal
- ✛ Copper
- ○ Bauxite
- ▲ Nickel
- ✳ Lead
- △ Zinc

**ECONOMIC**

- Dairy farming
- Commercial grain
- Livestock ranching
- Livestock, crop farming
- Plantation agriculture
- Specialized horticulture
- Mediterranean agriculture
- Shifting cultivation
- Rudimental sedentary agriculture
- Subsistence crop and livestock farming
- Nomadic herding
- Non agriculture
- Industrial areas

Longitude West of Greenwich

N-GDS20000-D1- -2-2-2

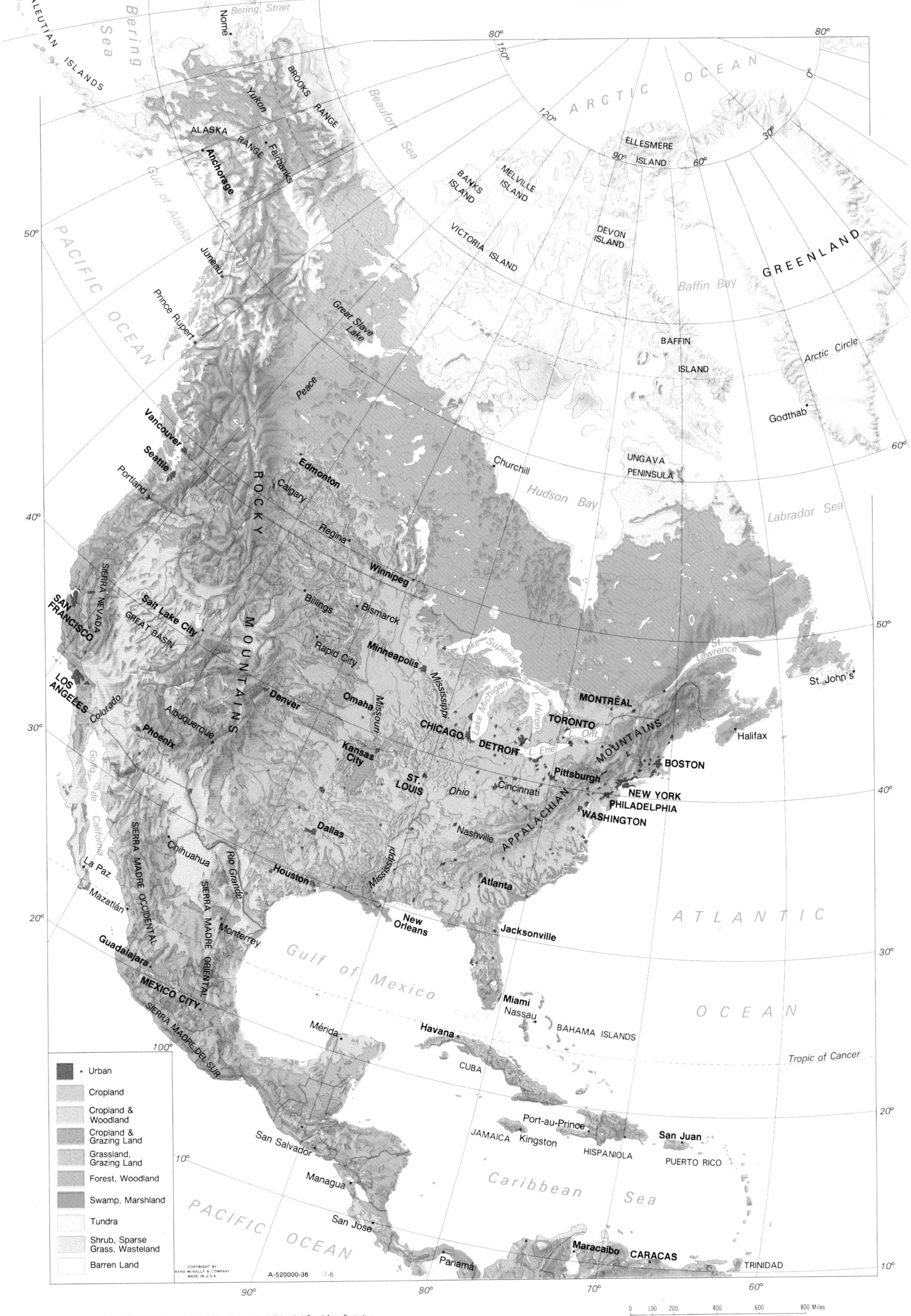

ALEUTIAN ISLANDS

Bering Sea

Bering Strait

Nome

BROOKS RANGE

Yukon

ALASKA RANGE

Fairbanks

Anchorage

Gulf of Alaska

Juneau

Prince Rupert

ARCTIC OCEAN

ELLESMERE ISLAND

BANKS ISLAND

MELVILLE ISLAND

DEVON ISLAND

VICTORIA ISLAND

Beaufort Sea

GREENLAND

Baffin Bay

BAFFIN ISLAND

Arctic Circle

Godthab

PACIFIC OCEAN

ROCKY MOUNTAINS

Vancouver

Seattle

Portland

Edmonton

Calgary

Regina

Winnipeg

Great Slave Lake

Peace

Churchill

Hudson Bay

UNGAVA PENINSULA

Labrador Sea

SIERRA NEVADA

SAN FRANCISCO

Salt Lake City

GREAT BASIN

Billings

Bismarck

Rapid City

Minneapolis

Lake Superior

St. Lawrence

St. John's

LOS ANGELES

Colorado

Denver

Omaha

Missouri

Mississippi

Lake Michigan

CHICAGO

Huron

MONTRÉAL

TORONTO

Ont.

Halifax

Phoenix

Albuquerque

Kansas City

ST. LOUIS

DETROIT

L. Erie

Pittsburgh

Cincinnati

Ohio

APPALACHIAN MOUNTAINS

BOSTON

NEW YORK

PHILADELPHIA

WASHINGTON

Gulf of California

SIERRA MADRE OCCIDENTAL

Chihuahua

Rio Grande

Dallas

Nashville

Atlanta

La Paz

Mazatlán

Monterrey

SIERRA MADRE ORIENTAL

Houston

Mississippi

New Orleans

Jacksonville

ATLANTIC OCEAN

Guadalajara

Gulf of Mexico

MEXICO CITY

SIERRA MADRE DEL SUR

Mérida

Havana

CUBA

Miami

Nassau

BAHAMA ISLANDS

Tropic of Cancer

San Salvador

Port-au-Prince

JAMAICA

Kingston

HISPANIOLA

San Juan

PUERTO RICO

Managua

Caribbean Sea

PACIFIC OCEAN

San Jose

Panamá

Maracaibo

CARACAS

TRINIDAD

**Legend**

- Urban
- Cropland
- Cropland & Woodland
- Cropland & Grazing Land
- Grassland, Grazing Land
- Forest, Woodland
- Swamp, Marshland
- Tundra
- Shrub, Sparse Grass, Wasteland
- Barren Land

COPYRIGHT BY
RAND McNALLY & COMPANY
MADE IN U.S.A.

A-520000-36  2-6

Scale 1:36,000,000; one inch to 570 miles. Lambert Azimuthal Equal-Area Projection

0 100 200 400 600 800 Miles

0 150 300 600 900 1200 Kilometers

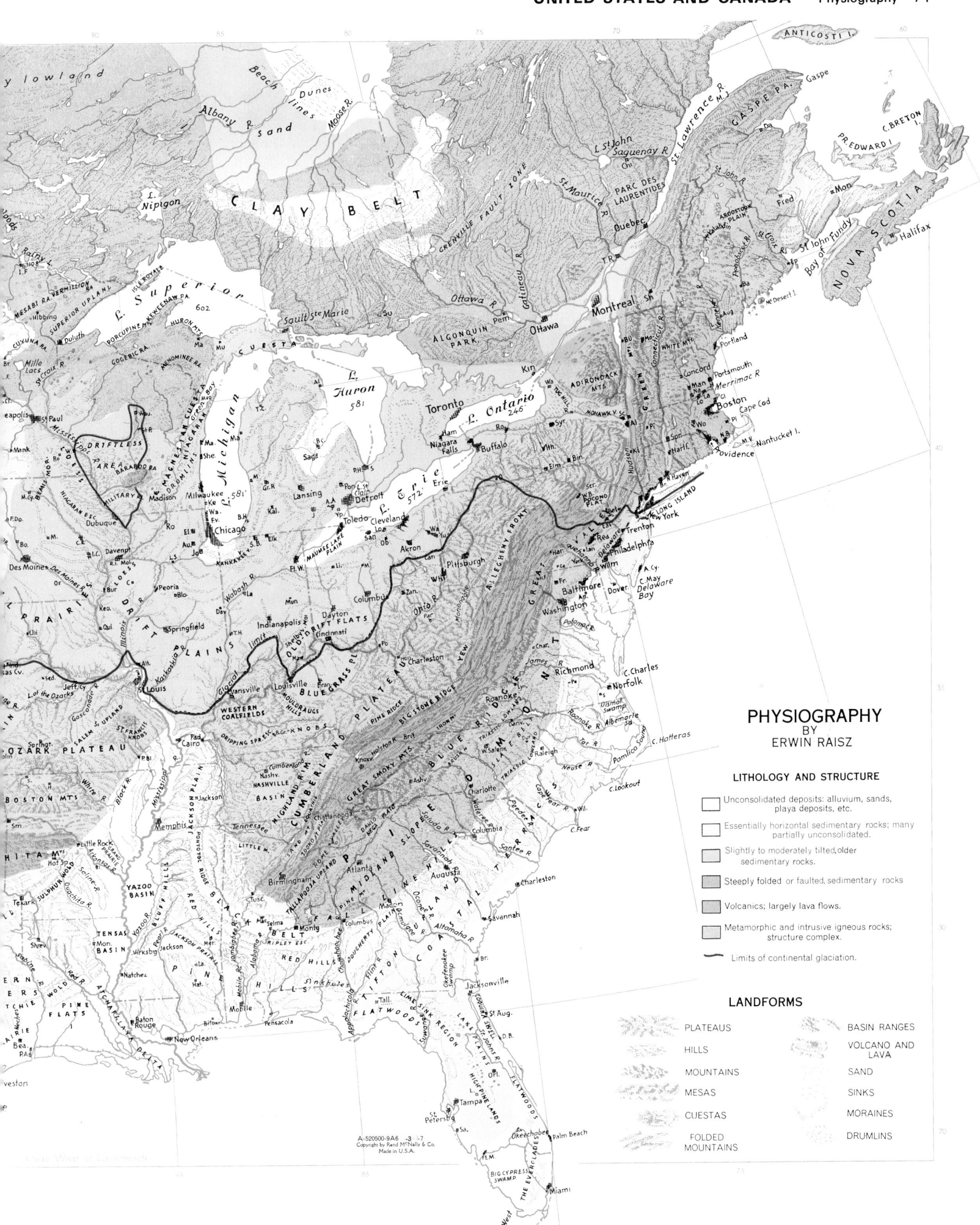

PHYSIOGRAPHY
BY
ERWIN RAISZ

LITHOLOGY AND STRUCTURE

Unconsolidated deposits: alluvium, sands, playa deposits, etc.

Essentially horizontal sedimentary rocks; many partially unconsolidated.

Slightly to moderately tilted, older sedimentary rocks.

Steeply folded or faulted, sedimentary rocks

Volcanics; largely lava flows.

Metamorphic and intrusive igneous rocks; structure complex.

Limits of continental glaciation.

LANDFORMS

PLATEAUS

HILLS

MOUNTAINS

MESAS

CUESTAS

FOLDED MOUNTAINS

BASIN RANGES

VOLCANO AND LAVA

SAND

SINKS

MORAINES

DRUMLINS

A-520500-9A6  -3 -7
Copyright by Rand McNally & Co.
Made in U.S.A.

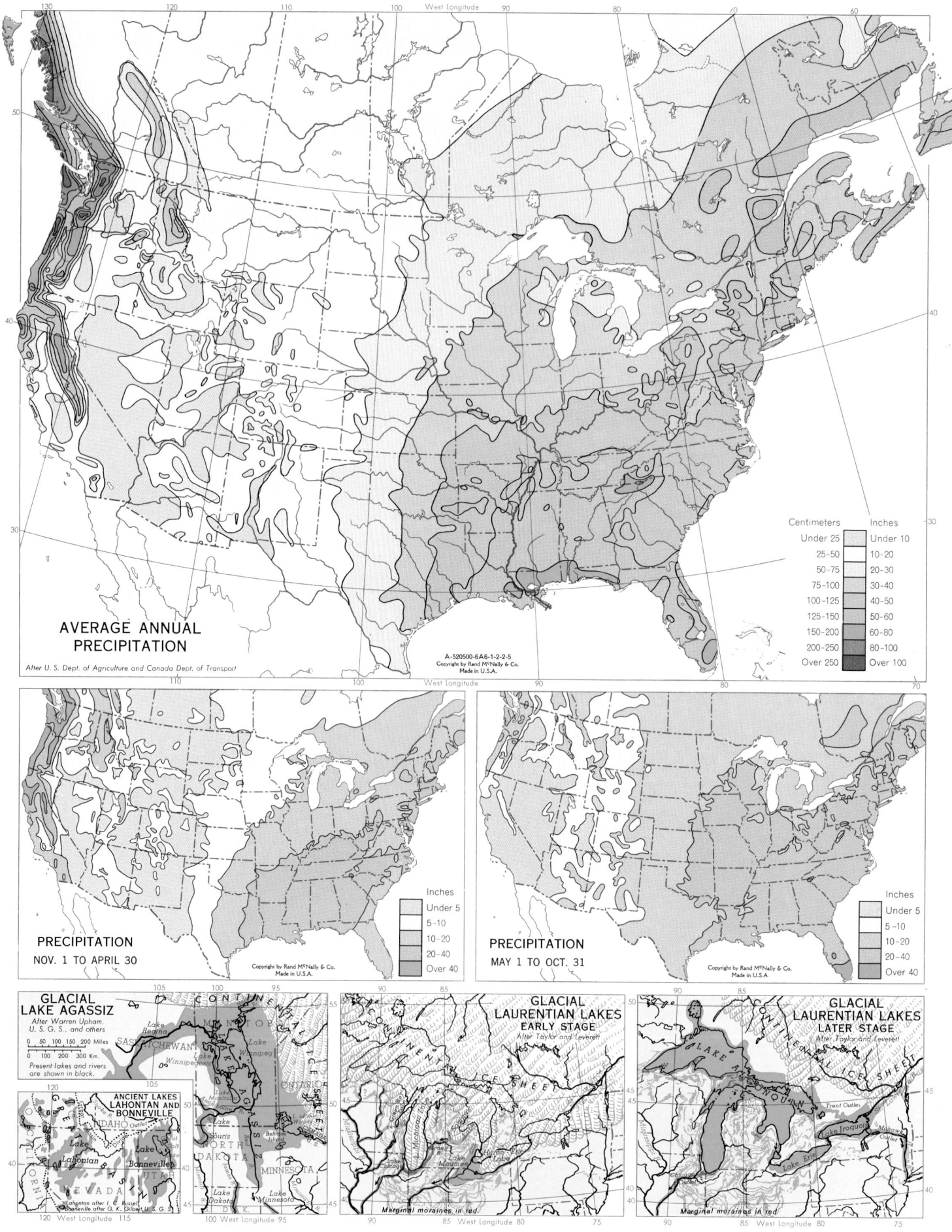

## AVERAGE ANNUAL PRECIPITATION

*After U. S. Dept. of Agriculture and Canada Dept. of Transport*

A-520500-6A6-1-2-2-5
Copyright by Rand McNally & Co.
Made in U.S.A.

| Centimeters | Inches |
|---|---|
| Under 25 | Under 10 |
| 25–50 | 10–20 |
| 50–75 | 20–30 |
| 75–100 | 30–40 |
| 100–125 | 40–50 |
| 125–150 | 50–60 |
| 150–200 | 60–80 |
| 200–250 | 80–100 |
| Over 250 | Over 100 |

## PRECIPITATION

NOV. 1 TO APRIL 30

Copyright by Rand McNally & Co.
Made in U.S.A.

| Inches |
|---|
| Under 5 |
| 5–10 |
| 10–20 |
| 20–40 |
| Over 40 |

## PRECIPITATION

MAY 1 TO OCT. 31

Copyright by Rand McNally & Co.
Made in U.S.A.

| Inches |
|---|
| Under 5 |
| 5–10 |
| 10–20 |
| 20–40 |
| Over 40 |

## GLACIAL LAKE AGASSIZ

*After Warren Upham, U. S. G. S., and others*

0   50  100 150  200 Miles
0   100   200   300 Km.

*Present lakes and rivers are shown in block.*

### ANCIENT LAKES LAHONTAN AND BONNEVILLE

*Lahontan after I. C. Russell
Bonneville after G. K. Gilbert, U. S. G. S.*

## GLACIAL LAURENTIAN LAKES

EARLY STAGE

*After Taylor and Leverett*

Marginal moraines in red

## GLACIAL LAURENTIAN LAKES

LATER STAGE

*After Taylor and Leverett*

Marginal moraines in red

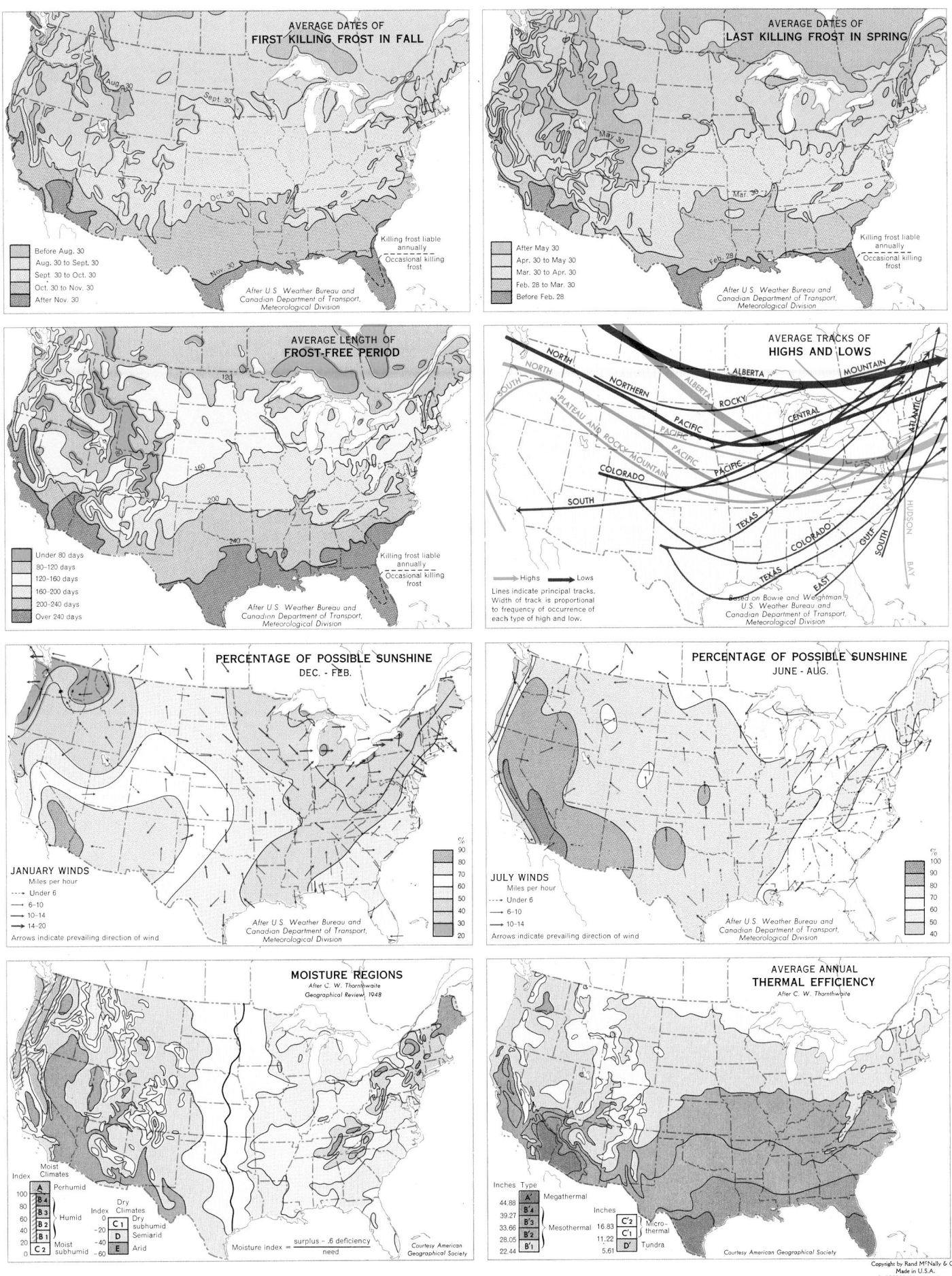

**AVERAGE DATES OF**
**FIRST KILLING FROST IN FALL**

Aug. 30
Sept. 30
Oct. 30
Nov. 30

Before Aug. 30
Aug. 30 to Sept. 30
Sept. 30 to Oct. 30
Oct. 30 to Nov. 30
After Nov. 30

Killing frost liable
annually
Occasional killing
frost

After U.S. Weather Bureau and
Canadian Department of Transport,
Meteorological Division

**AVERAGE DATES OF**
**LAST KILLING FROST IN SPRING**

May 30
Mar. 30
Feb. 28

After May 30
Apr. 30 to May 30
Mar. 30 to Apr. 30
Feb. 28 to Mar. 30
Before Feb. 28

Killing frost liable
annually
Occasional killing
frost

After U.S. Weather Bureau and
Canadian Department of Transport,
Meteorological Division

**AVERAGE LENGTH OF**
**FROST-FREE PERIOD**

120
160
200
240

Under 80 days
80–120 days
120–160 days
160–200 days
200–240 days
Over 240 days

Killing frost liable
annually
Occasional killing
frost

After U.S. Weather Bureau and
Canadian Department of Transport,
Meteorological Division

**AVERAGE TRACKS OF**
**HIGHS AND LOWS**

NORTH
NORTH
SOUTH
NORTHERN
PLATEAU AND ROCKY MOUNTAIN
PACIFIC
PACIFIC
PACIFIC
COLORADO
SOUTH
ALBERTA
ALBERTA ROCKY
CENTRAL
MOUNTAIN
ATLANTIC
TEXAS
COLORADO
GULF
SOUTH
EAST
HUDSON BAY
TEXAS

→ Highs    → Lows

Lines indicate principal tracks.
Width of track is proportional
to frequency of occurrence of
each type of high and low.

Based on Bowie and Weightman,
U.S. Weather Bureau and
Canadian Department of Transport,
Meteorological Division

**PERCENTAGE OF POSSIBLE SUNSHINE**
**DEC. - FEB.**

%
90
80
70
60
50
40
30
20

JANUARY WINDS
Miles per hour
---- Under 6
→ 6–10
→ 10–14
→ 14–20
Arrows indicate prevailing direction of wind

After U.S. Weather Bureau and
Canadian Department of Transport,
Meteorological Division

**PERCENTAGE OF POSSIBLE SUNSHINE**
**JUNE - AUG.**

%
100
90
80
70
60
50
40

JULY WINDS
Miles per hour
---- Under 6
→ 6–10
→ 10–14
Arrows indicate prevailing direction of wind

After U.S. Weather Bureau and
Canadian Department of Transport,
Meteorological Division

**MOISTURE REGIONS**
After C. W. Thornthwaite
Geographical Review, 1948

| Index | Moist Climates | | Index | Dry Climates | |
|---|---|---|---|---|---|
| 100 | A | Perhumid | | C1 | Dry subhumid |
| 80 | B4 | Humid | -20 | D | Semiarid |
| 60 | B3 | | -40 | E | Arid |
| 40 | B2 | | | | |
| 20 | B1 | | | | |
| 0 | C2 | Moist subhumid | | | |

Moisture index = $\dfrac{\text{surplus} - .6\ \text{deficiency}}{\text{need}}$

Courtesy American
Geographical Society

**AVERAGE ANNUAL**
**THERMAL EFFICIENCY**
After C. W. Thornthwaite

| Inches | Type | | | Inches | |
|---|---|---|---|---|---|
| 44.88 | A' | Megathermal | | | |
| 39.27 | B'4 | | | | |
| 33.66 | B'3 | Mesothermal | 16.83 | C'2 | Microthermal |
| 28.05 | B'2 | | 11.22 | C'1 | |
| 22.44 | B'1 | | 5.61 | D' | Tundra |

Courtesy American Geographical Society

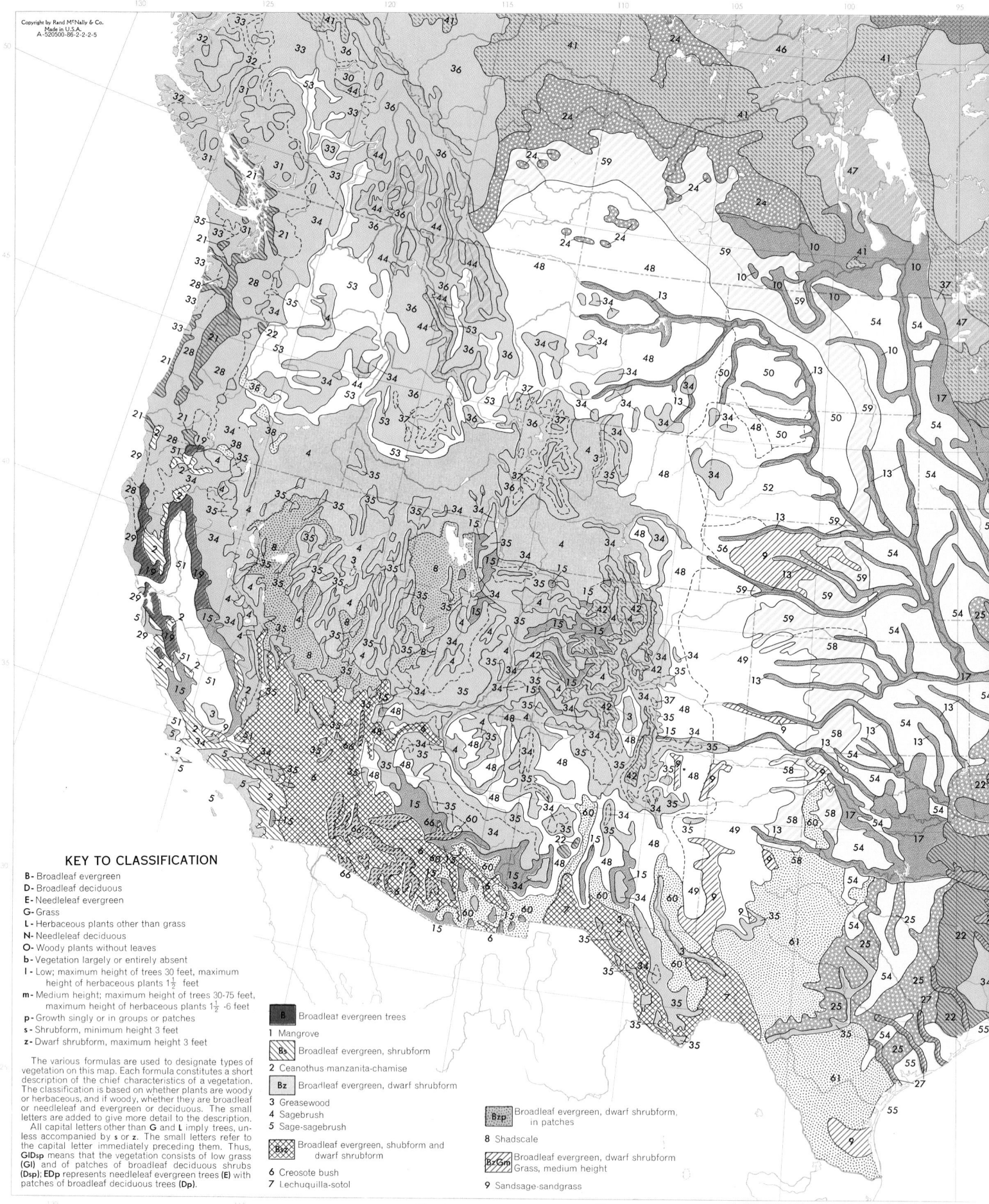

Copyright by Rand McNally & Co.
Made in U.S.A.
A-520500-86-2-2-5

## KEY TO CLASSIFICATION

B - Broadleaf evergreen
D - Broadleaf deciduous
E - Needleleaf evergreen
G - Grass
L - Herbaceous plants other than grass
N - Needleleaf deciduous
O - Woody plants without leaves
b - Vegetation largely or entirely absent
l - Low; maximum height of trees 30 feet, maximum
    height of herbaceous plants 1½ feet
m - Medium height; maximum height of trees 30-75 feet,
    maximum height of herbaceous plants 1½ -6 feet
p - Growth singly or in groups or patches
s - Shrubform, minimum height 3 feet
z - Dwarf shrubform, maximum height 3 feet

The various formulas are used to designate types of
vegetation on this map. Each formula constitutes a short
description of the chief characteristics of a vegetation.
The classification is based on whether plants are woody
or herbaceous, and if woody, whether they are broadleaf
or needleleaf and evergreen or deciduous. The small
letters are added to give more detail to the description.

All capital letters other than G and L imply trees, unless
accompanied by s or z. The small letters refer to
the capital letter immediately preceding them. Thus,
GlDsp means that the vegetation consists of low grass
(Gl) and of patches of broadleaf deciduous shrubs
(Dsp); EDp represents needleleaf evergreen trees (E) with
patches of broadleaf deciduous trees (Dp).

| B | Broadleaf evergreen trees |
| --- | --- |

1 Mangrove

| Bs | Broadleaf evergreen, shrubform |

2 Ceanothus-manzanita-chamise

| Bz | Broadleaf evergreen, dwarf shrubform |

3 Greasewood
4 Sagebrush
5 Sage-sagebrush

| Bsz | Broadleaf evergreen, shubform and dwarf shrubform |

6 Creosote bush
7 Lechuquilla-sotol

| Bzp | Broadleaf evergreen, dwarf shrubform, in patches |

8 Shadscale

| BzGm | Broadleaf evergreen, dwarf shrubform Grass, medium height |

9 Sandsage-sandgrass

Scale 1:14 000 000;   One inch to 220 miles.

0  25  50  75  100    200        300        400        500 Miles

0  50  100    200        400        600        800 Kilometers

# NATURAL VEGETATION

BY A. W. KÜCHLER

Based on "A Physiognomic Classification of Vegetation"
Annals of the Assoc. of American Geographers, Vol. 39, September, 1949

| D | Broadleaf deciduous trees |

10 Aspen-oak
11 Beech-maple
12 Beech-tulip tree-maple-basswood
13 Cottonwood-willow
14 Maple-basswood
15 Oak
16 Oak-ash-maple
17 Oak-hickory
18 Oak-tulip tree

| DB | Broadleaf deciduous trees / Broadleaf evergreen trees |

19 Oak-madrone

| DE | Broadleaf deciduous trees / Needleleaf evergreen trees |

20 Maple-yellow birch-hemlock-pine
21 Oak-Douglas fir
22 Oak-pine
23 Maple-beech-hemlock

| D / Gmp | Broadleaf deciduous trees / Grass, medium height, in patches |

24 Aspen-needle grass-wheat grass
25 Oak-hickory-bluestem

| DN | Broadleaf deciduous trees / Needleleaf deciduous trees |

26 Bay trees-bald cypress
27 Tupelo-gum-bald cypress

| E | Needleleaf evergreen trees |

28 Douglas fir
29 Douglas fir-redwood
30 Hemlock-arbor vitae
31 Hemlock-arbor vitae-Douglas fir
32 Hemlock-arbor vitae-fir
33 Hemlock-spruce
34 Pine
35 Pine-juniper
36 Pine-spruce
37 Spruce-fir

| Esp | Needleleaf evergreen, shrubform, in patches |

38 Juniper

| EDp | Needleleaf evergreen trees / Broadleaf deciduous trees, in patches |

39 Douglas fir-pine-aspen
40 Pine-spruce-birch
41 Spruce-aspen
42 Spruce-fir-aspen
43 Spruce-poplar-birch

| EN | Needleleaf evergreen trees / Needleleaf deciduous trees |

44 Hemlock-arbor vitae-Douglas fir-larch
45 Pine-bald cypress
46 Pine-spruce-larch
47 Spruce-larch

| Gl | Grass, low |

48 Grama grass
49 Grama grass-buffalo grass
50 Grama grass-needle grass
51 Needle grass-blue grass
52 Wheat grass
53 Wheat grass-blue grass

| Gm | Grass, medium height |

54 Bluestem
55 Broom grass-water grass
56 Marsh grass
57 Saw grass

| Gml | Grass, medium and low height |

58 Bluestem-bunch grass
59 Needle grass-wheat grass

| Gl / Dsp | Grass, low / Broadleaf deciduous, shrubform, in patches |

60 Bunch grass-oak

| Gm / Dsp | Grass, medium height / Broadleaf deciduous, shrubform, in patches |

61 Mesquite grass-mesquite

| L | Herbaceous plants other than grass |

62 Lichens, etc.

| LEp | Herbaceous plants other than grass / Needleleaf evergreen trees, in patches |

63 Lichens-spruce

| LEp / Np | Herbaceous plants other than grass / Needleleaf evergreen trees, in patches / Needleleaf deciduous trees, in patches |

64 Lichens-spruce-larch

| N | Needleleaf deciduous trees |

65 Bald cypress

| Op | Woody plants without leaves, in patches |

66 Palo verde-cacti-ocotillo

| b | Vegetation largely or entirely absent |

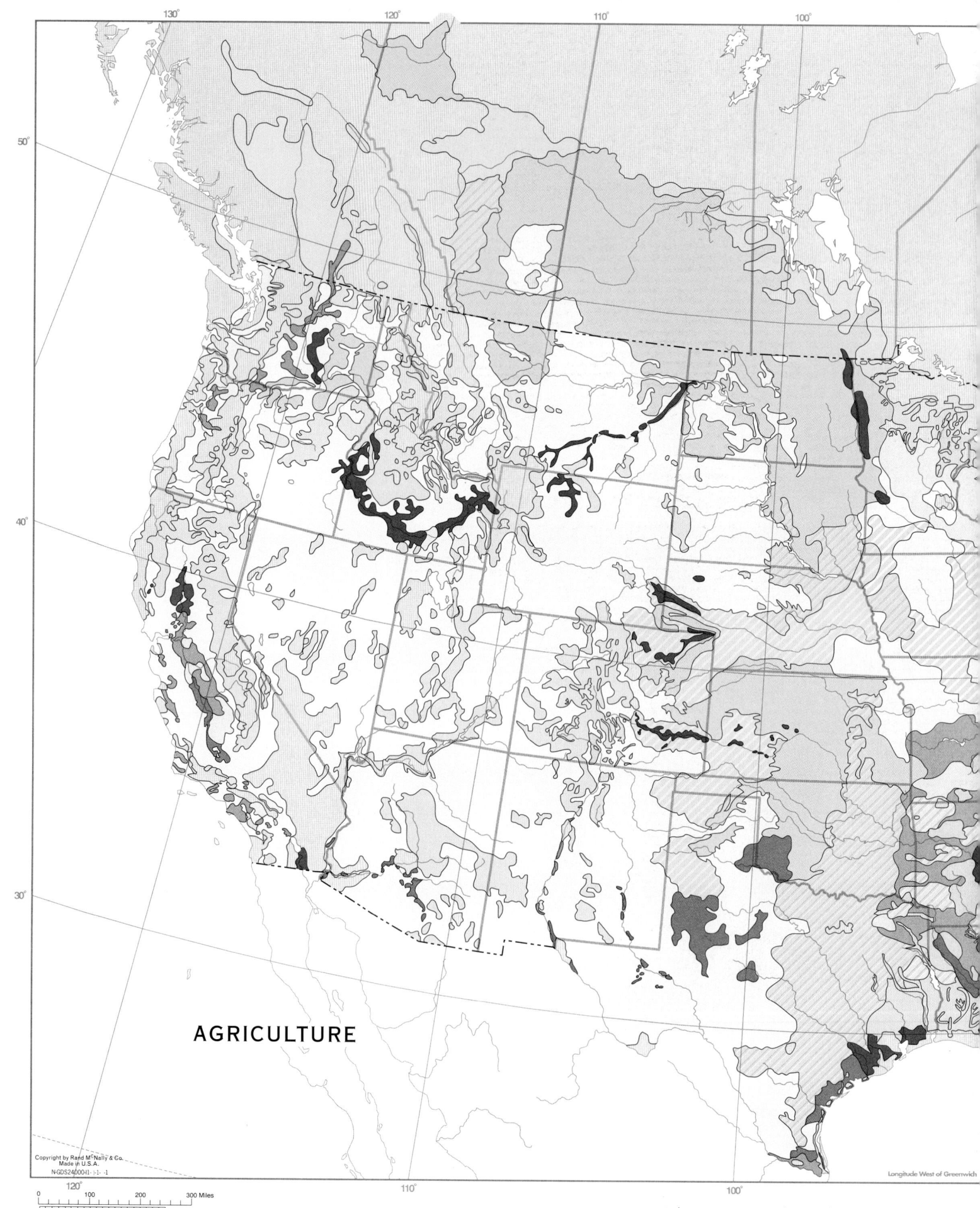

AGRICULTURE

Longitude West of Greenwich

0    100    200    300 Miles

0    100    200    300    400 Kilometers

Scale 1:15,000,000;  One inch to 237 miles. One centimeter to 150 kilometers.

Dairying

Fruits and Vegetables

Wheat, Barley, and Oilseeds

Cash Corn and Soybeans

Tobacco

Cotton

Livestock and Feed Grains: Beef

Livestock and Feed Grains: Hogs

Livestock and Feed Grains: Poultry

Livestock and Feed Grains: Mixed

Specialty Crops (Peanuts, Potatoes, Rice, Sugar)

Western Livestock Ranching

Western Feedlots

Agriculture and Forestry

Non-Agricultural Areas

Tropic of Cancer

ALBERS CONIC PROJECTION

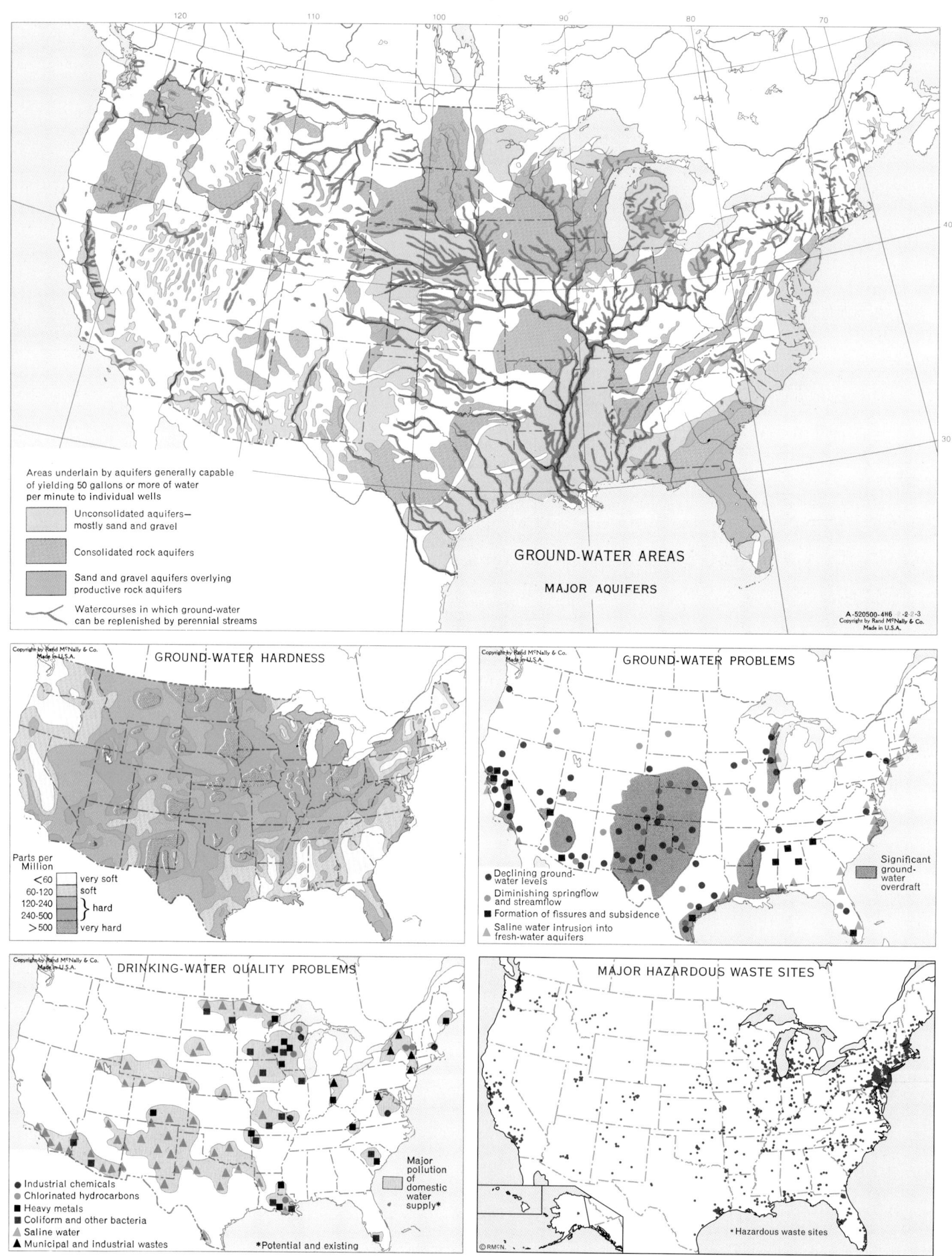

**GROUND-WATER AREAS**

**MAJOR AQUIFERS**

Areas underlain by aquifers generally capable of yielding 50 gallons or more of water per minute to individual wells

Unconsolidated aquifers— mostly sand and gravel

Consolidated rock aquifers

Sand and gravel aquifers overlying productive rock aquifers

Watercourses in which ground-water can be replenished by perennial streams

A-520500-4H6 8-2-2-3
Copyright by Rand McNally & Co.
Made in U.S.A.

**GROUND-WATER HARDNESS**

Parts per Million
<60   very soft
60-120   soft
120-240 } hard
240-500
>500   very hard

**GROUND-WATER PROBLEMS**

● Declining ground-water levels
● Diminishing springflow and streamflow
■ Formation of fissures and subsidence
▲ Saline water intrusion into fresh-water aquifers

Significant ground-water overdraft

**DRINKING-WATER QUALITY PROBLEMS**

● Industrial chemicals
● Chlorinated hydrocarbons
■ Heavy metals
■ Coliform and other bacteria
▲ Saline water
▲ Municipal and industrial wastes

Major pollution of domestic water supply*

*Potential and existing

**MAJOR HAZARDOUS WASTE SITES**

• Hazardous waste sites

©RMcN.

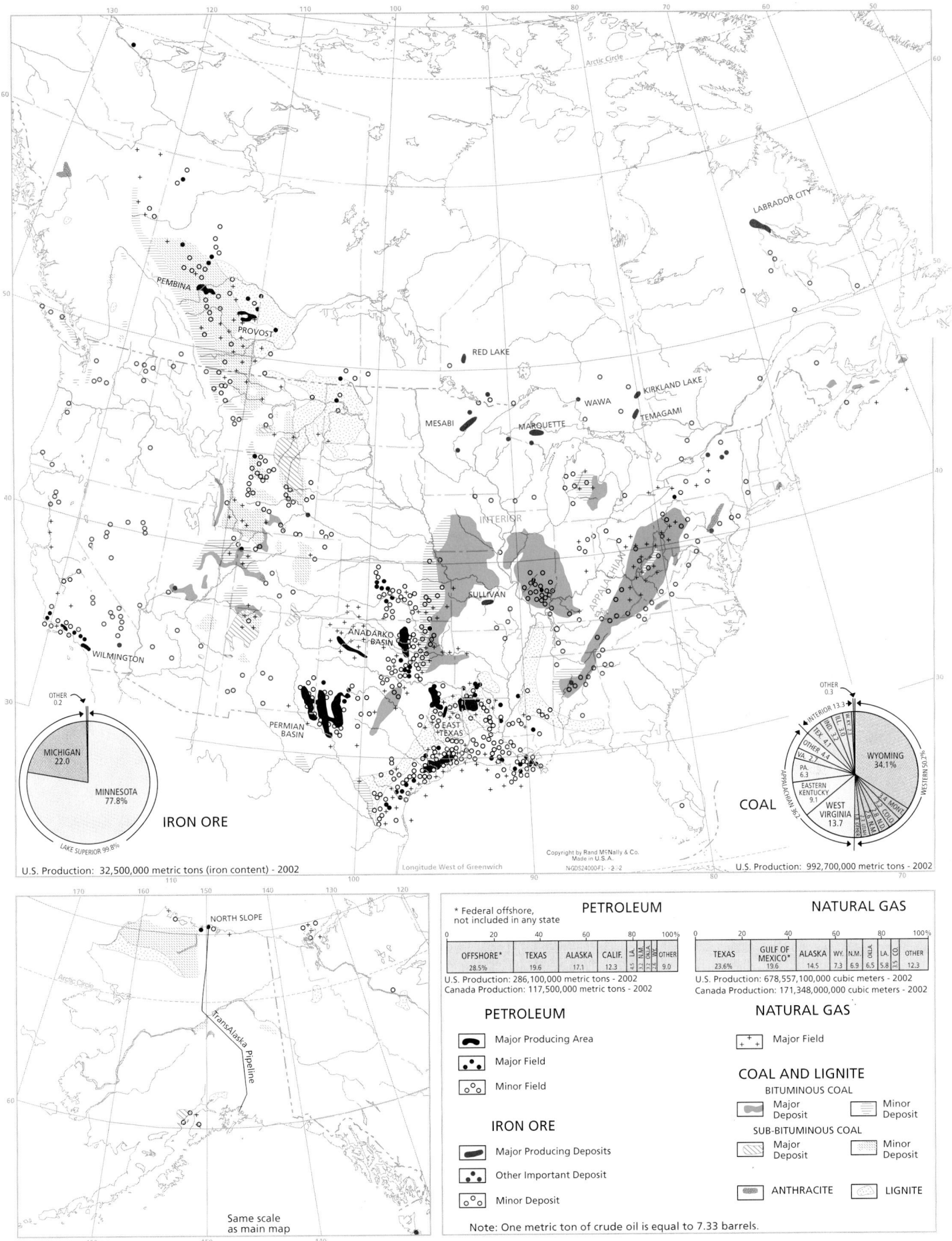

IRON ORE

OTHER
0.2

MICHIGAN
22.0

MINNESOTA
77.8%

LAKE SUPERIOR 99.8%

U.S. Production: 32,500,000 metric tons (iron content) - 2002

COAL

OTHER
0.3

INTERIOR 13.3

ILL. 7.7

IND. 3.2

TEX. 4.4

OTHER 4.4

VA. 2.5

PA.
6.3

EASTERN
KENTUCKY
9.1

WEST
VIRGINIA
13.7

APPALACHIAN 36.3

WYOMING
34.1%

WESTERN 50.2%

N.D. 3.3

MONT.

COLO.

UTAH

N.M.

ARIZ.

U.S. Production: 992,700,000 metric tons - 2002

PEMBINA

PROVOST

RED LAKE

MESABI

MARQUETTE

WAWA

KIRKLAND LAKE

TEMAGAMI

LABRADOR CITY

INTERIOR

APPALACHIAN

SULLIVAN

ANADARKO
BASIN

WILMINGTON

PERMIAN
BASIN

EAST
TEXAS

Copyright by Rand McNally & Co.
Made in U.S.A.

Longitude West of Greenwich

N-GDS24000-F1- -2- -2

NORTH SLOPE

TransAlaska Pipeline

Same scale
as main map

* Federal offshore,
not included in any state

### PETROLEUM

| | | | | | | | | |
|---|---|---|---|---|---|---|---|---|
| 0 | 20 | 40 | 60 | 80 | 100% | | | |
| OFFSHORE*
28.5% | TEXAS
19.6 | ALASKA
17.1 | CALIF.
12.3 | LA. 4.5 | N.M. 3.3 | OKLA. 2.7 | OTHER
9.0 | |

U.S. Production: 286,100,000 metric tons - 2002
Canada Production: 117,500,000 metric tons - 2002

### NATURAL GAS

| | | | | | | | |
|---|---|---|---|---|---|---|---|
| 0 | 20 | 40 | 60 | 80 | 100% | | |
| TEXAS
23.6% | GULF OF
MEXICO*
19.6 | ALASKA
14.5 | WY.
7.3 | N.M.
6.9 | OKLA. 6.5 | CO. 3.5 | OTHER
12.3 |

U.S. Production: 678,557,100,000 cubic meters - 2002
Canada Production: 171,348,000,000 cubic meters - 2002

### PETROLEUM

⬛ Major Producing Area

⬛•• Major Field

○°○ Minor Field

### IRON ORE

⬛ Major Producing Deposits

•⬛• Other Important Deposit

○°○ Minor Deposit

### NATURAL GAS

+⁺+ Major Field

### COAL AND LIGNITE

BITUMINOUS COAL

▨ Major
Deposit

▨ Minor
Deposit

SUB-BITUMINOUS COAL

▨ Major
Deposit

▨ Minor
Deposit

▨ ANTHRACITE

○ LIGNITE

Note: One metric ton of crude oil is equal to 7.33 barrels.

Scale 1:29,000,000; One inch to 457 miles. ALBERS CONIC PROJECTION

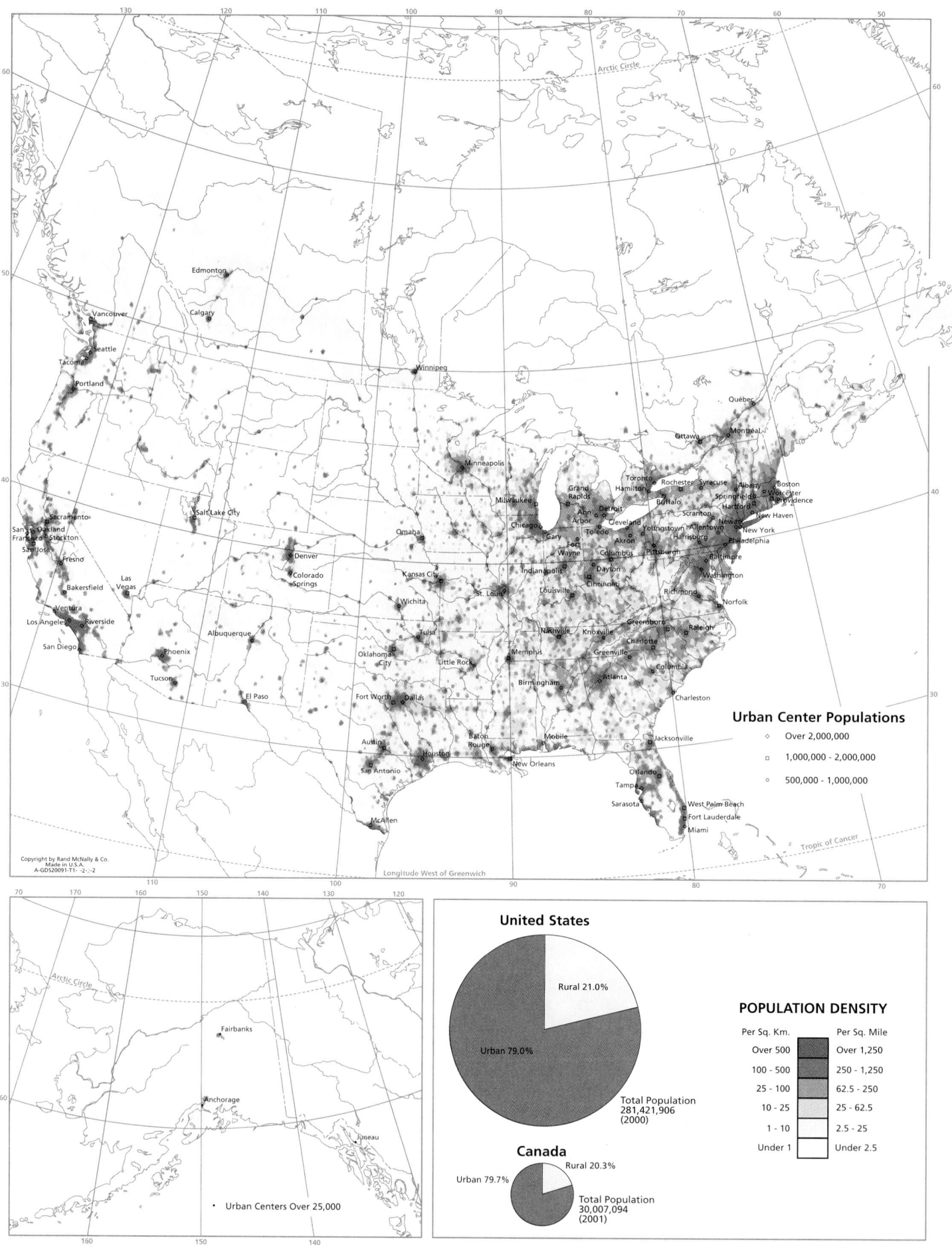

Copyright by Rand McNally & Co.
Made in U.S.A.
A-GDS20091-T1- -2-/--2

Longitude West of Greenwich

**Urban Center Populations**

◇ Over 2,000,000

□ 1,000,000 - 2,000,000

○ 500,000 - 1,000,000

• Urban Centers Over 25,000

**United States**

Rural 21.0%

Urban 79.0%

Total Population
281,421,906
(2000)

**Canada**

Rural 20.3%

Urban 79.7%

Total Population
30,007,094
(2001)

**POPULATION DENSITY**

| Per Sq. Km. | Per Sq. Mile |
|---|---|
| Over 500 | Over 1,250 |
| 100 - 500 | 250 - 1,250 |
| 25 - 100 | 62.5 - 250 |
| 10 - 25 | 25 - 62.5 |
| 1 - 10 | 2.5 - 25 |
| Under 1 | Under 2.5 |

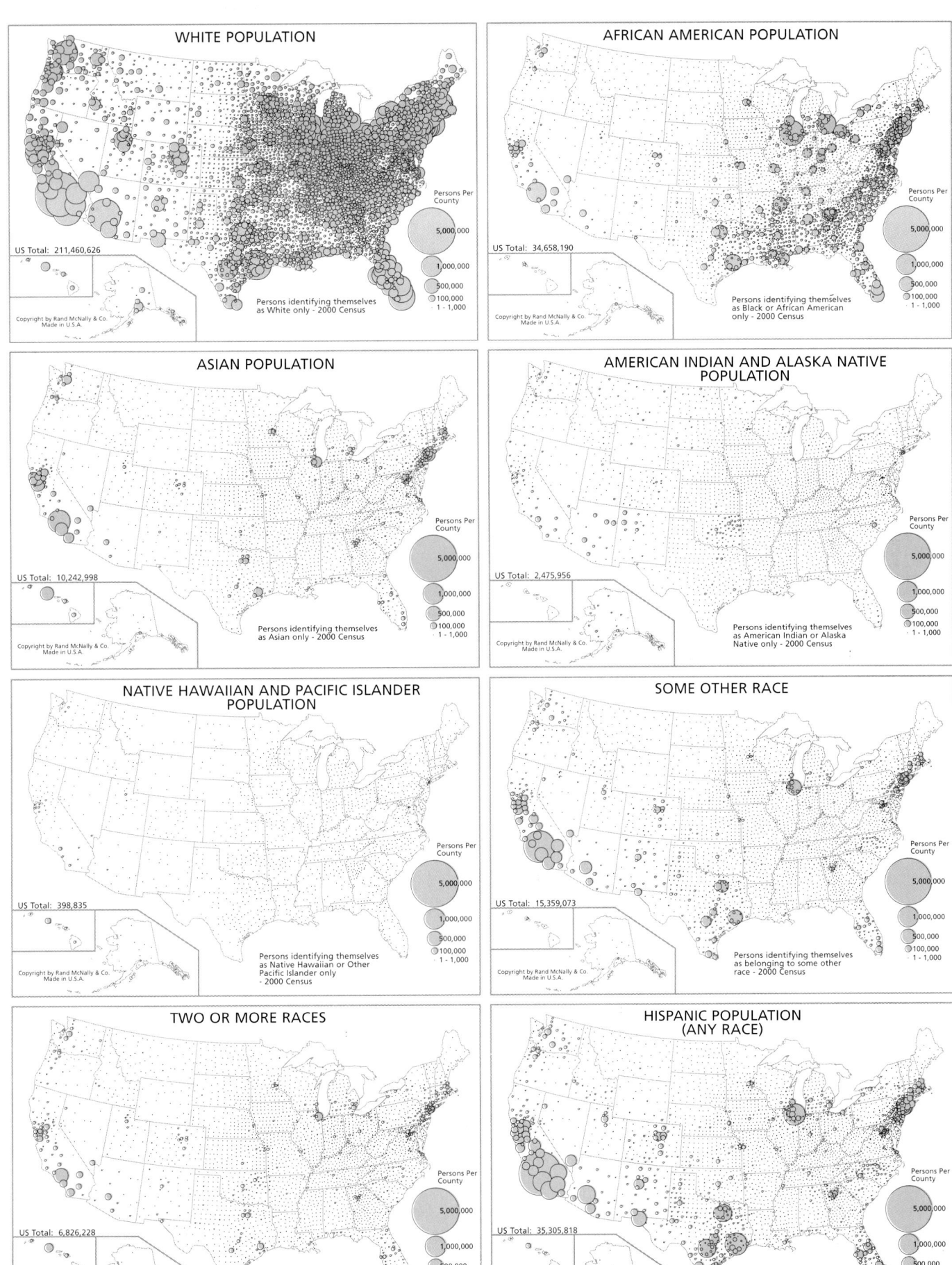

WHITE POPULATION

US Total: 211,460,626

Copyright by Rand McNally & Co.
Made in U.S.A.

Persons Per County

5,000,000
1,000,000
500,000
100,000
1 - 1,000

Persons identifying themselves as White only - 2000 Census

AFRICAN AMERICAN POPULATION

US Total: 34,658,190

Copyright by Rand McNally & Co.
Made in U.S.A.

Persons Per County

5,000,000
1,000,000
500,000
100,000
1 - 1,000

Persons identifying themselves as Black or African American only - 2000 Census

ASIAN POPULATION

US Total: 10,242,998

Copyright by Rand McNally & Co.
Made in U.S.A.

Persons Per County

5,000,000
1,000,000
500,000
100,000
1 - 1,000

Persons identifying themselves as Asian only - 2000 Census

AMERICAN INDIAN AND ALASKA NATIVE POPULATION

US Total: 2,475,956

Copyright by Rand McNally & Co.
Made in U.S.A.

Persons Per County

5,000,000
1,000,000
500,000
100,000
1 - 1,000

Persons identifying themselves as American Indian or Alaska Native only - 2000 Census

NATIVE HAWAIIAN AND PACIFIC ISLANDER POPULATION

US Total: 398,835

Copyright by Rand McNally & Co.
Made in U.S.A.

Persons Per County

5,000,000
1,000,000
500,000
100,000
1 - 1,000

Persons identifying themselves as Native Hawaiian or Other Pacific Islander only - 2000 Census

SOME OTHER RACE

US Total: 15,359,073

Copyright by Rand McNally & Co.
Made in U.S.A.

Persons Per County

5,000,000
1,000,000
500,000
100,000
1 - 1,000

Persons identifying themselves as belonging to some other race - 2000 Census

TWO OR MORE RACES

US Total: 6,826,228

Copyright by Rand McNally & Co.
Made in U.S.A.

Persons Per County

5,000,000
1,000,000
500,000
100,000
1 - 1,000

Persons identifying themselves as belonging to two or more races - 2000 Census

HISPANIC POPULATION (ANY RACE)

US Total: 35,305,818

Copyright by Rand McNally & Co.
Made in U.S.A.
A-GDS24000-U4- - - ·3

Persons Per County

5,000,000
1,000,000
500,000
100,000
1 - 1,000

Persons identifying themselves as Hispanic or Latino (any race) - 2000 Census

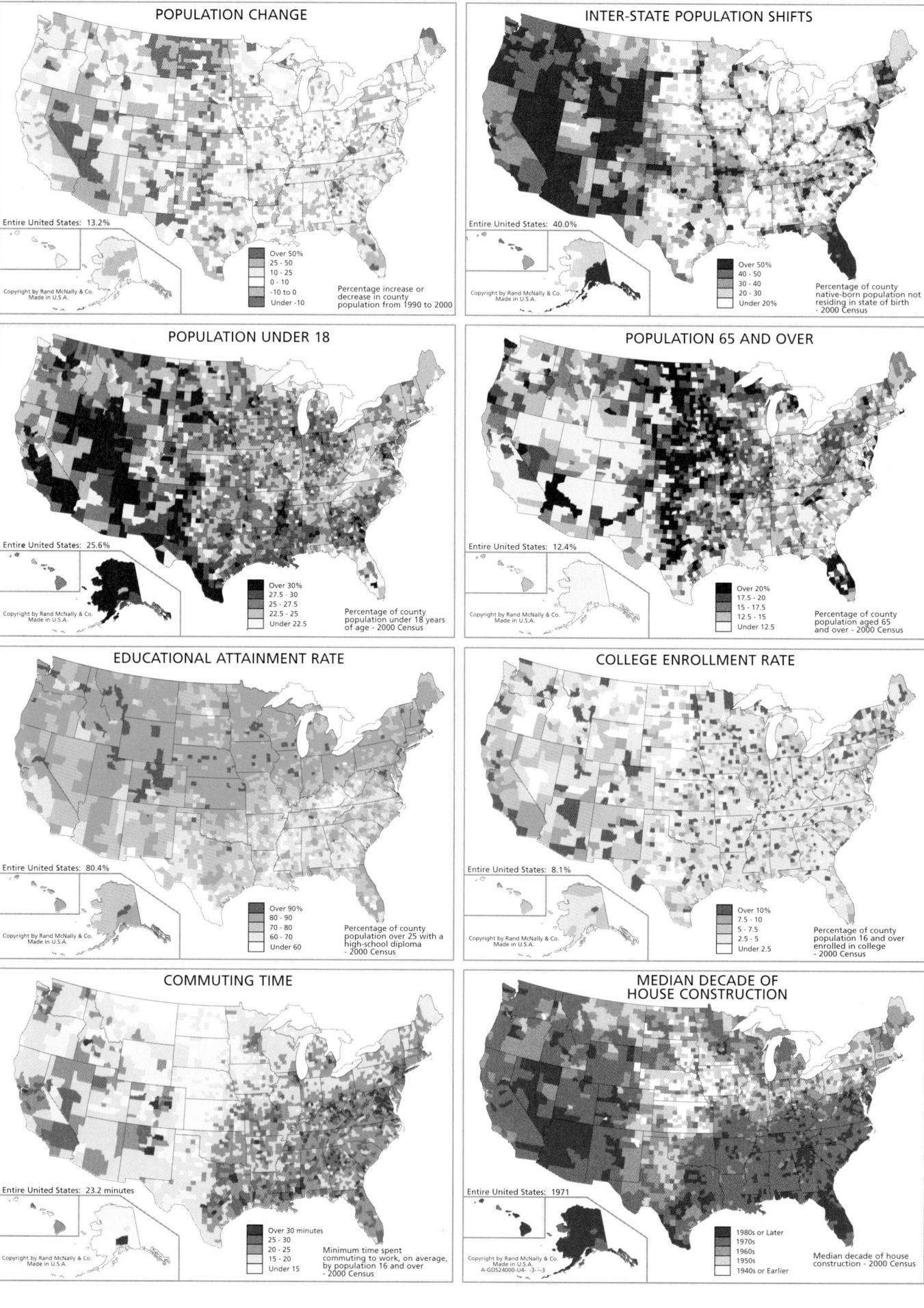

### POPULATION CHANGE

Entire United States: 13.2%

- Over 50%
- 25 - 50
- 10 - 25
- 0 - 10
- -10 to 0
- Under -10

Copyright by Rand McNally & Co.
Made in U.S.A.

Percentage increase or decrease in county population from 1990 to 2000

### INTER-STATE POPULATION SHIFTS

Entire United States: 40.0%

- Over 50%
- 40 - 50
- 30 - 40
- 20 - 30
- Under 20%

Copyright by Rand McNally & Co.
Made in U.S.A.

Percentage of county native-born population not residing in state of birth - 2000 Census

### POPULATION UNDER 18

Entire United States: 25.6%

- Over 30%
- 27.5 - 30
- 25 - 27.5
- 22.5 - 25
- Under 22.5

Copyright by Rand McNally & Co.
Made in U.S.A.

Percentage of county population under 18 years of age - 2000 Census

### POPULATION 65 AND OVER

Entire United States: 12.4%

- Over 20%
- 17.5 - 20
- 15 - 17.5
- 12.5 - 15
- Under 12.5

Copyright by Rand McNally & Co.
Made in U.S.A.

Percentage of county population aged 65 and over - 2000 Census

### EDUCATIONAL ATTAINMENT RATE

Entire United States: 80.4%

- Over 90%
- 80 - 90
- 70 - 80
- 60 - 70
- Under 60

Copyright by Rand McNally & Co.
Made in U.S.A.

Percentage of county population over 25 with a high-school diploma - 2000 Census

### COLLEGE ENROLLMENT RATE

Entire United States: 8.1%

- Over 10%
- 7.5 - 10
- 5 - 7.5
- 2.5 - 5
- Under 2.5

Copyright by Rand McNally & Co.
Made in U.S.A.

Percentage of county population 16 and over enrolled in college - 2000 Census

### COMMUTING TIME

Entire United States: 23.2 minutes

- Over 30 minutes
- 25 - 30
- 20 - 25
- 15 - 20
- Under 15

Copyright by Rand McNally & Co.
Made in U.S.A.

Minimum time spent commuting to work, on average, by population 16 and over - 2000 Census

### MEDIAN DECADE OF HOUSE CONSTRUCTION

Entire United States: 1971

- 1980s or Later
- 1970s
- 1960s
- 1950s
- 1940s or Earlier

Copyright by Rand McNally & Co.
Made in U.S.A.
A-GDS24000-U4- -3- -l-3

Median decade of house construction - 2000 Census

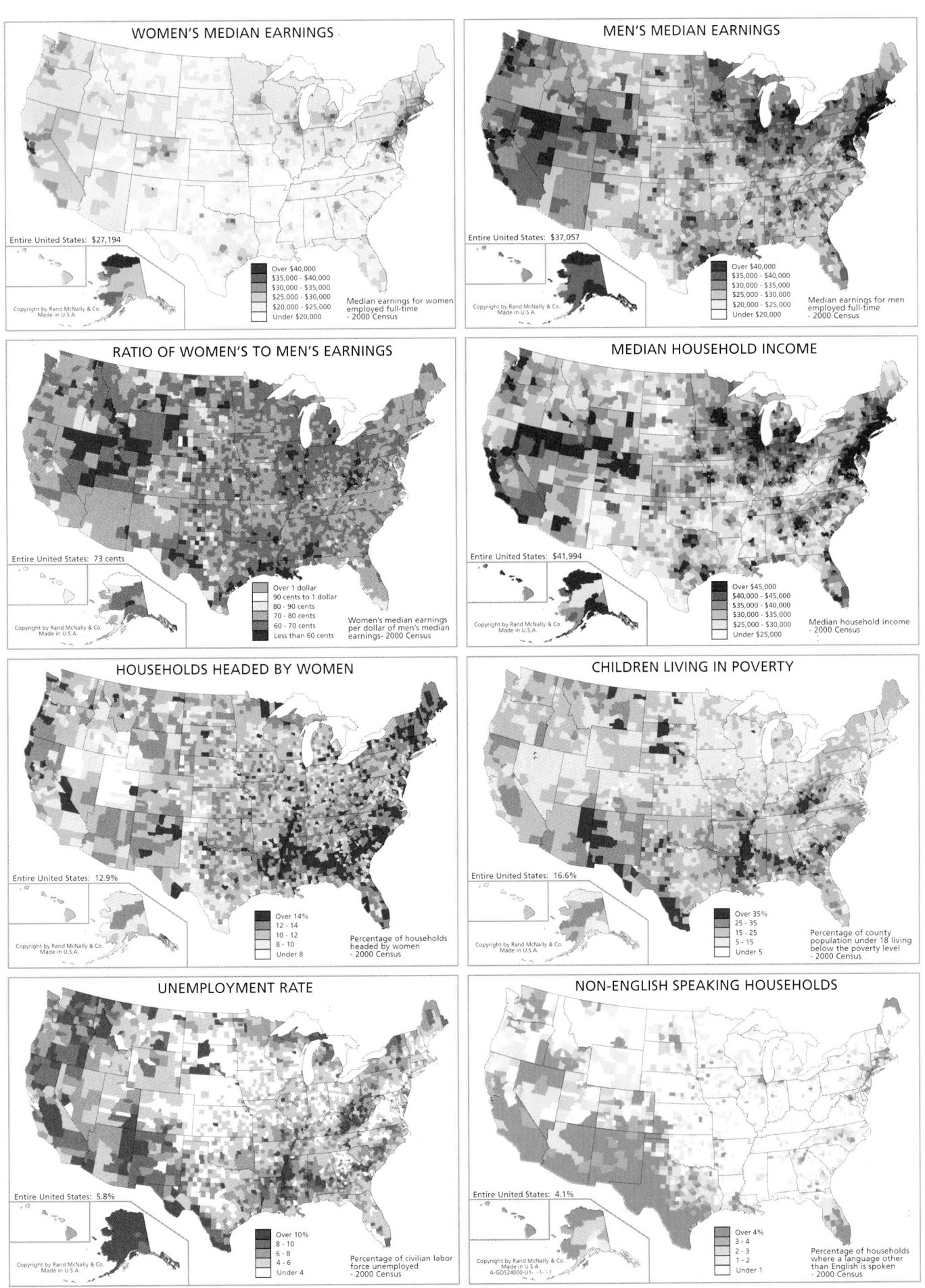

## WOMEN'S MEDIAN EARNINGS

Entire United States: $27,194

Over $40,000
$35,000 - $40,000
$30,000 - $35,000
$25,000 - $30,000
$20,000 - $25,000
Under $20,000

Median earnings for women employed full-time - 2000 Census

Copyright by Rand McNally & Co. Made in U.S.A.

## MEN'S MEDIAN EARNINGS

Entire United States: $37,057

Over $40,000
$35,000 - $40,000
$30,000 - $35,000
$25,000 - $30,000
$20,000 - $25,000
Under $20,000

Median earnings for men employed full-time - 2000 Census

Copyright by Rand McNally & Co. Made in U.S.A.

## RATIO OF WOMEN'S TO MEN'S EARNINGS

Entire United States: 73 cents

Over 1 dollar
90 cents to 1 dollar
80 - 90 cents
70 - 80 cents
60 - 70 cents
Less than 60 cents

Women's median earnings per dollar of men's median earnings- 2000 Census

Copyright by Rand McNally & Co. Made in U.S.A.

## MEDIAN HOUSEHOLD INCOME

Entire United States: $41,994

Over $45,000
$40,000 - $45,000
$35,000 - $40,000
$30,000 - $35,000
$25,000 - $30,000
Under $25,000

Median household income - 2000 Census

Copyright by Rand McNally & Co. Made in U.S.A.

## HOUSEHOLDS HEADED BY WOMEN

Entire United States: 12.9%

Over 14%
12 - 14
10 - 12
8 - 10
Under 8

Percentage of households headed by women - 2000 Census

Copyright by Rand McNally & Co. Made in U.S.A.

## CHILDREN LIVING IN POVERTY

Entire United States: 16.6%

Over 35%
25 - 35
15 - 25
5 - 15
Under 5

Percentage of county population under 18 living below the poverty level - 2000 Census

Copyright by Rand McNally & Co. Made in U.S.A.

## UNEMPLOYMENT RATE

Entire United States: 5.8%

Over 10%
8 - 10
6 - 8
4 - 6
Under 4

Percentage of civilian labor force unemployed - 2000 Census

Copyright by Rand McNally & Co. Made in U.S.A.

## NON-ENGLISH SPEAKING HOUSEHOLDS

Entire United States: 4.1%

Over 4%
3 - 4
2 - 3
1 - 2
Under 1

Percentage of households where a language other than English is spoken - 2000 Census

Copyright by Rand McNally & Co. Made in U.S.A. A-GD524000-U1- -1- '-1

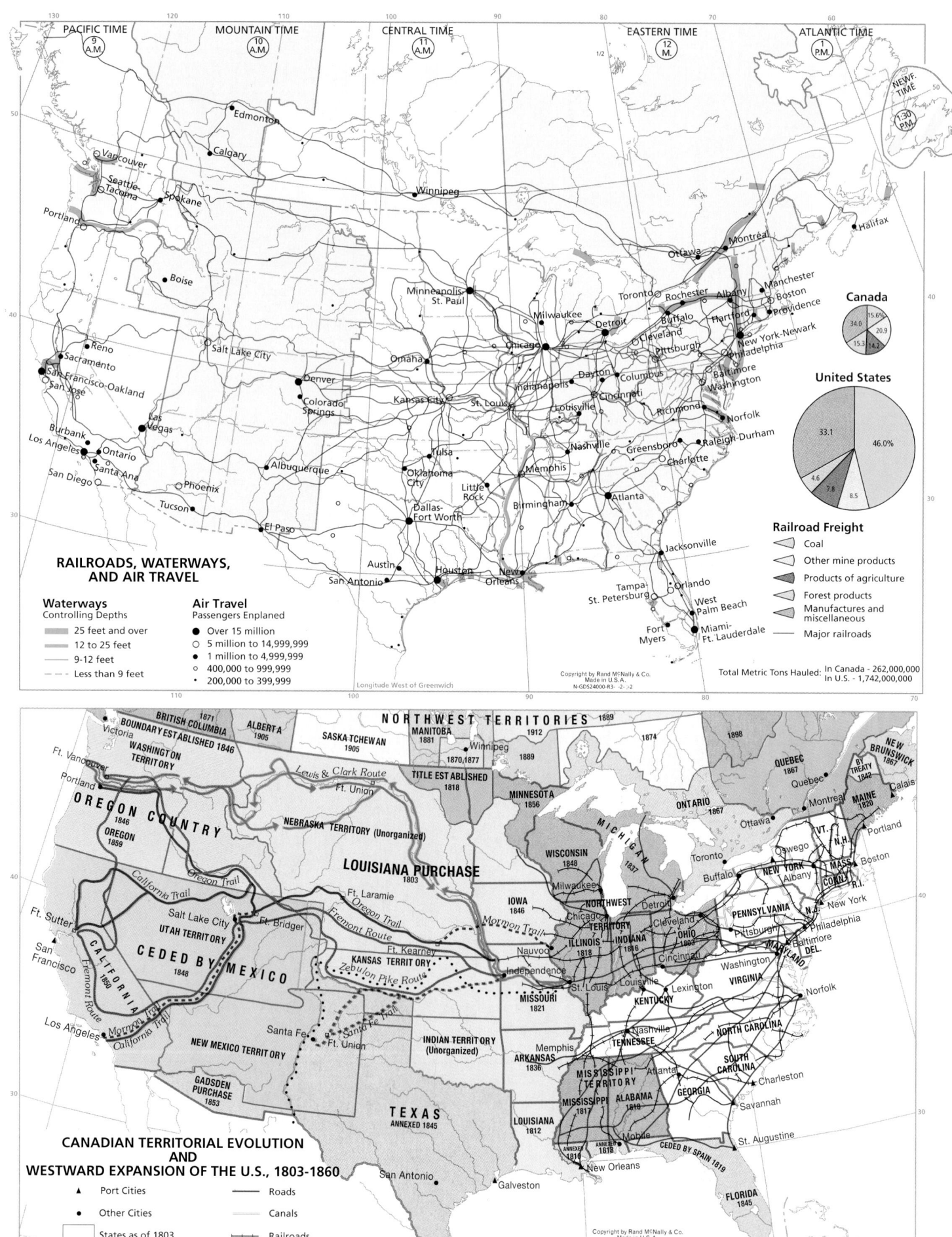

## RAILROADS, WATERWAYS, AND AIR TRAVEL

**Waterways**
Controlling Depths
- 25 feet and over
- 12 to 25 feet
- 9-12 feet
- Less than 9 feet

**Air Travel**
Passengers Enplaned
- Over 15 million
- 5 million to 14,999,999
- 1 million to 4,999,999
- 400,000 to 999,999
- 200,000 to 399,999

**Railroad Freight**
- Coal
- Other mine products
- Products of agriculture
- Forest products
- Manufactures and miscellaneous
- Major railroads

**Canada**
34.0  15.6%  20.9  15.3  14.2

**United States**
46.0%  33.1  4.6  7.8  8.5

Total Metric Tons Hauled: In Canada - 262,000,000
In U.S. - 1,742,000,000

Copyright by Rand McNally & Co.
Made in U.S.A.
N-GDS24000-R3- -2- -2

## CANADIAN TERRITORIAL EVOLUTION AND WESTWARD EXPANSION OF THE U.S., 1803-1860

- ▲ Port Cities
- ● Other Cities
- ▭ States as of 1803
- —— Roads
- —— Canals
- —|—|— Railroads

Copyright by Rand McNally & Co.
Made in U.S.A.
H-GDS24000-B6- -1- -2

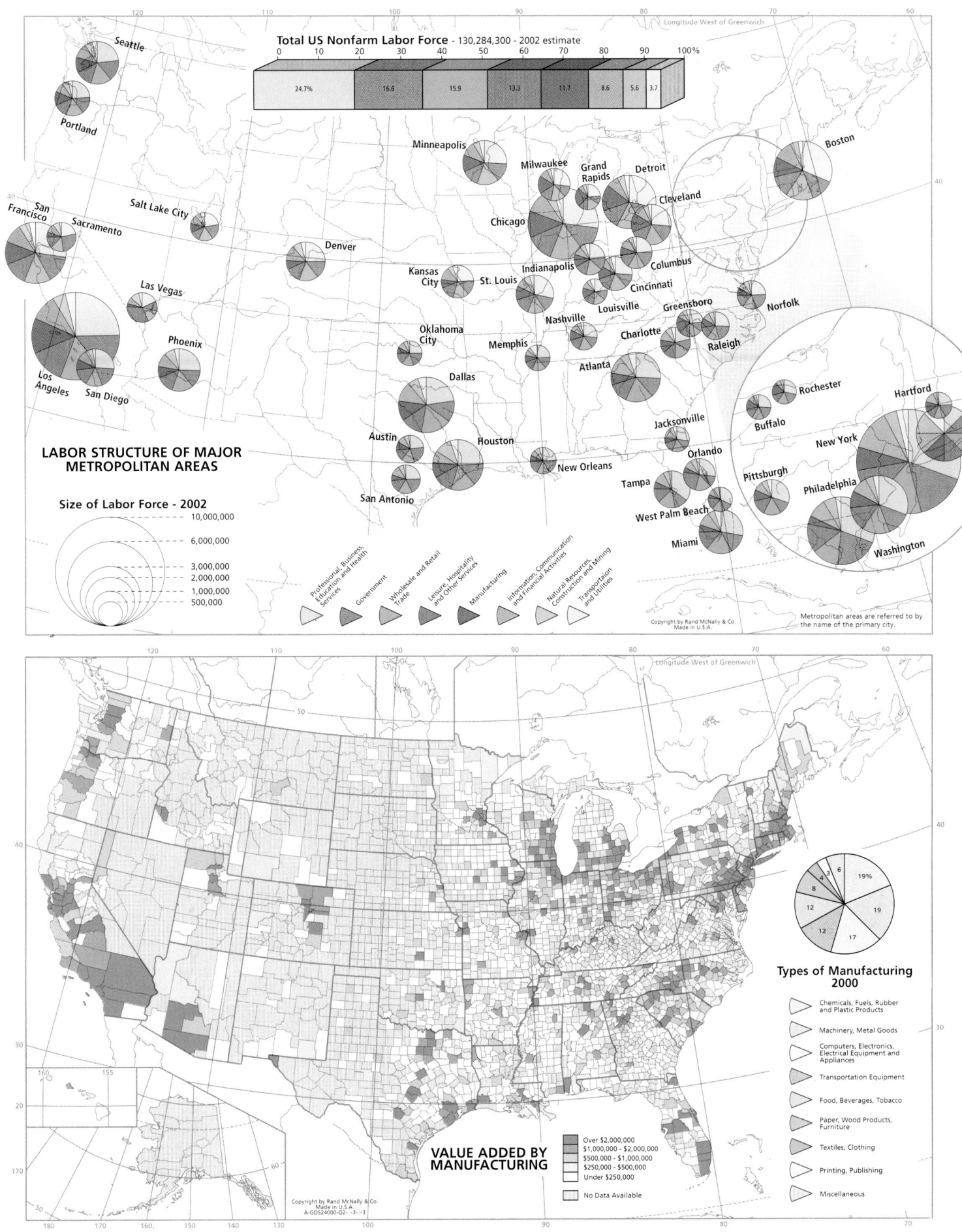

Total US Nonfarm Labor Force - 130,284,300 - 2002 estimate

| 24.7% | 16.6 | 15.9 | 13.3 | 11.7 | 8.6 | 5.6 | 3.7 |

**LABOR STRUCTURE OF MAJOR METROPOLITAN AREAS**

Size of Labor Force - 2002

10,000,000
6,000,000
3,000,000
2,000,000
1,000,000
500,000

Professional, Business, Education and Health Services

Government

Wholesale and Retail Trade

Leisure, Hospitality and Other Services

Manufacturing

Information, Communication and Financial Activities

Natural Resources, Construction and Mining

Transportation and Utilities

Copyright by Rand McNally & Co.
Made in U.S.A.

Metropolitan areas are referred to by the name of the primary city.

**Types of Manufacturing 2000**

Chemicals, Fuels, Rubber and Plastic Products

Machinery, Metal Goods

Computers, Electronics, Electrical Equipment and Appliances

Transportation Equipment

Food, Beverages, Tobacco

Paper, Wood Products, Furniture

Textiles, Clothing

Printing, Publishing

Miscellaneous

**VALUE ADDED BY MANUFACTURING**

Over $2,000,000
$1,000,000 - $2,000,000
$500,000 - $1,000,000
$250,000 - $500,000
Under $250,000
No Data Available

Copyright by Rand McNally & Co.
Made in U.S.A.
A-GDS24000-Q2--3--3

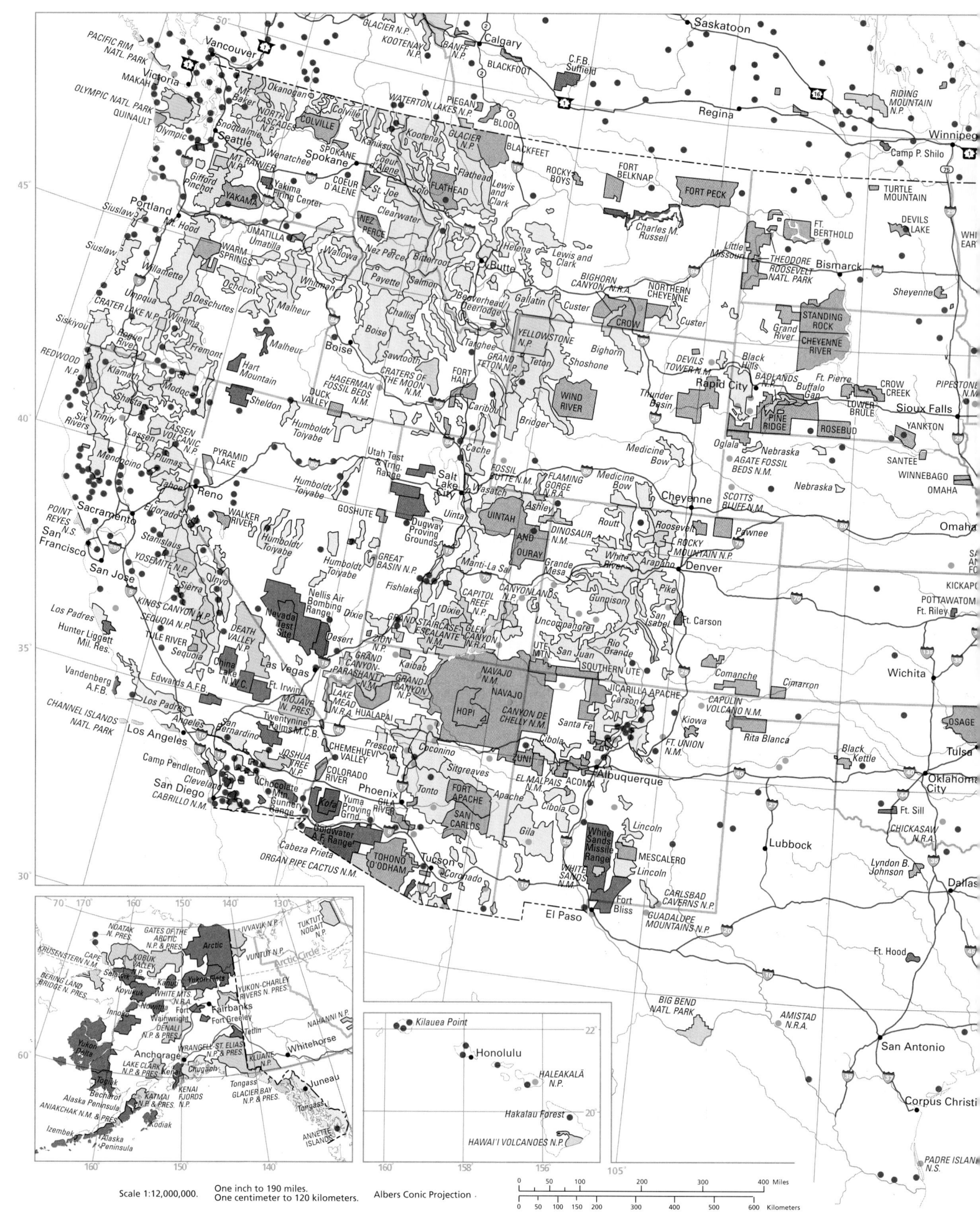

Scale 1:12,000,000.
One inch to 190 miles.
One centimeter to 120 kilometers.
Albers Conic Projection

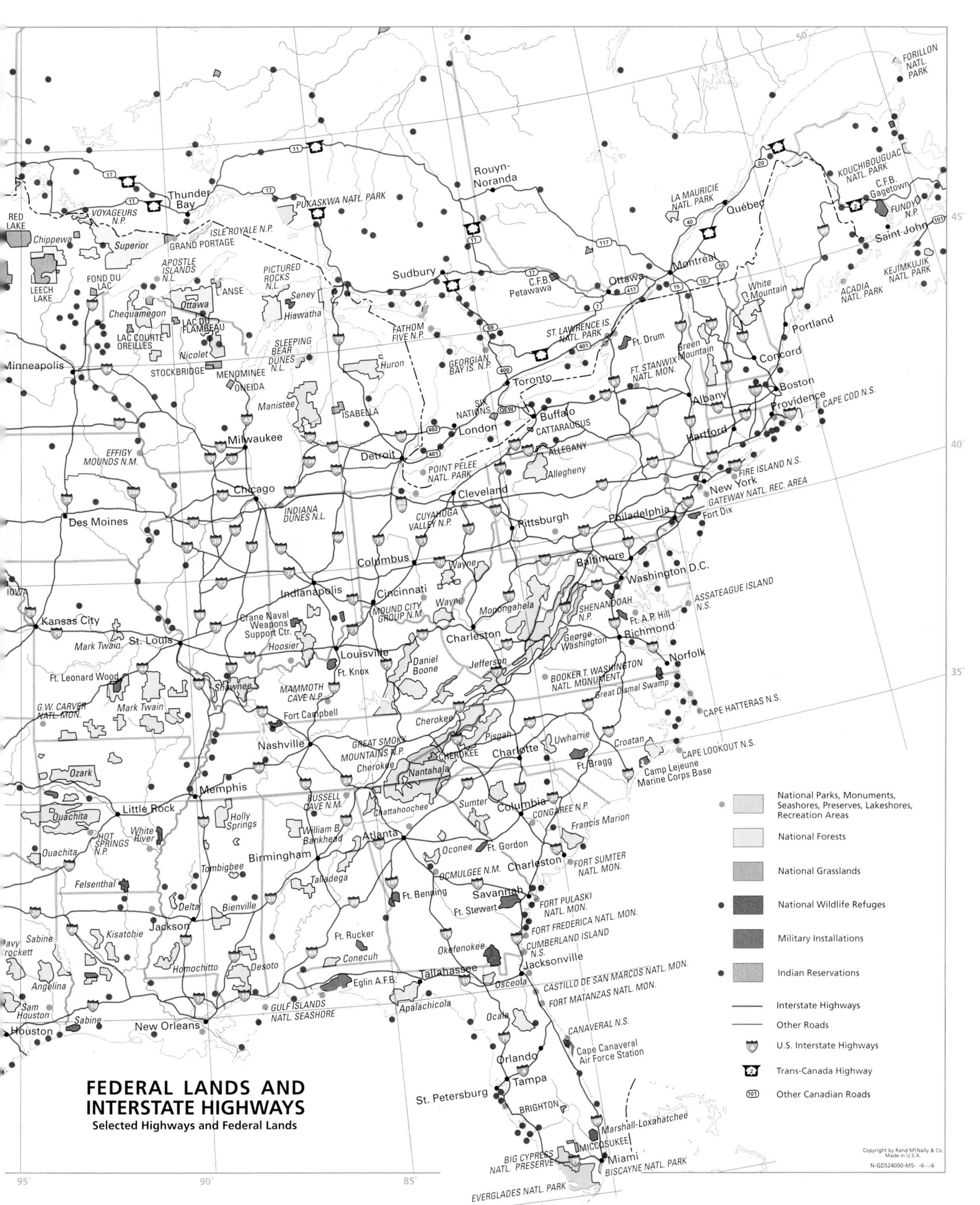

# FEDERAL LANDS AND INTERSTATE HIGHWAYS
Selected Highways and Federal Lands

| | |
|---|---|
| | National Parks, Monuments, Seashores, Preserves, Lakeshores, Recreation Areas |
| | National Forests |
| | National Grasslands |
| | National Wildlife Refuges |
| | Military Installations |
| | Indian Reservations |
| | Interstate Highways |
| | Other Roads |
| | U.S. Interstate Highways |
| | Trans-Canada Highway |
| | Other Canadian Roads |

Copyright by Rand McNally & Co.
Made in U.S.A.
N-GDS24000-M5- -6- -6

A-520000-26 -5-5-18
COPYRIGHT BY
RAND McNALLY & COMPANY
MADE IN U.S.A.

40,000 SQ MI
AREA

0        300        600
Miles

Scale 1:40 000 000; one inch to 630 miles. Lambert's Azimuthal Equal Area Projection
Elevations and depressions are given in feet

0    200    400    600    800    1000 Miles
0    400    800    1200    1600 Kilometers

Longitude    West    of    Greenwich

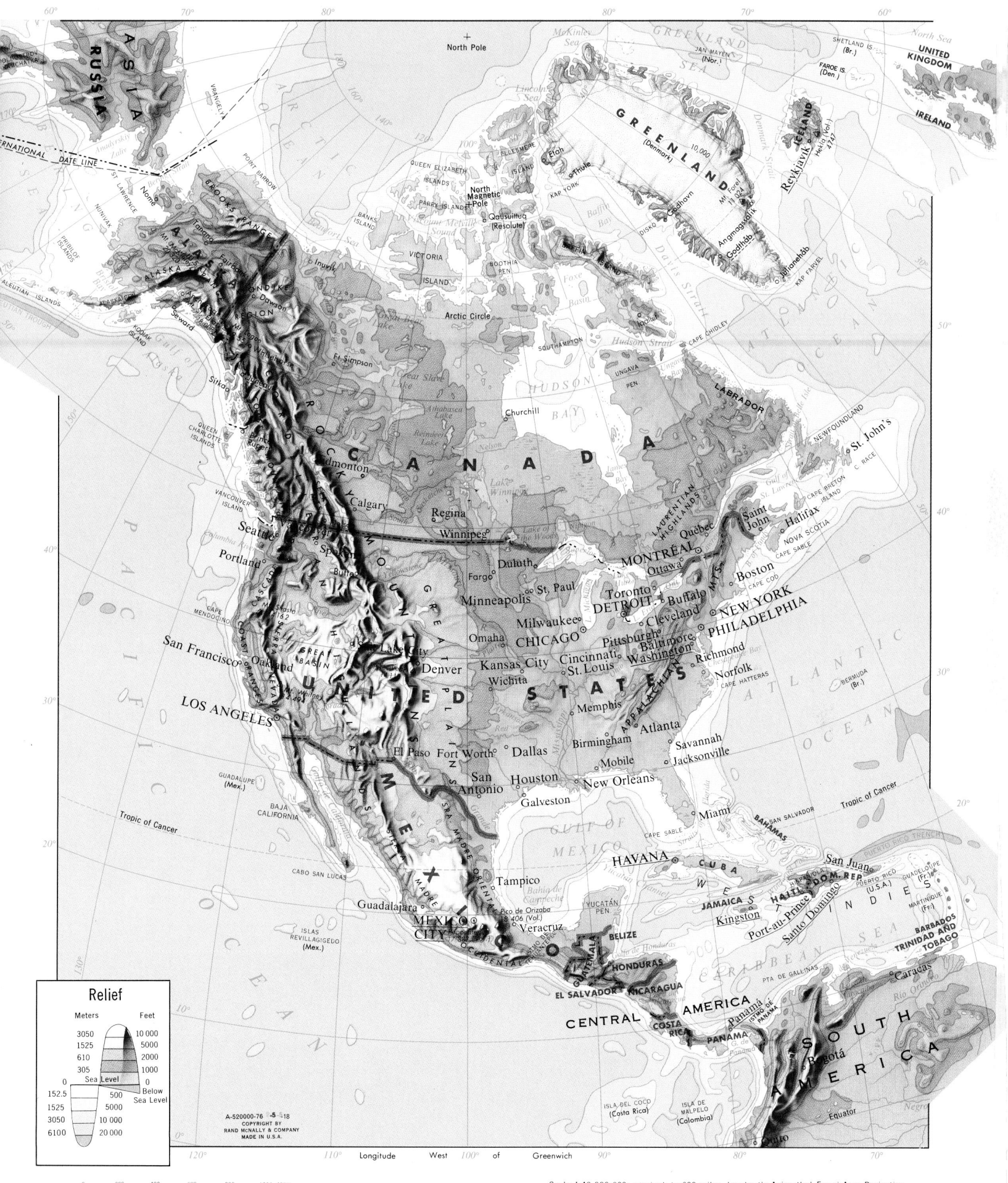

North Pole

RUSSIA
ASIA
UNITED
KINGDOM
IRELAND

GREENLAND
(Denmark)
ICELAND
Reykjavik

ALASKA
BROOKS RANGE
Nome
Fairbanks
Seward
KODIAK ISLAND
ALEUTIAN ISLANDS

Arctic Circle

CANADA

Edmonton
Calgary
Regina
Winnipeg

VANCOUVER ISLAND
Seattle
Spokane
Portland
Buffalo

Churchill

St. John's
NEWFOUNDLAND

LABRADOR

HUDSON BAY

Saint John
Halifax
NOVA SCOTIA

Québec
MONTRÉAL
Ottawa
Toronto
DETROIT
Cleveland
Buffalo
NEW YORK
PHILADELPHIA
Boston

Duluth
Fargo
Minneapolis
St. Paul
Milwaukee
CHICAGO
Omaha
Pittsburgh
Baltimore
Washington
Richmond
Cincinnati
St. Louis
Kansas City
Denver
Wichita
Norfolk

San Francisco
Oakland
GREAT BASIN
Lake City

LOS ANGELES

UNITED STATES

Memphis

APPALACHIAN MTS.
CAPE HATTERAS

El Paso  Fort Worth  Dallas
San Antonio
Houston
Galveston
New Orleans
Mobile
Birmingham
Atlanta
Savannah
Jacksonville
Miami

Tropic of Cancer

BAJA CALIFORNIA

GUADALUPE (Mex.)

CABO SAN LUCAS

MEXICO

Guadalajara
MEXICO CITY
Pico de Orizaba
Veracruz
Tampico

GULF OF MEXICO

BAHAMAS
SAN SALVADOR

HAVANA
CUBA
JAMAICA
Kingston
HAITI
Port-au-Prince
DOM. REP.
Santo Domingo
San Juan
PUERTO RICO (U.S.A.)

WEST INDIES

CENTRAL AMERICA
GUATEMALA
BELIZE
EL SALVADOR
HONDURAS
NICARAGUA
COSTA RICA
PANAMA

CARIBBEAN SEA

BARBADOS
TRINIDAD AND TOBAGO

Caracas

SOUTH AMERICA
Bogotá
Quito

PACIFIC OCEAN

ATLANTIC OCEAN

**Relief**

| Meters | | Feet |
|---|---|---|
| 3050 | | 10 000 |
| 1525 | | 5000 |
| 610 | | 2000 |
| 305 | | 1000 |
| 0 | Sea Level | 0 |
| 152.5 | | 500 Below Sea Level |
| 1525 | | 5000 |
| 3050 | | 10 000 |
| 6100 | | 20 000 |

A-520000-76 -5- 18
COPYRIGHT BY
RAND McNALLY & COMPANY
MADE IN U.S.A.

Longitude   West   of   Greenwich

0   200   400   600   800   1000 Miles
0   400   800   1200   1600 Kilometers

Scale 1:40 000 000; one inch to 630 miles. Lambert's Azimuthal Equal Area Projection
Elevations and depressions are given in feet

Continued on pages 104-105

Longitude West of Greenwich

Scale 1: 12 000 000; one inch to 190 miles. Conic Projection
Elevations and depressions are given in feet

Continued on pages 106-107

Longitude West of Greenwich
Scale 1: 12 000 000; one inch to 190 miles. Conic Projection
Elevations and depressions are given in feet

134°   132°   130°   128°   126°   124°

54°

52°

50°

48°

PRINCE
OF
WALES
ISLAND

Klawock
Hydaburg
△Copper Mtn.
9916
Metlakatla
Ketchikan
ANNETTE
ISLAND

DALL
ISLAND

Mt. Reid
4870
REVILLAGIGEDO
ISLAND

SKEENA
MOUNTAINS
Shean Pk.
8750△

OMINECA
MOUNTAINS

Williston
Lake

Alice Arm

HAZELTON

Hazelton

Mt. Thomlinson
△8050

Tchentlo
Lake

McLeod Lake

UNITED STATES
CANADA

Dixon Entrance

DUNDAS
ISLAND

Terrace

Smithers

Babine
Lake

Fort
St. James

CAPE KNOX

CHATHAM
SOUND

Prince Rupert

BULKLEY
RANGES

Hawson Pk.
9050

Burns Lake

Stuart
Lake

NECHAKO

CLEVELAND
PENINSULA

Masset

PORCHER
ISLAND

KITIMAT

Kitimat

Morice Lake

Endako

Vanderhoof

QUEEN

Skidegate Inlet

GRAHAM ISLAND

Hecate

BANKS
ISLAND

PITT
ISLAND

Hartley Bay

Ootsa
Lake

Michel Pk.
△7396

Nechako
Reservoir

PLATEAU

KENNEY DAM

NECHAKO
RANGE

CHARLOTTE

MORESBY ISLAND

Mount Kermode
△3550

Strait

ESTEVAN
GROUP

PRINCESS
ROYAL
ISLAND

Whitesail
Lake

Eutsuk Lake

Tetachuck
Lake

West Road

ISLANDS

QUEEN CHARLOTTE RANGES

ARISTAZABAL
ISLAND

Mt. Parry △
3450

RODERICK
ISLAND

POOLEY
ISLAND

West Road

CAPE ST. JAMES

SWINDLE
ISLAND

Ocean Falls

Bella Coola

Charlotte
Lake

Redstone

COLUMBIA

FRASER

Queen

Bella Bella

Monarch Mtn.
11590 △

BRITISH

Namu

Rivers Inlet

CALVERT ISLAND

Charlotte

Silverthrone Mtn.
9700

Razorback Mtn.
10432△

Mt. Waddington
△3163

Mt. Tatlow
△10058

PLATEAU

Sound

CAPE
CAUTION

Mt. Queen Bess
△10791

Good Hope Mtn.
△10613 △

Monmouth Mtn.
△10480

Bull Harbour

CAPE SCOTT

Queen Charlotte Strait

GEORGE
ISLAND

Simood
Sound

Mt. Gilbert
△3109

PACIFIC

Port Hardy

REDONDA
ISLANDS

Wedge Mtn
△948

OCEAN

Quatsino Sound

Port Alice

Kelsey Bay

RANGES

Mt. Garibaldi
△8787

CAPE COOK

Victoria Pk.
7095 △

Bloedel

Powell River

Bralorne

VANCOUVER

Golden Hinde
△7291

Campbell
River

Squamish

VANCOUVER

NOOTKA
ISLAND

Courtenay

Comox

TEXADA
ISLAND

ISLAND

Nootka
Sound

ISLAND

Tofino

Port Alberni

Nanaimo

North Vancouver
VANCOUVER
BURNABY
New Westminster
Ladner
White Rock

PACIFIC RIM
NATIONAL PARK

RANGES

Mt. Whymper
△5056

Ladysmith

Barkley
Sound
CAPE BEALE

Lake Cowichan

Duncan

Sidney

PACIFIC

CAPE FLATTERY

Esquimalt

Strait of Juan de Fuca

Victoria

Oak Bay

OLYMPIC
NATIONAL
PARK

OLYMPIC
NATIONAL
PARK

Port
Angeles

Port
Townse

130°   128°   126°   124°

132°

Relief

| Meters | Feet |
|---|---|
| 3050 | 10 000 |
| 1525 | 5000 |
| 610 | 2000 |
| 305 | 1000 |
| 152.5 | 500 |
| Sea Level | 0 |
| 152.5 | 500 |
| 1525 | 5000 |

A-520220-76   6-9
COPYRIGHT BY
RAND McNALLY & COMPANY
MADE IN U.S.A.

Continued on pages 114-115

Longitude West of Greenwich

Scale 1:4 000 000; one inch to 64 miles. Conic Projection
Elevations and depressions are given in feet.

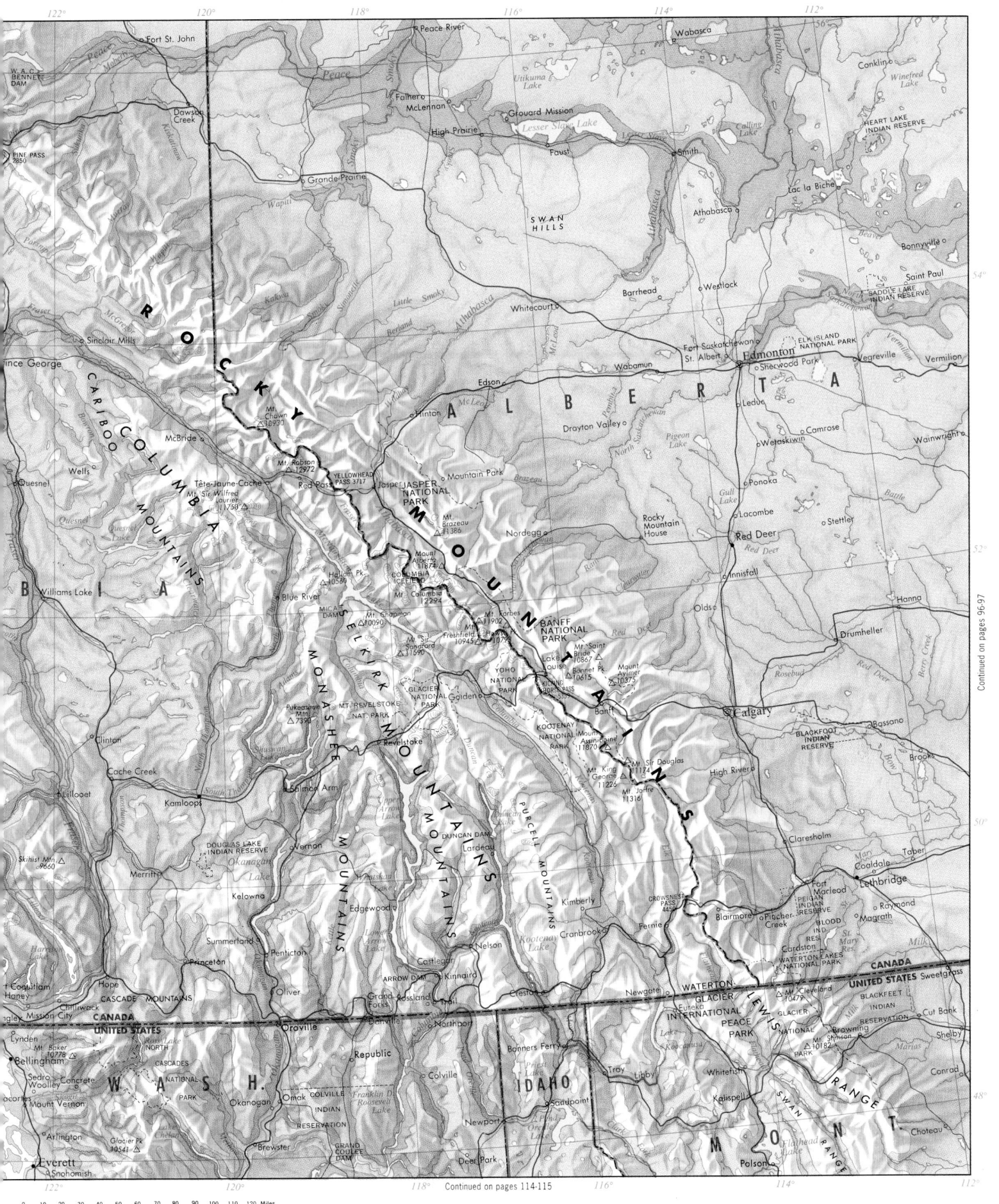

Continued on pages 96-97

Continued on pages 114-115

0 10 20 30 40 50 60 70 80 90 100 110 120 Miles
0 20 40 60 80 100 120 140 160 180 200 Kilometers

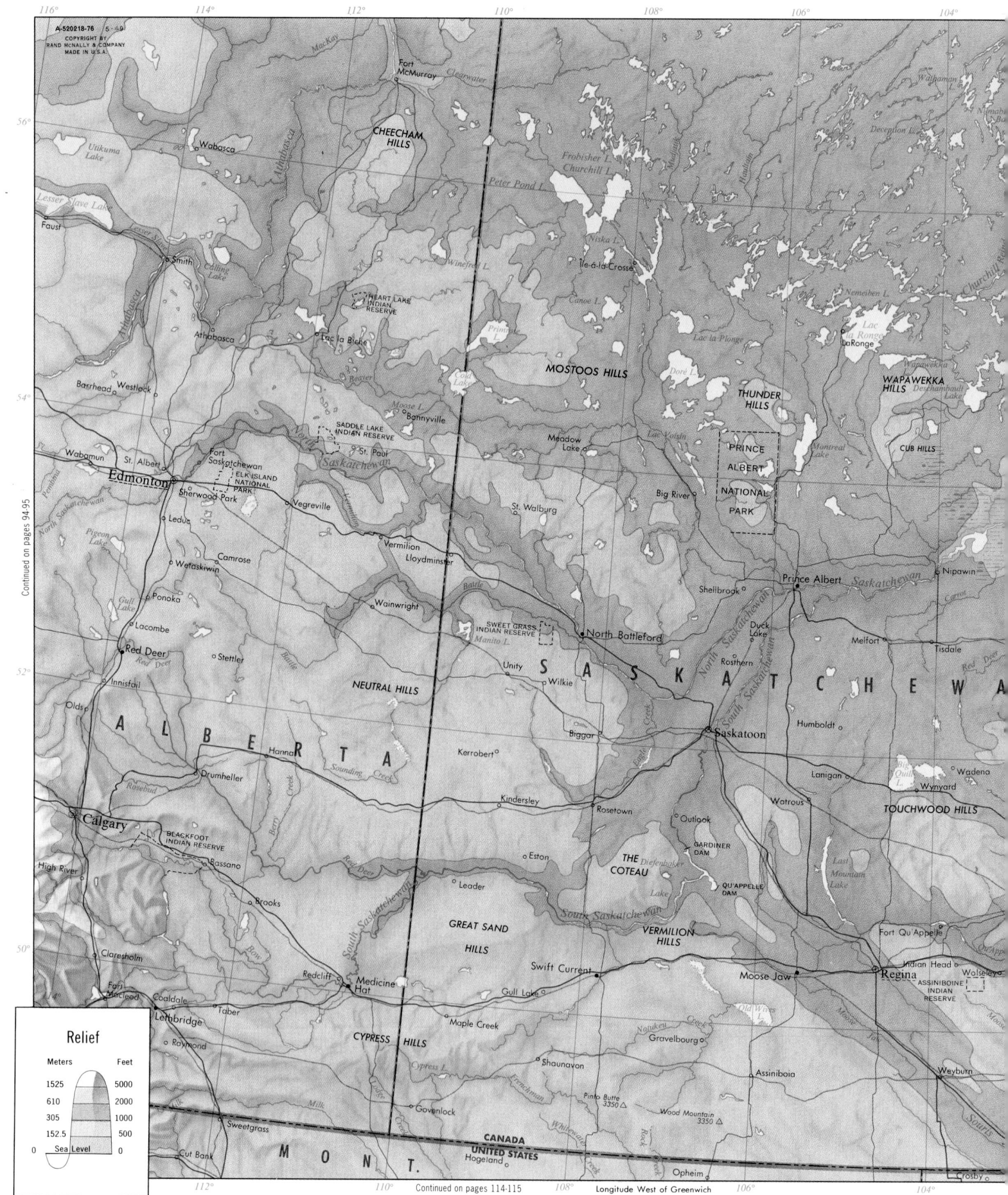

A-520218-76  5-69
COPYRIGHT BY
RAND McNALLY & COMPANY
MADE IN U.S.A.

Continued on pages 94-95

**Relief**

| Meters | | Feet |
|--------|--|------|
| 1525 | | 5000 |
| 610 | | 2000 |
| 305 | | 1000 |
| 152.5 | | 500 |
| 0 | Sea Level | 0 |

Fort McMurray
Clearwater
CHEECHAM HILLS
Frobisher L.
Churchill L.
Utikuma Lake
Wabasca
Athabasca
Peter Pond L.
Deception L.
Lesser Slave Lake
Faust
Smith
Calling Lake
Winefred L.
Ile-à-la-Crosse
Canoe L.
Niska L.
Nemeiben L.
Lac la Ronge
Wapawekka
Churchill
HEART LAKE INDIAN RESERVE
Lac la Biche
Primrose L.
Doré L.
Lac la Plonge
LaRonge
Wapawekka
Barrhead
Westlock
Moose L.
Bonnyville
Cold Lake
MOSTOOS HILLS
THUNDER HILLS
WAPAWEKKA HILLS
Deschambault
CUB HILLS
Wabamun
St. Albert
Fort Saskatchewan
SADDLE LAKE INDIAN RESERVE
St. Paul
Meadow Lake
Lac Voisin
PRINCE ALBERT NATIONAL PARK
Edmonton
ELK ISLAND NATIONAL PARK
Sherwood Park
North Saskatchewan
St. Walburg
Big River
Montreal Lake
Pigeon Lake
Ledue
Vegreville
Shellbrook
Prince Albert
Saskatchewan
Nipawin
Wetaskiwin
Camrose
Vermilion
Lloydminster
Battle
Duck Lake
Melfort
Tisdale
Ponoka
Wainwright
SWEET GRASS INDIAN RESERVE
Rosthern
Carrot
Gull Lake
Lacombe
Red Deer
Manito L.
North Battleford
SASKATCHEWAN
Humboldt
Innisfail
Stettler
Unity
Wilkie
Biggar
Saskatoon
Big Quill L.
Wadena
Olds
NEUTRAL HILLS
ALBERTA
Kerrobert
Lanigan
Wynyard
Hanna
Sounding Creek
Watrous
TOUCHWOOD HILLS
Drumheller
Kindersley
Rosetown
Outlook
Rosebud
Berry Creek
GARDINER DAM
Calgary
BLACKFOOT INDIAN RESERVE
Eston
THE COTEAU
Diefenbaker Lake
QU'APPELLE DAM
Last Mountain Lake
High River
Bassano
Leader
South Saskatchewan
Fort Qu'Appelle
Brooks
GREAT SAND HILLS
VERMILION HILLS
Claresholm
Swift Current
Moose Jaw
Regina
Indian Head
Wolseley
Fort Macleod
Redcliff
Medicine Hat
Gull Lake
ASSINIBOINE INDIAN RESERVE
Coaldale
Taber
Maple Creek
Lethbridge
CYPRESS HILLS
Gravelbourg
Weyburn
Raymond
Cypress L.
Shaunavon
Nonkeu Creek
Assiniboia
Old Wives
Milk
Govenlock
Frenchman
Pinto Butte 3350△
Wood Mountain 3350△
Sweetgrass
CANADA
UNITED STATES
Hogeland
Cut Bank
M O N T.
Opheim
Crosby

Continued on pages 114-115

Longitude West of Greenwich

Scale 1:4 000 000; one inch to 64 miles. Conic Projection
Elevations and depressions are given in feet.

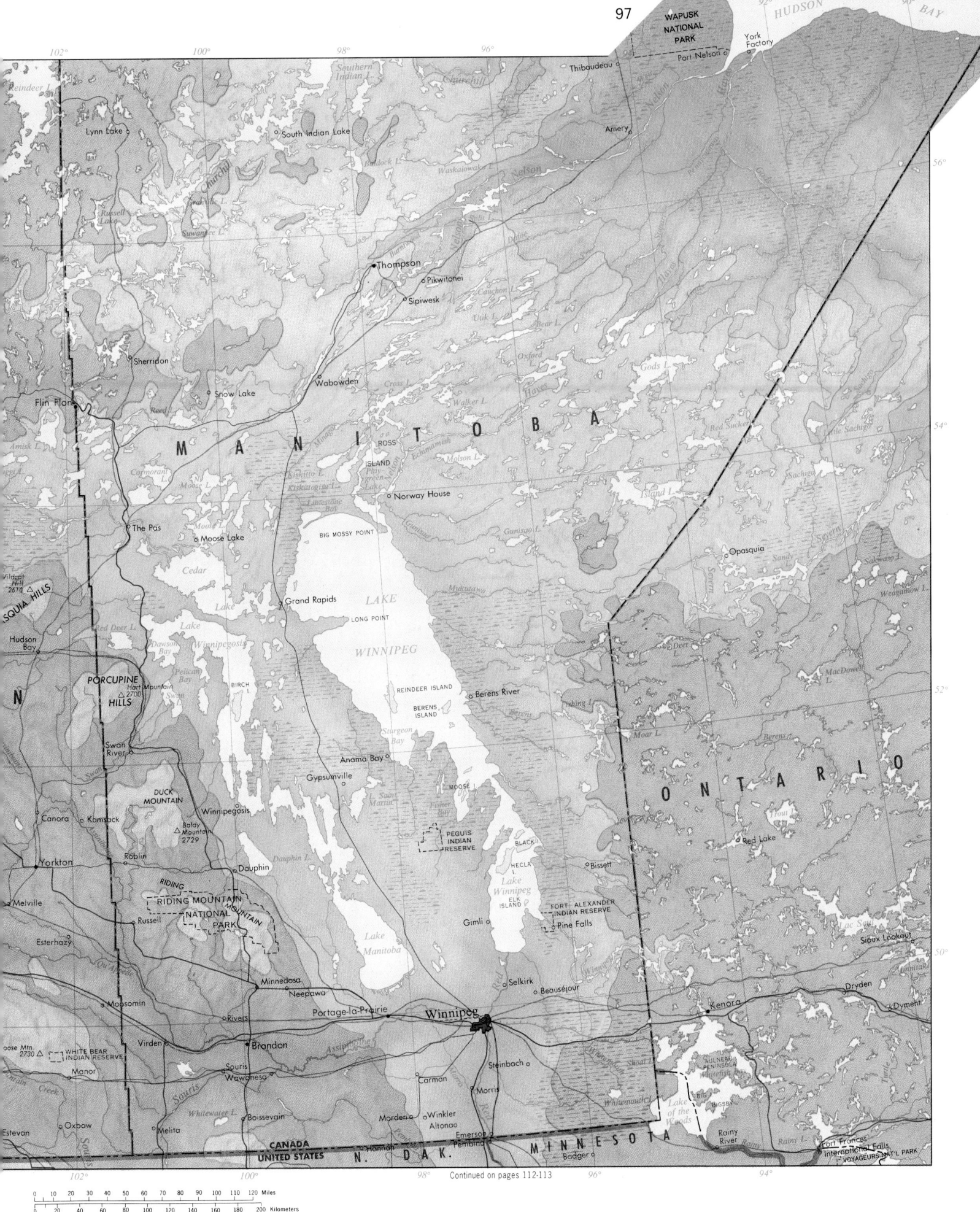

Continued on pages 112-113

0  10  20  30  40  50  60  70  80  90  100  110  120  Miles

0  20  40  60  80  100  120  140  160  180  200  Kilometers

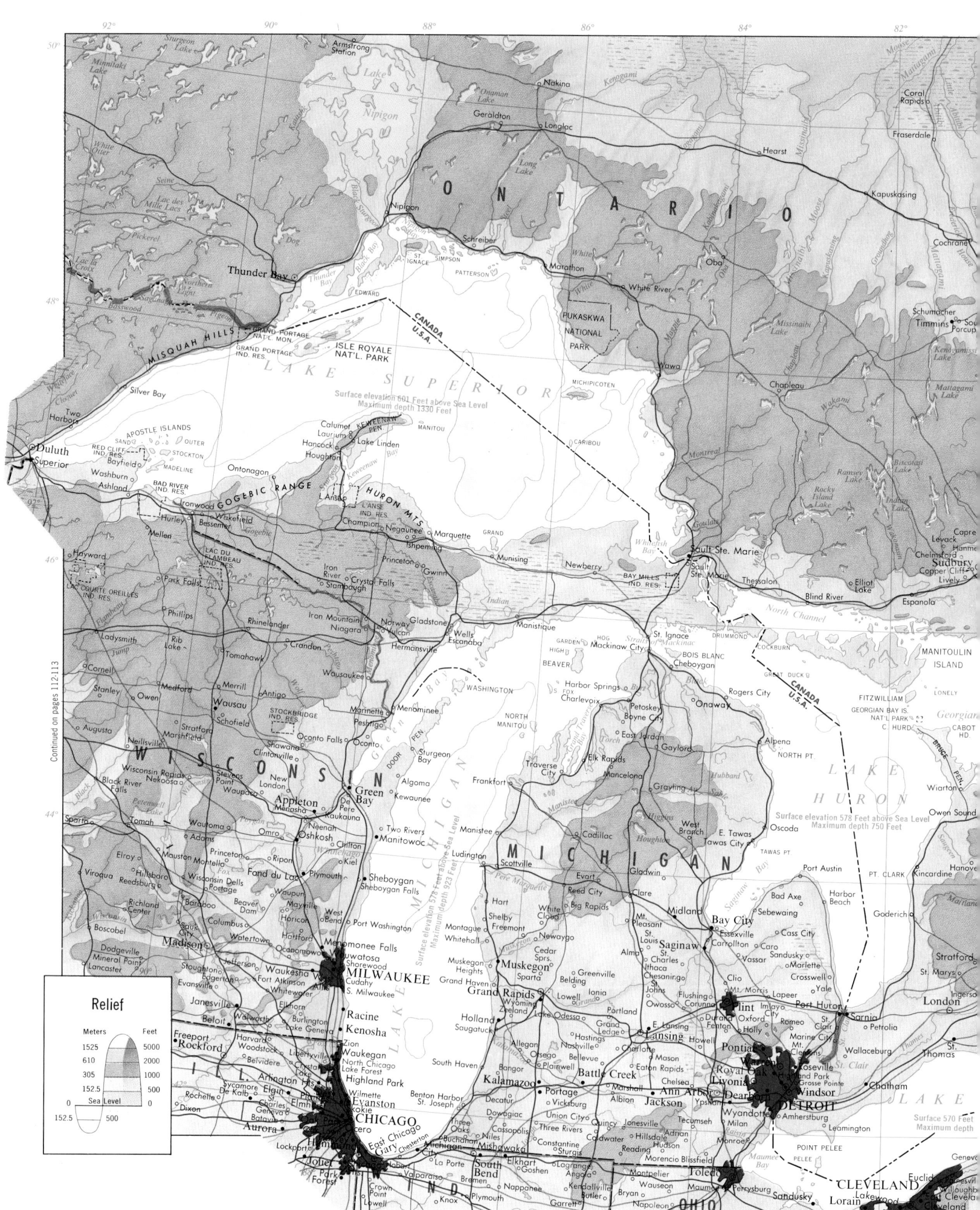

Continued on pages 112-113

Relief

| Meters | | Feet |
|---|---|---|
| 1525 | | 5000 |
| 610 | | 2000 |
| 305 | | 1000 |
| 152.5 | | 500 |
| 0 | Sea Level | 0 |
| 152.5 | | 500 |

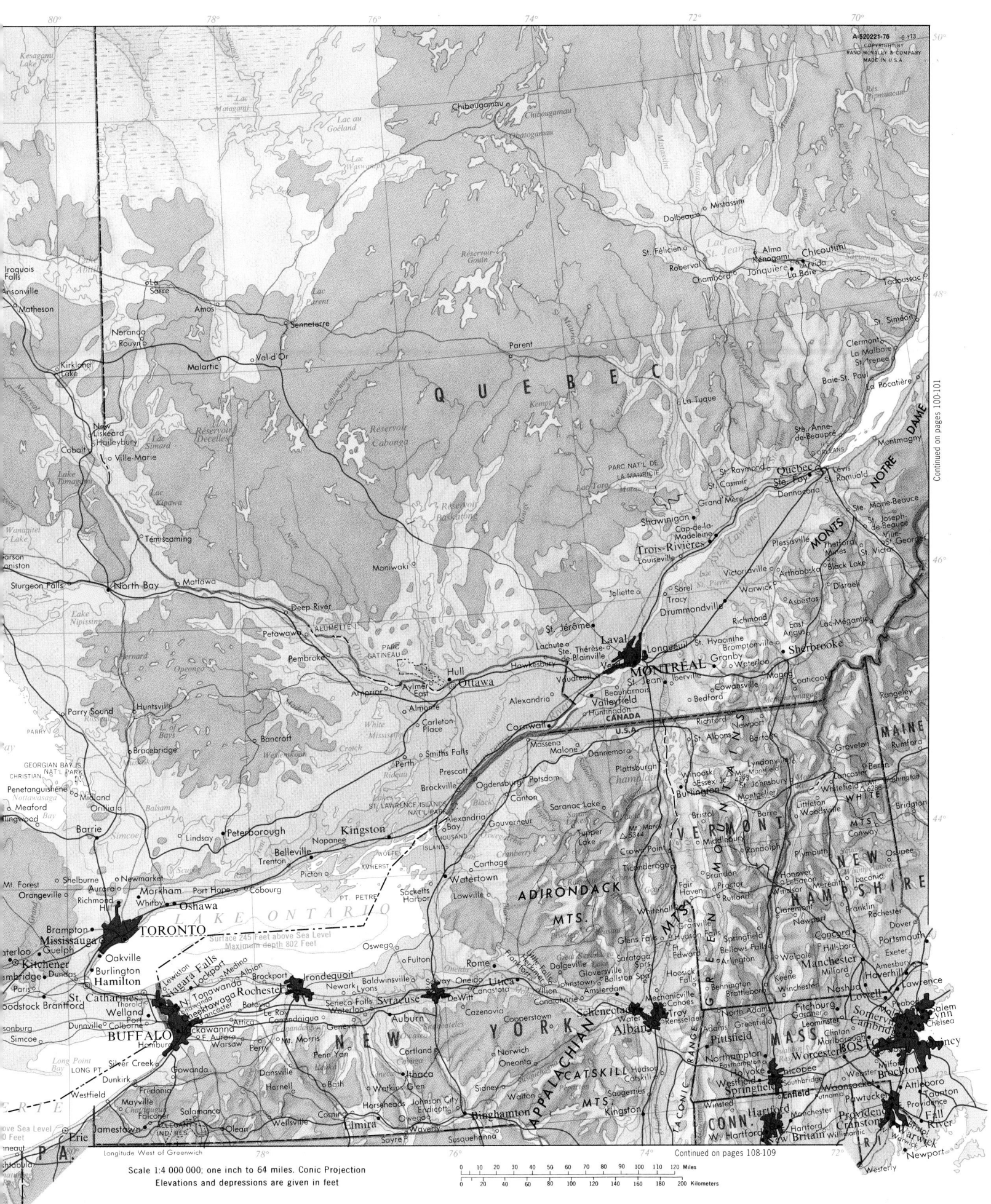

Continued on pages 100-101

Continued on pages 108-109

Scale 1:4 000 000; one inch to 64 miles. Conic Projection
Elevations and depressions are given in feet

Longitude West of Greenwich

0  10  20  30  40  50  60  70  80  90  100  110  120 Miles

0  20  40  60  80  100  120  140  160  180  200 Kilometers

Continued on pages 98-99

Continued on pages 108-109

Longitude West of Greenwich

Scale 1:4 000 000; one inch to 64 miles. Conic Projection
Elevations and depressions are given in feet.

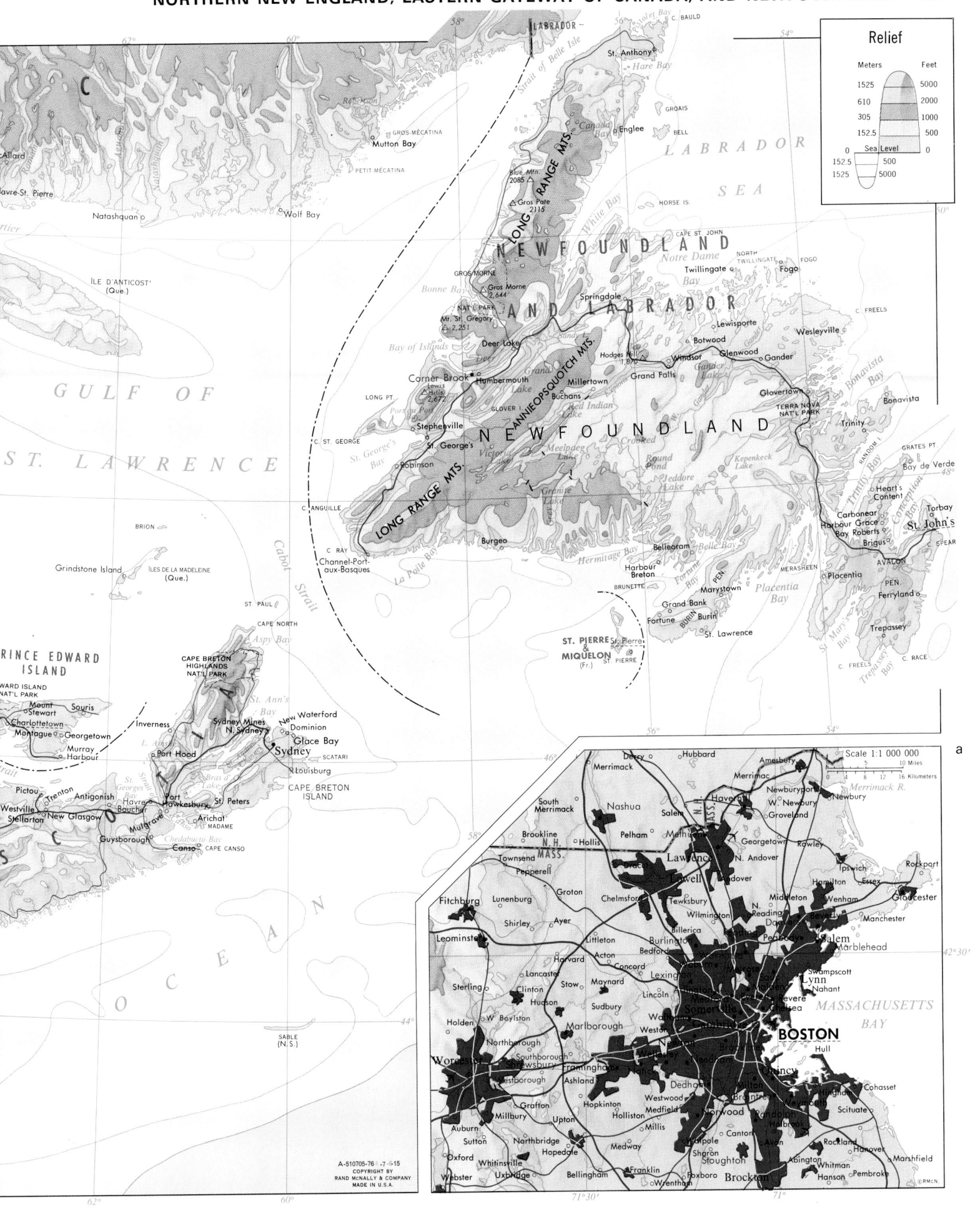

Relief

| Meters | Feet |
|--------|------|
| 1525 | 5000 |
| 610 | 2000 |
| 305 | 1000 |
| 152.5 | 500 |
| Sea Level | 0 |
| 152.5 | 500 |
| 1525 | 5000 |

LABRADOR

C. BAULD

St. Anthony

Hare Bay

Strait of Belle Isle

Red Island

Mutton Bay

PETIT MÉCATINA

GROS-MÉCATINA

Canada Bay

Englee

GROAIS

BELL

LABRADOR

Blue Mtn. 2085

△Gros Pate 2115

HORSE IS.

SEA

Natashquan

Wolf Bay

ÎLE D'ANTICOSTI (Que.)

LONG RANGE MTS.

NEWFOUNDLAND

Notre Dame

Twillingate

Fogo

CAPE ST. JOHN

NORTH TWILLINGATE

FOGO

GROS MORNE

Springdale

Lewisporte

C. FREELS

Wesleyville

AND LABRADOR

Bonne Bay

Gros Morne 2,644

NAT'L PARK

Mt. St. Gregory 2,251

Deer Lake

Botwood

Glenwood

Gander

Bonavista Bay

Bay of Islands

Hodges Hill

Windsor

GULF OF

LONG PT.

Corner Brook

Humbermouth

Millertown

Grand Falls

Glovertown

Bonavista

ST. LAWRENCE

Lewis Hills 2,672

Grand Lake

Buchans

TERRA NOVA NAT'L PARK

Trinity

C. ST. GEORGE

GLOVER MTS.

Red Indian Lake

Round Pond

GRATES PT.

Bay de Verde

ANNIEOPSQUOTCH MTS.

Stephenville

St. George's

Robinson

NEWFOUNDLAND

Heart's Content

Carbonear

Harbour Grace

Bay Roberts

Conception Bay

Torbay

St. John's

C. SPEAR

St. George's Bay

Victoria

Meelpaeg Lake

Kepenkeck Lake

Crooked

Brigus

AVALON

Jeddore Lake

PEN.

C. ANGUILLE

Granite Lake

LONG RANGE MTS.

Burgeo

Placentia

PEN.

Ferryland

C. RAY

Channel-Port-aux-Basques

La Poile Bay

Hermitage Bay

Belleoram

Belle Bay

MERASHEEN

Marystown

Placentia Bay

Trepassey

La Moine

Harbour Breton

Fortune Bay

BURIN PEN.

C. FREELS

C. RACE

BRUNETTE

Grand Bank

Burin

GRINDSTONE Island

ÎLES DE LA MADELEINE (Que.)

BRION

Fortune

Burin

St. Lawrence

ST. PIERRE & MIQUELON (Fr.)

St. Pierre

St. Pierre

ST. PAUL

CAPE NORTH

PRINCE EDWARD ISLAND

WARD ISLAND NAT'L PARK

Aspy Bay

CAPE BRETON HIGHLANDS NAT'L PARK

Mount Stewart

Souris

St. Ann's Bay

Inverness

Sydney Mines

N. Sydney

New Waterford

Dominion

Charlottetown

Montague

Georgetown

Port Hood

Glace Bay

Murray Harbour

L. Ainslie

Sydney

SCATARI

Louisburg

Pictou

Trenton

Antigonish

St. George's Bay

Bras d'Or Lake

St. Peters

CAPE BRETON ISLAND

Westville

Stellarton

New Glasgow

Havre Boucher

Port Hawkesbury

ISLE MADAME

Arichat

S.

Mulgrave

Guysborough

Canso

CAPE CANSO

Chedabucto Bay

OCEAN

SABLE (N.S.)

A-510705-76 7 15

COPYRIGHT BY

RAND McNALLY & COMPANY

MADE IN U.S.A.

| 0 | 10 | 20 | 30 | 40 | 50 | 60 | 70 | 80 | 90 | 100 | 110 | 120 Miles |
| 0 | 20 | 40 | 60 | 80 | 100 | 120 | 140 | 160 | 180 | 200 Kilometers |

Scale 1:1 000 000

0   5   12   10 Miles

Merrimack R.

Derry

Hubbard

Amesbury

Merrimack

Newburyport

Newbury

South Merrimack

Nashua

Salem

Haverhill

W. Newbury

Brookline

Pelham

Methuen

Georgetown

Rowley

Ipswich

Rockport

Townsend

MASS.

Pepperell

Dracut

Lawrence

N. Andover

Andover

Hamilton

Essex

Gloucester

Fitchburg

Lunenburg

Groton

Chelmsford

Tewksbury

Wilmington

Middleton

Wenham

Manchester

Leominster

Shirley

Ayer

Littleton

Burlington

N. Reading

Danvers

Peabody

Salem

Marblehead

Harvard

Acton

Concord

Lexington

Swampscott

Lynn

Nahant

Sterling

Clinton

Stow

Maynard

Lincoln

MASSACHUSETTS BAY

Holden

Hudson

Sudbury

Revere

Chelsea

W. Boylston

Marlborough

Weston

Somerville

BOSTON

Hull

Worcester

Shrewsbury

Framingham

Natick

Dedham

Milton

Quincy

Westborough

Ashland

Westwood

Braintree

Cohasset

Northborough

Southborough

Hopkinton

Medfield

Norwood

Scituate

Grafton

Millbury

Upton

Holliston

Millis

Canton

Avon

Rockland

Hanover

Auburn

Sutton

Northbridge

Hopedale

Medway

Sharon

Stoughton

Abington

Marshfield

Webster

Uxbridge

Whitinsville

Bellingham

Franklin

Foxboro

Brockton

Whitman

Hanson

Pembroke

Oxford

Northbridge

Wrentham

©RMCN.

a

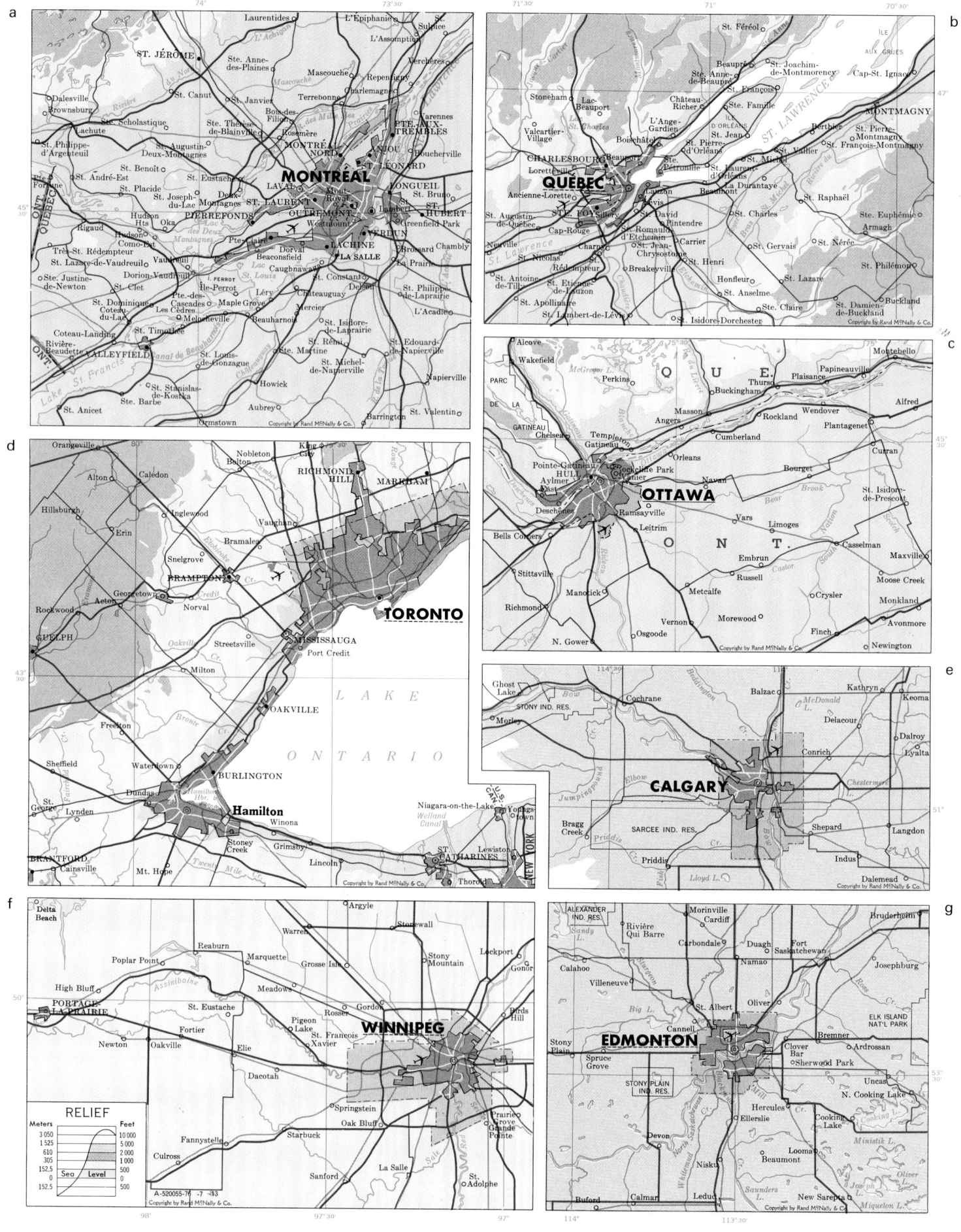

Scale 1:1 000 000; One inch to 16 miles.
Elevations and depressions are given in feet.

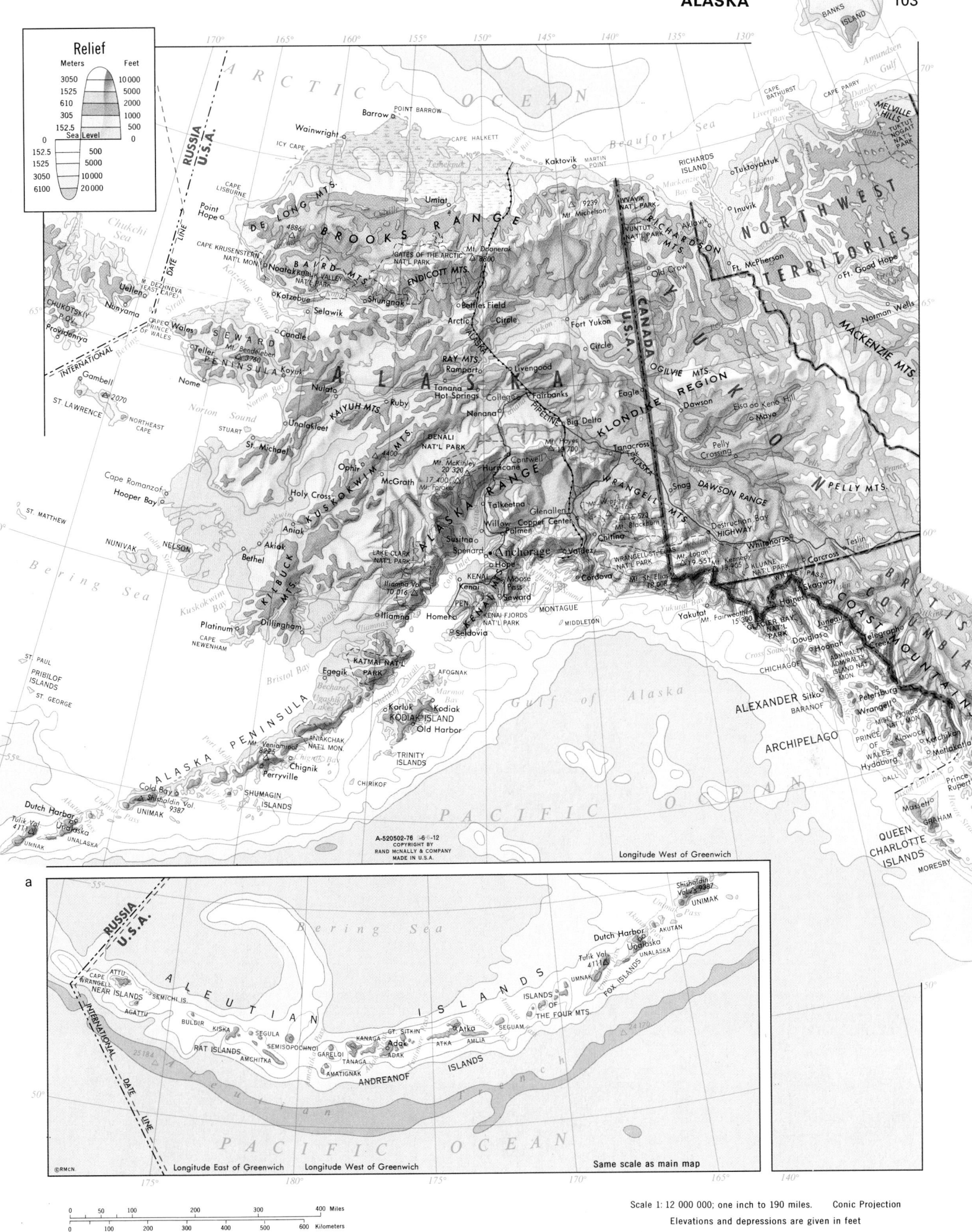

Relief

| Meters | Feet |
|---|---|
| 3050 | 10 000 |
| 1525 | 5000 |
| 610 | 2000 |
| 305 | 1000 |
| 152.5 | 500 |
| Sea Level | 0 |
| 152.5 | 500 |
| 1525 | 5000 |
| 3050 | 10 000 |
| 6100 | 20 000 |

A-520502-76 -6 6 -12
COPYRIGHT BY
RAND McNALLY & COMPANY
MADE IN U.S.A.

Longitude West of Greenwich

a

Same scale as main map

Longitude East of Greenwich    Longitude West of Greenwich

Scale 1: 12 000 000; one inch to 190 miles.    Conic Projection

Elevations and depressions are given in feet

Continued on pages 90-91

Scale 1:12 000 000; one inch to 190 miles. Polyconic Projection
Elevations and depressions are given in feet

A-520500-26

COPYRIGHT BY
RAND MCNALLY & COMPANY
MADE IN U.S.A.

a

Scale 1: 36 000 000

b

Scale 1: 36 000 000
One inch to 570 miles

c

Longitude West of Greenwich

d

Scale 1: 3 400 000

Same scale as main map

Longitude West of Greenwich

Cities
and
Towns

0 to 50,000 ○    500,000 to 1,000,000 ◎

50,000 to 500,000 ⊙    1,000,000 and over

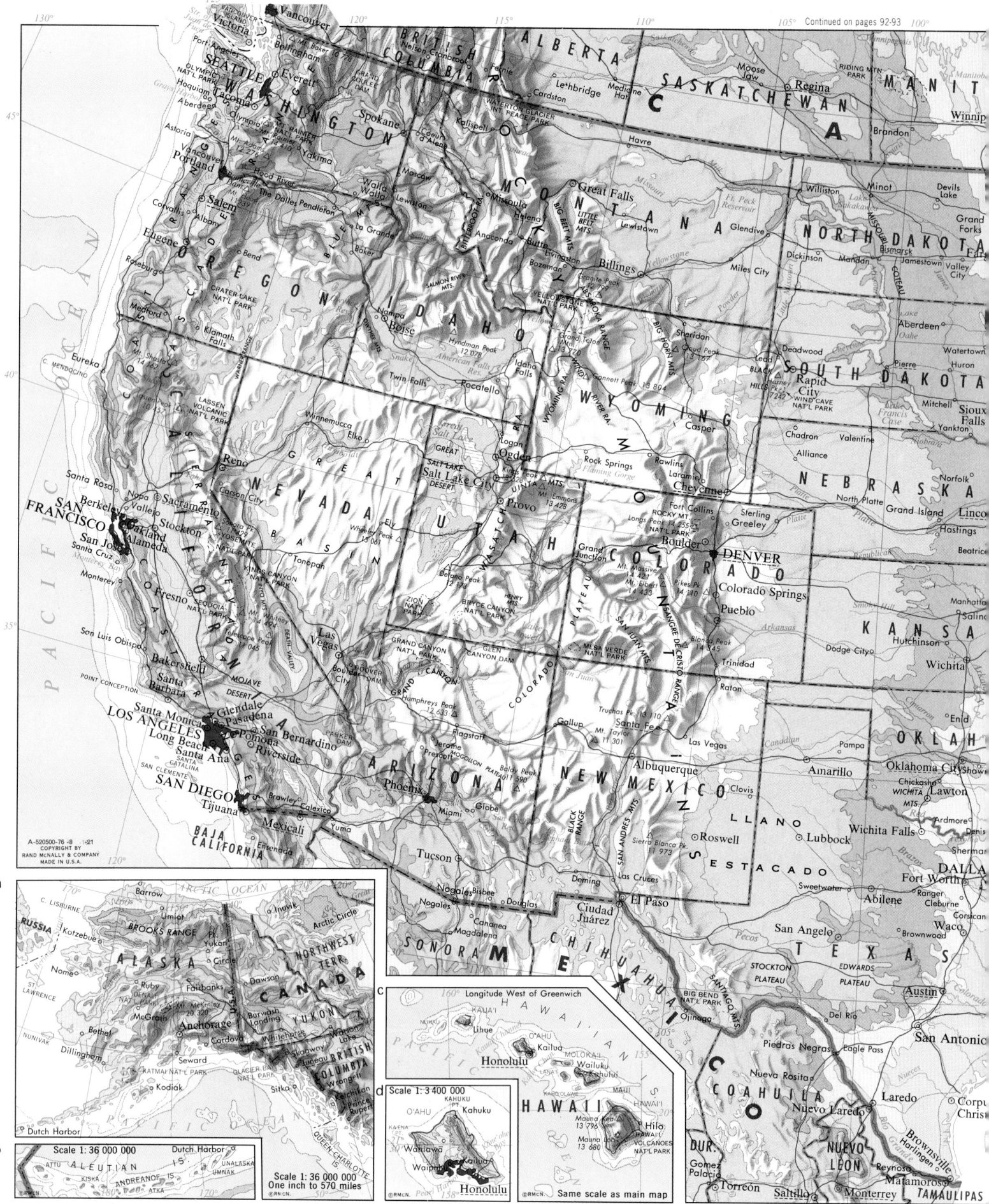

Continued on pages 92-93

A-520500-76-8 ·1·21
COPYRIGHT BY
RAND McNALLY & COMPANY
MADE IN U.S.A.

a

b  Scale 1: 36 000 000
One inch to 570 miles

c

d  Scale 1: 3 400 000

Scale 1: 36 000 000

HAWAII  Same scale as main map

Scale 1:12 000 000; one inch to 190 miles. Polyconic Projection
Elevations and depressions are given in feet

WISCONSIN

MICHIGAN

ILLINOIS

INDIANA

OHIO

KENTUCKY

WEST V

LAKE HURON
Surface 579 Feet above Sea Level
maximum depth 750 Feet

LAKE ER
Surface 570 Feet above Sea Level
maximum depth 210 Feet

MILWAUKEE

CHICAGO

DETROIT

CLEVELAND

CINCINNATI

ST LOUIS

Continued on pages 112-113

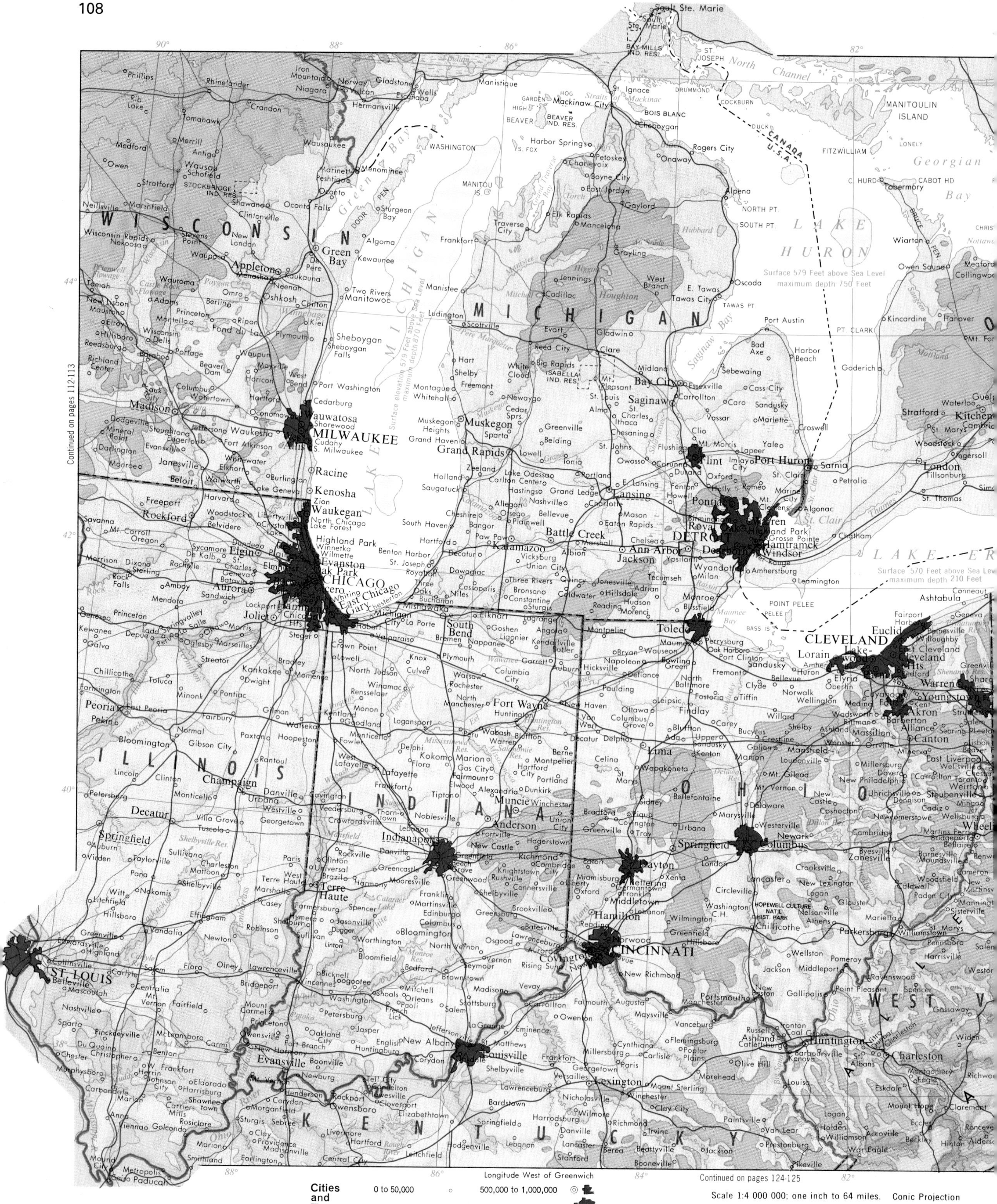

Continued on pages 124-125

Longitude West of Greenwich

| Cities and Towns | | | |
|---|---|---|---|
| 0 to 50,000 | ○ | 500,000 to 1,000,000 | |
| 50,000 to 500,000 | ⊙ | 1,000,000 and over | |

Scale 1:4 000 000; one inch to 64 miles.  Conic Projection
Elevations and depressions are given in feet

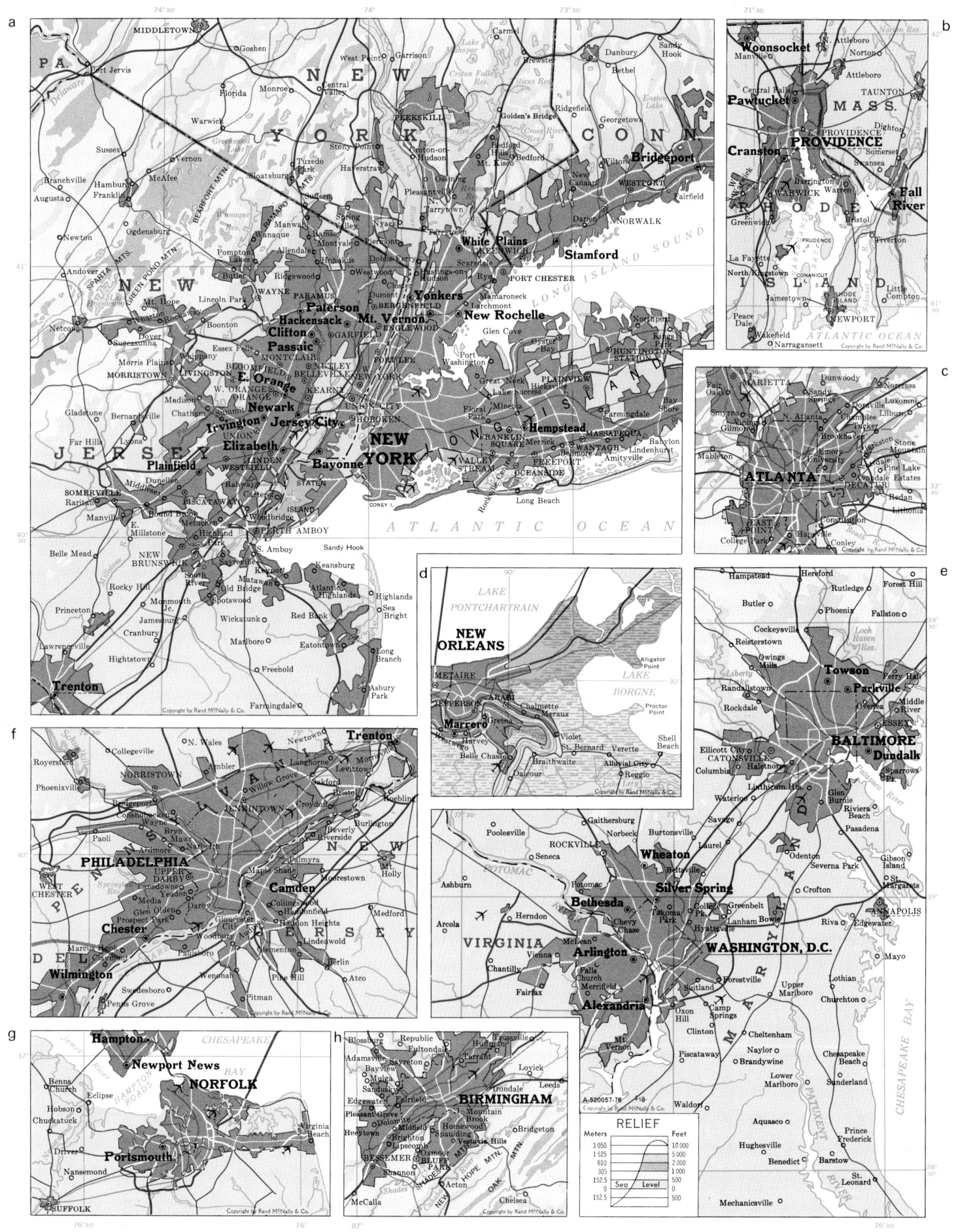

Scale 1:1 000 000; One inch to 16 miles.
Elevations and depressions are given in feet.

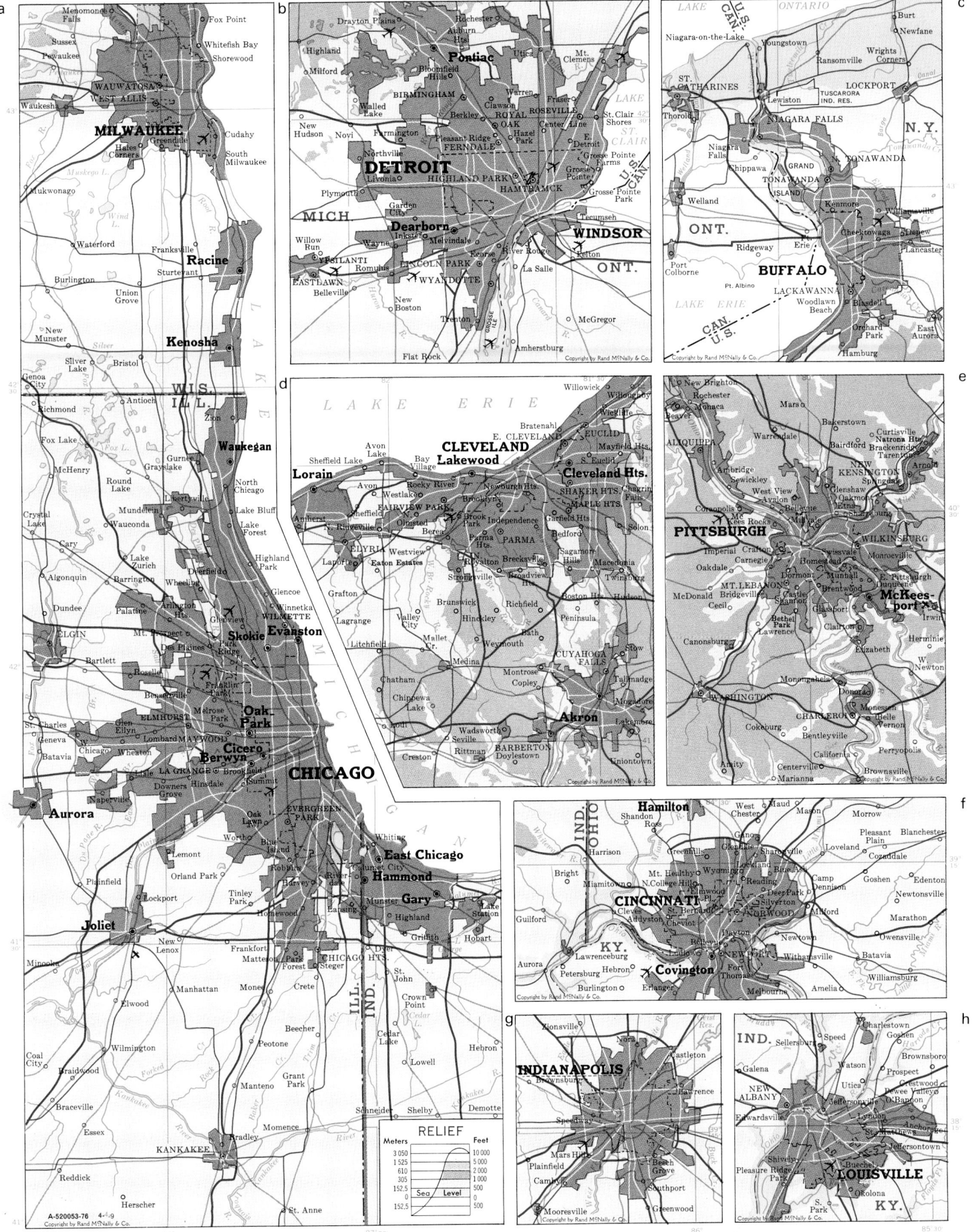

Menomonee Falls
Sussex
Pewaukee
Fox Point
Whitefish Bay
Shorewood
WAUWATOSA
WEST ALLIS
Waukesha
**MILWAUKEE**
Cudahy
Hales Corners
Greendale
South Milwaukee
Mukwonago
Waterford
Franksville
**Racine**
Burlington
Union Grove
Sturtevant
New Munster
**Kenosha**
Silver Lake
Bristol
Genoa City
WIS.
ILL.
Richmond
Antioch
Zion
Fox Lake
Round Lake
Gurnee
Grayslake
**Waukegan**
McHenry
Mundelein
Wauconda
North Chicago
Crystal Lake
Cary
Lake Zurich
Libertyville
Lake Bluff
Lake Forest
Algonquin
Barrington
Deerfield
Highland Park
Dundee
Palatine
Wheeling
Arlington Hts.
Glencoe
Winnetka
WILMETTE
**ELGIN**
Mt. Prospect
Glenview
**Skokie** **Evanston**
Bartlett
Roselle
Des Plaines
Elk Grove
St. Charles
Geneva
Glen Ellyn
Franklin Park
Bensenville
W. Chicago
Wheaton
Lombard MAYWOOD
ELMHURST
Melrose Park
**Oak Park**
Batavia
Lisle
LA GRANGE
Brookfield
**Cicero**
**Berwyn**
Downers Grove
Hinsdale
Summit
**CHICAGO**
**Aurora**
Naperville
Oak Lawn
EVERGREEN PARK
Plainfield
Lemont
Worth
Blue Island
Whiting
**East Chicago**
**Joliet**
Lockport
Orland Park
Tinley Park
Harvey
Robbins
Riverdale
Calumet City
**Hammond**
Homewood
Munster
**Gary**
New Lenox
Frankfort
Matteson
Park Forest
Steger
CHICAGO HTS.
Dyer
Griffith
Hobart
Minooka
Manhattan
Elwood
Monee
Crete
St. John
Lake Station
Highland
Crown Point
Cedar Lake
Lowell
Coal City
Wilmington
Beecher
Peotone
Grant Park
Schneider
Shelby
Demotte
Braceville
Manteno
Braidwood
Essex
**KANKAKEE**
Bradley
Reddick
Herscher
St. Anne
A-520053-76  4-1-59
Copyright by Rand McNally & Co.

Drayton Plains
Rochester
Auburn Hts.
Highland
Utica
Mt. Clemens
Milford
**Pontiac**
Warren
Walled Lake
BIRMINGHAM
Fraser
ROSEVILLE
New Hudson
Novi
Berkley
Clawson
ROYAL OAK
St. Clair Shores
Northville
Farmington
Pleasant Ridge
FERNDALE
Hazel Park
Center Line
E. Detroit
Grosse Pointe Shores
Plymouth
Livonia
HIGHLAND PARK
HAMTRAMCK
Grosse Pointe Farms
**DETROIT**
MICH.
Garden City
Grosse Pointe Park
Willow Run
**Dearborn**
Wayne
Inkster
Melvindale
**WINDSOR**
YPSILANTI
Romulus
LINCOLN PARK
Kearny
River Rouge
Belton
ONT.
EASTLAWN
Belleville
**WYANDOTTE**
La Salle
New Boston
Trenton
McGregor
Flat Rock
Amherstburg
Copyright by Rand McNally & Co.

LAKE  ONTARIO
U.S. CAN.
Burt
Newfane
Niagara-on-the-Lake
Youngstown
Ransomville
Wrights Corners
ST. CATHARINES
Lewiston
LOCKPORT
Thorold
NIAGARA FALLS
TUSCARORA IND. RES.
N.Y.
Niagara Falls
Chippawa
GRAND
TONAWANDA
Welland
ISLAND
TONAWANDA
Kenmore
Williamsville
Ridgeway
Erie
Cheektowaga
Depew
Port Colborne
Lancaster
ONT.
Pt. Albino
**BUFFALO**
LACKAWANNA
Woodlawn Beach
Blasdell
CAN. U.S.
LAKE ERIE
Orchard Park
East Aurora
Hamburg

LAKE  ERIE
Willowick
Willoughby
Wickliffe
New Brighton
Rochester
Monaca
Mars
Bratenahl
E. CLEVELAND
EUCLID
Beaver
Bakerstown
Curtisville
Natrona Hts.
Avon Lake
Bay Village
**CLEVELAND**
Mayfield Hts.
Euclid
ALIQUIPPA
Warrendale
Bairdford
Brackenridge
Tarentum
Sheffield Lake
**Lakewood**
Ambridge
Sewickley
NEW KENSINGTON
Arnold
**Lorain**
Rocky River
Brooklyn
Newburgh Hts.
SHAKER HTS.
Chagrin Falls
West View
Avalon
Glenshaw
Oakmont
Springdale
Avon
Westlake
Fairview Park
MAPLE HTS.
Coraopolis
Bellevue
Etna
Amherst
Sheffield
Olmsted
Berea
Brook Park
Independence
Garfield Hts.
Solon
**PITTSBURGH**
Wilkinsburg
Lapoorte
ELYRIA
Eaton Estates
Westview
Parma Hts.
Royalton
PARMA
Bedford
Imperial
Crafton
Swissvale
Monroeville
Grafton
Strongsville
Broadview Hts.
Sagamore Hills
Macedonia
Oakdale
Carnegie
Homestead
E. Pittsburgh
Duquesne
Lagrange
Brunswick
Richfield
Twinsburg
McDonald
MT. LEBANON
Munhall
Braddock
Litchfield
Valley City
Hinckley
Boston Hts.
Hudson
Bridgeville
Castle Shannon
Brentwood
**McKees-port**
Mallet Cr.
Weymouth
Bath
Cecil
Bethel Park
Glassport
Irwin
Chatham
Medina
CUYAHOGA FALLS
Canonsburg
Lawrence
Clairton
Hermine
Chippewa Lake
Montrose
Copley
Tallmadge
Elizabeth
W. Newton
Mogadore
Monongahela
Donora
Creston
Wadsworth
Seville
Rittman
BARBERTON
Doylestown
**Akron**
Lakemore
WASHINGTON
CHARLEROI
Monessen
Belle Vernon
Uniontown
Cokeburg
Bentleyville
Perryopolis
California
Amity
Centerville
Brownsville
Marianna
Copyright by Rand McNally & Co.

**f**

IND.
OHIO
**Hamilton**
West Chester
Maud
Mason
Morrow
Shandon
Ross
Camp
Greenhills
Pleasant Plain
Blanchester
Harrison
Mt. Healthy
Wyoming
Lockland Reading
Loveland
Cozaddale
Bright
Miamitown
N.College Hill
Silverton
Camp Dennison
Goshen
Edenton
Guilford
Cleves
Elmwood
St. Bernard
**CINCINNATI**
NORWOOD
Milford
Newtonsville
Addyston
Cheviot
Marathon
Aurora
KY.
Dayton
Newtown
Owensville
Lawrenceburg
Ludlow
**NEWPORT**
Withamsville
Batavia
Petersburg
Hebron
Bellevue
Fort Thomas
Williamsburg
Burlington
**Covington**
Erlanger
Melbourne
Amelia

**g**

Zionsville
Nora
Castleton
**INDIANAPOLIS**
Brownsburg
Lawrence
Speedway
Mars Hill
Beech Grove
Plainfield
Camby
Southport
Mooresville
Greenwood
Copyright by Rand McNally & Co.

**h**

IND.
Charlestown
Speed
Goshen
Sellersburg
Watson
Brownsboro
Galena
Utica
Prospect
**NEW ALBANY**
Jeffersonville
Crestwood
Pewee Valley
Clarksville
Lyndon
St. Matthews
Jeffersontown
Pleasure Ridge Park
Shively
Buechel
S. Park
**LOUISVILLE**
Okolona
KY.
Copyright by Rand McNally & Co.

**RELIEF**

| Meters | | Feet |
|---|---|---|
| 3 050 | | 10 000 |
| 1 525 | | 5 000 |
| 610 | | 2 000 |
| 305 | | 1 000 |
| 152.5 | | 500 |
| 0 | Sea Level | 0 |
| 152.5 | | 500 |

0 2 4 6 8 10 12 14 16 18 20 22 24  Miles
0 4 8 12 16 20 24 28 32 36 40  Kilometers

Scale 1:1 000 000; One inch to 16 miles.
Elevations and depressions are given in feet.

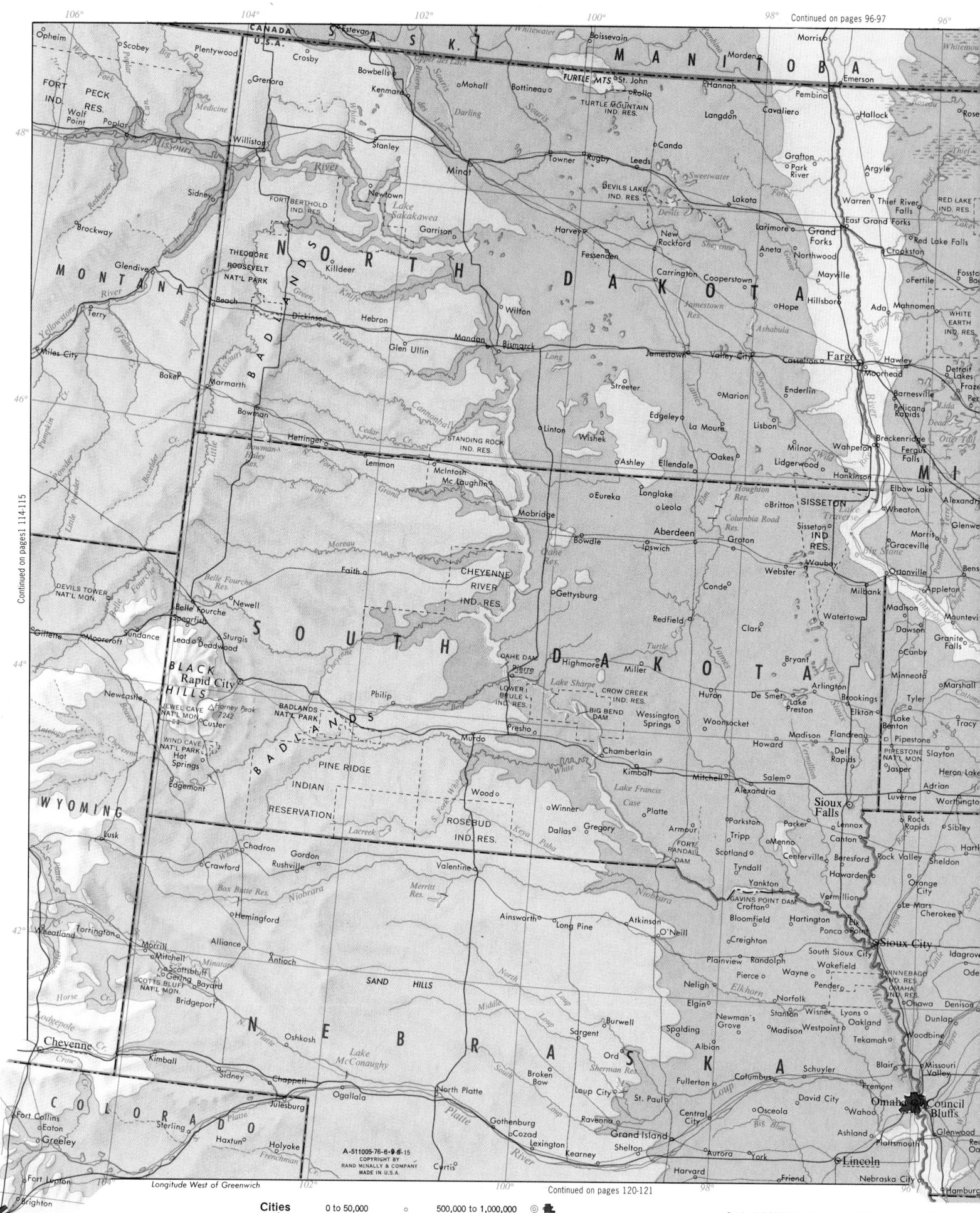

Continued on pages 96-97

Continued on pages 114-115

Continued on pages 120-121

CANADA
U.S.A.
SASK. MANITOBA

MONTANA

NORTH DAKOTA

SOUTH DAKOTA

WYOMING

NEBRASKA

COLORADO

DENVER

Longitude West of Greenwich

A-511005-76-6-9-8-15
COPYRIGHT BY
RAND MCNALLY & COMPANY
MADE IN U.S.A.

**Cities and Towns**

| | | | |
|---|---|---|---|
| 0 to 50,000 | o | 500,000 to 1,000,000 | ◉ |
| 50,000 to 500,000 | ⊙ | 1,000,000 and over | |

Scale 1:4 000 000; one inch to 64 miles. Conic Projection
Elevations and depressions are given in feet

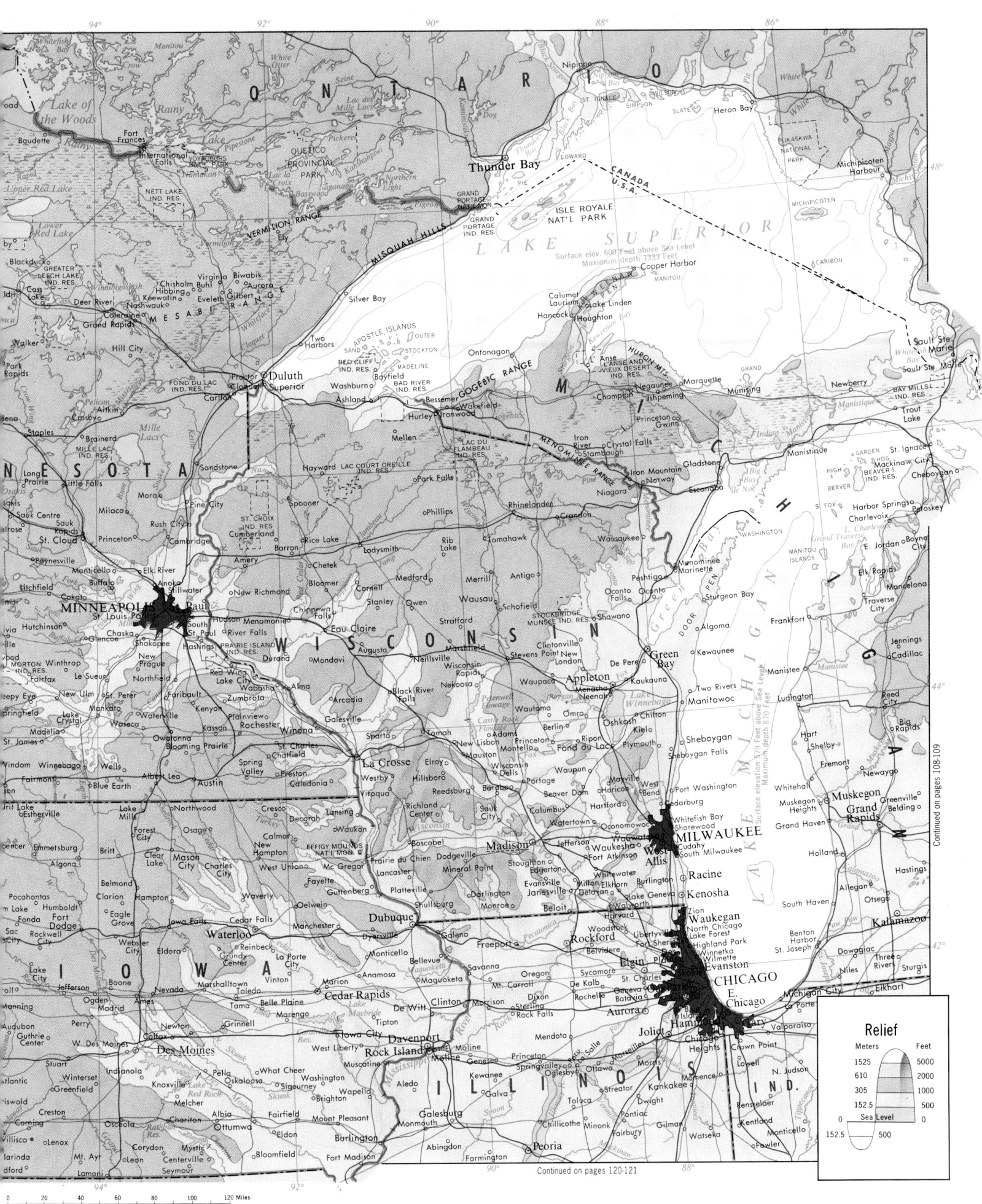

Continued on pages 108-109

Continued on pages 120-121

**Relief**

| Meters | | Feet |
|---|---|---|
| 1525 | | 5000 |
| 610 | | 2000 |
| 305 | | 1000 |
| 152.5 | | 500 |
| 0 | Sea Level | 0 |
| 152.5 | | 500 |

0   20   40   60   80   100   120 Miles
0   20   40   60   80   100   120   140   160   180   200 Kilometers

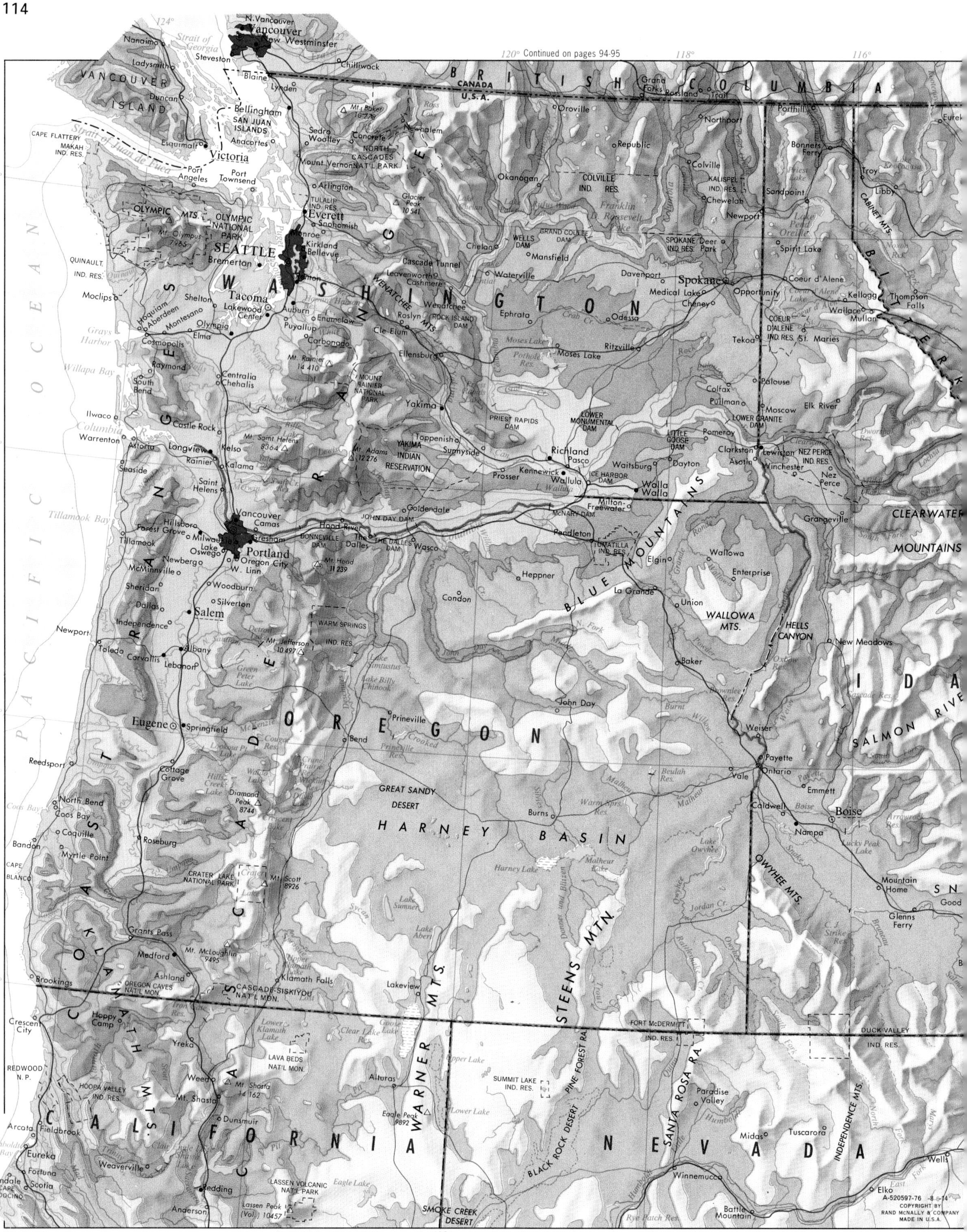

Continued on pages 94-95
Continued on pages 118-119
Longitude West of Greenwich
124°
122°
120°
118°
116°
48°
46°
44°
42°
BRITISH COLUMBIA
CANADA
U.S.A.
VANCOUVER ISLAND
WASHINGTON
OREGON
IDAHO
CALIFORNIA
NEVADA
PACIFIC OCEAN
COAST RANGES
CASCADE RANGE
KLAMATH MTS.
OLYMPIC MTS.
BLUE MOUNTAINS
WALLOWA MTS.
HELLS CANYON
CLEARWATER MOUNTAINS
SALMON RIVER
BITTERROOT
CABINET MTS.
OWYHEE MTS.
STEENS MTN.
WARNER MTS.
PINE FOREST RA.
SANTA ROSA RA.
INDEPENDENCE MTS.
BLACK ROCK DESERT
SMOKE CREEK DESERT
GREAT SANDY DESERT
HARNEY BASIN
WENATCHEE MTS.
Strait of Georgia
Strait of Juan de Fuca
Puget Sound
Grays Harbor
Willapa Bay
Columbia R.
Tillamook Bay
Coos Bay
Humboldt Bay
CAPE FLATTERY
CAPE BLANCO
CAPE MENDOCINO
N. Vancouver
Vancouver
New Westminster
Nanaimo
Ladysmith
Duncan
Esquimalt
Victoria
Steveston
Chilliwack
Blaine
Lynden
Bellingham
SAN JUAN ISLANDS
Anacortes
Sedro Woolley
Concrete
Newhalem
Mt. Baker 10 778
NORTH CASCADES NAT'L PARK
Mount Vernon
Arlington
TULALIP IND. RES.
Everett
Snohomish
Monroe
Kirkland
Bellevue
SEATTLE
Bremerton
Renton
Tacoma
Lakewood Center
Auburn
Puyallup
Enumclaw
Carbonado
Glacier Peak 10 541
MAKAH IND. RES.
Port Angeles
Port Townsend
OLYMPIC NATIONAL PARK
Mt. Olympus 7965
QUINAULT IND. RES.
Moclips
Shelton
Hoquiam
Aberdeen
Montesano
Olympia
Elma
Cosmopolis
Raymond
South Bend
Centralia
Chehalis
Mt. Rainier 14 410
MOUNT RAINIER NATIONAL PARK
Ilwaco
Castle Rock
Warrenton
Astoria
Longview
Kelso
Rainier
Kalama
Mt. Saint Helens 8364
Mt. Adams 12 276
Seaside
Saint Helens
Vancouver
Camas
Portland
Gresham
Hillsboro
Forest Grove
Milwaukie
Lake Oswego
Tillamook
Newberg
McMinnville
Oregon City
W. Linn
Sheridan
Dallas
Woodburn
Silverton
Salem
Independence
Newport
Toledo
Corvallis
Albany
Lebanon
Mt. Hood 11 239
Mt. Jefferson 10 497
WARM SPRINGS IND. RES.
Green Peter Lake
Lake Simtustus
Lake Billy Chinook
Eugene
Springfield
Cougar Res.
Reedsport
Cottage Grove
Hills Creek Lake
Diamond Peak 8744
North Bend
Coos Bay
Coquille
Bandon
Myrtle Point
Roseburg
CRATER LAKE NATIONAL PARK
Mt. Scott 8926
Grants Pass
Medford
Ashland
Mt. McLoughlin 9495
OREGON CAVES NAT'L MON.
CASCADE-SISKIYOU NAT'L MON.
Klamath Falls
Brookings
Crescent City
Happy Camp
Yreka
REDWOOD N.P.
HOOPA VALLEY IND. RES.
Weed
Mt. Shasta
Mt. Shasta 14 162
Dunsmuir
Arcata
Fieldbrook
Eureka
Fortuna
Scotia
Ferndale
Weaverville
Redding
Anderson
LASSEN VOLCANIC NAT'L PARK
Lassen Peak (Vol.) 10457
Eagle Lake
LAVA BEDS NAT'L MON.
Lower Klamath Lake
Clear Lake Res.
Goose Lake
Alturas
Eagle Peak 9892
Upper Lake
Lower Lake
Lakeview
Lake Abert
Lake Sumner
Sycan
Crescent Lake
Bend
Prineville
Prineville Res.
Crooked
Leavenworth
Cashmere
Wenatchee
Cascade Tunnel
Roslyn
Cle Elum
ROCK ISLAND DAM
Ellensburg
Yakima
YAKIMA INDIAN RESERVATION
Toppenish
Sunnyside
Prosser
PRIEST RAPIDS DAM
Chelan
Lake Chelan
WELLS DAM
GRAND COULEE DAM
Mansfield
Waterville
Ephrata
Moses Lake
Potholes Res.
Odessa
Ritzville
Okanogan
COLVILLE IND. RES.
Franklin D. Roosevelt Lake
Oroville
Republic
Colville
Chewelah
KALISPEL IND. RES.
Newport
SPOKANE IND. RES.
Deer Park
Davenport
Spokane
Opportunity
Medical Lake
Cheney
Grand Forks
Rossland
Trail
Northport
Ross Lake
Richland
Pasco
Kennewick
Wallula
LOWER MONUMENTAL DAM
ICE HARBOR DAM
LITTLE GOOSE DAM
Waitsburg
Dayton
Walla Walla
Pomeroy
Colfax
Pullman
Palouse
Moscow
LOWER GRANITE DAM
Clarkston
Asotin
Lewiston
NEZ PERCE IND. RES.
Nez Perce
Winchester
Elk River
Grangeville
Tekoa
Coeur d'Alene
COEUR D'ALENE IND. RES.
St. Maries
Kellogg
Wallace
Mullan
Thompson Falls
Spirit Lake
Pend Oreille Lake
Priest Lake
Sandpoint
Bonners Ferry
Porthill
Troy
Libby
Eureka
Goldendale
JOHN DAY DAM
McNARY DAM
Milton-Freewater
Hood River
The Dalles
THE DALLES DAM
BONNEVILLE DAM
Wasco
Pendleton
UMATILLA IND. RES.
Heppner
Condon
Elgin
La Grande
Wallowa
Enterprise
Union
Baker
John Day
Burns
Harney Lake
Malheur Lake
Warm Sprs. Res.
Beulah Res.
Brownlee Res.
Oxbow Res.
Vale
Ontario
Payette
Weiser
New Meadows
Cascade Res.
Emmett
Caldwell
Nampa
Boise
Lucky Peak Lake
Arrowrock Res.
Lake Owyhee
Jordan Cr.
Mountain Home
Glenns Ferry
C. J. Strike Res.
FORT McDERMITT IND. RES.
DUCK VALLEY IND. RES.
SUMMIT LAKE IND. RES.
Paradise Valley
Midas
Tuscarora
Winnemucca
Battle Mountain
Rye Patch Res.
Elko
Wells
A-520597-76 -8-6-14
COPYRIGHT BY RAND McNALLY & COMPANY MADE IN U.S.A.

Scale 1: 4,000 000; one inch to 64 miles. Conic Projection
Elevations and depressions are given in feet

Continued on pages 96-97
Continued on pages 112-113
Continued on pages 118-119

ALBERTA
CANADA
U.S.A.
SASKATCHEWAN

MONTANA
WYOMING
UTAH
IDAHO
N. DAK.
COLO.

ROCKY MOUNTAIN RANGE
SWAN RANGE
LEWIS RANGE
BIG BELT MTS.
LITTLE BELT MTS.
CRAZY MTS.
ABSAROKA RANGE
WIND RIVER RANGE
BIGHORN MOUNTAINS
LEMHI RANGE
LOST RIVER RA.
PIONEER MTS.
BEAVERHEAD MTS.
SNAKE RIVER PLAIN
WASATCH RANGE
UINTA MTS.
WYOMING RANGE
SALT RIVER RANGE
PARK RANGE

WATERTON GLACIER INTERNATIONAL PEACE PARK
BLACKFEET IND. RES.
FLATHEAD INDIAN RESERVATION
NATIONAL BISON RANGE
ROCKY BOYS IND. RES.
FT. BELKNAP IND. RES.
FORT PECK IND. RES.
CROW IND. RES.
NORTHERN CHEYENNE IND. RES.
FORT HALL IND. RES.
WIND RIVER IND. RES.
UINTAH AND OURAY IND. RES.

BIG HOLE NAT'L BATTLEFIELD
CRATERS OF THE MOON NAT'L MON.
YELLOWSTONE NATIONAL PARK
GRAND TETON NAT'L PARK
LITTLE BIGHORN BATTLEFIELD NAT'L MON.
DEVILS TOWER NAT'L MON.
DINOSAUR NAT'L MON.

GREAT SALT LAKE DESERT
GREAT SALT LAKE
GREAT DIVIDE BASIN

Cities and towns:
Whitefish, Kalispell, Missoula, Lolo, Stevensville, Hamilton, Philipsburg, Anaconda, Ronan, Browning, Cut Bank, Shelby, Sunburst, Valier, Conrad, Choteau, Great Falls, Belt, Neihart, White Sulphur Spgs., Harlowton, Lewistown, Winifred, Winnett, Roundup, Fort Benton, Hogeland, Chinook, Harlem, Malta, Glasgow, Ft. Peck, Wolf Point, Poplar, Sidney, Williston, Opheim, Scobey, Plentywood, Grenora, Beach, Glendive, Terry, Miles City, Baker, Marmarth, Forsyth, Colstrip, Hardin, Crow Agency, Lame Deer, Billings, Laurel, Columbus, Big Timber, Livingston, Bozeman, Three Forks, Townsend, Helena, East Helena, Walkerville, Butte, Deer Lodge, Twin Bridges, Dillon, Salmon, Mackay, Arco, Shoshone, Rupert, Burley, Oakley, Twin Falls, Idaho Falls, Shelley, Blackfoot, Pocatello, Soda Springs, Lava Hot Spgs., American Falls, St. Anthony, Ashton, Rexburg, Rigby, Montpelier, Afton, Kemmerer, Green River, Rock Springs, Granger, Superior, Rawlins, Evanston, Wendover, Lucin, Tooele, Murray, Salt Lake City, Midvale, Heber City, Park City, Bountiful, Farmington, Ogden, Morgan, Brigham, Huntsville, Wellsville, Logan, Providence, Richmond, Smithfield, Garland, Lewiston, Preston, Malad City, Montpelier, Vernal, Craig, Steamboat Spgs., Oak Creek, Craigo, Hanna, Wheatland, Douglas, Orin, Casper, Glenrock, Midwest, Powder River, Lander, Riverton, Shoshoni, Thermopolis, Worland, Ten Sleep, Gebo, Basin, Greybull, Cody, Powell, Lovell, Greybull, Kaycee, Buffalo, Gillette, Moorcroft, Sundance, Sheridan, Devils Tower

Peaks:
Homer Youngs Peak 10 621
Borah Pk. 12 662
Boulder Peak 10 981
Hyndman Peak 12 009
Electric Peak 10 992
Mt. Washburn 10 243
Granite Peak
Grand Teton 13 770
Garnett Peak 13 804
Fremont Peak 13 745
Gannett Peak
Cloud Peak 13 167
Meade Peak 9957
Kings Peak 13 528
Mt. Emmons 13 440

Rivers and waters:
Missouri, Yellowstone, Snake, Bear, Green, Wind, Bighorn, Milk, Marias, Teton, Sun, Jefferson, Madison, Gallatin, Musselshell, Powder, Platte, North Platte, Sweetwater, Clark Fork, Bitterroot, Flathead Lake, Lake Elwell, Fort Peck Lake, Hebgen Lake, Jackson Lake, Shoshone Lake, Bighorn Lake, Boysen Res., American Falls, Blackfoot Reservoir, Meade Res., Flaming Gorge Res., Fontenelle Res., Pathfinder Res., Seminoe Res., Alcova Res., Medicine Lake

7733 ft above sea level

| Relief | | |
| --- | --- | --- |
| Meters | | Feet |
| 3050 | | 10000 |
| 1525 | | 5000 |
| 610 | | 2000 |
| 305 | | 1000 |
| 152.5 | | 500 |
| 0 | Sea Level | 0 |
| 1525 | | 500 |

0 20 40 60 80 100 120 Miles
0 20 40 60 80 100 120 140 160 180 200 Kilometers

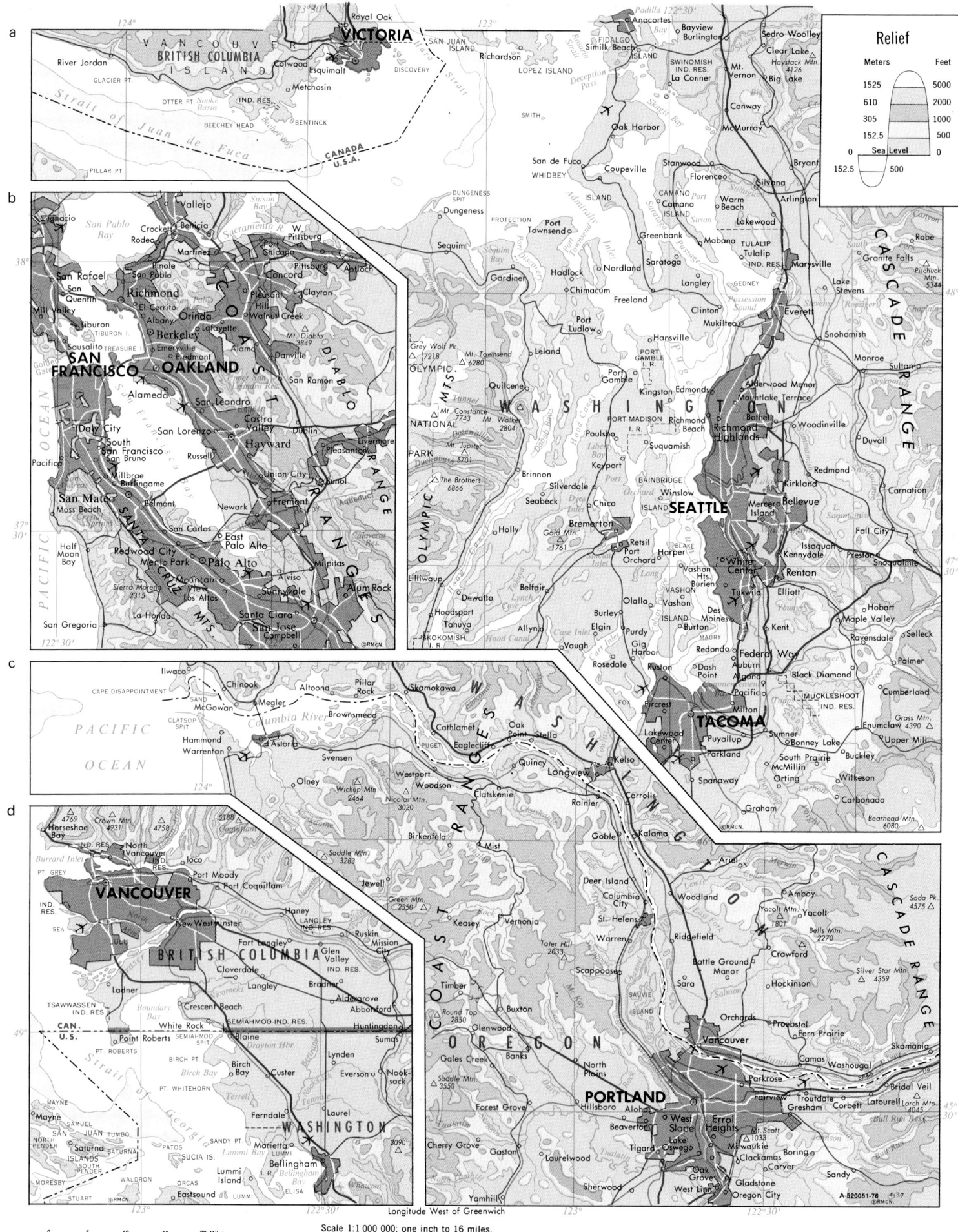

Scale 1:1 000 000; one inch to 16 miles.
Elevations and depressions are given in feet.

Longitude West of Greenwich

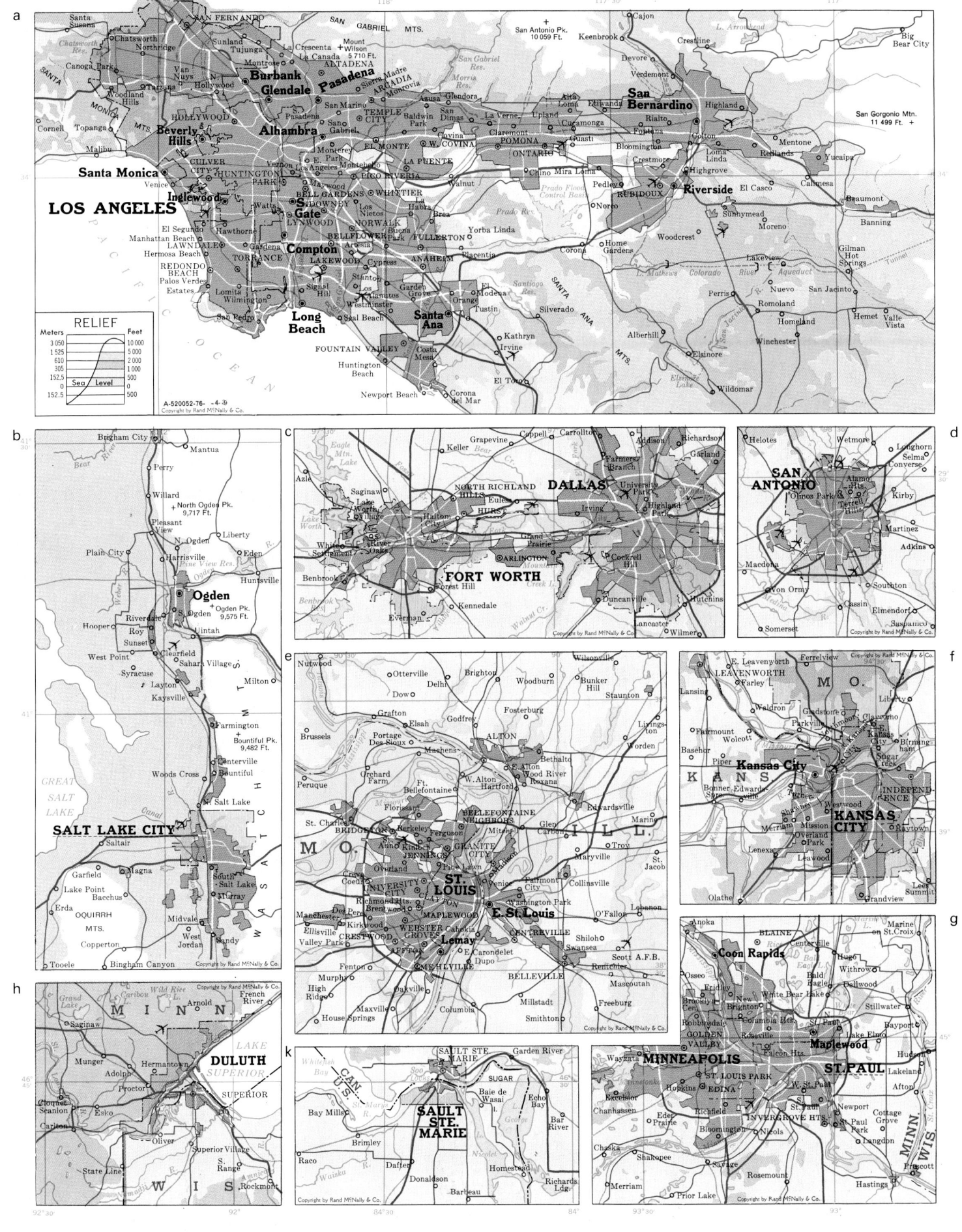

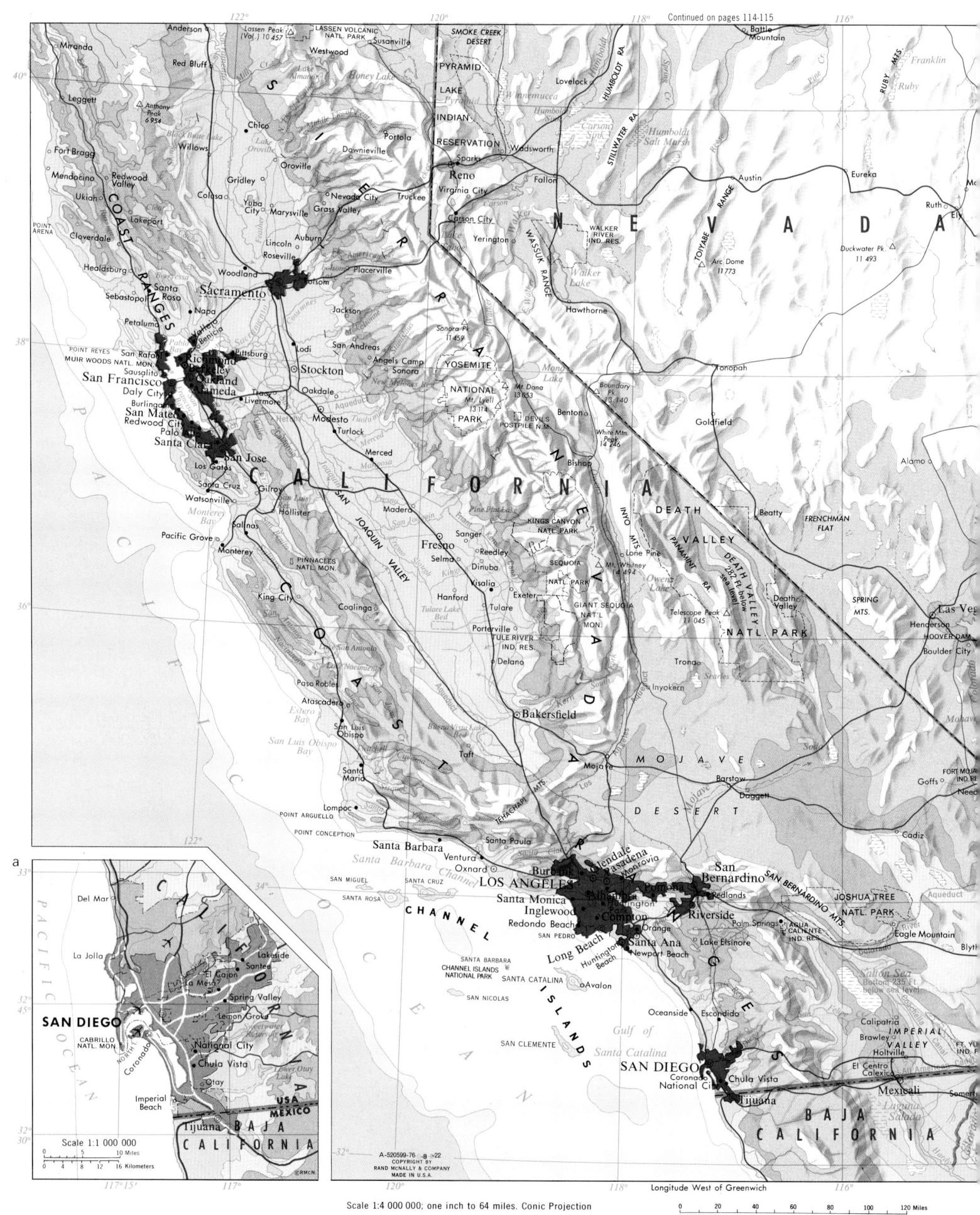

Continued on pages 114-115

Scale 1:4 000 000; one inch to 64 miles. Conic Projection
Elevations and depressions are given in feet

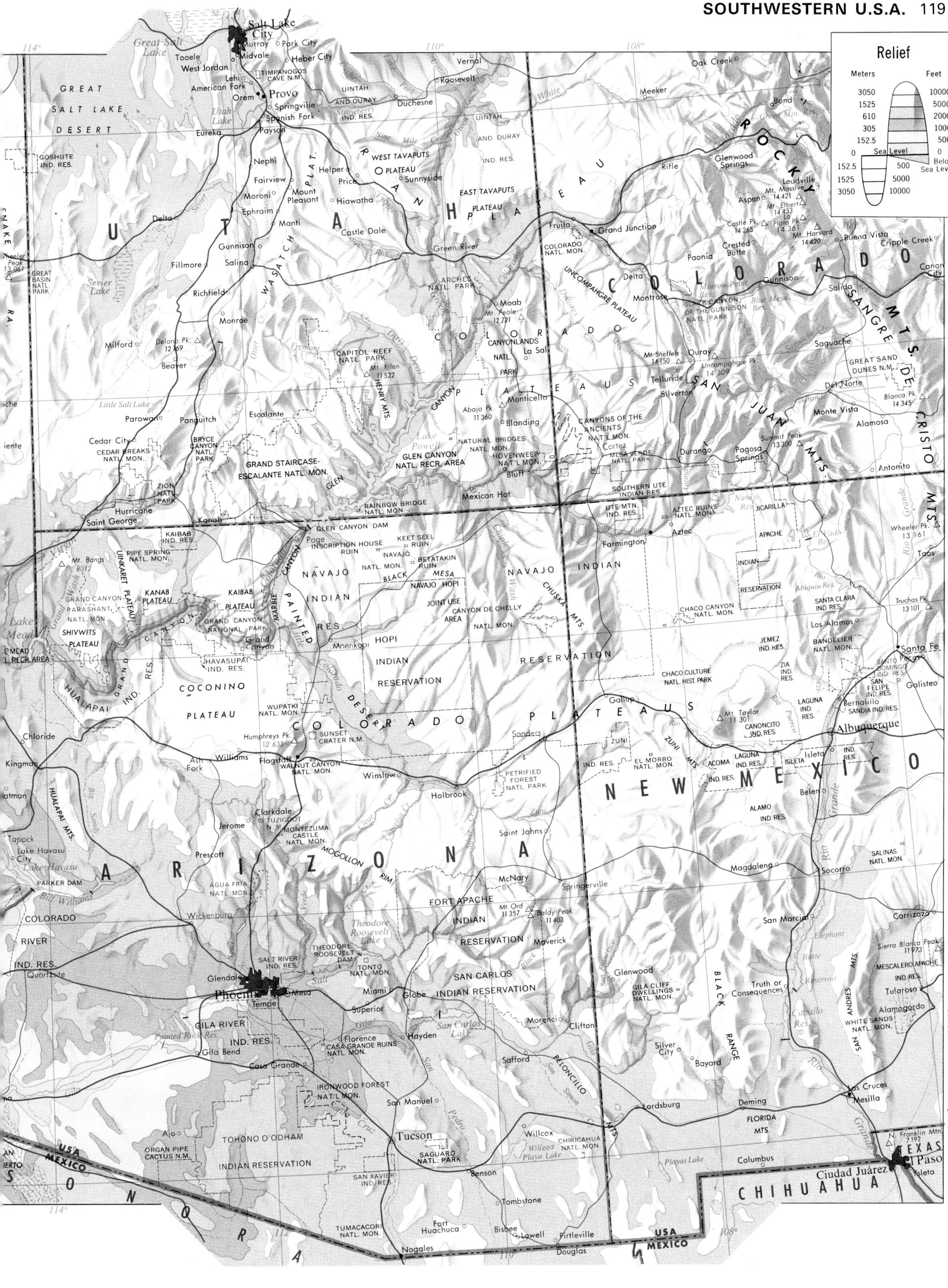

**Relief**

| Meters | Feet |
|---|---|
| 3050 | 10000 |
| 1525 | 5000 |
| 610 | 2000 |
| 305 | 1000 |
| 152.5 | 500 |
| Sea Level | 0 |
| 152.5 | 500 Below Sea Level |
| 1525 | 5000 |
| 3050 | 10000 |

GREAT SALT LAKE DESERT

GOSHUTE IND. RES.

Great Salt Lake

Salt Lake City
Tooele
West Jordan
Murray
Midvale
Lehi
American Fork
Orem
Provo
Springville
Spanish Fork
Payson
Nephi
Park City
Heber City
TIMPANOGOS CAVE N.M.
UINTAH
AND OURAY IND. RES.
Duchesne
Roosevelt
Vernal
Meeker
Oak Creek
Bond

Eureka
Utah Lake
Fairview
Mount Pleasant
Moroni
Ephraim
Manti
Gunnison
Salina
Delta
Fillmore
Richfield
Monroe

UTAH
WASATCH PLAT.
WEST TAVAPUTS PLATEAU
EAST TAVAPUTS PLATEAU
Price
Helper
Sunnyside
Hiawatha
Castle Dale
Green River

UINTA BASIN
Strawberry Res.
White
Rifle
Glenwood Springs
ROCKY
Leadville
Mt. Massive 14 421
Aspen
Mt. Elbert 14 433

Fruita
Grand Junction
COLORADO NATL. MON.
Castle Pk. 14 265
Mt. Harvard 14 420
Buena Vista
Cripple Creek

Delta
Montrose
Paonia
Crested Butte
Gunnison
Salida
Cañon City

COLORADO

UNCOMPAHGRE PLATEAU
Mt. Sneffels 14 150
Ouray
Uncompahgre Pk. 14 309
Telluride
Silverton
SAN JUAN MTS.
Saguache
GREAT SAND DUNES N.M.
Del Norte
Monte Vista
Alamosa

Milford
Delano Pk. 12 169
Beaver
Little Salt Lake
Parowan
Panguitch
Escalante
Sevier Lake

CAPITOL REEF NATL. PARK
Mt. Ellen 11 522
HENRY MTS.
Abajo Pk. 11 360
Monticello
Blanding

CANYONLANDS NATL. PARK
Moab
Mt. Peale 12 721
La Sal

CANYON PLATEAUS

Cedar City
CEDAR BREAKS NATL. MON.
BRYCE CANYON NATL. PARK
ZION NATL. PARK
GRAND STAIRCASE-ESCALANTE NATL. MON.
Saint George
Hurricane
Kanab
Lake Powell
GLEN CANYON NATL. RECR. AREA
NATURAL BRIDGES NATL. MON.
HOVENWEEP NATL. MON.
Bluff
Mexican Hat
CANYONS OF THE ANCIENTS NATL. MON.
Cortez
MESA VERDE NATL. PARK
Durango
Pagosa Springs
Summit Peak 13 300
Antonito

SANGRE DE CRISTO MTS.
Blanca Pk. 14 345

Mt. Bangs 8012
PIPE SPRING NATL. MON.
KAIBAB IND. RES.
Page
GLEN CANYON DAM
INSCRIPTION HOUSE RUIN
KEET SEEL RUIN
BETATAKIN RUIN
NAVAJO NATL. MON.
Farmington
Aztec
AZTEC RUINS NATL. MON.
UTE MTN. IND. RES.
SOUTHERN UTE INDIAN RES.
Wheeler Pk. 13 161
Taos
JICARILLA APACHE IND. RES.

GRAND CANYON PARASHANT NATL. MON.
KANAB PLATEAU
KAIBAB PLATEAU
MARBLE CANYON
PAINTED DESERT
NAVAJO INDIAN RES.
BLACK MESA
NAVAJO
HOPI
JOINT USE AREA
CANYON DE CHELLY NATL. MON.
CHUSKA MTS.
NAVAJO INDIAN RESERVATION
CHACO CANYON NATL. MON.
APACHE
Truchas Pk. 13 101
Santa Fe
Los Alamos
BANDELIER NATL. MON.

Lake Mead
LAKE MEAD NATL. RECR. AREA
SHIVWITS PLATEAU
HUALAPAI IND. RES.
GRAND CANYON NATIONAL PARK
Grand Canyon
HAVASUPAI IND. RES.
Moenkopi
HOPI INDIAN RESERVATION
COCONINO PLATEAU
CHACO CULTURE NATL. HIST. PARK
JEMEZ IND. RES.
ZIA IND. RES.
SANTO DOMINGO IND. RES.
SANTA CLARA IND. RES.
SAN FELIPE IND. RES.
Galisteo

Chloride
Kingman
Hualapai
Humphreys Pk. 12 633
WUPATKI NATL. MON.
SUNSET CRATER N.M.
Williams
Flagstaff
WALNUT CANYON NATL. MON.
Winslow
Holbrook
Sanders
PETRIFIED FOREST NATL. PARK
Gallup
ZUNI
ZUNI MTS.
EL MORRO NATL. MON.
ACOMA
LAGUNA IND. RES.
CANONCITO IND. RES.
SANDIA IND. RES.
Bernalillo
Albuquerque
ISLETA IND. RES.
Belen
Mt. Taylor 11 301

NEW MEXICO

Oatman
HUALAPAI MTS.
Tapock
Lake Havasu City
Lake Havasu
PARKER DAM
Clarkdale
TUZIGOOT
Jerome
MONTEZUMA CASTLE NATL. MON.
Prescott
MOGOLLON RIM
Saint Johns
Springerville
McNary
FORT APACHE INDIAN RESERVATION
Mt. Ord 11 357
Baldy Peak 11 403
Maverick
ALAMO IND. RES.
Magdalena
Socorro
SALINAS NATL. MON.

COLORADO RIVER
IND. RES.
Quartzsite
AGUA FRIA NATL. MON.
Wickenburg
THEODORE ROOSEVELT LAKE
THEODORE ROOSEVELT DAM
SALT RIVER IND. RES.
Glendale
Phoenix
Tempe
Mesa
TONTO NATL. MON.
Miami
Globe
SAN CARLOS INDIAN RESERVATION
Glenwood
GILA CLIFF DWELLINGS NATL. MON.
Truth or Consequences
Sierra Blanca Peak 11 973
MESCALERO APACHE IND. RES.
Tularosa
Alamogordo

ARIZONA

GILA RIVER IND. RES.
Superior
Florence
CASA GRANDE RUINS NATL. MON.
Hayden
Casa Grande
Gila Bend
Painted Rock Res.
Morenci
Clifton
Safford
Silver City
Bayard
BLACK RANGE
Caballo Res.
WHITE SANDS NATL. MON.

Ajo
ORGAN PIPE CACTUS N.M.
IRONWOOD FOREST NATL. MON.
San Manuel
TOHONO O'ODHAM INDIAN RESERVATION
Tucson
SAGUARO NATL. PARK
SAN XAVIER IND. RES.
Benson
Willcox
Willcox Playa Lake
CHIRICAHUA NATL. MON.
Playas Lake
Columbus
Lordsburg
Deming
FLORIDA MTS.
Las Cruces
Mesilla
Franklin Mtn. 7192
El Paso
Isleta
Ciudad Juárez

USA MEXICO
SONORA
CHIHUAHUA
TEXAS

Nogales
TUMACACORI NATL. MON.
Fort Huachuca
Bisbee
Lowell
Pirtleville
Douglas
Tombstone

Continued on pages 120-121
Continued on pages 122-123

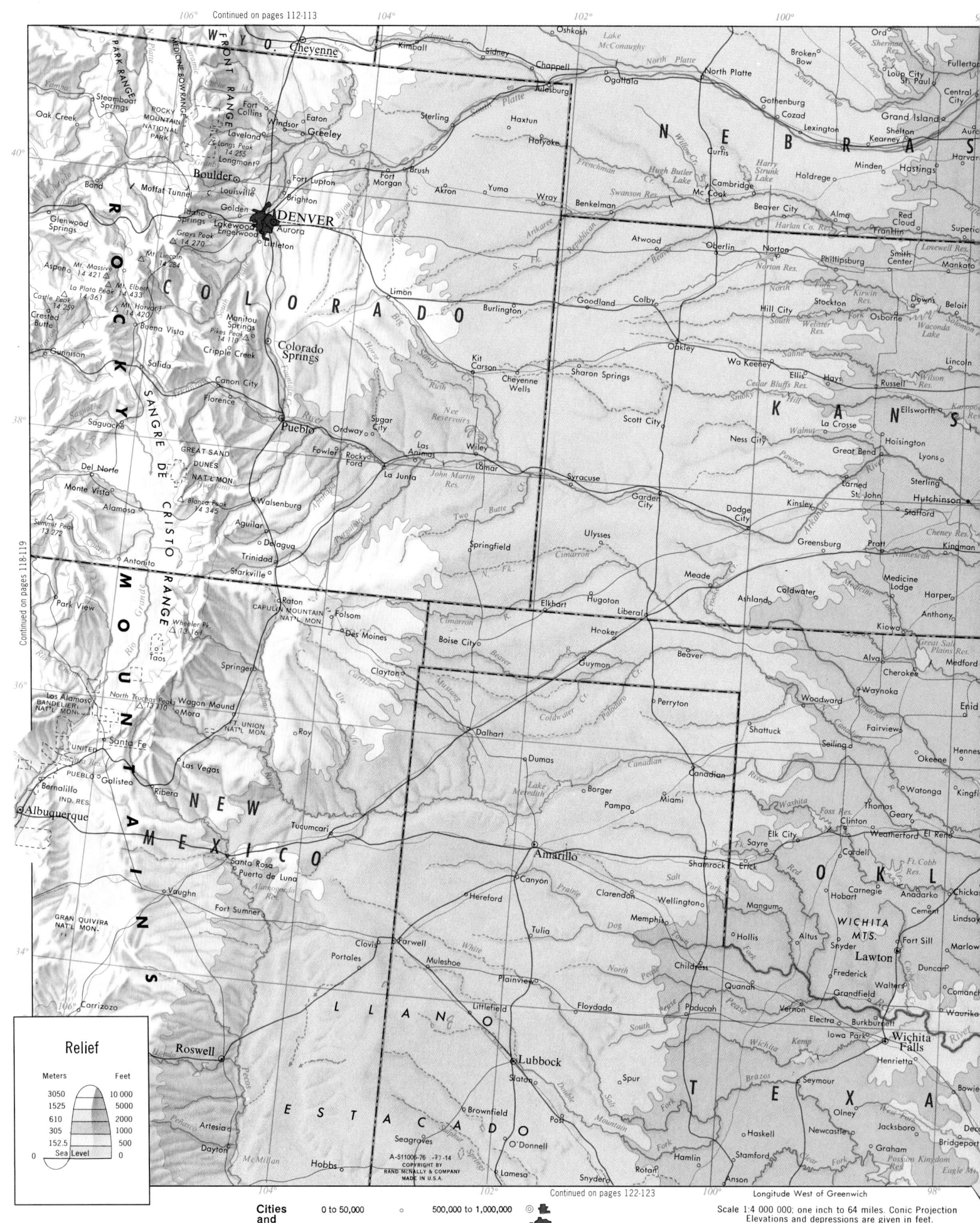

120

Continued on pages 112-113

106°    104°    102°    100°

W Y O.    Cheyenne

PARK RANGE

MEDICINE BOW RANGE

FRONT RANGE

ROCKY MOUNTAIN NATIONAL PARK

Oak Creek
Steamboat Springs
Bond
Glenwood Springs
Aspen ▲Mt. Massive
14 421
▲Mt. Elbert
14 433
Castle Peak
14 259
Crested Butte
Gunnison
▲La Plata Peak
14 361
▲Mt. Harvard
14 420
Buena Vista
▲Mt. Lincoln
14 284
Pikes Peak
14 110
Saguache
Salida
Del Norte
Monte Vista
Alamosa
Summit Peak
13 272
Antonito
Park View
Taos
North Truchas Peaks
13 310
Wheeler Pk.
13 161

Fort Collins
Loveland
Windsor    Eaton    Greeley
▲Longs Peak
14 255
Longmont
Boulder
Moffat Tunnel
Louisville
Idaho Springs
Golden
Lakewood
Engelwood
Littleton
▲Grays Peak
14 270
Manitou Springs
Colorado Springs
Cripple Creek
Canon City
Florence
Pueblo
Walsenburg
Blanca Peak
14 345
Aguilar
Delagua
Trinidad
Starkville
Raton
CAPULIN MOUNTAIN NAT'L MON.

Brighton
Fort Lupton
Fort Morgan
Brush
Akron
Limon
Ordway
Sugar City
Fowler
Rocky Ford
La Junta
Lamar
Wiley
Las Animas

C O L O R A D O

R O C K Y

S A N G R E   D E   C R I S T O   R A N G E

M O U N T A I N S

Cheyenne
Kimball    Sidney    Oshkosh
Chappell
Julesburg
Ogallala
Sterling
Haxtun
Holyoke
Yuma
Wray
Benkelman
Burlington
Goodland
Colby
Kit Carson
Cheyenne Wells
Sharon Springs
Scott City
Wa Keeney
Garden City
Dodge City
Syracuse
Springfield
Ulysses
Meade
Elkhart
Hugoton
Liberal

Lake McConaughy
North Platte
Ogallala
North Platte
Gothenburg
Cozad
Lexington
Kearney
Curtis
Frenchman
Hugh Butler Lake
Swanson Res.
Mc Cook
Cambridge
Beaver City
Alma
Atwood
Oberlin
Norton
Norton Res.
Phillipsburg
Smith Center
Hill City
Stockton
Osborne
Oakley
Hays
Russell
Ellsworth
Ness City
La Crosse
Great Bend
Larned
St. John
Hoisington
Lyons
Sterling
Hutchinson
Stafford
Greensburg
Pratt
Kinsley
Kingman
Coldwater
Medicine Lodge
Harper
Anthony
Ashland
Kiowa
Alva
Cherokee

N E B R A S

Ord
Broken Bow
Loup City    St. Paul
Grand Island
Shelton
Minden
Hastings
Holdrege
Red Cloud
Franklin
Smith Center
Mankato
Beloit
Lincoln
Waconda Lake
Wilson Lake

K A N S A S

Woodward
Waynoka
Fairview
Okeene
Watonga
Kingfisher
Thomas
Clinton
Weatherford
El Reno
Cordell
Cardell
Carnegie
Anadarko
Cement

Capulin
Folsom
Des Moines
Clayton
Springer
Wagon Mound
Mora
Roy
FT. UNION NAT'L MON.
Los Alamos
BANDELIER NAT'L MON.
Santa Fe
UNITED PUEBLO IND. RES.
Bernalillo
Galisteo
Albuquerque
GRAN QUIVIRA NAT'L MON.
Carrizozo
Vaughn
Santa Rosa
Puerto de Luna
Fort Sumner
Las Vegas
Ribera

N E W   M E X I C O

Boise City
Hooker
Guymon
Beaver
Dalhart
Dumas
Borger
Pampa
Miami
Perryton
Canadian
Amarillo
Canyon
Hereford
Clarendon
Wellington
Memphis
Tulia
Shamrock
Erick
Elk City
Sayre
Mangum
Hobart
Altus
Hollis
Snyder
Lawton
Frederick
Walters
Fort Sill
WICHITA MTS.

O K L A

Enid
Hennessey
Fairview
Kingfisher
Marlow
Duncan
Grandfield
Vernon
Electra
Iowa Park
Burkburnett
Wichita Falls
Henrietta
Seymour

Tucumcari
Clovis
Portales
Farwell
Muleshoe
Plainview
Littlefield
Floydada
Paducah
Quanah
Childress

L L A N O    E S T A C A D O

Roswell
Lubbock
Slaton
Spur
Brownfield
Post
Artesia
Seagroves
O'Donnell
Lamesa
Snyder
McMillan
Hobbs
Dayton

T E X A S

Olney
Jacksboro
Haskell
Stamford
Anson
Hamlin
Rotan

Seymour
Olney
Bridgeport
Bowie
Decatur

Continued on pages 118-119

40°

38°

36°

34°

106°    104°    102°    100°    98°

Continued on pages 122-123    Longitude West of Greenwich

## Relief

| Meters | | Feet |
|---|---|---|
| 3050 | | 10 000 |
| 1525 | | 5000 |
| 610 | | 2000 |
| 305 | | 1000 |
| 152.5 | | 500 |
| 0 | Sea Level | 0 |

**Cities and Towns**

| 0 to 50,000 | ○ | 500,000 to 1,000,000 | ◉ |
|---|---|---|---|
| 50,000 to 500,000 | ⊙ | 1,000,000 and over | |

A-511006-76 -77-14
COPYRIGHT BY
RAND MCNALLY & COMPANY
MADE IN U.S.A.

Scale 1:4 000 000; one inch to 64 miles. Conic Projection
Elevations and depressions are given in feet.

CHICAGO
Aurora
Joliet

Continued on pages 112-113

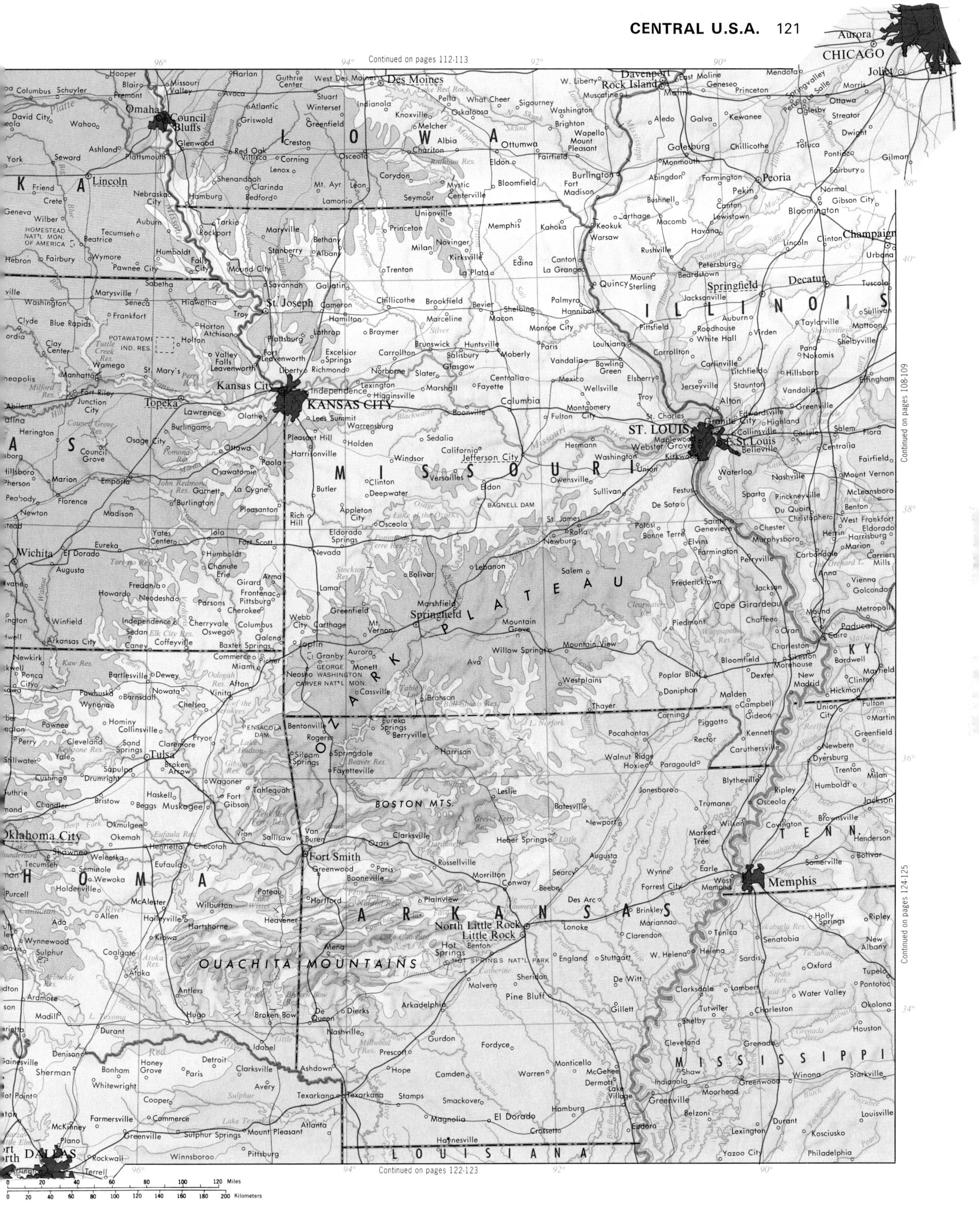

Continued on pages 108-109

Continued on pages 124-125

Continued on pages 122-123

I O W A

ILLINOIS

M I S S O U R I

K A N S A S

O K L A H O M A

A R K A N S A S

TENN.

MISSISSIPPI

LOUISIANA

KY.

O Z A R K   P L A T E A U

BOSTON MTS.

OUACHITA MOUNTAINS

Omaha
Council Bluffs
Lincoln
Des Moines
Davenport
Rock Island
Peoria
Champaign
St. Joseph
Kansas City
KANSAS CITY
Topeka
Wichita
Tulsa
Oklahoma City
ST. LOUIS
E. St. Louis
Springfield
Decatur
Jefferson City
Columbia
Springfield
Fort Smith
North Little Rock
Little Rock
Hot Springs
Memphis
West Memphis
DALLAS

Quincy
Hannibal
Cape Girardeau
Cairo
Paducah
New Madrid
Jonesboro
Pine Bluff
Texarkana
El Dorado

BAGNELL DAM
Lake of the Ozarks
PENSACOLA DAM
HOT SPRINGS NAT'L PARK
GEORGE WASHINGTON CARVER NAT'L MON.
HOMESTEAD NAT'L MON. OF AMERICA

Miles
0   20   40   60   80   100   120
Kilometers
0   20   40   60   80   100   120   140   160   180   200

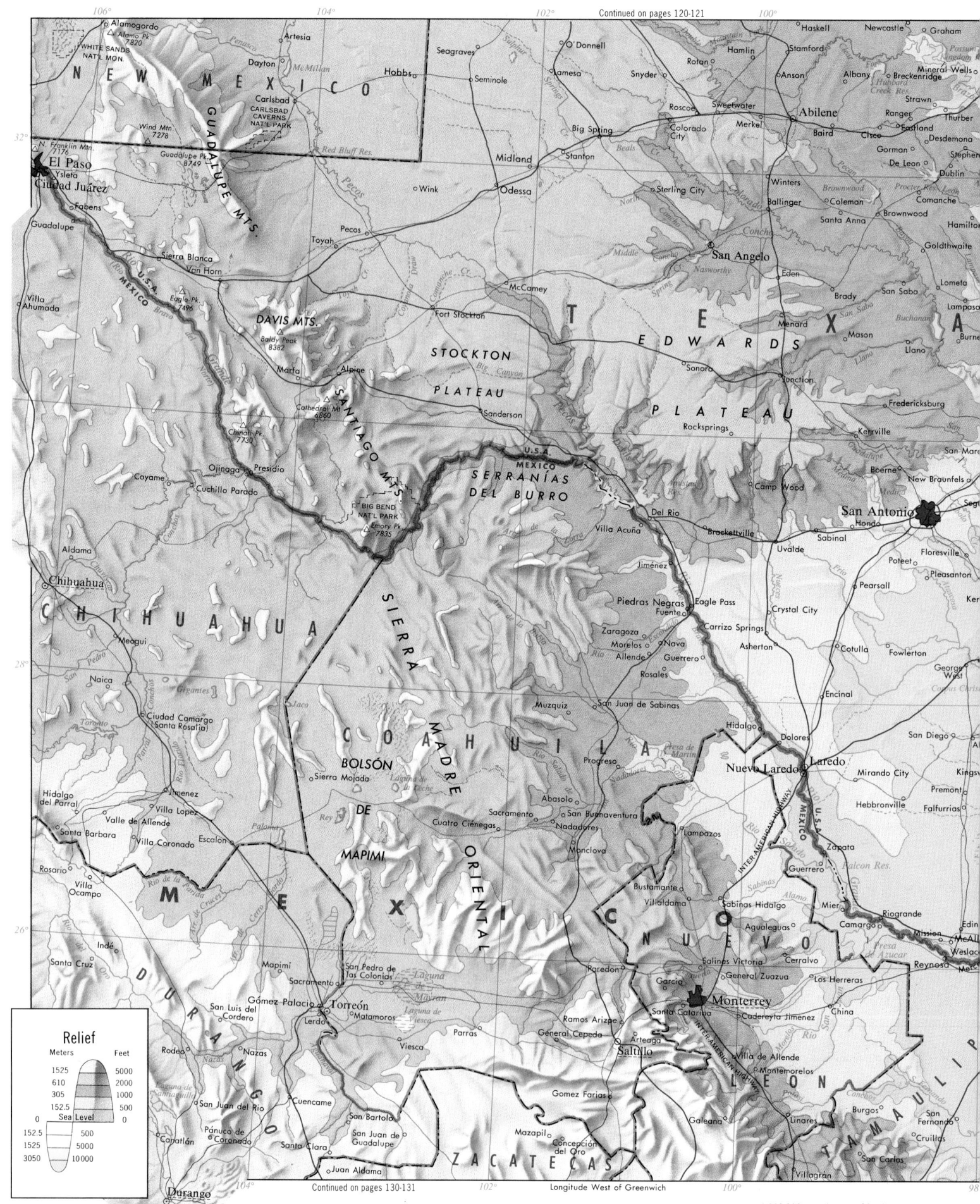

Continued on pages 120-121

NEW MEXICO

Alamogordo
Alamo Pk. 7820
WHITE SANDS NAT'L MON.
Artesia
Dayton
McMillan
Seagraves
O'Donnell
Haskell
Newcastle
Graham
Wind Mtn. 7278
Carlsbad
CARLSBAD CAVERNS NAT'L PARK
Hobbs
Lamesa
Seminole
Snyder
Rotan
Hamlin
Stamford
Albany
Breckenridge
Mineral Wells

32°
N. Franklin Mtn. 7176
El Paso
Ysleta
Ciudad Juárez
Fabens
GUADALUPE MTS.
Guadalupe Pk. 8749
Red Bluff Res.
Midland
Stanton
Big Spring
Colorado City
Sweetwater
Merkel
Abilene
Baird
Clsee
Ranger
Eastland
Thurber
Desdemona
Stephen

Guadalupe
Sierra Blanca
Van Horn
Pecos
Toyah
Wink
Odessa
Sterling City
North
Winters
Ballinger
Coleman
Santa Anna
Brownwood
Comanche
De Leon
Gorman
Dublin

Villa Ahumada
Eagle Pk. 7496
DAVIS MTS.
Baldy Peak 8382
Marfa
Alpine
Fort Stockton
STOCKTON PLATEAU
McCamey
San Angelo
Nasworthy
Eden
Menard
Brady
San Saba
Goldthwaite
Lometa
Lampasas

Cathedral Mt. 6860
Chinati Pk. 7730
SANTIAGO MTS.
Sanderson
Big Canyon
Sonora
Junction
Rocksprings
Kerrville
Fredericksburg

Ojinaga
Presidio
Coyame
Cuchillo Parado
BIG BEND NAT'L PARK
Emory Pk. 7835
U.S.A. MEXICO
SERRANÍAS DEL BURRO
Del Rio
Villa Acuña
Brackettville
Camp Wood
Boerne
New Braunfels
San Antonio
Honda
Uvalde
Sabinal

Aldama
Chihuahua
Meoqui
Naica
Gigantes
Jaco
CHIHUAHUA
Jimenez
Piedras Negras
Fuente
Eagle Pass
Crystal City
Pearsall
Floresville
Poteet
Pleasanton
Ker

28°
Ciudad Camargo (Santa Rosalia)
Zaragoza
Morelos
Nava
Allende
Guerrero
Rosales
Muzquiz
San Juan de Sabinas
Carrizo Springs
Asherton
Cotulla
Fowlerton
George West

SIERRA MADRE ORIENTAL
COAHUILA
Sierra Mojada
BOLSÓN DE MAPIMI
Laguna de la Leche
Cuatro Ciénegas
Sacramento
Abasolo
San Buenaventura
Nadadores
Monclova
Progreso
Presa de la Martin
Hidalgo
Dolores
San Diego
Encinal

Hidalgo del Parral
Jimenez
Villa Lopez
Valle de Allende
Santa Barbara
Villa Coronado
Escalon
DURANGO
Rosario
Villa Ocampo
Indé
Santa Cruz
Rodeo
Nazas
Palomas
Rey
Laguna de Mayran
Presa Don Martin
Nuevo Laredo
Laredo
Mirando City
Hebbronville
Premont
Falfurrias
Bustamante
Villaldama
Sabinas Hidalgo
Mier
Camargo
Riogrande
Zapata
Guerrero
Falcon Res.

26°
Mapimi
Sacramento
San Pedro de las Colonias
Laguna de Tlahualilo
Lampazos
Aqualeguas
Cerralvo
General Zuazua
Los Herreras
China
Mission
McAll
Weslac
Reynosa

Gómez Palacio
Torreón
Lerdo
Matamoros
Laguna de Viesca
Viesca
Parras
Paredon
Salinas Victoria
Garcia
Santa Catarina
Monterrey
Cadereyta Jimenez

San Juan del Rio
Cuencamé
San Pedro de las Colonias
Ramos Arizpe
General Cepeda
Arteaga
Saltillo
Villa de Allende
Montemorels
NUEVO LEÓN

Canatlán
Panuco de Coronado
San Luis del Cordero
San Juan de Guadalupe
Gomez Farias
Galeana
Linares
Burgos
San Fernando
Cruillas

Rodeo
Nazas
Mazapil
Concepcion del Oro
ZACATECAS
San Carlos
Villagran
TAMAULIPAS

Durango
Longitude West of Greenwich

104°
102°
100°
98°

Scale 1:4 000 000; one inch to 64 miles. Conic Projection
Elevations and depressions are given in feet

Relief

| Meters | | Feet |
|---|---|---|
| 1525 | | 5000 |
| 610 | | 2000 |
| 305 | | 1000 |
| 152.5 | | 500 |
| 0 | Sea Level | 0 |
| 152.5 | | 500 |
| 1525 | | 5000 |
| 3050 | | 10 000 |

Continued on pages 120-121

Continued on pages 124-125

Scale 1:1 000 000

0   5   10 Miles
0  4  8  12  16 Kilometers

A-511007-76 5⅛-8
COPYRIGHT BY
RAND MCNALLY & COMPANY
MADE IN U.S.A.

0   20   40   60   80   100   120 Miles
0  20  40  60  80  100  120  140  160  180  200 Kilometers

**Cities and Towns**

| 0 to 50,000 | ○ | 500,000 to 1,000,000 | ◎ |
| 50,000 to 500,000 | ⊙ | 1,000,000 and over | ● |

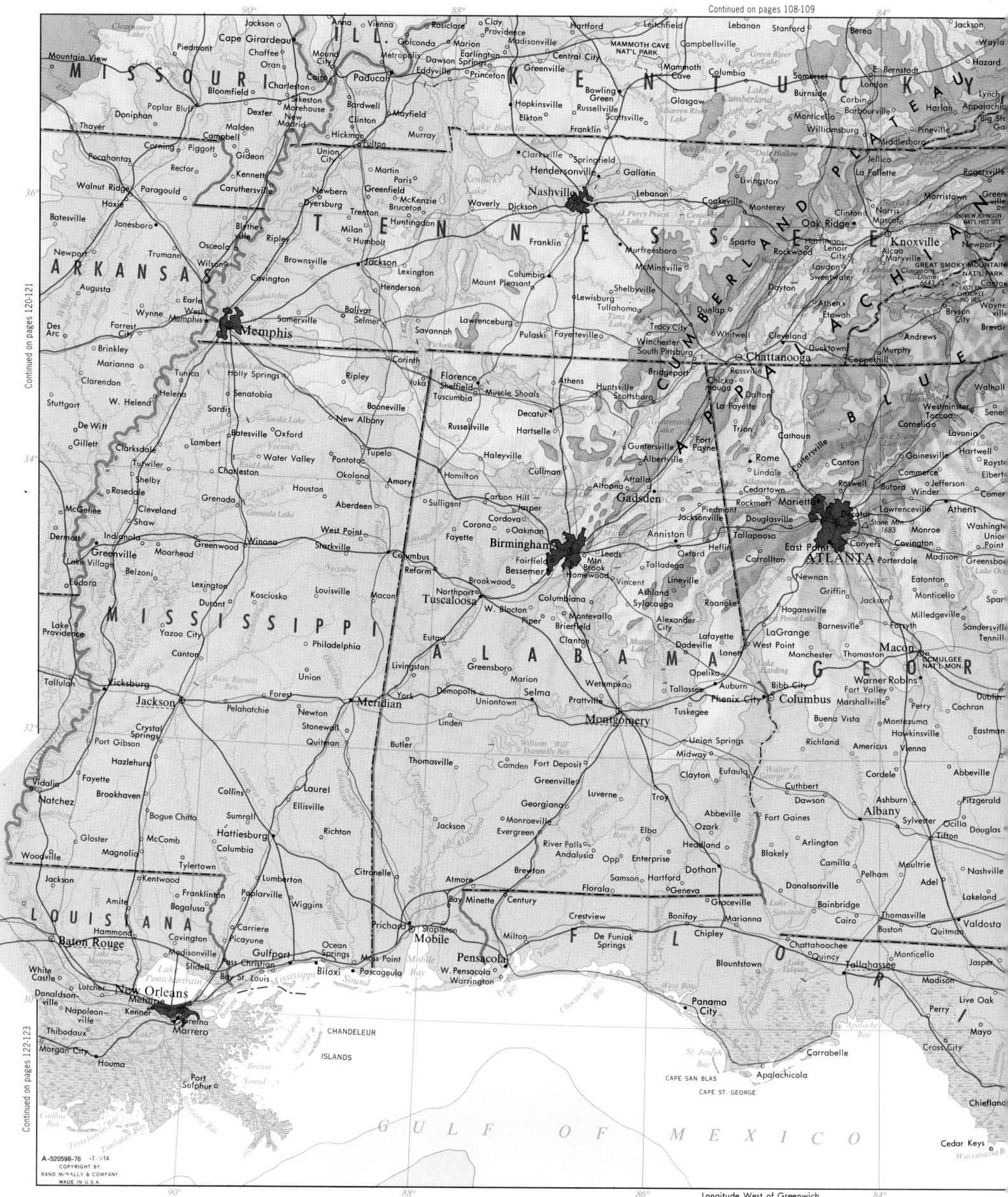

Continued on pages 108-109

Continued on pages 120-121

Continued on pages 122-123

A-520598-76  -7-7-14
COPYRIGHT BY
RAND McNALLY & COMPANY
MADE IN U.S.A.

Longitude West of Greenwich

Scale 1:4 000 000; one inch to 64 miles. Conic Projection
Elevations and depressions are given in feet

Relief

| Meters | | Feet |
|---|---|---|
| 1525 | | 5000 |
| 610 | | 2000 |
| 305 | | 1000 |
| 152.5 | | 500 |
| 0 | Sea Level | 0 |
| 152.5 | | 500 |
| 1525 | | 5000 |

Same scale as main map

a

0  20  40  60  80  100  120 Miles
0  20  40  60  80  100  120  140  160  180  200 Kilometers

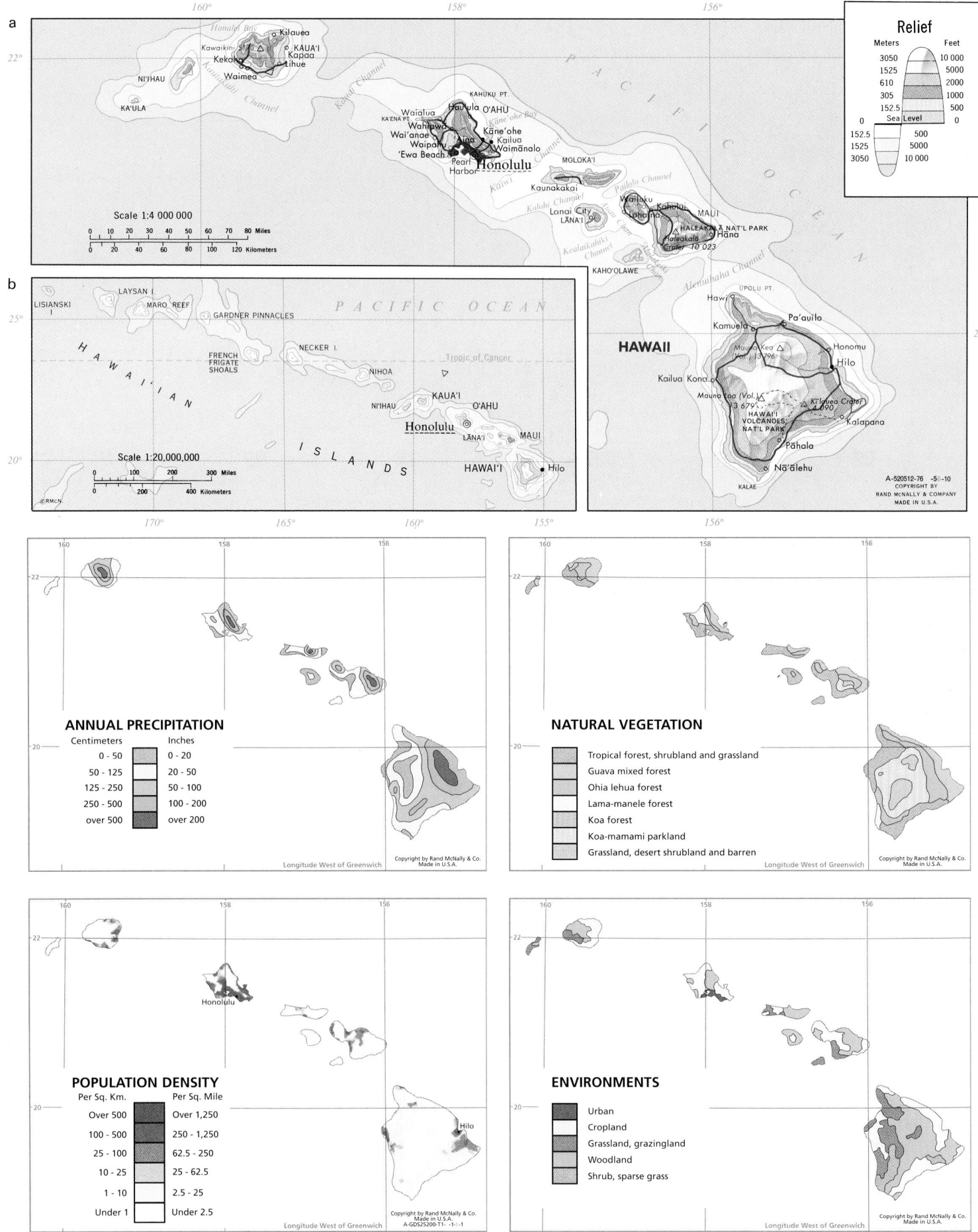

a

**Relief**

| Meters | | Feet |
|---|---|---|
| 3050 | | 10 000 |
| 1525 | | 5000 |
| 610 | | 2000 |
| 305 | | 1000 |
| 152.5 | | 500 |
| 0 | Sea Level | 0 |
| 152.5 | | 500 |
| 1525 | | 5000 |
| 3050 | | 10 000 |

Scale 1:4 000 000

b

Scale 1:20,000,000

HAWAII

**ANNUAL PRECIPITATION**

| Centimeters | Inches |
|---|---|
| 0 - 50 | 0 - 20 |
| 50 - 125 | 20 - 50 |
| 125 - 250 | 50 - 100 |
| 250 - 500 | 100 - 200 |
| over 500 | over 200 |

**NATURAL VEGETATION**

Tropical forest, shrubland and grassland
Guava mixed forest
Ohia lehua forest
Lama-manele forest
Koa forest
Koa-mamami parkland
Grassland, desert shrubland and barren

**POPULATION DENSITY**

| Per Sq. Km. | Per Sq. Mile |
|---|---|
| Over 500 | Over 1,250 |
| 100 - 500 | 250 - 1,250 |
| 25 - 100 | 62.5 - 250 |
| 10 - 25 | 25 - 62.5 |
| 1 - 10 | 2.5 - 25 |
| Under 1 | Under 2.5 |

**ENVIRONMENTS**

Urban
Cropland
Grassland, grazingland
Woodland
Shrub, sparse grass

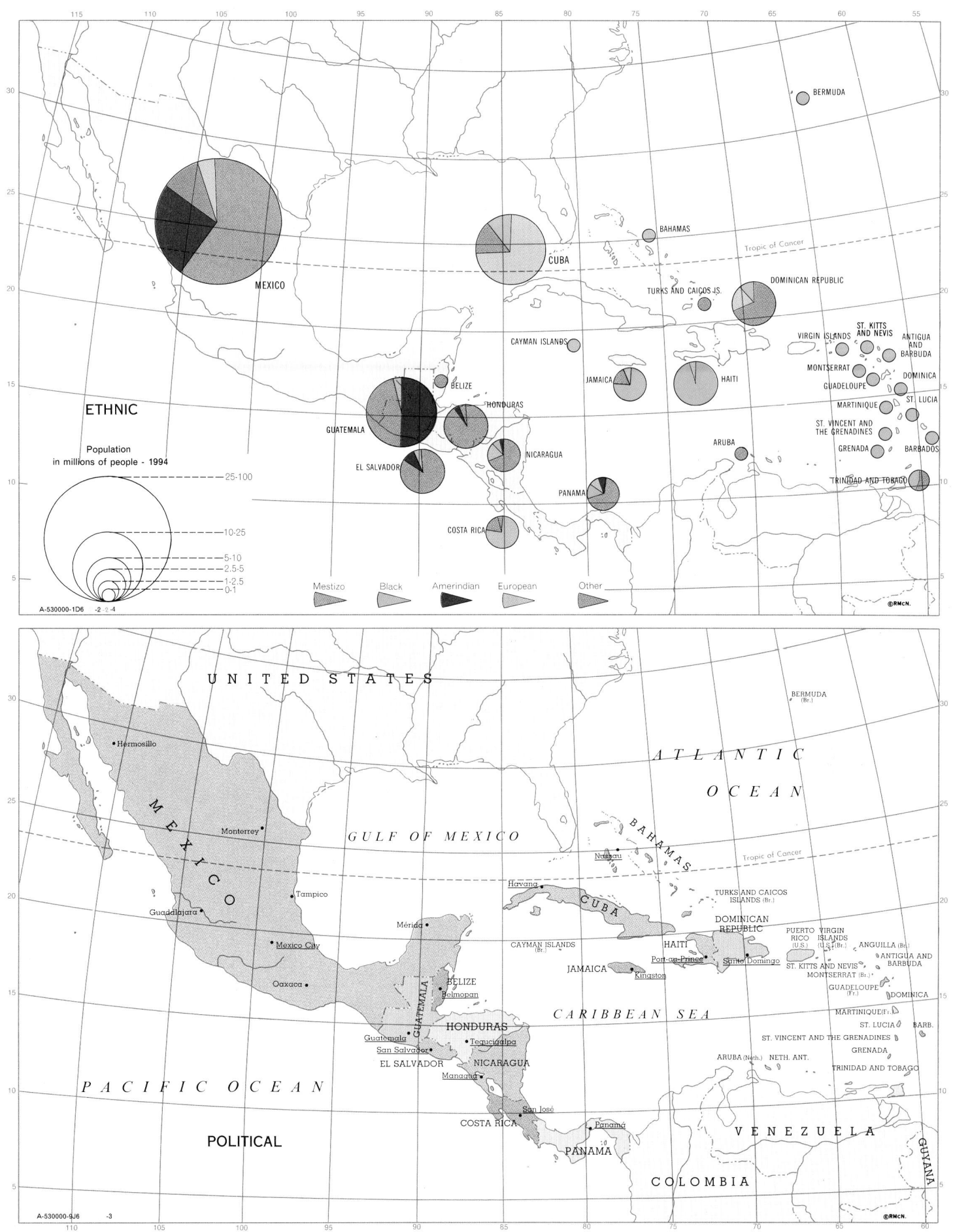

ETHNIC

Population
in millions of people - 1994

25-100
10-25
5-10
2.5-5
1-2.5
0-1

A-530000-1D6    -2 -2 -4

Mestizo    Black    Amerindian    European    Other

MEXICO

BERMUDA

BAHAMAS

CUBA

TURKS AND CAICOS IS.

DOMINICAN REPUBLIC

CAYMAN ISLANDS

VIRGIN ISLANDS    ST. KITTS
AND NEVIS    ANTIGUA
AND
BARBUDA

BELIZE

HONDURAS

GUATEMALA

EL SALVADOR

NICARAGUA

JAMAICA

HAITI

MONTSERRAT    DOMINICA
GUADELOUPE
MARTINIQUE    ST. LUCIA
ST. VINCENT AND
THE GRENADINES
GRENADA    BARBADOS

PANAMA

ARUBA

TRINIDAD AND TOBAGO

COSTA RICA

©RMCN.

POLITICAL

UNITED STATES

• Hermosillo

M E X I C O

• Monterrey

GULF OF MEXICO

BERMUDA
(Br.)

ATLANTIC

OCEAN

• Tampico

• Guadalajara

• Mexico City

• Mérida

• Oaxaca

Nassau

BAHAMAS

Tropic of Cancer

Havana

CUBA

TURKS AND CAICOS
ISLANDS (Br.)

CAYMAN ISLANDS
(Br.)

JAMAICA

HAITI

Port-au-Prince

DOMINICAN
REPUBLIC

Santo Domingo

Kingston

PUERTO    VIRGIN
RICO    ISLANDS
(U.S.)    (U.S.)(Br.)

ST. KITTS AND NEVIS (Br.)

ANGUILLA (Br.)

ANTIGUA AND
BARBUDA

MONTSERRAT (Br.)

GUADELOUPE
(Fr.)

DOMINICA

CARIBBEAN SEA

MARTINIQUE(Fr.)

ST. LUCIA    BARB.

ST. VINCENT AND THE GRENADINES

GRENADA

BELIZE
Belmopan

GUATEMALA

HONDURAS

• Tegucigalpa

Guatemala
San Salvador
EL SALVADOR    NICARAGUA

Managua

PACIFIC OCEAN

COSTA RICA

San José

ARUBA (Neth.)    NETH. ANT.

TRINIDAD AND TOBAGO

V E N E Z U E L A

Panamá

PANAMA

COLOMBIA

G
U
Y
A
N
A

A-530000-9J6    -3    ©RMCN.

128

Scale 1:16 000 000; one inch to 250 miles. Polyconic Projection
Elevations and depressions are given in feet

b

c

Continued on pages 142-143

**Relief**

| Meters | Feet |
|---|---|
| 3050 | 10 000 |
| 1525 | 5000 |
| 610 | 2000 |
| 305 | 1000 |
| 152.5 | 500 |
| Sea Level | 0 |
| 152.5 | 500 |
| 1525 | 5000 |
| 3050 | 10 000 |
| 6100 | 20 000 |

**Cities and Towns**

| | |
|---|---|
| 0 to 50,000 | ○ |
| 50,000 to 500,000 | ⊙ |
| 500,000 to 1,000,000 | ◎ |
| 1,000,000 and over | |

Continued on pages 122-123

**Relief**

| Meters | | Feet |
|---|---|---|
| 3050 | | 10 000 |
| 1525 | | 5000 |
| 610 | | 2000 |
| 305 | | 1000 |
| 152.5 | | 500 |
| 0 | Sea Level | 0 |
| 152.5 | | 500 |
| 1525 | | 5000 |
| 3050 | | 10 000 |

A-531695-76  6-15
COPYRIGHT BY
RAND MCNALLY & COMPANY
MADE IN U.S.A.

Longitude West of Greenwich

**Cities and Towns**

0 to 50,000  o
50,000 to 500,000  ⊙
500,000 to 1,000,000  ◎
1,000,000 and over

Scale 1:4 000 000; one inch to 64 miles. Conic Projection
Elevations and depressions are given in feet

a

Continued on pages 132-133

## Inset map (Mexico City area)

MÉXICO

Morelos
Nicolás Romero
Cuautitlán
Tutitlán
Tecamac
Teotihuacán
Otumba
HIDALGO
Cahuacán
Coacalco
Acolman
Chiconautla
Pyramids of Teotihuacán
San Bartolo
Atizapán
Tlalnepantla
Tepexpan
Calpulalpan
Ixtlahuaca
Jiquipilco
Cerro La Catedral 13 000
Mazatla
Tulpetlac
Tepetlaoxtoc
TLAXCALA
Temoaya
Atzcapotzalco
Naucalpan de Juárez
Gustavo A. Madero
San Jerónimo
Texcoco
Nanacamilpa
Mimiapan
Chimalpa
**MEXICO CITY**
Coatlinchán
Chicoloapan
Mexicaltzingo
Toluca
Huixquilucan
Cuajimalpa
Ixtacalco
Ixtapalapa
Los Reyes
Nezahualcóyotl
Río Frío
HY
Lerma
Capultitlán
Villa Obregón
Contreras
Ayotla
Ixtapaluca
INTER-AMERICAN
Texmelucan
Metepec
Mexicalcingo
Tlalpan
Xochimilco
Tláhuac
Chalco
Tlalmanalco
PUEBLA
Ajusco
San Andrés
Cerro Muneca 12 655
Almoloya
DISTRITO FEDERAL
Topilejo
Tecómitl
Milpa Alta
Iztaccihuatl 17 343
Nevado de Toluca 14 409
Cerro Ajusco 12 850
Oxtotepec
Tenango
Amecameca
Coatepec
Tenango
Tres Cumbres
Ozumba
Volcán Popocatépetl 17 887
Huitzilac
Tepoztlán
Tlalnepantla
MORELOS
Tlayacapan
Cuernavaca

Scale 1:1 000 000
0 5 10 Miles
0 4 8 12 16 Kilometers
©RMcN.

## Main map

Tropic of Cancer
Laguna Almagre
PTA JEREZ
Laguna de San Andres
Altamira
Ciudad Madero
Tampico
Villa Cuauhtémoc
Tampico Alto
Laguna Tamiahua
zuluama
Tancoco
Tamiahua
CABO ROJO
ARRECIFE BLANQUILLA
ISLA DE LOBOS
ARRECIFE TANQUIJO
ARRECIFE TÚXPAN
Tihuatlán
Alamo
Túxpan
Poza Rica
Tecolutla
Gutiérrez Zamora
capalapa
Furbero
Nautla
Coyutla
Coxquihui
eytlapan
Vega de Alatorre
Cuetzalan del Progreso
Tlapacoyan
capoaxtla
Atempan
Teziutlán
Juilacingo
Misantla
Las Vigas
Altotonga
Perote
Naolinco
Libres
Xalapa
14 048 Cofre de Perote
BAHÍA DE CAMPECHE
PUNTA ZEMPOALA
Coatepec
amantla
Teocelo
Antigua Veracruz
San Juan Ixtenco
Huatusco
Ciudad Serdán
Coscomatepec
Pico de Orizaba (Vol.) 18 406
Veracruz
ARRECIFE CABEZA
eaca
Orizaba
Córdoba
Medellín
Acatzingo de Hidalgo
Heroica Nogales
Omealca
Tlalixcoyan
Atoyatempan
Maltrata
Cotaxtla
Tlacotepec
Tehuacan
Tierra Blanca
ISLA DEL CARMEN
CAMPECHE
San Gabriel Chilac
Ajalpan
San Martín (Vol.) 6000
PTA. ZAPOTITLÁN
San Pedro
Ciudad del Carmen
Chicbul
Zoquitlán
Tlacotalpan
Santiago Tuxtla
PUNTA FONTERA
Chazumba
Huatla de Jiménez
Ojitlán (S. Lucas)
San Andrés Tuxtla
Paraíso
Frontera
Mamantel
Palizada
Pátlacingo
S. Miguel Teotitlán del Camino
Jalapa de Díaz (San Felipe)
Tuxtepec
Catemaco
Pajapan
Cosamaloápan
Chacaltianguis
Coatzacoalcos (Puerto México)
Comalcalco
Jalpa
Januta
Huajuapan de León
Tesechoacan
Soteapan
Cosoleacaque
Cunduacán
Cárdenas
Coixtlahuaca
Tejúpan (Santiago)
San Juan Evangelista
Jaltipan
Minatitlán
Texistepec
Villahermosa
San Carlos
Balancán
mazulapan
el Progreso
Cuicatlán
Acayucan
Sayula
Huimanguillo
Tacotalpa
Emiliano Zapata
MEXICO
Pedro y San Pablo
Nochixtlán (Asunción)
Playa Vicente
Pichucalco
Teapa
Palenque
Tenosique
GUATEMALA
Tlaxiaco
Sta. María Asunción
Ixtlán de Juárez
Villa Alta (San Ildefonso)
Talea de Castro (San Miguel)
Jesús Carranza
Puebla Viejo
Chapultenango
Yajalón
Hidalgo Yalalag
Zempoaltepetl 11 142
Zacatepec (Santiago)
ISTMO
Tecpatán
Pantepec
Simojovel
Bachajón
tla de uerrero
Chalcatongo
San Mateo (Etlatongo)
Oaxaca
Tlacolula de Matamoros
Mazatlán (San Juan)
Guichicovi (San Juan)
DE
Berriozabal
Compainá
Jitotol
Ococingo
Yosonotu
Zaachila
Zimatlán de Alvarez
Ocotlán de Morelos
Tuxtla Gutiérrez
9400
Cancuc
Oxchuc
San Cristóbal de las Casas
MESETA DE AGUA ESCONDIDA
ndujia Sta. Cruz
Sola de Vega (S. Miguel)
Táviche
INTER-AMERICAN HY
Ixtepec
Ixtaltepec (Asunción)
Zanatepec (Sto. Domingo)
Unión Hidalgo
Cintalapa
Las Cruces
TEHUANTEPEC
Orozocoautla
Chiapa de Corzo
Acala
Amatenango
CHIAPAS
uazolotitlán (Sta. Marta)
omiltepec
Ejutla de Crespo
Jalapa del Marqués
Las Vacas
Juchitán de Zaragoza
Tehuantepec Sto. Domingo
Ixhuatán (San Francisco)
6202
Villa Flores
Venustiano Carranza
Las Rosas
Teopisca
Comitán
SIERRA DE OAXACA
Miahuatlán
Laguna Superior
Laguna Inferior
Tapanatepec
Arriaga
La Concordia
Socoltenango
Trinitaria
Loxicha (Sta. Catarina)
Salina Cruz
Golfo de Tehuantepec
Tonalá
SIERRA MADRE
SA CUCHUMATANES
Pluma Hidalgo
Pochutla (San Pedro)
Puerto Ángel
CORD. DE CHIAPAS
Cuauhtémoc
Jacatenango
GUATEMALA
Pijijiapan
Mapastepec

YUCATÁN
Sisal
Hunucmá
Maxcanú
Halachó
Calkiní
Dzitbalché
Hecelchakán
Lerma
Campeche
Seybaplaya
Champotón
Pustunich
Sabancuy
Palenque

0 20 40 60 80 100 120 Miles
0 20 40 60 80 100 120 140 160 180 200 Kilometers

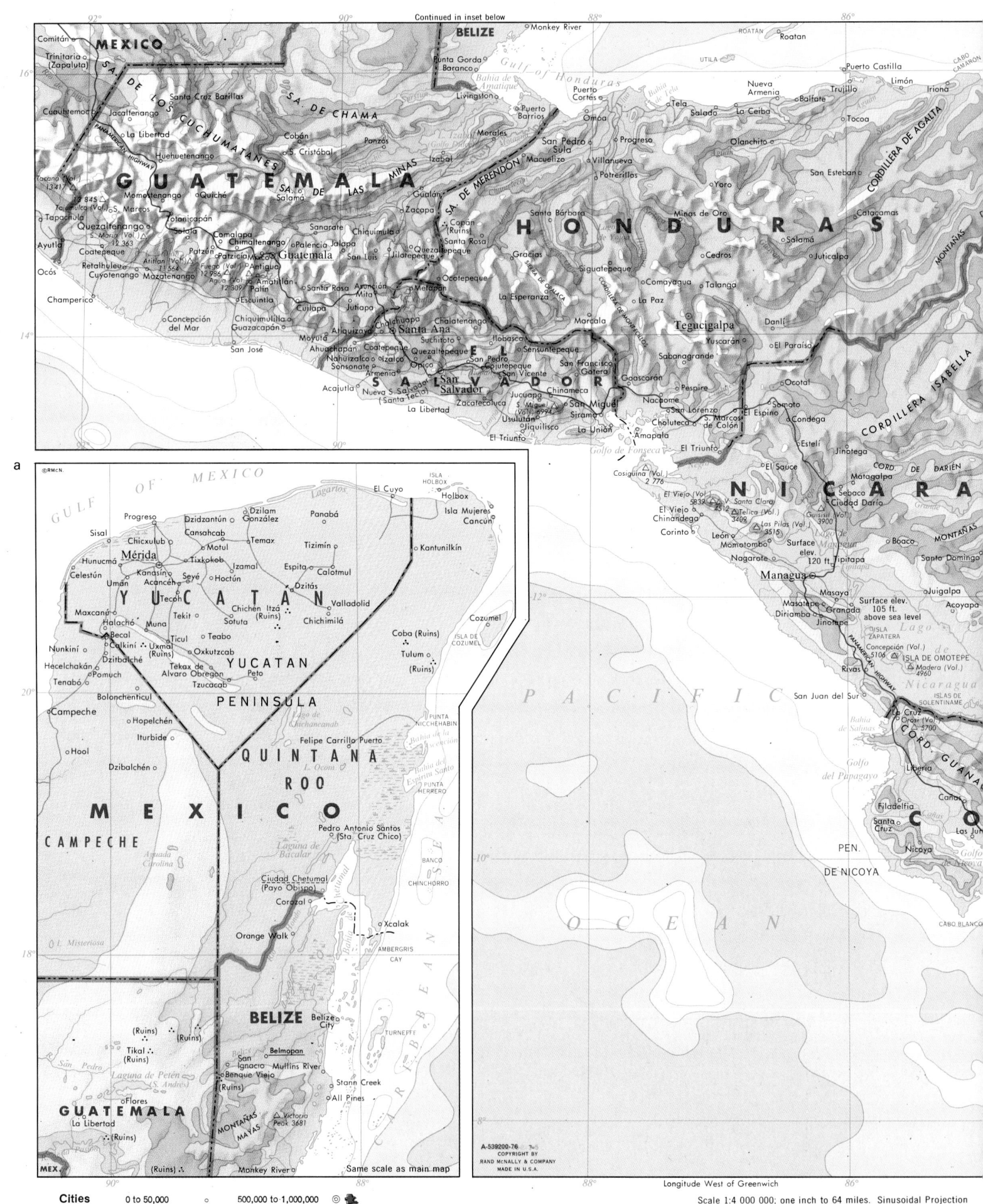

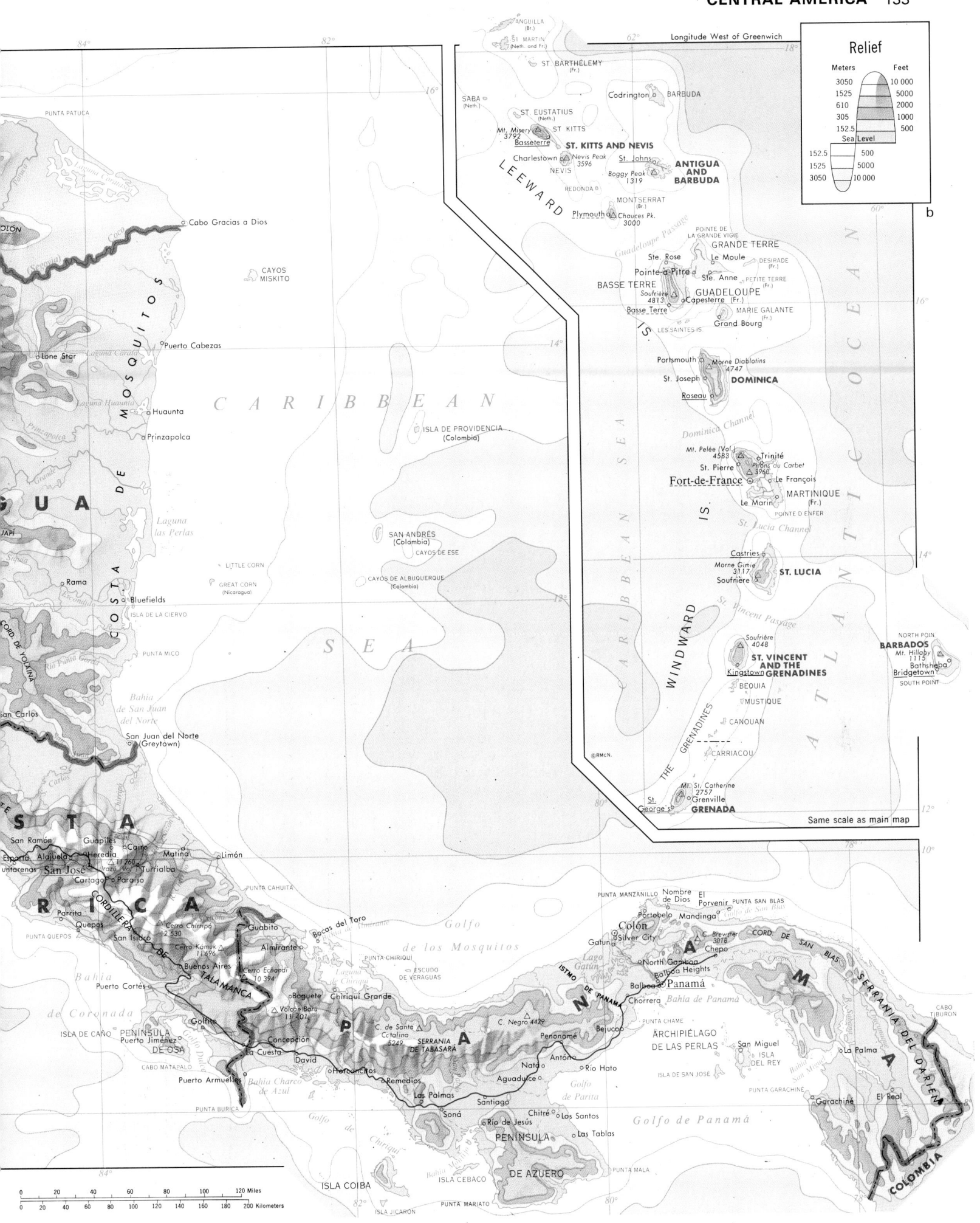

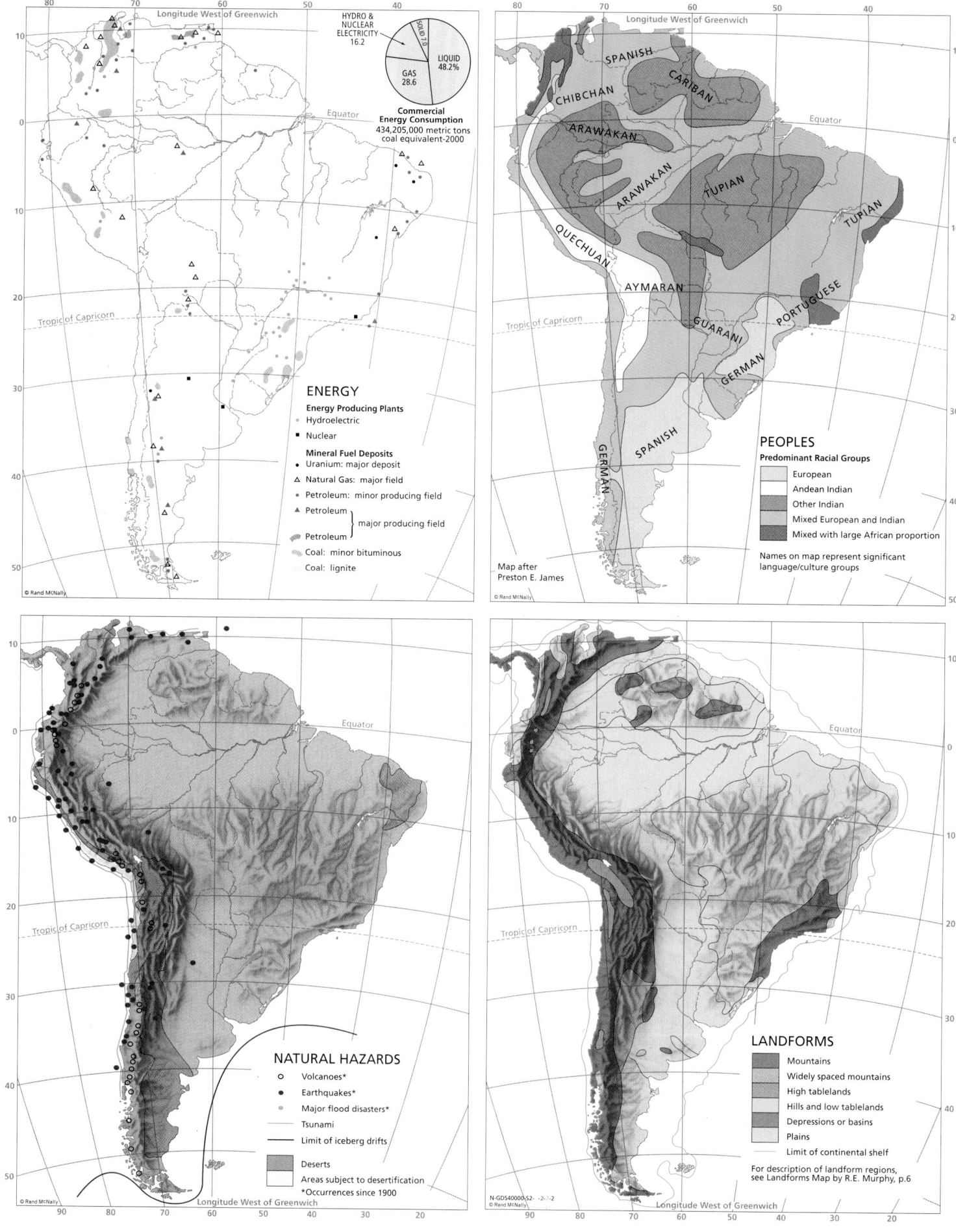

## ENERGY

**Energy Producing Plants**
- Hydroelectric
■ Nuclear

**Mineral Fuel Deposits**
• Uranium: major deposit
△ Natural Gas: major field
• Petroleum: minor producing field
▲ Petroleum } major producing field
Petroleum
Coal: minor bituminous
Coal: lignite

HYDRO & NUCLEAR ELECTRICITY 16.2
SOLID 7.0
LIQUID 48.2%
GAS 28.6

**Commercial Energy Consumption**
434,205,000 metric tons coal equivalent-2000

© Rand McNally

## PEOPLES

**Predominant Racial Groups**
- European
- Andean Indian
- Other Indian
- Mixed European and Indian
- Mixed with large African proportion

Names on map represent significant language/culture groups

Map after Preston E. James

© Rand McNally

SPANISH
CHIBCHAN
CARIBAN
ARAWAKAN
ARAWAKAN
TUPIAN
TUPIAN
QUECHUAN
AYMARAN
GUARANI
PORTUGUESE
GERMAN
GERMAN
SPANISH

## NATURAL HAZARDS

○ Volcanoes*
● Earthquakes*
● Major flood disasters*
Tsunami
Limit of iceberg drifts
Deserts
Areas subject to desertification
*Occurrences since 1900

© Rand McNally

## LANDFORMS

- Mountains
- Widely spaced mountains
- High tablelands
- Hills and low tablelands
- Depressions or basins
- Plains
- Limit of continental shelf

For description of landform regions, see Landforms Map by R.E. Murphy, p.6

N-GDS40000-S2- -2->-2
© Rand McNally

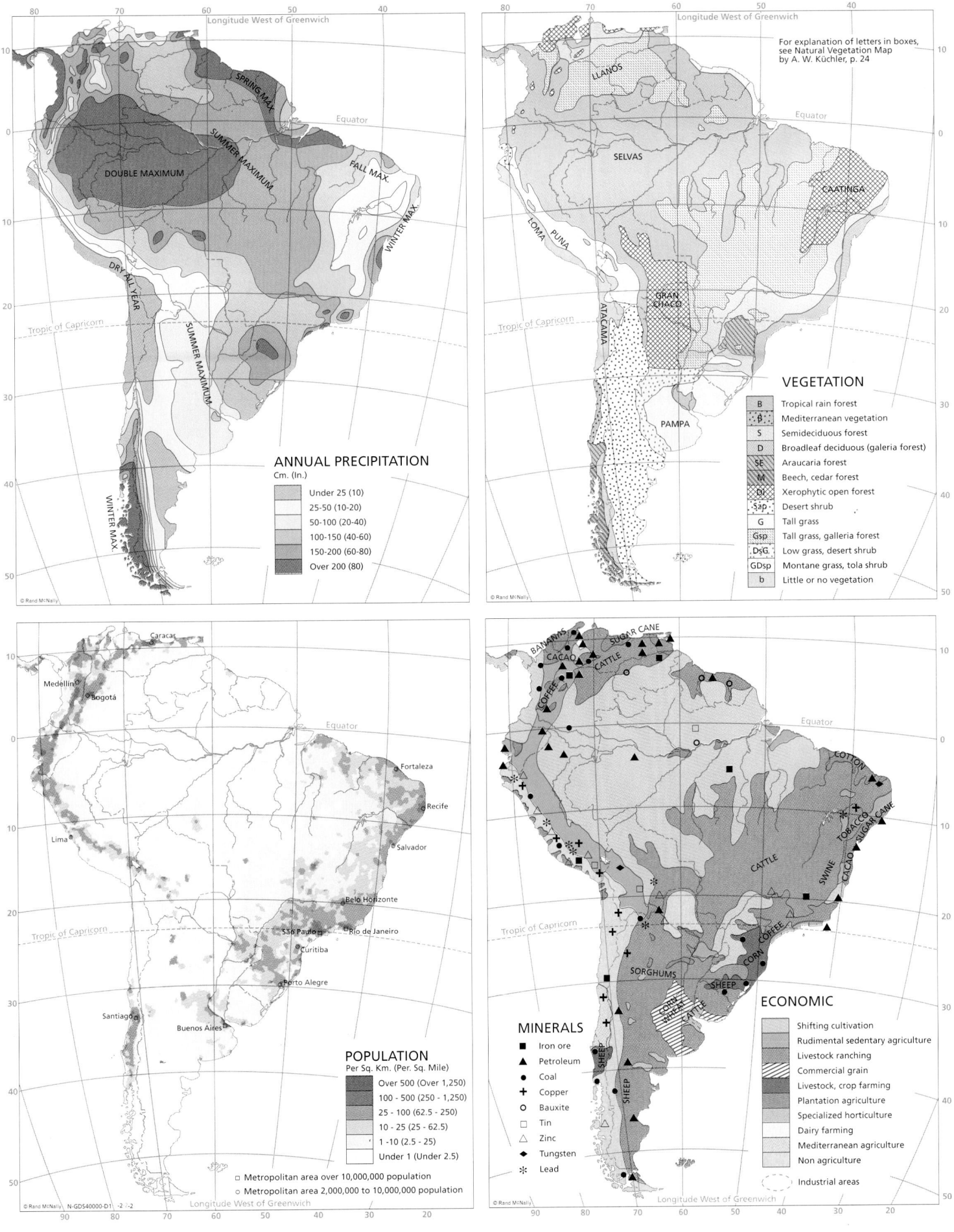

## ANNUAL PRECIPITATION
Cm. (In.)

- Under 25 (10)
- 25-50 (10-20)
- 50-100 (20-40)
- 100-150 (40-60)
- 150-200 (60-80)
- Over 200 (80)

SPRING MAX.
SUMMER MAXIMUM
FALL MAX.
WINTER MAX.
DOUBLE MAXIMUM
DRY ALL YEAR
SUMMER MAXIMUM
WINTER MAX.

© Rand McNally

## VEGETATION

For explanation of letters in boxes, see Natural Vegetation Map by A. W. Küchler, p. 24

| B | Tropical rain forest |
| β | Mediterranean vegetation |
| S | Semideciduous forest |
| D | Broadleaf deciduous (galeria forest) |
| SE | Araucaria forest |
| M | Beech, cedar forest |
| Dl | Xerophytic open forest |
| Sap | Desert shrub |
| G | Tall grass |
| Gsp | Tall grass, galleria forest |
| DsG | Low grass, desert shrub |
| GDsp | Montane grass, tola shrub |
| b | Little or no vegetation |

LLANOS
SELVAS
CAATINGA
LOMA
PUNA
ATACAMA
GRAN CHACO
PAMPA

© Rand McNally

## POPULATION
Per Sq. Km. (Per. Sq. Mile)

- Over 500 (Over 1,250)
- 100 - 500 (250 - 1,250)
- 25 - 100 (62.5 - 250)
- 10 - 25 (25 - 62.5)
- 1 -10 (2.5 - 25)
- Under 1 (Under 2.5)

□ Metropolitan area over 10,000,000 population
○ Metropolitan area 2,000,000 to 10,000,000 population

Caracas
Medellín
Bogotá
Lima
Fortaleza
Recife
Salvador
Belo Horizonte
São Paulo
Rio de Janeiro
Curitiba
Santiago
Porto Alegre
Buenos Aires

© Rand McNally   N-GDS40000-D1

## MINERALS

- ■ Iron ore
- ▲ Petroleum
- ● Coal
- + Copper
- ○ Bauxite
- □ Tin
- △ Zinc
- ◆ Tungsten
- ✳ Lead

## ECONOMIC

- Shifting cultivation
- Rudimental sedentary agriculture
- Livestock ranching
- Commercial grain
- Livestock, crop farming
- Plantation agriculture
- Specialized horticulture
- Dairy farming
- Mediterranean agriculture
- Non agriculture
- Industrial areas

BANANAS
CACAO
COFFEE
SUGAR CANE
CATTLE
COTTON
TOBACCO
SUGAR CANE
CACAO
SWINE
CATTLE
COFFEE
CORN
SORGHUMS
SHEEP
CORN WHEAT
CATTLE
SHEEP

© Rand McNally

HAVANA

NORTH AMERICAN BASIN

Tropic of Cancer

Bahía de Campeche

PEN. DE YUCATÁN

Yucatán Channel

Windward Passage

HISPANIOLA

San Juan
PUERTO RICO
(U.S.A.)

PUERTO RICO TRENCH

GUADELOUPE (Fr.)
MARTINIQUE (Fr.)

BARBADOS

ATLANTIC
OCEAN

JAMAICA

Gulf of Honduras

CARIBBEAN   SEA

W E S T   I N D I E S

CENTRAL

Lago de Nicaragua

Panamá
IST. DE PAN.

Golfo del Darién

Golfo de Panamá

Barranquilla
Cartagena

PUNTA DE GALLINAS

Maracaibo
La Guaira

Golfo de Venezuela

Valencia   CARACAS

TRINIDAD AND TOBAGO
Port of Spain

AMERICA

ISLA DEL COCO
(Costa Rica)

ISLA DE MALPELO
(Colombia)

Mérida

LLANOS

Ciudad Bolívar

Orinoco

VENEZUELA

Georgetown
Paramaribo

Medellín
Nevado del Tolima
17 110

BOGOTÁ

Cerro Icutú
7800

GUYANA

SURINAME   FR. GUIANA

Cayenne

COLOMBIA

Boa Vista do Rio Branco

GUIANA   HIGHLANDS

Quito

Guaviare

ILHA DE MARAJÓ

Equator

ROCEDOS SÃO PEDRO E SÃO PAULO
(Brazil)

ECUADOR
Cotopaxi 19 347

Japurá

Negro

Manaus
(Manáos)

Amazon (Amazonas)

Belém
(Pará)

São Luís
(Maranhão)

ARCHIPIÉLAGO DE COLÓN
(GALÁPAGOS ISLANDS)
(Ec.)

Guayaquil   Chimborazo 20 702

Golfo de Guayaquil

Iquitos

Letícia

(Solimões)

Juruá

Purús

Madeira

Tapajós

Xingu

Fortaleza
(Ceará)

ARQUIPÉLAGO FERNANDO DE NORONHA
(Brazil)

Chiclayo

Trujillo
Nevs. Huascarán 22 133

P E R U

A N D E S

LIMA

Río Branco

Porto Velho

Tocantins

Rio

Teresina

Natal
João Pessoa (Paraíba)

CABO DE SÃO ROQUE

B R A Z I L

SERRA DO PIAUÍ

RECIFE (Pernambuco)

Callao   Cusco

CHAPADA DE MATO GROSSO

B R A Z I L I A N

Salto São Apolo

Maceió

Arequipa
Volcán Misti

La Paz
Nev. Illimani
20 741

BOLIVIA

Cuiabá

Brasília

Salvador
(Bahía)

Mollendo

Sucre
Potosí

Pilcomayo

H I G H L A N D S

Diamantina

Belo Horizonte

Pico da Bandeira

ISLA DE SAN FÉLIX
(Chile)

ISLA DE SAN AMBROSIO
(Chile)

Iquique

Lago de Titicaca

GRAN CHACO

PARAGUAY

Bermejo

SÃO PAULO

Vitória

Tropic of Capricorn

Antofagasta

DESIERTO DE ATACAMA

Salta

Asunción

Santos

CABO FRIO

RIO DE JANEIRO

PARAGUAY

Cerro Azufre 19 947

Tucumán

Paraná

Corrientes

Iguassú Falls

Florianópolis

Copiapó

FRENCH

A R G E N T I N A

Coquimbo

Córdoba

Santa Fe

Salto

Porto Alegre

Cerro Aconcagua 22 867

Valparaíso

Mendoza

Rosario

URUGUAY

Rio Grande

SANTIAGO

C H I L E

BUENOS AIRES

MONTEVIDEO

La Plata

Río de la Plata

Concepción

PAMPAS

A N D E S

Colorado

Bahía Blanca

Valdivia

Viedma

Puerto Montt

Golfo San Matías

ISLA DE CHILOÉ

ARCHIPIÉLAGO DE LOS CHONOS

A R G E N T I N A

Comodoro Rivadavia

Golfo San Jorge

Monte Valentín 13 314

FALKLAND IS.
(ISLAS MALVINAS)
(Br.)

WELLINGTON

Río Gallegos

Stanley

HANOVER

Estrecho de Magallanes

Punta Arenas

DESOLACIÓN

TIERRA DEL FUEGO

Mt. Sarmiento 8100

ISLA DE LOS ESTADOS

CABO DE HORNOS
(CAPE HORN)

SOUTH GEORGIA
(Br.)

Drake   Passage

SOUTH ORKNEY IS.
(Br.)

SOUTH SANDWICH ISLANDS
(Br.)

SOUTH SANDWICH TRENCH

40,000 SQ MI
AREA

0      300      600
Miles

SOUTH SHETLAND ISLANDS

JOINVILLE

ANTARCTIC PENINSULA

JAMES ROSS

Antarctic Circle

A-540000-26  -4-7-16
COPYRIGHT BY
RAND McNALLY & COMPANY
MADE IN U.S.A.

Longitude West of Greenwich

0    200    400    600    800    1000  Miles
0    400    800    1200   1600  Kilometers

Scale 1:40 000 000; one inch to 630 miles. Lambert's Azimuthal. Equal Area Projection
Elevations and depressions are given in feet

HAVANA

CENTRAL

AMERICA

ATLANTIC

OCEAN

Bahía de Campeche

PEN. DE YUCATÁN

Golfo de Honduras

HISPANIOLA

San Juan

PUERTO RICO (U.S.A.)

JAMAICA

GUADELOUPE (Fr.)

MARTINIQUE (Fr.)

W E S T

I N D I E S

CARIBBEAN SEA

NORTH AMERICAN BASIN

PUERTO RICO TRENCH

BARBADOS

PUNTA DE GALLINAS

Barranquilla

Cartagena

Maracaibo

La Guaira

Valencia

Mérida

VENEZUELA

Ciudad Bolívar

Cerro Yaví 7800

TRINIDAD AND TOBAGO

Port of Spain

CARACAS

Panamá

IST. DE PAN.

Golfo de Panamá

Medellín

BOGOTÁ

Nevado del Tolima 17 110

Georgetown

Paramaribo

Cayenne

GUYANA

SURINAME

FR. GUIANA

ISLA DEL COCO (Costa Rica)

ISLA DE MALPELO (Colombia)

COLOMBIA

Boa Vista do Rio Branco

GUIANA HIGHLANDS

ILHA DE MARAJÓ

Belém (Pará)

São Luís (Maranhão)

Equator

ROCEDOS SÃO PEDRO E SÃO PAULO (Brazil)

ARCHIPIÉLAGO DE COLÓN (GALÁPAGOS ISLANDS) (Ec.)

Quito

Cotopaxi 19 347

ECUADOR

Chimborazo 20 702

Guayaquil

Golfo de Guayaquil

Iquitos

Leticia

Manaus (Manáos)

Amazon (Amazonas)

Fortaleza (Ceará)

ARQUIPÉLAGO FERNANDO DE NORONHA (Brazil)

Chiclayo

Trujillo

Nevs. Huascarán 22 133

PERU

LIMA

Callao

Cusco

A N D E S

Porto Velho

Rio Branco

Teresina

CABO DE SÃO ROQUE

Natal

João Pessoa (Paraíba)

RECIFE (Pernambuco)

Maceió

B R A Z I L

CHAPADA DE MATO GROSSO

Cuiabá

Brasília

Diamantina

Belo Horizonte

Salvador (Bahia)

B R A Z I L I A N   H I G H L A N D S

Volcán Misti 19 101

Arequipa

Mollendo

La Paz

Nev. Illiman 20 741

BOLIVIA

Sucre

Potosí

Vitória

Pico da Bandeira 9482

PACIFIC

OCEAN

ISLA DE SAN FÉLIX (Chile)

ISLA DE SAN AMBROSIO (Chile)

Tropic of Capricorn

Antofagasta

Salta

Tucumán

GRAN CHACO

PARAGUAY

Asunción

Corrientes

Iguassú Falls

SÃO PAULO

Santos

RIO DE JANEIRO

CABO FRIO

Florianópolis

Copiapó

Coquimbo

Córdoba

Rosario

Santa Fe

Salto

URUGUAY

Rio Grande

Porto Alegre

ISLAS DE JUAN FERNÁNDEZ (Chile)

Valparaíso

SANTIAGO

Mendoza

BUENOS AIRES

La Plata

MONTEVIDEO

Cerro Aconcagua 22 831

A R G E N T I N A

PAMPAS

Concepción

Bahía Blanca

Valdivia

Viedma

Golfo San Matías

Puerto Montt

ISLA DE CHILOÉ

A N D E S   M T S.

Comodoro Rivadavia

Golfo San Jorge

ARCHIPIÉLAGO DE LOS CHONOS

Monte Valentín 13 314

ATLANTIC

OCEAN

WELLINGTON

HANOVER

DESOLACIÓN

Punta Arenas

Estrecho de Magallanes

Mt. Sarmiento 8100

Río Gallegos

FALKLAND IS. (ISLAS MALVINAS) (Br.)

Stanley

TIERRA DEL FUEGO

ISLA DE LOS ESTADOS

CABO DE HORNOS (CAPE HORN)

Drake Passage

SOUTH GEORGIA (Br.)

SOUTH SANDWICH ISLANDS (Br.)

SOUTH ORKNEY IS. (Br.)

SOUTH SHETLAND ISLANDS (Br.)

JOINVILLE

JAMES ROSS

Antarctic Circle

| Relief | | |
|---|---|---|
| Meters | | Feet |
| 3050 | | 10 000 |
| 1525 | | 5000 |
| 610 | | 2000 |
| 305 | | 1000 |
| 0 | Sea Level | 0 |
| 152.5 | | 500 |
| 1525 | | 5000 |
| 3050 | | 10 000 |
| 6100 | | 20 000 |

A-540000-76-3- -16

COPYRIGHT BY

RAND MCNALLY & COMPANY

MADE IN U.S.A.

Longitude West of Greenwich

0 200 400 600 800 1000 Miles

0 400 800 1200 1600 Kilometers

Scale 1:40 000 000; one inch to 630 miles. Lambert's Azimuthal, Equal Area Projection

Elevations and depressions are given in feet

ATLANTIC OCEAN

CUBA
JAMAICA
Kingston
HISPANIOLA
San Juan
PUERTO RICO

Caribbean Sea

Barranquilla
Maracaibo
CARACAS
Port of Spain
TRINIDAD
Panamá
LLANOS
Orinoco
Georgetown
BOGOTÁ
Quito
Negro
Equator
Belém
Iquitos
Amazon
Manaus
Fortaleza
S E L V A S
A
N
D
E
S
Rio Branco
São Francisco
Recife
LIMA
La Paz
Cuiabá
M A T O
G R O S S O
Brasília
Salvador
Iquique
G R A N   C H A C O
Belo Horizonte
Paraná
SÃO PAULO
Asunción
RIO DE JANEIRO
Tropic of Capricorn
San Miguel
de Tucumán
A
N
D
E
S
Porto Alegre
Córdoba
SANTIAGO
BUENOS AIRES
Montevideo
PACIFIC OCEAN
PAMPA
Bahía Blanca
ATLANTIC OCEAN
P
A
T
A
G
O
N
I
A
Puerto Montt
FALKLAND ISLANDS
Punta Arenas
TIERRA DEL FUEGO
SOUTH GEORGIA
Drake Passage

Urban
Cropland
Cropland & Woodland
Cropland & Grazing Land
Grassland, Grazing Land
Forest, Woodland
Swamp, Marshland
Shrub, Sparse Grass, Wasteland
Barren Land

A-540000-36
COPYRIGHT BY
RAND MCNALLY & COMPANY
MADE IN U.S.A.

Scale 1:36,000,000; one inch to 570 miles  Lambert Azimuthal Equal-Area Projection

0   100   200        400        600        800 Miles

0   150   300      600        900      1200 Kilometers

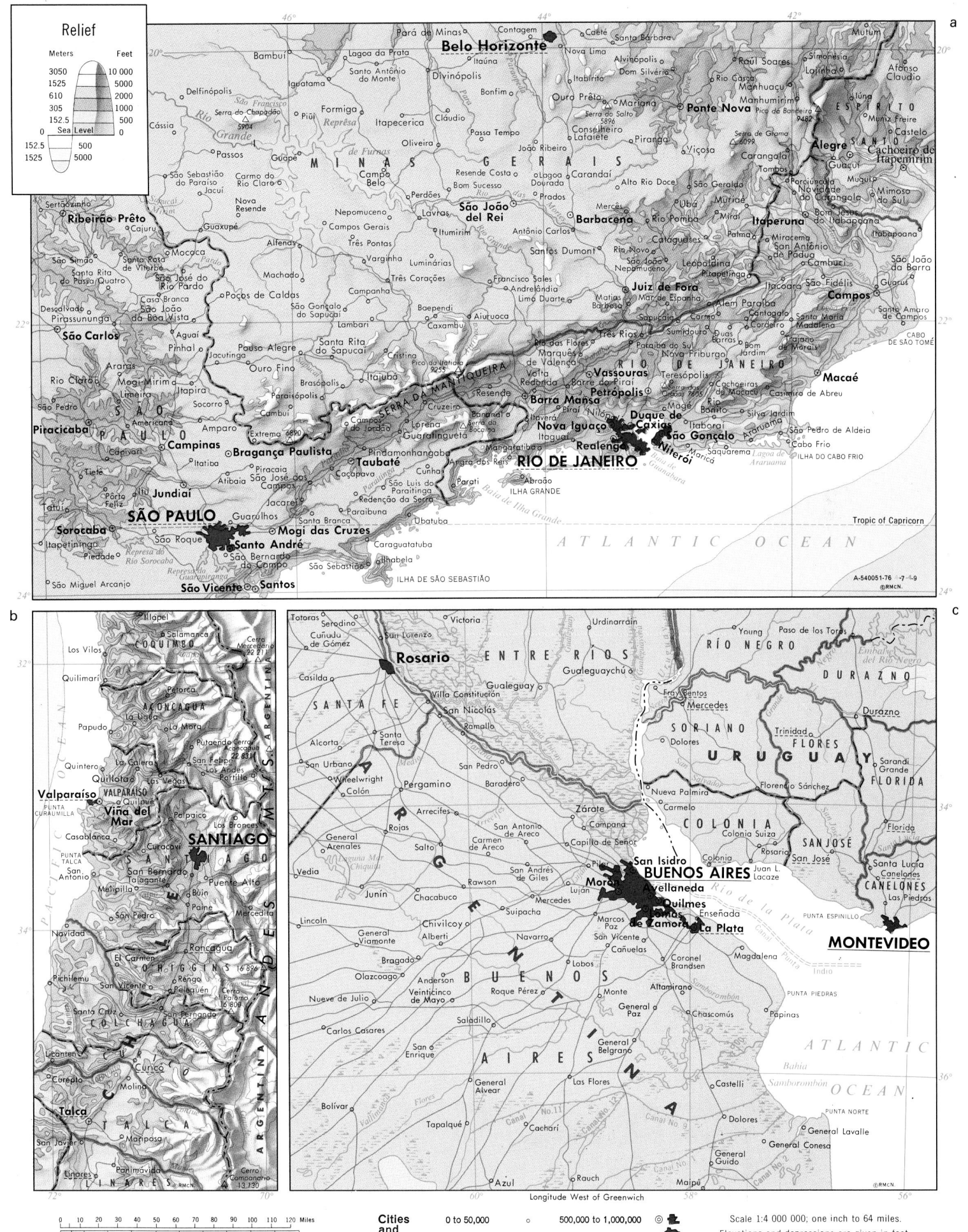

**Relief**

| Meters | Feet |
|---|---|
| 3050 | 10 000 |
| 1525 | 5000 |
| 610 | 2000 |
| 305 | 1000 |
| 152.5 | 500 |
| 0 Sea Level | 0 |
| 152.5 | 500 |
| 1525 | 5000 |

3904

a

0  10  20  30  40  50  60  70  80  90  100  110  120 Miles
0   20    40    60    80   100   120   140   160   180  200 Kilometers

**Cities and Towns**

0 to 50,000 ○
50,000 to 500,000 ⊙
500,000 to 1,000,000 ◉
1,000,000 and over

Scale 1:4 000 000; one inch to 64 miles.
Elevations and depressions are given in feet.

Longitude West of Greenwich

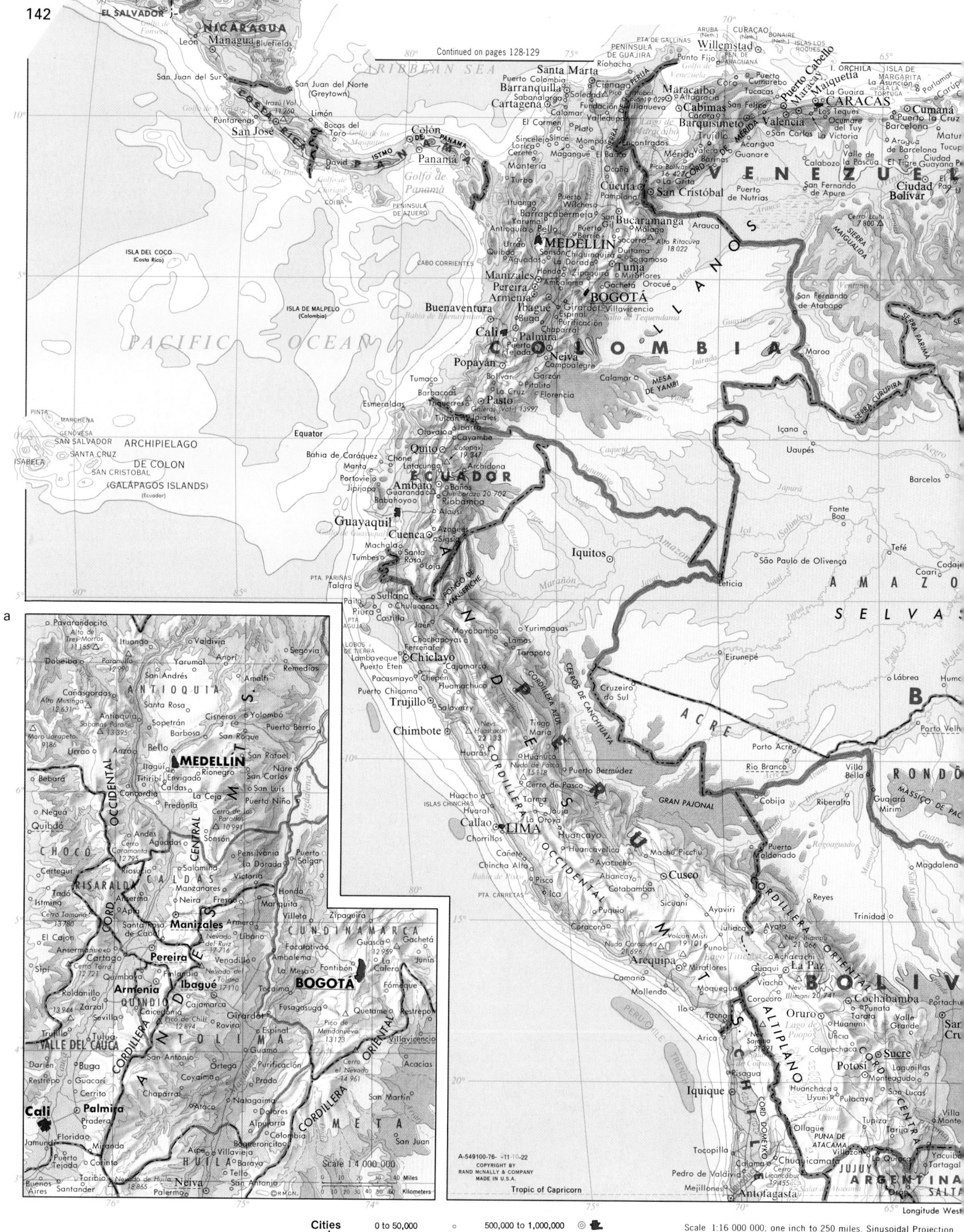

EL SALVADOR

NICARAGUA

Managua
León
Bluefields

San Juan del Sur

San Juan del Norte
(Greytown)

CARIBBEAN SEA

Continued on pages 128-129

Puntarenas
Irazú (Vol.)
11 260

San José

Limón

COSTA RICA

Bocas del Toro

Golfo de los Mosquitos

Colón
PANAMA
Panamá

Golfó de Panamá

PENINSULA DE AZUERO

COIBA

CABO CORRIENTES

ISLA DEL COCO
(Costa Rica)

ISLA DE MALPELO
(Colombia)

PACIFIC OCEAN

PINTA
MARCHENA
GENOVESA
SAN SALVADOR
SANTA CRUZ
SAN CRISTOBAL
ISABELA

ARCHIPIELAGO DE COLON
(GALÁPAGOS ISLANDS)
(Ecuador)

Equator

PTA. GALLINAS
PENÍNSULA DE GUAJIRA

ARUBA (Neth.)
CURAÇAO (Neth.)
BONAIRE (Neth.)
ISLAS LOS ROQUES
I. ORCHILA
ISLA DE MARGARITA

Willemstad
Punto Fijo
PEN. DE PARAGUANÁ

Santa Marta
Riohacha
Puerto Colombia
Barranquilla
Sabanalarga
Cartagena
Calamar

Cumarebo
Pico Cristóbal
Fundación
Valledupar
El Carmen
Plato
Sincelejo
Magangué
El Banco
Lorica
Cereté
Mompós
Montería
Turbo

Maracaibo
Altagracia
Cabimas
San Felipe
Coro

La Asunción
La Guaira
Maiquetía

Puerto Cabello
Maracay
CARACAS
Los Teques

Cumaná
Puerto La Cruz
Barcelona

Barquisimeto
Valencia
San Carlos
La Victoria

Acarigua
Guanare
Calabozo
Valle de la Pascua
El Tigre
Ciudad Guayana

VENEZUELA

Ituango
Barrancabermeja
Bello
Antioquia
Quibdó

MEDELLÍN
Sonsón
Chiquinquirá
La Dorada
Aguadas
Honda

Bucaramanga
Málaga
Arauca
Puerto Berrío
Socorro
Duitama
Alto Ritacuva 18 022

Cúcuta
Pamplona
San Cristóbal
Puerto de Nutrias

San Fernando de Apure

Ciudad Bolívar

Manizales
Pereira
Armenia
Ambalema

Buenaventura

Cali
Palmira

Tunja
Gachetá
Orocué
Girardot
Villavicencio
BOGOTÁ
Espinal
Salto de Tequendama

COLOMBIA

San Fernando de Atabapo

Maroa

Popayán
Bolívar
Neiva
Campoalegre
Garzón
Pitalito
Florencia

Calamar

MESA DE YAMBI

Tumaco
Barbacoas
Túquerres
Pasto
Cruz
Esmeraldas
Galeras (Vol.) 13997

Inírida

Içana

Uaupés

Tulcán
Ipiales
Otavalo
Ibarra
Cayambe

Quito
Latacunga
Manta
Ambato
Guaranda
Riobamba
Chimborazo 20 702
Alausí

ECUADOR

Cotopaxi 19 347
Baños
Archidona

Caquetá

Japurá

Negro

Fonte Boa

Barcelos

Bahía de Caráquez
Chone
Portoviejo
Jipijapa
Bababoyo

Guayaquil

Cuenca
Machala
Santa Rosa
Tumbes

Azogues
Sígsig
Loja

Iquitos

Tefé
São Paulo de Olivença

AMAZO
SELVAS

PTA. PARIÑAS
Talara

Sullana
Paita
Piura
Castilla

PONGO DE MANSERICHE

PTA. AGUJA

LOBOS DE TIERRA

Chulucanas

Jaén
Chachapoyas
Moyobamba
Yurimaguas
Lamas
Tarapoto

Leticia

Eirunepé

Lábrea

Lambayeque
Ferreñafe
Chiclayo
Puerto Eten
Cajamarca

Pacasmayo
Chepén
Puerto Chicama
Huamachuco
Trujillo
Salaverry

Cruzeiro do Sul

ACRE

Porto Velho

Chimbote

Nev. Huascarán 22 133
Huarás

Tingo María
Huánuco
Cerro de Pasco
Nudo de Pasco 15 118

Rio Branco

Porto Acre
Cobija

Villa Bella

RONDO

ISLAS CHINCHAS
Huaral
Huacho

Tarma
La Oroya

Puerto Bermúdez

GRAN PAJONAL

Riberalta

Guajará
Mirim

MASSIÇO DE PAC

Callao
LIMA
Chorrillos

Huancayo
Huancavelica
Ayacucho
Cañete

Machu Picchu
Abancay
Cusco

Puerto Maldonado

Magdalena

Rogoaguado

PERU

Chincha Alta
Pisco
Ica

Cotabambas
Puquio
Coracora

Sicuani
Ayaviri

Reyes

Trinidad

PTA. CARRETAS

Nudo Carapuna 21 696
Arequipa
Volcán Misti 19 101

Juliaca
Lago Titicaca
Ayata
Nev. Illampu 21 066
Achacachi
Guaqui
Viacha
LA PAZ

BOLIV

Camaná
Mollendo

Moquegua
Corocoro
Nev. Illimani 20 741

Cochabamba
Punata
Valle
Grande

Sar
Cru

Ilo
Tacna
Arica

Oruro
Huanuni

ALTIPLANO

Lago de Poopó

Colquechaca

Sucre
Potosí
Lagunillas
Monteagudo
San Lucas

Iquique

Pisagua

Huanchaca
Uyuni
Pulacayo

Tupiza
Tarija

PUNA DE ATACAMA

Tocopilla

Ollagüe
Calama
Chuquicamata
Pedro de Valdivia
Mejillones
Antofagasta

Cobija

JUJUY
SALTA

ARGENTINA

Tropic of Capricorn

A-549100-76- -11-10-22

COPYRIGHT BY
RAND McNALLY & COMPANY
MADE IN U.S.A.

Scale 1:16 000 000; one inch to 250 miles. Sinusoidal Projection
Elevations and depressions are given in feet

Longitude West

a

Pavarandocito
Alto de Tres Morros 11 155
Dabeiba
Ituango
Valdivia
Segovia

Paramillo 12 990
San Andrés
Yarumal
Anorí
Remedios

Cañasgordas
Alto Musinga 12 631
ANTIOQUIA
Santa Rosa
Amalfi
Yolombó

Antioquia
Sopetrán
Sabanas Paramo 13 395
Cisneros
Barbosa
San Roque
Puerto Berrío

Urrao
Anzá
Bello
Ilaguí
Rionegro
Nare
San Rafael

Maro Urapeta 9186
MEDELLÍN
Titiribí
Envigado
San Luis

Negua
Quibdó
Caldas
La Ceja
Puerto Niño

CHOCÓ
Concordia
Fredonia
Cerro de los Paraúbos 10 991

Certeguí
Andes
Aguadas
Sonsón

Tadó
Caramanta 12 299
Pensilvania
Puerto
Salgar

RISARALDA
Riosucio
Salamina
La Dorada
Victoria

Istmina
Apía
Manzanares

Cerro Tatama 13 780
Santa Rosa de Cabal
Neira
Fresno

El Cajón
Armero
Villeta
Zipaquira

Ansermanuevo
CALDAS
Nevado del Ruiz 17 716
Líbano

Anserma
Cerro Tarro 12 721
Manizales
Armenia

CUNDINAMARCA
Guasca
Gachetá

Sipí
Quimbaya
Finlandia
Venadillo
Ambalema
La Mesa
La Calera
Junín

Roldanillo
Zarzal
Pereira
Nevado de Tolima 17 110
Tocaima
Facatativá
BOGOTÁ
Fómeque

Cerro Tamang 13 944
Sevilla
QUINDÍO
Ibagué
Cajamarca
Girardot
Fusagasugá
Quetame
Restrepo

Trujillo
Tuluá
Caicedonia
Pico de Chilí 12 894
Rovira
Espinal
Cerro el Nevado 14 961
Pico de Mendonuevo 13 123
Villavicencio

VALLE DEL CAUCA
Darién
Buga
San Antonio
Ortega
Prado

Restrepo
Guacarí
Cerrito
Coyaima
Purificación
TOLIMA
Acacías

Cali
Palmira
Pradera
Chaparral
Ataco
Natagaima
Dolores
Alpujarra
San Martín

Florida
Miranda
Corinto
HUILA
META

Jamundí
Puerto Tejada
Villarica
Baraya

Buenos
Aires
Santander
Toribío
Nevado de Huila 18 865
Tello
San Antonio

CORDILLERA OCCIDENTAL
CORDILLERA CENTRAL
CORDILLERA ORIENTAL
ANDES MTS.

Magdalena

Scale 1:4 000 000

0  10  20  30  40 Miles
0 10 20 30 40 50 60 Kilometers

©R.M.C.N.

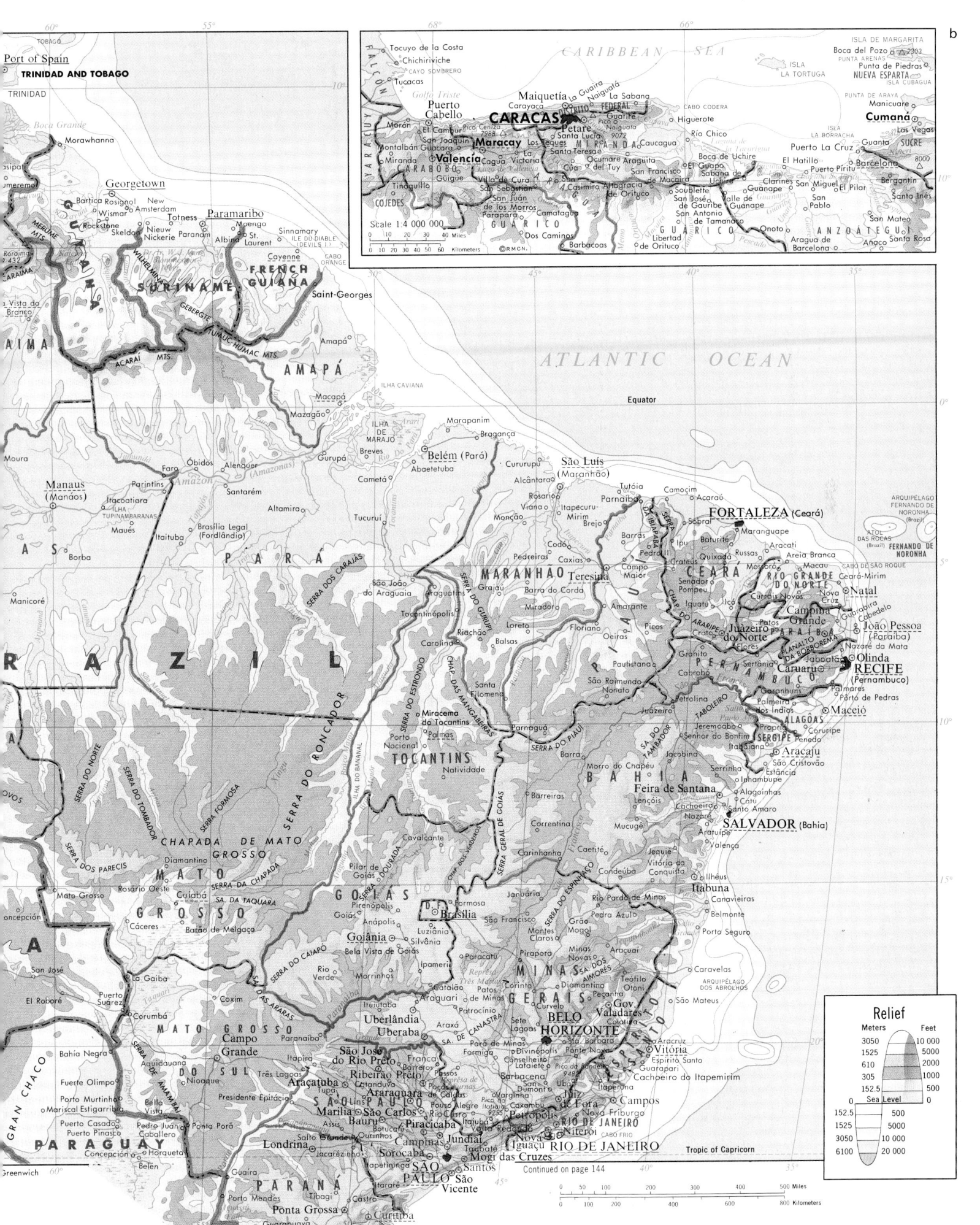

b

**TRINIDAD AND TOBAGO**

Port of Spain

TRINIDAD

Tobago

Boca Grande

Morawhanna

Georgetown

Bartica Rosignol
New Amsterdam
Wismar Nieuw Nickerie Totness Paramaribo
Rockstone Skeldon Paranam Moengo
Nieuw Amsterdam St. Laurent Albina
Sinnamary
ILE DU DIABLE
(DEVIL'S I.)

Cayenne

**FRENCH GUIANA**

**SURINAME**

Saint-Georges

CABO ORANGE

**AMAPÁ**

Amapá

Macapá

Mazagão

ILHA DE MARAJO

Breves

Belém (Pará)

Cururupú

São Luís (Maranhão)

Alcântara

Parnaíba

**FORTALEZA** (Ceará)

Sobral

Maranguape

ATLANTIC OCEAN

Equator

ARQUIPÉLAGO
FERNANDO DE
NORONHA

ATOL
DAS ROCAS
(Brazil)

FERNANDO DE
NORONHA

**Caribbean inset (Scale 1:4 000 000)**

CARIBBEAN SEA

ISLA DE MARGARITA

NUEVA ESPARTA

**CARACAS**

**Maracay**

**Valencia**

Puerto Cabello

**Cumaná**

SUCRE

Barcelona

MIRANDA

CARABOBO

COJEDES

GUÁRICO

ANZOÁTEGUI

Scale 1:4 000 000

0  10  20  30  40 Miles

0  10  20  30 40 50  60 Kilometers

©RMcN.

**Main map — Brazil**

Manaus (Manáos)

Moura

Manicoré

**B R A Z I L**

**P A R Á**

Santarém

Altamira

Tucuruí

Óbidos

Faro

**MARANHÃO** Teresina

Codó

Caxias

Grajaú

Barra do Corda

Floriano

Oeiras

Picos

**CEARÁ**

Russas

Quixadá

Crateús

Iguatú

Juàzeiro do Norte
Crato

**RIO GRANDE
DO NORTE**

Natal

Currais Novos

Campina Grande

**PARAÍBA**

João Pessoa (Paraíba)

Olinda

**RECIFE** (Pernambuco)

**PERNAMBUCO**

Caruaru

**ALAGÔAS**

Maceió

**TOCANTINS**

Palmas

Porto Nacional

Natividade

Barreiras

**BAHIA**

Feira de Santana

**SALVADOR** (Bahia)

**SERGIPE**

**Aracaju**

Jacobina

Morro do Chapéu

Lençóis

Mucugê

Ilhéus

Itabuna

**MATO
GROSSO**

Cuiabá

CHAPADA DE MATO
GROSSO

Diamantino

**GOIÁS**

Goiânia

D.F. Brasília

Anápolis

Formosa

**MINAS
GERAIS**

Patos de Minas

Paracatú

Araguari

Uberlândia

Uberaba

Corinto

Curvelo

**BELO
HORIZONTE**

Pirapora

Montes Claros

Governador
Valadares

**ESPÍRITO
SANTO**

Vitória

Guarapari

Cachoeiro do Itapemirim

Campos

**RIO DE JANEIRO**

Niterói

Nova Iguaçu

CABO FRIO

Juiz de Fora

Petrópolis

**MATO
GROSSO
DO SUL**

Campo
Grande

Corumbá

**PARAGUAY**

GRAN CHACO

Concepción

**PARANÁ**

Londrina

**SÃO
PAULO**

**SÃO
PAULO**

Santos

São Vicente

Curitiba

Ponta Grossa

São José
do Rio Prêto

Ribeirão Prêto

Araçatuba

Marília

Bauru

Piracicaba

**Campinas** Jundiaí

Sorocaba

Mogi das Cruzes

Tropic of Capricorn

**Relief**

| Meters | Feet |
|---|---|
| 3050 | 10 000 |
| 1525 | 5000 |
| 610 | 2000 |
| 305 | 1000 |
| 152.5 | 500 |
| Sea Level | 0 |
| 152.5 | 500 |
| 1525 | 5000 |
| 3050 | 10 000 |
| 6100 | 20 000 |

Continued on page 144

0  100  200  300  400  500 Miles

0  100  200  400  600  800 Kilometers

Continued on pages 142-143

a

**BUENOS AIRES**

Scale 1:1 000 000

0       5       10 Miles
0   4   8   12   16 Kilometers
©RMCN.

b

**RIO DE JANEIRO**

Scale 1:1 000 000

0       5       10 Miles
0   4   8   12   16 Kilometers
©rmcn.

**Relief**

| Meters | Feet |
|---|---|
| 3050 | 10 000 |
| 1525 | 5000 |
| 610 | 2000 |
| 305 | 1000 |
| 152.5 | 500 |
| 0 Sea Level | 0 |
| 152.5 | 500 |
| 1525 | 5000 Below |
| 3050 | 10 000 Sea Level |
| 6100 | 20 000 |

A-549200-76  -11-  14
COPYRIGHT BY
RAND McNALLY & COMPANY
MADE IN U.S.A.

0   50   100        200        300        400        500 Miles
0   100   200        400        600        800 Kilometers

Scale 1:16 000 000; one inch to 250 miles. Sinusoidal Projection
Elevations and depressions are given in feet

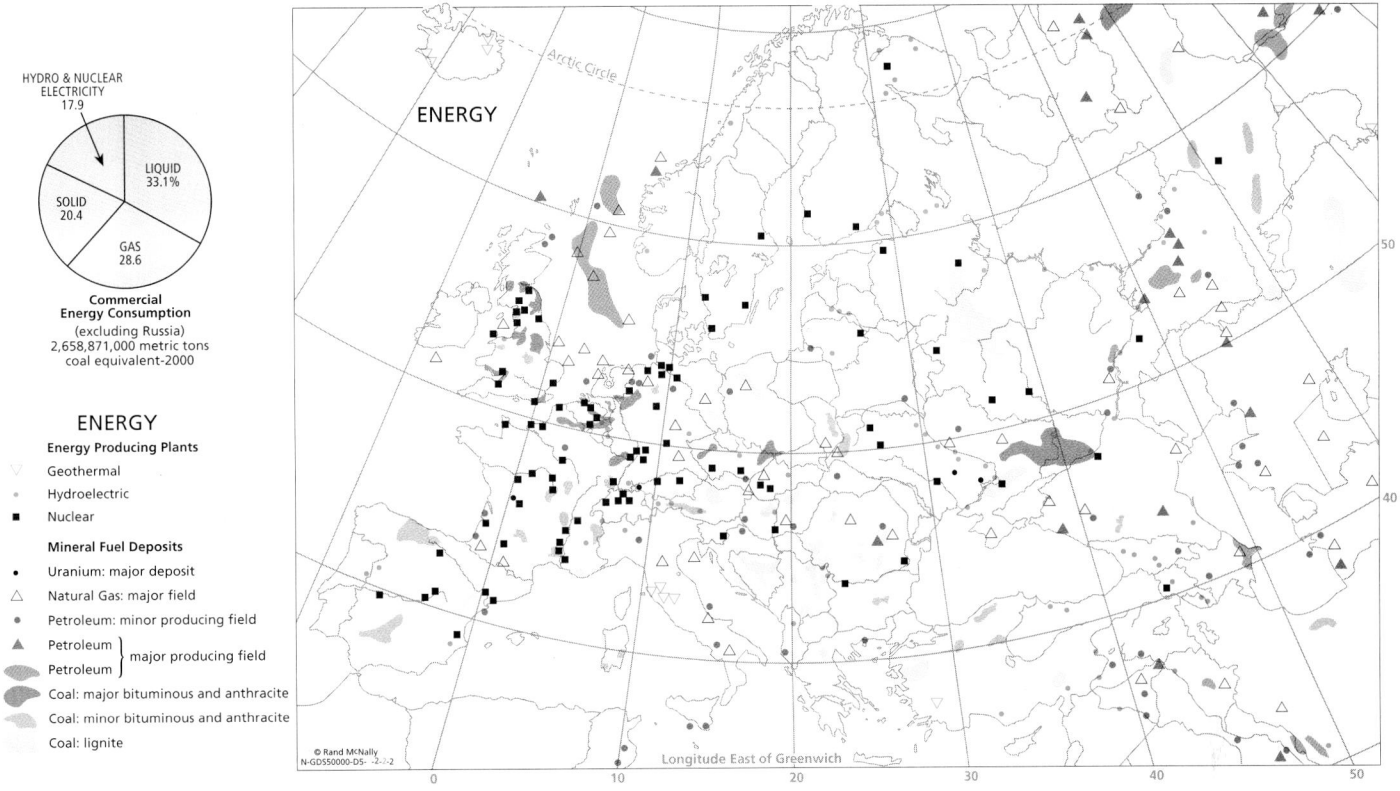

HYDRO & NUCLEAR
ELECTRICITY
17.9

LIQUID
33.1%

SOLID
20.4

GAS
28.6

**Commercial
Energy Consumption**
(excluding Russia)
2,658,871,000 metric tons
coal equivalent-2000

ENERGY

## ENERGY

**Energy Producing Plants**

▽ Geothermal
• Hydroelectric
■ Nuclear

**Mineral Fuel Deposits**

• Uranium: major deposit
△ Natural Gas: major field
• Petroleum: minor producing field
▲ Petroleum } major producing field
Petroleum }
Coal: major bituminous and anthracite
Coal: minor bituminous and anthracite
Coal: lignite

© Rand McNally
N-GDS50000-D5-  -2-?-2

Longitude East of Greenwich

NATURAL HAZARDS

## NATURAL HAZARDS

○ Volcanoes*
● Earthquakes*
● Major flood disasters*
—— Tsunamis
—— Limit of iceburg drift
☐ Temporary pack ice
▨ Areas subject to desertification

*Occurrences since 1900

Longitude East of Greenwich

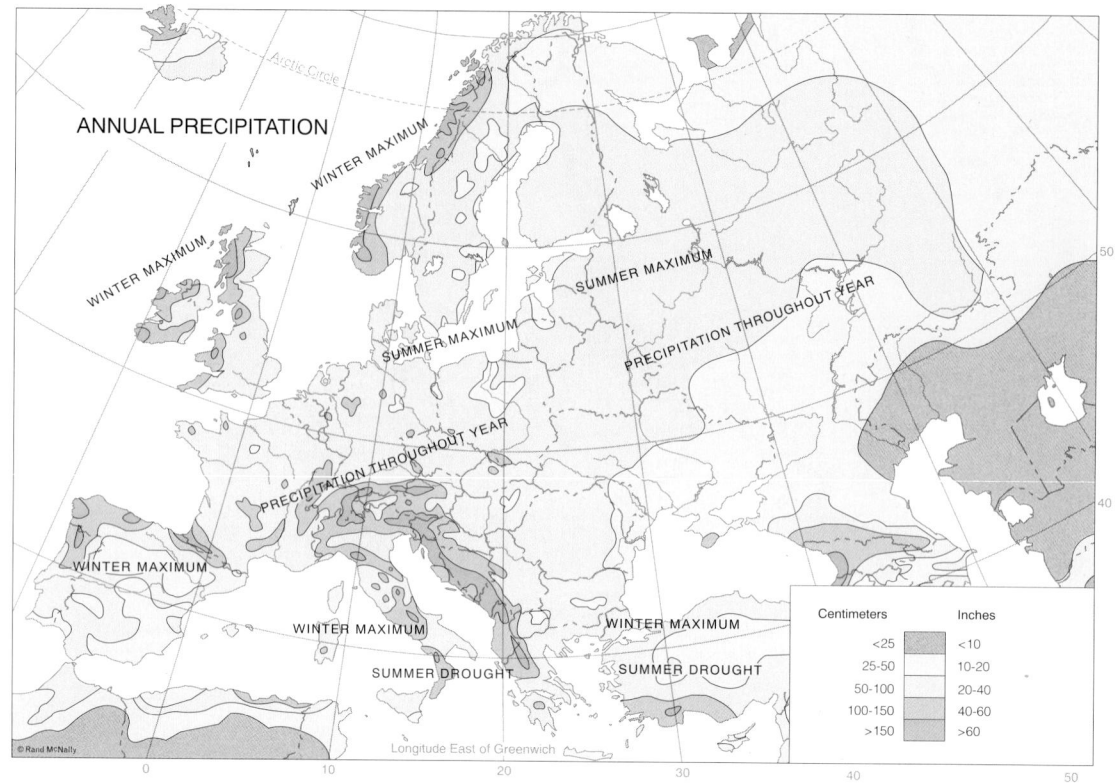

ANNUAL PRECIPITATION

| Centimeters | | Inches |
|---|---|---|
| <25 | | <10 |
| 25-50 | | 10-20 |
| 50-100 | | 20-40 |
| 100-150 | | 40-60 |
| >150 | | >60 |

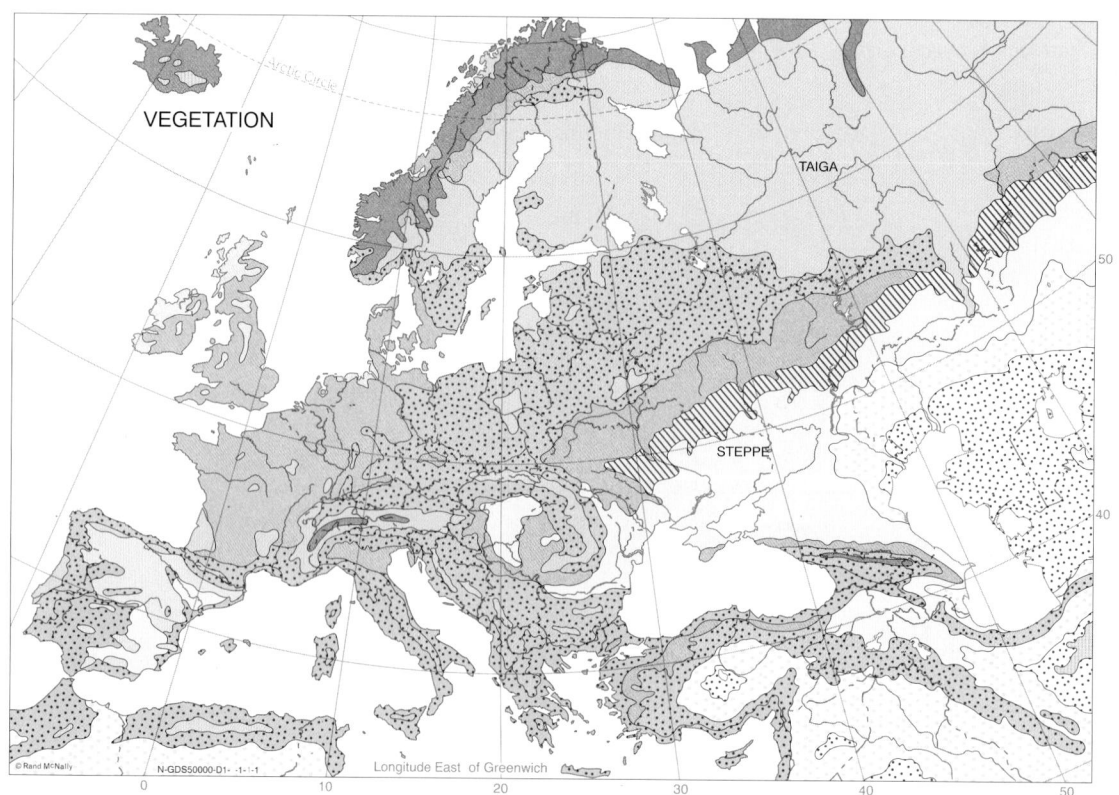

VEGETATION

VEGETATION

| E | Coniferous forest |
|---|---|
| B,Bs | Mediterranean vegetation |
| M | Mixed forest: coniferous-deciduous |
| S | Semi-deciduous forest |
| D | Deciduous forest |
| | Wooded steppe |
| G | Grass (steppe) |
| Gp | Short grass |
| Den | Desert shrub |
| L | Heath and moor |
| L | Alpine vegetation, tundra |
| b | Little or no vegetation |

For explanation of letters in boxes,
see Natural Vegetation Map
by A. W. Kuchler, p. 24

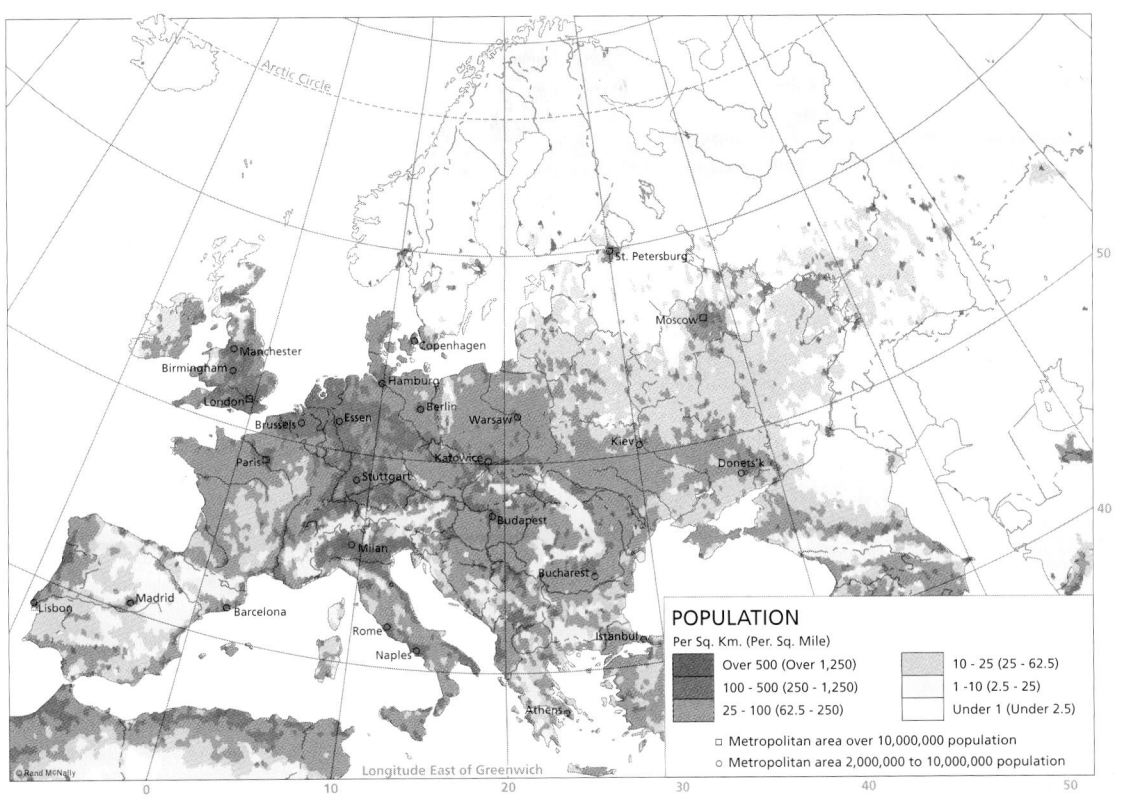

## POPULATION

Per Sq. Km. (Per. Sq. Mile)

| | |
|---|---|
| Over 500 (Over 1,250) | 10 - 25 (25 - 62.5) |
| 100 - 500 (250 - 1,250) | 1 -10 (2.5 - 25) |
| 25 - 100 (62.5 - 250) | Under 1 (Under 2.5) |

□ Metropolitan area over 10,000,000 population
o Metropolitan area 2,000,000 to 10,000,000 population

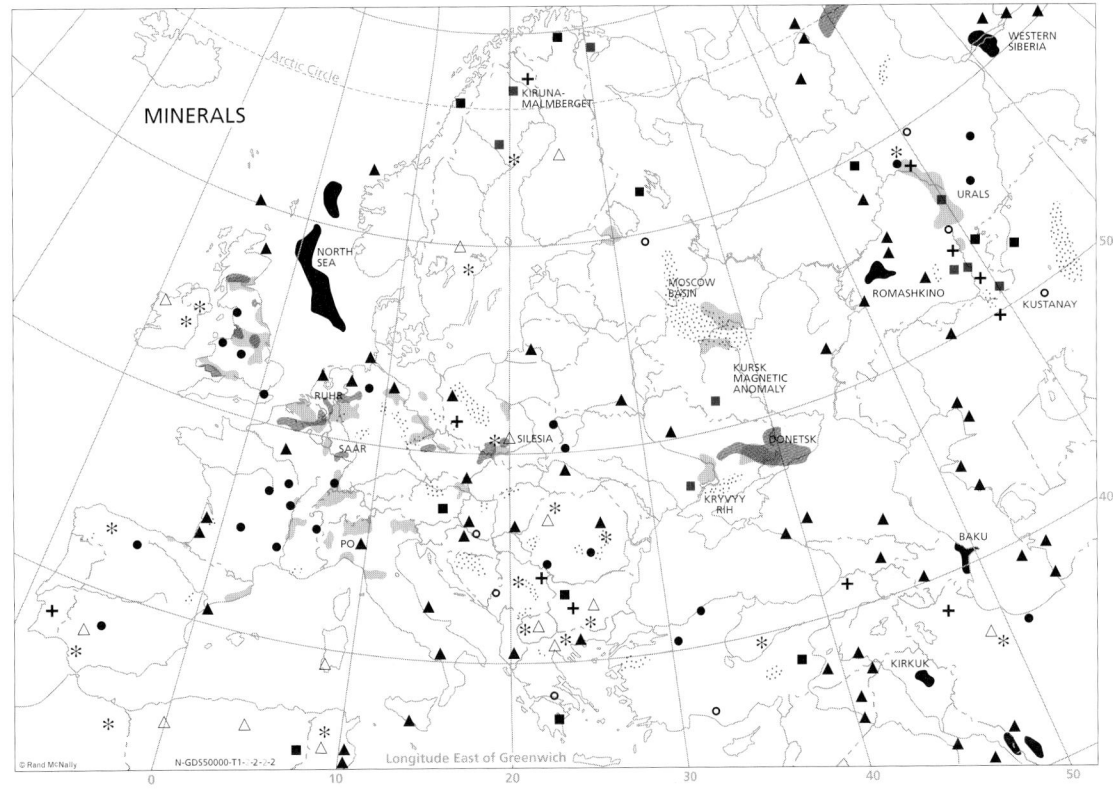

## MINERALS

- Industrial areas
- Major coal deposits
- Major petroleum deposits
- Lignite deposits
- ▲ Minor petroleum deposits
- ● Minor coal deposits
- ■ Major iron ore
- ■ Minor iron ore
- ✳ Lead
- o Bauxite
- △ Zinc
- + Copper

148

Urban

Cropland

Cropland & Woodland

Cropland & Grazing Land

Grassland, Grazing Land

Forest, Woodland

Swamp, Marshland

Tundra

Shrub, Sparse Grass,
Wasteland (pattern)

Barren Land

Oasis

ATLANTIC

OCEAN

North

Sea

Baltic Sea

Gulf of Bothnia

Reykjavik

Narvik

Murmansk

Trondheim

Bergen

Oslo

Helsinki

ST. PETERSBURG

Tallinn

Stockholm

Göteborg

Rīga

Copenhagen

Vilnius

Kaliningrad

Minsk

Glasgow

Belfast

MANCHESTER

Dublin

Hamburg

Elbe

BERLIN

Warsaw

Pripet

Amsterdam

Oder

LONDON

Antwerp

Essen

Leipzig

Kraków

L'viv

Frankfurt

Prague

Brest

PARIS

Seine

Strasbourg

Rhine

Danube

VIENNA

CARPATHIANS

Loire

Munich

Dnies

A Coruña

Bay of Biscay

Zürich

BUDAPEST

Tisza

Bordeaux

Lyon

ALPS

Bilbao

Garonne

Rhône

MILAN

Zagreb

Sava

Belgrade

Duero

PYRENEES

Venice

Bucharest

Lisbon

MADRID

Ebro

Marseille

Genoa

Adriatic

Danube

BARCELONA

CORSICA

Sofia

Sevilla

ROME

Tiranë

Tanger

SARDINIA

Tyrrhenian Sea

Aegean Sea

ISLAS BALEARES

Oran

Algiers

Naples

Athens

Casablanca

ATLAS

MOUNTAINS

Tunis

Palermo

SICILY

Mediterranean Sea

MALTA

CRETE

Longitude West of Greenwich   0°   Longitude East of Greenwich

Scale 1: 16,000,000; one inch to 250 miles. Conic Projection

0   50   100   200   300   400   500 Miles

0   100   200   400   600   800 Kilometers

150

ICELAND
Lava
Ice
Red
Arctic Circle

Nord Cape

LAPPLAND
Narvik
Kiruna
Inari Basin
Knobs Knob
Gäl.
Dunes
LOWLAND
Muskeg Region
Rov.
Kan.
Rock and Drift
Northern Driftland
Elongated
Lakes
Faeröerne

656 feet

Sogne Fiord
Bergen
Hardanger Fiord

Trondh.
Sylarna
Östersund
Dovre
Um.
Granite Upland
Morain
L.
Vätter Massiv
Moraine
Helsinki
Gulf of Finland
Narva
L. Peipsi

Shetland Is.
Orkney Is.
NW. HIGHL'DS
GRAMPIAN Mts.
Bonn
Ed.
SO. HIGHLANDS

Stav.
Hallingdal
Humdal
Oslo
Guldbrandsdalen
Osterdalen
Orsa Ring
Vänern Basin
Glacial Channel
Non.
Lowland
Malar Basin Channel
Stockholm
Southern
Driftland
Gotland

NORTH
SEA

Skagerrak
Kattegat

Cuestas
Riga
Lowland
Daugava R.

Shannon Va.
Wicklow
Snow.
Pennine Chain
Lake Dist.

Welsh
Highlds
Cotswold
Exmoor

Limit of Glaciation

Chiltern Hills
E. Anglian Hi.
London
N. Downs
Dartmoor
S. Downs

Copenhagen
Skåne Plain
Öland

Kiel
Hamb.
Lübeck
BALTIC LAKE PLAINS
Mazurian Lakes

Niemen R.
BALTIC SEA
Kau.
Lowland
Vilnius
Minsk

English Channel

Cotentin
C. Penins.
Seine R.
LH.

Amsterdam
The Hague
Br.
Ant.
Rhine
NETHERLANDS
Flandrian Plain
Dunes
Weser R.
Elbe R.
Oder R.
Berlin
Pos.
Mazovian Plain
Warsaw
Brest
POLES
SWAM

ARMORICAN MASSIVE
Loire R.
Nan.
Br.

Ou B
Es.
A Con.
Ardenne
Eifel
Westerwald
Sauerland
Taunus
Vogelsbg.
Harz
Thuringian for.
ORE
Dr.
L.
SILESIAN PLAIN
SUDETES
Wr.
Lódz
Lyso Gory
Lublin
Galician Basin
Cracow
Pr.
PODOLIAN
Moraine

PARIS BASIN
Paris
Orl.
CHAMPAGNE LOWLD
Hunsruck
Lorrain Basin
M.
Nur.
Prague
Bohemian Pl.
Bohemian FOR.
Moravian Hills
Pr.

LOIRE BASIN
Goronne R.
AQUITANIAN LOWLD
Dunes Landes
Bordeaux

MORVAN PLAT.
LANGRES PLAT.
Str. Forest
Black Forest
Schwabian Jura
Frankf.
Reg.
Stu.
Rhon
Tatry
BIHARM
Cluj

CENTRAL MASSIVE
Lyons
CAUSSES PLAT.
CEVENNES
Tou.
Carc.

JURA
Ins.
Mun.
SWISS
BAVARIAN BASIN
Austrian Plain
Vienna
Little Alföld
Budapest
Bakony
L. Balaton
Mecsek
Transylvanian Basin
Maros

Bay of Biscay
CANTABRIAN Mts.
Douro R.
S. de Estrela

LEON-OLD CASTILIAN BASIN
Bu.
IBERIAN Mts.
EBRO BASIN
Zar.
CATALAN Mts.
COSTA BRAVA
Barcelona
Tar.
Ebro R.

Turin
Milan
PO VALLEY
Po R.
Triest
Venice
Trieste
Zagreb
Sava R.
Papuk
Belgrade
HUNGARIAN (Alföld)
BASIN
KAPELA
DINARIC ALPS
KARST
VELEBIT
WALLACHIAN PLAIN
Bucharest
Iron Gate
Danube R.
Danubian Plateau
Var.
Nis.

Lisbon
Tagus R.
SA. MORENA
Guadiana R.
ANDALUSIAN LOWLAND
Seville
Cor.
S. de Segura
S. de Pila
Valencia

NEW CAST. BASIN
LA MANCHA BASIN
Toledo
S. de Gredos
Madrid
Guadarrama
Cuenca

BALEARIC ISLANDS

CORSICA

SARDINIA

VOLCANIC BELT
Rome
M. Gargano
Naples
Vesuvius
APULIAN V.
MURGE PLAT.
Dur.

ABRUZZI
ADRIATIC SEA
Kosovo Polje
Skoplje
Rila M.
Sof.
ANTIBALKANS
RODOPE Mts.
BALKAN RA.
PINDUS Mts.

Guadalete R.
Seville
Gr.
S. Nevada
Mal.
Cart.
Strait of Gibraltar
Tangiers
Ce.
Gib.

656 feet

Marseilles
Riviera
Monaco
Genoa

MEDITERRANEAN

TYRRHENIAN SEA

Lipari Volcanoes
Palermo
SICILY
Etna
Cat.
CALABRIAN
IONIAN SEA

Olympus
Struma R.
Vardar R.
Maritsa R.
Tekir.
Dardanelles
Larisa
Athens
CRETE

Rabat
Fes
RIF ATLAS
S.RIF
M.
COASTAL PLAIN
Mel.
Oran
TELL ATLAS
Algiers
Bône
Biz.
Tunis
Malta

Morocco Meseta
MIDDLE ATLAS
MOULOUYA BASIN
HIGH PLATEAUS
SAHARAN ATLAS
Const.
B.S.
TUNISIAN ATLAS
Sousse

HIGH ATLAS
JEB. AURES
Biskra

Scale 1:16 000 000; one inch to 250 miles. Conic Projection
Elevations and depressions are given in feet.

## PHYSIOGRAPHIC PROVINCES

0        400
Miles

Western Uplands (Mostly old rocks) | Great European Plain | Central Uplands | Alpine System

## EUROPE DURING THE ICE AGE

Tundra | Forest | Steppe

## PHYSIOGRAPHY
### BY
### ERWIN RAISZ

### LITHOLOGY AND STRUCTURE

Unconsolidated deposits: alluvium, sands, bottom lands.

Essentially horizontal sediments, also uplands and terraces in the plains.

Moderately folded sedimentary rocks.

Strongly folded and faulted rocks. The "Younger Series" in Norway.

Metamorphic and intrusive igneous rocks.

volcanics, lava flows, basalts, etc.

### LANDFORMS

PLATEAUS | CUESTAS | SAND
HILLS | FOLDED MOUNTAINS | SINKS
MOUNTAINS | BASIN RANGES | MORAINES
MESAS | VOLCANO AND LAVA | DRUMLINS

0   50  100      200        300        400       500 Miles
0    100     200        400        600        800 Kilometers

# EUROPE LANGUAGES
## BY
### BOGDAN ZABORSKI

Arctic Circle

Longitude West of Greenwich Longitude East of Greenwich

B-550000-1C6-1-1-1-4
COPYRIGHT BY
RAND McNALLY & COMPANY
MADE IN U.S.A.

| 0 | 100 | 200 | 300 | 400 | 500 | 600 | Miles |

| 0 | 200 | 400 | 600 | 800 | 1000 | Kilometers |

Scale 1:16,500,000; one inch to 260 miles Conic Projection

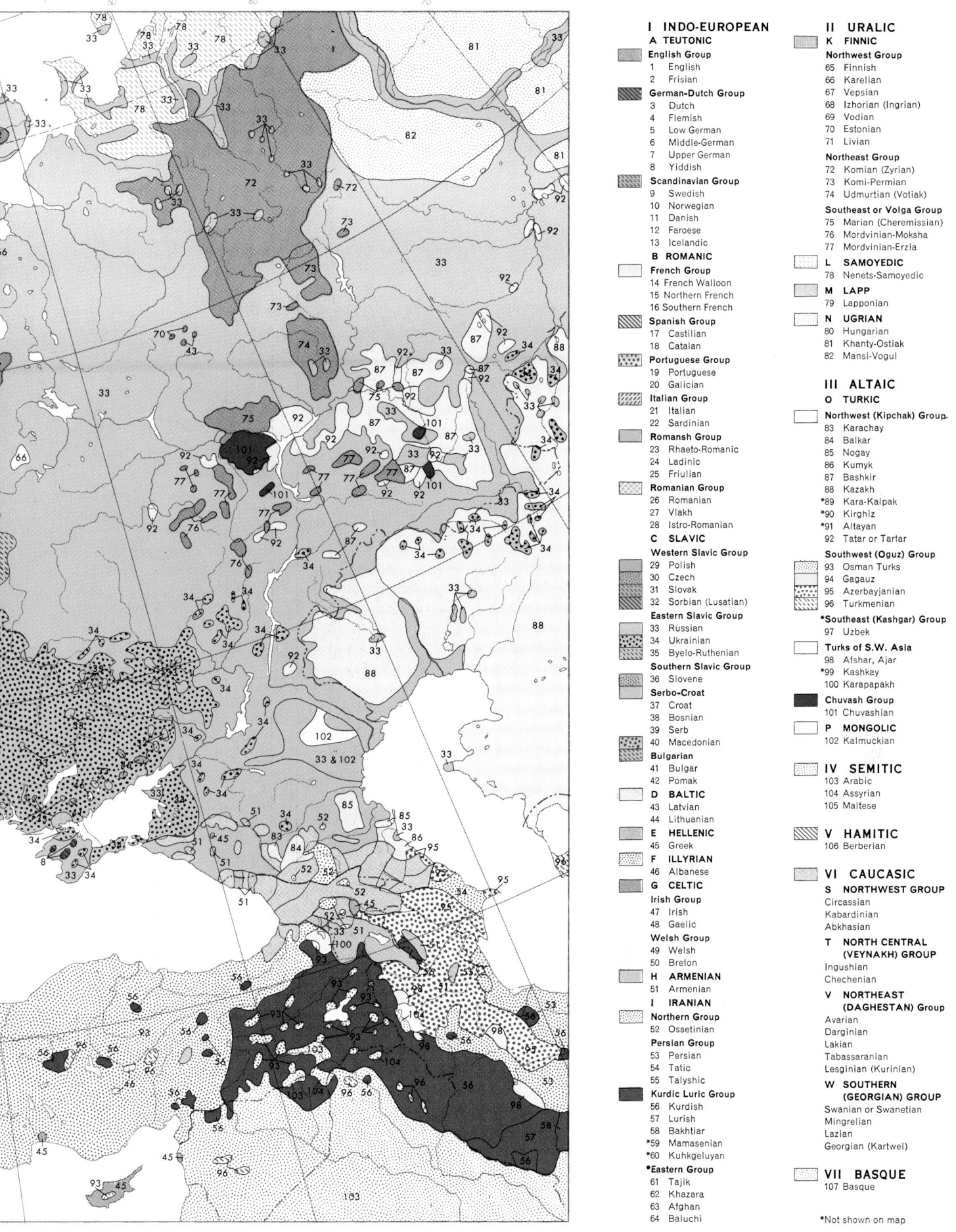

**I INDO-EUROPEAN**

**A TEUTONIC**

English Group
1 English
2 Frisian

German-Dutch Group
3 Dutch
4 Flemish
5 Low German
6 Middle-German
7 Upper German
8 Yiddish

Scandinavian Group
9 Swedish
10 Norwegian
11 Danish
12 Faroese
13 Icelandic

**B ROMANIC**

French Group
14 French Walloon
15 Northern French
16 Southern French

Spanish Group
17 Castilian
18 Catalan

Portuguese Group
19 Portuguese
20 Galician

Italian Group
21 Italian
22 Sardinian

Romansh Group
23 Rhaeto-Romanic
24 Ladinic
25 Friulian

Romanian Group
26 Romanian
27 Vlakh
28 Istro-Romanian

**C SLAVIC**

Western Slavic Group
29 Polish
30 Czech
31 Slovak
32 Sorbian (Lusatian)

Eastern Slavic Group
33 Russian
34 Ukrainian
35 Byelo-Ruthenian

Southern Slavic Group
36 Slovene

Serbo-Croat
37 Croat
38 Bosnian
39 Serb
40 Macedonian

Bulgarian
41 Bulgar
42 Pomak

**D BALTIC**
43 Latvian
44 Lithuanian

**E HELLENIC**
45 Greek

**F ILLYRIAN**
46 Albanese

**G CELTIC**

Irish Group
47 Irish
48 Gaelic

Welsh Group
49 Welsh
50 Breton

**H ARMENIAN**
51 Armenian

**I IRANIAN**

Northern Group
52 Ossetinian

Persian Group
53 Persian
54 Tatic
55 Talyshic

Kurdic Luric Group
56 Kurdish
57 Lurish
58 Bakhtiar
*59 Mamasenian
*60 Kuhkgeluyan

*Eastern Group
61 Tajik
62 Khazara
63 Afghan
64 Baluchi

**II URALIC**

**K FINNIC**

Northwest Group
65 Finnish
66 Karelian
67 Vepsian
68 Izhorian (Ingrian)
69 Vodian
70 Estonian
71 Livian

Northeast Group
72 Komian (Zyrian)
73 Komi-Permian
74 Udmurtian (Votiak)

Southeast or Volga Group
75 Marian (Cheremissian)
76 Mordvinian-Moksha
77 Mordvinian-Erzia

**L SAMOYEDIC**
78 Nenets-Samoyedic

**M LAPP**
79 Lapponian

**N UGRIAN**
80 Hungarian
81 Khanty-Ostiak
82 Mansi-Vogul

**III ALTAIC**

**O TURKIC**

Northwest (Kipchak) Group
83 Karachay
84 Balkar
85 Nogay
86 Kumyk
87 Bashkir
88 Kazakh
*89 Kara-Kalpak
*90 Kirghiz
*91 Altayan
92 Tatar or Tartar

Southwest (Oguz) Group
93 Osman Turks
94 Gagauz
95 Azerbayjanian
96 Turkmenian

*Southeast (Kashgar) Group
97 Uzbek

Turks of S.W. Asia
98 Afshar, Ajar
*99 Kashkay
100 Karapapakh

Chuvash Group
101 Chuvashian

**P MONGOLIC**
102 Kalmuckian

**IV SEMITIC**
103 Arabic
104 Assyrian
105 Maltese

**V HAMITIC**
106 Berberian

**VI CAUCASIC**

**S NORTHWEST GROUP**
Circassian
Kabardinian
Abkhasian

**T NORTH CENTRAL (VEYNAKH) GROUP**
Ingushian
Chechenian

**V NORTHEAST (DAGHESTAN) Group**
Avarian
Darginian
Lakian
Tabassaranian
Lesginian (Kurinian)

**W SOUTHERN (GEORGIAN) GROUP**
Swanian or Swanetian
Mingrelian
Lazian
Georgian (Kartwel)

**VII BASQUE**
107 Basque

*Not shown on map

Scale 1: 16 000 000; one inch to 250 miles. Conic Projection

Elevations and depressions are given in feet

Continued on pages 194-195

A-519697-26 -13  -35
COPYRIGHT BY
RAND McNALLY & COMPANY
MADE IN U.S.A.

Relief

| Meters | | Feet |
|---|---|---|
| 3050 | | 10 000 |
| 1525 | | 5000 |
| 610 | | 2000 |
| 305 | | 1000 |
| 152.5 | | 500 |
| 0 | Sea Level | 0 |
| 152.5 | | 500 |
| 1525 | | 5000 Below |
| 3050 | | 10 000 Sea Level |

Longitude West of Greenwich    Longitude East of Greenwich

Continued on pages 230-231

Scale 1: 16 000 000; one inch to 250 miles. Conic Projection

Elevations and depressions are given in feet

| 0 | 50 | 100 | 200 | 300 | 400 | 500 Miles |
|---|---|---|---|---|---|---|
| 0 | 100 | 200 | 400 | 600 | 800 Kilometers | |

Continued on pages 184-185

Continued on pages 198-199

A-519697-76  13-16-35
COPYRIGHT BY
RAND McNALLY & COMPANY
MADE IN U.S.A.

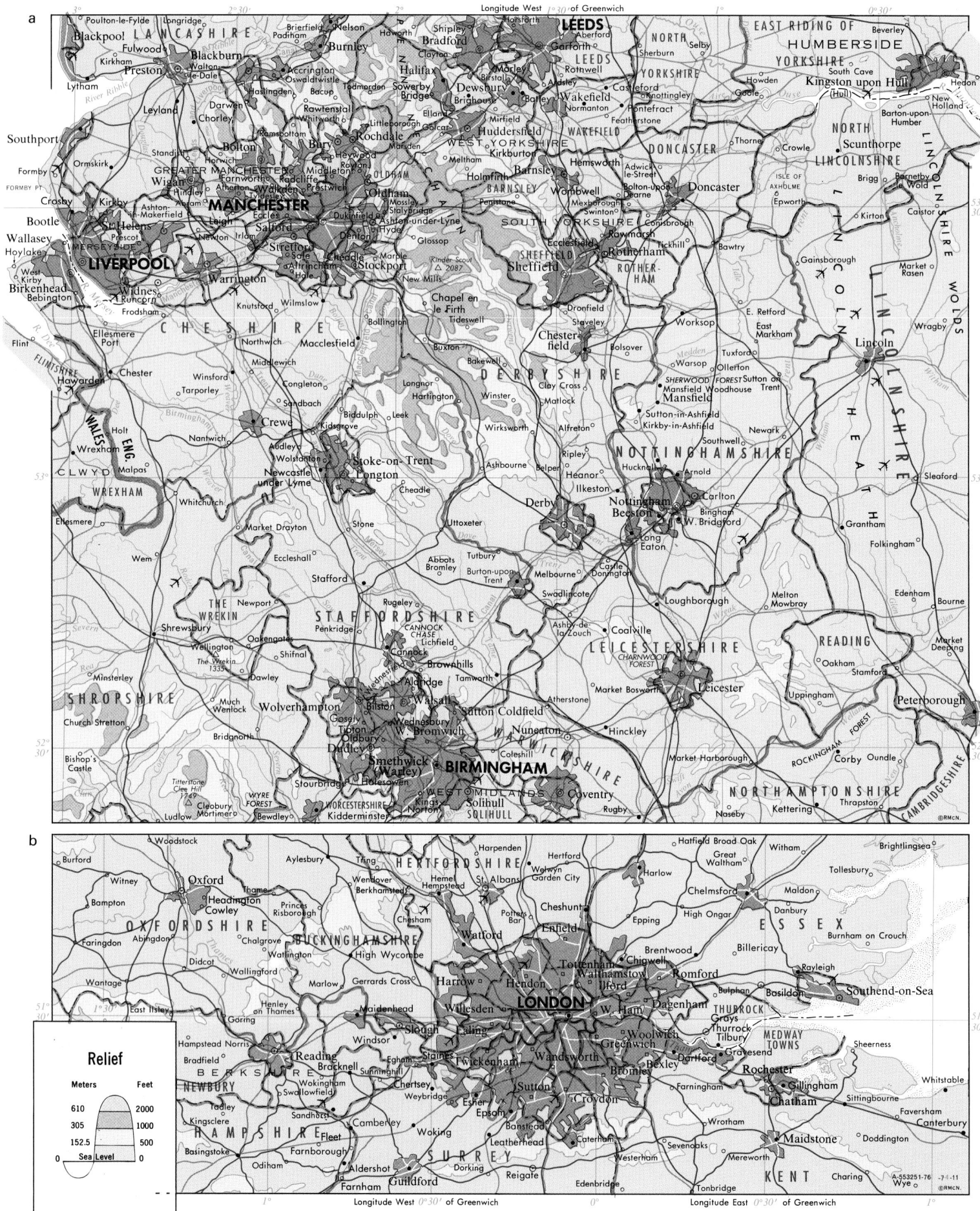

a

b

**Relief**

| Meters | Feet |
|--------|------|
| 610 | 2000 |
| 305 | 1000 |
| 152.5 | 500 |
| 0 Sea Level | 0 |

Scale 1:1 000 000; one inch to 16 miles.
Elevations and depressions are given in feet.

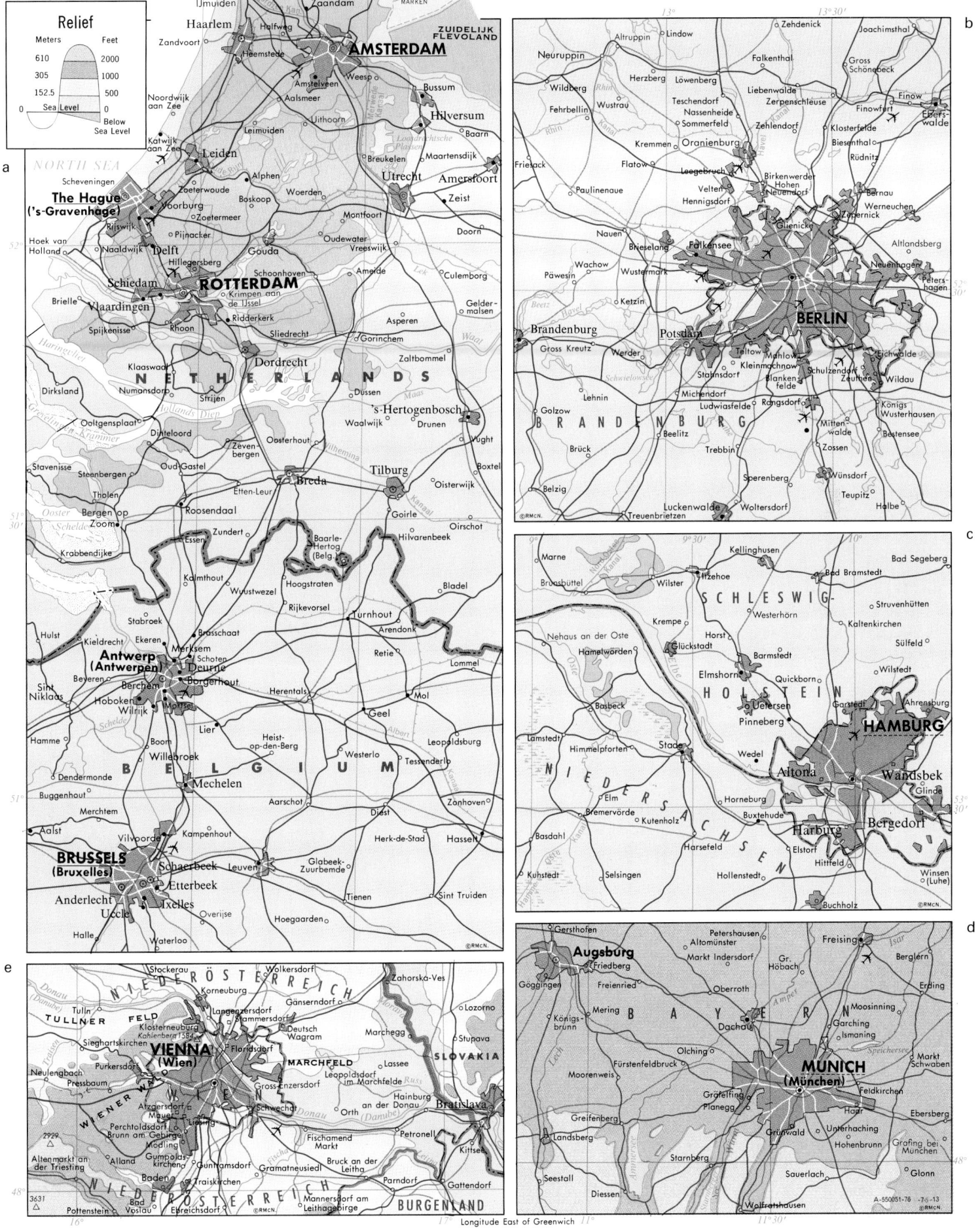

Scale 1:1 000 000; one inch to 16 miles.

Elevations and depressions are given in feet.

Longitude East of Greenwich

A-550051-76  -7-5-13

Continued on pages 180-181

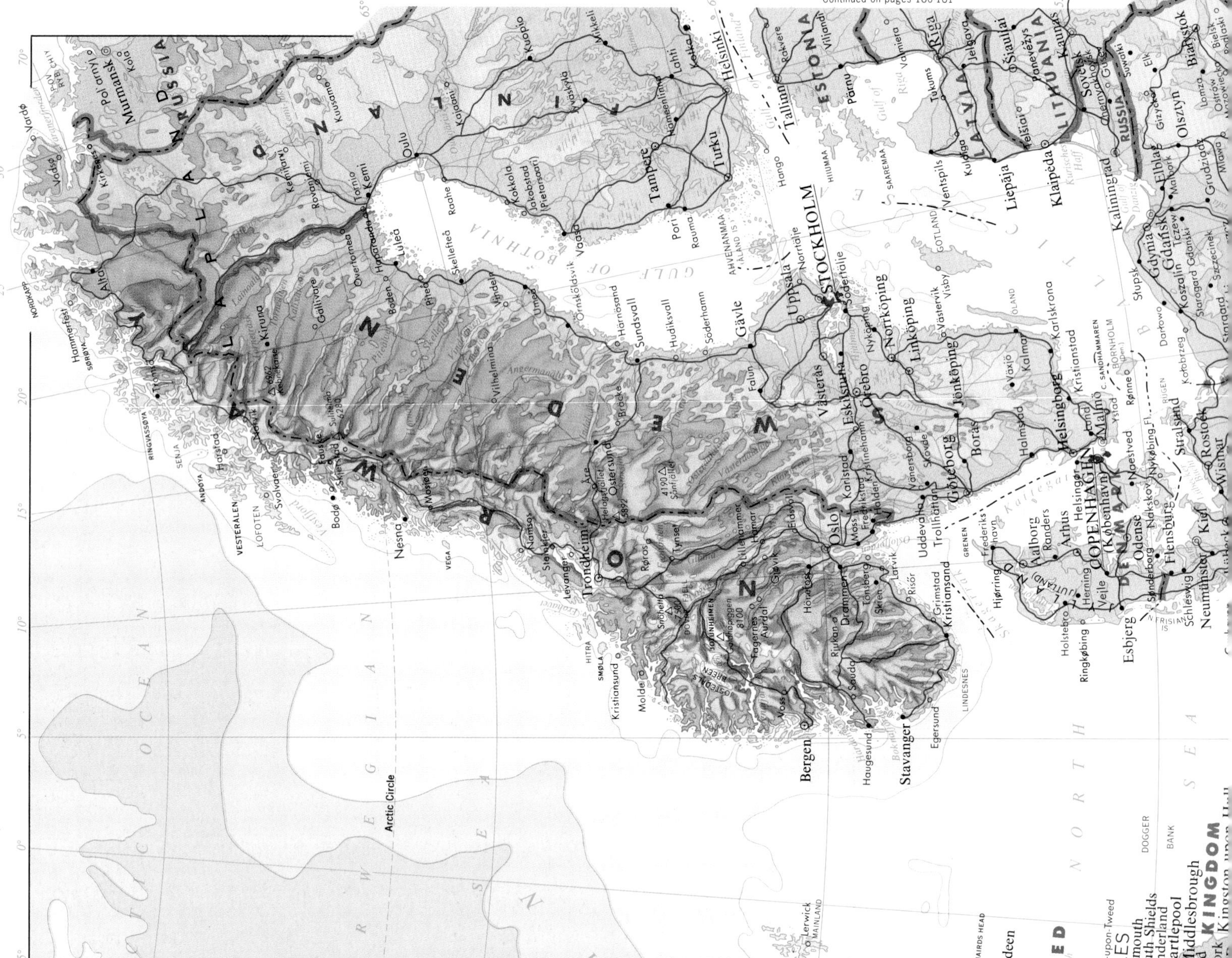

BELARUS

RUSSIA
Murmansk
Kola

LAPLAND

FINLAND

ESTONIA
Tallinn
Pärnu

LATVIA
Ventspils
Liepāja
Klaipėda

LITHUANIA
Šiauliai
Panevėžys
Kaunas
Vilnius

RUSSIA
Kaliningrad

GULF OF BOTHNIA

STOCKHOLM
Uppsala
Norrköping
Linköping
Jönköping

SWEDEN

Kiruna
Gällivare
Luleå
Skellefteå
Umeå
Sundsvall
Gävle
Falun
Västerås
Örebro

Oslo
Drammen
Trondheim
Bergen
Stavanger
Haugesund
Egersund

NORWAY

DENMARK
COPENHAGEN (København)
Odense
Esbjerg
Aalborg
Århus

NORTH SEA

UNITED KINGDOM

SCOTLAND
Aberdeen
Dundee
Edinburgh
Glasgow
GLASGOW

BRITISH ISLES

IRELAND
Belfast
Dublin

SHETLAND IS. (Br.)
Lerwick

ORKNEY IS. (Br.)
Kirkwall

FAROE IS. (Den.)
Tórshavn

ICELAND
Reykjavík

JAN MAYEN (Nor.)

ARCTIC OCEAN

NORWEGIAN SEA

Arctic Circle

## Relief

| Meters | Feet | |
|---|---|---|
| 3050 | 10 000 | |
| 1525 | 5000 | |
| 610 | 2000 | |
| 305 | 1000 | |
| 152.5 | 500 | |
| 0 | 0 | Sea Level |
| | Below Sea Level | |
| 152.5 | 500 | |
| 1525 | 5000 | |
| 3050 | 10 000 | |

Scale 1: 10 000 000; one inch to 160 miles. Conic Projection

Elevations and depressions are given in feet

LONDON
PARIS
MADRID
ROME
LISBON
BARCELONA
NAPLES
BRUSSELS
AMSTERDAM
The Hague
BERLIN
PRAGUE (Praha)
VIENNA
MUNICH
BUDAPEST
MILAN
TURIN
GENOA
Marseille
Lyon
Toulouse
Bordeaux
València
Sevilla
Algiers
Tunis
CORSICA (Fr.)
SARDINIA (It.)
BALEARS (Sp.)
TYRRHENIAN SEA
LIGURIAN SEA
BAY OF BISCAY
Longitude West of Greenwich
Longitude East of Greenwich
0 50 100 150 200 250 300 Miles
0 100 200 300 400 500 Kilometers
COPYRIGHT BY RAND McNALLY & COMPANY MADE IN U.S.A.

Continued on pages 160-161

Relief

| Meters | | Feet |
|---|---|---|
| 3050 | | 10000 |
| 1525 | | 5000 |
| 610 | | 2000 |
| 305 | | 1000 |
| 152.5 | | 500 |
| 0 | Sea Level | 0 |
| | | Below |
| 152.5 | | 500 | Sea Level |
| 1525 | | 5000 |
| 3050 | | 10000 |

A-558300-76
COPYRIGHT BY
RAND McNALLY & COMPANY
MADE IN U.S.A.

Longitude West of Greenwich 0° Longitude East of Greenwich

Scale 1:10 000 000; one inch to 160 miles. Bonne's Projection
Elevations and depressions are given in feet

Continued on pages 180-181

The Turkish Republic of Northern Cyprus
unilaterally declared its independence
on Nov. 15, 1983.

Areas occupied by Israel since 1967.

0   50   100   150   200   250   300 Miles
0   100   200   300   400   500 Kilometers

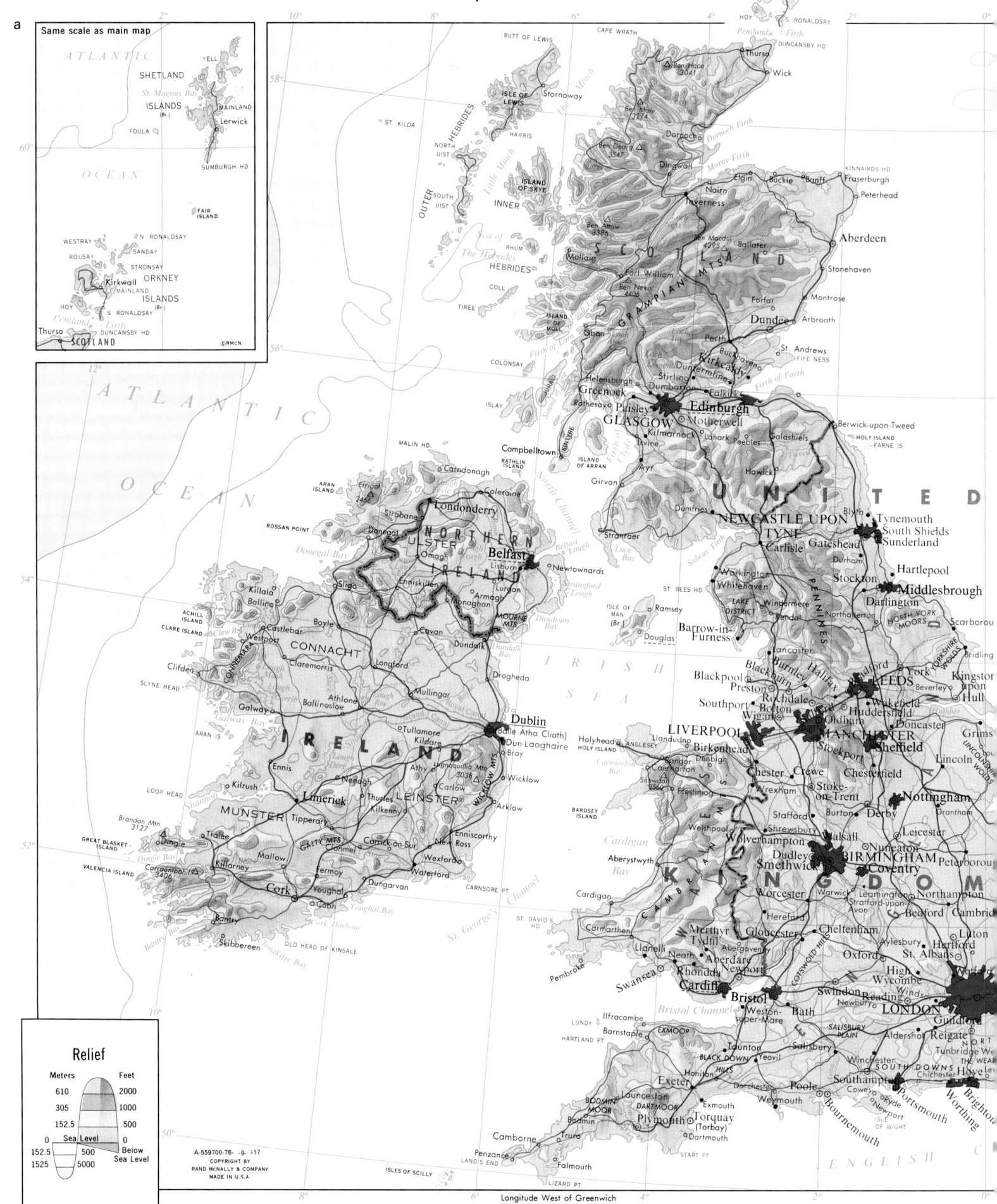

a

Same scale as main map

ATLANTIC OCEAN

SHETLAND
ISLANDS
(Br.)
YELL
FOULA
MAINLAND
Lerwick
St. Magnus Bay
SUMBURGH HD.

FAIR ISLAND

WESTRAY
ROUSAY
N. RONALDSAY
SANDAY
STRONSAY
ORKNEY
ISLANDS
(Br.)
Kirkwall
MAINLAND
HOY
S. RONALDSAY
Pentland Firth
DUNCANSBY HD.
Thurso
SCOTLAND
©RMCN.

ATLANTIC OCEAN

Relief

| Meters | Feet |
|---|---|
| 610 | 2000 |
| 305 | 1000 |
| 152.5 | 500 |
| 0 Sea Level | 0 |
| 152.5 | 500 |
| 1525 | 5000 |
| | Below Sea Level |

A-559700-76- -9- 717
COPYRIGHT BY
RAND McNALLY & COMPANY
MADE IN U.S.A

HOY
S RONALDSAY
Pentland Firth
DUNCANSBY HD.
BUTT OF LEWIS
CAPE WRATH
Ben Hope
3041
Thurso
Wick

ISLE OF LEWIS
Stornoway
HEBRIDES
HARRIS
NORTH UIST
ISLAND OF SKYE
INNER
SOUTH UIST
The Minch
Little Minch
Sea of the Hebrides
RHUM
COLL
TIREE
ISLAND OF MULL
Oban
ST KILDA
OUTER HEBRIDES

Ben Dearg
3547
Dingwall
Moray Firth
Nairn
Inverness
Ben Attow
3386
Ben Macdui
4295
Ballater
Fort William
Ben Nevis
4406
Elgin
Buckie
Banff
Fraserburgh
Peterhead
KINNAIRDS HD.
Aberdeen
Stonehaven
Montrose
Arbroath
Forfar
Dundee
Perth
St. Andrews
FIFE NESS
Kirkcaldy
Dunfermline
Stirling
Falkirk
Firth of Forth
EDINBURGH
Berwick-upon-Tweed
HOLY ISLAND
FARNE IS.

SCOTLAND
GRAMPIAN MTS.

Helensburgh
Greenock
Rothesay
Paisley
GLASGOW
Motherwell
Dumbarton
Kilmarnock
Lanark
Peebles
Galashiels
Irvine
Hawick
Ayr
Girvan
KINTYRE
ISLAND OF ARRAN
Campbeltown
RATHLIN ISLAND
ISLAY

MALIN HD.
Carndonagh
Coleraine
Londonderry
Strabane
Donegal
Omagh
NORTHERN IRELAND
ULSTER
Enniskillen
Sligo
Ballina
Killala
ACHILL ISLAND
CLARE ISLAND
Westport
Castlebar
CONNEMARA
CONNACHT
Clifden
SLYNE HEAD
Galway
ARAN IS.
Claremorris
Boyle
Longford
Athlone
Ballinasloe
Mullingar
Royal Canal
Grand Canal

ARAN ISLAND
Errigal 2466
ROSSAN POINT
Donegal Bay
Lisburn
BELFAST
Newtownards
Belfast Lough
Strangford Lough
Armagh
Monaghan
Lurgan
Cavan
MOURNE MTS.
Dundalk
Dundalk Bay
Drogheda
Carlingford
Dundrum Bay

Stranraer
Solway Firth
Luce Bay
Dumfries
Workington
Whitehaven
ST BEES HD.
Windermere
LAKE DISTRICT
Kendal
Barrow-in-Furness
Lancaster
ISLE OF MAN (Br.)
Ramsey
Douglas
NORTH CHANNEL
IRISH SEA

UNITED
NEWCASTLE UPON TYNE
Tynemouth
South Shields
Gateshead
Sunderland
Carlisle
Durham
Hartlepool
Stockton
Darlington
Middlesbrough
Northallerton
NORTH YORK MOORS
Scarborough
PENNINES

Dublin
Baile Atha Cliath
Dun Laoghaire
Bray
Tullamore
Kildare
Athy
Carlow
Wicklow
Arklow
Enniscorthy
New Ross
Wexford
CARNSORE PT.
Lugnaquillia Mtn. 3038
WICKLOW MTS.
LEINSTER
Kilkenny
Thurles
Nenagh
IRELAND
Ennis
Limerick
Tipperary
MUNSTER
GALTY MTS.
Carrick-on-Suir
Clonmel
Fermoy
Mallow
Cork
Youghal
Cobh
Dungarvan
Waterford
Cork Harbour
Youghal Bay

LOOP HEAD
Kilrush
Shannon
Brandon Mtn. 3127
Tralee
GREAT BLASKET ISLAND
Dingle
Dingle Bay
Corrauntoohil 3406
VALENCIA ISLAND
Killarney
Bantry
Bantry Bay
Skibbereen
Clonakilty Bay
OLD HEAD OF KINSALE

Holyhead
HOLY ISLAND
ANGLESEY
Llandudno
Caernarfon
Bangor
Denbigh
Snowdon 3560
Caernarfon Bay
Ffestiniog
Cardigan Bay
BARDSEY ISLAND
Aberystwyth
Cardigan
Welshpool
CAMBRIAN MTS.
Carmarthen
Llanelli
Pembroke
Neath
Swansea
Merthyr Tydfil
Aberdare
Rhondda
Abergavenny
CARDIFF
Newport
ST DAVID'S HD.
St. George's Channel

Blackpool
Southport
Preston
Blackburn
Burnley
Bolton
Wigan
LIVERPOOL
Birkenhead
Chester
Crewe
Wrexham
Stoke-on-Trent
Rochdale
Oldham
MANCHESTER
Stockport
Halifax
Huddersfield
Wakefield
Bradford
LEEDS
Sheffield
Chesterfield
York
YORKSHIRE WOLDS
Beverley
Kingston upon Hull
Grimsby
Doncaster
Burton
Derby
Nottingham
Grantham
LINCOLN WOLDS
Lincoln

UNITED KINGDOM
Stafford
Shrewsbury
Wolverhampton
Dudley
Smethwick
Walsall
BIRMINGHAM
Coventry
Nuneaton
Leamington
Warwick
Stratford-upon-Avon
Worcester
Hereford
Gloucester
Cheltenham
Leicester
Peterborough
Northampton
Bedford
Cambridge
Luton
Hertford
St. Albans
Aylesbury
Oxford
High Wycombe
Watford
LONDON
Guildford
Reigate
Aldershot
THE WEALD
Tunbridge Wells
NORTH DOWNS

COTSWOLD HILLS
Swindon
Newbury
Reading
Windsor
Gloucester

Bristol
Bath
Weston-super-Mare
Bristol Channel
LUNDY
Ilfracombe
Barnstaple
EXMOOR
HARTLAND PT.
Taunton
Yeovil
SALISBURY PLAIN
Salisbury
Winchester
BLACK DOWN HILLS
Honiton
Dorchester
Weymouth
Poole
Bournemouth
Southampton
Cowes
ISLE OF WIGHT
Ryde
Newport
Portsmouth
Chichester
SOUTH DOWNS
Worthing
Hove
Brighton

Exeter
DARTMOOR
Launceston
Exmouth
Torquay (Torbay)
Dartmouth
START PT.
BODMIN MOOR
Bodmin
Plymouth
Camborne
Truro
Penzance
Falmouth
LAND'S END
ISLES OF SCILLY
LIZARD PT.
ENGLISH CHANNEL

Longitude West of Greenwich

Scale 1: 4 000 000; one inch to 64 miles. Conic Projection
Elevations and depressions are given in feet

Continued on pages 166-167

Continued on pages 168-169

Continued on pages 170-171

Longitude East of Greenwich

0 10 20 30 40 50 60 70 80 90 100 110 120 Miles

0 20 40 60 80 100 120 140 160 180 200 Kilometers

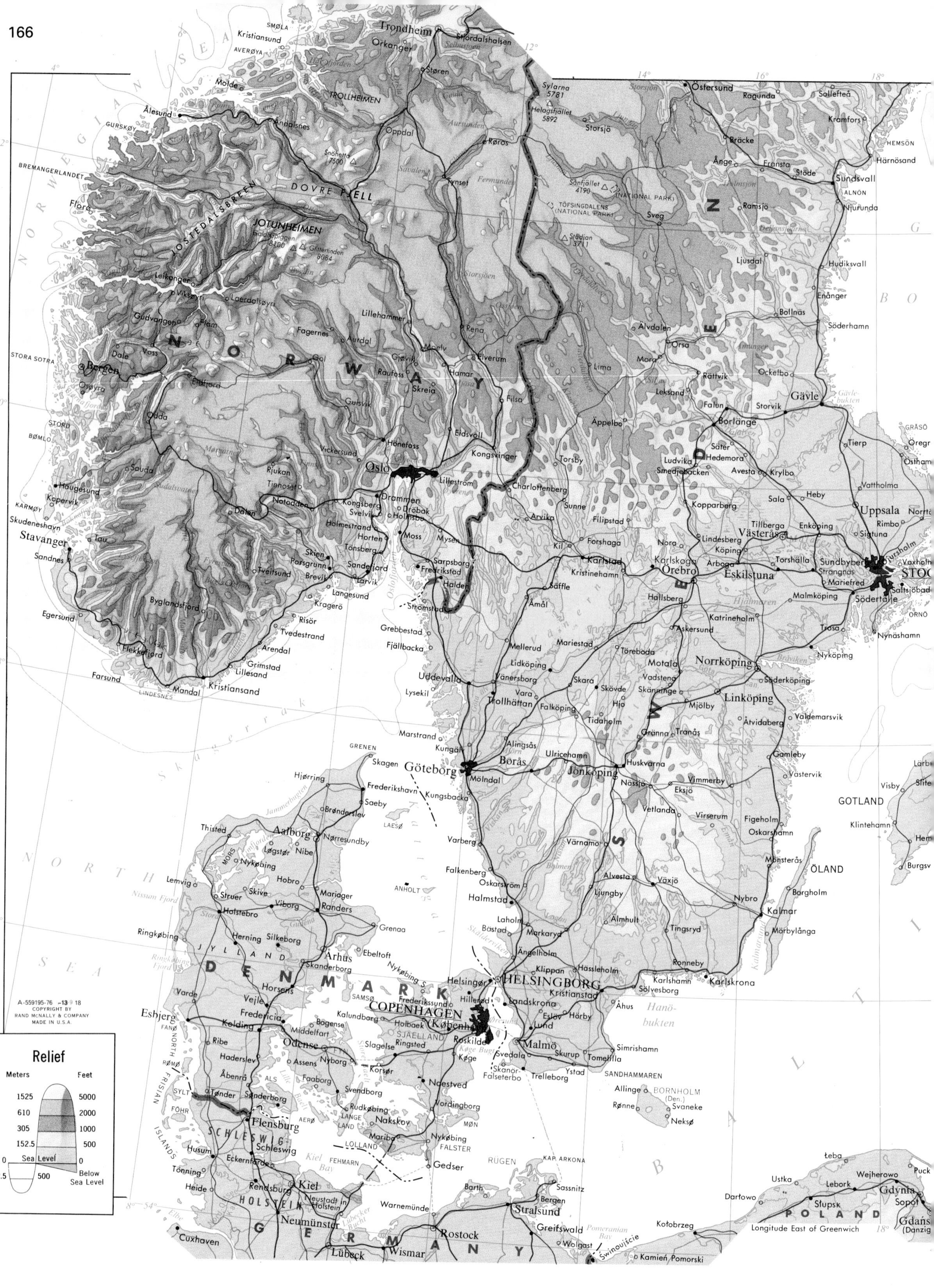

NORWEGIAN SEA

SMØLA
Kristiansund
Trondheim
Orkanger
Stjørdalshalsen
Averøya
Molde
Åndalsnes
TROLLHEIMEN
Oppdal
Støren
Ålesund
Snøhetta 7500
DOVRE FJELL
Røros
Tynset
Sylarna 5781
Helagsfjället 5892
Storsjö
Östersund
Ragunda
Sollefteå
Kramfors
HEMSÖ
Härnösand
Bräcke
Ånge
Fransta
Stöde
Sundsvall
ALNÖN
Njurunda
Ramsjö
Sänfjället 4190 (NATIONAL PARK)
Töfsingdalens (NATIONAL PARK)
Sveg
Städjan 3711

GURSKØY
Flora
JOSTEDALSBREEN
JOTUNHEIMEN
Galdhøpiggen 8100
Glittertinden 8084
BREMANGERLANDET
Leikanger
Vik
Gudvangen
Flåm
Dale
Voss
STORA SOTRA
Bergen
Osøyra
STORD
BØMLO
Odda
Haugesund
Kopervik
KARMØY
Skudeneshavn
Tau
Stavanger
Sandnes
Egersund
Farsund
Flekkefjord
Mandal
Kristiansand
LINDESNES

Lærdalsøyri
Fagernes
Aurdal
Lillehammer
Rena
Gjøvik
Raufoss
Hamar
Elverum
Skreia
Filsa
Eldsvoll
Hønefoss
Kongsvinger
Oslo
Drammen
Lillestrøm
Charlottenberg
Rjukan
Tinnoset
Kongsberg
Svelvik
Holmsbu
Drøbak
Notodden
Dalen
Holmestrand
Horten
Moss
Mysen
Skien
Tønsberg
Porsgrunn
Sandefjord
Brevik
Larvik
Langesund
Kragerø
Risør
Tvedestrand
Arendal
Grimstad
Lillesand
Byglandsfjord
Tveitsund
Sarpsborg
Fredrikstad
Halden
Strömstad
Grebbestad
Fjällbacka
Uddevalla
Lysekil

NORWAY

Storsjön
Älvdalen
Orsa
Mora
Lima
Äppelbo
Rättvik
Ockelbo
Gävle
Gävlebukten
Leksand
Falun
Storvik
Borlänge
Säter
Hedemora
Ludvika
Smedjebacken
Avesta
Krylbo
Kopparberg
Tierp
Sala
Heby
Vattholma
Uppsala
Rimbo
Norrtälje
Sigtuna
Enköping
Tillberga
Västerås
Lindesberg
Köping
Arboga
Sundbyberg
Torshälla
Strängnäs
Mariefred
STOCKHOLM
Örebro
Eskilstuna
Södertälje
Saltsjöbad
ORNÖ
Malmköping
Katrineholm
Askersund
Hallsberg
Trosa
Nynäshamn
Nyköping
Söderköping
Norrköping
Motala
Vadstena
Skänninge
Linköping
Mjölby
Gränna
Tranås
Åtvidaberg
Valdemarsvik
Gamleby
Västervik
Vimmerby
Eksjö
Nässjö
Huskvarna
Jönköping
Vetlanda
Virserum
Figeholm
Oskarshamn
Mönsterås
GOTLAND
Visby
Slite
Klintehamn
ÖLAND
Borgholm
Kalmar
Mörbylånga

Karlstad
Kristinehamn
Säffle
Åmål
Kil
Forshaga
Sunne
Arvika
Filipstad
Nora
Karlskoga
Mariestad
Töreboda
Lidköping
Skara
Skövde
Tidaholm
Falköping
Vara
Hjo
Vänern
Vänersborg
Trollhättan
Alingsås
Ulricehamn
Borås
Mölndal
Göteborg
Kungsbacka
Kungälv
Marstrand
Varberg
Falkenberg
Oskarström
Halmstad
Laholm
Båstad
Markaryd
Ängelholm
Klippan
Hässleholm
Kristianstad
Åhus
Hanöbukten
Sölvesborg
Karlshamn
Karlskrona
Ronneby
Värnamo
Alvesta
Växjö
Nybro
Ljungby
Almhult
Tingsryd
Simrishamn
SANDHAMMAREN
Ystad
Trelleborg
Skurup
Tomelilla
ALLINGE
BORNHOLM (Den.)
Svaneke
Rønne
Neksø

Göta
Hjørring
Skagen
GRENEN
Frederikshavn
Sæby
Brønderslev
Kungsbacka
LÆSØ
Thisted
Aalborg
Nørresundby
Løgstør
Nibe
MORS
Nykøbing
Hobro
Lemvig
Struer
Skive
Viborg
Mariager
Randers
Grenaa
ANHOLT
Holstebro
Ringkøbing
Herning
Silkeborg
Århus
Ebeltoft
Skanderborg
JYLLAND
DENMARK
Varde
Horsens
Vejle
Esbjerg
FANØ
Kolding
Fredericia
Middelfart
Bogense
Assens
Odense
Ribe
Haderslev
Åbenrå
SYLT
Tønder
Sønderborg
ALS
FØHR
FRISIAN ISLANDS
SCHLESWIG
Flensburg
Husum
Eckernförde
Schleswig
FEHMARN
Rendsburg
Kiel
HOLSTEIN
Neustadt in Holstein
Neumünster
Heide
Tönning
Cuxhaven
Elbe
GERMANY

NORTH SEA

Frederikssund
Hillerød
Helsingør
Helsingborg
Landskrona
COPENHAGEN
København
Roskilde
Holbæk
SJÆLLAND
Slagelse
Ringsted
Køge
Køge Bugt
Lund
Eslöv
Hörby
Malmö
Svedala
Skanör
Falsterbo
Kalundborg
Nyborg
Korsør
Næstved
Vordingborg
MØN
Svendborg
Rudkøbing
LANGELAND
Nakskov
Maribo
Nykøbing FALSTER
LOLLAND
AERØ
Faaborg
Gedser
RÜGEN
KAP ARKONA
Sassnitz
Bergen
Stralsund
Greifswald
Barth
Warnemünde
Rostock
Wismar
Lübeck
Kiel Bucht
Lübecker Bucht
Pomeranian Bay
Wolgast
Swinoujscie
Kamień Pomorski
Kołobrzeg
POLAND
Słupsk
Ustka
Darłowo
Łeba
Lębork
Wejherowo
Puck
Gdynia
Sopot
Gdańsk (Danzig)
Longitude East of Greenwich

SKAGERRAK
KATTEGAT
BALTIC SEA
Hanöbukten

A-559195-76 –13-9-18
COPYRIGHT BY
RAND MCNALLY & COMPANY
MADE IN U.S.A.

**Relief**

| Meters | | Feet |
|---|---|---|
| 1525 | | 5000 |
| 610 | | 2000 |
| 305 | | 1000 |
| 152.5 | | 500 |
| 0 | Sea Level | 0 |
| 152.5 | | 500 Below Sea Level |

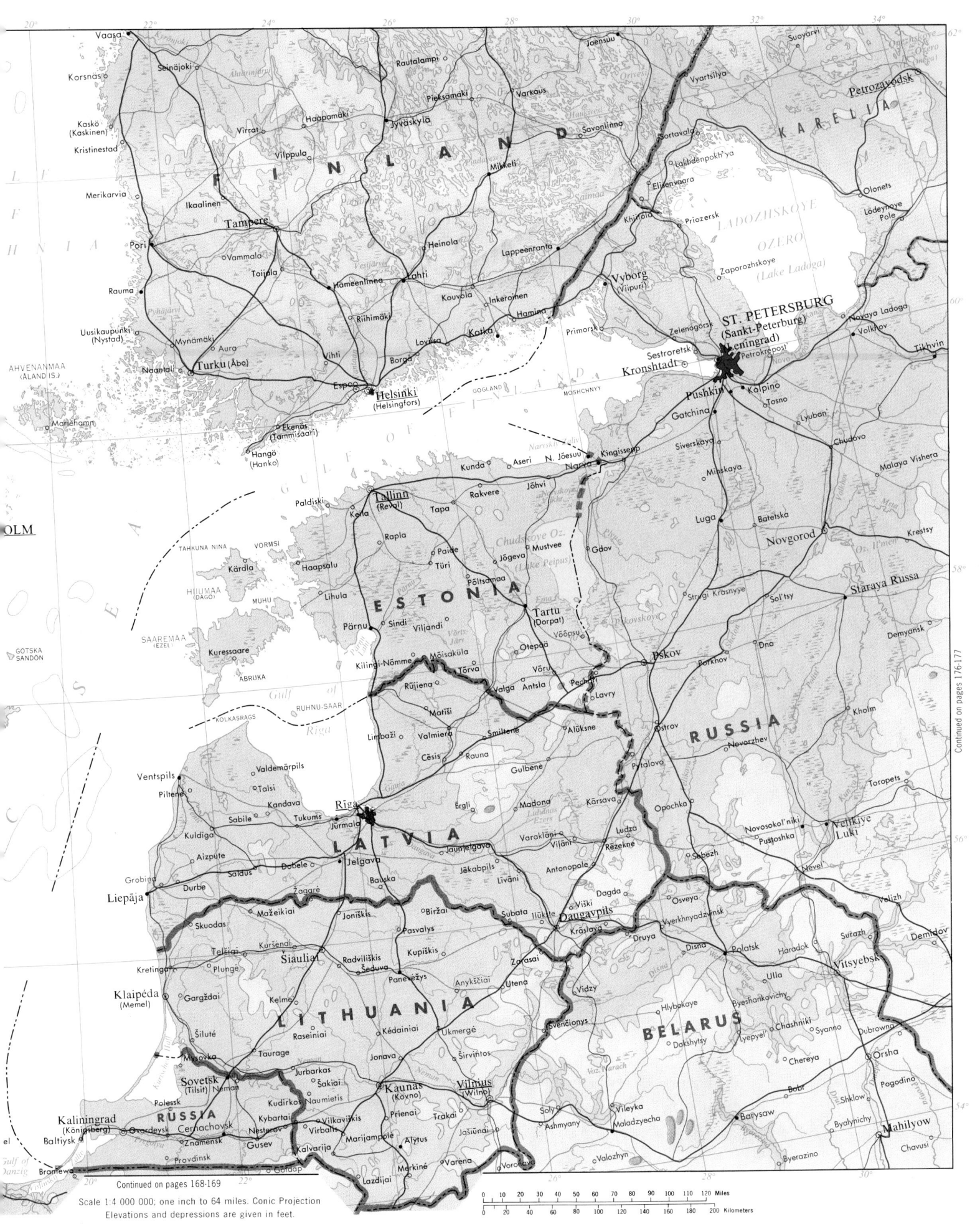

OLM

Vaasa
Korsnäs
Seinäjoki
Kaskö (Kaskinen)
Kristinestad
Merikarvia
Ikaalinen
Pori
Rauma
Uusikaupunki (Nystad)
AHVENANMAA (ÅLAND IS.)
Mariehamn
Mynämäki
Naantali
Aura
Turku (Åbo)

F I N L A N D

Rautalampi
Pieksämäki
Varkaus
Jyväskylä
Haapamäki
Virrat
Vilppula
Tampere
Vammala
Toijala
Hämeenlinna
Riihimäki
Vihti
Espoo
Borga
Helsinki (Helsingfors)
Ekenäs (Tammisaari)
Hangö (Hanko)

Joensuu
Vyartsilya
Petrozavodsk
K A R E L I A
Sortavala
Lakhdenpokh'ya
Elisenvaara
Olonets
Khitola
Priozersk
Lödeynoye Pole
Zaporozhskoye (Lake Ladoga)
L A D O Z H S K O Y E   O Z E R O

Mikkeli
Savonlinna
Heinola
Lahti
Lappeenranta
Kouvola
Inkeroinen
Hamina
Lovisa
Kotka
Primorsk
Vyborg (Viipuri)
Zelenogorsk
Sestroretsk
Kronshtadt
ST. PETERSBURG (Sankt-Peterburg) (Leningrad)
Petrokrepost
Pushkin
Gatchina
Kolpino
Tosno
Lyuban
Chudovo
Novaya Ladoga
Volkhov
Tikhvin

GULF OF FINLAND
GOGLAND
MOSHCHNYY

Kunda
Aseri
N. Jõesuu
Narva
Jõhvi
Kingissepp
Siverskaya
Luga
Minskaya
Bateskaya
Malaya Vishera

TAHKUNA NINA
VORMSI
Paldiski
Kärla
Tallinn (Reval)
Tapa
Rakvere
Rapla
Paide
HIIUMAA (DAGO)
MUHU
Kärdla
Haapsalu
Türi
Lihula
E S T O N I A
Pärnu
Sindi
Viljandi
Jõgeva
Mustvee
Gdov
Novgorod
Krestsy
Staraya Russa
Demyansk
Dno
Oz. Il'men'
Sol'tsy
Strugi Krasnye
Chudskoye Oz. (Lake Peipus)
SAAREMAA (EZEL)
Kuressaare
ABRUKA
Põltsamaa
Võrtsjärv
Otepää
Tartu (Dorpat)
Võõpsu
Pskovskoye
GOTSKA SANDÖN
RUHNU-SAAR
Gulf of Riga
KOLKASRAGS
Kilingi-Nõmme
Mõisaküla
Tõrva
Rüjiena
Valga
Antsla
Võru
Pechory
Lavry
Matiši
Smiltene
Alūksne
Ostrov
Novorzhev
Kholm
R U S S I A
Limbaži
Valmiera
Cēsis
Rauna
Gulbene
Pytalovo
Toropets
Ventspils
Piltene
Valdemārpils
Talsi
Kandava
Sabile
Rīga
Tukums
Jūrmala
Ērgli
Madona
Kārsava
Opochka
Novosokol'niki
Velikiye Luki
Kuldīga
Aizpute
Saldus
Dobele
Jelgava
L A T V I A
Jaunjelgava
Varakļāni
Vilāni
Rēzekne
Ludza
Sebezh
Pustoshka
Nevel
Grobiņa
Durbe
Žagarē
Bauska
Jēkabpils
Līvāni
Antonopole
Dagda
Osveya
Liepāja
Mažeikiai
Joniškis
Pasvalys
Subata
Ilūkste
Daugavpils
Krāslava
Druya
Disna
Polatsk
Haradok
Vitsyebsk
Skuodas
Birži
Kupiškis
Zarasai
Vyerkhnyadzvinsk
Telšiai
Kuršėnai
Radviliškis
Šeduva
Utena
Vidzy
Ulla
Kretinga
Plungė
Šiauliai
Panevėžys
Anykščiai
Druya
Demidov
Surazh
Klaipėda (Memel)
Gargždai
Kelmė
Kėdainiai
Ukmergė
Širvintos
Švenčionys
Hlybokaye
Dokshytsy
Lyepyel
Chashniki
Syanno
Dubrowna
Orsha
L I T H U A N I A
Raseiniai
Jonava
Vilnius (Wilno)
B E L A R U S
Mysovka
Taurage
Jurbarkas
Šakiai
Kaunas (Kovno)
Trakai
Soly
Ashmyany
Maladzyechna
Vileyka
Barysaw
Byelynichy
Mahilyow
Sovetsk (Tilsit)
Neman
Kudirkos Naumiestis
Prienai
Jašiūnai
Vievis
Valozhyn
Smalyavichy
Pahost
Chavusi
Kaliningrad (Königsberg)
Ovardeysk
Černachovsk
Kybartai
Vilkaviškis
Virbalis
Marijampolė
Alytus
Varena
Voronava
Bobr
Shklow
Pogodino
Baltiysk
Znamensk
Gusev
Provdinsk
Goldap
Kalvarija
Merkinė
Varėna
Byerazino
Byalynichy
Polessk
R U S S I A
Gulf of Danzig
Braniewo
Lazdijai
Continued on pages 168-169

Continued on pages 176-177

Scale 1:4 000 000; one inch to 64 miles. Conic Projection
Elevations and depressions are given in feet.

0  10  20  30  40  50  60  70  80  90  100  110  120 Miles
0  20  40  60  80  100  120  140  160  180  200 Kilometers

Continued on pages 166-167

NORTH SEA

BALTIC

DENMARK

Svendborg
Langeland
Nakskov
MØN
Tønder
Flensburg
Sønderborg
Rudkøbing
Nykøbing
FALSTER
SCHLESWIG
Schleswig
Eckernförde
Kiel
Gedser
FÖHR
Husum
Heide
Rendsburg
HOLSTEIN
Kiel Bay
Sassnitz
RÜGEN
Bergen
Stralsund
Greifswald
Wolgast
Demmin
Anklam
Rostock
Wismar
Schwerin
MECKLENBURG
Güstrow
Teterow
Waren
Neubrandenburg
Pasewalk
Ueckermünde

FRISIAN ISLANDS
NORDERNEY
WANGEROOGE
Cuxhaven
Bremerhaven
Stade
HAMBURG
Lübeck
Bad Oldesloe
Neumünster
Itzehoe

VLIELAND
TERSCHELLING
AMELAND
BORKUM
Norden
Emden
Wilhelmshaven
Jadebusen
Bremen
Delmenhorst
Oldenburg
Papenburg
Leer

NETHERLANDS
Den Helder
Alkmaar
Leeuwarden
Groningen
Delfzijl
Emmen
Meppen
Lingen
Nordhorn
LÜNEBURGER HEIDE
Lüneburg
Soltau
Uelzen
Salzwedel
Stendal
Gardelegen
Tangermünde
Genthin
Brandenburg
Potsdam
BERLIN
Oranienburg
Eberswalde
Bernau
Strausberg
Frankfurt an der Oder

AMSTERDAM
Zwolle
Deventer
Apeldoorn
Hengelo
Almelo
Enschede
Gronau
Rheine
Osnabrück
Minden
Hannover
Braunschweig
Hildesheim
Wolfsburg
Celle
Magdeburg
Schönebeck
Zerbst
Dessau
Wittenberg
Lübben
Cottbus
Forst
Spremberg

Utrecht
Arnhem
Nijmegen
Kleve
s-Hertogenbosch
Münster
Bielefeld
Herford
Detmold
Paderborn
Gütersloh
Hameln
Göttingen
Northeim
Nordhausen
Eisleben
Halle
Merseburg
Leipzig
Eilenburg
Wurzen
Riesa
Grossenhain
Meissen
Dresden
Bautzen
Görlitz

Tilburg
Eindhoven
Duisburg
Gelsenkirchen
Dortmund
Bochum
Hamm
Soest
Lippstadt
Kassel
BELGIUM
Mönchengladbach
DÜSSELDORF
ESSEN
Wuppertal
Solingen
Hagen
Gummersbach
WESTFALEN
Marburg an der Lahn
Hersfeld
Eschwege
Mühlhausen
Sondershausen
Sangerhausen
THÜRINGEN
Weimar
Gera
Altenburg
Zwickau
Chemnitz
Freiberg
Pirna
GERMANY

Heerlen
Aachen
COLOGNE
(Köln)
Bonn
Siegen
Ahrweiler
WESTERWALD
Wetzlar
Giessen
HESSEN
Fulda
Meiningen
Zella-Mehlis
Suhl
Saalfeld
Plauen
Hof
CZECH REPUBLIC

Liège
Verviers
Spa
Malmedy
EIFEL
Andernach
Neuwied
Koblenz
Limburg an der Lahn
RHEINLAND
FRANKFURT AM MAIN
Wiesbaden
Hanau
Offenbach
Aschaffenburg
Schweinfurt
Würzburg
Bamberg
Bayreuth
Weiden
Amberg
BOHEMIA
Plzeň
Rakovník
Kladno
PRAGUE
(Praha)
Hradec Králové
Pardubice

LUXEMBOURG
Trier
Bingen
Mainz
Darmstadt
Worms
Bensheim
ODENWALD
MANNHEIM
Heidelberg
Würzburg
Rothenburg
Ansbach
Erlangen
Fürth
Nürnberg
Neumarkt
Schwandorf
Regensburg
BÖHMERWALD
České Budějovice
Třeboň
Jindřichův Hradec
Písek

Luxembourg
Longwy
Thionville
Metz
Saarbrücken
Kaiserslautern
Neustadt
Landau
Speyer
Ludwigshafen
Pirmasens
Karlsruhe
Bruchsal
Heilbronn
Schwäbisch Hall
Ellwangen
Nördlingen
Weissenburg
Eichstätt
Ingolstadt
Straubing
BAYERN
(BAVARIA)
Landshut
Passau
Deggendorf
Linz

Nancy
Sarreguemines
Saarbourg
Strasbourg
Haguenau
Rastatt
Baden-Baden
Pforzheim
Ludwigsburg
STUTTGART
Esslingen
Göppingen
Aalen
Heidenheim
Ulm
Neu-Ulm
Augsburg
Dachau
Freising
Mühldorf
Braunau
Ried
Wels
St. Pölten
VIENNA
(Wien)

ALSACE
Colmar
Freiburg
Offenburg
Lahr
Rottweil
Tübingen
Reutlingen
SCHWÄBISCHE ALB
Biberach
Memmingen
Landsberg
Kaufbeuren
Weilheim
Rosenheim
Traunstein
Salzburg
Bad Ischl

FRANCE
Mulhouse
Belfort
Basel
Lörrach
Schaffhausen
Konstanz
Bodensee
Friedrichshafen
Ravensburg
Kempten
Garmisch-Partenkirchen
Innsbruck
Schwaz
Kufstein
Wörgl
Wiener Neustadt
Neunkirchen

SWITZERLAND
Zürich
Winterthur
Sankt Gallen
Feldkirch
Bludenz
LIECHTENSTEIN
Dornbirn
Arlberg Tunnel
HOHE TAUERN
NIEDERE TAUERN
Leoben
Bruck
Graz
Szombathely

La Chaux-de-Fonds
Neuchâtel
Biel
Bern
Solothurn
Luzern
Glarus
Davos
Merano
Bolzano
Villach
Klagenfurt
Maribor
SLOVENIA

Lausanne
Geneva
(Genève)
BERNER ALPEN
GOTTHARD
PENNINE ALPS
Bressanone
CARNIC ALPS
KARAWANKEN
Celje
CROATIA
Udine

A L P S

Scale 1:4 000 000; one inch to 64 miles. Conic Projection
Elevations and depressions are given in feet.

Continued on pages 170-171
Continued on pages 174-175

Longitude East of Greenwich

COPYRIGHT BY
RAND McNALLY & COMPANY
MADE IN U.S.A.

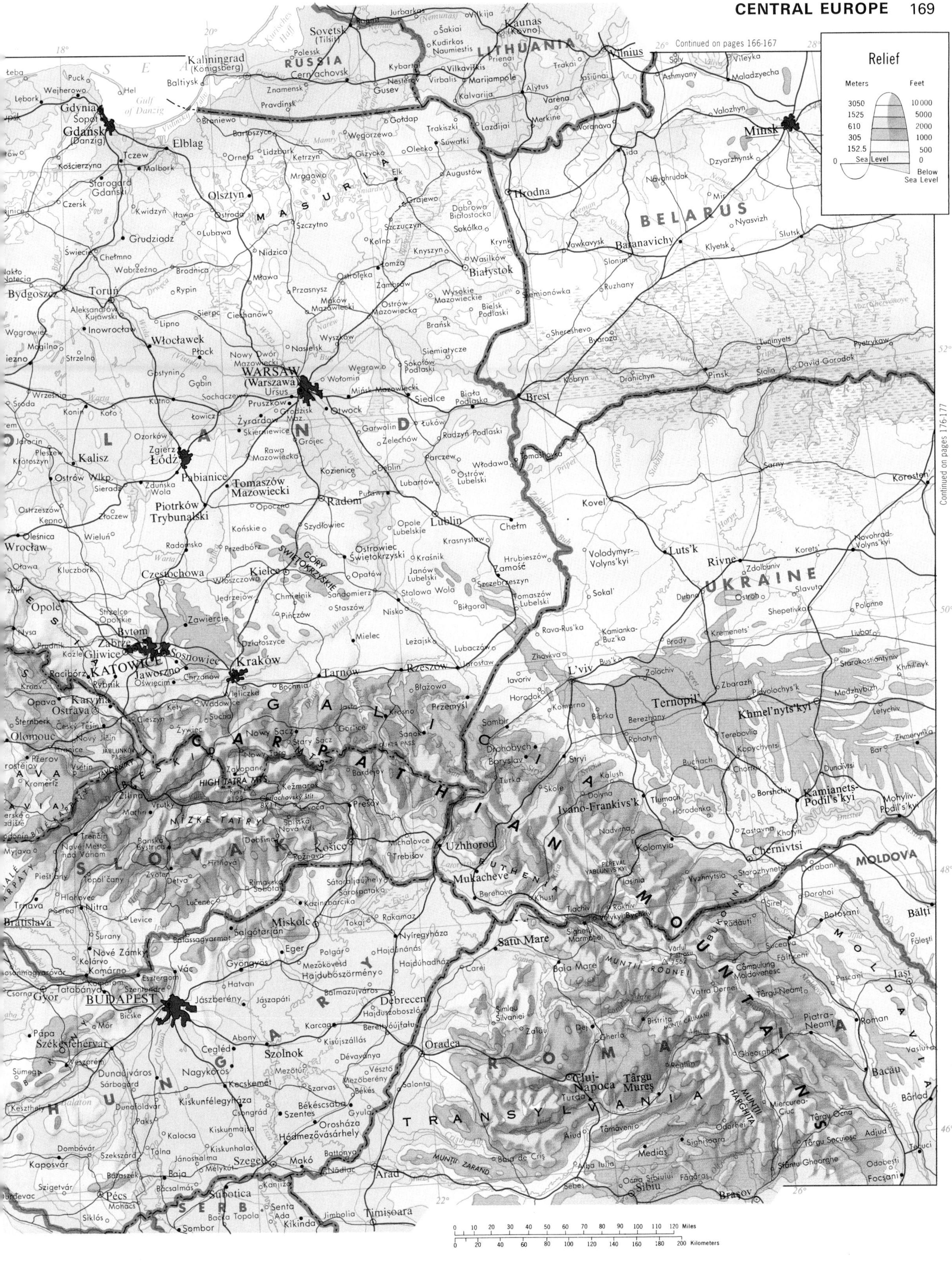

Continued on pages 166-167

Continued on pages 176-177

**Relief**

| Meters | | Feet |
|---|---|---|
| 3050 | | 10 000 |
| 1525 | | 5000 |
| 610 | | 2000 |
| 305 | | 1000 |
| 152.5 | | 500 |
| Sea Level | | 0 |
| | | Below Sea Level |

RUSSIA

LITHUANIA

BELARUS

POLAND

UKRAINE

SLOVAKIA

HUNGARY

ROMANIA

MOLDOVA

SERBIA

GALICIA

CARPATHIAN MOUNTAINS

TRANSYLVANIA

MASURIA

RUTHENIA

HIGH TATRA MTS.

NIZKE TATRY

MUNTII RODNEI

MUNTII CALIMANI

MUNTII HARGHITA

MUNTII ZARAND

Gdańsk (Danzig)
Gdynia
Sopot
Warsaw (Warszawa)
Łódź
Kraków
Katowice
Wrocław
Poznań
Bydgoszcz
Toruń
Lublin
Białystok
Minsk
Vilnius
Kaunas (Kovno)
Kaliningrad (Königsberg)
L'viv
Ternopil'
Ivano-Frankivs'k
Chernivtsi
Kamianets-Podil's'kyi
Bratislava
Košice
BUDAPEST
Miskolc
Debrecen
Satu Mare
Oradea
Cluj-Napoca
Târgu Mureș
Sibiu
Brașov
Bacău
Iași
Bălți

Gulf of Danzig

BALTIC SEA

0 10 20 30 40 50 60 70 80 90 100 110 120 Miles

0 20 40 60 80 100 120 140 160 180 200 Kilometers

Continued on pages 164-165

### Relief

| Meters | Feet |
|---|---|
| 3050 | 10 000 |
| 1525 | 5000 |
| 610 | 2000 |
| 305 | 1000 |
| 152.5 | 500 |
| Sea Level | 0 |
| 152.5 | 500 |
| 1525 | 5000 |

A-550900-76   -76-14
COPYRIGHT BY
RAND McNALLY & COMPANY
MADE IN U.S.A.

**a**

Marseille

Scale 1:1 000 000

0   5   10 Miles

0   4   8   12   16 Kilometers

Continued on pages 172-173

Longitude West of Greenwich    Longitude East of Greenwich

Scale 1:4 000 000; one inch to 64 miles. Conic Projection
Elevations and depressions are given in feet

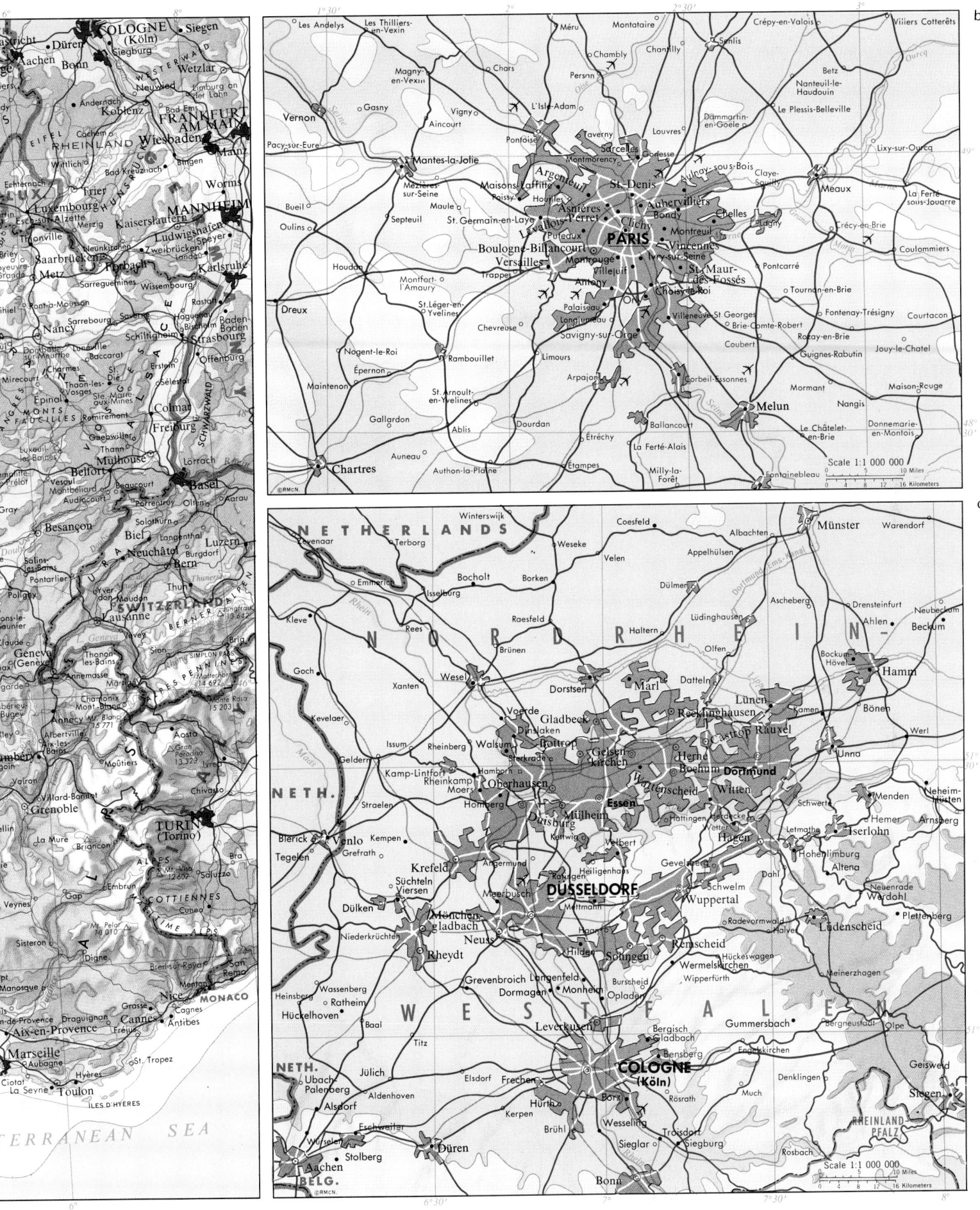

b

c

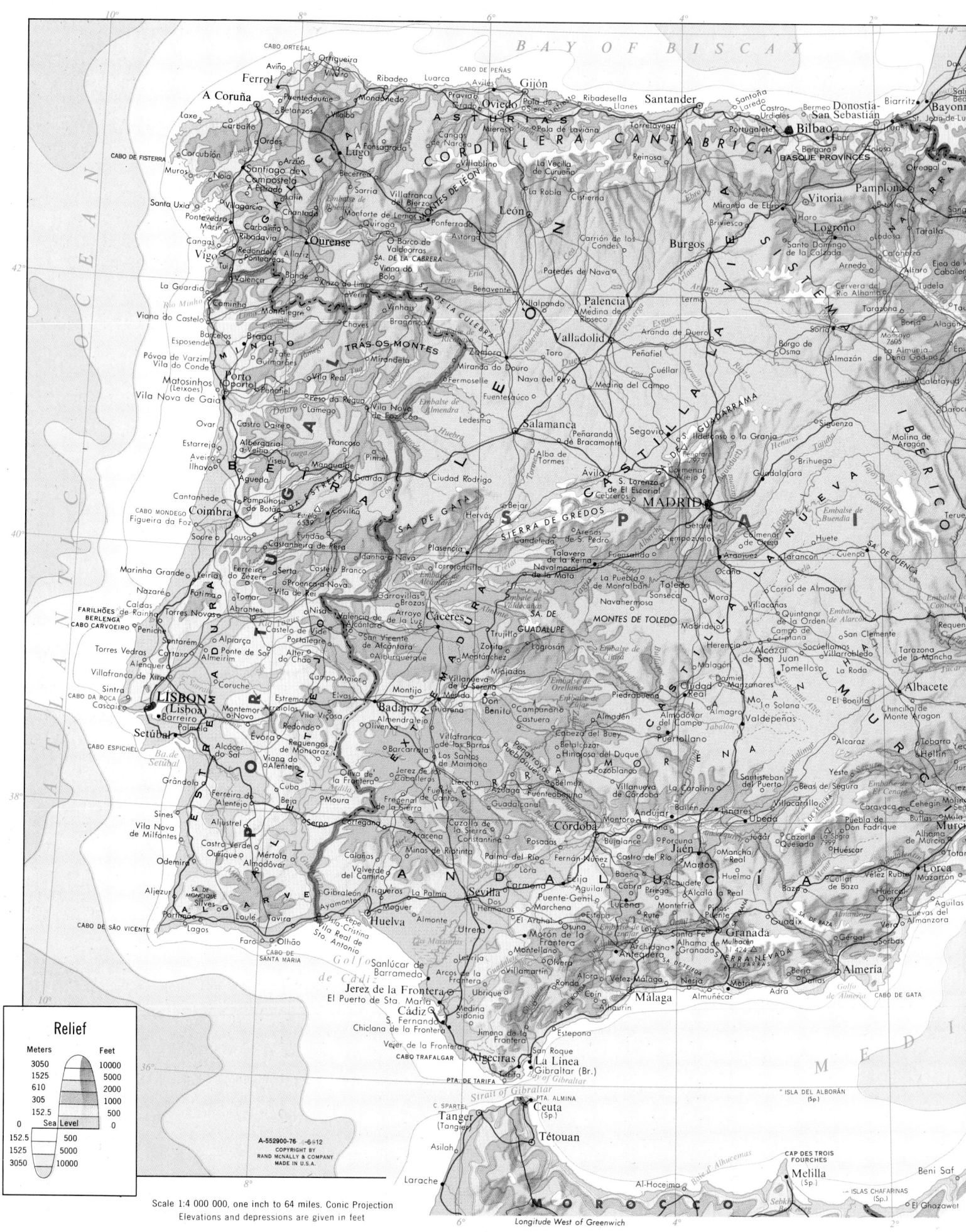

Continued on pages 170-171

**a**

SA. DEL HOYO
4606
S. Lorenzo de
El Escorial
Colmenar
Viejo
Galapagar
El Escorial
Valdemorillo
Las Rozas
de Madrid
El Pardo
Barajas
de Madrid
Torrejón
de Ardoz
Alcalá de
Henares
Pozuela de Alarcón
Fuencarral
MADRID
Vicálvaro
S. Fernando de Henares
Brunete
Alcorcón
Leganés
Móstoles
Getafe
Vallecas
Arganda
Campo Real
Navalcarnero
Valdilecha
Carabaña
Parla
Pinto
S. Martín
de la Vega
Morata
de Tajuña
Perales
de Tajuña
Scale 1:1 000 000

**b**

Mafra
Cheleiros
Alhandra
Samora Correia
São João
das Lampas
Montelavar
Alverca
Alcabideche
Sintra
Odivelas
Touros
Sacavém
Moscavide
Alcochete
Queluz
Barcarena
Amadora
Carnaxide
LISBON
(Lisboa)
Montijo
Cascais
Oeiras
Estoril
ATLANTIC
Almada
Barreiro
OCEAN
Costa de Caparica
Seixal
Albufeira
Vedras
Moita
Pinhal Novo
Coina
Palmela
Setúbal
Ba. de
Setúbal
Sesimbra
CABO ESPICHEL
Comporta
Scale 1:1 000 000

**c**

Frattamaggiore
Acerra
Nola
Avellino
Marano di Napoli
Afragola
Pomigliano d'Arco
Montefreda
Irpino
Somma Vesuviana
NAPLES
(Napoli)
Vesuvio
S. Giuseppe
Vesuviano
Mercato
Severino
Pozzuoli
Portici
Torre
del Greco
Sarno
Bacoli
Torre Annunziata
Nocera Inf.
C. MISENO
Pompeii Ruins
Cava de'
Tirreni
Forio
Ischia
Golfo di Napoli
Castellammare
di Stabia
Angri
Gragnano
Salerno
I. D'ISCHIA
Amalfi
TYRRHENIAN
Sorrento
SEA
Golfo di Salerno
PUNTA
CAMPANELLA
I. DI CAPRI
Capri
Scale 1:1 000 000

**d**

Monterotondo
Pyrgi
Caere
Veio
Mentana
Guidonia
Cerveteri
Ladispoli
ROME
(Roma)
Tivoli
Villa
Adriana
VATICAN CITY
Fregene
Zagarolo
Fiumicino
Frascati
Marino
COLLI ALBANI
Ostia Antica
Albano Laziale
Genzano di Roma
Lido di Roma
Laurentum
Velletri
Lanuvio
Pomezia
Aprília
TYRRHENIAN
Cisterna
di Latina
SEA
Nettuno
Anzio
Scale 1:1 000 000

Longitude East of Greenwich

Continued on pages 168-169

Continued on pages 170-171

**Countries / Regions:** AUSTRIA, SLOVENIA, CROATIA, BOSNIA, SWITZERLAND, FRANCE, MONACO

**Italian regions:** TRENTINO-ALTO ADIGE, FRIULI-VENEZIA GIULIA, LOMBARDY, EMILIA, ROMAGNA, TOSCANA, UMBRIA, MARCHE, ABRUZZI E MOLISE, LAZIO, CAMPANIA, PUGLIA, BASILICATA, CALABRIA, SICILY, SARDINIA, CORSICA

**Seas:** LIGURIAN SEA, TYRRHENIAN SEA, ADRIATIC, Gulf of Venice, AEGEAN SEA, MEDITERRANEAN SEA

**Cities and towns:**
Brenner Pass, Lienz, Maribor, Klagenfurt, Villach, Dravograd, Čakovec, Koprivnica, Szigetvár, Merano, Bolzano, Bressanone, Pieve di Cadore, Tolmezzo, Kranj, Celje, Varaždin, Đurđevac, Bjelovar, Virovitica
Trento, Belluno, Udine, Pordenone, Gorizia, Ljubljana, Zagreb, Čazma, Daruvar
Varese, Como, Bergamo, Brescia, Vicenza, Verona, Treviso, Mestre, Venice (Venezia), Trieste, Rijeka (Fiume), Ogulin, Sisak, Petrinja, Kutina
Busto Arsizio, Monza, MILAN (Milano), Novara, Lodi, Crema, Cremona, Padova (Padua), Rovigo, Chioggia, Pula
TURIN (Torino), Pavia, Piacenza, Mantova (Mantua), Adria, Cavarzere, Cres, Rovinj, Poreč, Pazin, Banja Luka, Bosanski Novi
Casale, Monferrato, Asti, Alessandria, Voghera, Tortona, Parma, Reggio nell'Emilia, Modena, Ferrara, Comacchio, Zadar, Bosanski Gradiška
Cuneo, Savona, Genoa (Genova), La Spezia, Bologna, Ravenna, Faenza, Forlì, Cesena, Rimini, Pesaro, Fano, Senigallia, Ancona, Šibenik, Split
Nice, Ventimiglia, Imperia, Albenga, Carrara, Massa, Pistoia, Prato, Florence (Firenze), San Marino, Urbino, Recanati, Fermo, Knin, Trogir, Livno
S. Remo, Pisa, Lucca, Livorno (Leghorn), Siena, Arezzo, Perugia, Macerata, Fabriano, San Benedetto del Tronto, Ascoli Piceno, Teramo
Piombino, Grosseto, Orvieto, Foligno, Spoleto, Terni, Rieti, L'Aquila, Chieti, Pescara, Vasto, Termoli, Vieste, Manfredonia
Civitavecchia, Viterbo, Tivoli, Avezzano, Sulmona, Monte Sant'Angelo, Foggia, Barletta, Trani, Molfetta, Bari
VATICAN CITY, ROME (Roma), Frascati, Frosinone, Cassino, Benevento, Andria, Corato, Ruvo, Bitonto, Gioia del Colle
Anzio, Terracina, Gaeta, Capua, Caserta, Avellino, Potenza, Altamura, Matera, Gravina, Ginosa, Taranto
NAPLES (Napoli), Pozzuoli, Torre del Greco, Sorrento, Salerno, Eboli, Sala Consilina, Metaponto
Sassari, Olbia, Nuoro, Oristano, Cagliari, Iglesias, Carbonia, Catanzaro, Cosenza, Crotone, Rossano
Palermo, Trapani, Marsala, Mazara del Vallo, Agrigento, Caltanissetta, Enna, Catania, Messina, Reggio di Calabria, Siracusa, Augusta
Vibo Valentia, Polistena, Bagnara, Milazzo, Taormina, Acireale

**Crete inset:**
Same scale as main map
AEGEAN SEA, CRETE (Greece), Khaniá, Iráklion (Candia), Kissamos, Khóra Sfakíon, Neápoli, Sitía, Ierápetra, GÁVDHOS, MEDITERRANEAN SEA

Scale 1:4 000 000; one inch to 64 miles. Conic Projection
Elevations and depressions are given in feet

©RMcN.

Continued on pages 166-167

Scale 1:4 000 000; one inch to 64 miles. Conic Projection
Elevations and depressions are given in feet

Scale 1:20 000 000; one inch to 315 miles.
Lambert's Azimuthal, Equal Area Projection
Elevations and depressions are given in feet

**Relief**

| Meters | | Feet |
|---|---|---|
| 3050 | | 10 000 |
| 1525 | | 5000 |
| 610 | | 2000 |
| 305 | | 1000 |
| 152.5 | | 500 |
| 0 | Sea Level | 0 |
| 152.5 | | 500 |
| 1525 | | 5000 | Below Sea Level |
| 3050 | | 10 000 |

A R C T I C   O C E A N

P-OV GORY
TAYMYR
BYRRANGA

SEVERNAYA ZEMLYA
(NORTHERN LAND)

M. CHELYUSKIN

BOL'SHOY
BEGICHEV

Nordvik

Khatanskiy
Zaliv

Khatanga

Ust'-Olenek

Tiksi

Bulun

KOTEL'NYY

NOVOSIBIRSKIYE O-VA
(NEW SIBERIAN ISLANDS)
MALYY LYAKHOVSKIYE
LYAKHOVSKIYE

FADDEYA

NOVAYA SIBIR

DE-LONGA

L A P T E V   S E A

E A S T   S I B E R I A N   S E A

VRANGELYA
(WRANGEL)

M. SHELAGSKIY

Ambarchik

Arctic Circle

Nizhne-Kolymsk

Sredne-
Kolymsk

Markovo

Penzhino

Anadyr'

Chukotskiy

CHUKOTSKOYE NAGOR'YE

KORYAKSKIY KHREBET

M. Olyutorskiy

P-OV
KAMCHATKA

Ust'-Kamchatsk

Verkhne-Kamchatsk

Petropavlovsk-
Kamchatskiy

Ust'-Bol'sheretsk

S E A   O F   O K H O T S K

Magadan

Okhotsk

KHREBET GYDAN (KOLYMSKIY)

KHREBET CHERSKOGO

VERKHOYANSKIY KHREBET

Zashiversk

Zyryanka

Alazeya

Verkhoyansk

Gora Chen
10 171

Oymyakon

M. BUOR-
KHAYA

Kozach'ye

Zhigansk

Yana

DZHUGDZHUR KHREBET

Ayan

SHANTAR

M. ALEVINA

M. TERPENIYA

SAKHALIN

Aleksandrovsk

Poronaysk

Uglegorsk

Yuzhno-Sakhalinsk

Korsakov

Kholmsk

Okha

S A K H A L I N

S I B E R I A

Noril'sk

GORY PUTORANA

Turukhansk

Baykit

Nizhnaya Tunguska

Podkamennaya Tunguska

Tura

Polkan 3543

Yartsevo

Yeniseysk

Kirensk

Ilimsk

Nizhne-Angarsk

Zhigalovo

Kachuga

Baykal (Baikal)

Barguzin

Surface elev.1535 ft.
above sea level

PATOM PLATEAU

Golets Purpula 537

Bodaybo

Golets Skalistyy 9180

Peleduy

Vitim

Muktuya

Olekminsk

Yakutsk

Suntar

Vilyuysk

Vilyuy

Lena

Aldan

Amga

Tommot

Aldan

Ust'-Maya

Nel'kan

Nel'kan

Chumikan

Nikolayevsk-na-Amure

STANOVOY KHREBET

Tyndinskiy

Zeya

Skovorodino

Svobodnyy

Belogorsk

Ust' Tyrma

Bureya

Komsomol'sk-
na-Amure

Sovetskaya Gavan'

KHREBET BUREINSKIY

SIKHOTE ALIN

Aldanskoye

Tommot

R U S S I A

Krasnoyarsk

Kansk

Tayshet

Bratsk

Tulun

Bratskoye Vdkhr.

Nizhneudinsk

Pyramida 10801

Minusinsk

Abakan

KHREBET SAYAN

Munku Sardyk 11457

Kyzyl

Kyren

TANNU-OLA

Uvs Nuur

Har Us Nuur

Cheremkhovo

Kutulik

Angarsk

Irkutsk

Ulan-Ude

Aginskoye

Gorodok

Kyakhta

Selenge

Petrovsk-Zabaykal'skiy

Kuznetski

Bogotol

Balakhta

YABLONOVYY KHREBET

BAYKAL'SKIY KHREBET

Sretensk

Nerchinsk

Chita

Aksha

Borzya

Nerchinskiy Zavod

NERCHINSKIY KHREBET

Blagoveshchensk

Nenjiang

Goukou

Hailun

Suihua

LESSER KHINGAN RANGE

Birobidzhan

Khabarovsk

Spassk-
Dal'niy

Ussuriysk

Arsen'ev

Partizansk

Nakhodka

Vladivostok

Ol'ga

Dal'nerechensk

KHREBET USSURIYSKIY

HOKKAIDŌ

Wakkanai

Otaru

Sapporo

Esashi

J A P A N

Qiqihar

HARBIN

Mudanjiang

Boli

M A N C H U R I A

Jilin

Changchun

Fuyu

Tao an

Jarud Qi

Wenquan

Kerulen

Ondorhaan

GREATER KHINGAN RANGE

Shuangliao

Dunhua

Hunchun

Najin

Chŏngjin

S E A   O F   J A P A N

Mergen

HONSHŪ

Kanazawa

Tottori

Matsue

KYOTO

KŌBE

Okayama

OSAKA

Kōchi

Hiroshima

M O N G O L I A

Ulan Bator
(Ulaanbaatar)

HANGAYN NURUU

KHANGAYN

Uliastay

Hovd

Tsast Bogd 13 419

Sayr Usa

ALTAI MTS

G O B I   O R   S H A M O
(DESERT)

Hami

C H I N A

Chifeng

Weichang

Chengde

Zhangjiakou

Fengzhen

BEIJING

TIANJIN

Baoding

Lüshun

Dalian

SHANDONG BANDAO

Y E L L O W   S E A

Korea Bay

Bo Hai

FUSHUN

SHENYANG

Chengde

Pyongyang

NORTH KOREA

Kaesŏng

SEOUL

SOUTH KOREA

Inch'ŏn

Taejŏn

Andong

Taegu

PUSAN

Tottori

Matsue

Longitude East of Greenwich

0  100  200  300  400  500  600 Miles

0  200  400  600  800  1000 Kilometers

A-570000-76 · 17-38
COPYRIGHT BY
RAND McNALLY & COMPANY
MADE IN U.S.A.

Cities
and
Towns

0 to 50,000    ○    500,000 to 1,000,000    ◎

50,000 to 500,000    ⊙    1,000,000 and over

Obskaya Guba

WESTERN SIBERIAN LOWLAND

KARA SEA

NOVAYA ZEMLYA

BARENTS SEA

ARCTIC OCEAN

KHREBET PAY-KHOY

PECHORA BASIN

MALOZEMEL'SKAYA TUNDRA

KOLGUYEV

P-OV KANIN

U R A L S

YEKATERINBURG

BASHKORTOSTAN

Ufa

Krasnouralsk

Nizhniy Tagil

Perm'

Chelyabinsk

Zlatoust

Magnitogorsk

UDMURTIA

Izhevsk

Kirov

TATARSTAN

Kazan'

Syktyvkar

MARI EL

Yoshkar-Ola

CHUVASHIA

Cheboksary

NIZHNIY NOVGOROD

MORDVINIA

Saransk

Arkhangel'sk
(Archangel)

Vologda

Kostroma

Yaroslavl'

Rybinsk

Cherepovets

R U S S I A

Murmansk

Monchegorsk

Kandalaksha

Kirovsk

KARELIA

Petrozavodsk

LAPLAND

NORWAY

NORD KAPP

MAGERØYA

Hammerfest

SWEDEN

FINLAND

Oulu

Helsinki

Tampere

Turku

Vyborg

ST. PETERSBURG
(Sankt-Peterburg) (Leningrad)

Kronshtadt

Pushkin

Novgorod

Pskov

MOSCOW
(Moskva)

Tula

Ryazan'

Vladimir

Murom

Ivanovo

Smolensk

ESTONIA

Tallinn

Tartu

Narva

LATVIA

Riga

Daugavpils

LITHUANIA

Vilnius

Kaunas

Klaipėda

Šiauliai

BELARUS

Minsk

Mahilyow

GULF OF FINLAND

BALTIC SEA

GULF OF RIGA

Relief

| Meters | Feet | |
|---|---|---|
| 3050 | 10000 | |
| 1525 | 5000 | |
| 610 | 2000 | |
| 305 | 1000 | |
| 152.5 | 500 | |
| 0 | Sea Level | Sea Level |
| 152.5 | 500 | Below Sea Level |
| 1525 | 5000 | |
| 3050 | 10000 | |

0  50  100  150  200  250  300 Miles

0  100  200  300  400  500 Kilometers

Continued on pages 160-161

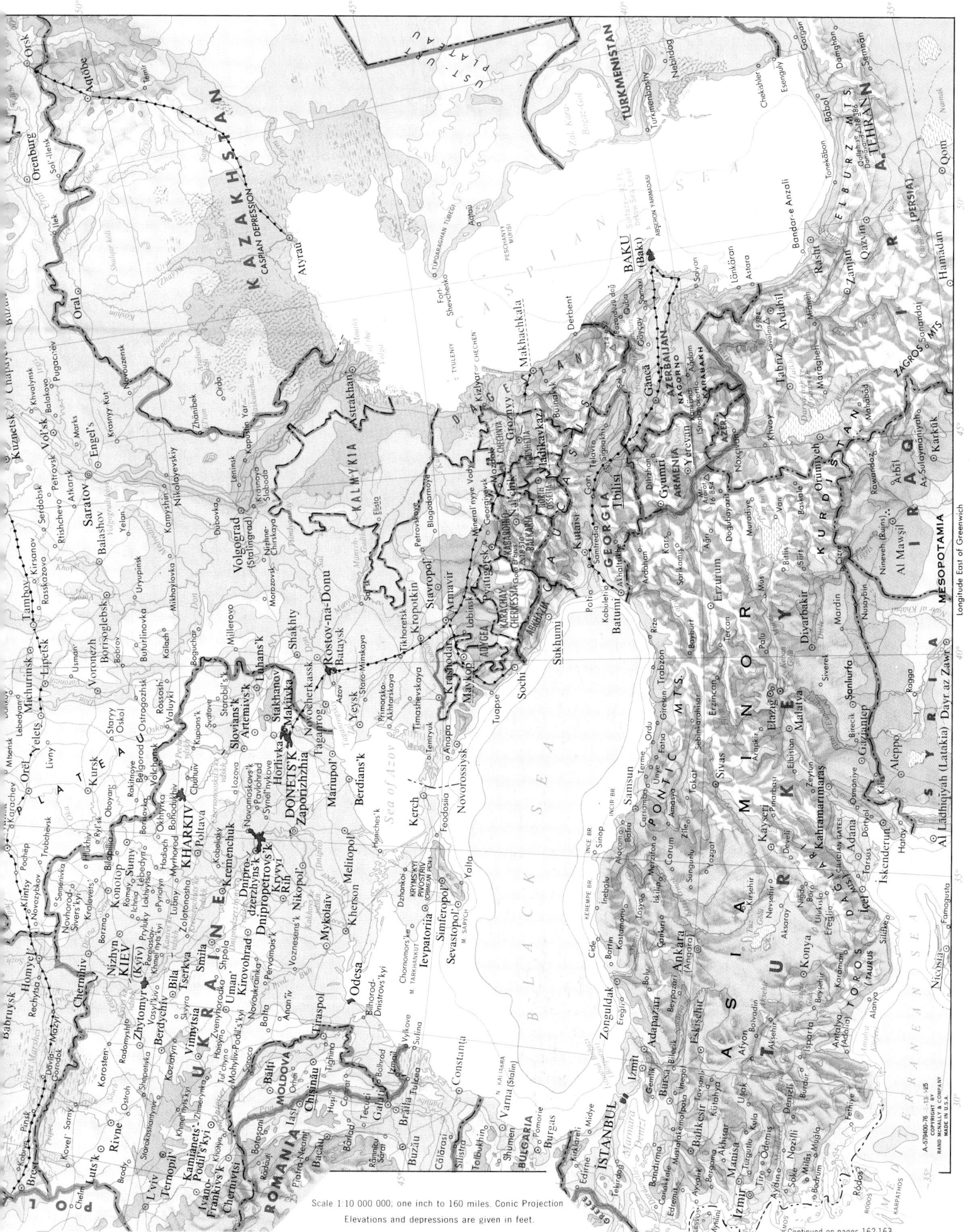

Scale 1:10 000 000; one inch to 160 miles. Conic Projection

Elevations and depressions are given in feet.

Continued on pages 162-163

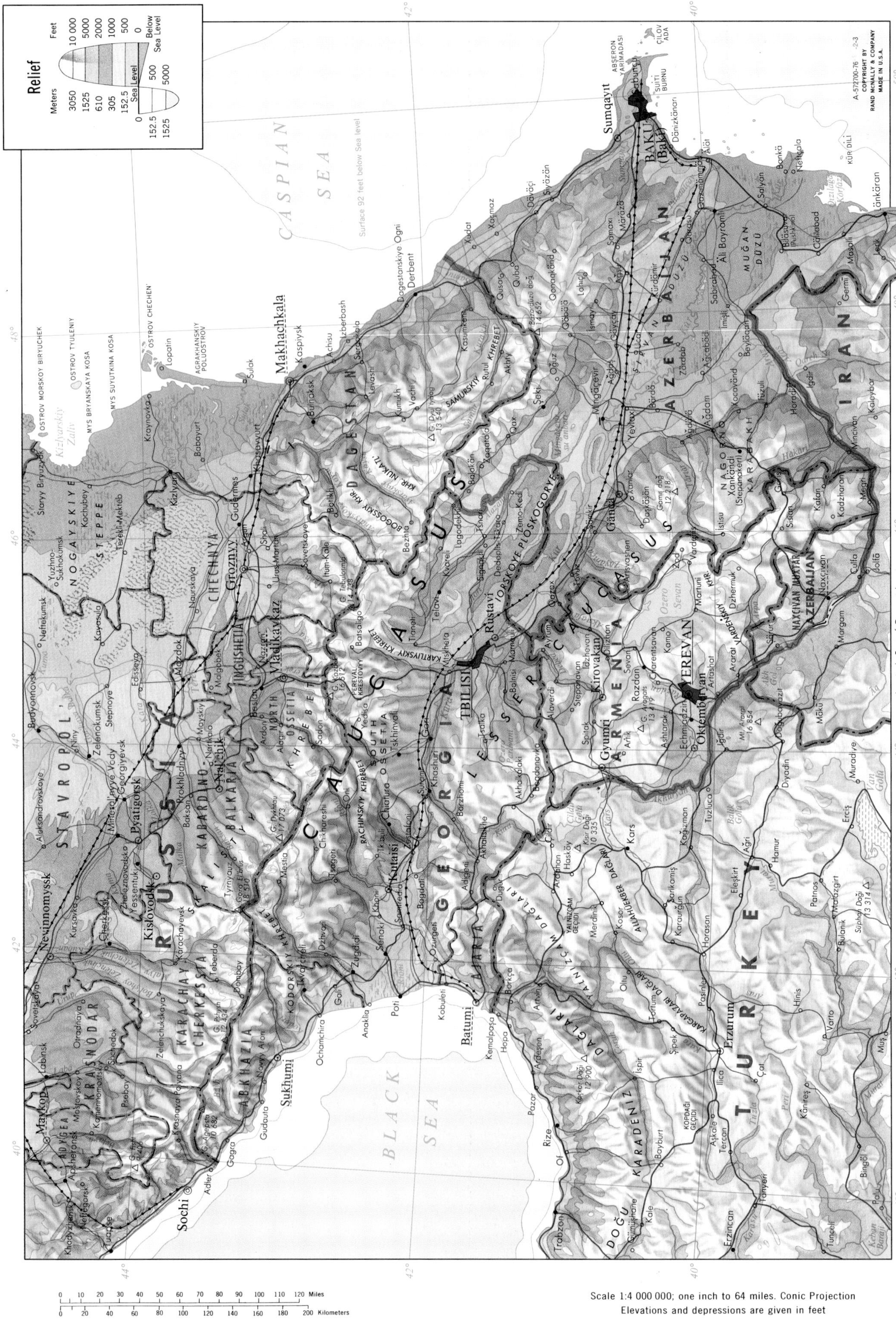

**Relief**

| Feet | Meters |
|---|---|
| 10 000 | 3050 |
| 5000 | 1525 |
| 2000 | 610 |
| 1000 | 305 |
| 500 | 152.5 |
| 0 Sea Level | 0 Sea Level |
| 500 | 152.5 |
| 5000 | 1525 |
| Below Sea Level | |

CASPIAN SEA

Surface 92 feet below sea level

BLACK SEA

ABŞERON YARIMADASI

ÇILOV ADA

Sumqayıt

BAKU (Bakı)

SUJTI BURNU

KÜR DILI

IRAN

Makhachkala

DAGESTAN

Derbent

CHECHNYA

Groznyy

INGUSHETIA

Vladikavkaz

NORTH OSSETIA

SOUTH OSSETIA

Tskhinvali

KABARDINO-BALKARIA

KARACHAY-CHERKESSIA

ABKHAZIA

Sukhumi

Sochi

STAVROPOL'

Nevinnomyssk

Kislovodsk

Pyatigorsk

Mineral'nyye Vody

Georgiyevsk

KRASNODAR

Maykop

ADYGEA

R U S S I A

NOGAYSKIYE STEPPE

Kizlyar

Mozdok

G R E A T E R   C A U C A S U S

L E S S E R   C A U C A S U S

T R A N S C A U C A S I A

GEORGIA

TBILISI

Rustavi

Kutaisi

Batumi

Poti

ADJARA

KARTLIYSKIY KHREBET

RACHINSKIY KHREBET

ARMENIA

YEREVAN

Gyumri

Kirovakan

Oktemberyan

Ečmiadzin

Ozero Sevan

AZERBAIJAN

Mingäçevir

Gäncä

Salyan

Länkäran

NAGORNO-KARABAKH

Xankändi (Stepanakert)

NAXÇIVAN MUXTAR ZERBAIJAN

Naxçıvan

TURKEY

Erzurum

Kars

Ağrı

Trabzon

DOĞU KARADENIZ DAĞLARI

KARGAPAZARI DAĞLARI

Longitude East of Greenwich

A-572700-76

COPYRIGHT BY RAND McNALLY & COMPANY

MADE IN U.S.A.

2-3

Scale 1:4 000 000; one inch to 64 miles. Conic Projection

Elevations and depressions are given in feet

0 10 20 30 40 50 60 70 80 90 100 110 120 Miles

0 20 40 60 80 100 120 140 160 180 200 Kilometers

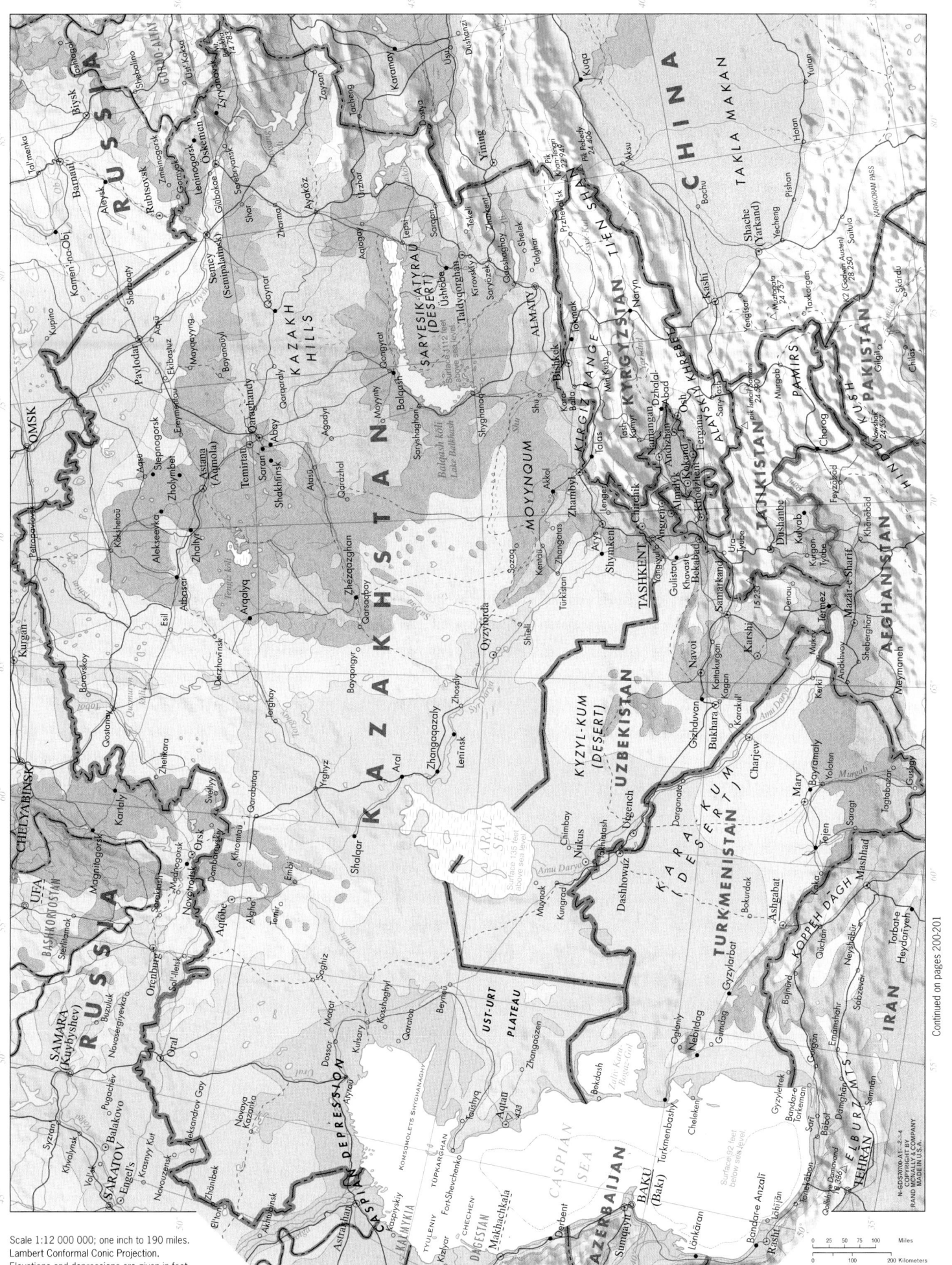

Scale 1:12 000 000; one inch to 190 miles.
Lambert Conformal Conic Projection.
Elevations and depressions are given in feet.

Continued on pages 200-201

RUSSIA

GORNO-ALTAY

Mt. Belukha
14,783

KAZAKHSTAN

KAZAKH HILLS

SARYESIK-ATYRAÜ (DESERT)
Surface 1112 feet
above sea level

CHINA

TAKLA MAKAN

TIEN SHAN

Pik Pobedy
24,406

Khan-Tengri
22,949

K2 (Qogir Feng)
28,250

Muztagata
24,757

Nowshak
24,557

PAKISTAN

HINDU KUSH

PAMIRS

Pik Ismail Samani
24,590

TAJIKISTAN

KIRGIZ RANGE

KYRGYZSTAN

ALAYSKIY KHREBET

15,233

MOYYNQUM

Balqash Köli
Lake Balkhash

ARAL SEA
Surface 135 feet
above sea level

KYZYL-KUM (DESERT)

UZBEKISTAN

KARA-KUM (DESERT)

TURKMENISTAN

UST-URT PLATEAU

CASPIAN DEPRESSION

433

CASPIAN SEA
Surface 92 feet
below sea level

KOPPEH DAGH

IRAN

ELBURZ MTS.

TEHRAN

AFGHANISTAN

AZERBAIJAN

BASHKORTOSTAN

SAMARA
(Kuybyshev)

KALMYKIA

DAGESTAN

CHECHEN

ALMATY

TASHKENT

BISHKEK

N-GDS70700-A1-2-4
COPYRIGHT BY
RAND MCNALLY & COMPANY
MADE IN U.S.A.

0   25   50   75   100   Miles
0        100        200 Kilometers

Continued on pages 156-157

Continued on pages 198-199

FINLAND

KARELIA

RARENTS SEA

NOVAYA ZEMLYA

KARSKOYE MORE
(Kara Sea)

SERGEYA
KIROVA

Murmansk
Polyarny
Kirovsk
KOL'SKIY P-OV

Kandalaksha

Kem

Arctic Circle

KANIN
P-OV

KOLGUYEV

P-OV
YAMAL

P-OV
GYDANSKIY

TUNDRA

P-OV

GORY

Dikson

ST. PETERSBURG
(Sankt-Peterburg) (Leningrad)

Kron-
shtadt

Novgorod

Petrozavodsk

Arkhangel'sk
(Archangel)

PECHORA
BASIN

Vorkuta

Salekhard

Ust'-Port

Dudinka

Noril'sk

GORY PUTORAN

Igarka

Vyshny
Volochëk

Tver

MOSCOW
(Moskva)

KOMI

Syktyvkar

Vorkuta

Berëzovo

WESTERN

R

U

S

Turukhansk

Baykit

NIZHNIY
NOVGOROD

MORDOVIA

Kazan

TATARSTAN

UDMURTIA

Perm

YEKATERINBURG

U
R
A
L

Khanty-Mansiysk

Surgut

SIBERIAN

Yartsevo

Yeniseysk

SAMARA

UFA

BASHKOR-
TOSTAN

Chelyabinsk

Tyumen'

Tobol'sk

LOWLAND

Narym

KAZAKHSTAN

Orenburg

Orsk

Qostanay

Petropavlovsk

Omsk

Tatarsk

Barabinsk

Tomsk

NOVOSIBIRSK

KUZNETSK
BASIN

Kemerovo

Anzhero-Sudzhensk

Achinsk

Kansk

Krasnoyarsk

Tayshet

Brats

ARAL
SEA

KAZAKH

STEPPE

Astana
(Aqmola)

Pavlodar

Barnaul

Biysk

GORNO-ALTAY

Novokuz-
netsk

KHAKASSIA

Abakan

Minusinsk

Nizhneudinsk

Tulun

Zima

Cheremkhovo

Angarsk

Irkuts

KIRGIZ

Qyzylorda

Semey
(Semipalatinsk)

Oskemen

GORNO-ALTAY

SAYAN

KHREBET

TUVA
TANNU-OLA

Kyzyl

UZBEKISTAN

TASHKENT

Shymkent

Zhambyl

Bishkek

Almaty

Yining

XINJIANG
(SINKIANG)

CHINA

MONGOLIA

HANGAYN
NURUU

TAJIKISTAN

Dushanbe

KYRGYZSTAN

Osh

Fergana

TIEN SHAN

Kashi

AFGHANISTAN

GORNO-
BADAKHSHAN
AUTONOMOUS
OBLAST'

**Cities
and
Towns**

0 to 50,000  ○

50,000 to 500,000  ◉

500,000 to 1,000,000  ◎

1,000,000 and over

Longitude East of Greenwich

Scale 1:16 000 000; one inch to 250 miles  Conic Projection

Elevations and depressions are given in feet.

Bering Strait

SEVERNAYA ZEMLYA
(NORTHERN LAND)
MALYY TAMIR
M. CHELYUSKIN

VRANGELYA
(WRANGEL)
M. SHELASSKIY
AYON

CHUKOTSKIY
P-OV

NOVOSIBIRSKIYE O-VA
(NEW SIBERIAN ISLANDS)
FADDEYA
NOVAYA SIBIR

DE LONGA

Anadyr'

ANADYRSKIY
ZALIV

BYRRANGA
TAYMYR

BOLSHOY
BEGICHEV

Nordvik

KOTEL NYY
BEL KOVSKIY
MALYY
L'YAKHOVSKIYE
LYAKHOVSKIYE

STOLBOVOY

M. SVYATOY
NOS

Ambarchik

Nizhne-Kolymsk

Arctic Circle

Mankovo

KORYAKSKIY KHREBET

Tilichki

Khatanga

Ust'-Olenek

Tiksi

Kazach'ye

Allaykha

Sredne-
Kolymsk

Penzhino

Ust'-Penzhino

Gizhiga

M. OLYUTORSKIY

Bulun

M. BUOR
KHAYA

Guba
Buor
Khaya

Abyy

KHREBET
KULAR

Verkhoyansk

VERKHOYANSKIY

Zashiversk

Zyryanka

Magadan

Yamsk

Palana

POLUOSTROV

Zhigansk

KHREBET CHERSKOGO

Gora Chen
10 171

Oymyakon

Kolyma

KHREBET GYDAN
(KOLYMSKIY)

M. TAYGONOS

ZALIV
SHELEKHOVA

M. ALEVINA

Verkhne-
Kamchatsk

Ust'-Kamchatsk

KAMCHATKA

Vol'y
15 584

SIBERIA

SAKHA
(YAKUTIA)

Yakutsk

Vilyuysk

Aldanskaya

Okhotsk

SEA OF OKHOTSK

Petropavlovsk-
Kamchatskiy

Suntar

Amga

Ust'-Maya

Nel'kan

M. ELIZAVETY

Ust'-Bol'sheretsk

Olëkminsk

Tommot

DZHUGDZHUR KHREBET

Ayon

Okha

Mukhtuya

ALDAN
PLATEAU

Aldan

SHANTAR

KURIL ISLANDS
(Russia)

Peleduy

Vitim

PATOM
1377

Golets Purpula
PLATEAU

Badaybo

Golets Skalistyy
9186

STANOVOY KHREBET

Chumikan

SAKHALIN
(Russia)

Kirensk

Nizhne-Angarsk

Tyndinskiy

Uda

Zeya

Nikolayevsk-
na-Amure

Aleksandrovsk

Poronaysk

M. TERPENIYA

Zhigalovo

Kachuga

Barguzin

BURYATIA

YABLONOVYY KHREBET

Skovorodina

Bekatova

Zeya

Komsomol'sk-
na-Amure

Malmyzh

Uglegorsk

Dolinsk

Yuzhno-Sakhalinsk

TATAR STRAIT

Ulan-Ude

Petrovsk-
Zabaykal'skiy

Chita

Nerchinsk

Sretensk

Baley

NERCHINSKIY
ZAVOD

Svobodnyy

Belogorsk

Ust'-Tyrma

Sovetskaya
Gavan'

Khabarovsk

Kholmsk

Korsakov

A-579300-76
RAND McNALLY & COMPANY
MADE IN U.S.A.

Babushkin

Kyakhta

Aginskoye

Aksha

Borzya

NERCHINSKIY KHREBET

MANJ

Zavitinsk

Bureya

Raychikhinsk

Birobidzhan

KHREBET BUREINSKIY

Dalnerechensk

SIKHOTE ALIN'

USSURIYSKIY KHREBET

SEA OF JAPAN

Relief

Ulan Bator

Ondorhaan

NEI
MONGGOL

Blagoveshchensk

Aihui

GREATER KHINGAN RANGE

LESSER KHINGAN RANGE

Longzhen

Goukou

Spassk-Dal'niy

Arsen'yev

HOKKAIDO

Meters  Feet
3050    10 000
1525    5000
610     2000
305     1000
152.5   500
0       Sea Level  0
152.5   500
1525    5000
3050    10 000

Manzhouli

Hailar

Qiqihar

Qiqihar

HEILUNGKIANG

Hulan

HARBIN

Yilan

Ning'an

Ussuriysk

Artëm

Nakhodka

Vladivostok

JAPAN

Continued on pages 204-205

0  50  100   200    300    400    500 Miles
0  100  200      400      600       800 Kilometers

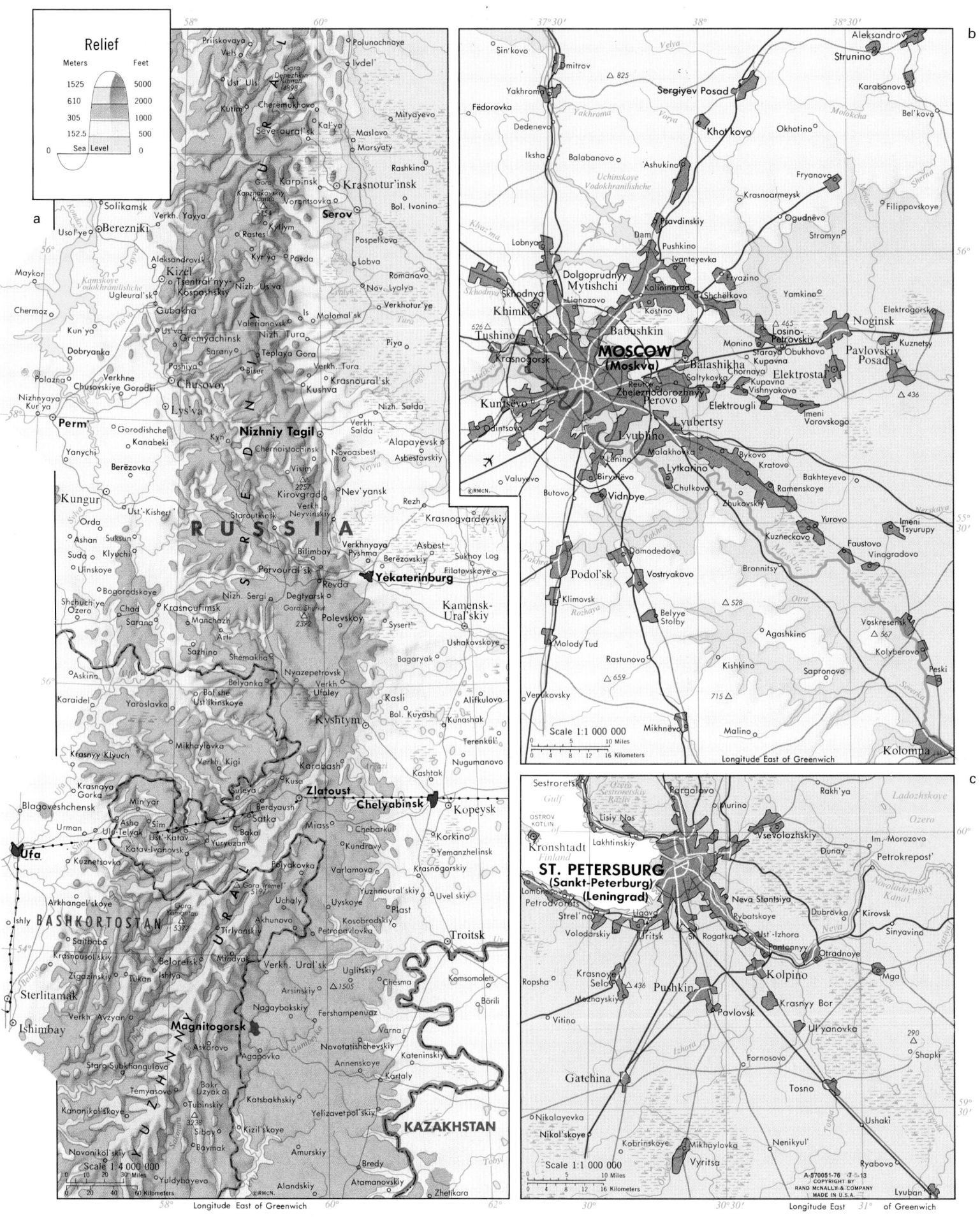

Relief

| Meters | Feet |
|--------|------|
| 1525 | 5000 |
| 610 | 2000 |
| 305 | 1000 |
| 152.5 | 500 |
| Sea Level | 0 |

Scale 1:1 000 000

Scale 1:4 000 000

Scale 1:1 000 000

Longitude East of Greenwich

**Cities and Towns**

0 to 50,000    500,000 to 1,000,000

50,000 to 500,000    1,000,000 and over

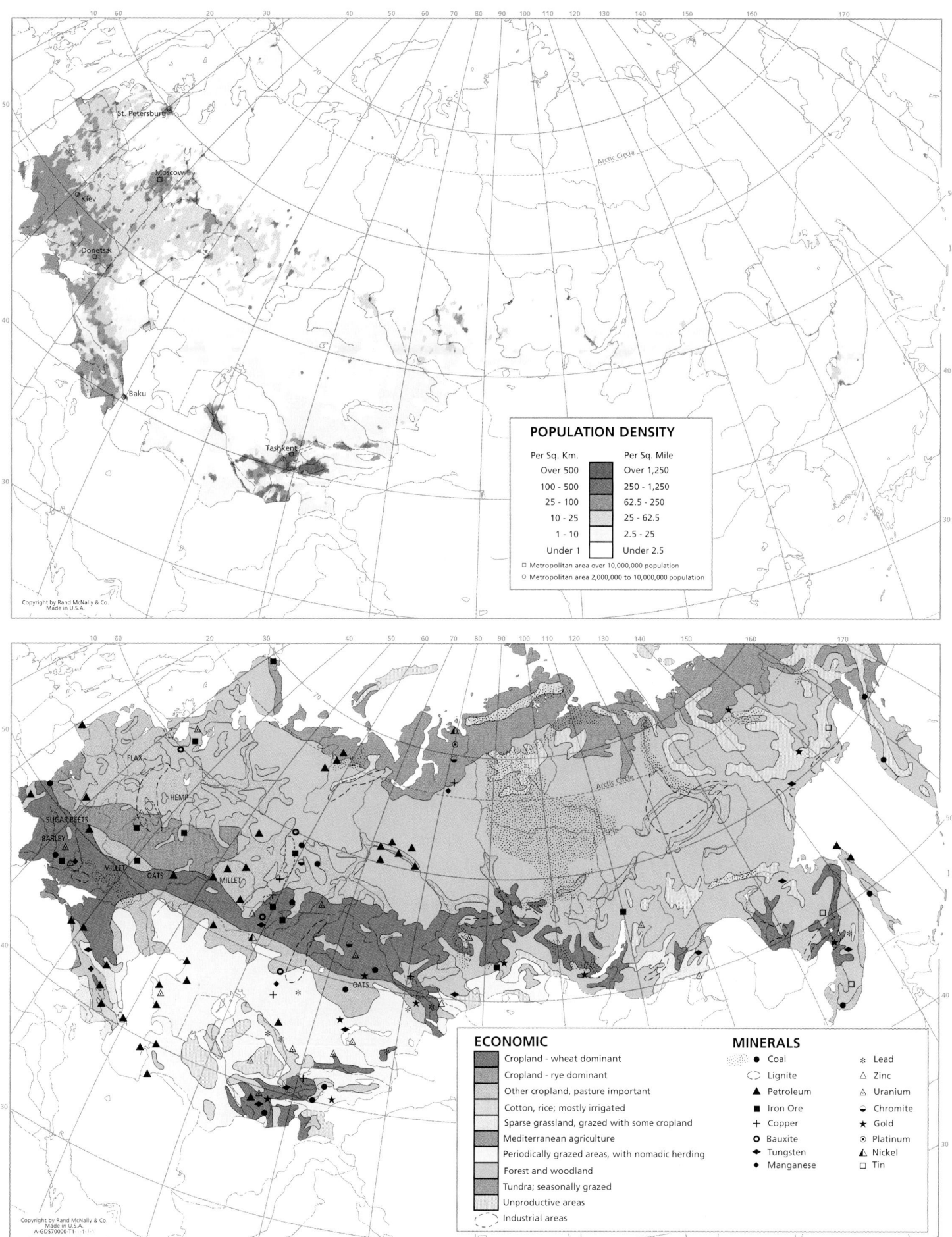

**POPULATION DENSITY**

| Per Sq. Km. | Per Sq. Mile |
|---|---|
| Over 500 | Over 1,250 |
| 100 - 500 | 250 - 1,250 |
| 25 - 100 | 62.5 - 250 |
| 10 - 25 | 25 - 62.5 |
| 1 - 10 | 2.5 - 25 |
| Under 1 | Under 2.5 |

□ Metropolitan area over 10,000,000 population
○ Metropolitan area 2,000,000 to 10,000,000 population

Copyright by Rand McNally & Co.
Made in U.S.A.

**ECONOMIC**

- Cropland - wheat dominant
- Cropland - rye dominant
- Other cropland, pasture important
- Cotton, rice; mostly irrigated
- Sparse grassland, grazed with some cropland
- Mediterranean agriculture
- Periodically grazed areas, with nomadic herding
- Forest and woodland
- Tundra; seasonally grazed
- Unproductive areas
- Industrial areas

**MINERALS**

| | | |
|---|---|---|
| ● Coal | | ☀ Lead |
| ◡ Lignite | | △ Zinc |
| ▲ Petroleum | | △ Uranium |
| ■ Iron Ore | | ◠ Chromite |
| + Copper | | ★ Gold |
| ○ Bauxite | | ◉ Platinum |
| ◆ Tungsten | | ▲ Nickel |
| ◆ Manganese | | □ Tin |

Copyright by Rand McNally & Co.
Made in U.S.A.
A-GDS70000-T1- -1- -1

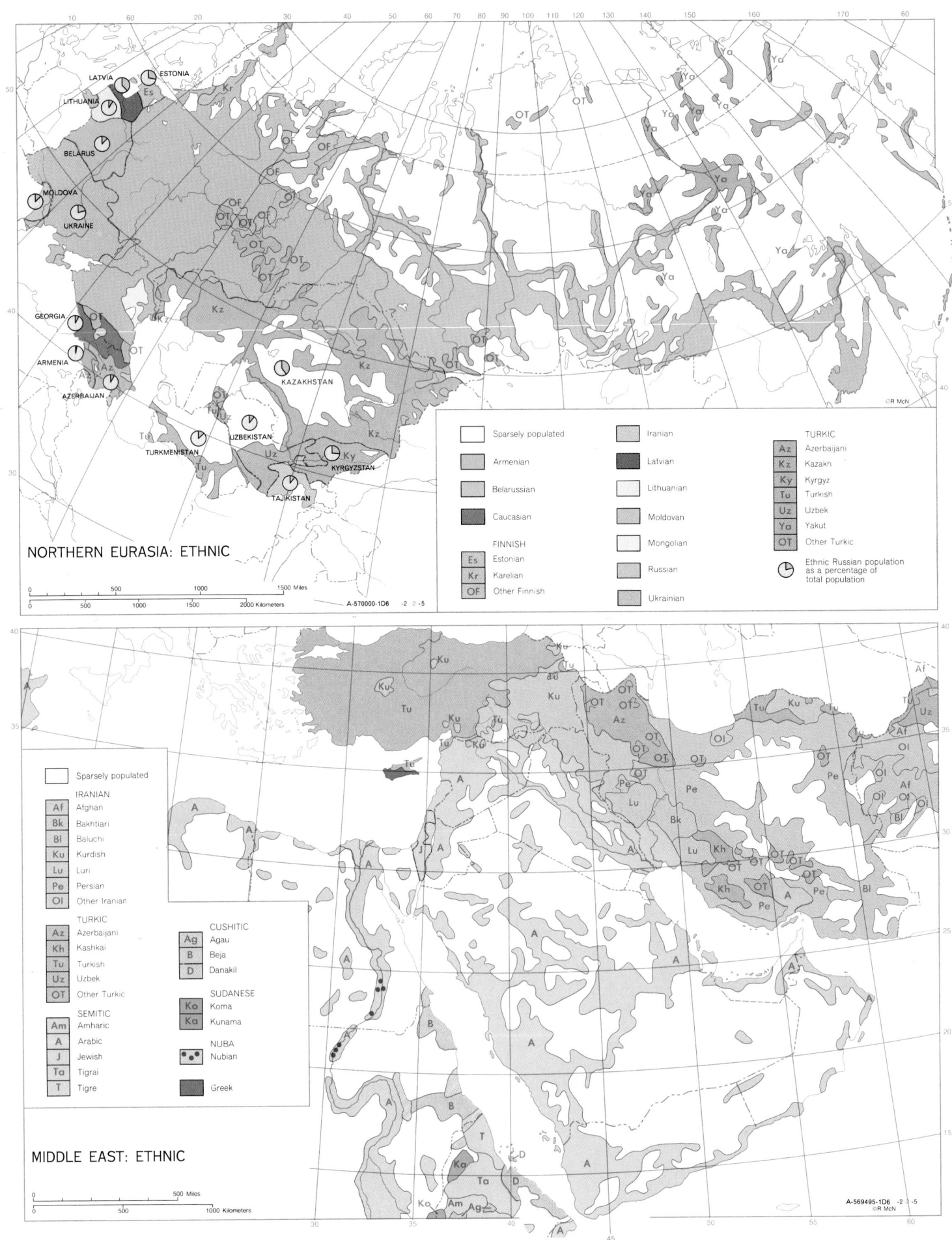

NORTHERN EURASIA: ETHNIC

| | Sparsely populated | | Iranian | | | TURKIC |
|---|---|---|---|---|---|---|
| | Armenian | | Latvian | Az | Azerbaijani |
| | Belarussian | | Lithuanian | Kz | Kazakh |
| | Caucasian | | Moldovan | Ky | Kyrgyz |
| | | | Mongolian | Tu | Turkish |
| | FINNISH | | Russian | Uz | Uzbek |
| Es | Estonian | | Ukrainian | Ya | Yakut |
| Kr | Karelian | | | OT | Other Turkic |
| OF | Other Finnish | | | | Ethnic Russian population as a percentage of total population |

MIDDLE EAST: ETHNIC

| | Sparsely populated |
|---|---|
| | IRANIAN |
| Af | Afghan |
| Bk | Bakhtiari |
| Bl | Baluchi |
| Ku | Kurdish |
| Lu | Luri |
| Pe | Persian |
| OI | Other Iranian |
| | TURKIC |
| Az | Azerbaijani |
| Kh | Kashkai |
| Tu | Turkish |
| Uz | Uzbek |
| OT | Other Turkic |
| | SEMITIC |
| Am | Amharic |
| A | Arabic |
| J | Jewish |
| Ta | Tigrai |
| T | Tigre |

| | CUSHITIC |
|---|---|
| Ag | Agau |
| B | Beja |
| D | Danakil |
| | SUDANESE |
| Ko | Koma |
| Ka | Kunama |
| | NUBA |
| | Nubian |
| | Greek |

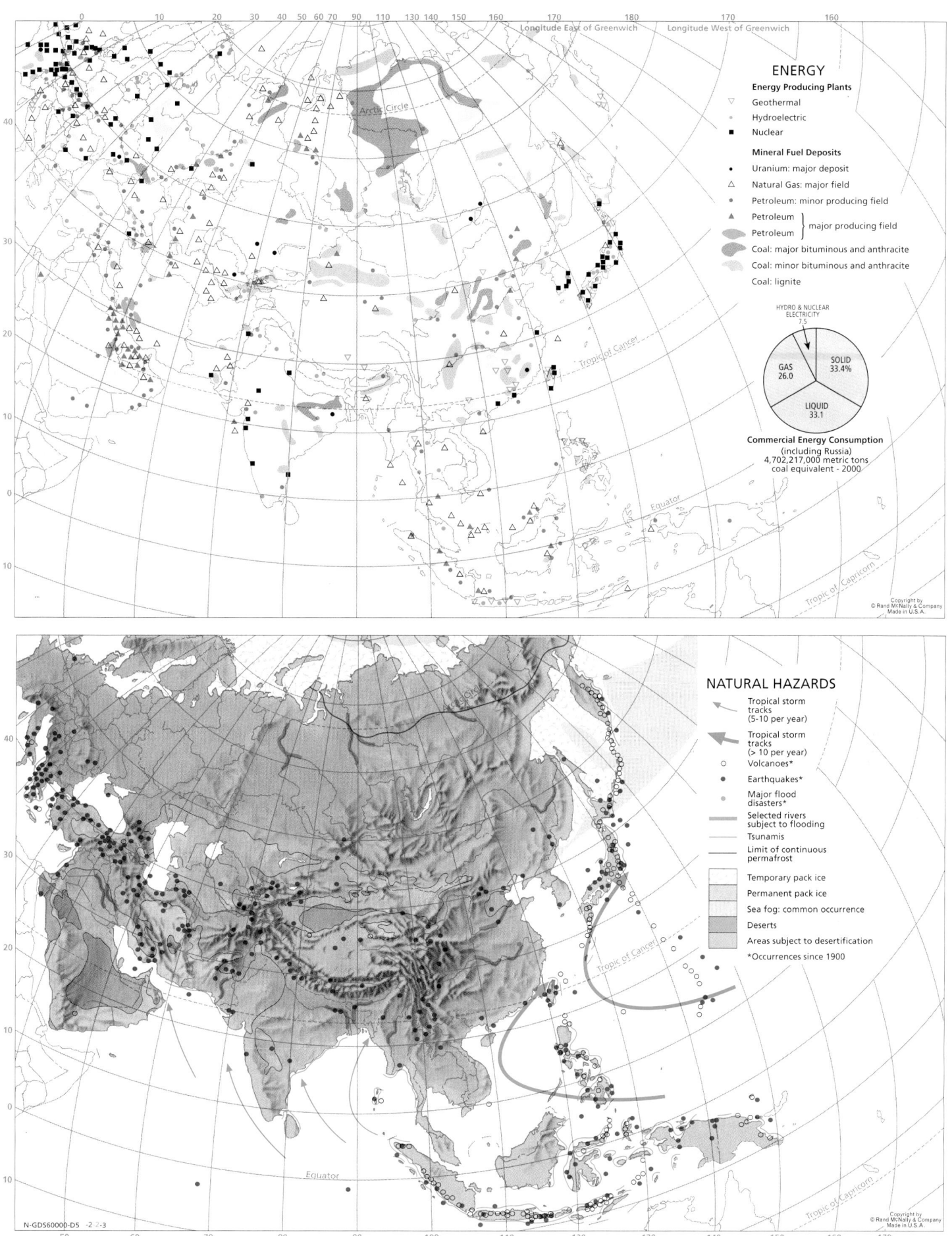

ENERGY

**Energy Producing Plants**
▽ Geothermal
• Hydroelectric
■ Nuclear

**Mineral Fuel Deposits**
• Uranium: major deposit
△ Natural Gas: major field
• Petroleum: minor producing field
▲ Petroleum } major producing field
  Petroleum }
  Coal: major bituminous and anthracite
  Coal: minor bituminous and anthracite
  Coal: lignite

HYDRO & NUCLEAR
ELECTRICITY
7.5

GAS
26.0

SOLID
33.4%

LIQUID
33.1

**Commercial Energy Consumption**
(including Russia)
4,702,217,000 metric tons
coal equivalent - 2000

Copyright by
© Rand McNally & Company
Made in U.S.A.

NATURAL HAZARDS

Tropical storm
tracks
(5-10 per year)

Tropical storm
tracks
(> 10 per year)

○ Volcanoes*
● Earthquakes*
● Major flood
disasters*

Selected rivers
subject to flooding

Tsunamis

Limit of continuous
permafrost

Temporary pack ice
Permanent pack ice
Sea fog: common occurrence
Deserts
Areas subject to desertification

*Occurrences since 1900

N-GDS60000-D5  -2-2-3

Copyright by
© Rand McNally & Company
Made in U.S.A.

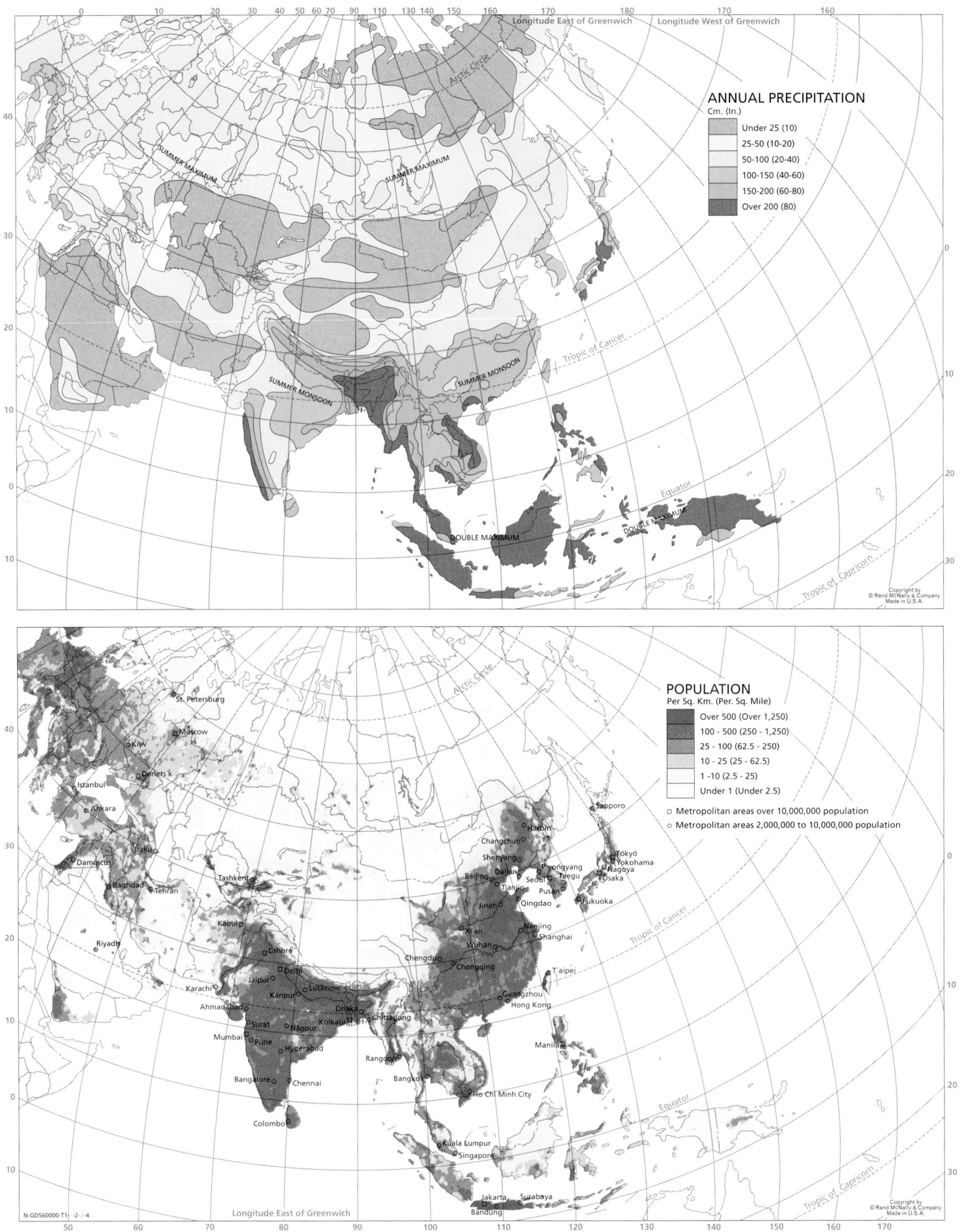

ANNUAL PRECIPITATION
Cm. (In.)

- Under 25 (10)
- 25-50 (10-20)
- 50-100 (20-40)
- 100-150 (40-60)
- 150-200 (60-80)
- Over 200 (80)

POPULATION
Per Sq. Km. (Per. Sq. Mile)

- Over 500 (Over 1,250)
- 100 - 500 (250 - 1,250)
- 25 - 100 (62.5 - 250)
- 10 - 25 (25 - 62.5)
- 1 -10 (2.5 - 25)
- Under 1 (Under 2.5)

□ Metropolitan areas over 10,000,000 population
○ Metropolitan areas 2,000,000 to 10,000,000 population

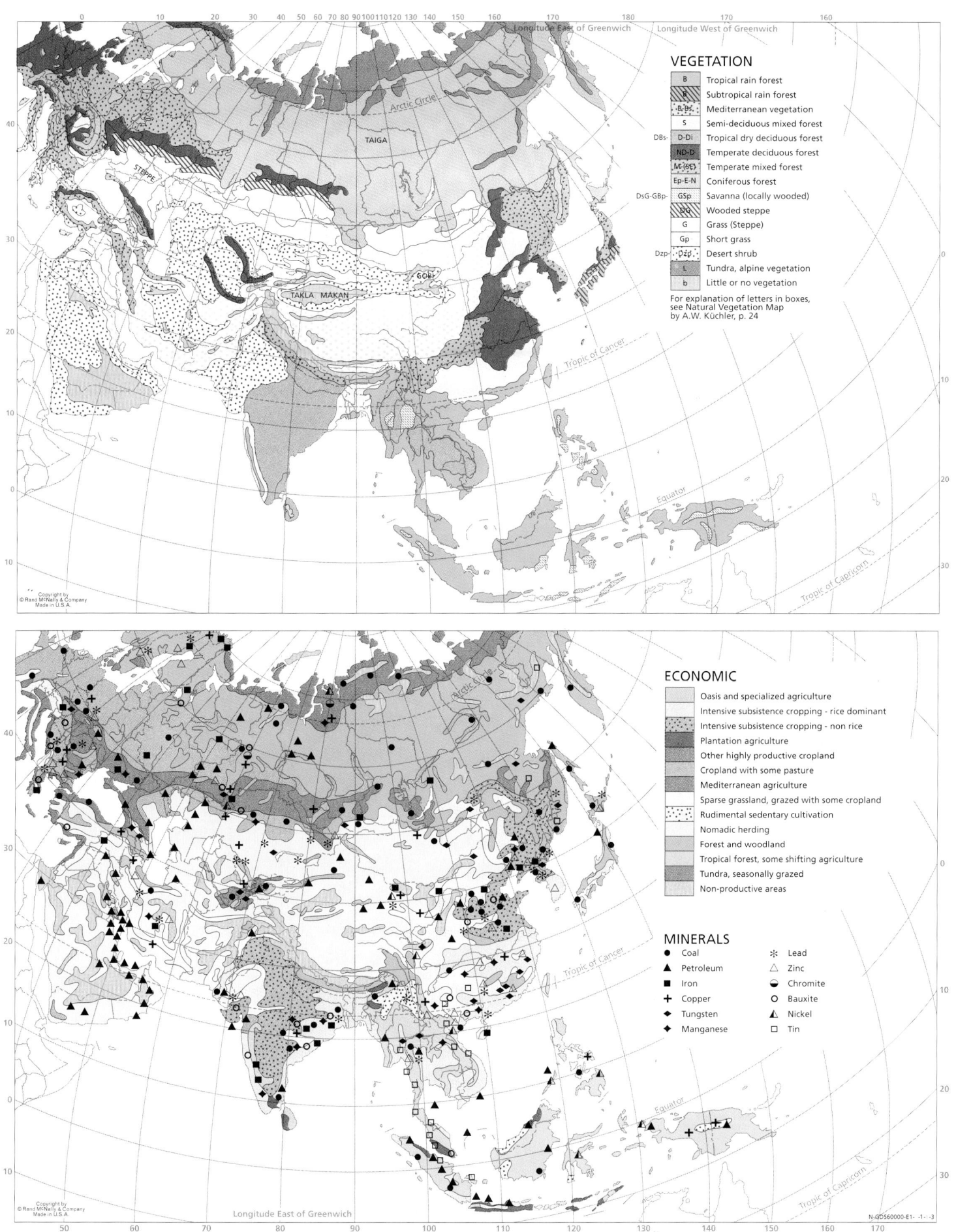

**VEGETATION**

| | |
|---|---|
| B | Tropical rain forest |
| R | Subtropical rain forest |
| R-Rs | Mediterranean vegetation |
| S | Semi-deciduous mixed forest |
| DBs- D-Di | Tropical dry deciduous forest |
| ND-D | Temperate deciduous forest |
| M-(6S) | Temperate mixed forest |
| Ep-E-N | Coniferous forest |
| DsG-GBp- GSp | Savanna (locally wooded) |
| DG | Wooded steppe |
| G | Grass (Steppe) |
| Gp | Short grass |
| Dzp- Dzp | Desert shrub |
| L | Tundra, alpine vegetation |
| b | Little or no vegetation |

For explanation of letters in boxes,
see Natural Vegetation Map
by A.W. Küchler, p. 24

**ECONOMIC**

| | |
|---|---|
| | Oasis and specialized agriculture |
| | Intensive subsistence cropping - rice dominant |
| | Intensive subsistence cropping - non rice |
| | Plantation agriculture |
| | Other highly productive cropland |
| | Cropland with some pasture |
| | Mediterranean agriculture |
| | Sparse grassland, grazed with some cropland |
| | Rudimental sedentary cultivation |
| | Nomadic herding |
| | Forest and woodland |
| | Tropical forest, some shifting agriculture |
| | Tundra, seasonally grazed |
| | Non-productive areas |

**MINERALS**

| | | | |
|---|---|---|---|
| ● | Coal | ✳ | Lead |
| ▲ | Petroleum | △ | Zinc |
| ■ | Iron | ◖ | Chromite |
| ✚ | Copper | ○ | Bauxite |
| ◆ | Tungsten | ◭ | Nickel |
| ◆ | Manganese | □ | Tin |

N-GDS60000-E1- -1- -3

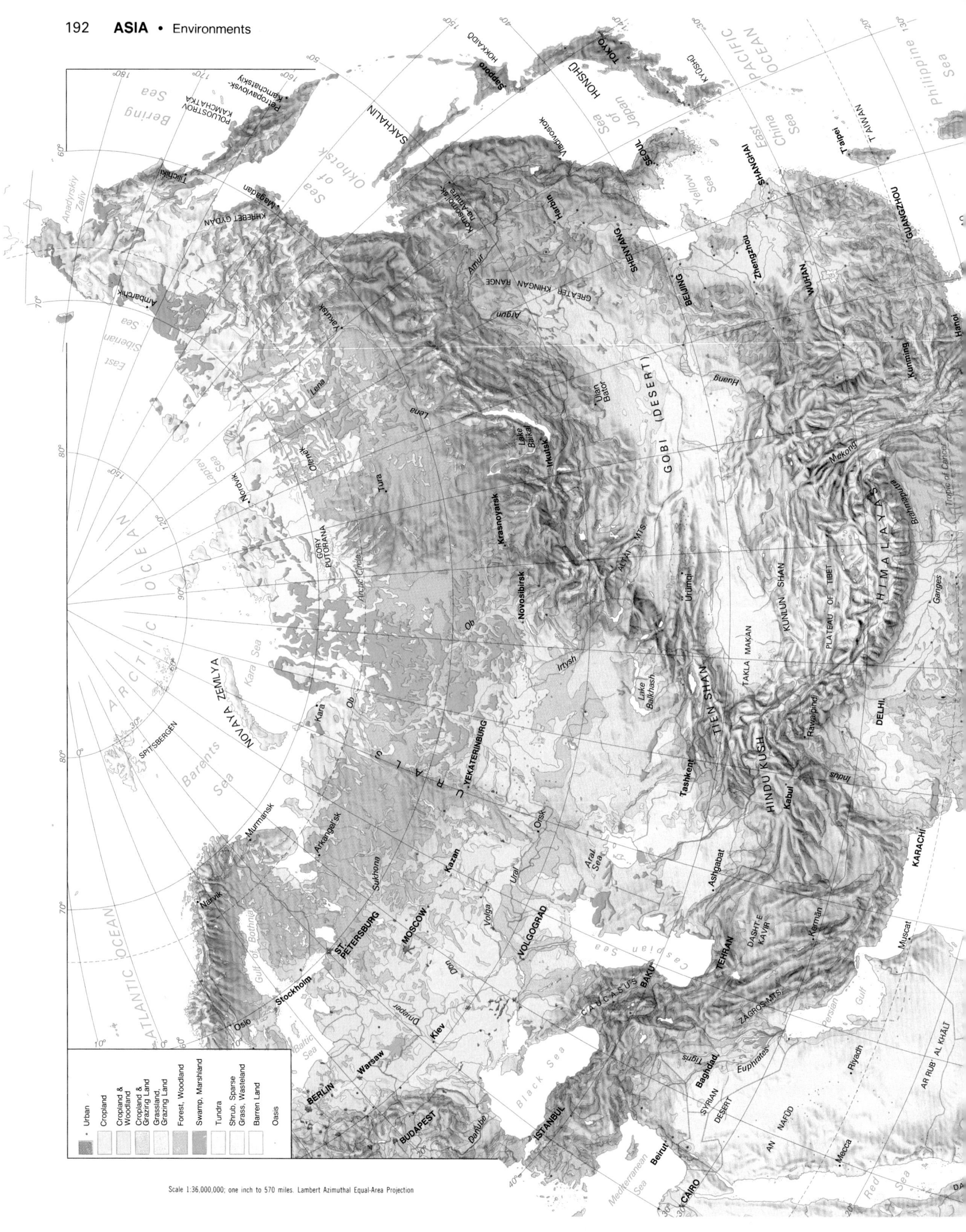

Scale 1:36,000,000; one inch to 570 miles. Lambert Azimuthal Equal-Area Projection

Urban
• Cropland
Cropland & Woodland
Cropland & Grazing Land
Grassland, Grazing Land
Forest, Woodland
Swamp, Marshland
Tundra
Shrub, Sparse Grass, Wasteland
Barren Land
Oasis

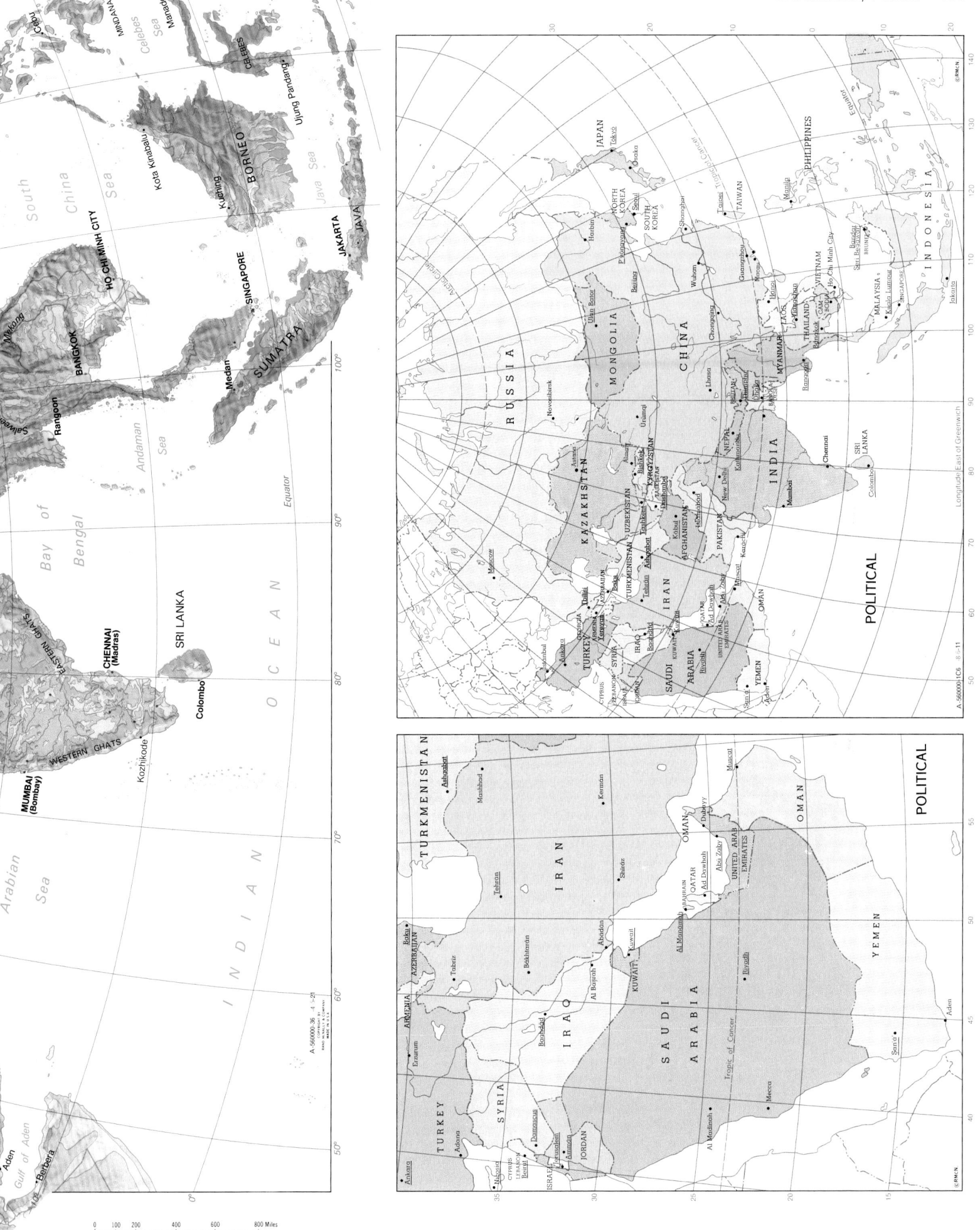

MINDANAO

Manado

Celebes
Sea

CELEBES

Ujung Pandang

Kota Kinabalu

Kuching

BORNEO

Java Sea

JAVA

JAKARTA

SINGAPORE

Medan

SUMATRA

HO CHI MINH CITY

BANGKOK

Rangoon

Mekong

Salween

Andaman
Sea

South
China
Sea

Equator

SRI LANKA

Colombo

CHENNAI
(Madras)

Kozhikode

WESTERN GHATS

EASTERN GHATS

MUMBAI
(Bombay)

Bay
of
Bengal

INDIAN

OCEAN

Arabian
Sea

Gulf of Aden

Aden

Berbera

A-560000-36  -4  i-21

0   100   200   400   600   800 Miles
0   150   300   600   900   1200 Kilometers

RUSSIA

MONGOLIA

Ulan Bator

Novosibirsk

Moscow

KAZAKHSTAN

UZBEKISTAN

Almaty

Bishkek

KYRGYZSTAN

Tashkent

TAJIKISTAN

Dushanbe

TURKMENISTAN

Ashgabat

Tehran

IRAN

AFGHANISTAN

Kabul

PAKISTAN

CHINA

Ürümqi

Lhasa

NEPAL

Kathmandu

New Delhi

Ahmadabad

Mumbai

INDIA

Chennai

SRI
LANKA

Colombo

Karachi

Muscat

OMAN

UNITED ARAB
EMIRATES

Abu Dhabi

Ad Dawhah

QATAR

Kuwait

Riyadh

SAUDI
ARABIA

YEMEN

Aden

Sana

Baghdad

IRAQ

SYRIA

Istanbul

Ankara

TURKEY

CYPRUS

LEBANON

ISRAEL

Jerusalem

GEORGIA

Tbilisi

ARMENIA

Yerevan

AZERBAIJAN

Baku

Beijing

Harbin

Shanghai

Chongqing

Wuhan

Guangzhou

Hong Kong

Hanoi

VIETNAM

LAOS

THAILAND

Bangkok

MYANMAR

Yangon

BANGLADESH

Dhaka

BHUTAN

Ho Chi Minh City

CAMBODIA

MALAYSIA

Kuala Lumpur

SINGAPORE

Jakarta

INDONESIA

Brunei

Bandar Seri Begawan

PHILIPPINES

Manila

TAIWAN

Taipei

NORTH
KOREA

Pyongyang

SOUTH
KOREA

Seoul

JAPAN

Tokyo

Osaka

Arctic Circle

Equator

Tropic of Cancer

Longitude East of Greenwich

POLITICAL

A-560000-1C6  -8 i-11

©RMCN

TURKMENISTAN

Ashgabat

Mashhad

Kerman

IRAN

Tehran

ARMENIA

AZERBAIJAN

Baku

Tabriz

Bakhtaran

Abadan

Al Basrah

IRAQ

Baghdad

Erzurum

TURKEY

Adana

SYRIA

Damascus

Amman

JORDAN

CYPRUS

LEBANON

Beirut

ISRAEL

Jerusalem

Nicosia

Al Madinah

Mecca

Tropic of Cancer

SAUDI
ARABIA

Riyadh

Kuwait

KUWAIT

Al Manamah

BAHRAIN

QATAR

Ad Dawhah

Abu Zaby

UNITED ARAB
EMIRATES

Dubayy

Muscat

OMAN

OMAN

YEMEN

Aden

Sana

POLITICAL

©RMCN

194

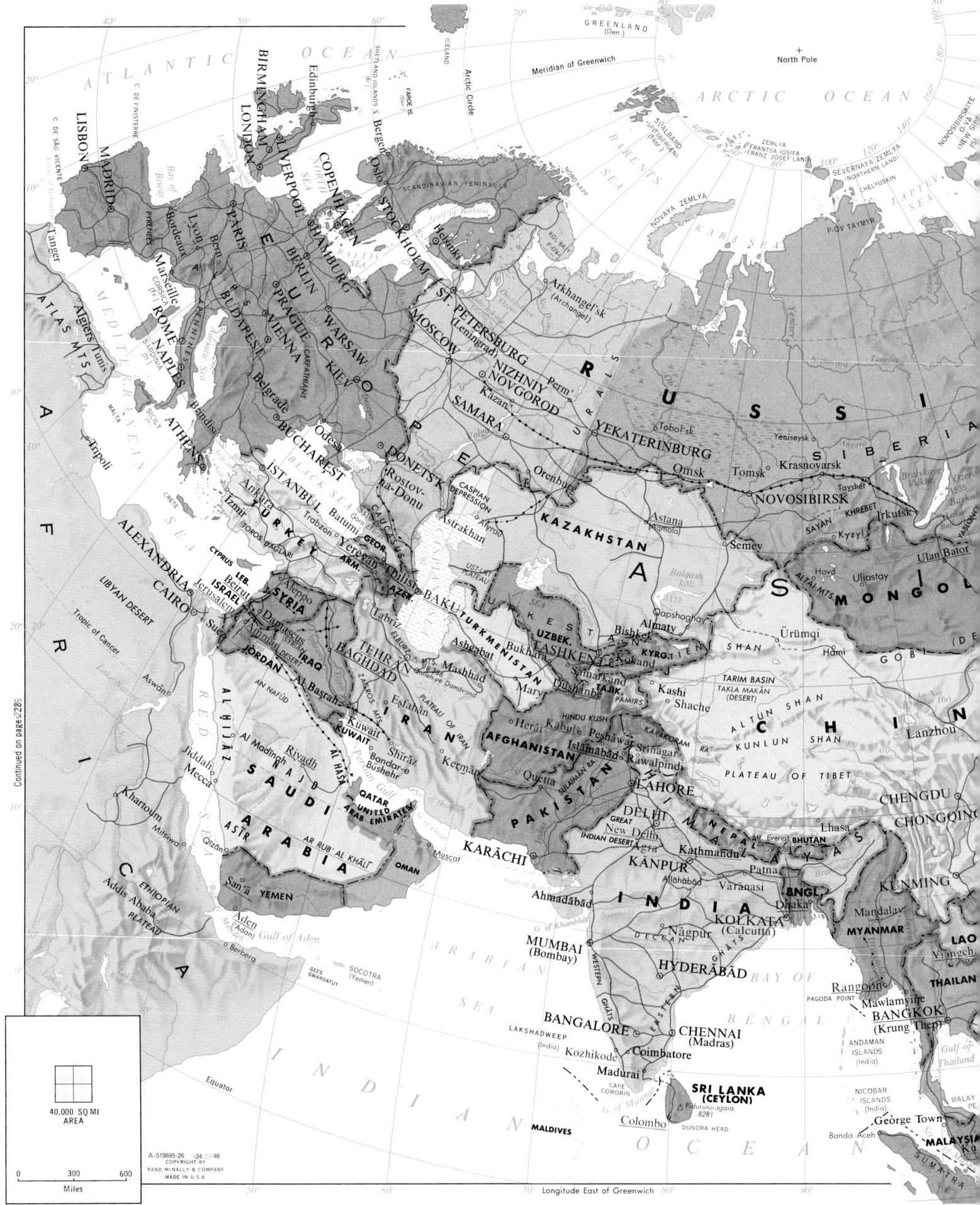

Continued on page 228

40,000 SQ MI
AREA

0        300        600
Miles

A-519695-26   -24 20 46
COPYRIGHT BY
RAND MCNALLY & COMPANY
MADE IN U.S.A.

Scale 1:40 000 000; one inch to 630 miles. Lambert's Azimuthal, Equal Area Projection
Elevations and depressions are given in feet

ATLANTIC OCEAN

ARCTIC OCEAN

GREENLAND
(Den.)

North Pole

Meridian of Greenwich

ICELAND

Arctic Circle

BARENTS SEA

KARA SEA

LAPTEV SEA

SVALBARD
(SPITSBERGEN)
(Nor.)

ZEMLYA
FRANTSA-IOSIFA
(FRANZ
JOSEF LAND)

SEVERNAYA ZEMLYA
(NORTHERN LAND)

NOVAYA ZEMLYA

CHELYUSKIN

P. OV TAYMYR

LISBON
MADRID
ROME
NAPLES
BIRMINGHAM
LONDON
LIVERPOOL
COPENHAGEN
HAMBURG
BERLIN
PARIS
PRAGUE
VIENNA
WARSAW
BUDAPEST
BUCHAREST
KIEV
ATHENS
ISTANBUL
ANKARA
MOSCOW
ST. PETERSBURG
(Leningrad)
NIZHNIY
NOVGOROD
SAMARA
YEKATERINBURG
NOVOSIBIRSK

Edinburgh
Oslo
Helsinki
Stockholm
Bergen
Bordeaux
Lyon
Bern
Marseille
Belgrade
Odesa
Kazan
Perm'
Tobol'sk
Orenburg
Omsk
Tomsk
Krasnoyarsk
Tayshet
Irkutsk
Kyzyl
Semey
Astana
(Aqmola)
Almaty
Bishkek

RUSSIA
SIBERIA
URALS
EUROPE
CASPIAN DEPRESSION
KAZAKHSTAN
MONGOLIA
Ulan Bator
Uliastay
Hovd
Ürümqi
Hami

TURKEY
SYRIA
ISRAEL
LEB.
CYPRUS
JORDAN
IRAQ
IRAN
BAGHDAD
TEHRAN
Beirut
Damascus
Amman
Aleppo
Tabriz
Yerevan
Tbilisi
Baku
GEOR.
ARM.
AZER.
TURKMENISTAN
Ashgabat
UZBEK.
TASHKENT
Bukhara
Samarkand
Mary
TAJIK.
Dushanbe
KYRG.
Kokand
Kashi
Shache
PAMIRS
TARIM BASIN
TAKLA MAKAN
(DESERT)
ALTUN SHAN
KUNLUN SHAN
PLATEAU OF TIBET
CHINA
Lanzhou
CHENGDU
CHONGQING
KUNMING

ALEXANDRIA
CAIRO
Jerusalem
Suez
Aswan
LIBYAN DESERT
SAUDI ARABIA
AL HIJAZ
NAJD
ASIR
Mecca
Jiddah
Al Madinah
Riyadh
Kuwait
KUWAIT
QATAR
UNITED ARAB EMIRATES
OMAN
Muscat
YEMEN
San'a
Aden
(Adan)
GEES GWARDAFUY
(Yemen)
SOCOTRA
(Yemen)
Khartoum
Addis Ababa
ETHIOPIAN PLATEAU
Berbera
Misrawa
Al Qizan

AFGHANISTAN
Kabul
Herat
Quetta
PAKISTAN
Islamabad
Rawalpindi
Peshawar
Srinagar
LAHORE
KARACHI
DELHI
New Delhi
Agra
NEPAL
Kathmandu
BHUTAN
Mt. Everest
Lhasa
KANPUR
Allahabad
Patna
Varanasi
BNGL.
Dhaka
MYANMAR
Mandalay
LAOS
THAILAND
BANGKOK
(Krung Thep)
Rangoon
Mawlamyine
INDIA
Ahmadabad
Nagpur
HYDERABAD
MUMBAI
(Bombay)
BANGALORE
CHENNAI
(Madras)
KOLKATA
(Calcutta)
DECCAN
WESTERN GHATS
EASTERN GHATS
Coimbatore
Kozhikode
Madurai
CAPE COMORIN
LAKSHADWEEP
(India)
MALDIVES
SRI LANKA
(CEYLON)
Colombo
ANDAMAN ISLANDS
(India)
NICOBAR ISLANDS
(India)
George Town
Banda Aceh
MALAYSIA
SUMATRA
PAGODA POINT
DONDRA HEAD
Gulf of Thailand
BAY OF BENGAL
ARABIAN SEA
INDIAN OCEAN
Equator
Tropic of Cancer
MEDITERRANEAN SEA
ATLAS MTS.
Algiers
Tunis
Tripoli
RED SEA
Gulf of Aden
Persian Gulf
Gulf of Oman
CAUCASUS MTS.
ZAGROS MTS.
ELBURZ MTS.
HINDU KUSH
KARAKORAM
HIMALAYAS
GOBI (DESERT)
ALTAI MTS.
SAYAN
TIEN SHAN
BLACK SEA
CASPIAN SEA
Astrakhan
Rostov-na-Donu
DONETS'K
Balqash koli

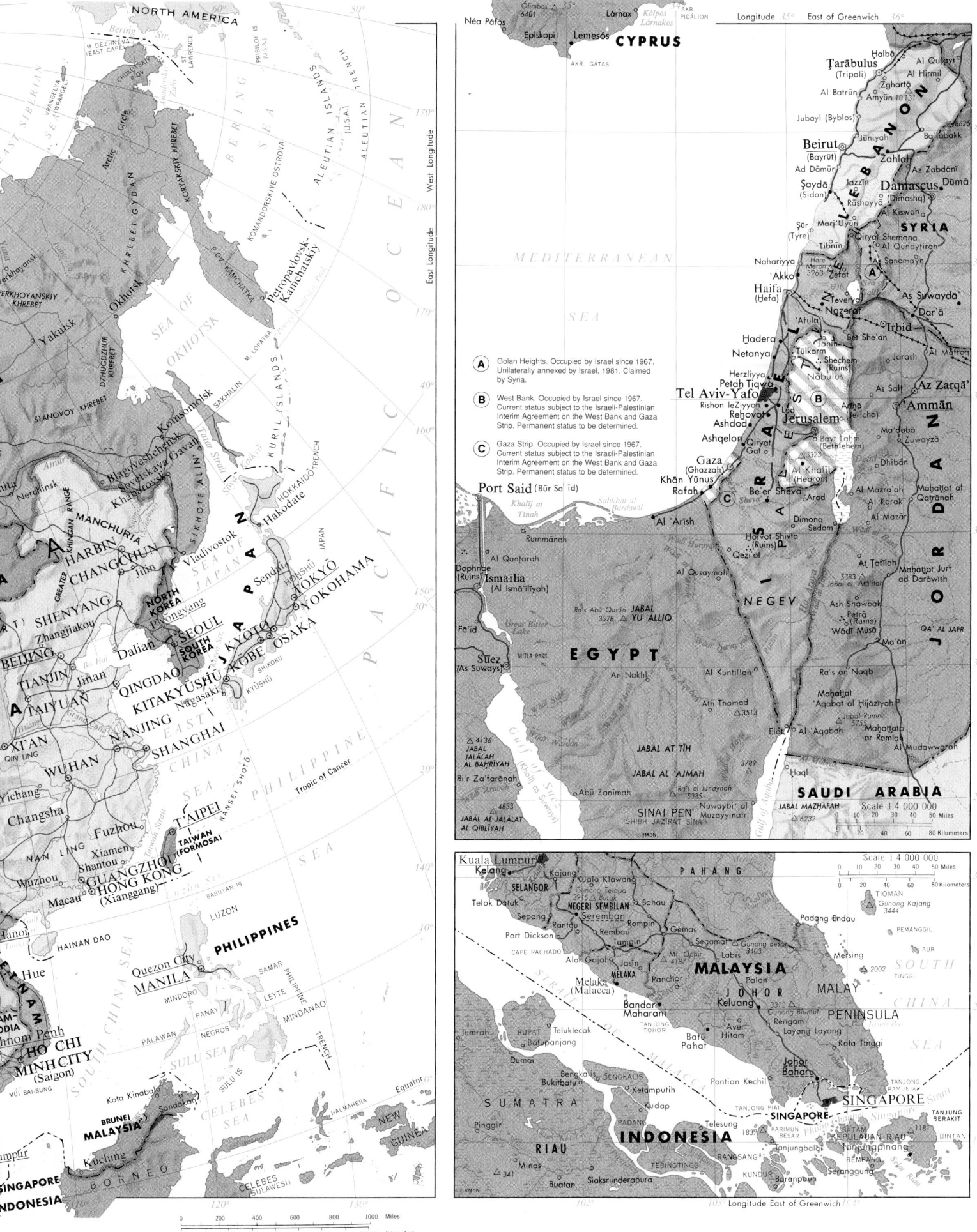

CYPRUS

Ólimbos 6401
Néa Páfos
Episkopi    Lemesós
AKR GÁTAS
Kólpos Lárnax Lárnakos AKR PIDÁLION
Longitude 35° East of Greenwich 36°

MEDITERRANEAN

SEA

**Ṭarābulus (Tripoli)**
Al Qusayr
Halbā
Al Hirmil
Al Batrūn
Amyūn 10131
Zgharta
Jubayl (Byblos)
Jūniyah
Ba'labakk
**Beirut (Bayrūt)**
Zahlah
Az Zabdānī
Shaydā (Sidon)
Jazzīn
Rāshayyā
**Damascus (Dimashq)**
Dūmā
Şūr (Tyre)
Marj 'Uyūn
Al Kiswah
**SYRIA**
Tibnīn
Qiryat Shemona
Al Qunayţirah
Nahariyya
Merom 3963 Zefat
As Sanamayn
'Akko
Teverya
As Suwaydā'
Haifa (Hefa)
'Afula
Nazerat
Dar'ā
Hadera
Janin
Irbid
Netanya
Tulkarm
Jarash
Al Mafraq
Herzliyya
Shechem (Ruins) Nābulus
As Salt
Petah Tiqwa
'Ammān
Tel Aviv-Yafo
Rishon leZiyyon
Arīḥā (Jericho)
Az Zarqā'
Rehovot
**Jerusalem**
Ma'dāba
Zuwayzā
Ashdod
Qiryat Gat
Bayt Lahm (Bethlehem)
Ashqelon
Al Khalīl (Hebron)
Mahattat al Qaṭrānah
**Gaza (Ghazzah)**
Be'er Sheva
Al Mazra'ah
Al Karak
Khān Yūnus
Arad
Dhībān
Rafah
Dimona
Sedom
Al Mazār

**A** Golan Heights. Occupied by Israel since 1967.
Unilaterally annexed by Israel, 1981. Claimed
by Syria.

**B** West Bank. Occupied by Israel since 1967.
Current status subject to the Israeli-Palestinian
Interim Agreement on the West Bank and Gaza
Strip. Permanent status to be determined.

**C** Gaza Strip. Occupied by Israel since 1967.
Current status subject to the Israeli-Palestinian
Interim Agreement on the West Bank and Gaza
Strip. Permanent status to be determined.

**Port Said (Būr Sa'īd)**
Khalīj at Tīnah
Sabkhat al Bardawīl
Rummānah
Al 'Arīsh
Al Qanţarah
Horvot Shiva (Ruins)
At Tafilah
Daphnae (Ruins)
**Ismailia (Al Ismā'īlīyah)**
Qezi ot
Mahattat Jurt ad Darāwīsh
Fā'id
Al Qusaymah
Ra's Abū Qurūn JABAL 3578 △ YU 'ALLIQ
Ash Shawbak
Petrā (Ruins)
Wādī Mūsā
**Suez (As Suways)**
MITLA PASS
**EGYPT**
**NEGEV**
Ma'ān
An Nakhl
Al Kuntillah
Ra's an Naqb
JABAL 4136 JALĀLAH AL BAḤRĪYAH
Mahattat 'Aqabat al Ḥijāzīyah
Bi'r Za'farānah
Ath Thamad 3513
3789
Elat
Al 'Aqabah
Mahattat ar Ramlah
Abū Zanīmah
Ra's al Junaynah 5335
Haql
Al Mudawwarah
JABAL AT TĪH
Nuwaybi' al Muzayyinah
JABAL MAZḤAFAH
4833
SINAI PEN (SHIBH JAZIRAT SĪNA) 6232
JABAL AL JALĀLAT AL QIBLĪYAH
JABAL AL 'AJMAH
**SAUDI ARABIA**
Scale 1:4 000 000
0  10  20  30  40  50 Miles
0  20  40  60  80 Kilometers

Kuala Lumpur
Kelang
Kajang
Kuala Klawang
**PAHANG**
Scale 1:4 000 000
0  10  20  30  40  50 Miles
0  20  40  60  80 Kilometers
**SELANGOR**
Gunong Telapa 3915 △ Burat
Bahau
Telok Datok
Sepang
Rantau
Rompin
Gemas
Segamat △ Gunong Besar 3403
Padang Endau
**NEGERI SEMBILAN**
Seremban
Rembau
Tampin
Mersing
Port Dickson
TIOMAN
Gunong Kajang 3444
CAPE RACHADO
Alor Gajah
Jasin
Labis
Mt. Ophir △ 4187
**MALAYSIA**
2002 AUR
**MELAKA**
Panchor
Palah
**Melaka (Malacca)**
**JOHOR**
**MALAY**
Bandar Maharani
Keluang
Gunong Blumut 3312
Ayer Hitam
Rengam
Layang Layang
**PENINSULA**
Jumrah
**RUPAT**
Teluklecak
TANJONG TOHOR
Batu Pahat
Kota Tinggi
Dumai
Pontian Kechil
TANJONG PIAI
Johor Baharu
TANJUNG RAMUNIA
**SUMATRA**
Bengkalis
**BENGKALIS**
Ketamputih
TANJONG PIAI
**SINGAPORE**
TANJUNG BERAKIT
Bukitbatu
Pinggir
Telesung
KARIMUN BESAR
**SINGAPORE**
Singapore
Kudap
Padang
**RIAU**
Tanjungbalai
BINTAN
**INDONESIA**
Minas
341
Buatan
Siaksriindrapura
RANGSANG
Tanjungpinang
**KEPULAUAN RIAU**
TEBINGTINGGI
Seranggung
KUNDUR
Baranpuih
Longitude East of Greenwich 103°

**NORTH AMERICA**
Bering Str.
M. DEZHNEVA (EAST CAPE)
ST. LAWRENCE
PRIBILOF IS (USA)
KOMANDORSKIYE OSTROVA
ALEUTIAN ISLANDS (USA)
Arctic Circle
P. OV. KAMCHATKA
**PACIFIC OCEAN**
West Longitude
East Longitude
KHREBET GYDAN
VRANGELYA (WRANGEL)
KORYAKSKIY KHREBET
Petropavlovsk-Kamchatskiy
Verkhoyansk
Yakutsk
Okhotsk
KHREBET DZHUGDZHUR
SAKHALIN
**SEA OF OKHOTSK**
KURIL ISLANDS
Nerchinsk
Komsomolsk
Sovetskaya Gavan
HOKKAIDŌ TRENCH
Hakodate
Blagoveshchensk
Khabarovsk
SIKHOTE ALIN
Vladivostok
**SEA OF JAPAN**
Sendai
**JAPAN**
HONSHŪ
**TOKYO**
**YOKOHAMA**
GREATER KHINGAN RANGE
**MANCHURIA**
**HARBIN**
**CHANGCHUN**
Jilin
**NORTH KOREA**
Pyongyang
**KYOTO**
**KOBE OSAKA**
SHIKOKU
**SHENYANG**
Zhangjiakou
Dalian
**SEOUL**
**SOUTH KOREA**
**KITAKYUSHŪ**
KYŪSHŪ
Nagasaki
**BEIJING**
**TIANJIN**
Jinan
Bo Hai
**QINGDAO**
NANSEI SHOTŌ
**TAIYUAN**
Huang
**XI'AN**
QIN LING
**NANJING**
**SHANGHAI**
**EAST CHINA SEA**
Tropic of Cancer
**WUHAN**
Yichang
**PHILIPPINE SEA**
Changsha
**TAIPEI**
**TAIWAN (FORMOSA)**
NAN LING
Fuzhou
Taiwan Strait
Xiamen
Wuzhou
Shantou
**GUANGZHOU**
**HONG KONG (Xianggang)**
Macau
LUZON
BABUYAN IS
HAINAN DAO
**PHILIPPINES**
Hue
Quezon City
**MANILA**
SAMAR
MINDORO
LEYTE
PHILIPPINE TRENCH
**HO CHI MINH CITY (Saigon)**
PANAY
NEGROS
MINDANAO
PALAWAN
MŨI BAI BUNG
Phnom Penh
**CAMBODIA**
**SULU SEA**
SULU IS
Koto Kinabalu
Sandakan
Equator
**BRUNEI**
**MALAYSIA**
Kuching
**BORNEO**
**CELEBES SEA (SULAWESI)**
HALMAHERA
**NEW GUINEA**
Lumpur
**SINGAPORE**
**INDONESIA**

0  200  400  600  800  1000 Miles
0  400  800  1200  1600 Kilometers

Continued on pages 229

Relief

| Meters | | Feet |
|---|---|---|
| 3050 | | 10 000 |
| 1525 | | 5000 |
| 610 | | 2000 |
| 305 | | 1000 |
| 0 | Sea Level | 0 |
| | | Below |
| | | Sea Level |
| 152.5 | | 500 |
| 1525 | | 5000 |
| 3050 | | 10 000 |
| 6100 | | 20 000 |

A-519695-76 -24- 2946
COPYRIGHT BY
RAND McNALLY & COMPANY
MADE IN U.S.A.

Longitude East of Greenwich

Scale 1:40 000 000; one inch to 630 miles. Lambert's Azimuthal, Equal Area Projection
Elevations and depressions are given in feet

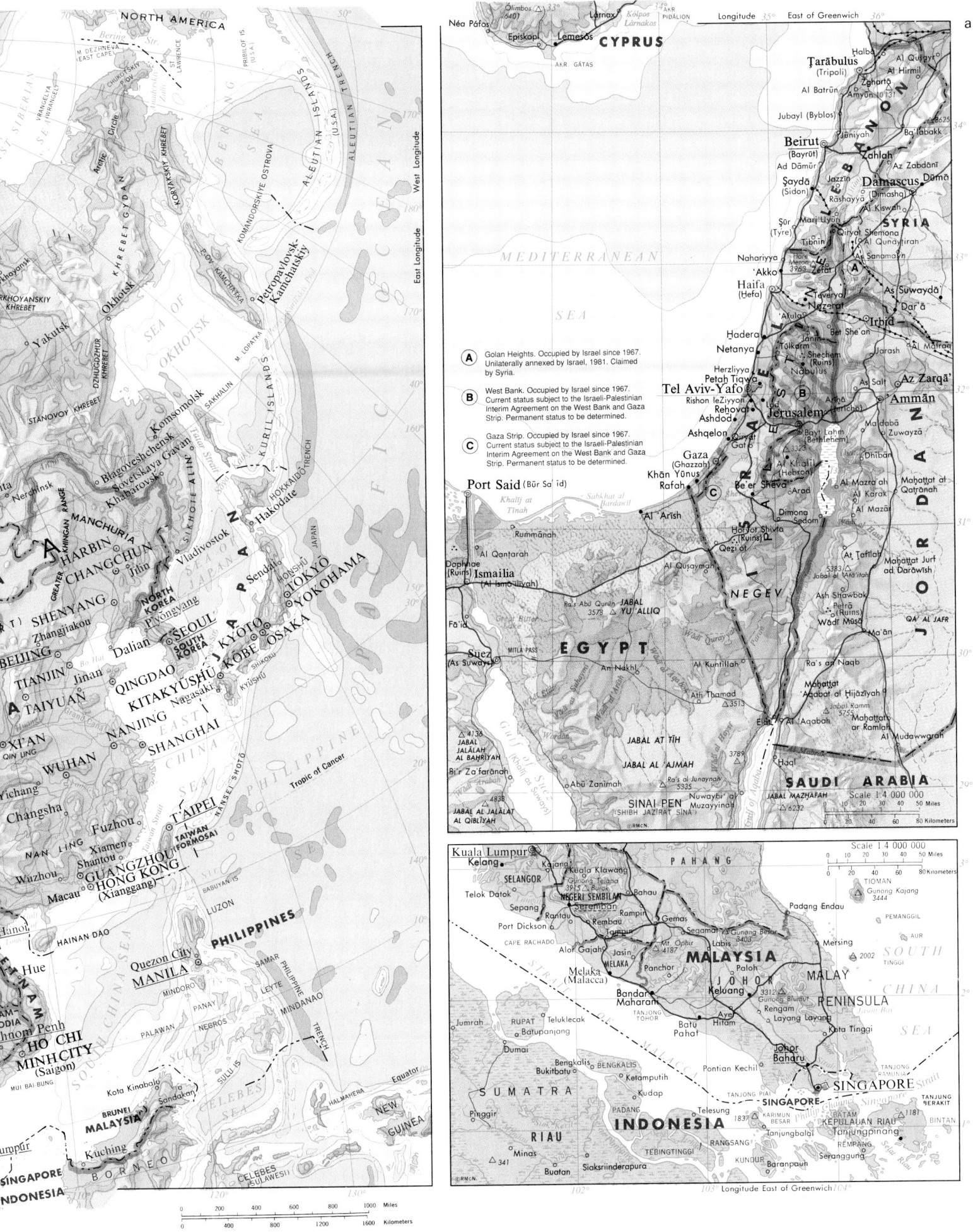

**a**

NORTH AMERICA

M. DEZHNEVA
(EAST CAPE)
Bering Str.
Arctic Circle

CYPRUS

Néa Páfos
Episkopi
Lemesos
Larnax
Kólpos
Lárnakos
AKR. GÁTAS
AKR. PIDÁLION
Longitude  35°  East of Greenwich  36°
Olimbos
6407
AKR

Halba
Al Qusayr
Al Hirmil
Ṭarābulus
(Tripoli)
Al Batrūn
Zgharta
Amyūn
Ba'labakk
Jubayl (Byblos)
Jūniyah
2625
Beirut
(Bayrūt)
Ad Dāmūr
Zahlah
Az Zabdānī
Şaydā
(Sidon)
Jazzīn
Rāshayyā
Al Kiswah
Damascus
(Dimashq)
Dūmā
Şūr
(Tyre)
Marj Uyūn
Qiryat Shemona
SYRIA
Tibnīn
Al Qunayṭirah
Nahariyya
Meron
3963
Zefat
As Sanamayn
A
Akko
Ṭaveryā
As Suwaydā
Haifa
(Hefa)
Nazerat
Dar'ā
'Afula
Irbid
Bet She'an
Hadera
Jānīn
Jarash
Al Mafraq
Netanya
Ṭūlkarm
Shechem
(Ruins)
Herzliyya
Nablus
As Salt
Az Zarqā'
Petah Tiqwa
Amman
Tel Aviv-Yafo
B
Ariḥa
(Jericho)
Rishon leZiyyon
Lod
Jerusalem
Maldabā
Zuwayzā
Rehovot
Qiryat
Gat
Bayt Laḥm
(Bethlehem)
Dhibān
Ashdod
Ashqelon
Al Khalīl
(Hebron)
Al Mazra'ah
Gaza
(Ghazzah)
Be'er Sheva
Arad
Al Karak
Maḥaṭṭat at Qaṭrānah
Khān Yūnus
Rafah
C
Port Said (Būr Sa'īd)
Khalīj at
Tīnah
Sabkhat al
Bardawīl
Al 'Arīsh
Ḥorfor Shiṿta
(Ruins)
Dimona
Sedom
Al Mazār
Rummānah
Qezi'ot
At Ṭafīlah
Al Qantarah
Maḥaṭṭat Jurf
ad Darāwīsh
Daphnae
(Ruins)
Ismailia
(Al Ismā'īlīya)
Al Qusaymah
5383
Jabal 'Ata'ītah
Ash Shawbak
Fā'id
Ra's Abū Qurūn
JABAL
YU'ALLIQ
3578
NEGEV
Petra
(Ruins)
Wādī Mūsā
Ma'ān
QA' AL JAFR
Suez
(As Suways)
An-Nakhl
Wādī Quray
Mitla Pass
EGYPT
Al Kuntillah
Ra's an Naqb
Ath Thamad
3513
Maḥaṭṭat
'Aqabat al Ḥijāzīyah
4136
JABAL
JALĀLAH
AL BAḤRĪYAH
Bi'r Za'farānah
Jabal Ramm
5755
Elat
Al 'Aqabah
Maḥaṭṭat
ar Ramlah
3789
Al Mudawwarah
Ḥaql
JABAL AT TĪH
SAUDI ARABIA
JABAL AL AJMAH
Scale 1:4 000 000
Abū Zanimah
Ra's al Junaynah
5335
JABAL AL JALĀLAT
AL QIBLĪYAH
4838
SINAI PEN
(SHIBH JAZĪRAT SĪNĀ)
Nuwaybi' al
Muzayyinah
JABAL MAZHAFAH
6232
©RMCN
0  10  20  30  40  50 Miles
0  20  40  60  80 Kilometers

VOSTOCHNO-
SIBIRSKIY
VRANGELYA
(WRANGEL I.)
CHUKCHI
SEA
KHREBET GYDAN
KORYAKSKIY KHREBET
KOMANDORSKIYE OSTROVA
ALEUTIAN ISLANDS
PRIBILOF IS.
(U.S.A.)
LAWRENCE
ST.
ALEUTIAN TRENCH
West Longitude
170°
180°
East Longitude
170°
Petropavlovsk-
Kamchatskiy
M. LOPATKA
50°
Okhotsk
Komsomolsk
SEA OF
OKHOTSK
KURIL ISLANDS
KURIL TRENCH
40°
DZHUGDZHUR KHREBET
STANOVOY KHREBET
Blagoveshchensk
Sovetskaya Gavan
Khabarovsk
SAKHALIN
Tatar Strait
HOKKAIDŌ
Hakodate
HOKKAIDŌ TRENCH
SIKHOTE ALIN
MANCHURIA
Vladivostok
GREATER KHINGAN RANGE
HARBIN
CHANGCHUN
Jilin
Komsomolsk
JAPAN
Sendai
Monshū
TŌKYŌ
YOKOHAMA
SHENYANG
NORTH KOREA
SŌUL
SEOUL
Pyongyang
SHIKOKU
KYŌTO
KŌBE
OSAKA
BEIJING
Zhangjiakou
Dalian
SOUTH KOREA
QINGDAO
KITAKYŪSHŪ
Nagasaki
KYŪSHŪ
TIANJIN
Jinan
Bo Hai
TAIYUAN
NANJING
SHANGHAI
EAST CHINA SEA
NANSEI SHOTŌ
XI'AN
QIN LING
WUHAN
Yichang
Changsha
NAN LING
Fuzhou
Xiamen
Shantou
T'AIPEI
TAIWAN
(FORMOSA)
GUANGZHOU
HONG KONG
(Xianggang)
Macau
Wuzhou
Tropic of Cancer
PHILIPPINE SEA
BABUYAN IS.
LUZON
PHILIPPINE TRENCH
Hanoi
HAINAN DAO
PHILIPPINES
Quezon City
MANILA
Mindoro
Samar
Leyte
PHILIPPINE TRENCH
Hue
VIETNAM
CAMBODIA
Phnom Penh
HO CHI
MINH CITY
(Saigon)
MUI BAI BUNG
Panay
Negros
PALAWAN
Mindanao
SULU IS.
SOUTH CHINA SEA
Kota Kinabalu
Sandakan
SULU SEA
CELEBES SEA
CELEBES
(SULAWESI)
Equator
HALMAHERA
NEW GUINEA
lumpur
SINGAPORE
INDONESIA
BRUNEI
MALAYSIA
Kuching
BORNEO
130°
120°
0  200  400  600  800  1000 Miles
0  400  800  1200  1600 Kilometers

**b**

Scale 1:4 000 000
0  10  20  30  40  50 Miles
0  20  40  60  80 Kilometers

Kuala Lumpur
Kelang
PAHANG
Kajang
Kuala Klawang
SELANGOR
Gunong Telapa
3915
Burok
Bahau
TIOMAN
Gunong Kajang
3444
Telok Datok
Sepang
NEGERI SEMBILAN
Seremban
Rantau
Rembau
Rampin
Gemas
Segamat
Gunong Besar
3403
Padang Endau
PEMANGGIL
Port Dickson
Tampin
AUR
CAPE RACHADO
Alor Gajah
Jasin
Mt. Ophir
4187
Labis
MALAYSIA
Paloh
Mersing
2002
TINGGI
Melaka
(Malacca)
MELAKA
Panchor
JOHOR
MALAY
PENINSULA
SOUTH CHINA SEA
Bandar
Maharam
Keluang
Gunong Blumut
3312
Rengam
Layang Layang
Kota Tinggi
Ayer Hitam
Batu Pahat
TANJONG TOHOR
Jumrah
RUPAT
Teluklecak
Dumai
BENGKALIS
Bengkalis
Bukitbatu
Ketamputih
Kudap
SUMATRA
Pinggir
PADANG
Telesung
1837
Johor
Baharu
Pontian Kechil
TANJONG PIAI
Phillip
KEPULAUAN
RIAU
SINGAPORE
Singapore Strait
BATAM
KARIMUN
BESAR
BULAN
RANGSANG
Tanjungbalai
Tanjungpinang
BINTAN
TANJUNG
BERAKIT
RIAU
INDONESIA
Minas
341
Buatan
Siaksriinderapura
REMPANG
KUNDUR
Baranpauh
Seranggung
©RMCN
102°
103°  Longitude East of Greenwich  104°

A  Golan Heights. Occupied by Israel since 1967.
Unilaterally annexed by Israel, 1981. Claimed
by Syria.

B  West Bank. Occupied by Israel since 1967.
Current status subject to the Israeli-Palestinian
Interim Agreement on the West Bank and Gaza
Strip. Permanent status to be determined.

C  Gaza Strip. Occupied by Israel since 1967.
Current status subject to the Israeli-Palestinian
Interim Agreement on the West Bank and Gaza
Strip. Permanent status to be determined.

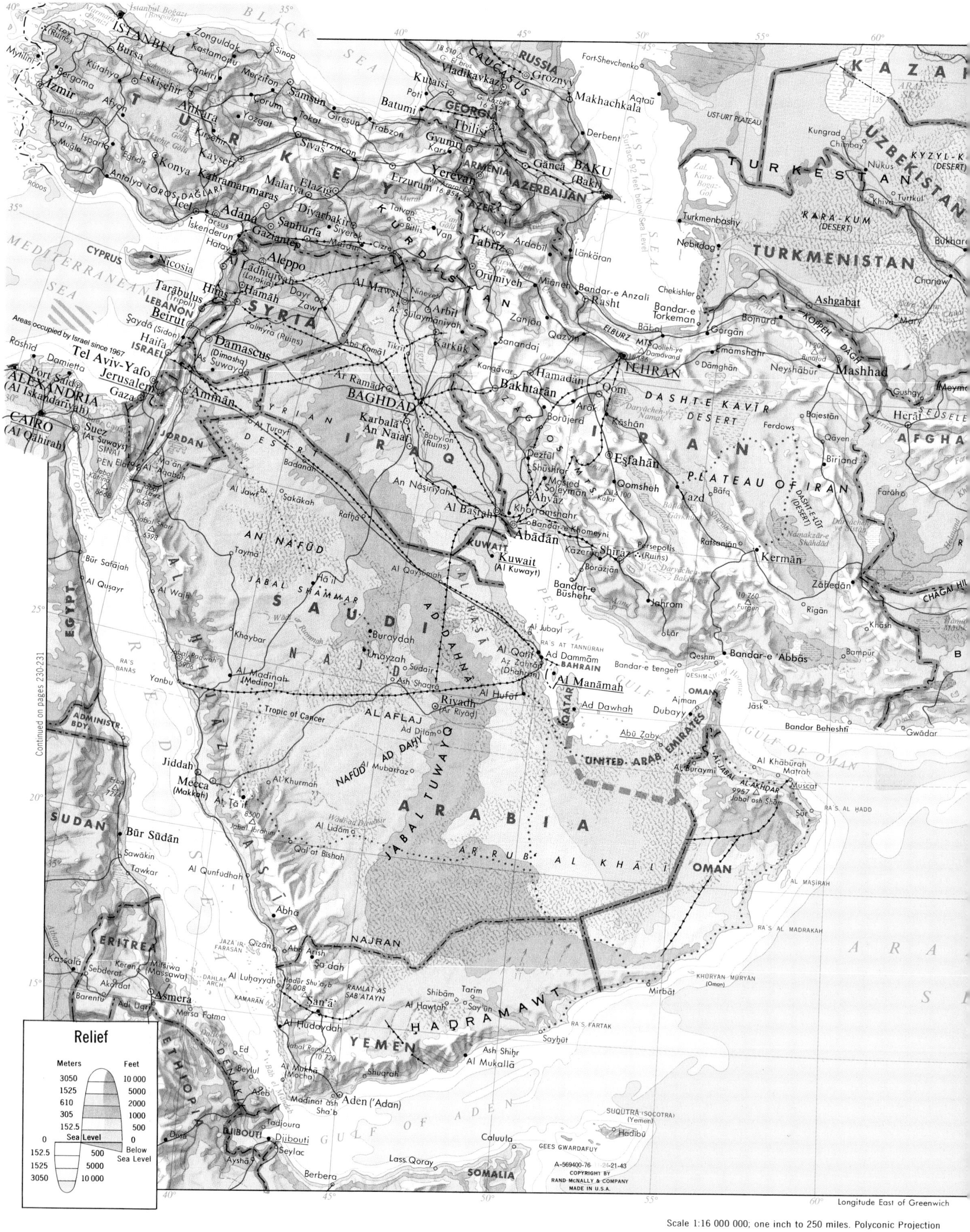

BLACK SEA

İstanbul Boğazı (Bosphorus)
ISTANBUL
Zonguldak
Kastamonu
Sinop
Samsun
Bursa
Eskişehir
Çankırı
Çorum
Merzifon
Giresun
Trabzon
RUSSIA
Grozny
Fort-Shevchenko
Aqtaū
KAZA
Kütahya
Ankara
Yozgat
Tokat
Sivas
Kırşehir
Kayseri
Batumi
Poti
Kutaisi
Vladikavkaz
Makhachkala
Derbent
CAUCASUS
GEORGIA
Tbilisi
UST-URT PLATEAU
Kungrad
Chimbay
Nukus
UZBEKISTAN
KYZYL-K (DESERT)
Izmir
Bergama
Mytilini
Afyon
Aydın
Muğla
Rodos
Antalya
TOROS DAĞLARI
Tarsus
Iceli
İskenderun
Adana
Kahramanmaraş
Malatya
Elazığ
Diyarbakır
Siverek
Şanlıurfa
Gaziantep
Hatay
TURKEY
Erzincan
Sivas
Erzurum
Kars
Gyumri
Yerevan
ARMENIA
Gänca
BAKU (Bakı)
AZERBAIJAN
Tabrīz
Ardabīl
Lānkārān
Bandar-e Anzalī
Rasht
Bandar-e Torkeman
Gorgān
Turkmenbashy
Nebitdag
Chekishler
TURKMENISTAN
Ashgabat
Bojnūrd
KOPPEH DAGH
Gushgy
Mashhad
Neyshābūr
Dāmghān
Semnān
Charjew

CYPRUS
Nicosia
MEDITERRANEAN SEA
Tarābulus (Tripoli)
Ḩimş
Ḩamāh
Aleppo
Al Lādhiqīyah (Latakia)
Dayr az Zawr
SYRIA
Al Mawşil
Nineveh
Arbīl
As Sulaymānīyah
KURDISTAN
Van
Bitlis
Khvoy
Orūmīyeh
Mīāneh
Zanjān
Qazvīn
Qollleh-ye Damāvand
ELBURZ MTS.
TEHRĀN
Karaj
Qom
DASHT-E KAVIR DESERT
Dāmghān
Herāt
AFGHA

Beirut
LEBANON
Şaydā (Sidon)
ISRAEL
Haifa
Tel Aviv-Yafo
Jerusalem
Gaza
Damascus (Dimashq)
As Suwaydā
Palmyra (Ruins)
Abū Kamāl
Tikrīt
Karkūk
Sanandaj
Kangāvar
Hamadān
Bakhtarān
Arāk
Borūjerd
Kāshān
Esfahān
Qomsheh
Yazd
Bāfq
PLATEAU OF IRAN
Farāh
Areas occupied by Israel since 1967
Rashīd
Damietta
ALEXANDRIA (Al Iskandarīyah)
Port Said
Suez (As Suways)
CAIRO (Al Qāhirah)
Amman
JORDAN
Al Tutayf
SYRIAN DESERT
Ar Ramādī
BAGHDAD
Karbalā
An Najaf
Babylon (Ruins)
IRAQ
Dezfūl
Shūshtar
Masjed Soleymān
Ahvāz
Khorramshahr
ZAGROS MTS.
Borūjen
Qomsheh
Persepolis (Ruins)
Shīrāz
Kerman
Rafsanjān
Zāhedān
CHAGAI HILLS

SINAI
PEN.
Elat (Al 'Aqabah)
Jabal Katrīnah
8668
Al 'Aqabah
Ma'ān
Al Jawf
Sakākah
An Nāşirīyah
Al Başrah
Bandar-e Khomeynī
Abādān
KUWAIT
Kuwait (Al Kuwayt)
Kāzerūn
Borāzjān
Bandar-e Būshehr
Jahrom
Lār
Fūrgun
10 760
Rīgān
Khāsh
EGYPT
Bur Safajah
Al Qusayr
AN NAFŪD
Taymā'
Ha'il
JABAL SHAMMAR
Al Jubayl
Ra's At Tannūrah
Bandar-e Lengeh
Bandar-e 'Abbās
Bampūr
Jāsk

RA'S BANAS
Khaybar
Al Wajh
Buraydah
'Unayzah
Sudair
Ash Shaqrā'
ADDAHNA
Al Qatīf
Az Zahrān (Dhahran)
Ad Dammām
BAHRAIN
Al Manāmah
Qeshm
QESHM
STR. OF HORMUZ
OMAN
Bandar Beheshtī
Gwādar

ADMINISTR. BDY.
AL HIJAZ
Al Madīnah (Medina)
Yanbu'
NAJD
Riyadh (Ar Riyāḍ)
Al Hufūf
QATAR
Ad Dawhah
Abū Zaby
Dubayy
Ajman
UNITED ARAB EMIRATES
Al Buraymī
AL JABAL AL AKHDAR
Al Khābūrah
Matrah
Muscat
RA'S AL HADD

Tropic of Cancer
AL AFLAJ
Ad Dilam
NAFŪD
Mubarraz
AD DAHY
Jiddah
Mecca (Makkah)
At Tā'if
Al Khurmah
Al Lidām
SAUDI ARABIA
JABAL TUWAYQ
AR RUB' AL KHĀLĪ
OMAN
RA'S AL MADRAKAH

Erba
7274
Būr Sūdān
SUDAN
Sawākin
Al Qunfudhah
Abhā
Qal'at Bīshah
Jabal Ibrāhīm
Jabal ash Shām
9957
Şūr
KHŪRYAN MŪRYAN (Oman)
RA'S AL HADD

Kassalā
Sebderat
ERITREA
Keren
Akordat
Barentu
Adī Ugrī
Asmera
ETHIOPIA
Mitsiwa (Massawa)
DAHLAK ARCH.
KAMARĀN
NAJRAN
JAZĀ'IR FARASAN
Qizān
Abu 'Arīsh
Şa'dah
Al Luhayyah
Ḩajjah
Ḩodur Shu'ayb
2008
San'ā
RAMLAT AS SAB'ATAYN
Shibām
Tarīm
Say'ūn
Al Ḩawṭah
HADRAMAWT
Mirbat
RA'S FARTAK

Keftya
Beylul
Mersa Fatma
DENAKIL
Al Ḩudaydah
Al Mukhā (Mocha)
YEMEN
Jabal Ḩaraz
10 729
Shuqrah
Ash Shiḥr
Al Mukallā
Sayḩūt
GEES GWARDAFUY

Ed
Tadjoura
DJIBOUTI
Djibouti
Seylac
Aysha
Madīnat ash Sha'b
Aden ('Adan)
GULF OF ADEN
Caluula
SUQUTRA (SOCOTRA) (Yemen)
Hadibū
Berbera
Lass Qoray
SOMALIA

---

**Relief**

| Meters | Feet |
|---|---|
| 3050 | 10 000 |
| 1525 | 5000 |
| 610 | 2000 |
| 305 | 1000 |
| 152.5 | 500 |
| 0 Sea Level | 0 |
| 152.5 | 500 Below Sea Level |
| 1525 | 5000 |
| 3050 | 10 000 |

A-569400-76    24-21-43
COPYRIGHT BY
RAND-McNALLY & COMPANY
MADE IN U.S.A.

Longitude East of Greenwich

Scale 1:16 000 000; one inch to 250 miles. Polyconic Projection
Elevations and depressions are given in feet

Continued on pages 230/231

Continued on pages 184-185

**a**

PAKISTAN

AFGHANISTAN

Jalālābād
Dargai
Chārsadda
KHYBER PASS
14 930
MORGA RA.
Peshāwar

Scale 1:4 000 000

0  10  20  30   40 Miles
0  20   40    60 Kilometers
©RMCN.

**b**

Scale 1:40 000 000

©RMCN

AFGHANISTAN

PAKISTAN

JAMMU AND KASHMIR

C H I N A

HIMACHAL PRADESH

XIZAGN (TIBET)

PUNJAB
UTTARANCHAL

HARYANA

NEPAL
SIKKIM
BHUTAN
ARUNACHAL PRADESH

RĀJASTHĀN
UTTAR PRADESH
BIHAR
ASSAM
NAGALAND
MEGHALAYA
MIZORAM

Tropic of Cancer

GUJARAT
MADHYA PRADESH
JHARKHAND
WEST BENGAL
ORISSA
BANGLADESH
MYANMAR

ARABIAN SEA

MAHĀRĀSHTRA
CHHATTISGARH

BAY OF BENGAL

KARNATAKA
ANDHRA PRADESH

KERALA
TAMIL NADU

SRI LANKA (CEYLON)

**INDIA · POLITICAL**

1-TRIPURA
2-MANIPUR
3-LAKSHADWEEP
4-DELHI
5-DĀDRA AND NAGAR HAVELI
6-PONDICHERRY
7-GOA, DAMĀN, AND DIU

Continued on pages 204-206

**c**

Tiruchchirāppalli
Ernākulam
Thanjāvūr  TAMIL NADU
Nāgappattinam

KERALA
Madurai
Jaffna
Alleppey
Tuticorin
Mannar
Trincomalee
Quilon
Tirunelveli
Thiruvananthapuram
Puttalam
Anuradhapura
CAPE COMORIN

SRI LANKA (CEYLON)
Kandy
Colombo
Pidurutalagala 8281

INDIAN OCEAN
Galle
Matara
DONDRA HEAD

Same scale as main map

**A** Area occupied by Pakistan and claimed by India.

**B** Area claimed and occupied by India; status disputed by Pakistan.

**C** Area occupied by China and claimed by India.

**D** Area occupied by India and claimed by China.

0  50  100   200   300   400   500 Miles
0   100   200    400    600    800 Kilometers

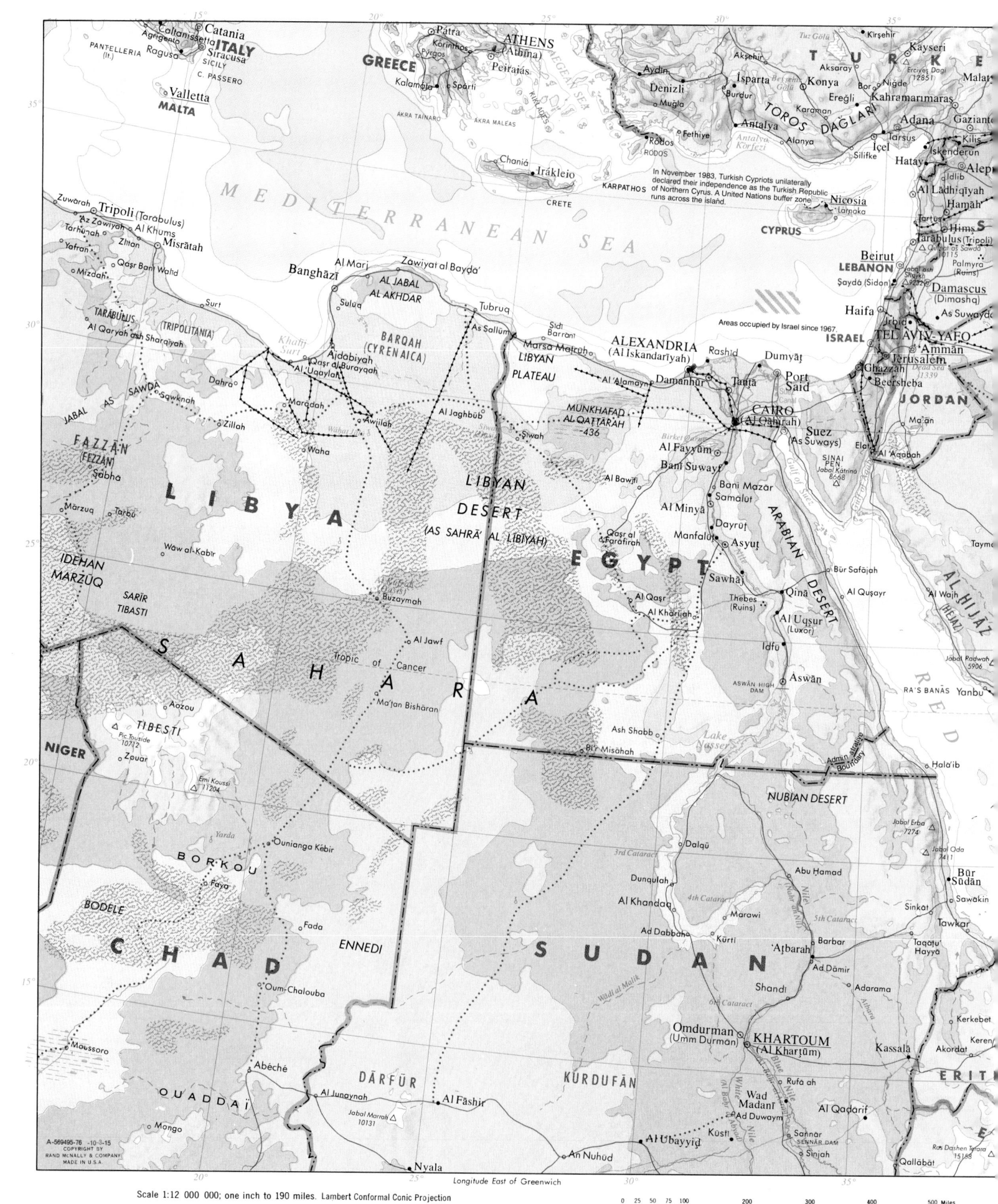

In November 1983, Turkish Cypriots unilaterally
declared their independence as the Turkish Republic
of Northern Cyrus. A United Nations buffer zone
runs across the island.

Areas occupied by Israel since 1967

Scale 1:12 000 000; one inch to 190 miles. Lambert Conformal Conic Projection

Elevations and depressions are given in feet

A-569495-76 -10-3-15
COPYRIGHT BY
RAND MCNALLY & COMPANY
MADE IN U.S.A.

Longitude East of Greenwich

0  25  50  75  100        200        300        400        500 Miles

0      100      200      300      400      500      600      700      800 Kilometers

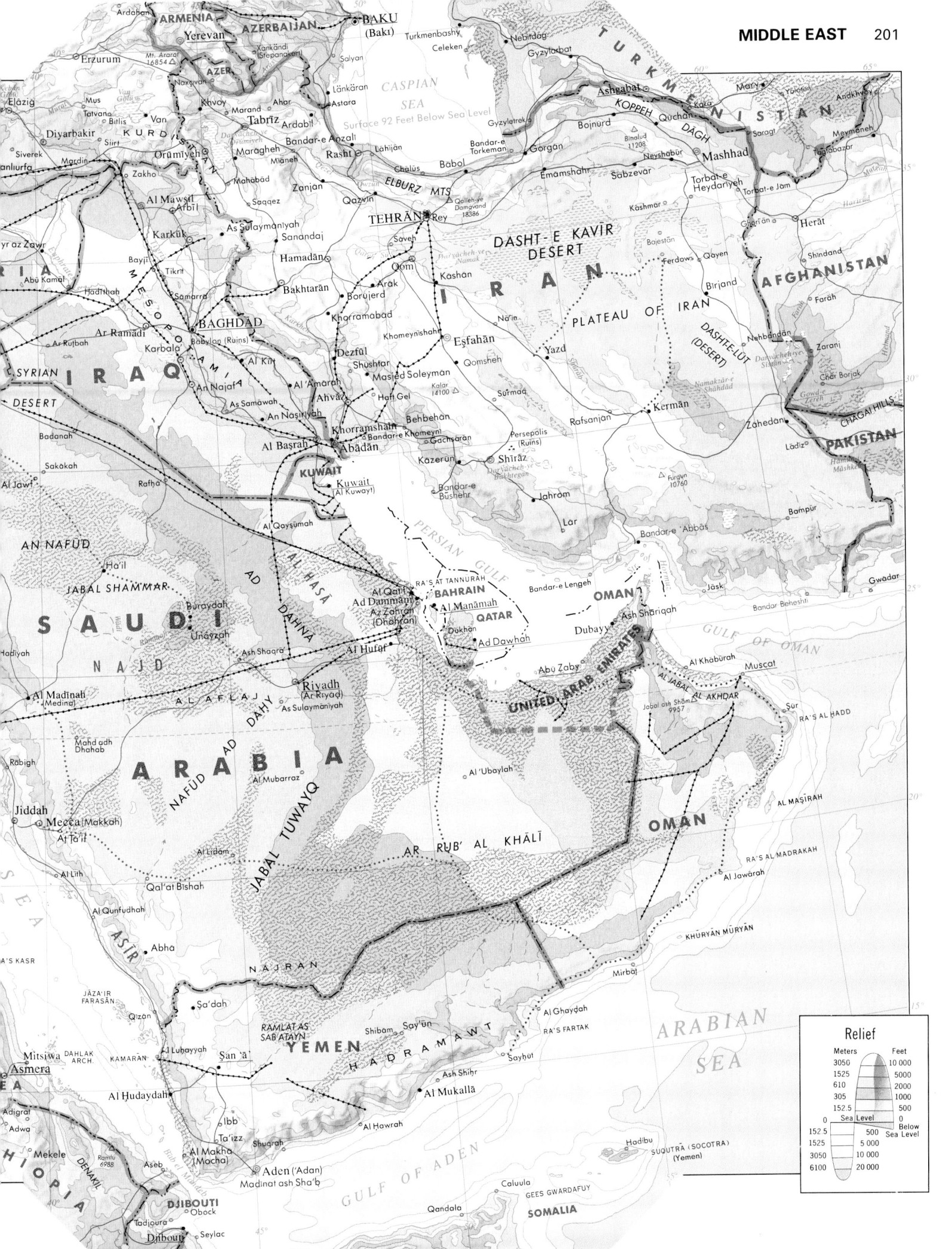

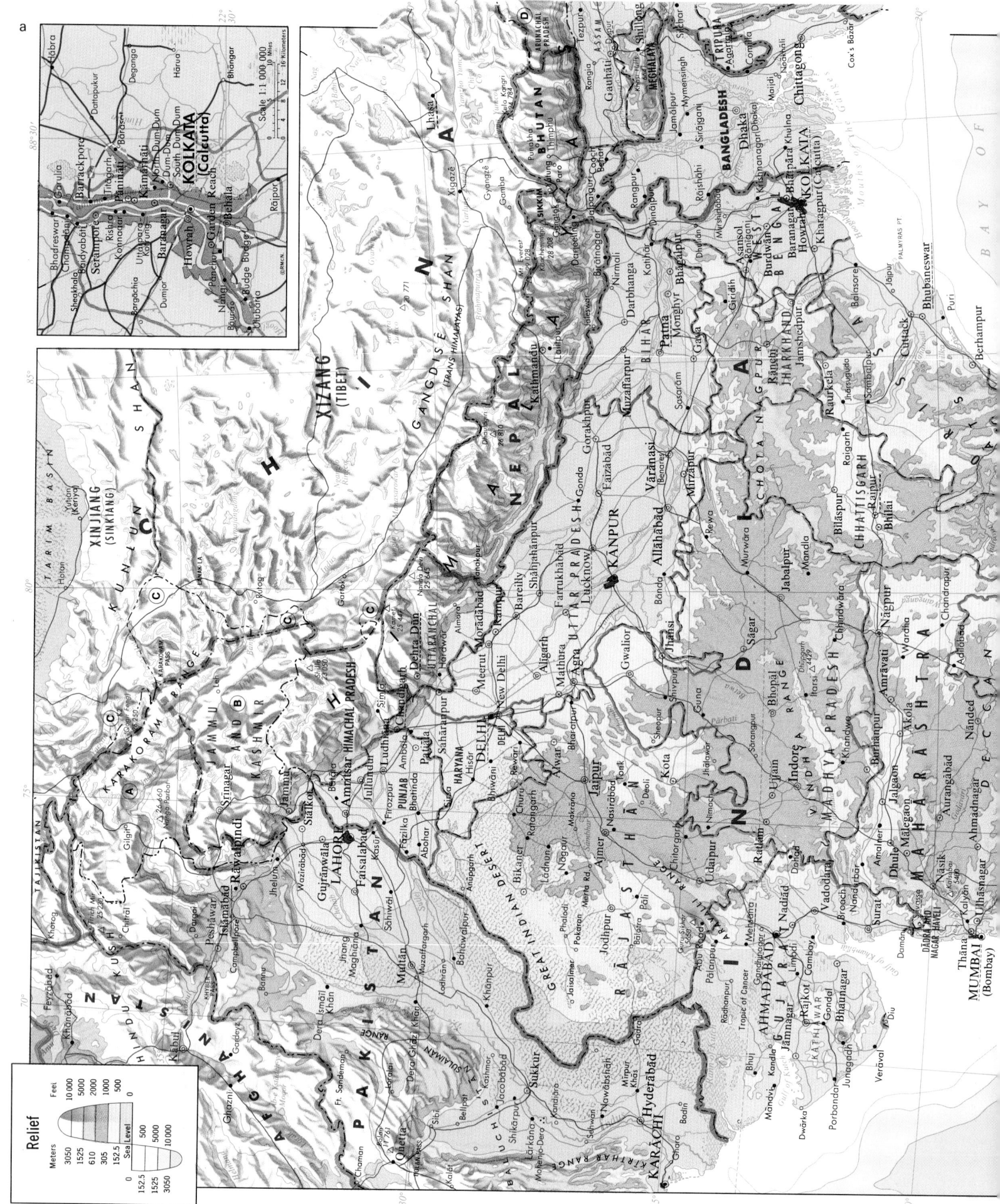

a

KOLKATA
(Calcutta)

Scale 1:1 000 000

Relief

| Meters | Feet |
|---|---|
| 3050 | 10 000 |
| 1525 | 5000 |
| 610 | 2000 |
| 305 | 1000 |
| 152.5 | 500 |
| | Sea Level |

500
5000
10 000

152.5
1525
3050

Scale 1:10 000 000; one inch to 160 miles. Lambert Conformal Conic Projection
Elevations and depressions are given in feet

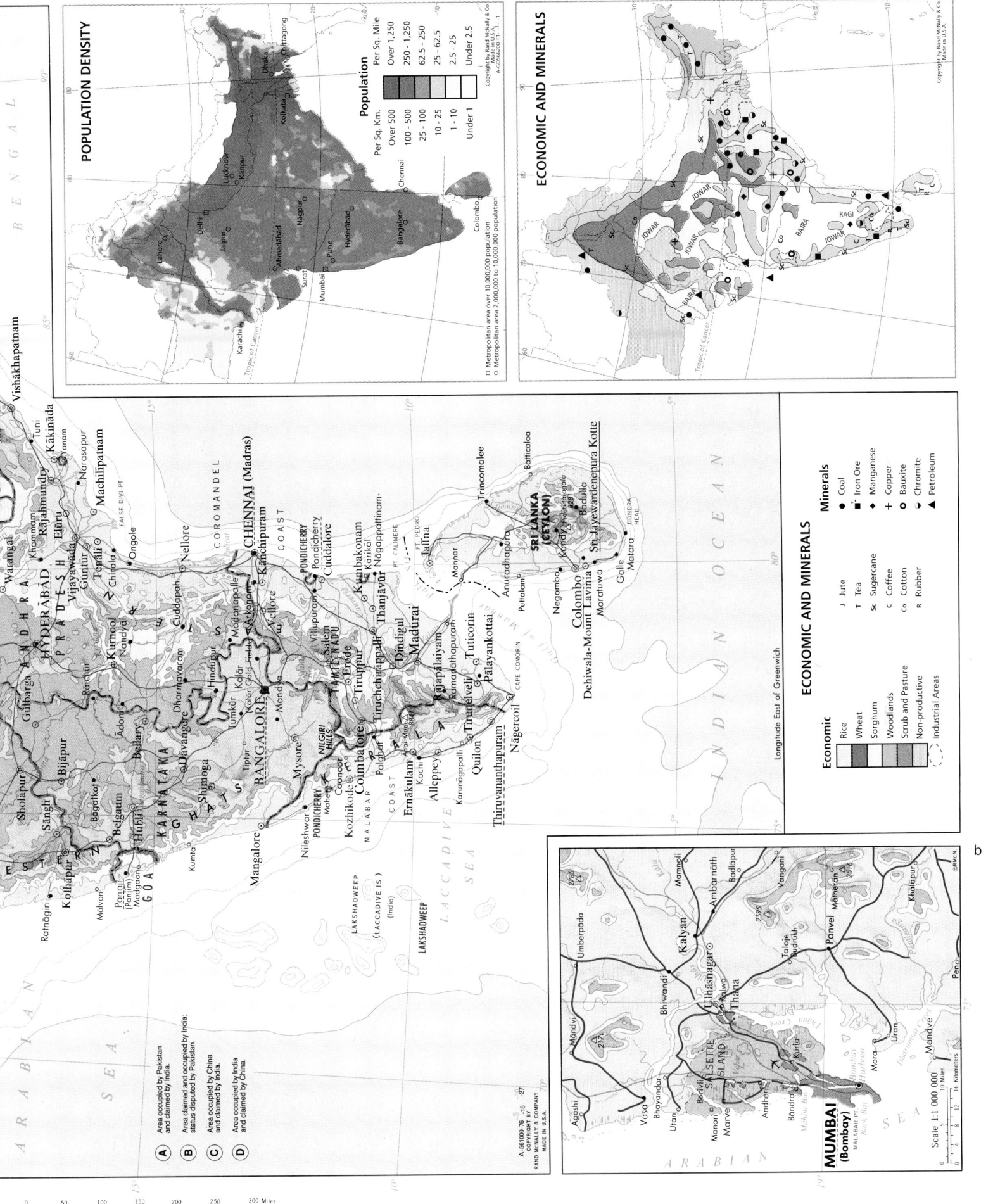

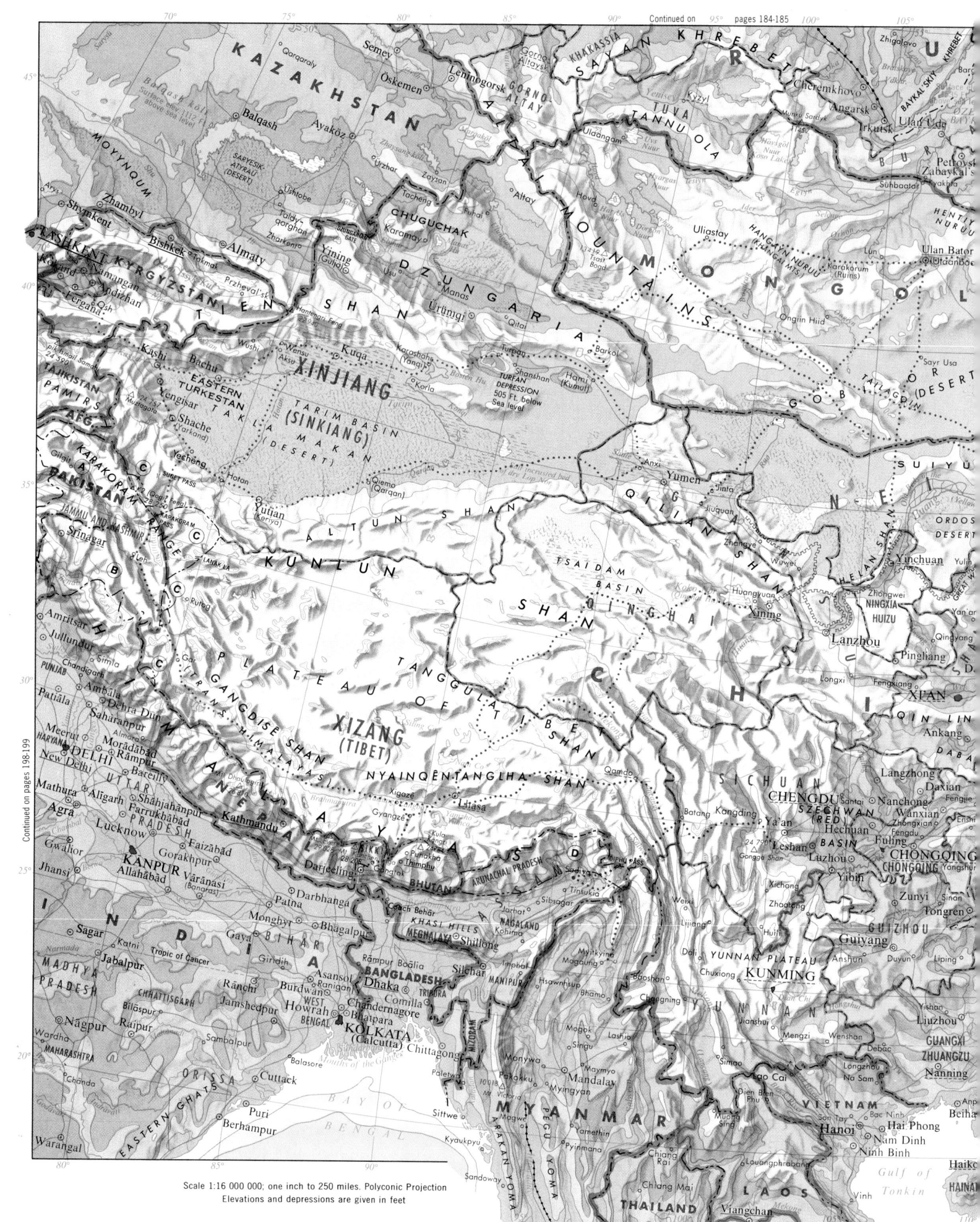

Continued on pages 184-185

KAZAKHSTAN

Semey
Qarqaraly
Balqash kôl
Surface elev. 1112 ft.
above sea level
Öskemen
Leninogorsk-Altay
GORNO-
ALTAY
SAYAN KHREBET
KHAKASSIA
Zhigalovo
Cheremkhovo
Angarsk
Irkutsk
Ulan Ude

Balqash
Ayaköz
Zaysan
Altay
Hovd
TUVA
TANNU OLA
Kyzyl
BAYKAL SKIY KHREBET
Petrovsk
Zabaykal's
yakha

MOYNQUM
SARYESIK-
ATYRAÜ
(DESERT)
Uştobe
Urzhar
Tacheng
DZUNGARIAN
GATE
Ulaangom
Uvs
Nuur
HANGAYN NURUU
KHANGAI MTS
Ulan Bator
Ulaanbaatar

Shymkent
Zhambyl
Taldy-
qorghan
Zharkent
CHUGUCHAK
Karamay
MONGOLIA

Bishkek
Almaty
Yining
(Gulja)
DZUNGARIA
Altay
Uliastay
Karakorum
(Ruins)

KYRGYZSTAN
TIEN SHAN
Usu
Manas
Ürümqi
Qitai
Turpan
Shanshan
Hami
(Kumul)
Barkol

TAJIKISTAN
Kashi
Bachu
Kuqa
Karashahr
(Yanqi)
Korla
TURFAN
DEPRESSION
505 ft. below
sea level
GOBI
(DESERT)

PAMIRS
XINJIANG
TARIM BASIN
(SINKIANG)
TAKLA MAKAN
(DESERT)
Bosten Hu
Anxi
Yumen
Jinta
Jiuquan
QILIAN SHAN
SUIYU

PAKISTAN
EASTERN
TURKESTAN
Yengisar
Shache
Yecheng
Hotan
Qiemo
(Qarqan)
Dry Lop Nor
Incrusted bed

Srinagar
KARAKORAM RANGE
Yutian
(Keriya)
ALTUN SHAN
Zhangye
Wuwei
Yinchuan
ORDOS
DESERT
NINGXIA
HUIZU

JAMMU AND KASHMIR
KARAKORAM
KUNLUN
TSAIDAM
BASIN
Huangyuan
Xining
Zhongwei
Lanzhou

Amritsar
LANAK LA
Ruoq
SHAN
QINGHAI
Koko nor
Longxi
Qingyang

Jullundur
PLATEAU
TANGGULA
SHAN
Fengxiang
Pingliang

PUNJAB
Chandigarh
Simla
GAR
GANGDISE SHAN
XIZANG
(TIBET)
OF TIBET
Qamdo
XI'AN
QIN LING
Ankang
DABA

Delhi
Meerut
HARYANA
Morādābād
Rāmpur
HIMALAYAS
NYAINQÊNTANGLHA SHAN
Lhasa
Batang
Kangding
SICHUAN
SZECHWAN
(RED)
Langzhong
Nanchong
Daxian
Fengjie

New Delhi
UTTAR
Bareilly
Xigaze
Gyangze
Ya'an
BASIN
Wanxian
Enshi

Mathura
Aligarh
Shāhjahānpur
Farrukhābād
PRADESH
Kathmandu
SIKKIM
Thimphu
ARUNACHAL PRADESH
DIPHU PASS
Leshan
Gongga Shan
Luzhou
Fuling
CHONGQING
CHONGQING

Agra
Gwalior
Lucknow
Faizābād
Gorakhpur
Darjeeling
BHUTAN
ASSAM
Gonga Shan
Xichang
Yibin
Yongshun
Zunyi

Jhansi
KĀNPUR
Allahābād
Vārānasi
(Banaras)
Patna
Darbhanga
Coach Behar
NAGALAND
Kohima
Weixi
Zhaotong
Sinan
Tongren

Sagar
Katni
Tropic of Cancer
Gaya
BIHAR
Bhagalpur
Monghyr
KHASI HILLS
MEGHALAYA
Shillong
MANIPUR
Myitkyina
Lijiang
Huili
GUIZHOU
Guiyang
Liping

Jabalpur
MADHYA
PRADESH
Ranchi
Asansol
Burdwan
Ranigani
Rāmpur
Bogra
Silchar
Imphal
Dali
YUNNAN PLATEAU
Anshun
Duyun
Liuzhou

Nagpur
CHHATTISGARH
Bilāspur
Raipur
Jamshedpur
WEST
BENGAL
Howrah
Chandernagore
Bhatpara
BANGLADESH
Dhaka
Comilla
TRIPURA
Chuxiong
KUNMING
YUNNAN
Mengzi
Wenshan
GUANGXI
ZHUANGZU
Nanning

Wardha
MAHARASHTRA
Sambalpur
KOLKATA
(Calcutta)
Chittagong
MIZORAM
Mogok
Lashio
Jianshui
Debao
Longzhou
Yishan

ORISSA
Chanda
Cuttack
Balasore
Mouths of the Ganges
Paletwa
Monywa
Singu
Simao
Gao Cai
Na Sam

Warangal
EASTERN GHATS
Puri
Berhampur
BAY OF
BENGAL
Sittwe
ARAKAN YOMA
Mandalay
Myingyan
VIETNAM
Longzhou
Beihai

Godavari
Sandoway
Kyaukpyu
Victoria
PEGU YOMA
Pakokku
Maymyo
Pyinmana
Muong
Sing
Dien Bien
Phu
Bac Ninh
Hanoi
Hai Phong
Nam Dinh
Ninh Binh

MYANMAR
Chiang
Rai
Chiang Mai
Luangphrabang
LAOS
Vinh
Gulf of
Tonkin
HAINAN

THAILAND
Viangchan

Continued on pages 198-199

Chinese Provinces,
Autonomous Regions (AR),
Special Administrative Regions (SAR),
and Municipalities (M)

| Conventional Form | Pinyin Form |
| --- | --- |
| Anhwei | Anhui |
| Chekiang | Zhenjiang |
| Chungking | Chongqing |
| Fukien | Fujian |
| Heilungkiang | Heilongjiang |
| Honan | Henan |
| Hong Kong (SAR) | Xianggang |
| Hopeh | Hebei |
| Hunan | Hunan |
| Hupeh | Hubei |
| Inner Mongolia (AR) | Nei Monggol |
| Kansu | Gansu |
| Kiangsi | Jiangxi |
| Kiangsu | Jiangsu |
| Kirin | Jilin |
| Kwangsi (AR) | Guangxi Zhuangzu |
| Kwangtung | Guangdong |
| Kweichow | Guizhou |
| Liaoning | Liaoning |
| Macau (SAR) | Aomen |
| Ningsia Hui (AR) | Ningxia Huizu |
| Peking (M) | Beijing |
| Shanghai (M) | Shanghai |
| Shansi | Shanxi |
| Shantung | Shandong |
| Shensi | Shaanxi |
| Sinkiang (AR) | Xinjiang |
| Szechwan | Sichuan |
| Tibet (AR) | Xizang |
| Tientsin (M) | Tianjin |
| Tsinghai | Qinghai |
| Yunnan | Yunnan |

(A) Area occupied by Pakistan
and claimed by India.

(B) Area claimed and occupied by India;
status disputed by Pakistan.

(C) Area occupied by China
and claimed by India.

(D) Area occupied by India
and claimed by China.

A-569700-76-|-17-|-32
COPYRIGHT BY
RAND McNALLY & COMPANY
MADE IN U.S.A.

**Relief**

| Meters | | Feet |
| --- | --- | --- |
| 3050 | | 10 000 |
| 1525 | | 5000 |
| 610 | | 2000 |
| 305 | | 1000 |
| 152.5 | | 500 |
| 0 | Sea Level | Sea Level |
| | | Below |
| 152.5 | | 500 |
| 1525 | | 5000 |
| 3050 | | 10 000 |
| 6100 | | 20 000 |

Continued on pages 212-213

Longitude East of Greenwich

0  50  100    200    300    400    500 Miles
0  100  200    400    600    800 Kilometers

**Cities
and
Towns**

| 0 to 50,000 | ○ | 500,000 to 1,000,000 |
| 50,000 to 500,000 | ⊙ | 1,000,000 and over |

Habomai, Shikotan,
Kunashiri, and Etorofu,
occupied since 1945,
are claimed by Japan
pending a final peace
treaty.

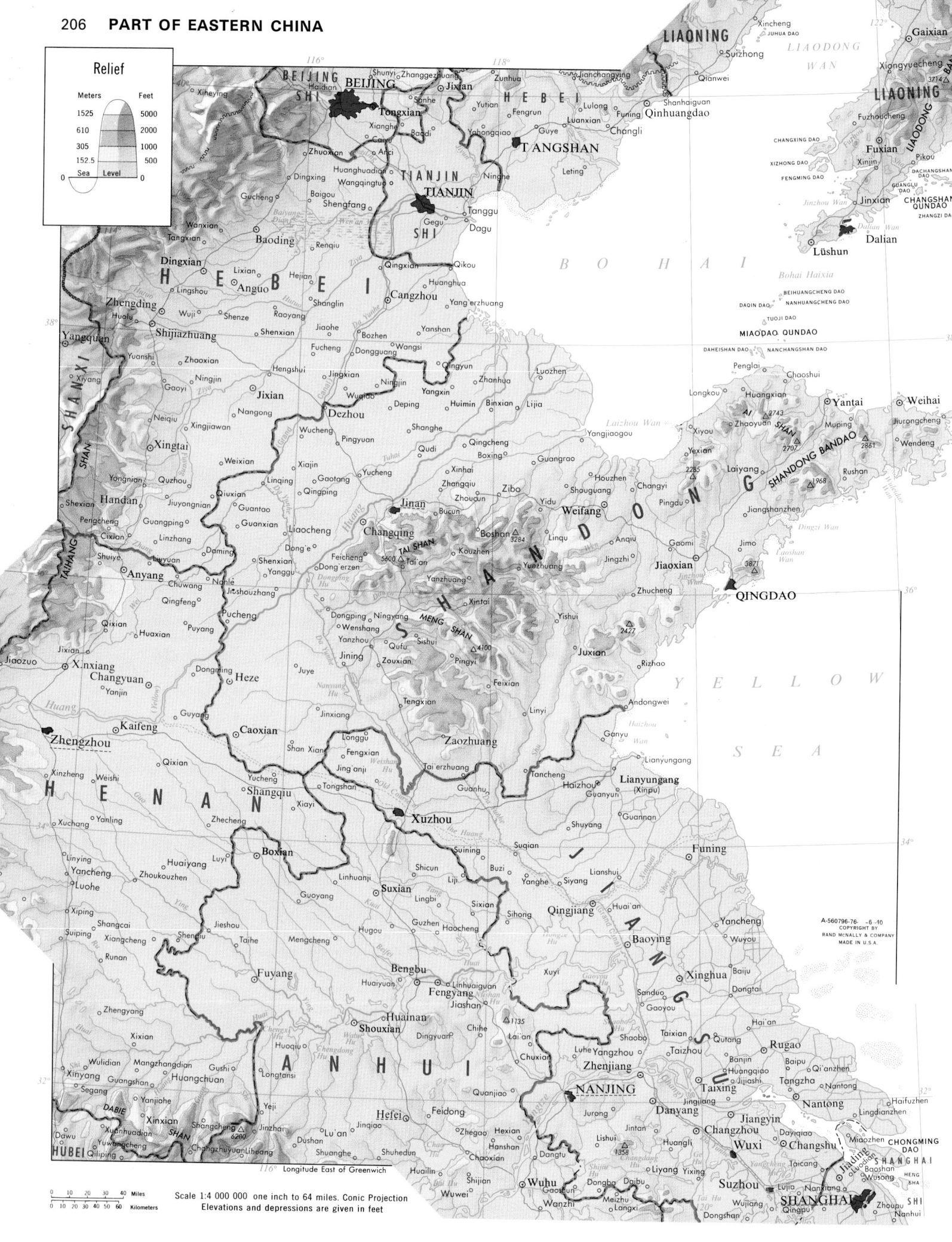

**Relief**

| Meters | Feet |
|---|---|
| 1525 | 5000 |
| 610 | 2000 |
| 305 | 1000 |
| 152.5 | 500 |
| Sea Level | 0 |

Scale 1:4 000 000 one inch to 64 miles. Conic Projection
Elevations and depressions are given in feet

0 10 20 30 40 Miles
0 10 20 30 40 50 60 Kilometers

Longitude East of Greenwich

A-560796-76- -6-10
COPYRIGHT BY
RAND McNALLY & COMPANY
MADE IN U.S.A.

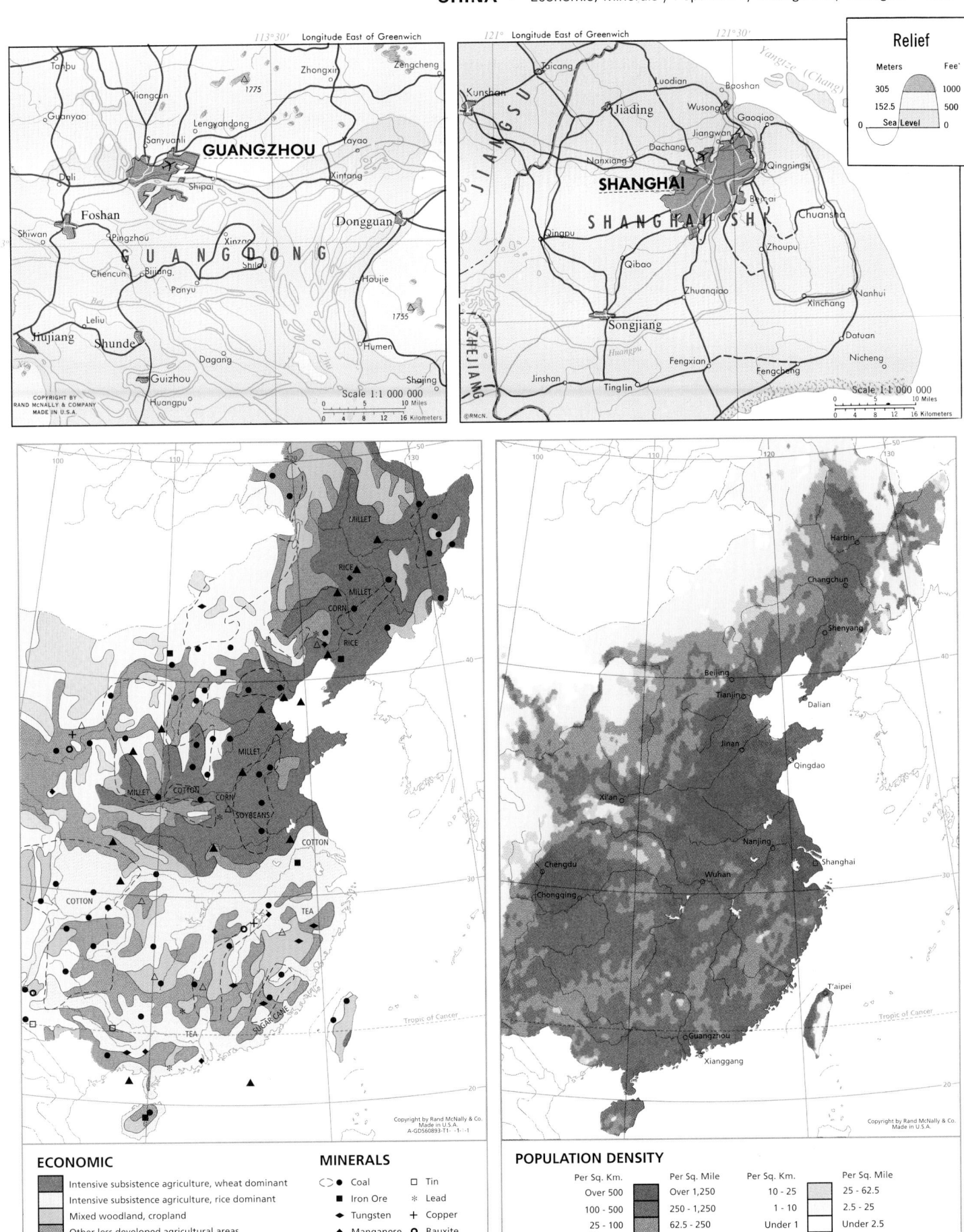

Relief

| Meters | Feet |
|---|---|
| 305 | 1000 |
| 152.5 | 500 |
| 0 | Sea Level | 0 |

Longitude East of Greenwich

113°30'

Tanbu
Zhongxin
Zengcheng
1775
Jiangcun
Guanyao
Lengyandong
Yayao
Sanyuanli
**GUANGZHOU**
Dali
Shipai
Xintang
Foshan
Pingzhou
Xinzao
Dongguan
Shiwan
Chencun
Bijiang
Shilou
Houjie
Panyu
**GUANGDONG**
Lijiang
Leliu
Dagang
Humen
Hujiang
Shunde
Guizhou
1755
Shajing
Huangpu

COPYRIGHT BY
RAND McNALLY & COMPANY
MADE IN U.S.A.

Scale 1:1 000 000

121° Longitude East of Greenwich 121°30'

Yangtze (Chang)
Taicang
Luodian
Baoshan
Kunshan
Jiading
Wusong
Gaoqiao
Nanxiang
Dachang
Jiangwan
**SHANGHAI**
Qingningsi
**JIANGSU**
Qingpu
**SHANGHAI SHI**
Chuansha
Qibao
Zhoupu
**ZHEJIANG**
Zhuangqiao
Xinchang
Nanhui
Songjiang
Datuan
Huangpu
Fengxian
Fengcheng
Nicheng
Jinshan
Tinglin

©RMCN.

Scale 1:1 000 000

## ECONOMIC

- Intensive subsistence agriculture, wheat dominant
- Intensive subsistence agriculture, rice dominant
- Mixed woodland, cropland
- Other less developed agricultural areas
- Nomadic herding
- Non-productive

## MINERALS

- ◖● Coal
- ■ Iron Ore
- ◆ Tungsten
- ◆ Manganese
- △ Zinc
- □ Tin
- ✳ Lead
- ✚ Copper
- ◯ Bauxite
- ▲ Petroleum

## POPULATION DENSITY

| Per Sq. Km. | Per Sq. Mile | Per Sq. Km. | Per Sq. Mile |
|---|---|---|---|
| Over 500 | Over 1,250 | 10 - 25 | 25 - 62.5 |
| 100 - 500 | 250 - 1,250 | 1 - 10 | 2.5 - 25 |
| 25 - 100 | 62.5 - 250 | Under 1 | Under 2.5 |

- □ Metropolitan area over 10,000,000 population
- ◯ Metropolitan area 2,000,000 to 10,000,000 population

Continued on page 210

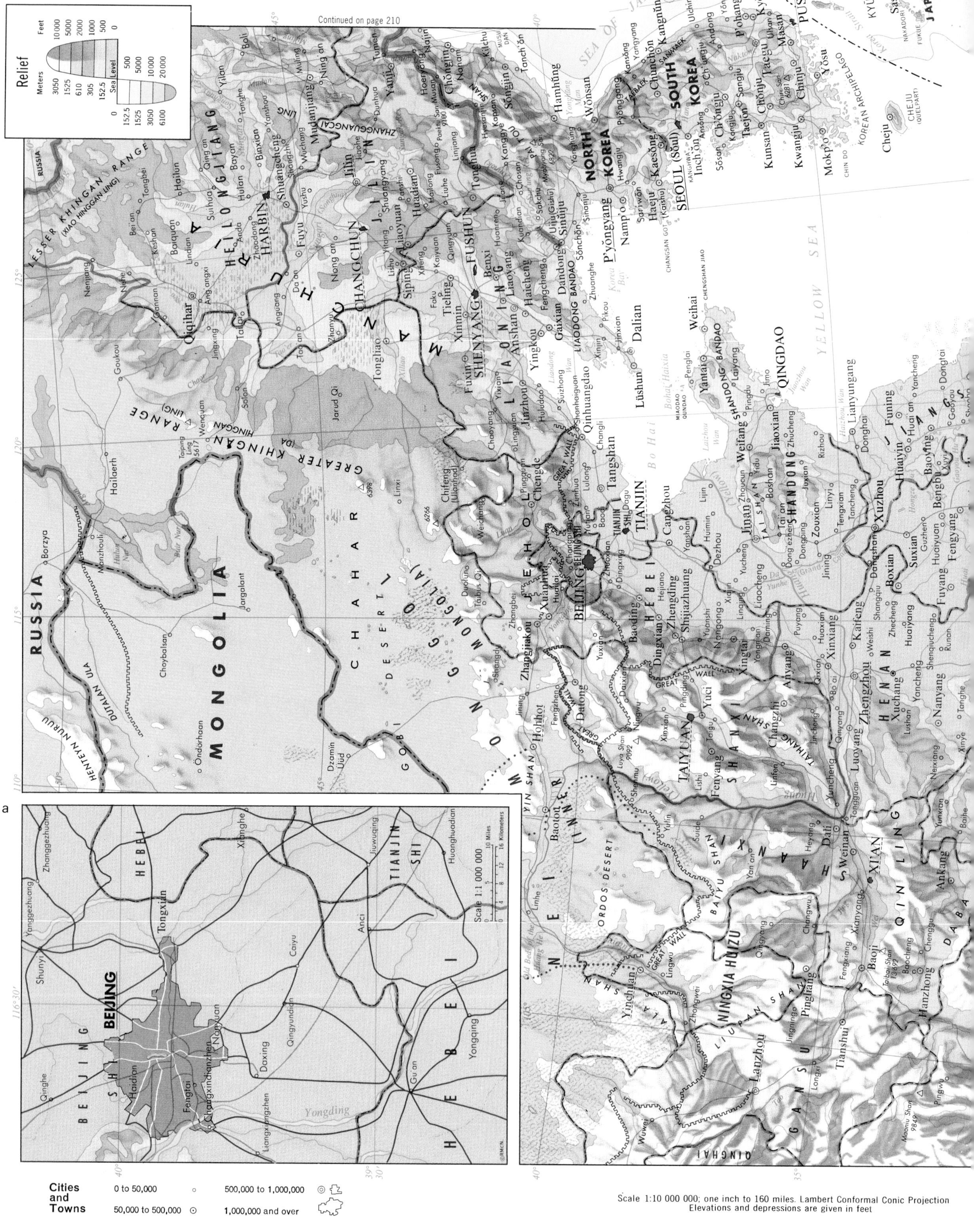

Relief

| Meters | Feet |
|---|---|
| 3050 | 10,000 |
| 1525 | 5000 |
| 610 | 2000 |
| 305 | 1000 |
| 152.5 | 500 |
| 0 | Sea Level |

| | 500 |
| | 5000 |
| | 10,000 |
| | 20,000 |

| 0 | 152.5 |
| 1525 | |
| 3050 | |
| 6100 | |

RUSSIA

LESSER KHINGAN RANGE (XIAO HINGGAN LING)

HEILONGJIANG

HARBIN

Qiqihar

CHINA

JILIN

CHANGCHUN

Tongliao

GREATER KHINGAN RANGE (DA HINGGAN LING)

MONGOLIA

GOBI DESERT

CHAHAR

INNER MONGOLIA

Hailaer

Manzhouli

Borzya

Choybalsan

Öndörhaan

Dzamin Üüd

HENTIYN NURUU

DUTALAN ULA

SEA OF JAPAN

NORTH KOREA

Pʻyŏngyang

Nampo

SOUTH KOREA

SEOUL (Sŏul)

Inchʻon

PUSAN

JAPAN

KYUSHU

CHEJU (QUELPART)

Cheju

KOREAN ARCHIPELAGO

YELLOW SEA

SHENYANG

FUSHUN

LIAONING

Anshan

Dalian

Lüshun

Qinhuangdao

LIAODONG BANDAO

Bo Hai

SHANDONG BANDAO

QINGDAO

Yantai

Weihai

SHANDONG

Jinan

TIANJIN

BEIJING

HEBEI

Tangshan

Baoding

Shijiazhuang

GREAT WALL

TAIYUAN

SHANXI

TAIHANG SHAN

NEI MONGOL

ORDOS DESERT

Baotou

YIN SHAN

NINGXIA HUIZU

Yinchuan

LIUPAN SHAN

GANSU

Lanzhou

Tianshui

QINGHAI

XIAN

SHAANXI

QIN LING

DABA

HENAN

Zhengzhou

Luoyang

Kaifeng

Xuchang

Nanyang

JIANGSU

Xuzhou

Lianyungang

Bo Hai

Cities and Towns

| 0 to 50,000 | ○ |
| 50,000 to 500,000 | ◎ |
| 500,000 to 1,000,000 | ◎ |
| 1,000,000 and over | |

Scale 1:10 000 000; one inch to 160 miles. Lambert Conformal Conic Projection
Elevations and depressions are given in feet

a

BEIJING

BEIJING SHI

HEBEI

TIANJIN SHI

Tongxian

Haidian

Fengtai

Changxindianzhen

Daxing

Anci

Yongding

Scale 1:1 000 000

| 0 | 5 | 10 Miles |
| 0 | 4 8 12 16 Kilometers |

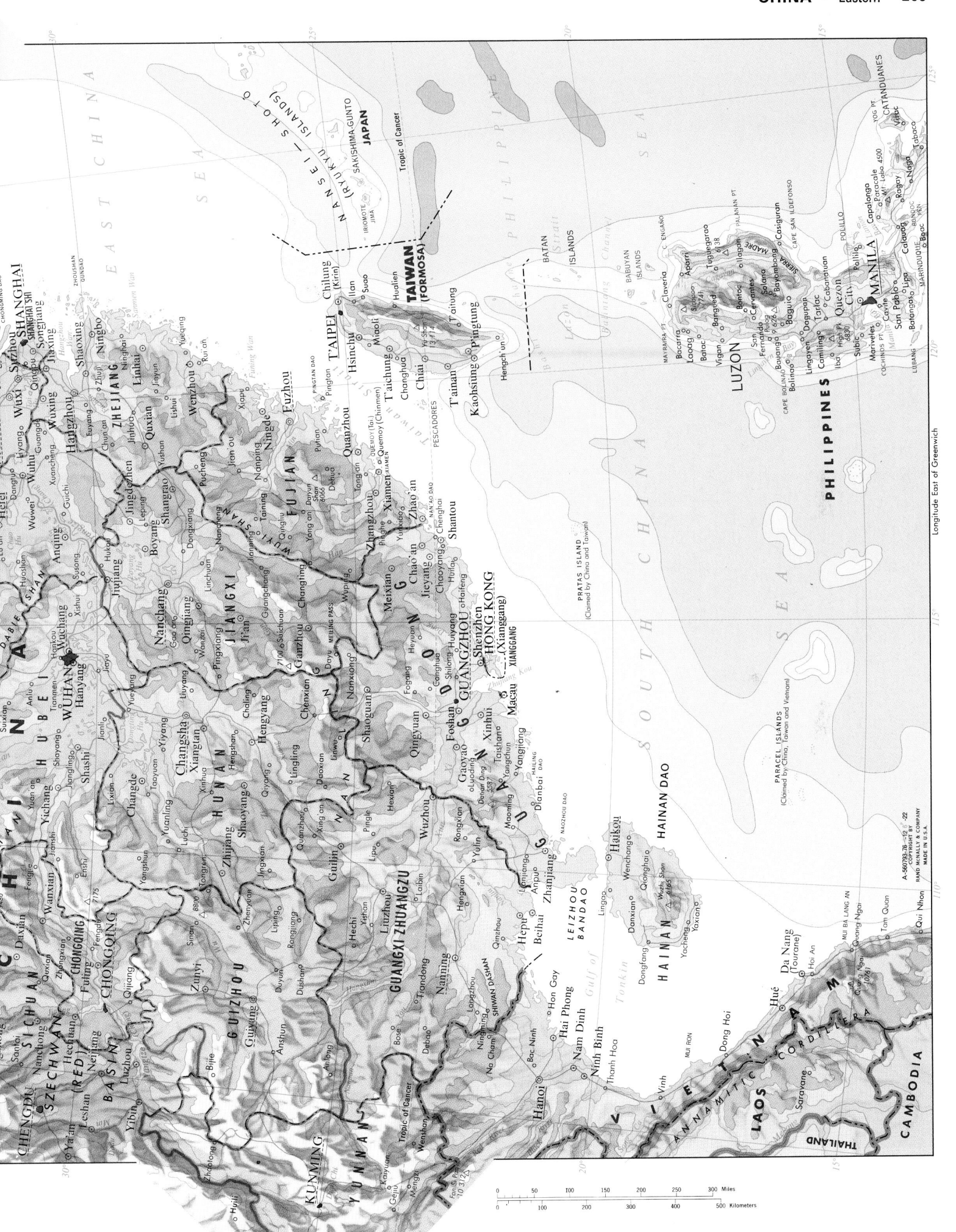

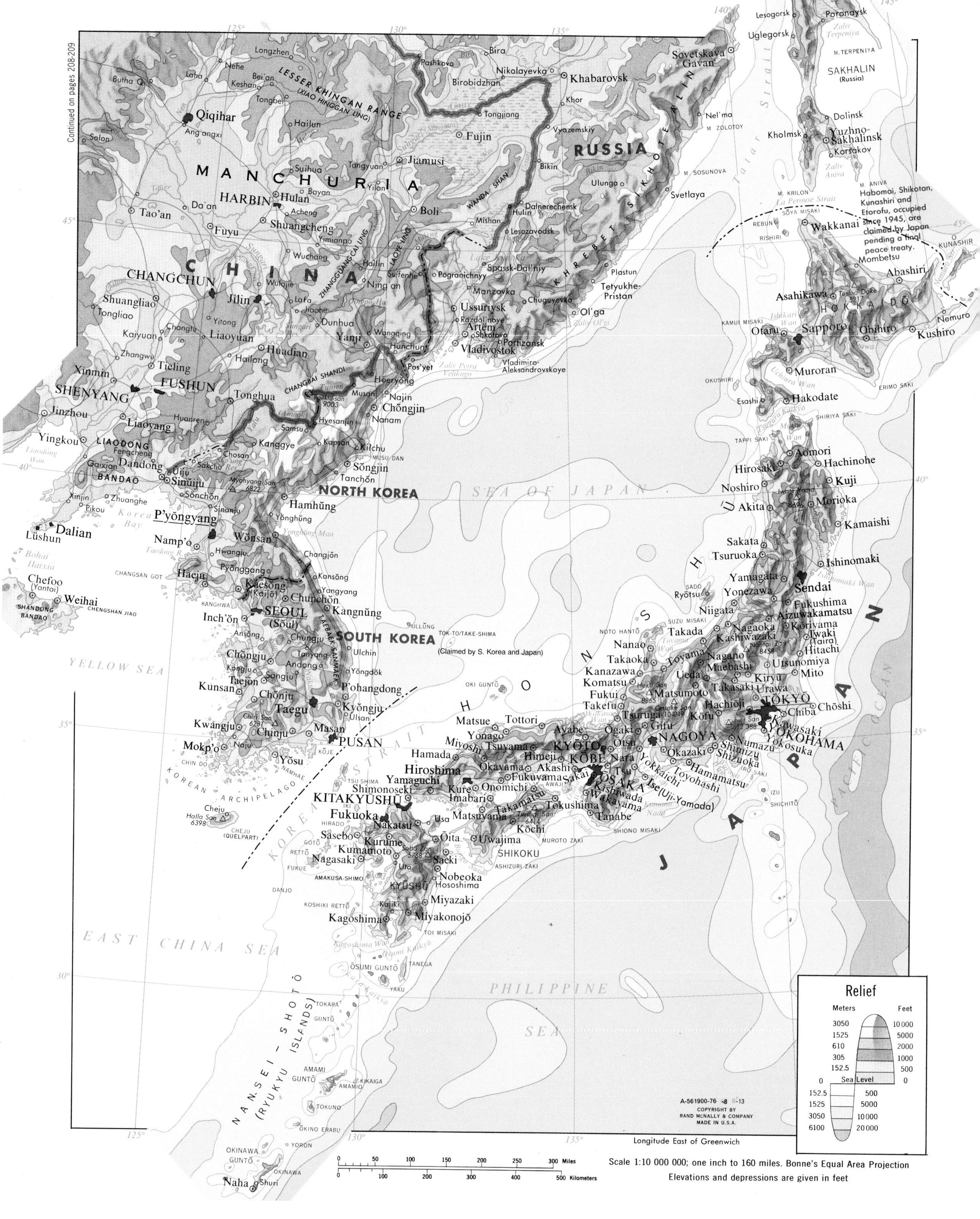

Continued on pages 208-209

RUSSIA

SAKHALIN (Russia)

MANCHURIA

LESSER KHINGAN RANGE (XIAO HINGGAN LING)

Qiqihar

Butha Qi
Nehe
Longzhen
Laba
Bei'an
Keshan
Tongbei
Hailun
Suihua
Bayan
Acheng
Harbin
Hulan
Tao'an
Da'an
Fuyu
Shuangcheng
Ang'angxi
Solon
Tieli
Yichun
Tangyuan
Jiamusi
Yilan
Boli
Huachuan
Fujin
Tongjiang

Bira
Pashkovo
Nikolayevka
Birobidzhan
Khabarovsk
Khor
Vyazemskiy
Bikin
Dalnerechensk
Hulin
Lesozavodsk
Mishan

Soyetskaya Gavan'
M. Terpeniya
Zaliv Terpeniya

KHREBET SIKHOTE-ALIN

WANDA SHAN

CHINA

CHANGCHUN
Shuangliao
Tongliao
Kaiyuan
Zhangwu
Tieling
FUSHUN
Jilin
Jiaohe
Dunhua
Huadian
Liaoyuan
Yitong
Changtu
SHENYANG
Jinzhou
Liaoyang
LIAODONG
Fengcheng
Dandong
Gaixian
Yingkou
Xinmin
BANDAO
Zhuanghe
Pikou
Dalian
Lüshun
Chefoo (Yantai)
Weihai
SHANDONG BANDAO
CHENGSHAN JIAO

CHANGBAI SHANDI

Yanji
Wangqing
Hunchun
Pos'yet
Ussuriysk
Razdol'noye
Artëm
Shkotovo
Portzansk
Vladivostok

Zaliv Petra Velikogo

Ussuriysk
Spassk-Dal'niy
Pogranichnyy
Manzovka
Chuguyevka
Ol'ga
Plastun
Tetyukhe-Pristan'
M. Zolotoy
Ulunga
Svetlaya

SAKHALIN
Lesogorsk
Uglegorsk
Poronaysk
Kholmsk
Dolinsk
Yuzhno-Sakhalinsk
Korsakov
M. Krilon
M. Aniva
Zaliv Aniva

La Perouse Strait
SOYA MISAKI
Wakkanai
Rebun
Rishiri

HOKKAIDO
Asahikawa
Otaru
Sapporo
Obihiro
Kushiro
Muroran
Hakodate
Esashi
Abashiri
Nemuro
KUNASHIR

Habomai, Shikotan, Kunashiri and Etorofu, occupied since 1945, are claimed by Japan pending a final peace treaty.
Mombetsu

NORTH KOREA
P'yŏngyang
Namp'o
Haeju
Wŏnsan
Hamhŭng
Kanggye
Chosan
Hyesanjin
Samsu
Kilchu
Songjin
Tanch'on
Ch'ŏngjin
Nanam
Najin
Hoeryŏng
Musan
Kapsan

SEA OF JAPAN

SOUTH KOREA
SEOUL (Sŏul)
Inch'ŏn
Suwŏn
Ch'ŏngju
Taejŏn
Chŏnju
Kunsan
Kwangju
Mokp'o
Chinju
Taegu
Masan
PUSAN
Chŏngju
Kyŏngju
Ulsan
Ulchin
Yŏngdŏk
P'ohangdong
Yŏsu
Chinhae

Cheju (QUELPART)
Halla San 6398

TOK-TO/TAKE-SHIMA (Claimed by S. Korea and Japan)

HONSHU
JAPAN
TOKYO
YOKOHAMA
Kawasaki
Chiba
NAGOYA
KYOTO
OSAKA
KOBE
Hiroshima
KITAKYUSHU
Fukuoka
Nagasaki
Kumamoto
Kagoshima
Miyazaki
KYUSHU
SHIKOKU

Niigata
Nagaoka
Kanazawa
Toyama
Takada
Nagano
Matsumoto
Takasaki
Maebashi
Utsunomiya
Mito
Sendai
Yamagata
Aizuwakamatsu
Koriyama
Fukushima
Iwaki (Taira)
Hitachi
Aomori
Hachinohe
Kuji
Morioka
Kamaishi
Akita
Noshiro
Hirosaki
Ishinomaki
Sakata
Tsuruoka
Yonezawa

Matsue
Tottori
Yonago
Okayama
Fukuyama
Onomichi
Imabari
Matsuyama
Takamatsu
Tokushima
Kōchi
Uwajima
Ōita
Nobeoka

EAST CHINA SEA

PHILIPPINE SEA

PACIFIC OCEAN

NANSEI-SHOTO (RYUKYU ISLANDS)
ŌSUMI GUNTŌ
TANEGA
YAKU
TOKARA GUNTŌ
AMAMI GUNTŌ
OKINAWA GUNTŌ
OKINAWA
Naha
Shuri

**Relief**

| Meters | | Feet |
|---|---|---|
| 3050 | | 10 000 |
| 1525 | | 5000 |
| 610 | | 2000 |
| 305 | | 1000 |
| 152.5 | | 500 |
| 0 | Sea Level | 0 |
| 152.5 | | 500 |
| 1525 | | 5000 |
| 3050 | | 10 000 |
| 6100 | | 20 000 |

A-561900-76 -8 6-13
COPYRIGHT BY
RAND McNALLY & COMPANY
MADE IN U.S.A.

Longitude East of Greenwich

Scale 1:10 000 000; one inch to 160 miles. Bonne's Equal Area Projection
Elevations and depressions are given in feet

0 50 100 150 200 250 300 Miles
0 100 200 300 400 500 Kilometers

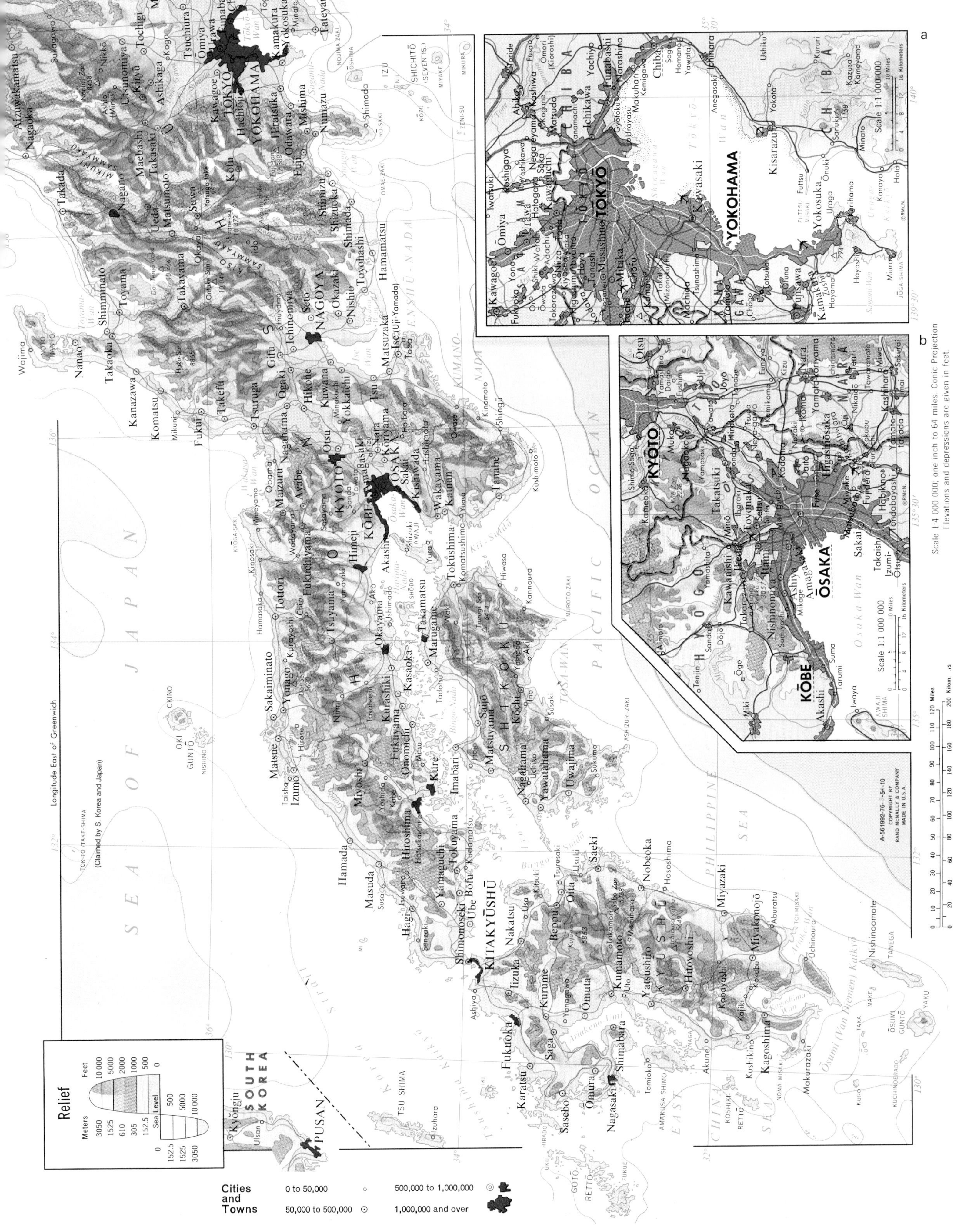

a

Scale 1:1 000 000

**TŌKYŌ**

**YOKOHAMA**

b

**KYŌTO**

**ŌSAKA**

**KŌBE**

Scale 1:1 000 000

Scale 1:4 000 000; one inch to 64 miles. Conic Projection
Elevations and depressions are given in feet

A-561992-76-¾-10
COPYRIGHT BY
RAND MCNALLY & COMPANY
MADE IN U.S.A.

S E A   O F   J A P A N

P A C I F I C   O C E A N

PHILIPPINE SEA

EAST CHINA SEA

TŌKYŌ
YOKOHAMA
NAGOYA
KYŌTO
ŌSAKA
KŌBE
SHIKOKU
KYŪSHŪ
KITAKYŪSHŪ

SOUTH KOREA
PUSAN
Kyongju
Ulsan

Longitude East of Greenwich

TOK-TO (TAKE-SHIMA)
(Claimed by S. Korea and Japan)

OKI GUNTŌ
NISHINO

Fukuoka
Saga
Kurume
Kumamoto
Nagasaki
Sasebo
Ōmura
Karatsu
Beppu
Ōita
Miyazaki
Kagoshima

Hiroshima
Kure
Okayama
Himeji
Matsue
Tottori
Takamatsu
Kōchi
Matsuyama

Relief

| Meters | Feet |
|---|---|
| 3050 | 10 000 |
| 1525 | 5000 |
| 610 | 2000 |
| 305 | 1000 |
| 152.5 | 500 |
| 0 | Sea Level |
| 152.5 | 500 |
| 305 | 1000 |
| 1525 | 5000 |
| 3050 | 10 000 |

Cities and Towns

0 to 50,000
50,000 to 500,000
500,000 to 1,000,000
1,000,000 and over

Scale 1:16 000 000; one inch to 250 miles. Polyconic Projection
Elevations and depressions are given in feet

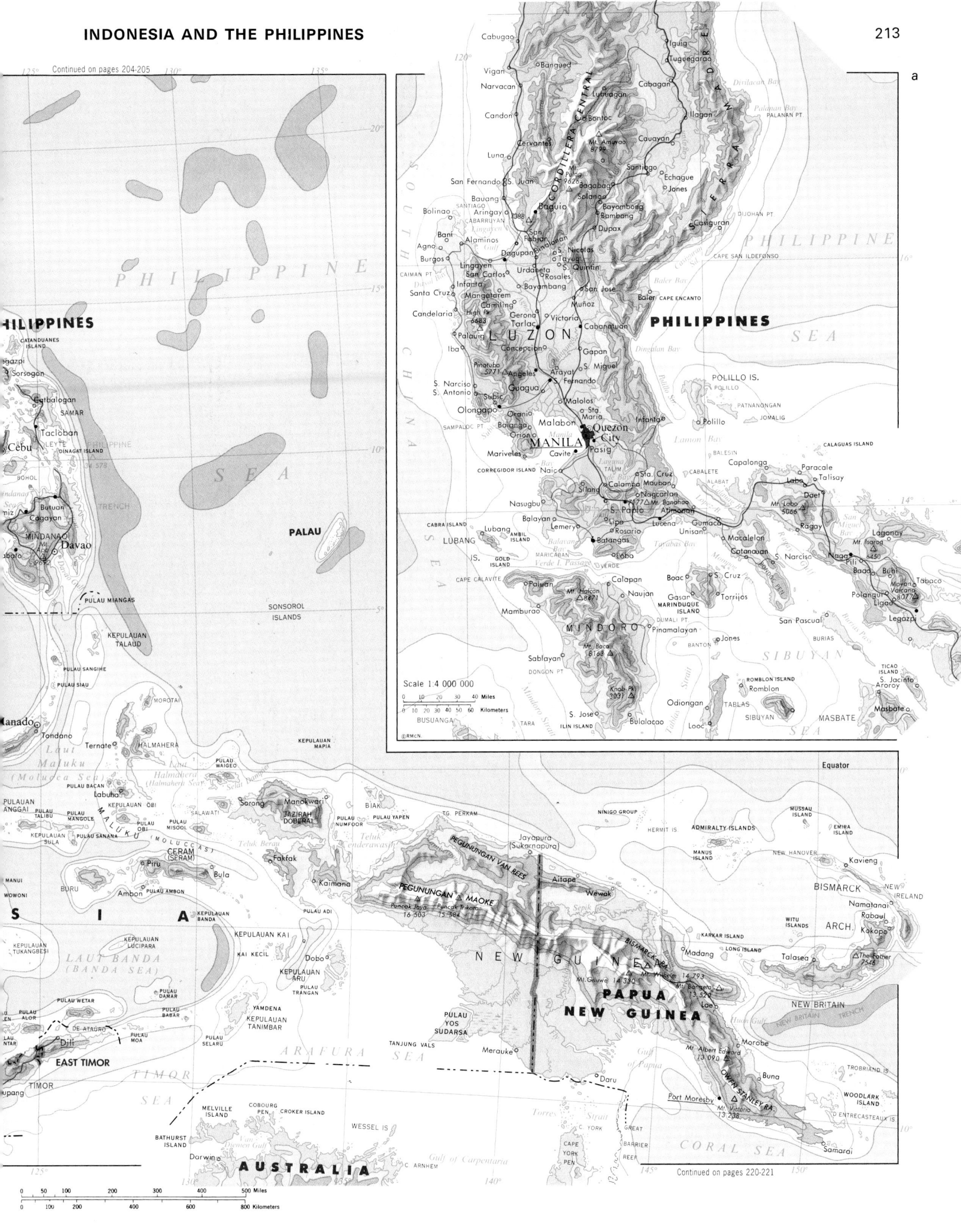

a

Continued on pages 204–205

PHILIPPINES

PHILIPPINE

SEA

PHILIPPINES

PALAU

CATANDUANES ISLAND

Sorsogon

Calbalogan

SAMAR

Tacloban

Cebu

LEYTE

DINAGAT ISLAND

BOHOL

Butuan

Cagayan

MINDANAO

Davao

PULAU MIANGAS

SONSOROL ISLANDS

KEPULAUAN TALAUD

PULAU SANGIHE

PULAU SIAU

MOROTAI

Manado

Tondano

Ternate

HALMAHERA

KEPULAUAN MAPIA

Laut Maluku
(Molucca Sea)

Laut Halmahera
(Halmahera Sea)

PULAU WAIGEO

## LUZON

Cabugao
Vigan
Narvacan
Candon
Luna

Bangued
CORDILLERA CENTRAL
Lubuagan
Bontoc
Cervantes
Mt. Amuyao 8795
Mt. Pulag 9626

Iguig
Tuguegarao
Cabagan
Ilagan
Cauayan
Santiago
Echague
Jones

San Fernando S. Juan
Bauang
Baguio
Aringay
Bolinao
CABARRUYAN
Bani
Alaminos
Agno
Burgos
CAIMAN PT.
Lingayen
San Carlos
Infanta
Santa Cruz
Mangatarem
Camiling
Candelaria
High Pk. 6683
Palauig
Iba
Concepcion
Pinatubo 5771
Angeles
S. Narciso
S. Antonio
Subic
Olongapo
SAMPALOC PT.
Orani
Orion
Balanga
Mariveles
CORREGIDOR ISLAND
Naic

Solana
Bayombong
Bambang
Dupax

Dagupan
Urdaneta
Rosales
Bayambang
Gerona
Tarlac
Victoria
Cabanatuan

Nicolas
S. Quintin
San Jose
Muñoz
Gapan
S. Miguel
Arayat
S. Fernando
Guagua
Malolos
Sta. Maria
Malabon
MANILA
Cavite
Pasig
Quezon City
Laguna de Bay

CAPE SAN ILDEFONSO
Baler Bay
Baler CAPE ENCANTO
Dingalan Bay
Infanta
POLILLO IS.
POLILLO
PATNANONGAN
JOMALIG
Polillo
CALAGUAS ISLAND
Capalonga
Paracale
Talisay
Labo
Daet
Mt. Labo 5066

DIVILACAN BAY
PALANAN BAY
PALANAN PT.
DIJOHAN PT.

PHILIPPINE SEA

Lamon Bay

BALESIN
CABALETE
ALABAT
San Miguel Bay
Lagonay
Naga
Mt. Isarog 6450
Pili
Baao
Buhi
Tabaco
Mayon Volcano 8077
Polangui
Ligao
Legazpi

Sta. Cruz
Mauban
Calamba
Nagcarlan
S. Pablo
Mt. Banahao 7177
Lipa
Rosario
Lucena
Gumaca
Macalelon
Catanauan
S. Narciso

Nasugbu
Silang
Balayan
Lemery
Lubang
AMBIL ISLAND
LUBANG IS.
GOLD ISLAND
CABRA ISLAND
Batangas
Lobo
MARICABAN ISLAND
Verde I. Passage
VERDE
CAPE CALAVITE
Paluan

Boac
Gasar
MARINDUQUE ISLAND
Torrijos
Cruz
Unisan
Lopez

Mt. Halcon 8481
Calapan
Naujan

Mamburao
MINDORO
Mt. Baco 8163

Sablayan
DONGON PT.
DUMALI PT.
Pinamalayan
Jones
BANTON
San Pascual
BURIAS
SIBUYAN SEA

Knob Pk. 3031
S. Jose
ILIN ISLAND
Bulalacao
BUSUANGA
TARA

ROMBLON ISLAND
Romblon
Odiongan
TABLAS
SIBUYAN
TICAO ISLAND
S. Jacinto
Aroroy
MASBATE

Scale 1:4 000 000

0  10  20  30  40 Miles
0  10  20  30  40  50  60 Kilometers

©RMCN.

Equator

PULAUAN ANGGAI
PULAU TALIBU
PULAU MANGOLE
KEPULAUAN SULA
KEPULAUAN OBI
PULAU OBI
PULAU MISOOL
PULAU SANANA
MALUKU

Sorong
Manokwari
JAZIRAH DOBERAI
PULAU SALAWATI
BIAK
PULAU NUMFOOR
PULAU YAPEN
TG. PERKAM
NINIGO GROUP
HERMIT IS.
ADMIRALTY ISLANDS
MUSSAU ISLAND
EMIRA ISLAND

Teluk Berau
Teluk Cenderawasih
PEGUNUNGAN VAN REES
Jayapura (Sukarnapura)
Aitape
Wewak
MANUS ISLAND
NEW HANOVER
Kavieng

MANUI
WOWONI
BURU
Piru
CERAM (SERAM)
Bula
Fakfak
Kaimana
PEGUNUNGAN MAOKE
Puncak Jaya 16 503
Puncak Trikora 15 584
Sepik
BISMARCK
NEW IRELAND
Namatanai
Rabaul
ARCH.
Kokopo

SIA

Ambon
PULAU AMBON
KEPULAUAN BANDA
PULAU ADI
KEPULAUAN KAI
KAI KECIL
Dobo
KEPULAUAN ARU
PULAU TRANGAN
NEW GUINEA
Mt. Wilhelm 14 793
Mt. Giluwe 14 330
Mt. Bangeta 13 529
Madang
KARKAR ISLAND
LONG ISLAND
WITU ISLANDS
Talasea
The Father 7545
BISMARCK RANGE
Lae
NEW BRITAIN
BISMARCK SEA

KEPULAUAN TUKANGBESI
KEPULAUAN LUCIPARA
Laut Banda
(Banda Sea)
KEPULAUAN BANDA
PULAU DAMAR
YAMDENA
KEPULAUAN TANIMBAR
PULAU SELARU
PULAU YOS SUDARSA
TANJUNG VALS
Merauke
PAPUA NEW GUINEA
Mt. Albert Edward 13 090
Morobe
Buna
TROBRIAND IS.
NEW BRITAIN TRENCH

PULAU WETAR
PULAU ALOR
DE ATAÚRO
PULAU MOA
PULAU BABAR
PULAU MOA
PULAU SELARU
ARAFURA SEA
Daru
Gulf of Papua
Port Moresby
Mt. Victoria 13 238
OWEN STANLEY RA.
Samarai
WOODLARK ISLAND
D'ENTRECASTEAUX IS.
CORAL SEA

Dili
EAST TIMOR
TIMOR
Kupang
TIMOR SEA

MELVILLE ISLAND
COBOURG PEN.
CROKER ISLAND
WESSEL IS.
BATHURST ISLAND
Darwin
Van Diemen Gulf
C. ARNHEM
Gulf of Carpentaria
CAPE YORK
C. YORK
Torres Strait
GREAT BARRIER REEF

# AUSTRALIA

Continued on pages 220–221

0  50  100  200  300  400  500 Miles
0  100  200  400  600  800 Kilometers

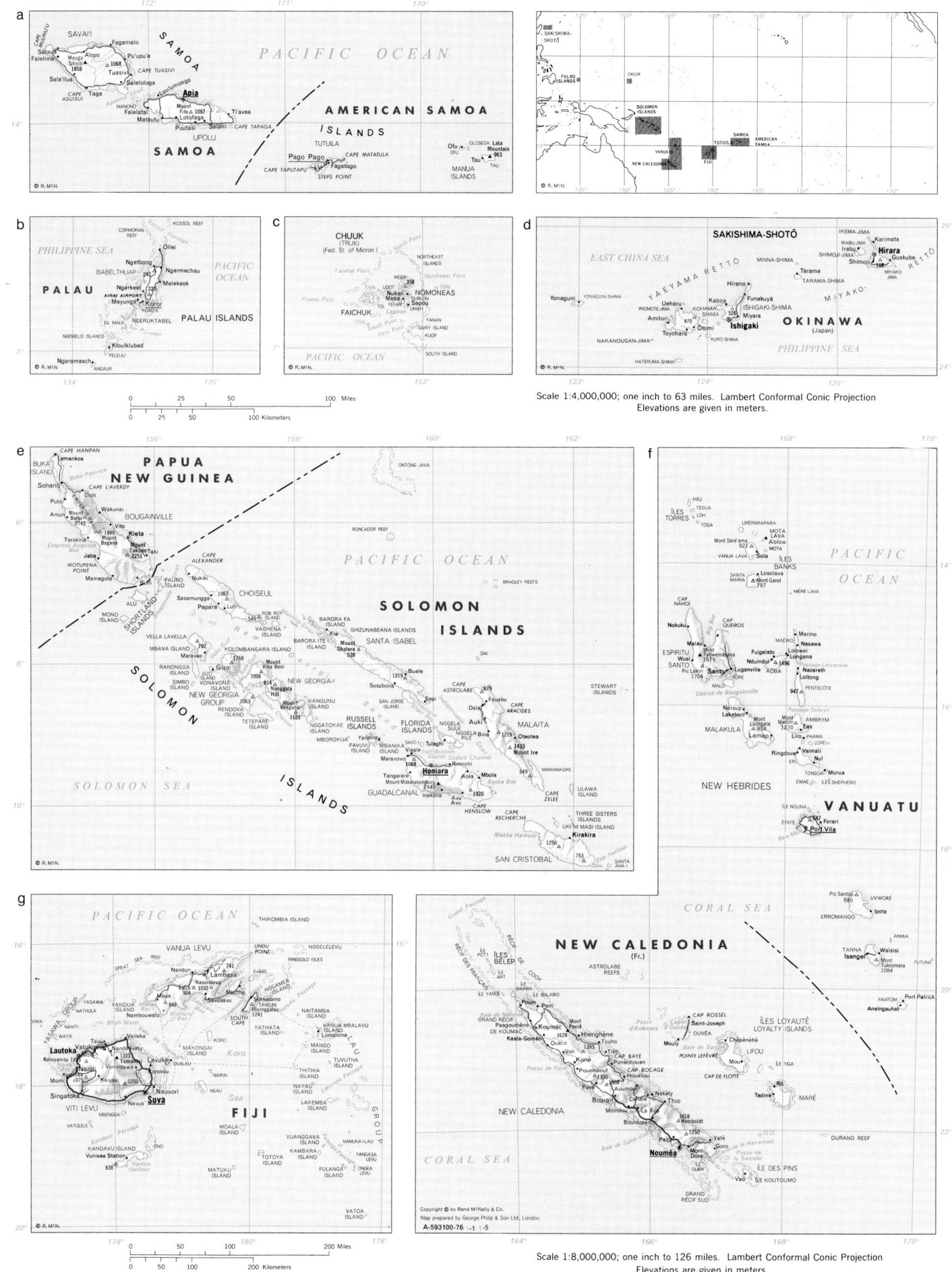

**a**

SAVAI'I
CAPE MULINU'U
Sataua
Falelima    Fagamalo    Mauga    A'opo    Pu'upu'a    CAPE TUASIVI
Sili    Sfili 1068
Sala'ilua    1858    Tuasivi    PACIFIC OCEAN
Taga    Salelologa
CAPE ASUISUI    MANONO    Leulumoega    Apia    AMERICAN SAMOA
CAPE    Matautu    Mount    Ti'avea
Falelatai    Fito 1097    Lotofaga    ISLANDS
UPOLU    Poutasi    Salani    CAPE TAPAGA
14°    SAMOA    TUTUILA    OFU OLOSEGA    Lata Mountain
Pago Pago    CAPE MATATULA    OFU    Tau    963
CAPE TAPUTAPU    Fagatogo    TAU    MANUA
STEPS POINT    ISLANDS

SAMOA

SAKISHIMA-SHOTŌ
PALAU ISLANDS    CHUUK
SOLOMON ISLANDS
NEW CALEDONIA    VANUATU    FIJI    TUTUILA SAMOA    AMERICAN SAMOA

**b**

PHILIPPINE SEA    CORMORAN REEF    KOSSOL REEF
Ngetbun    Ollei    PACIFIC OCEAN
BABELTHUAP    242    Ngermechau
Ngerkeai    Melekeok
AIRAI AIRPORT    225
PALAU    Meyungs    Koror    KOROR    PALAU ISLANDS
EIL MALK    NGERUKTABEL
NGEMELIS ISLANDS
Ngaramasch    Kloulklubed
PELELIU
ANGAUR

**c**

CHUUK
(TRUK)
(Fed. St. of Micron.)
North Pass
Tsalap Pass    NORTHEAST ISLANDS
Northeast Pass
Piaanu Pass    MOEN    UDOT    TOL    NUKAN    NOMONEAS
Meen    FEFAN    Sapou
FAICHUK    UMAN    FANAN
(566)    South Pass    GIIRY ISLAND
KUOP
PACIFIC OCEAN    SOUTH ISLAND

**d**

SAKISHIMA-SHOTŌ    IKEMA-JIMA
IRABU-JIMA    Karimata
EAST CHINA SEA    YAEYAMA RETTO    MINNA-SHIMA    SHIMOJI-JIMA    Hirara
Tarama    TARAMA-SHIMA    Shimoji    Guskube
Yonaguni    YONAGUNI-SHIMA    Hirano    Funakuya    MIYAKO-JIMA    RETTO
Ueharu    Kabira    ISHIGAKI-SHIMA    Miyara    MIYAKO-
IROMOTE-JIMA    KOHAMA    520    Miyara
Amitori    470    Ōtomi    Ishigaki    OKINAWA
NAKANOUGAN-JIMA    Toyohara    KURO SHIMA    (Japan)
PHILIPPINE SEA
HATERUMA-SHIMA

Scale 1:4,000,000; one inch to 63 miles. Lambert Conformal Conic Projection
Elevations are given in meters.

0    25    50    100    Miles
0    25    50    100    Kilometers

**e**

CAPE HANPAN
BUKA ISLAND    Lemankoa
Buka Passage
Sohano    PAPUA
Puto    CAPE L'AVERDY    NEW GUINEA
Amun    Wakunai
Torokina    Mount Balbi    BOUGAINVILLE
2743    1999    Kieta
Jaba    Mount Bagana    Mount Takuan    2251
Empress Augusta Bay    Taki
MOTUPENA POINT    Mamagota
ALU    FAURO ISLAND    Nukiki    PACIFIC OCEAN
MONO ISLAND    SHORTLAND ISLANDS    Sasamungga    1067    CHOISEUL
Maravari    Papara    Luti
SOLOMON    RANONGGA ISLAND    549    ROB ROY ISLAND
SIMBO    VELLA LAVELLA    VAGHENA ISLAND    Kia
ISLAND    792    KOLOMBANGARA ISLAND    BARORA FA ISLAND
Gizo    Mount    BARORA ITE ISLAND    GHIZUNABEANA ISLANDS
1006    Vila Roni    1768    Kolombangara    SANTA ISABEL
NEW GEORGIA    614    Nanggala Hill    Buala    SOLOMON
GROUP    Mount    NEW GEORGIA    1219    ISLANDS
Vangunu    ISLAND    Susubona    CAPE ASTROLABE    679
RENDOVA    1123    NGGATOKAE ISLAND    Sepi    FAUABU    CAPE
ISLAND    VANGUNU ISLAND    SAN JORGE ISLAND    Dala    ARACIDES
TETEPARE ISLAND    MBOROKUA    Yandina    Oteotea
RUSSELL ISLANDS    NGELLA SULE    Auki    MALAITA
PAVUVU    MBANIKA    Visale    NGELLA PILE    Bina    1433    Mount Ire
SAVO    Tulaghi    Rororoni    Oloburi
Maravovo    1068    Tangarare    Honiara    Aola    Mbola    549
Mount Makarakomburu    ULAWA ISLAND
SOLOMON SEA    GUADALCANAL    2447    Avu    1920    CAPE ZELEE
Inakona    Avu    CAPE HENSLOW
ISLANDS    THREE SISTERS ISLANDS
UKI NI MASI ISLAND
Makira Harbour    1250    Kirakira
SAN CRISTOBAL    753    SANTA ANA I.

ONTONG JAVA

RONCADOR REEF

BRADLEY REEFS

STEWART ISLANDS

MARAMASIKE

**f**

ÎLES    HIU    TEGUA
TORRES    LOH
TOGA    UREPARAPARA    MOTA LAVA
Mont Séré'ama    Ablow    Longana
921    VANUA LAVA    Sola    MOTA    ÎLES
SANTA    Losolava    BANKS    PACIFIC
MARIA    Mont Garet    MÈRÈ LAVA    OCEAN
797
CAP    MÈRÈ LAVA
NAHOI    Marino
Nokuku    CAP    Nasawa
QUEROS    MAEWO    Fuigalato    Lolowai
ESPIRITU    Wusi    Mont Tawemenbuta    1436    Loltong
SANTO    Pic Lakiri    1879    Santo    AOBA    PENTECÔTE
1704    Luganville    947    Nazareth
MALO    Passage Lolivarou
Norsup    Passage Selwyn
Lakatoro    Mont    AMBRYM
MALAKULA    Lambele    1270    Eas
854    Lamap    Liro    PAAMA    LOPEVI
Ringdove    Vaimali    ÎLES SHEPHERD
EPI    Nui    EMAE    Morua
NEW HEBRIDES    ÎLE NGUNA    VANUATU
EFATE    Forari    847
Port Vila

**g**

PACIFIC OCEAN    THIKOMBIA ISLAND
16°    VANUA LEVU
GREAT    SEA    UNDU POINT    NGGELELEVU
NATHULA    REEF    NGGELELEVU ISLES
YASAWA    Nandi    741    RINGGOLD ISLES
GROUP    Mbua    Lambasa    RAMI
NAVITI    Nasorolevu    1032    NGAMEA ISLAND
Mbua    849    Savusavu    Waiyevo    TAVEUNI ISLAND
Shishusomo    1241    NAITAMBA ISLAND
NAMBOUWALU    ULUNGGELEVU    VANUA MBALAVU ISLAND
SOUTH CAPE    YATHATA ISLAND    Lomaloma
Bligh Water    MAKONGAI ISLAND    MANGO ISLAND
Tavua    NATHULA    TUVUTHA ISLAND
Lautoka    Vatukoula    1323    Vaileka    Levuka
Koroyanitu 1195    Tavua    OVALAU    NAIRAI    THITHIA ISLAND
Nandi    1032    Vunindawa    Korovou    Koro    NAYAU ISLAND
MbenggUi    Navua    1075    Keiyasi    1203    Nausori    LAKEMBA ISLAND
Singatoka    VITI LEVU    Suva    NGAU    NGAU
838    MBENGGA    FIJI    MOALA ISLAND
Vunisea Station    Kandavu Passage    VANUA    VUANGGAVA ISLAND
VATULELE    KANDAVU ISLAND    TOTOYA ISLAND    NAMUKA-I-LAU    YANGASA LEVU
Nggaloa Harbour    MATUKU ISLAND    FULANGA LEVU    VATOA ISLAND

NEW CALEDONIA
(Fr.)
CORAL SEA    Pic Santo    UVWORE
886    ERROMANGO    Ipota
RECIF    Grand Passage    GRAND RÉCIF
ÎLES BÉLEP    TANNA    Isangel    Waisisi    FUTUNA
POTT    ÎLE BAABA    Tukosméra
ASTROLABE REEFS    1084
LE YANDÉ    ÎLE BALABO    CAP ROSSEL    ANATOM    Port Patrick
Poum    Pam    Saint-Joseph    Aneingauhat
Koumac    1628    Hienghène    OUVÉA    ÎLES LOYAUTÉ
Kaala-Gomen    1383    Touho    Mouly    LOYALTY ISLANDS
Quaco    Koné    CAP BAYE    Baie du Santal
Poembout    CAP BOCAGE    Chepenehe    LIFOU
Pova    1330    Koumo    POINTE LEFÈVRE    ÎLE TIGA
Bourail    Nakety    La Foa    Mou    CAP DE FLOTTE
Moindou    Thio    1618    Ro    Tadine    MARÉ
NEW CALEDONIA    Boulouparis    Humboldt    Tinuei    1212
Paita    1250    Goro    Baie de la Havannah
Boulari    Yaté    ÎLE DES PINS
Nouméa    Mont Dore    Passe de la Sarcelle
Dumbea    Vao    ÎLE KOUTOUMO
GRAND RÉCIF SUD    DURAND REEF

Copyright © by Rand McNally & Co.
Map prepared by George Philip & Son Ltd, London.
A-593100-76  -1 1-5

Scale 1:8,000,000; one inch to 126 miles. Lambert Conformal Conic Projection
Elevations are given in meters.

0    50    100    200    Miles
0    50    100    200    Kilometers

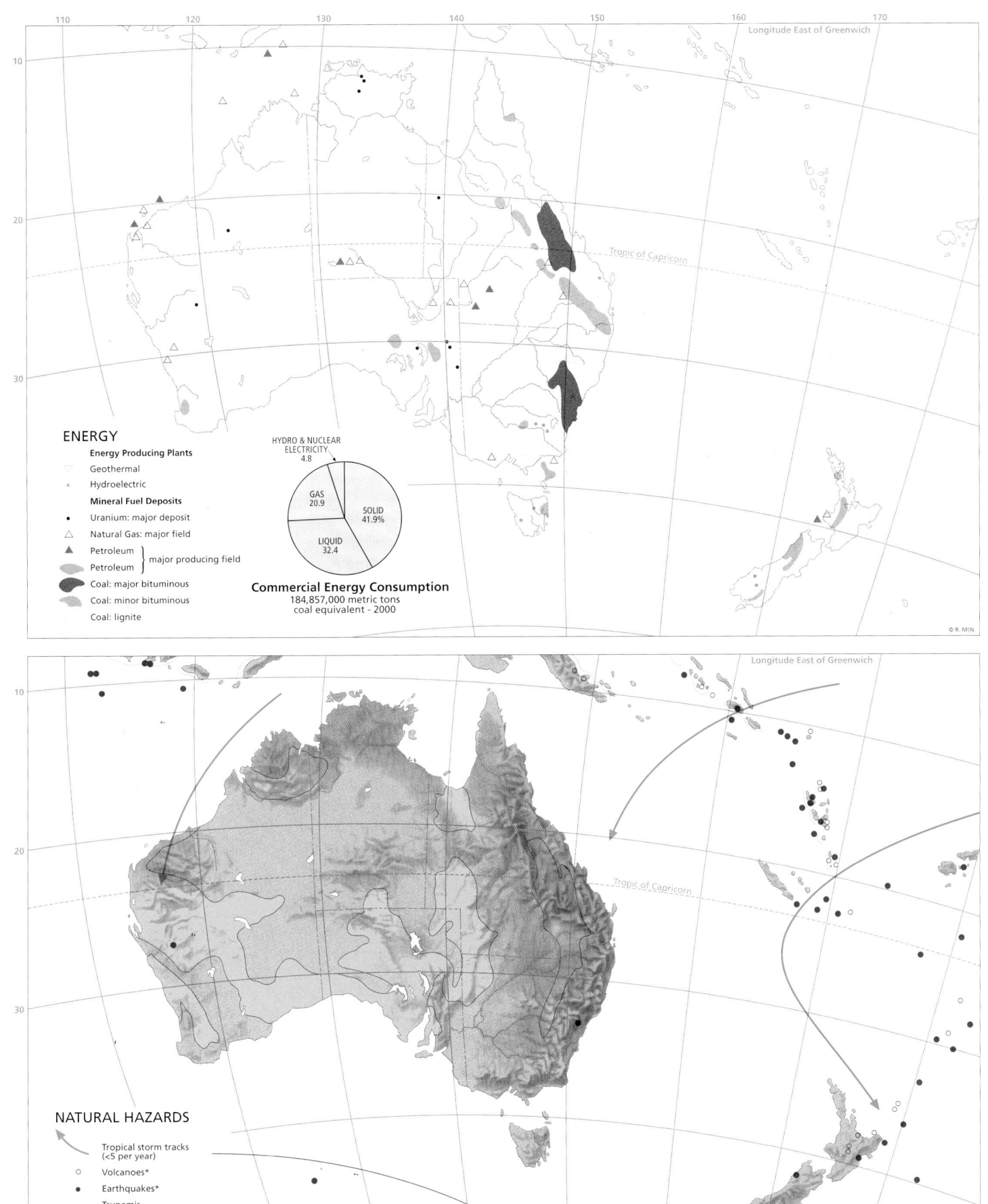

## ENERGY

**Energy Producing Plants**

▽ Geothermal

▪ Hydroelectric

**Mineral Fuel Deposits**

• Uranium: major deposit

△ Natural Gas: major field

▲ Petroleum

◢ Petroleum } major producing field

◼ Coal: major bituminous

◼ Coal: minor bituminous

Coal: lignite

HYDRO & NUCLEAR
ELECTRICITY
4.8

GAS
20.9

SOLID
41.9%

LIQUID
32.4

**Commercial Energy Consumption**
184,857,000 metric tons
coal equivalent - 2000

© R. McN.

## NATURAL HAZARDS

↖ Tropical storm tracks
(<5 per year)

○ Volcanoes*

● Earthquakes*

Tsunamis

Limit of iceberg drift

▨ Areas subject to desertification

*Occurrences since 1900

© R. McN.  N-GD595000-D5 -2 2-2

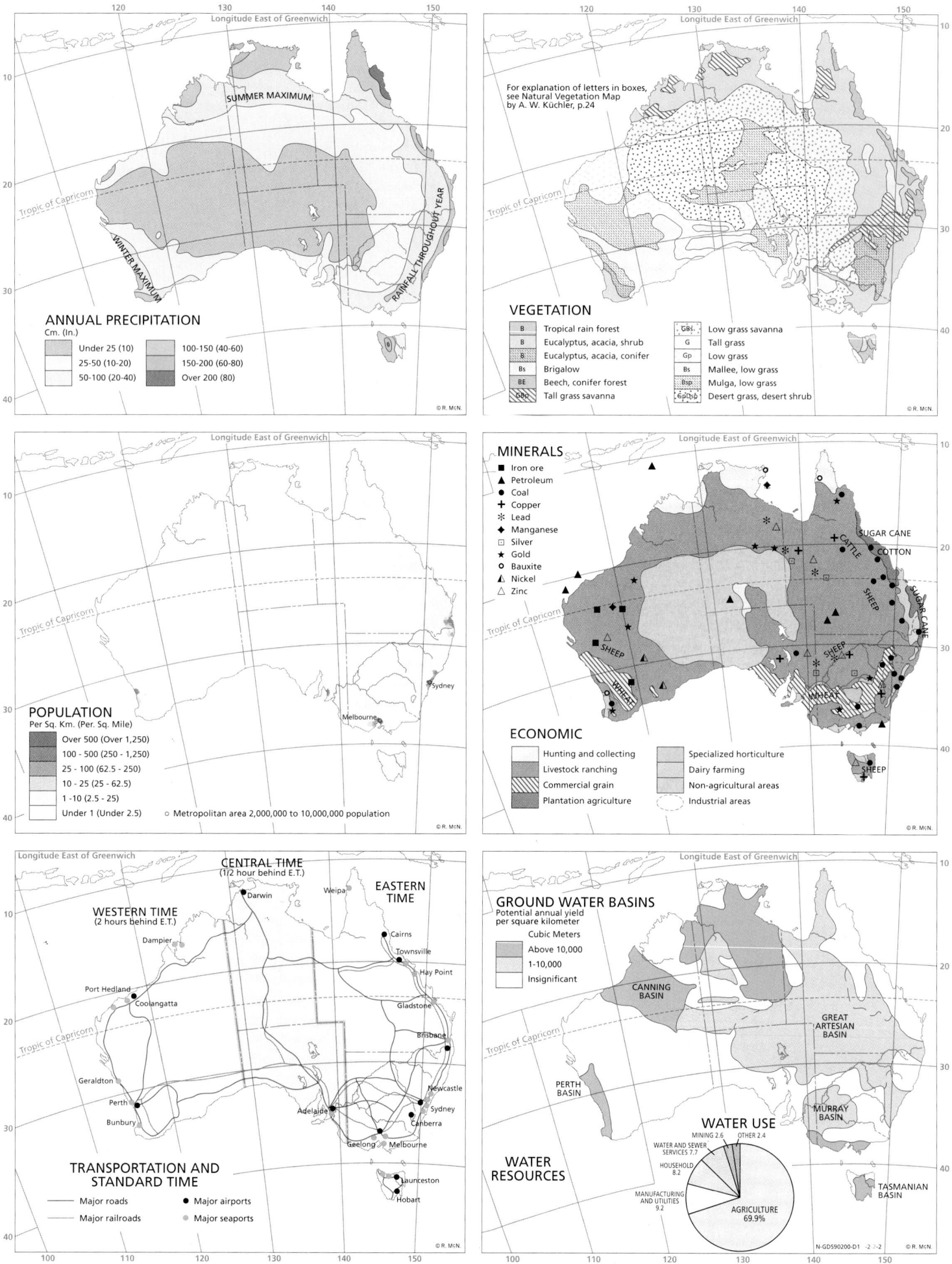

## ANNUAL PRECIPITATION
Cm. (In.)

| | |
|---|---|
| Under 25 (10) | 100-150 (40-60) |
| 25-50 (10-20) | 150-200 (60-80) |
| 50-100 (20-40) | Over 200 (80) |

SUMMER MAXIMUM
RAINFALL THROUGHOUT YEAR
WINTER MAXIMUM

## VEGETATION

For explanation of letters in boxes,
see Natural Vegetation Map
by A. W. Küchler, p.24

| | | | |
|---|---|---|---|
| B | Tropical rain forest | GBs | Low grass savanna |
| B | Eucalyptus, acacia, shrub | G | Tall grass |
| B | Eucalyptus, acacia, conifer | Gp | Low grass |
| Bs | Brigalow | Bs | Mallee, low grass |
| BE | Beech, conifer forest | Bsp | Mulga, low grass |
| GBp | Tall grass savanna | GpBsb | Desert grass, desert shrub |

## POPULATION
Per Sq. Km. (Per. Sq. Mile)

| | |
|---|---|
| | Over 500 (Over 1,250) |
| | 100 - 500 (250 - 1,250) |
| | 25 - 100 (62.5 - 250) |
| | 10 - 25 (25 - 62.5) |
| | 1 - 10 (2.5 - 25) |
| | Under 1 (Under 2.5) |

o Metropolitan area 2,000,000 to 10,000,000 population

Sydney
Melbourne

## MINERALS
- ■ Iron ore
- ▲ Petroleum
- ● Coal
- ＋ Copper
- ✳ Lead
- ◆ Manganese
- ▣ Silver
- ★ Gold
- ○ Bauxite
- ◢ Nickel
- △ Zinc

SUGAR CANE
CATTLE
COTTON
SHEEP
SUGAR CANE
SHEEP
WHEAT
SHEEP
WHEAT
SHEEP

## ECONOMIC

| | | | |
|---|---|---|---|
| | Hunting and collecting | | Specialized horticulture |
| | Livestock ranching | | Dairy farming |
| | Commercial grain | | Non-agricultural areas |
| | Plantation agriculture | | Industrial areas |

## TRANSPORTATION AND STANDARD TIME

CENTRAL TIME
(1/2 hour behind E.T.)
WESTERN TIME
(2 hours behind E.T.)
EASTERN TIME

Darwin
Weipa
Cairns
Townsville
Hay Point
Dampier
Port Hedland
Coolangatta
Gladstone
Brisbane
Geraldton
Newcastle
Perth
Sydney
Bunbury
Adelaide
Canberra
Geelong Melbourne
Launceston
Hobart

| | | | |
|---|---|---|---|
| —— | Major roads | ● | Major airports |
| —— | Major railroads | ● | Major seaports |

## WATER RESOURCES

### GROUND WATER BASINS
Potential annual yield
per square kilometer

Cubic Meters

| | |
|---|---|
| | Above 10,000 |
| | 1-10,000 |
| | Insignificant |

CANNING BASIN
GREAT ARTESIAN BASIN
PERTH BASIN
MURRAY BASIN
TASMANIAN BASIN

### WATER USE
MINING 2.6   OTHER 2.4
WATER AND SEWER SERVICES 7.7
HOUSEHOLD 8.2
MANUFACTURING AND UTILITIES 9.2
AGRICULTURE 69.9%

N-GDS90200-D1 -2 2-2

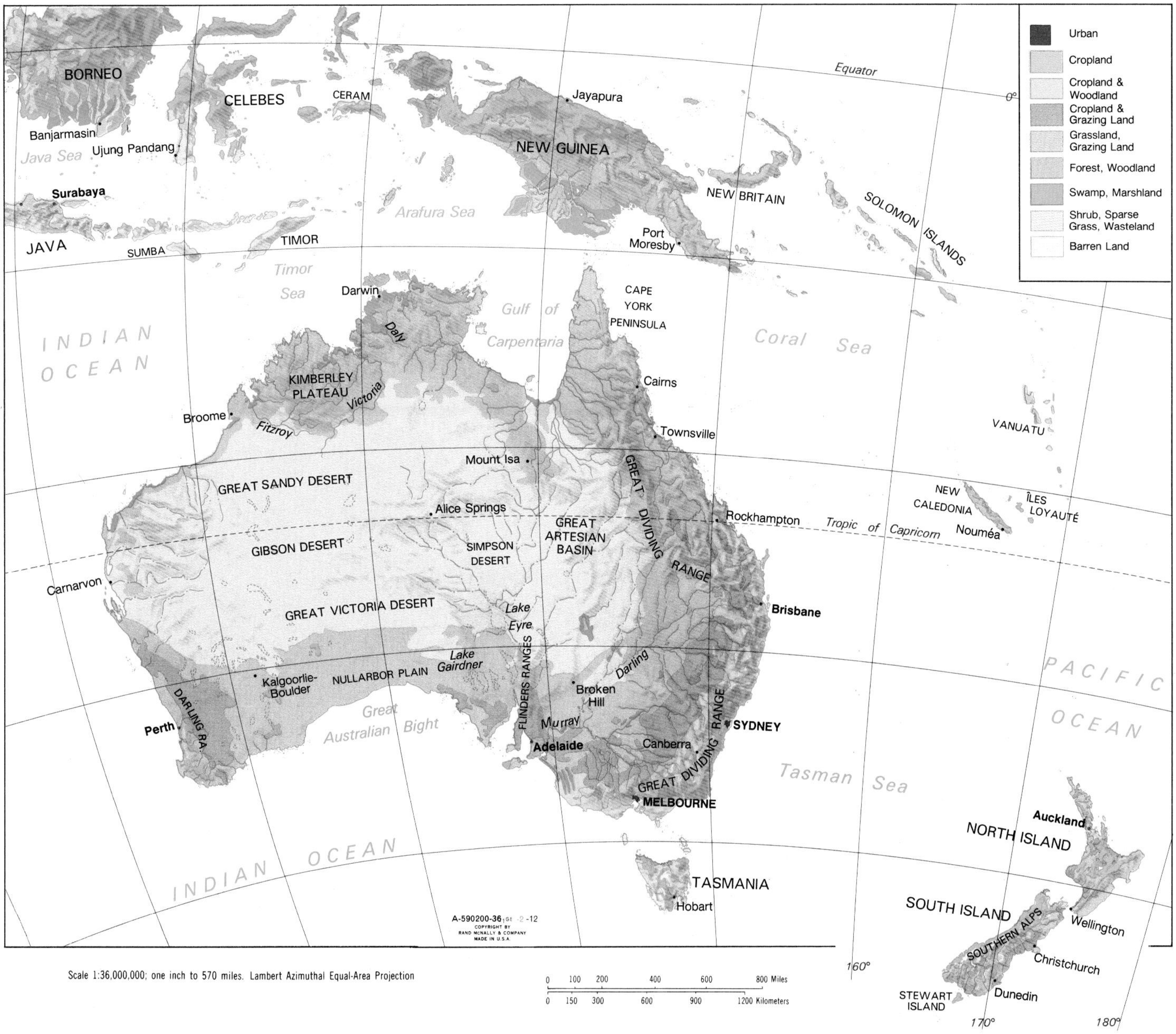

BORNEO

CELEBES

CERAM

Banjarmasin

*Java Sea* Ujung Pandang

**Surabaya**

JAVA SUMBA TIMOR

*Timor Sea*

Darwin

Jayapura

NEW GUINEA

NEW BRITAIN

Port Moresby

SOLOMON ISLANDS

*Arafura Sea*

CAPE YORK PENINSULA

Gulf of Carpentaria

*Coral Sea*

Cairns

*INDIAN OCEAN*

KIMBERLEY PLATEAU

*Daly*

*Victoria*

Broome

*Fitzroy*

Mount Isa

GREAT SANDY DESERT

Alice Springs

SIMPSON DESERT

GREAT ARTESIAN BASIN

Townsville

VANUATU

GIBSON DESERT

GREAT VICTORIA DESERT

*Lake Eyre*

*Lake Gairdner*

Carnarvon

Kalgoorlie-Boulder NULLARBOR PLAIN

FLINDERS RANGES

Broken Hill

*Murray*

*Darling*

Brisbane

Rockhampton *Tropic of Capricorn*

NEW CALEDONIA

Nouméa

ÎLES LOYAUTÉ

GREAT DIVIDING RANGE

**SYDNEY**

GREAT DIVIDING RANGE

*PACIFIC OCEAN*

*DARLING RA.*

**Perth**

*Great Australian Bight*

Adelaide

Canberra

Broken Hill

*Tasman Sea*

Auckland

NORTH ISLAND

*INDIAN OCEAN*

GREAT DIVIDING RANGE

**MELBOURNE**

TASMANIA

Hobart

SOUTH ISLAND

SOUTHERN ALPS

Wellington

Christchurch

STEWART ISLAND

Dunedin

160°

170°

180°

| | |
|---|---|
| ▮ | Urban |
| | Cropland |
| | Cropland & Woodland |
| | Cropland & Grazing Land |
| | Grassland, Grazing Land |
| | Forest, Woodland |
| | Swamp, Marshland |
| | Shrub, Sparse Grass, Wasteland |
| | Barren Land |

A-590200-36
COPYRIGHT BY
RAND MCNALLY & COMPANY
MADE IN U.S.A.

Scale 1:36,000,000; one inch to 570 miles. Lambert Azimuthal Equal-Area Projection

0 100 200 400 600 800 Miles

0 150 300 600 900 1200 Kilometers

a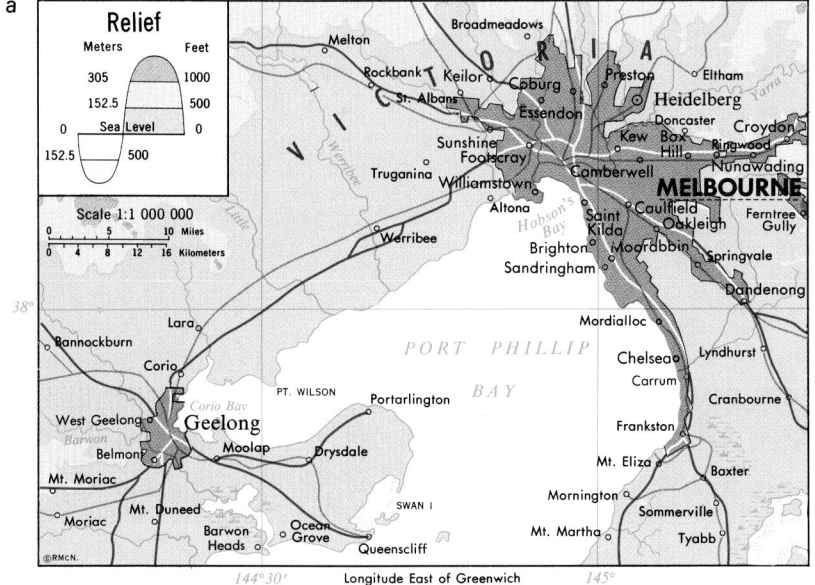

**Relief**

| Meters | | Feet |
|---|---|---|
| 305 | | 1000 |
| 152.5 | | 500 |
| 0 | Sea Level | 0 |
| 152.5 | | 500 |

Scale 1:1 000 000

0 5 10 Miles
0 4 8 12 16 Kilometers

Melton

Broadmeadows

Rockbank Keilor

St. Albans

Coburg

Essendon

Preston

Eltham

Heidelberg

Sunshine

Footscray

Doncaster

Kew Box Hill

Croydon

Ringwood

Nunawading

Truganina

Williamstown

Camberwell

**MELBOURNE**

*Hobson's Bay*

Caulfield

Altona

Saint Kilda

Oakleigh

Moorabbin

Ferntree Gully

Werribee

Brighton

Sandringham

Springvale

Dandenong

Lara

Bannockburn

Corio

*PORT PHILLIP BAY*

Mordialloc

PT. WILSON

Portarlington

Chelsea

Carrum

Lyndhurst

*Corio Bay*

**Geelong**

West Geelong

Belmont

Moolap

Drysdale

Frankston

Cranbourne

Mt. Moriac

Mt. Duneed

Ocean Grove

SWAN I.

Mt. Eliza

Baxter

Moriac

Barwon Heads

Queenscliff

Mornington

Sommerville

Mt. Martha

Tyabb

VICTORIA

*Werribee*

*Yarra*

*Barwon*

*Little*

38°

144°30' Longitude East of Greenwich 145°

b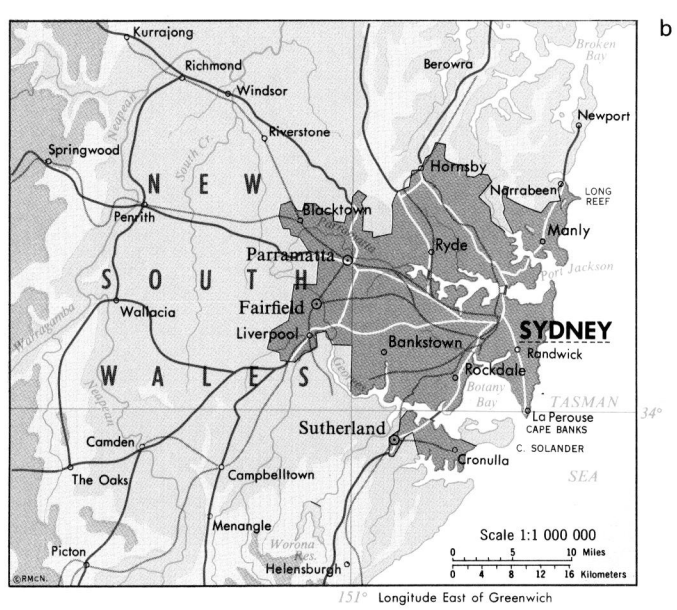

Kurrajong

Richmond

Windsor

Berowra

*Broken Bay*

Springwood

Riverstone

Newport

Penrith

Hornsby

Narrabeen

LONG REEF

Blacktown

Parramatta

Ryde

Manly

Wallacia

Fairfield

*Port Jackson*

**SYDNEY**

Liverpool

Bankstown

Randwick

Rockdale

*Botany Bay*

Camden

Sutherland

La Perouse

CAPE BANKS

C. SOLANDER

The Oaks

Campbelltown

Cronulla

*TASMAN SEA*

Menangle

Picton

Helensburgh

NEW SOUTH WALES

*Nepean*

*Hawkesbury*

*Georges*

*Woronora Res.*

34°

Scale 1:1 000 000

0 5 10 Miles
0 4 8 12 16 Kilometers

151° Longitude East of Greenwich

Scale 1:16 000 000; one inch to 250 miles. Lambert's Azimuthal, Equal Area Projection
Elevations and depressions are given in feet

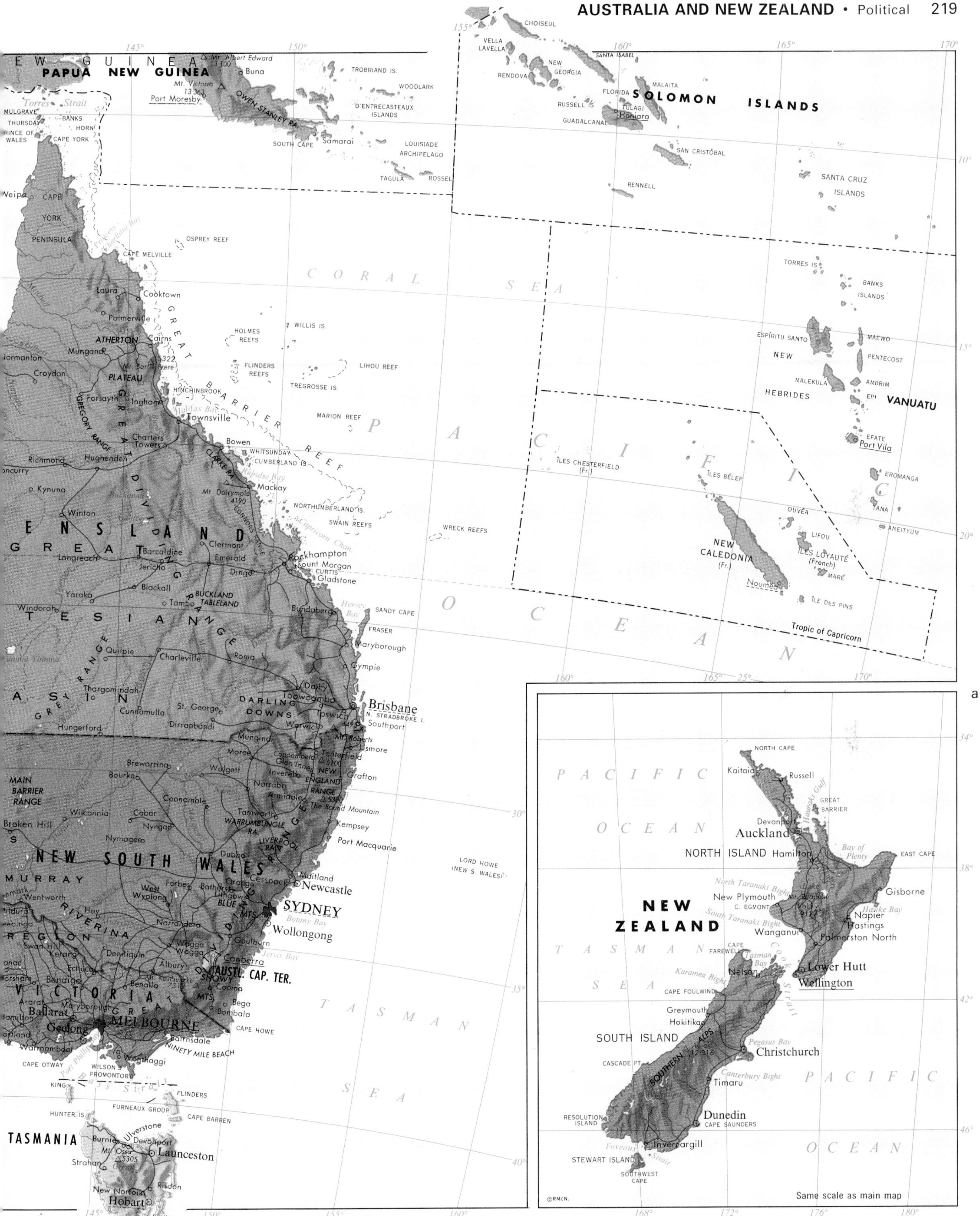

CHOISEUL

VELLA LAVELLA

SANTA ISABEL

NEW GEORGIA

RENDOVA

FLORIDA MALAITA

RUSSELL IS. TULAGI

Honiara

GUADALCANAL

SOLOMON ISLANDS

SAN CRISTÓBAL

RENNELL

SANTA CRUZ ISLANDS

TORRES IS.

BANKS ISLANDS

ESPÍRITU SANTO MAEWO

NEW PENTECOST

MALEKULA AMBRIM

HEBRIDES EPI VANUATU

EFATE

Port Vila

EROMANGA

ÎLES CHESTERFIELD (Fr.)

ÎLES BÉLEP

OUVÉA

LIFOU TANA

ANEITYUM

NEW CALEDONIA (Fr.)

ÎLES LOYAUTÉ (French)

Nouméa MARÉ

ÎLE DES PINS

Tropic of Capricorn

CORAL SEA

PACIFIC OCEAN

**NEW GUINEA**

**PAPUA NEW GUINEA**

Mt. Albert Edward 13,100

Buna

TROBRIAND IS.

Mt. Victoria 13,363

Port Moresby

OWEN STANLEY RA.

WOODLARK

D'ENTRECASTEAUX ISLANDS

Torres Strait

MULGRAVE

THURSDAY BANKS HORN

PRINCE OF WALES CAPE YORK

SOUTH CAPE

Samarai

LOUISIADE ARCHIPELAGO

TAGULA ROSSEL

Weipa CAPE YORK

PENINSULA

OSPREY REEF

CAPE MELVILLE

HOLMES REEFS

WILLIS IS.

Laura Cooktown

ATHERTON Cairns

Palmerville

PLATEAU

FLINDERS REEFS

TREGROSSE IS.

LIHOU REEF

Mungana 5322

Forsayth Ingham

Croydon

HINCHINBROOK

MARION REEF

Townsville

Charters Towers

Hughenden

Bowen

WHITSUNDAY

CUMBERLAND IS.

Mt. Dalrymple 4190

Mackay

NORTHUMBERLAND IS.

SWAIN REEFS

WRECK REEFS

QUEENSLAND

GREAT DIVIDING RANGE

Richmond

Winton

Clermont

Barcaldine

Longreach

Emerald

Jericho

Dingo

Rockhampton

Mount Morgan

CURTIS

Gladstone

Capricorn Chan.

Yaraka

Blackall

BUCKLAND TABLELAND

Tambo

Bundaberg

Hervey Bay

SANDY CAPE

WESTERN

GREAT DIVIDING RANGE

Windorah

Quilpie

Charleville

Roma

FRASER

Maryborough

Thargomindah

Cunnamulla

St. George

Gympie

Dalby

Toowoomba

Ipswich

**Brisbane**

N. STRADBROKE I.

Southport

Hungerford

DARLING DOWNS

Warwick

Dirranbandi

Mt. Roberts

Lismore

MAIN BARRIER RANGE

Bourke

Brewarrina

Walgett

Mungindi

Moree

Tenterfield

Glen Innes

NEW ENGLAND RANGE

Grafton

Wilcannia

Cobar

Coonamble

Narrabri

Inverell

Armidale

Broken Hill

Nyngan

Tamworth

WARRUMBUNGLE RA.

LIVERPOOL RA.

Kempsey

Port Macquarie

NEW SOUTH WALES

MURRAY

Wentworth

RIVERINA

Hay

Nymagee

Forbes

Bathurst

Lithgow

Orange

BLUE MTS.

Maitland

**Newcastle**

Cessnock

REGION

Swan Hill

Deniliquin

West Wyalong

Narrandera

Wagga Wagga

Goulburn

**SYDNEY**

Wollongong

Botany Bay

Jervis Bay

Kerang

Echuca

Albury

Canberra

AUSTL. CAP. TER.

Bega

Bombala

CAPE HOWE

Bendigo

Benalla

Mt. Kosciusko 7316

SNOWY MTS.

Cooma

VICTORIA

Ararat

Maryborough

Ballarat

**MELBOURNE**

Geelong

Bairnsdale

NINETY MILE BEACH

CAPE OTWAY

WILSONS PROMONTORY

Warrnambool

Wonthaggi

Port Phillip

KING IS.

Bass Strait

FLINDERS

FURNEAUX GROUP

HUNTER IS.

CAPE BARREN

**TASMANIA**

Burnie Ulverstone

Devonport

Mt. Ossa 5305

Launceston

Strahan

New Norfolk

**Hobart**

Risdon

BRUNY

SOUTH EAST CAPE

TASMAN SEA

LORD HOWE (NEW S. WALES)

| 0 | 50 | 100 | 200 | 300 | 400 | 500 Miles |
| 0 | 100 | 200 | 400 | 600 | 800 Kilometers |

a

PACIFIC OCEAN

NORTH CAPE

Kaitaia

Russell

GREAT BARRIER

Devonport

**Auckland**

NORTH ISLAND

Hamilton

Bay of Plenty

EAST CAPE

**NEW ZEALAND**

North Taranaki Bight

New Plymouth

C. EGMONT

South Taranaki Bight

Gisborne

Napier

Hastings

Wanganui

Palmerston North

CAPE FAREWELL

Tasman Bay

Nelson

Cook Strait

**Lower Hutt**

**Wellington**

Karamea Bight

CAPE FOULWIND

Greymouth

Hokitika

SOUTH ISLAND

SOUTHERN ALPS

12,318

Pegasus Bay

**Christchurch**

CASCADE PT.

Canterbury Bight

Timaru

RESOLUTION ISLAND

**Dunedin**

CAPE SAUNDERS

Foveaux Strait

Invercargill

STEWART ISLAND

SOUTHWEST CAPE

TASMAN SEA

PACIFIC OCEAN

Same scale as main map

©RMcN.

| Cities and Towns | 0 to 50,000 | ○ | 500,000 to 1,000,000 | ◎ |
| | 50,000 to 500,000 | ⊙ | 1,000,000 and over | |

Continued on pages 212-213

115°

120°

125°

130°

135°

146

**INDONESIA**

Pasuruan

A 10 932
G. Mahameru
12 060
G. Raung

JAVA

Singaraja

Rinjani
12 225

BALI

LOMBOK

Sumbawa
Besar

Raba

SUMBAWA

FLORES

Savu
Sea

LOMBLEN PANTAR

ALOR

Dili

**EAST TIMOR**

SELARU

TANJUNG VALS

SUNDA

S U N D A

I S L A N D S

Waingapu

SUMBA

SAWU

ROTI

Kupang

TIMOR

A R A F U R A

S E A

**Dundas Strait**

Croker

C. VAN DIEMEN

MELVILLE

Van Diemen Gulf

Clarence Str

COBURG PEN.

WESSEL IS.

CAPE ARNHEM

10°

BATHURST

Darwin

**ARNHEM LAND**

Blue Mud Bay

GROOTE
EYLANDT

GULF OF

Pine Creek

Anson Bay

Katherine

Limmen
Bight

CARPENTARIA

I N D I A N

TIMOR

SEA

CAPE
LONDONDERRY

Joseph
Bonaparte Gulf

Daly

SIR EDWARD PELLEW
GROUP

WELLESLEY

Queen Ch

Wyndham

Victoria River
Downs

Birdum

Borroloola

Burketown

15°

O C E A N

BUCCANEER
ARCH.

CAPE LEVEQUE

Mt. Hann
2800

KING
LEOPOLD
RANGES

Derby

**DAMPIER
LAND**

Broome

GEIKIE
RANGE

Fitzroy
Crossing

Halls Creek

Daly Waters

Newcastle Waters

Victoria

Sturt Cr.

**NORTHERN**

Alexandria

BARKLY TABLELAND

Dobbyn

Camooweal

Roebuck Bay

LaGrange

EIGHTY MILE BEACH

Tanami

Tennant Creek

Mount Isa

Malbo

Duc

Dajarra

LARREY POINT

DAMPIER
ARCH.

Port Hedland

RIPON

De Grey

GREAT SANDY DESERT

Mackay

**T E R R I T O R Y**

Barrow Creek

**QU**

20°

MONTE BELLO IS.

BARROW

Roebourne

Marble Bar

Nullagine

Mt. Ziel
4955

Artunga

NORTH WEST CAPE

Millstream

Onslow

**HAMERSLEY RANGE**

Mt. Bruce
4052

Jiggalong

Disappointment

**W E S T E R N**

**GIBSON DESERT**

MACDONNELL

RANGES

Alice Springs

JAMES RANGE

SIMPSON

POINT CLOATES

Tropic of Capricorn

CAPE FARQUHAR

Peak Hill

Carnarvon

Nabberu

Carnegie

Gillen

Wells

Uluru
(Ayers Rock)

Charlotte
Waters

**DESERT**

Birdsville

A

BERNIER

DORRE

Shark Bay

Meekatharra

Nannine

Wiluna

MUSGRAVE RANGES
Mt. Woodroffe
4724

EVERARD RANGES

Oodnadatta

25°

DIRK HARTOG

STEEP POINT

Cue

Sandstone

Mount
Magnet

Ajana

Northampton

HOUTMAN ROCKS

Geraldton

Mingenew

**A U S T R A L I A**

Laverton

Everard

**SOUTH   AUSTRALIA**

STUART RANGE

William Creek

Marree

FLINDERS RANGES

Parachilna

Dongara

**GREAT VICTORIA DESERT**

Menzies

Kalgoorlie-Boulder

Coolgardie

Hughes

Rawlinna

Ooldea Station

**NULLARBOR**

**PLAIN**

Penong

Ceduna

POINT FOWLER

Woomera

Pimba

Farina

Whyalla

Port Augusta

30°

**DARLING RANGE**

Pithara

Miling

Moora

Lake Brown

Southern Cross

**SWANLAND**

Norseman

Dundas

Salmon Gums

Eucla

Eyre

Port Pirie

Peterboro

EYRE
PENINSULA

Moonta

Wallaroo

Gladstone

Port Lincoln

Gawler

Port Wakefield

**Perth**

Fremantle

Northam

York

Ravensthorpe

Esperance

**GREAT   AUSTRALIAN   BIGHT**

**Adela**

Murr

Narrogin

COLLIE

Bunbury

Katanning

Hopetoun

ARCHIPELAGO
OF THE RECHERCHE

KANGAROO

Bridg

CAPE NATURALISTE

Bussleton

Nornalup

Albany

Naracoo

Kingston

CAPE JAFFA

CAPE LEEUWIN

PT. D'ENTRECASTEAUX

WEST CAPE HOWE

King George Sd.

35°

Mt. Gamb

I N D I A N

O C E A N

**Relief**

| Meters | | Feet |
|---|---|---|
| 3050 | | 10 000 |
| 1525 | | 5000 |
| 610 | | 2000 |
| 305 | | 1000 |
| 152.5 | | 500 |
| 0 | Sea Level | 0 |
| 152.5 | | 500 |
| 1525 | | 5000 |
| 3050 | | 10 000 |
| 6100 | | 20 000 |

Below
Sea Level

A-590200-76   7-18
COPYRIGHT BY
RAND McNALLY & COMPANY
MADE IN U.S.A.

110°

115°

120°

125°

130°

135°

40°

Longitude    East of Greenwich

Scale 1:16 000 000; one inch to 250 miles. Lambert's Azimuthal, Equal Area Projection
Elevations and depressions are given in feet

PAPUA NEW GUINEA

NEW GUINEA

Mt. Albert Edward 13,100
Mt. Victoria 13,363
Port Moresby
OWEN STANLEY RA.
Buna
TROBRIAND IS.
WOODLARK
D'ENTRECASTEAUX ISLANDS
SOUTH CAPE
Samarai
LOUISIADE ARCHIPELAGO
TAGULA
ROSSEL

CHOISEUL
VELLA LAVELLA
NEW GEORGIA
RENDOVA
SANTA ISABEL
FLORIDA
RUSSELL IS.
TULAGI Honiara
GUADALCANAL
SAN CRISTÓBAL
RENNELL
SOLOMON ISLANDS

Torres Strait
MULGRAVE
THURSDAY
BANKS
HORN
PRINCE OF WALES
CAPE YORK

SANTA CRUZ ISLANDS

Weipa
CAPE YORK PENINSULA
Normanton
CAPE MELVILLE
OSPREY REEF
TORRES IS.
BANKS ISLANDS

ESPÍRITU SANTO
MAEWO
NEW
PENTECOST
HEBRIDES
MALEKULA
AMBRIM
EPI
VANUATU

Laura
Cooktown
HOLMES REEFS
WILLIS IS.
LIHOU REEF
ATHERTON
Cairns
Mt. Bartle Frere 5322
PLATEAU
Mungana
Forsayth
Ingham
FLINDERS REEFS
TREGROSSE IS.
Halifax Bay
Townsville
MARION REEF
CORAL SEA
ÎLES CHESTERFIELD (Fr.)
ÎLES BÉLEP
OUVÉA
MAEWO
EROMANGA
EFATE
Port Vila
TANA
ANEITYUM

Richmond
Hughenden
Charters Towers
Bowen
WHITSUNDAY
CUMBERLAND IS.
Repulse Bay
Mackay
NORTHUMBERLAND IS.
SWAIN REEFS
WRECK REEFS
NEW CALEDONIA
ÎLES LOYAUTÉ (French)
LIFOU
MARÉ
Nouméa
ÎLE DES PINS

Normanton
Croydon
Kynuna
CLARKE RA.
Mt. Dalrymple 4190
CONNORS RANGE
GREAT DIVIDING RANGE
GREAT BARRIER REEF

QUEENSLAND
Winton
Barcaldine
Jericho
Clermont
Emerald
Dingo
Rockhampton
Mount Morgan
CURTIS
Gladstone

PACIFIC OCEAN

Longreach
Blackall
Tambo
BUCKLAND TABLELAND
Bundaberg
Hervey Bay
SANDY CAPE
FRASER

Yaraka
Windorah
Quilpie
Charleville
Roma
Maryborough
Gympie

Tropic of Capricorn

GREAT
DIVIDING
RANGE
ARTESIAN
BASIN

Thargomindah
Cunnamulla
St. George
Dirranbandi
DARLING DOWNS
Toowoomba
Dalby
Warwick
Ipswich
Brisbane
N. STRADBROKE I.
Southport
4495

Hungerford
Mungindi
Moree
Mt. Roberts
Tenterfield
Lismore
NEW ENGLAND RANGE
Grafton

MAIN BARRIER RANGE
Brewarrina
Bourke
Walgett
Narrabri
Capoompeta 5100
Glen Innes
Inverell
Armidale
5300
The Round Mountain

Broken Hill
Wilcannia
Cobar
Nyngan
Coonamble
Tamworth
WARRUMBUNGLE RA.
LIVERPOOL RANGE
Kempsey
Port Macquarie

NEW SOUTH WALES
Nymagee
Dubbo
Gilgandra
LORD HOWE I. (NEW S. WALES)

MURRAY
West Wyalong
Forbes
Bathurst
Orange
Lithgow
BLUE MTS.
Cessnock
Maitland
Newcastle

RIVERINA REGION
Hay
Narrandera
Wagga Wagga
Albury
Cootamundra
Goulburn
Canberra
AUSTL. CAP. TER.
SYDNEY
Wollongong
Botany Bay

Mildura
Swan Hill
Deniliquin
Mt. Kosciusko 7316
SNOWY MTS.
Cooma
Bombala
Bega
TASMAN SEA

VICTORIA
Bendigo
Benalla
GREAT DIVIDING RANGE
Bairnsdale
NINETY MILE BEACH
CAPE HOWE

Ararat
Ballarat
Maryborough
Geelong
MELBOURNE
Warrnambool
CAPE OTWAY
WILSON'S PROMONTORY

KING I.
FLINDERS
FURNEAUX GROUP
CAPE BARREN
BASS STRAIT
HUNTER IS.

TASMANIA
Burnie
Ulverstone
Devonport
Launceston
Strahan
Mt. Ossa 5305
New Norfolk
Hobart
BRUNY
SOUTH EAST CAPE

**NEW ZEALAND**

PACIFIC OCEAN
NORTH CAPE
Kaitaia
Russell
GREAT BARRIER
Devonport
Auckland
NORTH ISLAND
Hamilton
Bay of Plenty
EAST CAPE

New Plymouth
C. EGMONT
Mt. Egmont
Wanganui
Napier
Hastings
Palmerston North
Gisborne

CAPE FAREWELL
Nelson
Lower Hutt
Wellington

Greymouth
Hokitika
SOUTH ISLAND
SOUTHERN ALPS
12,318
Christchurch
Pegasus Bay

CASCADE PT.
Timaru
Canterbury Bight

RESOLUTION ISLAND
Dunedin
CAPE SAUNDERS
Invercargill
STEWART ISLAND
SOUTHWEST CAPE

Same scale as main map

| Cities and Towns | 0 to 50,000 | 500,000 to 1,000,000 |
|---|---|---|
| | 50,000 to 500,000 | 1,000,000 and over |

0  50  100    200    300    400    500 Miles
0   100   200    400    600    800 Kilometers

a

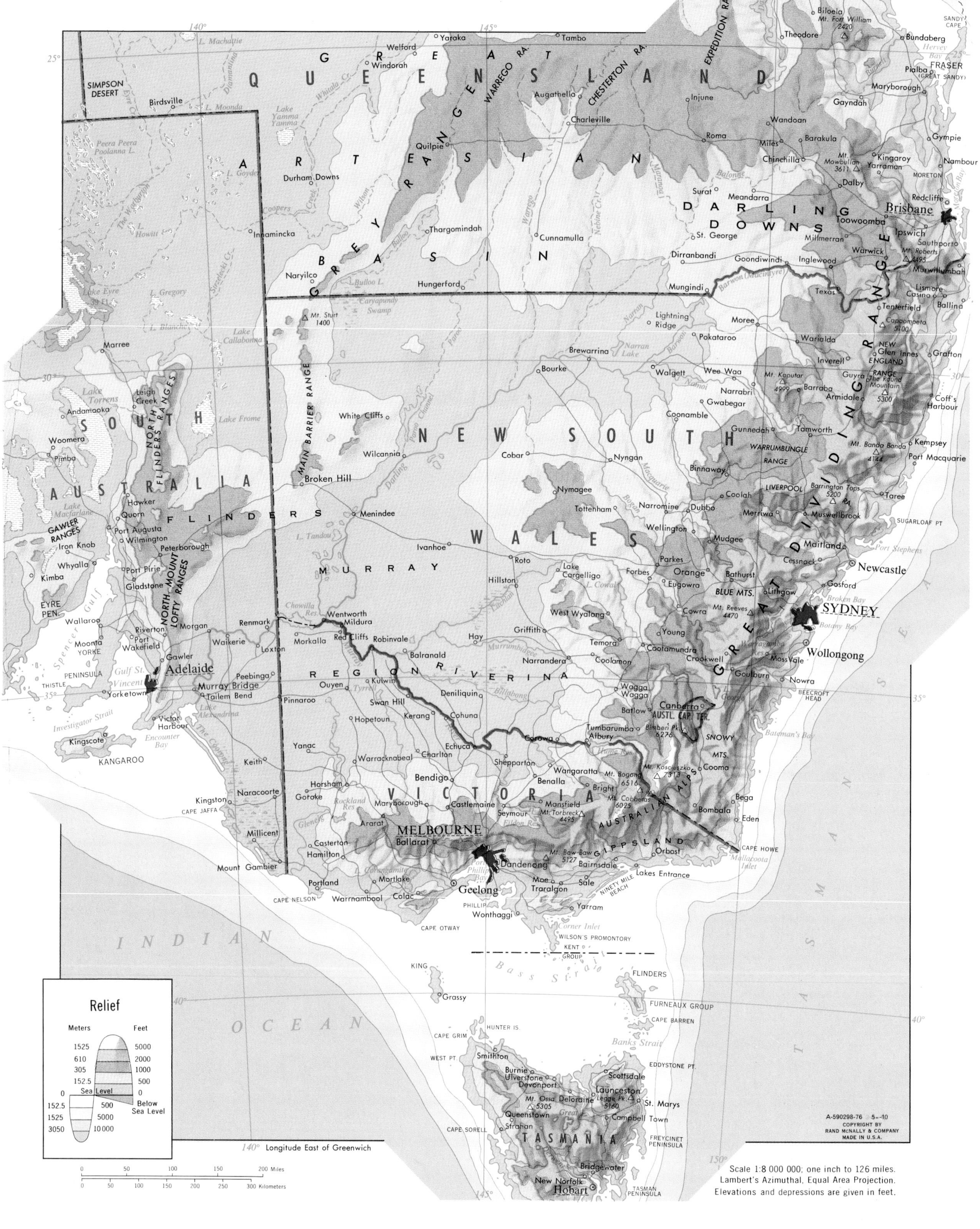

QUEENSLAND

SIMPSON DESERT

Gladstone
Biloela
Mt. Fort William 2420
Bundaberg
Pialba
FRASER (GREAT SANDY)
SANDY CAPE
Theodore
Maryborough
Gayndah
Gympie
Nambour
MORETON
Welford
Windorah
Yaraka
Tambo
EXPEDITION RA.
Injune
Wandoan
Barakula
Kingaroy
Yarraman
Mt. Mowbullan 3611
Dalby
Chinchilla
Miles
Roma
Durham Downs
Augathella
Charleville
Surat
Meandarra
Millmerran
Toowoomba
Brisbane
Ipswich
Southporto
WARREGO RA.
CHESTERTON RA.
Quilpie
Cunnamulla
St. George
Dirranbandi
Goondiwindi
Inglewood
Warwick
Mt. Roberts 4495
Murwillumbah
Birdsville
L. Machattie
L. Yamma Yamma
Lake Yamma Yamma
Thargomindah
Naryilco
Hungerford
Mungindi
Texas
Tenterfield
Lismore
Casino
Ballina
Barwon (Macintyre)

GREAT ARTESIAN BASIN
DARLING DOWNS

Coopers
Innamincka
L. Goyder
Mt. Sturt 1400
Lightning Ridge
Moree
Warialda
Glen Innes
NEW ENGLAND
Grafton
Coff's Harbour
GREAT DIVIDING RANGE
Inverell
Capcompeta 5100
Marree
L. Blanche
Caryapundy Swamp
Brewarrina
Narran Lake
Pokataroo
Guyra
Blue Round Mountain
Mt. Kaputar 4999
Barraba
Armidale 5300

SOUTH AUSTRALIA
Lake Eyre
L. Gregory
Andamooka
Leigh Creek
NORTH FLINDERS RANGES
Bourke
Walgett
Wee Waa
Coonamble
Narrabri
Gwabegar
Gunnedah
Tamworth
Mt. Banda Banda 4144
Kempsey
Port Macquarie

Woomera
Pimba
Hawker
Quorn
FLINDERS RANGES
Broken Hill
Wilcannia
White Cliffs
NEW SOUTH
Cobar
Nyngan
Nymagee
Tottenham
Narromine
Dubbo
Wellington
Mudgee
Merriwa
Coolah
WARRUMBUNGLE RANGE
LIVERPOOL RANGE
Barrington Tops 5200
Muswellbrook
Taree
SUGARLOAF PT.

GAWLER RANGES
Iron Knob
Port Augusta
Wilmington
Peterborough
NORTH MOUNT LOFTY RANGES
FLINDERS
Menindee
L. Tandou
Ivanhoe
Roto
Lake Cargelligo
L. Cowal
Forbes
Parkes
Orange
Bathurst
BLUE MTS.
Mt. Reeves 4470
Lithgow
Maitland
Cessnock
Newcastle
Gosford
Port Stephens
Broken Bay

Whyalla
Kimba
EYRE PEN.
Wallaroo
Moonta
YORKE PENINSULA
Port Pirie
Gladstone
MURRAY
Hillston
Griffith
West Wyalong
Young
Cowra
Eugowra
Temora
Coolamundra
SYDNEY
Wollongong
Moss Vale
BEECROFT HEAD
Botany Bay

Kimba
Riverton
Gawler
Adelaide
Peebinga
REGION RIVERINA
Hay
Narrandera
Coolamon
Wagga Wagga
Crookwell
Goulburn
Nowra

Thistle
Gulf St. Vincent
Yorketown
Murray Bridge
Tailem Bend
Pinnaroo
Ouyen
Kulwin
Balranald
Deniliquin
Batlow
Canberra
AUSTL. CAP. TER.
Bimberi Pk. 6276
SNOWY MTS.
Cooma

Kingscote
KANGAROO
Victor Harbour
Encounter Bay
The Coorong
Lake Alexandrina
Swan Hill
Kerang
Cohuna
Corowa
Tumbarumba
Albury
AUSTRALIAN ALPS
Mt. Kosciusko 7313
Bega
Bombala
Eden

Kingston
CAPE JAFFA
Naracoorte
Keith
Yanac
Warracknabeal
Charlton
Echuca
Shepparton
Wangaratta
Benalla
Mt. Bogong 6516
Mt. Cobberas 6025
Cooma

Millicent
Mount Gambier
Casterton
Hamilton
Horsham
Gotoke
Rockland Res.
Maryborough
Castlemaine
VICTORIA
Mansfield
Mt. Torbreck 4495
Seymour
Fildon Res.
Mt. Baw Baw 5127
GIPPSLAND
Orbost
CAPE HOWE
Mallacoota Inlet

Portland
CAPE NELSON
Warrnambool
Colac
Mortlake
Ararat
Ballarat
MELBOURNE
Dandenong
Geelong
Moe
Traralgon
Sale
Bairnsdale
Lakes Entrance
NINETY MILE BEACH

CAPE OTWAY
PHILLIP IS.
Port Phillip Bay
Wonthaggi
Yarram
Corner Inlet
Wilson's Promontory
KENT GROUP

INDIAN OCEAN

KING IS.
Grassy
CAPE GRIM
HUNTER IS.
CAPE BARREN
FURNEAUX GROUP
FLINDERS
Banks Strait
Bass Strait

WEST PT.
Smithton
Burnie
Ulverstone
Devonport
Scottsdale
EDDYSTONE PT.
Launceston
St. Marys

Mt. Ossa 5305
Deloraine
Legge Pk. 5160
Campbell Town
Queenstown
Strahan
TASMANIA
CAPE SORELL
FREYCINET PENINSULA

Bridgewater
New Norfolk
Hobart
TASMAN PENINSULA

TASMAN SEA

Relief

| Meters | | Feet |
|---|---|---|
| 1525 | | 5000 |
| 610 | | 2000 |
| 305 | | 1000 |
| 152.5 | | 500 |
| 0 | Sea Level | 0 |
| 152.5 | | 500 Below Sea Level |
| 1525 | | 5000 |
| 3050 | | 10 000 |

140° Longitude East of Greenwich

0   50   100   150   200 Miles
0   50   100   150   200   250   300 Kilometers

A-590298-76  5--10
COPYRIGHT BY
RAND McNALLY & COMPANY
MADE IN U.S.A.

Scale 1:8 000 000; one inch to 126 miles.
Lambert's Azimuthal, Equal Area Projection.
Elevations and depressions are given in feet.

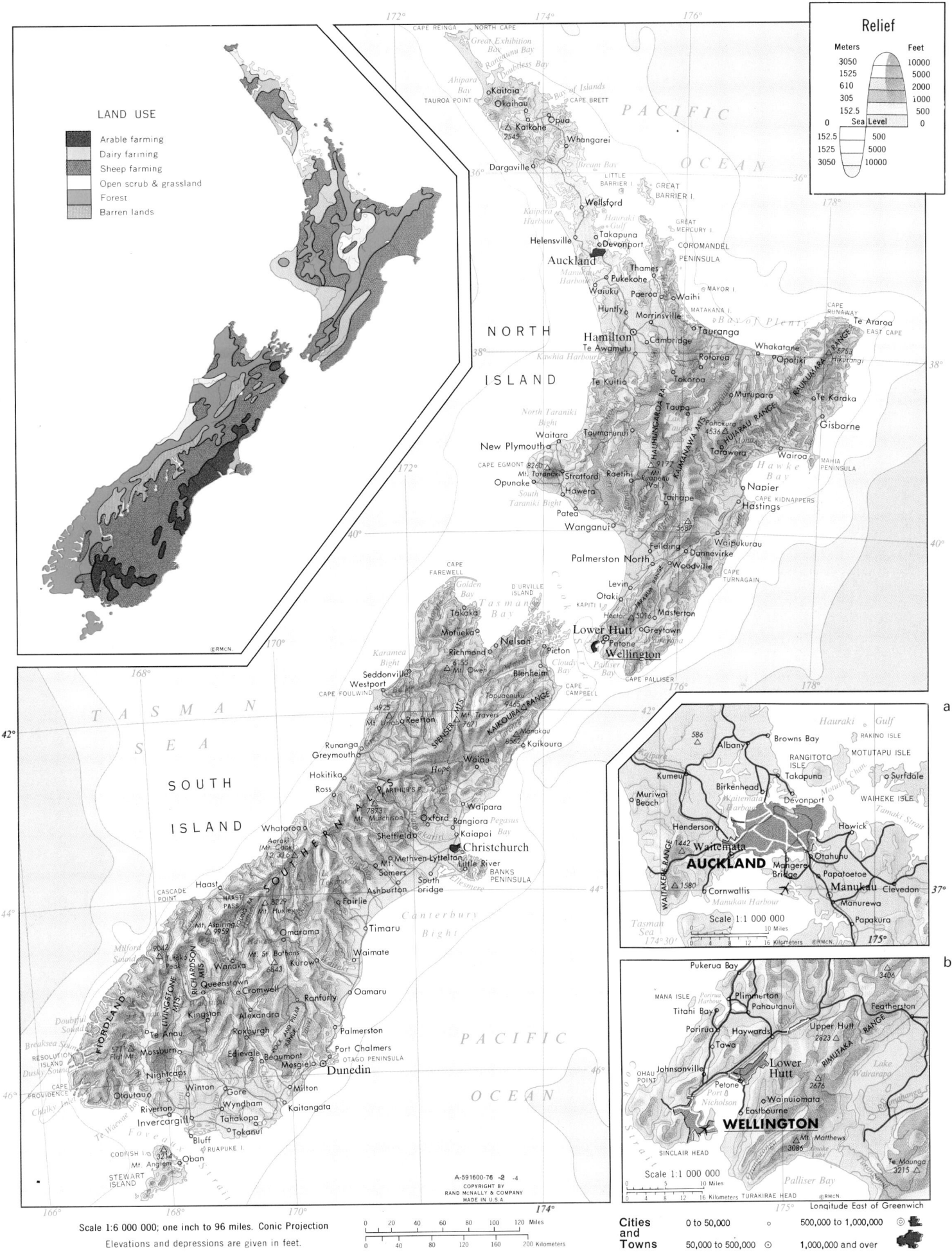

Relief

| Meters | | Feet |
|---|---|---|
| 3050 | | 10000 |
| 1525 | | 5000 |
| 610 | | 2000 |
| 305 | | 1000 |
| 152.5 | | 500 |
| 0 | Sea Level | 0 |
| 152.5 | | 500 |
| 1525 | | 5000 |
| 3050 | | 10000 |

LAND USE

- Arable farming
- Dairy farming
- Sheep farming
- Open scrub & grassland
- Forest
- Barren lands

©RMCN

Scale 1:6 000 000; one inch to 96 miles. Conic Projection
Elevations and depressions are given in feet.

0  20  40  60  80  100  120  Miles
0  40  80  120  160  200  Kilometers

A-591600-76 -2 -4
COPYRIGHT BY
RAND McNALLY & COMPANY
MADE IN U.S.A.

Scale 1:1 000 000 (a)
Scale 1:1 000 000 (b)

Longitude East of Greenwich

**Cities and Towns**

| | |
|---|---|
| 0 to 50,000 ○ | 500,000 to 1,000,000 ◎ |
| 50,000 to 500,000 ⊙ | 1,000,000 and over |

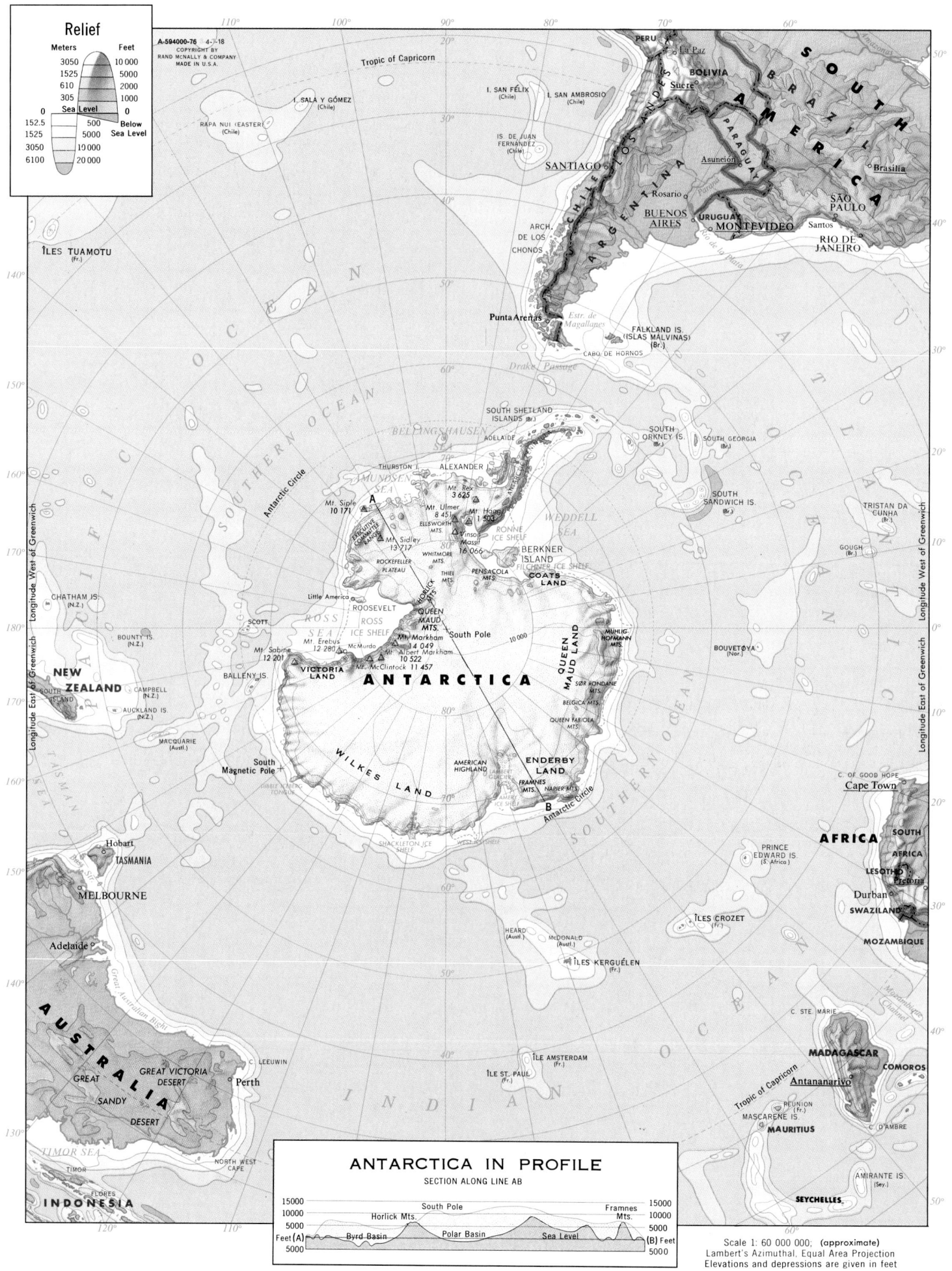

Relief

| Meters | | Feet |
|---|---|---|
| 3050 | | 10 000 |
| 1525 | | 5000 |
| 610 | | 2000 |
| 305 | | 1000 |
| 0 | Sea Level | 0 |
| 152.5 | | 500 Below |
| 1525 | | 5000 Sea Level |
| 3050 | | 19 000 |
| 6100 | | 20 000 |

A-594000-76  4-7-18
COPYRIGHT BY
RAND McNALLY & COMPANY
MADE IN U.S.A.

Tropic of Capricorn

SOUTH AMERICA

PERU
La Paz
BOLIVIA
Sucre
PARAGUAY
Asunción
SANTIAGO
Rosario
BUENOS
AIRES
URUGUAY
MONTEVIDEO
Santos
RIO DE
JANEIRO
ARCH.
DE LOS
CHONOS

BRAZIL
SÃO
PAULO
Brasília

I. SALA Y GÓMEZ (Chile)
I. SAN FÉLIX (Chile)
I. SAN AMBROSIO (Chile)
RAPA NUI (EASTER) (Chile)
IS. DE JUAN FERNÁNDEZ (Chile)
ÎLES TUAMOTU (Fr.)

Punta Arenas
Estr. de Magallanes
FALKLAND IS. (ISLAS MALVINAS) (Br.)
CABO DE HORNOS

Drake Passage

SOUTH SHETLAND ISLANDS (Br.)
ADELAIDE
SOUTH ORKNEY (S.) (Br.)
SOUTH GEORGIA (Br.)
SOUTH SANDWICH IS. (Br.)
TRISTAN DA CUNHA (Br.)
GOUGH (Br.)

BELLINGSHAUSEN
THURSTON I.
ALEXANDER
Mt. Rex 3 625
Mt. Ulmer 8 451
Mt. Hagg 1 503
EXECUTIVE COMMITTEE RANGE
Mt. Siple 10 171
Mt. Sidley 13 717
ELLSWORTH MTS.
Vinson Massif 16 066
WHITMORE MTS.
ROCKEFELLER PLATEAU
THIEL MTS.
PENSACOLA MTS.
WEDDELL SEA
RONNE ICE SHELF
BERKNER ISLAND
FILCHNER ICE SHELF
COATS LAND
BOUVETØYA (Nor.)

AMUNDSEN SEA

Little America
Roosevelt
SCOTT
ROSS SEA
ROSS ICE SHELF
HORLICK MTS.
QUEEN MAUD MTS.
South Pole
10 000
ANTARCTICA
QUEEN MAUD LAND
MÜHLIG-HOFMANN MTS.
SØR RONDANE MTS.
BELGICA MTS.
QUEEN FABIOLA MTS.

CHATHAM IS. (N.Z.)
BOUNTY IS. (N.Z.)

NEW ZEALAND
SOUTH ISLAND
CAMPBELL (N.Z.)
AUCKLAND IS. (N.Z.)
MACQUARIE (Austl.)

Mt. Erebus 12 280
McMurdo
Mt. Sabine 12 201
VICTORIA LAND
Mt. Markham 14 049
Mt. Albert Markham 10 522
Mt. McClintock 11 457
BALLENY IS.

South Magnetic Pole
DIBBLE ICEBERG TONGUE
WILKES LAND
AMERICAN HIGHLAND
LAMBERT GLACIER
ENDERBY LAND
FRAMNES MTS.
NAPIER MTS.
B
Antarctic Circle

AFRICA
C. OF GOOD HOPE
Cape Town
SOUTH AFRICA
LESOTHO
Pretoria
Durban
SWAZILAND
MOZAMBIQUE

PRINCE EDWARD IS. (S. Africa)
ÎLES CROZET (Fr.)

SHACKLETON ICE SHELF
WEST ICE SHELF
HEARD (Austl.)
McDONALD (Austl.)
ÎLES KERGUÉLEN (Fr.)

Hobart
TASMANIA
MELBOURNE
Adelaide

AUSTRALIA
GREAT AUSTRALIAN BIGHT
GREAT VICTORIA DESERT
GREAT SANDY DESERT
Perth
C. LEEUWIN
NORTH WEST CAPE

C. STE. MARIE
MADAGASCAR
COMOROS

ÎLE AMSTERDAM (Fr.)
ÎLE ST. PAUL (Fr.)
Tropic of Capricorn
RÉUNION (Fr.)
MASCARENE IS.
Antananarivo
C. D'AMBRE
MAURITIUS

TIMOR SEA
TIMOR
FLORES
INDONESIA

AMIRANTE IS. (Sey.)
SEYCHELLES

**ANTARCTICA IN PROFILE**
SECTION ALONG LINE AB

| Feet (A) | | | | | | Feet (B) |
|---|---|---|---|---|---|---|
| 15000 | South Pole | | | | Framnes Mts. | 15000 |
| 10000 | Horlick Mts. | | | | | 10000 |
| 5000 | | | | | | 5000 |
| | Byrd Basin | Polar Basin | Sea Level | | | |
| 5000 | | | | | | 5000 |

Scale 1: 60 000 000;  (approximate)
Lambert's Azimuthal, Equal Area Projection
Elevations and depressions are given in feet

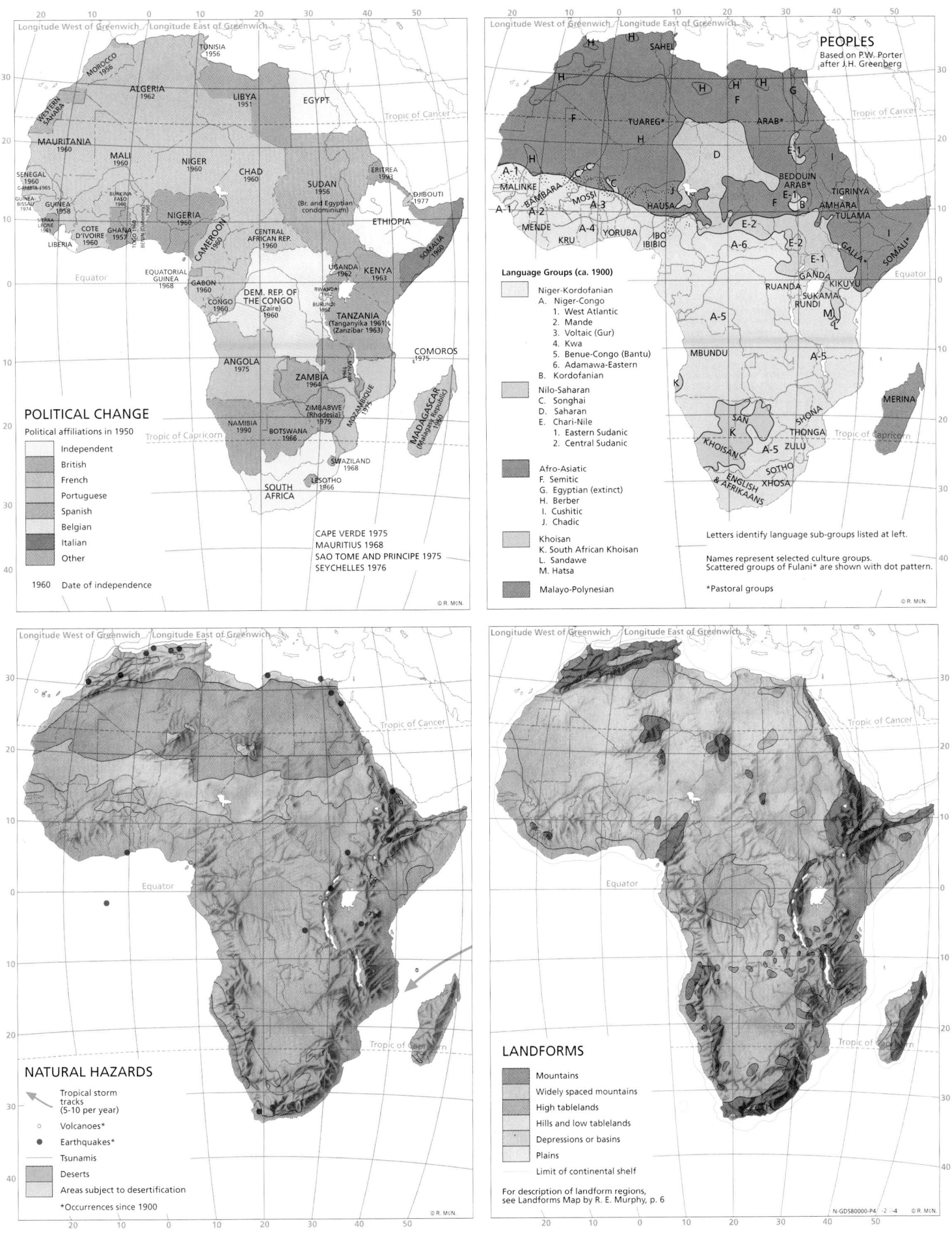

## POLITICAL CHANGE

Political affiliations in 1950

- Independent
- British
- French
- Portuguese
- Spanish
- Belgian
- Italian
- Other

1960   Date of independence

CAPE VERDE 1975
MAURITIUS 1968
SAO TOME AND PRINCIPE 1975
SEYCHELLES 1976

© R. McN.

## PEOPLES

Based on P.W. Porter
after J.H. Greenberg

**Language Groups (ca. 1900)**

- Niger-Kordofanian
  - A.  Niger-Congo
    - 1.  West Atlantic
    - 2.  Mande
    - 3.  Voltaic (Gur)
    - 4.  Kwa
    - 5.  Benue-Congo (Bantu)
    - 6.  Adamawa-Eastern
  - B.  Kordofanian
- Nilo-Saharan
  - C.  Songhai
  - D.  Saharan
  - E.  Chari-Nile
    - 1.  Eastern Sudanic
    - 2.  Central Sudanic
- Afro-Asiatic
  - F.  Semitic
  - G.  Egyptian (extinct)
  - H.  Berber
  - I.  Cushitic
  - J.  Chadic
- Khoisan
  - K.  South African Khoisan
  - L.  Sandawe
  - M.  Hatsa
- Malayo-Polynesian

Letters identify language sub-groups listed at left.

Names represent selected culture groups.
Scattered groups of Fulani* are shown with dot pattern.

*Pastoral groups

© R. McN.

## NATURAL HAZARDS

- → Tropical storm tracks (5-10 per year)
- ○ Volcanoes*
- ● Earthquakes*
- Tsunamis
- Deserts
- Areas subject to desertification

*Occurrences since 1900

© R. McN.

## LANDFORMS

- Mountains
- Widely spaced mountains
- High tablelands
- Hills and low tablelands
- Depressions or basins
- Plains
- Limit of continental shelf

For description of landform regions,
see Landforms Map by R. E. Murphy, p. 6

N-GDS80000-P4  -2  -4     © R. McN.

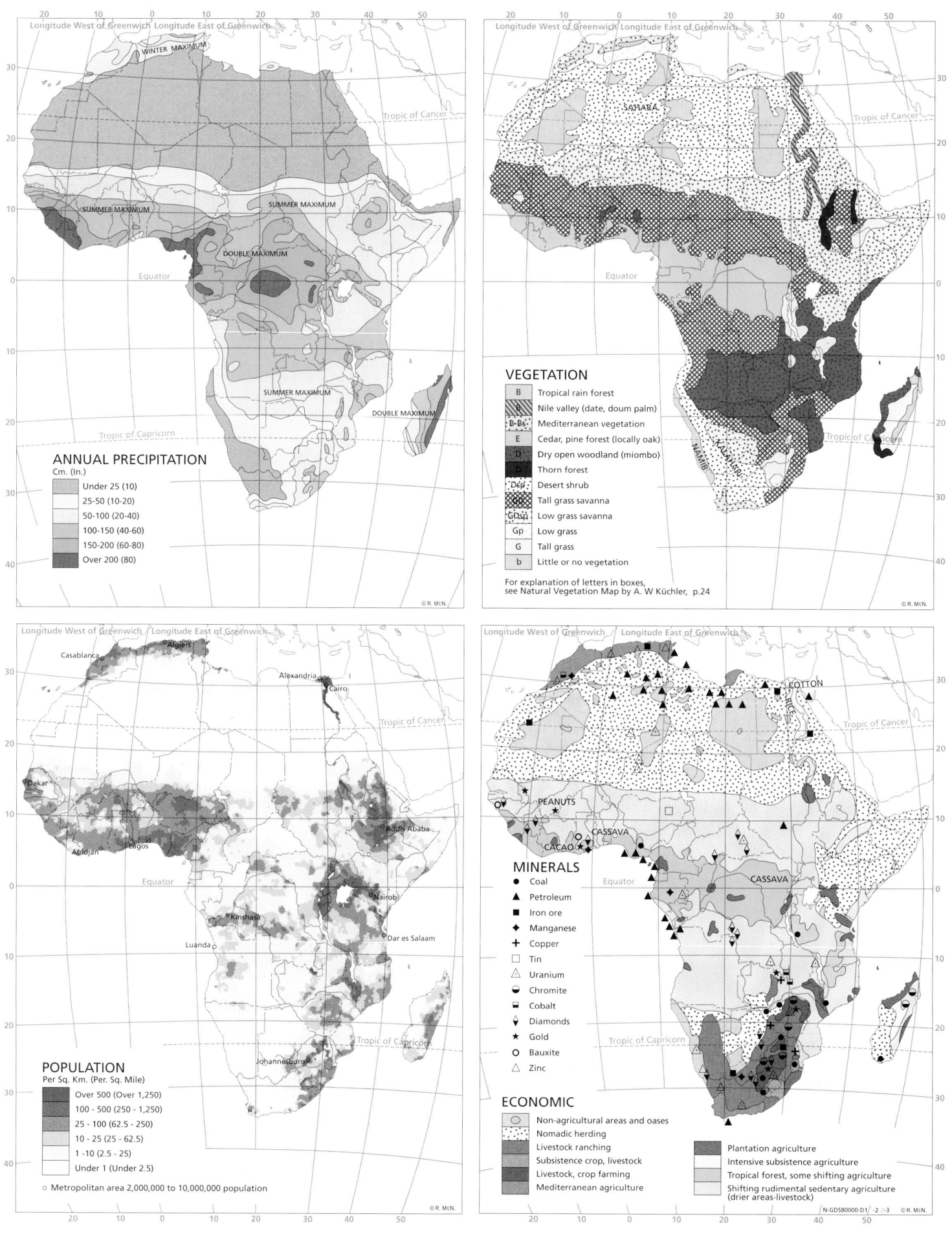

## ANNUAL PRECIPITATION
Cm. (In.)

- Under 25 (10)
- 25-50 (10-20)
- 50-100 (20-40)
- 100-150 (40-60)
- 150-200 (60-80)
- Over 200 (80)

WINTER MAXIMUM
SUMMER MAXIMUM
SUMMER MAXIMUM
DOUBLE MAXIMUM
SUMMER MAXIMUM
DOUBLE MAXIMUM

Tropic of Cancer
Equator
Tropic of Capricorn

© R. McN.

## VEGETATION

| | |
|---|---|
| B | Tropical rain forest |
| B | Nile valley (date, doum palm) |
| B–Bs | Mediterranean vegetation |
| E | Cedar, pine forest (locally oak) |
| D | Dry open woodland (miombo) |
| D | Thorn forest |
| Dsp | Desert shrub |
| | Tall grass savanna |
| GDsp | Low grass savanna |
| Gp | Low grass |
| G | Tall grass |
| b | Little or no vegetation |

For explanation of letters in boxes,
see Natural Vegetation Map by A. W Küchler, p.24

SAHARA
KALAHARI
NAMIB

© R. McN.

## POPULATION
Per Sq. Km. (Per. Sq. Mile)

- Over 500 (Over 1,250)
- 100 - 500 (250 - 1,250)
- 25 - 100 (62.5 - 250)
- 10 - 25 (25 - 62.5)
- 1 - 10 (2.5 - 25)
- Under 1 (Under 2.5)

○ Metropolitan area 2,000,000 to 10,000,000 population

Casablanca
Algiers
Alexandria
Cairo
Dakar
Abidjan
Lagos
Addis Ababa
Nairobi
Kinshasa
Luanda
Dar es Salaam
Johannesburg

© R. McN.

## MINERALS

- ● Coal
- ▲ Petroleum
- ■ Iron ore
- ◆ Manganese
- + Copper
- □ Tin
- △ Uranium
- ⬡ Chromite
- ⬠ Cobalt
- ⬧ Diamonds
- ★ Gold
- ○ Bauxite
- △ Zinc

COTTON
RICE
PEANUTS
CASSAVA
CACAO
CASSAVA

## ECONOMIC

| | |
|---|---|
| | Non-agricultural areas and oases |
| | Nomadic herding |
| | Livestock ranching |
| | Subsistence crop, livestock |
| | Livestock, crop farming |
| | Mediterranean agriculture |
| | Plantation agriculture |
| | Intensive subsistence agriculture |
| | Tropical forest, some shifting agriculture |
| | Shifting rudimental sedentary agriculture (drier areas-livestock) |

N-GDS80000-D1/ -2-:-3    © R. McN.

ATLANTIC
OCEAN

MADRID

CORSICA

ROME

İSTANBUL

BAKU

SARDINIA

SICILY

Athens

TEHRAN

Mediterranean Sea

Algiers

Tunis

MALTA

CRETE

CYPRUS

Beirut

Baghdad

Casablanca

ATLAS   MOUNTAINS

Tripoli

Banghāzī

Alexandria

SYRIAN
DESERT

Euphrates

CANARY ISLANDS

Tropic of Cancer

GRAND ERG OCCIDENTAL

GRAND ERG ORIENTAL

CAIRO

Nile

ARABIAN   DESERT

Tigris

AN NAFŪD

El Aaíun

EL DJOUF

AHAGGAR

LIBYAN
DESERT

Lake Nasser

Riyadh

Red Sea

Mecca

Tamenghest

S   A   H   A   R   A

TIBESTI

NUBIAN DESERT

ADRAR
DES IFÔGHAS

ENNEDI

Khartoum

Asmera

Tombouctou

S   U   D   A   N

Al-Fāshir

Nile

DANAKIL

Aden

Gulf of Aden

Dakar

Niger

Lake Chad

White   Nile

Berbera

Bamako

Kano

N'Djamena

Blue Nile

Freetown

Niger

Addis Ababa

Lake Volta

Lagos

Yaoundé

Bangui

Uele

Mountain Nile

Mogadishu

Abidjan

Gulf of Guinea

Ubangi

Congo

Kisangani

Equator

Lake
Victoria

Nairobi

INDIAN
OCEAN

Congo

Kasai

Luanda

Kinshasa

Lake
Tanganyika

Dar es Salaam

ATLANTIC   OCEAN

Lubumbashi

COMORO ISLANDS

Lake Nyasa

Lusaka

Zambezi

Blantyre

Moçambique

Harare

MADAGASCAR

Mozambique Channel

Antananarivo

NAMIB DESERT

Tropic of Capricorn

Windhoek

KALAHARI
DESERT

Limpopo

Orange

Johannesburg

Orange

Durban

Cape
Town

INDIAN   OCEAN

| | |
|---|---|
| ■ | Urban |
| | Cropland |
| | Cropland & Woodland |
| | Cropland & Grazing Land |
| | Grassland, Grazing Land |
| | Forest, Woodland |
| | Swamp, Marshland |
| | Shrub, Sparse Grass, Wasteland |
| | Barren Land |
| • | Oasis |

A-580000-36   -2  3-13

Scale 1:36,000,000; one inch to 570 miles.   Lambert Azimuthal Equal-Area Projection

0   100   200   400   600   800 Miles

0   150   300   600   900   1200 Kilometers

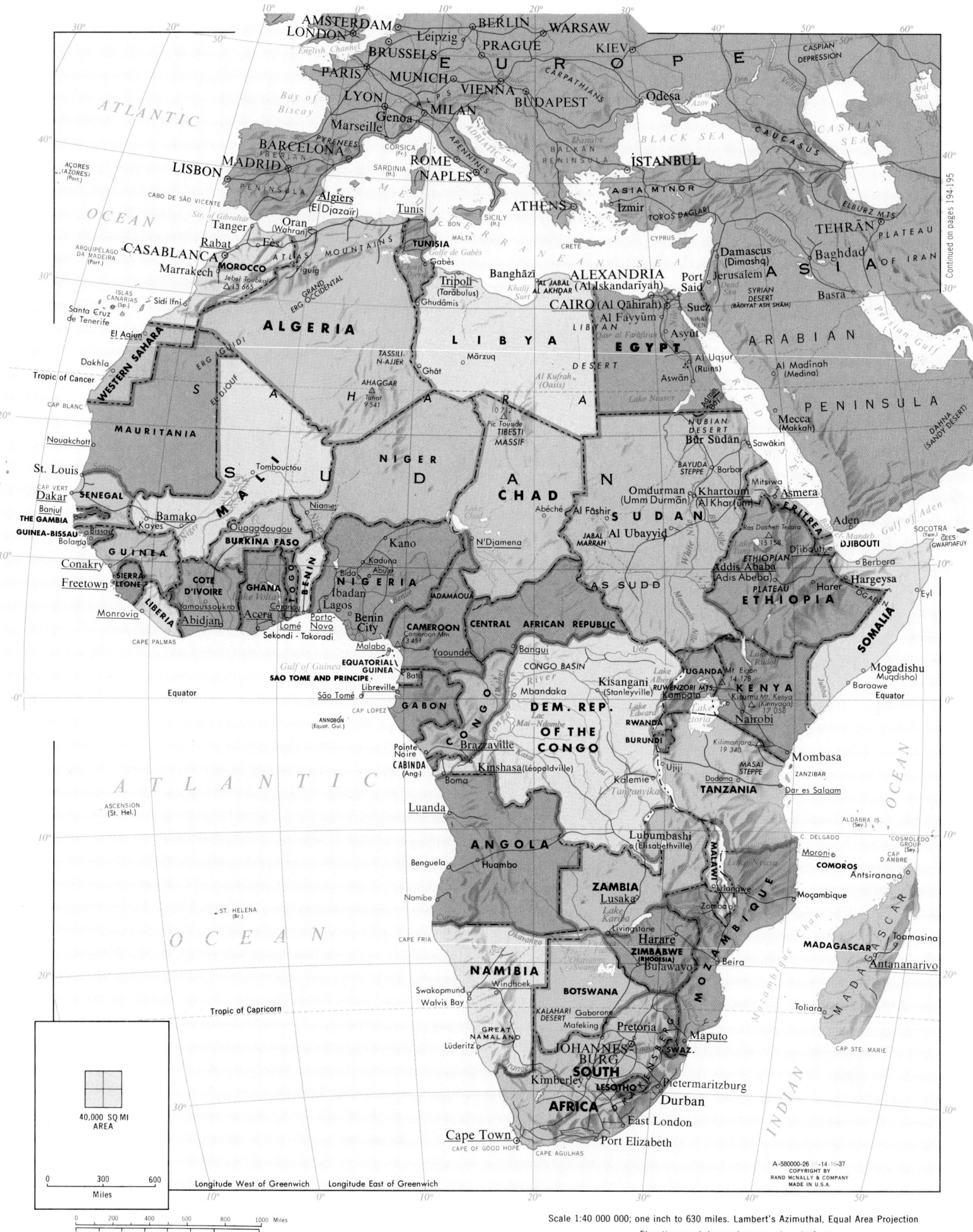

Scale 1:40 000 000; one inch to 630 miles. Lambert's Azimuthal, Equal Area Projection

Elevations and depressions are given in feet.

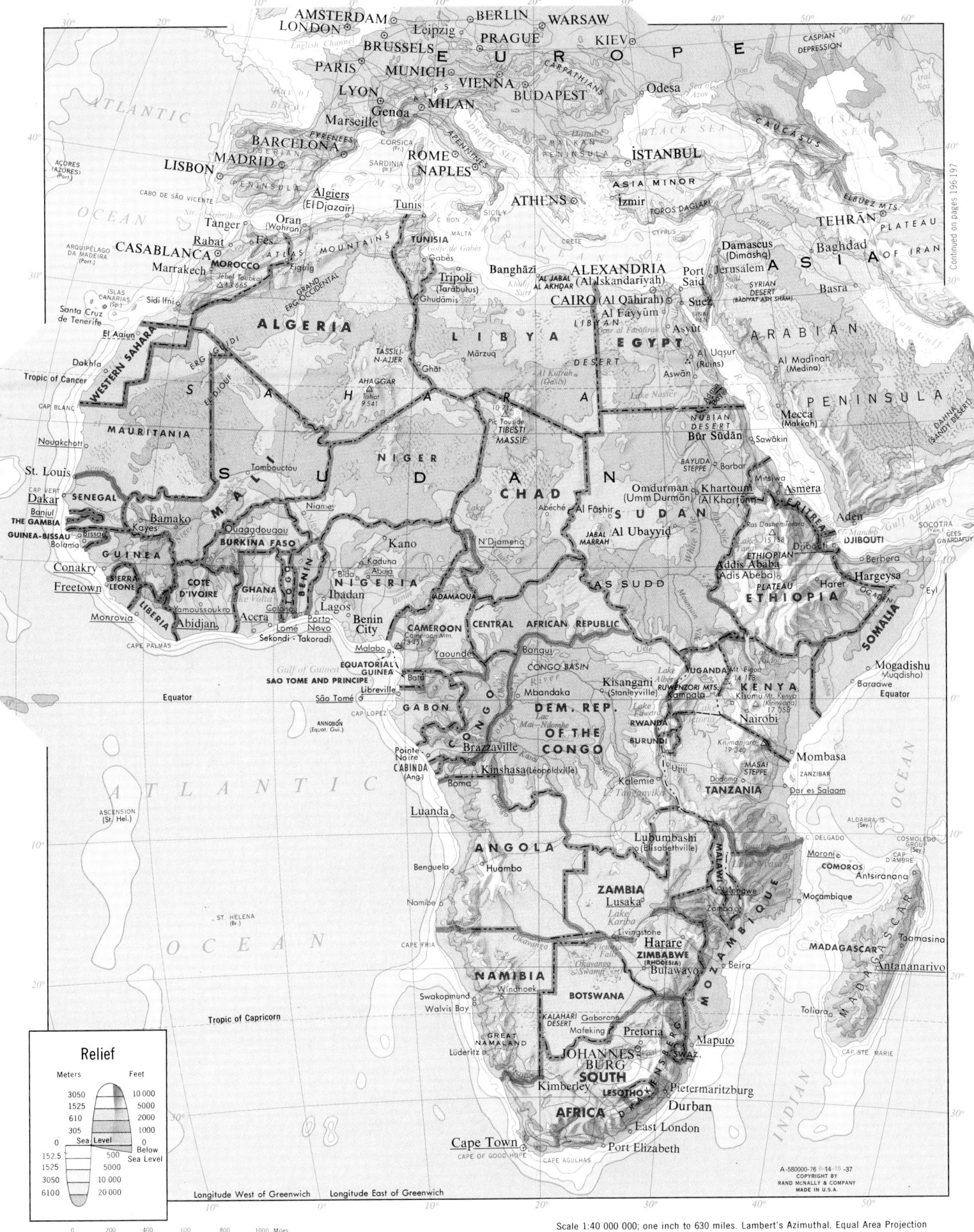

Continued on pages 196-197

Relief

| Meters | | Feet |
|---|---|---|
| 3050 | | 10 000 |
| 1525 | | 5000 |
| 610 | | 2000 |
| 305 | | 1000 |
| 0 | Sea Level | 0 |
| 152.5 | | 500 Below |
| 1525 | | 5000 Sea Level |
| 3050 | | 10 000 |
| 6100 | | 20 000 |

Longitude West of Greenwich    Longitude East of Greenwich

0    200    400    600    800    1000 Miles
0    400    800    1200    1600 Kilometers

Scale 1:40 000 000; one inch to 630 miles. Lambert's Azimuthal, Equal Area Projection
Elevations and depressions are given in feet.

A-580000-76 8-14-16 -37
COPYRIGHT BY
RAND McNALLY & COMPANY
MADE IN U.S.A.

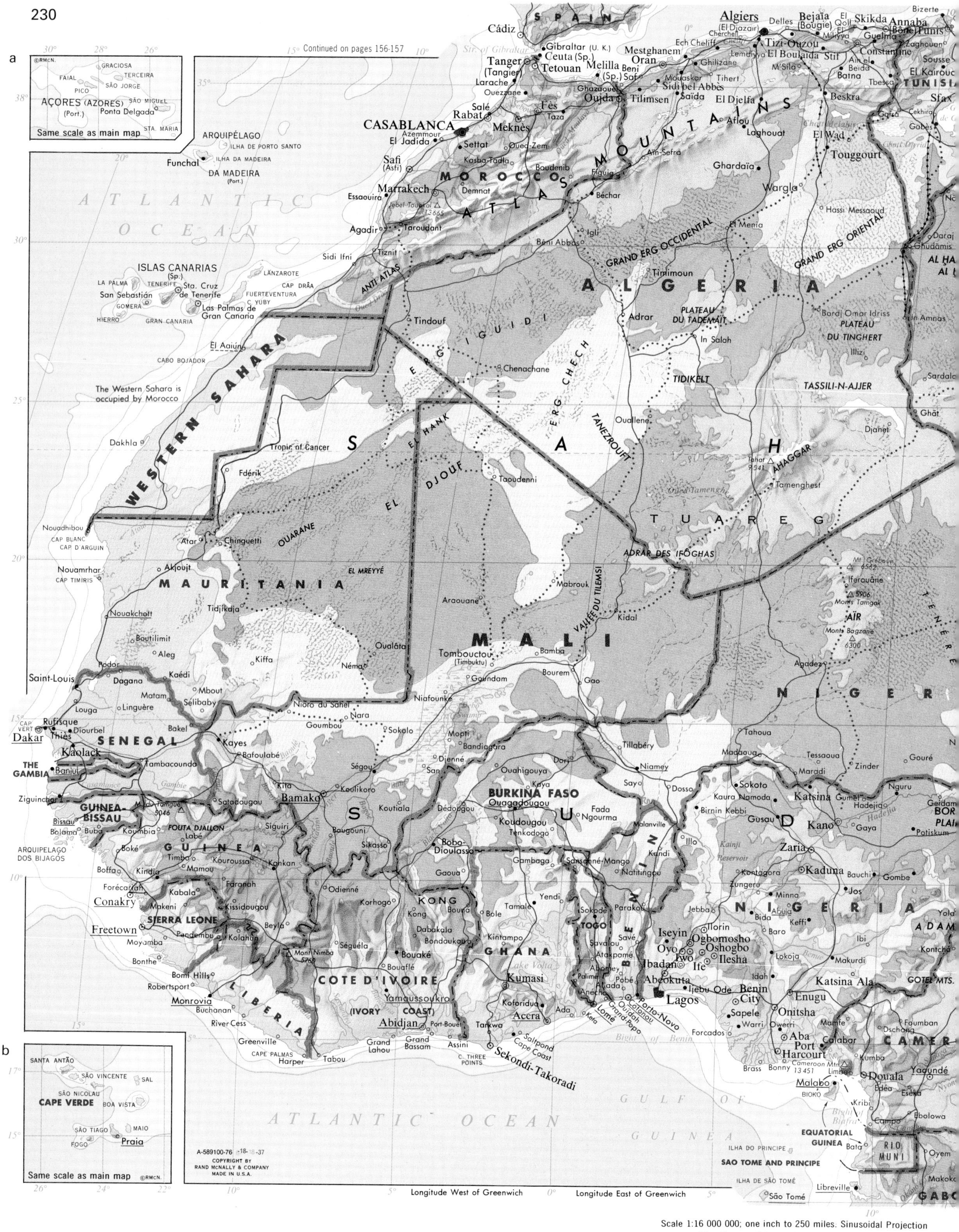

230

Continued on pages 156-157

**a**

30° 28° 26°
FAIAL GRACIOSA
TERCEIRA
PICO SÃO JORGE
38° AÇORES (AZORES) SÃO MIGUEL
(Port.) Ponta Delgada
STA. MARIA
Same scale as main map

**SPAIN**
Cádiz
Gibraltar (U.K.)
Tanger (Tangier) Ceuta (Sp.)
Larache Tetouan Melilla (Sp.)
Salé Fes
35° Rabat Meknès Taza
CASABLANCA
El Jadida Azemmour Settat Oued-Zem Kasba-Tadla
Safi (Asfi) Boudenib
Marrakech MOROCCO Demnat
Essaouira Jebel Toubkal 13665
Agadir Taroudant

Algiers (El Djazair) Delles Bejaïa (Bougie)
Cherchell Tizi-Ouzou Skikda Annaba (Bône) Tunis
Ech Cheliff Lemdiya El Boulaïda Stif Constantine TUNISIA
Mestghanem Oran Ghilizane Aïn Beida Sousse
Mouaskar Sidi bel Abbès M'Sila Batna El Kairouan Sfax
Oujda Tilimsen Saïda El Djelfa Beskra
Aïn-Sefra Laghouat Touggourt El Wad
Figuig Béchar Ghardaïa Wargla Hassi Messaoud
GRAND ERG OCCIDENTAL El Menia GRAND ERG ORIENTAL
Timimoun ALGERIA Bordj Omar Idriss In Amnas
Adrar PLATEAU DU TADEMAÏT PLATEAU DU TINGHERT
In Salah TIDIKELT Illizi
TASSILI-N-AJJER

ISLAS CANARIAS (Sp.)
LA PALMA TENERIFE LANZAROTE
San Sebastián Sta. Cruz de Tenerife FUERTEVENTURA
GOMERA Las Palmas de Gran Canaria C. YUBY
HIERRO GRAN CANARIA
30° CABO BOJADOR
Sidi Ifni Tiznit ANTI ATLAS
ATLAS MOUNTAINS

WESTERN SAHARA
El Aaiún
Tindouf Chenachane
ERG IGUIDI ERG CHECH
Tropic of Cancer
Dakhla Fdérik S A EL HANK Taoudenni
EL DJOUF TANEZROUFT Ouallene
Ahaggar 9541 Djanet
Tamanghest Ghat

Nouadhibou CAP BLANC CAP D'ARGUIN
Atar Chinguetti OUARANE
Nouamghar CAP TIMIRIS EL MREYYÉ
MAURITANIA Mabrouk T U A R E G
Nouakchott Tidjikdja ADRAR DES IFÔGHAS
Boutilimit Araouane Kidal AÏR
Aleg Kiffa Oualâta Tombouctou (Timbuktu) Agadez
Saint-Louis Rosso Kaédi Néma Bamba
Dagana Matam Mbout Niafounké Gao NIGER
Louga Linguère Sélibaby Nioro du Sahel M A L I Bourem Tahoua
Diourbel Bakel Nara Goundam
Dakar Thiès SENEGAL Kayes Goumbou Sokolo Mopti
Kaolack Tambacounda Bafoulabé Diénné Bandiagara Niamey Madaoua Tessaoua Zinder
THE GAMBIA Banjul Kita Ségou San Ouahigouya Dori Tillabéry Maradi Gouré
Ziguinchor GUINEA-BISSAU Bamako Koulikoro Say Dosso Birnin Kebbi Katsina Hadejia
Bissau FOUTA DJALON Siguiri Koutiala BURKINA FASO Sokoto Gusau Kano
Bolama Labé Sikasso Dédougou Ouagadougou Fada Ngourma Gaya Zaria Potiskum
Buba Boké Bafing Bougouni Bobo-Dioulasso Koudougou Malanville Kontagora Kaduna Bauchi Gombe
GUINEA Timbo Kankan Gaoua Gambaga Illo Zungeru Minna Jos
Boffa Kindia Mamou Odienné Kandi Jebba NIGERIA Abuja
Conakry Forécariah Faranah Korhogo Kong Tamale Yendi Parakou Baro Keffi
Makeni Kissidougou Boundoukou Bole Bida Yola
SIERRA LEONE Beyla KONG Dabakala Kintampo Sokode Savalou Ilorin Ibi
Freetown Pendembu Kolahun Séguéla Bouaké GHANA Atakpamé Ogbomosho Oyo Oshogbo Lokoja Makurdi
Moyamba Mont Nimba 5748 Bouaflé Abomey Iseyin Ife Ilesha ADAMAWA
Bonthe Bomi Hills COTE D'IVOIRE Kumasi Palimé TOGO Oyo Ibadan Abeokuta Idah Katsina Ala GOTEL MTS.
Robertsport (IVORY COAST) Yamoussoukro Koforidua Ijebu-Ode Benin City Enugu
Monrovia LIBERIA Abidjan Accra Lome Porto-Novo Onitsha Mamfe
Buchanan River Cess Grand Bassam Lagos Sapele Warri Aba Calabar CAMEROON
Greenville Grand Lahou C. THREE POINTS Cotonou Owerri Port Harcourt Kumba
CAPE PALMAS Harper Tabou Sekondi-Takoradi Cameroon Mtn 13451 Douala
Brass Bonny Malabo BIOKO Edéa Yaoundé
EQUATORIAL GUINEA Bata RIO MUNI
SAO TOME AND PRINCIPE ILHA DO PRINCIPE Kribi
ILHA DE SÃO TOMÉ Libreville GABON
São Tomé

**b**
SANTO ANTÃO
SÃO VICENTE SAL
SÃO NICOLAU
CAPE VERDE BOA VISTA
SÃO TIAGO MAIO
FOGO Praia
Same scale as main map

ATLANTIC OCEAN
GULF OF GUINEA
Bight of Benin
Bight of Biafra

A-589100-76 18-18-37
COPYRIGHT BY RAND MCNALLY & COMPANY MADE IN U.S.A.

Longitude West of Greenwich / Longitude East of Greenwich

Scale 1:16 000 000; one inch to 250 miles. Sinusoidal Projection
Elevations and depressions are given in feet

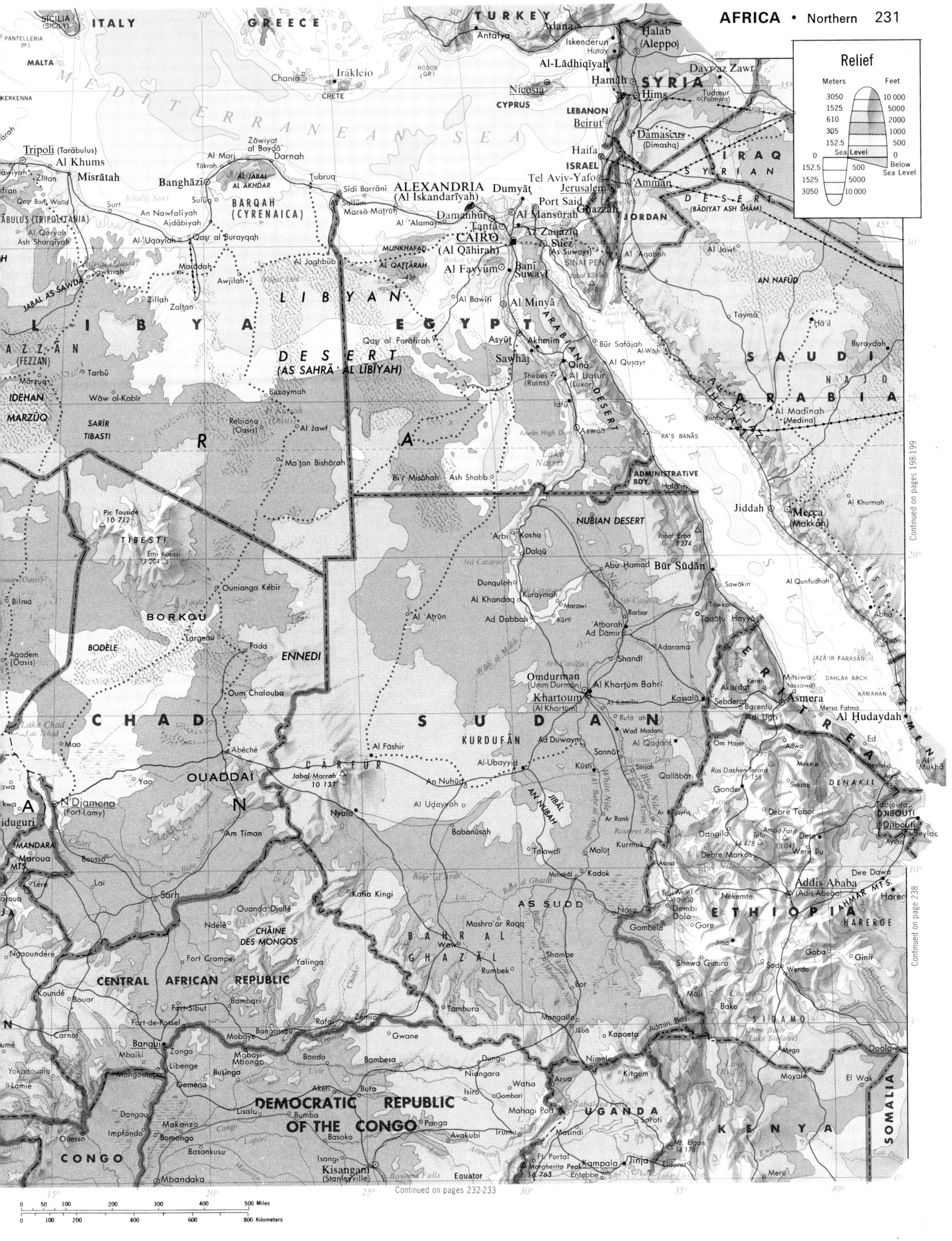

Relief

| Meters | Feet |
|--------|------|
| 3050 | 10 000 |
| 1525 | 5000 |
| 610 | 2000 |
| 305 | 1000 |
| 152.5 | 500 |
| 0 Sea Level | 0 |
| 152.5 | 500 Below |
| 1525 | 5000 Sea Level |
| 3050 | 10 000 |

SICILIA (SICILY)    ITALY    GREECE    TURKEY

PANTELLERIA (It.)

MALTA

KERKENNA

Antalya    Adana    Iskenderun    Hatay    Ḩalab (Aleppo)

Irákleio    Chania    RODOS (GR)    CRETE    Nicosia    Al-Lādhiqīyah    Ḩamāh    SYRIA    Dayr az Zawr

CYPRUS    Ḩimṣ    Tudmur (Palmyra)

LEBANON    Beirut

M E D I T E R R A N E A N   S E A    Damascus (Dimashq)    IRAQ

Tripoli (Ṭarābulus)    Al Khums    Haifa    Amman    S Y R I A N

Zlitan    Misrātah    Tel Aviv-Yafo    Jerusalem    JORDAN    D E S E R T    (BĀDIYAT ASH SHĀM)

Zāwiyat al Bayḍā    Darnah    ISRAEL    Ghazzah    Al 'Aqabah    Al Jawf

Qaṣr Banī Walīd    Al Marj    Tūkrah    AL JABAL AL AKHDAR    Tubruq    Sīdī Barrānī    ALEXANDRIA (Al Iskandarīyah)    Dumyāṭ    Port Said    AN NAFŪD

ṬABULUS (TRIPOLITANIA)    Banghāzī    As Sallūm    Marsā Maṭrūḩ    Damanhūr    Al Manṣūrah    Suez (As Suways)    SAUDI

Al Qaryah Ash Sharqīyah    Sulūq    BARQAH (CYRENAICA)    Al 'Alamayn    Tanṭā    Al Zaqāzīq    SINAI PEN.    Jabal Kātrīnā    Taymā'    Ḩā'il    Buraydah

Al-'Uqaylah    Ajdābiyā    Qaṣr al Burayqah    An Nawfalīyah    CAIRO (Al Qāhirah)    Bani Suwayf    Al Fayyūm    8668    ARABIA

Surt    Khalīj Surt    MUNKHAFAD    Birket Qārūn    NAJD

Sawknah    Marādah    Awjilah    Al Jaghbūb    AL QATTĀRAH -436    Al Bawīṭī    Al Minyā    Al Madīnah (Medina)    Yanbu'

JABAL AS SAWDA    Zillah    Zaltan    LIBYAN    Asyūṭ    Akhmīm    Būr Safājah    Al-Wajh

IDEHAN    Tarbū    DESERT (AS SAHRĀ' AL LĪBĪYAH)    Sawhāj    Qinā    Al Quṣayr    THE HIJĀZ

MARZŪQ    Wāw al-Kabīr    Thebes (Ruins)    Al Uqṣur (Luxor)    Idfū    Aswān High Dam    Aswān    Jiddah    Mecca (Makkah)    Al Khurmah

SARĪR TIBESTI    Rebiana (Oasis)    Al Jawf    Ma'tan Bishārah    Bīr Misāḩah    Ash Shabb    Lake Nasser    ADMINISTRATIVE BDY.    Ḩalā'ib    Al Qunfudhah

FEZZĀN    Pic Touside 10 712    RA'S BĀNĀS

AZZĀN (FEZZAN)    Buzaymah    NUBIAN DESERT    'Arbi    Kosha    Jabal Erba 7 274

TIBESTI    Emi Koussi 11 204    Dalqū    Jiddah    Abha

Bilma    Ounianga Kébir    Dunqulah    Abu Hamad    Būr Sūdān    Sawākin    Qizan

BORKOU    Fada    Kuraymah    Marawi    JAZĀ'IR FARASĀN

BODÉLE    Largeau    ENNEDI    Al 'Aṭrūn    Al Khandaq    Barbar    Tawkar    Taqāṭu Ḩayya    DAHLAK ARCH.    KAMARAN

Agadem (Oasis)    Ad Dabbah    Kūrtī    Atbarah    Ad Dāmir    Adarama    Akordat    Mitsiwa    Al Ḩudaydah

Oum Chalouba    Shandī    Mersa Fatma

C H A D    Omdurman (Umm Durmān)    Al Khartūm Baḥrī    Kassalā    Sebderat    ERITREA    Asmera

Lake Chad Lac Tchad    Mao    Khartoum (Al Khartūm)    As Sudd    Adi Ugrī    Al Ḩudaydah

Abéché    Al Fāshir    DĀRFŪR    Ad Duwaym    Wad Madanī    Al Qaḍārif    Om Hajer    Adwa    Ed    YEMEN

N'Djamena (Fort-Lamy)    OUADDAÏ    Jabal Marrah 10 131    KURDUFAN    Al-Ubayyid    Kūstī    Sinjah    Qallābāt    Mekele    DENAKIL    Al Mukhā

Yao    An Nuhūd    Ras Dashen Terara 5 158    Gonder    Sekota

Am Timan    Nyala    Al Uḍayyah    JIBĀL AN NUBAH    AN NĪL    Sannār    Roseires Res.    Dangila    Debre Tabor    Dire Dawa

Bousso    Babanūsah    Talawdi    Malūṭ    Asosa    Ambo Farīt 4 478    Debre Markos    DJIBOUTI

Sarh    Kafia Kingi    AS SUDD    Kurmuk    Dangila    Harer    Djibouti    Seylac

Fort Crampel    Ouanda Djallé    Mashra'ar Raqq    Nasir    Gambela    ETHIOPIA    HARERGE

CHÂINE DES MONGOS    BAHR AL GHAZĀL    Shambe    Gore    Addis Ababa (Ādīs Ābeba)    AHMAR MTS.    Aysha

CENTRAL AFRICAN REPUBLIC    Ndélé    Wāw    Rumbek    Dembi Dolo    Jima    Goba    Ginir

Koundé    Bouar    Fort-Sibut    Yalinga    Bor    Maji    Shewa Gimira    SIDAMO

Ngaoundéré    Bambari    Tambura    Mongalla    Jūba    Sodo    Wendo    Doolow

CONGO    Carnot    Fort-de-Rossel    Rafai    Zémio    Juba    Kapoeta    Admin. Bdy.    Bako    Mega

Bangui    Mobaye    Gwane    Nimule    Lake Rudolf    Moyale    El Wak    SOMALIA

Yokadouma    Zonga    Mbaïki    Bangassou    Bondo    Dungu    Arua    Kitgum    Moyale

Lomie    Libenge    Gemena    Bambesa    Niangara    Soroti    Mt Elgon 4 178    Meru

Lisala    Businga    Akeli    Isiro    Gombari    UGANDA    Kampala    KENYA

DEMOCRATIC REPUBLIC OF THE CONGO    Bumba    Panga    Avakubi    Buta    Irumu    Masindi    Jinja    Eldoret

Bomongo    Basoko    Margherita Peak 16 763    Ft Portal    Entebbe    Equator

Mbandaka    Isangi    Kisangani (Stanleyville)    Bovuma Falls    Lake Victoria

Continued on pages 198·199

Continued on page 238

Continued on pages 232-233

0  50  100    200    300    400    500 Miles
0    100    200    400    600    800 Kilometers

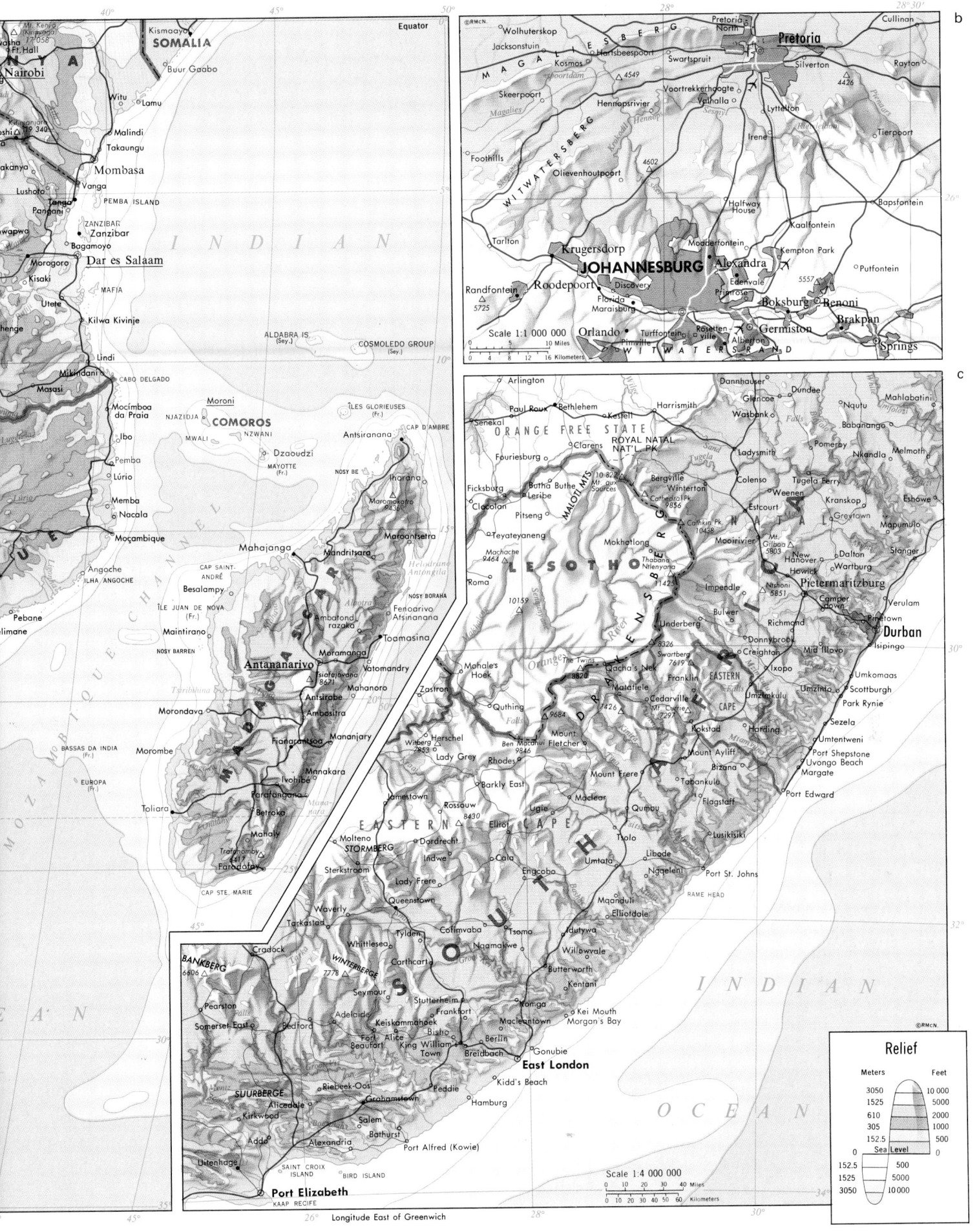

b

**Scale 1:1 000 000**

Witwatersrand map inset labels:
Wolhuterskop, Jacksonstuin, Pretoria North, Pretoria, Cullinan, Magaliesberg, Hartbeespoort, Kosmos, Skeerpoort, Swartspruit, Silverton, Rayton, Henropsrivier, Valhalla, Lyttelton, Tierpoort, Foothills, Olievenhoutpoort, Voortrekkerhoogte, Irene, Halfway House, Bapsfontein, Tarlton, Krugersdorp, Modderfontein, Kaalfontein, Kempton Park, Putfontein, Randfontein, Roodepoort, **JOHANNESBURG**, Discovery, Alexandra, Edenvale, Florida, Maraisburg, Primrose, Boksburg, Renoni, Brakpan, Orlando, Turffontein, Rosetten-ville, Germiston, Springs, Pimville, Alberton, **WITWATERSRAND**

c

Inset map of Madagascar, Comoros, and Southern Africa labels:
SOMALIA, Nairobi, Kismaayo, Buur Gaabo, Witu, Lamu, Takaungu, Mombasa, Vanga, PEMBA ISLAND, Tanga, Pangani, Zanzibar, Bagamoyo, Dar es Salaam, Morogoro, Kisaki, MAFIA, Utete, Kilwa Kivinje, Lindi, Mikindani, CABO DELGADO, Masasi, Mocímboa da Praia, COMOROS, Moroni, NJAZIDJA, MWALI, NZWANI, MAYOTTE, ÎLES GLORIEUSES, CAP D'AMBRE, Antsiranana, Ibo, Pemba, NOSY BE, Iharana, Memba, Nacala, Maromokotra, Moçambique, Mahajanga, Mandritsara, Maroantsetra, Angoche, ILHA ANGOCHE, CAP SAINT-ANDRÉ, Helodrano Antongila, NOSY BORAHA, Besalampy, Fenoarivo Atsinanana, Pebane, ÎLE JUAN DE NOVA, Ambatond-razaka, Atsinanana, Quelimane, MADAGASCAR, Maintirano, Toamasina, NOSY BARREN, Moramanga, Antananarivo, Tsiafajavona, Vatomandry, NORONO, Morondava, Antsirabe, Mahanoro, Zastron, Ambositra, Mananjary, MOZAMBIQUE CHANNEL, Fianarantsoa, Manakara, BASSAS DA INDIA, Ivohibe, EUROPA, Parafangana, Toliara, Betroko, Mahaly, Trafonomby, Faradofay, CAP STE. MARIE

Southern Africa mainland labels:
Arlington, Paul Roux, Bethlehem, Harrismith, Dannhauser, Dundee, Nqutu, Mahlabatini, Senekal, Kestell, Glencoe, Wasbank, Babanango, ORANGE FREE STATE, ROYAL NATAL NAT'L PK, Ladysmith, Pomeroy, Nkandla, Melmoth, Fouriesburg, Clarens, Ficksburg, Butha Buthe, Bergville, Winterton, Colenso, Tugela Ferry, Kranskop, Eshowe, Clocolan, Leribe, Cathedral Pk, Weenen, Greytown, Pitseng, MALOTI MTS, Estcourt, Mapumulo, Teyateyaneng, Mooirivier, New Hanover, Dalton, Wartburg, Stanger, Machache, Mokhotlong, Thabana Ntlenyana, LESOTHO, Howick, Roma, Impendle, Bulwer, Pietermaritzburg, Verulam, Underberg, Richmond, Camperdown, Pinetown, Durban, Mohale's Hoek, The Twins, Swartberg, Creighton, Isipingo, Qacha's Nek, Franklin, Donnybrook, Mid Illovo, Matatiele, EASTERN CAPE, Ixopo, Quthing, Cedarville, Umzimkulu, Scottburgh, Mt. Currie, Kokstad, Harding, Park Rynie, Mount Fletcher, Sezela, Ben Macdhui, Umtentweni, Witberg, Herschel, Rhodes, Mount Ayliff, Port Shepstone, Lady Grey, Bizana, Uvongo Beach, Mount Frere, Tabankulu, Margate, Barkly East, Flagstaff, Port Edward, Jamestown, Rossouw, Ugie, Maclear, Qumbu, Lusikisiki, Molteno, Dordrecht, Elliot, Tsolo, Libode, Ngqeleni, Port St. Johns, Sterkstroom, Indwe, Cala, Engcobo, Umtata, Mqanduli, RAME HEAD, Waverly, Lady Frere, Queenstown, Elliotdale, Tarkastad, Cofimvaba, Tsomo, Idutywa, STORMBERG, Tylden, Ngamakwe, Willowvale, Whittlesea, Carthcart, Butterworth, SOUTH, Cradock, WINTERBERG, Seymour, Stutterheim, Kentani, BANKBERG, Frankfort, Nxuba, Kei Mouth, Pearston, Adelaide, Keiskammahoek, Macleantown, Morgan's Bay, Somerset East, Bedford, Fort Beaufort, Fort Alice, Bisho, Berlin, Breidbach, Gonubie, King William's Town, East London, SUURBERG, Riebeek-Oos, Peddie, Kidd's Beach, Alicedale, Grahamstown, Hamburg, Kirkwood, Addo, Salem, Bathurst, Alexandria, Port Alfred (Kowie), Uitenhage, SAINT CROIX ISLAND, BIRD ISLAND, Port Elizabeth, KAAP RECIFE, INDIAN OCEAN

**Scale 1:4 000 000**

**Relief**

| Meters | Feet |
|--------|------|
| 3050 | 10 000 |
| 1525 | 5000 |
| 610 | 2000 |
| 305 | 1000 |
| 152.5 | 500 |
| Sea Level | 0 |
| 152.5 | 500 |
| 1525 | 5000 |
| 3050 | 10 000 |

Longitude East of Greenwich

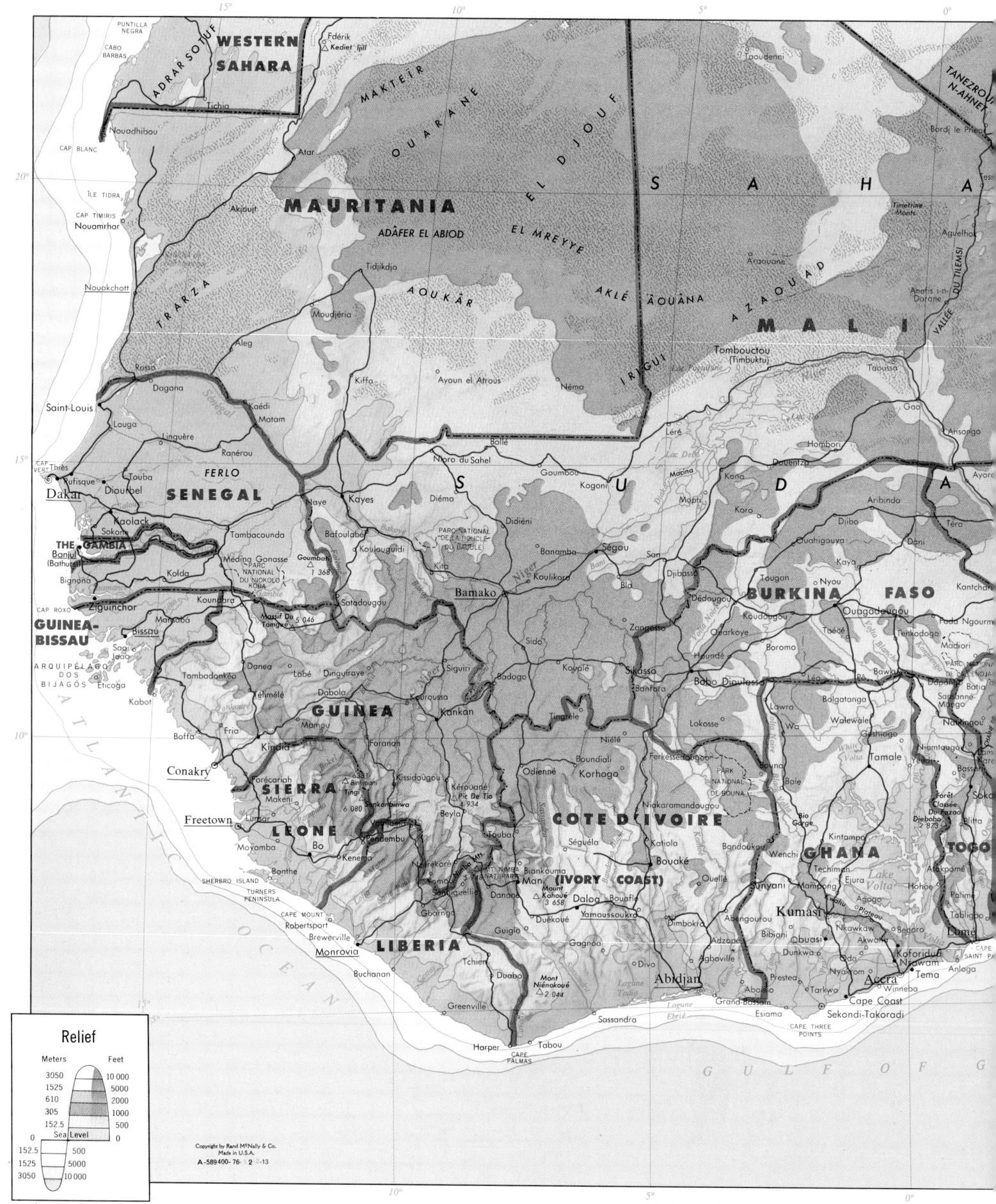

CAP BLANC

PUNTILLA
NEGRA

CABO
BARBAS

ADRAR SOTIUF

WESTERN
SAHARA

Fdérik
Kediet Ijill

Nouadhibou

ÎLE TIDRA

CAP TIMIRIS

Nouamrhar

Atar

MAKTEÏR

OUARANE

EL DJOUF

SAHA

Taoudenni

Bordj le Prieur

TANEZROU
N.-AHNET

20°

MAURITANIA

ADÂFER EL ABIOD

EL MREYYE

Timetrine
Monts

Aguelhok

Nouakchott

Tidjikdja

AOUKÂR

AKLÉ ÂOUÂNA

Araouane

AZAOUAD

M A L I

Anefis i-n-
Darane

VALLÉE DU TILEMSI

TRARZA

Moudjéria

Aleg

IRIGUI

Lac Faguibine

Tombouctou
(Timbuktu)

Taoussa

Rosso

Dagana

Kiffa

Ayoun el Atrous

Néma

Gao

Ansongo

Saint-Louis

Louga

Kaédi
Matam

Diéma

Balé

Nioro du Sahel

Léré

Lac Débo

Hombori

15°

CAP VERT Thiès

Rufisque

Touba

Diourbel

Linguère

Ranérou

FERLO

Naye

Kayes

Goumbou

Kogoni

Macina

Kona

Douentza

S          U          D          A

Dakar

Kaolack

Sokone

SENEGAL

Diéma

Didiéni

Ségou

Moptu

Karo

Aribinda

Djibo

Téra

Dori

THE GAMBIA

Banjul
(Bathurst)

Tambacounda

Bafoulabé

Koulouguidi

PARC NATIONAL
DE LA BOUCLE
DU BAOULÉ

Banamba

San

Djibasso

Dédougou

BURKINA          FASO

Ouahigouya

Kaya

Kantch

Bignona

Kolda

MÉDINA GONASSE

PARC
NATIONAL
DU NIOKOLO
KOBA

Goumbati
1 368

Kita

Koulikoro

Bla

Zangasso

Koudougou

Ouagadougou

Toécé

Fada Ngourma

Tenkodogo

Madiori

CAP ROXO

Ziguinchor

Mansaba

Koundara

Satadougou

Bamako

Sido

Sikasso

Houndé

Boromo

Oaarkoye

Bobo Dioulasso

Léo

Bawk

PARC NATIONAL
DE LA PENDJARI

GUINEA-
BISSAU

Bissau

Saoi
Joaa

ARQUIPÉLAGO
DOS
BIJAGÓS

Tombadonkéa

Eticoga

Kabot

Danéa

Téhmélé

Labé

Dingyiraye

Siguiri

Badogo

Kayalé

Banfora

Lokosse

Wa

Lawra

Balgatanga

Gishiego

Niamtougou

Naringou

Dabola

Kouroussa

Kankan

Tingréla

Niélé

Boundiali

Bole

White Volta

Tamale

Bassin

MASSIF DU
TAMGUÉ 5 046

Mamou

Fria

GUINEA

Farandh

Odienné

Korhogo

PARK
NATIONAL
DE BOUNA

10°

Boffa

Kindia

Forécariah

Birimian
Tingi 3 311

Kissidougou

Kérouané
Pic De Tio
1 934

Séguéla

Katiola

Bondoukou

Bio
Gorge

Kintampo

Wenchi

GHANA

TOGO

FORÊT
CLASSÉE
DU FAZAO
2 873

Blitta

Conakry

SIERRA

Makeni

Sankanbiriwa
6 080

Beyla

COTE D'IVOIRE

Bouaké

Techiman

Ejura

Lake Volta

Hohoe

Soka

LEONE

Lumba

Bo

Touba

Mano

(IVORY COAST)

Ouellé

Sunyani

Mampong

Agogo

Palime

Freetown

Moyamba

Kenema

Biankouma

Mont
Kahoué
3 658

Daloa

Bouaflé

Dimbokra

Abengourou

Kumasi

Nkawkaw

Begoro

Lome

SHERBRO ISLAND

Bonthe

Njarekoré

MTS NIMBA
NAT. PARK

Man

Danané

Duékoué

Yamoussoukro

Adzopé

Bibiani

Obuasi

Dunkwa

Oda

Nyakrom

Akwatia

Koforidua

Nsawam

TURNERS
PENINSULA

Gbarnga

Guiglo

Gagnoa

Agboville

Prestea

Tarkwa

Accra

Tema

CAP SAINT PA

CAPE MOUNT

Robertsport

Tchien

Duabo

Mont
Niénokoué
2 044

Divo

Aboisso

Winneba

Anloga

Brewerville

LIBERIA

Abidjan

Grand-Bassam

Esiama

Cape Coast

Monrovia

Buchanan

Lagune
Tado

Lagune
Ebrié

Sassandra

CAPE THREE
POINTS

Sekondi-Takoradi

15°

Greenville

Tabou

Harper

CAPE
PALMAS

GULF OF G

ATLANTIC          OCEAN

Relief

| Meters | | Feet |
|---|---|---|
| 3050 | | 10 000 |
| 1525 | | 5000 |
| 610 | | 2000 |
| 305 | | 1000 |
| 152.5 | | 500 |
| 0 | Sea Level | 0 |
| 152.5 | | 500 |
| 1525 | | 5000 |
| 3050 | | 10 000 |

Scale 1:10,000,000; one inch to 160 miles. Lambert Azimuthal Equal Area Projection
Elevations and depressions are given in feet.

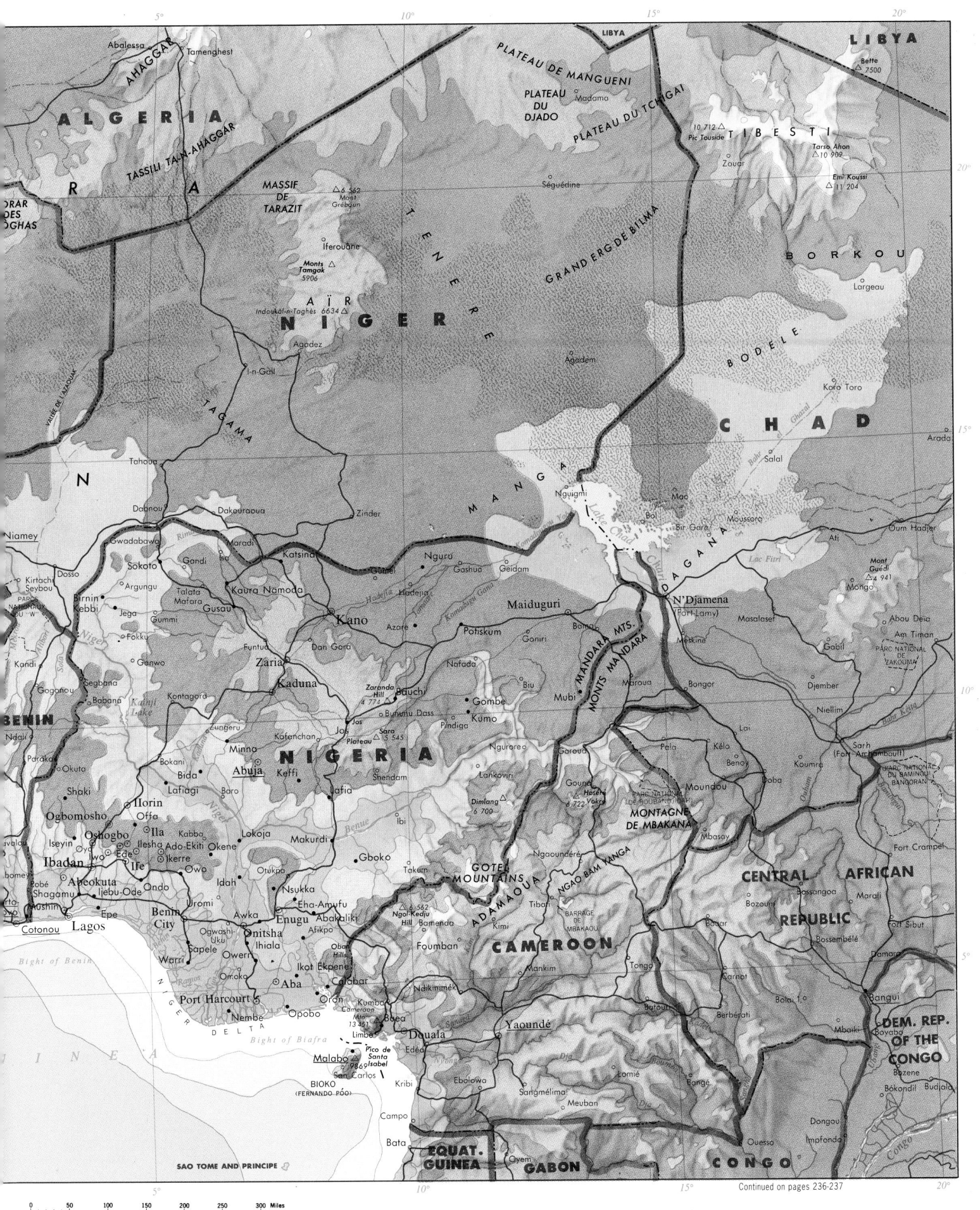

Continued on pages 236-237

Continued on pages 234-235

NIGERIA

• Opobo

Bight of Biafra

Cameroon Mtn.
13 451 △

Douala

Bata

Buea

Edéa

• Yaoundé

CAMEROON

Malabo

San Carlos

BIOKO
(FERNANDO PÓO)

EQUATORIAL GUINEA

SAO TOME AND PRINCIPE

PRÍNCIPE

CABO SAN JUAN

ISLA DE CORISCO

São Tomé
SÃO TOMÉ

Libreville

Kango

Ebolowa

Campo

Kribi

Sangmélima

Meuban

Lomié

Bangé

Doumé

Batouri

Berbérati

Bangui

MONTS DE CRISTAL

Makokou

Mekambo

Souanké

Ouesso

Impfondo

CENTRAL AFRICAN REPUBLIC

Fort de Possel

Boali

Mbaiki

Mongoumba

Boyabo

Bosobolo

Mobaye

Yakoma

Kongbo

Bangassou

Zemio

Gitamet

Bozene

Gemena

Businga

Bodalang

Yandongi

Bumba

Lisala

Aketi

Banalia

Isangi

Bengamisa

Kisangani
(Stanleyville)

GABON

CONGO

Port-Gentil

CAP LOPEZ

Booué

Bifoun

Lambaréné

3360 △

Koula-Moutou

Moulla

Mbinda

Franceville

Gamboma

Owando

St. François de Baundji

Djokoumatombi

Loka

Mbandaka
Coquilhatville

Bikoro

Mange

Boende

Bokungu

Ekoli

Lifanga

Simba

DEMOCRATIC REP. OF THE CONGO (ZAIRE)

Yayama

Litoko

Omboué

Petit Loango

Djambala

Mossendjo

Tchibanga

Kindanba

Mayumba

Madingo

Madingou

Sibiti

Brazzaville

Kinshasa
(Léopoldville)

Makaw

Inongo

Lac Mai-Ndombe

Monkoto

Lokolama

Ekanga

Katopa

Kiri

Dekese

Tiebo (Port-Francqui)

Domionge

Esombo

Bandundu

Masi-Manimba

Kikwit

Lusambo

Mbuji-Mayi
(Bakwanga)

Loubomo

Pointe-Noire

Tshela

Kisanfu

Mbanza-Ngungu

Popokabaka

Kikwit

Kilembe

Djokupunda

Bulunga

Tshikapa

Kananga
(Luluabourg)

Damba

Kanda-Kanda

Kabir

CABINDA
(Ang.)

Cabinda

Boma

Matadi

Nóqui

Kimvula

Kitenda

Kahemba

Chitata

PONTA DO PADRÃO

Soyo

M'banza Congo

Quimbele

Damba

Kibenga

Marimba

SERRA DO CONGO

N'zeto

Mobaia

Uíge

Quimbonge

Caluango

Sambungo

Kapanga

Kamina

N'dalatando

Caxito

Catete

Ambriz

Luanda

Kalandula

Quela

Cuilo

Kahemba

Katanga

Kangowa

PONTA DAS PALMEIRINHAS

Malanje

Cacólo

Malanga

Nasondoy

PARQUE NACIONAL DE QUICAMA

Dondo

Cambundi-Catembo

Luao

Lucano

CABO DAS TRÊS PONTAS

Porto Amboim

Mussende

Saútar

ANGOLA

PARQUE NACIONAL DA CAMEIA

Lumwand

Sumbe

Gabela

Waku Kunda

Calucinga

Coemba

Luena

Curunga

Calunda

KASHIJI PLAIN

Covelo

Wama

Kuito

Chitokoloki

Lobito

Benguela

SERRA CAMBONDA

Serra do Môco
8596 △

Coemba

Cangamba

LIUWA PLAIN

Huambo
(Nova Lisboa)

Chitembo

Chá Pungana

Mussuma

Ninda

SERRE DO CHILENGUE

Caconda

Cuando

Mongu

Caculama

SERRA DA NEVE

CABO DE SANTA MARTA

Bentiaba

Caluquembe

Cacula

Menongue

Lunga

BAROTSE PLAIN

Lubango

Namibe

PARQUE NACIONAL DO BIKUAR

Folgares

Cassinga

Mavinga

Caiundo

Catula

SILOANA PLAINS

PONTA ALBINA

Tômbua

Chiange

Caconda

Nangweshi

PONTA DA MARCA

PARQUE NACIONAL DO IONA

Baía dos Tigres

Cahama

Cuangar

Oncocua

Cuamato

CAPRIVI STRIP

Foz do Cunene

Ruacaná

Melunga

NAMIBIA

Cuangar

BOTS.

CHOBE NAT'L PARK

Sambusu

Shakawe

ATLANTIC OCEAN

## Relief

| Meters | | Feet |
|--------|--|------|
| 3050 | | 10 000 |
| 1525 | | 5000 |
| 610 | | 2000 |
| 305 | | 1000 |
| 152.5 | | 500 |
| 0 | Sea Level | 0 |
| 152.5 | | 500 |
| 1525 | | 5000 |
| 3050 | | 10 000 |

Scale 1:10,000,000; one inch to 160 miles. Lambert Azimuthal Equal Area Projection
Elevations and depressions are given in feet.

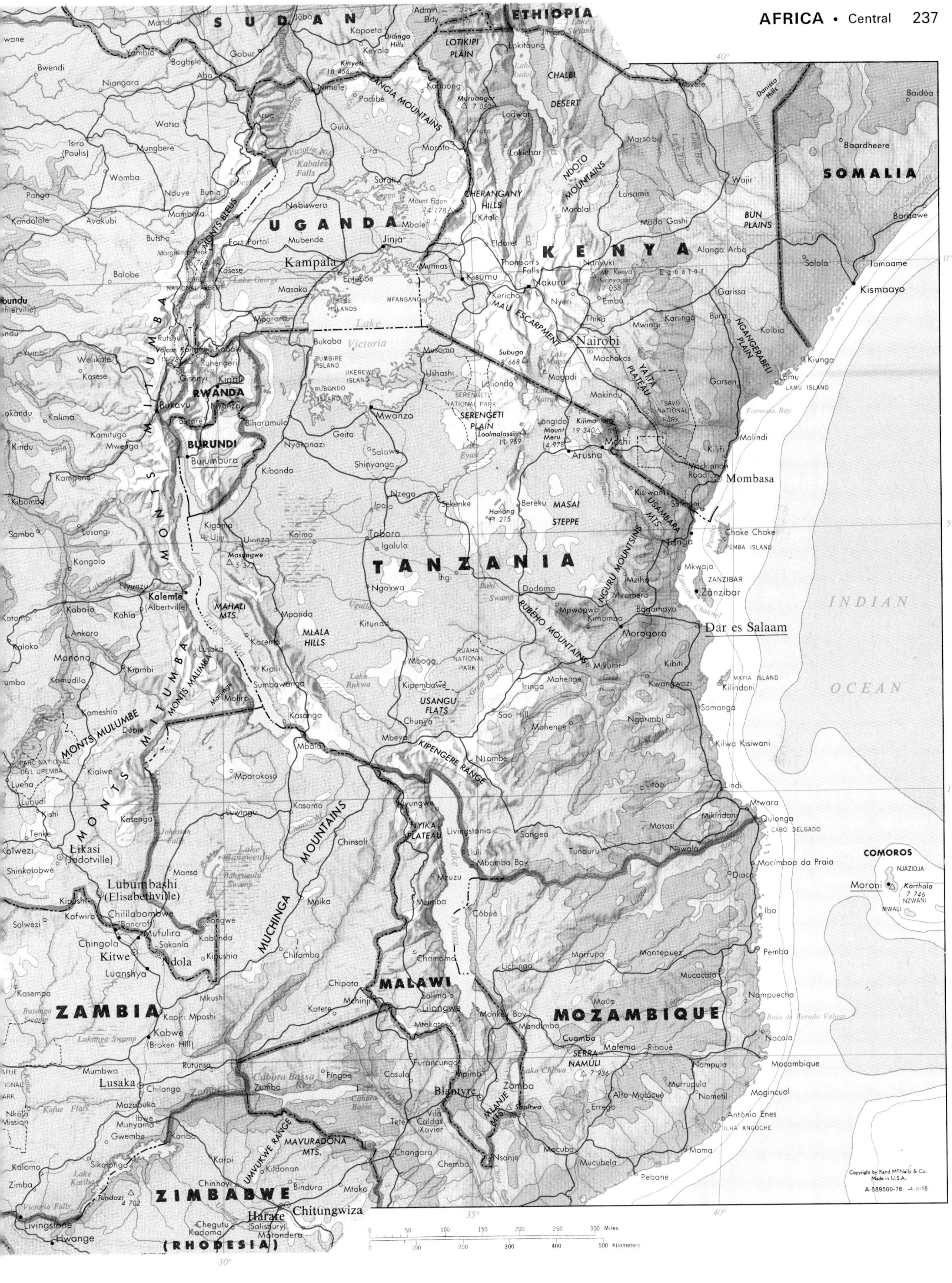

SUDAN
ETHIOPIA
SOMALIA
UGANDA
KENYA
RWANDA
BURUNDI
TANZANIA
ZAMBIA
MALAWI
MOZAMBIQUE
COMOROS
ZIMBABWE
(RHODESIA)

INDIAN OCEAN

LOTIKIPI PLAIN
CHALBI DESERT
CHERANGANY HILLS
NDOTO MOUNTAINS
BUN PLAINS
MAU ESCARPMENT
YATTA PLATEAU
TSAVO NATIONAL PARK
NGANGERABELI PLAIN
SERENGETI NATIONAL PARK
SERENGETI PLAIN
MASAI STEPPE
MAHALI MTS.
MLALA HILLS
RUAHA NATIONAL PARK
USANGU FLATS
NGURU MOUNTAINS
RUBEHO MOUNTAINS
USAMBARA MTS.
KIPENGERE RANGE
NYIKA PLATEAU
MUCHINGA MOUNTAINS
MONTS MITUMBA
MONTS MALIMBA
MONTS MULUMBE
PARC NATIONAL DE L'UPEMBA
UMVUKWE RANGE
MAVURADONA MTS.
SERRA NAMULI
MLANJE MTS.

Maridi Jūbā Kapoeta Admin Bdy
Kampala Entebbe Jinja Mbale
Nairobi Machakos Magadi Makindu
Mombasa Zanzibar Dar es Salaam
Dodoma Morogoro
Tabora Igalula Ngowwa
Mwanza Musoma Arusha Moshi
Lubumbashi (Elisabethville)
Kitwe Ndola Luanshya
Lusaka Kabwe (Broken Hill)
Lilongwe Blantyre Zomba
Harare (Salisbury) Chitungwiza
Livingstone Hwange

Mt. Kenya (Kirinyaga) 17 058
Kilimanjaro 19 340
Mount Meru 14 978
Mount Elgon 14 178
Margherita Peak
Karthala 7 746

Scale
0 50 100 150 200 250 300 Miles
0 100 200 300 400 500 Kilometers

Copyright by Rand McNally & Co.
Made in U.S.A.
A-589500-76 -4-6-16

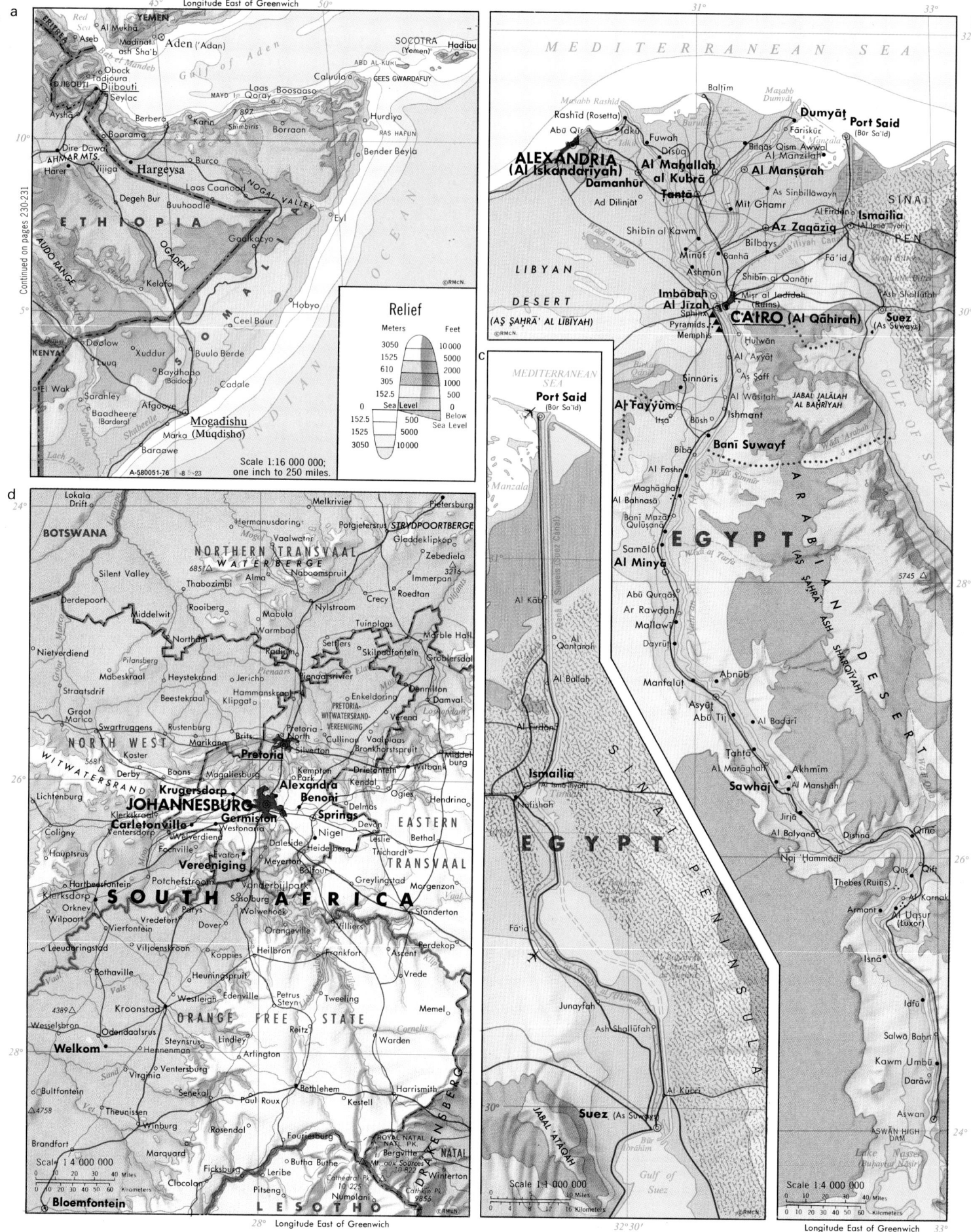

**a**

45° Longitude East of Greenwich 50°

Red Sea
YEMEN
Al Mukha
Madinat ash Sha'b    Aden ('Adan)
ERITREA
Aseb
SOCOTRA (Yemen)
Hadibu
ABD AL KURI
GEES GWARDAFUY
Gulf of Aden
Obock
Tadjoura
DJIBOUTI
Djibouti
Seylac
Berbera
Karin
Laas Qoray
Hurdiyo
RAS HAFUN
MAYD
7 897
Shimbiris
Borraan
Bender Beyla
Aysha
Dire Dawa
AHMAR MTS.
Harer
Jijiga
Hargeysa
Burco
Laas Caanood
NOGAL VALLEY
Degeh Bur
Buuhoodle
Eyl
ETHIOPIA
OGADEN
Gaalkacyo
Kelafo
INDIAN OCEAN
Hobyo
KENYA
Doolow
Luuq
Xuddur
Baydhabo (Baidoa)
Ceel Buur
Buulo Berde
Cadale
El Wak
Saranley
Baraawe
Baadheere (Bardera)
Afgooye
Mogadishu
Marka (Muqdisho)
Numolani
Baraawe

**Relief**

| Meters | | Feet |
|---|---|---|
| 3050 | | 10 000 |
| 1525 | | 5000 |
| 610 | | 2000 |
| 305 | | 1000 |
| 152.5 | | 500 |
| 0 | Sea Level | 0 |
| 152.5 | | Below Sea Level |
| 1525 | | 500 |
| 3050 | | 5000 |
|  | | 10 000 |

Scale 1:16 000 000;
one inch to 250 miles.
A-580051-76  -8 5-23

Continued on pages 230-231

**b**

31°    33°
32°
MEDITERRANEAN SEA

Masabb Rashid
Baltim
Masabb Dumyat
Rashid (Rosetta)
Abu Qir
Idku
Fuwah
Fariskur
Dumyat
Port Said (Bur Sa'id)
Burullus
ALEXANDRIA (Al Iskandariyah)
Idku
Disuq
Bilqas Qism Awwal
Al Manzilah
Al Mahallah al Kubra
As Sinbillawayn
Damanhur
Ad Dilinjat
Tanta
Mit Ghamr
Al Mansurah
Al Firdan
Ismailia (Al Isma'iliyah)
SINAI PEN.
Shibin al Kawm
Az Zaqaziq
Bilbays
Fa'id
LIBYAN
Minuf
Banha
Isma'iliyah Canal
Ashmun
Shibin al Qanatir
Ash Shallufah
DESERT
Imbabah
Misr al Jadidah (Ruins)
Al Jizah
Suez (As Suways)
(AS SAHRA' AL LIBIYAH)
Pyramids
CAIRO (Al Qahirah)
Memphis
Hulwan
Al 'Ayyat
Birkat Qarun
Sinnuris
Aş Şaff
Al Fayyum
Itsa
Al Wasitah
JABAL JALALAH AL BAHRIYAH
Bush
Bani Suwayf
Biba
Wadi 'Arabah
Al Fashn
Maghaghah
Wadi Sannur
Al Bahnasa
Bani Mazar
Qulusana
E G Y P T
Samalut
Al Minya
5745
Abu Qurqas
Ar Rawdah
Mallawi
Dayrut
Manfalut
Abnub
Asyut
Abu Tij
Al Badari
Tahta
Al Maraghah
Akhmim
Sawhaj
Al Manshah
Jirja
Al Balyana
Dishna
Naj' Hammadi
Thebes (Ruins)
Qus
Qift
Armant
Uqsur (Luxor)
Al Karnak
Isna
Idfu
Salwa Bahri
Kawm Umbu
Daraw
ASWAN HIGH DAM
Aswan
Lake Nasser (Buhayrat Nasir)

28°
ARABIAN DESERT (AS SAHRA' ASH SHARQIYAH)
GULF OF SUEZ
26°
24°

**c**

MEDITERRANEAN SEA
Port Said (Bur Sa'id)
Manzala
Al Kab
Al Qantarah
Al Ballah
Bahr as Suways (Suez Canal)
Al Firdan
Ismailia (Al Isma'iliyah)
Nafishah
SINAI PENINSULA
Fa'id
E G Y P T
Junayfah
Ash Shallufah
JABAL ATAQAH
Al Kubri
Suez (As Suways)
Bur Ibrahim
Gulf of Suez

Scale 1:4 000 000
0  10  20  30 Miles
0  10  20  30  40 Kilometers

32°30'
Longitude East of Greenwich

**d**

24°
Lokala Drift
Melkrivier
Pietersburg
BOTSWANA
Hermanusdoring
Potgietersrus
STRYDPOORTBERGE
Vaalwater
Gladdeklipkop
NORTHERN TRANSVAAL
WATERBERGE
Zebediela
Immerpan
685
3216
Thabazimbi
Alma
Naboomspruit
Silent Valley
Rooiberg
Crecy
Roedtan
Derdepoort
Mabula
Nylstroom
Middelwit
Warmbad
Tuinplaas
Northam
Radium
Settlers
Marble Hall
Pilansberg
Jericho
Skilpadfontein
Groblersdal
Mabeskraal
Heystekrand
Pienaars
Pienaarsrivier
Enkeldoring
Denilton
Straatsdrif
Hammanskraal
Klipgat
PRETORIA-WITWATERSRAND-VEREENIGING
Damval
NORTH WEST
Rustenburg
Brits
Pretoria North
Verena
Groot Marico
Swartruggens
Marikana
Silverton
Vadplaas
Bronkhorstspruit
Koster
568
Pretoria
Cullinan
Middelburg
Derby
Magaliesburg
Boons
Kempton Park
Witbank
Lichtenburg
Krugersdorp
JOHANNESBURG
Alexandra
Benoni
Kendal
EASTERN
Coligny
Klerkskraal
Germiston
Springs
Ogies
Hendrina
Carletonville
Westonaria
Devon
Leslie
Hauptrus
Welverdiend
Nigel
Bethal
Thichardt
Fochville
Evaton
Meyerton
TRANSVAAL
WITWATERSRAND
Vereeniging
Heidelberg
Balfour
Greylingstad
Morgenzon
SOUTH AFRICA
Vanderbijlpark
Standerton
Sasolburg
Wolwehoek
Villiers
Klerksdorp
Parys
Vredefort
Dover
Perdekop
Orkney
Vierfontein
Orangeville
Memel
Wilpoort
Koppies
Heilbron
Frankfort
Vrede
Leeudoringstad
Viljoenskroon
Ascent
ORANGE FREE STATE
Cornelis
Bothaville
Tweeling
Warden
Wesselsbron
4389
Kroonstad
Westleigh
Edenville
Reitz
Virginia
Steynsrus
Lindley
Welkom
Hennenman
Arlington
Harrismith
Bultfontein
Odendaalsrus
Ventersburg
4758
Theunissen
Senekal
Kestell
Brandfort
Winburg
Paul Roux
Bethlehem
DRAKENSBERG
NATAL
Marquard
Rosendal
Fouriesburg
ROYAL NATAL NATL. PK.
Bergville
Winterton
Bloemfontein
Ficksburg
Leribe
Clocolan
Pitseng
Butha Buthe
Cathedral Pk. 10 225
Cathkin Pk. 3056
LESOTHO

26°
28°

Scale 1:4 000 000
0  20  40 Miles
0  20  40  60 Kilometers

28° Longitude East of Greenwich

Scale 1:4 000 000
0  10  20  30 Miles
0  10  20  30  40  50  60 Kilometers
33°
Longitude East of Greenwich

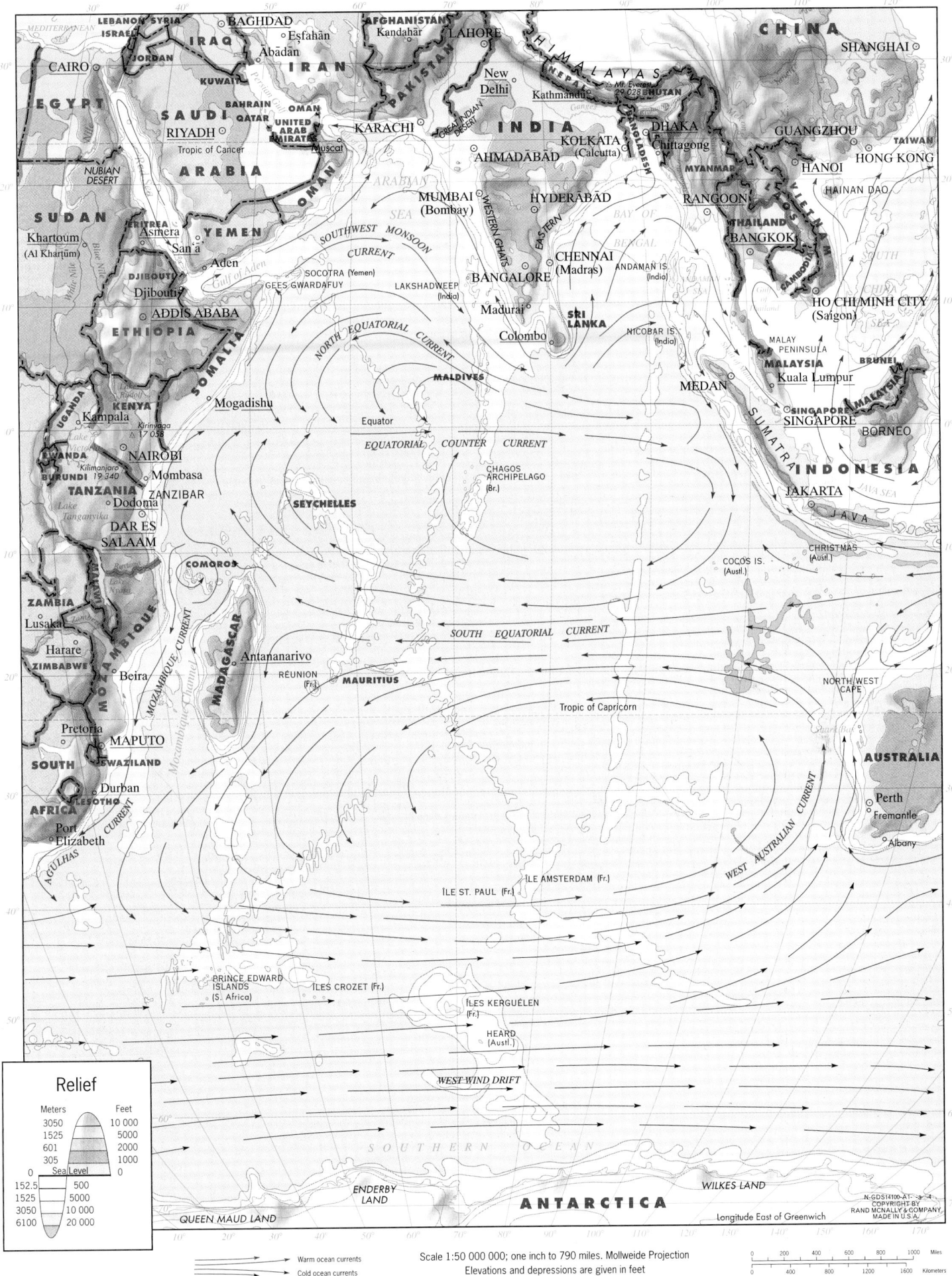

Scale 1:50 000 000; one inch to 790 miles. Mollweide Projection
Elevations and depressions are given in feet

Longitude East of Greenwich

N-GDS14100-AT-→-4
COPYRIGHT BY
RAND McNALLY & COMPANY
MADE IN U.S.A.

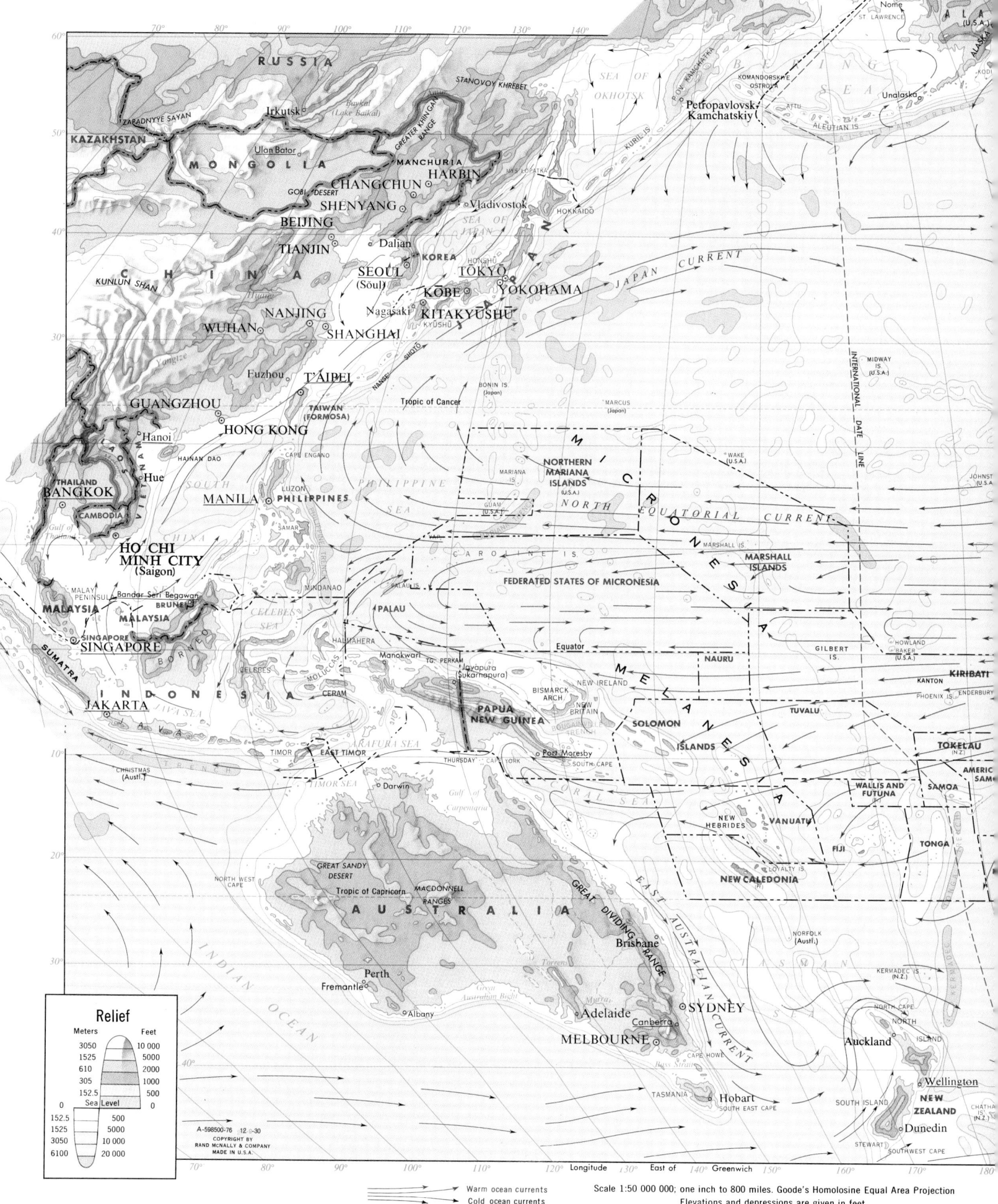

Relief

| Meters | | Feet |
|---|---|---|
| 3050 | | 10 000 |
| 1525 | | 5000 |
| 610 | | 2000 |
| 305 | | 1000 |
| 152.5 | | 500 |
| 0 | Sea Level | 0 |
| 152.5 | | 500 |
| 1525 | | 5000 |
| 3050 | | 10 000 |
| 6100 | | 20 000 |

A-598500-76  12.0-30
COPYRIGHT BY
RAND McNALLY & COMPANY
MADE IN U.S.A.

→ Warm ocean currents
→ Cold ocean currents

Scale 1:50 000 000; one inch to 800 miles. Goode's Homolosine Equal Area Projection
Elevations and depressions are given in feet

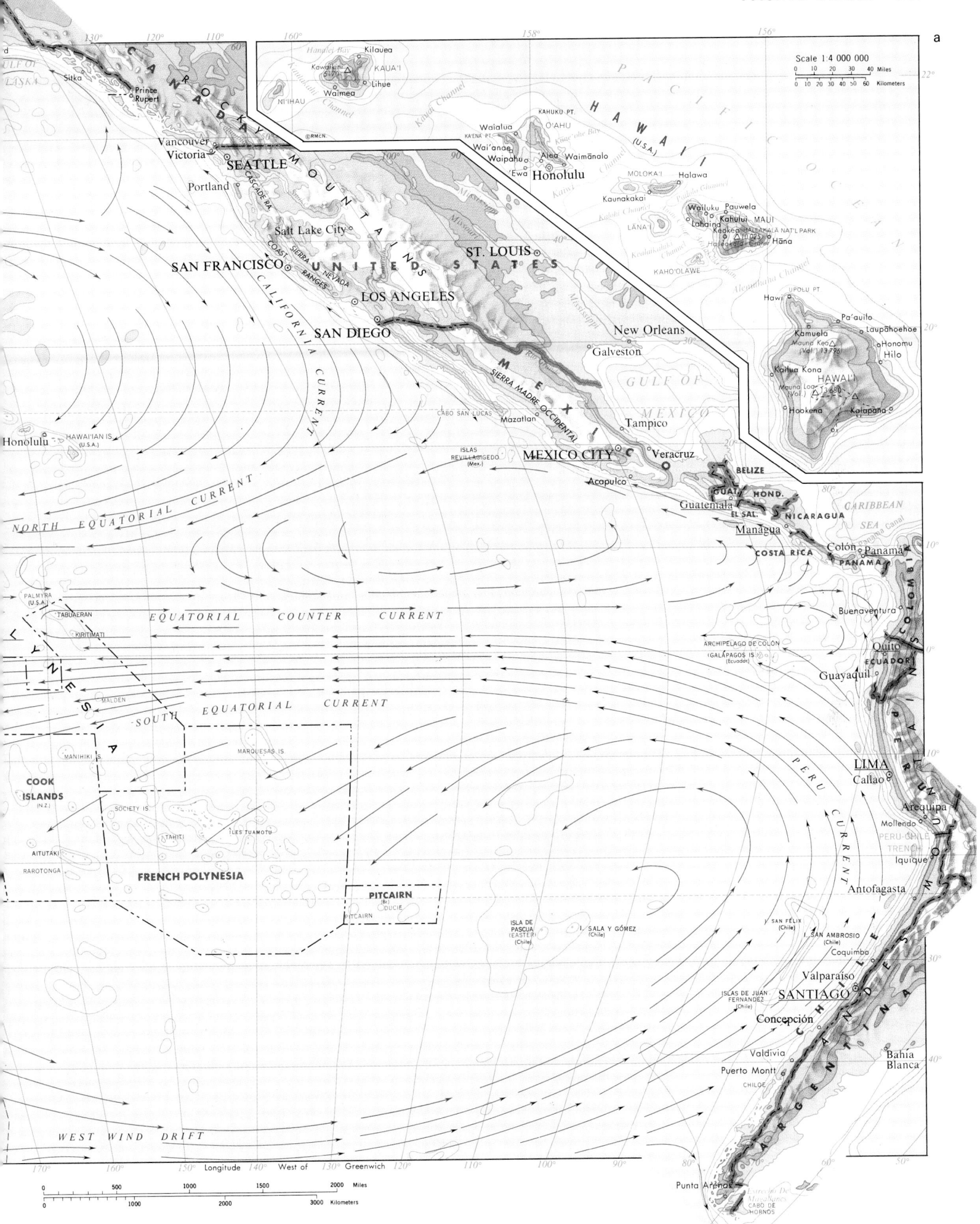

a

Scale 1:4 000 000

0   10   20   30   40 Miles

0  10 20 30 40 50 60 Kilometers

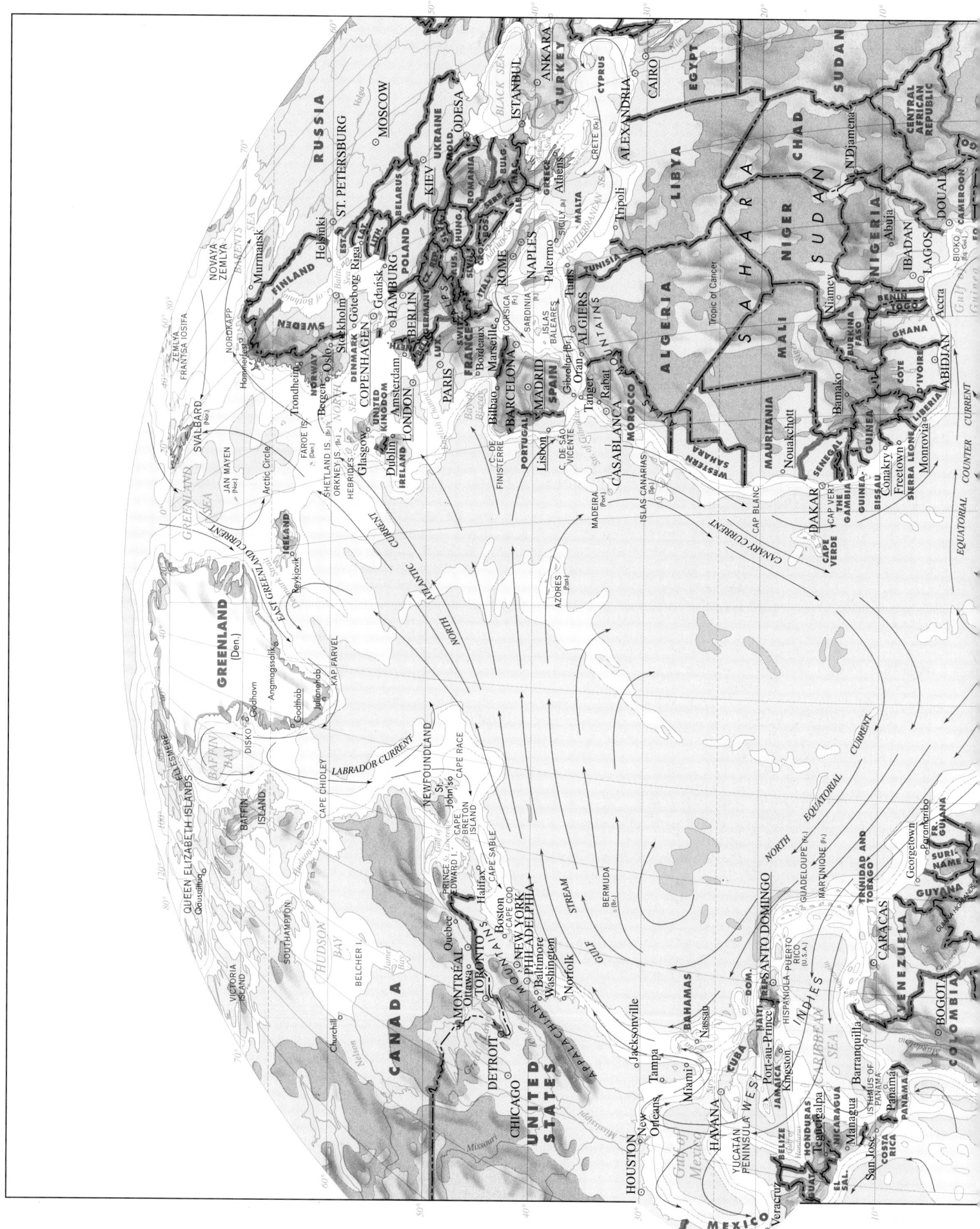

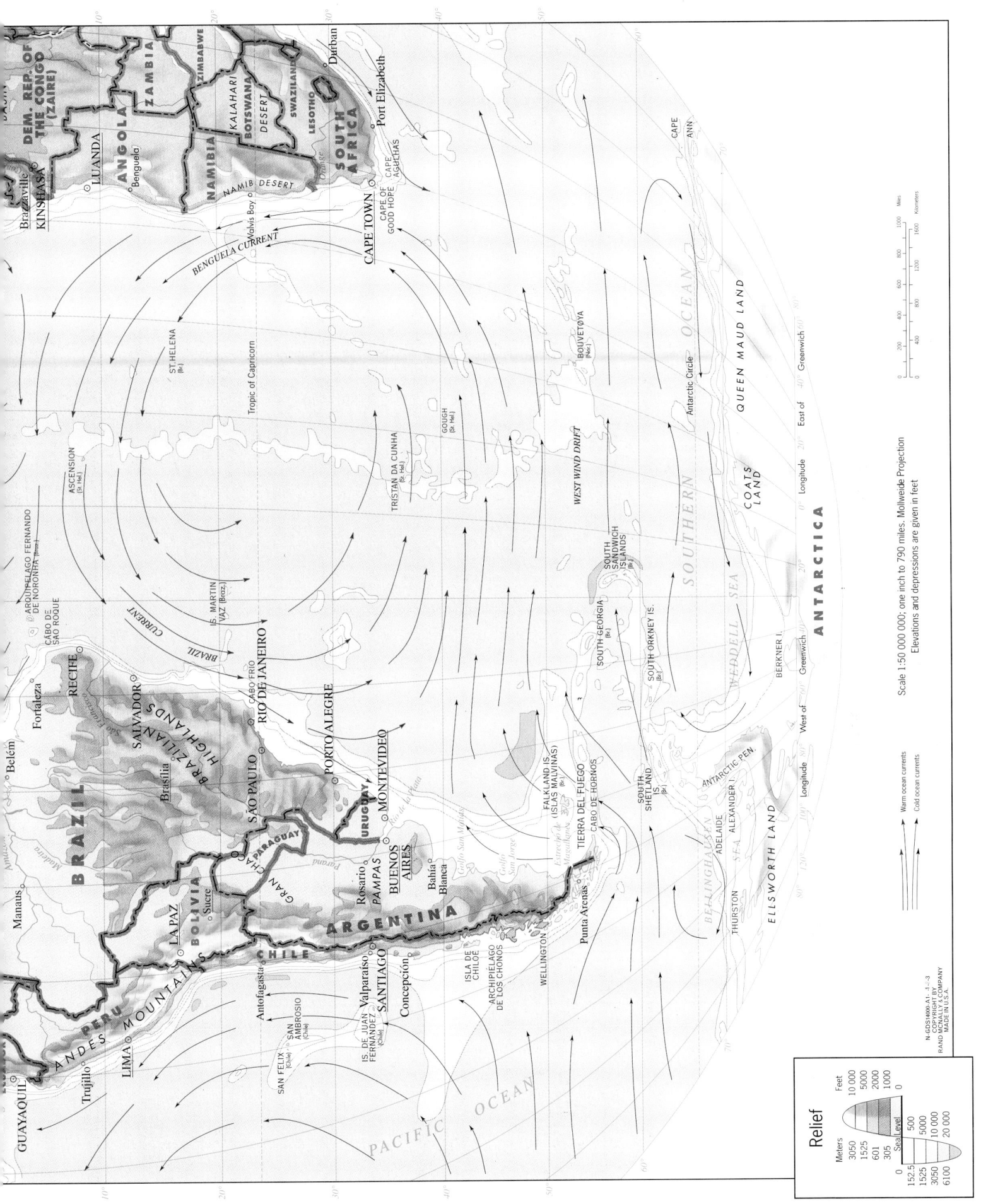

Scale 1:50 000 000; one inch to 790 miles. Mollweide Projection
Elevations and depressions are given in feet

Warm ocean currents
Cold ocean currents

Relief

| Meters | Feet |
|---|---|
| 3050 | 10 000 |
| 1525 | 5000 |
| 601 | 2000 |
| 305 | 1000 |
| 0 | Sea Level |
| 152.5 | 500 |
| 1525 | 5000 |
| 3050 | 10 000 |
| 6100 | 20 000 |

Miles
Kilometers

N-GDS4000-A1 -1--3
COPYRIGHT BY
RAND McNALLY & COMPANY
MADE IN U.S.A.

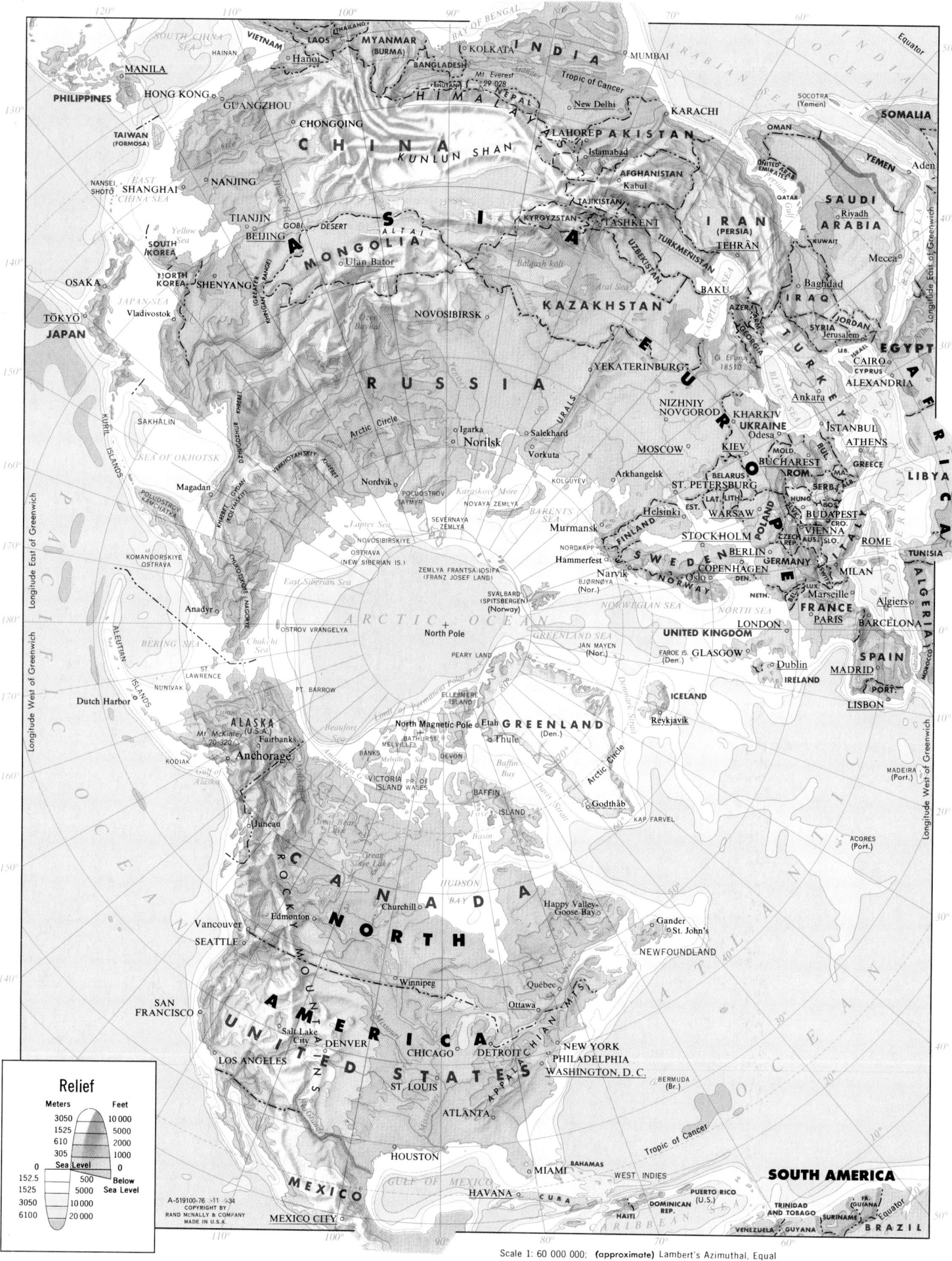

Relief

| Meters | Feet |
|---|---|
| 3050 | 10 000 |
| 1525 | 5000 |
| 610 | 2000 |
| 305 | 1000 |
| Sea Level | 0 |
| | Below |
| | Sea Level |

| 152.5 | 500 |
| 1525 | 5000 |
| 3050 | 10 000 |
| 6100 | 20 000 |

A-519100-76 -11 -534
COPYRIGHT BY
RAND MCNALLY & COMPANY
MADE IN U.S.A.

Scale 1: 60 000 000; (approximate) Lambert's Azimuthal, Equal
Area Projection    Elevations and depressions are given in feet

# WORLD POLITICAL INFORMATION TABLE

This table gives the area, population, population density, political status, capital, and predominant languages for every country in the world. The political units listed are categorized by political status in the form of government column of the table, as follows: A—independent countries; B—internally independent political entities which are under the protection of another country in matters of defense and foreign affairs; C—colonies and other dependent political units; and D—the major administrative subdivisions

of Australia, Canada, China, the United Kingdom, and the United States. For comparison, the table also includes the continents and the world. All footnotes appear at the end of the table.

The populations are estimates for January 1, 2004, made by Rand McNally on the basis of official data, United States Census Bureau estimates, and other available information. Area figures include inland water.

| REGION OR POLITICAL DIVISION | Area Sq. Mi. | Est. Pop. 1/1/04 | Pop. Per Sq. Mi. | Form of Government and Ruling Power | Capital | Predominant Languages | International Organizations |
|---|---|---|---|---|---|---|---|
| Afars and Issas see Djibouti | | | | | | | |
| Afghanistan | 251,773 | 29,205,000 | 116 | Transitional ............................ A | Kābul | Dari, Pashto, Uzbek, Turkmen | UN |
| Africa | 11,700,000 | 866,305,000 | 74 | ............................................ D | | | |
| Alabama | 52,419 | 4,515,000 | 86 | State (U.S.) ............................ D | Montgomery | English | |
| Alaska | 663,267 | 650,000 | 1.0 | State (U.S.) ............................ D | Juneau | English, indigenous | |
| Albania | 11,100 | 3,535,000 | 318 | Republic .............................. A | Tiranë | Albanian, Greek | NATO/PP, UN |
| Alberta | 255,541 | 3,215,000 | 13 | Province (Canada) .................... D | Edmonton | English | |
| Algeria | 919,595 | 33,090,000 | 36 | Republic .............................. A | Algiers (El Djazaïr) | Arabic, Berber dialects, French | AL, AU, OPEC, UN |
| American Samoa | 77 | 58,000 | 753 | Unincorporated territory (U.S.) ........ C | Pago Pago | Samoan, English | |
| Andorra | 181 | 70,000 | 387 | Parliamentary co-principality (Spanish and French) ................. B | Andorra | Catalan, Spanish (Castilian), French, Portuguese | UN |
| Angola | 481,354 | 10,875,000 | 23 | Republic .............................. A | Luanda | Portuguese, indigenous | AU, COMESA, UN |
| Anguilla | 37 | 13,000 | 351 | Overseas territory (U.K.) .............. C | The Valley | English | |
| Anhui | 53,668 | 61,215,000 | 1,141 | Province (China) ...................... D | Hefei | Chinese (Mandarin) | |
| Antarctica | 5,400,000 | (¹) | | | | | |
| Antigua and Barbuda | 171 | 68,000 | 398 | Parliamentary state ................... A | St. John's | English, local dialects | OAS, UN |
| Aomen (Macau) | 6.9 | 445,000 | 64,493 | Special administrative region (China) ........ D | Macau (Aomen) | Chinese (Cantonese), Portuguese | |
| Argentina | 1,073,519 | 38,945,000 | 36 | Republic .............................. A | Buenos Aires | Spanish, English, Italian, German, French | MERCOSUR, OAS, UN |
| Arizona | 113,998 | 5,600,000 | 49 | State (U.S.) ............................ D | Phoenix | English | |
| Arkansas | 53,179 | 2,735,000 | 51 | State (U.S.) ............................ D | Little Rock | English | |
| Armenia | 11,506 | 3,325,000 | 289 | Republic .............................. A | Yerevan | Armenian, Russian | CIS, NATO/PP, UN |
| Aruba | 75 | 71,000 | 947 | Self-governing territory (Netherlands protection) ........ B | Oranjestad | Dutch, Papiamento, English, Spanish | |
| Ascension | 34 | 1,000 | 29 | Dependency (St. Helena) .............. C | Georgetown | English | |
| Asia | 17,300,000 | 3,839,320,000 | 222 | | | | |
| Australia | 2,969,910 | 19,825,000 | 6.7 | Federal parliamentary state ........... A | Canberra | English, indigenous | ANZUS, UN |
| Australian Capital Territory | 911 | 325,000 | 357 | Territory (Australia) .................. D | Canberra | English | |
| Austria | 32,378 | 8,170,000 | 252 | Federal republic ...................... A | Vienna (Wien) | German | EU, NATO/PP, UN |
| Azerbaijan | 33,437 | 7,850,000 | 235 | Republic .............................. A | Baku (Bakı) | Azeri, Russian, Armenian | CIS, NATO/PP, UN |
| Bahamas | 5,382 | 300,000 | 56 | Parliamentary state ................... A | Nassau | English, Creole | OAS, UN |
| Bahrain | 267 | 675,000 | 2,528 | Monarchy ............................ A | Al Manāmah | Arabic, English, Persian, Urdu | AL, UN |
| Bangladesh | 55,598 | 139,875,000 | 2,516 | Republic .............................. A | Dkaha (Dacca) | Bangla, English | UN |
| Barbados | 166 | 280,000 | 1,687 | Parliamentary state ................... A | Bridgetown | English | OAS, UN |
| Beijing (Peking) | 6,487 | 14,135,000 | 2,179 | Autonomous city (China) .............. D | Beijing (Peking) | Chinese (Mandarin) | |
| Belarus | 80,155 | 10,315,000 | 129 | Republic .............................. A | Minsk | Belarussian, Russian | CIS, NATO/PP, UN |
| Belau see Palau | | | | | | | |
| Belgium | 11,787 | 10,340,000 | 877 | Constitutional monarchy .............. A | Brussels (Bruxelles) | Dutch (Flemish), French, German | EU, NATO, UN |
| Belize | 8,867 | 270,000 | 30 | Parliamentary state ................... A | Belmopan | English, Spanish, Mayan, Garifuna, Creole | OAS, UN |
| Benin | 43,484 | 7,145,000 | 164 | Republic .............................. A | Porto-Novo and Cotonou | French, Fon, Yoruba, indigenous | AU, UN |
| Bermuda | 21 | 65,000 | 3,095 | Overseas territory (U.K. protection) ........... B | Hamilton | English, Portuguese | |
| Bhutan | 17,954 | 2,160,000 | 120 | Monarchy (Indian protection) ......... B | Thimphu | Dzongkha, Tibetan and Nepalese dialects | UN |
| Bolivia | 424,165 | 8,655,000 | 20 | Republic .............................. A | La Paz and Sucre | Aymara, Quechua, Spanish | OAS, UN |
| Bosnia and Herzegovina | 19,767 | 4,000,000 | 202 | Republic .............................. A | Sarajevo | Bosnian, Serbian, Croatian | UN |
| Botswana | 224,607 | 1,570,000 | 7.0 | Republic .............................. A | Gaborone | English, Tswana | AU, UN |
| Brazil | 3,300,172 | 183,080,000 | 55 | Federal republic ...................... A | Brasília | Portuguese, Spanish, English, French | MERCOSUR, OAS, UN |
| British Columbia | 364,764 | 4,245,000 | 12 | Province (Canada) .................... D | Victoria | English | |
| British Indian Ocean Territory | 23 | (¹) | | Overseas territory (U.K.) .............. C | | English | |
| British Virgin Islands | 58 | 22,000 | 379 | Overseas territory (U.K.) .............. C | Road Town | English | |
| Brunei | 2,226 | 360,000 | 162 | Monarchy ............................ A | Bandar Seri Begawan | Malay, English, Chinese | ASEAN, UN |
| Bulgaria | 42,855 | 7,550,000 | 176 | Republic .............................. A | Sofia (Sofiya) | Bulgarian, Turkish | NATO, UN |
| Burkina Faso | 105,869 | 13,400,000 | 127 | Republic .............................. A | Ouagadougou | French, indigenous | AU, UN |
| Burma see Myanmar | | | | | | | |
| Burundi | 10,745 | 6,165,000 | 574 | Republic .............................. A | Bujumbura | French, Kirundi, Swahili | AU, COMESA, UN |
| California | 163,696 | 35,590,000 | 217 | State (U.S.) ............................ D | Sacramento | English | |
| Cambodia | 69,898 | 13,245,000 | 189 | Constitutional monarchy .............. A | Phnom Penh (Phnum Pénh) | Khmer, French, English | ASEAN, UN |
| Cameroon | 183,568 | 15,905,000 | 87 | Republic .............................. A | Yaoundé | English, French, indigenous | AU, UN |
| Canada | 3,855,103 | 32,360,000 | 8.4 | Federal parliamentary state ........... A | Ottawa | English, French, other | NAFTA, NATO, OAS, UN |
| Cape Verde | 1,557 | 415,000 | 267 | Republic .............................. A | Praia | Portuguese, Crioulo | AU, UN |
| Cayman Islands | 102 | 43,000 | 422 | Overseas territory (U.K.) .............. C | George Town | English | |
| Central African Republic | 240,536 | 3,715,000 | 15 | Republic .............................. A | Bangui | French, Sango, indigenous | AU, UN |
| Ceylon see Sri Lanka | | | | | | | |
| Chad | 495,755 | 9,395,000 | 19 | Republic .............................. A | N'Djamena | Arabic, French, indigenous | AU, UN |
| Channel Islands | 75 | 155,000 | 2,067 | Two crown dependencies (U.K. protection) ..... | | English, French | |
| Chile | 291,930 | 15,745,000 | 54 | Republic .............................. A | Santiago | Spanish | OAS, UN |
| China (excl. Taiwan) | 3,690,045 | 1,298,720,000 | 352 | Socialist republic .................... A | Beijing (Peking) | Chinese dialects | UN |
| Chongqing | 31,815 | 31,600,000 | 993 | Autonomous city (China) .............. D | Chongqing (Chungking) | Chinese (Mandarin) | |
| Christmas Island | 52 | 400 | 7.7 | External territory (Australia) ........... C | Settlement | English, Chinese, Malay | |
| Cocos (Keeling) Islands | 5.4 | 600 | 111 | External territory (Australia) ........... C | West Island | English, Cocos-Malay | |
| Colombia | 439,737 | 41,985,000 | 95 | Republic .............................. A | Bogotá | Spanish | OAS, UN |
| Colorado | 104,094 | 4,565,000 | 44 | State (U.S.) ............................ D | Denver | English | |
| Comoros (excl. Mayotte) | 863 | 640,000 | 742 | Republic .............................. A | Moroni | Arabic, French, Shikomoro | AL, AU, COMESA, UN |
| Congo | 132,047 | 2,975,000 | 23 | Republic .............................. A | Brazzaville | French, Lingala, Monokutuba, indigenous | AU, UN |
| Congo, Democratic Republic of the (Zaire) | 905,446 | 57,445,000 | 63 | Republic .............................. A | Kinshasa | French, Lingala, indigenous | AU, COMESA, UN |
| Connecticut | 5,543 | 3,495,000 | 631 | State (U.S.) ............................ D | Hartford | English | |

| REGION OR POLITICAL DIVISION | Area Sq. Mi. | Est. Pop. 1/1/04 | Pop. Per Sq. Mi. | Form of Government and Ruling Power | Capital | Predominant Languages | International Organizations |
|---|---|---|---|---|---|---|---|
| Cook Islands | 91 | 21,000 | 231 | Self-governing territory (New Zealand protection) ... B | Avarua | English, Maori | |
| Costa Rica | 19,730 | 3,925,000 | 199 | Republic ... A | San José | Spanish, English | OAS, UN |
| Cote d'Ivoire (Ivory Coast) | 124,504 | 17,145,000 | 138 | Republic ... A | Abidjan and Yamoussoukro | French, Dioula and other indigenous | AU, UN |
| Croatia | 21,829 | 4,430,000 | 203 | Republic ... A | Zagreb | Croatian | NATO/PP, UN |
| Cuba | 42,804 | 11,290,000 | 264 | Socialist republic ... A | Havana (La Habana) | Spanish | OAS, UN |
| Cyprus | 3,572 | 775,000 | 217 | Republic ... A | Nicosia | Greek, Turkish, English | EU, UN |
| Czech Republic | 30,450 | 10,250,000 | 337 | Republic ... A | Prague (Praha) | Czech | EU, NATO, UN |
| Delaware | 2,489 | 820,000 | 329 | State (U.S.) ... D | Dover | English | |
| Denmark | 16,640 | 5,405,000 | 325 | Constitutional monarchy ... A | Copenhagen (København) | Danish | EU, NATO, UN |
| District of Columbia | 68 | 565,000 | 8,309 | Federal district (U.S.) ... D | Washington | English | |
| Djibouti | 8,958 | 460,000 | 51 | Republic ... A | Djibouti | French, Arabic, Somali, Afar | AL, AU, COMESA, UN |
| Dominica | 290 | 69,000 | 238 | Republic ... A | Roseau | English, French | OAS, UN |
| Dominican Republic | 18,730 | 8,775,000 | 468 | Republic ... A | Santo Domingo | Spanish | OAS, UN |
| East Timor | 5,743 | 1,010,000 | 176 | Republic ... A | Dili | Portuguese, Tetum, Bahasa Indonesia (Malay), English | UN |
| Ecuador | 109,484 | 13,840,000 | 126 | Republic ... A | Quito | Spanish, Quechua, indigenous | OAS, UN |
| Egypt | 386,662 | 75,420,000 | 195 | Republic ... A | Cairo (Al Qāhirah) | Arabic | AL, AU, CAEU, COMESA, UN |
| Ellice Islands see Tuvalu | | | | | | | |
| El Salvador | 8,124 | 6,530,000 | 804 | Republic ... A | San Salvador | Spanish, Nahua | OAS, UN |
| England | 50,356 | 50,360,000 | 1,000 | Administrative division (U.K.) ... D | London | English | |
| Equatorial Guinea | 10,831 | 515,000 | 48 | Republic ... A | Malabo | French, Spanish, indigenous, English | AU, UN |
| Eritrea | 45,406 | 4,390,000 | 97 | Republic ... A | Asmera | Afar, Arabic, Tigre, Kunama, Tigrinya, other | AU, COMESA, UN |
| Estonia | 17,462 | 1,405,000 | 80 | Republic ... A | Tallinn | Estonian, Russian, Ukrainian, Finnish, other | EU, NATO, UN |
| Ethiopia | 426,373 | 67,210,000 | 158 | Federal republic ... A | Addis Ababa (Adis Abeba) | Amharic, Tigrinya, Orominga, Guaraginga, Somali, Arabic | AU, COMESA, UN |
| Europe | 3,800,000 | 729,330,000 | 192 | | | | |
| Falkland Islands (²) | 4,700 | 3,000 | 0.6 | Overseas territory (U.K.) ... C | Stanley | English | |
| Faroe Islands | 540 | 47,000 | 87 | Self-governing territory (Danish protection) ... B | Tórshavn | Danish, Faroese | |
| Fiji | 7,056 | 875,000 | 124 | Republic ... A | Suva | English, Fijian, Hindustani | UN |
| Finland | 130,559 | 5,210,000 | 40 | Republic ... A | Helsinki (Helsingfors) | Finnish, Swedish, Sami, Russian | EU, NATO/PP, UN |
| Florida | 65,755 | 17,070,000 | 260 | State (U.S.) ... D | Tallahassee | English | |
| France (excl. Overseas Departments) | 208,482 | 60,305,000 | 289 | Republic ... A | Paris | French | EU, NATO, UN |
| French Guiana | 32,253 | 190,000 | 5.9 | Overseas department (France) ... C | Cayenne | French | |
| French Polynesia | 1,544 | 265,000 | 172 | Overseas territory (France) ... C | Papeete | French, Tahitian | |
| Fujian | 46,332 | 35,495,000 | 766 | Province (China) ... D | Fuzhou | Chinese dialects | |
| Gabon | 103,347 | 1,340,000 | 13 | Republic ... A | Libreville | French, Fang, indigenous | AU, UN |
| Gambia, The | 4,127 | 1,525,000 | 370 | Republic ... A | Banjul | English, Malinke, Wolof, Fula, indigenous | AU, UN |
| Gansu | 173,746 | 26,200,000 | 151 | Province (China) ... D | Lanzhou | Chinese (Mandarin), Mongolian, Tibetan dialects | |
| Gaza Strip | 139 | 1,300,000 | 9,353 | Israeli territory with limited self-government | | Arabic, Hebrew | (⁴) |
| Georgia | 59,425 | 8,710,000 | 147 | State (U.S.) ... D | Atlanta | English | |
| Georgia | 26,911 | 4,920,000 | 183 | Republic ... A | Tbilisi | Georgian, Russian, Armenian, Azeri, other | NATO/PP, UN |
| Germany | 137,847 | 82,415,000 | 598 | Federal republic ... A | Berlin | German | EU, NATO, UN |
| Ghana | 92,098 | 20,615,000 | 224 | Republic ... A | Accra | English, Akan and other indigenous | AU, UN |
| Gibraltar (²) | 2.3 | 28,000 | 12,174 | Overseas territory (U.K.) ... C | Gibraltar | English, Spanish, Italian, Portuguese | |
| Gilbert Islands see Kiribati | | | | | | | |
| Golan Heights | 454 | 37,000 | 81 | Occupied by Israel | | Arabic, Hebrew | |
| Great Britain see United Kingdom | | | | | | | |
| Greece | 50,949 | 10,635,000 | 209 | Republic ... A | Athens (Athína) | Greek, English, French | EU, NATO, UN |
| Greenland | 836,331 | 56,000 | 0.07 | Self-governing territory (Danish protection) ... B | Godthåb (Nuuk) | Danish, Greenlandic, English | |
| Grenada | 133 | 89,000 | 669 | Parliamentary state ... A | St. George's | English, French | OAS, UN |
| Guadeloupe (incl. Dependencies) | 687 | 440,000 | 640 | Overseas department (France) ... C | Basse-Terre | French, Creole | |
| Guam | 212 | 165,000 | 778 | Unincorporated territory (U.S.) ... C | Hagåtña (Agana) | English, Chamorro, Japanese | |
| Guangdong | 68,649 | 88,375,000 | 1,287 | Province (China) ... D | Guangzhou (Canton) | Chinese dialects, Miao-Yao | |
| Guangxi Zhuangzu | 91,236 | 45,905,000 | 503 | Autonomous region (China) ... D | Nanning | Chinese dialects, Thai, Miao-Yao | |
| Guatemala | 42,042 | 14,095,000 | 335 | Republic ... A | Guatemala | Spanish, indigenous | OAS, UN |
| Guernsey (incl. Dependencies) | 30 | 65,000 | 2,167 | Crown dependency (U.K. protection) ... B | St. Peter Port | English, French | |
| Guinea | 94,926 | 9,135,000 | 96 | Republic ... A | Conakry | French, indigenous | AU, UN |
| Guinea-Bissau | 13,948 | 1,375,000 | 99 | Republic ... A | Bissau | Portuguese, Crioulo, indigenous | AU, UN |
| Guizhou | 65,637 | 36,045,000 | 549 | Province (China) ... D | Guiyang | Chinese (Mandarin), Thai, Miao-Yao | |
| Guyana | 83,000 | 705,000 | 8.5 | Republic ... A | Georgetown | English, indigenous, Creole, Hindi, Urdu | OAS, UN |
| Hainan | 13,205 | 8,050,000 | 610 | Province (China) ... D | Haikou | Chinese, Min, Tai | |
| Haiti | 10,714 | 7,590,000 | 708 | Republic ... A | Port-au-Prince | Creole, French | OAS, UN |
| Hawaii | 10,931 | 1,260,000 | 115 | State (U.S.) ... D | Honolulu | English, Hawaiian, Japanese | |
| Hebei | 73,359 | 68,965,000 | 940 | Province (China) ... D | Shijiazhuang | Chinese (Mandarin) | |
| Heilongjiang | 181,082 | 37,725,000 | 208 | Province (China) ... D | Harbin | Chinese dialects, Mongolian, Tungus | |
| Henan | 64,479 | 94,655,000 | 1,468 | Province (China) ... D | Zhengzhou | Chinese (Mandarin) | |
| Holland see Netherlands | | | | | | | |
| Honduras | 43,277 | 6,745,000 | 156 | Republic ... A | Tegucigalpa | Spanish, indigenous | OAS, UN |
| Hubei | 72,356 | 61,645,000 | 852 | Province (China) ... D | Wuhan | Chinese dialects | |
| Hunan | 81,082 | 65,855,000 | 812 | Province (China) ... D | Changsha | Chinese dialects, Miao-Yao | |
| Hungary | 35,919 | 10,045,000 | 280 | Republic ... A | Budapest | Hungarian | EU, NATO, UN |
| Iceland | 39,769 | 280,000 | 7.0 | Republic ... A | Reykjavík | Icelandic, English, other | EFTA, NATO, UN |
| Idaho | 83,570 | 1,370,000 | 16 | State (U.S.) ... D | Boise | English | |
| Illinois | 57,914 | 12,690,000 | 219 | State (U.S.) ... D | Springfield | English | |
| India (incl. part of Jammu and Kashmir) | 1,222,510 | 1,057,415,000 | 865 | Federal republic ... A | New Delhi | English, Hindi, Telugu, Bengali, indigenous | UN |
| Indiana | 36,418 | 6,215,000 | 171 | State (U.S.) ... D | Indianapolis | English | |
| Indonesia | 735,310 | 236,680,000 | 322 | Republic ... A | Jakarta | Bahasa Indonesia (Malay), English, Dutch, indigenous | ASEAN, OPEC, UN |
| Iowa | 56,272 | 2,955,000 | 53 | State (U.S.) ... D | Des Moines | English | |
| Iran | 636,372 | 68,650,000 | 108 | Islamic republic ... A | Tehrān | Persian, Turkish dialects, Kurdish, other | OPEC, UN |
| Iraq | 169,235 | 25,025,000 | 148 | Republic ... A | Baghdād | Arabic, Kurdish, Assyrian, Armenian | AL, CAEU, OPEC, UN |
| Ireland | 27,133 | 3,945,000 | 145 | Republic ... A | Dublin (Baile Átha Cliath) | English, Irish Gaelic | EU, NATO/PP, UN |
| Isle of Man | 221 | 74,000 | 335 | Crown dependency (U.K. protection) ... B | Douglas | English, Manx Gaelic | |

| REGION OR POLITICAL DIVISION | Area Sq. Mi. | Est. Pop. 1/1/04 | Pop. Per Sq. Mi. | Form of Government and Ruling Power | Capital | Predominant Languages | International Organizations |
|---|---|---|---|---|---|---|---|
| Israel (excl. Occupied Areas) | 8,019 | 6,160,000 | 768 | Republic A | Jerusalem (Yerushalayim) | Hebrew, Arabic | UN |
| Italy | 116,342 | 58,030,000 | 499 | Republic A | Rome (Roma) | Italian, German, French, Slovene | EU, NATO, UN |
| Ivory Coast see Cote d'Ivoire | | | | | | | |
| Jamaica | 4,244 | 2,705,000 | 637 | Parliamentary state A | Kingston | English, Creole | OAS, UN |
| Japan | 145,850 | 127,285,000 | 873 | Constitutional monarchy A | Tōkyō | Japanese | UN |
| Jersey | 45 | 90,000 | 2,000 | Crown dependency (U.K. protection) B | St. Helier | English, French | |
| Jiangsu | 39,614 | 76,065,000 | 1,920 | Province (China) D | Nanjing (Nanking) | Chinese dialects | |
| Jiangxi | 64,325 | 42,335,000 | 658 | Province (China) D | Nanchang | Chinese dialects | |
| Jilin | 72,201 | 27,895,000 | 386 | Province (China) D | Changchun | Chinese (Mandarin), Mongolian, Korean | |
| Jordan | 34,495 | 5,535,000 | 160 | Constitutional monarchy A | 'Ammān | Arabic | AL, CAEU, UN |
| Kansas | 82,277 | 2,730,000 | 33 | State (U.S.) D | Topeka | English | |
| Kazakhstan | 1,049,156 | 16,780,000 | 16 | Republic A | Astana (Aqmola) | Kazakh, Russian | CIS, NATO/PP, UN |
| Kentucky | 40,409 | 4,130,000 | 102 | State (U.S.) D | Frankfort | English | |
| Kenya | 224,961 | 31,840,000 | 142 | Republic A | Nairobi | English, Swahili, indigenous | AU, COMESA, UN |
| Kiribati | 313 | 100,000 | 319 | Republic A | Bairiki | English, I-Kiribati | UN |
| Korea, North | 46,540 | 22,585,000 | 485 | Socialist republic A | P'yŏngyang | Korean | UN |
| Korea, South | 38,328 | 48,450,000 | 1,264 | Republic A | Seoul (Sŏul) | Korean | UN |
| Kuwait | 6,880 | 2,220,000 | 323 | Constitutional monarchy A | Kuwait (Al Kuwayt) | Arabic, English | AL, CAEU, OPEC, UN |
| Kyrgyzstan | 77,182 | 4,930,000 | 64 | Republic A | Bishkek | Kirghiz, Russian | CIS, NATO/PP, UN |
| Laos | 91,429 | 5,995,000 | 66 | Socialist republic A | Viangchan (Vientiane) | Lao, French, English | ASEAN, UN |
| Latvia | 24,942 | 2,340,000 | 94 | Republic A | Rīga | Latvian, Lithuanian, Russian, other | EU, NATO, UN |
| Lebanon | 4,016 | 3,755,000 | 935 | Republic A | Beirut (Bayrūt) | Arabic, French, Armenian, English | AL, UN |
| Lesotho | 11,720 | 1,865,000 | 159 | Constitutional monarchy A | Maseru | English, Sesotho, Zulu, Xhosa | AU, UN |
| Liaoning | 56,255 | 43,340,000 | 770 | Province (China) D | Shenyang (Mukden) | Chinese (Mandarin), Mongolian | |
| Liberia | 43,000 | 3,345,000 | 78 | Republic A | Monrovia | English, indigenous | AU, UN |
| Libya | 679,362 | 5,565,000 | 8.2 | Socialist republic A | Tripoli (Ṭarābulus) | Arabic | AL, AU, CAEU, OPEC, UN |
| Liechtenstein | 62 | 33,000 | 532 | Constitutional monarchy A | Vaduz | German | EFTA, UN |
| Lithuania | 25,213 | 3,590,000 | 142 | Republic A | Vilnius | Lithuanian, Polish, Russian | EU, NATO, UN |
| Louisiana | 51,840 | 4,510,000 | 87 | State (U.S.) D | Baton Rouge | English | |
| Luxembourg | 999 | 460,000 | 460 | Constitutional monarchy A | Luxembourg | French, Luxembourgish, German | EU, NATO, UN |
| Macedonia | 9,928 | 2,065,000 | 208 | Republic A | Skopje | Macedonian, Albanian, other | NATO/PP, UN |
| Madagascar | 226,658 | 17,235,000 | 76 | Republic A | Antananarivo | French, Malagasy | AU, COMESA, UN |
| Maine | 35,385 | 1,310,000 | 37 | State (U.S.) D | Augusta | English | |
| Malawi | 45,747 | 11,780,000 | 258 | Republic A | Lilongwe | Chichewa, English, indigenous | AU, COMESA, UN |
| Malaysia | 127,320 | 23,310,000 | 183 | Federal constitutional monarchy A | Kuala Lumpur and Putrajaya (1) | Bahasa Melayu, Chinese dialects, English, other | ASEAN, UN |
| Maldives | 115 | 335,000 | 2,913 | Republic A | Male' | Dhivehi | UN |
| Mali | 478,841 | 11,790,000 | 25 | Republic A | Bamako | French, Bambara, indigenous | AU, UN |
| Malta | 122 | 400,000 | 3,279 | Republic A | Valletta | English, Maltese | EU, UN |
| Manitoba | 250,116 | 1,190,000 | 4.8 | Province (Canada) D | Winnipeg | English | |
| Marshall Islands | 70 | 57,000 | 814 | Republic (U.S. protection) B | Majuro (island) | English, indigenous, Japanese | UN |
| Martinique | 425 | 430,000 | 1,012 | Overseas department (France) C | Fort-de-France | French, Creole | |
| Maryland | 12,407 | 5,525,000 | 445 | State (U.S.) D | Annapolis | English | |
| Massachusetts | 10,555 | 6,455,000 | 612 | State (U.S.) D | Boston | English | |
| Mauritania | 397,956 | 2,955,000 | 7.4 | Republic A | Nouakchott | Arabic, Wolof, Pular, Soninke, French | AL, AU, CAEU, UN |
| Mauritius (incl. Dependencies) | 788 | 1,215,000 | 1,542 | Republic A | Port Louis | English, French, Creole, other | AU, COMESA, UN |
| Mayotte (6) | 144 | 180,000 | 1,250 | Departmental collectivity (France) C | Mamoutzou | French, Swahili (Mahorian) | |
| Mexico | 758,452 | 104,340,000 | 138 | Federal republic A | Mexico City (Ciudad de México) | Spanish, indigenous | NAFTA, OAS, UN |
| Michigan | 96,716 | 10,110,000 | 105 | State (U.S.) D | Lansing | English | |
| Micronesia, Federated States of | 271 | 110,000 | 406 | Republic (U.S. protection) B | Palikir | English, indigenous | UN |
| Midway Islands | 2.0 | (1) | | Unincorporated territory (U.S.) C | | English | |
| Minnesota | 86,939 | 5,075,000 | 58 | State (U.S.) D | St. Paul | English | |
| Mississippi | 48,430 | 2,890,000 | 60 | State (U.S.) D | Jackson | English | |
| Missouri | 69,704 | 5,720,000 | 82 | State (U.S.) D | Jefferson City | English | |
| Moldova | 13,070 | 4,440,000 | 340 | Republic A | Chişinău (Kishinev) | Romanian (Moldovan), Russian, Gagauz | CIS, NATO/PP, UN |
| Monaco | 0.8 | 32,000 | 40,000 | Constitutional monarchy A | Monaco | French, English, Italian, Monegasque | UN |
| Mongolia | 604,829 | 2,730,000 | 4.5 | Republic A | Ulan Bator (Ulaanbaatar) | Khalkha Mongol, Turkish dialects, Russian | UN |
| Montana | 4,095 | 920,000 | 225 | State (U.S.) D | Helena | English | |
| Montserrat | 39 | 9,000 | 231 | Overseas territory (U.K.) C | Plymouth | English | |
| Morocco (excl. Western Sahara) | 172,414 | 31,950,000 | 185 | Constitutional monarchy A | Rabat | Arabic, Berber dialects, French | AL, UN |
| Mozambique | 309,496 | 18,695,000 | 60 | Republic A | Maputo | Portuguese, indigenous | AU, UN |
| Myanmar (Burma) | 261,228 | 42,620,000 | 163 | Provisional military government A | Rangoon (Yangon) | Burmese, indigenous | ASEAN, UN |
| Namibia | 317,818 | 1,940,000 | 6.1 | Republic A | Windhoek | English, Afrikaans, German, indigenous | AU, COMESA, UN |
| Nauru | 8.1 | 13,000 | 1,605 | Republic A | Yaren District | Nauruan, English | UN |
| Nebraska | 77,354 | 1,745,000 | 23 | State (U.S.) D | Lincoln | English | |
| Nei Mongol (Inner Mongolia) | 456,759 | 24,295,000 | 53 | Autonomous region (China) D | Hohhot | Mongolian | |
| Nepal | 56,827 | 26,770,000 | 471 | Constitutional monarchy A | Kathmandu | Nepali, indigenous | UN |
| Netherlands | 16,164 | 16,270,000 | 1,007 | Constitutional monarchy A | Amsterdam and The Hague ('s-Gravenhage) | Dutch, Frisian | EU, NATO, UN |
| Netherlands Antilles | 309 | 215,000 | 696 | Self-governing territory (Netherlands protection) B | Willemstad | Dutch, Papiamento, English, Spanish | |
| Nevada | 110,561 | 2,250,000 | 20 | State (U.S.) D | Carson City | English | |
| New Brunswick | 28,150 | 770,000 | 27 | Province (Canada) D | Fredericton | English, French | |
| New Caledonia | 7,172 | 210,000 | 29 | Territorial collectivity (France) C | Nouméa | French, indigenous | |
| Newfoundland and Labrador | 156,453 | 535,000 | 3.4 | Province (Canada) D | St. John's | English | |
| New Hampshire | 9,350 | 1,290,000 | 138 | State (U.S.) D | Concord | English | |
| New Hebrides see Vanuatu | | | | | | | |
| New Jersey | 8,721 | 8,665,000 | 994 | State (U.S.) D | Trenton | English | |
| New Mexico | 121,590 | 1,880,000 | 15 | State (U.S.) D | Santa Fe | English, Spanish | |
| New South Wales | 309,129 | 6,665,000 | 22 | State (Australia) D | Sydney | English | |
| New York | 54,556 | 19,245,000 | 353 | State (U.S.) D | Albany | English | |
| New Zealand | 104,454 | 3,975,000 | 38 | Parliamentary state A | Wellington | English, Maori | ANZUS, UN |
| Nicaragua | 50,054 | 5,180,000 | 103 | Republic A | Managua | Spanish, English, indigenous | OAS, UN |
| Niger | 489,192 | 11,210,000 | 23 | Republic A | Niamey | French, Hausa, Djerma, indigenous | AU, UN |
| Nigeria | 356,669 | 135,570,000 | 380 | Transitional military government A | Abuja | English, Hausa, Fulani, Yorbua, Ibo, indigenous | AU, OPEC, UN |
| Ningxia Huizu | 25,637 | 5,745,000 | 224 | Autonomous region (China) D | Yinchuan | Chinese (Mandarin) | |
| Niue | 100 | 2,000 | 20 | Self-governing territory (New Zealand protection) B | Alofi | Niuean, English | |
| Norfolk Island | 14 | 2,000 | 143 | External territory (Australia) C | Kingston | English, Norfolk | |

| REGION OR POLITICAL DIVISION | Area Sq. Mi. | Est. Pop. 1/1/04 | Pop. Per Sq. Mi. | Form of Government and Ruling Power | Capital | Predominant Languages | International Organizations |
|---|---|---|---|---|---|---|---|
| North America | 9,500,000 | 505,780,000 | 53 | | | | |
| North Carolina | 53,819 | 8,430,000 | 157 | State (U.S.) D | Raleigh | English | |
| North Dakota | 70,700 | 635,000 | 9.0 | State (U.S.) D | Bismarck | English | |
| Northern Ireland | 5,242 | 1,725,000 | 329 | Administrative division (U.K.) D | Belfast | English | |
| Northern Mariana Islands | 179 | 77,000 | 430 | Commonwealth (U.S. protection) B | Saipan (island) | English, Chamorro, Carolinian | |
| Northern Territory | 520,902 | 200,000 | 0.4 | Territory (Australia) D | Darwin | English, indigenous | |
| Northwest Territories | 519,735 | 43,000 | 0.08 | Territory (Canada) D | Yellowknife | English, indigenous | |
| Norway (incl. Svalbard and Jan Mayen) | 125,050 | 4,565,000 | 37 | Constitutional monarchy A | Oslo | Norwegian, Sami, Finnish | EFTA, NATO, UN |
| Nova Scotia | 21,345 | 965,000 | 45 | Province (Canada) D | Halifax | English | |
| Nunavut | 808,185 | 30,000 | 0.04 | Territory (Canada) D | Iqaluit | English, indigenous | |
| Oceania (incl. Australia) | 3,300,000 | 32,170,000 | 9.7 | | | | |
| Ohio | 44,825 | 11,470,000 | 256 | State (U.S.) D | Columbus | English | |
| Oklahoma | 69,898 | 3,520,000 | 50 | State (U.S.) D | Oklahoma City | English | |
| Oman | 119,499 | 2,855,000 | 24 | Monarchy A | Muscat (Masqat) | Arabic, English, Baluchi, Urdu, Indian dialects | AL, UN |
| Ontario | 415,599 | 12,495,000 | 30 | Province (Canada) D | Toronto | English | |
| Oregon | 98,381 | 3,570,000 | 36 | State (U.S.) D | Salem | English | |
| Pakistan (incl. part of Jammu and Kashmir) | 339,732 | 152,210,000 | 448 | Federal Islamic republic A | Islāmābād | English, Urdu, Punjabi, Sindhi, Pashto, other | UN |
| Palau (Belau) | 188 | 20,000 | 106 | Republic (U.S. protection) B | Koror and Melekeok (¹) | Angaur, English, Japanese, Palauan, Sonsorolese, Tobi | UN |
| Panama | 29,157 | 2,980,000 | 102 | Republic A | Panamá | Spanish, English | OAS, UN |
| Papua New Guinea | 178,704 | 5,360,000 | 30 | Parliamentary state A | Port Moresby | English, Motu, Pidgin, indigenous | UN |
| Paraguay | 157,048 | 6,115,000 | 39 | Republic A | Asunción | Guarani, Spanish | MERCOSUR, OAS, UN |
| Pennsylvania | 46,055 | 12,400,000 | 269 | State (U.S.) D | Harrisburg | English | |
| Peru | 496,225 | 28,640,000 | 58 | Republic A | Lima | Quechua, Spanish, Aymara | OAS, UN |
| Philippines | 115,831 | 85,430,000 | 738 | Republic A | Manila | English, Filipino, indigenous | ASEAN, UN |
| Pitcairn Islands (incl. Dependencies) | 19 | 100 | 5.3 | Overseas territory (U.K.) C | Adamstown | English, Pitcairnese | |
| Poland | 120,728 | 38,625,000 | 320 | Republic A | Warsaw (Warszawa) | Polish | EU, NATO, UN |
| Portugal | 35,516 | 10,110,000 | 285 | Republic A | Lisbon (Lisboa) | Portuguese, Mirandese | EU, NATO, UN |
| Prince Edward Island | 2,185 | 140,000 | 64 | Province (Canada) D | Charlottetown | English | |
| Puerto Rico | 3,515 | 3,890,000 | 1,107 | Commonwealth (U.S. protection) B | San Juan | Spanish, English | |
| Qatar | 4,412 | 830,000 | 188 | Monarchy A | Ad Dawḥah (Doha) | Arabic | AL, OPEC, UN |
| Qinghai | 277,994 | 5,295,000 | 19 | Province (China) D | Xining | Tibetan dialects, Mongolian, Turkish dialects, Chinese (Mandarin) | |
| Quebec | 595,391 | 7,675,000 | 13 | Province (Canada) D | Québec | French, English | |
| Queensland | 668,208 | 3,785,000 | 5.7 | State (Australia) D | Brisbane | English | |
| Reunion | 969 | 760,000 | 784 | Overseas department (France) C | Saint-Denis | French, Creole | |
| Rhode Island | 1,545 | 1,080,000 | 699 | State (U.S.) D | Providence | English | |
| Rhodesia see Zimbabwe | | | | | | | |
| Romania | 91,699 | 22,370,000 | 244 | Republic A | Bucharest (Bucureşti) | Romanian, Hungarian, German | NATO, UN |
| Russia | 6,592,849 | 144,310,000 | 22 | Federal republic A | Moscow (Moskva) | Russian, other | CIS, NATO/PP, UN |
| Rwanda | 10,169 | 7,880,000 | 775 | Republic A | Kigali | English, French, Kinyarwanda, Kiswahili | AU, COMESA, UN |
| St. Helena (incl. Dependencies) | 121 | 7,500 | 62 | Overseas territory (U.K.) C | Jamestown | English | |
| St. Kitts and Nevis | 101 | 39,000 | 386 | Parliamentary state A | Basseterre | English | OAS, UN |
| St. Lucia | 238 | 165,000 | 693 | Parliamentary state A | Castries | English, French | OAS, UN |
| St. Pierre and Miquelon | 93 | 7,000 | 75 | Territorial collectivity (France) C | Saint-Pierre | French | |
| St. Vincent and the Grenadines | 150 | 115,000 | 767 | Parliamentary state A | Kingstown | English, French | OAS, UN |
| Samoa | 1,093 | 180,000 | 165 | Constitutional monarchy A | Apia | English, Samoan | UN |
| San Marino | 24 | 28,000 | 1,167 | Republic A | San Marino | Italian | UN |
| Sao Tome and Principe | 372 | 180,000 | 484 | Republic A | São Tomé | Portuguese | AU, UN |
| Saskatchewan | 251,366 | 1,025,000 | 4.1 | Province (Canada) D | Regina | English | |
| Saudi Arabia | 830,000 | 24,690,000 | 30 | Monarchy A | Riyadh (Ar Riyāḍ) | Arabic | AL, OPEC, UN |
| Scotland | 30,167 | 5,135,000 | 170 | Administrative division (U.K.) D | Edinburgh | English, Scots Gaelic | |
| Senegal | 75,951 | 10,715,000 | 141 | Republic A | Dakar | French, Wolof and other indigenous | AU, UN |
| Serbia and Montenegro (Yugoslavia) | 39,449 | 10,660,000 | 270 | Republic A | Belgrade (Beograd) | Serbian, Albanian | UN |
| Seychelles | 176 | 81,000 | 460 | Republic A | Victoria | English, French, Creole | AU, COMESA, UN |
| Shaanxi | 79,151 | 36,865,000 | 466 | Province (China) D | Xi'an (Sian) | Chinese (Mandarin) | |
| Shandong | 59,074 | 92,845,000 | 1,572 | Province (China) D | Jinan | Chinese (Mandarin) | |
| Shanghai | 2,394 | 17,120,000 | 7,151 | Autonomous city (China) D | Shanghai | Chinese (Wu) | |
| Shanxi | 60,232 | 33,715,000 | 560 | Province (China) D | Taiyuan | Chinese (Mandarin) | |
| Sichuan | 188,263 | 85,175,000 | 452 | Province (China) D | Chengdu | Chinese (Mandarin), Tibetan dialects, Miao-Yao | |
| Sierra Leone | 27,699 | 5,815,000 | 210 | Republic A | Freetown | English, Krio, Mende, Temne, indigenous | AU, UN |
| Singapore | 264 | 4,685,000 | 17,746 | Republic A | Singapore | Chinese (Mandarin), English, Malay, Tamil | ASEAN, UN |
| Slovakia | 18,924 | 5,420,000 | 286 | Republic A | Bratislava | Slovak, Hungarian | EU, NATO, UN |
| Slovenia | 7,821 | 1,935,000 | 247 | Republic A | Ljubljana | Slovenian, Croatian, Serbian | EU, NATO, UN |
| Solomon Islands | 10,954 | 515,000 | 47 | Parliamentary state A | Honiara | English, indigenous | UN |
| Somalia | 246,201 | 8,165,000 | 33 | Transitional A | Mogadishu (Muqdisho) | Arabic, Somali, English, Italian | AL, AU, CAEU, UN |
| South Africa | 470,693 | 42,770,000 | 91 | Republic A | Pretoria, Cape Town, and Bloemfontein | Afrikaans, English, Xhosa, Zulu, other indigenous | AU, UN |
| South America | 6,900,000 | 366,600,000 | 53 | | | | |
| South Australia | 379,724 | 1,525,000 | 4.0 | State (Australia) D | Adelaide | English | |
| South Carolina | 32,020 | 4,160,000 | 130 | State (U.S.) D | Columbia | English | |
| South Dakota | 77,117 | 765,000 | 9.9 | State (U.S.) D | Pierre | English | |
| South Georgia and the South Sandwich Islands (²) | 1,450 | (¹) | | Overseas territory (U.K.) C | | English | |
| South West Africa see Namibia | | | | | | | |
| Spain | 194,885 | 40,250,000 | 207 | Constitutional monarchy A | Madrid | Spanish (Castilian), Catalan, Galician, Basque | EU, NATO, UN |
| Spanish North Africa (³) | 12 | 140,000 | 11,667 | Five possessions (Spain) C | | Spanish, Arabic, Berber dialects | |
| Spanish Sahara see Western Sahara | | | | | | | |
| Sri Lanka | 25,332 | 19,825,000 | 783 | Socialist republic A | Colombo and Sri Jayewardenepura Kotte | English, Sinhala, Tamil | UN |
| Sudan | 967,500 | 38,630,000 | 40 | Provisional military government A | Khartoum (Al Kharṭūm) | Arabic, Nubian, and other indigenous, English | AL, AU, CAEU, COMESA, UN |
| Suriname | 63,037 | 435,000 | 6.9 | Republic A | Paramaribo | Dutch, Sranan Tongo, English, Hindustani, Javanese | OAS, UN |

| REGION OR POLITICAL DIVISION | Area Sq. Mi. | Est. Pop. 1/1/04 | Pop. Per Sq. Mi. | Form of Government and Ruling Power | Capital | Predominant Languages | International Organizations |
|---|---|---|---|---|---|---|---|
| Swaziland | 6,704 | 1,165,000 | 174 | Monarchy............................A | Mbabane and Lobamba..... | English, siSwati................. | AU, COMESA, UN |
| Sweden | 173,732 | 8,980,000 | 52 | Constitutional monarchy ...................A | Stockholm ............... | Swedish, Sami, Finnish............ | EU, NATO/PP, UN |
| Switzerland | 15,943 | 7,430,000 | 466 | Federal republic.......................A | Bern (Berne) ..... | German, French, Italian, Romansch .... | EFTA, NATO/PP, UN |
| Syria | 71,498 | 17,800,000 | 249 | Republic............................A | Damascus (Dimashq)........ | Arabic, Kurdish, Armenian, Aramaic, Circassian...................... | AL, CAEU, UN |
| Taiwan | 13,901 | 22,675,000 | 1,631 | Republic............................A | T'aipei ................ | Chinese (Mandarin), Taiwanese (Min), Hakka ........ | ................. |
| Tajikistan | 55,251 | 6,935,000 | 126 | Republic............................A | Dushanbe................ | Tajik, Russian ............. | CIS, NATO/PP, UN |
| Tanzania | 364,900 | 36,230,000 | 99 | Republic............................A | Dar es Salaam and Dodoma.. | English, Swahili, indigenous .......... | AU, UN |
| Tasmania | 26,409 | 475,000 | 18 | State (Australia).....................D | Hobart .... | English .... | ................. |
| Tennessee | 42,143 | 5,860,000 | 139 | State (U.S.).........................D | Nashville ....... | English .... | ................. |
| Texas | 268,581 | 22,185,000 | 83 | State (U.S.).........................D | Austin.... | English, Spanish ........ | ................. |
| Thailand | 198,115 | 64,570,000 | 326 | Constitutional monarchy ...............A | Bangkok (Krung Thep) ...... | Thai, indigenous ... | ASEAN, UN |
| Tianjin (Tientsin) | 4,363 | 10,235,000 | 2,346 | Autonomous city (China) .............D | Tianjin (Tientsin) ........... | Chinese (Mandarin) ... | ................. |
| Togo | 21,925 | 5,495,000 | 251 | Republic............................A | Lomé .... | French, Ewe, Mina, Kabye, Dagomba .. | AU, UN |
| Tokelau | 4.6 | 1,500 | 326 | Island territory (New Zealand) ........C | ......... | English, Tokelauan.............. | ................. |
| Tonga | 251 | 110,000 | 438 | Constitutional monarchy ...............A | Nuku'alofa....... | Tongan, English ... | UN |
| Trinidad and Tobago | 1,980 | 1,100,000 | 556 | Republic............................A | Port of Spain .... | English, Hindi, French, Spanish, Chinese | OAS, UN |
| Tristan da Cunha | 40 | 300 | 7.5 | Dependency (St. Helena)...............C | Edinburgh .... | English ... | ................. |
| Tunisia | 63,170 | 9,980,000 | 158 | Republic............................A | Tunis.... | Arabic, French ... | AL, AU, UN |
| Turkey | 302,541 | 68,505,000 | 226 | Republic............................A | Ankara.... | Turkish, Kurdish, Arabic, Armenian, Greek...................... | NATO, UN |
| Turkmenistan | 188,457 | 4,820,000 | 26 | Republic............................A | Ashgabat (Ashkhabad)...... | Turkmen, Russian, Uzbek ........... | CIS, NATO/PP, UN |
| Turks and Caicos Islands | 166 | 20,000 | 120 | Overseas territory (U.K.) .............C | Grand Turk... | English ... | ................. |
| Tuvalu | 10 | 11,000 | 1,100 | Parliamentary state ..................A | Funafuti............ | Tuvaluan, English, Samoan, I-Kiribati... | UN |
| Uganda | 93,065 | 26,010,000 | 279 | Republic............................A | Kampala.... | English, Luganda, Swahili, indigenous, Arabic ........ | AU, COMESA, UN |
| Ukraine | 233,090 | 47,890,000 | 205 | Republic............................A | Kiev (Kyïv) .... | Ukrainian, Russian, Romanian, Polish, Hungarian .......... | CIS, NATO/PP, UN |
| United Arab Emirates | 32,278 | 2,505,000 | 78 | Federation of monarchs ...............A | Abū Ẓaby (Abu Dhabi) ...... | Arabic, Persian, English, Hindi, Urdu ... | AL, CAEU, OPEC, UN |
| United Kingdom | 93,788 | 60,185,000 | 642 | Constitutional monarchy ...............A | London.... | English, Welsh, Scots Gaelic ........ | EU, NATO, UN |
| United States | 3,794,083 | 291,680,000 | 77 | Federal republic.....................A | Washington.... | English, Spanish ........ | ANZUS, NAFTA, NATO, OAS, UN |
| Upper Volta see Burkina Faso | ......... | ......... | ...... | ................................... | ......... | ................. | ................. |
| Uruguay | 67,574 | 3,425,000 | 51 | Republic............................A | Montevideo.... | Spanish ... | MERCOSUR, OAS, UN |
| Utah | 84,899 | 2,360,000 | 28 | State (U.S.).........................D | Salt Lake City.... | English ... | ................. |
| Uzbekistan | 172,742 | 26,195,000 | 152 | Republic............................A | Tashkent (Toshkent) ....... | Uzbek, Russian, Tajik ... | CIS, NATO/PP, UN |
| Vanuatu | 4,707 | 200,000 | 42 | Republic............................A | Port Vila.... | Bislama, English, French ............. | UN |
| Vatican City | 0.2 | 900 | 4,500 | Ecclesiastical state ..................A | Vatican City .... | Italian, Latin, French, other.......... | ................. |
| Venezuela | 352,145 | 24,835,000 | 71 | Federal republic.....................A | Caracas.... | Spanish, indigenous.............. | OAS, OPEC, UN |
| Vermont | 9,614 | 620,000 | 64 | State (U.S.).........................D | Montpelier.... | English ... | ................. |
| Victoria | 87,807 | 4,905,000 | 56 | State (Australia).....................D | Melbourne.... | English ... | ................. |
| Vietnam | 128,066 | 82,150,000 | 641 | Socialist republic ....................A | Hanoi .... | Vietnamese, English, French, Chinese, Khmer, indigenous .............. | ASEAN, UN |
| Virginia | 42,774 | 7,410,000 | 173 | State (U.S.).........................D | Richmond.... | English ... | ................. |
| Virgin Islands (U.S.) | 134 | 110,000 | 821 | Unincorporated territory (U.S.)..............C | Charlotte Amalie.......... | English, Spanish, Creole ... | ................. |
| Wake Island | 3.0 | ... | ...... | Unincorporated territory (U.S.).............C | ......... | English ... | ................. |
| Wales | 8,023 | 2,965,000 | 370 | Administrative division (U.K.)..............D | Cardiff .... | English, Welsh Gaelic............. | ................. |
| Wallis and Futuna | 99 | 16,000 | 162 | Overseas territory (France) ...........C | Mata-Utu.... | French, Wallisian ... | ................. |
| Washington | 71,300 | 6,150,000 | 86 | State (U.S.).........................D | Olympia.... | English ... | ................. |
| West Bank (incl. Jericho and East Jerusalem) | 2,263 | 2,275,000 | 1,005 | Israeli territory with limited self-government .... | ......... | Arabic, Hebrew .............. | (⁴) |
| Western Australia | 976,792 | 1,945,000 | 2.0 | State (Australia).....................D | Perth .... | English ... | ................. |
| Western Sahara | 102,703 | 265,000 | 2.6 | Occupied by Morocco ................C | ......... | Arabic ... | ................. |
| West Virginia | 24,230 | 1,815,000 | 75 | State (U.S.).........................D | Charleston.... | English ... | ................. |
| Wisconsin | 65,498 | 5,490,000 | 84 | State (U.S.).........................D | Madison.... | English ... | ................. |
| Wyoming | 97,814 | 505,000 | 5.2 | State (U.S.).........................D | Cheyenne.... | English ... | ................. |
| Xianggang (Hong Kong) | 425 | 7,440,000 | 17,506 | Special administrative region (China) ....D | Hong Kong (Xianggang) .... | Chinese (Cantonese), English ......... | ................. |
| Xinjiang Uygur (Sinkiang) | 617,764 | 19,685,000 | 32 | Autonomous region (China)..............D | Ürümqi.... | Turkish dialects, Mongolian, Tungus, English.... | ................. |
| Xizang (Tibet) | 471,045 | 2,680,000 | 5.7 | Autonomous region (China)..............D | Lhasa.... | Tibetan dialects ... | ................. |
| Yemen | 203,850 | 19,680,000 | 97 | Republic............................A | Ṣan'ā' (Sanaa) .... | Arabic ... | AL, CAEU, UN |
| Yugoslavia see Serbia and Montenegro | ......... | ......... | ...... | ................................... | ......... | ................. | ................. |
| Yukon Territory | 186,272 | 32,000 | 0.2 | Territory (Canada) ...................D | Whitehorse.... | English, Inuktitut, indigenous......... | ................. |
| Yunnan | 152,124 | 43,850,000 | 288 | Province (China)......................D | Kunming.... | Chinese (Mandarin), Tibetan dialects, Khmer, Miao-Yao .............. | ................. |
| Zaire see Congo, Democratic Republic of the | ......... | ......... | ...... | ................................... | ......... | ................. | ................. |
| Zambia | 290,586 | 10,385,000 | 36 | Republic............................A | Lusaka.... | English, indigenous ................. | AU, COMESA, UN |
| Zhejiang | 39,305 | 47,830,000 | 1,217 | Province (China)......................D | Hangzhou .... | Chinese dialects ... | ................. |
| Zimbabwe | 150,873 | 12,630,000 | 84 | Republic............................A | Harare (Salisbury) ......... | English, indigenous ................. | AU, COMESA, UN |
| WORLD | 57,900,000 | 6,339,505,000 | 109 | ................................... | ......... | ................. | ................. |

... None, or not applicable
(1) No permanent population
(2) Claimed by Argentina
(3) Claimed by Spain
(4) The Palestinian Liberation Organization (PLO) is a member of AL and CAEU
(5) Future capital
(6) Claimed by Comoros
(7) Comprises Ceuta, Melilla, and several small islands

| | |
|---|---|
| AL | Arab League (League of Arab States) |
| ANZUS | Australia-New Zealand-U.S. Security Treaty |
| ASEAN | Association of Southeast Asian Nations |
| AU | African Union |
| CAEU | Council of Arab Unity |
| CIS | Commonwealth of Independent States |
| COMESA | Common Market for Eastern and Southern Africa |
| EFTA | European Free Trade Association |
| EU | European Union |
| MERCOSUR | Southern Common Market |
| NAFTA | North American Free Trade Agreement |
| NATO | North Atlantic Treaty Organization |
| NATO/PP | NATO-Partnership for Peace Program |
| OAS | Organization of American States |
| OPEC | Organization of Petroleum Exporting Countries |

# WORLD DEMOGRAPHIC TABLE

| CONTINENT/Country | Population Estimate 2004 | Pop. Per Sq. Mile 2004 | Percent Urban[1] 2001 | Crude Birth Rate per 1,000[2] 2003 | Crude Death Rate per 1,000[2] 2003 | Natural Increase Percent[2] 2003 | Fertility Rate (Children born/Woman)[3] 2003 | Infant Mortality Rate per 1,000[3] 2003 | Median Age[2] 2002 | Life Expectancy Male[2] 2003 | Life Expectancy Female[2] 2003 |
|---|---|---|---|---|---|---|---|---|---|---|---|
| **NORTH AMERICA** | | | | | | | | | | | |
| Bahamas | 300,000 | 56 | 64.7 | 19 | 9 | 1.0% | 2 | 26 | 27 | 62 | 69 |
| Belize | 270,000 | 30 | 48.1 | 30 | 6 | 2.4% | 4 | 27 | 19 | 65 | 70 |
| Canada | 32,360,000 | 8 | 78.9 | 11 | 8 | 0.3% | 2 | 5 | 38 | 76 | 83 |
| Costa Rica | 3,925,000 | 199 | 59.5 | 19 | 4 | 1.5% | 2 | 11 | 25 | 74 | 79 |
| Cuba | 11,290,000 | 264 | 75.5 | 12 | 7 | 0.5% | 2 | 7 | 35 | 75 | 79 |
| Dominica | 69,000 | 238 | 71.4 | 17 | 7 | 1.0% | 2 | 15 | 28 | 71 | 77 |
| Dominican Republic | 8,775,000 | 468 | 66.0 | 24 | 7 | 1.7% | 3 | 34 | 24 | 66 | 70 |
| El Salvador | 6,530,000 | 804 | 61.5 | 28 | 6 | 2.2% | 3 | 27 | 21 | 67 | 74 |
| Guatemala | 14,095,000 | 335 | 39.9 | 35 | 7 | 2.8% | 5 | 38 | 18 | 64 | 66 |
| Haiti | 7,590,000 | 708 | 36.3 | 34 | 13 | 2.1% | 5 | 76 | 18 | 50 | 53 |
| Honduras | 6,745,000 | 156 | 53.7 | 32 | 6 | 2.5% | 4 | 30 | 19 | 65 | 68 |
| Jamaica | 2,705,000 | 637 | 56.6 | 17 | 5 | 1.2% | 2 | 13 | 27 | 74 | 78 |
| Mexico | 104,340,000 | 138 | 74.6 | 22 | 5 | 1.7% | 3 | 22 | 24 | 72 | 78 |
| Nicaragua | 5,180,000 | 103 | 56.5 | 26 | 5 | 2.2% | 3 | 31 | 20 | 68 | 72 |
| Panama | 2,980,000 | 102 | 56.5 | 21 | 6 | 1.5% | 3 | 21 | 26 | 70 | 75 |
| St. Lucia | 165,000 | 693 | 38.0 | 21 | 5 | 1.6% | 2 | 14 | 24 | 70 | 77 |
| Trinidad and Tobago | 1,100,000 | 556 | 74.5 | 13 | 9 | 0.4% | 2 | 25 | 30 | 67 | 72 |
| United States | 291,680,000 | 77 | 77.4 | 14 | 8 | 0.6% | 2 | 7 | 36 | 74 | 80 |
| **SOUTH AMERICA** | | | | | | | | | | | |
| Argentina | 38,945,000 | 36 | 88.3 | 17 | 8 | 1.0% | 2 | 16 | 29 | 72 | 79 |
| Bolivia | 8,655,000 | 20 | 62.9 | 26 | 8 | 1.8% | 3 | 56 | 21 | 62 | 67 |
| Brazil | 183,080,000 | 55 | 81.7 | 18 | 6 | 1.2% | 2 | 32 | 27 | 67 | 75 |
| Chile | 15,745,000 | 54 | 86.1 | 16 | 6 | 1.0% | 2 | 9 | 30 | 73 | 80 |
| Colombia | 41,985,000 | 95 | 75.5 | 22 | 6 | 1.6% | 3 | 22 | 26 | 67 | 75 |
| Ecuador | 13,840,000 | 126 | 63.4 | 25 | 5 | 2.0% | 3 | 32 | 23 | 69 | 75 |
| Guyana | 705,000 | 9 | 36.7 | 18 | 9 | 0.9% | 2 | 38 | 26 | 61 | 66 |
| Paraguay | 6,115,000 | 39 | 56.7 | 30 | 5 | 2.6% | 4 | 28 | 21 | 72 | 77 |
| Peru | 28,640,000 | 58 | 73.1 | 23 | 6 | 1.7% | 3 | 37 | 24 | 68 | 73 |
| Suriname | 435,000 | 7 | 74.8 | 19 | 7 | 1.3% | 2 | 25 | 26 | 67 | 72 |
| Uruguay | 3,425,000 | 51 | 92.1 | 17 | 9 | 0.8% | 2 | 14 | 32 | 73 | 79 |
| Venezuela | 24,835,000 | 71 | 87.2 | 20 | 5 | 1.5% | 2 | 24 | 25 | 71 | 77 |
| **EUROPE** | | | | | | | | | | | |
| Albania | 3,535,000 | 318 | 42.9 | 15 | 5 | 1.0% | 2 | 23 | 27 | 74 | 80 |
| Austria | 8,170,000 | 252 | 67.4 | 9 | 9 | 0% | 1 | 5 | 39 | 76 | 82 |
| Belarus | 10,315,000 | 129 | 69.6 | 10 | 14 | -0.4% | 1 | 14 | 37 | 63 | 75 |
| Belgium | 10,340,000 | 877 | 97.4 | 11 | 10 | 0.1% | 2 | 5 | 40 | 75 | 82 |
| Bosnia and Herzegovina | 4,000,000 | 202 | 43.4 | 13 | 8 | 0.4% | 2 | 23 | 36 | 70 | 75 |
| Bulgaria | 7,550,000 | 176 | 67.4 | 10 | 14 | -0.5% | 1 | 22 | 41 | 68 | 75 |
| Croatia | 4,430,000 | 203 | 58.1 | 13 | 11 | 0.2% | 2 | 7 | 39 | 71 | 78 |
| Czech Republic | 10,250,000 | 337 | 74.5 | 9 | 11 | -0.1% | 1 | 4 | 38 | 72 | 79 |
| Denmark | 5,405,000 | 325 | 85.1 | 12 | 11 | 0.1% | 2 | 5 | 39 | 75 | 80 |
| Estonia | 1,405,000 | 80 | 69.4 | 9 | 13 | -0.4% | 1 | 12 | 38 | 64 | 77 |
| Finland | 5,210,000 | 40 | 58.5 | 11 | 10 | 0.1% | 2 | 4 | 40 | 75 | 82 |
| France | 60,305,000 | 289 | 75.5 | 13 | 9 | 0.3% | 2 | 4 | 38 | 76 | 83 |
| Germany | 82,415,000 | 598 | 87.7 | 9 | 10 | -0.2% | 1 | 4 | 41 | 75 | 82 |
| Greece | 10,635,000 | 209 | 60.3 | 10 | 10 | 0% | 1 | 6 | 40 | 76 | 81 |
| Hungary | 10,045,000 | 280 | 64.8 | 10 | 13 | -0.3% | 1 | 9 | 38 | 68 | 77 |
| Iceland | 280,000 | 7 | 92.7 | 14 | 7 | 0.7% | 2 | 4 | 34 | 78 | 82 |
| Ireland | 3,945,000 | 145 | 59.3 | 14 | 8 | 0.6% | 2 | 6 | 33 | 75 | 80 |
| Italy | 58,030,000 | 499 | 67.1 | 9 | 10 | -0.1% | 1 | 6 | 41 | 76 | 83 |
| Latvia | 2,340,000 | 94 | 59.8 | 9 | 15 | -0.6% | 1 | 15 | 39 | 63 | 75 |
| Lithuania | 3,590,000 | 142 | 68.6 | 10 | 13 | -0.2% | 1 | 14 | 37 | 64 | 76 |
| Luxembourg | 460,000 | 460 | 91.9 | 12 | 8 | 0.4% | 2 | 5 | 38 | 75 | 82 |
| Macedonia | 2,065,000 | 208 | 59.4 | 13 | 8 | 0.5% | 2 | 12 | 33 | 72 | 77 |
| Moldova | 4,440,000 | 340 | 41.4 | 14 | 13 | 0.2% | 2 | 42 | 32 | 61 | 69 |
| Netherlands | 16,270,000 | 1,007 | 89.6 | 12 | 9 | 0.3% | 2 | 5 | 39 | 76 | 81 |
| Norway | 4,565,000 | 37 | 75.0 | 12 | 10 | 0.3% | 2 | 4 | 38 | 77 | 82 |
| Poland | 38,625,000 | 320 | 62.5 | 10 | 10 | 0.1% | 1 | 9 | 36 | 70 | 78 |
| Portugal | 10,110,000 | 285 | 65.8 | 11 | 10 | 0.1% | 1 | 6 | 38 | 73 | 80 |
| Romania | 22,370,000 | 244 | 55.2 | 11 | 12 | -0.1% | 1 | 28 | 35 | 67 | 75 |
| Serbia and Montenegro | 10,660,000 | 270 | 51.7 | 13 | 11 | 0.2% | 2 | 17 | 36 | 71 | 77 |
| Slovakia | 5,420,000 | 286 | 57.6 | 10 | 10 | 0.1% | 1 | 8 | 35 | 70 | 78 |
| Slovenia | 1,935,000 | 247 | 49.1 | 9 | 10 | -0.1% | 1 | 4 | 39 | 72 | 80 |
| Spain | 40,250,000 | 207 | 77.8 | 10 | 9 | 0.1% | 1 | 5 | 39 | 76 | 83 |
| Sweden | 8,980,000 | 52 | 83.3 | 11 | 10 | 0% | 2 | 3 | 40 | 78 | 83 |
| Switzerland | 7,430,000 | 466 | 67.3 | 10 | 8 | 0.1% | 1 | 4 | 40 | 77 | 83 |
| Ukraine | 47,890,000 | 205 | 68.0 | 10 | 16 | -0.7% | 1 | 21 | 38 | 61 | 72 |
| United Kingdom | 60,185,000 | 642 | 89.5 | 11 | 10 | 0.1% | 2 | 5 | 38 | 76 | 81 |
| Russia | 144,310,000 | 22 | 72.9 | 10 | 14 | -0.4% | 1 | 20 | 38 | 62 | 73 |
| **ASIA** | | | | | | | | | | | |
| Afghanistan | 29,205,000 | 116 | 22.3 | 41 | 17 | 2.3% | 6 | 142 | 19 | 48 | 46 |
| Armenia | 3,325,000 | 289 | 67.2 | 13 | 10 | 0.2% | 2 | 41 | 32 | 62 | 71 |
| Azerbaijan | 7,850,000 | 235 | 51.8 | 19 | 10 | 1.0% | 2 | 82 | 27 | 59 | 68 |
| Bahrain | 675,000 | 2,528 | 92.5 | 19 | 4 | 1.5% | 3 | 19 | 29 | 71 | 76 |
| Bangladesh | 139,875,000 | 2,516 | 25.6 | 30 | 9 | 2.1% | 3 | 66 | 21 | 61 | 61 |
| Brunei | 360,000 | 162 | 72.8 | 20 | 3 | 1.6% | 2 | 14 | 26 | 72 | 77 |
| Cambodia | 13,245,000 | 189 | 17.5 | 27 | 9 | 1.8% | 4 | 76 | 19 | 55 | 60 |
| China | 1,298,720,000 | 352 | 37.1 | 13 | 7 | 0.6% | 2 | 25 | 32 | 70 | 74 |
| Cyprus | 775,000 | 217 | 70.2 | 13 | 8 | 0.5% | 2 | 8 | 34 | 75 | 80 |
| East Timor | 1,010,000 | 176 | 7.5 | 28 | 6 | 2.1% | 4 | 50 | 20 | 63 | 68 |
| Georgia | 4,920,000 | 183 | 56.5 | 12 | 15 | -0.3% | 2 | 51 | 35 | 61 | 68 |
| India | 1,057,415,000 | 865 | 27.9 | 23 | 8 | 1.5% | 3 | 60 | 24 | 63 | 64 |
| Indonesia | 236,680,000 | 322 | 42.1 | 21 | 6 | 1.5% | 3 | 38 | 26 | 67 | 71 |
| Iran | 68,650,000 | 108 | 64.7 | 17 | 6 | 1.2% | 2 | 44 | 23 | 68 | 71 |
| Iraq | 25,025,000 | 148 | 67.4 | 34 | 6 | 2.8% | 5 | 55 | 19 | 67 | 69 |
| Israel | 6,160,000 | 768 | 91.8 | 19 | 6 | 1.2% | 3 | 7 | 29 | 77 | 81 |
| Japan | 127,285,000 | 873 | 78.9 | 10 | 9 | 0.1% | 1 | 3 | 42 | 78 | 84 |
| Jordan | 5,535,000 | 160 | 78.7 | 24 | 3 | 2.1% | 3 | 19 | 22 | 75 | 81 |
| Kazakhstan | 16,780,000 | 16 | 55.8 | 18 | 11 | 0.8% | 2 | 59 | 28 | 58 | 69 |
| Korea, North | 22,585,000 | 485 | 60.5 | 18 | 7 | 1.1% | 2 | 26 | 31 | 68 | 74 |
| Korea, South | 48,450,000 | 1,264 | 82.5 | 13 | 6 | 0.7% | 2 | 7 | 33 | 72 | 79 |
| Kuwait | 2,220,000 | 323 | 96.1 | 22 | 2 | 1.9% | 3 | 11 | 26 | 76 | 78 |

| CONTINENT/Country | Population Estimate 2004 | Pop. Per Sq. Mile 2004 | Percent Urban[1] 2001 | Crude Birth Rate per 1,000[2] 2003 | Crude Death Rate per 1,000[2] 2003 | Natural Increase Percent[2] 2003 | Fertility Rate (Children born/Woman)[3] 2003 | Infant Mortality Rate per 1,000[3] 2003 | Median Age[2] 2002 | Life Expectancy Male[2] 2003 | Life Expectancy Female[2] 2003 |
|---|---|---|---|---|---|---|---|---|---|---|---|
| Kyrgyzstan | 4,930,000 | 64 | 34.3 | 26 | 9 | 1.7% | 3 | 75 | 23 | 59 | 68 |
| Laos | 5,995,000 | 66 | 19.7 | 37 | 12 | 2.5% | 5 | 89 | 19 | 52 | 56 |
| Lebanon | 3,755,000 | 935 | 90.1 | 20 | 6 | 1.3% | 2 | 26 | 26 | 70 | 75 |
| Malaysia | 23,310,000 | 183 | 58.1 | 24 | 5 | 1.9% | 3 | 19 | 24 | 69 | 75 |
| Mongolia | 2,730,000 | 5 | 56.6 | 21 | 7 | 1.4% | 2 | 57 | 24 | 62 | 66 |
| Myanmar | 42,620,000 | 163 | 28.1 | 19 | 12 | 0.7% | 2 | 70 | 25 | 54 | 58 |
| Nepal | 26,770,000 | 471 | 12.2 | 32 | 10 | 2.3% | 4 | 71 | 20 | 59 | 59 |
| Oman | 2,855,000 | 24 | 76.5 | 37 | 4 | 3.4% | 6 | 21 | 19 | 70 | 75 |
| Pakistan | 152,210,000 | 448 | 33.4 | 30 | 9 | 2.1% | 4 | 77 | 20 | 61 | 63 |
| Philippines | 85,430,000 | 738 | 59.4 | 26 | 6 | 2.1% | 3 | 25 | 22 | 66 | 72 |
| Qatar | 830,000 | 188 | 92.9 | 16 | 4 | 1.1% | 3 | 20 | 31 | 71 | 76 |
| Saudi Arabia | 24,690,000 | 30 | 86.7 | 37 | 6 | 3.1% | 6 | 48 | 19 | 67 | 71 |
| Singapore | 4,685,000 | 17,746 | 100.0 | 13 | 4 | 0.8% | 1 | 4 | 35 | 77 | 84 |
| Sri Lanka | 19,825,000 | 783 | 23.1 | 16 | 6 | 1.0% | 2 | 15 | 29 | 70 | 75 |
| Syria | 17,800,000 | 249 | 51.8 | 30 | 5 | 2.5% | 4 | 32 | 20 | 68 | 71 |
| Taiwan | 22,675,000 | 1,631 | [5] | 13 | 6 | 0.7% | 2 | 7 | 33 | 74 | 80 |
| Tajikistan | 6,935,000 | 126 | 27.7 | 33 | 8 | 2.4% | 4 | 113 | 19 | 61 | 68 |
| Thailand | 64,570,000 | 326 | 20.0 | 16 | 7 | 1.0% | 2 | 22 | 30 | 69 | 74 |
| Turkey | 68,505,000 | 226 | 66.2 | 18 | 6 | 1.2% | 2 | 44 | 27 | 69 | 74 |
| Turkmenistan | 4,820,000 | 26 | 44.9 | 28 | 9 | 1.9% | 4 | 73 | 21 | 58 | 65 |
| United Arab Emirates | 2,505,000 | 78 | 87.2 | 18 | 4 | 1.4% | 3 | 16 | 28 | 72 | 77 |
| Uzbekistan | 26,195,000 | 152 | 36.6 | 26 | 8 | 1.8% | 3 | 72 | 22 | 61 | 68 |
| Vietnam | 82,150,000 | 641 | 24.5 | 20 | 6 | 1.3% | 2 | 31 | 25 | 68 | 73 |
| Yemen | 19,680,000 | 97 | 25.0 | 43 | 9 | 3.4% | 7 | 65 | 16 | 59 | 63 |
| **AFRICA** | | | | | | | | | | | |
| Algeria | 33,090,000 | 36 | 57.7 | 22 | 5 | 1.7% | 3 | 38 | 23 | 69 | 72 |
| Angola | 10,875,000 | 23 | 34.9 | 46 | 26 | 2.0% | 6 | 194 | 18 | 36 | 38 |
| Benin | 7,145,000 | 164 | 43.0 | 43 | 14 | 3.0% | 6 | 87 | 16 | 50 | 52 |
| Botswana | 1,570,000 | 7 | 49.4 | 26 | 31 | -0.6% | 3 | 67 | 19 | 32 | 32 |
| Burkina Faso | 13,400,000 | 127 | 16.9 | 45 | 19 | 2.6% | 6 | 100 | 17 | 43 | 46 |
| Burundi | 6,165,000 | 574 | 9.3 | 40 | 18 | 2.2% | 6 | 72 | 16 | 43 | 44 |
| Cameroon | 15,905,000 | 87 | 49.7 | 35 | 15 | 2.0% | 5 | 70 | 18 | 47 | 49 |
| Cape Verde | 415,000 | 267 | 63.5 | 27 | 7 | 2.0% | 4 | 51 | 19 | 67 | 73 |
| Central African Republic | 3,715,000 | 15 | 41.7 | 36 | 20 | 1.6% | 5 | 93 | 18 | 40 | 43 |
| Chad | 9,395,000 | 19 | 24.1 | 47 | 16 | 3.1% | 6 | 96 | 16 | 47 | 50 |
| Comoros | 640,000 | 742 | 33.8 | 39 | 9 | 3.0% | 5 | 80 | 19 | 59 | 64 |
| Congo | 2,975,000 | 23 | 66.1 | 29 | 14 | 1.5% | 4 | 95 | 20 | 49 | 51 |
| Congo, Democratic Republic of the | 57,445,000 | 63 | 30.7 | 45 | 15 | 3.0% | 7 | 97 | 16 | 47 | 51 |
| Cote d'Ivoire | 17,145,000 | 138 | 44.0 | 40 | 18 | 2.2% | 6 | 98 | 17 | 40 | 45 |
| Djibouti | 460,000 | 51 | 84.2 | 41 | 19 | 2.1% | 6 | 107 | 18 | 42 | 44 |
| Egypt | 75,420,000 | 195 | 42.7 | 24 | 5 | 1.9% | 3 | 35 | 23 | 68 | 73 |
| Equatorial Guinea | 515,000 | 48 | 49.3 | 37 | 13 | 2.4% | 5 | 89 | 19 | 53 | 57 |
| Eritrea | 4,390,000 | 97 | 19.1 | 39 | 13 | 2.6% | 6 | 76 | 18 | 51 | 55 |
| Ethiopia | 67,210,000 | 158 | 15.9 | 40 | 20 | 2.0% | 6 | 103 | 17 | 40 | 42 |
| Gabon | 1,340,000 | 13 | 82.3 | 37 | 11 | 2.5% | 5 | 55 | 19 | 55 | 59 |
| Gambia, The | 1,525,000 | 370 | 31.3 | 41 | 12 | 2.8% | 6 | 75 | 17 | 52 | 56 |
| Ghana | 20,615,000 | 224 | 36.4 | 26 | 11 | 1.5% | 3 | 53 | 20 | 56 | 57 |
| Guinea | 9,135,000 | 96 | 27.9 | 43 | 16 | 2.7% | 6 | 93 | 18 | 48 | 51 |
| Guinea-Bissau | 1,375,000 | 99 | 32.3 | 38 | 17 | 2.2% | 5 | 110 | 19 | 45 | 49 |
| Kenya | 31,840,000 | 142 | 34.4 | 29 | 16 | 1.3% | 3 | 63 | 18 | 45 | 45 |
| Lesotho | 1,865,000 | 159 | 28.8 | 27 | 25 | 0.3% | 4 | 86 | 20 | 37 | 37 |
| Liberia | 3,345,000 | 78 | 45.5 | 45 | 18 | 2.7% | 6 | 132 | 18 | 47 | 49 |
| Libya | 5,565,000 | 8 | 88.0 | 27 | 3 | 2.4% | 3 | 27 | 22 | 74 | 78 |
| Madagascar | 17,235,000 | 76 | 30.1 | 42 | 12 | 3.0% | 6 | 80 | 17 | 54 | 59 |
| Malawi | 11,780,000 | 258 | 15.1 | 45 | 23 | 2.2% | 6 | 105 | 16 | 38 | 38 |
| Mali | 11,790,000 | 25 | 30.9 | 48 | 19 | 2.9% | 7 | 119 | 16 | 45 | 46 |
| Mauritania | 2,955,000 | 7 | 59.1 | 42 | 13 | 2.9% | 6 | 74 | 17 | 50 | 54 |
| Mauritius | 1,215,000 | 1,542 | 41.6 | 16 | 7 | 0.9% | 2 | 16 | 30 | 68 | 76 |
| Morocco | 31,950,000 | 185 | 56.1 | 23 | 6 | 1.7% | 3 | 45 | 23 | 68 | 72 |
| Mozambique | 18,695,000 | 60 | 33.3 | 37 | 23 | 1.4% | 5 | 138 | 19 | 39 | 37 |
| Namibia | 1,940,000 | 6 | 31.4 | 34 | 19 | 1.5% | 5 | 68 | 18 | 44 | 41 |
| Niger | 11,210,000 | 23 | 21.1 | 50 | 22 | 2.8% | 7 | 124 | 16 | 42 | 42 |
| Nigeria | 135,570,000 | 380 | 44.9 | 39 | 14 | 2.5% | 5 | 71 | 18 | 51 | 51 |
| Rwanda | 7,880,000 | 775 | 6.3 | 40 | 22 | 1.8% | 6 | 103 | 18 | 39 | 40 |
| Sao Tome and Principe | 180,000 | 484 | 47.7 | 42 | 7 | 3.5% | 6 | 46 | 16 | 65 | 68 |
| Senegal | 10,715,000 | 141 | 48.2 | 36 | 11 | 2.5% | 5 | 58 | 18 | 55 | 58 |
| Sierra Leone | 5,815,000 | 210 | 37.3 | 44 | 21 | 2.3% | 6 | 147 | 18 | 40 | 45 |
| Somalia | 8,165,000 | 33 | 27.9 | 46 | 18 | 2.9% | 7 | 120 | 18 | 46 | 49 |
| South Africa | 42,770,000 | 91 | 57.7 | 19 | 18 | 0% | 2 | 61 | 25 | 47 | 47 |
| Sudan | 38,630,000 | 40 | 37.1 | 36 | 10 | 2.7% | 5 | 66 | 18 | 57 | 59 |
| Swaziland | 1,165,000 | 174 | 26.7 | 29 | 21 | 0.8% | 4 | 67 | 19 | 41 | 38 |
| Tanzania | 36,230,000 | 99 | 33.3 | 40 | 17 | 2.2% | 5 | 104 | 18 | 43 | 46 |
| Togo | 5,495,000 | 251 | 33.9 | 35 | 12 | 2.4% | 5 | 69 | 17 | 51 | 55 |
| Tunisia | 9,980,000 | 158 | 66.2 | 17 | 5 | 1.2% | 2 | 27 | 26 | 73 | 76 |
| Uganda | 26,010,000 | 279 | 14.5 | 47 | 17 | 3.0% | 7 | 88 | 15 | 43 | 46 |
| Zambia | 10,385,000 | 36 | 39.8 | 40 | 24 | 1.5% | 5 | 99 | 17 | 35 | 35 |
| Zimbabwe | 12,630,000 | 84 | 36.0 | 30 | 22 | 0.8% | 4 | 66 | 19 | 40 | 38 |
| **OCEANIA** | | | | | | | | | | | |
| Australia | 19,825,000 | 7 | 91.2 | 13 | 7 | 0.5% | 2 | 5 | 36 | 77 | 83 |
| Fiji | 875,000 | 124 | 50.2 | 23 | 6 | 1.7% | 3 | 13 | 24 | 66 | 71 |
| Kiribati | 100,000 | 319 | 38.6 | 31 | 9 | 2.3% | 4 | 51 | 20 | 58 | 64 |
| Micronesia, Federated States of | 110,000 | 406 | 28.6 | 26 | 5 | 2.1% | 4 | 32 | 19[4] | 67 | 71 |
| New Zealand | 3,975,000 | 38 | 85.9 | 14 | 8 | 0.7% | 2 | 6 | 33 | 75 | 81 |
| Papua New Guinea | 5,360,000 | 30 | 17.6 | 31 | 8 | 2.3% | 4 | 55 | 21 | 62 | 66 |
| Samoa | 180,000 | 165 | 22.3 | 15 | 6 | 0.9% | 3 | 30 | 24 | 67 | 73 |
| Solomon Islands | 515,000 | 47 | 20.2 | 32 | 4 | 2.8% | 4 | 23 | 18 | 70 | 75 |
| Tonga | 110,000 | 438 | 33.0 | 25 | 6 | 1.9% | 3 | 13 | 20 | 66 | 71 |
| Vanuatu | 200,000 | 42 | 22.1 | 24 | 8 | 1.6% | 3 | 58 | 22 | 60 | 63 |

This table presents data for most independent nations having an area greater than 200 square miles
(1) Source: United Nations World Urbanization Prospects
(2) Source: United States Census Bureau International Database
(3) Source: United States Central Intelligence Agency World Factbook
(4) 2000 Census preliminary count from www.fsmgov.org/info/people.html
(5) Data for Taiwan is included with China

# WORLD AGRICULTURE TABLE

| CONTINENT/Country | Total Area Sq. Miles | Cropland Area[1] Sq. Miles | Cropland Area[1] % | Pasture Area[1] Sq. Miles | Pasture Area[1] % | Wheat[1] 1,000 metric tons | Rice[1] 1,000 metric tons | Corn[1] 1,000 metric tons | Cattle[1] 1,000 | Pigs[1] 1,000 | Sheep[1] 1,000 |
|---|---|---|---|---|---|---|---|---|---|---|---|
| **NORTH AMERICA** | | | | | | | | | | | |
| Bahamas | 5,382 | 46 | 0.9% | 8 | 0.1% | - | - | - | 1 | 5 | 6 |
| Belize | 8,867 | 402 | 4.5% | 193 | 2.2% | - | 12 | 36 | 52 | 25 | 4 |
| Canada | 3,855,103 | 177,144 | 4.6% | 111,970 | 2.9% | 24,676 | - | 8,168 | 13,340 | 12,970 | 819 |
| Costa Rica | 19,730 | 2,027 | 10.3% | 9,035 | 45.8% | - | 267 | 20 | 1,358 | 438 | 3 |
| Cuba | 42,804 | 17,239 | 40.3% | 8,494 | 19.8% | - | 342 | 207 | 4,305 | 2,600 | 310 |
| Dominica | 290 | 77 | 26.6% | 8 | 2.7% | - | - | - | 13 | 5 | 8 |
| Dominican Republic | 18,730 | 6,162 | 32.9% | 8,108 | 43.3% | - | 615 | 30 | 2,026 | 548 | 106 |
| El Salvador | 8,124 | 3,514 | 43.2% | 3,066 | 37.7% | - | 47 | 605 | 1,190 | 195 | 5 |
| Guatemala | 42,042 | 7,355 | 17.5% | 10,046 | 23.9% | 9 | 46 | 1,057 | 2,500 | 1,417 | 270 |
| Haiti | 10,714 | 4,247 | 39.6% | 1,892 | 17.7% | - | 111 | 211 | 1,390 | 934 | 147 |
| Honduras | 43,277 | 5,514 | 12.7% | 5,822 | 13.5% | 1 | 9 | 509 | 1,737 | 474 | 14 |
| Jamaica | 4,244 | 1,097 | 25.8% | 884 | 20.8% | - | - | 2 | 400 | 180 | 1 |
| Mexico | 758,452 | 105,406 | 13.9% | 308,882 | 40.7% | 3,263 | 324 | 18,466 | 30,428 | 16,112 | 6,048 |
| Nicaragua | 50,054 | 8,382 | 16.7% | 18,591 | 37.1% | - | 234 | 374 | 2,008 | 402 | 4 |
| Panama | 29,157 | 2,683 | 9.2% | 5,927 | 20.3% | - | 237 | 71 | 1,348 | 279 | - |
| St. Lucia | 238 | 69 | 29.2% | 8 | 3.2% | - | - | - | 12 | 15 | 13 |
| Trinidad and Tobago | 1,980 | 471 | 23.8% | 42 | 2.1% | - | 13 | 5 | 36 | 41 | 12 |
| United States | 3,794,083 | 684,401 | 18.0% | 903,479 | 23.8% | 58,862 | 9,222 | 244,296 | 98,197 | 60,229 | 7,071 |
| **SOUTH AMERICA** | | | | | | | | | | | |
| Argentina | 1,073,519 | 135,136 | 12.6% | 548,265 | 51.1% | 15,642 | 1,140 | 15,217 | 49,299 | 4,200 | 13,588 |
| Bolivia | 424,165 | 11,973 | 2.8% | 130,618 | 30.8% | 121 | 281 | 607 | 6,715 | 2,786 | 8,743 |
| Brazil | 3,300,172 | 256,623 | 7.8% | 760,621 | 23.0% | 2,461 | 10,998 | 35,119 | 170,295 | 30,608 | 14,728 |
| Chile | 291,930 | 8,880 | 3.0% | 49,942 | 17.1% | 1,490 | 113 | 685 | 4,117 | 2,395 | 4,153 |
| Colombia | 439,737 | 16,405 | 3.7% | 161,391 | 36.7% | 37 | 2,262 | 1,128 | 25,274 | 2,726 | 2,247 |
| Ecuador | 109,484 | 11,525 | 10.5% | 19,653 | 18.0% | 19 | 1,340 | 483 | 5,261 | 2,654 | 2,214 |
| Guyana | 83,000 | 1,969 | 2.4% | 4,749 | 5.7% | - | 560 | 3 | 220 | 20 | 130 |
| Paraguay | 157,048 | 12,008 | 7.6% | 83,784 | 53.3% | 256 | 112 | 804 | 9,758 | 2,633 | 402 |
| Peru | 496,225 | 16,255 | 3.3% | 104,634 | 21.1% | 180 | 1,963 | 1,205 | 4,936 | 2,795 | 14,414 |
| Suriname | 63,037 | 259 | 0.4% | 81 | 0.1% | - | 178 | - | 128 | 22 | 8 |
| Uruguay | 67,574 | 5,174 | 7.7% | 52,290 | 77.4% | 284 | 1,189 | 190 | 10,446 | 375 | 13,257 |
| Venezuela | 352,145 | 13,158 | 3.7% | 70,425 | 20.0% | 1 | 696 | 1,547 | 14,620 | 5,555 | 780 |
| **EUROPE** | | | | | | | | | | | |
| Albania | 11,100 | 2,699 | 24.3% | 1,699 | 15.3% | 298 | - | 203 | 719 | 96 | 1,929 |
| Austria | 32,378 | 5,676 | 17.5% | 7,413 | 22.9% | 1,412 | - | 1,774 | 2,166 | 3,556 | 357 |
| Belarus | 80,155 | 24,151 | 30.1% | 11,564 | 14.4% | 903 | - | 13 | 4,411 | 3,565 | 96 |
| Belgium | 11,787 | 3,344[2] | 26.2%[2] | 2,618[2] | 20.5%[2] | 1,535 | - | 420 | 3,165 | 7,462 | 150 |
| Bosnia and Herzegovina | 19,767 | 3,243 | 16.4% | 4,633 | 23.4% | 289 | - | 656 | 448 | 345 | 645 |
| Bulgaria | 42,855 | 17,900 | 41.8% | 6,236 | 14.6% | 3,071 | 8 | 1,137 | 664 | 1,459 | 2,536 |
| Croatia | 21,829 | 6,124 | 28.1% | 6,035 | 27.6% | 852 | - | 1,958 | 435 | 1,276 | 519 |
| Czech Republic | 30,450 | 12,788 | 42.0% | 3,730 | 12.2% | 4,196 | - | 324 | 1,604 | 3,761 | 87 |
| Denmark | 16,640 | 8,880 | 53.4% | 1,452 | 8.7% | 4,683 | - | - | 1,887 | 12,052 | 147 |
| Estonia | 17,462 | 2,691 | 15.4% | 745 | 4.3% | 123 | - | - | 276 | 304 | 29 |
| Finland | 130,559 | 8,490 | 6.5% | 77 | 0.1% | 427 | - | - | 1,060 | 1,303 | 101 |
| France | 208,482 | 75,618 | 36.3% | 38,788 | 18.6% | 35,327 | 110 | 15,928 | 20,377 | 14,693 | 9,754 |
| Germany | 137,847 | 46,409 | 33.7% | 19,355 | 14.0% | 21,358 | - | 3,362 | 14,723 | 26,021 | 2,746 |
| Greece | 50,949 | 14,873 | 29.2% | 17,954 | 35.2% | 2,111 | 153 | 2,007 | 584 | 925 | 8,977 |
| Hungary | 35,919 | 18,548 | 51.6% | 4,097 | 11.4% | 3,843 | 9 | 6,664 | 845 | 5,216 | 991 |
| Iceland | 39,769 | 27 | 0.1% | 8,780 | 22.1% | - | - | - | 72 | 44 | 477 |
| Ireland | 27,133 | 4,050 | 14.9% | 12,934 | 47.7% | 688 | - | - | 6,613 | 1,765 | 5,311 |
| Italy | 116,342 | 42,379 | 36.4% | 16,907 | 14.5% | 7,239 | 1,310 | 10,222 | 7,167 | 8,356 | 11,000 |
| Latvia | 24,942 | 7,220 | 28.9% | 2,355 | 9.4% | 410 | - | - | 393 | 407 | 28 |
| Lithuania | 25,213 | 11,541 | 45.8% | 1,923 | 7.6% | 1,062 | - | - | 856 | 984 | 14 |
| Luxembourg | 999 | [3] | [3] | [3] | [3] | - | - | 2 | 134 | - | - |
| Macedonia | 9,928 | 2,363 | 23.8% | 2,432 | 24.5% | 308 | 20 | 135 | 267 | 209 | 1,285 |
| Moldova | 13,070 | 8,398 | 64.3% | 1,483 | 11.3% | 902 | - | 1,096 | 423 | 646 | 929 |
| Netherlands | 16,164 | 3,622 | 22.4% | 3,834 | 23.7% | 995 | - | 148 | 4,108 | 13,253 | 1,335 |
| Norway | 125,050 | 3,398 | 2.7% | 625 | 0.5% | 265 | - | - | 1,017 | 414 | 2,342 |
| Poland | 120,728 | 55,267 | 45.8% | 15,745 | 13.0% | 8,946 | - | 962 | 6,124 | 17,588 | 366 |
| Portugal | 35,516 | 10,444 | 29.4% | 5,548 | 15.6% | 295 | 146 | 907 | 1,415 | 2,346 | 4,337 |
| Romania | 91,699 | 38,305 | 41.8% | 19,039 | 20.8% | 5,610 | 3 | 8,317 | 3,021 | 5,946 | 8,062 |
| Serbia and Montenegro | 39,449 | 14,394 | 36.5% | 7,197 | 18.2% | 2,207 | - | 5,013 | 1,550 | 4,012 | 1,853 |
| Slovakia | 18,924 | 6,085 | 32.2% | 3,375 | 17.8% | 1,445 | - | 612 | 671 | 1,548 | 344 |
| Slovenia | 7,821 | 784 | 10.0% | 1,185 | 15.2% | 153 | - | 283 | 473 | 585 | 80 |
| Spain | 194,885 | 69,298 | 35.6% | 44,209 | 22.7% | 5,785 | 844 | 4,208 | 6,140 | 22,079 | 24,185 |
| Sweden | 173,732 | 10,413 | 6.0% | 1,726 | 1.0% | 2,135 | - | - | 1,683 | 1,975 | 440 |
| Switzerland | 15,943 | 1,683 | 10.6% | 4,417 | 27.7% | 535 | - | 214 | 1,603 | 1,499 | 421 |
| Ukraine | 233,090 | 129,321 | 55.5% | 30,541 | 13.1% | 15,043 | 74 | 3,075 | 10,591 | 9,270 | 1,074 |
| United Kingdom | 93,788 | 22,019 | 23.5% | 43,440 | 46.3% | 14,380 | - | - | 11,052 | 6,537 | 41,205 |
| Russia | 6,592,849 | 485,400 | 7.4% | 351,905 | 5.3% | 37,455 | 509 | 1,133 | 27,936 | 17,076 | 12,954 |
| **ASIA** | | | | | | | | | | | |
| Afghanistan | 251,773 | 31,097 | 12.4% | 115,831 | 46.0% | 1,821 | 205 | 172 | 2,600 | - | 12,762 |
| Armenia | 11,506 | 2,162 | 18.8% | 3,089 | 26.8% | 211 | - | 9 | 478 | 75 | 515 |
| Azerbaijan | 33,437 | 7,471 | 22.3% | 10,039 | 30.0% | 1,172 | 19 | 107 | 1,965 | 21 | 5,321 |
| Bahrain | 267 | 23 | 8.7% | 15 | 5.8% | - | - | - | 12 | - | 17 |
| Bangladesh | 55,598 | 32,761 | 58.9% | 2,317 | 4.2% | 1,807 | 36,909 | 8 | 23,817 | - | 1,128 |
| Brunei | 2,226 | 27 | 1.2% | 23 | 1.0% | - | - | - | 2 | 6 | 2 |
| Cambodia | 69,898 | 14,699 | 21.0% | 5,792 | 8.3% | - | 4,035 | 146 | 2,896 | 2,079 | - |
| China | 3,690,045 | 599,520[4] | 16.2%[4] | 1,544,412[4] | 41.9%[4] | 102,463[4] | 189,840[4] | 116,240[4] | 104,179[4] | 440,384[4] | 130,536[4] |
| Cyprus | 3,572 | 436 | 12.2% | 15 | 0.4% | 12 | - | - | 55 | 419 | 240 |
| East Timor | 5,743 | 309 | 5.4% | 579 | 10.1% | - | 33 | 93 | 173 | 300 | 36 |
| Georgia | 26,911 | 4,104 | 15.3% | 7,490 | 27.8% | 207 | - | 358 | 1,117 | 433 | 541 |
| India | 1,222,510 | 655,987 | 53.7% | 42,124 | 3.4% | 72,140 | 132,818 | 12,285 | 217,773 | 17,000 | 57,900 |
| Indonesia | 735,310 | 129,730 | 17.6% | 43,155 | 5.9% | - | 50,953 | 9,409 | 11,370 | 6,098 | 7,316 |
| Iran | 636,372 | 63,892 | 10.0% | 169,885 | 26.7% | 8,740 | 2,103 | 1,113 | 8,273 | - | 53,900 |
| Iraq | 169,235 | 23,514 | 13.9% | 15,444 | 9.1% | 667 | 110 | 73 | 1,342 | - | 6,770 |
| Israel | 8,019 | 1,637 | 20.4% | 548 | 6.8% | 94 | - | 73 | 393 | 138 | 373 |
| Japan | 145,850 | 18,510 | 12.7% | 1,564 | 1.1% | 657 | 11,551 | - | 4,592 | 9,823 | 11 |
| Jordan | 34,495 | 1,544 | 4.5% | 2,865 | 8.3% | 18 | - | 13 | 66 | - | 1,900 |
| Kazakhstan | 1,049,156 | 83,672 | 8.0% | 714,667 | 68.1% | 10,938 | 225 | 256 | 4,021 | 984 | 8,785 |
| Korea, North | 46,540 | 10,811 | 23.2% | 193 | 0.4% | 88 | 2,031 | 1,253 | 575 | 3,076 | 186 |
| Korea, South | 38,328 | 7,293 | 19.0% | 208 | 0.5% | 4 | 7,204 | 67 | 2,191 | 8,266 | 1 |
| Kuwait | 6,880 | 58 | 0.8% | 525 | 7.6% | - | - | - | 19 | - | 543 |

| CONTINENT/Country | Agricultural Area 2001 Total Area Sq. Miles | Cropland Area[1] Sq. Miles | Cropland Area[1] % | Pasture Area[1] Sq. Miles | Pasture Area[1] % | Average Production 1999-2001 Wheat[1] 1,000 metric tons | Rice[1] 1,000 metric tons | Corn[1] 1,000 metric tons | Average 1999-2001 Cattle[1] 1,000 | Pigs[1] 1,000 | Sheep[1] 1,000 |
|---|---|---|---|---|---|---|---|---|---|---|---|
| Kyrgyzstan | 77,182 | 5,664 | 7.3% | 35,873 | 46.5% | 1,113 | 17 | 363 | 942 | 98 | 3,101 |
| Laos | 91,429 | 3,699 | 4.0% | 3,390 | 3.7% | - | 2,213 | 108 | 1,106 | 1,390 | - |
| Lebanon | 4,016 | 1,208 | 30.1% | 62 | 1.5% | 60 | - | 4 | 76 | 63 | 354 |
| Malaysia | 127,320 | 29,286 | 23.0% | 1,100 | 0.9% | - | 2,170 | 63 | 744 | 1,943 | 167 |
| Mongolia | 604,829 | 4,633 | 0.8% | 499,230 | 82.5% | 148 | - | - | 2,997 | 17 | 14,587 |
| Myanmar | 261,228 | 41,023 | 15.7% | 1,212 | 0.5% | 105 | 20,683 | 413 | 10,974 | 3,923 | 390 |
| Nepal | 56,827 | 12,324 | 21.7% | 6,784 | 11.9% | 1,143 | 4,137 | 1,528 | 7,012 | 872 | 852 |
| Oman | 119,499 | 313 | 0.3% | 3,861 | 3.2% | 1 | - | - | 299 | - | 342 |
| Pakistan | 339,732 | 85,560 | 25.2% | 19,305 | 5.7% | 19,319 | 6,920 | 1,653 | 22,007 | - | 24,067 |
| Philippines | 115,831 | 41,120 | 35.5% | 4,942 | 4.3% | - | 12,377 | 4,540 | 2,467 | 10,724 | 30 |
| Qatar | 4,412 | 81 | 1.8% | 193 | 4.4% | - | - | 1 | 15 | - | 214 |
| Saudi Arabia | 830,000 | 14,649 | 1.8% | 656,373 | 79.1% | 1,871 | - | 5 | 304 | - | 7,848 |
| Singapore | 264 | 4 | 1.5% | - | 0.0% | - | - | - | - | 190 | - |
| Sri Lanka | 25,332 | 7,378 | 29.1% | 1,699 | 6.7% | - | 2,804 | 30 | 1,580 | 71 | 12 |
| Syria | 71,498 | 21,043 | 29.4% | 31,942 | 44.7% | 3,514 | - | 196 | 933 | - | 13,288 |
| Taiwan | 13,901 | (5) | (5) | (5) | (5) | (5) | (5) | (5) | (5) | (5) | (5) |
| Tajikistan | 55,251 | 4,093 | 7.4% | 13,514 | 24.5% | 375 | 67 | 38 | 1,045 | 1 | 1,481 |
| Thailand | 198,115 | 70,657 | 35.7% | 3,089 | 1.6% | 1 | 25,578 | 4,405 | 4,973 | 6,539 | 40 |
| Turkey | 302,541 | 101,757 | 33.6% | 47,792 | 15.8% | 19,341 | 350 | 2,266 | 10,949 | 4 | 29,394 |
| Turkmenistan | 188,457 | 7,008 | 3.7% | 118,533 | 62.9% | 1,472 | 33 | 9 | 863 | 46 | 5,750 |
| United Arab Emirates | 32,278 | 919 | 2.8% | 1,178 | 3.6% | - | - | - | 94 | - | 504 |
| Uzbekistan | 172,742 | 18,649 | 10.8% | 88,031 | 51.0% | 3,637 | 219 | 133 | 5,279 | 83 | 7,980 |
| Vietnam | 128,066 | 32,579 | 25.4% | 2,479 | 1.9% | - | 31,964 | 1,961 | 4,029 | 20,273 | - |
| Yemen | 203,850 | 6,158 | 3.0% | 62,027 | 30.4% | 145 | - | 48 | 1,320 | - | 4,758 |
| **AFRICA** | | | | | | | | | | | |
| Algeria | 919,595 | 31,861 | 3.5% | 122,780 | 13.4% | 1,414 | - | 1 | 1,667 | 6 | 19,000 |
| Angola | 481,354 | 12,741 | 2.6% | 208,495 | 43.3% | 4 | 16 | 417 | 3,995 | 800 | 345 |
| Benin | 43,484 | 8,745 | 20.1% | 2,124 | 4.9% | - | 46 | 740 | 1,486 | 463 | 650 |
| Botswana | 224,607 | 1,440 | 0.6% | 98,842 | 44.0% | 1 | - | 8 | 2,035 | 6 | 347 |
| Burkina Faso | 105,869 | 15,444 | 14.6% | 23,166 | 21.9% | - | 102 | 500 | 4,767 | 621 | 6,722 |
| Burundi | 10,745 | 4,865 | 45.3% | 3,610 | 33.6% | 7 | 57 | 124 | 321 | 67 | 215 |
| Cameroon | 183,568 | 27,645 | 15.1% | 7,722 | 4.2% | - | 69 | 759 | 5,761 | 1,232 | 3,734 |
| Cape Verde | 1,557 | 158 | 10.2% | 97 | 6.2% | - | - | 27 | 22 | 195 | 9 |
| Central African Republic | 240,536 | 7,799 | 3.2% | 12,066 | 5.0% | 3 | 23 | 101 | 3,096 | 669 | 218 |
| Chad | 495,755 | 14,016 | 2.8% | 173,746 | 35.0% | 3 | 114 | 88 | 5,852 | 22 | 2,374 |
| Comoros | 863 | 510 | 59.1% | 58 | 6.7% | - | 17 | 4 | 51 | - | 21 |
| Congo | 132,047 | 849 | 0.6% | 38,610 | 29.2% | - | 1 | 6 | 87 | 46 | 102 |
| Congo, Democratic Republic of the | 905,446 | 30,425 | 3.4% | 57,915 | 6.4% | 9 | 338 | 1,184 | 823 | 1,050 | 925 |
| Cote d'Ivoire | 124,504 | 28,958 | 23.3% | 50,193 | 40.3% | - | 1,217 | 693 | 1,398 | 333 | 1,439 |
| Djibouti | 8,958 | 4 | 0.0% | 5,019 | 56.0% | - | - | - | 269 | - | 465 |
| Egypt | 386,662 | 12,888 | 3.3% | - | 0.0% | 6,388 | 5,681 | 6,487 | 3,583 | 29 | 4,510 |
| Equatorial Guinea | 10,831 | 888 | 8.2% | 402 | 3.7% | - | - | 13 | 5 | 6 | 37 |
| Eritrea | 45,406 | 1,942 | 4.3% | 26,900 | 59.2% | 32 | - | - | 2,150 | - | 1,570 |
| Ethiopia | 426,373 | 44,255 | 10.4% | 77,220 | 18.1% | 1,340 | - | 2,938 | 35,025 | 25 | 22,333 |
| Gabon | 103,347 | 1,911 | 1.8% | 18,012 | 17.4% | - | 1 | 26 | 36 | 213 | 197 |
| Gambia, The | 4,127 | 985 | 23.9% | 1,772 | 42.9% | - | 28 | 24 | 350 | 12 | 115 |
| Ghana | 92,098 | 22,780 | 24.7% | 32,240 | 35.0% | - | 244 | 988 | 1,297 | 327 | 2,715 |
| Guinea | 94,926 | 5,888 | 6.2% | 41,313 | 43.5% | - | 830 | 96 | 2,576 | 93 | 824 |
| Guinea-Bissau | 13,948 | 2,116 | 15.2% | 4,170 | 29.9% | - | 95 | 26 | 509 | 347 | 283 |
| Kenya | 224,961 | 19,923 | 8.9% | 82,240 | 36.6% | 184 | 58 | 2,419 | 13,229 | 311 | 7,000 |
| Lesotho | 11,720 | 1,290 | 11.0% | 7,722 | 65.9% | 39 | - | 128 | 547 | 63 | 839 |
| Liberia | 43,000 | 2,317 | 5.4% | 7,722 | 18.0% | - | 188 | - | 36 | 127 | 210 |
| Libya | 679,362 | 8,301 | 1.2% | 51,352 | 7.6% | 128 | - | - | 207 | - | 5,100 |
| Madagascar | 226,658 | 13,707 | 6.0% | 92,664 | 40.9% | 9 | 2,412 | 175 | 10,339 | 1,267 | 793 |
| Malawi | 45,747 | 9,035 | 19.7% | 7,143 | 15.6% | 2 | 86 | 2,190 | 741 | 450 | 110 |
| Mali | 478,841 | 18,147 | 3.8% | 115,831 | 24.2% | 8 | 801 | 378 | 6,594 | 72 | 6,282 |
| Mauritania | 397,956 | 1,931 | 0.5% | 151,545 | 38.1% | - | 65 | 7 | 1,470 | - | 7,437 |
| Mauritius | 788 | 409 | 51.9% | 27 | 3.4% | - | - | - | 27 | 12 | 10 |
| Morocco | 172,414 | 37,529 | 21.8% | 81,081 | 47.0% | 2,284 | 33 | 95 | 2,629 | 8 | 17,059 |
| Mozambique | 309,496 | 16,351 | 5.3% | 169,885 | 54.9% | 1 | 168 | 1,136 | 1,317 | 179 | 125 |
| Namibia | 317,818 | 3,166 | 1.0% | 146,719 | 46.2% | 4 | - | 26 | 2,436 | 21 | 2,330 |
| Niger | 489,192 | 17,375 | 3.6% | 46,332 | 9.5% | 10 | 66 | 5 | 2,217 | 39 | 4,386 |
| Nigeria | 356,669 | 120,464 | 33.8% | 151,352 | 42.4% | 75 | 3,109 | 4,734 | 19,677 | 5,000 | 20,833 |
| Rwanda | 10,169 | 5,019 | 49.4% | 2,124 | 20.9% | 6 | 13 | 66 | 766 | 172 | 264 |
| Sao Tome and Principe | 372 | 205 | 55.0% | 4 | 1.0% | - | - | 2 | 4 | 2 | 3 |
| Senegal | 75,951 | 9,653 | 12.7% | 21,815 | 28.7% | - | 229 | 84 | 3,076 | 263 | 4,619 |
| Sierra Leone | 27,699 | 2,178 | 7.9% | 8,494 | 30.7% | - | 215 | 9 | 413 | 52 | 365 |
| Somalia | 246,201 | 4,135 | 1.7% | 166,024 | 67.4% | 1 | 2 | 188 | 5,133 | 4 | 13,100 |
| South Africa | 470,693 | 60,664 | 12.9% | 324,048 | 68.8% | 2,200 | 3 | 9,147 | 13,594 | 1,542 | 28,677 |
| Sudan | 967,500 | 64,298 | 6.6% | 452,434 | 46.8% | 230 | 8 | 48 | 37,081 | - | 45,980 |
| Swaziland | 6,704 | 734 | 10.9% | 4,633 | 69.1% | - | - | 94 | 613 | 32 | 27 |
| Tanzania | 364,900 | 19,112 | 5.2% | 135,136 | 37.0% | 87 | 509 | 2,567 | 17,350 | 449 | 3,513 |
| Togo | 21,925 | 10,154 | 46.3% | 3,861 | 17.6% | - | 69 | 480 | 277 | 287 | 1,528 |
| Tunisia | 63,170 | 18,954 | 30.0% | 15,792 | 25.0% | 1,111 | - | - | 760 | 6 | 6,862 |
| Uganda | 93,065 | 27,799 | 29.9% | 19,738 | 21.2% | 12 | 106 | 1,108 | 5,977 | 1,540 | 1,065 |
| Zambia | 290,586 | 20,386 | 7.0% | 115,831 | 39.9% | 80 | 11 | 768 | 2,709 | 324 | 137 |
| Zimbabwe | 150,873 | 12,934 | 8.6% | 66,410 | 44.0% | 282 | - | 1,698 | 5,840 | 494 | 602 |
| **OCEANIA** | | | | | | | | | | | |
| Australia | 2,969,910 | 195,368 | 6.6% | 1,563,327 | 52.6% | 23,654 | 1,417 | 363 | 27,645 | 2,607 | 116,736 |
| Fiji | 7,056 | 1,100 | 15.6% | 676 | 9.6% | - | 16 | 1 | 335 | 139 | 7 |
| Kiribati | 313 | 151 | 48.1% | - | 0.0% | - | - | - | - | 10 | - |
| Micronesia, Federated States of | 271 | 139 | 51.3% | 42 | 15.7% | - | - | - | 14 | 32 | - |
| New Zealand | 104,454 | 13,019 | 12.5% | 53,525 | 51.2% | 337 | - | 185 | 9,025 | 364 | 45,114 |
| Papua New Guinea | 178,704 | 3,320 | 1.9% | 676 | 0.4% | - | 1 | 7 | 87 | 1,583 | 6 |
| Samoa | 1,093 | 498 | 45.6% | 8 | 0.7% | - | - | - | 28 | 179 | - |
| Solomon Islands | 10,954 | 286 | 2.6% | 154 | 1.4% | - | 5 | - | 11 | 63 | - |
| Tonga | 251 | 185 | 73.8% | 15 | 6.2% | - | - | - | 11 | 81 | - |
| Vanuatu | 4,707 | 463 | 9.8% | 162 | 3.4% | - | - | 1 | 151 | 62 | - |

This table presents data for most independent nations having an area greater than 200 square miles
- Zero, insignificant, or not available
(1) Source: United Nations Food and Agriculture Organization
(2) Includes data for Luxembourg
(3) Data for Luxembourg is included with Belgium
(4) Includes data for Taiwan
(5) Data for Taiwan is included with China

# WORLD ECONOMIC TABLE

| CONTINENT/Country | GDP 2002 | | Trade | | Commercial Energy Production Avg. 2000[2] | | | | | Average Production 1999-2001 in Metric Tons | | | |
|---|---|---|---|---|---|---|---|---|---|---|---|---|---|
| | Total GDP[1] | GDP Per Capita[1] | Value of Exports[1] | Value of Imports[1] | Total (1,000 Metric Tons of Coal Equiv.) | Solid % | Liquid % | Gas % | Hydro & Nuclear % | Coal[3] | Petroleum[3] | Iron Ore[4] | Bauxite[4] |
| **NORTH AMERICA** | | | | | | | | | | | | | |
| Bahamas | $4,590,000,000 | $17,000 | $560,700,000 | $1,860,000,000 | - | - | - | - | - | - | - | - | - |
| Belize | $1,280,000,000 | $4,900 | $290,000,000 | $430,000,000 | 12 | - | - | - | 100% | - | - | - | - |
| Canada | $934,100,000,000 | $29,400 | $260,500,000,000 | $229,000,000,000 | 507,218 | 10% | 33% | 43% | 14% | 70,711,084 | 97,834,913 | 20,527,000 | - |
| Costa Rica | $32,000,000,000 | $8,500 | $5,100,000,000 | $6,400,000,000 | 1,937 | - | - | - | 100% | - | - | - | - |
| Cuba | $30,690,000,000 | $2,300 | $1,800,000,000 | $4,800,000,000 | 4,626 | - | 83% | 17% | - | - | 2,134,520 | - | - |
| Dominica | $380,000,000 | $5,400 | $50,000,000 | $135,000,000 | 4 | - | - | - | 100% | - | - | - | - |
| Dominican Republic | $53,780,000,000 | $6,100 | $5,300,000,000 | $8,700,000,000 | 115 | - | - | - | 100% | - | - | - | - |
| El Salvador | $29,410,000,000 | $4,700 | $3,000,000,000 | $4,900,000,000 | 1,110 | - | - | - | 100% | - | - | - | - |
| Guatemala | $53,200,000,000 | $3,700 | $2,700,000,000 | $5,600,000,000 | 1,822 | - | 81% | 1% | 18% | - | 1,076,526 | 9,000 | - |
| Haiti | $10,600,000,000 | $1,700 | $298,000,000 | $1,140,000,000 | 33 | - | - | - | 100% | - | - | - | - |
| Honduras | $16,290,000,000 | $2,600 | $1,300,000,000 | $2,700,000,000 | 347 | - | - | - | 100% | - | - | - | - |
| Jamaica | $10,080,000,000 | $3,900 | $1,400,000,000 | $3,100,000,000 | 18 | - | - | - | 100% | - | - | - | 11,728,000 |
| Mexico | $924,400,000,000 | $9,000 | $158,400,000,000 | $168,400,000,000 | 340,594 | 1% | 79% | 16% | 4% | 11,097,943 | 150,165,451 | 6,860,000 | - |
| Nicaragua | $11,160,000,000 | $2,500 | $637,000,000 | $1,700,000,000 | 706 | - | - | - | 100% | - | - | - | - |
| Panama | $18,060,000,000 | $6,000 | $5,800,000,000 | $6,700,000,000 | 418 | - | - | - | 100% | - | - | - | - |
| St. Lucia | $866,000,000 | $5,400 | $68,300,000 | $319,400,000 | - | - | - | - | - | - | - | - | - |
| Trinidad and Tobago | $11,070,000,000 | $9,500 | $4,200,000,000 | $3,800,000,000 | 22,768 | - | 39% | 61% | - | - | 5,964,991 | - | - |
| United States | $10,450,000,000,000 | $37,600 | $733,900,000,000 | $1,194,100,000,000 | 2,342,228 | 33% | 22% | 30% | 14% | 996,498,186 | 289,640,487 | 35,178,000 | - |
| **SOUTH AMERICA** | | | | | | | | | | | | | |
| Argentina | $403,800,000,000 | $10,200 | $25,300,000,000 | $9,000,000,000 | 118,739 | - | 50% | 45% | 5% | 260,299 | 38,783,798 | - | - |
| Bolivia | $21,150,000,000 | $2,500 | $1,300,000,000 | $1,600,000,000 | 7,732 | - | 33% | 64% | 3% | - | 1,599,401 | - | - |
| Brazil | $1,376,000,000,000 | $7,600 | $59,400,000,000 | $46,200,000,000 | 143,640 | 3% | 63% | 6% | 28% | 4,446,477 | 61,155,586 | 124,667,000 | 13,654,000 |
| Chile | $156,100,000,000 | $10,000 | $17,800,000,000 | $15,600,000,000 | 6,180 | 6% | 11% | 45% | 38% | 475,484 | 349,201 | 5,523,000 | - |
| Colombia | $251,600,000,000 | $6,500 | $12,900,000,000 | $12,500,000,000 | 99,513 | 36% | 52% | 9% | 4% | 38,112,136 | 34,896,672 | 348,000 | - |
| Ecuador | $42,650,000,000 | $3,100 | $4,900,000,000 | $6,000,000,000 | 32,171 | - | 94% | 3% | 3% | - | 19,520,185 | - | - |
| Guyana | $2,628,000,000 | $4,000 | $500,000,000 | $575,000,000 | 1 | - | - | - | 100% | - | - | - | 2,272,000 |
| Paraguay | $25,190,000,000 | $4,200 | $2,000,000,000 | $2,400,000,000 | 6,577 | - | - | - | 100% | - | - | - | - |
| Peru | $138,800,000,000 | $4,800 | $7,600,000,000 | $7,300,000,000 | 10,933 | - | 73% | 9% | 18% | 52,297 | 4,932,561 | 2,701,000 | - |
| Suriname | $1,469,000,000 | $3,500 | $445,000,000 | $300,000,000 | 1,022 | - | 84% | - | 16% | - | 496,400 | - | 3,946,000 |
| Uruguay | $26,820,000,000 | $7,800 | $2,100,000,000 | $1,870,000,000 | 867 | - | - | - | 100% | - | - | - | - |
| Venezuela | $131,700,000,000 | $5,500 | $28,600,000,000 | $18,800,000,000 | 311,899 | 3% | 81% | 14% | 2% | 7,482,998 | 146,621,238 | 10,497,000 | 4,309,000 |
| **EUROPE** | | | | | | | | | | | | | |
| Albania | $15,690,000,000 | $4,500 | $340,000,000 | $1,500,000,000 | 1,089 | 1% | 42% | 2% | 55% | 32,666 | 284,321 | - | - |
| Austria | $227,700,000,000 | $27,700 | $70,000,000,000 | $74,000,000,000 | 9,611 | 5% | 15% | 24% | 56% | 1,197,660 | 921,120 | 525,000 | - |
| Belarus | $90,190,000,000 | $8,200 | $7,700,000,000 | $8,800,000,000 | 3,644 | 18% | 73% | 9% | - | - | 1,830,872 | - | - |
| Belgium | $299,700,000,000 | $29,000 | $162,000,000,000 | $152,000,000,000 | 18,451 | 2% | - | - | 98% | 318,998 | - | - | - |
| Bosnia and Herzegovina | $7,300,000,000 | $1,900 | $1,150,000,000 | $2,800,000,000 | 6,553 | 90% | - | - | 10% | 8,414,623 | - | 50,000 | 75,000 |
| Bulgaria | $49,230,000,000 | $6,600 | $5,300,000,000 | $6,900,000,000 | 13,500 | 46% | - | - | 53% | 28,841,963 | 37,048 | 310,000 | - |
| Croatia | $43,120,000,000 | $8,800 | $4,900,000,000 | $10,700,000,000 | 4,962 | - | 42% | 43% | 15% | 5,104 | 1,191,360 | - | - |
| Czech Republic | $157,100,000,000 | $15,300 | $40,800,000,000 | $43,200,000,000 | 39,843 | 85% | 1% | 1% | 14% | 63,466,671 | 283,097 | - | - |
| Denmark | $155,300,000,000 | $29,000 | $56,300,000,000 | $47,900,000,000 | 36,502 | - | 70% | 29% | 2% | - | 16,701,163 | - | - |
| Estonia | $15,520,000,000 | $10,900 | $3,400,000,000 | $4,400,000,000 | 3,892 | 100% | - | - | - | - | - | - | - |
| Finland | $133,800,000,000 | $26,200 | $40,100,000,000 | $31,800,000,000 | 11,933 | 15% | - | - | 85% | - | - | - | - |
| France | $1,558,000,000,000 | $25,700 | $307,800,000,000 | $303,700,000,000 | 175,306 | 2% | 4% | 1% | 93% | 3,616,981 | 1,446,228 | 12,000 | - |
| Germany | $2,160,000,000,000 | $26,600 | $608,000,000,000 | $487,300,000,000 | 181,697 | 47% | 2% | 13% | 38% | 204,685,080 | 3,044,206 | 5,000 | - |
| Greece | $203,300,000,000 | $19,000 | $12,600,000,000 | $31,400,000,000 | 12,988 | 92% | 3% | 1% | 4% | 64,503,999 | 166,807 | 583,000 | 1,975,000 |
| Hungary | $134,000,000,000 | $13,300 | $31,400,000,000 | $33,900,000,000 | 16,319 | 25% | 19% | 24% | 32% | 14,796,257 | 1,301,710 | - | 994,000 |
| Iceland | $8,444,000,000 | $25,000 | $2,300,000,000 | $2,100,000,000 | 1,638 | - | - | - | 100% | - | - | - | - |
| Ireland | $113,700,000,000 | $30,500 | $86,600,000,000 | $48,600,000,000 | 3,232 | 47% | - | 47% | 6% | - | - | - | - |
| Italy | $1,455,000,000,000 | $25,000 | $259,200,000,000 | $238,200,000,000 | 40,332 | - | 16% | 54% | 30% | 47,666 | 4,144,278 | - | - |
| Latvia | $20,990,000,000 | $8,300 | $2,300,000,000 | $3,900,000,000 | 369 | 6% | - | - | 94% | - | - | - | - |
| Lithuania | $30,080,000,000 | $8,400 | $5,400,000,000 | $6,800,000,000 | 3,677 | - | 12% | - | 87% | - | 251,824 | - | - |
| Luxembourg | $21,940,000,000 | $44,000 | $10,100,000,000 | $13,250,000,000 | 113 | - | - | - | 100% | - | - | - | - |
| Macedonia | $10,570,000,000 | $5,000 | $1,100,000,000 | $1,900,000,000 | 3,038 | 95% | - | - | 5% | 7,463,628 | - | 9,000 | - |
| Moldova | $11,510,000,000 | $2,500 | $590,000,000 | $980,000,000 | 7 | - | - | - | 100% | - | - | - | - |
| Netherlands | $437,800,000,000 | $26,900 | $243,300,000,000 | $201,100,000,000 | 87,974 | - | 4% | 94% | 2% | - | 1,437,293 | - | - |
| Norway | $149,100,000,000 | $31,800 | $68,200,000,000 | $37,300,000,000 | 324,396 | - | 72% | 22% | 5% | 847,996 | 154,419,533 | 355,000 | - |
| Poland | $373,200,000,000 | $9,500 | $32,400,000,000 | $43,400,000,000 | 108,277 | 94% | 1% | 5% | - | 164,737,813 | 645,072 | - | - |
| Portugal | $195,200,000,000 | $18,000 | $25,900,000,000 | $39,000,000,000 | 1,560 | - | - | - | 100% | - | - | 6,000 | - |
| Romania | $169,300,000,000 | $7,400 | $13,700,000,000 | $16,700,000,000 | 37,598 | 19% | 24% | 46% | 10% | 27,392,191 | 6,038,110 | 24,000 | - |
| Serbia and Montenegro | $23,150,000,000 | $2,370 | $2,400,000,000 | $6,300,000,000 | 14,188 | 74% | 8% | 8% | 10% | 34,480,488 | 810,787 | 10,000 | 580,000 |
| Slovakia | $67,340,000,000 | $12,200 | $12,900,000,000 | $15,400,000,000 | 8,813 | 17% | 1% | 2% | 79% | 3,606,648 | 48,134 | 200,000 | - |
| Slovenia | $37,060,000,000 | $18,000 | $10,300,000,000 | $11,100,000,000 | 3,644 | 38% | - | - | 62% | 4,391,644 | 991 | - | - |
| Spain | $850,700,000,000 | $20,700 | $122,200,000,000 | $156,600,000,000 | 40,444 | 28% | 2% | 1% | 68% | 23,479,212 | 296,665 | - | - |
| Sweden | $230,700,000,000 | $25,400 | $80,600,000,000 | $68,600,000,000 | 31,413 | 1% | - | - | 99% | - | - | 12,114,000 | - |
| Switzerland | $233,400,000,000 | $31,700 | $100,300,000,000 | $94,400,000,000 | 14,710 | - | - | - | 100% | - | - | - | - |
| Ukraine | $218,000,000,000 | $4,500 | $18,100,000,000 | $18,000,000,000 | 118,973 | 50% | 5% | 20% | 25% | 81,998,575 | 3,747,936 | 28,933,000 | - |
| United Kingdom | $1,528,000,000,000 | $25,300 | $286,300,000,000 | $330,100,000,000 | 397,906 | 7% | 47% | 38% | 8% | 32,758,497 | 119,820,635 | 1,000 | - |
| Russia | $1,409,000,000,000 | $9,300 | $104,600,000,000 | $60,700,000,000 | 1,412,286 | 10% | 33% | 52% | 5% | 253,376,954 | 324,436,632 | 48,300,000 | 3,983,000 |
| **ASIA** | | | | | | | | | | | | | |
| Afghanistan | $19,000,000,000 | $700 | $1,200,000,000 | $1,300,000,000 | 195 | 1% | - | 79% | 20% | 1,000 | - | - | - |
| Armenia | $12,130,000,000 | $3,800 | $525,000,000 | $991,000,000 | 901 | - | - | - | 100% | - | - | - | - |
| Azerbaijan | $28,610,000,000 | $3,500 | $2,000,000,000 | $1,800,000,000 | 27,748 | - | 72% | 27% | 1% | - | 14,183,985 | - | - |
| Bahrain | $9,910,000,000 | $14,000 | $5,800,000,000 | $4,200,000,000 | 14,442 | - | 22% | 78% | - | - | 1,827,397 | - | - |
| Bangladesh | $238,200,000,000 | $1,700 | $6,200,000,000 | $8,500,000,000 | 11,713 | - | - | 99% | 1% | - | 120,476 | - | - |
| Brunei | $6,500,000,000 | $18,600 | $3,000,000,000 | $1,400,000,000 | 27,922 | - | 49% | 51% | - | - | 9,435,323 | - | - |
| Cambodia | $20,420,000,000 | $1,500 | $1,380,000,000 | $1,730,000,000 | 10 | - | - | - | 100% | - | - | - | - |
| China | $5,989,000,000,000 | $4,400 | $658,260,000,000 | $618,930,000,000 | 1,023,314[5] | 70%[5] | 23%[5] | 4%[5] | 3%[5] | 1,251,423,183 | 161,226,848 | 72,967,000 | 9,000,000 |
| Cyprus | $9,400,000,000 | $15,000 | $1,030,000,000 | $3,900,000,000 | - | - | - | - | - | - | - | - | - |
| East Timor | $440,000,000 | $500 | $8,000,000 | $237,000,000 | - | - | - | - | - | - | - | - | - |
| Georgia | $16,050,000,000 | $3,100 | $515,000,000 | $750,000,000 | 963 | 1% | 16% | 8% | 75% | 10,000 | 102,258 | - | - |
| India | $2,664,000,000,000 | $2,540 | $44,500,000,000 | $53,800,000,000 | 367,807 | 73% | 14% | 8% | 4% | 304,842,421 | 32,123,682 | 48,080,000 | 7,554,000 |
| Indonesia | $714,200,000,000 | $3,100 | $52,300,000,000 | $32,100,000,000 | 279,695 | 27% | 45% | 26% | 2% | 79,664,587 | 70,565,213 | 282,000 | 1,168,000 |
| Iran | $458,300,000,000 | $7,000 | $24,800,000,000 | $21,800,000,000 | 350,729 | - | 77% | 23% | - | 1,376,993 | 181,632,777 | 5,367,000 | 136,000 |
| Iraq | $58,000,000,000 | $2,400 | $13,000,000,000 | $7,800,000,000 | 186,519 | - | 97% | 3% | - | - | 124,281,583 | - | - |
| Israel | $117,400,000,000 | $19,000 | $28,100,000,000 | $30,800,000,000 | 334 | 94% | 2% | 4% | 1% | - | 5,957 | - | - |
| Japan | $3,651,000,000,000 | $28,000 | $383,800,000,000 | $292,100,000,000 | 142,731 | 2% | 1% | 2% | 95% | 3,286,983 | 351,650 | 1,000 | - |
| Jordan | $22,630,000,000 | $4,300 | $2,500,000,000 | $4,400,000,000 | 316 | - | 1% | 97% | 2% | - | 1,986 | - | - |
| Kazakhstan | $120,000,000,000 | $6,300 | $10,300,000,000 | $9,600,000,000 | 113,390 | 40% | 45% | 14% | 1% | 70,311,969 | 30,508,827 | 7,467,000 | 3,668,000 |
| Korea, North | $22,260,000,000 | $1,000 | $842,000,000 | $1,314,000,000 | 65,932 | 96% | - | - | 4% | 94,174,845 | - | 3,000,000 | - |
| Korea, South | $941,500,000,000 | $19,400 | $162,600,000,000 | $148,400,000,000 | 43,892 | 6% | - | - | 94% | 4,054,646 | - | 175,000 | - |
| Kuwait | $36,850,000,000 | $15,000 | $16,000,000,000 | $7,300,000,000 | 161,322 | - | 92% | 8% | - | - | 98,844,823 | - | - |

| CONTINENT/Country | Total GDP[1] | GDP Per Capita[1] | Value of Exports[1] | Value of Imports[1] | Total (1,000 Metric Tons of Coal Equiv.) | Solid % | Liquid % | Gas % | Hydro & Nuclear % | Coal[3] | Petroleum[3] | Iron Ore[4] | Bauxite[4] |
|---|---|---|---|---|---|---|---|---|---|---|---|---|---|
| **GDP 2002** | | | **Trade** | | **Commercial Energy Production Avg. 2000[2]** | | | | | **Average Production 1999-2001 in Metric Tons** | | | |
| Kyrgyzstan | $13,880,000,000 | $2,800 | $488,000,000 | $587,000,000 | 2,026 | 9% | 5% | 2% | 83% | 423,664 | 91,503 | - | - |
| Laos | $10,400,000,000 | $1,700 | $345,000,000 | $555,000,000 | 146 | 1% | - | - | 99% | 1,000 | - | - | - |
| Lebanon | $17,610,000,000 | $5,400 | $1,000,000,000 | $6,000,000,000 | 55 | - | - | - | 100% | - | - | - | - |
| Malaysia | $198,400,000,000 | $9,300 | $95,200,000,000 | $76,800,000,000 | 110,069 | - | 41% | 58% | 1% | 314,332 | 33,792,132 | 208,000 | 137,000 |
| Mongolia | $5,060,000,000 | $1,840 | $501,000,000 | $659,000,000 | 2,212 | 100% | - | - | - | 5,099,640 | - | - | - |
| Myanmar | $73,690,000,000 | $1,660 | $2,700,000,000 | $2,500,000,000 | 9,297 | 3% | 6% | 88% | 2% | 358,331 | 587,374 | - | - |
| Nepal | $37,320,000,000 | $1,400 | $720,000,000 | $1,600,000,000 | 172 | 10% | - | - | 90% | 9,667 | - | - | - |
| Oman | $22,400,000,000 | $8,300 | $10,600,000,000 | $5,500,000,000 | 74,376 | - | 92% | 8% | - | - | 46,989,489 | - | - |
| Pakistan | $295,300,000,000 | $2,100 | $9,800,000,000 | $11,100,000,000 | 33,773 | 6% | 12% | 74% | 7% | 3,247,391 | 2,768,108 | - | 10,000 |
| Philippines | $379,700,000,000 | $4,200 | $35,100,000,000 | $33,500,000,000 | 16,244 | 6% | - | - | 94% | 1,306,993 | 173,128 | - | - |
| Qatar | $15,910,000,000 | $21,500 | $10,900,000,000 | $3,900,000,000 | 92,237 | - | 57% | 43% | - | - | 35,018,538 | - | - |
| Saudi Arabia | $268,900,000,000 | $10,500 | $71,000,000,000 | $39,500,000,000 | 736,996 | - | 91% | 9% | - | - | 401,559,222 | - | - |
| Singapore | $112,400,000,000 | $24,000 | $127,000,000,000 | $113,000,000,000 | - | - | - | - | - | - | - | - | - |
| Sri Lanka | $73,700,000,000 | $3,700 | $4,600,000,000 | $5,400,000,000 | 394 | - | - | - | 100% | - | - | - | - |
| Syria | $63,480,000,000 | $3,500 | $6,200,000,000 | $4,900,000,000 | 47,898 | - | 83% | 15% | 2% | - | 26,119,029 | - | - |
| Taiwan | $406,000,000,000 | $18,000 | $130,000,000,000 | $113,000,000,000 | [6] | [6] | [6] | [6] | [6] | 58,284 | 38,686 | - | - |
| Tajikistan | $8,476,000,000 | $1,250 | $710,000,000 | $830,000,000 | 1,790 | - | 1% | 3% | 95% | 20,667 | 16,613 | - | - |
| Thailand | $445,800,000,000 | $6,900 | $67,700,000,000 | $58,100,000,000 | 44,127 | 25% | 24% | 50% | 2% | 18,551,756 | 5,080,720 | 20,000 | - |
| Turkey | $489,700,000,000 | $7,000 | $35,100,000,000 | $50,800,000,000 | 28,167 | 69% | 14% | 3% | 14% | 65,334,995 | 2,642,106 | 2,300,000 | 303,000 |
| Turkmenistan | $31,340,000,000 | $5,500 | $2,970,000,000 | $2,250,000,000 | 71,764 | - | 15% | 85% | - | - | 7,139,688 | - | - |
| United Arab Emirates | $53,970,000,000 | $22,000 | $44,900,000,000 | $30,800,000,000 | 199,656 | - | 83% | 17% | - | - | 112,737,023 | - | - |
| Uzbekistan | $66,060,000,000 | $2,500 | $2,800,000,000 | $2,500,000,000 | 85,806 | 1% | 13% | 85% | 1% | 2,736,319 | 4,419,300 | - | - |
| Vietnam | $183,800,000,000 | $2,250 | $16,500,000,000 | $16,800,000,000 | 39,300 | 30% | 59% | 5% | 7% | 9,688,950 | 15,926,911 | - | - |
| Yemen | $15,070,000,000 | $840 | $3,400,000,000 | $2,900,000,000 | 30,622 | - | 100% | - | - | - | 21,304,264 | - | - |
| **AFRICA** | | | | | | | | | | | | | |
| Algeria | $173,800,000,000 | $5,300 | $19,500,000,000 | $10,600,000,000 | 222,648 | - | 47% | 53% | - | 24,000 | 61,651,110 | 757,000 | - |
| Angola | $18,360,000,000 | $1,600 | $8,600,000,000 | $4,100,000,000 | 53,315 | - | 98% | 1% | - | - | 36,961,745 | - | - |
| Benin | $7,380,000,000 | $1,070 | $207,000,000 | $479,000,000 | 69 | - | 100% | - | - | - | 39,547 | - | - |
| Botswana | $13,480,000,000 | $9,500 | $2,400,000,000 | $1,900,000,000 | [7] | [7] | [7] | [7] | [7] | 956,767 | - | - | - |
| Burkina Faso | $14,510,000,000 | $1,080 | $250,000,000 | $525,000,000 | 15 | - | - | - | 100% | - | - | - | - |
| Burundi | $3,146,000,000 | $600 | $26,000,000 | $135,000,000 | 21 | 29% | - | - | 71% | 1,000 | - | - | - |
| Cameroon | $26,840,000,000 | $1,700 | $1,900,000,000 | $1,700,000,000 | 10,722 | - | 96% | - | 4% | - | 4,326,440 | - | - |
| Cape Verde | $600,000,000 | $1,400 | $30,000,000 | $220,000,000 | - | - | - | - | - | - | - | - | - |
| Central African Republic | $4,296,000,000 | $1,300 | $134,000,000 | $102,000,000 | 10 | - | - | - | 100% | - | - | - | - |
| Chad | $9,297,000,000 | $1,100 | $197,000,000 | $570,000,000 | - | - | - | - | - | - | - | - | - |
| Comoros | $441,000,000 | $720 | $16,300,000 | $39,800,000 | - | - | - | - | - | - | - | - | - |
| Congo | $2,500,000,000 | $900 | $2,400,000,000 | $73,000,000 | 19,097 | - | 99% | 1% | - | - | 13,651,000 | - | - |
| Congo, Democratic Republic of the | $34,000,000,000 | $610 | $1,200,000,000 | $890,000,000 | 2,630 | 4% | 71% | - | 25% | 96,000 | 1,194,669 | - | - |
| Cote d'Ivoire | $24,030,000,000 | $1,500 | $4,400,000,000 | $2,500,000,000 | 4,439 | - | 50% | 45% | 5% | - | 620,450 | - | - |
| Djibouti | $619,000,000 | $1,300 | $70,000,000 | $255,000,000 | - | - | - | - | - | - | - | - | - |
| Egypt | $289,800,000,000 | $3,900 | $7,000,000,000 | $15,200,000,000 | 86,315 | - | 65% | 32% | 2% | - | 38,024,058 | 1,283,000 | - |
| Equatorial Guinea | $1,270,000,000 | $2,700 | $2,500,000,000 | $562,000,000 | 7,531 | - | 100% | - | - | - | 7,461,521 | - | - |
| Eritrea | $3,300,000,000 | $740 | $20,000,000 | $500,000,000 | - | - | - | - | - | - | - | - | - |
| Ethiopia | $48,530,000,000 | $750 | $433,000,000 | $1,630,000,000 | 211 | - | - | - | 100% | - | - | - | - |
| Gabon | $8,354,000,000 | $5,700 | $2,600,000,000 | $1,100,000,000 | 23,273 | - | 95% | 5% | - | - | 15,674,359 | - | - |
| Gambia, The | $2,582,000,000 | $1,800 | $138,000,000 | $225,000,000 | - | - | - | - | - | - | - | - | - |
| Ghana | $41,250,000,000 | $2,100 | $2,200,000,000 | $2,800,000,000 | 830 | - | 2% | - | 98% | - | 330,933 | - | 525,000 |
| Guinea | $18,690,000,000 | $2,000 | $835,000,000 | $670,000,000 | 25 | - | - | - | 100% | - | - | - | 15,663,000 |
| Guinea-Bissau | $901,400,000 | $800 | $71,000,000 | $59,000,000 | - | - | - | - | - | - | - | - | - |
| Kenya | $32,890,000,000 | $1,020 | $2,100,000,000 | $3,000,000,000 | 642 | - | - | - | 100% | - | - | - | - |
| Lesotho | $5,106,000,000 | $2,700 | $422,000,000 | $738,000,000 | [7] | [7] | [7] | [7] | [7] | - | - | - | - |
| Liberia | $3,116,000,000 | $1,100 | $110,000,000 | $165,000,000 | 24 | - | - | - | 100% | - | - | - | - |
| Libya | $33,360,000,000 | $7,600 | $11,800,000,000 | $6,300,000,000 | 103,205 | - | 92% | 8% | - | - | 67,767,436 | - | - |
| Madagascar | $12,590,000,000 | $760 | $700,000,000 | $985,000,000 | 64 | - | - | - | 100% | - | - | - | - |
| Malawi | $6,811,000,000 | $670 | $435,000,000 | $505,000,000 | 107 | - | - | - | 100% | - | - | - | - |
| Mali | $9,775,000,000 | $860 | $680,000,000 | $630,000,000 | 29 | - | - | - | 100% | - | - | - | - |
| Mauritania | $4,891,000,000 | $1,900 | $355,000,000 | $360,000,000 | 4 | - | - | - | 100% | - | - | 7,492,000 | - |
| Mauritius | $12,150,000,000 | $11,000 | $1,600,000,000 | $1,800,000,000 | 12 | - | - | - | 100% | - | - | - | - |
| Morocco | $121,800,000,000 | $3,900 | $7,500,000,000 | $10,400,000,000 | 201 | 14% | 9% | 33% | 43% | 61,000 | 15,223 | 4,000 | - |
| Mozambique | $19,520,000,000 | $1,000 | $680,000,000 | $1,180,000,000 | 874 | 2% | - | - | 98% | 18,667 | - | - | 8,000 |
| Namibia | $13,150,000,000 | $6,900 | $1,210,000,000 | $1,380,000,000 | [7] | [7] | [7] | [7] | [7] | - | - | - | - |
| Niger | $8,713,000,000 | $830 | $293,000,000 | $368,000,000 | 175 | 100% | - | - | - | 151,666 | - | - | - |
| Nigeria | $112,500,000,000 | $875 | $17,300,000,000 | $13,600,000,000 | 172,641 | - | 90% | 10% | - | 61,000 | 108,397,478 | - | - |
| Rwanda | $8,920,000,000 | $1,200 | $68,000,000 | $253,000,000 | 20 | - | - | - | 100% | - | - | - | - |
| Sao Tome and Principe | $200,000,000 | $1,200 | $5,500,000 | $24,800,000 | 1 | - | - | - | 100% | - | - | - | - |
| Senegal | $15,640,000,000 | $1,500 | $1,150,000,000 | $1,460,000,000 | 1 | - | - | 100% | - | - | - | - | - |
| Sierra Leone | $2,826,000,000 | $580 | $35,000,000 | $190,000,000 | [7] | [7] | [7] | [7] | [7] | - | - | - | - |
| Somalia | $4,270,000,000 | $550 | $126,000,000 | $343,000,000 | - | - | - | - | - | - | - | - | - |
| South Africa | $427,700,000,000 | $10,000 | $31,800,000,000 | $26,600,000,000 | 245,195[8] | 92%[8] | 5%[8] | 1%[8] | 2%[8] | 224,286,505 | 1,277,485 | 20,751,000 | - |
| Sudan | $52,900,000,000 | $1,420 | $1,800,000,000 | $1,500,000,000 | 13,436 | - | 99% | - | 1% | - | 7,679,837 | - | - |
| Swaziland | $5,542,000,000 | $4,400 | $820,000,000 | $938,000,000 | [7] | [7] | [7] | [7] | [7] | 288,665 | - | - | - |
| Tanzania | $20,420,000,000 | $630 | $863,000,000 | $1,670,000,000 | 343 | 23% | - | - | 77% | 5,000 | - | - | - |
| Togo | $7,594,000,000 | $1,500 | $449,000,000 | $561,000,000 | - | - | - | - | - | - | - | - | - |
| Tunisia | $67,130,000,000 | $6,500 | $6,800,000,000 | $8,700,000,000 | 8,065 | - | 66% | 34% | - | - | 3,826,400 | 105,000 | - |
| Uganda | $30,490,000,000 | $1,260 | $476,000,000 | $1,140,000,000 | 193 | - | - | - | 100% | - | - | 3,000 | - |
| Zambia | $8,240,000,000 | $890 | $709,000,000 | $1,123,000,000 | 1,117 | 15% | - | - | 85% | 192,358 | - | - | - |
| Zimbabwe | $26,070,000,000 | $2,400 | $1,570,000,000 | $1,739,000,000 | 4,801 | 92% | - | - | 8% | 4,508,643 | - | 237,000 | - |
| **OCEANIA** | | | | | | | | | | | | | |
| Australia | $525,500,000,000 | $27,000 | $66,300,000,000 | $68,000,000,000 | 331,923 | 71% | 14% | 14% | 1% | 307,176,075 | 31,728,994 | 104,014,000 | 51,834,000 |
| Fiji | $4,822,000,000 | $5,500 | $442,000,000 | $642,000,000 | 53 | - | - | - | 100% | - | - | - | - |
| Kiribati | $79,000,000 | $840 | $6,000,000 | $44,000,000 | - | - | - | - | - | - | - | - | - |
| Micronesia, Federated States of | $277,000,000 | $2,000 | $22,000,000 | $149,000,000 | - | - | - | - | - | - | - | - | - |
| New Zealand | $78,400,000,000 | $20,200 | $15,000,000,000 | $12,500,000,000 | 19,812 | 14% | 13% | 40% | 33% | 3,452,315 | 1,839,394 | 660,000 | - |
| Papua New Guinea | $10,860,000,000 | $2,300 | $1,800,000,000 | $1,100,000,000 | 5,864 | - | 96% | 2% | 2% | - | 3,874,601 | - | - |
| Samoa | $1,000,000,000 | $5,600 | $15,500,000 | $130,100,000 | 3 | - | - | - | 100% | - | - | - | - |
| Solomon Islands | $800,000,000 | $1,700 | $47,000,000 | $82,000,000 | - | - | - | - | - | - | - | - | - |
| Tonga | $236,000,000 | $2,200 | $8,900,000 | $70,000,000 | - | - | - | - | - | - | - | - | - |
| Vanuatu | $563,000,000 | $2,900 | $22,000,000 | $93,000,000 | - | - | - | - | - | - | - | - | - |

This table presents data for most independent nations having an area greater than 200 square miles
- Zero, insignificant, or not available
(1) Source: United States Central Intelligence Agency World Factbook
(2) Source: United Nations Energy Statistics Yearbook
(3) Source: United States Energy Information Administration International Energy Annual
(4) Source: United States Geological Survey Minerals Yearbook
(5) Includes data for Taiwan
(6) Data for Taiwan is included with China
(7) Data for countries in the South Africa Customs Union are included with South Africa
(8) Includes data for countries in the South Africa Customs Union

# WORLD ENVIRONMENT TABLE

| CONTINENT/Country | Total Area Sq. Miles | Protected Area 2002[1,2] Sq. Miles | % | Mammal | Bird | Endangered Species 2003[3] Reptile | Amphib. | Fish | Invrt. | Forest Cover[4] Sq. Miles 2000 | Percent Change 1990-2000 |
|---|---|---|---|---|---|---|---|---|---|---|---|
| **NORTH AMERICA** | | | | | | | | | | | |
| Bahamas | 5,382 | - | - | 5 | 4 | 6 | 0 | 15 | 1 | 3,251 | |
| Belize | 8,867 | 3,999 | 45.1% | 5 | 2 | 4 | 0 | 17 | 1 | 5,205 | -20.9% |
| Canada | 3,855,103 | 427,916 | 11.1% | 16 | 8 | 2 | 1 | 25 | 11 | 944,294 | |
| Costa Rica | 19,730 | 4,538 | 23.0% | 13 | 13 | 7 | 1 | 13 | 9 | 7,598 | -7.4% |
| Cuba | 42,804 | 29,578 | 69.1% | 11 | 18 | 7 | 0 | 23 | 3 | 9,066 | 13.4% |
| Dominica | 290 | - | - | 1 | 3 | 4 | 0 | 11 | 0 | 178 | -8.0% |
| Dominican Republic | 18,730 | 9,721 | 51.9% | 5 | 15 | 10 | 1 | 10 | 2 | 5,313 | |
| El Salvador | 8,124 | 33 | 0.4% | 2 | 0 | 4 | 0 | 5 | 1 | 467 | -37.3% |
| Guatemala | 42,042 | 8,408 | 20.0% | 7 | 6 | 8 | 0 | 14 | 8 | 11,004 | -15.9% |
| Haiti | 10,714 | 43 | 0.4% | 4 | 14 | 8 | 1 | 12 | 2 | 340 | -44.3% |
| Honduras | 43,277 | 2,770 | 6.4% | 10 | 5 | 6 | 0 | 14 | 2 | 20,784 | -9.9% |
| Jamaica | 4,244 | 3,590 | 84.6% | 5 | 12 | 8 | 4 | 12 | 5 | 1,255 | -14.2% |
| Mexico | 758,452 | 77,362 | 10.2% | 72 | 40 | 18 | 4 | 106 | 41 | 213,148 | -10.3% |
| Nicaragua | 50,054 | 8,910 | 17.8% | 6 | 5 | 7 | 0 | 17 | 2 | 12,656 | -26.3% |
| Panama | 29,157 | 6,327 | 21.7% | 17 | 16 | 7 | 0 | 17 | 2 | 11,104 | -15.3% |
| St. Lucia | 238 | - | - | 2 | 5 | 6 | 0 | 10 | 0 | 35 | -35.7% |
| Trinidad and Tobago | 1,980 | 119 | 6.0% | 1 | 1 | 5 | 0 | 15 | 0 | 1,000 | -7.8% |
| United States | 3,794,083 | 982,668 | 25.9% | 39 | 56 | 27 | 25 | 155 | 557 | 872,563 | 1.7% |
| **SOUTH AMERICA** | | | | | | | | | | | |
| Argentina | 1,073,519 | 70,852 | 6.6% | 32 | 39 | 5 | 5 | 9 | 10 | 133,777 | -7.6% |
| Bolivia | 424,165 | 56,838 | 13.4% | 25 | 28 | 2 | 1 | 0 | 1 | 204,897 | -2.9% |
| Brazil | 3,300,172 | 221,112 | 6.7% | 74 | 113 | 22 | 6 | 33 | 34 | 2,100,028 | -4.1% |
| Chile | 291,930 | 55,175 | 18.9% | 21 | 22 | 0 | 3 | 9 | 0 | 59,985 | -1.3% |
| Colombia | 439,737 | 44,853 | 10.2% | 39 | 78 | 14 | 0 | 23 | 0 | 191,510 | -3.7% |
| Ecuador | 109,484 | 20,036 | 18.3% | 34 | 62 | 10 | 0 | 11 | 48 | 40,761 | -11.5% |
| Guyana | 83,000 | 249 | 0.3% | 13 | 2 | 6 | 0 | 13 | 1 | 65,170 | -2.8% |
| Paraguay | 157,048 | 5,497 | 3.5% | 10 | 26 | 2 | 0 | 0 | 0 | 90,240 | -5.0% |
| Peru | 496,225 | 30,270 | 6.1% | 46 | 76 | 6 | 1 | 8 | 2 | 251,796 | -4.0% |
| Suriname | 63,037 | 3,089 | 4.9% | 12 | 1 | 6 | 0 | 12 | 0 | 54,491 | |
| Uruguay | 67,574 | 203 | 0.3% | 6 | 11 | 3 | 0 | 8 | 1 | 4,988 | 63.3% |
| Venezuela | 352,145 | 224,669 | 63.8% | 26 | 24 | 13 | 0 | 19 | 1 | 191,144 | -4.2% |
| **EUROPE** | | | | | | | | | | | |
| Albania | 11,100 | 422 | 3.8% | 3 | 3 | 4 | 0 | 16 | 4 | 3,826 | -7.3% |
| Austria | 32,378 | 10,685 | 33.0% | 7 | 3 | 0 | 0 | 7 | 44 | 15,004 | 2.0% |
| Belarus | 80,155 | 5,050 | 6.3% | 7 | 3 | 0 | 0 | 0 | 5 | 36,301 | 37.5% |
| Belgium | 11,787 | - | - | 11 | 2 | 0 | 0 | 7 | 11 | 2,811 | -1.8% |
| Bosnia and Herzegovina | 19,767 | 99 | 0.5% | 10 | 3 | 1 | 1 | 10 | 10 | 8,776 | |
| Bulgaria | 42,855 | 1,928 | 4.5% | 14 | 10 | 2 | 0 | 10 | 9 | 14,247 | 5.9% |
| Croatia | 21,829 | 1,637 | 7.5% | 9 | 4 | 1 | 1 | 26 | 11 | 6,884 | 1.1% |
| Czech Republic | 30,450 | 4,902 | 16.1% | 8 | 2 | 0 | 0 | 7 | 19 | 10,162 | 0.2% |
| Denmark | 16,640 | 5,658 | 34.0% | 5 | 1 | 0 | 0 | 7 | 11 | 1,757 | 2.2% |
| Estonia | 17,462 | 2,061 | 11.8% | 5 | 3 | 0 | 0 | 1 | 4 | 7,954 | 6.5% |
| Finland | 130,559 | 12,142 | 9.3% | 4 | 3 | 0 | 0 | 1 | 10 | 84,691 | 0.4% |
| France | 208,482 | 27,728 | 13.3% | 18 | 5 | 3 | 2 | 15 | 65 | 59,232 | 4.2% |
| Germany | 137,847 | 43,973 | 31.9% | 11 | 5 | 0 | 0 | 12 | 31 | 41,467 | |
| Greece | 50,949 | 1,834 | 3.6% | 13 | 7 | 6 | 1 | 26 | 11 | 13,896 | 9.1% |
| Hungary | 35,919 | 2,514 | 7.0% | 9 | 8 | 1 | 0 | 8 | 25 | 7,104 | 4.1% |
| Iceland | 39,769 | 3,897 | 9.8% | 7 | 0 | 0 | 0 | 8 | 0 | 120 | 24.0% |
| Ireland | 27,133 | 461 | 1.7% | 6 | 1 | 0 | 0 | 6 | 3 | 2,544 | 34.8% |
| Italy | 116,342 | 9,191 | 7.9% | 14 | 5 | 4 | 4 | 16 | 58 | 38,622 | 3.0% |
| Latvia | 24,942 | 3,342 | 13.4% | 5 | 3 | 0 | 0 | 3 | 8 | 11,286 | 4.5% |
| Lithuania | 25,213 | 2,597 | 10.3% | 6 | 4 | 0 | 0 | 3 | 5 | 7,699 | 2.5% |
| Luxembourg | 999 | - | - | 3 | 1 | 0 | 0 | 0 | 4 | | |
| Macedonia | 9,928 | 705 | 7.1% | 11 | 3 | 2 | 0 | 4 | 5 | 3,498 | |
| Moldova | 13,070 | 183 | 1.4% | 6 | 5 | 1 | 0 | 9 | 5 | 1,255 | 2.2% |
| Netherlands | 16,164 | 2,295 | 14.2% | 10 | 4 | 0 | 0 | 7 | 7 | 1,448 | 2.7% |
| Norway | 125,050 | 8,503 | 6.8% | 10 | 2 | 0 | 0 | 7 | 9 | 34,240 | 3.6% |
| Poland | 120,728 | 14,970 | 12.4% | 14 | 4 | 0 | 0 | 3 | 15 | 34,931 | 2.0% |
| Portugal | 35,516 | 2,344 | 6.6% | 17 | 7 | 0 | 1 | 19 | 82 | 14,154 | 18.4% |
| Romania | 91,699 | 4,310 | 4.7% | 17 | 8 | 2 | 0 | 10 | 22 | 24,896 | 2.3% |
| Serbia and Montenegro | 39,449 | 1,302 | 3.3% | 12 | 5 | 1 | 0 | 19 | 19 | 11,147 | -0.5% |
| Slovakia | 18,924 | 4,315 | 22.8% | 9 | 4 | 1 | 0 | 8 | 19 | 8,405 | 9.0% |
| Slovenia | 7,821 | 469 | 6.0% | 9 | 1 | 0 | 1 | 15 | 42 | 4,274 | 2.0% |
| Spain | 194,885 | 16,565 | 8.5% | 24 | 7 | 7 | 3 | 23 | 63 | 55,483 | 6.4% |
| Sweden | 173,732 | 15,810 | 9.1% | 6 | 2 | 0 | 0 | 6 | 13 | 104,765 | |
| Switzerland | 15,943 | 4,783 | 30.0% | 5 | 2 | 0 | 0 | 4 | 30 | 4,629 | 3.7% |
| Ukraine | 233,090 | 9,091 | 3.9% | 16 | 8 | 2 | 0 | 11 | 14 | 37,004 | 3.3% |
| United Kingdom | 93,788 | 19,602 | 20.9% | 12 | 2 | 0 | 0 | 11 | 10 | 10,788 | 6.5% |
| Russia | 6,592,849 | 514,242 | 7.8% | 45 | 38 | 6 | 0 | 18 | 30 | 3,287,242 | 0.2% |
| **ASIA** | | | | | | | | | | | |
| Afghanistan | 251,773 | 755 | 0.3% | 13 | 11 | 1 | 1 | 0 | 1 | 5,216 | - |
| Armenia | 11,506 | 874 | 7.6% | 11 | 4 | 5 | 0 | 1 | 7 | 1,355 | 13.6% |
| Azerbaijan | 33,437 | 2,040 | 6.1% | 13 | 8 | 5 | 0 | 5 | 6 | 4,224 | 13.5% |
| Bahrain | 267 | - | - | 1 | 6 | 0 | 0 | 6 | 0 | | |
| Bangladesh | 55,598 | 445 | 0.8% | 22 | 23 | 20 | 0 | 8 | 0 | 5,151 | 14.1% |
| Brunei | 2,226 | - | - | 11 | 14 | 4 | 0 | 6 | 0 | 1,707 | -2.2% |
| Cambodia | 69,898 | 12,931 | 18.5% | 24 | 19 | 10 | 0 | 11 | 0 | 36,043 | -5.7% |
| China | 3,690,045 | 287,824 | 7.8% | 81 | 75 | 31 | 1 | 46 | 4 | 631,200 | 12.4% |
| Cyprus | 3,572 | - | - | 3 | 3 | 3 | 0 | 6 | 0 | 664 | 44.5% |
| East Timor | 5,743 | | | 0 | 6 | 0 | 0 | 2 | 0 | 1,958 | -6.3% |
| Georgia | 26,911 | 619 | 2.3% | 13 | 3 | 7 | 1 | 6 | 10 | 11,537 | |
| India | 1,222,510 | 63,571 | 5.2% | 86 | 72 | 25 | 3 | 27 | 23 | 247,542 | 0.6% |
| Indonesia | 735,310 | 151,474 | 20.6% | 147 | 114 | 28 | 0 | 91 | 31 | 405,353 | -11.1% |
| Iran | 636,372 | 30,546 | 4.8% | 22 | 13 | 8 | 2 | 14 | 3 | 28,182 | |
| Iraq | 169,235 | | | 11 | 11 | 2 | 0 | 3 | 2 | 3,085 | |
| Israel | 8,019 | 1,267 | 15.8% | 15 | 12 | 4 | 0 | 10 | 10 | 510 | 61.0% |
| Japan | 145,850 | 9,918 | 6.8% | 37 | 35 | 11 | 10 | 27 | 45 | 92,977 | 0.1% |
| Jordan | 34,495 | 1,173 | 3.4% | 9 | 8 | 1 | 0 | 5 | 3 | 332 | |
| Kazakhstan | 1,049,156 | 28,327 | 2.7% | 17 | 15 | 2 | 1 | 7 | 4 | 46,904 | 24.5% |
| Korea, North | 46,540 | 1,210 | 2.6% | 13 | 19 | 0 | 0 | 5 | 1 | 31,699 | |
| Korea, South | 38,328 | 2,645 | 6.9% | 13 | 25 | 0 | 0 | 7 | 1 | 24,124 | -0.8% |

| CONTINENT/Country | Total Area Sq. Miles | Protected Area 2002[1,2] Sq. Miles | % | Mammal | Bird | Reptile | Amphib. | Fish | Invrt. | Forest Cover[4] Sq. Miles 2000 | Percent Change 1990-2000 |
|---|---|---|---|---|---|---|---|---|---|---|---|
| Kuwait | 6,880 | 103 | 1.5% | 1 | 7 | 1 | 0 | 6 | 0 | 19 | 66.7% |
| Kyrgyzstan | 77,182 | 2,779 | 3.6% | 7 | 4 | 2 | 0 | 0 | 3 | 3,873 | 29.4% |
| Laos | 91,429 | 11,429 | 12.5% | 31 | 20 | 11 | 0 | 6 | 0 | 48,498 | -4.0% |
| Lebanon | 4,016 | 20 | 0.5% | 6 | 7 | 1 | 0 | 8 | 1 | 139 | -2.7% |
| Malaysia | 127,320 | 7,257 | 5.7% | 50 | 37 | 21 | 0 | 34 | 3 | 74,487 | 52.4% |
| Mongolia | 604,829 | 69,555 | 11.5% | 14 | 16 | 0 | 0 | 1 | 3 | 41,101 | -5.3% |
| Myanmar | 261,228 | 784 | 0.3% | 39 | 35 | 20 | 0 | 7 | 2 | 132,892 | -13.1% |
| Nepal | 56,827 | 5,058 | 8.9% | 29 | 25 | 6 | 0 | 0 | 1 | 15,058 | -16.7% |
| Oman | 119,499 | 16,730 | 14.0% | 11 | 10 | 4 | 0 | 17 | 1 | 4 | - |
| Pakistan | 339,732 | 16,647 | 4.9% | 17 | 17 | 9 | 0 | 14 | 0 | 9,116 | -14.3% |
| Philippines | 115,831 | 6,602 | 5.7% | 50 | 67 | 8 | 23 | 48 | 19 | 22,351 | -13.3% |
| Qatar | 4,412 | - | - | 0 | 6 | 1 | 0 | 4 | 0 | - | - |
| Saudi Arabia | 830,000 | 317,890 | 38.3% | 9 | 15 | 2 | 0 | 8 | 1 | 5,807 | - |
| Singapore | 264 | 13 | 4.9% | 3 | 7 | 3 | 0 | 12 | 1 | 8 | - |
| Sri Lanka | 25,332 | 3,420 | 13.5% | 22 | 14 | 8 | 0 | 22 | 2 | 7,490 | -15.2% |
| Syria | 71,498 | - | - | 4 | 8 | 3 | 0 | 8 | 3 | 1,780 | - |
| Taiwan | 13,901 | - | - | 12 | 21 | 8 | 0 | 23 | 0 | - | - |
| Tajikistan | 55,251 | 2,321 | 4.2% | 9 | 7 | 1 | 0 | 3 | 2 | 1,544 | 5.3% |
| Thailand | 198,115 | 27,538 | 13.9% | 37 | 37 | 19 | 0 | 35 | 1 | 56,996 | -7.1% |
| Turkey | 302,541 | 4,841 | 1.6% | 17 | 11 | 12 | 3 | 29 | 13 | 39,479 | 2.2% |
| Turkmenistan | 188,457 | 7,915 | 4.2% | 13 | 6 | 2 | 0 | 8 | 5 | 14,498 | - |
| United Arab Emirates | 32,278 | - | - | 4 | 8 | 1 | 0 | 6 | 0 | 1,239 | 32.1% |
| Uzbekistan | 172,742 | 3,455 | 2.0% | 9 | 9 | 2 | 0 | 4 | 1 | 7,602 | 2.4% |
| Vietnam | 128,066 | 4,738 | 3.7% | 42 | 37 | 24 | 1 | 22 | 0 | 37,911 | 5.5% |
| Yemen | 203,850 | - | - | 6 | 12 | 2 | 0 | 10 | 2 | 1,734 | -17.0% |
| | | | | | | | | | | | |
| **AFRICA** | | | | | | | | | | | |
| Algeria | 919,595 | 45,980 | 5.0% | 13 | 6 | 2 | 0 | 9 | 12 | 8,282 | 14.2% |
| Angola | 481,354 | 31,769 | 6.6% | 19 | 15 | 4 | 0 | 8 | 6 | 269,329 | -1.7% |
| Benin | 43,484 | 4,957 | 11.4% | 9 | 2 | 1 | 0 | 7 | 0 | 10,232 | -20.9% |
| Botswana | 224,607 | 41,552 | 18.5% | 7 | 7 | 0 | 0 | 0 | 0 | 47,981 | -8.7% |
| Burkina Faso | 105,869 | 12,175 | 11.5% | 7 | 2 | 1 | 0 | 0 | 3 | 27,371 | -2.1% |
| Burundi | 10,745 | 612 | 5.7% | 6 | 7 | 0 | 0 | 0 | 0 | 363 | -61.0% |
| Cameroon | 183,568 | 8,261 | 4.5% | 38 | 15 | 1 | 1 | 34 | 4 | 92,116 | -8.5% |
| Cape Verde | 1,557 | - | - | 3 | 2 | 0 | 0 | 13 | 0 | 328 | 142.9% |
| Central African Republic | 240,536 | 20,927 | 8.7% | 14 | 3 | 1 | 0 | 0 | 0 | 88,444 | -1.3% |
| Chad | 495,755 | 45,114 | 9.1% | 15 | 5 | 1 | 0 | 0 | 1 | 49,004 | -6.0% |
| Comoros | 863 | - | - | 2 | 9 | 2 | 0 | 3 | 4 | 31 | -33.3% |
| Congo | 132,047 | 6,602 | 5.0% | 15 | 3 | 1 | 0 | 9 | 1 | 85,174 | -0.8% |
| Congo, Democratic Republic of the | 905,446 | 58,854 | 6.5% | 40 | 28 | 2 | 0 | 9 | 45 | 522,037 | -3.8% |
| Cote d'Ivoire | 124,504 | 7,470 | 6.0% | 19 | 12 | 2 | 1 | 10 | 1 | 27,479 | -27.1% |
| Djibouti | 8,958 | - | - | 5 | 5 | 0 | 0 | 9 | 0 | 23 | - |
| Egypt | 386,662 | 37,506 | 9.7% | 13 | 7 | 6 | 0 | 13 | 1 | 278 | 38.5% |
| Equatorial Guinea | 10,831 | - | - | 16 | 5 | 2 | 1 | 7 | 2 | 6,765 | -5.7% |
| Eritrea | 45,406 | 1,952 | 4.3% | 12 | 7 | 6 | 0 | 8 | 0 | 6,120 | -3.3% |
| Ethiopia | 426,373 | 72,057 | 16.9% | 35 | 16 | 1 | 0 | 0 | 4 | 17,734 | -8.1% |
| Gabon | 103,347 | 723 | 0.7% | 14 | 5 | 1 | 0 | 11 | 1 | 84,271 | -0.5% |
| Gambia, The | 4,127 | 95 | 2.3% | 3 | 2 | 1 | 0 | 10 | 0 | 1,857 | 10.3% |
| Ghana | 92,098 | 5,157 | 5.6% | 14 | 8 | 2 | 0 | 7 | 0 | 24,460 | -15.9% |
| Guinea | 94,926 | 664 | 0.7% | 12 | 10 | 1 | 1 | 7 | 3 | 26,753 | -4.8% |
| Guinea-Bissau | 13,948 | - | - | 3 | 0 | 1 | 0 | 9 | 1 | 8,444 | -9.0% |
| Kenya | 224,961 | 17,997 | 8.0% | 50 | 24 | 5 | 0 | 27 | 15 | 66,008 | -5.2% |
| Lesotho | 11,720 | 23 | 0.2% | 6 | 7 | 0 | 0 | 1 | 1 | 54 | - |
| Liberia | 43,000 | 731 | 1.7% | 16 | 11 | 2 | 0 | 7 | 2 | 13,440 | -17.9% |
| Libya | 679,362 | 679 | 0.1% | 8 | 1 | 3 | 0 | 8 | 0 | 1,382 | 15.1% |
| Madagascar | 226,658 | 9,746 | 4.3% | 50 | 27 | 18 | 2 | 25 | 32 | 45,278 | -9.1% |
| Malawi | 45,747 | 5,124 | 11.2% | 8 | 11 | 0 | 0 | 0 | 8 | 9,892 | -21.6% |
| Mali | 478,841 | 17,717 | 3.7% | 13 | 4 | 1 | 0 | 1 | 0 | 50,911 | -7.0% |
| Mauritania | 397,956 | 6,765 | 1.7% | 10 | 2 | 2 | 0 | 10 | 1 | 1,224 | -23.6% |
| Mauritius | 788 | - | - | 3 | 9 | 4 | 0 | 7 | 32 | 62 | -5.9% |
| Morocco | 172,414 | 1,207 | 0.7% | 16 | 9 | 2 | 0 | 10 | 8 | 11,680 | -0.4% |
| Mozambique | 309,496 | 25,998 | 8.4% | 15 | 16 | 5 | 0 | 19 | 7 | 118,151 | -2.0% |
| Namibia | 317,818 | 43,223 | 13.6% | 14 | 11 | 3 | 1 | 11 | 1 | 31,043 | -8.4% |
| Niger | 489,192 | 37,668 | 7.7% | 11 | 3 | 0 | 0 | 0 | 1 | 5,127 | -31.7% |
| Nigeria | 356,669 | 11,770 | 3.3% | 27 | 9 | 2 | 0 | 11 | 1 | 52,189 | -22.8% |
| Rwanda | 10,169 | 630 | 6.2% | 8 | 9 | 0 | 0 | 0 | 2 | 1,185 | -32.8% |
| Sao Tome and Principe | 372 | - | - | 3 | 9 | 1 | 0 | 6 | 2 | 104 | - |
| Senegal | 75,951 | 8,810 | 11.6% | 12 | 4 | 6 | 0 | 17 | 0 | 23,958 | -6.8% |
| Sierra Leone | 27,699 | 582 | 2.1% | 12 | 10 | 3 | 0 | 7 | 4 | 4,073 | -25.5% |
| Somalia | 246,201 | 1,970 | 0.8% | 19 | 10 | 2 | 0 | 16 | 1 | 29,016 | -9.3% |
| South Africa | 470,693 | 25,888 | 5.5% | 36 | 28 | 19 | 9 | 47 | 113 | 34,429 | -0.9% |
| Sudan | 967,500 | 50,310 | 5.2% | 22 | 6 | 2 | 0 | 7 | 1 | 237,943 | -13.5% |
| Swaziland | 6,704 | - | - | 5 | 5 | 0 | 0 | 0 | 0 | 2,015 | 12.5% |
| Tanzania | 364,900 | 108,740 | 29.8% | 41 | 33 | 5 | 0 | 26 | 47 | 149,850 | -2.3% |
| Togo | 21,925 | 1,732 | 7.9% | 9 | 0 | 2 | 0 | 7 | 0 | 1,969 | -29.1% |
| Tunisia | 63,170 | 190 | 0.3% | 11 | 5 | 3 | 0 | 8 | 5 | 1,969 | 2.2% |
| Uganda | 93,065 | 22,894 | 24.6% | 20 | 13 | 0 | 0 | 27 | 10 | 16,178 | -17.9% |
| Zambia | 290,586 | 92,697 | 31.9% | 11 | 11 | 0 | 0 | 0 | 6 | 120,641 | -21.4% |
| Zimbabwe | 150,873 | 18,256 | 12.1% | 11 | 10 | 0 | 0 | 0 | 2 | 73,514 | -14.4% |
| | | | | | | | | | | | |
| **OCEANIA** | | | | | | | | | | | |
| Australia | 2,969,910 | 397,968 | 13.4% | 63 | 35 | 38 | 35 | 74 | 282 | 596,678 | -1.8% |
| Fiji | 7,056 | 78 | 1.1% | 5 | 13 | 6 | 1 | 8 | 2 | 3,147 | -2.0% |
| Kiribati | 313 | - | - | 0 | 4 | 1 | 0 | 4 | 1 | 108 | - |
| Micronesia, Federated States of ... | 271 | - | - | 6 | 5 | 2 | 0 | 6 | 4 | 58 | -37.5% |
| New Zealand | 104,454 | 30,918 | 29.6% | 8 | 63 | 11 | 1 | 16 | 13 | 30,680 | 5.2% |
| Papua New Guinea | 178,704 | 4,110 | 2.3% | 58 | 32 | 9 | 0 | 31 | 12 | 118,151 | -3.6% |
| Samoa | 1,093 | - | - | 3 | 8 | 1 | 0 | 4 | 1 | 405 | -19.2% |
| Solomon Islands | 10,954 | 33 | 0.3% | 20 | 23 | 4 | 0 | 4 | 6 | 9,792 | -1.7% |
| Tonga | 251 | - | - | 2 | 3 | 2 | 0 | 3 | 2 | 15 | - |
| Vanuatu | 4,707 | - | - | 5 | 8 | 2 | 0 | 4 | 0 | 1,726 | 1.4% |

This table presents data for most independent nations having an area greater than 200 square miles
- Zero, insignificant, or not available
(1) Source: World Resources Institute, 2003. Earth Trends: The Environmental Information Portal. Available at http://earthtrends.wri.org. Washington D. C. World Resources Institute
(2) Source: United Nations Environment Programme - World Conservation Monitoring Centre (UNEP-WCMC); World Database on Protected Areas
(3) Source: International Union of Conservation of Nature and Natural Resources; IUCN 2003 Red List of Threatened Species <www.redlist.org>
(4) Source: United Nations Food and Agriculture Organization; Global Forest Resources Assessment 2000

# WORLD COMPARISONS

## General Information

Equatorial diameter of the earth, 7,926.38 miles.
Polar diameter of the earth, 7,899.80 miles.
Mean diameter of the earth, 7,917.52 miles.
Equatorial circumference of the earth, 24,901.46 miles.
Polar circumference of the earth, 24,855.34 miles.
Mean distance from the earth to the sun, 93,020,000 miles.
Mean distance from the earth to the moon, 238,857 miles.
Total area of the earth, 197,000,000 sq. miles.

Highest elevation on the earth's surface, Mt. Everest, Asia, 29,028 ft.
Lowest elevation on the earth's land surface, shores of the Dead Sea, Asia, 1,339 ft. below sea level.
Greatest known depth of the ocean, southwest of Guam, Pacific Ocean, 35,810 ft.
Total land area of the earth (incl. inland water and Antarctica), 57,900,000 sq. miles.

Area of Africa, 11,700,000 sq. miles.
Area of Antarctica, 5,400,000 sq. miles.
Area of Asia, 17,300,000 sq. miles.
Area of Europe, 3,800,000 sq. miles.
Area of North America, 9,500,000 sq. miles.
Area of Oceania (incl. Australia) 3,300,000 sq. miles.
Area of South America, 6,900,000 sq. miles.
Population of the earth (est. 1/1/04), 6,339,505,000.

## Principal Islands and Their Areas

| ISLAND | Area (Sq. Mi.) |
|---|---|
| **Baffin I.**, Canada | 195,928 |
| **Banks I.**, Canada | 27,038 |
| **Borneo** (Kalimantan), Asia | 287,300 |
| **Bougainville**, Papua New Guinea | 3,591 |
| **Cape Breton I.**, Canada | 3,981 |
| **Celebes** (Sulawesi), Indonesia | 73,057 |
| **Ceram** (Seram), Indonesia | 7,191 |
| **Corsica**, France | 3,367 |
| **Crete**, Greece | 3,189 |
| **Cuba**, N. America | 42,780 |
| **Cyprus**, Asia | 3,572 |
| **Devon I.**, Canada | 21,331 |
| **Ellesmere I.**, Canada | 75,767 |
| **Flores**, Indonesia | 5,502 |
| **Great Britain**, U.K. | 88,795 |
| **Greenland**, N. America | 840,000 |
| **Guadalcanal**, Solomon Is. | 2,060 |
| **Hainan Dao**, China | 13,127 |
| **Hawaii**, U.S. | 4,028 |
| **Hispaniola**, N. America | 29,300 |
| **Hokkaidō**, Japan | 32,245 |
| **Honshū**, Japan | 89,176 |
| **Iceland**, Europe | 39,769 |
| **Ireland**, Europe | 32,587 |
| **Jamaica**, N. America | 4,247 |
| **Java** (Jawa), Indonesia | 51,038 |
| **Kodiak I.**, U.S. | 3,670 |
| **Kyūshū**, Japan | 17,129 |
| **Lyete**, Philippines | 2,785 |
| **Long Island**, U.S. | 1,377 |
| **Luzon**, Philippines | 40,420 |
| **Madagascar**, Africa | 226,642 |
| **Melville I.**, Canada | 16,274 |
| **Mindanao**, Philippines | 36,537 |
| **Mindoro**, Philippines | 3,759 |
| **Negros**, Philippines | 4,907 |
| **New Britain**, Papua New Guinea | 14,093 |
| **New Caledonia**, Oceania | 6,252 |
| **Newfoundland**, Canada | 42,031 |
| **New Guinea**, Asia-Oceania | 308,882 |
| **New Ireland**, Papua New Guinea | 3,475 |
| **North East Land**, Norway | 6,350 |
| **North I.**, New Zealand | 44,333 |
| **Novaya Zemlya**, Russia | 31,892 |
| **Palawan**, Philippines | 4,550 |
| **Panay**, Philippines | 4,446 |
| **Prince of Wales I.**, Canada | 12,872 |
| **Puerto Rico**, N. America | 3,514 |
| **Sakhalin**, Russia | 29,498 |
| **Samar**, Philippines | 5,050 |
| **Sardinia**, Italy | 9,301 |
| **Shikoku**, Japan | 7,258 |
| **Sicily**, Italy | 9,926 |
| **Somerset I.**, Canada | 9,570 |
| **Southampton I.**, Canada | 15,913 |
| **South I.**, New Zealand | 57,708 |
| **Spitsbergen**, Norway | 15,260 |
| **Sri Lanka**, Asia | 24,942 |
| **Sumatra** (Sumatera), Indonesia | 182,860 |
| **Taiwan**, Asia | 13,900 |
| **Tasmania**, Australia | 26,178 |
| **Tierra del Fuego**, S. America | 18,600 |
| **Timor**, Asia | 5,743 |
| **Vancouver I.**, Canada | 12,079 |
| **Victoria I.**, Canada | 83,897 |
| **Vrangelya** (Wrangel), Russia | 2,819 |

## Principal Lakes, Oceans, Seas, and Their Areas

| LAKE Country | Area (Sq. Mi.) |
|---|---|
| **Arabian Sea** | 1,492,000 |
| **Aral Sea**, Kazakhstan-Uzbekistan | 13,000 |
| **Arctic Ocean** | 5,400,000 |
| **Athabasca, L.**, Canada | 3,064 |
| **Atlantic Ocean** | 29,600,000 |
| **Balqash köli** (L. Balkhash), Kazakhstan | 7,027 |
| **Baltic Sea**, Europe | 163,000 |
| **Baykal, Ozero** (L. Baikal), Russia | 12,162 |
| **Bering Sea**, Asia-N.A. | 876,000 |
| **Black Sea**, Europe-Asia | 178,000 |
| **Caribbean Sea**, N.A.-S.A. | 1,063,000 |
| **Caspian Sea**, Asia-Europe | 144,402 |
| **Chad, L.**, Cameroon-Chad-Nigeria | 595 |
| **Erie, L.**, Canada-U.S. | 9,910 |
| **Eyre, L.**, Australia | 3,668 |
| **Gairdner, L.**, Australia | 1,076 |
| **Great Bear Lake**, Canada | 12,096 |
| **Great Salt Lake**, U.S. | 1,700 |
| **Great Slave Lake**, Canada | 11,030 |
| **Hudson Bay**, Canada | 475,000 |
| **Huron, L.**, Canada-U.S. | 23,000 |
| **Indian Ocean** | 26,500,000 |
| **Japan, Sea of**, Asia | 389,000 |
| **Koko Nor** (Qinghai Hu), China | 1,722 |
| **Ladozhskoye Ozero** (L. Ladoga), Russia | 7,002 |
| **Manitoba, L.**, Canada | 1,785 |
| **Mediterranean Sea**, Europe-Africa-Asia | 967,000 |
| **Mexico, Gulf of**, N. America | 596,000 |
| **Michigan, L.**, U.S. | 22,300 |
| **Nicaragua, Lago de**, Nicaragua | 3,147 |
| **North Sea**, Europe | 222,000 |
| **Nyasa, L.**, Malawi-Mozambique-Tanzania | 11,120 |
| **Onezhskoye Ozero** (L. Onega), Russia | 3,819 |
| **Ontario, L.**, Canada-U.S. | 7,340 |
| **Pacific Ocean** | 60,100,000 |
| **Red Sea**, Africa-Asia | 169,000 |
| **Rudolf, L.**, Ethiopia-Kenya | 2,471 |
| **Southern Ocean** | 7,800,000 |
| **Superior, L.**, Canada-U.S. | 31,700 |
| **Tanganyika, L.**, Africa | 12,355 |
| **Titicaca, Lago**, Bolivia-Peru | 3,232 |
| **Torrens, L.**, Australia | 1,076 |
| **Vänern (L.)**, Sweden | 2,181 |
| **Van Gölü (L.)**, Turkey | 1,434 |
| **Victoria, L.**, Kenya-Tanzania-Uganda | 26,564 |
| **Winnipeg, L.**, Canada | 9,416 |
| **Winnipegosis, L.**, Canada | 2,075 |
| **Yellow Sea**, China-Korea | 480,000 |

## Principal Mountains and Their Heights

| MOUNTAIN Country | Elev. (Ft.) |
|---|---|
| **Aconcagua, Cerro**, Argentina | 22,831 |
| **Annapurna**, Nepal | 26,504 |
| **Aoraki**, New Zealand | 12,316 |
| **Api**, Nepal | 23,399 |
| **Apo**, Philippines | 9,692 |
| **Ararat, Mt.**, Turkey | 16,854 |
| **Barú, Volcán**, Panama | 11,401 |
| **Bangueta, Mt.**, Papua New Guinea | 13,520 |
| **Belukha, Mt.**, Kazakhstan-Russia | 14,783 |
| **Bia, Phou**, Laos | 9,249 |
| **Blanc, Mont** (Monte Bianco), France-Italy | 15,771 |
| **Blanca Pk.**, Colorado, U.S. | 14,345 |
| **Bolívar, Pico**, Venezuela | 16,427 |
| **Bonete, Cerro**, Argentina | 22,546 |
| **Borah Pk.**, Idaho, U.S. | 12,662 |
| **Boundary Pk.**, Nevada, U.S. | 13,140 |
| **Cameroon Mtn.**, Cameroon | 13,451 |
| **Carrauntoohil**, Ireland | 3,406 |
| **Chaltel, Cerro** (Monte Fitzroy), Argentina-Chile | 10,958 |
| **Chimborazo**, Ecuador | 20,702 |
| **Chirripó, Cerro**, Costa Rica | 12,530 |
| **Colima, Nevado de**, Mexico | 13,911 |
| **Cotopaxi**, Ecuador | 19,347 |
| **Cristóbal Colón, Pico**, Colombia | 19,029 |
| **Damāvand, Qolleh-ye**, Iran | 18,386 |
| **Dhawalāgiri**, Nepal | 26,810 |
| **Duarte, Pico**, Dominican Rep. | 10,417 |
| **Dufourspitze** (Monte Rosa), Italy-Switzerland | 15,203 |
| **Elbert, Mt.**, Colorado, U.S. | 14,433 |
| **El'brus, Gora**, Russia | 18,510 |
| **Elgon, Mt.**, Kenya-Uganda | 14,178 |
| **Erciyeş, Dağı**, Turkey | 12,848 |
| **Etna, Mt.**, Italy | 10,902 |
| **Everest, Mt.**, China-Nepal | 29,028 |
| **Fairweather, Mt.**, Alaska-Canada | 15,300 |
| **Folādī, Koh-e**, Afghanistan | 16,847 |
| **Foraker, Mt.**, Alaska, U.S. | 17,400 |
| **Fuji San**, Japan | 12,388 |
| **Galdhøpiggen**, Norway | 8,100 |
| **Gannett Pk.**, Wyoming, U.S. | 13,804 |
| **Gasherbrum**, China-Pakistan | 26,470 |
| **Gerlachovský štít**, Slovakia | 8,711 |
| **Giluwe, Mt.**, Papua New Guinea | 14,331 |
| **Gongga Shan**, China | 24,790 |
| **Grand Teton**, Wyoming, U.S. | 13,770 |
| **Grossglockner**, Austria | 12,457 |
| **Hadūr Shu'ayb**, Yemen | 12,008 |
| **Haleakalā Crater**, Hawaii, U.S. | 10,023 |
| **Hekla**, Iceland | 4,892 |
| **Hood, Mt.**, Oregon, U.S. | 11,239 |
| **Huascarán, Nevado**, Peru | 22,133 |
| **Huila, Nevado de**, Colombia | 18,865 |
| **Hvannadalshnúkur**, Iceland | 6,952 |
| **Illampu, Nevado**, Bolivia | 21,066 |
| **Illimani, Nevado**, Bolivia | 20,741 |
| **Ismail Samani, pik**, Tajikistan | 24,590 |
| **Iztaccíhuatl**, Mexico | 17,159 |
| **Jaya, Puncak**, Indonesia | 16,503 |
| **Jungfrau**, Switzerland | 13,642 |
| **K2** (Qogir Feng), China-Pakistan | 28,250 |
| **Kāmet**, China-India | 25,447 |
| **Kānchenjunga**, India-Nepal | 28,208 |
| **Kātrīnā, Jabal**, Egypt | 8,668 |
| **Kebnekaise**, Sweden | 6,926 |
| **Kenya, Mt.** (Kirinyaga), Kenya | 17,058 |
| **Kerinci, Gunung**, Indonesia | 12,467 |
| **Kilimanjaro**, Tanzania | 19,340 |
| **Kinabalu, Gunong**, Malaysia | 13,455 |
| **Klyuchevskaya**, Russia | 15,584 |
| **Kosciuszko, Mt.**, Australia | 7,313 |
| **Koussi, Emi**, Chad | 11,204 |
| **Kula Kangri**, Bhutan | 24,784 |
| **La Selle, Massif de**, Haiti | 8,793 |
| **Lassen Pk.**, California, U.S. | 10,457 |
| **Llullaillaco, Volcán**, Argentina-Chile | 22,110 |
| **Logan, Mt.**, Canada | 19,551 |
| **Longs Pk.**, Colorado, U.S. | 14,255 |
| **Makālu**, China-Nepal | 27,825 |
| **Margherita Peak**, Dem. Rep. of the Congo-Uganda | 16,763 |
| **Markham, Mt.**, Antarctica | 14,049 |
| **Maromokotro**, Madagascar | 9,436 |
| **Massive, Mt.**, Colorado, U.S. | 14,421 |
| **Matterhorn**, Italy-Switzerland | 14,692 |
| **Mauna Kea**, Hawaii, U.S. | 13,796 |
| **Mauna Loa**, Hawaii, U.S. | 13,679 |
| **Mayon Volcano**, Philippines | 8,077 |
| **McKinley, Mt.**, Alaska, U.S. | 20,320 |
| **Meron, Hare**, Israel | 3,963 |
| **Meru, Mt.**, Tanzania | 14,978 |
| **Misti, Volcán**, Peru | 19,101 |
| **Mitchell, Mt.**, North Carolina, U.S. | 6,684 |
| **Môco, Serra do**, Angola | 8,596 |
| **Moldoveanu**, Romania | 8,346 |
| **Mulhacén**, Spain | 11,424 |
| **Musala**, Bulgaria | 9,596 |
| **Muztag**, China | 25,338 |
| **Muztagata**, China | 24,757 |
| **Namjagbarwa Feng**, China | 25,446 |
| **Nanda Devi**, India | 25,645 |
| **Nanga Parbat**, Pakistan | 26,660 |
| **Narodnaya, Gora**, Russia | 6,217 |
| **Nevis, Ben**, United Kingdom | 4,406 |
| **Ojos del Salado, Nevado**, Argentina-Chile | 22,615 |
| **Ólimbos**, Cyprus | 6,401 |
| **Ólympos**, Greece | 9,570 |
| **Olympus, Mt.**, Washington, U.S. | 7,965 |
| **Orizaba, Pico de**, Mexico | 18,406 |
| **Paektu San**, North Korea-China | 9,003 |
| **Paricutín**, Mexico | 9,186 |
| **Parnassós**, Greece | 8,061 |
| **Pelée, Montagne**, Martinique | 4,583 |
| **Pidurutalagala**, Sri Lanka | 8,281 |
| **Pikes Pk.**, Colorado, U.S. | 14,110 |
| **Pobedy, pik**, China-Kyrgyzstan | 24,406 |
| **Popocatépetl, Volcán**, Mexico | 17,930 |
| **Pulog, Mt.**, Philippines | 9,626 |
| **Rainier, Mt.**, Washington, U.S. | 14,410 |
| **Ramm, Jabal**, Jordan | 5,755 |
| **Ras Dashen Terara**, Ethiopia | 15,158 |
| **Rinjani, Gunung**, Indonesia | 12,224 |
| **Robson, Mt.**, Canada | 12,972 |
| **Roraima, Mt.**, Brazil-Guyana-Venezuela | 9,432 |
| **Ruapehu, Mt.**, New Zealand | 9,177 |
| **St. Elias, Mt.**, Alaska, U.S.-Canada | 18,008 |
| **Sajama, Nevado**, Bolivia | 21,391 |
| **Semeru, Gunung**, Indonesia | 12,060 |
| **Shām, Jabal ash**, Oman | 9,957 |
| **Shasta, Mt.**, California, U.S. | 14,162 |
| **Snowdon**, United Kingdom | 3,560 |
| **Tahat**, Algeria | 9,541 |
| **Tajumulco**, Guatemala | 13,845 |
| **Taranaki, Mt.**, New Zealand | 8,260 |
| **Tirich Mīr**, Pakistan | 25,230 |
| **Tomanivi** (Victoria), Fiji | 4,341 |
| **Toubkal, Jebel**, Morocco | 13,665 |
| **Triglav**, Slovenia | 9,396 |
| **Trikora, Puncak**, Indonesia | 15,584 |
| **Tupungato, Cerro**, Argentina-Chile | 21,555 |
| **Turquino, Pico**, Cuba | 6,470 |
| **Uluru** (Ayers Rock), Australia | 2,844 |
| **Uncompahgre Pk**, Colorado, U.S. | 14,309 |
| **Vesuvio** (Vesuvius), Italy | 4,190 |
| **Victoria, Mt.**, Papua New Guinea | 13,238 |
| **Vinson Massif**, Antarctica | 16,066 |
| **Waddington, Mt.**, Canada | 13,163 |
| **Washington, Mt.**, New Hampshire, U.S. | 6,288 |
| **Whitney, Mt.**, California, U.S. | 14,494 |
| **Wilhelm, Mt.**, Papua New Guinea | 14,793 |
| **Wrangell, Mt.**, Alaska, U.S. | 14,163 |
| **Xixabangma Feng** (Gosainthan), China | 26,286 |
| **Yü Shan**, Taiwan | 13,114 |
| **Zugspitze**, Austria-Germany | 9,718 |

## Principal Rivers and Their Lengths

| RIVER Continent | Length (Mi.) |
|---|---|
| **Albany**, N. America | 610 |
| **Aldan**, Asia | 1,412 |
| **Amazonas-Ucayali**, S. America | 4,000 |
| **Amu Darya**, Asia | 1,578 |
| **Amur**, Asia | 1,752 |
| **Araguaia**, S. America | 1,367 |
| **Arkansas**, N. America | 1,460 |
| **Atchafalaya**, N. America | 1,420 |
| **Athabasca**, N. America | 765 |
| **Brahmaputra**, Asia | 1,770 |
| **Brazos**, N. America | 1,280 |
| **Canadian**, N. America | 906 |
| **Churchill**, N. America | 1,000 |
| **Colorado**, N. America (U.S.-Mexico) | 1,450 |
| **Colorado**, N. America (Texas) | 862 |
| **Columbia**, N. America | 1,240 |
| **Congo** (Zaïre), Africa | 2,715 |
| **Danube**, Europe | 1,777 |
| **Darling**, Australia | 864 |
| **Dnieper** (Dnipro), Europe | 1,367 |
| **Don**, Europe | 1,162 |
| **Elbe**, Europe | 690 |
| **Essequibo**, S. America | 603 |
| **Euphrates**, Asia | 1,510 |
| **Fraser**, N. America | 851 |
| **Ganges**, Asia | 1,864 |
| **Gila**, N. America | 649 |
| **Godāvari**, Asia | 932 |
| **Huang** (Yellow), Asia | 2,902 |
| **Indigirka**, Asia | 1,072 |
| **Indus**, Asia | 1,118 |
| **Irrawaddy**, Asia | 1,300 |
| **Juruá**, S. America | 1,250 |
| **Kama**, Europe | 1,122 |
| **Kasai**, Africa | 1,338 |
| **Kolyma**, Asia | 1,323 |
| **Lena**, Asia | 2,734 |
| **Limpopo**, Africa | 1,100 |
| **Loire**, Europe | 690 |
| **Mackenzie**, N. America | 2,635 |
| **Madeira**, S. America | 2,013 |
| **Magdalena**, S. America | 951 |
| **Marañón**, S. America | 1,000 |
| **Mekong**, Asia | 2,796 |
| **Meuse**, Europe | 575 |
| **Mississippi**, N. America | 2,340 |
| **Mississippi-Missouri**, N. America | 3,710 |
| **Missouri**, N. America | 2,540 |
| **Murray-Darling**, Australia | 2,169 |
| **Negro**, S. America | 1,305 |
| **Nelson**, N. America | 1,600 |
| **Niger**, Africa | 2,585 |
| **Nile**, Africa | 4,132 |
| **Ob'**, Asia | 2,268 |
| **Oder**, Europe | 565 |
| **Ohio**, N. America | 1,310 |
| **Oka**, Europe | 932 |
| **Orange**, Africa | 1,300 |
| **Orinoco**, S. America | 1,703 |
| **Ottawa**, N. America | 790 |
| **Paraguay**, S. America | 1,610 |
| **Parnaíba**, S. America | 901 |
| **Peace**, N. America | 1,195 |
| **Pechora**, Europe | 1,125 |
| **Pecos**, N. America | 926 |
| **Pilcomayo**, S. America | 1,550 |
| **Plata-Paraná**, S. America | 2,920 |
| **Platte**, N. America | 990 |
| **Purús**, S. America | 1,860 |
| **Red**, N. America | 1,290 |
| **Rhine**, Europe | 820 |
| **Rhône**, Europe | 503 |
| **Rio Grande**, N. America | 1,900 |
| **Roosevelt**, S. America | 950 |
| **St. Lawrence**, N. America | 1,900 |
| **Salado**, S. America | 870 |
| **Salween** (Nu), Asia | 1,750 |
| **São Francisco**, S. America | 1,740 |
| **Saskatchewan-Bow**, N. America | 1,205 |
| **Severnaya Dvina** (Northern Dvina), Europe | 462 |
| **Snake**, N. America | 1,040 |
| **Sungari** (Songhua), Asia | 1,140 |
| **Syr Darya**, Asia | 1,370 |
| **Tagus**, Europe | 625 |
| **Tarim**, Asia | 1,328 |
| **Tennessee**, N. America | 886 |
| **Tigris**, Asia | 1,180 |
| **Tisa**, Europe | 607 |
| **Tocantins**, S. America | 1,640 |
| **Ucayali**, S. America | 1,220 |
| **Ural**, Asia | 1,509 |
| **Uruguay**, S. America | 1,025 |
| **Verkhnyaya Tunguska** (Angara), Asia | 1,105 |
| **Vilyuy**, Asia | 1,647 |
| **Volga**, Europe | 2,082 |
| **Volta**, Africa | 994 |
| **Wisła (Vistula)**, Europe | 630 |
| **Xiang**, Asia | 930 |
| **Xingu**, S. America | 1,230 |
| **Yangtze** (Chang), Asia | 3,915 |
| **Yellowstone**, N. America | 692 |
| **Yenisey**, Asia | 2,169 |
| **Yukon**, N. America | 1,980 |
| **Zambezi**, Africa | 1,653 |

# PRINCIPAL CITIES OF THE WORLD

**Abidjan**, Cote d'Ivoire . . . 1,929,079
**Abū Ẓaby (Abu Dhabi)**, United Arab Emirates . . . 242,975
**Accra**, Ghana (1,390,000) . . . 949,113
**Addis Ababa**, Ethiopia . . . 2,424,000
**Ahmadābād**, India (4,519,278) . . . 3,515,361
**Aleppo (Ḩalab)**, Syria (1,640,000) . . . 1,591,400
**Alexandria (Al Iskandarīyah)**, Egypt (3,350,000) . . . 3,339,076
**Algiers (El Djazaïr)**, Algeria (2,547,983) . . . 1,507,241
**Al Jīzah (Giza)**, Egypt (*Al Qāhirah) . . . 2,221,817
**Almaty**, Kazakhstan (1,190,000) . . . 1,129,356
**'Ammān**, Jordan (1,500,000) . . . 1,147,447
**Amsterdam**, Netherlands (1,121,303) . . . 727,053
**Ankara**, Turkey (3,294,220) . . . 2,984,099
**Antananarivo**, Madagascar . . . 1,250,000
**Antwerp (Antwerpen)**, Belgium (1,135,000) . . . 453,030
**Ashgabat (Ashkhabad)**, Turkmenistan . . . 557,600
**Asmera**, Eritrea . . . 358,100
**Astana (Aqmola)**, Kazakhstan (319,324) . . . 312,965
**Asunción**, Paraguay (700,000) . . . 546,637
**Athens (Athína)**, Greece (3,150,000) . . 772,072
**Atlanta**, Georgia, U.S. (4,112,198) . . . 416,474
**Auckland**, New Zealand (1,074,510) . . 367,737
**Baghdād**, Iraq . . . 3,841,268
**Baku (Bakı)**, Azerbaijan (2,020,000) . . . 1,792,300
**Bamako**, Mali . . . 658,275
**Bandung**, Indonesia . . . 5,919,400
**Bangalore**, India (5,686,844) . . . 4,292,223
**Banghāzī**, Libya . . . 800,000
**Bangkok (Krung Thep)**, Thailand (7,060,000) . . . 5,620,591
**Bangui**, Central African Republic . . . 451,690
**Barcelona**, Spain (4,000,000) . . . 1,496,266
**Beijing**, China (7,320,000) . . . 6,690,000
**Beirut (Bayrūt)**, Lebanon (1,675,000) . 509,000
**Belfast**, N. Ireland, U.K. (730,000) . . . 297,300
**Belgrade (Beograd)**, Serbia and Montenegro . . . 1,594,483
**Belo Horizonte**, Brazil (4,055,000) . . 1,366,301
**Berlin**, Germany (4,220,000) . . . 3,386,667
**Birmingham**, England, U.K. (2,705,000) . . . 1,020,589
**Bishkek**, Kyrgyzstan . . . 753,400
**Bogotá**, Colombia . . . 6,422,198
**Bonn**, Germany (600,000) . . . 301,048
**Boston**, Massachusetts, U.S. (5,819,100) . . . 589,141
**Brasília**, Brazil . . . 1,947,133
**Bratislava**, Slovakia . . . 451,395
**Brazzaville**, Congo . . . 693,712
**Brisbane**, Australia (1,627,535) . . . 888,449
**Brussels (Bruxelles)**, Belgium (2,390,000) . . . 133,845
**Bucharest (Bucureşti)**, Romania (2,300,000) . . . 2,016,131
**Budapest**, Hungary (2,450,000) . . . 1,825,153
**Buenos Aires**, Argentina (11,000,000) . . . 2,960,976
**Cairo (Al Qāhirah)**, Egypt (9,300,000) . . . 6,800,992
**Calgary**, Alberta, Canada (951,395) . . . 878,866
**Cali**, Colombia . . . 2,128,920
**Canberra**, Australia (342,798) . . . 311,518
**Cape Town**, South Africa (1,900,000) . . . 854,616
**Caracas**, Venezuela (4,000,000) . . . 1,822,465
**Cardiff**, Wales, U.K. (645,000) . . . 315,040
**Casablanca**, Morocco (3,400,000) . . . 3,022,000
**Changchun**, China . . . 2,470,000
**Chelyabinsk**, Russia (1,320,000) . . . 1,086,300
**Chengdu**, China . . . 2,760,000
**Chennai (Madras)**, India (6,424,624) . . . 4,216,268
**Chicago**, Illinois, U.S. (9,157,540) . . . 2,896,016
**Chişinău (Kishinev)**, Moldova (746,500) . . . 658,300
**Chittagong**, Bangladesh (2,342,662) . . . 1,566,070
**Chongqing**, China . . . 3,870,000
**Cincinnati**, Ohio, U.S. (1,979,202) . . . 331,285
**Cleveland**, Ohio, U.S. (2,945,831) . . . 478,403
**Cologne (Köln)**, Germany (1,830,000) . . . 962,507
**Colombo**, Sri Lanka (2,050,000) . . . 615,000
**Conakry**, Guinea . . . 950,000
**Copenhagen (København)**, Denmark (2,030,000) . . . 499,148
**Córdoba**, Argentina (1,260,000) . . . 1,179,067
**Cotonou**, Benin . . . 650,660
**Curitiba**, Brazil (2,595,000) . . . 1,586,848
**Dakar**, Senegal (1,976,533) . . . 879,703
**Dalian**, China . . . 2,400,000
**Dallas**, Texas, U.S. (5,221,801) . . . 1,188,580
**Damascus (Dimashq)**, Syria (2,230,000) . . . 1,549,932
**Dar es Salaam**, Tanzania . . . 1,360,850
**Delhi**, India (12,791,458) . . . 9,817,439
**Denver**, Colorado, U.S. (2,581,506) . . . 554,636
**Detroit**, Michigan, U.S. (5,456,428) . . . 951,270
**Dhaka (Dacca)**, Bangladesh (6,537,308) . . . 3,637,892
**Djibouti**, Djibouti . . . 329,337
**Dnipropetrovs'k**, Ukraine (1,590,000) . . . 1,108,682
**Donets'k**, Ukraine (2,090,000) . . . 1,050,369
**Douala**, Cameroon . . . 712,251
**Dublin (Baile Átha Cliath)**, Ireland (1,175,000) . . . 481,854
**Durban**, South Africa (1,740,000) . . . 669,242
**Dushanbe**, Tajikistan (700,000) . . . 528,600
**Düsseldorf**, Germany (1,200,000) . . . 568,855
**Edinburgh**, Scotland, U.K. (640,000) . . 448,850
**Edmonton**, Alberta, Canada (937,845) . . . 666,104
**Eşfahān**, Iran (1,525,000) . . . 1,266,072
**Essen**, Germany (5,040,000) . . . 599,515
**Fortaleza**, Brazil (2,780,000) . . . 788,956
**Frankfurt am Main**, Germany (1,960,000) . . . 643,821
**Fukuoka**, Japan (2,000,000) . . . 1,341,489
**Geneva (Génève)**, Switzerland (450,592) . . . 172,598
**Glasgow**, Scotland, U.K. (1,870,000) . . 616,430
**Goiânia**, Brazil . . . 1,075,761
**Guadalajara**, Mexico (3,669,021) . . . 1,646,183
**Guangzhou (Canton)**, China . . . 3,750,000
**Guatemala**, Guatemala (1,500,000) . . . 1,006,954
**Guayaquil**, Ecuador . . . 2,117,553
**Halifax**, Nova Scotia, Canada (359,183) . . . 119,300
**Hamburg**, Germany (2,460,000) . . . 1,704,735
**Hannover**, Germany (1,015,000) . . . 514,718
**Hanoi**, Vietnam (1,275,000) . . . 1,073,760
**Harare**, Zimbabwe (1,470,000) . . . 1,189,103
**Harbin**, China . . . 3,120,000
**Havana (La Habana)**, Cuba (2,285,000) . . . 2,189,716
**Helsinki**, Finland (939,697) . . . 548,720
**Hiroshima**, Japan (1,600,000) . . . 1,126,282
**Ho Chi Minh City (Saigon)**, Vietnam (3,300,000) . . . 3,015,743
**Hong Kong (Xianggang)**, China (4,770,000) . . . 1,250,993
**Honolulu**, Hawaii, U.S. (876,156) . . . 371,657
**Houston**, Texas, U.S. (4,669,571) . . . 1,953,631
**Hyderābād**, India (5,533,640) . . . 3,449,878
**Ibadan**, Nigeria . . . 1,144,000
**Islāmābād**, Pakistan (*Rāwalpindi) . . . 529,180
**İstanbul**, Turkey (8,506,026) . . . 8,260,438
**İzmir**, Turkey (2,554,363) . . . 2,081,556
**Jaipur**, India . . . 2,324,319
**Jakarta**, Indonesia (10,200,000) . . . 9,373,900
**Jerusalem (Yerushalayim)**, Israel (685,000) . . . 633,700
**Jiddah**, Saudi Arabia . . . 1,450,000
**Jinan**, China . . . 2,150,000
**Johannesburg**, South Africa (4,000,000) . . . 752,349
**Kābul**, Afghanistan . . . 1,424,400
**Kampala**, Uganda . . . 773,463
**Kānpur**, India (2,690,486) . . . 2,540,069
**Kaohsiung**, Taiwan (1,845,000) . . . 1,468,586
**Karāchi**, Pakistan . . . 9,339,023
**Katowice**, Poland (2,755,000) . . . 343,158
**Kharkiv**, Ukraine (1,950,000) . . . 1,494,235
**Khartoum (Al Kharţūm)**, Sudan (1,450,000) . . . 947,483
**Kiev (Kyïv)**, Ukraine (3,250,000) . . . 2,589,541
**Kingston**, Jamaica (830,000) . . . 516,500
**Kinshasa**, Dem. Rep. of the Congo . . . 3,000,000
**Kitakyūshū**, Japan (1,550,000) . . . 1,011,491
**Kolkata (Calcutta)**, India (13,216,546) . . . 4,580,544
**Kuala Lumpur**, Malaysia (2,500,000) . . . 1,297,526
**Kuwait (Al Kuwayt)**, Kuwait (1,126,000) . . . 28,859
**Lagos**, Nigeria (3,800,000) . . . 1,213,000
**Lahore**, Pakistan . . . 5,143,495
**La Paz**, Bolivia (1,487,854) . . . 792,611
**Libreville**, Gabon (418,616) . . . 362,386
**Lilongwe**, Malawi . . . 435,964
**Lima**, Peru (6,321,173) . . . 340,422
**Lisbon (Lisboa)**, Portugal (2,350,000) . . 563,210
**Liverpool**, England, U.K. (1,515,000) . . 467,995
**Ljubljana**, Slovenia . . . 263,832
**Lomé**, Togo . . . 450,000
**London**, England, U.K. (12,000,000) . . . 7,074,265
**Los Angeles**, California, U.S. (16,373,645) . . . 3,694,820
**Luanda**, Angola . . . 1,459,900
**Lucknow**, India (2,266,933) . . . 2,207,340
**Lusaka**, Zambia . . . 1,269,848
**Lyon**, France (1,648,216) . . . 445,452
**Madrid**, Spain (4,690,000) . . . 2,882,860
**Managua**, Nicaragua . . . 864,201
**Manaus**, Brazil . . . 1,394,724
**Manchester**, England, U.K. (2,760,000) . . . 430,818
**Manila**, Philippines (11,200,000) . . . 1,654,761
**Mannheim**, Germany (1,525,000) . . . 307,730
**Maputo**, Mozambique . . . 966,837
**Maracaibo**, Venezuela . . . 1,249,670
**Marseille**, France (1,516,340) . . . 798,430
**Mashhad**, Iran . . . 1,887,405
**Mecca (Makkah)**, Saudi Arabia . . . 630,000
**Medan**, Indonesia . . . 1,988,200
**Medellín**, Colombia (2,290,000) . . . 1,885,001
**Melbourne**, Australia (3,366,542) . . . 67,784
**Mexico City (Ciudad de México)**, Mexico (17,786,983) . . . 8,605,239
**Miami**, Florida, U.S. (3,876,380) . . . 362,470
**Milan (Milano)**, Italy (3,790,000) . . . 1,305,591
**Milwaukee**, Wisconsin, U.S. (1,689,572) . . . 596,974
**Minneapolis**, Minnesota, U.S. (2,968,806) . . . 382,618
**Minsk**, Belarus (1,680,567) . . . 1,677,137
**Mogadishu (Muqdisho)**, Somalia . . . 600,000
**Monrovia**, Liberia . . . 465,000
**Monterrey**, Mexico (3,236,604) . . . 1,110,909
**Montevideo**, Uruguay (1,650,000) . . 1,303,182
**Montréal**, Quebec, Canada (3,426,350) . . . 1,039,534
**Moscow (Moskva)**, Russia (12,850,000) . . . 8,389,700
**Mumbai (Bombay)**, India (16,368,084) . . . 11,914,398
**Munich (München)**, Germany (1,930,000) . . . 1,194,560
**Nagoya**, Japan (5,250,000) . . . 2,171,378
**Nāgpur**, India (2,122,965) . . . 2,051,320
**Nairobi**, Kenya . . . 2,143,254
**Nanjing**, China . . . 2,490,000
**Naples (Napoli)**, Italy (3,150,000) . . . 1,046,987
**N'Djamena**, Chad . . . 546,572
**Newcastle upon Tyne**, England, U.K. (1,350,000) . . . 282,338
**New Delhi**, India (*Delhi) . . . 294,783
**New York**, New York, U.S. (21,199,865) . . . 8,008,278
**Niamey**, Niger . . . 392,165
**Nizhniy Novgorod**, Russia (1,950,000) . . . 1,364,900
**Nouakchott**, Mauritania . . . 393,325
**Novosibirsk**, Russia (1,505,000) . . . 1,402,400
**Nürnberg**, Germany (1,065,000) . . . 486,628
**Odesa**, Ukraine (1,150,000) . . . 1,002,246
**Omsk**, Russia (1,190,000) . . . 1,157,600
**Ōsaka**, Japan (17,050,000) . . . 2,598,589
**Oslo**, Norway (773,498) . . . 504,040
**Ottawa**, Ontario, Canada (1,063,664) . . . 774,072
**Ouagadougou**, Burkina Faso . . . 634,479
**Palembang**, Indonesia . . . 1,415,500
**Panamá**, Panama (995,000) . . . 415,964
**Paris**, France (11,174,743) . . . 2,125,246
**Patna**, India (1,707,429) . . . 1,376,950
**Perm'**, Russia (1,110,000) . . . 1,017,100
**Perth**, Australia (1,244,320) . . . 10,195
**Philadelphia**, Pennsylvania, U.S. (6,188,463) . . . 1,517,550
**Phnom Penh (Phnum Pénh)**, Cambodia . . . 570,155
**Phoenix**, Arizona, U.S. (3,251,876) . . 1,321,045
**Port Moresby**, Papua New Guinea . . . 246,664
**Port-au-Prince**, Haiti (1,425,594) . . . 990,558
**Portland**, Oregon, U.S. (2,265,223) . . . 529,121
**Porto**, Portugal (1,230,000) . . . 273,060
**Porto Alegre**, Brazil (3,375,000) . . . 1,304,998
**Prague (Praha)**, Czech Republic (1,328,000) . . . 1,193,270
**Pretoria**, South Africa (1,100,000) . . . 692,348
**Pune**, India (3,755,525) . . . 2,540,069
**Pusan**, South Korea . . . 3,814,325
**P'yŏngyang**, North Korea . . . 2,741,260
**Qingdao**, China . . . 2,300,000
**Québec**, Quebec, Canada (682,757) . . . 169,076
**Quezon City**, Philippines (*Manila) . . . 1,989,419
**Quito**, Ecuador . . . 1,615,809
**Rabat**, Morocco (1,200,000) . . . 717,000
**Rangoon (Yangon)**, Myanmar (2,800,000) . . . 2,705,039
**Recife**, Brazil (3,160,000) . . . 1,421,993
**Regina**, Saskatchewan, Canada (192,800) . . . 178,225
**Reykjavík**, Iceland (166,015) . . . 107,684
**Rīga**, Latvia (1,000,000) . . . 792,508
**Rio de Janeiro**, Brazil (10,465,000) . . 5,851,914
**Riyadh (Ar Riyāḑ)**, Saudi Arabia . . . 1,800,000
**Rome (Roma)**, Italy (3,235,000) . . . 2,649,765
**Rosario**, Argentina (1,190,000) . . . 894,645
**Rostov-na-Donu**, Russia (1,160,000) . . . 1,017,300
**Rotterdam**, Netherlands (1,089,979) . . 539,000
**Sacramento**, California, U.S. (1,796,857) . . . 407,018
**St. Louis**, Missouri, U.S. (2,603,607) . . . 348,189
**St. Petersburg (Leningrad)**, Russia (6,000,000) . . . 4,728,200
**Salvador**, Brazil (2,855,000) . . . 2,439,823
**Samara**, Russia (1,450,000) . . . 1,168,000
**San Diego**, California, U.S. (2,813,833) . . . 1,223,400
**San Francisco**, California, U.S. (7,039,362) . . . 776,733
**San José**, Costa Rica (996,194) . . . 309,672
**San Juan**, Puerto Rico (1,967,627) . . . 421,958
**San Salvador**, El Salvador (1,908,921) . . . 473,372
**Santiago**, Chile . . . 4,788,543
**Santo Domingo**, Dominican Republic . . . 2,677,056
**São Paulo**, Brazil (17,380,000) . . . 9,713,692
**Sapporo**, Japan (2,000,000) . . . 1,822,300
**Sarajevo**, Bosnia and Herzegovina . . . 367,703
**Saratov**, Russia (1,135,000) . . . 881,000
**Seattle**, Washington, U.S. (3,554,760) . . . 563,374
**Seoul (Sŏul)**, South Korea (15,850,000) . . . 10,231,217
**Shanghai**, China (11,010,000) . . . 8,930,000
**Shenyang (Mukden)**, China . . . 4,050,000
**Singapore**, Singapore (4,400,000) . . . 4,017,700
**Skopje**, Macedonia . . . 440,577
**Sofia (Sofiya)**, Bulgaria (1,189,794) . . 1,138,629
**Stockholm**, Sweden (1,643,366) . . . 743,703
**Stuttgart**, Germany (2,020,000) . . . 582,443
**Surabaya**, Indonesia . . . 2,801,300
**Sūrat**, India (2,811,466) . . . 2,433,787
**Sydney**, Australia (3,741,290) . . . 11,115
**T'aipei**, Taiwan (6,200,000) . . . 2,640,322
**Tallinn**, Estonia . . . 403,981
**Tashkent (Toshkent)**, Uzbekistan (2,325,000) . . . 2,142,700
**Tbilisi**, Georgia (1,460,000) . . . 1,279,000
**Tegucigalpa**, Honduras . . . 576,661
**Tehrān**, Iran (8,800,000) . . . 6,758,845
**Tel Aviv-Yafo**, Israel (1,890,000) . . . 348,100
**Tianjin (Tientsin)**, China . . . 5,000,000
**Tiranë**, Albania . . . 244,153
**Tōkyō**, Japan (30,300,000) . . . 8,130,408
**Toronto**, Ontario, Canada (4,682,897) . . . 2,481,494
**Tripoli (Ţarābulus)**, Libya . . . 1,500,000
**Tunis**, Tunisia (1,300,000) . . . 702,330
**Turin (Torino)**, Italy (1,550,000) . . . 921,485
**Ufa**, Russia (1,110,000) . . . 1,088,900
**Ulan Bator (Ulaanbaatar)**, Mongolia . . . 672,882
**Ürümqi**, China . . . 1,130,000
**València**, Spain (1,340,000) . . . 739,014
**Vancouver**, British Columbia, Canada (1,986,965) . . . 545,671
**Viangchan (Vientiane)**, Laos . . . 464,000
**Vienna (Wien)**, Austria (1,950,000) . . 1,609,631
**Vilnius**, Lithuania . . . 578,334
**Volgograd (Stalingrad)**, Russia (1,358,000) . . . 1,000,000
**Warsaw (Warszawa)**, Poland (2,300,000) . . . 1,615,369
**Washington**, D.C., U.S. (7,608,070) . . . 572,059
**Wellington**, New Zealand (346,500) . . 167,400
**Winnipeg**, Manitoba, Canada (671,274) . . . 619,544
**Wuhan**, China . . . 3,870,000
**Xi'an**, China . . . 2,410,000
**Yekaterinburg**, Russia (1,530,000) . . 1,272,900
**Yerevan**, Armenia (1,315,000) . . . 1,249,202
**Yokohama**, Japan (*Tōkyō) . . . 3,426,506
**Zagreb**, Croatia . . . 867,865
**Zürich**, Switzerland (932,681) . . . 337,553

Metropolitan area populations are shown in parentheses.
* City is located within the metropolitan area of another city; for example, Yokohama, Japan is located in the Tōkyō metropolitan area.

# GLOSSARY OF FOREIGN GEOGRAPHICAL TERMS

Annam . . . Annamese
Arab . . . Arabic
Bantu . . . Bantu
Bur . . . Burmese
Camb . . . Cambodian
Celt . . . Celtic
Chn . . . Chinese
Czech . . . Czech
Dan . . . Danish
Du . . . Dutch
Fin . . . Finnish
Fr . . . French
Ger . . . German
Gr . . . Greek
Hung . . . Hungarian
Ice . . . Icelandic
India . . . India
Indian . . . American Indian
Indon . . . Indonesian
It . . . Italian
Jap . . . Japanese
Kor . . . Korean
Mal . . . Malayan
Mong . . . Mongolian
Nor . . . Norwegian
Per . . . Persian
Pol . . . Polish
Port . . . Portuguese
Rom . . . Romanian
Rus . . . Russian
Siam . . . Siamese
So. Slav . . . Southern Slavonic
Sp . . . Spanish
Swe . . . Swedish
Tib . . . Tibetan
Tur . . . Turkish
Yugo . . . Yugoslav

**å**, Nor., Swe . . . brook, river
**aa**, Dan., Nor . . . brook
**aas**, Dan., Nor . . . ridge
**āb**, Per . . . water, river
**abad**, India, Per . . . town, city
**ada**, Tur . . . island
**adrar**, Berber . . . mountain
**air**, Indon . . . stream
**akrotírion**, Gr . . . cape
**älf**, Swe . . . river
**alp**, Ger . . . mountain
**altipiano**, It . . . plateau
**alto**, Sp . . . height
**archipel**, Fr . . . archipelago
**archipiélago**, Sp . . . archipelago
**arquipélago**, Port . . . archipelago
**arroyo**, Sp . . . brook, stream
**ås**, Nor., Swe . . . ridge
**austral**, Sp . . . southern
**baai**, Du . . . bay
**bab**, Arab . . . gate, port
**bach**, Ger . . . brook, stream
**backe**, Swe . . . hill
**bad**, Ger . . . bath, spa
**bahía**, Sp . . . bay, gulf
**bahr**, Arab . . . river, sea, lake
**baia**, It . . . bay, gulf
**baía**, Port . . . bay
**baie**, Fr . . . bay, gulf
**bajo**, Sp . . . depression
**bak**, Indon . . . stream
**bakke**, Dan., Nor . . . hill
**balkan**, Tur . . . mountain range
**bana**, Jap . . . point, cape
**banco**, Sp . . . bank
**bandar**, Mal., Per. . . . town, port, harbor
**bang**, Siam . . . village
**bassin**, Fr . . . basin
**batang**, Indon., Mal . . . river
**ben**, Celt . . . mountain, summit
**bender**, Arab . . . harbor, port
**bereg**, Rus . . . coast, shore
**berg**, Du., Ger., Nor., Swe. . . . mountain, hill
**bir**, Arab . . . well
**birkat**, Arab . . . lake, pond, pool
**bit**, Arab . . . house
**bjaerg**, Dan., Nor . . . mountain
**bocche**, It . . . mouth
**boğazı**, Tur . . . strait
**bois**, Fr . . . forest, wood
**boloto**, Rus . . . marsh
**bolsón**, Sp. . . . flat-floored desert valley
**boreal**, Sp . . . northern
**borg**, Dan., Nor., Swe . . . castle, town
**borgo**, It . . . town, suburb
**bosch**, Du . . . forest, wood
**bouche**, Fr . . . river mouth
**bourg**, Fr . . . town, borough
**bro**, Dan., Nor., Swe . . . bridge
**brücke**, Ger . . . bridge
**bucht**, Ger . . . bay, bight
**bugt**, Dan., Nor., Swe . . . bay, gulf
**bulu**, Indon . . . mountain
**burg**, Du., Ger . . . castle, town
**buri**, Siam . . . town
**burun, burnu**, Tur . . . cape
**by**, Dan., Nor., Swe . . . village
**caatinga**, Port. (Brazil) . . . open brushland
**cabezo**, Sp . . . summit
**cabo**, Port., Sp . . . cape
**campo**, It., Port., Sp . . . plain, field
**campos**, Port. (Brazil) . . . plains
**cañón**, Sp . . . canyon
**cap**, Fr . . . cape
**capo**, It . . . cape
**casa**, It., Port., Sp . . . house
**castello**, It., Port . . . castle, fort
**castillo**, Sp . . . castle
**càte**, Fr . . . hill
**çay**, Tur . . . stream, river
**cayo**, Sp . . . rock, shoal, islet
**cerro**, Sp . . . mountain, hill
**champ**, Fr . . . field
**chang**, Chn . . . village, middle
**château**, Fr . . . castle
**chen**, Chn . . . market town
**chiang**, Chn . . . river
**chott**, Arab . . . salt lake
**chou**, Chn. . . . capital of district; island
**chu**, Tib . . . water, stream
**cidade**, Port . . . town, city
**cima**, Sp . . . summit, peak
**città**, It . . . town, city
**ciudad**, Sp . . . town, city
**cochilha**, Port . . . ridge
**col**, Fr . . . pass
**colina**, Sp . . . hill
**cordillera**, Sp . . . mountain chain
**costa**, It., Port., Sp . . . coast
**côte**, Fr . . . coast
**cuchilla**, Sp . . . mountain ridge
**dağ**, Tur . . . mountain(s)
**dake**, Jap . . . peak, summit
**dal**, Dan., Du., Nor., Swe . . . valley
**dan**, Kor . . . point, cape
**danau**, Indon . . . lake
**dar**, Arab . . . house, abode, country
**darya**, Per . . . river, sea
**dasht**, Per . . . plain, desert
**deniz**, Tur . . . sea
**désert**, Fr . . . desert
**deserto**, It . . . desert
**desierto**, Sp . . . desert
**détroit**, Fr . . . strait
**dijk**, Du . . . dam, dike
**djebel**, Arab . . . mountain
**do**, Kor . . . island
**dorf**, Ger . . . village
**dorp**, Du . . . village
**duin**, Du . . . dune
**dzong**, Tib. . . . fort, administrative capital
**eau**, Fr . . . water
**ecuador**, Sp . . . equator
**eiland**, Du . . . island
**elv**, Dan., Nor . . . river, stream
**embalse**, Sp . . . reservoir
**erg**, Arab . . . dune, sandy desert
**est**, Fr., It . . . east
**estado**, Sp . . . state
**este**, Port., Sp . . . east
**estrecho**, Sp . . . strait
**étang**, Fr . . . pond, lake
**état**, Fr . . . state
**eyjar**, Ice . . . islands
**feld**, Ger . . . field, plain
**festung**, Ger . . . fortress
**fiume**, It . . . river
**fjäll**, Swe . . . mountain
**fjärd**, Swe . . . bay, inlet
**fjeld**, Nor . . . mountain, hill
**fjord**, Dan., Nor . . . fiord, inlet
**fjördur**, Ice . . . fiord, inlet
**fleuve**, Fr . . . river
**flod**, Dan., Swe . . . river
**flói**, Ice . . . bay, marshland
**fluss**, Ger . . . river
**foce**, It . . . river mouth
**fontein**, Du . . . a spring
**forêt**, Fr . . . forest
**fors**, Swe . . . waterfall
**forst**, Ger . . . forest
**fos**, Dan., Nor . . . waterfall
**fu**, Chn . . . town, residence
**fuente**, Sp . . . spring, fountain
**fuerte**, Sp . . . fort
**furt**, Ger . . . ford
**gang**, Kor . . . stream, river
**gangri**, Tib . . . mountain
**gat**, Dan., Nor . . . channel
**gàve**, Fr . . . stream
**gawa**, Jap . . . river
**gebergte**, Du . . . mountain range
**gebiet**, Ger . . . district, territory
**gebirge**, Ger . . . mountains
**ghat**, India . . . pass, mountain range
**gobi**, Mong . . . desert
**gol**, Mong . . . river
**göl, gölü**, Tur . . . lake
**golf**, Du., Ger . . . gulf, bay
**golfe**, Fr . . . gulf, bay
**golfo**, It., Port., Sp . . . gulf, bay
**gomba, gompa**, Tib . . . monastery
**gora**, Rus., So. Slav . . . mountain
**góra**, Pol . . . mountain
**gorod**, Rus . . . town
**grad**, Rus., So. Slav . . . town
**guba**, Rus . . . bay, gulf
**gundung**, Indon . . . mountain
**guntō**, Jap . . . archipelago
**gunung**, Mal . . . mountain
**haf**, Swe . . . sea, ocean
**hafen**, Ger . . . port, harbor
**haff**, Ger . . . gulf, inland sea
**hai**, Chn . . . sea, lake
**hama**, Jap . . . beach, shore
**hamada**, Arab . . . rocky plateau
**hamn**, Swe . . . harbor
**hāmūn**, Per . . . swampy lake, plain
**hantō**, Jap . . . peninsula
**hassi**, Arab . . . well, spring
**haus**, Ger . . . house
**haut**, Fr . . . summit, top
**hav**, Dan., Nor . . . sea, ocean
**havn**, Dan., Nor . . . harbor, port
**havre**, Fr . . . harbor, port
**háza**, Hung . . . house, dwelling of
**heim**, Ger . . . hamlet, home
**hem**, Swe . . . hamlet, home
**higashi**, Jap . . . east
**hisar**, Tur . . . fortress
**hissar**, Arab . . . fort
**ho**, Chn . . . river
**hoek**, Du . . . cape
**hof**, Ger . . . court, farmhouse
**höfn**, Ice . . . harbor
**hoku**, Jap . . . north
**holm**, Dan., Nor., Swe . . . island
**hora**, Czech . . . mountain
**horn**, Ger . . . peak
**hoved**, Dan., Nor . . . cape
**hsien**, Chn . . . district, district capital
**hu**, Chn . . . lake
**hügel**, Ger . . . hill
**huk**, Dan., Swe . . . point
**hus**, Dan., Nor., Swe . . . house
**île**, Fr . . . island
**ilha**, Port . . . island
**indsö**, Dan., Nor . . . lake
**insel**, Ger . . . island
**insjö**, Swe . . . lake
**irmak, irmagi**, Tur . . . river
**isla**, Sp . . . island
**isola**, It . . . island
**istmo**, It., Sp . . . isthmus
**järvi, jaur**, Fin . . . lake
**jebel**, Arab . . . mountain
**jima**, Jap . . . island
**jökel**, Nor . . . glacier
**joki**, Fin . . . river
**jökull**, Ice . . . glacier
**kaap**, Du . . . cape
**kai**, Jap . . . bay, gulf, sea
**kaikyō**, Jap . . . channel, strait
**kalat**, Per . . . castle, fortress
**kale**, Tur . . . fort
**kali**, Mal . . . creek, river
**kand**, Per . . . village
**kang**, Chn . . . mountain ridge; village
**kap**, Dan., Ger . . . cape
**kapp**, Nor., Swe . . . cape
**kasr**, Arab . . . fort, castle
**kawa**, Jap . . . river
**kefr**, Arab . . . village
**kei**, Jap . . . creek, river
**ken**, Jap . . . prefecture
**khor**, Arab . . . bay, inlet
**khrebet**, Rus . . . mountain range
**kiang**, Chn . . . large river
**king**, Chn . . . capital city, town
**kita**, Jap . . . north
**ko**, Jap . . . lake
**köbstad**, Dan . . . market-town
**kol**, Mong . . . lake
**kólpos**, Gr . . . gulf
**kong**, Chn . . . river
**kopf**, Ger . . . head, summit, peak
**köpstad**, Swe . . . market-town
**körfezi**, Tur . . . gulf
**kosa**, Rus . . . spit
**kou**, Chn . . . river mouth
**köy**, Tur . . . village
**kraal**, Du. (Africa) . . . native village
**ksar**, Arab . . . fortified village
**kuala**, Mal . . . bay, river mouth
**kuh**, Per . . . mountain
**kum**, Tur . . . sand
**kuppe**, Ger . . . summit
**küste**, Ger . . . coast
**kyo**, Jap . . . town, capital
**la**, Tib . . . mountain pass
**labuan**, Mal . . . anchorage, port
**lac**, Fr . . . lake
**lago**, It., Port., Sp . . . lake
**lagoa**, Port . . . lake, marsh
**laguna**, It., Port., Sp . . . lagoon, lake
**lahti**, Fin . . . bay, gulf
**län**, Swe . . . county
**landsby**, Dan., Nor . . . village
**liehtao**, Chn . . . archipelago
**liman**, Tur . . . bay, port
**ling**, Chn . . . pass, ridge, mountain
**llanos**, Sp . . . plains
**loch**, Celt. (Scotland) . . . lake, bay
**loma**, Sp . . . long, low hill
**lough**, Celt. (Ireland) . . . lake, bay
**machi**, Jap . . . town
**man**, Kor . . . bay
**mar**, Port., Sp . . . sea
**mare**, It., Rom . . . sea
**marisma**, Sp . . . marsh, swamp
**mark**, Ger . . . boundary, limit
**massif**, Fr . . . block of mountains
**mato**, Port . . . forest, thicket
**me**, Siam . . . river
**meer**, Du., Ger . . . lake, sea
**mer**, Fr . . . sea
**mesa**, Sp . . . flat-topped mountain
**meseta**, Sp . . . plateau
**mina**, Port., Sp . . . mine
**minami**, Jap . . . south
**minato**, Jap . . . harbor, haven
**misaki**, Jap . . . cape, headland
**mont**, Fr . . . mount, mountain
**montagna**, It . . . mountain
**montagne**, Fr . . . mountain
**montaña**, Sp . . . mountain
**monte**, It., Port., Sp. . . . mount, mountain
**more**, Rus., So. Slav . . . sea
**morro**, Port., Sp . . . hill, bluff
**mühle**, Ger . . . mill
**mund**, Ger . . . mouth, opening
**mündung**, Ger . . . river mouth
**mura**, Jap . . . township
**myit**, Bur . . . river
**mys**, Rus . . . cape
**nada**, Jap . . . sea
**nadi**, India . . . river, creek
**naes**, Dan., Nor . . . cape
**nafud**, Arab . . . desert of sand dunes
**nagar**, India . . . town, city
**nahr**, Arab . . . river
**nam**, Siam . . . river, water
**nan**, Chn., Jap . . . south
**näs**, Nor., Swe . . . cape
**nez**, Fr . . . point, cape
**nishi, nisi**, Jap . . . west
**njarga**, Fin . . . peninsula
**nong**, Siam . . . marsh
**noord**, Du . . . north
**nor**, Mong . . . lake
**nord**, Dan., Fr., Ger., It., Nor., Swe . . . north
**norte**, Port., Sp . . . north
**nos**, Rus . . . cape
**nyasa**, Bantu . . . lake
**ö**, Dan., Nor., Swe . . . island
**occidental**, Sp . . . western
**ocna**, Rom . . . salt mine
**odde**, Dan., Nor . . . point, cape
**oeste**, Port., Sp . . . west
**oka**, Jap . . . hill
**oost**, Du . . . east
**oriental**, Sp . . . eastern
**óros**, Gr . . . mountain
**ost**, Ger., Swe . . . east
**öster**, Dan., Nor., Swe . . . eastern
**ostrov**, Rus . . . island
**oued**, Arab . . . river, stream
**ouest**, Fr . . . west
**ozero**, Rus . . . lake
**pää**, Fin . . . mountain
**padang**, Mal . . . plain, field
**pampas**, Sp. (Argentina) . . . grassy plains
**pará**, Indian (Brazil) . . . river
**pas**, Fr . . . channel, passage
**paso**, Sp . . . mountain pass, passage
**passo**, It., Port. mountain pass, passage, strait
**patam**, India . . . city, town
**pei**, Chn . . . north
**pélagos**, Gr . . . open sea
**pegunungan**, Indon . . . mountains
**peña**, Sp . . . rock
**peresheyek**, Rus . . . isthmus
**pertuis**, Fr . . . strait
**peski**, Rus . . . desert
**pic**, Fr . . . mountain peak
**pico**, Port., Sp . . . mountain peak
**piedra**, Sp . . . stone, rock
**ping**, Chn . . . plain, flat
**planalto**, Port . . . plateau
**planina**, Yugo . . . mountains
**playa**, Sp . . . shore, beach
**pnom**, Camb . . . mountain
**pointe**, Fr . . . point
**polder**, Du., Ger . . . reclaimed marsh
**polje**, So. Slav . . . plain, field
**poluostrov**, Rus . . . peninsula
**pont**, Fr . . . bridge
**ponta**, Port . . . point, headland
**ponte**, It., Port . . . bridge
**pore**, India . . . city, town
**porthmós**, Gr . . . strait
**porto**, It., Port . . . port, harbor
**potamós**, Gr . . . river
**p'ov**, Rus . . . peninsula
**prado**, Sp . . . field, meadow
**presqu'île**, Fr . . . peninsula
**proliv**, Rus . . . strait
**pu**, Chn . . . commercial village
**pueblo**, Sp . . . town, village
**puerto**, Sp . . . port, harbor
**pulau**, Indon . . . island
**punkt**, Ger . . . point
**punt**, Du . . . point
**punta**, It., Sp . . . point
**pur**, India . . . city, town
**puy**, Fr . . . peak
**qal'a, qal'at**, Arab . . . fort, village
**qasr**, Arab . . . fort, castle
**rann**, India . . . wasteland
**ra's**, Arab . . . cape, head
**reka**, Rus., So. Slav . . . river
**reprêsa**, Port . . . reservoir
**rettō**, Jap . . . island chain
**ría**, Sp . . . estuary
**ribeira**, Port . . . stream
**ribeirão**, Port . . . river
**rio**, It., Port . . . stream, river
**río**, Sp . . . river
**rivière**, Fr . . . river
**roca**, Sp . . . rock
**rt**, Yugo . . . cape
**rūd**, Per . . . river
**saari**, Fin . . . island
**sable**, Fr . . . sand
**sahara**, Arab . . . desert, plain
**saki**, Jap . . . cape
**sal**, Sp . . . salt
**salar**, Sp . . . salt flat, salt lake
**salto**, Sp . . . waterfall
**san**, Jap., Kor . . . mountain, hill
**sat, satul**, Rom . . . village
**schloss**, Ger . . . castle
**sebkha**, Arab . . . salt marsh
**see**, Ger . . . lake, sea
**şehir**, Tur . . . town, city
**selat**, Indon . . . stream
**selvas**, Port. (Brazil) . . . tropical rain forests
**seno**, Sp . . . bay
**serra**, Port . . . mountain chain
**serranía**, Sp . . . mountain ridge
**seto**, Jap . . . strait
**severnaya**, Rus . . . northern
**shahr**, Per . . . town, city
**shan**, Chn . . . mountain, hill, island
**shatt**, Arab . . . river
**shi**, Jap . . . city
**shima**, Jap . . . island
**shōtō**, Jap . . . archipelago
**si**, Chn . . . west, western
**sierra**, Sp . . . mountain range
**sjö**, Nor., Swe . . . lake, sea
**sö**, Dan., Nor . . . lake, sea
**söder, södra**, Swe . . . south
**song**, Annam . . . river
**sopka**, Rus . . . peak, volcano
**source**, Fr . . . a spring
**spitze**, Ger . . . summit, point
**staat**, Ger . . . state
**stad**, Dan., Du., Nor., Swe. . . . city, town
**stadt**, Ger . . . city, town
**stato**, It . . . state
**step'**, Rus . . . treeless plain, steppe
**straat**, Du . . . strait
**strand**, Dan., Du., Ger., Nor., Swe . . . shore, beach
**stretto**, It . . . strait
**strom**, Ger . . . river, stream
**ström**, Dan., Nor., Swe. . . . stream, river
**stroom**, Du . . . stream, river
**su, suyu**, Tur . . . water, river
**sud**, Fr., Sp . . . south
**süd**, Ger . . . south
**suidō**, Jap . . . channel
**sul**, Port . . . south
**sund**, Dan., Nor., Swe . . . sound
**sungai, sungei**, Indon., Mal . . . river
**sur**, Sp . . . south
**syd**, Dan., Nor., Swe . . . south
**tafelland**, Ger . . . plateau
**take**, Jap . . . peak, summit
**tal**, Ger . . . valley
**tanjung, tanjong**, Mal . . . cape
**tao**, Chn . . . island
**târg, târgul**, Rom . . . market, town
**tell**, Arab . . . hill
**teluk**, Indon . . . bay, gulf
**terra**, It . . . land
**terre**, Fr . . . earth, land
**thal**, Ger . . . valley
**tierra**, Sp . . . earth, land
**tō**, Jap . . . east; island
**tonle**, Camb . . . river, lake
**top**, Du . . . peak
**torp**, Swe . . . hamlet, cottage
**tsangpo**, Tib . . . river
**tsi**, Chn . . . village, borough
**tso**, Tib . . . lake
**tsu**, Jap . . . harbor, port
**tundra**, Rus . . . treeless arctic plains
**tung**, Chn . . . east
**tuz**, Tur . . . salt
**udde**, Swe . . . cape
**ufer**, Ger . . . shore, riverbank
**ujung**, Indon . . . point, cape
**umi**, Jap . . . sea, gulf
**ura**, Jap . . . bay, coast, creek
**ust'ye**, Rus . . . river mouth
**valle**, It., Port., Sp . . . valley
**vallée**, Fr . . . valley
**valli**, It . . . lake
**vár**, Hung . . . fortress
**város**, Hung . . . town
**varoš**, So. Slav . . . town
**veld**, Du . . . open plain, field
**verkh**, Rus . . . top, summit
**ves**, Czech . . . village
**vest**, Dan., Nor., Swe . . . west
**vik**, Swe . . . cove, bay
**vila**, Port . . . town
**villa**, Sp . . . town
**villar**, Sp . . . village, hamlet
**ville**, Fr . . . town, city
**vostok**, Rus . . . east
**wad, wādī**, Arab. . . . intermittent stream
**wald**, Ger . . . forest, woodland
**wan**, Chn., Jap . . . bay, gulf
**weiler**, Ger . . . hamlet, village
**westersch**, Du . . . western
**wüste**, Ger . . . desert
**yama**, Jap . . . mountain
**yarimada**, Tur . . . peninsula
**yug**, Rus . . . south
**zaki**, Jap . . . cape
**zaliv**, Rus . . . bay, gulf
**zapad**, Rus . . . west
**zee**, Du . . . sea
**zemlya**, Rus . . . land
**zuid**, Du . . . south

# ABBREVIATIONS OF GEOGRAPHICAL NAMES AND TERMS

# PRONUNCIATION OF GEOGRAPHICAL NAMES

| | | |
|---|---|---|
| Afg. | Afghanistan |
| Afr. | Africa |
| Ak., U.S. | Alaska, U.S. |
| Al., U.S. | Alabama, U.S. |
| Alb. | Albania |
| Alg. | Algeria |
| Am. Sam. | American Samoa |
| And. | Andorra |
| Ang. | Angola |
| Ant. | Antarctica |
| Antig. | Antigua and Barbuda |
| aq. | Aqueduct |
| Ar., U.S. | Arkansas, U.S. |
| Arg. | Argentina |
| Arm. | Armenia |
| arpt. | Airport |
| Aus. | Austria |
| Austl. | Australia |
| Az., U.S. | Arizona, U.S. |
| Azer. | Azerbaijan |
| b. | Bay, Gulf, Inlet, Lagoon |
| Bah. | Bahamas |
| Bahr. | Bahrain |
| Barb. | Barbados |
| Bdi. | Burundi |
| Bel. | Belgium |
| Bela. | Belarus |
| Ber. | Bermuda |
| Bhu. | Bhutan |
| bk. | Undersea Bank |
| bldg. | Building |
| Blg. | Bulgaria |
| Bngl. | Bangladesh |
| Bol. | Bolivia |
| Bos. | Bosnia and Herzegovina |
| Bots. | Botswana |
| Braz. | Brazil |
| Bru. | Brunei |
| Br. Vir. Is. | British Virgin Islands |
| bt. | Bight |
| Burkina | Burkina Faso |
| c. | Cape, Point |
| Ca., U.S. | California, U.S. |
| Cam. | Cameroon |
| Camb. | Cambodia |
| can. | Canal |
| Can. | Canada |
| C.A.R. | Central African Republic |
| Cay. Is. | Cayman Islands |
| C. Iv. | Cote d'Ivoire |
| clf. | Cliff, Escarpment |
| co. | County, Parish |
| Co., U.S. | Colorado, U.S. |
| Col. | Colombia |
| Com. | Comoros |
| cont. | Continent |
| Cook Is. | Cook Islands |
| C.R. | Costa Rica |
| Cro. | Croatia |
| cst. | Coast, Beach |
| Ct., U.S. | Connecticut, U.S. |
| C.V. | Cape Verde |
| Cyp. | Cyprus |
| Czech Rep. | Czech Republic |
| d. | Delta |
| D.C., U.S. | District of Columbia, U.S. |
| De., U.S. | Delaware, U.S. |
| Den. | Denmark |
| dep. | Dependency, Colony |
| depr. | Depression |
| dept. | Department, District |
| des. | Desert |
| Dji. | Djibouti |
| Dom. | Dominica |
| Dom. Rep. | Dominican Republic |
| D.R.C. | Democratic Republic of the Congo |
| Ec. | Ecuador |
| educ. | Educational Facility |
| El Sal. | El Salvador |
| Eng., U.K. | England, U.K. |
| Eq. Gui. | Equatorial Guinea |
| Erit. | Eritrea |
| Est. | Estonia |
| est. | Estuary |
| Eth. | Ethiopia |
| E. Timor | East Timor |
| Eur. | Europe |
| Falk. Is. | Falkland Islands |
| Far. Is. | Faroe Islands |
| Fin. | Finland |
| fj. | Fjord |
| Fl., U.S. | Florida, U.S. |
| for. | Forest, Moor |
| Fr. | France |
| Fr. Gu. | French Guiana |
| Fr. Poly. | French Polynesia |
| Ga., U.S. | Georgia, U.S. |
| Gam. | The Gambia |
| Gaza | Gaza Strip |
| Geor. | Georgia |
| Ger. | Germany |
| Grc. | Greece |
| Gren. | Grenada |
| Grnld. | Greenland |
| Guad. | Guadeloupe |
| Guat. | Guatemala |
| Guern. | Guernsey |
| Gui. | Guinea |
| Gui.-B. | Guinea-Bissau |
| Guy. | Guyana |
| Hi., U.S. | Hawaii, U.S. |
| hist. | Historic Site, Ruins |
| hist. reg. | Historic Region |
| Hond. | Honduras |
| Hung. | Hungary |
| i. | Island |
| Ia., U.S. | Iowa, U.S. |
| ice | Ice Feature, Glacier |
| Ice. | Iceland |
| Id., U.S. | Idaho, U.S. |
| Il., U.S. | Illinois, U.S. |
| In., U.S. | Indiana, U.S. |
| Indon. | Indonesia |
| I. of Man | Isle of Man |
| I.R. | Indian Reservation |
| Ire. | Ireland |
| is. | Islands |
| Isr. | Israel |
| isth. | Isthmus |
| Jam. | Jamaica |
| Jord. | Jordan |
| Kaz. | Kazakhstan |
| Kir. | Kiribati |
| Kor., N. | Korea, North |
| Kor., S. | Korea, South |
| Ks., U.S. | Kansas, U.S. |
| Kuw. | Kuwait |
| Ky., U.S. | Kentucky, U.S. |
| Kyrg. | Kyrgyzstan |
| l. | Lake, Pond |
| La., U.S. | Louisiana, U.S. |
| Lat. | Latvia |
| Leb. | Lebanon |
| Leso. | Lesotho |
| Lib. | Liberia |
| Liech. | Liechtenstein |
| Lith. | Lithuania |
| Lux. | Luxembourg |
| Ma., U.S. | Massachusetts, U.S. |
| Mac. | Macedonia |
| Madag. | Madagascar |
| Malay. | Malaysia |
| Mald. | Maldives |
| Marsh. Is. | Marshall Islands |
| Mart. | Martinique |
| Maur. | Mauritania |
| May. | Mayotte |
| Md., U.S. | Maryland, U.S. |
| Me., U.S. | Maine, U.S. |
| Mex. | Mexico |
| Mi., U.S. | Michigan, U.S. |
| Micron. | Micronesia, Federated States of |
| Mn., U.S. | Minnesota, U.S. |
| Mo., U.S. | Missouri, U.S. |
| Mol. | Moldova |
| Mong. | Mongolia |
| Monts. | Montserrat |
| Mor. | Morocco |
| Moz. | Mozambique |
| Ms., U.S. | Mississippi, U.S. |
| Mt., U.S. | Montana, U.S. |
| mth. | River Mouth or Channel |
| mtn. | Mountain |
| mts. | Mountains |
| Mwi. | Malawi |
| Mya. | Myanmar |
| N.A. | North America |
| N.C., U.S. | North Carolina, U.S. |
| N. Cal. | New Caledonia |
| N.D., U.S. | North Dakota, U.S. |
| Ne., U.S. | Nebraska, U.S. |
| neigh. | Neighborhood |
| Neth. | Netherlands |
| Neth. Ant. | Netherlands Antilles |
| N.H., U.S. | New Hampshire, U.S. |
| Nic. | Nicaragua |
| Nig. | Nigeria |
| N. Ire., U.K. | Northern Ireland, U.K. |
| N.J., U.S. | New Jersey, U.S. |
| N.M., U.S. | New Mexico, U.S. |
| N. Mar. Is. | Northern Mariana Islands |
| Nmb. | Namibia |
| Nor. | Norway |
| Nv., U.S. | Nevada, U.S. |
| N.Y., U.S. | New York, U.S. |
| N.Z. | New Zealand |
| o. | Ocean |
| Oc. | Oceania |
| Oh., U.S. | Ohio, U.S. |
| Ok., U.S. | Oklahoma, U.S. |
| Or., U.S. | Oregon, U.S. |
| p. | Pass |
| Pa., U.S. | Pennsylvania, U.S. |
| Pak. | Pakistan |
| Pan. | Panama |
| Pap. N. Gui. | Papua New Guinea |
| Para. | Paraguay |
| pen. | Peninsula |
| Phil. | Philippines |
| Pit. | Pitcairn |
| pl. | Plain, Flat |
| plat. | Plateau, Highland |
| Pol. | Poland |
| Port. | Portugal |
| P.R. | Puerto Rico |
| prov. | Province, Region |
| pt. of i. | Point of Interest |
| r. | River, Creek |
| Reu. | Reunion |
| rec. | Recreational Site, Park |
| reg. | Physical Region |
| rel. | Religious Institution |
| res. | Reservoir |
| rf. | Reef, Shoal |
| R.I., U.S. | Rhode Island, U.S. |
| Rom. | Romania |
| Rw. | Rwanda |
| S.A. | South America |
| S. Afr. | South Africa |
| Sau. Ar. | Saudi Arabia |
| S.C., U.S. | South Carolina, U.S. |
| sci. | Scientific Station |
| Scot., U.K. | Scotland, U.K. |
| S.D., U.S. | South Dakota, U.S. |
| sea feat. | Undersea Feature |
| Sen. | Senegal |
| Serb. | Serbia and Montenegro |
| Sey. | Seychelles |
| S. Geor. | South Georgia |
| Sing. | Singapore |
| S.L. | Sierra Leone |
| Slvk. | Slovakia |
| Slvn. | Slovenia |
| S. Mar. | San Marino |
| Sol. Is. | Solomon Islands |
| Som. | Somalia |
| Sp. N. Afr. | Spanish North Africa |
| Sri L. | Sri Lanka |
| St. Hel. | St. Helena |
| St. K./N. | St. Kitts and Nevis |
| St. Luc. | St. Lucia |
| St. P./M. | St. Pierre and Miquelon |
| S. Tom./P. | Sao Tome and Principe |
| St. Vin. | St. Vincent and the Grenadines |
| Sur. | Suriname |
| Sval. | Svalbard |
| sw. | Swamp, Marsh |
| Swaz. | Swaziland |
| Swe. | Sweden |
| Switz. | Switzerland |
| Tai. | Taiwan |
| Taj. | Tajikistan |
| Tan. | Tanzania |
| T./C. Is. | Turks and Caicos Islands |
| ter. | Territory |
| Thai. | Thailand |
| Tn., U.S. | Tennessee, U.S. |
| trans. | Transportation Facility |
| Trin. | Trinidad and Tobago |
| Tun. | Tunisia |
| Tur. | Turkey |
| Turkmen. | Turkmenistan |
| Tx., U.S. | Texas, U.S. |
| U.A.E. | United Arab Emirates |
| Ug. | Uganda |
| U.K. | United Kingdom |
| Ukr. | Ukraine |
| Ur. | Uruguay |
| U.S. | United States |
| Ut., U.S. | Utah, U.S. |
| Uzb. | Uzbekistan |
| Va., U.S. | Virginia, U.S. |
| val. | Valley, Watercourse |
| Ven. | Venezuela |
| Viet. | Vietnam |
| V.I.U.S. | Virgin Islands (U.S.) |
| vol. | Volcano |
| Vt., U.S. | Vermont, U.S. |
| Wa., U.S. | Washington, U.S. |
| W.B. | West Bank |
| Wi., U.S. | Wisconsin, U.S. |
| W. Sah. | Western Sahara |
| wtfl. | Waterfall |
| W.V., U.S. | West Virginia, U.S. |
| Wy., U.S. | Wyoming, U.S. |
| Zam. | Zambia |
| Zimb. | Zimbabwe |

## Key to the Sound Values of Letters and Symbols Used in the Index to Indicate Pronunciation

ă-ăt; băttle
ȧ-finȧl; appeȧl
ā-rāte; elāte
å-senåte; inanimåte
ä-ärm; cälm
à-àsk; båth
a̤-sofa̤; ma̤rine (short neutral or indeterminate sound)
â-fâre; prepâre
ch-choose; church
dh-as th in other; either
ē-bē; ēve
ĕ-ĕvent; crĕate
ĕ-bĕt; ĕnd
ḙ-recḙnt (short neutral or indeterminate sound)
ẽ-cratẽr; cindẽr
g-gō; gāme
gh-guttural g
ĭ-bĭt; wĭll
ĩ-(short neutral or indeterminate sound)
ī-rīde; bīte
κ-gutteral k as ch in German ich
ng-sing
ŋ-baŋk; liŋger
N-indicates nasalized
ŏ-nŏd; ŏdd
ọ-cọmmit; cọnnect
ō-ōld; bōld
ô-ôbey; hôtel
ô-ôrder; nôrth
oi-boil
o͞o-fo͞od; ro͞ot
ȯ-as oo in foot; wood
ou-out; thou
s-soft; so; sane
sh-dish; finish
th-thin; thick
ū-pūre; cūre
ů-ůnite; ůsůrp
û-ûrn; fûr
ŭ-stŭd; ŭp
u̇-circu̇s; su̇bmit
ü-as in French tu
zh-as z in azure
'-indeterminate vowel sound

In many cases the spelling of foreign geographical names does not even remotely indicate the pronunciation to an American, i.e., Słupsk in Poland is pronounced swȯpsk; Jujuy in Argentina is pronounced ho͞ohwē', La Spezia in Italy is lä-spĕ'zyä.

This condition is hardly surprising, however, when we consider that in our own language Worcester, Massachusetts, is pronounced wȯs'tẽr; Sioux City, Iowa, so͞o sī'tĭ; Schuylkill Haven, Pennsylvania, sko͞ol'kĭl hä-vĕn; Poughkeepsie, New York, pō-kĭp'sĕ.

The indication of pronunciation of geographic names presents several peculiar problems:

1. Many foreign tongues use sounds that are not present in the English language and which an American cannot normally articulate. Thus, though the nearest English equivalent sound has been indicated, only approximate results are possible.

2. There are several dialects in each foreign tongue which cause variation in the local pronunciation of names. This also occurs in identical names in the various divisions of a great language group, as the Slavic or the Latin.

3. Within the United States there are marked differences in pronunciation, not only of local geographic names, but also of common words, indicating that the sound and tone values for letters as well as the placing of the emphasis vary considerably from one part of the country to another.

4. A number of different letters and diacritical combinations could be used to indicate essentially the same or approximate pronunciations.

Some variation in pronunciation other than that indicated in this index may be encountered, but such a difference does not necessarily indicate that either is in error, and in many cases it is a matter of individual choice as to which is preferred. In fact, an exact indication of pronunciation of many foreign names using English letters and diacritical marks is extremely difficult and sometimes impossible.

# PRONOUNCING INDEX

This universal index includes in a single alphabetical list approximately 30,000 names of features that appear on the reference maps. Each name is followed by a page reference and geographical coordinates.

**Abbreviation and Capitalization** Abbreviations of names on the maps have been standardized as much as possible. Names that are abbreviated on the maps are generally spelled out in full in the index. Periods are used after all abbreviations regardless of local practice. The abbreviation "St." is used only for "Saint". "Sankt" and other forms of this term are spelled out.

Most initial letters of names are capitalized, except for a few Dutch names, such as "s-Gravenhage". Capitalization of noninitial words in a name generally follows local practice.

**Alphabetization** Names are alphabetized in the order of the letters of the English alphabet. Spanish *ll* and *ch*, for example, are not treated as direct letters. Furthermore, diacritical marks are disregarded in alphabetization — German or Scandinavian *ä* or *ö* are treated as *a* or *o*.

The names of physical features may appear inverted, since they are always alphabetized under the proper, not the generic, part of the name, thus: "Gibraltar, Strait of". Otherwise every entry, whether consisting of one word or more, is alphabetized as a single continuous entity. "Lakeland", for example, appears after "La Crosse" and before "La Salle". Names beginning with articles (Le Harve, Den Helder, Al Manāmah, Ad Dawhah) are not inverted.

In the case of identical names, towns are listed first, then political divisions, then physical features.

**Generic Terms** Except for cities, the names of all features are followed by terms that represent broad classes of features, for example, Mississippi, r. or Alabama, state. A list of all abbreviations used in the index is on page 261.

Country names and the names of features that extend beyond the boundaries of one county are followed by the name of the continent in which each is located. Country designations follow the names of all other places in the index. The locations of places in the United States and the United Kingdom are further defined by abbreviations that include the state or political division in which each is located.

**Pronunciations** Pronunciations are included for most names listed. An explanation of the pronunciation system used appears on page 261.

**Page References and Geographical Coordinates** The geographical coordinates and page references are found in the last columns of each entry.

If a page contains several maps or insets, a lowercase letter identifies the specific map or inset.

Latitude and longitude coordinates for point features, such as cities and mountain peaks, indicate the location of the symbols. For extensive areal features, such as countries or mountain ranges, or linear features, such as canals and rivers, locations are given for the position of the type as it appears on the map.

| PLACE (Pronunciation) | PAGE | LAT. | LONG. |
|---|---|---|---|
| **A** | | | |
| Aachen, Ger. (ä′kĕn) | 161 | 50°46′N | 6°07′E |
| Aalborg, Den. (ôl′bôr) | 154 | 57°02′N | 9°55′E |
| Aalen, Ger. (ä′lĕn) | 168 | 48°49′N | 10°08′E |
| Aalsmeer, Neth. | 159a | 52°16′N | 4°44′E |
| Aalst, Bel. | 165 | 50°58′N | 4°00′E |
| Aarau, Switz. (ärou) | 161 | 47°22′N | 8°03′E |
| Aarschot, Bel. | 159a | 50°59′N | 4°51′E |
| Aba, D.R.C. | 237 | 3°52′N | 30°14′E |
| Aba, Nig. | 230 | 5°06′N | 7°21′E |
| Ābādān, Iran (ä-bǔ-dän′) | 198 | 30°15′N | 48°30′E |
| Abaetetuba, Braz. (ä′bä̇-tĕ-tōo′bä) | 143 | 1°44′S | 48°45′W |
| Abajo Peak, mtn., Ut., U.S. (ä-bä′hō) | 119 | 37°51′N | 109°28′W |
| Abakaliki, Nig. | 235 | 6°21′N | 8°06′E |
| Abakan, Russia (ŭ-bá-kän′) | 179 | 53°43′N | 91°28′E |
| Abakan, r., Russia (u-bá-kän′) | 184 | 53°00′N | 91°06′E |
| Abancay, Peru (ä-bän-kä′ė) | 142 | 13°44′S | 72°46′W |
| Abashiri, Japan (ä-bä-shē′rē) | 210 | 44°00′N | 144°13′E |
| Abasolo, Mex. (ä-bä-sō′lô) | 130 | 24°05′N | 98°24′W |
| Abasolo, Mex. (ä-bä-sō′lô) | 122 | 27°13′N | 101°25′W |
| Abaya, Lake, l., Eth. (ä-bä′yä) | 231 | 6°24′N | 38°22′E |
| 'Abbāsah, Tur'at al, can., Egypt | 238d | 30°45′N | 32°15′E |
| Abbeville, Fr. (áb-vēl′) | 161 | 50°08′N | 1°49′E |
| Abbeville, Al., U.S. (ăb′ê-vĭl) | 124 | 31°35′N | 85°15′W |
| Abbeville, Ga., U.S. (ăb′ê-vĭl) | 124 | 31°53′N | 83°23′W |
| Abbeville, La., U.S. | 123 | 29°59′N | 92°07′W |
| Abbeville, S.C., U.S. | 125 | 34°09′N | 82°25′W |
| Abbiategrasso, Italy (äb-byä′tå-gräs′sō) | 174 | 45°23′N | 8°52′E |
| Abbots Bromley, Eng., U.K. (ăb′ŭts brŭm′lê) | 158a | 52°49′N | 1°52′W |
| Abbotsford, Can. (ăb′ŭts-fĕrd) | 116d | 49°03′N | 122°17′W |
| 'Abd al Kūrī, i., Yemen (ăbd-ĕl-kò′rê) | 238a | 12°12′N | 51°00′E |
| Abdulino, Russia (ăb-dò-lē′nō) | 180 | 53°42′N | 53°40′E |
| Abengourou, C. Iv. | 234 | 6°44′N | 3°29′W |
| Abeokuta, Nig. (ä-bå-ô-kōo′tä) | 230 | 7°10′N | 3°26′E |
| Abercorn *see* Mbala, Zam. | 232 | 8°50′S | 31°22′E |
| Aberdare, Wales, U.K. (ăb-ĕr-dâr′) | 164 | 51°45′N | 3°35′W |
| Aberdeen, Scot., U.K. | 154 | 57°10′N | 2°05′W |
| Aberdeen, Ms., U.S. | 124 | 33°49′N | 88°33′W |
| Aberdeen, S.D., U.S. (ăb-ĕr-dēn′) | 104 | 45°28′N | 98°29′W |
| Aberdeen, Wa., U.S. | 104 | 47°00′N | 123°48′W |
| Aberford, Eng., U.K. (ăb′ĕr-fĕrd) | 158a | 53°49′N | 1°21′W |
| Abergavenny, Wales, U.K. (ăb′ĕr-gá-vĕn′ĭ) | 164 | 51°45′N | 3°05′W |
| Abert, Lake, l., Or., U.S. (ā′bĕrt) | 114 | 42°39′N | 120°24′W |
| Aberystwyth, Wales, U.K. (ă-bĕr-ĭst′wĭth) | 164 | 52°25′N | 4°04′W |
| Abidjan, C. Iv. (ä-bēd-zhän′) | 230 | 5°19′N | 4°02′W |
| Abiko, Japan (ä-bē-kō) | 211a | 35°53′N | 140°01′E |
| Abilene, Ks., U.S. (ăb′ī-lēn) | 121 | 38°54′N | 97°12′W |
| Abilene, Tx., U.S. | 104 | 32°25′N | 99°45′W |
| Abingdon, Eng., U.K. | 158b | 51°38′N | 1°17′W |
| Abingdon, Il., U.S. (ăb′ĭng-dŭn) | 113 | 40°48′N | 90°21′W |
| Abingdon, Va., U.S. | 125 | 36°42′N | 81°57′W |
| Abington, Ma., U.S. (ăb′ĭng-tŭn) | 101a | 42°07′N | 70°57′W |
| Abiquiu Reservoir, res., N.M., U.S. | 119 | 36°31′N | 106°42′W |
| Abitibi, l., Can. (ăb-ĭ-tĭb′ĭ) | 93 | 48°27′N | 80°20′W |
| Abitibi, r., Can. | 93 | 49°30′N | 81°10′W |
| Abkhazia, state, Geor. | 181 | 43°10′N | 40°45′E |
| Ablis, Fr. (á-blē′) | 171b | 48°31′N | 1°50′E |
| Abnūb, Egypt (äb-nōob′) | 238b | 27°18′N | 31°11′E |
| Ābo *see* Turku, Fin. | 154 | 60°28′N | 22°12′E |
| Abohar, India | 202 | 30°12′N | 74°13′E |
| Aboisso, C. Iv. | 234 | 5°28′N | 3°12′W |
| Abomey, Benin (áb-ô-mā′) | 230 | 7°11′N | 1°59′E |
| Abony, Hung. (ŏ′bô-ny′) | 169 | 47°12′N | 20°00′E |
| Abou Deïa, Chad | 235 | 11°27′N | 19°17′E |
| Abra, r., Phil. (ä′brä) | 213a | 17°16′N | 120°38′E |
| Abraão, Braz. (äbrå-oun′) | 141a | 23°10′S | 44°10′W |
| Abraham's Bay, b., Bah. | 135 | 22°20′N | 73°50′W |
| Abram, Eng., U.K. (ā′brăm) | 158a | 53°31′N | 2°36′W |
| Abrantes, Port. (á-brän′tĕs) | 172 | 39°28′N | 8°13′W |
| Abrolhos, Arquipélago dos, is., Braz. | 143 | 17°58′S | 38°40′W |
| Abruka, i., Est. (á-brô′kà) | 167 | 58°09′N | 22°30′E |
| Abruzzi e Molise, hist. reg., Italy | 174 | 42°10′N | 13°55′E |
| Absaroka Range, mts., U.S. (äb-sǎ-rō-kǎ) | 106 | 44°50′N | 109°47′W |
| Abşeron Yarımadası, pen., Azer. | 181 | 40°20′N | 50°30′E |
| Abū Arish, Sau. Ar. (ä-bōō á-rēsh′) | 198 | 16°48′N | 43°00′E |
| Abu Dhabi *see* Abū Ẓaby, U.A.E. | 198 | 24°15′N | 54°28′E |
| Abū Ḥamad, Sudan (ä′bōō hä′-mĕd) | 231 | 19°37′N | 33°21′E |
| Abuja, Nig. | 230 | 9°12′N | 7°11′E |
| Abū Kamāl, Syria | 198 | 34°45′N | 40°46′E |
| Abunã, r., S.A. (ä-boō-nä′) | 142 | 10°25′S | 67°00′W |
| Abū Qīr, Egypt (ä′boō kēr′) | 238b | 31°18′N | 30°06′E |
| Abū Qurūn, Ra's, mtn., Egypt | 197a | 30°22′N | 33°32′E |
| Aburatsu, Japan (ä-bò-rät′soō) | 211 | 31°33′N | 131°20′E |
| Abu Road, India (á′boō) | 199 | 24°38′N | 72°45′E |
| Abū Tīj, Egypt | 238b | 27°03′N | 31°19′E |
| Abū Ẓaby, U.A.E. | 198 | 24°15′N | 54°28′E |
| Abū Zanīmah, Egypt | 197a | 29°03′N | 33°08′E |
| Abyy, Russia | 179 | 68°24′N | 134°00′E |
| Acacias, Col. (á-ká′sëäs) | 142a | 3°59′N | 73°44′W |
| Acadia National Park, rec., Me., U.S. (ä-kā′dǐ-á) | 107 | 44°19′N | 68°01′W |
| Acajutla, El Sal. (ä-kä-hōōt′lä) | 132 | 13°37′N | 89°50′W |
| Acala, Mex. (ä-kä′lä) | 131 | 16°38′N | 92°49′W |
| Acalayong, Eq. Gui. | 236 | 1°05′N | 9°40′E |
| Acámbaro, Mex. (ä-käm′bä-rō) | 130 | 20°03′N | 100°42′W |
| Acancéh, Mex. (ä-kän-sĕ′) | 132a | 20°50′N | 89°27′W |
| Acapetlahuaya, Mex. (ä-kä-pĕt′lä-hwä′yä) | 130 | 18°24′N | 100°04′W |
| Acaponeta, Mex. (ä-kä-pô-nä′tä) | 130 | 22°31′N | 105°25′W |
| Acaponeta, r., Mex. (ä-kä-pô-nä′tä) | 130 | 22°47′N | 105°23′W |
| Acapulco, Mex. (ä-kä-pōōl′kō) | 128 | 16°49′N | 99°57′W |
| Acaraí Mountains, mts., S.A. | 143 | 1°30′N | 57°40′W |
| Acarigua, Ven. (ä-kä-rē′gwä) | 142 | 9°29′N | 69°11′W |
| Acatlán de Osorio, Mex. (ä-kät-län′dä ô-sō′rē-ō) | 130 | 18°11′N | 98°04′W |
| Acatzingo de Hidalgo, Mex. | 131 | 18°58′N | 97°47′W |
| Acayucan, Mex. (ä-kä-yōō′kän) | 131 | 17°56′N | 94°55′W |
| Accoville, W.V., U.S. (ăk′kô-vĭl) | 108 | 37°45′N | 81°50′W |
| Accra, Ghana (ä′krà) | 230 | 5°33′N | 0°13′W |
| Accrington, Eng., U.K. (ăk′rĭng-tŭn) | 158a | 53°45′N | 2°22′W |
| Acerra, Italy (ä-chĕ′r-rä) | 173c | 40°42′N | 14°22′E |
| Achacachi, Bol. (ä-chä-kä′chê) | 142 | 16°11′S | 68°32′W |
| Achelóos, r., Grc. | 175 | 38°45′N | 21°26′E |
| Achill Island, i., Ire. (ä-chĭl′) | 160 | 53°55′N | 10°05′W |
| Achinsk, Russia (á-chênsk′) | 184 | 56°13′N | 90°32′E |
| Acireale, Italy (ä-chê-rä-ä′lä) | 174 | 37°37′N | 15°12′E |
| Acklins, i., Bah. (ăk′lĭns) | 129 | 22°30′N | 73°55′W |
| Acklins, The Bight of, b., Bah. (ăk′lĭns) | 135 | 22°35′N | 74°20′W |
| Acolman, Mex. (ä-kōl-mä′n) | 131a | 19°38′N | 98°56′W |
| Acoma Indian Reservation, I.R., N.M., U.S. | 119 | 34°52′N | 107°40′W |
| Aconcagua, prov., Chile (ä-kôn-kä′gwä) | 141b | 32°20′S | 71°00′W |
| Aconcagua, r., Chile (ä-kôn-kä′gwä) | 141b | 32°43′S | 70°53′W |
| Aconcagua, Cerro, mtn., Arg. (ä-kôn-kä′gwä) | 144 | 32°38′S | 70°00′W |
| Açores (Azores), is., Port. | 229 | 37°44′N | 29°25′W |
| A Coruña, Spain | 154 | 43°20′N | 8°20′W |
| Acoyapa, Nic. (ä-kô-yä′pä) | 132 | 11°54′N | 85°11′W |
| Acqui, Italy (äk′kwē) | 174 | 44°41′N | 8°22′W |
| Acre, state, Braz. (ä′krä) | 142 | 8°40′S | 70°45′W |
| Acre, r., S.A. | 142 | 10°33′S | 68°34′W |
| Acton, Can. (ăk′tŭn) | 102d | 43°38′N | 80°02′W |
| Acton, Al., U.S. (ăk′tŭn) | 110h | 33°21′N | 86°49′W |
| Acton, Ma., U.S. (ăk′tŭn) | 101a | 42°29′N | 71°26′W |
| Actopan, Mex. (äk-tô-pän′) | 130 | 20°16′N | 98°57′W |
| Actópan, r., Mex. (äk-tô′pän) | 131 | 19°25′N | 96°31′W |
| Acuitzio del Canje, Mex. (ä-kwēt′zē-ō dĕl kän′hä) | 130 | 19°28′N | 101°21′W |
| Acul, Baie de l', b., Haiti (ä-kōol′) | 135 | 19°55′N | 72°20′W |
| Ada, Mn., U.S. (ā′dŭ) | 112 | 47°17′N | 96°32′W |
| Ada, Oh., U.S. (ā′dŭ) | 108 | 40°45′N | 83°45′W |
| Ada, Ok., U.S. (ā′dŭ) | 121 | 34°45′N | 96°43′W |

ăt; fìnal; rāte; senåte; ärm; àsk; sofà; fâre; ch-choose; dh-as th in other; bē; ĕvent; bĕt; recĕnt; cratĕr; g-gō; gh-guttural g; bīt; ĭ-short neutral; rīde; к-guttural k as ch in German ich;

| PLACE (Pronunciation) | PAGE | LAT. | LONG. |
|---|---|---|---|
| Ada, Serb. (ä'dä) | 175 | 45°48'N | 20°06'E |
| Adachi, Japan | 211a | 35°50'N | 39°36'E |
| Adak, Ak., U.S. (ä-dăk') | 103a | 56°50'N | 176°48'W |
| Adak, i., Ak., U.S. (ä-dăk') | 103a | 51°40'N | 176°28'W |
| Adak Strait, strt., Ak., U.S. (ä-dăk') | 103a | 51°42'N | 177°16'W |
| Adamaoua, mts., Afr. | 230 | 6°30'N | 11°50'E |
| Adams, Ma., U.S. (ăd'ămz) | 109 | 42°35'N | 73°10'W |
| Adams, Wi., U.S. (ăd'ămz) | 113 | 43°55'N | 89°48'W |
| Adams, r., Can. (ăd'ămz) | 95 | 51°30'N | 119°20'W |
| Adams, Mount, mtn., Wa., U.S. (ăd'ămz) | 106 | 46°15'N | 121°19'W |
| Adamsville, Al., U.S. (ăd'ămz-vĭl) | 110h | 33°36'N | 86°57'W |
| Adana, Tur. (ä'dä-nä) | 198 | 37°05'N | 35°20'E |
| Adapazarı, Tur. (ä-dä-pä-zä'rē) | 163 | 40°45'N | 30°20'E |
| Adarama, Sudan (ä-dä-rä'mä) | 231 | 17°11'N | 34°56'E |
| Adda, r., Italy (äd'dä) | 174 | 45°43'N | 9°31'E |
| Ad Dabbah, Sudan | 231 | 18°04'N | 30°58'E |
| Ad Dahnā, des., Sau. Ar. | 198 | 26°05'N | 47°15'E |
| Ad-Dāmir, Sudan (ad-dä'mĕr) | 231 | 17°38'N | 33°57'E |
| Ad Dammām, Sau. Ar. | 198 | 26°27'N | 49°59'E |
| Ad Dāmūr, Leb. | 197a | 33°44'N | 35°27'E |
| Ad Dawhah, Qatar | 198 | 25°02'N | 51°28'E |
| Ad Dilam, Sau. Ar. | 198 | 23°47'N | 47°03'E |
| Ad Dilinjāt, Egypt | 238b | 30°48'N | 30°32'E |
| Addis Ababa, Eth. | 231 | 9°00'N | 38°44'E |
| Addison, Tx., U.S. (ă'dĭ-sŭn) | 117c | 32°58'N | 96°50'W |
| Addo, S. Afr. (ădō) | 233c | 33°33'S | 25°43'E |
| Ad Duwaym, Sudan (ad-dò-ām') | 231 | 13°56'N | 32°22'E |
| Addyston, Oh., U.S. (ăd'ē-stŭn) | 111f | 39°09'N | 84°42'W |
| Adel, Ga., U.S. (ā-dĕl') | 124 | 31°08'N | 83°55'W |
| Adelaide, Austl. (ăd'ē-lād) | 218 | 34°46'S | 139°08'E |
| Adelaide, S. Afr. (ăd-ĕl'ăd) | 233c | 32°41'S | 26°07'E |
| Adelaide Island, i., Ant. (ăd'ē-lād) | 224 | 67°15'S | 68°40'W |
| Aden ('Adan), Yemen (ä'dĕn) | 198 | 12°48'N | 45°00'E |
| Aden, Gulf of, b. | 198 | 11°45'N | 45°45'E |
| Adi, Pulau, i., Indon. (ä'dē) | 213 | 4°25'S | 133°52'E |
| Adige, r., Italy (ä'dē-jā) | 162 | 46°38'N | 10°43'E |
| Adigrat, Eth. | 201 | 14°17'N | 39°28'E |
| Adilābād, India (ŭ-dĭl-ä-băd') | 202 | 19°47'N | 78°30'E |
| Adirondack Mountains, mts., N.Y., U.S. (ăd-ĭ-rŏn'dăk) | 107 | 43°45'N | 74°40'W |
| Adis Abeba see Addis Ababa, Eth. | 231 | 9°00'N | 38°44'E |
| Adi Ugri, Erit. (ä-dē ōō'grē) | 231 | 14°54'N | 38°52'E |
| Adjud, Rom. (äd'zhòd) | 169 | 46°05'N | 27°12'E |
| Adkins, Tx., U.S. | 117d | 29°22'N | 98°18'W |
| Admiralty, i., Ak., U.S. (ăd'mĭ-răl-tē) | 103 | 57°50'N | 133°50'W |
| Admiralty Inlet, Wa., U.S. (ăd'mĭ-răl-tē) | 116a | 48°10'N | 122°45'W |
| Admiralty Island National Monument, rec., Ak., U.S. (ăd'mĭ-răl-tē) | 103 | 57°50'N | 137°30'W |
| Admiralty Islands, is., Pap. N. Gui. (ăd'mĭ-răl-tē) | 213 | 1°40'S | 146°45'E |
| Ado-Ekiti, Nig. | 235 | 7°38'N | 5°12'E |
| Adolph, Mn., U.S. (ā'dolf) | 117h | 46°47'N | 92°17'W |
| Ādoni, India | 203 | 15°42'N | 77°18'E |
| Adour, r., Fr. (à-dōōr') | 161 | 43°43'N | 0°38'W |
| Adra, Spain (ä'drä) | 172 | 36°45'N | 3°02'W |
| Adrano, Italy (ä-drä'nō) | 174 | 37°42'N | 14°52'E |
| Adrar, Alg. | 230 | 27°53'N | 0°15'W |
| Adria, Italy (ä'drē-ä) | 174 | 45°03'N | 12°01'E |
| Adrian, Mi., U.S. (ā'drĭ-ăn) | 108 | 41°55'N | 84°00'W |
| Adrian, Mn., U.S. (ā'drĭ-ăn) | 112 | 43°39'N | 95°56'W |
| Adrianople see Edirne, Tur. | 154 | 41°41'N | 26°35'E |
| Adriatic Sea, sea, Eur. | 156 | 43°30'N | 14°27'E |
| Adwa, Eth. | 231 | 14°02'N | 38°58'E |
| Adwick-le-Street, Eng., U.K. (ăd'wĭk-lē-strēt') | 158a | 53°35'N | 1°11'W |
| Adycha, r., Russia (ä'dĭ-chà) | 185 | 66°11'N | 136°45'E |
| Adygea, prov., Russia | 180 | 45°00'N | 40°00'E |
| Adz'va, r., Russia (ädz'vá) | 180 | 67°00'N | 59°20'E |
| Aegean Sea, sea (ē-jē'ăn) | 156 | 39°04'N | 24°56'E |
| A Estrada, Spain | 172 | 42°42'N | 8°29'W |
| Affton, Mo., U.S. | 117e | 38°33'N | 90°20'W |
| Afghanistan, nation, Asia (ăf-găn-ĭ-stăn') | 198 | 33°00'N | 63°00'E |
| Afgooye, Som. (äf-gô'ī) | 238a | 2°08'N | 45°08'E |
| Afikpo, Nig. | 235 | 5°53'N | 7°56'E |
| Aflou, Alg. (ä-flōō') | 230 | 33°59'N | 2°04'E |
| Afognak, i., Ak., U.S. (ä-fŏg-năk') | 103 | 58°28'N | 151°35'W |
| A Fonsagrada, Spain | 172 | 43°08'N | 7°07'W |
| Afonso Claudio, Braz. (äl-fōn'sō-klou'dēō) | 141a | 20°05'S | 41°05'W |
| Afragola, Italy (ä-frà'gō-lä) | 173c | 40°40'N | 14°19'E |
| Africa, cont. | 229 | 10°00'N | 22°00'E |
| Afton, Mn., U.S. (ăf'tŭn) | 117g | 44°54'N | 92°47'W |
| Afton, Ok., U.S. (ăf'tŭn) | 121 | 36°42'N | 94°56'W |
| Afton, Wy., U.S. (ăf'tŭn) | 115 | 42°42'N | 110°52'W |
| 'Afula, Isr. (ä-fò'là) | 197a | 32°36'N | 35°17'E |
| Afyon, Tur. (ä-fē-ōn) | 198 | 38°45'N | 30°20'E |
| Agadem, Niger (ä'gá-dĕm) | 231 | 16°50'N | 13°17'E |
| Agadez, Niger (ä'gá-dĕs) | 230 | 16°58'N | 7°59'E |
| Agadir, Mor. (ä-gá-dēr) | 230 | 30°30'N | 9°37'W |
| Agalta, Cordillera de, mts., Hond. (kôr-dēl-yĕ'rä-dĕ-ä-gä'l-tä) | 132 | 15°15'N | 85°42'W |
| Agapovka, Russia (ä-gä-pôv'kä) | 186a | 53°18'N | 59°10'E |
| Agartala, India | 202 | 23°53'N | 91°22'E |
| Agāshi, India | 203b | 19°28'N | 72°46'E |
| Agashkino, Russia (á-gäsh'kĭ-nô) | 186b | 55°18'N | 38°13'E |
| Agattu, i., Ak., U.S. (á'gä-tōō) | 103a | 52°14'N | 173°40'E |
| Agboville, C. Iv. | 234 | 5°56'N | 4°13'W |
| Ağdam, Azer. (äg'dām) | 181 | 40°00'N | 47°00'E |
| Agde, Fr. (ägd) | 170 | 43°19'N | 3°30'E |
| Agen, Fr. (à-zhäN') | 161 | 44°13'N | 0°31'E |
| Agiásos, Grc. | 175 | 39°06'N | 26°25'E |
| Aginskoye, Russia (ä-hĭn'skô-yĕ) | 179 | 51°15'N | 113°15'E |

| PLACE (Pronunciation) | PAGE | LAT. | LONG. |
|---|---|---|---|
| Ágios Efstrátios, i., Grc. | 163 | 39°30'N | 24°58'E |
| Agíou Órous, Kólpos, b., Grc. | 175 | 40°15'N | 24°00'E |
| Agno, Phil. (äg'nō) | 213a | 16°07'N | 119°49'E |
| Agno, r., Phil. | 213a | 15°42'N | 120°28'E |
| Agnone, Italy (än-yō'nā) | 174 | 41°49'N | 14°23'E |
| Agogo, Ghana | 234 | 6°47'N | 1°04'W |
| Agra, India (ä'grä) | 199 | 27°18'N | 78°00'E |
| Ağrı, Tur. | 181 | 39°50'N | 43°10'E |
| Agri, r., Italy (ä'grē) | 174 | 40°15'N | 16°21'E |
| Agrínio, Grc. | 163 | 38°38'N | 21°06'E |
| Agua, vol., Guat. (ä'gwä) | 132 | 14°28'N | 90°43'W |
| Agua Blanca, Río, r., Mex. (rē'ō-ä-gwä-blä'n-kä) | 130 | 21°46'N | 102°54'W |
| Agua Brava, Laguna de, l., Mex. | 130 | 22°04'N | 105°40'W |
| Agua Caliente Indian Reservation, I.R., Ca., U.S. (ä'gwä kal-yĕn'tä) | 118 | 33°50'N | 116°24'W |
| Aguada, Cuba (ä-gwä'dȧ) | 134 | 22°25'N | 80°50'W |
| Aguada, l., Mex. (ä-gwä'dȧ) | 132a | 18°46'N | 89°40'W |
| Aguadas, Col. (ä-gwä'dás) | 142 | 5°37'N | 75°27'W |
| Aguadilla, P.R. (ä-gwä-dēl'yä) | 129b | 18°27'N | 67°10'W |
| Aguadulce, Pan. (ä-gwä-dōōl'sā) | 133 | 8°15'N | 80°33'W |
| Agua Escondida, Meseta de, plat., Mex. | 131 | 16°54'N | 91°35'W |
| Agua Fria, r., Az., U.S. (ä'gwä frē-ä) | 119 | 33°43'N | 112°22'W |
| Agua Fria National Monument, rec., Az., U.S. | 119 | 34°13'N | 112°03'W |
| Aguai, Braz. (ägwä-ē') | 141a | 22°04'S | 46°57'W |
| Agualeguas, Mex. (ä-gwä-lā'gwäs) | 122 | 26°19'N | 99°33'W |
| Aguán, r., Hond. (ä-gwä'n) | 132 | 15°22'N | 87°00'W |
| Aguanaval, r., Mex. (á-guä-nä-väl') | 122 | 25°12'N | 103°28'W |
| Aguanus, r., Can. (á-gwä'nŭs) | 101 | 50°45'N | 62°03'W |
| Aguascalientes, Mex. (ä'gwäs-käl-yĕn'tās) | 128 | 21°52'N | 102°17'W |
| Aguascalientes, state, Mex. (ä'gwäs-käl-yĕn'tās) | 130 | 22°00'N | 102°18'W |
| Águeda, Port. (ä-gwä'dȧ) | 172 | 40°36'N | 8°26'W |
| Agueda, r., Eur. (ä-gē-dä) | 172 | 40°50'N | 6°44'W |
| Aguelhok, Mali | 234 | 19°28'N | 0°52'E |
| Aguilar, Spain | 172 | 37°32'N | 4°39'W |
| Aguilar, Co., U.S. (ä-gē-lär') | 120 | 37°24'N | 104°38'W |
| Aguilas, Spain (ä-gē-läs) | 162 | 37°26'N | 1°35'W |
| Aguililla, Mex. (ä-gē-lēl-yä) | 130 | 18°44'N | 102°44'W |
| Aguililla, r., Mex. (ä-gē-lēl-yä) | 130 | 18°30'N | 102°48'W |
| Aguja, Punta, c., Peru (pŭn'tȧ ȧ-gōō' hä) | 142 | 6°00'S | 81°15'W |
| Agulhas, Cape, c., S. Afr. (ä-gōōl'yäs) | 232 | 34°47'S | 20°00'E |
| Agusan, r., Phil. (ä-gōō'sän) | 213 | 8°12'N | 126°07'E |
| Ahaggar, mts., Alg. (á-há-gär') | 230 | 23°14'N | 6°00'E |
| Ahar, Iran | 201 | 38°28'N | 47°04'E |
| Ahlen, Ger. (ä'lĕn) | 168 | 51°45'N | 7°52'E |
| Ahmadābād, India (ŭ-mĕd-ä-bäd') | 199 | 23°04'N | 72°38'E |
| Ahmadnagar, India (ä'mûd-nû-gûr) | 199 | 19°09'N | 74°45'E |
| Ahmar Mountains, mts., Eth. | 231 | 9°22'N | 42°00'E |
| Ahoskie, N.C., U.S. (ā-hŏs'kē) | 125 | 36°15'N | 77°00'W |
| Ahrensburg, Ger. (ä'rĕns-bòrg) | 159c | 53°40'N | 10°14'E |
| Ahrweiler, Ger. (är'vī-lĕr) | 168 | 50°34'N | 7°05'E |
| Ähtärinjärvi, l., Fin. | 167 | 62°46'N | 24°25'E |
| Ahuacatlán, Mex. (ä-wä-kät-län') | 130 | 21°05'N | 104°28'W |
| Ahuachapán, El Sal. (ä-wä-chä-pän') | 132 | 13°57'N | 89°53'W |
| Ahualulco, Mex. (ä-wä-lōōl'kō) | 130 | 20°43'N | 103°57'W |
| Ahuatempan, Mex. (ä-wä-tĕm-pän) | 130 | 18°11'N | 98°02'W |
| Åhus, Swe. (ô'hòs) | 166 | 55°56'N | 14°19'E |
| Ahvāz, Iran | 198 | 31°15'N | 48°54'E |
| Ahvenanmaa (Åland), is., Fin. (ä'vĕ-nàn-mô) (ô'lănd) | 160 | 60°36'N | 19°55'E |
| 'Aiea, Hi., U.S. | 126a | 21°18'N | 157°52'W |
| Aígina, Grc. | 175 | 37°43'N | 23°35'E |
| Aígina, i., Grc. | 175 | 37°43'N | 23°35'E |
| Aígio, Grc. | 175 | 38°13'N | 22°04'E |
| Aiken, S.C., U.S. (ā'kĕn) | 125 | 33°32'N | 81°43'W |
| Aimorès, Serra dos, mts., Braz. (sĕ'r-rä-dôs-ī-mō-rĕ's) | 143 | 17°40'S | 42°38'W |
| Aimoto, Japan (ī-mô-tō) | 211b | 34°59'N | 135°09'E |
| Aincourt, Fr. (ăN-kōō'r) | 171b | 49°04'N | 1°47'E |
| Aïn el Beïda, Alg. | 230 | 35°57'N | 7°25'E |
| Ainsworth, Ne., U.S. (ānz'wûrth) | 112 | 42°32'N | 99°51'W |
| Aïn Témouchent, Alg. (ä'ĕntĕ-mōō-shaN') | 162 | 35°20'N | 1°23'W |
| Aïn Wessara, Alg. (ĕn ōō-sä-rà) | 173 | 35°25'N | 2°50'E |
| Aipe, Col. (ī'pĕ) | 142a | 3°13'N | 75°15'W |
| Aïr, mts., Niger | 230 | 18°00'N | 8°30'E |
| Aire, r., Eng., U.K. (âr) | 158a | 53°42'N | 1°00'W |
| Aire-sur-l'Adour, Fr. (âr) | 170 | 43°42'N | 0°17'W |
| Airhitam, Selat, strt., Indon. | 197b | 0°58'N | 102°38'E |
| Ai Shan, mts., China (äī'shän) | 206 | 37°27'N | 120°35'E |
| Aisne, r., Fr. (ĕn) | 161 | 49°28'N | 3°32'E |
| Aitape, Pap. N. Gui. (ä-ē-tä'pȧ) | 213 | 3°00'S | 142°10'E |
| Aitkin, Mn., U.S. (āt'kĭn) | 113 | 46°32'N | 93°43'W |
| Aitolikó, Grc. | 175 | 38°27'N | 21°21'E |
| Aitos, Blg. (ä-ē'tōs) | 175 | 42°42'N | 27°17'E |
| Aitutaki, i., Cook Is. (ī-tōō-tä'kē) | 241 | 19°00'S | 162°00'W |
| Aiud, Rom. (ä'ē-òd) | 163 | 46°19'N | 23°40'E |
| Aiuruoca, Braz. (äē'ōō-rōōō'-kà) | 141a | 21°57'S | 44°36'W |
| Aiuruoca, r., Braz. | 141a | 22°11'S | 44°35'W |
| Aix-en-Provence, Fr. (ĕks-prô-văNs) | 161 | 43°32'N | 5°27'E |
| Aix-les-Bains, Fr. (ĕks'-lā-băN') | 171 | 45°42'N | 5°56'E |
| Aizpute, Lat. (ä'ĕz-pōō-tĕ) | 167 | 56°44'N | 21°37'E |
| Aizuwakamatsu, Japan | 210 | 37°27'N | 139°51'E |
| Ajaccio, Fr. (ä-yät'chō) | 154 | 41°55'N | 8°42'E |
| Ajalpan, Mex. (ä-häl'pän) | 131 | 18°21'N | 97°14'W |
| Ajana, Austl. (ăj-än'ĕr) | 218 | 28°00'S | 114°45'E |
| Ajaria, state, Geor. | 182 | 41°40'N | 42°00'E |
| Ajdābiyah, Libya | 231 | 30°56'N | 20°16'E |
| Ajjer, Tassili-n-, plat., Alg. | 230 | 25°40'N | 6°57'E |

| PLACE (Pronunciation) | PAGE | LAT. | LONG. |
|---|---|---|---|
| Ajmah, Jabal al, mts., Egypt | 197a | 29°12'N | 34°03'E |
| Ajman, U.A.E. | 198 | 25°15'N | 54°30'E |
| Ajmer, India (ŭj-mēr') | 199 | 26°26'N | 74°42'E |
| Ajo, Az., U.S. (ä'hō) | 119 | 32°20'N | 112°55'W |
| Ajuchitlán del Progreso, Mex. (ä-hōō-chet-lån) | 130 | 18°11'N | 100°32'W |
| Ajusco, Mex. (ä-hōō's-kō) | 131a | 19°13'N | 99°12'W |
| Ajusco, Cerro, mtn., Mex. (sĕ'r-rô-ä-hōō's-kō) | 131a | 19°12'N | 99°16'W |
| Akaishi-dake, mtn., Japan (ä-kī-shē dä'kā) | 211 | 35°30'N | 138°00'E |
| Akashi, Japan (ä'kä-shē) | 210 | 34°38'N | 134°59'E |
| Aketi, D.R.C. (ä-kå-tē) | 231 | 2°44'N | 23°46'E |
| Akhaltsikhe, Geor. (äkà'l-tsĭ-kĕ) | 181 | 41°40'N | 42°50'E |
| Akhdar, Al Jabal al, mts., Libya | 231 | 32°00'N | 22°00'E |
| Akhḑar, Al Jabal al, mts., Oman | 198 | 23°30'N | 56°43'W |
| Akhisar, Tur. (äk-hĭs-sär') | 163 | 38°58'N | 27°58'E |
| Akhtarskaya, Bukhta, b., Russia (bōōk'tȧ ák-tär'skȧ-yȧ) | 177 | 45°53'N | 38°22'E |
| Akhtopol, Blg. (äx'tô-pōl) | 175 | 42°08'N | 27°54'E |
| Akhunovo, Russia (ä-kŭ'nô-vô) | 186a | 54°13'N | 59°36'E |
| Aki, Japan (ä'kē) | 211 | 33°31'N | 133°51'E |
| Akiak, Ak., U.S. (äk'yak) | 103 | 61°00'N | 161°02'W |
| Akimiski, i., Can. (ä-kĭ-mĭ'skĭ) | 93 | 52°54'N | 80°22'W |
| Akita, Japan (ä'kē-tä) | 205 | 39°40'N | 140°12'E |
| Akjoujt, Maur. | 230 | 19°45'N | 14°23'W |
| 'Akko, Isr. | 197a | 32°56'N | 35°05'E |
| Aklavik, Can. (äk'lä-vĭk) | 90 | 68°28'N | 135°26'W |
| 'Aklé'Âouâna, dunes, Afr. | 234 | 18°07'N | 6°00'W |
| Ako, Japan (ä'kô) | 211 | 34°44'N | 134°22'E |
| Akola, India (ä-kō'lä) | 199 | 20°47'N | 77°00'E |
| Akordat, Erit. | 231 | 15°34'N | 37°54'E |
| Akpatok, i., Can. (ák'pá-tŏk) | 93 | 60°30'N | 67°10'W |
| Akranes, Ice. | 160 | 64°18'N | 21°40'W |
| Akron, Co., U.S. (ăk'rŭn) | 120 | 40°09'N | 103°14'W |
| Akron, Oh., U.S. (ăk'rŭn) | 105 | 41°05'N | 81°30'W |
| Aksaray, Tur. (äk-sá-rī') | 163 | 38°30'N | 34°05'E |
| Akşehir, Tur. (äk'shå-hĕr) | 163 | 38°20'N | 31°20'E |
| Akşehır Gölü, l., Tur. (äk'shå-hĕr) | 198 | 38°40'N | 31°30'E |
| Aksha, Russia (äk'shà) | 179 | 50°28'N | 113°00'E |
| Aksu, China (ä-kŭ-sōō) | 204 | 41°29'N | 80°15'E |
| Akune, Japan (ä'kò-nå) | 211 | 32°03'N | 130°16'E |
| Akureyri, Ice. (ä-kò-rä'rē) | 160 | 65°39'N | 18°01'W |
| Akutan, i., Ak., U.S. (ä-kōō-tän') | 103a | 53°58'N | 169°54'W |
| Akwatia, Ghana | 234 | 6°04'N | 0°49'W |
| Alabama, state, U.S. (ăl-ȧ-băm'ȧ) | 105 | 32°50'N | 87°30'W |
| Alabama, r., Al., U.S. (ăl-ȧ-băm'ȧ) | 107 | 31°20'N | 87°39'W |
| Alabat, i., Phil. (ä-lä-bät') | 213a | 14°14'N | 122°05'E |
| Alacam, Tur. (ä-lä-chäm') | 181 | 41°30'N | 35°40'E |
| Alacant, Spain | 162 | 38°20'N | 0°30'W |
| Alacranes, Cuba (ä-lä-krä'nås) | 134 | 22°45'N | 81°35'W |
| Al Aflaj, des., Sau. Ar. | 198 | 24°00'N | 44°47'E |
| Alagôas, state, Braz. (ä-lä-gō'äzh) | 143 | 9°50'S | 36°33'W |
| Alagoinhas, Braz. (ä-lä-gō-ēn'yäzh) | 143 | 12°13'S | 38°12'W |
| Alagón, Spain (ä-lä-gōn') | 172 | 41°46'N | 1°07'W |
| Alagón, r., Spain (ä-lä-gōn') | 172 | 39°53'N | 6°42'W |
| Alahuatán, r., Mex. (ä-lä-wä-tá'n) | 130 | 18°30'N | 100°00'W |
| Alajuela, C.R. (ä-lä-hwa'lä) | 133 | 10°01'N | 84°14'W |
| Alajuela, Lago, l., Pan. (ä-lä-hwa'lä) | 128a | 9°15'N | 79°34'W |
| Alaköl, l., Kaz. | 183 | 45°45'N | 81°13'E |
| 'Alalakeiki Channel, strt., Hi., U.S. (ä-lä-lä-kā'kē) | 126a | 20°40'N | 156°30'W |
| Al 'Alamayn, Egypt | 231 | 30°53'N | 28°52'E |
| Al 'Amārah, Iraq | 201 | 31°50'N | 47°09'E |
| Alameda, Ca., U.S. (ăl-ȧ-mā'dȧ) | 104 | 37°46'N | 122°15'W |
| Alameda, r., Ca., U.S. (ăl-ȧ-mā'dȧ) | 116b | 37°36'N | 122°02'W |
| Alaminos, Phil. (ä-lä-mē'nôs) | 213a | 16°09'N | 119°58'E |
| Al 'Amirīyah, Egypt | 163 | 31°01'N | 29°52'E |
| Alamo, Mex. (ä'lä-mô) | 131 | 20°55'N | 97°41'W |
| Alamo, Ca., U.S. (ă'lȧ-mō) | 116b | 37°51'N | 122°02'W |
| Alamo, Nv., U.S. (ă'là-mō) | 118 | 37°22'N | 115°10'W |
| Alamo, r., Mex. (ä'lä-mô) | 122 | 26°33'N | 99°35'W |
| Alamogordo, N.M., U.S. (ăl-ȧ-mō-gôr'dō) | 119 | 32°55'N | 106°00'W |
| Alamo Heights, Tx., U.S. (ă'lá-mō) | 117d | 29°28'N | 98°27'W |
| Alamo Indian Reservation, I.R., N.M., U.S. | 119 | 34°30'N | 107°30'W |
| Alamo Peak, mtn., N.M., U.S. (ă'lȧ-mō pēk) | 122 | 32°50'N | 105°55'W |
| Alamosa, Co., U.S. (ăl-ȧ-mō'sȧ) | 119 | 37°25'N | 105°50'W |
| Åland see Ahvenanmaa, is., Fin. | 160 | 60°36'N | 19°55'E |
| Alandskiy, Russia (ä-länt'skĭ) | 186a | 52°14'N | 59°48'E |
| Alanga Arba, Kenya | 237 | 0°07'N | 40°25'E |
| Alanya, Tur. | 163 | 36°40'N | 32°10'E |
| Alaotra, l., Madag. (ä-lä-ō'trȧ) | 233 | 17°15'S | 48°17'E |
| Alapayevsk, Russia (ä-lä-pä'yĕfsk) | 178 | 57°50'N | 61°35'E |
| Al 'Aqabah, Jord. | 198 | 29°32'N | 35°00'E |
| Alaquines, Mex. (ä-lä-kē'nås) | 130 | 22°07'N | 99°35'W |
| Al 'Arīsh, Egypt (ä-rēsh') | 197a | 31°08'N | 33°48'E |
| Alaska, state, U.S. (ȧ-lăs'kȧ) | 106a | 64°00'N | 150°00'W |
| Alaska, Gulf of, b., Ak., U.S. (ȧ-lăs'kȧ) | 103 | 57°42'N | 147°40'W |
| Alaska Highway, Ak., U.S. (ȧ-lăs'kȧ) | 103 | 63°00'N | 142°00'W |
| Alaska Peninsula, pen., Ak., U.S. (ȧ-lăs'kȧ) | 103 | 55°50'N | 162°10'W |
| Alaska Range, mts., Ak., U.S. (ȧ-lăs'kȧ) | 103 | 62°00'N | 152°18'W |
| Al 'Atrūn, Sudan | 231 | 18°13'N | 26°44'E |
| Alatyr', Russia (ä'lä-tür) | 178 | 54°55'N | 46°30'E |
| Alazani, r., Asia | 182 | 41°05'N | 46°40'E |
| Alba, Italy (äl'bä) | 174 | 44°41'N | 8°02'E |
| Albacete, Spain (äl-bä-thā'tā) | 162 | 39°00'N | 1°49'W |
| Albachten, Ger. (äl-bá'κ-tĕn) | 171c | 51°55'N | 7°31'E |
| Alba de Tormes, Spain (äl-bä dā tôr'măs) | 172 | 40°48'N | 5°28'W |
| Alba Iulia, Rom. (äl-bä yōō'lyá) | 163 | 46°05'N | 23°32'E |


ng-sing; ŋ-baŋk; N-nasalized n; nŏd; cŏmmit; ōld; ôbey; ôrder; oi-boil; fōōd; ò-as oo in foot; ou-out; s-soft; sh-dish; th-thin; pūre; ûnite; ûrn; stŭd; circŭs; ü-as in French tu; '-indeterminate vowel.

ăt; finăl; rāte; senăte; ärm; ȧsk; sofȧ; fâre; ch-choose; dh-as th in other; bē; ĕvent; bĕt; recĕnt; cratĕr; g-gō; gh-guttural g; bĭt; ĭ-short neutral; rīde; ᴋ-guttural k as ch in German ich;

PRONOUNCING INDEX

Almendra – Andrelândia 265


| PLACE (Pronunciation) | PAGE | LAT. | LONG. |
| --- | --- | --- | --- |
| Almendra, Embalse de, res., Spain | 172 | 41°15′N | 6°10′W |
| Almendralejo, Spain (äl-mān-drä-lā′hō) | 172 | 38°43′N | 6°24′W |
| Almería, Spain (äl-mā-rē′ä) | 154 | 36°52′N | 2°28′W |
| Almería, Golfo de, b., Spain (gôl-fô-dĕ-äl-māĭ-reN′) | 172 | 36°45′N | 2°26′W |
| Älmhult, Swe. (älm′hoolt) | 166 | 56°35′N | 14°08′E |
| Almina, Punta, c., Mor. (äl-mē′nä) | 172 | 35°58′N | 5°17′W |
| Al Minyā, Egypt | 231 | 28°06′N | 30°45′E |
| Almirante, Pan. (äl-mē-rän′tā) | 133 | 9°18′N | 82°24′W |
| Almirante, Bahía de, b., Pan. | 133 | 9°22′N | 82°07′W |
| Almodóvar del Campo, Spain (äl-mō-dhō′vär) | 172 | 38°43′N | 4°10′W |
| Almoloya, Mex. (äl-mō-lō′yä) | 130 | 19°32′N | 99°44′W |
| Almoloya, Mex. (äl-mō-lō′yä) | 131a | 19°11′N | 99°28′W |
| Almonte, Can. (ăl-mŏn′tē) | 99 | 45°15′N | 76°15′W |
| Almonte, Spain (äl-mōn′tā) | 172 | 37°16′N | 6°32′W |
| Almonte, r., Spain (äl-mōn′tā) | 172 | 39°35′N | 5°50′W |
| Almora, India | 199 | 29°20′N | 79°40′E |
| Al Mubarraz, Sau. Ar. | 198 | 22°31′N | 46°27′E |
| Al Mudawwarah, Jord. | 197a | 29°20′N | 36°01′E |
| Al Mukhā (Mocha), Yemen | 198 | 13°11′N | 43°20′E |
| Almuñécar, Spain (äl-moon-yā′kär) | 172 | 36°44′N | 3°43′W |
| Almyrós, Grc. | 175 | 39°13′N | 22°47′E |
| Alnön, i., Swe. | 166 | 62°20′N | 17°39′E |
| Aloha, Or., U.S. (ä′lō-hā) | 116c | 45°29′N | 122°52′W |
| Alor, Pulau, i., Indon. (ä′lōr) | 213 | 8°07′S | 125°00′E |
| Álora, Spain (ä′lō-rä) | 172 | 36°49′N | 4°42′W |
| Alor Gajah, Malay. | 197b | 2°23′N | 102°13′E |
| Alor Setar, Malay. (ä′lōr stär) | 212 | 6°10′N | 100°16′E |
| Alouette, r., Can. (ä-loo-ĕt′) | 116d | 49°16′N | 122°32′W |
| Alpena, Mi., U.S. (ăl-pē′nȧ) | 105 | 45°05′N | 83°30′W |
| Alpes Cotiennes, mts., Eur. | 171 | 44°46′N | 7°02′E |
| Alphen, Neth. | 159a | 52°07′N | 4°38′E |
| Alpiarça, Port. (äl-pyär′sȧ) | 172 | 39°38′N | 8°37′W |
| Alpine, Tx., U.S. (ăl′pīn) | 122 | 30°21′N | 103°41′W |
| Alps, mts., Eur. (ălps) | 156 | 46°18′N | 8°42′E |
| Alpujarra, Col. (ȧl-poo-Kȧ′rȧ) | 142a | 3°23′N | 74°56′W |
| Al Qaḑārif, Sudan | 231 | 14°03′N | 35°11′E |
| Al Qāhirah *see* Cairo, Egypt | 231 | 30°00′N | 31°17′E |
| Al Qanţarah, Egypt | 238d | 30°51′N | 32°20′E |
| Al Qaryah Ash Sharqīyah, Libya | 231 | 30°36′N | 13°13′E |
| Al Qaşr, Egypt | 200 | 25°42′N | 28°53′E |
| Al Qaţīf, Sau. Ar. | 198 | 26°30′N | 50°00′E |
| Al Qayşūmah, Sau. Ar. | 198 | 28°15′N | 46°20′E |
| Al Qunaytirah, Syria | 197a | 33°09′N | 35°49′E |
| Al Qunfudhah, Sau. Ar. | 198 | 19°08′N | 41°05′E |
| Al Quşaymah, Egypt | 197a | 30°40′N | 34°23′E |
| Al Quşayr, Egypt | 231 | 26°14′N | 34°11′E |
| Al Qusayr, Syria | 197a | 34°32′N | 36°33′E |
| Als, i., Den. (äls) | 166 | 55°06′N | 9°40′E |
| Alsace, hist. reg., Fr. (äl-sȧ′s) | 171 | 48°25′N | 7°24′E |
| Altadena, Ca., U.S. (ăl-tă-dē′nä) | 117a | 34°12′N | 118°08′W |
| Alta Gracia, Arg. (äl′tä grä′sē-a) | 144 | 31°41′S | 64°19′W |
| Altagracia, Ven. | 142 | 10°42′N | 71°34′W |
| Altagracia de Orituco, Ven. | 143b | 9°53′N | 66°22′W |
| Altai Mountains, mts., Asia (äl′tī′) | 204 | 49°11′N | 87°15′E |
| Alta Loma, Ca., U.S. (ăl′tă lō′mä) | 117a | 34°07′N | 117°35′W |
| Alta Loma, Tx., U.S. (ăl′tȧ lō-mȧ) | 123a | 29°22′N | 95°05′W |
| Altamaha, r., Ga., U.S. (ôl-tȧ-mȧ-hô′) | 125 | 31°50′N | 82°00′W |
| Altamira, Braz. (äl-tä-mē′rä) | 143 | 3°13′S | 52°14′W |
| Altamira, Mex. | 131 | 22°25′N | 97°55′W |
| Altamirano, Arg. (äl-tä-mē-rā′nō) | 144 | 35°26′S | 58°12′W |
| Altamura, Italy (äl-tä-moo′rä) | 163 | 40°40′N | 16°35′E |
| Altavista, Va., U.S. (äl-tä-vĭs′tȧ) | 125 | 37°08′N | 79°14′W |
| Altay, China (äl-tā) | 204 | 47°52′N | 86°50′E |
| Altenburg, Ger. (äl-tĕn-boorgh) | 168 | 50°59′N | 12°27′E |
| Altenmarkt an der Triesting, Aus. | 159e | 48°02′N | 16°00′E |
| Alter do Chão, Port. (äl-tĕr′dȯ shäN′ōN) | 172 | 39°13′N | 7°38′W |
| Altiplano, pl., Bol. (äl-tē-plȧ′nō) | 142 | 18°38′S | 68°20′W |
| Altlandsberg, Ger. (ält länts′bĕrgh) | 159b | 52°34′N | 13°44′E |
| Alto, La., U.S. (ăl′tō) | 123 | 32°21′N | 91°52′W |
| Alto Marañón, r., Peru (ȧl′tô-mä-rän-yŏ′n) | 142 | 8°18′S | 77°13′W |
| Altomünster, Ger. (äl′tō-mün′stĕr) | 159d | 48°24′N | 11°16′E |
| Alton, Can. (ôl′tŭn) | 102d | 43°52′N | 80°05′W |
| Alton, Il., U.S. (ôl′tŭn) | 105 | 38°53′N | 90°11′W |
| Altona, Austl. | 217a | 37°52′S | 144°50′E |
| Altona, Can. | 97 | 49°06′N | 97°33′W |
| Altona, Ger. (äl′tō-nȧ) | 159c | 53°33′N | 9°54′E |
| Altoona, Al., U.S. (ăl-too′nȧ) | 124 | 34°01′N | 86°15′W |
| Altoona, Pa., U.S. (ăl-too′nȧ) | 105 | 40°25′N | 78°25′W |
| Altoona, Wa., U.S. (ăl-too′nȧ) | 116c | 46°16′N | 123°39′W |
| Alto Rio Doce, Braz. (äl′tō-rē′ō-dō′sĕ) | 141a | 21°02′S | 43°23′W |
| Alto Songo, Cuba (äl-fō-sôŋ′gō) | 135 | 20°10′N | 75°45′W |
| Altotonga, Mex. (ȧl-tō-tôŋ′gä) | 131 | 19°44′N | 97°13′W |
| Alto Velo, i., Dom. Rep. (äl-tō-vĕ′lō) | 135 | 17°30′N | 71°35′W |
| Altrincham, Eng., U.K. (ôl′trĭng-ăm) | 158a | 53°18′N | 2°21′W |
| Altruppin, Ger. (ält roo′ppēn) | 159b | 52°56′N | 12°50′E |
| Altun Shan, mts., China (äl-tȯn shän) | 204 | 36°58′N | 85°09′E |
| Alturas, Ca., U.S. (ăl-too′rȧs) | 114 | 41°29′N | 120°33′W |
| Altus, Ok., U.S. (ăl′tŭs) | 120 | 34°38′N | 99°20′W |
| Al ‘Ubaylah, Sau. Ar. | 201 | 21°59′N | 50°57′E |
| Al-Uḑayyah, Sudan | 231 | 12°06′N | 28°16′E |
| Alūksne, Lat. (ä′lȯks-nĕ) | 180 | 57°24′N | 27°04′E |
| Alumette Island, i., Can. (ȧ-lü-mĕt′) | 99 | 45°50′N | 77°00′W |
| Alum Rock, Ca., U.S. | 116b | 37°23′N | 121°50′W |
| Al ‘Uqaylah, Libya | 231 | 30°15′N | 19°07′E |
| Al Uqşur, Egypt | 231 | 25°38′N | 32°59′E |
| Alushta, Ukr. (ä′lshȯ-tȧ) | 177 | 44°39′N | 34°23′E |
| Alva, Ok., U.S. (ăl′vȧ) | 120 | 36°46′N | 98°41′W |
| Alvarado, Mex. (äl-vä-rä′dhō) | 131 | 18°48′N | 95°45′W |
| Alvarado, Luguna de, l., Mex. (lä-gȯ′nä-dĕ-äl-vä-rȧ′dō) | 131 | 18°44′N | 95°45′W |
| Älvdalen, Swe. (ĕlv′dä-lĕn) | 166 | 61°14′N | 14°04′E |
| Alverca, Port. (al-vĕr′kȧ) | 173b | 38°53′N | 9°02′W |
| Alvesta, Swe. (äl-vĕs′tä) | 166 | 56°55′N | 14°29′E |
| Alvin, Tx., U.S. (ăl′vĭn) | 123a | 29°25′N | 95°14′W |
| Alvinópolis, Braz. (äl-vēnō′pō-lēs) | 141a | 20°07′S | 43°03′W |
| Alviso, Ca., U.S. (ăl-vī′sō) | 116b | 37°26′N | 121°59′W |
| Al Wajh, Sau. Ar. | 198 | 26°15′N | 36°32′E |
| Alwar, India (ŭl′wŭr) | 199 | 27°39′N | 76°39′E |
| Al Wāsiţah, Egypt | 238b | 29°21′N | 31°15′E |
| Alytus, Lith. (ä′lē-tȯs) | 167 | 54°25′N | 24°05′E |
| Amacuzac, r., Mex. (ä-mä-koo-zȧk) | 130 | 18°00′N | 99°03′W |
| Amadeus, l., Austl. (ăm-ȧ-dē′ŭs) | 220 | 24°30′S | 131°25′E |
| Amadjuak, l., Can. (ä-mädj′wäk) | 93 | 64°50′N | 69°20′W |
| Amadora, Port. | 173b | 38°45′N | 9°14′W |
| Amagasaki, Japan (ä′mä-gä-sä′kē) | 211 | 34°43′N | 135°25′E |
| Amakusa-Shimo, i., Japan (ämä-koo′sä shē-mō) | 210 | 32°24′N | 129°35′E |
| Åmål, Swe. (ô′môl) | 166 | 59°05′N | 12°40′E |
| Amalfi, Col. (ä′mȧ′l-fē) | 142a | 6°55′N | 75°04′W |
| Amalfi, Italy (ä-mä′l-fē) | 173c | 40°23′N | 14°36′E |
| Amaliáda, Grc. | 175 | 37°48′N | 21°23′E |
| Amalner, India | 202 | 21°07′N | 75°06′E |
| Amambai, Serra de, mts., S.A. | 143 | 20°06′S | 57°08′W |
| Amami, i., Japan | 205 | 28°10′N | 129°55′E |
| Amapala, Hond. (ä-mä-pä′lä) | 132 | 13°16′N | 87°39′W |
| Amarante, Braz. (ä-mä-rän′tā) | 143 | 6°17′S | 42°43′W |
| Amargosa, r., Ca., U.S. (ȧ′mär-gō′sȧ) | 118 | 35°55′N | 116°45′W |
| Amarillo, Tx., U.S. (ăm-ȧ-rĭl′ō) | 104 | 35°14′N | 101°49′W |
| Amaro, Mount, mtn., Italy (ä-mä′rō) | 162 | 42°07′N | 14°07′E |
| Amasya, Tur. (ä-mä′sē-ȧ) | 163 | 40°40′N | 35°50′E |
| Amatenango, Mex. (ä-mä-tā-naŋ′gō) | 131 | 16°30′N | 92°29′W |
| Amatignak, i., Ak., U.S. (ä-mȧ′tē-näk) | 103a | 51°12′N | 178°30′W |
| Amatique, Bahía de, b., N.A. (bä-ē′ä-dĕ-ä-mä-tē′kā) | 132 | 15°58′N | 88°50′W |
| Amatitlán, Guat. (ä-mä-tē-tlän′) | 132 | 14°27′N | 90°39′W |
| Amatlán de Cañas, Mex. (ä-mät-län′dā kän-yäs) | 130 | 20°50′N | 104°22′W |
| Amazon (Amazonas) (Solimões), r., S.A. | 143 | 2°03′S | 53°18′W |
| Amazonas, state, Braz. (ä-mä-thō′näs) | 142 | 4°15′S | 64°30′W |
| Ambāla, India (ŭm-bä′lŭ) | 199 | 30°31′N | 76°48′E |
| Ambalema, Col. (äm-bä-lā′mä) | 142 | 4°47′N | 74°45′W |
| Ambarchik, Russia (ŭm-bär′chĭk) | 179 | 69°39′N | 162°18′E |
| Ambarnāth, India | 203b | 19°12′N | 73°10′E |
| Ambato, Ec. (äm-bä′tō) | 142 | 1°15′S | 78°30′W |
| Ambatondrazaka, Madag. | 233 | 17°58′S | 48°43′E |
| Amberg, Ger. (äm′bĕrgh) | 168 | 49°26′N | 11°51′E |
| Ambergris Cay, i., Belize (ăm′bēr-grēs kāz) | 132a | 18°04′N | 87°43′W |
| Ambergris Cays, is., T./C. Is. | 135 | 21°20′N | 71°40′W |
| Ambérieu-en-Bugey, Fr. (äN-bā-rē-u′) | 171 | 45°57′N | 5°21′E |
| Ambert, Fr. (äN-bĕr′) | 170 | 45°32′N | 3°41′E |
| Ambil Island, i., Phil. (äm′bēl) | 213a | 13°51′N | 120°25′E |
| Ambler, Pa., U.S. (ăm′blēr) | 110f | 40°09′N | 75°13′W |
| Amboise, Fr. (äN-bwăz′) | 170 | 47°25′N | 0°56′E |
| Ambon, Indon. | 213 | 3°45′S | 128°17′E |
| Ambon, Pulau, i., Indon. | 213 | 4°50′S | 128°45′E |
| Ambositra, Madag. (äN-bō-sē′trä) | 233 | 20°31′S | 47°28′E |
| Amboy, Il., U.S. (ăm′boi) | 108 | 41°41′N | 89°15′W |
| Amboy, Wa., U.S. (ăm′boi) | 116c | 45°55′N | 122°27′W |
| Ambre, Cap d′, c., Madag. | 233 | 12°06′S | 49°15′E |
| Ambridge, Pa., U.S. (ăm′brĭdj) | 111e | 40°36′N | 80°13′W |
| Ambrim, i., Vanuatu | 221 | 16°25′S | 168°15′E |
| Ambriz, Ang. | 232 | 7°50′S | 13°06′E |
| Amchitka, i., Ak., U.S. (ăm-chĭt′kȧ) | 103a | 51°25′N | 178°10′E |
| Amchitka Passage, strt., Ak., U.S. (ăm-chĭt′kȧ) | 103a | 51°30′N | 179°36′W |
| Amealco, Mex. (ä-mā-äl′kō) | 130 | 20°12′N | 100°08′W |
| Ameca, Mex. (ä-mĕ′kä) | 128 | 20°34′N | 104°02′W |
| Amecameca, Mex. (ä-mȧ-kä-mā′kä) | 130 | 19°06′N | 98°46′W |
| Ameide, Neth. | 159a | 51°57′N | 4°57′E |
| Ameland, i., Neth. | 165 | 53°29′N | 5°54′E |
| Amelia, Oh., U.S. (ȧ-mēl′yā) | 111f | 39°01′N | 84°12′W |
| American, South Fork, r., Ca., U.S. (ȧ-mĕr′ĭ-kăn) | 118 | 38°43′N | 120°45′W |
| Americana, Braz. (ä-mĕ-rē-kȧ′nȧ) | 141a | 22°46′S | 47°19′W |
| American Falls, Id., U.S. (ȧ-mĕr′ĭ-kăn-fâls′) | 115 | 42°45′N | 112°53′W |
| American Falls Reservoir, res., Id., U.S. (ȧ-mĕr′ĭ-kăn-fâls′) | 106 | 42°56′N | 113°18′W |
| American Fork, Ut., U.S. | 119 | 40°20′N | 111°50′W |
| American Highland, plat., Ant. | 224 | 72°00′S | 79°00′E |
| American Samoa, dep., Oc. | 2 | 14°20′S | 170°00′W |
| Americus, Ga., U.S. (ȧ-mĕr′ĭ-kŭs) | 105 | 32°04′N | 84°15′W |
| Amersfoort, Neth. (ä′mĕrz-fōrt) | 159a | 52°08′N | 5°23′E |
| Amery, Can. (ā′mēr-ē) | 91 | 56°34′N | 94°03′W |
| Amery, Wi., U.S. | 113 | 45°19′N | 92°24′W |
| Ames, Ia., U.S. (āmz) | 113 | 42°00′N | 93°36′W |
| Amesbury, Ma., U.S. (āmz′bēr-ē) | 101a | 42°51′N | 70°56′W |
| Amfissa, Grc. (ȧm-fĭ′sȧ) | 175 | 38°32′N | 22°26′E |
| Amga, Russia (ŭm-gä′) | 179 | 61°08′N | 132°09′E |
| Amga, r., Russia | 185 | 61°41′N | 133°11′E |
| Amgun′, r., Russia | 185 | 52°30′N | 138°00′E |
| Amherst, Can. (ăm′hērst) | 91 | 45°49′N | 64°14′W |
| Amherst, Oh., U.S. | 111d | 41°24′N | 82°13′W |
| Amherst, i., Can. (ăm′hērst) | 99 | 44°08′N | 76°45′W |
| Amiens, Fr. (ä-myäN′) | 161 | 49°54′N | 2°18′E |
| Amirante Islands, is., Sey. | 5 | 6°02′S | 52°30′E |
| Amisk Lake, l., Can. | 97 | 54°35′N | 102°13′W |
| Amistad Reservoir, res., N.A. | 122 | 29°20′N | 101°00′W |
| Amite, La., U.S. (ă-mēt′) | 123 | 30°43′N | 90°32′W |
| Amite, r., La., U.S. | 123 | 30°45′N | 90°48′W |
| Amity, Pa., U.S. (ăm′ĭ-tĭ) | 111e | 40°02′N | 80°11′W |
| Amityville, N.Y., U.S. (ăm′ĭ-tĭ-vĭl) | 110a | 40°41′N | 73°24′W |
| Amlia, i., Ak., U.S. (ȧ′mlēȧ) | 103a | 52°00′N | 173°28′W |
| ‘Ammān, Jord. (äm′mȧn) | 198 | 31°57′N | 35°57′E |
| Ammersee, l., Ger. (äm′mĕr) | 159d | 48°00′N | 11°08′E |
| Amnicon, r., Wi., U.S. (ăm′nė-kŏn) | 117h | 46°35′N | 91°56′W |
| Amorgós, i., Grc. (ä-môr′gōs) | 163 | 36°47′N | 25°47′E |
| Amory, Ms., U.S. (āmō-rē) | 124 | 33°58′N | 88°27′W |
| Amos, Can. (ā′mŭs) | 91 | 48°31′N | 78°04′W |
| Amoy *see* Xiamen, China | 205 | 24°30′N | 118°10′E |
| Amparo, Braz. (äm-pȧ′-rô) | 141a | 22°43′S | 46°44′W |
| Amper, r., Ger. (äm′pĕr) | 159d | 48°18′N | 11°32′E |
| Amposta, Spain (äm-pōs′tä) | 173 | 40°42′N | 0°34′E |
| Amqui, Can. | 100 | 48°28′N | 67°28′W |
| Amrāvati, India | 199 | 20°58′N | 77°47′E |
| Amritsar, India (ŭm-rĭt′sŭr) | 199 | 31°43′N | 74°52′E |
| Amstelveen, Neth. | 159a | 52°18′N | 4°51′E |
| Amsterdam, Neth. (äm-stēr-däm′) | 154 | 52°21′N | 4°52′E |
| Amsterdam, N.Y., U.S. (ăm′stĕr-dăm) | 109 | 42°55′N | 74°10′W |
| Amsterdam, Île, i., Afr. | 224 | 37°52′S | 77°32′E |
| Amstetten, Aus. (äm′stĕt-ĕn) | 168 | 48°09′N | 14°53′E |
| Am Timan, Chad (äm′tē-män′) | 231 | 11°18′N | 20°30′E |
| Amu Darya, r., Asia (ä-mȯ-dä′rēä) | 178 | 38°30′N | 64°00′E |
| Amukta Passage, strt., Ak., U.S. (ä-mook′tȧ) | 103a | 52°30′N | 172°00′W |
| Amundsen Gulf, b., Can. (ä′mŭn-sĕn-gŭlf′) | 92 | 70°17′N | 123°28′W |
| Amundsen Sea, sea, Ant. (ä′mŭn-sĕn-sē′) | 224 | 72°00′S | 110°00′W |
| Amungen, l., Swe. | 166 | 61°07′N | 16°00′E |
| Amur, r., Asia | 179 | 49°00′N | 136°00′E |
| Amurskiy, Russia (ä-mûr′skĭ) | 186a | 52°35′N | 59°36′E |
| Amurskiy, Zaliv, b., Russia (zä′lĭf ä-mȯr′skĭ) | 210 | 43°20′N | 131°40′E |
| Amusgos, Mex. | 130 | 16°39′N | 98°09′W |
| Amuyao, Mount, mtn., Phil. (ä-moo-yä′ō) | 213a | 17°04′N | 121°09′E |
| Amvrakikos Kólpos, b., Grc. | 175 | 39°00′N | 21°00′E |
| Amyun, Leb. | 197a | 34°18′N | 35°48′E |
| Anabar, r., Russia (ăn-ȧ-bär′) | 185 | 71°15′N | 113°00′E |
| Anaco, Ven. (ä-nȧ′kô) | 143b | 9°29′N | 64°27′W |
| Anaconda, Mt., U.S. (ăn-ȧ-kŏn′dȧ) | 104 | 46°07′N | 112°55′W |
| Anacortes, Wa., U.S. (ăn-ȧ-kôr′tĕz) | 116a | 48°30′N | 122°37′W |
| Anadarko, Ok., U.S. (ăn-ȧ-där′kō) | 120 | 35°05′N | 98°14′W |
| Anadyr′, Russia (ŭ-nȧ-dĭr′) | 179 | 64°47′N | 177°01′E |
| Anadyr, r., Russia | 185 | 65°30′N | 172°45′E |
| Anadyrskiy Zaliv, b., Russia | 178 | 64°10′N | 178°00′W |
| Anaheim, Ca., U.S. (ăn′ȧ-hīm) | 117a | 33°50′N | 117°55′W |
| Anahuac, Tx., U.S. (ä-nä′wäk) | 123a | 29°46′N | 94°41′W |
| Ānai Mudi, mtn., India | 203 | 10°10′N | 77°00′E |
| Anama Bay, Can. | 97 | 51°56′N | 98°05′W |
| Ana María, Cayos, is., Cuba | 134 | 21°25′N | 78°50′W |
| Anambas, Kepulauan, is., Indon. (ä-näm-bäs) | 212 | 2°41′N | 106°38′E |
| Anamosa, Ia., U.S. (ăn-ȧ-mō′sȧ) | 113 | 42°06′N | 91°18′W |
| Anan′ïv, Ukr. | 181 | 47°43′N | 29°59′E |
| Anapa, Russia (ȧ-nä′pä) | 181 | 44°54′N | 37°19′E |
| Anápolis, Braz. (ä-nȧ′pō-lēs) | 143 | 16°17′S | 48°47′W |
| Añatuya, Arg. (ȧ-nyä-too′yȧ) | 144 | 28°22′S | 62°45′W |
| Anchieta, Braz. (ȧn-chyĕ′tä) | 144b | 22°49′S | 43°24′W |
| Ancholme, r., Eng., U.K. (ăn′chŭm) | 158a | 53°28′N | 0°27′W |
| Anchorage, Ak., U.S. (ăŋ′kēr-ȧj) | 106a | 61°12′N | 149°48′W |
| Anchorage, Ky., U.S. | 111h | 38°16′N | 85°32′W |
| Anci, China (än-tsŭ) | 206 | 39°31′N | 116°41′E |
| Ancienne-Lorette, Can. (äN-syĕn′ lō-rĕt′) | 102b | 46°48′N | 71°21′W |
| Ancon, Pan. (ăŋ-kōn′) | 128a | 8°55′N | 79°32′W |
| Ancona, Italy (än-kō′nä) | 154 | 43°37′N | 13°32′E |
| Ancud, Chile (äŋ-koodh′) | 144 | 41°52′S | 73°45′W |
| Ancud, Golfo de, b., Chile (gôl-fô-dĕ-äŋ-koodh′) | 144 | 41°15′S | 73°00′W |
| Anda, China | 208 | 46°20′N | 125°20′E |
| Åndalsnes, Nor. | 166 | 62°33′N | 7°46′E |
| Andalucia, hist. reg., Spain (än-dä-loo-sē′ä) | 172 | 37°35′N | 5°40′W |
| Andalusia, Al., U.S. (ăn-dȧ-loo′zhĭȧ) | 124 | 31°19′N | 86°19′W |
| Andaman Islands, is., India (ăn-dȧ-măn′) | 212 | 11°38′N | 92°17′E |
| Andaman Sea, sea, Asia | 212 | 12°44′N | 95°45′E |
| Andarax, r., Spain | 172 | 37°00′N | 2°40′W |
| Anderlecht, Bel. (än′dēr-lĕkt) | 159a | 50°49′N | 4°16′E |
| Andernach, Ger. (än′dēr-näk) | 168 | 50°25′N | 7°23′E |
| Anderson, Arg. (ȧ′n-dĕr-sōn) | 141c | 35°15′S | 60°15′W |
| Anderson, Ca., U.S. (ăn′dēr-sŭn) | 114 | 40°28′N | 122°19′W |
| Anderson, In., U.S. (ăn′dēr-sŭn) | 108 | 40°05′N | 85°50′W |
| Anderson, S.C., U.S. (ăn′dēr-sŭn) | 105 | 34°30′N | 82°40′W |
| Anderson, r., Can. (ăn′dēr-sŭn) | 92 | 68°32′N | 125°12′W |
| Andes Mountains, mts., S.A. (ăn′dēz) (än′dās) | 139 | 13°00′S | 75°00′W |
| Andheri, neigh., India | 203b | 19°08′N | 72°50′E |
| Andhra Pradesh, state, India | 199 | 16°00′N | 79°00′E |
| Andikýthira, i., Grc. | 163 | 35°50′N | 23°20′E |
| Andizhan, Uzb. (än-dē-zhän′) | 183 | 40°45′N | 72°22′E |
| Andong, Kor., S. (än′dŭng′) | 205 | 36°31′N | 128°42′E |
| Andongwei, China (än-dōŋ-wā) | 206 | 35°08′N | 119°19′E |
| Andorra, And. (än-dôr′rä) | 173 | 42°38′N | 1°30′E |
| Andorra, nation, Eur. (än-dôr′rä) | 154 | 42°30′N | 2°00′E |
| Andover, Ma., U.S. (ăn′dō-vēr) | 101a | 42°39′N | 71°08′W |
| Andover, N.J., U.S. (ăn′dō-vēr) | 110a | 40°59′N | 74°45′W |
| Andøya, i., Nor. (änd-ûē) | 160 | 69°12′N | 14°58′E |
| Andreanof Islands, is., Ak., U.S. (än-drȧ-ä′nôf-ī′ăndz) | 106b | 51°10′N | 177°00′W |
| Andrelândia, Braz. (än-drĕ-lȧ′n-dyȧ) | 141a | 21°45′S | 44°18′W |


ng-sing; ŋ-baŋk; N-nasalized n; nŏd; cŏmmit; ōld; ôbey; ôrder; oi-boil; food; ȯ-as oo in foot; ou-out; s-soft; sh-dish; th-thin; pūre; ůnite; ûrn; stŭd; circŭs; ü-as in French tu; ′-indeterminate vowel.

266 Andrew Johnson National Historic Site – Archidona PRONOUNCING INDEX


| PLACE (Pronunciation) | PAGE | LAT. | LONG. |
|---|---|---|---|
| Andrew Johnson National Historic Site, rec., Tn., U.S. (ăn′drōō jŏn′sŭn) | 125 | 36°15′N | 82°55′W |
| Andrews, N.C., U.S. (ăn′drōōz) | 124 | 35°12′N | 83°48′W |
| Andrews, S.C., U.S. (ăn′drōōz) | 125 | 33°25′N | 79°32′W |
| Andria, Italy (än′drē-ä) | 163 | 41°17′N | 15°55′E |
| Andros, Grc. (àn′dhrôs) | 175 | 37°50′N | 24°54′E |
| Ándros, i., Grc. (àn′drŏs) | 163 | 37°59′N | 24°55′E |
| Androscoggin, r., Me., U.S. (ăn-drŭs-kŏg′ĭn) | 100 | 44°25′N | 70°45′W |
| Andros Island, i., Bah. (ăn′drŏs) | 129 | 24°30′N | 78°00′W |
| Anefis i-n-Darane, Mali | 234 | 18°03′N | 0°36′E |
| Anegasaki, Japan (ä′nå-gä-sä′kė) | 211a | 35°29′N | 140°02′E |
| Aneityum, i., Vanuatu (ä-nå-ē′tē-ŭm) | 221 | 20°15′S | 169°49′E |
| Aneta, N.D., U.S. (ă-nē′tá) | 112 | 47°41′N | 97°57′W |
| Aneto, Pico de, mtn., Spain (pē′kō-dĕ-ä-nĕ′tō) | 156 | 42°35′N | 0°38′E |
| Angamacutiro, Mex. (äṅ′gä-mä-kōō-tē′rō) | 130 | 20°08′N | 101°44′W |
| Angangueo, Mex. (än-gäṅ′gwå-ō) | 130 | 19°36′N | 100°18′W |
| Ang'angxi, China (äŋ-äŋ-shyē) | 205 | 47°05′N | 123°58′E |
| Angarsk, Russia | 179 | 52°48′N | 104°15′E |
| Ånge, Swe. (ông′ă) | 166 | 62°31′N | 15°39′E |
| Angel, Salto, wtfl., Ven. (säl′tō-á′n-hĕl) | 142 | 5°44′N | 62°27′W |
| Ángel de la Guarda, i., Mex. (á′n-hĕl-dĕ-lä-gwä′r-dä) | 128 | 29°30′N | 113°00′W |
| Angeles, Phil. (än′hâ-lās) | 213a | 15°09′N | 120°35′E |
| Ängelholm, Swe. (ĕng′ĕl-hôlm) | 166 | 56°14′N | 12°50′E |
| Angelina, r., Tx., U.S. (ăn-jē lē′ná) | 123 | 31°30′N | 94°53′W |
| Angels Camp, Ca., U.S. (ān′jĕls kămp′) | 118 | 38°03′N | 120°33′W |
| Ångermanälven, r., Swe. | 160 | 64°10′N | 17°30′E |
| Angermund, Ger. (án′ngĕr-mŭnd) | 171c | 51°20′N | 6°47′E |
| Angermünde, Ger. (äng′ĕr-mûn-dĕ) | 168 | 53°02′N | 14°00′E |
| Angers, Can. (äN-zhā′) | 102c | 45°31′N | 75°29′W |
| Angers, Fr. | 170 | 47°29′N | 0°36′W |
| Angkor, hist., Camb. (äng′kôr) | 212 | 13°52′N | 103°50′E |
| Anglesey, i., Wales, U.K. (ăŋ′g′l-sė) | 164 | 53°35′N | 4°28′W |
| Angleton, Tx., U.S. (aŋ′g′l-tŭn) | 123a | 29°10′N | 95°25′W |
| Angmagssalik, Grnld. (aŋ-má′sá-lĭk) | 89 | 65°40′N | 37°40′W |
| Angoche, Ilha, i., Moz. (ē′lä-ăn-gō′chå) | 233 | 16°20′S | 40°00′E |
| Angol, Chile (aŋ-gōl′) | 144 | 37°47′S | 72°43′W |
| Angola, In., U.S. (ăŋ-gō′lá) | 108 | 41°35′S | 85°00′W |
| Angola, nation, Afr. (ăŋ-gō′lá) | 232 | 14°15′S | 16°00′E |
| Angora see Ankara, Tur. | 198 | 39°55′N | 32°50′E |
| Angoulême, Fr. (äN′gōō-lâm′) | 170 | 45°40′N | 0°09′E |
| Angra dos Reis, Braz. (aŋ′grä dōs rā′ēs) | 141a | 23°01′S | 44°17′W |
| Angri, Italy (ä′n-grē) | 173c | 40°30′N | 14°35′E |
| Anguang, China (än-gůäŋ) | 208 | 45°28′N | 123°42′E |
| Anguilla, dep., N.A. | 129 | 18°15′N | 62°54′W |
| Anguilla Cays, is., Bah. (ăŋ-gwĭl′á) | 134 | 23°30′N | 79°35′W |
| Anguille, Cape, c., Can. (kāp′-äŋ-gē′yĕ) | 101 | 47°55′N | 59°25′W |
| Anguo, China (än-gwô) | 206 | 38°27′N | 115°19′E |
| Anholt, i., Den. (än′hŏlt) | 166 | 56°43′N | 11°34′E |
| Anhui, prov., China (än-hwā) | 205 | 31°30′N | 117°15′E |
| Aniak, Ak., U.S. (ä-nyà′k) | 103 | 61°32′N | 159°35′W |
| Aniakchak National Monument, rec., Ak., U.S. | 104 | 56°50′N | 157°50′W |
| Animas, r., Co., U.S. (ä′nė-más) | 119 | 37°03′N | 107°50′W |
| Anina, Rom. (ä-nē′nä) | 175 | 45°03′N | 21°50′E |
| Anita, Pa., U.S. (à-nē′á) | 109 | 41°05′N | 79°00′W |
| Aniva, Mys, c., Russia (mĭs á-nē′vá) | 210 | 46°08′N | 143°13′E |
| Aniva, Zaliv, b., Russia (zä′lĭf á-nē′vá) | 210 | 46°30′N | 143°00′E |
| Anjou, Can. | 102a | 45°37′N | 73°33′W |
| Ankang, China (än-käŋ) | 204 | 32°38′N | 109°10′E |
| Ankara, Tur. (än′ká-rá) | 198 | 39°55′N | 32°50′E |
| Anklam, Ger. (än′kläm) | 168 | 53°52′N | 13°43′E |
| Ankoro, D.R.C. (ăŋ-kō′rō) | 232 | 6°45′S | 26°57′E |
| Anloga, Ghana | 234 | 5°47′N | 0°50′E |
| Anlong, China (än-loŋ) | 209 | 25°01′N | 105°32′E |
| Anlu, China (än′lōō′) | 209 | 31°18′N | 113°40′E |
| Ann, Cape, c., Ma., U.S. (kāp′ăn′) | 109 | 42°40′N | 70°40′W |
| Anna, Russia (än′ä) | 177 | 51°31′N | 40°27′E |
| Anna, Il., U.S. (ăn′á) | 121 | 37°28′N | 89°15′W |
| Annaba, Alg. | 230 | 36°57′N | 7°39′E |
| Annaberg-Bucholz, Ger. (än′ä-bĕrgh) | 168 | 50°35′N | 13°02′E |
| An Nafūd, des., Sau. Ar. | 198 | 28°30′N | 40°30′E |
| An Najaf, Iraq (än nä-jäf′) | 198 | 32°00′N | 44°25′E |
| An Nakhl, Egypt | 197a | 29°55′N | 33°45′E |
| Annamese Cordillera, mts., Asia | 212 | 17°34′N | 105°38′E |
| Annapolis, Md., U.S. (ă-năp′ô-lĭs) | 105 | 39°00′N | 76°25′W |
| Annapolis Royal, Can. | 100 | 44°45′N | 65°31′W |
| Ann Arbor, Mi., U.S. (ăn är′bĕr) | 105 | 42°15′N | 83°45′W |
| An Nāşirīyah, Iraq | 198 | 31°08′N | 46°15′E |
| An Nawfalīyah, Libya | 231 | 30°57′N | 17°38′E |
| Annecy, Fr. (àn sē′) | 171 | 45°54′N | 6°07′E |
| Annemasse, Fr. (än′mäs′) | 171 | 46°09′N | 6°13′E |
| Annette Island, i., Ak., U.S. | 94 | 55°13′N | 131°30′W |
| An Nhon, Viet. | 212 | 13°55′N | 109°00′E |
| Annieopsquotch Mountains, mts., Can. | 101 | 48°37′N | 57°17′W |
| Anniston, Al., U.S. (ăn′ĭs-tŭn) | 105 | 33°39′N | 85°47′W |
| Annobón, i., Eq. Gui. | 229 | 2°00′S | 3°30′E |
| Annonay, Fr. (àn′ĭs-tsiŭn) | 170 | 45°16′N | 4°36′E |
| Annotto Bay, Jam. (än-nō′tō) | 134 | 18°15′N | 76°45′W |
| An Nuhūd, Sudan | 231 | 12°39′N | 28°18′E |
| Anoka, Mn., U.S. (á-nō′ká) | 117g | 45°12′N | 93°24′W |
| Anori, Col. (á-nō′rē) | 142a | 7°01′N | 75°09′W |
| Áno Viánnos, Grc. | 174a | 35°02′N | 25°26′E |
| Anpu, China (än-pōō) | 204 | 21°28′N | 110°00′E |
| Anqiu, China (än-chyô) | 206 | 36°26′N | 119°12′E |
| Ansbach, Ger. (äns′bäk) | 168 | 49°18′N | 10°35′E |

| PLACE (Pronunciation) | PAGE | LAT. | LONG. |
|---|---|---|---|
| Anse à Veau, Haiti (äNs′ ä-vō′) | 135 | 18°30′N | 73°25′W |
| Anse d'Hainault, Haiti (äns′dĕnō) | 135 | 18°30′N | 74°25′W |
| Anserma, Col. (á′n-sĕ′r-má) | 142a | 5°13′N | 75°47′W |
| Ansermanuevo, Col. (á′n-sĕ′r-má-nwĕ′vō) | 142a | 4°47′N | 75°59′W |
| Anshan, China | 208 | 41°00′N | 123°00′E |
| Anshun, China (än-shōōn′) | 204 | 26°12′N | 105°50′E |
| Anson, Tx., U.S. (ăn′sŭn) | 122 | 32°45′N | 99°52′W |
| Anson Bay, b., Austl. | 220 | 13°10′S | 130°00′E |
| Ansŏng, Kor., S. (än′sŭng′) | 210 | 37°00′N | 127°12′E |
| Ansongo, Mali | 234 | 15°40′N | 0°30′E |
| Ansonia, Ct., U.S. (ăn-sōnĭ-á) | 109 | 41°20′N | 73°05′W |
| Antalya, Tur. (än-tä′lē-ä) (ä-dä′lē-ä) | 163 | 37°00′N | 30°50′E |
| Antalya Körfezi, b., Tur. | 163 | 36°40′N | 31°20′E |
| Antananarivo, Madag. | 233 | 18°51′S | 47°40′E |
| Antarctica, cont. | 224 | 80°15′S | 127°00′E |
| Antarctic Peninsula, pen., Ant. | 224 | 70°00′S | 65°00′W |
| Antelope Creek, r., Wy., U.S. (ăn′tē-lōp) | 115 | 43°29′N | 105°42′W |
| Antequera, Spain (än-tĕ-kĕ′rä) | 162 | 37°01′N | 4°34′W |
| Anthony, Ks., U.S. (ăn′thō-nē) | 120 | 37°08′N | 98°01′W |
| Anthony Peak, mtn., Ca., U.S. | 118 | 39°51′N | 122°58′W |
| Anti Atlas, mts., Mor. | 230 | 28°45′N | 9°30′W |
| Antibes, Fr. (äN-tēb′) | 171 | 43°36′N | 7°12′E |
| Anticosti, Île d', i., Can. (ăn-tĭ-kŏs′tē) | 93 | 49°30′N | 62°00′W |
| Antigo, Wi., U.S. (ăn′tĭ-gō) | 113 | 45°09′N | 89°11′W |
| Antigonish, Can. (ăn-tĭ-gō-nêsh′) | 101 | 45°35′N | 61°55′W |
| Antigua, Guat. (än-tē′gwä) | 128 | 14°32′N | 90°43′W |
| Antigua, r., Mex. | 131 | 19°16′N | 96°36′W |
| Antigua and Barbuda, nation, N.A. | 129 | 17°15′N | 61°15′W |
| Antigua Veracruz, Mex. (än-tē′gwä vā-rä-krōōz′) | 131 | 19°18′N | 96°17′W |
| Antilla, Cuba (än-tē′lyä) | 135 | 20°50′N | 75°50′W |
| Antioch, Ca., U.S. (ăn′tĭ-ŏk) | 116b | 38°00′N | 121°48′W |
| Antioch, Il., U.S. | 111a | 42°29′N | 88°06′W |
| Antioch, Ne., U.S. | 112 | 42°05′N | 102°36′W |
| Antioquia, Col. (än-tė-ō′kėä) | 142 | 6°34′N | 75°49′W |
| Antioquia, dept., Col. | 142a | 6°48′N | 75°42′W |
| Antlers, Ok., U.S. (ănt′lērz) | 121 | 34°14′N | 95°38′W |
| Antofagasta, Chile (än-tô-fä-gäs′tä) | 144 | 23°32′S | 70°21′W |
| Antofalla, Salar de, pl., Arg. (sá-lár′de án′tō-fä′lä) | 144 | 26°00′S | 67°52′W |
| Antón, Pan. (än-tōn′) | 129 | 8°24′N | 80°15′W |
| Antongila, Helodrano, b., Madag. | 233 | 16°15′S | 50°15′E |
| Antônio Carlos, Braz. (än-tō′nėō-ká′r-lôs) | 141a | 21°19′S | 43°45′W |
| António Enes, Moz. (än-to′nyō ĕn′ēs) | 233 | 16°14′S | 39°58′E |
| Antonito, Co., U.S. (ăn-tô-nē′tō) | 120 | 37°04′N | 106°01′W |
| Antonopole, Lat. (än′tō-nō-pō lyĕ) | 167 | 56°19′N | 27°11′E |
| Antony, Fr. | 171b | 48°45′N | 2°18′E |
| Antsirabe, Madag. (änt-sė-rä′bā) | 233 | 19°49′S | 47°16′E |
| Antsiranana, Madag. | 233 | 12°18′S | 49°16′E |
| Antsla, Est. (änt′slá) | 167 | 57°49′N | 26°29′E |
| Antuco, vol., S.A. (än-tōō′kō) | 144 | 37°30′S | 72°30′W |
| Antwerp, Bel. | 154 | 51°13′N | 4°24′E |
| Antwerpen see Antwerp, Bel. | 154 | 51°13′N | 4°24′E |
| Anūpgarh, India (ŭ-nòp′gŭr) | 202 | 29°22′N | 73°20′E |
| Anuradhapura, Sri L. (ŭ-nōō′rä-dŭ-pōō′rŭ) | 203 | 8°24′N | 80°25′E |
| Anxi, China (än-shyē) | 204 | 40°36′N | 95°49′E |
| Anyang, China (än′yäng) | 205 | 36°05′N | 114°22′E |
| Anykščiai, Lith. (aniksh-chá′ê) | 167 | 55°34′N | 25°04′E |
| Anzhero-Sudzhensk, Russia (än′zhâ-rô-sòd′zhĕnsk) | 178 | 56°08′N | 86°08′E |
| Anzio, Italy (änt′zē-ō) | 174 | 41°28′N | 12°39′E |
| Anzoátegui, dept., Ven. (án-zŏá′tĕ-gė) | 143b | 9°38′N | 64°45′W |
| Aoba, i., Vanuatu | 214f | 15°25′S | 167°50′E |
| Aomori, Japan (äō-mō′rė) | 205 | 40°45′N | 140°52′E |
| Aoraki (Cook, Mount), mtn., N.Z. | 221a | 43°27′S | 170°13′E |
| Aosta, Italy (ä-ôs′tä) | 174 | 45°45′N | 7°20′E |
| Aouk, Bahr, r., Afr. (ä-ōk′) | 231 | 9°30′N | 20°45′E |
| Aoukâr, reg., Maur. | 234 | 18°00′N | 9°40′W |
| Apalachicola, Fl., U.S. (ăp-á-lăch-ĭ-kō′lá) | 124 | 29°43′N | 84°59′W |
| Apan, Mex. (ä-pá′n) | 130 | 19°43′N | 98°27′W |
| Apango, Mex. (ä-päŋ′gō) | 130 | 17°41′N | 99°22′W |
| Apaporis, r., S.A. (ä-pä-pō′rĭs) | 142 | 0°48′N | 72°32′W |
| Aparri, Phil. (ä-pär′rē) | 212 | 18°15′N | 121°40′E |
| Apasco, Mex. (ä-pá′s-kō) | 130 | 20°33′N | 100°43′W |
| Apatin, Serb. (ŏ′pŏ-tĭn) | 175 | 45°40′N | 19°00′E |
| Apatzingán de la Constitución, Mex. | 130 | 19°07′N | 102°21′W |
| Apeldoorn, Neth. (ä′pĕl-dōōrn) | 161 | 52°14′N | 5°55′E |
| Apennines see Appennino, mts., Italy | 156 | 43°48′N | 11°06′E |
| Apía, Col. (à-pē′ä) | 142a | 5°07′N | 75°58′W |
| Apia, Samoa | 214a | 13°50′S | 171°44′W |
| Apipilulco, Mex. (ä-pĭ-pĭ-lōōl′kō) | 130 | 18°09′N | 99°40′W |
| Apishapa, r., Co., U.S. (ăp-ĭ-shä′pá) | 120 | 37°40′N | 104°08′W |
| Apizaco, Mex. (ä-pė-zä′kō) | 130 | 19°18′N | 98°11′W |
| Apo, Mount, mtn., Phil. (ä′pō) | 213 | 6°56′N | 125°05′E |
| Apopka, Fl., U.S. (ä-pŏp′ká) | 125a | 28°37′N | 81°30′W |
| Apopka, Lake, l., Fl., U.S. | 125a | 28°38′N | 81°50′W |
| Apostle Islands, is., Wi., U.S. (á-pŏs′l) | 113 | 47°05′N | 90°55′W |
| Appalachia, Va., U.S. (ăpá-lăch′ĭ-á) | 125 | 36°54′N | 82°49′W |
| Appalachian Mountains, mts., N.A. (ăp-á-lăch′ĭ-án) | 107 | 37°20′N | 82°00′W |
| Appalachicola, r., Fl., U.S. (ăpá-lăch′ĭ-cōlä) | 107 | 30°11′N | 85°00′W |
| Äppelbo, Swe. (ĕp-ĕl-bōō) | 166 | 60°30′N | 14°02′E |
| Appelhülsen, Ger. (ä′pĕl-hül′sĕn) | 171c | 51°55′N | 7°26′E |
| Appennino, mts., Italy (äp-pĕn-nē′nô) | 156 | 43°48′N | 11°06′E |
| Appleton, Mn., U.S. (ăp′l-tŭn) | 112 | 45°10′N | 96°01′W |
| Appleton, Wi., U.S. | 105 | 44°14′N | 88°27′W |
| Appleton City, Mo., U.S. | 121 | 38°10′N | 94°02′W |

| PLACE (Pronunciation) | PAGE | LAT. | LONG. |
|---|---|---|---|
| Appomattox, r., Va., U.S. (ăp-ô-măt′ŭks) | 125 | 37°22′N | 78°09′W |
| Aprilia, Italy (á-prē′lyá) | 174 | 41°36′N | 12°40′E |
| Apsheronsk, Russia | 182 | 44°28′N | 39°44′E |
| Apt, Fr. (äpt) | 171 | 43°54′N | 5°19′E |
| Apure, r., Ven. (ä-pōō′rä) | 142 | 8°08′N | 68°46′W |
| Apurimac, r., Peru (ä-pōō-rē-mäk′) | 142 | 11°39′S | 73°48′W |
| Aqaba, Gulf of, b. (ä′ká-bá) | 198 | 28°30′N | 34°40′E |
| Aqabah, Wādī al, r., Egypt | 197a | 29°48′N | 34°05′E |
| Aqmola see Astana, Kaz. | 183 | 51°10′N | 71°43′E |
| Aqtaū, Kaz. | 183 | 43°35′N | 51°05′E |
| Aqtöbe, Kaz. | 183 | 50°20′N | 57°00′E |
| Aquasco, Md., U.S. (á′gwá′scô) | 110e | 38°35′N | 76°44′W |
| Aquidauana, Braz. (ä-kē-däwä′nä) | 143 | 20°24′S | 55°46′W |
| Aquin, Haiti (ä-kăn′) | 135 | 18°20′N | 73°25′W |
| Ara, r., Japan (ä-rä) | 211a | 35°40′N | 139°52′E |
| Arab, Baḩr al, r., Sudan | 231 | 9°46′N | 26°52′E |
| ʻArabah, Wādī, val., Egypt | 238b | 29°02′N | 32°10′E |
| Arabats'ka Strilka (Tongue of Arabat), spit, Ukr. | 177 | 45°50′N | 35°05′E |
| Arabi, La., U.S. | 110d | 29°58′N | 90°01′W |
| Arabian Desert, des., Egypt (á-rā′bĭ-ăn) | 231 | 27°06′N | 32°49′E |
| Arabian Sea, sea (á-rā′bĭ-ăn) | 196 | 16°00′N | 65°15′E |
| Aracaju, Braz. (ä-rä′kä-zhōō′) | 143 | 11°00′S | 37°01′W |
| Aracati, Braz. (ä-rä′kä-tē′) | 143 | 4°31′S | 37°41′W |
| Araçatuba, Braz. (ä-rä-sá-tōō′bä) | 143 | 21°14′S | 50°19′W |
| Aracena, Spain | 172 | 37°53′N | 6°34′W |
| Arachthos, r., Grc. (är′äκ-thôs) | 175 | 39°10′N | 21°05′E |
| Aracruz, Braz. (ä-rä-krōō′s) | 143 | 19°58′S | 40°11′W |
| ʻArad, Isr. | 197a | 31°20′N | 35°15′E |
| Arad, Rom. (ŏ′rŏd) | 163 | 46°10′N | 21°18′E |
| Arafura Sea, sea (ä-rä-fōō′rä) | 213 | 8°40′S | 130°00′E |
| Aragats, Gora, mtn., Arm. | 182 | 40°32′N | 44°14′E |
| Aragon, hist. reg., Spain (ä-rä-gōn′) | 173 | 40°55′N | 0°45′W |
| Aragón, r., Spain | 172 | 42°35′N | 1°10′W |
| Aragua, dept., Ven. (ä-rä′gwä) | 143b | 10°00′N | 67°05′W |
| Aragua de Barcelona, Ven. | 142 | 9°29′N | 64°48′W |
| Araguaía, r., Braz. (ä-rä-gwä′yä) | 143 | 8°37′S | 49°43′W |
| Araguari, Braz. (ä-rä-gwä′rē) | 143 | 18°43′S | 48°03′W |
| Araguatins, Braz. (ä-rä-gwä-tēns) | 143 | 5°41′S | 48°04′W |
| Aragüita, Ven. (ärá-gwē′tá) | 143b | 10°13′N | 66°28′W |
| Araj, oasis, Egypt (ä-räj′) | 163 | 29°05′N | 26°51′E |
| Arāk, Iran | 198 | 34°08′N | 49°57′E |
| Arakan Yoma, mts., Mya. (ŭ-rŭ-kŭn′yō′má) | 199 | 19°51′N | 94°13′E |
| Aral, Kaz. | 183 | 46°47′N | 62°00′E |
| Aral Sea, sea, Asia | 178 | 45°17′N | 60°02′E |
| Aralsor köli, l., Kaz. (á-räl′sôr′) | 181 | 49°00′N | 48°20′E |
| Aramberri, Mex. (ä-räm-bĕr-rē′) | 130 | 24°05′N | 99°47′W |
| Arana, Sierra, mts., Spain | 172 | 37°17′N | 3°28′W |
| Aranda de Duero, Spain (ä-rän′dä dā dwā′rō) | 172 | 41°43′N | 3°45′W |
| Arandas, Mex. (ä-rän′dās) | 130 | 20°43′N | 102°18′W |
| Aran Island, i., Ire. (ăr′ăn) | 164 | 54°58′N | 8°33′W |
| Aran Islands, is., Ire. | 160 | 53°04′N | 9°59′W |
| Aranjuez, Spain (ä-rän-hwāth′) | 162 | 40°02′N | 3°24′W |
| Aransas Pass, Tx., U.S. (á-răn′sás pás) | 123 | 27°55′N | 97°09′W |
| Araouane, Mali | 230 | 18°54′N | 3°33′W |
| Arapkir, Tur. (ä-räp-kēr′) | 163 | 39°00′N | 38°10′E |
| Araraquara, Braz. (ä-rä-rä-kwä′rä) | 143 | 21°47′S | 48°08′W |
| Araras, Braz. (ä-rá′räs) | 141a | 22°21′S | 47°22′W |
| Araras, Serra das, mts., Braz. (sĕ′r-rä-däs-ä-rä′räs) | 143 | 18°03′S | 53°23′W |
| Araras, Serra das, mts., Braz. | 144b | 22°24′S | 43°15′W |
| Araras, Serra das, mts., Braz. (sĕ′r-rä-däs-ä-rä′räs) | 144 | 23°30′S | 53°00′W |
| Ararat, Austl. (ăr′ărăt) | 219 | 37°17′S | 142°56′E |
| Ararat, Mount, mtn., Tur. | 198 | 39°50′N | 44°20′E |
| Arari, l., Braz. (ä-rá′rē) | 143 | 0°30′S | 48°50′W |
| Araripe, Chapada do, hills, Braz. (shä-pä′dä-dō-ä-rä-rē′pĕ) | 143 | 5°55′S | 40°42′W |
| Araruama, Braz. (ä-rä-rōō-ä′mä) | 141a | 22°53′S | 42°19′W |
| Araruama, Lagoa de, l., Braz. | 141a | 23°00′S | 42°15′W |
| Aras, r., Asia (á-räs) | 198 | 39°15′N | 47°10′E |
| Aratuípe, Braz. (ä-rä-tōō-ē′pĕ) | 143 | 13°12′S | 38°58′W |
| Arauca, Col. (ä-rou′kä) | 142 | 6°56′N | 70°45′W |
| Arauca, r., S.A. | 142 | 7°13′N | 68°43′W |
| Aravalli Range, mts., India (ä-rä′vŭ-lė) | 199 | 24°15′N | 72°40′E |
| Araya, Punta de, c., Ven. (pŭn′tá-dĕ-ä-rä′yá) | 143b | 10°40′N | 64°15′W |
| Arayat, Phil. (ä-rä′yät) | 213a | 15°10′N | 120°44′E |
| ʻArbi, Sudan | 231 | 20°36′N | 29°57′E |
| Arbīl, Iraq | 198 | 36°10′N | 44°00′E |
| Arboga, Swe. (är-bō′gä) | 166 | 59°26′N | 15°50′E |
| Arborea, Italy (är-bō-rĕ′ä) | 174 | 39°50′N | 8°36′E |
| Arbroath, Scot., U.K. (är-brōth′) | 164 | 56°36′N | 2°25′W |
| Arcachon, Fr. (är-kä-shôN′) | 161 | 44°39′N | 1°12′W |
| Arcachon, Bassin d', Fr. (bä-sĕn′ där-kä-shôn′) | 170 | 44°42′N | 1°50′W |
| Arcadia, Ca., U.S. (är-kā′dĭ-á) | 117a | 34°08′N | 118°02′W |
| Arcadia, Fl., U.S. | 125a | 27°12′N | 81°51′W |
| Arcadia, La., U.S. | 123 | 32°33′N | 92°56′W |
| Arcadia, Wi., U.S. | 113 | 44°15′N | 91°30′W |
| Arcata, Ca., U.S. (är-ká′tá) | 114 | 40°54′N | 124°05′W |
| Arc Dome Mountain, mtn., Nv., U.S. (ärk dōm) | 118 | 38°51′N | 117°21′W |
| Arcelia, Mex. (är-sä′lē-ä) | 130 | 18°19′N | 100°14′W |
| Archbald, Pa., U.S. (ärch′bôld) | 109 | 41°30′N | 75°35′W |
| Arches National Park, rec., Ut., U.S. (är′ches) | 119 | 38°45′N | 109°35′W |
| Archidona, Ec. (är-chē-do′nä) | 142 | 1°01′S | 77°49′W |
| Archidona, Spain (är-chē-dô′nä) | 172 | 37°08′N | 4°24′W |


ăt; finăl; rāte; senâte; ärm; ȧsk; sofá; fâre; ch-choose; dh-as th in other; bē; ėvent; bĕt; recĕnt; cratẽr; g-gō; gh-guttural g; bĭt; ĭ-short neutral; rīde; κ-guttural k as ch in German ich;

| PLACE (Pronunciation) | PAGE | LAT. | LONG. |
|---|---|---|---|
| Arcis-sur-Aube, Fr. (är-sēs´sür-ōb´) | 170 | 48°31´N | 4°04´E |
| Arco, Id., U.S. (är´kō) | 115 | 43°39´N | 113°15´W |
| Arcola, Tx., U.S. | 123a | 29°30´N | 95°28´W |
| Arcola, Va., U.S. (är´cōlà) | 110e | 38°57´N | 77°32´W |
| Arcos de la Frontera, Spain (är´kōs-dĕ-lä-frōn-tĕ´rä) | 172 | 36°44´N | 5°48´W |
| Arctic Ocean, o. | 244 | 85°00´N | 170°00´E |
| Arda, r., Blg. (är´dä) | 175 | 41°36´N | 25°18´E |
| Ardabīl, Iran | 198 | 38°15´N | 48°00´E |
| Ardahan, Tur. (är-dá-hän´) | 181 | 41°10´N | 42°40´E |
| Ardatov, Russia (är-dá-tôf´) | 180 | 54°58´N | 46°10´E |
| Ardennes, mts., Eur. (är-dĕn´) | 161 | 50°01´N | 5°12´E |
| Ardila, r., Eur. (är-dē´lä) | 172 | 38°10´N | 7°15´W |
| Ardmore, Ok., U.S. (ärd´mōr) | 104 | 34°10´N | 97°08´W |
| Ardmore, Pa., U.S. | 110f | 40°01´N | 75°18´W |
| Ardrossan, Can. (är-dros´án) | 102g | 53°33´N | 113°08´W |
| Ardsley, Eng., U.K. (ärdz´lĕ) | 158a | 53°43´N | 1°33´W |
| Åre, Swe. | 160 | 63°12´N | 13°12´E |
| Arecibo, P.R. (ä-rå-sē´bō) | 129b | 18°28´N | 66°45´W |
| Areia Branca, Braz. (ä-rĕ´yä-brä´n-kä) | 143 | 4°58´S | 37°02´W |
| Arena, Point, c., Ca., U.S. (ä-rā´nà) | 118 | 38°57´N | 123°40´W |
| Arenas, Punta, c., Ven. (pón´tä-rē´näs) | 143b | 10°57´N | 64°24´W |
| Arenas de San Pedro, Spain | 172 | 40°12´N | 5°04´W |
| Arendal, Nor. (ä´rĕn-däl) | 166 | 58°29´N | 8°44´E |
| Arendonk, Bel. | 159a | 51°19´N | 5°07´E |
| Arequipa, Peru (ä-rå-kē´pä) | 142 | 16°27´S | 71°30´W |
| Arezzo, Italy (ä-rĕt´sō) | 162 | 43°28´N | 11°54´E |
| Arga, r., Spain (är´gä) | 172 | 42°35´N | 1°55´W |
| Arganda, Spain (är-gän´dä) | 173a | 40°18´N | 3°27´W |
| Argazi, l., Russia (är-gä-zī) | 186a | 55°24´N | 60°37´E |
| Argazi, r., Russia | 186a | 55°33´N | 57°30´E |
| Argentan, Fr. (är-zhän-tän´) | 170 | 48°45´N | 0°01´W |
| Argentat, Fr. (är-zhän-tä´) | 170 | 45°07´N | 1°57´E |
| Argenteuil, Fr. (är-zhän-tü´y´) | 170 | 48°56´N | 2°15´E |
| Argentina, nation, S.A. (är-jĕn-tē´nà) | 144 | 35°30´S | 67°00´W |
| Argentino, l., Arg. (är-kĕn-tē´nō) | 144 | 50°15´S | 72°45´W |
| Argenton-sur-Creuse, Fr. (är-zhän´tôn-sür-krôs) | 170 | 46°34´N | 1°28´E |
| Argolikós Kólpos, b., Grc. | 175 | 37°20´N | 23°00´E |
| Argonne, mts., Fr. (ä´r-gôn) | 171 | 49°21´N | 5°54´E |
| Argos, Grc. (är´gôs) | 175 | 37°38´N | 22°45´E |
| Argostóli, Grc. | 175 | 38°10´N | 20°30´E |
| Arguello, Point, c., Ca., U.S. (är-gwäl´yō) | 118 | 34°35´N | 120°40´W |
| Arguin, Cap d´, c., Maur. | 230 | 20°28´N | 17°46´W |
| Argun´, r., Asia (är-gōōn´) | 179 | 50°00´N | 119°00´E |
| Argungu, Nig. | 235 | 12°45´N | 4°31´E |
| Argyle, Can. (är´gīl) | 102f | 50°11´N | 97°27´W |
| Argyle, Mn., U.S. | 112 | 48°21´N | 96°48´W |
| Århus, Den. (ôr´hōōs) | 160 | 56°09´N | 10°10´E |
| Ariakeno-Umi, b., Japan (ä-rē´ä-kä´nō ōō´mē) | 211 | 33°03´N | 130°18´E |
| Ariake-Wan, b., Japan (ä´rē-ä´kå wän) | 211 | 31°19´N | 131°15´E |
| Ariano, Italy (ä-rē-ä´nō) | 174 | 41°09´N | 15°11´E |
| Ariari, r., Col. (ä-ryá´rē) | 142a | 3°34´N | 73°42´W |
| Aribinda, Burkina | 234 | 14°14´N | 0°52´W |
| Arica, Chile (ä-rē´kä) | 142 | 18°34´S | 70°14´W |
| Arichat, Can. (ä-rĭ-shät´) | 101 | 45°31´N | 61°01´W |
| Ariège, r., Fr. (ä-rē-ĕzh´) | 170 | 43°26´N | 1°29´E |
| Ariel, Wa., U.S. (ä´rĭ-ĕl) | 116c | 45°57´N | 122°34´W |
| Arieș, r., Rom. | 169 | 46°25´N | 23°15´E |
| Ariguanabo, Lago de, l., Cuba (lä´gô-dĕ-ä-rē-gwä-nä´bô) | 135a | 22°52´N | 82°33´W |
| Arikaree, r., Co., U.S. (ä-rĭ-kä-rē´) | 120 | 39°51´N | 102°18´W |
| Arima, Japan (ä´rē-mä´) | 211b | 34°48´N | 135°16´E |
| Aringay, Phil. (ä-rĭn-gä´ē) | 213a | 16°25´N | 120°20´E |
| Arinos, r., Braz. (ä-rē´nōzsh) | 143 | 12°09´S | 56°49´W |
| Aripuanã, r., Braz. (á-rē-pwän´yá) | 143 | 7°06´S | 60°29´W |
| ´Arīsh, Wādī al, r., Egypt (á-rēsh´) | 197a | 30°36´N | 34°07´E |
| Aristazabal Island, i., Can. | 94 | 52°30´N | 129°20´W |
| Arizona, state, U.S. (är-ĭ-zō´nà) | 104 | 34°00´N | 113°00´W |
| Arjona, Spain (är-hō´nä) | 172 | 37°58´N | 4°03´W |
| Arka, r., Russia | 185 | 60°45´N | 142°30´E |
| Arkabutla Lake, res., Ms., U.S. (är-ká-bŭt´là) | 124 | 34°48´N | 90°00´W |
| Arkadelphia, Ar., U.S. (är-ká-dĕl´fĭ-á) | 121 | 34°06´N | 93°05´W |
| Arkansas, state, U.S. (är´kăn-sô) (är-kăn´sás) | 105 | 34°50´N | 93°40´W |
| Arkansas, r., U.S. | 106 | 37°30´N | 97°00´W |
| Arkansas City, Ks., U.S. | 121 | 37°04´N | 97°02´W |
| Arkhangelsk (Archangel), Russia (ár-kän´gĕlsk) | 178 | 64°30´N | 40°25´E |
| Arkhangel´skoye, Russia (ár-kän-gĕl´skô-yĕ) | 186a | 54°25´N | 56°48´E |
| Arklow, Ire. (ärk´lō) | 164 | 52°47´N | 6°10´W |
| Arkonam, India (är-kō-näm´) | 203 | 13°05´N | 79°43´E |
| Arlanza, r., Spain (är-län-thä´) | 172 | 42°08´N | 3°45´W |
| Arlanzón, r., Spain (är-län-thōn´) | 172 | 42°12´N | 3°58´W |
| Arlberg Tunnel, trans., Aus. (ärl´bĕrgh) | 168 | 47°05´N | 10°15´E |
| Arles, Fr. (ärl) | 170 | 43°42´N | 4°38´E |
| Arlington, S. Afr. | 238c | 28°02´S | 27°52´E |
| Arlington, Ga., U.S. (är´lĭng-tun) | 124 | 31°25´N | 84°42´W |
| Arlington, Ma., U.S. | 101a | 42°26´N | 71°13´W |
| Arlington, S.D., U.S. | 112 | 44°23´N | 97°09´W |
| Arlington, Tx., U.S. (är´lĭng-tun) | 117c | 32°44´N | 97°07´W |
| Arlington, Va., U.S. | 110e | 38°55´N | 77°10´W |
| Arlington, Vt., U.S. | 109 | 43°05´N | 73°05´W |
| Arlington, Wa., U.S. | 116a | 48°11´N | 122°08´W |
| Arlington Heights, Il., U.S. (är´lĕng-tun-hī´ts) | 111a | 42°05´N | 87°59´W |
| Arltunga, Austl. (ärl-tòn´gà) | 218 | 23°19´S | 134°45´E |
| Arma, Ks., U.S. (är´mà) | 121 | 37°34´N | 94°43´W |
| Armagh, Can. (är-mä´) (är-mäk´) | 102b | 46°45´N | 70°36´W |
| Armagh, N. Ire., U.K. | 160 | 54°21´N | 6°25´W |
| Armant, Egypt (är-mänt´) | 238b | 25°37´N | 32°32´E |
| Armaro, Col. (är-mä´rō) | 142a | 4°58´N | 74°54´W |
| Armavir, Russia (är-mä-vīr´) | 178 | 45°00´N | 41°00´E |
| Armenia, Col. (är-mĕ´nêá) | 142 | 4°33´N | 75°40´W |
| Armenia, El Sal. (är-mä´nê-ä) | 132 | 13°44´N | 89°31´W |
| Armenia, nation, Asia | 178 | 41°00´N | 44°39´E |
| Armentières, Fr. (àr-män-tyär´) | 170 | 50°43´N | 2°53´E |
| Armeria, Río de, r., Mex. (rē´ō-dĕ-är-mä-rē´ä) | 130 | 19°36´N | 104°10´W |
| Armherstburg, Can. (ärm´hĕrst-bōōrgh) | 98 | 42°06´N | 83°06´W |
| Armians´k, Ukr. | 177 | 46°06´N | 33°42´E |
| Armidale, Austl. (är´mĭ-dāl) | 219 | 30°27´S | 151°50´E |
| Armour, S.D., U.S. (är´mēr) | 112 | 43°18´N | 98°21´W |
| Armstrong Station, Can. (ärm´strŏng) | 91 | 50°21´N | 89°00´W |
| Arnedo, Spain (är-nä´dō) | 172 | 42°12´N | 2°03´W |
| Arnhem, Neth. (ärn´hĕm) | 161 | 51°58´N | 5°56´E |
| Arnhem, Cape, c., Austl. | 220 | 12°15´S | 137°00´E |
| Arnhem Land, reg., Austl. (ärn´hĕm-länd) | 220 | 13°15´S | 133°00´E |
| Arno, r., Italy (ä´r-nò) | 162 | 43°30´N | 11°00´E |
| Arnold, Eng., U.K. (är´nŭld) | 158a | 53°00´N | 1°08´W |
| Arnold, Mn., U.S. (är´nŭld) | 117h | 46°53´N | 92°06´W |
| Arnold, Pa., U.S. | 111e | 40°35´N | 79°45´W |
| Arnprior, Can. (ärn-prī´ēr) | 99 | 45°25´N | 76°20´W |
| Arnsberg, Ger. (ärns´bĕrgh) | 171c | 51°25´N | 8°02´E |
| Arnstadt, Ger. (ärn´shtät) | 168 | 50°51´N | 10°57´E |
| Aroab, Nmb. (är´ō-áb) | 232 | 25°40´S | 19°45´E |
| Aroostook, r., Me., U.S. (á-rós´tók) | 100 | 46°44´N | 68°15´W |
| Aroroy, Phil. (ä-rô-rō´ē) | 213a | 12°30´N | 123°24´E |
| Arpajon, Fr. (är-pä-jō´n) | 171b | 48°35´N | 2°15´E |
| Arpoador, Ponta do, c., Braz. (pô´n-tä-dō-är´pôá-dō´r) | 144b | 22°59´S | 43°11´W |
| Arraiolos, Port. (är-rī-ō´lōzh) | 172 | 38°47´N | 7°59´W |
| Ar Ramādī, Iraq | 198 | 33°26´N | 43°19´E |
| Arran, Island of, Scot., U.K. (a´rán) | 164 | 55°25´N | 5°25´W |
| Ar Rank, Sudan | 231 | 11°45´N | 32°53´E |
| Arras, Fr. (à-räs´) | 161 | 50°21´N | 2°40´E |
| Ar Rawḍah, Egypt | 238b | 27°47´N | 30°52´E |
| Arrecifes, Arg. (är-rå-sē´fäs) | 141c | 34°03´S | 60°05´W |
| Arrecifes, r., Arg. | 141c | 34°07´S | 59°50´W |
| Arrée, Monts d´, mts., Fr. (är-rā´) | 170 | 48°27´N | 4°00´W |
| Arriaga, Mex. (är-rēä´gä) | 131 | 16°15´N | 93°54´W |
| Arriaga, Mex. (är-rēä´gä) | 130 | 21°55´N | 101°22´W |
| Arrone, r., Italy | 173d | 41°57´N | 12°17´E |
| Arrow Creek, r., Mt., U.S. (ăr´ō) | 115 | 47°29´N | 109°53´W |
| Arrowhead, Lake, l., Ca., U.S. (lăk är´ōhĕd) | 117a | 34°17´N | 117°13´W |
| Arrowrock Reservoir, res., Id., U.S. (ăr´ō-rŏk) | 114 | 43°40´N | 115°30´W |
| Arroyo Arena, Cuba (är-rō´yä-rē´nä) | 135a | 23°01´N | 82°30´W |
| Arroyo de la Luz, Spain (är-rō´yō-dĕ-lä-lōō´z) | 172 | 39°39´N | 6°46´W |
| Arroyo Seco, Mex. (är-rō´yō sä´kō) | 130 | 21°31´N | 99°44´W |
| Ar Rub´ al Khālī, des., Asia | 198 | 20°00´N | 51°00´E |
| Ar Ruṭbah, Iraq | 201 | 33°02´N | 40°17´E |
| Arsen´yev, Russia | 179 | 44°13´N | 133°32´E |
| Arsinskiy, Russia (är-sĭn´skĭ) | 186a | 53°46´N | 59°54´E |
| Árta, Grc. (är´tä) | 163 | 39°08´N | 21°02´E |
| Arteaga, Mex. (är-tä-ä´gä) | 122 | 25°28´N | 100°50´W |
| Artëm, Russia (ar-tyòm´) | 179 | 43°28´N | 132°29´E |
| Artemisa, Cuba (är-tå-mē´sä) | 134 | 22°50´N | 82°45´W |
| Artemivs´k, Ukr. | 181 | 48°37´N | 38°00´E |
| Artesia, N.M., U.S. (är-tē´sĭ-á) | 120 | 32°44´N | 104°23´W |
| Arthabaska, Can. | 99 | 46°03´N | 71°54´W |
| Arthur´s Town, Bah. | 135 | 24°40´N | 75°40´W |
| Arti, Russia (är´tĭ) | 186a | 56°20´N | 58°38´E |
| Artibonite, r., N.A. (är-tē-bô-nē´tå) | 135 | 19°00´N | 72°25´W |
| Aru, Kepulauan, is., Indon. | 213 | 6°20´S | 133°00´E |
| Arua, Ug. (ä´rōō-ä) | 231 | 3°01´N | 30°55´E |
| Aruba, i., Aruba (ä-rōō´bä) | 129 | 12°29´N | 70°00´W |
| Arunachal Pradesh, state, India | 199 | 27°35´N | 92°56´E |
| Arusha, Tan. (á-rōō´shä) | 232 | 3°22´S | 36°41´E |
| Arvida, Can. | 91 | 48°26´N | 71°11´W |
| Arvika, Swe. (är-vē´kä) | 166 | 59°41´N | 12°35´E |
| Arzamas, Russia (är-zä-mäs´) | 180 | 55°20´N | 43°52´E |
| Arziw, Alg. | 162 | 35°50´N | 0°20´W |
| Arzúa, Spain | 172 | 42°54´N | 8°19´W |
| Aš, Czech Rep. (äsh´) | 168 | 50°12´N | 12°13´E |
| Asahi-Gawa, r., Japan (à-sä´hĕ-gä´wä) | 211 | 35°01´N | 133°40´E |
| Asahikawa, Japan | 205 | 43°50´N | 142°09´E |
| Asaka, Japan (ä-sä´kä) | 211a | 35°47´N | 139°36´E |
| Asansol, India | 199 | 23°45´N | 86°58´E |
| Asbest, Russia (äs-bĕst´) | 180 | 57°02´N | 61°28´E |
| Asbestos, Can. (äs-bĕs´tōs) | 99 | 45°49´N | 71°52´W |
| Asbestovskiy, Russia | 186a | 57°46´N | 61°23´E |
| Asbury Park, N.J., U.S. (ăz´bĕr-ĭ) | 110a | 40°13´N | 74°01´W |
| Ascención, Bahía de la, b., Mex. | 132a | 19°39´N | 87°30´W |
| Ascención, Mex. (äs-sĕn-sĕ-ōn´) | 130 | 24°21´N | 99°54´W |
| Ascension, i., St. Hel. (á-sĕn´shŭn) | 229 | 8°00´S | 13°00´W |
| Ascent, S. Afr. (äs-ĕnt´) | 238c | 27°14´S | 29°06´E |
| Aschaffenburg, Ger. (ä-shäf´ĕn-bŏrgh) | 168 | 49°58´N | 9°12´E |
| Ascheberg, Ger. (ä´shĕ-bĕrg) | 171c | 51°47´N | 7°38´E |
| Aschersleben, Ger. (äsh´ĕrs-lä-bĕn) | 168 | 51°46´N | 11°28´E |
| Ascoli Piceno, Italy (äs´kô-lēpē-chā´nō) | 174 | 42°50´N | 13°55´E |
| Aseb, Erit. | 231 | 12°52´N | 43°39´E |
| Asenovgrad, Blg. | 175 | 42°00´N | 24°49´E |
| Aseri, Est. (à´sĕ-rī) | 167 | 59°26´N | 26°58´E |
| Asha, Russia (ä´shä) | 186a | 55°01´N | 57°17´E |
| Ashabula, l., N.D., U.S. (ăsh´á-bū-lä) | 112 | 47°07´N | 97°51´W |
| Ashan, Russia (ä´shän) | 186a | 57°08´N | 56°25´E |
| Ashbourne, Eng., U.K. (ăsh´bŭrn) | 158a | 53°01´N | 1°44´W |
| Ashburn, Ga., U.S. (ăsh´bŭrn) | 124 | 31°42´N | 83°42´W |
| Ashburn, Va., U.S. | 110e | 39°02´N | 77°30´W |
| Ashburton, r., Austl. (ăsh´bŭr-tŭn) | 220 | 22°30´S | 115°30´E |
| Ashby-de-la-Zouch, Eng., U.K. (ăsh´bĭ-dĕ-là zōōsh´) | 158a | 52°44´N | 1°23´W |
| Ashdod, Isr. | 197a | 31°46´N | 34°39´E |
| Ashdown, Ar., U.S. (ăsh´doun) | 121 | 33°41´N | 94°07´W |
| Asheboro, N.C., U.S. (ăsh´bŭr-ô) | 125 | 35°41´N | 79°50´W |
| Asherton, Tx., U.S. (ăsh´ēr-tŭn) | 122 | 28°26´N | 99°45´W |
| Asheville, N.C., U.S. (ăsh´vĭl) | 105 | 35°35´N | 82°35´W |
| Ash Fork, Az., U.S. | 119 | 35°13´N | 112°29´W |
| Ashgabat, Turkmen. | 183 | 37°57´N | 58°23´E |
| Ashikaga, Japan (ä´shē-kä´gä) | 211 | 36°22´N | 139°26´E |
| Ashiya, Japan (ä´shē-yä´) | 211 | 33°54´N | 130°40´E |
| Ashiya, Japan | 211b | 34°44´N | 135°18´E |
| Ashizuri-Zaki, c., Japan (ä-shē-zò-rē zä-kē) | 210 | 32°43´N | 133°04´E |
| Ashland, Al., U.S. (ăsh´lánd) | 124 | 33°15´N | 85°50´W |
| Ashland, Ks., U.S. | 120 | 37°11´N | 99°46´W |
| Ashland, Ky., U.S. | 108 | 38°25´N | 82°40´W |
| Ashland, Ma., U.S. | 101a | 42°16´N | 71°28´W |
| Ashland, Me., U.S. | 100 | 46°37´N | 68°26´W |
| Ashland, Ne., U.S. | 112 | 41°02´N | 96°23´W |
| Ashland, Oh., U.S. | 108 | 40°50´N | 82°15´W |
| Ashland, Or., U.S. | 114 | 42°12´N | 122°42´W |
| Ashland, Pa., U.S. | 109 | 40°45´N | 76°20´W |
| Ashland, Wi., U.S. | 105 | 46°34´N | 90°55´W |
| Ashley, N.D., U.S. (ăsh´lĕ) | 112 | 46°03´N | 99°23´W |
| Ashley, Pa., U.S. | 109 | 41°15´N | 75°55´W |
| Ashmūn, Egypt (ăsh-mōōn´) | 238b | 30°19´N | 30°57´E |
| Ashmyany, Bela. | 167 | 54°27´N | 25°55´E |
| Ashqelon, Isr. (ăsh´kĕ-lōn) | 197a | 31°40´N | 34°36´E |
| Ash Shabb, Egypt (shĕb) | 231 | 22°34´N | 29°52´E |
| Ash Shallūfah, Egypt (shäl´lò-fà) | 238b | 30°09´N | 32°33´E |
| Ash Shaqrā´, Sau. Ar. | 198 | 25°10´N | 45°08´E |
| Ash Shāriqah, U.A.E. | 201 | 25°22´N | 55°23´E |
| Ash Shawbak, Jord. | 197a | 30°31´N | 35°35´E |
| Ash Shiḥr, Yemen | 198 | 14°45´N | 49°32´E |
| Ashtabula, Oh., U.S. (ăsh-tá-bū´lá) | 105 | 41°55´N | 80°50´W |
| Ashton, Id., U.S. (ăsh´tŭn) | 115 | 44°04´N | 111°28´W |
| Ashton-in-Makerfield, Eng., U.K. (ăsh´tŭn-ĭn-māk´ĕr-fēld) | 158a | 53°29´N | 2°39´W |
| Ashton-under-Lyne, Eng., U.K. (ăsh´tŭn-ŭn-dĕr-līn´) | 158a | 53°29´N | 2°04´W |
| Ashuanipi, l., Can. (ăsh-wå-nĭp´ĭ) | 93 | 52°40´N | 67°42´W |
| Ashukino, Russia (á-shōō´kinò) | 186b | 56°10´N | 37°57´E |
| Asia, cont. | 196 | 50°00´N | 100°00´E |
| Asia Minor, reg., Tur. (ā´zhá) | 157 | 38°18´N | 31°18´E |
| Asientos, Mex. (ä-sĕ-ĕn´tōs) | 130 | 22°13´N | 102°05´W |
| Asilah, Mor. | 172 | 35°30´N | 6°05´W |
| Asinara, i., Italy | 174 | 41°02´N | 8°22´E |
| Asinara, Golfo dell´, b., Italy (gòl´fô-dĕl-ä-sē-nä´rä) | 174 | 40°58´N | 8°28´E |
| Asīr, reg., Sau. Ar. (ä-sēr´) | 198 | 19°30´N | 42°00´E |
| Askarovo, Russia (äs-kä-rō´vò) | 186a | 53°21´N | 58°32´E |
| Askersund, Swe. (äs´kĕr-sònd) | 166 | 58°43´N | 14°53´E |
| Askino, Russia (äs´kĕ-lōn) | 186a | 56°06´N | 56°29´E |
| Asmara see Asmera, Erit. | 230 | 15°17´N | 38°56´E |
| Asmera, Erit. (äs-mä´rä) | 231 | 15°17´N | 38°56´E |
| Asnieres, Fr. (ä-nyär´) | 171b | 48°55´N | 2°18´E |
| Asosa, Eth. | 231 | 10°13´N | 34°28´E |
| Asotin, Wa., U.S. (á-sō´tĭn) | 114 | 46°19´N | 117°01´W |
| Aspen, Co., U.S. (ăs´pĕn) | 119 | 39°15´N | 106°55´W |
| Asperen, Neth. | 159a | 51°52´N | 5°07´E |
| Aspy Bay, b., Can. (ăs´pē) | 101 | 46°56´N | 60°25´W |
| Aş Şaff, Egypt | 238b | 29°33´N | 31°23´E |
| As Sallūm, Egypt | 231 | 31°35´N | 25°05´E |
| As Salt, Jord. | 197a | 32°02´N | 35°44´E |
| Assam, state, India (äs-säm´) | 199 | 26°00´N | 91°00´E |
| As Samāwah, Iraq | 201 | 31°18´N | 45°17´E |
| Assens, Den. (äs´sĕns) | 166 | 55°16´N | 9°54´E |
| As Sinbillāwayn, Egypt | 238b | 30°53´N | 31°37´E |
| Assini, C. Iv. (ä-sē-nē´) | 230 | 4°52´N | 3°16´W |
| Assiniboia, Can. | 90 | 49°38´N | 105°59´W |
| Assiniboine, r., Can. (ä-sĭn´ĭ-boin) | 87 | 50°03´N | 97°57´W |
| Assiniboine, Mount, mtn., Can. | 95 | 50°52´N | 115°39´W |
| Assis, Braz. (ä-sē´s) | 143 | 22°39´S | 50°21´W |
| Assisi, Italy | 162 | 43°04´N | 12°37´E |
| As-Sudd, reg., Sudan | 231 | 8°45´N | 30°45´E |
| As Sulaymānīyah, Iraq | 198 | 35°47´N | 45°23´E |
| As Sulaymānīyah, Sau. Ar. | 201 | 24°09´N | 46°19´E |
| As Suwaydā´, Syria | 198 | 32°41´N | 36°41´E |
| Astakós, Grc. (äs´tä-kôs) | 175 | 38°42´N | 21°00´E |
| Astana (Aqmola), Kaz. | 183 | 51°10´N | 71°43´E |
| Astara, Azer. | 181 | 38°30´N | 48°50´E |
| Asti, Italy (äs´tē) | 162 | 44°54´N | 8°12´E |
| Astorga, Spain (äs-tôr´gä) | 172 | 42°28´N | 6°03´W |
| Astoria, Or., U.S. (äs-tō´rĭ-á) | 104 | 46°11´N | 123°51´W |
| Astrakhan´, Russia (äs-trá-kän´) | 178 | 46°15´N | 48°00´E |
| Astrida, Rw. (äs-trē´dä) | 232 | 2°37´S | 29°48´E |
| Asturias, hist. reg., Spain (äs-tōō´ryäs) | 172 | 43°21´N | 6°00´W |
| Astypalaia, i., Grc. | 163 | 36°31´N | 26°19´E |
| Asunción see Ixtaltepec, Mex. | 131 | 16°33´N | 95°04´W |
| Asunción see Nochistlán, Mex. | 130 | 21°23´N | 102°52´W |
| Asunción, Para. (ä-sōōn-syōn´) | 144 | 25°25´S | 57°30´W |
| Asunción Mita, Guat. (ä-sōōn-syō´n-mē´tä) | 132 | 14°19´N | 89°43´W |
| Aswān, Egypt (ä-swän´) | 231 | 24°05´N | 32°57´E |
| Aswān High Dam, dam, Egypt | 231 | 23°58´N | 32°53´E |
| Atacama, Desierto de, des., Chile (dĕ-syĕ´r-tô-dĕ-ä-tä-kä´mä) | 139 | 23°50´S | 69°00´W |

268 Atacama – Babylon

PRONOUNCING INDEX


| PLACE (Pronunciation) | PAGE | LAT. | LONG. |
|---|---|---|---|
| Atacama, Puna de, plat., Bol. (po͞o′nä-dĕ-ä-tä-kȧ′mä) | 142 | 21°35′S | 66°58′W |
| Atacama, Puna de, reg., Chile (po͞o′nä-dĕ-ȧtä-kȧ′mä) | 144 | 23°15′S | 68°45′W |
| Atacama, Salar de, l., Chile (sȧ-lär′dĕ-ȧtä-kȧ′mä) | 144 | 23°38′S | 68°15′W |
| Ataco, Col. (ä-tȧ′kō) | 142a | 3°36′N | 75°22′W |
| Atacora, Chaîne de l′, mts., Benin | 234 | 10°15′N | 1°15′E |
| Atā ′itah, Jabal al, mtn., Jord. | 197a | 30°48′N | 35°19′E |
| Atamanovskiy, Russia (ä-tä-mä′nôv-skĭ) | 186a | 52°15′N | 60°47′E |
| ′Atāqah, Jabal, mts., Egypt | 238d | 29°59′N | 32°20′E |
| Atar, Maur. (ä-tär′) | 230 | 20°45′N | 13°16′W |
| Atascadero, Ca., U.S. (ăt-ăs-kȧ-dâ′rō) | 118 | 35°29′N | 120°40′W |
| Atascosa, r., Tx., U.S. (ăt-ăs-kō′sȧ) | 122 | 28°50′N | 98°17′W |
| Atauro, Ilha de, i., E. Timor (dĕ-ä-tä′o͞o-rô) | 213 | 8°20′S | 126°15′E |
| Atbara, r., Afr. | 231 | 17°14′N | 34°27′E |
| ′Aṭbarah, Sudan (ät′bȧ-rä) | 231 | 17°45′N | 33°15′E |
| Atbasar, Kaz. (ät′bä-sär′) | 183 | 51°42′N | 68°28′E |
| Atchafalaya, r., La., U.S. | 123 | 30°53′N | 91°51′W |
| Atchafalaya Bay, b., La., U.S. (ăch-ȧ-fȧ-lī′ȧ) | 123 | 29°25′N | 91°30′W |
| Atchison, Ks., U.S. (ăch′ĭ-sŭn) | 105 | 39°33′N | 95°08′W |
| Atco, N.J., U.S. (ăt′kō) | 110f | 39°46′N | 74°53′W |
| Atempan, Mex. (ä-tĕm-pä′n) | 131 | 19°49′N | 97°25′W |
| Atenguillo, r., Mex. (ä-tĕn-gē′l-yô) | 130 | 20°18′N | 104°35′W |
| Athabasca, Can. (ăth-ȧ-băs′kȧ) | 90 | 54°43′N | 113°17′W |
| Athabasca, l., Can. | 92 | 59°04′N | 109°10′W |
| Athabasca, r., Can. | 92 | 57°30′N | 112°00′W |
| Athens (Athína), Grc. | 175 | 38°00′N | 23°38′E |
| Athens, Al., U.S. (ăth′ĕnz) | 124 | 34°47′N | 86°58′W |
| Athens, Ga., U.S. | 105 | 33°55′N | 83°24′W |
| Athens, Oh., U.S. | 108 | 39°20′N | 82°10′W |
| Athens, Pa., U.S. | 109 | 42°00′N | 76°30′W |
| Athens, Tn., U.S. | 124 | 35°26′N | 84°36′W |
| Athens, Tx., U.S. | 123 | 32°13′N | 95°51′W |
| Atherstone, Eng., U.K. (ăth′ĕr-stŭn) | 158a | 52°34′N | 1°33′W |
| Atherton, Eng., U.K. (ăth′ĕr-tŭn) | 158a | 53°32′N | 2°29′W |
| Atherton Plateau, plat., Austl. (ădh-ĕr-tŏn) | 221 | 17°00′S | 144°30′E |
| Athi, r., Kenya (ä′tē) | 233 | 2°43′S | 38°30′E |
| Athína see Athens, Grc. | 154 | 38°00′N | 23°38′E |
| Athlone, Ire. (ăth-lōn′) | 160 | 53°24′N | 7°30′W |
| Áthos, mtn., Grc. (ăth′ŏs) | 175 | 40°10′N | 24°15′E |
| Ath Thamad, Egypt | 197a | 29°41′N | 34°17′E |
| Athy, Ire. (ȧ-thī) | 164 | 52°59′N | 7°08′W |
| Ati, Chad | 235 | 13°13′N | 18°20′E |
| Atibaia, Braz. (ä-tē-bȧ′yȧ) | 141a | 23°08′S | 46°32′W |
| Atikonak, l., Can. | 93 | 52°34′N | 63°49′W |
| Atimonan, Phil. (ä-tē-mō′nän) | 213a | 13°59′N | 121°56′E |
| Atiquizaya, El Sal. (ä′tē-kē-zä′yä) | 132 | 14°00′N | 89°42′W |
| Atitlan, vol., Guat. (ä-tē-tlän′) | 132 | 14°35′N | 91°11′W |
| Atitlan, Lago, l., Guat. (ä-tē-tlän′) | 132 | 14°38′N | 91°23′W |
| Atizapán, Mex. (ä′tē-zȧ-pän′) | 131a | 19°33′N | 99°16′W |
| Atka, Ak., U.S. (ăt′kȧ) | 103a | 52°18′N | 174°18′W |
| Atka, i., Ak., U.S. | 106b | 51°58′N | 174°30′W |
| Atkarsk, Russia (ät-kärsk′) | 181 | 51°50′N | 45°00′E |
| Atkinson, Ne., U.S. (ăt′kĭn-sŭn) | 112 | 42°32′N | 98°58′W |
| Atlanta, Ga., U.S. (ăt-lăn′tȧ) | 105 | 33°45′N | 84°23′W |
| Atlanta, Tx., U.S. | 121 | 33°09′N | 94°09′W |
| Atlantic, Ia., U.S. (ăt-lăn′tĭk) | 113 | 41°23′N | 94°58′W |
| Atlantic, N.C., U.S. | 125 | 34°54′N | 76°20′W |
| Atlantic City, N.J., U.S. | 105 | 39°20′N | 74°30′W |
| Atlantic Highlands, N.J., U.S. | 110a | 40°25′N | 74°04′W |
| Atlantic Ocean, o. | 4 | 5°00′S | 25°00′W |
| Atlas Mountains, mts., Afr. (ăt′lăs) | 230 | 31°22′N | 4°57′W |
| Atliaca, Mex. (ät-lê-ä′kä) | 130 | 17°38′N | 99°24′W |
| Atlin, l., Can. (ăt′lĭn) | 92 | 59°34′N | 133°20′W |
| Atlixco, Mex. (ät-lēz′kō) | 130 | 18°52′N | 98°27′W |
| Atmore, Al., U.S. (ăt′mōr) | 124 | 31°01′N | 87°31′W |
| Atoka, Ok., U.S. (ȧ-tō′kȧ) | 121 | 34°23′N | 96°07′W |
| Atoka Reservoir, res., Ok., U.S. | 121 | 34°30′N | 96°05′W |
| Atotonilco el Alto, Mex. | 130 | 20°35′N | 102°32′W |
| Atotonilco el Grande, Mex. | 130 | 20°17′N | 98°41′W |
| Atoui, r., Afr. (ȧ-to͞o-ē′) | 230 | 21°00′N | 15°32′W |
| Atoyac, Mex. (ä-tô-yäk′) | 130 | 20°01′N | 103°28′W |
| Atoyac, r., Mex. | 130 | 18°35′N | 98°16′W |
| Atoyac, r., Mex. | 131 | 16°27′N | 97°28′W |
| Atoyac de Alvarez, Mex. (ä-tô-yäk′dā äl′vä-rāz) | 130 | 17°13′N | 100°29′W |
| Atoyatempan, Mex. (ä-tō′yȧ-tĕm-pän′) | 131 | 18°47′N | 97°54′W |
| Atrak, r., Asia | 198 | 37°45′N | 56°30′E |
| Åtran, r., Swe. | 166 | 57°02′N | 12°43′E |
| Atrato, Río, r., Col. (rē′ō-ä-trä′tō) | 142 | 7°15′N | 77°18′W |
| Aṭ Ṭafīlah, Jord. (tä-fē′lȧ) | 197a | 30°50′N | 35°36′E |
| Aṭ Ṭā′if, Sau. Ar. | 198 | 21°03′N | 41°00′E |
| Attalla, Al., U.S. (ȧ-tăl′yȧ) | 124 | 34°01′N | 86°05′W |
| Attawapiskat, r., Can. (ăt′ȧ-wȧ-pĭs′kăt) | 93 | 52°31′N | 86°22′W |
| Attersee, l., Aus. | 168 | 47°57′N | 13°25′E |
| Attica, N.Y., U.S. (ăt′ĭ-kȧ) | 109 | 42°55′N | 78°15′W |
| Attleboro, Ma., U.S. (ăt′′l-bŭr-ô) | 110b | 41°56′N | 71°15′W |
| Attow, Ben, mtn., Scot., U.K. (bĕn ăt′tô) | 164 | 57°15′N | 5°25′W |
| Attoyac Bay, Tx., U.S. (ă-toi′yăk) | 123 | 31°45′N | 94°23′W |
| Attu, i., Ak., U.S. (ät-to͞o′) | 106b | 53°08′N | 173°18′E |
| Aṭ Ṭūr, Egypt | 163 | 28°09′N | 33°47′E |
| Aṭ Ṭurayf, Sau. Ar. | 198 | 31°32′N | 38°30′E |
| Åtvidaberg, Swe. (ôt-vē′dȧ-bĕrgh) | 166 | 58°12′N | 15°55′E |
| Atwood, Ks., U.S. (ăt′wŏŏd) | 120 | 39°48′N | 101°06′W |
| Atyraū, Kaz. | 183 | 47°10′N | 51°50′E |
| Atzcapotzalco, Mex. (ät′zkä-pô-tzäl′kō) | 130 | 19°29′N | 99°11′W |
| Atzgersdorf, Aus. | 159e | 48°10′N | 16°17′E |
| Auau Channel, strt., Hi., U.S. (ä′ô-ä′ôo) | 126a | 20°55′N | 156°50′W |
| Aubagne, Fr. (ō-bän′y′) | 171 | 43°18′N | 5°34′E |
| Aube, r., Fr. (ōb) | 170 | 48°42′N | 3°49′E |
| Aubenas, Fr. (ōb-nä′) | 170 | 44°37′N | 4°22′E |
| Aubervilliers, Fr. (ō-bĕr-vē-yā′) | 171b | 48°54′N | 2°23′E |
| Aubin, Fr. (ō-băN′) | 170 | 44°29′N | 2°12′E |
| Aubrey, Can. (ô-brē′) | 102a | 45°08′N | 73°47′W |
| Auburn, Al., U.S. (ô′bûrn) | 124 | 32°35′N | 85°26′W |
| Auburn, Ca., U.S. | 118 | 38°52′N | 121°05′W |
| Auburn, Il., U.S. | 121 | 39°36′N | 89°46′W |
| Auburn, In., U.S. | 108 | 41°20′N | 85°05′W |
| Auburn, Ma., U.S. | 101a | 42°11′N | 71°51′W |
| Auburn, Me., U.S. | 105 | 44°04′N | 70°24′W |
| Auburn, Ne., U.S. | 121 | 40°23′N | 95°50′W |
| Auburn, N.Y., U.S. | 109 | 42°55′N | 76°35′W |
| Auburn, Wa., U.S. | 116a | 47°18′N | 122°14′W |
| Auburn Heights, Mi., U.S. | 111b | 42°37′N | 83°13′W |
| Aubusson, Fr. (ō-bü-sôN′) | 170 | 45°57′N | 2°10′E |
| Auch, Fr. (ōsh) | 161 | 43°38′N | 0°35′E |
| Aucilla, r., Fl., U.S. (ô-sĭl′ȧ) | 124 | 30°15′N | 83°55′W |
| Auckland, N.Z. (ôk′lănd) | 221a | 36°53′S | 174°45′E |
| Auckland Islands, is., N.Z. | 3 | 50°30′S | 166°30′E |
| Aude, r., Fr. (ōd) | 170 | 42°55′N | 2°08′E |
| Audierne, Fr. (ō-dyĕrn′) | 170 | 48°02′N | 4°31′W |
| Audincourt, Fr. (ō-dăn-ko͞or′) | 171 | 47°30′N | 6°49′E |
| Audley, Eng., U.K. (ôd′lĭ) | 158a | 53°03′N | 2°18′W |
| Audo Range, mts., Eth. | 238a | 6°58′N | 41°18′E |
| Audubon, Ia., U.S. (ô′dȯ-bŏn) | 113 | 41°43′N | 94°57′W |
| Audubon, N.J., U.S. | 110f | 39°54′N | 75°04′W |
| Aue, Ger. (ou′ĕ) | 168 | 50°35′N | 12°44′E |
| Augathella, Austl. (ôr′gȧ′thĕ-lȧ) | 222 | 25°49′S | 146°40′E |
| Augrabiesvalle, wtfl., S. Afr. | 232 | 28°30′S | 20°00′E |
| Augsburg, Ger. (ouks′bŏrgh) | 161 | 48°23′N | 10°55′E |
| Augusta, Ar., U.S. (ô-gŭs′tȧ) | 121 | 35°16′N | 91°21′W |
| Augusta, Ga., U.S. | 105 | 33°26′N | 82°00′W |
| Augusta, Ks., U.S. | 121 | 37°41′N | 96°58′W |
| Augusta, Ky., U.S. | 108 | 38°45′N | 84°00′W |
| Augusta, Me., U.S. | 105 | 44°19′N | 69°42′W |
| Augusta, N.J., U.S. | 110a | 41°07′N | 74°44′W |
| Augusta, Wi., U.S. | 113 | 44°40′N | 91°09′W |
| Augustow, Pol. (ou-gŏs′tŏf) | 169 | 53°52′N | 23°00′E |
| Auki, Sol. Is. | 214e | 8°46′S | 160°42′E |
| Aulnay-sous-Bois, Fr. (ō-nĕ′so͞o-bwä′) | 171b | 48°56′N | 2°30′E |
| Aulne, r., Fr. (ōn) | 170 | 48°08′N | 3°53′W |
| Auneau, Fr. (ō-nĕü) | 171b | 48°28′N | 1°45′E |
| Auob, r., Afr. (ä′wŏb) | 232 | 25°00′S | 19°00′E |
| Aur, i., Malay. | 197b | 2°27′N | 104°51′E |
| Aura, Fin. | 167 | 60°38′N | 22°32′E |
| Aurangābād, India (ou-rŭŋ-gä-bäd′) | 199 | 19°56′N | 75°19′E |
| Aurdal, Nor. (äŭr-däl) | 160 | 60°54′N | 9°24′E |
| Aurès, Massif de l′, mts., Alg. | 162 | 35°16′N | 5°53′E |
| Aurillac, Fr. (ō-rē-yȧk′) | 161 | 44°57′N | 2°27′E |
| Aurora, Can. | 99 | 43°59′N | 79°25′W |
| Aurora, Co., U.S. | 120 | 39°44′N | 104°50′W |
| Aurora, Il., U.S. (ô-rō′rȧ) | 105 | 41°45′N | 88°18′W |
| Aurora, In., U.S. | 111f | 39°04′N | 84°55′W |
| Aurora, Mn., U.S. | 113 | 47°31′N | 92°17′W |
| Aurora, Mo., U.S. | 121 | 36°58′N | 93°42′W |
| Aurora, Ne., U.S. | 120 | 40°54′N | 98°01′W |
| Aursunden, l., Nor. (äûr-sûndĕn) | 166 | 62°42′N | 11°10′E |
| Au Sable, r., Mi., U.S. (ô-să′b′l) | 108 | 44°40′N | 84°25′W |
| Ausable, r., N.Y., U.S. | 109 | 44°25′N | 73°50′W |
| Austin, Mn., U.S. (ôs′tĭn) | 113 | 43°40′N | 92°58′W |
| Austin, Nv., U.S. | 118 | 39°30′N | 117°05′W |
| Austin, Tx., U.S. | 104 | 30°15′N | 97°42′W |
| Austin, l., Austl. | 220 | 27°45′S | 117°30′E |
| Austin Bayou, Tx., U.S. (ôs′tĭn bī-o͞o′) | 123a | 29°17′N | 95°21′W |
| Australia, nation, Oc. | 218 | 25°00′S | 135°00′E |
| Australian Alps, mts., Austl. | 222 | 37°10′S | 147°55′E |
| Australian Capital Territory, ter., Austl. (ôs-trā′lĭ-ăn) | 219 | 35°30′S | 148°40′E |
| Austria, nation, Eur. (ôs′trĭ-ȧ) | 154 | 47°15′N | 11°53′E |
| Authon-la-Plaine, Fr. (ō-tôN-lä-plĕ′n) | 171b | 48°27′N | 1°58′E |
| Autlán, Mex. (ä-o͞ot-län′) | 128 | 19°47′N | 104°24′W |
| Autun, Fr. (ō-tŭN′) | 170 | 46°58′N | 4°14′E |
| Auvergne, mts., Fr. (ō-vĕrn′y′) | 170 | 45°12′N | 2°31′E |
| Auxerre, Fr. (ō-sâr′) | 161 | 47°48′N | 3°32′E |
| Ava, Mo., U.S. (ā′vȧ) | 121 | 36°56′N | 92°40′W |
| Avakubi, D.R.C. (ä-vȧ-ko͞o′bē) | 231 | 1°20′N | 27°34′E |
| Avallon, Fr. (ȧ-vȧ-lôN′) | 170 | 47°30′N | 3°58′E |
| Avalon, Ca., U.S. | 118 | 33°21′N | 118°22′W |
| Avalon, Pa., U.S. (ăv′ȧ-lŏn) | 111e | 40°31′N | 80°05′W |
| Aveiro, Port. (ä-vā′rô) | 162 | 40°38′N | 8°38′W |
| Avelar, Braz. (ä′vĕ-lȧ′r) | 144b | 22°20′S | 43°25′W |
| Avellaneda, Arg. (ä-vĕl-yä-nā′dhä) | 144 | 34°40′S | 58°23′W |
| Avellino, Italy (ä-vĕl-lē′nō) | 174 | 40°40′N | 14°46′E |
| Averøya, i., Nor. (ävĕr-ûê) | 166 | 63°40′N | 7°16′E |
| Aversa, Italy (ä-vĕr′sä) | 174 | 40°58′N | 14°13′E |
| Avery, Tx., U.S. (ā′vĕr-ĭ) | 121 | 33°34′N | 94°46′W |
| Avesta, Swe. (ä-vĕs′tä) | 166 | 60°16′N | 16°09′E |
| Aveyron, r., Fr. (ä-vâ-rôN) | 170 | 44°07′N | 1°45′E |
| Avezzano, Italy (ä-vāt-sä′nō) | 174 | 42°03′N | 13°27′E |
| Avigliano, Italy (ä-vēl-yä′nō) | 174 | 40°45′N | 15°44′E |
| Avignon, Fr. (ȧ-vē-nyôN′) | 161 | 43°55′N | 4°50′E |
| Ávila, Spain (ä-vê-lä) | 172 | 40°39′N | 4°42′W |
| Avilés, Spain (ä-vē-lās′) | 162 | 43°33′N | 5°55′W |
| Aviño, Spain | 172 | 43°36′N | 8°05′W |
| Avoca, Ia., U.S. (ȧ-vō′kȧ) | 121 | 41°29′N | 95°16′W |
| Avon, Ct., U.S. (ā′vŏn) | 109 | 41°40′N | 72°50′W |
| Avon, Ma., U.S. (ā′vŏn) | 101a | 42°08′N | 71°03′W |
| Avon, Oh., U.S. | 111d | 41°27′N | 82°02′W |
| Avon, r., Eng., U.K. (ā′vŭn) | 164 | 52°05′N | 1°55′W |
| Avondale, Ga., U.S. | 110c | 33°47′N | 84°16′W |
| Avon Lake, Oh., U.S. | 111d | 41°31′N | 82°01′W |
| Avonmore, Can. (ā′vŏN-mōr) | 102c | 45°11′N | 74°58′W |
| Avon Park, Fl., U.S. (ā′vŏn pärk′) | 125a | 27°35′N | 81°29′W |
| Avranches, Fr. (ȧ-vräNsh′) | 170 | 48°43′N | 1°34′W |
| Awaji-Shima, i., Japan | 210 | 34°32′N | 135°02′E |
| Awe, Loch, l., Scot., U.K. (lŏĸ ôr) | 164 | 56°22′N | 5°04′W |
| Awjilah, Libya | 231 | 29°07′N | 21°21′E |
| Ax-les-Thermes, Fr. (äks′lā tĕrm′) | 170 | 42°43′N | 1°50′E |
| Axochiapan, Mex. (äks-ō-chyä′pän) | 130 | 18°29′N | 98°49′W |
| Ay, r., Russia | 180 | 55°55′N | 57°55′E |
| Ayabe, Japan (ä′yä-bĕ) | 210 | 35°16′N | 135°17′E |
| Ayachi, Arin′, mtn., Mor. | 162 | 32°29′N | 4°57′W |
| Ayacucho, Arg. (ä-yä-ko͞o′chō) | 144 | 37°05′S | 58°30′W |
| Ayacucho, Peru | 142 | 13°12′S | 74°03′W |
| Ayaköz, Kaz. | 183 | 48°00′N | 80°12′E |
| Ayamonte, Spain (ä-yä-mŏ′n-tĕ) | 162 | 37°14′N | 7°28′W |
| Ayan, Russia (ä-yän′) | 179 | 56°26′N | 138°18′E |
| Ayata, Bol. (ä-yä′tä) | 142 | 15°17′S | 68°43′W |
| Ayaviri, Peru (ä-yä-vē′rē) | 142 | 14°46′S | 70°38′W |
| Aydar, r., Eur. (ī-där′) | 177 | 49°15′N | 38°48′E |
| Ayden, N.C., U.S. (ā′dĕn) | 125 | 35°27′N | 77°25′W |
| Aydın, Tur. (āīy-dĕn) | 198 | 37°40′N | 27°40′E |
| Ayer, Ma., U.S. (âr) | 101a | 42°33′N | 71°36′W |
| Ayer Hitam, Malay. | 197b | 1°55′N | 103°11′E |
| Ayers Rock see Uluru, mtn., Austl. | 220 | 25°23′S | 131°05′E |
| Aylesbury, Eng., U.K. (ālz′bĕr-ĭ) | 164 | 51°47′N | 0°49′W |
| Aylmer, l., Can. (āl′mēr) | 92 | 64°27′N | 108°22′W |
| Aylmer, Mount, mtn., Can. | 95 | 51°19′N | 115°26′W |
| Aylmer East, Can. (āl′mēr) | 99 | 45°24′N | 75°50′W |
| Ayo el Chico, Mex. (ä′yô el chē′kō) | 130 | 20°31′N | 102°21′W |
| Ayon, i., Russia (ī-ôn′) | 179 | 69°50′N | 168°40′E |
| Ayorou, Niger | 234 | 14°44′N | 0°55′E |
| Ayotla, Mex. (ä-yōt′lä) | 131a | 19°18′N | 98°55′W |
| Ayoun el Atrous, Maur. | 234 | 16°40′N | 9°37′W |
| Ayr, Scot., U.K. (âr) | 164 | 55°27′N | 4°40′W |
| Aysha, Eth. | 231 | 10°48′N | 42°32′E |
| Ayutla, Guat. (ȧ-yo͞ot′lä) | 132 | 14°44′N | 92°11′W |
| Ayutla, Mex. | 130 | 16°50′N | 99°16′W |
| Ayutla, Mex. | 130 | 20°09′N | 104°20′W |
| Ayvalık, Tur. (āīy-wä-lĭk) | 163 | 39°19′N | 26°40′E |
| Azaouad, reg., Mali | 234 | 18°00′N | 3°20′W |
| Azaouak, Vallée de l′, val., Afr. | 235 | 15°50′N | 3°10′E |
| Azare, Nig. | 235 | 11°40′N | 10°11′E |
| Azemmour, Mor. (ȧ-zē-mo͞or′) | 230 | 33°20′N | 8°21′W |
| Azerbaijan, nation, Asia | 178 | 40°30′N | 47°30′E |
| Azle, Tx., U.S. (āz′lē) | 117c | 35°54′N | 97°33′W |
| Azogues, Ec. (ä-sō′gās) | 142 | 2°47′S | 78°45′W |
| Azores see Açores, is., Port. | 229 | 37°44′N | 29°25′W |
| Azov, Russia (ȧ-zôf′) (ä-zôf) | 181 | 47°07′N | 39°19′E |
| Azov, Sea of, sea, Eur. | 178 | 46°00′N | 36°20′E |
| Aztec, N.M., U.S. (ăz′tĕk) | 119 | 36°40′N | 108°00′W |
| Aztec Ruins National Monument, rec., N.M., U.S. | 119 | 36°50′N | 108°00′W |
| Azua, Dom. Rep. (ä′swä) | 135 | 18°30′N | 70°45′W |
| Azuaga, Spain (ä-thwä′gä) | 172 | 38°15′N | 5°42′W |
| Azucar, Presa de, res., Mex. | 122 | 26°06′N | 98°44′W |
| Azuero, Península de, pen., Pan. | 129 | 7°30′N | 80°34′W |
| Azufre, Cerro (Copiapó), mtn., Chile | 144 | 27°10′S | 69°00′W |
| Azul, Arg. (ä-so͞ol′) | 144 | 36°46′S | 59°51′W |
| Azul, Cordillera, mts., Peru | 142 | 7°15′S | 75°30′W |
| Azul, Sierra, mts., Mex. | 130 | 23°20′N | 98°28′W |
| Azusa, Ca., U.S. (ȧ-zo͞o′sȧ) | 117a | 34°08′N | 117°55′W |
| Aẓ Ẓahrān (Dhahran), Sau. Ar. | 198 | 26°13′N | 50°00′E |
| Az Zaqāzīq, Egypt | 231 | 30°36′N | 31°36′E |
| Az Zarqā′, Jord. | 197a | 32°03′N | 36°07′E |
| Az Zāwiyah, Libya | 230 | 32°28′N | 11°55′E |


# B


| PLACE (Pronunciation) | PAGE | LAT. | LONG. |
|---|---|---|---|
| Baadheere (Bardera), Som. | 238a | 2°13′N | 42°24′E |
| Baal, Ger. (bäl) | 171c | 51°02′N | 6°17′E |
| Baao, Phil. (bä′ō) | 213a | 13°27′N | 123°22′E |
| Baarle-Hertog, Bel. | 159a | 51°26′N | 4°57′E |
| Baarn, Neth. | 159a | 52°12′N | 5°18′E |
| Babaeski, Tur. (bä′bä-ĕs′kĭ) | 175 | 41°25′N | 27°05′E |
| Babahoyo, Ec. (bä-bä-ō′yō) | 142 | 1°56′S | 79°24′W |
| Babana, Nig. | 235 | 10°36′N | 3°50′E |
| Babanango, S. Afr. | 233c | 28°24′S | 31°11′E |
| Babanūsah, Sudan | 231 | 11°30′N | 27°55′E |
| Babar, Pulau, i., Indon. (bä′bär) | 213 | 7°50′S | 129°15′E |
| Bab-el-Mandeb see Mandeb, Bab-el-, strt. | 198 | 13°17′N | 42°49′E |
| Babelthuap, i., Palau | 214b | 7°30′N | 134°36′E |
| Babia, Arroyo de la, r., Mex. | 122 | 28°26′N | 101°50′W |
| Babine, r., Can. | 94 | 55°10′N | 127°00′W |
| Babine Lake, l., Can. (băb′ēn) | 92 | 54°45′N | 126°00′W |
| Bābol, Iran | 198 | 36°30′N | 52°48′E |
| Babruysk, Bela. | 180 | 53°07′N | 29°13′E |
| Babushkin, Russia (bä′bŏsh-kĭn) | 184 | 51°47′N | 106°08′W |
| Babushkin, Russia | 176 | 55°52′N | 37°42′E |
| Babuyan Islands, is., Phil. (bä-bo͞o-yän′) | 212 | 19°30′N | 122°38′E |
| Babyak, Blg. (bäb′zhȧk) | 175 | 41°59′N | 23°42′E |
| Babylon, N.Y., U.S. (băb′ĭ-lŏn) | 110a | 40°42′N | 73°19′W |
| Babylon, hist., Iraq | 198 | 32°15′N | 45°23′E |

PRONOUNCING INDEX

Bacalar – Bangor 269


| PLACE (Pronunciation) | PAGE | LAT. | LONG. |
|---|---|---|---|
| Bacalar, Laguna de, l., Mex. (lä-gōō-nä-dĕ-bä-kä-lär′) | 132a | 18°50′N | 88°31′W |
| Bacan, Pulau, i., Indon. | 213 | 0°30′S | 127°00′E |
| Bacarra, Phil. (bä-kär′rä) | 209 | 18°22′N | 120°40′E |
| Bacău, Rom. | 163 | 46°34′N | 27°00′E |
| Baccarat, Fr. (bȧ-kȧ-rȧ′) | 171 | 48°29′N | 6°42′E |
| Bacchus, Ut., U.S. (băk′ŭs) | 117b | 40°40′N | 112°06′W |
| Bachajón, Mex. (bä-chä-hōn′) | 131 | 17°08′N | 92°18′W |
| Bachu, China (bä-chōō) | 204 | 39°50′N | 78°23′E |
| Back, r., Can. | 92 | 65°30′N | 104°15′W |
| Bačka Palanka, Serb. (bäch′kä pälän-kä) | 175 | 45°14′N | 19°24′E |
| Bačka Topola, Serb. (bäch′kä tô′pô-lä′) | 175 | 45°48′N | 19°38′E |
| Back Bay, India (băk) | 203b | 18°55′N | 72°45′E |
| Backstairs Passage, strt., Austl. (băk-stârs′) | 220 | 35°50′S | 138°15′E |
| Bac Lieu, Viet. | 212 | 9°45′N | 105°50′E |
| Bac Ninh, Viet. (bäk′nēn′′) | 209 | 21°10′N | 106°02′E |
| Baco, Mount, mtn., Phil. (bä′kô) | 213a | 12°50′N | 121°11′E |
| Bacoli, Italy (bä-kō-lē′) | 173c | 40°33′N | 14°05′E |
| Bacolod, Phil. (bä-kō′lôd) | 213 | 10°42′N | 123°03′E |
| Bácsalmás, Hung. (bäch′ôl-mäs) | 169 | 46°07′N | 19°18′E |
| Bacup, Eng., U.K. (băk′ŭp) | 158a | 53°42′N | 2°12′W |
| Bad, r., S.D., U.S. (băd) | 112 | 44°04′N | 100°58′W |
| Badajoz, Spain (bȧ-dhä-hōth′) | 162 | 38°52′N | 6°56′W |
| Badalona, Spain (bä-dhä-lō′nä) | 173 | 41°27′N | 2°15′E |
| Badanah, Sau. Ar. | 198 | 30°49′N | 40°45′E |
| Bad Axe, Mi., U.S. (băd′ ăks) | 108 | 43°50′N | 82°55′W |
| Bad Bramstedt, Ger. (bät bräm′shtĕt) | 159c | 53°55′N | 9°53′E |
| Baden, Aus. (bä′dĕn) | 168 | 48°00′N | 16°14′E |
| Baden, Switz. | 168 | 47°28′N | 8°17′E |
| Baden-Baden, Ger. (bä′dĕn-bä′dĕn) | 161 | 48°46′N | 8°11′E |
| Bad Freienwalde, Ger. (bät frī′ĕn-väl′dĕ) | 168 | 52°47′N | 14°00′E |
| Bad Hersfeld, Ger. (bät hĕrsh′fĕlt) | 168 | 50°53′N | 9°43′E |
| Badīn, Pak. | 202 | 24°47′N | 69°51′E |
| Bad Ischl, Aus. (bät ĭsh′′l) | 168 | 47°46′N | 13°37′E |
| Bad Kissingen, Ger. (bät kĭs′ĭng-ĕn) | 168 | 50°12′N | 10°05′E |
| Bad Kreuznach, Ger. (bät kroits′näk) | 168 | 49°52′N | 7°53′E |
| Badlands, reg., N.D., U.S. (băd′ lănds) | 112 | 46°43′N | 103°22′W |
| Badlands, reg., S.D., U.S. | 112 | 43°43′N | 102°36′W |
| Badlands National Park, rec., S.D., U.S. | 112 | 43°56′N | 102°37′W |
| Badlāpur, India | 203b | 19°12′N | 73°12′E |
| Badogo, Mali | 234 | 11°02′N | 8°13′W |
| Bad Oldesloe, Ger. (bät ôl′dĕs-lōē) | 168 | 53°48′N | 10°21′E |
| Bad Reichenhall, Ger. (bät rī′kĕn-häl) | 168 | 47°43′N | 12°53′E |
| Bad River Indian Reservation, I.R., Wi., U.S. (băd) | 113 | 46°41′N | 90°36′W |
| Bad Segeberg, Ger. (bät sĕ′gĕ-bōōrgh) | 159c | 53°56′N | 10°18′E |
| Bad Tölz, Ger. (bät tûltz) | 168 | 47°46′N | 11°35′E |
| Badulla, Sri L. | 203 | 6°55′N | 81°07′E |
| Bad Vöslau, Aus. | 159e | 47°58′N | 16°13′E |
| Badwater Creek, r., Wy., U.S. (băd′wô-tēr) | 115 | 43°13′N | 107°55′W |
| Baena, Spain (bä-ā′nä) | 162 | 37°38′N | 4°20′W |
| Baependi, Braz. (bä-å-pĕn′dĭ) | 141a | 21°57′S | 44°51′W |
| Baffin Bay, b., N.A. (băf′ĭn) | 89 | 72°00′N | 65°00′W |
| Baffin Bay, b., Tx., U.S. | 123 | 27°11′N | 97°35′W |
| Baffin Island, i., Can. | 89 | 67°20′N | 71°00′W |
| Bāfq, Iran (bäfk) | 198 | 31°48′N | 55°23′E |
| Bafra, Tur. (bäf′rä) | 163 | 41°30′N | 35°50′E |
| Bagabag, Phil. (bä-gä-bäg′) | 213a | 16°38′N | 121°16′E |
| Bāgalkot, India | 203 | 16°14′N | 75°40′E |
| Bagamoyo, Tan. (bä-gä-mō′yō) | 233 | 6°26′S | 38°54′E |
| Bagaryak, Russia (bȧ-gȧr-yäk′) | 186a | 56°13′N | 61°32′E |
| Bagbele, D.R.C. | 237 | 4°21′N | 29°17′E |
| Bagdad see Baghdād, Iraq | 198 | 33°14′N | 44°22′E |
| Baghdād, Iraq (bȧgh-dȧd′) (băg′dăd) | 198 | 33°14′N | 44°22′E |
| Bagheria, Italy (bä-gå-rē′ä) | 174 | 38°03′N | 13°32′E |
| Bagley, Mn., U.S. (băg′lē) | 112 | 47°31′N | 95°24′W |
| Bagnara, Italy (bän-yä′rä) | 174 | 38°17′N | 15°52′E |
| Bagnell Dam, Mo., U.S. (băg′nĕl) | 121 | 38°13′N | 92°40′W |
| Bagnères-de-Bigorre, Fr. (bän-yâr′dĕ-bē-gor′) | 170 | 43°04′N | 0°09′E |
| Bagnères-de-Luchon, Fr. (bän-yâr′ dĕ-lu chôn′) | 170 | 42°46′N | 0°36′E |
| Bagnols-sur-Ceze, Fr. (bä-nyôl′) | 170 | 44°09′N | 4°37′E |
| Bago, Mya. | 212 | 17°17′N | 96°29′E |
| Bagoé, r., Mali (bȧ-gō′å) | 230 | 12°22′N | 6°34′W |
| Baguio, Phil. (bä-gē-ō′) | 212 | 16°24′N | 120°36′E |
| Bagzane, Monts, mtn., Niger | 230 | 18°40′N | 8°40′E |
| Bahamas, nation, N.A. (bȧ-hä′mȧs) | 129 | 26°15′N | 76°00′W |
| Bahau, Malay. | 197b | 2°48′N | 102°25′E |
| Bahāwalpur, Pak. (bŭ-hä′wŭl-pōōr) | 199 | 29°29′N | 71°41′E |
| Bahia, state, Braz. | 143 | 11°05′S | 43°00′W |
| Bahía, Islas de la, i., Hond. (ē′s-läs-dĕ-lä-bä-ē′ä) | 128 | 16°15′N | 86°30′W |
| Bahia Blanca, Arg. (bä-ē′ä bläŋ′kä) | 144 | 38°45′S | 62°07′W |
| Bahía de Caráquez, Ec. (bä-ē′ä dā kä-rä′kĕz) | 142 | 0°45′S | 80°29′W |
| Bahía Negra, Para. (bä-ē′ä nā′grä) | 143 | 20°11′S | 58°05′W |
| Bahi Swamp, sw., Tan. | 237 | 6°05′S | 35°10′E |
| Bahoruco, Sierra de, mts., Dom. Rep. (sē-ĕ′r-rä-dĕ-bä-ō-rōō′kô) | 135 | 18°10′N | 71°25′W |
| Bahrain, nation, Asia (bä-rān′) | 198 | 26°15′N | 51°17′E |
| Baḥr al Ghazāl, hist. reg., Sudan (bär ĕl ghä-zäl′) | 231 | 7°56′N | 27°15′E |
| Baḥrīyah, oasis, Egypt (bȧ-hȧ-rē′yä) | 163 | 28°34′N | 29°01′E |
| Baía dos Tigres, Ang. | 236 | 16°36′S | 11°43′E |
| Baia Mare, Rom. (bä′yä mä′rä) | 163 | 47°40′N | 23°35′E |

| PLACE (Pronunciation) | PAGE | LAT. | LONG. |
|---|---|---|---|
| Baidyabāti, India | 202a | 22°47′N | 88°21′E |
| Baie-Comeau, Can. | 100 | 49°13′N | 68°10′W |
| Baie de Wasai, Mi., U.S. (bā dē wä-sä′ē) | 117k | 46°27′N | 84°15′W |
| Baie-Saint Paul, Can. (bā′sånt-pôl′) | 91 | 47°27′N | 70°30′W |
| Baigou, China (bī-gō) | 206 | 39°08′N | 116°02′E |
| Baihe, China (bī-hŭ) | 208 | 32°30′N | 110°15′E |
| Bai Hu, l., China (bī-hōō) | 206 | 31°22′N | 117°38′E |
| Baiju, China (bī-jyōō) | 206 | 33°04′N | 120°17′E |
| Baikal, Lake see Baykal, Ozero, l., Russia | 179 | 53°00′N | 109°28′E |
| Bailén, Spain (bä-ē-lān′) | 172 | 38°05′N | 3°48′W |
| Băileşti, Rom. (bȧ-ī-lĕsh′tē) | 175 | 44°01′N | 23°21′E |
| Bainbridge, Ga., U.S. (bān′brĭj) | 124 | 30°52′N | 84°35′W |
| Bainbridge Island, i., Wa., U.S. | 116a | 47°39′N | 122°32′W |
| Baipu, China (bī-pōō) | 206 | 32°15′N | 120°47′E |
| Baiquan, China (bī-chyuän) | 208 | 47°22′N | 126°00′E |
| Baird, Tx., U.S. (bârd) | 122 | 32°22′N | 99°28′W |
| Bairdford, Pa., U.S. (bârd′fōrd) | 111e | 40°37′N | 79°53′W |
| Baird Mountains, mts., Ak., U.S. | 103 | 67°35′N | 160°10′W |
| Bairnsdale, Austl. (bârnz′dāl) | 219 | 37°50′S | 147°39′E |
| Baïse, r., Fr. (bä-ēz′) | 170 | 43°52′N | 0°23′E |
| Baiyang Dian, l., China (bī-yäŋ-dĭĕn) | 206 | 39°00′N | 115°45′E |
| Baiyu Shan, mts., China (bī-yōō shän) | 208 | 37°02′N | 108°30′E |
| Baja, Hung. (bŏ′yŏ) | 169 | 46°11′N | 18°55′E |
| Baja California, state, Mex. (bä-hä) | 128 | 30°15′N | 117°25′W |
| Baja California, pen., Mex. | 89 | 28°00′N | 113°30′W |
| Baja California Sur, state, Mex. | 128 | 26°00′N | 113°30′W |
| Bajo, Canal, can., Spain | 173a | 40°36′N | 3°41′W |
| Bakal, Russia (bä′kȧl) | 186a | 54°57′N | 58°50′E |
| Baker, Mt., U.S. (bā′kēr) | 115 | 46°21′N | 104°12′W |
| Baker, Or., U.S. | 104 | 44°46′N | 117°52′W |
| Baker, i., Oc. | 2 | 1°00′N | 176°00′W |
| Baker, l., Can. | 92 | 63°51′N | 96°10′W |
| Baker, Mount, mtn., Wa., U.S. | 106 | 48°46′N | 121°52′W |
| Baker Creek, r., Il., U.S. | 111a | 41°13′N | 87°47′W |
| Bakersfield, Ca., U.S. (bā′kērz-fēld) | 104 | 35°23′N | 119°00′W |
| Bakerstown, Pa., U.S. (bā′kerz-toun) | 111e | 40°39′N | 79°56′W |
| Bakewell, Eng., U.K. (băk′wĕl) | 158a | 53°12′N | 1°40′W |
| Bakhchysarai, Ukr. | 177 | 44°46′N | 33°54′E |
| Bakhmach, Ukr. (bȧk-mäch′) | 177 | 51°09′N | 32°47′E |
| Bakhtarān, Iran | 198 | 34°01′N | 47°00′E |
| Bakhtegan, Daryācheh-ye, l., Iran | 198 | 29°29′N | 54°31′E |
| Bakhteyevo, Russia | 186b | 55°35′N | 38°32′E |
| Bako, Eth. (bä′kō) | 231 | 5°47′N | 36°39′E |
| Bakony, mts., Hung. (bȧ-kōn′y′) | 169 | 46°57′N | 17°30′E |
| Bakoye, r., Afr. (bȧ-kô′ē) | 230 | 12°47′N | 9°35′W |
| Bakr Uzyak, Russia (bákr ōōz′yák) | 186a | 52°59′N | 58°43′E |
| Baku (Bakı), Azer. (bȧ-kōō′) | 178 | 40°28′N | 49°45′E |
| Bakwanga see Mbuji-Mayi, D.R.C. | 236 | 6°09′S | 23°28′E |
| Balabac Island, i., Phil. (bä′lä-bäk) | 212 | 8°00′N | 116°28′E |
| Balabac Strait, strt., Asia | 212 | 7°23′N | 116°30′E |
| Ba′labakk, Leb. | 197a | 34°00′N | 36°13′E |
| Balabanovo, Russia (bȧ-lȧ-bä′nô-vô) | 186b | 56°10′N | 37°44′E |
| Balagansk, Russia (bä-lä-gänsk′) | 184 | 53°58′N | 103°09′E |
| Balaguer, Spain (bä-lä-gĕr′) | 173 | 41°48′N | 0°50′E |
| Balakhta, Russia (bȧ′lȧk-tȧ′) | 179 | 55°22′N | 91°43′E |
| Balakliia, Ukr. | 177 | 49°28′N | 36°51′E |
| Balakovo, Russia (bȧ′lȧ-kô′vô) | 181 | 52°00′N | 47°40′E |
| Balancán, Mex. (bä-läŋ-kän′) | 131 | 17°47′N | 91°32′W |
| Balanga, Phil. (bä-läŋ′gä) | 213a | 14°41′N | 120°31′E |
| Ba Lang An, Mui, c., Viet. | 209 | 15°18′N | 109°10′E |
| Balashikha, Russia (bȧ-lä′shĭ-kȧ) | 186b | 55°48′N | 37°58′E |
| Balashov, Russia (bȧ′lȧ-shôf) | 181 | 51°30′N | 43°00′E |
| Balasore, India (bä-lȧ-sōr′) | 199 | 21°38′N | 86°59′E |
| Balassagyarmat, Hung. (bô′lôsh-shô-dyôr′môt) | 169 | 48°04′N | 19°19′E |
| Balaton Lake, l., Hung. (bô′lô-tôn) | 163 | 46°47′N | 17°55′E |
| Balayan, Phil. (bä-lä-yän′) | 213a | 13°56′N | 120°44′E |
| Balayan Bay, b., Phil. | 213a | 13°46′N | 120°46′E |
| Balboa Heights, Pan. (bäl-bō′ä) | 133 | 8°59′N | 79°33′W |
| Balboa Mountain, mtn., Pan. | 128a | 9°05′N | 79°44′W |
| Balcarce, Arg. (bäl-kär′sā) | 144 | 37°49′S | 58°17′W |
| Balchik, Blg. | 175 | 43°24′N | 28°13′E |
| Bald Eagle, Mn., U.S. (bôld ē′g′l) | 117g | 45°06′N | 93°01′W |
| Bald Eagle Lake, l., Mn., U.S. | 117g | 45°08′N | 93°03′W |
| Baldock Lake, l., Can. | 97 | 56°33′N | 97°57′W |
| Baldwin Park, Ca., U.S. (bôld′wĭn) | 117a | 34°05′N | 117°58′W |
| Baldwinsville, N.Y., U.S. (bôld′wĭns-vĭl) | 109 | 43°10′N | 76°20′W |
| Baldy Mountain, mtn., Can. | 97 | 51°28′N | 100°44′W |
| Baldy Peak, mtn., Az., U.S. (bôl′dē) | 106 | 33°55′N | 109°35′W |
| Baldy Peak, mtn., Tx., U.S. (bôl′dē pĕk) | 122 | 30°38′N | 104°11′W |
| Balearic Islands see Balears, Illes, is., Spain | 156 | 39°25′N | 1°28′E |
| Balearic Sea, sea, Spain (băl-ē-ăr′ĭk) | 173 | 39°40′N | 1°05′E |
| Balears, Illes, is., Spain | 156 | 39°25′N | 1°28′E |
| Baleine, Grande Rivière de la, r., Can. | 93 | 55°00′N | 75°30′W |
| Baler, Phil. (bä-lar′) | 213a | 15°46′N | 121°33′E |
| Baler Bay, b., Phil. | 213a | 15°51′N | 121°40′E |
| Balesin, i., Phil. | 213a | 14°28′N | 122°10′E |
| Baley, Russia (bȧl-yä′) | 185 | 51°29′N | 116°12′E |
| Balfate, Hond. (bäl-fä′tē) | 132 | 15°48′N | 86°24′W |
| Balfour, S. Afr. (băl′fŏr) | 238c | 26°41′S | 28°37′E |
| Bali, i., Indon. (bä′lē) | 212 | 8°00′S | 115°22′E |
| Balıkeşir, Tur. (balĭk′ĭysĭr) | 181 | 39°40′N | 27°50′E |
| Balikpapan, Indon. (bä′lēk-pä′pän) | 212 | 1°13′S | 116°52′E |
| Balintang Channel, strt., Phil. (bä-lĭn-täng′) | 212 | 19°50′N | 121°08′E |
| Balkan Mountains see Stara Planina, mts., Blg. | 156 | 42°50′N | 24°45′E |
| Balkh, Afg. (bälk) | 199 | 36°48′N | 66°50′E |
| Balkhash, Lake see Balqash köli, l., Kaz. | 183 | 45°58′N | 72°15′E |

| PLACE (Pronunciation) | PAGE | LAT. | LONG. |
|---|---|---|---|
| Ballancourt, Fr. (bä-äN-kôr′) | 171b | 48°31′N | 2°23′E |
| Ballarat, Austl. (băl′ȧ-răt) | 219 | 37°37′S | 144°00′E |
| Ballard, l., Austl. (băl′ȧrd) | 220 | 29°15′S | 120°45′E |
| Ballater, Scot., U.K. (băl′ȧ-tēr) | 164 | 57°05′N | 3°06′W |
| Balleny Islands, is., Ant. (băl′ĕ nē) | 224 | 67°00′S | 164°00′E |
| Ballina, Austl. (băl-ĭ-nä′) | 222 | 28°50′S | 153°35′E |
| Ballina, Ire. | 164 | 54°06′N | 9°05′W |
| Ballinasloe, Ire. (băl′ĭ-nȧ-slō′) | 164 | 53°20′N | 8°09′W |
| Ballinger, Tx., U.S. (băl′ĭn-jēr) | 122 | 31°45′N | 99°58′W |
| Ballston Spa, N.Y., U.S. (bôls′tŭn spä′) | 109 | 43°05′N | 73°50′W |
| Balmazújváros, Hung. (bŏl′mŏz-ōō′y′vä′rôsh) | 169 | 47°35′N | 21°23′E |
| Balobe, D.R.C. | 237 | 0°05′N | 28°00′E |
| Balonne, r., Austl. (băl-ōn′) | 221 | 27°00′S | 149°10′E |
| Bālotra, India | 202 | 25°56′N | 72°12′E |
| Balqash, Kaz. | 183 | 46°58′N | 75°00′E |
| Balqash köli, l., Kaz. | 183 | 45°58′N | 72°15′E |
| Balranald, Austl. (băl′-rȧn-ăld) | 222 | 34°42′S | 143°30′E |
| Balsam, l., Can. (bôl′sȧm) | 99 | 44°30′N | 78°50′W |
| Balsas, Braz. (bäl′säs) | 143 | 7°09′S | 46°04′W |
| Balsas, r., Mex. | 128 | 18°00′N | 101°00′W |
| Balta, Ukr. (bäl′tȧ) | 181 | 47°57′N | 29°38′E |
| Bălți, Mol. | 181 | 47°47′N | 27°57′E |
| Baltic Sea, sea, Eur. (bôl′tĭk) | 156 | 55°20′N | 16°50′E |
| Baltīm, Egypt (bål-tēm′) | 238b | 31°33′N | 31°04′E |
| Baltimore, Md., U.S. (bôl′tĭ-môr) | 105 | 39°20′N | 76°38′W |
| Baltiysk, Russia (bäl-tēysk′) | 167 | 54°40′N | 19°55′E |
| Baluarte, Río del, Mex. (rē′ō-dĕl-bä-lōō′r-tĕ) | 130 | 23°09′N | 105°42′W |
| Baluchistān, hist. reg., Asia (bȧ-lò-chĭ-stän′) | 199 | 27°30′N | 65°30′E |
| Balzac, Can. (bôl′zăk) | 102e | 51°10′N | 114°01′W |
| Bama, Nig. | 235 | 11°30′N | 13°41′E |
| Bamako, Mali (bä-mä-kō′) | 230 | 12°39′N | 8°00′W |
| Bambang, Phil. (bäm-bäng′) | 213a | 16°24′N | 121°08′E |
| Bambari, C.A.R. (bäm-bȧ-rē) | 231 | 5°44′N | 20°40′E |
| Bamberg, Ger. (bäm′bĕrgh) | 161 | 49°53′N | 10°52′E |
| Bamberg, S.C., U.S. (băm′bûrg) | 125 | 33°17′N | 81°04′W |
| Bamenda, Cam. | 235 | 5°56′N | 10°10′E |
| Bamingui, r., C.A.R. | 235 | 7°35′N | 19°45′E |
| Bampton, Eng., U.K. (băm′tŭn) | 158b | 51°42′N | 1°33′W |
| Bampūr, Iran (bŭm-pōōr′) | 198 | 27°15′N | 60°22′E |
| Bam Yanga, Ngao, mts., Cam. | 235 | 8°20′N | 14°40′E |
| Banahao, Mount, mtn., Phil. (bä-nä-hä′ô) | 213a | 14°04′N | 121°45′E |
| Banalia, D.R.C. | 237 | 1°33′N | 25°20′E |
| Banamba, Mali | 234 | 13°33′N | 7°27′W |
| Bananal, Braz. (bä-nä-näl′) | 141a | 22°42′S | 44°17′W |
| Bananal, Ilha do, i., Braz. (ē′lä-dô-bä-nä-näl′) | 143 | 12°09′S | 50°27′W |
| Banās, r., India (băn-äs′) | 199 | 25°20′N | 75°20′E |
| Banās, Ra's, c., Egypt | 231 | 23°48′N | 36°39′E |
| Banat, reg., Rom. (bä-nät′) | 175 | 45°35′N | 21°05′E |
| Bancroft, Can. (băn′krŏft) | 91 | 45°05′N | 77°55′W |
| Bancroft see Chililabombwe, Zam. | 237 | 12°18′S | 27°43′E |
| Bānda, India (bän′dä) | 199 | 25°36′N | 80°21′E |
| Banda, Kepulauan, is., Indon. | 213 | 4°40′S | 129°56′E |
| Banda, Laut (Banda Sea), sea, Indon. | 213 | 6°05′S | 127°28′E |
| Banda Aceh, Indon. | 212 | 5°10′N | 95°10′E |
| Banda Banda, Mount, mtn., Austl. (băn′dȧ băn′dȧ) | 222 | 31°09′S | 152°15′E |
| Bandama Blanc, r., C. Iv. (bän-dä′mä) | 234 | 6°15′N | 5°00′W |
| Bandar Beheshtī, Iran | 198 | 25°18′N | 60°45′E |
| Bandar-e ′Abbās, Iran (bän-där′ ȧb-bäs′) | 198 | 27°04′N | 56°22′E |
| Bandar-e Būshehr, Iran | 198 | 28°48′N | 50°53′E |
| Bandar-e Lengeh, Iran | 198 | 26°44′N | 54°47′E |
| Bandar-e Torkeman, Iran | 198 | 37°05′N | 54°08′E |
| Bandar Lampung, Indon. | 212 | 5°16′S | 105°06′E |
| Bandar Maharani, Malay. (bän-där′ mä-hä-rä′nē) | 197b | 2°02′N | 102°34′E |
| Bandar Seri Begawan, Bru. | 212 | 5°00′N | 114°59′E |
| Bande, Spain | 172 | 42°02′N | 7°58′W |
| Bandeira, Pico da, mtn., Braz. (pē′kō dä bän dā′rä) | 143 | 20°27′S | 41°47′W |
| Bandelier National Monument, rec., N.M., U.S. (băn-dĕ-lēr′) | 119 | 35°50′N | 106°45′W |
| Banderas, Bahía de, b., Mex. (bä-ē′ä dĕ bän-dĕ′räs) | 130 | 20°38′N | 105°35′W |
| Bandirma, Tur. (bän-dĭr′mȧ) | 163 | 40°25′N | 27°50′E |
| Bandon, Or., U.S. (băn′dŭn) | 114 | 43°06′N | 124°25′W |
| Bāndra, India | 203b | 19°04′N | 72°49′E |
| Bandundu, D.R.C. | 232 | 3°18′S | 17°20′E |
| Bandung, Indon. | 212 | 7°00′S | 107°22′E |
| Banes, Cuba (bä′näs) | 135 | 21°00′N | 75°45′W |
| Banff, Can. (bănf) | 90 | 51°10′N | 115°34′W |
| Banff, Scot., U.K. | 164 | 57°39′N | 2°37′W |
| Banff National Park, rec., Can. | 92 | 51°38′N | 116°22′W |
| Bánfield, Arg. (bá′n-fyĕ′ld) | 144a | 34°44′S | 58°24′W |
| Banfora, Burkina | 234 | 10°38′N | 4°46′W |
| Bangalore, India (băŋ′gȧ′lôr) | 199 | 13°03′N | 77°39′E |
| Bangassou, C.A.R. (bäN-gȧ-sōō′) | 231 | 4°47′N | 22°49′E |
| Bangeta, Mount, mtn., Pap. N. Gui. | 213 | 6°20′S | 147°00′E |
| Banggai, Kepulauan, is., Indon. (bäng-gī′) | 213 | 1°05′S | 123°45′E |
| Banggi, Pulau, i., Malay. | 212 | 7°12′N | 117°10′E |
| Banghāzī, Libya | 231 | 32°07′N | 20°04′E |
| Bangka, i., Indon. (bäŋ′kȧ) | 212 | 2°24′S | 106°55′E |
| Bangkalan, Indon. (bäng-kȧ-län′) | 212 | 6°07′S | 112°50′E |
| Bangkok, Thai. | 212 | 13°50′N | 100°29′E |
| Bangladesh, nation, Asia | 199 | 24°15′N | 90°00′E |
| Bangong Co, l., Asia (bäŋ-gôŋ tswo) | 202 | 33°40′N | 79°30′E |
| Bangor, Wales, U.K. (băŋ′ōr) | 164 | 53°13′N | 4°05′W |
| Bangor, Me., U.S. (băn′gēr) | 105 | 44°47′N | 68°47′W |

270 Bangor – Bayard PRONOUNCING INDEX


| PLACE (Pronunciation) | PAGE | LAT. | LONG. |
|---|---|---|---|
| Bangor, Mi., U.S. | 108 | 42°20'N | 86°05'W |
| Bangor, Pa., U.S. | 109 | 40°55'N | 75°10'W |
| Bangs, Mount, mtn., Az., U.S. (băngs) | 119 | 36°45'N | 113°50'W |
| Bangued, Phil. (bän-gād′) | 213a | 17°36'N | 120°38'E |
| Bangui, C.A.R. (bäɴ-gē′) | 231 | 4°22'N | 18°35'E |
| Bangweulu, Lake, l., Zam. (băng-wė-o͞o′lo͞o) | 232 | 10°55'S | 30°10'E |
| Bangweulu Swamp, sw., Zam. | 237 | 11°25'S | 30°10'E |
| Bani, Dom. Rep. (bä′-nė) | 135 | 18°15'N | 70°25'W |
| Bani, Phil. (bä′nē) | 213a | 16°11'N | 119°51'E |
| Bani, r., Mali | 230 | 13°00'N | 5°30'W |
| Bánica, Dom. Rep. (bä′-nē-kä) | 135 | 19°00'N | 71°35'W |
| Banī Mazār, Egypt | 200 | 28°29'N | 30°48'E |
| Banister, r., Va., U.S. (băn′ĭs-tẽr) | 125 | 36°45'N | 79°17'W |
| Banī Suwayf, Egypt | 231 | 29°05'N | 31°06'E |
| Banja Luka, Bos. (bän-yä-lo͞o′kȧ) | 163 | 44°45'N | 17°11'E |
| Banjarmasin, Indon. (bän-jẽr-mä′sėn) | 212 | 3°18'S | 114°32'E |
| Banjin, China (bän-jyĭn) | 206 | 32°23'N | 120°14'E |
| Banjul, Gam. | 230 | 13°28'N | 16°39'W |
| Bankberg, mts., S. Afr. (bȧŋk′bûrg) | 233c | 32°18'S | 25°15'E |
| Banks, Or., U.S. (bănks) | 116c | 45°37'N | 123°07'W |
| Banks, i., Austl. | 221 | 10°10'S | 143°08'E |
| Banks, Cape, c., Austl. | 217b | 34°01'S | 151°17'E |
| Banks Island, i., Can. | 89 | 73°00'N | 123°00'W |
| Banks Island, i., Can. | 94 | 53°25'N | 130°10'W |
| Banks Islands, is., Vanuatu | 221 | 13°38'S | 168°23'E |
| Banks Peninsula, pen., N.Z. | 223 | 43°45'S | 172°20'E |
| Banks Strait, strt., Austl. | 222 | 40°45'S | 148°00'E |
| Bankstown, Austl. | 217b | 33°55'S | 151°02'E |
| Bann, r., N. Ire., U.K. (băn) | 164 | 54°50'N | 6°29'W |
| Banning, Ca., U.S. (băn′ĭng) | 117a | 33°56'N | 116°53'W |
| Bannockburn, Austl. | 217a | 38°03'S | 144°11'E |
| Bannu, Pak. | 202 | 33°03'N | 70°39'E |
| Baños, Ec. (bä′-nyỏs) | 142 | 1°30'S | 78°22'W |
| Banská Bystrica, Slvk. (bän′skä bė′strė-tzä) | 161 | 48°46'N | 19°10'E |
| Bansko, Blg. (bän′skō) | 175 | 41°51'N | 23°33'E |
| Banstead, Eng., U.K. (băn′stĕd) | 158b | 51°18'N | 0°09'W |
| Banton, i., Phil. (bän-tōn′) | 213a | 12°54'N | 121°55'E |
| Bantry, Ire. (băn′trĭ) | 164 | 51°39'N | 9°30'W |
| Bantry Bay, b., Ire. | 164 | 51°25'N | 10°09'W |
| Banyak, Kepulauan, is., Indon. | 212 | 2°08'N | 97°15'E |
| Banyuwangi, Indon. (bän-jȯ-wäŋ′gė) | 212 | 8°15'S | 114°15'E |
| Baocheng, China (bou-chŭŋ) | 208 | 33°15'N | 106°58'E |
| Baodi, China (bou-dē) | 208 | 39°44'N | 117°19'E |
| Baoding, China (bou-dĭŋ) | 205 | 38°52'N | 115°31'E |
| Baoji, China (bou-jyē) | 208 | 34°10'N | 106°58'E |
| Baoshan, China (bou-shän) | 204 | 25°14'N | 99°03'E |
| Baoshan, China | 206 | 31°25'N | 121°29'E |
| Baotou, China (bou-tō) | 205 | 40°28'N | 110°10'E |
| Baoying, China (bou-yĭŋ) | 208 | 33°14'N | 119°20'E |
| Bapsfontein, S. Afr. (băps-fŏn-tān′) | 233b | 26°01'S | 28°26'E |
| Baqueroncito, Col. (bä-kĕ-rỏ′n-sē-tỏ) | 142a | 3°18'N | 74°40'W |
| Baraawe, Som. | 238a | 1°20'N | 44°00'E |
| Barabinsk, Russia (bȧ′rȧ-bĭnsk) | 184 | 55°18'N | 78°00'E |
| Baraboo, Wi., U.S. (bâr′ȧ-bo͞o) | 113 | 43°29'N | 89°44'W |
| Baracoa, Cuba (bä-rä-kō′ä) | 135 | 20°20'N | 74°25'W |
| Baracoa, Cuba | 135a | 23°03'N | 82°34'W |
| Baradères, Baie des, b., Haiti (bä-rä-dâr′) | 135 | 18°35'N | 73°35'W |
| Baradero, Arg. (bä-rä-dĕ′ŏ) | 141c | 33°50'S | 59°30'W |
| Barahona, Dom. Rep. (bä-rä-ô′nä) | 135 | 18°15'N | 71°10'W |
| Barajas de Madrid, Spain (bä-rȧ′häs dā mä-drēdh′) | 173a | 40°28'N | 3°35'W |
| Baranagar, India | 202 | 22°38'N | 88°25'E |
| Baranavichy, Bela. (bä′rä-nỏ-vē′chė) | 180 | 53°08'N | 25°59'E |
| Baranco, Belize (bä-räŋ′kō) | 132 | 16°01'N | 88°55'W |
| Baranof, i., Ak., U.S. (bä-rä′nỏf) | 103 | 56°48'N | 136°08'W |
| Baranpauh, Indon. | 197b | 0°40'N | 103°28'E |
| Barão de Melgaço, Braz. (bä-rouɴ-dĕ-mĕl-gä′sỏ) | 143 | 16°12'S | 55°48'W |
| Bārāsat, India | 202a | 22°42'N | 88°29'E |
| Barataria Bay, b., La., U.S. | 123 | 29°13'N | 89°50'W |
| Baraya, Col. (bä-rȧ′yä) | 142a | 3°10'N | 75°04'W |
| Barbacena, Braz. (bär-bä-sā′nȧ) | 143 | 21°15'S | 43°46'W |
| Barbacoas, Col. (bär-bä-kō′äs) | 142 | 1°39'N | 78°12'W |
| Barbacoas, Ven. (bä-bä-kô′ȧs) | 143b | 9°30'N | 66°58'W |
| Barbados, nation, N.A. (bär-bā′dōz) | 129 | 13°30'N | 59°00'W |
| Barbar, Sudan | 231 | 18°11'N | 34°00'E |
| Barbastro, Spain (bär-bäs′trō) | 173 | 42°05'N | 0°05'E |
| Barbeau, Mi., U.S. (bȧr-bō′) | 117k | 46°17'N | 84°16'W |
| Barberton, S. Afr. | 232 | 25°48'S | 31°04'E |
| Barberton, Oh., U.S. (bär′bẽr-tŭn) | 111d | 41°01'N | 81°37'W |
| Barbezieux, Fr. (bärb′zyû′) | 170 | 45°30'N | 0°11'W |
| Barbosa, Col. (bär-bỏ′-sȧ) | 142a | 6°26'N | 75°19'W |
| Barboursville, W.V., U.S. (bär′bẽrs-vĭl) | 108 | 38°20'N | 82°20'W |
| Barbourville, Ky., U.S. | 124 | 36°52'N | 83°58'W |
| Barbuda, i., Antig. (bär-bo͞o′dȧ) | 129 | 17°45'N | 61°15'W |
| Barcaldine, Austl. (bär′kôl-dīn) | 219 | 23°33'S | 145°17'E |
| Barcarrota, Spain (bär-kär-rō′tä) | 172 | 38°31'N | 6°50'W |
| Barcellona, Italy (bä-chĕl-lō′nä) | 174 | 38°07'N | 15°15'E |
| Barcelona, Spain (bär-thȧ-lō′nä) | 154 | 41°25'N | 2°08'E |
| Barcelona, Ven. (bär-sȧ-lō′nä) | 142 | 10°09'N | 64°41'W |
| Barcelos, Braz. (bär-sĕ′lỏs) | 142 | 1°04'S | 63°00'W |
| Barcelos, Port. (bär-thå′lōs) | 172 | 41°34'N | 8°39'W |
| Bardawīl, Sabkhat al, b., Egypt | 197a | 31°20'N | 33°24'E |
| Bardejov, Czech Rep. (bär′dyĕ-yôf) | 169 | 49°18'N | 21°18'E |
| Bardsey Island, i., Wales, U.K. (bärd′sė) | 164 | 52°45'N | 4°50'W |
| Bardstown, Ky., U.S. (bärds′toun) | 108 | 37°50'N | 85°30'W |
| Bardwell, Ky., U.S. (bärd′wĕl) | 124 | 36°51'N | 88°57'W |
| Bareilly, India | 199 | 28°21'N | 79°25'E |
| Barents Sea, sea, Eur. (bä′rĕnts) | 178 | 72°14'N | 37°28'E |
| Barentu, Erit. (bä-rĕn′to͞o) | 231 | 15°06'N | 37°39'E |
| Barfleur, Pointe de, c., Fr. (bȧr-flûr′) | 170 | 49°43'N | 1°17'W |
| Barguzin, Russia (bär′go͞o-zĭn) | 179 | 53°44'N | 109°28'E |
| Bar Harbor, Me., U.S. (bär här′bẽr) | 100 | 44°22'N | 68°13'W |
| Bari, Italy (bä′rē) | 154 | 41°08'N | 16°53'E |
| Barinas, Ven. (bä-rē′näs) | 142 | 8°36'N | 70°14'W |
| Baring, Cape, c., Can. (bâr′ĭng) | 92 | 70°07'N | 119°48'W |
| Barisan, Pegunungan, mts., Indon. (bä-rė-sän′) | 212 | 2°38'S | 101°45'E |
| Barito, r., Indon. (bä-rē′tō) | 212 | 2°10'S | 114°38'E |
| Barka, r., Afr. | 231 | 16°44'N | 37°34'E |
| Barkley Sound, strt., Can. | 94 | 48°53'N | 125°20'W |
| Barkly East, S. Afr. (bärk′lē ēst) | 233c | 30°58'S | 27°37'E |
| Barkly Tableland, plat., Austl. (bär′klė) | 220 | 18°15'S | 137°05'E |
| Barkol, China (bär-kůl) | 204 | 43°43'N | 92°50'E |
| Bârlad, Rom. | 163 | 46°15'N | 27°43'E |
| Bar-le-Duc, Fr. (băr-lē-dük′) | 171 | 48°47'N | 5°05'E |
| Barlee, l., Austl. (bär-lē′) | 220 | 29°45'S | 119°00'E |
| Barletta, Italy (bär-lĕt′tä) | 163 | 41°19'N | 16°20'E |
| Barmstedt, Ger. (bärm′shtĕt) | 159c | 53°47'N | 9°46'E |
| Barnaul, Russia (bär-nä-ȯl′) | 178 | 53°18'N | 83°23'E |
| Barnesboro, Pa., U.S. (bärnz′bẽr-ỏ) | 109 | 40°45'N | 78°50'W |
| Barnesville, Ga., U.S. (bärnz′vĭl) | 124 | 33°03'N | 84°10'W |
| Barnesville, Mn., U.S. | 112 | 46°38'N | 96°25'W |
| Barnesville, Oh., U.S. | 108 | 39°55'N | 81°10'W |
| Barnet, Vt., U.S. (bär′nĕt) | 109 | 44°20'N | 72°00'W |
| Barnetby le Wold, Eng., U.K. (bär′nĕt-bī) | 158a | 53°34'N | 0°26'W |
| Barnett Harbor, b., Bah. | 134 | 25°40'N | 79°20'W |
| Barnsdall, Ok., U.S. (bärnz′dôl) | 121 | 36°38'N | 96°14'W |
| Barnsley, Eng., U.K. (bärnz′lĭ) | 158a | 53°33'N | 1°29'W |
| Barnsley, co., Eng., U.K. | 158a | 53°33'N | 1°30'W |
| Barnstaple, Eng., U.K. (bärn′stā-p'l) | 164 | 51°06'N | 4°05'W |
| Barnwell, S.C., U.S. (bärn′wĕl) | 125 | 33°14'N | 81°23'W |
| Baro, Nig. (bä′rỏ) | 230 | 8°37'N | 6°25'E |
| Baroda, India (bär-rō′dä) | 199 | 22°21'N | 73°12'E |
| Barotse Plain, pl., Zam. | 236 | 15°50'S | 22°55'E |
| Barqah (Cyrenaica), hist. reg., Libya | 231 | 31°09'N | 21°45'E |
| Barquisimeto, Ven. (bär-kē-sė-mā′tō) | 142 | 10°04'N | 69°16'W |
| Barra, Braz. (bär′rä) | 143 | 11°04'S | 43°11'W |
| Barraba, Austl. | 222 | 30°22'S | 150°36'E |
| Barrackpore, India | 202a | 22°46'N | 88°21'E |
| Barra do Corda, Braz. (bär′rä dȯ cōr-dä) | 143 | 5°33'S | 45°13'W |
| Barra Mansa, Braz. (bär′rä män′sä) | 141a | 22°35'S | 44°09'W |
| Barrancabermeja, Col. (bär-räŋ′kä-bēr-mā′hä) | 142 | 7°06'N | 73°49'W |
| Barranquilla, Col. (bär-rän-kēl′yä) | 142 | 10°57'N | 75°00'W |
| Barras, Braz. (bȧ′r-räs) | 143 | 4°13'S | 42°14'W |
| Barre, Vt., U.S. (băr′ė) | 109 | 44°15'N | 72°30'W |
| Barreiras, Braz. (bär-rā′räs) | 143 | 12°13'S | 44°59'W |
| Barreiro, Port. (bär-rĕ′ė-rȯ) | 162 | 38°39'N | 9°05'W |
| Barren, r., Ky., U.S. | 124 | 37°00'N | 86°20'W |
| Barren, Cape, c., Austl. (băr′ĕn) | 221 | 40°20'S | 149°00'E |
| Barren, Nosy, is., Madag. | 233 | 18°18'S | 43°57'E |
| Barren River Lake, res., Ky., U.S. | 124 | 36°45'N | 86°02'W |
| Barretos, Braz. (bär-rā′tōs) | 143 | 20°40'S | 48°36'W |
| Barrhead, Can. (băr′ĭd) | 90 | 54°08'N | 114°24'W |
| Barrie, Can. (băr′ĭ) | 91 | 44°25'N | 79°45'W |
| Barrington, Can. (bă-rĕng-tŏn) | 102a | 45°07'N | 73°35'W |
| Barrington, Il., U.S. | 111a | 42°09'N | 88°08'W |
| Barrington, R.I., U.S. | 110b | 41°44'N | 71°16'W |
| Barrington Tops, mtn., Austl. | 222 | 32°00'S | 151°25'E |
| Bar River, Can. (băr) | 117k | 46°27'N | 84°02'W |
| Barron, Wi., U.S. (băr′ŭn) | 113 | 45°24'N | 91°51'W |
| Barrow, Ak., U.S. (băr′ō) | 106a | 71°20'N | 156°00'W |
| Barrow, i., Austl. | 220 | 20°50'S | 115°00'E |
| Barrow, r., Ire. (bȧ-rå) | 164 | 52°35'N | 7°05'W |
| Barrow, Point, c., Ak., U.S. | 103 | 71°20'N | 156°00'W |
| Barrow Creek, Austl. | 218 | 21°23'S | 133°55'E |
| Barrow-in-Furness, Eng., U.K. | 160 | 54°10'N | 3°15'W |
| Barstow, Ca., U.S. (bär′stō) | 118 | 34°53'N | 117°03'W |
| Barstow, Md., U.S. | 110e | 38°32'N | 76°37'W |
| Barth, Ger. (bärt) | 168 | 54°20'N | 12°43'E |
| Bartholomew Bayou, r., U.S. (bär-thŏl′ỏ-mū bī-o͞o′) | 121 | 33°53'N | 91°45'W |
| Barthurst, Can. (băr-thŭrst′) | 91 | 47°38'N | 65°40'W |
| Bartica, Guy. (bär′tĭ-kȧ) | 143 | 6°23'N | 58°32'W |
| Bartın, Tur. (bär′tĭn) | 163 | 41°35'N | 32°12'E |
| Bartle Frere, Mount, mtn., Austl. (bärt′'l frēr′) | 221 | 17°30'S | 145°46'E |
| Bartlesville, Ok., U.S. (bär′tlz-vil) | 121 | 36°44'N | 95°58'W |
| Bartlett, Il., U.S. (bärt′lĕt) | 111a | 41°59'N | 88°11'W |
| Bartlett, Tx., U.S. | 123 | 30°48'N | 97°25'W |
| Barton, Vt., U.S. (bär′tŭn) | 109 | 44°45'N | 72°05'W |
| Barton-upon-Humber, Eng., U.K. (bär′tŭn-ŭp′ŏn-hŭm′bẽr) | 158a | 53°41'N | 0°26'W |
| Bartoszyce, Pol. (bär-tỏ-shĭ′tså) | 169 | 54°15'N | 20°50'E |
| Bartow, Fl., U.S. (bär′tō) | 125a | 27°51'N | 81°50'W |
| Barvinkove, Ukr. | 177 | 48°55'N | 36°59'E |
| Barwon, r., Austl. (bär′wŭn) | 221 | 30°00'S | 147°30'E |
| Barwon Heads, Austl. | 217a | 38°17'S | 144°29'E |
| Barycz, r., Pol. (bä′rĭch) | 168 | 51°30'N | 16°38'E |
| Barysaw, Bela. | 180 | 54°16'N | 28°33'E |
| Basankusu, D.R.C. (bä-sän-ko͞o′so͞o) | 231 | 1°14'N | 19°45'E |
| Basbeck, Ger. (bäs′bĕk) | 159c | 53°40'N | 9°11'E |
| Basdahl, Ger. (bäs′däl) | 159c | 53°27'N | 9°00'E |
| Basehor, Ks., U.S. (bās′hôr) | 117f | 39°08'N | 94°55'W |
| Basel, Switz. (bä′z'l) | 161 | 47°32'N | 7°35'E |
| Bashee, r., S. Afr. (bă-shē′) | 233c | 31°47'S | 28°25'E |
| Bashi Channel, strt., Asia (bäsh′ė) | 205 | 21°20'N | 120°22'E |
| Bashkortostan, prov., Russia | 180 | 54°12'N | 57°15'E |
| Bashtanka, Ukr. (bȧsh-tän′kȧ) | 177 | 47°32'N | 32°31'E |
| Basilan Island, i., Phil. | 212 | 6°37'N | 122°07'E |
| Basildon, Eng., U.K. | 165 | 51°35'N | 0°25'E |
| Basilicata, hist. reg., Italy (bä-zē-lė-kä′tä) | 174 | 40°30'N | 15°55'E |
| Basin, Wy., U.S. (bā′sĭn) | 115 | 44°22'N | 108°02'W |
| Basingstoke, Eng., U.K. (bā′zĭng-stōk) | 158b | 51°14'N | 1°06'W |
| Baška, Cro. (bäsh′ka) | 174 | 44°58'N | 14°44'E |
| Baskale, Tur. (bäsh-kä′lĕ) | 181 | 38°10'N | 44°00'E |
| Baskatong, Réservoir, res., Can. | 99 | 46°50'N | 75°50'W |
| Baskunchak, l., Russia | 181 | 48°20'N | 46°40'E |
| Basoko, D.R.C. (bȧ-sō′kō) | 231 | 0°52'N | 23°50'E |
| Basque Provinces, hist. reg., Spain | 172 | 43°00'N | 2°46'W |
| Basra *see* Al Başrah, Iraq | 198 | 30°35'N | 47°59'E |
| Bassano, Can. (bäs-sän′ō) | 90 | 50°47'N | 112°28'W |
| Bassano del Grappa, Italy | 174 | 45°46'N | 11°44'E |
| Bassari, Togo | 234 | 9°15'N | 0°47'E |
| Bassas da India, i., Reu. (bäs′säs dä ēn′dė-ȧ) | 233 | 21°23'S | 39°42'E |
| Basse Terre, Guad. (bȧs′ târ′) | 129 | 16°00'N | 61°43'W |
| Basseterre, St. K./N. | 133b | 17°20'N | 62°42'W |
| Basse Terre, i., Guad. | 133b | 16°10'N | 62°14'W |
| Bassett, Va., U.S. (băs′sĕt) | 125 | 36°45'N | 81°58'W |
| Bass Islands, is., Oh., U.S. (băs) | 108 | 41°40'N | 82°50'W |
| Bass Strait, strt., Austl. | 221 | 39°40'S | 145°40'E |
| Basswood, l., N.A. (băs′wȯd) | 113 | 48°10'N | 91°36'W |
| Båstad, Swe. (bỏ′stät) | 166 | 56°26'N | 12°46'E |
| Bastia, Fr. (bäs′tē-ä) | 161 | 42°43'N | 9°27'E |
| Bastogne, Bel. (băs-tỏn′y′) | 165 | 50°02'N | 5°45'E |
| Bastrop, La., U.S. (băs′trŭp) | 123 | 32°47'N | 91°55'W |
| Bastrop, Tx., U.S. | 123 | 30°08'N | 97°18'W |
| Bastrop Bayou, Tx., U.S. | 123a | 29°07'N | 95°22'W |
| Bata, Eq. Gui. (bä′tä) | 230 | 1°51'N | 9°45'E |
| Batabano, Golfo de, b., Cuba (gỏl-fô-dĕ-bä-tä-bȧ′nỏ) | 134 | 22°10'N | 83°05'W |
| Batāla, India | 202 | 31°54'N | 75°18'E |
| Batam, i., Indon. (bä-täm′) | 197b | 1°03'N | 104°00'E |
| Batang, China (bä-täŋ) | 204 | 30°08'N | 99°00'E |
| Batangas, Phil. (bä-tän′gäs) | 212 | 13°45'N | 121°04'E |
| Batan Islands, is., Phil. (bä-tän′) | 212 | 20°58'N | 122°20'E |
| Bátaszék, Hung. (bä′tȧ-sĕk) | 169 | 46°07'N | 18°40'E |
| Batavia, Il., U.S. (bȧ-tā′vĭ-ȧ) | 111a | 41°51'N | 88°18'W |
| Batavia, N.Y., U.S. | 109 | 43°00'N | 78°15'W |
| Batavia, Oh., U.S. | 111f | 39°05'N | 84°10'W |
| Bataysk, Russia (bȧ-tīsk′) | 181 | 47°08'N | 39°44'E |
| Bātdâmbâng, Camb. (bȧt-tȧm-bāng′) | 212 | 13°14'N | 103°15'E |
| Batesburg, S.C., U.S. (bāts′bûrg) | 125 | 33°53'N | 81°34'W |
| Batesville, Ar., U.S. (bāts′vĭl) | 121 | 35°46'N | 91°39'W |
| Batesville, In., U.S. | 108 | 39°15'N | 85°15'W |
| Batesville, Ms., U.S. | 124 | 34°17'N | 89°55'W |
| Batetska, Russia (bȧ-tĕ′tskȧ) | 176 | 58°36'N | 30°21'E |
| Bath, Can. (bȧth) | 100 | 46°31'N | 67°36'W |
| Bath, Eng., U.K. | 161 | 51°24'N | 2°20'W |
| Bath, Me., U.S. | 100 | 43°54'N | 69°50'W |
| Bath, N.Y., U.S. | 109 | 42°25'N | 77°20'W |
| Bath, Oh., U.S. | 111d | 41°11'N | 81°38'W |
| Bathsheba, Barb. | 133b | 13°13'N | 60°30'W |
| Bathurst, Austl. (bȧth′ŭrst) | 219 | 33°28'S | 149°30'E |
| Bathurst *see* Banjul, Gam. | 230 | 13°28'N | 16°39'W |
| Bathurst, S. Afr. (băt-hûrst) | 233c | 33°26'S | 26°53'E |
| Bathurst, i., Austl. | 220 | 11°19'S | 130°13'E |
| Bathurst, Cape, c., Can. (bath′-ûrst) | 92 | 70°33'N | 127°55'W |
| Bathurst Inlet, b., Can. | 92 | 68°10'N | 108°00'W |
| Batia, Benin | 234 | 10°54'N | 1°29'E |
| Batley, Eng., U.K. (băt′lĭ) | 158a | 53°43'N | 1°37'W |
| Batna, Alg. (bät′nä) | 230 | 35°41'N | 6°12'E |
| Baton Rouge, La., U.S. (băt′ŭn ro͞ozh′) | 105 | 30°28'N | 91°10'W |
| Batticaloa, Sri L. | 203 | 7°40'N | 81°10'E |
| Battle, r., Can. | 96 | 52°20'N | 111°59'W |
| Battle Creek, Mi., U.S. (băt′'l krēk′) | 105 | 42°20'N | 85°15'W |
| Battle Ground, Wa., U.S. (băt′'l ground) | 116c | 45°47'N | 122°32'W |
| Battle Harbour, Can. (băt′'l här′bẽr) | 91 | 52°17'N | 55°33'W |
| Battle Mountain, Nv., U.S. | 114 | 40°40'N | 116°56'W |
| Battonya, Hung. (bät-tỏ′nyä) | 169 | 46°17'N | 21°00'E |
| Batu, Kepulauan, is., Indon. (bä′to͞o) | 212 | 0°10'S | 98°00'E |
| Batumi, Geor. (bŭ-to͞o′mē) | 178 | 41°40'N | 41°30'E |
| Batu Pahat, Malay. | 212 | 1°51'N | 102°56'E |
| Batupanjang, Indon. | 197b | 1°42'N | 101°35'E |
| Bauang, Phil. (bä′wäng) | 213a | 16°31'N | 120°19'E |
| Bauchi, Nig. (bȧ-o͞o′chė) | 230 | 10°19'N | 9°50'E |
| Bauld, Cape, c., Can. | 93a | 51°38'N | 55°25'W |
| Bāuria, India | 202a | 22°29'N | 88°08'E |
| Bauru, Braz. (bou-ro͞o′) | 143 | 22°21'S | 48°57'W |
| Bauska, Lat. (bou′skȧ) | 167 | 56°24'N | 24°12'E |
| Bauta, Cuba (bȧ′o͞o-tä) | 135a | 22°59'N | 82°33'W |
| Bautzen, Ger. (bout′sĕn) | 161 | 51°11'N | 14°27'E |
| Bavaria *see* Bayern, hist. reg., Ger. | 168 | 49°00'N | 11°16'E |
| Baw Baw, Mount, mtn., Austl. | 222 | 37°50'S | 146°17'E |
| Bawean, Pulau, i., Indon. (bȧ′vē-än) | 212 | 5°50'S | 112°40'E |
| Bawtry, Eng., U.K. (bôtrĭ) | 158a | 53°26'N | 1°01'W |
| Baxley, Ga., U.S. (băks′lĭ) | 125 | 31°47'N | 82°22'W |
| Baxter, Austl. | 217a | 38°12'S | 145°10'E |
| Baxter Springs, Ks., U.S. (băks′tẽr sprĭngs′) | 121 | 37°01'N | 94°44'W |
| Bay, Laguna de, l., Phil. (lă-go͞o′nă dȧ bä′ė) | 213a | 14°24'N | 121°13'E |
| Bayaguana, Dom. Rep. (bä-yä-gwä′nä) | 135 | 18°45'N | 69°40'W |
| Bay al Kabīr, Wadi, val., Libya | 162 | 29°52'N | 14°28'E |
| Bayambang, Phil. (bä-yäm-bäng′) | 213a | 15°50'N | 120°26'E |
| Bayamo, Cuba (bä-yä′mō) | 134 | 20°25'N | 76°35'W |
| Bayamón, P.R. | 129b | 18°27'N | 66°13'W |
| Bayan, China (bä-yän) | 208 | 46°00'N | 127°20'E |
| Bayanaūyl, Kaz. | 183 | 50°43'N | 75°37'E |
| Bayard, Ne., U.S. (bā′ẽrd) | 112 | 41°45'N | 103°20'W |


ăt; finăl; rāte; senåte; ärm; ȧsk; sofȧ; fâre; ch-choose; dh-as th in other; bē; ėvent; bĕt; recĕnt; cratẽr; g-gō; gh-guttural g; bĭt; ĭ-short neutral; rīde; ᴋ-guttural k as ch in German ich;

PRONOUNCING INDEX

Bayard – Bengamisa 271


| PLACE (Pronunciation) | PAGE | LAT. | LONG. |
|---|---|---|---|
| Bayard, N.M., U.S. | 119 | 32°45'N | 108°07'W |
| Bayard, W.V., U.S. | 109 | 39°15'N | 79°20'W |
| Bayburt, Tur. (bä'ĭ-bŏrt) | 181 | 40°15'N | 40°10'E |
| Bay City, Mi., U.S. (bā) | 105 | 43°35'N | 83°55'W |
| Bay City, Tx., U.S. | 123 | 28°59'N | 95°58'W |
| Baydaratskaya Guba, b., Russia | 180 | 69°20'N | 66°10'E |
| Bay de Verde, Can. | 101 | 48°05'N | 52°54'W |
| Baydhabo (Baidoa), Som. | 238a | 3°19'N | 44°20'E |
| Baydrag, r., Mong. | 204 | 46°09'N | 98°52'E |
| Bayern, state, Ger. | 159d | 48°05'N | 11°30'E |
| Bayern (Bavaria), hist. reg., Ger. (bī'ērn) (bå-vâ-rĭ-å) | 168 | 49°00'N | 11°16'E |
| Bayeux, Fr. (bå-yû') | 161 | 49°19'N | 0°41'W |
| Bayfield, Wi., U.S. (bā'fēld) | 113 | 46°48'N | 90°51'W |
| Baykal, Ozero (Lake Baikal), l., Russia | 179 | 53°00'N | 109°28'E |
| Baykal'skiy Khrebet, mts., Russia | 179 | 53°30'N | 107°30'E |
| Baykit, Russia (bī-kēt') | 179 | 61°43'N | 96°39'E |
| Baymak, Russia (báy'mäk) | 186a | 52°35'N | 58°21'E |
| Bay Mills, Mi., U.S. (bā mĭlls) | 117k | 46°27'N | 84°36'W |
| Bay Mills Indian Reservation, I.R., Mi., U.S. | 113 | 46°19'N | 85°03'W |
| Bay Minette, Al., U.S. (bā'mĭn-ĕt') | 124 | 30°52'N | 87°44'W |
| Bayombong, Phil. (bä-yôm-bŏng') | 213a | 16°28'N | 121°09'E |
| Bayonne, Fr. (bá-yŏn') | 154 | 43°28'N | 1°30'W |
| Bayonne, N.J., U.S. (bā-yōn') | 110a | 40°40'N | 74°07'W |
| Bayou Bodcau Reservoir, res., La., U.S. (bī'yōō bŏd'kō) | 107 | 32°49'N | 93°22'W |
| Bayport, Mn., U.S. (bā'pōrt) | 117g | 45°02'N | 92°46'W |
| Bayqongyr, Kaz. | 183 | 47°46'N | 66°11'E |
| Bayramiç, Tur. | 175 | 39°48'N | 26°35'E |
| Bayreuth, Ger. (bī-roit') | 168 | 49°56'N | 11°35'E |
| Bay Roberts, Can. (bā rŏb'ērts) | 101 | 47°36'N | 53°16'W |
| Bays, Lake of, l., Can. (bās) | 99 | 45°15'N | 79°00'W |
| Bay Saint Louis, Ms., U.S. (bā' sânt lōō'ĭs) | 124 | 30°19'N | 89°20'W |
| Bay Shore, N.Y., U.S. (bā' shôr) | 110a | 40°44'N | 73°15'W |
| Bayt Lahm, W.B. (bĕth'lê-hĕm) | 197a | 31°42'N | 35°13'E |
| Baytown, Tx., U.S. (bā'town) | 123a | 29°44'N | 95°01'W |
| Bayview, Al., U.S. (bā'vū) | 110h | 33°34'N | 86°59'W |
| Bayview, Wa., U.S. | 116a | 48°29'N | 122°28'W |
| Bay Village, Oh., U.S. (bā) | 111d | 41°29'N | 81°56'W |
| Baza, Spain (bä'thä) | 162 | 37°29'N | 2°46'W |
| Baza, Sierra de, mts., Spain | 172 | 37°19'N | 2°48'W |
| Bazar-Dyuzi, mtn., Azer. (bä'zär-dyōōz'ĕ) | 181 | 41°20'N | 47°40'E |
| Bazaruto, Ilha do, i., Moz. (bá-zá-rōō'tō) | 232 | 21°42'S | 36°10'E |
| Baziège, Fr. | 170 | 43°25'N | 1°41'E |
| Be, Nosy, i., Madag. | 233 | 13°14'S | 47°28'E |
| Beach, N.D., U.S. (bēch) | 112 | 46°55'N | 104°00'W |
| Beachy Head, c., Eng., U.K. (bēchē hĕd) | 165 | 50°40'N | 0°25'E |
| Beacon, N.Y., U.S. (bē'kŭn) | 109 | 41°30'N | 73°55'W |
| Beaconsfield, Can. (bē'kŭnz-fēld) | 102a | 45°26'N | 73°51'W |
| Beals Creek, r., Tx., U.S. (bēls) | 122 | 32°10'N | 101°14'W |
| Bear, r., Ut., U.S. | 117b | 41°28'N | 112°10'W |
| Bear, r., U.S. | 115 | 42°17'N | 111°42'W |
| Bear Brook, r., Can. | 102c | 45°24'N | 75°15'W |
| Bear Creek, Mt., U.S. (bâr krēk) | 115 | 45°11'N | 109°07'W |
| Bear Creek, r., Al., U.S. (bâr) | 124 | 34°27'N | 88°00'W |
| Bear Creek, r., Tx., U.S. | 117c | 32°56'N | 97°09'W |
| Beardstown, Il., U.S. (bērds'toun) | 121 | 40°01'N | 90°26'W |
| Bearfort Mountain, mtn., N.J., U.S. (bē'fōrt) | 110a | 41°08'N | 74°23'W |
| Bearhead Mountain, mtn., Wa., U.S. (bâr'hĕd) | 116a | 47°01'N | 121°49'W |
| Bear Lake, l., Can. | 97 | 55°08'N | 96°00'W |
| Bear Lake, l., Id., U.S. | 115 | 41°56'N | 111°10'W |
| Bear River Range, mts., U.S. | 115 | 41°50'N | 111°30'W |
| Beas de Segura, Spain (bā'äs dā sä-gōō'rä) | 172 | 38°16'N | 2°53'W |
| Beata, i., Dom. Rep. (bĕ-ä'tä) | 135 | 17°40'N | 71°40'W |
| Beata, Cabo, c., Dom. Rep. (ká'bô-bĕ-ä'tä) | 135 | 17°40'N | 71°20'W |
| Beatrice, Ne., U.S. (bē'ă-trĭs) | 104 | 40°16'N | 96°45'W |
| Beatty, Nv., U.S. (bēt'ê) | 118 | 36°58'N | 116°48'W |
| Beattyville, Ky., U.S. (bēt'ê-vĭl) | 108 | 37°35'N | 83°40'W |
| Beaucaire, Fr. (bō-kâr') | 170 | 43°49'N | 4°37'E |
| Beaucourt, Fr. (bō-kōōr') | 171 | 47°30'N | 6°54'E |
| Beaufort, N.C., U.S. (bō'frt) | 125 | 34°43'N | 76°40'W |
| Beaufort, S.C., U.S. | 125 | 32°25'N | 80°40'W |
| Beaufort Sea, sea, N.A. | 103 | 70°30'N | 138°40'W |
| Beaufort West, S. Afr. | 232 | 32°20'S | 22°45'E |
| Beauharnois, Can. (bō-är-nwä') | 99 | 45°23'N | 73°52'W |
| Beaumont, Can. | 102b | 46°50'N | 71°01'W |
| Beaumont, Can. | 102g | 53°22'N | 113°18'W |
| Beaumont, Ca., U.S. (bō'mŏnt) | 117a | 33°57'N | 116°57'W |
| Beaumont, Tx., U.S. | 105 | 30°05'N | 94°06'W |
| Beaune, Fr. (bōn) | 170 | 47°02'N | 4°49'E |
| Beauport, Can. (bō-pôr') | 102b | 46°52'N | 71°11'W |
| Beauséjour, Can. | 90 | 50°04'N | 96°33'W |
| Beauvais, Fr. (bō-vĕ') | 170 | 49°25'N | 2°05'E |
| Beaver, Ok., U.S. (bē'vēr) | 120 | 36°46'N | 100°31'W |
| Beaver, Pa., U.S. | 111e | 40°42'N | 80°18'W |
| Beaver, Ut., U.S. | 119 | 38°15'N | 112°40'W |
| Beaver, i., Mi., U.S. | 108 | 45°40'N | 85°30'W |
| Beaver, r., Can. | 92 | 54°20'N | 111°10'W |
| Beaver City, Ne., U.S. | 120 | 40°08'N | 99°52'W |
| Beaver Creek, r., Co., U.S. | 120 | 39°42'N | 103°37'W |
| Beaver Creek, r., Ks., U.S. | 120 | 39°44'N | 101°05'W |
| Beaver Creek, r., Mt., U.S. | 112 | 46°45'N | 104°18'W |
| Beaver Creek, r., Wy., U.S. | 112 | 43°46'N | 104°25'W |
| Beaver Dam, Wi., U.S. | 113 | 43°29'N | 88°50'W |
| Beaverhead, r., Mt., U.S. | 115 | 45°25'N | 112°35'W |
| Beaverhead Mountains, mts., Mt., U.S. (bē'vēr-hĕd) | 115 | 44°33'N | 112°59'W |
| Beaver Indian Reservation, I.R., Mi., U.S. | 108 | 45°40'N | 85°30'W |
| Beaverton, Or., U.S. (bē'vēr-tŭn) | 116c | 45°29'N | 122°49'W |
| Bebington, Eng., U.K. (bē'bĭng-tŭn) | 158a | 53°20'N | 2°59'W |
| Bečej, Serb. (bĕ'chā) | 175 | 45°36'N | 20°03'E |
| Béchar, Alg. | 230 | 31°39'N | 2°14'W |
| Becharof, l., Ak., U.S. (bĕk-å-rôf) | 103 | 57°58'N | 156°58'W |
| Becher Bay, b., Can. (bēch'ēr) | 116a | 48°18'N | 123°37'W |
| Beckley, W.V., U.S. (bĕk'lĭ) | 108 | 37°40'N | 81°15'W |
| Bédarieux, Fr. (bā-dá-ryû') | 170 | 43°36'N | 3°11'E |
| Beddington Creek, r., Can. (bĕd'ĕng tŭn) | 102e | 51°14'N | 114°13'W |
| Bedford, Can. (bĕd'fērd) | 99 | 45°10'N | 73°00'W |
| Bedford, S. Afr. | 233c | 32°43'S | 26°19'E |
| Bedford, Eng., U.K. | 161 | 52°10'N | 0°25'W |
| Bedford, Ia., U.S. | 113 | 40°40'N | 94°41'W |
| Bedford, In., U.S. | 108 | 38°50'N | 86°30'W |
| Bedford, Ma., U.S. | 101a | 42°30'N | 71°17'W |
| Bedford, N.Y., U.S. | 110a | 41°12'N | 73°38'W |
| Bedford, Oh., U.S. | 111d | 41°23'N | 81°32'W |
| Bedford, Pa., U.S. | 109 | 40°05'N | 78°20'W |
| Bedford, Va., U.S. | 125 | 37°19'N | 79°27'W |
| Bedford Hills, N.Y., U.S. | 110a | 41°14'N | 73°41'W |
| Beebe, Ar., U.S. (bē'bē) | 121 | 35°04'N | 91°54'W |
| Beecher, Il., U.S. (bē'chûr) | 111a | 41°20'N | 87°38'W |
| Beechey Head, c., Can. (bē'chĭ hĕd) | 116a | 48°19'N | 123°40'W |
| Beech Grove, In., U.S. (bēch grōv) | 111g | 39°43'N | 86°05'W |
| Beecroft Head, c., Austl. (bē'krŭft) | 222 | 35°03'S | 151°15'E |
| Beelitz, Ger. (bĕ'lētz) | 159b | 52°14'N | 12°59'E |
| Be'er Sheva', Isr. (bēr-shē'bá) | 197a | 31°15'N | 34°48'E |
| Be'er Sheva', r., Isr. | 197a | 31°23'N | 34°30'E |
| Beestekraal, S. Afr. | 238c | 25°22'S | 27°34'E |
| Beeston, Eng., U.K. (bēs't'n) | 158a | 52°55'N | 1°11'W |
| Beetz, r., Ger. (bĕtz) | 159b | 52°28'N | 12°37'E |
| Beeville, Tx., U.S. (bē'vĭl) | 123 | 28°24'N | 97°44'W |
| Bega, Austl. (bā'gă) | 219 | 36°50'S | 149°49'E |
| Beggs, Ok., U.S. (bĕgz) | 121 | 35°46'N | 96°06'W |
| Bègles, Fr. (bĕ'gl') | 170 | 44°47'N | 0°34'W |
| Begoro, Ghana | 234 | 6°23'N | 0°23'W |
| Behala, India | 202a | 22°31'N | 88°19'E |
| Behbehān, Iran | 201 | 30°35'N | 50°14'E |
| Behm Canal, can., Ak., U.S. | 94 | 55°41'N | 131°35'W |
| Bei, r., China (bā) | 207a | 22°54'N | 113°08'E |
| Bei'an, China (bā-än) | 208 | 48°05'N | 126°26'E |
| Beicai, China (bā-tsī) | 207b | 31°12'N | 121°33'E |
| Beifei, r., China (bā-fā) | 206 | 33°14'N | 117°03'E |
| Beihai, China (bā-hī) | 204 | 21°30'N | 109°10'E |
| Beihuangcheng Dao, i., China (bā-hûäŋ-chŭŋ dou) | 206 | 38°23'N | 120°55'E |
| Beijing, China | 205 | 39°55'N | 116°23'E |
| Beijing Shi, prov., China (bā-jyĭŋ shr) | 208 | 40°07'N | 116°00'E |
| Beira, Moz. (bā'rá) | 232 | 19°45'S | 34°58'E |
| Beira, hist. reg., Port. (bĕ'y-rä) | 172 | 40°38'N | 8°00'W |
| Beirut, Leb. (bā-rōōt') | 198 | 33°53'N | 35°30'E |
| Beja, Port. (bä'zhä) | 162 | 38°03'N | 7°53'W |
| Béja, Tun. | 162 | 36°52'N | 9°20'E |
| Bejaïa (Bougie), Alg. | 230 | 36°46'N | 5°00'E |
| Bejar, Spain | 172 | 40°25'N | 5°43'W |
| Bejestān, Iran | 198 | 34°30'N | 58°22'E |
| Bejucal, Cuba (bā-hōō-käl') | 134 | 22°56'N | 82°23'W |
| Bejuco, Pan. (bĕ-kōō'kō) | 133 | 8°37'N | 79°54'W |
| Békés, Hung. (bā'kāsh) | 169 | 46°45'N | 21°08'E |
| Békéscsaba, Hung. (bā'kāsh-chô'bô) | 163 | 46°39'N | 21°06'E |
| Beketova, Russia (bĕkĕ-to'vá) | 185 | 53°23'N | 125°21'E |
| Bela Crkva, Serb. (bĕ'lä tsĕrk'vä) | 175 | 44°53'N | 21°25'E |
| Belalcázar, Spain (bāl-å-kä'thär) | 172 | 38°35'N | 5°12'W |
| Belarus, nation, Eur. | 178 | 53°30'N | 25°33'E |
| Belau *see* Palau, nation, Oc. | 3 | 7°15'N | 134°30'E |
| Bela Vista de Goiás, Braz. | 143 | 16°57'S | 48°47'W |
| Belawan, Indon. (bå-lä'wan) | 212 | 3°43'N | 98°43'E |
| Belaya, r., Russia (byĕ'lĭ-yå) | 181 | 52°30'N | 56°15'E |
| Belcher Islands, is., Can. (bĕl'chēr) | 93 | 56°20'N | 80°40'W |
| Belding, Mi., U.S. (bĕl'dĭng) | 108 | 43°05'N | 85°25'W |
| Belebey, Russia (byĕ'lĕ-bā'ĭ) | 180 | 54°00'N | 54°10'E |
| Belém, Braz. (bå-lĕN') | 143 | 1°18'S | 48°27'W |
| Belén, Para. (bā-lān') | 144 | 23°30'S | 57°09'W |
| Belen, N.M., U.S. (bĕ-lån') | 119 | 34°40'N | 106°45'W |
| Bélep, Îles, is., N. Cal. | 221 | 19°30'S | 164°00'E |
| Belëv, Russia (byĕl'yĕf) | 180 | 53°49'N | 36°06'E |
| Belfair, Wa., U.S. (bĕl'far) | 116a | 47°27'N | 122°50'W |
| Belfast, N. Ire., U.K. | 154 | 54°36'N | 5°45'W |
| Belfast, Me., U.S. (bĕl'fäst) | 100 | 44°25'N | 69°01'W |
| Belfast, Lough, b., N. Ire., U.K. (lŏk bĕl'fäst) | 164 | 54°45'N | 6°00'W |
| Belford Roxo, Braz. | 144b | 22°46'S | 43°24'W |
| Belfort, Fr. (bā-fôr') | 161 | 47°40'N | 7°50'E |
| Belgaum, India | 199 | 15°57'N | 74°32'E |
| Belgium, nation, Eur. (bĕl'jĭ-ŭm) | 154 | 51°00'N | 2°52'E |
| Belgorod, Russia (byĕl'gŭ-rut) | 181 | 50°36'N | 36°32'E |
| Belgorod, prov., Russia | 177 | 50°40'N | 36°42'E |
| Belgrade (Beograd), Serb. | 154 | 44°48'N | 20°32'E |
| Belhaven, N.C., U.S. (bĕl'hā-vĕn) | 125 | 35°33'N | 76°37'W |
| Belington, W.V., U.S. (bĕl'ĭng-tŭn) | 109 | 39°00'N | 79°55'W |
| Belitung, i., Indon. | 212 | 3°30'S | 107°30'E |
| Belize, nation, N.A. | 128 | 17°00'N | 88°40'W |
| Belize, r., Belize | 132a | 17°16'N | 88°56'W |
| Belize City, Belize (bĕ-lēz') | 128 | 17°31'N | 88°10'W |
| Bel'kovo, Russia (byĕl'kô-vô) | 186b | 56°15'N | 38°49'E |
| Bel'kovskiy, i., Russia (byĕl-kôf'skĭ) | 185 | 75°45'N | 137°00'E |
| Bell, i., Can. (bĕl) | 101 | 50°45'N | 55°35'W |
| Bell, r., Can. | 99 | 49°25'N | 77°15'W |
| Bella Bella, Can. | 94 | 52°10'N | 128°07'W |
| Bella Coola, Can. | 94 | 52°22'N | 126°46'W |
| Bellaire, Oh., U.S. (bĕl-âr') | 108 | 40°00'N | 80°45'W |
| Bellaire, Tx., U.S. | 123a | 29°43'N | 95°28'W |
| Bellary, India (bĕl-lä'rē) | 199 | 15°15'N | 76°56'E |
| Bella Union, Ur. (bĕ'l-yä-ōō-nyô'n) | 144 | 30°18'S | 57°26'W |
| Bella Vista, Arg. (bä'lyå vēs'tà) | 144 | 27°07'S | 65°14'W |
| Bella Vista, Arg. | 144 | 28°35'S | 58°53'W |
| Bella Vista, Arg. | 144a | 34°35'S | 58°41'W |
| Bella Vista, Para. | 143 | 22°16'S | 56°14'W |
| Belle-Anse, Haiti | 135 | 18°15'N | 72°00'W |
| Belle Bay, b., Can. (bĕl) | 101 | 47°35'N | 55°15'W |
| Belle Chasse, La., U.S. (bĕl shäs') | 110d | 29°52'N | 90°00'W |
| Bellefontaine, Oh., U.S. (bel-fōn'tān) | 108 | 40°25'N | 83°50'W |
| Bellefontaine Neighbors, Mo., U.S. | 117e | 38°46'N | 90°13'W |
| Belle Fourche, S.D., U.S. (bĕl' fōōrsh') | 112 | 44°28'N | 103°50'W |
| Belle Fourche, r., Wy., U.S. | 112 | 44°29'N | 104°40'W |
| Belle Fourche Reservoir, res., S.D., U.S. | 112 | 44°51'N | 103°44'W |
| Bellegarde, Fr. (bĕl-gärd') | 171 | 46°06'N | 5°50'E |
| Belle Glade, Fl., U.S. (bĕl glād) | 125a | 26°39'N | 80°37'W |
| Belle-Île, i., Fr. (bĕlēl') | 161 | 47°15'N | 3°30'W |
| Belle Isle, Strait of, strt., Can. | 93 | 51°35'N | 56°30'W |
| Belle Mead, N.J., U.S. (bĕl mēd) | 110a | 40°28'N | 74°40'W |
| Belleoram, Can. | 101 | 47°31'N | 55°25'W |
| Belle Plaine, Ia., U.S. (bĕl plān') | 113 | 41°52'N | 92°19'W |
| Belle Vernon, Pa., U.S. (bĕl vûr'nŭn) | 111e | 40°08'N | 79°52'W |
| Belleville, Can. (bĕl'vĭl) | 99 | 44°15'N | 77°25'W |
| Belleville, Il., U.S. | 117e | 38°31'N | 89°59'W |
| Belleville, Ks., U.S. | 121 | 39°49'N | 97°37'W |
| Belleville, Mi., U.S. | 111b | 42°12'N | 83°29'W |
| Belleville, N.J., U.S. | 110a | 40°47'N | 74°09'W |
| Bellevue, Ia., U.S. (bĕl'vū) | 113 | 42°14'N | 90°26'W |
| Bellevue, Ky., U.S. | 111f | 39°06'N | 84°29'W |
| Bellevue, Mi., U.S. | 108 | 42°30'N | 85°00'W |
| Bellevue, Oh., U.S. | 108 | 41°15'N | 82°45'W |
| Bellevue, Pa., U.S. | 111e | 40°30'N | 80°04'W |
| Bellevue, Wa., U.S. | 116a | 47°37'N | 122°12'W |
| Belley, Fr. (bĕ-lē') | 171 | 45°46'N | 5°41'E |
| Bellflower, Ca., U.S. (bĕl-flou'ēr) | 117a | 33°53'N | 118°08'W |
| Bell Gardens, Ca., U.S. | 117a | 33°59'N | 118°11'W |
| Bellingham, Ma., U.S. (bĕl'ĭng-hăm) | 101a | 42°05'N | 71°28'W |
| Bellingham, Wa., U.S. | 104 | 48°46'N | 122°29'W |
| Bellingham Bay, b., Wa., U.S. | 116d | 48°44'N | 122°34'W |
| Bellingshausen Sea, sea, Ant. (bĕl'ĭngz houz'n) | 224 | 72°00'S | 80°30'W |
| Bellinzona, Switz. (bĕl-ĭn-tsō'nä) | 168 | 46°10'N | 9°09'E |
| Bellmore, N.Y., U.S. (bĕl-mōr) | 110a | 40°40'N | 73°31'W |
| Bello, Col. (bĕ'l-yô) | 142 | 6°20'N | 75°33'W |
| Bellow Falls, Vt., U.S. (bĕl'ōz fôls) | 109 | 43°10'N | 72°30'W |
| Bellpat, Pak. | 202 | 29°08'N | 68°00'E |
| Bell Peninsula, pen., Can. | 93 | 63°50'N | 81°16'W |
| Bells Corners, Can. | 102c | 45°20'N | 75°49'W |
| Bells Mountain, mtn., Wa., U.S. (bĕls) | 116c | 45°50'N | 122°21'W |
| Belluno, Italy (bĕl-lōō'nō) | 174 | 46°08'N | 12°14'E |
| Bell Ville, Arg. (bĕl vēl') | 144 | 32°33'S | 62°36'W |
| Bellville, S. Afr. | 232a | 33°54'S | 18°38'E |
| Bellville, Tx., U.S. (bĕl'vĭl) | 123 | 29°57'N | 96°15'W |
| Bélmez, Spain (bĕl'mĕth) | 172 | 38°17'N | 5°17'W |
| Belmond, Ia., U.S. (bĕl'mŏnd) | 113 | 42°49'N | 93°37'W |
| Belmont, Ca., U.S. | 116b | 37°34'N | 122°18'W |
| Belmonte, Braz. (bĕl-mōn'tå) | 143 | 15°58'S | 38°47'W |
| Belmopan, Belize | 128 | 17°15'N | 88°47'W |
| Belogorsk, Russia | 179 | 51°09'N | 128°32'E |
| Belo Horizonte, Braz. (bĕ'lôre-sô'n-tĕ) | 143 | 19°54'S | 43°56'W |
| Beloit, Ks., U.S. (bē-loit') | 120 | 39°26'N | 98°06'W |
| Beloit, Wi., U.S. | 105 | 42°31'N | 89°04'W |
| Belomorsk, Russia (byĕl-ô-môrsk') | 180 | 64°30'N | 34°42'E |
| Beloretsk, Russia (byĕ'lō-rĕtsk) | 180 | 53°58'N | 58°25'E |
| Belosarayskaya, Kosa, c., Ukr. | 177 | 46°43'N | 37°18'E |
| Belovo, Russia (byĕ'lŭ-vû) | 184 | 54°25'N | 86°18'E |
| Beloye, l., Russia | 180 | 60°10'N | 38°05'E |
| Belozersk, Russia (byĕ-lŭ-zyôrsk') | 180 | 60°00'N | 38°00'E |
| Belper, Eng., U.K. (bĕl'pēr) | 158a | 53°01'N | 1°28'W |
| Belt, Mt., U.S. (bĕlt) | 115 | 47°11'N | 110°58'W |
| Belt Creek, r., Mt., U.S. | 115 | 47°19'N | 110°58'W |
| Belton, Tx., U.S. (bĕl'tŭn) | 123 | 31°04'N | 97°27'W |
| Belton Lake, l., Tx., U.S. | 123 | 31°15'N | 97°35'W |
| Beltsville, Md., U.S. (belts-vĭl) | 110e | 39°03'N | 76°56'W |
| Belukha, Mount, mtn., Asia | 178 | 49°47'N | 86°23'E |
| Belvidere, Il., U.S. (bĕl-vĕ-dēr') | 113 | 42°14'N | 88°52'W |
| Belvidere, N.J., U.S. | 109 | 40°50'N | 75°05'W |
| Belyando, r., Austl. (bĕl-yän'dō) | 221 | 22°09'S | 146°48'E |
| Belyanka, Russia (byĕl'yan-kå) | 186a | 56°04'N | 59°16'E |
| Belyy, Russia (byĕ'lē) | 180 | 55°52'N | 32°58'E |
| Belyy, i., Russia | 178 | 73°19'N | 72°00'E |
| Belyye Stolby, Russia (byĕ'lĭ-ye stôl'bĭ) | 186b | 55°20'N | 37°52'E |
| Belzig, Ger. (bĕl'tsēg) | 159b | 52°08'N | 12°35'E |
| Belzoni, Ms., U.S. (bĕl-zō'nê) | 124 | 33°09'N | 90°30'W |
| Bembe, Ang. (bĕN'bĕ) | 232 | 7°00'S | 14°20'E |
| Bembézar, r., Spain (bĕm-bā-thär') | 172 | 38°00'N | 5°18'W |
| Bemidji, Mn., U.S. (bê-mĭj'ĭ) | 113 | 47°28'N | 94°54'W |
| Bena Dibele, D.R.C. (bĕn'å dē-bĕ'lĕ) | 232 | 4°00'S | 22°49'E |
| Benalla, Austl. (bĕn-ăl'å) | 219 | 36°30'S | 146°00'E |
| Benares *see* Vārānasi, India | 199 | 25°25'N | 83°00'E |
| Benavente, Spain (bā-nä-vĕn'tā) | 162 | 42°01'N | 5°43'W |
| Benbrook, Tx., U.S. (bĕn'brŏŏk) | 117c | 32°41'N | 97°27'W |
| Benbrook Reservoir, res., Tx., U.S. | 117c | 32°35'N | 97°30'W |
| Bend, Or., U.S. (bĕnd) | 104 | 44°04'N | 121°17'W |
| Bendeleben, Mount, mtn., Ak., U.S. (bĕn-dĕl-bĕn) | 103 | 65°18'N | 163°45'W |
| Bender Beyla, Som. | 238a | 9°40'N | 50°45'E |
| Bendigo, Austl. (bĕn'dĭ-gō) | 219 | 36°39'S | 144°20'E |
| Benedict, Md., U.S. (bĕnĕ'dĭct) | 110e | 38°31'N | 76°41'W |
| Benešov, Czech Rep. (bĕn'ĕ-shôf) | 168 | 49°48'N | 14°40'E |
| Benevento, Italy (bā-nā-vĕn'tō) | 162 | 41°08'N | 14°46'E |
| Bengal, Bay of, b., Asia (bĕn-gôl') | 196 | 17°30'N | 87°00'E |
| Bengamisa, D.R.C. | 237 | 0°57'N | 25°10'E |


ng-sing; ŋ-baŋk; N-nasalized n; nŏd; cŏmmit; ōld; ôbey; ôrder; oi-boil; fōōd; ŏŏ-as oo in foot; ou-out; s-soft; sh-dish; th-thin; pūre; ûnite; ûrn; stŭd; circŭs; ü-as in French tu; '-indeterminate vowel.

272 Bengbu – Bijou Creek PRONOUNCING INDEX


| PLACE (Pronunciation) | PAGE | LAT. | LONG. |
|---|---|---|---|
| Bengbu, China (bŭŋ-bōō) | 205 | 32°52'N | 117°22'E |
| Benghazi *see* Banghāzī, Libya | 230 | 32°07'N | 20°04'E |
| Bengkalis, Indon. (bĕng-kä'lĭs) | 212 | 1°29'N | 102°06'E |
| Bengkulu, Indon. | 212 | 3°46'S | 102°18'E |
| Benguela, Ang. (bĕn-gĕl'ȧ) | 232 | 12°35'S | 13°25'E |
| Beni, r., Bol. (bā'nē) | 142 | 13°41'S | 67°30'W |
| Béni-Abbas, Alg. (bā'nē ä-bĕs') | 230 | 30°11'N | 2°13'W |
| Benicia, Ca., U.S. (bē-nĭsh'ĭ-ȧ) | 116b | 38°03'N | 122°09'W |
| Benin, nation, Afr. | 230 | 8°00'N | 2°00'E |
| Benin, r., Nig. (bĕn-ēn') | 235 | 5°55'N | 5°15'E |
| Benin, Bight of, b., Afr. | 230 | 5°30'N | 3°00'E |
| Benin City, Nig. | 230 | 6°19'N | 5°41'E |
| Beni Saf, Alg. (bā'nē säf') | 230 | 35°23'N | 1°20'W |
| Benito, r., Eq. Gui. | 236 | 1°35'N | 10°45'E |
| Benkelman, Ne., U.S. (bĕn-kĕl-mȧn) | 120 | 40°05'N | 101°35'W |
| Benkovac, Cro. (bĕn'kō-vȧts) | 174 | 44°02'N | 15°41'E |
| Bennettsville, S.C., U.S. (bĕn'ĕts vĭl) | 125 | 34°35'N | 79°41'W |
| Bennington, Vt., U.S. (bĕn'ĭng-tŭn) | 109 | 42°55'N | 73°15'W |
| Benns Church, Va., U.S. (bĕnz' chûrch') | 110g | 36°47'N | 76°35'W |
| Benoni, S. Afr. (bĕ-nō'nī) | 232 | 26°11'S | 28°19'E |
| Benoy, Chad | 235 | 8°59'N | 16°19'E |
| Benque Viejo, Belize (bĕn-kĕ bĭĕ'hō) | 132a | 17°07'N | 89°07'W |
| Bensberg, Ger. | 171c | 50°58'N | 7°09'E |
| Bensenville, Il., U.S. (bĕn'sĕn-vĭl) | 111a | 41°57'N | 87°56'W |
| Bensheim, Ger. (bĕns-hīm) | 168 | 49°42'N | 8°38'E |
| Benson, Az., U.S. (bĕn-sŭn) | 119 | 32°00'N | 110°20'W |
| Benson, Mn., U.S. | 112 | 45°18'N | 95°36'W |
| Bentiaba, Ang. | 236 | 14°15'S | 12°21'E |
| Bentleyville, Pa., U.S. (bent'lē vĭl) | 111e | 40°07'N | 80°01'W |
| Benton, Can. | 100 | 45°59'N | 67°36'W |
| Benton, Ar., U.S. (bĕn'tŭn) | 121 | 34°34'N | 92°34'W |
| Benton, Ca., U.S. | 118 | 37°44'N | 118°22'W |
| Benton, Il., U.S. | 108 | 38°00'N | 88°55'W |
| Benton Harbor, Mi., U.S. (bĕn'tŭn här'bẽr) | 108 | 42°05'N | 86°30'W |
| Bentonville, Ar., U.S. (bĕn'tŭn-vĭl) | 121 | 36°22'N | 94°11'W |
| Benue, r., Afr. (bā'nōō-å) | 230 | 8°00'N | 8°00'E |
| Benut, r., Malay. | 197b | 1°43'N | 103°20'E |
| Benwood, W.V., U.S. (bĕn-wŏd) | 108 | 39°55'N | 80°45'W |
| Benxi, China (bŭn-shyē) | 208 | 41°25'N | 123°50'E |
| Beograd *see* Belgrade, Serb. | 154 | 44°48'N | 20°32'E |
| Beppu, Japan (bĕ'pōō) | 211 | 33°16'N | 131°30'E |
| Bequia Island, i., St. Vin. (bĕk-ē'ä) | 133b | 13°00'N | 61°08'W |
| Berakit, Tanjung, c., Indon. | 197b | 1°16'N | 104°44'E |
| Berat, Alb. (bĕ-rät') | 175 | 40°43'N | 19°59'E |
| Berau, Teluk, b., Indon. | 213 | 2°22'S | 131°40'E |
| Berazategui, Arg. (bĕ-rä-zà'tĕ-gē) | 144a | 34°46'S | 58°14'W |
| Berbera, Som. (bûr'bûr-ȧ) | 238a | 10°25'N | 45°05'E |
| Berbérati, C.A.R. | 235 | 4°16'N | 15°47'E |
| Berck, Fr. (bĕrk) | 170 | 50°26'N | 1°36'E |
| Berdians'k, Ukr. | 181 | 46°45'N | 36°47'E |
| Berdians'ka kosa, c., Ukr. | 177 | 46°38'N | 36°42'E |
| Berdyaush, Russia (bĕr'dyȧûsh) | 186a | 55°10'N | 59°12'E |
| Berdychiv, Ukr. | 178 | 49°53'N | 28°32'E |
| Berea, Ky., U.S. (bē-rē'ȧ) | 124 | 37°30'N | 84°19'W |
| Berea, Oh., U.S. | 111d | 41°22'N | 81°51'W |
| Berehove, Ukr. | 169 | 48°13'N | 22°40'E |
| Bereku, Tan. | 237 | 4°27'S | 35°44'E |
| Berens, r., Can. (bĕrĕnz) | 97 | 52°15'N | 96°30'W |
| Berens Island, i., Can. | 97 | 52°18'N | 97°40'W |
| Berens River, Can. | 90 | 52°22'N | 97°02'W |
| Beresford, S.D., U.S. (bĕr'ĕs-fẽrd) | 112 | 43°05'N | 96°46'W |
| Berettyóújfalu, Hung. (bĕ'rĕt-tyō-ōō'y'fō-lōō) | 169 | 47°14'N | 21°33'E |
| Berezhany, Ukr. (bĕr-yĕ'zhȧ-nĕ) | 169 | 49°25'N | 24°58'E |
| Berezivka, Ukr. | 177 | 47°12'N | 30°56'E |
| Berezna, Ukr. (bĕr-yôz'nȧ) | 177 | 51°32'N | 31°47'E |
| Bereznehuvate, Ukr. | 177 | 47°19'N | 32°58'E |
| Berezniki, Russia (bĕr-yôz'nyē-kē) | 180 | 59°25'N | 56°46'E |
| Berëzovka, Russia | 186a | 57°35'N | 57°19'E |
| Berëzovo, Russia (bĭr-yô'zē-vû) | 178 | 64°10'N | 65°10'E |
| Berëzovskiy, Russia (bĕr-yô'zôf-skĭ) | 186a | 56°54'N | 60°47'E |
| Berga, Spain (bĕr'gä) | 173 | 42°05'N | 1°52'E |
| Bergama, Tur. (bĕr'gä-mä) | 198 | 39°08'N | 27°09'E |
| Bergamo, Italy (bĕr'gä-mō) | 162 | 45°43'N | 9°41'E |
| Bergantin, Ven. (bĕr-gän-tē'n) | 143b | 10°04'N | 64°23'W |
| Bergara, Spain | 172 | 43°08'N | 2°23'W |
| Bergedorf, Ger. (bĕr'gē-dôrf) | 159c | 53°29'N | 10°12'E |
| Bergen, Ger. (bĕr'gĕn) | 168 | 54°26'N | 13°26'E |
| Bergen, Nor. | 154 | 60°24'N | 5°20'E |
| Bergenfield, N.J., U.S. | 110a | 40°55'N | 73°59'W |
| Bergen op Zoom, Neth. | 165 | 51°29'N | 4°16'E |
| Bergerac, Fr. (bĕr-zhē-råk') | 161 | 44°49'N | 0°28'E |
| Bergisch Gladbach, Ger. (bĕrg'ĭsh-glät'bäk) | 171c | 50°59'N | 7°08'E |
| Berglern, Ger. (bĕrgh'lĕrn) | 159d | 48°24'N | 11°55'E |
| Bergneustadt, Ger. | 171c | 51°01'N | 7°39'E |
| Bergville, S. Afr. (bĕrg'vĭl) | 233c | 28°46'S | 29°22'E |
| Berhampur, India | 199 | 19°19'N | 84°48'E |
| Bering Sea, sea (bē'rĭng) | 240 | 58°00'N | 175°00'W |
| Bering Strait, strt. | 106a | 64°50'N | 169°50'W |
| Berja, Spain (bĕr'hä) | 172 | 36°50'N | 2°56'W |
| Berkeley, Ca., U.S. (bûrk'lĭ) | 104 | 37°52'N | 122°17'W |
| Berkeley, Mo., U.S. | 117e | 38°45'N | 90°20'W |
| Berkeley Springs, W.V., U.S. (bûrk'lĭ sprĭngz) | 109 | 39°40'N | 78°10'W |
| Berkhamsted, Eng., U.K. (bĕk'hȧm'stĕd) | 158b | 51°44'N | 0°34'W |
| Berkley, Mi., U.S. (bûrk'lĭ) | 111b | 42°30'N | 83°10'W |
| Berkovitsa, Blg. (bĕ-kō'vē-tsȧ) | 175 | 43°14'N | 23°08'E |
| Berkshire, hist. reg., Eng., U.K. | 158b | 51°23'N | 1°07'W |
| Berland, r., Can. | 95 | 54°00'N | 117°10'W |
| Berlenga, is., Port. (bĕr-lĕn'gäzh) | 172 | 39°25'N | 9°33'W |
| Berlin, Ger. (bĕr-lēn') | 154 | 52°31'N | 13°28'E |
| Berlin, S. Afr. (bẽr-lĭn) | 233c | 32°53'S | 27°36'E |
| Berlin, N.H., U.S. (bûr-lĭn) | 109 | 44°25'N | 71°10'W |
| Berlin, N.J., U.S. | 110f | 39°47'N | 74°56'W |
| Berlin, Wi., U.S. (bûr-lĭn') | 113 | 43°58'N | 88°58'W |
| Bermejo, r., S.A. (bĕr-mā'hō) | 144 | 25°05'S | 61°00'W |
| Bermeo, Spain (bĕr-mā'yō) | 172 | 43°23'N | 2°43'W |
| Bermuda, dep., N.A. | 129 | 32°20'N | 65°45'W |
| Bern, Switz. (bĕrn) | 154 | 46°55'N | 7°25'E |
| Bernal, Arg. (bĕr-näl') | 144a | 34°43'S | 58°17'W |
| Bernalillo, N.M., U.S. (bĕr-nä-lē'yō) | 119 | 35°20'N | 106°30'W |
| Bernard, l., Can. (bẽr-närd') | 109 | 45°45'N | 79°25'W |
| Bernardsville, N.J., U.S. (bŭr nårds'vĭl) | 110a | 40°43'N | 74°34'W |
| Bernau, Ger. (bĕr'nou) | 168 | 52°40'N | 13°35'E |
| Bernburg, Ger. (bĕrn'bŏrgh) | 168 | 51°48'N | 11°43'E |
| Berndorf, Aus. (bĕrn'dôrf) | 168 | 47°57'N | 16°05'E |
| Berne, In., U.S. (bûrn) | 108 | 40°40'N | 84°55'W |
| Berner Alpen, mts., Switz. | 168 | 46°29'N | 7°30'E |
| Bernier, i., Austl. (bẽr-nēr') | 220 | 24°58'S | 113°15'E |
| Bernina, Pizzo, mtn., Eur. | 168 | 46°23'N | 9°58'E |
| Bero, r., Ang. | 236 | 15°10'S | 12°20'E |
| Beroun, Czech Rep. (bā'rōn) | 168 | 49°57'N | 14°03'E |
| Berounka, r., Czech Rep. (bĕ-rōn'kȧ) | 168 | 49°53'N | 13°40'E |
| Berowra, Austl. | 217b | 33°36'S | 151°10'E |
| Berre, Étang de, l., Fr. (ā-tôn' dē bâr') | 170a | 43°27'N | 5°07'E |
| Berre-l'Étang, Fr. (bâr'lā-tôn') | 170a | 43°28'N | 5°11'E |
| Berriozabal, Mex. (bā'rēō-zä-bäl') | 131 | 16°47'N | 93°16'W |
| Berriyyane, Alg. | 162 | 32°50'N | 3°49'E |
| Berry Creek, r., Can. | 96 | 51°15'N | 111°40'W |
| Berryessa, r., Ca., U.S. (bĕ'rĭ ĕs'ȧ) | 118 | 38°35'N | 122°33'W |
| Berry Islands, is., Bah. | 134 | 25°40'N | 77°50'W |
| Berryville, Ar., U.S. (bĕr'ē-vĭl) | 121 | 36°21'N | 93°34'W |
| Bershad', Ukr. (byĕr'shät) | 177 | 48°22'N | 29°31'E |
| Berthier, Can. | 102b | 46°56'N | 70°44'W |
| Bertrand, r., Wa., U.S. (bûr'trȧnd) | 116d | 48°58'N | 122°31'W |
| Berwick, Pa., U.S. (bûr'wĭk) | 109 | 41°05'N | 76°10'W |
| Berwick-upon-Tweed, Eng., U.K. (bûr'ĭk) | 160 | 55°45'N | 2°01'W |
| Berwyn, Il., U.S. (bûr'wĭn) | 111a | 41°49'N | 87°47'W |
| Beryslav, Ukr. | 177 | 46°49'N | 33°24'E |
| Besalampy, Madag. (bĕz-ȧ-lȧm-pē') | 233 | 16°48'S | 44°40'E |
| Besançon, Fr. (bē-sän-sôn) | 161 | 47°14'N | 6°02'E |
| Besar, Gunong, mtn., Malay. | 197b | 2°31'N | 103°09'E |
| Besed', r., Eur. (byĕ'syĕt) | 176 | 52°58'N | 31°36'E |
| Beskid Mountains, mts., Eur. | 169 | 49°23'N | 19°00'E |
| Beskra, Alg. | 230 | 34°52'N | 5°39'E |
| Beslan, Russia | 182 | 43°12'N | 44°33'E |
| Bessarabia, hist. reg., Mol. | 177 | 47°00'N | 28°30'E |
| Bességes, Fr. (bĕ-sĕzh') | 170 | 44°20'N | 4°07'E |
| Bessemer, Al., U.S. (bĕs'ē-mẽr) | 110h | 33°24'N | 86°58'W |
| Bessemer, Mi., U.S. | 113 | 46°29'N | 90°04'W |
| Bessemer City, N.C., U.S. | 125 | 35°16'N | 81°17'W |
| Bestensee, Ger. (bĕs'tĕn-zā) | 159b | 52°15'N | 13°39'E |
| Betanzos, Spain (bĕ-tän'thōs) | 172 | 43°18'N | 8°14'W |
| Betatakin Ruin, Az., U.S. (bĕt-ȧ-tăk'ĭn) | 119 | 36°40'N | 110°29'W |
| Bethal, S. Afr. (bĕth'ăl) | 238c | 26°27'S | 29°28'E |
| Bethalto, Il., U.S. (bȧ-thăl'tō) | 117e | 38°54'N | 90°03'W |
| Bethanien, Nmb. | 232 | 26°20'S | 16°10'E |
| Bethany, Mo., U.S. | 121 | 40°15'N | 94°04'W |
| Bethel, Ak., U.S. (bĕth'ĕl) | 106a | 60°50'N | 161°50'W |
| Bethel, Ct., U.S. | 110a | 41°22'N | 73°24'W |
| Bethel, Vt., U.S. | 109 | 43°50'N | 72°40'W |
| Bethel Park, Pa., U.S. | 111e | 40°19'N | 80°02'W |
| Bethesda, Md., U.S. (bĕ-thĕs'dȧ) | 110e | 39°00'N | 77°10'W |
| Bethlehem, S. Afr. | 232 | 28°14'S | 28°18'E |
| Bethlehem, Pa., U.S. (bĕth'lē-hĕm) | 109 | 40°40'N | 75°25'W |
| Bethlehem *see* Bayt Lahm, W.B. | 197a | 31°42'N | 35°13'E |
| Béthune, Fr. (bā-tün') | 170 | 50°32'N | 2°37'E |
| Betroka, Madag. (bĕ-trōk'ȧ) | 233 | 23°13'S | 46°17'E |
| Bet She'an, Isr. | 197a | 32°30'N | 35°30'E |
| Betsiamites, Can. | 91 | 48°57'N | 68°36'W |
| Betsiamites, r., Can. | 100 | 49°11'N | 69°20'W |
| Betsiboka, r., Madag. (bĕt-sĭ-bō'kȧ) | 233 | 16°47'S | 46°45'E |
| Bettles Field, Ak., U.S. (bĕt'tŭls) | 103 | 66°58'N | 151°48'W |
| Betwa, r., India (bĕt'wȧ) | 199 | 25°00'N | 78°00'E |
| Betz, Fr. (bĕ) | 171b | 49°09'N | 2°58'E |
| Beveren, Bel. | 159a | 51°13'N | 4°14'E |
| B. Everett Jordan Lake, res., N.C., U.S. | 125 | 35°45'N | 79°00'W |
| Beverly, Ma., U.S. | 101a | 42°34'N | 70°53'W |
| Beverly, N.J., U.S. | 110f | 40°03'N | 74°56'W |
| Beverly Hills, Ca., U.S. | 117a | 34°05'N | 118°24'W |
| Bevier, Mo., U.S. (bē-vēr') | 121 | 39°44'N | 92°36'W |
| Bewdley, Eng., U.K. (būd'lĭ) | 158a | 52°22'N | 2°19'W |
| Bexhill, Eng., U.K. (bĕks'hĭl) | 165 | 50°49'N | 0°25'E |
| Bexley, Eng., U.K. (bĕks'ly) | 158b | 51°26'N | 0°09'E |
| Beyla, Gui. (bā'lȧ) | 230 | 8°41'N | 8°37'W |
| Beylul, Erit. | 231 | 13°15'N | 42°21'E |
| Beypazari, Tur. (bā-pȧ-zä'rĭ) | 163 | 40°10'N | 31°40'E |
| Beyşehir, Tur. | 181 | 38°00'N | 31°45'E |
| Beysugskiy, Liman, b., Russia (lĭ-män' bĕy-sōōg'skĭ) | 177 | 46°07'N | 38°35'E |
| Bezhetsk, Russia (byĕ-zhĕtsk') | 180 | 57°46'N | 36°40'E |
| Bezhitsa, Russia (byĕ-zhĭ'tsȧ) | 180 | 53°19'N | 34°18'E |
| Béziers, Fr. (bā-zyā') | 161 | 43°21'N | 3°12'E |
| Bhadreswar, India | 202a | 22°49'N | 88°22'E |
| Bhāgalpur, India (bä'gŭl-pŏr) | 199 | 25°15'N | 86°59'E |
| Bhamo, Mya. (bŭ-mō') | 199 | 24°00'N | 96°15'E |
| Bhāngar, India | 202a | 22°30'N | 88°36'E |
| Bharatpur, India (bẽrt'pŏr) | 199 | 27°21'N | 77°33'E |
| Bhatinda, India (bŭ-tĭn-dȧ) | 199 | 30°19'N | 74°56'E |
| Bhātpāra, India | 199 | 22°52'N | 88°24'E |
| Bhaunagar, India (bäv-nŭg'ŭr) | 199 | 21°45'N | 72°58'E |
| Bhayandar, India | 203b | 19°20'N | 72°50'E |
| Bhilai, India | 202 | 21°14'N | 81°23'E |
| Bhīma, r., India (bē'mȧ) | 199 | 18°00'N | 74°45'E |
| Bhiwandi, India | 203b | 19°18'N | 73°03'E |
| Bhiwāni, India | 202 | 28°53'N | 76°08'E |
| Bhopāl, India (bŏ-päl) | 199 | 23°20'N | 77°25'E |
| Bhubaneswar, India (bŏ-bŏ-năsh'vŭr) | 199 | 20°21'N | 85°53'E |
| Bhuj, India (bōōj) | 199 | 23°22'N | 69°39'E |
| Bhutan, nation, Asia (bōō-tän') | 199 | 27°15'N | 90°30'E |
| Biafra, Bight of, b., Afr. | 230 | 4°05'N | 7°10'E |
| Biak, i., Indon. (bē'ăk) | 213 | 1°00'S | 136°00'E |
| Biała Podlaska, Pol. (byä'wä pŏd-läs'kä) | 169 | 52°01'N | 23°08'E |
| Białograd, Pol. | 168 | 54°00'N | 16°01'E |
| Bialystok, Pol. (byä-wĭs'tŏk) | 154 | 53°08'N | 23°12'E |
| Biankouma, C. Iv. | 234 | 7°44'N | 7°37'W |
| Biarritz, Fr. (byä-rēts') | 161 | 43°27'N | 1°39'W |
| Bibb City, Ga., U.S. (bĭb' sĭ'tē) | 124 | 32°31'N | 84°56'W |
| Biberach, Ger. (bē'bĕräk) | 168 | 48°06'N | 9°49'E |
| Bibiani, Ghana | 234 | 6°28'N | 2°20'W |
| Bic, Can. (bĭk) | 100 | 48°22'N | 68°42'W |
| Bicknell, In., U.S. (bĭk'nĕl) | 108 | 38°45'N | 87°20'W |
| Bicske, Hung. (bĭsh'kē) | 169 | 47°29'N | 18°38'E |
| Bida, Nig. (bē'dä) | 230 | 9°05'N | 6°01'E |
| Biddeford, Me., U.S. (bĭd'ē-fẽrd) | 100 | 43°29'N | 70°29'W |
| Biddulph, Eng., U.K. (bĭd'ŭlf) | 158a | 53°07'N | 2°10'W |
| Biebrza, r., Pol. (byĕb'zhȧ) | 169 | 53°18'N | 22°25'E |
| Biel, Switz. (bēl) | 168 | 47°09'N | 7°12'E |
| Bielefeld, Ger. (bē'lē-fĕlt) | 161 | 52°01'N | 8°35'E |
| Biella, Italy (byĕl'lä) | 174 | 45°34'N | 8°05'E |
| Bielsk Podlaski, Pol. (byĕlsk pŭd-lä'skĭ) | 161 | 52°47'N | 23°14'E |
| Bien Hoa, Viet. | 212 | 10°59'N | 106°49'E |
| Bienville, Lac, l., Can. | 93 | 55°32'N | 72°45'W |
| Biesenthal, Ger. (bē'sĕn-täl) | 159b | 52°46'N | 13°38'E |
| Biferno, r., Italy (bē-fĕr'nō) | 174 | 41°49'N | 14°46'E |
| Bifoum, Gabon | 236 | 0°22'S | 10°23'E |
| Biga, Tur. (bē'ghȧ) | 175 | 40°13'N | 27°14'E |
| Big Bay de Noc, Mi., U.S. (bĭg bā dē nŏk') | 113 | 45°48'N | 86°41'W |
| Big Bayou, Ar., U.S. (bĭg'bī'yōō) | 121 | 33°04'N | 91°28'W |
| Big Bear City, Ca., U.S. (bĭg bâr) | 117a | 34°16'N | 116°51'W |
| Big Belt Mountains, mts., Mt., U.S. (bĭg bĕlt) | 106 | 46°53'N | 111°43'W |
| Big Bend Dam, S.D., U.S. (bĭg bĕnd) | 112 | 44°11'N | 99°33'W |
| Big Bend National Park, rec., Tx., U.S. | 106 | 29°15'N | 103°15'W |
| Big Black, r., Ms., U.S. (bĭg blăk) | 124 | 32°05'N | 90°49'W |
| Big Blue, r., Ne., U.S. (bĭg blōō) | 121 | 40°53'N | 97°00'W |
| Big Canyon, Tx., U.S. (bĭg kăn'yŭn) | 122 | 30°27'N | 102°19'W |
| Big Cypress Indian Reservation, I.R., Fl., U.S. | 125a | 26°19'N | 81°11'W |
| Big Cypress Swamp, sw., Fl., U.S. (bĭg sī'prĕs) | 125a | 26°02'N | 81°20'W |
| Big Delta, Ak., U.S. (bĭg dĕl'tȧ) | 103 | 64°08'N | 145°48'W |
| Big Fork, r., Mn., U.S. (bĭg fôrk) | 113 | 48°08'N | 93°47'W |
| Biggar, Can. | 90 | 52°04'N | 108°00'W |
| Big Hole, r., Mt., U.S. (bĭg hōl) | 115 | 45°53'N | 113°15'W |
| Big Hole National Battlefield, Mt., U.S. (bĭg hōl băt''l-fēld) | 115 | 45°44'N | 113°35'W |
| Bighorn, r., U.S. | 106 | 45°30'N | 108°00'W |
| Bighorn Lake, res., Mt., U.S. | 115 | 45°00'N | 108°10'W |
| Bighorn Mountains, mts., U.S. (bĭg hôrn) | 106 | 44°47'N | 107°40'W |
| Big Island, i., Can. | 97 | 49°10'N | 94°40'W |
| Big Lake, Wa., U.S. (bĭg lăk) | 116a | 48°24'N | 122°14'W |
| Big Lake, l., Can. | 102g | 53°35'N | 113°47'W |
| Big Lake, l., Wa., U.S. | 116a | 48°24'N | 122°14'W |
| Big Lost, r., Id., U.S. (lôst) | 115 | 43°56'N | 113°38'W |
| Big Mossy Point, c., Can. | 97 | 53°45'N | 97°50'W |
| Big Muddy, r., Il., U.S. | 108 | 37°50'N | 89°00'W |
| Big Muddy Creek, r., Mt., U.S. (bĭg mud'ĭ) | 115 | 48°53'N | 105°02'W |
| Bignona, Sen. | 234 | 12°49'N | 16°14'W |
| Big Porcupine Creek, r., Mt., U.S. (pôr'kū-pīn) | 115 | 46°38'N | 107°04'W |
| Big Quill Lake, l., Can. | 92 | 51°55'N | 104°22'W |
| Big Rapids, Mi., U.S. (bĭg răp'ĭdz) | 108 | 43°40'N | 85°30'W |
| Big River, Can. | 90 | 53°50'N | 107°01'W |
| Big Sandy, r., Az., U.S. (bĭg sănd'ē) | 119 | 34°59'N | 113°36'W |
| Big Sandy, r., Ky., U.S. | 108 | 38°15'N | 82°35'W |
| Big Sandy, r., Wy., U.S. | 115 | 42°08'N | 109°35'W |
| Big Sandy Creek, r., Co., U.S. | 120 | 39°08'N | 103°36'W |
| Big Sandy Creek, r., Mt., U.S. | 115 | 48°20'N | 110°08'W |
| Bigsby Island, i., Can. | 97 | 49°04'N | 94°35'W |
| Big Sioux, r., U.S. (bĭg sōō) | 112 | 44°34'N | 97°00'W |
| Big Spring, Tx., U.S. (bĭg sprĭng) | 122 | 32°15'N | 101°28'W |
| Big Stone, l., Mn., U.S. (bĭg stōn) | 112 | 45°29'N | 96°40'W |
| Big Stone Gap, Va., U.S. | 125 | 36°50'N | 82°50'W |
| Big Sunflower, r., Ms., U.S. (sŭn-flou'ẽr) | 124 | 32°57'N | 90°40'W |
| Big Timber, Mt., U.S. (bĭg'tĭm-bẽr) | 115 | 45°50'N | 109°57'W |
| Big Wood, r., Id., U.S. (bĭg wŏd) | 115 | 43°02'N | 114°30'W |
| Bihār, state, India (bē-här') | 199 | 25°30'N | 87°00'E |
| Biharamulo, Tan. (bē-hä-rä-mōō'lō) | 232 | 2°38'S | 31°20'E |
| Bihorului, Munţii, mts., Rom. | 169 | 46°37'N | 22°37'E |
| Bijagós, Arquipélago dos, is., Gui.-B. | 230 | 11°20'N | 17°10'W |
| Bijāpur, India | 203 | 16°53'N | 75°42'E |
| Bijeljina, Bos. | 175 | 44°44'N | 19°15'E |
| Bijelo Polje, Serb. (bē'yĕ-lō pō'lyĕ) | 175 | 43°02'N | 19°48'E |
| Bijiang, China (bē-jyän) | 207a | 22°57'N | 113°15'E |
| Bijie, China (bē-jyĕ) | 209 | 27°20'N | 105°18'E |
| Bijou Creek, r., Co., U.S. (bē'zhōō) | 120 | 39°41'N | 104°13'W |


ăt; finăl; rāte; senāte; ärm; åsk; sofȧ; fâre; ch-choose; dh-as th in other; bē; ēvent; bĕt; recĕnt; cratẽr; g-gō; gh-guttural g; bĭt; ĭ-short neutral; rīde; ĸ-guttural k as ch in German ich;

| PLACE (Pronunciation) | PAGE | LAT. | LONG. |
|---|---|---|---|
| Bīkaner, India (bĭ-kă′nûr) | 199 | 28°07'N | 73°19'E |
| Bikin, Russia (bė-kēn′) | 210 | 46°41'N | 134°29'E |
| Bikin, r., Russia | 210 | 46°37'N | 135°55'E |
| Bikoro, D.R.C. (bė-kō′rṓ) | 232 | 0°45'S | 18°07'E |
| Bikuar, Parque Nacional do, rec., Ang. | 236 | 15°07'S | 14°40'E |
| Bilāspur, India (bė-läs′pōōr) | 199 | 22°08'N | 82°12'E |
| Bila Tserkva, Ukr. | 181 | 49°48'N | 30°09'E |
| Bilauktaung, mts., Asia | 212 | 14°40'N | 98°50'E |
| Bilbao, Spain (bĭl-bä′ō) | 154 | 43°12'N | 2°48'W |
| Bilbays, Egypt | 238b | 30°26'N | 31°37'E |
| Bileća, Bos. (bē′lĕ-chä) | 175 | 42°52'N | 18°26'E |
| Bilecik, Tur. (bē-lĕd-zhēk′) | 163 | 40°10'N | 29°58'E |
| Bilé Karpaty, mts., Eur. | 169 | 48°53'N | 17°35'E |
| Biłgoraj, Pol. (bēw-gō′rī) | 169 | 50°31'N | 22°43'E |
| Bilhorod-Dnistrovs'kyi, Ukr. | 181 | 46°09'N | 30°19'E |
| Bilimbay, Russia (bē′lĭm-bȧy) | 186a | 56°59'N | 59°53'E |
| Billabong, r., Austl. (bĭl′ă-bŏng) | 221 | 35°15'S | 145°20'E |
| Billerica, Ma., U.S. (bĭl′rĭk-ȧ) | 101a | 42°33'N | 71°16'W |
| Billericay, Eng., U.K. | 158b | 51°38'N | 0°25'E |
| Billings, Mt., U.S. (bĭl′ĭngz) | 104 | 45°47'N | 108°29'W |
| Bill Williams, r., Az., U.S. (bĭl-wĭl′yumz) | 119 | 34°10'N | 113°50'W |
| Bilma, Niger (bēl′mä) | 231 | 18°41'N | 13°20'E |
| Bilopillia, Ukr. | 181 | 51°10'N | 34°19'E |
| Bilovods'k, Ukr. | 177 | 49°12'N | 39°36'E |
| Biloxi, Ms., U.S. (bĭ-lŏk′sĭ) | 105 | 30°24'N | 88°50'W |
| Bilqās Qism Awwal, Egypt | 238b | 31°14'N | 31°25'E |
| Bimberi Peak, mtn., Austl. (bĭm′bĕrĭ) | 222 | 35°45'S | 148°50'E |
| Binalonan, Phil. (bē-nä-lô′nän) | 213a | 16°03'N | 120°35'E |
| Bingen, Ger. (bĭn′gĕn) | 168 | 49°57'N | 7°54'E |
| Bingham, Eng., U.K. (bĭng′ăm) | 158a | 52°57'N | 0°57'W |
| Bingham, Me., U.S. | 100 | 45°03'N | 69°51'W |
| Bingham Canyon, Ut., U.S. | 117b | 40°33'N | 112°09'W |
| Binghamton, N.Y., U.S. (bĭng′ȧm-tŭn) | 105 | 42°05'N | 75°55'W |
| Bingo-Nada, b., Japan (bĭn′gō nä-dä) | 211 | 34°06'N | 133°14'E |
| Binjai, Indon. | 212 | 3°59'N | 108°00'E |
| Binnaway, Austl. (bĭn′ă-wā) | 222 | 31°42'S | 149°22'E |
| Bintan, i., Indon. (bĭn′tän) | 197b | 1°09'N | 104°43'E |
| Bintimani, mtn., S.L. | 234 | 9°13'N | 11°07'W |
| Bintulu, Malay. (bēn′tōō-lōō) | 212 | 3°07'N | 113°06'E |
| Binxian, China | 208 | 45°40'N | 127°20'E |
| Binxian, China (bĭn-shyän) | 206 | 37°27'N | 117°58'E |
| Bio Gorge, val., Ghana | 234 | 8°30'N | 2°05'W |
| Bioko (Fernando Póo), i., Eq. Gui. | 230 | 3°35'N | 7°45'E |
| Bira, Russia (bē′rȧ) | 210 | 49°00'N | 133°18'E |
| Bira, r., Russia | 210 | 48°55'N | 132°25'E |
| Birātnagar, Nepal (bĭ-rät′nŭ-gŭr) | 202 | 26°35'N | 87°18'E |
| Birbka, Ukr. | 169 | 49°36'N | 24°18'E |
| Birch Bay, Wa., U.S. (bûrch) | 116d | 48°55'N | 122°45'W |
| Birch Bay, b., Wa., U.S. | 116d | 48°55'N | 122°52'W |
| Birch Island, i., Can. | 97 | 52°25'N | 99°55'W |
| Birch Mountains, mts., Can. | 92 | 57°36'N | 113°10'W |
| Birch Point, c., Wa., U.S. | 116d | 48°57'N | 122°50'W |
| Bird Island, i., S. Afr. (bẽrd) | 233c | 33°51'S | 26°21'E |
| Bird Rock, i., Bah. (bŭrd) | 135 | 22°50'N | 74°20'W |
| Birds Hill, Can. (bûrds) | 102f | 49°58'N | 97°00'W |
| Birdsville, Austl. (bûrdz′vĭl) | 218 | 25°50'S | 139°31'E |
| Birdum, Austl. (bûrd′ŭm) | 218 | 15°45'S | 133°25'E |
| Birecik, Tur. (bē-rĕd-zhēk′) | 163 | 37°10'N | 37°50'E |
| Bir Gara, Chad | 235 | 13°11'N | 15°58'E |
| Bīrjand, Iran (bēr′jänd) | 198 | 33°07'N | 59°16'E |
| Birkenfeld, Or., U.S. | 116c | 45°59'N | 123°20'W |
| Birkenhead, Eng., U.K. (bûr′kĕn-hĕd) | 164 | 53°23'N | 3°02'W |
| Birkenwerder, Ger. (bēr′kĕn-vĕr-dĕr) | 159b | 52°41'N | 13°22'E |
| Birmingham, Eng., U.K. | 154 | 52°29'N | 1°53'W |
| Birmingham, Al., U.S. (bûr′mĭng-häm) | 105 | 33°31'N | 86°49'W |
| Birmingham, Mi., U.S. | 111b | 42°32'N | 83°13'W |
| Birmingham, Mo., U.S. | 117f | 39°10'N | 94°22'W |
| Birmingham Canal, can., Eng., U.K. | 158a | 53°07'N | 2°40'W |
| Bi'r Misāhah, Egypt | 231 | 22°16'N | 28°04'E |
| Birnin Kebbi, Nig. | 230 | 12°32'N | 4°12'E |
| Birobidzhan, Russia (bē′rṓ-bė-jän′) | 179 | 48°42'N | 133°28'E |
| Birsk, Russia (bĭrsk) | 178 | 55°25'N | 55°30'E |
| Birstall, Eng., U.K. (bûr′stôl) | 158a | 53°44'N | 1°39'W |
| Biryulëvo, Russia (bēr-yōōl′yô-vô) | 186b | 55°35'N | 37°39'E |
| Biryusa, r., Russia (bēr-yōō′sä) | 184 | 56°43'N | 97°30'E |
| Bi'r Za'farānah, Egypt | 197a | 29°07'N | 32°38'E |
| Biržai, Lith. (bėr-zhä′ė) | 167 | 56°11'N | 24°45'E |
| Bisbee, Az., U.S. (bĭz′bē) | 104 | 31°30'N | 109°55'W |
| Biscay, Bay of, b., Eur. (bĭs′kā′) | 156 | 45°19'N | 3°51'W |
| Biscayne Bay, b., Fl., U.S. (bĭs-kān′) | 125a | 25°22'N | 80°15'W |
| Bischeim, Fr. (bĭsh′hīm) | 171 | 48°40'N | 7°48'E |
| Biscotasi Lake, l., Can. | 98 | 47°20'N | 81°55'W |
| Biser, Russia (bē′sĕr) | 186a | 58°24'N | 58°54'E |
| Biševo, is., Serb. (bē′shĕ-vō) | 174 | 42°58'N | 15°50'E |
| Bishkek, Kyrg. | 183 | 42°49'N | 74°42'E |
| Bisho, S. Afr. | 232 | 32°50'S | 27°20'E |
| Bishop, Ca., U.S. (bĭsh′ŭp) | 118 | 37°22'N | 118°25'W |
| Bishop, Tx., U.S. | 123 | 27°35'N | 97°46'W |
| Bishop's Castle, Eng., U.K. (bĭsh′ŏps käs′l) | 158a | 52°29'N | 2°57'W |
| Bishopville, S.C., U.S. (bĭsh′ŭp-vĭl) | 125 | 34°11'N | 80°13'W |
| Bismarck, N.D., U.S. (bĭz′märk) | 104 | 46°48'N | 100°46'W |
| Bismarck Archipelago, is., Pap. N. Gui. | 213 | 3°15'S | 150°45'E |
| Bismarck Range, mts., Pap. N. Gui. | 213 | 5°15'S | 144°15'E |
| Bissau, Gui.-B. (bė-sa′ōō) | 234 | 11°51'N | 15°35'W |
| Bissett, Can. | 97 | 51°01'N | 95°45'W |
| Bistineau, l., La., U.S. (bĭs-tĭ-nō′) | 123 | 32°19'N | 93°45'W |
| Bistrita, Rom. (bĭs-trĭt-sȧ) | 163 | 47°09'N | 24°29'E |
| Bistrita, r., Rom. | 169 | 47°08'N | 25°47'E |
| Bitlis, Tur. (bĭt-lēs′) | 198 | 38°30'N | 42°00'E |
| Bitola, Mac. (bė′tô-lä) (mṓ′nä-stėr) | 174 | 41°02'N | 21°22'E |
| Bitonto, Italy (bė-tôn′tō) | 174 | 41°08'N | 16°42'E |
| Bitter Creek, r., Wy., U.S. (bĭt′ẽr) | 115 | 41°36'N | 108°29'W |
| Bitterfeld, Ger. (bĭt′ẽr-fĕlt) | 168 | 51°39'N | 12°19'E |
| Bitterroot, r., Mt., U.S. | 115 | 46°28'N | 114°10'W |
| Bitterroot Range, mts., U.S. (bĭt′ẽr-ōōt) | 106 | 47°15'N | 115°13'W |
| Bityug, r., Russia (bĭt′yōōg) | 177 | 51°23'N | 40°33'E |
| Biu, Nig. | 235 | 10°35'N | 12°13'E |
| Biwabik, Mn., U.S. (bė-wä′bĭk) | 113 | 47°32'N | 92°24'W |
| Biwa-ko, l., Japan (bė-wä′kō) | 211 | 35°03'N | 135°51'E |
| Biya, r., Russia (bĭ′yȧ) | 184 | 52°22'N | 87°28'E |
| Biysk, Russia (bēsk) | 178 | 52°32'N | 85°28'E |
| Bizana, S. Afr. (bĭz-änä) | 233c | 30°51'S | 29°54'E |
| Bizerte, Tun. (bė-zĕrt′) | 230 | 37°23'N | 9°52'E |
| Bjelovar, Cro. (byĕ-lō′vär) | 174 | 45°54'N | 16°53'E |
| Bjørnafjorden, b., Nor. | 166 | 60°11'N | 5°26'E |
| Bla, Mali | 234 | 12°57'N | 5°46'W |
| Black, l., Mi., U.S. (blăk) | 108 | 45°25'N | 84°15'W |
| Black, l., N.Y., U.S. | 109 | 44°30'N | 75°35'W |
| Black, r., Asia | 212 | 21°00'N | 103°30'E |
| Black, r., Can. | 98 | 49°20'N | 81°15'W |
| Black, r., Az., U.S. | 119 | 33°35'N | 109°35'W |
| Black, r., N.Y., U.S. | 109 | 43°45'N | 75°20'W |
| Black, r., S.C., U.S. | 125 | 33°55'N | 80°10'W |
| Black, r., Wi., U.S. | 113 | 44°07'N | 90°56'W |
| Black, r., U.S. | 121 | 35°47'N | 91°22'W |
| Blackall, Austl. (blăk′ŭl) | 219 | 24°23'S | 145°37'E |
| Black Bay, b., Can. (blăk) | 98 | 48°36'N | 88°32'W |
| Blackburn, Eng., U.K. (blăk′bûrn) | 164 | 53°45'N | 2°28'W |
| Blackburn Mount, mtn., Ak., U.S. | 103 | 61°50'N | 143°12'W |
| Black Butte Lake, res., Ca., U.S. | 118 | 39°45'N | 122°20'W |
| Black Canyon of the Gunnison National Park, rec., Co., U.S. | 119 | 38°34'N | 107°43'W |
| Black Diamond, Wa., U.S. (dī′mŭnd) | 116a | 47°19'N | 122°00'W |
| Black Down Hills, hills, Eng., U.K. (blăk′doun) | 164 | 50°58'N | 3°19'W |
| Blackduck, Mn., U.S. (blăk′dŭk) | 113 | 47°41'N | 94°33'W |
| Blackfeet Indian Reservation, I.R., Mt., U.S. | 115 | 48°40'N | 113°00'W |
| Blackfoot, Id., U.S. (blăk′fŏt) | 115 | 43°11'N | 112°23'W |
| Blackfoot, r., Mt., U.S. | 115 | 46°53'N | 113°33'W |
| Blackfoot Indian Reservation, I.R., Mt., U.S. | 115 | 48°49'N | 112°53'W |
| Blackfoot Indian Reserve, I.R., Can. | 95 | 50°45'N | 113°00'W |
| Blackfoot Reservoir, res., Id., U.S. | 115 | 42°53'N | 111°23'W |
| Black Forest *see* Schwarzwald, for., Ger. | 168 | 47°54'N | 7°57'E |
| Black Hills, mts., U.S. | 106 | 44°08'N | 103°47'W |
| Black Island, i., Can. | 97 | 51°10'N | 96°30'W |
| Black Lake, Can. | 99 | 46°02'N | 71°24'W |
| Black Mesa, Az., U.S. (blăk māsȧ) | 119 | 36°33'N | 110°40'W |
| Blackmud Creek, r., Can. (blăk′mŭd) | 102g | 53°28'N | 113°34'W |
| Blackpool, Eng., U.K. (blăk′pōōl) | 164 | 53°49'N | 3°02'W |
| Black Range, mts., N.M., U.S. | 106 | 33°15'N | 107°55'W |
| Black River, Jam. (blăk′) | 134 | 18°00'N | 77°50'W |
| Black River Falls, Wi., U.S. | 113 | 44°18'N | 90°51'W |
| Black Rock Desert, des., Nv., U.S. (rŏk) | 114 | 40°55'N | 119°00'W |
| Blacksburg, S.C., U.S. (blăks′bûrg) | 125 | 35°09'N | 81°30'W |
| Black Sea, sea | 157 | 43°01'N | 32°16'E |
| Blackshear, Ga., U.S. (blăk′shĭr) | 125 | 31°20'N | 82°15'W |
| Blackstone, Va., U.S. (blăk′stṓn) | 125 | 37°04'N | 78°00'W |
| Black Sturgeon, r., Can. (stû′jŭn) | 98 | 49°12'N | 88°41'W |
| Blacktown, Austl. (blăk′toun) | 217b | 33°47'S | 150°55'E |
| Blackville, Can. (blăk′vĭl) | 100 | 46°44'N | 65°50'W |
| Blackville, S.C., U.S. | 125 | 33°21'N | 81°19'W |
| Black Volta (Volta Noire), r., Afr. | 230 | 11°30'N | 4°00'W |
| Black Warrior, r., Al., U.S. (blăk wŏr′ĭ-ẽr) | 124 | 32°37'N | 87°42'W |
| Blackwater, r., Ire. (blăk-wô′tẽr) | 164 | 52°05'N | 9°02'W |
| Blackwater, r., Mo., U.S. | 121 | 38°53'N | 93°22'W |
| Blackwater, r., Va., U.S. | 125 | 37°07'N | 77°10'W |
| Blackwell, Ok., U.S. (blăk′wĕl) | 121 | 36°47'N | 97°19'W |
| Bladel, Neth. | 159a | 51°22'N | 5°15'E |
| Blagodarnoye, Russia (blä′gṓ-där-nō′yĕ) | 181 | 45°00'N | 43°30'E |
| Blagoevgrad, Blg. | 175 | 42°01'N | 23°06'E |
| Blagoveshchensk, Russia (blä′gŏ-vyĕsh′chĕnsk) | 179 | 50°16'N | 127°47'E |
| Blagoveshchensk, Russia | 186a | 55°03'N | 56°00'E |
| Blaine, Mn., U.S. (blān) | 117g | 45°11'N | 93°14'W |
| Blaine, Wa., U.S. | 116d | 48°59'N | 122°49'W |
| Blaine, W.V., U.S. | 109 | 39°25'N | 79°10'W |
| Blair, Ne., U.S. (blâr) | 112 | 41°33'N | 96°09'W |
| Blairmore, Can. | 95 | 49°38'N | 114°25'W |
| Blairsville, Pa., U.S. (blârs′vĭl) | 109 | 40°30'N | 79°40'W |
| Blake, i., Wa., U.S. (blāk) | 116a | 47°37'N | 122°28'W |
| Blakely, Ga., U.S. (blāk′lė) | 124 | 31°22'N | 84°55'W |
| Blanc, Cap, c., Afr. | 230 | 20°39'N | 18°08'W |
| Blanc, Mont, mtn., Eur. (môɴ bläɴ) | 156 | 45°50'N | 6°53'E |
| Blanca, Bahía, b., Arg. (bä-ē′ä-blȧn′kä) | 144 | 39°30'S | 61°00'W |
| Blanca Peak, mtn., Co., U.S. (blăŋ′kȧ) | 106 | 37°36'N | 105°22'W |
| Blanche, r., Can. | 102c | 45°34'N | 75°38'W |
| Blanche, Lake, l., Austl. (blănch) | 222 | 29°20'S | 139°12'E |
| Blanchester, Oh., U.S. (blăn′chĕs-tẽr) | 111f | 39°18'N | 83°58'W |
| Blanco, r., Mex. | 130 | 24°05'N | 99°21'W |
| Blanco, r., Mex. | 131 | 18°42'N | 96°03'W |
| Blanco, Cabo, c., Arg. (bläŋ′kṓ) | 144 | 47°08'S | 65°47'W |
| Blanco, Cabo, c., C.R. (kȧ′bṓ-blăŋ′kō) | 132 | 9°29'N | 85°15'W |
| Blanco, Cape, c., Or., U.S. (blăn′kō) | 114 | 42°53'N | 124°38'W |
| Blancos, Cayo, i., Cuba (kä′yō-blăŋ′kōs) | 134 | 23°15'N | 80°55'W |
| Blanding, Ut., U.S. | 119 | 37°40'N | 109°31'W |
| Blankenfelde, Ger. (blän′kĕn-fĕl-dĕ) | 159b | 52°20'N | 13°24'E |
| Blanquefort, Fr. | 170 | 44°53'N | 0°38'W |
| Blanquilla, Arrecife, i., Mex. (är-rĕ-sē′fĕ-blän-kė′l-yä) | 131 | 21°32'N | 97°14'W |
| Blantyre, Mwi. (blăn-tĭyr) | 232 | 15°47'S | 35°00'E |
| Blasdell, N.Y., U.S. (blāz′dĕl) | 111c | 42°48'N | 78°51'W |
| Blato, Cro. (blä′tō) | 174 | 42°55'N | 16°47'E |
| Blaye-et-Sainte Luce, Fr. (blā′ā-săɴt-lüs′) | 170 | 45°08'N | 0°40'W |
| Blażowa, Pol. (bwä-zhō′vȧ) | 169 | 49°51'N | 22°05'E |
| Bleus, Monts, mts., D.R.C. | 237 | 1°10'N | 30°10'E |
| Blind River, Can. (blīnd) | 91 | 46°10'N | 83°09'W |
| Blissfield, Mi., U.S. (blĭs-fēld) | 108 | 41°50'N | 83°50'W |
| Blithe, r., Eng., U.K. (blĭth) | 158a | 52°22'N | 1°49'W |
| Blitta, Togo | 234 | 8°19'N | 0°59'E |
| Block, i., R.I., U.S. (blŏk) | 109 | 41°05'N | 71°35'W |
| Bloedel, Can. | 94 | 50°07'N | 125°23'W |
| Bloemfontein, S. Afr. (blōōm′fŏn-tān) | 232 | 29°09'S | 26°16'E |
| Blois, Fr. (blwä) | 161 | 47°36'N | 1°21'E |
| Blood Indian Reserve, I.R., Can. | 95 | 49°30'N | 113°10'W |
| Bloomer, Wi., U.S. (blōōm′ẽr) | 113 | 45°07'N | 91°30'W |
| Bloomfield, Ia., U.S. | 113 | 40°44'N | 92°21'W |
| Bloomfield, In., U.S. (blōōm′fēld) | 108 | 39°00'N | 86°55'W |
| Bloomfield, Mo., U.S. | 121 | 36°54'N | 89°55'W |
| Bloomfield, Ne., U.S. | 112 | 42°36'N | 97°40'W |
| Bloomfield, N.J., U.S. | 110a | 40°48'N | 74°12'W |
| Bloomfield Hills, Mi., U.S. | 111b | 42°35'N | 83°15'W |
| Blooming Prairie, Mn., U.S. (blōōm′ĭng prā′rĭ) | 113 | 43°52'N | 93°04'W |
| Bloomington, Ca., U.S. (blōōm′ĭng-tŭn) | 117a | 34°04'N | 117°24'W |
| Bloomington, Il., U.S. | 105 | 40°30'N | 89°00'W |
| Bloomington, In., U.S. | 108 | 39°10'N | 86°35'W |
| Bloomington, Mn., U.S. | 117g | 44°50'N | 93°18'W |
| Bloomsburg, Pa., U.S. (blōōmz′bûrg) | 109 | 41°00'N | 76°25'W |
| Blossburg, Al., U.S. (blŏs′bûrg) | 110h | 33°38'N | 86°57'W |
| Blossburg, Pa., U.S. | 109 | 41°45'N | 77°00'W |
| Bloubergstrand, S. Afr. | 232a | 33°48'S | 18°28'E |
| Blountstown, Fl., U.S. (blŭnts′tun) | 124 | 30°24'N | 85°02'W |
| Bludenz, Aus. (blōō-dĕnts′) | 168 | 47°09'N | 9°50'E |
| Blue Ash, Oh., U.S. (blōō ăsh) | 111f | 39°14'N | 84°23'W |
| Blue Earth, Mn., U.S. (blōō ûrth) | 113 | 43°38'N | 94°05'W |
| Blue Earth, r., Mn., U.S. | 113 | 43°55'N | 94°16'W |
| Bluefield, W.V., U.S. (blōō′fēld) | 125 | 37°15'N | 81°11'W |
| Bluefields, Nic. (blōō′fēldz) | 129 | 12°03'N | 83°45'W |
| Blue Island, Il., U.S. | 111a | 41°39'N | 87°41'W |
| Blue Mesa Reservoir, res., Co., U.S. | 119 | 38°25'N | 107°00'W |
| Blue Mountain, mtn., Can. | 101 | 50°28'N | 57°11'W |
| Blue Mountains, mts., Austl. | 221 | 33°35'S | 149°00'E |
| Blue Mountains, mts., Jam. | 134 | 18°05'N | 76°35'W |
| Blue Mountains, mts., U.S. | 106 | 45°15'N | 118°50'W |
| Blue Mud Bay, b., Austl. (bōō mŭd) | 220 | 13°20'S | 136°45'E |
| Blue Nile, r., Afr. | 231 | 12°30'N | 34°00'E |
| Blue Rapids, Ks., U.S. (blōō răp′ĭdz) | 121 | 39°40'N | 96°41'W |
| Blue Ridge, mtn., U.S. (blōō rĭj) | 107 | 35°30'N | 82°50'W |
| Blue River, Can. | 90 | 52°05'N | 119°17'W |
| Blue River, r., Mo., U.S. | 117f | 38°55'N | 94°33'W |
| Bluff, Ut., U.S. | 119 | 37°18'N | 109°34'W |
| Bluff Park, Al., U.S. | 110h | 33°24'N | 86°52'W |
| Bluffton, In., U.S. (blŭf-tŭn) | 108 | 40°40'N | 85°15'W |
| Bluffton, Oh., U.S. | 108 | 40°50'N | 83°55'W |
| Blumenau, Braz. (blōō′mĕn-ou) | 144 | 26°53'S | 48°58'W |
| Blumut, Gunong, mtn., Malay. | 197b | 2°03'N | 103°34'E |
| Blyth, Eng., U.K. (blīth) | 164 | 55°03'N | 1°34'W |
| Blythe, Ca., U.S. | 119 | 33°37'N | 114°37'W |
| Blytheville, Ar., U.S. (blīth′vĭl) | 121 | 35°55'N | 89°51'W |
| Bo, S.L. | 234 | 7°56'N | 11°21'W |
| Boac, Phil. | 213a | 13°26'N | 121°50'E |
| Boaco, Nic. (bṓ-ä′kō) | 132 | 12°24'N | 85°41'W |
| Bo'ai, China (bwo-ī) | 208 | 35°10'N | 113°08'E |
| Boa Vista, i., C.V. (bō-ä-vēsh′tȧ) | 230b | 16°01'N | 23°52'W |
| Boa Vista do Rio Branco, Braz. | 143 | 2°46'N | 60°45'W |
| Bobo Dioulasso, Burkina (bō′bṓ-dyōō-lȧs-sō′) | 230 | 11°12'N | 4°18'W |
| Bobr, Bela. (bṓ′b'r) | 176 | 54°19'N | 29°11'E |
| Bóbr, r., Pol. (bŭ′br) | 168 | 51°44'N | 15°13'E |
| Bobrov, Russia (bŭb-rôf′) | 181 | 51°07'N | 40°01'E |
| Bobrovyts'a, Ukr. | 177 | 50°43'N | 31°27'E |
| Bobrynets', Ukr. | 177 | 48°04'N | 32°10'E |
| Boca del Pozo, Ven. (bô-kä-dĕl-pṓ′zŏ) | 143b | 11°00'N | 64°21'W |
| Boca de Uchire, Ven. (bô-kä-dĕ-ōō-chē′rĕ) | 143b | 10°09'N | 65°27'W |
| Bocaina, Serra da, mtn., Braz. (sĕ′r-rä-dȧ-bṓ-kä′ē-nä) | 141a | 22°47'S | 44°39'W |
| Bocas, Mex. (bō′käs) | 130 | 22°29'N | 101°03'W |
| Bocas del Toro, Pan. (bō′käs dĕl tō′rō) | 133 | 9°24'N | 82°15'W |
| Bochnia, Pol. (bōĸ′nyä) | 169 | 49°58'N | 20°28'E |
| Bocholt, Ger. (bō′ĸōlt) | 171c | 51°50'N | 6°37'E |
| Bochum, Ger. | 168 | 51°29'N | 7°13'E |
| Bockum-Hövel, Ger. (bō′ĸȯm-hû′fĕl) | 171c | 51°41'N | 7°45'E |
| Bodalang, D.R.C. | 236 | 3°14'N | 22°14'E |
| Bodaybo, Russia (bō-dī′bō) | 179 | 57°12'N | 114°46'E |
| Bodele, depr., Chad (bō-dȧ-lā′) | 231 | 16°45'N | 17°05'E |
| Boden, Swe. | 160 | 65°51'N | 21°29'E |
| Bodensee, l., Eur. (bō′dĕn zā) | 156 | 47°48'N | 9°22'E |
| Bodmin, Eng., U.K. (bŏd′mĭn) | 164 | 50°29'N | 4°45'W |
| Bodmin Moor, Eng., U.K. (bŏd′mĭn mȯr) | 164 | 50°36'N | 4°43'W |
| Bodrum, Tur. | 181 | 37°10'N | 27°07'E |
| Boende, D.R.C. (bô-ĕn′dȧ) | 232 | 0°13'S | 20°52'E |
| Boerne, Tx., U.S. (bō′ẽrn) | 122 | 29°49'N | 98°44'W |
| Boesmans, r., S. Afr. | 233c | 33°29'S | 26°09'E |
| Boeuf, r., U.S. (bĕf) | 123 | 32°23'N | 91°57'W |


ng-sing; ŋ-baŋk; ɴ-nasalized n; nŏd; cŏmmit; ōld; ôbey; ôrder; oi-boil; fōōd; ȯ-as oo in foot; ou-out; s-soft; sh-dish; th-thin; pūre; ůnite; ûrn; stŭd; circŭs; ü-as in French tu; ′-indeterminate vowel.

274 Boffa – Bowie PRONOUNCING INDEX


| PLACE (Pronunciation) | PAGE | LAT. | LONG. |
|---|---|---|---|
| Boffa, Gui. (bôf'á) | 230 | 10°10'N | 14°02'W |
| Bōfu, Japan (bō'fōō) | 211 | 34°03'N | 131°35'E |
| Bogalusa, La., U.S. (bō-gȧ-lōō'sȧ) | 123 | 30°48'N | 89°52'W |
| Bogan, r., Austl. (bŏ'gĕn) | 222 | 32°10'S | 147°40'E |
| Bogense, Den. (bō'gĕn-sĕ) | 166 | 55°34'N | 10°09'E |
| Boggy Peak, mtn., Antig. (bŏg'ĭ-pēk) | 133b | 17°03'N | 61°50'W |
| Bogong, Mount, mtn., Austl. | 222 | 36°50'S | 147°15'E |
| Bogor, Indon. | 212 | 6°45'S | 106°45'E |
| Bogoroditsk, Russia (bŏ-gŏ'rŏ-dĭtsk) | 176 | 53°48'N | 38°06'E |
| Bogorodsk, Russia | 180 | 56°02'N | 43°40'E |
| Bogorodskoye, Russia (bô-gô-rôd'skô-yĕ) | 186a | 56°43'N | 56°53'E |
| Bogotá, Col. | 142 | 4°36'N | 74°05'W |
| Bogotol, Russia (bŏ'gō-tŏl) | 179 | 56°15'N | 89°45'E |
| Boguchar, Russia (bō'gō-chär) | 181 | 49°40'N | 41°00'E |
| Bogue Chitto, Ms., U.S. (nôr'fēld) | 124 | 31°26'N | 90°25'W |
| Boguete, Pan. (bŏ-gĕ'tĕ) | 133 | 8°54'N | 82°29'W |
| Bo Hai, b., China | 205 | 38°30'N | 120°00'E |
| Bohai Haixia, strt., China (bwo-hī hī-shyä) | 208 | 38°05'N | 121°40'E |
| Bohain-en-Vermandois, Fr. (bō-ăn-ŏn-vâr-män-dwä') | 170 | 49°58'N | 3°22'E |
| Bohemia see Čechy, hist. reg., Czech Rep. | 168 | 49°51'N | 13°55'E |
| Bohemian Forest, mts., Eur. (bō-hē'mĭ-ăn) | 156 | 49°35'N | 12°27'E |
| Bohodukhiv, Ukr. | 181 | 50°10'N | 35°31'E |
| Bohol, i., Phil. (bō-hôl') | 213 | 9°28'N | 124°35'E |
| Bohom, Mex. (bŏ-ô'm) | 131 | 16°47'N | 92°42'W |
| Bohuslav, Ukr. | 177 | 49°34'N | 30°51'W |
| Boiestown, Can. (boiz'toun) | 100 | 46°27'N | 66°25'W |
| Bois Blanc, i., Mi., U.S. (boi' blăŋk) | 108 | 45°45'N | 84°30'W |
| Boischâtel, Can. (bwä-shä-tĕl') | 102b | 46°54'N | 71°08'W |
| Bois-des-Filion, Can. (bōō-ä'dĕ-fē-yŏn') | 102a | 45°40'N | 73°46'W |
| Boise, Id., U.S. (boi'zē) | 104 | 43°38'N | 116°12'W |
| Boise, r., Id., U.S. | 114 | 43°43'N | 116°30'W |
| Boise City, Ok., U.S. | 120 | 36°42'N | 102°30'W |
| Boissevain, Can. (bois'vān) | 90 | 49°14'N | 100°03'W |
| Bojador, Cabo, c., W. Sah. | 230 | 26°21'N | 16°08'W |
| Bojnūrd, Iran | 198 | 37°29'N | 57°13'E |
| Bokani, Nig. | 235 | 9°26'N | 5°13'E |
| Boknafjorden, b., Nor. | 160 | 59°12'N | 5°37'E |
| Boksburg, S. Afr. (bŏks'bûrgh) | 233b | 26°13'N | 28°15'E |
| Bokungu, D.R.C. | 236 | 0°41'S | 22°19'E |
| Bol, Chad | 235 | 13°28'N | 14°43'E |
| Bolai I, C.A.R. | 235 | 4°20'N | 17°21'E |
| Bolama, Gui.-B. (bō-lä'mä) | 230 | 11°34'S | 15°41'W |
| Bolan, mtn., Pak. (bō-län') | 202 | 30°13'N | 67°09'E |
| Bolaños, Mex. (bō-län'yŏs) | 130 | 21°40'N | 103°48'W |
| Bolaños, r., Mex. | 130 | 21°26'N | 103°54'W |
| Bolan Pass, p., Pak. | 199 | 29°50'N | 67°10'E |
| Bolbec, Fr. (bōl-bĕk') | 170 | 49°37'N | 0°26'E |
| Bole, Ghana (bō'lā) | 230 | 9°02'N | 2°29'W |
| Bolesławiec, Pol. (bō-lĕ-slä'vyĕts) | 168 | 51°15'N | 15°35'E |
| Bolgatanga, Ghana | 234 | 10°46'N | 0°52'W |
| Bolhrad, Ukr. | 181 | 45°41'N | 28°38'E |
| Boli, China (bwo-lē) | 205 | 45°40'N | 130°38'E |
| Bolinao, Phil. (bō-lē-nä'ō) | 213a | 16°24'N | 119°53'E |
| Bolívar, Arg. (bō-lē'vär) | 144 | 36°15'S | 61°05'W |
| Bolívar, Col. | 142 | 1°46'N | 76°58'W |
| Bolivar, Mo., U.S. (bŏl'ĭ-vȧr) | 121 | 37°37'N | 93°22'W |
| Bolivar, Tn., U.S. | 124 | 35°14'N | 88°56'W |
| Bolívar, Pico, mtn., Ven. | 142 | 8°44'N | 70°54'W |
| Bolivar Peninsula, pen., Tx., U.S. (bŏl'ĭ-vȧr) | 123a | 29°25'N | 94°40'W |
| Bolivia, nation, S.A. (bō-lĭv'ĭ-ȧ) | 142 | 17°00'S | 64°00'W |
| Bolkhov, Russia (bōl-kôf') | 180 | 53°27'N | 35°59'E |
| Bollin, r., Eng., U.K. (bŏl'ĭn) | 158a | 53°18'N | 2°11'W |
| Bollington, Eng., U.K. (bôl'ĭng-tŭn) | 158a | 53°18'N | 2°06'W |
| Bollnäs, Swe. (bôl'nĕs) | 166 | 61°22'N | 16°20'E |
| Bolmen, l., Swe. (bôl'mĕn) | 166 | 56°58'N | 13°25'E |
| Bolobo, D.R.C. (bō'lō-bō) | 232 | 2°14'S | 16°18'E |
| Bologna, Italy (bō-lōn'yä) | 154 | 44°30'N | 11°18'E |
| Bologoye, Russia (bŏ-lŏ-gô'yĕ) | 180 | 57°52'N | 34°02'E |
| Bolonchenticul, Mex. (bô-lôn-chĕn-tē-kōō'l) | 132a | 20°03'N | 89°47'W |
| Bolondrón, Cuba (bō-lôn-drōn') | 134 | 22°45'N | 81°25'W |
| Bolseno, Lago di, l., Italy (lä'gō-dē-bôl-sä'nō) | 174 | 42°35'N | 11°40'E |
| Bol'shaya Anyuy, r., Russia | 185 | 67°58'N | 161°15'E |
| Bol'shaya Chuya, r., Russia | 185 | 58°15'N | 111°40'E |
| Bol'shaya Kinel', r., Russia | 180 | 53°20'N | 52°40'E |
| Bol'she Ust'ikinskoye, Russia (bôl'she ŏs-tyĭ-kēn'skô-yĕ) | 186a | 55°58'N | 58°18'E |
| Bol'shoy Begichëv, i., Russia | 179 | 74°30'N | 114°40'E |
| Bol'shoye Ivonino, Russia (ĭ-vô'nĭ-nō) | 186a | 59°41'N | 61°12'E |
| Bol'shoy Kuyash, Russia (bôl'-shôy kōō'yȧsh) | 186a | 55°52'N | 61°07'E |
| Bolsover, Eng., U.K. (bōl'zō-vẽr) | 158a | 53°14'N | 1°17'W |
| Boltaña, Spain (bôl-tä'nä) | 173 | 42°28'N | 0°03'E |
| Bolton, Can. (bōl'tŭn) | 102d | 43°53'N | 79°44'W |
| Bolton, Eng., U.K. | 164 | 53°35'N | 2°26'W |
| Bolton-upon-Dearne, Eng., U.K. (bōl'tŭn-ŭp'ŏn-dûrn) | 158a | 53°31'N | 1°19'W |
| Bolu, Tur. (bō'lŏ) | 163 | 40°45'N | 31°45'E |
| Bolva, r., Russia (bôl'vä) | 176 | 53°30'N | 34°30'E |
| Bolvadin, Tur. (bōl-vä-dēn') | 163 | 38°50'N | 30°50'E |
| Bolzano, Italy (bôl-tsä'nō) | 162 | 46°31'N | 11°22'E |
| Boma, D.R.C. (bō'mä) | 232 | 5°51'S | 13°03'E |
| Bombala, Austl. (bŭm-bä'lȧ) | 219 | 36°55'S | 149°07'E |
| Bombay see Mumbai, India | 199 | 18°58'N | 72°50'E |
| Bombay Harbour, b., India | 203b | 18°55'N | 72°52'E |
| Bomi Hills, Lib. | 230 | 7°00'N | 11°00'W |
| Bom Jardim, Braz. (bôn zhär-dēn') | 141a | 22°10'S | 42°25'W |
| Bom Jesus do Itabapoana, Braz. | 141a | 21°08'S | 41°51'W |
| Bømlo, i., Nor. (bûmlô) | 166 | 59°47'N | 4°57'E |
| Bomongo, D.R.C. | 231 | 1°22'N | 18°21'E |
| Bom Sucesso, Braz. (bôn-sōō-sĕ'sō) | 141a | 21°02'S | 44°44'W |
| Bomu see Mbomou, r., Afr. | 231 | 4°50'N | 24°00'E |
| Bon, Cap, c., Tun. (bôn) | 162 | 37°04'N | 11°13'E |
| Bonaire, i., Neth. Ant. (bō-nâr') | 142 | 12°10'N | 68°15'W |
| Bonavista, Can. (bŏ-nȧ-vĭs'tȧ) | 93a | 48°39'N | 53°07'W |
| Bonavista Bay, b., Can. | 93a | 48°45'N | 53°20'W |
| Bond, Co., U.S. (bŏnd) | 120 | 39°53'N | 106°40'W |
| Bondo, D.R.C. (bôn'dō) | 184 | 3°49'N | 23°40'E |
| Bondoc Peninsula, pen., Phil. (bôn-dŏk') | 213a | 13°24'N | 122°30'E |
| Bondoukou, C. Iv. (bŏn-dōō'kōō) | 230 | 8°02'N | 2°48'W |
| Bonds Cay, i., Bah. (bŏnds kē) | 134 | 25°30'N | 77°45'W |
| Bondy, Fr. | 171b | 48°54'N | 2°28'E |
| Bône see Annaba, Alg. | 230 | 36°57'N | 7°39'E |
| Bone, Teluk, b., Indon. | 212 | 4°09'S | 121°00'E |
| Bonete, Cerro, mtn., Arg. (bô'nĕtĕh çĕrrō) | 144 | 27°50'S | 68°35'W |
| Bonfim, Braz. (bôn-fē'n) | 141a | 20°20'S | 44°15'W |
| Bongor, Chad | 235 | 10°17'N | 15°22'E |
| Bonham, Tx., U.S. (bŏn'ăm) | 121 | 33°35'N | 96°09'W |
| Bonhomme, Pic, mtn., Haiti | 135 | 19°10'N | 72°20'W |
| Bonifacio, Fr. (bō-nē-fä'chō) | 174 | 41°23'N | 9°10'E |
| Bonifacio, Strait of, strt., Eur. | 162 | 41°14'N | 9°02'E |
| Bonifay, Fl., U.S. (bŏn-ĭ-fā') | 124 | 30°46'N | 85°40'W |
| Bonin Islands, is., Japan (bō'nĭn) | 241 | 26°30'N | 141°00'E |
| Bonn, Ger. (bōn) | 154 | 50°44'N | 7°06'E |
| Bonne Bay, b., Can. (bŏn) | 101 | 49°33'N | 57°55'W |
| Bonners Ferry, Id., U.S. (bonẽrz fĕr'ĭ) | 114 | 48°41'N | 116°19'W |
| Bonner Springs, Ks., U.S. (bŏn'ẽr sprĭngz) | 117f | 39°04'N | 94°52'W |
| Bonne Terre, Mo., U.S. (bŏn târ') | 121 | 37°55'N | 90°32'W |
| Bonnet Peak, mtn., Can. (bŏn'ĭt) | 95 | 51°26'N | 115°53'W |
| Bonneville Dam, dam, U.S. (bôn'ĕ-vĭl) | 114 | 45°37'N | 121°57'W |
| Bonny, Nig. (bŏn'ē) | 230 | 4°29'N | 7°13'E |
| Bonny Lake, Wa., U.S. (bŏn'ē lăk) | 116a | 47°11'N | 122°11'W |
| Bonnyville, Can. (bŏnē-vĭl) | 95 | 54°16'N | 110°44'W |
| Bonorva, Italy (bō-nôr'vä) | 174 | 40°26'N | 8°46'E |
| Bonthain, Indon. (bôn-tīn') | 212 | 5°30'S | 119°52'E |
| Bonthe, S.L. | 230 | 7°32'N | 12°30'W |
| Bontoc, Phil. (bŏn-tŏk') | 213a | 17°10'N | 121°01'E |
| Booby Rocks, is., Bah. (bōō'bĭ rŏks) | 134 | 23°55'N | 77°00'W |
| Booker T. Washington National Monument, rec., Va., U.S. (bŏŏk'ẽr tē wŏsh'ĭng-tŭn) | 125 | 37°07'N | 79°45'W |
| Boom, Bel. | 159a | 51°05'N | 4°22'E |
| Boone, Ia., U.S. (bōōn) | 113 | 42°04'N | 93°51'W |
| Booneville, Ar., U.S. (bōōn'vĭl) | 121 | 35°09'N | 93°54'W |
| Booneville, Ky., U.S. | 108 | 37°25'N | 83°40'W |
| Booneville, Ms., U.S. | 124 | 34°37'N | 88°35'W |
| Boons, S. Afr. | 238c | 25°59'S | 27°15'E |
| Boonton, N.J., U.S. (bōōn'tŭn) | 110a | 40°54'N | 74°24'W |
| Boonville, In., U.S. | 108 | 38°00'N | 87°15'W |
| Boonville, Mo., U.S. | 121 | 38°57'N | 92°44'W |
| Boorama, Som. | 238a | 10°05'N | 43°08'E |
| Boosaaso, Som. | 238a | 11°19'N | 49°10'E |
| Boothbay Harbor, Me., U.S. (bōōth'bā här'bẽr) | 100 | 43°51'N | 69°39'W |
| Boothia, Gulf of, b., Can. (bōō'thĭ-ȧ) | 93 | 69°04'N | 86°04'W |
| Boothia Peninsula, pen., Can. | 89 | 73°30'N | 95°00'W |
| Bootle, Eng., U.K. (bōōt'l) | 158a | 53°29'N | 3°02'W |
| Bor, Sudan (bôr) | 231 | 6°13'N | 31°35'E |
| Bor, Tur. (bōr) | 181 | 37°50'N | 34°40'E |
| Boraha, Nosy, i., Madag. | 233 | 16°58'S | 50°15'E |
| Borah Peak, mtn., Id., U.S. (bō'rä) | 115 | 44°12'N | 113°47'W |
| Borås, Swe. (bō'rōs) | 160 | 57°43'N | 12°55'E |
| Borāzjān, Iran (bō-räz-jän') | 198 | 29°13'N | 51°13'E |
| Borba, Braz. (bŏr'bä) | 143 | 4°23'S | 59°31'W |
| Borborema, Planalto da, plat., Braz. (plä-nàl'tō-dä-bôr-bō-rĕ'mä) | 143 | 7°35'S | 36°40'W |
| Bordeaux, Fr. (bôr-dō') | 154 | 44°50'N | 0°37'W |
| Bordentown, N.J., U.S. (bôr'dĕn-toun) | 109 | 40°05'N | 74°40'W |
| Bordj-bou-Arréridj, Alg. (bôrj-bōō-ȧ-rā-rēj') | 162 | 36°03'N | 4°48'E |
| Bordj Omar Idriss, Alg. | 230 | 28°06'N | 6°34'E |
| Borgarnes, Ice. | 160 | 64°31'N | 21°40'W |
| Borger, Tx., U.S. (bôr'gẽr) | 120 | 35°40'N | 101°23'W |
| Borgholm, Swe. (bôrg-hōlm') | 166 | 56°52'N | 16°40'E |
| Borgne, l., La., U.S. (bôrn'y') | 123 | 30°03'N | 89°36'W |
| Borgomanero, Italy (bôr'gō-mä-nā'rō) | 174 | 45°40'N | 8°28'E |
| Borgo Val di Taro, Italy (bô'r-zhō-väl-dē-tá'rō) | 174 | 44°29'N | 9°44'E |
| Börili, Kaz. | 186a | 53°36'N | 61°55'E |
| Boring, Or., U.S. (bōring) | 116c | 45°26'N | 122°22'W |
| Borisoglebsk, Russia (bŏ-rē sŏ-glyĕpsk') | 178 | 51°20'N | 42°00'E |
| Borisovka, Russia (bŏ-rē-sôf'kȧ) | 181 | 50°38'N | 36°00'E |
| Borivli, India | 203b | 19°15'N | 72°48'E |
| Borja, Spain (bôr'hä) | 172 | 41°50'N | 1°33'W |
| Borken, Ger. (bōr'kĕn) | 171c | 51°50'N | 6°51'E |
| Borkou, reg., Chad (bôr-kōō') | 231 | 18°11'N | 18°28'E |
| Borkum, i., Ger. (bōr'kōōm) | 168 | 53°31'N | 6°50'E |
| Borlänge, Swe. (bôr-lĕŋ'gĕ) | 166 | 60°30'N | 15°24'E |
| Borneo, i., Asia | 212 | 0°25'N | 112°39'E |
| Bornholm, i., Den. (bôrn-hôlm) | 156 | 55°16'N | 15°15'E |
| Boromlia, Ukr. | 177 | 50°36'N | 34°58'E |
| Boromo, Burkina | 234 | 11°45'N | 2°56'W |
| Borovan, Blg. (bō-rō-vän') | 175 | 43°24'N | 23°47'E |
| Borovichi, Russia (bō-rô-vē'chē) | 178 | 58°22'N | 33°56'E |
| Borovsk, Russia (bô'rŏvsk) | 176 | 55°13'N | 36°26'E |
| Borraan, Som. | 238a | 10°38'N | 48°30'E |
| Borracha, Isla la, i., Ven. (ē's-lä-lȧ-bôr-rä'chä) | 143b | 10°18'N | 64°44'W |
| Borriana, Spain | 162 | 39°53'N | 0°05'W |
| Borroloola, Austl. (bŏr-rō-lōō'lȧ) | 218 | 16°15'S | 136°19'E |
| Borshchiv, Ukr. | 169 | 48°47'N | 26°04'E |
| Bort-les-Orgues, Fr. (bôr-lā-zôrg) | 170 | 45°26'N | 2°26'E |
| Borūjerd, Iran | 198 | 33°45'N | 48°53'E |
| Boryslav, Ukr. | 169 | 49°17'N | 23°24'E |
| Boryspil', Ukr. | 177 | 50°17'N | 30°54'E |
| Borzna, Ukr. (bôrz'nȧ) | 181 | 51°15'N | 32°26'E |
| Borzya, Russia (bôrz'yȧ) | 179 | 50°37'N | 116°53'E |
| Bosa, Italy (bō'sä) | 174 | 40°18'N | 8°34'E |
| Bosanska Dubica, Bos. (bō'sän-skä dōō'bĭt-sä) | 174 | 45°10'N | 16°49'E |
| Bosanska Gradiška, Bos. (bō'sän-skä grä-dĭsh'kä) | 175 | 45°08'N | 17°15'E |
| Bosanski Novi, Bos. (bō's sän-skĭ nō'vē) | 174 | 45°00'N | 16°22'E |
| Bosanski Petrovac, Bos. (bō'sän-skĭ pĕt'rō-väts) | 174 | 44°33'N | 16°23'E |
| Bosanski Šamac, Bos. (bō'sän-skĭ shä'mȧts) | 175 | 45°03'N | 18°30'E |
| Boscobel, Wi., U.S. (bŏs'kō-bĕl) | 113 | 43°08'N | 90°44'W |
| Bose, China (bwo-sŭ) | 209 | 24°00'N | 106°38'E |
| Boshan, China (bwo-shan) | 205 | 36°32'N | 117°51'E |
| Boskoop, Neth. | 159a | 52°04'N | 4°39'E |
| Boskovice, Czech Rep. (bŏs'kō-vē-tsĕ) | 168 | 49°26'N | 16°37'E |
| Bosna, r., Serb. | 175 | 44°19'N | 17°54'E |
| Bosnia and Herzegovina, nation, Eur. | 175 | 44°15'N | 17°30'E |
| Bosobolo, D.R.C. | 236 | 4°11'N | 19°54'E |
| Bosporus see İstanbul Boğazı, strt., Tur. | 198 | 41°10'N | 29°10'E |
| Bossangoa, C.A.R. | 235 | 6°29'N | 17°27'E |
| Bossier City, La., U.S. (bŏsh'ẽr) | 123 | 32°31'N | 93°42'W |
| Bosten Hu, l., China (bwo-stŭn hōō) | 204 | 42°06'N | 88°01'E |
| Boston, Ga., U.S. (bôs'tŭn) | 124 | 30°47'N | 83°47'W |
| Boston, Ma., U.S. | 105 | 42°15'N | 71°07'W |
| Boston Heights, Oh., U.S. | 111d | 41°15'N | 81°30'W |
| Boston Mountains, mts., Ar., U.S. | 107 | 35°46'N | 93°32'W |
| Botany Bay, b., Austl. (bŏt'ȧ-nĭ) | 221 | 33°58'S | 151°11'E |
| Botevgrad, Blg. | 175 | 42°54'N | 23°41'E |
| Bothaville, S. Afr. (bō'tä-vĭl) | 238c | 27°24'S | 26°38'E |
| Bothell, Wa., U.S. (bŏth'ĕl) | 116a | 47°46'N | 122°12'W |
| Bothnia, Gulf of, b., Eur. (bŏth'nĭ-ȧ) | 156 | 63°40'N | 21°30'E |
| Botoşani, Rom. (bō-tō-shàn'ĭ) | 169 | 47°46'N | 26°40'E |
| Botswana, nation, Afr. (bŏtswănă) | 232 | 22°10'S | 23°13'E |
| Bottineau, N.D., U.S. (bŏt-ĭ-nō') | 112 | 48°48'N | 100°28'W |
| Bottrop, Ger. (bōt'trōp) | 168 | 51°31'N | 6°56'E |
| Botwood, Can. (bŏt'wŏd) | 93a | 49°08'N | 55°21'W |
| Bouafle, C. Iv. (bŏ-ȧ-flā') | 230 | 6°59'N | 5°45'W |
| Bouar, C.A.R. (bōō-är) | 231 | 5°57'N | 15°36'E |
| Bou Areg, Sebkha, Mor. | 172 | 35°09'N | 3°02'W |
| Boubandjidah, Parc National de, rec., Cam. | 235 | 8°20'N | 14°40'E |
| Boucherville, Can. (bōō-shä-vēl') | 102a | 45°37'N | 73°27'W |
| Boudenib, Mor. (bōō-dĕ-nēb') | 230 | 32°14'N | 3°04'W |
| Boudette, Mn., U.S. (bōō-dĕt) | 113 | 48°42'N | 94°34'W |
| Boudouaou, Alg. | 173 | 36°44'N | 3°25'E |
| Boufarik, Alg. (bōō-fȧ-rēk') | 173 | 36°35'N | 2°55'E |
| Bougainville, i., Pap. N. Gui. | 214e | 6°00'S | 155°00'E |
| Bougainville Trench, deep (bōō-găn-vēl') | 241 | 7°00'S | 152°00'E |
| Bougie see Bejaïa, Alg. | 230 | 36°46'N | 5°00'E |
| Bougouni, Mali (bōō-gōō-nē') | 230 | 11°27'N | 7°30'W |
| Bouïra, Alg. (boo-ē'rȧ) | 162 | 36°25'N | 3°55'E |
| Bouïra-Sahary, Alg. (bwē-rȧ sȧ'ȧ-rē) | 173 | 35°16'N | 3°23'E |
| Bouka, r., Gui. | 234 | 11°05'N | 10°40'W |
| Boulder, Co., U.S. | 104 | 40°02'N | 105°19'W |
| Boulder, r., Mt., U.S. | 115 | 46°10'N | 112°07'W |
| Boulder City, Nv., U.S. | 104 | 35°57'N | 114°50'W |
| Boulder Peak, mtn., Id., U.S. | 115 | 43°53'N | 114°33'W |
| Boulogne-Billancourt, Fr. (bōō-lôn'y'-bē-yän-kōōr') | 170 | 48°50'N | 2°14'E |
| Boulogne-sur-Mer, Fr. (bōō-lôn'y-sür-mâr') | 161 | 50°44'N | 1°37'E |
| Boumba, r., Cam. | 235 | 3°20'N | 14°40'E |
| Bouna, C. Iv. (bōō-nä') | 230 | 9°16'N | 3°00'W |
| Bouna, Parc National de, rec., C. Iv. | 234 | 9°20'N | 3°35'W |
| Boundary Bay, b., N.A. (boun'dȧ-rĭ) | 116d | 49°03'N | 122°59'W |
| Boundary Peak, mtn., Nv., U.S. | 118 | 37°52'N | 118°20'W |
| Bound Brook, N.J., U.S. (bound brŏk) | 110a | 40°34'N | 74°32'W |
| Bountiful, Ut., U.S. (boun'tĭ-fŏl) | 117b | 40°55'N | 111°53'W |
| Bountiful Peak, mtn., Ut., U.S. (boun'tĭ-fŏl) | 117b | 40°58'N | 111°49'W |
| Bounty Islands, is., N.Z. | 5 | 47°42'S | 179°05'E |
| Bourail, N. Cal. | 214f | 21°34'S | 165°30'E |
| Bourem, Mali (bōō-rĕm') | 230 | 16°43'N | 0°15'W |
| Bourg-en-Bresse, Fr. (bōōr-gĕn-brĕs') | 161 | 46°12'N | 5°13'E |
| Bourges, Fr. (bōōrzh) | 161 | 47°06'N | 2°22'E |
| Bourget, Can. (bōōr-zhĕ') | 102c | 45°26'N | 75°09'W |
| Bourgoin, Fr. (bōōr-gwăn') | 171 | 45°46'N | 5°17'E |
| Bourke, Austl. (bŭrk) | 219 | 30°10'S | 146°00'E |
| Bourne, Eng., U.K. (bōrn) | 158a | 52°46'N | 0°22'W |
| Bournemouth, Eng., U.K. (bôrn'mŭth) | 164 | 50°44'N | 1°55'W |
| Bou Saâda, Alg. (bōō-sä'dä) | 162 | 35°13'N | 4°17'E |
| Bousso, Chad (bōō-sō') | 231 | 10°33'N | 16°45'E |
| Boutilimit, Maur. | 230 | 17°30'N | 14°54'W |
| Bouvetøya, i., Ant. | 3 | 55°00'S | 3°00'E |
| Bow, r., Can. (bō) | 92 | 50°35'N | 112°15'W |
| Bowbells, N.D., U.S. (bō'bĕls) | 112 | 48°50'N | 102°16'W |
| Bowdle, S.D., U.S. (bōd''l) | 112 | 45°28'N | 99°42'W |
| Bowen, Austl. (bō'ĕn) | 219 | 20°02'S | 148°14'E |
| Bowie, Md., U.S. (bōō'ĭ) (bō'ē) | 110e | 38°59'N | 76°47'W |
| Bowie, Tx., U.S. | 121 | 33°34'N | 97°50'W |

PRONOUNCING INDEX
Bowling Green – Brownsville 275


| PLACE (Pronunciation) | PAGE | LAT. | LONG. |
|---|---|---|---|
| Bowling Green, Ky., U.S. (bōlĭng grēn) | 105 | 37°00′N | 86°26′W |
| Bowling Green, Mo., U.S. | 121 | 39°19′N | 91°09′W |
| Bowling Green, Oh., U.S. | 108 | 41°25′N | 83°40′W |
| Bowman, N.D., U.S. (bō′măn) | 112 | 46°11′N | 103°23′W |
| Bowron, r., Can. (bō′rŭn) | 95 | 53°20′N | 121°10′W |
| Boxelder Creek, r., Mt., U.S. (bŏks′ĕl-dẽr) | 112 | 45°35′N | 104°28′W |
| Box Elder Creek, r., Mt., U.S. | 115 | 47°17′N | 108°37′W |
| Box Hill, Austl. | 217a | 37°49′S | 145°08′E |
| Boxian, China (bwo shyĕn) | 208 | 33°52′N | 115°47′E |
| Boxing, China (bwo-shyĭŋ) | 206 | 37°09′N | 118°08′E |
| Boxtel, Neth. | 159a | 51°40′N | 5°21′E |
| Boyabo, D.R.C. | 236 | 3°43′N | 18°46′E |
| Boyang, China (bwo-yäŋ) | 209 | 29°00′N | 116°42′E |
| Boyer, r., Can. (boi′ẽr) | 102b | 46°45′N | 70°56′W |
| Boyer, r., Ia., U.S. | 112 | 41°45′N | 95°36′W |
| Boyle, Ire. (boil) | 164 | 53°59′N | 8°15′W |
| Boyne, r., Ire. (boin) | 164 | 53°40′N | 6°40′W |
| Boyne City, Mi., U.S. | 108 | 45°15′N | 85°05′W |
| Boyoma Falls, wtfl., D.R.C. | 231 | 0°30′N | 25°12′E |
| Boysen Reservoir, res., Wy., U.S. | 115 | 43°19′N | 108°11′W |
| Bozcaada, Tur. (bōz-cä′dä) | 175 | 39°50′N | 26°05′E |
| Bozca Ada, i., Tur. | 175 | 39°50′N | 26°00′E |
| Bozeman, Mt., U.S. (bōz′măn) | 104 | 45°41′N | 111°00′W |
| Bozene, D.R.C. | 236 | 2°56′N | 19°12′E |
| Bozhen, China (bwo-jŭn) | 206 | 38°05′N | 116°35′E |
| Bozoum, C.A.R. | 235 | 6°19′N | 16°23′E |
| Bra, Italy (brä) | 174 | 44°41′N | 7°52′E |
| Bracciano, Lago di, l., Italy (lä′gō-dē-brä-chä′nō) | 174 | 42°05′N | 12°00′E |
| Bracebridge, Can. (brās′brĭj) | 99 | 45°05′N | 79°20′W |
| Braceville, Il., U.S. (brās′vĭl) | 111a | 41°13′N | 88°16′W |
| Bräcke, Swe. (brĕk′kĕ) | 160 | 62°44′N | 15°28′E |
| Brackenridge, Pa., U.S. (brăk′ĕn-rĭj) | 111e | 40°37′N | 79°44′W |
| Brackettville, Tx., U.S. (brăk′ĕt-vĭl) | 122 | 29°19′N | 100°24′W |
| Braço Maior, mth., Braz. | 143 | 11°00′S | 51°00′W |
| Braço Menor, mth., Braz. (brä′zô-mĕ-nō′r) | 143 | 11°38′S | 50°00′W |
| Bradano, r., Italy (brä-dä′nō) | 174 | 40°43′N | 16°22′E |
| Bradenton, Fl., U.S. (brā′dĕn-tŭn) | 125a | 27°28′N | 82°35′W |
| Bradfield, Eng., U.K. (brâd′fēld) | 158b | 51°25′N | 1°08′W |
| Bradford, Eng., U.K. (brăd′fẽrd) | 160 | 53°47′N | 1°44′W |
| Bradford, Oh., U.S. | 108 | 40°10′N | 84°30′W |
| Bradford, Pa., U.S. | 109 | 42°00′N | 78°40′W |
| Bradley, Il., U.S. (brăd′lĭ) | 111a | 41°09′N | 87°52′W |
| Bradner, Can. (brăd′nẽr) | 116d | 49°05′N | 122°26′W |
| Brady, Tx., U.S. (brā′dĭ) | 122 | 31°09′N | 99°21′W |
| Braga, Port. (brä′gä) | 162 | 41°20′N | 8°25′W |
| Bragado, Arg. (brä-gä′dō) | 144 | 35°07′S | 60°28′W |
| Bragança, Braz. (brä-gän′sä) | 143 | 1°02′S | 46°50′W |
| Bragança, Port. | 172 | 41°48′N | 6°46′W |
| Bragança Paulista, Braz. (brä-gän′sä-pä′o͞oo-lē′s-tȧ) | 144 | 22°58′S | 46°31′W |
| Bragg Creek, Can. (brăg) | 102e | 50°57′N | 114°35′W |
| Brahmaputra, r., Asia (brä′mȧ-po͞o′trȧ) | 199 | 26°45′N | 92°45′E |
| Brāhui, mts., Pak. | 199 | 28°32′N | 66°15′E |
| Braidwood, Il., U.S. (brād′wȯd) | 111a | 41°16′N | 88°13′W |
| Brăila, Rom. (brē′ēlȧ) | 154 | 45°15′N | 27°58′E |
| Brainerd, Mn., U.S. (brān′ẽrd) | 113 | 46°20′N | 94°09′W |
| Braintree, Ma., U.S. (brān′trē) | 101a | 42°14′N | 71°00′W |
| Braithwaite, La., U.S. (brīth′wīt) | 110d | 29°52′N | 89°57′W |
| Brakpan, S. Afr. (brăk′păn) | 233b | 26°15′S | 28°22′E |
| Bralorne, Can. (brā′lôrn) | 95 | 50°47′N | 122°49′W |
| Bramalea, Can. | 102d | 43°48′N | 79°41′W |
| Brampton, Can. (brămp′tŭn) | 99 | 43°41′N | 79°46′W |
| Branca, Pedra, mtn., Braz. (pĕ′drä-brȧ′ɴ-kä) | 144b | 22°55′S | 43°28′W |
| Branchville, N.J., U.S. (brȧnch′vĭl) | 110a | 41°09′S | 74°44′W |
| Branchville, S.C., U.S. | 125 | 33°17′N | 80°48′W |
| Branco, r., Braz. (bräŋ′kō) | 143 | 2°21′N | 60°38′W |
| Brandberg, mtn., Nmb. | 232 | 21°15′S | 14°15′E |
| Brandenburg, Ger. (brän′dĕn-bȯrgh) | 161 | 52°25′N | 12°33′E |
| Brandenburg, state, Ger. | 159b | 52°15′N | 13°00′E |
| Brandenburg, hist. reg., Ger. | 168 | 52°12′N | 13°31′E |
| Brandfort, S. Afr. (brăn′d-fôrt) | 238c | 28°42′S | 26°29′E |
| Brandon, Can. (brăn′dŭn) | 90 | 49°50′N | 99°57′W |
| Brandon, Vt., U.S. | 109 | 43°45′N | 73°05′W |
| Brandon Mountain, mtn., Ire. (brăn-dŏn) | 164 | 52°15′N | 10°12′W |
| Brandywine, Md., U.S. (brăndĭ′wīn) | 110e | 38°42′N | 76°51′W |
| Branford, Ct., U.S. (brăn′fẽrd) | 109 | 41°15′N | 72°50′W |
| Braniewo, Pol. (brä-nyĕ′vô) | 169 | 54°23′N | 19°50′E |
| Brańsk, Pol. (brän′ sk) | 169 | 52°44′N | 22°51′E |
| Branson, Mo., U.S. | 121 | 36°39′N | 93°13′W |
| Brantford, Can. (brănt′fẽrd) | 99 | 43°09′N | 80°17′W |
| Bras d'Or Lake, l., Can. (brä-dôr′) | 101 | 45°52′N | 60°50′W |
| Brasília, Braz. (brä-sē′lvä) | 143 | 15°49′S | 47°39′W |
| Brasilia Legal, Braz. | 143 | 3°45′S | 55°46′W |
| Brasópolis, Braz. (brä-sô′pô-lĕs) | 141a | 22°30′S | 45°36′W |
| Braşov, Rom. | 163 | 45°39′N | 25°35′E |
| Brass, Nig. (brăs) | 230 | 4°28′N | 6°28′E |
| Brasschaat, Bel. (bräs′ĸät) | 159a | 51°19′N | 4°30′E |
| Bratenahl, Oh., U.S. (bră′tĕn-ôl) | 111d | 41°34′N | 81°36′W |
| Bratislava, Slvk. (brä′tĭs-lä-vä) | 154 | 48°09′N | 17°07′E |
| Bratsk, Russia (brätsk) | 179 | 56°10′N | 102°04′E |
| Bratskoye Vodokhranilishche, res., Russia | 179 | 56°10′N | 102°05′E |
| Bratslav, Ukr. (brät′slȧf) | 177 | 48°48′N | 28°59′E |
| Brattleboro, Vt., U.S. (brăt′'l-bŭr-ô) | 109 | 42°50′N | 72°35′W |
| Braunau, Aus. (brou′nou) | 168 | 48°15′N | 13°05′E |
| Braunschweig, Ger. (broun′shvīgh) | 161 | 52°16′N | 10°32′E |
| Bråviken, r., Swe. | 166 | 58°40′N | 16°40′E |
| Brawley, Ca., U.S. (brô′lĭ) | 104 | 32°59′N | 115°32′W |
| Bray, Ire. (brā) | 164 | 53°10′N | 6°05′W |
| Braymer, Mo., U.S. (brā′mẽr) | 121 | 39°34′N | 93°47′W |
| Brays Bay, Tx., U.S. (brās′bī′yo͞o) | 123a | 29°41′N | 95°33′W |
| Brazeau, r., Can. | 95 | 52°55′N | 116°10′W |
| Brazeau, Mount, mtn., Can. (bră-zō′) | 95 | 52°33′N | 117°21′W |
| Brazil, In., U.S. (brȧ-zĭl′) | 108 | 39°30′N | 87°00′W |
| Brazil, nation, S.A. | 143 | 9°00′S | 53°00′W |
| Brazilian Highlands, mts., Braz. (brȧ zĭl yȧn hī-lȧndz) | 139 | 14°00′S | 48°00′W |
| Brazos, r., Tx., U.S. (brä′zōs) | 106 | 33°10′N | 98°50′W |
| Brazos, Clear Fork, r., Tx., U.S. | 122 | 32°56′N | 99°14′W |
| Brazos, Double Mountain Fork, r., Tx., U.S. | 120 | 33°23′N | 101°21′W |
| Brazos, Salt Fork, r., Tx., U.S. (sôlt fôrk) | 120 | 33°20′N | 101°57′W |
| Brazzaville, Congo (brȧ-zȧ-vēl′) | 232 | 4°16′S | 15°17′E |
| Brčko, Bos. (bĕrch′kô) | 175 | 44°54′N | 18°46′E |
| Brda, r., Pol. (bĕr-dä) | 169 | 53°18′N | 17°55′E |
| Brea, Ca., U.S. (brē′ȧ) | 117a | 33°55′N | 117°54′W |
| Breakeyville, Can. | 102b | 46°40′N | 71°13′W |
| Breckenridge, Mn., U.S. (brĕk′ĕn-rĭj) | 112 | 46°17′N | 96°35′W |
| Breckenridge, Tx., U.S. | 122 | 32°46′N | 98°53′W |
| Brecksville, Oh., U.S. (brĕks′vĭl) | 111d | 41°19′N | 81°38′W |
| Břeclav, Czech Rep. (brzhĕl′lȧf) | 168 | 48°46′N | 16°54′E |
| Breda, Neth. (brā-dä′) | 165 | 51°35′N | 4°47′E |
| Bredasdorp, S. Afr. (brā′das-dôrp) | 232 | 34°15′S | 20°00′E |
| Bredy, Russia (brĕ′dĭ) | 186a | 52°25′N | 60°23′E |
| Bregenz, Aus. (brā′gĕnts) | 168 | 47°30′N | 9°46′E |
| Bregovo, Blg. (brĕ′gô-vô) | 175 | 44°07′N | 22°45′E |
| Breidafjördur, b., Ice. | 160 | 65°15′N | 22°50′W |
| Breidbach, S. Afr. (brēd′băk) | 233c | 32°54′S | 27°26′E |
| Breil-sur-Roya, Fr. (brê′y') | 171 | 43°57′N | 7°36′E |
| Brejo, Braz. (brå′zhȯ) | 143 | 3°33′S | 42°46′W |
| Bremangerlandet, i., Nor. | 166 | 61°51′N | 4°25′E |
| Bremen, Ger. (brā-mĕn) | 154 | 53°05′N | 8°50′E |
| Bremen, In., U.S. (brē′mĕn) | 108 | 41°25′N | 86°05′W |
| Bremerhaven, Ger. (brām-ẽr-hä′fĕn) | 160 | 53°33′N | 8°38′E |
| Bremerton, Wa., U.S. (brĕm′ẽr-tŭn) | 114 | 47°34′N | 122°38′W |
| Bremervörde, Ger. (brĕ′mĕr-fûr-dĕ) | 159c | 53°29′N | 9°09′E |
| Bremner, Can. (brĕm′nẽr) | 102g | 53°34′N | 113°14′W |
| Bremond, Tx., U.S. (brĕm′ŭnd) | 123 | 31°11′N | 96°40′W |
| Brenham, Tx., U.S. (brĕn′ăm) | 123 | 30°10′N | 96°24′W |
| Brenner Pass, p., Eur. (brĕn′ẽr) | 161 | 47°00′N | 11°30′E |
| Brentwood, Eng., U.K. (brĕnt′wȯd) | 165 | 51°37′N | 0°18′E |
| Brentwood, Md., U.S. | 109 | 39°00′N | 76°55′W |
| Brentwood, Mo., U.S. | 117e | 38°37′N | 90°21′W |
| Brentwood, Pa., U.S. | 111e | 40°22′N | 79°59′W |
| Brescia, Italy (brā′shä) | 162 | 45°33′N | 10°15′E |
| Bressanone, Italy (brĕs-sä-nō′nā) | 174 | 46°42′N | 11°40′E |
| Bressuire, Fr. (grĕ-swēr′) | 170 | 46°49′N | 0°14′W |
| Brest, Bela. | 178 | 52°06′N | 23°43′E |
| Brest, Fr. (brĕst) | 154 | 48°24′N | 4°30′W |
| Brest, prov., Bela. | 176 | 52°30′N | 26°50′E |
| Bretagne, hist. reg., Fr. (brĕ-täɴ′yĕ) | 170 | 48°00′N | 3°00′W |
| Breton, Pertuis, strt., Fr. (pâr-twē′brĕ-tôɴ′) | 170 | 46°18′N | 1°43′W |
| Breton Sound, strt., La., U.S. (brĕt′ŭn) | 124 | 29°38′N | 89°15′W |
| Breukelen, Neth. | 159a | 52°09′N | 5°00′E |
| Brevard, N.C., U.S. (brė-värd′) | 125 | 35°14′N | 82°45′W |
| Breves, Braz. (brā′vĕzh) | 143 | 1°32′S | 50°13′W |
| Brevik, Nor. (brĕ′vĕk) | 166 | 59°04′N | 9°39′E |
| Brewarrina, Austl. (bro͞o-ẽr-rē′nȧ) | 219 | 29°54′S | 146°50′E |
| Brewer, Me., U.S. (bro͞o′ẽr) | 100 | 44°46′N | 68°46′W |
| Brewerville, Lib. | 234 | 6°26′N | 10°47′W |
| Brewster, N.Y., U.S. (bro͞o′stẽr) | 110a | 41°23′N | 73°38′W |
| Brewster, Cerro, mtn., Pan. (sĕ′r-rô-bro͞o′stẽr) | 133 | 9°19′N | 79°15′W |
| Brewton, Al., U.S. (bro͞o′tŭn) | 124 | 31°06′N | 87°04′W |
| Brežice, Slvn. (brĕ′zhė-tsĕ) | 174 | 45°55′N | 15°37′E |
| Breznik, Blg. (brĕs′nėk) | 175 | 42°44′N | 22°55′E |
| Briancon, Fr. (brē-äɴ-sôɴ′) | 171 | 44°54′N | 6°39′E |
| Briare, Fr. (brē-är′) | 170 | 47°40′N | 2°46′E |
| Bridal Veil, Or., U.S. (brīd′ȧl vāl) | 116c | 45°33′N | 122°10′W |
| Bridge Point, c., Bah. (brĭj) | 134 | 25°35′N | 76°40′W |
| Bridgeport, Al., U.S. (brĭj′pôrt) | 124 | 34°55′N | 85°42′W |
| Bridgeport, Ct., U.S. | 105 | 41°12′N | 73°12′W |
| Bridgeport, Il., U.S. | 108 | 38°40′N | 87°45′W |
| Bridgeport, Ne., U.S. | 112 | 41°40′N | 103°06′W |
| Bridgeport, Oh., U.S. | 108 | 40°00′N | 80°45′W |
| Bridgeport, Pa., U.S. | 110f | 40°06′N | 75°21′W |
| Bridgeport, Tx., U.S. | 121 | 33°13′N | 97°46′W |
| Bridgeton, Al., U.S. (brĭj′tŭn) | 110h | 33°27′N | 86°39′W |
| Bridgeton, Mo., U.S. | 117e | 38°45′N | 90°23′W |
| Bridgeton, N.J., U.S. | 109 | 39°30′N | 75°15′W |
| Bridgetown, Barb. (brĭj′ toun) | 129 | 13°08′N | 59°37′W |
| Bridgetown, Can. | 100 | 44°51′N | 65°18′W |
| Bridgeville, Pa., U.S. (brĭj′vĭl) | 111e | 40°22′N | 80°07′W |
| Bridgewater, Austl. (brĭj′wô-tẽr) | 222 | 42°50′S | 147°28′E |
| Bridgewater, Can. | 91 | 44°23′N | 64°31′W |
| Bridgnorth, Eng., U.K. (brĭj′nôrth) | 158a | 52°32′N | 2°25′W |
| Bridgton, Me., U.S. (brĭj′tŭn) | 100 | 44°04′N | 70°45′W |
| Bridlington, Eng., U.K. (brĭd′lĭng-tŭn) | 164 | 54°06′N | 0°10′W |
| Brie-Comte-Robert, Fr. (brē-ĸôɴt-ĕ-rō-bâr′) | 171b | 48°42′N | 2°37′E |
| Brielle, Neth. | 159a | 51°54′N | 4°08′E |
| Brierfield, Eng., U.K. (brī′ẽr fēld) | 158a | 53°49′N | 2°14′W |
| Brierfield, Al., U.S. (brī′ẽr-fēld) | 124 | 33°01′N | 86°55′W |
| Brier Island, i., Can. (brī′ẽr) | 100 | 44°16′N | 66°24′W |
| Brieselang, Ger. (brē′zĕ-läng) | 159b | 52°36′N | 12°59′E |
| Briey, Fr. (brē-ĕ′) | 171 | 49°15′N | 5°57′E |
| Brig, Switz. (brēg) | 161 | 46°17′N | 7°59′E |
| Brigg, Eng., U.K. (brĭg) | 158a | 53°33′N | 0°29′W |
| Brigham City, Ut., U.S. (brĭg′ăm) | 117b | 41°31′N | 112°01′W |
| Brighouse, Eng., U.K. (brĭg′hous) | 158a | 53°42′N | 1°47′W |
| Bright, Austl. (brīt) | 222 | 36°43′S | 147°00′E |
| Bright, In., U.S. (brīt) | 111f | 39°13′N | 84°51′W |
| Brightlingsea, Eng., U.K. (brī′t-lĭng-sē) | 158b | 51°50′N | 1°00′E |
| Brighton, Austl. | 217a | 37°55′S | 145°00′E |
| Brighton, Eng., U.K. | 161 | 50°47′N | 0°07′W |
| Brighton, Al., U.S. (brīt′ŭn) | 110h | 33°27′N | 86°56′W |
| Brighton, Co., U.S. | 120 | 39°58′N | 104°49′W |
| Brighton, Ia., U.S. | 113 | 41°11′N | 91°47′W |
| Brighton, Il., U.S. | 117e | 39°03′N | 90°08′W |
| Brighton Indian Reservation, I.R., Fl., U.S. | 125a | 27°05′N | 81°25′W |
| Brihuega, Spain (brė-wā′gä) | 172 | 40°32′N | 2°52′W |
| Brimley, Mi., U.S. (brĭm′lē) | 117k | 46°24′N | 84°34′W |
| Brindisi, Italy (brēn′dē-zē) | 154 | 40°38′N | 17°57′E |
| Brinje, Cro. (brēn′yĕ) | 174 | 45°00′N | 15°08′E |
| Brinkley, Ar., U.S. (brĭŋk′lĭ) | 121 | 34°52′N | 91°12′W |
| Brinnon, Wa., U.S. (brĭn′ŭn) | 116a | 47°41′N | 122°54′W |
| Brion, i., Can. (brē-ôɴ′) | 101 | 47°47′N | 61°29′W |
| Brioude, Fr. (brē-o͞od′) | 170 | 45°18′N | 3°22′E |
| Brisbane, Austl. (brĭz′bån) | 222 | 27°30′S | 153°10′E |
| Bristol, Eng., U.K. | 161 | 51°29′N | 2°39′W |
| Bristol, Ct., U.S. (brĭs′tŭl) | 109 | 41°40′N | 72°55′W |
| Bristol, Pa., U.S. | 110f | 40°06′N | 74°51′W |
| Bristol, R.I., U.S. | 110b | 41°41′N | 71°14′W |
| Bristol, Tn., U.S. | 105 | 36°35′N | 82°10′W |
| Bristol, Va., U.S. | 105 | 36°36′N | 82°00′W |
| Bristol, Vt., U.S. | 109 | 44°10′N | 73°00′W |
| Bristol, Wi., U.S. | 111a | 42°32′N | 88°04′W |
| Bristol Bay, b., Ak., U.S. | 103 | 58°05′N | 158°54′W |
| Bristol Channel, strt., Eng., U.K. | 161 | 51°20′N | 3°47′W |
| Bristow, Ok., U.S. (brĭs′tō) | 121 | 35°50′N | 96°25′W |
| British Columbia, prov., Can. (brĭt′ĭsh kŏl′ŭm-bĭ-ȧ) | 90 | 56°00′N | 124°53′W |
| British Indian Ocean Territory, dep., Afr. | 2 | 7°00′S | 72°00′E |
| British Isles, is., Eur. | 156 | 54°00′N | 4°00′W |
| Brits, S. Afr. | 238c | 25°39′S | 27°47′E |
| Britstown, S. Afr. (brĭts′toun) | 232 | 30°30′S | 23°40′E |
| Britt, Ia., U.S. (brĭt) | 113 | 43°05′N | 93°47′W |
| Brittany *see* Bretagne, hist. reg., Fr. | 170 | 48°00′N | 3°00′W |
| Britton, S.D., U.S. (brĭt′ŭn) | 112 | 45°47′N | 97°44′W |
| Brive-la-Gaillarde, Fr. (brēv-lä-gī-yärd′ĕ) | 161 | 45°10′N | 1°31′E |
| Briviesca, Spain (brė-vyās′kȧ) | 172 | 42°34′N | 3°21′W |
| Brno, Czech Rep. (b'r′nô) | 154 | 49°18′N | 16°37′E |
| Broa, Ensenada de la, b., Cuba | 134 | 22°30′N | 82°00′W |
| Broach, India | 202 | 21°47′N | 72°58′E |
| Broad, r., Ga., U.S. (brôd) | 124 | 34°15′N | 83°14′W |
| Broad, r., N.C., U.S. | 125 | 35°38′N | 82°40′W |
| Broadmeadows, Austl. (brôd′mĕd-ōz) | 217a | 37°40′S | 144°53′E |
| Broadview Heights, Oh., U.S. (brôd′vū) | 111d | 41°18′N | 81°41′W |
| Brockport, N.Y., U.S. (brŏk′pōrt) | 109 | 43°15′N | 77°55′W |
| Brockton, Ma., U.S. (brŏk′tŭn) | 101a | 42°04′N | 71°01′W |
| Brockville, Can. (brŏk′vĭl) | 91 | 44°35′N | 75°40′W |
| Brockway, Mt., U.S. (brŏk′wā) | 115 | 47°24′N | 105°41′W |
| Brodnica, Pol. (brôd′nĭt-sȧ) | 169 | 53°16′N | 19°26′E |
| Brody, Ukr. (brô′dĭ) | 181 | 50°05′N | 25°10′E |
| Broken Arrow, Ok., U.S. (brō′kĕn ăr′ō) | 121 | 36°03′N | 95°48′W |
| Broken Bay, b., Austl. | 222 | 33°34′S | 151°20′E |
| Broken Bow, Ne., U.S. (brō′kĕn bō) | 112 | 41°24′N | 99°37′W |
| Broken Bow, Ok., U.S. | 121 | 34°02′N | 94°43′W |
| Broken Hill, Austl. (brōk′ĕn) | 219 | 31°55′S | 141°35′E |
| Broken Hill *see* Kabwe, Zam. | 232 | 14°27′S | 28°27′E |
| Bromley, Eng., U.K. (brŭm′lĭ) | 158b | 51°23′N | 0°01′E |
| Bromptonville, Can. (brŭmp′tŭn-vĭl) | 99 | 45°30′N | 72°00′W |
| Brønderslev, Den. (brûn′dẽr-slĕv) | 166 | 57°15′N | 9°56′E |
| Bronkhorstspruit, S. Afr. | 238c | 25°50′S | 28°48′E |
| Bronnitsy, Russia (brô-nyĭ′tsĭ) | 176 | 55°26′N | 38°16′E |
| Bronson, Mi., U.S. (brŏn′sŭn) | 108 | 41°55′N | 85°15′W |
| Bronte Creek, r., Can. | 102d | 43°25′N | 79°53′W |
| Brood, r., S.C., U.S. (bro͞od) | 125 | 34°46′N | 81°25′W |
| Brookfield, Il., U.S. (brȯk′fēld) | 111a | 41°49′N | 87°51′W |
| Brookfield, Mo., U.S. | 121 | 39°45′N | 93°04′W |
| Brookhaven, Ga., U.S. (brȯk′hāv'n) | 110c | 33°52′N | 84°21′W |
| Brookhaven, Ms., U.S. | 124 | 31°35′N | 90°26′W |
| Brookings, Or., U.S. (brȯk′ĭngs) | 114 | 42°04′N | 124°16′W |
| Brookings, S.D., U.S. | 112 | 44°18′N | 96°47′W |
| Brookline, Ma., U.S. (brȯk′līn) | 101a | 42°20′N | 71°08′W |
| Brookline, N.H., U.S. | 101a | 42°44′N | 71°37′W |
| Brooklyn, Oh., U.S. (brȯk′lĭn) | 111d | 41°26′N | 81°44′W |
| Brooklyn Center, Mn., U.S. | 117g | 45°05′N | 93°21′W |
| Brook Park, Oh., U.S. (brȯk) | 111d | 41°24′N | 81°50′W |
| Brooks, Can. | 95 | 50°35′N | 111°53′W |
| Brooks Range, mts., Ak., U.S. (brȯks) | 106a | 68°20′N | 159°00′W |
| Brooksville, Fl., U.S. (brȯks′vĭl) | 125a | 28°32′N | 82°28′W |
| Brookville, In., U.S. (brȯk′vĭl) | 108 | 39°20′N | 85°00′W |
| Brookville, Pa., U.S. | 109 | 41°10′N | 79°00′W |
| Brookwood, Al., U.S. (brȯk′wȯd) | 124 | 33°15′N | 87°17′W |
| Broome, Austl. (bro͞om) | 218 | 18°00′S | 122°15′E |
| Brossard, Can. | 102a | 45°26′N | 73°28′W |
| Brothers, is., Bah. (brŭd′hẽrs) | 134 | 26°05′N | 79°00′W |
| Broumov, Czech Rep. (bro͞o′môf) | 168 | 50°33′N | 15°55′E |
| Brown Bank, bk. | 135 | 21°30′N | 74°35′W |
| Brownfield, Tx., U.S. (broun′fēld) | 120 | 33°11′N | 102°16′W |
| Browning, Mt., U.S. (broun′ĭng) | 115 | 48°37′N | 113°05′W |
| Brownsboro, Ky., U.S. (brounz′bô-rô) | 111h | 38°22′N | 85°30′W |
| Brownsburg, Can. (brouns′bûrg) | 102a | 45°40′N | 74°24′W |
| Brownsburg, In., U.S. | 111g | 39°51′N | 86°23′W |
| Brownsmead, Or., U.S. (brounz′-mēd) | 116c | 46°13′N | 123°33′W |
| Brownstown, In., U.S. (brounz′toun) | 108 | 38°50′N | 86°00′W |
| Brownsville, Pa., U.S. (brounz′vĭl) | 111e | 40°01′N | 79°53′W |
| Brownsville, Tn., U.S. | 124 | 35°35′N | 89°15′W |


ng-sing; ŋ-baŋk; ɴ-nasalized n; nŏd; cŏmmit; ōld; ôbey; ôrder; oi-boil; fo͞od; ȯ-as oo in foot; ou-out; s-soft; sh-dish; th-thin; pūre; ůnite; ûrn; stŭd; circŭs; ü-as in French tu; ′-indeterminate vowel.

PRONOUNCING INDEX

Byesville – Camp Indian Reservation 277


| PLACE (Pronunciation) | PAGE | LAT. | LONG. |
|---|---|---|---|
| Byesville, Oh., U.S. (bīz-vĭl) | 108 | 39°55'N | 81°35'W |
| Bygdin, l., Nor. (bügh-dĕn') | 166 | 61°24'N | 8°31'E |
| Byglandsfjord, Nor. (bügh'lānds-fyôr) | 166 | 58°40'N | 7°49'E |
| Bykhaw, Bela. | 176 | 53°32'N | 30°15'E |
| Bykovo, Russia (bĭ-kô'vô) | 186b | 55°38'N | 38°05'E |
| Byrranga, Gory, mts., Russia | 184 | 74°15'N | 94°28'E |
| Bytantay, r., Russia (byän'tāy) | 185 | 68°15'N | 132°15'E |
| Bytom, Pol. (bĭ'tŭm) | 161 | 50°21'N | 18°55'E |
| Bytosh', Russia (bĭ-tôsh') | 176 | 53°48'N | 34°06'E |
| Bytow, Pol. (bĭ'tŭf) | 169 | 54°10'N | 17°30'E |

# C

| PLACE (Pronunciation) | PAGE | LAT. | LONG. |
|---|---|---|---|
| Cabagan, Phil. (kä-bä-gän') | 213a | 17°27'N | 121°50'E |
| Cabalete, i., Phil. (kä-bä-lā'tå) | 213a | 14°19'N | 122°00'E |
| Caballones, Canal de, strt., Cuba (kä-nä'l-dĕ-kä-bäl-yō'nĕs) | 134 | 20°45'N | 79°20'W |
| Caballo Reservoir, res., N.M., U.S. (kä-bä-lyō') | 119 | 33°00'N | 107°20'W |
| Cabanatuan, Phil. (kä-bä-nä-twän') | 213a | 15°30'N | 120°56'E |
| Cabano, Can. (kä-bä-nō') | 100 | 47°41'N | 68°54'W |
| Cabarruyan, i., Phil. (kä-bä-rōō'yän) | 213a | 16°21'N | 120°10'E |
| Cabedelo, Braz. (kä-bē-dā'lo) | 143 | 6°58'S | 34°49'W |
| Cabeza, Arrecife, i., Mex. | 131 | 19°07'N | 95°52'W |
| Cabeza del Buey, Spain (kä-bā'thä dĕl bwā') | 172 | 38°43'N | 5°18'W |
| Cabimas, Ven. (kä-bē'mäs) | 142 | 10°21'N | 71°27'W |
| Cabinda, Ang. | 232 | 5°33'S | 12°12'E |
| Cabinda, hist. reg., Ang. (kä-bĭn'dȧ) | 232 | 5°10'S | 10°00'E |
| Cabinet Mountains, mts., Mt., U.S. (kăb'ĭ-nĕt) | 114 | 48°13'N | 115°52'W |
| Cabo Frio, Braz. (kä'bô-frē'ô) | 141a | 22°53'S | 42°02'W |
| Cabo Frio, Ilha do, Braz. (ē'lä-dô-kä'bô frē'ô) | 141a | 23°01'S | 42°00'W |
| Cabo Gracias a Dios, Hond. (kà'bô-grä-syäs-ä-dyô's) | 133 | 15°00'N | 83°13'W |
| Cabonga, Réservoir, res., Can. | 99 | 47°25'N | 76°35'W |
| Cabora Bassa Reservoir, res., Moz. | 232 | 15°45'S | 32°00'E |
| Cabot Head, c., Can. (kăb'ŭt) | 98 | 45°15'N | 81°20'W |
| Cabot Strait, strt., Can. (kăb'ŭt) | 93a | 47°35'N | 60°00'W |
| Cabra, Spain (käb'rä) | 172 | 37°28'N | 4°29'W |
| Cabra, i., Phil. | 213a | 13°55'N | 119°55'E |
| Cabrera, Illa de, i., Spain | 173 | 39°08'N | 2°57'E |
| Cabrera, Sierra de la, mts., Spain | 172 | 42°15'N | 6°45'W |
| Cabriel, r., Spain (kä-brē-ĕl') | 172 | 39°25'N | 1°20'W |
| Cabrillo National Monument, rec., Ca., U.S. (kä-brēl'yō) | 118a | 32°41'N | 117°03'W |
| Cabuçu, r., Braz. (kä-bōō'-sōō) | 144b | 22°57'S | 43°36'W |
| Cabugao, Phil. (kä-bōō'gä-ô) | 213a | 17°48'N | 120°28'E |
| Čačak, Serb. (chä'chäk) | 175 | 43°51'N | 20°22'E |
| Caçapava, Braz. (kä'sä-pä'vä) | 141a | 23°05'S | 45°52'W |
| Cáceres, Braz. (kä'sĕ-rĕs) | 143 | 16°11'S | 57°32'W |
| Cáceres, Spain (ká'thå-rās) | 162 | 39°28'N | 6°20'W |
| Cachapoal, r., Chile (kä-chä-pô-ä'l) | 141b | 34°23'S | 70°19'W |
| Cache, r., Ar., U.S. (kash) | 121 | 35°24'N | 91°12'W |
| Cache Creek, Can. | 95 | 50°48'N | 121°19'W |
| Cache Creek, r., Ca., U.S. (kăsh) | 118 | 38°53'N | 122°24'W |
| Cache la Poudre, r., Co., U.S. (kash lȧ pōōd'r') | 120 | 40°43'N | 105°39'W |
| Cachi, Nevados de, mtn., Arg. (nĕ-vä'dôs-dĕ-kȧ'chē) | 144 | 25°05'S | 66°40'W |
| Cachinal, Chile (kä-chē-näl') | 144 | 24°57'S | 69°33'W |
| Cachoeira, Braz. (kä-shô-ā'rä) | 143 | 12°32'S | 38°47'W |
| Cachoeirá do Sul, Braz. (kä-shô-ā'rä-dô-sōō'l) | 144 | 30°02'S | 52°49'W |
| Cachoeiras de Macacu, Braz. (kä-shô-ā'räs-dĕ-mä-kȧ'kōō) | 141a | 22°28'S | 42°39'W |
| Cachoeiro de Itapemirim, Braz. | 143 | 20°51'S | 41°06'W |
| Cacólo, Ang. | 236 | 10°07'S | 19°17'E |
| Caconda, Ang. (kä-kōn'dä) | 232 | 13°43'S | 15°06'E |
| Cacouna, Can. | 100 | 47°54'N | 69°31'W |
| Cacula, Ang. | 236 | 14°29'S | 14°10'E |
| Cadale, Som. | 238a | 2°45'N | 46°15'E |
| Caddo, l., La., U.S. (kăd'ō) | 123 | 32°37'N | 94°15'W |
| Cadereyta, Mex. (kä-dȧ-rā'tä) | 130 | 20°42'N | 99°47'W |
| Cadereyta Jimenez, Mex. (kä-dä-rā'tä hē-mā'nāz) | 122 | 25°36'N | 99°59'W |
| Cadi, Sierra de, mts., Spain (sē-ĕ'r-rä-dĕ-kä'dē) | 173 | 42°17'N | 1°34'E |
| Cadillac, Mi., U.S. (kăd'ĭ-lăk) | 108 | 44°15'N | 85°25'W |
| Cádiz, Spain (kȧ'dēz) | 154 | 36°34'N | 6°20'W |
| Cadiz, Ca., U.S. (kā'dĭz) | 118 | 34°33'N | 115°30'W |
| Cadiz, Oh., U.S. | 108 | 40°15'N | 81°00'W |
| Cádiz, Golfo de, b., Spain (gôl-fô-dĕ-kȧ'dēz) | 162 | 36°50'N | 7°00'W |
| Caen, Fr. (käN) | 161 | 49°13'N | 0°22'W |
| Caernarfon, Wales, U.K. | 160 | 53°08'N | 4°17'W |
| Caernarfon Bay, b., Wales, U.K. | 164 | 53°09'N | 4°56'W |
| Cagayan, Phil. (kä-gä-yän') | 213 | 8°13'N | 124°30'E |
| Cagayan, r., Phil. | 212 | 16°45'N | 121°55'E |
| Cagayan Islands, is., Phil. | 212 | 9°40'N | 120°30'E |
| Cagayan Sulu, i., Phil. (kä-gä-yän sōō'lōō) | 212 | 7°00'N | 118°30'E |
| Cagli, Italy (käl'yē) | 174 | 43°35'N | 12°40'E |
| Cagliari, Italy (käl'yä-rē) | 154 | 39°16'N | 9°08'E |
| Cagliari, Golfo di, b., Italy (gôl-fô-dē-käl'yä-rē) | 162 | 39°08'N | 9°12'E |
| Cagnes, Fr. (kän'y') | 171 | 43°40'N | 7°14'E |
| Cagua, Ven. (kä'gwä) | 143b | 10°12'N | 67°27'W |
| Caguas, P.R. (kä'gwäs) | 129b | 18°12'N | 66°01'W |
| Cahaba, r., Al., U.S. (kȧ hä-bä) | 124 | 32°50'N | 87°15'W |
| Cahama, Ang. (kä-ȧ'mä) | 232 | 16°17'S | 14°19'E |
| Cahokia, Il., U.S. (kȧ-hō'kĭ-ȧ) | 117e | 38°34'N | 90°11'W |
| Cahora-Bassa, wtfl., Moz. | 237 | 15°40'S | 32°50'E |
| Cahors, Fr. (kȧ-ôr') | 161 | 44°27'N | 1°27'E |
| Cahuacán, Mex. (kä-wä-kä'n) | 131a | 19°38'N | 99°25'W |
| Cahuita, Punta, c., C.R. (pōō'n-tä-kä-wē'tȧ) | 133 | 9°47'N | 82°41'W |
| Cahul, Mol. | 177 | 45°49'N | 28°17'E |
| Caibarién, Cuba (kī-bä-rē-ĕn') | 134 | 22°35'N | 79°30'W |
| Caicedonia, Col. (kī-sĕ-dô-nêȧ) | 142a | 4°21'N | 75°48'W |
| Caicos Bank, bk. (kī'kōs) | 135 | 21°35'N | 72°00'W |
| Caicos Islands, is., T./C. Is. | 129 | 21°45'N | 71°50'W |
| Caicos Passage, strt., N.A. | 135 | 21°55'N | 72°45'W |
| Caillou Bay, b., La., U.S. (kȧ-yōō') | 123 | 29°07'N | 91°00'W |
| Caimanera, Cuba (kī-mä-nā'rä) | 135 | 20°00'N | 75°10'W |
| Caiman Point, c., Phil. (kī'mán) | 213a | 15°56'N | 119°33'E |
| Caimito, r., Pan. (kä-ē-mē'tô) | 128a | 8°50'N | 79°45'W |
| Caimito del Guayabal, Cuba (kä-ē-mē'tô-dĕl-gwä-yä-bä'l) | 135a | 22°57'N | 82°36'W |
| Cairns, Austl. (kârnz) | 219 | 17°02'S | 145°49'E |
| Cairo, C.R. (kī'rô) | 133 | 10°06'N | 83°47'W |
| Cairo, Egypt | 231 | 30°00'N | 31°17'E |
| Cairo, Ga., U.S. (kā'rō) | 124 | 30°48'N | 84°12'W |
| Cairo, Il., U.S. | 105 | 36°59'N | 89°11'W |
| Caistor, Eng., U.K. (kâs'tẽr) | 158a | 53°30'N | 0°20'W |
| Caiundo, Ang. | 236 | 15°46'S | 17°28'E |
| Caiyu, China (tsī-yōō) | 206 | 39°39'N | 116°36'E |
| Cajamarca, Col. (kä-kä-mȧ'r-kä) | 142a | 4°25'N | 75°25'W |
| Cajamarca, Peru (kä-hä-mär'kä) | 142 | 7°16'S | 78°30'W |
| Čajniče, Bos. (chī'nĭ-chĕ) | 175 | 43°32'N | 19°04'E |
| Cajon, Ca., U.S. (kȧ-hōn') | 117a | 34°18'N | 117°28'W |
| Cajuru, Braz. (kȧ-zhōō'rōō) | 141a | 21°17'S | 47°17'W |
| Čakovec, Cro. (chȧ'kō-vĕts) | 174 | 46°23'N | 16°27'E |
| Cala, S. Afr. (cä-lȧ) | 233c | 31°33'S | 27°41'E |
| Calabar, Nig. (kăl-ȧ-bär') | 230 | 4°57'N | 8°19'E |
| Calabazar, Cuba (kä-lä-bä-zä'r) | 135a | 23°02'N | 82°25'W |
| Calabozo, Ven. (kä-lä-bō'zō) | 142 | 8°48'N | 67°27'W |
| Calabria, hist. reg., Italy (kä-lä'brē-ä) | 174 | 39°26'N | 16°23'E |
| Calafat, Rom. (kȧ-lȧ-fät') | 175 | 43°59'N | 22°56'E |
| Calaguas Islands, is., Phil. (kä-läg'wäs) | 213a | 14°30'N | 123°06'E |
| Calahoo, Can. (kă-lȧ-hōō') | 102g | 53°42'N | 113°58'W |
| Calahorra, Spain (kä-lä-ôr'rä) | 162 | 42°18'N | 1°58'W |
| Calais, Fr. (kȧ-lĕ') | 154 | 50°56'N | 1°51'E |
| Calais, Me., U.S. | 105 | 45°11'N | 67°15'W |
| Calama, Chile (kä-lä'mä) | 144 | 22°17'S | 68°58'W |
| Calamar, Col. (kä-lä-mär') | 142 | 10°24'N | 75°00'W |
| Calamar, Col. | 142 | 1°55'N | 72°33'W |
| Calamba, Phil. (kä-läm'bä) | 213a | 14°12'N | 121°10'E |
| Calamian Group, is., Phil. (kä-lä-myän') | 212 | 12°14'N | 118°38'E |
| Calañas, Spain (kä-län'yäs) | 172 | 37°41'N | 6°52'W |
| Calanda, Spain | 173 | 40°53'N | 0°20'W |
| Calapan, Phil. (kä-lä-pän') | 213a | 13°25'N | 121°11'E |
| Călăraşi, Rom. (kŭ-lŭ-rásh'ĭ) | 163 | 44°09'N | 27°20'E |
| Calatayud, Spain (kä-lä-tä-yōōdh') | 162 | 41°23'N | 1°37'W |
| Calauag Bay, b., Phil. | 213a | 14°07'N | 122°10'E |
| Calaveras Reservoir, res., Ca., U.S. (kăl-ȧ-vĕr'ăs) | 116b | 37°29'N | 121°47'W |
| Calavite, Cape, c., Phil. (kä-lä-vē'tä) | 213a | 13°29'N | 120°00'E |
| Calcasieu, r., La., U.S. (kăl'kȧ-shū) | 123 | 30°22'N | 93°08'W |
| Calcasieu Lake, l., La., U.S. | 123 | 29°58'N | 93°08'W |
| Calcutta *see* Kolkata, India (kăl-kŭt'ȧ) | 199 | 22°32'N | 88°22'E |
| Caldas, Col. (kà'l-däs) | 142a | 6°06'N | 75°38'W |
| Caldas, dept., Col. | 142a | 5°20'N | 75°38'W |
| Caldas da Rainha, Port. (käl'däs dä rīn'yȧ) | 172 | 39°25'N | 9°08'W |
| Calder, r., Eng., U.K. (kôl'dẽr) | 158a | 53°39'N | 1°30'W |
| Caldera, Chile (käl-dā'rä) | 144 | 27°02'S | 70°53'W |
| Calder Canal, can., Eng., U.K. | 158a | 53°48'N | 2°25'W |
| Caldwell, Id., U.S. (kôld'wĕl) | 114 | 43°40'N | 116°43'W |
| Caldwell, Ks., U.S. | 121 | 37°04'N | 97°36'W |
| Caldwell, Oh., U.S. | 108 | 39°40'N | 81°30'W |
| Caldwell, Tx., U.S. | 123 | 30°30'N | 96°40'W |
| Caledon, Can. (kăl'ē-dŏn) | 102d | 43°52'N | 79°59'W |
| Caledonia, Mn., U.S. (kăl-ē-dō'nĭ-ȧ) | 113 | 43°38'N | 91°31'W |
| Calella, Spain (kä-lĕl'yä) | 173 | 41°37'N | 2°39'E |
| Calera Victor Rosales, Mex. (kä-lā'rä-vē'k-tôr-rô-sà'lĕs) | 130 | 22°57'N | 102°42'W |
| Calexico, Ca., U.S. (kȧ-lĕk'sĭ-kō) | 104 | 32°41'N | 115°30'W |
| Calgary, Can. (kăl'gȧ-rĭ) | 90 | 51°03'N | 114°05'W |
| Calhoun, Ga., U.S. (kăl-hōōn') | 124 | 34°30'N | 84°56'W |
| Cali, Col. (kä'lē) | 142 | 3°26'N | 76°30'W |
| Caliente, Nv., U.S. (käl-yĕn'tä) | 119 | 37°38'N | 114°30'W |
| California, Mo., U.S. (kăl-ĭ-fôr'nĭ-ȧ) | 121 | 38°38'N | 92°38'W |
| California, Pa., U.S. | 111e | 40°03'N | 79°53'W |
| California, state, U.S. | 104 | 38°10'N | 121°20'W |
| California, Golfo de, b., Mex. (gôl-fô-dĕ-kä-lē-fôr-nyä) | 128 | 30°30'N | 113°45'W |
| California Aqueduct, aq., Ca., U.S. | 118 | 37°10'N | 121°10'W |
| Călimani, Munţii, mts., Rom. | 169 | 47°05'N | 24°47'E |
| Calimere, Point, c., India | 203 | 10°20'N | 80°20'E |
| Calimesa, Ca., U.S. (kă-lĭ-mā'sȧ) | 117a | 34°00'N | 117°04'W |
| Calipatria, Ca., U.S. (kăl-ĭ-pát'rĭ-ȧ) | 118 | 33°03'N | 115°30'W |
| Calkini, Mex. (käl-kē-nē') | 131 | 20°21'N | 90°06'W |
| Callabonna, Lake, l., Austl. (călă'bŏnȧ) | 222 | 29°35'S | 140°28'E |
| Callao, Peru (käl-yä'ô) | 142 | 12°02'S | 77°07'W |
| Calling, l., Can. (kôl'ĭng) | 95 | 55°15'N | 113°12'W |
| Calmar, Can. (kăl'mär) | 102g | 53°16'N | 113°49'W |
| Calmar, Ia., U.S. | 113 | 43°12'N | 91°54'W |
| Caloosahatchee, r., Fl., U.S. (kȧ-loo-sȧ-hăch'ē) | 125a | 26°45'N | 81°41'W |
| Calotmul, Mex. (kä-lôt-mōōl) | 132a | 20°58'N | 88°11'W |
| Calpulalpan, Mex. (käl-pōō-läl'pän) | 130 | 19°35'N | 98°33'W |
| Caltagirone, Italy (käl-tä-jē-rō'nå) | 162 | 37°14'N | 14°32'E |
| Caltanissetta, Italy (käl-tä-nē-sĕt'tä) | 162 | 37°30'N | 14°02'E |
| Caluango, Ang. | 236 | 8°21'S | 19°40'E |
| Calucinga, Ang. | 236 | 11°18'S | 16°12'E |
| Calumet, Mi., U.S. (kă-lū-mĕt') | 113 | 47°15'N | 88°29'W |
| Calumet, Lake, l., Il., U.S. | 111a | 41°43'N | 87°36'W |
| Calumet City, Il., U.S. | 111a | 41°37'N | 87°33'W |
| Calunda, Ang. | 236 | 12°06'S | 23°23'E |
| Caluquembe, Ang. | 236 | 13°47'S | 14°44'E |
| Caluula, Som. | 238a | 11°53'N | 50°40'E |
| Calvert, Tx., U.S. (kăl'vẽrt) | 123 | 30°59'N | 96°41'W |
| Calvert Island, i., Can. | 92 | 51°35'N | 128°00'W |
| Calvi, Fr. (käl'vē) | 174 | 42°33'N | 8°35'E |
| Calvillo, Mex. (käl-vēl'yō) | 131 | 21°51'N | 102°44'E |
| Calvinia, S. Afr. (kăl-vĭn'ĭ-ȧ) | 232 | 31°20'S | 19°50'E |
| Cam, r., Eng., U.K. (kăm) | 165 | 52°15'N | 0°05'E |
| Camagüey, Cuba (kä-mä-gwā') | 129 | 21°25'N | 78°00'W |
| Camagüey, prov., Cuba | 134 | 21°30'N | 78°10'W |
| Camajuani, Cuba (kä-mä-hwä'nē) | 134 | 22°25'N | 79°50'W |
| Camano, Wa., U.S. (kä-mä'no) | 116a | 48°10'N | 122°32'W |
| Camano Island, i., Wa., U.S. | 116a | 48°11'N | 122°29'W |
| Camargo, Mex. (kä-mär gō) | 122 | 26°19'N | 98°49'W |
| Camarón, Cabo, c., Hond. (kȧ'bô-kä-mä-rōn') | 132 | 16°06'N | 85°05'W |
| Camas, Wa., U.S. (kăm'ȧs) | 116c | 45°36'N | 122°24'W |
| Camas Creek, r., Id., U.S. | 115 | 44°10'N | 112°09'W |
| Camatagua, Ven. (kä-mä-tȧ'gwä) | 143b | 9°49'N | 66°55'W |
| Ca Mau, Mui, c., Viet. | 212 | 8°36'N | 104°43'E |
| Cambay, India (kăm-bā') | 202 | 22°22'N | 72°39'E |
| Cambodia, nation, Asia | 212 | 12°15'N | 104°00'E |
| Cambonda, Serra, mts., Ang. | 236 | 12°10'S | 14°15'E |
| Camborne, Eng., U.K. (kăm'bôrn) | 164 | 50°15'N | 5°28'W |
| Cambrai, Fr. (käN-brĕ') | 161 | 50°10'N | 3°15'E |
| Cambrian Mountains, mts., Wales, U.K. (kăm'brĭ-ăn) | 164 | 52°05'N | 4°05'W |
| Cambridge, Can. | 99 | 43°22'N | 80°19'W |
| Cambridge, Eng., U.K. (kăm'brĭj) | 161 | 52°12'N | 0°11'E |
| Cambridge, Ma., U.S. | 101a | 42°23'N | 71°07'W |
| Cambridge, Md., U.S. | 109 | 38°35'N | 76°10'W |
| Cambridge, Mn., U.S. | 113 | 45°35'N | 93°14'W |
| Cambridge, Ne., U.S. | 120 | 40°17'N | 100°10'W |
| Cambridge, Oh., U.S. | 108 | 40°00'N | 81°35'W |
| Cambridge Bay *see* Kaluktutiak, Can. | 92 | 69°15'N | 105°00'W |
| Cambridge City, In., U.S. | 108 | 39°45'N | 85°15'W |
| Cambridgeshire, co., Eng., U.K. | 158a | 52°26'N | 0°19'W |
| Cambuci, Braz. (käm-bōō'sē) | 141a | 21°35'S | 41°54'W |
| Cambundi-Catembo, Ang. | 236 | 10°09'S | 17°31'E |
| Camby, In., U.S. (kăm'bē) | 111g | 39°40'N | 86°19'W |
| Camden, Austl. | 217b | 34°03'S | 150°42'E |
| Camden, Al., U.S. (kăm'dĕn) | 124 | 31°58'N | 87°15'W |
| Camden, Ar., U.S. | 121 | 33°36'N | 92°49'W |
| Camden, Me., U.S. | 100 | 44°11'N | 69°05'W |
| Camden, N.J., U.S. | 105 | 39°56'N | 75°06'W |
| Camden, S.C., U.S. | 125 | 34°14'N | 80°37'W |
| Cameia, Parque Nacional da, rec., Ang. | 236 | 11°40'S | 21°20'E |
| Camenca, Mol. | 177 | 48°02'N | 28°43'E |
| Cameron, Mo., U.S. (kăm'ẽr-ŭn) | 121 | 39°44'N | 94°14'W |
| Cameron, Tx., U.S. | 123 | 30°52'N | 96°57'W |
| Cameron, W.V., U.S. | 108 | 39°40'N | 80°35'W |
| Cameron Hills, hills, Can. | 92 | 60°13'N | 120°20'W |
| Cameroon, nation, Afr. | 230 | 5°48'N | 11°00'E |
| Cameroon Mountain, mtn., Cam. | 230 | 4°12'N | 9°11'E |
| Camiling, Phil. (kä-mē-lĭng') | 213a | 15°42'N | 120°24'E |
| Camilla, Ga., U.S. (kȧ-mĭl'ȧ) | 124 | 31°13'N | 84°12'W |
| Caminha, Port. (kä-mĭn'yȧ) | 172 | 41°52'N | 8°44'W |
| Camoçim, Braz. (kä-mô-sēN') | 143 | 2°56'S | 40°55'W |
| Camooweal, Austl. | 218 | 20°00'S | 138°13'E |
| Campana, Arg. (käm-pä'nä) | 141c | 34°10'S | 58°58'W |
| Campana, i., Chile (käm-pän'yä) | 144 | 48°20'S | 75°15'W |
| Campanario, Spain (kä-pä-nä'rē-ō) | 172 | 38°51'N | 5°36'W |
| Campanella, Punta, c., Italy (pò'n-tä-käm-pä-nĕ'lä) | 173c | 40°20'N | 14°21'E |
| Campanha, Braz. (käm-pän-yäN') | 141a | 21°51'S | 45°24'W |
| Campania, hist. reg., Italy (käm-pän'yä) | 174 | 41°00'N | 14°40'E |
| Campbell, Ca., U.S. (kăm'bĕl) | 116b | 37°17'N | 121°57'W |
| Campbell, Mo., U.S. | 121 | 36°29'N | 90°04'W |
| Campbell, is., N.Z. | 3 | 52°30'S | 169°00'E |
| Campbellpore, Pak. | 202 | 33°49'N | 72°24'E |
| Campbell River, Can. | 90 | 50°01'N | 125°15'W |
| Campbellsville, Ky., U.S. (kăm'bĕlz-vĭl) | 124 | 37°19'N | 85°20'W |
| Campbellton, Can. (kăm'bĕl-tŭn) | 91 | 48°00'N | 66°40'W |
| Campbelltown, Austl. (kăm'bĕl-toun) | 217b | 34°04'S | 150°49'E |
| Campbelltown, Scot., U.K. (kăm'b'l-toun) | 164 | 55°25'N | 5°50'W |
| Camp Dennison, Oh., U.S. (dĕ'nĭ-sŏn) | 111f | 39°12'N | 84°17'W |
| Campeche, Mex. (käm-pā'chȧ) | 128 | 19°51'N | 90°32'W |
| Campeche, state, Mex. | 128 | 18°55'N | 90°20'W |
| Campeche, Bahía de, b., Mex. (bä-ē'ä-dĕ-käm-pā'chä) | 128 | 19°30'N | 93°40'W |
| Campechuela, Cuba (käm-pä-chwā'lä) | 134 | 20°15'N | 77°15'W |
| Camperdown, S. Afr. (kăm'pẽr-doun) | 233c | 29°44'S | 30°33'E |
| Câmpina, Rom. | 175 | 45°08'N | 25°47'E |
| Campina Grande, Braz. (käm-pē'nä grän'dĕ) | 143 | 7°15'S | 35°49'W |
| Campinas, Braz. (käm-pē'näzh) | 143 | 22°53'S | 47°03'W |
| Camp Indian Reservation, I.R., Ca., U.S. (kămp) | 118 | 32°39'N | 116°26'W |


ng-sing; ŋ-baŋk; N-nasalized n; nŏd; cŏmmit; ōld; ôbey; ôrder; oi-boil; fōōd; ŏŏ-as oo in foot; ou-out; s-soft; sh-dish; th-thin; pūre; ûnite; ûrn; stŭd; circŭs; ü-as in French tu; '-indeterminate vowel.

| PLACE (Pronunciation) | PAGE | LAT. | LONG. |
|---|---|---|---|
| Campo, Cam. (käm′pō) | 230 | 2°22′N | 9°49′E |
| Campoalegre, Col. (kä′m-pô-àlĕ′grĕ) | 142 | 2°34′N | 75°20′W |
| Campobasso, Italy (käm′pô-bäs′sō) | 174 | 41°35′N | 14°39′E |
| Campo Belo, Braz. | 141a | 20°52′S | 45°15′W |
| Campo de Criptana, Spain (käm′pō dā krēp-tä′nä) | 172 | 39°24′N | 3°09′W |
| Campo Florido, Cuba (kä′m-pō flō-rē′dō) | 135a | 23°07′N | 82°07′W |
| Campo Grande, Braz. (käm-pô grän′dĕ) | 143 | 20°28′S | 54°32′W |
| Campo Grande, Braz. | 144b | 22°54′S | 43°33′W |
| Campo Maior, Braz. (käm-pô mä-yôr′) | 143 | 4°48′S | 42°12′W |
| Campo Maior, Port. | 172 | 39°03′N | 7°06′W |
| Campo Real, Spain (käm′pô rå-äl′) | 173a | 40°21′N | 3°23′W |
| Campos, Braz. (kä′m-pôs) | 143 | 21°46′S | 41°19′W |
| Campos do Jordão, Braz. (kä′m-pôs-dô-zhôr-dou′ɴ) | 141a | 22°45′S | 45°35′W |
| Campos Gerais, Braz. (kä′m-pôs-zhĕ-ràĕs) | 141a | 21°17′S | 45°43′W |
| Camps Bay, S. Afr. (kămps) | 232a | 33°57′S | 18°22′E |
| Camp Springs, Md., U.S. (cămp sprĭngz) | 110e | 38°48′N | 76°55′W |
| Câmpulung, Rom. | 163 | 45°15′N | 25°03′E |
| Câmpulung Moldovenesc, Rom. | 169 | 47°31′N | 25°36′E |
| Camp Wood, Tx., U.S. (kămp wŏod) | 122 | 29°39′N | 100°02′W |
| Camrose, Can. (kăm-rōz) | 90 | 53°01′N | 112°50′W |
| Camu, r., Dom. Rep. (kä′mōō) | 135 | 19°05′N | 70°15′W |
| Canada, nation, N.A. (kăn′á-dá) | 90 | 50°00′N | 100°00′W |
| Canada Bay, b., Can. | 101 | 50°43′N | 56°10′W |
| Cañada de Gómez, Arg. (kä-nyä′dä-dĕ-gô′mĕz) | 144 | 32°49′S | 61°24′W |
| Canadian, Tx., U.S. (ká-nā′dĭ-ăn) | 120 | 35°54′N | 100°24′W |
| Canadian, r., U.S. | 106 | 35°30′N | 102°30′W |
| Canajoharie, N.Y., U.S. (kăn-á-jô-hăr′ē) | 109 | 42°55′N | 74°35′W |
| Çanakkale, Tur. (chä-näk-kä′lĕ) | 163 | 40°10′N | 26°26′E |
| Çanakkale Boğazi (Dardanelles), strt., Tur. | 163 | 40°05′N | 25°50′E |
| Canandaigua, N.Y., U.S. (kăn-ăn-dā′gwá) | 109 | 42°55′N | 77°20′W |
| Canandaigua, l., N.Y., U.S. | 109 | 42°45′N | 77°20′W |
| Cananea, Mex. (kä-nä-nĕ′ä) | 128 | 31°00′N | 110°20′W |
| Canarias, Islas (Canary Is.), is., Spain (ē′s-läs-kä-nä′ryäs) | 229 | 29°15′N | 16°30′W |
| Canarreos, Archipiélago de los, is., Cuba | 134 | 21°35′N | 82°20′W |
| Canary Islands *see* Canarias, Islas, is., Spain | 229 | 29°15′N | 16°30′W |
| Cañas, C.R. (kä′-nyäs) | 132 | 10°26′N | 85°06′W |
| Cañas, r., C.R. | 132 | 10°20′N | 85°21′W |
| Cañasgordas, Col. (kä′nyäs-gô′r-däs) | 142a | 6°44′N | 76°01′W |
| Canastota, N.Y., U.S. (kăn-ás-tō′tá) | 109 | 43°05′N | 75°45′W |
| Canastra, Serra de, mts., Braz. (sĕ′r-rä-dĕ-kä-nä′s-trä) | 143 | 19°53′S | 46°57′W |
| Canatlán, Mex. (kä-nät-län′) | 122 | 24°30′N | 104°45′W |
| Canaveral, Cape, c., Fl., U.S. | 107 | 28°30′N | 80°23′W |
| Canavieiras, Braz. (kä-ná-vē-ā′räs) | 143 | 15°40′S | 38°49′W |
| Canberra, Austl. (kăn′bĕr-á) | 219 | 35°21′S | 149°10′E |
| Canby, Mn., U.S. (kăn′bĭ) | 112 | 44°43′N | 96°15′W |
| Canchyuaya, Cerros de, mts., Peru (sĕ′r-rôs-dĕ-kän-chōō-á′īä) | 142 | 7°30′S | 74°30′W |
| Cancuc, Mex. (kän-kōōk) | 131 | 16°58′N | 92°17′W |
| Cancún, Mex. | 132a | 21°25′N | 86°50′W |
| Candelaria, Cuba (kän-dĕ-lä′ryä) | 134 | 22°45′N | 82°55′W |
| Candelaria, Phil. (kän-då-lä′rē-ä) | 213a | 15°39′N | 119°55′E |
| Candelaria, r., Mex. (kän-dĕ-lä-ryä) | 131 | 18°25′N | 91°21′W |
| Candeleda, Spain (kän-dhå-lā′dhä) | 172 | 40°09′N | 5°18′W |
| Candia *see* Iráklion, Grc. | 154 | 35°20′N | 25°10′E |
| Candle, Ak., U.S. (kăn′d′l) | 103 | 65°00′N | 162°04′W |
| Cando, N.D., U.S. (kăn′dō) | 112 | 48°27′N | 99°13′W |
| Candon, Phil. (kän-dōn′) | 213a | 17°13′N | 120°26′E |
| Canelones, Ur. (kä-nĕ-lô-nĕs) | 141c | 34°32′S | 56°19′W |
| Canelones, dept., Ur. | 141c | 34°34′S | 56°15′W |
| Cañete, Peru (kän-yā′tå) | 142 | 13°06′S | 76°17′W |
| Caney, Cuba (kä-nā′) (kā′nĭ) | 135 | 20°05′N | 75°45′W |
| Caney, Ks., U.S. (kā′nĭ) | 121 | 37°00′N | 95°57′W |
| Caney Fork, r., Tn., U.S. | 124 | 36°10′N | 85°50′W |
| Cangamba, Ang. | 232 | 13°40′S | 19°54′E |
| Cangas, Spain (kän′gäs) | 172 | 42°15′N | 8°43′W |
| Cangas de Narcea, Spain (kä′n-gäs-dĕ-när-sĕ-ä) | 172 | 43°08′N | 6°36′W |
| Cangzhou, China (tsäŋ-jō) | 208 | 38°21′N | 116°53′E |
| Caniapiscau, l., Can. | 93 | 54°10′N | 71°13′E |
| Caniapiscau, r., Can. | 93 | 57°00′N | 68°45′W |
| Canicatti, Italy (kä-nē-kät′tē) | 174 | 37°18′N | 13°58′E |
| Cañitas, Mex. (kän-yē′täs) | 130 | 23°38′N | 102°44′W |
| Cannell, Can. | 102g | 53°35′N | 113°38′W |
| Cannelton, In., U.S. (kăn′ĕl-tŭn) | 108 | 37°55′N | 86°45′W |
| Cannes, Fr. (kån) | 161 | 43°34′N | 7°05′E |
| Canning, Can. (kăn′ĭng) | 100 | 45°09′N | 64°25′W |
| Cannock, Eng., U.K. (kăn′ŭk) | 158a | 52°41′N | 2°02′W |
| Cannock Chase, reg., Eng., U.K. (kăn′ŭk chās) | 158a | 52°43′N | 1°54′W |
| Cannon, r., Mn., U.S. (kăn′ŭn) | 113 | 44°18′N | 93°24′W |
| Cannonball, r., N.D., U.S. (kăn′ŭn-bäl) | 112 | 46°17′N | 101°35′W |
| Caño, Isla de, i., C.R. (ē′s-lä-dĕ-kä′nō) | 133 | 8°38′N | 84°00′W |
| Canoga Park, Ca., U.S. (kä-nō′gá) | 117a | 34°07′N | 118°36′W |
| Canoncito Indian Reservation, I.R., N.M., U.S. | 119 | 35°00′N | 107°05′W |
| Canon City, Co., U.S. (kăn′yŭn) | 120 | 38°27′N | 105°16′W |
| Canonsburg, Pa., U.S. (kăn′ŭnz-bûrg) | 111e | 40°16′N | 80°11′W |
| Canoochee, r., Ga., U.S. (ká-nōō′chē) | 125 | 32°25′N | 82°11′W |
| Canora, Can. (ká-nōrá) | 90 | 51°37′N | 102°26′W |
| Canosa, Italy (kä-nō′sä) | 174 | 41°14′N | 16°03′E |
| Canouan, i., St. Vin. | 133b | 12°44′N | 61°10′W |
| Cansahcab, Mex. | 132a | 21°11′N | 89°05′W |
| Canso, Can. (kăn′sō) | 101 | 45°20′N | 61°00′W |
| Canso, Cape, c., Can. | 101 | 45°21′N | 60°46′W |
| Canso, Strait of, strt., Can. | 101 | 45°37′N | 61°25′W |
| Cantabrica, Cordillera, mts., Spain | 156 | 43°05′N | 6°05′W |
| Cantagalo, Braz. (kän-tä-gá′lo) | 141a | 21°59′S | 42°22′W |
| Cantanhede, Port. (kän-täɴ-yā′då) | 172 | 40°22′N | 8°35′W |
| Canterbury, Eng., U.K. (kăn′tĕr-bĕr-ē) | 165 | 51°17′N | 1°06′E |
| Canterbury Bight, b., N.Z. | 221a | 44°15′S | 172°08′E |
| Cantiles, Cayo, i., Cuba (ky-ō-kän-tē′lås) | 134 | 21°40′N | 82°00′W |
| Canton *see* Guangzhou, China | 205 | 23°07′N | 113°15′E |
| Canton, Ga., U.S. | 124 | 34°13′N | 84°29′W |
| Canton, Il., U.S. | 121 | 40°34′N | 90°02′W |
| Canton, Ma., U.S. | 101a | 42°09′N | 71°09′W |
| Canton, Mo., U.S. | 121 | 40°08′N | 91°33′W |
| Canton, Ms., U.S. | 124 | 32°36′N | 90°01′W |
| Canton, N.C., U.S. | 125 | 35°32′N | 82°50′W |
| Canton, Oh., U.S. | 105 | 40°50′N | 81°25′W |
| Canton, Pa., U.S. | 109 | 41°50′N | 76°45′W |
| Canton, S.D., U.S. | 112 | 43°17′N | 96°37′W |
| Cantu, Italy (kän-tōō′) | 174 | 45°43′N | 9°09′E |
| Cañuelas, Arg. (kä-nyōĕ′-läs) | 141c | 35°03′S | 58°45′W |
| Canyon, Tx., U.S. (kăn′yŭn) | 120 | 34°59′N | 101°57′W |
| Canyon, r., Wa., U.S. | 116a | 48°09′N | 121°48′W |
| Canyon de Chelly National Monument, rec., Az., U.S. | 119 | 36°14′N | 110°00′W |
| Canyon Ferry Lake, res., Mt., U.S. | 115 | 46°33′N | 111°37′W |
| Canyonlands National Park, rec., Ut., U.S. | 119 | 38°10′N | 110°00′W |
| Canyons of the Ancients National Monument, rec., Co., U.S. | 119 | 37°30′N | 108°50′W |
| Caoxian, China (tsou shyĕn) | 206 | 34°48′N | 115°33′E |
| Capalonga, Phil. (kä-pä-lôŋ′gä) | 213a | 14°20′N | 122°30′E |
| Capannori, Italy (kä-pän′nô-rē) | 174 | 43°50′N | 10°30′E |
| Capaya, r., Ven. (kä-pä-īä) | 143b | 10°28′N | 66°15′W |
| Cap-Chat, Can. (kåp-shä′) | 91 | 48°02′N | 65°20′W |
| Cap-de-la-Madeleine, Can. (kåp dē lå må-d′lĕn′) | 99 | 46°23′N | 72°30′W |
| Cape Breton, i., Can. (kāp brĕt′ŭn) | 101 | 45°48′N | 59°50′W |
| Cape Breton Highlands National Park, rec., Can. | 91 | 46°45′N | 60°45′W |
| Cape Charles, Va., U.S. (kāp chärlz) | 125 | 37°13′N | 76°02′W |
| Cape Coast, Ghana | 230 | 5°05′N | 1°15′W |
| Cape Fear, r., N.C., U.S. (kāp fēr) | 107 | 35°00′N | 79°00′W |
| Cape Flats, pl., S. Afr. (kāp flăts) | 232a | 34°01′S | 18°37′E |
| Cape Girardeau, Mo., U.S. (jē-rär-dō′) | 105 | 37°17′N | 89°32′W |
| Cape Krusenstern National Monument, rec., Ak., U.S. | 103 | 67°30′N | 163°40′W |
| Cape May, N.J., U.S. (kāp mā) | 109 | 38°55′N | 74°50′W |
| Cape May Court House, N.J., U.S. | 109 | 39°05′N | 75°00′W |
| Cape Romanzof, Ak., U.S. (rō′ măn zôf) | 103 | 61°50′N | 165°45′W |
| Capesterre, Guad. | 133b | 16°02′N | 61°37′W |
| Cape Tormentine, Can. | 100 | 46°08′N | 63°47′W |
| Cape Town, S. Afr. (kāp toun) | 232 | 33°48′S | 18°28′E |
| Cape Verde, nation, Afr. | 230b | 15°48′N | 26°02′W |
| Cape York Peninsula, pen., Austl. (kāp yôrk) | 221 | 12°30′S | 142°35′E |
| Cap-Haïtien, Haiti (kåp à-ē-syăn′) | 129 | 19°45′N | 72°15′W |
| Capilla de Señor, Arg. (kä-pēl′yä dā sān-yôr′) | 141c | 34°18′S | 59°07′W |
| Capitachouane, r., Can. | 99 | 47°50′N | 76°45′W |
| Capitol Reef National Park, rec., Ut., U.S. (kăp′ĭ-tŏl) | 119 | 38°15′N | 111°10′W |
| Capivari, Braz. (kä-pē-vá′rē) | 141a | 22°59′S | 47°29′W |
| Capivari, r., Braz. | 144b | 22°39′S | 43°19′W |
| Capoompeta, mtn., Austl. (ká-pōōm-pē′tá) | 221 | 29°15′S | 152°12′E |
| Capraia, i., Italy (kä-prä′yä) | 162 | 43°02′N | 9°51′E |
| Caprara Point, c., Italy (kä-prä′rä) | 174 | 41°08′N | 8°20′E |
| Capreol, Can. | 99 | 46°43′N | 80°56′W |
| Caprera, i., Italy (kä-prâ′rä) | 174 | 41°12′N | 9°28′E |
| Capri, Italy | 173c | 40°18′N | 14°16′E |
| Capri, Isola di, i., Italy (ē′s-sō-lä-dē-kä′prē) | 173c | 40°19′N | 14°10′E |
| Capricorn Channel, strt., Austl. (kăp′rĭ-kôrn) | 221 | 22°27′S | 151°24′E |
| Caprivi Strip, hist. reg., Nmb. | 232 | 18°00′S | 22°00′E |
| Cap-Rouge, Can. (kåp rōōzh′) | 102b | 46°45′N | 71°21′W |
| Cap-Saint Ignace, Can. (kĭp săɴ-tē-nyås′) | 102b | 47°02′N | 70°27′W |
| Capua, Italy (kä′pwä) | 162 | 41°07′N | 14°14′E |
| Capulhuac, Mex. (kä-pôl-hwäk′) | 130 | 19°33′N | 99°43′W |
| Capulin Mountain National Monument, rec., N.M., U.S. (kä-pū′lĭn) | 120 | 36°15′N | 103°58′W |
| Capultitlán, Mex. (kä-pô′l-tē-tlá′n) | 131a | 19°15′N | 99°40′W |
| Caquetá (Japurá), r., S.A. | 142 | 0°20′S | 73°00′W |
| Carabaña, Spain (kä-rä-bän′yä) | 173a | 40°16′N | 3°15′W |
| Carabelle, Fl., U.S. (kăr′á-bĕl) | 124 | 29°50′N | 84°40′W |
| Carabobo, dept., Ven. (kä-rä-bô′-bô) | 143b | 10°07′N | 68°06′W |
| Caracal, Rom. (kå-rå-kál′) | 175 | 44°06′N | 24°22′E |
| Caracas, Ven. (kä-rä′käs) | 142 | 10°30′N | 66°58′W |
| Carácuaro de Morelos, Mex. (kä-rä′kwä-rō-dĕ-mô-rĕ-lôs) | 130 | 18°44′N | 101°04′W |
| Caraguatatuba, Braz. (kä-rä-gwä-tá-tōō′bä) | 141a | 23°37′S | 45°26′W |
| Carajás, Serra dos, mts., Braz. (sĕ′r-rä-dôs-kä-rä-zhá′s) | 143 | 5°58′S | 51°45′W |
| Caramanta, Cerro, mtn., Col. (sĕ′r-rô-kä-rä-má′n-tä) | 142a | 5°29′N | 76°01′W |
| Carangola, Braz. (kä-rán′gō′lä) | 141a | 20°46′S | 42°02′W |
| Caraquet, Can. (kă-rá-kĕt′) | 91 | 47°48′N | 64°57′W |
| Carata, Laguna, l., Nic. (lä-gô′nä-kä-rä′tä) | 133 | 13°59′N | 83°41′W |
| Caratasca, Laguna, l., Hond. (lä-gô′nä-kä-rä-täs′kä) | 133 | 15°20′N | 83°45′W |
| Caravaca, Spain (kä-rä-vä′kä) | 172 | 38°05′N | 1°51′W |
| Caravelas, Braz. (ká-rä-vĕl′äzh) | 143 | 17°46′S | 39°06′W |
| Carayaca, Ven. (kå-rä-īá′kä) | 143b | 10°32′N | 67°07′W |
| Caràzinho, Braz. (kä-rá′zē-nyŏ) | 144 | 28°22′S | 52°33′W |
| Carballiño, Spain | 162 | 42°26′N | 8°04′W |
| Carballo, Spain (kär-bäl′yō) | 172 | 43°13′N | 8°40′W |
| Carbet, Pitons du, mtn., Mart. | 133b | 14°40′N | 61°05′W |
| Carbon, r., Wa., U.S. (kär′bŏn) | 116a | 47°06′N | 122°08′W |
| Carbonado, Wa., U.S. (kär-bō-nā′dō) | 116a | 47°05′N | 122°03′W |
| Carbonara, Cape, c., Italy (kär-bō-nä′rä) | 162 | 39°08′N | 9°33′E |
| Carbondale, Can. (kär′bŏn-dāl) | 102g | 53°45′N | 113°32′W |
| Carbondale, Il., U.S. | 108 | 37°42′N | 89°12′W |
| Carbondale, Pa., U.S. | 109 | 41°35′N | 75°30′W |
| Carbonear, Can. (kär-bô-nēr′) | 101 | 47°45′N | 53°14′W |
| Carbon Hill, Al., U.S. (kär′bŏn hĭl) | 124 | 33°53′N | 87°34′W |
| Carcaixent, Spain | 173 | 39°09′N | 0°29′W |
| Carcans, Étang de, l., Fr. (ā-taɴ-dĕ-kär-kän) | 170 | 45°12′N | 1°00′W |
| Carcassonne, Fr. (kár-ká-sôn′) | 161 | 43°12′N | 2°23′E |
| Carcross, Can. (kär′krôs) | 90 | 60°18′N | 134°54′W |
| Cárdenas, Cuba (kär′då-näs) | 129 | 23°00′N | 81°10′W |
| Cárdenas, Mex. (ká′r-dĕ-näs) | 131 | 17°59′N | 93°23′W |
| Cárdenas, Mex. | 130 | 22°01′N | 99°38′W |
| Cárdenas, Bahía de, b., Cuba (bä-ē′ä-dĕ-kär′då-näs) | 134 | 23°10′N | 81°10′W |
| Cardiff, Can. (kär′dĭf) | 102g | 53°46′N | 113°36′W |
| Cardiff, Wales, U.K. | 161 | 51°30′N | 3°18′W |
| Cardigan, Wales, U.K. (kär′dĭ-găn) | 161 | 52°05′N | 4°40′W |
| Cardigan Bay, b., Wales, U.K. | 161 | 52°35′N | 4°40′W |
| Cardston, Can. (kärds′tŭn) | 90 | 49°12′N | 113°18′W |
| Carei, Rom. (kä-rē′) | 169 | 47°42′N | 22°28′E |
| Carentan, Fr. (kä-rôɴ-täɴ′) | 170 | 49°19′N | 1°14′W |
| Carey, Oh., U.S. (kā′rē) | 108 | 40°55′N | 83°25′W |
| Carey, l., Austl. (kâr′ē) | 220 | 29°20′S | 123°35′E |
| Carhaix-Plouguer, Fr. (kär-ĕ′) | 170 | 48°17′N | 3°37′W |
| Caribbean Sea, sea (kăr-ĭ-bē′ăn) | 129 | 14°30′N | 75°30′W |
| Caribe, Arroyo, r., Mex. (är-ro′ī-kä-rē′bĕ) | 131 | 18°18′N | 90°38′W |
| Cariboo Mountains, mts., Can. (kă′rĭ-bōō) | 92 | 53°00′N | 121°00′W |
| Caribou, Me., U.S. | 100 | 46°51′N | 68°01′W |
| Caribou, i., Can. | 98 | 47°22′N | 85°42′W |
| Caribou Lake, l., Mn., U.S. | 117h | 46°54′N | 92°16′W |
| Caribou Mountains, mts., Can. | 92 | 59°20′N | 115°30′W |
| Carinhanha, Braz. (kä-rĭ-nyän′yä) | 143 | 14°14′S | 43°44′W |
| Carini, Italy (kä-rē′nē) | 174 | 38°09′N | 13°10′E |
| Carleton Place, Can. (kärl′tŭn) | 99 | 45°15′N | 76°10′W |
| Carletonville, S. Afr. | 238c | 26°20′S | 27°23′E |
| Carlinville, Il., U.S. (kär′lĭn-vĭl) | 121 | 39°16′N | 89°52′W |
| Carlisle, Eng., U.K. (kär-līl′) | 154 | 54°54′N | 3°03′W |
| Carlisle, Ky., U.S. | 108 | 38°20′N | 84°00′W |
| Carlisle, Pa., U.S. | 109 | 40°10′N | 77°15′W |
| Carloforte, Italy (kär′lô-fôr-tå) | 174 | 39°11′N | 8°28′E |
| Carlos Casares, Arg. (kär-lôs-kä-sá′rĕs) | 144 | 35°38′S | 61°17′W |
| Carlow, Ire. (kär′lō) | 164 | 52°50′N | 7°00′W |
| Carlsbad, N.M., U.S. (kärlz′băd) | 122 | 32°24′N | 104°12′W |
| Carlsbad Caverns National Park, rec., N.M., U.S. | 122 | 32°08′N | 104°30′W |
| Carlton, Eng., U.K. (kärl′tŭn) | 158a | 52°58′N | 1°05′W |
| Carlton, Mn., U.S. | 117h | 46°40′N | 92°26′W |
| Carlton Center, Mi., U.S. (kärl′tŭn sĕn′tĕr) | 108 | 42°45′N | 85°20′W |
| Carlyle, Il., U.S. (kärlīl′) | 121 | 38°37′N | 89°23′W |
| Carmagnola, Italy (kär-mä-nyô′lä) | 174 | 44°52′N | 7°48′E |
| Carman, Can. (kär′mán) | 90 | 49°32′N | 98°00′W |
| Carmarthen, Wales, U.K. (kär-mär′thĕn) | 164 | 51°50′N | 4°20′W |
| Carmaux, Fr. (kár-mō′) | 170 | 44°05′N | 2°09′E |
| Carmel, N.Y., U.S. (kär′mĕl) | 110a | 41°25′N | 73°42′W |
| Carmelo, Ur. (kär-mĕ′lo) | 141c | 33°59′S | 58°15′W |
| Carmen, Isla del, i., Mex. (ē′s-lä-dĕl-ká′r-mĕn) | 131 | 18°43′N | 91°40′W |
| Carmen, Laguna del, l., Mex. (lä-gô′nä-dĕl-ká′r-mĕn) | 131 | 18°15′N | 93°26′W |
| Carmen de Areco, Arg. (kär′mĕn′ dā ä-rā′kō) | 141c | 34°21′S | 59°50′W |
| Carmen de Patagones, Arg. (ká′r-mĕn-dĕ-pä-tä-gô′nĕs) | 144 | 41°00′S | 63°00′W |
| Carmi, Il., U.S. (kär′mī) | 108 | 38°05′N | 88°10′W |
| Carmo, Braz. (ká′r-mô) | 141a | 21°57′S | 42°45′W |
| Carmo do Rio Clara, Braz. (ká′r-mô-dô-rē′ô-klä′rä) | 141a | 20°57′S | 46°04′W |
| Carmona, Spain | 172 | 37°28′N | 5°38′W |
| Carnarvon, Austl. (kär-när′vŭn) | 218 | 24°45′S | 113°45′E |
| Carnarvon, S. Afr. | 232 | 31°00′S | 22°15′E |
| Carnation, Wa., U.S. (kär-nā′shŭn) | 116a | 47°39′N | 121°55′W |
| Carnaxide, Port. (kär-nä-shē′dĕ) | 173b | 38°44′N | 9°15′W |
| Carndonagh, Ire. (kärn-dō-nä′) | 164 | 55°15′N | 7°15′W |
| Carnegie, Ok., U.S. (kär-nĕg′ĭ) | 120 | 35°06′N | 98°38′W |
| Carnegie, Pa., U.S. | 111e | 40°24′N | 80°06′W |
| Carneys Point, N.J., U.S. (kär′nĕs) | 109 | 39°45′N | 75°25′W |
| Carnic Alps, mts., Eur. | 161 | 46°43′N | 12°38′E |
| Carnot, Alg. (kär nō′) | 173 | 36°15′N | 1°40′E |
| Carnot, C.A.R. | 231 | 5°00′N | 15°52′E |
| Carnsore Point, c., Ire. (kärn′sôr) | 164 | 52°10′N | 6°16′W |
| Caro, Mi., U.S. (kâ′rō) | 108 | 43°30′N | 83°25′W |
| Carolina, Braz. (kä-rô-lē′nä) | 143 | 7°26′S | 47°16′W |


ăt; finăl; rāte; senåte; ärm; åsk; sofá; fâre; ch-choose; dh-as th in other; bē; ēvent; bĕt; recĕnt; cratĕr; g-gō; gh-guttural g; bĭt; ĭ-short neutral; rīde; ᴋ-guttural k as ch in German ich;

ng-sing;  ŋ-bank;  N-nasalized n;  nŏd;  cŏmmit;  ōld;  ôbey;  ôrder;  oi-boil;  fŏŏd;  ò-as oo in foot;  ou-out;  s-soft;  sh-dish;  th-thin;  pūre;  ûnite;  ûrn;  stŭd;  circŭs;  ü-as in French tu;  '-indeterminate vowel.

| PLACE (Pronunciation) | PAGE | LAT. | LONG. |
|---|---|---|---|
| Celina, Oh., U.S. (sẻlī′na) | 108 | 40°30′N | 84°35′W |
| Celje, Slvn. (tsĕl′yĕ) | 174 | 46°13′N | 15°17′E |
| Celle, Ger. (tsĕl′ē) | 161 | 52°37′N | 10°05′E |
| Cement, Ok., U.S. (sẻ-mĕnt′) | 120 | 34°56′N | 98°07′W |
| Cenderawasih, Teluk, b., Indon. | 213 | 2°20′S | 135°30′E |
| Ceniza, Pico, mtn., Ven. (pē′kỏ-sĕ-nē′zä) | 143b | 10°24′N | 67°26′W |
| Center, Tx., U.S. (sĕn′tẽr) | 123 | 31°50′N | 94°10′W |
| Center Hill Lake, res., Tn., U.S. (sĕn′tẽr-hĭl) | 124 | 36°02′N | 86°00′W |
| Center Line, Mi., U.S. (sĕn′tẽr līn) | 111b | 42°29′N | 83°01′W |
| Centerville, Ia., U.S. (sĕn′tẽr-vĭl) | 113 | 40°44′N | 92°48′W |
| Centerville, Mn., U.S. | 117g | 45°10′N | 93°03′W |
| Centerville, Pa., U.S. | 111e | 40°02′N | 79°58′W |
| Centerville, S.D., U.S. | 112 | 43°07′N | 96°56′W |
| Centerville, Ut., U.S. | 117b | 40°55′N | 111°53′W |
| Central, Cordillera, mts., Bol. (kỏr-dēl-yĕ′rä-sĕn-trȧ′l) | 142 | 19°18′S | 65°29′W |
| Central, Cordillera, mts., Col. | 142a | 3°58′N | 75°55′W |
| Central, Cordillera, mts., Dom. Rep. | 135 | 19°05′N | 71°30′W |
| Central, Cordillera, mts., Phil. (kỏr-dēl-yĕ′rä-sĕn′träl) | 213a | 17°05′N | 120°55′E |
| Central African Republic, nation, Afr. | 231 | 7°50′N | 21°00′E |
| Central America, reg., N.A. (ä-mĕr′ĭ-kȧ) | 128 | 10°45′N | 87°15′W |
| Central City, Ky., U.S. (sĕn′trȧl) | 124 | 37°15′N | 87°09′W |
| Central City, Ne., U.S. (sĕn′trȧl sĭ′tĭ) | 112 | 41°07′N | 98°00′W |
| Central Falls, R.I., U.S. (sĕn′trȧl fôlz) | 110b | 41°54′N | 71°23′W |
| Centralia, Il., U.S. (sĕn-trā′lĭ-ȧ) | 108 | 38°35′N | 89°05′W |
| Centralia, Mo., U.S. | 121 | 39°11′N | 92°07′W |
| Centralia, Wa., U.S. | 114 | 46°42′N | 122°58′W |
| Central Plateau, plat., Russia | 180 | 55°00′N | 33°30′E |
| Central Valley, N.Y., U.S. | 110a | 41°19′N | 74°07′W |
| Centreville, Il., U.S. (sĕn′tẽr-vĭl) | 117e | 38°33′N | 90°06′W |
| Centreville, Md., U.S. | 109 | 39°05′N | 76°05′W |
| Century, Fl., U.S. (sĕn′tů-rĭ) | 124 | 30°57′N | 87°15′W |
| Ceram (Seram), i., Indon. | 213 | 2°45′S | 129°30′E |
| Céret, Fr. | 170 | 42°29′N | 2°47′E |
| Cerignola, Italy (chā-rẻ-nyô′lä) | 174 | 41°16′N | 15°55′E |
| Cerknica, Slvn. (tsĕr′knẻ-tsȧ) | 174 | 45°48′N | 14°21′E |
| Cern'achovsk, Russia (chĕr-nyä′ĸôfsk) | 180 | 54°38′N | 21°49′E |
| Cerralvo, Mex. (sĕr-räl′vō) | 122 | 26°05′N | 99°37′W |
| Cerralvo, i., Mex. | 128 | 24°00′N | 109°59′W |
| Cerrito, Col. (sĕr-rē′-tỏ) | 142a | 3°41′N | 76°17′W |
| Cerritos, Mex. (sĕr-rē′tỏs) | 130 | 22°26′N | 100°16′W |
| Cerro de Pasco, Peru (sĕr′rō dā päs′kō) | 142 | 10°45′S | 76°14′W |
| Cerro Gordo, Arroyo de, r., Mex. (är-rô-yŏ-dĕ-sĕ′r-rỏ-gôr-dŏ) | 122 | 26°12′N | 104°06′W |
| Certegui, Col. (sĕr-tĕ′gē) | 142a | 5°21′N | 76°35′W |
| Cervantes, Phil. (sĕr-vän′tās) | 213a | 16°59′N | 120°42′E |
| Cervera del Río Alhama, Spain | 172 | 42°02′N | 1°55′W |
| Cerveteri, Italy (chĕr-vĕ′tĕ-rē) | 173d | 42°00′N | 12°06′E |
| Cesena, Italy (chĕ′sĕ-nä) | 174 | 44°08′N | 12°16′E |
| Çēsis, Lat. (sā′sĭs) | 167 | 57°19′N | 25°17′E |
| Česká Lípa, Czech Rep. (chĕs′kä lē′pa) | 168 | 50°41′N | 14°31′E |
| České Budějovice, Czech Rep. (chĕs′kā bōō′dyĕ-yỏ-vēt-sĕ) | 161 | 49°00′N | 14°30′E |
| Českomoravská Vysočina, hills, Czech Rep. | 168 | 49°21′N | 15°40′E |
| Český Těšín, Czech Rep. | 169 | 49°43′N | 18°22′E |
| Çeşme, Tur. (chĕsh′mĕ) | 175 | 38°20′N | 26°20′E |
| Cessnock, Austl. | 219 | 32°58′S | 151°15′E |
| Cestos, r., Lib. | 234 | 5°40′N | 9°25′W |
| Cetinje, Serb. (tsĕt′in-yĕ) | 154 | 42°23′N | 18°55′E |
| Ceuta, Sp. N. Afr. (thā-ōō′tä) | 230 | 36°04′N | 5°36′W |
| Cévennes, reg., Fr. (sā-vĕn′) | 161 | 44°20′N | 3°48′E |
| Ceylon *see* Sri Lanka, nation, Asia | 203 | 8°45′N | 82°30′E |
| Chabot, Lake, l., Ca., U.S. (sha′bŏt) | 116b | 37°44′N | 122°06′W |
| Chacabuco, Arg. (chä-kä-bōō′kō) | 141c | 34°37′S | 60°27′W |
| Chacaltianguis, Mex. (chä-käl-tẻ-äŋ′gwẻs) | 131 | 18°18′N | 95°50′W |
| Chachapoyas, Peru (chä-chä-poi′yäs) | 142 | 6°16′S | 77°48′W |
| Chaco, prov., Arg. (chä′kō) | 144 | 26°00′S | 60°45′W |
| Chaco Culture National Historic Park, rec., N.M., U.S. (chä′kỏ) | 119 | 36°05′N | 108°00′W |
| Chad, Russia (chäd) | 186a | 56°33′N | 57°11′E |
| Chad, nation, Afr. | 231 | 17°48′N | 19°00′E |
| Chad, Lake, l., Afr. | 231 | 13°55′N | 13°40′E |
| Chadbourn, N.C., U.S. (chăd′bŭrn) | 125 | 34°19′N | 78°55′W |
| Chadron, Ne., U.S. (chăd′rŭn) | 104 | 42°50′N | 103°10′W |
| Chafarinas, Islas, is., Sp. N. Afr. | 172 | 35°08′N | 2°20′W |
| Chaffee, Mo., U.S. (chăf′ẻ) | 121 | 37°10′N | 89°39′W |
| Chāgal Hills, hills, Afg. | 198 | 29°15′N | 63°28′E |
| Chagodoshcha, r., Russia (chä-gō-dôsh-chä) | 176 | 59°08′N | 35°13′E |
| Chagres, r., Pan. (chä′grĕs) | 133 | 9°18′N | 79°22′W |
| Chagrin, r., Oh., U.S. (shȧ′grĭn) | 111d | 41°34′N | 81°24′W |
| Chagrin Falls, Oh., U.S. (shȧ′grĭn fôls) | 111d | 41°26′N | 81°23′W |
| Chahar, hist. reg., China (chä-här) | 205 | 44°25′N | 115°00′E |
| Chake Chake, Tan. | 237 | 5°15′S | 39°46′E |
| Chalatenango, El Sal. (chäl-ä-tĕ-näŋ′gō) | 132 | 14°04′N | 88°54′W |
| Chalbi Desert, des., Kenya | 237 | 3°40′N | 36°50′E |
| Chalcatongo, Mex. (chäl-kä-tôŋ′gō) | 131 | 17°04′N | 97°41′W |
| Chalchihuites, Mex. (chäl-chẻ-wē′tås) | 130 | 23°28′N | 103°57′W |
| Chalchuapa, El Sal. (chäl-chwä′pä) | 132 | 14°01′N | 89°39′W |
| Chalco, Mex. (chäl-kō) | 131a | 19°15′N | 98°54′W |
| Chaleur Bay, b., Can. (shȧ-lûr′) | 93 | 47°58′N | 65°33′W |
| Chalgrove, Eng., U.K. (chăl′grỏv) | 158b | 51°38′N | 1°05′W |
| Chaling, China (chä′lĭng) | 209 | 27°00′N | 113°31′E |
| Chalkída, Grc. | 163 | 38°28′N | 23°38′E |
| Chalmette, La., U.S. (shăl-mĕt′) | 110d | 29°57′N | 89°57′W |
| Châlons-sur-Marne, Fr. (shȧ-lôɴ′sür-märn) | 161 | 48°57′N | 4°23′E |
| Chalon-sur-Saône, Fr. | 161 | 46°47′N | 4°54′E |
| Chaltel, Cerro (Monte Fitzroy), mtn., S.A. (sĕ′r-rỏ-chäl′tĕl) | 144 | 48°10′S | 73°18′W |
| Chālūs, Iran | 201 | 36°38′N | 51°26′E |
| Chama, Rio, r., N.M., U.S. (chä′mä) | 119 | 36°19′N | 106°31′W |
| Chama, Sierra de, mts., Guat. (sē-ĕ′r-rä-dĕ-chä-mä) | 132 | 15°48′N | 90°20′W |
| Chamama, Mwi. | 237 | 12°55′S | 33°43′E |
| Chaman, Pak. (chŭm-än′) | 199 | 30°58′N | 66°21′E |
| Chambal, r., India (chŭm-bäl′) | 199 | 24°30′N | 75°30′E |
| Chamberlain, S.D., U.S. (chäm′bẽr-lĭn) | 112 | 43°48′N | 99°21′W |
| Chamberlain, l., Me., U.S. | 100 | 46°15′N | 69°10′W |
| Chambersburg, Pa., U.S. (chām′bẽrz-bûrg) | 109 | 40°00′N | 77°40′W |
| Chambéry, Fr. (shäm-bā-rē′) | 161 | 45°35′N | 5°54′E |
| Chambeshi, r., Zam. | 237 | 10°35′S | 31°20′E |
| Chamblee, Ga., U.S. (chăm-blē′) | 110c | 33°55′N | 84°18′W |
| Chambly, Can. (shäɴ-blē′) | 102a | 45°27′N | 73°17′W |
| Chambly, Fr. | 171b | 49°11′N | 2°14′E |
| Chambord, Can. | 91 | 48°22′N | 72°01′W |
| Chame, Punta, c., Pan. (pỏ′n-tä-chä′må) | 133 | 8°41′N | 79°27′W |
| Chamelecón, r., Hond. (chä-mĕ-lĕ-kô′n) | 132 | 15°09′N | 88°42′W |
| Chamo, l., Eth. | 231 | 5°58′N | 37°00′E |
| Chamonix-Mont-Blanc, Fr. (shȧ-mỏ-nē′) | 171 | 45°55′N | 6°50′E |
| Champagne, reg., Fr. (shäm-pän′yē) | 170 | 48°53′N | 4°48′E |
| Champaign, Il., U.S. (shăm-pān′) | 105 | 40°10′N | 88°15′W |
| Champdāni, India | 202a | 22°48′N | 88°21′E |
| Champerico, Guat. (chăm-på-rē′kō) | 132 | 14°18′N | 91°55′W |
| Champion, Mi., U.S. (chăm′pĭ-ŭn) | 113 | 46°30′N | 87°59′W |
| Champlain, Lake, l., N.A. (shăm-plān′) | 107 | 44°45′N | 73°20′W |
| Champlitte-et-le-Prálot, Fr. (shäɴ-plēt′) | 171 | 47°38′N | 5°28′E |
| Champotón, Mex. (chäm-pō-tōn′) | 131 | 19°21′N | 90°43′W |
| Champotón, r., Mex. | 131 | 19°19′N | 90°15′W |
| Chañaral, Chile (chän-yä-räl′) | 144 | 26°20′S | 70°46′W |
| Chances Peak, vol., Monts. | 133b | 16°43′N | 62°10′W |
| Chandeleur Islands, is., La., U.S. (shăn-dẽ-lōōr′) | 124 | 29°53′N | 88°35′W |
| Chandeleur Sound, strt., La., U.S. | 124 | 29°47′N | 89°08′W |
| Chandīgarh, India | 199 | 30°51′N | 77°13′E |
| Chandler, Can. (chăn′dlẽr) | 91 | 48°21′N | 64°41′W |
| Chandler, Ok., U.S. | 121 | 35°42′N | 96°52′W |
| Chandrapur, India | 199 | 19°58′N | 79°21′E |
| Chang *see* Yangtze, r., China | 205 | 30°30′N | 117°25′E |
| Changane, r., Moz. | 232 | 22°42′S | 32°46′E |
| Changara, Moz. | 237 | 16°54′S | 33°14′E |
| Changchun, China (chäŋ-chỏn) | 205 | 43°55′N | 125°25′E |
| Changdang Hu, l., China (chäŋ-däŋ hōō) | 206 | 31°37′N | 119°29′E |
| Changde, China (chäŋ-dŭ) | 205 | 29°00′N | 111°38′E |
| Changhua, Tai. (chäng′hwä′) | 209 | 24°02′N | 120°32′E |
| Changjŏn, Kor., N. (chäng′jŭn′) | 210 | 38°40′N | 128°05′E |
| Changli, China (chäŋ-lē) | 208 | 39°46′N | 119°10′E |
| Changning, China (chäŋ-nĭŋ) | 204 | 24°34′N | 99°49′E |
| Changping, China (chäŋ-pĭŋ) | 208 | 40°12′N | 116°10′E |
| Changqing, China (chäŋ-chyĭŋ) | 206 | 36°33′N | 116°42′E |
| Changsan Got, c., Kor., N. | 210 | 38°06′N | 124°50′E |
| Changsha, China (chäŋ-shä) | 205 | 28°20′N | 113°00′E |
| Changshan Qundao, is., China (chäŋ-shän chyỏn-dou) | 206 | 39°08′N | 122°26′E |
| Changshu, China (chäŋ-shōō) | 206 | 31°40′N | 120°45′E |
| Changting, China | 209 | 25°50′N | 116°18′E |
| Changwu, China (chäng′wōō′) | 208 | 35°12′N | 107°45′E |
| Changxindianzhen, China (chäŋ-shyĭn-dĭĕn-jŭn) | 208a | 39°49′N | 116°12′E |
| Changxing Dao, i., China (chäŋ-shyĭŋ dou) | 206 | 39°38′N | 121°10′E |
| Changyi, China (chäŋ-yē) | 206 | 36°51′N | 119°23′E |
| Changyuan, China (chyäŋ-yuän) | 206 | 35°10′N | 114°41′E |
| Changzhi, China (chäŋ-jr) | 208 | 35°58′N | 112°58′E |
| Changzhou, China (chäŋ-jō) | 205 | 31°47′N | 119°56′E |
| Changzhuyuan, China (chäŋ-jōō-yuän) | 206 | 31°33′N | 115°17′E |
| Chanhassen, Mn., U.S. (shān′hās-sĕn) | 117g | 44°52′N | 93°32′W |
| Chaniá, Grc. | 162 | 35°31′N | 24°01′E |
| Channel Islands, is., Eur. (chăn′ĕl) | 156 | 49°15′N | 3°30′W |
| Channel Islands, is., Ca., U.S. | 118 | 33°30′N | 119°15′W |
| Channel-Port-aux-Basques, Can. | 91 | 47°35′N | 59°11′W |
| Channelview, Tx., U.S. (chănẻlvū) | 123a | 29°46′N | 95°07′W |
| Chantada, Spain (chän-tä′dä) | 172 | 42°38′N | 7°36′W |
| Chanthaburi, Thai. | 212 | 12°37′N | 102°04′E |
| Chantilly, Fr. (shäɴ-tẻ-yē′) | 171b | 49°12′N | 2°30′E |
| Chantilly, Va., U.S. (shăn′tĭlē) | 110e | 38°53′N | 77°26′W |
| Chantrey Inlet, b., Can. (chăn-trē) | 92 | 67°49′N | 95°00′W |
| Chanute, Ks., U.S. (shȧ-nōōt′) | 105 | 37°41′N | 95°27′W |
| Chany, l., Russia (chä′nẻ) | 178 | 54°15′N | 77°31′E |
| Chao'an, China (chou-än) | 205 | 23°48′N | 116°35′E |
| Chao Hu, l., China | 209 | 31°45′N | 116°59′E |
| Chao Phraya, r., Thai. | 212 | 16°13′N | 99°33′E |
| Chaor, r., China (chou-r) | 208 | 47°20′N | 121°40′E |
| Chaoshui, China (chou-shwā) | 206 | 37°43′N | 120°56′E |
| Chaoxian, China (chou shyĕn) | 206 | 31°37′N | 117°50′E |
| Chaoyang, China | 205 | 41°32′N | 120°20′E |
| Chaoyang, China (chou-yäŋ) | 209 | 23°18′N | 116°32′E |
| Chapada, Serra da, mts., Braz. (sĕ′r-rä-dä-shä-pä′dä) | 143 | 14°57′S | 54°34′W |
| Chapadão, Serra do, mtn., Braz. (sĕ′r-rä-dỏ-shä-pȧ-dou′ɴ) | 141a | 20°31′S | 46°20′W |
| Chapala, Mex. (chä-pä′lä) | 130 | 20°18′N | 103°10′W |
| Chapala, Lago de, l., Mex. (lä′gô-dĕ-chä-pä′lä) | 128 | 20°14′N | 103°02′W |
| Chapalagana, r., Mex. (chä-pä-lä-gȧ′nä) | 130 | 22°11′N | 104°09′W |
| Chaparral, Col. (chä-pär-rȧ′l) | 142 | 3°44′N | 75°28′W |
| Chapayevsk, Russia (châ-pī′ĕfsk) | 180 | 53°00′N | 49°30′E |
| Chapel Hill, N.C., U.S. (chăp′′l hĭl) | 125 | 35°55′N | 79°05′W |
| Chaplain, l., Wa., U.S. (chăp′lĭn) | 116a | 47°58′N | 121°50′W |
| Chapleau, Can. (chăp-lō′) | 91 | 47°43′N | 83°28′W |
| Chapman, Mount, mtn., Can. (chăp′mȧn) | 95 | 51°50′N | 118°20′W |
| Chapman's Bay, b., S. Afr. (chăp′mȧns bă) | 232a | 34°06′S | 18°17′E |
| Chappell, Ne., U.S. (chă-pĕl′) | 112 | 41°06′N | 102°29′W |
| Chapultenango, Mex. (chä-pỏl-tē-näŋ′gō) | 131 | 17°19′N | 93°08′W |
| Chá Pungana, Ang. | 236 | 13°44′S | 18°39′E |
| Chār Borjak, Afg. | 201 | 30°17′N | 62°03′E |
| Charcas, Mex. (chär′käs) | 130 | 23°09′N | 101°09′W |
| Charco de Azul, Bahía, b., Pan. | 133 | 8°14′N | 82°45′W |
| Charente, r., Fr. (shȧ-räɴt′) | 170 | 45°48′N | 0°28′W |
| Chari, r., Afr. (shä-rē′) | 235 | 12°45′N | 14°55′E |
| Charing, Eng., U.K. (chă′rĭng) | 158b | 51°13′N | 0°49′E |
| Chariton, Ia., U.S. (châr′ĭ-tŭn) | 113 | 41°02′N | 93°16′W |
| Chariton, r., Mo., U.S. | 121 | 40°24′N | 92°38′W |
| Charjew, Turkmen. | 183 | 38°52′N | 63°37′E |
| Charlemagne, Can. (shärl-mäny′) | 102a | 45°43′N | 73°29′W |
| Charleroi, Bel. (shȧr-lē-rwä′) | 161 | 50°25′N | 4°35′E |
| Charleroi, Pa., U.S. (shär′lē-roi) | 111e | 40°08′N | 79°54′W |
| Charles, Cape, c., Va., U.S. (chärlz) | 109 | 37°05′N | 75°48′W |
| Charlesbourg, Can. (shȧrl-bōōr′) | 102b | 46°51′N | 71°16′W |
| Charles City, Ia., U.S. (chärlz) | 113 | 43°03′N | 92°40′W |
| Charleston, Il., U.S. (chärlz′tŭn) | 108 | 39°30′N | 88°10′W |
| Charleston, Mo., U.S. | 121 | 36°53′N | 89°20′W |
| Charleston, Ms., U.S. | 124 | 34°00′N | 90°02′W |
| Charleston, S.C., U.S. | 105 | 32°47′N | 79°56′W |
| Charleston, W.V., U.S. | 105 | 38°20′N | 81°35′W |
| Charlestown, St. K./N. | 133b | 17°10′N | 62°32′W |
| Charlestown, In., U.S. (chärlz′toun) | 111h | 38°46′N | 85°39′W |
| Charleville, Austl. (chär′lẻ-vĭl) | 219 | 26°16′S | 146°28′E |
| Charleville Mézières, Fr. (shärl-vēl′) | 170 | 49°48′N | 4°41′E |
| Charlevoix, Mi., U.S. (shär′lē-voi) | 108 | 45°20′N | 85°15′W |
| Charlevoix, Lake, l., Mi., U.S. | 113 | 45°17′N | 85°43′W |
| Charlotte, Mi., U.S. (shär′lŏt) | 108 | 42°35′N | 84°50′W |
| Charlotte, N.C., U.S. | 105 | 35°15′N | 80°50′W |
| Charlotte Amalie, V.I.U.S. (shär-lŏt′ĕ ä-mä′lĭ-ȧ) | 129 | 18°21′N | 64°54′W |
| Charlotte Harbor, b., Fl., U.S. | 125a | 26°49′N | 82°00′W |
| Charlotte Lake, l., Can. | 94 | 52°07′N | 125°30′W |
| Charlottenberg, Swe. (shär-lŭt′ĕn-bĕrg) | 166 | 59°53′N | 12°17′E |
| Charlottesville, Va., U.S. (shär′lŏtz-vĭl) | 105 | 38°00′N | 78°25′W |
| Charlottetown, Can. (shär′lŏt-toun) | 91 | 46°14′N | 63°08′W |
| Charlotte Waters, Austl. (shär′lŏt) | 218 | 26°00′S | 134°50′E |
| Charmes, Fr. (shärm) | 171 | 48°23′N | 6°19′E |
| Charnwood Forest, for., Eng., U.K. (chärn′wỏd) | 158a | 52°42′N | 1°15′W |
| Charny, Can. (shär-nē′) | 102b | 46°43′N | 71°16′W |
| Chars, Fr. (shär) | 171b | 49°09′N | 1°57′E |
| Chārsadda, Pak. (chŭr-sä′dä) | 199a | 34°17′N | 71°43′E |
| Charters Towers, Austl. (chär′tẽrz) | 219 | 20°03′S | 146°20′E |
| Chartres, Fr. (shärt′r′) | 161 | 48°26′N | 1°29′E |
| Chascomús, Arg. (chäs-kō-mōōs′) | 144 | 35°32′S | 58°01′W |
| Chase City, Va., U.S. (chās) | 125 | 36°45′N | 78°27′W |
| Chashniki, Bela. (chäsh′nyẻ-kē) | 176 | 54°51′N | 29°08′E |
| Chaska, Mn., U.S. (chăs′kȧ) | 117g | 44°48′N | 93°36′W |
| Châteaudun, Fr. (shä-tō-dȧɴ′) | 170 | 48°04′N | 1°23′E |
| Château-Gontier, Fr. (chȧ-tō′gôɴ′tyā′) | 170 | 47°48′N | 0°43′W |
| Châteauguay, Can. (chȧ-tō-gā) | 102a | 45°22′N | 73°45′W |
| Châteauguay, r., N.A. | 102a | 45°13′N | 73°51′W |
| Châteauneaut, Fr. | 170a | 43°23′N | 5°11′E |
| Château-Renault, Fr. (shȧ-tō-rẽ-nō′) | 170 | 47°36′N | 0°57′E |
| Château-Richer, Can. (shȧ-tō′rē-shā′) | 102b | 47°00′N | 71°01′W |
| Châteauroux, Fr. (shȧ-tō-rōō′) | 161 | 46°47′N | 1°39′E |
| Château-Thierry, Fr. (shȧ-tō′ty-ĕr-rē′) | 170 | 49°03′N | 3°22′E |
| Châtellerault, Fr. (shä-tĕl-rō′) | 161 | 46°48′N | 0°31′E |
| Chatfield, Mn., U.S. (chăt′fēld) | 113 | 43°50′N | 92°10′W |
| Chatham, Can. (chăt′ȧm) | 91 | 42°25′N | 82°10′W |
| Chatham, Can. | 91 | 47°02′N | 65°28′W |
| Chatham, Eng., U.K. (chăt′ŭm) | 165 | 51°23′N | 0°32′E |
| Chatham, N.J., U.S. (chăt′ȧm) | 110a | 40°44′N | 74°23′W |
| Chatham, Oh., U.S. | 111d | 41°06′N | 82°01′W |
| Chatham Islands, is., N.Z. | 2 | 44°00′S | 178°00′W |
| Chatham Sound, strt., Can. | 94 | 54°32′N | 130°35′W |
| Chatham Strait, strt., Ak., U.S. | 103 | 57°00′N | 134°40′W |
| Chatsworth, Ca., U.S. (chătz′wûrth) | 117a | 34°16′N | 118°36′W |
| Chatsworth Reservoir, res., Ca., U.S. | 117a | 34°15′N | 118°41′W |
| Chattahoochee, Fl., U.S. (chăt-tȧ-hōō′ cheē) | 124 | 30°42′N | 84°47′W |
| Chattahoochee, r., U.S. | 107 | 32°00′N | 85°10′W |
| Chattanooga, Tn., U.S. (chăt-ȧ-nōō′gȧ) | 105 | 35°01′N | 85°15′W |
| Chattooga, r., Ga., U.S. (chă-tōō′gȧ) | 124 | 34°47′N | 83°13′W |
| Chaudière, r., Can. (shō-dyĕr′) | 99 | 46°26′N | 71°10′W |
| Chaumont, Fr. (shō-môɴ′) | 161 | 48°08′N | 5°07′E |
| Chaunskaya Guba, b., Russia | 185 | 69°15′N | 170°00′E |
| Chauny, Fr. (shō-nē′) | 170 | 49°40′N | 3°09′E |
| Chau-phu, Viet. | 212 | 10°49′N | 104°57′E |

PRONOUNCING INDEX

Chautauqua – Chippewa Lake 281


| PLACE (Pronunciation) | PAGE | LAT. | LONG. |
|---|---|---|---|
| Chautauqua, l., N.Y., U.S. (shá-tô´kwá) | 109 | 42°10'N | 79°25'W |
| Chavaniga, Russia | 180 | 66°02'N | 37°50'E |
| Chaves, Port. (chä´vězh) | 172 | 41°44'N | 7°30'W |
| Chavinda, Mex. (chä-vē´n-dä) | 130 | 20°01'N | 102°27'W |
| Chavusi, Bela. | 176 | 53°57'N | 30°58'E |
| Chazumba, Mex. (chä-zōm´bä) | 131 | 18°11'N | 97°41'W |
| Cheadle, Eng., U.K. (chē´d'l) | 158a | 52°59'N | 1°59'W |
| Cheat, W.V., U.S. (chēt) | 109 | 39°35'N | 79°40'W |
| Cheb, Czech Rep. (kĕb) | 168 | 50°05'N | 12°23'E |
| Chebarkul', Russia (chĕ-bár-kûl´) | 186a | 54°59'N | 60°22'E |
| Cheboksary, Russia (chyĕ-bôk-sä´rê) | 180 | 56°00'N | 47°20'E |
| Cheboygan, Mi., U.S. (shê-boi´găn) | 108 | 45°40'N | 84°30'W |
| Chech, Erg, des., Alg. | 230 | 24°45'N | 2°07'W |
| Chechen', i., Russia (chyĕch´ĕn) | 181 | 44°00'N | 48°10'E |
| Chechnya, prov., Russia | 182 | 43°30'N | 45°50'E |
| Checotah, Ok., U.S. (chê-kō´tá) | 121 | 35°27'N | 95°32'W |
| Chedabucto Bay, b., Can. (chĕd-á-bŭk-tō) | 101 | 45°23'N | 61°10'W |
| Cheduba Island, i., Mya. | 212 | 18°45'N | 93°01'E |
| Cheecham Hills, hills, Can. (chēē´hăm) | 96 | 56°20'N | 111°10'W |
| Cheektowaga, N.Y., U.S. (chēk-tō-wä´gá) | 111c | 42°54'N | 78°46'W |
| Chefoo see Yantai, China | 205 | 37°32'N | 121°22'E |
| Chegutu, Zimb. | 232 | 18°18'S | 30°10'E |
| Chehalis, Wa., U.S. (chê-hā´lĭs) | 114 | 46°39'N | 122°58'W |
| Chehalis, r., Wa., U.S. | 114 | 46°47'N | 123°17'W |
| Cheju, Kor., S. (chĕ´jōō´) | 210 | 33°29'N | 126°40'E |
| Cheju (Quelpart), i., Kor., S. | 210 | 33°20'N | 126°25'E |
| Chekalin, Russia (chĕ-kä´lĭn) | 176 | 54°05'N | 36°13'E |
| Chela, Serra da, mts., Ang. (sĕr´rá dä shā´lá) | 232 | 15°30'S | 13°30'E |
| Chelan, Wa., U.S. (chê-lăn´) | 114 | 47°51'N | 119°59'W |
| Chelan, Lake, l., Wa., U.S. | 114 | 48°09'N | 120°20'W |
| Cheleiros, Port. (shĕ-la´rōzh) | 173b | 38°54'N | 9°19'W |
| Chéliff, r., Alg. (shā-lēf) | 230 | 36°00'N | 2°00'E |
| Chelles, Fr. | 171b | 48°53'N | 2°36'E |
| Chełm, Pol. (kĕlm) | 161 | 51°08'N | 23°30'E |
| Chełmno, Pol. (kĕlm´nō) | 169 | 53°20'N | 18°25'E |
| Chelmsford, Can. | 98 | 46°35'N | 81°12'W |
| Chelmsford, Eng., U.K. (chĕlm´s-fērd) | 165 | 51°44'N | 0°28'E |
| Chelmsford, Ma., U.S. | 101a | 42°36'N | 71°21'W |
| Chelsea, Austl. | 217a | 38°05'S | 145°08'E |
| Chelsea, Can. | 102c | 45°30'N | 75°46'W |
| Chelsea, Al., U.S. (chĕl´sê) | 110h | 33°20'N | 86°38'W |
| Chelsea, Ma., U.S. | 101a | 42°23'N | 71°02'W |
| Chelsea, Mi., U.S. | 108 | 42°20'N | 84°00'W |
| Chelsea, Ok., U.S. | 121 | 36°32'N | 95°23'W |
| Cheltenham, Eng., U.K. (chĕlt´nŭm) | 164 | 51°57'N | 2°06'W |
| Cheltenham, Md., U.S. (chĕltĕn-hăm) | 110e | 38°45'N | 76°50'W |
| Chelyabinsk, Russia (chĕl-yä-bênsk´) | 178 | 55°10'N | 61°25'E |
| Chelyuskin, Mys, c., Russia (chĕl-yòs´-kĭn) | 179 | 77°45'N | 104°45'E |
| Chemba, Moz. | 237 | 17°08'S | 34°52'E |
| Chemnitz, Ger. | 161 | 50°48'N | 12°53'E |
| Chemung, r., N.Y., U.S. (shê-mŭng) | 109 | 42°20'N | 77°25'W |
| Chën, Gora, mtn., Russia | 179 | 65°13'N | 142°12'E |
| Chenāb, r., Asia (chê-näb) | 199 | 30°30'N | 71°30'E |
| Chenachane, Alg. (shĕ-ná-shän´) | 230 | 26°14'N | 4°14'W |
| Chencun, China (chŭn-tsòn) | 207a | 22°58'N | 113°14'E |
| Cheney, Wa., U.S. (chē´nâ) | 114 | 47°29'N | 117°34'W |
| Chengde, China (chŭŋ-dŭ) | 205 | 40°50'N | 117°50'E |
| Chengdong Hu, l., China (chŭŋ-dôŋ hōō) | 206 | 32°22'N | 116°32'E |
| Chengdu, China (chŭŋ-dōō) | 204 | 30°30'N | 104°10'E |
| Chenggu, China (chŭŋ-gōō) | 208 | 33°05'N | 107°25'E |
| Chenghai, China (chŭŋ-hī) | 209 | 23°22'N | 116°40'E |
| Chengshan Jiao, c., China (jyou chŭŋ-shän) | 208 | 37°28'N | 122°40'E |
| Chengxi Hu, l., China (chŭŋ-shyē hōō) | 206 | 32°31'N | 116°04'E |
| Chennai (Madras), India | 199 | 13°08'N | 80°15'E |
| Chenxian, China (chŭn-shyĕn) | 209 | 25°40'N | 113°00'E |
| Chepén, Peru (chĕ-pĕ´n) | 142 | 7°17'S | 79°24'W |
| Chepo, Pan. (chā´pō) | 133 | 9°12'N | 79°06'W |
| Chepo, r., Pan. | 133 | 9°10'N | 78°36'W |
| Cher, r., Fr. (shâr) | 161 | 47°14'N | 1°34'E |
| Cherán, Mex. (chā-rän´) | 130 | 19°41'N | 101°54'W |
| Cherangany Hills, hills, Kenya | 237 | 1°25'N | 35°20'E |
| Cheraw, S.C., U.S. (chē´rô) | 125 | 34°40'N | 79°52'W |
| Cherbourg, Fr. (shär-bōr´) | 154 | 49°39'N | 1°43'W |
| Cherdyn', Russia (chĕr-dyĕn´) | 178 | 60°25'N | 56°32'E |
| Cheremkhovo, Russia (chĕr´yĕm-kô-vō) | 179 | 52°58'N | 103°18'E |
| Cherëmukhovo, Russia (chĕr-yĕ-mû-kô-vô) | 186a | 60°20'N | 60°00'E |
| Cherepanovo, Russia (chĕr´yĕ pä-nô´vō) | 178 | 54°13'N | 83°22'E |
| Cherepovets, Russia (chĕr-yĕ-pô´vyĕtz) | 178 | 59°08'N | 37°59'E |
| Chereya, Bela. (chĕr-ā´yä) | 176 | 54°38'N | 29°16'E |
| Chergui, i., Tun. | 162 | 34°50'N | 11°40'E |
| Chergui, Chott ech, l., Alg. (chĕr gē) | 162 | 34°12'N | 0°10'W |
| Cherkasy, Ukr. | 177 | 49°26'N | 32°03'E |
| Cherkasy, prov., Ukr. | 177 | 48°58'N | 30°55'E |
| Cherkessk, Russia | 182 | 44°14'N | 42°04'E |
| Cherlak, Russia (chĭr-läk´) | 178 | 54°04'N | 74°28'E |
| Chermoz, Russia (chĕr-môz´) | 180 | 58°47'N | 56°08'E |
| Chern', Russia (chĕrn) | 176 | 53°28'N | 36°49'E |
| Chërnaya Kalitva, r., Russia (chôr´ná yá kå-lēt´vá) | 177 | 50°15'N | 39°16'E |
| Chernihiv, Ukr. | 181 | 51°23'N | 31°15'E |
| Chernihiv, prov., Ukr. | 177 | 51°28'N | 31°18'E |
| Chernihivka, Ukr. | 177 | 47°08'N | 36°20'E |
| Chernivtsi, Ukr. | 178 | 48°18'N | 25°56'E |
| Chernobyl' see Chornobai, Ukr. | 176 | 51°17'N | 30°14'E |
| Chernogorsk, Russia (chĕr-nŏ-gôrsk´) | 184 | 54°01'N | 91°07'E |
| Chernoistochinsk, Russia (chĕr-nôy-stô´chĭnsk) | 186a | 57°44'N | 59°55'E |
| Chernyanka, Russia (chĕrn-yäŋ´kä) | 177 | 50°56'N | 37°48'E |
| Cherokee, Ia., U.S. (chĕr-ô-kē´) | 112 | 42°43'N | 95°33'W |
| Cherokee, Ks., U.S. | 121 | 37°21'N | 94°50'W |
| Cherokee, Ok., U.S. | 120 | 36°44'N | 98°22'W |
| Cherokee Lake, res., Tn., U.S. | 124 | 36°22'N | 83°22'W |
| Cherokees, Lake of the, res., Ok., U.S. (chĕr-ô-kēz´) | 107 | 36°32'N | 95°14'W |
| Cherokee Sound, Bah. | 134 | 26°15'N | 76°55'W |
| Cherryfield, Me., U.S. (chĕr´ĭ-fēld) | 100 | 44°37'N | 67°56'W |
| Cherry Grove, Or., U.S. | 116c | 45°27'N | 123°15'W |
| Cherryvale, Ks., U.S. | 121 | 37°16'N | 95°33'W |
| Cherryville, N.C., U.S. (chĕr´ĭ-vĭl) | 125 | 35°32'N | 81°22'W |
| Cherskogo, Khrebet, mts., Russia | 179 | 67°15'N | 140°00'E |
| Chertsey, Eng., U.K. | 158b | 51°24'N | 0°30'W |
| Chervonoye, Vozyera, l., Bela. (chĕr-vō´nô-yĕ) | 176 | 52°24'N | 28°00'E |
| Chervyen', Bela. (chĕr´vyĕn) | 176 | 53°43'N | 28°26'E |
| Cherykaw, Bela. | 176 | 53°34'N | 31°22'E |
| Chesaning, Mi., U.S. (chĕs´á-nĭng) | 108 | 43°10'N | 84°10'W |
| Chesapeake, Va., U.S. (chĕs´á-pēk) | 110g | 36°48'N | 76°16'W |
| Chesapeake Bay, b., U.S. | 107 | 38°20'N | 76°15'W |
| Chesapeake Beach, Md., U.S. | 110e | 38°42'N | 76°33'W |
| Chesham, Eng., U.K. (chĕsh´ŭm) | 158b | 51°41'N | 0°37'W |
| Cheshire, Mi., U.S. (chĕsh´ĭr) | 108 | 42°25'N | 86°00'W |
| Cheshire, co., Eng., U.K. | 158a | 53°16'N | 2°30'W |
| Chëshskaya Guba, b., Russia | 178 | 67°25'N | 46°00'E |
| Cheshunt, Eng., U.K. | 158b | 51°43'N | 0°02'W |
| Chesma, Russia (chĕs´má) | 186a | 53°50'N | 60°42'E |
| Chesnokovka, Russia (chĕs-nŏ-kôf´ká) | 178 | 53°28'N | 83°41'E |
| Chester, Eng., U.K. (chĕs´tĕr) | 164 | 53°12'N | 2°53'W |
| Chester, Il., U.S. | 121 | 37°54'N | 89°48'W |
| Chester, Pa., U.S. | 110f | 39°51'N | 75°22'W |
| Chester, S.C., U.S. | 125 | 34°42'N | 81°11'W |
| Chester, Va., U.S. | 125 | 37°20'N | 77°24'W |
| Chester, W.V., U.S. | 108 | 40°35'N | 80°30'W |
| Chesterfield, Eng., U.K. (chĕs´tĕr-fēld) | 164 | 53°14'N | 1°26'W |
| Chesterfield, Îles, is., N. Cal. | 221 | 19°38'S | 160°08'E |
| Chesterfield Inlet see Igluligaarjuk, Can. | 92 | 63°19'N | 91°11'W |
| Chesterfield Inlet, b., Can. | 93 | 63°59'N | 92°09'W |
| Chestermere Lake, l., Can. (chĕs´tē-mēr) | 102e | 51°03'N | 113°45'W |
| Chesterton, In., U.S. (chĕs´tĕr-tŭn) | 108 | 41°35'N | 87°05'W |
| Chestertown, Md., U.S. (chĕs´tĕr-toun) | 109 | 39°15'N | 76°05'W |
| Chesuncook, l., Me., U.S. (chĕs´ŭn-kòk) | 100 | 46°03'N | 69°40'W |
| Chetek, Wi., U.S. (chĕ´tĕk) | 113 | 45°18'N | 91°41'W |
| Chetumal, Bahía de, b., N.A. (bä-ē-ä dĕ chĕt-ōō-mäl´) | 128 | 18°07'N | 88°05'W |
| Chevelon Creek, r., Az., U.S. (shĕv´á-lŏn) | 119 | 34°35'N | 111°00'W |
| Cheviot, Oh., U.S. (shĕv´ĭ-ŭt) | 111f | 39°10'N | 84°37'W |
| Chevreuse, Fr. (shĕ-vrûz´) | 171b | 48°42'N | 2°02'E |
| Chevy Chase, Md., U.S. (shĕvĭ chās) | 110e | 38°58'N | 77°06'W |
| Chew Bahir, Afr. (stĕf-a-nē) | 231 | 4°46'N | 37°31'E |
| Chewelah, Wa., U.S. (chē-wē´lä) | 114 | 48°17'N | 117°42'W |
| Cheyenne, Wy., U.S. (shī-ĕn´) | 104 | 41°10'N | 104°49'W |
| Cheyenne, r., U.S. | 106 | 44°20'N | 102°15'W |
| Cheyenne River Indian Reservation, I.R., S.D., U.S. | 112 | 45°07'N | 100°46'W |
| Cheyenne Wells, Co., U.S. | 120 | 38°46'N | 102°21'W |
| Chhattisgarh, state, India | 199 | 23°00'N | 83°00'E |
| Chhindwāra, India | 202 | 22°08'N | 78°57'E |
| Chiai, Tai. (chī´ī´) | 209 | 23°28'N | 120°28'E |
| Chiange, Ang. | 236 | 15°45'S | 13°48'E |
| Chiang Mai, Thai. | 212 | 18°38'N | 98°44'E |
| Chiang Rai, Thai. | 212 | 19°53'N | 99°48'E |
| Chiapa, Río de, r., Mex. | 132 | 16°00'N | 92°20'W |
| Chiapa de Corzo, Mex. (chê-ä´pä dā kôr´zō) | 131 | 16°44'N | 93°01'W |
| Chiapas, state, Mex. (chê-ä´päs) | 128 | 17°10'N | 93°00'W |
| Chiapas, Cordilla de, mts., Mex. (kôr-dēl-yĕ´rä-dĕ-chyá´räs) | 131 | 15°55'N | 93°15'W |
| Chiari, Italy (kyä´rē) | 174 | 45°31'N | 9°57'E |
| Chiasso, Switz. | 168 | 45°50'N | 8°57'E |
| Chiatura, Geor. | 182 | 42°17'N | 43°17'E |
| Chiautla, Mex. (chyä-ōōt´lä) | 130 | 18°16'N | 98°37'W |
| Chiavari, Italy (kyä-vä´rē) | 174 | 44°18'N | 9°21'E |
| Chiba, Japan (chē´bá) | 205 | 35°37'N | 140°08'E |
| Chiba, dept., Japan | 211a | 35°47'N | 140°02'E |
| Chibougamau, Can. (chē-bōō´gä-mou) | 91 | 49°57'N | 74°23'W |
| Chibougamau, l., Can. | 99 | 49°53'N | 74°21'W |
| Chicago, Il., U.S. (shĭ-kô-gō) (chĭ-kä´gō) | 105 | 41°49'N | 87°37'W |
| Chicago Heights, Il., U.S. | 111a | 41°30'N | 87°38'W |
| Chicapa, r., Afr. (chē-kä´pä) | 232 | 7°45'S | 20°25'E |
| Chicbul, Mex. (chēk-bōō´l) | 131 | 18°45'N | 90°56'W |
| Chic-Chocs, Monts, mts., Can. | 93 | 48°38'N | 66°37'W |
| Chichagof, i., Ak., U.S. (chê-chä´gôf) | 103 | 57°50'N | 137°00'W |
| Chichancanab, Lago de, l., Mex. (lä´gô-dĕ-chē-chän-kä-nä´b) | 132a | 19°50'N | 88°28'W |
| Chichén Itzá, hist., Mex. | 132a | 20°40'N | 88°35'W |
| Chichester, Eng., U.K. (chĭch´ĕs-tĕr) | 164 | 50°50'N | 0°55'W |
| Chichimilá, Mex. (chē-chē-mê´lä) | 132a | 20°36'N | 88°14'W |
| Chichiriviche, Ven. (chē-chē-rē-vē-chĕ) | 143b | 10°56'N | 68°17'W |
| Chickamauga, Ga., U.S. (chĭk-á-mô´gá) | 124 | 34°50'N | 85°15'W |
| Chickamauga Lake, res., Tn., U.S. | 124 | 35°18'N | 85°22'W |
| Chickasawhay, r., Ms., U.S. (chĭk-á-sô´wā) | 124 | 31°45'N | 88°45'W |
| Chickasha, Ok., U.S. (chĭk´á-shā) | 104 | 35°04'N | 97°56'W |
| Chiclana de la Frontera, Spain (chê-klä´nä) | 172 | 36°25'N | 6°09'W |
| Chiclayo, Peru (chê-klä´yō) | 142 | 6°46'S | 79°50'W |
| Chico, Ca., U.S. (chē´kō) | 118 | 39°43'N | 121°51'W |
| Chico, Wa., U.S. | 116a | 47°37'N | 122°43'W |
| Chico, r., Arg. | 144 | 44°30'S | 66°00'W |
| Chico, r., Arg. | 144 | 49°15'S | 69°30'W |
| Chico, r., Phil. | 213a | 17°33'N | 121°24'E |
| Chicoloapan, Mex. (chê-kō-lwä´pän) | 131a | 19°24'N | 98°54'W |
| Chiconautla, Mex. | 131a | 19°39'N | 99°01'W |
| Chicontepec, Mex. (chê-kōn´tĕ-pĕk´) | 130 | 20°58'N | 98°08'W |
| Chicopee, Ma., U.S. (chĭk´ô-pē) | 109 | 42°10'N | 72°35'W |
| Chicoutimi, Can. (shē-kōō´tē-mē´) | 91 | 48°26'N | 71°04'W |
| Chicxulub, Mex. (chēk-sōō-lōō´b) | 132a | 21°10'N | 89°30'W |
| Chiefland, Fl., U.S. (chēf´lánd) | 125 | 29°30'N | 82°50'W |
| Chiemsee, l., Ger. (kēm zā) | 168 | 47°58'N | 12°20'E |
| Chieri, Italy (kyâ´rē) | 174 | 45°03'N | 7°48'E |
| Chieti, Italy (kyĕ´tē) | 162 | 42°22'N | 14°22'E |
| Chifeng, China (chr-fŭŋ) | 205 | 42°18'N | 118°52'E |
| Chignanuapan, Mex. (chē´g-nä-nwä-pá´n) | 130 | 19°49'N | 98°02'W |
| Chignecto Bay, b., Can. (shĭg-nĕk´tō) | 100 | 45°33'N | 64°50'W |
| Chignik, Ak., U.S. (chĭg´nĭk) | 103 | 56°14'N | 158°12'W |
| Chignik Bay, b., Ak., U.S. | 103 | 56°18'N | 157°22'W |
| Chigu Co, l., China (chr-gōō tswo) | 202 | 28°55'N | 91°47'E |
| Chigwell, Eng., U.K. | 158b | 51°38'N | 0°05'E |
| Chihe, China (chr-hŭ) | 206 | 32°32'N | 117°57'E |
| Chihuahua, Mex. (chê-wä´wä) | 128 | 28°37'N | 106°06'W |
| Chihuahua, state, Mex. | 128 | 29°00'N | 107°30'W |
| Chikishlyar, Turkmen. (chê-kêsh-lyär´) | 183 | 37°40'N | 53°50'E |
| Chilanga, Zam. | 237 | 15°34'S | 28°17'E |
| Chilapa, Mex. (chê-lä´pä) | 130 | 17°34'N | 99°14'W |
| Chilchota, Mex. (chêl-chō´tä) | 130 | 19°40'N | 102°04'W |
| Chilcotin, r., Can. (chĭl-kō´tĭn) | 94 | 52°20'N | 124°15'W |
| Childress, Tx., U.S. (chīld´rĕs) | 120 | 34°26'N | 100°11'W |
| Chile, nation, S.A. (chē´lā) | 144 | 35°00'S | 72°00'W |
| Chilecito, Arg. (chē-lā-sē´tō) | 144 | 29°06'S | 67°25'W |
| Chilengue, Serra do, mts., Ang. | 236 | 13°20'S | 15°00'E |
| Chilibre, Pan. (chē-lê´brĕ) | 128a | 9°09'N | 79°37'W |
| Chililabombwe, Zam. | 237 | 12°18'S | 27°43'E |
| Chilka, l., India | 202 | 19°26'N | 85°42'E |
| Chilko, r., Can. (chĭl´kō) | 94 | 51°53'N | 123°53'W |
| Chilko Lake, l., Can. | 94 | 51°20'N | 124°05'W |
| Chillán, Chile (chēl-yän´) | 144 | 36°44'S | 72°06'W |
| Chillicothe, Il., U.S. (chĭl-ĭ-kŏth´ê) | 108 | 41°55'N | 89°30'W |
| Chillicothe, Mo., U.S. | 121 | 39°46'N | 93°32'W |
| Chillicothe, Oh., U.S. | 108 | 39°20'N | 83°00'W |
| Chilliwack, Can. (chĭl´ĭ-wăk) | 90 | 49°10'N | 121°57'W |
| Chiloé, Isla de, i., Chile | 144 | 42°30'S | 73°55'W |
| Chilpancingo de los Bravo, Mex. | 128 | 17°32'N | 99°30'W |
| Chilton, Wi., U.S. (chĭl´tŭn) | 113 | 44°00'N | 88°12'W |
| Chilung, Tai. (chĭ´lung) | 205 | 25°02'N | 121°48'E |
| Chilwa, Lake, l., Afr. | 232 | 15°12'S | 36°30'E |
| Chimacum, Wa., U.S. (chĭm´ă-kŭm) | 116a | 48°01'N | 122°47'W |
| Chimalpa, Mex. (chē-mäl´pä) | 131a | 19°26'N | 99°22'W |
| Chimaltenango, Guat. (chê-mäl-tå-näŋ´gō) | 132 | 14°39'N | 90°48'W |
| Chimaltitan, Mex. (chêmäl-tē-tän´) | 130 | 21°36'N | 103°50'W |
| Chimbay, Uzb. (chĭm-bī´) | 183 | 43°00'N | 59°44'E |
| Chimborazo, mtn., Ec. (chêm-bô-rä´zō) | 142 | 1°35'S | 78°45'W |
| Chimbote, Peru (chêm-bō´tå) | 142 | 9°02'S | 78°33'W |
| China, Mex. (chē´nä) | 122 | 25°43'N | 99°13'W |
| China, nation, Asia (chī´ná) | 204 | 36°45'N | 93°00'E |
| Chinameca, El Sal. (Chē-nä-mä´kä) | 132 | 13°31'N | 88°18'W |
| Chinandega, Nic. (chē-nän-dä´gä) | 132 | 12°38'N | 87°08'W |
| Chinati Peak, mtn., Tx., U.S. (chĭ-nä´tē) | 122 | 29°56'N | 104°29'W |
| Chincha Alta, Peru (chĭn´chä äl´tä) | 142 | 13°24'S | 76°04'W |
| Chinchas, Islas, is., Peru (ē´s-läs-chē´n-chäs) | 142 | 11°27'S | 79°05'W |
| Chinchilla, Austl. (chĭn-chĭl´á) | 222 | 26°44'S | 150°36'E |
| Chinchorro, Banco, bk., Mex. (bä´n-kô-chēn-chô´r-rō) | 132a | 18°43'N | 87°25'W |
| Chincilla de Monte Aragon, Spain | 172 | 38°54'N | 1°43'W |
| Chinde, Moz. (shĕn´dĕ) | 232 | 17°39'S | 36°34'E |
| Chin Do, i., Kor., S. | 210 | 34°30'N | 125°43'E |
| Chindwin, r., Mya. (chĭn-dwĭn) | 199 | 23°30'N | 94°34'E |
| Chingola, Zam. (chĭng-gōlä) | 232 | 12°32'S | 27°52'E |
| Chinguar, Ang. (chĭng-gär) | 232 | 12°35'S | 16°15'E |
| Chinguetti, Maur. (chêŋ-gĕt´ê) | 230 | 20°34'N | 12°34'W |
| Chinhoyi, Zimb. | 232 | 17°22'S | 30°12'E |
| Chinju, Kor., S. (chĭn´jōō) | 210 | 35°13'N | 128°10'E |
| Chinko, r., C.A.R. (shĭn´kō) | 231 | 6°37'N | 24°31'E |
| Chinmen see Quemoy, Tai. | 209 | 24°30'N | 118°20'E |
| Chino, Ca., U.S. (chē´nō) | 117a | 34°01'N | 117°42'W |
| Chinon, Fr. (shē-nôN´) | 170 | 47°09'N | 0°13'E |
| Chinook, Mt., U.S. (shĭn-òk´) | 115 | 48°35'N | 109°15'W |
| Chinsali, Zam. | 237 | 10°34'S | 32°03'E |
| Chinteche, Mwi. (chĭn-tĕ´chĕ) | 232 | 11°48'S | 34°14'E |
| Chioggia, Italy (kyôd´jä) | 174 | 45°12'N | 12°17'E |
| Chíos, Grc. (kē´ôs) | 163 | 38°23'N | 26°09'E |
| Chíos, i., Grc. | 163 | 38°20'N | 25°45'E |
| Chipata, Zam. | 232 | 13°39'S | 32°40'E |
| Chipera, Moz. (zhê-pĕ´rä) | 232 | 15°16'S | 32°30'E |
| Chipley, Fl., U.S. (chĭp´lĭ) | 124 | 30°45'N | 85°33'W |
| Chipman, Can. (chĭp´mán) | 100 | 46°11'N | 65°53'W |
| Chipola, r., Fl., U.S. (chĭ-pō´lá) | 124 | 30°40'N | 85°14'W |
| Chippawa, Can. (chĭp´ê-wä) | 111c | 43°03'N | 79°03'W |
| Chippewa, r., Mn., U.S. (chĭp´ê-wä) | 112 | 45°07'N | 95°41'W |
| Chippewa, r., Wi., U.S. | 113 | 45°07'N | 91°19'W |
| Chippewa Falls, Wi., U.S. | 113 | 44°55'N | 91°26'W |
| Chippewa Lake, Oh., U.S. | 111d | 41°04'N | 81°54'W |


ng-sing; ŋ-baŋk; N-nasalized n; nŏd; cŏmmit; ōld; ôbey; ôrder; oi-boil; fōōd; ò-as oo in foot; ou-out; s-soft; sh-dish; th-thin; pūre; ûnite; ûrn; stŭd; circŭs; ü-as in French tu; ´-indeterminate vowel.

ăt; fin*a*l; rāte; senåte; ärm; åsk; sof*à*; fâre; ch-choose; dh-as th in other; bē; ĕvent; bĕt; recĕnt; cratẽr; g-gō; gh-guttural g; bĭt; ĭ-short neutral; rīde; к-guttural k as ch in German ich;

PRONOUNCING INDEX

Clearwater – Comacchio 283


| PLACE (Pronunciation) | PAGE | LAT. | LONG. |
|---|---|---|---|
| Clearwater, Middle Fork, r., Id., U.S. | 114 | 46°10'N | 115°48'W |
| Clearwater, North Fork, r., Id., U.S. | 114 | 46°34'N | 116°08'W |
| Clearwater, South Fork, r., Id., U.S. | 114 | 45°46'N | 115°53'W |
| Clearwater Mountains, mts., Id., U.S. | 114 | 45°56'N | 115°15'W |
| Cleburne, Tx., U.S. (klē'bŭrn) | 104 | 32°21'N | 97°23'W |
| Cle Elum, Wa., U.S. (klē ĕl'ŭm) | 114 | 47°12'N | 120°55'W |
| Clementon, N.J., U.S. (klē'mĕn-tŭn) | 110f | 39°49'N | 75°00'W |
| Cleobury Mortimer, Eng., U.K. (klēȯ-bĕr'ĭ môr'tĭ-mĕr) | 158a | 52°22'N | 2°29'W |
| Clermont, Austl. (klĕr'mŏnt) | 219 | 23°02'S | 147°46'E |
| Clermont, Can. | 99 | 47°45'N | 70°20'W |
| Clermont-Ferrand, Fr. (klĕr-môɴ'fĕr-răɴ') | 154 | 45°47'N | 3°03'E |
| Cleveland, Ms., U.S. (klēv'lănd) | 124 | 33°45'N | 90°42'W |
| Cleveland, Oh., U.S. | 105 | 41°30'N | 81°42'W |
| Cleveland, Ok., U.S. | 121 | 36°18'N | 96°28'W |
| Cleveland, Tn., U.S. | 124 | 35°09'N | 84°52'W |
| Cleveland, Tx., U.S. | 123 | 30°18'N | 95°05'W |
| Cleveland Heights, Oh., U.S. | 111d | 41°30'N | 81°35'W |
| Cleveland Peninsula, pen., Ak., U.S. | 94 | 55°45'N | 132°00'W |
| Cleves, Oh., U.S. (klē'vĕs) | 111f | 39°10'N | 84°45'W |
| Clew Bay, b., Ire. (kloo͞) | 164 | 53°47'N | 9°45'W |
| Clewiston, Fl., U.S. (klē'wis-tŭn) | 125a | 26°44'N | 80°55'W |
| Clichy, Fr. (klē-shē) | 170 | 48°54'N | 2°18'E |
| Clifden, Ire. (klĭf'dĕn) | 164 | 53°31'N | 10°04'W |
| Clifton, Az., U.S. (klĭf'tŭn) | 119 | 33°05'N | 109°20'W |
| Clifton, N.J., U.S. | 110a | 40°52'N | 74°09'W |
| Clifton, S.C., U.S. | 125 | 35°00'N | 81°47'W |
| Clifton, Tx., U.S. | 123 | 31°45'N | 97°31'W |
| Clifton Forge, Va., U.S. | 109 | 37°50'N | 79°50'W |
| Clinch, r., Tn., U.S. (klĭnch) | 124 | 36°30'N | 83°19'W |
| Clingmans Dome, mtn., U.S. (klĭng'măns dōm) | 124 | 35°37'N | 83°26'W |
| Clinton, Can. (klĭn-'tŭn) | 90 | 51°05'N | 121°35'W |
| Clinton, Ia., U.S. | 113 | 41°50'N | 90°13'W |
| Clinton, Il., U.S. | 108 | 40°10'N | 88°55'W |
| Clinton, In., U.S. | 108 | 39°40'N | 87°25'W |
| Clinton, Ky., U.S. | 124 | 36°39'N | 88°56'W |
| Clinton, Ma., U.S. | 101a | 42°25'N | 71°41'W |
| Clinton, Md., U.S. | 110e | 38°46'N | 76°54'W |
| Clinton, Mo., U.S. | 121 | 38°23'N | 93°46'W |
| Clinton, N.C., U.S. | 125 | 34°58'N | 78°20'W |
| Clinton, Ok., U.S. | 120 | 35°31'N | 98°56'W |
| Clinton, S.C., U.S. | 125 | 34°27'N | 81°53'W |
| Clinton, Tn., U.S. | 124 | 36°05'N | 84°08'W |
| Clinton, Wa., U.S. | 116a | 47°59'N | 122°22'W |
| Clinton, r., Mi., U.S. | 111b | 42°36'N | 83°00'W |
| Clinton-Colden, l., Can. | 92 | 63°58'N | 106°34'W |
| Clintonville, Wi., U.S. (klĭn'tŭn-vĭl) | 113 | 44°37'N | 88°46'W |
| Clio, Mi., U.S. (klē'ō) | 108 | 43°10'N | 83°45'W |
| Cloates, Point, c., Austl. (klōts) | 220 | 22°47'S | 113°45'E |
| Clocolan, S. Afr. | 238c | 28°56'S | 27°35'E |
| Clonakilty Bay, b., Ire. (klŏn-ȧ-kĭltē) | 164 | 51°30'N | 8°50'W |
| Cloncurry, Austl. (klŏn-kŭr'ė) | 218 | 20°58'S | 140°42'E |
| Clonmel, Ire. (klŏn-mĕl) | 164 | 52°21'N | 7°45'W |
| Cloquet, Mn., U.S. (klȯ-kā') | 117h | 46°42'N | 92°28'W |
| Closter, N.J., U.S. (klōs'tĕr) | 110a | 40°58'N | 73°57'W |
| Cloud Peak, mtn., Wy., U.S. (kloud) | 106 | 44°23'N | 107°11'W |
| Clover, S.C., U.S. (klō'vẽr) | 125 | 35°08'N | 81°08'W |
| Clover Bar, Can. (klō'vẽr bär) | 102g | 53°34'N | 113°20'W |
| Cloverdale, Can. | 116d | 49°06'N | 122°44'W |
| Cloverdale, Ca., U.S. (klō'vẽr-dāl) | 118 | 38°47'N | 123°03'W |
| Cloverport, Ky., U.S. (klō'vẽr pōrt) | 108 | 37°50'N | 86°35'W |
| Clovis, N.M., U.S. (klō'vĭs) | 104 | 34°24'N | 103°11'W |
| Cluj-Napoca, Rom. | 154 | 46°46'N | 23°34'E |
| Clun, r., Eng., U.K. (klŭn) | 158a | 52°25'N | 2°56'W |
| Cluny, Fr. (klü-nē') | 170 | 46°27'N | 4°40'E |
| Clutha, r., N.Z. (kloo͞'thȧ) | 221a | 45°52'S | 169°30'E |
| Clwyd, hist. reg., Wales, U.K. | 158a | 53°01'N | 2°59'W |
| Clyde, Ks., U.S. | 121 | 39°34'N | 97°23'W |
| Clyde, Oh., U.S. | 108 | 41°15'N | 83°00'W |
| Clyde, r., Scot., U.K. | 164 | 55°35'N | 3°50'W |
| Clyde, Firth of, b., Scot., U.K. (fûrth ŏv klīd) | 164 | 55°28'N | 5°01'W |
| Côa, r., Port. (kô'ä) | 172 | 40°28'N | 6°55'W |
| Coacalco, Mex. (kō-ä-käl'kō) | 131a | 19°37'N | 99°06'W |
| Coachella, Canal, can., Ca., U.S. (kō'chĕl-lȧ) | 118 | 33°15'N | 115°25'W |
| Coahuayana, Río de, r., Mex. (rė'ō-dĕ-kô-ä-wä-yȧ'nä) | 130 | 19°00'N | 103°33'W |
| Coahuayutla, Mex. (kō'ä-wī-yoo͞t'lȧ) | 130 | 18°19'N | 101°44'W |
| Coahuila, state, Mex. (kō-ä-wē'lȧ) | 128 | 27°30'N | 103°00'W |
| Coal City, Il., U.S. (kōl sĭ'tĭ) | 111a | 41°17'N | 88°17'W |
| Coalcomán, Río de, r., Mex. (rė'ō-dĕ-kō-äl-kō-män') | 130 | 18°45'N | 103°15'W |
| Coalcomán, Sierra de, mts., Mex. | 130 | 18°30'N | 102°45'W |
| Coalcomán de Matamoros, Mex. | 130 | 18°46'N | 103°10'W |
| Coaldale, Can. (kōl'dāl) | 95 | 49°43'N | 112°37'W |
| Coalgate, Ok., U.S. (kōl'gāt) | 121 | 34°44'N | 96°13'W |
| Coal Grove, Oh., U.S. (kōl grōv) | 108 | 38°20'N | 82°40'W |
| Coalinga, Ca., U.S. (kō-ȧ-lĭŋ'gȧ) | 118 | 36°09'N | 120°23'W |
| Coalville, Eng., U.K. (kōl'vĭl) | 158a | 52°43'N | 1°21'W |
| Coamo, P.R. (kō-ä'mō) | 129b | 18°05'N | 66°21'W |
| Coari, Braz. (kō-är'ė) | 142 | 4°06'S | 63°10'W |
| Coast Mountains, mts., N.A. (kōst) | 92 | 54°10'N | 128°00'W |
| Coast Ranges, mts., U.S. | 106 | 41°28'N | 123°30'W |
| Coatepec, Mex. (kō-ä-tā-pĕk) | 130 | 19°23'N | 98°44'W |
| Coatepec, Mex. | 131a | 19°08'N | 99°25'W |
| Coatepec, Mex. | 131 | 19°26'N | 96°56'W |
| Coatepeque, El Sal. | 132 | 13°56'N | 89°30'W |
| Coatepeque, Guat. (kō-ä-tå-pā'kå) | 132 | 14°40'N | 91°52'W |
| Coatesville, Pa., U.S. (kōts'vĭl) | 109 | 40°00'N | 75°50'W |
| Coatetelco, Mex. (kō-ä-tå-tĕl'kō) | 130 | 18°43'N | 99°17'W |
| Coaticook, Can. (kō'tĭ-kŏŏk) | 99 | 45°10'N | 71°55'W |
| Coatlinchán, Mex. (kô-ä-tlē'n-chä'n) | 131a | 19°26'N | 98°52'W |
| Coats, i., Can. (kōts) | 93 | 62°23'N | 82°11'W |
| Coats Land, reg., Ant. | 224 | 74°00'S | 30°00'W |
| Coatzacoalcos, Mex. | 128 | 18°09'N | 94°26'W |
| Coatzacoalcos, r., Mex. | 131 | 17°40'N | 94°41'W |
| Coba, hist., Mex. (kô'bä) | 132a | 20°23'N | 87°23'W |
| Cobalt, Can. (kō'bôlt) | 91 | 47°21'N | 79°40'W |
| Cobán, Guat. (kō-bän') | 128 | 15°28'N | 90°19'W |
| Cobar, Austl. | 219 | 31°28'S | 145°50'E |
| Cobberas, Mount, mtn., Austl. (cŏ-bĕr-ăs) | 222 | 36°45'S | 148°15'E |
| Cobequid Mountains, mts., Can. | 100 | 45°35'N | 64°10'W |
| Cobh, Ire. (kȯv) | 154 | 51°52'N | 8°09'W |
| Cobija, Bol. (kô-bē'hä) | 142 | 11°12'S | 68°49'W |
| Cobourg, Can. (kō'bŏŏrgh) | 91 | 43°55'N | 78°05'W |
| Cobre, r., Jam. (kō'brā) | 134 | 18°05'N | 77°00'W |
| Coburg, Austl. | 217a | 37°45'S | 144°58'E |
| Coburg, Ger. (kō'boo͞rg) | 168 | 50°16'N | 10°57'E |
| Cocentaina, Spain (kō-thån-tä-ē'nȧ) | 173 | 38°44'N | 0°27'W |
| Cochabamba, Bol. | 142 | 17°24'S | 66°09'W |
| Cochinos, Bahía, b., Cuba (bä-ē'ä-kȯ-chė'nōs) | 134 | 22°05'N | 81°10'W |
| Cochinos Banks, bk. | 134 | 22°20'N | 76°15'W |
| Cochiti Indian Reservation, I.R., N.M., U.S. | 119 | 35°37'N | 106°20'W |
| Cochran, Ga., U.S. (kŏk'răn) | 124 | 32°23'N | 83°23'W |
| Cochrane, Can. (kŏk'răn) | 91 | 49°01'N | 81°06'W |
| Cochrane, Can. | 102e | 51°11'N | 114°28'W |
| Cockburn, i., Can. (kŏk-bûrn) | 98 | 45°55'N | 83°25'W |
| Cockeysville, Md., U.S. (kŏk'ĭz-vĭl) | 110e | 39°30'N | 76°40'W |
| Cockrell Hill, Tx., U.S. (kŏk'rĕl) | 117c | 32°44'N | 96°53'W |
| Coco, r., N.A. | 129 | 14°55'N | 83°45'W |
| Coco, Cayo, i., Cuba (kä'-yō-kȯ'kȯ) | 134 | 22°30'S | 78°30'W |
| Coco, Isla del, i., C.R. (ė's-lä-dĕl-kȯ-kȯ) | 128 | 5°33'N | 87°02'W |
| Cocoa, Fl., U.S. (kō'kō) | 125a | 28°21'N | 80°44'W |
| Cocoa Beach, Fl., U.S. | 125a | 28°20'N | 80°35'W |
| Cocoli, Pan. (kŏ-kô'lē) | 128a | 8°58'N | 79°36'W |
| Coconino, Plateau, plat., Az., U.S. (kō kō nė'nō) | 119 | 35°45'N | 112°28'W |
| Cocos (Keeling) Islands, is., Oc. (kō'kōs) (kē'ling) | 3 | 11°50'S | 90°50'E |
| Coco Solito, Pan. (kô-kô-sŏ-lē'tŏ) | 128a | 9°21'N | 79°53'W |
| Cocula, Mex. (kō-koo͞'lä) | 130 | 20°23'N | 103°47'W |
| Cocula, r., Mex. | 130 | 18°17'N | 99°45'W |
| Cod, Cape, pen., Ma., U.S. | 107 | 41°42'N | 70°15'W |
| Codajás, Braz. (kō-dä-häzh') | 142 | 3°44'S | 62°09'W |
| Codera, Cabo, c., Ven. (kȧ'bȯ-kō-dĕ'rä) | 143b | 10°35'N | 66°06'W |
| Codogno, Italy (kȯ-dō'nyō) | 174 | 45°08'N | 9°43'E |
| Codrington, Antig. (kŏd'rĭng-tŭn) | 133b | 17°39'N | 61°49'W |
| Cody, Wy., U.S. (kō'dĭ) | 115 | 44°31'N | 109°02'W |
| Coelho da Rocha, Braz. | 144b | 22°47'S | 43°23'W |
| Coemba, Ang. | 236 | 12°08'S | 18°05'E |
| Coesfeld, Ger. (kûs'fĕld) | 171c | 51°56'N | 7°10'E |
| Coeur d'Alene, Id., U.S. (kûr dȧ-lān') | 104 | 47°43'N | 116°35'W |
| Coeur d'Alene, r., Id., U.S. | 114 | 47°26'N | 116°35'W |
| Coeur d'Alene Indian Reservation, I.R., Id., U.S. | 114 | 47°18'N | 116°45'W |
| Coeur d'Alene Lake, l., Id., U.S. | 114 | 47°32'N | 116°39'W |
| Coffeyville, Ks., U.S. (kŏf'ĭ-vĭl) | 105 | 37°01'N | 95°38'W |
| Coff's Harbour, Austl. | 222 | 30°20'S | 153°10'E |
| Cofimvaba, S. Afr. (căfĭm'vä-bȧ) | 233c | 32°01'S | 27°37'E |
| Coghinas, r., Italy (kō'gē-nȧs) | 174 | 40°31'N | 9°00'E |
| Cognac, Fr. (kȯn-yak') | 161 | 45°41'N | 0°22'W |
| Cohasset, Ma., U.S. (kȯ-hăs'ĕt) | 101a | 42°14'N | 70°48'W |
| Cohoes, N.Y., U.S. (kô-hōz') | 109 | 42°50'N | 73°40'W |
| Coig, r., Arg. (kȯ'ėk) | 144 | 51°15'N | 71°00'W |
| Coimbatore, India (kȯ-ēm-bȧ-tȯr') | 199 | 11°03'N | 76°56'E |
| Coimbra, Port. (kȯ-ēm'brä) | 154 | 40°14'N | 8°23'W |
| Coín, Spain (kȯ-ēn') | 172 | 36°40'N | 4°45'W |
| Coina, Port. (kȯ-ē'nȧ) | 173b | 38°35'N | 9°03'W |
| Coina, r., Port. (kȯ'y-nä) | 173b | 38°35'N | 9°02'W |
| Coipasa, Salar de, pl., Bol. (sä-lä'r-dĕ-koi-pä'-sä) | 142 | 19°12'S | 69°13'W |
| Coixtlahuaca, Mex. (kō-ēks'tlä-wä'kä) | 131 | 17°42'N | 97°17'W |
| Cojedes, dept., Ven. (kȯ-kĕ'dĕs) | 143b | 9°50'N | 68°21'W |
| Cojimar, Cuba (kō-hė-mär') | 135a | 23°10'N | 82°19'W |
| Cojutepeque, El Sal. (kȯ-hȯ-tĕ-pā'kȧ) | 132 | 13°45'N | 88°50'W |
| Cokato, Mn., U.S. (kȯ-kā'tō) | 113 | 45°03'N | 94°11'W |
| Cokeburg, Pa., U.S. (kōk bŭgh) | 111e | 40°06'N | 80°03'W |
| Colac, Austl. (kŏ'lȧc) | 222 | 38°25'S | 143°40'E |
| Colares, Port. (kȯ-lä'rĕs) | 173b | 38°47'N | 9°27'W |
| Colatina, Braz. (kô-lä-tė'nä) | 143 | 19°33'S | 40°42'W |
| Colby, Ks., U.S. (kōl'bĭ) | 120 | 39°23'N | 101°04'W |
| Colchagua, prov., Chile (kȯl-chȧ'gwä) | 141b | 34°42'S | 71°24'W |
| Colchester, Eng., U.K. (kōl'chĕs-tēr) | 165 | 51°52'N | 0°50'E |
| Cold Lake, l., Can. (kōld) | 96 | 54°33'N | 110°05'W |
| Coldwater, Ks., U.S. (kōld'wô-tēr) | 120 | 37°14'N | 99°21'W |
| Coldwater, Mi., U.S. | 108 | 41°55'N | 85°00'W |
| Coldwater, r., Ms., U.S. | 124 | 34°25'N | 90°12'W |
| Coldwater Creek, r., Tx., U.S. | 120 | 36°10'N | 101°45'W |
| Coleman, Tx., U.S. (kōl'mȧn) | 122 | 31°50'N | 99°25'W |
| Colenso, S. Afr. (kŏ-lĕnz'ȯ) | 233c | 28°48'S | 29°49'E |
| Coleraine, N. Ire., U.K. | 164 | 55°08'N | 6°40'W |
| Coleraine, Mn., U.S. (kōl-rān') | 113 | 47°16'N | 93°29'W |
| Coleshill, Eng., U.K. (kōlz'hĭl) | 158a | 52°30'N | 1°42'W |
| Colfax, Ia., U.S. (kōl'făks) | 113 | 41°40'N | 93°13'W |
| Colfax, La., U.S. | 123 | 31°31'N | 92°42'W |
| Colfax, Wa., U.S. | 114 | 46°53'N | 117°21'W |
| Colhué Huapi, l., Arg. (kȯl-wā'ȯȧ'pė) | 144 | 45°30'S | 68°45'W |
| Coligny, S. Afr. | 238c | 26°20'S | 26°18'E |
| Colima, Mex. (kōlē'mä) | 128 | 19°13'N | 103°45'W |
| Colima, state, Mex. | 130 | 19°10'N | 104°00'W |
| Colima, Nevado de, mtn., Mex. (nĕ-vä'dȯ-dĕ-kȯ-lē'mä) | 128 | 19°30'N | 103°38'W |
| Coll, i., Scot., U.K. (kōl) | 164 | 56°42'N | 6°23'W |
| College, Ak., U.S. | 103 | 64°43'N | 147°50'W |
| College Park, Ga., U.S. (kŏl'ĕj) | 110c | 33°39'N | 84°27'W |
| College Park, Md., U.S. | 110e | 38°59'N | 76°58'W |
| Collegeville, Pa., U.S. (kŏl'ĕj-vĭl) | 110f | 40°11'N | 75°27'W |
| Collie, Austl. (kŏl'ė) | 218 | 33°20'S | 116°20'E |
| Collier Bay, b., Austl. (kŏl-yēr) | 220 | 15°30'S | 123°30'E |
| Collingswood, N.J., U.S. (kŏl'ĭngz-wŏŏd) | 110f | 39°54'N | 75°04'W |
| Collingwood, Can. | 99 | 44°30'N | 80°20'W |
| Collins, Ms., U.S. (kŏl'ĭns) | 124 | 31°40'N | 89°34'W |
| Collinsville, Il., U.S. (kŏl'ĭnz-vĭl) | 117e | 38°41'N | 89°59'W |
| Collinsville, Ok., U.S. | 121 | 36°21'N | 95°50'W |
| Colmar, Fr. (kȯl'mär) | 161 | 48°03'N | 7°25'E |
| Colmenar de Oreja, Spain (kȯl-mā-när'dāōrā'hä) | 172 | 40°06'N | 3°25'W |
| Colmenar Viejo, Spain (kȯl-mā-när'vyā'hō) | 172 | 40°40'N | 3°46'W |
| Cologne, Ger. | 154 | 50°56'N | 6°57'E |
| Colombia, Col. (kȯ-lȯm'bė-ä) | 142a | 3°23'N | 74°48'W |
| Colombia, nation, S.A. | 142 | 3°30'N | 72°30'W |
| Colombo, Sri L. (kȯ-lȯm'bō) | 203 | 6°58'N | 79°52'E |
| Colón, Arg. (kō-lōn') | 141c | 33°55'S | 61°08'W |
| Colón, Cuba (kȯ-lȯ'n) | 134 | 22°45'N | 80°55'W |
| Colón, Mex. (kō-lōn') | 130 | 20°46'N | 100°02'W |
| Colón, Pan. (kŏ-lô'n) | 129 | 9°22'N | 79°54'W |
| Colón, Archipiélago de, is., Ec. | 142 | 0°10'S | 87°45'W |
| Colón, Montañas de, mts., Hond. (môn-tä'n-yäs-dĕ-kŏ-lô'n) | 133 | 14°58'N | 84°39'W |
| Colonia, Ur. (kō-lō'nė-ä) | 144 | 34°27'S | 57°50'W |
| Colonia, dept., Ur. | 141c | 34°08'S | 57°50'W |
| Colonia Suiza, Ur. (kȯ-lô'nėä-sȯē'zä) | 141c | 34°17'S | 57°15'W |
| Colonna, Capo, c., Italy | 175 | 39°02'N | 17°15'E |
| Colonsay, i., Scot., U.K. (kŏl-ŏn-sā') | 165 | 56°08'N | 6°08'E |
| Coloradas, Lomas, Arg. (lȯ'mäs-kō-lō-rä'däs) | 144 | 43°30'S | 68°00'W |
| Colorado, state, U.S. | 104 | 39°30'N | 106°55'W |
| Colorado, r., Arg. | 144 | 38°30'S | 66°00'W |
| Colorado, r., N.A. | 106 | 36°00'N | 113°30'W |
| Colorado, r., Tx., U.S. | 106 | 30°08'N | 97°33'W |
| Colorado City, Tx., U.S. (kŏl-ȯ-rä'dō sĭ'tĭ) | 122 | 32°24'N | 100°50'W |
| Colorado National Monument, rec., Co., U.S. | 119 | 39°00'N | 108°40'W |
| Colorado Plateau, plat., U.S. | 106 | 36°20'N | 109°25'W |
| Colorado River Aqueduct, aq., Ca., U.S. | 118 | 33°38'N | 115°43'W |
| Colorado River Indian Reservation, I.R., Az., U.S. | 119 | 34°03'N | 114°02'W |
| Colorados, Archipiélago de los, is., Cuba | 134 | 22°25'N | 84°25'W |
| Colorado Springs, Co., U.S. (kŏl-ȯ-rä'dō) | 104 | 38°49'N | 104°48'W |
| Colotepec, r., Mex. (kô-lȯ'tĕ-pĕk) | 131 | 15°56'N | 96°57'W |
| Colotlán, Mex. (kȯ-lȯ-tlän') | 130 | 22°06'N | 103°14'W |
| Colotlán, r., Mex. | 130 | 22°09'N | 103°17'W |
| Colquechaca, Bol. (kȯl-kā-chä'kä) | 142 | 18°47'S | 66°02'W |
| Colstrip, Mt., U.S. (kōl'strip) | 115 | 45°54'N | 106°38'W |
| Colton, Ca., U.S. (kōl'tŭn) | 117a | 34°04'N | 117°20'W |
| Columbia, Il., U.S. (kȯ-lŭm'bĭ-ȧ) | 117e | 38°26'N | 90°12'W |
| Columbia, Ky., U.S. | 124 | 37°06'N | 85°15'W |
| Columbia, Md., U.S. | 110e | 39°15'N | 76°51'W |
| Columbia, Mo., U.S. | 105 | 38°55'N | 92°19'W |
| Columbia, Ms., U.S. | 124 | 31°15'N | 89°49'W |
| Columbia, Pa., U.S. | 109 | 40°00'N | 76°25'W |
| Columbia, S.C., U.S. | 105 | 34°00'N | 81°00'W |
| Columbia, Tn., U.S. | 124 | 35°36'N | 87°02'W |
| Columbia, r., N.A. | 92 | 46°00'N | 120°00'W |
| Columbia, Mount, mtn., Can. | 95 | 52°09'N | 117°25'W |
| Columbia City, In., U.S. | 108 | 41°10'N | 85°30'W |
| Columbia City, Or., U.S. | 116c | 45°53'N | 112°49'W |
| Columbia Heights, Mn., U.S. | 117g | 45°03'N | 93°15'W |
| Columbia Icefield, ice, Can. | 95 | 52°08'N | 117°26'W |
| Columbia Mountains, mts., N.A. | 95 | 51°30'N | 118°30'W |
| Columbiana, Al., U.S. (kô-ŭm-bĭ-ă'nȧ) | 124 | 33°10'N | 86°35'W |
| Columbretes, is., Spain (kȯ-loo͞m-brĕ'tĕs) | 173 | 39°54'N | 0°54'E |
| Columbus, Ga., U.S. (kȯ-lŭm'bŭs) | 105 | 32°29'N | 84°56'W |
| Columbus, In., U.S. | 108 | 39°15'N | 85°55'W |
| Columbus, Ks., U.S. | 121 | 37°10'N | 94°50'W |
| Columbus, Ms., U.S. | 124 | 33°30'N | 88°25'W |
| Columbus, Mt., U.S. | 115 | 45°39'N | 109°15'W |
| Columbus, Ne., U.S. | 112 | 41°25'N | 97°25'W |
| Columbus, N.M., U.S. | 119 | 31°50'N | 107°40'W |
| Columbus, Oh., U.S. | 105 | 40°00'N | 83°00'W |
| Columbus, Tx., U.S. | 123 | 29°44'N | 96°34'W |
| Columbus, Wi., U.S. | 113 | 43°20'N | 89°01'W |
| Columbus Bank, bk. (kȯ-lŭm'büs) | 135 | 22°05'N | 75°30'W |
| Columbus Grove, Oh., U.S. | 108 | 40°55'N | 84°05'W |
| Columbus Point, c., Bah. | 135 | 24°10'N | 75°15'W |
| Colusa, Ca., U.S. (kȯ-lū'sȧ) | 118 | 39°12'N | 122°01'W |
| Colville, Wa., U.S. (kŏl'vĭl) | 114 | 48°33'N | 117°53'W |
| Colville, r., Ak., U.S. | 103 | 69°00'N | 156°25'W |
| Colville Indian Reservation, I.R., Wa., U.S. | 114 | 48°15'N | 119°00'W |
| Colville R, Wa., U.S. | 114 | 48°25'N | 117°58'W |
| Colvos Passage, strt., Wa., U.S. (kōl'vōs) | 116a | 47°24'N | 122°32'W |
| Colwood, Can. (kŏl'wŏŏd) | 116a | 48°26'N | 123°30'W |
| Comacchio, Italy (kȯ-mäk'kyō) | 174 | 44°42'N | 12°12'E |


ng-sing; ŋ-baŋk; ɴ-nasalized n; nŏd; cŏmmit; ōld; ȯbey; ôrder; oi-boil; fo͞od; ȯ-as oo in foot; ou-out; s-soft; sh-dish; th-thin; pūre; ůnite; ûrn; stŭd; circŭs; ü-as in French tu; '-indeterminate vowel.

284 Comala – Cosamaloápan
PRONOUNCING INDEX


| PLACE (Pronunciation) | PAGE | LAT. | LONG. |
|---|---|---|---|
| Comala, Mex. (kō-mä-lä′) | 130 | 19°22′N | 103°47′W |
| Comalapa, Guat. (kō-mä-lä′-pä) | 132 | 14°43′N | 90°56′W |
| Comalcalco, Mex. (kō-mäl-käl′kō) | 131 | 18°16′N | 93°13′W |
| Comanche, Ok., U.S. (kō-măn′chē) | 121 | 34°20′N | 97°58′W |
| Comanche, Tx., U.S. | 122 | 31°54′N | 98°37′W |
| Comanche Creek, r., Tx., U.S. | 122 | 31°02′N | 102°47′W |
| Comayagua, Hond. (kō-mä-yä′gwä) | 128 | 14°24′N | 87°36′W |
| Combahee, r., S.C., U.S. (kŏm-bȧ-hē′) | 125 | 32°42′N | 80°40′W |
| Comer, Ga., U.S. (kŭm′ẽr) | 124 | 34°02′N | 83°07′W |
| Comete, Cape, c., T./C. Is. (kō-mā′tā) | 135 | 21°45′N | 71°25′W |
| Comilla, Bngl. (kō-mĭl′ä) | 199 | 23°33′N | 91°17′E |
| Comino, Cape, c., Italy (kô-mē′nō) | 174 | 40°30′N | 9°48′E |
| Comitán, Mex. (kô-mē-tän′) | 128 | 16°16′N | 92°09′W |
| Commencement Bay, b., Wa., U.S. (kŏ-mĕns′mĕnt bā) | 116a | 47°17′N | 122°21′W |
| Commentry, Fr. (kô-mäɴ-trē′) | 170 | 46°16′N | 2°44′E |
| Commerce, Ga., U.S. (kŏm′ẽrs) | 124 | 34°10′N | 83°27′W |
| Commerce, Ok., U.S. | 121 | 36°57′N | 94°54′W |
| Commerce, Tx., U.S. | 121 | 33°15′N | 95°52′W |
| Como, Italy (kō′mō) | 162 | 45°48′N | 9°03′E |
| Como, Lago di, l., Italy (lä′gō-dē-kō′mō) | 162 | 46°00′N | 9°30′E |
| Comodoro Rivadavia, Arg. | 144 | 45°47′S | 67°31′W |
| Como-Est, Can. | 102a | 45°27′N | 74°08′W |
| Comonfort, Mex. (kô-mōn-fô′rt) | 130 | 20°43′N | 100°47′W |
| Comorin, Cape, c., India (kŏ′mô-rĭn) | 203 | 8°05′N | 78°05′E |
| Comoros, nation, Afr. | 233 | 12°30′S | 42°45′E |
| Comox, Can. (kō′mŏks) | 94 | 49°40′N | 124°55′W |
| Companario, Cerro, mtn., S.A. (sĕ′r-rô-kôm-pä-nä′ryō) | 141b | 35°54′S | 70°23′W |
| Compiègne, Fr. (kôɴ-pyĕn′y′) | 161 | 49°25′N | 2°49′E |
| Comporta, Port. (kôm-pôr′tȧ) | 173b | 38°24′N | 8°48′W |
| Compostela, Mex. (kōm-pô-stā′lä) | 130 | 21°14′N | 104°54′W |
| Compton, Ca., U.S. (kŏmpt′tŭn) | 117a | 33°54′N | 118°14′W |
| Comrat, Mol. (kôm-rät′) | 181 | 46°17′N | 28°38′E |
| Conakry, Gui. (kô-nȧ-krē′) | 230 | 9°31′N | 13°43′W |
| Conanicut, i., R.I., U.S. (kŏn′ȧ-nĭ-kŭt) | 110b | 41°34′N | 71°20′W |
| Conasauga, r., Ga., U.S. (kō-nȧ) | 124 | 34°40′N | 84°51′W |
| Concarneau, Fr. (kôɴ-kär-nō′) | 170 | 47°54′N | 3°52′W |
| Concepción, Bol. (kôn-sĕp′syōn′) | 143 | 15°47′S | 61°08′W |
| Concepción, Chile | 144 | 36°51′S | 72°59′W |
| Concepción, Pan. | 133 | 8°31′N | 82°38′W |
| Concepción, Para. | 144 | 23°29′S | 57°18′W |
| Concepcion, Phil. | 213a | 15°19′N | 120°40′E |
| Concepción, vol., Nic. | 132 | 11°36′N | 85°43′W |
| Concepción, r., Mex. | 128 | 30°25′N | 112°20′W |
| Concepción del Mar, Guat. (kôn-sĕp-syōn′dĕl mär′) | 132 | 14°07′N | 91°23′W |
| Concepción del Oro, Mex. (kôn-sĕp-syōn′ dĕl ō′rō) | 128 | 24°39′N | 101°24′W |
| Concepción del Uruguay, Arg. (kôn-sĕp-syō′n-dĕl-ōō-rōō-gwī′) | 144 | 32°31′S | 58°10′W |
| Conception, i., Bah. | 135 | 23°50′N | 75°05′W |
| Conception, Point, c., Ca., U.S. | 106 | 34°27′N | 120°28′W |
| Conception Bay, b., Can. (kŏn-sĕp′shŭn) | 101 | 47°50′N | 52°50′W |
| Concho, r., Tx., U.S. (kŏn′chō) | 122 | 31°34′N | 100°00′W |
| Conchos, r., Mex. | 128 | 29°30′N | 105°00′W |
| Conchos, r., Mex. (kōn′chōs) | 122 | 25°03′N | 99°00′W |
| Concord, Ca., U.S. (kŏŋ′kẽrd) | 116b | 37°58′N | 122°02′W |
| Concord, Ma., U.S. | 101a | 42°28′N | 71°21′W |
| Concord, N.C., U.S. | 125 | 35°23′N | 80°11′W |
| Concord, N.H., U.S. | 105 | 43°10′N | 71°30′W |
| Concordia, Arg. (kŏn-kôr′dĭ-ȧ) | 144 | 31°18′S | 57°59′W |
| Concordia, Col. | 142a | 6°04′N | 75°54′W |
| Concordia, Mex. (kôn-kô′r-dyä) | 130 | 23°17′N | 106°06′W |
| Concordia, Ks., U.S. | 121 | 39°32′N | 97°39′W |
| Concrete, Wa., U.S. (kŏn-′krēt) | 114 | 48°33′N | 121°44′W |
| Conde, Fr. | 170 | 48°50′N | 0°36′W |
| Conde, S.D., U.S. (kŏn-dē′) | 112 | 45°10′N | 98°06′W |
| Condega, Nic. (kŏn-dĕ′gä) | 132 | 13°20′N | 86°27′W |
| Condeúba, Braz. (kōn-dā-ōō′bä) | 143 | 14°47′S | 41°44′W |
| Condom, Fr. | 170 | 43°58′N | 0°22′E |
| Condon, Or., U.S. (kŏn′dŭn) | 114 | 45°14′N | 120°10′W |
| Conecun, r., Al., U.S. (kô-nē′kŭ) | 124 | 31°05′N | 86°52′W |
| Conegliano, Italy (kō-nāl-yä′nō) | 174 | 45°59′N | 12°17′E |
| Conejos, r., Co., U.S. (kô-nā′hōs) | 119 | 37°07′N | 106°19′W |
| Conemaugh, Pa., U.S. (kŏn′ē-mô) | 109 | 40°25′N | 78°50′W |
| Coney Island, i., N.Y., U.S. (kō′nĭ) | 110a | 40°34′N | 73°27′W |
| Confolens, Fr. (kôɴ-fā-läɴ′) | 170 | 46°01′N | 0°41′E |
| Congaree, r., S.C., U.S. (kŏŋ-gȧ-rē′) | 125 | 33°53′N | 80°55′W |
| Conghua, China (tsôŋ-hwä) | 209 | 23°30′N | 113°40′E |
| Congleton, Eng., U.K. (kŏŋ′g′l-tŭn) | 158a | 53°10′N | 2°13′W |
| Congo, nation, Afr. (kŏn′gō) | 232 | 3°00′S | 13°48′E |
| Congo (Zaire), r., Afr. (kŏn′gō) | 229 | 2°00′S | 17°00′E |
| Congo, Democratic Republic of the (Zaire), nation, Afr. | 232 | 1°00′S | 22°15′E |
| Congo, Serra do, mts., Ang. | 236 | 6°25′S | 13°30′E |
| Congo Basin, basin, D.R.C. | 229 | 2°47′N | 20°58′E |
| Conisbrough, Eng., U.K. (kŏn′ĭs-bŭr-ô) | 158a | 53°29′N | 1°13′W |
| Coniston, Can. | 99 | 46°29′N | 80°51′W |
| Conklin, Can. (kŏŋk′lĭn) | 95 | 55°38′N | 111°05′W |
| Conley, Ga., U.S. (kŏn′lĭ) | 110c | 33°38′N | 84°19′W |
| Conn, Lough, l., Ire. (lŏk kŏn) | 164 | 53°56′N | 9°25′W |
| Connacht, hist. reg., Ire. (cŏn′ăt) | 164 | 53°50′N | 8°45′W |
| Conneaut, Oh., U.S. (kŏn-ê-ôt′) | 108 | 41°55′N | 80°35′W |
| Connecticut, state, U.S. (kŏ-nĕt′ĭ-kŭt) | 105 | 41°40′N | 73°10′W |
| Connecticut, r., U.S. | 107 | 43°55′N | 72°15′W |
| Connellsville, Pa., U.S. (kŏn′nĕlz-vĭl) | 109 | 40°00′N | 79°40′W |
| Connemara, mts., Ire. (kŏn-nē-mȧ′rȧ) | 164 | 53°30′N | 9°54′W |
| Connersville, In., U.S. (kŏn′ẽrz-vĭl) | 108 | 39°35′N | 85°10′W |
| Connors Range, mts., Austl. (kŏn′nŏrs) | 221 | 22°15′S | 149°00′E |
| Conrad, Mt., U.S. (kŏn′răd) | 115 | 48°11′N | 111°56′W |
| Conrich, Can. (kŏn′rĭch) | 102e | 51°06′N | 113°51′W |
| Conroe, Tx., U.S. (kŏn′rō) | 123 | 30°18′N | 95°23′W |
| Conselheiro Lafaiete, Braz. | 143 | 20°40′S | 43°46′W |
| Conshohocken, Pa., U.S. (kŏn-shō-hŏk′ĕn) | 110f | 40°04′N | 75°18′W |
| Consolación del Sur, Cuba (kōn-sô-lä-syōn′) | 134 | 22°30′N | 83°55′W |
| Con Son, is., Viet. | 212 | 8°30′N | 106°28′E |
| Constance, Mount, mtn., Wa., U.S. (kŏn′stăns) | 116a | 47°46′N | 123°08′W |
| Constanţa, Rom. (kōn-stȧn′tsȧ) | 154 | 44°12′N | 28°36′E |
| Constantina, Spain (kŏn-stän-tē′nä) | 172 | 37°52′N | 5°39′W |
| Constantine, Alg. (kôɴ-stäɴ′tēn′) | 230 | 36°28′N | 6°38′E |
| Constantine, Mi., U.S. (kŏn′stăn-tēn) | 108 | 41°50′N | 85°40′W |
| Constitución, Chile (kōn′stĭ-tōō-syōn′) | 144 | 35°24′S | 72°25′W |
| Constitution, Ga., U.S. (kŏn-stĭ-tū′shŭn) | 110c | 33°41′N | 84°20′W |
| Contagem, Braz. (kōn-tá′zhĕm) | 141a | 19°54′S | 44°05′W |
| Contepec, Mex. (kōn-tĕ-pĕk′) | 130 | 20°04′N | 100°07′W |
| Contreras, Mex. (kôn-trĕ′räs) | 131a | 19°18′N | 99°14′W |
| Contwoyto, l., Can. | 92 | 65°42′N | 110°50′W |
| Converse, Tx., U.S. (kŏn′vẽrs) | 117d | 29°31′N | 98°17′W |
| Conway, Ar., U.S. (kŏn′wā) | 121 | 35°06′N | 92°27′W |
| Conway, N.H., U.S. | 109 | 44°00′N | 71°10′W |
| Conway, S.C., U.S. | 125 | 33°49′N | 79°01′W |
| Conway, Wa., U.S. | 116a | 48°20′N | 122°20′W |
| Conyers, Ga., U.S. (kŏn′yẽrz) | 124 | 33°41′N | 84°01′W |
| Cooch Behār, India (kōōch bē-här′) | 199 | 26°25′N | 89°34′E |
| Cook, Cape, c., Can. (kŏŏk) | 94 | 50°08′N | 127°55′W |
| Cook, Mount *see* Aoraki, mtn., N.Z. | 221a | 43°27′S | 170°13′E |
| Cookeville, Tn., U.S. (kŏŏk′vĭl) | 124 | 36°07′N | 85°30′W |
| Cooking Lake, Can. (kŏŏk′ĭng) | 102g | 53°25′N | 113°08′W |
| Cooking Lake, l., Can. | 102g | 53°25′N | 113°02′W |
| Cook Inlet, b., Ak., U.S. | 103 | 60°50′N | 151°38′W |
| Cook Islands, dep., Oc. | 2 | 20°00′S | 158°00′W |
| Cook Strait, strt., N.Z. | 221a | 40°37′S | 174°15′E |
| Cooktown, Austl. (kŏŏk′toun) | 219 | 15°40′S | 145°20′E |
| Cooleemee, N.C., U.S. (kōō-lē′mē) | 125 | 35°50′N | 80°32′W |
| Coolgardie, Austl. (kōōl-gär′dē) | 218 | 31°00′S | 121°25′E |
| Cooma, Austl. (kōō′mȧ) | 219 | 36°22′S | 149°10′E |
| Coonamble, Austl. (kōō-năm′b′l) | 219 | 31°00′S | 148°30′E |
| Coonoor, India | 203 | 10°22′N | 76°15′E |
| Coon Rapids, Mn., U.S. (kōōn) | 117g | 45°09′N | 93°17′W |
| Cooper, Tx., U.S. (kōōp′ẽr) | 121 | 33°23′N | 95°40′W |
| Cooper Center, Ak., U.S. | 103 | 61°54′N | 15°30′W |
| Coopers Creek, r., Austl. (kōō′pẽrz) | 221 | 27°32′N | 141°19′E |
| Cooperstown, N.D., U.S. | 112 | 47°26′N | 98°07′W |
| Cooperstown, N.Y., U.S. (kōōp′ẽrs-toun) | 109 | 42°45′N | 74°55′W |
| Coosa, Al., U.S. (kōō′sȧ) | 124 | 32°43′N | 86°25′W |
| Coosa, r., U.S. | 107 | 34°00′N | 86°00′W |
| Coosawattee, r., Ga., U.S. | 124 | 34°37′N | 84°45′W |
| Coos Bay, Or., U.S. (kōōs) | 114 | 43°21′N | 124°12′W |
| Coos Bay, b., Or., U.S. | 114 | 43°19′N | 124°40′W |
| Cootamundra, Austl. (kŏŏtȧ-mŭnd′rȧ) | 222 | 34°25′S | 148°00′E |
| Copacabana, Braz. (kō′pä-kȧ-bá′nä) | 144b | 22°57′S | 43°11′W |
| Copalita, r., Mex. (kō-pä-lē′tä) | 131 | 15°55′N | 96°06′W |
| Copán, hist., Hond. (kō-pän′) | 132 | 14°50′N | 89°10′W |
| Copano Bay, b., Tx., U.S. (kō-pän′ō) | 123 | 28°08′N | 97°25′W |
| Copenhagen (København), Den. | 154 | 55°43′N | 12°27′E |
| Copiapó, Chile (kō-pyä-pō′) | 144 | 27°16′S | 70°28′W |
| Copley, Oh., U.S. (kŏp′lē) | 111d | 41°06′N | 81°38′W |
| Copparo, Italy (kôp-pä′rō) | 174 | 44°53′N | 11°50′E |
| Coppell, Tx., U.S. (kŏp′pĕl) | 117c | 32°57′N | 97°00′W |
| Copper, r., Ak., U.S. (kŏp′ẽr) | 103 | 62°38′N | 145°00′W |
| Copper Cliff, Can. | 98 | 46°28′N | 81°04′W |
| Copper Harbor, Mi., U.S. | 113 | 47°27′N | 87°53′W |
| Copperhill, Tn., U.S. (kŏp′ẽr hĭl) | 124 | 35°00′N | 84°22′W |
| Coppermine *see* Kugluktuk, Can. | 92 | 67°46′N | 115°19′W |
| Coppermine, r., Can. | 92 | 66°48′N | 114°59′W |
| Copper Mountain, mtn., Ak., U.S. | 94 | 55°14′N | 132°36′W |
| Copperton, Ut., U.S. (kŏp′ẽr-tŭn) | 117b | 40°34′N | 112°06′W |
| Coquilee, Or., U.S. (kô-kēl′) | 114 | 43°11′N | 124°11′W |
| Coquilhatville *see* Mbandaka, D.R.C. | 232 | 0°04′N | 18°16′E |
| Coquimbo, Chile (kô-kēm′bō) | 144 | 29°58′S | 71°31′W |
| Coquimbo, prov., Chile | 141b | 31°50′S | 71°05′W |
| Coquitlam Lake, l., Can. (kō-kwĭt-lȧm) | 116d | 49°23′N | 122°44′W |
| Corabia, Rom. (kô-rä′bĭ-ȧ) | 163 | 43°45′N | 24°29′E |
| Coracora, Peru (kō′rä-kō′rä) | 142 | 15°12′S | 73°42′W |
| Coral Gables, Fl., U.S. | 125a | 25°43′N | 80°14′W |
| Coral Rapids, Can. (kŏr′ăl) | 91 | 50°18′N | 81°49′W |
| Coral Sea, sea, Oc. (kŏr′ăl) | 221 | 13°30′S | 150°00′E |
| Coralville Reservoir, res., Ia., U.S. | 113 | 41°45′N | 91°50′W |
| Corangamite, Lake, l., Austl. (cŏr-ăŋg′ȧ-mīt) | 222 | 38°05′S | 142°55′E |
| Coraopolis, Pa., U.S. (kō-rä-ŏp′ō-lĭs) | 111e | 40°30′N | 80°09′W |
| Corato, Italy (kō′rä-tō) | 174 | 41°08′N | 16°28′E |
| Corbeil-Essonnes, Fr. (kôr-bâ′yĕ-sŏn′) | 170 | 48°31′N | 2°29′E |
| Corbett, Or., U.S. (kôr′bĕt) | 116c | 45°31′N | 122°17′W |
| Corbie, Fr. (kôr-bē′) | 170 | 49°55′N | 2°27′E |
| Corbin, Ky., U.S. (kôr′bĭn) | 124 | 36°55′N | 84°06′W |
| Corby, Eng., U.K. (kôr′bĭ) | 158a | 52°29′N | 0°38′W |
| Corcovado, mtn., Braz. (kôr-kô-vä′dō) | 144b | 22°57′S | 43°13′W |
| Corcovado, Golfo, b., Chile (kôr-kô-vä′dhō) | 144 | 43°40′S | 75°00′W |
| Cordeiro, Braz. (kôr-dā′rō) | 141a | 22°03′S | 42°22′W |
| Cordele, Ga., U.S. (kôr-dēl′) | 124 | 31°55′N | 83°50′W |
| Cordell, Ok., U.S. (kôr-dĕl′) | 120 | 35°19′N | 98°58′W |
| Córdoba, Arg. (kôr′dô-vä) | 144 | 30°20′S | 64°03′W |
| Córdoba, Mex. (kô′r-dô-bä) | 128 | 18°53′N | 96°54′W |
| Córdoba, Spain (kô′r-dô-bä) | 172 | 37°55′N | 4°45′W |
| Córdoba, prov., Arg. (kôr′dô-vä) | 144 | 32°00′S | 64°00′W |
| Córdoba, Sierra de, mts., Arg. | 144 | 31°15′S | 64°30′W |
| Cordova, Ak., U.S. (kôr′dō-vä) | 106a | 60°34′N | 145°38′W |
| Cordova, Al., U.S. (kôr′dō-vȧ) | 124 | 33°45′N | 86°22′W |
| Cordova Bay, b., Ak., U.S. | 94 | 54°55′N | 132°35′W |
| Corfu *see* Kérkira, i., Grc. | 156 | 39°33′N | 19°36′E |
| Corigliano, Italy (kō-rē-lyä′nō) | 174 | 39°35′N | 16°30′E |
| Corinth *see* Kórinthos, Grc. | 154 | 37°56′N | 22°54′E |
| Corinth, Ms., U.S. (kŏr′ĭnth) | 124 | 34°55′N | 88°30′W |
| Corinto, Braz. (kô-rē′n-tō) | 143 | 18°20′S | 44°16′W |
| Corinto, Col. | 142a | 3°09′N | 76°12′W |
| Corinto, Nic. (kŏr-ĭn′tō) | 132 | 12°30′N | 87°12′W |
| Corio, Austl. | 217a | 38°05′S | 144°22′E |
| Corio Bay, b., Austl. | 217a | 38°07′S | 144°25′E |
| Corisco, Isla de, i., Eq. Gui. | 236 | 0°50′N | 8°40′E |
| Cork, Ire. (kôrk) | 154 | 51°54′N | 8°25′W |
| Cork Harbour, b., Ire. | 164 | 51°44′N | 8°15′W |
| Corleone, Italy (kôr-lå-ō′nā) | 174 | 37°48′N | 13°18′E |
| Cormorant Lake, l., Can. | 97 | 54°13′N | 100°47′W |
| Cornelia, Ga., U.S. (kôr-nē′lyȧ) | 124 | 34°31′N | 83°30′W |
| Cornelis, r., S. Afr. (kôr-nē′lĭs) | 238c | 27°48′S | 29°15′E |
| Cornell, Ca., U.S. (kôr-nĕl′) | 117a | 34°06′N | 118°46′W |
| Cornell, Wi., U.S. | 113 | 45°10′N | 91°10′W |
| Corner Brook, Can. (kôr′nẽr) | 91 | 48°57′N | 57°57′W |
| Corner Inlet, b., Austl. | 222 | 38°55′S | 146°45′E |
| Corning, Ar., U.S. (kôr′nĭng) | 121 | 36°26′N | 90°35′W |
| Corning, Ia., U.S. | 113 | 40°58′N | 94°40′W |
| Corning, N.Y., U.S. | 109 | 42°10′N | 77°05′W |
| Corno, Monte, mtn., Italy (kôr′nō) | 162 | 42°28′N | 13°37′E |
| Cornwall, Bah. | 134 | 25°55′N | 77°15′W |
| Cornwall, Can. (kôrn′wôl) | 99 | 45°05′N | 74°35′W |
| Coro, Ven. (kō′rō) | 142 | 11°22′N | 69°43′W |
| Corocoro, Bol. (kō-rō-kō′rō) | 142 | 17°15′S | 68°21′W |
| Coromandel Coast, cst., India (kŏr-ō-man′dĕl) | 199 | 13°30′N | 80°30′E |
| Coromandel Peninsula, pen., N.Z. | 223 | 36°50′S | 176°00′E |
| Corona, Al., U.S. (kō-rō′nȧ) | 124 | 33°42′N | 87°28′W |
| Corona, Ca., U.S. | 117a | 33°52′N | 117°34′W |
| Coronada, Bahía de, b., C.R. (bä-ē′ä-dĕ-kô-rō-nä′dō) | 133 | 8°47′N | 84°04′W |
| Corona del Mar, Ca., U.S. (kô-rō′nȧ dĕl măr) | 117a | 33°36′N | 117°53′W |
| Coronado, Ca., U.S. (kŏr-ō-nä′dō) | 118a | 32°42′N | 117°12′W |
| Coronation Gulf, b., Can. (kŏr-ō-nā′shŭn) | 92 | 68°07′N | 112°50′W |
| Coronel, Chile (kō-rō-nĕl′) | 144 | 37°00′S | 73°10′W |
| Coronel Brandsen, Arg. (kŏ-rō-nĕl-brá′nd-sĕn) | 141c | 35°09′S | 58°15′W |
| Coronel Dorrego, Arg. (kŏ-rō-nĕl-dôr-rĕ′gô) | 144 | 38°43′S | 61°16′W |
| Coronel Oviedo, Para. (kŏ-rō-nĕl-ô-vĕē′dō) | 144 | 25°28′S | 56°22′W |
| Coronel Pringles, Arg. (kŏ-rō-nĕl-prēn′glĕs) | 144 | 37°54′S | 61°22′W |
| Coronel Suárez, Arg. (kŏ-rō-nĕl-swä′rās) | 144 | 37°27′S | 61°49′W |
| Corowa, Austl. (cŏr-ôwȧ) | 222 | 36°02′S | 146°23′E |
| Corozal, Belize (cŏr-ŏth-ăl′) | 132a | 18°25′N | 88°23′W |
| Corpus Christi, Tx., U.S. (kôr′pŭs krĭstē) | 104 | 27°48′N | 97°24′W |
| Corpus Christi Bay, b., Tx., U.S. | 123 | 27°47′N | 97°14′W |
| Corpus Christi Lake, l., Tx., U.S. | 122 | 28°08′N | 98°20′W |
| Corral, Chile (kô-räl′) | 144 | 39°57′S | 73°15′W |
| Corral de Almaguer, Spain (kô-räl′dā äl-mä-gâr′) | 172 | 39°45′N | 3°10′W |
| Corralillo, Cuba (kô-rä-lē-yō) | 134 | 23°00′N | 80°40′W |
| Corregidor Island, i., Phil. (kō-rā-hē-dōr′) | 213a | 14°21′N | 120°25′E |
| Correntina, Braz. (kô-rĕn-tē-nȧ) | 143 | 13°18′S | 44°33′W |
| Corrib, Lough, l., Ire. (lŏk kŏr′ĭb) | 164 | 53°25′N | 9°19′W |
| Corrientes, Arg. (kō-ryĕn′täs) | 144 | 27°25′S | 58°39′W |
| Corrientes, prov., Arg. | 144 | 28°45′S | 58°00′W |
| Corrientes, Cabo, c., Col. (kȧ′bô-kō-ryĕn′tās) | 142 | 5°34′N | 77°35′W |
| Corrientes, Cabo, c., Cuba (kȧ′bô-kôr-rē-ĕn′tĕs) | 134 | 21°50′N | 84°25′W |
| Corrientes, Cabo, c., Mex. | 128 | 20°25′N | 105°41′W |
| Corry, Pa., U.S. (kŏr′ĭ) | 109 | 41°55′N | 79°40′W |
| Corse, Cap, c., Fr. (kôrs) | 161 | 42°59′N | 9°19′E |
| Corsica, i., Fr. (kô′r-sē-kä) | 156 | 42°10′N | 8°55′E |
| Corsicana, Tx., U.S. (kôr-sĭ-kăn′ȧ) | 104 | 32°06′N | 96°28′W |
| Cortazar, Mex. (kôr-tä-zär) | 130 | 20°30′N | 100°57′W |
| Corte, Fr. (kôr′tā) | 174 | 42°18′N | 9°10′E |
| Cortegana, Spain (kôr-tå-gä′nä) | 172 | 37°54′N | 6°48′W |
| Cortés, Ensendada de, b., Cuba (ĕn-sĕ-nä-dä-dĕ-kôr-tās′) | 134 | 22°05′N | 83°45′W |
| Cortez, Co., U.S. | 119 | 37°21′N | 108°35′W |
| Cortland, N.Y., U.S. (kôrt′lănd) | 109 | 42°35′N | 76°10′W |
| Cortona, Italy (kôr-tō′nä) | 174 | 43°16′N | 12°00′E |
| Corubal, r., Gui.-B. | 234 | 11°43′N | 14°40′W |
| Coruche, Port. (kô-rōō′she) | 172 | 38°58′N | 8°34′W |
| Çoruh, r., Asia (chō-rōōk′) | 181 | 40°30′N | 41°10′E |
| Çorum, Tur. (chô-rōōm′) | 198 | 40°34′N | 34°45′E |
| Corunna, Mi., U.S. (kô-rŭn′ȧ) | 108 | 43°00′N | 84°05′W |
| Coruripe, Braz. (kô-rô-rē′pĭ) | 143 | 10°09′S | 36°13′W |
| Corvallis, Or., U.S. (kŏr-văl′ĭs) | 104 | 44°34′N | 123°17′W |
| Corve, r., Eng., U.K. (kôr′vê) | 158a | 52°28′N | 2°43′W |
| Corydon, Ia., U.S. | 113 | 40°45′N | 93°20′W |
| Corydon, In., U.S. (kŏr′ĭ-dŭn) | 108 | 38°10′N | 86°05′W |
| Corydon, Ky., U.S. | 108 | 37°45′N | 87°40′W |
| Cosamaloápan, Mex. (kô-sä-mä-lwä′pän) | 131 | 18°21′N | 95°48′W |


ăt; finăl; rāte; senâte; ärm; ȧsk; sofȧ; fâre; ch-choose; dh-as th in other; bē; ēvent; bĕt; recĕnt; cratẽr; g-gō; gh-guttural g; bĭt; ĭ-short neutral; rīde; ĸ-guttural k as ch in German ich;

PRONOUNCING INDEX

Coscomatepec – Cuilo 285


| PLACE (Pronunciation) | PAGE | LAT. | LONG. |
|---|---|---|---|
| Coscomatepec, Mex. (kôs′kōmä-tě-pěk′) | 131 | 19°04′N | 97°03′W |
| Cosenza, Italy (kō-zěnt′sä) | 163 | 39°18′N | 16°15′E |
| Coshocton, Oh., U.S. (kō-shŏk′tŭn) | 108 | 40°15′N | 81°55′W |
| Cosigüina, vol., Nic. | 132 | 12°59′N | 87°35′W |
| Cosmoledo Group, is., Sey. (kŏs-mô-lā′dō) | 233 | 9°42′S | 47°45′E |
| Cosmopolis, Wa., U.S. (kŏz-mŏp′ô-lĭs) | 114 | 46°58′N | 123°47′W |
| Cosne-sur-Loire, Fr. (kōn-sür-lwär′) | 170 | 47°25′N | 2°57′E |
| Cosoleacaque, Mex. (kō sō lā-ä-kä′kē) | 131 | 18°01′N | 94°38′W |
| Costa de Caparica, Port. | 173b | 38°40′N | 9°12′W |
| Costa Mesa, Ca., U.S. (kŏs′tá mā′sá) | 117a | 33°39′N | 118°54′W |
| Costa Rica, nation, N.A. (kŏs′tá rē′ká) | 129 | 10°30′N | 84°30′W |
| Cosumnes, r., Ca., U.S. (kō-sŭm′nĕz) | 118 | 38°21′N | 121°17′W |
| Cotabambas, Peru (kô-tä-bám′bäs) | 142 | 13°49′S | 72°17′W |
| Cotabato, Phil. (kō-tä-bä′tō) | 213 | 7°06′N | 124°13′E |
| Cotaxtla, Mex. (kō-täs′tlä) | 131 | 18°49′N | 96°22′W |
| Cotaxtla, r., Mex. | 131 | 18°54′N | 96°21′W |
| Coteau-du-Lac, Can. (cō-tō′dü-läk) | 102a | 45°17′N | 74°11′W |
| Coteau-Landing, Can. | 102a | 45°15′N | 74°13′W |
| Coteaux, Haiti | 135 | 18°15′N | 74°05′W |
| Cote d'Ivoire (Ivory Coast), nation, Afr. | 230 | 7°43′N | 6°30′W |
| Côte d'Or, reg., Fr. | 170 | 47°02′N | 4°35′E |
| Cotija de la Paz, Mex. (kō-tē′-kä-dě-lä-pá′z) | 130 | 19°46′N | 102°43′W |
| Cotonou, Benin (kō-tō-nōō′) | 230 | 6°21′N | 2°26′E |
| Cotopaxi, mtn., Ec. (kō-tō-päk′sē) | 142 | 0°40′S | 78°26′W |
| Cotorro, Cuba (kō-tōr-rō) | 135a | 23°03′N | 82°17′W |
| Cotswold Hills, hills, Eng., U.K. (kŭtz′wōld) | 164 | 51°35′N | 2°16′W |
| Cottage Grove, Mn., U.S. (kŏt′ǎj grōv) | 117g | 44°50′N | 92°52′W |
| Cottage Grove, Or., U.S. | 114 | 43°48′N | 123°04′W |
| Cottbus, Ger. (kōtt′bōōs) | 161 | 51°47′N | 14°20′E |
| Cottonwood, r., Mn., U.S. (kŏt′ŭn-wŏŏd) | 112 | 44°25′N | 95°35′W |
| Cotulla, Tx., U.S. (kō-tŭl′lá) | 122 | 28°26′N | 99°14′W |
| Coubert, Fr. (kōō-bâr′) | 171b | 48°40′N | 2°43′E |
| Coudersport, Pa., U.S. (kou′dẽrz-port) | 109 | 41°45′N | 78°00′W |
| Coudres, Île aux, i., Can. | 100 | 47°17′N | 70°12′W |
| Coulommiers, Fr. (kōō-lô-myā′) | 171b | 48°49′N | 3°05′E |
| Coulto, Serra do, mts., Braz. (sĕ′r-rä-dô-kô-ô′tô) | 144b | 22°33′S | 43°27′W |
| Council Bluffs, Ia., U.S. (koun′sĭl blŭf) | 105 | 41°16′N | 95°53′W |
| Council Grove, Ks., U.S. (koun′sĭl grōv) | 121 | 38°39′N | 96°30′W |
| Coupeville, Wa., U.S. (kōōp′vĭl) | 116a | 48°13′N | 122°41′W |
| Courantyne, r., S.A. (kôr′ǎntīn) | 143 | 4°28′N | 57°42′W |
| Courtenay, Can. (cōōrt-nā′) | 90 | 49°41′N | 125°00′W |
| Coushatta, La., U.S. (kou-shăt′á) | 123 | 32°02′N | 93°21′W |
| Coutras, Fr. (kōō-trá′) | 170 | 45°02′N | 0°07′W |
| Covelo, Ang. | 236 | 12°06′S | 13°55′E |
| Coventry, Eng., U.K. (kŭv′ĕn-trĭ) | 164 | 52°25′N | 1°29′W |
| Covina, Ca., U.S. (kô-vē′ná) | 117a | 34°06′N | 117°54′W |
| Covington, Ga., U.S. (kŭv′ĭng-tŭn) | 124 | 33°36′N | 83°50′W |
| Covington, In., U.S. | 108 | 40°10′N | 87°15′W |
| Covington, Ky., U.S. | 105 | 39°05′N | 84°31′W |
| Covington, La., U.S. | 123 | 30°30′N | 90°06′W |
| Covington, Oh., U.S. | 108 | 40°10′N | 84°20′W |
| Covington, Ok., U.S. | 121 | 36°18′N | 97°32′W |
| Covington, Tn., U.S. | 124 | 35°33′N | 89°40′W |
| Covington, Va., U.S. | 108 | 37°50′N | 80°00′W |
| Cowal, Lake, l., Austl. (kou′ǎl) | 222 | 33°30′S | 147°10′E |
| Cowan, l., Austl. (kou′ǎn) | 220 | 32°00′S | 122°30′E |
| Cowansville, Can. | 99 | 45°13′N | 72°47′W |
| Cow Creek, r., Or., U.S. (kou) | 114 | 42°45′N | 123°35′W |
| Cowes, Eng., U.K. (kouz) | 164 | 50°43′N | 1°25′W |
| Cowichan Lake, l., Can. | 94 | 48°54′N | 124°20′W |
| Cowlitz, r., Wa., U.S. (kou′lĭts) | 114 | 46°30′N | 122°45′W |
| Cowra, Austl. (kou′rá) | 222 | 33°50′S | 148°33′E |
| Coxim, Braz. (kō-shēN′) | 143 | 18°32′S | 54°43′W |
| Coxquihui, Mex. (kōz-kē-wē′) | 131 | 20°10′N | 97°34′W |
| Cox's Bāzār, Bngl. | 202 | 21°32′N | 92°00′E |
| Coyaima, Col. (kō-yäē′mä) | 142a | 3°48′N | 75°11′W |
| Coyame, Mex. (kō-yä′mā) | 122 | 29°26′N | 105°05′W |
| Coyanosa Draw, Tx., U.S. (kō yá-nō′sä) | 122 | 30°55′N | 103°07′W |
| Coyoacán, Mex. (kô-yô-á-kän′) | 130 | 19°21′N | 99°10′W |
| Coyote, r., Ca., U.S. (kī′ōt) | 116b | 37°37′N | 121°57′W |
| Coyuca de Benítez, Mex. (kō-yōō′kä dā bā-nē′tāz) | 130 | 17°04′N | 100°06′W |
| Coyuca de Catalán, Mex. (kō-yōō′kä dā kä-tä-län′) | 130 | 18°19′N | 100°41′W |
| Coyutla, Mex. (kō-yōō′tlä) | 131 | 20°13′N | 97°40′W |
| Cozad, Ne., U.S. (kō′zăd) | 120 | 40°53′N | 99°59′W |
| Cozaddale, Oh., U.S. (kō-zăd-dāl) | 111f | 39°16′N | 84°09′W |
| Cozoyoapan, Mex. (kô-zō-yô-ä-pá′n) | 130 | 16°45′N | 98°17′W |
| Cozumel, Mex. (kŏ-zōō-mĕ′l) | 132a | 20°31′N | 86°55′W |
| Cozumel, Isla de, i., Mex. (ē′s-lä-dě-kŏ-zōō-mĕ′l) | 128 | 20°26′N | 87°10′W |
| Crab Creek, r., Wa., U.S. (krăb) | 114 | 46°47′N | 119°43′W |
| Crab Creek, r., Wa., U.S. | 114 | 47°21′N | 119°09′W |
| Cradock, S. Afr. (kră′dŭk) | 232 | 32°12′S | 25°38′E |
| Crafton, Pa., U.S. (krăf′tŭn) | 111e | 40°26′N | 80°04′W |
| Craig, Co., U.S. (krāg) | 115 | 40°32′N | 107°31′W |
| Craiova, Rom. (krá-yō′vá) | 163 | 44°18′N | 23°50′E |
| Cranberry, l., N.Y., U.S. (krăn′bĕr-ĭ) | 109 | 44°10′N | 74°50′W |
| Cranbourne, Austl. | 217a | 38°07′S | 145°16′E |
| Cranbrook, Can. (krăn′brŏŏk) | 90 | 49°31′N | 115°46′W |
| Cranbury, N.J., U.S. (krăn′bĕ-rĭ) | 110a | 40°19′N | 74°31′W |
| Crandon, Wi., U.S. (krăn′dŭn) | 113 | 45°35′N | 88°55′W |
| Crane Prairie Reservoir, res., Or., U.S. | 114 | 43°50′N | 121°55′W |
| Cranston, R.I., U.S. (krăns′tŭn) | 110b | 41°46′N | 71°25′W |
| Crater Lake, l., Or., U.S. (krā′tẽr) | 114 | 43°00′N | 122°08′W |
| Crater Lake National Park, rec., Or., U.S. | 114 | 42°58′N | 122°40′W |
| Craters of the Moon National Monument, rec., Id., U.S. (krā′tẽr) | 115 | 43°28′N | 113°15′W |
| Crateús, Braz. (krä-tå-ōōzh′) | 143 | 5°09′S | 40°35′W |
| Crato, Braz. (krä′tŏŏ) | 143 | 7°19′S | 39°13′W |
| Crawford, Ne., U.S. (krô′fẽrd) | 112 | 42°41′N | 103°25′W |
| Crawford, Wa., U.S. | 116c | 45°49′N | 122°24′W |
| Crawfordsville, In., U.S. (krô′fẽrdz-vĭl) | 108 | 40°00′N | 86°55′W |
| Crazy Mountains, mts., Mt., U.S. (krā′zĭ) | 115 | 46°11′N | 110°25′W |
| Crazy Woman Creek, r., Wy., U.S. | 115 | 44°08′N | 106°40′W |
| Crecy, S. Afr. (krĕ-sē) | 238c | 24°38′S | 28°52′E |
| Crécy-en-Brie, Fr. (krā-sē′-ĕN-brē′) | 171b | 48°52′N | 2°55′E |
| Crécy-en-Ponthieu, Fr. | 170 | 50°13′N | 1°48′E |
| Credit, r., Can. | 102d | 43°41′N | 79°55′W |
| Cree, l., Can. (krē) | 92 | 57°35′N | 107°52′W |
| Creighton, S. Afr. (cre-tŏn) | 233c | 30°02′S | 29°52′E |
| Creighton, Ne., U.S. (krā′tŭn) | 112 | 42°27′N | 97°54′W |
| Creil, Fr. (krĕ′y′) | 170 | 49°18′N | 2°28′E |
| Crema, Italy (krā′mä) | 174 | 45°21′N | 9°53′E |
| Cremona, Italy (krā-mō′nä) | 162 | 45°09′N | 10°02′E |
| Crépy-en-Valois, Fr. (krā-pē′ĕN-vä-lwä′) | 171b | 49°14′N | 2°53′E |
| Cres, Cro. (tsrĕs) | 174 | 44°58′N | 14°21′E |
| Crescent Beach, Can. | 116d | 49°03′N | 122°58′W |
| Crescent City, Ca., U.S. (krĕs′ĕnt) | 114 | 41°46′N | 124°13′W |
| Crescent City, Fl., U.S. | 125 | 29°26′N | 81°35′W |
| Crescent Lake, l., Fl., U.S. (krĕs′ĕnt) | 125 | 29°33′N | 81°30′W |
| Crescent Lake, l., Or., U.S. | 114 | 43°25′N | 121°58′W |
| Cresco, Ia., U.S. (krĕs′kō) | 113 | 43°23′N | 92°07′W |
| Crested Butte, Co., U.S. (krĕst′ĕd būt) | 119 | 38°50′N | 107°00′W |
| Crestline, Ca., U.S. (krĕst-līn) | 117a | 34°15′N | 117°17′W |
| Crestline, Oh., U.S. | 108 | 40°50′N | 82°40′W |
| Crestmore, Ca., U.S. (krĕst′môr) | 117a | 34°02′N | 117°23′W |
| Creston, Can. (krĕs′tŭn) | 90 | 49°06′N | 116°31′W |
| Creston, Ia., U.S. | 113 | 41°04′N | 94°22′W |
| Creston, Oh., U.S. | 111d | 40°59′N | 81°54′W |
| Crestview, Fl., U.S. (krĕst′vū) | 124 | 30°44′N | 86°35′W |
| Crestwood, Ky., U.S. (krĕst′wŏŏd) | 111h | 38°20′N | 85°28′W |
| Crestwood, Mo., U.S. | 117e | 38°33′N | 90°23′W |
| Crete, Il., U.S. (krēt) | 111a | 41°26′N | 87°38′W |
| Crete, Ne., U.S. | 121 | 40°38′N | 96°56′W |
| Crete, i., Grc. | 156 | 35°15′N | 24°30′E |
| Creus, Cap de, c., Spain | 173 | 42°16′N | 3°18′E |
| Creuse, r., Fr. (krûz) | 170 | 46°51′N | 0°49′E |
| Creve Coeur, Mo., U.S. (krēv kôr) | 117e | 38°40′N | 90°27′W |
| Crevillent, Spain | 173 | 38°12′N | 0°48′W |
| Crewe, Eng., U.K. (krōō) | 164 | 53°06′N | 2°27′W |
| Crewe, Va., U.S. | 125 | 37°09′N | 78°08′W |
| Crimean Peninsula *see* Kryms′kyi Pivostriv, pen., Ukr. | 181 | 45°18′N | 33°30′E |
| Crimmitschau, Ger. (krĭm′ĭt-shou) | 168 | 50°49′N | 12°22′E |
| Cripple Creek, Co., U.S. (krĭp′′l) | 120 | 38°44′N | 105°12′W |
| Crisfield, Md., U.S. (krĭs-fēld) | 109 | 38°00′N | 75°50′W |
| Cristal, Monts de, mts., Gabon | 236 | 0°50′N | 10°30′E |
| Cristina, Braz. (krēs-tē′-nä) | 141a | 22°13′S | 45°15′W |
| Cristóbal Colón, Pico, mtn., Col. (pē′kô-krēs-tô′bäl-kō-lôn′) | 142 | 11°00′N | 74°00′W |
| Crişul Alb, r., Rom. (krē′shōōl älb) | 169 | 46°20′N | 22°15′E |
| Crna, r., Serb. (ts′r′nà) | 175 | 41°03′N | 21°46′E |
| Crna Gora (Montenegro), state, Serb. | 175 | 42°55′N | 18°52′E |
| Črnomelj, Slvn. (ch′r′nō-māl′) | 174 | 45°35′N | 15°11′E |
| Croatia, nation, Eur. | 174 | 45°24′N | 15°18′E |
| Crockett, Ca., U.S. (krŏk′ĕt) | 116b | 38°03′N | 122°14′W |
| Crockett, Tx., U.S. | 123 | 31°19′N | 95°28′W |
| Crofton, Md., U.S. | 110e | 39°01′N | 76°43′W |
| Crofton, Ne., U.S. | 112 | 42°44′N | 97°32′W |
| Croix, Lac la, l., N.A. (läk lä krōō-ä′) | 113 | 48°19′N | 91°53′W |
| Croker, i., Austl. (krō′ká) | 220 | 10°45′S | 132°25′E |
| Cronulla, Austl. (krō-nŭl′á) | 217b | 34°03′S | 151°09′E |
| Crooked, i., Bah. | 135 | 22°45′N | 74°10′W |
| Crooked, l., Can. | 101 | 48°25′N | 56°05′W |
| Crooked, r., Can. | 95 | 54°30′N | 122°55′W |
| Crooked, r., Or., U.S. | 114 | 44°07′N | 120°30′W |
| Crooked Creek, r., Il., U.S. (krŏŏk′ĕd) | 121 | 40°21′N | 90°49′W |
| Crooked Island Passage, strt., Bah. | 135 | 22°40′N | 74°50′W |
| Crookston, Mn., U.S. (krŏŏks′tŭn) | 112 | 47°44′N | 96°35′W |
| Crooksville, Oh., U.S. (krŏŏks′vĭl) | 108 | 39°45′N | 82°05′W |
| Crosby, Eng., U.K. | 158a | 53°30′N | 3°02′W |
| Crosby, Mn., U.S. (krôz′bĭ) | 113 | 46°29′N | 93°58′W |
| Crosby, N.D., U.S. | 112 | 48°55′N | 103°18′W |
| Crosby, Tx., U.S. | 123a | 29°55′N | 95°04′W |
| Cross, l., La., U.S. | 123 | 32°33′N | 93°58′W |
| Cross, r., Nig. | 235 | 5°35′N | 8°05′E |
| Cross City, Fl., U.S. | 124 | 29°55′N | 83°25′W |
| Crossett, Ar., U.S. (krôs′ĕt) | 121 | 33°08′N | 92°00′W |
| Cross Lake, l., Can. | 92 | 54°45′N | 97°30′W |
| Cross River Reservoir, res., N.Y., U.S. (krôs) | 110a | 41°14′N | 73°34′W |
| Cross Sound, strt., Ak., U.S. (krŏs) | 103 | 58°12′N | 137°20′W |
| Crosswell, Mi., U.S. (krŏz′wĕl) | 108 | 43°15′N | 82°35′W |
| Croswell, i., Serb. | 174 | 44°50′N | 14°31′E |
| Crotch, l., Can. | 99 | 44°55′N | 76°55′W |
| Crotone, Italy (krō-tō′nĕ) | 175 | 39°05′N | 17°08′E |
| Croton Falls Reservoir, res., N.Y., U.S. (krōtŭn) | 110a | 41°22′N | 73°44′W |
| Croton-on-Hudson, N.Y., U.S. (krō′tŭn-ŏn hŭd′sŭn) | 110a | 41°12′N | 73°53′W |
| Crow, l., Can. | 113 | 49°13′N | 93°29′W |
| Crow Agency, Mt., U.S. | 115 | 45°36′N | 107°27′W |
| Crow Creek, r., Co., U.S. | 120 | 41°08′N | 104°25′W |
| Crow Creek Indian Reservation, I.R., S.D., U.S. | 112 | 44°17′N | 99°17′W |
| Crow Indian Reservation, I.R., Mt., U.S. (krō) | 115 | 45°26′N | 108°12′W |
| Crowle, Eng., U.K. (kroul) | 158a | 53°36′N | 0°49′W |
| Crowley, La., U.S. (krou′lē) | 123 | 30°13′N | 92°22′W |
| Crown Mountain, mtn., Can. (kroun) | 116d | 49°24′N | 123°05′W |
| Crown Mountain, mtn., V.I.U.S. | 129c | 18°22′N | 64°58′W |
| Crown Point, In., U.S. (kroun point′) | 111a | 41°25′N | 87°22′W |
| Crown Point, N.Y., U.S. | 109 | 44°00′N | 73°25′W |
| Crowsnest Pass, p., Can. | 95 | 49°39′N | 114°45′W |
| Crow Wing, r., Mn., U.S. (krō) | 113 | 44°50′N | 94°01′W |
| Crow Wing, r., Mn., U.S. | 113 | 46°42′N | 94°48′W |
| Crow Wing, North Fork, r., Mn., U.S. | 113 | 45°16′N | 94°28′W |
| Crow Wing, South Fork, r., Mn., U.S. | 113 | 44°59′N | 94°42′W |
| Croydon, Austl. (kroi′dŭn) | 219 | 18°15′S | 142°15′E |
| Croydon, Austl. | 217a | 37°48′S | 145°17′E |
| Croydon, Eng., U.K. | 161 | 51°22′N | 0°06′W |
| Croydon, Pa., U.S. | 110f | 40°05′N | 74°55′W |
| Crozet, Îles, is., Afr. (krô-zĕ′) | 3 | 46°20′S | 51°30′E |
| Cruces, Cuba (krōō′sás) | 134 | 22°20′N | 80°20′W |
| Cruces, Arroyo de, r., Mex. (är-rō′yô-dĕ-krōō′sĕs) | 122 | 26°17′N | 104°32′W |
| Cruillas, Mex. (krōō-ēl′yäs) | 122 | 24°45′N | 98°31′W |
| Cruz, Cabo, c., Cuba (ká′-bô-krōōz) | 129 | 19°50′N | 77°45′W |
| Cruz, Cayo, i., Cuba (kä′yō-krōōz) | 134 | 22°15′N | 77°50′W |
| Cruz Alta, Braz. (krōōz äl′tä) | 144 | 28°41′S | 54°02′W |
| Cruz del Eje, Arg. (krōō′s-dĕl-ĕ-kĕ) | 144 | 30°46′S | 64°45′W |
| Cruzeiro, Braz. (krōō-zā′rō) | 141a | 22°36′S | 44°57′W |
| Cruzeiro do Sul, Braz. (krōō-zā′rō dŏŏ sōōl) | 142 | 7°34′S | 72°40′W |
| Crysler, Can. | 102c | 45°13′N | 75°09′W |
| Crystal City, Tx., U.S. (krĭs′tăl sĭ′tĭ) | 122 | 28°40′N | 99°50′W |
| Crystal Falls, Mi., U.S. (krĭs′tăl fôls) | 113 | 46°06′N | 88°21′W |
| Crystal Lake, Il., U.S. (krĭs′tăl lăk) | 111a | 42°15′N | 88°18′W |
| Crystal Springs, Ms., U.S. (krĭs′tăl sprĭngz) | 124 | 31°58′N | 90°20′W |
| Crystal Springs, oasis, Ca., U.S. | 116b | 37°31′N | 122°26′W |
| Csongrád, Hung. (chôn′gräd) | 169 | 46°42′N | 20°09′E |
| Csorna, Hung. (chôr′nä) | 169 | 47°39′N | 17°11′E |
| Cúa, Ven. (kōō′ä) | 143b | 10°10′N | 66°54′W |
| Cuajimalpa, Mex. (kwä-hē-mäl′pä) | 131a | 19°21′N | 99°18′W |
| Cuale, Sierra del, mts., Mex. (sē-ĕ′r-rä-dĕl-kwá′lĕ) | 130 | 20°20′N | 104°58′W |
| Cuamato, Ang. (kwä-mä′tō) | 236 | 17°05′S | 15°09′E |
| Cuamba, Moz. | 237 | 14°49′S | 36°33′E |
| Cuando, Ang. (kwän′dō) | 236 | 16°32′S | 22°07′E |
| Cuando, r., Afr. | 232 | 14°30′S | 20°00′E |
| Cuangar, Ang. | 236 | 17°36′S | 18°39′E |
| Cuango, r., Afr. | 232 | 9°00′S | 18°00′E |
| Cuanza, r., Ang. (kwän′zä) | 232 | 9°45′S | 15°00′E |
| Cuarto, r., Arg. | 144 | 33°00′S | 63°25′W |
| Cuatro Caminos, Cuba (kwä′trô-kä-mē′nôs) | 135a | 23°01′N | 82°13′W |
| Cuatro Ciénegas, Mex. (kwä′trō syā′nä-gäs) | 122 | 26°59′N | 102°03′W |
| Cuauhtemoc, Mex. (kwä-ōō-tě-mōk′) | 131 | 15°43′N | 91°57′W |
| Cuautepec, Mex. (kwä-ōō-tě-pěk) | 130 | 16°41′N | 99°04′W |
| Cuautepec, Mex. | 130 | 20°01′N | 98°19′W |
| Cuautitlán, Mex. (kwä-ōō-tēt-län′) | 131a | 19°40′N | 99°12′W |
| Cuautla, Mex. (kwä-ōō′tlá) | 130 | 18°47′N | 98°57′W |
| Cuba, Port. (kōō′bá) | 172 | 38°10′N | 7°55′W |
| Cuba, nation, N.A. (kū′bá) | 129 | 22°00′N | 79°00′W |
| Cubagua, Isla, i., Ven. (ē′s-lä-kōō-bä′gwä) | 143b | 10°48′N | 64°10′W |
| Cubango (Okavango), r., Afr. (kōō-bäŋ′gō) | 232 | 17°10′S | 18°20′E |
| Cub Hills, hills, Can. (kŭb) | 96 | 54°20′N | 104°30′W |
| Cucamonga, Ca., U.S. (kōō-ká-mŏŋ′gá) | 117a | 34°05′N | 117°35′W |
| Cuchi, Ang. | 232 | 14°40′S | 16°50′E |
| Cuchillo Parado, Mex. (kōō-chē′lyô pä-rä′dō) | 122 | 29°26′N | 104°52′W |
| Cuchumatanes, Sierra de los, mts., Guat. | 132 | 15°35′N | 91°10′W |
| Cúcuta, Col. (kōō′kōō-tä) | 142 | 7°56′N | 72°30′W |
| Cudahy, Wi., U.S. (kŭd′á-hī) | 111a | 42°57′N | 87°52′W |
| Cuddalore, India (kŭd á-lōr′) | 199 | 11°49′N | 79°46′E |
| Cuddapah, India (kŭd′á-pä) | 199 | 14°31′N | 78°52′E |
| Cue, Austl. (kū) | 218 | 27°30′S | 118°10′E |
| Cuéllar, Spain (kwā′lyär′) | 172 | 41°24′N | 4°15′W |
| Cuenca, Ec. (kwěn′kä) | 142 | 2°52′S | 78°54′W |
| Cuenca, Spain | 162 | 40°05′N | 2°07′W |
| Cuenca, Sierra de, mts., Spain (sē-ĕ′r-rä-dĕ-kwĕ′n-kä) | 172 | 40°02′N | 1°50′W |
| Cuencame, Mex. (kwěn-kä-mā′) | 122 | 24°52′N | 103°42′W |
| Cuerámaro, Mex. (kwā-rä′mä-rō) | 130 | 20°39′N | 101°44′W |
| Cuernavaca, Mex. (kwĕr-nä-vä′kä) | 128 | 18°55′N | 99°15′W |
| Cuero, Tx., U.S. (kwā′rō) | 123 | 29°05′N | 97°16′W |
| Cuetzalá del Progreso, Mex. (kwĕt-zä-lä dĕl prō-grā′sō) | 130 | 18°07′N | 99°51′W |
| Cuetzalan del Progreso, Mex. | 131 | 20°02′N | 97°33′W |
| Cuevas del Almanzora, Spain (kwĕ′väs-dĕl-äl-män-zō-rä) | 162 | 37°19′N | 1°54′W |
| Cuglieri, Italy (kōō-lyā′rē) | 174 | 40°11′N | 8°37′E |
| Cuicatlán, Mex. (kwē-kä-tlän′) | 131 | 17°46′N | 96°57′W |
| Cuilapa, Guat. (kô-ē-lä′pä) | 132 | 14°16′N | 90°20′W |
| Cuilo (Kwilu), r., Afr. | 236 | 9°15′S | 19°30′E |


ng-sing; ŋ-baŋk; N-nasalized n; nŏd; cŏmmit; ōld; ōbey; ôrder; oi-boil; fōōd; ŏŏ-as oo in foot; ou-out; s-soft; sh-dish; th-thin; pūre; ûnite; ûrn; stŭd; circŭs; ü-as in French tu; ′-indeterminate vowel.

286 Cuito – Davenport PRONOUNCING INDEX


| PLACE (Pronunciation) | PAGE | LAT. | LONG. |
|---|---|---|---|
| Cuito, r., Ang. (ko͞o-ē-'tō) | 232 | 14°45'S | 19°00'E |
| Cuitzeo, Mex. (kwēt'zä-ō) | 130 | 19°57'N | 101°11'W |
| Cuitzeo, Laguna de, l., Mex. (lä-ó'nä-dĕ-kwēt'zä-ō) | 130 | 19°58'N | 101°05'W |
| Cul de Sac, pl., Haiti (ko͞o'l-dĕ-sä'k) | 135 | 18°35'N | 72°05'W |
| Culebra, i., P.R. (ko͞o-lä'brä) | 129b | 18°19'N | 65°32'W |
| Culebra, Sierra de la, mts., Spain (sē-ĕ'r-rä-dĕ-lä-ko͞o-lĕ-brä) | 172 | 41°52'N | 6°21'W |
| Culemborg, Neth. | 159a | 51°57'N | 5°14'E |
| Culfa, Azer. | 182 | 38°58'N | 45°38'E |
| Culgoa, r., Austl. (kŭl-gō'à) | 221 | 29°21'S | 147°00'E |
| Culiacán, Mex. (ko͞o-lyä-kà'n) | 128 | 24°45'N | 107°30'W |
| Culion, Phil. (ko͞o-lē-ōn') | 212 | 11°43'N | 119°58'E |
| Cúllar de Baza, Spain (ko͞o'l-yär-dĕ-bä'zä) | 172 | 37°36'N | 2°35'W |
| Cullera, Spain (ko͞o-lyā'rä) | 162 | 39°12'N | 0°15'W |
| Cullinan, S. Afr. (kŏ'lĭ-năn) | 238c | 25°41'S | 28°32'E |
| Cullman, Al., U.S. (kŭl'măn) | 124 | 34°10'N | 86°50'W |
| Culpeper, Va., U.S. (kŭl'pĕp-ẽr) | 109 | 38°30'N | 77°55'W |
| Culross, Can. (kŭl'rôs) | 102f | 49°43'N | 97°54'W |
| Culver, In., U.S. (kŭl'vẽr) | 108 | 41°15'N | 86°25'W |
| Culver City, Ca., U.S. | 117a | 34°00'N | 118°23'W |
| Cumaná, Ven. | 142 | 10°28'N | 64°10'W |
| Cumberland, Can. (kŭm'bẽr-lănd) | 102c | 45°31'N | 75°25'W |
| Cumberland, Md., U.S. | 105 | 39°40'N | 78°40'W |
| Cumberland, Wa., U.S. | 116a | 47°17'N | 121°55'W |
| Cumberland, Wi., U.S. | 113 | 45°31'N | 92°01'W |
| Cumberland, r., U.S. | 124 | 36°45'N | 85°33'W |
| Cumberland, Lake, res., Ky., U.S. | 107 | 36°55'N | 85°20'W |
| Cumberland Islands, is., Austl. | 221 | 20°20'S | 149°46'E |
| Cumberland Peninsula, pen., Can. | 93 | 65°59'N | 64°05'W |
| Cumberland Plateau, plat., U.S. | 124 | 35°25'N | 85°30'W |
| Cumberland Sound, strt., Can. | 93 | 65°27'N | 65°44'W |
| Cundinamarca, dept., Col. (ko͞on-dē-nä-mä'r-kä) | 142a | 4°57'N | 74°27'W |
| Cunduacán, Mex. (kŏn-do͞o-à-kän') | 131 | 18°04'N | 93°23'W |
| Cunene (Kunene), r., Afr. | 232 | 17°05'S | 12°35'E |
| Cuneo, Italy (ko͞o'nā-ō) | 174 | 44°24'N | 7°31'E |
| Cunha, Braz. (ko͞o'nyà) | 141a | 23°05'S | 44°56'W |
| Cunnamulla, Austl. (kŭn-à-mŭl-à) | 219 | 28°00'S | 145°55'E |
| Cupula, Pico, mtn., Mex. (pē'kō-ko͞o'po͞o-lä) | 128 | 24°45'N | 111°10'W |
| Cuquío, Mex. (ko͞o-kē'ō) | 130 | 20°55'N | 103°03'W |
| Curaçao, i., Neth. Ant. (ko͞o-rä-sä'ō) | 142 | 12°12'N | 68°58'W |
| Curacautín, Chile (kä-rä-kä-o͞o-tē'n) | 144 | 38°25'S | 71°53'W |
| Curaumilla, Punta, c., Chile (ko͞o-rou-mē'lyä) | 141b | 33°05'S | 71°44'W |
| Curepto, Chile (ko͞o-rĕp-tō) | 141b | 35°06'S | 72°02'W |
| Curitiba, Braz. (ko͞o-rē-tē'bà) | 143 | 25°20'S | 49°15'W |
| Curly Cut Cays, is., Bah. | 134 | 23°40'N | 77°40'W |
| Currais Novos, Braz. (ko͞or-rä'ēs nō-vōs) | 143 | 6°02'S | 36°39'W |
| Curran, Can. (kü-răɴ') | 102c | 45°30'N | 74°59'W |
| Current, i., Bah. (kŭ-rĕnt) | 134 | 25°20'N | 76°50'W |
| Current, r., Mo., U.S. (kûr'ĕnt) | 121 | 37°18'N | 91°21'W |
| Currie, Mount, mtn., S. Afr. (kŭ-rē) | 233c | 30°28'S | 29°23'E |
| Currituck Sound, strt., N.C., U.S. (kûr'ĭ-tŭk) | 125 | 36°27'N | 75°42'W |
| Curtis, Ne., U.S. (kûr'tĭs) | 120 | 40°36'N | 100°29'W |
| Curtis, i., Austl. | 221 | 23°38'S | 151°43'E |
| Curtisville, Pa., U.S. (kûr'tĭs-vĭl) | 111e | 40°38'N | 79°50'W |
| Čurug, Serb. (cho͞o'rŏg) | 175 | 45°27'N | 20°03'E |
| Curunga, Ang. | 236 | 12°51'S | 21°12'E |
| Curupira, Serra, mts., S.A. (sĕr'rà ko͞o-ro͞o-pē'rà) | 142 | 1°00'N | 65°30'W |
| Cururupu, Braz. (ko͞o-ro͞o-rō-po͞o') | 143 | 1°40'S | 44°56'W |
| Curvelo, Braz. (kŏr-vĕl'ō) | 143 | 18°47'S | 44°14'W |
| Cusco, Peru | 142 | 13°36'S | 71°52'W |
| Cushing, Ok., U.S. (kŭsh'ĭng) | 121 | 35°58'N | 96°46'W |
| Custer, S.D., U.S. (kŭs'tẽr) | 112 | 43°46'N | 103°36'W |
| Custer, Wa., U.S. | 116d | 48°55'N | 122°39'W |
| Cut Bank, Mt., U.S. (kŭt bănk) | 115 | 48°38'N | 112°19'W |
| Cuthbert, Ga., U.S. (kŭth'bẽrt) | 124 | 31°47'N | 84°48'W |
| Cuttack, India (kŭ-tăk') | 199 | 20°38'N | 85°53'E |
| Cutzamala, r., Mex. (ko͞o-tzä-mä-lä') | 130 | 18°57'N | 100°41'W |
| Cutzamalá de Pinzón, Mex. (ko͞o-tzä-mä-lä'dĕ-pēn-zō'n) | 130 | 18°28'N | 100°36'W |
| Cuvo, r., Ang. (ko͞o'vō) | 232 | 11°00'S | 14°30'E |
| Cuxhaven, Ger. (kŏŏks'hä-fĕn) | 160 | 53°51'N | 8°43'E |
| Cuyahoga, r., Oh., U.S. (kī-à-hō'gà) | 111d | 41°22'N | 81°38'W |
| Cuyahoga Falls, Oh., U.S. | 111d | 41°08'N | 81°29'W |
| Cuyapaire Indian Reservation, I.R., Ca., U.S. (kū-yà-pâr) | 118 | 32°46'N | 116°20'W |
| Cuyo Islands, is., Phil. (ko͞o'yō) | 212 | 10°54'N | 120°08'E |
| Cuyotenango, Guat. (ko͞o-yō-tĕ-năn'gō) | 132 | 14°30'N | 91°35'W |
| Cuyuni, r., S.A. (ko͞o-yo͞o'nē) | 143 | 6°40'N | 60°44'W |
| Cuyutlán, Mex. (ko͞o-yo͞o-tlän') | 130 | 18°54'N | 104°04'W |
| Cyclades *see* Kikládhes, is., Grc. | 156 | 37°30'N | 24°45'E |
| Cynthiana, Ky., U.S. (sĭn-thĭ-ăn'à) | 108 | 38°20'N | 84°20'W |
| Cypress, Ca., U.S. (sī'prĕs) | 117a | 33°50'N | 118°03'W |
| Cypress Hills, hills, Can. | 96 | 49°40'N | 110°20'W |
| Cypress Lake, l., Can. | 96 | 49°28'N | 109°43'W |
| Cyprus, nation, Asia (sī'prŭs) | 198 | 35°00'N | 31°00'E |
| Cyrenaica *see* Barqah, hist. reg., Libya | 231 | 31°09'N | 21°45'E |
| Czech Republic, nation, Eur. | 154 | 50°00'N | 15°00'E |
| Czersk, Pol. (chĕrsk) | 169 | 53°47'N | 17°58'E |
| Częstochowa, Pol. (chăɴ-stō kō'vä) | 161 | 50°49'N | 19°10'E |

# D

| PLACE (Pronunciation) | PAGE | LAT. | LONG. |
|---|---|---|---|
| Da'an, China (dä-än) | 208 | 45°25'N | 124°22'E |
| Dabakala, C. Iv. (dä-bä-kä'lä) | 230 | 8°16'N | 4°36'W |
| Daba Shan, mts., China (dä-bä shän) | 204 | 32°25'N | 108°20'E |
| Dabeiba, Col. (dà-bā'bä) | 142a | 7°01'N | 76°16'W |
| Dabie Shan, mts., China (dä-bĭē shän) | 205 | 31°40'N | 114°50'E |
| Dabnou, Niger | 235 | 14°09'N | 5°22'E |
| Dabob Bay, b., Wa., U.S. (dā'bŏb) | 116a | 47°50'N | 122°50'W |
| Dabola, Gui. | 234 | 10°45'N | 11°07'W |
| Dąbrowa Białostocka, Pol. | 169 | 53°37'N | 23°18'E |
| Dacca *see* Dhaka, Bngl. | 198 | 23°45'N | 90°29'E |
| Dachang, China (dä-chäŋ) | 207b | 31°18'N | 121°25'E |
| Dachangshan Dao, i., China (dä-chäŋ-shän dou) | 206 | 39°21'N | 122°31'E |
| Dachau, Ger. (dä'κou) | 168 | 48°16'N | 11°26'E |
| Dacotah, Can. (dà-kō'tà) | 102f | 49°52'N | 97°38'W |
| Dade City, Fl., U.S. (dād) | 125a | 28°22'N | 82°09'W |
| Dadeville, Al., U.S. (dād'vĭl) | 124 | 32°48'N | 85°44'W |
| Dādra & Nagar Haveli, India | 199 | 20°00'N | 73°00'E |
| Dadu, r., China (dä-do͞o) | 209 | 29°20'N | 103°03'E |
| Daet, mtn., Phil. (dä'ât) | 213a | 14°07'N | 122°59'E |
| Dafoe, r., Can. | 97 | 55°50'N | 95°50'W |
| Dafter, Mi., U.S. (dăf'tẽr) | 117k | 46°21'N | 84°26'W |
| Dagana, Sen. (dä-gä'nä) | 230 | 16°31'N | 15°30'W |
| Dagana, reg., Chad | 235 | 12°20'N | 15°15'E |
| Dagang, China (dä-gäŋ) | 207a | 22°48'N | 113°24'E |
| Dagda, Lat. (dåg'dà) | 167 | 56°04'N | 27°30'E |
| Dagenham, Eng., U.K. (dăg'ĕn-ăm) | 158b | 51°32'N | 0°09'E |
| Dagestan, prov., Russia (dä-gĕs-tän') | 181 | 43°40'N | 46°10'E |
| Daggett, Ca., U.S. (dăg'ĕt) | 118 | 34°50'N | 116°52'W |
| Dagu, China (dä-go͞o) | 208 | 39°00'N | 117°42'E |
| Dagu, r., China | 206 | 36°29'N | 120°06'W |
| Dagupan, Phil. (dä-go͞o'pän) | 213a | 16°02'N | 120°20'E |
| Daheishan Dao, i., China (dä-hā-shän dou) | 206 | 37°57'N | 120°37'E |
| Dahl, Ger. (däl) | 171c | 51°18'N | 7°33'E |
| Dahlak Archipelago, is., Erit. | 231 | 15°45'N | 40°30'E |
| Dahomey *see* Benin, nation, Afr. | 230 | 8°00'N | 2°00'E |
| Dahra, Libya | 200 | 29°34'N | 17°50'E |
| Daibu, China (dī-bo͞o) | 206 | 31°22'N | 119°29'E |
| Daigo, Japan (dī-gō) | 211b | 34°57'N | 135°49'E |
| Daimiel Manzanares, Spain (dī-myĕl'män-zä-nä'rĕs) | 172 | 39°05'N | 3°36'W |
| Dairen *see* Dalian, China | 204 | 38°54'N | 121°35'E |
| Dairy, r., Or., U.S. (dâr'ĭ) | 116c | 45°33'N | 123°04'W |
| Dai-Sen, mtn., Japan (dī'sĕn') | 211 | 35°22'N | 133°35'E |
| Dai-Tenjo-dake, mtn., Japan (dī-tĕn'jō dä-kä) | 211 | 36°21'N | 137°38'E |
| Daiyun Shan, mtn., China (dī-yŏn shän) | 209 | 25°40'N | 118°08'E |
| Dajabón, Dom. Rep. (dä-κä-bō'n) | 135 | 19°35'N | 71°40'W |
| Dajarra, Austl. (dà-jär'à) | 218 | 21°45'S | 139°30'E |
| Dakar, Sen. (dà-kär') | 230 | 14°40'N | 17°26'W |
| Dakhla, W. Sah. | 230 | 23°45'N | 16°04'W |
| Dakouraoua, Niger | 235 | 13°58'N | 6°15'E |
| Dakovica, Serb. | 175 | 42°33'N | 20°28'E |
| Dalälven, r., Swe. | 156 | 60°26'N | 15°50'E |
| Dalby, Austl. (dôl'bē) | 219 | 27°10'S | 151°15'E |
| Dalcour, La., U.S. (dăl-kour) | 110d | 29°49'N | 89°59'W |
| Dale, Nor. (dä'lĕ) | 166 | 60°35'N | 5°55'E |
| Dale Hollow Lake, res., Tn., U.S. (dāl hŏl'ō) | 107 | 36°33'N | 85°03'W |
| Dalemead, Can. (dä'lĕ-mēd) | 102e | 50°53'N | 113°38'W |
| Dalen, Nor. (dä'lĕn) | 166 | 59°28'N | 8°01'E |
| Daleside, S. Afr. (dāl'sīd) | 238c | 26°30'S | 28°03'E |
| Dalesville, Can. (dălz'vĭl) | 102a | 45°42'N | 74°23'W |
| Daley Waters, Austl. (dā lē) | 218 | 16°15'N | 133°30'E |
| Dalhart, Tx., U.S. (dăl härt) | 120 | 36°04'N | 102°32'W |
| Dalhousie, Can. (dăl-ho͞o'zē) | 100 | 48°04'N | 66°23'W |
| Dali, China (dä-lē) | 207a | 23°07'N | 113°06'E |
| Dali, China | 204 | 26°00'N | 100°08'E |
| Dali, China | 204 | 35°00'N | 109°38'E |
| Dalian, China (lů-dä) | 205 | 38°54'N | 121°35'E |
| Dalian Wan, b., China (dä-lĭĕn wän) | 206 | 38°55'N | 121°50'E |
| Dalías, Spain (dä-lē'ás) | 172 | 36°49'N | 2°50'W |
| Dall, i., Ak., U.S. (dăl) | 103 | 54°50'N | 133°10'W |
| Dallas, Or., U.S. (dăl'lås) | 114 | 44°55'N | 123°20'W |
| Dallas, S.D., U.S. | 112 | 43°13'N | 99°34'W |
| Dallas, Tx., U.S. | 104 | 32°45'N | 96°48'W |
| Dalles Dam, Or., U.S. | 114 | 45°36'N | 121°08'W |
| Dall Island, i., Ak., U.S. | 94 | 54°50'N | 132°55'W |
| Dalmacija, hist. reg., Serb. (däl-mä'tsē-yä) | 174 | 43°25'N | 16°37'E |
| Dalnerechensk, Russia | 179 | 46°07'N | 133°21'E |
| Daloa, C. Iv. | 234 | 6°53'N | 6°27'W |
| Dalroy, Can. (dăl'roi) | 102e | 51°07'N | 113°39'W |
| Dalrymple, Mount, mtn., Austl. (dăl'rĭm-p'l) | 221 | 21°14'S | 148°46'E |
| Dalton, S. Afr. (dŏl'tŏn) | 233c | 29°21'S | 30°41'E |
| Dalton, Ga., U.S. (dôl'tŭn) | 124 | 34°46'N | 84°58'W |
| Daly, r., Austl. (dā'lĭ) | 220 | 14°15'S | 131°15'E |
| Daly City, Ca., U.S. (dā'lē) | 116b | 37°42'N | 122°27'W |
| Damān, India | 199 | 20°32'N | 72°53'E |
| Damanhūr, Egypt (dä-män-ho͞or') | 231 | 30°59'N | 30°31'E |
| Damar, Pulau, i., Indon. | 213 | 7°15'S | 129°15'E |
| Damara, C.A.R. | 235 | 4°58'N | 18°42'E |
| Damaraland, hist. reg., Nmb. (dă'nà-rà-lănd) | 232 | 22°15'S | 16°15'E |
| Damas Cays, is., Bah. (dä'mäs) | 134 | 23°50'N | 79°50'W |
| Damascus, Syria | 198 | 33°30'N | 36°18'E |
| Damāvand, Qolleh-ye, mtn., Iran | 198 | 36°05'N | 52°05'E |
| Damba, Ang. (däm'bä) | 232 | 6°41'S | 15°08'E |
| Dâmbovița, r., Rom. | 175 | 44°43'N | 25°41'E |
| Dame Marie, Cap, c., Haiti (dām mȧrē') | 135 | 18°35'N | 74°50'W |
| Dāmghān, Iran (dām-gän') | 198 | 35°50'N | 54°15'E |
| Daming, China (dä-mĭŋ) | 208 | 36°15'N | 115°09'E |
| Dammartin-en-Goële, Fr. (däɴ-mär-tăɴ-äɴ-gô-ĕl') | 171b | 49°03'N | 2°40'E |
| Dampier, Selat, strt., Indon. (dăm'pēr) | 213 | 0°40'S | 131°15'E |
| Dampier Archipelago, is., Austl. | 220 | 20°15'S | 116°25'E |
| Dampier Land, reg., Austl. | 220 | 17°30'S | 122°25'E |
| Dan, r., N.C., U.S. (dăn) | 125 | 36°26'N | 79°40'W |
| Dana, Mount, mtn., Ca., U.S. | 118 | 37°54'N | 119°13'W |
| Da Nang, Viet. | 212 | 16°08'N | 108°22'E |
| Danbury, Eng., U.K. | 158b | 51°42'N | 0°34'E |
| Danbury, Ct., U.S. (dăn'bẽr-ĭ) | 110a | 41°23'N | 73°27'W |
| Danbury, Tx., U.S. | 123a | 29°14'N | 95°22'W |
| Dandenong, Austl. (dăn'dē-nông) | 222 | 37°59'S | 145°13'E |
| Dandong, China (dän-dôŋ) | 205 | 40°10'N | 124°30'E |
| Dane, r., Eng., U.K. (dān) | 158a | 53°11'N | 2°14'W |
| Danea, Gui. | 234 | 11°27'N | 13°12'W |
| Danforth, Me., U.S. | 100 | 45°38'N | 67°53'W |
| Dan Gora, Nig. | 235 | 11°30'N | 8°09'E |
| Dangtu, China (däŋ-to͞o) | 209 | 31°35'N | 118°28'E |
| Dani, Burkina | 230 | 13°43'N | 0°10'W |
| Dania, Fl., U.S. (dā'nĭ-à) | 125a | 26°01'N | 80°10'W |
| Danilov, Russia (dä'nē-lôf) | 180 | 58°12'N | 40°08'E |
| Danissa Hills, hills, Kenya | 237 | 3°20'N | 40°55'E |
| Dānizkānarı, Azer. | 182 | 40°13'N | 49°33'E |
| Dankov, Russia (däŋ'kôf) | 180 | 53°17'N | 39°09'E |
| Dannemora, N.Y., U.S. (dăn-ē-mō'rà) | 109 | 44°45'N | 73°45'W |
| Dannhauser, S. Afr. (dän'hou-zẽr) | 233c | 28°07'S | 30°04'E |
| Dansville, N.Y., U.S. (dănz'vĭl) | 109 | 42°30'N | 77°40'W |
| Danube, r., Eur. | 156 | 43°00'N | 24°00'E |
| Danube, Mouths of the, mth., Rom. (dăn'ub) | 177 | 45°13'N | 29°37'E |
| Danvers, Ma., U.S. (dăn'vẽrz) | 101a | 42°34'N | 70°57'W |
| Danville, Ca., U.S. (dăn'vĭl) | 116b | 37°49'N | 122°00'W |
| Danville, Il., U.S. | 108 | 40°10'N | 87°35'W |
| Danville, In., U.S. | 108 | 39°45'N | 86°30'W |
| Danville, Ky., U.S. | 108 | 37°35'N | 84°50'W |
| Danville, Pa., U.S. | 109 | 41°00'N | 76°35'W |
| Danville, Va., U.S. | 105 | 36°35'N | 79°24'W |
| Danxian, China (dän shyĕn) | 209 | 19°30'N | 109°38'E |
| Danyang, China (dän-yäŋ) | 206 | 32°01'N | 119°32'E |
| Danzig *see* Gdańsk, Pol. | 154 | 54°20'N | 18°40'E |
| Danzig, Gulf of, b., Eur. (dán'tsĭk) | 160 | 54°41'N | 19°01'E |
| Daoxian, China (dou shyĕn) | 209 | 25°35'N | 111°27'E |
| Dapango, Togo | 234 | 10°52'N | 0°12'E |
| Daphnae, hist., Egypt | 197a | 30°43'N | 32°12'E |
| Daqin Dao, i., China (dä-chyĭn dou) | 206 | 38°18'N | 120°50'E |
| Darabani, Rom. (dă-rä-băn'ĭ) | 169 | 48°13'N | 26°38'E |
| Daraj, Libya | 230 | 30°12'N | 10°14'E |
| Darāw, Egypt (dà-rä'o͞o) | 238b | 24°24'N | 32°56'E |
| Darbhanga, India (dŭr-bŭŋ'gä) | 199 | 26°03'N | 85°09'E |
| Darby, Pa., U.S. (där'bĭ) | 110f | 39°55'N | 75°16'W |
| Darby, i., Bah. | 134 | 23°50'N | 76°20'W |
| Dardanelles *see* Çanakkale Boğazi, strt., Tur. | 163 | 40°05'N | 25°50'E |
| Dar es Salaam, Tan. (där ĕs sà-läm') | 233 | 6°48'S | 39°17'E |
| Dārfūr, hist. reg., Sudan (där-fo͞or') | 231 | 13°21'N | 23°46'E |
| Dargai, Pak. (dŭr-gä'ē) | 202 | 34°35'N | 72°00'E |
| Darien, Col. (dā-rĭ-ĕn') | 142a | 3°56'N | 76°30'W |
| Darien, Ct., U.S. (dâ-rē-ĕn') | 110a | 41°04'N | 73°28'W |
| Darién, Cordillera de, mts., Nic. | 132 | 13°00'N | 85°42'W |
| Darien, Serranía del, mts. | 133 | 8°13'N | 77°28'W |
| Darjeeling, India (dŭr-jē'lĭng) | 199 | 27°05'N | 88°16'E |
| Darling, r., Austl. | 221 | 31°50'S | 143°20'E |
| Darling Downs, reg., Austl. | 221 | 27°22'S | 150°00'E |
| Darling Range, mts., Austl. | 220 | 30°30'S | 115°45'E |
| Darlington, Eng., U.K. (där'lĭng-tŭn) | 164 | 54°32'N | 1°35'W |
| Darlington, S.C., U.S. | 125 | 34°15'N | 79°52'W |
| Darlington, Wi., U.S. | 113 | 42°41'N | 90°06'W |
| Darłowo, Pol. (där-lô'vô) | 168 | 54°26'N | 16°23'E |
| Darmstadt, Ger. (därm'shtät) | 161 | 49°53'N | 8°40'E |
| Darnah, Libya | 231 | 32°44'N | 22°41'E |
| Darnley Bay, b., Ak., U.S. (därn'lē) | 103 | 70°00'N | 124°00'W |
| Daroca, Spain (dä-rō-kä) | 172 | 41°08'N | 1°24'W |
| Dartford, Eng., U.K. | 158b | 51°27'N | 0°14'E |
| Dartmoor, for., Eng., U.K. (därt'mo͞or) | 164 | 50°35'N | 4°05'W |
| Dartmouth, Can. (därt'mŭth) | 91 | 44°40'N | 63°34'W |
| Dartmouth, Eng., U.K. | 164 | 50°33'N | 3°28'W |
| Daru, Pap. N. Gui. (dä'ro͞o) | 213 | 9°04'S | 143°21'E |
| Daruvar, Cro. (där'ro͞o-vär) | 175 | 45°37'N | 17°16'E |
| Darwen, Eng., U.K. (där'wĕn) | 158a | 53°42'N | 2°28'W |
| Darwin, Austl. (där'wĭn) | 218 | 12°25'S | 131°00'E |
| Darwin, Cordillera, mts., Chile (kôr-dēl-yĕ'rä-där'wĕn) | 144 | 54°40'S | 69°30'W |
| Dashhowuz, Turkmen. | 183 | 41°50'N | 59°45'E |
| Dash Point, Wa., U.S. (dăsh) | 116a | 47°19'N | 122°25'W |
| Dasht, r., Pak. (dŭsht) | 198 | 25°30'N | 62°30'E |
| Dasol Bay, b., Phil. (dä-sōl') | 213a | 15°53'N | 119°40'E |
| Datian Ding, mtn., China (dä-tĭĕn dĭŋ) | 209 | 22°25'N | 111°20'E |
| Datong, China (dä-tôŋ) | 208 | 40°00'N | 113°30'E |
| Dattapukur, India | 202a | 22°45'N | 88°32'E |
| Datteln, Ger. (dät'tĕln) | 171c | 51°39'N | 7°20'E |
| Datu, Tandjung, c., Asia | 212 | 2°08'N | 110°15'E |
| Datuan, China (dä-tůän) | 207b | 30°57'N | 121°43'E |
| Daugava (Zapadnaya Dvina), r., Eur. | 167 | 56°40'N | 24°40'E |
| Daugavpils, Lat. (dä'ŏ-gäv-pēls) | 180 | 55°52'N | 26°32'E |
| Dauphin, Can. (dô'fĭn) | 90 | 51°09'N | 100°00'W |
| Dauphin Lake, l., Can. | 97 | 51°17'N | 99°48'W |
| Dāvangere, India | 203 | 14°30'N | 75°55'E |
| Davao, Phil. (dä'vä-ō) | 213 | 7°05'N | 125°30'E |
| Davao Gulf, b., Phil. | 213 | 6°30'N | 125°45'E |
| Davenport, Ia., U.S. (dăv'ĕn-pōrt) | 105 | 41°34'N | 90°38'W |


ăt; finăl; rāte; senāte; ärm; ȧsk; sofȧ; fâre; ch-choose; dh-as th in other; bē; ēvent; bĕt; recĕnt; cratẽr; g-gō; gh-guttural g; bĭt; ĭ-short neutral; rīde; κ-guttural k as ch in German ich;

PRONOUNCING INDEX

Davenport – Diablotins 287


| PLACE (Pronunciation) | PAGE | LAT. | LONG. |
|---|---|---|---|
| Davenport, Wa., U.S. | 114 | 47°39'N | 118°07'W |
| David, Pan. (dá-vēdh') | 129 | 8°27'N | 82°27'W |
| David City, Ne., U.S. (dā'vĭd) | 112 | 41°15'N | 97°10'W |
| David-Gorodok, Bela. (dá-vět' gō-rō'dôk) | 181 | 52°02'N | 27°14'E |
| Davis, Ok., U.S. (dā'vĭs) | 121 | 34°34'N | 97°08'W |
| Davis, W.V., U.S. | 109 | 39°15'N | 79°25'W |
| Davis Lake, l., Or., U.S. | 114 | 43°38'N | 121°43'W |
| Davis Mountains, mts., Tx., U.S. | 122 | 30°45'N | 104°17'W |
| Davis Strait, strt., N.A. | 89 | 66°00'N | 60°00'W |
| Davlekanovo, Russia | 180 | 54°15'N | 55°05'E |
| Davos, Switz. (dä'vōs) | 168 | 46°47'N | 9°50'E |
| Dawa, r., Afr. | 231 | 4°30'N | 40°30'E |
| Dawāsir, Wādī ad, val., Sau. Ar. | 198 | 20°48'N | 44°07'E |
| Dawei, Mya. | 212 | 14°04'N | 98°19'E |
| Dawen, r., China (dä-wŭn) | 206 | 35°58'N | 116°53'E |
| Dawley, Eng., U.K. (dô'lĭ) | 158a | 52°38'N | 2°28'W |
| Dawna Range, mts., Mya. (dô'ná) | 212 | 17°02'N | 98°01'E |
| Dawson, Can. (dô'sŭn) | 90 | 64°04'N | 139°22'W |
| Dawson, Ga., U.S. | 124 | 31°45'N | 84°29'W |
| Dawson, Mn., U.S. | 112 | 44°54'N | 96°03'W |
| Dawson, r., Austl. | 221 | 24°20'S | 149°45'E |
| Dawson Bay, b., Can. | 97 | 52°55'N | 100°50'W |
| Dawson Creek, Can. | 90 | 55°46'N | 120°14'W |
| Dawson Range, mts., Can. | 103 | 62°15'N | 138°10'W |
| Dawson Springs, Ky., U.S. | 124 | 37°10'N | 87°40'W |
| Dawu, China (dä-wōō) | 206 | 31°33'N | 114°07'E |
| Dax, Fr. (dàks) | 161 | 43°42'N | 1°06'W |
| Daxian, China (dä-shyĕn) | 204 | 31°12'N | 107°30'E |
| Daxing, China (dä-shyĭŋ) | 208a | 39°44'N | 116°19'E |
| Dayiqiao, China (dä-yē-chyou) | 206 | 31°43'N | 120°40'E |
| Dayr az Zawr, Syria (då-ērěz-zôr') | 198 | 35°15'N | 40°01'E |
| Dayton, Ky., U.S. (dā'tŭn) | 111f | 39°07'N | 84°28'W |
| Dayton, N.M., U.S. | 120 | 32°44'N | 104°23'W |
| Dayton, Oh., U.S. | 105 | 39°54'N | 84°15'W |
| Dayton, Tn., U.S. | 124 | 35°30'N | 85°00'W |
| Dayton, Tx., U.S. | 123 | 30°03'N | 94°53'W |
| Dayton, Wa., U.S. | 114 | 46°18'N | 117°59'W |
| Daytona Beach, Fl., U.S. (dā-tō'nȧ) | 105 | 29°11'N | 81°02'W |
| Dayu, China (dä-yōō) | 209 | 25°20'N | 114°20'E |
| Da Yunhe (Grand Canal), can., China (dä yòn-hŭ) | 205 | 35°00'N | 117°00'E |
| Dayville, Ct., U.S. (dā'vĭl) | 109 | 41°50'N | 71°55'W |
| De Aar, S. Afr. (dē-är') | 232 | 30°45'S | 24°05'E |
| Dead, l., Mn., U.S. (dĕd) | 112 | 46°28'N | 96°00'W |
| Dead Sea, l., Asia | 198 | 31°30'N | 35°30'E |
| Deadwood, S.D., U.S. (dĕd'wȯd) | 104 | 44°23'N | 103°43'W |
| Deal Island, Md., U.S. (dēl-ī'lȧnd) | 109 | 38°10'N | 75°55'W |
| Dean, r., Can. (dēn) | 94 | 52°45'N | 125°30'W |
| Dean Channel, strt., Can. | 94 | 52°33'N | 127°13'W |
| Deán Funes, Arg. (dĕ-á'n-fōō-nĕs) | 144 | 30°26'S | 64°12'W |
| Dearborn, Mi., U.S. (dēr'bŭrn) | 111b | 42°18'N | 83°15'W |
| Dearg, Ben, mtn., Scot., U.K. (bĕn dŭrg) | 164 | 57°48'N | 4°59'W |
| Dease Strait, strt., Can. (dēz) | 92 | 68°50'N | 108°20'W |
| Death Valley, Ca., U.S. | 118 | 36°18'N | 116°26'W |
| Death Valley, val., Ca., U.S. | 106 | 36°30'N | 117°00'W |
| Death Valley National Park, rec., U.S. | 118 | 36°34'N | 117°00'W |
| Debal'tseve, Ukr. | 177 | 48°23'N | 38°29'E |
| Debao, China (dŭ-bou) | 204 | 23°18'N | 106°40'E |
| Debar, Mac. (dĕ'bär) (dā'brä) | 175 | 41°31'N | 20°32'E |
| Dęblin, Pol. (däɴ'blĭn) | 169 | 51°34'N | 21°49'E |
| Dębno, Pol. (dĕb-nō') | 168 | 52°47'N | 13°43'E |
| Debo, Lac, l., Mali | 234 | 15°15'N | 4°40'W |
| Debrecen, Hung. (dĕ'brĕ-tsĕn) | 154 | 47°32'N | 21°40'E |
| Debre Markos, Eth. | 231 | 10°15'N | 37°45'E |
| Debre Tabor, Eth. | 231 | 11°57'N | 38°09'E |
| Decatur, Al., U.S. (dē-kā'tŭr) | 124 | 34°35'N | 87°00'W |
| Decatur, Ga., U.S. | 110c | 33°47'N | 84°18'W |
| Decatur, Il., U.S. | 105 | 39°50'N | 88°59'W |
| Decatur, In., U.S. | 108 | 40°50'N | 84°55'W |
| Decatur, Mi., U.S. | 108 | 42°10'N | 86°00'W |
| Decatur, Tx., U.S. | 121 | 33°14'N | 97°33'W |
| Decazeville, Fr. (dē-käz'vēl') | 161 | 44°33'N | 2°16'E |
| Deccan, plat., India (dĕk'ăn) | 199 | 19°05'N | 76°40'E |
| Deception Lake, l., Can. | 96 | 56°33'N | 104°15'W |
| Deception Pass, p., Wa., U.S. (dē-sĕp'shŭn) | 116a | 48°24'N | 122°44'W |
| Děčín, Czech Rep. (dyĕ'chēn) | 168 | 50°47'N | 14°14'E |
| Decorah, Ia., U.S. (dē-kō'rȧ) | 113 | 43°18'N | 91°48'W |
| Dedenevo, Russia (dyĕ-dyĕ'nyĕ-vô) | 186b | 56°14'N | 37°31'E |
| Dedham, Ma., U.S. (dĕd'ăm) | 101a | 42°15'N | 71°11'W |
| Dedo do Deus, mtn., Braz. (dĕ-dô-dô-dĕ'ōōs) | 144b | 22°30'S | 43°02'W |
| Dédougou, Burkina (dā-dò-gōō') | 230 | 12°38'N | 3°28'W |
| Dee, r., Scot., U.K. | 164 | 57°05'N | 2°25'W |
| Dee, r., U.K. | 158a | 53°15'N | 3°05'E |
| Deep, r., N.C., U.S. (dēp) | 125 | 35°36'N | 79°32'W |
| Deep Fork, r., Ok., U.S. | 121 | 35°35'N | 96°42'W |
| Deep River, Can. | 99 | 46°06'N | 77°20'W |
| Deepwater, Mo., U.S. (dep-wô-tēr) | 121 | 38°15'N | 93°46'W |
| Deer, i., Me., U.S. | 100 | 44°07'N | 68°38'W |
| Deerfield, Il., U.S. (dēr'fēld) | 111a | 42°10'N | 87°51'W |
| Deer Island, Or., U.S. | 116c | 45°56'N | 122°51'W |
| Deer Lake, Can. | 93a | 49°10'N | 57°25'W |
| Deer Lake, l., Can. | 97 | 52°40'N | 94°30'W |
| Deer Lodge, Mt., U.S. (dēr lŏj) | 115 | 46°23'N | 112°42'W |
| Deer Park, Oh., U.S. | 111f | 39°12'N | 84°24'W |
| Deer Park, Wa., U.S. | 114 | 47°58'N | 117°28'W |
| Deer River, Mn., U.S. | 113 | 47°20'N | 93°49'W |
| Defiance, Oh., U.S. (dē-fī'ăns) | 108 | 41°15'N | 84°20'W |
| DeFuniak Springs, Fl., U.S. (dē fū'nĭ-ăk) | 124 | 30°42'N | 86°06'W |
| Deganga, India | 202a | 22°41'N | 88°41'E |
| Degeh Bur, Eth. | 238a | 8°10'N | 43°25'E |
| Deggendorf, Ger. (dĕ'ghĕn-dôrf) | 168 | 48°50'N | 12°59'E |
| Degollado, Mex. (dā-gō-lyä'dō) | 130 | 20°27'N | 102°11'W |
| DeGrey, r., Austl. (dē grā') | 220 | 20°20'S | 119°25'E |
| Degtyarsk, Russia (dĕg-ty'arsk) | 186a | 56°42'N | 60°05'E |
| Dehiwala-Mount Lavinia, Sri L. | 203 | 6°47'N | 79°55'E |
| Dehra Dūn, India (dā'rŭ) | 199 | 30°09'N | 78°07'E |
| Dehua, China (dŭ-hwä) | 209 | 25°30'N | 118°15'E |
| Dej, Rom. (dāzh) | 163 | 47°09'N | 23°53'E |
| De Kalb, Il., U.S. (dē kălb') | 108 | 41°54'N | 88°46'W |
| Dekese, D.R.C. | 236 | 3°27'S | 21°24'E |
| Delacour, Can. (dĕ-lä-kōōr') | 102e | 51°09'N | 113°45'W |
| Delagua, Co., U.S. (dĕl-ä'gwä) | 120 | 37°19'N | 104°42'W |
| De Land, Fl., U.S. (dē lănd') | 125 | 29°00'N | 81°19'W |
| Delano, Ca., U.S. (dĕl'ȧ-nō) | 118 | 35°47'N | 119°15'W |
| Delano Peak, mtn., Ut., U.S. | 106 | 38°25'N | 112°25'W |
| Delavan, Wi., U.S. (dĕl'ȧ-văn) | 113 | 42°39'N | 88°38'W |
| Delaware, Oh., U.S. (dĕl'ȧ-wâr) | 108 | 40°15'N | 83°05'W |
| Delaware, state, U.S. | 105 | 38°40'N | 75°30'W |
| Delaware, r., Ks., U.S. | 121 | 39°45'N | 95°47'W |
| Delaware, r., U.S. | 109 | 41°50'N | 75°20'W |
| Delaware Bay, b., U.S. | 107 | 39°05'N | 75°10'W |
| Delaware Reservoir, res., Oh., U.S. | 109 | 40°30'N | 83°05'E |
| Delémont, Switz. (dē-lā-môɴ') | 168 | 47°21'N | 7°18'E |
| De Leon, Tx., U.S. (dē lē-ŏn') | 122 | 32°06'N | 98°33'W |
| Delft, Neth. (dĕlft) | 165 | 52°01'N | 4°20'E |
| Delfzijl, Neth. | 165 | 53°20'N | 6°50'E |
| Delgada, Punta, c., Arg. (pōō'n-tä-dĕl-gä'dä) | 144 | 43°46'S | 63°46'W |
| Delgado, Cabo, c., Moz. (kä'bô-dĕl-gä'dō) | 233 | 10°40'S | 40°35'E |
| Delhi, India | 199 | 28°54'N | 77°13'E |
| Delhi, Il., U.S. (dĕl'hī) | 117e | 39°03'N | 90°16'W |
| Delhi, La., U.S. | 123 | 32°26'N | 91°29'W |
| Delhi, state, India | 199 | 28°30'N | 76°50'E |
| Delitzsch, Ger. (dā'lĭch) | 168 | 51°32'N | 12°18'E |
| Dellansjöarna, l., Swe. | 166 | 61°57'N | 16°25'E |
| Delles, Alg. (dĕ'lĕs') | 230 | 36°59'N | 3°40'E |
| Dell Rapids, S.D., U.S. (dĕl) | 112 | 43°50'N | 96°43'W |
| Dellwood, Mn., U.S. (dĕl'wȯd) | 117g | 45°05'N | 92°58'W |
| Del Mar, Ca., U.S. (dĕl mär') | 118a | 32°57'N | 117°16'W |
| Delmas, S. Afr. (dĕl'mȧs) | 238c | 26°08'S | 28°43'E |
| Delmenhorst, Ger. (dĕl'mĕn-hôrst) | 168 | 53°03'N | 8°38'E |
| Del Norte, Co., U.S. (dĕl nôrt') | 119 | 37°40'N | 106°25'W |
| De-Longa, i., Russia | 179 | 76°21'N | 148°56'E |
| De Long Mountains, mts., Ak., U.S. (dē'lŏng) | 103 | 68°38'N | 162°30'W |
| Deloraine, Austl. (dĕ-lŭ-rān) | 222 | 41°30'S | 146°40'E |
| Delphi, In., U.S. (dĕl'fī) | 108 | 40°35'N | 86°40'W |
| Delphos, Oh., U.S. (dĕl'fŏs) | 108 | 40°50'N | 84°20'W |
| Delray Beach, Fl., U.S. (dĕl-rā') | 125a | 26°27'N | 80°05'W |
| Del Rio, Tx., U.S. (dĕl rē'ō) | 104 | 29°21'N | 100°52'W |
| Delson, Can. (dĕl'sŭn) | 102a | 45°24'N | 73°32'W |
| Delta, Co., U.S. | 119 | 38°45'N | 108°05'W |
| Delta, Ut., U.S. | 119 | 39°20'N | 112°35'W |
| Delta Beach, Can. | 102f | 50°10'N | 98°20'W |
| Delvine, Alb. (dĕl'vē-ná) | 175 | 39°58'N | 20°10'E |
| Dëma, r., Russia (dyĕm'ä) | 180 | 53°40'N | 54°30'E |
| Demba, D.R.C. | 236 | 5°30'S | 22°16'E |
| Dembi Dolo, Eth. | 231 | 8°46'N | 34°46'E |
| Demidov, Russia (dzyĕ'mē-dô'f) | 176 | 55°16'N | 31°32'E |
| Deming, N.M., U.S. (dĕm'ĭng) | 104 | 32°15'N | 107°45'W |
| Demmin, Ger. (dĕm'mēn) | 168 | 53°54'N | 13°04'E |
| Demnat, Mor. (dĕm-nät) | 230 | 31°58'N | 7°03'W |
| Demopolis, Al., U.S. (dē-mŏp'ō-lĭs) | 124 | 32°30'N | 87°50'W |
| Demotte, In., U.S. (dē'mŏt) | 111a | 41°12'N | 87°13'W |
| Dempo, Gunung, mtn., Indon. (dĕm'pō) | 212 | 4°04'S | 103°11'E |
| Dem'yanka, r., Russia (dyĕm-yän'kä) | 184 | 59°07'N | 72°58'E |
| Demyansk, Russia (dyĕm-yänsk') | 176 | 57°39'N | 32°26'E |
| Denain, Fr. (dē-näɴ') | 170 | 50°23'N | 3°21'E |
| Denakil Plain, pl., Eth. | 231 | 12°45'N | 41°01'E |
| Denali National Park, rec., Ak., U.S. | 106a | 63°48'N | 153°02'W |
| Denbigh, Wales, U.K. (dĕn'bĭ) | 164 | 53°15'N | 3°25'W |
| Dendermonde, Bel. | 159a | 51°02'N | 4°04'E |
| Dendron, Va., U.S. (dĕn'drŭn) | 125 | 37°02'N | 76°53'W |
| Denezhkin Kamen, Gora, mtn., Russia (dzyē-ŋĕ'zhkĭn kämĭēŋ) | 186a | 60°26'N | 59°35'E |
| Denham, Mount, mtn., Jam. | 129 | 18°20'N | 77°30'W |
| Den Helder, Neth. (dĕn hĕl'dĕr) | 165 | 52°55'N | 5°45'E |
| Dénia, Spain | 173 | 38°48'N | 0°06'E |
| Deniliquin, Austl. (dĕ-nĭl'ĭ-kwĭn) | 219 | 35°20'S | 144°52'E |
| Denison, Ia., U.S. (dĕn'ĭ-sŭn) | 112 | 42°01'N | 95°22'W |
| Denison, Tx., U.S. | 104 | 33°45'N | 97°02'W |
| Denizli, Tur. (dĕn-ĭz-lē') | 163 | 37°40'N | 29°10'E |
| Denklingen, Ger. (dĕn'klĕn-gĕn) | 171c | 50°54'N | 7°40'E |
| Denmark, S.C., U.S. (dĕn'märk) | 125 | 33°18'N | 81°09'W |
| Denmark, nation, Eur. | 154 | 56°14'N | 8°30'E |
| Denmark Strait, strt., Eur. | 89 | 66°30'N | 27°00'W |
| Dennilton, S. Afr. (dĕn-ĭl-tŭn) | 238c | 25°18'S | 29°13'E |
| Dennison, Oh., U.S. (dĕn'ĭ-sŭn) | 108 | 40°25'N | 81°20'W |
| Denpasar, Indon. | 212 | 8°35'S | 115°10'E |
| Denton, Eng., U.K. (dĕn'tŭn) | 158a | 53°27'N | 2°07'W |
| Denton, Md., U.S. | 109 | 38°55'N | 75°50'W |
| Denton, Tx., U.S. | 121 | 33°12'N | 97°06'W |
| D'Entrecasteaux, Point, c., Austl. (däɴ-tr'-kȧs-tō') | 220 | 34°50'S | 114°45'E |
| D'Entrecasteaux Islands, is., Pap. N. Gui. (däɴ-tr'-kȧs-tō') | 213 | 9°45'S | 152°00'E |
| Denver, Co., U.S. (dĕn'vĕr) | 104 | 39°44'N | 104°59'W |
| Deoli, India | 202 | 25°52'N | 75°23'E |
| De Pere, Wi., U.S. (dē pēr') | 113 | 44°25'N | 88°04'W |
| Depew, N.Y., U.S. (dē-pū') | 111c | 42°55'N | 78°43'W |
| Deping, China (dŭ-pĭŋ) | 206 | 37°28'N | 116°57'E |
| Depue, Il., U.S. (dē pū) | 108 | 41°15'N | 89°55'W |
| De Queen, Ar., U.S. (dē kwēn') | 121 | 34°02'N | 94°21'W |
| De Quincy, La., U.S. (dē kwĭn'sĭ) | 123 | 30°27'N | 93°27'W |
| Dera, Lach, r., Afr. (läk dā'rä) | 238a | 0°45'N | 41°26'E |
| Dera, Lak, r., Afr. | 231 | 0°45'N | 41°30'E |
| Dera Ghāzi Khān, Pak. (dā'rŭ gä-zē' ĸan') | 199 | 30°09'N | 70°39'E |
| Dera Ismāīl Khān, Pak. (dā'rŭ ĭs-mä-ēl' ĸän') | 202 | 31°55'N | 70°51'E |
| Derbent, Russia (dĕr-bĕnt') | 181 | 42°00'N | 48°10'E |
| Derby, Austl. (där'bē) (dûr'bē) | 218 | 17°20'S | 123°40'E |
| Derby, S. Afr. (där'bĭ) | 238c | 25°55'S | 27°02'E |
| Derby, Eng., U.K. (där'bē) | 161 | 52°55'N | 1°29'W |
| Derby, Ct., U.S. (dûr'bē) | 109 | 41°20'N | 73°05'W |
| Derbyshire, co., Eng., U.K. | 158a | 53°11'N | 1°30'W |
| Derdepoort, S. Afr. | 238c | 24°39'S | 26°21'E |
| Derg, Lough, l., Ire. (lŏk dĕrg) | 164 | 53°00'N | 8°09'W |
| De Ridder, La., U.S. (dē rĭd'ĕr) | 123 | 30°50'N | 93°18'W |
| Dermott, Ar., U.S. (dûr'mŏt) | 121 | 33°32'N | 91°24'W |
| Derry, N.H., U.S. (dâr'ĭ) | 101a | 42°53'N | 71°22'W |
| Derventa, Bos. (dĕr'ven-tȧ) | 175 | 44°58'N | 17°58'E |
| Derwent, r., Austl. (dĕr'wĕnt) | 222 | 42°21'S | 146°30'E |
| Derwent, r., Eng., U.K. | 158a | 52°54'N | 1°24'W |
| Des Arc, Ar., U.S. (dāz ärk') | 121 | 34°59'N | 91°31'W |
| Descalvado, Braz. (dĕs-käl-vá-dô) | 141a | 21°55'S | 47°37'W |
| Descartes, Fr. | 170 | 46°58'N | 0°42'E |
| Deschambault Lake, l., Can. | 96 | 54°40'N | 103°35'W |
| Deschênes, Can. | 102c | 45°23'N | 75°47'W |
| Deschenes, Lake, l., Can. | 102c | 45°25'N | 75°53'W |
| Deschutes, r., Or., U.S. (dā-shōōt') | 114 | 44°25'N | 121°21'W |
| Desdemona, Tx., U.S. (dĕz-dē-mō'nȧ) | 122 | 32°16'N | 98°33'W |
| Dese, Eth. | 231 | 11°00'N | 39°51'E |
| Deseado, r., Arg. (dā-sā-ä'dhō) | 144 | 46°50'S | 67°45'W |
| Desirade Island, i., Guad. (dā-zē-räs') | 133b | 16°21'N | 60°51'W |
| De Smet, S.D., U.S. (dē smĕt') | 112 | 44°23'N | 97°33'W |
| Des Moines, Ia., U.S. (dē moin') | 105 | 41°35'N | 93°37'W |
| Des Moines, N.M., U.S. | 120 | 36°42'N | 103°48'W |
| Des Moines, Wa., U.S. | 116a | 46°24'N | 122°20'W |
| Des Moines, r., U.S. | 107 | 42°30'N | 94°20'W |
| Desna, r., Eur. (dyĕs-ná') | 181 | 51°55'N | 31°45'E |
| Desolación, i., Chile (dĕ-sô-lä-syō'n) | 144 | 53°05'S | 74°00'W |
| De Soto, Mo., U.S. (dē sō'tō) | 121 | 38°07'N | 90°32'W |
| Des Peres, Mo., U.S. (dĕs pĕr'ĕs) | 117e | 38°36'N | 90°26'W |
| Des Plaines, Il., U.S. (dĕs plānz') | 111a | 42°02'N | 87°54'W |
| Des Plaines, r., U.S. | 111a | 41°39'N | 87°56'W |
| Dessau, Ger. (dĕsôu) | 161 | 51°50'N | 12°15'E |
| Detmold, Ger. (dĕt'mōld) | 168 | 51°57'N | 8°55'E |
| Detroit, Mi., U.S. (dē-troit') | 105 | 42°22'N | 83°10'W |
| Detroit, Tx., U.S. | 121 | 33°41'N | 95°16'W |
| Detroit Lake, res., Or., U.S. | 114 | 44°42'N | 122°10'W |
| Detroit Lakes, Mn., U.S. (dē-troit'lăkz) | 112 | 46°48'N | 95°51'W |
| Detva, Slvk. (dyĕt'vá) | 169 | 48°32'N | 19°21'E |
| Deurne, Bel. | 159a | 51°13'N | 4°27'E |
| Deutsch Wagram, Aus. | 159e | 48°19'N | 16°34'E |
| Deux-Montagnes, Can. | 102a | 45°33'N | 73°53'W |
| Deux Montagnes, Lac des, l., Can. | 102a | 45°28'N | 74°00'W |
| Deva, Rom. (dā'vä) | 163 | 45°52'N | 22°52'E |
| Dévaványa, Hung. (dā'vô-vän-yô) | 169 | 47°01'N | 20°58'E |
| Develi, Tur. (dĕ'vå-lē) | 181 | 38°20'N | 35°10'E |
| Deventer, Neth. (dĕv'ĕn-tĕr) | 165 | 52°14'N | 6°07'E |
| Devils, r., Tx., U.S. | 122 | 29°55'N | 101°10'W |
| Devils Island *see* Diable, Île du, i., Fr. Gu. | 143 | 5°15'N | 52°40'W |
| Devils Lake, N.D., U.S. | 104 | 48°10'N | 98°55'W |
| Devils Lake, l., N.D., U.S. (dĕv''lz) | 112 | 47°57'N | 99°04'W |
| Devils Lake Indian Reservation, I.R., N.D., U.S. | 112 | 48°08'N | 99°40'W |
| Devils Postpile National Monument, rec., Ca., U.S. | 118 | 37°42'N | 119°12'W |
| Devils Tower National Monument, rec., Wy., U.S. | 115 | 44°38'N | 105°07'W |
| Devoll, r., Alb. | 175 | 40°55'N | 20°10'E |
| Devon, Can. | 102g | 53°23'N | 113°43'W |
| Devon, S. Afr. (dĕv'ŭn) | 238c | 26°23'S | 28°47'E |
| Devonport, Austl. (dĕv'ŭn-pôrt) | 219 | 41°20'S | 146°30'E |
| Devonport, N.Z. | 221a | 36°50'S | 174°45'E |
| Devore, Ca., U.S. (dē-vôr') | 117a | 34°13'N | 117°24'W |
| Dewatto, Wa., U.S. (dē-wät'ô) | 116a | 47°27'N | 123°04'W |
| Dewey, Ok., U.S. (dū'ĭ) | 121 | 36°48'N | 95°55'W |
| De Witt, Ar., U.S. (dē wĭt') | 121 | 34°17'N | 91°22'W |
| De Witt, Ia., U.S. | 113 | 41°46'N | 90°34'W |
| Dewsbury, Eng., U.K. (dūz'bĕr-ĭ) | 158a | 53°42'N | 1°39'W |
| Dexter, Me., U.S. (dĕks'tĕr) | 100 | 45°01'N | 69°19'W |
| Dexter, Mo., U.S. | 121 | 36°46'N | 89°56'W |
| Dezfūl, Iran | 198 | 32°14'N | 48°37'E |
| Dezhnëva, Mys, c., Russia (dyĕzh'nyĭf) | 196 | 68°00'N | 172°00'W |
| Dezhou, China (dŭ-jō) | 208 | 37°28'N | 116°17'E |
| Dhahran *see* Aẓ Ẓahrān, Sau. Ar. | 198 | 26°13'N | 50°00'E |
| Dhaka, Bngl. (dä'kä) (dăk'á) | 199 | 23°45'N | 90°29'E |
| Dharamtar Creek, r., India | 203b | 18°49'N | 72°54'E |
| Dharmavaram, India | 203 | 14°32'N | 77°43'E |
| Dhawalāgiri, mtn., Nepal | 199 | 28°42'N | 83°31'E |
| Dhībān, Jord. | 197a | 31°30'N | 35°46'E |
| Dhidhimótikhon, Grc. | 175 | 41°20'N | 26°27'E |
| Dhule, India | 199 | 20°58'N | 74°43'E |
| Día, i., Grc. (dē'ä) | 174a | 35°27'N | 25°17'E |
| Diable, Île du, i., Fr. Gu. | 143 | 5°15'N | 52°40'W |
| Diablo, Mount, mtn., Ca., U.S. (dyä'blô) | 116b | 37°52'N | 121°55'W |
| Diablo Heights, Pan. (dyá'blō) | 128a | 8°58'N | 79°34'W |
| Diablo Range, mts., Ca., U.S. | 116b | 37°47'N | 121°50'W |
| Diablotins, Morne, mtn., Dom. | 133b | 15°31'N | 61°24'W |


ng-sing; ŋ-baŋk; ɴ-nasalized n; nŏd; cŏmmit; ōld; ôbey; ôrder; oi-boil; fōōd; ȯ-as oo in foot; ou-out; s-soft; sh-dish; th-thin; pūre; ůnite; ûrn; stŭd; circŭs; ü-as in French tu; '-indeterminate vowel.

| PLACE (Pronunciation) | PAGE | LAT. | LONG. |
|---|---|---|---|
| Diaca, Moz. | 237 | 11°30'S | 39°59'E |
| Diaka, r., Mali | 235 | 14°40'N | 5°00'E |
| Diamantina, Braz. | 143 | 18°14'S | 43°32'W |
| Diamantina, r., Austl. (dī'man-tē'nȧ) | 220 | 25°38'S | 139°53'E |
| Diamantino, Braz. (dē-ȧ-män-tē'no) | 143 | 14°22'S | 56°23'W |
| Diamond Peak, mtn., Or., U.S. | 114 | 43°32'N | 122°08'W |
| Diana Bank, bk. (dī'ăn'ȧ) | 135 | 22°30'N | 74°45'W |
| Dianbai, China (dĭěn-bī) | 209 | 21°30'N | 111°20'E |
| Dian Chi, l., China (dĭěn chē) | 204 | 24°58'N | 103°18'E |
| Dickinson, N.D., U.S. (dĭk'ĭn-sŭn) | 104 | 46°52'N | 102°49'W |
| Dickinson, Tx., U.S. (dĭk'ĭn-sŭn) | 123a | 29°28'N | 95°02'W |
| Dickinson Bayou, Tx., U.S. | 123a | 29°26'N | 95°08'W |
| Dickson, Tn., U.S. (dĭk'sŭn) | 124 | 36°03'N | 87°24'W |
| Dickson City, Pa., U.S. | 109 | 41°25'N | 75°40'W |
| Didcot, Eng., U.K. (dĭd'cŏt) | 158b | 51°35'N | 1°15'W |
| Didiéni, Mali | 234 | 13°53'N | 8°06'W |
| Die, Fr. (dē) | 171 | 44°45'N | 5°22'E |
| Diefenbaker, res., Can. | 92 | 51°20'N | 108°10'W |
| Diego de Ocampo, Pico, mtn., Dom. Rep. (pē'-kô-dyě'gô-dě-ŏ-kä'm-pô) | 135 | 19°40'N | 70°45'W |
| Diego Ramirez, Islas, is., Chile (dě ä'gō rä-mē'räz) | 144 | 56°15'S | 70°15'W |
| Diéma, Mali | 234 | 14°32'N | 9°12'W |
| Dien Bien Phu, Viet. | 204 | 21°38'N | 102°49'E |
| Dieppe, Can. (dē-ĕp') | 100 | 46°06'N | 64°45'W |
| Dieppe, Fr. | 161 | 49°54'N | 1°05'E |
| Dierks, Ar., U.S. (dērks) | 121 | 34°06'N | 94°02'W |
| Diessen, Ger. (dēs'sĕn) | 159d | 47°57'N | 11°06'E |
| Diest, Bel. | 159a | 50°59'N | 5°05'E |
| Digby, Can. (dĭg'bĭ) | 91 | 44°37'N | 65°46'W |
| Dighton, Ma., U.S. (dī-tŭn) | 110b | 41°49'N | 71°05'W |
| Digne, Fr. (dēn'y') | 171 | 44°07'N | 6°16'E |
| Digoin, Fr. (dē-gwăn') | 170 | 46°28'N | 4°06'E |
| Digul, r., Indon. | 213 | 7°00'S | 140°27'E |
| Dijohan Point, c., Phil. (dē-kô-än) | 213a | 16°24'N | 122°25'E |
| Dijon, Fr. (dē-zhôn') | 154 | 47°21'N | 5°02'E |
| Dikson, Russia (dĭk'sŏn) | 178 | 73°30'N | 80°35'E |
| Dikwa, Nig. (dē'kwȧ) | 231 | 12°06'N | 13°53'E |
| Dili, E. Timor (dĭl'ē) | 213 | 8°35'S | 125°35'E |
| Di Linosa Island, i., Italy (dē-lē-nô'sä) | 162 | 36°01'N | 12°43'E |
| Dilizhan, Arm. | 181 | 40°45'N | 45°00'E |
| Dillingham, Ak., U.S. (dĭl'ĭng-hăm) | 106a | 59°10'N | 158°38'W |
| Dillon, Mt., U.S. (dĭl'ŭn) | 115 | 45°12'N | 112°40'W |
| Dillon, S.C., U.S. | 125 | 34°24'N | 79°28'W |
| Dillon Reservoir, res., Oh., U.S. | 108 | 40°05'N | 82°05'W |
| Dilolo, D.R.C. (dē-lō'lō) | 232 | 10°19'S | 22°23'E |
| Dimashq *see* Damascus, Syria | 198 | 33°31'N | 36°18'E |
| Dimbokro, C. Iv. | 234 | 6°39'N | 4°42'W |
| Dimitrovo *see* Pernik, Blg. | 163 | 42°36'N | 23°04'E |
| Dimlang, mtn., Nig. | 235 | 8°24'N | 11°47'E |
| Dimona, Isr. | 197a | 31°03'N | 35°01'E |
| Dinagat Island, i., Phil. | 213 | 10°15'N | 126°15'E |
| Dinājpur, Bngl. | 202 | 25°38'N | 87°39'E |
| Dinan, Fr. (dē-näN') | 170 | 48°27'N | 2°03'W |
| Dinant, Bel. (dē-näN') | 165 | 50°17'N | 4°50'E |
| Dinara, mts., Serb. (dē'nä-rä) | 163 | 43°50'N | 16°15'E |
| Dinard, Fr. | 170 | 48°38'N | 2°04'W |
| Dindigul, India | 203 | 10°25'N | 78°03'E |
| Dingalan Bay, b., Phil. (dĭŋ-gä'län) | 213a | 15°19'N | 121°33'E |
| Dingle, Ire. (dĭng''l) | 164 | 52°10'N | 10°13'W |
| Dingle Bay, b., Ire. | 161 | 52°02'N | 10°15'W |
| Dingo, Austl. (dĭŋ'gō) | 219 | 23°45'S | 149°26'E |
| Dinguiraye, Gui. | 234 | 11°18'N | 10°43'W |
| Dingwall, Scot., U.K. (dĭng'wôl) | 164 | 57°37'N | 4°23'W |
| Dingxian, China (dĭŋ shyĕn) | 208 | 38°30'N | 115°00'E |
| Dingxing, China (dĭŋ-shyĭŋ) | 208 | 39°18'N | 115°50'E |
| Dingyuan, China (dĭŋ-yủän) | 206 | 32°32'N | 117°40'E |
| Dingzi Wan, b., China | 206 | 36°33'N | 121°06'E |
| Dinosaur National Monument, rec., Co., U.S. (dī'nô-sôr) | 115 | 40°45'N | 109°17'W |
| Dinslaken, Ger. (dēns'lä-kĕn) | 171c | 51°33'N | 6°44'E |
| Dinteloord, Neth. | 159a | 51°38'N | 4°21'E |
| Dinuba, Ca., U.S. (dĭ-nū'bȧ) | 118 | 36°33'N | 119°29'W |
| Dios, Cayo de, i., Cuba (kä'yō-dě-dē-ōs') | 134 | 22°05'N | 83°05'W |
| Diourbel, Sen. (dē-ōōr-bĕl') | 230 | 14°40'N | 16°15'W |
| Diphu Pass, p., Asia (dĭ-pōō) | 204 | 28°15'N | 96°45'E |
| Diquis, r., C.R. (dē-kēs') | 133 | 8°59'N | 83°24'W |
| Dire Dawa, Eth. | 231 | 9°40'N | 41°47'E |
| Diriamba, Nic. (dēr-yäm'bä) | 132 | 11°52'N | 86°15'W |
| Dirk Hartog, i., Austl. | 220 | 26°25'S | 113°15'E |
| Dirksland, Neth. | 159a | 51°45'N | 4°04'E |
| Dirranbandi, Austl. (dĭ-rȧ-băn'dē) | 219 | 28°24'S | 148°29'E |
| Dirty Devil, r., Ut., U.S. (dûr'tĭ dĕv''l) | 119 | 38°20'N | 110°30'W |
| Disappointment, l., Austl. | 220 | 23°20'S | 123°00'E |
| Disappointment, Cape, c., Wa., U.S. (dĭs'ȧ-point'ment) | 116c | 46°16'N | 124°11'W |
| Discovery, S. Afr. (dĭs-kŭv'ēr-ĭ) | 233b | 26°10'S | 27°53'E |
| Discovery, is., Can. (dĭs-kŭv'ēr-ē) | 116a | 48°25'N | 123°13'W |
| Disko, i., Grnld. (dĭs'kō) | 89 | 70°00'N | 54°00'W |
| Disna, Bela. (dēs'nȧ) | 180 | 55°34'N | 28°15'E |
| Dispur, India | 202 | 26°00'N | 91°50'E |
| Disraëli, Can. (dĭs-rä'lĭ) | 99 | 45°53'N | 71°23'W |
| District of Columbia, dept., U.S. | 105 | 38°50'N | 77°00'W |
| Distrito Federal, dept., Braz. (dēs-trē'tô-fĕ-dĕ-rä'l) | 143 | 15°49'S | 47°39'W |
| Distrito Federal, dept., Mex. | 130 | 19°14'N | 99°08'W |
| Disūq, Egypt (dē-sōōk') | 238b | 31°07'N | 30°41'E |
| Diu, India (dē'ōō) | 199 | 20°48'N | 70°58'E |
| Divilacan Bay, b., Phil. (dē-vē-lä'kän) | 213a | 17°26'N | 122°25'E |
| Divinópolis, Braz. (dē-vē-nô'pō-lēs) | 143 | 20°10'S | 44°53'W |
| Divo, C. Iv. | 234 | 5°50'N | 5°22'W |
| Dixon, Il., U.S. (dĭks'ŭn) | 113 | 41°50'N | 89°30'W |

| PLACE (Pronunciation) | PAGE | LAT. | LONG. |
|---|---|---|---|
| Dixon Entrance, strt., N.A. | 92 | 54°25'N | 132°00'W |
| Diyarbakir, Tur. (dē-yär-bĕk'ĭr) | 198 | 38°00'N | 40°10'E |
| Dja, r., Afr. | 231 | 2°30'N | 14°00'E |
| Djambala, Congo | 236 | 2°33'S | 14°45'E |
| Djanet, Alg. | 230 | 24°29'N | 9°26'E |
| Djebobo, mtn., Ghana | 234 | 8°20'N | 0°37'E |
| Djedi, Oued, r., Alg. | 162 | 34°18'N | 4°39'E |
| Djember, Chad | 235 | 10°25'N | 17°50'E |
| Djerba, Île de, i., Tun. | 162 | 33°53'N | 11°26'E |
| Djerid, Chott, l., Tun. (jĕr'ĭd) | 230 | 33°15'N | 8°29'E |
| Djibasso, Burkina | 234 | 13°07'N | 4°10'W |
| Djibo, Burkina | 234 | 14°06'N | 1°38'W |
| Djibouti, Dji. (jē-bōō-tē') | 238a | 11°34'N | 43°00'E |
| Djibouti, nation, Afr. | 238a | 11°35'N | 48°08'E |
| Djokoumatombi, Congo | 236 | 0°47'N | 15°22'E |
| Djokupunda, D.R.C. | 232 | 5°27'S | 20°58'E |
| Djoua, r., Afr. | 236 | 1°25'N | 13°40'E |
| Djursholm, Swe. (djōōrs'hōlm) | 166 | 59°26'N | 18°01'E |
| Dmitriyev-L'govskiy, Russia (d'mē'trĭ-yĕf l'gôf'skĭ) | 176 | 52°07'N | 35°05'E |
| Dmitrov, Russia (d'mē'trôf) | 176 | 56°21'N | 37°32'E |
| Dmitrovsk, Russia (d'mē'trôfsk) | 176 | 52°30'N | 35°10'E |
| Dmytrivka, Ukr. | 177 | 47°57'N | 38°56'E |
| Dnepropetrovsk *see* Dnipropetrovs'k, Ukr. | 178 | 48°15'N | 34°08'E |
| Dnieper (Dnipro), r., Eur. | 181 | 46°45'N | 33°40'E |
| Dniester, r., Eur. | 181 | 48°21'N | 28°10'E |
| Dniprodzerzhyns'k, Ukr. | 181 | 48°32'N | 34°38'E |
| Dniprodzerzhyns'ke vodoskhovyshche, res., Ukr. | 178 | 49°00'N | 34°10'E |
| Dnipropetrovs'k, Ukr. | 178 | 48°15'N | 34°08'E |
| Dnipropetrovs'k, prov., Ukr. | 177 | 48°15'N | 34°10'E |
| Dniprovs'kyi lyman, b., Ukr. | 177 | 46°33'N | 31°45'E |
| Dnistrovs'kyi lyman, l., Ukr. | 177 | 46°13'N | 29°50'E |
| Dno, Russia (d'nô') | 176 | 57°49'N | 29°59'E |
| Do, Lac, l., Mali | 234 | 15°50'N | 2°20'W |
| Doba, Chad | 235 | 8°39'N | 16°51'E |
| Dobbs Ferry, N.Y., U.S. (dŏbz fĕ'rē) | 110a | 41°01'N | 73°53'W |
| Dobbyn, Austl. (dôb'ĭn) | 218 | 19°45'S | 140°02'E |
| Dobele, Lat. (dô'bĕ-lĕ) | 167 | 56°37'N | 23°18'E |
| Doberai, Jazirah, pen., Indon. | 213 | 1°25'S | 133°15'E |
| Dobo, Indon. | 213 | 6°00'S | 134°18'E |
| Doboj, Bos. (dō'boi) | 175 | 44°42'N | 18°04'E |
| Dobrich, Blg. | 163 | 43°33'N | 27°52'E |
| Dobryanka, Russia (dôb-ryän'kȧ) | 186a | 58°27'N | 56°26'E |
| Dobšina, Slvk. (dôp'shē-nä) | 169 | 48°48'N | 20°25'E |
| Doce, r., Braz. (dō'sā) | 143 | 19°01'S | 42°14'W |
| Doce, Canal Numero, can., Arg. | 141c | 36°47'S | 59°00'W |
| Doce Leguas, Cayos de las, is., Cuba | 134 | 20°55'N | 79°05'W |
| Doctor Arroyo, Mex. (dōk-tōr' är-rō'yō) | 130 | 23°41'N | 100°10'W |
| Doddington, Eng., U.K. (dŏd'dĭng-tŏn) | 158b | 51°17'N | 0°47'E |
| Dodecanese *see* Dodekanisoy, is., Grc. | 175 | 38°00'N | 26°10'E |
| Dodekanisoy (Dodecanese), is., Grc. | 175 | 38°00'N | 26°10'E |
| Dodge City, Ks., U.S. (dŏj) | 104 | 37°44'N | 100°01'W |
| Dodgeville, Wi., U.S. (dŏj'vĭl) | 113 | 42°58'N | 90°07'W |
| Dodoma, Tan. (dō'dô-mȧ) | 232 | 6°11'S | 35°45'E |
| Dog, l., Can. (dŏg) | 98 | 48°42'N | 89°24'W |
| Dogger Bank, bk. (dŏg'gēr) | 165 | 55°07'N | 2°25'E |
| Dogubayazit, Tur. | 181 | 39°35'N | 44°00'E |
| Doha *see* Ad Dawhah, Qatar | 198 | 25°02'N | 51°28'E |
| Dohad, India | 202 | 22°52'N | 74°18'E |
| Dokshytsy, Bela. (dôk-shētsĕ) | 176 | 54°53'N | 27°49'E |
| Dolbeau, Can. | 91 | 48°52'N | 72°16'W |
| Dole, Fr. (dōl) | 161 | 47°07'N | 5°28'E |
| Dolgaya, Kosa, c., Russia (kô'sȧ dôl-gä'yä) | 177 | 46°42'N | 37°42'E |
| Dolgeville, N.Y., U.S. | 109 | 43°10'N | 74°45'W |
| Dolgiy, i., Russia | 180 | 69°20'N | 59°20'E |
| Dolgoprudnyy, Russia | 186b | 55°57'N | 37°33'E |
| Dolinsk, Russia (dȧ-lēnsk') | 185 | 47°29'N | 142°31'E |
| Dollar Harbor, b., Bah. | 134 | 25°30'N | 79°15'W |
| Dolomite, Al., U.S. (dŏl'ô-mīt) | 110h | 33°28'N | 86°57'W |
| Dolomiti, mts., Italy | 174 | 46°16'N | 11°43'E |
| Dolores, Arg. (dô-lō'rĕs) | 144 | 36°20'S | 57°42'W |
| Dolores, Col. | 142a | 3°33'N | 74°54'W |
| Dolores, Ur. | 141c | 33°32'S | 58°15'W |
| Dolores, Tx., U.S. (dô-lō'rĕs) | 122 | 27°42'N | 99°47'W |
| Dolores, r., Co., U.S. | 119 | 38°35'N | 108°50'W |
| Dolores Hidalgo, Mex. (dô-lô'rĕs-ē-däl'gō) | 130 | 21°09'N | 100°56'W |
| Dolphin and Union Strait, strt., Can. (dŏl'fĭn ūn'yŭn) | 92 | 69°22'N | 117°10'W |
| Dolyna, Ukr. | 169 | 48°57'N | 24°01'E |
| Domažlice, Czech Rep. (dō'mäzh-lē-tsĕ) | 168 | 49°27'N | 12°55'E |
| Dombasle-sur-Meurthe, Fr. (dôN-bäl') | 171 | 48°38'N | 6°18'E |
| Dombóvár, Hung. (dŏm'bō-vär) | 169 | 46°22'N | 18°08'E |
| Domeyko, Cordillera, mts., Chile (kôr-dēl-yĕ'rä-dô-mā'kô) | 142 | 20°50'S | 69°02'W |
| Dominica, nation, N.A. (dŏ-mĭ-nē'kȧ) | 129 | 15°30'N | 60°45'W |
| Dominica Channel, strt., N.A. | 133b | 15°00'N | 61°30'W |
| Dominican Republic, nation, N.A. (dô-mĭn'ĭ-kăn) | 129 | 19°00'N | 70°45'W |
| Dominion, Can. (dô-mĭn'yŭn) | 101 | 46°13'N | 60°01'W |
| Domiongo, D.R.C. | 236 | 4°37'S | 21°15'E |
| Domodedovo, Russia (dô-mô-dyĕ'do-vô) | 186b | 55°27'N | 37°45'E |
| Dom Silvério, Braz. (doN-sēl-vĕ'ryō) | 141a | 20°09'S | 42°57'W |
| Don, r., Russia | 178 | 49°50'N | 41°30'E |
| Don, r., Eng., U.K. | 158a | 53°39'N | 0°58'W |
| Don, r., Scot., U.K. | 164 | 57°19'N | 2°39'W |
| Donaldson, Mi., U.S. (dŏn'ăl-sŭn) | 117k | 46°19'N | 84°22'W |

| PLACE (Pronunciation) | PAGE | LAT. | LONG. |
|---|---|---|---|
| Donaldsonville, La., U.S. (dŏn'ăld-sŭn-vĭl) | 123 | 30°05'N | 90°58'W |
| Donalsonville, Ga., U.S. | 124 | 31°02'N | 84°50'W |
| Donawitz, Aus. (dō'nȧ-vĭts) | 168 | 47°23'N | 15°05'E |
| Don Benito, Spain (dōn'bå-nē'tō) | 172 | 38°55'N | 5°52'W |
| Doncaster, Austl. (doŋ'kăs-tēr) | 217a | 37°47'S | 145°08'E |
| Doncaster, Eng., U.K. (doŋ'kăs-tēr) | 164 | 53°32'N | 1°07'W |
| Doncaster, co., Eng., U.K. | 158a | 53°35'N | 1°10'W |
| Dondo, Ang. (dōn'dō) | 232 | 9°38'S | 14°25'E |
| Dondo, Moz. | 232 | 19°33'S | 34°47'E |
| Dondra Head, c., Sri L. | 203 | 5°52'N | 80°52'E |
| Donegal, Ire. (dŏn-ē-gôl') | 164 | 54°44'N | 8°05'W |
| Donegal Bay, Ire. (dŏn-ĕ-gôl') | 160 | 54°35'N | 8°36'W |
| Donets Coal Basin, reg., Ukr. (dō-nyĕts') | 177 | 48°15'N | 38°50'E |
| Donets'k, Ukr. | 178 | 48°00'N | 37°35'E |
| Donets'k, prov., Ukr. | 177 | 47°55'N | 37°40'E |
| Dong, r., China (dôŋ) | 205 | 24°13'N | 115°08'E |
| Dongara, Austl. (dôn-gă'rȧ) | 218 | 29°15'S | 115°00'E |
| Dongba, China (dôŋ-bä) | 206 | 31°40'N | 119°02'E |
| Dong'e, China (dôŋ-ŭ) | 206 | 36°21'N | 116°14'E |
| Dong'ezhen, China | 208 | 36°11'N | 116°16'E |
| Dongfang, China (dôŋ-fäŋ) | 209 | 19°08'N | 108°42'E |
| Donggala, Indon. (dôn-gä'lä) | 212 | 0°45'S | 119°32'E |
| Dongguan, China (dôŋ-gůän) | 207a | 23°03'N | 113°46'E |
| Dongguang, China (dôŋ-gůäŋ) | 206 | 37°54'N | 116°33'E |
| Donghai, China (dôŋ-hī) | 208 | 34°35'N | 119°05'E |
| Dong Hoi, Viet. (dông-hô-ĕ') | 212 | 17°25'N | 106°42'E |
| Dongila, Eth. | 231 | 11°17'N | 37°00'E |
| Dongming, China (dôŋ-mĭŋ) | 206 | 35°16'N | 115°06'E |
| Dongo, Ang. (dôŋ'gō) | 232 | 14°45'S | 15°30'E |
| Dongon Point, c., Phil. (dŏng-ôn') | 213a | 12°43'N | 120°35'E |
| Dongou, Congo (dôŋ-gōō') | 231 | 2°02'N | 18°04'E |
| Dongping, China (dôŋ-pĭŋ) | 208 | 35°50'N | 116°24'E |
| Dongping Hu, l., China (dôŋ-pĭŋ hōō) | 206 | 36°06'N | 116°24'E |
| Dongshan, China (doŋ-shän) | 206 | 31°05'N | 120°24'E |
| Dongtai, China | 206 | 32°51'N | 120°20'E |
| Dongting Hu, l., China (dôŋ-tĭŋ hōō) | 205 | 29°10'N | 112°30'E |
| Dongxiang, China (dôŋ-shyän) | 209 | 28°18'N | 116°38'E |
| Doniphan, Mo., U.S. (dŏn'ĭ-făn) | 121 | 36°37'N | 90°50'W |
| Donji Vakuf, Bos. (dōn'yĭ väk'ōōf) | 175 | 44°08'N | 17°25'E |
| Don Martin, Presa de, res., Mex. (prĕ'sä-dĕ-dôn-mär-tē'n) | 122 | 27°35'N | 100°38'W |
| Donnacona, Can. | 99 | 46°40'N | 71°46'W |
| Donnemarie-en-Montois, Fr. (dôn-mä-rē'ĕN-môN-twä') | 171b | 48°29'N | 3°09'E |
| Donner und Blitzen, r., Or., U.S. (dŏn'ēr ȯnt'blĭ'tsĕn) | 114 | 42°45'N | 118°57'W |
| Donnybrook, S. Afr. (dŏ-nĭ-brŏk) | 233c | 29°56'S | 29°54'E |
| Donora, Pa., U.S. (dŏ-nō'rȧ) | 111e | 40°10'N | 79°51'W |
| Donostia-San Sebastián, Spain | 154 | 43°19'N | 1°59'W |
| Donoússa, i., Grc. | 175 | 37°09'N | 25°53'E |
| Doolow, Som. | 238a | 4°10'N | 42°05'E |
| Doonerak, Mount, mtn., Ak., U.S. (dōō'nē-răk) | 103 | 68°00'N | 150°34'W |
| Doorn, Neth. | 159a | 52°02'N | 5°21'E |
| Door Peninsula, pen., Wi., U.S. (dōr) | 113 | 44°40'N | 87°36'W |
| Dora Baltea, r., Italy (dō'rä bäl'tā-ä) | 174 | 45°40'N | 7°34'E |
| Doraville, Ga., U.S. (dō'rȧ-vĭl) | 110c | 33°54'N | 84°17'W |
| Dorchester, Eng., U.K. (dôr'chĕs-tēr) | 164 | 50°45'N | 2°34'W |
| Dordogne, r., Fr. (dôr-dôn'yĕ) | 156 | 44°53'N | 0°16'E |
| Dordrecht, Neth. (dôr'drĕkt) | 165 | 51°48'N | 4°39'E |
| Dordrecht, S. Afr. (dô'drĕkt) | 233c | 31°24'S | 27°06'E |
| Doré Lake, l., Can. | 96 | 54°31'N | 107°06'W |
| Dorgali, Italy (dôr'gä-lē) | 174 | 40°18'N | 9°37'E |
| Dörgön Nuur, l., Mong. | 204 | 47°47'N | 94°01'E |
| Dorion-Vaudreuil, Can. (dôr-yō) | 102a | 45°23'N | 74°01'W |
| Dorking, Eng., U.K. (dôr'kĭng) | 158b | 51°12'N | 0°20'W |
| Dormont, Pa., U.S. (dôr'mŏnt) | 111e | 40°24'N | 80°02'W |
| Dornbirn, Aus. (dŏrn'bĕrn) | 168 | 47°24'N | 9°45'E |
| Dornoch, Scot., U.K. (dôr'nŏK) | 160 | 57°55'N | 4°01'W |
| Dornoch Firth, b., Scot., U.K. (dôr'nŏK fûrth) | 164 | 57°55'N | 3°55'W |
| Dorogobuzh, Russia (dôrôgô'-bōō'zh) | 176 | 54°57'N | 33°18'E |
| Dorohoi, Rom. (dō-rô-hoi') | 169 | 47°57'N | 26°28'E |
| Dorre Island, i., Austl. (dôr) | 220 | 25°19'S | 113°10'E |
| Dorstsen, Ger. | 171c | 51°40'N | 6°58'E |
| Dortmund, Ger. (dôrt'mȯnt) | 161 | 51°31'N | 7°28'E |
| Dortmund-Ems-Kanal, can., Ger. (dôrt'mōōnd-ĕms'kä-näl') | 171c | 51°50'N | 7°25'E |
| Dörtyol, Tur. (dûrt'yōl) | 163 | 36°50'N | 36°20'E |
| Dorval, Can. (dôr-vàl') | 102a | 45°26'N | 73°44'W |
| Dos Bahías, Cabo, c., Arg. (kȧ'bô-dôs-bä-ē'äs) | 144 | 44°55'S | 65°35'W |
| Dos Caminos, Ven. (dôs-kä-mē'nôs) | 143b | 9°38'N | 67°17'W |
| Dosewallips, r., Wa., U.S. (dō'sē-wäl'lĭps) | 116a | 47°45'N | 123°04'W |
| Dos Hermanas, Spain (dōsĕr-mä'näs) | 172 | 37°17'N | 5°56'W |
| Dosso, Niger (dôs-ō') | 230 | 13°03'N | 3°12'E |
| Dothan, Al., U.S. (dō'thăn) | 105 | 31°13'N | 85°23'W |
| Douai, Fr. (dōō-å') | 161 | 50°23'N | 3°04'E |
| Douala, Cam. (dōō-ä'lä) | 230 | 4°03'N | 9°42'E |
| Douarnenez, Fr. (dōō-är-nē-nĕs') | 170 | 48°06'N | 4°18'W |
| Double Bayou, Tx., U.S. (dŭb''l bī'yōō) | 123a | 29°40'N | 94°38'W |
| Doubs, r., Eur. | 171 | 46°15'N | 5°50'E |
| Douentza, Mali | 234 | 15°00'N | 2°57'W |
| Douglas, I. of Man (dŭg'lăs) | 164 | 54°10'N | 4°24'W |
| Douglas, Ak., U.S. (dŭg'lăs) | 103 | 58°18'N | 134°35'W |
| Douglas, Az., U.S. | 104 | 31°20'N | 109°30'W |
| Douglas, Ga., U.S. | 125 | 31°30'N | 82°53'W |
| Douglas, Wy., U.S. (dŭg'lăs) | 115 | 42°45'N | 105°21'W |
| Douglas, r., Eng., U.K. (dŭg'lăs) | 158a | 53°38'N | 2°48'W |


ăt; finăl; rāte; senāte; ärm; åsk; sofȧ; fâre; ch-choose; dh-as th in other; bē; ēvent; bĕt; recĕnt; cratēr; g-gō; gh-guttural g; bĭt; ĭ-short neutral; rīde; K-guttural k as ch in German ich;

PRONOUNCING INDEX

Douglas Channel – East Cleveland 289


| PLACE (Pronunciation) | PAGE | LAT. | LONG. |
|---|---|---|---|
| Douglas Channel, strt., Can. | 94 | 53°30'N | 129°12'W |
| Douglas Lake, res., Tn., U.S. (dŭg'lăs) | 124 | 36°00'N | 83°35'W |
| Douglas Lake Indian Reserve, I.R., Can. | 95 | 50°10'N | 120°49'W |
| Douglasville, Ga., U.S. (dŭg'lăs-vĭl) | 124 | 33°45'N | 84°47'W |
| Dourada, Serra, mts., Braz. (sĕ'r-rä-dôōō-rá'dă) | 143 | 15°11'S | 49°57'W |
| Dourdan, Fr. (dōōr-däN') | 171b | 48°32'N | 2°01'E |
| Douro, r., Port. (dô'ò-rò) | 172 | 41°03'N | 8°12'W |
| Dove, r., Eng., U.K. (dŭv) | 158a | 52°53'N | 1°47'W |
| Dover, S. Afr. | 238c | 27°05'S | 27°44'E |
| Dover, Eng., U.K. | 154 | 51°08'N | 1°19'E |
| Dover, De., U.S. (dō vẽr) | 105 | 39°10'N | 75°30'W |
| Dover, N.H., U.S. | 109 | 43°15'N | 71°00'W |
| Dover, N.J., U.S. | 110a | 40°53'N | 74°33'W |
| Dover, Oh., U.S. | 108 | 40°35'N | 81°30'W |
| Dover, Strait of, strt., Eur. | 156 | 50°50'N | 1°15'W |
| Dover-Foxcroft, Me., U.S. (dō'vẽr fôks'krôft) | 100 | 45°10'N | 69°15'W |
| Dovre Fjell, mts., Nor. (dŏv'rĕ fyĕl') | 156 | 62°03'N | 8°36'E |
| Dow, Il., U.S. (dou) | 117e | 39°01'N | 90°20'W |
| Dowagiac, Mi., U.S. (dò-wô'jăk) | 108 | 42°00'N | 86°05'W |
| Downers Grove, Il., U.S. (dou'nẽrz grōv) | 111a | 41°48'N | 88°00'W |
| Downey, Ca., U.S. (dou'nĭ) | 117a | 33°56'N | 118°08'W |
| Downieville, Ca., U.S. (dou'nĭ-nĭl) | 118 | 39°35'N | 120°48'W |
| Downs, Ks., U.S. (dounz) | 120 | 39°29'N | 98°32'W |
| Doylestown, Oh., U.S. (doilz'toun) | 111d | 40°58'N | 81°43'W |
| Drâa, Cap, c., Mor. (drá) | 230 | 28°39'N | 12°15'W |
| Drâa, Oued, r., Afr. | 230 | 28°00'N | 9°31'W |
| Drabiv, Ukr. | 177 | 49°57'N | 32°14'E |
| Drac, r., Fr. (dräk) | 171 | 44°50'N | 5°47'E |
| Dracut, Ma., U.S. (dră'kŭt) | 101a | 42°40'N | 71°19'W |
| Draganovo, Blg. (drä-gä-nō'vô) | 175 | 43°13'N | 25°45'E |
| Drăgăşani, Rom. (drä-gá-shän'ĭ) | 175 | 44°39'N | 24°18'E |
| Draguignan, Fr. (drä-gēn-yäN') | 171 | 43°35'N | 6°28'E |
| Drahichyn, Bela. | 169 | 52°10'N | 25°11'E |
| Drakensberg, mts., Afr. (drä'kĕnz-bĕrgh) | 232 | 29°15'S | 29°07'E |
| Drake Passage, strt. (drāk păs'ĭj) | 139 | 57°00'S | 65°00'W |
| Dráma, Grc. (drä'mä) | 163 | 41°09'N | 24°10'E |
| Drammen, Nor. (dräm'ĕn) | 160 | 59°45'N | 10°15'E |
| Drau (Drava), r., Eur. (drou) | 168 | 46°44'N | 13°45'E |
| Drava, r., Eur. (drä'vä) | 156 | 45°45'N | 17°30'E |
| Dravograd, Slvn. (drä'vô-gräd') | 174 | 46°37'N | 15°01'E |
| Drawsko Pomorskie, Pol. (dräv'skō pō-mōr'skyĕ) | 168 | 53°31'N | 15°50'E |
| Drayton Harbor, b., Wa., U.S. (drā'tŭn) | 116d | 48°58'N | 122°40'W |
| Drayton Plains, Mi., U.S. | 111b | 42°41'N | 83°23'W |
| Drayton Valley, Can. | 95 | 53°13'N | 114°59'W |
| Drensteinfurt, Ger. (drĕn'shtīn-fōōrt) | 171c | 51°47'N | 7°44'E |
| Dresden, Ger. (drās'dĕn) | 154 | 51°05'N | 13°45'E |
| Dreux, Fr. (drû) | 170 | 48°44'N | 1°24'E |
| Driefontein, S. Afr. | 238c | 25°53'S | 29°10'E |
| Drin, r., Alb. (drēn) | 175 | 42°13'N | 20°13'E |
| Drina, r., Serb. (drē'nä) | 163 | 44°09'N | 19°30'E |
| Drinit, Pellg i, b., Alb. | 175 | 41°42'N | 19°17'E |
| Dr. Ir. W. J. van Blommestein Meer, res., Sur. | 143 | 4°45'N | 55°05'W |
| Drissa, r., Eur. | 176 | 55°44'N | 28°58'E |
| Driver, Va., U.S. | 110g | 36°50'N | 76°30'W |
| Dröbak, Nor. (drû'bäk) | 166 | 59°40'N | 10°35'E |
| Drobeta-Turnu Severin, Rom. | 163 | 43°54'N | 24°49'E |
| Drogheda, Ire. (drŏ'hē-dȧ) | 160 | 53°43'N | 6°15'W |
| Drohobych, Ukr. | 169 | 49°21'N | 23°31'E |
| Drôme, r., Fr. (drōm) | 170 | 44°42'N | 4°53'E |
| Dronfield, Eng., U.K. (drŏn'fēld) | 158a | 53°18'N | 1°28'W |
| Drumheller, Can. (drŭm-hĕl-ẽr) | 90 | 51°28'N | 112°42'W |
| Drummond, i., Mi., U.S. (drŭm'ŭnd) | 108 | 46°00'N | 83°50'W |
| Drummondville, Can. (drŭm'ŭnd-vĭl) | 91 | 45°53'N | 72°33'W |
| Drumright, Ok., U.S. (drŭm'rīt) | 121 | 35°59'N | 96°37'W |
| Drunen, Neth. | 159a | 51°41'N | 5°10'E |
| Drut', r., Bela. (drōōt) | 176 | 53°40'N | 29°45'E |
| Druya, Bela. (drò'yȧ) | 176 | 55°45'N | 27°26'E |
| Drwęca, r., Pol. (d'r-văn'tsȧ) | 169 | 53°06'N | 19°13'E |
| Dryden, Can. (drī-dĕn) | 91 | 49°47'N | 92°50'W |
| Drysdale, Austl. | 217a | 38°11'S | 144°34'E |
| Dry Tortugas, is., Fl., U.S. (tôr-tōō'gäz) | 125a | 24°37'N | 82°45'W |
| Dry Tortugas National Park, rec., Fl., U.S. | 125a | 24°42'N | 83°02'W |
| Dschang, Cam. (dshäng) | 230 | 5°34'N | 10°09'E |
| Duabo, Lib. | 234 | 5°40'N | 8°05'W |
| Duagh, Can. | 102g | 53°43'N | 113°24'W |
| Duarte, Pico, mtn., Dom. Rep. (dĭŭ'ärtĕh pēcô) | 129 | 19°00'N | 71°00'W |
| Duas Barras, Braz. (dōō'äs-bä'r-räs) | 141a | 22°03'S | 42°30'W |
| Dubai *see* Dubayy, U.A.E. | 198 | 25°18'N | 55°26'E |
| Dubăsari, Mol. | 177 | 47°16'N | 29°11'E |
| Dubawnt, l., Can. (dōō-bônt') | 92 | 63°27'N | 103°30'W |
| Dubawnt, r., Can. | 92 | 61°30'N | 103°49'W |
| Dubayy, U.A.E. | 198 | 25°18'N | 55°26'E |
| Dubbo, Austl. (dŭb'ō) | 219 | 32°20'S | 148°42'E |
| Dubie, D.R.C. | 237 | 8°33'S | 28°32'E |
| Dublin, Ire. | 154 | 53°20'N | 6°15'W |
| Dublin, Ca., U.S. (dŭb'lĭn) | 116b | 37°42'N | 121°56'W |
| Dublin, Ga., U.S. | 125 | 32°33'N | 82°55'W |
| Dublin, Tx., U.S. | 122 | 32°05'N | 98°20'W |
| Dubna, Russia | 176 | 56°44'N | 37°10'E |
| Dubno, Ukr. (dōō'b-nô) | 169 | 50°24'N | 25°44'E |
| Du Bois, Pa., U.S. (dò-bois') | 109 | 41°10'N | 78°45'W |
| Dubovka, Russia (dò-bôf'kȧ) | 181 | 49°00'N | 44°50'E |
| Dubrovka, Russia (dōō-brôf'kȧ) | 186c | 59°51'N | 30°56'E |

| PLACE (Pronunciation) | PAGE | LAT. | LONG. |
|---|---|---|---|
| Dubrovnik, Cro. (dò'brôv-nĕk) (rä-gōō'sä) | 154 | 42°40'N | 18°10'E |
| Dubrowna, Bela. | 176 | 54°39'N | 30°54'E |
| Dubuque, Ia., U.S. (dò-būk') | 105 | 42°30'N | 90°43'W |
| Duchesne, Ut., U.S. (dò-shān') | 119 | 40°12'N | 110°23'W |
| Duchesne, r., Ut., U.S. | 119 | 40°20'N | 110°50'W |
| Duchess, Austl. (dŭch'ĕs) | 218 | 21°30'S | 139°55'E |
| Ducie Island, i., Pit. (dü-sē') | 2 | 25°30'S | 126°20'W |
| Duck, r., Tn., U.S. | 124 | 35°55'N | 87°40'W |
| Duckabush, r., Wa., U.S. (dŭk'ȧ-bòsh) | 116a | 47°41'N | 123°09'W |
| Duck Lake, Can. | 96 | 52°47'N | 106°13'W |
| Duck Mountain, mtn., Can. | 97 | 51°35'N | 101°00'W |
| Ducktown, Tn., U.S. (dŭk'toun) | 124 | 35°03'N | 84°20'W |
| Duck Valley Indian Reservation, I.R., Id., U.S. | 114 | 42°02'N | 115°49'W |
| Duckwater Peak, mtn., Nv., U.S. (dŭk-wô-tẽr) | 118 | 39°00'N | 115°31'W |
| Duda, r., Col. (dōō'dä) | 142a | 3°25'N | 74°23'W |
| Dudinka, Russia (dōō-dĭn'kȧ) | 178 | 69°15'N | 85°42'E |
| Dudley, Eng., U.K. (dŭd'lĭ) | 161 | 52°28'N | 2°07'E |
| Duero, r., Eur. | 156 | 41°30'N | 4°30'W |
| Dufourspitze, mtn., Eur. | 168 | 45°55'N | 7°52'E |
| Dugger, In., U.S. (dŭg'ẽr) | 108 | 39°00'N | 87°10'W |
| Dugi Otok, i., Serb. (dōō'gē o'tòk) | 174 | 44°03'N | 14°40'E |
| Duisburg, Ger. (dōō'ĭs-bòrgh) | 161 | 51°26'N | 6°46'E |
| Dukhān, Qatar | 201 | 25°25'N | 50°48'E |
| Dukhovshchina, Russia (dōō-kôfsh-'chē̆nȧ) | 176 | 55°13'N | 32°26'E |
| Dukinfield, Eng., U.K. (dŭk'ĭn-fēld) | 158a | 53°28'N | 2°05'W |
| Dukla Pass, p., Eur. (dò'klä) | 161 | 49°25'N | 21°44'E |
| Dulce, Golfo, b., C.R. (gōl'fō dōōl'sä) | 129 | 8°25'N | 83°13'W |
| Dülken, Ger. (dül'kĕn) | 171c | 51°15'N | 6°21'E |
| Dülmen, Ger. (dül'mĕn) | 171c | 51°50'N | 7°17'E |
| Duluth, Mn., U.S. (dò-lōōth') | 105 | 46°50'N | 92°07'W |
| Dumai, Indon. | 197b | 1°39'N | 101°30'E |
| Dumali Point, c., Phil. (dōō-mä'lē) | 213a | 13°07'N | 121°42'E |
| Dumas, Tx., U.S. | 120 | 35°52'N | 101°58'W |
| Dumbarton, Scot., U.K. (dŭm'bär-tŭn) | 164 | 56°00'N | 4°35'W |
| Dum-Dum, India | 202a | 22°37'N | 88°25'E |
| Dumfries, Scot., U.K. (dŭm-frēs') | 164 | 55°05'N | 3°40'W |
| Dumjor, India | 202a | 22°37'N | 88°14'E |
| Dumont, N.J., U.S. (dōō'mŏnt) | 110a | 40°56'N | 74°00'W |
| Dumyāt, Egypt | 231 | 31°22'N | 31°50'E |
| Dunaföldvär, Hung. (dò'nô-fûld'vär) | 169 | 46°48'N | 18°55'E |
| Dunaïvtsi, Ukr. | 177 | 48°52'N | 26°51'E |
| Dunajec, r., Pol. (dò-nä'yĕts) | 169 | 49°52'N | 20°53'E |
| Dunaújváros, Hung. | 169 | 46°57'N | 18°55'E |
| Dunay, Russia (dōō'nĭ) | 186c | 59°59'N | 30°57'E |
| Dunbar, W.V., U.S. | 108 | 38°20'N | 81°45'W |
| Duncan, Can. (dŭŋ'kăn) | 90 | 48°47'N | 123°42'W |
| Duncan, Ok., U.S. | 121 | 34°29'N | 97°56'W |
| Duncan, r., Can. | 95 | 50°30'N | 116°45'W |
| Duncan Dam, dam, Can. | 95 | 50°15'N | 116°55'W |
| Duncan Lake, l., Can. | 95 | 50°20'N | 117°00'W |
| Duncansby Head, c., Scot., U.K. (dŭn'kănz-bĭ) | 164 | 58°40'N | 3°01'W |
| Duncanville, Tx., U.S. (dŭn'kăn-vĭl) | 117c | 32°39'N | 96°55'W |
| Dundalk, Ire. (dŭn'kôk) | 160 | 54°00'N | 6°18'W |
| Dundalk, Md., U.S. | 110e | 39°16'N | 76°31'W |
| Dundalk Bay, b., Ire. (dŭn'dôk) | 164 | 53°55'N | 6°15'W |
| Dundas, Can. (dŭn-dăs') | 99 | 43°16'N | 79°58'W |
| Dundas, l., Austl. (dŭn-dăs) | 220 | 32°15'S | 122°00'E |
| Dundas Island, i., Can. | 94 | 54°33'N | 130°55'W |
| Dundas Strait, strt., Austl. | 220 | 10°35'S | 131°15'E |
| Dundedin, Fl., U.S. (dŭn-ē'dĭn) | 125a | 28°00'N | 82°43'W |
| Dundee, S. Afr. | 233c | 28°14'S | 30°16'E |
| Dundee, Scot., U.K. | 154 | 56°30'N | 2°55'W |
| Dundee, Il., U.S. (dŭn-dē) | 111a | 42°06'N | 88°17'W |
| Dundrum Bay, b., N. Ire., U.K. (dŭn-drŭm') | 164 | 54°13'N | 5°47'W |
| Dunedin, N.Z. | 221a | 45°48'S | 170°32'E |
| Dunellen, N.J., U.S. (dŭn-ĕl'l'n) | 110a | 40°36'N | 74°28'W |
| Dunfermline, Scot., U.K. (dŭn-fẽrm'lĭn) | 164 | 56°05'N | 3°30'W |
| Dungarvan, Ire. (dŭn-gär'vă̆n) | 164 | 52°06'N | 7°50'W |
| Dungeness, Wa., U.S. (dŭnj-nĕs') | 116a | 48°09'N | 123°07'W |
| Dungeness, r., Wa., U.S. | 116a | 48°03'N | 123°10'W |
| Dungeness Spit, Wa., U.S. | 116a | 48°11'N | 123°03'W |
| Dunhua, China (dòn-hwä) | 205 | 43°18'N | 128°10'E |
| Dunkerque, Fr. (dŭn-kĕrk') | 161 | 51°02'N | 2°37'E |
| Dunkirk, In., U.S. (dŭn'kûrk) | 108 | 40°20'N | 85°25'W |
| Dunkwa, Ghana | 234 | 5°22'N | 1°12'W |
| Dun Laoghaire, Ire. (dŭn-lā'rĕ) | 160 | 53°16'N | 6°09'W |
| Dunlap, Ia., U.S. (dŭn'lăp) | 112 | 41°53'N | 95°33'W |
| Dunlap, Tn., U.S. | 124 | 35°23'N | 85°23'W |
| Dunmore, Pa., U.S. (dŭn'mōr) | 109 | 41°25'N | 75°30'W |
| Dunn, N.C., U.S. (dŭn) | 125 | 35°18'N | 78°37'W |
| Dunnellon, Fl., U.S. (dŭn-ĕl'ŏn) | 125 | 29°02'N | 82°28'W |
| Dunnville, Can. (dŭn'vĭl) | 99 | 42°55'N | 79°40'W |
| Dunqulah, Sudan | 231 | 19°21'N | 30°19'E |
| Dunsmuir, Ca., U.S. (dŭnz'mūr) | 114 | 41°08'N | 122°17'W |
| Dunwoody, Ga., U.S. (dŭn-wòd'ĭ) | 110c | 33°57'N | 84°20'W |
| Duolun, China (dwô-lōōn) | 205 | 42°12'N | 116°15'E |
| Du Page, r., Il., U.S. (dōō pāj) | 111a | 41°41'N | 88°11'W |
| Du Page, East Branch, r., Il., U.S. | 111a | 41°42'N | 88°09'W |
| Du Page, West Branch, r., Il., U.S. | 111a | 41°42'N | 88°09'W |
| Dupax, Phil. (dōō'päks) | 213a | 16°16'N | 121°06'E |
| Dupo, Il., U.S. (dū'pō) | 117e | 38°31'N | 90°12'W |
| Duque de Caxias, Braz. (dōō'kĕ-dĕ-kȧ'shyás) | 141a | 22°46'S | 43°18'W |
| Duquesne, Pa., U.S. (dò-kān') | 111e | 40°22'N | 79°51'W |
| Du Quoin, Il., U.S. (dò-kwoin') | 121 | 38°01'N | 89°14'W |
| Durance, r., Fr. (dü-räNs') | 161 | 43°46'N | 5°52'E |

| PLACE (Pronunciation) | PAGE | LAT. | LONG. |
|---|---|---|---|
| Durand, Mi., U.S. (dů-rănd') | 108 | 42°50'N | 84°00'W |
| Durand, Wi., U.S. | 113 | 44°37'N | 91°58'W |
| Durango, Mex. (dōō-rä'n-gô) | 128 | 24°02'N | 104°42'W |
| Durango, Co., U.S. (dò-răŋ'gō) | 119 | 37°15'N | 107°55'W |
| Durango, state, Mex. | 128 | 25°00'N | 106°00'W |
| Durant, Ms., U.S. (dů-rănt') | 124 | 33°05'N | 89°50'W |
| Durant, Ok., U.S. | 121 | 33°59'N | 96°23'W |
| Duratón, r., Spain (dōō-rä-tōn') | 172 | 41°30'N | 3°55'W |
| Durazno, Ur. (dōō-räz'nō) | 144 | 33°21'S | 56°31'W |
| Durazno, dept., Ur. | 141c | 33°00'S | 56°35'W |
| Durban, S. Afr. (dûr'băn) | 232 | 29°48'S | 31°00'E |
| Durbanville, S. Afr. (dûr-băn'vĭl) | 232a | 33°50'S | 18°39'E |
| Durbe, Lat. (dōōr'bĕ) | 167 | 56°36'N | 21°24'E |
| Đurđevac, Cro. | 163 | 46°03'N | 17°03'E |
| Düren, Ger. (dü'rĕn) | 171c | 50°48'N | 6°30'E |
| Durham, Eng., U.K. (dûr'ăm) | 164 | 54°47'N | 1°46'W |
| Durham, N.C., U.S. | 105 | 36°00'N | 78°55'W |
| Durham Downs, Austl. | 222 | 27°30'S | 141°55'E |
| Durrës, Alb. (dòr'ĕs) | 154 | 41°19'N | 19°27'E |
| Duryea, Pa., U.S. (dōōr-yā') | 109 | 41°20'N | 75°50'W |
| Dushan, China | 206 | 31°38'N | 116°16'E |
| Dushan, China (dōō-shän) | 209 | 25°50'N | 107°42'E |
| Dushanbe, Taj. | 183 | 38°30'N | 68°45'E |
| Düsseldorf, Ger. (düs'ĕl-dôrf) | 161 | 51°14'N | 6°47'E |
| Dussen, Neth. | 159a | 51°43'N | 4°58'E |
| Dutalan Ula, mts., Mong. | 208 | 49°25'N | 112°40'E |
| Dutch Harbor, Ak., U.S. (dŭch här'bẽr) | 106a | 53°58'N | 166°30'W |
| Duvall, Wa., U.S. (dōō'vâl) | 116a | 47°44'N | 121°59'W |
| Duwamish, r., Wa., U.S. (dōō-wăm'ĭsh) | 116a | 47°24'N | 122°18'W |
| Duyun, China (dōō-yòn) | 204 | 26°18'N | 107°40'E |
| Dvinskaya Guba, b., Russia | 180 | 65°10'N | 38°40'E |
| Dwārka, India | 202 | 22°18'N | 68°59'E |
| Dwight, Il., U.S. (dwīt) | 108 | 41°00'N | 88°20'W |
| Dworshak Res, Id., U.S. | 114 | 46°45'N | 115°50'W |
| Dyat'kovo, Russia (dyät'kō-vō) | 176 | 53°36'N | 34°19'E |
| Dyer, In., U.S. (dī'ẽr) | 111a | 41°30'N | 87°31'W |
| Dyersburg, Tn., U.S. (dī'ẽrz-bûrg) | 124 | 36°02'N | 89°23'W |
| Dyersville, Ia., U.S. (dī'ẽrz-vĭl) | 113 | 42°28'N | 91°09'W |
| Dyes Inlet, Wa., U.S. (dīz) | 116a | 47°37'N | 122°45'W |
| Dykhtau, Gora, mtn., Russia | 182 | 43°03'N | 43°08'E |
| Dyment, Can. (dī'mĕnt) | 97 | 49°37'N | 92°19'W |
| Dzamïn Üüd, Mong. | 205 | 44°38'N | 111°32'E |
| Dzaoudzi, May. (dzou'dzĭ) | 233 | 12°44'S | 45°15'E |
| Dzavhan, r., Mong. | 204 | 48°19'N | 94°08'E |
| Dzerzhinsk, Russia | 180 | 56°20'N | 43°50'E |
| Dzerzhyns'k, Ukr. | 177 | 48°26'N | 37°50'E |
| Dzhalal-Abad, Kyrg. (jȧ-läl'ȧ-bät') | 183 | 40°56'N | 73°00'E |
| Dzhambul *see* Zhambyl, Kaz. | 183 | 42°51'N | 71°29'E |
| Dzhankoi, Ukr. | 181 | 45°43'N | 34°22'E |
| Dzhizak, Uzb. (dzhĕ'zäk) | 183 | 40°13'N | 67°58'E |
| Dzhugdzhur Khrebet, mts., Russia (jòg-jōōr') | 179 | 56°15'N | 137°00'E |
| Działoszyce, Pol. (jyä-wō-shē'tsĕ) | 169 | 50°21'N | 20°22'E |
| Dzibalchén, Mex. (zē-bäl-chĕ'n) | 132a | 19°25'N | 89°39'W |
| Dzidzantún, Mex. (zēd-zän-tōō'n) | 132a | 21°18'N | 89°00'W |
| Dzierżoniów, Pol. (dzyĕr-zhôn'yŭf) | 168 | 50°44'N | 16°38'E |
| Dzilam González, Mex. (zē-lä'm-gôn-zä'lĕz) | 132a | 21°21'N | 88°53'W |
| Dzitás, Mex. (zē-tá's) | 132a | 20°47'N | 88°32'W |
| Dzungaria, reg., China (dzòŋ-gä'rĭ-ȧ) | 204 | 44°39'N | 86°13'E |
| Dzungarian Gate, p., Asia | 204 | 45°00'N | 88°00'E |
| Dzyarzhynsk, Bela. | 176 | 53°41'N | 27°14'E |


# E


| PLACE (Pronunciation) | PAGE | LAT. | LONG. |
|---|---|---|---|
| Eagle, W.V., U.S. | 108 | 38°10'N | 81°20'W |
| Eagle, r., Co., U.S. | 119 | 39°32'N | 106°28'W |
| Eaglecliff, Wa., U.S. (ē'gl-klĭf) | 116c | 46°10'N | 123°13'W |
| Eagle Creek, r., In., U.S. | 111g | 39°54'N | 86°17'W |
| Eagle Grove, Ia., U.S. | 113 | 42°39'N | 93°55'W |
| Eagle Lake, Me., U.S. | 100 | 47°03'N | 68°38'W |
| Eagle Lake, Tx., U.S. | 123 | 29°37'N | 96°20'W |
| Eagle Lake, l., Ca., U.S. | 114 | 40°45'N | 120°52'W |
| Eagle Mountain, Ca., U.S. | 118 | 33°49'N | 115°27'W |
| Eagle Mountain L, Tx., U.S. | 117c | 32°56'N | 97°27'W |
| Eagle Pass, Tx., U.S. | 104 | 28°49'N | 100°30'W |
| Eagle Pk, Ca., U.S. | 114 | 41°18'N | 120°11'W |
| Ealing, Eng., U.K. (ē'lĭng) | 158b | 51°29'N | 0°19'W |
| Earle, Ar., U.S. (ûrl) | 121 | 35°14'N | 90°28'W |
| Earlington, Ky., U.S. (ûr'lĭng-tŭn) | 124 | 37°15'N | 87°31'W |
| Easley, S.C., U.S. (ēz'lĭ) | 125 | 34°48'N | 82°37'W |
| East, Mount, mtn., Pan. | 128a | 9°09'N | 79°46'W |
| East Alton, Il., U.S. (ôl'tŭn) | 117e | 38°53'N | 90°08'W |
| East Angus, Can. (ăŋ'gŭs) | 99 | 45°35'N | 71°40'W |
| East Aurora, N.Y., U.S. (ô-rō'rȧ) | 111c | 42°46'N | 78°38'W |
| East Bay, b., Tx., U.S. | 123a | 29°30'N | 94°41'W |
| East Bernstadt, Ky., U.S. (bûrn'stát) | 124 | 37°09'N | 84°08'W |
| Eastbourne, Eng., U.K. (ēst'bôrn) | 165 | 50°48'N | 0°16'E |
| East Caicos, i., T./C. Is. (kī'kōs) | 135 | 21°40'N | 71°35'W |
| East Cape, c., N.Z. | 221a | 37°37'S | 178°33'E |
| East Cape *see* Dezhnëva, Mys, c., Russia | 196 | 68°00'N | 172°00'W |
| East Carondelet, Il., U.S. (kȧ-rŏn'dĕ-lĕt) | 117e | 38°33'N | 90°14'W |
| East Cherokee Indian Reservation, I.R., N.C., U.S. | 124 | 35°33'N | 83°12'W |
| East Chicago, In., U.S. (shĭ-kô'gō) | 111a | 41°39'N | 87°29'W |
| East China Sea, sea, Asia | 205 | 30°28'N | 125°52'E |
| East Cleveland, Oh., U.S. (klēv'lănd) | 111d | 41°33'N | 81°35'W |

290 East Cote Blanche Bay – Ellice Islands
PRONOUNCING INDEX


| PLACE (Pronunciation) | PAGE | LAT. | LONG. |
|---|---|---|---|
| East Cote Blanche Bay, b., La., U.S. (kōt blänsh´) | 123 | 29°30'N | 92°07'W |
| East Des Moines, r., Ia., U.S. (dē moin´) | 113 | 42°57'N | 94°17'W |
| East Detroit, Mi., U.S. (dē-troit´) | 111b | 42°28'N | 82°57'W |
| Easter Island *see* Pascua, Isla de, i., Chile | 241 | 26°50'S | 109°00'W |
| Eastern Ghāts, mts., India | 199 | 13°50'N | 78°45'E |
| Eastern Turkestan, hist. reg., China (tòr-kĕ-stän´)(tûr-kĕ-stăn´) | 204 | 39°40'N | 78°20'E |
| East Grand Forks, Mn., U.S. (grănd fôrks) | 112 | 47°56'N | 97°02'W |
| East Greenwich, R.I., U.S. (grĭn´ĭj) | 110b | 41°40'N | 71°27'W |
| Easthampton, Ma., U.S. (ēst-hămp´tŭn) | 109 | 42°15'N | 72°45'W |
| East Hartford, Ct., U.S. (härt´fērd) | 109 | 41°45'N | 72°35'W |
| East Helena, Mt., U.S. (hĕ-hē´nȧ) | 115 | 46°31'N | 111°50'W |
| East Ilsley, Eng., U.K. (ĭl´slē) | 158b | 51°30'N | 1°18'W |
| East Jordan, Mi., U.S. (jôr´dăn) | 108 | 45°05'N | 85°05'W |
| East Kansas City, Mo., U.S. (kăn´zȧs) | 117f | 39°09'N | 94°30'W |
| Eastland, Tx., U.S. (ēst´lănd) | 122 | 32°24'N | 98°47'W |
| East Lansing, Mi., U.S. (lăn´sĭng) | 108 | 42°45'N | 84°30'W |
| Eastlawn, Mi., U.S. | 111b | 42°15'N | 83°35'W |
| East Leavenworth, Mo., U.S. (lĕv´ĕn-wûrth) | 117f | 39°18'N | 94°50'W |
| East Liverpool, Oh., U.S. (lĭv´ēr-pōōl) | 108 | 40°40'N | 80°35'W |
| East London, S. Afr. (lŭn´dŭn) | 232 | 33°02'S | 27°54'E |
| East Los Angeles, Ca., U.S. (lōs ăŋ´hå-lās) | 117a | 34°01'N | 118°09'W |
| Eastmain, r., Can. (ēst´mān) | 93 | 52°12'N | 73°19'W |
| Eastman, Ga., U.S. (ēst´măn) | 124 | 32°10'N | 83°11'W |
| East Millstone, N.J., U.S. (mĭl´stōn) | 110a | 40°30'N | 74°35'W |
| East Moline, Il., U.S. (mō-lēn´) | 113 | 41°31'N | 90°28'W |
| East Nishnabotna, r., Ia., U.S. (nĭsh-nȧ-bŏt´nȧ) | 112 | 40°53'N | 95°23'W |
| Easton, Md., U.S. (ēs´tŭn) | 109 | 38°45'N | 76°05'W |
| Easton, Pa., U.S. | 109 | 40°45'N | 75°15'W |
| Easton L, Ct., U.S. | 110a | 41°18'N | 73°17'W |
| East Orange, N.J., U.S. (ŏr´ĕnj) | 110a | 40°46'N | 74°12'W |
| East Pakistan *see* Bangladesh, nation, Asia | 199 | 24°15'N | 90°00'E |
| East Palo Alto, Ca., U.S. | 116b | 37°27'N | 122°07'W |
| East Peoria, Il., U.S. (pē-ō´rĭ-ȧ) | 108 | 40°40'N | 89°30'W |
| East Pittsburgh, Pa., U.S. (pĭts´bûrg) | 111e | 40°24'N | 79°50'W |
| East Point, Ga., U.S. | 110c | 33°41'N | 84°27'W |
| Eastport, Me., U.S. (ēst´pōrt) | 100 | 44°53'N | 67°01'W |
| East Providence, R.I., U.S. (prŏv´ĭ-dĕns) | 110b | 41°49'N | 71°22'W |
| East Retford, Eng., U.K. (rĕt´fērd) | 158a | 53°19'N | 0°56'W |
| East Riding of Yorkshire, co., Eng., U.K. | 158a | 53°45'N | 0°40'W |
| East Rochester, N.Y., U.S. (rŏch´ĕs-tēr) | 109 | 43°10'N | 77°30'W |
| East Saint Louis, Il., U.S. | 105 | 38°38'N | 90°10'W |
| East Siberian Sea, sea, Russia (sī-bĭr´y´n) | 179 | 73°00'N | 153°28'E |
| Eastsound, Wa., U.S. (ēst-sound) | 116d | 48°42'N | 122°42'W |
| East Stroudsburg, Pa., U.S. (stroudz´bûrg) | 109 | 41°00'N | 75°10'W |
| East Syracuse, N.Y., U.S. (sĭr´ȧ-kūs) | 109 | 43°05'N | 76°00'W |
| East Tavaputs Plateau, plat., Ut., U.S. (tă-vă´-pŭts) | 119 | 39°25'N | 109°45'W |
| East Tawas, Mi., U.S. (tô´wȧs) | 108 | 44°15'N | 83°30'W |
| East Timor, nation, Asia | 213 | 9°00'S | 125°30'E |
| East Walker, r., U.S. (wôk´ēr) | 118 | 38°36'N | 119°02'W |
| Eaton, Co., U.S. (ē´tŭn) | 120 | 40°31'N | 104°42'W |
| Eaton, Oh., U.S. | 108 | 39°45'N | 84°40'W |
| Eaton Estates, Oh., U.S. | 111d | 41°19'N | 82°01'W |
| Eaton Rapids, Mi., U.S. (răp´ĭdz) | 108 | 42°30'N | 84°40'W |
| Eatonton, Ga., U.S. (ē´tŭn-tŭn) | 124 | 33°20'N | 83°24'W |
| Eatontown, N.J., U.S. (ē´tŭn-toun) | 110a | 40°18'N | 74°04'W |
| Eau Claire, Wi., U.S. (ō klâr´) | 105 | 44°47'N | 91°32'W |
| Ebeltoft, Den. (ĕ´bĕl-tŭft) | 166 | 56°11'N | 10°39'E |
| Ebensburg, Pa., U.S. (ĕ´bĕnz-bûrg) | 109 | 40°29'N | 78°44'W |
| Ebersberg, Ger. (ĕ´bĕrs-bĕrgh) | 159d | 48°05'N | 11°58'E |
| Ebingen, Ger. (ā´bĭng-ĕn) | 168 | 48°13'N | 9°04'E |
| Eboli, Italy (ĕb´ō-lē) | 174 | 40°38'N | 15°04'E |
| Ebolowa, Cam. | 230 | 2°54'N | 11°09'E |
| Ebreichsdorf, Aus. | 159e | 47°58'N | 16°24'E |
| Ebrié, Lagune, b., C. Iv. | 234 | 5°20'N | 4°50'W |
| Ebro, r., Spain (ā´brō) | 156 | 42°00'N | 2°00'W |
| Eccles, Eng., U.K. (ĕk´'lz) | 158a | 53°29'N | 2°20'W |
| Eccles, W.V., U.S. | 108 | 37°45'N | 81°10'W |
| Eccleshall, Eng., U.K. | 158a | 52°51'N | 2°15'W |
| Eceabat, Tur. | 175 | 40°10'N | 26°21'E |
| Echague, Phil. (ā-chä´gwä) | 213a | 16°43'N | 121°40'E |
| Echandi, Cerro, mtn., N.A. (sĕ´r-rō-ĕ-chä´nd) | 133 | 9°05'N | 82°51'W |
| Ech Cheliff, Alg. | 230 | 36°14'N | 1°32'E |
| Echimamish, r., Can. | 97 | 54°15'N | 97°30'W |
| Echmiadzin, Arm. | 182 | 40°10'N | 44°18'E |
| Echo Bay, Can. (ĕk´ō) | 117k | 46°29'N | 84°04'W |
| Echoing, r., Can. (ĕk´ō-ĭng) | 97 | 55°15'N | 91°30'W |
| Echternach, Lux. (ĕk´tēr-näk) | 171 | 49°48'N | 6°25'E |
| Echuca, Austl. (ē-chōō´kȧ) | 219 | 36°10'S | 144°47'E |
| Ecija, Spain (ā´thē-hä) | 162 | 37°20'N | 5°07'W |
| Eckernförde, Ger. | 168 | 54°27'N | 9°51'E |
| Eclipse, Va., U.S. (ē-klĭps´) | 110g | 36°55'N | 76°29'W |
| Ecorse, Mi., U.S. (ē-kôrs´) | 111b | 42°15'N | 83°09'W |
| Ecuador, nation, S.A. (ĕk´wȧ-dôr) | 142 | 0°00'N | 78°30'W |
| Ed, Erit. | 231 | 13°57'N | 41°37'E |
| Eddyville, Ky., U.S. (ĕd´ĭ-vĭl) | 124 | 37°03'N | 88°03'W |
| Ede, Nig. | 235 | 7°44'N | 4°27'E |
| Edéa, Cam. (ĕ-dā´ä) | 230 | 3°48'N | 10°08'E |

| PLACE (Pronunciation) | PAGE | LAT. | LONG. |
|---|---|---|---|
| Eden, Tx., U.S. | 122 | 31°13'N | 99°51'W |
| Eden, Ut., U.S. | 117b | 41°18'N | 111°49'W |
| Eden, r., Eng., U.K. (ē´dĕn) | 164 | 54°40'N | 2°35'W |
| Edenbridge, Eng., U.K. (ē´dĕn-brĭj) | 158b | 51°11'N | 0°05'E |
| Edenham, Eng., U.K. (ē´d'n-ăm) | 158a | 52°46'N | 0°25'W |
| Eden Prairie, Mn., U.S. (prâr´ĭ) | 117g | 44°51'N | 93°29'W |
| Edenton, N.C., U.S. (ē´dĕn-tŭn) | 125 | 36°02'N | 76°37'W |
| Edenton, Oh., U.S. | 111f | 39°14'N | 84°02'W |
| Edenvale, S. Afr. (ēd´ĕn-vāl) | 233b | 26°09'S | 28°10'E |
| Edenville, S. Afr. (ē´d'n-vĭl) | 238c | 27°33'S | 27°42'E |
| Eder, r., Ger. (ā´dēr) | 168 | 51°05'N | 8°52'E |
| Édessa, Grc. | 163 | 40°48'N | 22°04'E |
| Edgefield, S.C., U.S. (ĕj´fēld) | 125 | 33°52'N | 81°55'W |
| Edgeley, N.D., U.S. (ĕj´lĭ) | 112 | 46°24'N | 98°43'W |
| Edgemont, S.D., U.S. (ĕj´mŏnt) | 112 | 43°19'N | 103°50'W |
| Edgerton, Wi., U.S. (ĕj´ēr-tŭn) | 113 | 42°49'N | 89°06'W |
| Edgewater, Al., U.S. (ĕj-wô-tēr) | 110h | 33°31'N | 86°52'W |
| Edgewater, Md., U.S. | 110e | 38°58'N | 76°35'W |
| Edgewood, Can. (ĕj´wŏŏd) | 95 | 49°47'N | 118°08'W |
| Edina, Mn., U.S. (ē-dī´nȧ) | 117g | 44°55'N | 93°20'W |
| Edina, Mo., U.S. | 121 | 40°10'N | 92°11'W |
| Edinburg, In., U.S. (ĕd´'n-bûrg) | 108 | 39°20'N | 85°55'W |
| Edinburg, Tx., U.S. | 122 | 26°18'N | 98°08'W |
| Edinburgh, Scot., U.K. (ĕd´'n-bŭr-ō) | 154 | 55°57'N | 3°10'W |
| Edirne, Tur. | 175 | 41°41'N | 26°35'E |
| Edisto, r., S.C., U.S. (ĕd´ĭs-tō) | 125 | 33°10'N | 80°50'W |
| Edisto, North Fork, r., S.C., U.S. | 125 | 33°42'N | 81°24'W |
| Edisto, South Fork, r., S.C., U.S. | 125 | 33°43'N | 81°35'W |
| Edisto Island, S.C., U.S. | 125 | 32°32'N | 80°20'W |
| Edmond, Ok., U.S. (ĕd´mŭnd) | 121 | 35°39'N | 97°29'W |
| Edmonds, Wa., U.S. (ĕd´mŭndz) | 116a | 47°49'N | 122°23'W |
| Edmonton, Can. | 90 | 53°33'N | 113°28'W |
| Edmundston, Can. (ĕd´mŭn-stŭn) | 91 | 47°22'N | 68°20'W |
| Edna, Tx., U.S. (ĕd´nȧ) | 123 | 28°59'N | 96°39'W |
| Edremit, Tur. (ĕd-rĕ-mēt´) | 163 | 39°35'N | 27°00'E |
| Edremit Körfezi, b., Tur. | 175 | 39°28'N | 26°35'E |
| Edson, Can. (ĕd´sŭn) | 90 | 53°35'N | 116°26'W |
| Edward, i., Can. (ĕd´wērd) | 98 | 48°21'N | 88°29'W |
| Edward, l., Afr. | 232 | 0°25'S | 29°40'E |
| Edwardsville, Il., U.S. (ĕd´wērdz-vĭl) | 117e | 38°49'N | 89°58'W |
| Edwardsville, In., U.S. | 111h | 38°17'N | 85°53'W |
| Edwardsville, Ks., U.S. | 117f | 39°04'N | 94°49'W |
| Eel, r., Ca., U.S. (ēl) | 114 | 40°39'N | 124°15'W |
| Eel, r., In., U.S. | 108 | 40°50'N | 85°55'W |
| Efate, i., Vanuatu (å-fä´tä) | 221 | 18°02'S | 168°29'E |
| Effigy Mounds National Monument, rec., Ia., U.S. (ĕf´ĭ-jŭ mounds) | 113 | 43°04'N | 91°15'W |
| Effingham, Il., U.S. (ĕf´ĭng-hăm) | 108 | 39°05'N | 88°30'W |
| Ega, r., Spain (ā´gä) | 172 | 42°40'N | 2°20'W |
| Egadi, Isole, is., Italy (ĕ´sō-lĕ-ĕ´gä-dē) | 162 | 38°01'N | 12°00'E |
| Egegik, Ak., U.S. (ĕg´ĕ-jĭt) | 103 | 58°10'N | 157°22'W |
| Eger, Hung. (ĕ gĕr) | 169 | 47°53'N | 20°24'E |
| Egersund, Nor. (ĕ´ghĕr-sòn´) | 160 | 58°29'N | 6°01'E |
| Egg Harbor, N.J., U.S. (ĕg här´bēr) | 109 | 39°30'N | 74°35'W |
| Egham, Eng., U.K. (ĕg´ŭm) | 158b | 51°24'N | 0°33'W |
| Egiyn, r., Mong. | 204 | 49°41'N | 100°40'E |
| Egmont, Cape, c., N.Z. (ĕg´mŏnt) | 221a | 39°18'S | 173°49'E |
| Egypt, nation, Afr. (ē´jĭpt) | 231 | 26°58'N | 27°01'E |
| Eha-Amufu, Nig. | 235 | 6°40'N | 7°46'E |
| Eibar, Spain (ā´ē-bär) | 172 | 43°12'N | 2°20'W |
| Eichstätt, Ger. (īk´shtät) | 168 | 48°54'N | 11°14'E |
| Eichwalde, Ger. (īk´väl-dĕ) | 159b | 52°22'N | 13°37'E |
| Eidfjord, Nor. (ĕĭd´fyôr) | 166 | 60°28'N | 7°04'E |
| Eidsvoll, Nor. (ĭdhs´vôl) | 160 | 60°19'N | 11°15'E |
| Eifel, mts., Ger. (ī´fĕl) | 168 | 50°08'N | 6°30'E |
| Eighty Mile Beach, cst., Austl. | 220 | 19°00'S | 121°00'E |
| Eilenburg, Ger. (ī´lĕn-bòrgh) | 168 | 51°27'N | 12°38'E |
| Einbeck, Ger. (īn´bĕk) | 168 | 51°49'N | 9°52'E |
| Eindhoven, Neth. (īnd´hō-vĕn) | 165 | 51°29'N | 5°20'E |
| Eisenach, Ger. (ī´zĕn-äĸ) | 161 | 50°58'N | 10°18'E |
| Eisenhüttenstadt, Ger. | 168 | 52°08'N | 14°40'E |
| Eivissa, Spain | 173 | 38°55'N | 1°24'E |
| Eivissa, i., Spain | 156 | 38°55'N | 1°24'E |
| Ejea de los Caballeros, Spain | 172 | 42°07'N | 1°05'W |
| Ejura, Ghana | 234 | 7°23'N | 1°22'W |
| Ejutla de Crespo, Mex. (å-hōōt´lä dā kräs´pō) | 131 | 16°34'N | 96°44'W |
| Ekanga, D.R.C. | 236 | 2°23'S | 23°14'E |
| Ekenäs, Fin. (ĕ´kĕ-nâs) | 167 | 59°59'N | 23°25'E |
| Ekeren, Bel. | 159a | 51°17'N | 4°27'E |
| Ekoli, D.R.C. | 236 | 0°23'S | 24°16'E |
| El Aaiún, W. Sah. | 230 | 26°45'N | 13°15'W |
| El Affroun, Alg. (ĕl ȧf-froun´) | 173 | 36°28'N | 2°38'E |
| Elands, r., S. Afr. (ēlănds) | 233c | 31°48'S | 26°09'E |
| Elands, r., S. Afr. | 238c | 25°11'S | 28°52'E |
| El Arahal, Spain (ĕl ä-rä-äl´) | 172 | 37°17'N | 5°32'W |
| El Arba, Alg. | 173 | 36°35'N | 3°10'E |
| Elat, Isr. | 198 | 29°34'N | 34°57'E |
| Elazığ, Tur. (ĕl-ä´zĕz) | 198 | 38°40'N | 39°00'E |
| Elba, Al., U.S. (ĕl´bȧ) | 124 | 31°25'N | 86°01'W |
| Elba, Isola d', i., Italy (ē-sō lä-d-ĕl´bȧ) | 162 | 42°42'N | 10°25'E |
| El Banco, Col. (ĕl băn´cō) | 142 | 8°58'N | 74°01'W |
| Elbansan, Alb. (ĕl-bä-sän´) | 163 | 41°08'N | 20°05'E |
| Elbe (Labe), r., Eur. (ĕl´bĕ)(lä´bĕ) | 156 | 52°30'N | 11°30'E |
| Elbert, Mount, mtn., Co., U.S. (ĕl´bērt) | 106 | 39°05'N | 106°25'W |
| Elberton, Ga., U.S. (ĕl´bēr-tŭn) | 125 | 34°05'N | 82°53'W |
| Elbeuf, Fr. (ĕl-bûf´) | 161 | 49°16'N | 0°59'E |
| El Beyadh, Alg. | 162 | 33°42'N | 1°06'E |
| Elbistan, Tur. (ĕl-bē-stän´) | 163 | 38°20'N | 37°10'E |
| Elblag, Pol. (ĕl´blăng) | 160 | 54°11'N | 19°25'E |
| El Bonillo, Spain (ĕl bō-nēl´yō) | 172 | 38°56'N | 2°31'W |
| El Boulaïda, Alg. | 230 | 36°33'N | 2°45'E |
| Elbow, r., Can. (ĕl´bō) | 102e | 51°03'N | 114°24'W |

| PLACE (Pronunciation) | PAGE | LAT. | LONG. |
|---|---|---|---|
| Elbow Cay, i., Bah. | 134 | 26°25'N | 76°55'W |
| Elbow Lake, Mn., U.S. | 112 | 46°00'N | 95°59'W |
| El'brus, Gora, mtn., Russia (ĕl´brôs´) | 178 | 43°20'N | 42°25'E |
| Elbrus, Mount *see* El'brus, Gora, mtn., Russia | 178 | 43°20'N | 42°25'E |
| Elburz Mountains, mts., Iran (ĕl´bòrz´) | 198 | 36°30'N | 51°00'E |
| El Cajon, Col. (ĕl-kä-kô´n) | 142a | 4°50'N | 76°35'W |
| El Cajon, Ca., U.S. | 118a | 32°48'N | 116°58'W |
| El Cambur, Ven. (käm-bōōr´) | 143b | 10°24'N | 68°06'W |
| El Campo, Tx., U.S. (kăm´pō) | 123 | 29°13'N | 96°17'W |
| El Carmen, Chile (kå´r-mĕn) | 141b | 34°14'S | 71°23'W |
| El Carmen, Col. (kå´r-mĕn) | 142 | 9°54'N | 75°12'W |
| El Casco, Ca., U.S. (kăs´kō) | 117a | 33°59'N | 117°08'W |
| El Centro, Ca., U.S. (sĕn´trō) | 118 | 32°47'N | 115°33'W |
| El Cerrito, Ca., U.S. (sĕr-rē´tō) | 116b | 37°55'N | 122°19'W |
| El Cuyo, Mex. | 132a | 21°30'N | 87°42'W |
| Elda, Spain (ĕl´dä) | 173 | 38°28'N | 0°44'W |
| El Djelfa, Alg. | 230 | 34°40'N | 3°17'E |
| El Djouf, des., Afr. (ĕl djōōf) | 230 | 21°45'N | 7°05'W |
| Eldon, Ia., U.S. (ĕl-dŭn) | 113 | 40°55'N | 92°15'W |
| Eldon, Mo., U.S. | 121 | 38°21'N | 92°36'W |
| Eldora, Ia., U.S. (ĕl-dō´rȧ) | 113 | 42°21'N | 93°08'W |
| El Dorado, Ar., U.S. (ĕl dô-rä´dō) | 105 | 33°13'N | 92°39'W |
| Eldorado, Il., U.S. | 108 | 37°50'N | 88°30'W |
| El Dorado, Ks., U.S. | 121 | 37°49'N | 96°51'W |
| Eldorado Springs, Mo., U.S. (sprĭngz) | 121 | 37°51'N | 94°02'W |
| Eldoret, Kenya (ĕl-dô-rĕt´) | 237 | 0°31'N | 35°17'E |
| El Ebano, Mex. (ā-bä´nō) | 130 | 22°13'N | 98°26'W |
| Electra, Tx., U.S. (ē-lĕk´trȧ) | 120 | 34°02'N | 98°54'W |
| Electric Peak, mtn., Mt., U.S. (ē-lĕk´trĭk) | 115 | 45°03'N | 110°52'W |
| Elek, r. | 181 | 51°20'N | 53°10'E |
| Elektrogorsk, Russia (ĕl-yĕk´trô-gôrsk) | 186b | 55°53'N | 38°48'E |
| Elektrostal', Russia (ĕl-yĕk´trō-stál) | 186b | 55°47'N | 38°27'E |
| Elektrougli, Russia | 186b | 55°43'N | 38°13'E |
| Elephant Butte Reservoir, res., N.M., U.S. (ĕl´ē-fănt būt) | 106 | 33°25'N | 107°10'W |
| El Escorial, Spain (ĕl-ĕs-kō-ryä´l) | 173a | 40°38'N | 4°08'W |
| El Espino, Nic. (ĕl-ĕs-pē´nō) | 132 | 13°26'N | 86°48'W |
| Eleuthera, i., Bah. (ē-lū´thēr-ȧ) | 129 | 25°05'N | 76°10'W |
| Eleuthera Point, c., Bah. | 134 | 24°35'N | 76°05'W |
| Eleven Point, r., Mo., U.S. (ē-lĕv´ĕn) | 121 | 36°53'N | 91°39'W |
| Elgin, Scot., U.K. | 164 | 57°40'N | 3°30'W |
| Elgin, Il., U.S. (ĕl´jĭn) | 111a | 42°03'N | 88°16'W |
| Elgin, Ne., U.S. | 112 | 41°58'N | 98°04'W |
| Elgin, Or., U.S. | 114 | 45°34'N | 117°58'W |
| Elgin, Tx., U.S. | 123 | 30°21'N | 97°22'W |
| Elgin, Wa., U.S. | 116a | 47°23'N | 122°42'W |
| Elgon, Mount, mtn., Afr. (ĕl´gŏn) | 231 | 1°00'N | 34°25'E |
| El Grara, Alg. | 162 | 32°50'N | 4°26'E |
| El Grullo, Mex. (grōōl-yō) | 130 | 19°46'N | 104°10'W |
| El Guapo, Ven. (gwá´pō) | 143b | 10°07'N | 66°00'W |
| El Hank, reg., Afr. | 230 | 23°44'N | 6°45'W |
| El Hatillo, Ven. (ä-tē´l-yō) | 143b | 10°08'N | 65°13'W |
| Elie, Can. (ē´lē) | 102f | 49°55'N | 97°45'W |
| Elila, r., D.R.C. (ĕ-lē´lȧ) | 232 | 3°30'S | 28°00'E |
| Elisa, i., Wa., U.S. (ē-lī´sȧ) | 116d | 48°43'N | 122°37'W |
| Élisabethville *see* Lubumbashi, D.R.C. | 232 | 11°40'S | 27°28'E |
| Elisenvaara, Russia (ā-lē´sĕn-vä´rȧ) | 167 | 61°25'N | 29°46'E |
| Elizabeth, La., U.S. (ē-lĭz´ȧ-bĕth) | 123 | 30°50'N | 92°47'W |
| Elizabeth, N.J., U.S. | 110a | 40°40'N | 74°13'W |
| Elizabeth, Pa., U.S. | 111e | 40°16'N | 79°53'W |
| Elizabeth City, N.C., U.S. | 125 | 36°15'N | 76°15'W |
| Elizabethton, Tn., U.S. (ē-lĭz-ȧ-bĕth´tŭn) | 125 | 36°19'N | 82°12'W |
| Elizabethtown, Ky., U.S. (ē-lĭz´ȧ-bĕth-toun) | 108 | 37°40'N | 85°55'W |
| El Jadida, Mor. | 230 | 33°14'N | 8°34'W |
| Elk, Pol. | 160 | 53°53'N | 22°23'E |
| Elk, r., Can. | 95 | 50°00'N | 115°00'W |
| Elk, r., Tn., U.S. | 124 | 35°05'N | 86°36'W |
| Elk, r., W.V., U.S. | 108 | 38°30'N | 81°05'W |
| El Kairouan, Tun. (kĕr-ō-än) | 230 | 35°46'N | 10°04'E |
| Elk City, Ok., U.S. (ĕlk) | 120 | 35°23'N | 99°23'W |
| El Kef, Tun. (ĸĕf´) | 162 | 36°14'N | 8°42'E |
| Elkhart, In., U.S. (ĕlk´härt) | 108 | 41°40'N | 86°00'W |
| Elkhart, Ks., U.S. | 120 | 37°00'N | 101°54'W |
| Elkhart, Tx., U.S. | 123 | 31°38'N | 95°35'W |
| Elkhorn, Wi., U.S. (ĕlk´hôrn) | 113 | 42°39'N | 88°32'W |
| Elkhorn, r., Ne., U.S. | 112 | 42°06'N | 97°46'W |
| Elkin, N.C., U.S. (ĕl´kĭn) | 125 | 36°15'N | 80°50'W |
| Elk Island, i., Can. | 97 | 50°45'N | 96°32'W |
| Elk Island National Park, rec., Can. (ĕlk ī´lănd) | 92 | 53°37'N | 112°45'W |
| Elko, Nv., U.S. (ĕl´kō) | 104 | 40°51'N | 115°46'W |
| Elk Point, S.D., U.S. | 112 | 42°41'N | 96°41'W |
| Elk Rapids, Mi., U.S. (răp´ĭdz) | 108 | 44°55'N | 85°25'W |
| Elk River, Id., U.S. (rĭv´ēr) | 114 | 46°47'N | 116°11'W |
| Elk River, Mn., U.S. | 113 | 45°17'N | 93°33'W |
| Elkton, Ky., U.S. (ĕlk´tŭn) | 124 | 36°47'N | 87°08'W |
| Elkton, Md., U.S. | 109 | 39°35'N | 75°50'W |
| Elkton, S.D., U.S. | 112 | 44°15'N | 96°28'W |
| Elland, Eng., U.K. (el´ănd) | 158a | 53°41'N | 1°50'W |
| Ellen, Mount, mtn., Ut., U.S. (ĕl´ĕn) | 119 | 38°05'N | 110°50'W |
| Ellendale, N.D., U.S. (ĕl´ĕn-dāl) | 112 | 46°01'N | 98°33'W |
| Ellensburg, Wa., U.S. (ĕl´ĕnz-bûrg) | 114 | 47°00'N | 120°31'W |
| Ellenville, N.Y., U.S. (ĕl´ĕn-vĭl) | 109 | 41°40'N | 74°25'W |
| Ellerslie, Can. (ĕl´ērz-lē) | 102g | 53°25'N | 113°30'W |
| Ellesmere, Eng., U.K. (ĕlz´mēr) | 158a | 52°55'N | 2°54'W |
| Ellesmere Island, i., Can. | 88 | 81°00'N | 80°00'W |
| Ellesmere Port, Eng., U.K. | 158a | 53°17'N | 2°54'W |
| Ellice Islands *see* Tuvalu, nation, Oc. | 3 | 5°20'S | 174°00'E |


ăt; finăl; rāte; senåte; ärm; åsk; sofȧ; fâre; ch-choose; dh-as th in other; bē; ēvent; bĕt; recĕnt; cratēr; g-gō; gh-guttural g; bĭt; ĭ-short neutral; rīde; ĸ-guttural k as ch in German ich;

ng-sing;   ŋ-baŋk;   ɴ-nasalized n;   nŏd; cŏmmit; ōld; ôbey; ôrder; oi-boil; fōōd; ò-as oo in foot; ou-out;   s-soft; sh-dish;   th-thin;   pūre; ûnite; ûrn; stŭd; circŭs; ü-as in French tu;   ´-indeterminate vowel.

292 Estats – Felipe Carrillo Puerto

PRONOUNCING INDEX


| PLACE (Pronunciation) | PAGE | LAT. | LONG. |
|---|---|---|---|
| Estats, Pique d', mtn., Eur. | 173 | 42°43'N | 1°30'E |
| Estcourt, S. Afr. (ĕst-coort) | 233c | 29°04'S | 29°53'E |
| Este, Italy (ĕs´tā) | 174 | 45°13'N | 11°40'E |
| Estella, Spain (ĕs-tāl´yä) | 172 | 42°40'N | 2°01'W |
| Estepa, Spain (ĕs-tā´pä) | 172 | 37°18'N | 4°54'W |
| Estepona, Spain (ĕs-tå-pō´nä) | 172 | 36°26'N | 5°08'W |
| Esterhazy, Can. (ĕs´tẽr-hā-zē) | 97 | 50°40'N | 102°08'W |
| Estero Bay, b., Ca., U.S. (ĕs-tā´rōs) | 118 | 35°22'N | 121°04'W |
| Estevan, Can. (ĕ-stē´vă̈n) | 90 | 49°07'N | 103°05'W |
| Estevan Group, is., Can. | 94 | 53°05'N | 129°40'W |
| Estherville, Ia., U.S. (ĕs´tẽr-vĭl) | 113 | 43°24'N | 94°49'W |
| Estill, S.C., U.S. (ĕs´tĭl) | 125 | 32°46'N | 81°15'W |
| Eston, Can. | 96 | 51°10'N | 108°45'W |
| Estonia, nation, Eur. | 178 | 59°10'N | 25°00'E |
| Estoril, Port. (ĕs-tô-rēl´) | 173b | 38°45'N | 9°24'W |
| Estrêla, mtn., Port. (mäl-you´ɴ-dä-ĕs-trĕ´lä) | 172 | 40°20'N | 7°38'W |
| Estrêla, r., Braz. (ĕs-trĕ´lȧ) | 144b | 22°39'S | 43°16'W |
| Estrêla, Serra da, mts., Port. (sĕr´rȧ dä ĕs-trā´lȧ) | 172 | 40°25'N | 7°45'W |
| Estremadura, hist. reg., Port. (ĕs-trā-mä-dōō´rȧ) | 172 | 39°00'N | 8°36'W |
| Estremoz, Port. (ĕs-trā-mōzh´) | 172 | 38°50'N | 7°35'W |
| Estrondo, Serra do, mts., Braz. (sĕr´-rȧ dȯ ĕs-trôn´-dȯ) | 143 | 9°52'S | 48°56'W |
| Esumba, Île, i., D.R.C. | 236 | 2°00'N | 21°12'E |
| Esztergom, Hung. (ĕs´tẽr-gōm) | 169 | 47°46'N | 18°45'E |
| Etah, Grnld. (ē´tă) | 89 | 78°20'N | 72°42'W |
| Étampes, Fr. (ā-tänp´) | 170 | 48°26'N | 2°09'E |
| Étaples, Fr. (ā-täp´l') | 170 | 50°32'N | 1°38'E |
| Etchemin, r., Can. (ĕch´ĕ-mĭn) | 102b | 46°39'N | 71°03'W |
| Ethiopa, nation, Afr. (ē-thē-ō´pē-ȧ) | 231 | 7°53'N | 37°55'E |
| Eticoga, Gui.-B. | 234 | 11°09'N | 16°08'W |
| Etiwanda, Ca., U.S. (ĕ-tĭ-wän´dȧ) | 117a | 34°07'N | 117°31'W |
| Etna, Pa., U.S. (ĕt´nȧ) | 111e | 40°30'N | 79°55'W |
| Etna, Mount, vol., Italy | 156 | 37°48'N | 15°00'E |
| Etobicoke Creek, r., Can. | 102d | 43°44'N | 79°48'W |
| Etolin Strait, strt., Ak., U.S. (ĕt ō lĭn) | 103 | 60°35'S | 165°40'W |
| Etoshapan, pl., Nmb. (ētō´shä) | 232 | 19°07'S | 15°30'E |
| Etowah, Tn., U.S. (ĕt´ō-wä) | 124 | 35°18'N | 84°31'W |
| Etowah, r., Ga., U.S. | 124 | 34°23'N | 84°19'W |
| Étréchy, Fr. (ā-trā-shē´) | 171b | 48°29'N | 2°12'E |
| Etten-Leur, Neth. | 159a | 51°34'N | 4°38'E |
| Etterbeek, Bel. (ĕt´ẽr-bāk) | 159a | 50°51'N | 4°24'E |
| Etzatlán, Mex. (ĕt-zä-tlän´) | 130 | 20°44'N | 104°04'W |
| Eucla, Austl. (ū´klȧ) | 218 | 31°45'S | 128°50'E |
| Euclid, Oh., U.S. (ū´klĭd) | 111d | 41°34'N | 81°32'W |
| Eudora, Ar., U.S. (u-dō´rȧ) | 121 | 33°07'N | 91°16'W |
| Eufaula, Al., U.S. (ů-fô´lȧ) | 124 | 31°53'N | 85°09'W |
| Eufaula, Ok., U.S. | 121 | 35°16'N | 95°35'W |
| Eufaula Reservoir, res., Ok., U.S. | 121 | 35°00'N | 94°45'W |
| Eugene, Or., U.S. (ů-jēn´) | 104 | 44°02'N | 123°06'W |
| Euless, Tx., U.S. (ū´lĕs) | 117c | 32°50'N | 97°05'W |
| Eunice, La., U.S. (ū´nĭs) | 123 | 30°30'N | 92°25'W |
| Eupen, Bel. (oi´pĕn) | 165 | 50°39'N | 6°05'E |
| Euphrates, r., Asia (ů-frā´tēz) | 198 | 36°00'N | 40°00'E |
| Eure, r., Fr. (ûr) | 170 | 49°03'N | 1°22'E |
| Eureka, Ca., U.S. (û-rē´kȧ) | 104 | 40°45'N | 124°10'W |
| Eureka, Ks., U.S. | 121 | 37°48'N | 96°17'W |
| Eureka, Mt., U.S. | 114 | 48°53'N | 115°07'W |
| Eureka, Nv., U.S. | 118 | 39°33'N | 115°58'W |
| Eureka, S.D., U.S. | 112 | 45°46'N | 99°38'W |
| Eureka, Ut., U.S. | 119 | 39°55'N | 112°10'W |
| Eureka Springs, Ar., U.S. | 121 | 36°24'N | 93°43'W |
| Europe, cont. (ū´rŭp) | 156 | 50°00'N | 15°00'E |
| Eustis, Fl., U.S. (ūs´tĭs) | 125 | 28°50'N | 81°41'W |
| Eutaw, Al., U.S. (ū-tȧ) | 124 | 32°48'N | 87°50'W |
| Eutsuk Lake, l., Can. (ōōt´sŭk) | 94 | 53°20'N | 126°44'W |
| Evanston, Il., U.S. (ĕv´ă̈n-stŭn) | 105 | 42°03'N | 87°41'W |
| Evanston, Wy., U.S. | 115 | 41°17'N | 111°02'W |
| Evansville, In., U.S. (ĕv´ă̈nz-vĭl) | 105 | 38°00'N | 87°30'W |
| Evansville, Wi., U.S. | 113 | 42°46'N | 89°19'W |
| Evart, Mi., U.S. (ĕv´ẽrt) | 108 | 43°55'N | 85°10'W |
| Evaton, S. Afr. (ĕv´ȧ-tŏ̈n) | 238c | 26°32'S | 27°53'E |
| Eveleth, Mn., U.S. (ĕv´ē-lĕth) | 113 | 47°27'N | 92°35'W |
| Everard, l., Austl. (ĕv´ẽr-ȧrd) | 220 | 31°20'S | 134°10'E |
| Everard Ranges, mts., Austl. | 220 | 27°15'S | 132°00'E |
| Everest, Mount, mtn., Asia (ĕv´ẽr-ĕst) | 199 | 28°00'N | 86°57'E |
| Everett, Ma., U.S. (ĕv´ẽr-ĕt) | 101a | 42°24'N | 71°03'W |
| Everett, Wa., U.S. (ĕv´ẽr-ĕt) | 104 | 47°59'N | 122°11'W |
| Everett Mountains, mts., Can. | 93 | 62°34'N | 68°00'W |
| Everglades, The, sw., Fl., U.S. | 125a | 25°35'N | 80°55'W |
| Everglades City, Fl., U.S. (ĕv´ẽr-glādz) | 125a | 25°50'N | 81°25'W |
| Everglades National Park, rec., Fl., U.S. | 107 | 25°39'N | 80°57'W |
| Evergreen, Al., U.S. (ĕv´ẽr-grēn) | 124 | 31°25'N | 87°56'W |
| Evergreen Park, Il., U.S. | 111a | 41°44'N | 87°42'W |
| Everman, Tx., U.S. (ĕv´ẽr-măn) | 117c | 32°38'N | 97°17'W |
| Everson, Wa., U.S. (ĕv´ẽr-sŭ̈n) | 116d | 48°55'N | 122°21'W |
| Évora, Port. (ĕv´ō-rä) | 162 | 38°35'N | 7°54'W |
| Évreux, Fr. (ā-vrû´) | 161 | 49°02'N | 1°11'E |
| Evrótas, r., Grc. (ĕv-rō´täs) | 175 | 37°15'N | 22°17'E |
| Évvoia, i., Grc. | 163 | 38°38'N | 23°45'E |
| 'Ewa Beach, Hi., U.S. (ē´wä) | 126a | 21°17'N | 158°03'W |
| Ewaso Ng'iro, r., Kenya | 231 | 0°59'N | 37°47'E |
| Excelsior, Mn., U.S. (ĕk-sel´sĭ-ŏr) | 117g | 44°54'N | 93°35'W |
| Excelsior Springs, Mo., U.S. | 121 | 39°20'N | 94°13'W |
| Exe, r., Eng., U.K. (ĕks) | 164 | 50°57'N | 3°37'W |
| Exeter, Eng., U.K. | 161 | 50°45'N | 3°33'W |
| Exeter, Ca., U.S. (ĕk´sē-tẽr) | 118 | 36°18'N | 119°09'W |
| Exeter, N.H., U.S. | 109 | 43°00'N | 71°00'W |
| Exmoor, for., Eng., U.K. (ĕks´mȯr) | 164 | 51°10'N | 3°55'W |
| Exmouth, Eng., U.K. (ĕks´mŭ̈th) | 164 | 50°40'N | 3°20'W |
| Exmouth Gulf, b., Austl. | 220 | 21°45'S | 114°30'E |
| Exploits, r., Can. (ĕks-ploits´) | 101 | 48°50'N | 56°15'W |
| Extórrax, r., Mex. (ĕx-tó´ràx) | 130 | 21°04'N | 99°39'W |
| Extrema, Braz. (ĕsh-trĕ´mä) | 141a | 22°52'S | 46°19'W |
| Extremadura, hist. reg., Spain (ĕks-trā-mä-doo´rä) | 172 | 38°43'N | 6°30'W |
| Exuma Sound, strt., Bah. (ĕk-sōō´mä) | 134 | 24°20'N | 76°20'W |
| Eyasi, Lake, l., Tan. (å-yä´sē) | 232 | 3°25'S | 34°55'E |
| Eyjafjördur, b., Ice. | 160 | 66°21'N | 18°20'W |
| Eyl, Som. | 238a | 7°53'N | 49°45'E |
| Eyrarbakki, Ice. | 160 | 63°51'N | 20°52'W |
| Eyre, Austl. (âr) | 218 | 32°15'S | 126°20'E |
| Eyre, l., Austl. | 220 | 28°43'S | 137°50'E |
| Eyre Peninsula, pen., Austl. | 220 | 33°30'S | 136°00'E |
| Ezeiza, Arg. (ĕ-zā´zä) | 144a | 34°52'S | 58°31'W |
| Ezine, Tur. (å´zĭ-nå) | 175 | 39°47'N | 26°18'E |


# F


| PLACE (Pronunciation) | PAGE | LAT. | LONG. |
|---|---|---|---|
| Faaborg, Den. (fô´bôrg) | 166 | 55°06'N | 10°19'E |
| Fabens, Tx., U.S. (fā´bĕnz) | 122 | 31°30'N | 106°07'W |
| Fabriano, Italy (fä-brē-ä´nō) | 174 | 43°20'N | 12°55'E |
| Fada, Chad (fä´dä) | 231 | 17°06'N | 21°18'E |
| Fada Ngourma, Burkina (fä´dä´'n gōōr´mä) | 230 | 12°04'N | 0°21'E |
| Faddeya, i., Russia (fȧd-yä´) | 179 | 76°12'N | 145°00'E |
| Faenza, Italy (fä-ĕnd´zä) | 174 | 44°16'N | 11°53'E |
| Fafe, Port. (fä´fā) | 172 | 41°30'N | 8°10'W |
| Fafen, r., Eth. | 238a | 8°15'N | 42°40'E |
| Făgăras, Rom. (fȧ-gä´räsh) | 175 | 45°50'N | 24°55'E |
| Fagerness, Nor. (fä´ghẽr-nĕs) | 160 | 61°00'N | 9°10'E |
| Fagnano, l., S.A. (fäk-nä´nō) | 144 | 54°35'S | 68°20'W |
| Faguibine, Lac, l., Mali | 234 | 16°50'N | 4°20'W |
| Faial, i., Port. (fä-yä´l) | 230a | 38°40'N | 29°19'W |
| Fā'id, Egypt (fä-yēd´) | 238d | 30°19'N | 32°18'E |
| Fairbanks, Ak., U.S. (fâr´bănks) | 106a | 64°50'N | 147°48'W |
| Fairbury, Il., U.S. (fâr´bĕr-ĭ) | 108 | 40°45'N | 88°25'W |
| Fairbury, Ne., U.S. | 121 | 40°09'N | 97°11'W |
| Fairchild Creek, r., Can. (fâr´chīld) | 102d | 43°18'N | 80°10'W |
| Fairfax, Mn., U.S. (fâr´făks) | 113 | 44°29'N | 94°44'W |
| Fairfax, S.C., U.S. | 125 | 32°29'N | 81°13'W |
| Fairfax, Va., U.S. | 110e | 38°51'N | 77°20'W |
| Fairfield, Austl. | 217b | 33°52'S | 150°57'E |
| Fairfield, Al., U.S. (fâr´fēld) | 110h | 33°30'N | 86°50'W |
| Fairfield, Ct., U.S. | 110a | 41°08'N | 73°22'W |
| Fairfield, Ia., U.S. | 113 | 41°00'N | 91°59'W |
| Fairfield, Il., U.S. | 108 | 38°25'N | 88°20'W |
| Fairfield, Me., U.S. | 100 | 44°35'N | 69°38'W |
| Fairhaven, Ma., U.S. (fâr-hā´vĕ̈n) | 109 | 41°35'N | 70°55'W |
| Fair Haven, Vt., U.S. | 109 | 43°35'N | 73°15'W |
| Fair Island, i., Scot., U.K. (fâr) | 164a | 59°34'N | 1°41'W |
| Fairmont, Mn., U.S. (fâr´mŏnt) | 113 | 43°39'N | 94°26'W |
| Fairmont, W.V., U.S. | 108 | 39°30'N | 80°10'W |
| Fairmont City, Il., U.S. | 117e | 38°39'N | 90°05'W |
| Fairmount, In., U.S. | 108 | 40°25'N | 85°45'W |
| Fairmount, Ks., U.S. | 117f | 39°12'N | 95°55'W |
| Fair Oaks, Ga., U.S. (fâr ōks) | 110c | 33°56'N | 84°33'W |
| Fairport, N.Y., U.S. (fâr´pōrt) | 109 | 43°05'N | 77°30'W |
| Fairport Harbor, Oh., U.S. | 108 | 41°45'N | 81°15'W |
| Fairview, Ok., U.S. (fâr´vū) | 120 | 36°16'N | 98°28'W |
| Fairview, Or., U.S. | 116c | 45°32'N | 112°26'W |
| Fairview, Ut., U.S. | 119 | 39°35'N | 111°30'W |
| Fairview Park, Oh., U.S. | 111d | 41°27'N | 81°52'W |
| Fairweather, Mount, mtn., N.A. (fâr-wĕdh´ẽr) | 103 | 59°12'N | 137°22'W |
| Faisalabad, Pak. | 199 | 31°29'N | 73°06'E |
| Faith, S.D., U.S. (fāth) | 112 | 45°02'N | 120°02'W |
| Faizābād, India | 199 | 26°50'N | 82°17'E |
| Fajardo, P.R. | 129b | 18°20'N | 65°40'W |
| Fakfak, Indon. | 213 | 2°56'S | 132°25'E |
| Faku, China (fä-kōō) | 208 | 42°28'N | 123°20'E |
| Falcón, dept., Ven. (fäl-kô´n) | 143b | 11°00'N | 68°28'W |
| Falconer, N.Y., U.S. (fô´k'n-ẽr) | 109 | 42°10'N | 79°10'W |
| Falcon Heights, Mn., U.S. (fô´k'n) | 117g | 44°59'N | 93°10'W |
| Falcon Reservoir, res., N.A. (fôk'n) | 122 | 26°47'N | 99°03'W |
| Făleşti, Mol. | 177 | 47°33'N | 27°46'E |
| Falfurrias, Tx., U.S. (făl´fōō-rē´ȧs) | 122 | 27°15'N | 98°08'W |
| Falher, Can. (făl´ẽr) | 95 | 55°44'N | 117°12'W |
| Falkenberg, Swe. (fäl´kĕn-bĕrgh) | 166 | 56°54'N | 12°25'E |
| Falkensee, Ger. (fäl´kĕn-zā) | 159b | 52°34'N | 13°05'E |
| Falkenthal, Ger. (fäl´kĕn-täl) | 159b | 52°54'N | 13°18'E |
| Falkirk, Scot., U.K. (fôl´kûrk) | 164 | 55°59'N | 3°55'W |
| Falkland Islands, dep., S.A. (fôk´lă̈nd) | 144 | 50°45'S | 61°00'W |
| Falköping, Swe. (fäl´chûp-ĭng) | 166 | 58°09'N | 13°30'E |
| Fall City, Wa., U.S. | 116a | 47°34'N | 121°53'W |
| Fall Creek, r., In., U.S. (fôl) | 111g | 39°52'N | 86°04'W |
| Fallon, Nv., U.S. (făl´ŭ̈n) | 118 | 39°30'N | 118°48'W |
| Fall River, Ma., U.S. | 105 | 41°42'N | 71°07'W |
| Falls Church, Va., U.S. (fălz chûrch) | 110e | 38°53'N | 77°10'W |
| Falls City, Ne., U.S. | 121 | 40°04'N | 95°37'W |
| Fallston, Md., U.S. (făls´ton) | 110e | 39°32'N | 76°26'W |
| Falmouth, Jam. | 134 | 18°30'N | 77°40'W |
| Falmouth, Eng., U.K. (făl´mŭ̈th) | 164 | 50°08'N | 5°04'W |
| Falmouth, Ky., U.S. | 108 | 38°40'N | 84°20'W |
| False Divi Point, c., India | 203 | 15°45'N | 80°50'E |
| Falster, i., Den. (fäls´tĕr) | 166 | 54°48'N | 11°58'E |
| Fălticeni, Rom. (fŭl-tē-chån´y') | 169 | 47°27'N | 26°17'E |
| Falun, Swe. (fä-lōōn´) | 160 | 60°38'N | 15°35'E |
| Famagusta, Cyp. (fä-mä-gōōs´tä) | 163 | 35°08'N | 33°59'E |
| Famatina, Sierra de, mts., Arg. | 144 | 29°00'S | 67°50'W |
| Fangxian, China (fäŋ-shyĕn) | 208 | 32°05'N | 110°45'E |
| Fanning, i., Can. | 102f | 49°45'N | 97°46'W |
| Fano, Italy (fä´nō) | 174 | 43°49'N | 13°01'E |
| Fanø, i., Den. (fän´û) | 166 | 55°24'N | 8°10'E |
| Fan Si Pan, mtn., Viet. | 209 | 22°25'N | 103°50'E |
| Farafangana, Madag. (fä-rä-fäŋ-gä´nä) | 233 | 23°18'S | 47°59'E |
| Farāh, Afg. (fä-rä´) | 198 | 32°15'N | 62°13'E |
| Farallón, Punta, c., Mex. (pŏ´n-tä-fä-rä-lōn) | 130 | 19°21'N | 105°03'W |
| Faranah, Gui. (fä-rä´nä) | 230 | 10°02'N | 10°44'W |
| Farasān, Jaza'ir, is., Sau. Ar. | 198 | 16°45'N | 41°08'E |
| Faregh, Wadi al, r., Libya (wädē ĕl fä-rĕg´) | 163 | 30°10'N | 19°34'E |
| Farewell, Cape, c., N.Z. (fâr-wĕl´) | 221a | 40°37'S | 172°40'E |
| Fargo, N.D., U.S. (fär´gō) | 104 | 46°53'N | 96°48'W |
| Far Hills, N.J., U.S. (fär hĭlz) | 110a | 40°41'N | 74°38'W |
| Faribault, Mn., U.S. (fâ´rĭ-bō) | 113 | 44°19'N | 93°16'W |
| Farilhões, is., Port. (fä-rē-lyôɴzh´) | 172 | 39°28'N | 9°32'W |
| Faringdon, Eng., U.K. (fă´rĭng-dŏ̈n) | 158b | 51°38'N | 1°35'W |
| Fāriskūr, Egypt (fä-rēs-kōōr´) | 238b | 31°19'N | 31°46'E |
| Farit, Amba, mtn., Eth. | 231 | 10°51'N | 37°52'E |
| Farley, Mo., U.S. (fär´lē) | 117f | 39°16'N | 94°49'W |
| Farmers Branch, Tx., U.S. | 117c | 32°56'N | 96°53'W |
| Farmersburg, In., U.S. (fär´mẽrz-bûrg) | 108 | 39°15'N | 87°25'W |
| Farmersville, Tx., U.S. (fär´mẽrz-vĭl) | 121 | 33°11'N | 96°22'W |
| Farmingdale, N.J., U.S. (färm´ĕng-dāl) | 110a | 40°11'N | 74°10'W |
| Farmingdale, N.Y., U.S. | 110a | 40°44'N | 73°26'W |
| Farmingham, Ma., U.S. (färm-ĭng-hăm) | 101a | 42°17'N | 71°25'W |
| Farmington, Il., U.S. (färm-ĭng-tŭn) | 121 | 40°42'N | 90°01'W |
| Farmington, Me., U.S. | 100 | 44°40'N | 70°10'W |
| Farmington, Mi., U.S. | 111b | 42°28'N | 83°23'W |
| Farmington, Mo., U.S. | 121 | 37°46'N | 90°26'W |
| Farmington, N.M., U.S. | 119 | 36°40'N | 108°10'W |
| Farmington, Ut., U.S. | 117b | 40°59'N | 111°53'W |
| Farmville, N.C., U.S. (färm-vĭl) | 125 | 35°35'N | 77°35'W |
| Farmville, Va., U.S. | 125 | 37°15'N | 78°23'W |
| Farnborough, Eng., U.K. (färn´bŭ̈r-ō) | 158b | 51°15'N | 0°45'W |
| Farne Islands, is., Eng., U.K. (färn) | 164 | 55°40'N | 1°32'W |
| Farnham, Can. (fär´nă̈m) | 109 | 45°15'N | 72°55'W |
| Farningham, Eng., U.K. (fär´nĭng-ŭm) | 158b | 51°22'N | 0°14'E |
| Farnworth, Eng., U.K. (färn´wŭ̈rth) | 158a | 53°34'N | 2°24'W |
| Faro, Braz. (fä´rȯ) | 143 | 2°05'S | 56°32'W |
| Faro, Port. | 162 | 37°01'N | 7°57'W |
| Farodofay, Madag. | 233 | 24°59'S | 46°58'E |
| Faroe Islands, is., Eur. | 156 | 62°00'N | 5°45'W |
| Fårön, i., Swe. | 167 | 57°57'N | 19°10'E |
| Farquhar, Cape, c., Austl. (fär´kwȧr) | 220 | 23°50'S | 112°55'E |
| Farrell, Pa., U.S. (făr´ĕl) | 108 | 41°10'N | 80°30'W |
| Farrukhābād, India (fŭ̈-rȯk-hä-bäd´) | 199 | 27°29'N | 79°35'E |
| Fársala, Grc. | 175 | 39°18'N | 22°25'E |
| Farsund, Nor. (fär´sȯn) | 166 | 58°05'N | 6°47'E |
| Fartak, Ra's, c., Yemen | 198 | 15°43'N | 52°17'E |
| Fartura, Serra da, mts., Braz. (sĕ´r-rä-dȧ-fär-tōō´rä) | 144 | 26°40'S | 53°15'W |
| Farvel, Kap, c., Grnld. | 89 | 60°00'N | 44°00'W |
| Farwell, Tx., U.S. (fär´wĕ̈l) | 120 | 34°24'N | 103°03'W |
| Fasano, Italy (fä-zä´nō) | 175 | 40°50'N | 17°22'E |
| Fastiv, Ukr. | 177 | 50°04'N | 29°57'E |
| Fatëzh, Russia | 176 | 52°06'N | 35°51'E |
| Fatima, Port. | 173 | 39°36'N | 9°36'E |
| Fatsa, Tur. (făt´sä) | 163 | 40°50'N | 37°30'E |
| Faucilles, Monts, mts., Fr. (môɴ´ fō-sēl´) | 171 | 48°07'N | 6°13'E |
| Fauske, Nor. | 160 | 67°15'N | 15°24'E |
| Faust, Can. (foust) | 95 | 55°19'N | 115°38'W |
| Faustovo, Russia | 186b | 55°27'N | 38°29'E |
| Faversham, Eng., U.K. (fă´vẽr-sh'm) | 158b | 51°19'N | 0°54'E |
| Faxaflói, b., Ice. | 160 | 64°33'N | 22°40'W |
| Fayette, Al., U.S. (få-yĕt´) | 124 | 33°40'N | 87°54'W |
| Fayette, Ia., U.S. | 113 | 42°49'N | 91°49'W |
| Fayette, Mo., U.S. | 121 | 39°09'N | 92°41'W |
| Fayette, Ms., U.S. | 124 | 31°43'N | 91°00'W |
| Fayetteville, Ar., U.S. (få-yĕt´vĭl) | 121 | 36°03'N | 94°08'W |
| Fayetteville, N.C., U.S. | 125 | 35°02'N | 78°54'W |
| Fayetteville, Tn., U.S. | 124 | 35°10'N | 86°33'W |
| Fazao, Forêt Classée du, for., Togo | 234 | 8°50'N | 0°40'E |
| Fazilka, India | 202 | 30°30'N | 74°02'E |
| Fazzān (Fezzan), hist. reg., Libya | 231 | 26°45'N | 13°01'E |
| Fdérik, Maur. | 230 | 22°45'N | 12°38'W |
| Fear, Cape, c., N.C., U.S. (fēr) | 125 | 33°52'N | 77°48'W |
| Feather, r., Ca., U.S. (fĕth´ẽr) | 118 | 38°56'N | 121°41'W |
| Feather, Middle Fork of, r., Ca., U.S. | 118 | 39°49'N | 121°10'W |
| Feather, North Fork of, r., Ca., U.S. | 118 | 40°00'N | 121°20'W |
| Featherstone, Eng., U.K. (fĕdh´ẽr stŭ̈n) | 158a | 53°39'N | 1°21'W |
| Fécamp, Fr. (fā-käɴ´) | 161 | 49°45'N | 0°20'E |
| Federal, Distrito, dept., Ven. (dēs-trē´tō-fĕ-dĕ-rä´l) | 143b | 10°34'N | 66°55'W |
| Federal Way, Wa., U.S. | 116a | 47°20'N | 122°20'W |
| Fëdorovka, Russia (fyô´dō-rôf-kȧ) | 186b | 56°15'N | 37°14'E |
| Fehmarn, i., Ger. (fā´märn) | 168 | 54°28'N | 11°15'E |
| Fehrbellin, Ger. (fĕr´bĕl-lēn) | 159b | 52°49'N | 12°46'E |
| Feia, Logoa, l., Braz. (lō-gôä-fĕ´yä) | 141a | 21°54'S | 41°15'W |
| Feicheng, China (fā-chŭŋ) | 206 | 36°18'N | 116°45'E |
| Feidong, China (fā-dōŋ) | 206 | 31°53'N | 117°28'E |
| Feira de Santana, Braz. (fĕ´ê-rä dā sänt-än´ä) | 143 | 12°16'S | 38°46'W |
| Feixian, China (fā-shyĕn) | 206 | 35°17'N | 117°59'E |
| Felanitx, Spain (fā-lä-nēch´) | 162 | 39°29'N | 3°09'E |
| Feldkirch, Aus. (fĕlt´kĭrk) | 168 | 47°15'N | 9°36'E |
| Feldkirchen, Ger. (fĕld´kēr-ĸĕn) | 159d | 48°09'N | 11°44'E |
| Felipe Carrillo Puerto, Mex. | 132a | 19°36'N | 88°04'W |


ăt; finăl; rāte; senåte; ärm; åsk; sofȧ; fâre; ch-choose; dh-as th in other; bē; ēvent; bĕt; recĕnt; cratẽr; g-gō; gh-guttural g; bĭt; ĭ-short neutral; rīde; ĸ-guttural k as ch in German ich;

PRONOUNCING INDEX

Feltre – Fort Bellefontaine 293


| PLACE (Pronunciation) | PAGE | LAT. | LONG. |
|---|---|---|---|
| Feltre, Italy (fĕl′trā) | 174 | 46°02′N | 11°56′E |
| Femunden, l., Nor. | 160 | 62°17′N | 11°40′E |
| Fengcheng, China (fŭŋ-chŭŋ) | 208 | 40°28′N | 124°03′E |
| Fengcheng, China | 207b | 30°55′N | 121°38′E |
| Fengdu, China (fŭŋ-dōō) | 204 | 29°58′N | 107°50′E |
| Fengjie, China (fŭŋ-jyĕ) | 204 | 31°02′N | 109°30′E |
| Fengming Dao, i., China (fŭŋ-mĭŋ dou) | 206 | 39°19′N | 121°15′E |
| Fengrun, China (fŭŋ-ròn) | 206 | 39°51′N | 118°06′E |
| Fengtai, China (fŭŋ-tī) | 208a | 39°51′N | 116°19′E |
| Fengxian, China (fŭŋ-shyĕn) | 207b | 30°55′N | 121°26′E |
| Fengxian, China | 206 | 34°41′N | 116°36′E |
| Fengxiang, China (fŭŋ-shyäŋ) | 204 | 34°25′N | 107°20′E |
| Fengyang, China (fŭng′yäng′) | 208 | 32°55′N | 117°32′E |
| Fengzhen, China (fŭŋ-jŭn) | 205 | 40°28′N | 113°20′E |
| Fennimore Pass, strt., Ak., U.S. (fĕn-ĭ-mōr) | 103a | 51°40′N | 175°38′W |
| Fenoarivo Atsinanana, Madag. | 233 | 17°30′S | 49°31′E |
| Fenton, Mi., U.S. (fĕn-tŭn) | 108 | 42°50′N | 83°40′W |
| Fenton, Mo., U.S. | 117e | 38°31′N | 90°27′W |
| Fenyang, China | 205 | 37°20′N | 111°48′E |
| Feodosiia, Ukr. | 181 | 45°02′N | 35°21′E |
| Ferdows, Iran | 198 | 34°00′N | 58°13′E |
| Ferentino, Italy (fā-rĕn-tē′nō) | 174 | 41°42′N | 13°18′E |
| Fergana, Uzb. | 183 | 40°23′N | 71°46′E |
| Fergus Falls, Mn., U.S. (fûr′gŭs) | 104 | 46°17′N | 96°03′W |
| Ferguson, Mo., U.S. (fûr-gŭ-sŭn) | 117e | 38°45′N | 90°18′W |
| Ferkéssédougou, C. Iv. | 234 | 9°36′N | 5°12′W |
| Fermo, Italy (fĕr′mō) | 174 | 43°10′N | 13°43′E |
| Fermoselle, Spain (fĕr-mō-säl′yā) | 172 | 41°20′N | 6°23′W |
| Fermoy, Ire. (fûr-moi′) | 164 | 52°05′N | 8°06′W |
| Fernandina Beach, Fl., U.S. (fûr-năn-dē′nȧ) | 125 | 30°38′N | 81°29′W |
| Fernando de Noronha, Arquipélago, is., Braz. | 143 | 3°51′S | 32°25′W |
| Fernando Póo *see* Bioko, i., Eq. Gui. | 230 | 3°35′N | 7°45′E |
| Fernán-Núñez, Spain (fĕr-nän′nōōn′yāth) | 172 | 37°42′N | 4°43′W |
| Fernão Veloso, Baia de, b., Moz. | 237 | 14°20′S | 40°55′E |
| Ferndale, Ca., U.S. (fûrn′dāl) | 114 | 40°34′N | 124°18′W |
| Ferndale, Mi., U.S. | 111b | 42°27′N | 83°08′W |
| Ferndale, Wa., U.S. | 116d | 48°51′N | 122°36′W |
| Fernie, Can. (fûr′nĭ) | 90 | 49°30′N | 115°03′W |
| Fern Prairie, Wa., U.S. (fûrn prâr′ĭ) | 116c | 45°38′N | 122°25′W |
| Ferrara, Italy (fĕr-rä′rä) | 162 | 44°50′N | 11°37′E |
| Ferrat, Cap, c., Alg. (kăp fĕr-rät) | 173 | 35°49′N | 0°29′W |
| Ferreira do Alentejo, Port. | 172 | 38°03′N | 8°06′W |
| Ferreira do Zezere, Port. (fĕr-rĕ′ē-rä dò zā-zā′rĕ) | 172 | 39°49′N | 8°17′W |
| Ferrelview, Mo., U.S. (fĕr′rĕl-vū) | 117f | 39°18′N | 94°40′W |
| Ferreñafe, Peru (fĕr-rĕn-yä′fĕ) | 142 | 6°38′S | 79°48′W |
| Ferriday, La., U.S. (fĕr′ĭ-dā) | 123 | 31°38′N | 91°33′W |
| Ferrol, Spain | 154 | 43°30′N | 8°12′W |
| Fershampenuaz, Russia (fĕr-shàm′pĕn-wäz) | 186a | 53°32′N | 59°50′E |
| Fertile, Mn., U.S. (fur′tĭl) | 112 | 47°33′N | 96°18′W |
| Fès, Mor. (fĕs) | 230 | 34°08′N | 5°00′W |
| Fessenden, N.D., U.S. (fĕs′ĕn-dĕn) | 112 | 47°39′N | 99°40′W |
| Festus, Mo., U.S. (fĕst′ŭs) | 121 | 38°12′N | 90°22′W |
| Fethiye, Tur. (fĕt-hē′yĕ) | 163 | 36°40′N | 29°05′E |
| Feuilles, Rivière aux, r., Can. | 93 | 58°30′N | 70°50′W |
| Ffestiniog, Wales, U.K. | 164 | 52°59′N | 3°58′W |
| Fianarantsoa, Madag. (fyȧ-nä′rȧn-tsō′ȧ) | 233 | 21°21′S | 47°15′E |
| Ficksburg, S. Afr. (fĭks′bûrg) | 238c | 28°53′S | 27°53′E |
| Fidalgo Island, i., Wa., U.S. (fĭ-dăl′gō) | 116a | 48°28′N | 122°39′W |
| Fieldbrook, Ca., U.S. (fēld′brŏŏk) | 114 | 40°59′N | 124°02′W |
| Fier, Alb. (fyĕr) | 175 | 40°43′N | 19°34′E |
| Fife Ness, c., Scot., U.K. (fīf′nes′) | 164 | 56°15′N | 2°19′W |
| Fifth Cataract, wtfl., Sudan | 231 | 18°27′N | 33°38′E |
| Figeac, Fr. (fē-zhàk′) | 170 | 44°37′N | 2°02′E |
| Figeholm, Swe. (fē-ghĕ-hōlm) | 166 | 57°24′N | 16°33′E |
| Figueira da Foz, Port. (fē-gwĕy-rä-dä-fō′z) | 172 | 40°10′N | 8°50′W |
| Figuig, Mor. | 230 | 32°20′N | 1°30′W |
| Fiji, nation, Oc. (fē′jē) | 3 | 18°40′S | 175°00′E |
| Filadelfia, C.R. (fĭl-ȧ-dĕl′fĭ-ȧ) | 132 | 10°26′N | 85°37′W |
| Filatovskoye, Russia (fĭ-lä′tôf-skô-yĕ) | 186a | 56°49′N | 62°20′E |
| Filchner Ice Shelf, ice, Ant. (fĭlk′nĕr) | 224 | 80°00′S | 35°00′W |
| Filicudi, i., Italy (fē′le-kōō′dē) | 174 | 38°34′N | 14°39′E |
| Filippovskoye, Russia (fĭ-lĭ-pôf′skô-yĕ) | 186b | 56°06′N | 38°38′E |
| Filipstad, Swe. (fĭl′ĭps-städh) | 166 | 59°44′N | 14°09′E |
| Fillmore, Ut., U.S. (fĭl′môr) | 119 | 39°00′N | 112°20′W |
| Filsa, Nor. | 166 | 60°35′N | 12°03′E |
| Fimi, r., D.R.C. | 232 | 2°43′S | 17°50′E |
| Finch, Can. (fĭnch) | 102c | 45°09′N | 75°06′W |
| Findlay, Oh., U.S. (fĭnd′lå) | 108 | 41°05′N | 83°40′W |
| Fingoe, Moz. | 237 | 15°12′S | 31°50′E |
| Finke, r., Austl. (fĭŋ′kē) | 220 | 25°25′S | 134°30′E |
| Finland, nation, Eur. (fĭn′lănd) | 154 | 62°45′N | 26°13′E |
| Finland, Gulf of, b., Eur. (fĭn′lănd) | 156 | 59°35′N | 23°35′E |
| Finlandia, Col. (fēn-lä′n-dēä) | 142a | 4°38′N | 75°39′W |
| Finlay, r., Can. (fĭn′lā) | 92 | 57°45′N | 125°30′W |
| Finow, Ger. (fē′nōv) | 159b | 52°50′N | 13°44′E |
| Finowfurt, Ger. (fē′nō-fōōrt) | 159b | 52°50′N | 13°41′E |
| Fircrest, Wa., U.S. (fûr′krĕst) | 116a | 47°14′N | 122°31′W |
| Firenze *see* Florence, Italy | 154 | 43°47′N | 11°15′E |
| Firenzuola, Italy (fē-rĕnt-swô′lä) | 174 | 44°08′N | 11°21′E |
| Firozpur, India | 199 | 30°58′N | 74°39′E |
| Fischa, r., Aus. | 159e | 48°04′N | 16°33′E |
| Fischamend Markt, Aus. | 159e | 48°07′N | 16°37′E |
| Fish, r., Nmb. (fĭsh) | 232 | 28°00′S | 17°30′E |
| Fish Cay, i., Bah. | 135 | 22°30′N | 74°20′W |
| Fish Creek, r., Can. (fĭsh) | 102e | 50°52′N | 114°21′W |
| Fisher, La., U.S. (fĭsh′ĕr) | 123 | 31°28′N | 93°30′W |
| Fisher Bay, b., Can. | 97 | 51°30′N | 97°16′W |
| Fisher Channel, strt., Can. | 94 | 52°10′N | 127°42′W |
| Fisher Strait, strt., Can. | 93 | 62°43′N | 84°28′W |
| Fisterra, Cabo de, c., Spain | 156 | 42°52′N | 9°48′W |
| Fitchburg, Ma., U.S. (fĭch′bûrg) | 109 | 42°35′N | 71°48′W |
| Fitri, Lac, l., Chad | 235 | 12°50′N | 17°28′E |
| Fitzgerald, Ga., U.S. (fĭts-jĕr′ăld) | 124 | 31°42′N | 83°17′W |
| Fitz Hugh Sound, strt., Can. (fĭts hū) | 94 | 51°40′N | 127°57′W |
| Fitzroy, r., Austl. (fĭts-roi′) | 220 | 18°00′S | 124°05′E |
| Fitzroy, r., Austl. | 221 | 23°45′S | 150°02′E |
| Fitzroy, Monte (Cerro Chaltel), mtn., S.A. | 144 | 48°10′S | 73°18′W |
| Fitzroy Crossing, Austl. | 218 | 18°08′S | 126°00′E |
| Fitzwilliam, i., Can. (fĭts-wĭl′yŭm) | 98 | 45°30′N | 81°45′W |
| Fiume *see* Rijeka, Cro. | 162 | 45°22′N | 14°24′E |
| Fiumicino, Italy (fyōō-mē-chē′nō) | 173d | 41°47′N | 12°19′E |
| Fjällbacka, Swe. (fyĕl′bäk-å) | 166 | 58°37′N | 11°17′E |
| Flagstaff, S. Afr. (flăg′stäf) | 233c | 31°06′S | 29°31′E |
| Flagstaff, Az., U.S. (flăg-stàf) | 104 | 35°15′N | 111°40′W |
| Flagstaff, l., Me., U.S. (flăg-stàf) | 109 | 45°05′N | 70°30′W |
| Flåm, Nor. (flôm) | 166 | 60°50′N | 7°00′E |
| Flambeau, r., Wi., U.S. (flăm-bō′) | 113 | 45°32′N | 91°05′W |
| Flaming Gorge Reservoir, res., U.S. | 106 | 41°13′N | 109°30′W |
| Flamingo, Fl., U.S. (flȧ-mĭŋ′gō) | 125 | 25°10′N | 80°55′W |
| Flamingo Cay, i., Bah. (flȧ-mĭŋ′gō) | 135 | 22°50′N | 75°50′W |
| Flamingo Point, c., V.I.U.S. | 129c | 18°19′N | 65°00′W |
| Flanders, hist. reg., Fr. (flăn′dĕrz) | 165 | 50°53′N | 2°29′E |
| Flandreau, S.D., U.S. (flăn′drō) | 112 | 44°02′N | 96°35′W |
| Flathead, r., N.A. | 95 | 49°30′N | 114°30′W |
| Flathead, Middle Fork, r., Mt., U.S. | 115 | 48°30′N | 113°47′W |
| Flathead, North Fork, r., N.A. | 115 | 48°45′N | 114°20′W |
| Flathead, South Fork, r., Mt., U.S. | 115 | 48°05′N | 113°45′W |
| Flathead Indian Reservation, I.R., Mt., U.S. | 115 | 47°30′N | 114°25′W |
| Flathead Lake, l., Mt., U.S. (flăt′hĕd) | 106 | 47°57′N | 114°20′W |
| Flatow, Ger. | 159b | 52°44′N | 12°58′E |
| Flat Rock, Mi., U.S. (flăt rŏk) | 111b | 42°06′N | 83°17′W |
| Flattery, Cape, c., Wa., U.S. (flăt′ẽr-ĭ) | 114 | 48°22′N | 124°45′W |
| Flatwillow Creek, r., Mt., U.S. (flat wĭl′ō) | 115 | 46°45′N | 108°47′W |
| Flekkefjord, Nor. (flăk′kĕ-fyôr) | 166 | 58°19′N | 6°38′E |
| Flemingsburg, Ky., U.S. (flĕm′ĭngz-bûrg) | 108 | 38°25′N | 83°45′W |
| Flensburg, Ger. (flĕns′bòrgh) | 160 | 54°48′N | 9°27′E |
| Flers, Fr. (flĕr) | 161 | 48°43′N | 0°37′W |
| Fletcher, N.C., U.S. | 125 | 35°26′N | 82°30′W |
| Flinders, i., Austl. | 221 | 39°35′S | 148°10′E |
| Flinders, r., Austl. | 221 | 18°48′S | 141°07′E |
| Flinders, reg., Austl. (flĭn′dẽrz) | 220 | 32°15′S | 138°45′E |
| Flinders Reefs, rf., Austl. | 221 | 17°30′S | 149°02′E |
| Flin Flon, Can. (flĭn flŏn) | 90 | 54°46′N | 101°53′W |
| Flint, Wales, U.K. | 158a | 53°15′N | 3°07′W |
| Flint, Mi., U.S. | 105 | 43°00′N | 83°45′W |
| Flint, r., Ga., U.S. (flĭnt) | 107 | 31°25′N | 84°15′W |
| Flintshire, co., Wales, U.K. | 158a | 53°13′N | 3°00′W |
| Flora, Il., U.S. (flō′rȧ) | 108 | 38°40′N | 88°25′W |
| Flora, In., U.S. | 108 | 40°25′N | 86°30′W |
| Florala, Al., U.S. (flŏr-ăl′ȧ) | 124 | 31°01′N | 86°19′W |
| Floral Park, N.Y., U.S. (flôr′ăl pärk) | 110a | 40°42′N | 73°42′W |
| Florence, Italy | 154 | 43°47′N | 11°15′E |
| Florence, Al., U.S. (flŏr′ĕns) | 105 | 34°46′N | 87°40′W |
| Florence, Az., U.S. | 119 | 33°00′N | 111°25′W |
| Florence, Co., U.S. | 120 | 38°23′N | 105°08′W |
| Florence, Ks., U.S. | 121 | 38°14′N | 96°56′W |
| Florence, S.C., U.S. | 125 | 34°10′N | 79°45′W |
| Florence, Wa., U.S. | 116a | 48°13′N | 122°21′W |
| Florencia, Col. (flō-rĕn′sē-ȧ) | 142 | 1°31′N | 75°13′W |
| Florencio Sánchez, Ur. (flō-rĕn-sēō-sȧ′n-chĕz) | 141c | 33°52′S | 57°24′W |
| Florencio Varela, Arg. (flō-rĕn′sē-o vä-rā′lä) | 144a | 34°50′S | 58°16′W |
| Flores, Braz. (flō′rĕzh) | 143 | 7°57′S | 37°48′W |
| Flores, Guat. | 132a | 16°53′N | 89°54′W |
| Flores, dept., Ur. | 141c | 33°33′S | 57°00′W |
| Flores, i., Indon. | 212 | 8°14′S | 121°08′E |
| Flores, r., Arg. | 141c | 36°13′S | 60°28′W |
| Flores, Laut (Flores Sea), sea, Indon. | 212 | 7°09′S | 120°30′E |
| Floresville, Tx., U.S. (flō′rĕs-vĭl) | 122 | 29°10′N | 98°08′W |
| Floriano, Braz. (flō-rȧ-ä′nò) | 143 | 6°17′S | 42°58′W |
| Florianópolis, Braz. (flō-rē-ä-nō′pō-lēs) | 144 | 27°30′S | 48°30′W |
| Florida, Col. (flō-rē′dä) | 142a | 3°20′N | 76°12′W |
| Florida, Cuba | 134 | 22°10′N | 79°50′W |
| Florida, S. Afr. | 233b | 26°11′S | 27°56′E |
| Florida, Ur. (flō-rē-dhä) | 144 | 34°06′S | 56°14′W |
| Florida, N.Y., U.S. (flŏr′ĭ-dȧ) | 110a | 41°20′N | 74°21′W |
| Florida, state, U.S. (flŏr′ĭ-dȧ) | 105 | 30°30′N | 84°40′W |
| Florida, dept., Ur. (flō-rē′dhä) | 141c | 33°48′S | 56°15′W |
| Florida, i., Sol. Is. | 221 | 8°56′S | 159°45′E |
| Florida, Straits of, strt., N.A. | 129 | 24°10′N | 81°00′W |
| Florida Bay, b., Fl., U.S. (flŏr′ĭ-dȧ) | 125a | 24°55′N | 80°55′W |
| Florida Keys, is., Fl., U.S. | 107 | 24°33′N | 81°20′W |
| Florida Mountains, mts., N.M., U.S. | 119 | 32°10′N | 107°35′W |
| Florido, Río, r., Mex. (flō-rē′dō) | 122 | 27°21′N | 104°48′W |
| Floridsdorf, Aus. (flō′rĭds-dôrf) | 159e | 48°16′N | 16°25′E |
| Florina, Grc. (flō-rē′nä) | 163 | 40°48′N | 21°24′E |
| Florissant, Mo., U.S. (flŏr′ĭ-sȧnt) | 117e | 38°47′N | 90°20′W |
| Floyd, r., Ia., U.S. (floid) | 112 | 42°38′N | 96°15′W |
| Floydada, Tx., U.S. (floi-dā′dȧ) | 120 | 33°59′N | 101°19′W |
| Floyds Fork, r., Ky., U.S. (floi-dz) | 111h | 38°08′N | 85°30′W |
| Flumendosa, r., Italy | 174 | 39°45′N | 9°18′E |
| Flushing, Mi., U.S. (flûsh′ĭng) | 108 | 43°05′N | 83°50′W |
| Fly, r. (flī) | 213 | 8°00′S | 141°45′E |
| Foča, Bos. (fō′chä) | 175 | 43°29′N | 18°48′E |
| Fochville, S. Afr. (fŏk′vĭl) | 238c | 26°29′S | 27°29′E |
| Focşani, Rom. (fōk-shä′nĕ) | 169 | 45°41′N | 27°17′E |
| Fogang, China (fwo-gäŋ) | 209 | 23°50′N | 113°35′E |
| Foggia, Italy (fôd′jä) | 163 | 41°30′N | 15°34′E |
| Fogo, Can. (fō′gō) | 101 | 49°43′N | 54°17′W |
| Fogo, i., Can. | 99 | 49°40′N | 54°13′W |
| Fogo, i., C.V. | 230b | 14°46′N | 24°51′W |
| Fohnsdorf, Aus. (fōns′dôrf) | 168 | 47°13′N | 14°40′E |
| Föhr, i., Ger. (fûr) | 168 | 54°47′N | 8°30′E |
| Foix, Fr. (fwä) | 170 | 42°58′N | 1°34′E |
| Fokku, Nig. | 235 | 11°40′N | 4°31′E |
| Foladī, Koh-e, mtn., Afg. | 199 | 34°38′N | 67°32′E |
| Folgares, Ang. | 236 | 14°54′S | 15°08′E |
| Foligno, Italy (fō-lēn′yō) | 174 | 42°58′N | 12°41′E |
| Folkeston, Eng., U.K. | 165 | 51°05′N | 1°18′E |
| Folkingham, Eng., U.K. (fō′kĭng-ȧm) | 158a | 52°53′N | 0°24′W |
| Folkston, Ga., U.S. | 125 | 30°50′N | 82°01′W |
| Folsom, Ca., U.S. | 118 | 38°40′N | 121°10′W |
| Folsom, N.M., U.S. (fōl′sŭm) | 120 | 36°47′N | 103°56′W |
| Fomento, Cuba (fō-mĕ′n-tō) | 134 | 21°35′N | 78°20′W |
| Fómeque, Col. (fō′mĕ-kĕ) | 142a | 4°29′N | 73°52′W |
| Fonda, Ia., U.S. (fŏn′dȧ) | 113 | 42°33′N | 94°51′W |
| Fond du Lac, Wi., U.S. (fŏn dū lăk′) | 105 | 43°47′N | 88°29′W |
| Fond du Lac Indian Reservation, I.R., Mn., U.S. | 113 | 46°44′N | 93°04′W |
| Fondi, Italy (fōn′dē) | 174 | 41°23′N | 13°25′E |
| Fonseca, Golfo de, b., N.A. (gôl-fô-dĕ-fōn-sā′kä) | 128 | 13°09′N | 87°55′W |
| Fontainebleau, Fr. (fôN-tĕn-blō′) | 161 | 48°24′N | 2°42′E |
| Fontana, Ca., U.S. (fŏn-tă′nȧ) | 117a | 34°06′N | 117°27′W |
| Fonte Boa, Braz. (fōn′tȧ bō′ȧ) | 142 | 2°32′S | 66°05′W |
| Fontenay-le-Comte, Fr. (fônt-nĕ′lē-kônt′) | 170 | 46°28′N | 0°53′W |
| Fontenay-Trésigny, Fr. (fôN-te-nā′ tra-sēn-yē′) | 171b | 48°43′N | 2°53′E |
| Fontenelle Reservoir, res., Wy., U.S. | 115 | 42°05′N | 110°05′W |
| Fontera, Punta, c., Mex. (pōō′n-tä-fōn-tĕ′rä) | 131 | 18°36′N | 92°43′W |
| Fontibón, Col. (fōn-tē-bôn′) | 142a | 4°42′N | 74°09′W |
| Fontur, c., Ice. | 156 | 66°21′N | 14°02′W |
| Foothills, S. Afr. (fòt-hĭls) | 233b | 25°55′S | 27°36′E |
| Footscray, Austl. | 217a | 37°48′S | 144°54′E |
| Foraker, Mount, mtn., Ak., U.S. (fôr′á-kẽr) | 103 | 62°40′N | 152°40′W |
| Forbach, Fr. (fôr′bäk) | 171 | 49°12′N | 6°54′E |
| Forbes, Austl. (fôrbz) | 219 | 33°24′S | 148°05′E |
| Forbes, Mount, mtn., Can. | 95 | 51°52′N | 116°56′W |
| Forchheim, Ger. (fôrk′hīm) | 168 | 49°43′N | 11°05′E |
| Fordyce, Ar., U.S. (fôr′dīs) | 121 | 33°48′N | 92°24′W |
| Forécariah, Gui. (fôr-kà-rē′ä′) | 230 | 9°26′N | 13°06′W |
| Forel, Mont, mtn., Grnld. | 89 | 65°50′N | 37°41′W |
| Forest, Ms., U.S. (fŏr′ĕst) | 124 | 32°22′N | 89°29′W |
| Forest, r., N.D., U.S. | 112 | 48°08′N | 97°45′W |
| Forest City, Ia., U.S. | 113 | 43°14′N | 93°40′W |
| Forest City, N.C., U.S. | 125 | 35°20′N | 81°52′W |
| Forest City, Pa., U.S. | 109 | 41°35′N | 75°30′W |
| Forest Grove, Or., U.S. (grōv) | 116c | 45°31′N | 123°07′W |
| Forest Hill, Md., U.S. | 110e | 39°35′N | 76°26′W |
| Forest Hill, Tx., U.S. | 117c | 32°40′N | 97°16′W |
| Forestville, Can. (fŏr′ĕst-vĭl) | 100 | 48°45′N | 69°06′W |
| Forestville, Md., U.S. | 110e | 38°51′N | 76°55′W |
| Forez, Monts du, mts., Fr. (môN dū fō-rā′) | 170 | 44°55′N | 3°43′E |
| Forfar, Scot., U.K. (fôr′fȧr) | 164 | 57°10′N | 2°55′W |
| Forillon, Parc National, rec., Can. | 100 | 48°50′N | 64°05′W |
| Forio, mtn., Italy (fô′ryō) | 173c | 40°29′N | 13°55′E |
| Forked Creek, r., Il., U.S. (fôrk′d) | 111a | 41°16′N | 88°01′W |
| Forked Deer, r., Tn., U.S. | 124 | 35°53′N | 89°29′W |
| Forli, Italy (fôr-lē′) | 162 | 44°13′N | 12°03′E |
| Formby, Eng., U.K. (fôrm′bē) | 158a | 53°34′N | 3°04′W |
| Formby Point, c., Eng., U.K. | 158a | 53°33′N | 3°06′W |
| Formentera, Isla de, i., Spain (ē′s-lä-dĕ-fôr-mĕn-tā′rä) | 162 | 38°43′N | 1°25′E |
| Formiga, Braz. (fôr-mē′gȧ) | 143 | 20°27′S | 45°25′W |
| Formigas Bank, bk. (fôr-mē′gäs) | 135 | 18°30′N | 75°40′W |
| Formosa, Arg. (fôr-mō′sä) | 144 | 27°25′S | 58°12′W |
| Formosa, Braz. | 143 | 15°32′S | 47°10′W |
| Formosa, prov., Arg. | 144 | 24°30′S | 60°45′W |
| Formosa, Serra, mts., Braz. (sĕ′r-rä) | 143 | 12°59′S | 55°11′W |
| Formosa Bay, b., Kenya | 237 | 2°45′S | 40°30′E |
| Formosa Strait *see* Taiwan Strait, strt., Asia | 205 | 24°30′N | 120°00′E |
| Fornosovo, Russia (fôr-nô′sô vô) | 186c | 59°35′N | 30°34′E |
| Forrest City, Ar., U.S. (for′ĕst sĭ′tĭ) | 121 | 35°00′N | 90°46′W |
| Forsayth, Austl. (fôr-sīth′) | 219 | 18°33′S | 143°42′E |
| Forshaga, Swe. (fôrs′hä′gä) | 166 | 59°34′N | 13°25′E |
| Forst, Ger. (fôrst) | 161 | 51°45′N | 14°38′E |
| Forsyth, Ga., U.S. (fôr-sīth′) | 124 | 33°02′N | 83°56′W |
| Forsyth, Mt., U.S. | 115 | 46°15′N | 106°41′W |
| Fort Albany, Can. (fôrt ôl′bȧ nĭ) | 91 | 52°20′N | 81°30′W |
| Fort Alexander Indian Reserve, I.R., Can. | 97 | 50°27′N | 96°15′W |
| Fortaleza, Braz. (fôr′tä-lā′zȧ) | 143 | 3°35′S | 38°31′W |
| Fort Apache Indian Reservation, I.R., Az., U.S. (ȧ-păch′ē) | 119 | 34°02′N | 110°27′W |
| Fort Atkinson, Wi., U.S. (ăt′kĭn-sŭn) | 113 | 42°55′N | 88°46′W |
| Fort Beaufort, S. Afr. (bō′fôrt) | 233c | 32°47′S | 26°39′E |
| Fort Belknap Indian Reservation, I.R., Mt., U.S. | 115 | 48°16′N | 108°38′W |
| Fort Bellefontaine, Mo., U.S. (bĕl-fōn-tān′) | 117f | 38°50′N | 90°15′W |

294 Fort Benton – Fryazino PRONOUNCING INDEX


| PLACE (Pronunciation) | PAGE | LAT. | LONG. |
|---|---|---|---|
| Fort Benton, Mt., U.S. (bĕn′tŭn) | 115 | 47°51′N | 110°40′W |
| Fort Berthold Indian Reservation, I.R., N.D., U.S. (bĕrth′ôld) | 112 | 47°47′N | 103°28′W |
| Fort Bragg, Ca., U.S. | 118 | 39°26′N | 123°48′W |
| Fort Branch, In., U.S. (brănch) | 108 | 38°15′N | 87°35′W |
| Fort Chipewyan, Can. | 90 | 58°46′N | 111°15′W |
| Fort Cobb Reservoir, res., Ok., U.S. | 120 | 35°12′N | 98°28′W |
| Fort Collins, Co., U.S. (kŏl′ĭns) | 104 | 40°36′N | 105°04′W |
| Fort Crampel, C.A.R. (kràm-pĕl′) | 231 | 6°59′N | 19°11′E |
| Fort-de-France, Mart. (dē fräns) | 129 | 14°37′N | 61°06′W |
| Fort Deposit, Al., U.S. (dē-pŏz′ĭt) | 124 | 31°58′N | 86°35′W |
| Fort-de-Possel, C.A.R. (dē pô-sĕl′) | 231 | 5°03′N | 19°11′E |
| Fort Dodge, Ia., U.S. (dŏj) | 105 | 42°31′N | 94°10′W |
| Fort Edward, N.Y., U.S. (wẽrd) | 109 | 43°15′N | 73°30′W |
| Fort Erie, Can. (ē′rĭ) | 111c | 42°55′N | 78°56′W |
| Fortescue, r., Austl. (fôr′tĕs-kū) | 220 | 21°25′S | 116°50′E |
| Fort Fairfield, Me., U.S. (fâr′fēld) | 100 | 46°46′N | 67°53′W |
| Fort Fitzgerald, Can. (fĭts-jĕr′ăld) | 90 | 59°48′N | 111°50′W |
| Fort Frances, Can. (frăn′sĕs) | 91 | 48°36′N | 93°24′W |
| Fort Frederica National Monument, rec., Ga., U.S. (frĕd′ĕ-rī-kā) | 124 | 31°13′N | 85°25′W |
| Fort Gaines, Ga., U.S. (gānz) | 124 | 31°35′N | 85°03′W |
| Fort Gibson, Ok., U.S. (gĭb′sŭn) | 121 | 35°50′N | 95°13′W |
| Fort Good Hope, Can. (go͝od hōp) | 90 | 66°19′N | 128°52′W |
| Forth, Firth of, b., Scot., U.K. (fûrth ŏv fôrth) | 156 | 56°04′N | 3°03′W |
| Fort Hall, Kenya (hôl) | 233 | 0°47′S | 37°13′E |
| Fort Hall Indian Reservation, I.R., Id., U.S. | 115 | 43°02′N | 112°21′W |
| Fort Huachuca, Az., U.S. (wä-cho͞o′kä) | 119 | 31°30′N | 110°25′W |
| Fortier, Can. (fôr′tyā′) | 102f | 49°56′N | 97°55′W |
| Fort Kent, Me., U.S. (kĕnt) | 100 | 47°14′N | 68°37′W |
| Fort Langley, Can. (lăng′lĭ) | 116d | 49°10′N | 122°35′W |
| Fort Lauderdale, Fl., U.S. (lô′dẽr-dāl) | 125a | 26°07′N | 80°09′W |
| Fort Lee, N.J., U.S. | 110a | 40°50′N | 73°58′W |
| Fort Liard, Can. | 90 | 60°16′N | 123°34′W |
| Fort Loudoun Lake, res., Tn., U.S. (fōrt lou′dĕn) | 124 | 35°52′N | 84°10′W |
| Fort Lupton, Co., U.S. (lŭp′tŭn) | 120 | 40°04′N | 104°54′W |
| Fort Macleod, Can. (mă-kloud′) | 90 | 49°43′N | 113°25′W |
| Fort Madison, Ia., U.S. (măd′ĭ-sŭn) | 113 | 40°40′N | 91°17′W |
| Fort Matanzas, Fl., U.S. (mä-tän′zäs) | 125 | 29°39′N | 81°17′W |
| Fort McDermitt Indian Reservation, I.R., Or., U.S. (măk dẽr′mĭt) | 114 | 42°04′N | 118°07′W |
| Fort McMurray, Can. (măk-mŭr′ĭ) | 90 | 56°44′N | 111°23′W |
| Fort McPherson, Can. (măk-fŭr′s′n) | 90 | 67°37′N | 134°59′W |
| Fort Meade, Fl., U.S. (mēd) | 125a | 27°45′N | 81°48′W |
| Fort Mill, S.C., U.S. (mĭl) | 125 | 35°03′N | 80°57′W |
| Fort Mojave Indian Reservation, I.R., Ca., U.S. (mô-hä′vâ) | 118 | 34°59′N | 115°02′W |
| Fort Morgan, Co., U.S. (môr′găn) | 120 | 40°14′N | 103°49′W |
| Fort Myers, Fl., U.S. (mī′ẽrz) | 125a | 26°36′N | 81°45′W |
| Fort Nelson, Can. (nĕl′sŭn) | 90 | 58°57′N | 122°30′W |
| Fort Nelson, r., Can. (nĕl′sŭn) | 92 | 58°44′N | 122°20′W |
| Fort Payne, Al., U.S. (pān) | 124 | 34°26′N | 85°41′W |
| Fort Peck, Mt., U.S. (pĕk) | 115 | 47°58′N | 106°30′W |
| Fort Peck Indian Reservation, I.R., Mt., U.S. | 112 | 48°22′N | 105°40′W |
| Fort Peck Lake, res., Mt., U.S. | 106 | 47°52′N | 106°59′W |
| Fort Pierce, Fl., U.S. (pērs) | 125a | 27°25′N | 80°20′W |
| Fort Portal, Ug. (pôr′tál) | 231 | 0°40′N | 30°16′E |
| Fort Providence, Can. (prŏv′ĭ-dĕns) | 90 | 61°27′N | 117°59′W |
| Fort Pulaski National Monument, rec., Ga., U.S. (pu-lăs′kĭ) | 125 | 31°59′N | 80°56′W |
| Fort Qu'Appelle, Can. | 96 | 50°46′N | 103°55′W |
| Fort Randall Dam, dam, S.D., U.S. | 112 | 42°48′N | 98°35′W |
| Fort Resolution, Can. (rĕz′ō-lū′shŭn) | 90 | 61°08′N | 113°42′W |
| Fort Riley, Ks., U.S. (rī′lĭ) | 121 | 39°05′N | 96°46′W |
| Fort Saint James, Can. (fôrt sānt jāmz) | 90 | 54°26′N | 124°15′W |
| Fort Saint John, Can. (sānt jŏn) | 90 | 56°15′N | 120°51′W |
| Fort Sandeman, Pak. (săn′da-măn) | 199 | 31°28′N | 69°29′E |
| Fort Saskatchewan, Can. (săs-kăt′cho͞o-ån) | 102g | 53°43′N | 113°13′W |
| Fort Scott, Ks., U.S. (skŏt) | 105 | 37°50′N | 94°43′W |
| Fort Severn, Can. (sĕv′ẽrn) | 91 | 55°58′N | 87°50′W |
| Fort-Shevchenko, Kaz. (shĕv-chĕn′kô) | 183 | 44°30′N | 50°18′E |
| Fort Sibut, C.A.R. (fôr sē-bü′) | 231 | 5°44′N | 19°05′E |
| Fort Sill, Ok., U.S. (fôrt sĭl) | 120 | 34°41′N | 98°25′W |
| Fort Simpson, Can. (sĭmp′sŭn) | 90 | 61°52′N | 121°48′W |
| Fort Smith, Can. | 90 | 60°09′N | 112°08′W |
| Fort Smith, Ar., U.S. (smĭth) | 105 | 35°23′N | 94°24′W |
| Fort Stockton, Tx., U.S. (stŏk′tŭn) | 122 | 30°54′N | 102°51′W |
| Fort Sumner, N.M., U.S. (sŭm′nẽr) | 120 | 34°30′N | 104°17′W |
| Fort Sumter National Monument, rec., S.C., U.S. (sŭm′tẽr) | 125 | 32°43′N | 79°54′W |
| Fort Thomas, Ky., U.S. (tŏm′ăs) | 111f | 39°05′N | 84°27′W |
| Fortuna, Ca., U.S. (fôr-tū′nȧ) | 114 | 40°36′N | 124°10′W |
| Fortune, Can. (fôr′tŭn) | 101 | 47°04′N | 55°51′W |
| Fortune, i., Bah. | 135 | 22°35′N | 74°20′W |
| Fortune Bay, b., Can. | 93a | 47°25′N | 55°25′W |
| Fort Union National Monument, rec., N.M., U.S. (ūn′yŭn) | 120 | 35°51′N | 104°57′W |
| Fort Valley, Ga., U.S. (văl′ĭ) | 124 | 32°33′N | 83°53′W |
| Fort Vermilion, Can. (vẽr-mĭl′yŭn) | 90 | 58°23′N | 115°50′W |
| Fort Victoria see Masvingo, Zimb. | 232 | 20°07′S | 30°47′E |
| Fort Wayne, In., U.S. (wān) | 105 | 41°00′N | 85°10′W |
| Fort William, Scot., U.K. (wĭl′yăm) | 164 | 56°50′N | 3°00′W |
| Fort William, Mount, mtn., Austl. (wĭ′ĭ-ăm) | 222 | 24°45′S | 151°15′E |
| Fort Worth, Tx., U.S. (wûrth) | 104 | 32°45′N | 97°20′W |
| Fort Yukon, Ak., U.S. (yo͞o′kŏn) | 106a | 66°30′N | 145°00′W |
| Fort Yuma Indian Reservation, I.R., Ca., U.S. (yo͞o′mä) | 119 | 32°54′N | 114°47′W |
| Foshan, China | 205 | 23°02′N | 113°07′E |
| Fossano, Italy (fôs-sä′nō) | 174 | 44°34′N | 7°42′E |
| Fossil Creek, r., Tx., U.S. (fŏs-ĭl) | 117c | 32°53′N | 97°19′W |
| Fossombrone, Italy (fôs-sôm-brō′nā) | 174 | 43°41′N | 12°48′E |
| Foss Res, Ok., U.S. | 120 | 35°38′N | 99°11′W |
| Fosston, Mn., U.S. (fôs′tŭn) | 112 | 47°34′N | 95°44′W |
| Fosterburg, Il., U.S. (fŏs′tẽr-bûrg) | 117e | 38°58′N | 90°04′W |
| Fostoria, Oh., U.S. (fŏs-tō′rĭ-ȧ) | 108 | 41°10′N | 83°20′W |
| Fougéres, Fr. (fo͞o-zhâr′) | 161 | 48°23′N | 1°14′W |
| Foula, i., Scot., U.K. (fou′lȧ) | 164a | 60°08′N | 2°04′W |
| Foulwind, Cape, c., N.Z. (foul′wĭnd) | 221a | 41°45′S | 171°00′E |
| Foumban, Cam. (fo͞om-bän′) | 230 | 5°43′N | 10°55′E |
| Fountain Creek, r., Co., U.S. (foun′tĭn) | 120 | 38°36′N | 104°37′W |
| Fountain Valley, Ca., U.S. | 117a | 33°42′N | 117°57′W |
| Fourche la Fave, r., Ar., U.S. (fo͞orsh lä fäv′) | 121 | 34°46′N | 93°45′W |
| Fouriesburg, S. Afr. (fō′rēz-bûrg) | 238c | 28°38′S | 28°13′E |
| Fourmies, Fr. (fo͞or-mē′) | 170 | 50°01′N | 4°01′E |
| Four Mountains, Islands of the, is., Ak., U.S. | 103a | 52°58′N | 170°40′W |
| Fourth Cataract, wtfl., Sudan | 231 | 18°52′N | 32°07′E |
| Fouta Djallon, mts., Gui. (fo͞o′tä jä-lôɴ) | 230 | 11°37′N | 12°29′W |
| Foveaux Strait, strt., N.Z. (fō-vō′) | 221a | 46°30′S | 167°43′E |
| Fowler, Co., U.S. (foul′ẽr) | 120 | 38°04′N | 104°02′W |
| Fowler, In., U.S. | 108 | 40°35′N | 87°20′W |
| Fowler, Point, c., Austl. | 220 | 32°05′S | 132°30′E |
| Fowlerton, Tx., U.S. (foul′ẽr-tŭn) | 122 | 28°26′N | 98°48′W |
| Fox, i., Wa., U.S. (fŏks) | 116a | 47°15′N | 122°08′W |
| Fox, r., Il., U.S. | 113 | 41°35′N | 88°43′W |
| Fox, r., Wi., U.S. | 113 | 44°18′N | 88°23′W |
| Foxboro, Ma., U.S. (fŏks′bŭrō) | 101a | 42°04′N | 71°15′W |
| Foxe Basin, b., Can. (fŏks) | 93 | 67°35′N | 79°21′W |
| Foxe Channel, strt., Can. | 93 | 64°30′N | 79°23′W |
| Foxe Peninsula, pen., Can. | 93 | 64°57′N | 77°26′W |
| Fox Islands, is., Ak., U.S. (fŏks) | 103a | 53°04′N | 167°30′W |
| Fox Lake, Il., U.S. (lăk) | 111a | 42°24′N | 88°11′W |
| Fox Lake, l., Il., U.S. | 111a | 42°24′N | 88°07′W |
| Fox Point, Wi., U.S. | 111a | 43°10′N | 87°54′W |
| Foyle, Lough, b., Eur. (lŏk foil′) | 164 | 55°07′N | 7°08′W |
| Foz do Cunene, Ang. | 236 | 17°16′S | 11°50′E |
| Fraga, Spain (frä′gä) | 173 | 41°31′N | 0°20′E |
| Fragoso, Cayo, i., Cuba (kä′yō-frä-gō′sō) | 134 | 22°45′N | 79°30′W |
| Framnes Mountains, mts., Ant. | 224 | 67°50′S | 62°35′E |
| Franca, Braz. (frä′n-kä) | 143 | 20°28′S | 47°20′W |
| Francavilla, Italy (främ-kä-vēl′lä) | 175 | 40°32′N | 17°37′E |
| France, nation, Eur. (fråns) | 154 | 46°39′N | 0°47′E |
| Frances, l., Can. (frăn′sĭs) | 92 | 61°27′N | 128°28′W |
| Frances, Cabo, c., Cuba (kä′bō-frän-sĕ′s) | 134 | 21°55′N | 84°05′W |
| Frances, Punta, c., Cuba (po͞o′n-tä-frän-sĕ′s) | 134 | 21°45′N | 83°10′W |
| Francés Viejo, Cabo, c., Dom. Rep. (kȧ′bō-frän′sås vyā′hō) | 135 | 19°40′N | 69°35′W |
| Franceville, Gabon (fräɴs-vēl′) | 232 | 1°38′S | 13°35′E |
| Francis Case, Lake, res., S.D., U.S. (frăn′sĭs) | 106 | 43°15′N | 99°00′W |
| Francisco Sales, Braz. (frän-sē′s-kô-sȧ′lĕs) | 141a | 21°42′S | 44°26′W |
| Francistown, Bots. (från′sĭs-toun) | 232 | 21°17′S | 27°28′E |
| Frankfort, S. Afr. (frănk′fŏrt) | 233c | 32°43′S | 27°28′E |
| Frankfort, S. Afr. | 238c | 27°17′S | 28°30′E |
| Frankfort, Il., U.S. (frăŋk′fŭrt) | 111a | 41°30′N | 87°51′W |
| Frankfort, In., U.S. | 108 | 40°15′N | 86°30′W |
| Frankfort, Ks., U.S. | 121 | 39°42′N | 96°27′W |
| Frankfort, Ky., U.S. | 105 | 38°10′N | 84°55′W |
| Frankfort, Mi., U.S. | 108 | 44°40′N | 86°15′W |
| Frankfort, N.Y., U.S. | 109 | 43°05′N | 75°05′W |
| Frankfurt am Main, Ger. | 154 | 50°07′N | 8°40′E |
| Frankfurt an der Oder, Ger. | 161 | 52°20′N | 14°31′E |
| Franklin, S. Afr. | 233c | 30°19′S | 29°28′E |
| Franklin, In., U.S. (frănk′lĭn) | 108 | 39°25′N | 86°00′W |
| Franklin, Ky., U.S. | 124 | 36°42′N | 86°34′W |
| Franklin, La., U.S. | 123 | 29°47′N | 91°31′W |
| Franklin, Ma., U.S. | 101a | 42°05′N | 71°24′W |
| Franklin, Ne., U.S. | 120 | 40°06′N | 99°01′W |
| Franklin, N.H., U.S. | 109 | 43°25′N | 71°40′W |
| Franklin, N.J., U.S. | 110a | 41°08′N | 74°35′W |
| Franklin, Oh., U.S. | 108 | 39°30′N | 84°20′W |
| Franklin, Pa., U.S. | 109 | 41°25′N | 79°50′W |
| Franklin, Tn., U.S. | 124 | 35°54′N | 86°54′W |
| Franklin, Va., U.S. | 125 | 36°41′N | 76°57′W |
| Franklin, l., Nv., U.S. | 118 | 40°23′N | 115°10′W |
| Franklin D. Roosevelt Lake, res., Wa., U.S. | 114 | 48°12′N | 118°43′W |
| Franklin Mountains, mts., Can. | 92 | 65°36′N | 125°55′W |
| Franklin Park, Il., U.S. | 111a | 41°56′N | 87°53′W |
| Franklin Square, N.Y., U.S. | 110a | 40°43′N | 73°40′W |
| Franklinton, La., U.S. (frăŋk′lĭn-tŭn) | 123 | 30°49′N | 90°09′W |
| Frankston, Austl. | 217a | 38°09′S | 145°08′E |
| Franksville, Wi., U.S. (frănkz′vĭl) | 111a | 42°46′N | 87°55′W |
| Fransta, Swe. | 166 | 62°30′N | 16°04′E |
| Franz Josef Land see Zemlya Frantsa-Iosifa, is., Russia | 178 | 81°32′N | 40°00′E |
| Frascati, Italy (fräs-kä′tē) | 174 | 41°49′N | 12°45′E |
| Fraser, Mi., U.S. (frā′zẽr) | 111b | 42°32′N | 82°57′W |
| Fraser, i., Austl. | 221 | 25°12′S | 153°00′E |
| Fraser, r., Can. | 92 | 51°30′N | 122°00′W |
| Fraserburgh, Scot., U.K. (frā′zẽr-bûrg) | 164 | 57°40′N | 2°01′W |
| Fraser Plateau, plat., Can. | 95 | 51°30′N | 122°00′W |
| Frattamaggiore, Italy (frät-tä-mäg-zhyō′rĕ) | 173c | 40°41′N | 14°16′E |
| Fray Bentos, Ur. (frī bĕn′tōs) | 144 | 33°10′S | 58°19′W |
| Frazee, Mn., U.S. (frå-zē′) | 112 | 46°42′N | 95°43′W |
| Fraziers Hog Cay, i., Bah. | 134 | 25°25′N | 77°55′W |
| Frechen, Ger. (frĕ′ĸĕn) | 171c | 50°54′N | 6°49′E |
| Fredericia, Den. (frĕdh-ĕ-rē′tsē-à) | 166 | 55°35′N | 9°45′E |
| Frederick, Md., U.S. (frĕd′ẽr-ĭk) | 105 | 39°25′N | 77°25′W |
| Frederick, Ok., U.S. | 120 | 34°23′N | 99°01′W |
| Frederick House, r., Can. | 98 | 49°05′N | 81°20′W |
| Fredericksburg, Tx., U.S. (frĕd′ẽr-ĭkz-bûrg) | 122 | 30°16′N | 98°52′W |
| Fredericksburg, Va., U.S. | 109 | 38°20′N | 77°30′W |
| Fredericktown, Mo., U.S. (frĕd′ẽr-ĭk-toun) | 121 | 37°32′N | 90°16′W |
| Fredericton, Can. (frĕd′-ẽr-ĭk-tŭn) | 91 | 45°48′N | 66°39′W |
| Frederikshavn, Den. (frĕdh′ĕ-rĕks-houn) | 160 | 57°27′N | 10°31′E |
| Frederikssund, Den. (frĕdh′ĕ-rĕks-sōn) | 166 | 55°51′N | 12°04′E |
| Fredonia, Col. (frĕ-dō′nyà) | 142a | 5°55′N | 75°40′W |
| Fredonia, Ks., U.S. (frē-dō′nĭ-ȧ) | 121 | 36°31′N | 95°50′W |
| Fredonia, N.Y., U.S. | 109 | 42°25′N | 79°20′W |
| Fredrikstad, Nor. (frådh′rĕks-städ) | 160 | 59°14′N | 10°58′E |
| Freeburg, Il., U.S. (frē′bûrg) | 117e | 38°26′N | 89°59′W |
| Freehold, N.J., U.S. (frē′hōld) | 110a | 40°15′N | 74°16′W |
| Freeland, Pa., U.S. (frē′lȧnd) | 109 | 41°00′N | 75°50′W |
| Freeland, Wa., U.S. | 116a | 48°01′N | 122°32′W |
| Freels, Cape, c., Can. (frēlz) | 101 | 46°37′N | 53°45′W |
| Freelton, Can. (frēl′tŭn) | 102d | 43°24′N | 80°02′W |
| Freeport, Bah. | 134 | 26°30′N | 78°45′W |
| Freeport, Il., U.S. (frē′pōrt) | 105 | 42°19′N | 89°30′W |
| Freeport, N.Y., U.S. | 110a | 40°39′N | 73°35′W |
| Freeport, Tx., U.S. | 123 | 28°56′N | 95°21′W |
| Freetown, S.L. (frē′toun) | 230 | 8°30′N | 13°15′W |
| Fregenal de la Sierra, Spain (frā-hå-näl′ dā lä syĕr′rä) | 172 | 38°09′N | 6°40′W |
| Fregene, Italy (frĕ-zhĕ′-nĕ) | 173d | 41°52′N | 12°12′E |
| Freiberg, Ger. (frī′bĕrgh) | 161 | 50°54′N | 13°18′E |
| Freiburg, Ger. | 161 | 48°00′N | 7°50′E |
| Freienried, Ger. (frī′ĕn-rēd) | 159d | 48°20′N | 11°08′E |
| Freirina, Chile (frå-ĭ-rē′nä) | 144 | 28°35′S | 71°26′W |
| Freising, Ger. (frī′zĭng) | 168 | 48°25′N | 11°45′E |
| Fréjus, Fr. (frā-zhüs′) | 171 | 43°28′N | 6°46′E |
| Fremantle, Austl. (frē′măn-t′l) | 218 | 32°03′S | 116°05′E |
| Fremont, Ca., U.S. (frē-mŏnt′) | 116b | 37°33′N | 122°00′W |
| Fremont, Mi., U.S. | 108 | 43°25′N | 85°55′W |
| Fremont, Ne., U.S. | 112 | 41°26′N | 96°30′W |
| Fremont, Oh., U.S. | 108 | 41°20′N | 83°05′W |
| Fremont, r., Ut., U.S. | 119 | 38°20′N | 111°30′W |
| Fremont Peak, mtn., Wy., U.S. | 115 | 43°05′N | 109°35′W |
| French Broad, r., Tn., U.S. (frĕnch brôd) | 124 | 35°59′N | 83°01′W |
| French Frigate Shoals, Hi., U.S. | 126b | 23°30′N | 167°10′W |
| French Guiana, dep., S.A. (gē-ä′nä) | 143 | 4°20′N | 53°00′W |
| French Lick, In., U.S. (frĕnch lĭk) | 108 | 38°35′N | 86°35′W |
| Frenchman, r., N.A. | 96 | 49°25′N | 108°30′W |
| Frenchman Creek, r., Mt., U.S. (frĕnch-măn) | 115 | 48°51′N | 107°20′W |
| Frenchman Creek, r., Ne., U.S. | 120 | 40°24′N | 101°50′W |
| Frenchman Flat, Nv., U.S. | 118 | 36°55′N | 116°11′W |
| French Polynesia, dep., Oc. | 2 | 15°00′S | 140°00′W |
| French River, Mn., U.S. | 117h | 46°54′N | 91°54′W |
| Freshfield, Mount, mtn., Can. (frĕsh′fēld) | 95 | 51°44′N | 116°57′W |
| Fresnillo, Mex. (frås-nēl′yō) | 128 | 23°10′N | 102°52′W |
| Fresno, Col. (frĕs′nō) | 142a | 5°10′N | 75°01′W |
| Fresno, Ca., U.S. | 104 | 36°44′N | 119°46′W |
| Fresno, r., Ca., U.S. (frĕz′nō) | 118 | 37°00′N | 120°24′W |
| Fresno Slough, Ca., U.S. | 118 | 36°39′N | 120°12′W |
| Freudenstadt, Ger. (froi′den-shtät) | 168 | 48°28′N | 8°26′E |
| Freycinet Peninsula, pen., Austl. (frā-sē-nĕ′) | 222 | 42°13′S | 148°56′E |
| Fria, Gui. | 234 | 10°05′N | 13°32′W |
| Fria, r., Az., U.S. (frē-ä) | 119 | 34°03′N | 112°12′W |
| Fria, Cape, c., Nmb. (frīȧ) | 232 | 18°15′S | 12°10′E |
| Friant-Kern Canal, can., Ca., U.S. (kûrn) | 118 | 36°57′N | 119°37′W |
| Frias, Arg. (frē-äs) | 144 | 28°43′S | 65°03′W |
| Fribourg, Switz. (frē-bo͞or′) | 161 | 46°48′N | 7°07′E |
| Fridley, Mn., U.S. (frĭd′lĭ) | 117g | 45°05′N | 93°16′W |
| Friedberg, Ger. (frēd′bĕrgh) | 159d | 48°22′N | 11°00′E |
| Friedland, Ger. (frēt′länt) | 168 | 53°39′N | 13°34′E |
| Friedrichshafen, Ger. (frē-drēks-häf′ĕn) | 168 | 47°39′N | 9°28′E |
| Friend, Ne., U.S. (frĕnd) | 121 | 40°40′N | 97°16′W |
| Friendswood, Tx., U.S. (frĕnds′wŏd) | 123a | 29°31′N | 95°11′W |
| Fries, Va., U.S. (frēz) | 125 | 36°42′N | 80°59′W |
| Friesack, Ger. (frē′săk) | 159b | 52°44′N | 12°35′E |
| Frio, Cabo, c., Braz. (kä′bō-frē′ō) | 143 | 22°58′S | 42°08′W |
| Frio R, Tx., U.S. | 122 | 29°00′N | 99°15′W |
| Frisian Islands, is., Neth. (frĭ′zhăn) | 160 | 53°30′N | 5°20′E |
| Friuli-Venezia Giulia, hist. reg., Italy | 174 | 46°20′N | 13°20′E |
| Frobisher Bay, b., Can. | 93 | 62°49′N | 66°41′W |
| Frobisher Lake, l., Can. (frŏb′ĭsh-ẽr) | 92 | 56°25′N | 108°20′W |
| Frodsham, Eng., U.K. (frŏdz′ăm) | 158a | 53°18′N | 2°48′W |
| Frohavet, b., Nor. | 160 | 63°49′N | 9°12′E |
| Frome, Lake, l., Austl. (fro͞om) | 220 | 30°40′S | 140°13′E |
| Frontenac, Ks., U.S. (frŏn′tē-năk) | 121 | 37°27′N | 94°41′W |
| Frontera, Mex. (frôn-tā′rä) | 131 | 18°34′N | 92°38′W |
| Front Range, mts., Co., U.S. (frŭnt) | 120 | 40°59′N | 105°29′W |
| Front Royal, Va., U.S. (frŭnt) | 109 | 38°55′N | 78°10′W |
| Frosinone, Italy (frō-zē-nō′nā) | 174 | 41°38′N | 13°22′E |
| Frostburg, Md., U.S. (frôst′bûrg) | 109 | 39°40′N | 78°55′W |
| Fruita, Co., U.S. (fro͞ot-ȧ) | 119 | 39°10′N | 108°45′W |
| Frunze see Bishkek, Kyrg. | 183 | 42°49′N | 74°42′E |
| Fryanovo, Russia (f′ryä′nô-vô) | 186b | 56°08′N | 38°28′E |
| Fryazino, Russia (f′ryä′zĭ-nô) | 186b | 55°58′N | 38°05′E |


ăt; finăl; rāte; senåte; ärm; åsk; sofȧ; fâre; ch-choose; dh-as th in other; bē; ēvent; bĕt; recĕnt; cratẽr; g-gō; gh-guttural g; bĭt; ĭ-short neutral; rīde; ĸ-guttural k as ch in German ich;

PRONOUNCING INDEX

Frydlant – Gattendorf 295


| PLACE (Pronunciation) | PAGE | LAT. | LONG. |
|---|---|---|---|
| Frydlant, Czech Rep. (frēd'länt) | 168 | 50°56'N | 15°05'E |
| Fucheng, China (fo͞o-chŭŋ) | 206 | 37°53'N | 116°08'E |
| Fuchu, Japan (fo͞o'cho͞o) | 211a | 35°41'N | 139°29'E |
| Fuchun, r., China (fo͞o-chòn) | 209 | 29°50'N | 120°00'E |
| Fuego, vol., Guat. (fwā'gō) | 132 | 14°29'N | 90°52'W |
| Fuencarral, Spain (fuān-kär-räl') | 173a | 40°29'N | 3°42'W |
| Fuensalida, Spain (fwān-sä-lē'dä) | 172 | 40°04'N | 4°15'W |
| Fuente, Mex. (fwĕ'n-tĕ') | 122 | 28°39'N | 100°34'W |
| Fuente de Cantos, Spain (fwĕn'tå dā kän'tōs) | 172 | 38°15'N | 6°18'W |
| Fuente el Saz, Spain (fwĕn'tå ĕl säth') | 173a | 40°39'N | 3°30'W |
| Fuenteobejuna, Spain | 172 | 38°15'N | 5°30'W |
| Fuentesaúco, Spain (fwĕn-tå-sä-o͞o'kō) | 172 | 41°18'N | 5°25'W |
| Fuerte, Río del, r., Mex. (rē'ō-dĕl-fo͞o-ĕ'r-tĕ) | 128 | 26°15'N | 108°50'W |
| Fuerte Olimpo, Para. (fwĕr'tå ō-lēm-pō) | 144 | 21°10'S | 57°49'W |
| Fuerteventura Island, i., Spain (fwĕr'tå-vĕn-to͞o'rä) | 230 | 28°24'N | 13°21'W |
| Fuhai, China | 204 | 47°01'N | 87°07'E |
| Fuji, Japan (jo͞o'jē) | 211 | 35°11'N | 138°44'E |
| Fuji, r., Japan | 211 | 35°20'N | 138°23'E |
| Fujian, prov., China (fo͞o-jyĕn) | 205 | 25°40'N | 117°30'E |
| Fujidera, Japan | 211b | 34°34'N | 135°37'E |
| Fujin, China (fo͞o-jyĭn) | 205 | 47°13'N | 132°11'E |
| Fuji San, mtn., Japan (fo͞o'jē sän) | 205 | 35°23'N | 138°44'E |
| Fujisawa, Japan (fo͞o'jē-sä'wa) | 211a | 35°20'N | 139°29'E |
| Fujiyama *see* Fuji San, mtn., Japan | 205 | 35°23'N | 138°44'E |
| Fukuchiyama, Japan (fò'kò-chē-yä'ma) | 211 | 35°18'N | 135°07'E |
| Fukue, i., Japan (fò-ko͞o'ä) | 210 | 32°40'N | 129°02'E |
| Fukui, Japan (fo͞o'ko͞o-ē) | 205 | 36°05'N | 136°14'E |
| Fukuoka, Japan (fo͞o'kò-ō'kà) | 205 | 33°35'N | 130°23'E |
| Fukuoka, Japan | 211a | 35°52'N | 139°31'E |
| Fukushima, Japan (fo͞o'kò-shē'mà) | 210 | 37°45'N | 140°29'E |
| Fukuyama, Japan (fo͞o'kò-yä'mà) | 210 | 34°31'N | 133°21'E |
| Fulda, Ger. | 161 | 50°33'N | 9°41'E |
| Fulda, r., Ger. (fòl'dä) | 168 | 51°05'N | 9°40'E |
| Fuling, China (fo͞o-lĭŋ) | 204 | 29°40'N | 107°30'E |
| Fullerton, Ca., U.S. (fòl'ĕr-tŭn) | 117a | 33°53'N | 117°56'W |
| Fullerton, La., U.S. | 123 | 31°00'N | 93°00'W |
| Fullerton, Ne., U.S. | 112 | 41°21'N | 97°59'W |
| Fulton, Ky., U.S. (fŭl'tŭn) | 124 | 36°30'N | 88°53'W |
| Fulton, Mo., U.S. | 121 | 38°51'N | 91°56'W |
| Fulton, N.Y., U.S. | 109 | 43°20'N | 76°25'W |
| Fultondale, Al., U.S. (fŭl'tŭn-dāl) | 110h | 33°37'N | 86°48'W |
| Funabashi, Japan (fo͞o'nà-bä'shē) | 211 | 35°43'N | 139°59'E |
| Funaya, Japan (fo͞o-nä'yä) | 211b | 34°45'N | 135°52'E |
| Funchal, Port. (fòn-shäl') | 230 | 32°41'N | 16°15'W |
| Fundación, Col. (fo͞on-dä-syō'n) | 142 | 10°43'N | 74°13'W |
| Fundão, Port. (fòn-douN') | 172 | 40°08'N | 7°32'W |
| Fundy, Bay of, b., Can. (fŭn'dĭ) | 93 | 45°00'N | 66°00'W |
| Fundy National Park, rec., Can. | 93 | 45°38'N | 65°00'W |
| Funing, China (fo͞o-nĭŋ) | 208 | 33°55'N | 119°54'E |
| Funing, China | 206 | 39°55'N | 119°16'E |
| Funing Wan, b., China | 209 | 26°48'N | 120°35'E |
| Funtua, Nig. | 235 | 11°31'N | 7°17'E |
| Furancungo, Moz. | 237 | 14°55'S | 33°35'E |
| Furbero, Mex. (fo͞or-bĕ'rô) | 131 | 20°21'N | 97°32'W |
| Furgun, mtn., Iran | 198 | 28°47'N | 57°00'E |
| Furmanov, Russia (fûr-mä'nôf) | 180 | 57°14'N | 41°11'E |
| Furnas, Represa de, res., Braz. | 143 | 21°00'S | 46°00'W |
| Furneaux Group, is., Austl. (fûr'nō) | 221 | 40°15'S | 146°27'E |
| Fürstenfeld, Aus. (für'stĕn-fĕlt) | 168 | 47°02'N | 16°03'E |
| Fürstenfeldbruck, Ger. (fur'stĕn-fĕld'bro͞ok) | 159d | 48°11'N | 11°16'E |
| Fürstenwalde, Ger. (für'stĕn-väl-dĕ) | 168 | 52°21'N | 14°04'E |
| Fürth, Ger. (fürt) | 161 | 49°28'N | 11°03'E |
| Furuichi, Japan (fo͞o'rò-ē'chē) | 211b | 34°33'N | 135°37'E |
| Fusa, Japan (fo͞o'sä) | 211a | 35°52'N | 140°08'E |
| Fuse, Japan | 211b | 34°40'N | 135°33'E |
| Fushimi, Japan (fo͞o'shē-mē) | 211b | 34°57'N | 135°47'E |
| Fushun, China (fo͞o'sho͞on') | 205 | 41°50'N | 124°00'E |
| Fusong, China (fo͞o-soŋ) | 208 | 42°12'N | 127°12'E |
| Futtsu, Japan (fo͞o'tso͞o') | 211a | 35°19'N | 139°49'E |
| Futtsu Misaki, c., Japan (fo͞ot'tso͞o' mē-sä'kē) | 211a | 35°19'N | 139°46'E |
| Fuwah, Egypt (fo͞o'wà) | 238b | 31°13'N | 30°35'E |
| Fuxian, China (fo͞o shyĕn) | 206 | 39°36'N | 121°59'E |
| Fuxin, China (fo͞o-shyĭn) | 208 | 42°05'N | 121°40'E |
| Fuyang, China (fo͞o-yäŋ) | 205 | 32°53'N | 115°48'E |
| Fuyang, China | 209 | 30°10'N | 119°58'E |
| Fuyang, r., China (fo͞o-yäŋ) | 206 | 36°59'N | 114°48'E |
| Fuyu, China (fo͞o-yo͞o) | 205 | 45°20'N | 125°00'E |
| Fuzhou, China (fo͞o-jō) | 205 | 26°02'N | 119°18'E |
| Fuzhou, r., China | 206 | 39°38'N | 121°43'E |
| Fuzhoucheng, China (fo͞o-jō-chŭŋ) | 206 | 39°46'N | 121°44'E |
| Fyn, i., Den. (fü'n) | 166 | 55°24'N | 10°33'E |
| Fyne, Loch, l., Scot., U.K. (fīn) | 164 | 56°14'N | 5°10'W |
| Fyresvatn, l., Nor. | 166 | 59°04'N | 7°55'E |


# G


| PLACE (Pronunciation) | PAGE | LAT. | LONG. |
|---|---|---|---|
| Gaalkacyo, Som. | 238a | 7°00'N | 47°30'E |
| Gabela, Ang. | 236 | 10°48'S | 14°20'E |
| Gabès, Tun. (gä'bĕs) | 230 | 33°51'N | 10°04'E |
| Gabès, Golfe de, b., Tun. | 230 | 32°22'N | 10°59'E |
| Gabil, Chad | 235 | 11°09'N | 18°12'E |
| Gąbin, Pol. (gôN'bēn) | 169 | 52°23'N | 19°47'E |
| Gabon, nation, Afr. (gà-bôN') | 232 | 0°30'S | 10°45'E |
| Gaborone, Bots. | 232 | 24°28'S | 25°59'E |
| Gabriel, r., Tx., U.S. (gā'brĭ-ĕl) | 123 | 30°38'N | 97°15'W |
| Gabrovo, Blg. (gäb'rô-vō) | 175 | 42°52'N | 25°19'E |
| Gachsārān, Iran | 201 | 30°12'N | 50°47'E |
| Gacko, Bos. (gäts'kô) | 175 | 43°10'N | 18°34'E |
| Gadsden, Al., U.S. (gădz'dĕn) | 105 | 34°00'N | 86°00'W |
| Găeşti, Rom. (gä-yĕsh'tē) | 175 | 44°43'N | 25°21'E |
| Gaeta, Italy (gä-å'tä) | 174 | 41°18'N | 13°34'E |
| Gaffney, S.C., U.S. (găf'nĭ) | 125 | 35°04'N | 81°47'W |
| Gafsa, Tun. (găf'sä) | 230 | 34°16'N | 8°37'E |
| Gagarin, Russia | 176 | 55°32'N | 34°58'E |
| Gagnoa, C. Iv. | 234 | 6°08'N | 5°56'W |
| Gagra, Geor. | 182 | 43°20'N | 40°15'E |
| Gaillac-sur-Tarn, Fr. (gà-yäk'sür-tärn') | 170 | 43°54'N | 1°52'E |
| Gaillard Cut, reg., Pan. (gä-ēl-yä'rd) | 128a | 9°03'N | 79°42'W |
| Gainesville, Fl., U.S. (gānz'vĭl) | 105 | 29°40'N | 82°20'W |
| Gainesville, Ga., U.S. | 124 | 34°16'N | 83°48'W |
| Gainesville, Tx., U.S. | 121 | 33°38'N | 97°08'W |
| Gainsborough, Eng., U.K. (gānz'bŭr-ô) | 158a | 53°23'N | 0°46'W |
| Gairdner, Lake, l., Austl. (gård'nĕr) | 220 | 32°20'S | 136°30'E |
| Gaithersburg, Md., U.S. (gā'thĕrs'bûrg) | 110e | 39°08'N | 77°13'W |
| Gaixian, China (gī-shyĕn) | 208 | 40°25'N | 122°20'E |
| Galana, r., Kenya | 237 | 3°00'S | 39°30'E |
| Galapagar, Spain (gä-lä-pä-gär') | 173a | 40°36'N | 4°00'W |
| Galapagos Islands *see* Colón, Archipiélago de, is., Ec. | 142 | 0°10'S | 87°45'W |
| Galaria, r., Italy | 173d | 41°58'N | 12°21'E |
| Galashiels, Scot., U.K. (găl-à-shēlz) | 164 | 55°40'N | 2°57'W |
| Galaţi, Rom. | 154 | 45°25'N | 28°05'E |
| Galatina, Italy (gä-lä-tē'nä) | 175 | 40°10'N | 18°12'E |
| Galaxídi, Grc. | 175 | 38°26'N | 22°22'E |
| Galdhøpiggen, mtn., Nor. | 166 | 61°37'N | 8°17'E |
| Galeana, Mex. (gä-lå-ä'nä) | 122 | 24°50'N | 100°04'W |
| Galena, Il., U.S. (gà-lē'nà) | 113 | 42°26'N | 90°27'W |
| Galena, In., U.S. | 111h | 38°21'N | 85°55'W |
| Galena Peak, mtn., Tx., U.S. | 123a | 29°44'N | 95°14'W |
| Galera, Cerro, mtn., Pan. (sĕ'r-rô-gä-lĕ'rä) | 128a | 8°55'N | 79°38'W |
| Galeras, vol., Col. (gä-lĕ'räs) | 142 | 0°57'N | 77°27'W |
| Gales, r., Or., U.S. (gālz) | 116c | 45°33'N | 123°11'W |
| Galesburg, Il., U.S. (gālz'bûrg) | 105 | 40°56'N | 90°21'W |
| Galesville, Wi., U.S. (gālz'vĭl) | 113 | 44°04'N | 91°22'W |
| Galeton, Pa., U.S. (gāl'tŭn) | 109 | 41°45'N | 77°40'W |
| Galich, Russia (gál'ĭch) | 180 | 58°20'N | 42°38'E |
| Galicia, hist. reg., Pol. (gà-lĭsh'ĭ-à) | 169 | 49°48'N | 21°05'E |
| Galicia, hist. reg., Spain (gä-lē'thyä) | 172 | 43°35'N | 8°03'W |
| Galilee, l., Austl. (găl'ĭ-lē) | 221 | 22°23'S | 145°09'E |
| Galilee, Sea of, l., Isr. | 197a | 32°53'N | 35°45'E |
| Galina Point, c., Jam. (gä-lē'nä) | 134 | 18°25'N | 76°50'W |
| Galion, Oh., U.S. (găl'ĭ-ŭn) | 108 | 40°45'N | 82°50'W |
| Galisteo, N.M., U.S. (gä-lĭs-tā'ō) | 120 | 35°20'N | 106°00'W |
| Gallarate, Italy (gäl-lä-rä'tä) | 174 | 45°37'N | 8°48'E |
| Gallardon, Fr. (gä-lär-dôN') | 171b | 48°31'N | 1°40'E |
| Gallatin, Mo., U.S. (găl'à-tĭn) | 121 | 39°55'N | 93°58'W |
| Gallatin, Tn., U.S. | 124 | 36°23'N | 86°28'W |
| Gallatin, r., Mt., U.S. | 115 | 45°12'N | 111°10'W |
| Galle, Sri L. (gäl) | 203 | 6°13'N | 80°10'E |
| Gállego, r., Spain (gäl-yā'gō) | 173 | 42°27'N | 0°37'W |
| Gallinas, Punta de, c., Col. (gä-lyē'näs) | 142 | 12°10'N | 72°10'W |
| Gallipoli, Italy (gäl-lē'pô-lē) | 175 | 40°03'N | 17°58'E |
| Gallipoli *see* Gelibolu, Tur. (gäl-lē'pô-lē) | 163 | 40°25'N | 26°40'E |
| Gallipoli Peninsula, pen., Tur. | 175 | 40°23'N | 25°10'E |
| Gallipolis, Oh., U.S. (găl-ĭ-pô-lēs) | 108 | 38°50'N | 82°10'W |
| Gällivare, Swe. (yĕl-ĭ-vär'ĕ) | 160 | 68°06'N | 20°29'E |
| Gallo, r., Spain (gäl'yō) | 172 | 40°43'N | 1°42'W |
| Gallup, N.M., U.S. (găl'ŭp) | 104 | 35°30'N | 108°45'W |
| Galty Mountains, mts., Ire. | 164 | 52°19'N | 8°20'W |
| Galva, Il., U.S. (găl'và) | 121 | 41°11'N | 90°02'W |
| Galveston, Tx., U.S. (găl'vĕs-tŭn) | 105 | 29°18'N | 94°48'W |
| Galveston Bay, b., Tx., U.S. | 107 | 29°39'N | 94°45'W |
| Galveston I, Tx., U.S. | 123a | 29°12'N | 94°53'W |
| Galway, Ire. | 154 | 53°16'N | 9°05'W |
| Galway Bay, b., Ire. (gôl'wā) | 164 | 53°10'N | 9°47'W |
| Gamba, China (gäm-bä) | 202 | 28°23'N | 89°42'E |
| Gambaga, Ghana (gäm-bä'gä) | 230 | 10°32'N | 0°26'W |
| Gambela, Eth. (gäm-bā'là) | 235 | 8°15'N | 34°33'E |
| Gambia (Gambie), r., Afr. | 234 | 13°20'N | 15°55'W |
| Gambia, The, nation, Afr. | 230 | 13°38'N | 19°38'W |
| Gambie, r., Afr. | 230 | 12°30'N | 13°00'W |
| Gamboma, Congo (gäm-bō'mä) | 232 | 1°53'S | 15°51'E |
| Gamleby, Swe. (gäm'lĕ-bü) | 166 | 57°54'N | 16°20'E |
| Gan, r., China (gän) | 209 | 26°50'N | 115°00'E |
| Gäncä, Azer. | 180 | 40°40'N | 46°22'E |
| Gandak, r., India | 202 | 26°37'N | 84°22'E |
| Gander, Can. (găn'dēr) | 91 | 48°57'N | 54°34'W |
| Gander, r., Can. | 101 | 49°10'N | 54°35'W |
| Gander Lake, l., Can. | 101 | 48°55'N | 55°40'W |
| Gandhinagar, India | 202 | 23°30'N | 72°47'E |
| Gandi, Nig. | 235 | 12°55'N | 5°49'E |
| Gandía, Spain (gän-dē'ä) | 173 | 38°56'N | 0°10'W |
| Gangdisê Shan (Trans Himalayas), mts., China | 204 | 30°25'N | 83°43'E |
| Ganges, r., Asia (găn'jēz) | 199 | 24°00'N | 89°30'E |
| Ganges, Mouths of the, mth., Asia (găn'jēz) | 199 | 21°18'N | 88°40'E |
| Gangi, Italy (gän'jē) | 174 | 37°48'N | 14°15'E |
| Gangtok, India | 199 | 27°15'N | 88°30'E |
| Gannan, China (gän-nän) | 208 | 47°50'N | 123°30'E |
| Gannett Peak, mtn., Wy., U.S. (găn'ĕt) | 106 | 43°10'N | 109°38'W |
| Gano, Oh., U.S. (ă'nō) | 111f | 39°18'N | 84°24'W |
| Gänserndorf, Aus. | 159e | 48°21'N | 16°43'E |
| Gansu, prov., China (gän-so͞o) | 204 | 38°50'N | 101°10'E |
| Ganwo, Nig. | 235 | 11°13'N | 4°42'E |
| Ganyu, China (gän-yo͞o) | 206 | 34°52'N | 119°07'E |
| Ganzhou, China (gän-jō) | 205 | 25°50'N | 114°30'E |
| Gao, Mali (gä'ō) | 230 | 16°16'N | 0°03'W |
| Gao'an, China (gou-än) | 209 | 28°30'N | 115°02'E |
| Gaomi, China (gou-mē) | 206 | 36°23'N | 119°46'E |
| Gaoqiao, China (gou-chyou) | 207b | 31°21'N | 121°35'E |
| Gaoshun, China (gou-shòn) | 206 | 31°22'N | 118°50'E |
| Gaotang, China (gou-täŋ) | 206 | 36°52'N | 116°12'E |
| Gaoyao, China (gou-you) | 209 | 23°08'N | 112°25'E |
| Gaoyi, China (gou-yē) | 206 | 37°37'N | 114°39'E |
| Gaoyou, China (gou-yō) | 208 | 32°46'N | 119°26'E |
| Gaoyou Hu, l., China (kä'ō-yo͞o'ho͞o) | 205 | 32°42'N | 118°40'E |
| Gap, Fr. (gàp) | 161 | 44°34'N | 6°08'E |
| Gapan, Phil. (gä-pän) | 213a | 15°18'N | 120°56'E |
| Gar, China | 204 | 31°11'N | 80°35'E |
| Garanhuns, Braz. (gä-rän-yòNsh') | 143 | 8°49'S | 36°28'W |
| Garber, Ok., U.S. (gär'bĕr) | 121 | 36°28'N | 97°35'W |
| Garching, Ger. (gär'κĕng) | 159d | 48°15'N | 11°39'E |
| Garcia, Mex. (gär-sē'ä) | 122 | 25°50'N | 100°37'W |
| García de la Cadena, Mex. | 130 | 21°14'N | 103°26'W |
| Garda, Lago di, l., Italy (lä-gō-dē-gär'dä) | 162 | 45°43'N | 10°26'E |
| Gardanne, Fr. (gàr-dän') | 170a | 43°28'N | 5°29'E |
| Gardelegen, Ger. (gär-dē-lā'ghĕn) | 168 | 52°32'N | 11°22'E |
| Garden, i., Mi., U.S. (gär'd'n) | 108 | 45°50'N | 85°50'W |
| Gardena, Ca., U.S. (gär-dē'nà) | 117a | 33°53'N | 118°19'W |
| Garden City, Ks., U.S. | 120 | 37°58'N | 100°52'W |
| Garden City, Mi., U.S. | 111b | 42°20'N | 83°21'W |
| Garden Grove, Ca., U.S. (gär'd'n grōv) | 117a | 33°47'N | 117°56'W |
| Garden Reach, India | 202a | 22°33'N | 88°17'E |
| Garden River, Can. | 117k | 46°33'N | 84°10'W |
| Gardeyz, Afg. | 202 | 33°43'N | 69°09'E |
| Gardiner, Me., U.S. (gärd'nĕr) | 100 | 44°12'N | 69°46'W |
| Gardiner, Mt., U.S. | 115 | 45°03'N | 110°43'W |
| Gardiner, Wa., U.S. | 116a | 48°03'N | 122°55'W |
| Gardiner Dam, dam, Can. | 96 | 51°17'N | 106°51'W |
| Gardner, Ma., U.S. | 109 | 42°35'N | 72°00'W |
| Gardner Canal, strt., Can. | 94 | 53°28'N | 128°15'W |
| Gardner Pinnacles, Hi., U.S. | 126b | 25°10'N | 167°00'W |
| Gareloi, i., Ak., U.S. (gär-lo͞o-ä') | 103a | 51°40'N | 178°48'W |
| Garfield, N.J., U.S. (gär'fēld) | 110a | 40°53'N | 74°06'W |
| Garfield, Ut., U.S. | 117b | 40°45'N | 112°10'W |
| Garfield Heights, Oh., U.S. | 111d | 41°25'N | 81°36'W |
| Gargaliánoi, Grc. (gär-gä-lyä'nĕ) | 175 | 37°07'N | 21°50'E |
| Gargždai, Lith. (gärgzh'dī) | 167 | 55°43'N | 20°09'E |
| Garibaldi, Mount, mtn., Can. (găr-ĭ-băl'dē) | 94 | 49°51'N | 123°01'W |
| Garin, Arg. (gä-rē'n) | 144a | 34°25'S | 58°44'W |
| Garissa, Kenya | 237 | 0°28'S | 39°38'E |
| Garland, Tx., U.S. (gär'lănd) | 117c | 32°55'N | 96°39'W |
| Garland, Ut., U.S. | 115 | 41°45'N | 112°10'W |
| Garm, Taj. | 183 | 39°12'N | 70°28'E |
| Garmisch-Partenkirchen, Ger. (gär'mēsh pär'tĕn-kĕr'κĕn) | 168 | 47°38'N | 11°10'E |
| Garnett, Ks., U.S. (gär'nĕt) | 121 | 38°16'N | 95°15'W |
| Garonne, r., Fr. (gà-rôn) | 156 | 44°00'N | 1°00'E |
| Garoua, Cam. (gär'wä) | 231 | 9°18'N | 13°24'E |
| Garrett, In., U.S. (găr'ĕt) | 108 | 41°20'N | 85°10'W |
| Garrison, N.D., U.S. | 112 | 47°38'N | 101°24'W |
| Garrison, N.Y., U.S. (găr'ĭ-sŭn) | 110a | 41°23'N | 73°57'W |
| Garrovillas, Spain (gä-rô-vēl'yäs) | 172 | 39°42'N | 6°30'W |
| Garry, l., Can. (găr'ĭ) | 92 | 66°16'N | 99°23'W |
| Garsen, Kenya | 237 | 2°16'S | 40°07'E |
| Garson, Can. | 99 | 46°34'N | 80°52'W |
| Garstedt, Ger. (gär'shtĕt) | 159c | 53°40'N | 9°58'E |
| Garulia, India | 202a | 22°48'N | 88°23'E |
| Garwolin, Pol. (gär-vō'lēn) | 169 | 51°54'N | 21°40'E |
| Gary, In., U.S. (gā'rĭ) | 105 | 41°35'N | 87°21'W |
| Gary, W.V., U.S. (fĭl'bĕrt) | 125 | 37°21'N | 81°33'W |
| Garzón, Col. (gär-thōn') | 142 | 2°13'N | 75°44'W |
| Gasan, Phil. (gä-sän') | 213a | 13°19'N | 121°52'E |
| Gasan-Kuli, Turkmen. | 183 | 37°25'N | 53°55'E |
| Gas City, In., U.S. (găs) | 108 | 40°30'N | 85°40'W |
| Gascogne, reg., Fr. (gäs-kôn'yĕ) | 170 | 43°45'N | 1°49'W |
| Gasconade, r., Mo., U.S. (găs-kô-nād') | 121 | 37°46'N | 92°15'W |
| Gascoyne, r., Austl. (găs-koin') | 220 | 25°15'S | 117°00'E |
| Gashland, Mo., U.S. (găsh'-lănd) | 117f | 39°15'N | 94°35'W |
| Gashua, Nig. | 235 | 12°54'N | 11°00'E |
| Gasny, Fr. (gäs-nē') | 171b | 49°05'N | 1°36'E |
| Gaspé, Can. | 91 | 48°50'N | 64°29'W |
| Gaspé, Péninsule de, pen., Can. | 93 | 48°30'N | 65°00'W |
| Gasper Hernández, Dom. Rep. (gäs-pär' ĕr-nän'dāth) | 135 | 19°40'N | 70°15'W |
| Gassaway, W.V., U.S. (găs'à-wā) | 108 | 38°40'N | 80°45'W |
| Gaston, Or., U.S. (găs'tŭn) | 116c | 45°26'N | 123°08'W |
| Gastonia, N.C., U.S. (găs-tô'nĭ-à) | 125 | 35°15'N | 81°14'W |
| Gastre, Arg. (gäs-trĕ) | 144 | 42°12'S | 68°50'W |
| Gata, Cabo de, c., Spain (kä'bō-dĕ-gä'tä) | 162 | 36°42'N | 2°00'W |
| Gata, Sierra de, mts., Spain (syĕr'rà dā gä'tä) | 162 | 40°12'N | 6°39'W |
| Gatchina, Russia (gä-chē'nà) | 180 | 59°33'N | 30°08'E |
| Gátes, Akrotírion, c., Cyp. | 197a | 34°30'N | 33°15'E |
| Gateshead, Eng., U.K. (gāts'hĕd) | 164 | 54°56'N | 1°38'W |
| Gates of the Arctic National Park, rec., Ak., U.S. | 103 | 67°45'N | 153°30'W |
| Gatesville, Tx., U.S. (gāts'vĭl) | 123 | 31°26'N | 97°34'W |
| Gâtine, Hauteurs de, hills, Fr. | 170 | 46°40'N | 0°50'W |
| Gatineau, Can. (gà'tē-nō) | 102c | 45°29'N | 75°38'W |
| Gatineau, r., Can. | 99 | 45°45'N | 75°50'W |
| Gatineau, Parc de la, rec., Can. | 99 | 45°32'N | 75°53'W |
| Gattendorf, Aus. | 159e | 48°01'N | 17°00'E |

| PLACE (Pronunciation) | PAGE | LAT. | LONG. |
|---|---|---|---|
| Gatun, Pan. (gä-tōōn′) | 133 | 9°16′N | 79°25′W |
| Gatun, r., Pan. | 128a | 9°21′N | 79°40′W |
| Gatún, Lago, l., Pan. | 133 | 9°13′N | 79°24′W |
| Gatun Locks, trans., Pan. | 128a | 9°16′N | 79°57′W |
| Gauhāti, India | 199 | 26°09′N | 91°51′E |
| Gauja, r., Lat. (gà′ō-yà) | 167 | 57°10′N | 24°30′E |
| Gaula, r., Nor. | 166 | 62°55′N | 10°45′E |
| Gávdos, i., Grc. (gäv′dôs) | 163 | 34°48′N | 24°08′E |
| Gavins Point Dam, Ne., U.S. (gă′-vĭns) | 112 | 42°47′N | 97°47′W |
| Gāvkhūnī, Bātlāq-e, l., Iran | 198 | 31°40′N | 52°48′E |
| Gävle, Swe. (yĕv′lĕ) | 154 | 60°40′N | 17°07′E |
| Gävlebukten, b., Swe. | 166 | 60°45′N | 17°30′E |
| Gavrilov Posad, Russia (gà′vrê-lôf′ka po-sàt) | 176 | 56°34′N | 40°09′E |
| Gavrilov-Yam, Russia (gà′vrê-lôf yäm′) | 176 | 57°17′N | 39°49′E |
| Gawler, Austl. (gô′lẽr) | 218 | 34°35′S | 138°47′E |
| Gawler Ranges, mts., Austl. | 222 | 32°35′S | 136°30′E |
| Gaya, India (gŭ′yä)(gī′à) | 199 | 24°53′N | 85°00′E |
| Gaya, Nig. (gä′yä) | 230 | 11°58′N | 9°05′E |
| Gaylord, Mi., U.S. (gā′lôrd) | 108 | 45°00′N | 84°35′W |
| Gayndah, Austl. (gān′dăh) | 222 | 25°43′S | 151°33′E |
| Gaza, Gaza | 198 | 31°30′N | 34°29′E |
| Gaziantep, Tur. (gä-zē-än′tĕp) | 198 | 37°10′N | 37°30′E |
| Gbarnga, Lib. | 234 | 7°00′N | 9°29′W |
| Gdańsk, Pol. (g′dänsk) | 154 | 54°20′N | 18°40′E |
| Gdov, Russia (g′dôf′) | 180 | 58°44′N | 27°51′E |
| Gdynia, Pol. (g′dēn′yä) | 160 | 54°29′N | 18°30′E |
| Geary, Ok., U.S. (gē′rĭ) | 120 | 35°36′N | 98°19′W |
| Géba, r., Gui.-B. | 234 | 12°25′N | 14°35′W |
| Gebo, Wy., U.S. (gĕb′ō) | 115 | 43°49′N | 108°13′W |
| Ged, La., U.S. (gĕd) | 123 | 30°07′N | 93°36′W |
| Gediz, r., Tur. | 163 | 38°44′N | 28°45′E |
| Gedney, i., Wa., U.S. (gĕd-nê) | 116a | 48°01′N | 122°18′W |
| Gedser, Den. | 166 | 54°35′N | 12°08′E |
| Geel, Bel. | 159a | 51°09′N | 5°01′E |
| Geelong, Austl. (jē-lông′) | 219 | 38°06′S | 144°13′E |
| Gegu, China (gŭ-gōō) | 206 | 39°00′N | 117°30′E |
| Ge Hu, l., China (gŭ hōō) | 206 | 31°37′N | 119°57′E |
| Geidam, Nig. | 230 | 12°57′N | 11°57′E |
| Geikie Range, mts., Austl. (gē′kê) | 220 | 17°35′S | 125°32′E |
| Geislingen, Ger. (gis′lĭng-ĕn) | 168 | 48°37′N | 9°52′E |
| Geist Reservoir, res., In., U.S. (gēst) | 111g | 39°57′N | 85°59′W |
| Geita, Tan. | 237 | 2°52′S | 32°10′E |
| Gejiu, China (gŭ-jĭo) | 209 | 23°32′N | 102°50′E |
| Geldermalsen, Neth. | 159a | 51°53′N | 5°18′E |
| Geldern, Ger. (gĕl′dĕrn) | 171c | 51°31′N | 6°20′E |
| Gelibolu, Tur. (gĕ-lĭb′ō-lò) | 163 | 40°25′N | 26°40′E |
| Gelsenkirchen, Ger. (gĕl-zĕn-kĭrk-ĕn) | 168 | 51°31′N | 7°05′E |
| Gemas, Malay. (jĕm′ás) | 197b | 2°35′N | 102°37′E |
| Gemena, D.R.C. | 231 | 3°15′N | 19°46′E |
| Gemlik, Tur. (gĕm′lĭk) | 163 | 40°30′N | 29°10′E |
| Genale (Jubba), r., Afr. | 238a | 5°15′N | 41°00′E |
| General Alvear, Arg. (gĕ-nĕ-ràl′ál-vĕ-á′r) | 141c | 36°04′S | 60°02′W |
| General Arenales, Arg. (ä-rĕ-nä′lĕs) | 141c | 34°19′S | 61°16′W |
| General Belgrano, Arg. (bĕl-grá′nô) | 141c | 35°45′S | 58°32′W |
| General Cepeda, Mex. (sĕ-pĕ′dä) | 122 | 25°24′N | 101°29′W |
| General Conesa, Arg. (kô-nĕ′sä) | 141c | 36°30′S | 57°19′W |
| General Guido, Arg. (gē′dô) | 141c | 36°41′S | 57°48′W |
| General Lavalle, Arg. (là-vá′l-yĕ) | 141c | 36°25′S | 56°55′W |
| General Madariaga, Arg. (män-dà-rêä′gä) | 144 | 36°59′S | 57°14′W |
| General Paz, Arg. (pà′z) | 141c | 35°30′S | 58°20′W |
| General Pedro Antonio Santos, Mex. | 130 | 21°37′N | 98°58′W |
| General Pico, Arg. (pē′kô) | 144 | 36°46′S | 63°44′W |
| General Roca, Arg. (rô-kä) | 144 | 39°01′S | 67°31′W |
| General San Martín, Arg. (sän-màr-tē′n) | 144a | 34°35′S | 58°32′W |
| General Sarmiento (San Miguel), Arg. | 144a | 34°33′S | 58°43′W |
| General Viamonte, Arg. (vēä′môn-tĕ) | 141c | 35°01′S | 60°59′W |
| General Zuazua, Mex. (zwä′zwä) | 122 | 25°54′N | 100°07′W |
| Genesee, r., N.Y., U.S. (jĕn-ê-sē′) | 109 | 42°25′N | 78°10′W |
| Geneseo, Il., U.S. (jē-nĕsēō) | 108 | 41°28′N | 90°11′W |
| Geneva (Genève), Switz. | 154 | 46°14′N | 6°04′E |
| Geneva, Al., U.S. (jê-nē′và) | 124 | 31°03′N | 85°50′W |
| Geneva, Il., U.S. | 111a | 41°53′N | 88°18′W |
| Geneva, Ne., U.S. | 121 | 40°32′N | 97°37′W |
| Geneva, N.Y., U.S. | 109 | 42°50′N | 77°00′W |
| Geneva, Oh., U.S. | 108 | 41°45′N | 80°55′W |
| Geneva, Lake, l., Switz. | 161 | 46°28′N | 6°30′E |
| Genève *see* Geneva, Switz. | 154 | 46°14′N | 6°04′E |
| Genil, r., Spain (hå-nēl′) | 172 | 37°15′N | 4°05′W |
| Genoa, Italy | 154 | 44°23′N | 9°52′E |
| Genoa, Ne., U.S. (jen′ô-à) | 121 | 41°26′N | 97°43′W |
| Genoa City, Wi., U.S. | 111a | 42°31′N | 88°19′W |
| Genova, Golfo di, b., Italy (gôl-fō-dē-jĕn′ō-vä) | 156 | 44°10′N | 8°45′E |
| Genovesa, i., Ec. (ĕ′s-lä-gĕ-nō-vĕ-sä) | 142 | 0°08′N | 90°15′W |
| Gent, Bel. | 161 | 51°05′N | 3°40′E |
| Genthin, Ger. (gĕn-tēn′) | 168 | 52°24′N | 12°10′E |
| Genzano di Roma, Italy (gzhĕnt-zä′-nô-dē-rô′mä) | 173d | 41°43′N | 12°49′E |
| Geographe Bay, b., Austl. (jē-ô-graf′) | 220 | 33°00′S | 114°00′E |
| Geographe Channel, strt., Austl. (jēô′grā-fĭk) | 220 | 24°15′S | 112°50′E |
| George, l., N.Y., U.S. (jôrj) | 109 | 43°40′N | 73°30′W |
| George, Lake, l., N.A. (jôrg) | 117k | 46°26′N | 84°09′W |
| George, Lake, l., Ug. | 237 | 0°02′N | 30°25′E |
| George, Lake, l., Fl., U.S. (jôr-ĭj) | 125 | 29°10′N | 81°50′W |
| George, Lake, l., In., U.S. | 111a | 41°31′N | 87°17′W |
| Georges, r., Austl. | 217b | 33°57′S | 151°00′E |
| George Town, Bah. | 135 | 23°30′N | 75°50′W |
| Georgetown, Can. (jôrg-toun) | 102d | 43°39′N | 79°56′W |
| Georgetown, Can. (jôr-ĭj-toun) | 101 | 46°11′N | 62°32′W |
| George Town, Cay. Is. | 134 | 19°20′N | 81°20′W |
| Georgetown, Guy. (jôrj′toun) | 143 | 7°45′N | 58°04′W |
| George Town, Malay. | 212 | 5°21′N | 100°09′E |
| Georgetown, Ct., U.S. | 110a | 41°15′N | 73°25′W |
| Georgetown, De., U.S. | 109 | 38°40′N | 75°20′W |
| Georgetown, Il., U.S. | 108 | 40°00′N | 87°40′W |
| Georgetown, Ky., U.S. | 108 | 38°10′N | 84°35′W |
| Georgetown, Ma., U.S. (jôrg-toun) | 101a | 42°43′N | 71°00′W |
| Georgetown, Md., U.S. | 109 | 39°25′N | 75°55′W |
| Georgetown, S.C., U.S. (jôr-ĭj-toun) | 125 | 33°22′N | 79°17′W |
| Georgetown, Tx., U.S. (jôrg-toun) | 123 | 30°37′N | 97°40′W |
| George Washington Birthplace National Monument, rec., Va., U.S. (jôrj wŏsh′ĭng-tŭn) | 109 | 38°10′N | 77°00′W |
| George Washington Carver National Monument, rec., Mo., U.S. (jôrg wăsh-ĭng-tŭn kär′vẽr) | 121 | 36°58′N | 94°21′W |
| George West, Tx., U.S. | 122 | 28°20′N | 98°07′W |
| Georgia, nation, Asia | 178 | 42°17′N | 43°00′E |
| Georgia, state, U.S. (jôr′ji-ă) | 105 | 32°40′N | 83°50′W |
| Georgia, Strait of, strt., N.A. | 94 | 49°20′N | 124°00′W |
| Georgiana, Al., U.S. (jôr-jē-än′à) | 124 | 31°39′N | 86°44′W |
| Georgian Bay, b., Can. | 93 | 45°15′N | 80°50′W |
| Georgian Bay Islands National Park, rec., Can. | 98 | 45°20′N | 81°40′W |
| Georgina, r., Austl. (jôr-jē′nà) | 220 | 22°00′S | 138°15′E |
| Georgiyevsk, Russia (gyôr-gyĕfsk′) | 181 | 44°05′N | 43°30′E |
| Gera, Ger. (gā′rä) | 161 | 50°52′N | 12°06′E |
| Geral, Serra, mts., Braz. (sĕr′rà zhà-räl′) | 144 | 28°30′S | 51°00′W |
| Geral de Goiás, Serra, mts., Braz. (zhà-räl′-dĕ-gô-yà′s) | 143 | 14°22′S | 45°40′W |
| Geraldton, Austl. (jĕr′ăld-tŭn) | 218 | 28°40′S | 114°35′E |
| Geraldton, Can. | 91 | 49°43′N | 87°00′W |
| Gérgal, Spain (gĕr′gäl) | 172 | 37°08′N | 2°29′W |
| Gering, Ne., U.S. (gē′rĭng) | 112 | 41°49′N | 103°41′W |
| Gerlachovský štít, mtn., Slvk. | 169 | 49°12′N | 20°08′E |
| Germantown, Oh., U.S. (jûr′măn-toun) | 108 | 39°35′N | 84°25′W |
| Germany, nation, Eur. (jûr′mà-nĭ) | 154 | 51°00′N | 10°00′E |
| Germiston, S. Afr. (jûr′mĭs-tŭn) | 232 | 26°19′S | 28°11′E |
| Gerona, Phil. (hā-rō′nä) | 213a | 15°36′N | 120°36′E |
| Gerrards Cross, Eng., U.K. (jĕrărds krôs) | 158b | 51°34′N | 0°33′W |
| Gers, r., Fr. (zhĕr) | 173 | 43°25′N | 0°30′E |
| Gersthofen, Ger. (gĕrst-hō′fĕn) | 159d | 48°26′N | 10°54′E |
| Getafe, Spain (hā-tä′fā) | 172 | 40°19′N | 3°44′W |
| Gettysburg, Pa., U.S. (gĕt′ĭs-bûrg) | 109 | 39°50′N | 77°15′W |
| Gettysburg, S.D., U.S. | 112 | 45°01′N | 99°59′W |
| Gevelsberg, Ger. (gĕ-fĕls′bĕrgh) | 171c | 51°18′N | 7°20′E |
| Ghāghra, r., India | 199 | 26°00′N | 83°00′E |
| Ghana, nation, Afr. (gän′ä) | 230 | 8°00′N | 2°00′W |
| Ghanzi, Bots. (gän′zē) | 232 | 21°30′S | 22°00′E |
| Ghardaïa, Alg. (gär-dä′ê-ä) | 230 | 32°29′N | 3°38′E |
| Gharo, Pak. | 202 | 24°50′N | 68°35′E |
| Ghāt, Libya | 230 | 24°52′N | 10°16′E |
| Ghazāl, Bahr al-, r., Sudan | 231 | 9°30′N | 30°00′E |
| Ghazal, Bahr el, r., Chad (bär ĕl ghä-zäl′) | 235 | 14°30′N | 17°00′E |
| Ghazzah *see* Gaza, Gaza | 198 | 31°30′N | 34°29′E |
| Gheorgheni, Rom. | 163 | 46°48′N | 25°30′E |
| Gherla, Rom. (gĕr′lä) | 169 | 47°01′N | 23°55′E |
| Ghilizane, Alg. | 230 | 35°43′N | 0°43′E |
| Ghorīān, Afg. | 201 | 34°21′N | 61°30′E |
| Ghost Lake, Can. | 102e | 51°15′N | 114°46′W |
| Ghudāmis, Libya | 230 | 30°07′N | 9°26′E |
| Giannitsá, Grc. | 175 | 40°47′N | 22°26′E |
| Giannutri, Isola di, i., Italy (jän-nōō′trē) | 174 | 42°15′N | 11°06′E |
| Giant Sequoia National Monument, rec., Ca., U.S. | 118 | 36°10′N | 118°35′W |
| Gibara, Cuba (hē-bä′rä) | 134 | 21°05′N | 76°10′W |
| Gibeon, Nmb. (gĭb′ê-ŭn) | 232 | 25°15′S | 17°30′E |
| Gibraleón, Spain (hē-brä-lå-ōn′) | 172 | 37°24′N | 7°00′W |
| Gibraltar, dep., Eur. (gĭ-bräl-tä′r) | 154 | 36°08′N | 5°22′W |
| Gibraltar, Strait of, strt. | 156 | 35°55′N | 5°45′W |
| Gibson City, Il., U.S. (gĭb′sŭn) | 108 | 40°25′N | 88°20′W |
| Gibson Desert, des., Austl. | 220 | 24°45′S | 123°15′E |
| Gibson Island, Md., U.S. | 110e | 39°05′N | 76°26′W |
| Gibson Reservoir, res., Ok., U.S. | 121 | 36°07′N | 95°08′W |
| Giddings, Tx., U.S. (gĭd′ĭngz) | 123 | 30°11′N | 96°55′W |
| Gideon, Mo., U.S. (gĭd′ê-ŭn) | 121 | 36°27′N | 89°56′W |
| Gien, Fr. (zhē-ăn′) | 161 | 47°43′N | 2°37′E |
| Giessen, Ger. (gēs′sĕn) | 168 | 50°35′N | 8°40′E |
| Gifu, Japan (gē′fōō) | 205 | 35°25′N | 136°45′E |
| Gig Harbor, Wa., U.S. (gĭg) | 116a | 47°20′N | 122°36′W |
| Giglio, Isola del, i., Italy (jēl′yō) | 174 | 42°23′N | 10°55′E |
| Gijón, Spain (hê-hōn′) | 154 | 43°33′N | 5°37′W |
| Gila, r., U.S. (hē′là) | 106 | 33°00′N | 110°00′W |
| Gila Bend, Az., U.S. | 119 | 32°59′N | 112°41′W |
| Gila Cliff Dwellings National Monument, rec., N.M., U.S. | 119 | 33°15′N | 108°20′W |
| Gila River Indian Reservation, I.R., Az., U.S. | 119 | 33°11′N | 112°38′W |
| Gilbert, Mn., U.S. (gĭl′bẽrt) | 113 | 47°27′N | 92°29′W |
| Gilbert, r., Austl. (gĭl-bẽrt) | 221 | 17°15′S | 142°09′E |
| Gilbert, Mount, mtn., Can. | 94 | 50°51′N | 124°20′W |
| Gilbert Islands, is., Kir. | 241 | 0°30′S | 174°00′E |
| Gilboa, Mount, mtn., S. Afr. (gĭl-bōà) | 233c | 29°13′N | 30°17′W |
| Gilford Island, i., Can. (gĭl′fẽrd) | 94 | 50°45′N | 126°25′W |
| Gilgit, Pak. (gĭl′gĭt) | 199 | 35°58′N | 73°48′E |
| Gil Island, i., Can. (gĭl) | 94 | 53°13′N | 129°15′W |
| Gillen, l., Austl. (jĭl′ĕn) | 220 | 26°15′S | 125°15′E |
| Gillett, Ar., U.S. (jĭ-lĕt′) | 121 | 34°07′N | 91°22′W |
| Gillette, Wy., U.S. | 115 | 44°17′N | 105°30′W |
| Gillingham, Eng., U.K. (gĭl′ĭng ăm) | 165 | 51°23′N | 0°33′E |
| Gilman, Il., U.S. (gĭl′măn) | 108 | 40°45′N | 87°55′W |
| Gilman Hot Springs, Ca., U.S. | 117a | 33°49′N | 116°57′W |
| Gilmer, Tx., U.S. (gĭl′mẽr) | 123 | 32°43′N | 94°57′W |
| Gilmore, Ga., U.S. (gĭl′môr) | 110c | 33°51′N | 84°29′W |
| Gilo, r., Eth. | 231 | 7°40′N | 34°17′E |
| Gilroy, Ca., U.S. (gĭl-roi′) | 118 | 37°00′N | 121°34′W |
| Giluwe, Mount, mtn., Pap. N. Gui. | 213 | 6°04′S | 144°00′E |
| Gimli, Can. (gĭm′lē) | 97 | 50°39′N | 97°00′W |
| Gimone, r., Fr. (zhē-mōn′) | 170 | 43°26′N | 0°36′E |
| Gīnīr, Eth. | 231 | 7°13′N | 40°44′E |
| Ginosa, Italy (jê-nō′zä) | 174 | 40°35′N | 16°48′E |
| Gioia del Colle, Italy (jô′yä dĕl kôl′lā) | 174 | 40°48′N | 16°55′E |
| Girard, Ks., U.S. (jĭ-rärd′) | 121 | 37°30′N | 94°50′W |
| Girardot, Col. (hē-rär-dōt′) | 142 | 4°19′N | 74°47′W |
| Giresun, Tur. (ghĕr′ĕ-sòn′) | 198 | 40°55′N | 38°20′E |
| Giridih, India (jē-rê-dê) | 199 | 24°12′N | 86°18′E |
| Girona, Spain | 162 | 41°55′N | 2°48′E |
| Gironde, r., Fr. (zhē-rôɴd′) | 156 | 45°31′N | 1°00′W |
| Girvan, Scot., U.K. (gûr′văn) | 164 | 55°15′N | 5°01′W |
| Gisborne, N.Z. (gĭz′bŭrn) | 221a | 38°40′S | 178°08′E |
| Gisenyi, Rw. | 232 | 1°43′S | 29°15′E |
| Gisors, Fr. (zhē-zôr′) | 170 | 49°19′N | 1°47′E |
| Gitambo, D.R.C. | 236 | 4°21′N | 24°45′E |
| Gitega, Bdi. | 232 | 3°39′S | 30°05′E |
| Giurgiu, Rom. (jòr′jò) | 175 | 43°53′N | 25°58′E |
| Givet, Fr. (zhē-vĕ′) | 170 | 50°08′N | 4°47′E |
| Givors, Fr. (zhē-vôr′) | 170 | 45°35′N | 4°46′E |
| Giza *see* Al Jīzah, Egypt | 238b | 30°01′N | 31°12′E |
| Gizhiga, Russia (gē′zhi-gà) | 179 | 61°59′N | 160°46′E |
| Gizo, Sol. Is. | 214e | 8°06′S | 156°51′E |
| Gizycko, Pol. (gĭ′zhĭ-ko) | 160 | 54°03′N | 21°48′E |
| Gjirokastër, Alb. | 163 | 40°04′N | 20°10′E |
| Gjøvik, Nor. (gyû′vêk) | 160 | 60°47′N | 10°36′E |
| Glabeek-Zuurbemde, Bel. | 159a | 50°52′N | 4°59′E |
| Glace Bay, Can. (glās bā) | 101 | 46°12′N | 59°57′W |
| Glacier Bay National Park, rec., Ak., U.S. (glā′shẽr) | 106a | 58°40′N | 136°50′W |
| Glacier National Park, rec., Can. | 92 | 51°45′N | 117°35′W |
| Glacier Peak, mtn., Wa., U.S. | 114 | 48°07′N | 121°10′W |
| Glacier Point, c., Can. | 116a | 48°24′N | 123°59′W |
| Gladbeck, Ger. (gläd′bĕk) | 168 | 51°35′N | 6°59′E |
| Gladdeklipkop, S. Afr. | 238c | 24°17′S | 29°36′E |
| Gladstone, Austl. (glăd′stōn) | 219 | 23°45′S | 152°00′E |
| Gladstone, Austl. | 218 | 33°15′S | 138°20′E |
| Gladstone, Mi., U.S. | 113 | 45°50′N | 87°04′W |
| Gladstone, N.J., U.S. | 110a | 40°43′N | 74°39′W |
| Gladstone, Or., U.S. | 116c | 45°23′N | 122°36′W |
| Gladwin, Mi., U.S. (glăd′wĭn) | 108 | 44°00′N | 84°25′W |
| Glåma, r., Nor. | 156 | 61°30′N | 10°30′E |
| Glarus, Switz. (glä′rós) | 168 | 47°02′N | 9°03′E |
| Glasgow, Scot., U.K. (glás′gō) | 154 | 55°54′N | 4°25′W |
| Glasgow, Ky., U.S. | 124 | 37°00′N | 85°55′W |
| Glasgow, Mo., U.S. | 121 | 39°14′N | 92°48′W |
| Glasgow, Mt., U.S. | 115 | 48°14′N | 106°39′W |
| Glassport, Pa., U.S. (glás′pōrt) | 111e | 40°19′N | 79°53′W |
| Glauchau, Ger. (glou′kou) | 168 | 50°51′N | 12°28′E |
| Glazov, Russia (glä′zôf) | 178 | 58°05′N | 52°52′E |
| Glen, r., Eng., U.K. (glĕn) | 158a | 52°44′N | 0°18′W |
| Glénan, Îles de, is., Fr. (ĕl-dĕ-glā-nän′) | 170 | 47°43′N | 4°42′W |
| Glen Burnie, Md., U.S. (bûr′nê) | 110e | 39°10′N | 76°38′W |
| Glen Canyon, p., Ut., U.S. | 119 | 37°10′N | 110°50′W |
| Glen Canyon Dam, dam, Az., U.S. (glĕn kăn′yŭn) | 106 | 36°57′N | 111°25′W |
| Glen Canyon National Recreation Area, rec., U.S. | 119 | 37°00′N | 111°20′W |
| Glen Carbon, Il., U.S. (kär′bŏn) | 117e | 38°45′N | 89°59′W |
| Glencoe, S. Afr. (glĕn-cō) | 233c | 28°14′S | 30°09′E |
| Glencoe, Il., U.S. | 111a | 42°08′N | 87°45′W |
| Glencoe, Mn., U.S. (glĕn′kō) | 113 | 44°44′N | 94°07′W |
| Glen Cove, N.Y., U.S. (kōv) | 110a | 40°51′N | 73°38′W |
| Glendale, Az., U.S. (glĕn′dāl) | 119 | 33°30′N | 112°15′W |
| Glendale, Ca., U.S. | 104 | 34°09′N | 118°15′W |
| Glendale, Oh., U.S. | 111f | 31°16′N | 84°22′W |
| Glendive, Mt., U.S. (glĕn′dīv) | 104 | 47°08′N | 104°41′W |
| Glendo, Wy., U.S. | 115 | 42°32′N | 104°54′W |
| Glendora, Ca., U.S. (glĕn-dō′rà) | 117a | 34°08′N | 117°52′W |
| Glenelg, r., Austl. | 222 | 37°20′S | 141°30′E |
| Glen Ellyn, Il., U.S. (glĕn ĕl′-lĕn) | 111a | 41°53′N | 88°04′W |
| Glen Innes, Austl. (ĭn′ĕs) | 219 | 29°45′S | 152°02′E |
| Glenns Ferry, Id., U.S. (fĕr′ĭ) | 114 | 42°58′N | 115°21′W |
| Glen Olden, Pa., U.S. (ōl′d′n) | 110f | 39°54′N | 75°17′W |
| Glenomra, La., U.S. (glĕn-mō′rà) | 123 | 30°58′N | 92°36′W |
| Glenrock, Wy., U.S. (glĕn′rŏk) | 115 | 42°50′N | 105°53′W |
| Glens Falls, N.Y., U.S. (glĕnz fôlz) | 109 | 43°20′N | 73°40′W |
| Glenshaw, Pa., U.S. (glĕn′shô) | 111e | 40°33′N | 79°57′W |
| Glen Valley, Can. | 116d | 49°09′N | 122°30′W |
| Glenview, Il., U.S. (glĕn′vū) | 111a | 42°04′N | 87°48′W |
| Glenville, Ga., U.S. (glĕn′vĭl) | 125 | 31°55′N | 81°56′W |
| Glenwood, Ia., U.S. | 112 | 41°03′N | 95°44′W |
| Glenwood, Mn., U.S. | 112 | 45°39′N | 95°23′W |
| Glenwood, N.M., U.S. | 119 | 33°19′N | 108°52′W |
| Glenwood Springs, Co., U.S. | 119 | 39°35′N | 107°20′W |
| Glienicke, Ger. (glē′nē-kĕ) | 159b | 52°38′N | 13°19′E |
| Glinde, Ger. (glĕn′dĕ) | 159c | 53°32′N | 10°13′E |
| Glittertinden, mtn., Nor. | 166 | 61°39′N | 8°33′E |
| Gliwice, Pol. (gwĭ-wĭt′sĕ) | 161 | 50°18′N | 18°40′E |
| Globe, Az., U.S. (glōb) | 104 | 33°20′N | 110°50′W |
| Głogów, Pol. (gwō′gōōv) | 161 | 51°40′N | 16°04′E |
| Glommen, r., Nor. (glôm′ĕn) | 166 | 60°03′N | 11°15′E |
| Glonn, Ger. (glônn) | 159d | 47°59′N | 11°52′E |

298 Grand-Riviere – Guadalajara

PRONOUNCING INDEX


| PLACE (Pronunciation) | PAGE | LAT. | LONG. |
|---|---|---|---|
| Grand-Riviere, Can. | 100 | 48°26'N | 64°30'W |
| Grand Staircase-Escalante National Monument, rec., Ut., U.S. | 119 | 37°25'N | 111°30'W |
| Grand Teton, mtn., Wy., U.S. | 106 | 43°46'N | 110°50'W |
| Grand Teton National Park, rec., Wy., U.S. (tē'tŏn) | 115 | 43°54'N | 110°15'W |
| Grand Traverse Bay, b., Mi., U.S. (trăv'ērs) | 108 | 45°00'N | 85°30'W |
| Grand Turk, T./C. Is. (tûrk) | 135 | 21°30'N | 71°10'W |
| Grand Turk, i., T./C. Is. | 135 | 21°30'N | 71°10'W |
| Grandview, Mo., U.S. (grănd'vyōō) | 117f | 38°53'N | 94°32'W |
| Granger, Wy., U.S. (grān'jēr) | 115 | 41°37'N | 109°58'W |
| Grangeville, Id., U.S. (grānj'vĭl) | 114 | 45°56'N | 116°08'W |
| Granite City, Il., U.S. (grăn'ĭt sĭt'ĭ) | 117e | 38°42'N | 90°09'W |
| Granite Falls, Mn., U.S. (fôlz) | 112 | 44°46'N | 95°34'W |
| Granite Falls, N.C., U.S. | 125 | 35°49'N | 81°25'W |
| Granite Falls, Wa., U.S. | 116a | 48°05'N | 121°59'W |
| Granite Lake, l., Can. | 101 | 48°01'N | 57°00'W |
| Granite Peak, mtn., Mt., U.S. | 106 | 45°13'N | 109°48'W |
| Graniteville, S.C., U.S. (grăn'ĭt-vĭl) | 125 | 33°35'N | 81°50'W |
| Granito, Braz. (grä-nē'tō) | 143 | 7°39'S | 39°34'W |
| Granma, prov., Cuba | 134 | 20°10'N | 76°50'W |
| Gränna, Swe. (grĕn'à) | 166 | 58°02'N | 14°38'E |
| Granollers, Spain (grä-nôl-yĕrs') | 173 | 41°36'N | 2°19'E |
| Gran Pajonal, reg., Peru (grä'n-pä-kô-näl') | 142 | 11°14'S | 71°45'W |
| Gran Paradiso, mtn., Italy | 174 | 45°32'N | 7°16'E |
| Gran Piedra, mtn., Cuba (grän-pyĕ'drä) | 135 | 20°00'N | 75°40'W |
| Grantham, Eng., U.K. (grăn'tăm) | 164 | 52°54'N | 0°38'W |
| Grant Park, Il., U.S. (grănt pärk) | 111a | 41°14'N | 87°39'W |
| Grants Pass, Or., U.S. (grȧnts pȧs) | 114 | 42°26'N | 123°20'W |
| Granville, Fr. (grän-vēl') | 161 | 48°52'N | 1°35'W |
| Granville, N.Y., U.S. (grăn'vĭl) | 109 | 43°25'N | 73°15'W |
| Granville, l., Can. | 92 | 56°18'N | 100°30'W |
| Grão Mogol, Braz. (groun' mō-gôl') | 143 | 16°34'S | 42°35'W |
| Grapevine, Tx., U.S. (grāp'vīn) | 117c | 32°56'N | 97°05'W |
| Gräso, i., Swe. | 166 | 60°30'N | 18°35'E |
| Grass, r., N.Y., U.S. | 109 | 44°45'N | 75°10'W |
| Grass Cay, i., V.I.U.S. | 129c | 18°22'N | 64°50'W |
| Grasse, Fr. (gräs) | 171 | 43°39'N | 6°57'E |
| Grass Mountain, mtn., Wa., U.S. (grȧs) | 116a | 47°13'N | 121°48'W |
| Grates Point, c., Can. (grāts) | 101 | 48°09'N | 52°57'W |
| Gravelbourg, Can. (grăv'ĕl-bôrg) | 90 | 49°53'N | 106°34'W |
| Gravesend, Eng., U.K. (grāvz'ĕnd') | 158b | 51°26'N | 0°22'E |
| Gravina, Italy (grä-vē'nä) | 174 | 40°48'N | 16°27'E |
| Gravois, Pointe à, c., Haiti (grȧ-vwä') | 135 | 18°00'N | 74°20'W |
| Gray, Fr. (grȧ) | 171 | 47°26'N | 5°35'E |
| Grayling, Mi., U.S. (grā'lĭng) | 108 | 44°40'N | 84°40'W |
| Grays Harbor, b., Wa., U.S. (grās) | 106 | 46°55'N | 124°23'W |
| Grayslake, Il., U.S. (grāz'lāk) | 111a | 42°20'N | 88°20'W |
| Grays Peak, mtn., Co., U.S. (grāz) | 120 | 39°29'N | 105°52'W |
| Grays Thurrock, Eng., U.K. (thŭ'rŏk) | 158b | 51°28'N | 0°19'E |
| Grayvoron, Russia (grȧ-ē'vô-rôn) | 177 | 50°28'N | 35°41'E |
| Graz, Aus. (gräts) | 154 | 47°05'N | 15°26'E |
| Great Abaco, i., Bah. (ä'bä-kō) | 129 | 26°30'N | 77°05'W |
| Great Artesian Basin, basin, Austl. (är-tēzh-ăn bā-sĭn) | 221 | 23°16'S | 143°37'E |
| Great Australian Bight, b., Austl. (ôs-trā'lĭ-ăn bīt) | 220 | 33°30'S | 127°00'E |
| Great Bahama Bank, bk. (bȧ-hā'mȧ) | 134 | 25°00'N | 78°50'W |
| Great Barrier, i., N.Z. (băr'ĭ-ēr) | 221a | 36°10'S | 175°30'E |
| Great Barrier Reef, rf., Austl. (bȧ-rĭ-ēr rēf) | 221 | 16°43'S | 146°34'E |
| Great Basin, basin, U.S. (grāt bā's'n) | 106 | 40°08'N | 117°10'W |
| Great Bear Lake, l., Can. (bâr) | 92 | 66°10'N | 119°53'W |
| Great Bend, Ks., U.S. (bĕnd) | 120 | 38°41'N | 98°46'W |
| Great Bitter Lake, l., Egypt | 238b | 30°24'N | 32°27'E |
| Great Blasket Island, i., Ire. (blăs'kĕt) | 164 | 52°05'N | 10°55'W |
| Great Corn Island, i., Nic. | 133 | 12°10'N | 82°54'W |
| Great Dismal Swamp, sw., U.S. (dĭz'măl) | 125 | 36°35'N | 76°34'W |
| Great Divide Basin, basin, Wy., U.S. (dĭ-vīd' bā's'n) | 115 | 42°10'N | 108°10'W |
| Great Dividing Range, mts., Austl. (dĭ-vī-dĭng rānj) | 221 | 35°16'S | 146°38'E |
| Great Duck, i., Can. (dŭk) | 98 | 45°40'N | 83°22'W |
| Greater Antilles, is., N.A. | 129 | 20°30'N | 79°15'W |
| Greater Khingan Range, mts., China (dä hĭŋ-gän lĭŋ) | 205 | 46°30'N | 120°00'E |
| Greater Leech Indian Reservation, I.R., Mn., U.S. (grāt'ēr lēch) | 113 | 47°39'N | 94°27'W |
| Greater Manchester, hist. reg., Eng., U.K. | 158a | 53°34'N | 2°41'W |
| Greater Sunda Islands, is., Asia | 212 | 4°00'S | 108°00'E |
| Great Exuma, i., Bah. (ĕk-sōō'mä) | 134 | 23°35'N | 76°00'W |
| Great Falls, Mt., U.S. (fôlz) | 104 | 47°30'N | 111°15'W |
| Great Falls, S.C., U.S. | 125 | 34°32'N | 80°53'W |
| Great Guana Cay, i., Bah. (gwä'nä) | 134 | 24°00'N | 76°20'W |
| Great Harbor Cay, i., Bah. (kē) | 134 | 25°45'N | 77°50'W |
| Great Inagua, i., Bah. (ē-nä'gwä) | 129 | 21°00'N | 73°15'W |
| Great Indian Desert, des., Asia | 199 | 27°35'N | 71°37'E |
| Great Isaac, i., Bah. (ī'zăk) | 134 | 26°05'N | 79°05'W |
| Great Karroo, plat., S. Afr. (grāt kä'rōō) | 232 | 32°45'S | 22°00'E |
| Great Limpopo Transfrontier Park, rec., Afr. | 232 | 22°00'S | 31°30'E |
| Great Namaland, hist. reg., Nmb. | 232 | 25°45'S | 16°15'E |
| Great Neck, N.Y., U.S. (nĕk) | 110a | 40°48'N | 73°44'W |
| Great Nicobar Island, i., India (nĭk-ô-bär') | 212 | 7°00'N | 94°18'E |
| Great Pedro Bluff, c., Jam. | 134 | 17°50'N | 78°05'W |
| Great Pee Dee, r., S.C., U.S. (pē-dē') | 107 | 34°01'N | 79°26'W |
| Great Plains, pl., N.A. (plāns) | 89 | 45°00'N | 104°00'W |
| Great Ragged, i., Bah. | 135 | 22°10'N | 75°45'W |
| Great Ruaha, r., Tan. | 232 | 7°30'S | 37°00'E |
| Great Salt Lake, l., Ut., U.S. (sôlt lāk) | 106 | 41°19'N | 112°48'W |
| Great Salt Lake Desert, des., Ut., U.S. | 106 | 41°00'N | 113°30'W |
| Great Salt Plains Reservoir, res., Ok., U.S. | 120 | 36°56'N | 98°14'W |
| Great Sand Dunes National Monument, rec., Co., U.S. | 120 | 37°56'N | 105°25'W |
| Great Sand Hills, hills, Can. (sănd) | 96 | 50°35'N | 109°05'W |
| Great Sandy Desert, des., Austl. (săn'dē) | 220 | 21°50'S | 123°10'E |
| Great Sandy Desert, des., Or., U.S. (săn'dĭ) | 114 | 43°43'N | 120°44'W |
| Great Sitkin, i., Ak., U.S. (sĭt-kĭn) | 103a | 52°18'N | 176°22'W |
| Great Slave Lake, l., Can. (slāv) | 92 | 61°37'N | 114°58'W |
| Great Smoky Mountains National Park, rec., U.S. (smōk-ē) | 107 | 35°43'N | 83°20'W |
| Great Stirrup Cay, i., Bah. (stĭr-ŭp) | 134 | 25°50'N | 77°55'W |
| Great Victoria Desert, des., Austl. (vĭk-tō'rĭ-ȧ) | 220 | 29°45'S | 124°30'E |
| Great Wall, hist., China | 204 | 38°00'N | 109°00'E |
| Great Waltham, Eng., U.K. (wôl'thŭm) | 158b | 51°47'N | 0°27'E |
| Great Yarmouth, Eng., U.K. (yär-mŭth) | 161 | 52°35'N | 1°45'E |
| Grebbestad, Swe. (grĕb-bĕ-städh) | 166 | 58°42'N | 11°15'E |
| Gréboun, Mont, mtn., Niger | 230 | 20°00'N | 8°35'E |
| Gredos, Sierra de, mts., Spain (syĕr'rä dā grā'dōs) | 172 | 40°13'N | 5°30'W |
| Greece, nation, Eur. (grēs) | 154 | 39°00'N | 21°30'E |
| Greeley, Co., U.S. (grē'lĭ) | 104 | 40°25'N | 104°41'W |
| Green, r., Ky., U.S. (grēn) | 124 | 37°13'N | 86°30'W |
| Green, r., N.D., U.S. | 112 | 47°05'N | 103°05'W |
| Green, r., Ut., U.S. | 119 | 38°30'N | 110°05'W |
| Green, r., Wa., U.S. | 116a | 47°17'N | 121°57'W |
| Green, r., Wy., U.S. | 115 | 41°08'N | 110°27'W |
| Green, r., U.S. | 106 | 38°30'N | 110°10'W |
| Greenbank, Wa., U.S. (grēn'bănk) | 116a | 48°06'N | 122°35'W |
| Green Bay, Wi., U.S. | 105 | 44°30'N | 88°04'W |
| Green Bay, b., U.S. | 107 | 44°55'N | 87°40'W |
| Green Bayou, Tx., U.S. | 123a | 29°53'N | 95°13'W |
| Greenbelt, Md., U.S. (grēn'bĕlt) | 110e | 38°59'N | 76°53'W |
| Greencastle, In., U.S. (grēn-kȧs''l) | 108 | 39°40'N | 86°50'W |
| Green Cay, i., Bah. | 134 | 24°05'N | 77°10'W |
| Green Cove Springs, Fl., U.S. (kōv) | 125 | 29°56'N | 81°42'W |
| Greendale, Wi., U.S. (grēn'dāl) | 111a | 42°56'N | 87°59'W |
| Greenfield, Ia., U.S. | 113 | 41°16'N | 94°30'W |
| Greenfield, In., U.S. (grēn'fēld) | 108 | 39°45'N | 85°40'W |
| Greenfield, Ma., U.S. | 109 | 42°35'N | 72°35'W |
| Greenfield, Mo., U.S. | 121 | 37°23'N | 93°48'W |
| Greenfield, Oh., U.S. | 108 | 39°15'N | 83°25'W |
| Greenfield, Tn., U.S. | 124 | 36°08'N | 88°45'W |
| Greenfield Park, Can. | 102a | 45°29'N | 73°29'W |
| Greenhills, Oh., U.S. (grēn-hĭls) | 111f | 39°16'N | 84°31'W |
| Greenland, dep., N.A. (grēn'lănd) | 89 | 74°00'N | 40°00'W |
| Greenland Sea, sea | 244 | 77°00'N | 1°00'W |
| Green Mountain, mtn., Or., U.S. | 116c | 45°52'N | 123°24'W |
| Green Mountain Reservoir, res., Co., U.S. | 119 | 39°50'N | 106°20'W |
| Green Mountains, mts., N.A. | 107 | 43°10'N | 73°05'W |
| Greenock, Scot., U.K. (grēn'ŭk) | 160 | 55°55'N | 4°45'W |
| Green Peter Lake, res., Or., U.S. | 114 | 44°28'N | 122°30'W |
| Green Pond Mountain, mtn., N.J., U.S. (pŏnd) | 110a | 41°00'N | 74°32'W |
| Greenport, N.Y., U.S. | 109 | 41°06'N | 72°22'W |
| Green River, Ut., U.S. (grēn rĭv'ēr) | 119 | 39°00'N | 110°05'W |
| Green River, Wy., U.S. | 115 | 41°32'N | 109°26'W |
| Green River Lake, res., Ky., U.S. | 124 | 37°15'N | 85°15'W |
| Greensboro, Al., U.S. (grēnz'bŭro) | 124 | 32°42'N | 87°36'W |
| Greensboro, Ga., U.S. (grēns-bûr'ō) | 124 | 33°34'N | 83°11'W |
| Greensboro, N.C., U.S. | 105 | 36°04'N | 79°45'W |
| Greensburg, In., U.S. (grēnz'bûrg) | 108 | 39°20'N | 85°30'W |
| Greensburg, Ks., U.S. (grēns-bûrg) | 120 | 37°36'N | 99°17'W |
| Greensburg, Pa., U.S. | 109 | 40°20'N | 79°30'W |
| Greenville, Lib. | 230 | 5°01'N | 9°03'W |
| Greenville, Al., U.S. (grēn'vĭl) | 124 | 31°49'N | 86°39'W |
| Greenville, Il., U.S. | 121 | 38°52'N | 89°22'W |
| Greenville, Ky., U.S. | 124 | 37°11'N | 87°11'W |
| Greenville, Me., U.S. | 100 | 45°26'N | 69°35'W |
| Greenville, Mi., U.S. | 108 | 43°10'N | 85°25'W |
| Greenville, Ms., U.S. | 105 | 33°25'N | 91°00'W |
| Greenville, N.C., U.S. | 125 | 35°35'N | 77°22'W |
| Greenville, Oh., U.S. | 108 | 40°05'N | 84°35'W |
| Greenville, Pa., U.S. | 108 | 41°20'N | 80°25'W |
| Greenville, S.C., U.S. | 105 | 34°50'N | 82°25'W |
| Greenville, Tn., U.S. | 125 | 36°08'N | 82°50'W |
| Greenville, Tx., U.S. | 123 | 33°09'N | 96°07'W |
| Greenwich, Eng., U.K. | 158b | 51°28'N | 0°00' |
| Greenwich, Ct., U.S. | 110a | 41°01'N | 73°37'W |
| Greenwood, Ar., U.S. (grēn-wŏŏd) | 121 | 35°13'N | 94°15'W |
| Greenwood, In., U.S. | 111g | 39°37'N | 86°07'W |
| Greenwood, Ms., U.S. | 124 | 33°30'N | 90°09'W |
| Greenwood, S.C., U.S. | 125 | 34°10'N | 82°10'W |
| Greenwood, Lake, res., S.C., U.S. | 125 | 34°17'N | 81°55'W |
| Greenwood Lake, l., N.Y., U.S. | 110a | 41°13'N | 74°20'W |
| Greer, S.C., U.S. (grēr) | 125 | 34°55'N | 81°56'W |
| Grefrath, Ger. (grĕf'rät) | 171c | 51°20'N | 6°21'E |
| Gregory, S.D., U.S. (grĕg'ō-rĭ) | 112 | 43°12'N | 99°27'W |
| Gregory, Lake, l., Austl. (grĕg'ō-rē) | 220 | 28°47'S | 139°15'E |
| Gregory Range, mts., Austl. | 221 | 19°23'S | 143°45'E |
| Greifenberg, Ger. (grī'fĕn-bĕrgh) | 159d | 48°04'N | 11°06'E |
| Greifswald, Ger. (grīfs'vält) | 168 | 54°05'N | 13°24'E |
| Greiz, Ger. (grīts) | 168 | 50°39'N | 12°14'E |
| Gremyachinsk, Russia (grâ'myȧ-chĭnsk) | 186a | 58°35'N | 57°53'E |
| Grenada, Ms., U.S. (grē-nä'da) | 124 | 33°45'N | 89°47'W |
| Grenada, nation, N.A. | 129 | 12°02'N | 61°15'W |
| Grenada Lake, res., Ms., U.S. | 124 | 33°52'N | 89°30'W |
| Grenadines, The, is., N.A. (grĕn'ȧ-dēnz) | 133b | 12°37'N | 61°35'W |
| Grenen, c., Den. | 160 | 57°43'N | 10°31'E |
| Grenoble, Fr. (grē-nô'bl') | 161 | 45°14'N | 5°45'E |
| Grenora, N.D., U.S. (grē-nō'rȧ) | 112 | 48°38'N | 103°55'W |
| Grenville, Can. (grĕn'vĭl) | 109 | 45°40'N | 74°35'W |
| Grenville, Gren. | 133b | 12°07'N | 61°38'W |
| Gresham, Or., U.S. (grĕsh'ăm) | 116c | 45°30'N | 122°25'W |
| Gretna, La., U.S. (grĕt'nȧ) | 110d | 29°56'N | 90°03'W |
| Grevelingen Krammer, r., Neth. | 159a | 51°42'N | 4°03'E |
| Grevenbroich, Ger. (grĕ'fen-broik) | 171c | 51°05'N | 6°36'E |
| Grey, r., Can. (grā) | 101 | 47°53'N | 57°00'W |
| Grey, Point, c., Can. | 116d | 49°22'N | 123°16'W |
| Greybull, Wy., U.S. (grā'bŏŏl) | 115 | 44°28'N | 108°05'W |
| Greybull, r., Wy., U.S. | 115 | 44°13'N | 108°43'W |
| Greylingstad, S. Afr. (grā-lĭng'shtȧt) | 238c | 26°40'S | 29°13'E |
| Greymouth, N.Z. (grā'mouth) | 221a | 42°27'S | 171°17'E |
| Grey Range, mts., Austl. | 221 | 28°40'S | 142°05'E |
| Greytown, S. Afr. (grā'toun) | 233c | 29°07'S | 30°38'E |
| Grey Wolf Peak, mtn., Wa., U.S. (grā wŏlf) | 116a | 48°53'N | 123°12'W |
| Gridley, Ca., U.S. (grĭd'lĭ) | 118 | 39°22'N | 121°43'W |
| Griffin, Ga., U.S. (grĭf'ĭn) | 124 | 33°15'N | 84°16'W |
| Griffith, Austl. (grĭf-ĭth) | 222 | 34°16'S | 146°10'E |
| Griffith, In., U.S. | 111a | 41°31'N | 87°26'W |
| Grigoriopol', Mol. (grĭ'gor-i-ô'pôl) | 177 | 47°09'N | 29°18'E |
| Grijalva, r., Mex. (grē-häl'vä) | 131 | 17°25'N | 93°23'W |
| Grim, Cape, c., Austl. (grĭm) | 222 | 40°43'S | 144°30'E |
| Grimma, Ger. (grĭm'ȧ) | 168 | 51°14'N | 12°43'E |
| Grimsby, Can. (grĭmz'bĭ) | 102d | 43°11'N | 79°33'W |
| Grimsby, Eng., U.K. | 160 | 53°35'N | 0°05'W |
| Grímsey, i., Ice. (grĭms'ȧ) | 160 | 66°30'N | 17°50'W |
| Grimstad, Nor. (grĭm-städh) | 160 | 58°21'N | 8°30'E |
| Grindstone Island, Can. | 101 | 47°25'N | 61°51'W |
| Grinnel, Ia., U.S. (grĭ-nĕl') | 113 | 41°44'N | 92°44'W |
| Griswold, Ia., U.S. (grĭz'wŭld) | 112 | 41°11'N | 95°05'W |
| Groais Island, i., Can. | 101 | 50°57'N | 55°35'W |
| Grobina, Lat. (grō'bĭnĭa) | 167 | 56°35'N | 21°10'E |
| Groblersdal, S. Afr. | 238c | 25°11'S | 29°25'E |
| Grodzisk, Pol. (grō'jĕsk) | 168 | 52°14'N | 16°22'E |
| Grodzisk Masowiecki, Pol. (grō'jĕsk mä-zō-vyĕts'ke) | 169 | 52°06'N | 20°40'E |
| Groesbeck, Tx., U.S. (grōs'bĕk) | 123 | 31°32'N | 96°31'W |
| Groix, Île de, i., Fr. (ēl dē grwä') | 170 | 47°39'N | 3°28'W |
| Grójec, Pol. (grō'yĕts) | 169 | 51°53'N | 20°52'E |
| Gronau, Ger. (grō'nou) | 168 | 52°12'N | 7°05'E |
| Groningen, Neth. (grō'nĭng-ĕn) | 160 | 53°13'N | 6°30'E |
| Groote Eylandt, i., Austl. (grō'tē ī'länt) | 220 | 13°50'S | 137°30'E |
| Grootfontein, Nmb. (grōt'fōn-tān') | 232 | 19°30'S | 18°15'E |
| Groot-Kei, r., Afr. (kē) | 233c | 32°17'S | 27°30'E |
| Grootkop, mtn., S. Afr. | 232a | 34°11'S | 18°23'E |
| Groot Marico, S. Afr. | 238c | 25°36'S | 26°23'E |
| Groot Marico, r., Afr. | 238c | 25°13'S | 26°20'E |
| Groot-Vis, r., S. Afr. | 233c | 33°04'S | 26°08'E |
| Groot Vloer, pl., S. Afr. (grōt' vlôr') | 232 | 30°00'S | 21°00'E |
| Gros-Mécatina, i., Can. | 101 | 50°50'N | 58°33'W |
| Gros Morne, mtn., Can. (grō môrn') | 101 | 49°36'N | 57°48'W |
| Gros Morne National Park, rec., Can. | 93a | 49°45'N | 59°15'W |
| Gros Pate, mtn., Can. | 101 | 50°16'N | 57°25'W |
| Grosse Island, i., Mi., U.S. (grōs) | 111b | 42°08'N | 83°09'W |
| Grosse Isle, Can. (īl') | 102f | 50°04'N | 97°27'W |
| Grossenhain, Ger. (grōs'ĕn-hīn) | 168 | 51°17'N | 13°33'E |
| Gross-Enzersdorf, Aus. | 159e | 48°13'N | 16°33'E |
| Grosse Pointe, Mi., U.S. (point') | 111b | 42°23'N | 82°54'W |
| Grosse Pointe Farms, Mi., U.S. (färm) | 111b | 42°25'N | 82°53'W |
| Grosse Pointe Park, Mi., U.S. (pärk) | 111b | 42°23'N | 82°55'W |
| Grosseto, Italy (grôs-sā'tō) | 174 | 42°46'N | 11°09'E |
| Grossglockner, mtn., Aus. | 161 | 47°06'N | 12°45'E |
| Gross Höbach, Ger. (hû'bäk) | 159d | 48°21'N | 11°36'E |
| Gross Kreutz, Ger. (kroitz) | 159b | 52°24'N | 12°47'E |
| Gross Schönebeck, Ger. (shō'nĕ-bĕk) | 159b | 52°54'N | 13°32'E |
| Gros Ventre, r., Wy., U.S. (grōvĕn't'r) | 115 | 43°38'N | 110°34'W |
| Groton, Ct., U.S. (grŏt'ŭn) | 109 | 41°20'N | 72°00'W |
| Groton, Ma., U.S. | 101a | 42°37'N | 71°34'W |
| Groton, S.D., U.S. | 112 | 45°25'N | 98°04'W |
| Grottaglie, Italy (grôt-täl'yā) | 175 | 40°32'N | 17°26'E |
| Grouard Mission, Can. | 90 | 55°31'N | 116°09'W |
| Groveland, Ma., U.S. (grōv'lănd) | 101a | 42°25'N | 71°02'W |
| Groveton, N.H., U.S. (grōv'tŭn) | 109 | 44°35'N | 71°30'W |
| Groveton, Tx., U.S. | 123 | 31°04'N | 95°07'W |
| Groznyy, Russia (grŏz'nĭ) | 178 | 43°20'N | 45°40'E |
| Grudziądz, Pol. (grō'jyŏnts) | 160 | 53°30'N | 18°48'E |
| Grues, Île aux, i., Can. (ō grü) | 102b | 47°05'N | 70°32'W |
| Grundy Center, Ia., U.S. (grŭn'dĭ sĕn'tēr) | 113 | 42°22'N | 92°45'W |
| Gruñidora, Mex. (grōō-nyē-dô'rō) | 130 | 24°10'N | 101°49'W |
| Grünwald, Ger. (grōōn'väld) | 159d | 48°04'N | 11°34'E |
| Gryazi, Russia (gryä'zĭ) | 176 | 52°31'N | 39°59'E |
| Gryazovets, Russia (gryä'zō-vĕts) | 180 | 58°52'N | 40°14'E |
| Gryfice, Pol. (grĭ'fĭ-tsĕ) | 168 | 53°55'N | 15°11'E |
| Gryfino, Pol. (grĭ'fē-nō) | 168 | 53°16'N | 14°30'E |
| Guabito, Pan. (gwä-bē'tō) | 133 | 9°30'N | 82°33'W |
| Guacanayabo, Golfo de, b., Cuba (gôl-fô-dĕ-gwä-kä-nä-yä'bō) | 134 | 20°30'N | 77°40'W |
| Guacara, Ven. (gwá'kä-rä) | 143b | 10°16'N | 67°48'W |
| Guadalajara, Mex. (gwä-dhä-lä-hä'rä) | 128 | 20°41'N | 103°21'W |


ăt; finăl; rāte; senāte; ärm; ȧsk; sofȧ; fâre; ch-choose; dh-as th in other; bē; ēvent; bĕt; recĕnt; cratēr; g-gō; gh-guttural g; bĭt; ĭ-short neutral; rīde; ĸ-guttural k as ch in German ich;

PRONOUNCING INDEX
Guadalajara – Haines City 299


| PLACE (Pronunciation) | PAGE | LAT. | LONG. |
|---|---|---|---|
| Guadalajara, Spain (gwä-dä-lä-kä'rä) | 162 | 40°37'N | 3°10'W |
| Guadalcanal, Spain (gwä-dhäl-kä-näl') | 172 | 38°05'N | 5°48'W |
| Guadalcanal, i., Sol. Is. | 221 | 9°48'S | 158°43'E |
| Guadalcázar, Mex. (gwä-dhäl-kä'zär) | 130 | 22°38'N | 100°24'W |
| Guadalete, r., Spain (gwä-dhä-lā'tå) | 172 | 36°53'N | 5°38'W |
| Guadalhorce, r., Spain (gwä-dhäl-ôr'thā) | 172 | 37°05'N | 4°50'W |
| Guadalimar, r., Spain (gwä-dhä-lē-mär') | 172 | 38°29'N | 2°53'W |
| Guadalope, r., Spain (gwä-dä-lô-pā) | 173 | 40°48'N | 0°10'W |
| Guadalquivir, Río, r., Spain (rē'ō-gwä-dhäl-kē-vēr') | 156 | 37°30'N | 5°00'W |
| Guadalupe, Mex. | 122 | 31°23'N | 106°06'W |
| Guadalupe, i., Mex. | 128 | 29°00'N | 118°45'W |
| Guadalupe, r., Tx., U.S. (gwä-dhä-lōō'pä) | 122 | 29°54'N | 99°03'W |
| Guadalupe, Sierra de, mts., Spain (syĕr'rä dā gwä-dhä-lōō'pä) | 162 | 39°30'N | 5°25'W |
| Guadalupe Mountains, mts., N.M., U.S. | 122 | 32°00'N | 104°55'W |
| Guadalupe Peak, mtn., Tx., U.S. | 122 | 31°55'N | 104°55'W |
| Guadarrama, r., Spain (gwä-dhär-rä'mä) | 173a | 40°34'N | 3°58'W |
| Guadarrama, Sierra de, mts., Spain (gwä-dhär-rä'mä) | 156 | 41°00'N | 3°40'W |
| Guadatentin, r., Spain | 172 | 37°43'N | 1°58'W |
| Guadeloupe, dep., N.A. (gwä-dē-lōōp') | 129 | 16°40'N | 61°10'W |
| Guadeloupe Passage, strt., N.A. | 133b | 16°26'N | 62°00'W |
| Guadiana, r., Eur. (gwä-dvä'nä) | 156 | 39°00'N | 6°00'W |
| Guadiana, Bahía de, b., Cuba (bä-ē'ä-dĕ-gwä-dhē-ä'nä) | 134 | 22°10'N | 84°35'W |
| Guadiana Alto, r., Spain (äl'tō) | 172 | 39°02'N | 2°52'W |
| Guadiana Menor, r., Spain (mā'nôr) | 172 | 37°43'N | 2°45'W |
| Guadiaro, r., Spain (gwä-dhē-ä rō) | 172 | 36°38'N | 5°25'W |
| Guadiela, r., Spain (gwä-dhē-ā'lä) | 172 | 40°27'N | 2°05'W |
| Guadix, Spain (gwä-dēsh') | 172 | 37°18'N | 3°09'W |
| Guaira, Braz. (gwä-ē-rä) | 143 | 24°03'S | 54°02'W |
| Guaire, r., Ven. (gwī'rĕ) | 143b | 10°25'N | 66°43'W |
| Guajaba, Cayo, i., Cuba (kä'yō-gwä-hä'bä) | 134 | 21°50'N | 77°35'W |
| Guajará Mirim, Braz. (gwä-zhä-rä'mē-rēN') | 142 | 10°58'S | 65°12'W |
| Guajira, Península de, pen., S.A. | 142 | 12°35'N | 73°00'W |
| Gualán, Guat. (gwä-län') | 132 | 15°08'N | 89°21'W |
| Gualeguay, Arg. (gwä-lĕ-gwä'y) | 144 | 33°10'S | 59°20'W |
| Gualeguay, r., Arg. | 144 | 32°49'S | 59°05'W |
| Gualicho, Salina, l., Arg. (sä-lē'nä-gwä-lē'chō) | 144 | 40°20'S | 65°15'W |
| Guam, i., Oc. (gwäm) | 3 | 14°00'N | 143°20'E |
| Guamo, Col. (gwá'mō) | 142a | 4°02'N | 74°58'W |
| Gu'an, China (gōō-än) | 208a | 39°25'N | 116°18'E |
| Guan, r., China (gůän) | 206 | 31°56'N | 115°19'E |
| Guanabacoa, Cuba (gwä-nä-bä-kō'ä) | 129 | 23°08'N | 82°19'W |
| Guanabara, Baía de, b., Braz. | 141a | 22°44'S | 43°09'W |
| Guanacaste, Cordillera, mts., C.R. | 132 | 10°54'N | 85°27'W |
| Guanacevi, Mex. (gwä-nä-sĕ-vē') | 128 | 25°30'N | 105°45'W |
| Guanahacabibes, Península de, pen., Cuba | 134 | 21°55'N | 84°35'W |
| Guanajay, Cuba (gwä-ŋä-hī') | 134 | 22°55'N | 82°40'W |
| Guanajuato, Mex. (gwä-nä-hwä'tō) | 128 | 21°01'N | 101°16'W |
| Guanajuato, state, Mex. | 128 | 21°00'N | 101°00'W |
| Guanape, Ven. (gwä-nä'pĕ) | 143b | 9°55'N | 65°32'W |
| Guanape, r., Ven. | 143b | 9°52'N | 65°20'W |
| Guanare, Ven. (gwä-nä'rå) | 142 | 8°57'N | 69°47'W |
| Guanduçu, r., Braz. (gwä'n-dōō'sōō) | 144b | 22°50'S | 43°40'W |
| Guane, Cuba (gwä'nå) | 134 | 22°10'N | 84°05'W |
| Guangchang, China (gůäŋ-chäŋ) | 209 | 26°50'N | 116°18'E |
| Guangde, China (gůäŋ-dŭ) | 209 | 30°40'N | 119°20'E |
| Guangdong, prov., China (gůäŋ-dôŋ) | 205 | 23°45'N | 113°15'E |
| Guanglu Dao, i., China (gůäŋ-lōō dou) | 206 | 39°13'N | 122°21'E |
| Guangping, China (gůäŋ-pĭŋ) | 206 | 36°30'N | 114°57'E |
| Guangrao, China (gůaŋ-rou) | 206 | 37°04'N | 118°24'E |
| Guangshan, China (gůäŋ-shän) | 206 | 32°02'N | 114°53'E |
| Guangxi Zhuangzu, prov., China (gůäŋ-shyē) | 204 | 24°00'N | 108°30'E |
| Guangzhou, China | 204 | 23°07'N | 113°15'W |
| Guanhu, China (gůän-hōō) | 206 | 34°26'N | 117°59'E |
| Guannan, China (gůän-nän) | 206 | 34°17'N | 119°17'E |
| Guanta, Ven. (gwän'tä) | 143b | 10°15'N | 64°35'W |
| Guantánamo, Cuba (gwän-tä'nä-mô) | 135 | 20°10'N | 75°10'W |
| Guantánamo, prov., Cuba | 135 | 20°10'N | 75°05'W |
| Guantánamo, Bahía de, b., Cuba | 135 | 19°35'N | 75°35'W |
| Guantao, China (gůän-tou) | 206 | 36°39'N | 115°25'E |
| Guanxian, China (gůän-shyĕn) | 206 | 36°30'N | 115°28'E |
| Guanyao, China (gůän-you) | 207a | 23°13'N | 113°04'E |
| Guanyun, China (gůän-yòn) | 206 | 34°28'N | 119°16'E |
| Guapiles, C.R. (gwä-pē-lĕs) | 133 | 10°05'N | 83°54'W |
| Guapimirim, Braz. (gwä-pē-mē-rē'N) | 144b | 22°31'S | 42°59'W |
| Guaporé, r., S.A. (gwä-pô-rā') | 142 | 12°11'S | 63°47'W |
| Guaqui, Bol. (guä'kē) | 142 | 16°42'S | 68°47'W |
| Guara, Sierra de, mts., Spain (sē-ĕ'r-rä-dĕ-gwä'rä) | 173 | 42°24'N | 0°15'W |
| Guarabira, Braz. (gwä-rä-bē'rå) | 143 | 6°49'S | 35°27'W |
| Guaranda, Ec. (gwä-ràn'dä) | 142 | 1°39'S | 78°57'W |
| Guarapari, Braz. (gwä-rä-pä'rē) | 143 | 20°34'S | 40°31'W |
| Guarapiranga, Represa do, res., Braz. | 141a | 23°45'S | 46°44'W |
| Guarapuava, Braz. (gwä-rä-pwä'vå) | 144 | 25°29'S | 51°26'W |
| Guarda, Port. (gwär'dä) | 172 | 40°32'N | 7°17'W |
| Guardiato, r., Spain | 172 | 38°10'N | 5°05'W |
| Guarena, Spain (gwä-rā'nyä) | 172 | 38°52'N | 6°08'W |
| Guaribe, r., Ven. (gwä-rē'bĕ) | 143b | 9°48'N | 65°17'W |
| Guárico, dept., Ven. | 143b | 9°42'N | 67°25'W |
| Guarulhos, Braz. (gwå-rò'l-yôs) | 141a | 23°28'S | 46°30'W |
| Guarus, Braz. (gwá'rōōs) | 141a | 21°44'S | 41°19'W |
| Guasca, Col. (gwäs'kä) | 142a | 4°52'N | 73°52'W |
| Guasipati, Ven. (gwä-sē-pä'tē) | 143 | 7°26'N | 61°57'W |
| Guastalla, Italy (gwäs-täl'lä) | 174 | 44°53'N | 10°39'E |
| Guasti, Ca., U.S. (gwäs'tĭ) | 117a | 34°04'N | 117°35'W |
| Guatemala, Guat. (guä-tå-mä'lä) | 128 | 14°37'N | 90°32'W |
| Guatemala, nation, N.A. | 128 | 15°45'N | 91°45'W |
| Guatire, Ven. (gwä-tē'rĕ) | 143b | 10°28'N | 66°34'W |
| Guaviare, r., Col. | 142 | 3°35'N | 69°28'W |
| Guayabal, Cuba (gwä-yä-bä'l) | 134 | 20°40'N | 77°40'W |
| Guayalejo, r., Mex. (gwä-yä-lĕ'hô) | 130 | 23°24'N | 99°09'W |
| Guayama, P.R. (gwä-yä'mä) | 129b | 18°00'N | 66°08'W |
| Guayamouc, r., Haiti | 135 | 19°05'N | 72°00'W |
| Guayaquil, Ec. (gwī-ä-kēl') | 142 | 2°16'S | 79°53'W |
| Guayaquil, Golfo de, b., Ec. (gôl-fô-dĕ) | 142 | 3°03'S | 82°12'W |
| Guaymas, Mex. (gwá'y-mäs) | 128 | 27°49'N | 110°58'W |
| Guayubin, Dom. Rep. (gwá-yōō-bē'n) | 135 | 19°40'N | 71°25'W |
| Guazacapán, Guat. (gwä-zä-kä-pän') | 132 | 14°04'N | 90°26'W |
| Gubakha, Russia (gōō-bä'kå) | 178 | 58°53'N | 57°35'E |
| Gubbio, Italy (gōōb'byô) | 174 | 43°23'N | 12°36'E |
| Guben, Ger. | 168 | 51°57'N | 14°43'E |
| Gucheng, China (gōō-chŭŋ) | 206 | 39°09'N | 115°43'E |
| Gúdar, Sierra de, mts., Spain | 173 | 40°28'N | 0°47'W |
| Gudena, r., Den. | 166 | 56°20'N | 9°47'E |
| Gudermes, Russia | 182 | 43°20'N | 46°08'E |
| Gudvangen, Nor. (gōōdh'väŋ-gĕn) | 166 | 60°52'N | 6°45'E |
| Guebwiller, Fr. (gĕb-vē-lâr') | 171 | 47°53'N | 7°10'E |
| Guédi, Mont, mtn., Chad | 235 | 12°14'N | 18°58'E |
| Guelma, Alg. (gwĕl'mä) | 230 | 36°32'N | 7°17'E |
| Guelph, Can. (gwĕlf) | 99 | 43°33'N | 80°15'W |
| Güere, r., Ven. (gwĕ'rĕ) | 143b | 9°39'N | 65°00'W |
| Guéret, Fr. (gā-rĕ') | 170 | 46°09'N | 1°52'E |
| Guernsey, dep., Eur. | 170 | 49°28'N | 2°35'W |
| Guernsey, i., Guern. (gûrn'zĭ) | 161 | 49°27'N | 2°36'W |
| Guerrero, Mex. (gĕr-rā'rō) | 122 | 26°47'N | 99°20'W |
| Guerrero, Mex. | 122 | 28°20'N | 100°24'W |
| Guerrero, state, Mex. | 128 | 17°45'N | 100°15'W |
| Gueydan, La., U.S. (gā'dǎn) | 123 | 30°01'N | 92°31'W |
| Guia de Pacobaíba, Braz. (gwē'ä-dĕ-pä'kō-bī'bä) | 144b | 22°42'S | 43°10'W |
| Guiana Highlands, mts., S.A. | 139 | 3°20'N | 60°00'W |
| Guichi, China (gwā-chr) | 209 | 30°35'N | 117°28'E |
| Guichicovi, Mex. (gwē-chē-kō'vē) | 131 | 16°58'N | 95°10'W |
| Guidonia, Italy (gwē-dō'nyà) | 174 | 42°00'N | 12°45'E |
| Guiglo, C. Iv. | 234 | 6°33'N | 7°29'W |
| Guignes-Rabutin, Fr. (gēN'yĕ) | 171b | 48°38'N | 2°48'E |
| Güigüe, Ven. (gwē'gwĕ) | 143b | 10°05'N | 67°48'W |
| Guija, Lago, l., N.A. (gē'hä) | 132 | 14°16'N | 89°21'W |
| Guildford, Eng., U.K. (gĭl'fērd) | 164 | 51°13'N | 0°34'W |
| Guilford, In., U.S. (gĭl'fērd) | 111f | 39°10'N | 84°55'W |
| Guilin, China (gwā-lĭn) | 205 | 25°18'N | 110°22'E |
| Guimarães, Port. (gē-mä-rănsh') | 172 | 41°27'N | 8°22'W |
| Guinea, nation, Afr. (gĭn'ē) | 230 | 10°48'N | 12°28'W |
| Guinea, Gulf of, b., Afr. | 230 | 2°00'N | 1°00'E |
| Guinea-Bissau, nation, Afr. (gĭn'ē) | 230 | 12°00'N | 20°00'W |
| Guingamp, Fr. (găn-gän') | 170 | 48°35'N | 3°10'W |
| Guir, r., Mor. | 162 | 31°55'N | 2°48'W |
| Güira de Melena, Cuba (gwē'rä dā må-lā'nä) | 134 | 22°45'N | 82°30'W |
| Güiria, Ven. (gwē-rē'ä) | 142 | 10°43'N | 62°16'W |
| Guise, Fr. (guēz) | 170 | 49°54'N | 3°37'E |
| Guisisil, vol., Nic. (gē-sē-sēl') | 132 | 12°40'N | 86°11'W |
| Guiyang, China (gwā-yäŋ) | 204 | 26°45'N | 107°00'E |
| Guizhou, China (gwā-jō) | 207a | 22°46'N | 113°15'E |
| Guizhou, prov., China | 204 | 27°00'N | 106°10'E |
| Gujānwāla, Pak. (gòj-rän'va-lå) | 199 | 32°08'N | 74°14'E |
| Gujarat, India | 199 | 22°54'N | 72°00'E |
| Gulbarga, India (gòl-bûr'gà) | 199 | 17°25'N | 76°52'E |
| Gulbene, Lat. (gòl-bā'nĕ) | 167 | 57°09'N | 26°49'E |
| Gulfport, Ms., U.S. (gŭlf'pōrt) | 124 | 30°24'N | 89°05'W |
| Gulja *see* Yining, China | 204 | 43°58'N | 80°40'E |
| Gull Lake, Can. | 96 | 50°10'N | 108°25'W |
| Gull Lake, l., Can. | 95 | 52°35'N | 114°00'W |
| Gulu, Ug. | 237 | 2°47'N | 32°18'E |
| Gumaca, Phil. (gōō-mä-kä') | 213a | 13°55'N | 122°06'E |
| Gumbeyka, r., Russia (gòm-bĕy'kà) | 186a | 53°20'N | 59°42'E |
| Gumel, Nig. | 230 | 12°39'N | 9°22'E |
| Gummersbach, Ger. (gòm'ĕrs-bäk) | 168 | 51°02'N | 7°34'E |
| Gummi, Nig. | 235 | 12°09'N | 5°09'E |
| Gumpoldskirchen, Aus. | 159e | 48°04'N | 16°15'E |
| Guna, India | 202 | 24°44'N | 77°17'E |
| Gunisao, r., Can. (gŭn-ĭ-sä'ō) | 97 | 53°40'N | 97°35'W |
| Gunisao Lake, l., Can. | 97 | 53°35'N | 96°10'W |
| Gunnedah, Austl. (gŭ'nē-dä) | 222 | 31°00'S | 150°10'E |
| Gunnison, Co., U.S. (gŭn'ĭ-sŭn) | 119 | 38°33'N | 106°56'W |
| Gunnison, Ut., U.S. | 119 | 39°10'N | 111°50'W |
| Gunnison, r., Co., U.S. | 119 | 38°45'N | 108°20'W |
| Guntersville, Al., U.S. (gŭn'tērz-vĭl) | 124 | 34°20'N | 86°19'W |
| Guntersville Lake, res., Al., U.S. | 124 | 34°30'N | 86°20'W |
| Guntramsdorf, Aus. | 159e | 48°04'N | 16°19'E |
| Guntūr, India (gòn'tōōr) | 199 | 16°22'N | 80°29'E |
| Guoyang, China (gwô-yäŋ) | 206 | 33°32'N | 116°10'E |
| Gurdon, Ar., U.S. (gûr'dǎn) | 121 | 33°56'N | 93°10'W |
| Gurgueia, r., Braz. | 143 | 8°12'S | 43°49'W |
| Guri, Embalse, res., Ven. | 142 | 7°30'N | 63°00'W |
| Gurnee, Il., U.S. (gûr'nē) | 111a | 42°22'N | 87°55'W |
| Gurskøy, i., Nor. (gōōrskûē) | 166 | 62°18'N | 5°20'E |
| Gurupi, Serra do, mts., Braz. (sĕ'r-rä-dô-gōō-rōō-pē') | 143 | 5°32'S | 47°02'W |
| Guru Sikhar, mtn., India | 202 | 29°42'N | 72°50'E |
| Gur'yevsk, Russia (gōōr-yĭfsk') | 178 | 54°17'N | 85°56'E |
| Gusau, Nig. (gōō-zä'ōō) | 230 | 12°12'N | 6°40'E |
| Gusev, Russia (gōō'sĕf) | 167 | 54°35'N | 22°15'E |
| Gushi, China (gōō-shr) | 206 | 32°11'N | 115°39'E |
| Gushiago, Ghana | 234 | 9°55'N | 0°12'W |
| Gusinje, Serb. (gōō-sēn'yĕ) | 175 | 42°34'N | 19°54'E |
| Gus'-Khrustal'nyy, Russia (gōōs-krōō-stäl'ny') | 180 | 55°39'N | 40°41'E |
| Gustavo A. Madero, Mex. (gōōs-tä'vô-à-mä-dĕ'rô) | 130 | 19°29'N | 99°07'W |
| Güstrow, Ger. (güs'trō) | 168 | 53°48'N | 12°12'E |
| Gütersloh, Ger. (gü'tĕrs-lo) | 168 | 51°54'N | 8°22'E |
| Guthrie, Ok., U.S. (gŭth'rĭ) | 121 | 35°52'N | 97°26'W |
| Guthrie Center, Ia., U.S. | 113 | 41°41'N | 94°33'W |
| Gutiérrez Zamora, Mex. (gōō-tĭ-âr'rāz zä-mō'rä) | 131 | 20°27'N | 97°17'W |
| Guttenberg, Ia., U.S. (gŭt'ĕn-bûrg) | 113 | 42°48'N | 91°09'W |
| Guyana, nation, S.A. (güy'ănă) | 143 | 7°45'N | 59°00'W |
| Guyang, China (gōō-yän) | 206 | 34°56'N | 114°57'E |
| Guye, China (gōō-yŭ) | 206 | 39°46'N | 118°23'E |
| Guymon, Ok., U.S. (gī'mŏn) | 120 | 36°41'N | 101°29'W |
| Guysborough, Can. (gīz'bŭr-ô) | 101 | 45°23'N | 61°30'W |
| Guzhen, China (gōō-jŭn) | 208 | 33°20'N | 117°18'E |
| Gvardeysk, Russia (gvår-dĕysk') | 167 | 54°39'N | 21°11'E |
| Gwadabawa, Nig. | 235 | 13°20'N | 5°15'E |
| Gwādar, Pak. (gwä'dŭr) | 198 | 25°15'N | 62°29'E |
| Gwalior, India | 199 | 26°13'N | 78°10'E |
| Gwane, D.R.C. (gwän) | 231 | 4°43'N | 25°50'E |
| Gwardafuy, Gees, c., Som. | 238a | 11°55'N | 51°30'E |
| Gwda, r., Pol. | 168 | 53°27'N | 16°52'E |
| Gwembe, Zam. | 237 | 16°30'S | 27°35'E |
| Gweru, Zimb. | 232 | 19°15'S | 29°48'E |
| Gwinn, Mi., U.S. (gwĭn) | 113 | 46°15'N | 87°30'W |
| Gyaring Co, l., China | 202 | 30°37'N | 88°33'E |
| Gydan, Khrebet (Kolymskiy), mts., Russia | 179 | 61°45'N | 155°00'E |
| Gydanskiy Poluostrov, pen., Russia | 178 | 70°42'N | 76°03'E |
| Gympie, Austl. (gĭm'pē) | 219 | 26°20'S | 152°50'E |
| Gyöngyös, Hung. (dyûn'dyûsh) | 163 | 47°47'N | 19°55'E |
| Györ, Hung. (dyûr) | 163 | 47°40'N | 17°37'E |
| Gyōtoku, Japan (gyō'tō-kōō') | 211a | 35°42'N | 139°56'E |
| Gypsumville, Can. (jĭp'sŭm-vĭl) | 90 | 51°45'N | 98°35'W |
| Gýtheio, Grc. | 175 | 36°50'N | 22°37'E |
| Gyula, Hung. (dyò'lä) | 169 | 46°38'N | 21°18'E |
| Gyumri, Arm. | 181 | 40°40'N | 43°50'E |
| Gyzylarbat, Turkmen. | 183 | 38°55'N | 56°33'E |


# H


| PLACE (Pronunciation) | PAGE | LAT. | LONG. |
|---|---|---|---|
| Haan, Ger. (hän) | 171c | 51°12'N | 7°00'E |
| Haapamäki, Fin. (häp'ä-mĕ-kē) | 167 | 62°16'N | 24°20'E |
| Haapsalu, Est. (häp'sä-lò) | 167 | 58°56'N | 23°33'E |
| Haar, Ger. (här) | 159d | 48°06'N | 11°44'E |
| Ha'Arava (Wādī al Jayb), val., Asia | 197a | 30°33'N | 35°10'E |
| Haarlem, Neth. (här'lĕm) | 165 | 52°22'N | 4°37'E |
| Habana, prov., Cuba (hä-vä'nä) | 134 | 22°45'N | 82°25'W |
| Hābra, India | 202a | 22°49'N | 88°38'E |
| Hachinohe, Japan (hä'chē-nō'hå) | 210 | 40°29'N | 141°40'E |
| Hachiōji, Japan (hä'chē-ō'jē) | 210 | 35°39'N | 139°18'E |
| Hackensack, N.J., U.S. (hăk'ĕn-săk) | 110a | 40°54'N | 74°03'W |
| Ḩadd, Ra's al, c., Oman | 198 | 22°29'N | 59°46'E |
| Haddonfield, N.J., U.S. (hăd'ŭn-fēld) | 110f | 39°53'N | 75°02'W |
| Haddon Heights, N.J., U.S. (hăd'ŭn hīts) | 110f | 39°53'N | 75°03'W |
| Hadejia, Nig. (hä-dā'jä) | 230 | 12°30'N | 9°59'E |
| Hadejia, r., Nig. | 230 | 12°15'N | 10°00'E |
| Ḩadera, Isr. (ĸå-dĕ'rà) | 197a | 32°26'N | 34°55'E |
| Haderslev, Den. (hä'dhĕrs-lĕv) | 166 | 55°17'N | 9°28'E |
| Hadiach, Ukr. | 181 | 50°22'N | 33°59'E |
| Ḩadīdū, Yemen | 198 | 12°40'N | 53°50'E |
| Hadlock, Wa., U.S. (hăd'lŏk) | 116a | 48°02'N | 122°46'W |
| Ḩaḑramawt, reg., Yemen | 198 | 15°22'N | 48°40'E |
| Hadūr Shu'ayb, mtn., Yemen | 198 | 15°45'N | 43°45'E |
| Haeju, Kor., N. (hä'ĕ-jŭ) | 210 | 38°03'N | 125°42'E |
| Hafnarfjördur, Ice. | 160 | 64°02'N | 21°32'W |
| Haft Gel, Iran | 201 | 31°27'N | 49°27'E |
| Hafun, Ras, c., Som. (hä-fōōn') | 238a | 10°15'N | 51°35'E |
| Hageland, Mt., U.S. (hăge'lănd) | 115 | 48°53'N | 108°43'W |
| Hagen, Ger. (hä'gĕn) | 168 | 51°21'N | 7°29'E |
| Hagerstown, In., U.S. (hā'gĕrz-toun) | 108 | 39°55'N | 85°10'W |
| Hagerstown, Md., U.S. | 105 | 39°40'N | 77°45'W |
| Hagi, Japan (hä'gĭ) | 211 | 34°25'N | 131°25'E |
| Hague, Cap de la, c., Fr. (dē lá äg') | 170 | 49°44'N | 1°55'W |
| Haguenau, Fr. (åg'nō') | 171 | 48°47'N | 7°48'E |
| Hai'an, China (hī-än) | 206 | 32°35'N | 120°25'E |
| Haibara, Japan (hä'ē-bä'rä) | 211 | 34°29'N | 135°57'E |
| Haicheng, China (hī-chŭŋ) | 208 | 40°58'N | 122°45'E |
| Haidian, China (hī-dĭĕn) | 206 | 39°59'N | 116°17'E |
| Haifa, Isr. (hä'ē-fà) | 198 | 32°48'N | 35°00'E |
| Haifeng, China (hä'ē-fĕng') | 209 | 23°00'N | 115°20'E |
| Haifuzhen, China (hī-fōō-jŭn) | 206 | 31°57'N | 121°48'E |
| Haikou, China (hī-kō) | 209 | 20°00'N | 110°20'E |
| Ḩā'il, Sau. Ar. | 198 | 27°30'N | 41°47'E |
| Hailar, China | 205 | 49°10'N | 118°40'E |
| Hailey, Id., U.S. (hā'lĭ) | 115 | 43°31'N | 114°19'W |
| Haileybury, Can. | 99 | 47°27'N | 79°38'W |
| Haileyville, Ok., U.S. (hā'lĭ-vĭl) | 121 | 34°51'N | 95°34'W |
| Hailing Dao, i., China (hī-lĭŋ dou) | 209 | 21°30'N | 112°15'E |
| Hailong, China (hī-loŋ) | 208 | 42°32'N | 125°52'E |
| Hailun, China (hä'ē-lōōn') | 205 | 47°18'N | 126°50'E |
| Hainan, prov., China | 204 | 19°00'N | 109°30'E |
| Hainan Dao, i., China (hī-nän dou) | 205 | 19°00'N | 111°10'E |
| Hainburg, Aus. | 168 | 48°09'N | 16°57'E |
| Haines, Ak., U.S. (hānz) | 103 | 59°10'N | 135°38'W |
| Haines City, Fl., U.S. | 125a | 28°05'N | 81°38'W |

| PLACE (Pronunciation) | PAGE | LAT. | LONG. |
|---|---|---|---|
| Hai Phong, Viet. (hī'fông')(hä'ēp-hŏng) | 212 | 20°52'N | 106°40'E |
| Haisyn, Ukr. | 181 | 48°46'N | 29°22'E |
| Haiti, nation, N.A. (hā'tĭ) | 129 | 19°00'N | 72°15'W |
| Haizhou, China | 206 | 34°34'N | 119°11'E |
| Haizhou Wan, b., China | 208 | 34°49'N | 120°35'E |
| Hajdúböszormény, Hung. (hô'ĭ-dŏ-bû'sûr-män') | 169 | 47°41'N | 21°30'E |
| Hajdúhadház, Hung. (hô'ĭ-dŏ-hôd'häz) | 169 | 47°32'N | 21°32'E |
| Hajdúnánás, Hung. (hô'ĭ-dŏ-nä'näsh) | 169 | 47°52'N | 21°27'E |
| Hakodate, Japan (hä-kō-dä't å) | 205 | 41°46'N | 140°42'E |
| Haku-San, mtn., Japan (hä'kōō-sän') | 210 | 36°11'N | 136°45'E |
| Halā'ib, Egypt (hä-lä'ēb) | 231 | 22°10'N | 36°40'E |
| Halbe, Ger. (häl'bē) | 159b | 52°07'N | 13°43'E |
| Halberstadt, Ger. (häl'bĕr-shtät) | 168 | 51°54'N | 11°07'E |
| Halcon, Mount, mtn., Phil. (häl-kōn') | 213a | 13°19'N | 120°55'E |
| Halden, Nor. (häl'dĕn) | 160 | 59°10'N | 11°21'E |
| Haldensleben, Ger. | 168 | 52°18'N | 11°23'E |
| Hale, Eng., U.K. (hāl) | 158a | 53°22'N | 2°20'W |
| Haleakalā Crater, depr., Hi., U.S. (hä'lä-ä'kä-lä) | 126a | 20°44'N | 156°15'W |
| Haleakalā National Park, rec., Hi., U.S. | 126a | 20°46'N | 156°00'W |
| Hales Corners, Wi., U.S. (hālz kŏr'nērz) | 111a | 42°56'N | 88°03'W |
| Halesowen, Eng., U.K. (hālz'ō-wĕn) | 158a | 52°26'N | 2°03'W |
| Halethorpe, Md., U.S. (hāl-thôrp) | 110e | 39°15'N | 76°40'W |
| Haleyville, Al., U.S. (hā'lĭ-vĭl) | 124 | 34°11'N | 87°36'W |
| Half Moon Bay, Ca., U.S. (häf'mōōn) | 116b | 37°28'N | 122°26'W |
| Halfway House, S. Afr. (häf-wā hous) | 233b | 26°00'S | 28°08'E |
| Halfweg, Neth. | 159a | 52°23'N | 4°45'E |
| Halifax, Can. (hăl'ĭ-făks) | 91 | 44°39'N | 63°36'W |
| Halifax, Eng., U.K. | 164 | 53°44'N | 1°52'W |
| Halifax Bay, b., Austl. (hăl'ĭ-făx) | 221 | 18°56'S | 147°07'E |
| Halifax Harbour, b., Can. | 100 | 44°35'N | 63°31'W |
| Halkett, Cape, c., Ak., U.S. | 103 | 70°50'N | 151°15'W |
| Hallam Peak, mtn., Can. | 95 | 52°11'N | 118°46'E |
| Halla San, mtn., Kor., S. (häl'lä-sän) | 210 | 33°20'N | 126°37'E |
| Halle, Bel. (häl'lĕ) | 159a | 50°45'N | 4°13'E |
| Halle, Ger. | 161 | 51°30'N | 11°59'E |
| Hallettsville, Tx., U.S. (hăl'ĕts-vĭl) | 123 | 29°26'N | 96°55'W |
| Hallock, Mn., U.S. (hăl'ŭk) | 112 | 48°46'N | 96°57'W |
| Hall Peninsula, pen., Can. (hôl) | 93 | 63°14'N | 65°40'W |
| Halls Bayou, Tx., U.S. | 123a | 29°55'N | 95°23'W |
| Hallsberg, Swe. (häls'bĕrgh) | 166 | 59°04'N | 15°04'E |
| Halls Creek, Austl. (hôlz) | 218 | 18°15'S | 127°45'E |
| Halmahera, i., Indon. (häl-mä-hä'rä) | 213 | 0°45'N | 128°45'E |
| Halmahera, Laut, Indon. | 213 | 1°00'S | 129°00'E |
| Halmstad, Swe. (hälm'städ) | 160 | 56°40'N | 12°46'E |
| Halsafjorden, b., Nor. (häl'sĕ fyôrd) | 166 | 63°03'N | 8°23'E |
| Halstead, Ks., U.S. (hôl'stĕd) | 121 | 38°02'N | 97°36'W |
| Haltern, Ger. (häl'tĕrn) | 171c | 51°45'N | 7°10'E |
| Haltom City, Tx., U.S. (hôl'tŏm) | 117c | 32°48'N | 97°13'W |
| Halver, Ger. | 171c | 51°11'N | 7°30'E |
| Hamada, Japan | 210 | 34°53'N | 132°05'E |
| Hamadān, Iran (hŭ-mŭ-dän') | 198 | 34°45'N | 48°07'E |
| Ḩamāh, Syria (hä'mä) | 198 | 35°08'N | 36°53'E |
| Hamamatsu, Japan (hä'mä-mät'sŏ) | 210 | 34°41'N | 137°43'E |
| Hamar, Nor. (hä'mär) | 160 | 60°49'N | 11°05'E |
| Hamasaka, Japan (hä'mà-sä'kà) | 211 | 35°57'N | 134°27'E |
| Hamborn, Ger. (häm'bōrn) | 171c | 51°30'N | 6°43'E |
| Hamburg, Ger. (häm'bŏŏrgh) | 154 | 53°34'N | 10°02'E |
| Hamburg, S. Afr. (hăm'bûrg) | 233c | 33°18'S | 27°28'E |
| Hamburg, Ar., U.S. (hăm'bûrg) | 121 | 33°15'N | 91°49'W |
| Hamburg, N.J., U.S. | 110a | 41°09'N | 74°35'W |
| Hamburg, N.Y., U.S. | 111c | 42°44'N | 78°51'W |
| Hamden, Ct., U.S. (hăm'dĕn) | 109 | 41°20'N | 72°55'W |
| Hämeenlinna, Fin. (hĕ'mân-lĭn-nà) | 160 | 61°00'N | 24°29'E |
| Hameln, Ger. (hä'mĕln) | 168 | 52°06'N | 9°23'E |
| Hamelwörden, Ger. (hä'mĕl-vûr-dĕn) | 159c | 53°47'N | 9°19'E |
| Hamersley Range, mts., Austl. (hăm'ērz-lē) | 220 | 22°15'S | 117°50'E |
| Hamhŭng, Kor., N. (häm'hông') | 205 | 39°57'N | 127°35'E |
| Hami, China (hä-mē) | 204 | 42°58'N | 93°14'E |
| Hamilton, Austl. (hăm'ĭl-tŭn) | 219 | 37°50'S | 142°10'E |
| Hamilton, Can. | 91 | 43°15'N | 79°52'W |
| Hamilton, N.Z. | 221a | 37°45'S | 175°28'E |
| Hamilton, Al., U.S. | 124 | 34°09'N | 88°01'W |
| Hamilton, Ma., U.S. | 101a | 42°37'N | 70°52'W |
| Hamilton, Mo., U.S. | 121 | 39°43'N | 93°59'W |
| Hamilton, Mt., U.S. | 115 | 46°15'N | 114°09'W |
| Hamilton, Oh., U.S. | 105 | 39°22'N | 84°33'W |
| Hamilton, Tx., U.S. | 122 | 31°42'N | 98°07'W |
| Hamilton, Lake, l., Ar., U.S. | 121 | 34°25'N | 93°32'W |
| Hamilton Harbour, b., Can. | 102d | 43°17'N | 79°50'W |
| Hamilton Inlet, b., Can. | 93 | 54°20'N | 56°57'W |
| Hamina, Fin. (hà'mē-nà) | 167 | 60°34'N | 27°15'E |
| Hamlet, N.C., U.S. (hăm'lĕt) | 125 | 34°53'N | 79°42'W |
| Hamlin, Tx., U.S. (hăm'lĭn) | 120 | 32°54'N | 100°08'W |
| Hamm, Ger. (häm) | 168 | 51°40'N | 7°48'E |
| Hammanskraal, S. Afr. (hä-măns-kräl') | 238c | 25°24'S | 28°17'E |
| Hamme, Bel. | 159a | 51°06'N | 4°07'E |
| Hamme-Oste Kanal, can., Ger. (hä'mĕ-ōs'tĕ kä-näl) | 159c | 53°20'N | 8°59'E |
| Hammerfest, Nor. (hä'mĕr-fĕst) | 154 | 70°38'N | 23°59'E |
| Hammond, In., U.S. (hăm'ŭnd) | 105 | 41°37'N | 87°31'W |
| Hammond, La., U.S. | 123 | 30°30'N | 90°28'W |
| Hammond, Or., U.S. | 116c | 46°12'N | 123°57'W |
| Hammonton, N.J., U.S. (hăm'ŭn-tŭn) | 109 | 39°40'N | 74°45'W |
| Hampden, Me., U.S. (hăm'dĕn) | 100 | 44°44'N | 68°51'W |
| Hampstead, Md., U.S. | 110e | 39°36'N | 76°54'W |
| Hampstead Norris, Eng., U.K. (hămp-stĕd nŏ'rĭs) | 158b | 51°27'N | 1°14'W |
| Hampton, Can. (hămp'tŭn) | 100 | 45°32'N | 65°51'W |
| Hampton, Ia., U.S. | 113 | 42°43'N | 93°15'W |
| Hampton, Va., U.S. | 109 | 37°02'N | 76°21'W |
| Hampton Roads, b., Va., U.S. | 110g | 36°56'N | 76°23'W |
| Hams Fork, r., Wy., U.S. | 115 | 41°55'N | 110°40'W |
| Hamtramck, Mi., U.S. (hăm-trăm'ĭk) | 111b | 42°24'N | 83°03'W |
| Han, r., China (hän) | 209 | 25°00'N | 116°35'E |
| Han, r., China | 205 | 31°40'N | 112°04'E |
| Han, r., Kor., S. | 210 | 37°10'N | 127°40'E |
| Hāna, Hi., U.S. (hä'nä) | 126a | 20°43'N | 155°59'W |
| Hanábana, r., Cuba (hä-nä-bä'nä) | 134 | 22°30'N | 80°55'W |
| Hanalei Bay, b., Hi., U.S. (hä-nä-lā'ē) | 126a | 22°15'N | 159°40'W |
| Hanang, mtn., Tan. | 237 | 4°26'S | 35°24'E |
| Hanau, Ger. (hä'nou) | 168 | 50°08'N | 8°56'E |
| Hancock, Mi., U.S. (hăn'kŏk) | 105 | 47°08'N | 88°37'W |
| Handan, China (hän-dän) | 206 | 36°37'N | 114°30'E |
| Haney, Can. (hā-nē) | 95 | 49°13'N | 122°36'W |
| Hanford, Ca., U.S. (hăn'fērd) | 118 | 36°20'N | 119°38'W |
| Hangayn Nuruu, mts., Mong. | 204 | 48°03'N | 99°45'E |
| Hango, Fin. (häŋ'gû) | 154 | 59°49'N | 22°56'E |
| Hangzhou, China (häng'chō') | 205 | 30°17'N | 120°12'E |
| Hangzhou Wan, b., China (häŋ-jō wän) | 209 | 30°20'N | 121°25'E |
| Hankamer, Tx., U.S. (hăn'kà-mēr) | 123a | 29°52'N | 94°42'W |
| Hankinson, N.D., U.S. (häŋ'kĭn-sŭn) | 112 | 46°04'N | 96°54'W |
| Hankou, China (hän-kō) | 209 | 30°42'N | 114°22'E |
| Hann, Mount, mtn., Austl. (hän) | 220 | 16°05'S | 126°07'E |
| Hanna, Can. (hăn'à) | 90 | 51°38'N | 111°54'W |
| Hanna, Wy., U.S. | 115 | 41°51'N | 106°34'W |
| Hannah, N.D., U.S. | 112 | 48°58'N | 98°42'W |
| Hannibal, Mo., U.S. (hăn'ĭ băl) | 105 | 39°42'N | 91°22'W |
| Hannover, Ger. (hän-ō'vĕr) | 154 | 52°22'N | 9°45'E |
| Hannover, hist. reg., Ger. | 168 | 52°52'N | 8°27'E |
| Hanöbukten, b., Swe. | 166 | 55°54'N | 14°55'E |
| Hanoi, Viet. (hä-noi') | 212 | 21°04'N | 105°50'E |
| Hanover, Can. (hăn'ô-vēr) | 98 | 44°10'N | 81°05'W |
| Hanover, Ma., U.S. | 101a | 42°07'N | 70°49'W |
| Hanover, N.H., U.S. | 109 | 43°45'N | 72°15'W |
| Hanover, Pa., U.S. | 109 | 39°50'N | 77°00'W |
| Hanover, i., Chile | 144 | 51°00'S | 74°45'W |
| Hanshan, China (hän'shän') | 206 | 31°43'N | 118°06'E |
| Hans Lollick, i., V.I.U.S. (häns'lôl'ĭk) | 129c | 18°24'N | 64°55'W |
| Hanson, Ma., U.S. (hăn'sŭn) | 101a | 42°04'N | 70°53'W |
| Hansville, Wa., U.S. (hăns'-vĭl) | 116a | 47°55'N | 122°33'W |
| Hantengri Feng, mtn., Asia (hän-tŭŋ-rē fŭŋ) | 204 | 42°10'N | 80°20'E |
| Hantsport, Can. (hănts'pōrt) | 100 | 45°04'N | 64°11'W |
| Hanyang, China (han'yäng') | 205 | 30°30'N | 114°10'E |
| Hanzhong, China (hän-jôŋ) | 208 | 33°02'N | 107°00'E |
| Haocheng, China (hou-chŭŋ) | 206 | 33°19'N | 117°33'E |
| Haparanda, Swe. (hä-pa-rän'dä) | 160 | 65°54'N | 23°57'E |
| Hapeville, Ga., U.S. (hāp'vĭl) | 110c | 33°39'N | 84°25'W |
| Happy Camp, Ca., U.S. | 114 | 41°47'N | 123°22'W |
| Happy Valley-Goose Bay, Can. | 91 | 53°19'N | 60°33'W |
| Ḩaql, Sau. Ar. | 197a | 29°15'N | 34°57'E |
| Har, Laga, r., Kenya | 237 | 2°15'N | 39°30'E |
| Haradok, Bela. | 176 | 55°27'N | 29°58'E |
| Harare, Zimb. | 232 | 17°50'S | 31°03'E |
| Harbin, China | 205 | 45°40'N | 126°30'E |
| Harbor Beach, Mi., U.S. (här'bēr bēch) | 108 | 43°50'N | 82°40'W |
| Harbor Springs, Mi., U.S. | 108 | 45°25'N | 85°05'W |
| Harbour Breton, Can. (brĕt'ŭn) (brē-tôN') | 101 | 47°29'N | 55°48'W |
| Harbour Grace, Can. (grās) | 101 | 47°32'N | 53°13'W |
| Harburg, Ger. (här-bŏrgh) | 159c | 53°28'N | 9°58'E |
| Hardangerfjorden, Nor. (här-däng'ēr fyôrd) | 160 | 59°58'N | 6°30'E |
| Hardin, Mt., U.S. (här'dĭn) | 115 | 45°44'N | 107°36'W |
| Harding, S. Afr. (här'dĭng) | 232 | 30°34'S | 29°54'E |
| Harding, Lake, res., U.S. | 124 | 32°43'N | 85°00'W |
| Hardwār, India (hŭr'dvär) | 199 | 29°56'N | 78°06'E |
| Hardy, r., Mex. (här'dĭ) | 118 | 32°04'N | 115°10'W |
| Hare Bay, b., Can. (hâr) | 101 | 51°18'N | 55°50'W |
| Harer, Eth. | 231 | 9°43'N | 42°10'E |
| Harerge, hist. reg., Eth. | 231 | 8°15'N | 41°00'E |
| Hargeysa, Som. (här-gä'ē-sà) | 238a | 9°20'N | 43°57'E |
| Harghita, Munţii, mts., Rom. | 169 | 46°25'N | 25°40'E |
| Harima-Nada, b., Japan (hä'rē-mä nä-dä) | 211 | 34°34'N | 134°37'E |
| Haringvliet, r., Neth. | 159a | 51°49'N | 4°03'E |
| Harīrūd, r., Asia | 198 | 34°29'N | 61°16'E |
| Harlan, Ia., U.S. (här'lăn) | 121 | 41°40'N | 95°10'W |
| Harlan, Ky., U.S. | 124 | 36°50'N | 83°19'W |
| Harlan County Reservoir, res., Ne., U.S. | 120 | 40°03'N | 99°51'W |
| Harlem, Mt., U.S. (hár'lĕm) | 115 | 48°33'N | 108°50'W |
| Harlingen, Neth. (här'lĭng-ĕn) | 165 | 53°10'N | 5°24'E |
| Harlingen, Tx., U.S. | 104 | 26°12'N | 97°42'W |
| Harlow, Eng., U.K. (här'lō) | 158b | 51°46'N | 0°08'E |
| Harlowton, Mt., U.S. (hár'lō-tun) | 115 | 46°26'N | 109°50'W |
| Harmony, In., U.S. (här'mō-nĭ) | 108 | 39°35'N | 87°00'W |
| Harney Basin, Or., U.S. (här'nĭ) | 114 | 43°26'N | 120°19'W |
| Harney Lake, l., Or., U.S. | 114 | 43°11'N | 119°23'W |
| Harney Peak, mtn., S.D., U.S. | 106 | 43°52'N | 103°32'W |
| Härnösand, Swe. (hĕr-nû-sänd) | 160 | 62°37'N | 17°54'E |
| Haro, Spain (ä'rō) | 172 | 42°35'N | 2°49'W |
| Haro Strait, strt., N.A. (hă'rō) | 116a | 48°27'N | 123°11'W |
| Harpenden, Eng., U.K. (här'pĕn-d'n) | 158b | 51°48'N | 0°22'W |
| Harper, Lib. | 230 | 4°25'N | 7°43'W |
| Harper, Ks., U.S. (här'pēr) | 120 | 37°17'N | 98°02'W |
| Harper, Wa., U.S. | 116a | 47°31'N | 122°32'W |
| Harpers Ferry, W.V., U.S. (här'pērz) | 109 | 39°20'N | 77°45'W |
| Harricana, r., Can. | 99 | 50°10'N | 78°50'W |
| Harriman, Tn., U.S. (hă'ĭ-măn) | 124 | 35°55'N | 84°34'W |
| Harrington, De., U.S. (hăr'ĭng-tŭn) | 109 | 38°55'N | 75°35'W |
| Harris, i., Scot., U.K. (hăr'ĭs) | 164 | 57°55'N | 6°40'W |
| Harris, Lake, l., Fl., U.S. | 125a | 28°43'N | 81°40'W |
| Harrisburg, Il., U.S. (hăr'ĭs-bûrg) | 108 | 37°45'N | 88°35'W |
| Harrisburg, Pa., U.S. | 105 | 40°15'N | 76°50'W |
| Harrismith, S. Afr. (hă-rĭs'mĭth) | 238c | 28°17'S | 29°08'E |
| Harrison, Ar., U.S. (hăr'ĭ-sŭn) | 121 | 36°13'N | 93°06'W |
| Harrison, Oh., U.S. | 111f | 39°16'N | 84°45'W |
| Harrisonburg, Va., U.S. (hăr'ĭ-sŭn-bûrg) | 109 | 38°30'N | 78°50'W |
| Harrison Lake, l., Can. | 95 | 49°31'N | 121°59'W |
| Harrisonville, Mo., U.S. (hăr-ĭ-sŭn-vĭl) | 121 | 38°39'N | 94°21'W |
| Harrisville, Ut., U.S. (hăr'ĭs-vĭl) | 117b | 41°17'N | 112°00'W |
| Harrisville, W.V., U.S. | 108 | 39°10'N | 81°05'W |
| Harrodsburg, Ky., U.S. (hăr'ŭdz-bûrg) | 108 | 37°45'N | 84°50'W |
| Harrods Creek, r., Ky., U.S. (hăr'ŭdz) | 111h | 38°24'N | 85°33'W |
| Harrow, Eng., U.K. (hăr'ō) | 158b | 51°34'N | 0°21'W |
| Harsefeld, Ger. (här'zĕ-fĕld') | 159c | 53°27'N | 9°30'E |
| Harstad, Nor. (här'städh) | 160 | 68°49'N | 16°10'E |
| Hart, Mi., U.S. (härt) | 108 | 43°40'N | 86°25'W |
| Hartbeesfontein, S. Afr. | 238c | 26°46'S | 26°25'E |
| Hartbeespoortdam, res., S. Afr. | 233b | 25°47'S | 27°43'E |
| Hartford, Al., U.S. (härt'fērd) | 124 | 31°05'N | 85°42'W |
| Hartford, Ar., U.S. | 121 | 35°01'N | 94°21'W |
| Hartford, Ct., U.S. | 105 | 41°45'N | 72°40'W |
| Hartford, Il., U.S. | 117e | 38°50'N | 90°06'W |
| Hartford, Ky., U.S. | 124 | 37°25'N | 86°50'W |
| Hartford, Mi., U.S. | 108 | 42°15'N | 86°15'W |
| Hartford, Wi., U.S. | 113 | 43°19'N | 88°25'W |
| Hartford City, In., U.S. | 108 | 40°35'N | 85°25'W |
| Hartington, Eng., U.K. (härt'ĭng-tŭn) | 158a | 53°08'N | 1°48'W |
| Hartington, Ne., U.S. | 112 | 42°37'N | 97°18'W |
| Hartland Point, c., Eng., U.K. | 164 | 51°03'N | 4°40'W |
| Hartlepool, Eng., U.K. (här't'l-pōōl) | 160 | 54°40'N | 1°12'W |
| Hartley, Ia., U.S. (härt'lĭ) | 112 | 43°12'N | 95°29'W |
| Hartley Bay, Can. | 94 | 53°25'N | 129°15'W |
| Hart Mountain, mtn., Can. (härt) | 97 | 52°25'N | 101°30'W |
| Hartsbeespoort, S. Afr. | 233b | 25°44'S | 27°51'E |
| Hartselle, Al., U.S. (härt'sĕl) | 124 | 34°24'N | 86°55'W |
| Hartshorne, Ok., U.S. (härts'hôrn) | 121 | 34°49'N | 95°34'W |
| Hartsville, S.C., U.S. (härts'vĭl) | 125 | 34°20'N | 80°04'W |
| Hartwell, Ga., U.S. (härt'wĕl) | 125 | 34°21'N | 82°56'W |
| Hartwell Lake, res., U.S. | 107 | 34°30'N | 83°00'W |
| Hārua, India | 202a | 22°36'N | 88°40'E |
| Harvard, Il., U.S. (här'vàrd) | 113 | 42°25'N | 88°39'W |
| Harvard, Ma., U.S. | 101a | 42°30'N | 71°35'W |
| Harvard, Ne., U.S. | 120 | 40°36'N | 98°08'W |
| Harvard, Mount, mtn., Co., U.S. | 119 | 38°55'N | 106°20'W |
| Harvey, Can. | 100 | 45°44'N | 64°46'W |
| Harvey, Il., U.S. | 111a | 41°37'N | 87°39'W |
| Harvey, La., U.S. | 110d | 29°54'N | 90°05'W |
| Harvey, N.D., U.S. | 112 | 47°46'N | 99°55'W |
| Harwich, Eng., U.K. (här'wĭch) | 165 | 51°53'N | 1°13'E |
| Haryana, state, India | 199 | 29°00'N | 75°45'E |
| Harz Mountains, mts., Ger. (härts) | 168 | 51°42'N | 10°50'E |
| Hashimoto, Japan (hä'shē-mō'tō) | 211 | 34°19'N | 135°37'E |
| Haskell, Ok., U.S. (hăs'kĕl) | 121 | 35°49'N | 95°41'W |
| Haskell, Tx., U.S. | 120 | 33°09'N | 99°43'W |
| Haslingden, Eng., U.K. (hăz'lĭng dĕn) | 158a | 53°43'N | 2°19'W |
| Hassi Messaoud, Alg. | 230 | 31°17'N | 6°13'E |
| Hässleholm, Swe. (hĕs'lĕ-hōlm) | 166 | 56°10'N | 13°44'E |
| Hastings, N.Z. | 221a | 39°33'S | 176°53'E |
| Hastings, Eng., U.K. (hās'tĭngz) | 161 | 50°52'N | 0°28'E |
| Hastings, Mi., U.S. | 108 | 42°40'N | 85°20'W |
| Hastings, Mn., U.S. | 117g | 44°44'N | 92°51'W |
| Hastings, Ne., U.S. | 104 | 40°34'N | 98°42'W |
| Hastings-on-Hudson, N.Y., U.S. (ŏn-hŭd'sŭn) | 110a | 40°59'N | 75°53'W |
| Hatay, Tur. | 198 | 36°20'N | 36°10'E |
| Hatchie, r., Tn., U.S. (hăch'ē) | 124 | 35°28'N | 89°14'W |
| Haţeg, Rom. (kät-säg') | 175 | 45°35'N | 22°57'E |
| Hatfield Broad Oak, Eng., U.K. (hăt-fēld brôd ōk) | 158b | 51°50'N | 0°14'E |
| Hatogaya, Japan (hä'tō-gä-yä) | 211a | 35°50'N | 139°45'E |
| Hatsukaichi, Japan (hät'sōō-kà'ē-chē) | 211 | 34°22'N | 132°19'E |
| Hatteras, Cape, c., N.C., U.S. (hăt'ēr-ás) | 107 | 35°15'N | 75°24'W |
| Hattiesburg, Ms., U.S. (hăt'ĭz-bûrg) | 105 | 31°20'N | 89°18'W |
| Hattingen, Ger. (hä'tĕn-gĕn) | 171c | 51°24'N | 7°11'E |
| Hatvan, Hung. (hôt'vôn) | 169 | 47°39'N | 19°44'E |
| Hat Yai, Thai. | 212 | 7°01'N | 100°29'E |
| Haugesund, Nor. (hou'gĕ-soon') | 160 | 59°26'N | 5°20'E |
| Haukivesi, l., Fin. (hou'kē-vĕ'sē) | 167 | 62°02'N | 29°02'E |
| Haultain, r., Can. | 96 | 56°15'N | 106°35'W |
| Hauptsrus, S. Afr. | 238c | 26°35'S | 26°16'E |
| Hauraki Gulf, b., N.Z. (hä-ōō-rä'kē) | 221a | 36°30'S | 175°00'E |
| Haut, Isle au, Me., U.S. (hō) | 100 | 44°03'N | 68°13'W |
| Haut Atlas, mts., Mor. | 162 | 32°10'N | 5°49'W |
| Hauterive, Can. | 100 | 49°11'N | 68°16'W |
| Hau'ula, Hi., U.S. | 126a | 21°37'N | 157°45'W |
| Havana, Cuba | 129 | 23°08'N | 82°23'W |
| Havana, Il., U.S. (hà-vă'nà) | 121 | 40°17'N | 90°02'W |
| Havasu, Lake, res., U.S. (hăv'à-sōō) | 119 | 34°26'N | 114°09'W |
| Havel, r., Ger. (hä'fĕl) | 168 | 53°09'N | 13°10'E |
| Havel-Kanal, can., Ger. | 159b | 52°36'N | 13°12'E |
| Haverhill, Ma., U.S. (hā'vēr-hĭl) | 101a | 42°46'N | 71°05'W |
| Haverhill, N.H., U.S. | 109 | 44°00'N | 72°05'W |
| Haverstraw, N.Y., U.S. (hā'vēr-strô) | 110a | 41°11'N | 73°58'W |
| Havlíčkův Brod, Czech Rep. | 161 | 49°38'N | 15°34'E |
| Havre, Mt., U.S. (hăv'ēr) | 104 | 48°34'N | 109°42'W |
| Havre-Boucher, Can. (hăv'rā-bōō-shā') | 101 | 45°42'N | 61°30'W |
| Havre de Grace, Md., U.S. (hăv'ēr dē gräs') | 109 | 39°35'N | 76°05'W |
| Havre-Saint Pierre, Can. | 100 | 50°15'N | 63°36'W |
| Haw, r., N.C., U.S. (hô) | 125 | 36°17'N | 79°46'W |


ăt; finăl; rāte; senāte; ärm; àsk; sofá; fâre; ch-choose; dh-as th in other; bē; ēvent; bĕt; recĕnt; cratĕr; g-gō; gh-guttural g; bĭt; ĭ-short neutral; rīde; ĸ-guttural k as ch in German ich;

PRONOUNCING INDEX

Hawaii – Hindupur 301


| PLACE (Pronunciation) | PAGE | LAT. | LONG. |
|---|---|---|---|
| Hawaii, state, U.S. | 106c | 20°00'N | 157°40'W |
| Hawai'i, i., Hi., U.S. (häw wī'ē) | 106c | 19°30'N | 155°30'W |
| Hawai'ian Islands, is., Hi., U.S. (hä-wī'ǎn) | 106c | 22°00'N | 158°00'W |
| Hawai'i Volcanoes National Park, rec., Hi., U.S. | 106c | 19°30'N | 155°25'W |
| Hawarden, Ia., U.S. (hā'wàr-dĕn) | 112 | 43°00'N | 96°28'W |
| Hawi, Hi., U.S. (hä'wē) | 126a | 20°16'N | 155°48'W |
| Hawick, Scot., U.K. (hô'ĭk) | 164 | 55°25'N | 2°55'W |
| Hawke Bay, b., N.Z. (hôk) | 221a | 39°17'S | 177°20'E |
| Hawker, Austl. (hô'kẽr) | 222 | 31°58'S | 138°12'E |
| Hawkesbury, Can. (hôks'bĕr-ĭ) | 99 | 45°35'N | 74°35'W |
| Hawkinsville, Ga., U.S. (hô'kĭnz-vĭl) | 124 | 32°15'N | 83°30'W |
| Hawks Nest Point, c., Bah. | 135 | 24°05'N | 75°30'W |
| Hawley, Mn., U.S. (hô'lĭ) | 112 | 46°52'N | 96°18'W |
| Haworth, Eng., U.K. (hā'wûrth) | 158a | 53°50'N | 1°57'W |
| Hawthorne, Ca., U.S. (hô'thôrn) | 117a | 33°55'N | 118°22'W |
| Hawthorne, Nv., U.S. | 118 | 38°33'N | 118°39'W |
| Haxtun, Co., U.S. (hăks'tŭn) | 120 | 40°39'N | 102°38'W |
| Hay, r., Austl. (hā) | 220 | 23°00'S | 136°45'E |
| Hay, r., Can. | 92 | 60°21'N | 117°14'W |
| Hayama, Japan (hä-yä'mä) | 211a | 35°16'N | 139°35'E |
| Hayashi, Japan (hä-yä'shē) | 211a | 35°13'N | 139°38'E |
| Hayden, Az., U.S. (hā'dĕn) | 119 | 33°00'N | 110°50'W |
| Hayes, r., Can. | 93 | 55°25'N | 93°55'W |
| Hayes, Mount, mtn., Ak., U.S. (hāz) | 103 | 63°32'N | 146°40'W |
| Haynesville, La., U.S. (hānz'vĭl) | 123 | 32°55'N | 93°08'W |
| Hayrabolu, Tur. | 175 | 41°14'N | 27°05'E |
| Hay River, Can. | 90 | 60°50'N | 115°53'W |
| Hays, Ks., U.S. (hāz) | 120 | 38°51'N | 99°20'W |
| Haystack Mountain, mtn., Wa., U.S. (hā-stăk') | 116a | 48°26'N | 122°07'W |
| Hayward, Ca., U.S. (hā'wẽrd) | 116b | 37°40'N | 122°06'W |
| Hayward, Wi., U.S. | 113 | 46°01'N | 91°31'W |
| Hazard, Ky., U.S. (hăz'ǎrd) | 124 | 37°13'N | 83°10'W |
| Hazelhurst, Ga., U.S. (hā'z'l-hûrst) | 125 | 31°50'N | 82°36'W |
| Hazelhurst, Ms., U.S. | 124 | 31°52'N | 90°23'W |
| Hazel Park, Mi., U.S. | 111b | 42°28'N | 83°06'W |
| Hazelton, Can. (hā'z'l-tŭn) | 90 | 55°15'N | 127°40'W |
| Hazelton Mountains, mts., Can. | 94 | 55°00'N | 128°00'W |
| Hazleton, Pa., U.S. | 109 | 41°00'N | 76°00'W |
| Headland, Al., U.S. (hĕd'lǎnd) | 124 | 31°22'N | 85°20'W |
| Healdsburg, Ca., U.S. (hēldz'bûrg) | 118 | 38°37'N | 122°52'W |
| Healdton, Ok., U.S. (hēld'tŭn) | 121 | 34°13'N | 97°28'W |
| Heanor, Eng., U.K. (hēn'ŏr) | 158a | 53°01'N | 1°22'W |
| Heard Island, i., Austl. (hûrd) | 3 | 53°10'S | 74°35'E |
| Hearne, Tx., U.S. (hûrn) | 123 | 30°53'N | 96°35'W |
| Hearst, Can. (hûrst) | 91 | 49°36'N | 83°40'W |
| Heart, r., N.D., U.S. (härt) | 112 | 46°46'N | 102°34'W |
| Heart Lake Indian Reserve, I.R., Can. | 95 | 55°02'N | 111°30'W |
| Heart's Content, Can. (härts kŏn'tĕnt) | 101 | 47°52'N | 53°22'W. |
| Heavener, Ok., U.S. (hēv'nẽr) | 121 | 34°52'N | 94°36'W |
| Hebbronville, Tx., U.S. (hē'brŭn-vĭl) | 122 | 27°18'N | 98°40'W |
| Hebei, prov., China (hŭ-bā) | 205 | 39°15'N | 115°40'E |
| Heber City, Ut., U.S. (hē'bẽr) | 119 | 40°30'N | 111°25'W |
| Heber Springs, Ar., U.S. | 121 | 35°28'N | 91°59'W |
| Hebgen Lake, res., Mt., U.S. (hĕb'gĕn) | 115 | 44°47'N | 111°38'W |
| Hebrides, is., Scot., U.K. | 156 | 57°00'N | 6°30'W |
| Hebrides, Sea of the, sea, Scot., U.K. | 164 | 57°00'N | 7°00'W |
| Hebron, Can. (hĕb'rŭn) | 91 | 58°11'N | 62°56'W |
| Hebron, In., U.S. | 111a | 41°19'N | 87°13'W |
| Hebron, Ky., U.S. | 111f | 39°04'N | 84°43'W |
| Hebron, N.D., U.S. | 112 | 46°54'N | 102°04'W |
| Hebron, Ne., U.S. | 121 | 40°11'N | 97°36'W |
| Hebron *see* Al Khalīl, W.B. | 197a | 31°31'N | 35°07'E |
| Heby, Swe. (hĭ'bü) | 166 | 59°56'N | 16°48'E |
| Hecate Strait, strt., Can. (hĕk'ǎ-tē) | 92 | 53°00'N | 131°00'W |
| Hecelchakán, Mex. (ā-sĕl-chä-kän') | 131 | 20°10'N | 90°09'W |
| Hechi, China (hŭ-chr) | 209 | 24°50'N | 108°18'E |
| Hechuan, China (hŭ-chyuän) | 204 | 30°00'N | 106°20'E |
| Hecla Island, i., Can. | 97 | 51°08'N | 96°45'W |
| Hedemora, Swe. (hĭ-dĕ-mō'rä) | 166 | 60°16'N | 15°55'E |
| Hedon, Eng., U.K. (hĕ-dŭn) | 158a | 53°44'N | 0°12'W |
| Heemstede, Neth. | 159a | 52°20'N | 4°36'E |
| Heerlen, Neth. | 165 | 50°55'N | 5°58'E |
| Hefei, China (hŭ-fā) | 205 | 31°51'N | 117°15'E |
| Heflin, Al., U.S. (hĕf'lĭn) | 124 | 33°40'N | 85°33'W |
| Heide, Ger. (hī'dĕ) | 168 | 54°13'N | 9°06'E |
| Heidelberg, Austl. (hī'dĕl-bûrg) | 217a | 37°45'S | 145°04'E |
| Heidelberg, Ger. (hīdĕl-bĕrgh) | 161 | 49°24'N | 8°43'E |
| Heidelberg, S. Afr. | 238c | 26°32'S | 28°22'E |
| Heidenheim, Ger. (hī'dĕn-hīm) | 168 | 48°41'N | 10°09'E |
| Heilbron, S. Afr. (hīl'brōn) | 238c | 27°17'S | 27°58'E |
| Heilbronn, Ger. (hīl'brōn) | 161 | 49°09'N | 9°16'E |
| Heiligenhaus, Ger. (hī'lē-gĕn-houz) | 171c | 51°19'N | 6°58'E |
| Heiligenstadt, Ger. (hī'lē-gĕn-shtät) | 168 | 51°21'N | 10°10'E |
| Heilongjiang, prov., China (hā-lôŋ-jyäŋ) | 205 | 46°36'N | 128°07'E |
| Heinola, Fin. (hå-nō'lå) | 167 | 61°13'N | 26°03'E |
| Heinsberg, Ger. (hīnz'bĕrgh) | 171c | 51°04'N | 6°07'E |
| Heist-op-den-Berg, Bel. | 159a | 51°05'N | 4°14'E |
| Hejaz *see* Al Ḩijāz, reg., Sau. Ar. | 198 | 23°45'N | 39°08'E |
| Hejian, China (hŭ-jyĕn) | 208 | 38°28'N | 116°05'E |
| Hekla, vol., Ice. | 156 | 63°53'N | 19°37'W |
| Hel, Pol. (hāl) | 169 | 54°37'N | 18°53'E |
| Helagsfjället, mtn., Swe. | 160 | 62°54'N | 12°24'E |
| Helan Shan, mts., China (hŭ-län shän) | 204 | 38°02'N | 105°20'E |
| Helena, Ar., U.S. (hē-lē'nà) | 105 | 34°33'N | 90°35'W |
| Helena, Mt., U.S. (hĕ-lē'nǎ) | 104 | 46°35'N | 112°01'W |
| Helensburgh, Austl. (hĕl'ĕnz-bŭr-ô) | 217b | 34°11'S | 150°59'E |
| Helensburgh, Scot., U.K. | 164 | 56°01'N | 4°53'W |
| Helgoland, i., Ger. (hĕl'gô-länd) | 168 | 54°13'N | 7°30'E |
| Hellier, Ky., U.S. (hĕl'yẽr) | 125 | 37°16'N | 82°27'W |

| PLACE (Pronunciation) | PAGE | LAT. | LONG. |
|---|---|---|---|
| Hellín, Spain (ĕl-yén') | 162 | 38°30'N | 1°40'W |
| Hells Canyon, p., U.S. | 114 | 45°20'N | 116°45'W |
| Helmand, r., Afg. (hĕl'mŭnd) | 198 | 31°00'N | 63°48'E |
| Hel'miaziv, Ukr. | 177 | 49°49'N | 31°54'E |
| Helmond, Neth. (hĕl'mŏnt) (ĕl'môɴ') | 165 | 51°35'N | 5°04'E |
| Helmstedt, Ger. (hĕlm'shtĕt) | 168 | 52°14'N | 11°03'E |
| Helotes, Tx., U.S. (hē'lōts) | 117d | 29°35'N | 98°41'W |
| Helper, Ut., U.S. (hĕlp'ẽr) | 119 | 39°40'N | 110°55'W |
| Helsingborg, Swe. (hĕl'sĭng-bôrgh) | 160 | 56°04'N | 12°40'E |
| Helsingfors *see* Helsinki, Fin. | 154 | 60°10'N | 24°53'E |
| Helsingør, Den. (hĕl-sĭng-ŭr') | 160 | 56°03'N | 12°33'E |
| Helsinki, Fin. (hĕl'sĕn-kē) | 154 | 60°10'N | 24°53'E |
| Hemel Hempstead, Eng., U.K. (hĕm'ĕl hĕmp'stĕd) | 158b | 51°43'N | 0°29'W |
| Hemer, Ger. | 171c | 51°22'N | 7°46'E |
| Hemet, Ca., U.S. (hĕm'ĕt) | 117a | 33°45'N | 116°57'W |
| Hemingford, Ne., U.S. (hĕm'ĭng-fẽrd) | 112 | 42°21'N | 103°30'W |
| Hemphill, Tx., U.S. (hĕmp'hĭl) | 123 | 31°20'N | 93°48'W |
| Hempstead, N.Y., U.S. (hĕmp'stĕd) | 110a | 40°42'N | 73°37'W |
| Hempstead, Tx., U.S. | 123 | 30°07'N | 96°05'W |
| Hemse, Swe. (hĕm'sĕ) | 166 | 57°15'N | 18°25'E |
| Hemsön, i., Swe. | 166 | 62°43'N | 18°22'E |
| Henan, prov., China (hŭ-nän) | 205 | 33°58'N | 112°33'E |
| Henares, r., Spain (å-nä'rås) | 172 | 40°50'N | 2°55'W |
| Henderson, Ky., U.S. (hĕn'dẽr-sŭn) | 108 | 37°50'N | 87°30'W |
| Henderson, N.C., U.S. | 125 | 36°18'N | 78°24'W |
| Henderson, Nv., U.S. | 118 | 36°09'N | 115°04'W |
| Henderson, Tn., U.S. | 124 | 35°25'N | 88°40'W |
| Henderson, Tx., U.S. | 123 | 32°09'N | 94°48'W |
| Hendersonville, N.C., U.S. (hĕn'dẽr-sŭn-vĭl) | 125 | 35°17'N | 82°28'W |
| Hendersonville, Tn., U.S. | 124 | 36°18'N | 86°37'W |
| Hendon, Eng., U.K. (hĕn'dŭn) | 158b | 51°34'N | 0°13'W |
| Hendrina, S. Afr. (hĕn-drē'nǎ) | 238c | 26°10'S | 29°44'E |
| Hengch'un, Tai. (hĕng'chŭn') | 209 | 22°00'N | 120°42'E |
| Hengelo, Neth. (hĕngĕ-lō) | 165 | 52°20'N | 6°45'E |
| Hengshan, China (hĕng'shän') | 209 | 27°20'N | 112°40'E |
| Hengshui, China (hĕng'shōō-ē') | 206 | 37°43'N | 115°42'E |
| Hengxian, China (hŭŋ shyĕn) | 209 | 22°40'N | 109°20'E |
| Hengyang, China | 205 | 26°58'N | 112°30'E |
| Heniches'k, Ukr. | 181 | 46°11'N | 34°47'E |
| Henley on Thames, Eng., U.K. (hĕn'lē ŏn tĕmz) | 158b | 51°31'N | 0°54'W |
| Henlopen, Cape, c., De., U.S. (hĕn-lō'pĕn) | 109 | 38°45'N | 75°05'W |
| Hennebont, Fr. (ĕn-bôɴ') | 170 | 47°47'N | 3°16'W |
| Hennenman, S. Afr. | 238c | 27°59'S | 27°03'E |
| Hennessey, Ok., U.S. (hĕn'ĕ-sĭ) | 121 | 36°04'N | 97°53'W |
| Hennigsdorf, Ger. (hĕ'nēngz-dōrf)) | 159b | 52°39'N | 13°12'E |
| Hennops, r., S. Afr. (hĕn'ŏps) | 233b | 25°51'S | 27°57'E |
| Hennopsrivier, S. Afr. | 233b | 25°50'S | 27°59'E |
| Henrietta, Ok., U.S. (hĕn-rĭ-ĕt'ǎ) | 121 | 35°25'N | 95°58'W |
| Henrietta, Tx., U.S. (hen-rĭ-ĕ'tǎ) | 120 | 33°47'N | 98°11'W |
| Henrietta Maria, Cape, c., Can. (hĕn-rĭ-ĕt'ǎ) | 93 | 55°10'N | 82°20'W |
| Henry Mountains, mts., Ut., U.S. (hĕn'rĭ) | 106 | 37°55'N | 110°45'W |
| Henrys Fork, r., Id., U.S. | 115 | 43°52'N | 111°55'W |
| Henteyn Nuruu, mtn., Russia | 208 | 49°40'N | 111°00'E |
| Hentiyn Nuruu, mts., Mong. | 204 | 49°25'N | 107°51'E |
| Henzada, Mya. | 199 | 17°38'N | 95°28'E |
| Heppner, Or., U.S. (hĕp'nẽr) | 114 | 45°21'N | 119°33'W |
| Hepu, China (hŭ-pōō) | 209 | 21°28'N | 109°10'E |
| Herāt, Afg. (hĕ-rät') | 198 | 34°28'N | 62°13'E |
| Hercules, Can. | 102g | 53°27'N | 113°20'W |
| Herdecke, Ger. (hĕr'dĕ-kĕ) | 171c | 51°24'N | 7°26'E |
| Heredia, C.R. (ā-rā'dhē-ä) | 133 | 10°04'N | 84°06'W |
| Hereford, Eng., U.K. (hĕrĕ'fẽrd) | 164 | 52°05'N | 2°44'W |
| Hereford, Md., U.S. | 110e | 39°35'N | 76°42'W |
| Hereford, Tx., U.S. (hĕr'ĕ-fẽrd) | 120 | 34°47'N | 102°25'W |
| Hereford and Worcester, co., Eng., U.K. | 158a | 52°24'N | 2°15'W |
| Herencia, Spain (å-rān'thē-ä) | 172 | 39°23'N | 3°22'W |
| Herentals, Bel. | 159a | 51°10'N | 4°51'E |
| Herford, Ger. (hĕr'fōrt) | 168 | 52°06'N | 8°42'E |
| Herington, Ks., U.S. (hĕr'ĭng-tŭn) | 121 | 38°41'N | 96°57'W |
| Herisau, Switz. (hā'rē-zou) | 168 | 47°23'N | 9°18'E |
| Herk-de-Stad, Bel. | 159a | 50°56'N | 5°13'E |
| Herkimer, N.Y., U.S. (hûr'kĭ-mẽr) | 109 | 43°05'N | 75°00'W |
| Hermansville, Mi., U.S. (hûr'mǎns-vĭl) | 108 | 45°40'N | 87°35'W |
| Hermantown, Mn., U.S. (hẽr'mǎn-toun) | 117h | 46°46'N | 92°12'W |
| Hermanusdorings, S. Afr. | 238c | 24°08'S | 27°46'E |
| Herminie, Pa., U.S. (hûr-mī'nē) | 111e | 40°16'N | 79°45'W |
| Hermitage Bay, b., Can. (hûr'mĭ-tĕj) | 101 | 47°35'N | 56°05'W |
| Hermit Islands, is., Pap. N. Gui. (hûr'mĭt) | 213 | 1°48'S | 144°55'E |
| Hermosa Beach, Ca., U.S. (hẽr-mō'sà) | 117a | 33°51'N | 118°24'W |
| Hermosillo, Mex. (ĕr-mô-sē'l-yō) | 128 | 29°00'N | 110°57'W |
| Herndon, Va., U.S. (hĕrn'don) | 110e | 38°58'N | 77°22'W |
| Herne, Ger. (hĕr'nĕ) | 171c | 51°32'N | 7°13'E |
| Herning, Den. (hĕr'nĭng) | 160 | 56°08'N | 8°55'E |
| Heron, l., Mn., U.S. (hĕr'ŭn) | 112 | 43°42'N | 95°23'W |
| Heron Lake, Mn., U.S. | 112 | 43°48'N | 95°20'W |
| Herrero, Punta, Mex. (pŏ'n-tä-ĕr-rĕ'rô) | 132a | 19°18'N | 87°24'W |
| Herrin, Il., U.S. (hĕr'ĭn) | 108 | 37°50'N | 89°00'W |
| Herschel, S. Afr. (hĕr-shĕl) | 233c | 30°37'S | 27°12'E |
| Herscher, Il., U.S. (hĕr'shẽr) | 111a | 41°03'N | 88°06'W |
| Herstal, Bel. (hĕr'stäl) | 165 | 50°42'N | 5°32'E |
| Hertford, Eng., U.K. | 164 | 51°48'N | 0°05'W |
| Hertford, N.C., U.S. (hûrt'fẽrd) | 125 | 36°10'N | 76°30'W |
| Hertfordshire, co., Eng., U.K. | 158b | 51°46'N | 0°05'W |
| Hertzberg, Ger. (hĕrtz'bĕrgh) | 159b | 52°54'N | 12°58'E |

| PLACE (Pronunciation) | PAGE | LAT. | LONG. |
|---|---|---|---|
| Hervás, Spain | 172 | 40°16'N | 5°51'W |
| Herzliyya, Isr. | 197a | 32°10'N | 34°49'E |
| Hessen, hist. reg., Ger. (hĕs'ĕn) | 168 | 50°42'N | 9°00'E |
| Hetch Hetchy Aqueduct, Ca., U.S. (hĕtch hĕt'chĭ ǎk'wē-dŭkt) | 118 | 37°27'N | 120°54'W |
| Hettinger, N.D., U.S. (hĕt'ĭn-jẽr) | 112 | 45°58'N | 102°36'W |
| Heuningspruit, S. Afr. | 238c | 27°28'S | 27°26'E |
| Hexian, China (hŭ shyĕn) | 209 | 24°20'N | 111°28'E |
| Hexian, China | 206 | 31°44'N | 118°20'E |
| Heyang, China (hŭ-yäŋ) | 208 | 35°18'N | 110°18'E |
| Heystekrand, S. Afr. | 238c | 25°16'S | 27°14'E |
| Heyuan, China (hŭ-yůän) | 209 | 23°48'N | 114°45'E |
| Heywood, Eng., U.K. (hā'wŏd) | 158a | 53°36'N | 2°12'W |
| Heze, China (hŭ-dzŭ) | 206 | 35°13'N | 115°28'E |
| Hialeah, Fl., U.S. (hī-à-lē'äh) | 125a | 25°49'N | 80°18'W |
| Hiawatha, Ks., U.S. (hī-ǎ-wô'thǎ) | 121 | 39°50'N | 95°33'W |
| Hiawatha, Ut., U.S. | 119 | 39°25'N | 111°05'W |
| Hibbing, Mn., U.S. (hĭb'ĭng) | 105 | 47°26'N | 92°58'W |
| Hickman, Ky., U.S. (hĭk'mǎn) | 124 | 34°33'N | 89°10'W |
| Hickory, N.C., U.S. (hĭk'ô-rĭ) | 125 | 35°43'N | 81°21'W |
| Hicksville, N.Y., U.S. | 108 | 41°15'N | 84°45'W |
| Hicksville, N.Y., U.S. (hĭks'vĭl) | 110a | 40°47'N | 73°25'W |
| Hico, Tx., U.S. (hī'kō) | 122 | 32°00'N | 98°02'W |
| Hidalgo, Mex. (ē-dhäl'gō) | 130 | 24°14'N | 99°25'W |
| Hidalgo, Mex. | 122 | 27°49'N | 99°53'W |
| Hidalgo, state, Mex. | 128 | 20°45'N | 99°30'W |
| Hidalgo del Parral, Mex. (ē-dä'l-gō-dĕl-pär-rá'l) | 128 | 26°55'N | 105°40'W |
| Hidalgo Yalalag, Mex. (ē-dhäl'gō-yä-lä-läg) | 131 | 17°12'N | 96°11'W |
| Hierro Island, i., Spain (yĕ'r-rô) | 230 | 27°37'N | 18°29'W |
| Higashimurayama, Japan | 211a | 35°46'N | 139°28'E |
| Higashiōsaka, Japan | 211b | 34°40'N | 135°44'E |
| Higgins, l., Mi., U.S. (hĭg'ĭnz) | 108 | 44°20'N | 84°45'W |
| Higginsville, Mo., U.S. (hĭg'ĭnz-vĭl) | 121 | 39°05'N | 93°44'W |
| High, i., Mi., U.S. | 108 | 45°45'N | 85°45'W |
| High Bluff, Can. | 102f | 50°01'N | 98°08'W |
| Highborne Cay, i., Bah. (hībôrn kē) | 134 | 24°45'N | 76°50'W |
| Highgrove, Ca., U.S. (hī'grōv) | 117a | 34°01'N | 117°20'W |
| High Island, Tx., U.S. | 123a | 29°34'N | 94°24'W |
| Highland, Ca., U.S. (hī'lǎnd) | 117a | 34°08'N | 117°13'W |
| Highland, Il., U.S. | 121 | 38°44'N | 89°41'W |
| Highland, In., U.S. | 111a | 41°33'N | 87°28'W |
| Highland, Mi., U.S. | 111b | 42°38'N | 83°37'W |
| Highland Park, Il., U.S. | 111a | 42°11'N | 87°47'W |
| Highland Park, Mi., U.S. | 111b | 42°24'N | 83°06'W |
| Highland Park, N.J., U.S. | 110a | 40°30'N | 74°25'W |
| Highland Park, Tx., U.S. | 117c | 32°49'N | 96°48'W |
| Highlands, N.J., U.S. (hī-lǎndz) | 110a | 40°24'N | 73°59'W |
| Highlands, Tx., U.S. | 123a | 29°49'N | 95°01'W |
| Highmore, S.D., U.S. (hī'mōr) | 112 | 44°30'N | 99°26'W |
| High Ongar, Eng., U.K. (on'gẽr) | 158b | 51°43'N | 0°15'E |
| High Peak, mtn., Phil. | 213a | 15°38'N | 120°05'E |
| High Point, N.C., U.S. | 125 | 35°55'N | 80°00'W |
| High Prairie, Can. | 90 | 55°26'N | 116°29'W |
| High Ridge, Mo., U.S. | 117e | 38°27'N | 90°32'W |
| High River, Can. | 90 | 50°35'N | 113°52'W |
| High Rock Lake, res., N.C., U.S. (hī'-rŏk) | 125 | 35°40'N | 80°15'W |
| High Springs, Fl., U.S. | 125 | 29°48'N | 82°38'W |
| High Tatra Mountains, mts., Eur. | 169 | 49°15'N | 19°40'E |
| Hightstown, N.J., U.S. (hīts-toun) | 110a | 40°16'N | 74°32'W |
| High Wycombe, Eng., U.K. (wĭ-kŭm) | 164 | 51°36'N | 0°45'W |
| Higuero, Punta, c., P.R. | 129b | 18°21'N | 67°11'W |
| Higuerote, Ven. (ē-gĕ-rô'tĕ) | 143b | 10°29'N | 66°06'W |
| Higüey, Dom. Rep. (ē-gwĕ'y) | 135 | 18°40'N | 68°45'W |
| Hiiumaa, i., Est. (hē'ŏm-ô) | 180 | 58°47'N | 22°05'E |
| Hikone, Japan (hē'kō-nĕ) | 211 | 35°15'N | 136°15'E |
| Hildburghausen, Ger. (hĭld'bŏrg hou-zĕn) | 168 | 50°26'N | 10°45'E |
| Hilden, Ger. (hĕl'dĕn) | 171c | 51°10'N | 6°56'E |
| Hildesheim, Ger. (hĭl'dĕs-hīm) | 161 | 52°08'N | 9°56'E |
| Hillaby, Mount, mtn., Barb. (hĭl'ǎ-bĭ) | 133b | 13°15'N | 59°35'W |
| Hill City, Ks., U.S. (hĭl) | 120 | 39°22'N | 99°54'W |
| Hill City, Mn., U.S. | 113 | 46°58'N | 93°38'W |
| Hillegersberg, Neth. | 159a | 51°57'N | 4°29'E |
| Hillerød, Den. (hē'lĕ-rûdh) | 166 | 55°56'N | 12°17'E |
| Hillsboro, Il., U.S. (hĭlz'bŭr-ō) | 121 | 39°09'N | 89°28'W |
| Hillsboro, Ks., U.S. | 121 | 38°22'N | 97°11'W |
| Hillsboro, N.D., U.S. | 112 | 47°23'N | 97°05'W |
| Hillsboro, N.H., U.S. | 109 | 43°05'N | 71°55'W |
| Hillsboro, Oh., U.S. | 108 | 39°10'N | 83°40'W |
| Hillsboro, Or., U.S. | 116c | 45°31'N | 122°59'W |
| Hillsboro, Tx., U.S. | 123 | 32°01'N | 97°06'W |
| Hillsboro, Wi., U.S. | 113 | 43°39'N | 90°20'W |
| Hillsburgh, Can. (hĭlz'bûrg) | 102d | 43°48'N | 80°09'W |
| Hills Creek Lake, res., Or., U.S. | 114 | 43°41'N | 122°26'W |
| Hillsdale, Mi., U.S. (hĭls-dāl) | 119 | 41°55'N | 84°35'W |
| Hilo, Hi., U.S. (hē'lō) | 106c | 19°44'N | 155°01'W |
| Hilvarenbeek, Neth. | 159a | 51°29'N | 5°10'E |
| Hilversum, Neth. (hĭl'vẽr-sŭm) | 159a | 52°13'N | 5°10'E |
| Himachal Pradesh, India | 199 | 32°00'N | 77°30'E |
| Himalayas, mts., Asia | 199 | 29°30'N | 85°02'E |
| Himeji, Japan (hē'mā-jē) | 210 | 34°50'N | 134°42'E |
| Himmelpforten, Ger. (hē'mĕl-pfōr-tĕn) | 159c | 53°37'N | 9°19'E |
| Ḩimş, Syria | 198 | 34°44'N | 36°43'E |
| Hinche, Haiti (hēn'chå) (ǎnsh) | 135 | 19°10'N | 72°05'W |
| Hinchinbrook, i., Austl. (hĭn-chĭn-brŏŏk) | 220 | 18°23'S | 146°57'W |
| Hinckley, Eng., U.K. (hĭnk'lĭ) | 158a | 52°32'N | 1°21'W |
| Hindley, Eng., U.K. (hĭnd'lĭ) | 158a | 53°32'N | 2°35'W |
| Hindu Kush, mts., Asia (hĭn'dōō kōōsh') | 199 | 35°15'N | 68°44'E |
| Hindupur, India (hĭn'dōō-pōōr) | 203 | 13°52'N | 77°34'E |


ng-sing; ŋ-baŋk; ɴ-nasalized n; nŏd; cŏmmit; ōld; ôbey; ôrder; oi-boil; fōōd; ŏ-as oo in foot; ou-out; s-soft; sh-dish; th-thin; pūre; ûnite; ûrn; stŭd; circŭs; ü-as in French tu; '-indeterminate vowel.

302 Hingham – Hualapai Mountains PRONOUNCING INDEX


| PLACE (Pronunciation) | PAGE | LAT. | LONG. |
|---|---|---|---|
| Hingham, Ma., U.S. (hĭng′ăm) | 101a | 42°14′N | 70°53′W |
| Hinkley, Oh., U.S. (hĭnk′-lĭ) | 111d | 41°14′N | 81°45′W |
| Hinojosa del Duque, Spain (ē-nô-kô′sä) | 172 | 38°30′N | 5°09′W |
| Hinsdale, Il., U.S. (hĭnz′dāl) | 111a | 41°48′N | 87°56′W |
| Hinton, Can. (hĭn′tŭn) | 95 | 53°25′N | 117°34′W |
| Hinton, W.V., U.S. (hĭn′tŭn) | 108 | 37°40′N | 80°55′W |
| Hirado, i., Japan (hē′rä-dō) | 210 | 33°19′N | 129°18′E |
| Hirakata, Japan (hē′rä-kä′tä) | 211b | 34°49′N | 135°40′E |
| Hirara, Japan | 214d | 24°48′N | 125°17′E |
| Hiratsuka, Japan (hē-rät-sōō′kȧ) | 211 | 35°20′N | 139°19′E |
| Hirosaki, Japan (hē′rô-sä′kē) | 205 | 40°31′N | 140°38′E |
| Hirose, Japan (hē′rô-sä) | 211 | 35°20′N | 133°11′E |
| Hiroshima, Japan (hē-rô-shē′mȧ) | 205 | 34°22′N | 132°25′E |
| Hirson, Fr. (ēr-sôN′) | 170 | 49°54′N | 4°00′E |
| Hisar, India | 202 | 29°15′N | 75°47′E |
| Hispaniola, i., N.A. (hĭ′spăn-ĭ-ō-lȧ) | 129 | 17°30′N | 73°15′W |
| Hitachi, Japan (hē-tä′chē) | 210 | 36°42′N | 140°47′E |
| Hitchcock, Tx., U.S. (hĭch′kŏk) | 123a | 29°21′N | 95°01′W |
| Hitoyoshi, Japan (hē′tô-yō′shē) | 211 | 32°13′N | 130°45′E |
| Hitra, i., Nor. (hĭträ) | 160 | 63°34′N | 7°37′E |
| Hittefeld, Ger. (hē′tĕ-fĕld) | 159c | 53°23′N | 9°59′E |
| Hiwasa, Japan (hē′wȧ-sä) | 211 | 33°44′N | 134°31′E |
| Hiwassee, r., Tn., U.S. (hī-wôs′sē) | 124 | 35°10′N | 84°35′W |
| Hjälmaren, l., Swe. | 160 | 59°07′N | 16°05′E |
| Hjo, Swe. (yō) | 166 | 58°19′N | 14°11′E |
| Hjørring, Den. (jûr′ĭng) | 160 | 57°27′N | 9°59′E |
| Hlobyne, Ukr. | 177 | 49°22′N | 33°17′E |
| Hlohovec, Slvk. (hlō′ho-vĕts) | 169 | 48°24′N | 17°49′E |
| Hlukhiv, Ukr. | 181 | 51°42′N | 33°52′E |
| Hlybokaye, Bela. | 180 | 55°08′N | 27°44′E |
| Hobart, Austl. (hō′bȧrt) | 219 | 43°00′S | 147°30′E |
| Hobart, In., U.S. | 111a | 41°31′N | 87°15′W |
| Hobart, Ok., U.S. | 120 | 35°02′N | 99°06′W |
| Hobart, Wa., U.S. | 116a | 47°25′N | 121°58′W |
| Hobbs, N.M., U.S. (hŏbs) | 120 | 32°41′N | 103°15′W |
| Hoboken, Bel. (hō′bō-kĕn) | 159a | 51°11′N | 4°20′E |
| Hoboken, N.J., U.S. | 110a | 40°43′N | 74°03′W |
| Hobro, Den. (hô-brô′) | 166 | 56°38′N | 9°47′E |
| Hobson, Va., U.S. (hŏb′sŭn) | 110g | 36°54′N | 76°31′W |
| Hobson's Bay, b., Austl. (hŏb′sŭnz) | 217a | 37°54′S | 144°45′E |
| Hobyo, Som. | 238a | 5°24′N | 48°28′E |
| Ho Chi Minh City, Viet. | 212 | 10°46′N | 106°34′E |
| Hockinson, Wa., U.S. (hŏk′ĭn-sŭn) | 116c | 45°44′N | 122°29′W |
| Hoctún, Mex. (ôk-tōō′n) | 132a | 20°52′N | 89°10′W |
| Hodgenville, Ky., U.S. (hŏj′ĕn-vĭl) | 108 | 37°35′N | 85°45′W |
| Hodges Hill, mtn., Can. (hŏj′ĕz) | 101 | 49°04′N | 55°53′W |
| Hódmezövásárhely, Hung. (hōd′mĕ-zû-vô′shôr-hĕl-y′) | 169 | 46°24′N | 20°21′E |
| Hodna, Chott el, l., Alg. | 162 | 35°20′N | 3°27′E |
| Hodonin, Czech Rep. (hē′dô-nén) | 169 | 48°50′N | 17°06′E |
| Hoegaarden, Bel. | 159a | 50°46′N | 4°55′E |
| Hoek van Holland, Neth. | 159a | 51°59′N | 4°05′E |
| Hoeryŏng, Kor., N. (hwĕr′yŭng) | 210 | 42°28′N | 129°39′E |
| Hof, Ger. (hōf) | 168 | 50°19′N | 11°55′E |
| Hofsjökull, ice, Ice. (hôfs′yü′kōōl) | 160 | 64°55′N | 18°40′W |
| Hog, i., Mi., U.S. | 108 | 45°50′N | 85°20′W |
| Hogansville, Ga., U.S. (hō′gănz-vĭl) | 124 | 33°10′N | 84°54′W |
| Hog Cay, i., Bah. | 135 | 23°35′N | 75°30′W |
| Hogsty Reef, rf., Bah. | 135 | 21°45′N | 73°50′W |
| Hohenbrunn, Ger. (hō′hĕn-brōōn) | 159d | 48°03′N | 11°42′E |
| Hohenlimburg, Ger. (hō′hĕn lēm′bōōrg) | 171c | 51°20′N | 7°35′E |
| Hohen Neuendorf, Ger. (hō′hĕn noi′ĕn-dōrf) | 159b | 52°40′N | 13°22′E |
| Hohe Tauern, mts., Aus. (hō′ĕ tou′ĕrn) | 168 | 47°11′N | 12°12′E |
| Hohhot, China (hŭ-hōō-tŭ) | 205 | 41°05′N | 111°50′E |
| Hohoe, Ghana | 234 | 7°09′N | 0°28′E |
| Hohokus, N.J., U.S. (hō-hō-kŭs) | 110a | 41°01′N | 74°08′W |
| Hoi An, Viet. | 209 | 15°48′N | 108°30′E |
| Hoisington, Ks., U.S. (hoi′zĭng-tŭn) | 120 | 38°30′N | 98°46′W |
| Hojo, Japan (hō′jô) | 211 | 33°58′N | 132°50′E |
| Hokitika, N.Z. (hō-kĭ-tē′kä) | 221a | 42°43′S | 170°59′E |
| Hokkaidō, i., Japan (hôk′kī-dō) | 210 | 43°30′N | 142°45′E |
| Holbaek, Den. (hôl′bĕk) | 166 | 55°42′N | 11°40′E |
| Holbox, Mex. (ôl-bŏ′x) | 132a | 21°33′N | 87°19′W |
| Holbox, Isla, i., Mex. (ē′s-lä-ôl-bŏ′x) | 132a | 21°40′N | 87°21′W |
| Holbrook, Az., U.S. (hōl′brŏŏk) | 119 | 34°55′N | 110°15′W |
| Holbrook, Ma., U.S. | 101a | 42°10′N | 71°01′W |
| Holden, Ma., U.S. (hōl′dĕn) | 101a | 42°21′N | 71°51′W |
| Holden, Mo., U.S. | 121 | 38°42′N | 94°00′W |
| Holden, W.V., U.S. | 108 | 37°45′N | 82°05′W |
| Holdenville, Ok., U.S. (hōl′dĕn-vĭl) | 121 | 35°05′N | 96°25′W |
| Holdrege, Ne., U.S. (hōl′drĕj) | 120 | 40°25′N | 99°28′W |
| Holguín, Cuba (ôl-gēn′) | 129 | 20°55′N | 76°15′W |
| Holguín, prov., Cuba | 134 | 20°40′N | 76°15′W |
| Holidaysburg, Pa., U.S. (hŏl′ĭ-dāz-bûrg) | 109 | 40°30′N | 78°30′W |
| Hollabrunn, Aus. | 168 | 48°33′N | 16°04′E |
| Holland, Mi., U.S. (hŏl′ănd) | 108 | 42°45′N | 86°10′W |
| Hollands Diep, strt., Neth. | 159a | 51°43′N | 4°25′E |
| Hollenstedt, Ger. (hō′lĕn-shtĕt) | 159c | 53°22′N | 9°43′E |
| Hollis, N.H., U.S. (hŏl′ĭs) | 101a | 42°30′N | 71°29′W |
| Hollis, Ok., U.S. | 120 | 34°39′N | 99°56′W |
| Hollister, Ca., U.S. (hŏl′ĭs-tēr) | 118 | 36°50′N | 121°25′W |
| Holliston, Ma., U.S. (hŏl′ĭs-tŭn) | 101a | 42°12′N | 71°25′W |
| Holly, Mi., U.S. (hŏl′ĭ) | 108 | 42°45′N | 83°30′W |
| Holly, Wa., U.S. | 116a | 47°34′N | 122°58′W |
| Holly Springs, Ms., U.S. (hŏl′ĭ sprĭngz) | 124 | 34°45′N | 89°28′W |
| Hollywood, Ca., U.S. (hŏl′ē-wŏŏd) | 117a | 34°06′N | 118°20′W |
| Hollywood, Fl., U.S. | 125a | 26°00′N | 80°11′W |
| Holmes Reefs, rf., Austl. (hōmz) | 221 | 16°33′S | 148°43′E |
| Holmestrand, Nor. (hôl′mĕ-strän) | 166 | 59°29′N | 10°17′E |
| Holmsbu, Nor. (hôlms′bōō) | 166 | 59°36′N | 10°26′E |
| Holmsjön, l., Swe. | 166 | 62°23′N | 15°43′E |
| Holstebro, Den. (hôl′stĕ-brô) | 160 | 56°22′N | 8°39′E |
| Holstein, hist. reg., Ger. | 168 | 54°10′N | 9°40′E |
| Holston, r., Tn., U.S. (hōl′stŭn) | 124 | 36°02′N | 83°42′W |
| Holt, Eng., U.K. (hōlt) | 158a | 53°05′N | 2°53′W |
| Holton, Ks., U.S. (hōl′tŭn) | 121 | 39°27′N | 95°43′W |
| Holy Cross, Ak., U.S. (hō′lĭ krôs) | 103 | 62°10′N | 159°40′W |
| Holyhead, Wales, U.K. (hŏl′ē-hĕd) | 164 | 53°18′N | 4°45′W |
| Holy Island, i., Eng., U.K. | 164 | 55°43′N | 1°48′W |
| Holy Island, i., Wales, U.K. (hō′lĭ) | 164 | 53°15′N | 4°45′W |
| Holyoke, Co., U.S. (hōl′yōk) | 120 | 40°36′N | 102°18′W |
| Holyoke, Ma., U.S. | 109 | 42°10′N | 72°40′W |
| Homano, Japan (hō-mä′nō) | 211a | 35°33′N | 140°08′E |
| Homberg, Ger. (hōm′bĕrgh) | 171c | 51°27′N | 6°42′E |
| Hombori, Mali | 234 | 15°17′N | 1°42′W |
| Home Gardens, Ca., U.S. (hōm gär′d′nz) | 117a | 33°53′N | 117°32′W |
| Homeland, Ca., U.S. (hōm′lănd) | 117a | 33°44′N | 117°07′W |
| Homer, Ak., U.S. (hō′mēr) | 103 | 59°42′N | 151°30′W |
| Homer, La., U.S. | 123 | 32°46′N | 93°05′W |
| Homer Youngs Peak, mtn., Mt., U.S. | 115 | 45°19′N | 113°41′W |
| Homestead, Fl., U.S. (hōm′stĕd) | 125a | 25°27′N | 80°28′W |
| Homestead, Mi., U.S. | 117k | 46°20′N | 84°07′W |
| Homestead, Pa., U.S. | 111e | 40°29′N | 79°55′W |
| Homestead National Monument of America, rec., Ne., U.S. | 121 | 40°16′N | 96°51′W |
| Homewood, Al., U.S. (hōm′wŏŏd) | 110h | 33°28′N | 86°48′W |
| Homewood, Il., U.S. | 111a | 41°34′N | 87°40′W |
| Hominy, Ok., U.S. (hŏm′ĭ-nĭ) | 121 | 36°25′N | 96°24′W |
| Homochitto, r., Ms., U.S. (hō-mō-chĭt′ō) | 124 | 31°23′N | 91°15′W |
| Homyel′, Bela. | 180 | 52°20′N | 31°03′E |
| Homyel′, prov., Bela. | 176 | 52°18′N | 29°00′E |
| Honda, Col. (hōn′dȧ) | 142 | 5°13′N | 74°45′W |
| Honda, Bahía, b., Cuba (bä-ē′ä-ô′n-dä) | 134 | 23°10′N | 83°20′W |
| Hondo, Tx., U.S. | 122 | 29°20′N | 99°08′W |
| Hondo, r., N.M., U.S. | 120 | 33°22′N | 105°06′W |
| Hondo, Río, r., N.A. (hon-dō′) | 132a | 18°16′N | 88°32′W |
| Honduras, nation, N.A. (hŏn-dōō′rȧs) | 128 | 14°30′N | 88°00′W |
| Honduras, Gulf of, b., N.A. | 128 | 16°30′N | 87°30′W |
| Honea Path, S.C., U.S. (hŭn′ĭ păth) | 125 | 34°25′N | 82°16′W |
| Hönefoss, Nor. (hē′nē-fôs) | 160 | 60°10′N | 10°15′E |
| Honesdale, Pa., U.S. (hōnz′dāl) | 109 | 41°30′N | 75°15′W |
| Honey Grove, Tx., U.S. (hŭn′ĭ grōv) | 121 | 33°35′N | 95°54′W |
| Honey Lake, l., Ca., U.S. (hŭn′ĭ) | 118 | 40°11′N | 120°34′W |
| Honfleur, Can. (ôN-flûr′) | 102b | 46°39′N | 70°53′W |
| Honfleur, Fr. (ôN-flûr′) | 170 | 49°26′N | 0°13′E |
| Hon Gay, Viet. | 209 | 20°58′N | 107°10′E |
| Hong Kong (Xianggang), China | 205 | 21°45′N | 115°00′E |
| Hongshui, r., China (hôŋ-shwā) | 204 | 24°30′N | 105°00′E |
| Honguedo, Détroit d′, strt., Can. | 100 | 49°08′N | 63°45′W |
| Hongze Hu, l., China | 205 | 33°17′N | 118°37′E |
| Honiara, Sol. Is. | 219 | 9°26′S | 159°57′E |
| Honiton, Eng., U.K. (hŏn′ĭ-tŏn) | 164 | 50°49′N | 3°10′W |
| Honolulu, Hi., U.S. (hŏn-ô-lōō′lōō) | 106c | 21°18′N | 157°50′W |
| Honomu, Hi., U.S. (hŏn′ō-mōō) | 126a | 19°50′N | 155°04′W |
| Honshū, i., Japan | 205 | 36°00′N | 138°00′E |
| Hood, Mount, mtn., Or., U.S. | 106 | 45°20′N | 121°43′W |
| Hood Canal, b., Wa., U.S. (hŏŏd) | 116a | 47°45′N | 122°45′W |
| Hood River, Or., U.S. | 104 | 45°42′N | 121°30′W |
| Hoodsport, Wa., U.S. (hŏŏdz′pōrt) | 116a | 47°25′N | 123°09′W |
| Hoogly, r., India (hōōg′lĭ) | 199 | 21°35′N | 87°50′E |
| Hoogstraten, Bel. | 159a | 51°24′N | 4°46′E |
| Hooker, Ok., U.S. (hŏŏk′ēr) | 120 | 36°49′N | 101°13′W |
| Hool, Mex. (ōō′l) | 132a | 19°32′N | 90°22′W |
| Hoonah, Ak., U.S. (hōō′nä) | 103 | 58°05′N | 135°25′W |
| Hoopa Valley Indian Reservation, I.R., Ca., U.S. | 114 | 41°18′N | 123°35′W |
| Hooper, Ne., U.S. (hŏŏp′ēr) | 121 | 41°37′N | 96°31′W |
| Hooper, Ut., U.S. | 117b | 41°10′N | 112°08′W |
| Hooper Bay, Ak., U.S. | 103 | 61°32′N | 166°02′W |
| Hoopeston, Il., U.S. (hōōps′tŭn) | 108 | 40°35′N | 87°40′W |
| Hoosick Falls, N.Y., U.S. (hōō′sĭk) | 109 | 42°55′N | 73°15′W |
| Hoover Dam, Nv., U.S. (hōō′vēr) | 118 | 36°00′N | 115°06′W |
| Hoover Dam, dam, U.S. | 106 | 36°00′N | 114°27′W |
| Hopatcong, Lake, l., N.J., U.S. (hō-păt′kong) | 110a | 40°57′N | 74°38′W |
| Hope, Ak., U.S. (hōp) | 103 | 60°54′N | 149°48′W |
| Hope, Ar., U.S. | 121 | 33°41′N | 93°35′W |
| Hope, N.D., U.S. | 112 | 47°17′N | 97°45′W |
| Hope, Ben, mtn., Scot., U.K. (bĕn hōp) | 164 | 58°25′N | 4°25′W |
| Hopedale, Can. (hōp′dāl) | 91 | 55°26′N | 60°11′W |
| Hopedale, Ma., U.S. (hōp′dāl) | 101a | 42°08′N | 71°33′W |
| Hopelchén, Mex. (o-pĕl-chĕ′n) | 132a | 19°47′N | 89°51′W |
| Hopes Advance, Cap, c., Can. (hōps ăd-vans′) | 93 | 61°05′N | 69°35′W |
| Hopetoun, Austl. (hōp′toun) | 218 | 33°50′S | 120°15′E |
| Hopetown, S. Afr. (hōp′toun) | 232 | 29°35′S | 24°10′E |
| Hopewell, Va., U.S. (hōp′wĕl) | 125 | 37°14′N | 77°15′W |
| Hopewell Culture National Historical Park, rec., Oh., U.S. | 108 | 39°25′N | 83°00′W |
| Hopi Indian Reservation, I.R., Az., U.S. (hō′pē) | 119 | 36°20′N | 110°30′W |
| Hopkins, Mn., U.S. (hŏp′kĭns) | 117g | 44°55′N | 93°24′W |
| Hopkinsville, Ky., U.S. (hŏp′kĭns-vĭl) | 105 | 36°50′N | 87°28′W |
| Hopkinton, Ma., U.S. (hŏp′kĭn-tŭn) | 101a | 42°14′N | 71°31′W |
| Hoquiam, Wa., U.S. (hō′kwĭ-ăm) | 104 | 47°00′N | 123°53′W |
| Horconcitos, Pan. (ŏr-kôn-sē′-tôs) | 133 | 8°18′N | 82°11′W |
| Horgen, Switz. (hôr′gĕn) | 168 | 47°16′N | 8°35′E |
| Horicon, Wi., U.S. (hŏr′ĭ-kŏn) | 113 | 43°26′N | 88°40′W |
| Horlivka, Ukr. | 181 | 48°17′N | 38°03′E |
| Hormuz, Strait of, strt., Asia (hôr′mŭz′) | 198 | 26°30′N | 56°30′E |
| Horn, i., Austl. (hôrn) | 221 | 10°30′S | 143°30′E |
| Horn, Cape *see* Hornos, Cabo de, c., Chile | 144 | 56°00′S | 67°00′W |
| Hornavan, l., Swe. | 160 | 65°54′N | 16°17′E |
| Horneburg, Ger. (hôr′nĕ-bōrgh) | 159c | 53°30′N | 9°35′E |
| Hornell, N.Y., U.S. (hôr-nĕl′) | 109 | 42°20′N | 77°40′W |
| Hornos, Cabo de, c., Chile | 144 | 56°00′S | 67°00′W |
| Horn Plateau, plat., Can. | 92 | 62°12′N | 120°29′W |
| Hornsby, Austl. (hôrnz′bĭ) | 217b | 33°43′S | 151°06′E |
| Horodenka, Ukr. | 169 | 48°40′N | 25°30′E |
| Horodnia, Ukr. | 177 | 51°54′N | 31°31′E |
| Horodok, Ukr. | 169 | 49°47′N | 23°39′E |
| Horqueta, Para. (ŏr-kĕ′tä) | 144 | 23°20′S | 57°00′W |
| Horse Creek, r., Co., U.S. (hôrs) | 120 | 38°49′N | 103°48′W |
| Horse Creek, r., Wy., U.S. | 112 | 41°33′N | 104°39′W |
| Horse Islands, is., Can. | 101 | 50°11′N | 55°45′W |
| Horsens, Den. (hôrs′ĕns) | 166 | 55°50′N | 9°49′E |
| Horseshoe Bay, Can. (hôrs-shōō) | 116d | 49°23′N | 123°16′W |
| Horsforth, Eng., U.K. (hôrs′fûrth) | 158a | 53°50′N | 1°38′W |
| Horsham, Austl. (hôr′shăm) (hôrs′ăm) | 219 | 36°42′S | 142°17′E |
| Horst, Ger. (hôrst) | 159c | 53°49′N | 9°37′E |
| Horten, Nor. (hŏr′tĕn) | 166 | 59°26′N | 10°27′E |
| Horton, Ks., U.S. (hôr′tŭn) | 121 | 39°38′N | 95°32′W |
| Horton, r., Ak., U.S. (hôr′tŭn) | 103 | 68°38′N | 122°00′W |
| Horwich, Eng., U.K. (hŏr′ĭch) | 158a | 53°36′N | 2°33′W |
| Horyn′, r., Eur. (gō′rĕn′) | 169 | 50°55′N | 26°07′E |
| Hososhima, Japan (hō′sō-shē′mä) | 210 | 32°25′N | 131°40′E |
| Hoste, i., Chile (ŏs′tā) | 144 | 55°20′S | 70°45′W |
| Hostotipaquillo, Mex. (ôs-tō′tĭ-pä-kēl′yō) | 130 | 21°09′N | 104°05′W |
| Hota, Japan (hō′tä) | 211a | 35°08′N | 139°50′E |
| Hotan, China (hwō-tän) | 204 | 37°11′N | 79°50′E |
| Hotan, r., China | 204 | 39°09′N | 81°08′E |
| Hoto Mayor, Dom. Rep. (ô-tô-mä-yô′r) | 135 | 18°45′N | 69°10′W |
| Hot Springs, Ak., U.S. (hŏt sprĭngs) | 103 | 65°00′N | 150°20′W |
| Hot Springs, Ar., U.S. | 105 | 34°29′N | 93°02′W |
| Hot Springs, S.D., U.S. | 112 | 43°28′N | 103°32′W |
| Hot Springs, Va., U.S. | 109 | 38°00′N | 79°55′W |
| Hot Springs National Park, rec., Ar., U.S. | 107 | 34°30′N | 93°00′W |
| Hotte, Massif de la, mts., Haiti | 135 | 18°25′N | 74°00′W |
| Hotville, Ca., U.S. (hŏt′vĭl) | 118 | 32°50′N | 115°24′W |
| Houdan, Fr. (ōō-däN′) | 171b | 48°47′N | 1°36′E |
| Houghton, Mi., U.S. (hō′tŭn) | 113 | 47°06′N | 88°36′W |
| Houghton, l., Mi., U.S. | 108 | 44°20′N | 84°45′W |
| Houilles, Fr. (ōō-yĕs′) | 171b | 48°55′N | 2°11′E |
| Houjie, China (hwō-jyĕ) | 207a | 22°58′N | 113°39′E |
| Houlton, Me., U.S. (hōl′tŭn) | 100 | 46°07′N | 67°50′W |
| Houma, La., U.S. (hōō′mȧ) | 123 | 29°36′N | 90°43′W |
| Housatonic, r., U.S. (hōō-sȧ-tŏn′ĭk) | 109 | 41°50′N | 73°25′W |
| House Springs, Mo., U.S. (hous sprĭngs) | 117e | 38°24′N | 90°34′W |
| Houston, Ms., U.S. (hūs′tŭn) | 124 | 33°53′N | 89°00′W |
| Houston, Tx., U.S. | 105 | 29°46′N | 95°21′W |
| Houston Ship Channel, strt., Tx., U.S. | 123a | 29°38′N | 94°57′W |
| Houtbaai, S. Afr. | 232a | 34°03′S | 18°22′E |
| Houtman Rocks, is., Austl. (hout′män) | 220 | 28°15′S | 112°45′E |
| Houzhen, China (hwō-jŭn) | 206 | 36°59′N | 118°59′E |
| Hovd, Mong. | 204 | 48°08′N | 91°40′E |
| Hovd Gol, r., Mong. | 204 | 49°06′N | 91°16′E |
| Hove, Eng., U.K. (hōv) | 164 | 50°50′N | 0°09′W |
| Hövsgöl Nuur, l., Mong. | 204 | 51°11′N | 99°11′E |
| Howard, Ks., U.S. (hou′ȧrd) | 121 | 37°27′N | 96°10′W |
| Howard, S.D., U.S. | 112 | 44°01′N | 97°31′W |
| Howden, Eng., U.K. (hou′dĕn) | 158a | 53°44′N | 0°52′W |
| Howe, Cape, c., Austl. (hou) | 221 | 37°30′S | 150°40′E |
| Howell, Mi., U.S. (hou′ĕl) | 108 | 42°40′N | 84°00′W |
| Howe Sound, strt., Can. | 94 | 49°22′N | 123°18′W |
| Howick, Can. (hou′ĭk) | 102a | 45°11′N | 73°51′W |
| Howick, S. Afr. | 233c | 29°29′S | 30°16′E |
| Howland, i., Oc. (hou′lănd) | 2 | 1°00′N | 176°00′W |
| Howrah, India (hou′rä) | 199 | 22°33′N | 88°20′E |
| Howse Peak, mtn., Can. | 95 | 51°30′N | 116°40′W |
| Howson Peak, mtn., Can. | 94 | 54°25′N | 127°45′W |
| Hoxie, Ar., U.S. (kŏh′sĭ) | 121 | 36°03′N | 91°00′W |
| Hoy, i., Scot., U.K. (hoi) | 164a | 58°53′N | 3°10′W |
| Hōya, Japan | 211a | 35°45′N | 139°35′E |
| Hoylake, Eng., U.K. (hoi-lāk′) | 158a | 53°23′N | 3°11′W |
| Hoyo, Sierra del, mts., Spain (sē-ĕ′r-rä-dĕl-ô′yō) | 173a | 40°39′N | 3°56′W |
| Hradec Králové, Czech Rep. | 161 | 50°12′N | 15°50′E |
| Hradyz′k, Ukr. | 177 | 49°12′N | 33°06′E |
| Hranice, Czech Rep. (hrän′yĕ-tsĕ) | 169 | 49°33′N | 17°45′E |
| Hröby, Swe. (hûr′bü) | 166 | 55°50′N | 13°41′E |
| Hrodna, Bela. | 180 | 53°40′N | 23°49′E |
| Hron, r., Slvk. | 169 | 48°22′N | 18°42′E |
| Hrubieszów, Pol. (hrōō-byā′shōōf) | 169 | 50°48′N | 23°54′E |
| Hsawnhsup, Mya. | 204 | 24°29′N | 94°45′E |
| Hsinchu, Tai. (hsĭn′chōō′) | 209 | 24°48′N | 121°00′E |
| Huadian, China (hwä-dĭĕn) | 208 | 42°38′N | 126°45′E |
| Huai, r., China (hwī) | 205 | 32°07′N | 114°38′E |
| Huai′an, China (hwī-än) | 208 | 33°31′N | 119°11′E |
| Huailai, China | 208 | 40°20′N | 115°45′E |
| Huailin, China (hwī-lĭn) | 206 | 31°27′N | 117°36′E |
| Huainan, China | 206 | 32°38′N | 117°02′E |
| Huaiyang, China (hōōäī′yang) | 208 | 33°45′N | 114°54′E |
| Huaiyuan, China (hwī-yüän) | 208 | 32°53′N | 117°13′E |
| Huajicori, Mex. (wä-jē-kō′rē) | 130 | 22°41′N | 105°24′W |
| Huajuapan de León, Mex. (wäj-wä′pän dā lā-ón′) | 131 | 17°46′N | 97°45′W |
| Hualapai Indian Reservation, I.R., Az., U.S. (wälăpī) | 119 | 35°41′N | 113°38′W |
| Hualapai Mountains, mts., Az., U.S. | 119 | 34°53′N | 113°54′W |


ăt; finăl; rāte; senāte; ärm; åsk; sofȧ; fâre; ch-choose; dh-as th in other; bē; ēvent; bĕt; recĕnt; cratẽr; g-gō; gh-guttural g; bĭt; ĭ-short neutral; rīde; K-guttural k as ch in German ich;

| PLACE (Pronunciation) | PAGE | LAT. | LONG. |
|---|---|---|---|
| Hualien, Tai. (hwä´lyĕn´) | 209 | 23°58′N | 121°58′E |
| Huallaga, r., Peru (wäl-yä´gä) | 142 | 8°12′S | 76°34′W |
| Huamachuco, Peru (wä-mä-chōō´kō) | 142 | 7°52′S | 78°11′W |
| Huamantla, Mex. (wä-män´tlä) | 131 | 19°18′N | 97°54′W |
| Huambo, Ang. | 232 | 12°44′S | 15°47′E |
| Huamuxtitlán, Mex. (wä-mōōs-tē-tlän´) | 130 | 17°49′N | 98°38′W |
| Huancavelica, Peru (wän´kä-vä-lē´kä) | 142 | 12°47′S | 75°02′W |
| Huancayo, Peru (wän-kä´yō) | 142 | 12°09′S | 75°04′W |
| Huanchaca, Bol. (wän-chä´kä) | 142 | 20°09′S | 66°40′W |
| Huang (Yellow), r., China | 205 | 35°06′N | 113°39′E |
| Huang, Old Beds of the, mth., China | 204 | 40°28′N | 106°34′E |
| Huang, Old Course of the, r., China | 206 | 34°28′N | 116°59′E |
| Huangchuan, China (hŭän-chüän) | 208 | 32°07′N | 115°01′E |
| Huanghua, China (hŭän-hwä) | 206 | 38°28′N | 117°18′E |
| Huanghuadian, China (hŭän-hwä-dīĕn) | 206 | 39°22′N | 116°53′E |
| Huangli, China (hōōäng´lē) | 206 | 31°39′N | 119°42′E |
| Huangpu, China (hŭän-pōō) | 207a | 22°44′N | 113°20′E |
| Huangpu, r., China | 207b | 30°56′N | 121°16′E |
| Huangqiao, China (hŭän-chyou) | 206 | 32°15′N | 120°13′E |
| Huangxian, China (hŭän shyĕn) | 206 | 37°39′N | 120°32′E |
| Huangyuan, China (hŭän-yŭän) | 204 | 37°00′N | 101°01′E |
| Huanren, China (hŭän-rŭn) | 208 | 41°10′N | 125°30′E |
| Huánuco, Peru (wä-nōō´kō) | 142 | 9°50′S | 76°17′W |
| Huánuni, Bol. (wä-nōō´nē) | 142 | 18°11′S | 66°43′W |
| Huaquechula, Mex. (wä-kĕ-chōō´lä) | 130 | 18°44′N | 98°37′W |
| Huaral, Peru (wä-rä´l) | 142 | 11°28′S | 77°11′W |
| Huarás, Peru (öä´rä´s) | 142 | 9°32′S | 77°29′W |
| Huascarán, Nevados, mts., Peru (wäs-kä-rän´) | 142 | 9°05′S | 77°50′W |
| Huasco, Chile (wäs´kō) | 144 | 28°32′S | 71°16′W |
| Huatla de Jiménez, Mex. (wä´tlä-dĕ-κē-mĕ´nĕz) | 131 | 18°08′N | 96°49′W |
| Huatlatlauch, Mex. (wä´tlä-tlä-ōō´ch) | 130 | 18°40′N | 98°04′W |
| Huatusco, Mex. (wä-tōōs´kō) | 131 | 19°09′N | 96°57′W |
| Huauchinango, Mex. (wä-ōō-chē-nän´gō) | 130 | 20°09′N | 98°03′W |
| Huaunta, Nic. (wä-ō´n-tä) | 133 | 13°30′N | 83°32′W |
| Huaunta, Laguna, l., Nic. (lä-gô´nä-wä-ó´n-tä) | 133 | 13°35′N | 83°46′W |
| Huautla, Mex. (wä-ōō´tlä) | 130 | 21°04′N | 98°13′W |
| Huaxian, China (hwä shyĕn) | 208 | 35°34′N | 114°32′E |
| Huaynamota, Río de, r., Mex. (rĕ´ō-dĕ-wäy-nä-mō´tä) | 130 | 22°10′N | 104°36′W |
| Huazolotitlán, Mex. (wäzô-lô-tē-tlän´) | 131 | 16°18′N | 97°55′W |
| Hubbard, N.H., U.S. (hŭb´ĕrd) | 101a | 42°53′N | 71°12′W |
| Hubbard, Tx., U.S. | 123 | 31°53′N | 96°46′W |
| Hubbard, l., Mi., U.S. | 108 | 44°45′N | 83°30′W |
| Hubbard Creek Reservoir, res., Tx., U.S. | 122 | 32°50′N | 98°55′W |
| Hubei, prov., China (hōō-bā) | 205 | 31°20′N | 111°58′E |
| Hubli, India (hó´blĕ) | 199 | 15°25′N | 75°09′E |
| Hückeswagen, Ger. (hü´kĕs-vä´gĕn) | 171c | 51°09′N | 7°20′E |
| Hucknall, Eng., U.K. (hŭk´nál) | 158a | 53°02′N | 1°12′W |
| Huddersfield, Eng., U.K. (hŭd´ērz-fēld) | 164 | 53°39′N | 1°47′W |
| Hudiksvall, Swe. (hōō´dĭks-väl) | 160 | 61°44′N | 17°05′E |
| Hudson, Can. (hŭd´sŭn) | 102a | 45°26′N | 74°08′W |
| Hudson, Ma., U.S. | 101a | 42°24′N | 71°34′W |
| Hudson, Mi., U.S. | 108 | 41°50′N | 84°15′W |
| Hudson, N.Y., U.S. | 109 | 42°15′N | 73°45′W |
| Hudson, Oh., U.S. | 111d | 41°15′N | 81°27′W |
| Hudson, Wi., U.S. | 117g | 44°59′N | 92°45′W |
| Hudson, r., U.S. | 107 | 42°30′N | 73°55′W |
| Hudson Bay, Can. | 97 | 52°52′N | 102°25′W |
| Hudson Bay, b., Can. | 93 | 60°15′N | 85°30′W |
| Hudson Falls, N.Y., U.S. | 109 | 43°20′N | 73°30′W |
| Hudson Heights, Can. | 102a | 45°28′N | 74°09′W |
| Hudson Strait, strt., Can. | 93 | 63°25′N | 74°05′W |
| Hue, Viet. (ü-ā´) | 212 | 16°28′N | 107°42′E |
| Huebra, r., Spain (wĕ´brä) | 172 | 40°44′N | 6°17′W |
| Huehuetenango, Guat. (wä-wä-tå-näŋ´gō) | 132 | 15°19′N | 91°26′W |
| Huejotzingo, Mex. (wä-hô-tzĭŋ´gō) | 130 | 19°09′N | 98°24′W |
| Huejúcar, Mex. (wä-hōō´kär) | 130 | 22°26′N | 103°12′W |
| Huejuquilla el Alto, Mex. (wä-hōō-kēl´yä ĕl äl´tō) | 130 | 22°42′N | 103°54′W |
| Huejutla, Mex. (wä-hōō´tlä) | 130 | 21°08′N | 98°26′W |
| Huelma, Spain (wĕl´mä) | 172 | 37°39′N | 3°36′W |
| Huelva, Spain (wĕl´vä) | 162 | 37°16′N | 6°58′W |
| Huércal-Overa, Spain (wĕr-käl´ ō-vä´rä) | 172 | 37°12′N | 1°58′W |
| Huerfano, r., Co., U.S. (wâr´fá-nō) | 120 | 37°41′N | 105°13′W |
| Huesca, Spain (wĕs-kä) | 162 | 42°07′N | 0°25′W |
| Huéscar, Spain (wäs´kär) | 172 | 37°50′N | 2°34′W |
| Huetamo de Núñez, Mex. | 130 | 18°34′N | 100°53′W |
| Huete, Spain (wä´tá) | 172 | 40°09′N | 2°42′W |
| Hueycatenango, Mex. (wĕy-kä-tĕ-nä´n-gô) | 130 | 17°31′N | 99°10′W |
| Hueytlalpan, Mex. (wä´ĭ-tläl´pän) | 131 | 20°03′N | 97°41′W |
| Hueytown, Al., U.S. | 110h | 33°28′N | 86°59′W |
| Huffman, Al., U.S. (hŭf´mán) | 110h | 33°36′N | 86°42′W |
| Hugh Butler, l., Ne., U.S. | 120 | 40°21′N | 100°40′W |
| Hughenden, Austl. | 219 | 20°58′S | 144°13′E |
| Hughes, Austl. (hūz) | 218 | 30°45′S | 129°30′E |
| Hughesville, Md., U.S. | 110e | 38°32′N | 76°48′W |
| Hugo, Mn., U.S. (hū´gō) | 117g | 45°10′N | 93°00′W |
| Hugo, Ok., U.S. | 121 | 34°01′N | 95°32′W |
| Hugoton, Ks., U.S. (hū´gō-tŭn) | 120 | 37°10′N | 101°28′W |
| Hugou, China (hōō-gō) | 206 | 33°22′N | 117°07′E |
| Huichapan, Mex. (wē-chä-pän´) | 130 | 20°22′N | 99°39′W |
| Huila, dept., Col. | 142a | 3°10′N | 75°20′W |
| Huila, Nevado de, mtn., Col. (nĕ-vä-dô-de-wē´lä) | 142a | 2°59′N | 76°01′W |

| PLACE (Pronunciation) | PAGE | LAT. | LONG. |
|---|---|---|---|
| Huilai, China | 209 | 23°02′N | 116°18′E |
| Huili, China | 204 | 26°48′N | 102°20′E |
| Huimanguillo, Mex. (wē-män-gēl´yō) | 131 | 17°50′N | 93°16′W |
| Huimin, China (hōōĭ mĭn) | 205 | 37°29′N | 117°32′E |
| Huitzilac, Mex. (ȯē´t-zē-lä´k) | 131a | 19°01′N | 99°16′W |
| Huitzitzilingo, Mex. (wē-tzē-tzē-lē´n-go) | 130 | 21°11′N | 98°42′W |
| Huitzuco, Mex. (wē-tzōō´kō) | 130 | 18°16′N | 99°20′W |
| Huixquilucan, Mex. (ȯē´x-kē-lōō-kä´n) | 131a | 19°21′N | 99°22′W |
| Huiyang, China | 209 | 23°05′N | 114°25′E |
| Hukou, China (hōō-kō) | 205 | 29°58′N | 116°20′E |
| Hulan, China (hōō´län´) | 205 | 45°58′N | 126°32′E |
| Hulan, r., China | 208 | 47°20′N | 126°32′E |
| Huliaipole, Ukr. | 177 | 47°39′N | 36°12′E |
| Hulin, China (hōō´lĭn´) | 210 | 45°45′N | 133°25′E |
| Hull, Can. (hŭl) | 91 | 45°26′N | 75°43′W |
| Hull, Ma., U.S. | 101a | 42°18′N | 70°54′W |
| Hull, r., Eng., U.K. | 158a | 53°47′N | 0°20′W |
| Hulst, Neth. (hȯlst) | 159a | 51°17′N | 4°01′E |
| Huludao, China (hōō-lōō-dou) | 205 | 40°40′N | 120°55′E |
| Hulun Nur, l., China (hōō-lòn nòr) | 205 | 48°50′N | 116°45′E |
| Humacao, P.R. (ōō-mä-kä´ō) | 129b | 18°09′N | 65°49′W |
| Humansdorp, S. Afr. (hōō´mäns-dȯrp) | 232 | 33°57′S | 24°45′E |
| Humbe, Ang. (hòm´bä) | 232 | 16°50′S | 14°55′E |
| Humber, r., Can. | 102d | 43°53′N | 79°40′W |
| Humber, r., Eng., U.K. (hŭm´bĕr) | 160 | 53°30′N | 0°30′E |
| Humbermouth, Can. (hŭm´bĕr-mŭth) | 101 | 48°58′N | 57°55′W |
| Humberside, hist. reg., Eng., U.K. | 158a | 53°47′N | 0°36′W |
| Humble, Tx., U.S. (hŭm´b´l) | 123 | 29°58′N | 95°15′W |
| Humboldt, Ia., U.S. | 113 | 42°43′N | 94°11′W |
| Humboldt, Ks., U.S. | 121 | 37°48′N | 95°26′W |
| Humboldt, Ne., U.S. | 121 | 40°10′N | 95°57′W |
| Humboldt, r., Nv., U.S. | 106 | 40°30′N | 116°50′W |
| Humboldt, East Fork, r., Nv., U.S. | 114 | 40°59′N | 115°21′W |
| Humboldt, North Fork, r., Nv., U.S. | 114 | 41°25′N | 115°45′W |
| Humboldt Bay, b., Ca., U.S. | 114 | 40°48′N | 124°25′W |
| Humboldt Range, mts., Nv., U.S. | 118 | 40°12′N | 118°16′W |
| Humbolt, Tn., U.S. | 124 | 35°47′N | 88°55′W |
| Humbolt Salt Marsh, Nv., U.S. | 118 | 39°49′N | 117°41′W |
| Humbolt Sink, Nv., U.S. | 118 | 39°58′N | 118°54′W |
| Humen, China (hōō-mŭn) | 207a | 22°49′N | 113°39′E |
| Humphreys Peak, mtn., Az., U.S. (hŭm´frĭs) | 106 | 35°20′N | 111°40′W |
| Humpolec, Czech Rep. (hŏm´pō-lěts) | 168 | 49°33′N | 15°21′E |
| Humuya, r., Hond. (ōō-mōō´yä) | 132 | 14°38′N | 87°36′W |
| Hunaflói, b., Ice. (hōō´nä-flō´ĭ) | 160 | 65°41′N | 20°40′W |
| Hunan, prov., China (hōō´nän´) | 205 | 28°08′N | 111°25′E |
| Hunchun, China (hòn-chŭn) | 205 | 42°53′N | 130°34′E |
| Hunedoara, Rom. (hōō´nĕd-wä´rä) | 175 | 45°45′N | 22°54′E |
| Hungary, nation, Eur. (hŭn´gà-rĭ) | 154 | 46°44′N | 17°55′E |
| Hungerford, Austl. (hŭn´gĕr-fĕrd) | 219 | 28°50′S | 144°32′E |
| Hungry Horse Reservoir, res., Mt., U.S. (hŭn´grà-rĭ hȯrs) | 115 | 48°11′N | 113°30′W |
| Hunsrück, mts., Ger. (hōōns´rŭk) | 154 | 49°43′N | 7°12′E |
| Hunte, r., Ger. (hòn´tĕ) | 168 | 52°45′N | 8°26′E |
| Hunter Islands, is., Austl. (hŭn-tĕr) | 221 | 40°33′S | 143°36′E |
| Huntingburg, In., U.S. (hŭnt´ĭng-bûrg) | 108 | 38°15′N | 86°55′W |
| Huntingdon, Can. (hŭnt´ĭng-dŭn) | 99 | 45°00′N | 74°10′W |
| Huntingdon, Can. | 116d | 49°00′N | 122°16′W |
| Huntingdon, Tn., U.S. | 124 | 36°00′N | 88°23′W |
| Huntington, In., U.S. | 108 | 40°55′N | 85°30′W |
| Huntington, Pa., U.S. | 109 | 40°30′N | 78°00′W |
| Huntington, W.V., U.S. | 105 | 38°25′N | 82°25′W |
| Huntington Beach, Ca., U.S. | 117a | 33°39′N | 118°00′W |
| Huntington Park, Ca., U.S. | 117a | 33°59′N | 118°14′W |
| Huntington Station, N.Y., U.S. | 110a | 40°51′N | 73°25′W |
| Huntley, Mt., U.S. | 115 | 45°54′N | 108°01′W |
| Huntsville, Can. | 91 | 45°20′N | 79°15′W |
| Huntsville, Al., U.S. (hŭnts´vĭl) | 124 | 34°44′N | 86°36′W |
| Huntsville, Mo., U.S. | 121 | 39°24′N | 92°32′W |
| Huntsville, Tx., U.S. | 123 | 30°44′N | 95°35′W |
| Huntsville, Ut., U.S. | 117b | 41°16′N | 111°46′W |
| Huolu, China (hōō lōō) | 205 | 38°05′N | 114°22′E |
| Huon Gulf, b., Pap. N. Gui. | 213 | 7°15′S | 147°45′E |
| Huoqiu, China (hwȯ-chyȯ) | 206 | 32°19′N | 116°17′E |
| Huoshan, China (hwȯ-shän) | 209 | 31°30′N | 116°25′E |
| Huraydīn, Wādī, r., Egypt | 197a | 30°55′N | 34°12′E |
| Hurd, Cape, c., Can. (hŭrd) | 98 | 45°15′N | 81°45′W |
| Hurdiyo, Som. | 238a | 10°43′N | 51°05′E |
| Hurley, Wi., U.S. (hûr´lĭ) | 113 | 46°26′N | 90°11′W |
| Hurlingham, Arg. (hȯr´lēn-gäm) | 144a | 34°36′S | 58°38′W |
| Huron, Oh., U.S. (hū´rŏn) | 108 | 41°20′N | 82°35′W |
| Huron, S.D., U.S. | 104 | 44°22′N | 98°15′W |
| Huron, r., Mi., U.S. | 111b | 42°22′N | 83°26′W |
| Huron, Lake, l., N.A. (hū´rŏn) | 107 | 45°15′N | 82°40′W |
| Huron Mountains, mts., Mi., U.S. (hū´rŏn) | 113 | 46°47′N | 87°52′W |
| Hurricane, Ak., U.S. (hûr´ĭ-kān) | 103 | 63°00′N | 149°30′W |
| Hurricane, Ut., U.S. | 119 | 37°10′N | 113°20′W |
| Hurricane Flats, bk. (hŭ-rĭ-kán flāts) | 134 | 23°35′N | 78°30′W |
| Hurst, Tx., U.S. | 117c | 32°48′N | 97°12′W |
| Húsavik, Ice. | 160 | 66°00′N | 17°10′W |
| Huşi, Rom. (kòsh´) | 177 | 46°52′N | 28°04′E |
| Huskvarna, Swe. (hōsk-vär´nä) | 166 | 57°48′N | 14°16′E |
| Husum, Ger. (hōō´zòm) | 168 | 54°29′N | 9°04′E |
| Hutchinson, Ks., U.S. (hŭch´ĭn-sŭn) | 104 | 38°02′N | 97°56′W |
| Hutchinson, Mn., U.S. | 113 | 44°53′N | 94°23′W |
| Hutuo, r., China | 208 | 38°10′N | 114°00′E |
| Huy, Bel. (ü-ē´) (hü´ē) | 165 | 50°33′N | 5°14′E |
| Hvannadalshnúkur, mtn., Ice. | 160 | 64°09′N | 16°46′W |

| PLACE (Pronunciation) | PAGE | LAT. | LONG. |
|---|---|---|---|
| Hvar, i., Serb. (khvär) | 174 | 43°08′N | 16°28′E |
| Hwange, Zimb. | 232 | 18°22′S | 26°29′E |
| Hwangju, Kor., N. (hwäng´jōō´) | 210 | 38°39′N | 125°49′E |
| Hyargas Nuur, l., Mong. | 204 | 48°00′N | 92°32′E |
| Hyattsville, Md., U.S. (hī´ăt´s-vĭl) | 110e | 38°57′N | 76°58′W |
| Hyco Lake, res., N.C., U.S. (rŏks´ bŭr-ȯ) | 125 | 36°22′N | 78°58′W |
| Hydaburg, Ak., U.S. (hī-dä´bûrg) | 103 | 55°12′N | 132°49′W |
| Hyde, Eng., U.K. (hīd) | 158a | 53°27′N | 2°05′W |
| Hyderābād, India (hī-dĕr-à-bäd´) | 199 | 17°29′N | 78°28′E |
| Hyderabad, India | 199 | 18°30′N | 76°50′E |
| Hyderābād, Pak. | 199 | 25°29′N | 68°28′E |
| Hyères, Fr. (ē-âr´) | 161 | 43°09′N | 6°08′E |
| Hyères, Îles d', is., Fr. (ēl´dyâr´) | 161 | 42°57′N | 6°17′E |
| Hyesanjin, Kor., N. (hyĕ´sän-jĭn´) | 210 | 41°11′N | 128°12′E |
| Hymera, In., U.S. (hī-mē´rà) | 108 | 39°10′N | 87°20′W |
| Hyndman Peak, mtn., Id., U.S. (hīnd´măn) | 106 | 43°38′N | 114°04′W |
| Hyōgo, dept., Japan (hĭyō´gō) | 211b | 34°54′N | 135°15′E |

## I

| PLACE (Pronunciation) | PAGE | LAT. | LONG. |
|---|---|---|---|
| Ia, r., Japan (ē´ä) | 211b | 34°54′N | 135°34′E |
| Iahotyn, Ukr. | 177 | 50°18′N | 31°46′E |
| Ialomiţa, r., Rom. | 175 | 44°37′N | 26°42′E |
| Iaşi, Rom. (yä´shĕ) | 154 | 47°10′N | 27°40′E |
| Iasinia, Ukr. | 169 | 48°17′N | 24°21′E |
| Iavoriv, Ukr. | 169 | 49°56′N | 23°24′E |
| Iba, Phil. (ē´bä) | 213a | 15°20′N | 119°59′E |
| Ibadan, Nig. (ē-bä´dän) | 230 | 7°17′N | 3°30′E |
| Ibagué, Col. | 142 | 4°27′N | 75°14′W |
| Ibar, r., Serb. (ē´bär) | 175 | 43°22′N | 20°35′E |
| Ibaraki, Japan (ē-bä´rä-gē) | 211b | 34°49′N | 135°35′E |
| Ibarra, Ec. (ē-bär´rä) | 142 | 0°19′N | 78°08′W |
| Ibb, Yemen | 201 | 14°01′N | 44°10′E |
| Iberville, Can. (ē-bår-vēl´)(ī´bĕr-vĭl) | 99 | 45°14′N | 73°01′W |
| Ibi, Spain (ē´bĕ) | 230 | 8°12′N | 9°45′E |
| Ibiapaba, Serra da, mts., Braz. (sē´r-rä-dä-ē-byä-pá´bä) | 143 | 3°30′S | 40°55′W |
| Ibiza see Eivissa, i., Spain | 156 | 38°55′N | 1°24′E |
| Ibo, Moz. (ē´bō) | 233 | 12°20′S | 40°35′E |
| Ibrāhīm, Būr, b., Egypt | 238d | 29°57′N | 32°33′E |
| Ibrahim, Jabal, mtn., Sau. Ar. | 198 | 20°31′N | 41°17′E |
| Ibwe Munyama, Zam. | 237 | 16°09′S | 28°34′E |
| Ica, Peru (ē´kä) | 142 | 14°09′S | 75°42′W |
| Icá (Putumayo), r., S.A. | 142 | 3°00′S | 69°00′W |
| Içana, Braz. (ē-sä´nä) | 142 | 0°15′N | 67°19′W |
| Ice Harbor Dam, Wa., U.S. | 114 | 46°15′N | 118°54′W |
| İçel, Tur. | 198 | 37°00′N | 34°40′E |
| Iceland, nation, Eur. (īs´lánd) | 154 | 65°12′N | 19°45′W |
| Ichibusayama, mtn., Japan (ē´chĕ-bōō´sá-yä´mä) | 211 | 32°19′N | 131°08′E |
| Ichihara, Japan | 211a | 35°31′N | 140°05′E |
| Ichikawa, Japan (ē´chĕ-kä´wä) | 211a | 35°44′N | 139°54′E |
| Ichinomiya, Japan (ē´chē-nō-mē´yä) | 211 | 35°19′N | 136°49′E |
| Ichinomoto, Japan (ē-chē´nō-mō-tō´) | 211b | 34°37′N | 135°50′E |
| Ichnia, Ukr. | 181 | 50°47′N | 32°23′E |
| Icy Cape, c., Ak., U.S. (ī´sī) | 103 | 70°20′N | 161°40′W |
| Idabel, Ok., U.S. (ī´dá-bĕl) | 121 | 33°52′N | 94°47′W |
| Idagrove, Ia., U.S. (ī´dá-grōv) | 112 | 42°22′N | 95°29′W |
| Idah, Nig. (ē´dä) | 230 | 7°07′N | 6°43′E |
| Idaho, state, U.S. (ī´dá-hō) | 104 | 44°00′N | 115°10′W |
| Idaho Falls, Id., U.S. | 104 | 43°30′N | 112°01′W |
| Idaho Springs, Co., U.S. | 120 | 39°43′N | 105°32′W |
| Idanha-a-Nova, Port. (ē-dän´yä-ä-nō´vä) | 172 | 39°58′N | 7°13′W |
| Ider, r., Mong. | 204 | 48°58′N | 98°38′E |
| Idi, Indon. (ē´dē) | 212 | 4°58′N | 97°47′E |
| Idkū Lake, l., Egypt | 238b | 31°13′N | 30°22′E |
| Idle, r., Eng., U.K. (īd´'l) | 158a | 53°22′N | 0°56′W |
| Idlib, Syria | 200 | 35°55′N | 36°38′E |
| Idriaj, Slvn. (ē´drĕ-ä) | 174 | 46°01′N | 14°01′E |
| Idutywa, S. Afr. (ē-dò-tī´wá) | 233c | 32°06′S | 28°18′E |
| Ienakiieve, Ukr. | 177 | 48°14′N | 38°12′E |
| Ieper, Bel. | 165 | 50°50′N | 2°53′E |
| Ierápetra, Grc. | 174a | 35°01′N | 25°48′E |
| Iesi, Italy (yä´sĕ) | 174 | 43°37′N | 13°20′E |
| Ievpatoriia, Ukr. | 181 | 45°13′N | 33°22′E |
| Ife, Nig. | 230 | 7°30′N | 4°30′E |
| Iferouâne, Niger (ēf´rō-än´) | 230 | 19°04′N | 8°24′E |
| Ifôghas, Adrar des, plat., Afr. | 230 | 19°55′N | 2°00′E |
| Igalula, Tan. | 237 | 5°14′S | 33°00′E |
| Igarka, Russia (ē-gär´kä) | 178 | 67°22′N | 86°16′E |
| Iglesias, Italy (ē-lĕ´syôs) | 162 | 39°20′N | 8°34′E |
| Igli, Alg. (ē-glē´) | 230 | 30°32′N | 2°15′W |
| Igluligaarjuk (Chesterfield Inlet), Can. | 91 | 63°19′N | 91°11′W |
| Iglulik, Can. | 91 | 69°33′N | 81°18′W |
| Ignacio, Ca., U.S. (ĭg-nä´cĭ-ō) | 116b | 38°05′N | 122°32′W |
| Iguaçu, r., Braz. (ē-gwä-sōō´) | 144b | 22°42′S | 43°19′W |
| Iguala, Mex. (ē-gwä´lä) | 130 | 18°18′N | 99°34′W |
| Igualada, Spain (ē-gwä-lä´dä) | 173 | 41°35′N | 1°38′E |
| Iguassu, r., S.A. (ē-gwä-sōō´) | 144 | 25°45′S | 52°30′W |
| Iguassu Falls, wtfl., S.A. | 143 | 25°40′S | 54°16′W |
| Iguatama, Braz. (ē-gwä-tá´mä) | 141a | 20°13′S | 45°40′W |
| Iguatu, Braz. (ē-gwä-tōō´) | 143 | 6°22′S | 39°17′W |
| Iguidi, Erg, Afr. | 230 | 26°22′N | 6°53′W |
| Iguig, Phil. (ē-gēg´) | 213a | 17°46′N | 121°44′E |
| Iharana, Madag. | 233 | 13°35′S | 50°05′E |
| Ihiala, Nig. | 235 | 5°51′N | 6°51′E |
| Iida, Japan (ē´ē-dä) | 211 | 35°39′N | 137°53′E |

304 Iijoki – Isla-Cristina

PRONOUNCING INDEX


| PLACE (Pronunciation) | PAGE | LAT. | LONG. |
|---|---|---|---|
| Iijoki, r., Fin. (ē′yō′kĭ) | 180 | 65°28′N | 27°00′E |
| Iizuka, Japan (ē′ē-zò-kà) | 211 | 33°39′N | 130°39′E |
| Ijebu-Ode, Nig. (ė-jĕ′bōō ōdå) | 230 | 6°50′N | 3°56′E |
| IJmuiden, Neth. | 159a | 52°27′N | 4°36′E |
| IJsselmeer, l., Neth. (ĭ′sĕl-mär) | 165 | 52°46′N | 5°14′E |
| Ikaalinen, Fin. (ē′kä-lĭ-nĕn) | 167 | 61°47′N | 22°55′E |
| Ikaría, i., Grc. (ē-kä′ryà) | 175 | 37°43′N | 26°07′E |
| Ikeda, Japan (ē′kå-dä) | 211b | 34°49′N | 135°26′E |
| Ikerre, Nig. | 235 | 7°31′N | 5°14′E |
| Ikhtiman, Blg. (ėk′tė-män) | 175 | 42°26′N | 23°49′E |
| Iki, i., Japan (ē′kė) | 210 | 33°46′N | 129°44′E |
| Ikoma, Japan | 211b | 34°41′N | 135°43′E |
| Ikoma, Tan. (ė-kō′mä) | 232 | 2°08′S | 34°47′E |
| Iksha, Russia (ĭk′shá) | 186b | 56°10′N | 37°30′E |
| Ila, Nig. | 235 | 8°01′N | 4°55′E |
| Ilagan, Phil. | 213a | 17°09′N | 121°52′E |
| Ilan, Tai. (ē′län′) | 209 | 24°50′N | 121°42′E |
| Iława, Pol. (ė-lä′vå) | 169 | 53°35′N | 19°36′E |
| Île-á-la-Crosse, Can. | 96 | 55°34′N | 108°00′W |
| Ilebo, D.R.C. | 232 | 4°19′S | 20°35′E |
| Ilek, Russia (ē′lyĕk) | 181 | 51°30′N | 53°10′E |
| Île-Perrot, Can. (yl-pĕ-rōt′) | 102a | 45°21′N | 73°54′W |
| Ilesha, Nig. | 230 | 7°38′N | 4°45′E |
| Ilford, Eng., U.K. (ĭl′fērd) | 158b | 51°33′N | 0°06′E |
| Ilfracombe, Eng., U.K. (ĭl-fră-kōōm′) | 164 | 51°13′N | 4°08′W |
| Ilhabela, Braz. (ē′lä-bĕ′lä) | 141a | 23°47′S | 45°21′W |
| Ilha Grande, Baía de, b., Braz. (ēl′yà grän′dĕ) | 141a | 23°17′S | 44°25′W |
| Ílhavo, Port. (ēl′yá-vō) | 162 | 40°36′N | 8°41′W |
| Ilhéus, Braz. (ē-lĕ′ōōs) | 143 | 14°52′S | 39°00′W |
| Ili, r., Asia | 184 | 44°30′N | 76°45′E |
| Iliamna, Ak., U.S. (ē-lė-ăm′nȧ) | 103 | 59°45′N | 155°05′W |
| Iliamna, Ak., U.S. | 103 | 60°18′N | 153°25′W |
| Iliamna, l., Ak., U.S. | 103 | 59°25′N | 155°30′W |
| Ilim, r., Russia (ė-lyĕm′) | 184 | 57°28′N | 103°00′E |
| Ilimsk, Russia (ė-lyĕmsk′) | 179 | 56°47′N | 103°43′E |
| Ilin Island, i., Phil. (ė-lyēn′) | 213a | 12°16′N | 120°57′E |
| Ilion, N.Y., U.S. (ĭl′ĭ-ŭn) | 109 | 43°00′N | 75°05′W |
| Ilkeston, Eng., U.K. (ĭl′kĕs-tŭn) | 158a | 52°58′N | 1°19′W |
| Illampu, Nevado, mtn., Bol. (nĕ-vá′dô-ēl-yäm-pōō′) | 142 | 15°50′S | 68°15′W |
| Illapel, Chile (ē-zhä-pĕ′l) | 144 | 31°37′S | 71°10′W |
| Iller, r., Ger. (ĭlēr) | 168 | 47°52′N | 10°06′E |
| Illimani, Nevado, mtn., Bol. (nĕ-vá′dô-ēl-yė-mä′nė) | 142 | 16°50′S | 67°38′W |
| Illinois, state, U.S. (ĭl-ĭ-noi′) (ĭl-ĭ-noiz′) | 105 | 40°25′N | 90°40′W |
| Illinois, r., Il., U.S. | 107 | 39°00′N | 90°30′W |
| Illintsi, Ukr. | 177 | 49°07′N | 29°13′E |
| Illizi, Alg. | 230 | 26°35′N | 8°24′E |
| Il′men, l., Russia (ô′zē-rô el′′men′′) (ĭl′mĕn) | 180 | 58°18′N | 32°00′E |
| Ilo, Peru | 142 | 17°46′S | 71°13′W |
| Ilobasco, El Sal. (ė-lô-bäs′kô) | 132 | 13°57′N | 88°46′W |
| Iloilo, Phil. (ē-lô-ē′lō) | 212 | 10°49′N | 122°33′E |
| Ilopango, Lago, l., El Sal. (ē-lô-pāŋ′gō) | 132 | 13°48′N | 88°50′W |
| Ilorin, Nig. (ē-lô-rēn′) | 230 | 8°30′N | 4°32′E |
| Ilūkste, Lat. | 167 | 55°59′N | 26°20′E |
| Ilwaco, Wa., U.S. (ĭl-wă′kô) | 116c | 46°19′N | 124°02′W |
| Ilych, r., Russia (ē′l′ĭch) | 180 | 62°30′N | 57°30′E |
| Imabari, Japan (ē′mä-bä′rė) | 210 | 34°05′N | 132°58′E |
| Imai, Japan (ė-mī′) | 211b | 34°30′N | 135°47′E |
| Iman, r., Russia (ė-män′) | 210 | 45°40′N | 134°31′E |
| Imandra, l., Russia (ē-män′drȧ) | 180 | 67°40′N | 32°30′E |
| Imbābah, Egypt (ēm-bä′bȧ) | 238b | 30°06′N | 31°09′E |
| Imeni Morozova, Russia (ĭm-yĕ′nyĭ mô rô′zô vȧ) | 186c | 59°58′N | 31°02′E |
| Imeni Moskvy, Kanal (Moscow Canal), can., Russia (kȧ-näl′ĭm-yă′nĭ mŏs-kvĭ) | 176 | 56°33′N | 37°15′E |
| Imeni Tsyurupy, Russia | 186b | 55°30′N | 38°39′E |
| Imeni Vorovskogo, Russia | 186b | 55°43′N | 38°21′E |
| Imlay City, Mi., U.S. (ĭm′lā) | 108 | 43°00′N | 83°15′W |
| Immenstadt, Ger. (ĭm′ĕn-shtät) | 168 | 47°34′N | 10°12′E |
| Immerpan, S. Afr. (ĭmĕr-pän) | 238c | 24°29′S | 29°14′E |
| Imola, Italy (ē′mô-lä) | 174 | 44°19′N | 11°43′E |
| Imotski, Cro. (ė-môts′kė) | 175 | 43°25′N | 17°15′E |
| Impameri, Braz. | 143 | 17°44′S | 48°03′W |
| Impendle, S. Afr. (ĭm-pĕnd′lȧ) | 233c | 29°38′S | 29°54′E |
| Imperia, Italy (ėm-pä′rė-ä) | 162 | 43°52′N | 8°00′E |
| Imperial, Pa., U.S. (ĭm-pē′rĭ-ăl) | 111e | 40°27′N | 80°15′W |
| Imperial Beach, Ca., U.S. | 118a | 32°34′N | 117°08′W |
| Imperial Valley, Ca., U.S. | 118 | 33°00′N | 115°22′W |
| Impfondo, Congo (ĭmp-fōn′dô) | 231 | 1°37′N | 18°04′E |
| Imphāl, India (ĭmp′hŭl) | 199 | 24°42′N | 94°00′E |
| Ina, r., Japan (ė-nä′) | 211b | 34°56′N | 135°21′E |
| Inaja Indian Reservation, I.R., Ca., U.S. (ė-nä′hä) | 118 | 32°56′N | 116°37′W |
| Inari, l., Fin. | 160 | 69°02′N | 26°22′E |
| Inca, Spain (ėŋ′kä) | 173 | 39°43′N | 2°53′E |
| Ince Burun, c., Tur. (ĭn′jȧ) | 163 | 42°00′N | 35°00′E |
| Inch′ŏn, Kor., S. (ĭn′chŭn) | 205 | 37°26′N | 126°46′E |
| Incudine, Monte, mtn., Fr. (ēn-kōō-dē′nȧ) (ăɴ-kü-dēn′) | 174 | 41°53′N | 9°17′E |
| Indalsälven, r., Swe. | 160 | 62°50′N | 16°50′E |
| Independence, Ks., U.S. (ĭn-dė-pĕn′dĕns) | 121 | 37°14′N | 95°42′W |
| Independence, Mo., U.S. | 117f | 39°06′N | 94°26′W |
| Independence, Oh., U.S. | 111d | 41°23′N | 81°39′W |
| Independence, Or., U.S. | 114 | 44°49′N | 123°13′W |
| Independence Mountains, mts., Nv., U.S. | 114 | 41°15′N | 116°02′W |
| Inder köli, l., Kaz. | 181 | 48°20′N | 52°10′E |
| India, nation, Asia (ĭn′dĭ-ȧ) | 199 | 23°00′N | 77°30′E |

| PLACE (Pronunciation) | PAGE | LAT. | LONG. |
|---|---|---|---|
| Indian, l., Mi., U.S. (ĭn′dĭ-ăn) | 113 | 46°04′N | 86°34′W |
| Indian, r., N.Y., U.S. | 109 | 44°05′N | 75°45′W |
| Indiana, Pa., U.S. (ĭn-dĭ-ăn′ȧ) | 109 | 40°40′N | 79°10′W |
| Indiana, state, U.S. | 105 | 39°50′N | 86°45′W |
| Indianapolis, In., U.S. (ĭn-dĭ-ăn-ăp′ô-lĭs) | 105 | 39°45′N | 86°08′W |
| Indian Arm, b., Can. (ĭn′dĭ-ăn ärm) | 116d | 49°21′N | 122°55′W |
| Indian Head, Can. | 90 | 50°29′N | 103°44′W |
| Indian Lake, l., Can. | 98 | 47°00′N | 82°00′W |
| Indian Ocean, o. | 5 | 10°00′S | 70°00′E |
| Indianola, Ia., U.S. (ĭn-dĭ-ăn-ō′lȧ) | 113 | 41°22′N | 93°33′W |
| Indianola, Ms., U.S. | 124 | 33°29′N | 90°35′W |
| Indigirka, r., Russia (ėn-dė-gēr′kȧ) | 185 | 67°45′N | 145°45′E |
| Indio, r., Pan. (ē′n-dyô) | 128a | 9°13′N | 79°28′W |
| Indochina, reg., Asia (ĭn-dô-chī′nȧ) | 212 | 17°22′N | 105°18′E |
| Indonesia, nation, Asia (ĭn′dô-nė-zhȧ) | 212 | 4°38′S | 118°45′E |
| Indore, India (ĭn-dōr′) | 199 | 22°48′N | 76°51′E |
| Indragiri, r., Indon. (ĭn-drȧ-jē′rė) | 212 | 0°27′S | 102°05′E |
| Indrāvati, r., India (ĭn-drŭ-vä′tė) | 199 | 19°00′N | 82°00′E |
| Indre, r., Fr. (ăɴ′dr′) | 170 | 47°13′N | 0°29′E |
| Indus, Can. (ĭn′dŭs) | 102e | 50°55′N | 113°45′W |
| Indus, r., Asia | 199 | 26°43′N | 67°41′E |
| Indwe, S. Afr. (ĭnd′wȧ) | 233c | 31°30′S | 27°21′E |
| Inebolu, Tur. (ė-nȧ-bō′lōō) | 163 | 41°50′N | 33°40′E |
| Inego, Tur. (ē′nȧ-gü) | 181 | 40°05′N | 29°20′E |
| Infanta, Phil. (ėn-fän′tä) | 213a | 14°44′N | 121°39′E |
| Infanta, Phil. | 213a | 15°50′N | 119°53′E |
| Inferror, Laguna, l., Mex. (lä-gò′nä-ēn-fĕr-rôr) | 131 | 16°18′N | 94°40′W |
| Infiernillo, Presa de, res., Mex. | 130 | 18°50′N | 101°50′W |
| Infiesto, Spain (ēn-fyĕ′s-tô) | 172 | 43°21′N | 5°24′W |
| I-n-Gall, Niger | 235 | 16°47′N | 6°56′E |
| Ingersoll, Can. (ĭn′gēr-sŏl) | 98 | 43°05′N | 81°00′W |
| Ingham, Austl. (ĭng′ăm) | 219 | 18°45′S | 146°14′E |
| Ingles, Cayos, is., Cuba (kä-yōs-ē′n-glĕ′s) | 134 | 21°55′N | 82°35′W |
| Inglewood, Can. | 102d | 43°48′N | 79°56′W |
| Inglewood, Ca., U.S. (ĭn′g′l-wòd) | 117a | 33°57′N | 118°22′W |
| Ingoda, r., Russia (ėn-gō′dȧ) | 185 | 51°29′N | 112°32′E |
| Ingolstadt, Ger. (ĭŋ′gôl-shtät) | 168 | 48°46′N | 11°27′E |
| Ingur, r., Geor. (ėn-gòr′) | 181 | 42°30′N | 42°00′E |
| Ingushetia, prov., Russia | 182 | 43°15′N | 45°00′E |
| Inhambane, Moz. (ėn-äm-bä′-nĕ) | 232 | 23°47′S | 35°28′E |
| Inhambupe, Braz. (ėn-yäm-bōō′pä) | 143 | 11°47′S | 38°13′W |
| Inharrime, Moz. (ėn-yär-rē′mä) | 232 | 24°17′S | 35°07′E |
| Inhomirim, Braz. (ē-nô-mė-rē′ɴ) | 144b | 22°34′S | 43°11′W |
| Inhul, r., Ukr. | 177 | 47°22′N | 32°52′E |
| Inhulets′, r., Ukr. | 177 | 47°12′N | 33°12′E |
| Inírida, r., Col. (ē-nė-rē′dä) | 142 | 2°25′N | 70°38′W |
| Injune, Austl. (ĭn′jòn) | 222 | 25°52′S | 148°30′E |
| Inkeroinem, Fin. (ĭn′kēr-oi-nĕn) | 167 | 60°42′N | 26°50′E |
| Inkster, Mi., U.S. (ĭngk′stēr) | 111b | 42°18′N | 83°19′W |
| Inn, r., Eur. (ĭn) | 161 | 48°00′N | 12°00′E |
| Innamincka, Austl. (ĭnn-ȧ′mĭn-kȧ) | 222 | 27°50′S | 140°48′E |
| Inner Brass, i., V.I.U.S. (bräs) | 129c | 18°23′N | 64°58′W |
| Inner Hebrides, is., Scot., U.K. | 164 | 57°20′N | 6°20′W |
| Inner Mongolia see Nei Monggol, prov., China | 204 | 40°15′N | 105°00′E |
| Innisfail, Can. | 90 | 52°02′N | 113°57′W |
| Innsbruck, Aus. (ĭns′bròk) | 161 | 47°15′N | 11°25′E |
| Ino, Japan (ē′nô) | 211 | 33°34′N | 133°23′E |
| Inongo, D.R.C. (ė-nôŋ′gō) | 232 | 1°57′S | 18°16′E |
| Inowrocław, Pol. (ē-nô-vrôts′läf) | 169 | 52°48′N | 18°16′E |
| In Salah, Alg. | 230 | 27°13′N | 2°22′E |
| Inscription House Ruin, Az., U.S. (ĭn′skrĭp-shŭn hous rōō′ĭn) | 119 | 36°45′N | 110°47′W |
| International Falls, Mn., U.S. (ĭn′tēr-năsh′ŭn-ăl fôlz) | 105 | 48°34′N | 93°26′W |
| Inuvik, Can. | 90 | 68°40′N | 134°10′W |
| Inuyama, Japan (ē′nōō-yä′mä) | 211 | 35°24′N | 137°01′E |
| Invercargil, N.Z. (ĭn-vēr-kär′gĭl) | 223 | 46°25′S | 168°27′E |
| Inverel, Austl. (ĭn-vēr-el′) | 219 | 29°50′S | 151°32′E |
| Invergrove Heights, Mn., U.S. (ĭn′vēr-grōv) | 117g | 44°51′N | 93°01′W |
| Inverness, Can. (ĭn-vēr-nĕs′) | 101 | 46°14′N | 61°18′W |
| Inverness, Scot., U.K. | 160 | 57°30′N | 4°07′W |
| Inverness, Fl., U.S. | 125 | 28°48′N | 82°22′W |
| Investigator Strait, strt., Austl. (ĭn-vĕst′ĭ′gā-tôr) | 222 | 35°33′S | 137°00′E |
| Inyangani, mtn., Zimb. (ėn-yän-gä′nė) | 232 | 18°06′S | 32°37′E |
| Inyokern, Ca., U.S. | 118 | 35°39′N | 117°51′W |
| Inyo Mountains, mts., Ca., U.S. (ĭn′yō) | 106 | 36°55′N | 118°04′W |
| Inzer, r., Russia (ĭn′zĕr) | 186a | 54°24′N | 57°17′E |
| Inzia, r., D.R.C. | 236 | 5°55′S | 17°50′E |
| Ioánnina, Grc. (yô-ä′nė-nȧ) | 163 | 39°39′N | 20°52′E |
| Ioco, Can. | 116d | 49°18′N | 122°53′W |
| Iola, Ks., U.S. (ī-ō′lȧ) | 121 | 37°55′N | 95°23′W |
| Iôna, Parque Nacional do, rec., Ang. | 236 | 16°35′S | 12°00′E |
| Ionia, Mi., U.S. (ī-ō′nĭ-ȧ) | 108 | 43°00′N | 85°10′W |
| Ionian Islands, is., Grc. (ī-ō′nĭ-ăn) | 163 | 39°10′N | 20°05′E |
| Ionian Sea, sea, Eur. | 156 | 38°59′N | 18°48′E |
| Iori, r., Asia | 182 | 41°03′N | 46°17′E |
| Íos, i., Grc. (ī′ŏs) | 175 | 36°48′N | 25°25′E |
| Iowa, state, U.S. (ī′ô-wȧ) | 105 | 42°05′N | 94°20′W |
| Iowa, r., Ia., U.S. | 113 | 41°55′N | 92°20′W |
| Iowa City, Ia., U.S. | 105 | 41°39′N | 91°31′W |
| Iowa Falls, Ia., U.S. | 113 | 42°32′N | 93°16′W |
| Iowa Park, Tx., U.S. | 120 | 33°57′N | 98°39′W |
| Ipala, Tan. | 237 | 4°30′S | 32°53′E |
| Ipeirus, hist. reg., Grc. | 175 | 39°35′N | 20°45′E |
| Ipel′, r., Eur. (ė′pĕl) | 169 | 48°08′N | 19°00′E |
| Ipiales, Col. (ē-pė-ä′lås) | 142 | 0°48′N | 77°45′W |
| Ipoh, Malay. | 212 | 4°45′N | 101°05′E |

| PLACE (Pronunciation) | PAGE | LAT. | LONG. |
|---|---|---|---|
| Ipswich, Austl. (ĭps′wĭch) | 219 | 27°40′S | 152°50′E |
| Ipswich, Eng., U.K. | 161 | 52°05′N | 1°05′E |
| Ipswich, Ma., U.S. | 101a | 42°41′N | 70°50′W |
| Ipswich, S.D., U.S. | 112 | 45°26′N | 99°01′W |
| Ipu, Braz. (ē-pōō) | 143 | 4°11′S | 40°45′W |
| Iput′, r., Eur. (ė-pòt′) | 181 | 52°53′N | 31°57′E |
| Iqaluit, Can. | 91 | 63°48′N | 68°31′W |
| Iquique, Chile (ē-kē′kĕ) | 142 | 20°16′S | 70°07′W |
| Iquitos, Peru (ė-kē′tōs) | 142 | 3°39′S | 73°18′W |
| Irákleio, Grc. | 154 | 35°20′N | 25°10′E |
| Iran, nation, Asia (ē-rän′) | 198 | 31°15′N | 53°30′E |
| Iran, Plateau of, plat., Iran | 198 | 32°28′N | 58°00′E |
| Iran Mountains, mts., Asia | 212 | 2°30′N | 114°30′E |
| Irapuato, Mex. (ē-rä-pwä′tō) | 130 | 20°41′N | 101°24′W |
| Iraq, nation, Asia (ē-räk′) | 198 | 32°00′N | 42°30′E |
| Irazú, vol., C.R. (ē-rä-zōō′) | 133 | 9°58′N | 83°54′W |
| Irbid, Jord. (ėr-bēd′) | 200 | 32°33′N | 35°51′E |
| Irbit, Russia (ėr-bēt′) | 178 | 57°40′N | 63°10′E |
| Irébou, D.R.C. (ē-rā′bōō) | 232 | 0°40′S | 17°48′E |
| Ireland, nation, Eur. (īr-lănd) | 154 | 53°33′N | 8°00′W |
| Iremel′, Gora, mtn., Russia (gȧ-rä′ĭ-rĕ′mĕl) | 186a | 54°32′N | 58°52′E |
| Irene, S. Afr. (ĭ-rē-nē) | 233b | 25°53′S | 28°13′E |
| Irîgui, reg., Mali | 234 | 16°45′N | 5°35′W |
| Iriklinskoye Vodokhranilishche, res., Russia | 181 | 52°20′N | 58°50′E |
| Iringa, Tan. (ė-rĭŋ′gä) | 232 | 7°46′S | 35°42′E |
| Iriomote Jima, i., Japan (ērē′-ō-mō-tä) | 205 | 24°20′N | 123°30′E |
| Iriona, Hond. (ė-rė-ō′nä) | 132 | 15°53′N | 85°12′W |
| Irish Sea, sea, Eur. (ī′rĭsh) | 156 | 53°55′N | 5°25′W |
| Irkutsk, Russia (ĭr-kòtsk′) | 179 | 52°16′N | 104°00′E |
| Irlam, Eng., U.K. (ûr′lăm) | 158a | 53°26′N | 2°26′W |
| Irois, Cap des, c., Haiti | 135 | 18°25′N | 74°50′W |
| Iron Bottom Sound, strt., Sol. Is. | 214e | 9°15′S | 160°00′E |
| Irondale, Al., U.S. (ī′ērn-dăl) | 110h | 33°32′N | 86°43′W |
| Iron Gate, val., Eur. | 175 | 44°43′N | 22°32′E |
| Iron Knob, Austl. (ī-ăn nŏb) | 222 | 32°47′S | 137°10′E |
| Iron Mountain, Mi., U.S. (ī′ērn) | 113 | 45°49′N | 88°04′W |
| Iron River, Mi., U.S. | 113 | 46°09′N | 88°39′W |
| Ironton, Oh., U.S. (ī′ērn-tŭn) | 108 | 38°30′N | 82°45′W |
| Ironwood, Mi., U.S. (ī′ērn-wòd) | 113 | 46°28′N | 90°10′W |
| Ironwood Forest National Monument, rec., Az., U.S. | 119 | 32°30′N | 111°25′W |
| Iroquois, r., Il., U.S. (ĭr′ô-kwoi) | 108 | 40°55′N | 87°20′W |
| Iroquois Falls, Can. | 91 | 48°41′N | 80°39′W |
| Irō-Saki, c., Japan (ē′rō sä′kē) | 210 | 34°35′N | 138°54′E |
| Irpin, r., Ukr. | 177 | 50°13′N | 29°55′E |
| Irrawaddy, r., Mya. (ĭr-ȧ-wäd′ė) | 199 | 23°27′N | 96°25′E |
| Irtysh, r., Asia (ĭr-tĭsh′) | 178 | 59°00′N | 69°00′E |
| Irumu, D.R.C. (ė-rō′mōō) | 231 | 1°30′N | 29°52′E |
| Irun, Spain (ė-rōōn′) | 172 | 43°20′N | 1°47′W |
| Irvine, Scot., U.K. | 164 | 55°39′N | 4°40′W |
| Irvine, Ca., U.S. (ûr′vĭn) | 117a | 33°40′N | 117°45′W |
| Irvine, Ky., U.S. | 108 | 37°40′N | 84°00′W |
| Irving, Tx., U.S. (ûr′vēng) | 117c | 32°49′N | 96°57′W |
| Irvington, N.J., U.S. (ûr′vēng-tŭn) | 110a | 40°43′N | 74°15′W |
| Irwin, Pa., U.S. (ûr′wĭn) | 111e | 40°19′N | 79°42′W |
| Is, Russia (ēs) | 186a | 58°48′N | 59°44′E |
| Isa, Nig. | 235 | 13°14′N | 6°24′E |
| Isaacs, Mount, mtn., Pan. (ē-sä-ä′ks) | 128a | 9°22′N | 79°31′W |
| Isabela, i., Ec. (ē-sä-bā′lä) | 142 | 0°47′S | 91°35′W |
| Isabela, Cabo, c., Dom. Rep. (kä′bō-ē-sä-bĕ′lä) | 135 | 20°00′N | 71°00′W |
| Isabella, Cordillera, mts., Nic. (kôr-dēl-yĕ′rä-ē-sä-bĕlä) | 132 | 13°20′N | 85°37′W |
| Isabella Indian Reservation, I.R., Mi., U.S. (ĭs-ȧ-bĕl′-lȧ) | 108 | 43°35′N | 84°55′W |
| Isaccea, Rom. (ė-säk′chä) | 177 | 45°16′N | 28°26′E |
| Ísafjördur, Ice. (ēs′ä-fy̆r-dòr) | 160 | 66°09′N | 22°39′W |
| Isangi, D.R.C. (ė-säŋ′gē) | 204 | 0°46′N | 24°15′E |
| Isar, r., Ger. (ē′zär) | 161 | 48°30′N | 12°30′E |
| Isarco, r., Italy (ė-sär′kō) | 174 | 46°37′N | 11°25′E |
| Isarog, Mount, mtn., Phil. (ē-sä-rô-g) | 213a | 13°40′N | 123°23′E |
| Ischia, Italy (ēs′kyä) | 173c | 40°29′N | 13°58′E |
| Ischia, Isola d′, i., Italy (dĕ′sh-kyä) | 162 | 40°26′N | 13°55′E |
| Ise, Japan (ĭs′hė) (ū′gē-yä′mä′dȧ) | 210 | 34°30′N | 136°43′E |
| Iseo, Lago d′, l., Italy (lä-′gō-dē-ė-zĕ′ō) | 174 | 45°50′N | 9°55′E |
| Isére, r., Fr. (ė-zâr′) | 161 | 45°15′N | 5°15′E |
| Iserlohn, Ger. (ē′zĕr-lōn) | 171c | 51°22′N | 7°42′E |
| Isernia, Italy (ė-zĕr′nyä) | 174 | 41°35′N | 14°14′E |
| Ise-Wan, b., Japan (ē′sĕ wän) | 210 | 34°49′N | 136°44′E |
| Iseyin, Nig. | 230 | 7°58′N | 3°36′E |
| Ishigaki, Japan | 214d | 24°20′N | 124°09′E |
| Ishikari Wan, b., Japan (ē′shė-kä-rē wän) | 210 | 43°30′N | 141°05′E |
| Ishim, Russia (ĭsh-ėm′) | 178 | 56°07′N | 69°13′E |
| Ishim, r., Asia | 178 | 53°17′N | 67°45′E |
| Ishimbay, Russia (ē-shēm-bī′) | 186a | 53°28′N | 56°02′E |
| Ishinomaki, Japan (ĭsh-nō-mä′kē) | 205 | 38°22′N | 141°22′E |
| Ishinomaki Wan, b., Japan (ē-shē-nō-mä′kē wän) | 210 | 38°10′N | 141°40′E |
| Ishly, Russia (ĭsh′lĭ) | 186a | 54°13′N | 55°55′E |
| Ishlya, Russia (ĭsh′lyȧ) | 186a | 53°54′N | 57°48′E |
| Ishmant, Egypt | 238b | 29°17′N | 31°15′E |
| Ishpeming, Mi., U.S. (ĭsh′pė-mĭng) | 113 | 46°28′N | 87°42′W |
| Isipingo, S. Afr. (ĭs-ĭ-pĭŋg-gô) | 233c | 29°59′S | 30°58′E |
| Isiro, D.R.C. | 231 | 2°47′N | 27°37′E |
| İskenderun, Tur. (ĭs-kĕn′dĕr-ōōn) | 198 | 36°45′N | 36°15′E |
| İskenderun Körfezi, b., Tur. | 163 | 36°22′N | 35°25′E |
| İskilip, Tur. (ès′kĭ-lĕp′) | 163 | 40°40′N | 34°30′E |
| Iskŭr, r., Blg. (ĭs′k′r) | 175 | 43°05′N | 23°37′E |
| Isla-Cristina, Spain (ī′lä-krė-stē′nä) | 172 | 37°13′N | 7°20′W |


ăt; finăl; rāte; senåte; ärm; ȧsk; sofȧ; fâre; ch-choose; dh-as th in other; bē; ėvent; bĕt; recĕnt; cratẽr; g-gō; gh-guttural g; bĭt; ĭ-short neutral; rīde; ᴋ-guttural k as ch in German ich;

| PLACE (Pronunciation) | PAGE | LAT. | LONG. |
|---|---|---|---|
| Islāmābād, Pak. | 199 | 33°55'N | 73°05'E |
| Isla Mujeres, Mex. (ē's-lä-moo-kĕ'rĕs) | 132a | 21°25'N | 86°53'W |
| Island Lake, l., Can. | 93 | 53°47'N | 94°25'W |
| Islands, Bay of, b., Can. (ī'lăndz) | 101 | 49°10'N | 58°15'W |
| Islay, i., Scot., U.K. (ī'lā) | 160 | 55°55'N | 6°35'W |
| Isle, r., Fr. (ēl) | 170 | 45°02'N | 0°29'E |
| Isle of Axholme, reg., Eng., U.K. (ăks'-hōm) | 158a | 53°33'N | 0°48'W |
| Isle of Man, dep., Eur. (măn) | 164 | 54°26'N | 4°21'W |
| Isle Royale National Park, rec., Mi., U.S. (īl'roi-ăl') | 107 | 47°57'N | 88°37'W |
| Isleta, N.M., U.S. (ēs-lā'tȧ) (ī-lē'tȧ) | 119 | 34°55'N | 106°45'W |
| Isleta Indian Reservation, I.R., N.M., U.S. | 119 | 34°55'N | 106°45'W |
| Ismailia, Egypt (ēs-mä-ēl'ēȧ) | 238b | 30°35'N | 32°17'E |
| Ismā'īlīyah Canal, can., Egypt | 238b | 30°25'N | 31°45'E |
| Ismail Samani, pik, mtn., Taj. | 183 | 38°57'N | 72°01'E |
| Ismaning, Ger. (ēz'mä-nēng) | 159d | 48°14'N | 11°41'E |
| Isparta, Tur. (ē-spär'tȧ) | 198 | 37°50'N | 30°40'E |
| Israel, nation, Asia | 198 | 32°40'N | 34°00'E |
| Issaquah, Wa., U.S. (ĭz'să-kwăh) | 116a | 47°32'N | 122°02'W |
| Isselburg, Ger. (ē'sĕl-boorg) | 171c | 51°50'N | 6°28'E |
| Issoire, Fr. (ē-swȧr') | 170 | 45°32'N | 3°13'E |
| Issoudun, Fr. (ē-soo-dăN') | 170 | 46°56'N | 2°00'E |
| Issum, Ger. (ē'soom) | 171c | 51°32'N | 6°24'E |
| Issyk-Kul, Ozero, l., Kyrg. | 183 | 42°13'N | 76°12'E |
| İstanbul, Tur. (ē-stän-bool') | 198 | 41°02'N | 29°00'E |
| İstanbul Boğazı (Bosporus), strt., Tur. | 198 | 41°10'N | 29°10'E |
| Istiaía, Grc. (ĭs-tyī'yä) | 175 | 38°58'N | 23°11'E |
| Istmina, Col. (ēst-mē'nä) | 142a | 5°10'N | 76°40'W |
| Istokpoga, Lake, l., Fl., U.S. (ĭs-tŏk-pō'gȧ) | 125a | 27°20'N | 81°33'W |
| Istra, pen., Serb. (ē-strä) | 174 | 45°18'N | 13°48'E |
| Istranca Dağlari, mts., Eur. (ĭ-strän'jȧ) | 175 | 41°50'N | 27°25'E |
| Istres, Fr. (ēs'tr') | 170a | 43°30'N | 5°00'E |
| Itabaiana, Braz. (ē-tä-bä-yȧ-nä) | 143 | 10°42'S | 37°17'W |
| Itabapoana, Braz. (ē-tä'-bä-pôä'nä) | 141a | 21°19'S | 40°58'W |
| Itabapoana, r., Braz. | 141a | 21°11'S | 41°18'W |
| Itabirito, Braz. (ē-tä-bē-rē'tô) | 141a | 20°15'S | 43°46'W |
| Itabuna, Braz. (ē-tä-boo'nȧ) | 143 | 14°47'S | 39°17'W |
| Itacoara, Braz. (ē-tä-kô'ä-rä) | 141a | 21°41'S | 42°04'W |
| Itacoatiara, Braz. (ē-tȧ-kwȧ-tyȧ'rȧ) | 143 | 3°03'S | 58°18'W |
| Itagüí, Col. (ē-tä'gwē) | 142a | 6°11'N | 75°36'W |
| Itagui, r., Braz. | 144b | 22°53'S | 43°43'W |
| Itaipava, Braz. (ē-tī-pȧ'-vä) | 144b | 22°23'S | 43°09'W |
| Itaipu, Braz. (ē-tī'poo) | 144b | 22°58'S | 43°02'W |
| Itaituba, Braz. (ē-tä'ī-too'bȧ) | 143 | 4°12'S | 56°00'W |
| Itajái, Braz. (ē-tä-zhī') | 144 | 26°52'S | 48°39'W |
| Italy, Tx., U.S. | 123 | 32°11'N | 96°51'W |
| Italy, nation, Eur. (ĭt'ȧ-lē) | 154 | 43°58'N | 11°14'E |
| Itambi, Braz. (ē-tä'm-bē) | 144b | 22°44'S | 42°57'W |
| Itami, Japan (ē'tä'mē') | 211b | 34°47'N | 135°25'E |
| Itapecerica, Braz. (ē-tä-pĕ-sĕ-rē'kȧ) | 141a | 20°29'S | 45°08'W |
| Itapecuru-Mirim, Braz. (ē-tä-pĕ'koo-roo-mē-rēN') | 143 | 3°17'S | 44°15'W |
| Itaperuna, Braz. (ē-tȧ'pâ-roo'nä) | 143 | 21°12'S | 41°53'W |
| Itapetininga, Braz. (ē-tä-pĕ-tē-nē'N-gä) | 143 | 23°37'S | 48°03'W |
| Itapira, Braz. (ē-tȧ-pē'rȧ) | 143 | 20°42'S | 51°19'W |
| Itapira, Braz. | 141a | 22°27'S | 46°47'W |
| Itarsi, India | 202 | 22°43'N | 77°45'E |
| Itasca, Tx., U.S. (ĭ-tăs'kȧ) | 123 | 32°09'N | 97°08'W |
| Itasca, l., Mn., U.S. | 112 | 47°13'N | 95°14'W |
| Itatiaia, Pico da, mtn., Braz. (pē'-kô-dȧ-ē-tä-tyȧ'ēä) | 143 | 22°18'S | 44°41'W |
| Itatiba, Braz. (ē-tä-tē'bä) | 141a | 23°01'S | 46°48'W |
| Itaúna, Braz. (ē-tä-oo'nä) | 141a | 20°05'S | 44°35'W |
| Ithaca, Mi., U.S. (ĭth'ȧ-kȧ) | 108 | 43°20'N | 84°35'W |
| Ithaca, N.Y., U.S. | 105 | 42°25'N | 76°30'W |
| Itháka, i., Grc. (ē'thä-kē) | 175 | 38°27'N | 20°48'E |
| Itigi, Tan. | 237 | 5°42'S | 34°29'E |
| Itimbiri, r., D.R.C. | 236 | 2°40'N | 23°30'E |
| Itoko, D.R.C. (ē-tō'kō) | 232 | 1°13'S | 22°07'E |
| Itu, Braz. (ē-too') | 141a | 23°16'S | 47°16'W |
| Ituango, Col. (ē-twän'gō) | 142 | 7°07'N | 75°44'W |
| Ituiutaba, Braz. (ē-too-ēoo-tä'bä) | 143 | 18°56'S | 49°17'W |
| Itumirim, Braz. (ē-too-mē-rē'N) | 141a | 21°20'S | 44°51'W |
| Itundujia Santa Cruz, Mex. (ē-toon-doo-hē'ä sä'n-tä kroo'z) | 131 | 16°50'N | 97°43'W |
| Iturbide, Mex. (ē'toor-bē'dhä) | 132a | 19°38'N | 89°31'W |
| Iturup, i., Russia (ē-too-roop') | 185 | 45°35'N | 147°15'E |
| Ituzaingo, Arg. (ē-too-zä-ē'n-gô) | 144a | 34°40'S | 58°40'W |
| Itzehoe, Ger. (ē'tzĕ-hō) | 168 | 53°55'N | 9°31'E |
| Iuka, Ms., U.S. (ī-ū'kȧ) | 124 | 34°47'N | 88°10'W |
| Iúna, Braz. (ē-oo'-nä) | 141a | 20°22'S | 41°32'W |
| Ivanhoe, Austl. (ĭv'ăn-hō) | 222 | 32°53'S | 144°10'E |
| Ivanivka, Ukr. | 176 | 46°43'N | 34°33'E |
| Ivano-Frankivs'k, Ukr. | 181 | 48°53'N | 24°46'E |
| Ivanopil', Ukr. | 177 | 49°51'N | 28°11'E |
| Ivanovo, Russia (ē-vä'nô-vō) | 178 | 57°02'N | 41°54'E |
| Ivanovo, prov., Russia | 176 | 56°55'N | 40°30'E |
| Ivanteyevka, Russia (ē-vȧn-tyĕ'yĕf-kȧ) | 186b | 55°58'N | 37°56'E |
| Ivdel', Russia (ĭv'dyĕl) | 186a | 60°42'N | 60°27'E |
| Iviza *see* Eivissa, i., Spain | 156 | 38°55'N | 1°24'E |
| Ivohibé, Madag. (ē-vō-hē-bā') | 233 | 22°28'S | 46°59'E |
| Ivory Coast *see* Cote d'Ivoire, nation, Afr. | 230 | 7°43'N | 6°30'W |
| Ivrea, Italy (ē-vrĕ'ä) | 162 | 45°25'N | 7°54'E |
| Ivry-sur-Seine, Fr. | 171b | 48°49'N | 2°23'E |
| Ivujivik, Can. | 91 | 62°17'N | 77°52'W |
| Ivvavik National Park, rec., Can. | 103 | 69°10'N | 139°30'W |
| Iwaki, Japan | 210 | 37°03'N | 140°57'E |
| Iwate Yama, mtn., Japan (ē-wä-tĕ-yä'mä) | 210 | 39°50'N | 140°56'E |
| Iwatsuki, Japan | 211a | 35°48'N | 139°43'E |
| Iwaya, Japan (ē'wȧ-yȧ) | 211b | 34°35'N | 135°01'E |
| Iwo, Nig. | 230 | 7°38'N | 4°11'E |
| Ixcateopán, Mex. (ēs-kä-tä-ō-pän') | 130 | 18°29'N | 99°49'W |
| Ixelles, Bel. | 159a | 50°49'N | 4°23'E |
| Ixhautlán, Mex. (ēs-wȧt-län') | 130 | 20°41'N | 98°01'W |
| Ixhuatán, Mex. (ēs-hwä-tän') | 131 | 16°19'N | 94°30'W |
| Ixmiquilpan, Mex. (ēs-mē-kēl'pän) | 130 | 20°30'N | 99°12'W |
| Ixopo, S. Afr. | 233c | 30°10'S | 30°04'E |
| Ixtacalco, Mex. (ēs-tȧ-käl'kō) | 131a | 19°23'N | 99°07'W |
| Ixtaltepec, Mex. (ēs-täl-tĕ-pĕk') | 131 | 16°33'N | 95°04'W |
| Ixtapalapa, Mex. (ēs'tä-pä-lä'pä) | 131a | 19°21'N | 99°06'W |
| Ixtapaluca, Mex. (ēs'tä-pä-loo'kä) | 131a | 19°18'N | 98°53'W |
| Ixtepec, Mex. (ēks-tĕ'pĕk) | 131 | 16°37'N | 95°09'W |
| Ixtlahuaca, Mex. (ēs-tlä-wä'kä) | 130 | 19°34'N | 99°46'W |
| Ixtlán de Juárez, Mex. (ēs-tlän' dā hwä'rāz) | 131 | 17°20'N | 96°29'W |
| Ixtlán del Río, Mex. (ēs-tlän'dĕl rē'ō) | 130 | 21°05'N | 104°22'W |
| Iya, r., Russia | 184 | 53°45'N | 99°30'E |
| Iyo-Nada, b., Japan (ē'yō nä-dä) | 211 | 33°33'N | 132°07'E |
| Izabal, Guat. (ē'zä-bäl') | 132 | 15°23'N | 89°10'W |
| Izabal, Lago, l., Guat. | 132 | 15°30'N | 89°04'W |
| Izalco, El Sal. (ē-zäl'kō) | 132 | 13°50'N | 89°40'W |
| Izamal, Mex. (ē-zä-mä'l) | 132a | 20°55'N | 89°00'W |
| Izberbash, Russia | 182 | 42°33'N | 47°52'E |
| Izhevsk, Russia (ē-zhyĕfsk') | 178 | 56°50'N | 53°15'E |
| Izhma, Russia (ĭzh'mȧ) | 180 | 65°00'N | 54°05'E |
| Izhma, r., Russia | 180 | 64°00'N | 53°00'E |
| Izhora, r., Russia (ēz'hô-rȧ) | 186c | 59°36'N | 30°20'E |
| Izmail, Ukr. | 181 | 45°00'N | 28°49'E |
| İzmir, Tur. (ĭz-mēr') | 198 | 38°25'N | 27°05'E |
| İzmit, Tur. (ĭz-mēt') | 163 | 40°45'N | 29°45'E |
| Iznajar, Embalse de, res., Spain | 172 | 37°15'N | 4°30'W |
| Iztaccíhuatl, mtn., Mex. | 130 | 19°10'N | 98°38'W |
| Izuhara, Japan (ē'zoo-hä'rä) | 211 | 34°11'N | 129°18'E |
| Izumi-Ōtsu, Japan (ē'zoo-moo ō'tsoo) | 211b | 34°30'N | 135°24'E |
| Izumo, Japan (ē'zoo-mō) | 211 | 35°22'N | 132°45'E |
| Izu Shichitō, is., Japan | 205 | 34°32'N | 139°25'E |


## J


| PLACE (Pronunciation) | PAGE | LAT. | LONG. |
|---|---|---|---|
| Jabal, Bahr al, r., Sudan | 231 | 7°30'N | 31°00'E |
| Jabalpur, India | 199 | 23°18'N | 79°59'E |
| Jablonec nad Nisou, Czech Rep. (yäb'lô-nyĕts) | 168 | 50°43'N | 15°12'E |
| Jablunkov Pass, p., Eur. (yäb'lôn-kôf) | 169 | 49°31'N | 18°35'E |
| Jaboatão, Braz. (zhä-bô-ä-touN) | 143 | 8°14'S | 35°08'W |
| Jaca, Spain (hä'kä) | 173 | 42°35'N | 0°30'W |
| Jacala, Mex. (hä-kä'lä) | 130 | 21°01'N | 99°11'W |
| Jacaltenango, Guat. (hä-käl-tĕ-nàn'gō) | 132 | 15°39'N | 91°41'W |
| Jacarézinho, Braz. (zhä-kä-rĕ'zē-nyō) | 143 | 23°13'S | 49°58'W |
| Jachymov, Czech Rep. (yä'chĭ-môf) | 168 | 50°22'N | 12°51'E |
| Jacinto City, Tx., U.S. (hä-sēn'tō) (jȧ-sĭn'tō) | 123a | 29°45'N | 95°14'W |
| Jacksboro, Tx., U.S. (jăks'bŭr-ō) | 120 | 33°13'N | 98°11'W |
| Jackson, Al., U.S. (jăk'sŭn) | 124 | 31°31'N | 87°52'W |
| Jackson, Ca., U.S. | 118 | 38°22'N | 120°47'W |
| Jackson, Ga., U.S. | 124 | 33°19'N | 83°55'W |
| Jackson, Ky., U.S. | 124 | 37°32'N | 83°17'W |
| Jackson, La., U.S. | 123 | 30°50'N | 91°13'W |
| Jackson, Mi., U.S. | 105 | 42°15'N | 84°25'W |
| Jackson, Mn., U.S. | 112 | 43°37'N | 95°00'W |
| Jackson, Mo., U.S. | 121 | 37°23'N | 89°40'W |
| Jackson, Ms., U.S. | 105 | 32°17'N | 90°10'W |
| Jackson, Oh., U.S. | 108 | 39°00'N | 82°40'W |
| Jackson, Tn., U.S. | 105 | 35°37'N | 88°49'W |
| Jackson, Port, b., Austl. | 217b | 33°50'S | 151°18'E |
| Jackson Lake, l., Wy., U.S. | 115 | 43°57'N | 110°28'W |
| Jacksonville, Al., U.S. (jăk'sŭn-vĭl) | 124 | 33°52'N | 85°45'W |
| Jacksonville, Fl., U.S. | 105 | 30°20'N | 81°40'W |
| Jacksonville, Il., U.S. | 105 | 39°43'N | 90°12'W |
| Jacksonville, Tx., U.S. | 123 | 31°58'N | 95°18'W |
| Jacksonville Beach, Fl., U.S. | 125 | 31°18'N | 81°25'W |
| Jacmel, Haiti (zhȧk-mĕl') | 135 | 18°15'N | 72°30'W |
| Jaco, l., Mex. (hä'kō) | 122 | 27°51'N | 103°50'W |
| Jacobābād, Pak. | 202 | 28°22'N | 68°30'E |
| Jacobina, Braz. (zhä-kô-bē'nȧ) | 143 | 11°13'S | 40°30'W |
| Jacques-Cartier, r., Can. | 102b | 47°04'N | 71°28'W |
| Jacques Cartier, Détroit de, strt., Can. | 100 | 50°07'S | 63°58'W |
| Jacques-Cartier, Mont, mtn., Can. | 100 | 48°59'N | 66°00'W |
| Jacquet River, Can. (zhȧ-kĕ') | 100 | 47°55'N | 66°00'W |
| Jacutinga, Braz. (zhȧ-koo-tēn'gä) | 141a | 22°17'S | 46°36'W |
| Jadebusen, b., Ger. | 168 | 53°28'N | 8°17'E |
| Jadotville *see* Likasi, D.R.C. | 232 | 10°59'S | 26°44'E |
| Jaén, Peru (kä-ĕ'n) | 142 | 5°38'S | 78°49'W |
| Jaen, Spain | 162 | 37°45'N | 3°48'W |
| Jaffa, Cape, c., Austl. (jăf'ȧ) | 220 | 36°58'S | 139°29'E |
| Jaffna, Sri L. (jăf'nȧ) | 203 | 9°44'N | 80°09'E |
| Jagüey Grande, Cuba (hä'gwā grän'dā) | 134 | 22°35'N | 81°05'W |
| Jahore Strait, strt., Asia | 197b | 1°22'N | 103°37'E |
| Jahrom, Iran | 198 | 28°30'N | 53°28'E |
| Jaibo, r., Cuba (hä-ē'bō) | 135 | 20°10'N | 75°20'W |
| Jaipur, India | 199 | 27°00'N | 75°50'E |
| Jaisalmer, India | 202 | 27°00'N | 70°54'E |
| Jajce, Bos. (yī'tsĕ) | 175 | 44°20'N | 17°19'E |
| Jajpur, India | 199 | 20°49'N | 86°37'E |
| Jakarta, Indon. (yä-kär'tä) | 212 | 6°17'S | 106°45'E |
| Jakobstad, Fin. (yȧ'kôb-stȧdh) | 160 | 63°33'N | 22°31'E |
| Jalacingo, Mex. (hä-lä-sĭŋ'gō) | 131 | 19°47'N | 97°16'W |
| Jalālābād, Afg. (jŭ-lä-lȧ-bäd) | 199a | 34°25'N | 70°27'E |
| Jalālah al Baḩrīyah, Jabal, mts., Egypt | 238b | 29°20'N | 32°00'E |
| Jalapa, Guat. (hä-lä'pȧ) | 132 | 14°38'N | 89°58'W |
| Jalapa de Díaz, Mex. | 131 | 18°06'N | 96°33'W |
| Jalapa del Marqués, Mex. (dĕl mär-kās') | 131 | 16°30'N | 95°29'W |
| Jaleswar, Nepal | 202 | 26°50'N | 85°55'E |
| Jalgaon, India | 202 | 21°08'N | 75°33'E |
| Jalisco, Mex. (hä-lēs'kō) | 130 | 21°27'N | 104°54'W |
| Jalisco, state, Mex. | 128 | 20°07'N | 104°45'W |
| Jalón, r., Spain (hä-lōn') | 172 | 41°22'N | 1°46'W |
| Jalostotitlán, Mex. (hä-lōs-tē-tlán') | 130 | 21°09'N | 102°30'W |
| Jalpa, Mex. (häl'pȧ) | 131 | 18°12'N | 93°06'W |
| Jalpa, Mex. (häl'pä) | 130 | 21°40'N | 103°04'W |
| Jalpan, Mex. (häl'pän) | 130 | 21°13'N | 99°31'W |
| Jaltepec, Mex. (häl-tȧ-pĕk') | 131 | 17°20'N | 95°15'W |
| Jaltipan, Mex. (häl-tȧ-pän') | 131 | 17°59'N | 94°42'W |
| Jaltocan, Mex. (häl-tô-kän') | 130 | 21°08'N | 98°32'W |
| Jamaare, r., Nig. | 235 | 11°50'N | 10°10'E |
| Jamaica, nation, N.A. | 129 | 17°45'N | 78°00'W |
| Jamaica Cay, i., Bah. | 135 | 22°45'N | 75°55'W |
| Jamālpur, Bngl. | 202 | 24°56'N | 89°58'E |
| Jamay, Mex. (hä-mī') | 130 | 20°16'N | 102°43'W |
| Jambi, Indon. (mäm'bē) | 212 | 1°45'S | 103°28'E |
| James, r., Mo., U.S. | 121 | 36°51'N | 93°22'W |
| James, r., Va., U.S. | 107 | 37°35'N | 77°50'W |
| James, r., U.S. | 106 | 46°25'N | 98°55'W |
| James, Lake, res., N.C., U.S. | 125 | 36°07'N | 81°48'W |
| James Bay, b., Can. (jāmz) | 93 | 53°53'N | 80°40'W |
| Jamesburg, N.J., U.S. (jāmz'bûrg) | 110a | 40°21'N | 74°26'W |
| James Point, c., Bah. | 134 | 25°20'N | 76°30'W |
| James Range, mts., Austl. | 220 | 24°15'S | 133°30'E |
| James Ross, i., Ant. | 139 | 64°20'S | 58°20'W |
| Jamestown, S. Afr. | 233c | 31°07'S | 26°49'E |
| Jamestown, N.D., U.S. | 104 | 46°54'N | 98°42'W |
| Jamestown, N.Y., U.S. (jāmz'toun) | 105 | 42°05'N | 79°15'W |
| Jamestown, R.I., U.S. | 110b | 41°30'N | 71°21'W |
| Jamestown Reservoir, res., N.D., U.S. | 112 | 47°16'N | 98°40'W |
| Jamiltepec, Mex. (hä-mēl-tȧ-pĕk) | 131 | 16°16'N | 97°54'W |
| Jammerbugten, b., Den. | 166 | 57°20'N | 9°28'E |
| Jammu, India | 199 | 32°50'N | 74°52'E |
| Jammu and Kashmir, state, India (kȧsh-mēr') | 199 | 34°30'N | 76°00'E |
| Jammu and Kashmīr, hist. reg., Asia (kȧsh-mēr') | 199 | 39°10'N | 75°05'E |
| Jāmnagar, India (jäm-nû'gŭr) | 199 | 22°33'N | 70°03'E |
| Jamshedpur, India (jäm'shĕd-poor) | 199 | 22°52'N | 86°11'E |
| Jándula, r., Spain (hän'doo-lȧ) | 172 | 38°28'N | 3°52'W |
| Janesville, Wi., U.S. (jānz'vĭl) | 113 | 42°41'N | 89°03'W |
| Janin, W.B. | 197a | 32°27'N | 35°19'E |
| Jan Mayen, i., Nor. (yän mī'ĕn) | 160 | 70°59'N | 8°05'W |
| Jánoshalma, Hung. (yä'nôsh-hôl-mô) | 169 | 46°17'N | 19°18'E |
| Janów Lubelski, Pol. (yä'noof lŭ-bĕl'skĭ) | 169 | 50°40'N | 22°25'E |
| Januária, Braz. (zhä-nwä'rē-ä) | 143 | 15°31'S | 44°17'W |
| Japan, nation, Asia (jȧ-păn') | 205 | 36°30'N | 133°30'E |
| Japan, Sea of, sea, Asia (jȧ-păn') | 205 | 40°08'N | 132°55'E |
| Japeri, Braz. (zhȧ-pĕ'rē) | 144b | 22°38'S | 43°40'W |
| Japurá (Caquetá), r., S.A. | 142 | 2°00'S | 68°00'W |
| Jarabacoa, Dom. Rep. (kä-rä-bä-kō'ä) | 135 | 19°05'N | 70°40'W |
| Jaral del Progreso, Mex. (hä-räl dĕl prô-grā'sō) | 130 | 20°21'N | 101°05'W |
| Jarama, r., Spain (hä-rä'mä) | 172 | 40°33'N | 3°30'W |
| Jarash, Jord. | 197a | 32°17'N | 35°53'E |
| Jardines, Banco, bk., Cuba (bä'n-kō-här-dē'nâs) | 134 | 21°45'N | 81°40'W |
| Jargalant, Mong. | 208 | 46°28'N | 115°10'E |
| Jari, r., Braz. (zhä-rē) | 143 | 0°28'N | 53°00'W |
| Jarocin, Pol. (yä-rō'tsyēn) | 169 | 51°58'N | 17°31'E |
| Jarosław, Pol. (yȧ-rôs-wȧf) | 161 | 50°01'N | 22°41'E |
| Jarud Qi, China (jya-loo-tŭ shyē) | 205 | 44°35'N | 120°40'E |
| Jasin, Malay. | 197b | 2°19'N | 102°26'E |
| Jašiūnai, Lith. (dzȧ-shoo-nȧ'yē) | 167 | 54°27'N | 25°25'E |
| Jāsk, Iran (jäsk) | 198 | 25°46'N | 57°48'E |
| Jasło, Pol. (yȧs'wō) | 169 | 49°44'N | 21°28'E |
| Jason Bay, b., Malay. | 197b | 1°53'N | 104°14'E |
| Jasonville, In., U.S. (jā'sŭn-vĭl) | 108 | 39°10'N | 87°15'W |
| Jasper, Can. | 90 | 52°53'N | 118°05'W |
| Jasper, Al., U.S. (jăs'pēr) | 124 | 33°50'N | 87°17'W |
| Jasper, Fl., U.S. | 125 | 30°30'N | 82°56'W |
| Jasper, In., U.S. | 108 | 38°20'N | 86°55'W |
| Jasper, Mn., U.S. | 112 | 43°51'N | 96°22'W |
| Jasper, Tx., U.S. | 123 | 30°55'N | 93°59'W |
| Jasper National Park, rec., Can. | 92 | 53°09'N | 117°45'W |
| Jászapáti, Hung. (yäs'ō-pä-tē) | 169 | 47°29'N | 20°10'E |
| Jászberény, Hung. | 169 | 47°30'N | 19°56'E |
| Jatibonico, Cuba (hä-tē-bō-nē'kō) | 134 | 22°00'N | 79°15'W |
| Jauja, Peru (kä-ō'k) | 142 | 11°43'S | 75°32'W |
| Jaumave, Mex. (hou-mä'vȧ) | 130 | 23°23'N | 99°24'W |
| Jaunjelgava, Lat. (youn'yĕl'gȧ-vȧ) | 180 | 56°37'N | 25°06'E |
| Java (Jawa), i., Indon. | 212 | 8°35'S | 111°11'E |
| Javari, r., S.A. (kȧ-vä-rē) | 142 | 4°25'S | 72°07'W |
| Java Trench, deep | 212 | 9°45'S | 107°30'E |
| Jawa, Laut (Java Sea), sea, Indon. | 212 | 5°10'S | 110°30'E |
| Jawor, Pol. (yä'vôr) | 168 | 51°04'N | 16°12'E |
| Jaworzno, Pol. (yä-vōzh'nō) | 169 | 50°11'N | 19°18'E |
| Jaya, Puncak, mtn., Indon. | 213 | 4°00'S | 137°00'E |
| Jayapura, Indon. | 212 | 2°30'S | 140°45'E |
| Jayb, Wādī al (Ha'Arava), val., Asia | 197a | 30°33'N | 35°10'E |


ng-sing; ŋ-baŋk; N-nasalized n; nŏd; cŏmmit; ōld; ôbey; ôrder; oi-boil; fōōd; ŏ-as oo in foot; ou-out; s-soft; sh-dish; th-thin; pūre; ûnite; ûrn; stŭd; circŭs; ü-as in French tu; '-indeterminate vowel.

| PLACE (Pronunciation) | PAGE | LAT. | LONG. |
|---|---|---|---|
| Jazzīn, Leb. | 197a | 33°34′N | 35°37′E |
| Jeanerette, La., U.S. (jĕn-ēr-et′) (zhän-rĕt′) | 123 | 29°54′N | 91°41′W |
| Jebba, Nig. (jĕb′á) | 230 | 9°07′N | 4°46′E |
| Jeddore Lake, l., Can. | 101 | 48°07′N | 55°35′W |
| Jędrzejów, Pol. (yăN-dzhā′yóf) | 169 | 50°38′N | 20°18′E |
| Jefferson, Ga., U.S. (jĕf′ēr-sŭn) | 124 | 34°05′N | 83°35′W |
| Jefferson, Ia., U.S. | 113 | 42°10′N | 94°22′W |
| Jefferson, La., U.S. | 110d | 29°57′N | 90°04′W |
| Jefferson, Tx., U.S. | 123 | 32°47′N | 94°21′W |
| Jefferson, Wi., U.S. | 113 | 42°59′N | 88°45′W |
| Jefferson, r., Mt., U.S. | 115 | 45°37′N | 112°22′W |
| Jefferson, Mount, mtn., Or., U.S. | 114 | 44°41′N | 121°50′W |
| Jefferson City, Mo., U.S. | 105 | 38°34′N | 92°10′W |
| Jeffersontown, Ky., U.S. (jĕf′ēr-sŭn-toun) | 111h | 38°11′N | 85°34′W |
| Jeffersonville, In., U.S. (jĕf′ēr-sŭn-vĭl) | 111h | 38°17′N | 85°44′W |
| Jega, Nig. | 235 | 12°15′N | 4°23′E |
| Jehol, hist. reg., China (jĕ-hŏl) | 205 | 42°31′N | 118°12′E |
| Jēkabpils, Lat. (yĕk′áb-pĭls) | 180 | 56°29′N | 25°50′E |
| Jelenia Góra, Pol. (yĕ-lĕn′yá gō′rá) | 168 | 50°53′N | 15°43′E |
| Jelgava, Lat. | 167 | 56°39′N | 23°42′E |
| Jellico, Tn., U.S. (jĕl′ĭ-kō) | 124 | 36°34′N | 84°06′W |
| Jemez Indian Reservation, I.R., N.M., U.S. | 119 | 35°35′N | 106°45′W |
| Jena, Ger. (yā′nä) | 161 | 50°55′N | 11°37′E |
| Jenkins, Ky., U.S. (jĕŋ′kĭnz) | 125 | 37°09′N | 82°38′W |
| Jenkintown, Pa., U.S. (jĕŋ′kĭn-toun) | 110f | 40°06′N | 75°08′W |
| Jennings, La., U.S. (jĕn′ĭngz) | 123 | 30°14′N | 92°40′W |
| Jennings, Mi., U.S. | 108 | 44°20′N | 85°20′W |
| Jennings, Mo., U.S. | 117e | 38°43′N | 90°16′W |
| Jequitinhonha, r., Braz. (zhĕ-kē-tēŋ-ō′n-yä) | 143 | 16°47′S | 41°19′W |
| Jérémie, Haiti (zhā-rá-mē′) | 135 | 18°40′N | 74°10′W |
| Jeremoabo, Braz. (zhĕ-rā-mō-á′bō) | 143 | 10°03′S | 38°13′W |
| Jerez, Punta, c., Mex. (pōō′n-tä-ĸĕ-räz′) | 131 | 23°04′N | 97°44′W |
| Jerez de la Frontera, Spain | 162 | 36°42′N | 6°09′W |
| Jerez de los Caballeros, Spain | 172 | 38°20′N | 6°45′W |
| Jericho, Austl. (jĕr′ĭ-kō) | 219 | 23°38′S | 146°24′E |
| Jericho, S. Afr. (jĕr-ĭkô) | 238c | 25°16′N | 27°47′E |
| Jericho see Arīḥā, W.B. | 197a | 31°51′N | 35°28′E |
| Jerome, Az., U.S. (jĕ-rōm′) | 104 | 34°45′N | 112°10′W |
| Jerome, Id., U.S. | 115 | 42°44′N | 114°31′W |
| Jersey, dep., Eur. | 170 | 49°15′N | 2°10′W |
| Jersey, i., Jersey (jûr′zĭ) | 161 | 49°13′N | 2°07′W |
| Jersey City, N.J., U.S. | 105 | 40°43′N | 74°05′W |
| Jersey Shore, Pa., U.S. | 109 | 41°10′N | 77°15′W |
| Jerseyville, Il., U.S. (jēr′zē-vĭl) | 121 | 39°07′N | 90°18′W |
| Jerusalem, Isr. (jē-rōō′sá-lĕm) | 198 | 31°46′N | 35°14′E |
| Jesup, Ga., U.S. (jĕs′ŭp) | 125 | 31°36′N | 81°53′W |
| Jesús Carranza, Mex. (hē-sōō′s-kär-rá′n-zä) | 131 | 17°26′N | 95°01′W |
| Jewel, Or., U.S. (jū′ĕl) | 116c | 45°56′N | 123°30′W |
| Jewel Cave National Monument, rec., S.D., U.S. | 112 | 43°44′N | 103°52′W |
| Jhālawār, India | 199 | 24°30′N | 76°00′E |
| Jhang Maghiāna, Pak. | 202 | 31°21′N | 72°19′E |
| Jhānsi, India (jän′sē) | 199 | 25°29′N | 78°32′E |
| Jharkhand, state, India | 199 | 23°30′N | 85°00′E |
| Jhārsuguda, India | 202 | 22°51′N | 84°13′E |
| Jhelum, Pak. | 199 | 32°59′N | 73°43′E |
| Jhelum, r., Asia (jā′lŭm) | 199 | 31°40′N | 71°51′E |
| Jiading, China (jyä-dĭŋ) | 206 | 31°23′N | 121°15′E |
| Jialing, r., China (jyä-lĭŋ) | 204 | 32°30′N | 105°30′E |
| Jiamusi, China | 210 | 46°50′N | 130°21′E |
| Ji'an, China (jyē-än) | 205 | 27°15′N | 115°10′E |
| Ji'an, China | 208 | 41°00′N | 126°04′E |
| Jianchangying, China (jyĕn-chäŋ-yĭŋ) | 206 | 40°09′N | 118°47′E |
| Jiangcun, China (jyän-tsòn) | 207a | 23°16′N | 113°14′E |
| Jiangling, China (jyäŋ-lĭŋ) | 205 | 30°30′N | 112°10′E |
| Jiangshanzhen, China (jyäŋ-shän-jŭn) | 206 | 36°39′N | 120°31′E |
| Jiangsu, prov., China (jyäŋ-sōō) | 205 | 33°45′N | 120°30′E |
| Jiangwan, China (jyäŋ-wän) | 207b | 31°18′N | 121°29′E |
| Jiangxi, prov., China (jyäŋ-shyē) | 205 | 28°15′N | 116°00′E |
| Jiangyin, China (jyäŋ-yĭn) | 209 | 31°54′N | 120°15′E |
| Jianli, China (jyĕn-lē) | 209 | 29°50′N | 112°52′E |
| Jianning, China (jyĕn-nĭŋ) | 209 | 26°50′N | 116°55′E |
| Jian'ou, China (jyĕn-ō) | 209 | 27°10′N | 118°18′E |
| Jianshi, China (jyĕn-shr) | 209 | 30°40′N | 109°45′E |
| Jiaohe, China | 208 | 38°03′N | 116°18′E |
| Jiaohe, China (jyou-hŭ) | 208 | 43°40′N | 127°20′E |
| Jiaoxian, China (jyou shyĕn) | 205 | 36°18′N | 120°01′E |
| Jiaozuo, China (jyou-dzwô) | 206 | 35°15′N | 113°18′E |
| Jiashan, China (jyä-shän) | 206 | 32°41′N | 118°00′E |
| Jiaxing, China (jyä-shyĭŋ) | 205 | 30°45′N | 120°50′E |
| Jiayu, China (jyä-yōō) | 209 | 30°00′N | 114°00′E |
| Jiazhou Wan, b., China (jyä-jō wän) | 205 | 36°10′N | 119°55′E |
| Jicarilla Apache Indian Reservation, I.R., N.M., U.S. | 119 | 36°45′N | 107°00′W |
| Jicarón, Isla, i., Pan. (ĸē-kä-rōn′) | 133 | 7°14′N | 81°41′W |
| Jiddah, Sau. Ar. | 198 | 21°30′N | 39°15′E |
| Jieshou, China | 206 | 33°17′N | 115°20′E |
| Jieyang, China (jyĕ-yäŋ) | 205 | 23°38′N | 116°20′E |
| Jiggalong, Austl. (jĭg′á-lông) | 218 | 23°20′S | 120°45′E |
| Jiguani, Cuba (ĸē-gwä-nē′) | 134 | 20°20′N | 76°30′W |
| Jigüey, Bahía, b., Cuba (bä-ē′ä-ĸĕ-gwā) | 134 | 22°15′N | 78°10′W |
| Jihlava, Czech Rep. (yē′hlá-vá) | 161 | 49°23′N | 15°33′E |
| Jijel, Alg. | 161 | 36°49′N | 5°47′E |
| Jijia, r., Rom. | 169 | 47°35′N | 27°02′E |
| Jijiashi, China (jyē-jyä-shr) | 206 | 32°10′N | 120°17′E |
| Jijiga, Eth. | 238a | 9°15′N | 42°48′E |
| Jilin, China (jyē-lĭn) | 205 | 43°58′N | 126°40′E |
| Jilin, prov., China | 205 | 44°20′N | 124°50′E |
| Jiloca, r., Spain (ĸē-lō′kä) | 172 | 41°13′N | 1°30′W |
| Jilotepeque, Guat. (ĸē-lō-tĕ-pĕ′kĕ) | 132 | 14°39′N | 89°36′W |
| Jima, Eth. | 231 | 7°41′N | 36°52′E |
| Jimbolia, Rom. (zhĭm-bô′lyä) | 175 | 45°45′N | 20°44′E |
| Jiménez, Mex. (ĸē-mā′nâz) | 130 | 24°12′N | 98°29′W |
| Jiménez, Mex. | 122 | 27°09′N | 104°55′W |
| Jiménez, Mex. | 122 | 29°03′N | 100°42′W |
| Jiménez del Téul, Mex. (tĕ-ōō′l) | 130 | 21°28′N | 103°51′W |
| Jimo, China (jyē-mwo) | 208 | 36°22′N | 120°28′E |
| Jim Thorpe, Pa., U.S. (jĭm′ thôrp′) | 109 | 40°50′N | 75°45′W |
| Jinan, China (jyē-nän) | 205 | 36°40′N | 117°01′E |
| Jincheng, China (jyĭn-chŭŋ) | 208 | 35°30′N | 112°50′E |
| Jindřichův Hradec, Czech Rep. (yēn′d′r-zhĭ-kōōf hrä′dĕts) | 168 | 49°09′N | 15°02′E |
| Jing, r., China (jyĭŋ) | 208 | 34°40′N | 108°20′E |
| Jing'anji, China (jyĭŋ-än-jē) | 206 | 34°30′N | 116°55′E |
| Jingdezhen, China (jyĭŋ-dŭ-jŭn) | 209 | 29°18′N | 117°18′E |
| Jingjiang, China (jyĭŋ-jyäŋ) | 206 | 32°02′N | 120°15′E |
| Jingning, China (jyĭŋ-nĭŋ) | 208 | 35°28′N | 105°50′E |
| Jingpo Hu, l., China (jyĭŋ-pwo hōō) | 208 | 44°10′N | 129°00′E |
| Jingxian, China (jyĭŋ shyĕn) | 209 | 26°32′N | 109°45′E |
| Jingxian, China | 206 | 37°43′N | 116°17′E |
| Jingxing, China (jyĭŋ-shyĭŋ) | 208 | 47°00′N | 123°00′E |
| Jingzhi, China (jyĭŋ-jr) | 206 | 36°19′N | 119°23′E |
| Jinhua, China (jyĭn-hwä) | 205 | 29°10′N | 119°42′E |
| Jining, China (jyē-nĭŋ) | 205 | 35°26′N | 116°34′E |
| Jining, China | 208 | 41°00′N | 113°10′E |
| Jinja, Ug. (jĭn′jä) | 231 | 0°26′N | 33°12′E |
| Jinotega, Nic. (kē-nô-tā′gä) | 132 | 13°07′N | 86°00′W |
| Jinotepe, Nic. (kē-nô-tā′på) | 132 | 11°52′N | 86°12′W |
| Jinqiao, China (jyĭn-chyou) | 206 | 31°46′N | 116°46′E |
| Jinshan, China (jyĭn-shän) | 207b | 30°53′N | 121°09′E |
| Jinta, China (jyĭn-tä) | 204 | 40°11′N | 98°45′E |
| Jintan, China (jyĭn-tän) | 206 | 31°47′N | 119°34′E |
| Jin Xian, China (jyĭn shyĕn) | 208 | 39°04′N | 121°40′E |
| Jinxiang, China (jyĭn-shyäŋ) | 206 | 35°03′N | 116°20′E |
| Jinyun, China (jyĭn-yòn) | 209 | 28°40′N | 120°08′E |
| Jinzhai, China (jyĭn-jī) | 206 | 31°41′N | 115°51′E |
| Jinzhou, China (jyĭn-jō) | 205 | 41°00′N | 121°00′E |
| Jinzhou Wan, b., China (jyĭn-jō wän) | 206 | 39°07′N | 121°17′E |
| Jinzū-Gawa, r., Japan (jĕn′zōō gä′wä) | 211 | 36°26′N | 137°18′E |
| Jipijapa, Ec. (kē-pē-hä′pä) | 142 | 1°36′S | 80°52′W |
| Jiquilisco, El Sal. (ĸē-kē-lē′s-kô) | 132 | 13°18′N | 88°32′W |
| Jiquilpan de Juárez, Mex. (ĸē-kēl′pän dā hwä′räz) | 130 | 20°00′N | 102°43′W |
| Jiquipilco, Mex. (hē-kē-pē′l-kô) | 131a | 19°32′N | 99°37′W |
| Jitotol, Mex. (ĸē-tô-tōl′) | 131 | 17°03′N | 92°54′W |
| Jiu, r., Rom. | 175 | 44°45′N | 23°17′E |
| Jiujiang, China (jyô-jyän) | 207a | 22°50′N | 113°02′E |
| Jiujiang, China | 205 | 29°43′N | 116°00′E |
| Jiuquan, China (jyô-chyän) | 204 | 39°46′N | 98°26′E |
| Jiurongcheng, China (jyô-rôŋ-chŭŋ) | 206 | 37°23′N | 122°31′E |
| Jiushouzhang, China (jyô-shō-jäŋ) | 206 | 35°59′N | 115°52′E |
| Jiuwuqing, China (jyô-wōō-chyĭŋ) | 208a | 32°31′N | 116°51′E |
| Jiuyongnian, China (jyô-yôŋ-nĭĕn) | 206 | 36°41′N | 114°46′E |
| Jixian, China (jyē shyĕn) | 206 | 35°25′N | 114°03′E |
| Jixian, China | 206 | 37°37′N | 115°33′E |
| Jixian, China | 206 | 40°03′N | 117°25′E |
| Jiyun, r., China (jyē-yōōn) | 206 | 39°35′N | 117°34′E |
| Joachimsthal, Ger. | 159b | 52°58′N | 13°45′E |
| João Pessoa, Braz. | 143 | 7°09′S | 34°45′W |
| João Ribeiro, Braz. (zhô-un-rē-bā′rō) | 141a | 20°42′S | 44°03′W |
| Jobabo, r., Cuba (hō-bä′bä) | 134 | 20°50′N | 77°15′W |
| Jock, r., Can. (jŏk) | 102c | 45°08′N | 75°51′W |
| Jocotepec, Mex. (jô-kō-tä-pĕk′) | 130 | 20°17′N | 103°26′W |
| Jodar, Spain (hō′där) | 172 | 37°54′N | 3°20′W |
| Jodhpur, India (jŏd′pōōr) | 199 | 26°23′N | 73°00′E |
| Joensuu, Fin. (yô-ĕn′sōō) | 167 | 62°35′N | 29°46′E |
| Joffre, Mount, mtn., Can. (jŏ′f′r) | 95 | 50°32′N | 115°13′W |
| Jõgeva, Est. (yû′gĕ-vá) | 167 | 58°45′N | 26°23′E |
| Joggins, Can. (jŏ′gĭnz) | 100 | 45°42′N | 64°27′W |
| Johannesburg, S. Afr. (yô-hän′ĕs-bôrgh) | 232 | 26°08′S | 27°54′E |
| John Day, r., Or., U.S. (jŏn′dā) | 114 | 44°46′N | 120°15′W |
| John Day, Middle Fork, r., Or., U.S. | 114 | 44°53′N | 119°04′W |
| John Day, North Fork, r., Or., U.S. | 114 | 45°03′N | 118°50′W |
| John Day Dam, Or., U.S. | 114 | 45°40′N | 120°15′W |
| John H. Kerr Reservoir, res., U.S. | 107 | 36°30′N | 78°38′W |
| John Martin Reservoir, res., Co., U.S. (jŏn mär′tĭn) | 120 | 37°57′N | 103°04′W |
| Johnson, r., Or., U.S. (jŏn′sŭn) | 116c | 45°27′N | 122°20′W |
| Johnsonburg, Pa., U.S. (jŏn′sŭn-bûrg) | 109 | 41°30′N | 78°40′W |
| Johnson City, Il., U.S. (jŏn′sŭn) | 108 | 37°50′N | 88°55′W |
| Johnson City, N.Y., U.S. | 109 | 42°10′N | 76°00′W |
| Johnson City, Tn., U.S. | 105 | 36°17′N | 82°23′W |
| Johnston, i., Oc. (jŏn′stŭn) | 2 | 17°00′N | 168°00′W |
| Johnstone Strait, strt., Can. | 94 | 50°25′N | 126°00′W |
| Johnston Falls, wtfl., Afr. | 237 | 10°35′S | 28°50′E |
| Johnstown, N.Y., U.S. (jonz′toun) | 109 | 43°00′N | 74°20′W |
| Johnstown, Pa., U.S. | 105 | 40°20′N | 78°50′W |
| Johor, r., Malay. (jŭ-hōr′) | 197b | 1°39′N | 103°52′E |
| Johor Baharu, Malay. | 212 | 1°28′N | 103°46′E |
| Jõhvi, Est. (yû′vĭ) | 167 | 59°21′N | 27°21′E |
| Joigny, Fr. (zhwán-yē′) | 170 | 47°58′N | 3°26′E |
| Joinville, Braz. (zhwăN-vĕl′) | 144 | 26°18′S | 48°47′W |
| Joinville, Fr. | 171 | 48°28′N | 5°05′E |
| Joinville, i., Ant. | 139 | 63°00′S | 53°30′W |
| Jojutla, Mex. (hō-hōō′tlá) | 130 | 18°39′N | 99°11′W |
| Jola, Mex. (kō′lä) | 130 | 21°08′N | 104°26′W |
| Joliet, Il., U.S. (jō-lĭ-ĕt′) | 111a | 41°32′N | 88°05′W |
| Joliette, Can. (zhô-lyĕt′) | 91 | 46°01′N | 73°30′W |
| Jolo, Phil. (hō-lō) | 212 | 5°59′N | 121°05′E |
| Jolo Island, i., Phil. | 212 | 5°55′N | 121°15′E |
| Jomalig, i., Phil. (hô-mä′lēg) | 213a | 14°44′N | 122°34′E |
| Jomulco, Mex. (hô-mōōl′kô) | 130 | 21°08′N | 104°24′W |
| Jonacatepec, Mex. | 130 | 18°39′N | 98°46′W |
| Jonava, Lith. (yō-nä′vá) | 167 | 55°05′N | 24°15′E |
| Jones, Phil. (jōnz) | 213a | 12°56′N | 122°05′E |
| Jones, Phil. | 213a | 16°35′N | 121°39′E |
| Jonesboro, Ar., U.S. (jōnz′bûro) | 105 | 35°49′N | 90°42′W |
| Jonesboro, La., U.S. | 123 | 32°14′N | 92°43′W |
| Jonesville, La., U.S. (jōnz′vĭl) | 123 | 31°35′N | 91°50′W |
| Jonesville, Mi., U.S. | 108 | 42°00′N | 84°45′W |
| Jong, r., S.L. | 234 | 8°10′N | 12°10′W |
| Joniškis, Lith. (yô′nĭsh-kĭs) | 167 | 56°14′N | 23°36′E |
| Jönköping, Swe. (yûn′chû-pĭng) | 160 | 57°47′N | 14°10′E |
| Jonquiere, Can. (zhôN-kyâr′) | 91 | 48°25′N | 71°15′W |
| Jonuta, Mex. (hô-nōō′tä) | 131 | 18°07′N | 92°09′W |
| Jonzac, Fr. (zhôN-zák′) | 170 | 45°27′N | 0°27′W |
| Joplin, Mo., U.S. (jŏp′lĭn) | 105 | 37°05′N | 94°31′W |
| Jordan, nation, Asia (jôr′dăn) | 198 | 30°15′N | 38°00′E |
| Jordan, r., Asia | 197a | 32°05′N | 35°35′E |
| Jordan, r., Ut., U.S. | 117b | 40°42′N | 111°56′W |
| Jorhāt, India (jôr-hät′) | 199 | 26°43′N | 94°16′E |
| Jorullo, Volcán de, vol., Mex. (vôl-ká′n-dĕ-hô-rōōl′yō) | 130 | 18°54′N | 101°38′W |
| José C. Paz, Arg. | 144a | 34°32′S | 58°44′W |
| Joseph Bonaparte Gulf, b., Austl. (jô′sĕf bō′ná-pärt) | 220 | 13°30′S | 128°40′E |
| Josephburg, Can. | 102g | 53°45′N | 113°06′W |
| Joseph Lake, l., Can. (jô′sĕf lāk) | 102g | 53°18′N | 113°06′W |
| Joshua Tree National Park, rec., Ca., U.S. (jô′shū-á trē) | 118 | 34°02′N | 115°53′W |
| Jos Plateau, plat., Nig. (jŏs) | 235 | 9°53′N | 9°05′E |
| Jostedalsbreen, ice, Nor. (yôstĕ-däls-brĕĕn) | 160 | 61°40′N | 6°55′E |
| Jotunheimen, mts., Nor. | 160 | 61°44′N | 8°11′E |
| Joulter's Cays, is., Bah. (jōl′tērz) | 134 | 25°20′N | 78°10′W |
| Jouy-le-Chatel, Fr. (zhwē-lĕ-shä-tĕl′) | 171b | 48°40′N | 3°07′E |
| Jovellanos, Cuba (hō-vĕl-yä′nōs) | 134 | 22°50′N | 81°10′W |
| J. Percy Priest Lake, res., Tn., U.S. | 124 | 36°00′N | 86°45′W |
| Juan Aldama, Mex. (kòá′n-äl-dá′mä) | 130 | 24°16′N | 103°21′W |
| Juan de Fuca, Strait of, strt., N.A. (hwän′ dā fōō′kä) | 92 | 48°25′N | 124°37′W |
| Juan de Nova, Île, i., Reu. | 233 | 17°18′S | 43°07′E |
| Juan Diaz, r., Pan. (ĸōōá′n-dē′äz) | 128a | 9°05′N | 79°30′W |
| Juan Fernández, Islas de, is., Chile | 139 | 33°30′S | 79°00′W |
| Juan L. Lacaze, Ur. (hōōá′n-ĕ′lĕ-lä-kä′zĕ) | 141c | 34°25′S | 57°28′W |
| Juan Luis, Cayos de, is., Cuba (ka-yōs-dĕ-hwän lōō-ēs′) | 134 | 22°15′N | 82°00′W |
| Juárez, Arg. (hōōá′rĕz) | 144 | 37°42′S | 59°46′W |
| Juázeiro, Braz. (zhōōá′zā′rô) | 143 | 9°27′S | 40°28′W |
| Juazeiro do Norte, Braz. (zhōōá′zā′rô-dô-nôr-tĕ) | 143 | 7°16′S | 38°57′W |
| Jubayl, Leb. (jōō-bīl′) | 197a | 34°07′N | 35°38′E |
| Jubba (Genale), r., Afr. | 238a | 1°30′N | 42°25′E |
| Juby, Cap, c., Mor. (yōō′bē) | 230 | 28°01′N | 13°21′W |
| Júcar, r., Spain (hōō′kär) | 162 | 39°10′N | 1°22′W |
| Júcaro, Cuba (hōō′ká-rō) | 134 | 21°40′N | 78°50′W |
| Juchipila, Mex. (hōō-chē-pē′lá) | 130 | 21°26′N | 103°09′W |
| Juchitán, Mex. (hōō-chē-tän′) | 128 | 16°15′N | 95°00′W |
| Juchitlán, Mex. (hōō-chē-tlän) | 130 | 20°05′N | 104°07′W |
| Jucuapa, El Sal. (ĸōō-kwá′pä) | 132 | 13°30′N | 88°24′W |
| Judenburg, Aus. (jōō′dĕn-bûrg) | 168 | 47°10′N | 14°40′E |
| Judith, r., Mt., U.S. (jōō′dĭth) | 115 | 47°20′N | 109°36′W |
| Juhua Dao, i., China (jyōō-hwä dou) | 206 | 40°30′N | 120°47′E |
| Juigalpa, Nic. (hwē-gäl′pä) | 132 | 12°02′N | 85°24′W |
| Juiz de Fora, Braz. (zhò-ēzh′ dā fō′rä) | 143 | 21°47′S | 43°20′W |
| Jujuy, Arg. (hōō-hwē′) | 144 | 24°14′S | 65°15′W |
| Jujuy, prov., Arg. (hōō-hwē′) | 144 | 23°00′S | 65°45′W |
| Jukskei, r., S. Afr. | 233b | 25°58′S | 27°58′E |
| Julesburg, Co., U.S. (jōōlz′bûrg) | 120 | 40°59′N | 102°16′W |
| Juliaca, Peru (hōō-lē-ä′kä) | 142 | 15°26′S | 70°12′W |
| Julian Alps, mts., Serb. | 162 | 46°05′N | 14°05′E |
| Julianehåb, Grnld. | 89 | 60°07′N | 46°20′W |
| Jülich, Ger. (yü′lĕk) | 171c | 50°55′N | 6°22′E |
| Jullundur, India | 199 | 31°29′N | 75°39′E |
| Julpaiguri, India | 202 | 26°35′N | 88°48′E |
| Jumento Cays, is., Bah. (hōō-mĕn′tō) | 135 | 23°05′N | 75°40′W |
| Jumilla, Spain (hōō-mēl′yä) | 172 | 38°28′N | 1°20′W |
| Jump, r., Wi., U.S. (jŭmp) | 113 | 45°18′N | 90°53′W |
| Jumpingpound Creek, r., Can. (jŭmp-ĭng-pound) | 102e | 51°01′N | 114°34′W |
| Jumrah, Indon. | 197b | 1°48′N | 101°04′E |
| Junagādh, India (jò-nä′gŭd) | 199 | 21°33′N | 70°25′E |
| Junayfah, Egypt | 238d | 30°11′N | 32°26′E |
| Junaynah, Ra's al, mtn., Egypt | 197a | 29°02′N | 33°58′E |
| Junction, Tx., U.S. (jŭŋk′shŭn) | 122 | 30°29′N | 99°48′W |
| Junction City, Ks., U.S. | 121 | 39°01′N | 96°49′W |
| Jundiaí, Braz. | 143 | 23°11′S | 46°52′W |
| Juneau, Ak., U.S. (jōō′nō) | 106a | 58°25′N | 134°30′W |
| Jungfrau, mtn., Switz. (yòng′frou) | 168 | 46°30′N | 7°59′E |
| Junín, Arg. (hōō-nē′n) | 144 | 34°35′S | 60°56′W |
| Junín, Col. | 142a | 4°47′N | 73°39′W |
| Juniyah, Leb. (jōō-nē′ĕ) | 197a | 33°59′N | 35°38′E |
| Jupiter, r., Can. | 100 | 49°40′N | 63°20′W |
| Jupiter, Mount, mtn., Wa., U.S. | 116a | 47°42′N | 123°04′W |
| Jur, r., Sudan (jòr) | 231 | 6°38′N | 27°52′E |
| Jura, mts., Eur. (zhü-rá′) | 161 | 46°55′N | 6°49′E |
| Jura, i., Scot., U.K. (jōō′rá) | 164 | 56°09′N | 6°45′W |
| Jura, Sound of, strt., Scot., U.K. (jōō′rá) | 164 | 55°45′N | 5°55′W |
| Jurbarkas, Lith. (yōōr-bär′käs) | 167 | 55°06′N | 22°50′E |
| Jūrmala, Lat. | 167 | 56°57′N | 23°37′E |
| Jurong, China (jyōō-roŋ) | 206 | 31°58′N | 119°12′E |
| Juruá, r., S.A. | 142 | 5°30′S | 67°30′W |
| Juruena, r., Braz. (zhōō-rōōĕ′nä) | 143 | 12°22′S | 58°34′W |

PRONOUNCING INDEX

Jutiapa – Kara-Kum 307


| PLACE (Pronunciation) | PAGE | LAT. | LONG. |
|---|---|---|---|
| Jutiapa, Guat. (ho͞o-tē-ä′pä) | 132 | 14°16′N | 89°55′W |
| Juticalpa, Hond. (ho͞o-tē-käl′pä) | 128 | 14°35′N | 86°17′W |
| Jutland *see* Jylland, reg., Den. | 160 | 56°04′N | 9°00′E |
| Juventino Rosas, Mex. | 130 | 20°38′N | 101°02′W |
| Juventud, Isla de la, i., Cuba | 129 | 21°40′N | 82°45′W |
| Juxian, China (jyo͞o shyĕn) | 208 | 35°35′N | 118°50′E |
| Juxtlahuaca, Mex. (ho͞os-tlä-hwä′kä) | 130 | 17°20′N | 98°02′W |
| Juye, China (jyo͞o-yŭ) | 206 | 35°25′N | 116°05′E |
| Južna Morava, r., Serb. (ŭ′zhnä mô′rä-vä) | 175 | 42°30′N | 22°00′E |
| Jylland, reg., Den. | 160 | 56°04′N | 9°00′E |
| **K** | | | |
| K2 (Qogir Feng), mtn., Asia | 199 | 36°06′N | 76°38′E |
| Kaabong, Ug. | 237 | 3°31′N | 34°08′E |
| Kaalfontein, S. Afr. (kärl-fŏn-tān) | 233b | 26°02′S | 28°16′E |
| Kaappunt, c., S. Afr. | 232a | 34°21′S | 18°30′E |
| Kabaena, Pulau, i., Indon. (kä-bä-ā′nä) | 212 | 5°35′S | 121°07′E |
| Kabala, S.L. (kȧ-bä′lȧ) | 230 | 9°43′N | 11°39′W |
| Kabale, Ug. | 237 | 1°15′S | 29°59′E |
| Kabalega Falls, wtfl., Ug. | 231 | 2°15′N | 31°41′E |
| Kabalo, D.R.C. (kä-bä′lō) | 232 | 6°03′S | 26°55′E |
| Kabambare, D.R.C. (kä-bäm-bä′rȧ) | 232 | 4°47′S | 27°45′E |
| Kabardino-Balkaria, prov., Russia | 180 | 43°30′N | 43°30′E |
| Kabba, Nig. | 235 | 7°50′N | 6°03′E |
| Kabe, Japan (kä′bā) | 211 | 34°32′N | 132°30′E |
| Kabinakagami, r., Can. | 98 | 49°00′N | 84°15′W |
| Kabinda, D.R.C. (kä-bĕn′dä) | 232 | 6°08′S | 24°29′E |
| Kabompo, r., Zam. (kȧ-bôm′pō) | 232 | 14°00′S | 23°40′E |
| Kabongo, D.R.C. (kȧ-bông′ō) | 232 | 7°58′S | 25°10′E |
| Kabot, Gui. | 234 | 10°48′N | 14°57′W |
| Kaboudia, Ra′s, c., Tun. | 162 | 35°17′N | 11°28′E |
| Kābul, Afg. (kä′bo͝ol) | 199 | 34°39′N | 69°14′E |
| Kabul, r., Asia (kä′bo͝ol) | 199 | 34°44′N | 69°43′E |
| Kabunda, D.R.C. | 237 | 12°25′S | 29°22′E |
| Kabwe, Zam. | 232 | 14°27′S | 28°27′E |
| Kachuga, Russia (kȧ-cho͞o-gȧ) | 179 | 54°09′N | 105°43′E |
| Kadei, r., Afr. | 235 | 4°00′N | 15°10′E |
| Kadnikov, Russia (käd′nê-kôf) | 180 | 59°30′N | 40°10′E |
| Kadoma, Japan | 211b | 34°43′N | 135°36′E |
| Kadoma, Zimb. | 232 | 18°21′S | 29°55′E |
| Kaduna, Nig. (kä-do͞o′nä) | 230 | 10°33′N | 7°27′E |
| Kaduna, r., Nig. | 235 | 9°30′N | 6°00′E |
| Kaédi, Maur. (kä-ā-dē′) | 230 | 16°09′N | 13°30′W |
| Ka′ena Point, c., Hi., U.S. (kä′ā-nä) | 106d | 21°33′N | 158°19′W |
| Kaesŏng, Kor., N. (kä′ĕ-sŭng) (kĭ′jō) | 205 | 38°00′N | 126°35′E |
| Kafanchan, Nig. | 235 | 9°36′N | 8°17′E |
| Kafia Kingi, Sudan (kä′fê-ȧ kĭŋ′gê) | 231 | 9°17′N | 24°28′E |
| Kafue, Zam. (kä′fo͞o) | 232 | 15°45′S | 28°17′E |
| Kafue, r., Zam. | 232 | 15°45′S | 26°30′E |
| Kafue Flats, sw., Zam. | 237 | 16°15′S | 26°30′E |
| Kafue National Park, rec., Zam. | 237 | 15°00′S | 25°35′E |
| Kafwira, D.R.C. | 237 | 12°10′S | 27°33′E |
| Kagal′nik, r., Russia (kä-gäl′′nêk) | 177 | 46°58′N | 39°25′E |
| Kagera, r., Afr. (kä-gā′rȧ) | 232 | 1°10′S | 31°10′E |
| Kagoshima, Japan (kä′gô-shē′mȧ) | 205 | 31°35′N | 130°31′E |
| Kagoshima-Wan, b., Japan (kä′gô-shē′mä wän) | 210 | 31°24′N | 130°39′E |
| Kahayan, r., Indon. | 212 | 1°45′S | 113°40′E |
| Kahemba, D.R.C. | 236 | 7°17′S | 19°00′E |
| Kahia, D.R.C. | 237 | 6°21′S | 28°24′E |
| Kahoka, Mo., U.S. (kȧ-hō′kȧ) | 121 | 40°26′N | 91°42′W |
| Kaho′olawe, i., Hi., U.S. (kä-ho͞o-lä′wē) | 106c | 20°28′N | 156°48′W |
| Kahramanmaraş, Tur. | 198 | 37°40′N | 36°50′W |
| Kahshahpiwi, r., Can. | 113 | 48°24′N | 90°56′W |
| Kahuku Point, c., Hi., U.S. (kä-ho͞o′ko͞o) | 106d | 21°50′N | 157°50′W |
| Kahului, Hi., U.S. | 106c | 20°53′N | 156°28′W |
| Kai, Kepulauan, is., Indon. | 213 | 5°35′S | 132°45′E |
| Kaiang, Malay. | 197b | 3°00′N | 101°47′E |
| Kaiashk, r., Can. | 98 | 49°40′N | 89°30′W |
| Kaibab Indian Reservation, I.R., Az., U.S. (kä′ē-bȧb) | 119 | 36°55′N | 112°45′W |
| Kaibab Plat, Az., U.S. | 119 | 36°30′N | 112°10′W |
| Kaidu, r., China (kī-do͞o) | 204 | 42°35′N | 84°04′E |
| Kaieteur Fall, wtfl., Guy. (kī-ĕ-to͞or′) | 143 | 4°48′N | 59°24′W |
| Kaifeng, China (kī-fŭŋ) | 205 | 34°48′N | 114°22′E |
| Kai Kecil, i., Indon. | 213 | 5°45′S | 132°40′E |
| Kailua, Hi., U.S. (kä′ē-lo͞o′ä) | 106c | 21°18′N | 157°43′W |
| Kailua Kona, Hi., U.S. | 126a | 19°49′N | 155°59′W |
| Kaimana, Indon. | 213 | 3°32′S | 133°47′E |
| Kaimanawa Mountains, mts., N.Z. | 223 | 39°10′S | 176°00′E |
| Kainan, Japan (kä′ē-nȧn′) | 211 | 34°09′N | 135°14′E |
| Kainji Lake, res., Nig. | 230 | 10°25′N | 4°50′E |
| Kaiserslautern, Ger. (kī-zĕrs-lou′tĕrn) | 161 | 49°26′N | 7°46′E |
| Kaitaia, N.Z. (kä-ē-tä′ē-ä) | 221a | 35°30′S | 173°28′E |
| Kaiwi Channel, strt., Hi., U.S. (käē-wē) | 106c | 21°10′N | 157°38′W |
| Kaiyuan, China (kū-yuän) | 209 | 23°42′N | 103°20′E |
| Kaiyuan, China | 208 | 42°30′N | 124°00′E |
| Kaiyuh Mountains, mts., Ak., U.S. (kī-yo͞o′) | 103 | 64°25′N | 157°38′W |
| Kajaani, Fin. (kä′yȧ-nē) | 160 | 64°15′N | 27°16′E |
| Kajang, Gunong, mtn., Malay. | 197b | 2°47′N | 104°05′E |
| Kajiki, Japan (kä′jē-kē) | 210 | 31°44′N | 130°41′E |
| Kakhovka, Ukr. (kä-kôf′kȧ) | 177 | 46°46′N | 33°32′E |
| Kakhovs′ke vodoskhovyshche, res., Ukr. | 178 | 47°21′N | 33°33′E |
| Kākināda, India | 199 | 16°58′N | 82°18′E |
| Kaktovik, Ak., U.S. (käk-tō′vĭk) | 103 | 70°08′N | 143°51′W |
| Kakwa, r., Can. (käk′wȧ) | 95 | 54°00′N | 118°55′W |
| Kalach, Russia (kȧ-lȧch′) | 181 | 50°15′N | 40°55′E |
| Kaladan, r., Asia | 204 | 21°07′N | 93°04′E |
| Kalae, c., Hi., U.S. | 126a | 18°55′N | 155°41′W |
| Kalahari Desert, des., Afr. (kä-lä-hä′rē) | 232 | 23°00′S | 22°03′E |
| Kalama, Wa., U.S. (kȧ-lăm′ȧ) | 116c | 46°01′N | 122°50′W |
| Kalama, r., Wa., U.S. | 116c | 46°03′N | 122°47′W |
| Kalamáta, Grc. | 154 | 37°04′N | 22°08′E |
| Kalamazoo, Mi., U.S. (kăl-ȧ-mȧ-zo͞o′) | 105 | 42°20′N | 85°40′W |
| Kalamazoo, r., Mi., U.S. | 108 | 42°35′N | 86°00′W |
| Kalanchak, Ukr. (kä-län-chäk′) | 177 | 46°17′N | 33°14′E |
| Kalandula, Ang. (do͞o′kȧ dȧ brä-gäɴ′sä) | 232 | 9°06′S | 15°57′E |
| Kalaotoa, Pulau, i., Indon. | 212 | 7°22′S | 122°30′E |
| Kalapana, Hi., U.S. (kä-lä-pá′nä) | 126a | 19°25′N | 155°00′W |
| Kalar, mtn., Iran | 198 | 31°43′N | 51°41′E |
| Kalāt, Pak. (kŭ-lät′) | 199 | 29°05′N | 66°36′E |
| Kalemie, D.R.C. | 232 | 5°56′S | 29°12′E |
| Kalgan *see* Zhangjiakou, China | 205 | 40°45′N | 114°58′E |
| Kalgoorlie-Boulder, Austl. (kăl-go͞or′lē) | 218 | 30°45′S | 121°35′E |
| Kaliakra, Nos, c., Blg. | 163 | 43°25′N | 28°42′E |
| Kalima, D.R.C. | 237 | 2°34′S | 26°37′E |
| Kaliningrad, Russia | 178 | 54°42′N | 20°32′E |
| Kaliningrad, Russia (kä-lē-nēn′grät) | 186b | 55°55′N | 37°49′E |
| Kalinkavichy, Bela. | 176 | 52°07′N | 29°19′E |
| Kalispel Indian Reservation, I.R., Wa., U.S. (kăl-ĭ-spĕl′) | 114 | 48°25′N | 117°30′W |
| Kalispell, Mt., U.S. (kăl′ĭ-spĕl) | 104 | 48°12′N | 114°18′W |
| Kalisz, Pol. (kä′lēsh) | 161 | 51°45′N | 18°05′E |
| Kaliua, Tan. | 237 | 5°04′S | 31°48′E |
| Kalixälven, r., Swe. | 160 | 67°12′N | 22°00′E |
| Kalmar, Swe. (käl′mär) | 160 | 56°40′N | 16°19′E |
| Kalmarsund, strt., Swe. (käl′mär) | 166 | 56°30′N | 16°17′E |
| Kal′mius, r., Ukr. (käl′′myo͞os) | 177 | 47°15′N | 37°38′E |
| Kalmykia, prov., Russia | 181 | 46°56′N | 46°00′E |
| Kalocsa, Hung. (kä′lô-chä) | 169 | 46°32′N | 19°00′E |
| Kalohi Channel, strt., Hi., U.S. (kä-lō′hī) | 126a | 20°55′N | 157°15′W |
| Kaloko, D.R.C. | 237 | 6°47′S | 25°48′E |
| Kalomo, Zam. (kä-lō′mō) | 232 | 17°02′S | 26°30′E |
| Kalsubai Mount, mtn., India | 202 | 19°43′N | 73°47′E |
| Kaltenkirchen, Ger. (käl′tĕn-kĕr-kĕn) | 159c | 53°50′N | 9°57′E |
| Kālu, r., India | 203b | 19°18′N | 73°14′E |
| Kaluga, Russia (kȧ-lo͞o′gä) | 178 | 54°29′N | 36°12′E |
| Kaluga, prov., Russia | 176 | 54°10′N | 35°00′E |
| Kaluktutiak (Cambridge Bay), Can. | 90 | 69°15′N | 105°00′W |
| Kalundborg, Den. (kȧ-lo͝on′′bôr′) | 166 | 55°42′N | 11°07′E |
| Kalush, Ukr. (kä′lo͝osh) | 169 | 49°02′N | 24°24′E |
| Kalvarija, Lith. (käl-vä-rē′yȧ) | 167 | 54°24′N | 23°17′E |
| Kalwa, India | 203b | 19°12′N | 72°59′E |
| Kal′ya, Russia (käl′yȧ) | 186a | 60°17′N | 59°58′E |
| Kalyān, India | 202 | 19°16′N | 73°07′E |
| Kalyazin, Russia (käl-yȧ′zĕn) | 176 | 57°13′N | 37°55′E |
| Kama, r., Russia (kä′mä) | 178 | 56°10′N | 53°50′E |
| Kamaishi, Japan (kä′mä-ē′shē) | 210 | 39°16′N | 142°03′E |
| Kamakura, Japan (kä′mä-ko͞o′rä) | 211 | 35°19′N | 139°33′E |
| Kamarān, i., Yemen | 198 | 15°19′N | 41°47′E |
| Kāmārhāti, India | 202a | 22°41′N | 88°23′E |
| Kambove, D.R.C. (käm-bō′vē) | 232 | 10°58′S | 26°43′E |
| Kamchatka, r., Russia | 185 | 54°15′N | 158°38′E |
| Kamchatka, Poluostrov, pen., Russia | 185 | 55°19′N | 157°45′E |
| Kamen, Ger. (kä′mĕn) | 171c | 51°35′N | 7°40′E |
| Kamenjak, Rt, c., Cro. (kä′mĕ-nyäk) | 174 | 44°45′N | 13°57′E |
| Kamen′-na-Obi, Russia (kä-mĭny′nŭ ô′bē) | 178 | 53°43′N | 81°28′E |
| Kamensk-Shakhtinskiy, Russia (kä′mĕnsk shäk′tĭn-skĭ) | 177 | 48°17′N | 40°16′E |
| Kamensk-Ural′skiy, Russia (kä′mĕnsk o͞o-räl′skĭ) | 180 | 56°27′N | 61°55′E |
| Kamenz, Ger. (kä′mĕnts) | 168 | 51°16′N | 14°05′E |
| Kameoka, Japan (kä′mā-ōkä) | 211b | 35°01′N | 135°35′E |
| Kāmet, mtn., Asia | 202 | 30°50′N | 79°42′E |
| Kamianets′-Podil′s′kyi, Ukr. | 181 | 48°41′N | 26°34′E |
| Kamianka-Buz′ka, Ukr. | 169 | 50°06′N | 24°20′E |
| Kamień Pomorski, Pol. | 168 | 53°57′N | 14°48′E |
| Kamikoma, Japan (kä′mē-kō′mä) | 211b | 34°45′N | 135°50′E |
| Kamina, D.R.C. | 232 | 8°44′S | 25°00′E |
| Kaministikwia, r., Can. (kȧ-mĭ-nĭ-stĭk′wĭ-ȧ) | 113 | 48°40′N | 89°41′W |
| Kamituga, D.R.C. | 237 | 3°04′S | 28°11′E |
| Kamloops, Can. (kăm′lo͞ops) | 90 | 50°40′N | 120°20′W |
| Kamp, r., Aus. (kămp) | 168 | 48°30′N | 15°45′E |
| Kampala, Ug. (käm-pä′lä) | 231 | 0°19′N | 32°25′E |
| Kampar, r., Indon. (käm′pär) | 212 | 0°30′N | 101°30′E |
| Kampene, D.R.C. | 237 | 3°36′S | 26°40′E |
| Kampenhout, Bel. | 159a | 50°56′N | 4°33′E |
| Kamp-Lintfort, Ger. (kämp-lēnt′fôrt) | 171c | 51°30′N | 6°34′E |
| Kâmpóng Saôm, Camb. | 212 | 10°40′N | 103°50′E |
| Kâmpóng Thum, Camb. (kŏm′pŏng-tŏm) | 212 | 12°41′N | 104°29′E |
| Kâmpôt, Camb. (käm′pōt) | 212 | 10°41′N | 104°07′E |
| Kampuchea *see* Cambodia, nation, Asia | 212 | 12°15′N | 104°00′E |
| Kamsack, Can. (kăm′săk) | 90 | 51°34′N | 101°54′W |
| Kamskoye, res., Russia | 178 | 59°08′N | 56°30′E |
| Kamudilo, D.R.C. | 237 | 7°42′S | 27°18′E |
| Kamuela, Hi., U.S. | 126a | 20°01′N | 155°40′W |
| Kamui Misaki, c., Japan | 210 | 43°25′N | 139°35′E |
| Kámuk, Cerro, mtn., C.R. (sĕ′r-rô-kä-mo͞o′k) | 133 | 9°18′N | 83°02′W |
| Kamyshevatskaya, Russia | 177 | 46°24′N | 37°58′E |
| Kamyshin, Russia (kä-mwēsh′ĭn) | 178 | 50°08′N | 45°20′E |
| Kamyshlov, Russia (kä-mēsh′lôf) | 178 | 56°50′N | 62°32′E |
| Kan, r., Russia (kän) | 184 | 56°30′N | 94°17′E |
| Kanab, Ut., U.S. (kăn′ăb) | 119 | 37°00′N | 112°30′W |
| Kanabeki, Russia (kȧ-nä′byĕ-kĭ) | 186a | 57°48′N | 57°16′E |
| Kanab Plateau, plat., Az., U.S. | 119 | 36°31′N | 112°55′W |
| Kanaga, i., Ak., U.S. (kă-nä′gă) | 103a | 52°02′N | 177°38′W |
| Kanagawa, dept., Japan (kä′nä-gä′wä) | 211a | 35°29′N | 139°32′E |
| Kanā′is, Ra′s al, c., Egypt | 163 | 31°14′N | 28°08′E |
| Kanamachi, Japan (kä-nä-mä′chē) | 211a | 35°46′N | 139°52′E |
| Kananga, D.R.C. | 232 | 6°14′S | 22°17′E |
| Kananikol′skoye, Russia | 186a | 52°48′N | 57°29′E |
| Kanasín, Mex. (kä-nä-sē′n) | 132a | 20°54′N | 89°31′W |
| Kanatak, Ak., U.S. (kă-nă′tŏk) | 103 | 57°35′N | 155°48′W |
| Kanawha, r., W.V., U.S. (kȧ-nô′wȧ) | 107 | 37°55′N | 81°50′W |
| Kanaya, Japan (kä-nä′yä) | 211a | 35°10′N | 139°49′E |
| Kanazawa, Japan (kä′nȧ-zä′wȧ) | 205 | 36°34′N | 136°38′E |
| Kānchenjunga, mtn., Asia (kĭn-chĭn-jŏn′gȧ) | 199 | 27°30′N | 88°18′E |
| Kānchipuram, India | 199 | 12°55′N | 79°43′E |
| Kandahār, Afg. | 199 | 31°43′N | 65°58′E |
| Kanda Kanda, D.R.C. (kän′dȧ kän′dȧ) | 232 | 6°56′S | 23°36′E |
| Kandalaksha, Russia (kȧn-dȧ-lák′shȧ) | 178 | 67°10′N | 33°05′E |
| Kandalakshskiy Zaliv, b., Russia | 180 | 66°20′N | 35°00′E |
| Kandava, Lat. (kän′dȧ-vȧ) | 167 | 57°03′N | 22°45′E |
| Kandi, Benin (käɴ-dē′) | 230 | 11°08′N | 2°56′E |
| Kandiāro, Pak. | 202 | 27°09′N | 68°12′E |
| Kandla, India (kŭnd′lŭ) | 202 | 23°00′N | 70°20′E |
| Kandy, Sri L. (kän′dē) | 203 | 7°18′N | 80°42′E |
| Kane, Pa., U.S. (kān) | 109 | 41°40′N | 78°50′W |
| Kāne′ohe, Hi., U.S. (kä-nä-ō′hā) | 126a | 21°25′N | 157°47′W |
| Kāne′ohe Bay, b., Hi., U.S. | 106d | 21°32′N | 157°40′W |
| Kanevskaya, Russia (kȧ-nyĕf′skȧ) | 177 | 46°07′N | 38°58′E |
| Kangaroo, i., Austl. (kăŋ-gȧ-ro͞o′) | 220 | 36°05′S | 137°05′E |
| Kangāvar, Iran (kŭŋ′gā-vär) | 198 | 34°37′N | 46°45′E |
| Kangean, Kepulauan, is., Indon. (käŋ′gē-än) | 212 | 6°50′S | 116°22′E |
| Kanggye, Kor., N. (käng′gyĕ) | 205 | 40°55′N | 126°40′E |
| Kanghwa, i., Kor., S. (käng′hwä) | 210 | 37°38′N | 126°00′E |
| Kangnŭng, Kor., S. (käng′no͝o ng) | 210 | 37°42′N | 128°50′E |
| Kango, Gabon (käɴ-gō) | 232 | 0°09′N | 10°08′E |
| Kangowa, D.R.C. | 236 | 9°55′S | 22°48′E |
| Kanin, Poluostrov, pen., Russia | 178 | 68°00′N | 45°00′E |
| Kaningo, Kenya | 237 | 0°49′S | 38°32′E |
| Kanin Nos, Mys, c., Russia | 180 | 68°40′N | 44°00′E |
| Kaniv, Ukr. | 177 | 49°46′N | 31°27′E |
| Kanivs′ke vodoskhovyshche, res., Ukr. | 178 | 50°10′N | 30°40′E |
| Kanjiža, Serb. (kä′nyē-zhä) | 175 | 46°05′N | 20°02′E |
| Kankakee, Il., U.S. (kăŋ-kȧ-kē′) | 108 | 41°07′N | 87°53′W |
| Kankakee, r., Il., U.S. | 108 | 41°15′N | 88°15′W |
| Kankan, Gui. (käɴ-käɴ) (kän-kän′) | 230 | 10°23′N | 9°18′W |
| Kannapolis, N.C., U.S. (kăn-ăp′ô-lĭs) | 125 | 35°30′N | 80°38′W |
| Kannoura, Japan (kä′nō-o͞o′rä) | 211 | 33°34′N | 134°18′E |
| Kano, Nig. (kä′nō) | 230 | 12°00′N | 8°30′E |
| Kanonkop, mtn., S. Afr. | 232a | 33°49′S | 18°37′E |
| Kanopolis Reservoir, res., Ks., U.S. (kăn-ŏp′ô-lĭs) | 120 | 38°44′N | 98°01′W |
| Kānpur, India (kän′pûr) | 202 | 26°30′N | 80°10′E |
| Kansas, state, U.S. (kăn′zȧs) | 104 | 38°30′N | 99°40′W |
| Kansas, r., Ks., U.S. | 121 | 39°08′N | 95°52′W |
| Kansas City, Ks., U.S. | 105 | 39°06′N | 94°39′W |
| Kansas City, Mo., U.S. | 105 | 39°05′N | 94°35′W |
| Kansk, Russia | 179 | 56°14′N | 95°43′E |
| Kansŏng, Kor., S. | 210 | 38°09′N | 128°29′E |
| Kantang, Thai. (kän′täng′) | 212 | 7°26′N | 99°28′E |
| Kantchari, Burkina | 234 | 12°29′N | 1°31′E |
| Kanton, i., Kir. | 240 | 3°50′S | 174°00′W |
| Kantunilkin, Mex. (kän-to͞o-nēl-kē′n) | 132a | 21°07′N | 87°30′W |
| Kanzhakovskiy Kamen, Gora, mtn., Russia (kȧn-zhä′kôvs-kēē kämĭen) | 186a | 59°38′N | 59°12′E |
| Kaohsiung, Tai. (kä-ō-syóng′) | 205 | 22°35′N | 120°25′E |
| Kaolack, Sen. | 230 | 14°09′N | 16°04′W |
| Kaouar, oasis, Niger | 231 | 19°16′N | 13°09′E |
| Kapaa, Hi., U.S. | 126a | 22°06′N | 159°20′W |
| Kapanga, D.R.C. | 236 | 8°21′S | 22°35′E |
| Kapfenberg, Aus. (kȧp′fĕn-bĕrgh) | 168 | 47°27′N | 15°16′E |
| Kapiri Mposhi, Zam. | 237 | 13°58′S | 28°41′E |
| Kapoeta, Sudan | 231 | 4°45′N | 33°35′E |
| Kaposvár, Hung. (kô′pôsh-vär) | 169 | 46°21′N | 17°45′E |
| Kapsan, Kor., N. (käp′sän′) | 210 | 40°59′N | 128°22′E |
| Kapuskasing, Can. | 91 | 49°28′N | 82°22′W |
| Kapuskasing, r., Can. | 98 | 48°55′N | 82°55′W |
| Kapustin Yar, Russia (kä′pôs-tĕn yär′) | 181 | 48°30′N | 45°40′E |
| Kaputar, Mount, mtn., Austl. (kȧ-pû-tȧr) | 222 | 30°11′S | 150°11′E |
| Kapuvár, Hung. (kô′po͞o-vär) | 169 | 47°35′N | 17°02′E |
| Kara, Russia (kärȧ) | 178 | 68°42′N | 65°30′E |
| Kara, r., Russia | 180 | 68°30′N | 65°20′E |
| Karabalā′, Iraq (kŭr′bȧ-lä) | 198 | 32°31′N | 43°58′E |
| Karabanovo, Russia (kä′rȧ-bȧ-nō-vō) | 176 | 56°19′N | 38°43′E |
| Karabash, Russia (kó-rȧ-bäsh′) | 186a | 55°27′N | 60°14′E |
| Kara-Bogaz-Gol, Zaliv, b., Turkmen. (kȧ-rä′ bŭ-gäs′) | 183 | 41°30′N | 53°40′E |
| Karachay-Cherkessia, prov., Russia | 182 | 44°00′N | 42°00′E |
| Karachev, Russia (kȧ-rȧ-chôf′) | 180 | 53°08′N | 34°54′E |
| Karāchi, Pak. | 199 | 24°59′N | 68°56′E |
| Karaganda *see* Qaraghandy, Kaz. | 183 | 49°42′N | 73°18′E |
| Karaidel′, Russia (kä′rī-dĕl) | 186a | 55°52′N | 56°54′E |
| Karakoram Pass, p., Asia | 199 | 35°35′N | 77°45′E |
| Karakoram Range, mts., India (kä′rä kō′rȯm) | 199 | 35°24′N | 76°38′E |
| Karakorum, hist., Mong. | 204 | 47°25′N | 102°22′E |
| Kara-Kum, des., Turkmen. | 183 | 40°00′N | 57°00′E |


ng-sing; ŋ-baŋk; ɴ-nasalized n; nŏd; cŏmmit; ōld; ôbey; ôrder; oi-boil; fo͞od; o͝o-as oo in foot; ou-out; s-soft; sh-dish; th-thin; pūre; ûnite; ûrn; stŭd; circŭs; ü-as in French tu; ′-indeterminate vowel.

308 Kara Kum Canal – Keshan

PRONOUNCING INDEX


| PLACE (Pronunciation) | PAGE | LAT. | LONG. |
|---|---|---|---|
| Kara Kum Canal, can., Turkmen. | 183 | 37°35'N | 61°50'E |
| Karaman, Tur. (kä-rä-män') | 163 | 37°10'N | 33°00'E |
| Karamay, China (kär-äm-ä) | 204 | 45°37'N | 84°53'E |
| Karamea Bight, b., N.Z. (kȧ-rȧ-mē'ȧ bīt) | 221a | 41°20'S | 171°30'E |
| Kara Sea see Karskoye More, sea, Russia | 178 | 74°00'N | 68°00'E |
| Karashahr (Yanqui), China (kä-rä-shä-är) (yän-chyē) | 204 | 42°14'N | 86°28'E |
| Karatsu, Japan (kä'rȧ-tsōō) | 211 | 33°28'N | 129°59'E |
| Karaul, Russia (kä-rä-ōl') | 184 | 70°13'N | 83°46'E |
| Karawanken, mts., Eur. | 168 | 46°32'N | 14°07'E |
| Karcag, Hung. (kär'tsäg) | 169 | 47°18'N | 20°58'E |
| Kárditsa, Grc. | 175 | 39°23'N | 21°57'E |
| Kärdla, Est. (kĕrd'lȧ) | 167 | 58°59'N | 22°44'E |
| Karelia, prov., Russia | 184 | 62°30'N | 32°35'E |
| Karema, Tan. | 232 | 6°49'S | 30°26'E |
| Kargat, Russia (kär-gät') | 178 | 55°17'N | 80°07'E |
| Karghalik see Yecheng, China | 204 | 37°54'N | 77°25'E |
| Kargopol', Russia (kär-gō-pōl'') | 178 | 61°30'N | 38°50'E |
| Kariba, Lake, res., Afr. | 232 | 17°15'S | 27°55'E |
| Karibib, Nmb. (kȧr'ȧ-bĭb) | 232 | 21°55'S | 15°50'E |
| Kārikāl, India (kä-rē-käl') | 203 | 10°58'N | 79°49'E |
| Karimata, Kepulauan, is., Indon. (kä-rē-mä'tȧ) | 212 | 1°08'S | 108°10'E |
| Karimata, Selat, strt., Indon. | 212 | 1°00'S | 107°10'E |
| Karimun Besar, i., Indon. | 197b | 1°10'N | 103°28'E |
| Karimunjawa, Kepulauan, is., Indon. (kä'rē-mōōn-yä'vä) | 212 | 5°36'S | 110°15'E |
| Karin, Som. (kȧr'ĭn) | 238a | 10°43'N | 45°50'E |
| Karkar Island, i., Pap. N. Gui. (kär'kär) | 213 | 4°50'S | 146°45'E |
| Karkheh, r., Iran | 198 | 32°45'N | 47°50'E |
| Karkinits'ka zatoka, b., Ukr. | 177 | 45°50'N | 32°45'E |
| Karkūk, Iraq | 198 | 35°28'N | 44°22'E |
| Karlivka, Ukr. | 177 | 49°26'N | 35°08'E |
| Karlobag, Cro. (kär-lō-bäg') | 174 | 44°30'N | 15°03'E |
| Karlovac, Cro. (kär'lô-vȧts) | 163 | 45°29'N | 15°16'E |
| Karlovo, Blg. (kär'lô-vō) | 175 | 42°39'N | 24°48'E |
| Karlovy Vary, Czech Rep. (kär'lô-vē vä'rē) | 161 | 50°13'N | 12°53'E |
| Karlshamn, Swe. (kärls'häm) | 166 | 56°11'N | 14°50'E |
| Karlskrona, Swe. (kärls'krō-nä) | 160 | 56°10'N | 15°33'E |
| Karlsruhe, Ger. (kärls'rōō-ē) | 161 | 49°00'N | 8°23'E |
| Karlstad, Swe. (kärl'städ) | 154 | 59°25'N | 13°28'E |
| Karluk, Ak., U.S. (kär'lŭk) | 103 | 57°30'N | 154°22'W |
| Karmøy, i., Nor. (kärm-ûe) | 166 | 59°14'N | 5°00'E |
| Karnataka, state, India | 199 | 14°55'N | 75°00'E |
| Karnobat, Blg. (kär-nô'bät) | 175 | 42°39'N | 26°59'E |
| Karonga, Mwi. (kȧ-rōŋ'gȧ) | 232 | 9°52'S | 33°57'E |
| Kárpathos, i., Grc. | 163 | 35°34'N | 27°26'E |
| Karpinsk, Russia (kär'pĭnsk) | 186a | 59°46'N | 60°00'E |
| Kars, Tur. (kärs) | 198 | 40°35'N | 43°00'E |
| Kärsava, Lat. (kär'sȧ-vä) | 167 | 56°46'N | 27°39'E |
| Karshi, Uzb. (kär'shē) | 183 | 38°30'N | 66°08'E |
| Karskiye Vorota, Proliv, strt., Russia | 178 | 70°30'N | 58°07'E |
| Karskoye More (Kara Sea), sea, Russia | 178 | 74°00'N | 68°00'E |
| Kartaly, Russia (kȧr'tȧ lē) | 178 | 53°05'N | 60°40'E |
| Karunagapalli, India | 203 | 9°09'N | 76°34'E |
| Karvina, Czech Rep. | 169 | 49°50'N | 18°30'E |
| Kasai (Cassai), r., Afr. | 232 | 3°45'S | 19°10'E |
| Kasama, Zam. (kȧ-sä'mȧ) | 232 | 10°13'S | 31°12'E |
| Kasanga, Tan. (kȧ-säŋ'gȧ) | 232 | 8°28'S | 31°09'E |
| Kasaoka, Japan (kä'sȧ-ō'kȧ) | 211 | 34°33'N | 133°29'E |
| Kasba-Tadla, Mor. (käs'bȧ-täd'lȧ) | 230 | 32°37'N | 5°57'W |
| Kasempa, Zam. (kȧ-sĕm'pȧ) | 232 | 13°27'S | 25°50'E |
| Kasenga, D.R.C. (kȧ-seŋ'gȧ) | 232 | 10°22'S | 28°38'E |
| Kasese, D.R.C. | 237 | 1°38'S | 27°07'E |
| Kasese, Ug. | 237 | 0°10'N | 30°05'E |
| Kāshān, Iran (kā-shän') | 198 | 33°52'N | 51°15'E |
| Kashgar see Kashi, China | 204 | 39°29'N | 76°00'E |
| Kashi (Kashgar), China (kä-shr) (käsh-gär) | 204 | 39°29'N | 76°00'E |
| Kashihara, Japan (kä'shē-hä'rä) | 211b | 34°31'N | 135°48'E |
| Kashiji Plain, pl., Zam. | 236 | 13°25'S | 22°30'E |
| Kashin, Russia (kä-shēn') | 176 | 57°20'N | 37°38'E |
| Kashira, Russia (kä-shē'rȧ) | 176 | 54°49'N | 38°11'E |
| Kashiwa, Japan (kä'shē-wä) | 211a | 35°51'N | 139°58'E |
| Kashiwara, Japan | 211b | 34°35'N | 135°38'E |
| Kashiwazaki, Japan (kä'shē-wä-zä'kē) | 210 | 37°06'N | 138°17'E |
| Kāshmar, Iran | 201 | 35°12'N | 58°27'E |
| Kashmir see Jammu and Kashmir, state, India | 199 | 34°30'N | 76°00'E |
| Kashmor, Pak. | 202 | 28°33'N | 69°34'E |
| Kashtak, Russia (käsh'tȧk) | 186a | 55°18'N | 61°25'E |
| Kasimov, Russia (kȧ-sē'môf) | 180 | 54°56'N | 41°23'E |
| Kaskanak, Ak., U.S. (kăs-kă'năk) | 103 | 60°00'N | 158°00'W |
| Kaskaskia, r., Il., U.S. (kăs-kăs'kĭ-ȧ) | 108 | 39°10'N | 88°50'W |
| Kaskattama, r., Can. (kăs-kă-tä'mȧ) | 97 | 56°28'N | 90°55'W |
| Kaskö (Kaskinen), Fin. (käs'kû) (käs'kē-nĕn) | 167 | 62°24'N | 21°18'E |
| Kasli, Russia (käs'lĭ) | 180 | 55°53'N | 60°46'E |
| Kasongo, D.R.C. (kä-sôŋ'gō) | 232 | 4°31'S | 26°42'E |
| Kásos, i., Grc. | 163 | 35°20'N | 26°55'E |
| Kaspiysk, Russia | 182 | 42°52'N | 47°38'E |
| Kassándras, Kólpos, b., Grc. | 175 | 40°10'N | 23°35'E |
| Kassel, Ger. (käs'ĕl) | 161 | 51°19'N | 9°30'E |
| Kasson, Mn., U.S. (kăs'ŭn) | 113 | 44°01'N | 92°45'W |
| Kastamonu, Tur. (kä-stȧ-mō'nōō) | 198 | 41°20'N | 33°50'E |
| Kastoría, Grc. (kȧs-tō'rĭ-ȧ) | 163 | 40°28'N | 21°17'E |
| Kasūr, Pak. | 202 | 31°10'N | 74°29'E |
| Kataba, Zam. | 237 | 16°05'S | 25°10'E |
| Katahdin, Mount, mtn., Me., U.S. (kȧ-tä'dĭn) | 100 | 45°56'N | 68°57'W |
| Katanga, hist. reg., D.R.C. (kȧ-täŋ'gȧ) | 232 | 8°30'S | 25°00'E |
| Katanning, Austl. (kȧ-tăn'ĭng) | 218 | 33°45'S | 117°45'E |
| Katav-Ivanovsk, Russia (kä'tȧf ĭ-vä'nôfsk) | 186a | 54°46'N | 58°13'E |
| Kateninskiy, Russia (kȧtyĕ'nĭs-kĭ) | 186a | 53°12'N | 61°05'E |
| Kateríni, Grc. | 175 | 40°18'N | 22°36'E |
| Katete, Zam. | 237 | 14°05'S | 32°07'E |
| Katherine, Austl. (kăth'ẽr-ĭn) | 218 | 14°15'S | 132°20'E |
| Kāthiāwār, pen., India (kä'tyȧ-wär') | 199 | 22°10'N | 70°20'E |
| Kathmandu, Nepal (kăt-măn-dōō') | 199 | 27°49'N | 85°21'E |
| Kathryn, Can. (kăth'rĭn) | 102e | 51°13'N | 113°42'W |
| Kathryn, Ca., U.S. | 117a | 33°42'N | 117°45'W |
| Katihār, India | 202 | 25°39'N | 87°39'E |
| Katiola, C. Iv. | 234 | 8°08'N | 5°06'W |
| Katmai National Park, rec., Ak., U.S. (kăt'mī) | 106a | 58°38'N | 155°00'W |
| Katompi, D.R.C. | 237 | 6°11'S | 26°20'E |
| Katopa, D.R.C. | 237 | 2°45'S | 25°06'E |
| Katowice, Pol. | 154 | 50°15'N | 19°00'E |
| Katrineholm, Swe. (kȧ-trē'nĕ-hōlm) | 166 | 59°01'N | 16°10'E |
| Katsbakhskiy, Russia (kȧts-băk'skĭ) | 186a | 52°57'N | 59°37'E |
| Katsina, Nig. (kăt'sē-nȧ) | 230 | 13°00'N | 7°32'E |
| Katsina Ala, Nig. | 230 | 7°10'N | 9°17'E |
| Katsura, r., Japan (kä'tsò-rä) | 211b | 34°55'N | 135°43'E |
| Katta-Kurgan, Uzb. (kȧ-tȧ-kòr-gän') | 183 | 39°45'N | 66°42'E |
| Kattegat, strt., Eur. (kăt'ĕ-gät) | 156 | 56°57'N | 11°25'E |
| Katumba, D.R.C. | 237 | 7°45'S | 25°18'E |
| Katun', r., Russia (kȧ-tòn') | 184 | 51°30'N | 86°18'E |
| Katwijk aan Zee, Neth. | 159a | 52°12'N | 4°23'E |
| Kaua'i, i., Hi., U.S. | 106c | 22°09'N | 159°15'W |
| Kauai Channel, strt., Hi., U.S. (kä-ōō-ä'ē) | 106c | 21°35'N | 158°52'W |
| Kaufbeuren, Ger. (kouf'boi-rĕn) | 168 | 47°52'N | 10°38'E |
| Kaufman, Tx., U.S. (kôf'măn) | 123 | 32°36'N | 96°18'W |
| Kaukauna, Wi., U.S. (kô-kô'nȧ) | 113 | 44°17'N | 88°15'W |
| Kaulakahi Channel, strt., Hi., U.S. (kä'ōō-lȧ-kä'hē) | 126a | 22°00'N | 159°55'W |
| Kaunakakai, Hi., U.S. (kä'ōō-nȧ-kä'kī) | 126a | 21°06'N | 156°59'W |
| Kaunas, Lith. (kou'nȧs) (kôv'nô) | 178 | 54°42'N | 23°54'E |
| Kaura Namoda, Nig. | 230 | 12°35'N | 6°35'E |
| Kavála, Grc. (kä-vä'lä) | 163 | 40°55'N | 24°24'E |
| Kavieng, Pap. N. Gui. (kä-vē-ĕng') | 213 | 2°44'S | 151°02'E |
| Kavīr, Dasht-e, des., Iran (dŭsht-ē-ka-vēr') | 198 | 34°41'N | 53°30'E |
| Kawagoe, Japan (kä-wă-gō'ā) | 211 | 35°55'N | 139°29'E |
| Kawaguchi, Japan (kä-wä-gōō-chē) | 211a | 35°48'N | 139°44'E |
| Kawaikini, mtn., Hi., U.S. (kä-wä'ē-kĭ-nĭ) | 126a | 22°05'N | 159°33'W |
| Kawanishi, Japan (kä-wä'nē-shē) | 211b | 34°49'N | 135°26'E |
| Kawasaki, Japan (kä-wä-sä'kē) | 210 | 35°32'N | 139°43'E |
| Kaxgar, r., China | 204 | 39°30'N | 75°00'E |
| Kaya, Burkina (kä'yä) | 230 | 13°05'N | 1°05'W |
| Kayan, r., Indon. | 212 | 1°45'N | 115°38'E |
| Kaycee, Wy., U.S. (kā-sē') | 115 | 43°43'N | 106°38'W |
| Kayes, Mali (kāz) | 230 | 14°27'N | 11°26'W |
| Kayseri, Tur. (kī'sĕ-rē) | 198 | 38°45'N | 35°20'E |
| Kazach'ye, Russia | 179 | 70°46'N | 135°47'E |
| Kazakhstan, nation, Asia | 178 | 48°45'N | 59°00'E |
| Kazan', Russia (kȧ-zän') | 178 | 55°50'N | 49°18'E |
| Kazanka, Ukr. (kȧ-zän'kȧ) | 177 | 47°49'N | 32°50'E |
| Kazanlŭk, Blg. (kä'zȧn-lĕk) | 175 | 42°47'N | 25°23'E |
| Kazbek, Gora, mtn. (kȧz-bĕk') | 181 | 42°42'N | 44°31'E |
| Kāzerūn, Iran | 198 | 29°37'N | 51°44'E |
| Kazincbarcika, Hung. (kô'zĭnts-bôr-tsĭ-ko) | 169 | 48°15'N | 20°39'E |
| Kazungula, Zam. | 237 | 17°45'S | 25°20'E |
| Kazusa Kameyama, Japan (kä-zōō-sä kä-mȧ'yä-mä) | 211a | 35°14'N | 140°06'E |
| Kazym, r., Russia (kä-zēm') | 184 | 63°30'N | 67°41'E |
| Kéa, i., Grc. | 175 | 37°36'N | 24°13'E |
| Kealaikahiki Channel, strt., Hi., U.S. (kā-ä'lä-ē-kä-hē'kē) | 126a | 20°38'N | 157°00'W |
| Keansburg, N.J., U.S. (kēnz'bûrg) | 110a | 40°26'N | 74°08'W |
| Kearney, Ne., U.S. (kär'nĭ) | 112 | 40°42'N | 99°05'W |
| Kearny, N.J., U.S. | 110a | 40°46'N | 74°09'W |
| Keasey, Or., U.S. (kēz'ĭ) | 116c | 45°51'N | 123°20'W |
| Kebnekaise, mtn., Swe. (kĕp'nĕ-kȧ-ēs'ĕ) | 156 | 67°53'N | 18°10'E |
| Kecskemét, Hung. (kĕch'kĕ-māt) | 163 | 46°52'N | 19°42'E |
| Kedah, hist. reg., Malay. (kä'dä) | 212 | 6°00'N | 100°31'E |
| Kėdainiai, Lith. (kē-dī'nĭ-ī) | 167 | 55°16'N | 23°58'E |
| Kedgwick, Can. (kĕdj'wĭk) | 100 | 47°39'N | 67°21'W |
| Keenbrook, Ca., U.S. (kēn'bròk) | 117a | 34°16'N | 117°29'W |
| Keene, N.H., U.S. (kēn) | 109 | 42°55'N | 72°15'W |
| Keetmanshoop, Nmb. (kāt'mȧns-hōp) | 232 | 26°30'S | 18°05'E |
| Keet Seel Ruin, Az., U.S. (kēt sēl) | 119 | 36°46'N | 110°32'W |
| Keewatin, Mn., U.S. (kē-wä'tĭn) | 113 | 47°24'N | 93°03'W |
| Kefallonía, i., Grc. | 163 | 38°08'N | 20°58'E |
| Keffi, Nig. (kĕf'ē) | 230 | 8°51'N | 7°52'E |
| Ke Ga, Mui, c., Viet. | 212 | 12°58'N | 109°50'E |
| Kei, r., Afr. (kā) | 233c | 32°57'S | 26°50'E |
| Keila, Est. (kā'lȧ) | 167 | 59°19'N | 24°25'E |
| Keilor, Austl. | 217a | 37°43'S | 144°50'E |
| Kei Mouth, S. Afr. | 233c | 32°40'S | 28°23'E |
| Keiskammahoek, S. Afr. (kās'kämä-hōōk') | 233c | 32°42'S | 27°11'E |
| Kéita, Bahr, r., Chad | 235 | 9°30'N | 19°17'E |
| Keitele, l., Fin. (kā'tĕ-lĕ) | 167 | 62°50'N | 25°40'E |
| Kekaha, Hi., U.S. | 126a | 21°57'N | 159°42'W |
| Kelafo, Eth. | 238a | 5°40'N | 44°00'E |
| Kelang, Malay. | 212 | 3°20'N | 101°27'E |
| Kelang, r., Malay. | 197b | 3°00'N | 101°40'E |
| Kelkit, r., Tur. | 163 | 40°38'N | 37°03'E |
| Keller, Tx., U.S. (kĕl'ẽr) | 117c | 32°56'N | 97°15'W |
| Kellinghusen, Ger. (kĕ'lĕng-hōō-zĕn) | 159c | 53°57'N | 9°43'E |
| Kellogg, Id., U.S. (kĕl'ŏg) | 114 | 47°32'N | 116°07'W |
| Kelme', Lith. (kĕl-mȧ) | 167 | 55°36'N | 22°53'E |
| Kélo, Chad | 235 | 9°19'N | 15°48'E |
| Kelowna, Can. | 90 | 49°53'N | 119°29'W |
| Kelsey Bay, Can. (kĕl'sē) | 94 | 50°24'N | 125°57'W |
| Kelso, Wa., U.S. | 116c | 46°09'N | 122°54'W |
| Keluang, Malay. | 197b | 2°01'N | 103°19'E |
| Kem', Russia (kĕm) | 178 | 65°00'N | 34°48'E |
| Kemah, Tx., U.S. (kē'mȧ) | 123a | 29°32'N | 95°01'W |
| Kemerovo, Russia | 178 | 55°31'N | 86°05'E |
| Kemi, Fin. (kā'mē) | 160 | 65°48'N | 24°38'E |
| Kemi, r., Fin. | 160 | 67°02'N | 27°50'E |
| Kemigawa, Japan (kĕ'mē-gä'wä) | 211a | 35°38'N | 140°07'E |
| Kemijarvi, Fin. (kā'mē-yĕr-vē) | 160 | 66°48'N | 27°21'E |
| Kemi-joki, l., Fin. | 160 | 66°37'N | 28°13'E |
| Kemmerer, Wy., U.S. (kĕm'ẽr-ẽr) | 115 | 41°48'N | 110°36'W |
| Kemp, l., Tx., U.S. (kĕmp) | 120 | 33°55'N | 99°22'W |
| Kempen, Ger. (kĕm'pĕn) | 171c | 51°22'N | 6°25'E |
| Kempsey, Austl. (kĕmp'sē) | 219 | 30°59'S | 152°50'E |
| Kempt, l., Can. (kĕmpt) | 99 | 47°28'N | 74°00'W |
| Kempten, Ger. (kĕmp'tĕn) | 161 | 47°44'N | 10°17'E |
| Kempton Park, S. Afr. (kĕmp'tŏn pärk) | 238c | 26°07'S | 28°29'E |
| Ken, r., India | 202 | 25°00'N | 79°55'E |
| Kenai, Ak., U.S. (kĕ-nī') | 103 | 60°38'N | 151°18'W |
| Kenai Fjords National Park, rec., Ak., U.S. | 103 | 59°45'N | 150°00'W |
| Kenai Mountains, mts., Ak., U.S. | 103 | 60°00'N | 150°00'W |
| Kenai Pen, Ak., U.S. | 103 | 64°40'N | 150°18'W |
| Kendal, S. Afr. | 238c | 26°03'S | 28°58'E |
| Kendal, Eng., U.K. (kĕn'dȧl) | 164 | 54°20'N | 1°48'W |
| Kendallville, In., U.S. (kĕn'dăl-vĭl) | 108 | 41°25'N | 85°20'W |
| Kenedy, Tx., U.S. (kĕn'ĕ-dĭ) | 123 | 28°49'N | 97°50'W |
| Kenema, S.L. | 234 | 7°52'N | 11°12'W |
| Kenitra, Mor. (kĕ-nē'trȧ) | 162 | 34°21'N | 6°34'W |
| Kenmare, N.D., U.S. (kĕn-mâr') | 112 | 48°41'N | 102°05'W |
| Kenmore, N.Y., U.S. (kĕn'mōr) | 111c | 42°58'N | 78°53'W |
| Kennebec, r., Me., U.S. (kĕn-ē-bĕk') | 100 | 44°23'N | 69°48'W |
| Kennebunk, Me., U.S. (kĕn-ē-buŋk') | 100 | 43°24'N | 70°33'W |
| Kennedale, Tx., U.S. (kĕn'-ē-dāl) | 117c | 32°38'N | 97°13'W |
| Kennedy, Cape see Canaveral, Cape, c., Fl., U.S. | 107 | 28°30'N | 80°23'W |
| Kennedy, Mount, mtn., Can. | 103 | 60°25'N | 138°50'W |
| Kenner, La., U.S. (kĕn'ẽr) | 123 | 29°58'N | 90°15'W |
| Kennett, Mo., U.S. (kĕn'ĕt) | 121 | 36°14'N | 90°01'W |
| Kennewick, Wa., U.S. (kĕn'ē-wĭk) | 114 | 46°12'N | 119°06'W |
| Kenney Dam, dam, Can. | 94 | 53°37'N | 124°58'W |
| Kennydale, Wa., U.S. (kĕn-nē'dāl) | 116a | 47°31'N | 122°12'W |
| Kénogami, Can. (kĕn-ŏ'gä-mē) | 91 | 48°26'N | 71°14'W |
| Kenogamissi Lake, l., Can. | 98 | 48°15'N | 81°31'W |
| Keno Hill, Can. | 103 | 63°58'N | 135°18'W |
| Kenora, Can. (kē-nō'rȧ) | 91 | 49°47'N | 94°29'W |
| Kenosha, Wi., U.S. (kĕ-nō'shȧ) | 105 | 42°34'N | 87°50'W |
| Kenova, W.V., U.S. (kē-nō'vȧ) | 108 | 38°20'N | 82°35'W |
| Kensico Reservoir, res., N.Y., U.S. (kĕn'sĭ-kō) | 110a | 41°08'N | 73°45'W |
| Kent, Oh., U.S. (kĕnt) | 108 | 41°05'N | 81°20'W |
| Kent, Wa., U.S. | 116a | 47°23'N | 122°14'W |
| Kentani, S. Afr. (kĕnt-änĭ') | 233c | 32°31'S | 28°19'E |
| Kentland, In., U.S. (kĕnt'lănd) | 108 | 40°50'N | 87°25'W |
| Kenton, Oh., U.S. (kĕn'tŭn) | 108 | 40°40'N | 83°35'W |
| Kent Peninsula, pen., Can. | 92 | 68°28'N | 108°10'W |
| Kentucky, state, U.S. (kĕn-tŭk'ĭ) | 105 | 37°30'N | 87°35'W |
| Kentucky, res., U.S. | 107 | 36°20'N | 88°50'W |
| Kentucky, r., Ky., U.S. | 107 | 38°15'N | 85°01'W |
| Kentwood, La., U.S. (kĕnt'wòd) | 123 | 30°56'N | 90°31'W |
| Kenya, nation, Afr. (kĕn'yȧ) | 232 | 1°00'N | 36°53'E |
| Kenya, Mount (Kirinyaga), mtn., Kenya | 233 | 0°10'S | 37°20'E |
| Kenyon, Mn., U.S. (kĕn'yŭn) | 113 | 44°15'N | 92°58'W |
| Keokuk, Ia., U.S. (kē'ô-kŭk) | 105 | 40°24'N | 91°34'W |
| Keoma, Can. (kē-ō'mȧ) | 102e | 51°13'N | 113°39'W |
| Kepenkeck Lake, l., Can. | 101 | 48°13'N | 54°45'W |
| Kępno, Pol. (kăŋ'pnō) | 169 | 51°17'N | 17°59'E |
| Kerala, state, India | 199 | 16°38'N | 76°00'E |
| Kerang, Austl. (kē-răng') | 219 | 35°32'S | 143°58'E |
| Kerch, Ukr. | 178 | 45°20'N | 36°26'E |
| Kerchenskiy Proliv, strt., Eur. (kĕr-chĕn'skĭ prô'lĭf) | 177 | 45°08'N | 36°35'E |
| Kerempe Burun, c., Tur. | 163 | 42°00'N | 33°20'E |
| Keren, Erit. | 231 | 15°46'N | 38°28'E |
| Kerguélen, Îles, is., Afr. (kĕr'gā-lĕn) | 3 | 49°50'S | 69°30'E |
| Kericho, Kenya | 237 | 0°22'S | 35°17'E |
| Kerinci, Gunung, mtn., Indon. | 212 | 1°45'S | 101°18'E |
| Keriya see Yutian, China | 204 | 36°55'N | 81°39'E |
| Keriya, r., China (kē'rē-yä) | 204 | 37°13'N | 81°59'E |
| Kerkebet, Erit. | 200 | 16°18'N | 37°24'E |
| Kerkenna, Îles, i., Tun. (kĕr'kĕn-nä) | 230 | 34°49'N | 11°37'E |
| Kerki, Turkmen. (kĕr'kē) | 183 | 37°52'N | 65°15'E |
| Kérkyra, Grc. | 163 | 39°36'N | 19°56'E |
| Kérkyra, i., Grc. | 162 | 39°33'N | 19°36'E |
| Kermadec Islands, is., N.Z. (kẽr-mȧd'ĕk) | 3 | 30°30'S | 177°00'E |
| Kermān, Iran (kĕr-män') | 198 | 30°23'N | 57°08'E |
| Kermānshāh see Bakhtarān, Iran | 198 | 34°01'N | 47°00'E |
| Kern, r., Ca., U.S. | 118 | 35°31'N | 118°37'W |
| Kern, South Fork, r., Ca., U.S. | 118 | 35°40'N | 118°15'W |
| Kerpen, Ger. (kĕr'pĕn) | 171c | 50°52'N | 6°42'E |
| Kerrobert, Can. | 96 | 51°53'N | 109°13'W |
| Kerrville, Tx., U.S. (kûr'vĭl) | 122 | 30°02'N | 99°07'W |
| Kerulen, r., Asia (kĕr'ōō-lĕn) | 205 | 47°52'N | 113°22'E |
| Kesagami Lake, l., Can. | 99 | 50°23'N | 80°15'W |
| Keşan, Tur. (kĕ'shȧn) | 175 | 40°50'N | 26°37'E |
| Keshan, China (kŭ-shän) | 205 | 48°00'N | 126°30'E |

PRONOUNCING INDEX

Kesour – Kitgum 309


| PLACE (Pronunciation) | PAGE | LAT. | LONG. |
|---|---|---|---|
| Kesour, Monts des, mts., Alg. | 162 | 32°51'N | 0°30'W |
| Kestell, S. Afr. (kĕs'tĕl) | 238c | 28°19'S | 28°43'E |
| Keszthely, Hung. (kĕst'hĕl-lĭ) | 169 | 46°46'N | 17°12'E |
| Ket', r., Russia (kyĕt) | 184 | 58°30'N | 84°15'E |
| Keta, Ghana | 230 | 6°00'N | 1°00'E |
| Ketamputih, Indon. | 197b | 1°25'N | 102°19'E |
| Ketapang, Indon. (kĕ-tá-päng') | 212 | 2°00'S | 109°57'E |
| Ketchikan, Ak., U.S. (kĕch-ĭ-kăn') | 106a | 55°21'N | 131°35'W |
| Kętrzyn, Pol. (kăṉ't'r-zĭn) | 169 | 54°04'N | 21°24'E |
| Kettering, Eng., U.K. (kĕt'ĕr-ĭng) | 158a | 52°23'N | 0°43'W |
| Kettering, Oh., U.S. | 108 | 39°40'N | 84°15'W |
| Kettle, r., Can. | 95 | 49°40'N | 119°00'W |
| Kettle, r., Mn., U.S. (kĕt''l) | 113 | 46°20'N | 92°57'W |
| Kettwig, Ger. (kĕt'vēg) | 171c | 51°22'N | 6°56'E |
| Kęty, Pol. (kăṉ tĭ) | 169 | 49°54'N | 19°16'E |
| Ketzin, Ger. (kĕ'tzĕn) | 159b | 52°29'N | 12°51'E |
| Keuka, l., N.Y., U.S. (kē-ū'kȧ) | 109 | 42°30'N | 77°10'W |
| Kevelaer, Ger. (kĕ'fĕ-lăr) | 171c | 51°35'N | 6°15'E |
| Kew, Austl. | 217a | 37°49'S | 145°02'E |
| Kewanee, Il., U.S. (kē-wä'nē) | 113 | 41°15'N | 89°55'W |
| Kewaunee, Wi., U.S. (kē-wô'nē) | 113 | 44°27'N | 87°33'W |
| Keweenaw Bay, b., Mi., U.S. (kē'wē-nô) | 113 | 46°59'N | 88°15'W |
| Keweenaw Peninsula, pen., Mi., U.S. | 113 | 47°28'N | 88°12'W |
| Keya Paha, r., S.D., U.S. (kē-yȧ pä'hä) | 112 | 43°11'N | 100°10'W |
| Key Largo, i., Fl., U.S. | 125a | 25°11'N | 80°15'W |
| Keyport, N.J., U.S. (kē'pōrt) | 110a | 40°26'N | 74°12'W |
| Keyport, Wa., U.S. | 116a | 47°42'N | 122°38'W |
| Keyser, W.V., U.S. (kī'sẽr) | 109 | 39°25'N | 79°00'W |
| Key West, Fl., U.S. (kē wĕst') | 105 | 24°31'N | 81°47'W |
| Kežmarok, Slvk. (kĕzh'mà-rôk) | 169 | 49°10'N | 20°27'E |
| Khabarovo, Russia (kŭ-bȧr-ôvô) | 178 | 69°31'N | 60°41'E |
| Khabarovsk, Russia (kä-bä'rôfsk) | 179 | 48°35'N | 135°12'E |
| Khakassia, prov., Russia | 184 | 52°32'N | 89°33'E |
| Khālāpur, India | 203b | 18°48'N | 73°17'E |
| Khalkidhikí, pen., Grc. | 175 | 40°30'N | 23°18'E |
| Khal'mer-Yu, Russia (kŭl-myĕr'-yōō') | 178 | 67°52'N | 64°25'E |
| Khalturin, Russia (käl'tōō-rēn) | 180 | 58°28'N | 49°00'E |
| Khambhāt, Gulf of, b., India | 199 | 21°20'N | 72°27'E |
| Khammam, India | 203 | 17°09'N | 80°13'E |
| Khānābād, Afg. | 202 | 36°43'N | 69°11'E |
| Khandwa, India | 202 | 21°53'N | 76°22'E |
| Khaníon, Kólpos, b., Grc. | 174a | 35°35'N | 23°55'E |
| Khanka, l., Asia (kän'kà) | 179 | 45°09'N | 133°28'E |
| Khānpur, Pak. | 202 | 28°42'N | 70°42'E |
| Khanty-Mansiysk, Russia (kŭn-te'mŭn-sēsk') | 178 | 61°02'N | 69°01'E |
| Khān Yūnus, Gaza | 197a | 31°21'N | 34°19'E |
| Kharagpur, India (kŭ-rŭg'pòr) | 199 | 22°26'N | 87°21'E |
| Kharkiv, Ukr. | 178 | 50°00'N | 36°10'E |
| Kharkiv, prov., Ukr. | 177 | 49°33'N | 35°55'E |
| Kharkov see Kharkiv, Ukr. | 178 | 50°00'N | 36°10'E |
| Kharlovka, Russia | 180 | 68°47'N | 37°20'E |
| Kharmanli, Blg. (kȧr-män'lē) | 175 | 41°54'N | 25°55'E |
| Khartoum, Sudan | 231 | 15°34'N | 32°36'E |
| Khasavyurt, Russia | 182 | 43°15'N | 46°37'E |
| Khāsh, Iran | 198 | 28°08'N | 61°08'E |
| Khāsh, r., Afg. | 198 | 32°30'N | 64°27'E |
| Khasi Hills, hills, India | 199 | 25°38'N | 91°55'E |
| Khaskovo, Blg. (kás'kô-vô) | 163 | 41°56'N | 25°32'E |
| Khatanga, Russia (kȧ-tän'gȧ) | 179 | 71°48'N | 101°47'E |
| Khatangskiy Zaliv, b., Russia (kä-täṉ'g-skē) | 179 | 73°45'N | 108°30'E |
| Khaybar, Sau. Ar. | 198 | 25°45'N | 39°28'E |
| Kherson, Ukr. (kĕr-sôn') | 181 | 46°38'N | 32°34'E |
| Kherson, prov., Ukr. | 177 | 46°32'N | 32°55'E |
| Khiitola, Russia (khē'tō-là) | 167 | 61°14'N | 29°40'E |
| Khimki, Russia (kēm'kĭ) | 186b | 55°54'N | 37°27'E |
| Khmel'nyts'kyi, Ukr. | 181 | 49°29'N | 26°54'E |
| Khmel'nyts'kyy, prov., Ukr. | 177 | 49°27'N | 26°30'E |
| Khmil'nyk, Ukr. | 177 | 49°34'N | 27°58'E |
| Kholm, Russia (kôlm) | 176 | 57°09'N | 31°07'E |
| Kholmsk, Russia (kŭlmsk) | 179 | 47°09'N | 142°33'E |
| Khomeynīshahr, Iran | 201 | 32°41'N | 51°31'E |
| Khon Kaen, Thai. | 212 | 16°37'N | 102°41'E |
| Khopër, r., Russia (kô'pēr) | 181 | 52°00'N | 43°00'E |
| Khor, Russia (kôr') | 210 | 47°50'N | 134°52'E |
| Khor, r., Russia | 210 | 47°23'N | 135°20'E |
| Khóra Sfakíon, Grc. | 174a | 35°12'N | 24°10'E |
| Khorog, Taj. | 183 | 37°30'N | 71°36'E |
| Khorol, Ukr. (kô'rôl) | 177 | 49°48'N | 33°17'E |
| Khorol, r., Ukr. | 177 | 49°50'N | 33°21'E |
| Khorramābād, Iran | 201 | 33°30'N | 48°20'E |
| Khorramshahr, Iran (kô-ram'shär) | 198 | 30°36'N | 48°15'E |
| Khot'kovo, Russia | 186b | 56°15'N | 38°00'E |
| Khotyn, Ukr. | 181 | 48°29'N | 26°32'E |
| Khoyniki, Bela. | 177 | 51°54'N | 30°00'E |
| Khudzhand, Taj. | 183 | 40°17'N | 69°37'E |
| Khulna, Bngl. | 199 | 22°50'N | 89°38'E |
| Khūryān Mūryān, is., Oman | 198 | 17°27'N | 56°02'E |
| Khust, Ukr. (kŏost) | 169 | 48°10'N | 23°18'E |
| Khvalynsk, Russia (kvá-lĭnsk') | 181 | 52°30'N | 48°00'E |
| Khvoy, Iran | 198 | 38°32'N | 45°01'E |
| Khyber Pass, p., Asia (kī'bẽr) | 199 | 34°28'N | 71°18'E |
| Kialwe, D.R.C. | 237 | 9°22'S | 27°08'E |
| Kiambi, D.R.C. (kyäm'bē) | 232 | 7°20'S | 28°01'E |
| Kiamichi, r., Ok., U.S. (kyȧ-mē'chē) | 121 | 34°31'N | 95°34'W |
| Kianta, l., Fin. (kyán'tà) | 180 | 65°00'N | 28°15'E |
| Kibenga, D.R.C. | 236 | 7°55'S | 17°35'E |
| Kibiti, Tan. | 237 | 7°44'S | 38°57'E |
| Kibombo, D.R.C. | 237 | 3°54'S | 25°55'E |
| Kibondo, Tan. | 237 | 3°35'S | 30°42'E |
| Kičevo, Mac. (kē'chĕ-vô) | 175 | 41°30'N | 20°59'E |
| Kickapoo, r., Wi., U.S. (kĭk'á-pōō) | 113 | 43°20'N | 90°55'W |

| PLACE (Pronunciation) | PAGE | LAT. | LONG. |
|---|---|---|---|
| Kicking Horse Pass, p., Can. | 95 | 51°25'N | 116°10'W |
| Kidal, Mali (kē-dàl') | 230 | 18°33'N | 1°00'E |
| Kidderminster, Eng., U.K. (kĭd'ẽr-mĭn-stẽr) | 158a | 52°23'N | 2°14'W |
| Kidd's Beach, S. Afr. (kĭdz) | 233c | 33°09'S | 27°43'E |
| Kidsgrove, Eng., U.K. (kĭdz'grōv) | 158a | 53°05'N | 2°15'W |
| Kiel, Ger. (kēl) | 154 | 54°19'N | 10°08'E |
| Kiel, Wi., U.S. | 113 | 43°52'N | 88°04'W |
| Kiel Bay, b., Ger. | 168 | 54°33'N | 10°19'E |
| Kiel Canal see Nord-Ostsee Kanal, can., Ger. | 168 | 54°03'N | 9°23'E |
| Kielce, Pol. (kyĕl'tsĕ) | 169 | 50°50'N | 20°41'E |
| Kieldrecht, Bel. (kēl'drĕκt) | 159a | 51°17'N | 4°09'E |
| Kiev (Kyïv), Ukr. | 178 | 50°27'N | 30°30'E |
| Kiffa, Maur. (kēf'á) | 230 | 16°37'N | 11°24'W |
| Kigali, Rw. (kē-gä'lē) | 232 | 1°59'S | 30°05'E |
| Kigoma, Tan. (kē-gō'mä) | 232 | 4°57'S | 29°38'E |
| Kii-Suido, strt., Japan (kē sōō-ē'dō) | 210 | 33°53'N | 134°55'E |
| Kikaiga, i., Japan | 210 | 28°25'N | 130°10'E |
| Kikinda, Serb. (kē'kēn-dä) | 175 | 45°49'N | 20°30'E |
| Kikládes, is., Grc. | 162 | 37°30'N | 24°45'E |
| Kikwit, D.R.C. (kē'kwēt) | 232 | 5°02'S | 18°49'E |
| Kil, Swe. (kēl) | 166 | 59°30'N | 13°15'E |
| Kilauea, Hi., U.S. (kē-lä-ōō-ā'ä) | 126a | 22°12'N | 159°25'W |
| Kilauea Crater, depr., Hi., U.S. | 126a | 19°28'N | 155°18'W |
| Kilbuck Mountains, mts., Ak., U.S. (kĭl-bŭk) | 103 | 60°05'N | 160°00'W |
| Kilchu, Kor., N. (kĭl'chò) | 210 | 40°59'N | 129°23'E |
| Kildare, Ire. (kĭl-dār') | 164 | 53°09'N | 7°05'W |
| Kilembe, D.R.C. | 236 | 5°42'S | 19°55'E |
| Kilgore, Tx., U.S. | 123 | 32°23'N | 94°53'W |
| Kilia, Ukr. | 177 | 45°28'N | 29°17'E |
| Kilifi, Kenya | 237 | 3°38'S | 39°51'E |
| Kilimanjaro, mtn., Tan. (kyl-ē-măn-jä'rô) | 233 | 3°09'S | 37°19'E |
| Kilimatinde, Tan. (kĭl-ē-mä-tĭn'dȧ) | 232 | 5°48'S | 34°58'E |
| Kilindoni, Tan. | 237 | 7°55'S | 39°39'E |
| Kilingi-Nõmme, Est. (kē'lĭn-gē-nôm'mĕ) | 167 | 58°08'N | 25°03'E |
| Kilis, Tur. (kē'lēs) | 163 | 36°50'N | 37°20'E |
| Kilkenny, Ire. (kĭl-kĕn-ĭ) | 161 | 52°40'N | 7°30'W |
| Kilkís, Grc. (kĭl'kĭs) | 175 | 40°59'N | 22°51'E |
| Killala, Ire. (kĭ-lä'lȧ) | 164 | 54°11'N | 9°10'W |
| Killarney, Ire. | 164 | 52°03'N | 9°05'W |
| Killdeer, N.D., U.S. (kĭl'dẽr) | 112 | 47°22'N | 102°45'W |
| Killiniq Island, i., Can. | 93 | 60°32'N | 63°56'W |
| Kilmarnock, Scot., U.K. (kĭl-mär'nŭk) | 164 | 55°38'N | 4°25'W |
| Kilrush, Ire. (kĭl'rŭsh) | 164 | 52°40'N | 9°16'W |
| Kilwa Kisiwani, Tan. | 237 | 8°58'S | 39°30'E |
| Kilwa Kivinje, Tan. | 233 | 8°43'S | 39°18'E |
| Kim, r., Cam. | 235 | 5°40'N | 11°17'E |
| Kimamba, Tan. | 237 | 6°47'S | 37°08'E |
| Kimba, Austl. (kĭm'bȧ) | 222 | 33°08'S | 136°25'E |
| Kimball, Ne., U.S. (kĭm-bȧl) | 112 | 41°14'N | 103°41'W |
| Kimball, S.D., U.S. | 112 | 43°44'N | 98°58'W |
| Kimberley, Can. (kĭm'bẽr-lĭ) | 90 | 49°41'N | 115°59'W |
| Kimberley, S. Afr. | 232 | 28°40'S | 24°50'E |
| Kimi, Cam. | 235 | 6°05'N | 11°30'E |
| Kimmirut (Lake Harbour), Can. | 91 | 62°43'N | 69°40'W |
| Kímolos, i., Grc. (kē'mô-lôs) | 175 | 36°52'N | 24°20'E |
| Kimry, Russia (kĭm'rē) | 180 | 56°53'N | 37°24'E |
| Kimvula, D.R.C. | 236 | 5°44'S | 15°58'E |
| Kinabalu, Gunong, mtn., Malay. | 212 | 5°45'N | 115°26'E |
| Kincardine, Can. (kĭn-kär'dĭn) | 91 | 44°10'N | 81°15'W |
| Kinda, D.R.C. | 237 | 9°18'S | 25°04'E |
| Kindanba, Congo | 236 | 3°44'S | 14°31'E |
| Kinder, La., U.S. (kĭn'dẽr) | 123 | 30°30'N | 92°50'W |
| Kindersley, Can. (kĭn'dẽrz-lē) | 90 | 51°27'N | 109°10'W |
| Kindia, Gui. (kĭn'dē-ȧ) | 230 | 10°04'N | 12°51'W |
| Kindu, D.R.C. | 232 | 2°57'S | 25°56'E |
| Kinel'-Cherkassy, Russia | 180 | 53°32'N | 51°32'E |
| Kineshma, Russia (kē-nĕsh'mȧ) | 180 | 57°27'N | 41°02'E |
| King, i., Austl. (kĭng) | 221 | 39°35'S | 143°40'E |
| Kingaroy, Austl. (kĭŋ'gă-roi) | 222 | 26°37'S | 151°50'E |
| King City, Can. | 102d | 43°56'N | 79°32'W |
| King City, Ca., U.S. (kĭng sĭ'tĭ) | 118 | 36°12'N | 121°08'W |
| Kingcome Inlet, b., Can. (kĭng'kŭm) | 94 | 50°50'N | 126°10'W |
| Kingfisher, Ok., U.S. (kĭng'fĭsh-ẽr) | 121 | 35°51'N | 97°55'W |
| King George Sound, strt., Austl. (jôrj) | 220 | 35°17'S | 118°30'E |
| Kingisepp, Russia (kĭŋ-gē-sep') | 180 | 59°22'N | 28°38'E |
| King Leopold Ranges, mts., Austl. (lē'ô-pōld) | 220 | 16°25'S | 125°00'E |
| Kingman, Az., U.S. (kĭng'măn) | 119 | 35°10'N | 114°05'W |
| Kingman, Ks., U.S. (kĭng'măn) | 120 | 37°38'N | 98°07'W |
| Kings, r., Ca., U.S. | 118 | 36°28'N | 119°43'W |
| Kings Canyon National Park, rec., Ca., U.S. (kăn'yŭn) | 106 | 36°52'N | 118°53'W |
| Kingsclere, Eng., U.K. (kĭngs-clēr) | 158b | 51°18'N | 1°15'W |
| Kingscote, Austl. (kĭngz'kŭt) | 222 | 35°45'S | 137°32'E |
| King's Lynn, Eng., U.K. (kĭngz lĭn') | 165 | 52°45'N | 0°20'E |
| Kings Mountain, N.C., U.S. | 125 | 35°13'N | 81°30'W |
| Kings Norton, Eng., U.K. (nôr'tŭn) | 158a | 52°25'N | 1°54'W |
| King Sound, strt., Austl. | 220 | 16°50'S | 123°35'E |
| Kings Park, N.Y., U.S. (kĭngz pärk) | 110a | 40°53'N | 73°16'W |
| Kings Peak, mtn., Ut., U.S. | 106 | 40°46'N | 110°20'W |
| Kingsport, Tn., U.S. (kĭngz'pōrt) | 125 | 36°33'N | 82°36'W |
| Kingston, Austl. (kĭngz'tŭn) | 218 | 37°52'S | 139°52'E |
| Kingston, Can. | 91 | 44°15'N | 76°30'W |
| Kingston, Jam. | 129 | 18°00'N | 76°45'W |
| Kingston, N.Y., U.S. | 105 | 42°00'N | 74°00'W |
| Kingston, Pa., U.S. | 109 | 41°15'N | 75°50'W |
| Kingston, Wa., U.S. | 116a | 47°04'N | 122°29'W |
| Kingston upon Hull, Eng., U.K. | 154 | 53°45'N | 0°25'W |
| Kingstown, St. Vin. (kĭngz'toun) | 129 | 13°10'N | 61°14'W |

| PLACE (Pronunciation) | PAGE | LAT. | LONG. |
|---|---|---|---|
| Kingstree, S.C., U.S. (kĭngz'trē) | 125 | 33°30'N | 79°50'W |
| Kingsville, Tx., U.S. (kĭngz'vĭl) | 123 | 27°32'N | 97°52'W |
| King William Island, i., Can. (kĭng wĭl'yăm) | 92 | 69°25'N | 97°00'W |
| King William's Town, S. Afr. (kĭng-wĭl'-yŭmz-toun) | 233c | 32°53'S | 27°24'E |
| Kinira, r., S. Afr. | 233c | 30°37'S | 28°52'E |
| Kinloch, Mo., U.S. (kĭn-lŏk) | 117e | 38°44'N | 90°19'W |
| Kinnaird, Can. (kĭn-ärd') | 95 | 49°17'N | 117°39'W |
| Kinnairds Head, c., Scot., U.K. (kĭn-års'hĕd) | 160 | 57°42'N | 3°55'W |
| Kinomoto, Japan (kē'nō-mōtō) | 211 | 33°53'N | 136°07'E |
| Kinosaki, Japan (kē'nō-sä'kē) | 211 | 35°38'N | 134°47'E |
| Kinshasa, D.R.C. | 232 | 4°18'S | 15°18'E |
| Kinsley, Ks., U.S. (kĭnz'lĭ) | 120 | 37°55'N | 99°24'W |
| Kinston, N.C., U.S. (kĭnz'tŭn) | 125 | 35°15'N | 77°35'W |
| Kintampo, Ghana (kēn-täm'pō) | 230 | 8°03'N | 1°43'W |
| Kintyre, pen., Scot., U.K. | 164 | 55°50'N | 5°40'W |
| Kiowa, Ks., U.S. (kī'ô-wȧ) | 120 | 37°01'N | 98°30'W |
| Kiowa, Ok., U.S. | 121 | 34°42'N | 95°53'W |
| Kipawa, Lac, l., Can. | 99 | 46°55'N | 79°00'W |
| Kipembawe, Tan. (kē-pĕm-bä'wȧ) | 232 | 7°39'S | 33°24'E |
| Kipengere Range, mts., Tan. | 237 | 9°10'S | 34°00'E |
| Kipili, Tan. | 237 | 7°26'S | 30°36'E |
| Kipushi, D.R.C. | 237 | 11°46'S | 27°14'E |
| Kirakira, Sol. Is. | 214e | 10°27'S | 161°55'E |
| Kirby, Tx., U.S. (kŭr'bĭ) | 117d | 29°29'N | 98°23'W |
| Kirbyville, Tx., U.S. (kŭr'bĭ-vĭl) | 123 | 30°39'N | 93°54'W |
| Kirenga, r., Russia (kē-rĕŋ'gȧ) | 185 | 56°30'N | 108°18'E |
| Kirensk, Russia (kē-rĕnsk') | 179 | 57°47'N | 108°22'E |
| Kirgiz Range, mts., Asia | 183 | 42°30'N | 74°00'E |
| Kiri, D.R.C. | 236 | 1°27'S | 19°00'E |
| Kiribati, nation, Oc. | 3 | 1°30'S | 173°00'E |
| Kirin see Chilung, Tai. | 205 | 25°02'N | 121°48'E |
| Kiritimati, i., Kir. | 2 | 2°20'N | 157°40'W |
| Kirkby, Eng., U.K. | 158a | 53°29'N | 2°54'W |
| Kirkby-in-Ashfield, Eng., U.K. (kûrk'bē-ĭn-ăsh'fēld) | 158a | 53°06'N | 1°16'W |
| Kirkcaldy, Scot., U.K. (kẽr-kô'dĭ) | 164 | 56°06'N | 3°15'W |
| Kirkenes, Nor. | 160 | 69°40'N | 30°03'E |
| Kirkham, Eng., U.K. (kûrk'ăm) | 158a | 53°47'N | 2°53'W |
| Kirkland, Wa., U.S. (kûrk'lănd) | 116a | 47°41'N | 122°12'W |
| Kirklareli, Tur. (kērk'lär-ĕ'lē) | 163 | 41°44'N | 27°15'E |
| Kirksville, Mo., U.S. (kûrks'vĭl) | 105 | 40°12'N | 92°35'W |
| Kirkwall, Scot., U.K. (kûrk'wôl) | 160 | 58°58'N | 2°59'W |
| Kirkwood, S. Afr. | 233c | 33°26'S | 25°24'E |
| Kirkwood, Mo., U.S. (kûrk'wòd) | 117e | 38°35'N | 90°24'W |
| Kirn, Ger. (kērn) | 168 | 49°47'N | 7°23'E |
| Kirov, Russia | 176 | 54°04'N | 34°19'E |
| Kirov, Russia | 178 | 58°35'N | 49°35'E |
| Kirovakan, Arm. | 182 | 40°48'N | 44°30'E |
| Kirovgrad, Russia (kē'rŭ-vŭ-grad) | 186a | 57°26'N | 60°03'E |
| Kirovohrad, Ukr. | 181 | 48°33'N | 32°17'E |
| Kirovohrad, prov., Ukr. | 177 | 48°23'N | 31°10'E |
| Kirovsk, Russia (kē-rôfsk') | 186c | 59°52'N | 30°59'E |
| Kirovsk, Russia | 178 | 67°40'N | 33°58'E |
| Kirsanov, Russia (kēr-sá'nôf) | 181 | 52°40'N | 42°40'E |
| Kırşehir, Tur. (kẽr-shĕ'hĕr) | 198 | 39°10'N | 34°00'E |
| Kirtachi Seybou, Niger | 235 | 12°48'N | 2°29'E |
| Kirthar Range, mts., Pak. (kĭr-tŭr) | 199 | 27°00'N | 67°10'E |
| Kirton, Eng., U.K. (kûr'tŭn) | 158a | 53°29'N | 0°35'W |
| Kiruna, Swe. (kē-rōō'nä) | 160 | 67°49'N | 20°08'E |
| Kirundu, D.R.C. | 237 | 0°44'S | 25°32'E |
| Kirwin Reservoir, res., Ks., U.S. (kûr'wĭn) | 120 | 39°34'N | 99°04'W |
| Kiryū, Japan | 210 | 36°24'N | 139°20'E |
| Kirzhach, Russia (kēr-zhák') | 176 | 56°08'N | 38°53'E |
| Kisaki, Tan. (kē-sä'kē) | 233 | 7°37'S | 37°43'E |
| Kisangani, D.R.C. | 231 | 0°30'N | 25°12'E |
| Kisarazu, Japan (kē'sä-rä'zōō) | 211a | 35°23'N | 139°55'E |
| Kiselëvsk, Russia (kē-sĭ-lyôfsk') | 178 | 54°00'N | 86°39'E |
| Kishinev see Chişinău, Mol. | 178 | 47°02'N | 28°52'E |
| Kishiwada, Japan (kē'shē-wä'dä) | 210 | 34°25'N | 135°18'E |
| Kishkino, Russia (kĕsh'kĭ-nô) | 186b | 55°15'N | 38°04'E |
| Kisiwani, Tan. | 237 | 4°08'S | 37°57'E |
| Kiska, i., Ak., U.S. (kĭs'kä) | 106b | 52°08'N | 177°10'E |
| Kiskatinaw, r., Can. | 95 | 55°10'N | 120°20'W |
| Kiskittogisu Lake, l., Can. | 97 | 54°05'N | 99°00'W |
| Kiskitto Lake, l., Can. (kĭs-kĭ'tō) | 97 | 54°16'N | 98°34'W |
| Kiskunfélegyháza, Hung. (kĭsh'kòn-fā'lĕd-y'hä'zô) | 169 | 46°42'N | 19°52'E |
| Kiskunhalas, Hung. (kĭsh'kòn-hô'lôsh) | 169 | 46°24'N | 19°26'E |
| Kiskunmajsa, Hung. (kĭsh'kòn-mī'shô) | 169 | 46°29'N | 19°42'E |
| Kislovodsk, Russia | 182 | 43°55'N | 42°44'E |
| Kismaayo, Som. | 233 | 0°18'S | 42°30'E |
| Kiso-Gawa, r., Japan (kē'sō-gä'wä) | 211 | 35°29'N | 137°12'E |
| Kiso-Sammyaku, mts., Japan (kē'sō säm'myà-kōō) | 211 | 35°47'N | 137°39'E |
| Kissamos, Grc. | 174a | 35°13'N | 23°35'E |
| Kissidougou, Gui. (kē'sē-dōō'gōō) | 230 | 9°11'N | 10°06'W |
| Kissimmee, Fl., U.S. (kĭ-sĭm'ē) | 125a | 28°17'N | 81°25'W |
| Kissimmee, r., Fl., U.S. | 125a | 27°45'N | 81°07'W |
| Kissimmee, Lake, l., Fl., U.S. | 125a | 27°58'N | 81°17'W |
| Kisujszallás, Hung. | 169 | 47°12'N | 20°47'E |
| Kisumu, Kenya (kē'sōō-mōō) | 232 | 0°06'S | 34°45'E |
| Kita, Mali (kē'tȧ) | 230 | 13°03'N | 9°29'W |
| Kitakami Gawa, r., Japan | 210 | 39°20'N | 141°10'E |
| Kitakyūshū, Japan | 205 | 33°53'N | 130°50'E |
| Kitale, Kenya | 237 | 1°01'N | 35°00'E |
| Kit Carson, Co., U.S. | 120 | 38°46'N | 102°48'W |
| Kitchener, Can. (kĭch'ĕ-nẽr) | 91 | 43°25'N | 80°35'W |
| Kitenda, D.R.C. | 236 | 6°53'S | 17°21'E |
| Kitgum, Ug. (kĭt'gòm) | 231 | 3°29'N | 33°04'E |

310 Kitimat – Kozhikode
PRONOUNCING INDEX


| PLACE (Pronunciation) | PAGE | LAT. | LONG. |
|---|---|---|---|
| Kitimat, Can. (kĭ'tĭ-măt) | 90 | 54°03'N | 128°33'W |
| Kitimat, r., Can. | 94 | 53°50'N | 129°00'W |
| Kitimat Ranges, mts., Can. | 94 | 53°30'N | 128°50'W |
| Kitlope, r., Can. (kĭt'lōp) | 94 | 53°00'N | 128°00'W |
| Kitsuki, Japan (kēt'sò-kê) | 211 | 33°24'N | 131°35'E |
| Kittanning, Pa., U.S. (kĭ-tăn'ĭng) | 109 | 40°50'N | 79°30'W |
| Kittatinny Mountains, mts., N.J., U.S. (kĭ-tă-tĭ'nê) | 110a | 41°16'N | 74°44'W |
| Kittery, Me., U.S. (kĭt'ēr-ĭ) | 100 | 43°07'N | 70°45'W |
| Kittsee, Aus. | 159e | 48°05'N | 17°05'E |
| Kitty Hawk, N.C., U.S. (kĭt'tê hôk) | 125 | 36°04'N | 75°42'W |
| Kitunda, Tan. | 237 | 6°48'S | 33°13'E |
| Kitwe, Zam. | 237 | 12°49'S | 28°13'E |
| Kitzingen, Ger. (kĭt'zĭng-ĕn) | 168 | 49°44'N | 10°08'E |
| Kiunga, Kenya | 237 | 1°45'S | 41°29'E |
| Kivu, Lac, l., Afr. | 232 | 1°45'S | 28°55'E |
| Kīyose, Japan | 211a | 35°47'N | 139°32'E |
| Kizel, Russia (kē'zĕl) | 180 | 59°05'N | 57°42'E |
| Kızıl, r., Tur. | 198 | 40°00'N | 34°00'E |
| Kizil'skoye, Russia (kĭz'ĭl-skô-yĕ) | 186a | 52°43'N | 58°53'E |
| Kizlyar, Russia (kĭz-lyär') | 181 | 44°00'N | 46°50'E |
| Kizlyarskiy Zaliv, b., Russia | 182 | 44°33'N | 46°55'E |
| Kizu, Japan (kē'zōō) | 211 | 34°43'N | 135°49'E |
| Klaas Smits, r., S. Afr. | 233c | 31°45'S | 26°33'E |
| Klaaswaal, Neth. | 159a | 51°46'N | 4°25'E |
| Kladno, Czech Rep. (kläd'nō) | 168 | 50°10'N | 14°05'E |
| Klagenfurt, Aus. (klä'gĕn-fòrt) | 161 | 46°38'N | 14°19'E |
| Klaipėda, Lith. (klī'pā-dȧ) | 180 | 55°43'N | 21°10'E |
| Klamath, r., U.S. | 114 | 41°40'N | 123°25'W |
| Klamath Falls, Or., U.S. | 104 | 42°13'N | 121°49'W |
| Klamath Mountains, mts., Ca., U.S. | 114 | 42°00'N | 123°25'W |
| Klarälven, r., Swe. | 160 | 60°40'N | 13°00'E |
| Klaskanine, r., Or., U.S. (klăs'kȧ-nīn) | 116c | 46°02'N | 123°43'W |
| Klatovy, Czech Rep. (klä'tô-vê) | 161 | 49°23'N | 13°18'E |
| Klawock, Ak., U.S. (klā'wăk) | 103 | 55°32'N | 133°10'W |
| Kleinmachnow, Ger. (klīn-mäĸ'nō) | 159b | 52°22'N | 13°12'E |
| Klerksdorp, S. Afr. (klĕrks'dôrp) | 238c | 26°52'S | 26°40'E |
| Klerksraal, S. Afr. (klĕrks'kräl) | 238c | 26°15'N | 27°10'E |
| Kletnya, Russia (klyĕt'nyȧ) | 176 | 53°19'N | 33°14'E |
| Kleve, Ger. (klĕ'fĕ) | 168 | 51°47'N | 6°09'E |
| Klickitat, r., Wa., U.S. | 114 | 46°01'N | 121°07'W |
| Klimovichi, Bela. (klē-mô-vē'chê) | 176 | 53°37'N | 31°21'E |
| Klimovsk, Russia (klĭ'môfsk) | 186b | 55°21'N | 37°32'E |
| Klin, Russia (klēn) | 176 | 56°18'N | 36°43'E |
| Klintehamn, Swe. (klēn'tē-häm) | 166 | 57°24'N | 18°14'E |
| Klintsy, Russia (klĭn'tsĭ) | 181 | 52°46'N | 32°14'E |
| Klip, r., S. Afr. (klĭp) | 238c | 27°18'N | 29°25'E |
| Klipgat, S. Afr. | 238c | 25°26'S | 27°57'E |
| Klippan, Swe. (klyp'pán) | 166 | 56°08'N | 13°09'E |
| Kłodzko, Pol. (klôd'skô) | 168 | 50°26'N | 16°38'E |
| Klondike Region, hist. reg., N.A. (klŏn'dīk) | 90 | 64°12'N | 142°38'W |
| Klosterfelde, Ger. (klōs'tĕr-fĕl-dĕ) | 159b | 52°47'N | 13°29'E |
| Klosterneuburg, Aus. (klōs-tĕr-noi'bŏŏrgh) | 159e | 48°19'N | 16°20'E |
| Kluane, l., Can. | 92 | 61°15'N | 138°40'W |
| Kluane National Park, rec., Can. | 92 | 60°25'N | 137°53'W |
| Kluczbork, Pol. (klŏŏch'bŏrk) | 169 | 50°59'N | 18°15'E |
| Klyaz'ma, r., Russia (klyäz'mȧ) | 176 | 55°49'N | 39°19'E |
| Klyetsk, Bela. (klĕtsk) | 176 | 53°04'N | 26°43'E |
| Klyuchevskaya, vol., Russia (klyŏŏ-chĕfskä'yä) | 179 | 56°13'N | 160°00'E |
| Klyuchi, Russia (klyŏŏ'chĭ) | 186a | 57°03'N | 57°20'E |
| Knezha, Blg. (knyā'zhȧ) | 163 | 43°27'N | 24°03'E |
| Knife, r., N.D., U.S. (nīf) | 112 | 47°06'N | 102°33'W |
| Knight Inlet, b., Can. (nīt) | 94 | 50°41'N | 125°40'W |
| Knightstown, In., U.S. (nīts'toun) | 108 | 39°45'N | 85°30'W |
| Knin, Cro. (knēn) | 174 | 44°02'N | 16°14'E |
| Knittelfeld, Aus. | 161 | 47°13'N | 14°50'E |
| Knob Peak, mtn., Phil. (nŏb) | 213a | 12°30'N | 121°20'E |
| Knottingley, Eng., U.K. (nŏt'ĭng-lĭ) | 158a | 53°42'N | 1°14'W |
| Knox, In., U.S. (nŏks) | 108 | 41°15'N | 86°40'W |
| Knox, Cape, c., Can. | 94 | 54°12'N | 133°20'W |
| Knoxville, Ia., U.S. (nŏks'vĭl) | 113 | 41°19'N | 93°05'W |
| Knoxville, Tn., U.S. | 105 | 35°58'N | 83°55'W |
| Knutsford, Eng., U.K. (nŭts'fērd) | 158a | 53°18'N | 2°22'W |
| Knyszyn, Pol. (knĭ'shĭn) | 169 | 53°16'N | 22°59'E |
| Kobayashi, Japan (kō'bȧ-yä'shê) | 211 | 31°58'N | 130°59'E |
| Kōbe, Japan (kō'bĕ) | 205 | 34°30'N | 135°10'E |
| Kobeliaky, Ukr. | 181 | 49°11'N | 34°12'E |
| København see Copenhagen, Den. | 154 | 55°43'N | 12°27'E |
| Koblenz, Ger. (kō'blĕntz) | 161 | 50°18'N | 7°36'E |
| Kobozha, r., Russia (kô-bō'zhȧ) | 176 | 58°55'N | 35°18'E |
| Kobrinskoye, Russia (kô-brĭn'skô-yĕ) | 186c | 59°25'N | 30°07'E |
| Kobryn, Bela. (kō'brĕn') | 181 | 52°13'N | 24°23'E |
| Kobuk, r., Ak., U.S. (kō'bŭk) | 103 | 66°58'N | 158°48'W |
| Kobuk Valley National Park, rec., Ak., U.S. | 103 | 67°20'N | 159°00'W |
| Kobuleti, Geor. (kô-bò-lyā'tē) | 181 | 41°50'N | 41°40'E |
| Kočani, Mac. (kô'chä-nĕ) | 175 | 41°54'N | 22°25'E |
| Kočevje, Slvn. (kô'chäv-ye) | 174 | 45°38'N | 14°51'E |
| Kocher, r., Ger. (kôĸ'ēr) | 168 | 49°00'N | 9°52'E |
| Kochi, India | 203 | 9°58'N | 76°19'E |
| Kōchi, Japan (kō'chê) | 205 | 33°35'N | 133°32'E |
| Kodaira, Japan | 211a | 35°43'N | 139°29'E |
| Kodiak, Ak., U.S. (kō'dyăk) | 106a | 57°50'N | 152°30'W |
| Kodiak Island, i., Ak., U.S. | 103 | 57°24'N | 153°32'W |
| Kodok, Sudan (ko'dŏk) | 231 | 9°57'N | 32°08'E |
| Koforidua, Ghana (kō fō-rĭ-dōō'ȧ) | 230 | 6°03'N | 0°17'W |
| Kōfu, Japan (kō'fōō') | 210 | 35°41'N | 138°34'E |
| Koga, Japan (kō'gȧ) | 211 | 36°13'N | 139°40'E |
| Kogan, r., Gui. | 234 | 11°30'N | 14°05'W |
| Kogane, Japan (kō'gä-nå) | 211a | 35°50'N | 139°56'E |
| Koganei, Japan (kō'gä-nā) | 211a | 35°42'N | 139°31'E |
| Køge, Den. (kû'gĕ) | 166 | 55°27'N | 12°09'E |
| Køge Bugt, b., Den. | 166 | 55°30'N | 12°25'E |
| Kogoni, Mali | 234 | 14°44'N | 6°02'W |
| Kohīma, India (kô-ē'mȧ) | 199 | 25°45'N | 94°41'E |
| Kohyl'nyk, r., Eur. | 177 | 46°08'N | 29°10'E |
| Koito, r., Japan (kô'ê-tō) | 211a | 35°19'N | 139°58'E |
| Kŏje, i., Kor., S. (kû'jĕ) | 210 | 34°53'N | 129°00'E |
| Kokand, Uzb. (kô-känt') | 183 | 40°27'N | 71°07'E |
| Kokemäenjoki, r., Fin. | 167 | 61°23'N | 22°03'E |
| Kokhma, Russia (kôĸ'mȧ) | 176 | 56°57'N | 41°08'E |
| Kokkola, Fin. (kô'kô-lȧ) | 160 | 63°47'N | 22°58'E |
| Kokomo, In., U.S. (kō'kô-mō) | 108 | 40°30'N | 86°20'W |
| Koko Nor (Qinghai Hu), l., China (kō'kô nor) (chyĭŋ-hī hōō) | 204 | 37°26'N | 98°30'E |
| Kokopo, Pap. N. Gui. (kô-kô'pō) | 213 | 4°25'S | 152°27'E |
| Kökshetaū, Kaz. | 183 | 53°15'N | 69°13'E |
| Koksoak, r., Can. (kôk'sô-ăk) | 93 | 57°42'N | 69°50'W |
| Kokstad, S. Afr. (kôk'shtät) | 233c | 30°33'S | 29°27'E |
| Kokubu, Japan (kō'kōō-bōō) | 211 | 31°42'N | 130°46'E |
| Kokuou, Japan (kô'kōō-ô'ōō) | 211b | 34°34'N | 135°39'E |
| Kola Peninsula see Kol'skiy Poluostrov, pen., Russia | 178 | 67°15'N | 37°40'E |
| Kolār (Kolār Gold Fields), India (kōl-är') | 199 | 13°39'N | 78°33'E |
| Kolárvo, Slvk. (kôl-árōvō) | 169 | 47°54'N | 17°59'E |
| Kolbio, Kenya | 237 | 1°10'S | 41°15'E |
| Kol'chugino, Russia (kôl-chò'gē-nô) | 176 | 56°19'N | 39°29'E |
| Kolda, Sen. | 234 | 12°53'N | 14°57'W |
| Kolding, Den. (kŭl'dĭng) | 166 | 55°29'N | 9°24'E |
| Kole, D.R.C. (kō'lā) | 232 | 3°19'S | 22°46'E |
| Kolguyev, i., Russia (kôl-gò'yĕf) | 178 | 69°00'N | 49°00'E |
| Kolhāpur, India | 203 | 16°48'N | 74°15'E |
| Kolín, Czech Rep. (kō'lēn) | 168 | 50°01'N | 15°11'E |
| Kolkasrags, c., Lat. (kôl-käs'rágz) | 167 | 57°46'N | 22°39'E |
| Kolkata (Calcutta), India | 199 | 22°32'N | 88°22'E |
| Köln see Cologne, Ger. | 171c | 50°56'N | 6°57'E |
| Kolno, Pol. (kôw'nô) | 169 | 53°23'N | 21°56'E |
| Koło, Pol. (kō'wô) | 169 | 52°11'N | 18°37'E |
| Kołobrzeg, Pol. (kô-lô'b'zhĕk) | 160 | 54°10'N | 15°35'E |
| Kolomna, Russia (kál-ôm'nȧ) | 180 | 55°06'N | 38°47'E |
| Kolomyia, Ukr. | 169 | 48°32'N | 25°04'E |
| Kolp', r., Russia (kôlp) | 176 | 59°18'N | 35°32'E |
| Kolpashevo, Russia (kŭl pá shô'vȧ) | 178 | 58°16'N | 82°43'E |
| Kolpino, Russia (kôl'pē-nô) | 180 | 59°45'N | 30°37'E |
| Kolpny, Russia (kôlp'nyê) | 176 | 52°14'N | 36°54'E |
| Kol'skiy Poluostrov, pen., Russia | 178 | 67°15'N | 37°40'E |
| Kolva, r., Russia | 180 | 61°00'N | 57°00'E |
| Kolwezi, D.R.C. (kōl-wĕ'zē) | 232 | 10°43'S | 25°28'E |
| Kolyberovo, Russia (kô-lĭ-byâ'rô-vô) | 186b | 55°16'N | 38°45'E |
| Kolyma, r., Russia | 179 | 66°30'N | 151°45'E |
| Kolymskiy Mountains see Gydan, Khrebet, mts., Russia | 179 | 61°45'N | 155°00'E |
| Kom, r., Afr. | 236 | 2°15'N | 12°05'E |
| Komadugu Gana, r., Nig. | 235 | 12°15'N | 11°10'E |
| Komae, Japan | 211a | 35°37'N | 139°35'E |
| Komandorskiye Ostrova, is., Russia | 197 | 55°40'N | 167°13'E |
| Komárno, Slvk. (kô'mär-nô) | 169 | 47°46'N | 18°08'E |
| Komarno, Ukr. | 169 | 49°38'N | 23°42'E |
| Komárom, Hung. (kô'mä-rôm) | 169 | 47°45'N | 18°06'E |
| Komatipoort, S. Afr. (kō-mä'tē-pōrt) | 232 | 25°21'S | 32°00'E |
| Komatsu, Japan (kō-mät'sōō) | 210 | 36°23'N | 136°26'E |
| Komatsushima, Japan (kō-mät'sōō-shê'mä) | 211 | 34°04'N | 134°32'E |
| Komeshia, D.R.C. | 237 | 8°01'S | 27°07'E |
| Komga, S. Afr. (kōm'gȧ) | 233c | 32°36'S | 27°54'E |
| Komi, prov., Russia (kômê) | 184 | 63°00'N | 55°00'E |
| Kommetijie, S. Afr. | 232a | 34°09'S | 18°19'E |
| Komoé, r., C. Iv. | 234 | 5°40'N | 3°40'W |
| Komsomolets, Kaz. | 186a | 53°45'N | 62°04'E |
| Komsomol'sk-na-Amure, Russia | 179 | 50°46'N | 137°14'E |
| Kona, Mali | 234 | 14°57'N | 3°53'W |
| Konda, r., Russia (kôn'dȧ) | 180 | 60°50'N | 64°00'E |
| Kondas, r., Russia (kôn'dȧs) | 186a | 59°30'N | 56°28'E |
| Kondoa, Tan. (kôn-dō'ȧ) | 232 | 4°52'S | 36°00'E |
| Kondolole, D.R.C. | 237 | 1°20'N | 25°58'E |
| Koné, N. Cal. | 214f | 21°04'S | 164°52'E |
| Kong, C. Iv. (kông) | 230 | 9°05'N | 4°41'W |
| Kongbo, C.A.R. | 236 | 4°44'N | 21°23'E |
| Kongolo, D.R.C. (kôŋ'gō'lō) | 232 | 5°23'S | 27°00'E |
| Kongsberg, Nor. (kŭngs'bĕrg) | 166 | 59°40'N | 9°36'E |
| Kongsvinger, Nor. (kŭngs'vĭŋ-gĕr) | 166 | 60°12'N | 12°00'E |
| Koni, D.R.C. (kō'nē) | 232 | 10°32'S | 27°27'E |
| Königsberg see Kaliningrad, Russia | 178 | 54°42'N | 20°32'E |
| Königsbrunn, Ger. (kû'nēgs-brōōn) | 159d | 48°16'N | 10°53'E |
| Königs Wusterhausen, Ger. (kû'nēgs vōōs'tēr-hou-zĕn) | 159b | 52°18'N | 13°38'E |
| Konin, Pol. (kô'nyĕn) | 161 | 52°11'N | 18°17'E |
| Kónitsa, Grc. (kô'nyē'tsȧ) | 175 | 40°03'N | 20°46'E |
| Konjic, Bos. (kôn'yēts) | 175 | 43°38'N | 17°59'E |
| Konju, Kor., S. | 210 | 36°21'N | 127°05'E |
| Konnagar, India | 202a | 22°41'N | 88°22'E |
| Konotop, Ukr. (kô-nô-tôp') | 181 | 51°13'N | 33°14'E |
| Konpienga, r., Burkina | 234 | 11°15'N | 0°35'E |
| Konqi, r., China (kôn-chyē) | 204 | 41°09'N | 87°46'E |
| Końskie, Pol. (koin''skyĕ) | 169 | 51°12'N | 20°26'E |
| Konstanz, Ger. (kôn'shtänts) | 168 | 47°39'N | 9°10'E |
| Kontagora, Nig. (kōn-tȧ-gō'rä) | 230 | 10°24'N | 5°28'E |
| Konya, Tur. (kōn'yȧ) | 198 | 36°55'N | 32°25'E |
| Koocanusa, Lake, res., N.A. | 114 | 49°00'N | 115°10'W |
| Kootenay (Kootenai), r., N.A. | 95 | 49°45'N | 117°05'W |
| Kootenay Lake, l., Can. | 95 | 49°35'N | 116°50'W |
| Kootenay National Park, rec., Can. (kōō'tē-nâ) | 90 | 51°06'N | 117°02'W |
| Kōō-zan, mtn., Japan (kōō'zän) | 211b | 34°53'N | 135°32'E |
| Kopervik, Nor. (kô'pĕr-vêk) | 166 | 59°18'N | 5°20'E |
| Kopeysk, Russia (kô-pāsk') | 184 | 55°07'N | 61°37'E |
| Köping, Swe. (chû'pĭng) | 166 | 59°32'N | 15°58'E |
| Kopparberg, Swe. (kŏp'pár-bĕrgh) | 166 | 59°53'N | 15°00'E |
| Koppeh Dāgh, mts., Asia | 198 | 37°28'N | 58°29'E |
| Koppies, S. Afr. | 238c | 27°15'S | 27°35'E |
| Koprivnica, Cro. (kô'prēv-nē'tsá) | 174 | 46°10'N | 16°48'E |
| Kopychyntsi, Ukr. | 169 | 49°06'N | 25°55'E |
| Korčula, i., Serb. (kôr'chōō-lȧ) | 175 | 42°50'N | 17°05'E |
| Korea, North, nation, Asia | 205 | 40°00'N | 127°00'E |
| Korea, South, nation, Asia | 205 | 36°30'N | 128°00'E |
| Korea Bay, b., Asia | 208 | 39°18'N | 123°50'E |
| Korean Archipelago, is., Kor., S. | 205 | 34°05'N | 125°35'E |
| Korea Strait, strt., Asia | 205 | 33°30'N | 128°30'E |
| Korets', Ukr. | 169 | 50°35'N | 27°13'E |
| Korhogo, C. Iv. (kôr-hō'gō) | 230 | 9°27'N | 5°38'W |
| Korinthiakós Kólpos, b., Grc. | 163 | 38°15'N | 22°33'E |
| Kórinthos, Grc. (kô-rēn'thôs) (kŏr'ĭnth) | 154 | 37°56'N | 22°54'E |
| Koriukivka, Ukr. | 177 | 51°44'N | 32°24'E |
| Kōriyama, Japan (kō'rē-yä'mä) | 210 | 37°18'N | 140°25'E |
| Korkino, Russia (kôr'kē-nŭ) | 186a | 54°53'N | 61°25'E |
| Korla, China (kōr-lä) | 204 | 41°37'N | 86°03'E |
| Körmend, Hung. (kûr'mĕnt) | 168 | 47°02'N | 16°36'E |
| Kornat, i., Serb. (kôr-nät') | 174 | 43°46'N | 15°10'E |
| Korneuburg, Aus. (kôr'noi-bòrgh) | 159e | 48°22'N | 16°21'E |
| Koro, Mali | 234 | 14°04'N | 3°05'W |
| Korocha, Russia (kô-rō'chȧ) | 177 | 50°50'N | 37°13'E |
| Korop, Ukr. (kō'rôp) | 177 | 51°33'N | 32°54'E |
| Koro Sea, sea, Fiji | 214g | 18°00'S | 179°50'E |
| Korosten', Ukr. (kô'rôs-tĕn) | 181 | 50°51'N | 28°39'E |
| Korostyshiv, Ukr. | 177 | 50°19'N | 29°05'E |
| Koro Toro, Chad | 235 | 16°05'N | 18°30'E |
| Korotoyak, Russia (kô'rô-tô-yák') | 177 | 51°00'N | 39°06'E |
| Korsakov, Russia (kôr'sȧ-kôf') | 179 | 46°42'N | 143°16'E |
| Korsnäs, Fin. (kôrs'nĕs) | 167 | 62°51'N | 21°17'E |
| Korsør, Den. (kôrs'ûr') | 166 | 55°19'N | 11°08'E |
| Kortrijk, Bel. | 165 | 50°49'N | 3°10'E |
| Koryakskiy Khrebet, mts., Russia | 179 | 62°00'N | 168°45'E |
| Kosa Biryuchyi ostriv, i., Ukr. | 177 | 46°07'N | 35°12'E |
| Kościan, Pol. (kŭsh'tsyán) | 168 | 52°05'N | 16°38'E |
| Kościerzyna, Pol. (kŭsh-tsyĕ-zhē'nȧ) | 169 | 54°08'N | 17°59'E |
| Kosciusko, Ms., U.S. (kŏs-ĭ-ŭs'kō) | 124 | 33°04'N | 89°35'W |
| Kosciuszko, Mount, mtn., Austl. | 221 | 36°26'S | 148°20'E |
| Kosha, Sudan | 231 | 20°49'N | 30°27'E |
| Koshigaya, Japan (kō'shê-gä'yä) | 211a | 35°53'N | 139°48'E |
| Kōshim, r., Kaz. | 181 | 50°30'N | 50°40'E |
| Kosi, r., India (kô'sē) | 202 | 26°00'N | 86°20'E |
| Košice, Slvk. (kō'shē-tsĕ') | 161 | 48°43'N | 21°17'E |
| Kosmos, S. Afr. (kŏz'mŏs) | 233b | 25°45'S | 27°51'E |
| Kosobrodskiy, Russia (kä-sô'brôd-skĭ) | 186a | 54°14'N | 60°53'E |
| Kosovo, hist. reg., Serb. | 175 | 42°35'N | 21°00'E |
| Kosovska Mitrovica, Serb. (kô'sôv-skä' mē'trô-vē-tsä') | 175 | 42°51'N | 20°50'E |
| Kostajnica, Cro. (kôs'tä-ê-nē'tsá) | 174 | 45°14'N | 16°32'E |
| Koster, S. Afr. | 238c | 25°52'S | 26°52'E |
| Kostiantynivka, Ukr. | 177 | 48°33'N | 37°42'E |
| Kostino, Russia (kôs'tĭ-nô) | 186b | 55°54'N | 37°51'E |
| Kostroma, Russia (kôs-trô-mà') | 178 | 57°46'N | 40°55'E |
| Kostroma, prov., Russia | 176 | 57°50'N | 41°10'E |
| Kostrzyn, Pol. (kôst'chĕn) | 161 | 52°35'N | 14°38'E |
| Kos'va, r., Russia (kôs'vȧ) | 186a | 58°44'N | 57°08'E |
| Koszalin, Pol. (kô-shä'lĭn) | 160 | 54°12'N | 16°10'E |
| Kőszeg, Hung. (kû'sĕg) | 168 | 47°21'N | 16°32'E |
| Kota, India | 199 | 25°17'N | 75°49'E |
| Kota Baharu, Malay. (kō'tä bä'rōō) | 212 | 6°15'N | 102°23'E |
| Kotabaru, Indon. | 212 | 3°22'S | 116°15'E |
| Kota Kinabalu, Malay. | 212 | 5°55'N | 116°05'E |
| Kota Tinggi, Malay. | 197b | 1°43'N | 103°54'E |
| Kotel, Blg. (kô-tĕl') | 175 | 42°54'N | 26°28'E |
| Kotel'nich, Russia (kô-tyĕl'nĕch) | 180 | 58°15'N | 48°20'E |
| Kotel'nyy, i., Russia (kô-tyĕl'nĕ) | 179 | 74°51'N | 134°09'E |
| Kotka, Fin. (kŏt'kȧ) | 160 | 60°28'N | 26°56'E |
| Kotlas, Russia (kôt'lás) | 180 | 61°10'N | 46°50'E |
| Kotlin, Ostrov, i., Russia (ôs-trôf' kôt'lĭn) | 186c | 60°02'N | 29°49'E |
| Kotor, Serb. | 175 | 42°25'N | 18°46'E |
| Kotorosl', r., Russia (kô-tô'rôsl) | 176 | 57°18'N | 39°08'E |
| Kotovs'k, Ukr. | 177 | 47°49'N | 29°31'E |
| Kotto, r., C.A.R. | 231 | 5°17'N | 22°04'E |
| Kotuy, r., Russia (kô-tōō') | 184 | 71°00'N | 103°15'E |
| Kotzebue, Ak., U.S. (kŏt'sē-bōō) | 106a | 66°48'N | 162°42'W |
| Kotzebue Sound, strt., Ak., U.S. | 103 | 67°00'N | 164°28'W |
| Kouchibouguac National Park, rec., Can. | 100 | 46°53'N | 65°35'W |
| Koudougou, Burkina (kōō-dōō'gōō) | 230 | 12°15'N | 2°22'W |
| Kouilou, r., Congo | 232 | 4°30'S | 12°00'E |
| Koula-Moutou, Gabon | 236 | 1°08'S | 12°29'E |
| Koulikoro, Mali (kōō-lê-kō'rô) | 230 | 12°53'N | 7°33'W |
| Koulouguidi, Mali | 235 | 13°27'N | 17°33'E |
| Koumac, N. Cal. | 214f | 20°33'S | 164°17'E |
| Koumra, Chad | 235 | 8°55'N | 17°33'E |
| Koundara, Gui. | 234 | 12°29'N | 13°18'W |
| Kouroussa, Gui. (kōō-rōō'sä) | 230 | 10°39'N | 9°53'W |
| Koutiala, Mali (kōō-tê-ä'lä) | 230 | 12°29'N | 5°29'W |
| Kouvola, Fin. (kō'ô-vô-lä) | 167 | 60°51'N | 26°40'E |
| Kouzhen, China (kō-jŭn) | 206 | 36°19'N | 117°37'E |
| Kovda, l., Russia (kôv'dá) | 180 | 66°45'N | 32°00'E |
| Kovel', Ukr. (kō'vĕl) | 181 | 51°13'N | 24°45'E |
| Kovno see Kaunas, Lith. | 178 | 54°42'N | 23°54'E |
| Kovrov, Russia (kôv-rôf') | 180 | 56°23'N | 41°21'E |
| Koyuk, Ak., U.S. (kô-yōōk') | 103 | 65°00'N | 161°18'W |
| Koyukuk, r., Ak., U.S. (kô-yōō'kŏk) | 103 | 66°25'N | 153°50'W |
| Kozáni, Grc. | 163 | 40°16'N | 21°51'E |
| Kozelets', Ukr. (kôzĕ-lyĕts) | 177 | 50°53'N | 31°07'E |
| Kozel'sk, Russia (kô-zĕlsk') | 176 | 54°01'N | 35°49'E |
| Kozhikode, India | 199 | 11°19'N | 75°49'E |


ăt; finăl; rāte; senâte; ärm; àsk; sofȧ; fâre; ch-choose; dh-as th in other; bē; ēvent; bĕt; recĕnt; cratēr; g-gō; gh-guttural g; bĭt; ĭ-short neutral; rīde; ĸ-guttural k as ch in German ich;

ăt; fināl; rāte; senāte; ärm; ȧsk; sofȧ; fâre; ch-choose; dh-as th in other; bē; ĕvent; bĕt; recĕnt; cratĕr; g-gō; gh-guttural g; bǐt; ī-short neutral; rīde; ĸ-guttural k as ch in German ich;

PRONOUNCING INDEX

L'Anse and Vieux Desert – Leivádia 313


| PLACE (Pronunciation) | PAGE | LAT. | LONG. |
|---|---|---|---|
| L'Anse and Vieux Desert Indian Reservation, I.R., Mi., U.S. | 113 | 46°41'N | 88°12'W |
| Lansford, Pa., U.S. (lănz'fērd) | 109 | 40°50'N | 75°50'W |
| Lansing, Ia., U.S. | 113 | 43°22'N | 91°16'W |
| Lansing, Il., U.S. | 111a | 41°34'N | 87°33'W |
| Lansing, Ks., U.S. | 117f | 39°15'N | 94°53'W |
| Lansing, Mi., U.S. | 105 | 42°45'N | 84°35'W |
| Lanús, Arg. (lä-no͞os') | 144a | 34°42'S | 58°24'W |
| Lanusei, Italy (lä-no͞o-sĕ'y) | 174 | 39°51'N | 9°34'E |
| Lanúvio, Italy (lä-no͞o'vyô) | 173d | 41°41'N | 12°42'E |
| Lanzarote Island, i., Spain (län-zá-rō'tä) | 230 | 29°04'N | 13°03'W |
| Lanzhou, China (län-jō) | 204 | 35°55'N | 103°55'E |
| Laoag, Phil. (lä-wäg') | 212 | 18°13'N | 120°38'E |
| Laon, Fr. (läɴ) | 170 | 49°36'N | 3°35'E |
| La Oroya, Peru (lä-ô-rō'yä) | 142 | 11°30'S | 76°00'W |
| Laos, nation, Asia (lä-ōs) (lá-ōs') | 212 | 20°15'N | 102°00'E |
| Laoshan Wan, b., China (lou-shän wän) | 206 | 36°21'N | 120°48'E |
| La Palma, Pan. (lä-päl'mä) | 133 | 8°25'N | 78°07'W |
| La Palma, Spain | 172 | 37°24'N | 6°36'W |
| La Palma Island, i., Spain | 230 | 28°42'N | 19°03'W |
| La Pampa, prov., Arg. | 144 | 37°25'S | 67°00'W |
| Lapa Rio Negro, Braz. (lä-pä-rē'ō-nĕ'grō) | 144 | 26°12'S | 49°56'W |
| La Paz, Arg. (lä päz') | 144 | 30°48'S | 59°47'W |
| La Paz, Bol. | 142 | 16°31'S | 68°03'W |
| La Paz, Hond. | 132 | 14°15'N | 87°40'W |
| La Paz, Mex. (lä-pá'z) | 130 | 23°39'N | 100°44'W |
| La Paz, Mex. | 128 | 24°00'N | 110°15'W |
| Lapeer, Mi., U.S. (lá-pēr') | 108 | 43°05'N | 83°15'W |
| La-Penne-sur-Huveaune, Fr. (la-pĕn'sür-ü-vōn') | 170a | 43°18'N | 5°33'E |
| La Perouse, Austl. | 217b | 33°59'S | 151°14'E |
| La Piedad Cabadas, Mex. (lä pyå-dhädh' kä-bä'dhäs) | 130 | 20°20'N | 102°04'W |
| Lapland, hist. reg., Eur. (lăp'lănd) | 154 | 68°20'N | 22°00'E |
| La Plata, Arg. (lä plä'tä) | 144 | 34°54'S | 57°57'W |
| La Plata, Mo., U.S. (lá plā'tá) | 121 | 40°03'N | 92°28'W |
| La Plata Peak, mtn., Co., U.S. | 119 | 39°00'N | 106°25'W |
| La Pocatière, Can. (lá pô-ká-tyår') | 99 | 47°24'N | 70°01'W |
| La Poile Bay, b., Can. (lá pwäl') | 101 | 47°38'N | 58°20'W |
| La Porte, In., U.S. (lá pōrt') | 108 | 41°35'N | 86°45'W |
| Laporte, Oh., U.S. | 111d | 41°19'N | 82°05'W |
| La Porte, Tx., U.S. | 123a | 29°40'N | 95°01'W |
| La Porte City, Ia., U.S. | 113 | 42°20'N | 92°10'W |
| Lappeenranta, Fin. (lä'pēn-rän'tä) | 167 | 61°04'N | 28°08'E |
| La Prairie, Can. (lá-prå-rē') | 102a | 45°24'N | 73°30'W |
| Lâpseki, Tur. (läp'sá-kē) | 175 | 40°20'N | 26°41'E |
| Laptev Sea, sea, Russia (läp'tyĭf) | 179 | 75°39'N | 120°00'E |
| La Puebla de Montalbán, Spain | 172 | 39°54'N | 4°21'W |
| La Puente, Ca., U.S. (pwĕn'tē) | 117a | 34°01'N | 117°57'W |
| Lapuşul, r., Rom. (lä'po͞o-sho͞ol) | 169 | 47°29'N | 23°46'E |
| La Quiaca, Arg. (lä kē-ä'kä) | 144 | 22°15'S | 65°44'W |
| L'Aquila, Italy (lá'kē-lä) | 162 | 42°22'N | 13°24'E |
| Lār, Iran (lär) | 198 | 27°31'N | 54°12'E |
| Lara, Austl. | 217a | 38°02'S | 144°24'E |
| Larache, Mor. (lä-räsh') | 230 | 35°15'N | 6°09'W |
| Laramie, Wy., U.S. (lăr'á-mĭ) | 104 | 41°20'N | 105°40'W |
| Laramie, r., Co., U.S. | 120 | 40°56'N | 105°55'W |
| Larchmont, N.Y., U.S. (lärch'mŏnt) | 110a | 40°56'N | 73°46'W |
| Larch Mountain, mtn., Or., U.S. (lärch) | 116c | 45°32'N | 122°06'W |
| Laredo, Spain (lá-rā'dhō) | 172 | 43°24'N | 3°24'W |
| Laredo, Tx., U.S. | 104 | 27°31'N | 99°29'W |
| La Réole, Fr. (lá rå-ōl') | 170 | 44°37'N | 0°03'W |
| Largeau, Chad (lär-zhō') | 231 | 17°55'N | 19°07'E |
| Largo, Cayo, Cuba (kä'yō-lär'gō) | 134 | 21°40'N | 81°30'W |
| Larimore, N.D., U.S. (lăr'ĭ-môr) | 112 | 47°53'N | 97°38'W |
| Larino, Italy (lä-rē'nô) | 174 | 41°48'N | 14°54'E |
| La Rioja, Arg. (lä rē-ōhä) | 144 | 29°18'S | 67°42'W |
| La Rioja, prov., Arg. (lä-rê-ô'kä) | 144 | 28°45'S | 68°00'W |
| Lárisa, Grc. (lä'rē-sá) | 163 | 39°38'N | 22°25'E |
| Lārkāna, Pak. | 202 | 27°40'N | 68°12'E |
| Larnaka, Cyp. | 163 | 34°55'N | 33°37'E |
| Lárnakos, Kólpos, b., Cyp. | 197a | 36°50'N | 33°45'E |
| Larned, Ks., U.S. (lär'nĕd) | 120 | 38°09'N | 99°07'W |
| La Robla, Spain (lä rōb'lä) | 172 | 42°48'N | 5°36'W |
| La Rochelle, Fr. (lá rô-shĕl') | 154 | 46°10'N | 1°09'W |
| La Roche-sur-Yon, Fr. (lá rôsh'sûr-yôɴ') | 161 | 46°39'N | 1°27'W |
| La Roda, Spain (lä rō'dä) | 172 | 39°13'N | 2°08'W |
| La Romona, Dom. Rep. (lä-rä-mō'nä) | 135 | 18°25'N | 69°00'W |
| Larrey Point, c., Austl. (lăr'ē) | 220 | 19°15'S | 118°15'E |
| Laruns, Fr. (lá-räɴs') | 170 | 42°58'N | 0°28'W |
| Larvik, Nor. (lär'vēk) | 160 | 59°06'N | 10°03'E |
| La Sabana, Ven. (lä-sä-bá'nä) | 143b | 10°38'N | 66°24'W |
| La Sabina, Cuba (lä-sä-bē'nä) | 135a | 22°51'N | 82°05'W |
| La Sagra, mtn., Spain (lä sä'grä) | 162 | 37°56'N | 2°35'W |
| La Sal, Ut., U.S. (lá sál') | 119 | 38°10'N | 109°20'W |
| La Salle, Can. (lá säl') | 111b | 42°14'N | 83°06'W |
| La Salle, Can. | 102a | 45°26'N | 73°39'W |
| La Salle, Can. | 102f | 49°41'N | 97°16'W |
| La Salle, Il., U.S. | 108 | 41°20'N | 89°05'W |
| Las Animas, Co., U.S. (lás ă'nĭ-más) | 120 | 38°03'N | 103°16'W |
| La Sarre, Can. | 91 | 48°43'N | 79°12'W |
| Lascahobas, Haiti (läs-kä-ō'bås) | 135 | 19°00'N | 71°55'W |
| Las Cruces, Mex. (läs-kro͞o'sĕs) | 131 | 16°37'N | 93°54'W |
| Las Cruces, N.M., U.S. | 104 | 32°20'N | 106°50'W |
| La Selle, Massif de, mtn., Haiti (lä'sĕl') | 135 | 18°25'N | 72°05'W |
| La Serena, Chile (lä-sĕ-rē'nä) | 144 | 29°55'S | 71°24'W |
| La Seyne, Fr. (lä-sån') | 161 | 43°07'N | 5°52'E |
| Las Flores, Arg. (läs flo'rês) | 144 | 36°01'S | 59°07'W |
| Lashio, Mya. (lăsh'ē-ō) | 204 | 22°58'N | 98°03'E |
| Las Juntas, C.R. (läs-ĸo͞o'n-täs) | 132 | 10°15'N | 85°00'W |
| Las Maismas, sw., Spain (läs-mī's-mäs) | 172 | 37°05'N | 6°25'W |
| La Solana, Spain (lä-sô-lä-nä) | 172 | 38°56'N | 3°13'W |
| Las Palmas, Pan. | 133 | 8°08'N | 81°30'W |
| Las Palmas de Gran Canaria, Spain (läs päl'mäs) | 230 | 28°07'N | 15°28'W |
| La Spezia, Italy (lä-spĕ'zyä) | 154 | 44°07'N | 9°48'E |
| Las Piedras, Ur. (läs-pyĕ'drás) | 141c | 34°42'S | 56°08'W |
| Las Pilas, vol., Nic. (läs-pē'läs) | 132 | 12°32'N | 86°43'W |
| Las Rosas, Mex. (läs rō thäs) | 131 | 16°24'N | 92°23'W |
| Las Rozas de Madrid, Spain (läs rō'thas dā mä-dhrēd') | 173a | 40°29'N | 3°53'W |
| Lassee, Aus. | 159e | 48°14'N | 16°50'E |
| Lassen Peak, mtn., Ca., U.S. (lăs'ĕn) | 106 | 40°30'N | 121°32'W |
| Lassen Volcanic National Park, rec., Ca., U.S. | 106 | 40°43'N | 121°35'W |
| L'Assomption, Can. (lás-sôm-syôɴ) | 102a | 45°50'N | 73°25'W |
| Lass Qoray, Som. | 238a | 11°13'N | 48°19'E |
| Las Tablas, Pan. (läs tä'bläs) | 133 | 7°48'N | 80°16'W |
| Last Mountain, l., Can. (lást moun'tĭn) | 92 | 51°05'N | 105°10'W |
| Lastoursville, Gabon (lás-to͞or-vēl') | 232 | 1°00'S | 12°49'E |
| Las Tres Vírgenes, Volcán, vol., Mex. (vē'r-hĕ-nĕs) | 128 | 26°00'N | 111°45'W |
| Las Tunas, prov., Cuba | 134 | 21°05'N | 77°00'W |
| Las Vacas, Mex. (läs-vá'käs) | 131 | 16°24'N | 95°48'W |
| Las Vegas, Chile (läs-vĕ'gäs) | 141b | 32°50'S | 70°59'W |
| Las Vegas, N.M., U.S. | 104 | 35°36'N | 105°13'W |
| Las Vegas, Nv., U.S. (läs vā'gäs) | 104 | 36°12'N | 115°10'W |
| Las Vegas, Ven. (läs-vĕ'gäs) | 143b | 10°26'N | 64°08'W |
| Las Vigas, Mex. | 131 | 19°38'N | 97°03'W |
| Las Vizcachas, Meseta de, plat., Arg. | 144 | 49°35'S | 71°00'W |
| Latacunga, Ec. (lä-tä-kôŋ'gä) | 142 | 1°02'S | 78°33'W |
| Latakia *see* Al Lādhiqīyah, Syria | 198 | 35°32'N | 35°51'E |
| La Teste-de-Buch, Fr. (lä-tĕst-dē-büsh) | 170 | 44°38'N | 1°11'W |
| Lathrop, Mo., U.S. (lā'thrŭp) | 121 | 39°32'N | 94°21'W |
| La Tortuga, Isla, i., Ven. (ē's-lä-lä-tôr-to͞o'gä) | 142 | 10°55'N | 65°18'W |
| Latorytsia, r., Eur. | 169 | 48°27'N | 22°30'E |
| Latourell, Or., U.S. (lá-tou'rĕl) | 116c | 45°32'N | 122°13'W |
| La Tremblade, Fr. (lä-trĕɴ-bläd') | 170 | 45°45'N | 1°12'W |
| Latrobe, Pa., U.S. (lá-trōb') | 109 | 40°25'N | 79°15'W |
| La Tuque, Can. (lá'tük') | 91 | 47°27'N | 72°49'W |
| Lātūr, India (lä-to͞or') | 202 | 18°20'N | 76°35'E |
| Latvia, nation, Eur. | 178 | 57°28'N | 24°29'E |
| Lau Group, is., Fiji | 214g | 18°20'S | 178°30'W |
| Launceston, Austl. (lôn'sĕs-tŭn) | 219 | 41°35'S | 147°22'E |
| Launceston, Eng., U.K. (lôrn'stŏn) | 164 | 50°38'N | 4°26'W |
| La Unión, Chile (lä-o͞o-nyō'n) | 144 | 40°15'S | 73°04'W |
| La Unión, El Sal. | 132 | 13°18'N | 87°51'W |
| La Unión, Mex. (lä o͞on-nyōn') | 130 | 17°59'N | 101°48'W |
| La Unión, Spain | 162 | 37°38'N | 0°50'W |
| Laura, Austl. (lôrá) | 219 | 15°40'S | 144°45'E |
| Laurel, De., U.S. (lô'rĕl) | 109 | 38°30'N | 75°40'W |
| Laurel, Md., U.S. | 110e | 39°06'N | 76°51'W |
| Laurel, Ms., U.S. | 105 | 31°42'N | 89°07'W |
| Laurel, Mt., U.S. | 115 | 45°41'N | 108°45'W |
| Laurel, Wa., U.S. | 116d | 48°52'N | 122°29'W |
| Laurelwood, Or., U.S. (lô'rĕl-wŏd) | 116c | 45°25'N | 123°05'W |
| Laurens, S.C., U.S. (lô'rĕnz) | 125 | 34°29'N | 82°03'W |
| Laurentian Highlands, hills, Can. (lô'rĕn-tĭ-ăn) | 89 | 49°00'N | 74°50'W |
| Laurentides, Can. (lô'rĕn-tīdz) | 102a | 45°51'N | 73°46'W |
| Lauria, Italy (lou'rē-ä) | 163 | 40°03'N | 15°02'E |
| Laurinburg, N.C., U.S. (lô'rĭn-bûrg) | 125 | 34°45'N | 79°27'W |
| Laurium, Mi., U.S. (lô'rĭ-ŭm) | 113 | 47°13'N | 88°28'W |
| Lausanne, Switz. (lō-zán') | 154 | 46°32'N | 6°35'E |
| Laut, Pulau, i., Indon. | 212 | 3°39'S | 116°07'E |
| Lautaro, Chile (lou-tä'rô) | 144 | 38°40'S | 72°24'W |
| Laut Kecil, Kepulauan, is., Indon. | 212 | 4°44'S | 115°43'E |
| Lautoka, Fiji | 214g | 17°37'S | 177°27'E |
| Lauzon, Can. (lō-zōɴ') | 102b | 46°50'N | 71°10'W |
| Lava Beds National Monument, rec., Ca., U.S. (lä'vá bĕds) | 114 | 41°38'N | 121°44'W |
| Lavaca, r., Tx., U.S. (lá-văk'á) | 123 | 29°05'N | 96°50'W |
| Lava Hot Springs, Id., U.S. | 115 | 42°37'N | 111°58'W |
| Laval, Can. | 91 | 45°31'N | 73°44'W |
| Laval, Fr. (lä-väl') | 161 | 48°05'N | 0°47'W |
| La Vecilla de Curueño, Spain | 172 | 42°53'N | 5°18'W |
| La Vega, Dom. Rep. (lä-vĕ'gä) | 135 | 19°15'N | 70°35'W |
| Lavello, Italy (lä-vĕl'lô) | 174 | 41°05'N | 15°50'E |
| La Verne, Ca., U.S. (lá vûrn') | 117a | 34°06'N | 117°46'W |
| Laverton, Austl. (lā'vēr-tŭn) | 218 | 28°45'S | 122°30'E |
| La Victoria, Ven. (lä vēk-tō'rê-ä) | 142 | 10°14'N | 67°20'W |
| La Vila Joiosa, Spain | 173 | 38°30'N | 0°14'W |
| Lavonia, Ga., U.S. (lá-vō'nĭ-á) | 124 | 34°26'N | 83°05'W |
| Lavon Reservoir, res., Tx., U.S. | 123 | 33°06'N | 96°20'W |
| Lavras, Braz. (lá'vräzh) | 141a | 21°15'S | 44°59'W |
| Lávrio, Grc. | 175 | 37°44'N | 24°05'E |
| Lavry, Russia (lou'rá) | 176 | 57°35'N | 27°28'E |
| Lawndale, Ca., U.S. (lôn'dāl) | 117a | 33°54'N | 118°22'W |
| Lawra, Ghana | 234 | 10°39'N | 2°52'W |
| Lawrence, In., U.S. (lô'rĕns) | 111g | 39°59'N | 86°01'W |
| Lawrence, Ks., U.S. | 105 | 38°57'N | 95°13'W |
| Lawrence, Ma., U.S. | 101a | 42°42'N | 71°09'W |
| Lawrence, Pa., U.S. | 111e | 40°18'N | 80°07'W |
| Lawrenceburg, In., U.S. (lô'rĕns-bûrg) | 111f | 39°06'N | 84°47'W |
| Lawrenceburg, Ky., U.S. | 108 | 38°00'N | 85°00'W |
| Lawrenceburg, Tn., U.S. | 124 | 35°13'N | 87°20'W |
| Lawrenceville, Ga., U.S. (lô-rĕns-vĭl) | 124 | 33°56'N | 83°57'W |
| Lawrenceville, Il., U.S. | 108 | 38°45'N | 87°45'W |
| Lawrenceville, N.J., U.S. | 110a | 40°17'N | 74°44'W |
| Lawrenceville, Va., U.S. | 125 | 36°43'N | 77°52'W |
| Lawsonia, Md., U.S. (lô-sō'nĭ-á) | 109 | 38°00'N | 75°50'W |
| Lawton, Ok., U.S. (lô'tŭn) | 104 | 34°36'N | 98°25'W |
| Lawz, Jabal al, mtn., Sau. Ar. | 198 | 28°46'N | 35°37'E |
| Layang Layang, Malay. (lä-yäng' lä-yäng') | 197b | 1°49'N | 103°28'E |
| Laysan, i., Hi., U.S. | 126b | 26°00'N | 171°00'W |
| Layton, Ut., U.S. (lā'tŭn) | 117b | 41°04'N | 111°58'W |
| Lazdijai, Lith. (läzh'dē-yī') | 167 | 54°12'N | 23°35'E |
| Lazio (Latium), hist. reg., Italy | 174 | 42°05'N | 12°25'E |
| Lead, S.D., U.S. (lēd) | 104 | 44°22'N | 103°47'W |
| Leader, Can. | 96 | 50°55'N | 109°32'W |
| Leadville, Co., U.S. (lĕd'vĭl) | 120 | 39°14'N | 106°18'W |
| Leaf, r., Ms., U.S. (lēf) | 124 | 31°43'N | 89°20'W |
| League City, Tx., U.S. (lēg) | 123a | 29°31'N | 95°05'W |
| Leamington, Can. (lĕm'ĭng-tŭn) | 98 | 42°05'N | 82°35'W |
| Leamington, Eng., U.K. (lĕ'mĭng-tŭn) | 164 | 52°17'N | 1°25'W |
| Leatherhead, Eng., U.K. (lĕdh'ēr-hĕd') | 158b | 51°17'N | 0°20'W |
| Leavenworth, Ks., U.S. (lĕv'ĕn-wûrth) | 105 | 39°19'N | 94°54'W |
| Leavenworth, Wa., U.S. | 114 | 47°35'N | 120°39'W |
| Leawood, Ks., U.S. (lē'wŏd) | 117f | 38°58'N | 94°37'W |
| Łeba, Pol. (lā'bä) | 169 | 54°45'N | 17°34'E |
| Lebam, r., Malay. | 197b | 1°35'N | 104°09'E |
| Lebango, Congo | 236 | 0°22'N | 14°49'E |
| Lebanon, Il., U.S. (lĕb'á-nŭn) | 117e | 38°36'N | 89°49'W |
| Lebanon, In., U.S. | 108 | 40°00'N | 86°30'W |
| Lebanon, Ky., U.S. | 124 | 37°32'N | 85°15'W |
| Lebanon, Mo., U.S. | 121 | 37°40'N | 92°43'W |
| Lebanon, N.H., U.S. | 109 | 43°40'N | 72°15'W |
| Lebanon, Oh., U.S. | 108 | 39°25'N | 84°10'W |
| Lebanon, Or., U.S. | 114 | 44°31'N | 122°53'W |
| Lebanon, Pa., U.S. | 109 | 40°20'N | 76°20'W |
| Lebanon, Tn., U.S. | 124 | 36°10'N | 86°16'W |
| Lebanon, nation, Asia | 198 | 34°00'N | 34°00'E |
| Lebedyan', Russia (lyĕ'bĕ-dyän') | 180 | 53°03'N | 39°08'E |
| Lebedyn, Ukr. | 181 | 50°34'N | 34°27'E |
| Le Blanc, Fr. (lĕ-bläɴ') | 170 | 46°38'N | 0°59'E |
| Le Borgne, Haiti (lĕ bōrn'y') | 135 | 19°50'N | 72°30'W |
| Lębork, Pol. (lăɴ-bòrk') | 169 | 54°33'N | 17°46'E |
| Lebrija, Spain (lå-brē'hä) | 172 | 36°55'N | 6°06'W |
| Lecce, Italy (lĕt'chā) | 163 | 40°22'N | 18°11'E |
| Lecco, Italy (lĕk'kō) | 174 | 45°52'N | 9°28'E |
| Lech, r., Ger. (lĕk) | 168 | 47°41'N | 10°52'E |
| Le Châtelet-en-Brie, Fr. (lĕ-shä-tĕ-lā'ĕɴ-brē') | 171b | 48°29'N | 2°50'E |
| Leche, Laguna de, l., Cuba (lä-gò'nä-dĕ-lĕ'chĕ) | 134 | 22°10'N | 78°30'W |
| Leche, Laguna de la, l., Mex. | 122 | 27°16'N | 102°45'W |
| Lecompte, La., U.S. | 123 | 31°06'N | 92°25'W |
| Le Creusot, Fr. (lĕkrû-zô) | 161 | 46°48'N | 4°23'E |
| Ledesma, Spain (lå-dĕs'mä) | 172 | 41°05'N | 5°59'W |
| Leduc, Can. (lē-do͝ok') | 95 | 53°16'N | 113°33'W |
| Leech, l., Mn., U.S. (lēch) | 113 | 47°06'N | 94°16'W |
| Leeds, Eng., U.K. | 154 | 53°48'N | 1°33'W |
| Leeds, Al., U.S. (lēdz) | 110h | 33°33'N | 86°33'W |
| Leeds, N.D., U.S. | 112 | 48°18'N | 99°24'W |
| Leeds, co., Eng., U.K. | 158a | 53°50'N | 1°30'W |
| Leeds and Liverpool Canal, can., Eng., U.K. (lĭv'ēr-po͞ol) | 158a | 53°36'N | 2°38'W |
| Leegebruch, Ger. (lĕh'gĕn-bro͝ok) | 159b | 52°43'N | 13°12'E |
| Leek, Eng., U.K. (lēk) | 158a | 53°06'N | 2°01'W |
| Leer, Ger. (lār) | 168 | 53°14'N | 7°27'E |
| Leesburg, Fl., U.S. (lēz'bûrg) | 125 | 28°49'N | 81°53'W |
| Leesburg, Va., U.S. | 109 | 39°10'N | 77°30'W |
| Lees Summit, Mo., U.S. | 117f | 38°55'N | 94°23'W |
| Lee Stocking, i., Bah. | 134 | 23°45'N | 76°05'W |
| Leesville, La., U.S. (lēz'vĭl) | 123 | 31°09'N | 93°17'W |
| Leetonia, Oh., U.S. (lē-tō'nĭ-á) | 108 | 40°50'N | 80°45'W |
| Leeuwarden, Neth. (lā'wär-dĕn) | 161 | 52°12'N | 5°50'E |
| Leeuwin, Cape, c., Austl. (lo͞o'wĭn) | 220 | 34°15'S | 114°30'E |
| Leeward Islands, is., N.A. (lē'wērd) | 123 | 17°00'N | 62°15'W |
| Lefkáda, Grc. | 175 | 38°49'N | 20°43'E |
| Lefkáda, i., Grc. | 163 | 38°42'N | 20°22'E |
| Le François, Mart. | 133b | 14°37'N | 60°55'W |
| Lefroy, l., Austl. (lē-froi') | 220 | 31°30'S | 122°00'E |
| Leganés, Spain (lå-gä'nås) | 173a | 40°20'N | 3°46'W |
| Legazpi, Phil. (lå-gäs'pē) | 213 | 13°09'N | 123°44'E |
| Legge Peak, mtn., Austl. (lĕg) | 222 | 41°33'S | 148°10'E |
| Leggett, Ca., U.S. | 118 | 39°51'N | 123°42'W |
| Leghorn *see* Livorno, Italy | 154 | 43°32'N | 11°18'E |
| Legnano, Italy (lå-nyä'nō) | 174 | 45°35'N | 8°53'E |
| Legnica, Pol. (lĕk-nĭt'sá) | 161 | 51°13'N | 16°10'E |
| Leh, India (lā) | 202 | 34°10'N | 77°40'E |
| Le Havre, Fr. (lē áv'r') | 154 | 49°31'N | 0°07'E |
| Lehi, Ut., U.S. (lē'hī) | 119 | 40°25'N | 111°55'W |
| Lehman Caves National Monument, rec., Nv., U.S. (lē'măn) | 119 | 38°54'N | 114°08'W |
| Lehnin, Ger. (lĕh'nēn) | 159b | 52°19'N | 12°45'E |
| Leicester, Eng., U.K. (lĕs'tēr) | 154 | 52°37'N | 1°08'W |
| Leicestershire, co., Eng., U.K. | 158a | 52°40'N | 1°12'W |
| Leichhardt, r., Austl. (līk'härt) | 220 | 18°30'S | 139°45'E |
| Leiden, Neth. (lī'dĕn) | 165 | 52°09'N | 4°29'E |
| Leigh Creek, Austl. (lē krēk) | 222 | 30°33'S | 138°30'E |
| Leikanger, Nor. (lī'käŋ'gēr) | 166 | 61°11'N | 6°51'E |
| Leimuiden, Neth. | 159a | 52°13'N | 4°40'E |
| Leine, r., Ger. (lī'nē) | 168 | 51°58'N | 9°56'E |
| Leinster, hist. reg., Ire. (lĕn-stēr) | 164 | 52°45'N | 7°19'W |
| Leipsic, Oh., U.S. (lĭp'sĭk) | 108 | 41°05'N | 84°00'W |
| Leipzig, Ger. (līp'tsĭk) | 154 | 51°20'N | 12°24'E |
| Leiria, Port. (lā-rē'ä) | 172 | 39°45'N | 8°50'W |
| Leitchfield, Ky., U.S. (lēch'fēld) | 124 | 37°28'N | 86°20'W |
| Leitha, r., Aus. | 159e | 48°04'N | 16°57'E |
| Leitrim, Can. | 102c | 45°20'N | 75°36'W |
| Leivádia, Grc. | 175 | 38°25'N | 22°51'E |

314 Leizhou Bandao – Lincoln Park PRONOUNCING INDEX


| PLACE (Pronunciation) | PAGE | LAT. | LONG. |
|---|---|---|---|
| Leizhou Bandao, pen., China (lā-jō bän-dou) | 204 | 20°42'N | 109°10'E |
| Leksand, Swe. (lĕk'sänd) | 166 | 60°45'N | 14°56'E |
| Leland, Wa., U.S. (lē'lănd) | 116a | 47°54'N | 122°53'W |
| Leliu, China (lŭ-lĭō) | 207a | 22°52'N | 113°09'E |
| Le Locle, Switz. (lẽ lỏ'kl') | 168 | 47°03'N | 6°43'E |
| Le Maire, Estrecho de, strt., Arg. (ĕs-trĕ'chỏ-dĕ-lĕ-mī'rĕ) | 144 | 55°15'S | 65°30'W |
| Le Mans, Fr. (lẽ mäN') | 161 | 48°01'N | 0°12'E |
| Le Marin, Mart. | 133b | 14°28'N | 60°55'W |
| Le Mars, Ia., U.S. (lē märz') | 112 | 42°46'N | 96°09'W |
| Lemay, Mo., U.S. | 117e | 38°32'N | 90°17'W |
| Lemdiyya, Alg. | 230 | 36°18'N | 2°40'E |
| Lemery, Phil. (lā-mā-rē') | 213a | 13°51'S | 120°55'E |
| Lemhi, r., Id., U.S. | 115 | 44°40'N | 113°27'W |
| Lemhi Range, mts., Id., U.S. (lĕm'hī) | 115 | 44°35'N | 113°33'W |
| Lemmon, S.D., U.S. (lĕm'ŭn) | 112 | 45°55'N | 102°10'W |
| Le Môle, Haiti (lẽ mōl') | 135 | 19°50'N | 73°20'W |
| Lemon Grove, Ca., U.S. (lĕm'ŭn-grōv) | 118a | 32°44'N | 117°02'W |
| Le Moule, Guad. (lẽ mōōl') | 133b | 16°19'N | 61°22'W |
| Lempa, r., N.A. (lĕm'pä) | 132 | 13°20'N | 88°46'W |
| Lemvig, Den. (lĕm'vēgh) | 166 | 56°33'N | 8°16'E |
| Lena, r., Russia | 179 | 68°00'N | 123°00'E |
| Lençóes Paulista, Braz. (lĕN-sôNs' pou-lēs'tá) | 144 | 22°30'S | 48°45'W |
| Lençóis, Braz. (lĕn-sóis) | 143 | 12°38'S | 41°28'W |
| Lenexa, Ks., U.S. (lĕ'nĕx-ă) | 117f | 38°58'N | 99°44'W |
| Lengyandong, China (lŭŋ-yän-dôŋ) | 207a | 23°12'N | 113°21'E |
| Lenik, r., Malay. | 197b | 1°59'N | 102°51'E |
| Leningrad see Saint Petersburg, Russia | 178 | 59°57'N | 30°20'E |
| Leningrad, prov., Russia | 176 | 59°15'N | 30°30'E |
| Leningradskaya, Russia (lyĕ-nĭn-gräd'ská-yá) | 177 | 46°19'N | 39°23'E |
| Lenino, Russia (lyĕ'nĭ-nô) | 186b | 55°37'N | 37°41'E |
| Leninogorsk, Kaz. | 183 | 50°29'N | 83°25'E |
| Leninsk, Kaz. | 183 | 45°39'N | 63°19'E |
| Leninsk, Russia (lyĕ-nĕnsk') | 181 | 48°40'N | 45°10'E |
| Leninsk-Kuznetski, Russia (lyĕ-nĕnsk'kōōz-nyĕt'skĭ) | 178 | 54°28'N | 86°48'E |
| Lennox, S.D., U.S. (lĕn'ŭks) | 112 | 43°22'N | 96°53'W |
| Lenoir, N.C., U.S. (lė-nōr') | 125 | 35°54'N | 81°35'W |
| Lenoir City, Tn., U.S. | 124 | 35°47'N | 84°16'W |
| Lenox, Ia., U.S. | 113 | 40°51'N | 94°29'W |
| Léo, Burkina | 234 | 11°06'N | 2°06'W |
| Leoben, Aus. (lå-ō'bĕn) | 168 | 47°22'N | 15°09'E |
| Léogane, Haiti (lā-ô-gan') | 135 | 18°30'N | 72°35'W |
| Leola, S.D., U.S. (lė-ō'lá) | 112 | 45°43'N | 99°55'W |
| Leominster, Ma., U.S. (lĕm'ĭn-stẽr) | 109 | 42°32'N | 71°45'W |
| León, Mex. (lå-ōn') | 128 | 21°08'N | 101°41'W |
| León, Nic. (lĕ-ô'n) | 128 | 12°28'N | 86°53'W |
| León, Spain (lĕ-ô'n) | 162 | 42°38'N | 5°33'W |
| Leon, Ia., U.S. (lē'ŏn) | 113 | 40°43'N | 93°44'W |
| León, hist. reg., Spain | 172 | 41°18'N | 5°50'W |
| Leon, r., Tx., U.S. (lē'ŏn) | 122 | 31°54'N | 98°20'W |
| Leonforte, Italy (lā-ôn-fôr'tā) | 174 | 37°40'N | 14°27'E |
| Leopold II, Lac see Mai-Ndombe, Lac, I., D.R.C. | 232 | 2°16'S | 19°00'E |
| Leopoldina, Braz. (lā-ô-pôl-dē'nä) | 141a | 21°32'S | 42°38'W |
| Leopoldsburg, Bel. | 159a | 51°07'N | 5°18'E |
| Leopoldsdorf im Marchfelde, Aus. (lā'ô-pôlts-dôrf') | 159e | 48°14'N | 16°42'E |
| Léopoldville see Kinshasa, D.R.C. | 232 | 4°18'S | 15°18'E |
| Leova, Mol. | 177 | 46°30'N | 28°16'E |
| Lepe, Spain (lā'pā) | 172 | 37°15'N | 7°12'W |
| Leping, China (lŭ-pĭŋ) | 209 | 29°02'N | 117°12'E |
| L'Épiphanie, Can. (lā-pė-fä-nē') | 102a | 45°51'N | 73°29'W |
| Le Plessis-Belleville, Fr. (lẽ-plĕ-sē'bĕl-vēl') | 171b | 49°05'N | 2°46'E |
| Lepreau, Can. (lė-prō') | 100 | 45°10'N | 66°28'W |
| Le Puy, Fr. (lẽ pwē') | 161 | 45°02'N | 3°54'E |
| Lercara Friddi, Italy (lĕr-kä'rä) | 174 | 37°47'N | 13°36'E |
| Lerdo, Mex. (lĕr'dō) | 128 | 25°31'N | 103°30'W |
| Leribe, Leso. | 233c | 28°53'S | 28°02'E |
| Lerma, Mex. (lĕr'mä) | 131 | 19°49'N | 90°34'W |
| Lerma, Mex. | 131a | 19°17'N | 99°30'W |
| Lerma, Spain (lĕ'r-mä) | 172 | 42°03'N | 3°45'W |
| Lerma, r., Mex. | 130 | 20°14'N | 101°50'W |
| Le Roy, N.Y., U.S. (lė roi') | 109 | 43°00'N | 78°00'W |
| Lerwick, Scot., U.K. (lĕr'ĭk) (lûr'wĭk) | 154 | 60°08'N | 1°27'W |
| Léry, Can. (lā-rī') | 102a | 45°21'N | 73°49'W |
| Lery, Lake, l., La., U.S. (lĕ'rē) | 110d | 29°48'N | 89°45'W |
| Les Andelys, Fr. (lā-zäN-dē-lē') | 171b | 49°15'N | 1°25'E |
| Les Borges Blanques, Spain | 173 | 41°29'N | 0°53'E |
| Lesbos see Lésvos, i., Grc. | 156 | 39°15'N | 25°40'E |
| Les Cayes, Haiti | 135 | 18°15'N | 73°45'W |
| Les Cèdres, Can. (lā-sĕdr') | 102a | 45°18'N | 74°03'W |
| Lesh, Alb. (lĕshĕ) (ä-lā'sē-ō) | 175 | 41°47'N | 19°40'E |
| Leshan, China (lŭ-shän) | 204 | 29°40'N | 103°40'E |
| Lésina, Lago di, l., Italy (lā'gō dē lā'zē-nä) | 174 | 41°48'N | 15°12'E |
| Leskovac, Serb. (lĕs'kō-vàts) | 175 | 43°00'N | 21°58'E |
| Leslie, S. Afr. | 238c | 26°23'S | 28°57'E |
| Leslie, Ar., U.S. (lĕz'lĭ) | 121 | 35°49'N | 92°32'W |
| Lesnoy, Russia (lĕs'noi) | 180 | 66°45'N | 34°45'E |
| Lesogorsk, Russia (lyĕs'ô-gôrsk) | 210 | 49°28'N | 141°59'E |
| Lesotho, nation, Afr. (lĕsō'thō) | 232 | 29°45'S | 28°07'E |
| Lesozavodsk, Russia (lyĕ-sō-zá-vôdsk') | 210 | 45°21'N | 133°19'E |
| Les Sables-d'Olonne, Fr. (lā sá'bl'dō-lŭn') | 161 | 46°30'N | 1°47'W |
| Les Saintes Islands, is., Guad. (lā-săNt') | 133b | 15°50'N | 61°40'W |
| Lesser Antilles, is. | 129 | 12°15'N | 65°00'W |
| Lesser Caucasus, mts., Asia | 182 | 41°00'N | 44°35'E |
| Lesser Khingan Range, mts., China | 205 | 49°50'N | 129°26'E |
| Lesser Slave, r., Can. | 95 | 55°15'N | 114°30'W |
| Lesser Slave Lake, l., Can. (lĕs'ẽr slāv) | 92 | 55°25'N | 115°30'W |
| Lesser Sunda Islands, is., Indon. | 212 | 9°00'S | 120°00'E |
| L'Estaque, Fr. (lĕs-täl) | 170a | 43°22'N | 5°20'E |
| Les Thilliers-en-Vexin, Fr. (lā-tē-yā'ĕN-vĕ-săN') | 171b | 49°19'N | 1°36'E |
| Le Sueur, Mn., U.S. (lė sōōr') | 113 | 44°27'N | 93°53'W |
| Lésvos, i., Grc. | 156 | 39°15'N | 25°40'E |
| Leszno, Pol. (lĕsh'nō) | 161 | 51°51'N | 16°35'E |
| Le Teil, Fr. (lẽ tā'y') | 170 | 44°34'N | 4°39'E |
| Lethbridge, Can. (lĕth'brĭj) | 90 | 49°42'N | 112°50'W |
| Leticia, Col. (lĕ-tē'syá) | 142 | 4°04'S | 69°57'W |
| Leting, China (lŭ-tĭŋ) | 206 | 39°26'N | 118°53'E |
| Le Tréport, Fr. (lẽ-trā'pôr') | 170 | 50°03'N | 1°21'E |
| Letychiv, Ukr. | 177 | 49°22'N | 27°29'E |
| Leuven, Bel. | 165 | 50°53'N | 4°42'E |
| Levack, Can. | 98 | 46°38'N | 81°23'W |
| Levallois-Perret, Fr. (lẽ-vál-wä'pĕ-rĕ') | 171b | 48°53'N | 2°17'E |
| Levanger, Nor. (lĕ-väng'ẽr) | 160 | 63°42'N | 11°01'E |
| Levanna, mtn., Eur. (lå-vä'nä) | 174 | 45°25'N | 7°14'E |
| Leveque, Cape, c., Austl. (lė-vĕk') | 220 | 16°26'S | 123°08'E |
| Leverkusen, Ger. (lĕ'fĕr-kōō-zĕn) | 171c | 51°01'N | 6°59'E |
| Levice, Slvk. (lā'vėt-sĕ) | 169 | 48°13'N | 18°37'E |
| Levico, Italy (lā'vė-kō) | 174 | 46°02'N | 11°20'E |
| Le Vigan, Fr. (lẽ vē-gäN') | 170 | 43°59'N | 3°36'E |
| Lévis, Can. (lā-vē') (lē'vĭs) | 91 | 46°49'N | 71°11'W |
| Levittown, Pa., U.S. (lĕ'vĭt-toun) | 110f | 40°08'N | 74°50'W |
| Levoča, Slvk. (lā'vô-chá) | 169 | 49°03'N | 20°38'E |
| Levuka, Fiji | 214g | 17°41'S | 178°50'E |
| Lewes, Eng., U.K. | 165 | 50°51'N | 0°01'E |
| Lewes, De., U.S. (lōō'ĭs) | 109 | 38°45'N | 75°10'W |
| Lewis, r., Wa., U.S. | 114 | 46°05'N | 122°09'W |
| Lewis, East Fork, r., Wa., U.S. | 116c | 45°52'N | 122°40'W |
| Lewis, Island of, i., Scot., U.K. (lōō'ĭs) | 164 | 58°05'N | 6°07'W |
| Lewisburg, Tn., U.S. (lū'ĭs-bûrg) | 124 | 35°27'N | 86°47'W |
| Lewisburg, W.V., U.S. | 108 | 37°50'N | 80°20'W |
| Lewis Hills, hills, Can. | 101 | 48°48'N | 58°30'W |
| Lewisporte, Can. (lū'ĭs-pōrt) | 101 | 49°15'N | 55°04'W |
| Lewis Range, mts., Mt., U.S. (lū'ĭs) | 115 | 48°15'N | 113°20'W |
| Lewis Smith Lake, res., Al., U.S. | 124 | 34°05'N | 87°07'W |
| Lewiston, Id., U.S. (lū'ĭs-tŭn) | 104 | 46°24'N | 116°59'W |
| Lewiston, Me., U.S. | 105 | 44°05'N | 70°14'W |
| Lewiston, N.Y., U.S. | 111c | 43°11'N | 79°02'W |
| Lewiston, Ut., U.S. | 115 | 41°58'N | 111°51'W |
| Lewistown, Il., U.S. (lū'ĭs-toun) | 121 | 40°23'N | 90°06'W |
| Lewistown, Mt., U.S. | 104 | 47°05'N | 109°25'W |
| Lewistown, Pa., U.S. | 109 | 40°35'N | 77°30'W |
| Lexington, Ky., U.S. (lĕk'sĭng-tŭn) | 105 | 38°05'N | 84°30'W |
| Lexington, Ma., U.S. | 101a | 42°27'N | 71°14'W |
| Lexington, Mo., U.S. | 121 | 39°11'N | 93°52'W |
| Lexington, Ms., U.S. | 124 | 33°08'N | 90°02'W |
| Lexington, N.C., U.S. | 125 | 35°47'N | 80°15'W |
| Lexington, Ne., U.S. | 120 | 40°46'N | 99°44'W |
| Lexington, Tn., U.S. | 124 | 35°37'N | 88°24'W |
| Lexington, Va., U.S. | 109 | 37°45'N | 79°20'W |
| Leyte, i., Phil. (lā'tā) | 213 | 10°35'N | 125°35'E |
| Leżajsk, Pol. (lĕ'zhä-ĭsk) | 169 | 50°14'N | 22°25'E |
| Lezha, r., Russia (lĕ-zhä') | 176 | 58°59'N | 40°27'E |
| L'gov, Russia (lgôf) | 177 | 51°42'N | 35°15'E |
| Lhasa, China (läs'ä) | 204 | 29°41'N | 91°12'E |
| Liangxiangzhen, China (lĭäŋ-shyäŋ-jŭn) | 208a | 39°43'N | 116°08'E |
| Lianjiang, China (lĭĕn-jyäŋ) | 209 | 21°38'N | 110°15'E |
| Lianozovo, Russia (lĭ-a-nô'zô-vô) | 186b | 55°54'N | 37°36'E |
| Lianshui, China (lĭĕn-shwā) | 206 | 33°46'N | 119°15'E |
| Lianyungang, China (lĭĕn-yôn-gäŋ) | 205 | 34°35'N | 119°09'E |
| Liao, r., China | 208 | 41°40'N | 122°40'E |
| Liao, r., China | 205 | 43°37'N | 120°05'E |
| Liaocheng, China (lĭou-chŭŋ) | 208 | 36°27'N | 115°56'E |
| Liaodong Bandao, pen., China (lĭou-dôŋ bän-dou) | 205 | 39°45'N | 122°22'E |
| Liaodong Wan, b., China (lĭou-dôŋ wäŋ) | 208 | 40°25'N | 121°15'E |
| Liaoning, prov., China | 205 | 41°31'N | 122°11'E |
| Liaoyang, China (lyä'ô-yäng') | 205 | 41°18'N | 123°10'E |
| Liaoyuan, China (lĭou-yůän) | 208 | 43°00'N | 124°59'E |
| Liard, r., Can. (lė-är') | 92 | 59°43'N | 126°42'W |
| Libano, Col. (lē'bá-nō) | 142a | 4°55'N | 75°05'W |
| Libby, Mt., U.S. (lĭb'ē) | 114 | 48°27'N | 115°35'W |
| Libenge, D.R.C. (lė-bĕŋ'gä) | 231 | 3°39'N | 18°40'E |
| Liberal, Ks., U.S. (lĭb'ẽr-ăl) | 120 | 37°01'N | 100°56'W |
| Liberec, Czech Rep. (lē'bĕr-ĕts) | 161 | 50°45'N | 15°06'E |
| Liberia, C.R. | 132 | 10°38'N | 85°28'W |
| Liberia, nation, Afr. (lī-bē'rĭ-ă) | 230 | 6°30'N | 9°55'W |
| Libertad, Arg. | 144a | 34°42'S | 58°42'W |
| Libertad de Orituco, Ven. (lē-bĕr-tä'd-dĕ-ô-rē-tōō'kô) | 143b | 9°32'N | 66°24'W |
| Liberty, In., U.S. (lĭb'ẽr-tĭ) | 108 | 39°35'N | 84°55'W |
| Liberty, Mo., U.S. | 117f | 39°15'N | 94°25'W |
| Liberty, S.C., U.S. | 125 | 34°47'N | 82°41'W |
| Liberty, Tx., U.S. | 123 | 30°03'N | 94°46'W |
| Liberty, Ut., U.S. | 117b | 41°20'N | 111°52'W |
| Liberty Bay, b., Wa., U.S. | 116a | 47°43'N | 122°41'W |
| Liberty Lake, l., Md., U.S. | 110e | 39°25'N | 76°56'W |
| Libertyville, Il., U.S. (lĭb'ẽr-tĭ-vĭl) | 111a | 42°17'N | 87°57'W |
| Libode, S. Afr. (lĭ-bō'dĕ) | 233c | 31°33'S | 29°03'E |
| Libón, r., N.A. | 135 | 19°30'N | 71°45'W |
| Libourne, Fr. (lė-bōōrn') | 161 | 44°55'N | 0°12'W |
| Libres, Mex. (lē'brās) | 131 | 19°26'N | 97°41'W |
| Libreville, Gabon (lē-br'vēl') | 232 | 0°23'N | 9°27'E |
| Liburn, Ga., U.S. (lĭb'ûrn) | 110c | 33°53'N | 84°09'W |
| Libya, nation, Afr. (lĭb'ē-ä) | 231 | 27°38'N | 15°00'E |
| Libyan Desert, des., Afr. (lĭb'ē-ăn) | 231 | 28°23'N | 23°34'E |
| Libyan Plateau, plat., Afr. | 200 | 30°58'N | 26°20'E |
| Licancábur, Cerro, mtn., S.A. (sĕ'r-rô-lē-kän-kä'bōōr) | 144 | 22°45'S | 67°45'W |
| Licanten, Chile (lē-kän-tĕ'n) | 141b | 34°58'S | 72°00'W |
| Lichfield, Eng., U.K. (lĭch'fēld) | 158a | 52°41'N | 1°49'W |
| Lichinga, Moz. | 237 | 13°18'S | 35°14'E |
| Lichtenburg, S. Afr. (lĭk'tĕn-bĕrgh) | 238c | 26°09'S | 26°10'E |
| Lick Creek, r., In., U.S. (lĭk) | 111g | 39°43'N | 86°06'W |
| Licking, r., Ky., U.S. (lĭk'ĭng) | 108 | 38°30'N | 84°10'W |
| Lida, Bela. (lē'dá) | 169 | 53°53'N | 25°19'E |
| Lidgerwood, N.D., U.S. (lĭj'ẽr-wood) | 112 | 46°04'N | 97°10'W |
| Lidköping, Swe. (lēt'chû-pĭng) | 166 | 58°31'N | 13°06'E |
| Lido di Roma, Italy (lē'dô-dē-rô'mä) | 173d | 41°19'N | 12°17'E |
| Lidzbark, Pol. (lĭts'bärk) | 169 | 54°07'N | 20°36'E |
| Liebenbergsvlei, r., S. Afr. | 238c | 27°35'S | 28°25'E |
| Liebenwalde, Ger. (lē'bĕn-väl-dĕ) | 159b | 52°52'N | 13°24'E |
| Liechtenstein, nation, Eur. (lĕk'tĕn-shtĭn) | 161 | 47°10'N | 10°00'E |
| Liège, Bel. | 161 | 50°38'N | 5°34'E |
| Lienz, Aus. (lė-ĕnts') | 168 | 46°49'N | 12°45'E |
| Liepāja, Lat. (le'pä-yä') | 180 | 56°31'N | 20°59'E |
| Lier, Bel. | 159a | 51°08'N | 4°34'E |
| Liesing, Aus. (lē'sĭng) | 159e | 48°09'N | 16°17'E |
| Liestal, Switz. (lēs'täl) | 168 | 47°28'N | 7°44'E |
| Lifanga, D.R.C. | 236 | 0°19'N | 21°57'E |
| Lifou, i., N. Cal. | 221 | 21°15'S | 167°32'E |
| Ligao, Phil. (lė-gä'ō) | 213a | 13°14'N | 123°33'E |
| Lightning Ridge, Austl. | 222 | 29°23'S | 147°50'E |
| Ligonha, r., Moz. (lė-gō'nyă) | 233 | 16°14'S | 39°00'E |
| Ligonier, In., U.S. (lĭg-ô-nēr) | 108 | 41°30'N | 85°35'W |
| Ligovo, Russia (lē'gô-vô) | 186c | 59°51'N | 30°13'E |
| Liguria, hist. reg., Italy (lė-gōō-rė-ä) | 174 | 44°24'N | 8°27'E |
| Ligurian Sea, sea, Eur. (lĭ-gū'rĭ-ăn) | 162 | 43°42'N | 8°32'E |
| Lihou Reef, rf., Austl. (lė-hōō') | 221 | 17°23'S | 152°43'E |
| Lihuang, China (lē'hōōäng) | 206 | 31°32'N | 115°46'E |
| Lihue, Hi., U.S. (lė-hōō'ā) | 106c | 21°59'N | 159°23'W |
| Lihula, Est. (lē'hò-lá) | 167 | 58°41'N | 23°50'E |
| Liji, China (lē-jyē) | 206 | 33°47'N | 117°47'E |
| Lijiang, China (lē-jyäŋ) | 204 | 27°00'N | 100°08'E |
| Lijin, China (lē-jyĭn) | 208 | 37°30'N | 118°15'E |
| Likasi, D.R.C. | 232 | 10°59'S | 26°44'E |
| Likhoslavl', Russia (lyė-kôsläv''l) | 176 | 57°07'N | 35°27'E |
| Likouala, r., Congo | 236 | 0°10'S | 16°30'E |
| Lille, Fr. (lēl) | 154 | 50°38'N | 3°01'E |
| Lille Baelt, strt., Den. | 166 | 55°09'N | 9°53'E |
| Lillehammer, Nor. (lēl'ĕ-häm'mẽr) | 160 | 61°07'N | 10°25'E |
| Lillesand, Nor. (lēl'ĕ-sän') | 166 | 58°16'N | 8°19'E |
| Lilleström, Nor. (lēl'ĕ-strûm) | 166 | 59°56'N | 11°04'E |
| Lilliwaup, Wa., U.S. (lĭl'ĭ-wŏp) | 116a | 47°28'N | 123°07'W |
| Lillooet, Can. (lĭ'lōō-ĕt) | 90 | 50°30'N | 121°55'W |
| Lillooet, r., Can. | 95 | 49°50'N | 122°10'W |
| Lilongwe, Mwi. (lė-lô-än) | 232 | 13°59'S | 33°44'E |
| Lima, Peru (lē'mä) | 142 | 12°06'S | 76°55'W |
| Lima, Swe. | 166 | 60°54'N | 13°24'E |
| Lima, Oh., U.S. (lī'mă) | 105 | 40°40'N | 84°05'W |
| Lima, r., Eur. | 172 | 41°45'N | 8°22'W |
| Lima Duarte, Braz. (dwä'r-tĕ) | 141a | 21°52'S | 43°47'W |
| Lima Reservoir, res., Mt., U.S. | 115 | 44°45'N | 112°15'W |
| Limassol, Cyp. | 163 | 34°39'N | 33°02'E |
| Limay, r., Arg. (lē-mä'ė) | 144 | 39°50'S | 69°15'W |
| Limbazi, Lat. (lēm'bä-zĭ) | 167 | 57°32'N | 24°44'E |
| Limbdi, India | 202 | 22°37'N | 71°52'E |
| Limbe, Cam. | 230 | 4°01'N | 9°12'E |
| Limburg an der Lahn, Ger. (lem-bôrg') | 168 | 50°22'N | 8°03'E |
| Limeira, Braz. (lē-mā'rä) | 141a | 22°34'S | 47°24'W |
| Limerick, Ire. (lĭm'nák) | 161 | 52°39'N | 8°35'W |
| Limestone Bay, b., Can. (lĭm'stōn) | 97 | 53°50'N | 98°50'W |
| Limfjorden, Den. | 160 | 56°55'N | 8°56'E |
| Limmen Bight, b., Austl. (lĭm'ĕn) | 220 | 14°45'S | 136°00'E |
| Limnos, i., Grc. | 163 | 39°58'N | 24°48'E |
| Limoges, Can. (lė-môzh') | 102c | 45°20'N | 75°15'W |
| Limoges, Fr. | 161 | 45°50'N | 1°15'E |
| Limón, C.R. (lė-mōn') | 129 | 10°01'N | 83°02'W |
| Limón, Hond. (lē-mô'n) | 132 | 15°53'N | 85°34'W |
| Limon, Co., U.S. (lī'mŏn) | 120 | 39°15'N | 103°41'W |
| Limon, r., Dom. Rep. | 135 | 18°20'N | 71°40'W |
| Limón, Bahía, b., Pan. | 128a | 9°21'N | 79°58'W |
| Limours, Fr. (lē-mōōr') | 171b | 48°39'N | 2°05'E |
| Limousin, Plateaus du, plat., Fr. (plä-tō' dü lē-mōō-zăN') | 170 | 45°44'N | 1°09'E |
| Limoux, Fr. (lē-mōō') | 170 | 43°03'N | 2°14'E |
| Limpopo, r., Afr. (lĭm-pō'pō) | 232 | 23°15'S | 27°46'E |
| Linares, Chile (lė-nä'räs) | 144 | 35°51'S | 71°35'W |
| Linares, Mex. | 128 | 24°53'N | 99°34'W |
| Linares, Spain (lė-nä'rĕs) | 162 | 38°07'N | 3°38'W |
| Linares, prov., Chile | 141b | 35°53'S | 71°30'W |
| Linaro, Cape, c., Italy (lė-nä'rä) | 174 | 42°02'N | 11°53'E |
| Linchuan, China (lĭn-chůän) | 205 | 27°58'N | 116°18'E |
| Lincoln, Arg. (lĭŋ'kŭn) | 144 | 34°51'S | 61°29'W |
| Lincoln, Can. | 102d | 43°10'N | 79°29'W |
| Lincoln, Eng., U.K. | 160 | 53°14'N | 0°33'W |
| Lincoln, Ca., U.S. | 118 | 38°51'N | 121°19'W |
| Lincoln, Il., U.S. | 121 | 40°09'N | 89°21'W |
| Lincoln, Ks., U.S. | 120 | 39°02'N | 98°08'W |
| Lincoln, Ma., U.S. | 101a | 42°25'N | 71°19'W |
| Lincoln, Me., U.S. | 100 | 45°23'N | 68°31'W |
| Lincoln, Ne., U.S. | 104 | 40°49'N | 96°43'W |
| Lincoln, Mount, mtn., Co., U.S. | 120 | 39°20'N | 106°19'W |
| Lincoln Heath, reg., Eng., U.K. | 158a | 53°23'N | 0°39'W |
| Lincoln Park, Mi., U.S. | 111b | 42°14'N | 83°11'W |
| Lincoln Park, N.J., U.S. | 110a | 40°56'N | 74°18'W |


ăt; finăl; rāte; senåte; ärm; åsk; sofá; fâre; ch-choose; dh-as th in other; bē; ėvent; bĕt; recĕnt; cratẽr; g-gō; gh-guttural g; bĭt; ĭ-short neutral; rīde; K-guttural k as ch in German ich;

| PLACE (Pronunciation) | PAGE | LAT. | LONG. |
|---|---|---|---|
| Lincolnshire, co., Eng., U.K. | 158a | 53°12'N | 0°29'W |
| Lincolnshire Wolds, Eng., U.K. (woldz') | 164 | 53°25'N | 0°23'W |
| Lincolnton, N.C., U.S. (lĭŋ'kŭn-tŭn) | 125 | 35°27'N | 81°15'W |
| Lindale, Ga., U.S. (lĭn'dăl) | 124 | 34°10'N | 85°10'W |
| Lindau, Ger. (lĭn'dou) | 168 | 47°33'N | 9°40'E |
| Linden, Al., U.S. (lĭn'dĕn) | 124 | 32°16'N | 87°47'W |
| Linden, Mo., U.S. | 117f | 39°13'N | 94°35'W |
| Linden, N.J., U.S. | 110a | 40°39'N | 74°14'W |
| Lindenhurst, N.Y., U.S. (lĭn'dĕn-hûrst) | 110a | 40°41'N | 73°23'W |
| Lindenwold, N.J., U.S. (lĭn'dĕn-wôld) | 110f | 39°50'N | 75°00'W |
| Lindesberg, Swe. (lĭn'dĕs-bĕrgh) | 166 | 59°37'N | 15°14'E |
| Lindesnes, c., Nor. (lĭn'ĕs-nĕs) | 156 | 58°00'N | 7°05'E |
| Lindi, Tan. (lĭn'dē) | 233 | 10°00'S | 39°43'E |
| Lindi, r., D.R.C. | 231 | 1°00'N | 27°13'E |
| Lindian, China (lĭn-dĭĕn) | 208 | 47°08'N | 124°59'E |
| Lindley, S. Afr. (lĭnd'lē) | 238c | 27°52'S | 27°55'E |
| Lindow, Ger. (lēn'dōv) | 159b | 52°58'N | 12°59'E |
| Lindsay, Can. (lĭn'zē) | 99 | 44°20'N | 78°45'W |
| Lindsay, Ok., U.S. | 121 | 34°50'N | 97°38'W |
| Lindsborg, Ks., U.S. (lĭnz'bôrg) | 121 | 38°34'N | 97°42'W |
| Lineville, Al., U.S. (līn'vĭl) | 124 | 33°18'N | 85°45'W |
| Linfen, China | 205 | 36°00'N | 111°38'E |
| Linga, Kepulauan, is., Indon. | 212 | 0°35'S | 105°05'E |
| Lingao, China (lĭn-gou) | 209 | 19°58'N | 109°40'E |
| Lingayen, Phil. (lĭŋ'gä-yän') | 212 | 16°01'N | 120°13'E |
| Lingayen Gulf, b., Phil. | 213a | 16°18'N | 120°11'E |
| Lingdianzhen, China | 206 | 31°52'N | 121°28'E |
| Lingen, Ger. (lĭŋ'gĕn) | 168 | 52°32'N | 7°20'E |
| Lingling, China (lĭŋ-lĭŋ) | 209 | 26°10'N | 111°40'E |
| Lingshou, China (lĭŋ-shō) | 206 | 38°21'N | 114°41'E |
| Linguère, Sen. (lĭŋ-gĕr') | 230 | 15°24'N | 15°07'W |
| Lingwu, China | 208 | 38°05'N | 106°18'E |
| Lingyuan, China (lĭŋ-yůän) | 208 | 41°12'N | 119°20'E |
| Linhai, China | 209 | 28°52'N | 121°08'E |
| Linhe, China (lĭn-hŭ) | 208 | 40°49'N | 107°45'E |
| Linhuaiguan, China (lĭn-hwī-gůän) | 206 | 32°55'N | 117°38'E |
| Linhuanji, China | 206 | 33°42'N | 116°33'E |
| Linjiang, China (lĭn-jyäŋ) | 208 | 41°45'N | 127°00'E |
| Linköping, Swe. (lĭn'chû-pĭng) | 160 | 58°25'N | 15°35'E |
| Linnhe, Loch, b., Scot., U.K. (lĭn'ē) | 164 | 56°35'N | 4°30'W |
| Linqing, China (lĭn-chyĭŋ) | 205 | 36°49'N | 115°42'E |
| Linqu, China (lĭn-chyōō) | 206 | 36°31'N | 118°33'E |
| Lins, Braz. (lē'ɴs) | 143 | 21°42'S | 49°41'W |
| Linthicum Heights, Md., U.S. (lĭn'thĭ-kŭm) | 110e | 39°12'N | 76°39'W |
| Linton, In., U.S. (lĭn'tŭn) | 108 | 39°05'N | 87°15'W |
| Linton, N.D., U.S. | 112 | 46°16'N | 100°15'W |
| Linwu, China (lĭn'wōō') | 209 | 25°20'N | 112°30'E |
| Linxi, China (lĭn-shyē) | 208 | 43°30'N | 118°02'E |
| Linyi, China (lĭn-yē) | 205 | 35°04'N | 118°21'E |
| Linying, China (lĭn'yĭng') | 206 | 33°48'N | 113°56'E |
| Linz, Aus. (lĭnts) | 161 | 48°18'N | 14°18'E |
| Linzhang, China (lĭn-jäŋ) | 206 | 36°19'N | 114°40'E |
| Lion, Golfe du, b., Fin. | 156 | 43°00'N | 4°00'E |
| Lipa, Phil. (lē-pä') | 212 | 13°55'N | 121°10'E |
| Lipari, Italy (lē'pä-rē) | 174 | 38°29'N | 15°00'E |
| Lipari, i., Italy | 174 | 38°32'N | 15°04'E |
| Lipetsk, Russia (lyē'pĕtsk) | 178 | 52°26'N | 39°34'E |
| Lipetsk, prov., Russia | 176 | 52°18'N | 38°30'E |
| Liping, China (lē-pĭŋ) | 204 | 26°18'N | 109°00'E |
| Lipno, Pol. (lēp'nō) | 169 | 52°50'N | 19°12'E |
| Lippe, r., Ger. (lĭp'ĕ) | 171b | 51°36'N | 6°45'E |
| Lippstadt, Ger. (lĭp'shtät) | 168 | 51°39'N | 8°20'E |
| Lipscomb, Al., U.S. (lĭp'skŭm) | 110h | 33°26'N | 86°56'W |
| Lipu, China (lē-pōō) | 209 | 24°38'N | 110°35'E |
| Lira, Ug. | 237 | 2°15'N | 32°54'E |
| Liri, r., Italy (lē'rē) | 174 | 41°49'N | 13°30'E |
| Lisala, D.R.C. (lē-sä'lä) | 231 | 2°09'N | 21°31'E |
| Lisboa *see* Lisbon, Port. | 154 | 38°42'N | 9°05'W |
| Lisbon (Lisboa), Port. | 154 | 38°42'N | 9°05'W |
| Lisbon, N.D., U.S. | 112 | 46°21'N | 97°43'W |
| Lisbon, Oh., U.S. | 108 | 40°45'N | 80°50'W |
| Lisbon Falls, Me., U.S. | 100 | 43°59'N | 70°03'W |
| Lisburn, N. Ire., U.K. (lĭs'bŭrn) | 164 | 54°35'N | 6°05'W |
| Lisburne, Cape, c., Ak., U.S. | 106a | 68°20'N | 165°40'W |
| Lishi, China (lē-shr) | 208 | 37°32'N | 111°12'E |
| Lishu, China | 208 | 43°12'N | 124°18'E |
| Lishui, China (lĭ'shwĭ') | 206 | 31°41'N | 119°01'E |
| Lishui, China | 205 | 28°28'N | 120°00'E |
| Lisianski Island, i., Hi., U.S. | 126b | 25°30'N | 174°00'W |
| Lisieux, Fr. (lē-zyû') | 170 | 49°10'N | 0°13'E |
| Lisiy Nos, Russia (lĭ'sĭy-nôs) | 186c | 60°01'N | 30°00'E |
| Liski, Russia (lyēs'kē) | 177 | 50°56'N | 39°28'E |
| Lisle, Il., U.S. (lĭl) | 111a | 41°48'N | 88°04'W |
| L'Isle-Adam, Fr. (lēl-ädäɴ') | 171b | 49°05'N | 2°13'E |
| Lismore, Austl. (lĭz'môr) | 219 | 28°48'S | 153°18'E |
| Litani, r., Leb. | 197a | 33°28'N | 35°42'E |
| Litchfield, Il., U.S. (lĭch'fēld) | 121 | 39°10'N | 89°38'W |
| Litchfield, Mn., U.S. | 113 | 45°08'N | 94°34'W |
| Litchfield, Oh., U.S. | 111d | 41°10'N | 82°01'W |
| Lithgow, Austl. (lĭth'gō) | 219 | 33°23'S | 149°31'E |
| Lithinon, Akra, c., Grc. | 174a | 34°59'N | 24°35'E |
| Lithonia, Ga., U.S. (lĭ-thō'nĭ-ȧ) | 110c | 33°43'N | 84°07'W |
| Lithuania, nation, Eur. (lĭth-ů-ā'nĭ-ȧ) | 178 | 55°42'N | 23°30'E |
| Litóchoro, Grc. | 175 | 40°05'N | 22°29'E |
| Litoko, D.R.C. | 236 | 1°13'S | 24°47'E |
| Litoměřice, Czech Rep. (lē'tô-myĕr'zhĭ-tsĕ) | 168 | 50°33'N | 14°10'E |
| Litomyšl, Czech Rep. (lē'tô-mēsh'l) | 168 | 49°52'N | 16°14'E |
| Litoo, Tan. | 237 | 9°45'S | 38°24'E |
| Little, r., Austl. | 217a | 37°54'S | 144°27'E |
| Little, r., Tn., U.S. | 124 | 36°28'N | 89°39'W |
| Little, r., Tx., U.S. | 123 | 30°48'N | 96°50'W |
| Little Abaco, i., Bah. (ă'bä-kō) | 134 | 26°55'N | 77°45'W |
| Little Abitibi, r., Can. | 98 | 50°15'N | 81°30'W |
| Little America, sci., Ant. | 224 | 78°30'S | 161°30'W |
| Little Andaman, i., India (ăn-dȧ-măn') | 212 | 10°39'N | 93°08'E |
| Little Bahama Bank, bk. (bȧ-hā'mȧ) | 134 | 26°55'N | 78°40'W |
| Little Belt Mountains, mts., Mt., U.S. (bĕlt) | 106 | 47°00'N | 110°50'W |
| Little Bighorn, r., Mt., U.S. (bĭg-hôrn) | 115 | 45°08'N | 107°30'W |
| Little Bighorn Battlefield National Monument, rec., Mt., U.S. (bĭg-hôrn băt''l-fēld) | 115 | 45°44'N | 107°15'W |
| Little Bitter Lake, l., Egypt | 238b | 30°10'N | 32°36'E |
| Little Bitterroot, r., Mt., U.S. (bĭt'ĕr-ōōt) | 115 | 47°45'N | 114°45'W |
| Little Blue, r., Ia., U.S. (blōō) | 117f | 38°52'N | 94°25'W |
| Little Blue, r., Ne., U.S. | 120 | 40°15'N | 98°01'W |
| Littleborough, Eng., U.K. (lĭt''l-bŭr-ō) | 158a | 53°39'N | 2°06'W |
| Little Calumet, r., Il., U.S. (kăl-ů-mĕt') | 111a | 41°38'N | 87°38'W |
| Little Cayman, i., Cay. Is. (kā'mȧn) | 134 | 19°40'N | 80°05'W |
| Little Colorado, r., Az., U.S. (kŏl-ô-rä'dō) | 106 | 36°05'N | 111°35'W |
| Little Compton, R.I., U.S. (kŏmp'tŏn) | 110b | 41°31'N | 71°07'W |
| Little Corn Island, i., Nic. | 133 | 12°19'N | 82°50'W |
| Little Exuma, i., Bah. (ĕk-sōō'mä) | 135 | 23°25'N | 75°40'W |
| Little Falls, Mn., U.S. (fôlz) | 113 | 45°58'N | 94°23'W |
| Little Falls, N.Y., U.S. | 109 | 43°05'N | 74°55'W |
| Littlefield, Tx., U.S. (lĭt''l-fēld) | 120 | 33°55'N | 102°17'W |
| Little Fork, r., Mn., U.S. (fôrk) | 113 | 48°24'N | 93°30'W |
| Little Goose Dam, dam, Wa., U.S. | 114 | 46°35'N | 118°02'W |
| Little Hans Lollick, i., V.I.U.S. (häns lôl'ĭk) | 129c | 18°25'N | 64°54'W |
| Little Humboldt, r., Nv., U.S. (hŭm'bōlt) | 114 | 41°10'N | 117°40'W |
| Little Inagua, i., Bah. (ē-nä'gwä) | 135 | 21°30'N | 73°00'W |
| Little Isaac, i., Bah. (ī'zȧk) | 134 | 25°55'N | 79°00'W |
| Little Kanawha, r., W.V., U.S. (kȧ-nô'wȧ) | 108 | 39°05'N | 81°30'W |
| Little Karroo, plat., S. Afr. (kä-rōō) | 232 | 33°50'S | 21°02'E |
| Little Mecatina, r., Can. (mĕ cȧ tĭ nå) | 93 | 52°40'N | 62°21'W |
| Little Miami, r., Oh., U.S. (mī-ăm'ĭ) | 111f | 39°19'N | 84°15'W |
| Little Minch, strt., Scot., U.K. | 164 | 57°35'N | 6°45'W |
| Little Missouri, r., Ar., U.S. (mĭ-sōō'rĭ) | 121 | 34°15'N | 93°54'W |
| Little Missouri, r., U.S. | 106 | 46°00'N | 104°00'W |
| Little Pee Dee, r., S.C., U.S. (pē-dē') | 125 | 34°35'N | 79°21'W |
| Little Powder, r., Wy., U.S. (pou'dĕr) | 115 | 44°51'N | 105°20'W |
| Little Red, r., Ar., U.S. (rĕd) | 121 | 35°25'N | 91°55'W |
| Little Red, r., Ok., U.S. | 121 | 33°53'N | 94°38'W |
| Little Rock, Ar., U.S. (rôk) | 105 | 34°42'N | 92°16'W |
| Little Sachigo Lake, l., Can. (să'chĭ-gō) | 97 | 54°09'N | 92°11'W |
| Little Salt Lake, l., Ut., U.S. | 119 | 37°55'N | 112°53'W |
| Little San Salvador, i., Bah. (săn săl'vȧ-dôr) | 135 | 24°35'N | 75°55'W |
| Little Satilla, r., Ga., U.S. (sȧ-tĭl'ȧ) | 125 | 31°43'N | 82°47'W |
| Little Sioux, r., Ia., U.S. (sōō) | 112 | 42°22'N | 95°47'W |
| Little Smoky, r., Can. (smōk'ĭ) | 95 | 55°10'N | 116°55'W |
| Little Snake, r., Co., U.S. (snāk) | 115 | 40°40'N | 108°21'W |
| Little Tallapoosa, r., Al., U.S. (tăl-ȧ-pōō'sȧ) | 124 | 32°25'N | 85°28'W |
| Little Tennessee, r., Tn., U.S. (tĕn-ĕ-sē') | 124 | 35°36'N | 84°05'W |
| Littleton, Co., U.S. (lĭt''l-tŭn) | 120 | 39°34'N | 105°01'W |
| Littleton, Ma., U.S. | 101a | 42°32'N | 71°29'W |
| Littleton, N.H., U.S. | 109 | 44°15'N | 71°45'W |
| Little Wabash, r., Il., U.S. (wô'băsh) | 108 | 38°50'N | 88°30'W |
| Little Wood, r., Id., U.S. (wŏŏd) | 115 | 43°00'N | 114°08'W |
| Lityn, Ukr. | 177 | 49°16'N | 28°11'E |
| Liubar, Ukr. | 177 | 49°56'N | 27°44'E |
| Liuhe, China | 208 | 42°10'N | 125°38'E |
| Liuli, Tan. | 237 | 11°05'S | 34°38'E |
| Liupan Shan, mts., China | 208 | 36°20'N | 105°30'E |
| Liuwa Plain, pl., Zam. | 236 | 14°30'S | 22°40'E |
| Liuyang, China (lyōō'yäng') | 209 | 28°10'N | 113°35'E |
| Liuyuan, China (liô-yůän) | 206 | 36°09'N | 114°37'E |
| Liuzhou, China (liô-jō) | 204 | 24°25'N | 109°30'E |
| Līvāni, Lat. (lē'vȧ-nē) | 167 | 56°24'N | 26°12'E |
| Lively, Can. | 98 | 46°26'N | 81°09'W |
| Livengood, Ak., U.S. (lĭv'ĕn-gŏŏd) | 103 | 65°30'N | 148°35'W |
| Live Oak, Fl., U.S. (lĭv'ōk) | 124 | 30°15'N | 83°00'W |
| Livermore, Ca., U.S. (lĭv'ĕr-mōr) | 116b | 37°41'N | 121°46'W |
| Livermore, Ky., U.S. | 108 | 37°30'N | 87°05'W |
| Liverpool, Austl. (lĭv'ĕr-pōōl) | 217b | 33°55'S | 150°56'E |
| Liverpool, Can. | 91 | 44°02'N | 64°41'W |
| Liverpool, Eng., U.K. | 154 | 53°25'N | 2°52'W |
| Liverpool, Tx., U.S. | 123a | 29°18'N | 95°17'W |
| Liverpool Bay, b., Can. | 103 | 69°45'N | 130°00'W |
| Liverpool Range, mts., Austl. | 221 | 31°47'S | 151°00'E |
| Livindo, r., Afr. | 231 | 1°09'N | 13°30'E |
| Livingston, Guat. | 132 | 15°50'N | 88°45'W |
| Livingston, Al., U.S. (lĭv'ĭng-stŭn) | 124 | 32°35'N | 88°09'W |
| Livingston, Il., U.S. | 117e | 38°58'N | 89°51'W |
| Livingston, Mt., U.S. | 104 | 45°40'N | 110°35'W |
| Livingston, N.J., U.S. | 110a | 40°47'N | 74°20'W |
| Livingston, Tn., U.S. | 124 | 36°23'N | 85°20'W |
| Livingstone, Zam. (lĭv-ĭng-stôn) | 232 | 17°50'S | 25°53'E |
| Livingstone, Chutes de, wtfl., Afr. | 236 | 4°50'S | 14°30'E |
| Livingstonia, Mwi. (lĭv-ĭng-stō'nĭ-ȧ) | 232 | 10°36'S | 34°07'E |
| Livno, Bos. (lēv'nō) | 163 | 43°50'N | 17°03'E |
| Livny, Russia (lēv'nē) | 181 | 52°28'N | 37°36'E |
| Livonia, Mi., U.S. (lĭ-vō-nĭ-ȧ) | 111b | 42°25'N | 83°23'W |
| Livorno, Italy (lē-vôr'nō) (lĕg'hôrn) | 154 | 43°32'N | 11°18'E |
| Livramento, Braz. (lē-vrȧ-mĕ'n-tô) | 144 | 30°46'S | 55°21'W |
| Lixian, China (lē shyĕn) | 209 | 29°42'N | 111°40'E |
| Lixian, China | 206 | 38°30'N | 115°38'E |
| Liyang, China (lē'yäng') | 209 | 31°30'N | 119°29'E |
| Lizard Point, c., Eng., U.K. (lĭz'ȧrd) | 161 | 49°55'N | 5°09'W |
| Lizy-sur-Ourcq, Fr. (lēk-sē'sür-ōōrk') | 171b | 49°01'N | 3°02'E |
| Ljubljana, Slvn. (lyōō'blyȧ'na) | 154 | 46°04'N | 14°29'E |
| Ljubuški, Bos. (lyōō'bōsh-kē) | 175 | 43°11'N | 17°29'E |
| Ljungan, r., Swe. | 166 | 62°50'N | 13°45'E |
| Ljungby, Swe. (lyŏng'bü) | 166 | 56°49'N | 13°56'E |
| Ljusdal, Swe. (lyōōs'däl) | 166 | 61°50'N | 16°11'E |
| Ljusnan, r., Swe. | 160 | 61°55'N | 15°33'E |
| Llandudno, Wales, U.K. (lăn-düd'nō) | 164 | 53°20'N | 3°46'W |
| Llanelli, Wales, U.K. (lȧ-nĕl'ĭ) | 161 | 51°44'N | 4°09'W |
| Llanes, Spain (lyä'nās) | 162 | 43°25'N | 4°41'W |
| Llano, Tx., U.S. (lä'nō) (lyä'nō) | 122 | 30°45'N | 98°41'W |
| Llano, r., Tx., U.S. | 122 | 30°38'N | 99°04'W |
| Llanos, reg., S.A. (lyá'nōs) | 142 | 4°00'N | 71°15'W |
| Lleida, Spain | 162 | 41°38'N | 0°37'E |
| Llera, Mex. (lyā'rä) | 130 | 23°16'N | 99°03'W |
| Llerena, Spain (lyā-rā'nä) | 172 | 38°14'N | 6°02'W |
| Lliria, Spain | 173 | 39°35'N | 0°34'W |
| Llobregat, r., Spain (lyô-brĕ-gät') | 173 | 41°55'N | 1°55'E |
| Lloyd Lake, l., Can. (loid) | 102e | 50°52'N | 114°13'W |
| Lloydminster, Can. | 90 | 53°17'N | 110°00'W |
| Llucena, Spain | 173 | 40°08'N | 0°18'W |
| Llucmajor, Spain | 173 | 39°28'N | 2°53'E |
| Llullaillaco, Volcán, vol., S.A. (lyōō-lyī-lyä'kō) | 144 | 24°50'S | 68°30'W |
| Loange, r., Afr. (lô-äŋ'gȧ) | 232 | 5°00'S | 20°15'E |
| Lobamba, Swaz. | 232 | 26°27'S | 31°12'E |
| Lobatse, Bots. (lō-bä'tsē) | 232 | 25°13'S | 25°35'E |
| Lobería, Arg. (lô-bĕ'rē'ä) | 144 | 38°13'S | 58°48'W |
| Lobito, Ang. (lô-bē'tō) | 232 | 12°30'S | 13°34'E |
| Lobnya, Russia (lôb'nyȧ) | 186b | 56°01'N | 37°29'E |
| Lobo, Phil. | 213a | 13°39'N | 121°14'E |
| Lobos, Arg. (lō'bôs) | 141c | 35°10'S | 59°08'W |
| Lobos, Cayo, i., Bah. (lō'bôs) | 134 | 22°25'N | 77°40'W |
| Lobos, Isla de, i., Mex. (ē's-lä-dĕ-lô'bōs) | 131 | 21°24'N | 97°11'W |
| Lobos de Tierra, i., Peru (lô'bō-dĕ-tyĕ'r-rä) | 142 | 6°29'S | 80°55'W |
| Lobva, Russia (lôb'vȧ) | 186a | 59°12'N | 60°28'E |
| Lobva, r., Russia | 186a | 59°14'N | 60°17'E |
| Locarno, Switz. (lô-kär'nō) | 168 | 46°10'N | 8°43'E |
| Loches, Fr. (lôsh) | 170 | 47°08'N | 0°56'E |
| Loch Raven Reservoir, res., Md., U.S. | 110e | 39°28'N | 76°38'W |
| Lockeport, Can. | 100 | 43°42'N | 65°07'W |
| Lockhart, S.C., U.S. (lŏk'hȧrt) | 125 | 34°47'N | 81°30'W |
| Lockhart, Tx., U.S. | 123 | 29°54'N | 97°40'W |
| Lock Haven, Pa., U.S. (lŏk'hā-vĕn) | 109 | 41°05'N | 77°30'W |
| Lockland, Oh., U.S. (lŏk'lănd) | 111f | 39°14'N | 84°27'W |
| Lockport, Il., U.S. | 111a | 41°35'N | 88°04'W |
| Lockport, N.Y., U.S. | 109 | 43°11'N | 78°43'W |
| Loc Ninh, Viet. (lōk'nĭng') | 212 | 12°00'N | 106°30'E |
| Lod, Isr. (lôd) | 197a | 31°57'N | 34°55'E |
| Lodève, Fr. (lô-dĕv') | 170 | 43°43'N | 3°18'E |
| Lodeynoye Pole, Russia (lô-dĕy-nô'yĕ) | 180 | 60°43'N | 33°24'E |
| Lodge Creek, r., N.A. (lŏj) | 115 | 49°20'N | 110°20'W |
| Lodge Creek, r., Mt., U.S. | 115 | 48°51'N | 109°30'W |
| Lodgepole Creek, r., Wy., U.S. (lŏj'pōl) | 112 | 41°22'N | 104°48'W |
| Lodhran, Pak. | 202 | 29°40'N | 71°39'E |
| Lodi, Italy (lô'dē) | 174 | 45°18'N | 9°30'E |
| Lodi, Ca., U.S. (lō'dī) | 118 | 38°07'N | 121°17'W |
| Lodi, Oh., U.S. (lō'dī) | 111d | 41°02'N | 82°01'W |
| Lodosa, Spain (lô-dô'sä) | 172 | 42°27'N | 2°04'W |
| Lodwar, Kenya | 237 | 3°07'N | 35°36'E |
| Łódź, Pol. | 154 | 51°46'N | 19°30'E |
| Loeches, Spain (lô-āch'ĕs) | 173a | 40°22'N | 3°25'W |
| Loffa, r., Afr. | 234 | 7°10'N | 10°35'W |
| Lofoten, is., Nor. (lô'fō-tĕn) | 156 | 68°26'N | 13°42'E |
| Logan, Oh., U.S. (lō'gȧn) | 108 | 39°35'N | 82°25'W |
| Logan, Ut., U.S. | 104 | 41°46'N | 111°51'W |
| Logan, W.V., U.S. | 108 | 37°50'N | 82°00'W |
| Logan, Mount, mtn., Can. | 92 | 60°54'N | 140°33'W |
| Logansport, In., U.S. (lō'gănz-pōrt) | 105 | 40°45'N | 86°25'W |
| Logone, r., Afr. (lō-gō'nä) (lô-gôn') | 231 | 10°20'N | 15°30'E |
| Logroño, Spain (lô-grō'nyō) | 162 | 42°28'N | 2°25'W |
| Logrosán, Spain (lô-grô-sän') | 172 | 39°22'N | 5°29'W |
| Løgstør, Den. (lügh-stûr') | 166 | 56°56'N | 9°15'E |
| Loir, r., Fr. (lwȧr) | 170 | 47°40'N | 0°07'E |
| Loire, r., Fr. | 156 | 47°30'N | 2°00'E |
| Loja, Ec. (lō'hä) | 142 | 3°49'S | 79°13'W |
| Loja, Spain (lô'-kä) | 172 | 37°10'N | 4°11'W |
| Loka, D.R.C. | 236 | 0°20'N | 17°57'E |
| Lokala Drift, Bots. (lô'kä-lȧ drĭft) | 238c | 24°00'S | 26°38'E |
| Lokandu, D.R.C. | 237 | 2°31'S | 25°47'E |
| Lokhvytsia, Ukr. | 181 | 50°21'N | 33°16'E |
| Lokichar, Kenya | 237 | 2°23'N | 35°39'E |
| Lokitaung, Kenya | 237 | 4°16'N | 35°45'E |
| Lokofa-Bokolongo, D.R.C. | 236 | 0°12'N | 19°22'E |
| Lokoja, Nig. (lô-kō'yä) | 230 | 7°47'N | 6°45'E |
| Lokolama, D.R.C. | 236 | 2°34'S | 19°53'E |
| Lokosso, Burkina | 234 | 10°19'N | 3°40'W |
| Lol, r., Sudan (lōl) | 231 | 9°06'N | 28°09'E |
| Loliondo, Tan. | 237 | 2°03'S | 35°37'E |
| Lolland, i., Den. (lôl'än') | 166 | 54°41'N | 11°00'E |
| Lolo, Mt., U.S. | 115 | 46°45'N | 114°05'W |
| Lom, Blg. (lōm) | 163 | 43°48'N | 23°15'E |

ng-sing; ŋ-baŋk; ɴ-nasalized n; nŏd; cŏmmit; ōld; ôbey; ôrder; oi-boil; fōōd; ŏŏ-as oo in foot; ou-out; s-soft; sh-dish; th-thin; pūre; ůnite; ûrn; stŭd; circŭs; ü-as in French tu; '-indeterminate vowel.

ăt; final; rāte; senâte; ärm; àsk; sofá; fâre; ch-choose; dh-as th in other; bē; ěvent; bět; recěnt; crater; g-gō; gh-guttural g; bĭt; ī-short neutral; rīde; κ-guttural k as ch in German ich;

PRONOUNCING INDEX

Lukuga – Maḩaţţat Jurf ad Darāwīsh 317


| PLACE (Pronunciation) | PAGE | LAT. | LONG. |
|---|---|---|---|
| Lukuga, r., D.R.C. (lo͞o-ko͞o′gȧ) | 232 | 5°50′S | 27°35′E |
| Lüleburgaz, Tur. (lü′lĕ-bŏr-gäs′) | 175 | 41°25′N | 27°23′E |
| Luling, Tx., U.S. (lū′lĭng) | 123 | 29°41′N | 97°38′W |
| Lulong, China (lo͞o-lôŋ) | 205 | 39°54′N | 118°53′E |
| Lulonga, r., D.R.C. | 236 | 1°00′N | 18°37′E |
| Luluabourg see Kananga, D.R.C. | 232 | 6°14′S | 22°17′E |
| Lulu Island, i., Can. | 116d | 49°09′N | 123°05′W |
| Lulu Island, i., Ak., U.S. | 94 | 55°28′N | 133°30′W |
| Lumajangdong Co, l., China | 202 | 34°00′N | 81°47′E |
| Lumber, r., N.C., U.S. (lŭm′bẽr) | 125 | 34°45′N | 79°10′W |
| Lumberton, Ms., U.S. (lŭm′bẽr-tŭn) | 124 | 31°00′N | 89°25′W |
| Lumberton, N.C., U.S. | 125 | 34°47′N | 79°00′W |
| Luminárias, Braz. (lo͞o-mē-nä′ryäs) | 141a | 21°32′S | 44°53′W |
| Lummi, i., Wa., U.S. | 116d | 48°42′N | 122°43′W |
| Lummi Bay, b., Wa., U.S. (lŭm′ĭ) | 116d | 48°47′N | 122°44′W |
| Lummi Island, Wa., U.S. | 116d | 48°44′N | 122°42′W |
| Lumwana, Zam. | 237 | 11°50′S | 25°10′E |
| Lün, Mong. | 204 | 47°58′N | 104°52′E |
| Luna, Phil. (lo͞o′nä) | 213a | 16°51′N | 120°22′E |
| Lund, Swe. (lŭnd) | 160 | 55°42′N | 13°10′E |
| Lundy, i., Eng., U.K. (lŭn′dē) | 164 | 51°12′N | 4°50′W |
| Lüneburg, Ger. (lü′nē-bòrgh) | 168 | 53°16′N | 10°25′E |
| Lunel, Fr. (lü-nĕl′) | 170 | 43°41′N | 4°07′E |
| Lünen, Ger. (lü′nĕn) | 171c | 51°36′N | 7°30′E |
| Lunenburg, Can. (lo͞o′nĕn-bûrg) | 91 | 44°23′N | 64°19′W |
| Lunenburg, Ma., U.S. | 101a | 42°36′N | 71°44′W |
| Lunéville, Fr. (lü-nȧ-vel′) | 171 | 48°37′N | 6°29′E |
| Lunga, Ang. | 236 | 14°42′S | 18°32′E |
| Lungué-Bungo, r., Afr. | 232 | 13°00′S | 20°30′E |
| Lunsar, S.L. | 234 | 8°41′N | 12°32′W |
| Luodian, China (lwô-dĭĕn) | 206 | 31°25′N | 121°20′E |
| Luoding, China (lwô-dĭŋ) | 209 | 23°42′N | 111°35′E |
| Luohe, China (lwô-hŭ) | 206 | 33°35′N | 114°02′E |
| Luoyang, China (lwô-yäŋ) | 205 | 34°45′N | 112°32′E |
| Luozhen, China (lwô-jŭn) | 206 | 37°45′N | 118°29′E |
| Luque, Para. (loo′kā) | 144 | 25°18′S | 57°17′W |
| Luray, Va., U.S. (lū-rā′) | 109 | 38°40′N | 78°25′W |
| Lurgan, N. Ire., U.K. (lûr′găn) | 160 | 54°27′N | 6°28′W |
| Lúrio, Moz. (lo͞o′rē-ô) | 233 | 13°17′S | 40°29′E |
| Lúrio, Moz. | 233 | 14°00′S | 38°45′E |
| Lusaka, D.R.C. | 237 | 7°10′S | 29°27′E |
| Lusaka, Zam. (lò-sä′kȧ) | 232 | 15°25′S | 28°17′E |
| Lusambo, D.R.C. (lo͞o-säm′bō) | 232 | 4°58′S | 23°27′E |
| Lusanga, D.R.C. | 232 | 5°13′S | 18°43′E |
| Lusangi, D.R.C. | 237 | 4°37′S | 27°08′E |
| Lushan, China | 208 | 33°45′N | 113°00′E |
| Lushiko, r., Afr. | 236 | 6°35′S | 19°45′E |
| Lushoto, Tan. (lo͞o-shō′tō) | 233 | 4°47′S | 38°17′E |
| Lüshun, China (lü-shŭn) | 205 | 38°49′N | 121°15′E |
| Lusikisiki, S. Afr. (lo͞o-sē-kē-sē′kē) | 233c | 31°22′S | 29°37′E |
| Lusk, Wy., U.S. (lŭsk) | 112 | 42°46′N | 104°27′W |
| Lūt, Dasht-e, des., Iran (dä′sht-ē-lo͞ot) | 198 | 31°47′N | 58°38′E |
| Lutcher, La., U.S. (lŭch′ẽr) | 123 | 30°03′N | 90°43′W |
| Luton, Eng., U.K. (lū′tŭn) | 164 | 51°55′N | 0°28′W |
| Luts′k, Ukr. | 181 | 50°45′N | 25°20′E |
| Luuq, Som. | 238a | 3°38′N | 42°35′E |
| Luverne, Al., U.S. (lū-vûn′) | 124 | 31°42′N | 86°15′W |
| Luverne, Mn., U.S. | 112 | 43°40′N | 96°13′W |
| Luwingu, Zam. | 237 | 10°15′S | 29°55′E |
| Luxapallila Creek, r., U.S. (lŭk-sȧ-pôl′ĭ-lȧ) | 124 | 33°36′N | 88°08′W |
| Luxembourg, Lux. | 154 | 49°38′N | 6°30′E |
| Luxembourg, nation, Eur. | 154 | 49°30′N | 6°22′E |
| Luxeuil-les-Baines, Fr. | 171 | 47°49′N | 6°19′E |
| Luxomni, Ga., U.S. (lŭx′ŏm-nī) | 110c | 33°54′N | 84°07′W |
| Luxor see Al Uqşur, Egypt | 231 | 25°38′N | 32°59′E |
| Luya Shan, mtn., China | 208 | 38°50′N | 111°40′E |
| Luyi, China (lo͞o-yē) | 206 | 33°52′N | 115°32′E |
| Luzern, Switz. (lò-tsĕrn) | 161 | 47°03′N | 8°18′E |
| Luzhou, China (lo͞o-jō) | 204 | 28°58′N | 105°25′E |
| Luziânia, Braz. (lo͞o-zyȧ′nēȧ) | 143 | 16°17′S | 47°44′W |
| Luzon, i., Phil. (lo͞o-zŏn′) | 212 | 17°10′N | 119°45′E |
| Luzon Strait, strt., Asia | 209 | 20°40′N | 121°00′E |
| L′viv, Ukr. | 178 | 49°50′N | 24°00′E |
| L′vov see L′viv, Ukr. | 178 | 49°50′N | 24°00′E |
| Lyalta, Can. | 102e | 51°07′N | 113°36′W |
| Lyalya, r., Russia (lyȧ′lyȧ) | 186a | 58°58′N | 60°17′E |
| Lyaskovets, Blg. | 175 | 43°07′N | 25°41′E |
| Lydenburg, S. Afr. (lī′dĕn-bûrg) | 232 | 25°06′S | 30°21′E |
| Lyell, Mount, mtn., Ca., U.S. (lī′ĕl) | 118 | 37°44′N | 119°22′W |
| Lyepye′, Bela. (lyĕ-pĕl′) | 176 | 54°52′N | 28°41′E |
| Lykens, Pa., U.S. (lī′kĕnz) | 109 | 40°35′N | 76°45′W |
| Lykhivka, Ukr. | 177 | 48°52′N | 33°57′E |
| Lyna, r., Eur. (lĭn′ȧ) | 169 | 53°56′N | 20°30′E |
| Lynch, Ky., U.S. (lĭnch) | 125 | 36°56′N | 82°55′W |
| Lynchburg, Va., U.S. (lĭnch′bûrg) | 105 | 37°23′N | 79°08′W |
| Lynch Cove, Wa., U.S. (lĭnch) | 116a | 47°26′N | 122°54′W |
| Lynden, Can. (lĭn′dĕn) | 102d | 43°14′N | 80°08′W |
| Lynden, Wa., U.S. | 116d | 48°56′N | 122°27′W |
| Lyndhurst, Austl. | 217a | 38°03′S | 145°14′E |
| Lyndon, Ky., U.S. (lĭn′dŭn) | 111h | 38°15′N | 85°36′W |
| Lyndonville, Vt., U.S. (lĭn′dŭn-vĭl) | 109 | 44°35′N | 72°00′W |
| Lynn, Ma., U.S. (lĭn) | 105 | 42°28′N | 70°57′W |
| Lynn Lake, Can. (lāk) | 90 | 56°51′N | 101°05′W |
| Lynwood, Ca., U.S. (lĭn′wòd) | 117a | 33°56′N | 118°13′W |
| Lyon, Fr. (lē-ôn′) | 154 | 45°44′N | 4°52′E |
| Lyons, Ga., U.S. (lī′ŭnz) | 125 | 32°08′N | 82°19′W |
| Lyons, Ks., U.S. | 120 | 38°20′N | 98°11′W |
| Lyons, Ne., U.S. | 112 | 41°57′N | 96°28′W |
| Lyons, N.J., U.S. | 110a | 40°41′N | 74°33′W |
| Lyons, N.Y., U.S. | 109 | 43°05′N | 77°00′W |
| Lyptsi, Ukr. | 177 | 50°11′N | 36°25′E |
| Lysefjorden, b., Nor. | 166 | 58°59′N | 6°35′E |
| Lysekil, Swe. (lü′sĕ-kĕl) | 166 | 58°17′N | 11°22′E |
| Lys′va, Russia (lĭs′vȧ) | 180 | 58°07′N | 57°47′E |
| Lytham, Eng., U.K. (lĭth′ăm) | 158a | 53°44′N | 2°58′W |
| Lytkarino, Russia | 186b | 55°35′N | 37°55′E |
| Lyttelton, S. Afr. (lĭt′l′ton) | 233b | 25°51′S | 28°13′E |
| Lyuban′, Russia (lyo͞o′bȧn) | 176 | 59°21′N | 31°15′E |
| Lyubertsy, Russia (lyo͞o′bĕr-tsē) | 176 | 55°40′N | 37°55′E |
| Lyubim, Russia (lyo͞o-bēm′) | 176 | 58°24′N | 40°39′E |
| Lyublino, Russia (lyo͞ob′lĭ-nô) | 186b | 55°41′N | 37°45′E |
| Lyudinovo, Russia (lū-dē′novō) | 176 | 53°52′N | 34°28′E |


## M


| PLACE (Pronunciation) | PAGE | LAT. | LONG. |
|---|---|---|---|
| Ma′ān, Jord. (mä-än′) | 198 | 30°12′N | 35°45′E |
| Maartensdijk, Neth. | 159a | 52°09′N | 5°10′E |
| Maas (Meuse), r., Eur. | 165 | 51°50′N | 5°40′E |
| Maastricht, Neth. (mäs′trĭkt) | 165 | 50°51′N | 5°35′E |
| Mabaia, Ang. | 236 | 7°13′S | 14°03′E |
| Mabana, Wa., U.S. (mä-bä-nä) | 116a | 48°06′N | 122°25′W |
| Mabank, Tx., U.S. (mā′bănk) | 123 | 32°21′N | 96°05′W |
| Mabeskraal, S. Afr. | 238c | 25°12′S | 26°47′E |
| Mableton, Ga., U.S. (mā′b′l-tŭn) | 110c | 33°49′N | 84°34′W |
| Mabrouk, Mali | 230 | 19°27′N | 1°16′W |
| Mabula, S. Afr. (mä′bo͞o-la) | 238c | 24°49′S | 27°59′E |
| Macalelon, Phil. (mä-kä-lā-lōn′) | 213a | 13°46′N | 122°09′E |
| Macau, Braz. (mä-kà′ò) | 143 | 5°12′S | 36°34′W |
| Macau, China | 205 | 22°00′N | 113°00′E |
| Macaya, Pico de, mtn., Haiti | 135 | 18°25′N | 74°00′W |
| Macclesfield, Eng., U.K. (măk′′lz-fēld) | 158a | 53°15′N | 2°07′W |
| Macclesfield Canal, can., Eng., U.K. (măk′′lz-fēld) | 158a | 53°14′N | 2°07′W |
| Macdona, Tx., U.S. (măk-dō′nȧ) | 117d | 29°20′N | 98°42′W |
| Macdonald, l., Austl. (măk-dŏn′ăld) | 220 | 23°40′S | 127°40′E |
| Macdonnell Ranges, mts., Austl. (măk-dŏn′ĕl) | 220 | 23°40′S | 131°30′E |
| MacDowell Lake, l., Can. (măk-dou ĕl) | 97 | 52°15′N | 92°45′W |
| Macdui, Ben, mtn., Scot., U.K. (bĕn măk-do͞o′ē) | 160 | 57°06′N | 3°45′W |
| Macedonia, Oh., U.S. (măs-ê-dō′nĭ-ȧ) | 111d | 41°19′N | 81°30′E |
| Macedonia, nation, Eur. | 175 | 41°50′N | 22°00′E |
| Macedonia, hist. reg., Eur. (măs-ê-dō′nĭ-ȧ) | 163 | 41°05′N | 22°15′E |
| Maceió, Braz. | 143 | 9°40′S | 35°43′W |
| Macerata, Italy (mä-chȧ-rä′tä) | 174 | 43°18′N | 13°28′E |
| Macfarlane, Lake, l., Austl. (măc′fär-lān) | 222 | 32°10′S | 137°00′E |
| Machache, mtn., Leso. | 233c | 29°22′S | 27°53′E |
| Machado, Braz. (mä-shȧ-dô) | 141a | 21°42′S | 45°55′W |
| Machakos, Kenya | 237 | 1°31′S | 37°16′E |
| Machala, Ec. (mä-chá′lä) | 142 | 3°18′S | 78°54′W |
| Machens, Mo., U.S. (măk′ĕns) | 117e | 38°54′N | 90°20′W |
| Machias, Me., U.S. (mȧ-chī′ăs) | 100 | 44°22′N | 67°29′W |
| Machida, Japan (mä-chē′dä) | 211a | 35°32′N | 139°28′E |
| Machilīpatnam, India | 199 | 16°22′N | 81°10′E |
| Machu Picchu, Peru (mä′chò-pē′k-chò) | 142 | 13°07′S | 72°34′W |
| Măcin, Rom. (mȧ-chēn′) | 177 | 45°15′N | 28°09′E |
| Macina, reg., Mali | 234 | 14°50′N | 4°40′W |
| Mackay, Austl. (mă-kī′) | 219 | 21°15′S | 149°08′E |
| Mackay, Id., U.S. (măk-kā′) | 115 | 43°55′N | 113°38′W |
| Mackay, l., Austl. (mă-kī′) | 220 | 22°30′S | 127°45′E |
| MacKay, l., Can. (măk-kā′) | 92 | 64°10′N | 112°35′W |
| Mackenzie, r., Can. | 92 | 63°38′N | 124°23′W |
| Mackenzie Bay, b., Can. | 103 | 69°20′N | 137°10′W |
| Mackenzie Mountains, mts., Can. (mȧ-kĕn′zĭ) | 92 | 63°41′N | 129°27′W |
| Mackinaw, r., Il., U.S. | 108 | 40°35′N | 89°25′W |
| Mackinaw City, Mi., U.S. (măk′ĭ-nô) | 108 | 45°45′N | 84°45′W |
| Mackinnon Road, Kenya | 237 | 3°44′S | 39°03′E |
| Macleantown, S. Afr. (măk-lān′toun) | 233c | 32°48′S | 27°48′E |
| Maclear, S. Afr. (mȧ-klēr′) | 232 | 31°06′S | 28°23′E |
| Macomb, Il., U.S. (mȧ-ko͞om′) | 121 | 40°27′N | 90°40′W |
| Mâcon, Fr. (mä-kôn) | 161 | 46°19′N | 4°51′E |
| Macon, Ga., U.S. (mā′kŏn) | 105 | 32°49′N | 83°39′W |
| Macon, Mo., U.S. | 121 | 39°42′N | 92°29′W |
| Macon, Ms., U.S. | 124 | 32°07′N | 88°31′W |
| Macquarie, r., Austl. | 221 | 31°43′S | 148°04′E |
| Macquarie Islands, is., Austl. (mȧ-kwŏr′ē) | 3 | 54°36′S | 158°45′E |
| Macuelizo, Hond. (mä-kwĕ-lē′zō) | 132 | 15°22′N | 88°32′W |
| Mad, r., Ca., U.S. (măd) | 114 | 40°38′N | 123°37′W |
| Madagascar, nation, Afr. (măd-ȧ-găs′kăr) | 233 | 18°05′S | 43°12′E |
| Madame, i., Can. (mȧ-dàm′) | 101 | 45°33′N | 61°02′W |
| Madanapalle, India | 203 | 13°06′N | 78°09′E |
| Madang, Pap. N. Gui. (mä-däng′) | 213 | 5°15′S | 145°45′E |
| Madaoua, Niger (mȧ-dou′ȧ) | 230 | 14°04′N | 6°03′E |
| Madawaska, r., Can. (măd-ȧ-wôs′kȧ) | 99 | 45°20′N | 77°25′W |
| Madeira, r., S.A. | 142 | 6°48′S | 62°43′W |
| Madeira, Arquipélago da, is., Port. | 229 | 33°26′N | 16°44′W |
| Madeira, Ilha da, i., Port. (mȧ-dā′rä) | 230 | 32°41′N | 16°15′W |
| Madeleine, Îles de la, is., Can. | 93 | 47°30′N | 61°45′W |
| Madelia, Mn., U.S. (mȧ-dē′lĭ-ȧ) | 113 | 44°03′N | 94°23′W |
| Madeline, i., Wi., U.S. (măd′ĕ-lĭn) | 113 | 46°47′N | 91°30′W |
| Madera, Ca., U.S. (mȧ-dā′rȧ) | 118 | 36°57′N | 120°04′W |
| Madera, vol., Nic. | 132 | 11°27′N | 85°30′W |
| Madgaon, India | 203 | 15°09′N | 73°58′E |
| Madhya Pradesh, state, India (mŭd′vŭ prŭ-dăsh′) | 199 | 22°04′N | 77°48′E |
| Madill, Ok., U.S. (mȧ-dĭl′) | 121 | 34°04′N | 96°45′W |
| Madīnat ash Sha′b, Yemen | 198 | 12°45′N | 44°00′E |
| Madingo, Congo | 236 | 4°07′S | 11°22′E |
| Madingou, Congo | 236 | 4°09′S | 13°34′E |
| Madison, Fl., U.S. (măd′ĭ-sŭn) | 124 | 30°28′N | 83°25′W |
| Madison, Ga., U.S. | 124 | 33°34′N | 83°29′W |
| Madison, Il., U.S. | 117e | 38°40′N | 90°09′W |
| Madison, In., U.S. | 108 | 38°45′N | 85°25′W |
| Madison, Ks., U.S. | 121 | 38°08′N | 96°07′W |
| Madison, Me., U.S. | 100 | 44°47′N | 69°52′W |
| Madison, Mn., U.S. | 112 | 44°59′N | 96°13′W |
| Madison, N.C., U.S. | 125 | 36°22′N | 79°59′W |
| Madison, Ne., U.S. | 112 | 41°49′N | 97°27′W |
| Madison, N.J., U.S. | 110a | 40°46′N | 74°25′W |
| Madison, S.D., U.S. | 112 | 44°01′N | 97°08′W |
| Madison, Wi., U.S. | 105 | 43°05′N | 89°23′W |
| Madison Res, Mt., U.S. | 115 | 45°25′N | 111°28′W |
| Madisonville, Ky., U.S. (măd′ĭ-sŭn-vĭl) | 108 | 37°20′N | 87°30′W |
| Madisonville, La., U.S. | 123 | 30°22′N | 90°10′W |
| Madisonville, Tx., U.S. | 123 | 30°57′N | 95°55′W |
| Madjori, Burkina | 234 | 11°26′N | 1°15′E |
| Mado Gashi, Kenya | 237 | 0°44′N | 39°10′E |
| Madona, Lat. (mȧ′dō′nȧ) | 167 | 56°50′N | 26°14′E |
| Madrakah, Ra′s al, c., Oman | 198 | 18°53′N | 57°48′E |
| Madras see Chennai, India | 199 | 13°08′N | 80°15′E |
| Madre, Laguna, l., Mex. (lä-go͞o′nä mä′drā) | 123 | 25°08′N | 97°41′W |
| Madre, Sierra, mts., N.A. (sē-ĕ′r-rä-mȧ′drĕ) | 131 | 15°55′N | 92°40′W |
| Madre, Sierra, mts., Phil. | 213a | 16°40′N | 122°10′E |
| Madre de Dios, r., S.A. (mä′drā dā dē-ōs′) | 142 | 12°07′S | 68°02′W |
| Madre de Dios, Archipiélago, is., Chile (mä′drā dā dē-ōs′) | 144 | 50°40′S | 76°30′W |
| Madre del Sur, Sierra, mts., Mex. (sē-ĕ′r-rä-mä′drā dĕlso͞or′) | 128 | 17°35′N | 100°35′W |
| Madre Occidental, Sierra, mts., Mex. | 128 | 29°30′N | 107°30′W |
| Madre Oriental, Sierra, mts., Mex. | 128 | 25°30′N | 100°45′W |
| Madrid, Spain (mä-drē′d) | 154 | 40°26′N | 3°42′W |
| Madrid, Ia., U.S. (măd′rĭd) | 113 | 41°51′N | 93°48′W |
| Madridejos, Spain (mä-dhrē-dhā′hōs) | 172 | 39°29′N | 3°32′W |
| Madura, i., Indon. (mȧ-do͞o′rä) | 212 | 6°45′S | 113°30′E |
| Madurai, India (mä-do͞o′rī) | 199 | 9°57′N | 78°04′E |
| Madureira, Serra do, mtn., Braz. (sĕ′r-rä-dò-mä-do͞o-rā′rȧ) | 144b | 22°49′S | 43°30′W |
| Maebashi, Japan (mä-ĕ-bä′shē) | 205 | 36°26′N | 139°04′E |
| Maestra, Sierra, mts., Cuba (sē-ĕ′r-rȧ-mä-ās′trä) | 129 | 20°05′N | 77°05′W |
| Maewo, i., Vanuatu | 221 | 15°17′S | 168°16′E |
| Mafeking, S. Afr. (măf′ê′kĭng) | 232 | 25°46′S | 24°45′E |
| Mafra, Braz. (mä′frä) | 144 | 26°21′N | 49°59′W |
| Mafra, Port. (mäf′rȧ) | 173b | 38°56′N | 9°20′W |
| Magadan, Russia (mȧ-gȧ-dän′) | 179 | 59°39′N | 150°43′E |
| Magadan Oblast, Russia | 185 | 65°00′N | 160°00′E |
| Magadi, Kenya | 237 | 1°54′S | 36°17′E |
| Magalies, r., S. Afr. (mȧ-gä′lyĕs) | 233b | 25°51′S | 27°42′E |
| Magaliesberg, mts., S. Afr. | 233b | 25°45′S | 27°43′E |
| Magaliesburg, S. Afr. | 238c | 26°01′S | 27°32′E |
| Magallanes, Estrecho de, strt., S.A. | 144 | 52°30′S | 68°45′W |
| Magat, r., Phil. (mä-gät′) | 213a | 16°45′N | 121°16′E |
| Magdalena, Arg. (mäg-dä-lā′nä) | 141c | 35°05′S | 57°32′W |
| Magdalena, Bol. | 142 | 13°17′S | 63°57′W |
| Magdalena, Mex. | 104 | 30°34′N | 110°50′W |
| Magdalena, N.M., U.S. | 119 | 34°10′N | 107°45′W |
| Magdalena, i., Chile | 144 | 44°45′S | 73°15′W |
| Magdalena, r., Col. | 142 | 7°45′N | 74°04′W |
| Magdalena, Bahía, b., Mex. (bä-ē′ä-mäg-dä-lā′nä) | 128 | 24°30′N | 114°00′W |
| Magdeburg, Ger. (mäg′dĕ-bòrgh) | 154 | 52°07′N | 11°39′E |
| Magellan, Strait of see Magallanes, Estrecho de, strt., S.A. | 144 | 52°30′S | 68°45′W |
| Magenta, Italy (mȧ-jĕn′tȧ) | 174 | 45°26′N | 8°53′E |
| Magerøya, i., Nor. | 160 | 71°10′N | 24°11′E |
| Maggiore, Lago, l., Italy | 162 | 46°03′N | 8°25′E |
| Maghāghah, Egypt | 238b | 28°38′N | 30°50′W |
| Maghniyya, Alg. | 162 | 34°52′N | 1°40′W |
| Magiscatzin, Mex. (mä-kēs-kät-zēn′) | 130 | 22°48′N | 98°42′W |
| Maglaj, Bos. (mȧ′glä-ê) | 175 | 44°34′N | 18°12′E |
| Maglie, Italy (mäl′yā) | 175 | 40°06′N | 18°20′E |
| Magna, Ut., U.S. (măg′nȧ) | 117b | 40°43′N | 112°06′W |
| Magnitogorsk, Russia (mȧg-nyē′tô-gôrsk) | 178 | 53°26′N | 59°05′E |
| Magnolia, Ar., U.S. (măg-nō′lĭ-ȧ) | 121 | 33°16′N | 93°13′W |
| Magnolia, Ms., U.S. | 124 | 31°08′N | 90°27′W |
| Magny-en-Vexin, Fr. (män-nyē′ĕn-vĕ-săn′) | 171b | 49°09′N | 1°45′E |
| Magog, Can. (mȧ-gŏg′) | 99 | 45°15′N | 72°10′W |
| Magpie, r., Can. | 100 | 50°40′N | 64°30′W |
| Magpie, r., Can. | 98 | 48°13′N | 84°50′W |
| Magpie, Lac, l., Can. | 100 | 50°55′N | 64°39′W |
| Magrath, Can. | 90 | 49°25′N | 112°52′W |
| Magude, Moz. (mä-go͞o′dȧ) | 232 | 24°58′S | 32°39′E |
| Magwe, Mya. (mŭg-wā′) | 199 | 20°19′N | 94°57′E |
| Mahābād, Iran | 201 | 36°55′N | 45°50′E |
| Mahahi Port, D.R.C. (mä-hä′gē) | 231 | 2°14′N | 31°12′E |
| Mahajanga, Madag. | 233 | 15°12′S | 46°26′E |
| Mahakam, r., Indon. | 212 | 0°30′S | 116°15′E |
| Mahali Mountains, mts., Tan. | 237 | 6°20′S | 30°00′E |
| Mahaly, Madag. (mȧ-hȧl-ē′) | 233 | 24°09′S | 46°20′E |
| Mahanoro, Madag. (mȧ-hȧ-nō′rō) | 233 | 19°57′S | 48°47′E |
| Mahanoy City, Pa., U.S. (mä-hȧ-noi′) | 109 | 40°50′N | 76°10′W |
| Maḩaţţat al Qaţrānah, Jord. | 197a | 31°15′N | 36°04′E |
| Maḩaţţat ′Aqabat al Ḩijāzīyah, Jord. | 197a | 29°45′N | 35°55′E |
| Maḩaţţat ar Ramlah, Jord. | 197a | 29°31′N | 35°57′E |
| Maḩaţţat Jurf ad Darāwīsh, Jord. | 197a | 30°41′N | 35°51′E |


ng-sing; ŋ-baŋk; ɴ-nasalized n; nŏd; cŏmmit; ōld; ôbey; ôrder; oi-boil; fo͞od; ò-as oo in foot; ou-out; s-soft; sh-dish; th-thin; pūre; ûnite; ûrn; stŭd; circŭs; ü-as in French tu; ′-indeterminate vowel.

318 Mahd adh-Dhahab – Mansfield

PRONOUNCING INDEX


| PLACE (Pronunciation) | PAGE | LAT. | LONG. |
|---|---|---|---|
| Mahd adh-Dhahab, Sau. Ar. | 201 | 23°30'N | 40°52'E |
| Mahe, India (mä-ā') | 199 | 11°42'N | 75°39'E |
| Mahenge, Tan. (mä-hĕŋ'gå) | 232 | 7°38'S | 36°16'E |
| Mahi, r., India | 202 | 23°16'N | 73°20'E |
| Mahilyow, Bela. | 180 | 53°53'N | 30°22'E |
| Mahilyow, prov., Bela. | 176 | 53°28'N | 30°15'E |
| Māhim Bay, b., India | 203b | 19°03'N | 72°45'E |
| Mahlabatini, S. Afr. (mä'lå-bå-tē'nê) | 233c | 28°15'S | 31°29'E |
| Mahlow, Ger. (mä'lōv) | 159b | 52°23'N | 13°24'E |
| Mahnomen, Mn., U.S. (mô-nō'mĕn) | 112 | 47°18'N | 95°58'W |
| Mahone Bay, Can. (må-hōn') | 100 | 44°27'N | 64°23'W |
| Mahone Bay, b., Can. | 100 | 44°30'N | 64°15'W |
| Mahopac, Lake, l., N.Y., U.S. (mā-hō'păk) | 110a | 41°24'N | 73°45'W |
| Mahwah, N.J., U.S. (må-wä') | 110a | 41°05'N | 74°09'W |
| Maidenhead, Eng., U.K. (mād'ĕn-hĕd) | 158b | 51°30'N | 0°44'W |
| Maidstone, Eng., U.K. | 165 | 51°17'N | 0°32'E |
| Maiduguri, Nig. (mä'ē-då-gōō'rē) | 231 | 11°51'N | 13°10'E |
| Maigualida, Sierra, mts., Ven. (sē-ĕ'r-rå-mī-gwä'lē-dē) | 142 | 6°30'N | 65°50'W |
| Maijdi, Bngl. | 202 | 22°59'N | 91°08'E |
| Maikop *see* Maykop, Russia | 178 | 44°35'N | 40°07'E |
| Main, r., Ger. (mīn) | 168 | 49°49'N | 9°20'E |
| Main Barrier Range, mts., Austl. (băr'ĭ-ēr) | 221 | 31°25'S | 141°40'E |
| Mai-Ndombe, Lac, l., D.R.C. | 232 | 2°16'S | 19°00'E |
| Maine, state, U.S. (mān) | 105 | 45°25'N | 69°50'W |
| Mainland, i., Scot., U.K. (mān-lănd) | 160 | 60°19'N | 2°40'W |
| Maintenon, Fr. (măn-tĕ-nôn') | 171b | 48°35'N | 1°35'E |
| Maintirano, Madag. (mä'ēn-tē-rä'nō) | 233 | 18°05'S | 44°08'E |
| Mainz, Ger. (mīnts) | 154 | 49°59'N | 8°16'E |
| Maio, i., C.V. (mä'yo) | 230b | 15°15'N | 22°50'W |
| Maipo, S.A. | 144 | 34°08'S | 69°51'W |
| Maipo, r., Chile (mī'pô) | 141b | 33°45'S | 71°08'W |
| Maiquetía, Ven. (mī-kĕ-tē'ä) | 142 | 10°37'N | 66°56'W |
| Maison-Rouge, Fr. (mā-zôn-rōōzh') | 171b | 48°34'N | 3°09'E |
| Maisons-Laffitte, Fr. | 171b | 48°57'N | 2°09'E |
| Maitland, Austl. (māt'lănd) | 219 | 32°45'S | 151°40'E |
| Maizuru, Japan (mä-ĭ'zōō-rōō) | 211 | 35°26'N | 135°15'E |
| Majene, Indon. | 212 | 3°34'S | 119°00'E |
| Maji, Eth. | 231 | 6°14'N | 35°34'E |
| Majorca *see* Mallorca, i., Spain | 156 | 39°18'N | 2°22'E |
| Makah Indian Reservation, I.R., Wa., U.S. | 114 | 48°17'N | 124°52'W |
| Makanya, Tan. (mä-kän'yä) | 233 | 4°15'S | 37°49'E |
| Makanza, D.R.C. | 231 | 1°42'N | 19°08'E |
| Makarakomburu, Mount, mtn., Sol. Is. | 214e | 9°43'S | 160°02'E |
| Makarska, Cro. (mä'kär-skå) | 175 | 43°17'N | 17°05'E |
| Makar'yev, Russia | 180 | 57°50'N | 43°48'E |
| Makasar *see* Ujung Pandang, Indon. | 212 | 5°08'S | 119°28'E |
| Makasar, Selat (Makassar Strait), strt., Indon. | 212 | 2°00'S | 118°07'E |
| Makaw, D.R.C. | 236 | 3°29'S | 18°19'E |
| Make, i., Japan (mä'kå) | 211 | 30°43'N | 130°49'E |
| Makeni, S.L. | 230 | 8°53'N | 12°03'W |
| Makgadikgadi Pans, pl., Bots. | 232 | 20°38'S | 21°31'E |
| Makhachkala, Russia (mäk'äch-kä'lä) | 181 | 43°00'N | 47°40'E |
| Makhaleng, r., Leso. | 233c | 29°53'S | 27°33'E |
| Makiïvka, Ukr. | 181 | 48°03'N | 38°00'E |
| Makindu, Kenya | 237 | 2°17'S | 37°49'E |
| Makkah *see* Mecca, Sau. Ar. | 198 | 21°27'N | 39°45'E |
| Makkovik, Can. | 91 | 55°01'N | 59°10'W |
| Makokou, Gabon (må-kô-kōō') | 230 | 0°34'N | 12°52'E |
| Maków Mazowiecki, Pol. (mä'kōov mä-zō-vyĕts'kē) | 169 | 52°51'N | 21°07'E |
| Makuhari, Japan (mä-kōō-hä'rē) | 211a | 35°39'N | 140°04'E |
| Makurazaki, Japan (mä'kô-rä-zä'kê) | 211 | 31°16'N | 130°18'E |
| Makurdi, Nig. | 230 | 7°45'N | 8°32'E |
| Makushin, Ak., U.S. (mä-kô'shĭn) | 103 | 53°57'N | 166°28'W |
| Makushino, Russia (mä-kô-shēn'ô) | 178 | 55°03'N | 67°43'E |
| Mala, Punta, c., Pan. (pŏ'n-tä-mä'lä) | 133 | 7°32'N | 79°44'W |
| Malabar Coast, cst., India (măl'å-băr) | 203 | 11°19'N | 75°33'E |
| Malabar Point, c., India | 203b | 18°57'N | 72°47'E |
| Malabo, Eq. Gui. | 230 | 3°45'N | 8°47'E |
| Malabon, Phil. | 213a | 14°39'N | 120°57'E |
| Malacca, Strait of, strt., Asia (må-lăk'å) | 212 | 4°15'N | 99°44'E |
| Malad City, Id., U.S. (må-läd') | 115 | 42°11'N | 112°15'W |
| Maladzyecha, Bela. | 180 | 54°18'N | 26°57'E |
| Málaga, Col. (mä'lä-gå) | 142 | 6°41'N | 72°46'W |
| Málaga, Spain | 154 | 36°45'N | 4°25'W |
| Malagón, Spain (mä-lä-gōn') | 172 | 39°12'N | 3°52'W |
| Malaita, i., Sol. Is. (må-lä'ē-tå) | 221 | 8°38'S | 161°15'E |
| Malakāl, Sudan (må-lå-käl') | 231 | 9°46'N | 31°54'E |
| Malakhovka, Russia (må-läk'ôf-kå) | 186b | 55°38'N | 38°01'E |
| Malang, Indon. | 212 | 8°06'S | 112°50'E |
| Malanje, Ang. (mä-läŋ-gå) | 232 | 9°32'S | 16°20'E |
| Malanville, Benin | 230 | 12°04'N | 3°09'E |
| Mälaren, l., Swe. | 160 | 59°38'N | 16°55'E |
| Malartic, Can. | 91 | 48°07'N | 78°11'W |
| Malatya, Tur. (må-lä'tyå) | 198 | 38°30'N | 38°15'E |
| Malawi, nation, Afr. | 232 | 11°15'S | 33°45'E |
| Malawi, Lake *see* Nyasa, Lake, l., Afr. | 232 | 10°45'S | 34°30'E |
| Malaya Vishera, Russia (vê-shä'rä) | 178 | 58°51'N | 32°13'E |
| Malay Peninsula, pen., Asia (må-lā') (mā'lā) | 212 | 6°00'N | 101°00'E |
| Malaysia, nation, Asia (må-lā'zhå) | 212 | 4°10'N | 101°22'E |
| Malbon, Austl. (măl'bŭn) | 218 | 21°15'S | 140°30'E |
| Malbork, Pol. (mäl'bōrk) | 160 | 54°02'N | 19°04'E |
| Malcabran, r., Port. (mäl-kä-brän') | 173b | 38°47'N | 8°46'W |
| Malden, Ma., U.S. (môl'dĕn) | 101a | 42°26'N | 71°04'W |
| Malden, Mo., U.S. | 121 | 36°32'N | 89°56'W |
| Malden, i., Kir. | 2 | 4°20'S | 154°30'W |
| Maldives, nation, Asia | 194 | 4°30'N | 71°30'E |

| PLACE (Pronunciation) | PAGE | LAT. | LONG. |
|---|---|---|---|
| Maldon, Eng., U.K. (môrl'dŏn) | 158b | 51°44'N | 0°39'E |
| Maldonado, Ur. (mäl-dō-nä'dô) | 144 | 34°54'S | 54°57'W |
| Maldonado, Punta, c., Mex. (pōō'n-tä) | 130 | 16°18'N | 98°34'W |
| Maléas, Ákra, c., Grc. | 163 | 36°31'N | 23°13'E |
| Mālegaon, India | 202 | 20°35'N | 74°30'E |
| Malé Karpaty, mts., Slvk. | 169 | 48°31'N | 17°15'E |
| Malekula, i., Vanuatu (mä-lā-kōō'lä) | 221 | 16°44'S | 167°45'E |
| Malema, Moz. | 237 | 14°57'S | 37°20'E |
| Malheur, r., Or., U.S. (må-lōōr') | 114 | 43°45'N | 117°41'W |
| Malheur Lake, l., Or., U.S. (må-lōōr') | 114 | 43°16'N | 118°37'W |
| Mali, nation, Afr. | 230 | 15°45'N | 0°15'W |
| Malibu, Ca., U.S. (mă'lĭ-bōō) | 117a | 34°03'N | 118°38'W |
| Malik, Wādī al, r., Sudan | 231 | 16°48'N | 29°30'E |
| Malimba, Monts, mts., D.R.C. | 237 | 7°45'S | 29°15'E |
| Malinalco, Mex. (mä-lē-näl'kō) | 130 | 18°54'N | 99°31'W |
| Malinaltepec, Mex. (mä-lē-näl-tå-pĕk') | 130 | 17°01'N | 98°41'W |
| Malindi, Kenya (mä-lēn'dê) | 233 | 3°14'S | 40°04'E |
| Malin Head, c., Ire. | 160 | 55°23'N | 7°24'W |
| Malino, Russia (mä'lĭ-nô) | 186b | 55°07'N | 38°12'E |
| Malkara, Tur. (mäl'kå-rå) | 175 | 40°51'N | 26°52'E |
| Malko Tŭrnovo, Blg. (mäl'kō-t'r'nô-vå) | 175 | 41°59'N | 27°28'E |
| Mallaig, Scot., U.K. | 164 | 56°59'N | 5°55'W |
| Mallet Creek, Oh., U.S. (măl'ĕt) | 111d | 41°10'N | 81°55'W |
| Mallorca, i., Spain | 156 | 39°30'N | 3°00'E |
| Mallow, Ire. (măl'ō) | 164 | 52°07'N | 9°04'W |
| Malmédy, Bel. (mål-mā-dē') | 165 | 50°25'N | 6°01'E |
| Malmesbury, S. Afr. (mämz'bēr-ĭ) | 232 | 33°30'S | 18°35'E |
| Malmköping, Swe. (mälm'chû'pĭng) | 166 | 59°09'N | 16°39'E |
| Malmö, Swe. | 154 | 55°36'N | 13°00'E |
| Malmyzh, Russia (mål-mēzh') | 179 | 49°58'N | 137°07'E |
| Malmyzh, Russia | 180 | 56°30'N | 50°48'E |
| Maloarkhangelsk, Russia (mä'lō-år-kän'gĕlsk) | 176 | 52°26'N | 36°29'E |
| Malolos, Phil. (mä-lô'lôs) | 213a | 14°51'N | 120°49'E |
| Malomal'sk, Russia (må-lô-mälsk'') | 186a | 58°47'N | 59°55'E |
| Malone, N.Y., U.S. (må-lōn') | 109 | 44°50'N | 74°20'W |
| Malonga, D.R.C. | 236 | 10°24'S | 23°10'E |
| Maloti Mountains, mts., Leso. | 233c | 29°00'S | 28°29'E |
| Maloyaroslavets, Russia (mä'lô-yä-rô-slä-vyĕts) | 176 | 55°01'N | 36°25'E |
| Malozemel'skaya Tundra, reg., Russia | 180 | 67°30'N | 50°00'E |
| Malpas, Eng., U.K. (mål'påz) | 158a | 53°01'N | 2°46'W |
| Malpelo, Isla de, i., Col. (mäl-pä'lō) | 142 | 3°55'N | 81°30'W |
| Malpeque Bay, b., Can. (môl-pĕk') | 100 | 46°30'N | 63°47'W |
| Malta, Mt., U.S. (môl'tå) | 115 | 48°20'N | 107°50'W |
| Malta, nation, Eur. | 154 | 35°52'N | 13°30'E |
| Maltahöhe, Nmb. (mäl'tä-hō'ĕ) | 232 | 24°45'S | 16°45'E |
| Maltrata, Mex. (mäl-trä'tä) | 131 | 18°48'N | 97°16'W |
| Maluku (Moluccas), is., Indon. | 213 | 2°22'S | 128°25'E |
| Maluku, Laut (Molucca Sea), sea, Indon. | 213 | 0°15'N | 125°41'E |
| Malūţ, Sudan | 231 | 10°30'N | 32°17'E |
| Mālvan, India | 203 | 16°08'N | 73°32'E |
| Malvern, Ar., U.S. (măl'vērn) | 121 | 34°21'N | 92°47'W |
| Malyn, Ukr. | 177 | 50°44'N | 29°15'E |
| Malynivka, Ukr. | 177 | 49°50'N | 36°43'E |
| Malyy Anyuy, r., Russia | 185 | 67°52'N | 164°30'E |
| Malyy Tamir, i., Russia | 185 | 78°10'N | 107°30'E |
| Mamantel, Mex. (mä-mån-tĕl') | 131 | 18°36'N | 91°06'W |
| Mamaroneck, N.Y., U.S. (măm'å-rō-nĕk) | 110a | 40°57'N | 73°44'W |
| Mambasa, D.R.C. | 237 | 1°21'N | 29°03'E |
| Mamburao, Phil. (mäm-bōō'rä-ō) | 213a | 13°14'N | 120°35'E |
| Mamfe, Cam. (mäm'fĕ) | 230 | 5°46'N | 9°17'E |
| Mamihara, Japan (mä'mē-hä-rä) | 211 | 32°41'N | 131°12'E |
| Mammoth Cave, Ky., U.S. (măm'ŏth) | 124 | 37°10'N | 86°04'W |
| Mammoth Cave National Park, rec., Ky., U.S. | 107 | 37°20'N | 86°21'W |
| Mammoth Hot Springs, Wy., U.S. (măm'ŭth hôt sprĭngz) | 115 | 44°55'N | 110°50'W |
| Mamnoli, India | 203b | 19°17'N | 73°15'E |
| Mamoré, r., S.A. | 142 | 13°00'S | 65°20'W |
| Mamou, Gui. | 230 | 10°26'N | 12°07'W |
| Mampong, Ghana | 234 | 7°04'N | 1°24'W |
| Mamry, Jezioro, l., Pol. (mäm'rĭ) | 169 | 54°10'N | 21°28'E |
| Man, C. Iv. | 234 | 7°24'N | 7°33'W |
| Manacor, Spain (mä-nä-kôr') | 173 | 39°35'N | 3°15'E |
| Manado, Indon. | 213 | 1°29'N | 124°50'E |
| Managua, Cuba (mä-nä'gwä) | 135a | 22°58'N | 82°17'W |
| Managua, Nic. | 128 | 12°10'N | 86°16'W |
| Managua, Lago de, l., Nic. (lä'gô-dē) | 132 | 12°28'N | 86°10'W |
| Manakara, Madag. (mä-nä-kä'rŭ) | 233 | 22°17'S | 48°06'E |
| Manama *see* Al Manāmah, Bahr. | 198 | 26°01'N | 50°33'E |
| Mananara, r., Madag. (mä-nä-nä'rŭ) | 233 | 23°15'S | 48°15'E |
| Mananjary, Madag. (mä-nän-zhä'rē) | 233 | 20°16'S | 48°13'E |
| Manas, China | 204 | 44°30'N | 86°00'E |
| Manassas, Va., U.S. (må-năs'ås) | 109 | 38°45'N | 77°30'W |
| Manaus, Braz. (mä-nä'ōozh) | 143 | 3°01'S | 60°00'W |
| Mancelona, Mi., U.S. (măn-sē-lō'nå) | 108 | 44°50'N | 85°05'W |
| Mancha Real, Spain (män'chä rā-äl') | 172 | 37°48'N | 3°37'W |
| Manchazh, Russia (män'chåsh) | 186a | 56°30'N | 58°10'E |
| Manchester, Eng., U.K. | 154 | 53°28'N | 2°14'W |
| Manchester, Ct., U.S. (măn'chĕs-tēr) | 109 | 41°45'N | 72°30'W |
| Manchester, Ga., U.S. | 124 | 32°50'N | 84°37'W |
| Manchester, Ia., U.S. | 113 | 42°30'N | 91°30'W |
| Manchester, Ma., U.S. | 101a | 42°35'N | 70°47'W |
| Manchester, Mo., U.S. | 117e | 38°36'N | 90°31'W |
| Manchester, N.H., U.S. | 105 | 43°00'N | 71°30'W |
| Manchester, Oh., U.S. | 108 | 38°40'N | 83°35'W |
| Manchester Ship Canal, Eng., U.K. | 158a | 53°20'N | 2°40'W |

| PLACE (Pronunciation) | PAGE | LAT. | LONG. |
|---|---|---|---|
| Manchuria, hist. reg., China (măn-chōō'rē-å) | 205 | 48°00'N | 124°58'E |
| Mandal, Nor. (män'däl) | 166 | 58°03'N | 7°28'E |
| Mandalay, Mya. (măn'då-lā) | 199 | 22°00'N | 96°08'E |
| Mandalselva, r., Nor. | 166 | 58°25'N | 7°30'E |
| Mandan, N.D., U.S. (măn'dăn) | 104 | 46°49'N | 100°54'W |
| Mandara Mountains, mts., Afr. (män-dä'rä) | 231 | 10°15'N | 13°23'E |
| Mandau Siak, r., Indon. | 197b | 1°03'N | 101°25'E |
| Mandeb, Bab-el-, strt. (băb'ĕl män-dĕb') | 198 | 13°17'N | 42°49'E |
| Mandimba, Moz. | 237 | 14°21'S | 35°39'E |
| Mandinga, Pan. (män-dĭŋ'gä) | 133 | 9°32'N | 79°04'W |
| Mandla, India | 202 | 22°43'N | 80°23'E |
| Mándra, Grc. (män'drä) | 175 | 38°06'N | 23°32'E |
| Mandritsara, Madag. (mån-drēt-sä'rå) | 233 | 15°49'S | 48°47'E |
| Manduria, Italy (män-dōō'rē-ä) | 175 | 40°23'N | 17°41'E |
| Mandve, India | 203b | 18°47'N | 72°52'E |
| Māndvi, India (mŭnd'vē) | 203b | 19°29'N | 72°53'E |
| Māndvi, India (mŭnd'vē) | 199 | 22°54'N | 69°23'E |
| Mandya, India | 203 | 12°40'N | 77°00'E |
| Manfredonia, Italy (män-frå-dô'nyä) | 174 | 41°39'N | 15°55'E |
| Manfredónia, Golfo di, b., Italy (gôl-fô-dē) | 174 | 41°34'N | 16°05'E |
| Mangabeiras, Chapada das, pl., Braz. | 143 | 8°05'S | 47°32'W |
| Mangalore, India (mŭŋ-gŭ-lōr') | 199 | 12°53'N | 74°52'E |
| Mangaratiba, Braz. (män-gä-rä-tē'bå) | 141a | 22°56'S | 44°03'W |
| Mangatarem, Phil. (män'gå-tä'rĕm) | 213a | 15°48'N | 120°18'E |
| Mange, D.R.C. | 236 | 0°54'N | 20°30'E |
| Mangkalihat, Tanjung, c., Indon. | 212 | 1°25'N | 119°55'E |
| Mangles, Islas de, Cuba (ê's-läs-dē-mäŋ'glās) (măn'g'lz) | 134 | 22°05'N | 82°50'W |
| Mangoche, Mwi. | 232 | 14°16'S | 35°14'E |
| Mangoky, r., Madag. (män-gō'kē) | 233 | 22°02'S | 44°11'E |
| Mangole, Pulau, i., Indon. | 213 | 1°35'S | 126°22'E |
| Mangualde, Port. (män-gwäl'dĕ) | 172 | 40°38'N | 7°44'W |
| Mangueira, Lagoa da, l., Braz. | 144 | 33°15'S | 52°45'W |
| Mangum, Ok., U.S. (măŋ'gŭm) | 120 | 34°52'N | 99°31'W |
| Mangzhangdian, China (mäŋ-jäŋ-dĭĕn) | 206 | 32°07'N | 114°44'E |
| Manhattan, Il., U.S. | 111a | 41°25'N | 87°29'W |
| Manhattan, Ks., U.S. (măn-hăt'ăn) | 104 | 39°11'N | 96°34'W |
| Manhattan Beach, Ca., U.S. | 117a | 33°53'N | 118°24'W |
| Manhuaçu, Braz. (män-òå'sōō) | 141a | 20°17'S | 42°01'W |
| Manhumirim, Braz. (män-ōō-mē-rē'n) | 141a | 22°30'S | 41°57'W |
| Manicouagane, r., Can. | 93 | 50°00'N | 68°35'W |
| Manicouagane, Lac, res., Can. | 93 | 51°30'N | 68°19'W |
| Manicuare, Ven. (mä-nē-kwä'rē) | 143b | 10°35'N | 64°10'W |
| Manihiki Islands, is., Cook Is. (mä'nē-hē'kē) | 241 | 9°40'S | 158°00'W |
| Manila, Phil. | 212 | 14°37'N | 121°00'E |
| Manila Bay, b., Phil. (må-nĭl'å) | 213a | 14°38'N | 120°46'E |
| Manisa, Tur. (mä'nê-så) | 163 | 38°40'N | 27°30'E |
| Manistee, Mi., U.S. (măn-ĭs-tē') | 108 | 44°15'N | 86°20'W |
| Manistee, r., Mi., U.S. | 108 | 44°25'N | 85°45'W |
| Manistique, Mi., U.S. (măn-ĭs-tēk') | 113 | 45°58'N | 86°16'W |
| Manistique, l., Mi., U.S. | 113 | 46°14'N | 85°30'W |
| Manistique, r., Mi., U.S. | 113 | 46°05'N | 86°09'W |
| Manitoba, prov., Can. (măn-ĭ-tō'bå) | 90 | 55°12'N | 97°29'W |
| Manitoba, Lake, l., Can. | 92 | 51°00'N | 98°45'W |
| Manito Lake, l., Can. (măn'ĭ-tō) | 96 | 52°45'N | 109°45'W |
| Manitou, i., Mi., U.S. (măn'ĭ-tōō) | 113 | 47°21'N | 87°33'W |
| Manitou, l., Can. | 113 | 49°21'N | 93°01'W |
| Manitou Islands, is., Mi., U.S. | 108 | 45°05'N | 86°00'W |
| Manitoulin Island, i., Can. (măn-ĭ-tōō'lĭn) | 93 | 45°45'N | 81°30'W |
| Manitou Springs, Co., U.S. | 120 | 38°51'N | 104°58'W |
| Manitowoc, Wi., U.S. (măn-ĭ-tô-wŏk') | 113 | 44°05'N | 87°42'W |
| Manitqueira, Serra da, mts., Braz. | 141a | 22°40'S | 45°12'W |
| Maniwaki, Can. | 99 | 46°23'N | 76°00'W |
| Manizales, Col. (mä-nē-zä'lås) | 142 | 5°05'N | 75°31'W |
| Manjacaze, Moz. (man'yä-kä'zĕ) | 232 | 24°37'S | 33°49'E |
| Mankato, Ks., U.S. (măn-kā'tō) | 120 | 39°45'N | 98°12'W |
| Mankato, Mn., U.S. | 105 | 44°10'N | 93°59'W |
| Mankim, Cam. | 235 | 5°01'N | 12°00'E |
| Manlléu, Spain (män-lyā'ōō) | 173 | 42°00'N | 2°16'E |
| Mannar, Sri L. (må-när') | 203 | 9°48'N | 80°03'E |
| Mannar, Gulf of, b., Asia | 199 | 8°47'N | 78°33'E |
| Mannheim, Ger. (män'hīm) | 161 | 49°30'N | 8°31'E |
| Manning, Ia., U.S. (măn'ĭng) | 112 | 41°53'N | 95°04'W |
| Manning, S.C., U.S. | 125 | 33°41'N | 80°12'W |
| Mannington, W.V., U.S. (măn'ĭng-tŭn) | 108 | 39°30'N | 80°55'W |
| Mano, r., Afr. | 234 | 7°00'N | 11°25'W |
| Man of War Bay, b., Bah. | 135 | 21°05'N | 74°05'W |
| Man of War Channel, strt., Bah. | 134 | 22°45'N | 76°10'W |
| Manokwari, Indon. (må-nŏk-wä'rê) | 213 | 0°56'S | 134°10'E |
| Manono, D.R.C. | 237 | 7°18'S | 27°25'E |
| Manor, Can. (măn'ēr) | 97 | 49°36'N | 102°05'W |
| Manor, Wa., U.S. | 116c | 45°45'N | 122°36'W |
| Manori, neigh., India | 203b | 19°13'N | 72°43'E |
| Manosque, Fr. (må-nôsh') | 171 | 43°51'N | 5°48'E |
| Manotick, Can. | 102c | 45°13'N | 75°41'W |
| Manouane, r., Can. | 99 | 50°15'N | 70°30'W |
| Manouane, Lac, l., Can. (mä-nōō'än) | 100 | 50°36'N | 70°50'W |
| Manresa, Spain (män-rā'sä) | 162 | 41°44'N | 1°52'E |
| Mansa, Zam. | 232 | 11°12'S | 28°53'E |
| Mansel, i., Can. (măn'sĕl) | 93 | 61°56'N | 81°10'W |
| Manseriche, Pongo de, reg., Peru (pŏ'n-gô-dē-män-sē-rē'chē) | 142 | 4°15'S | 77°45'W |
| Mansfield, Eng., U.K. (mănz'fēld) | 158a | 53°08'N | 1°12'W |
| Mansfield, La., U.S. | 123 | 32°02'N | 93°43'W |
| Mansfield, Oh., U.S. | 108 | 40°45'N | 82°30'W |
| Mansfield, Wa., U.S. | 114 | 47°48'N | 119°39'W |
| Mansfield, Mount, mtn., Vt., U.S. | 109 | 44°30'N | 72°45'W |


ăt; finăl; rāte; senåte; ärm; åsk; sofå; fâre; ch-choose; dh-as th in other; bē; ēvent; bĕt; recĕnt; cratēr; g-gō; gh-guttural g; bĭt; ĭ-short neutral; rīde; ĸ-guttural k as ch in German ich;

PRONOUNCING INDEX

Mansfield Woodhouse – Marystown 319


| PLACE (Pronunciation) | PAGE | LAT. | LONG. |
|---|---|---|---|
| Mansfield Woodhouse, Eng., U.K. (wo͝od-hous) | 158a | 53°08'N | 1°12'W |
| Manta, Ec. (män'tä) | 142 | 1°03'S | 80°16'W |
| Manteno, Il., U.S. (măn-tē-nō) | 111a | 41°15'N | 87°50'W |
| Manteo, N.C., U.S. | 125 | 35°55'N | 75°40'W |
| Mantes-la-Jolie, Fr. (mäɴt-ĕ-lä-zhŏ-lē') | 170 | 48°59'N | 1°42'E |
| Manti, Ut., U.S. (măn'tī) | 119 | 39°15'N | 111°40'W |
| Mantova, Italy (män'tô-vä) (măn'tů-ȧ) | 162 | 45°09'N | 10°47'E |
| Mantua, Cuba (män-to͞o'ä) | 134 | 22°20'N | 84°15'W |
| Mantua see Mantova, Italy | 162 | 45°09'N | 10°47'E |
| Mantua, Ut., U.S. (măn'tů-ȧ) | 117b | 41°30'N | 111°57'W |
| Manua Islands, is., Am. Sam. | 214a | 14°13'S | 169°35'W |
| Manui, Pulau, i., Indon. (mä-no͞o'ē) | 213 | 3°35'S | 123°38'E |
| Manus Island, i., Pap. N. Gui. (mä'no͞os) | 213 | 2°22'S | 146°22'E |
| Manvel, Tx., U.S. (măn'vel) | 123a | 29°28'N | 95°22'W |
| Manville, N.J., U.S. (măn'vĭl) | 110a | 40°33'N | 74°36'W |
| Manville, R.I., U.S. | 110b | 41°57'N | 71°27'W |
| Manzala Lake, l., Egypt | 238b | 31°14'N | 32°04'E |
| Manzanares, Col. (män-sä-nä'rĕs) | 142a | 5°15'N | 75°09'W |
| Manzanares, r., Spain (mänz-nä'rĕs) | 173a | 40°36'N | 3°48'W |
| Manzanares, Canal del, Spain (kä-nä'l-dĕl-män-thä-nä'rĕs) | 173a | 40°20'N | 3°38'W |
| Manzanillo, Cuba (män'zä-nēl'yō) | 129 | 20°20'N | 77°05'W |
| Manzanillo, Mex. | 128 | 19°02'N | 104°21'W |
| Manzanillo, Bahía de, b., Mex. (bä-ē'ä-dĕ-män-zä-nē'l-yō) | 130 | 19°00'N | 104°38'W |
| Manzanillo, Bahía de, b., N.A. | 135 | 19°55'N | 71°50'W |
| Manzanillo, Punta, c., Pan. | 133 | 9°40'N | 79°33'W |
| Manzhouli, China (män-jō-lē) | 205 | 49°25'N | 117°15'E |
| Manzovka, Russia (mȧn-zhô'f-kȧ) | 210 | 44°16'N | 132°13'E |
| Mao, Chad (mä'ō) | 231 | 14°07'N | 15°19'E |
| Mao, Dom. Rep. | 135 | 19°35'N | 71°10'W |
| Maó, Spain | 162 | 39°52'N | 4°15'E |
| Maoke, Pegunungan, mts., Indon. | 213 | 4°00'S | 138°00'E |
| Maoming, China | 205 | 21°55'N | 110°40'E |
| Maoniu Shan, mtn., China (mou-nĭō shän) | 208 | 32°45'N | 104°09'E |
| Mapastepec, Mex. (ma-päs-tå-pĕk') | 131 | 15°24'N | 92°52'W |
| Mapia, Kepulauan, i., Indon. | 213 | 0°57'N | 134°22'E |
| Mapimí, Mex. (mä-pē-mē') | 122 | 25°50'N | 103°50'W |
| Mapimí, Bolsón de, des., Mex. (bôl-sŏ'n-dĕ-mä-pē'mē) | 122 | 27°27'N | 103°20'W |
| Maple Creek, Can. (mā'p'l) (crēk) | 90 | 49°55'N | 109°27'W |
| Maple Grove, Can. (grōv) | 102a | 45°19'N | 73°51'W |
| Maple Heights, Oh., U.S. | 111d | 41°25'N | 81°34'W |
| Maple Shade, N.J., U.S. (shād) | 110f | 39°57'N | 75°01'W |
| Maple Valley, Wa., U.S. (văl'ē) | 116a | 47°24'N | 122°02'W |
| Maplewood, Mn., U.S. (wo͝od) | 117g | 45°00'N | 93°03'W |
| Maplewood, Mo., U.S. | 117e | 38°37'N | 90°20'W |
| Mapumulo, S. Afr. (mä-pä-mo͞o'lō) | 233c | 29°12'S | 31°05'E |
| Maputo, Moz. | 232 | 26°50'S | 32°30'E |
| Maquela do Zombo, Ang. (mȧ-kā'lȧ dō zôm'bō) | 232 | 6°08'S | 15°15'E |
| Maquoketa, Ia., U.S. (mȧ-kō-kē-tȧ) | 113 | 42°04'N | 90°42'W |
| Maquoketa, r., Ia., U.S. | 113 | 42°08'N | 90°40'W |
| Mar, Serra do, mts., Braz. (sĕr'rȧ dō mär') | 144 | 26°30'S | 49°15'W |
| Maracaibo, Ven. (mä-rä-kī'bō) | 142 | 10°38'N | 71°45'W |
| Maracaibo, Lago de, l., Ven. (lä'gô-dĕ-mä-rä-kī'bō) | 142 | 9°55'N | 72°13'W |
| Maracay, Ven. (mä-rä-käy') | 142 | 10°15'N | 67°35'W |
| Marādah, Libya | 231 | 29°10'N | 19°07'E |
| Maradi, Niger (mȧ-rȧ-dē') | 230 | 13°29'N | 7°06'E |
| Marāgheh, Iran | 201 | 37°20'N | 46°10'E |
| Maraisburg, S. Afr. | 233b | 26°12'S | 27°57'E |
| Marais des Cygnes, r., Ks., U.S. | 121 | 38°30'N | 95°30'W |
| Marajó, Ilha de, i., Braz. | 143 | 1°00'S | 49°30'W |
| Maralal, Kenya | 237 | 1°06'N | 36°42'E |
| Marali, C.A.R. | 235 | 6°01'N | 18°24'E |
| Marand, Iran | 201 | 38°26'N | 45°46'E |
| Maranguape, Braz. (mä-rȧŋ-gwä'pĕ) | 143 | 3°48'S | 38°38'W |
| Maranhão, state, Braz. (mä-rän-youɴ) | 143 | 5°15'S | 45°52'W |
| Maranoa, r., Austl. (mä-rä-nō'ä) | 221 | 27°01'S | 148°03'E |
| Marano di Napoli, Italy (mä-rä'nô-dē-nä'pô-lē) | 173c | 40°39'N | 14°12'E |
| Marañón, r., Peru (mä-rä-nyōn') | 142 | 4°26'S | 75°08'W |
| Marapanim, Braz. (mä-rä-pä-nē'ɴ) | 143 | 0°45'S | 47°42'W |
| Marathon, Can. | 91 | 48°50'N | 86°10'W |
| Marathon, Fl., U.S. (măr'ȧ-thŏn) | 125a | 24°41'N | 81°06'W |
| Marathon, Oh., U.S. | 111f | 39°09'N | 83°59'W |
| Maravatio, Mex. (mä-rȧ-vä'tē-ō) | 130 | 19°54'N | 100°25'W |
| Marawi, Sudan | 231 | 18°07'N | 31°57'E |
| Marble Bar, Austl. (märb''l bär) | 218 | 21°15'S | 119°15'E |
| Marble Canal, can., Az., U.S. (mär'b'l) | 119 | 36°21'N | 111°48'W |
| Marblehead, Ma., U.S. (mär'b'l-hĕd) | 101a | 42°30'N | 70°51'W |
| Marburg an der Lahn, Ger. | 168 | 50°49'N | 8°46'E |
| Marca, Ponta da, c., Ang. | 236 | 16°31'S | 11°42'E |
| Marcala, Hond. (mär-kä-lä) | 132 | 14°08'N | 88°01'W |
| Marceline, Mo., U.S. (mär-sē-lēn') | 121 | 39°42'N | 92°56'W |
| Marche, hist. reg., Italy (mär'kā) | 174 | 43°35'N | 12°33'E |
| Marchegg, Aus. | 159e | 48°18'N | 16°55'E |
| Marchena, Spain (mär-chā'nä) | 162 | 37°20'N | 5°25'W |
| Marchena, i., Ec. (ē's-lä-mär-chē'nä) | 142 | 0°29'N | 90°31'W |
| Marchfeld, reg., Aus. | 159e | 48°14'N | 16°37'E |
| Mar Chiquita, Laguna, l., Arg. (lä-go͞o'nä-mär-chē-kē'tä) | 141c | 34°25'S | 61°10'W |
| Marcos Paz, Arg. (mär-kōs' päz) | 141c | 34°49'S | 58°51'W |
| Marcus, i., Japan (mär'kŭs) | 241 | 24°00'N | 155°00'E |
| Marcus Hook, Pa., U.S. (mär'kŭs ho͝ok) | 110f | 39°49'N | 75°25'W |
| Marcy, Mount, mtn., N.Y., U.S. (mär'sē) | 109 | 44°10'N | 73°55'W |

| PLACE (Pronunciation) | PAGE | LAT. | LONG. |
|---|---|---|---|
| Mar de Espanha, Braz. (mär-dĕ-ĕs-pä'nyȧ) | 141a | 21°53'S | 43°00'W |
| Mar del Plata, Arg. (mär dĕl- plä'ta) | 144 | 37°59'S | 57°35'W |
| Mardin, Tur. (mär-dēn') | 198 | 37°25'N | 40°40'E |
| Maré, i., N. Cal. (mȧ-rā') | 221 | 21°53'S | 168°30'E |
| Maree, Loch, b., Scot., U.K. (mä-rē') | 164 | 57°40'N | 5°44'W |
| Marengo, Ia., U.S. (mȧ-rĕŋ'gō) | 113 | 41°47'N | 92°04'W |
| Marennes, Fr. (mȧ-rĕn') | 170 | 45°49'N | 1°08'W |
| Marfa, Tx., U.S. (mär'fȧ) | 122 | 30°19'N | 104°01'W |
| Margarita, Pan. (mär-go͞o-rē'tä) | 128a | 9°20'N | 79°55'W |
| Margarita, Isla de, i., Ven. (mä-gȧ-rē'tȧ) | 142 | 11°00'N | 64°15'W |
| Margate, S. Afr. (mä-gāt') | 233c | 30°52'S | 30°21'E |
| Margate, Eng., U.K. (mär'gāt) | 165 | 51°21'N | 1°17'E |
| Margherita Peak, mtn., Afr. | 231 | 0°22'N | 29°51'E |
| Marguerite, r., Can. | 100 | 50°39'N | 66°42'W |
| Marhanets', Ukr. | 177 | 47°41'N | 34°33'E |
| Maria, Can. (mȧ-rē'ȧ) | 100 | 48°10'N | 66°04'W |
| Mariager, Den. (mä-rē-āgh'ĕr) | 166 | 56°38'N | 10°00'E |
| Mariana, Braz. (mä-ryä'nä) | 141a | 20°23'S | 43°24'W |
| Mariana Islands, is., Oc. | 5 | 16°00'N | 145°30'E |
| Marianao, Cuba (mä-rē-ä-nä'ō) | 129 | 23°05'N | 82°26'W |
| Mariana Trench, deep | 241 | 12°00'N | 144°00'E |
| Marianna, Ar., U.S. (mā-rī-ăn'ȧ) | 121 | 34°45'N | 90°45'W |
| Marianna, Fl., U.S. | 124 | 30°46'N | 85°14'W |
| Marianna, Pa., U.S. | 111e | 40°01'N | 80°05'W |
| Mariano Acosta, Arg. (mä-rēä'nō-ȧ-kōs'tä) | 144a | 34°28'S | 58°48'W |
| Mariánské Lázně, Czech Rep. (mär'yàn-skĕ'läz'nyĕ) | 168 | 49°58'N | 12°42'E |
| Marias, r., Mt., U.S. (mȧ-rī'ȧz) | 115 | 48°15'N | 110°50'W |
| Marias, Islas, is., Mex. (mä-rē'äs) | 128 | 21°30'N | 106°40'W |
| Mariato, Punta, c., Pan. | 133 | 7°17'N | 81°09'W |
| Maribo, Den. (mä'rē-bō) | 166 | 54°46'N | 11°29'E |
| Maribor, Slvn. (mä're-bôr) | 154 | 46°33'N | 15°37'E |
| Maricaban, i., Phil. (mä-rē-kä-bän') | 213a | 13°40'N | 120°44'E |
| Mariefred, Swe. (mä-rē'ĕ-frĭd) | 166 | 59°17'N | 17°09'E |
| Marie Galante, i., Guad. (mȧ-rē' gȧ-läɴt') | 133b | 15°58'N | 61°05'W |
| Mariehamn, Fin. (mȧ-rē'ĕ-häm''n) | 167 | 60°07'N | 19°57'E |
| Mari El, prov., Russia | 180 | 56°30'N | 48°00'E |
| Mariestad, Swe. (mä-rē'ĕ-städ') | 166 | 58°43'N | 13°45'E |
| Marietta, Ga., U.S. (mā-rĭ-ĕt'ȧ) | 110c | 33°57'N | 84°33'W |
| Marietta, Oh., U.S. | 108 | 39°25'N | 81°30'W |
| Marietta, Ok., U.S. | 121 | 33°53'N | 97°07'W |
| Marietta, Wa., U.S. | 116d | 48°48'N | 122°35'W |
| Mariinsk, Russia (mȧ-re'ĭnsk) | 184 | 56°15'N | 87°28'E |
| Marijampole, Lith. (mä-rē-yäm-pô'lĕ) | 167 | 54°33'N | 23°26'E |
| Marikana, S. Afr. (mă'-rĭ-kä-nȧ) | 238c | 25°40'S | 27°28'E |
| Marília, Braz. (mä-rē'lyȧ) | 143 | 22°02'S | 49°48'W |
| Marimba, Ang. | 236 | 8°28'S | 17°08'E |
| Marín, Spain | 172 | 42°24'N | 8°40'W |
| Marinduque Island, i., Phil. (mä-rēn-do͞o'kä) | 213a | 13°14'N | 121°45'E |
| Marine, Il., U.S. (mȧ-rēn') | 117e | 38°48'N | 89°47'W |
| Marine City, Mi., U.S. | 108 | 42°45'N | 82°30'W |
| Marine Lake, l., Mn., U.S. | 117g | 45°13'N | 92°55'W |
| Marine on Saint Croix, Mn., U.S. | 117g | 45°11'N | 92°47'W |
| Marinette, Wi., U.S. (măr-ĭ-nĕt') | 105 | 45°04'N | 87°40'W |
| Maringa, r., D.R.C. (mä-riŋ'gä) | 231 | 0°30'N | 21°00'E |
| Marinha Grande, Port. (mä-rēn'yȧ grän'dĕ) | 172 | 39°49'N | 8°53'W |
| Marion, Al., U.S. (măr'ĭ-ŭn) | 124 | 32°36'N | 87°19'W |
| Marion, Ia., U.S. | 113 | 42°01'N | 91°39'W |
| Marion, Il., U.S. | 108 | 37°40'N | 88°55'W |
| Marion, In., U.S. | 105 | 40°35'N | 85°45'W |
| Marion, Ks., U.S. | 121 | 38°21'N | 97°02'W |
| Marion, Ky., U.S. | 124 | 37°19'N | 88°05'W |
| Marion, N.C., U.S. | 125 | 35°40'N | 82°00'W |
| Marion, N.D., U.S. | 112 | 46°37'N | 98°20'W |
| Marion, Oh., U.S. | 108 | 40°35'N | 83°10'W |
| Marion, S.C., U.S. | 125 | 34°08'N | 79°23'W |
| Marion, Va., U.S. | 125 | 36°48'N | 81°33'W |
| Marion, Lake, res., S.C., U.S. | 125 | 33°25'N | 80°35'W |
| Marion Reef, rf., Austl. | 221 | 18°57'S | 151°31'E |
| Mariposa, Chile (mä-rē-pō'sä) | 141b | 35°33'S | 71°21'W |
| Mariposa Creek, r., Ca., U.S. | 118 | 37°14'N | 120°30'W |
| Mariquita, Col. (mä-rē-kē'tä) | 142a | 5°13'N | 74°52'W |
| Mariscal Estigarribia, Para. | 144 | 22°03'S | 60°28'W |
| Marisco, Ponta do, c., Braz. (pô'n-tä-dô-mä-rē's-kō) | 144b | 23°01'S | 43°17'W |
| Maritime Alps, mts., Eur. (mă'rĭ-tīm ălps) | 161 | 44°20'N | 7°02'E |
| Mariupol', Ukr. | 178 | 47°07'N | 37°32'E |
| Mariveles, Phil. | 213a | 14°27'N | 120°29'E |
| Marj Uyan, Leb. | 197a | 33°21'N | 35°36'E |
| Marka, Som. | 238a | 1°45'N | 44°47'E |
| Markaryd, Swe. (mär'kä-rüd) | 166 | 56°30'N | 13°34'E |
| Marked Tree, Ar., U.S. (märkt trē) | 121 | 35°31'N | 90°26'W |
| Marken, i., Neth. | 159a | 52°26'N | 5°08'E |
| Market Bosworth, Eng., U.K. (bŏz'wûrth) | 158a | 52°37'N | 1°23'W |
| Market Deeping, Eng., U.K. (dēp'ĭng) | 158a | 52°40'N | 0°19'W |
| Market Drayton, Eng., U.K. (drā'tŭn) | 158a | 52°54'N | 2°29'W |
| Market Harborough, Eng., U.K. (här'bŭr-ō) | 158a | 52°28'N | 0°55'W |
| Market Rasen, Eng., U.K. (rā'zĕn) | 158a | 53°23'N | 0°21'W |
| Markham, Can. (märk'ȧm) | 99 | 43°53'N | 79°15'W |
| Markham, Mount, mtn., Ant. | 224 | 82°59'S | 159°30'E |
| Markivka, Ukr. | 177 | 49°32'N | 39°34'E |
| Markovo, Russia (mär'kō-vō) | 179 | 64°46'N | 170°48'E |
| Markrāna, India | 202 | 27°08'N | 74°43'E |
| Marks, Russia | 181 | 51°42'N | 46°46'E |
| Marksville, La., U.S. (märks'vĭl) | 123 | 31°09'N | 92°05'W |

| PLACE (Pronunciation) | PAGE | LAT. | LONG. |
|---|---|---|---|
| Markt Indersdorf, Ger. (märkt ēn'dĕrs-dōrf) | 159d | 48°22'N | 11°23'E |
| Marktredwitz, Ger. (märk-rĕd'vēts) | 168 | 50°02'N | 12°05'E |
| Markt Schwaben, Ger. (märkt shvä'bĕn) | 159d | 48°12'N | 11°52'E |
| Marl, Ger. (märl) | 171c | 51°40'N | 7°05'E |
| Marlboro, N.J., U.S. | 110a | 40°18'N | 74°15'W |
| Marlborough, Ma., U.S. | 101a | 42°21'N | 71°33'W |
| Marlette, Mi., U.S. (mär-lĕt') | 108 | 43°25'N | 83°05'W |
| Marlin, Tx., U.S. (mär'lĭn) | 123 | 31°18'N | 96°52'W |
| Marlinton, W.V., U.S. (mär'lĭn-tŭn) | 108 | 38°15'N | 80°10'W |
| Marlow, Eng., U.K. (mär'lō) | 158b | 51°33'N | 0°46'W |
| Marlow, Ok., U.S. | 121 | 34°38'N | 97°56'W |
| Marls, The, b., Bah. (märls) | 134 | 26°30'N | 77°15'W |
| Marmande, Fr. (mȧr-mäɴd') | 170 | 44°30'N | 0°10'E |
| Marmara Denizi, sea, Tur. | 198 | 40°40'N | 28°00'E |
| Marmarth, N.D., U.S. (mär'mȧrth) | 112 | 46°19'N | 103°57'W |
| Mar Muerto, l., Mex. (mär-mōĕ'r-tô) | 131 | 16°13'N | 94°22'W |
| Marne, Ger. (mär'nĕ) | 159c | 53°57'N | 9°01'E |
| Marne, r., Fr. (märn) | 161 | 49°00'N | 4°30'E |
| Maroa, Ven. (mä-rō'ä) | 142 | 2°43'N | 67°37'W |
| Maroantsetra, Madag. (mȧ-rō-äŋ-tsā'trȧ) | 233 | 15°18'S | 49°48'E |
| Maro Jarapeto, mtn., Col. (mä-rō-hä-rä-pĕ'tō) | 142a | 6°29'N | 76°39'W |
| Maromokotro, mtn., Madag. | 233 | 14°00'S | 49°11'E |
| Marondera, Zimb. | 232 | 18°10'S | 31°36'E |
| Maroni, r., S.A. (mȧ-rō'nē) | 143 | 3°02'N | 53°54'W |
| Maro Reef, rf., Hi., U.S. | 126b | 25°15'N | 170°00'W |
| Maroua, Cam. (mär'wä) | 231 | 10°36'N | 14°20'E |
| Marple, Eng., U.K. (mär'p'l) | 158a | 53°24'N | 2°04'W |
| Marquard, S. Afr. | 238c | 28°41'S | 27°26'E |
| Marquesas Islands, is., Fr. Poly. (mär-kĕ'säs) | 2 | 8°50'S | 141°00'W |
| Marquesas Keys, is., Fl., U.S. (mȧr-kē'zȧs) | 125a | 24°37'N | 82°15'W |
| Marquês de Valença, Braz. (mȧr-kĕ's-dĕ-vä-lĕ'n-sȧ) | 141a | 22°16'S | 43°42'W |
| Marquette, Can. (mȧr-kĕt') | 102f | 50°04'N | 97°43'W |
| Marquette, Mi., U.S. | 105 | 46°32'N | 87°25'W |
| Marquez, Tx., U.S. (mär-kāz') | 123 | 31°14'N | 96°15'W |
| Marra, Jabal, mtn., Sudan (jĕb'ĕl mär'ä) | 231 | 13°00'N | 23°47'E |
| Marrakech, Mor. (mȧr-rä'kĕsh) | 230 | 31°38'N | 8°00'W |
| Marree, Austl. (mȧr'rē) | 218 | 29°38'S | 137°55'E |
| Marrero, La., U.S. | 110d | 29°55'N | 90°06'W |
| Marrupa, Moz. | 237 | 13°08'S | 37°30'E |
| Mars, Pa., U.S. (märz) | 111e | 40°42'N | 80°01'W |
| Marsabit, Kenya | 237 | 2°20'N | 37°59'E |
| Marsala, Italy (mär-sä'lä) | 162 | 37°48'N | 12°28'E |
| Marsden, Eng., U.K. (märz'dĕn) | 158a | 53°36'N | 1°55'W |
| Marseille, Fr. (mȧr-sâ'y') | 154 | 43°18'N | 5°25'E |
| Marseilles, Il., U.S. (mär-sĕlz') | 108 | 41°20'N | 88°40'W |
| Marshall, Il., U.S. (mär'shȧl) | 108 | 39°20'N | 87°40'W |
| Marshall, Mi., U.S. | 108 | 42°20'N | 84°55'W |
| Marshall, Mn., U.S. | 112 | 44°28'N | 95°49'W |
| Marshall, Mo., U.S. | 121 | 39°07'N | 93°12'W |
| Marshall, Tx., U.S. | 105 | 32°33'N | 94°22'W |
| Marshall Islands, nation, Oc. | 3 | 10°00'N | 165°00'E |
| Marshalltown, Ia., U.S. (mär'shȧl-toun) | 113 | 42°02'N | 92°55'W |
| Marshallville, Ga., U.S. (mär'shȧl-vĭl) | 124 | 32°29'N | 83°55'W |
| Marshfield, Ma., U.S. (märsh'fēld) | 101a | 42°06'N | 70°43'W |
| Marshfield, Mo., U.S. | 121 | 37°20'N | 92°53'W |
| Marshfield, Wi., U.S. | 113 | 44°40'N | 90°10'W |
| Marsh Harbour, Bah. | 134 | 26°30'N | 77°00'W |
| Mars Hill, In., U.S. (märz'hĭl') | 111g | 39°43'N | 86°15'W |
| Mars Hill, Me., U.S. | 100 | 46°34'N | 67°54'W |
| Marstrand, Swe. (mär'stränd) | 166 | 57°54'N | 11°33'E |
| Marsyaty, Russia (märs'yȧ-tĭ) | 186a | 60°03'N | 60°28'E |
| Mart, Tx., U.S. (märt) | 123 | 31°32'N | 96°49'W |
| Martaban, Gulf of, b., Mya. (mär-tŭ-bän') | 212 | 16°34'N | 96°58'E |
| Martapura, Indon. | 212 | 3°19'S | 114°45'E |
| Martha's Vineyard, i., Ma., U.S. (mär'thȧz vĭn'yȧrd) | 109 | 41°25'N | 70°35'W |
| Martigny, Switz. (mȧr-tē-nyē') | 168 | 46°06'N | 7°00'E |
| Martigues, Fr. | 171 | 43°24'N | 5°05'E |
| Martin, Tn., U.S. (mär'tĭn) | 124 | 36°20'N | 88°45'W |
| Martina Franca, Italy (mär-tē'nä frăŋ'kä) | 175 | 40°43'N | 17°21'E |
| Martinez, Ca., U.S. (mär-tē'nĕz) | 116b | 38°01'N | 122°08'W |
| Martinez, Tx., U.S. | 117d | 29°25'N | 98°20'W |
| Martinique, dep., N.A. (mȧr-tē-nēk') | 129 | 14°50'N | 60°40'W |
| Martin Lake, res., Al., U.S. | 124 | 32°40'N | 86°05'W |
| Martin Point, c., Ak., U.S. | 103 | 70°10'N | 142°00'W |
| Martinsburg, W.V., U.S. (mär'tĭnz-bûrg) | 109 | 39°30'N | 78°00'W |
| Martins Ferry, Oh., U.S. (mär'tĭnz) | 108 | 40°05'N | 80°45'W |
| Martinsville, In., U.S. (mär'tĭnz-vĭl) | 108 | 39°25'N | 86°25'W |
| Martinsville, Va., U.S. | 125 | 36°40'N | 79°53'W |
| Martos, Spain (mär'tōs) | 172 | 37°43'N | 3°58'W |
| Martre, Lac la, l., Can. (läk la märtr) | 92 | 63°24'N | 119°58'W |
| Marugame, Japan (mä'ro͞o-gä'mä) | 211 | 34°19'N | 133°48'E |
| Marungu, mts., D.R.C. | 237 | 7°50'S | 29°50'E |
| Marve, neigh., India | 203b | 19°12'N | 72°43'E |
| Mary, Turkmen. (mä'rē) | 183 | 37°45'N | 61°47'E |
| Mar'yanskaya, Russia (mȧr-yän'skȧ-yȧ) | 177 | 45°04'N | 38°39'E |
| Maryborough, Austl. (mā'rĭ-bŭr-ō) | 219 | 25°35'S | 152°40'E |
| Maryborough, Austl. | 219 | 37°00'S | 143°50'E |
| Maryland, state, U.S. (mĕr'ĭ-lănd) | 105 | 39°10'N | 76°25'W |
| Marys, r., Nv., U.S. (mā'rĭz) | 114 | 41°25'N | 115°10'W |
| Marystown, Can. (mâr'ĭz-toun) | 101 | 47°11'N | 55°10'W |


ng-sing; ŋ-baŋk; ɴ-nasalized n; nŏd; cŏmmit; ōld; ōbey; ôrder; oi-boil; fo͞od; o͝o-as oo in foot; ou-out; s-soft; sh-dish; th-thin; pūre; ûnite; ûrn; stŭd; circŭs; ü-as in French tu; '-indeterminate vowel.

āt; final; rāte; senåte; ärm; ásk; sofá; fåre; ch-choose; dh-as th in other; bē; ĕvent; bĕt; recĕnt; cratēr; g-gō; gh-guttural g; bīt; ĭ-short neutral; rīde; ĸ-guttural k as ch in German ich;

PRONOUNCING INDEX

Medanosa – Mezquitic 321


| PLACE (Pronunciation) | PAGE | LAT. | LONG. |
|---|---|---|---|
| Medanosa, Punta, c., Arg. (po͞o′n-tä-mĕ-dä-nô′sä) | 144 | 47°50′S | 65°53′W |
| Medden, r., Eng., U.K. (mĕd′ĕn) | 158a | 53°14′N | 1°05′W |
| Medellín, Col. (må-dhĕl-yēn′) | 142 | 6°15′N | 75°34′W |
| Medellin, Mex. (mĕ-dĕl-yē′n) | 131 | 19°03′N | 96°08′W |
| Medenine, Tun. (mā-dē-nēn′) | 162 | 33°22′N | 10°33′E |
| Medfeld, Ma., U.S. (mĕd′fēld) | 101a | 42°11′N | 71°19′W |
| Medford, Ma., U.S. (mĕd′fērd) | 101a | 42°25′N | 71°07′W |
| Medford, N.J., U.S. | 110f | 39°54′N | 74°50′W |
| Medford, Ok., U.S. | 121 | 36°47′N | 97°44′W |
| Medford, Or., U.S. | 104 | 42°19′N | 122°52′W |
| Medford, Wi., U.S. | 113 | 45°09′N | 90°22′W |
| Media, Pa., U.S. (mē′dĭ-å) | 110f | 39°55′N | 75°24′W |
| Mediaș, Rom. (mĕd-yäsh′) | 169 | 46°09′N | 24°21′E |
| Medical Lake, Wa., U.S. (mĕd′ĭ-kăl) | 114 | 47°34′N | 117°40′W |
| Medicine Bow, r., Wy., U.S. | 115 | 41°58′N | 106°30′W |
| Medicine Hat, Can. (mĕd′ĭ-sĭn hăt) | 90 | 50°03′N | 110°40′W |
| Medicine Lake, l., Mt., U.S. (mĕd′ĭ-sĭn) | 115 | 48°24′N | 104°15′W |
| Medicine Lodge, Ks., U.S. | 120 | 37°17′N | 98°37′W |
| Medicine Lodge, r., Ks., U.S. | 120 | 37°20′N | 98°57′W |
| Medina *see* Al Madīnah, Sau. Ar. | 198 | 24°26′N | 39°42′E |
| Medina, N.Y., U.S. (mē-dī′nȧ) | 109 | 43°15′N | 78°20′W |
| Medina, Oh., U.S. | 111d | 41°08′N | 81°52′W |
| Medina, r., Tx., U.S. | 122 | 29°45′N | 99°13′W |
| Medina del Campo, Spain (må-dē′nä dĕl käm′pō) | 162 | 41°18′N | 4°54′W |
| Medina de Ríoseco, Spain (må-dē′nä dā rē-ô-sā′kō) | 172 | 41°53′N | 5°05′W |
| Medina Lake, l., Tx., U.S. | 122 | 29°36′N | 98°47′W |
| Medina Sidonia, Spain | 172 | 36°28′N | 5°58′W |
| Mediterranean Sea, sea (mĕd-ĭ-tēr-ā′nē-ăn) | 162 | 36°22′N | 13°25′E |
| Medjerda, Oued, r., Afr. | 162 | 36°43′N | 9°54′E |
| Mednogorsk, Russia | 178 | 51°27′N | 57°22′E |
| Medveditsa, r., Russia (mĕd-vyĕ′dê tså) | 181 | 50°10′N | 43°40′E |
| Medvezhegorsk, Russia (mĕd-vyĕzh′yĕ-gôrsk′) | 180 | 63°00′N | 34°20′E |
| Medway, Ma., U.S. (mĕd′wā) | 101a | 42°08′N | 71°23′W |
| Medway Towns, co., Eng., U.K. | 158b | 51°27′N | 0°30′E |
| Medyn′, Russia (mĕ-dēn′) | 176 | 54°58′N | 35°53′E |
| Medzhybizh, Ukr. | 177 | 49°23′N | 27°29′E |
| Meekatharra, Austl. (mē-kȧ-thăr′ȧ) | 218 | 26°30′S | 118°38′E |
| Meeker, Co., U.S. (mēk′ēr) | 119 | 40°00′N | 107°55′W |
| Meelpaeg Lake, l., Can. (mēl′pȧ-ĕg) | 101 | 48°22′N | 56°52′W |
| Meerane, Ger. (mā-rä′nĕ) | 168 | 50°51′N | 12°27′E |
| Meerbusch, Ger. | 171c | 51°15′N | 6°41′E |
| Meerut, India (mē′rŏŏt) | 199 | 28°59′N | 77°43′E |
| Megalópoli, Grc. | 175 | 37°22′N | 22°08′E |
| Mégara, Grc. (mĕg′ȧ-rȧ) | 175 | 37°59′N | 23°21′E |
| Megget, S.C., U.S. (mĕg′ĕt) | 125 | 32°44′N | 80°15′W |
| Megler, Wa., U.S. (mĕg′lēr) | 116c | 46°15′N | 123°52′W |
| Mehanom, Mys, c., Ukr. | 177 | 44°48′N | 35°17′E |
| Meherrin, r., Va., U.S. (mê-hĕr′ĭn) | 125 | 36°40′N | 77°49′W |
| Mehlville, Mo., U.S. | 117e | 38°30′N | 90°19′W |
| Mehsāna, India | 202 | 23°42′N | 72°23′E |
| Mehun-sur-Yèvre, Fr. (mē-ŭɴ-sür-yĕvr′) | 170 | 47°11′N | 2°14′E |
| Meiling Pass, p., China (mā′lĭng′) | 205 | 25°22′N | 115°00′E |
| Meinerzhagen, Ger. (mī′nĕrts-hä-gĕn) | 171c | 51°06′N | 7°39′E |
| Meiningen, Ger. (mī′nĭng-ĕn) | 168 | 50°35′N | 10°25′E |
| Meiringen, Switz. | 168 | 46°45′N | 8°11′E |
| Meissen, Ger. | 168 | 51°11′N | 13°28′E |
| Meizhu, China (mā-jo͞o) | 206 | 31°17′N | 119°12′E |
| Mejillones, Chile (må-ĸē-lyō′nås) | 144 | 23°07′S | 70°31′W |
| Mekambo, Gabon | 236 | 1°01′N | 13°56′E |
| Mekele, Eth. | 231 | 13°31′N | 39°19′E |
| Meknès, Mor. (mĕk′nĕs) (mĕk-nĕs′) | 230 | 33°56′N | 5°44′W |
| Mekong, r., Asia | 212 | 18°00′N | 104°30′E |
| Melaka, Malay. | 212 | 2°11′N | 102°15′E |
| Melaka, state, Malay. | 197b | 2°19′N | 102°09′E |
| Melanesia, is., Oc. | 240 | 13°00′S | 164°00′E |
| Melbourne, Austl. (mĕl′bŭrn) | 219 | 37°52′S | 145°08′E |
| Melbourne, Eng., U.K. | 158a | 52°49′N | 1°26′W |
| Melbourne, Fl., U.S. | 125a | 28°05′N | 80°37′W |
| Melbourne, Ky., U.S. | 111f | 39°02′N | 84°22′W |
| Melcher, Ia., U.S. (mĕl′chĕr) | 113 | 41°13′N | 93°11′W |
| Melekess, Russia (mĕl-yĕk-ĕs) | 180 | 54°14′N | 49°39′E |
| Melenki, Russia (mĕ-lyĕŋ′kê) | 180 | 55°25′N | 41°34′E |
| Melfort, Can. (mĕl′fôrt) | 90 | 52°52′N | 104°36′W |
| Melghir, Chott, l., Alg. | 230 | 33°52′N | 5°22′E |
| Melilla, Sp. N. Afr. (mā-lēl′yä) | 230 | 35°24′N | 3°30′W |
| Melipilla, Chile (må-lê-pē′lyä) | 144 | 33°40′S | 71°12′W |
| Melita, Can. | 97 | 49°11′N | 101°09′W |
| Melitopol′, Ukr. (mā-lê-tô′pôl-y′) | 181 | 46°49′N | 35°19′E |
| Melívoia, Grc. | 175 | 39°42′N | 22°47′E |
| Melkrivier, S. Afr. | 238c | 24°01′S | 28°23′E |
| Mellen, Wi., U.S. (mĕl′ĕn) | 113 | 46°20′N | 90°40′W |
| Mellerud, Swe. (mål′ĕ-ro͞odh) | 166 | 58°43′N | 12°25′E |
| Melmoth, S. Afr. | 233c | 28°38′S | 31°26′E |
| Melo, Ur. (mā′lō) | 144 | 32°18′S | 54°07′W |
| Melocheville, Can. (mĕ-lôsh-vēl′) | 102a | 45°24′N | 73°56′W |
| Melozha, r., Russia (myĕ′lô-zhȧ) | 186b | 56°06′N | 38°34′E |
| Melrose, Ma., U.S. (mĕl′rōz) | 101a | 42°29′N | 71°06′W |
| Melrose, Mn., U.S. | 113 | 45°39′N | 94°49′W |
| Melrose Park, Il., U.S. | 111a | 41°54′N | 87°52′W |
| Meltham, Eng., U.K. (mĕl′thăm) | 158a | 53°35′N | 1°51′W |
| Melton, Austl. (mĕl′tŭn) | 217a | 37°41′S | 144°35′E |
| Melton Mowbray, Eng., U.K. (mō′brâ) | 158a | 52°45′N | 0°52′W |
| Melúli, r., Moz. | 237 | 16°10′S | 39°30′E |
| Melun, Fr. (mĕ-lŭɴ′) | 161 | 48°32′N | 2°40′E |
| Melunga, Ang. | 236 | 17°16′S | 16°24′E |
| Melville, Can. (mĕl′vĭl) | 90 | 50°55′N | 102°48′W |
| Melville, La., U.S. | 123 | 30°39′N | 91°45′W |
| Melville, i., Austl. | 220 | 11°30′S | 131°12′E |
| Melville, l., Can. | 93 | 53°46′N | 59°31′W |
| Melville, Cape, c., Austl. | 221 | 14°15′S | 145°50′E |
| Melville Hills, hills, Can. | 92 | 69°18′N | 124°57′W |
| Melville Peninsula, pen., Can. | 93 | 67°44′N | 84°09′W |
| Melvindale, Mi., U.S. (mĕl′vĭn-dāl) | 111b | 42°17′N | 83°11′W |
| Melyana, Alg. | 161 | 36°19′N | 1°56′E |
| Mélykút, Hung. (mā′l′ko͞ot) | 169 | 46°14′N | 19°21′E |
| Memba, Moz. (mĕm′bȧ) | 233 | 14°12′N | 40°35′E |
| Memel *see* Klaipėda, Lith. | 180 | 55°43′N | 21°10′E |
| Memel, S. Afr. (mĕ′mĕl) | 238c | 27°42′S | 29°35′E |
| Memmingen, Ger. (mĕm′ĭng-ĕn) | 168 | 47°59′N | 10°10′E |
| Memo, r., Ven. (mĕ′mō) | 143b | 9°32′N | 66°30′W |
| Memphis, Mo., U.S. (mĕm′fĭs) | 121 | 40°27′N | 92°11′W |
| Memphis, Tn., U.S. (mĕm′fĭs) | 105 | 35°07′N | 90°03′W |
| Memphis, Tx., U.S. | 120 | 34°42′N | 100°33′W |
| Memphis, hist., Egypt | 238b | 29°50′N | 31°12′E |
| Mena, Ukr. (mē-nȧ′) | 177 | 51°31′N | 32°14′E |
| Mena, Ar., U.S. (mē′nȧ) | 121 | 34°35′N | 94°09′W |
| Menangle, Austl. | 217b | 34°08′S | 150°48′E |
| Menard, Tx., U.S. (mê-närd′) | 122 | 30°56′N | 99°48′W |
| Menasha, Wi., U.S. (mê-năsh′ȧ) | 113 | 44°12′N | 88°29′W |
| Mende, Fr. (mäɴd) | 170 | 44°31′N | 3°30′E |
| Menden, Ger. (mĕn′dĕn) | 171c | 51°26′N | 7°47′E |
| Mendes, Braz. (mĕ′n-dĕs) | 144b | 22°32′S | 43°44′W |
| Mendocino, Ca., U.S. | 118 | 39°18′N | 123°47′W |
| Mendocino, Cape, c., Ca., U.S. (mĕn′dô-sē′nō) | 107 | 40°25′N | 12°42′W |
| Mendota, Il., U.S. (mĕn-dō′tȧ) | 113 | 41°34′N | 89°06′W |
| Mendota, l., Wi., U.S. | 113 | 43°09′N | 89°41′W |
| Mendoza, Arg. (mĕn-dō′sä) | 144 | 32°48′S | 68°45′W |
| Mendoza, prov., Arg. | 144 | 35°10′S | 69°00′W |
| Mengcheng, China (mŭŋ-chŭŋ) | 206 | 33°15′N | 116°34′E |
| Meng Shan, mts., China (mŭŋ shän) | 206 | 35°47′N | 117°23′E |
| Mengzi, China | 204 | 23°22′N | 103°20′E |
| Menindee, Austl. (mĕ-nĭn-dē) | 222 | 32°23′S | 142°30′E |
| Menlo Park, Ca., U.S. (mĕn′lō pärk) | 116b | 37°27′N | 122°11′W |
| Menno, S.D., U.S. (mĕn′ō) | 112 | 43°14′N | 97°34′W |
| Menominee, Mi., U.S. (mê-nŏm′ĭ-nē) | 113 | 45°08′N | 87°40′W |
| Menominee, r., Mi., U.S. | 113 | 45°37′N | 87°54′W |
| Menominee Falls, Wi., U.S. (fôls) | 111a | 43°11′N | 88°06′W |
| Menominee Ra, Mi., U.S. | 113 | 46°07′N | 88°53′W |
| Menomonee, r., Wi., U.S. | 111a | 43°09′N | 88°06′W |
| Menomonie, Wi., U.S. | 113 | 44°53′N | 91°55′W |
| Menongue, Ang. | 236 | 14°36′S | 17°48′E |
| Menorca (Minorca), i., Spain (mĕ-nô′r-kä) | 156 | 40°05′N | 3°58′E |
| Mentana, Italy (mĕn-tȧ′nä) | 173d | 42°02′N | 12°40′E |
| Mentawai, Kepulauan, is., Indon. (mĕn-tä-vī′) | 212 | 1°08′S | 98°10′E |
| Menton, Fr. (mäɴ-tôɴ′) | 171 | 43°46′N | 7°37′E |
| Mentone, Ca., U.S. (mĕn′tōne) | 117a | 34°05′N | 117°08′W |
| Mentz, l., S. Afr. (mĕnts) | 233c | 33°13′S | 25°15′E |
| Menzel Bourguiba, Tun. | 162 | 37°12′N | 9°51′E |
| Menzelinsk, Russia (mĕn′zyĕ-lĕnsk′) | 180 | 55°40′N | 53°15′E |
| Menzies, Austl. (mĕn′zēz) | 218 | 29°45′S | 122°15′E |
| Meogui, Mex. (må-ō′gē) | 122 | 28°17′N | 105°28′W |
| Meppel, Neth. (mĕp′ĕl) | 165 | 52°41′N | 6°08′E |
| Meppen, Ger. (mĕp′ĕn) | 168 | 52°40′N | 7°18′E |
| Merabéllou, Kólpos, b., Grc. | 174a | 35°16′N | 25°55′E |
| Meramec, r., Mo., U.S. (mĕr′ȧ-mĕk) | 121 | 38°06′N | 91°06′W |
| Merano, Italy (må-rä′nō) | 162 | 46°39′N | 11°10′E |
| Merasheen, i., Can. (mē′rȧ-shēn) | 101 | 47°30′N | 54°15′W |
| Merauke, Indon. (må-rou′kä) | 213 | 8°32′S | 140°17′E |
| Meraux, La., U.S. (mē-ro′) | 110d | 29°56′N | 89°56′W |
| Mercato San Severino, Italy | 173c | 40°34′N | 14°38′E |
| Merced, Ca., U.S. (mĕr-sĕd′) | 118 | 37°17′N | 120°30′W |
| Merced, r., Ca., U.S. | 118 | 37°25′N | 120°31′W |
| Mercedario, Cerro, mtn., Arg. (mĕr-så-dhä′rê-ō) | 144 | 31°58′S | 70°07′W |
| Mercedes, Arg. | 141c | 34°41′S | 59°26′W |
| Mercedes, Arg. (mĕr-sā′dhās) | 144 | 29°04′S | 58°01′W |
| Mercedes, Ur. | 144 | 33°17′S | 58°04′W |
| Mercedes, Tx., U.S. | 123 | 26°09′N | 97°55′W |
| Mercedita, Chile (mĕr-sĕ-dĕ′tä) | 141b | 33°51′S | 71°10′W |
| Mercer Island, Wa., U.S. (mûr′sēr) | 116a | 47°35′N | 122°15′W |
| Mercês, Braz. (mĕ-sĕ′s) | 141a | 21°13′S | 43°20′W |
| Merchtem, Bel. | 159a | 50°57′N | 4°13′E |
| Mercier, Can. | 102a | 45°19′N | 73°45′W |
| Mercy, Cape, c., Can. | 93 | 64°48′N | 63°22′W |
| Meredith, N.H., U.S. (mĕr′ê-dĭth) | 109 | 43°35′N | 71°35′W |
| Merefa, Ukr. (mĕ-rĕ′fȧ) | 177 | 49°49′N | 36°04′E |
| Merendón, Serranía de, mts., Hond. | 132 | 15°01′N | 89°05′W |
| Mereworth, Eng., U.K. (mĕ-rĕ wûrth) | 158b | 51°15′N | 0°23′E |
| Mergui, Mya. (mĕr-gē′) | 212 | 12°29′N | 98°39′E |
| Mergui Archipelago, is., Mya. | 212 | 12°04′N | 97°02′E |
| Meric (Maritsa), r., Eur. | 167 | 40°43′N | 26°19′E |
| Mérida, Mex. | 128 | 20°58′N | 89°37′W |
| Mérida, Ven. | 142 | 8°30′N | 71°15′W |
| Mérida, Cordillera de, mts., Ven. (mĕ′rē-dhä) | 142 | 8°30′N | 70°45′W |
| Meriden, Ct., U.S. (mĕr′ĭ-dĕn) | 109 | 41°30′N | 72°50′W |
| Meridian, Ms., U.S. (mê-rĭd-ĭ-ăn) | 105 | 32°21′N | 88°41′W |
| Meridian, Tx., U.S. | 123 | 31°56′N | 97°37′W |
| Mérignac, Fr. | 170 | 44°50′N | 0°40′W |
| Merikarvia, Fin. (mā′rē-kàr′vē-å) | 167 | 61°51′N | 21°30′E |
| Mering, Ger. (mĕ′rēng) | 159d | 48°16′N | 11°00′E |
| Merkel, Tx., U.S. (mûr′kĕl) | 122 | 32°26′N | 100°02′W |
| Merkinė, Lith. | 167 | 54°10′N | 24°10′E |
| Merksem, Bel. | 159a | 51°15′N | 4°27′E |
| Merkys, r., Lith. (măr′kĭs) | 169 | 54°23′N | 25°00′E |
| Merlo, Arg. (mĕr-lô) | 144a | 34°40′S | 58°44′W |
| Meron, Hare, mtn., Isr. | 197a | 32°58′N | 35°25′E |
| Merriam, Ks., U.S. (mĕr-rĭ-yăm) | 117f | 39°01′N | 94°42′W |
| Merriam, Mn., U.S. | 117g | 44°44′N | 93°36′W |
| Merrick, N.Y., U.S. (mĕr′ĭk) | 110a | 40°40′N | 73°33′W |
| Merrifield, Va., U.S. (mĕr′ĭ-fēld) | 110e | 38°50′N | 77°12′W |
| Merrill, Wi., U.S. (mĕr′ĭl) | 113 | 45°11′N | 89°42′W |
| Merrimac, Ma., U.S. (mĕr′ĭ-măk) | 101a | 45°20′N | 71°00′W |
| Merrimack, N.H., U.S. | 101a | 42°51′N | 71°25′W |
| Merrimack, r., Ma., U.S. (mĕr′ĭ-măk) | 109 | 43°10′N | 71°30′W |
| Merritt, Can. (mĕr′ĭt) | 90 | 50°07′N | 120°47′W |
| Merryville, La., U.S. (mĕr′ĭ-vĭl) | 123 | 30°46′N | 93°34′W |
| Mersa Fatma, Erit. | 231 | 14°54′N | 40°14′E |
| Merseburg, Ger. (mĕr′zĕ-bo͞orgh) | 168 | 51°21′N | 11°59′E |
| Mersey, r., Eng., U.K. (mûr′zê) | 158a | 53°20′N | 2°55′W |
| Merseyside, hist. reg., Eng., U.K. | 158a | 53°29′N | 2°59′W |
| Mersing, Malay. | 197b | 2°25′N | 103°51′E |
| Merta Road, India (măr′tŭ rōd) | 202 | 26°50′N | 73°54′E |
| Merthyr Tydfil, Wales, U.K. (mûr′thĕr tĭd′vĭl) | 164 | 51°46′N | 3°30′W |
| Mértola Almodóvar, Port. (mĕr-tô-lȧ-äl-mô-dô′vär) | 172 | 37°39′N | 8°04′W |
| Méru, Fr. (mā-rü′) | 170 | 49°14′N | 2°08′E |
| Meru, Kenya (mā′ro͞o) | 231 | 0°01′N | 37°45′E |
| Meru, Mount, mtn., Tan. | 237 | 3°15′S | 36°43′E |
| Merume Mountains, mts., Guy. (mĕr-ü′mē) | 143 | 5°45′N | 60°15′W |
| Merwede Kanaal, can., Neth. | 159a | 52°15′N | 5°01′E |
| Merwin, l., Wa., U.S. (mĕr′wĭn) | 116c | 45°58′N | 122°27′W |
| Merzifon, Tur. (mĕr′ze-fōn) | 198 | 40°50′N | 35°30′E |
| Mesa, Az., U.S. (mā′sȧ) | 119 | 33°25′N | 111°50′W |
| Mesabi Range, mts., Mn., U.S. (mā-sŏb′bē) | 113 | 47°17′N | 93°04′W |
| Mesagne, Italy (mā-sän′yå) | 175 | 40°34′N | 17°51′E |
| Mesa Verde National Park, rec., Co., U.S. (vĕr′dē) | 106 | 37°22′N | 108°27′W |
| Mescalero Apache Indian Reservation, I.R., N.M., U.S. (mĕs-kä-lā′rō) | 119 | 33°10′N | 105°45′W |
| Meshchovsk, Russia (myĕsh′chĕfsk) | 176 | 54°17′N | 35°19′E |
| Mesilla, N.M., U.S. (må-sē′yä) | 119 | 32°15′N | 106°45′W |
| Meskine, Chad | 235 | 11°25′N | 15°21′E |
| Mesolóngi, Grc. | 175 | 38°23′N | 21°28′E |
| Mesopotamia, hist. reg., Asia | 201 | 34°00′N | 44°00′E |
| Mesquita, Braz. | 144b | 22°48′S | 43°26′W |
| Messina, Italy (mĕ-sē′nȧ) | 154 | 38°11′N | 15°34′E |
| Messina, S. Afr. | 232 | 22°17′S | 30°13′E |
| Messina, Stretto di, strt., Italy (stĕ′t-tô dē) | 163 | 38°10′N | 15°34′E |
| Messíni, Grc. | 175 | 37°05′N | 22°00′E |
| Mestaganem, Alg. | 230 | 36°04′N | 0°11′E |
| Mestre, Italy (mĕs′trā) | 174 | 45°29′N | 12°15′E |
| Meta, dept., Col. (mĕ′tä) | 142a | 3°28′N | 74°07′W |
| Meta, r., S.A. | 142 | 4°33′N | 72°09′W |
| Métabetchouane, r., Can. (mĕ-tȧ-bĕt-cho͞o-ān′) | 99 | 47°45′N | 72°00′W |
| Metairie, La., U.S. | 123 | 30°00′N | 90°11′W |
| Metán, Arg. (mĕ-tá′n) | 144 | 25°32′S | 64°51′W |
| Metangula, Moz. | 232 | 12°42′S | 34°48′E |
| Metapán, El Sal. (må-täpän′) | 132 | 14°21′N | 89°26′W |
| Metcalfe, Can. (mĕt-käf) | 102c | 45°14′N | 75°27′W |
| Metchosin, Can. | 116a | 48°22′N | 123°33′W |
| Metepec, Mex. (må-tĕ-pĕk′) | 130 | 18°56′N | 98°31′W |
| Metepec, Mex. | 130 | 19°15′N | 99°36′W |
| Methow, r., Wa., U.S. (mĕt′hou) (mĕt hou′) | 114 | 48°26′N | 120°15′W |
| Methuen, Ma., U.S. (mê-thū′ĕn) | 101a | 42°44′N | 71°11′W |
| Metković, Cro. (mĕt′kô-vĭch) | 175 | 43°02′N | 17°40′E |
| Metlakatla, Ak., U.S. (mĕt-lȧ-kăt′lȧ) | 103 | 55°08′N | 131°35′W |
| Metropolis, Il., U.S. (mê-trŏp′ô-lĭs) | 121 | 37°09′N | 88°46′W |
| Metter, Ga., U.S. (mĕt′ĕr) | 125 | 32°21′N | 82°05′W |
| Mettmann, Ger. (mĕt′män) | 171c | 51°15′N | 6°58′E |
| Metuchen, N.J., U.S. (mĕ-tŭ′chĕn) | 110a | 40°32′N | 74°21′W |
| Metz, Fr. (mĕtz) | 161 | 49°08′N | 6°10′E |
| Metztitlán, Mex. (mĕtz-têt-län) | 130 | 20°36′N | 98°45′W |
| Meuban, Cam. | 235 | 2°27′N | 12°41′E |
| Meuse (Maas), r., Eur. (mûz) (mäs) | 165 | 50°32′N | 5°22′E |
| Mexborough, Eng., U.K. (mĕks′bŭr-ô) | 158a | 53°30′N | 1°17′W |
| Mexia, Tx., U.S. (må-hē′ä) | 123 | 31°32′N | 96°29′W |
| Mexian, China | 205 | 24°20′N | 116°10′E |
| Mexicalcingo, Mex. (mĕ-kē-käl-sēn′gō) | 131a | 19°13′N | 99°34′W |
| Mexicali, Mex. (mäk-sê-kä′lê) | 128 | 32°28′N | 115°29′W |
| Mexicana, Altiplanicie, plat., Mex. | 130 | 22°38′N | 102°33′W |
| Mexican Hat, Ut., U.S. (mĕk′sĭ-kăn hăt) | 119 | 37°10′N | 109°55′W |
| Mexico, Me., U.S. (mĕk′sĭ-kō) | 100 | 44°34′N | 70°33′W |
| Mexico, Mo., U.S. | 121 | 39°09′N | 91°51′W |
| Mexico, nation, N.A. | 128 | 23°45′N | 104°00′W |
| Mexico, Gulf of, b., N.A. | 128 | 25°15′N | 93°45′W |
| Mexico City, Mex. (mĕk′sĭ-kō) | 128 | 19°28′N | 99°09′W |
| Mexticacán, Mex. (mĕs′tê-kä-kän′) | 130 | 21°12′N | 102°43′W |
| Meyers Chuck, Ak., U.S. | 94 | 55°44′N | 132°15′W |
| Meyersdale, Pa., U.S. (mī′ĕrz-dāl) | 109 | 39°55′N | 79°00′W |
| Meyerton, S. Afr. (mī′ĕr-tŭn) | 238c | 26°35′S | 28°01′E |
| Meymaneh, Afg. | 198 | 35°53′N | 64°38′E |
| Mezen′, Russia | 178 | 65°50′N | 44°05′E |
| Mezen′, r., Russia | 180 | 65°20′N | 44°45′E |
| Mézenc, Mont, mtn., Fr. (mŏɴ-mā-zĕɴ′) | 170 | 44°55′N | 4°12′E |
| Mezha, r., Eur. (myā′zhȧ) | 176 | 55°53′N | 31°44′E |
| Mézieres-sur-Seine, Fr. (mā-zyâr′sür-sân′) | 171b | 48°58′N | 1°49′E |
| Mezőkövesd, Hung. (mĕ′zû-kû′vĕsht) | 169 | 47°49′N | 20°36′E |
| Mezötur, Hung. (mĕ′zû-to͞or) | 169 | 47°00′N | 20°36′E |
| Mezquital, Mex. (mäz-kê-täl′) | 130 | 23°30′N | 104°20′W |
| Mezquitic, Mex. (mäz-kê-tēk′) | 130 | 22°25′N | 103°43′W |
| Mezquitic, r., Mex. | 130 | 22°25′N | 103°45′W |


ng-sing; ŋ-baŋk; ɴ-nasalized n; nŏd; cŏmmit; ōld; ôbey; ôrder; oi-boil; fo͞od; ŏŏ-as oo in foot; ou-out; s-soft; sh-dish; th-thin; pūre; ûnite; ûrn; stŭd; circŭs; ü-as in French tu; ′-indeterminate vowel.

322 Mfangano Island – Mississippi

PRONOUNCING INDEX


| PLACE (Pronunciation) | PAGE | LAT. | LONG. |
|---|---|---|---|
| Mfangano Island, i., Kenya | 237 | 0°28'S | 33°35'E |
| Mga, Russia (m'gà) | 186c | 59°45'N | 31°04'E |
| Mglin, Russia (m'glĕn') | 176 | 53°03'N | 32°52'W |
| Mia, Oued, r., Alg. | 162 | 29°26'N | 3°15'E |
| Miacatlán, Mex. (mē'ä-kä-tlän') | 130 | 18°42'N | 99°17'W |
| Miahuatlán, Mex. (mē'ä-wä-tlän') | 131 | 16°20'N | 96°38'W |
| Miajadas, Spain (mē-ä-hä'däs) | 172 | 39°10'N | 5°53'W |
| Miami, Az., U.S. | 104 | 33°20'N | 110°55'W |
| Miami, Fl., U.S. | 105 | 25°45'N | 80°11'W |
| Miami, Ok., U.S. | 121 | 36°51'N | 94°51'W |
| Miami, Tx., U.S. | 120 | 35°41'N | 100°39'W |
| Miami Beach, Fl., U.S. | 125a | 25°47'N | 80°07'W |
| Miamisburg, Oh., U.S. (mī-ăm'iz-bûrg) | 108 | 39°40'N | 84°20'W |
| Miamitown, Oh., U.S. (mī-ăm'ĭ-toun) | 111f | 39°13'N | 84°43'W |
| Mīāneh, Iran | 198 | 37°15'N | 47°13'E |
| Miangas, Pulau, i., Indon. | 213 | 5°30'N | 127°00'E |
| Miaoli, Tai. (mē-ou'lĭ) | 209 | 24°30'N | 120°48'E |
| Miaozhen, China (miou-jŭn) | 206 | 31°44'N | 121°28'E |
| Miass, Russia (mī-äs') | 184 | 54°59'N | 60°06'E |
| Miastko, Pol. (myäst'kō) | 168 | 54°01'N | 17°00'E |
| Miccosukee Indian Reservation, I.R., Fl., U.S. | 125a | 26°10'N | 80°50'W |
| Michalovce, Slvk. (mē'ĸä-lôf'tsĕ) | 169 | 48°44'N | 21°56'E |
| Michel Peak, mtn., Can. | 94 | 53°35'N | 126°25'W |
| Michelson, Mount, mtn., Ak., U.S. (mĭch'ĕl-sŭn) | 103 | 69°11'N | 144°12'W |
| Michendorf, Ger. (mē'kĕn-dōrf) | 159b | 52°19'N | 13°02'E |
| Miches, Dom. Rep. (mē'chĕs) | 135 | 19°00'N | 69°05'W |
| Michigan, state, U.S. (mĭsh-ĭ-găn) | 105 | 45°55'N | 87°00'W |
| Michigan, Lake, l., U.S. | 107 | 43°20'N | 87°10'W |
| Michigan City, In., U.S. | 108 | 41°40'N | 86°55'W |
| Michipicoten, r., Can. | 113 | 47°56'N | 84°42'W |
| Michipicoten Harbour, Can. | 113 | 47°58'N | 84°58'W |
| Michurinsk, Russia (mĭ-chōō-rĭnsk') | 181 | 52°53'N | 40°32'E |
| Mico, Punta, c., Nic. (pōō'n-tä-mē'kô) | 133 | 11°38'N | 83°24'W |
| Micronesia, is., Oc. | 240 | 11°00'N | 159°00'E |
| Micronesia, Federated States of, nation, Oc. | 3 | 5°00'N | 152°00'E |
| Midas, Nv., U.S. (mī'dȧs) | 114 | 41°15'N | 116°50'W |
| Middelfart, Den. (mēd'''l-färt) | 166 | 55°30'N | 9°45'E |
| Middle, r., Can. | 94 | 55°00'N | 125°50'W |
| Middle Andaman, i., India (ăn-dȧ-măn') | 212 | 12°44'N | 93°21'E |
| Middle Bayou, Tx., U.S. | 123a | 29°38'N | 95°06'W |
| Middleburg, S. Afr. (mĭd'ĕl-bûrg) | 232 | 31°30'S | 25°00'E |
| Middleburg, S. Afr. | 238c | 25°47'S | 29°30'E |
| Middlebury, Vt., U.S. (mĭd'''l-bĕr-ĭ) | 109 | 44°00'N | 73°10'W |
| Middle Concho, Tx., U.S. (kōn'chō) | 122 | 31°21'N | 100°50'W |
| Middle River, Md., U.S. | 110e | 39°20'N | 76°27'W |
| Middlesboro, Ky., U.S. (mĭd'''lz-bŭr-ō) | 124 | 36°36'N | 83°42'W |
| Middlesbrough, Eng., U.K. (mĭd'''lz-brŭ) | 160 | 54°35'N | 1°18'W |
| Middlesex, N.J., U.S. (mĭd'''l-sĕks) | 110a | 40°34'N | 74°30'W |
| Middleton, Can. (mĭd'''l-tŭn) | 100 | 44°57'N | 65°04'W |
| Middleton, Eng., U.K. | 158a | 53°34'N | 2°12'W |
| Middletown, Ct., U.S. | 109 | 41°35'N | 72°40'W |
| Middletown, De., U.S. | 109 | 39°30'N | 75°40'W |
| Middletown, Ma., U.S. | 101a | 42°35'N | 71°01'W |
| Middletown, N.Y., U.S. | 109 | 41°26'N | 74°25'W |
| Middletown, Oh., U.S. | 108 | 39°30'N | 84°25'W |
| Middlewich, Eng., U.K. (mĭd'''l-wĭch) | 158a | 53°11'N | 2°27'W |
| Middlewit, S. Afr. (mĭd'l'wĭt) | 238c | 24°50'S | 27°00'E |
| Midfield, Al., U.S. | 110h | 33°28'N | 86°54'W |
| Midi, Canal du, Fr. (kä-näl-dü-mē-dē') | 161 | 43°22'N | 1°35'E |
| Mid Illovo, S. Afr. (mĭd ĭl'ō-vō) | 233c | 29°59'S | 30°32'E |
| Midland, Can. (mĭd'lănd) | 91 | 44°45'N | 79°50'W |
| Midland, Mi., U.S. | 108 | 43°40'N | 84°20'W |
| Midland, Tx., U.S. | 122 | 32°05'N | 102°05'W |
| Midvale, Ut., U.S. (mĭd'vāl) | 117b | 40°37'N | 111°54'W |
| Midway, Al., U.S. (mĭd'wā) | 124 | 32°03'N | 85°30'W |
| Midway Islands, is., Oc. | 2 | 28°00'N | 179°00'W |
| Midwest, Wy., U.S. (mĭd-wĕst') | 115 | 43°25'N | 106°15'W |
| Midye, Tur. (mēd'yĕ) | 181 | 41°35'N | 28°10'E |
| Międzyrzecz, Pol. (myăn-dzû'zhĕch) | 168 | 52°26'N | 15°35'E |
| Mielec, Pol. (myĕ'lĕts) | 169 | 50°17'N | 21°27'E |
| Mier, Mex. (myâr) | 122 | 26°26'N | 99°08'W |
| Mieres, Spain (myā'rās) | 172 | 43°14'N | 5°45'W |
| Mier y Noriega, Mex. (myâr'ē nō-rē-ā'gä) | 130 | 23°28'N | 100°08'W |
| Miguel Auza, Mex. | 130 | 24°17'N | 103°27'W |
| Miguel Pereira, Braz. | 144b | 22°27'S | 43°28'W |
| Mijares, r., Spain | 173 | 39°55'N | 0°01'W |
| Mikage, Japan (mē'kȧ-gȧ) | 211b | 34°42'N | 135°15'E |
| Mikawa-Wan, b., Japan (mē'kä-wä wän) | 211 | 34°43'N | 137°09'E |
| Mikhaylov, Russia (mē-ĸäy'lôf) | 180 | 54°14'N | 39°03'E |
| Mikhaylovka, Russia | 186a | 55°35'N | 57°57'E |
| Mikhaylovka, Russia | 186c | 59°20'N | 30°21'E |
| Mikhaylovka, Russia | 181 | 50°05'N | 43°10'E |
| Mikhnëvo, Russia (mĭk-nyô'vô) | 186b | 55°08'N | 37°57'E |
| Miki, Japan (mē'kē) | 211b | 34°47'N | 134°59'E |
| Mikindani, Tan. (mē-kēn-dä'nē) | 233 | 10°17'S | 40°07'E |
| Mikkeli, Fin. (mĕk'ĕ-lĭ) | 160 | 61°42'N | 27°14'E |
| Mikulov, Czech Rep. (mĭ'kōō-lôf) | 168 | 48°47'N | 16°39'E |
| Mikumi, Tan. | 237 | 7°24'S | 36°59'E |
| Mikuni, Japan (mē'kōō-nē) | 211 | 36°09'N | 136°14'E |
| Mikuni-Sammyaku, mts., Japan (säm'myä-kōō) | 211 | 36°51'N | 138°38'E |
| Mikura, i., Japan (mē'kōō-rȧ) | 211 | 33°53'N | 139°26'E |
| Milaca, Milaca, Mn., U.S. (mē-läk'ȧ) | 113 | 45°45'N | 93°41'W |
| Milan (Milano), Italy (mē-lä'nō) | 174 | 45°29'N | 9°12'E |
| Milan, Mi., U.S. (mĭ'lăn) | 108 | 42°05'N | 83°40'W |
| Milan, Mo., U.S. | 121 | 40°13'N | 93°07'W |
| Milan, Tn., U.S. | 124 | 35°54'N | 88°47'W |
| Milâs, Tur. (mē'läs) | 163 | 37°10'N | 27°25'E |
| Milazzo, Italy | 174 | 38°13'N | 15°17'E |
| Milbank, S.D., U.S. (mĭl'băŋĸ) | 112 | 45°13'N | 96°38'W |
| Mildura, Austl. (mĭl-dū'rȧ) | 219 | 34°10'S | 142°18'E |
| Miles City, Mt., U.S. (mīlz) | 104 | 46°24'N | 105°50'W |
| Milford, Ct., U.S. (mĭl'fērd) | 109 | 41°15'N | 73°05'W |
| Milford, De., U.S. | 109 | 38°55'N | 75°25'W |
| Milford, Ma., U.S. | 101a | 42°09'N | 71°31'W |
| Milford, Mi., U.S. | 111b | 42°35'N | 83°36'W |
| Milford, N.H., U.S. | 109 | 42°50'N | 71°40'W |
| Milford, Oh., U.S. | 111f | 39°11'N | 84°18'W |
| Milford, Ut., U.S. | 119 | 38°20'N | 113°05'W |
| Milford Sound, strt., N.Z. | 223 | 44°35'S | 167°47'E |
| Miling, Austl. (mĭl'' ng) | 218 | 30°30'S | 116°25'E |
| Milipitas, Ca., U.S. (mĭl-ĭ-pĭ'tăs) | 116b | 37°26'N | 121°54'W |
| Milk, r., N.A. | 106 | 48°30'N | 107°00'W |
| Millau, Fr. (mē-yō') | 161 | 44°06'N | 3°04'E |
| Millbrae, Ca., U.S. (mĭl'brā) | 116b | 37°36'N | 122°23'W |
| Millbury, Ma., U.S. (mĭl'bĕr-ĭ) | 101a | 42°12'N | 71°46'W |
| Mill Creek, r., Can. (mĭl) | 102g | 53°28'N | 113°25'W |
| Mill Creek, r., Ca., U.S. | 118 | 40°07'N | 121°55'W |
| Milledgeville, Ga., U.S. (mĭl'ĕj-vĭl) | 124 | 33°05'N | 83°15'W |
| Mille Îles, Rivière des, r., Can. (rē-vyâr' dā mĭl'ĭl') | 102a | 45°41'N | 73°40'W |
| Mille Lac Indian Reservation, I.R., Mn., U.S. (mĭl lăk') | 113 | 46°14'N | 94°13'W |
| Mille Lacs, l., Mn., U.S. | 113 | 46°25'N | 93°22'W |
| Mille Lacs, Lac des, l., Can. (läk dē mēl läks) | 98 | 48°52'N | 90°53'W |
| Millen, Ga., U.S. (mĭl'ĕn) | 125 | 32°47'N | 81°55'W |
| Miller, S.D., U.S. (mĭl'ēr) | 112 | 44°31'N | 99°00'W |
| Millerovo, Russia (mĭl'ĕ-rô-vô) | 181 | 48°58'N | 40°27'E |
| Millersburg, Ky., U.S. (mĭl'ērz-bûrg) | 108 | 38°15'N | 84°10'W |
| Millersburg, Oh., U.S. | 108 | 40°35'N | 81°55'W |
| Millersburg, Pa., U.S. | 109 | 40°35'N | 76°55'W |
| Millerton, Can. (mĭl'ēr-tŭn) | 100 | 46°56'N | 65°40'W |
| Millertown, Can. (mĭl'ēr-toun) | 101 | 48°49'N | 56°32'W |
| Millicent, Austl. (mĭl-ĭ-sĕnt) | 222 | 37°30'S | 140°20'E |
| Millinocket, Me., U.S. (mĭl-ĭ-nŏk'ĕt) | 100 | 45°40'N | 68°44'W |
| Millis, Ma., U.S. (mĭl-ĭs) | 101a | 42°10'N | 71°22'W |
| Millstadt, Il., U.S. (mĭl'stăt) | 117e | 38°27'N | 90°06'W |
| Millstone, r., N.J., U.S. (mĭl'stōn) | 110a | 40°27'N | 74°38'W |
| Millstream, Austl. (mĭl'strēm) | 218 | 21°45'S | 117°10'E |
| Milltown, Can. (mĭl'toun) | 100 | 45°13'N | 67°19'W |
| Mill Valley, Ca., U.S. (mĭl) | 116b | 37°54'N | 122°32'W |
| Millwood Reservoir, res., Ar., U.S. | 121 | 33°00'N | 94°00'W |
| Milly-la-Forêt, Fr. (mē-yē'-la-fō-rĕ') | 171b | 48°24'N | 2°28'E |
| Milnerton, S. Afr. (mĭl'nēr-tŭn) | 232a | 33°52'S | 18°30'E |
| Milnor, N.D., U.S. (mĭl'nēr) | 112 | 46°17'N | 97°29'W |
| Milo, Me., U.S. | 100 | 44°16'N | 69°01'W |
| Milos, i., Grc. (mē'lōs) | 163 | 36°45'N | 24°35'E |
| Milpa Alta, Mex. (mē'l-pä-ȧ'l-tä) | 131a | 19°11'N | 99°01'W |
| Milton, Can. | 102d | 43°31'N | 79°53'W |
| Milton, Fl., U.S. (mĭl'tŭn) | 124 | 30°37'N | 87°02'W |
| Milton, Pa., U.S. | 109 | 41°00'N | 76°50'W |
| Milton, Ut., U.S. | 117b | 41°04'N | 111°44'W |
| Milton, Wa., U.S. | 116a | 47°15'N | 122°20'W |
| Milton, Wi., U.S. | 113 | 42°45'N | 89°00'W |
| Milton-Freewater, Or., U.S. | 114 | 45°57'N | 118°25'W |
| Milvale, Pa., U.S. (mĭl'vāl) | 111e | 40°29'N | 79°58'W |
| Milville, N.J., U.S. (mĭl'vĭl) | 109 | 39°25'N | 75°00'W |
| Milwaukee, Wi., U.S. | 105 | 43°03'N | 87°55'W |
| Milwaukee, r., Wi., U.S. | 111a | 43°10'N | 87°56'W |
| Milwaukie, Or., U.S. (mĭl-wô'kē) | 114 | 45°27'N | 122°38'W |
| Mimiapan, Mex. (mē-myä-pȧn') | 131a | 19°26'N | 99°28'W |
| Mimoso do Sul, Braz. (mē-mō'sō-dō-sōō'l) | 141a | 21°03'S | 41°21'W |
| Min, r., China (mēn) | 205 | 26°03'N | 118°30'E |
| Min, r., China | 209 | 29°30'N | 104°00'E |
| Mina, r., Alg. (mē'nȧ) | 173 | 35°24'N | 0°51'E |
| Minago, r., Can. (mĭ-nä'gō) | 97 | 54°25'N | 98°45'W |
| Minakuchi, Japan (mē'nȧ-kōō'chē) | 211 | 34°59'N | 136°06'E |
| Minas, Cuba (mē'näs) | 134 | 21°30'N | 77°35'W |
| Minas, Indon. | 197b | 0°52'N | 101°29'E |
| Minas, Ur. (mē'näs) | 144 | 34°18'S | 55°12'W |
| Minas, Sierra de las, mts., Guat. (syĕr'rä dā läs mē'näs) | 132 | 15°08'N | 90°25'W |
| Minas Basin, b., Can. (mĭ'nȧs) | 100 | 45°20'N | 64°00'W |
| Minas Channel, strt., Can. | 100 | 45°15'N | 64°45'W |
| Minas de Oro, Hond. (mē'näs-dĕ-ō-rô) | 132 | 14°52'N | 87°19'W |
| Minas de Riotinto, Spain (mē'näs dā rē-ō-tēn'tō) | 172 | 37°43'N | 6°35'W |
| Minas Novas, Braz. (mē'näzh nō'vázh) | 143 | 17°20'S | 42°19'W |
| Minatare, l., Ne., U.S. (mĭn'ȧ-târ) | 112 | 41°56'N | 103°07'W |
| Minatitlán, Mex. (mē-nä-tē-tlän') | 128 | 17°59'N | 94°33'W |
| Minatitlán, Mex. | 130 | 19°21'N | 104°02'W |
| Minato, Japan (mē'nȧ-tô) | 211 | 35°13'N | 139°52'E |
| Minch, The, strt., Scot., U.K. | 156 | 58°04'N | 6°04'W |
| Mindanao, i., Phil. | 213 | 8°00'N | 125°00'E |
| Mindanao Sea, sea, Phil. | 213 | 8°55'N | 124°00'E |
| Minden, Ger. (mĭn'dĕn) | 168 | 52°17'N | 8°58'E |
| Minden, La., U.S. | 123 | 32°36'N | 93°19'W |
| Minden, Ne., U.S. | 120 | 40°30'N | 98°54'W |
| Mindoro, i., Phil. | 212 | 12°50'N | 121°05'E |
| Mindoro Strait, strt., Phil. | 213a | 12°28'N | 120°33'E |
| Mindyak, Russia (mēn'dyák) | 186a | 54°01'N | 58°48'E |
| Mineola, N.Y., U.S. (mĭn-ē-ō'lȧ) | 110a | 40°43'N | 73°38'W |
| Mineola, Tx., U.S. | 123 | 32°39'N | 95°31'W |
| Mineral del Chico, Mex. (mē-nȧ-räl'dĕl chē'kō) | 130 | 20°13'N | 98°46'W |
| Mineral del Monte, Mex. (mē-nȧ-räl dĕl mōn'tȧ) | 130 | 20°18'N | 98°39'W |
| Mineral'nyye Vody, Russia | 181 | 44°10'N | 43°15'E |
| Mineral Point, Wi., U.S. (mĭn'ēr-ăl) | 113 | 42°50'N | 90°10'W |
| Minerál Wells, Tx., U.S. (mĭn'ēr-ăl wĕlz) | 122 | 32°48'N | 98°06'W |
| Minerva, Oh., U.S. (mĭ-nur'vȧ) | 108 | 40°45'N | 81°10'W |
| Minervino, Italy (mē-nĕr-vē'nō) | 174 | 41°07'N | 16°05'E |
| Mineyama, Japan (mē-nĕ-yä'mä) | 211 | 35°38'N | 135°05'E |
| Mingäçevir, Azer. | 182 | 40°45'N | 47°03'E |
| Mingäçevir su anbarı, res., Azer. | 182 | 40°50'N | 46°50'E |
| Mingan, Can. | 91 | 50°18'N | 64°02'W |
| Mingenew, Austl. (mĭn'gĕ-nû) | 218 | 29°15'S | 115°45'E |
| Mingo Junction, Oh., U.S. (mĭŋ'gō) | 108 | 40°15'N | 80°40'W |
| Minho, hist. reg., Port. (mēn yò) | 172 | 41°32'N | 8°13'W |
| Minho (Miño), r., Eur. (mē'n-yō) | 172 | 41°28'N | 9°05'W |
| Ministik Lake, l., Can. (mĭ-nĭs'tĭk) | 102g | 53°23'N | 113°05'W |
| Minna, Nig. (mĭn'ȧ) | 230 | 9°37'N | 6°33'E |
| Minneapolis, Ks., U.S. (mĭn-ē-ăp'ō-lĭs) | 121 | 39°07'N | 97°41'W |
| Minneapolis, Mn., U.S. | 105 | 44°58'N | 93°15'W |
| Minnedosa, Can. (mĭn-ē-dō'sȧ) | 90 | 50°14'N | 99°51'W |
| Minneota, Mn., U.S. (mĭn-ē-ō'tȧ) | 112 | 44°34'N | 95°59'W |
| Minnesota, state, U.S. (mĭn-ē-sō'tȧ) | 105 | 46°10'N | 90°20'W |
| Minnesota, r., Mn., U.S. | 107 | 44°30'N | 95°00'W |
| Minnetonka, l., Mn., U.S. (mĭn-ē-tôŋ'kȧ) | 113 | 44°52'N | 93°34'W |
| Minnitaki Lake, l., Can. (mĭ'nĭ-tä'kē) | 97 | 49°58'N | 92°00'W |
| Mino, r., Japan | 211b | 34°56'N | 135°06'E |
| Minonk, Il., U.S. (mī'nŏnk) | 108 | 40°55'N | 89°00'W |
| Minooka, Il., U.S. (mĭ-nōō'kȧ) | 111a | 41°27'N | 88°15'W |
| Minot, N.D., U.S. | 104 | 48°13'N | 101°17'W |
| Minsk, Bela. (mēnsk) | 178 | 53°54'N | 27°35'E |
| Minsk, prov., Bela. | 176 | 53°50'N | 27°43'E |
| Mińsk Mazowiecki, Pol. (mēn'sk mä-zō-vyĕt'skĭ) | 169 | 52°10'N | 21°35'E |
| Minsterley, Eng., U.K. (mĭnstĕr-lē) | 158a | 52°38'N | 2°55'W |
| Minto, Can. | 100 | 46°05'N | 66°05'W |
| Minto, l., Can. | 93 | 57°18'N | 75°50'W |
| Minturno, Italy (mēn-tōōr'nō) | 174 | 41°17'N | 13°44'E |
| Minūf, Egypt (mē-nōōf') | 238b | 30°26'N | 30°55'E |
| Minusinsk, Russia (mē-nò-sēnsk') | 179 | 53°47'N | 91°45'E |
| Min'yar, Russia | 186a | 55°06'N | 57°33'E |
| Miquelon Lake, l., Can. (mĭ'kē-lôn) | 102g | 53°16'N | 112°55'W |
| Miquihuana, Mex. (mē-kē-wä'nä) | 130 | 23°36'N | 99°45'W |
| Mir, Bela. (mēr) | 169 | 53°27'N | 26°25'E |
| Miracema, Braz. (mē-rä-sĕ'mä) | 141a | 21°24'S | 42°10'W |
| Miracema do Tocantins, Braz. | 143 | 9°34'S | 48°24'W |
| Mirador, Braz. (mē-rȧ-dōr') | 143 | 6°19'S | 44°12'W |
| Miraflores, Col. (mē-rä-flō'rās) | 142 | 5°10'N | 73°13'W |
| Miraflores, Peru | 142 | 16°19'S | 71°20'W |
| Miraflores Locks, trans., Pan. | 128a | 9°00'N | 79°35'W |
| Miragoâne, Haiti (mē-rȧ-gwän') | 135 | 18°25'N | 73°05'W |
| Mira Loma, Ca., U.S. (mĭ'rȧ lō'mȧ) | 117a | 34°01'N | 117°32'W |
| Miramar, Ca., U.S. (mĭr'ȧ-mär) | 118a | 32°53'N | 117°08'W |
| Miramas, Fr. | 170 | 43°35'N | 5°00'E |
| Miramichi Bay, b., Can. (mĭr'ȧ-mē'shē) | 100 | 47°08'N | 65°08'W |
| Miranda, Col. (mē-rä'n-dä) | 142a | 3°14'N | 76°11'W |
| Miranda, Ca., U.S. | 118 | 40°14'N | 123°49'W |
| Miranda, Ven. | 143b | 10°09'N | 68°24'W |
| Miranda, dept., Ven. | 143b | 10°17'N | 66°41'W |
| Miranda de Ebro, Spain (mē-rä'n-dä-dĕ-ĕ'brô) | 172 | 42°42'N | 2°59'W |
| Miranda do Douro, Port. (mē-rän'dä dò-dwĕ'rô) | 172 | 41°30'N | 6°17'W |
| Mirandela, Port. (mē-rän-dā'lȧ) | 172 | 41°28'N | 7°10'W |
| Mirando City, Tx., U.S. (mĭr-ăn'dō) | 122 | 27°25'N | 99°03'W |
| Mira Por Vos Islets, is., Bah. (mē'rä pôr vōs) | 135 | 22°05'N | 74°30'W |
| Mira Por Vos Pass, strt., Bah. | 135 | 22°10'N | 74°35'W |
| Mirbāţ, Oman | 198 | 16°58'N | 54°42'E |
| Mirebalais, Haiti (mēr-bȧ-lĕ') | 135 | 18°50'N | 72°05'W |
| Mirecourt, Fr. (mēr-kōōr') | 171 | 48°20'N | 6°08'E |
| Mirfield, Eng., U.K. (mûr'fēld) | 158a | 53°41'N | 1°42'W |
| Miri, Malay. (mē'rē) | 212 | 4°13'N | 113°56'E |
| Mirim, Lagoa, l., S.A. (mē-rēɴ') | 144 | 33°00'S | 53°15'W |
| Miropol'ye, Ukr. (mē-rô-pôl'yĕ) | 177 | 51°02'N | 35°13'E |
| Mīrpur Khās, Pak. (mēr'pōōr ĸäs) | 202 | 25°36'N | 69°10'E |
| Mirzāpur, India (mēr'zä-pōōr) | 199 | 25°12'N | 82°38'E |
| Misantla, Mex. (mē-sän'tlä) | 131 | 19°55'N | 96°49'W |
| Miscou, i., Can. (mĭs'kō) | 100 | 47°58'N | 64°35'W |
| Miscou Point, c., Can. | 100 | 48°04'N | 64°32'W |
| Miseno, Cape, c., Italy (mē-zĕ'nō) | 173c | 40°33'N | 14°12'E |
| Misery, Mount, mtn., St. K./N. (mĭz'rē-ĭ) | 133b | 17°28'N | 62°47'W |
| Mishan, China (mĭ'shän) | 210 | 45°32'N | 132°19'E |
| Mishawaka, In., U.S. (mĭsh-ȧ-wôk'ȧ) | 108 | 41°45'N | 86°15'W |
| Mishina, Japan (mē'shē-mä) | 211 | 35°09'N | 138°56'E |
| Misiones, prov., Arg. (mē-syō'nās) | 144 | 27°00'S | 54°30'W |
| Miskito, Cayos, is., Nic. | 133 | 14°34'N | 82°30'W |
| Miskolc, Hung. (mĭsh'kôlts) | 154 | 48°07'N | 20°50'E |
| Misool, Pulau, i., Indon. (mē-sōl') | 213 | 2°00'S | 130°05'E |
| Misquah Hills, Mn., U.S. (mĭs-kwä' hĭlz) | 113 | 47°50'N | 90°30'W |
| Mişr al Jadīdah, Egypt | 238b | 30°06'N | 31°35'E |
| Misrātah, Libya | 231 | 32°23'N | 14°58'E |
| Missinaibi, r., Can. (mĭs'ĭn-ä'ē-bē) | 93 | 50°27'N | 83°01'W |
| Missinaibi Lake, l., Can. | 98 | 48°23'N | 83°40'W |
| Mission, Ks., U.S. (mĭsh'ŭn) | 117f | 39°02'N | 94°39'W |
| Mission, Tx., U.S. | 122 | 26°14'N | 98°19'W |
| Mission City, Can. (sĭ'tĭ) | 95 | 49°08'N | 112°18'W |
| Mississagi, r., Can. | 98 | 46°35'N | 83°30'W |
| Mississauga, Can. | 93 | 43°34'N | 79°37'W |
| Mississippi, state, U.S. (mĭs-ĭ-sĭp'ē) | 105 | 32°30'N | 89°45'W |
| Mississippi, l., Can. | 99 | 45°05'N | 76°15'W |
| Mississippi, r., U.S. | 107 | 32°00'N | 91°30'W |


ăt; finăl; rāte; senāte; ärm; ȧsk; sofȧ; fâre; ch-choose; dh-as th in other; bē; ēvent; bĕt; recĕnt; cratēr; g-gō; gh-guttural g; bĭt; ĭ-short neutral; rīde; ĸ-guttural k as ch in German ich;

PRONOUNCING INDEX

Mississippi Sound – Monterotondo 323


| PLACE (Pronunciation) | PAGE | LAT. | LONG. |
|---|---|---|---|
| Mississippi Sound, strt., Ms., U.S. | 124 | 34°16'N | 89°10'W |
| Missoula, Mt., U.S. (mĭ-zo͞o'lȧ) | 104 | 46°55'N | 114°00'W |
| Missouri, state, U.S. (mĭ-so͞o'rē) | 105 | 38°00'N | 93°40'W |
| Missouri, r., U.S. | 106 | 40°40'N | 96°00'W |
| Missouri City, Tx., U.S. | 123a | 29°37'N | 95°32'W |
| Missouri Coteau, hills, U.S. | 106 | 47°30'N | 101°00'W |
| Missouri Valley, Ia., U.S. | 112 | 41°35'N | 95°53'W |
| Mist, Or., U.S. (mĭst) | 116c | 46°00'N | 123°15'W |
| Mistassini, Can. (mĭs-tȧ-sĭ'nē) | 99 | 48°56'N | 71°55'W |
| Mistassini, l., Can. (mĭs-tȧ-sĭ'nē) | 93 | 50°48'N | 73°30'W |
| Mistelbach, Aus. (mĭs'tĕl-bäk) | 168 | 48°34'N | 16°33'E |
| Misteriosa, Lago, l., Mex. (mēs-tĕ-ryō'sä) | 132a | 18°05'N | 90°15'W |
| Misti, Volcán, vol., Peru | 142 | 16°04'S | 71°20'W |
| Mistretta, Italy (mē-strĕt'tä) | 174 | 37°54'N | 14°22'E |
| Misty Fjords National Monument, rec., Ak., U.S. | 103 | 51°00'N | 131°00'W |
| Mita, Punta de, c., Mex. (po͞o'n-tä-dĕ-mē'tä) | 130 | 20°44'N | 105°34'W |
| Mitaka, Japan (mē'tä-kä) | 211a | 35°42'N | 139°34'E |
| Mitchell, Il., U.S. (mĭch'ĕl) | 117e | 38°46'N | 90°05'W |
| Mitchell, In., U.S. | 108 | 38°45'N | 86°25'W |
| Mitchell, Ne., U.S. | 112 | 41°56'N | 103°49'W |
| Mitchell, S.D., U.S. | 104 | 43°42'N | 98°01'W |
| Mitchell, Mount, mtn., N.C., U.S. | 107 | 35°47'N | 82°15'W |
| Mīt Ghamr, Egypt | 238b | 30°43'N | 31°20'E |
| Mitla Pass, p., Egypt | 197a | 30°03'N | 32°40'E |
| Mito, Japan (mē'tō) | 210 | 36°20'N | 140°23'E |
| Mitsiwa, Erit. | 231 | 15°40'N | 39°19'E |
| Mitsu, Japan (mēt'sò) | 211 | 34°21'N | 132°49'E |
| Mittelland Kanal, can., Ger. (mĭt'ĕl-länd) | 168 | 52°18'N | 10°42'E |
| Mittenwalde, Ger. (mē'tĕn-väl-dĕ) | 159b | 52°16'N | 13°33'E |
| Mittweida, Ger. (mĭt-vī'dä) | 168 | 50°59'N | 12°58'E |
| Mitumba, Monts, mts., D.R.C. | 237 | 10°50'S | 27°00'E |
| Mityayevo, Russia (mĭt-yä'yĕ-vô) | 186a | 60°17'N | 61°02'E |
| Miura, Japan | 211a | 35°08'N | 139°37'E |
| Miwa, Japan (mē'wä) | 211b | 34°32'N | 135°51'E |
| Mixico, Guat. (mēs'kò) | 132 | 14°37'N | 90°37'W |
| Mixquiahuala, Mex. (mēs-kē-wä'lä) | 130 | 20°12'N | 99°13'W |
| Mixteco, r., Mex. (mēs-tä'kō) | 130 | 17°45'N | 98°10'W |
| Miyake, Japan (mē'yä-kå) | 211b | 34°35'N | 135°34'E |
| Miyake, i., Japan (mē'yä-kå) | 211 | 34°06'N | 139°21'E |
| Miyakonojō, Japan | 210 | 31°44'N | 131°04'E |
| Miyazaki, Japan (mē'yä-zä'kē) | 210 | 31°55'N | 131°27'E |
| Miyoshi, Japan (mē-yō'shē') | 210 | 34°48'N | 132°49'E |
| Mizdah, Libya (mēz'dä) | 200 | 31°29'N | 13°09'E |
| Mizil, Rom. (mē'zēl) | 175 | 45°01'N | 26°30'E |
| Mizoram, state, India | 199 | 23°25'N | 92°45'E |
| Mjölby, Swe. (myûl'bü) | 166 | 58°20'N | 15°09'E |
| Mjörn, l., Swe. | 166 | 57°55'N | 12°22'E |
| Mjösa, l., Nor. (myûsä) | 160 | 60°41'N | 11°25'E |
| Mkalama, Tan. | 232 | 4°07'S | 34°38'E |
| Mkushi, Zam. | 237 | 13°40'S | 29°20'E |
| Mkwaja, Tan. | 237 | 5°47'S | 38°51'E |
| Mladá Boleslav, Czech Rep. (mlä'dä bô'lĕ-slåf) | 168 | 50°26'N | 14°52'E |
| Mlala Hills, hills, Tan. | 237 | 6°47'S | 31°45'E |
| Mlanje Mountains, mts., Mwi. | 237 | 15°55'S | 35°30'E |
| Mława, Pol. (mwä'vȧ) | 160 | 53°07'N | 20°25'E |
| Mmabatho, S. Afr. | 232 | 25°42'S | 25°43'E |
| Moa, r., Afr. | 234 | 7°40'N | 11°15'W |
| Moa, Pulau, i., Indon. | 213 | 8°30'S | 128°30'E |
| Moab, Ut., U.S. (mō'ăb) | 119 | 38°35'N | 109°35'W |
| Moanda, Gabon | 232 | 1°37'S | 13°09'E |
| Moar Lake, l., Can. (môr) | 97 | 52°00'N | 95°09'W |
| Moba, D.R.C. | 232 | 7°12'S | 29°39'E |
| Mobaye, C.A.R. (mô-bä'y') | 231 | 4°19'N | 21°11'E |
| Mobayi-Mbongo, D.R.C. | 231 | 4°14'N | 21°11'E |
| Moberly, Mo., U.S. (mō'bēr-lĭ) | 105 | 39°24'N | 92°25'W |
| Mobile, Al., U.S. (mô-bēl') | 105 | 30°42'N | 88°03'W |
| Mobile, r., Al., U.S. | 124 | 31°15'N | 88°00'W |
| Mobile Bay, b., Al., U.S. | 107 | 30°26'N | 87°56'W |
| Mobridge, S.D., U.S. (mō'brĭj) | 112 | 45°32'N | 100°26'W |
| Moca, Dom. Rep. (mô'kä) | 135 | 19°25'N | 70°35'W |
| Moçambique, Moz. (mō-sän-bē'kĕ) | 237 | 15°03'S | 40°42'E |
| Moçâmedes, Ang. (mô-zá-mĕ-dĕs) | 232 | 15°10'S | 12°09'E |
| Moçâmedes, hist. reg., Ang. | 232 | 16°00'S | 12°15'E |
| Mochitlán, Mex. (mō-chē-tlän') | 130 | 17°10'N | 99°19'W |
| Mochudi, Bots. (mō-cho͞o'dē) | 232 | 24°13'S | 26°07'E |
| Mocímboa da Praia, Moz. (mô-sē'ēm-bô-ȧ prä'ēȧ) | 233 | 11°20'S | 40°21'E |
| Moclips, Wa., U.S. | 114 | 47°14'N | 124°13'W |
| Môco, Serra do, mtn., Ang. | 236 | 12°25'S | 15°10'E |
| Mococa, Braz. (mô-kô'kȧ) | 141a | 21°29'S | 46°58'W |
| Moctezuma, Mex. (mòk'tā-zo͞o'mä) | 130 | 22°44'N | 101°06'W |
| Mocuba, Moz. | 237 | 16°50'S | 36°59'E |
| Modderfontein, S. Afr. | 233b | 26°06'S | 28°10'E |
| Modena, Italy (mô'dĕ-nä) | 162 | 44°38'N | 10°54'E |
| Modesto, Ca., U.S. (mô-dĕs'tō) | 118 | 37°39'N | 121°00'W |
| Mödling, Aus. (mûd'lĭng) | 159e | 48°06'N | 16°17'E |
| Moelv, Nor. | 166 | 60°55'N | 10°40'E |
| Moengo, Sur. | 143 | 5°43'N | 54°19'W |
| Moenkopi, Az., U.S. | 119 | 36°07'N | 111°13'W |
| Moers, Ger. (mûrs) | 171c | 51°27'N | 6°38'E |
| Moffat Tunnel, trans., Co., U.S. (môf'ăt) | 120 | 39°52'N | 106°20'W |
| Mogadishu (Muqdisho), Som. | 238a | 2°08'N | 45°22'E |
| Mogadore, Oh., U.S. (mŏg-ȧ-dōr') | 111d | 41°04'N | 81°23'E |
| Mogaung, Mya. (mô-gä'òng) | 199 | 25°30'N | 96°52'E |
| Mogi das Cruzes, Braz. (mô-gē-däs-kro͞o'sĕs) | 143 | 23°33'S | 46°10'W |
| Mogi-Guaçu, r., Braz. (mô-gē-gwä'so͞o) | 141a | 22°06'S | 47°12'W |
| Mogilno, Pol. (mô-gēl'nô) | 168 | 52°38'N | 17°58'W |
| Mogi-Mirim, Braz. (mô-gē-mē-rē'n) | 141a | 22°26'S | 46°57'W |
| Mogok, Mya. (mô-gōk') | 199 | 23°14'N | 96°38'E |
| Mogol, r., S. Afr. (mô-gōl) | 238c | 24°12'S | 27°55'E |
| Mogollon Plateau, plat., Az., U.S. | 106 | 34°15'N | 110°45'W |
| Mogollon Rim, cliff, Az., U.S. (mō-gô-yōn') | 119 | 34°26'N | 111°17'W |
| Moguer, Spain (mô-gĕr') | 172 | 37°15'N | 6°50'W |
| Mohács, Hung. (mô'häch) | 169 | 45°59'N | 18°38'E |
| Mohale's Hoek, Leso. | 233c | 30°09'S | 27°28'E |
| Mohall, N.D., U.S. (mō'hôl) | 112 | 48°46'N | 101°29'W |
| Mohave, l., Nv., U.S. (mô-hä'vä) | 119 | 35°23'N | 114°40'W |
| Mohe, China (mwo-hŭ) | 205 | 53°33'N | 122°30'E |
| Mohenjo-Dero, hist., Pak. | 199 | 27°20'N | 68°10'E |
| Mohyliv-Podil's'kyi, Ukr. | 181 | 48°27'N | 27°51'E |
| Mõisaküla, Est. (mẽẽ'sȧ-kü'lä) | 167 | 58°07'N | 25°12'E |
| Moissac, Fr. (mwä-såk') | 170 | 44°07'N | 1°05'E |
| Moita, Port. (mô-ē'tȧ) | 173b | 38°39'N | 9°00'W |
| Mojave, Ca., U.S. | 118 | 35°06'N | 118°09'W |
| Mojave, r., Ca., U.S. (mô-hä'vä) | 118 | 34°46'N | 117°24'W |
| Mojave Desert, Ca., U.S. | 118 | 35°05'N | 117°30'W |
| Mojave Desert, des., Ca., U.S. | 106 | 35°00'N | 117°00'W |
| Mokhotlong, Leso. | 233c | 29°18'S | 29°06'E |
| Mokp'o, Kor., S. (mòk'pō') | 205 | 34°50'N | 126°30'E |
| Mol, Bel. | 159a | 51°21'N | 5°09'E |
| Moldavia *see* Moldova, nation, Eur. | 178 | 48°00'N | 28°00'E |
| Moldavia, hist. reg., Rom. | 169 | 47°20'N | 27°12'E |
| Molde, Nor. (môl'dĕ) | 160 | 62°44'N | 7°15'E |
| Moldova, nation, Eur. | 178 | 48°00'N | 28°00'E |
| Moldova, r., Rom. | 169 | 47°17'N | 26°27'E |
| Moldoveanu, Vârful, mtn., Rom. | 175 | 45°33'N | 24°38'E |
| Molepolole, Bots. (mō-lå-pô-lō'lå) | 232 | 24°15'S | 25°33'W |
| Molfetta, Italy (môl-fĕt'tä) | 163 | 41°11'N | 16°38'E |
| Molina, Chile (mŏ-lē'nä) | 141b | 35°07'S | 71°17'W |
| Molina de Aragón, Spain (mô-lē'nä dĕ ä-rä-gô'n) | 172 | 40°40'N | 1°54'W |
| Molína de Segura, Spain (mô-lē'nä dĕ sĕ-go͞o'rä) | 172 | 38°03'N | 1°07'W |
| Moline, Il., U.S. (mô-lēn') | 121 | 41°31'N | 90°34'W |
| Moliro, D.R.C. | 232 | 8°13'S | 30°34'E |
| Moliterno, Italy (môl-ē-tĕr'nō) | 174 | 40°13'N | 15°54'W |
| Mollendo, Peru (mô-lyĕn'dō) | 142 | 17°02'S | 71°59'W |
| Moller, Port, Ak., U.S. (pōrt mōl'ĕr) | 103 | 56°18'N | 161°30'W |
| Mölndal, Swe. (mûln'däl) | 166 | 57°39'N | 12°01'E |
| Molochna, r., Ukr. | 177 | 47°05'N | 35°22'E |
| Molochnyĭ lyman, l., Ukr. | 177 | 46°35'N | 35°32'E |
| Molody Tud, Russia (mō-lō-dô'ē to͞o'd) | 186b | 55°17'N | 37°31'E |
| Moloka'i, i., Hi., U.S. (mō-lō kä'ē) | 106c | 21°15'N | 157°05'W |
| Molokcha, r., Russia (mô'lôk-chä) | 186b | 56°15'N | 38°29'E |
| Molopo, r., Afr. (mō-lō-pô) | 232 | 27°45'S | 20°45'E |
| Molson Lake, l., Can. (mōl'sŭn) | 97 | 54°12'N | 96°45'W |
| Molteno, S. Afr. (môl-tā'nô) | 233c | 31°24'S | 26°23'E |
| Moluccas *see* Maluku, is., Indon. | 213 | 2°22'S | 128°25'E |
| Moma, Moz. | 237 | 16°44'S | 39°14'E |
| Mombasa, Kenya (mōm-bä'sä) | 233 | 4°03'S | 39°40'E |
| Mombetsu, Japan (môm'bĕt-so͞o') | 210 | 44°21'N | 142°48'E |
| Momence, Il., U.S. (mô-mĕns') | 111a | 41°09'N | 87°40'W |
| Momostenango, Guat. (mô-môs-tā-näŋ'gô) | 132 | 15°02'N | 91°25'W |
| Momotombo, Nic. | 132 | 12°25'N | 86°43'W |
| Mompog Pass, strt., Phil. (mōm-pōg') | 213a | 13°35'N | 122°09'E |
| Mompos, Col. (mōm-pōs') | 142 | 9°05'N | 74°30'W |
| Momtblanc, Spain | 173 | 41°20'N | 1°08'E |
| Møn, i., Den. (mûn) | 166 | 54°54'N | 12°30'E |
| Monaca, Pa., U.S. (mŏ-nȧ'kō) | 111e | 40°41'N | 80°17'W |
| Monaco, nation, Eur. (mŏn'ȧ-kō) | 154 | 43°43'N | 7°47'E |
| Monaghan, Ire. (mō'ȧ-găn) | 164 | 54°16'N | 7°20'W |
| Mona Passage, strt., N.A. (mō'nä) | 129 | 18°00'N | 68°10'W |
| Monarch Mountain, mtn., Can. (mŏn'ērk) | 94 | 51°41'N | 125°53'W |
| Monashee Mountains, mts., Can. (mŏ-nă'shē) | 95 | 50°30'N | 118°30'W |
| Monastir *see* Bitola, Mac. | 174 | 41°02'N | 21°22'E |
| Monastir, Tun. (mòn-ás-tēr') | 162 | 35°49'N | 10°56'E |
| Monastyrshchina, Russia (mô-nás-tērsh'chĭ-nȧ) | 176 | 54°19'N | 31°49'E |
| Monastyryshche, Ukr. | 177 | 48°57'N | 29°53'E |
| Monção, Braz. (mon-soun') | 143 | 3°39'S | 45°23'W |
| Moncayo, mtn., Spain (mòn-kä'yō) | 172 | 41°44'N | 1°48'W |
| Monchegorsk, Russia (mŏn'chĕ-gôrsk) | 180 | 69°00'N | 33°35'E |
| Mönchengladbach, Ger. (mûn'kĕn gläd'bäk) | 168 | 51°12'N | 6°28'E |
| Moncique, Serra de, mts., Port. (sĕr'rä dä mòn-chē'kĕ) | 172 | 37°22'N | 8°37'W |
| Monclova, Mex. (mòn-klō'vä) | 128 | 26°53'N | 101°25'W |
| Moncton, Can. (mŭngk'tŭn) | 91 | 46°06'N | 64°47'W |
| Mondêgo, r., Port. (mòn-dĕ'gō) | 172 | 40°10'N | 8°36'W |
| Mondego, Cabo, c., Port. (kä'bō mòn-dā'gò) | 172 | 40°12'N | 8°55'W |
| Mondombe, D.R.C. (mòn-dôm'bå) | 232 | 0°45'S | 23°06'E |
| Mondoñedo, Spain (mòn-dō-nyā'dō) | 172 | 43°35'N | 7°18'W |
| Mondovi, Wi., U.S. (mŏn-dō'vĭ) | 113 | 44°35'N | 91°42'W |
| Monee, Il., U.S. (mŏ-nĭ) | 111a | 41°25'N | 87°45'W |
| Monessen, Pa., U.S. (mō-nĕs'sen) | 111e | 40°09'N | 79°53'W |
| Monett, Mo., U.S. (mô-nĕt') | 121 | 36°55'N | 93°55'W |
| Monfalcone, Italy | 174 | 45°49'N | 13°30'E |
| Monforte de Lemos, Spain (môn-fôr'tä dĕ lĕ'môs) | 172 | 42°30'N | 7°30'W |
| Mongala, r., D.R.C. (mŏn-gäl'ȧ) | 231 | 3°20'N | 21°30'E |
| Mongalla, Sudan | 231 | 5°11'N | 31°46'E |
| Monghyr, India (mŏn-gēr') | 199 | 25°23'N | 86°34'E |
| Mongo, r., Afr. | 234 | 9°50'N | 11°50'W |
| Mongolia, nation, Asia (mŏŋ-gō'lĭ-ȧ) | 204 | 46°00'N | 100°00'E |
| Mongos, Chaîne des, mts., C.A.R. | 231 | 8°04'N | 21°59'E |
| Mongoumba, C.A.R. (mŏŋ-go͞om'bȧ) | 231 | 3°38'N | 18°36'E |
| Mongu, Zam. (mŏŋ-go͞o') | 232 | 15°15'S | 23°09'E |
| Monkey Bay, Mwi. | 237 | 14°05'S | 34°55'E |
| Monkey River, Belize (mŭŋ'kĭ) | 132a | 16°22'N | 88°33'W |
| Monkland, Can. (mŭngk-lănd) | 102c | 45°12'N | 74°52'W |
| Monkoto, D.R.C. (mòn-kō'tô) | 232 | 1°38'S | 20°39'E |
| Monmouth, Il., U.S. (mŏn'mŭth) (mŏn'mouth) | 121 | 40°54'N | 90°38'W |
| Monmouth Junction, N.J., U.S. (mŏn'mouth jŭngk'shŭn) | 110a | 40°23'N | 74°33'W |
| Monmouth Mountain, mtn., Can. (mŏn'mŭth) | 94 | 51°00'N | 123°47'W |
| Mono, r., Afr. | 234 | 7°20'N | 1°25'E |
| Mono Lake, l., Ca., U.S. (mō'nō) | 118 | 38°04'N | 119°00'W |
| Monon, In., U.S. (mō'nŏn) | 108 | 40°55'N | 86°55'W |
| Monongah, W.V., U.S. (mô-nŏŋ'gȧ) | 108 | 39°25'N | 80°10'W |
| Monongahela, Pa., U.S. (mô-nŏn-gȧ-hē'lȧ) | 111a | 40°11'N | 79°55'W |
| Monongahela, r., W.V., U.S. | 108 | 39°30'N | 80°10'W |
| Monopoli, Italy (mô-nô'pô-lē) | 175 | 40°55'N | 17°17'E |
| Monóvar, Spain (mô-nō'vär) | 173 | 38°26'N | 0°50'W |
| Monreale, Italy (mōn-rå-ä'lā) | 174 | 38°04'N | 13°15'E |
| Monroe, Ga., U.S. (mŭn-rō') | 124 | 33°47'N | 83°43'W |
| Monroe, La., U.S. | 105 | 32°30'N | 92°06'W |
| Monroe, Mi., U.S. | 108 | 41°55'N | 83°25'W |
| Monroe, N.C., U.S. | 125 | 34°58'N | 80°34'W |
| Monroe, N.Y., U.S. | 110a | 41°19'N | 74°11'W |
| Monroe, Ut., U.S. | 119 | 38°35'N | 112°10'W |
| Monroe, Wa., U.S. | 116a | 47°52'N | 121°58'W |
| Monroe, Wi., U.S. | 113 | 42°35'N | 89°40'W |
| Monroe, Lake, l., Fl., U.S. | 125 | 28°50'N | 81°15'W |
| Monroe City, Mo., U.S. | 121 | 39°38'N | 91°41'W |
| Monroeville, Al., U.S. (mŭn-rō'vĭl) | 124 | 31°33'N | 87°19'W |
| Monroeville, Pa., U.S. | 111e | 40°26'N | 79°46'W |
| Monrovia, Lib. | 230 | 6°18'N | 10°47'W |
| Monrovia, Ca., U.S. (mŏn-rō'vĭ-ȧ) | 117a | 34°09'N | 118°00'W |
| Mons, Bel. (môn') | 161 | 50°29'N | 3°55'E |
| Monson, Me., U.S. (mŏn'sŭn) | 100 | 45°17'N | 69°28'W |
| Mönsterås, Swe. (mŭn'stĕr-ôs) | 166 | 57°04'N | 16°24'E |
| Montagne Tremblant Provincial Park, rec., Can. | 107 | 46°30'N | 75°51'W |
| Montague, Can. (mŏn'tȧ-gū) | 101 | 46°10'N | 62°39'W |
| Montague, Mi., U.S. | 108 | 43°30'N | 86°25'W |
| Montague, i., Ak., U.S. | 103 | 60°10'N | 147°00'W |
| Montalbán, Ven. (mônt-äl-bän) | 143b | 10°14'N | 68°19'W |
| Montalegre, Port. (mōn-tä-lā'grĕ) | 172 | 41°49'N | 7°48'W |
| Montana, state, U.S. (mŏn-tăn'ȧ) | 104 | 47°10'N | 111°50'W |
| Montánchez, Spain (mòn-tän'chāth) | 172 | 39°18'N | 6°09'W |
| Montargis, Fr. (môn-tȧr-zhē') | 161 | 47°59'N | 2°42'E |
| Montataire, Fr. (môn-tȧ-târ) | 171b | 49°15'N | 2°26'E |
| Montauban, Fr. (môn-tô-bän') | 161 | 44°01'N | 1°22'E |
| Montauk, N.Y., U.S. | 109 | 41°03'N | 71°57'W |
| Montauk Point, c., N.Y., U.S. (mŏn-tôk') | 109 | 41°05'N | 71°55'W |
| Montbard, Fr. (môn-bȧr') | 170 | 47°40'N | 4°19'E |
| Montbéliard, Fr. (môn-bā-lyȧr') | 171 | 47°32'N | 6°45'E |
| Mont Belvieu, Tx., U.S. (mŏnt bĕl'vū) | 123a | 29°51'N | 94°53'W |
| Montbrison, Fr. (môn-brē-zon') | 170 | 45°38'N | 4°06'E |
| Montceau, Fr. (môn-sō') | 170 | 46°39'N | 4°22'E |
| Montclair, N.J., U.S. (mŏnt-klâr') | 110a | 40°49'N | 74°13'W |
| Mont-de-Marsan, Fr. (môn-dē-mȧr-sän') | 161 | 43°54'N | 0°32'W |
| Montdidier, Fr. (môn-dē-dyā') | 170 | 49°42'N | 2°33'E |
| Monte, Arg. (mô'n-tĕ) | 141c | 35°25'S | 58°49'W |
| Monteagudo, Bol. (mōn'tā-ä-go͞o'dhō) | 142 | 19°49'S | 63°48'W |
| Montebello, Can. | 102c | 45°40'N | 74°56'W |
| Montebello, Ca., U.S. (mŏn-tē-bĕl'ō) | 117a | 34°01'N | 118°06'W |
| Monte Bello Islands, is., Austl. | 220 | 20°30'S | 114°10'E |
| Monte Caseros, Arg. (mō'n-tĕ-kä-sĕ'rôs) | 144 | 30°16'S | 57°39'W |
| Montecillos, Cordillera de, mts., Hond. | 132 | 14°19'N | 87°52'W |
| Monte Cristi, Dom. Rep. (mô'n-tĕ-krē's-tē) | 135 | 19°50'N | 71°40'W |
| Montecristo, Isola di, i., Italy (mōn'tå-krēs'tō) | 174 | 42°20'N | 10°19'E |
| Monte Escobedo, Mex. (mōn'tå ĕs-kô-bā'dhō) | 130 | 22°18'N | 103°34'W |
| Monteforte Irpino, Italy (môn-tĕ-fô'r-tĕ ē'r-pē'nō) | 173c | 40°39'N | 14°42'E |
| Montefrío, Spain (mōn-tå-frē'ō) | 172 | 37°20'N | 4°02'W |
| Montego Bay, Jam. (mŏn-tē'gō) | 129 | 18°30'N | 77°55'W |
| Montelavar, Port. (mōn-tĕ-lä-vär') | 173b | 38°51'N | 9°20'W |
| Montélimar, Fr. (môn-tā-lē-mär') | 161 | 44°33'N | 4°47'E |
| Montellano, Spain (mōn-tå-lyä'nō) | 172 | 37°00'N | 5°34'W |
| Montello, Wi., U.S. (mŏn-tĕl'ō) | 113 | 43°47'N | 89°20'W |
| Montemorelos, Mex. (mōn'tå-mō-rā'lōs) | 128 | 25°14'N | 99°50'W |
| Montemor-o-Novo, Port. (mōn-tĕ-mōr'ō-nō'vò) | 172 | 38°39'N | 8°11'W |
| Montenegro *see* Crna Gora, state, Serb. | 175 | 42°55'N | 18°52'E |
| Montenegro, reg., Moz. | 237 | 13°07'S | 39°00'E |
| Montepulciano, Italy (mōn'tå-po͞ol-chä'nō) | 174 | 43°05'N | 11°48'E |
| Montereau-faut-Yonne, Fr. (môn-t'rō'fō-yôn') | 170 | 48°24'N | 2°57'E |
| Monterey, Ca., U.S. (mŏn-tĕ-rā') | 104 | 36°36'N | 121°53'W |
| Monterey, Tn., U.S. | 124 | 36°06'N | 85°15'W |
| Monterey Bay, b., Ca., U.S. | 106 | 36°48'N | 122°01'W |
| Monterey Park, Ca., U.S. | 117a | 34°04'N | 118°08'W |
| Montería, Col. (mōn-tā-rä'ä) | 142 | 8°47'N | 75°57'W |
| Monteros, Arg. (mōn-tĕ'rôs) | 144 | 27°14'S | 65°29'W |
| Monterotondo, Italy (môn-tĕ-rô-tô'n-dō) | 173d | 42°03'N | 12°39'E |


ng-sing; ŋ-baŋk; n-nasalized n; nŏd; cŏmmit; ōld; ôbey; ôrder; oi-boil; fo͞od; ò-as oo in foot; ou-out; s-soft; sh-dish; th-thin; pūre; ůnite; ûrn; stŭd; circŭs; ü-as in French tu; '-indeterminate vowel.

ăt; finăl; rāte; senăte; ärm; ásk; sofá; fâre;   ch-choose;   dh-as th in other;   bē; ĕvent; bĕt; recĕnt; cratĕr;   g-gō; gh-guttural g;   bĭt; ĭ-short neutral; rīde;   ĸ-guttural k as ch in German ich;

PRONOUNCING INDEX

Mount Moriac – Nabberu 325


| PLACE (Pronunciation) | PAGE | LAT. | LONG. |
|---|---|---|---|
| Mount Moriac, Austl. | 217a | 38°13′S | 144°12′E |
| Mount Morris, Mi., U.S. (mŏr′ĭs) | 108 | 43°10′N | 83°45′W |
| Mount Morris, N.Y., U.S. | 109 | 42°45′N | 77°50′W |
| Mount Nimba National Park, rec., C. Iv. | 234 | 7°35′N | 8°10′W |
| Mount Olive, N.C., U.S. (ŏl′ĭv) | 125 | 35°11′N | 78°05′W |
| Mount Peale, Ut., U.S. | 119 | 38°26′N | 109°16′W |
| Mount Pleasant, Ia., U.S. (plĕz′ănt) | 113 | 40°59′N | 91°34′W |
| Mount Pleasant, Mi., U.S. | 108 | 43°35′N | 84°45′W |
| Mount Pleasant, S.C., U.S. | 125 | 32°46′N | 79°51′W |
| Mount Pleasant, Tn., U.S. | 124 | 35°31′N | 87°12′W |
| Mount Pleasant, Tx., U.S. | 123 | 33°10′N | 94°56′W |
| Mount Pleasant, Ut., U.S. | 119 | 39°35′N | 111°20′W |
| Mount Prospect, Il., U.S. (prŏs′pĕkt) | 111a | 42°03′N | 87°56′W |
| Mount Rainier National Park, rec., Wa., U.S. (rā-nēr′) | 106 | 46°47′N | 121°17′W |
| Mount Revelstoke National Park, rec., Can. (rĕv′ĕl-stōk) | 90 | 51°22′N | 120°15′W |
| Mount Savage, Md., U.S. (săv′āj) | 109 | 39°45′N | 78°55′W |
| Mount Shasta, Ca., U.S. (shăs′tȧ) | 114 | 41°18′N | 122°17′W |
| Mount Sterling, Il., U.S. (stûr′lĭng) | 121 | 39°59′N | 90°44′W |
| Mount Sterling, Ky., U.S. | 108 | 38°05′N | 84°00′W |
| Mount Stewart, Can. (stū′ărt) | 101 | 46°22′N | 62°52′W |
| Mount Union, Pa., U.S. (ūn′yŭn) | 109 | 40°25′N | 77°50′W |
| Mount Vernon, Il., U.S. (vûr′nŭn) | 108 | 38°20′N | 88°50′W |
| Mount Vernon, In., U.S. | 108 | 37°55′N | 87°50′W |
| Mount Vernon, Mo., U.S. | 121 | 37°09′N | 93°48′W |
| Mount Vernon, N.Y., U.S. | 110a | 40°55′N | 73°51′W |
| Mount Vernon, Oh., U.S. | 108 | 40°25′N | 82°30′W |
| Mount Vernon, Va., U.S. | 110e | 38°43′N | 77°06′W |
| Mount Vernon, Wa., U.S. | 114 | 48°25′N | 122°20′W |
| Moura, Braz. (mō′rȧ) | 143 | 1°33′S | 61°38′W |
| Moura, Port. | 172 | 38°08′N | 7°28′W |
| Mourne Mountains, mts., N. Ire., U.K. (môrn) | 164 | 54°10′N | 6°09′W |
| Moussoro, Chad | 235 | 13°39′N | 16°29′E |
| Moûtiers, Fr. (mōō-tyâr′) | 171 | 45°31′N | 6°34′E |
| Mowbullan, Mount, mtn., Austl. | 222 | 26°50′S | 151°34′E |
| Moyahua, Mex. (mō-yä′wä) | 130 | 21°16′N | 103°10′W |
| Moyale, Kenya (mō-yä′lä) | 231 | 3°28′N | 39°04′E |
| Moyamba, S.L. (mō-yäm′bä) | 230 | 8°10′N | 12°26′W |
| Moyen Atlas, mts., Mor. | 162 | 32°49′N | 5°28′W |
| Moyeuvre-Grande, Fr. | 171 | 49°15′N | 6°26′E |
| Moyie, r., Id., U.S. (moi′yē) | 114 | 38°50′N | 116°10′W |
| Moyobamba, Peru (mō-yō-bäm′bä) | 142 | 6°12′S | 76°56′W |
| Moyuta, Guat. (mō-ē-ōō′tä) | 132 | 14°01′N | 90°05′W |
| Moyyero, r., Russia | 184 | 67°15′N | 104°10′E |
| Moyynqum, des., Kaz. | 183 | 44°30′N | 70°00′E |
| Mozambique, nation, Afr. (mō-zăm-bēk′) | 232 | 20°15′S | 33°53′E |
| Mozambique Channel, strt., Afr. (mō-zăm-bek′) | 233 | 24°00′S | 38°00′E |
| Mozdok, Russia (môz-dôk′) | 181 | 43°45′N | 44°35′E |
| Mozhaysk, Russia (mō-zhäysk′) | 176 | 55°31′N | 36°02′E |
| Mozhayskiy, Russia (mō-zhay′skĭ) | 186c | 59°42′N | 30°08′E |
| Mpanda, Tan. | 237 | 6°22′S | 31°02′E |
| Mpika, Zam. | 237 | 11°54′S | 31°26′E |
| Mpimbe, Mwi. | 237 | 15°18′S | 35°04′E |
| Mporokoso, Zam. (′m-pō-rō-kō′sō) | 232 | 9°23′S | 30°05′E |
| Mpwapwa, Tan. (′m-pwä′pwä) | 232 | 6°21′S | 36°29′E |
| Mqanduli, S. Afr. (′m-kän′dōō-lē) | 233c | 31°50′S | 28°42′E |
| Mrągowo, Pol. (mrän′gō-vō) | 169 | 53°52′N | 21°18′E |
| M'Sila, Alg. (m′sē′lȧ) | 230 | 35°47′N | 4°34′E |
| Msta, r., Russia (m′stá′) | 180 | 58°30′N | 33°00′E |
| Mstsislaw, Bela. | 176 | 54°01′N | 31°42′E |
| Mtakataka, Mwi. | 237 | 14°12′S | 34°32′E |
| Mtamvuna, r., Afr. | 233c | 30°43′S | 29°53′E |
| Mtata, r., S. Afr. | 233c | 31°48′S | 29°03′E |
| Mtsensk, Russia (m′tsĕnsk) | 180 | 53°17′N | 36°33′E |
| Mtwara, Tan. | 237 | 10°16′S | 40°11′E |
| Muar, r., Malay. | 197b | 2°18′N | 102°43′E |
| Mubende, Ug. | 237 | 0°35′N | 31°23′E |
| Mubi, Nig. | 235 | 10°18′N | 13°20′E |
| Mucacata, Moz. | 237 | 13°20′S | 39°59′E |
| Much, Ger. (mōōk) | 171c | 50°54′N | 7°24′E |
| Muchinga Mountains, mts., Zam. | 237 | 12°40′S | 30°50′E |
| Much Wenlock, Eng., U.K. (mŭch wĕn′lŏk) | 158a | 52°35′N | 2°33′W |
| Muckalee Creek, r., Ga., U.S. (mŭk′ȧ lē) | 124 | 31°55′N | 84°10′W |
| Muckleshoot Indian Reservation, I.R., Wa., U.S. (mŭck′′l-shōōt) | 116a | 47°21′N | 122°04′W |
| Mucubela, Moz. | 237 | 16°55′S | 37°52′E |
| Mud, l., Mi., U.S. (mŭd) | 113 | 46°12′N | 84°32′W |
| Mudan, r., China (mōō-dän) | 208 | 45°30′N | 129°40′E |
| Mudanjiang, China (mōō-dän-jyäŋ) | 208 | 44°28′N | 129°38′E |
| Muddy, r., Nv., U.S. (mŭd′ĭ) | 119 | 36°56′N | 114°42′W |
| Muddy Boggy Creek, r., Ok., U.S. (mud′ĭ bŏg′ĭ) | 121 | 34°42′N | 96°11′W |
| Muddy Creek, r., Ut., U.S. (mŭd′ĭ) | 119 | 38°45′N | 111°10′W |
| Mudgee, Austl. (mŭ-jē) | 222 | 32°47′S | 149°10′E |
| Mudjatik, r., Can. | 96 | 56°23′N | 107°40′W |
| Mufulira, Zam. | 237 | 12°33′S | 28°14′E |
| Muğla, Tur. (mōōg′lä) | 198 | 37°10′N | 28°20′E |
| Mühldorf, Ger. (mül-dôrf) | 168 | 48°15′N | 12°33′E |
| Mühlhausen, Ger. (mül′hou-zĕn) | 168 | 51°13′N | 10°25′E |
| Muhu, i., Est. (mōō′hōō) | 167 | 58°41′N | 22°55′E |
| Muir Woods National Monument, rec., Ca., U.S. (mūr) | 118 | 37°54′N | 123°22′W |
| Muizenberg, S. Afr. (mwĭz-ĕn-bûrg′) | 232a | 34°07′S | 18°28′E |
| Mukacheve, Ukr. | 169 | 48°25′N | 22°43′E |
| Mukden *see* Shenyang, China | 204 | 41°45′N | 123°22′E |
| Mukhtuya, Russia (mōk-tōō′yȧ) | 179 | 61°00′N | 113°00′E |
| Mukilteo, Wa., U.S. (mū-kĭl-tā′ō) | 116a | 47°57′N | 122°18′W |
| Muko, Japan (mōō′kō) | 211b | 34°57′N | 135°43′E |

| PLACE (Pronunciation) | PAGE | LAT. | LONG. |
|---|---|---|---|
| Muko, r., Japan (mōō′kō) | 211b | 34°52′N | 135°17′E |
| Mukutawa, r., Can. | 97 | 53°10′N | 97°28′W |
| Mukwonago, Wi., U.S. (mū-kwō-nȧ′gō) | 111a | 42°52′N | 88°19′W |
| Mula, Spain (mōō′lä) | 172 | 38°05′N | 1°12′W |
| Mula, Al., U.S. (mŭl′gȧ) | 110h | 33°33′N | 86°59′W |
| Mulde, r., Ger. (mōl′dĕ) | 168 | 50°30′N | 12°30′E |
| Muleros, Mex. (mōō-lā′rōs) | 130 | 23°44′N | 104°00′W |
| Muleshoe, Tx., U.S. | 120 | 34°13′N | 102°43′W |
| Mulgrave, Can. (mŭl′grāv) | 101 | 45°37′N | 61°23′W |
| Mulhacén, mtn., Spain | 162 | 37°04′N | 3°18′W |
| Mülheim, Ger. (mül′hīm) | 171c | 51°25′N | 6°53′E |
| Mulhouse, Fr. (mü-lōōz′) | 161 | 47°46′N | 7°20′E |
| Muling, China (mōō-lĭŋ) | 208 | 44°32′N | 130°18′E |
| Muling, r., China | 208 | 44°40′N | 130°30′E |
| Mull, Island of, i., Scot., U.K. (mŭl) | 164 | 56°40′N | 6°19′W |
| Mullan, Id., U.S. (mŭl′ăn) | 114 | 47°26′N | 115°50′W |
| Müller, Pegunungan, mts., Indon. (mül′ĕr) | 212 | 0°22′N | 113°05′E |
| Mullingar, Ire. (mŭl-ĭn-gär) | 164 | 53°31′N | 7°26′W |
| Mullins, S.C., U.S. (mŭl′ĭnz) | 125 | 34°11′N | 79°13′W |
| Mullins River, Belize | 132a | 17°08′N | 88°18′W |
| Multān, Pak. (mō-tän′) | 199 | 30°17′N | 71°13′E |
| Multnomah Channel, strt., Or., U.S. (mŭl nō mȧ) | 116c | 45°41′N | 122°53′W |
| Mulumbe, Monts, mts., D.R.C. | 237 | 8°47′S | 27°20′E |
| Mulvane, Ks., U.S. (mŭl-vān′) | 121 | 37°30′N | 97°13′W |
| Mumbai (Bombay), India | 199 | 18°58′N | 72°50′E |
| Mumbwa, Zam. (mōm′bwä) | 232 | 14°59′S | 27°04′E |
| Mumias, Kenya | 237 | 0°20′N | 34°29′E |
| Muna, Mex. (mōō′nȧ) | 132a | 20°28′N | 89°42′W |
| München *see* Munich, Ger. | 154 | 48°08′N | 11°35′E |
| Muncie, In., U.S. (mŭn′sĭ) | 105 | 40°10′N | 85°30′W |
| Mundelein, Il., U.S. (mŭn-dē-lĭn′) | 111a | 42°16′N | 88°00′W |
| Mundonueva, Pico de, mtn., Col. (pē′kō-dĕ-mōō′n-dō-nwĕ′vä) | 142a | 4°18′N | 74°12′W |
| Muneco, Cerro, mtn., Mex. (sĕ′r-rō-mōō-nĕ′kō) | 131a | 19°13′N | 99°20′W |
| Mungana, Austl. (mŭn-găn′ȧ) | 219 | 17°15′S | 144°18′E |
| Mungbere, D.R.C. | 237 | 2°38′N | 28°30′E |
| Munger, Mn., U.S. (mŭn′gẽr) | 117h | 46°48′N | 92°20′W |
| Mungindi, Austl. (mŭn-gĭn′dē) | 219 | 29°00′S | 148°45′E |
| Munhall, Pa., U.S. (mŭn′hôl) | 111e | 40°24′N | 79°53′W |
| Munhango, Ang. (mōn-hän′gȧ) | 232 | 12°15′S | 18°55′E |
| Munich, Ger. | 154 | 48°08′N | 11°35′E |
| Munising, Mi., U.S. (mū′nĭ-sĭng) | 113 | 46°24′N | 86°41′W |
| Muniz Freire, Braz. | 141a | 20°29′S | 41°25′W |
| Munku Sardyk, mtn., Asia (mōn′kō sär-dĭk′) | 179 | 51°45′N | 100°30′E |
| Muñoz, Phil. (mōōn-nyōth′) | 213a | 15°44′N | 120°53′E |
| Münster, Ger. (mün′stĕr) | 161 | 51°57′N | 7°38′E |
| Munster, In., U.S. (mŭn′stĕr) | 111a | 41°34′N | 87°31′W |
| Munster, hist. reg., Ire. (mŭn-stẽr) | 164 | 52°30′N | 9°24′W |
| Muntok, Indon. (mōn-tŏk′) | 212 | 2°05′S | 105°11′E |
| Muong Sing, Laos (mōō′ông-sĭng′) | 212 | 21°06′N | 101°17′E |
| Muping, China (mōō-pĭŋ) | 206 | 37°23′N | 121°36′E |
| Muqui, Braz. (mōō-kōē) | 141a | 20°56′S | 41°20′W |
| Mur, r., Eur. (mōōr) | 161 | 47°00′N | 15°00′E |
| Muradiye, Tur. (mōō-rä′dē-yĕ) | 181 | 39°00′N | 43°40′E |
| Murat, Fr. (mü-rä′) | 170 | 45°05′N | 2°56′E |
| Murat, r., Tur. (mōō-rät′) | 198 | 39°00′N | 42°00′E |
| Murchison, r., Austl. (mûr′chĭ-sŭn) | 220 | 26°45′S | 116°15′E |
| Murcia, Spain (mōōr′thyä) | 154 | 38°00′N | 1°10′W |
| Murcia, hist. reg., Spain | 172 | 38°35′N | 1°51′W |
| Murdo, S.D., U.S. (mûr′dō) | 112 | 43°53′N | 100°42′W |
| Mureş, r., Rom. (mōō′rĕsh) | 163 | 46°02′N | 21°50′E |
| Muret, Fr. (mü-rĕ′) | 170 | 43°28′N | 1°17′E |
| Murfreesboro, Tn., U.S. (mûr′frēz-bŭr-ō) | 124 | 35°50′N | 86°19′W |
| Murgab, Taj. | 183 | 38°10′N | 73°59′E |
| Murgab, r., Asia (mōōr-gäb′) | 198 | 37°07′N | 62°32′E |
| Muriaé, r., Braz. | 141a | 21°20′S | 41°40′W |
| Murino, Russia (mōō′rĭ-nō) | 186c | 60°03′N | 30°28′E |
| Müritz, l., Ger. (mür′its) | 168 | 53°20′N | 12°33′E |
| Murmansk, Russia (mōōr-mänsk′) | 178 | 69°00′N | 33°20′E |
| Murom, Russia (mōō′rŏm) | 178 | 55°30′N | 42°00′W |
| Muroran, Japan (mōō′rō-rän) | 205 | 42°21′N | 141°05′E |
| Muros, Spain (mōō′rōs) | 172 | 42°48′N | 9°00′W |
| Muroto-Zaki, c., Japan (mōō′rō-tō zä′kē) | 210 | 33°14′N | 134°12′E |
| Murphy, Mo., U.S. (mŭr′fĭ) | 117e | 38°29′N | 90°29′W |
| Murphy, N.C., U.S. | 124 | 35°05′N | 84°00′W |
| Murphysboro, Il., U.S. (mŭr′fĭz-bŭr-ō) | 121 | 37°46′N | 89°21′W |
| Murray, Ky., U.S. (mŭr′ĭ) | 124 | 36°39′N | 88°17′W |
| Murray, Ut., U.S. | 117b | 40°40′N | 111°53′W |
| Murray, r., Austl. | 220 | 34°20′S | 140°00′E |
| Murray, r., Can. | 95 | 55°00′N | 121°00′W |
| Murray, Lake, res., S.C., U.S. (mŭr′ĭ) | 125 | 34°07′N | 81°18′W |
| Murray Bridge, Austl. | 218 | 35°10′S | 139°35′E |
| Murray Harbour, Can. | 101 | 46°00′N | 62°31′W |
| Murray Region, reg., Austl. (mŭ′rē) | 221 | 33°20′S | 142°30′E |
| Murrumbidgee, r., Austl. (mŭr-ŭm-bĭd′jē) | 221 | 34°30′S | 145°20′E |
| Murrupula, Moz. | 237 | 15°27′S | 38°47′E |
| Murshidābād, India (mōr′shē-dä-bäd′) | 202 | 24°08′N | 88°11′E |
| Murska Sobota, Slvn. (mōōr′skä sō′bō-tä) | 174 | 46°40′N | 16°14′E |
| Muruasigar, mtn., Kenya | 237 | 3°08′N | 35°02′E |
| Murwāra, India | 199 | 23°54′N | 80°23′E |
| Murwillumbah, Austl. (mŭr-wĭl′lŭm-bŭ) | 222 | 28°15′S | 153°30′E |
| Mürz, r., Aus. (mürts) | 168 | 47°30′N | 15°21′E |
| Mürzzuschlag, Aus. (mürts′tsōō-shlägh) | 168 | 47°37′N | 15°41′E |

| PLACE (Pronunciation) | PAGE | LAT. | LONG. |
|---|---|---|---|
| Mus, Tur. (mōōsh) | 181 | 38°55′N | 41°30′E |
| Musala, mtn., Blg. | 175 | 42°05′N | 23°24′E |
| Musan, Kor., N. (mō′sän) | 205 | 41°11′N | 129°10′E |
| Musashino, Japan (mōō-sä′shē-nō) | 211a | 35°43′N | 139°35′E |
| Muscat, Oman (mŭs-kăt′) | 198 | 23°23′N | 58°30′E |
| Muscat and Oman *see* Oman, nation, Asia | 198 | 20°00′N | 57°45′E |
| Muscatine, Ia., U.S. (mŭs-kȧ-tēn) | 113 | 41°26′N | 91°00′W |
| Muscle Shoals, Al., U.S. (mŭs′′l shōlz) | 124 | 34°44′N | 87°38′W |
| Musgrave Ranges, mts., Austl. (mŭs′grāv) | 220 | 26°15′S | 131°15′E |
| Mushie, D.R.C. (mŭsh′ē) | 232 | 3°04′S | 16°50′E |
| Mushin, Nig. | 235 | 6°32′N | 3°22′E |
| Musi, r., Indon. (mōō′sē) | 212 | 2°40′S | 103°42′E |
| Musinga, Alto, mtn., Col. (ä′l-tō-mōō-sē′n-gä) | 142a | 6°40′N | 76°13′W |
| Muskego Lake, l., Wi., U.S. (mŭs-kē′gō) | 111a | 42°53′N | 88°10′W |
| Muskegon, Mi., U.S. (mŭs-kē′gŭn) | 105 | 43°15′N | 86°20′W |
| Muskegon, r., Mi., U.S. | 108 | 43°20′N | 85°55′W |
| Muskegon Heights, Mi., U.S. | 108 | 43°10′N | 86°20′W |
| Muskingum, r., Oh., U.S. (mŭs-kĭŋ′gŭm) | 108 | 39°45′N | 81°55′W |
| Muskogee, Ok., U.S. (mŭs-kō′gē) | 105 | 35°44′N | 95°21′W |
| Muskoka, l., Can. (mŭs-kō′kȧ) | 99 | 45°00′N | 79°30′W |
| Musoma, Tan. | 237 | 1°30′S | 33°48′E |
| Mussau Island, i., Pap. N. Gui. (mōō-sä′ōō) | 213 | 1°30′S | 149°32′E |
| Musselshell, r., Mt., U.S. (mŭs′′l-shĕl) | 115 | 46°25′N | 108°20′W |
| Mussende, Ang. | 236 | 10°32′S | 16°05′E |
| Mussuma, Ang. | 236 | 14°14′S | 21°59′E |
| Mustafakemalpaşa, Tur. | 163 | 40°05′N | 28°30′E |
| Mustang Bayou, Tx., U.S. | 123a | 29°22′N | 95°12′W |
| Mustang Creek, r., Tx., U.S. (mŭs′tăng) | 120 | 36°22′N | 102°46′W |
| Mustang Island, i., Tx., U.S. | 123 | 27°43′N | 97°00′W |
| Mustique, i., St. Vin. (müs-tēk′) | 133b | 12°53′N | 61°03′W |
| Mustvee, Est. (mōōst′vĕ-ĕ) | 167 | 58°50′N | 26°54′E |
| Musu Dan, c., Kor., N. (mō′sō dän) | 205 | 40°51′N | 130°00′E |
| Muswellbrook, Austl. (mŭs′wŭnl-brōk) | 222 | 32°15′S | 150°50′E |
| Mutare, Zimb. | 232 | 18°49′S | 32°39′E |
| Mutombo Mukulu, D.R.C. (mōō-tôm′bō mōō-kōō′lōō) | 232 | 8°12′S | 23°56′E |
| Mutsu Wan, b., Japan (mōōt′sōō wän) | 210 | 41°20′N | 140°55′E |
| Mutton Bay, Can. (mŭt′′n) | 101 | 50°48′N | 59°02′W |
| Mutum, Braz. (mōō-tōō′m) | 141a | 19°48′S | 41°24′W |
| Muzaffargarh, Pak. | 202 | 30°09′N | 71°15′E |
| Muzaffarpur, India | 202 | 26°13′N | 85°20′E |
| Muzon, Cape, c., Ak., U.S. | 94 | 54°41′N | 132°44′W |
| Muzquiz, Mex. (mōōz′kēz) | 122 | 27°53′N | 101°31′W |
| Muztagata, mtn., China | 204 | 38°20′N | 75°28′E |
| Mvomero, Tan. | 237 | 6°20′S | 37°25′E |
| Mvoti, r., S. Afr. | 233c | 29°18′S | 30°52′E |
| Mwali, i., Com. | 233 | 12°15′S | 43°45′E |
| Mwanza, Tan. (mwän′zä) | 232 | 2°31′S | 32°54′E |
| Mwaya, Tan. (mwä′yä) | 232 | 9°19′S | 33°51′E |
| Mwenga, D.R.C. | 237 | 3°02′S | 28°26′E |
| Mweru, l., Afr. | 232 | 8°50′S | 28°50′E |
| Mwingi, Kenya | 237 | 0°56′S | 38°04′E |
| Myanmar (Burma), nation, Asia | 194 | 21°00′N | 95°15′E |
| Myingyan, Mya. (myĭng-yŭn′) | 199 | 21°37′N | 95°26′E |
| Myitkyina, Mya. (myĭ′chē-nȧ) | 199 | 25°33′N | 97°25′E |
| Myjava, Slvk. (mûē′yȧ-vä) | 169 | 48°45′N | 17°33′E |
| Mykhailivka, Ukr. | 177 | 47°16′N | 35°12′E |
| Mykolaïv, Ukr. | 178 | 46°58′N | 32°02′E |
| Mykolaïv, prov., Ukr. | 177 | 47°27′N | 31°25′E |
| Mýkonos, i., Grc. | 175 | 37°26′N | 25°30′E |
| Mymensingh, Bngl. | 199 | 24°48′N | 90°28′E |
| Mynämäki, Fin. | 167 | 60°41′N | 21°58′E |
| Myohyang San, mtn., Kor., N. (myō′hyang) | 210 | 40°00′N | 126°12′E |
| Mýrdalsjökull, ice, Ice. (mür′däls-yû′kōl) | 160 | 63°34′N | 18°04′W |
| Myrhorod, Ukr. | 181 | 49°56′N | 33°36′E |
| Mýrina, Grc. | 175 | 39°52′N | 25°01′E |
| Myrtle Beach, S.C., U.S. (mûr′t′l) | 125 | 33°42′N | 78°53′W |
| Myrtle Point, Or., U.S. | 114 | 43°04′N | 124°08′W |
| Mysen, Nor. | 166 | 59°32′N | 11°16′E |
| Myshikino, Russia (mēsh′kē-nō) | 176 | 57°48′N | 38°21′E |
| Mysore, India (mī-sōr′) | 199 | 12°31′N | 76°42′E |
| Mysovka, Russia (mē′ sôf-kȧ) | 167 | 55°11′N | 21°17′E |
| Mystic, Ia., U.S. (mĭs′tĭk) | 113 | 40°47′N | 92°54′W |
| Mytilíni, Grc. | 163 | 39°09′N | 26°35′E |
| Mytishchi, Russia (mē-tēsh′chi) | 186b | 55°55′N | 37°46′E |
| Mziha, Tan. | 237 | 5°54′S | 37°47′E |
| Mzimba, Mwi. (′m-zĭm′bä) | 232 | 11°52′S | 33°34′E |
| Mzimkulu, r., Afr. | 233c | 30°12′S | 29°57′E |
| Mzimvubu, r., S. Afr. | 233c | 31°22′S | 29°20′E |
| Mzuzu, Mwi. | 237 | 11°30′S | 34°10′E |


## N


| | | | |
|---|---|---|---|
| Naab, r., Ger. (näp) | 168 | 49°38′N | 12°15′E |
| Naaldwijk, Neth. | 159a | 52°00′N | 4°11′E |
| Nā′ālehu, Hi., U.S. | 126a | 19°00′N | 155°35′W |
| Naantali, Fin. (nän′tȧ-lē) | 167 | 60°29′N | 22°03′E |
| Nabberu, l., Austl. (năb′ẽr-ōō) | 220 | 26°05′S | 120°35′E |


ng-sing; ŋ-baŋk; ɴ-nasalized n; nŏd; cŏmmit; ōld; ōbey; ôrder; oi-boil; fōōd; ō-as oo in foot; ou-out; s-soft; sh-dish; th-thin; pūre; ûnite; ûrn; stŭd; circŭs; ü-as in French tu; ′-indeterminate vowel.

326 Naberezhnyye Chelny – Nduye

PRONOUNCING INDEX


| PLACE (Pronunciation) | PAGE | LAT. | LONG. |
|---|---|---|---|
| Naberezhnyye Chelny, Russia | 178 | 55°42'N | 52°19'E |
| Nabeul, Tun. (nā-bûl') | 230 | 36°34'N | 10°45'E |
| Nabiswera, Ug. | 237 | 1°28'N | 32°16'E |
| Naboomspruit, S. Afr. | 238c | 24°32'S | 28°43'E |
| Nābulus, W.B. | 197a | 32°13'N | 35°16'E |
| Nacala, Moz. (nă-kà'lă) | 233 | 14°34'S | 40°41'E |
| Nacaome, Hond. (nä-kä-ō'mâ) | 132 | 13°32'N | 87°28'W |
| Na Cham, Viet. (nä chäm') | 209 | 22°02'N | 106°30'E |
| Naches, r., Wa., U.S. (năch'ĕz) | 114 | 46°51'N | 121°03'W |
| Náchod, Czech Rep. (näk'ôt) | 168 | 50°25'N | 16°08'E |
| Nacimiento, Lake, res., Ca., U.S. (nȧ-sĭ-myĕn'tô) | 118 | 35°50'N | 121°00'W |
| Nacogdoches, Tx., U.S. (năk'ō-dō'chĕz) | 123 | 31°36'N | 94°40'W |
| Nadadores, Mex. (nä-dä-dō'räs) | 122 | 27°04'N | 101°36'W |
| Nadiād, India | 202 | 22°45'N | 72°51'E |
| Nadir, V.I.U.S. | 129c | 18°19'N | 64°53'W |
| Nădlac, Rom. | 175 | 46°09'N | 20°52'E |
| Nadvirna, Ukr. | 169 | 48°37'N | 24°35'E |
| Nadym, r., Russia (ná'dĭm) | 184 | 64°30'N | 72°48'E |
| Naestved, Den. (nĕst'vĭdh) | 160 | 55°14'N | 11°46'E |
| Nafada, Nig. | 235 | 11°08'N | 11°20'E |
| Nafishah, Egypt | 238d | 30°34'N | 32°15'E |
| Náfplio, Grc. | 175 | 37°33'N | 22°46'E |
| Nafūd ad Daḩy, des., Sau. Ar. | 198 | 22°15'N | 44°15'E |
| Nag, Co, l., China | 202 | 31°38'N | 91°18'E |
| Naga, Phil. (nä'gä) | 213 | 13°37'N | 123°12'E |
| Naga, i., Japan | 211 | 32°09'N | 130°16'E |
| Nagahama, Japan (nä'gä-hä'mä) | 211 | 33°32'N | 132°29'E |
| Nagahama, Japan | 211 | 35°23'N | 136°16'E |
| Nagaland, India | 199 | 25°47'N | 94°15'E |
| Nagano, Japan (nä'gä-nô) | 205 | 36°42'N | 138°12'E |
| Nagaoka, Japan (nä'gà-ō'kà) | 205 | 37°22'N | 138°49'E |
| Nagaoka, Japan | 211b | 34°54'N | 135°42'E |
| Nāgappattinam, India | 199 | 10°48'N | 79°51'E |
| Nagarote, Nic. (nä-gä-rō'tĕ) | 132 | 12°17'N | 86°35'W |
| Nagasaki, Japan (nä'gà-sä'kê) | 205 | 32°48'N | 129°53'E |
| Nāgaur, India | 202 | 27°19'N | 73°41'E |
| Nagaybakskiy, Russia (nà-gày-bäk'skĭ) | 186a | 53°33'N | 59°33'E |
| Nagcarlan, Phil. (näg-kär-län') | 213a | 14°07'N | 121°24'E |
| Nāgercoil, India | 203 | 8°15'N | 77°29'E |
| Nagorno Karabakh, hist. reg., Azer. (nu-gôr'nŭ-kŭ-rŭ-bäk') | 181 | 40°10'N | 46°50'E |
| Nagoya, Japan | 205 | 35°09'N | 136°53'E |
| Nāgpur, India (näg'po͞or) | 199 | 21°12'N | 79°09'E |
| Nagua, Dom. Rep. (nä'gwä) | 135 | 19°20'N | 69°40'W |
| Nagykanizsa, Hung. (nôd'y'kô'nĕ-shô) | 163 | 46°27'N | 17°00'E |
| Nagykőrös, Hung. (nôd'y'kŭ-rûsh) | 169 | 47°02'N | 19°46'E |
| Naha, Japan (nä'hä) | 205 | 26°02'N | 127°43'E |
| Nahanni National Park, rec., Can. | 92 | 62°10'N | 125°15'W |
| Nahant, Ma., U.S. (nȧ-hănt) | 101a | 42°26'N | 70°55'W |
| Nahariyya, Isr. | 197a | 33°01'N | 35°06'E |
| Nahuel Huapi, l., Arg. (nä'wĕl wä'pê) | 144 | 41°00'S | 71°30'W |
| Nahuizalco, El Sal. (nä-wê-zäl'kō) | 132 | 13°50'N | 89°43'W |
| Naic, Phil. (nä-ēk) | 213a | 14°20'N | 120°46'E |
| Naica, Mex. (nä-ē'kä) | 122 | 27°53'N | 105°30'W |
| Naiguata, Pico, mtn., Ven. (pē'kô) | 143b | 10°32'N | 66°44'W |
| Nain, Can. (nīn) | 91 | 56°29'N | 61°52'W |
| Nā'īn, Iran | 201 | 32°52'N | 53°05'E |
| Nairn, Scot., U.K. (nârn) | 164 | 57°35'N | 3°54'W |
| Nairobi, Kenya (nī-rō'bē) | 232 | 1°17'S | 36°49'E |
| Naivasha, Kenya (nī-vä'shȧ) | 232 | 0°47'S | 36°29'E |
| Najd, hist. reg., Sau. Ar. | 198 | 25°18'N | 42°38'E |
| Najin, Kor., N. (nä'jĭn) | 205 | 42°04'N | 130°35'E |
| Najran, des., Sau. Ar. (nŭj-rän') | 198 | 17°29'N | 45°30'E |
| Naju, Kor., S. (nä'jo͞o') | 210 | 35°02'N | 126°42'E |
| Najusa, r., Cuba (nä-ho͞o'sä) | 134 | 20°55'N | 77°55'W |
| Nakatsu, Japan (nä'käts-o͞o) | 210 | 33°34'N | 131°10'E |
| Nakhodka, Russia (nŭ-κôt'kŭ) | 179 | 43°03'N | 133°08'E |
| Nakhon Ratchasima, Thai. | 212 | 14°56'N | 102°14'E |
| Nakhon Sawan, Thai. | 212 | 15°42'N | 100°06'E |
| Nakhon Si Thammarat, Thai. | 212 | 8°27'N | 99°58'E |
| Nakło nad Notecia, Pol. | 169 | 53°10'N | 17°35'E |
| Nakskov, Den. (näk'skou) | 160 | 54°51'N | 11°06'E |
| Naktong, r., Kor., S. (näk'tŭng) | 210 | 36°10'N | 128°30'E |
| Nal'chik, Russia (nál-chĕk') | 181 | 43°30'N | 43°35'E |
| Nalón, r., Spain (nä-lōn') | 172 | 43°15'N | 5°38'W |
| Nālūt, Libya (nä-lo͞ot') | 230 | 31°51'N | 10°49'E |
| Namak, Daryacheh-ye, l., Iran | 198 | 34°58'N | 51°33'E |
| Namakan, l., Mn., U.S. (nă'mȧ-kăn) | 113 | 48°20'N | 92°43'W |
| Namangan, Uzb. (nȧ-mȧn-gän') | 183 | 41°08'N | 71°59'E |
| Namao, Can. | 102g | 53°43'N | 113°30'W |
| Namatanai, Pap. N. Gui. (nä'mä-tȧ-nä'ē) | 213 | 3°43'S | 152°26'E |
| Nambour, Austl. (năm'bôr) | 222 | 26°48'S | 153°00'E |
| Nam Co, l., China (näm tswo) | 204 | 30°30'N | 91°10'E |
| Nam Dinh, Viet. (näm dēnκ') | 212 | 20°30'N | 106°10'E |
| Nametil, Moz. | 237 | 15°43'S | 39°21'E |
| Namhae, i., Kor., S. (näm'hī') | 210 | 34°23'N | 128°05'E |
| Namib Desert, des., Nmb. (nä-mēb') | 232 | 18°45'S | 12°45'E |
| Namibia, nation, Afr. | 232 | 19°30'S | 16°13'E |
| Namoi, r., Austl. (nămoi) | 221 | 30°10'S | 148°43'E |
| Namous, Oued en, r., Alg. (nà-mo͞os') | 162 | 31°48'N | 0°19'W |
| Nampa, Id., U.S. (năm'pȧ) | 104 | 43°35'N | 116°35'W |
| Namp'o, Kor., N. | 205 | 38°47'N | 125°28'E |
| Nampuecha, Moz. | 237 | 13°59'S | 40°18'E |
| Nampula, Moz. | 237 | 15°07'S | 39°15'E |
| Namsos, Nor. (näm'sôs) | 160 | 64°28'N | 11°14'E |
| Namu, Can. | 94 | 51°53'N | 127°50'W |
| Namuli, Serra, mts., Moz. | 237 | 15°05'S | 37°05'E |
| Namur, Bel. (nà-mür') | 161 | 50°29'N | 4°55'E |
| Namutoni, Nmb. (nä-mo͞o-tō'nē) | 232 | 18°45'S | 17°00'E |
| Nan, r., Thai. | 212 | 18°11'N | 100°29'E |
| Nanacamilpa, Mex. (nä-nä-kä-mē'l-pä) | 131a | 19°30'N | 98°33'W |
| Nanaimo, Can. (nȧ-nī'mō) | 90 | 49°10'N | 123°56'W |
| Nanam, Kor., N. (nä'năn') | 210 | 41°38'N | 129°37'E |
| Nanao, Japan (nä'nä-ō) | 210 | 37°03'N | 136°59'E |
| Nan'ao Dao, i., China (nän-ou dou) | 209 | 23°30'N | 117°30'E |
| Nanchang, China (nän'chäng') | 205 | 28°38'N | 115°48'E |
| Nanchangshan Dao, i., China (nän-chäŋ-shän dou) | 206 | 37°56'N | 120°42'E |
| Nancheng, China (nän-chäŋ) | 205 | 26°50'N | 116°40'E |
| Nanchong, China (nän-chôŋ) | 204 | 30°45'N | 106°05'E |
| Nancy, Fr. (näɴ-sē') | 161 | 48°42'N | 6°11'E |
| Nancy Creek, r., Ga., U.S. (năn'cē) | 110c | 33°51'N | 84°25'W |
| Nanda Devi, mtn., India (năn'dä dā'vē) | 199 | 30°30'N | 80°25'E |
| Nānded, India | 202 | 19°13'N | 77°21'E |
| Nandurbār, India | 202 | 21°29'N | 74°13'E |
| Nandyāl, India | 203 | 15°54'N | 78°09'E |
| Nanga Parbat, mtn., Pak. | 202 | 35°20'N | 74°35'E |
| Nangi, India | 202a | 22°30'N | 88°14'E |
| Nangis, Fr. (näɴ-zhē') | 171b | 48°33'N | 3°01'E |
| Nangong, China (nän-gôŋ) | 208 | 37°22'N | 115°22'E |
| Nangweshi, Zam. | 236 | 16°26'S | 23°17'E |
| Nanhuangcheng Dao, i., China (nän-hùäŋ-chŭŋ dou) | 206 | 38°22'N | 120°54'E |
| Nanhui, China | 206 | 31°03'N | 121°45'E |
| Nanjing, China (nän-jyĭŋ) | 205 | 32°04'N | 118°46'E |
| Nanjuma, r., China (nän-jyo͞o-mä) | 206 | 39°37'N | 115°45'E |
| Nanking *see* Nanjing, China | 204 | 32°04'N | 118°46'E |
| Nanle, China (nän-lŭ) | 206 | 36°03'N | 115°13'E |
| Nan Ling, mts., China | 205 | 25°15'N | 111°40'E |
| Nanliu, r., China (nän-lĭō) | 209 | 22°00'N | 109°18'E |
| Nannine, Austl. (nă-nēn') | 218 | 25°50'S | 118°30'E |
| Nanning, China (nän'nĭng') | 204 | 22°56'N | 108°10'E |
| Nanpan, r., China (nän-pän) | 209 | 24°50'N | 105°30'E |
| Nanping, China (nän-pĭŋ) | 205 | 26°40'N | 118°05'E |
| Nansei-shotō, is., Japan | 205 | 27°30'N | 127°00'E |
| Nansemond, Va., U.S. (năn'sē-mŭnd) | 110g | 36°46'N | 76°32'W |
| Nantai Zan, mtn., Japan (nän-tăē zän) | 210 | 36°47'N | 139°28'E |
| Nantes, Fr. (näɴt') | 154 | 47°13'N | 1°37'W |
| Nanteuil-le-Haudouin, Fr. (näɴ-tû-lĕ-ō-dwăɴ') | 171b | 49°08'N | 2°49'E |
| Nanticoke, Pa., U.S. (năn'tĭ-kōk) | 109 | 41°10'N | 76°00'W |
| Nantong, China (nän-tôŋ) | 206 | 32°02'N | 120°51'E |
| Nantong, China | 206 | 32°08'N | 121°06'E |
| Nantucket, i., Ma., U.S. (năn-tŭk'ĕt) | 107 | 41°15'N | 70°05'W |
| Nantwich, Eng., U.K. (nănt'wĭch) | 158a | 53°04'N | 2°31'W |
| Nanxiang, China (nän-shyäŋ) | 206 | 31°17'N | 121°17'E |
| Nanxiong, China (nän-shôŋ) | 209 | 25°10'N | 114°20'E |
| Nanyang, China | 205 | 33°00'N | 112°42'E |
| Nanyang Hu, l., China (nän-yäŋ ho͞o) | 206 | 35°14'N | 116°24'E |
| Nanyuan, China (nän-yüän) | 208a | 39°48'N | 116°24'E |
| Naolinco, Mex. (nä-o-lēŋ'kō) | 131 | 19°39'N | 96°50'W |
| Náousa, Grc. (nä'o͞o-sȧ) | 175 | 40°38'N | 22°05'E |
| Naozhou Dao, i., China (nou-jō dou) | 209 | 20°58'N | 110°58'E |
| Napa, Ca., U.S. (năp'ȧ) | 104 | 38°20'N | 122°17'W |
| Napanee, Can. (năp'ȧ-nē) | 99 | 44°15'N | 77°00'W |
| Naperville, Il., U.S. (nā'pēr-vĭl) | 111a | 41°46'N | 88°09'W |
| Napier, N.Z. (nā'pĭ-ēr) | 221a | 39°30'S | 177°00'E |
| Napierville, Can. (nā'pĭ-ē-vĭl) | 102a | 45°11'N | 73°24'W |
| Naples (Napoli), Italy | 154 | 40°37'N | 14°12'E |
| Naples, Fl., U.S. (nā'p'lz) | 125a | 26°07'N | 81°46'W |
| Napo, r., S.A. (nä'pō) | 142 | 1°49'S | 74°20'W |
| Napoleon, Oh., U.S. (nȧ-pō'lē-ŭn) | 108 | 41°20'N | 84°10'W |
| Napoleonville, La., U.S. (nȧ-pō'lē-ŭn-vĭl) | 123 | 29°56'N | 91°03'W |
| Napoli *see* Naples, Italy | 154 | 40°37'N | 14°12'E |
| Napoli, Golfo di, b., Italy | 162 | 40°29'N | 14°08'E |
| Nappanee, In., U.S. (năp'ȧ-nē) | 108 | 41°30'N | 86°00'W |
| Nara, Japan (nä'rä) | 205 | 34°41'N | 135°50'E |
| Nara, Mali | 230 | 15°09'N | 7°27'W |
| Nara, dept., Japan | 211b | 34°36'N | 135°49'E |
| Nara, r., Russia | 176 | 55°05'N | 37°16'E |
| Narach, Vozyera, l., Bela. | 176 | 54°51'N | 27°00'E |
| Naracoorte, Austl. (nȧ-rȧ-ko͞on'tē) | 218 | 36°50'S | 140°50'E |
| Narashino, Japan | 211a | 35°41'N | 140°01'E |
| Naraspur, India | 203 | 16°32'N | 81°43'E |
| Narberth, Pa., U.S. (när'bûrth) | 110f | 40°01'N | 75°17'W |
| Narbonne, Fr. (nȧr-bōn') | 161 | 43°12'N | 3°00'E |
| Nare, Col. (nä'rĕ) | 142a | 6°12'N | 74°37'W |
| Narew, r., Pol. (när'ĕf) | 169 | 52°43'N | 21°19'E |
| Narmada, r., India | 199 | 22°30'N | 75°30'E |
| Narodnaya, Gora, mtn., Russia (nȧ-rôd'nȧ-yȧ) | 178 | 65°10'N | 60°10'E |
| Naro-Fominsk, Russia (nä'rô-mĕnsk') | 180 | 55°23'N | 36°43'E |
| Narrabeen, Austl. (năr-ȧ-bĭn) | 217b | 33°44'S | 151°18'E |
| Narragansett, R.I., U.S. (năr-ă-găn'sĕt) | 110b | 41°26'N | 71°27'W |
| Narragansett Bay, b., R.I., U.S. | 109 | 41°20'N | 71°15'W |
| Narrandera, Austl. (nȧ-rȧn-dē'rȧ) | 219 | 34°40'S | 146°40'E |
| Narrogin, Austl. (năr'ō-gĭn) | 218 | 33°00'S | 117°15'E |
| Narva, Est. (när'vȧ) | 180 | 59°24'N | 28°12'E |
| Narvacan, Phil. (när-vä-kän') | 213a | 17°27'N | 120°29'E |
| Narva Jõesuu, Est. (nȧr'vȧ ô-ō-ă'so͞o-ô) | 167 | 59°26'N | 28°02'E |
| Narvik, Nor. (när'vêk) | 154 | 68°21'N | 17°18'E |
| Narvskiy Zaliv, b., Eur. (nȧr'vskĭ zä'lĭf) | 167 | 59°35'N | 27°25'E |
| Narvskoye, res., Eur. | 167 | 59°18'N | 28°14'E |
| Nar'yan-Mar, Russia (när'yȧn mär') | 178 | 67°42'N | 53°30'E |
| Naryilco, Austl. (năr-ĭl'kō) | 222 | 28°40'S | 141°50'E |
| Narym, Russia (nä-rēm') | 178 | 58°47'N | 82°05'E |
| Naryn, r., Asia (nŭ-rĭn') | 184 | 41°20'N | 76°00'E |
| Naseby, Eng., U.K. (nāz'bĭ) | 158a | 52°23'N | 0°59'W |
| Nashua, Mo., U.S. (năsh'ū-ȧ) | 117f | 39°18'N | 94°34'W |
| Nashua, N.H., U.S. | 105 | 42°47'N | 71°23'W |
| Nashville, Ar., U.S. (năsh'vĭl) | 121 | 33°56'N | 93°50'W |
| Nashville, Ga., U.S. | 124 | 31°12'N | 83°15'W |
| Nashville, Il., U.S. | 121 | 38°21'N | 89°42'W |
| Nashville, Mi., U.S. | 108 | 42°35'N | 85°50'W |
| Nashville, Tn., U.S. | 105 | 36°10'N | 86°48'W |
| Nashwauk, Mn., U.S. (năsh'wôk) | 113 | 47°21'N | 93°12'W |
| Näsi, l., Fin. | 160 | 61°42'N | 24°05'E |
| Našice, Cro. (nä'shĕ-tsĕ) | 163 | 45°29'N | 18°06'E |
| Nasielsk, Pol. (nä'syĕlsk) | 169 | 52°35'N | 20°50'E |
| Nāsik, India (nä'sĭk) | 199 | 20°02'N | 73°49'E |
| Nāşir, Sudan (nä-zēr') | 231 | 8°30'N | 33°06'E |
| Nasirabād, India | 202 | 26°13'N | 74°48'E |
| Naskaupi, r., Can. (näs'kô-pĭ) | 93 | 53°59'N | 61°10'W |
| Nasondoye, D.R.C. | 237 | 10°22'S | 25°06'E |
| Nass, r., Can. (năs) | 94 | 55°00'N | 129°30'W |
| Nassau, Bah. (năs'ô) | 129 | 25°05'N | 77°20'W |
| Nassenheide, Ger. (nä'sĕn-hī-dĕ) | 159b | 52°49'N | 13°13'E |
| Nasser, Lake, res., Egypt | 231 | 23°50'N | 32°50'E |
| Nasugbu, Phil. (nȧ-sòg-bo͞o') | 213a | 14°05'N | 120°37'E |
| Nasworthy Lake, l., Tx., U.S. (năz'wûr-thê) | 122 | 31°17'N | 100°30'W |
| Natagaima, Col. (nä-tä-gī'mä) | 142a | 3°38'N | 75°07'W |
| Natal, Braz. (nä-täl') | 143 | 6°00'S | 35°13'W |
| Natashquan, Can. (nä-täsh'kwän) | 91 | 50°11'N | 61°49'W |
| Natashquan, r., Can. | 101 | 50°35'N | 61°35'W |
| Natchez, Ms., U.S. (năch'ĕz) | 105 | 31°35'N | 91°20'W |
| Natchitoches, La., U.S. (năk'ĭ-tŏsh) (nách-ĭ-tŏsh') | 123 | 31°46'N | 93°06'W |
| Natick, Ma., U.S. (nā'tĭk) | 101a | 42°17'N | 71°21'W |
| National Bison Range, I.R., Mt., U.S. (năsh'ŭn-ăl bī's'n) | 115 | 47°18'N | 113°58'W |
| National City, Ca., U.S. | 118a | 32°38'N | 117°01'W |
| Natitingou, Benin | 230 | 10°19'N | 1°22'E |
| Natividade, Braz. (nä-tē-vē-dä'dĕ) | 143 | 11°43'S | 47°34'W |
| Natron, Lake, l., Tan. (nā'trŏn) | 232 | 2°17'S | 36°10'E |
| Natrona Heights, Pa., U.S. (nā'trō nȧ) | 111e | 40°38'N | 79°43'W |
| Naţrūn, Wādī an, val., Egypt | 238b | 30°33'N | 30°12'E |
| Natuna Besar, i., Indon. | 212 | 4°00'N | 106°50'E |
| Natural Bridges National Monument, rec., Ut., U.S. (năt'ū-răl brĭj'ĕs) | 119 | 37°20'N | 110°20'W |
| Naturaliste, Cape, c., Austl. (năt-ū-rȧ-lĭst') | 220 | 33°30'S | 115°10'E |
| Nau, Cap de la, c., Spain | 156 | 38°43'N | 0°14'E |
| Naucalpan de Juárez, Mex. | 131a | 19°28'N | 99°14'W |
| Nauchampatepetl, mtn., Mex. (nä'o͞o-chäm-pä-tĕ'pĕtl) | 131 | 19°32'N | 97°09'W |
| Nauen, Ger. (nou'ĕn) | 159b | 52°36'N | 12°53'E |
| Naugatuck, Ct., U.S. (nô'gȧ-tŭk) | 109 | 41°25'N | 73°05'W |
| Naujan, Phil. (nä-ò-hän') | 213a | 13°19'N | 121°17'E |
| Naumburg, Ger. (noum'bòrgh) | 168 | 51°10'N | 11°50'E |
| Nauru, nation, Oc. | 3 | 0°30'S | 167°00'E |
| Nautla, Mex. (nä-o͞ot'lä) | 128 | 20°14'N | 96°44'W |
| Nava, Mex. (nä'vä) | 122 | 28°25'N | 100°44'W |
| Nava del Rey, Spain (nä-vä dĕl rā'ê) | 172 | 41°22'N | 5°04'W |
| Navahermosa, Spain (nä-vä-ĕr-mō'sä) | 172 | 39°39'N | 4°28'W |
| Navajas, Cuba (nä-vä-häs') | 134 | 22°40'N | 81°20'W |
| Navajo Hopi Joint Use Area, I.R., Az., U.S. | 119 | 36°15'N | 110°30'W |
| Navajo Indian Reservation, I.R., U.S. (năv'ȧ-hō) | 119 | 36°31'N | 109°24'W |
| Navajo National Monument, rec., Az., U.S. | 119 | 36°43'N | 110°39'W |
| Navajo Reservoir, res., N.M., U.S. | 119 | 36°57'N | 107°26'W |
| Navalcarnero, Spain (nä-väl'kär-nā'rō) | 173a | 40°17'N | 4°05'W |
| Navalmoral de la Mata, Spain | 172 | 39°53'N | 5°32'W |
| Navan, Can. (nă'vȧn) | 102c | 45°25'N | 75°26'W |
| Navarino, i., Chile (nȧ-vä-rē'nô) | 144 | 55°30'S | 68°15'W |
| Navarra, hist. reg., Spain (nä-vär'rä) | 172 | 42°40'N | 1°35'W |
| Navarro, Arg. (nä-vá'r-rō) | 141c | 35°00'S | 59°16'W |
| Navasota, Tx., U.S. (năv-ȧ-sō'tȧ) | 123 | 30°24'N | 96°05'W |
| Navasota, r., Tx., U.S. | 123 | 31°03'N | 96°11'W |
| Navassa, i., N.A. (nȧ-văs'ȧ) | 135 | 18°25'N | 75°15'W |
| Navia, r., Spain (nä-vē'ä) | 172 | 43°10'N | 6°45'W |
| Navidad, Chile (nä-vē-dä'd) | 141b | 33°57'S | 71°51'W |
| Navidad Bank, bk. (nä-vē-dädh') | 135 | 20°05'N | 69°00'W |
| Navidade do Carangola, Braz. (nȧ-vē-dä'dô-kȧ-rän-gô'la) | 141a | 21°04'S | 41°58'W |
| Navojoa, Mex. (nä-vô-kô'ä) | 128 | 27°00'N | 109°40'W |
| Nawābshāh, Pak. (nȧ-wäb'shä) | 202 | 26°20'N | 68°30'E |
| Naxçıvan, Azer. | 181 | 39°10'N | 45°30'E |
| Naxçıvan Muxtar, state, Azer. | 182 | 39°20'N | 45°30'E |
| Náxos, i., Grc. (nák'sôs) | 163 | 37°15'N | 25°20'E |
| Nayarit, state, Mex. (nä-yä-rēt') | 128 | 22°00'N | 105°15'W |
| Nayarit, Sierra de, mts., Mex. (sē-ĕ'r-rä-dĕ) | 130 | 23°20'N | 105°07'W |
| Naye, Sen. | 234 | 14°25'N | 12°12'W |
| Naylor, Md., U.S. (nā'lōr) | 110e | 38°43'N | 76°46'W |
| Nazaré da Mata, Braz. (dä-mä-tä) | 143 | 7°46'S | 35°13'W |
| Nazas, Mex. (nä'zäs) | 122 | 25°14'N | 104°08'W |
| Nazas, r., Mex. | 128 | 25°30'N | 104°40'W |
| Nazerat, Isr. | 197a | 32°43'N | 35°19'E |
| Nazilli, Tur. (nà-zĭ-lē') | 181 | 37°40'N | 28°10'E |
| Naziya, r., Russia (ná-zē'yá) | 186c | 59°48'N | 31°18'E |
| Nazko, r., Can. | 94 | 52°35'N | 123°10'W |
| N'dalatando, Ang. | 236 | 9°18'S | 14°54'E |
| Ndali, Benin | 235 | 9°51'N | 2°43'E |
| Ndikiniméki, Cam. | 235 | 4°46'N | 10°50'E |
| N'Djamena, Chad | 231 | 12°07'N | 15°03'E |
| Ndola, Zam. (n'dō'lä) | 232 | 12°58'S | 28°38'E |
| Ndoto Mountains, mts., Kenya | 237 | 1°55'N | 37°05'E |
| Ndrhamcha, Sebkha de, l., Maur. | 234 | 18°50'N | 15°15'W |
| Nduye, D.R.C. | 237 | 1°50'N | 29°01'E |


ăt; finăl; rāte; senâte; ärm; ȧsk; sofȧ; fâre; ch-choose; dh-as th in other; bē; ēvent; bĕt; recĕnt; cratẽr; g-gō; gh-guttural g; bĭt; ĭ-short neutral; rīde; κ-guttural k as ch in German ich;

PRONOUNCING INDEX

Neagh – New Providence 327


| PLACE (Pronunciation) | PAGE | LAT. | LONG. |
|---|---|---|---|
| Neagh, Lough, l., N. Ire., U.K. (lŏk nā) | 160 | 54°40'N | 6°47'W |
| Néa Páfos, Cyp. | 197a | 34°46'N | 32°27'E |
| Neapean, r., Austl. | 217b | 33°40'S | 150°39'E |
| Neápoli, Grc. | 175 | 36°35'N | 23°08'E |
| Neápolis, Grc. | 174a | 35°17'N | 25°37'E |
| Near Islands, is., Ak., U.S. (nēr) | 103a | 52°20'N | 172°40'E |
| Neath, Wales, U.K. (nēth) | 164 | 51°41'N | 3°50'W |
| Nebine Creek, r., Austl. (nĕ-bēne′) | 222 | 27°50'S | 147°00'E |
| Nebitdag, Turkmen. | 183 | 39°30'N | 54°20'E |
| Nebraska, state, U.S. (nẻ-brăs′kȧ) | 104 | 41°45'N | 101°30'W |
| Nebraska City, Ne., U.S. | 121 | 40°40'N | 95°50'W |
| Nechako, r., Can. | 94 | 53°45'N | 124°55'W |
| Nechako Plateau, plat., Can. (nĭ-chă′kō) | 94 | 54°00'N | 124°30'W |
| Nechako Range, mts., Can. | 94 | 53°20'N | 124°30'W |
| Nechako Reservoir, res., Can. | 94 | 53°25'N | 125°10'W |
| Neches, r., Tx., U.S. (nĕch′ĕz) | 123 | 31°03'N | 94°40'W |
| Neckar, r., Ger. (nĕk′är) | 168 | 49°16'N | 9°06'E |
| Necker Island, i., Hi., U.S. | 126b | 24°00'N | 164°00'W |
| Necochea, Arg. (nā-kỏ-chā′ä) | 144 | 38°30'S | 58°45'W |
| Nedryhailiv, Ukr. | 177 | 50°49'N | 33°52'E |
| Needham, Ma., U.S. (nēd′ăm) | 101a | 42°17'N | 71°14'W |
| Needles, Ca., U.S. (nē′d'lz) | 119 | 34°51'N | 114°39'W |
| Neenah, Wi., U.S. (nē′nȧ) | 113 | 44°10'N | 88°30'W |
| Neepawa, Can. | 90 | 50°13'N | 99°29'W |
| Nee Reservoir, res., Co., U.S. (nee) | 120 | 38°26'N | 102°56'W |
| Negareyama, Japan (nå′gä-rå-yä′mä) | 211a | 35°52'N | 139°54'E |
| Negaunee, Mi., U.S. (nẻ-gô′nẻ) | 113 | 46°30'N | 87°37'W |
| Negeri Sembilan, state, Malay. (nā′grẻ-sĕm-bẻ-län′) | 197b | 2°46'N | 101°54'E |
| Negev, des., Isr. (nĕ′gĕv) | 197a | 30°34'N | 34°43'E |
| Negombo, Sri L. | 203 | 7°39'N | 79°49'E |
| Negotin, Serb. (nĕ′gỏ-tẻn) | 175 | 44°13'N | 22°33'E |
| Negro, r., Arg. | 144 | 39°50'S | 65°00'W |
| Negro, r., N.A. | 132 | 13°01'N | 87°10'W |
| Negro, r., S.A. | 141c | 33°17'S | 58°18'W |
| Negro, r., S.A. (nā′grȯ) | 142 | 0°18'S | 63°21'W |
| Negro, Cerro, mtn., Pan. (sĕ′-rrỏ-nā′grỏ) | 133 | 8°44'N | 80°37'W |
| Negros, i., Phil. (nā′grōs) | 212 | 9°50'N | 121°45'E |
| Nehalem, r., Or., U.S. (nẻ-hăl′ĕm) | 114 | 45°52'N | 123°37'W |
| Nehaus an der Oste, Ger. (noi′houz) (ōz′tĕ) | 159c | 53°48'N | 9°02'E |
| Nehbandān, Iran | 201 | 31°32'N | 60°02'E |
| Nehe, China (nŭ-hŭ) | 208 | 48°23'N | 124°58'E |
| Neheim-Hüsten, Ger. (nĕ′hīm) | 171c | 51°28'N | 7°58'E |
| Neiba, Dom. Rep. (nå-ē′bä) | 135 | 18°30'N | 71°20'W |
| Neiba, Bahía de, b., Dom. Rep. | 135 | 18°10'N | 71°00'W |
| Neiba, Sierra de, mts., Dom. Rep. (sē-ĕr′rä-dĕ) | 135 | 18°40'N | 71°40'W |
| Neihart, Mt., U.S. (nī′hȧrt) | 115 | 46°54'N | 110°39'W |
| Neijiang, China (nā-jyäŋ) | 209 | 29°38'N | 105°01'E |
| Neillsville, Wi., U.S. (nēlz′vĭl) | 113 | 44°35'N | 90°37'W |
| Nei Monggol (Inner Mongolia), state, China | 204 | 40°15'N | 105°00'E |
| Neiqiu, China (nā-chyō) | 206 | 37°17'N | 114°32'E |
| Neira, Col. (nā′rä) | 142a | 5°10'N | 75°32'W |
| Neisse, r., Eur. (nēs) | 168 | 51°30'N | 15°00'E |
| Neiva, Col. (nå-ē′vä) (nā′vä) | 142 | 2°55'N | 75°16'W |
| Neixiang, China (nā-shyäŋ) | 208 | 33°00'N | 111°38'E |
| Nekemte, Eth. | 231 | 9°09'N | 36°29'E |
| Nekoosa, Wi., U.S. (nẻ-kōō′sȧ) | 113 | 44°19'N | 89°54'W |
| Neligh, Ne., U.S. (nē′-lē) | 112 | 42°06'N | 98°02'W |
| Nel′kan, Russia (nĕl-kän′) | 179 | 57°45'N | 136°36'E |
| Nellore, India (nĕl-lōr′) | 199 | 14°28'N | 79°59'E |
| Nel′ma, Russia (nĕl-mä′) | 210 | 47°34'N | 139°05'E |
| Nelson, Can. (nĕl′sŭn) | 90 | 49°29'N | 117°17'W |
| Nelson, N.Z. | 221a | 41°15'S | 173°22'E |
| Nelson, Eng., U.K. | 158a | 53°50'N | 2°13'W |
| Nelson, i., Ak., U.S. | 103 | 60°38'N | 164°42'W |
| Nelson, r., Can. | 97 | 56°50'N | 93°40'W |
| Nelson, Cape, c., Austl. | 222 | 38°29'S | 141°20'E |
| Nelsonville, Oh., U.S. (nĕl′sŭn-vĭl) | 108 | 39°30'N | 82°15'W |
| Néma, Maur. (nā′mä) | 230 | 16°37'N | 7°15'W |
| Nemadji, r., Wi., U.S. (nĕ-măd′jẻ) | 117h | 46°33'N | 92°16'W |
| Neman, Russia (ŋĕ′-mån) | 167 | 55°02'N | 22°01'E |
| Neman, r., Eur. | 180 | 53°28'N | 24°45'E |
| Nembe, Nig. | 235 | 4°35'N | 6°26'E |
| Nemeiben Lake, l., Can. (nĕ-mē′bån) | 96 | 55°20'N | 105°20'W |
| Nemours, Fr. | 170 | 48°16'N | 2°41'E |
| Nemuro, Japan (nā′mȯ-rō) | 205 | 43°13'N | 145°10'E |
| Nemuro Strait, strt., Asia | 210 | 43°07'N | 145°10'E |
| Nemyriv, Ukr. | 177 | 48°56'N | 28°51'E |
| Nen, r., China (nŭn) | 205 | 47°07'N | 123°28'E |
| Nen, r., Eng., U.K. (nĕn) | 158a | 52°32'N | 0°19'W |
| Nenagh, Ire. (nē′nȧ) | 164 | 52°50'N | 8°05'W |
| Nenana, Ak., U.S. (nå-nä′nȧ) | 103 | 64°28'N | 149°18'W |
| Nenikyul′, Russia (nĕ-nyē′kyûl) | 186c | 59°26'N | 30°40'E |
| Nenjiang, China (nŭn-jyäŋ) | 205 | 49°02'N | 125°15'E |
| Neodesha, Ks., U.S. (nē-ỏ-dĕ-shô′) | 121 | 37°24'N | 95°41'W |
| Neosho, Mo., U.S. | 121 | 36°51'N | 94°22'W |
| Neosho, r., Ks., U.S. (nẻ-ō′shō) | 121 | 38°07'N | 95°40'W |
| Nepal, nation, Asia (nĕ-pôl′) | 199 | 28°45'N | 83°00'E |
| Nephi, Ut., U.S. (nē′fī) | 119 | 39°40'N | 111°50'W |
| Nepomuceno, Braz. (nĕ-pô-mōō-sĕ′no) | 141a | 21°15'S | 45°13'W |
| Nera, r., Italy (nā′rä) | 174 | 42°45'N | 12°54'E |
| Nérac, Fr. (nā-råk′) | 170 | 44°08'N | 0°19'E |
| Nerchinsk, Russia (nyĕr′ chẻnsk) | 179 | 51°47'N | 116°17'E |
| Nerchinskiy Khrebet, mts., Russia | 179 | 50°30'N | 118°30'E |
| Nerchinskiy Zavod, Russia (nyĕr′chẻn-skĭzȧ-vôt′) | 179 | 51°35'N | 119°46'E |
| Nerekhta, Russia (nyĕ-rĕĸ′tȧ) | 176 | 57°29'N | 40°34'E |
| Neretva, r., Serb. (nĕ′rĕt-vȧ) | 175 | 43°08'N | 17°50'E |
| Nerja, Spain (nĕr′hä) | 172 | 36°45'N | 3°53'W |
| Nerl′, r., Russia (nyĕrl) | 176 | 56°59'N | 37°57'E |
| Nerskaya, r., Russia (nyĕr′skȧ-yȧ) | 186b | 55°31'N | 38°46'E |
| Nerussa, r., Russia (nyå-rōō′sȧ) | 176 | 52°24'N | 34°20'E |
| Ness, Loch, l., Scot., U.K. (lŏĸ nĕs) | 164 | 57°23'N | 4°20'W |
| Ness City, Ks., U.S. (nĕs) | 120 | 38°27'N | 99°55'W |
| Nesterov, Russia (nyĕs-tă′rôf) | 167 | 54°39'N | 22°38'E |
| Néstos (Mesta), r., Eur. (nās′tōs) | 175 | 41°25'N | 24°12'E |
| Netanya, Isr. | 197a | 32°19'N | 34°52'E |
| Netcong, N.J., U.S. (nĕt′cŏnj) | 110a | 40°54'N | 74°42'W |
| Netherlands, nation, Eur. (nĕdh′ẽr-lăndz) | 154 | 53°01'N | 3°57'E |
| Netherlands Guiana *see* Suriname, nation, S.A. | 143 | 4°00'N | 56°00'W |
| Nettilling, l., Can. | 93 | 66°30'N | 70°40'W |
| Nett Lake Indian Reservation, I.R., Mn., U.S. (nĕt lāk) | 113 | 48°23'N | 93°19'W |
| Nettuno, Italy (nĕt-tōō′nô) | 173d | 41°28'N | 12°40'E |
| Neubeckum, Ger. (noi′bĕ-kōōm) | 171c | 51°48'N | 8°01'E |
| Neubrandenburg, Ger. (noi-brän′dĕn-bȯrgh) | 168 | 53°33'N | 13°16'E |
| Neuburg, Ger. (noi′bȯrgh) | 168 | 48°43'N | 11°12'E |
| Neuchâtel, Switz. (nû-shȧ-tĕl′) | 161 | 47°00'N | 6°52'E |
| Neuchâtel, Lac de, l., Switz. | 168 | 46°48'N | 6°53'E |
| Neuenhagen, Ger. (noi′ĕn-hä-gĕn) | 159b | 52°31'N | 13°41'E |
| Neuenrade, Ger. (noi′ĕn-rä-dĕ) | 171c | 51°17'N | 7°47'E |
| Neufchâtel-en-Bray, Fr. (nû-shä-tĕl′ĕɴ-brā′) | 170 | 49°43'N | 1°25'E |
| Neulengbach, Aus. | 159e | 48°13'N | 15°55'E |
| Neumarkt, Ger. (noi′märkt) | 168 | 49°17'N | 11°30'E |
| Neumünster, Ger. (noi′münstẽr) | 160 | 54°04'N | 10°00'E |
| Neunkirchen, Aus. (noin′kĭrĸ-ĕn) | 168 | 47°43'N | 16°05'E |
| Neuquén, Arg. (nĕ-ȯ-kān′) | 144 | 38°52'S | 68°12'W |
| Neuquén, prov., Arg. | 144 | 39°40'S | 70°45'W |
| Neuquén, r., Arg. | 144 | 38°45'S | 69°00'W |
| Neuruppin, Ger. (noi′rōō-pēn) | 168 | 52°55'N | 12°48'E |
| Neuse, r., N.C., U.S. (nūz) | 125 | 36°12'N | 78°50'W |
| Neusiedler See, l., Eur. (noi-zēd′lẽr) | 168 | 47°54'N | 16°31'E |
| Neuss, Ger. (nois) | 171c | 51°12'N | 6°41'E |
| Neustadt, Ger. (noi′shtät) | 168 | 49°21'N | 8°08'E |
| Neustadt bei Coburg, Ger. (bī kō′bōōrgh) | 168 | 50°20'N | 11°09'E |
| Neustadt in Holstein, Ger. | 168 | 54°06'N | 10°50'E |
| Neustrelitz, Ger. (noi-strā′lĭts) | 168 | 53°21'N | 13°05'E |
| Neutral Hills, hills, Can. (nū′trăl) | 96 | 52°10'N | 110°50'W |
| Neu Ulm, Ger. (noi ȯ lm′) | 168 | 48°23'N | 10°01'E |
| Neuville, Can. (nū′vĭl) | 102b | 46°39'N | 71°35'W |
| Neuwied, Ger. (noi′vēdt) | 168 | 50°26'N | 7°28'E |
| Neva, r., Russia (nyĕ-vä′) | 176 | 59°49'N | 30°54'E |
| Nevada, Ia., U.S. (nẻ-vä′dȧ) | 113 | 42°01'N | 93°27'W |
| Nevada, Mo., U.S. | 121 | 37°49'N | 94°21'W |
| Nevada, state, U.S. (nĕ vȧ′dȧ) | 104 | 39°30'N | 117°00'W |
| Nevada, Sierra, mts., Spain (syĕr′rä nā-vä′dhä) | 156 | 37°01'N | 3°28'W |
| Nevada, Sierra, mts., U.S. (sē-ĕ′r-rä nẻ-vä′dȧ) | 106 | 39°20'N | 120°05'W |
| Nevado, Cerro el, mtn., Col. (sĕ′r-rỏ-ĕl-nĕ-vä′dỏ) | 142a | 4°02'N | 74°08'W |
| Neva Stantsiya, Russia (nyĕ-vä′ stän′tsĭ-yȧ) | 186c | 59°53'N | 30°30'E |
| Neve, Serra da, mts., Ang. | 236 | 13°40'S | 13°20'E |
| Nevel′, Russia (nyĕ′vĕl) | 180 | 56°03'N | 29°57'E |
| Neveri, r., Ven. (nĕ-vĕ-rē) | 143b | 10°13'N | 64°18'W |
| Nevers, Fr. (nẽ-vår′) | 161 | 46°59'N | 3°10'E |
| Neves, Braz. | 144b | 22°51'S | 43°06'W |
| Nevesinje, Bos. (nĕ-vĕ′sẻn-yĕ) | 175 | 43°15'N | 18°08'E |
| Nevinnomiyssk, Russia | 182 | 44°38'N | 41°56'E |
| Nevis, i., St. K./N. (nē′vĭs) | 129 | 17°05'N | 62°38'W |
| Nevis, Ben, mtn., Scot., U.K. (bĕn) | 160 | 56°47'N | 5°00'W |
| Nevis Peak, mtn., St. K./N. | 133b | 17°11'N | 62°33'W |
| Nevşehir, Tur. (nĕv-shĕ′hẻr) | 163 | 38°40'N | 34°35'E |
| Nev′yansk, Russia (nĕv-yänsk′) | 178 | 57°29'N | 60°14'E |
| New, r., Va., U.S. (nū) | 125 | 37°20'N | 80°35'W |
| Newala, Tan. | 237 | 10°56'S | 39°18'E |
| New Albany, In., U.S. (nû ôl′bȧ-nĭ) | 111h | 38°17'N | 85°49'W |
| New Albany, Ms., U.S. | 125 | 34°28'N | 39°00'W |
| New Amsterdam, Guy. (ăm′stẽr-dăm) | 143 | 6°14'N | 57°30'W |
| Newark, Eng., U.K. (nū′ẽrk) | 158a | 53°04'N | 0°49'W |
| Newark, Ca., U.S. (nū′ẽrk) | 116b | 37°32'N | 122°02'W |
| Newark, De., U.S. (nōō′ärk) | 109 | 39°40'N | 75°45'W |
| Newark, N.J., U.S. (nōō′ûrk) | 105 | 40°44'N | 74°10'W |
| Newark, N.Y., U.S. (nū′ẽrk) | 109 | 43°05'N | 77°10'W |
| Newark, Oh., U.S. | 108 | 40°05'N | 82°25'W |
| Newaygo, Mi., U.S. (nū′wā-go) | 108 | 43°25'N | 85°50'W |
| New Bedford, Ma., U.S. (bĕd′fẽrd) | 105 | 41°35'N | 70°55'W |
| Newberg, Or., U.S. (nū′bûrg) | 108 | 45°17'N | 122°58'W |
| New Bern, N.C., U.S. (bûrn) | 105 | 35°05'N | 77°05'W |
| Newbern, Tn., U.S. | 124 | 36°05'N | 89°12'W |
| Newberry, Mi., U.S. (nū′bĕr-ĭ) | 113 | 46°22'N | 85°31'W |
| Newberry, S.C., U.S. | 125 | 34°15'N | 81°40'W |
| New Boston, Mi., U.S. (bôs′tŭn) | 111b | 42°10'N | 83°24'W |
| New Boston, Oh., U.S. | 108 | 38°45'N | 82°55'W |
| New Braunfels, Tx., U.S. (nū broun′fĕls) | 122 | 29°43'N | 98°07'W |
| New Brighton, Mn., U.S. (brī′tŭn) | 117g | 45°04'N | 93°12'W |
| New Brighton, Pa., U.S. | 111e | 40°34'N | 80°18'W |
| New Britain, Ct., U.S. (brĭt′'n) | 109 | 41°40'N | 72°45'W |
| New Britain, i., Pap. N. Gui. | 213 | 6°45'S | 149°38'E |
| New Brunswick, N.J., U.S. (brŭnz′wĭk) | 110a | 40°29'N | 74°27'W |
| New Brunswick, prov., Can. | 91 | 47°14'N | 66°30'W |
| Newburg, In., U.S. | 108 | 38°00'N | 87°25'W |
| Newburg, Mo., U.S. | 121 | 37°54'N | 91°53'W |
| Newburgh, N.Y., U.S. | 109 | 41°30'N | 74°00'W |
| Newburgh Heights, Oh., U.S. | 111d | 41°27'N | 81°40'W |
| Newbury, Eng., U.K. (nū′bẽr-ĭ) | 164 | 51°24'N | 1°26'W |
| Newbury, Ma., U.S. | 101a | 42°48'N | 70°52'W |
| Newbury, co., Eng., U.K. | 158b | 51°25'N | 1°15'W |
| Newburyport, Ma., U.S. (nū′bẽr-ĭ-pōrt) | 101a | 42°48'N | 70°53'W |
| New Caledonia, dep., Oc. | 219 | 21°28'S | 164°40'E |
| New Canaan, Ct., U.S. (kā-nȧn) | 110a | 41°06'N | 73°30'W |
| New Carlisle, Can. (kär-līl′) | 91 | 48°01'N | 65°20'W |
| Newcastle, Austl. (nū-kȧs′'l) | 222 | 33°00'S | 151°55'E |
| Newcastle, Can. | 91 | 47°00'N | 65°34'W |
| New Castle, De., U.S. | 109 | 39°40'N | 75°35'W |
| New Castle, In., U.S. | 108 | 39°55'N | 85°25'W |
| New Castle, Oh., U.S. | 108 | 40°20'N | 82°10'W |
| New Castle, Pa., U.S. | 108 | 41°00'N | 80°25'W |
| Newcastle, Tx., U.S. | 120 | 33°13'N | 98°44'W |
| Newcastle, Wy., U.S. | 112 | 43°51'N | 104°11'W |
| Newcastle under Lyme, Eng., U.K. (nů-kȧs′'l) (nů-käs′'l) | 158a | 53°01'N | 2°14'W |
| Newcastle upon Tyne, Eng., U.K. | 154 | 55°00'N | 1°45'W |
| Newcastle Waters, Austl. (wô′tẽrz) | 218 | 17°10'S | 133°25'E |
| Newcomerstown, Oh., U.S. (nū′kŭm-ẽrz-toun) | 108 | 40°15'N | 81°40'W |
| New Croton Reservoir, res., N.Y., U.S. (krŏ′tôn) | 110a | 41°15'N | 73°47'W |
| New Delhi, India (dĕl′hī) | 199 | 28°43'N | 77°18'E |
| Newell, S.D., U.S. (nū′ĕl) | 112 | 44°43'N | 103°26'W |
| New England Range, mts., Austl. (nů ĭŋ′glănd) | 221 | 29°32'S | 152°30'E |
| Newenham, Cape, c., Ak., U.S. (nū-ĕn-hăm) | 103 | 58°40'N | 162°32'W |
| Newfane, N.Y., U.S. (nū-fān) | 111c | 43°17'N | 78°44'W |
| Newfoundland, i., Can. | 93a | 48°30'N | 56°00'W |
| Newfoundland and Labrador, prov., Can. | 91 | 48°15'N | 56°53'W |
| Newgate, Can. (nů′gāt) | 95 | 49°01'N | 115°10'W |
| New Georgia, i., Sol. Is. (jôr′jĭ-ȧ) | 221 | 8°08'S | 158°00'E |
| New Georgia Group, is., Sol. Is. | 214e | 8°30'S | 157°20'E |
| New Georgia Sound, strt., Sol. Is. | 214e | 8°00'S | 158°10'E |
| New Glasgow, Can. (glȧs′gō) | 91 | 45°35'N | 62°36'W |
| New Guinea, i. (gĭne) | 213 | 5°45'S | 140°00'E |
| Newhalem, Wa., U.S. (nū hā′lŭm) | 114 | 48°44'N | 121°11'W |
| New Hampshire, state, U.S. (hămp′shĭr) | 105 | 43°55'N | 71°40'W |
| New Hampton, Ia., U.S. (hămp′tŭn) | 113 | 43°03'N | 92°20'W |
| New Hanover, S. Afr. (hăn′ỏvẽr) | 233c | 29°23'S | 30°32'E |
| New Hanover, i., Pap. N. Gui. | 213 | 2°37'S | 150°15'E |
| New Harmony, In., U.S. (nū här′mỏ-nĭ) | 108 | 38°10'N | 87°55'W |
| New Haven, Ct., U.S. (hā′vĕn) | 105 | 41°20'N | 72°55'W |
| New Haven, In., U.S. (nū hāv′'n) | 108 | 41°05'N | 85°00'W |
| New Hebrides, is., Vanuatu | 221 | 16°00'S | 167°00'E |
| New Holland, Eng., U.K. (hŏl′ănd) | 158a | 53°42'N | 0°21'W |
| New Holland, N.C., U.S. | 125 | 35°27'N | 76°14'W |
| New Hope Mountain, mtn., Al., U.S. (hōp) | 110h | 33°23'N | 86°45'W |
| New Hudson, Mi., U.S. (hŭd′sŭn) | 111b | 42°30'N | 83°36'W |
| New Iberia, La., U.S. (ī-bē′rĭ-ȧ) | 123 | 30°00'N | 91°50'W |
| Newington, Can. (nū′ẻng-tŏn) | 102c | 45°07'N | 75°00'W |
| New Ireland, i., Pap. N. Gui. (īr′lănd) | 213 | 3°15'S | 152°30'E |
| New Jersey, state, U.S. (jûr′zĭ) | 105 | 40°30'N | 74°50'W |
| New Kensington, Pa., U.S. (kĕn′zĭng-tŭn) | 111e | 40°34'N | 79°35'W |
| Newkirk, Ok., U.S. (nū′kûrk) | 121 | 36°52'N | 97°03'W |
| New Lenox, Il., U.S. (lĕn′ŭk) | 111a | 41°31'N | 87°58'W |
| New Lexington, Oh., U.S. (lĕk′sĭng-tŭn) | 108 | 39°40'N | 82°10'W |
| New Lisbon, Wi., U.S. (lĭz′bŭn) | 113 | 43°52'N | 90°11'W |
| New Liskeard, Can. | 99 | 47°30'N | 79°40'W |
| New London, Ct., U.S. (lŭn′dŭn) | 109 | 41°20'N | 72°05'W |
| New London, Wi., U.S. | 113 | 44°24'N | 88°45'W |
| New Madrid, Mo., U.S. (măd′rĭd) | 121 | 36°34'N | 89°31'W |
| Newman′s Grove, Ne., U.S. (nū′măn grōv) | 112 | 41°46'N | 97°44'W |
| Newmarket, Can. (nū′mär-kĕt) | 99 | 44°00'N | 79°30'W |
| New Martinsville, W.V., U.S. (mär′tĭnz-vĭl) | 108 | 39°35'N | 80°50'W |
| New Meadows, Id., U.S. | 114 | 44°58'N | 116°20'W |
| New Mexico, state, U.S. (mĕk′sĭ-kō) | 104 | 34°30'N | 107°10'W |
| New Mills, Eng., U.K. (mĭlz) | 158a | 53°22'N | 2°00'W |
| New Munster, Wi., U.S. (mŭn′stẽr) | 111a | 42°35'N | 88°13'W |
| Newnan, Ga., U.S. (nū′năn) | 124 | 33°22'N | 84°47'W |
| New Norfolk, Austl. (nôr′fŏk) | 219 | 42°50'S | 147°17'E |
| New Orleans, La., U.S. (ôr′lê-ănz) | 105 | 30°00'N | 90°05'W |
| New Philadelphia, Oh., U.S. (fĭl-ȧ-dĕl′fĭ-ȧ) | 108 | 40°30'N | 81°30'W |
| New Plymouth, N.Z. (plĭm′ūth) | 221a | 39°04'S | 174°13'E |
| Newport, Austl. | 217b | 33°39'S | 151°19'E |
| Newport, Eng., U.K. (nū-pôrt) | 164 | 50°41'N | 1°25'W |
| Newport, Eng., U.K. | 158a | 52°46'N | 2°22'W |
| Newport, Wales, U.K. | 161 | 51°36'N | 3°05'W |
| Newport, Ar., U.S. (nū′pōrt) | 121 | 35°35'N | 91°16'W |
| Newport, Ky., U.S. | 105 | 39°05'N | 84°30'W |
| Newport, Me., U.S. | 100 | 44°49'N | 69°20'W |
| Newport, Mn., U.S. | 117g | 44°52'N | 92°59'W |
| Newport, N.H., U.S. | 109 | 43°20'N | 72°10'W |
| Newport, Or., U.S. | 114 | 44°39'N | 124°02'W |
| Newport, R.I., U.S. | 109 | 41°29'N | 71°16'W |
| Newport, Tn., U.S. | 124 | 35°55'N | 83°12'W |
| Newport, Vt., U.S. | 109 | 44°55'N | 72°15'W |
| Newport, Wa., U.S. | 114 | 48°12'N | 117°01'W |
| Newport Beach, Ca., U.S. (bēch) | 117a | 33°36'N | 117°55'W |
| Newport News, Va., U.S. | 105 | 36°59'N | 76°24'W |
| New Prague, Mn., U.S. (nū prāg) | 113 | 44°33'N | 93°35'W |
| New Providence, i., Bah. (prŏv′ĭ-dĕns) | 134 | 25°00'N | 77°25'W |


ng-sing; ŋ-baŋk; ɴ-nasalized n; nŏd; cŏmmit; ōld; ỏbey; ôrder; oi-boil; fōōd; ȯ-as oo in foot; ou-out; s-soft; sh-dish; th-thin; pūre; ůnite; ûrn; stŭd; circŭs; ü-as in French tu; ′-indeterminate vowel.

328 New Richmond – Norman

PRONOUNCING INDEX


| PLACE (Pronunciation) | PAGE | LAT. | LONG. |
|---|---|---|---|
| New Richmond, Oh., U.S. (rĭch′mŭnd) | 108 | 38°55′N | 84°15′W |
| New Richmond, Wi., U.S. | 113 | 45°07′N | 92°34′W |
| New Roads, La., U.S. (rōds) | 123 | 30°42′N | 91°26′W |
| New Rochelle, N.Y., U.S. (rū-shĕl′) | 110a | 40°55′N | 73°47′W |
| New Rockford, N.D., U.S. (rŏk′fŏrd) | 112 | 47°40′N | 99°08′W |
| New Ross, Ire. (rôs) | 164 | 52°25′N | 6°55′W |
| New Sarepta, Can. | 102g | 53°17′N | 113°09′W |
| New Siberian Islands *see* Novosibirskiye Ostrova, is., Russia | 179 | 74°00′N | 140°30′E |
| New Smyrna Beach, Fl., U.S. (smûr′nȧ) | 125 | 29°00′N | 80°57′W |
| New South Wales, state, Austl. (wālz) | 219 | 32°45′S | 146°14′E |
| Newton, Can. (nū′tŭn) | 102f | 49°56′N | 98°04′W |
| Newton, Eng., U.K. | 158a | 53°27′N | 2°37′W |
| Newton, Ia., U.S. | 113 | 41°42′N | 93°04′W |
| Newton, Il., U.S. | 108 | 39°00′N | 88°10′W |
| Newton, Ks., U.S. | 121 | 38°03′N | 97°22′W |
| Newton, Ma., U.S. | 101a | 42°21′N | 71°13′W |
| Newton, Ms., U.S. | 124 | 32°18′N | 89°10′W |
| Newton, N.C., U.S. | 125 | 35°40′N | 81°19′W |
| Newton, N.J., U.S. | 110a | 41°03′N | 74°45′W |
| Newton, Tx., U.S. | 123 | 30°47′N | 93°45′W |
| Newtonsville, Oh., U.S. (nū′tŭnz-vĭl) | 111f | 39°11′N | 84°04′W |
| Newtown, N.D., U.S. (nū′toun) | 112 | 47°57′N | 102°25′W |
| Newtown, Oh., U.S. | 111f | 39°08′N | 84°22′W |
| Newtown, Pa., U.S. | 110f | 40°13′N | 74°56′W |
| Newtownards, N. Ire., U.K. (nu-t′n-ardz′) | 164 | 54°35′N | 5°39′W |
| New Ulm, Mn., U.S. (ŭlm) | 113 | 44°18′N | 94°27′W |
| New Waterford, Can. (wô′tẽr-fẽrd) | 91 | 46°15′N | 60°05′W |
| New Westminster, Can. (wĕst′mĭn-stẽr) | 95 | 49°12′N | 122°55′W |
| New York, N.Y., U.S. (yôrk) | 105 | 40°40′N | 73°58′W |
| New York, state, U.S. | 105 | 42°45′N | 78°05′W |
| New Zealand, nation, Oc. (zē′lănd) | 221a | 42°00′S | 175°00′E |
| Nexapa, r., Mex. (nĕks-ä′pä) | 130 | 18°32′N | 98°29′W |
| Neya-gawa, Japan (nā′yä gä′wä) | 211b | 34°47′N | 135°38′E |
| Neyshābūr, Iran | 198 | 36°06′N | 58°45′E |
| Neyva, r., Russia (nĕy′vȧ) | 186a | 57°39′N | 60°37′E |
| Nezahualcóyotl, Mex. | 131a | 19°27′N | 99°03′W |
| Nez Perce, Id., U.S. (nĕz′ pûrs′) | 114 | 46°16′N | 116°15′W |
| Nez Perce Indian Reservation, I.R., Id., U.S. | 114 | 46°20′N | 116°30′W |
| Ngami, l., Bots. (n′gä′mē) | 232 | 20°56′S | 22°31′E |
| Ngambangerabeli Plain, pl., Kenya | 237 | 1°20′S | 40°10′E |
| Ngangla Ringco, l., China (näŋ-lä rĭŋ-tswo) | 202 | 31°42′N | 82°53′E |
| Ngarimbi, Tan. | 237 | 8°28′S | 38°36′E |
| Ngoko, r., Afr. | 236 | 1°55′N | 15°53′E |
| Ngol-Kedju Hill, mtn., Cam. | 235 | 6°20′N | 9°45′E |
| Ngong, Kenya (′n-gông) | 232 | 1°27′S | 36°39′E |
| Ngounié, r., Gabon | 236 | 1°15′S | 10°43′E |
| Ngoywa, Tan. | 237 | 5°56′S | 32°48′E |
| Ngqeleni, S. Afr. (′ng-kĕ-lā′nē) | 233c | 31°41′S | 29°04′E |
| Nguigmi, Niger (′n-gĕg′mē) | 231 | 14°15′N | 13°07′E |
| Ngurore, Nig. | 235 | 9°18′N | 12°14′E |
| Nguru, Nig. (′n-gōō′rōō) | 230 | 12°53′N | 10°26′E |
| Nguru Mountains, mts., Tan. | 237 | 6°10′S | 37°35′E |
| Nha Trang, Viet. (nyä-träng′) | 212 | 12°08′N | 108°56′E |
| Niafounke, Mali | 230 | 16°03′N | 4°17′W |
| Niagara, Wi., U.S. (nī-ăg′ȧ-rȧ) | 113 | 45°45′N | 88°05′W |
| Niagara, r., N.A. | 111c | 43°12′N | 79°03′W |
| Niagara Falls, Can. | 111c | 43°05′N | 79°05′W |
| Niagara Falls, N.Y., U.S. | 105 | 43°06′N | 79°02′W |
| Niagara-on-the-Lake, Can. | 102d | 43°16′N | 79°05′W |
| Niakaramandougou, C. Iv. | 234 | 8°40′N | 5°17′W |
| Niamey, Niger (nē-ä-mā′) | 230 | 13°31′N | 2°07′E |
| Niamtougou, Togo | 234 | 9°46′N | 1°06′E |
| Niangara, D.R.C. (nē-äŋ-gä′rȧ) | 231 | 3°42′N | 27°52′E |
| Niangua, r., Mo., U.S. (nī-ăŋ′gwȧ) | 121 | 37°30′N | 93°05′W |
| Nias, Pulau, i., Indon. (nē′äs′) | 212 | 0°58′N | 97°43′E |
| Nibe, Den. (nē′bĕ) | 166 | 56°57′N | 9°36′E |
| Nicaragua, nation, N.A. (nĭk-ȧ-rä′gwȧ) | 128 | 12°45′N | 86°15′W |
| Nicaragua, Lago de, l., Nic. (lä′gô dĕ) | 128 | 11°45′N | 85°28′W |
| Nicastro, Italy (nē-käs′trō) | 163 | 38°39′N | 16°15′E |
| Nicchehabin, Punta, c., Mex. (pōō′n-tä-nĕk-chĕ-ä-bē′n) | 132a | 19°50′N | 87°20′W |
| Nice, Fr. (nēs) | 154 | 43°42′N | 7°21′E |
| Nicheng, China (nē-chŭŋ) | 207b | 30°54′N | 121°48′E |
| Nichicun, l., Can. (nĭch′ĭ-kŭn) | 93 | 53°07′N | 72°10′W |
| Nicholas Channel, strt., N.A. (nĭk′ô-lȧs) | 134 | 23°30′N | 80°20′W |
| Nicholasville, Ky., U.S. (nĭk′ô-lȧs-vĭl) | 108 | 37°55′N | 84°35′W |
| Nicobar Islands, is., India (nĭk-ô-bär′) | 212 | 8°28′N | 94°04′E |
| Nicolai Mountain, mtn., Or., U.S. (nē-cō lī′) | 116c | 46°05′N | 123°27′W |
| Nicolás Romero, Mex. (nē-kô-lá′s rô-mĕ′rô) | 131a | 19°38′N | 99°20′W |
| Nicolet, Lake, l., Mi., U.S. (nĭ′kō-lĕt) | 117k | 46°22′N | 84°14′W |
| Nicolls Town, Bah. | 134 | 25°10′N | 78°00′W |
| Nicols, Mn., U.S. (nĭk′ĕls) | 117g | 44°50′N | 93°12′W |
| Nicomeki, r., Can. | 116d | 49°04′N | 122°47′W |
| Nicosia, Cyp. (nē-kô-sē′ȧ) | 198 | 35°10′N | 33°22′E |
| Nicoya, C.R. (nē-kō′yä) | 132 | 10°08′N | 85°27′W |
| Nicoya, Golfo de, b., C.R. (gôl-fô-dĕ) | 132 | 10°03′N | 85°04′W |
| Nicoya, Península de, pen., C.R. | 132 | 10°05′N | 86°00′W |
| Nidzica, Pol. (nē-jēt′sä) | 169 | 53°21′N | 20°30′E |
| Niedere Tauern, mts., Aus. | 168 | 47°15′N | 13°41′E |
| Niederkrüchten, Ger. (nē′dĕr-krük-tĕn) | 171c | 51°12′N | 6°14′E |
| Niederösterreich, state, Aus. | 159e | 48°24′N | 16°20′E |
| Niedersachsen (Lower Saxony), state, Ger. (nē′dĕr-zäĸ-sĕn) | 159c | 53°30′N | 9°30′E |
| Niellim, Chad | 235 | 9°42′N | 17°49′E |
| Nienburg, Ger. (nē′ĕn-bôrgh) | 168 | 52°40′N | 9°15′E |
| Nietverdiend, S. Afr. | 238c | 25°02′S | 26°10′E |
| Nieuw Nickerie, Sur. (nē-nē′kĕ-rē′) | 143 | 5°51′N | 57°00′W |
| Nieves, Mex. (nyā′vås) | 130 | 24°00′N | 102°57′W |
| Niğde, Tur. (nĭg′dĕ) | 163 | 37°55′N | 34°40′E |
| Nigel, S. Afr. (nī′jĕl) | 238c | 26°26′S | 28°27′E |
| Niger, nation, Afr. (nī′jẽr) | 230 | 18°02′N | 8°30′E |
| Niger, r., Afr. | 230 | 8°00′N | 6°00′E |
| Niger Delta, d., Nig. | 235 | 4°45′N | 5°20′E |
| Nigeria, nation, Afr. (nī-jē′rĭ-ȧ) | 230 | 8°57′N | 6°30′E |
| Nihoa, i., Hi., U.S. | 126b | 23°15′N | 161°30′W |
| Nii, i., Japan (nē) | 211 | 34°26′N | 139°23′E |
| Niigata, Japan (nē′ē-gä′tȧ) | 205 | 37°47′N | 139°04′E |
| Ni′ihau, i., Hi., U.S. (nē′ē-hä′ōō) | 106c | 21°50′N | 160°05′W |
| Niimi, Japan (nē′mē) | 211 | 34°59′N | 133°28′E |
| Niiza, Japan | 211a | 35°48′N | 139°34′E |
| Nijmegen, Neth. (nī′mā-gĕn) | 165 | 51°50′N | 5°52′E |
| Nikitinka, Russia (nē-kĭ′tĭn-kȧ) | 176 | 55°33′N | 33°19′E |
| Nikolayevka, Russia (nē-kô-lä′yĕf-kȧ) | 186c | 59°29′N | 29°48′E |
| Nikolayevka, Russia | 210 | 48°37′N | 134°09′E |
| Nikolayevskiy, Russia | 181 | 50°00′N | 45°30′E |
| Nikolayevsk-na-Amure, Russia | 179 | 53°18′N | 140°49′E |
| Nikol′sk, Russia (nē-kôlsk′) | 178 | 59°30′N | 45°40′E |
| Nikol′skoye, Russia (nē-kôl′skô-yĕ) | 186c | 59°27′N | 30°00′E |
| Nikopol, Blg. (nē′kô-pōl′) | 163 | 43°41′N | 24°52′E |
| Nikopol′, Ukr. | 181 | 47°36′N | 34°24′E |
| Nilahue, r., Chile (nē-lȧ′wĕ) | 141b | 34°36′S | 71°50′W |
| Nile, r., Afr. (nīl) | 231 | 27°30′N | 31°00′E |
| Niles, Mi., U.S. (nīlz) | 108 | 41°50′N | 86°15′W |
| Niles, Oh., U.S. | 108 | 41°15′N | 80°45′W |
| Nileshwar, India | 203 | 12°08′N | 74°14′E |
| Nilgiri Hills, hills, India | 203 | 12°05′N | 76°22′E |
| Nilópolis, Braz. (nē-lô′pō-lēs) | 141a | 22°48′S | 43°25′W |
| Nīmach, India | 202 | 24°32′N | 74°51′E |
| Nimba, Mont, mtn., Afr. (nĭm′bȧ) | 230 | 7°40′N | 8°33′W |
| Nimba Mountains, mts., Afr. | 234 | 7°30′N | 8°35′W |
| Nîmes, Fr. (nēm) | 154 | 43°49′N | 4°22′E |
| Nimrod Reservoir, res., Ar., U.S. (nĭm′rŏd) | 121 | 34°58′N | 93°46′W |
| Nimule, Sudan (nē-mōō′lā) | 231 | 3°38′N | 32°12′E |
| Ninda, Ang. | 236 | 14°47′S | 21°24′E |
| Nine Mile Creek, r., Ut., U.S. (mīn′īmōd′) | 119 | 39°50′N | 110°30′W |
| Ninety Mile Beach, cst., Austl. | 221 | 38°20′S | 147°30′E |
| Nineveh, Iraq (nĭn′ĕ-vȧ) | 198 | 36°30′N | 43°10′E |
| Ning′an, China (nĭŋ-än) | 205 | 44°20′N | 129°20′E |
| Ningbo, China (nĭŋ-bwo) | 205 | 29°56′N | 121°30′E |
| Ningde, China (nĭŋ-dŭ) | 205 | 26°38′N | 119°33′E |
| Ninghai, China (nĭng′hī′) | 209 | 29°20′N | 121°20′E |
| Ninghe, China (nĭŋ-hŭ) | 206 | 39°20′N | 117°50′E |
| Ningjin, China (nĭŋ-jyĭn) | 206 | 37°39′N | 116°47′E |
| Ningjin, China | 206 | 37°37′N | 114°55′E |
| Ningming, China | 209 | 22°22′N | 107°06′E |
| Ningwu, China (nĭng′wōō′) | 205 | 39°00′N | 112°12′E |
| Ningxia Huizu, prov., China (nĭŋ-shyä) | 204 | 37°10′N | 106°00′E |
| Ningyang, China (nĭng′yäng′) | 206 | 35°46′N | 116°48′E |
| Ninh Binh, Viet. (nēn bĕnk′) | 212 | 20°22′N | 106°00′E |
| Ninigo Group, is., Pap. N. Gui. | 213 | 1°15′S | 143°30′E |
| Ninnescah, r., Ks., U.S. (nĭn′ĕs-kä) | 120 | 37°37′N | 98°31′W |
| Nioaque, Braz. (nēō-ȧ′-kĕ) | 143 | 21°14′S | 55°41′W |
| Niobrara, r., U.S. (nī-ô-brâr′ȧ) | 106 | 42°46′N | 98°46′W |
| Niokolo Koba, Parc National du, rec., Sen. | 234 | 13°05′N | 13°00′W |
| Nioro du Sahel, Mali (nē-ō′rō) | 230 | 15°15′N | 9°35′W |
| Nipawin, Can. | 90 | 53°22′N | 104°00′W |
| Nipe, Bahía de, b., Cuba (bä-ē′ä-dĕ-nē′pä) | 135 | 20°50′N | 75°30′W |
| Nipe, Sierra de, mts., Cuba (sē-ĕ′r-rȧ-dĕ) | 135 | 20°20′N | 75°50′W |
| Nipigon, Can. (nĭp′ĭ-gŏn) | 91 | 48°58′N | 88°17′W |
| Nipigon, l., Can. | 93 | 49°37′N | 89°55′W |
| Nipigon Bay, b., Can. | 98 | 48°56′N | 88°00′W |
| Nipisiguit, r., Can. (nĭ-pĭ′sĭ-kwĭt) | 100 | 47°26′N | 66°15′W |
| Nipissing, l., Can. (nĭp′ĭ-sĭng) | 93 | 45°59′N | 80°19′W |
| Niquero, Cuba (nē-kā′rō) | 134 | 20°00′N | 77°35′W |
| Nirmali, India | 202 | 26°30′N | 86°43′E |
| Niš, Serb. | 154 | 43°19′N | 21°54′E |
| Nisa, Port. (nē′sȧ) | 172 | 39°32′N | 7°41′W |
| Nišava, r., Eur. (nē′shȧ-vȧ) | 175 | 43°17′N | 22°17′E |
| Nishino, i., Japan (nēsh′ē-nô) | 211 | 36°06′N | 132°49′E |
| Nishinomiya, Japan (nēsh′ē-nô-mē′yȧ) | 211b | 34°44′N | 135°21′E |
| Nishio, Japan (nēsh′ē-ô) | 211 | 34°50′N | 137°01′E |
| Niska Lake, l., Can. (nĭs′kȧ) | 96 | 55°35′N | 108°38′W |
| Nisko, Pol. (nēs′kô) | 169 | 50°30′N | 22°07′E |
| Nisku, Can. (nĭs-kū′) | 102g | 53°21′N | 113°33′W |
| Nisqually, r., Wa., U.S. (nĭs-kwôl′ĭ) | 114 | 46°51′N | 122°33′W |
| Nissan, r., Swe. | 166 | 57°06′N | 13°22′E |
| Nisser, l., Nor. (nĭs′ẽr) | 166 | 59°14′N | 8°35′E |
| Nissum Fjord, b., Den. | 166 | 56°24′N | 7°35′E |
| Niterói, Braz. (nē-tĕ-rô′ĭ) | 143 | 22°53′S | 43°07′W |
| Nith, r., Scot., U.K. (nĭth) | 164 | 55°13′N | 3°55′W |
| Nitra, Slvk. (nē′trȧ) | 169 | 48°18′N | 18°04′E |
| Nitra, r., Slvk. | 169 | 48°13′N | 18°14′E |
| Nitro, W.V., U.S. (nī′trô) | 108 | 38°25′N | 81°50′W |
| Niue, dep., Oc. (nĭ′ô) | 241 | 19°50′S | 167°00′W |
| Nivelles, Bel. (nē′vĕl′) | 165 | 50°33′N | 4°17′E |
| Nixon, Tx., U.S. (nĭk′sŭn) | 123 | 29°16′N | 97°48′W |
| Nizāmābād, India | 199 | 18°48′N | 78°07′E |
| Nizhne-Angarsk, Russia (nyēzh′nyĭ-ŭngärsk′) | 179 | 55°49′N | 108°46′E |
| Nizhne-Chirskaya, Russia | 181 | 48°20′N | 42°50′E |
| Nizhne-Kolymsk, Russia (kô-lēmsk′) | 179 | 68°32′N | 160°56′E |
| Nizhneudinsk, Russia (nēzh′nyĭ-ōōdēnsk′) | 179 | 54°58′N | 99°15′E |
| Nizhniye Sergi, Russia (nyēzh′ nyē sĕr′gē) | 180 | 56°41′N | 59°19′E |
| Nizhniy Novgorod (Gor′kiy), Russia | 178 | 56°15′N | 44°05′E |
| Nizhniy Tagil, Russia (tŭgēl′) | 178 | 57°54′N | 59°59′E |
| Nizhnyaya Kur′ya, Russia (nyē′zhnyȧ-yȧ kōōr′yȧ) | 186a | 58°01′N | 56°00′E |
| Nizhnyaya Salda, Russia (nyē′zhnya′ya säl′dȧ′) | 186a | 58°05′N | 60°43′E |
| Nizhnyaya Taymyra, r., Russia | 184 | 72°30′N | 95°18′E |
| Nizhnyaya Tunguska, r., Russia | 179 | 64°13′N | 91°30′E |
| Nizhnyaya Tura, Russia (tōō′rȧ) | 186a | 58°38′N | 59°50′E |
| Nizhnyaya Us′va, Russia (ŏ′vȧ) | 186a | 59°05′N | 58°53′E |
| Nizhyn, Ukr. | 181 | 51°03′N | 31°52′E |
| Nízke Tatry, mts., Slvk. | 169 | 48°57′N | 19°18′E |
| Njazidja, i., Com. | 233 | 11°44′S | 42°38′E |
| Njombe, Tan. | 237 | 9°20′S | 34°46′E |
| Njurunda, Swe. (nyōō-rôn′dȧ) | 166 | 62°15′N | 17°24′E |
| Nkala Mission, Zam. | 237 | 15°55′S | 26°00′E |
| Nkandla, S. Afr. (′n-känd′lä) | 233c | 28°40′S | 31°06′E |
| Nkawkaw, Ghana | 234 | 6°33′N | 0°47′W |
| Nkhota, Mwi. (kō-tȧ kō-tȧ) | 232 | 12°52′S | 34°16′E |
| Noākhāli, Bngl. | 199 | 22°52′N | 91°08′E |
| Noatak, Ak., U.S. (nô-ȧ′tăk) | 103 | 67°22′N | 163°28′W |
| Noatak, r., Ak., U.S. | 103 | 67°58′N | 162°15′W |
| Nobeoka, Japan (nō-bȧ-ō′kȧ) | 210 | 32°36′N | 131°41′E |
| Noblesville, In., U.S. (nō′bl′z-vĭl) | 108 | 40°00′N | 86°00′W |
| Nobleton, Can. (nō′bl′tŭn) | 102d | 43°54′N | 79°39′W |
| Nocera Inferiore, Italy (ēn-fĕ-ryō′rĕ) | 173c | 40°30′N | 14°38′E |
| Nochistlán, Mex. (nô-chēs-tlän′) | 130 | 21°23′N | 102°52′W |
| Nochixtlón, Mex. (ä-sōn-syōn′) | 131 | 17°28′N | 97°12′W |
| Nogales, Mex. (nō-gä′lĕs) | 131 | 18°49′N | 97°09′W |
| Nogales, Mex. | 128 | 31°15′N | 111°00′W |
| Nogales, Az., U.S. (nô-gä′lĕs) | 104 | 31°20′N | 110°55′W |
| Nogal Valley, val., Som. (nô′găl) | 238a | 8°30′N | 47°50′E |
| Nogent-le-Roi, Fr. (nŏ-zhŏn-lĕ-rwä′) | 171b | 48°39′N | 1°32′E |
| Nogent-le-Rotrou, Fr. (rō-trōō′) | 170 | 48°22′N | 0°47′E |
| Noginsk, Russia (nô-gēnsk′) | 180 | 55°52′N | 38°28′E |
| Noguera Pallaresa, r., Spain | 173 | 42°18′N | 1°03′E |
| Noia, Spain | 172 | 42°46′N | 8°50′W |
| Noirmoutier, Île de, i., Fr. (nwȧr-mōō-tyā′) | 161 | 47°03′N | 3°08′W |
| Nojima-Zaki, c., Japan (nō′jē-mä zä-kē) | 211 | 34°54′N | 139°48′E |
| Nokomis, Il., U.S. (nô-kō′mĭs) | 108 | 39°15′N | 89°10′W |
| Nola, Italy (nô′lä) | 174 | 40°41′N | 14°32′E |
| Nolinsk, Russia (nô-lēnsk′) | 180 | 57°32′N | 49°50′E |
| Noma Misaki, c., Japan (nō′mä mē′sä-kē) | 211 | 31°25′N | 130°09′E |
| Nombre de Dios, Mex. (nôm-brĕ-dĕ-dyô′s) | 130 | 23°50′N | 104°14′W |
| Nombre de Dios, Pan. (nô′m-brĕ) | 133 | 9°34′N | 79°28′W |
| Nome, Ak., U.S. (nōm) | 106a | 64°30′N | 165°20′W |
| Nonacho, l., Can. | 92 | 61°48′N | 111°20′W |
| Nong′an, China (nôŋ-än) | 208 | 44°25′N | 125°10′E |
| Nongoma, S. Afr. (nŏn-gō′mȧ) | 232 | 27°48′S | 31°45′E |
| Nooksack, Wa., U.S. (nŏk′săk) | 116d | 48°55′N | 122°19′W |
| Nooksack, r., Wa., U.S. | 116d | 48°54′N | 122°31′W |
| Noordwijk aan Zee, Neth. | 159a | 52°14′N | 4°25′E |
| Noordzee Kanaal, can., Neth. | 159a | 52°27′N | 4°42′E |
| Nootka, i., Can. (nōōt′kȧ) | 92 | 49°32′N | 126°42′W |
| Nootka Sound, strt., Can. | 94 | 49°33′N | 126°38′W |
| Nóqui, Ang. (nô-kē′) | 232 | 5°51′S | 13°25′E |
| Nor, r., China (nou′) | 210 | 46°55′N | 132°45′E |
| Nora, Swe. | 166 | 59°32′N | 14°56′E |
| Nora, In., U.S. (nō′rȧ) | 111g | 39°54′N | 86°08′W |
| Noranda, Can. | 99 | 48°15′N | 79°01′W |
| Norbeck, Md., U.S. (nôr′bĕk) | 110e | 39°06′N | 77°05′W |
| Norborne, Mo., U.S. (nôr′bôrn) | 121 | 39°17′N | 93°39′W |
| Norco, Ca., U.S. (nôr′kô) | 117a | 33°57′N | 117°33′W |
| Norcross, Ga., U.S. (nôr′krôs) | 110c | 33°56′N | 84°13′W |
| Nord, Riviere du, Can. (rēv-yĕr′ dü nōr) | 102a | 45°45′N | 74°02′W |
| Nordegg, Can. (nûr′dĕg) | 95 | 52°28′N | 116°04′W |
| Norden, Ger. (nôr′dĕn) | 168 | 53°35′N | 7°14′E |
| Norderney, i., Ger. (nōr′dĕr-nĕy) | 168 | 53°45′N | 6°58′E |
| Nordfjord, b., Nor. (nô′fyôr) | 166 | 61°50′N | 5°35′E |
| Nordhausen, Ger. (nôrt′hau-zĕn) | 161 | 51°30′N | 10°48′E |
| Nordhorn, Ger. (nôrt′hôrn) | 168 | 52°26′N | 7°05′E |
| Nord Kapp, c., Nor. | 180 | 71°11′N | 25°48′E |
| Nordland, Wa., U.S. (nôrd′lȧnd) | 116a | 48°03′N | 122°41′W |
| Nördlingen, Ger. (nûrt′lĭng-ĕn) | 168 | 48°51′N | 10°30′E |
| Nord-Ostsee Kanal (Kiel Canal), can., Ger. (nōrd-ōzt-zā) (kēl) | 168 | 54°03′N | 9°23′E |
| Nordrhein-Westfalen (North Rhine-Westphalia), state, Ger. (nôrd′hīn-vĕst-fä-lĕn) | 171c | 51°40′N | 7°00′E |
| Nordvik, Russia (nôrd′vĕk) | 179 | 73°57′N | 111°15′E |
| Nore, r., Ire. (nōr) | 164 | 52°34′N | 7°15′W |
| Norfolk, Ma., U.S. (nôr′fŏk) | 101a | 42°07′N | 71°19′W |
| Norfolk, Ne., U.S. | 104 | 42°10′N | 97°25′W |
| Norfolk, Va., U.S. | 105 | 36°55′N | 76°15′W |
| Norfolk, i., Oc. | 241 | 27°10′S | 166°50′E |
| Norfork, Lake, l., Ar., U.S. | 121 | 36°25′N | 92°09′W |
| Noril′sk, Russia (nô rēlsk′) | 178 | 69°00′N | 87°11′E |
| Normal, Il., U.S. (nôr′mȧl) | 108 | 40°35′N | 89°00′W |
| Norman, r., Austl. | 221 | 18°27′S | 141°29′E |
| Norman, Lake, res., N.C., U.S. | 107 | 35°30′N | 80°53′W |


ăt; finȧl; rāte; senȧte; ärm; ȧsk; sofȧ; fâre; ch-choose; dh-as th in other; bē; ēvent; bĕt; recĕnt; cratẽr; g-gō; gh-guttural g; bĭt; ĭ-short neutral; rīde; ĸ-guttural k as ch in German ich;

PRONOUNCING INDEX

Normandie – Nowa Sól 329


| PLACE (Pronunciation) | PAGE | LAT. | LONG. |
|---|---|---|---|
| Normandie, hist. reg., Fr. (nôr-män-dē´) | 170 | 49°02′N | 0°17′E |
| Normandie, Collines de, hills, Fr. (kô-lēn´dĕ-nôr-män-dē´) | 170 | 48°46′N | 0°50′W |
| Normandy see Normandie, hist. reg., Fr. | 170 | 49°02′N | 0°17′E |
| Normanton, Austl. (nôr´măn-tŭn) | 219 | 17°45′S | 141°10′E |
| Normanton, Eng., U.K. | 158a | 53°40′N | 1°21′W |
| Norman Wells, Can. | 90 | 65°26′N | 127°00′W |
| Nornalup, Austl. (nôr-năl´ŭp) | 218 | 35°00′S | 117°00′E |
| Nørresundby, Den. (nû-rĕ-sòn´bü) | 166 | 57°04′N | 9°55′E |
| Norris, Tn., U.S. (nŏr´ĭs) | 124 | 36°09′N | 84°05′W |
| Norris Lake, res., Tn., U.S. | 107 | 36°17′N | 84°10′W |
| Norristown, Pa., U.S. (nŏr´ĭs-town) | 110f | 40°07′N | 75°21′W |
| Norrköping, Swe. (nôr´chûp´ĭng) | 154 | 58°37′N | 16°10′E |
| Norrtälje, Swe. (nôr-tĕl´yĕ) | 160 | 59°47′N | 18°39′E |
| Norseman, Austl. (nôrs´măn) | 218 | 32°15′S | 122°00′E |
| Norte, Punta, c., Arg. (pōō´n-tä-nôr´tĕ) | 141c | 36°17′S | 56°46′W |
| Norte, Serra do, mts., Braz. (sĕ´r-rä-dô-nôr´te) | 143 | 12°04′S | 59°08′W |
| North, Cape, c., Can. | 101 | 47°02′N | 60°25′W |
| North Adams, Ma., U.S. (ăd´ămz) | 109 | 42°40′N | 73°05′W |
| Northam, Austl. (nôr-dhăm) | 218 | 31°50′S | 116°45′E |
| Northam, S. Afr. (nôr´thăm) | 238c | 24°52′S | 27°16′E |
| North America, cont. | 89 | 45°00′N | 100°00′W |
| North American Basin, deep (á-mĕr´ĭ-kăn) | 4 | 23°45′N | 62°45′W |
| Northampton, Austl. (nôr-thămp´tŭn) | 218 | 28°22′S | 114°45′E |
| Northampton, Eng., U.K. (nôrth-ămp´tŭn) | 161 | 52°14′N | 0°56′W |
| Northampton, Ma., U.S. | 109 | 42°20′N | 72°45′W |
| Northampton, Pa., U.S. | 109 | 40°45′N | 75°30′W |
| Northamptonshire, co., Eng., U.K. | 158a | 52°25′N | 0°47′W |
| North Andaman Island, i., India (ăn-dá-măn´) | 212 | 13°15′N | 93°30′E |
| North Andover, Ma., U.S. (ăn´dô-vẽr) | 101a | 42°42′N | 71°07′W |
| North Arm, mth., Can. (ärm) | 116d | 49°13′N | 123°01′W |
| North Atlanta, Ga., U.S. (ăt-lăn´tá) | 110c | 33°52′N | 84°20′W |
| North Attleboro, Ma., U.S. (ăt´'l-bŭr-ô) | 110b | 41°59′N | 71°18′W |
| North Baltimore, Oh., U.S. (bôl´tĭ-môr) | 108 | 41°10′N | 83°40′W |
| North Basque, Tx., U.S. (băsk) | 122 | 31°56′N | 98°01′W |
| North Battleford, Can. (băt´'l-fẽrd) | 90 | 52°47′N | 108°17′W |
| North Bay, Can. | 91 | 46°13′N | 79°26′W |
| North Bend, Or., U.S. (bĕnd) | 114 | 43°23′N | 124°13′W |
| North Berwick, Me., U.S. (bûr´wĭk) | 100 | 43°18′N | 70°46′W |
| North Bight, b., Bah. (bīt) | 134 | 24°30′N | 77°40′W |
| North Bimini, i., Bah. (bĭ´mĭ-nē) | 134 | 25°45′N | 79°20′W |
| North Borneo see Sabah, hist. reg., Malay. | 212 | 5°10′N | 116°25′E |
| Northborough, Ma., U.S. | 101a | 42°19′N | 71°39′W |
| Northbridge, Ma., U.S. (nôrth´brĭj) | 101a | 42°09′N | 71°39′W |
| North Caicos, i., T./C. Is. (kī´kōs) | 135 | 21°55′N | 72°00′W |
| North Cape, c., N.Z. | 221a | 34°31′S | 173°02′E |
| North Carolina, state, U.S. (kăr-ô-lī´ná) | 105 | 35°40′N | 81°30′W |
| North Cascades National Park, rec., Wa., U.S. | 114 | 48°50′N | 120°50′W |
| North Cat Cay, i., Bah. | 134 | 25°35′N | 79°20′W |
| North Channel, strt., Can. | 98 | 46°10′N | 83°20′W |
| North Channel, strt., U.K. | 156 | 55°15′N | 7°56′W |
| North Charleston, S.C., U.S. (chärlz´tŭn) | 125 | 32°49′N | 79°57′W |
| North Chicago, Il., U.S. (shĭ-kô´gō) | 111a | 42°19′N | 87°51′W |
| North College Hill, Oh., U.S. (kŏl´ĕj hĭl) | 111f | 39°13′N | 84°33′W |
| North Concho, Tx., U.S. (kŏn´chō) | 122 | 31°40′N | 100°48′W |
| North Cooking Lake, Can. (kòk´ĭng lāk) | 102g | 53°28′N | 112°57′W |
| North Dakota, state, U.S. (dá-kō´tá) | 104 | 47°20′N | 101°55′W |
| North Downs, Eng., U.K. (dounz) | 164 | 51°11′N | 0°01′W |
| North Dum-Dum, India | 202a | 22°38′N | 88°23′E |
| Northeast Cape, c., Ak., U.S. (nôrth-ēst) | 103 | 63°15′N | 169°04′W |
| Northeast Point, c., Bah. | 135 | 21°25′N | 73°00′W |
| Northeast Point, c., Bah. | 135 | 22°45′N | 73°50′W |
| Northeast Providence Channel, strt., Bah. (prŏv´ĭ-dĕns) | 134 | 25°45′N | 77°00′W |
| Northeim, Ger. (nôrt´hīm) | 168 | 51°42′N | 9°59′E |
| North Elbow Cays, is., Bah. | 134 | 23°55′N | 80°30′W |
| Northern Cheyenne Indian Reservation, I.R., Mt., U.S. | 115 | 45°32′N | 106°43′W |
| Northern Dvina see Severnaya Dvina, r., Russia | 178 | 63°00′N | 42°40′E |
| Northern Ireland, state, U.K. (īr´lănd) | 154 | 54°48′N | 7°00′W |
| Northern Land see Severnaya Zemlya, is., Russia | 179 | 79°33′N | 101°15′E |
| Northern Mariana Islands, dep., Oc. (mä-rē-ä´nä) | 3 | 17°20′N | 145°00′E |
| Northern Territory, ter., Austl. | 218 | 18°15′S | 133°00′E |
| Northern Yukon National Park, rec., Can. | 103 | 69°00′N | 140°00′W |
| Northfield, Mn., U.S. (nôrth´fēld) | 113 | 44°28′N | 93°11′W |
| North Flinders Ranges, mts., Austl. (flĭn´dẽrz) | 222 | 31°55′S | 138°45′E |
| North Foreland, Eng., U.K. (nôrth-fōr´lănd) | 165 | 51°20′N | 1°30′E |
| North Franklin Mountain, mtn., Tx., U.S. (frăn´klĭn) | 122 | 31°55′N | 106°30′W |
| North Frisian Islands, is., Eur. | 160 | 55°16′N | 8°15′E |
| North Gamboa, Pan. (gäm-bô´ä) | 133 | 9°07′N | 79°40′W |
| North Gower, Can. (gŏw´ẽr) | 102c | 45°08′N | 75°43′W |
| North Hollywood, Ca., U.S. (hŏl´ē-wòd) | 117a | 34°10′N | 118°23′W |
| North Island, i., N.Z. | 221a | 37°20′S | 173°30′E |
| North Island, i., Ca., U.S. | 118a | 32°39′N | 117°14′W |
| North Judson, In., U.S. (jŭd´sŭn) | 108 | 41°15′N | 86°50′W |
| North Kansas City, Mo., U.S. (kăn´zás) | 117f | 39°08′N | 94°34′W |
| North Kingstown, R.I., U.S. | 110b | 41°34′N | 71°26′W |
| North Lincolnshire, co., Eng., U.K. | 158a | 53°40′N | 0°35′W |
| North Little Rock, Ar., U.S. (lĭt´'l rŏk) | 121 | 34°46′N | 92°13′W |
| North Loup, r., Ne., U.S. (lōōp) | 112 | 42°05′N | 100°10′W |
| North Magnetic Pole, pt. of i. | 244 | 77°19′N | 101°49′W |
| North Manchester, In., U.S. (măn´chĕs-tẽr) | 108 | 41°00′N | 85°45′W |
| Northmoor, Mo., U.S. (nôth´mōōr) | 117f | 39°10′N | 94°37′W |
| North Moose Lake, l., Can. | 97 | 54°09′N | 100°20′W |
| North Mount Lofty Ranges, mts., Austl. | 222 | 33°50′S | 138°30′E |
| North Ogden, Ut., U.S. (ŏg´dĕn) | 117b | 41°18′N | 111°58′W |
| North Ogden Peak, mtn., Ut., U.S. | 117b | 41°23′N | 111°59′W |
| North Olmsted, Oh., U.S. (ōlm-stĕd) | 111d | 41°25′N | 81°55′W |
| North Ossetia, prov., Russia | 180 | 43°00′N | 44°15′E |
| North Pease, r., Tx., U.S. (pēz) | 120 | 34°19′N | 100°58′W |
| North Pender, i., Can. (pĕn´dẽr) | 116d | 48°48′N | 123°16′W |
| North Plains, Or., U.S. (plānz) | 116c | 45°36′N | 123°00′W |
| North Platte, Ne., U.S. (plăt) | 104 | 41°08′N | 100°45′W |
| North Platte, r., U.S. | 106 | 41°20′N | 102°40′W |
| North Point, c., Barb. | 133b | 13°22′N | 59°36′W |
| North Point, c., Mi., U.S. | 108 | 45°00′N | 83°20′W |
| North Pole, pt. of i. | 244 | 90°00′N | 0°00′ |
| Northport, Al., U.S. (nôrth´pōrt) | 124 | 33°12′N | 87°35′W |
| Northport, N.Y., U.S. | 110a | 40°53′N | 73°20′W |
| Northport, Wa., U.S. | 114 | 48°53′N | 117°47′W |
| North Reading, Ma., U.S. (rĕd´ĭng) | 101a | 42°34′N | 71°04′W |
| North Richland Hills, Tx., U.S. | 117c | 32°50′N | 97°13′W |
| Northridge, Ca., U.S. (nôrth´ridj) | 117a | 34°14′N | 118°32′W |
| North Ridgeville, Oh., U.S. (rĭj-vĭl) | 111d | 41°23′N | 82°01′W |
| North Ronaldsay, i., Scot., U.K. | 164a | 59°21′N | 2°23′W |
| North Royalton, Oh., U.S. (roi´ăl-tŭn) | 111d | 41°19′N | 81°44′W |
| North Saint Paul, Mn., U.S. (sånt pôl´) | 113 | 45°01′N | 92°59′W |
| North Santiam, r., Or., U.S. (săn´tyăm) | 114 | 44°42′N | 122°50′W |
| North Saskatchewan, r., Can. (săn-kăch´ê-wän) | 92 | 54°00′N | 111°30′W |
| North Sea, Eur. | 154 | 56°09′N | 3°16′E |
| North Skunk, r., Ia., U.S. (skŭnk) | 113 | 41°39′N | 92°46′W |
| North Stradbroke Island, i., Austl. (străd´brōk) | 221 | 27°45′S | 154°18′E |
| North Sydney, Can. (sĭd´nē) | 101 | 46°13′N | 60°15′W |
| North Taranaki Bight, N.Z. (tá-rá-nä´kĭ bīt) | 221a | 38°40′S | 174°00′E |
| North Tarrytown, N.Y., U.S. (tăr´ĭ-toun) | 110a | 41°05′N | 73°52′W |
| North Thompson, r., Can. | 95 | 50°50′N | 120°10′W |
| North Tonawanda, N.Y., U.S. (tŏn-á-wŏn´dá) | 111c | 43°02′N | 78°53′W |
| North Truchas Peaks, mtn., N.M., U.S. (trōō´chäs) | 106 | 35°58′N | 105°40′W |
| North Twillingate, i., Can. (twĭl´ĭn-gāt) | 100 | 35°58′N | 105°37′W |
| North Uist, i., Scot., U.K. (û´ĭst) | 164 | 57°37′N | 7°22′W |
| Northumberland, N.H., U.S. | 109 | 44°30′N | 71°30′W |
| Northumberland Islands, is., Austl. | 221 | 21°42′S | 151°30′E |
| Northumberland Strait, strt., Can. (nôr thŭm´bẽr-lánd) | 100 | 46°25′N | 64°20′W |
| North Umpqua, r., Or., U.S. (ŭmp´kwá) | 114 | 43°20′N | 122°50′W |
| North Vancouver, Can. (văn-kōō´vẽr) | 90 | 49°19′N | 123°04′W |
| North Vernon, In., U.S. (vûr´nŭn) | 108 | 39°05′N | 85°45′W |
| Northville, Mi., U.S. (nôrth-vĭl) | 111b | 42°26′N | 83°28′W |
| North Wales, Pa., U.S. (wālz) | 110f | 40°12′N | 75°16′W |
| North West Cape, c., Austl. (nôrth´wĕst) | 220 | 21°50′S | 112°25′E |
| Northwest Cape Fear, r., N.C., U.S. (cāp fēr) | 125 | 34°34′N | 79°46′W |
| North West Gander, r., Can. (găn´dẽr) | 101 | 48°40′N | 55°15′W |
| Northwest Providence Channel, strt., Bah. (prŏv´ĭ-dĕns) | 134 | 26°15′N | 78°45′W |
| Northwest Territories, ter., Can. (tĕr´ĭ-tō´rĭs) | 90 | 65°00′N | 120°00′W |
| Northwich, Eng., U.K. (nôrth´wĭch) | 158a | 53°15′N | 2°31′W |
| North Wilkesboro, N.C., U.S. (wĭlks´bûrô) | 125 | 36°08′N | 81°10′W |
| Northwood, Ia., U.S. (nôrth´wòd) | 113 | 43°26′N | 93°13′W |
| Northwood, N.D., U.S. | 112 | 47°44′N | 97°36′W |
| North Yamhill, r., Or., U.S. (yăm´ hĭl) | 116c | 45°22′N | 123°21′W |
| North York, Can. | 99 | 43°47′N | 79°25′W |
| North York Moors, for., Eng., U.K. (yôrk mòrz´) | 164 | 54°20′N | 0°40′W |
| North Yorkshire, co., Eng., U.K. | 158a | 53°50′N | 1°10′W |
| Norton, Ks., U.S. (nôr´tŭn) | 120 | 39°40′N | 99°54′W |
| Norton, Ma., U.S. | 110b | 41°58′N | 71°08′W |
| Norton, Va., U.S. | 125 | 36°54′N | 82°36′W |
| Norton Bay, b., Ak., U.S. | 103 | 64°22′N | 162°18′W |
| Norton Reservoir, res., Ma., U.S. | 110b | 42°01′N | 71°07′W |
| Norton Sound, strt., Ak., U.S. | 103 | 63°48′N | 164°50′W |
| Norval, Can. (nôr´vál) | 102d | 43°39′N | 79°52′W |
| Norwalk, Ca., U.S. (nôr´wôk) | 117a | 33°54′N | 118°05′W |
| Norwalk, Ct., U.S. | 110a | 41°06′N | 73°25′W |
| Norwalk, Oh., U.S. | 108 | 41°15′N | 82°35′W |
| Norway, Me., U.S. | 100 | 44°11′N | 70°35′W |
| Norway, Mi., U.S. | 113 | 45°47′N | 87°55′W |
| Norway, nation, Eur. (nôr´wā) | 154 | 63°48′N | 11°17′E |
| Norway House, Can. | 90 | 53°59′N | 97°50′W |
| Norwegian Sea, sea, Eur. (nôr-wē´jăn) | 160 | 66°54′N | 1°43′E |
| Norwell, Ma., U.S. (nôr´wĕl) | 101a | 42°10′N | 70°47′W |
| Norwich, Eng., U.K. | 161 | 52°40′N | 1°15′E |
| Norwich, Ct., U.S. (nôr´wĭch) | 109 | 41°20′N | 72°00′W |
| Norwich, N.Y., U.S. | 109 | 42°35′N | 75°30′W |
| Norwood, Ma., U.S. (nôr´wòod) | 101a | 42°11′N | 71°13′W |
| Norwood, N.C., U.S. | 125 | 35°15′N | 80°08′W |
| Norwood, Oh., U.S. | 111f | 39°10′N | 84°27′W |
| Nose Creek, r., Can. (nōz) | 102e | 51°09′N | 114°02′W |
| Noshiro, Japan (nō´shē-rô) | 210 | 40°09′N | 140°02′E |
| Nosivka, Ukr. (nô´sôf-ká) | 177 | 50°54′N | 31°35′E |
| Nossob, r., Afr. (nô´sŏb) | 232 | 24°15′S | 19°10′E |
| Noteć, r., Pol. (nô´tĕcn) | 168 | 52°50′N | 16°19′E |
| Notodden, Nor. (nōt´ôd´n) | 166 | 59°35′N | 9°15′E |
| Notre Dame, Monts, mts., Can. | 100 | 46°35′N | 70°35′W |
| Notre Dame Bay, b., Can. (nō´t'r dám´) | 93a | 49°45′N | 55°15′W |
| Notre-Dame-du-Lac, Can. | 100 | 47°37′N | 68°51′W |
| Nottawasaga Bay, b., Can. (nŏt´á-wá-sä´gá) | 99 | 44°45′N | 80°35′W |
| Nottaway, r., Can. (nôt´á-wā) | 93 | 50°58′N | 78°02′W |
| Nottingham, Eng., U.K. (nŏt´ĭng-ăm) | 161 | 52°58′N | 1°09′W |
| Nottingham Island, i., Can. | 93 | 62°58′N | 78°53′W |
| Nottinghamshire, co., Eng., U.K. | 158a | 53°03′N | 1°05′W |
| Nottoway, r., Va., U.S. (nôt´á-wā) | 125 | 36°53′N | 77°47′W |
| Notukeu Creek, r., Can. | 96 | 49°55′N | 106°30′W |
| Nouadhibou, Maur. | 230 | 21°02′N | 17°09′W |
| Nouakchott, Maur. | 230 | 18°06′N | 15°57′W |
| Nouamrhar, Maur. | 230 | 19°22′N | 16°31′W |
| Nouméa, N. Cal. (nōō-mā´ä) | 219 | 22°16′S | 166°27′E |
| Nouvelle, Can. (nōō-vĕl´) | 100 | 48°09′N | 66°22′W |
| Nouvelle-France, Cap de, c., Can. | 93 | 62°03′N | 74°00′W |
| Nouzonville, Fr. (nōō-zôɴ-vēl´) | 170 | 49°51′N | 4°43′E |
| Nova Cruz, Braz. (nō´vá-krōō´z) | 143 | 6°22′S | 35°20′W |
| Nova Friburgo, Braz. (frĕ-bōōr´gò) | 143 | 22°18′S | 42°31′W |
| Nova Iguaçu, Braz. (nō´vä-ē-gwä-sōō´) | 143 | 22°45′S | 43°27′W |
| Nova Lima, Braz. (lē´mä) | 141a | 19°59′S | 43°51′W |
| Nova Lisboa see Huambo, Ang. | 232 | 12°44′S | 15°47′E |
| Nova Mambone, Moz. (nô´vá-mám-bō´nĕ) | 232 | 21°04′S | 35°13′E |
| Nova Odesa, Ukr. | 177 | 47°18′N | 31°48′E |
| Nova Praha, Ukr. | 177 | 48°34′N | 32°54′E |
| Novara, Italy (nô-vä´rä) | 162 | 45°24′N | 8°38′E |
| Nova Resende, Braz. | 141a | 21°12′S | 46°25′W |
| Nova Scotia, prov., Can. (skō´shá) | 91 | 44°28′N | 65°00′W |
| Nova Vodolaha, Ukr. | 177 | 49°43′N | 35°51′E |
| Novaya Ladoga, Russia (nô´vá-ya lá-dô-gá) | 167 | 60°06′N | 32°16′E |
| Novaya Lyalya, Russia (lyá´lyá) | 186a | 59°03′N | 60°36′E |
| Novaya Sibir, i., Russia (sē-bēr´) | 179 | 75°00′N | 149°00′E |
| Novaya Zemlya, i., Russia (zĕm-lyá´) | 178 | 72°00′N | 54°46′E |
| Nova Zagora, Blg. (zä´gô-rá) | 175 | 42°30′N | 26°01′E |
| Novelda, Spain (nō-vĕl´dá) | 173 | 38°22′N | 0°46′W |
| Nové Mesto nad Váhom, Slvk. (nô´vĕ myĕs´tô) | 169 | 48°44′N | 17°47′E |
| Nové Zámky, Slvk. (zám´kĕ) | 161 | 47°58′N | 18°10′E |
| Novgorod, Russia (nôv´gô-rŏt) | 180 | 58°32′N | 31°16′E |
| Novgorod, prov., Russia | 176 | 58°27′N | 31°55′E |
| Novhorod-Sivers'kyi, Ukr. | 181 | 52°01′N | 33°14′E |
| Novi, Mi., U.S. (nō´vĭ) | 111b | 42°29′N | 83°28′W |
| Novigrad, Cro. (nō´vĭ grád) | 174 | 44°09′N | 15°34′E |
| Novi Ligure, Italy (nô´vĕ) | 174 | 44°43′N | 8°48′E |
| Novinger, Mo., U.S. (nŏv´ĭn-jẽr) | 121 | 40°14′N | 92°43′W |
| Novi Pazar, Blg. (pä-zär´) | 175 | 43°22′N | 27°26′E |
| Novi Pazar, Serb. (pá-zär´) | 163 | 43°08′N | 20°30′E |
| Novi Sad, Serb. (säd´) | 154 | 45°15′N | 19°53′E |
| Novoaidar, Ukr. | 177 | 48°57′N | 39°01′E |
| Novoasbest, Russia (nô-vô-äs-bĕst´) | 186a | 57°43′N | 60°14′E |
| Novocherkassk, Russia (nô´vô-chĕr-kásk´) | 181 | 47°25′N | 40°04′E |
| Novokuznetsk, Russia (nô´vô-kô´z-nyĕ´tsk) (stá´lênsk) | 178 | 53°43′N | 86°59′E |
| Novo-Ladozhskiy Kanal, can., Russia (nô-vô-lä´dôzh-skĭ ká-näl´) | 167 | 59°54′N | 31°19′E |
| Novo Mesto, Slvn. (nôvô mās´tô) | 174 | 45°48′N | 15°13′E |
| Novomoskovsk, Russia (nô´vô-môs-kôfsk´) | 178 | 54°06′N | 38°08′E |
| Novomoskovs'k, Ukr. | 181 | 48°37′N | 35°12′E |
| Novomyrhorod, Ukr. | 177 | 48°46′N | 31°44′E |
| Novonikol'skiy, Russia (nô´vô-nyĭ-kôl´skĭ) | 186a | 52°28′N | 57°12′E |
| Novorossiysk, Russia (nô´vô-rô-sēsk´) | 178 | 44°43′N | 37°48′E |
| Novorzhev, Russia (nô´vô-rzhêv´) | 176 | 57°01′N | 29°17′E |
| Novo-Selo, Blg. (nô´vô-sĕ´lô) | 175 | 44°09′N | 22°46′E |
| Novosibirsk, Russia (nô´vô-sê-bērsk´) | 178 | 55°09′N | 82°58′E |
| Novosibirskiye Ostrova (New Siberian Islands), is., Russia | 179 | 74°00′N | 140°30′E |
| Novosil', Russia (nô´vô-sĭl) | 176 | 52°58′N | 37°03′E |
| Novosokol'niki, Russia (nô´vô-sô-kôl´nē-kē) | 176 | 56°18′N | 30°07′E |
| Novotatishchevskiy, Russia (nô´vô-tá-tyĭsh´chĕv-skĭ) | 186a | 53°22′N | 60°24′E |
| Novoukraïnka, Ukr. | 181 | 48°18′N | 31°33′E |
| Novouzensk, Russia (nô-vô-ò-zĕnsk´) | 181 | 50°40′N | 48°08′E |
| Novozybkov, Russia (nô´vô-zĕp´kôf) | 181 | 52°31′N | 31°54′E |
| Novyi Buh, Ukr. | 177 | 47°43′N | 32°33′E |
| Nový Jičín, Czech Rep. (nô´vē yē´chēn) | 169 | 49°36′N | 18°02′E |
| Novyy Oskol, Russia (ôs-kôl´) | 177 | 50°46′N | 37°53′E |
| Novyy Port, Russia (nô´vē) | 178 | 67°19′N | 72°28′E |
| Nowa Sól, Pol. (nô´vá sül´) | 168 | 51°49′N | 15°41′E |


ng-sing; ŋ-baŋk; ɴ-nasalized n; nŏd; cŏmmit; ōld; ôbey; ôrder; oi-boil; fōōd; ò-as oo in foot; ou-out; s-soft; sh-dish; th-thin; pūre; ûnite; ûrn; stŭd; circŭs; ü-as in French tu; ´-indeterminate vowel.

| PLACE (Pronunciation) | PAGE | LAT. | LONG. |
|---|---|---|---|
| Nowata, Ok., U.S. (nō-wä′tȧ) | 121 | 36°42′N | 95°38′W |
| Nowood Creek, r., Wy., U.S. | 115 | 44°02′N | 107°37′W |
| Nowra, Austl. (nou′rȧ) | 222 | 34°55′S | 150°45′E |
| Nowy Dwór Mazowiecki, Pol. (nō′vĭ dvōōr mä-zo-vyĕts′ke) | 169 | 52°26′N | 20°46′E |
| Nowy Sącz, Pol. (nō′vĕ sônch′) | 169 | 49°36′N | 20°42′E |
| Nowy Targ, Pol. (tärk′) | 169 | 49°29′N | 20°02′E |
| Noxon Reservoir, res., Mt., U.S. | 114 | 47°50′N | 115°40′W |
| Noxubee, r., Ms., U.S. (nŏks′ū-bē) | 124 | 33°20′N | 88°55′W |
| Noyes Island, i., Ak., U.S. (noiz) | 94 | 55°30′N | 133°40′W |
| Nozaki, Japan (nō′zä-kê) | 211b | 34°43′N | 135°39′E |
| Nqamakwe, S. Afr. (′n-gä-mä′kwå) | 233c | 32°13′S | 27°57′E |
| Nqutu, S. Afr. (′n-kōō′tōō) | 233c | 28°17′S | 30°41′E |
| Nsawam, Ghana | 234 | 5°50′N | 0°20′W |
| Ntshoni, mtn., S. Afr. | 233c | 29°34′S | 30°03′E |
| Ntwetwe Pan, pl., Bots. | 232 | 20°00′S | 24°18′E |
| Nubah, Jibāl an, mts., Sudan | 231 | 12°22′N | 30°39′E |
| Nubian Desert, des., Sudan (nōō′bĭ-ăn) | 231 | 21°13′N | 33°09′E |
| Nudo Coropuna, mtn., Peru (nōō′dō kō-rō-pōō′nä) | 142 | 15°53′S | 72°04′W |
| Nudo de Pasco, mtn., Peru (dĕ päs′kō) | 142 | 10°34′S | 76°12′W |
| Nueces, r., Tx., U.S. (nū-ā′sås) | 106 | 28°20′N | 98°08′W |
| Nueltin, l., Can. (nwĕl′tin) | 92 | 60°14′N | 101°00′W |
| Nueva Armenia, Hond. (nwā′vä är-mā′nê-ä) | 132 | 15°47′N | 86°32′W |
| Nueva Esparta, dept., Ven. (nwĕ′vä ĕs-pä′r-tä) | 143b | 10°50′N | 64°35′W |
| Nueva Gerona, Cuba (κĕ-rô′nä) | 134 | 21°55′N | 82°45′W |
| Nueva Palmira, Ur. (päl-mē′rä) | 141c | 33°53′S | 58°23′W |
| Nueva Rosita, Mex. (nòĕ′vä rô-sē′tä) | 104 | 27°55′N | 101°10′W |
| Nueva San Salvador, El Sal. | 132 | 13°41′N | 89°16′W |
| Nueve, Canal Numero, can., Arg. | 141c | 36°22′S | 58°19′W |
| Nueve de Julio, Arg. (nwā′vå dā hōō′lyô) | 144 | 35°26′S | 60°51′W |
| Nuevitas, Cuba (nwā-vē′täs) | 129 | 21°35′N | 77°15′W |
| Nuevitas, Bahía de, b., Cuba (bä-ē′ä dĕ nwā-vē′täs) | 134 | 21°30′N | 77°05′W |
| Nuevo, Ca., U.S. (nwā′vō) | 117a | 33°48′N | 117°09′W |
| Nuevo Laredo, Mex. (lä-rā′dhō) | 128 | 27°29′N | 99°30′W |
| Nuevo Leon, state, Mex. (lå-ōn′) | 128 | 26°00′N | 100°00′W |
| Nuevo San Juan, Pan. (nwĕ′vô sän κōō-ä′n) | 128a | 9°14′N | 79°43′W |
| Nugumanovo, Russia (nû-gû-mä′nô-vô) | 186a | 55°28′N | 61°50′E |
| Nulato, Ak., U.S. (nōō-lä′tō) | 103 | 64°40′N | 158°18′W |
| Nullagine, Austl. (nŭ-lă′jēn) | 218 | 22°00′S | 120°07′E |
| Nullarbor Plain, pl., Austl. (nŭ-lär′bôr) | 220 | 31°45′S | 126°30′E |
| Numabin Bay, b., Can. (nōō-mä′bĭn) | 96 | 56°30′N | 103°08′W |
| Numansdorp, Neth. | 159a | 51°43′N | 4°25′E |
| Numazu, Japan (nōō′mä-zōō) | 210 | 35°06′N | 138°55′E |
| Numfoor, Pulau, i., Indon. | 213 | 1°20′S | 134°48′E |
| Nun, r., Nig. | 235 | 5°05′N | 6°10′E |
| Nunavut, ter., Can. | 90 | 70°00′N | 95°00′W |
| Nunawading, Austl. | 217a | 37°49′S | 145°10′E |
| Nuneaton, Eng., U.K. (nŭn′ē-tŭn) | 164 | 52°31′N | 1°28′W |
| Nunivak, i., Ak., U.S. (nōō′nĭ-văk) | 106a | 60°25′N | 167°42′W |
| Nunyama, Russia (nûn-yä′mȧ) | 103 | 65°49′N | 170°32′W |
| Nuoro, Italy (nwô′rō) | 174 | 40°29′N | 9°20′E |
| Nura, r., Kaz. | 184 | 49°48′N | 73°54′E |
| Nurata, Uzb. (nōōr′ät′ä) | 183 | 40°33′N | 65°28′E |
| Nuremberg *see* Nürnberg, Ger. | 154 | 49°28′N | 11°07′E |
| Nürnberg, Ger. (nürn′bĕrgh) | 154 | 49°28′N | 11°07′E |
| Nurse Cay, i., Bah. | 135 | 22°30′N | 75°50′W |
| Nusabyin, Tur. (nōō′sī-bên) | 181 | 37°05′N | 41°10′E |
| Nushagak, r., Ak., U.S. (nū-shă-găk′) | 103 | 59°28′N | 157°40′W |
| Nushan Hu, l., China | 206 | 32°50′N | 117°59′E |
| Nushki, Pak. (nŭsh′kê) | 199 | 29°30′N | 66°02′E |
| Nuthe, r., Ger. (nōō′tê) | 159b | 52°15′N | 13°11′E |
| Nutley, N.J., U.S. (nŭt′lê) | 110a | 40°49′N | 74°09′W |
| Nutter Fort, W.V., U.S. (nŭt′ẽr fôrt) | 108 | 39°15′N | 80°15′W |
| Nutwood, Il., U.S. (nŭt′wŏŏd) | 117e | 39°05′N | 90°34′W |
| Nuwaybi ′al Muzayyinah, Egypt | 197a | 28°59′N | 34°40′E |
| Nuweland, S. Afr. | 232a | 33°58′S | 18°28′E |
| Nyack, N.Y., U.S. (nī′ăk) | 110a | 41°05′N | 73°55′W |
| Nyainqêntanglha Shan, mts., China (nyä-ĭn-chyŭn-täŋ-lä shän) | 204 | 29°55′N | 88°08′E |
| Nyakanazi, Tan. | 237 | 3°00′S | 31°15′E |
| Nyala, Sudan | 231 | 12°00′N | 24°52′E |
| Nyanga, r., Gabon | 236 | 2°45′S | 10°30′E |
| Nyanza, Rw. | 237 | 2°21′S | 29°45′E |
| Nyasa, Lake, l., Afr. (nyä′sä) | 232 | 10°45′S | 34°30′E |
| Nyasvizh, Bela. (nyĕs′vēsh) | 176 | 53°13′N | 26°44′E |
| Nyazepetrovsk, Russia (nyä′zĕ-pĕ-trôvsk′) | 186a | 56°04′N | 59°38′E |
| Nyborg, Den. (nü′bôr′′) | 166 | 55°20′N | 10°45′E |
| Nybro, Swe. (nü′brô) | 166 | 56°44′N | 15°56′E |
| Nyeri, Kenya | 237 | 0°25′S | 36°57′E |
| Nyika Plateau, plat., Mwi. | 237 | 10°30′S | 35°50′E |
| Nyíregyháza, Hung. (nyē′rĕd-y′hä′zä) | 163 | 47°58′N | 21°45′E |
| Nykøbing, Den. (nü′kû-bĭng) | 160 | 56°46′N | 8°47′E |
| Nykøbing, Den. | 166 | 54°45′N | 11°54′E |
| Nykøbing Sjaelland, Den. | 166 | 55°55′N | 11°37′E |
| Nyköping, Swe. (nü′chû-pĭng) | 160 | 58°46′N | 16°58′E |
| Nylstroom, S. Afr. (nĭl′strōm) | 232 | 24°42′S | 28°25′E |
| Nymagee, Austl. (nī-mȧ-gē′) | 219 | 32°17′S | 146°18′E |
| Nymburk, Czech Rep. (nĕm′bŏŏrk) | 161 | 50°12′N | 15°03′E |
| Nynäshamn, Swe. (nü-nĕs-häm′n) | 166 | 58°53′N | 17°55′E |
| Nyngan, Austl. (nĭŋ′găn) | 219 | 31°31′S | 147°25′E |
| Nyong, r., Cam. (nyông) | 230 | 4°00′N | 12°00′E |
| Nyou, Burkina | 234 | 12°46′N | 1°56′W |
| Nýřany, Czech Rep. (nêr-zhä′nê) | 168 | 49°43′N | 13°13′E |
| Nysa, Pol. (nē′sȧ) | 169 | 50°29′N | 17°20′E |
| Nytva, Russia | 180 | 58°00′N | 55°10′E |
| Nyungwe, Mwi. | 237 | 10°16′S | 34°07′E |
| Nyunzu, D.R.C. | 237 | 5°57′S | 28°01′E |
| Nyuya, r., Russia (nyōō′yȧ) | 185 | 60°30′N | 111°45′E |
| Nyzhni Sirohozy, Ukr. | 177 | 46°51′N | 34°25′E |
| Nzega, Tan. | 237 | 4°13′S | 33°11′E |
| N′zeto, Ang. | 232 | 7°14′S | 12°52′E |
| Nzi, r., C. Iv. | 234 | 7°00′N | 4°27′W |
| Nzwani, i., Com. (äN-zhwän) | 233 | 12°14′S | 44°47′E |


# O


| PLACE (Pronunciation) | PAGE | LAT. | LONG. |
|---|---|---|---|
| Oahe, Lake, res., U.S. | 106 | 45°20′N | 100°00′W |
| O′ahu, i., Hi., U.S. (ō-ä′hōō) (ō-ä′hü) | 106c | 21°38′N | 157°48′W |
| Oak Bay, Can. | 94 | 48°27′N | 123°18′W |
| Oak Bluff, Can. (ōk blŭf) | 102f | 49°47′N | 97°21′W |
| Oak Creek, Co., U.S. (ōk krēk′) | 115 | 40°20′N | 106°50′W |
| Oakdale, Ca., U.S. (ōk′dāl) | 118 | 37°45′N | 120°52′W |
| Oakdale, Ky., U.S. | 108 | 38°15′N | 85°50′W |
| Oakdale, La., U.S. | 123 | 30°49′N | 92°40′W |
| Oakdale, Pa., U.S. | 111e | 40°24′N | 80°11′W |
| Oakengates, Eng., U.K. (ōk′ĕn-gāts) | 158a | 52°41′N | 2°27′W |
| Oakes, N.D., U.S. (ōks) | 112 | 46°10′N | 98°50′W |
| Oakfield, Me., U.S. (ōk′fēld) | 100 | 46°08′N | 68°10′W |
| Oakford, Pa., U.S. (ōk′fŏrd) | 110f | 40°08′N | 74°58′W |
| Oak Grove, Or., U.S. (grōv) | 116c | 45°25′N | 122°38′W |
| Oakham, Eng., U.K. (ōk′ăm) | 158a | 52°40′N | 0°38′W |
| Oak Harbor, Oh., U.S. (ōk′här′bẽr) | 108 | 41°30′N | 83°05′W |
| Oak Harbor, Wa., U.S. | 116a | 48°18′N | 122°39′W |
| Oakland, Ca., U.S. (ōk′lănd) | 104 | 37°48′N | 122°16′W |
| Oakland, Ne., U.S. | 112 | 41°50′N | 96°28′W |
| Oakland City, In., U.S. | 108 | 38°20′N | 87°20′W |
| Oak Lawn, Il., U.S. | 111a | 41°43′N | 87°45′W |
| Oakleigh, Austl. (ōk′lȧ) | 217a | 37°54′S | 145°05′E |
| Oakley, Id., U.S. (ōk′lĭ) | 114 | 42°15′N | 135°53′W |
| Oakley, Ks., U.S. | 120 | 39°08′N | 100°49′W |
| Oakman, Al., U.S. (ōk′măn) | 124 | 33°42′N | 87°20′W |
| Oakmont, Pa., U.S. (ōk′mŏnt) | 111e | 40°31′N | 79°50′W |
| Oak Mountain, mtn., Al., U.S. | 110h | 33°22′N | 86°42′W |
| Oak Park, Il., U.S. (pärk) | 111a | 41°53′N | 87°48′W |
| Oak Point, Wa., U.S. | 116c | 46°11′N | 123°11′W |
| Oak Ridge, Tn., U.S. (rĭj) | 124 | 36°01′N | 84°15′W |
| Oakville, Can. (ōk′vĭl) | 99 | 43°27′N | 79°40′W |
| Oakville, Can. | 102f | 49°56′N | 97°58′W |
| Oakville, Mo., U.S. | 117e | 38°27′N | 90°18′W |
| Oakville Creek, r., Can. | 102d | 43°34′N | 79°54′W |
| Oakwood, Tx., U.S. (ōk′wŏŏd) | 123 | 31°36′N | 95°48′W |
| Oatman, Az., U.S. (ōt′măn) | 119 | 34°00′N | 114°25′W |
| Oaxaca, Mex. | 128 | 17°03′N | 96°42′W |
| Oaxaca, state, Mex. (wä-hä′kä) | 128 | 16°45′N | 97°00′W |
| Oaxaca, Sierra de, mts., Mex. (sē-ĕ′r-rä dĕ) | 131 | 16°15′N | 97°25′W |
| Ob′, r., Russia | 178 | 62°15′N | 67°00′E |
| Oba, Can. (ō′bȧ) | 91 | 48°58′N | 84°09′W |
| Obama, Japan (ō′bȧ-mä) | 211 | 35°29′N | 135°44′E |
| Oban, Scot., U.K. (ō′băn) | 164 | 56°25′N | 5°35′W |
| Oban Hills, hills, Nig. | 235 | 5°35′N | 8°30′E |
| O′Bannon, Ky., U.S. (ō-băn′nŏn) | 111h | 38°17′N | 85°30′W |
| O Barco de Valdeorras, Spain | 172 | 42°26′N | 6°58′W |
| Obatogamau, l., Can. (ō-bȧ-tō′găm-ô) | 99 | 49°38′N | 74°10′W |
| Oberhausen, Ger. (ō′bẽr-hou′zĕn) | 171c | 51°27′N | 6°51′E |
| Oberlin, Ks., U.S. (ō′bẽr-lĭn) | 120 | 39°49′N | 100°30′W |
| Oberlin, Oh., U.S. | 108 | 41°15′N | 82°15′W |
| Oberroth, Ger. (ō′bĕr-rōt) | 159d | 48°19′N | 11°20′E |
| Obi, Kepulauan, is., Indon. (ō′bê) | 213 | 1°25′S | 128°15′E |
| Obi, Pulau, i., Indon. | 213 | 1°30′S | 127°45′E |
| Óbidos, Braz. (ō′bê-dōzh) | 143 | 1°57′S | 55°32′W |
| Obihiro, Japan (ō′bē-hē′rō) | 210 | 42°55′N | 142°50′E |
| Obion, r., Tn., U.S. | 124 | 36°10′N | 89°25′W |
| Obion, North Fork, r., Tn., U.S. (ô-bī′ŏn) | 124 | 35°49′N | 89°06′W |
| Obitsu, r., Japan (ō′bēt′sōō) | 211a | 35°19′N | 140°03′E |
| Obock, Dji. (ō-bŏk′) | 238a | 11°55′N | 43°15′E |
| Obol′, r., Bela. (ô-bŏl′) | 176 | 55°24′N | 29°24′E |
| Oboyan′, Russia (ô-bô-yän′) | 181 | 51°14′N | 36°16′E |
| Obskaya Guba, b., Russia | 178 | 67°13′N | 73°45′E |
| Obuasi, Ghana | 234 | 6°14′N | 1°39′W |
| Obukhiv, Ukr. | 177 | 50°07′N | 30°36′E |
| Obukhovo, Russia | 186b | 55°50′N | 38°17′E |
| Obytichna kosa, spit, Ukr. | 177 | 46°32′N | 36°07′E |
| Ocala, Fl., U.S. (ô-kä′lȧ) | 125 | 29°11′N | 82°09′W |
| Ocampo, Mex. (ô-käm′pō) | 130 | 22°49′N | 99°23′W |
| Ocaña, Col. (ô-kän′yä) | 142 | 8°15′N | 73°37′W |
| Ocaña, Spain (ô-kä′n-yä) | 172 | 39°58′N | 3°31′W |
| Occidental, Cordillera, mts., Col. | 142a | 5°05′N | 76°04′W |
| Occidental, Cordillera, mts., Peru | 142 | 10°12′S | 76°58′W |
| Ocean Beach, Ca., U.S. (ō′shăn bēch) | 118a | 32°44′N | 117°14′W |
| Ocean Bight, b., Bah. | 135 | 21°15′N | 73°15′W |
| Ocean City, Md., U.S. | 109 | 38°20′N | 75°10′W |
| Ocean City, N.J., U.S. | 109 | 39°15′N | 74°35′W |
| Ocean Falls, Can. (Fôls) | 90 | 52°21′N | 127°40′W |
| Ocean Grove, Austl. | 217a | 38°16′S | 144°32′E |
| Ocean Grove, N.J., U.S. (grōv) | 109 | 40°10′N | 74°00′W |
| Oceanside, Ca., U.S. (ō′shăn-sīd) | 118 | 33°11′N | 117°22′W |
| Oceanside, N.Y., U.S. | 110a | 40°38′N | 73°39′W |
| Ocean Springs, Ms., U.S. (sprĭngs) | 124 | 30°25′N | 88°49′W |
| Ochakiv, Ukr. | 177 | 46°38′N | 31°33′E |
| Ochamchira, Geor. | 182 | 42°44′N | 41°28′E |
| Ochlockonee, r., Fl., U.S. (ŏk-lô-kō′nē) | 124 | 30°10′N | 84°38′W |
| Ocilla, Ga., U.S. (ô-sĭl′ȧ) | 124 | 31°36′N | 83°15′W |
| Ockelbo, Swe. (ŏk′ĕl-bō) | 166 | 60°54′N | 16°35′E |
| Ocklawaha, Lake, res., Fl., U.S. | 125 | 29°30′N | 81°50′W |
| Ocmulgee, r., Ga., U.S. | 124 | 32°25′N | 83°30′W |
| Ocmulgee National Monument, rec., Ga., U.S. (ôk-mŭl′gē) | 124 | 32°45′N | 83°28′W |
| Ocoa, Bahía de, b., Dom. Rep. | 135 | 18°20′N | 70°40′W |
| Ococingo, Mex. (ô-kô-sē′n-gô) | 131 | 17°03′N | 92°18′W |
| Ocom, Lago, l., Mex. (ô-kô′m) | 132a | 19°26′N | 88°18′W |
| Oconee, r., Ga., U.S. (ô-kō′nē) | 107 | 32°45′N | 83°00′W |
| Oconee, Lake, res., Ga., U.S. | 124 | 33°30′N | 83°15′W |
| Oconomowoc, Wi., U.S. (ô-kŏn′ô-mô-wŏk′) | 113 | 43°06′N | 88°24′W |
| Oconto, Wi., U.S. (ô-kŏn′tō) | 113 | 44°54′N | 87°55′W |
| Oconto, r., Wi., U.S. | 113 | 45°08′N | 88°24′W |
| Oconto Falls, Wi., U.S. | 113 | 44°53′N | 88°11′W |
| Ocós, Guat. (ô-kōs′) | 132 | 14°31′N | 92°12′W |
| Ocotal, Nic. (ō-kô-täl′) | 132 | 13°36′N | 86°31′W |
| Ocotepeque, Hond. (ô-kō-tå-pā′kå) | 132 | 14°25′N | 89°13′W |
| Ocotlán, Mex. (ō-kô-tlän′) | 130 | 20°19′N | 102°44′W |
| Ocotlán de Morelos, Mex. (dā mō-rā′lōs) | 131 | 16°46′N | 96°41′W |
| Ocozocoautla, Mex. (ô-kō′zô-kwä-ōō′tlä) | 131 | 16°44′N | 93°22′W |
| Ocumare del Tuy, Ven. (ō-kōō-mä′ra del twē′) | 142 | 10°07′N | 66°47′W |
| Oda, Ghana | 234 | 5°55′N | 0°59′W |
| Odawara, Japan (ō′dȧ-wä′rä) | 211 | 35°15′N | 139°10′E |
| Odda, Nor. (ôdh-ȧ) | 166 | 60°04′N | 6°30′E |
| Odebolt, Ia., U.S. (ō′dê-bōlt) | 112 | 42°20′N | 95°14′W |
| Odemira, Port. (ō-då-mē′rȧ) | 172 | 37°35′N | 8°40′W |
| Ödemiş, Tur. (û′dĕ-mēsh) | 163 | 38°12′N | 28°00′E |
| Odendaalsrus, S. Afr. (ō′dĕn-däls-rûs′) | 238c | 27°52′S | 26°41′E |
| Odense, Den. (ō′dhĕn-sĕ) | 160 | 55°24′N | 10°20′E |
| Odenton, Md., U.S. (ō′dĕn-tŭn) | 110e | 39°05′N | 76°43′W |
| Odenwald, for., Ger. (ō′dĕn-väld) | 168 | 49°39′N | 8°55′E |
| Oder, r., Eur. (ō′dẽr) | 156 | 52°40′N | 14°19′E |
| Oderhaff, l., Eur. | 168 | 53°47′N | 14°02′E |
| Odesa, Ukr. | 178 | 46°28′N | 30°44′E |
| Odesa, prov., Ukr. | 177 | 46°05′N | 29°48′E |
| Odessa, Tx., U.S. (ô-dĕs′ȧ) | 122 | 31°52′N | 102°21′W |
| Odessa, Wa., U.S. | 114 | 47°20′N | 118°42′W |
| Odiel, r., Spain (ō-dê-ĕl′) | 172 | 37°47′N | 6°42′W |
| Odiham, Eng., U.K. (ŏd′ē-ăm) | 158b | 51°14′N | 0°56′W |
| Odintsovo, Russia (ô-dēn′tsô-vô) | 186b | 55°40′N | 37°16′E |
| Odiongan, Phil. (ō-dê-ôŋ′gän) | 213a | 12°24′N | 121°59′E |
| Odivelas, Port. (ō-dê-vä′lyäs) | 173b | 38°47′N | 9°11′W |
| Odobeşti, Rom. (ō-dô-bĕsh′t′) | 169 | 45°46′N | 27°08′E |
| O′Donnell, Tx., U.S. (ō-dŏn′ĕl) | 120 | 32°59′N | 101°51′W |
| Odorhei, Rom. (ō-dôr-hā′) | 169 | 46°18′N | 25°17′E |
| Odra *see* Oder, r., Eur. (ō′drȧ) | 156 | 52°40′N | 14°19′E |
| Oeiras, Braz. (wå-ē-räzh′) | 143 | 7°05′S | 42°01′W |
| Oeirás, Port. (ô-ĕ′y-rà′s) | 173b | 38°42′N | 9°18′W |
| Oelwein, Ia., U.S. (ōl′wīn) | 113 | 42°40′N | 91°56′W |
| O′Fallon, Il., U.S. (ō-făl′ŭn) | 117e | 38°36′N | 89°55′W |
| O′Fallon Creek, r., Mt., U.S. | 115 | 46°25′N | 104°47′W |
| Ofanto, r., Italy (ô-făn′tō) | 174 | 41°08′N | 15°33′E |
| Offa, Nig. | 235 | 8°09′N | 4°44′E |
| Offenbach, Ger. (ôf′ĕn-bäk) | 168 | 50°06′N | 8°50′E |
| Offenburg, Ger. (ôf′ĕn-bŏŏrgh) | 168 | 48°28′N | 7°57′E |
| Ofuna, Japan (ō′fōō-nä) | 211a | 35°21′N | 139°32′E |
| Ogaden Plateau, plat., Eth. | 238a | 6°45′N | 44°53′E |
| Ogaki, Japan | 210 | 35°21′N | 136°36′E |
| Ogallala, Ne., U.S. (ō-gä-lä′lä) | 112 | 41°08′N | 101°44′W |
| Ogbomosho, Nig. (ŏg-bô-mō′shō) | 230 | 8°08′N | 4°15′E |
| Ogden, Ia., U.S. (ŏg′dĕn) | 113 | 42°10′N | 94°20′W |
| Ogden, Ut., U.S. | 104 | 41°14′N | 111°58′W |
| Ogden, r., Ut., U.S. | 117b | 41°16′N | 111°54′W |
| Ogden Peak, mtn., Ut., U.S. | 117b | 41°11′N | 111°51′W |
| Ogdensburg, N.J., U.S. (ŏg′dĕnz-bûrg) | 110a | 41°05′N | 74°36′W |
| Ogdensburg, N.Y., U.S. | 105 | 44°40′N | 75°30′W |
| Ogeechee, r., Ga., U.S. (ô-gē′chê) | 125 | 32°35′N | 81°50′W |
| Ogies, S. Afr. | 238c | 26°03′S | 29°04′E |
| Ogilvie Mountains, mts., Can. (ō′g′l-vĭ) | 92 | 64°45′N | 138°10′W |
| Oglesby, Il., U.S. (ō′g′lz-bĭ) | 108 | 41°20′N | 89°00′W |
| Oglio, r., Italy (ōl′yō) | 174 | 45°15′N | 10°19′E |
| Ōgo, Japan (ō′gô) | 211b | 34°49′N | 135°06′E |
| Ogou, r., Togo | 234 | 8°05′N | 1°30′E |
| Ogudnëvo, Russia (ôg-ŏŏd-nyô′vô) | 186b | 56°04′N | 38°17′E |
| Ogulin, Cro. (ō-gōō-lēn′) | 174 | 45°17′N | 15°11′E |
| Ogwashi-Uku, Nig. | 235 | 6°10′N | 6°31′E |
| O′Higgins, prov., Chile (ô-kē′gēns) | 141b | 34°17′S | 70°52′W |
| Ohio, state, U.S. (ô′hī′ō) | 105 | 40°30′N | 83°15′W |
| Ohio, r., U.S. | 107 | 37°25′N | 88°05′W |
| Ohoopee, r., Ga., U.S. (ô-hōō′pe-mc) | 125 | 32°32′N | 82°38′W |
| Ohře, r., Eur. (ōr′zhĕ) | 168 | 50°08′N | 12°45′E |
| Ohrid, Mac. (ō′krēd) | 175 | 41°08′N | 20°46′E |
| Ohrid, Lake, l., Eur. | 175 | 40°58′N | 20°35′E |
| Ōi, Japan (oi′) | 211a | 35°51′N | 139°31′E |
| Oi-Gawa, r., Japan (ō′ē-gä′wȧ) | 211 | 35°09′N | 138°05′E |
| Oil City, Pa., U.S. (oil sĭ′tĭ) | 109 | 41°25′N | 79°40′W |
| Oirschot, Neth. | 159a | 51°30′N | 5°20′E |
| Oise, r., Fr. (wäz) | 161 | 49°30′N | 2°56′E |
| Oisterwijk, Neth. | 159a | 51°34′N | 5°13′E |
| Oita, Japan (ō′ē-tä) | 210 | 33°14′N | 131°38′E |
| Oji, Japan (ō′jê) | 211b | 34°36′N | 135°43′E |
| Ojinaga, Mex. (ō-κê-nä′gä) | 128 | 29°34′N | 104°26′W |
| Ojitlán, Mex. (ôkê-tlän′) (sän-lōō′käs) | 131 | 18°04′N | 96°23′W |


ăt; finăl; rāte; senåte; ärm; åsk; sofȧ; fâre; ch-choose; dh-as th in other; bē; êvent; bĕt; recĕnt; cratẽr; g-gō; gh-guttural g; bĭt; ĭ-short neutral; rīde; κ-guttural k as ch in German ich;

PRONOUNCING INDEX

Ojo Caliente – Orikhiv 331


| PLACE (Pronunciation) | PAGE | LAT. | LONG. |
|---|---|---|---|
| Ojo Caliente, Mex. (ōκō käl-yĕn′tå) | 130 | 21°50′N | 100°43′W |
| Ojocaliente, Mex. (ō-κō-kä-lyĕ′n-tĕ) | 130 | 22°39′N | 102°15′W |
| Ojo del Toro, Pico, mtn., Cuba (pē′kô-ô-κō-dĕl-tô′rô) | 134 | 19°55′N | 77°25′W |
| Oka, Can. (ō-kä) | 102a | 45°28′N | 74°05′W |
| Oka, r., Russia (ô-kå′) | 180 | 55°10′N | 42°10′E |
| Oka, r., Russia (ō-kä′) | 184 | 53°28′N | 101°09′E |
| Oka, r., Russia (ô-kä′) | 181 | 52°10′N | 35°20′E |
| Okahandja, Nmb. | 232 | 21°50′S | 16°45′E |
| Okanagan (Okanogan), r., N.A. (ō′kȧ-näg′ȧn) | 95 | 49°06′N | 119°43′W |
| Okanagan Lake, l., Can. | 92 | 50°00′N | 119°28′W |
| Okano, r., Gabon (ô′kä′nō) | 230 | 0°15′N | 11°08′E |
| Okanogan, Wa., U.S. | 114 | 48°20′N | 119°34′W |
| Okanogan, r., Wa., U.S. | 114 | 48°36′N | 119°33′W |
| Okatibbee, r., Ms., U.S. (ō′kä-tĭb′ē) | 124 | 32°37′N | 88°54′W |
| Okatoma Creek, r., Ms., U.S. (ô-kȧ-tō′mă) | 124 | 31°43′N | 89°34′W |
| Okavango (Cubango), r., Afr. | 232 | 18°00′S | 20°00′E |
| Okavango Swamp, sw., Bots. | 232 | 19°30′S | 23°02′E |
| Okaya, Japan (ō′kȧ-yȧ) | 211 | 36°04′N | 138°01′E |
| Okayama, Japan (ō′kȧ-yä′mȧ) | 205 | 34°39′N | 133°54′E |
| Okazaki, Japan (ō′kȧ-zä′kē) | 210 | 34°58′N | 137°09′E |
| Okeechobee, Fl., U.S. (ō-kē-chō′bē) | 125 | 27°15′N | 80°50′W |
| Okeechobee, Lake, l., Fl., U.S. | 107 | 27°00′N | 80°49′W |
| Okeene, Ok., U.S. (ō-kēn′) | 120 | 36°06′N | 98°19′W |
| Okefenokee Swamp, sw., U.S. (ō′kē-fē-nō′kē) | 125 | 30°54′N | 82°20′W |
| Okemah, Ok., U.S. (ō-kē′mä) | 121 | 35°26′N | 96°18′W |
| Okene, Nig. | 235 | 7°33′N | 6°15′E |
| Okha, Russia (ŭ-κä′) | 179 | 53°44′N | 143°12′E |
| Okhotino, Russia (ō-κō′tĭ-nô) | 186b | 56°14′N | 38°24′E |
| Okhotsk, Russia (ô-κôtsk′) | 179 | 59°28′N | 143°32′E |
| Okhotsk, Sea of, sea, Asia (ô-kôtsk′) | 179 | 56°45′N | 146°00′E |
| Okhtyrka, Ukr. | 181 | 50°18′N | 34°53′E |
| Okinawa, i., Japan | 205 | 26°30′N | 128°00′E |
| Okino, i., Japan (ō′kē-nô) | 211 | 36°22′N | 133°27′E |
| Ōkino Erabu, i., Japan (ō-kē′nô-å-rä′bōō) | 210 | 27°18′N | 129°00′E |
| Oklahoma, state, U.S. (ô-klȧ-hō′mȧ) | 104 | 36°00′N | 98°20′W |
| Oklahoma City, Ok., U.S. | 104 | 35°27′N | 97°32′W |
| Oklawaha, r., Fl., U.S. (ŏk-lȧ-wô′hô) | 125 | 29°13′N | 82°00′W |
| Okmulgee, Ok., U.S. (ôk-mŭl′gē) | 121 | 35°37′N | 95°58′W |
| Okolona, Ky., U.S. (ō-kô-lō′nȧ) | 111h | 38°08′N | 85°41′W |
| Okolona, Ms., U.S. | 124 | 33°59′N | 88°43′W |
| Oktemberyan, Arm. | 182 | 40°09′N | 44°02′E |
| Okushiri, i., Japan (ō′kōō-shē′rē) | 210 | 42°12′N | 139°30′E |
| Okuta, Nig. | 235 | 9°14′N | 3°15′E |
| Olalla, Wa., U.S. (ō-lä′lȧ) | 116a | 47°26′N | 122°33′W |
| Olanchito, Hond. (ō′län-chē′tô) | 132 | 15°28′N | 86°35′W |
| Öland, i., Swe. (û-länd′) | 156 | 57°03′N | 17°15′E |
| Olathe, Ks., U.S. (ō-lā′thē) | 117f | 38°53′N | 94°49′W |
| Olavarría, Arg. (ō-lä-vär-rē′ä) | 144 | 36°49′N | 60°15′W |
| Oława, Pol. (ô-lä′vȧ) | 169 | 50°57′N | 17°18′E |
| Olazoago, Arg. (ō-läz-kôä′gô) | 141c | 35°14′S | 60°37′W |
| Olbia, Italy (ô′l-byä) | 174 | 40°55′N | 9°28′E |
| Olching, Ger. (ōl′κĕng) | 159d | 48°13′N | 11°21′E |
| Old Bahama Channel, strt., N.A. (bȧ-hā′mȧ) | 134 | 22°45′N | 78°30′W |
| Old Bight, Bah. | 135 | 24°15′N | 75°20′W |
| Old Bridge, N.J., U.S. (brĭj) | 110a | 40°24′N | 74°22′W |
| Old Crow, Can. (crō) | 90 | 67°51′N | 139°58′W |
| Oldenburg, Ger. (ôl′dĕn-bôrgh) | 160 | 53°09′N | 8°13′E |
| Old Forge, Pa., U.S. (fôrj) | 109 | 41°20′N | 75°50′W |
| Oldham, Eng., U.K. (ōld′ȧm) | 164 | 53°32′N | 2°07′W |
| Oldham, co., Eng., U.K. | 158a | 53°35′N | 2°05′W |
| Old Harbor, Ak., U.S. (här′bēr) | 103 | 57°18′N | 153°20′W |
| Old Head of Kinsale, c., Ire. (ōld hĕd ŏv kĭn-sāl) | 164 | 51°35′N | 8°35′W |
| Old R, Tx., U.S. | 123a | 29°54′N | 94°52′W |
| Olds, Can. (ōldz) | 90 | 51°47′N | 114°06′W |
| Old Tate, Bots. | 232 | 21°18′S | 27°43′E |
| Old Town, Me., U.S. (toun) | 100 | 44°55′N | 68°42′W |
| Old Wives Lake, l., Can. (wīvz) | 96 | 50°05′N | 106°00′W |
| Olean, N.Y., U.S. (ō-lē-ăn′) | 105 | 42°05′N | 78°25′W |
| Olecko, Pol. (ô-lĕt′skô) | 169 | 54°02′N | 22°29′E |
| Olekma, r., Russia (ô-lyĕk-mȧ′) | 185 | 55°41′N | 120°33′E |
| Olëkminsk, Russia (ô-lyĕk-mênsk′) | 179 | 60°39′N | 120°40′E |
| Oleksandriia, Ukr. | 176 | 48°40′N | 33°07′E |
| Olenëk, r., Russia (ô-lyĕ-nyôk′) | 179 | 68°00′N | 113°00′E |
| Oléron Île, d′, i., Fr. (ēl′ dō lā-rôn′) | 161 | 45°52′N | 1°58′W |
| Oleśnica, Pol. (ô-lĕsh-nĭ′tsȧ) | 161 | 51°13′N | 17°24′E |
| Olfen, Ger. (ōl′fĕn) | 171c | 51°43′N | 7°22′E |
| Ol′ga, Russia (ôl′gȧ) | 179 | 43°48′N | 135°44′E |
| Ol′gi, Zaliv, b., Russia (zä′lĭf ôl′gĭ) | 210 | 43°43′N | 135°25′E |
| Olhão, Port. (ôl-youN′) | 162 | 37°02′N | 7°54′W |
| Ol′hopil′, Ukr. | 177 | 48°11′N | 29°28′E |
| Olievenhoutpoort, S. Afr. | 233b | 25°58′S | 27°55′E |
| Ólimbos, mtn., Cyp. | 197a | 34°56′N | 32°52′E |
| Olinda, Braz. (ô-lē′n-dä) | 143 | 8°00′S | 34°58′W |
| Olinda, Braz. | 144b | 22°49′S | 43°25′W |
| Oliva, Spain (ô-lē′vä) | 173 | 38°54′N | 0°07′W |
| Oliva de la Frontera, Spain (ô-lē′vä dā) | 172 | 38°33′N | 6°55′W |
| Olive Hill, Ky., U.S. (ŏl′ĭv) | 108 | 38°15′N | 83°10′W |
| Oliveira, Braz. (ō-lē-vā′rȧ) | 141a | 20°42′S | 44°49′W |
| Olivenza, Spain (ō-lē-vĕn′thä) | 172 | 38°42′N | 7°06′W |
| Oliver, Can. (ŏ′lĭ-vēr) | 90 | 49°11′N | 119°33′W |
| Oliver, Can. | 102g | 53°38′N | 113°21′W |
| Oliver, Wi., U.S. (ŏ′lĭvēr) | 117h | 46°39′N | 92°12′W |
| Oliver Lake, l., Can. | 102g | 53°19′N | 113°00′W |
| Olivia, Mn., U.S. (ō-lĭv′ē-ȧ) | 112 | 44°46′N | 95°00′W |
| Olivos, Arg. (ōlē′vōs) | 144a | 34°30′S | 58°29′W |
| Ollagüe, Chile (ô-lyä′gå) | 142 | 21°17′S | 68°17′W |
| Ollerton, Eng., U.K. (ôl′ēr-tŭn) | 158a | 53°12′N | 1°02′W |
| Olmos Park, Tx., U.S. (ōl′mŭs pärk′) | 117d | 29°27′N | 98°32′W |
| Olney, Il., U.S. (ŏl′nĭ) | 108 | 38°45′N | 88°05′W |
| Olney, Or., U.S. (ŏl′nē) | 116c | 46°06′N | 123°45′W |
| Olney, Tx., U.S. | 120 | 33°24′N | 98°43′W |
| Olomane, r., Can. (ō′lô mȧ′nĕ) | 101 | 51°05′N | 60°50′W |
| Olomouc, Czech Rep. (ō′lô-mōts) | 161 | 49°37′N | 17°15′E |
| Olonets, Russia (ô-lô′nĕts) | 167 | 60°58′N | 32°54′E |
| Olongapo, Phil. | 212 | 14°49′S | 120°17′E |
| Oloron, Gave d′, r., Fr. (gäv-dō-lō-rôN′) | 170 | 43°21′N | 0°44′W |
| Oloron-Sainte Marie, Fr. (ō-lō-rôNt′sănt mȧ-rē′) | 170 | 43°11′N | 1°37′W |
| Olot, Spain (ô-lōt′) | 162 | 42°09′N | 2°30′E |
| Olpe, Ger. (ōl′pĕ) | 171c | 51°02′N | 7°51′E |
| Olsnitz, Ger. (ōlz′nētz) | 168 | 50°25′N | 12°11′E |
| Olsztyn, Pol. (ôl′shtĭn) | 160 | 53°47′N | 20°28′E |
| Olt, r., Rom. | 163 | 44°09′N | 24°40′E |
| Olten, Switz. (ôl′tĕn) | 168 | 47°20′N | 7°53′E |
| Oltenița, Rom. (ôl-tā′nĭ-tsȧ) | 175 | 44°05′N | 26°39′E |
| Olvera, Spain (ôl-vĕ′rä) | 172 | 36°55′N | 5°16′W |
| Olympia, Wa., U.S. (ô-lĭm′pĭ-ȧ) | 104 | 47°02′N | 122°52′W |
| Olympic Mountains, mts., Wa., U.S. | 114 | 47°54′N | 123°58′W |
| Olympic National Park, rec., Wa., U.S. (ô-lĭm′pĭk) | 106 | 47°54′N | 123°00′W |
| Ólympos, mtn., Grc. | 162 | 40°05′N | 22°21′E |
| Olympus, Mount, mtn., Wa., U.S. (ô-lĭm′pŭs) | 114 | 47°43′N | 123°30′W |
| Olyphant, Pa., U.S. (ŏl′ĭ-fănt) | 109 | 41°30′N | 75°40′W |
| Olyutorskiy, Mys, c., Russia (ŭl-yōō′tŏr-skē) | 179 | 59°49′N | 167°16′E |
| Omae-Zaki, c., Japan (ō′mä-å zä′kē) | 211 | 34°37′N | 138°15′E |
| Omagh, N. Ire., U.K. (ō′mä) | 164 | 54°35′N | 7°25′W |
| Omaha, Ne., U.S. (ō′mȧ-hä) | 105 | 41°18′N | 95°57′W |
| Omaha Indian Reservation, I.R., Ne., U.S. | 112 | 42°09′N | 96°08′W |
| Oman, nation, Asia | 198 | 20°00′N | 57°45′E |
| Oman, Gulf of, b., Asia | 198 | 24°24′N | 58°58′E |
| Omaruru, Nmb. (ō-mä-rōō′rōō) | 232 | 21°25′S | 16°50′E |
| Ombrone, r., Italy (ôm-brō′nä) | 174 | 42°48′N | 11°18′E |
| Omdurman, Sudan | 231 | 15°45′N | 32°30′E |
| Omealca, Mex. (ōmå-äl′kō) | 131 | 18°44′N | 96°45′W |
| Ometepec, Mex. (ō-mā-tå-pĕk′) | 130 | 16°41′N | 98°27′W |
| Om Hajer, Eth. | 231 | 14°06′N | 36°46′E |
| Omineca, r., Can. (ō-mĭ-nĕk′ȧ) | 94 | 55°50′N | 125°45′W |
| Omineca Mountains, mts., Can. | 94 | 56°00′N | 125°00′W |
| Ōmiya, Japan (ō′mē-yȧ) | 211 | 35°54′S | 139°38′E |
| Omo, r., Eth. (ō′mō) | 231 | 5°54′N | 36°09′E |
| Omoa, Hond. (ô-mō′rä) | 132 | 15°43′N | 88°03′W |
| Omoko, Nig. | 235 | 5°20′N | 6°39′E |
| Omolon, r., Russia (ō′mō) | 185 | 67°43′N | 159°15′E |
| Ōmori, Japan (ō′mô-rê) | 211a | 35°50′N | 140°09′E |
| Omotepe, Isla de, i., Nic. (ē′s-lä-dĕ-ō-mô-tå′på) | 132 | 11°32′N | 85°30′W |
| Omro, Wi., U.S. (ŏm′rō) | 113 | 44°01′N | 89°46′W |
| Omsk, Russia (ômsk) | 178 | 55°12′N | 73°19′E |
| Ōmura, Japan (ō′mōō-rȧ) | 211 | 32°56′N | 129°57′E |
| Ōmuta, Japan (ō-mō-tä) | 211 | 33°02′N | 130°28′E |
| Omutninsk, Russia (ō′mōō-tēnsk) | 180 | 58°38′N | 52°10′E |
| Onawa, Ia., U.S. (ŏn-ȧ-wȧ) | 112 | 42°02′N | 96°05′W |
| Onaway, Mi., U.S. | 108 | 45°25′N | 84°10′W |
| Oncócua, Ang. | 236 | 16°34′S | 13°28′E |
| Onda, Spain (ōn′dä) | 173 | 39°58′N | 0°13′W |
| Ondava, r., Slvk. (ōn′dȧ-vȧ) | 169 | 48°51′N | 21°40′E |
| Ondo, Nig. | 235 | 7°04′N | 4°47′E |
| Öndörhaan, Mong. | 205 | 47°20′N | 110°40′E |
| Onega, Russia (ô-nyĕ′gȧ) | 178 | 63°50′N | 38°08′E |
| Onega, r., Russia | 180 | 63°20′N | 39°20′E |
| Onega, Lake *see* Onezhskoye Ozero, l., Russia | 180 | 62°02′N | 34°35′E |
| Oneida, N.Y., U.S. (ō-nī′dȧ) | 109 | 43°05′N | 75°40′W |
| Oneida, l., N.Y., U.S. | 109 | 43°10′N | 76°00′W |
| O′Neill, Ne., U.S. (ō-nēl′) | 112 | 42°28′N | 98°38′W |
| Oneonta, N.Y., U.S. (ō-nê-ŏn′tȧ) | 109 | 42°25′N | 75°05′W |
| Onezhskaja Guba, b., Russia | 180 | 64°30′N | 36°00′E |
| Onezhskiy, Poluostrov, pen., Russia | 180 | 64°30′N | 37°40′E |
| Onezhskoye Ozero, Russia (ô-năsh′skô-yĕ ô′zĕ-rô) | 180 | 62°02′N | 34°35′E |
| Ongiin Hiid, Mong. | 204 | 46°00′N | 102°46′E |
| Ongole, India | 203 | 15°36′N | 80°03′E |
| Onilahy, r., Madag. | 233 | 23°41′S | 45°00′E |
| Onitsha, Nig. (ô-nĭt′shȧ) | 230 | 6°09′N | 6°47′W |
| Onomichi, Japan (ō′nô-mē′chê) | 210 | 34°27′N | 133°12′E |
| Onon, r., Asia (ō′nôn) | 179 | 49°00′N | 112°00′E |
| Onoto, Ven. (ô-nŏ′tô) | 143b | 9°38′N | 65°03′W |
| Onslow, Austl. (ŏnz′lō) | 218 | 21°53′S | 115°00′E |
| Onslow B, N.C., U.S. (ŏnz′lō) | 125 | 34°22′N | 77°35′W |
| Ontake San, mtn., Japan (ōn′tä-kå sän) | 210 | 35°55′N | 137°29′E |
| Ontario, Ca., U.S. (ŏn-tā′rĭ-ō) | 117a | 34°04′N | 117°39′E |
| Ontario, Or., U.S. | 114 | 44°02′N | 116°57′W |
| Ontario, prov., Can. | 91 | 50°47′N | 88°50′W |
| Ontario, Lake, l., N.A. | 107 | 43°35′N | 79°05′W |
| Ontinyent, Spain | 173 | 38°48′N | 0°35′W |
| Ontonagon, Mi., U.S. (ŏn-tô-năg′ŏn) | 113 | 46°50′N | 89°20′W |
| Ōnuki, Japan (ō′nōō-kê) | 211a | 35°17′N | 139°51′E |
| Oodnadatta, Austl. (ōōd′nȧ-dȧ′tȧ) | 218 | 27°38′S | 135°40′E |
| Ooldea Station, Austl. (ōōl-dā′ä) | 218 | 30°35′S | 132°08′E |
| Oologah Reservoir, res., Ok., U.S. | 107 | 36°43′N | 95°32′W |
| Ooltgensplaat, Neth. | 159a | 51°41′N | 4°19′E |
| Oostanaula, r., Ga., U.S. (ōō-stȧ-nô′lȧ) | 124 | 34°25′N | 85°10′W |
| Oostende, Bel. (ōst-ĕn′dē) | 161 | 51°14′N | 2°55′E |
| Oosterhout, Neth. | 159a | 51°38′N | 4°52′E |
| Ooster Schelde, r., Neth. | 159a | 51°40′N | 3°40′E |
| Ootsa Lake, l., Can. | 94 | 53°49′N | 126°18′W |
| Opalaca, Sierra de, mts., Hond. (sē-sē′r-rä-dē-ō-pä-lä′kä) | 132 | 14°30′N | 88°29′W |
| Opasquia, Can. (ō-păs′kwē-ȧ) | 97 | 53°16′N | 93°53′W |
| Opatów, Pol. (ô-pä′tōf) | 169 | 50°47′N | 21°25′E |
| Opava, Czech Rep. (ō′pä-vä) | 169 | 49°56′N | 17°52′E |
| Opelika, Al., U.S. (ŏp-ē-lī′kȧ) | 124 | 32°39′N | 85°23′W |
| Opelousas, La., U.S. (ŏp-ē-lōō′sȧs) | 123 | 30°33′N | 92°04′W |
| Opeongo, l., Can. (ŏp-ê-ôŋ′gō) | 99 | 45°40′N | 78°20′W |
| Opheim, Mt., U.S. (ô-fīm′) | 115 | 48°51′N | 106°19′W |
| Ophir, Ak., U.S. (ō′fēr) | 103 | 63°10′N | 156°28′W |
| Ophir, Mount, mtn., Malay. | 197b | 2°22′N | 102°37′E |
| Opico, El Sal. (ô-pē′kō) | 132 | 13°50′N | 89°23′W |
| Opinaca, r., Can. (ŏp-ĭ-nä′kȧ) | 93 | 52°28′N | 77°40′W |
| Opishnia, Ukr. | 177 | 49°57′N | 34°34′E |
| Opladen, Ger. (ŏp′lä-dĕn) | 171c | 51°04′N | 7°00′E |
| Opobo, Nig. | 235 | 4°34′N | 7°27′E |
| Opochka, Russia (ō-pôch′kȧ) | 180 | 56°43′N | 28°39′E |
| Opoczno, Pol. (ô-pôch′nô) | 169 | 51°22′N | 20°18′E |
| Opole, Pol. (ô-pôl′ä) | 161 | 50°42′N | 17°55′E |
| Opole Lubelskie, Pol. (ô-pō′lă lōō-bĕl′skyĕ) | 169 | 51°09′N | 21°58′E |
| Opp, Al., U.S. (ŏp) | 124 | 31°18′N | 86°15′W |
| Oppdal, Nor. (ôp′däl) | 166 | 62°37′N | 9°41′E |
| Opportunity, Wa., U.S. (ŏp-ŏr tū′nĭ tĭ) | 114 | 47°37′N | 117°20′W |
| Oquirrh Mountains, mts., Ut., U.S. (ō′kwēr) | 117b | 40°38′N | 112°11′W |
| Oradea, Rom. (ô-räd′yä) | 154 | 47°02′N | 21°55′E |
| Oral, Kaz. | 183 | 51°14′N | 51°22′E |
| Oran, Alg. (ō-rän) (ô-räN′) | 230 | 35°46′N | 0°45′W |
| Orán, Arg. (ô-rȧ′n) | 144 | 23°13′S | 64°17′W |
| Oran, Mo., U.S. (ŏr′ȧn) | 121 | 37°05′N | 89°39′W |
| Oran, Sebkha d′, l., Alg. | 173 | 35°28′N | 0°28′W |
| Orange, Austl. (ŏr′ĕnj) | 219 | 33°15′S | 149°08′E |
| Orange, Fr. (ô-raNzh′) | 161 | 44°08′N | 4°48′E |
| Orange, Ca., U.S. | 117a | 33°48′N | 117°51′W |
| Orange, Ct., U.S. | 109 | 41°15′N | 73°00′W |
| Orange, N.J., U.S. | 110a | 40°46′N | 74°14′W |
| Orange, Tx., U.S. | 121 | 30°07′N | 93°44′W |
| Orange, r., Afr. | 232 | 29°15′S | 17°30′E |
| Orange, Cabo, c., Braz. (kȧ-bô-rȧ′n-zhĕ) | 143 | 4°25′N | 51°30′W |
| Orangeburg, S.C., U.S. (ŏr′ĕnj-bûrg) | 125 | 33°30′N | 80°50′W |
| Orange Cay, i., Bah. (ŏr-ĕnj kē) | 134 | 24°55′N | 79°05′W |
| Orange City, Ia., U.S. | 112 | 43°01′N | 96°06′W |
| Orange Lake, l., Fl., U.S. | 125 | 29°30′N | 82°12′W |
| Orangeville, Can. (ŏr′ĕnj-vĭl) | 99 | 43°55′N | 80°06′W |
| Orangeville, S. Afr. | 238c | 27°05′S | 28°13′E |
| Orange Walk, Belize (wôl′′k) | 132a | 18°09′N | 88°32′W |
| Orani, Phil. (ō-rä′nē) | 213a | 14°47′N | 120°32′E |
| Oranienburg, Ger. (ō-rä′nê-ĕn-bôrgh) | 168 | 52°45′N | 13°14′E |
| Oranjemund, Nmb. | 232 | 28°33′S | 16°20′E |
| Orăștie, Rom. (ô-rûsh′tyå) | 175 | 45°50′N | 23°14′E |
| Orbetello, Italy (ôr-bȧ-tĕl′lō) | 174 | 42°27′N | 11°15′E |
| Orbigo, r., Spain (ôr-bē′gō) | 172 | 42°30′N | 5°55′W |
| Orbost, Austl. (ôr′bŭst) | 222 | 37°43′S | 148°20′E |
| Orcas, i., Wa., U.S. (ôr′kȧs) | 116d | 48°43′N | 122°52′W |
| Orchard Farm, Mo., U.S. (ôr′chērd färm) | 117e | 38°53′N | 90°27′W |
| Orchard Park, N.Y., U.S. | 111c | 42°46′N | 78°46′W |
| Orchards, Wa., U.S. (ôr′chĕdz) | 116c | 45°40′N | 122°33′W |
| Orchila, Isla, i., Ven. | 142 | 11°47′N | 66°34′W |
| Ord, Ne., U.S. (ôrd) | 112 | 41°35′N | 98°57′W |
| Ord, r., Austl. | 220 | 17°30′S | 128°40′E |
| Ord, Mount, mtn., Az., U.S. | 119 | 33°55′N | 109°40′W |
| Orda, Kaz. (ŏr′dȧ) | 181 | 48°50′N | 47°30′E |
| Orda, Russia (ôr′dȧ) | 186a | 57°10′N | 57°12′E |
| Ordes, Spain | 172 | 43°00′N | 8°24′W |
| Ordos Desert, des., China | 204 | 39°12′N | 108°10′E |
| Ordu, Tur. (ôr′dô) | 163 | 41°00′N | 37°50′E |
| Ordway, Co., U.S. (ôrd′wā) | 120 | 38°11′N | 103°46′W |
| Örebro, Swe. (û′rē-brō) | 160 | 59°16′N | 15°11′E |
| Oredezh, r., Russia (ô′rĕ-dĕzh) | 186c | 59°23′N | 30°21′E |
| Oregon, Il., U.S. | 113 | 42°01′N | 89°21′W |
| Oregon, state, U.S. | 104 | 43°40′N | 121°50′W |
| Oregon Caves National Monument, rec., Or., U.S. (cāvz) | 114 | 42°05′N | 123°13′W |
| Oregon City, Or., U.S. | 116c | 45°21′N | 122°36′W |
| Öregrund, Swe. (û-rĕ-grōnd) | 166 | 60°20′N | 18°26′E |
| Orekhovo, Blg. | 175 | 43°43′N | 23°59′E |
| Orekhovo-Zuyevo, Russia (ôr-yĕ′κô-vô zô′yĕ-vô) | 178 | 55°46′N | 39°00′E |
| Orël, Russia (ôr-yôl′) | 178 | 52°59′N | 36°05′E |
| Orël, prov., Russia | 176 | 52°35′N | 36°08′E |
| Orem, Ut., U.S. (ō′rĕm) | 119 | 40°15′N | 111°50′W |
| Ore Mountains *see* Erzgebirge, mts., Eur. | 156 | 50°29′N | 12°40′E |
| Orenburg, Russia (ô′rĕn-bōōrg) | 178 | 51°50′N | 55°05′E |
| Øresund, strt., Eur. | 166 | 55°50′N | 12°40′E |
| Órganos, Sierra de los, mts., Cuba (sē-ĕ′r-rä-dĕ-lôs-ŏ′r-gä-nôs) | 134 | 22°20′N | 84°10′W |
| Organ Pipe Cactus National Monument, rec., Az., U.S. (ôr′gȧn pīp kăk′tŭs) | 119 | 32°14′N | 113°05′W |
| Orgãos, Serra das, mtn., Braz. (sĕ′r-rä-däs-ôr-gouN′s) | 141a | 22°30′S | 43°01′W |
| Orhei, Mol. | 181 | 47°27′N | 28°49′E |
| Orhon, r., Mong. | 204 | 48°33′N | 103°07′E |
| Oriental, Cordillera, mts., Col. (kôr-dēl-yĕ′rä) | 142a | 3°30′N | 74°27′W |
| Oriental, Cordillera, mts., Dom. Rep. (kôr-dēl-yĕ′rä-ô-ryĕ′n-täl) | 135 | 18°55′N | 69°40′W |
| Oriental, Cordillera, mts., S.A. (kôr-dēl-yĕ′rä ō-rē-ĕn-täl′) | 142 | 14°00′S | 68°33′W |
| Orikhiv, Ukr. | 177 | 47°34′N | 35°51′E |


ng-sing; ŋ-baŋk; N-nasalized n; nŏd; cŏmmit; ōld; ôbey; ôrder; oi-boil; fōōd; ŏ-as oo in foot; ou-out; s-soft; sh-dish; th-thin; pūre; ûnite; ûrn; stŭd; circŭs; ü-as in French tu; ′-indeterminate vowel.

PRONOUNCING INDEX

Paarl – Paris 333


| PLACE (Pronunciation) | PAGE | LAT. | LONG. |
|---|---|---|---|
| **P** | | | |
| Paarl, S. Afr. (pärl) | 232 | 33°45'S | 18°55'E |
| Pa'auilo, Hi., U.S. (pä-ä-o͞o'ē-lō) | 126a | 20°03'N | 155°25'W |
| Pabianice, Pol. (pä-byȧ-nē'tsĕ) | 169 | 51°40'N | 19°29'E |
| Pacaás Novos, Massiço de, mts., Braz. | 142 | 11°03'S | 64°02'W |
| Pacaraima, Serra, mts., S.A. (sĕr'rȧ pä-kä-rä-ē'mȧ) | 142 | 3°45'N | 62°30'W |
| Pacasmayo, Peru (pä-käs-mä'yō) | 142 | 7°24'S | 79°30'W |
| Pachuca, Mex. (pä-cho͞o'kä) | 128 | 20°07'N | 98°43'W |
| Pacific, Wa., U.S. (pȧ-sĭf'ĭk) | 116a | 47°16'N | 122°15'W |
| Pacifica, Ca., U.S. (pȧ-sĭf'ĭ-kä) | 116b | 37°38'N | 122°29'W |
| Pacific Beach, Ca., U.S. | 118a | 32°47'N | 117°22'W |
| Pacific Grove, Ca., U.S. | 118 | 36°37'N | 121°54'W |
| Pacific Islands, Trust Territory of the *see* Palau, nation, Oc. | 3 | 7°15'N | 134°30'E |
| Pacific Ocean, o. | 2 | 0°00' | 170°00'W |
| Pacific Ranges, mts., Can. | 94 | 51°00'N | 125°30'W |
| Pacific Rim National Park, rec., Can. | 94 | 49°00'N | 126°00'W |
| Pacolet, r., S.C., U.S. (pă'cō-lĕt) | 125 | 34°55'N | 81°49'W |
| Pacy-sur-Eure, Fr. (pä-sē-sür-ûr') | 171b | 49°01'N | 1°24'E |
| Padang, Indon. (pä-däng') | 212 | 1°01'S | 100°28'E |
| Padang, i., Indon. | 197b | 1°12'N | 102°21'E |
| Padang Endau, Malay. | 197b | 2°39'N | 103°38'E |
| Paden City, W.V., U.S. (pā'dĕn) | 108 | 39°30'N | 80°55'W |
| Paderborn, Ger. (pä-dĕr-bôrn') | 168 | 51°43'N | 8°46'E |
| Padibe, Ug. | 237 | 3°28'N | 32°50'E |
| Padiham, Eng., U.K. (păd'ĭ-hăm) | 158a | 53°48'N | 2°19'W |
| Padilla, Mex. (pä-dēl'yä) | 130 | 24°00'N | 98°45'W |
| Padilla Bay, b., Wa., U.S. (pä-dĕl'lȧ) | 116a | 48°31'N | 122°34'W |
| Padova, Italy (pä'dô-vä)(păd'û-ȧ) | 162 | 45°24'N | 11°53'E |
| Padre Island, i., Tx., U.S. (pä'drā) | 123 | 27°09'N | 97°15'W |
| Padua *see* Padova, Italy | 162 | 45°24'N | 11°53'E |
| Paducah, Ky., U.S. | 105 | 37°05'N | 88°36'W |
| Paducah, Tx., U.S. | 120 | 34°01'N | 100°18'W |
| Paektu-san, mtn., Asia (pâk'to͞o-sän') | 210 | 42°00'N | 128°03'E |
| Pag, i., Serb. (päg) | 174 | 44°30'N | 14°48'E |
| Pagai Selatan, Pulau, i., Indon. | 212 | 2°48'S | 100°22'E |
| Pagai Utara, Pulau, i., Indon. | 212 | 2°45'S | 100°02'E |
| Pagasitikós Kólpos, b., Grc. | 175 | 39°15'N | 23°00'E |
| Page, Az., U.S. | 119 | 36°57'N | 111°27'W |
| Pago Pago, Am. Sam. | 214a | 14°16'S | 170°42'W |
| Pagosa Springs, Co., U.S. (pȧ-gō'sȧ) | 120 | 37°15'N | 107°05'W |
| Pāhala, Hi., U.S. (pä-hä'lä) | 126a | 19°11'N | 155°28'W |
| Pahang, state, Malay. | 197b | 3°02'N | 102°57'E |
| Pahang, r., Malay. | 212 | 3°39'N | 102°41'E |
| Pahokee, Fl., U.S. (pȧ-hō'kē) | 125a | 26°45'N | 80°40'W |
| Paide, Est. (pī'dĕ) | 167 | 58°54'N | 25°30'E |
| Päijänne, l., Fin. (pĕ'ē-yĕn-nĕ) | 160 | 61°38'N | 25°05'E |
| Pailolo Channel, strt., Hi., U.S. (pä-ē-lō'lō) | 126a | 21°05'N | 156°41'W |
| Paine, Chile (pī'nĕ) | 141b | 33°49'S | 70°44'W |
| Painesville, Oh., U.S. (pānz'vĭl) | 108 | 41°40'N | 81°15'W |
| Painted Desert, des., Az., U.S. (pānt'ĕd) | 120 | 36°15'N | 111°35'W |
| Painted Rock Reservoir, res., Az., U.S. | 119 | 33°00'N | 113°05'W |
| Paintsville, Ky., U.S. (pānts'vĭl) | 108 | 37°50'N | 82°50'W |
| Paisley, Scot., U.K. (pāz'lĭ) | 160 | 55°50'N | 4°30'W |
| Paita, Peru (pä-ē'tä) | 142 | 5°11'S | 81°12'W |
| Pai T'ou Shan, mts., Kor., N. | 205 | 40°30'N | 127°20'E |
| Paiute Indian Reservation, I.R., Ut., U.S. | 119 | 38°17'N | 113°50'W |
| Pajápan, Mex. (pä-hä'pän) | 131 | 18°16'N | 94°41'W |
| Pakanbaru, Indon. | 212 | 0°43'N | 101°15'E |
| Pakhra, r., Russia (päk'rȧ) | 186b | 55°29'N | 37°51'E |
| Pakistan, nation, Asia | 199 | 28°00'N | 67°30'E |
| Pakokku, Mya. (pȧ-kŏk'kö) | 204 | 21°29'N | 95°00'E |
| Paks, Hung. (pôksh) | 169 | 46°38'N | 18°53'E |
| Pala, Chad | 235 | 9°22'N | 14°54'E |
| Palacios, Tx., U.S. (pȧ-lä'syōs) | 123 | 28°42'N | 96°12'W |
| Palagruža, Otoci, is., Cro. | 174 | 42°20'N | 16°23'E |
| Palaiseau, Fr. (pȧ-lĕ-zō') | 171b | 48°44'N | 2°16'E |
| Palana, Russia | 179 | 59°07'N | 159°58'E |
| Palanan Bay, b., Phil. (pä-lä'nän) | 213a | 17°14'N | 122°35'E |
| Palanan Point, c., Phil. | 213a | 17°12'N | 122°40'E |
| Pālanpur, India (pä'lŭn-po͞or) | 199 | 24°08'N | 73°29'E |
| Palapye, Bots. (pȧ-läp'yĕ) | 232 | 22°34'S | 27°28'E |
| Palatine, Il., U.S. (păl'ȧ-tīn) | 111a | 42°07'N | 88°03'W |
| Palatka, Fl., U.S. (pȧ-lăt'kȧ) | 125 | 29°39'N | 81°40'W |
| Palau (Belau), nation, Oc. (pä-lä'ò) | 3 | 7°15'N | 134°30'E |
| Palauig, Phil. (pȧ-lou'ĕg) | 213a | 15°27'N | 119°54'E |
| Palawan, i., Phil. (pä-lä'wan) | 212 | 9°50'N | 117°38'E |
| Pālayankottai, India | 203 | 8°50'N | 77°50'E |
| Paldiski, Est. (päl'dĭ-skĭ) | 167 | 59°22'N | 24°04'E |
| Palembang, Indon. (pä-lĕm-bäng') | 212 | 2°57'S | 104°40'E |
| Palencia, Guat. (pä-lĕn'sē-ȧ) | 132 | 14°40'N | 90°22'W |
| Palencia, Spain (pä-lĕ'n-syä) | 162 | 42°02'N | 4°32'W |
| Palenque, Mex. (pä-lĕŋ'kā) | 131 | 17°34'N | 91°58'W |
| Palenque, Punta, c., Dom. Rep. (po͞o'n-tä) | 135 | 18°10'N | 70°10'W |
| Palermo, Col. (pä-lĕr'mô) | 142a | 2°53'N | 75°26'W |
| Palermo, Italy | 154 | 38°08'N | 13°24'E |
| Palestine, Tx., U.S. | 105 | 31°46'N | 95°38'W |
| Palestine, hist. reg., Asia (păl'ĕs-tīn) | 197a | 31°33'N | 35°00'E |
| Paletwa, Mya. (pŭ-lĕt'wä) | 199 | 21°19'N | 92°52'E |
| Palghāt, India | 203 | 10°49'N | 76°40'E |
| Pāli, India | 202 | 25°53'N | 73°18'E |
| Palín, Guat. (pä-lēn') | 132 | 14°42'N | 90°42'W |
| Palizada, Mex. (pä-lē-zä'dä) | 131 | 18°17'N | 92°04'W |
| Palk Strait, strt., Asia (pôk) | 199 | 10°00'N | 79°23'E |
| Palma, Braz. (päl'mä) | 141a | 21°23'S | 42°18'W |
| Palma, Spain | 154 | 39°35'N | 2°38'E |
| Palma, Bahía de, b., Spain | 173 | 39°24'N | 2°37'E |
| Palma del Río, Spain | 172 | 37°43'N | 5°19'W |
| Palmares, Braz. (päl-mä'rĕs) | 143 | 8°46'S | 35°28'W |
| Palmas, Braz. (päl'mäs) | 144 | 26°20'S | 51°56'W |
| Palmas, Braz. | 143 | 10°08'S | 48°18'W |
| Palmas, Cape, c., Lib. | 230 | 4°22'N | 7°44'W |
| Palma Soriano, Cuba (sô-ré-ä'nō) | 134 | 20°15'N | 76°00'W |
| Palm Beach, Fl., U.S. (päm bēch') | 125a | 26°43'N | 80°03'W |
| Palmeira dos Índios, Braz. (pä-mā'rä-dôs-ē'n-dyôs) | 143 | 9°26'S | 36°33'W |
| Palmeirinhas, Ponta das, c., Ang. | 236 | 9°05'S | 13°00'E |
| Palmela, Port. (päl-mā'lä) | 172 | 38°34'N | 8°54'W |
| Palmer, Ak., U.S. (päm'ẽr) | 103 | 61°38'N | 149°15'W |
| Palmer, Wa., U.S. | 116a | 47°19'N | 121°53'W |
| Palmerston North, N.Z. (päm'ẽr-stŭn) | 221a | 40°20'S | 175°35'E |
| Palmerville, Austl. (päm'ẽr-vĭl) | 219 | 16°08'S | 144°15'E |
| Palmetto, Fl., U.S. (pȧl-mĕt'ô) | 125a | 27°32'N | 82°34'W |
| Palmetto Point, c., Bah. | 135 | 21°15'N | 73°25'W |
| Palmi, Italy (päl'mē) | 174 | 38°21'N | 15°54'E |
| Palmira, Col. (päl-mē'rä) | 142 | 3°33'N | 76°17'W |
| Palmira, Cuba | 134 | 22°15'N | 80°25'W |
| Palmyra, Mo., U.S. (păl-mī'rȧ) | 121 | 39°45'N | 91°32'W |
| Palmyra, N.J., U.S. | 110f | 40°01'N | 75°00'W |
| Palmyra, i., Oc. | 2 | 6°00'N | 162°20'W |
| Palmyra, hist., Syria | 198 | 34°25'N | 38°28'E |
| Palmyras Point, c., India | 202 | 20°42'N | 87°45'E |
| Palo Alto, Ca., U.S. (pă'lō ăl'tō) | 116b | 37°27'N | 122°09'W |
| Paloduro Creek, r., Tx., U.S. (pā-lō-do͞o'rō) | 120 | 36°16'N | 101°12'W |
| Paloh, Malay. | 197b | 2°11'N | 103°12'E |
| Paloma, l., Mex. (pä-lō'mä) | 122 | 26°53'N | 104°02'W |
| Palomo, Cerro el, mtn., Chile (sĕ'r-rō-ĕl-pä-lō'mô) | 141b | 34°36'S | 70°20'W |
| Palos, Cabo de, c., Spain (kȧ'bô-dĕ-pä'lôs) | 162 | 39°38'N | 0°43'W |
| Palos Verdes Estates, Ca., U.S. (pă'lŭs vûr'dĭs) | 117a | 33°48'N | 118°24'W |
| Palouse, Wa., U.S. (pȧ-lo͞oz') | 114 | 46°54'N | 117°04'W |
| Palouse, r., Wa., U.S. | 114 | 47°02'N | 117°35'W |
| Palu, Tur. (pä-loo') | 181 | 38°55'N | 40°10'E |
| Paluan, Phil. (pä-lo͞o'än) | 213a | 13°25'N | 120°29'E |
| Pamiers, Fr. (pȧ-myā') | 161 | 43°07'N | 1°34'E |
| Pamirs, mts., Asia | 199 | 38°14'N | 72°27'E |
| Pamlico, r., N.C., U.S. (păm'lĭ-kō) | 125 | 35°25'N | 76°59'W |
| Pamlico Sound, strt., N.C., U.S. | 107 | 35°10'N | 76°10'W |
| Pampa, Tx., U.S. (păm'pȧ) | 104 | 35°32'N | 100°56'W |
| Pampa de Castillo, pl., Arg. (pä'm-pä-dĕ-käs-tē'l-yô) | 144 | 45°30'S | 67°30'W |
| Pampana, r., S.L. | 234 | 8°35'N | 11°55'W |
| Pampanga, r., Phil. (päm-päŋ'gä) | 213a | 15°20'N | 120°48'E |
| Pampas, reg., Arg. (päm'päs) | 144 | 37°00'S | 64°30'W |
| Pampilhosa do Botão, Port. (päm-pē-lyō'sȧ-dô-bō-toùn) | 172 | 40°21'N | 8°32'W |
| Pamplona, Col. (päm-plō'nä) | 142 | 7°19'N | 72°41'W |
| Pamplona, Spain (päm-plô'nä) | 162 | 42°49'N | 1°39'W |
| Pamunkey, r., Va., U.S. (pȧ-mŭŋ'kĭ) | 109 | 37°40'N | 77°20'W |
| Pana, Il., U.S. (pā'nȧ) | 108 | 39°25'N | 89°05'W |
| Panagyurishte, Blg. (pȧ-nȧ-gyo͞o'rēsh-tĕ) | 175 | 42°30'N | 24°11'E |
| Panaji (Panjim), India | 199 | 15°33'N | 73°52'E |
| Panamá, Pan. | 129 | 8°58'N | 79°32'W |
| Panama, nation, N.A. | 129 | 9°00'N | 80°00'W |
| Panamá, Istmo de, isth., Pan. | 129 | 9°00'N | 80°00'W |
| Panama Canal, can., Pan. | 128a | 9°20'N | 79°55'W |
| Panama City, Fl., U.S. (păn-ȧ mä' sĭ'tĭ) | 124 | 30°08'N | 85°39'W |
| Panamint Range, mts., Ca., U.S. (păn-ȧ-mĭnt') | 118 | 36°40'N | 117°30'W |
| Panarea, i., Italy (pä-nä'rē-a) | 174 | 38°37'N | 15°05'E |
| Panaro, r., Italy (pä-nä'rô) | 174 | 44°47'N | 11°06'E |
| Panay, i., Phil. (pä-nī') | 212 | 11°15'N | 121°38'E |
| Pančevo, Serb. (pȧn'chĕ-vô) | 163 | 44°52'N | 20°42'E |
| Panchor, Malay. | 197b | 2°11'N | 102°43'E |
| Pānchur, India | 202a | 22°31'N | 88°17'E |
| Panda, D.R.C. (pän'dä') | 232 | 10°59'S | 27°24'E |
| Pan de Guajaibon, mtn., Cuba (pän dā gwä-jȧ-bōn') | 134 | 22°50'N | 83°20'W |
| Panevėžys, Lith. (pä'nyĕ-vāzh'ĕs) | 180 | 55°44'N | 24°21'E |
| Panga, D.R.C. (päŋ'gä) | 231 | 1°51'N | 26°25'E |
| Pangani, Tan. (pän-gä'nē) | 233 | 5°28'S | 38°58'E |
| Pangani, r., Tan. | 237 | 4°40'S | 37°45'E |
| Pangkalpinang, Indon. (päng-käl'pē-näng') | 212 | 2°11'S | 106°04'E |
| Pangnirtung, Can. | 91 | 66°08'N | 65°26'W |
| Panguitch, Ut., U.S. (pän'gwĭch) | 119 | 37°50'N | 112°30'W |
| Panié, Mont, mtn., N. Cal. | 214f | 20°36'S | 164°46'E |
| Pānihāti, India | 202a | 22°42'N | 88°23'E |
| Panimávida, Chile (pä-nē-mȧ'vē-dä) | 141b | 35°44'S | 71°26'W |
| Panshi, China (pän-shē) | 208 | 42°50'N | 126°48'E |
| Pantar, Pulau, i., Indon. (pän'tär) | 213 | 8°40'N | 123°45'E |
| Pantelleria, i., Italy (pän-tĕl-lā-rē'ä) | 162 | 36°43'N | 11°59'E |
| Pantepec, Mex. (pän-tā-pĕk') | 131 | 17°11'N | 93°04'W |
| Panuco, Mex. (pä'no͞o-kô) | 130 | 22°04'N | 98°11'W |
| Pánuco, Mex. (pä'no͞o-kô) | 130 | 23°25'N | 105°55'W |
| Panuco, r., Mex. | 128 | 21°59'N | 98°20'W |
| Pánuco de Coronado, Mex. (pä'no͞o-kô dā kō-rô-nä'dhō) | 122 | 24°33'N | 104°20'W |
| Panvel, India | 203b | 18°59'N | 73°06'E |
| Panyu, China (pä-yo͞o) | 207a | 22°56'N | 113°22'E |
| Panzós, Guat. (pä-zós') | 132 | 15°26'N | 89°40'W |
| Pao, r., Ven. (pà'ō) | 143b | 9°52'N | 67°57'W |
| Paola, Ks., U.S. (pȧ-ō'lȧ) | 121 | 38°34'N | 94°51'W |
| Paoli, In., U.S. (pȧ-ō'lĭ) | 108 | 38°35'N | 86°30'W |
| Paoli, Pa., U.S. | 110f | 40°03'N | 75°29'W |
| Paonia, Co., U.S. (pā-ō'nyȧ) | 119 | 38°50'N | 107°40'W |
| Pápa, Hung. (pä'pô) | 163 | 47°18'N | 17°27'E |
| Papagayo, r., Mex. (pä-pä-gä'yō) | 130 | 16°52'N | 99°41'W |
| Papagayo, Golfo del, b., C.R. (gôl-fô-dĕl-pä-pä-gá'yō) | 132 | 10°44'N | 85°56'W |
| Papagayo, Laguna, l., Mex. (lä-ò-nä) | 130 | 16°44'N | 99°44'W |
| Papantla de Olarte, Mex. (pä-pän'tlä dā-ô-lä'r-tĕ) | 128 | 20°30'N | 97°15'W |
| Papatoapan, r., Mex. (pä-pä-tô-ā-pä'n) | 131 | 18°00'N | 96°22'W |
| Papenburg, Ger. (päp'ĕn-bòrgh) | 168 | 53°05'N | 7°23'E |
| Papinas, Arg. (pä-pē'näs) | 141c | 35°30'S | 57°19'W |
| Papineauville, Can. (pä-pē-nō'vēl) | 102c | 45°38'N | 75°01'W |
| Papua, Gulf of, b., Pap. N. Gui. (păp-o͞o-ȧ) | 213 | 8°20'S | 144°45'E |
| Papua New Guinea, nation, Oc. (păp-o͞o-ȧ)(gĭne) | 213 | 7°00'S | 142°15'E |
| Papudo, Chile (pä-po͞o'dô) | 141b | 32°30'S | 71°25'W |
| Paquequer Pequeno, Braz. (pä-kĕ-kĕ'r-pĕ-kĕ'nô) | 144b | 22°19'S | 43°02'W |
| Para, r., Russia | 176 | 53°45'N | 40°58'E |
| Paracale, Phil. (pä-rä-kä'lå) | 213a | 14°17'N | 122°47'E |
| Paracambi, Braz. | 144b | 22°36'S | 43°43'W |
| Paracatu, Braz. (pä-rä-kä-to͞o') | 143 | 17°17'S | 46°43'W |
| Paracel Islands, is., Asia | 212 | 16°40'N | 113°00'E |
| Paraćin, Serb. (pá'rä-chēn) | 163 | 43°51'N | 21°26'E |
| Para de Minas, Braz. (pä-rä-dĕ-mē'näs) | 143 | 19°52'S | 44°37'W |
| Paradise, i., Bah. | 134 | 25°05'N | 77°20'W |
| Paradise Valley, Nv., U.S. (păr'ȧ-dīs) | 114 | 41°28'N | 117°32'W |
| Parados, Cerro de los, mtn., Col. (sĕ'r-rō-dĕ-lôs-pä-rä'dôs) | 142a | 5°44'N | 75°13'W |
| Paragould, Ar., U.S. (păr'ȧ-go͞old) | 121 | 36°03'N | 90°29'W |
| Paraguaçu, r., Braz. (pä-rä-gwä-zo͞o') | 143 | 12°25'S | 39°46'W |
| Paraguay, nation, S.A. (păr'ȧ-gwā) | 144 | 24°00'S | 57°00'W |
| Paraguay, r., S.A. (pä-rä-gwä'y) | 144 | 21°12'S | 57°31'W |
| Paraíba, state, Braz. (pä-rä-ē'bä) | 143 | 7°11'S | 37°05'W |
| Paraíba, r., Braz. | 141a | 23°02'S | 45°43'W |
| Paraíba do Sul, Braz. (dô-so͞o'l) | 141a | 22°10'S | 43°18'W |
| Paraibuna, Braz. (pä-räē-bo͞o'nä) | 141a | 23°23'S | 45°38'W |
| Paraíso, C.R. | 133 | 9°50'N | 83°53'W |
| Paraíso, Mex. | 131 | 18°24'N | 93°11'W |
| Paraiso, Pan. (pä-rä-ē'sō) | 128a | 9°02'N | 79°38'W |
| Paraisópolis, Braz. (pä-räē-sô'pō-lēs) | 141a | 22°35'S | 45°45'W |
| Paraitinga, r., Braz. (pä-rä-ē-tē'n-gä) | 141a | 23°15'S | 45°24'W |
| Parakou, Benin (pȧ-rȧ-ko͞o') | 230 | 9°21'N | 2°37'E |
| Paramaribo, Sur. (pȧ-rȧ-mȧ'rē-bō) | 143 | 5°50'N | 55°15'W |
| Paramatta, Austl. (păr-ȧ-măt'ȧ) | 217b | 33°49'S | 150°59'E |
| Paramillo, mtn., Col. (pä-rä-mē'l-yō) | 142a | 7°06'N | 75°55'W |
| Paramus, N.J., U.S. | 110a | 40°56'N | 74°04'W |
| Paran, r., Asia | 197a | 30°05'N | 34°50'E |
| Paraná, Arg. | 144 | 31°44'S | 60°32'W |
| Paraná, r., S.A. | 144 | 24°00'S | 54°00'W |
| Paranaíba, Braz. (pä-rä-nȧ-ē'bȧ) | 143 | 19°43'S | 51°13'W |
| Paranaíba, r., Braz. | 143 | 18°58'S | 50°44'W |
| Paraná Ibicuy, r., Arg. | 141c | 33°27'S | 59°26'W |
| Paranam, Sur. | 143 | 5°39'N | 55°13'W |
| Paranápanema, r., Braz. (pä-rä'ná'pä-nĕ-mä) | 143 | 22°28'S | 52°15'W |
| Paraopeda, r., Braz. (pä-rä-o-pĕ'dä) | 141a | 20°09'S | 44°14'W |
| Parapara, Ven. (pä-rä-pä-rä) | 143b | 9°44'N | 67°17'W |
| Parati, Braz. (pä-rätē) | 141a | 23°14'S | 44°43'W |
| Paray-le-Monial, Fr. (pȧ-rĕ'lē-mô-nyäl') | 170 | 46°27'N | 4°14'E |
| Pārbati, r., India | 202 | 24°50'N | 76°44'E |
| Parchim, Ger. (par'kĭm) | 168 | 53°25'N | 11°52'E |
| Parczew, Pol. (pär'chĕf) | 169 | 51°38'N | 22°53'E |
| Pardo, r., Braz. (pär'dō) | 143 | 15°25'S | 39°40'W |
| Pardo, r., Braz. | 141a | 21°32'S | 46°40'W |
| Pardubice, Czech Rep. (pär'dò-bĭt-sĕ) | 168 | 50°02'N | 15°47'E |
| Parecis, Serra dos, mts., Braz. (sĕr'rȧ dôs pä-rä-sēzh') | 143 | 13°45'S | 59°28'W |
| Paredes de Nava, Spain (pä-rā'dās dā nä'vä) | 172 | 42°10'N | 4°41'W |
| Paredón, Mex. | 122 | 25°56'N | 100°58'W |
| Parent, Can. | 91 | 47°59'N | 74°30'W |
| Parent, Lac, l., Can. | 99 | 48°40'N | 77°00'W |
| Parepare, Indon. | 212 | 4°01'S | 119°38'E |
| Pargolovo, Russia (pȧr-gô'lô vô) | 186c | 60°04'N | 30°18'E |
| Paria, r., Az., U.S. | 119 | 37°07'N | 111°51'W |
| Paria, Golfo de, b. (gôl-fô-dĕ-br-pä-rē-ä) | 142 | 10°33'N | 62°14'W |
| Paricutín, Volcán, vol., Mex. | 130 | 19°27'N | 102°14'W |
| Parida, Río de la, r., Mex. (rē'ō-dĕ-lä-pä-rē'dä) | 122 | 26°23'N | 104°40'W |
| Parima, Serra, mts., S.A. (sĕr'rȧ pä-rē'mȧ) | 142 | 3°45'N | 64°00'W |
| Pariñas, Punta, c., Peru (po͞o'n-tä-pä-rē'n-yäs) | 142 | 4°30'S | 81°23'W |
| Parintins, Braz. (pä-rĭn-tĭnzh') | 143 | 2°34'S | 56°30'W |
| Paris, Can. | 99 | 43°15'N | 80°23'W |
| Paris, Fr. (pȧ-rē') | 154 | 48°51'N | 2°20'E |
| Paris, Ar., U.S. (păr'ĭs) | 121 | 35°17'N | 93°43'W |
| Paris, Il., U.S. | 108 | 39°35'N | 87°40'W |
| Paris, Ky., U.S. | 108 | 38°15'N | 84°15'W |
| Paris, Mo., U.S. | 121 | 39°27'N | 91°59'W |
| Paris, Tn., U.S. | 124 | 36°16'N | 88°20'W |
| Paris, Tx., U.S. | 105 | 33°39'N | 95°33'W |


ng-sing; ŋ-baŋk; ɴ-nasalized n; nŏd; cŏmmit; ōld; ôbey; ôrder; oi-boil; fo͞od; ŏ-as oo in foot; ou-out; s-soft; sh-dish; th-thin; pūre; ûnite; ûrn; stŭd; circŭs; ü-as in French tu; '-indeterminate vowel.

334 Parita – Penistone PRONOUNCING INDEX


| PLACE (Pronunciation) | PAGE | LAT. | LONG. |
|---|---|---|---|
| Parita, Golfo de, b., Pan. (gôl-fô-dĕ-pä-rē'tä) | 133 | 8°06'N | 80°10'W |
| Park City, Ut., U.S. | 115 | 40°39'N | 111°33'W |
| Parker, S.D., U.S. (pär'kẽr) | 112 | 43°24'N | 97°10'W |
| Parker Dam, dam, U.S. | 106 | 34°20'N | 114°00'W |
| Parkersburg, W.V., U.S. (pär'kẽrz-bûrg) | 105 | 39°15'N | 81°35'W |
| Parkes, Austl. (pärks) | 222 | 33°10'S | 148°10'E |
| Park Falls, Wi., U.S. (pärk) | 113 | 45°55'N | 90°29'W |
| Park Forest, Il., U.S. | 111a | 41°29'N | 87°41'W |
| Parkland, Wa., U.S. (pärk'lănd) | 116a | 47°09'N | 122°26'W |
| Park Range, mts., Co., U.S. | 115 | 40°54'N | 106°40'W |
| Park Rapids, Mn., U.S. | 112 | 46°53'N | 95°05'W |
| Park Ridge, Il., U.S. | 111a | 42°00'N | 87°50'W |
| Park River, N.D., U.S. | 112 | 48°22'N | 97°43'W |
| Parkrose, Or., U.S. (pärk'rōz) | 116c | 45°33'N | 122°33'W |
| Park Rynie, S. Afr. | 233c | 30°22'S | 30°43'E |
| Parkston, S.D., U.S. (pärks'tŭn) | 112 | 43°22'N | 97°59'W |
| Parkville, Md., U.S. | 110e | 39°22'N | 76°32'W |
| Parkville, Mo., U.S. | 117f | 39°12'N | 94°41'W |
| Parla, Spain (pär'lä) | 173a | 40°14'N | 3°46'W |
| Parma, Italy (pär'mä) | 162 | 44°48'N | 10°20'E |
| Parma, Oh., U.S. | 111d | 41°23'N | 81°44'W |
| Parma Heights, Oh., U.S. | 111d | 41°23'N | 81°36'W |
| Parnaíba, Braz. (pär-nä-ē'bä) | 143 | 3°00'S | 41°42'W |
| Parnaíba, r., Braz. | 143 | 3°57'S | 42°30'W |
| Parnassós, mtn., Grc. | 175 | 38°36'N | 22°35'E |
| Parndorf, Aus. | 159e | 48°00'N | 16°52'E |
| Pärnu, Est. (pĕr'nōō) | 180 | 58°24'N | 24°29'E |
| Pärnu, r., Est. | 167 | 58°40'N | 25°05'E |
| Pärnu Laht, b., Est. (läkt) | 167 | 58°15'N | 24°17'E |
| Paro, Bhu. (pä'rô) | 202 | 27°30'N | 89°30'E |
| Paroo, r., Austl. (pä'rōō) | 221 | 30°00'S | 144°00'E |
| Páros, Grc. (pä'rôs) (pā'rŏs) | 175 | 37°05'N | 25°14'E |
| Páros, i., Grc. | 163 | 37°11'N | 25°00'E |
| Parow, S. Afr. (pă'rō) | 232a | 33°54'S | 18°36'E |
| Parowan, Ut., U.S. (păr'ō-wăn) | 119 | 37°50'N | 112°50'W |
| Parral, Chile (pär-rä'l) | 144 | 36°07'S | 71°47'W |
| Parral, r., Mex. | 122 | 27°25'N | 105°08'W |
| Parramatta, r., Austl. (păr-à-măt'à) | 217b | 33°42'S | 150°58'E |
| Parras, Mex. (pär-räs') | 122 | 25°28'N | 102°08'W |
| Parrita, C.R. (pär-rē'tä) | 133 | 9°32'N | 84°17'W |
| Parrsboro, Can. (pärz'bŭr-ō) | 100 | 45°24'N | 64°20'W |
| Parry, i., Can. (păr'ĭ) | 99 | 45°15'N | 80°00'W |
| Parry, Mount, mtn., Can. | 94 | 52°53'N | 128°45'W |
| Parry Islands, is., Can. | 89 | 75°30'N | 110°00'W |
| Parry Sound, Can. | 91 | 45°20'N | 80°00'W |
| Parsnip, r., Can. (pärs'nĭp) | 95 | 54°45'N | 122°20'W |
| Parsons, Ks., U.S. (pär's'nz) | 105 | 37°20'N | 95°16'W |
| Parsons, W.V., U.S. | 109 | 39°05'N | 79°40'W |
| Parthenay, Fr. (pàr-t'nĕ') | 170 | 46°39'N | 0°16'W |
| Partinico, Italy (pär-tē'nê-kô) | 174 | 38°02'N | 13°11'E |
| Partizansk, Russia | 179 | 43°15'N | 133°19'E |
| Parys, S. Afr. (pà-rīs') | 238c | 26°53'S | 27°28'E |
| Pasadena, Ca., U.S. (păs-à-dē'nà) | 104 | 34°09'N | 118°09'W |
| Pasadena, Md., U.S. | 110e | 39°06'N | 76°35'W |
| Pasadena, Tx., U.S. | 123a | 29°43'N | 95°13'W |
| Pascagoula, Ms., U.S. (păs-kà-gōō'là) | 124 | 30°22'N | 88°33'W |
| Pascagoula, r., Ms., U.S. | 124 | 30°52'N | 88°48'W |
| Paşcani, Rom. (päsh-kän') | 169 | 47°46'N | 26°42'E |
| Pasco, Wa., U.S. (păs'kō) | 114 | 46°13'N | 119°04'W |
| Pascua, Isla de (Easter Island), i., Chile | 241 | 26°50'S | 109°00'W |
| Pasewalk, Ger. (pä'zĕ-välk) | 168 | 53°31'N | 14°01'E |
| Pashiya, Russia (pä'shĭ-yà) | 186a | 58°27'N | 58°17'E |
| Pashkovo, Russia (pàsh-kô'vô) | 210 | 48°52'N | 131°09'E |
| Pashkovskaya, Russia (pàsh-kôf'skà-yà) | 177 | 45°00'N | 39°04'E |
| Pasig, Phil. | 213a | 14°34'N | 121°05'E |
| Pasión, Río de la, r., Guat. (rē'ō-dĕ-lä-pä-syōn') | 132a | 16°31'N | 90°11'W |
| Paso de los Libres, Arg. (pä-sô-dĕ-lôs-lē'brĕs) | 144 | 29°33'S | 57°05'W |
| Paso de los Toros, Ur. (tō'rôs) | 141c | 32°43'S | 56°33'W |
| Paso Robles, Ca., U.S. (pă'sō rō'blĕs) | 118 | 35°38'N | 120°44'W |
| Pasquia Hills, hills, Can. (păs'kwē-à) | 97 | 53°13'N | 102°37'W |
| Passaic, N.J., U.S. (pă-sā'ĭk) | 110a | 40°52'N | 74°08'W |
| Passaic, r., N.J., U.S. | 110a | 40°42'N | 74°26'W |
| Passamaquoddy Bay, b., N.A. (păs'à-mà-kwŏd'ĭ) | 100 | 45°06'N | 66°59'W |
| Passa Tempo, Braz. (pä's-sä-tĕ'm-pô) | 141a | 20°40'S | 44°29'W |
| Passau, Ger. (päsou) | 161 | 48°34'N | 13°27'E |
| Pass Christian, Ms., U.S. (pàs krĭs'tyĕn) | 124 | 30°20'N | 89°15'W |
| Passero, Cape, c., Italy (päs-sĕ'rô) | 156 | 36°34'N | 15°13'E |
| Passo Fundo, Braz. (pä'sō fōō'n'dō) | 144 | 28°16'S | 52°13'W |
| Passos, Braz. (pä's-sōs) | 143 | 20°45'S | 46°37'W |
| Pastaza, r., S.A. (päs-tä'zä) | 142 | 3°05'S | 76°18'W |
| Pasto, Col. (päs'tō) | 142 | 1°15'N | 77°19'W |
| Pastora, Mex. (päs-tô-rä) | 130 | 22°08'N | 100°04'W |
| Pasuruan, Indon. | 212 | 7°45'S | 112°50'E |
| Pasvalys, Lith. (päs-vä-lēs') | 167 | 56°04'N | 24°23'E |
| Patagonia, reg., Arg. (păt-à-gō'nĭ-à) | 144 | 46°45'S | 69°30'W |
| Pātālganga, r., India | 203b | 18°52'N | 73°08'E |
| Patapsco, r., Md., U.S. (pà-tăps'kō) | 110e | 39°12'N | 76°30'W |
| Pateros, Lake, res., Wa., U.S. | 114 | 48°05'N | 119°45'W |
| Paterson, N.J., U.S. (păt'ẽr-sŭn) | 110a | 40°55'N | 74°10'W |
| Pathein, Mya. | 199 | 16°46'N | 94°47'E |
| Pathfinder Reservoir, res., Wy., U.S. (păth'fīn-dẽr) | 115 | 42°22'N | 107°10'W |
| Patiāla, India (pŭt-ē-ä'lŭ) | 199 | 30°25'N | 76°28'E |
| Pati do Alferes, Braz. (pä-tē-dô-äl-fĕ'rĕs) | 144b | 22°25'S | 43°25'W |
| Patna, India (pŭt'nŭ) | 199 | 25°33'N | 85°18'E |
| Patnanongan, i., Phil. (pät-nä-nôn'gän) | 213a | 14°50'N | 122°25'E |
| Patoka, r., In., U.S. (pà-tō'kà) | 108 | 38°25'N | 87°25'W |
| Patom Plateau, plat., Russia | 179 | 59°30'N | 115°00'E |
| Patos, Braz. (pä'tōzh) | 143 | 7°03'S | 37°14'W |
| Patos, Wa., U.S. (pä'tōs) | 116d | 48°47'N | 122°57'W |
| Patos, Lagoa dos, l., Braz. (lä'gō-à dozh pä'tōzh) | 144 | 31°15'S | 51°30'W |
| Patos de Minas, Braz. (dĕ-mē'näzh) | 143 | 18°39'S | 46°31'W |
| Pátra, Grc. | 163 | 38°15'N | 21°48'E |
| Patraïkós Kólpos, b., Grc. | 175 | 38°16'N | 21°19'E |
| Patras *see* Pátrai, Grc. | 163 | 38°15'N | 21°48'E |
| Patrocínio, Braz. (pä-trō-sē'nē-ō) | 143 | 18°48'S | 46°47'W |
| Pattani, Thai. (pät'à-nē) | 212 | 6°56'N | 101°13'E |
| Patten, Me., U.S. (păt''n) | 100 | 45°59'N | 68°27'W |
| Patterson, La., U.S. (păt'ẽr-sŭn) | 123 | 29°41'N | 91°20'W |
| Patterson, i., Can. | 98 | 48°38'N | 87°14'W |
| Patton, Pa., U.S. | 109 | 40°40'N | 78°45'W |
| Patuca, r., Hond. | 133 | 15°22'N | 84°31'W |
| Patuca, Punta, c., Hond. (pōō'n-tä-pä-tōō'kä) | 133 | 15°55'N | 84°05'W |
| Patuxent, r., Md., U.S. (pà-tŭk'sĕnt) | 109 | 39°10'N | 77°10'W |
| Pátzcuaro, Mex. (päts'kwä-rô) | 130 | 19°30'N | 101°36'W |
| Pátzcuaro, Lago de, l., Mex. (lä'gô-dĕ) | 130 | 19°36'N | 101°38'W |
| Patzicia, Guat. (pät-zē'syä) | 132 | 14°36'N | 90°57'W |
| Patzún, Guat. (pät-zōōn') | 132 | 14°40'N | 91°00'W |
| Pau, Fr. (pō) | 161 | 43°18'N | 0°23'W |
| Pau, Gave de, r., Fr. (gäv-dĕ) | 170 | 43°33'N | 0°51'W |
| Paulding, Oh., U.S. (pôl'dĭng) | 108 | 41°05'N | 84°35'W |
| Paulinenaue, Ger. (pou'lē-nĕ-nou-ĕ) | 159b | 52°40'N | 12°43'E |
| Paulistano, Braz. (pà'ô-lēs-tá-nä) | 143 | 8°13'S | 41°06'W |
| Paulo Afonso, Salto, wtfl., Braz. (säl-tô-pou'lô äf-fôn'sô) | 143 | 9°33'S | 38°32'W |
| Paul Roux, S. Afr. (pôrl rōō) | 238c | 28°18'S | 27°57'E |
| Paulsboro, N.J., U.S. (pôlz'bē-rô) | 110f | 39°50'N | 75°16'W |
| Pauls Valley, Ok., U.S. (pôlz văl'ē) | 121 | 34°43'N | 97°13'W |
| Pavarandocito, Col. (pä-vä-rän-dô-sē'tô) | 142a | 7°18'N | 76°32'W |
| Pavda, Russia (päv'da) | 186a | 59°16'N | 59°32'E |
| Pavia, Italy (pä-vē'ä) | 162 | 45°12'N | 9°11'E |
| Pavlodar, Kaz. (pàv-lô-dár') | 183 | 52°17'N | 77°23'E |
| Pavlof Bay, b., Ak., U.S. (păv-lŏf) | 103 | 55°20'N | 161°20'W |
| Pavlohrad, Ukr. | 181 | 48°32'N | 35°52'E |
| Pavlovsk, Russia (pàv-lôfsk') | 177 | 50°28'N | 40°05'E |
| Pavlovsk, Russia | 186c | 59°41'N | 30°27'E |
| Pavlovskiy Posad, Russia (pàv-lôf'skĭ pô-sàt') | 180 | 55°47'N | 38°39'E |
| Pavuna, Braz. (pä-vōō'nà) | 144b | 22°48'S | 43°21'W |
| Päwesin, Ger. (pă'vĕ-zēn) | 159b | 52°31'N | 12°44'E |
| Pawhuska, Ok., U.S. (pô-hŭs'kà) | 121 | 36°41'N | 96°20'W |
| Pawnee, Ok., U.S. (pô-nē') | 121 | 36°20'N | 96°47'W |
| Pawnee, r., Ks., U.S. | 120 | 38°18'N | 99°42'W |
| Pawnee City, Ne., U.S. | 121 | 40°08'N | 96°09'W |
| Paw Paw, Mi., U.S. (pô'pô) | 108 | 42°15'N | 85°55'W |
| Paw Paw, r., Mi., U.S. | 113 | 42°14'N | 86°21'W |
| Pawtucket, R.I., U.S. (pô-tŭk'ĕt) | 109 | 41°53'N | 71°23'W |
| Paxoi, i., Grc. | 175 | 39°14'N | 20°15'E |
| Paxton, Il., U.S. (păks'tŭn) | 108 | 40°35'N | 88°00'W |
| Payette, Id., U.S. (pâ-ĕt') | 114 | 44°05'N | 116°55'W |
| Payette, r., Id., U.S. | 114 | 43°57'N | 116°26'W |
| Payette, North Fork, r., Id., U.S. | 114 | 44°10'N | 116°10'W |
| Payette, South Fork, r., Id., U.S. | 114 | 44°07'N | 115°43'W |
| Pay-Khoy, Khrebet, mts., Russia | 180 | 68°08'N | 63°04'E |
| Payne, l., Can. (pān) | 93 | 59°22'N | 73°16'W |
| Paynesville, Mn., U.S. (pānz'vĭl) | 113 | 45°23'N | 94°43'W |
| Paysandú, Ur. (pī-sän-dōō') | 144 | 32°16'S | 57°55'W |
| Payson, Ut., U.S. (pā's'n) | 119 | 40°05'N | 111°45'W |
| Pazardzhik, Blg. (pä-zár-dzhek') | 163 | 42°10'N | 24°22'E |
| Pazin, Cro. (pä'zēn) | 174 | 45°14'N | 13°57'E |
| Peabody, Ks., U.S. (pē'bŏd-ĭ) | 121 | 38°09'N | 97°09'W |
| Peabody, Ma., U.S. | 101a | 42°32'N | 70°56'W |
| Peace, r., Can. | 92 | 57°30'N | 117°30'W |
| Peace Creek, r., Fl., U.S. (pēs) | 125a | 27°16'N | 81°53'W |
| Peace Dale, R.I., U.S. (dāl) | 110b | 41°27'N | 71°30'W |
| Peace River, Can. (rĭv'ẽr) | 90 | 56°14'N | 117°17'W |
| Peacock Hills, hills, Can. (pē-kŏk' hĭlz) | 92 | 66°08'N | 109°55'W |
| Peak Hill, Austl. | 218 | 25°38'S | 118°50'E |
| Pearl, r., U.S. (pûrl) | 107 | 30°30'N | 89°45'W |
| Pearland, Tx., U.S. (pûrl'ănd) | 123a | 29°34'N | 95°17'W |
| Pearl Harbor, Hi., U.S. | 126a | 21°20'N | 157°53'W |
| Pearl Harbor, b., Hi., U.S. | 106d | 21°22'N | 157°58'W |
| Pearsall, Tx., U.S. (pẽr'sôl) | 122 | 28°53'N | 99°06'W |
| Pearse Island, i., Can. (pērs) | 94 | 54°51'N | 130°21'W |
| Pearston, S. Afr. (pē'ẽrstŏn) | 233c | 32°36'S | 25°09'E |
| Peary Land, reg., Grnld. (pēr'ĭ) | 244 | 82°00'N | 40°00'W |
| Pease, r., Tx., U.S. (pēz) | 120 | 34°07'N | 99°53'W |
| Peason, La., U.S. (pē'z'n) | 123 | 31°25'N | 93°19'W |
| Pebane, Moz. (pĕ-bá'nĕ) | 233 | 17°10'S | 38°08'E |
| Pecan Bay, Tx., U.S. (pê-kăn') | 122 | 32°04'N | 99°15'W |
| Peçanha, Braz. (pā-kän'yà) | 143 | 18°37'S | 42°26'W |
| Pecatonica, r., Il., U.S. (pĕk-à-tŏn-ĭ-kà) | 113 | 42°21'N | 89°28'W |
| Pechenga, Russia (pyĕ'chĕn-gà) | 180 | 69°30'N | 31°10'E |
| Pechora, r., Russia | 178 | 66°00'N | 54°00'E |
| Pechora Basin, Russia (pyĕ-chô'rà) | 178 | 67°55'N | 58°37'E |
| Pechori, Russia (pĕt'sĕ-rĕ) | 176 | 57°48'N | 27°33'E |
| Pecos, N.M., U.S. (pā'kōs) | 119 | 35°29'N | 105°41'W |
| Pecos, Tx., U.S. | 122 | 31°26'N | 103°30'W |
| Pecos, r., U.S. | 106 | 31°10'N | 103°10'W |
| Pécs, Hung. (pāch) | 163 | 46°04'N | 18°15'E |
| Peddie, S. Afr. | 233c | 33°13'S | 27°09'E |
| Pedley, Ca., U.S. (pĕd'lē) | 117a | 33°59'N | 117°29'W |
| Pedra Azul, Braz. (pā'drä-zōō'l) | 143 | 16°03'S | 41°13'W |
| Pedreiras, Braz. (pĕ-drā'räs) | 143 | 4°30'S | 44°31'W |
| Pedro, Point, c., Sri L. (pē'drō) | 203 | 9°50'N | 80°14'E |
| Pedro Antonio Santos, Mex. | 132a | 18°55'N | 88°13'W |
| Pedro Betancourt, Cuba (bā-tän-kōrt') | 134 | 22°40'N | 81°15'W |
| Pedro de Valdivia, Chile (pĕ'drô-dĕ-väl-dē'vē-ä) | 144 | 22°32'S | 69°55'W |
| Pedro do Rio, Braz. (dô-rē'rô) | 144b | 22°20'S | 43°09'W |
| Pedro II, Braz. (pā'drò sĕ-gòn'dò) | 143 | 4°20'S | 41°27'W |
| Pedro Juan Caballero, Para. (hòà'n-kä-bäl-yĕ'rō) | 144 | 22°40'S | 55°42'W |
| Pedro Miguel, Pan. (mĕ-gāl') | 128a | 9°01'N | 79°36'W |
| Pedro Miguel Locks, trans., Pan. (mĕ-gāl') | 128a | 9°01'N | 79°36'W |
| Peebinga, Austl. (pē-bĭng'à) | 218 | 34°43'S | 140°55'E |
| Peebles, Scot., U.K. (pē'b'lz) | 164 | 55°40'N | 3°15'W |
| Peekskill, N.Y., U.S. (pēks'kĭl) | 110a | 41°17'N | 73°55'W |
| Pegasus Bay, b., N.Z. (pĕg'à-sŭs) | 221a | 43°18'S | 173°25'E |
| Pegnitz, r., Ger. (pĕgh-nēts) | 168 | 49°38'N | 11°40'E |
| Pego, Spain (pā'gō) | 173 | 38°50'N | 0°09'W |
| Peguis Indian Reserve, I.R., Can. | 97 | 51°20'N | 97°35'W |
| Pegu Yoma, mts., Mya. (pĕ-gōō'yō'mä) | 199 | 19°16'N | 95°59'E |
| Pehčevo, Mac. (pĕx'chĕ-vô) | 175 | 41°42'N | 22°57'E |
| Peigan Indian Reserve, I.R., Can. | 95 | 49°35'N | 113°40'W |
| Peipus, Lake *see* Chudskoye Ozero, l., Eur. | 180 | 58°43'N | 26°45'E |
| Peiraiás, Grc. | 163 | 37°57'N | 23°38'E |
| Pekin, Il., U.S. (pē'kĭn) | 108 | 40°35'N | 89°30'W |
| Peking *see* Beijing, China | 205 | 39°55'N | 116°23'E |
| Pelagie, Isole, is., Italy | 162 | 35°46'N | 12°32'E |
| Pélagos, i., Grc. | 175 | 39°17'N | 24°05'E |
| Pelahatchie, Ms., U.S. (pĕl-à-hăch'ē) | 124 | 32°17'N | 89°48'W |
| Pelat, Mont, mtn., Fr. (pē-là') | 161 | 44°16'N | 6°43'E |
| Peleduy, Russia (pyĕl-yĭ-dōō'ē) | 179 | 59°50'N | 112°47'E |
| Pelée, Mont, mtn., Mart. (pē-lā') | 133b | 14°49'N | 61°10'W |
| Pelee, Point, c., Can. | 98 | 41°55'N | 82°30'W |
| Pelee Island, i., Can. (pē'lē) | 98 | 41°45'N | 82°30'W |
| Pelequén, Chile (pĕ-lĕ-kĕ'n) | 141b | 34°26'S | 71°52'W |
| Pelham, Ga., U.S. (pĕl'hăm) | 124 | 31°07'N | 84°10'W |
| Pelham, N.H., U.S. | 101a | 42°43'N | 71°22'W |
| Pelican, l., Mn., U.S. | 113 | 46°36'N | 94°00'W |
| Pelican Bay, b., Can. | 97 | 52°45'N | 100°20'W |
| Pelican Harbor, b., Bah. (pĕl'ĭ-kăn) | 134 | 26°20'N | 76°45'W |
| Pelican Rapids, Mn., U.S. (pĕl'ĭ-kăn) | 112 | 46°34'N | 96°05'W |
| Pella, Ia., U.S. (pĕl'à) | 113 | 41°25'N | 92°50'W |
| Pellworm, i., Ger. (pĕl'vôrm) | 168 | 54°33'N | 8°25'E |
| Pelly, l., Can. | 92 | 66°08'N | 102°57'W |
| Pelly, r., Can. | 92 | 62°20'N | 133°00'W |
| Pelly Bay, b., Can. (pĕl'ĭ) | 93 | 68°57'N | 91°05'W |
| Pelly Crossing, Can. | 103 | 62°50'N | 136°50'W |
| Pelly Mountains, mts., Can. | 92 | 61°50'N | 133°05'W |
| Peloncillo Mountains, mts., Az., U.S. (pĕl-ôn-sĭl'lō) | 119 | 32°40'N | 109°20'W |
| Peloponnisos, pen., Grc. | 175 | 37°28'N | 22°14'E |
| Pelotas, Braz. (pâ-lō'tázh) | 144 | 31°45'S | 52°18'W |
| Pelton, Can. (pĕl'tŭn) | 111b | 42°15'N | 82°57'W |
| Pelym, r., Russia | 180 | 60°20'N | 63°05'E |
| Pelzer, S.C., U.S. (pĕl'zẽr) | 125 | 34°38'N | 82°30'W |
| Pemanggil, i., Malay. | 197b | 2°37'N | 104°41'E |
| Pematangsiantar, Indon. | 212 | 2°58'N | 99°03'E |
| Pemba, Moz. (pĕm'bà) | 233 | 12°58'S | 40°30'E |
| Pemba, Zam. | 232 | 15°29'S | 27°22'E |
| Pemba Channel, strt., Afr. | 237 | 5°10'S | 39°30'E |
| Pemba Island, i., Tan. | 237 | 5°20'S | 39°57'E |
| Pembina, N.D., U.S. (pĕm'bĭ-nà) | 112 | 48°58'N | 97°15'W |
| Pembina, r., Can. | 95 | 53°05'N | 114°30'W |
| Pembina, r., N.A. | 97 | 49°08'N | 98°20'W |
| Pembroke, Can. (pĕm' brŏk) | 91 | 45°50'N | 77°00'W |
| Pembroke, Wales, U.K. | 164 | 51°40'N | 5°00'W |
| Pembroke, Ma., U.S. (pĕm'brŏk) | 101a | 42°05'N | 70°49'W |
| Pen, India | 203b | 18°44'N | 73°06'E |
| Penafiel, Port. (pā-nà-fyĕl') | 172 | 41°12'N | 8°19'W |
| Peñafiel, Spain (pā-nyà-fyĕl') | 172 | 41°38'N | 4°08'W |
| Peñalara, mtn., Spain (pā-nyä-lä'rä) | 162 | 40°52'N | 3°57'W |
| Pena Nevada, Cerro, Mex. | 130 | 23°47'N | 99°52'W |
| Peñaranda de Bracamonte, Spain | 172 | 40°54'N | 5°11'W |
| Peñarroya-Pueblonuevo, Spain (pĕn-yär-rō'yä-pwĕ'blô-nwĕ'vô) | 172 | 38°18'N | 5°18'W |
| Peñas, Cabo de, c., Spain (kå'bô-dĕ-pā'nyäs) | 172 | 43°42'N | 6°12'W |
| Penas, Golfo de, b., Chile (gôl-fô-dĕ-pĕ'n-äs) | 144 | 47°15'S | 77°30'W |
| Penasco, r., Tx., U.S. (pā-nás'kō) | 122 | 32°50'N | 104°45'W |
| Pendembu, S.L. (pĕn-dĕm'bōō) | 230 | 8°06'N | 10°42'W |
| Pender, Ne., U.S. (pĕn'dẽr) | 112 | 42°08'N | 96°43'W |
| Penderisco, r., Col. (pĕn-dĕ-rē's-kô) | 142a | 6°30'N | 76°21'W |
| Pendjari, Parc National de la, rec., Benin | 234 | 11°25'N | 1°30'E |
| Pendleton, Or., U.S. (pĕn'd'l-tŭn) | 104 | 45°41'N | 118°47'W |
| Pend Oreille, r., Wa., U.S. | 114 | 48°44'N | 117°20'W |
| Pend Oreille, Lake, l., Id., U.S. (pŏn-dô-rā') (pĕn-dô-rĕl') | 106 | 48°09'N | 116°38'W |
| Penedo, Braz. (pā-nā'dô) | 143 | 10°17'S | 36°28'W |
| Penetanguishene, Can. (pĕn'ē-tăn-gĭ-shēn') | 99 | 44°45'N | 79°55'W |
| Pengcheng, China (pŭŋ-chŭŋ) | 206 | 36°24'N | 114°11'E |
| Penglai, China (pŭŋ-lī) | 208 | 37°49'N | 120°45'E |
| Peniche, Port. (pĕ-nē'chå) | 172 | 39°22'N | 9°24'W |
| Peninsula, Oh., U.S. (pĕn-ĭn'sū-là) | 111d | 41°14'N | 81°32'W |
| Penistone, Eng., U.K. (pĕn'ĭ-stŭn) | 158a | 53°31'N | 1°38'W |


ăt; finăl; rāte; senâte; ärm; àsk; sofà; fâre; ch-choose; dh-as th in other; bē; êvent; bĕt; recĕnt; cratẽr; g-gō; gh-guttural g; bĭt; ĭ-short neutral; rīde; κ-guttural k as ch in German ich;

PRONOUNCING INDEX
Penjamillo – Pillar Rocks 335


| PLACE (Pronunciation) | PAGE | LAT. | LONG. |
|---|---|---|---|
| Penjamillo, Mex. (pěn-hä-mēl′yō) | 130 | 20°06′N | 101°56′W |
| Pénjamo, Mex. (pān′hä-mō) | 130 | 20°27′N | 101°43′W |
| Penk, r., Eng., U.K. (pěnk) | 158a | 52°41′N | 2°10′W |
| Penkridge, Eng., U.K. (pěnk′rĭj) | 158a | 52°43′N | 2°07′W |
| Penne, Italy (pěn′nā) | 174 | 42°28′N | 13°57′E |
| Penner, r., India (pěn′ẽr) | 199 | 14°43′N | 79°09′E |
| Pennines, hills, Eng., U.K. (pěn-īn′) | 164 | 54°30′N | 2°10′W |
| Pennines, Alpes, mts., Eur. | 168 | 46°02′N | 7°07′E |
| Pennsboro, W.V., U.S. (pěnz′bŭr-ô) | 108 | 39°10′N | 81°00′W |
| Penns Grove, N.J., U.S. (pěnz grōv) | 110f | 39°44′N | 75°28′W |
| Pennsylvania, state, U.S. (pěn-sĭl-vā′nĭ-*ȧ*) | 105 | 41°00′N | 78°10′W |
| Penn Yan, N.Y., U.S. (pěn yăn′) | 109 | 42°40′N | 77°00′W |
| Pennycutaway, r., Can. | 97 | 56°10′N | 93°25′W |
| Peno, l., Russia (pā′nô) | 176 | 56°55′N | 32°28′E |
| Penobscot, r., Me., U.S. | 107 | 45°00′N | 68°36′W |
| Penobscot Bay, b., Me., U.S. (pě-nŏb′skŏt) | 100 | 44°20′N | 69°00′W |
| Penong, Austl. (pē-nông′) | 218 | 32°00′S | 133°00′E |
| Penrith, Austl. | 217b | 33°45′S | 150°42′E |
| Pensacola, Fl., U.S. (pěn-s*ȧ*-kō′l*ȧ*) | 105 | 30°25′N | 87°13′W |
| Pensacola Dam, Ok., U.S. | 121 | 36°27′N | 95°02′W |
| Pensilvania, Col. (pěn-sěl-vá′nyä) | 142a | 5°31′N | 75°05′W |
| Pentecost, i., Vanuatu (pěn′tē-kŏst) | 221 | 16°05′S | 168°28′E |
| Penticton, Can. | 90 | 49°30′N | 119°35′W |
| Pentland Firth, strt., Scot., U.K. (pěnt′l*ă*nd) | 164 | 58°44′N | 3°25′W |
| Penza, Russia (pěn′zȧ) | 178 | 53°10′N | 45°00′E |
| Penzance, Eng., U.K. (pěn-zăns′) | 164 | 50°07′N | 5°40′W |
| Penzberg, Ger. (pěnts′běrgh) | 168 | 47°43′N | 11°21′E |
| Penzhina, r., Russia (pyĭn-zē-nŭ) | 185 | 62°15′N | 166°30′E |
| Penzhino, Russia | 179 | 63°42′N | 168°00′E |
| Penzhinskaya Guba, b., Russia | 185 | 60°30′N | 161°30′E |
| Peoria, Il., U.S. (pē-ō′rĭ-*ȧ*) | 105 | 40°45′N | 89°35′W |
| Peotillos, Mex. (pā-ō-tel′yōs) | 130 | 22°30′N | 100°39′W |
| Peotone, Il., U.S. (pē′ō-tōn) | 111a | 41°20′N | 87°47′W |
| Pepacton Reservoir, res., N.Y., U.S. (pěp-ăc′t*ŭ*n) | 109 | 42°05′N | 74°40′W |
| Pepe, Cabo, c., Cuba (kä′bô-pě′pě) | 134 | 21°30′N | 83°10′W |
| Pepperell, Ma., U.S. (pěp′ẽr-ěl) | 101a | 42°40′N | 71°36′W |
| Peqin, Alb. (pě-kēn′) | 175 | 41°03′N | 19°48′E |
| Perales, r., Spain (pā-rä′lās) | 173a | 40°24′N | 4°07′W |
| Perales de Tajuña, Spain (dā tä-hōō′nyä) | 173a | 40°14′N | 3°22′W |
| Perche, Collines du, hills, Fr. | 170 | 48°25′N | 0°40′E |
| Perchtoldsdorf, Aus. (pěrk′tôlts-dôrf) | 159e | 48°07′N | 16°17′E |
| Perdekop, S. Afr. | 238c | 27°11′S | 29°38′E |
| Perdido, r., Al., U.S. (pěr-dī′dō) | 124 | 30°45′N | 87°38′W |
| Perdido, Monte, mtn., Spain (pěr-dē′dō) | 173 | 42°40′N | 0°00′ |
| Perdões, Braz. (pěr-dô′ěs) | 141a | 21°05′S | 45°05′W |
| Pereiaslav-Khmel′nyts′kyi, Ukr. | 181 | 50°05′N | 31°25′E |
| Pereira, Col. (på-rā′rä) | 142 | 4°49′N | 75°42′W |
| Pere Marquette, Mi., U.S. | 108 | 43°55′N | 86°10′W |
| Pereshchepyne, Ukr. | 177 | 49°02′N | 35°19′E |
| Pereslavl′-Zalesskiy, Russia (pâ-râ-sláv′′l zá-lyěs′kĭ) | 180 | 56°43′N | 38°52′E |
| Pergamino, Arg. (pěr-gä-mē′nō) | 144 | 33°53′S | 60°36′W |
| Perham, Mn., U.S. (pěr′h*ă*m) | 112 | 46°37′N | 95°35′W |
| Peribonca, r., Can. (pěr-ĭ-bŏŋ′ká) | 93 | 50°30′N | 71°00′W |
| Périgueux, Fr. (pā-rē-gû′) | 161 | 45°12′N | 0°43′E |
| Perija, Sierra de, mts., Col. (sē-ĕ′r-rá-dě-pě-rē′ĸä) | 142 | 9°25′N | 73°30′W |
| Perkam, Tanjung, c., Indon. | 213 | 1°20′S | 138°45′E |
| Perkins, Can. (pĕr′k*ĕ*ns) | 102c | 45°37′N | 75°37′W |
| Perlas, Archipiélago de las, is., Pan. | 133 | 8°29′N | 79°15′W |
| Perlas, Laguna las, l., Nic. (lä-gò′nä-dě-läs) | 133 | 12°34′N | 83°19′W |
| Perleberg, Ger. (pěr′lē-běrg) | 168 | 53°06′N | 11°51′E |
| Perm′, Russia (pěrm) | 178 | 58°00′N | 56°15′E |
| Pernambuco see Recife, Braz. | 143 | 8°09′S | 34°59′W |
| Pernambuco, state, Braz. (pěr-näm-bōō′kō) | 143 | 8°08′S | 38°54′W |
| Pernik, Blg. (pěr-nēk′) | 163 | 42°36′N | 23°04′E |
| Péronne, Fr. (pā-rôn′) | 170 | 49°57′N | 2°49′E |
| Perote, Mex. (pě-rō′tě) | 131 | 19°33′N | 97°13′W |
| Perovo, Russia (pâ′rô-vô) | 186b | 55°43′N | 37°47′E |
| Perpignan, Fr. (pěr-pē-nyäN′) | 161 | 42°42′N | 2°48′E |
| Perris, Ca., U.S. (pěr′ĭs) | 117a | 33°46′N | 117°14′W |
| Perros, Bahía, b., Cuba (bä-ē′ä-pā′rōs) | 134 | 22°25′N | 78°35′W |
| Perrot, Île, i., Can. | 102a | 45°23′N | 73°57′W |
| Perry, Fl., U.S. (pěr′ĭ) | 124 | 30°06′N | 83°35′W |
| Perry, Ga., U.S. | 124 | 32°27′N | 83°44′W |
| Perry, Ia., U.S. | 113 | 41°49′N | 94°40′W |
| Perry, N.Y., U.S. | 109 | 42°45′N | 78°00′W |
| Perry, Ok., U.S. | 121 | 36°17′N | 97°18′W |
| Perry, Ut., U.S. | 117b | 41°27′N | 112°02′W |
| Perry Hall, Md., U.S. | 110e | 39°24′N | 76°29′W |
| Perryopolis, Pa., U.S. (pě-rē-ŏ′pô-lĭs) | 111e | 40°05′N | 79°45′W |
| Perrysburg, Oh., U.S. (pěr′ĭz-bûrg) | 108 | 41°35′N | 83°35′W |
| Perryton, Tx., U.S. (pěr′ĭ-t*ŭ*n) | 120 | 36°23′N | 100°48′W |
| Perryville, Ak., U.S. (pěr-ĭ-vĭl) | 103 | 55°58′N | 159°28′W |
| Perryville, Mo., U.S. | 121 | 37°41′N | 89°52′W |
| Persan, Fr. (pěr-sän′) | 171b | 49°09′N | 2°15′E |
| Persepolis, hist., Iran (pēr-sěp′ô-lĭs) | 198 | 30°15′N | 53°08′E |
| Persian Gulf, b., Asia (pûr′zh*ă*n) | 198 | 27°38′N | 50°30′E |
| Perth, Austl. (pûrth) | 218 | 31°50′S | 116°10′E |
| Perth, Can. | 99 | 44°40′N | 76°15′W |
| Perth, Scot., U.K. | 160 | 56°24′N | 3°25′W |
| Perth Amboy, N.J., U.S. (ăm′boi) | 110a | 40°31′N | 74°16′W |
| Pertuis, Fr. (pěr-tüē′) | 171 | 43°43′N | 5°29′E |
| Peru, Il., U.S. (pē-rōō′) | 108 | 41°20′N | 89°10′W |
| Peru, In., U.S. | 108 | 40°45′N | 86°00′W |
| Peru, nation, S.A. | 142 | 10°00′S | 75°00′W |
| Peru-Chile Trench, deep | 139 | 25°00′S | 71°30′W |
| Perugia, Italy (pā-rōō′jä) | 162 | 43°08′N | 12°24′E |
| Peruque, Mo., U.S. (pě rō′kě) | 117e | 38°52′N | 90°36′W |
| Pervomais′k, Ukr. | 181 | 48°04′N | 30°52′E |
| Pervoural′sk, Russia (pěr-vô-ô-rálsk′) | 186a | 56°54′N | 59°58′E |
| Pesaro, Italy (pā′zä-rō) | 162 | 43°54′N | 12°55′E |
| Pescado, r., Ven. (pěs-kä′dō) | 143b | 9°33′N | 65°32′W |
| Pescara, Italy (pās-kä′rä) | 174 | 42°26′N | 14°15′E |
| Pescara, r., Italy | 174 | 42°18′N | 13°22′E |
| Peschanyy müyisi, c., Kaz. | 181 | 43°10′N | 51°20′E |
| Pescia, Italy (pā′shä) | 174 | 43°53′N | 11°42′E |
| Peshāwar, Pak. (pě-shä′w*ŭ*r) | 199 | 34°01′N | 71°34′E |
| Peshtera, Blg. | 175 | 42°03′N | 24°19′E |
| Peshtigo, Wi., U.S. (pěsh′tē-gō) | 113 | 45°03′N | 87°46′W |
| Peshtigo, r., Wi., U.S. | 113 | 45°15′N | 88°14′W |
| Peski, Russia (pyâs′kĭ) | 186b | 55°13′N | 38°48′E |
| Pêso da Régua, Port. (pā-sò-dä-rā′gwä) | 172 | 41°09′N | 7°47′W |
| Pespire, Hond. (pås-pē′rå) | 132 | 13°35′N | 87°20′W |
| Pesqueria, r., Mex. (pås-kå-rē′*ȧ*) | 122 | 25°55′N | 100°25′W |
| Pessac, Fr. | 170 | 44°48′N | 0°38′W |
| Petacalco, Bahía de, b., Mex. (bä-ē′ä-dě-pě-tä-kal′kô) | 130 | 17°55′N | 102°00′W |
| Petah Tiqwa, Isr. | 197a | 32°05′N | 34°53′E |
| Petaluma, Ca., U.S. (pét-*ȧ*-lò′m*ȧ*) | 118 | 38°15′N | 122°38′W |
| Petare, Ven. (pě-tä′rě) | 143b | 10°28′N | 66°48′W |
| Petatlán, Mex. (pā-tä-tlän′) | 130 | 17°31′N | 101°17′W |
| Petawawa, Can. | 99 | 45°54′N | 77°17′W |
| Petén, Laguna de, l., Guat. (lä-gò′nä-dě-på-tān′) | 132a | 17°05′N | 89°54′W |
| Petenwell Reservoir, res., Wi., U.S. | 113 | 44°10′N | 89°55′W |
| Peterborough, Austl. | 218 | 32°53′S | 138°58′E |
| Peterborough, Can. (pē′tẽr-bŭr-ô) | 91 | 44°20′N | 78°20′W |
| Peterborough, Eng., U.K. | 164 | 52°35′N | 0°14′W |
| Peterhead, Scot., U.K. (pē-tẽr-hěd′) | 164 | 57°36′N | 3°47′W |
| Peter Pond Lake, l., Can. (pŏnd) | 92 | 55°55′N | 108°44′W |
| Petersburg, Ak., U.S. (pē′tẽrz-bûrg) | 103 | 56°52′N | 133°10′W |
| Petersburg, Il., U.S. | 121 | 40°01′N | 89°51′W |
| Petersburg, In., U.S. | 108 | 38°30′N | 87°15′W |
| Petersburg, Ky., U.S. | 111f | 39°04′N | 84°52′W |
| Petersburg, Va., U.S. | 105 | 37°12′N | 77°30′W |
| Petershagen, Ger. (pě′těrs-hä-gěn) | 159b | 52°32′N | 13°46′E |
| Petershausen, Ger. (pě′těrs-hou-zěn) | 159d | 48°25′N | 11°29′E |
| Pétionville, Haiti | 135 | 18°30′N | 72°20′W |
| Petitcodiac, Can. (pē-tē-kō-dyák′) | 100 | 45°56′N | 65°10′W |
| Petite Terre, i., Guad. (pē-tēt′târ′) | 133b | 16°12′N | 61°00′W |
| Petit Goâve, Haiti (pē-tē′ gō-áv′) | 135 | 18°25′N | 72°50′W |
| Petit Jean Creek, r., Ar., U.S. (pē-tē′zhäN′) | 121 | 35°05′N | 93°55′W |
| Petit Loango, Gabon | 236 | 2°16′S | 9°35′E |
| Petlalcingo, Mex. (pě-tläl-sěŋ′gô) | 131 | 18°05′N | 97°53′W |
| Peto, Mex. (pě′tô) | 132a | 20°07′N | 88°49′W |
| Petorca, Chile (pā-tōr′kà) | 141b | 32°14′S | 70°55′W |
| Petoskey, Mi., U.S. (pě-tŏs-kĭ) | 108 | 45°25′N | 84°55′W |
| Petra, hist., Jord. | 197a | 30°21′N | 35°25′E |
| Petra Velikogo, Zaliv, b., Russia | 210 | 42°40′N | 131°50′E |
| Petre, Point, c., Can. | 99 | 43°50′N | 77°00′W |
| Petrich, Blg. (pā′trĭch) | 163 | 41°24′N | 23°13′E |
| Petrified Forest National Park, rec., Az., U.S. (pět′rĭ-fīd fôr′ěst) | 119 | 34°58′N | 109°35′W |
| Petrinja, Cro. (pā′trēn-yá) | 174 | 45°25′N | 16°17′E |
| Petrodvorets, Russia (pyě-trô-dvô-ryěts′) | 186c | 59°53′N | 29°55′E |
| Petrokrepost′, Russia (pyě′trô-krě-pôst) | 180 | 59°56′N | 31°03′E |
| Petrolia, Can. (pē-trō′lĭ-*ȧ*) | 98 | 42°50′N | 82°10′W |
| Petrolina, Braz. (pě-trō-lē′n*ȧ*) | 143 | 9°18′S | 40°28′W |
| Petronell, Aus. | 159e | 48°07′N | 16°52′E |
| Petropavlivka, Ukr. | 177 | 48°24′N | 36°23′E |
| Petropavlovka, Russia | 186a | 54°10′N | 59°50′E |
| Petropavlovsk, Kaz. | 183 | 54°44′N | 69°07′E |
| Petropavlovsk-Kamchatskiy, Russia (käm-chät′skĭ) | 179 | 53°13′N | 158°56′E |
| Petrópolis, Braz. (på-trô-pô-lēzh′) | 143 | 22°31′S | 43°10′W |
| Petroşani, Rom. | 175 | 45°24′N | 23°24′E |
| Petrovsk, Russia (pyě-trôfsk′) | 181 | 52°20′N | 45°15′E |
| Petrovskaya, Russia (pyě-trôf′ská-yá) | 177 | 45°25′N | 37°50′E |
| Petrovskoye, Russia | 181 | 45°20′N | 43°00′E |
| Petrovsk-Zabaykal′skiy, Russia (pyě-trôfskzä-bī-käl′skĭ) | 179 | 51°13′N | 109°08′E |
| Petrozavodsk, Russia (pyā′trô-zá-vôtsk′) | 178 | 61°46′N | 34°25′E |
| Petrus Steyn, S. Afr. | 238c | 27°40′S | 28°09′E |
| Petrykivka, Ukr. | 177 | 48°43′N | 34°29′E |
| Pewaukee, Wi., U.S. (pĭ-wô′kē) | 111a | 43°05′N | 88°15′W |
| Pewaukee Lake, l., Wi., U.S. | 111a | 43°03′N | 88°18′W |
| Pewee Valley, Ky., U.S. (pe wē) | 111h | 38°19′N | 85°29′W |
| Peza, r., Russia (pyå′zȧ) | 180 | 65°35′N | 46°50′E |
| Pézenas, Fr. (pā-zē-nä′) | 170 | 43°26′N | 3°24′E |
| Pforzheim, Ger. (pfôrts′hīm) | 161 | 48°52′N | 8°43′E |
| Phalodi, India | 202 | 27°13′N | 72°22′E |
| Phan Thiet, Viet. (p′hän′) | 212 | 11°30′N | 108°43′E |
| Phelps Lake, l., N.C., U.S. | 125 | 35°46′N | 76°27′W |
| Phenix City, Al., U.S. (fē′nĭks) | 124 | 32°29′N | 85°00′W |
| Philadelphia, Ms., U.S. (fĭl-*ȧ*-děl′phĭ-*ȧ*) | 124 | 32°45′N | 89°07′W |
| Philadelphia, Pa., U.S. | 105 | 40°00′N | 75°13′W |
| Philip, S.D., U.S. (fĭl′ĭp) | 112 | 44°03′N | 101°35′W |
| Philippeville see Skikda, Alg. | 230 | 36°58′N | 6°51′E |
| Philippines, nation, Asia (fĭl′ĭ-pēnz) | 213 | 14°25′N | 125°00′E |
| Philippine Sea, sea (fĭl′ĭ-pēn) | 241 | 16°00′N | 133°00′E |
| Philippine Trench, deep | 213 | 10°30′N | 127°15′E |
| Philipsburg, Pa., U.S. (fĭl′lĭps-bẽrg) | 109 | 40°55′N | 78°10′W |
| Philipsburg, Wy., U.S. | 115 | 46°19′N | 113°19′W |
| Phillip, i., Austl. (fĭl′ĭp) | 222 | 38°32′S | 145°10′E |
| Phillip Channel, strt., Indon. | 197b | 1°04′N | 103°40′E |
| Phillipi, W.V., U.S. (fĭ-lĭp′ĭ) | 108 | 39°10′N | 80°00′W |
| Phillips, Wi., U.S. (fĭl′ĭps) | 113 | 45°41′N | 90°24′W |
| Phillipsburg, Ks., U.S. (fĭl′lĭps-bẽrg) | 120 | 39°44′N | 99°19′W |
| Phillipsburg, N.J., U.S. | 109 | 40°45′N | 75°10′W |
| Phitsanulok, Thai. | 212 | 16°51′N | 100°15′E |
| Phnom Penh (Phnum Pénh), Camb. (nŏm′pěn′) | 212 | 11°39′N | 104°53′E |
| Phnum Pénh see Phnom Penh, Camb. | 212 | 11°39′N | 104°53′E |
| Phoenix, Az., U.S. (fē′nĭks) | 104 | 33°30′N | 112°00′W |
| Phoenix, Md., U.S. | 110e | 39°31′N | 76°40′W |
| Phoenix Islands, is., Kir. | 2 | 4°00′S | 174°00′W |
| Phoenixville, Pa., U.S. (fē′nĭks-vĭl) | 110f | 40°08′N | 75°31′W |
| Phou Bia, mtn., Laos | 212 | 19°36′N | 103°00′E |
| Phra Nakhon Si Ayutthaya, Thai. | 212 | 14°16′N | 100°37′E |
| Phuket, Thai. | 212 | 7°57′N | 98°19′E |
| Phu Quoc, Dao, i., Viet. | 212 | 10°13′N | 104°00′E |
| Pi, r., China (bē) | 206 | 32°06′N | 116°31′E |
| Piacenza, Italy (pyä-chěnt′sä) | 162 | 45°02′N | 9°42′E |
| Pianosa, i., Italy (pyä-nō′sä) | 174 | 42°13′N | 15°45′E |
| Piave, r., Italy (pyä′vā) | 174 | 45°45′N | 12°15′E |
| Piazza Armerina, Italy (pyät′sä är-mâ-rē′nä) | 174 | 37°23′N | 14°26′E |
| Pibor, r., Sudan (pē′bôr) | 231 | 7°21′N | 32°54′E |
| Pic, r., Can. (pěk) | 98 | 48°48′N | 86°28′W |
| Picara Point, c., V.I.U.S. (pê-kä′rä) | 129c | 18°23′N | 64°57′W |
| Picayune, Ms., U.S. (pĭk′á yōōn) | 124 | 30°32′N | 89°41′W |
| Picher, Ok., U.S. (pĭch′ẽr) | 121 | 36°58′N | 94°49′W |
| Pichilemu, Chile (pē-chē-lě′mōō) | 141b | 34°22′S | 72°01′W |
| Pichucalco, Mex. (pē-chōō-käl′kô) | 131 | 17°34′N | 93°06′W |
| Pickerel, l., Can. (pĭk′ẽr-ěl) | 98 | 48°35′N | 91°10′W |
| Pickwick Lake, res., U.S. (pĭk′wĭck) | 124 | 35°04′N | 88°05′W |
| Pico, Ca., U.S. (pē′kô) | 117a | 34°01′N | 118°05′W |
| Pico Island, i., Port. (pē′kô) | 230a | 38°16′N | 28°49′W |
| Pico Rivera, Ca., U.S. | 117a | 34°01′N | 118°05′W |
| Picos, Braz. (pē′kōzh) | 143 | 7°13′S | 41°23′W |
| Picton, Austl. (pĭk′t*ŭ*n) | 217b | 34°11′S | 150°37′E |
| Picton, Can. | 99 | 44°00′N | 77°15′W |
| Pictou, Can. (pĭk-tōō′) | 101 | 45°41′N | 62°43′W |
| Pidálion, Akrotírion, c., Cyp. | 197a | 34°50′N | 34°05′E |
| Pidurutalagala, mtn., Sri L. (pē′dò-rò-tä′lá-gä′lá) | 203 | 7°00′N | 80°46′E |
| Pidvolochys′k, Ukr. | 177 | 49°32′N | 26°16′E |
| Pie, i., Can. (pī) | 98 | 48°10′N | 89°07′W |
| Piedade, Braz. (pyā-dä′dě) | 141a | 23°42′S | 47°25′W |
| Piedmont, Al., U.S. (pēd′mŏnt) | 124 | 33°54′N | 85°36′W |
| Piedmont, Ca., U.S. | 116b | 37°50′N | 122°14′W |
| Piedmont, Mo., U.S. | 121 | 37°09′N | 90°42′W |
| Piedmont, S.C., U.S. | 125 | 34°40′N | 82°27′W |
| Piedmont, W.V., U.S. | 109 | 39°30′N | 79°05′W |
| Piedrabuena, Spain (pyā-drä-bwā′nä) | 172 | 39°01′N | 4°10′W |
| Piedras, Punta, c., Arg. (pōō′n-tä-pyě′dräs) | 141c | 35°25′S | 57°10′W |
| Piedras Negras, Mex. (pyā′dräs nā′gräs) | 128 | 28°41′N | 100°33′W |
| Pieksämäki, Fin. (pyěk′sě-mě-kē) | 167 | 62°18′N | 27°14′E |
| Piemonte, hist. reg., Italy (pyě-mô′n-tě) | 174 | 44°30′N | 7°42′E |
| Pienaars, r., S. Afr. | 238c | 25°13′S | 28°05′E |
| Pienaarsrivier, S. Afr. | 238c | 25°12′S | 28°18′E |
| Pierce, Ne., U.S. (pērs) | 112 | 42°11′N | 97°33′W |
| Pierce, W.V., U.S. | 109 | 39°15′N | 79°30′W |
| Piermont, N.Y., U.S. (pēr′mŏnt) | 110a | 41°03′N | 73°55′W |
| Pierre, S.D., U.S. (pēr) | 104 | 44°22′N | 100°20′W |
| Pierrefonds, Can. | 102a | 45°29′N | 73°52′W |
| Piešťany, Slvk. | 169 | 48°36′N | 17°48′E |
| Pietermaritzburg, S. Afr. (pē-tēr-mā-rĭts-bûrg) | 232 | 29°36′S | 30°23′E |
| Pietersburg, S. Afr. (pē′tẽrz-bûrg) | 232 | 23°56′S | 29°30′E |
| Piet Retief, S. Afr. (pēt rě-těf′) | 232 | 27°00′S | 30°58′E |
| Pietrosu, Vârful, mtn., Rom. | 169 | 47°35′N | 24°49′E |
| Pieve di Cadore, Italy (pyā′vå dē kä-dō′rå) | 162 | 46°26′N | 12°22′E |
| Pigeon, r., N.A. (pĭj′*ŭ*n) | 113 | 48°05′N | 90°13′W |
| Pigeon Lake, Can. | 102f | 49°57′N | 97°36′W |
| Pigeon Lake, l., Can. | 95 | 53°00′N | 114°00′W |
| Piggott, Ar., U.S. (pĭg-ŭt) | 121 | 36°22′N | 90°10′W |
| Pijijiapan, Mex. (pēĸē-kē-ä′pän) | 131 | 15°40′N | 93°12′W |
| Pijnacker, Neth. | 159a | 52°01′N | 4°25′E |
| Pikes Peak, mtn., Co., U.S. (pīks) | 106 | 38°49′N | 105°03′W |
| Pikeville, Ky., U.S. (pīk′vĭl) | 108 | 37°28′N | 82°31′W |
| Pikou, China (pē-kō) | 208 | 39°25′N | 122°19′E |
| Pikwitonei, Can. (pĭk′wĭ-tōn) | 97 | 55°35′N | 97°09′W |
| Piła, Pol. (pē′lá) | 168 | 53°09′N | 16°44′E |
| Pilansberg, mtn., S. Afr. (pē′*ă*ns′bûrg) | 238c | 25°08′S | 26°55′E |
| Pilar, Arg. (pē′lär) | 141c | 34°27′S | 58°55′W |
| Pilar, Para. | 144 | 27°00′S | 58°15′W |
| Pilar de Goiás, Braz. (dě-gô′yá′s) | 143 | 14°47′S | 49°33′W |
| Pilchuck, r., Wa., U.S. | 116a | 48°03′N | 121°58′W |
| Pilchuck Creek, r., Wa., U.S. (pĭl′chŭck) | 116a | 48°19′N | 122°11′W |
| Pilchuck Mountain, mtn., Wa., U.S. | 116a | 48°03′N | 121°48′W |
| Pilcomayo, r., S.A. (pēl-cō-mī′ô) | 144 | 24°45′S | 59°15′W |
| Pili, Phil. (pē′lē) | 213a | 13°34′N | 123°17′E |
| Pilica, r., Pol. (pē-lēt′sä) | 169 | 51°00′N | 19°48′E |
| Pillar Point, c., Wa., U.S. (pĭl′*ȧ*r) | 116a | 48°14′N | 124°06′W |
| Pillar Rocks, Wa., U.S. | 116c | 46°16′N | 123°35′W |


ng-sing; ŋ-baŋk; ɴ-nasalized n; nŏd; c*ŏ*mmit; ōld; ôbey; ôrder; oi-boil; fōōd; ò-as oo in foot; ou-out; s-soft; sh-dish; th-thin; pūre; ûnite; ûrn; stŭd; circ*ŭ*s; ü-as in French tu; ′-indeterminate vowel.

| PLACE (Pronunciation) | PAGE | LAT. | LONG. |
|---|---|---|---|
| Pilón, r., Mex. (pē-lōn′) | 130 | 24°13′N | 99°03′W |
| Pilot Point, Tx., U.S. (pī′lŭt) | 121 | 33°24′N | 97°00′W |
| Pilsen *see* Plzeň, Czech Rep. | 154 | 49°46′N | 13°25′E |
| Piltene, Lat. (pĭl′tĕ-nĕ) | 167 | 57°17′N | 21°40′E |
| Pimal, Cerra, mtn., Mex. (sĕ′r-rä-pē-mäl′) | 130 | 22°58′N | 104°19′W |
| Pimba, Austl. (pĭm′bȧ) | 218 | 31°15′S | 137°50′E |
| Pimville, neigh., S. Afr. (pĭm′vĭl) | 233b | 26°17′S | 27°54′E |
| Pinacate, Cerro, mtn., Mex. (sĕ′r-rô-pē-nä-kä′tĕ) | 128 | 31°45′N | 113°30′W |
| Pinamalayan, Phil. (pē-nä-mä-lä′yän) | 213a | 13°04′N | 121°31′E |
| Pinang *see* George Town, Malay. | 212 | 5°21′N | 100°09′E |
| Pınarbaşı, Tur. (pē′när-bä′shĭ) | 163 | 38°50′N | 36°10′E |
| Pinar del Río, Cuba (pē-när′ dĕl rē′ô) | 129 | 22°25′N | 83°35′W |
| Pinar del Río, prov., Cuba | 134 | 22°45′N | 83°25′W |
| Pinatubo, mtn., Phil. (pē-nä-tōō′bô) | 213a | 15°09′N | 120°19′E |
| Pincher Creek, Can. (pĭn′chẽr krēk) | 95 | 49°29′N | 113°57′W |
| Pinckneyville, Il., U.S. (pĭnk′nĭ-vĭl) | 121 | 38°06′N | 89°22′W |
| Pińczów, Pol. (pēn′′chôf) | 169 | 50°32′N | 20°33′E |
| Pindamonhangaba, Braz. (pē′n-dä-mōnyä′n-gä-bä) | 141a | 22°56′S | 45°26′W |
| Pinder Point, c., Bah. | 134 | 26°35′N | 78°35′W |
| Pindiga, Nig. | 235 | 9°59′N | 10°54′E |
| Píndos Óros, mts., Grc. | 156 | 39°48′N | 21°19′E |
| Pine, r., Can. (pīn) | 95 | 55°30′N | 122°20′W |
| Pine, r., Wi., U.S. | 113 | 45°50′N | 88°37′W |
| Pine Bluff, Ar., U.S. (pīn blŭf) | 105 | 34°13′N | 92°01′W |
| Pine City, Mn., U.S. (pīn) | 113 | 45°50′N | 93°01′W |
| Pine Creek, Austl. | 218 | 13°45′S | 132°00′E |
| Pine Creek, r., Nv., U.S. | 118 | 40°15′N | 116°17′W |
| Pine Falls, Can. | 97 | 50°35′N | 96°15′W |
| Pine Flat Lake, res., Ca., U.S. | 118 | 36°52′N | 119°18′W |
| Pine Forest Range, mts., Nv., U.S. | 114 | 41°35′N | 118°45′W |
| Pinega, Russia (pē-nyĕ′gȧ) | 178 | 64°40′N | 43°30′E |
| Pinega, r., Russia | 180 | 64°10′N | 42°30′E |
| Pine Hill, N.J., U.S. (pīn hĭl) | 110f | 39°47′N | 74°59′W |
| Pineiós, r., Grc. | 175 | 39°30′N | 21°40′E |
| Pine Island Sound, strt., Fl., U.S. | 125a | 26°32′N | 82°30′W |
| Pine Lake Estates, Ga., U.S. (lāk ĕs-tāts′) | 110c | 33°47′N | 84°13′W |
| Pinelands, S. Afr. (pīn′lănds) | 232a | 33°57′S | 18°30′E |
| Pine Lawn, Mo., U.S. (lôn) | 117e | 38°42′N | 90°17′W |
| Pine Pass, p., Can. | 95 | 55°22′N | 122°40′W |
| Pinerolo, Italy (pē-nȧ-rô′lō) | 174 | 44°47′N | 7°18′E |
| Pines, Lake o′ the, Tx., U.S. | 123 | 32°50′N | 94°40′W |
| Pinetown, S. Afr. (pīn′toun) | 233c | 29°47′S | 30°52′E |
| Pine View Reservoir, res., Ut., U.S. (vū) | 117b | 41°17′N | 111°54′W |
| Pineville, Ky., U.S. (pīn′vĭl) | 124 | 36°48′N | 83°43′W |
| Pineville, La., U.S. | 123 | 31°20′N | 92°25′W |
| Ping, r., Thai. | 212 | 17°54′N | 98°29′E |
| Pingding, China (pĭŋ-dĭŋ) | 208 | 37°50′N | 113°30′E |
| Pingdu, China (pĭŋ-dōō) | 208 | 36°46′N | 119°57′E |
| Pinggir, Indon. | 197b | 1°05′N | 101°12′E |
| Pinghe, China (pĭŋ-hŭ) | 209 | 24°30′N | 117°02′E |
| Pingle, China (pĭŋ-lŭ) | 209 | 24°30′N | 110°22′E |
| Pingliang, China (pĭng′lyäng′) | 204 | 35°12′N | 106°50′E |
| Pingquan, China (pĭŋ-chyüän) | 208 | 40°58′N | 118°40′E |
| Pingtan, China (pĭŋ-tän) | 209 | 25°30′N | 119°45′E |
| Pingtan Dao, i., China (pĭŋ-tän dou) | 209 | 25°40′N | 119°45′E |
| P′ingtung, Tai. | 209 | 22°40′N | 120°35′E |
| Pingwu, China (pĭŋ-wōō) | 208 | 32°20′N | 104°40′E |
| Pingxiang, China (pĭŋ-shyäŋ) | 209 | 27°40′N | 113°50′E |
| Pingyi, China (pĭŋ-yē) | 206 | 35°30′N | 117°38′E |
| Pingyuan, China (pĭŋ-yůän) | 206 | 37°11′N | 116°26′E |
| Pingzhou, China (pĭŋ-jō) | 207a | 23°01′N | 113°11′E |
| Pinhal, Braz. (pē-nyä′l) | 141a | 22°11′S | 46°43′W |
| Pinhal Novo, Port. (nô′vō) | 173b | 38°38′N | 8°54′W |
| Pinhel, Port. (pēn-yĕl′) | 172 | 40°45′N | 7°03′W |
| Pini, Pulau, i., Indon. | 212 | 0°07′S | 98°38′E |
| Pinnacles National Monument, rec., Ca., U.S. (pĭn′ȧ-k′lz) | 118 | 36°30′N | 121°00′W |
| Pinneberg, Ger. (pĭn′ĕ-bĕrg) | 159c | 53°40′N | 9°48′E |
| Pinole, Ca., U.S. (pĭ-nō′lē) | 116b | 38°01′N | 122°17′W |
| Pinos-Puente, Spain (pwān′tȧ) | 172 | 37°15′N | 3°43′W |
| Pinotepa Nacional, Mex. (pē-nô-tā′pä nä-syô-näl′) | 130 | 16°21′N | 98°04′W |
| Pins, Île des, i., N. Cal. | 221 | 22°44′S | 167°44′E |
| Pinsk, Bela. (pēn′sk) | 178 | 52°07′N | 26°05′E |
| Pinta, i., Ec. | 142 | 0°41′N | 90°47′W |
| Pintendre, Can. (pĕɴ-tăɴdr′) | 102b | 46°45′N | 71°07′W |
| Pinto, Spain (pēn′tō) | 173a | 40°14′N | 3°42′W |
| Pinto Butte, Can. (pĭn′tō) | 96 | 49°22′N | 107°25′W |
| Pioche, Nv., U.S. (pī-ō′chē) | 119 | 37°56′N | 114°28′W |
| Piombino, Italy (pyôm-bē′nō) | 162 | 42°56′N | 10°33′E |
| Pioneer Mountains, mts., Mt., U.S. (pī′ô-nēr′) | 115 | 45°23′N | 112°51′W |
| Piotrków Trybunalski, Pol. (pyōtr′kōōv trĭ-bōō-nal′skē) | 161 | 51°23′N | 19°44′E |
| Piper, Al., U.S. (pī′pēr) | 124 | 33°04′N | 87°00′W |
| Piper, Ks., U.S. | 117f | 39°09′N | 94°51′W |
| Pipe Spring National Monument, rec., Az., U.S. (pīp sprĭng) | 119 | 36°50′N | 112°45′W |
| Pipestone, Mn., U.S. (pīp′stōn) | 112 | 44°00′N | 96°19′W |
| Pipestone National Monument, rec., Mn., U.S. | 112 | 44°03′N | 96°24′W |
| Pipmuacan, Réservoir, res., Can. (pĭp-mä-kän′) | 99 | 49°45′N | 70°00′W |
| Piqua, Oh., U.S. (pĭk′wȧ) | 108 | 40°10′N | 84°15′W |
| Piracaia, Braz. (pē-rä-kȧ′yä) | 141a | 23°04′S | 46°20′W |
| Piracicaba, Braz. (pē-rä-sē-kä′bä) | 143 | 22°43′S | 47°39′W |
| Piraíba, r., Braz. (pä-rä-ē′bȧ) | 141a | 21°38′S | 41°29′W |
| Piramida, mtn., Russia | 179 | 54°00′N | 96°00′E |
| Piran, Slvn. (pē-rȧ′n) | 174 | 45°31′N | 13°34′E |
| Piranga, Braz. (pē-rä′n-gä) | 141a | 20°41′S | 43°17′W |
| Pirapetinga, Braz. (pē-rä-pĕ-tē′n-gä) | 141a | 21°40′S | 42°20′W |
| Pirapora, Braz. (pē-rȧ-pō′rȧ) | 143 | 17°39′S | 44°54′W |
| Pirassununga, Braz. (pē-rä-sōō-nōō′n-gä) | 141a | 22°00′S | 47°24′W |
| Pirenópolis, Braz. (pē-rĕ-nô′pō-lēs) | 143 | 15°56′S | 48°49′W |
| Piritu, Laguna de, l., Ven. (lä-gô′nä-dĕ-pē-rē′tōō) | 143b | 10°00′N | 64°57′W |
| Pirmasens, Ger. (pĭr-mä-zĕns′) | 168 | 49°12′N | 7°34′E |
| Pirna, Ger. (pĭr′nä) | 168 | 50°57′N | 13°56′E |
| Pirot, Serb. (pē′rōt) | 163 | 43°09′N | 22°35′E |
| Pirtleville, Az., U.S. (pûr′t′l-vĭl) | 119 | 31°25′N | 109°35′W |
| Piru, Indon. (pē-rōō′) | 213 | 3°15′S | 128°25′E |
| Pisa, Italy (pē′sä) | 162 | 43°52′N | 10°24′E |
| Pisagua, Chile (pē-sä′gwä) | 142 | 19°43′S | 70°12′W |
| Piscataway, Md., U.S. (pĭs-kȧ-tȧ-wā) | 110e | 38°42′N | 76°59′W |
| Piscataway, N.J., U.S. | 110a | 40°35′N | 74°27′W |
| Pisco, Peru (pēs′kō) | 142 | 13°43′S | 76°07′W |
| Pisco, Bahía de, b., Peru | 142 | 13°43′S | 77°48′W |
| Piseco, l., N.Y., U.S. (pĭ-sā′kô) | 109 | 43°25′N | 74°35′W |
| Pisek, Czech Rep. (pē′sĕk) | 161 | 49°18′N | 14°08′E |
| Pisticci, Italy (pēs-tē′chē) | 174 | 40°24′N | 16°34′E |
| Pistoia, Italy (pēs-tô′yä) | 162 | 43°57′N | 11°54′E |
| Pisuerga, r., Spain (pē-swĕr′gä) | 172 | 41°48′N | 4°28′W |
| Pit, r., Ca., U.S. (pĭt) | 114 | 40°58′N | 121°42′W |
| Pitalito, Col. (pē-tä-lē′tō) | 142 | 1°45′N | 75°09′W |
| Pitcairn, dep., Oc. | 2 | 25°04′S | 130°05′W |
| Piteälven, r., Swe. | 160 | 66°08′N | 18°51′E |
| Pitești, Rom. (pē-tĕsht′′) | 175 | 44°51′N | 24°51′E |
| Pithara, Austl. (pĭt′ărȧ) | 218 | 30°27′S | 116°45′E |
| Pithiviers, Fr. (pē-tē-vyā′) | 170 | 48°12′N | 2°14′E |
| Pitman, N.J., U.S. (pĭt′mȧn) | 110f | 39°44′N | 75°08′W |
| Pitseng, Leso. | 233c | 29°03′S | 28°13′E |
| Pitt, r., Can. | 116d | 49°19′N | 122°39′W |
| Pitt Island, i., Can. | 94 | 53°35′N | 129°45′W |
| Pittsburg, Ca., U.S. (pĭts′bûrg) | 116b | 38°01′N | 121°52′W |
| Pittsburg, Ks., U.S. | 105 | 37°25′N | 94°43′W |
| Pittsburg, Tx., U.S. | 121 | 32°00′N | 94°57′W |
| Pittsburgh, Pa., U.S. | 105 | 40°26′N | 80°01′W |
| Pittsfield, Il., U.S. (pĭts′fēld) | 121 | 39°37′N | 90°47′W |
| Pittsfield, Ma., U.S. | 109 | 42°25′N | 73°15′W |
| Pittsfield, Me., U.S. | 100 | 44°45′N | 69°44′W |
| Pittston, Pa., U.S. (pĭts′tŭn) | 109 | 41°20′N | 75°50′W |
| Piūi, Braz. (pē-ōō′ē) | 141a | 20°27′S | 45°57′W |
| Piura, Peru (pē-ōō′rä) | 142 | 5°13′S | 80°46′W |
| Pivdennyi Buh, r., Ukr. | 181 | 48°12′N | 30°13′E |
| Piya, Russia (pē′yȧ) | 186a | 58°34′N | 61°12′E |
| Placentia, Can. | 101 | 47°15′N | 53°58′W |
| Placentia, Ca., U.S. (plă-sĕn′shĭ-ȧ) | 117a | 33°52′N | 117°50′W |
| Placentia Bay, b., Can. | 93a | 47°14′N | 54°30′W |
| Placerville, Ca., U.S. (plăs′ẽr-vĭl) | 118 | 38°43′N | 120°47′W |
| Placetas, Cuba (plä-thā′täs) | 134 | 22°10′N | 79°40′W |
| Placid, l., N.Y., U.S. (plăs′ĭd) | 109 | 44°20′N | 74°00′W |
| Plain City, Ut., U.S. (plān) | 117b | 41°18′N | 112°06′W |
| Plainfield, Il., U.S. (plān′fēld) | 111a | 41°37′N | 88°12′W |
| Plainfield, In., U.S. | 111g | 39°42′N | 86°23′W |
| Plainfield, N.J., U.S. | 110a | 40°38′N | 74°25′W |
| Plainview, Ar., U.S. (plān′vū) | 121 | 34°59′N | 93°15′W |
| Plainview, Mn., U.S. | 113 | 44°09′N | 93°12′W |
| Plainview, Ne., U.S. | 112 | 42°20′N | 97°47′W |
| Plainview, Tx., U.S. | 120 | 34°11′N | 101°42′W |
| Plainwell, Mi., U.S. (plan′wĕl) | 108 | 42°25′N | 85°40′W |
| Plaisance, Can. (plĕ-zäɴs′) | 102c | 45°37′N | 75°07′W |
| Plana or Flat Cays, is., Bah. (plä′nä) | 135 | 22°35′N | 73°35′W |
| Planegg, Ger. (plä′nĕg) | 159d | 48°06′N | 11°27′E |
| Plano, Tx., U.S. (plä′nō) | 121 | 33°01′N | 96°42′W |
| Plantagenet, Can. (plăn-tăzh-nĕ′) | 102c | 45°33′N | 75°00′W |
| Plant City, Fl., U.S. (plȧnt sĭ′tĭ) | 125a | 28°00′N | 82°07′W |
| Plaquemine, La., U.S. (plăk′mēn′) | 123 | 30°17′N | 91°14′W |
| Plasencia, Spain (plä-sĕn′thē-ä) | 172 | 40°02′N | 6°07′W |
| Plast, Russia (plȧst) | 180 | 54°22′N | 60°48′E |
| Plaster Rock, Can. (plȧs′tẽr rŏk) | 100 | 46°54′N | 67°24′W |
| Plastun, Russia (plȧs-tōōn′) | 210 | 44°41′N | 136°08′E |
| Plata, Río de la, est., S.A. (dälä plä′tä) | 144 | 34°35′S | 58°15′W |
| Platani, r., Italy (plä-tä′nē) | 174 | 37°26′N | 13°28′E |
| Plateforme, Pointe, c., Haiti | 135 | 19°35′N | 73°50′W |
| Platinum, Ak., U.S. (plăt′ĭ-nŭm) | 103 | 59°00′N | 161°27′W |
| Plato, Col. (plä′tō) | 142 | 9°49′N | 74°48′W |
| Platón Sánchez, Mex. (plä-tōn′ sän′chĕz) | 130 | 21°14′N | 98°20′W |
| Platte, S.D., U.S. (plăt) | 112 | 43°22′N | 98°51′W |
| Platte, r., Mo., U.S. | 121 | 40°09′N | 94°40′W |
| Platte, r., Ne., U.S. | 106 | 40°50′N | 100°40′W |
| Platteville, Wi., U.S. (plăt′vĭl) | 113 | 42°44′N | 90°31′W |
| Plattsburg, Mo., U.S. (plăts′bûrg) | 121 | 39°33′N | 94°26′W |
| Plattsburg, N.Y., U.S. | 109 | 44°40′N | 73°30′W |
| Plattsmouth, Ne., U.S. (plăts′mŭth) | 112 | 41°00′N | 95°53′W |
| Plauen, Ger. (plou′ĕn) | 161 | 50°30′N | 12°08′E |
| Playa de Guanabo, Cuba (plä-yä-dĕ-gwä-nä′bô) | 135a | 23°10′N | 82°07′W |
| Playa de Santa Fé, Cuba | 135a | 23°05′N | 82°31′W |
| Playas Lake, l., N.M., U.S. (plä′yȧs) | 119 | 31°50′N | 108°30′W |
| Playa Vicente, Mex. (vē-sĕn′tā) | 131 | 17°49′N | 95°49′W |
| Playa Vicente, r., Mex. | 131 | 17°36′N | 96°13′W |
| Playgreen Lake, l., Can. (plā′grēn) | 97 | 54°00′N | 98°10′W |
| Pleasant, l., N.Y., U.S. (plĕz′ănt) | 109 | 43°25′N | 74°25′W |
| Pleasant Grove, Al., U.S. | 110h | 33°29′N | 86°57′W |
| Pleasant Hill, Ca., U.S. | 116b | 37°57′N | 122°04′W |
| Pleasant Hill, Mo., U.S. | 121 | 38°46′N | 94°18′W |
| Pleasanton, Ca., U.S. (plĕz′ăn-tŭn) | 116b | 37°40′N | 121°53′W |
| Pleasanton, Ks., U.S. | 121 | 38°10′N | 94°41′W |
| Pleasanton, Tx., U.S. | 122 | 28°58′N | 98°30′W |
| Pleasant Plain, Oh., U.S. (plĕz′ănt) | 111f | 39°17′N | 84°06′W |
| Pleasant Ridge, Mi., U.S. | 111b | 42°28′N | 83°09′W |
| Pleasant View, Ut., U.S. (plĕz′ănt vū) | 117b | 41°20′N | 112°02′W |
| Pleasantville, N.Y., U.S. (plĕz′ănt-vĭl) | 110a | 41°08′N | 73°47′W |
| Pleasure Ridge Park, Ky., U.S. (plĕzh′ẽr rĭj) | 111h | 38°09′N | 85°49′W |
| Plenty, Bay of, b., N.Z. (plĕn′tē) | 221a | 37°30′S | 177°10′E |
| Plentywood, Mt., U.S. (plĕn′tē-wŏŏd) | 115 | 48°47′N | 104°38′W |
| Ples, Russia (plyĕs) | 176 | 57°26′N | 41°29′E |
| Pleshcheyevo, l., Russia (plĕsh-chă′yĕ-vô) | 176 | 56°50′N | 38°22′E |
| Plessisville, Can. (plĕ-sē′vēl′) | 99 | 46°12′N | 71°47′W |
| Pleszew, Pol. (plĕ′zhĕf) | 169 | 51°54′N | 17°48′E |
| Plettenberg, Ger. (plĕ′tĕn-bĕrgh) | 171c | 51°13′N | 7°53′E |
| Pleven, Blg. (plĕ′vĕn) | 163 | 43°24′N | 24°26′E |
| Pljevlja, Serb. (plĕv′lyä) | 163 | 43°20′N | 19°21′E |
| Płock, Pol. (pwôtsk) | 161 | 52°32′N | 19°44′E |
| Ploërmel, Fr. (plô-ĕr-mĕl′) | 170 | 47°56′N | 2°25′W |
| Ploiești, Rom. (plô-yĕsht′′) | 154 | 44°56′N | 26°01′E |
| Plomári, Grc. | 175 | 38°51′N | 26°24′E |
| Plomb du Cantal, mtn., Fr. (plôɴ′dükäɴ-täl′) | 161 | 45°30′N | 2°49′E |
| Plonge, Lac la, l., Can. (plōɴzh) | 96 | 55°08′N | 107°25′W |
| Plovdiv, Blg. (plôv′dĭf) (fĭl-ĭp-ŏp′ô-lĭs) | 154 | 42°09′N | 24°43′E |
| Pluma Hidalgo, Mex. (plōō′mä ē-däl′gō) | 131 | 15°54′N | 96°23′W |
| Plunge, Lith. (plòn′gā) | 167 | 55°56′N | 21°45′E |
| Plymouth, Monts. | 133b | 16°43′N | 62°12′W |
| Plymouth, Eng., U.K. (plĭm′ŭth) | 161 | 50°25′N | 4°14′W |
| Plymouth, In., U.S. | 108 | 41°20′N | 86°20′W |
| Plymouth, Ma., U.S. | 109 | 42°00′N | 70°45′W |
| Plymouth, Mi., U.S. | 111b | 42°23′N | 83°27′W |
| Plymouth, N.C., U.S. | 125 | 35°50′N | 76°44′W |
| Plymouth, N.H., U.S. | 109 | 43°50′N | 71°40′W |
| Plymouth, Pa., U.S. | 109 | 41°15′N | 75°55′W |
| Plymouth, Wi., U.S. | 113 | 43°45′N | 87°59′W |
| Plyussa, r., Russia (plyōō′sȧ) | 176 | 58°33′N | 28°30′E |
| Plzeň, Czech Rep. | 154 | 49°45′N | 13°23′E |
| Po, r., Italy | 156 | 45°10′N | 11°00′E |
| Pocahontas, Ar., U.S. (pō-kȧ-hŏn′tȧs) | 121 | 36°15′N | 91°01′W |
| Pocahontas, Ia., U.S. | 113 | 42°43′N | 94°41′W |
| Pocatello, Id., U.S. (pō-kȧ-tĕl′ō) | 104 | 42°54′N | 112°30′W |
| Pochëp, Russia (pô-chĕp′) | 181 | 52°56′N | 33°27′E |
| Pochinok, Russia (pô-chē′nôk) | 176 | 54°14′N | 32°27′E |
| Pochinski, Russia | 180 | 54°40′N | 44°50′E |
| Pochotitán, Mex. (pô-chô-tē-tä′n) | 130 | 21°37′N | 104°33′W |
| Pochutla, Mex. | 131 | 15°46′N | 96°28′W |
| Pocomoke City, Md., U.S. (pō-kō-mōk′) | 109 | 38°05′N | 75°35′W |
| Pocono Mountains, mts., Pa., U.S. (pō-cō′nō) | 109 | 41°10′N | 75°30′W |
| Poços de Caldas, Braz. (pō-sôs-dĕ-käl′dȧs) | 143 | 21°48′S | 46°34′W |
| Poder, Sen. (pô-dôr′) | 230 | 16°35′N | 15°04′W |
| Podgorica, Serb. | 175 | 42°25′N | 19°15′E |
| Podkamennaya Tunguska, r., Russia | 179 | 61°43′N | 93°45′E |
| Podol′sk, Russia (pô-dôl′′sk) | 180 | 55°26′N | 37°33′E |
| Poggibonsi, Italy (pôd-jē-bôn′sē) | 174 | 43°27′N | 11°12′E |
| Pogodino, Bela. (pô-gô′dē-nô) | 180 | 54°17′N | 31°00′E |
| P′ohangdong, Kor., S. | 210 | 35°57′N | 129°23′E |
| Pointe-à-Pitre, Guad. (pwăɴt′ ȧ pē-tr′) | 129 | 16°15′N | 61°32′W |
| Pointe-aux-Trembles, Can. (pōō-ăɴt′ ō-tràɴbl) | 102a | 45°39′N | 73°30′W |
| Pointe Claire, Can. (pōō-ăɴt′ klĕr) | 102a | 45°27′N | 73°48′W |
| Pointe-des-Cascades, Can. (kăs-kädz′) | 102a | 45°19′N | 73°58′W |
| Pointe Fortune, Can. (fôr′tŭn) | 102a | 45°34′N | 74°23′W |
| Pointe-Gatineau, Can. (pōō-ăɴt′gä-tē-nō′) | 102c | 45°28′N | 75°42′W |
| Pointe Noire, Congo | 232 | 4°48′S | 11°51′E |
| Point Hope, Ak., U.S. (hōp) | 103 | 68°18′N | 166°38′W |
| Point Pleasant, W.V., U.S. (plĕz′ănt) | 108 | 38°50′N | 82°10′W |
| Point Roberts, Wa., U.S. (rŏb′ērts) | 116d | 48°59′N | 123°04′W |
| Poissy, Fr. (pwȧ-sē′) | 171b | 48°55′N | 2°02′E |
| Poitiers, Fr. (pwȧ-tyā′) | 161 | 46°35′N | 0°18′E |
| Pokaran, India (pō′kŭr-ŭn) | 202 | 27°00′N | 72°05′E |
| Pokrov, Russia (pô-krôf) | 176 | 55°56′N | 39°09′E |
| Pokrovskoye, Russia (pô-krôf′skô-yĕ) | 177 | 47°27′N | 38°54′E |
| Pola, r., Russia (pō′lä) | 176 | 57°44′N | 31°53′E |
| Pola de Laviana, Spain (dĕ-lä-vyä′nä) | 172 | 43°15′N | 5°29′W |
| Pola de Siero, Spain | 172 | 43°24′N | 5°39′W |
| Poland, nation, Eur. (pō′lȧnd) | 154 | 52°37′N | 17°01′E |
| Polangui, Phil. (pô-län′gē) | 213a | 13°18′N | 123°29′E |
| Polatsk, Bela. | 180 | 55°30′N | 28°48′E |
| Polazna, Russia (pô′láz-ná) | 186a | 58°18′N | 56°25′E |
| Polessk, Russia (pô′lĕsk) | 167 | 54°50′N | 21°14′E |
| Polevskoy, Russia (pô-lĕ′vs-kô′ĕ) | 186a | 56°28′N | 60°14′E |
| Polgár, Hung. (pôl′gär) | 169 | 47°54′N | 21°10′E |
| Policastro, Golfo di, b., Italy | 174 | 40°00′N | 13°23′E |
| Polichnítos, Grc. | 175 | 39°05′N | 26°11′E |
| Poligny, Fr. (pō-lē-nyē′) | 171 | 46°48′N | 5°42′E |
| Polillo, Phil. (pô-lēl′yō) | 213a | 14°42′N | 121°56′W |
| Polillo Islands, is., Phil. | 199 | 15°05′N | 122°15′E |
| Polillo Strait, strt., Phil. | 213a | 15°02′N | 121°40′E |
| Polist′, r., Russia (pô′lĭst) | 176 | 57°42′N | 31°02′E |
| Polistena, Italy (pō-lēs-tä′nä) | 174 | 38°25′N | 16°05′E |
| Polkan, Gora, mtn., Russia | 179 | 60°18′N | 92°08′E |
| Polochic, r., Guat. (pō-lô-chēk′) | 132 | 15°19′N | 89°45′W |
| Polonne, Ukr. | 177 | 50°07′N | 27°31′E |
| Polpaico, Chile (pōl-pȧ′y-kô) | 141b | 33°10′S | 70°53′W |
| Polson, Mt., U.S. (pōl′sŭn) | 115 | 47°40′N | 114°10′W |


ăt; finȧl; rāte; senȧte; ärm; ȧsk; sofȧ; fâre; ch-choose; dh-as th in other; bē; ēvent; bĕt; recĕnt; cratẽr; g-gō; gh-guttural g; bĭt; ĭ-short neutral; rīde; ĸ-guttural k as ch in German ich;

PRONOUNCING INDEX
Poltava – Pratas Island 337


| PLACE (Pronunciation) | PAGE | LAT. | LONG. |
|---|---|---|---|
| Poltava, Ukr. (pôl-tä'vä) | 178 | 49°35'N | 34°33'E |
| Poltava, prov., Ukr. | 177 | 49°53'N | 32°58'E |
| Põltsamaa, Est. (põlt'sà-mä) | 167 | 58°39'N | 26°00'E |
| Polunochnoye, Russia (pô-lōō-nô'ch-nô'yĕ) | 186a | 60°52'N | 60°27'E |
| Poluy, r., Russia (pôl'wē) | 184 | 65°45'N | 68°15'E |
| Polyakovka, Russia (pŭl-yä'kôv-kà) | 186a | 54°38'N | 59°42'E |
| Polyarnyy, Russia (pŭl-yär'nē) | 178 | 69°10'N | 33°30'E |
| Polygyros, Grc. | 175 | 40°23'N | 23°27'E |
| Polynesia, is., Oc. | 240 | 4°00'S | 156°00'W |
| Pomba, r., Braz. (pô'm-bà) | 141a | 21°28'S | 42°28'W |
| Pomerania, hist. reg., Pol. (pŏm-ē-rā'nĭ-ȧ) | 168 | 53°50'N | 15°20'E |
| Pomeroy, S. Afr. (pŏm'ēr-roi) | 233c | 28°36'S | 30°26'E |
| Pomeroy, Wa., U.S. (pŏm'ēr-oi) | 114 | 46°28'N | 117°35'W |
| Pomezia, Italy (pô-mĕ't-zyä) | 173d | 41°41'N | 12°31'E |
| Pomigliano d'Arco, Italy (pô-mē-lyä'nô-d-ä'r-kô) | 173c | 40°39'N | 14°23'E |
| Pomme de Terre, Mn., U.S. (pôm dē tĕr') | 112 | 45°22'N | 95°52'W |
| Pomona, Ca., U.S. (pô-mō'nȧ) | 104 | 34°04'N | 117°45'W |
| Pomorie, Blg. | 163 | 42°24'N | 27°41'E |
| Pompano Beach, Fl., U.S. (pŏm'pă-nō) | 125a | 26°12'N | 80°07'W |
| Pompeii Ruins, hist., Italy | 173c | 40°31'N | 14°29'E |
| Pompton Lakes, N.J., U.S. (pŏmp'tŏn) | 110a | 41°01'N | 74°16'W |
| Pomuch, Mex. (pô-mōō'ch) | 132a | 20°12'N | 90°10'W |
| Ponca, Ne., U.S. (pŏn'kȧ) | 112 | 42°34'N | 96°43'W |
| Ponca City, Ok., U.S. | 121 | 36°42'N | 97°07'W |
| Ponce, P.R. (pōn'sā) | 129 | 18°01'N | 66°43'W |
| Pondicherry, India | 199 | 11°58'N | 79°48'E |
| Pondicherry, state, India | 199 | 11°50'N | 74°50'E |
| Ponferrada, Spain (pôn-fĕr-rä'dhä) | 162 | 42°33'N | 6°38'W |
| Ponoka, Can. (pŏ-nō'kȧ) | 90 | 52°42'N | 113°35'W |
| Ponoy, Russia | 180 | 66°58'N | 41°00'E |
| Ponoy, r., Russia | 180 | 67°00'N | 39°00'E |
| Ponta Delgada, Port. (pōn'tȧ dĕl-gä'dȧ) | 230a | 37°40'N | 25°45'W |
| Ponta Grossa, Braz. (grō'sȧ) | 143 | 25°09'S | 50°05'W |
| Pont-à-Mousson, Fr. (pôN'tá-mōō-sôN') | 171 | 48°55'N | 6°02'E |
| Pontarlier, Fr. (pôN'tár-lyā') | 171 | 46°53'N | 6°22'E |
| Pont-Audemer, Fr. (pôN'tōd'mâr') | 170 | 49°23'N | 0°28'E |
| Pontchartrain Lake, l., La., U.S. (pôN-shár-trăn') | 123 | 30°10'N | 90°10'W |
| Ponteareas, Spain | 172 | 42°09'N | 8°23'W |
| Pontedera, Italy (pōn-tå-dā'rä) | 174 | 43°37'N | 10°37'E |
| Ponte de Sor, Port. | 172 | 39°14'N | 8°03'W |
| Pontefract, Eng., U.K. (pŏn'tē-frăkt) | 158a | 53°41'N | 1°18'W |
| Ponte Nova, Braz. (pô'n-tĕ-nô'vá) | 143 | 20°26'S | 42°52'W |
| Pontevedra, Spain (pôn-tĕ-vĕ-drä) | 162 | 42°28'N | 8°38'W |
| Ponthierville see Ubundi, D.R.C. | 232 | 0°21'S | 25°29'E |
| Pontiac, Il., U.S. (pŏn'tĭ-ăk) | 108 | 40°55'N | 88°35'W |
| Pontiac, Mi., U.S. | 105 | 42°37'N | 83°17'W |
| Pontianak, Indon. (pôn-tē-ä'nák) | 212 | 0°04'S | 109°20'E |
| Pontian Kechil, Malay. | 197b | 1°29'N | 103°24'E |
| Pontic Mountains, mts., Tur. | 181 | 41°20'N | 34°30'E |
| Pontivy, Fr. (pôN-tē-vē') | 170 | 48°05'N | 2°57'W |
| Pontoise, Fr. (pôN-twáz') | 170 | 49°03'N | 2°05'E |
| Pontonnyy, Russia (pôn'tôn-nyĭ) | 186c | 59°47'N | 30°39'E |
| Pontotoc, Ms., U.S. (pŏn-tô-tŏk') | 124 | 34°11'N | 88°59'W |
| Pontremoli, Italy (pôn-trĕm'ô-lē) | 174 | 44°21'N | 9°50'E |
| Ponziane, Isole, i., Italy (ē'sō-lĕ) | 162 | 40°55'N | 12°58'E |
| Poole, Eng., U.K. (pōōl) | 164 | 50°43'N | 2°00'W |
| Poolesville, Md., U.S. (poolēs-vĭl) | 110e | 39°08'N | 77°26'W |
| Pooley Island, i., Can. (pōō'lē) | 94 | 52°44'N | 128°16'W |
| Poopó, Lago de, l., Bol. | 142 | 18°45'S | 67°07'W |
| Popayán, Col. (pō-pä-yän') | 142 | 2°21'N | 76°43'W |
| Poplar, Mt., U.S. (pŏp'lēr) | 115 | 48°08'N | 105°10'W |
| Poplar, r., Mt., U.S. | 115 | 48°34'N | 105°20'W |
| Poplar, West Fork, r., Mt., U.S. | 115 | 48°59'N | 106°06'W |
| Poplar Bluff, Mo., U.S. (blŭf) | 121 | 36°43'N | 90°22'W |
| Poplar Plains, Ky., U.S. (plāns) | 108 | 38°20'N | 83°40'W |
| Poplar Point, Can. | 102f | 50°04'N | 97°57'W |
| Poplarville, Ms., U.S. (pŏp'lēr-vĭl) | 124 | 30°50'N | 89°33'W |
| Popocatépetl Volcán, Mex. (pô-pô-kä-tā'pĕ't'l) | 128 | 19°01'N | 98°38'W |
| Popokabaka, D.R.C. (pō'pô-kà-bä'kà) | 232 | 5°42'S | 16°35'E |
| Popovo, Blg. (pô'pô-vō) | 175 | 43°23'N | 26°17'E |
| Porbandar, India (pōr-bŭn'dŭr) | 199 | 21°44'N | 69°40'E |
| Porce, r., Col. (pôr-sĕ) | 142a | 7°11'N | 74°55'W |
| Porcher Island, i., Can. (pôr'kēr) | 94 | 53°57'N | 130°30'W |
| Porcuna, Spain (pôr-kōō'nä) | 172 | 37°54'N | 4°10'W |
| Porcupine, r., N.A. | 103 | 67°38'N | 140°07'W |
| Porcupine Creek, r., Mt., U.S. | 115 | 48°27'N | 106°24'W |
| Porcupine Hills, hills, Can. | 97 | 52°30'N | 101°45'W |
| Pordenone, Italy (pōr-dā-nō'nā) | 174 | 45°58'N | 12°38'E |
| Pori, Fin. (pō'rē) | 160 | 61°29'N | 21°45'E |
| Poriúncula, Braz. | 141a | 20°58'S | 42°02'W |
| Porkhov, Russia (pôr'kôf) | 180 | 57°46'N | 29°33'E |
| Porlamar, Ven. (pôr-lä-mär') | 142 | 11°00'N | 63°55'W |
| Pornic, Fr. (pôr-nēk') | 170 | 47°08'N | 2°07'W |
| Poronaysk, Russia (pô'rô-nīsk) | 179 | 49°21'N | 143°23'E |
| Porrentruy, Switz. (pô-räN-trüē') | 168 | 47°25'N | 7°02'E |
| Porsgrunn, Nor. (pôrs'grôn') | 166 | 59°09'N | 9°36'E |
| Portachuelo, Bol. (pôrt-ä-chwā'lō) | 142 | 17°20'S | 63°12'W |
| Portage, Pa., U.S. (pôr'tāj) | 109 | 40°25'N | 78°35'W |
| Portage, Wi., U.S. | 113 | 43°33'N | 89°29'W |
| Portage Des Sioux, Mo., U.S. (dē sōō) | 117e | 38°56'N | 90°21'W |
| Portage la Prairie, Can. (lä-prā'rĭ) | 90 | 49°57'N | 98°25'W |
| Port Alberni, Can. (pōr äl-bĕr-nē') | 90 | 49°14'N | 124°48'W |
| Portalegre, Port. (pôr-tä-lā'grĕ) | 162 | 39°18'N | 7°26'W |
| Portales, N.M., U.S. (pôr-tä'lĕs) | 120 | 34°10'N | 103°11'W |
| Port Alfred, S. Afr. | 232 | 33°36'S | 26°55'E |
| Port Alice, Can. (ăl'ĭs) | 90 | 50°23'N | 127°27'W |
| Port Allegany, Pa., U.S. (ăl-ē-gā'nĭ) | 109 | 41°50'N | 78°10'W |
| Port Angeles, Wa., U.S. (ăn'jē-lĕs) | 104 | 48°07'N | 123°26'W |
| Port Antonio, Jam. | 129 | 18°10'N | 76°25'W |
| Portarlington, Austl. | 217a | 38°07'S | 144°39'E |
| Port Arthur, Tx., U.S. | 105 | 29°52'N | 93°59'W |
| Port Augusta, Austl. (ô-gŭs'tă) | 222 | 32°28'S | 137°50'E |
| Port au Port Bay, b., Can. (pôr'tō pōr') | 101 | 48°41'N | 58°45'W |
| Port-au-Prince, Haiti (prăNs') | 129 | 18°35'N | 72°20'W |
| Port Austin, Mi., U.S. (ôs'tĭn) | 108 | 44°00'N | 83°00'W |
| Port Blair, India (blâr) | 212 | 12°07'N | 92°45'E |
| Port Bolivar, Tx., U.S. (bŏl'ĭ-vár) | 123a | 29°22'N | 94°46'W |
| Port Borden, Can. (bôr'dĕn) | 100 | 46°15'N | 63°42'W |
| Port-Bouët, C. Iv. | 230 | 5°24'N | 3°56'W |
| Port-Cartier, Can. | 100 | 50°01'N | 66°53'W |
| Port Chester, N.Y., U.S. (chĕs'tēr) | 110a | 40°59'N | 73°40'W |
| Port Chicago, Ca., U.S. (shĭ-kô'gō) | 116b | 38°03'N | 122°01'W |
| Port Clinton, Oh., U.S. (klĭn'tŭn) | 108 | 41°30'N | 83°00'W |
| Port Colborne, Can. | 99 | 42°53'N | 79°13'W |
| Port Coquitlam, Can. (kô-kwĭt'lăm) | 95 | 49°16'N | 122°46'W |
| Port Credit, Can. (krĕd'ĭt) | 102d | 43°33'N | 79°35'W |
| Port-de-Bouc, Fr. (pôr-dē-bōōk') | 170a | 43°24'N | 5°00'E |
| Port de Paix, Haiti (pĕ) | 135 | 19°55'N | 72°50'W |
| Port Dickson, Malay. (dĭk'sŭn) | 197b | 2°33'N | 101°49'E |
| Port Discovery, b., Wa., U.S. (dĭs-kŭv'ēr-ĭ) | 116a | 48°05'N | 122°55'W |
| Port Edward, S. Afr. (ĕd'wērd) | 233c | 31°04'S | 30°14'E |
| Port Elgin, Can. (ĕl'jĭn) | 100 | 46°03'N | 64°05'W |
| Port Elizabeth, S. Afr. (ē-lĭz'á-bĕth) | 232 | 33°57'S | 25°37'E |
| Porterdale, Ga., U.S. (pōr'tēr-dāl) | 124 | 33°34'N | 83°53'W |
| Porterville, Ca., U.S. (pōr'tēr-vĭl) | 118 | 36°03'N | 119°05'W |
| Port Francqui see Ilebo, D.R.C. | 232 | 4°19'S | 20°35'E |
| Port Gamble, Wa., U.S. (găm'bŭl) | 116a | 47°52'N | 122°36'W |
| Port Gamble Indian Reservation, I.R., Wa., U.S. | 116a | 47°54'N | 122°33'W |
| Port-Gentil, Gabon (zhäN-tē') | 232 | 0°43'S | 8°47'E |
| Port Gibson, Ms., U.S. | 124 | 31°56'N | 90°57'W |
| Port Harcourt, Nig. (här'kŭrt) | 230 | 4°43'N | 7°05'E |
| Port Hardy, Can. (här'dĭ) | 94 | 50°43'N | 127°29'W |
| Port Hawkesbury, Can. | 101 | 45°37'N | 61°21'W |
| Port Hedland, Austl. (hĕd'lănd) | 218 | 20°30'S | 118°30'E |
| Porthill, Id., U.S. | 114 | 49°00'N | 116°30'W |
| Port Hood, Can. (hŏd) | 101 | 46°01'N | 61°32'W |
| Port Hope, Can. (hōp) | 99 | 43°55'N | 78°10'W |
| Port Huron, Mi., U.S. (hū'rŏn) | 105 | 43°00'N | 82°30'W |
| Portici, Italy (pôr'tē-chē) | 173c | 40°34'N | 14°20'E |
| Portillo, Chile (pôr-tē'l-yô) | 141b | 32°51'S | 70°09'W |
| Portimão, Port. (pôr-tē-mouN) | 172 | 37°09'N | 8°34'W |
| Port Jervis, N.Y., U.S. (jûr'vĭs) | 110a | 41°22'N | 74°41'W |
| Portland, Austl. (pōrt'lănd) | 219 | 38°20'S | 142°40'E |
| Portland, In., U.S. | 108 | 40°25'N | 85°00'W |
| Portland, Me., U.S. | 105 | 43°40'N | 70°16'W |
| Portland, Mi., U.S. | 108 | 42°50'N | 85°00'W |
| Portland, Or., U.S. | 104 | 45°31'N | 122°41'W |
| Portland, Tx., U.S. | 123 | 27°53'N | 97°20'W |
| Portland Bight, b., Jam. | 134 | 17°45'N | 77°05'W |
| Portland Canal, can., Ak., U.S. | 94 | 55°10'N | 130°08'W |
| Portland Inlet, b., Can. | 94 | 54°50'N | 130°15'W |
| Portland Point, c., Jam. | 134 | 17°40'N | 77°20'W |
| Port Lavaca, Tx., U.S. (lá-vä'ká) | 123 | 28°36'N | 96°38'W |
| Port Lincoln, Austl. (lĭŋ-kŭn) | 218 | 34°39'S | 135°50'E |
| Port Ludlow, Wa., U.S. (lŭd'lō) | 116a | 47°26'N | 122°41'W |
| Port Macquarie, Austl. (mȧ-kwŏ'rĭ) | 219 | 31°25'S | 152°45'E |
| Port Madison Indian Reservation, I.R., Wa., U.S. (măd'ĭ-sŭn) | 116a | 47°46'N | 122°38'W |
| Port Maria, Jam. (mȧ-rī'ȧ) | 134 | 18°20'N | 76°55'W |
| Port Moody, Can. (mōōd'ĭ) | 95 | 49°17'N | 122°51'W |
| Port Moresby, Pap. N. Gui. (mōrz'bē) | 213 | 9°34'S | 147°20'E |
| Port Neches, Tx., U.S. (nĕch'ĕz) | 123 | 29°59'N | 93°57'W |
| Port Nelson, Can. (nĕl'sŭn) | 97 | 57°03'N | 92°36'W |
| Portneuf-Sur-Mer, Can. (pôr-nûf'sür mĕr) | 100 | 48°36'N | 69°06'W |
| Port Nolloth, S. Afr. (nŏl'ŏth) | 232 | 29°10'S | 17°00'E |
| Porto (Oporto), Port. (pōr'tô) | 154 | 41°10'N | 8°38'W |
| Porto Acre, Braz. (ä'krĕ) | 142 | 9°38'S | 67°34'W |
| Porto Alegre, Braz. (ä-lā'grĕ) | 144 | 29°58'S | 51°11'W |
| Porto Amboim, Ang. | 232 | 11°01'S | 13°45'E |
| Portobelo, Pan. (pôr'tô-bā'lô) | 129 | 9°32'N | 79°40'W |
| Pôrto de Pedras, Braz. (pā'dräzh) | 143 | 9°09'S | 35°20'W |
| Pôrto Feliz, Braz. (fē-lē's) | 141a | 23°12'S | 47°30'W |
| Portoferraio, Italy (pōr'tô-fĕr-rä'yō) | 174 | 42°47'N | 10°20'E |
| Port of Spain, Trin. (spān) | 143 | 10°44'N | 61°24'W |
| Portogruaro, Italy (pôr'tô-grô-ä'rō) | 174 | 45°48'N | 12°49'E |
| Portola, Ca., U.S. (pôr'tō-lá) | 118 | 39°47'N | 120°29'W |
| Porto Mendes, Braz. (mĕ'n-dĕs) | 143 | 24°41'S | 54°13'W |
| Porto Murtinho, Braz. (mòr-tēn'yô) | 143 | 21°43'S | 57°43'W |
| Porto Nacional, Braz. (ná-syô-näl') | 143 | 10°43'S | 48°14'W |
| Porto Novo, Benin (pōr'tô-nō'vō) | 230 | 6°29'N | 2°37'E |
| Port Orchard, Wa., U.S. (ôr'chērd) | 116a | 47°32'N | 122°38'W |
| Port Orchard, b., Wa., U.S. | 116a | 47°40'N | 122°39'W |
| Porto Santo, Ilha de, i., Port. (săN'tô) | 230 | 32°41'N | 16°15'W |
| Porto Seguro, Braz. (sā-gōō'rô) | 143 | 16°26'S | 38°59'W |
| Porto Torres, Italy (tôr'rĕs) | 174 | 40°49'N | 8°25'E |
| Porto-Vecchio, Fr. (vĕk'ē-ô) | 174 | 41°36'N | 9°17'E |
| Porto Velho, Braz. (vāl'yô) | 142 | 8°45'S | 63°43'W |
| Portoviejo, Ec. (pôr-tō-vyā'hō) | 142 | 1°11'S | 80°28'W |
| Port Phillip Bay, b., Austl. (fĭl'ĭp) | 221 | 37°57'S | 144°50'E |
| Port Pirie, Austl. (pĭ'rē) | 218 | 33°10'S | 138°00'E |
| Port Royal, b., Jam. (roi'ăl) | 134 | 17°50'N | 76°45'W |
| Port Said, Egypt | 238d | 31°15'N | 32°19'E |
| Port Saint Johns, S. Afr. (sānt jŏnz) | 232 | 31°37'S | 29°32'E |
| Port Saint Lucie, Fl., U.S. | 125a | 27°20'N | 80°20'W |
| Port Shepstone, S. Afr. (shĕps'tŭn) | 232 | 30°45'S | 30°23'E |
| Portsmouth, Dom. | 133b | 15°33'N | 61°28'W |
| Portsmouth, Eng., U.K. (pôrts'mŭth) | 154 | 50°45'N | 1°03'W |
| Portsmouth, N.H., U.S. | 105 | 43°05'N | 70°50'W |
| Portsmouth, Oh., U.S. | 105 | 38°45'N | 83°00'W |
| Portsmouth, Va., U.S. | 105 | 36°50'N | 76°19'W |
| Port Sulphur, La., U.S. (sŭl'fēr) | 124 | 29°28'N | 89°41'W |
| Port Susan, b., Wa., U.S. (sū-zán') | 116a | 48°11'N | 122°25'W |
| Port Townsend, Wa., U.S. (tounz'ĕnd) | 116a | 48°07'N | 122°46'W |
| Port Townsend, b., Wa., U.S. | 116a | 48°05'N | 122°47'W |
| Portugal, nation, Eur. (pōr'tu-găl) | 154 | 38°15'N | 8°08'W |
| Portugalete, Spain (pōr-tōō-gä-lā'tä) | 172 | 43°18'N | 3°05'W |
| Portuguese West Africa see Angola, nation, Ang. | 232 | 14°15'S | 16°00'E |
| Port Vendres, Fr. | 170 | 42°32'N | 3°07'E |
| Port Vila, Vanuatu | 219 | 17°44'S | 168°19'E |
| Port Wakefield, Austl. (wāk'fēld) | 218 | 34°12'S | 138°10'E |
| Port Washington, N.Y., U.S. (wôsh'ĭng-tŭn) | 110a | 40°49'N | 73°42'W |
| Port Washington, Wi., U.S. | 113 | 43°24'N | 87°52'W |
| Posadas, Arg. (pō-sä'dhäs) | 144 | 27°32'S | 55°56'W |
| Posadas, Spain (pô-sä-däs) | 172 | 37°48'N | 5°09'W |
| Poshekhon'ye Volodarsk, Russia (pô-shyĕ'kôn-yĕ vôl'ô-dàrsk) | 176 | 58°31'N | 39°07'E |
| Poso, Danau, l., Indon. (pō'sō) | 212 | 2°00'S | 119°40'E |
| Pospelokova, Russia (pôs-pyĕl'kô-vá) | 186a | 59°25'N | 60°50'E |
| Possession Sound, strt., Wa., U.S. (pŏ-zĕsh-ŭn) | 116a | 47°59'N | 122°17'W |
| Possum Kingdom Reservoir, res., Tx., U.S. (pŏs'ŭm kĭng'dŭm) | 122 | 32°58'N | 98°12'W |
| Post, Tx., U.S. (pōst) | 120 | 33°12'N | 101°21'W |
| Postojna, Slvn. (pōs-tōyná) | 174 | 45°45'N | 14°13'E |
| Pos'yet, Russia (pos-yĕt') | 210 | 42°27'N | 130°47'E |
| Potawatomi Indian Reservation, I.R., Ks., U.S. (pôt-å-wä'tō mē) | 121 | 39°30'N | 96°11'W |
| Potchefstroom, S. Afr. (pŏch'ĕf-strōm) | 232 | 26°42'S | 27°06'E |
| Poteau, Ok., U.S. (pô-tō') | 121 | 35°03'N | 94°37'W |
| Poteet, Tx., U.S. (pô-tēt) | 122 | 29°05'N | 98°35'W |
| Potenza, Italy (pô-tĕnt'sä) | 163 | 40°39'N | 15°49'E |
| Potenza, r., Italy | 174 | 43°09'N | 13°00'E |
| Potgietersrus, S. Afr. (pôt-kē'tērs-rûs) | 232 | 24°09'S | 29°04'E |
| Potholes Reservoir, res., Wa., U.S. | 114 | 47°00'N | 119°20'W |
| Poti, Geor. (pô'tē) | 181 | 42°10'N | 41°40'E |
| Potiskum, Nig. | 230 | 11°43'N | 11°05'E |
| Potomac, Md., U.S. (pô-tō'măk) | 110e | 39°01'N | 77°13'W |
| Potomac, r., U.S. (pô-tō'măk) | 107 | 38°15'N | 76°55'W |
| Potosí, Bol. | 142 | 19°35'S | 65°45'W |
| Potosi, Mo., U.S. (pŏ-tō'sĭ) | 121 | 37°56'N | 90°46'W |
| Potosí, r., Mex. (pō-tô-sē') | 122 | 25°04'N | 99°36'W |
| Potrerillos, Hond. (pō-trā-rēl'yôs) | 132 | 15°13'N | 87°58'W |
| Potsdam, Ger. (pôts'däm) | 161 | 52°24'N | 13°04'E |
| Potsdam, N.Y., U.S. (pŏts'dăm) | 109 | 44°40'N | 75°00'W |
| Pottenstein, Aus. | 159e | 47°58'N | 16°06'E |
| Potters Bar, Eng., U.K. (pŏt'ĕz bär) | 158b | 51°41'N | 0°12'W |
| Pottstown, Pa., U.S. (pŏts'toun) | 109 | 40°15'N | 75°40'W |
| Pottsville, Pa., U.S. (pôts'vĭl) | 109 | 40°40'N | 76°15'W |
| Poughkeepsie, N.Y., U.S. (pŏ-kĭp'sē) | 105 | 41°45'N | 73°55'W |
| Poulsbo, Wa., U.S. (pōlz'bò) | 116a | 47°44'N | 122°38'W |
| Poulton-le-Fylde, Eng., U.K. (pōl'tŭn-lē-fīld') | 158a | 53°52'N | 2°59'W |
| Pouso Alegre, Braz. (pō'zò ä-lā'grĕ) | 143 | 22°13'S | 45°56'W |
| Póvoa de Varzim, Port. (pō-vō'ȧ dā vär'zēN) | 162 | 41°23'N | 8°44'W |
| Powder, r., Or., U.S. | 114 | 44°55'N | 117°35'W |
| Powder, r., U.S. (pou'dēr) | 106 | 45°18'N | 105°37'W |
| Powder, South Fork, r., Wy., U.S. | 115 | 43°13'N | 106°54'W |
| Powder River, Wy., U.S. | 115 | 43°06'N | 106°55'W |
| Powell, Wy., U.S. (pou'ĕl) | 115 | 44°44'N | 108°44'W |
| Powell, Lake, res., U.S. | 106 | 37°26'N | 110°25'W |
| Powell Lake, l., Can. | 94 | 50°10'N | 124°13'W |
| Powell Point, c., Bah. | 134 | 24°50'N | 76°20'W |
| Powell Reservoir, res., Ky., U.S. | 124 | 36°30'N | 83°35'W |
| Powell River, Can. | 90 | 49°52'N | 124°33'W |
| Poyang Hu, l., China | 205 | 29°20'N | 116°28'E |
| Poygan, r., Wi., U.S. (poi'găn) | 113 | 44°10'N | 89°05'W |
| Požarevac, Serb. (pô'zhà'rĕ-vàts) | 175 | 44°38'N | 21°12'E |
| Poza Rica, Mex. (pô-zô-rē'kä) | 131 | 20°32'N | 97°25'W |
| Poznań, Pol. | 154 | 52°25'N | 16°55'E |
| Pozoblanco, Spain (pô-thō-bläŋ'kō) | 172 | 38°23'N | 4°50'W |
| Pozos, Mex. (pô'zōs) | 130 | 22°05'N | 100°50'W |
| Pozuelo de Alarcón, Spain (pô-thwā'lō dā ä-lär-kōn') | 173a | 40°27'N | 3°49'W |
| Pozzuoli, Italy (pôt-swô'lē) | 174 | 40°34'N | 14°08'E |
| Pra, r., Ghana (prà) | 234 | 5°45'N | 1°35'W |
| Pra, r., Russia | 176 | 55°00'N | 40°13'E |
| Prachin Buri, Thai. (prä'chĕn) | 212 | 13°59'N | 101°15'E |
| Pradera, Col. (prä-dĕ'rä) | 142a | 3°24'N | 76°13'W |
| Prades, Fr. (pråd) | 170 | 42°37'N | 2°23'E |
| Prado, Col. (prädô) | 142a | 3°44'N | 74°55'W |
| Prado Reservoir, res., Ca., U.S. (prä'dō) | 117a | 33°45'N | 117°40'W |
| Prados, Braz. (prá'dôs) | 141a | 21°05'S | 44°04'W |
| Prague, Czech Rep. | 168 | 50°05'N | 14°26'E |
| Praha see Prague, Czech Rep. | 154 | 50°05'N | 14°26'E |
| Praia, C.V. (prä'yà) | 230b | 15°00'N | 23°30'W |
| Praia Funda, Ponta da, c., Braz. (pôn'tä-dá-prä'yá-fōō'n-dä) | 144b | 23°04'S | 43°34'W |
| Prairie du Chien, Wi., U.S. (prā'rĭ dò shēn') | 113 | 43°02'N | 91°10'W |
| Prairie Grove, Can. (prā'rĭ grōv) | 102f | 49°48'N | 96°57'W |
| Prairie Island Indian Reservation, I.R., Mn., U.S. | 113 | 44°42'N | 92°32'W |
| Prairies, Rivière des, r., Can. (rē-vyâr' dā prå-rē') | 102a | 45°40'N | 73°34'W |
| Pratas Island, i., Asia | 209 | 20°40'N | 116°30'E |


ng-sing; ŋ-baŋk; N-nasalized n; nŏd; cŏmmit; ōld; ôbey; ôrder; oi-boil; fōōd; ò-as oo in foot; ou-out; s-soft; sh-dish; th-thin; pūre; ûnite; ûrn; stŭd; circŭs; ü-as in French tu; '-indeterminate vowel.

338 Prato – Purkersdorf PRONOUNCING INDEX


| PLACE (Pronunciation) | PAGE | LAT. | LONG. |
|---|---|---|---|
| Prato, Italy (prä'tō) | 174 | 43°53'N | 11°03'E |
| Pratt, Ks., U.S. (prăt) | 120 | 37°37'N | 98°43'W |
| Prattville, Al., U.S. (prăt'vĭl) | 124 | 32°28'N | 86°27'W |
| Pravdinsk, Russia | 167 | 54°26'N | 21°00'E |
| Pravdinskiy, Russia (pràv-dĕn'skĭ) | 186b | 56°03'N | 37°52'E |
| Pravia, Spain (prä'vē-ä) | 172 | 43°30'N | 6°08'W |
| Pregolya, r., Russia (prĕ-gô'lă) | 167 | 54°37'N | 20°50'E |
| Premont, Tx., U.S. (prē-mŏnt') | 122 | 27°20'N | 98°07'W |
| Prenzlau, Ger. (prĕnts'lou) | 168 | 53°19'N | 13°52'E |
| Přerov, Czech Rep. (przhĕ'rôf) | 161 | 49°28'N | 17°28'E |
| Prescot, Eng., U.K. (prĕs'kŭt) | 158a | 53°25'N | 2°48'W |
| Prescott, Can. (prĕs'kŭt) | 109 | 44°45'N | 75°35'W |
| Prescott, Ar., U.S. | 121 | 33°47'N | 93°23'W |
| Prescott, Az., U.S. (prĕs'kŏt) | 104 | 34°30'N | 112°30'W |
| Prescott, Wi., U.S. (prĕs'kŏt) | 117g | 44°45'N | 92°48'W |
| Presho, S.D., U.S. (prĕsh'ō) | 112 | 43°56'N | 100°04'W |
| Presidencia Rogue Sáenz Peña, Arg. | 144 | 26°52'S | 60°15'W |
| Presidente Epitácio, Braz. (prā-sē-dĕn'tĕ å-pē-tä'syō) | 143 | 21°56'S | 52°01'W |
| Presidio, Tx., U.S. (prĕ-sĭ'dĭ-ō) | 122 | 29°33'N | 104°23'W |
| Presidio, Río del, r., Mex. (rē'ō-dĕl-prĕ-sē'dyô) | 130 | 23°54'N | 105°44'W |
| Prešov, Slvk. (prĕ'shôf) | 161 | 49°00'N | 21°18'E |
| Prespa, Lake, l., Eur. (prĕs'pä) | 175 | 40°49'N | 20°50'E |
| Prespuntal, r., Ven. | 143b | 9°55'N | 64°32'W |
| Presque Isle, Me., U.S. (prĕsk'ēl') | 100 | 46°41'N | 68°03'W |
| Pressbaum, Aus. | 159e | 48°12'N | 16°06'E |
| Prestea, Ghana | 234 | 5°27'N | 2°08'W |
| Preston, Austl. | 217a | 37°45'S | 145°01'E |
| Preston, Eng., U.K. (prĕs'tŭn) | 164 | 53°46'N | 2°42'W |
| Preston, Id., U.S. (pres'tŭn) | 115 | 42°05'N | 111°54'W |
| Preston, Mn., U.S. (prĕs'tŭn) | 113 | 43°42'N | 92°06'W |
| Preston, Wa., U.S. | 116a | 47°31'N | 121°56'W |
| Prestonburg, Ky., U.S. (prĕs'tŭn-bûrg) | 108 | 37°35'N | 82°50'W |
| Prestwich, Eng., U.K. (prĕst'wĭch) | 158a | 53°32'N | 2°17'W |
| Pretoria, S. Afr. (prĕ-tō'rĭ-à) | 232 | 25°43'S | 28°16'E |
| Pretoria North, S. Afr. (prĕ-tō'rĭ-à nōōrd) | 238c | 25°41'S | 28°11'E |
| Préveza, Grc. (prĕ'vå-zä) | 175 | 38°58'N | 20°44'E |
| Pribilof Islands, is., Ak., U.S. (prĭ'bĭ-lof) | 103 | 57°00'N | 169°20'W |
| Priboj, Serb. (prē'boi) | 175 | 43°33'N | 19°33'E |
| Price, Ut., U.S. (prīs) | 119 | 39°35'N | 110°50'W |
| Price, r., Ut., U.S. | 119 | 39°21'N | 110°35'W |
| Prichard, Al., U.S. (prĭt'chârd) | 124 | 30°44'N | 88°04'W |
| Priddis, Can. (prĭd'dĭs) | 102e | 50°53'N | 114°20'W |
| Priddis Creek, r., Can. | 102e | 50°56'N | 114°32'W |
| Priego, Spain (prē-ā'gō) | 172 | 37°27'N | 4°13'W |
| Prienai, Lith. (prē-ĕn'ī) | 167 | 54°38'N | 23°56'E |
| Prieska, S. Afr. (prē-ĕs'kå) | 232 | 29°40'S | 22°50'E |
| Priest Lake, l., Id., U.S. (prēst) | 114 | 48°30'N | 116°43'W |
| Priest Rapids Dam, Wa., U.S. | 114 | 46°39'N | 119°55'W |
| Priest Rapids Lake, res., Wa., U.S. | 114 | 46°42'N | 119°58'W |
| Priiskovaya, Russia (prĭ-ĕs'kô-và-yà) | 186a | 60°50'N | 58°55'E |
| Prijedor, Bos. (prē'yĕ-dôr) | 174 | 44°58'N | 16°43'E |
| Prijepolje, Serb. (prē'yĕ-pô'lyĕ) | 175 | 43°22'N | 19°41'E |
| Prilep, Mac. (prē'lĕp) | 163 | 41°20'N | 21°35'E |
| Primorsk, Russia (prē-môrsk') | 167 | 60°24'N | 28°35'E |
| Primorsko-Akhtarskaya, Russia (prē-môr'skô äĸ-tär'skĭ-ē) | 181 | 46°03'N | 38°09'E |
| Primrose, S. Afr. | 233b | 26°11'S | 28°11'E |
| Primrose Lake, l., Can. | 96 | 54°55'N | 109°45'W |
| Prince Albert, Can. (prĭns ăl'bērt) | 90 | 53°12'N | 105°46'W |
| Prince Albert National Park, rec., Can. | 92 | 54°10'N | 105°25'W |
| Prince Albert Sound, strt., Can. | 92 | 70°23'N | 116°57'W |
| Prince Charles Island, i., Can. (chärlz) | 93 | 67°41'N | 74°10'W |
| Prince Edward Island, prov., Can. | 91 | 46°45'N | 63°10'W |
| Prince Edward Islands, is., S. Afr. | 224 | 46°36'S | 37°57'E |
| Prince Edward National Park, rec., Can. (ĕd'wērd) | 93 | 46°33'N | 63°35'W |
| Prince Edward Peninsula, pen., Can. | 109 | 44°00'N | 77°15'W |
| Prince Frederick, Md., U.S. (prĭnce frĕdĕrĭk) | 110e | 38°33'N | 76°35'W |
| Prince George, Can. (jôrj) | 90 | 53°51'N | 122°57'W |
| Prince of Wales, i., Austl. | 221 | 10°47'S | 142°15'E |
| Prince of Wales, i., Ak., U.S. | 103 | 55°47'N | 132°50'W |
| Prince of Wales, Cape, c., Ak., U.S. (wālz) | 103 | 65°48'N | 169°08'W |
| Prince Rupert, Can. (roo'pērt) | 90 | 54°19'N | 130°19'W |
| Princes Risborough, Eng., U.K. (prĭns'ĕz rĭz'brŭ) | 158b | 51°41'N | 0°51'W |
| Princess Charlotte Bay, b., Austl. (shär'lŏt) | 221 | 13°45'S | 144°15'E |
| Princess Royal Channel, strt., Can. (roi'ăl) | 94 | 53°10'N | 128°37'W |
| Princess Royal Island, i., Can. | 94 | 52°57'N | 128°49'W |
| Princeton, Can. (prĭns'tŭn) | 90 | 49°27'N | 120°31'W |
| Princeton, Il., U.S. | 108 | 41°20'N | 89°25'W |
| Princeton, In., U.S. | 108 | 38°20'N | 87°35'W |
| Princeton, Ky., U.S. | 124 | 37°07'N | 87°52'W |
| Princeton, Mi., U.S. | 113 | 46°16'N | 87°33'W |
| Princeton, Mn., U.S. | 113 | 45°34'N | 93°36'W |
| Princeton, Mo., U.S. | 121 | 40°23'N | 93°34'W |
| Princeton, N.J., U.S. | 109 | 40°21'N | 74°40'W |
| Princeton, Wi., U.S. | 113 | 43°50'N | 89°09'W |
| Princeton, W.V., U.S. | 125 | 37°21'N | 81°05'W |
| Prince William Sound, strt., Ak., U.S. (wĭl'yăm) | 103 | 60°40'N | 147°10'W |
| Príncipe, i., S. Tom./P. (prēn'sē-pĕ) | 230 | 1°37'N | 7°25'E |
| Principe Channel, strt., Can. (prĭn'sĭ-pē) | 94 | 53°28'N | 129°45'W |
| Prineville, Or., U.S. (prīn'vĭl) | 114 | 44°17'N | 120°48'W |
| Prineville Reservoir, res., Or., U.S. | 114 | 44°07'N | 120°45'W |
| Prinzapolca, Nic. (prēn-zä-pōl'kä) | 133 | 13°18'N | 83°35'W |
| Prinzapolca, r., Nic. | 133 | 13°23'N | 84°23'W |
| Prior Lake, Mn., U.S. (prī'ēr) | 117g | 44°43'N | 93°26'W |
| Priozërsk, Russia (prĭ-ô'zërsk) | 167 | 61°03'N | 30°08'E |
| Pripet, r., Eur. | 181 | 51°50'N | 29°45'E |
| Pripet Marshes, sw., Eur. | 181 | 52°10'N | 27°30'E |
| Priština, Serb. (prēsh'tĭ-nä) | 163 | 42°39'N | 21°12'E |
| Pritzwalk, Ger. (prēts'välk) | 168 | 53°09'N | 12°12'E |
| Privas, Fr. (prē-väs') | 170 | 44°44'N | 4°37'E |
| Prizren, Serb. (prē'zrĕn) | 163 | 42°11'N | 20°45'E |
| Procida, Italy (prô'chē-dä) | 173c | 40°31'N | 14°02'E |
| Procida, Isola di, i., Italy | 173c | 40°32'N | 13°57'E |
| Proctor, Mn., U.S. (prŏk'tēr) | 117h | 46°45'N | 92°14'W |
| Proctor, Vt., U.S. | 109 | 43°40'N | 73°00'W |
| Proebstel, Wa., U.S. (prōb'stĕl) | 116c | 45°40'N | 122°29'W |
| Proenca-a-Nova, Port. (prō-ăn'sá-ä-nō'vá) | 172 | 39°44'N | 7°55'W |
| Progreso, Hond. (prō-grĕ'sō) | 132 | 15°28'N | 87°49'W |
| Progreso, Mex. (prō-grā'sō) | 128 | 21°14'N | 89°39'W |
| Progreso, Mex. | 122 | 27°29'N | 101°05'W |
| Prokhladnyy, Russia | 182 | 43°46'N | 44°00'E |
| Prokop'yevsk, Russia | 184 | 53°53'N | 86°45'E |
| Prokuplje, Serb. (prô'kōp'l-yĕ) | 175 | 43°16'N | 21°40'E |
| Prome, Mya. | 212 | 18°46'N | 95°15'E |
| Pronya, r., Bela. (prô'nyä) | 176 | 54°08'N | 30°58'E |
| Pronya, r., Russia | 176 | 54°08'N | 39°30'E |
| Prospect, Ky., U.S. (prŏs'pĕkt) | 111h | 38°21'N | 85°36'W |
| Prospect Park, Pa., U.S. (prŏs'pĕkt pärk) | 110f | 39°53'N | 75°18'W |
| Prosser, Wa., U.S. (prŏs'ēr) | 114 | 46°10'N | 119°46'W |
| Prostějov, Czech Rep. (prôs'tyĕ-yôf) | 169 | 49°28'N | 17°08'E |
| Protection, i., Wa., U.S. (prō-tĕk'shŭn) | 116a | 48°07'N | 122°56'W |
| Protoka, r., Russia (prôt'ō-kà) | 176 | 55°00'N | 36°42'E |
| Provadiya, Blg. (prō-väd'ē-yà) | 175 | 43°13'N | 27°28'E |
| Providence, Ky., U.S. (prŏv'ĭ-dĕns) | 108 | 37°25'N | 87°45'W |
| Providence, R.I., U.S. | 105 | 41°50'N | 71°23'W |
| Providence, Ut., U.S. | 115 | 41°42'N | 111°50'W |
| Providencia, Isla de, i., Col. | 133 | 13°21'N | 80°55'W |
| Providenciales, i., T./C. Is. | 135 | 21°50'N | 72°15'W |
| Provideniya, Russia (prô-vĭ-dă'nĭ-yà) | 103 | 64°30'N | 172°54'W |
| Provincetown, Ma., U.S. | 109 | 42°03'N | 70°11'W |
| Provo, Ut., U.S. (prō'vō) | 104 | 40°15'N | 111°40'W |
| Prozor, Bos. (prô'zôr) | 175 | 43°48'N | 17°59'E |
| Prudence Island, i., R.I., U.S. (prōō'dĕns) | 110b | 41°38'N | 71°20'W |
| Prudhoe Bay, b., Ak., U.S. | 103 | 70°40'N | 147°25'W |
| Prudnik, Pol. (prŏd'nĭk) | 169 | 50°19'N | 17°34'E |
| Prussia, hist. reg., Eur. (prŭsh'á) | 168 | 50°43'N | 8°35'E |
| Pruszków, Pol. (prōsh'kōf) | 169 | 52°09'N | 20°50'E |
| Prut, r., Eur. (prōōt) | 156 | 48°05'N | 27°07'E |
| Pryluky, Ukr. | 181 | 50°36'N | 32°21'E |
| Prymors'k, Ukr. | 177 | 46°43'N | 36°21'E |
| Pryor, Ok., U.S. (prī'ēr) | 121 | 36°16'N | 95°19'W |
| Pryvil'ne, Ukr. | 177 | 47°30'N | 32°21'E |
| Przedbórz, Pol. | 169 | 51°05'N | 19°53'E |
| Przemyśl, Pol. (pzhĕ'mĭsh'l) | 154 | 49°47'N | 22°45'E |
| Przheval'sk, Kyrg. (p'r-zhĭ-välsk') | 183 | 42°29'N | 78°24'E |
| Psel, r., Eur. | 181 | 49°45'N | 33°42'E |
| Pskov, Russia (pskôf) | 178 | 57°48'N | 28°19'E |
| Pskov, prov., Russia | 176 | 57°33'N | 29°05'E |
| Pskovskoye Ozero, l., Eur. (p'skôv'skô'yĕ ôzē-rô) | 180 | 58°05'N | 28°15'E |
| Ptich', r., Bela. (p'tēch) | 180 | 53°17'N | 28°16'E |
| Ptuj, Slvn. (ptōō'ē) | 174 | 46°24'N | 15°54'E |
| Pucheng, China (pōō'chĕng') | 209 | 28°02'N | 118°25'E |
| Pucheng, China (pōō-chūŋ) | 206 | 35°43'N | 115°22'E |
| Puck, Pol. (pòtsk) | 169 | 54°43'N | 18°23'E |
| Pudozh, Russia (pōō'dôzh) | 180 | 61°50'N | 36°50'E |
| Puebla, Mex. (pwā'blä) | 128 | 19°02'N | 98°11'W |
| Puebla, state, Mex. | 131 | 19°00'N | 97°45'W |
| Puebla de Don Fadrique, Spain | 172 | 37°55'N | 2°55'W |
| Pueblo, Co., U.S. (pwā'blō) | 104 | 38°15'N | 104°36'W |
| Pueblo Nuevo, Mex. (nwā'vō) | 130 | 23°23'N | 105°21'W |
| Pueblo Viejo, Mex. (vyā'hō) | 131 | 17°23'N | 93°46'W |
| Puente Alto, Chile (pwĕ'n-tĕ àl'tô) | 141b | 33°36'S | 70°34'W |
| Puentedeume, Spain (pwĕn-tā-dhā-ōō'mā) | 172 | 43°28'N | 8°09'W |
| Puente-Genil, Spain (pwĕn'tå-hå-nēl') | 172 | 37°25'N | 4°18'W |
| Puerco, Rio, r., N.M., U.S. (pwĕr'kō) | 119 | 35°15'N | 107°05'W |
| Puerto Aisén, Chile (pwĕ'r-tō ā'y-sĕ'n) | 144 | 45°28'S | 72°44'W |
| Puerto Angel, Mex. (pwĕ'r-tō äŋ'hål) | 131 | 15°42'N | 96°32'W |
| Puerto Armuelles, Pan. (pwe'r-tô är-mōō-ā'lyās) | 133 | 8°18'N | 82°52'W |
| Puerto Barrios, Guat. (pwĕ'r-tô bär'rē-ôs) | 128 | 15°43'N | 88°36'W |
| Puerto Bermúdez, Peru (pwĕ'r-tō bĕr-mōō'dāz) | 142 | 10°17'S | 74°57'W |
| Puerto Berrío, Col. (pwĕ'r-tô bĕr-rē'ō) | 142 | 6°29'N | 74°27'W |
| Puerto Cabello, Ven. (pwĕ'r-tō kä-bĕl'yō) | 142 | 10°28'N | 68°01'W |
| Puerto Cabezas, Nic. (pwĕ'r-tō kä-bā'zäs) | 133 | 14°01'N | 83°26'W |
| Puerto Casado, Para. (pwĕ'r-tō kä-sä'dō) | 144 | 22°16'S | 57°57'W |
| Puerto Castilla, Hond. (pwĕ'r-tō käs-tēl'yō) | 132 | 16°01'N | 86°01'W |
| Puerto Chicama, Peru (pwĕ'r-tō chē-kä'mä) | 142 | 7°46'S | 79°18'W |
| Puerto Colombia, Col. (pwĕr'tō kō-lōm'bē-à) | 142 | 11°08'N | 75°09'W |
| Puerto Cortés, C.R. (pwĕ'r-tô kôr-tās') | 133 | 9°00'N | 83°37'W |
| Puerto Cortés, Hond. (pwĕ'r-tô kôr-tās') | 128 | 15°48'N | 87°57'W |
| Puerto Cumarebo, Ven. (pwĕ'r-tō kōō-mä-rĕ'bô) | 142 | 11°25'N | 69°17'W |
| Puerto de Luna, N.M., U.S. (pwĕr'tô då lōō'nä) | 120 | 34°49'N | 104°36'W |
| Puerto de Nutrias, Ven. (pwĕ'r-tō dĕ nōō-trē-äs') | 142 | 8°02'N | 69°19'W |
| Puerto Deseado, Arg. (pwĕ'r-tō dā-så-ä'dhō) | 144 | 47°38'S | 66°00'W |
| Puerto de Somport, p., Eur. | 173 | 42°51'N | 0°25'W |
| Puerto Eten, Peru (pwĕ'r-tō ĕ-tĕ'n) | 142 | 6°59'S | 79°51'W |
| Puerto Jiménez, C.R. (pwĕ'r-tō ĸē-mĕ'nĕz) | 133 | 8°35'N | 83°23'W |
| Puerto La Cruz, Ven. (pwĕ'r-tō lä krōō'z) | 142 | 10°14'N | 64°38'W |
| Puertollano, Spain (pwĕ-tôl-yä'nō) | 162 | 38°41'N | 4°05'W |
| Puerto Madryn, Arg. (pwĕ'r-tō mä-drĕn') | 144 | 42°45'S | 65°01'W |
| Puerto Maldonado, Peru (pwĕ'r-tō mäl-dō-nä'dô) | 142 | 12°43'S | 69°01'W |
| Puerto Miniso, Mex. (pwĕ'r-tō mē-nē'sô) | 130 | 16°06'N | 98°02'W |
| Puerto Montt, Chile (pwĕ'r-tō mô'nt) | 144 | 41°29'S | 73°00'W |
| Puerto Natales, Chile (pwĕ'r-tō nä-tà'lĕs) | 144 | 51°48'S | 72°01'W |
| Puerto Niño, Col. (pwĕ'r-tō nē'n-yô) | 142a | 5°57'N | 74°36'W |
| Puerto Padre, Cuba (pwĕ'r-tō pä'drā) | 134 | 21°10'N | 76°40'W |
| Puerto Peñasco, Mex. (pwĕ'r-tō pĕn-yä's-kô) | 128 | 31°39'N | 113°15'W |
| Puerto Pinasco, Para. (pwĕ'r-tō pē-nà's-kô) | 144 | 22°31'S | 57°50'W |
| Puerto Píritu, Ven. (pwĕ'r-tō pē'rē-tōō) | 143b | 10°05'N | 65°04'W |
| Puerto Plata, Dom. Rep. (pwĕ'r-tô plä'tä) | 129 | 19°50'N | 70°40'W |
| Puerto Princesa, Phil. (pwĕr-tô prēn-sā'sä) | 212 | 9°45'N | 118°41'E |
| Puerto Rico, dep., N.A. (pwĕr'tô rē'kō) | 129 | 18°16'N | 66°50'W |
| Puerto Rico Trench, deep | 129 | 19°45'N | 66°30'W |
| Puerto Salgar, Col. (pwĕ'r-tō säl-gär') | 142a | 5°30'N | 74°39'W |
| Puerto Santa Cruz, Arg. (pwĕ'r-tō sän'tä krōōz') | 144 | 50°04'S | 68°32'W |
| Puerto Suárez, Bol. (pwĕ'r-tō swä'råz) | 143 | 18°55'S | 57°39'W |
| Puerto Tejada, Col. (pwĕ'r-tō tĕ-ĸä'dä) | 142 | 3°13'N | 76°23'W |
| Puerto Vallarta, Mex. (pwĕ'r-tō väl-yär'tä) | 130 | 20°36'N | 105°13'W |
| Puerto Varas, Chile (pwĕ'r-tō vä'räs) | 144 | 41°16'S | 73°03'W |
| Puerto Wilches, Col. (pwĕ'r-tō vēl'c-hĕs) | 142 | 7°19'N | 73°54'W |
| Pugachëv, Russia (pōō'gà-chyôf) | 181 | 52°00'N | 48°40'E |
| Puget, Wa., U.S. (pū'jĕt) | 116c | 46°10'N | 123°23'W |
| Puget Sound, strt., Wa., U.S. | 114 | 47°49'N | 122°26'W |
| Puglia (Apulia), hist. reg., Italy (pōō'lyä) (ä-pōō'lyä) | 174 | 41°13'N | 16°10'E |
| Pukaskwa National Park, rec., Can. | 93 | 48°22'N | 85°55'W |
| Pukeashun Mountain, mtn., Can. | 95 | 51°12'N | 119°14'W |
| Pukin, r., Malay. | 197b | 2°53'N | 102°54'E |
| Pula, Cro. (pōō'lä) | 162 | 44°52'N | 13°55'E |
| Pulacayo, Bol. (pōō-lä-kä'yō) | 142 | 20°12'N | 66°33'W |
| Pulaski, Tn., U.S. (pŭ-lăs'kĭ) | 124 | 35°11'N | 87°03'W |
| Pulaski, Va., U.S. | 125 | 37°00'N | 81°45'W |
| Puławy, Pol. (pò-wä'vĕ) | 169 | 51°24'N | 21°59'E |
| Pulicat, r., India | 203 | 13°58'N | 79°52'E |
| Pullman, Wa., U.S. (pòl'măn) | 114 | 46°44'N | 117°10'W |
| Pulog, Mount, mtn., Phil. (pōō'lôg) | 213a | 16°38'N | 120°53'E |
| Puma Yumco, l., China (pōō-mä yōōm-tswo) | 202 | 28°30'N | 90°10'E |
| Pumpkin Creek, r., Mt., U.S. (pŭmp'kĭn) | 115 | 45°47'N | 105°35'W |
| Punakha, Bhu. (pōō-nŭk'ŭ) | 199 | 27°45'N | 89°59'E |
| Punata, Bol. (pōō-nä'tä) | 142 | 17°43'S | 65°43'W |
| Pune, India | 199 | 18°38'N | 73°53'E |
| Punjab, state, India (pŭn'jäb') | 199 | 31°00'N | 75°30'E |
| Puno, Peru (pōō'nō) | 142 | 15°58'S | 70°02'W |
| Punta Arenas, Chile (pōō'n-tä-rĕ'näs) | 144 | 53°09'S | 70°48'W |
| Punta de Piedras, Ven. (pōō'n-tä dĕ pyĕ'dräs) | 143b | 10°54'N | 64°06'W |
| Punta Gorda, Belize (pòn'tä gôr'dä) | 132 | 16°07'N | 88°50'W |
| Punta Gorda, Fl., U.S. (pŭn'tá gôr'dá) | 125a | 26°55'N | 82°02'W |
| Punta Gorda, Río, r., Nic. (pōō'n-tä gô'r-dä) | 133 | 11°34'N | 84°13'W |
| Punta Indio, Canal, strt., Arg. (pōō'n-tä-ē'n-dyô) | 141c | 34°56'S | 57°20'W |
| Puntarenas, C.R. (pònt-ä-rä'näs) | 129 | 9°59'N | 84°49'W |
| Punto Fijo, Ven. (pōō'n-tô fē'ĸō) | 142 | 11°48'N | 70°14'W |
| Punxsutawney, Pa., U.S. (pŭnk-sŭ-tô'nē) | 109 | 40°55'N | 79°00'W |
| Puquio, Peru (pōō'kyô) | 142 | 14°43'S | 74°02'W |
| Pur, r., Russia | 184 | 65°30'N | 77°30'E |
| Purcell, Ok., U.S. (pûr-sĕl') | 121 | 35°01'N | 97°22'W |
| Purcell Mountains, mts., N.A. (pûr-sĕl') | 95 | 50°00'N | 116°30'W |
| Purdy, Wa., U.S. (pûr'dē) | 116a | 47°23'N | 122°37'W |
| Purépero, Mex. (pōō-rā'på-rō) | 130 | 19°56'N | 102°02'W |
| Purgatoire, r., Co., U.S. (pûr-gà-twär') | 120 | 37°25'N | 103°53'W |
| Puri, India (pò'rē) | 199 | 19°52'N | 85°51'E |
| Purial, Sierra de, mts., Cuba (sē-ĕ'r-rà-dĕ-pōō-rē-äl') | 135 | 20°15'N | 74°40'W |
| Purificación, Col. (pōō-rē-fē-kä-syōn') | 142 | 3°52'N | 74°54'W |
| Purificación, Mex. (pōō-rē-fē-kä-syō'n) | 130 | 19°44'N | 104°38'W |
| Purificación, r., Mex. | 130 | 19°30'N | 104°54'W |
| Purkersdorf, Aus. | 159e | 48°13'N | 16°11'E |


ăt; finăl; rāte; senåte; ärm; åsk; sofá; fâre; ch-choose; dh-as th in other; bē; ėvent; bĕt; recĕnt; cratẽr; g-gō; gh-guttural g; bĭt; ĭ-short neutral; rīde; ĸ-guttural k as ch in German ich;

PRONOUNCING INDEX
Puruandiro – Ramanāthapuram 339


| PLACE (Pronunciation) | PAGE | LAT. | LONG. |
|---|---|---|---|
| Puruandiro, Mex. (pö-rōō-än'dē-rō) | 130 | 20°04'N | 101°33'W |
| Purús, r., S.A. (pōō-rōō's) | 142 | 6°45'S | 64°34'W |
| Pusan, Kor., S. | 205 | 35°08'N | 129°05'E |
| Pushkin, Russia (pŏsh'kĭn) | 180 | 59°43'N | 30°25'E |
| Pushkino, Russia (pōōsh'kē-nô) | 176 | 56°01'N | 37°51'E |
| Pustoshka, Russia (pûs-tôsh'kå) | 176 | 56°20'N | 29°33'E |
| Pustunich, Mex. (pōōs-tōō'nēch) | 131 | 19°10'N | 90°29'W |
| Putaendo, Chile (pōō-tä-ĕn-dô) | 141b | 32°37'S | 70°42'W |
| Puteaux, Fr. (pü-tō') | 171b | 48°52'N | 2°12'E |
| Putfontein, S. Afr. (pŏt'fŏn-tän) | 233b | 26°08'S | 28°24'E |
| Putian, China (pōō-tĭĕn) | 209 | 25°40'N | 119°02'E |
| Putla de Guerrero, Mex. (pōō'tlä-dē-gĕr-rĕ'rō) | 131 | 17°03'N | 97°55'W |
| Putnam, Ct., U.S. (pŭt'năm) | 109 | 41°55'N | 71°55'W |
| Putorana, Gory, mts., Russia | 179 | 68°45'N | 93°15'E |
| Puttalam, Sri L. | 203 | 8°02'N | 79°44'E |
| Putumayo, r., S.A. (pō-tōō-mä'yō) | 142 | 1°02'S | 73°50'W |
| Putung, Tanjung, c., Indon. | 212 | 3°35'S | 111°50'E |
| Putyvl', Ukr. | 177 | 51°21'N | 33°52'E |
| Puulavesi, l., Fin. | 167 | 61°49'N | 27°10'E |
| Puyallup, Wa., U.S. (pū-ăl'ŭp) | 116a | 47°12'N | 122°18'W |
| Puyang, China (pōō-yäŋ) | 208 | 35°42'N | 114°58'E |
| Pweto, D.R.C. (pwā'tō) | 232 | 8°29'S | 28°58'E |
| Pyasina, r., Russia (pyä-sē'nà) | 184 | 72°45'N | 87°37'E |
| Pyatigorsk, Russia (pyà-tē-gôrsk') | 181 | 44°00'N | 43°00'E |
| Pyetrykaw, Bela. | 176 | 52°09'N | 28°30'E |
| Pyhäjärvi, l., Fin. | 167 | 60°57'N | 21°50'E |
| Pyinmana, Mya. (pyēn-mä'nŭ) | 199 | 19°47'N | 96°15'E |
| Pymatuning Reservoir, res., Pa., U.S. (pī-mà-tūn'ĭng) | 108 | 41°40'N | 80°30'W |
| Pyŏnggang, Kor., N. (pyŭng'gäng') | 210 | 38°21'N | 127°18'E |
| P'yŏngyang, Kor., N. | 205 | 39°03'N | 125°48'E |
| Pyramid, l., Nv., U.S. (pĭ'rà-mĭd) | 118 | 40°02'N | 119°50'W |
| Pyramid Lake Indian Reservation, I.R., Nv., U.S. | 118 | 40°17'N | 119°52'W |
| Pyramids, hist., Egypt | 238b | 29°53'N | 31°10'E |
| Pyrenees, mts., Eur. (pĭr-e-nēz') | 156 | 43°00'N | 0°05'E |
| Pýrgos, Grc. | 163 | 37°51'N | 21°28'E |
| Pyriatyn, Ukr. | 181 | 50°13'N | 32°31'E |
| Pyrzyce, Pol. (pĕzhĭ'tsĕ) | 168 | 53°09'N | 14°53'E |


# Q


| PLACE (Pronunciation) | PAGE | LAT. | LONG. |
|---|---|---|---|
| Qal'at Bishah, Sau. Ar. | 198 | 20°01'N | 42°30'E |
| Qamdo, China (chyäm-dwō) | 204 | 31°06'N | 96°30'E |
| Qandala, Som. | 201 | 11°28'N | 49°52'E |
| Qaraghandy (Karaganda), Kaz. | 183 | 49°42'N | 73°18'E |
| Qaraözen, r. | 181 | 49°50'N | 49°35'E |
| Qarqan *see* Qiemo, China | 204 | 38°02'N | 85°16'E |
| Qarqan, r., China | 204 | 38°55'N | 87°15'E |
| Qarqaraly, Kaz. | 183 | 49°18'N | 75°28'E |
| Qārūn, Birket, l., Egypt | 231 | 29°34'N | 30°34'E |
| Qaşr al Burayqah, Libya | 231 | 30°25'N | 19°20'E |
| Qasr al-Farāfirah, Egypt | 231 | 27°04'N | 28°13'E |
| Qaşr Banī Walīd, Libya | 231 | 31°45'N | 14°04'E |
| Qasr el Boukhari, Alg. | 162 | 35°50'N | 2°48'E |
| Qatar, nation, Asia (kä'tår) | 198 | 25°00'N | 52°45'E |
| Qaţţārah, Munkhafaḍ al, depr., Egypt | 231 | 30°07'N | 27°30'E |
| Qausuittuq (Resolute), Can. | 89 | 74°41'N | 95°00'W |
| Qāyen, Iran | 198 | 33°45'N | 59°08'E |
| Qazvīn, Iran | 198 | 36°10'N | 49°59'E |
| Qeshm, Iran | 198 | 26°51'N | 56°10'E |
| Qeshm, i., Iran | 198 | 26°52'N | 56°15'E |
| Qezel Owzan, r., Iran | 198 | 36°30'N | 49°00'E |
| Qezi'ot, Isr. | 197a | 30°53'N | 34°28'E |
| Qianwei, China (chyĕn-wā) | 206 | 40°11'N | 120°05'E |
| Qi'anzhen, China (chyē-än-jŭn) | 206 | 32°16'N | 120°59'E |
| Qibao, China (chyē-bou) | 207b | 31°06'N | 121°16'E |
| Qiblīyah, Jabal al Jalālat al, mts., Egypt | 197a | 28°49'N | 32°21'E |
| Qijiang, China (chyē-jyäŋ) | 209 | 29°05'N | 106°40'E |
| Qikou, China (chyē-kō) | 206 | 38°37'N | 117°33'E |
| Qilian Shan, mts., China (chyē-lĭĕn shän) | 204 | 38°43'N | 98°00'E |
| Qiliping, China (chyē-lē-pĭŋ) | 206 | 31°28'N | 114°41'E |
| Qindao, China (chyĭn-dou) | 205 | 36°05'N | 120°10'E |
| Qing'an, China (chyĭŋ-än) | 208 | 46°50'N | 127°30'E |
| Qingcheng, China (chyĭŋ-chŭŋ) | 206 | 37°12'N | 117°43'E |
| Qingfeng, China (chyĭŋ-fŭŋ) | 206 | 35°52'N | 115°05'E |
| Qinghai, prov., China (chyĭŋ-hī) | 204 | 36°14'N | 95°30'E |
| Qinghai Hu *see* Koko Nor, l., China | 204 | 37°26'N | 98°30'E |
| Qinghe, China (chyĭŋ-hŭ) | 208a | 40°08'N | 116°16'E |
| Qingjiang, China (chyĭŋ-jyäŋ) | 209 | 28°00'N | 115°30'E |
| Qingjiang, China | 206 | 33°34'N | 118°58'E |
| Qingliu, China (chyĭŋ-lĭô) | 209 | 26°15'N | 116°50'E |
| Qingningsi, China (chyĭŋ-nĭŋ-sz) | 207b | 31°16'N | 121°33'E |
| Qingping, China (chyĭŋ-pĭŋ) | 206 | 36°46'N | 116°03'E |
| Qingpu, China (chyĭŋ-pōō) | 209 | 31°08'N | 121°06'E |
| Qingxian, China (chyĭŋ shyĕn) | 206 | 38°37'N | 116°48'E |
| Qingyang, China (chyĭŋ-yäŋ) | 206 | 36°02'N | 107°42'E |
| Qingyuan, China (chyĭŋ-yōän) | 209 | 23°43'N | 113°10'E |
| Qingyuan, China | 208 | 42°05'N | 125°00'E |
| Qingyun, China (chyĭŋ-yòn) | 206 | 37°52'N | 117°26'E |
| Qingyundian, China (chĭŋ-yòn-dĭĕn) | 208a | 39°41'N | 116°31'E |
| Qinhuangdao, China (chyĭn-huaŋ-dou) | 205 | 39°57'N | 119°34'E |
| Qin Ling, mts., China (chyĭn lĭŋ) | 204 | 33°25'N | 108°58'E |
| Qinyang, China (chyĭn-yäŋ) | 208 | 35°00'N | 112°55'E |
| Qinzhou, China (chyĭn-jō) | 209 | 22°00'N | 108°35'E |
| Qionghai, China (chyôŋ-hī) | 209 | 19°10'N | 110°28'E |
| Qiqian, China (chyē-chyĕn) | 205 | 52°23'N | 121°04'E |
| Qiqihar, China | 205 | 47°18'N | 124°00'E |
| Qiryat Gat, Isr. | 197a | 31°38'N | 34°36'E |
| Qiryat Shemona, Isr. | 197a | 33°12'N | 35°34'E |
| Qitai, China (chyē-tī) | 204 | 44°07'N | 89°04'E |
| Qiuxian, China (chyô shyĕn) | 206 | 36°43'N | 115°13'E |
| Qixian, China (chyē-shyĕn) | 206 | 34°33'N | 114°47'E |
| Qixian, China | 208 | 35°36'N | 114°13'E |
| Qiyang, China (chyē-yäŋ) | 209 | 26°40'N | 112°00'E |
| Qobda, r., Kaz. (kä-rà kôb'dà) | 181 | 50°40'N | 55°00'E |
| Qogir Feng *see* K2, mtn., Asia | 199 | 36°06'N | 76°38'E |
| Qom, Iran | 198 | 34°28'N | 50°53'E |
| Qongyrat, Kaz. | 183 | 47°25'N | 75°10'E |
| Qostanay, Kaz. | 183 | 53°10'N | 63°39'E |
| Quabbin Reservoir, res., Ma., U.S. (kwā'bĭn) | 109 | 42°20'N | 72°10'W |
| Quachita, Lake, l., Ar., U.S. (kwä shĭ'tô) | 121 | 34°47'N | 93°37'W |
| Quadra Island, i., Can. | 94 | 50°08'N | 125°16'W |
| Quakertown, Pa., U.S. (kwā'kēr-toun) | 109 | 40°30'N | 75°20'W |
| Quanah, Tx., U.S. (kwä'nà) | 120 | 34°19'N | 99°43'W |
| Quang Ngai, Viet. (kwäng n'gä'ē) | 212 | 15°05'N | 108°58'E |
| Quang Ngai, mtn., Viet. | 209 | 15°10'N | 108°20'E |
| Quanjiao, China (chyuän-jyou) | 206 | 32°06'N | 118°17'E |
| Quanzhou, China (chyuän-jō) | 205 | 24°58'N | 118°40'E |
| Quanzhou, China | 209 | 25°58'N | 111°02'E |
| Qu'Appelle, r., Can. | 92 | 50°30'N | 104°00'W |
| Qu'Appelle Dam, dam, Can. | 96 | 51°00'N | 106°25'W |
| Quartu Sant'Elena, Italy (kwär-tōō' sänt a'lå-nä) | 174 | 39°16'N | 9°12'E |
| Quartzsite, Az., U.S. | 119 | 33°40'N | 114°13'W |
| Quatsino Sound, strt., Can. (kwŏt-sē'nō) | 94 | 50°25'N | 128°10'W |
| Quba, Azer. (kōō'bā) | 181 | 41°05'N | 48°30'E |
| Qūchān, Iran | 201 | 37°06'N | 58°30'E |
| Qudi, China | 206 | 37°06'N | 117°15'E |
| Québec, Can. (kwê-bĕk') (kå-bĕk') | 102b | 46°49'N | 71°13'W |
| Quebec, prov., Can. | 91 | 51°07'N | 70°25'W |
| Quedlinburg, Ger. (kvĕd'lĕn-bōōrgh) | 168 | 51°45'N | 11°10'E |
| Queen Bess, Can. | 94 | 51°16'N | 124°34'W |
| Queen Charlotte Islands, is., Can. (kwēn shär'lŏt) | 92 | 53°30'N | 132°25'W |
| Queen Charlotte Ranges, mts., Can. | 94 | 53°00'N | 132°00'W |
| Queen Charlotte Sound, strt., Can. | 94 | 51°30'N | 129°30'W |
| Queen Charlotte Strait, strt., Can. (strāt) | 92 | 50°40'N | 127°25'W |
| Queen Elizabeth Islands, is., Can. (ē-lĭz'á-bĕth) | 89 | 78°20'N | 110°00'W |
| Queen Maud Gulf, b., Can. (mäd) | 92 | 68°27'N | 102°55'W |
| Queen Maud Land, reg., Ant. | 224 | 75°00'S | 10°00'E |
| Queen Maud Mountains, mts., Ant. | 224 | 85°00'S | 179°00'W |
| Queens Channel, strt., Austl. (kwēnz) | 220 | 14°25'S | 129°10'E |
| Queenscliff, Austl. | 217a | 38°16'S | 144°39'E |
| Queensland, state, Austl. (kwēnz'lănd) | 219 | 22°45'S | 141°01'E |
| Queenstown, Austl. (kwēnz'toun) | 222 | 42°00'S | 145°40'E |
| Queenstown, S. Afr. | 233c | 31°54'S | 26°53'E |
| Queimados, Braz. (kā-má'dôs) | 144b | 22°42'S | 43°34'W |
| Quela, Ang. | 236 | 9°16'S | 17°02'E |
| Quelimane, Moz. (kā-lē-mä'nĕ) | 233 | 17°48'S | 37°05'E |
| Queluz, Port. | 173b | 38°45'N | 9°15'W |
| Quemado de Güines, Cuba (kā-mä'dhä-dē-gwē'nĕs) | 134 | 22°45'N | 80°20'W |
| Quemoy, Tai. | 209 | 24°30'N | 118°20'E |
| Quemoy, i., Tai. | 209 | 24°27'N | 118°23'E |
| Quepos, C.R. (kā'pôs) | 133 | 9°26'N | 84°10'W |
| Quepos, Punta, c., C.R. (pōō'n-tä) | 133 | 9°23'N | 84°20'W |
| Querétaro, Mex. (kå-rā'tä-rō) | 128 | 20°37'N | 100°25'W |
| Querétaro, state, Mex. | 130 | 21°00'N | 100°00'W |
| Quesada, Spain (kå-sä'dhä) | 172 | 37°51'N | 3°04'W |
| Quesnel, Can. (kā-nĕl') | 90 | 52°59'N | 122°30'W |
| Quesnel, r., Can. | 95 | 52°15'N | 122°00'W |
| Quesnel Lake, l., Can. | 92 | 52°32'N | 121°05'W |
| Quetame, Col. (kĕ-tä'mĕ) | 142a | 4°20'N | 73°50'W |
| Quetta, Pak. (kwĕt'ä) | 199 | 30°19'N | 67°01'E |
| Quezaltenango, Guat. (kå-zäl'tå-näŋ'gō) | 128 | 14°50'N | 91°30'W |
| Quezaltepeque, El Sal. (kĕ-zäl'tĕ'pĕ-kĕ) | 132 | 13°50'N | 89°17'W |
| Quezaltepeque, Guat. (kå-zäl-tå-pä'kå) | 132 | 14°39'N | 89°26'W |
| Quezon City, Phil. (kā-zōn) | 212 | 14°40'N | 121°02'E |
| Qufu, China (chyōō-fōō) | 206 | 35°37'N | 116°54'E |
| Quibdo, Col. (kēb'dō) | 142 | 5°42'N | 76°41'W |
| Quiberon, Fr. (kē-bē-rôn') | 170 | 47°29'N | 3°08'W |
| Quiçama, Parque Nacional de, rec., Ang. | 236 | 10°00'S | 13°25'E |
| Quicksborn, Ger. (kvēks'bōrn) | 159c | 53°44'N | 9°54'E |
| Quilcene, Wa., U.S. (kwĭl-sēn') | 116a | 47°50'N | 122°53'W |
| Quilimari, Chile (kē-lē-mä'rē) | 141b | 32°06'S | 71°28'W |
| Quillan, Fr. (kē-yäN') | 170 | 42°53'N | 2°13'E |
| Quillota, Chile (kēl-yō'tä) | 144 | 32°52'S | 71°14'W |
| Quilmes, Arg. (kēl'mās) | 141c | 34°43'S | 58°16'W |
| Quilon, India (kwē-lōn') | 203 | 8°58'N | 76°16'E |
| Quilpie, Austl. (kwĭl'pē) | 219 | 26°34'S | 149°20'E |
| Quimbaya, Col. (kēm-bä'yä) | 142a | 4°38'N | 75°46'W |
| Quimbele, Ang. | 236 | 6°28'S | 16°13'E |
| Quimbonge, Ang. | 236 | 8°36'S | 18°30'E |
| Quimper, Fr. (kăN-pĕr') | 161 | 47°59'N | 4°04'W |
| Quinalt, r., Wa., U.S. | 114 | 47°23'N | 124°10'W |
| Quinault Indian Reservation, I.R., Wa., U.S. | 114 | 47°27'N | 124°34'W |
| Quincy, Fl., U.S. (kwĭn'sē) | 124 | 30°35'N | 84°35'W |
| Quincy, Il., U.S. | 105 | 39°55'N | 91°23'W |
| Quincy, Ma., U.S. | 101a | 42°15'N | 71°00'W |
| Quincy, Mi., U.S. | 108 | 42°00'N | 84°50'W |
| Quincy, Or., U.S. | 116c | 46°08'N | 123°10'W |
| Qui Nhon, Viet. (kwĭnyôn) | 212 | 13°51'N | 109°03'E |
| Quinn, r., Nv., U.S. (kwĭn) | 114 | 41°42'N | 117°45'W |
| Quintanar de la Orden, Spain (kēn-tä-när') | 172 | 39°36'N | 3°02'W |
| Quintana Roo, state, Mex. (rô'ô) | 128 | 19°30'N | 88°30'W |
| Quintero, Chile (kēn-tĕ'rô) | 141b | 32°48'S | 71°30'W |
| Quionga, Moz. | 237 | 10°37'S | 40°30'E |
| Quiroga, Mex. (kē-rō'gä) | 130 | 19°39'N | 101°30'W |
| Quiroga, Spain (kē-rō'gä) | 172 | 42°28'N | 7°18'W |
| Quitman, Ga., U.S. (kwĭt'măn) | 124 | 30°46'N | 83°35'W |
| Quitman, Ms., U.S. | 124 | 33°02'N | 88°43'W |
| Quito, Ec. (kē'tō) | 142 | 0°17'S | 78°32'W |
| Qumbu, S. Afr. (kòm'bōō) | 233c | 31°10'S | 28°48'E |
| Quorn, Austl. (kwôrn) | 222 | 32°20'S | 138°00'E |
| Qurayyah, Wādī, r., Egypt | 197a | 30°08'N | 34°27'E |
| Qusmuryn köli, l., Kaz. | 183 | 52°30'N | 64°15'E |
| Qutang, China (chyōō-täŋ) | 206 | 32°33'N | 120°07'E |
| Quthing, Leso. | 233c | 30°35'S | 27°42'E |
| Quxian, China (chyōō-shyĕn) | 205 | 28°58'N | 118°58'E |
| Quxian, China | 209 | 30°40'N | 106°48'E |
| Quzhou, China (chyoô-jō) | 206 | 36°47'N | 114°58'E |
| Qyzylorda, Kaz. | 183 | 44°58'N | 65°45'E |


# R


| PLACE (Pronunciation) | PAGE | LAT. | LONG. |
|---|---|---|---|
| Raab (Raba), r., Eur. (räp) | 168 | 46°55'N | 15°55'E |
| Raahe, Fin. (rä'ĕ) | 160 | 64°39'N | 24°22'E |
| Rab, i., Serb. (räb) | 174 | 44°45'N | 14°40'E |
| Raba, Indon. | 212 | 8°32'S | 118°49'E |
| Raba (Raab), r., Eur. | 169 | 47°28'N | 17°12'E |
| Rabat, Mor. (rà-bät') | 230 | 33°59'N | 6°47'W |
| Rabaul, Pap. N. Gui. (rä'boul) | 213 | 4°15'S | 152°19'E |
| Rābigh, Sau. Ar. | 201 | 22°48'N | 39°01'E |
| Raccoon, r., Ia., U.S. (ră-kōōn') | 113 | 42°07'N | 94°45'W |
| Raccoon Cay, i., Bah. | 135 | 22°25'N | 75°50'W |
| Race, Cape, c., Can. (rās) | 101 | 46°40'N | 53°10'W |
| Rachado, Cape, c., Malay. | 197b | 2°26'N | 101°29'E |
| Racibórz, Pol. (rä-chē'bōōzh) | 169 | 50°06'N | 18°14'E |
| Racine, Wi., U.S. (rà-sēn') | 105 | 42°43'N | 87°49'W |
| Raco, Mi., U.S. (rà cō) | 117k | 46°22'N | 84°43'W |
| Rădăuţi, Rom. | 163 | 47°53'N | 25°55'E |
| Radcliffe, Eng., U.K. (răd'klĭf) | 158a | 53°34'N | 2°20'W |
| Radevormwald, Ger. (rä'dĕ-fōrm-väld) | 171c | 51°12'N | 7°22'E |
| Radford, Va., U.S. (răd'fērd) | 125 | 37°06'N | 81°33'W |
| Rādhanpur, India | 202 | 23°57'N | 71°38'E |
| Radium, S. Afr. (rā'dĭ-ŭm) | 238c | 25°06'S | 28°18'E |
| Radom, Pol. (rä'dôm) | 161 | 51°24'N | 21°11'E |
| Radomir, Blg. (rä'dô-mêr) | 175 | 42°33'N | 22°58'E |
| Radomsko, Pol. (rä-dôm'skô) | 161 | 51°04'N | 19°27'E |
| Radomyshl, Ukr. (rä-dô-mēsh''l) | 181 | 50°30'N | 29°13'E |
| Radul', Ukr. (rå'dōōl) | 177 | 51°52'N | 30°46'E |
| Radviliškis, Lith. (råd'vē-lēsh'kēs) | 167 | 55°49'N | 23°31'E |
| Radwah, Jabal, mtn., Sau. Ar. | 198 | 24°44'N | 38°14'E |
| Radzyń Podlaski, Pol. (räd'zēn-y' pŭd-lä'skĭ) | 169 | 51°49'N | 22°40'E |
| Raeford, N.C., U.S. (rā'fērd) | 125 | 34°57'N | 79°15'W |
| Raesfeld, Ger. (răz'fĕld) | 171c | 51°46'N | 6°50'E |
| Raeside, l., Austl. (rā'sīd) | 220 | 29°20'S | 122°30'E |
| Rae Strait, strt., Can. (rā) | 92 | 68°40'N | 95°03'W |
| Rafaela, Arg. (rä-fä-å'lä) | 144 | 31°15'S | 61°21'W |
| Rafah, Pak. (rä'fä) | 197a | 31°14'N | 34°12'E |
| Rafsanjān, Iran | 198 | 30°45'N | 56°30'E |
| Raft, r., Id., U.S. (răft) | 115 | 42°20'N | 113°17'W |
| Ragay, Phil. (rä-gī') | 213a | 13°49'N | 122°45'E |
| Ragay Gulf, b., Phil. | 213a | 13°44'N | 122°38'E |
| Ragunda, .Swe. (rä-gòn'dä) | 166 | 63°07'N | 16°24'E |
| Ragusa, Italy (rä-gōō'sä) | 162 | 36°58'N | 14°41'E |
| Rahachow, Bela. | 180 | 53°07'N | 30°04'E |
| Rahway, N.J., U.S. (rô'wā) | 110a | 40°37'N | 74°16'W |
| Rāichūr, India (rä'ē-chōōr') | 199 | 16°23'N | 77°18'E |
| Raigarh, India (ri'gŭr) | 199 | 21°57'N | 83°32'E |
| Rainbow Bridge National Monument, rec., Ut., U.S. (rān'bō) | 119 | 37°05'N | 111°00'W |
| Rainbow City, Pan. | 128a | 9°20'N | 79°53'W |
| Rainier, Or., U.S. | 116c | 46°05'N | 122°56'W |
| Rainier, Mount, mtn., Wa., U.S. (rā-nēr') | 106 | 46°52'N | 121°46'W |
| Rainy, r., N.A. | 107 | 48°50'N | 94°41'W |
| Rainy Lake, l., N.A. (rān'ē) | 93 | 48°43'N | 94°29'W |
| Rainy River, Can. | 91 | 48°43'N | 94°29'W |
| Raipur, India (rä'jū-bōō-rē') | 202 | 21°25'N | 81°37'E |
| Raisin, r., Mi., U.S. (rā'zĭn) | 108 | 42°00'N | 83°35'W |
| Raitan, N.J., U.S. (rā-tăn) | 110a | 40°34'N | 74°40'W |
| Rājahmundry, India (räj-ŭ-mŭn'drē) | 199 | 17°03'N | 81°51'E |
| Rajang, r., Malay. | 212 | 2°10'N | 113°30'E |
| Rājapālaiyam, India | 203 | 9°30'N | 77°33'E |
| Rājasthān, state, India (rä'jŭs-tän) | 199 | 26°00'N | 72°00'E |
| Rājkot, India (räj'kōt) | 199 | 22°20'N | 70°48'E |
| Rājpur, India | 202a | 22°24'N | 88°25'E |
| Rājshāhi, Bngl. | 199 | 24°26'S | 88°39'E |
| Rakhiv, Ukr. | 169 | 48°02'N | 24°13'E |
| Rakh'oya, Russia (räk'yå) | 186c | 60°06'N | 30°50'E |
| Rakitnoye, Russia (rä-kēt'nô-yĕ) | 181 | 50°51'N | 35°53'E |
| Rakovník, Czech Rep. | 168 | 50°07'N | 13°45'E |
| Rakvere, Est. (rák'vĕ-rĕ) | 180 | 59°22'N | 26°14'E |
| Raleigh, N.C., U.S. (rô'lē) | 105 | 35°45'N | 78°39'W |
| Ram, r., Can. | 95 | 52°10'N | 115°05'W |
| Rama, Nic. (rä'mä) | 133 | 12°11'N | 84°14'W |
| Ramallo, Arg. (rä-mä'l-yô) | 141c | 33°28'S | 60°02'W |
| Ramanāthapuram, India | 203 | 9°13'N | 78°52'E |


ng-sing; ŋ-baŋk; N-nasalized n; nŏd; cŏmmit; ōld; ôbey; ôrder; oi-boil; fōōd; ò-as oo in foot; ou-out; s-soft; sh-dish; th-thin; pūre; ûnite; ûrn; stŭd; circŭs; ü-as in French tu; '-indeterminate vowel.

340 Rambouillet – Revda PRONOUNCING INDEX


| PLACE (Pronunciation) | PAGE | LAT. | LONG. |
|---|---|---|---|
| Rambouillet, Fr. (räN-bōō-yĕ') | 170 | 48°39'N | 1°49'E |
| Rame Head, c., S. Afr. | 233c | 31°48'S | 29°22'E |
| Ramenskoye, Russia (rá'mĕn-skô-yĕ) | 176 | 55°34'N | 38°15'E |
| Ramlat as Sab'atayn, reg., Asia | 198 | 16°08'N | 45°15'E |
| Ramm, Jabal, mtn., Jord. | 197a | 29°37'N | 35°32'E |
| Râmnicu Sărat, Rom. | 163 | 45°24'N | 27°06'E |
| Râmnicu Vâlcea, Rom. | 175 | 45°07'N | 24°22'E |
| Ramos, Mex. (rä'mōs) | 130 | 22°46'N | 101°52'W |
| Ramos, r., Nig. | 235 | 5°10'N | 5°40'E |
| Ramos Arizpe, Mex. (ä-rēz'pä) | 122 | 25°33'N | 100°57'W |
| Rampart, Ak., U.S. (răm'part) | 103 | 65°28'N | 150°18'W |
| Rampo Mountains, mts., N.J., U.S. (răm'pō) | 110a | 41°06'N | 72°12'W |
| Rāmpur, India (räm'pōōr) | 199 | 28°53'N | 79°03'E |
| Ramree Island, i., Mya. (räm'rē') | 212 | 19°01'N | 93°23'E |
| Ramsayville, Can. (răm'zē vĭl) | 102c | 45°23'N | 75°34'W |
| Ramsbottom, Eng., U.K. (rămz'bŏt-ŭm) | 158a | 53°39'N | 2°20'W |
| Ramsey, I. of Man (răm'zē) | 164 | 54°20'N | 4°25'W |
| Ramsey, N.J., U.S. | 110a | 41°03'N | 74°09'W |
| Ramsey Lake, l., Can. | 98 | 47°15'N | 82°16'W |
| Ramsgate, Eng., U.K. (rămz''gāt) | 165 | 51°19'N | 1°20'E |
| Ramu, r., Pap. N. Gui. (rä'mōō) | 213 | 5°35'S | 145°16'E |
| Rancagua, Chile (rän-kä'gwä) | 144 | 34°10'S | 70°43'W |
| Rance, r., Fr. (räNs) | 170 | 48°17'N | 2°30'W |
| Rānchī, India | 199 | 23°21'N | 85°20'E |
| Rancho Boyeros, Cuba (rä'n-chô-bô-yĕ'rôs) | 135a | 23°00'N | 82°23'W |
| Randallstown, Md., U.S. (răn'dălz-toun) | 110e | 39°22'N | 76°48'W |
| Randers, Den. (rän'ĕrs) | 160 | 56°28'N | 10°03'E |
| Randfontein, S. Afr. (rănt'fŏn-tān) | 233b | 26°10'S | 27°42'E |
| Randleman, N.C., U.S. (răn'd'l-măn) | 125 | 35°49'N | 79°50'W |
| Randolph, Ma., U.S. (răn'dôlf) | 101a | 42°10'N | 71°03'W |
| Randolph, Ne., U.S. | 112 | 42°22'N | 97°22'W |
| Randolph, Vt., U.S. | 109 | 43°55'N | 72°40'W |
| Random Island, i., Can. (răn'dŭm) | 101 | 48°12'N | 53°25'W |
| Randsfjorden, Nor. | 166 | 60°35'N | 10°10'E |
| Randwick, Austl. | 217b | 33°55'S | 151°15'E |
| Ranérou, Sen. | 234 | 15°18'N | 13°58'W |
| Rangeley, Me., U.S. (rānj'lē) | 100 | 44°56'N | 70°38'W |
| Rangeley, l., Me., U.S. | 100 | 45°00'N | 70°25'W |
| Ranger, Tx., U.S. (rān'jẽr) | 104 | 32°26'N | 98°41'W |
| Rangia, India | 202 | 26°32'N | 91°39'E |
| Rangoon (Yangon), Mya. (răŋ-gōōn') | 199 | 16°46'N | 96°09'E |
| Rangpur, Bngl. (rŭng'pōōr) | 199 | 25°48'N | 89°19'E |
| Rangsang, i., Indon. (räng'säng') | 197b | 0°53'N | 103°05'E |
| Rangsdorf, Ger. (rängs'dōrf) | 159b | 52°17'N | 13°25'E |
| Rānīganj, India (rä-nē-gŭnj') | 202 | 23°40'N | 87°08'E |
| Rankin Inlet, b., Can. (răŋ'kĕn) | 93 | 62°45'N | 94°27'W |
| Ranova, r., Russia (rä'nô-vá) | 176 | 53°55'N | 40°03'E |
| Rantau, Malay. | 197b | 2°35'N | 101°58'E |
| Rantekombola, Bulu, mtn., Indon. | 212 | 3°22'S | 119°50'E |
| Rantoul, Il., U.S. (răn-tōōl') | 108 | 40°25'N | 88°05'W |
| Raoyang, China (rou-yäŋ) | 206 | 38°16'N | 115°45'E |
| Rapallo, Italy (rä-päl'lô) | 174 | 44°21'N | 9°14'E |
| Rapel, r., Chile (rä-pål') | 141b | 34°05'S | 71°30'W |
| Rapid, r., Mn., U.S. (răp'ĭd) | 113 | 48°21'N | 94°50'W |
| Rapid City, S.D., U.S. | 104 | 44°06'N | 103°14'W |
| Rapla, Est. (räp'là) | 167 | 59°02'N | 24°46'E |
| Rappahannock, r., Va., U.S. (răp'ȧ-hăn'ŭk) | 109 | 38°20'N | 75°25'W |
| Raquette, l., N.Y., U.S. (răk'ĕt) | 109 | 43°50'N | 74°35'W |
| Raritan, r., N.J., U.S. (răr'ĭ-tăn) | 110a | 40°32'N | 74°27'W |
| Rarotonga, Cook Is. (rä'rō-tŏŋ'gȧ) | 2 | 20°40'S | 163°00'W |
| Ra's an Naqb, Jord. | 197a | 30°00'N | 35°29'E |
| Raşcov, Mol. | 177 | 47°55'N | 28°51'E |
| Ras Dashen Terara, mtn., Eth. (räs dä-shän') | 231 | 12°49'N | 38°14'E |
| Raseiniai, Lith. (rä-syā'nyĭ) | 167 | 55°23'N | 23°04'E |
| Rashayya, Leb. | 197a | 33°30'N | 35°50'E |
| Rashīd, Egypt (rä-shēd') (rō-zĕt'ȧ) | 200 | 31°22'N | 30°25'E |
| Rashīd, Masabb, mth., Egypt | 238b | 31°30'N | 29°58'E |
| Rashkina, Russia (rȧsh'kĭ-nȧ) | 186a | 59°57'N | 61°30'E |
| Rasht, Iran | 198 | 37°13'N | 49°45'E |
| Raška, Serb. (räsh'kȧ) | 175 | 43°16'N | 20°40'E |
| Rasskazovo, Russia (räs-kä'sô-vô) | 181 | 52°40'N | 41°40'E |
| Rastatt, Ger. (rä-shtät) | 168 | 48°51'N | 8°12'E |
| Rastes, Russia (rȧs'tĕs) | 186a | 59°24'N | 58°49'E |
| Rastunovo, Russia (rȧs-tōō'nô-vô) | 186b | 55°15'N | 37°50'E |
| Ratangarh, India (rŭ-tŭn'gŭr) | 202 | 28°10'N | 74°30'E |
| Ratcliff, Tx., U.S. (răt'klĭf) | 123 | 31°22'N | 95°09'W |
| Rathenow, Ger. (rä'tĕ-nō) | 168 | 52°36'N | 12°20'E |
| Rathlin Island, i., N. Ire., U.K. (răth-lĭn) | 164 | 55°18'N | 6°13'W |
| Ratingen, Ger. (rä'tēn-gĕn) | 171c | 51°18'N | 6°51'E |
| Rat Islands, is., Ak., U.S. (răt) | 103a | 51°35'N | 176°48'E |
| Ratlām, India | 202 | 23°19'N | 75°05'E |
| Ratnāgiri, India | 203 | 17°04'N | 73°24'E |
| Raton, N.M., U.S. (rȧ-tōn') | 104 | 36°52'N | 104°26'W |
| Rattlesnake Creek, r., Or., U.S. (răt''l snāk) | 114 | 42°38'N | 117°39'W |
| Rättvik, Swe. (rĕt'vēk) | 166 | 60°54'N | 15°07'E |
| Rauch, Arg. (rá'ōōch) | 144 | 36°47'S | 59°05'W |
| Raufoss, Nor. (rou'fôs) | 166 | 60°44'N | 10°30'E |
| Raúl Soares, Braz. (rä-ōō'l-sôä'rĕs) | 141a | 20°05'S | 42°28'W |
| Rauma, Fin. (rä'ô-mȧ) | 160 | 61°07'N | 21°31'E |
| Rauna, Lat. (rȧū'nȧ) | 167 | 57°21'N | 25°31'E |
| Raurkela, India | 199 | 22°15'N | 84°53'E |
| Rautalampi, Fin. (rä'ōō-tĕ-läm'pô) | 167 | 62°39'N | 26°25'E |
| Rava-Rus'ka, Ukr. | 169 | 50°14'N | 23°40'E |
| Ravenna, Italy (rä-vĕn'nä) | 162 | 44°27'N | 12°13'E |
| Ravenna, Ne., U.S. (rȧ-vĕn'ȧ) | 112 | 41°20'N | 98°50'W |
| Ravenna, Oh., U.S. | 108 | 41°10'N | 81°20'W |
| Ravensburg, Ger. (rä'vĕns-bōōrgh) | 168 | 47°48'N | 9°35'E |
| Ravensdale, Wa., U.S. (rā'vĕnz-dāl) | 116a | 47°22'N | 121°58'W |
| Ravensthorpe, Austl. (rā'vĕns-thôrp) | 218 | 33°30'S | 120°20'E |
| Ravenswood, W.V., U.S. (rā'vĕnz-wŏŏd) | 108 | 38°55'N | 81°50'W |
| Rāwalpindi, Pak. (rä-wŭl-pēn'dē) | 199 | 33°40'N | 73°10'E |
| Rawa Mazowiecka, Pol. | 169 | 51°46'N | 20°17'E |
| Rawandoz, Iraq | 181 | 36°37'N | 44°30'E |
| Rawicz, Pol. (rä'vēch) | 168 | 51°36'N | 16°51'E |
| Rawlina, Austl. (rôr-lēnȧ) | 218 | 31°13'S | 125°45'E |
| Rawlins, Wy., U.S. (rô'lĭnz) | 104 | 41°46'N | 107°15'W |
| Rawson, Arg. (rô'sŭn) | 144 | 43°16'S | 65°09'W |
| Rawson, Arg. | 141c | 34°36'S | 60°03'W |
| Rawtenstall, Eng., U.K. (rô'tĕn-stôl) | 158a | 53°42'N | 2°17'W |
| Ray, Cape, c., Can. (rā) | 93a | 47°40'N | 59°18'W |
| Raya, Bukit, mtn., Indon. | 212 | 0°45'S | 112°11'E |
| Raychikinsk, Russia (rī'chĭ-kēnsk) | 185 | 49°52'N | 129°17'E |
| Rayleigh, Eng., U.K. (rā'lē) | 158b | 51°35'N | 0°36'E |
| Raymond, Can. (rā'mŭnd) | 95 | 49°27'N | 112°39'W |
| Raymond, Wa., U.S. | 114 | 46°41'N | 123°42'W |
| Raymondville, Tx., U.S. (rā'mŭnd-vĭl) | 121 | 26°30'N | 97°46'W |
| Ray Mountains, mts., Ak., U.S. | 103 | 65°40'N | 151°45'W |
| Rayne, La., U.S. (rān) | 123 | 30°12'N | 92°15'W |
| Rayón, Mex. (rä-yōn') | 130 | 21°49'N | 99°39'W |
| Rayton, S. Afr. (rā'tŭn) | 233b | 25°45'S | 28°33'E |
| Raytown, Mo., U.S. (rā'toun) | 117f | 39°01'N | 94°48'W |
| Rayville, La., U.S. (rā-vĭl) | 123 | 32°28'N | 91°46'W |
| Raz, Pointe du, c., Fr. (pwănt dü rä) | 161 | 48°02'N | 4°43'W |
| Razdan, Arm. | 182 | 40°30'N | 44°46'E |
| Razdol'noye, Russia (räz-dôl'nô-yĕ) | 210 | 43°38'N | 131°58'E |
| Razgrad, Blg. | 163 | 43°32'N | 26°32'E |
| Razlog, Blg. (räz'lôk) | 175 | 41°54'N | 23°32'E |
| Razorback Mountain, mtn., Can. (rā'zẽr-băk) | 94 | 51°35'N | 124°42'W |
| Rea, r., Eng., U.K. (rē) | 158a | 52°25'N | 2°31'W |
| Reaburn, Can. (rā'bûrn) | 102f | 50°06'N | 97°53'W |
| Reading, Eng., U.K. (rĕd'ĭng) | 161 | 51°25'N | 0°58'W |
| Reading, Ma., U.S. | 101a | 42°32'N | 71°07'W |
| Reading, Mi., U.S. | 108 | 41°45'N | 84°45'W |
| Reading, Oh., U.S. | 111f | 39°14'N | 84°26'W |
| Reading, Pa., U.S. | 105 | 40°20'N | 75°55'W |
| Reading, co., Eng., U.K. | 158a | 52°37'N | 0°40'W |
| Realengo, Braz. (rĕ-ä-län-gô) | 141a | 23°50'S | 43°25'W |
| Rebiana, Libya | 231 | 24°10'N | 22°03'E |
| Rebun, i., Japan (rē'bōōn) | 210 | 45°25'N | 140°54'E |
| Recanati, Italy (rā-kä-nä'tē) | 174 | 43°25'N | 13°35'E |
| Recherche, Archipelago of the, is., Austl. (rē-shârsh') | 220 | 34°17'S | 122°30'E |
| Rechytsa, Bela. (ryĕ'chĕt-sȧ) | 181 | 52°22'N | 30°24'E |
| Recife, Braz. (rā-sē'fĕ) | 143 | 8°09'S | 34°59'W |
| Recife, Kapp, c., S. Afr. (rȧ-sē'fĕ) | 233c | 34°03'S | 25°43'E |
| Recklinghausen, Ger. (rĕk'lĭng-hou-zĕn) | 171c | 51°36'N | 7°13'E |
| Reconquista, Arg. (rā-kôn-kēs'tä) | 144 | 29°01'S | 59°41'W |
| Rector, Ar., U.S. (rĕk'tẽr) | 121 | 36°16'N | 90°21'W |
| Red, r., Asia | 212 | 21°00'N | 103°00'E |
| Red, r., N.A. (rĕd) | 106 | 48°00'N | 97°00'W |
| Red, r., Tn., U.S. | 124 | 36°35'N | 86°55'W |
| Red, r., U.S. | 107 | 31°40'N | 92°55'W |
| Red, North Fork, r., U.S. | 120 | 35°20'N | 100°08'W |
| Red, Prairie Dog Town Fork, r., U.S. (prā'rĭ) | 120 | 34°54'N | 101°31'W |
| Red, Salt Fork, r., U.S. | 120 | 35°04'N | 100°31'W |
| Redan, Ga., U.S. (rē-dăn') (rĕd'ăn) | 110c | 33°44'N | 84°09'W |
| Red Bank, N.J., U.S. (băngk) | 110a | 40°21'N | 74°06'W |
| Red Bluff Reservoir, res., Tx., U.S. | 122 | 32°03'N | 103°52'W |
| Redby, Mn., U.S. (rĕd'bē) | 113 | 47°52'N | 94°55'W |
| Red Cedar, r., Wi., U.S. (sē'dẽr) | 113 | 45°03'N | 91°48'W |
| Redcliff, Can. (rĕd'clĭf) | 90 | 50°05'N | 110°47'W |
| Redcliffe, Austl. (rĕd'clĭf) | 222 | 27°20'S | 153°12'E |
| Red Cliff Indian Reservation, I.R., Wi., U.S. | 113 | 46°48'N | 91°22'W |
| Red Cloud, Ne., U.S. (kloud) | 120 | 40°06'N | 98°32'W |
| Red Deer, Can. (dēr) | 90 | 52°16'N | 113°48'W |
| Red Deer, r., Can. | 92 | 51°00'N | 111°00'W |
| Red Deer, r., Can. | 97 | 52°55'N | 102°10'W |
| Red Deer Lake, l., Can. | 97 | 52°58'N | 101°28'W |
| Reddick, Il., U.S. (rĕd'ĭk) | 111a | 41°06'N | 88°16'W |
| Redding, Ca., U.S. (rĕd'ĭng) | 114 | 40°36'N | 122°25'W |
| Redenção da Serra, Braz. (rĕ-dĕn-soun-dä-sĕ'r-rä) | 141a | 23°17'S | 45°31'W |
| Redfield, S.D., U.S. (rĕd'fēld) | 112 | 44°53'N | 98°30'W |
| Red Fish Bar, Tx., U.S. | 123a | 29°29'N | 94°53'W |
| Red Indian Lake, l., Can. (ĭn'dĭ-ăn) | 93a | 48°40'N | 56°50'W |
| Red Lake, Can. (lāk) | 91 | 51°02'N | 93°49'W |
| Red Lake, r., Mn., U.S. | 112 | 48°02'N | 96°04'W |
| Red Lake Falls, Mn., U.S. (lāk fôls) | 112 | 47°52'N | 96°17'W |
| Red Lake Indian Reservation, I.R., Mn., U.S. | 112 | 48°09'N | 95°55'W |
| Redlands, Ca., U.S. (rĕd'lăndz) | 117a | 34°04'N | 117°11'W |
| Red Lion, Pa., U.S. (lī'ŭn) | 109 | 39°55'N | 76°30'W |
| Red Lodge, Mt., U.S. | 115 | 45°13'N | 107°16'W |
| Redmond, Wa., U.S. (rĕd'mŭnd) | 116a | 47°40'N | 122°07'W |
| Rednitz, r., Ger. (rĕd'nētz) | 168 | 49°10'N | 11°00'E |
| Red Oak, Ia., U.S. (ōk) | 112 | 41°00'N | 95°12'W |
| Redon, Fr. (rē-dôN') | 170 | 47°42'N | 2°03'W |
| Redonda, Isla, i., Braz. (ē's-lä-rĕ-dô'n-dä) | 144b | 23°05'S | 43°11'W |
| Redonda Island, i., Antig. (rĕ-dŏn'dȧ) | 133b | 16°55'N | 62°28'W |
| Redondela, Spain (rā-dhôn-dā'lä) | 172 | 42°16'N | 8°34'W |
| Redondo, Port. (rā-dôn'dō) | 172 | 38°40'N | 7°32'W |
| Redondo, Wa., U.S. (rē-dŏn'dō) | 116a | 47°21'N | 122°19'W |
| Redondo Beach, Ca., U.S. | 117a | 33°50'N | 118°23'W |
| Red Pass, Can. (pȧs) | 95 | 52°59'N | 118°59'W |
| Red Rock, r., Mt., U.S. | 115 | 44°54'N | 112°44'W |
| Red Sea, sea | 198 | 23°15'N | 37°00'E |
| Redstone, Can. (rĕd'stōn) | 94 | 52°08'N | 123°42'W |
| Red Sucker Lake, l., Can. (sŭk'ẽr) | 97 | 54°09'N | 93°40'W |
| Redwater, r., Mt., U.S. | 115 | 47°37'N | 105°25'W |
| Red Willow Creek, r., Ne., U.S. | 120 | 40°34'N | 100°48'W |
| Red Wing, Mn., U.S. | 113 | 44°34'N | 92°35'W |
| Redwood City, Ca., U.S. (rĕd' wŏŏd) | 116b | 37°29'N | 122°13'W |
| Redwood Falls, Mn., U.S. | 112 | 44°32'N | 95°06'W |
| Redwood National Park, rec., Ca., U.S. | 114 | 41°20'N | 124°00'W |
| Redwood Valley, Ca., U.S. | 118 | 39°15'N | 123°12'W |
| Ree, Lough, l., Ire. (lŏĸ'rē') | 160 | 53°30'N | 7°45'W |
| Reed City, Mi., U.S. (rēd) | 108 | 43°50'N | 85°35'W |
| Reed Lake, l., Can. | 97 | 54°37'N | 100°30'W |
| Reedley, Ca., U.S. (rēd'lē) | 118 | 36°37'N | 119°27'W |
| Reedsburg, Wi., U.S. (rēdz'bûrg) | 113 | 43°32'N | 90°01'W |
| Reedsport, Or., U.S. (rēdz'pôrt) | 114 | 43°42'N | 124°08'W |
| Reelfoot Lake, res., Tn., U.S. (rēl'fŏŏt) | 124 | 36°18'N | 89°20'W |
| Rees, Ger. (rĕz) | 171c | 51°46'N | 6°25'E |
| Reeves, Mount, mtn., Austl. (rēv's) | 222 | 33°50'S | 149°56'E |
| Reform, Al., U.S. (rē-fôrm') | 124 | 33°23'N | 88°00'W |
| Refugio, Tx., U.S. (rȧ-fōō'hyō) (rē-fū'jō) | 123 | 28°18'N | 97°15'W |
| Rega, r., Pol. (rĕ-gä) | 168 | 53°48'N | 15°30'E |
| Regen, r., Ger. (rā'ghĕn) | 168 | 49°09'N | 12°21'E |
| Regensburg, Ger. (rā'ghĕns-bŏrgh) | 161 | 49°02'N | 12°06'E |
| Reggio, La., U.S. (rĕg'jĭ-ō) | 110d | 29°50'N | 89°46'W |
| Reggio di Calabria, Italy (rĕ'jō dē kä-lä'brē-ä) | 163 | 38°07'N | 15°42'E |
| Reggio nell' Emilia, Italy | 162 | 44°43'N | 10°34'E |
| Reghin, Rom. (rā-gēn') | 169 | 46°47'N | 24°44'E |
| Regina, Can. (rē-jī'nȧ) | 96 | 50°25'N | 104°39'W |
| Regla, Cuba (rāg'lä) | 134 | 23°08'N | 82°20'W |
| Regnitz, r., Ger. (rĕg'nētz) | 168 | 49°50'N | 10°55'E |
| Reguengos de Monsaraz, Port. | 172 | 38°26'N | 7°30'W |
| Rehoboth, Nmb. | 232 | 23°10'S | 17°15'E |
| Reẖovot, Isr. | 197a | 31°53'N | 34°49'E |
| Reichenbach, Ger. (rī'kĕn-bäĸ) | 168 | 50°36'N | 12°18'E |
| Reidsville, N.C., U.S. (rēdz'vĭl) | 125 | 36°20'N | 79°37'W |
| Reigate, Eng., U.K. (rī'gāt) | 164 | 51°12'N | 0°12'W |
| Reims, Fr. (răNs) | 154 | 49°16'N | 4°00'E |
| Reina Adelaida, Archipiélago, is., Chile | 144 | 52°00'S | 74°15'W |
| Reinbeck, Ia., U.S. (rīn'bĕk) | 113 | 42°22'N | 92°34'W |
| Reindeer, l., Can. (rān'dēr) | 92 | 57°36'N | 101°23'W |
| Reindeer, r., Can. | 96 | 55°45'N | 103°30'W |
| Reindeer Island, i., Can. | 97 | 52°25'N | 98°00'W |
| Reinosa, Spain (rā-ê-nô'sä) | 172 | 43°01'N | 4°08'W |
| Reistertown, Md., U.S. (rēs'tẽr-toun) | 110e | 39°28'N | 76°50'W |
| Reitz, S. Afr. | 238c | 27°48'S | 28°25'E |
| Rema, Jabal, mtn., Yemen | 198 | 14°13'N | 44°38'E |
| Rembau, Malay. | 197b | 2°36'N | 102°06'E |
| Remedios, Col. (rĕ-mĕ'dyôs) | 142a | 7°03'N | 74°42'W |
| Remedios, Cuba (rā-mā'dhē-ōs) | 134 | 22°30'N | 79°35'W |
| Remedios, Pan. (rĕ-mĕ'dyôs) | 133 | 8°14'N | 81°46'W |
| Remiremont, Fr. (rē-mēr-môN') | 171 | 48°01'N | 6°35'E |
| Rempang, i., Indon. | 197b | 0°51'N | 104°04'E |
| Remscheid, Ger. (rĕm'shīt) | 171c | 51°10'N | 7°11'E |
| Rena, Nor. | 166 | 61°08'N | 11°17'E |
| Rendova, i., Sol. Is. (rĕn'dô-vȧ) | 221 | 8°38'S | 156°26'E |
| Rendsburg, Ger. (rĕnts'bôrgh) | 168 | 54°19'N | 9°39'E |
| Renfrew, Can. (rĕn'frōō) | 91 | 45°30'N | 76°30'W |
| Rengam, Malay. (rĕn'gäm') | 197b | 1°53'N | 103°24'E |
| Rengo, Chile (rĕn'gō) | 141b | 34°22'S | 70°50'W |
| Reni, Ukr. (ran') | 177 | 45°26'N | 28°18'E |
| Renmark, Austl. (rĕn'märk) | 218 | 34°10'S | 140°50'E |
| Rennel, i., Sol. Is. (rĕn-nĕl') | 221 | 11°50'S | 160°38'E |
| Rennes, Fr. (rĕn) | 154 | 48°07'N | 1°02'W |
| Reno, Nv., U.S. (rē'nō) | 104 | 39°32'N | 119°49'W |
| Reno, r., Italy (rā'nô) | 174 | 44°10'N | 10°55'E |
| Renovo, Pa., U.S. (rē-nō'vō) | 109 | 41°20'N | 77°50'W |
| Renqiu, China (rŭn-chyō) | 206 | 38°44'N | 116°05'E |
| Rensselaer, In., U.S. (rĕn'sē-lâr) | 108 | 41°00'N | 87°10'W |
| Rensselaer, N.Y., U.S. (rĕn'sē-lâr) | 109 | 42°40'N | 73°45'W |
| Rentchler, Il., U.S. (rĕnt'chlẽr) | 117e | 38°30'N | 89°52'W |
| Renton, Wa., U.S. (rĕn'tŭn) | 116a | 47°29'N | 122°13'W |
| Repentigny, Can. | 102a | 45°47'N | 73°26'W |
| Republic, Al., U.S. (rē-pŭb'lĭk) | 110h | 33°37'N | 86°54'W |
| Republic, Wa., U.S. | 114 | 48°38'N | 118°44'W |
| Republican, r., U.S. | 106 | 40°15'N | 100°00'W |
| Republican, South Fork, r., Co., U.S. (rē-pŭb'lĭ-kăn) | 120 | 39°35'N | 102°28'W |
| Repulse Bay, b., Austl. (rē-pŭls') | 221 | 20°56'S | 149°22'E |
| Requena, Spain (rā-kā'nä) | 162 | 39°29'N | 1°03'W |
| Resende, Braz. (rĕ-sĕ'n-dĕ) | 141a | 22°30'S | 44°26'W |
| Resende Costa, Braz. (kôs-tä) | 141a | 20°55'S | 44°12'W |
| Reshetylivka, Ukr. | 177 | 49°34'N | 34°04'E |
| Resistencia, Arg. (rā-sēs-tĕn'syä) | 144 | 27°24'S | 58°54'W |
| Reşiţa, Rom. (rå'shē-tȧ) | 175 | 45°18'N | 21°56'E |
| Resolute *see* Qausuittuq, Can. | 89 | 74°41'N | 95°00'W |
| Resolution, i., Can. (rĕz-ô-lū'shŭn) | 93 | 61°30'N | 63°58'W |
| Resolution Island, i., N.Z. (rĕz-ŏl-ûshûn) | 221a | 45°43'S | 166°20'E |
| Restigouche, r., Can. | 100 | 47°35'N | 67°35'W |
| Restrepo, Col. (rĕs-trĕ'pô) | 142a | 3°49'N | 76°31'W |
| Restrepo, Col. | 142a | 4°16'N | 73°32'W |
| Retalhuleu, Guat. (rā-täl-ōō-lān') | 132 | 14°31'N | 91°41'W |
| Rethel, Fr. (r-tl') | 170 | 49°34'N | 4°20'E |
| Réthimnon, Grc. | 174a | 35°21'N | 24°30'E |
| Retie, Bel. | 159a | 51°16'N | 5°08'E |
| Retsil, Wa., U.S. (rĕt'sĭl) | 116a | 47°33'N | 122°37'W |
| Reunion, dep., Afr. (rā-ü-nyôn') | 3 | 21°06'S | 55°36'E |
| Reus, Spain (rā'ōōs) | 162 | 41°08'N | 1°05'E |
| Reutlingen, Ger. (roit'lĭng-ĕn) | 168 | 48°29'N | 9°14'E |
| Reutov, Russia (rĕ-ōō'ôf) | 186b | 55°45'N | 37°52'E |
| Revda, Russia (ryâv'dȧ) | 186a | 56°48'N | 59°57'E |


ăt; finăl; rāte; senâte; ärm; àsk; sofȧ; fâre; ch-choose; dh-as th in other; bē; ēvent; bĕt; recĕnt; cratẽr; g-gō; gh-guttural g; bĭt; ĭ-short neutral; rīde; ĸ-guttural k as ch in German ich;

PRONOUNCING INDEX — Revelstoke – Rockingham Forest 341


| PLACE (Pronunciation) | PAGE | LAT. | LONG. |
|---|---|---|---|
| Revelstoke, Can. (rĕv′ĕl-stōk) | 90 | 51°00′N | 118°12′W |
| Reventazón, Río, r., C.R. (rā-vĕn-tä-zōn′) | 133 | 10°10′N | 83°30′W |
| Revere, Ma., U.S. (rē-vēr′) | 101a | 42°24′N | 71°01′W |
| Revillagigedo, Islas, is., Mex. (ē′s-läs-rĕ-vēl-yä-hĕ′gĕ-dō) | 128 | 18°45′N | 111°00′W |
| Revillagigedo Chan, Ak., U.S. (rĕ-vĭl′ă-gĭ-gē′dō) | 94 | 55°10′N | 131°13′W |
| Revillagigedo Island, i., Ak., U.S. | 94 | 55°35′N | 131°23′W |
| Revin, Fr. (rē-văN) | 170 | 49°56′N | 4°34′E |
| Rewa, India (rā′wä) | 199 | 24°41′N | 81°11′E |
| Rewāri, India | 202 | 28°19′N | 76°39′E |
| Rexburg, Id., U.S. (rĕks′bûrg) | 115 | 43°50′N | 111°48′W |
| Rey, Iran | 201 | 35°35′N | 51°25′E |
| Rey, l., Mex. (rā) | 122 | 27°00′N | 103°33′W |
| Rey, Isla del, i., Pan. (ē′s-lä-dĕl-rā′ē) | 133 | 8°20′N | 78°40′W |
| Reyes, Bol. (rā′yĕs) | 142 | 14°19′S | 67°16′W |
| Reyes, Point, c., Ca., U.S. | 118 | 38°00′N | 123°00′W |
| Reykjanes, c., Ice. (rā′kyá-nĕs) | 156 | 63°37′N | 24°33′W |
| Reykjavík, Ice. (rā′kyá-vēk) | 154 | 64°09′N | 21°39′W |
| Reynosa, Mex. (rā-ē-nō′sä) | 122 | 26°05′N | 98°21′W |
| Rēzekne, Lat. (rå′zĕk-nĕ) | 180 | 56°31′N | 27°19′E |
| Rezh, Russia (rĕzh′) | 186a | 57°22′N | 61°23′E |
| Rezina, Mol. (ryĕzh′ĕ-nĭ) | 177 | 47°44′N | 28°56′E |
| Rhaetian Alps, mts., Eur. | 168 | 46°30′N | 10°00′E |
| Rhaetien Alps, mts., Eur. | 174 | 46°22′N | 10°33′E |
| Rheinberg, Ger. (rīn′bĕrgh) | 171c | 51°33′N | 6°37′E |
| Rheine, Ger. (rī′nĕ) | 168 | 52°16′N | 7°26′E |
| Rheinkamp, Ger. | 171c | 51°30′N | 6°37′E |
| Rheinland, hist. reg., Ger. | 168 | 50°05′N | 6°40′E |
| Rheydt, Ger. (rĕ′yt) | 171c | 51°10′N | 6°28′E |
| Rhin, r., Ger. (rēn) | 159b | 52°52′N | 12°49′E |
| Rhine, r., Eur. | 156 | 50°34′N | 7°21′E |
| Rhinelander, Wi., U.S. (rīn′lăn-dẽr) | 113 | 45°39′N | 89°25′W |
| Rhin Kanal, can., Ger. (rēn kä-näl′) | 159b | 52°47′N | 12°40′E |
| Rhiou, r., Alg. | 173 | 35°45′N | 1°18′E |
| Rhode Island, state, U.S. (rōd ī′lănd) | 105 | 41°35′N | 71°40′W |
| Rhode Island, i., R.I., U.S. | 110b | 41°31′N | 71°14′W |
| Rhodes, S. Afr. (rōdz) | 233c | 30°48′S | 27°56′E |
| Rhodes *see* Ródhos, i., Grc. | 156 | 36°00′N | 28°29′E |
| Rhodesia *see* Zimbabwe, nation, Afr. | 232 | 17°50′S | 29°30′E |
| Rhodope Mountains, mts., Eur. (rô′dō-pĕ) | 156 | 42°00′N | 24°08′E |
| Rhondda, Wales, U.K. (rŏn′dhȧ) | 164 | 51°40′N | 3°40′W |
| Rhône, r., Fr. (rōn) | 156 | 44°30′N | 4°45′E |
| Rhoon, Neth. | 159a | 51°52′N | 4°24′E |
| Rhum, i., Scot., U.K. (rŭm) | 164 | 57°00′N | 6°20′W |
| Riachão, Braz. (rē-ä-chouN′) | 143 | 7°15′S | 46°30′W |
| Rialto, Ca., U.S. (rē-ăl′tō) | 117a | 34°06′N | 117°23′W |
| Riau, prov., Indon. | 197b | 0°56′N | 101°25′E |
| Riau, Kepulauan, is., Indon. | 212 | 0°30′N | 104°55′E |
| Riau, Selat, strt., Indon. | 197b | 0°40′N | 104°27′E |
| Riaza, r., Spain (rē-ä′thä) | 172 | 41°25′N | 3°25′W |
| Ribadavia, Spain (rē-bä-dhä′vē-ä) | 172 | 42°18′N | 8°06′W |
| Ribadeo, Spain (rē-bä-dhā′ō) | 172 | 43°32′N | 7°05′W |
| Ribadesella, Spain (rē′bä-dā-sāl′yä) | 172 | 43°30′N | 5°02′W |
| Ribe, Den. (rē′bĕ) | 166 | 55°20′N | 8°45′E |
| Ribeirão Prêto, Braz. (rē-bā-rouN-prĕ′tō) | 143 | 21°11′S | 47°47′W |
| Ribera, N.M., U.S. (rē-bē′rä) | 120 | 35°23′N | 105°27′W |
| Riberalta, Bol. (rē-bā-räl′tä) | 142 | 11°06′S | 66°02′W |
| Rib Lake, Wi., U.S. (rĭb lāk) | 113 | 45°20′N | 90°11′W |
| Ribniţa, Mol. | 177 | 47°45′N | 29°02′E |
| Rice, l., Can. | 99 | 44°05′N | 78°10′W |
| Rice Lake, Wi., U.S. | 113 | 45°30′N | 91°44′W |
| Rice Lake, l., Mn., U.S. | 117g | 45°10′N | 93°09′W |
| Richards Island, i., Can. (rĭch′ẽrds) | 103 | 69°45′N | 135°30′W |
| Richards Landing, Can. (lănd′ĭng) | 117k | 46°18′N | 84°02′W |
| Richardson, Tx., U.S. (rĭch′ẽrd-sŭn) | 117c | 32°56′N | 96°44′W |
| Richardson, Wa., U.S. | 116a | 48°27′N | 122°54′W |
| Richardson Mountains, mts., Can. | 92 | 66°58′N | 136°19′W |
| Richardson Mountains, mts., N.Z. | 223 | 44°50′S | 168°30′E |
| Richardson Park, De., U.S. (pärk) | 109 | 39°45′N | 75°35′W |
| Richelieu, r., Can. (rĕsh′lyû′) | 99 | 45°05′N | 73°25′W |
| Richfield, Mn., U.S. | 117g | 44°53′N | 93°17′W |
| Richfield, Oh., U.S. | 111d | 41°14′N | 81°38′W |
| Richfield, Ut., U.S. | 119 | 38°45′N | 112°05′W |
| Richford, Vt., U.S. (rĭch′fẽrd) | 109 | 45°00′N | 72°35′W |
| Rich Hill, Mo., U.S. (rĭch hĭl) | 121 | 38°05′N | 94°21′W |
| Richibucto, Can. (rĭ-chĭ-bŭk′tō) | 91 | 46°41′N | 64°52′W |
| Richland, Ga., U.S. (rĭch′lănd) | 124 | 32°05′N | 84°40′W |
| Richland, Wa., U.S. | 114 | 46°17′N | 119°19′W |
| Richland Center, Wi., U.S. (sĕn′tẽr) | 113 | 43°20′N | 90°25′W |
| Richmond, Austl. (rĭch′mŭnd) | 219 | 20°47′S | 143°14′E |
| Richmond, Austl. | 217b | 33°36′S | 150°45′E |
| Richmond, Can. | 102c | 45°12′N | 75°49′W |
| Richmond, Can. | 99 | 45°40′N | 72°07′W |
| Richmond, S. Afr. | 233c | 29°52′S | 30°17′E |
| Richmond, Il., U.S. | 111a | 42°29′N | 88°18′W |
| Richmond, In., U.S. | 108 | 39°50′N | 85°00′W |
| Richmond, Ky., U.S. | 108 | 37°45′N | 84°20′W |
| Richmond, Mo., U.S. | 121 | 39°16′N | 93°58′W |
| Richmond, Tx., U.S. | 123 | 29°35′N | 95°45′W |
| Richmond, Ut., U.S. | 115 | 41°55′N | 111°50′W |
| Richmond, Va., U.S. | 105 | 37°35′N | 77°30′W |
| Richmond Beach, Wa., U.S. | 116a | 47°47′N | 122°23′W |
| Richmond Heights, Mo., U.S. | 117e | 38°38′N | 90°20′W |
| Richmond Highlands, Wa., U.S. | 116a | 47°46′N | 122°22′W |
| Richmond Hill, Can. (hĭl) | 99 | 43°53′N | 79°26′W |
| Richton, Ms., U.S. (rĭch′tŭn) | 124 | 31°20′N | 89°54′W |
| Richwood, W.V., U.S. (rĭch′wŏŏd) | 108 | 38°10′N | 80°30′W |
| Ridderkerk, Neth. | 159a | 51°52′N | 4°35′E |
| Rideau, r., Can. | 102c | 45°17′N | 75°41′W |
| Rideau Lake, l., Can. (rē-dō′) | 99 | 44°40′N | 76°20′W |
| Ridgefield, Ct., U.S. (rĭj′fēld) | 110a | 41°16′N | 73°30′W |
| Ridgefield, Wa., U.S. | 116c | 45°49′N | 122°40′W |
| Ridgeway, Can. (rĭj′wā) | 111c | 42°53′N | 79°02′W |
| Ridgewood, N.J., U.S. (ridj′wŏŏd) | 110a | 40°59′N | 74°08′W |
| Ridgway, Pa., U.S. | 109 | 41°25′N | 78°40′W |
| Riding Mountain, mtn., Can. (rīd′ĭng) | 97 | 50°37′N | 99°37′W |
| Riding Mountain National Park, rec., Can. (rīd′ĭng) | 92 | 50°59′N | 99°19′W |
| Riding Rocks, is., Bah. | 134 | 25°20′N | 79°10′W |
| Riebeek-Oos, S. Afr. | 233c | 33°14′S | 26°09′E |
| Ried, Aus. (rēd) | 168 | 48°13′N | 13°30′E |
| Riesa, Ger. (rē′zȧ) | 168 | 51°17′N | 13°17′E |
| Rieti, Italy (rē-ā′tē) | 162 | 42°25′N | 12°51′E |
| Rievleidam, res., S. Afr. | 233b | 25°52′S | 28°18′E |
| Riffe Lake, res., Wa., U.S. | 114 | 46°20′N | 122°10′W |
| Rifle, Co., U.S. (rī′f′l) | 119 | 39°35′N | 107°50′W |
| Riga, Lat. (rē′gȧ) | 178 | 56°55′N | 24°05′E |
| Riga, Gulf of, b., Eur. | 180 | 57°56′N | 23°05′E |
| Rigān, Iran | 198 | 28°45′N | 58°55′E |
| Rigaud, Can. (rē-gō′) | 102a | 45°29′N | 74°18′W |
| Rigby, Id., U.S. (rĭg′bē) | 115 | 43°40′N | 111°55′W |
| Rigeley, W.V., U.S. (rĭj′lē) | 109 | 39°40′N | 78°45′W |
| Rīgestān, des., Afg. | 198 | 30°53′N | 64°42′E |
| Rigolet, Can. (rĭg-ō-lā′) | 91 | 54°10′N | 58°40′W |
| Riihimäki, Fin. | 167 | 60°44′N | 24°44′E |
| Rijeka, Cro. (rĭ-yĕ′kä) | 162 | 45°22′N | 14°24′E |
| Rijkevorsel, Bel. | 159a | 51°21′N | 4°46′E |
| Rijswijk, Neth. | 159a | 52°03′N | 4°19′E |
| Rika, r., Ukr. (rē′kȧ) | 169 | 48°21′N | 23°37′E |
| Rima, r., Nig. | 235 | 13°30′N | 5°50′E |
| Rimavska Sobota, Slvk. (rē′maf-skȧ sō′bō-tȧ) | 169 | 48°25′N | 20°01′E |
| Rimbo, Swe. (rēm′bō) | 166 | 59°45′N | 18°22′E |
| Rimini, Italy (rē′mē-nē) | 162 | 44°03′N | 12°33′E |
| Rimouski, Can. (rē-mōō′skē) | 91 | 48°27′N | 68°32′W |
| Rincón de Romos, Mex. (rēn-kōn dā rō-mōs′) | 130 | 22°13′N | 102°21′W |
| Ringkøbing, Den. (rĭng′kûb-ĭng) | 160 | 56°06′N | 8°14′E |
| Ringkøbing Fjord, b., Den. | 166 | 55°55′N | 8°04′E |
| Ringsted, Den. (rĭng′stĕdh) | 166 | 55°27′N | 11°49′E |
| Ringvassøya, i., Nor. (rĭng′väs-ûē) | 160 | 69°58′N | 16°43′E |
| Ringwood, Austl. | 217a | 37°49′S | 145°14′E |
| Rinjani, Gunung, mtn., Indon. | 212 | 8°39′S | 116°22′E |
| Río Abajo, Pan. (rē′ō-ä-bä′kō) | 128a | 9°01′N | 78°30′W |
| Río Balsas, Mex. (rē′ō-bäl-säs) | 130 | 17°59′N | 99°45′W |
| Riobamba, Ec. (rē′ō-bäm-bä) | 142 | 1°45′S | 78°37′W |
| Rio Bonito, Braz. (rē′ŏŏ bō-nē′tŏŏ) | 141a | 22°44′S | 42°38′W |
| Rio Branco, Braz. (rē′ŏŏ brän′kŏŏ) | 142 | 9°57′S | 67°50′W |
| Río Branco, Ur. (rīō brănċō) | 144 | 32°33′S | 53°29′W |
| Rio Casca, Braz. (rē′ō-kà′s-kä) | 141a | 20°15′S | 42°39′W |
| Río Chico, Ven. (rē′ō chē′kŏ) | 143b | 10°20′N | 65°58′W |
| Rio Claro, Braz. (rē′ŏŏ klä′rŏŏ) | 143 | 22°25′S | 47°33′W |
| Río Cuarto, Arg. (rē′ō kwär′tō) | 144 | 33°05′S | 64°15′W |
| Rio das Flores, Braz. (rē′ō-däs-flô-rĕs) | 141a | 22°10′S | 43°35′W |
| Rio de Janeiro, Braz. (rē′ŏŏ dā zhä-nā′ē-rŏŏ) | 144b | 22°50′S | 43°20′W |
| Rio de Janeiro, state, Braz. | 143 | 22°27′S | 42°43′W |
| Río de Jesús, Pan. | 133 | 7°54′N | 80°59′W |
| Río Frío, Mex. (rē′ō-frē′ō) | 131a | 19°21′N | 98°40′W |
| Río Gallegos, Arg. (rē′ō gä-lā′gōs) | 144 | 51°43′S | 69°15′W |
| Rio Grande, Braz. (rē′ŏŏ grän′dĕ) | 144 | 31°04′S | 52°14′W |
| Río Grande, Mex. (rē′ō grän′dā) | 130 | 23°51′N | 102°59′W |
| Riogrande, Tx., U.S. (rē′ō grăn-dā) | 122 | 26°23′N | 98°48′W |
| Rio Grande do Norte, state, Braz. | 143 | 5°26′S | 37°20′W |
| Rio Grande do Sul, state, Braz. (rē′ŏŏ grän′dĕ-dŏŏ-sōō′l) | 144 | 29°00′S | 54°00′W |
| Ríohacha, Col. (rē′ō-ä′chä) | 142 | 11°30′N | 72°54′W |
| Río Hato, Pan. (rē′ō-ä′tō) | 133 | 8°19′N | 80°11′W |
| Riom, Fr. (rē-ôN′) | 170 | 45°54′N | 3°08′E |
| Rio Muni, hist. reg., Eq. Gui. (rē′ō mōō′nē) | 230 | 1°47′N | 8°33′E |
| Rionegro, Col. (rē′ō-nĕ′grō) | 142a | 6°09′N | 75°22′W |
| Río Negro, prov., Arg. (rē′ō nā′grō) | 144 | 40°15′S | 68°15′W |
| Río Negro, dept., Ur. (rē′ō-nĕ′grō) | 141c | 32°48′S | 57°45′W |
| Río Negro, Embalse del, res., Ur. | 144 | 32°45′S | 55°50′W |
| Rionero, Italy (rē-ō-nā′rō) | 174 | 40°55′N | 15°42′E |
| Rioni, r., Geor. | 182 | 42°08′N | 41°39′E |
| Rio Novo, Braz. (rē′ō-nô′vō) | 141a | 21°30′S | 43°08′W |
| Rio Pardo de Minas, Braz. (rē′ō pär′dō-dĕ-mē′näs) | 143 | 15°43′S | 42°24′W |
| Rio Pombo, Braz. (rē′ō pôm′bä) | 141a | 21°17′S | 43°09′W |
| Rio Sorocaba, Represa do, res., Braz. | 141a | 23°37′S | 47°19′W |
| Ríosucio, Col. (rē′ō-sōō′syō) | 142a | 5°25′N | 75°41′W |
| Río Tercero, Arg. (rē′ō dĕr-sĕ′rō) | 144 | 32°12′S | 63°59′W |
| Rio Verde, Braz. (vĕr′dĕ) | 143 | 17°47′S | 50°49′W |
| Ríoverde, Mex. (rē′ō-vĕr′dā) | 128 | 21°54′N | 99°59′W |
| Ripley, Eng., U.K. (rĭp′lē) | 158a | 53°03′N | 1°24′W |
| Ripley, Ms., U.S. | 124 | 34°44′N | 88°55′W |
| Ripley, Tn., U.S. | 124 | 35°44′N | 89°34′W |
| Ripoll, Spain (rē-pōl′) | 173 | 42°10′N | 2°10′E |
| Ripon, Wi., U.S. (rĭp′ŏn) | 113 | 43°49′N | 88°50′W |
| Ripon, i., Austl. | 220 | 20°05′S | 118°10′E |
| Ripon Falls, wtfl., Ug. | 232 | 0°38′N | 33°02′E |
| Risaralda, dept., Col. | 142a | 5°15′N | 76°00′W |
| Risdon, Austl. (rĭz′dŭn) | 219 | 42°37′S | 147°32′E |
| Rishiri, i., Japan (rē-shē′rē) | 210 | 45°10′N | 141°08′E |
| Rishon le Ziyyon, Isr. | 197a | 31°57′N | 34°48′E |
| Rishra, India | 202a | 22°42′N | 88°22′E |
| Rising Sun, In., U.S. (rīz′ĭng sŭn) | 108 | 38°55′N | 84°55′W |
| Risør, Nor. (rēs′ûr) | 160 | 58°44′N | 9°10′E |
| Ritacuva, Alto, mtn., Col. (ä′l-tō-rē-tä-kōō′vä) | 142 | 6°22′N | 72°13′W |
| Rittman, Oh., U.S. (rĭt′năn) | 111d | 40°58′N | 81°47′W |
| Ritzville, Wa., U.S. (rĭts′vĭl) | 114 | 47°08′N | 118°23′W |
| Riva, Dom. Rep. (rē′vä) | 135 | 19°10′N | 69°55′W |
| Riva, Italy (rē′vä) | 174 | 45°54′N | 10°49′E |
| Riva, Md., U.S. (rī′vȧ) | 110e | 38°57′N | 76°36′W |
| Rivas, Nic. (rē′väs) | 132 | 11°25′N | 85°51′W |
| Rive-de-Gier, Fr. (rēv-dĕ-zhē-ā′) | 170 | 45°32′N | 4°37′E |
| Rivera, Ur. (rē-vā′rä) | 144 | 30°52′S | 55°32′W |
| River Cess, Lib. (rĭv′ẽr sĕs) | 230 | 5°46′N | 9°52′W |
| Riverdale, Il., U.S. (rĭv′ẽr dāl) | 111a | 41°38′N | 87°36′W |
| Riverdale, Ut., U.S. | 117b | 41°11′N | 112°00′W |
| River Falls, Al., U.S. | 124 | 31°20′N | 86°25′W |
| River Falls, Wi., U.S. | 113 | 44°48′N | 92°38′W |
| Riverhead, N.Y., U.S. (rĭv′ẽr hĕd) | 109 | 40°55′N | 72°40′W |
| Riverina, reg., Austl. (rĭv-ẽr-ē′nä) | 221 | 34°55′S | 144°30′E |
| River Jordan, Can. (jôr′dăn) | 116a | 48°25′N | 124°03′W |
| River Oaks, Tx., U.S. (ōkz) | 117c | 32°47′N | 97°24′W |
| River Rouge, Mi., U.S. (rōōzh) | 111b | 42°16′N | 83°09′W |
| Rivers, Can. | 97 | 50°01′N | 100°15′W |
| Riverside, Ca., U.S. (rĭv′ẽr-sīd) | 104 | 33°59′N | 117°21′W |
| Riverside, N.J., U.S. | 110f | 40°02′N | 74°58′W |
| Rivers Inlet, Can. | 94 | 51°45′N | 127°15′W |
| Riverstone, Austl. | 217b | 33°41′S | 150°52′E |
| Riverton, Va., U.S. | 109 | 39°00′N | 78°15′W |
| Riverton, Wy., U.S. | 115 | 43°02′N | 108°24′W |
| Rivesaltes, Fr. (rēv′zält′) | 170 | 42°48′N | 2°48′E |
| Riviera Beach, Fl., U.S. (rĭv-ĭ-ĕr′ȧ bēch) | 125a | 26°46′N | 80°04′W |
| Riviera Beach, Md., U.S. | 110e | 39°10′N | 76°32′W |
| Rivière-Beaudette, Can. | 102a | 45°14′N | 74°20′W |
| Rivière-du-Loup, Can. (rē-vyâr′ dü lōō′) | 91 | 47°50′N | 69°32′W |
| Rivière Qui Barre, Can. (rēv-yĕr′ kē-bär) | 102g | 53°47′N | 113°51′W |
| Rivière-Trois-Pistoles, Can. (trwä′pēs-tôl′) | 100 | 48°07′N | 69°10′W |
| Rivne, Ukr. | 177 | 48°11′N | 31°46′E |
| Rivne, Ukr. | 181 | 50°37′N | 26°17′E |
| Rivne, prov., Ukr. | 177 | 50°55′N | 27°00′E |
| Riyadh, Sau. Ar. | 198 | 24°31′N | 46°47′E |
| Rize, Tur. (rē′zĕ) | 163 | 41°00′N | 40°30′E |
| Rizhao, China (rē-jou) | 208 | 35°27′N | 119°28′E |
| Rizzuto, Cape, c., Italy (rēt-sōō′tō) | 175 | 38°53′N | 17°05′E |
| Rjukan, Nor. (ryōō′kän) | 160 | 59°53′N | 8°30′E |
| Roanne, Fr. (rō-än′) | 161 | 46°02′N | 4°04′E |
| Roanoke, Al., U.S. (rō′ȧ-nōk) | 124 | 33°08′N | 85°21′W |
| Roanoke, Va., U.S. | 105 | 37°16′N | 79°55′W |
| Roanoke, r., U.S. | 107 | 36°17′N | 77°22′W |
| Roanoke Rapids, N.C., U.S. | 125 | 36°25′N | 77°40′W |
| Roanoke Rapids Lake, res., N.C., U.S. | 125 | 36°28′N | 77°37′W |
| Roan Plateau, plat., Co., U.S. (rōn) | 119 | 39°25′N | 110°00′W |
| Roatan, Hond. (rō-ä-tän′) | 132 | 16°18′N | 86°33′W |
| Roatán, i., Hond. | 132 | 16°19′N | 86°46′W |
| Robbeneiland, i., S. Afr. | 232a | 33°48′S | 18°22′E |
| Robbins, Il., U.S. (rŏb′ĭnz) | 111a | 41°39′N | 87°42′W |
| Robbinsdale, Mn., U.S. (rŏb′ĭnz-dāl) | 117g | 45°03′N | 93°22′W |
| Robe, Wa., U.S. (rōb) | 116a | 48°06′N | 121°50′W |
| Roberts, Mount, mtn., Austl. (rŏb′ẽrts) | 221 | 28°05′S | 152°30′E |
| Roberts, Point, c., Wa., U.S. (rŏb′ẽrts) | 116d | 48°58′N | 123°05′W |
| Robertson, Lac, l., Can. | 101 | 51°00′N | 59°10′W |
| Robertsport, Lib. (rŏb′ẽrts-pōrt) | 230 | 6°45′N | 11°22′W |
| Roberval, Can. (rŏb′ẽr-văl) (rō-bĕr-vȧl′) | 91 | 48°32′N | 72°15′W |
| Robinson, Can. | 101 | 48°16′N | 58°50′W |
| Robinson, Il., U.S. (rŏb′ĭn-sŭn) | 108 | 39°00′N | 87°45′W |
| Robinvale, Austl. (rŏb-ĭn′văl) | 222 | 34°45′S | 142°45′E |
| Roblin, Can. | 97 | 51°15′N | 101°25′W |
| Robson, Mount, mtn., Can. (rŏb′sŭn) | 95 | 53°07′N | 119°09′W |
| Robstown, Tx., U.S. (rŏbz′toun) | 123 | 27°46′N | 97°41′W |
| Roca, Cabo da, c., Port. (kȧ′bō-dä-rō′kă) | 172 | 38°47′N | 9°30′W |
| Rocas, Atol das, atoll, Braz. (ä-tôl-däs-rō′kȧs) | 143 | 3°50′S | 33°46′W |
| Rocha, Ur. (rō′chȧs) | 144 | 34°26′S | 54°14′W |
| Rochdale, Eng., U.K. (rŏch′dāl) | 164 | 53°37′N | 2°09′W |
| Roche à Bateau, Haiti (rŏsh à bȧ-tō′) | 135 | 18°10′N | 74°00′W |
| Rochefort, Fr. (rōsh-fŏr′) | 161 | 45°55′N | 0°57′W |
| Rochelle, Il., U.S. (rō-shĕl′) | 113 | 41°53′N | 89°06′W |
| Rochester, Eng., U.K. | 158a | 51°24′N | 0°30′E |
| Rochester, In., U.S. (rŏch′ĕs-tẽr) | 108 | 41°05′N | 86°20′W |
| Rochester, Mi., U.S. | 111b | 42°41′N | 83°09′W |
| Rochester, Mn., U.S. | 105 | 44°01′N | 92°30′W |
| Rochester, N.H., U.S. | 109 | 43°20′N | 71°00′W |
| Rochester, N.Y., U.S. | 105 | 43°15′N | 77°35′W |
| Rochester, Pa., U.S. | 111e | 40°42′N | 80°16′W |
| Rock, r., Ia., U.S. | 112 | 43°17′N | 96°13′W |
| Rock, r., Or., U.S. | 116c | 45°34′N | 122°52′W |
| Rock, r., Or., U.S. | 116c | 45°52′N | 123°14′W |
| Rock, r., U.S. | 107 | 41°40′N | 90°00′W |
| Rockaway, N.J., U.S. (rŏck′ȧ-wā) | 110a | 40°54′N | 74°30′W |
| Rockbank, Austl. | 217a | 37°44′S | 144°40′E |
| Rockcliffe Park, Can. (rok′klĭf pärk) | 102c | 45°27′N | 75°40′W |
| Rock Creek, r., Can. (rŏk) | 115 | 49°01′N | 107°00′W |
| Rock Creek, r., Il., U.S. | 111a | 41°16′N | 87°54′W |
| Rock Creek, r., Mt., U.S. | 115 | 46°25′N | 113°40′W |
| Rock Creek, r., Or., U.S. | 114 | 45°30′N | 120°06′W |
| Rock Creek, r., Wa., U.S. | 114 | 47°09′N | 117°50′W |
| Rockdale, Austl. | 217b | 33°57′S | 151°08′E |
| Rockdale, Md., U.S. | 110e | 39°22′N | 76°49′W |
| Rockdale, Tx., U.S. (rŏk′dāl) | 123 | 30°39′N | 97°00′W |
| Rock Falls, Il., U.S. (rŏk fôlz) | 113 | 41°45′N | 89°42′W |
| Rockford, Il., U.S. (rŏk′fẽrd) | 105 | 42°16′N | 89°07′W |
| Rockhampton, Austl. (rŏk-hămp′tŭn) | 219 | 23°26′S | 150°29′E |
| Rock Hill, S.C., U.S. (rŏk′hĭl) | 105 | 34°55′N | 81°01′W |
| Rockingham, N.C., U.S. (rŏk′ĭng-hăm) | 125 | 34°54′N | 79°45′W |
| Rockingham Forest, for., Eng., U.K. (rok′ĭng-hăm) | 158a | 52°29′N | 0°43′W |


ng-sing; ŋ-baŋk; N-nasalized n; nŏd; cŏmmit; ōld; ôbey; ôrder; oi-boil; fōōd; ŏŏ-as oo in foot; ou-out; s-soft; sh-dish; th-thin; pūre; ůnite; ûrn; stŭd; circŭs; ü-as in French tu; ′-indeterminate vowel.

ăt; fĭnăl; rāte; senāte; ärm; àsk; sofá; fâre; ch-choose; dh-as th in other; bē; ĕvent; bĕt; recĕnt; cratĕr; g-gō; gh-guttural g; bĭt; ĭ-short neutral; rīde; к-guttural k as ch in German ich;

PRONOUNCING INDEX
Rum Cay – Saint George 343


| PLACE (Pronunciation) | PAGE | LAT. | LONG. |
|---|---|---|---|
| Rum Cay, i., Bah. | 135 | 23°40'N | 74°50'W |
| Rumford, Me., U.S. (rŭm'fẽrd) | 100 | 44°32'N | 70°35'W |
| Rummah, Wādī ar, val., Sau. Ar. | 198 | 26°17'N | 41°45'E |
| Rummānah, Egypt | 197a | 31°01'N | 32°39'E |
| Runan, China (rōō-nän) | 208 | 32°59'N | 114°22'E |
| Runcorn, Eng., U.K. (rŭŋ'kôrn) | 158a | 53°20'N | 2°44'W |
| Ruo, r., China (rwỏ) | 204 | 41°15'N | 100°46'E |
| Rupat, i., Indon. (rōō'pät) | 197b | 1°55'N | 101°35'E |
| Rupat, Selat, strt., Indon. | 197b | 1°55'N | 101°17'E |
| Rupert, Id., U.S. (rōō'pẽrt) | 115 | 42°36'N | 113°41'W |
| Rupert, Rivière de, r., Can. | 93 | 51°35'N | 76°30'W |
| Ruse, Blg. (rōō'sĕ) (rỏ'sĕ) | 154 | 43°50'N | 25°59'E |
| Rushan, China (rōō-shän) | 206 | 36°54'N | 121°31'E |
| Rush City, Mn., U.S. | 113 | 45°40'N | 92°59'W |
| Rushville, Il., U.S. (rŭsh'vĭl) | 121 | 40°08'N | 90°34'W |
| Rushville, In., U.S. | 108 | 39°35'N | 85°30'W |
| Rushville, Ne., U.S. | 112 | 42°43'N | 102°27'W |
| Rusizi, r., Afr. | 237 | 3°00'S | 29°05'E |
| Rusk, Tx., U.S. (rŭsk) | 123 | 31°49'N | 95°09'W |
| Ruskin, Can. (rŭs'kĭn) | 116d | 49°10'N | 122°25'W |
| Russ, r., Aus. | 159e | 48°12'N | 16°55'E |
| Russas, Braz. (rōō's-säs) | 143 | 4°48'S | 37°50'W |
| Russell, Can. (rŭs'ĕl) | 90 | 50°47'N | 101°15'W |
| Russell, Can. | 102c | 45°15'N | 75°22'W |
| Russell, Ca., U.S. | 116b | 37°39'N | 122°08'W |
| Russell, Ks., U.S. | 120 | 38°51'N | 98°51'W |
| Russell, Ky., U.S. | 108 | 38°30'N | 82°45'W |
| Russel Lake, l., Can. | 97 | 56°15'N | 101°30'W |
| Russell Islands, is., Sol. Is. | 221 | 9°16'S | 158°30'E |
| Russellville, Al., U.S. (rŭs'ĕl-vĭl) | 124 | 34°29'N | 87°44'W |
| Russellville, Ar., U.S. | 121 | 35°16'N | 93°08'W |
| Russelville, Ky., U.S. | 124 | 36°48'N | 86°51'W |
| Russia, nation, Russia | 178 | 61°00'N | 60°00'E |
| Russian, r., Ca., U.S. (rŭsh'ăn) | 118 | 38°59'N | 123°10'W |
| Rustavi, Geor. | 182 | 41°33'N | 45°02'E |
| Rustenburg, S. Afr. (rŭs'tĕn-bûrg) | 238c | 25°40'S | 27°15'E |
| Ruston, La., U.S. (rŭs'tŭn) | 123 | 32°32'N | 92°39'W |
| Ruston, Wa., U.S. | 116a | 47°18'N | 122°30'W |
| Rute, Spain (rōō'tā) | 172 | 38°20'N | 4°34'W |
| Ruth, Nv., U.S. (rōōth) | 118 | 39°17'N | 115°00'W |
| Ruthenia, hist. reg., Ukr. | 169 | 48°25'N | 23°00'E |
| Rutherfordton, N.C., U.S. (rŭdh'ẽr-fẽrd-tŭn) | 125 | 35°23'N | 81°58'W |
| Rutland, Vt., U.S. | 109 | 43°35'N | 72°55'W |
| Rutledge, Md., U.S. (rŭt'lĕdj) | 110e | 39°34'N | 76°33'W |
| Rutog, China | 204 | 33°29'N | 79°26'E |
| Rutshuru, D.R.C. (rōōt-shōō'rōō) | 232 | 1°11'S | 29°27'E |
| Ruvo, Italy (rōō'vỏ) | 174 | 41°07'N | 16°32'E |
| Ruvuma, r., Afr. | 232 | 11°30'S | 37°00'E |
| Ruza, Russia (rōō'zȧ) | 176 | 55°42'N | 36°12'E |
| Ruzhany, Bela. (rỏ-zhän'ĭ) | 169 | 52°49'N | 24°54'E |
| Rwanda, nation, Afr. | 232 | 2°10'S | 29°37'E |
| Ryabovo, Russia (ryä'bỏ-vỏ) | 186c | 59°24'N | 31°08'E |
| Ryazan', Russia (ryä-zän'') | 178 | 54°37'N | 39°43'E |
| Ryazan', prov., Russia | 176 | 54°10'N | 39°37'E |
| Ryazhsk, Russia (ryäzh'sk') | 180 | 53°43'N | 40°04'E |
| Rybachiy, Poluostrov, pen., Russia | 180 | 69°50'N | 33°20'E |
| Rybatskoye, Russia | 186c | 59°50'N | 30°31'E |
| Rybinsk, Russia | 178 | 58°02'N | 38°52'E |
| Rybinskoye, res., Russia | 178 | 58°23'N | 38°15'E |
| Rybnik, Pol. (rĭb'nĕk) | 169 | 50°06'N | 18°37'E |
| Ryde, Eng., U.K. (rīd) | 164 | 50°43'N | 1°16'W |
| Rye, N.Y., U.S. (rī) | 110a | 40°58'N | 73°42'W |
| Ryl'sk, Russia (rēl''sk) | 181 | 51°33'N | 34°42'E |
| Ryōtsu, Japan (ryōt'sōō) | 210 | 38°02'N | 138°23'E |
| Rypin, Pol. (rĭ'pĕn) | 169 | 53°04'N | 19°25'E |
| Rysy, mtn., Eur. | 169 | 49°12'N | 20°04'E |
| Ryukyu Islands *see* Nansei-shotō, is., Japan | 205 | 27°30'N | 127°00'E |
| Rzeszów, Pol. (zhä-shôf) | 161 | 50°02'N | 22°00'E |
| Rzhev, Russia ('r-zhĕf) | 178 | 56°16'N | 34°17'E |
| Rzhyshchiv, Ukr. | 177 | 49°58'N | 31°05'E |

# S

| PLACE (Pronunciation) | PAGE | LAT. | LONG. |
|---|---|---|---|
| Saale, r., Ger. (sä-lĕ) | 168 | 51°14'N | 11°52'E |
| Saalfeld, Ger. (säl'fĕlt) | 168 | 50°38'N | 11°20'E |
| Saarbrücken, Ger. (zähr'brü-kĕn) | 161 | 49°15'N | 7°01'E |
| Saaremaa, i., Est. | 180 | 58°25'N | 22°30'E |
| Saavedra, Arg. (sä-ä-vā'drä) | 144 | 37°45'S | 62°23'W |
| Saba, i., Neth. Ant. (sä'bä) | 133b | 17°39'N | 63°20'W |
| Šabac, Serb. (shä'bȧts) | 163 | 44°45'N | 19°49'E |
| Sabadell, Spain (sä-bä-dhāl') | 162 | 41°32'N | 2°07'E |
| Sabah, hist. reg., Malay. | 212 | 5°10'N | 116°25'E |
| Sabana, Archipiélago de, is., Cuba | 134 | 23°05'N | 80°00'W |
| Sabana, Río, r., Pan. (sä-bä'nä) | 133 | 8°40'N | 78°02'W |
| Sabana de la Mar, Dom. Rep. (sä-bä'nä dā lä mär') | 135 | 19°05'N | 69°30'W |
| Sabana de Uchire, Ven. (sä-bä'nä dĕ ōō-chē'rĕ) | 143b | 10°02'N | 65°32'W |
| Sabanagrande, Hond. (sä-bä-nä-grä'n-dĕ) | 132 | 13°47'N | 87°16'W |
| Sabanalarga, Col. (sä-bȧ'nä-lär'gä) | 142 | 10°38'N | 75°02'W |
| Sabanas Páramo, mtn., Col. (sä-bȧ'näs pȧ'rä-mỏ) | 142a | 6°28'N | 76°08'W |
| Sabancuy, Mex. (sä-bäŋ-kwē') | 131 | 18°58'N | 91°09'W |
| Sabang, Indon. (sä'bäng) | 212 | 5°52'N | 95°26'E |
| Sabaudia, Italy (sȧ-bou'dē-ä) | 174 | 41°19'N | 13°00'E |
| Sabetha, Ks., U.S. (sȧ-bĕth'ȧ) | 121 | 39°54'N | 95°49'W |
| Sabi (Rio Save), r., Afr. (sä'bē) | 232 | 20°18'S | 32°07'E |
| Sabile, Lat. (sȧ'bē-lĕ) | 167 | 57°03'N | 22°34'E |
| Sabinal, Tx., U.S. (sȧ-bī'nȧl) | 122 | 29°19'N | 99°27'W |
| Sabinal, Cayo, i., Cuba (kä'yō sä-bē-näl') | 134 | 21°40'N | 77°20'W |
| Sabinas, Mex. | 128 | 28°05'N | 101°30'W |
| Sabinas, r., Mex. (sä-bē'näs) | 122 | 26°37'N | 99°52'W |
| Sabinas, Río, r., Mex. (rē'ō sä-bē'näs) | 122 | 27°25'N | 100°33'W |
| Sabinas Hidalgo, Mex. (ē-däl'gỏ) | 122 | 26°30'N | 100°10'W |
| Sabine, Tx., U.S. (sȧ-bēn') | 123 | 29°44'N | 93°54'W |
| Sabine, r., U.S. | 107 | 32°00'N | 94°30'W |
| Sabine, Mount, mtn., Ant. | 224 | 72°05'S | 169°10'E |
| Sabine Lake, l., La., U.S. | 123 | 29°53'N | 93°41'W |
| Sablayan, Phil. (säb-lä-yän') | 213a | 12°49'N | 120°47'E |
| Sable, Cape, c., Can. (sā'b'l) | 93 | 43°25'N | 65°24'W |
| Sable, Cape, c., Fl., U.S. | 107 | 25°12'N | 81°10'W |
| Sables, Rivière aux, r., Can. | 99 | 49°00'N | 70°20'W |
| Sablé-sur-Sarthe, Fr. (säb-lā-sür-särt') | 170 | 47°50'N | 0°17'W |
| Sablya, Gora, mtn., Russia | 180 | 64°50'N | 59°00'E |
| Sàbor, r., Port. (sä-bōr') | 172 | 41°18'N | 6°54'W |
| Sabunchu, Azer. | 182 | 40°26'N | 49°56'E |
| Sabzevār, Iran | 201 | 36°13'N | 57°42'E |
| Sac, r., Mo., U.S. (sôk) | 121 | 38°11'N | 93°45'W |
| Sacandaga Reservoir, res., N.Y., U.S. (sä-kăn-dȧ'gȧ) | 109 | 43°10'N | 74°15'W |
| Sacavém, Port. (sä-kä-vĕN') | 173b | 38°47'N | 9°06'W |
| Sacavém, r., Port. | 173b | 38°52'N | 9°06'W |
| Sac City, Ia., U.S. (sŏk) | 112 | 42°25'N | 95°00'W |
| Sachigo Lake, l., Can. (săch'ĭ-gō) | 97 | 53°49'N | 92°08'W |
| Sachsen, hist. reg., Ger. (zäk'sĕn) | 168 | 50°45'N | 12°17'E |
| Sacketts Harbor, N.Y., U.S. (săk'ĕts) | 109 | 43°55'N | 76°05'W |
| Sackville, Can. (săk'vĭl) | 100 | 45°54'N | 64°22'W |
| Saco, Me., U.S. (sô'kỏ) | 100 | 43°30'N | 70°28'W |
| Saco, r., Braz. (sä'kỏ) | 144b | 22°20'S | 43°26'W |
| Saco, r., Me., U.S. | 100 | 43°53'N | 70°46'W |
| Sacramento, Mex. | 122 | 25°45'N | 103°22'W |
| Sacramento, Mex. | 122 | 27°05'N | 101°45'W |
| Sacramento, Ca., U.S. (săk-rȧ-mĕn'tō) | 104 | 38°35'N | 121°30'W |
| Sacramento, r., Ca., U.S. | 118 | 40°20'N | 122°07'W |
| Şa'dah, Yemen | 198 | 16°50'N | 43°45'E |
| Saddle Lake Indian Reserve, I.R., Can. | 95 | 54°00'N | 111°40'W |
| Saddle Mountain, mtn., Or., U.S. (săd''l) | 116c | 45°58'N | 123°40'W |
| Sadiya, India (sŭ-dē'yä) | 199 | 27°53'N | 95°35'E |
| Sado, i., Japan (sä'dō) | 205 | 38°05'N | 138°26'E |
| Sado, r., Port. (sä'dỏ) | 172 | 38°15'N | 8°20'W |
| Saeby, Den. (sĕ'bü) | 166 | 57°21'N | 10°29'E |
| Saeki, Japan (sä'ā-kē) | 210 | 32°56'N | 131°51'E |
| Säffle, Swe. | 166 | 59°10'N | 12°55'E |
| Safford, Az., U.S. (săf'fẽrd) | 119 | 32°50'N | 109°45'W |
| Safi, Mor. (sä'fē) (äs'fē) | 230 | 32°24'N | 9°09'W |
| Safīd Koh, Selseleh-ye, mts., Afg. | 198 | 34°45'N | 63°58'E |
| Saga, Japan (sä'gä) | 211 | 33°15'N | 130°18'E |
| Sagami-Nada, b., Japan (sä'gä'mē nä-dä) | 211 | 35°06'N | 139°24'E |
| Sagamore Hills, Oh., U.S. (săg'ȧ-môr hĭlz) | 111d | 41°19'N | 81°34'W |
| Saganaga, l., N.A. (să-gȧ-nä'gȧ) | 113 | 48°13'N | 91°17'W |
| Sāgar, India | 199 | 23°55'N | 78°45'E |
| Saghyz, r., Kaz. | 181 | 48°30'N | 56°10'E |
| Saginaw, Mi., U.S. (săg'ĭ-nô) | 105 | 43°25'N | 84°00'W |
| Saginaw, Mn., U.S. | 117h | 46°51'N | 92°26'W |
| Saginaw, Tx., U.S. | 117c | 32°52'N | 97°22'W |
| Saginaw Bay, b., Mi., U.S. | 107 | 43°50'N | 83°40'W |
| Saguache, Co., U.S. (sȧ-wăch') (sȧ-gwä'chē) | 119 | 38°05'N | 106°10'W |
| Saguache Creek, r., Co., U.S. | 108 | 38°05'N | 106°40'W |
| Sagua de Tánamo, Cuba (sä-gwä dĕ tä'nä-mō) | 135 | 20°40'N | 75°15'W |
| Sagua la Grande, Cuba (sä-gwä lä grä'n-dĕ) | 134 | 22°45'N | 80°05'W |
| Saguaro National Park, rec., Az., U.S. (säg-wä'rō) | 119 | 32°12'N | 110°40'W |
| Saguenay, r., Can. (săg-ē-nā') | 93 | 48°20'N | 70°15'W |
| Sagunt, Spain | 173 | 38°58'N | 1°29'E |
| Sagunto, Spain (sä-gōn'tō) | 162 | 39°40'N | 0°17'W |
| Sahara, des., Afr. (sȧ-hä'rȧ) | 230 | 23°44'N | 1°40'W |
| Saharan Atlas, mts., Afr. | 162 | 32°51'N | 1°02'W |
| Sahāranpur, India (sŭ-hä'rŭn-pōōr') | 199 | 29°58'N | 77°41'E |
| Sahara Village, Ut., U.S. (sȧ-hä'rȧ) | 117b | 41°06'N | 111°58'W |
| Sahel *see* Sudan, reg., Afr. | 230 | 15°00'N | 7°00'E |
| Sāhīwāl, Pak. | 202 | 30°43'N | 73°04'E |
| Sahuayo de Dias, Mex. | 130 | 20°03'N | 102°43'W |
| Saigon *see* Ho Chi Minh City, Viet. | 212 | 10°46'N | 106°34'E |
| Saijō, Japan (sä'ē-jō) | 211 | 33°55'N | 133°13'E |
| Saimaa, l., Fin. (sä'ĭ-mä) | 160 | 61°24'N | 28°45'E |
| Sain Alto, Mex. (sä-ēn' äl'tō) | 130 | 23°35'N | 103°13'W |
| Saint Adolphe, Can. (sânt a'dôlf) (săN' tȧ-dôlf') | 102f | 49°40'N | 97°07'W |
| Saint Afrique, Fr. (săN' tȧ-frēk') | 170 | 43°58'N | 2°52'E |
| Saint Albans, Austl. (sânt ôl'bănz) | 217a | 37°44'S | 144°47'E |
| Saint Albans, Eng., U.K. | 164 | 51°44'N | 0°20'W |
| Saint Albans, Vt., U.S. | 109 | 44°50'N | 73°05'W |
| Saint Albans, W.V., U.S. | 108 | 38°20'N | 81°50'W |
| Saint Albert, Can. (sânt ăl'bẽrt) | 95 | 53°38'N | 113°38'W |
| Saint Amand-Mont Rond, Fr. (săN't ȧ-mäN' môN-rôN') | 170 | 46°44'N | 2°28'E |
| Saint André-Est, Can. | 102a | 45°33'N | 74°19'W |
| Saint Andrews, Can. | 91 | 45°05'N | 67°03'W |
| Saint Andrews, Scot., U.K. | 164 | 56°20'N | 2°40'W |
| Saint Andrew's Channel, strt., Can. | 101 | 46°06'N | 60°28'W |
| Saint Anicet, Can. (sĕNt ȧ-nē-sĕ') | 102a | 45°07'N | 74°23'W |
| Saint Ann, Mo., U.S. (sânt ăn') | 117e | 38°44'N | 90°23'W |
| Sainte Anne, Guad. | 133b | 16°15'N | 61°23'W |
| Saint Anne, Il., U.S. | 111a | 41°01'N | 87°44'W |
| Sainte Anne, r., Can. (sănt ȧn') (sânt ăn') | 99 | 46°55'N | 71°46'W |
| Sainte-Anne, r., Can. | 102b | 47°07'N | 70°50'W |
| Sainte Anne-des-Plaines, Can. (dā plĕN) | 102a | 45°46'N | 73°49'W |
| Saint Ann's Bay, Jam. | 134 | 18°25'N | 77°15'W |
| Saint Anns Bay, b., Can. (ănz) | 101 | 46°20'N | 60°30'W |
| Saint Anselme, Can. (săN' tăN-sĕlm') | 102b | 46°37'N | 70°58'W |
| Saint Anthony, Can. (săN ăn'thỏ-nē) | 91 | 51°24'N | 55°35'W |
| Saint Anthony, Id., U.S. (sânt ăn'thỏ-nē) | 115 | 43°59'N | 111°42'W |
| Saint Antoine-de-Tilly, Can. | 102b | 46°40'N | 71°31'W |
| Saint Apollinaire, Can. (săN' tȧ-pỏl-ē-nâr') | 102b | 46°36'N | 71°30'W |
| Saint Arnoult-en-Yvelines, Fr. (sȧN-tär-nōō'ĕN-nēv-lēn') | 171b | 48°33'N | 1°55'E |
| Saint Augustin-de-Québec, Can. (sĕn tō-güs-tēn') | 102b | 46°45'N | 71°27'W |
| Saint Augustin-Deux-Montagnes, Can. | 102a | 45°38'N | 73°59'W |
| Saint Augustine, Fl., U.S. (sânt ô'gŭs-tēn) | 105 | 29°53'N | 81°21'W |
| Sainte Barbe, Can. (sănt bärb') | 102a | 45°14'N | 74°12'W |
| Saint Barthélemy, i., Guad. | 133b | 17°55'N | 62°32'W |
| Saint Bees Head, c., Eng., U.K. (sânt bēz' hĕd) | 164 | 54°30'N | 3°40'W |
| Saint Benoit, Can. (sĕN bĕ-nōō-ä') | 102a | 45°34'N | 74°05'W |
| Saint Bernard, La., U.S. (bẽr-närd') | 110d | 29°52'N | 89°52'W |
| Saint Bernard, Oh., U.S. | 111f | 39°10'N | 84°30'W |
| Saint Bride, Mount, mtn., Can. (sânt brīd) | 95 | 51°30'N | 115°57'W |
| Saint Brieuc, Fr. (săN' brēs') | 161 | 48°32'N | 2°47'W |
| Saint Bruno, Can. (brü'nō) | 102a | 45°31'N | 73°20'W |
| Saint Canut, Can. (săN' kȧ-nü') | 102a | 45°43'N | 74°04'W |
| Saint Casimir, Can. (kȧ-zē-mēr') | 99 | 46°45'N | 72°34'W |
| Saint Catharines, Can. (kăth'ȧ-rĭnz) | 91 | 43°10'N | 79°14'W |
| Saint Catherine, Mount, mtn., Gren. | 133b | 12°10'N | 61°42'W |
| Saint Chamas, Fr. (sȧN-shä-mä') | 170a | 43°32'N | 5°03'E |
| Saint Chamond, Fr. (săN' shȧ-môN') | 161 | 45°30'N | 4°17'E |
| Saint Charles, Can. (săN' shärlz') | 102b | 46°47'N | 70°57'W |
| Saint Charles, Il., U.S. (sânt chärlz') | 111a | 41°55'N | 88°19'W |
| Saint Charles, Mi., U.S. | 108 | 43°20'N | 84°10'W |
| Saint Charles, Mn., U.S. | 113 | 43°56'N | 92°05'W |
| Saint Charles, Mo., U.S. | 117e | 38°47'N | 90°29'W |
| Saint Charles, Lac, l., Can. | 102b | 46°56'N | 71°21'W |
| Saint Christopher-Nevis *see* Saint Kitts and Nevis, nation, N.A. | 128 | 17°24'N | 63°30'W |
| Saint Clair, Mi., U.S. (sânt klâr) | 108 | 42°55'N | 82°30'W |
| Saint Clair, l., Can. | 107 | 42°25'N | 82°30'W |
| Saint Clair, r., Can. | 98 | 42°45'N | 82°25'W |
| Sainte Claire, Can. | 102b | 46°36'N | 70°52'W |
| Saint Clair Shores, Mi., U.S. | 111b | 42°30'N | 82°54'W |
| Saint Claude, Fr. (săN' klōd') | 171 | 46°24'N | 5°53'E |
| Saint Clet, Can. (săNt' klā') | 102a | 45°22'N | 74°21'W |
| Saint Cloud, Fl., U.S. (sânt kloud') | 125a | 28°13'N | 81°17'W |
| Saint Cloud, Mn., U.S. | 105 | 45°33'N | 94°08'W |
| Saint Constant, Can. (kŏn'stănt) | 102a | 45°23'N | 73°34'W |
| Saint Croix, i., V.I.U.S. (sânt kroi') | 129 | 17°40'N | 64°43'W |
| Saint Croix, r., N.A. (kroi') | 100 | 45°28'N | 67°32'W |
| Saint Croix, r., U.S. (sânt kroi') | 107 | 45°45'N | 93°00'W |
| Saint Croix Indian Reservation, I.R., Wi., U.S. | 113 | 45°40'N | 92°21'W |
| Saint Croix Island, i., S. Afr. (săN krwă) | 233c | 33°48'S | 25°45'E |
| Saint Damien-de-Buckland, Can. (sânt dā'mē-ĕn) | 102b | 46°37'N | 70°39'W |
| Saint David, Can. (dā'vĭd) | 102b | 46°47'N | 71°11'W |
| Saint David's Head, c., Wales, U.K. | 164 | 51°54'N | 5°25'W |
| Saint-Denis, Fr. (săN'dē-nē') | 161 | 48°26'N | 2°22'E |
| Saint Dizier, Fr. (dē-zyā') | 161 | 48°49'N | 4°55'E |
| Saint Dominique, Can. (sĕN dō-mē-nēk') | 102a | 45°19'N | 74°09'W |
| Saint Edouard-de-Napierville, Can. (sĕN-tĕ-dōō-är') | 102a | 45°14'N | 73°31'W |
| Saint Elias, Mount, mtn., N.A. (sânt ē-lī'ăs) | 92 | 60°25'N | 141°00'W |
| Saint Étienne, Fr. | 161 | 45°26'N | 4°22'E |
| Saint Etienne-de-Lauzon, Can. (săN' tā-tyĕn') | 102b | 46°39'N | 71°19'W |
| Sainte Euphémie, Can. (sĕNt û-fē-mē') | 102b | 46°47'N | 70°27'W |
| Saint Eustache, Can. (săN' tû-stȧsh') | 102a | 45°34'N | 73°54'W |
| Saint Eustache, Can. | 102f | 49°58'N | 97°47'W |
| Sainte Famille, Can. (săN't fȧ-mē'y') | 102b | 46°58'N | 70°58'W |
| Saint Félicien, Can. (săN fā-lē-syăN') | 91 | 48°39'N | 72°28'W |
| Sainte Felicite, Can. | 100 | 48°54'N | 67°20'W |
| Saint Féréol, Can. (fa-rā-ôl') | 102b | 47°07'N | 70°52'W |
| Saint Florent-sur-Cher, Fr. (săN' flỏ-räN'sür-shâr') | 170 | 46°58'N | 2°15'E |
| Saint Flour, Fr. (săN flōōr') | 170 | 45°02'N | 3°09'E |
| Sainte Foy, Can. (sănt fwä) | 99 | 46°47'N | 71°18'W |
| Saint Francis, r., Ar., U.S. | 121 | 35°56'N | 90°27'W |
| Saint Francis Lake, l., Can. (săN frăn'sĭs) | 99 | 45°00'N | 74°20'W |
| Saint François, Can. (săN'frän-swä') | 102b | 47°01'N | 70°49'W |
| Saint François de Boundji, Congo | 236 | 1°03'S | 15°22'E |
| Saint Francois Xavier, Can. | 102f | 49°55'N | 97°32'W |
| Saint Gaudens, Fr. (gō-dăNs') | 170 | 43°07'N | 0°43'E |
| Sainte Genevieve, Mo., U.S. (sânt jĕn'ĕ-vēv) | 121 | 37°58'N | 90°02'W |
| Saint George, Austl. (sânt jôrj') | 219 | 28°02'S | 148°40'E |


ng-sing; ŋ-baŋk; N-nasalized n; nŏd; cŏmmit; ōld; ôbey; ôrder; oi-boil; fōōd; ỏ-as oo in foot; ou-out; s-soft; sh-dish; th-thin; pūre; ûnite; ûrn; stŭd; circŭs; ü-as in French tu; '-indeterminate vowel.

344 Saint George – Salem PRONOUNCING INDEX


| PLACE (Pronunciation) | PAGE | LAT. | LONG. |
|---|---|---|---|
| Saint George, Can. (săɴ jôrj′) | 91 | 45°08′N | 66°49′W |
| Saint George, Can. (săɴ′zhôrzh′) | 102d | 43°14′N | 80°15′W |
| Saint George, S.C., U.S. (sånt jôrj′) | 125 | 33°11′N | 80°35′W |
| Saint George, Ut., U.S. | 119 | 37°05′N | 113°40′W |
| Saint George, i., Ak., U.S. | 103 | 56°30′N | 169°40′W |
| Saint George, Cape, c., Can. | 93a | 48°28′N | 59°15′W |
| Saint George, Cape, c., Fl., U.S. | 124 | 29°30′N | 85°20′W |
| Saint George's, Can. (jôrj′ēs) | 91 | 48°26′N | 58°29′W |
| Saint Georges, Fr. Gu. | 143 | 3°48′N | 51°47′W |
| Saint George's, Gren. | 133b | 12°02′N | 61°57′W |
| Saint George's Bay, b., Can. | 93a | 48°20′N | 59°00′W |
| Saint Georges Bay, b., Can. | 101 | 45°49′N | 61°45′W |
| Saint George's Channel, strt., Eur. (jôr-jĕz) | 156 | 51°45′N | 6°30′W |
| Saint Germain-en-Laye, Fr. (săɴ′ zhĕr-măɴ-äɴ-lā′) | 170 | 48°53′N | 2°05′E |
| Saint Gervais, Can. (zhĕr-vĕ′) | 102b | 46°43′N | 70°53′W |
| Saint Girons, Fr. (zhē-rôɴ′) | 170 | 42°58′N | 1°08′E |
| Saint Gotthard Pass, p., Switz. | 168 | 46°33′N | 8°34′E |
| Saint Gregory, Mount, mtn., Can. (sånt grĕg′ẽr-ė) | 101 | 49°19′N | 58°13′W |
| Saint Helena, i., St. Hel. | 229 | 16°01′S | 5°16′W |
| Saint Helenabaai, b., S. Afr. | 232 | 32°25′S | 17°15′E |
| Saint Helens, Eng., U.K. (sånt hĕl′ĕnz) | 158a | 53°27′N | 2°44′W |
| Saint Helens, Or., U.S. (hĕl′ĕnz) | 116c | 45°52′N | 122°49′W |
| Saint Helens, Mount, vol., Wa., U.S. | 114 | 46°13′N | 122°10′W |
| Saint Helier, Jersey (hyĕl′yẽr) | 170 | 49°12′N | 2°06′W |
| Saint Henri, Can. (săɴ′ hĕn′rė) | 102b | 46°41′N | 71°04′W |
| Saint Hubert, Can. | 102a | 45°29′N | 73°24′W |
| Saint Hyacinthe, Can. | 91 | 45°35′N | 72°55′W |
| Saint Ignace, Mi., U.S. (sånt ĭg′nås) | 113 | 45°51′N | 84°39′W |
| Saint Ignace, i., Can. (săɴ′ ĭg′nås) | 98 | 48°47′N | 88°14′W |
| Saint Irenee, Can. (săɴ′ tē-rå-nā′) | 99 | 47°34′N | 70°15′W |
| Saint Isidore-de-Laprairie, Can. | 102a | 45°18′N | 73°41′W |
| Saint Isidore-de-Prescott, Can. (săɴ′ ĭz′ĭ-dôr-prĕs-kŏt) | 102c | 45°23′N | 74°54′W |
| Saint Isidore-Dorchester, Can. (dŏr-chĕs′tẽr) | 102b | 46°35′N | 71°05′W |
| Saint Jacob, Il., U.S. (jā-kŏb) | 117e | 38°43′N | 89°46′W |
| Saint James, Mn., U.S. (sånt jāmz′) | 113 | 43°58′N | 94°37′W |
| Saint James, Mo., U.S. | 121 | 37°59′N | 91°37′W |
| Saint James, Cape, c., Can. | 94 | 51°58′N | 131°00′W |
| Saint Janvier, Can. (săɴ′ zhän-vyā′) | 102a | 45°43′N | 73°56′W |
| Saint Jean, Can. (săɴ′ zhäɴ′) | 91 | 45°20′N | 73°15′W |
| Saint Jean, Can. | 102b | 46°55′N | 70°54′W |
| Saint Jean, Lac, l., Can. | 93 | 48°35′N | 72°00′W |
| Saint Jean-Chrysostome, Can. (krĭ-zōs-tōm′) | 102b | 46°43′N | 71°12′W |
| Saint Jean-d'Angely, Fr. (däɴ-zhå-lē′) | 170 | 45°56′N | 0°33′W |
| Saint Jean-de-Luz, Fr. (dĕ lüz′) | 170 | 43°23′N | 1°40′W |
| Saint Jérôme, Can. (sånt jĕ-rōm′) (săɴ zhā-rōm′) | 102a | 45°47′N | 74°00′W |
| Saint Joachim-de-Montmorency, Can. (sånt jō′ȧ-kĭm) | 102b | 47°04′N | 70°51′W |
| Saint John, Can. (sånt jŏn) | 91 | 45°16′N | 66°03′W |
| Saint John, In., U.S. | 111a | 41°27′N | 87°29′W |
| Saint John, Ks., U.S. | 120 | 37°59′N | 98°44′W |
| Saint John, N.D., U.S. | 112 | 48°57′N | 99°42′W |
| Saint John, i., V.I.U.S. | 129b | 18°16′N | 64°48′W |
| Saint John, r., N.A. | 93 | 47°00′N | 68°00′W |
| Saint John, Cape, c., Can. | 101 | 50°00′N | 55°32′W |
| Saint Johns, Antig. | 133b | 17°07′N | 61°50′W |
| Saint John's, Can. (jŏns) | 93a | 47°34′N | 52°43′W |
| Saint Johns, Az., U.S. (jŏnz) | 119 | 34°30′N | 109°25′W |
| Saint Johns, Mi., U.S. | 108 | 43°05′N | 84°35′W |
| Saint Johns, r., Fl., U.S. | 107 | 29°54′N | 81°32′W |
| Saint Johnsbury, Vt., U.S. (jŏnz′bĕr-ė) | 109 | 44°25′N | 72°00′W |
| Saint Joseph, Dom. | 133b | 15°25′N | 61°26′W |
| Saint Joseph, Mi., U.S. | 108 | 42°05′N | 86°30′W |
| Saint Joseph, Mo., U.S. (sånt jỏ-sĕf) | 105 | 39°44′N | 94°49′W |
| Saint Joseph, i., Can. | 108 | 46°15′N | 83°55′W |
| Saint Joseph, l., Can. (jō′zhûf) | 93 | 51°31′N | 90°40′W |
| Saint Joseph, r., Mi., U.S. (sånt jỏ′sĕf) | 108 | 41°45′N | 85°50′W |
| Saint Joseph Bay, b., Fl., U.S. (jō′zhûf) | 124 | 29°48′N | 85°26′W |
| Saint Joseph-de-Beauce, Can. (sĕɴ zhō-zĕf′dĕ bōs) | 99 | 46°18′N | 70°52′W |
| Saint Joseph-du-Lac, Can. (sĕɴ zhō-zĕf′ dü läk) | 102a | 45°32′N | 74°00′W |
| Saint Joseph Island, i., Tx., U.S. (sånt jỏ-sĕf) | 123 | 27°58′N | 96°50′W |
| Saint Junien, Fr. (săɴ′zhü-nyăɴ′) | 170 | 45°53′N | 0°54′E |
| Sainte Justine-de-Newton, Can. (sånt jŭs-tēn′) | 102a | 45°22′N | 74°22′W |
| Saint Kilda, Austl. | 217a | 37°52′S | 144°59′E |
| Saint Kilda, i., Scot., U.K. (kĭl′dȧ) | 164 | 57°50′N | 8°32′W |
| Saint Kitts, i., St. K./N. (sānt kĭtts) | 129 | 17°24′N | 63°30′W |
| Saint Kitts and Nevis, nation, N.A. | 129 | 17°24′N | 63°30′W |
| Saint Lambert, Can. | 109 | 45°29′N | 73°29′W |
| Saint Lambert-de-Lévis, Can. | 102b | 46°35′N | 71°12′W |
| Saint Laurent, Can. (săɴ′lō-rän) | 102a | 45°31′N | 73°41′W |
| Saint Laurent, Fr. Gu. | 143 | 5°27′N | 53°56′W |
| Saint Laurent-d'Orleans, Can. | 102b | 46°52′N | 71°00′W |
| Saint Lawrence, Can. (sānt lô′rĕns) | 101 | 46°55′N | 55°23′W |
| Saint Lawrence, i., Ak., U.S. (sånt lô′rĕns) | 106a | 63°10′N | 172°12′W |
| Saint Lawrence, r., N.A. | 93 | 48°24′N | 69°30′W |
| Saint Lawrence, Gulf of, b., Can. | 93 | 48°00′N | 62°00′W |
| Saint Lazare, Can. (săɴ′lȧ-zȧr′) | 102b | 46°39′N | 70°48′W |
| Saint Lazare-de-Vaudreuil, Can. | 102a | 45°24′N | 74°08′W |
| Saint Léger-en-Yvelines, Fr. (săɴ-lā-zhĕ′ĕɴ-nēv-lēn′) | 171b | 48°43′N | 1°45′E |

| PLACE (Pronunciation) | PAGE | LAT. | LONG. |
|---|---|---|---|
| Saint Leonard, Can. (sånt lĕn′ȧrd) | 100 | 47°10′N | 67°56′W |
| Saint Léonard, Can. | 102a | 45°36′N | 73°35′W |
| Saint Leonard, Md., U.S. | 110e | 38°29′N | 76°31′W |
| Saint Lô, Fr. | 161 | 49°07′N | 1°05′W |
| Saint-Louis, Sen. | 230 | 16°02′N | 16°30′W |
| Saint Louis, Mi., U.S. (sånt lo͞o′ĭs) | 108 | 43°25′N | 84°35′W |
| Saint Louis, Mo., U.S. (sånt lo͞o′ĭs) (lo͞o′ė) | 105 | 38°39′N | 90°15′W |
| Saint Louis, r., Mn., U.S. (sånt lo͞o′ĭs) | 113 | 46°57′N | 92°58′W |
| Saint Louis, Lac, l., Can. (săɴ′ lo͞o-ē′) | 102a | 45°24′N | 73°51′W |
| Saint Louis-de-Gonzague, Can. (săɴ′ lo͞o ē′) | 102a | 45°13′N | 74°00′W |
| Saint Louis Park, Mn., U.S. | 117g | 44°56′N | 93°21′W |
| Saint Lucia, nation, N.A. | 129 | 13°54′N | 60°40′W |
| Saint Lucia Channel, strt., N.A. (lū′shĭ-ȧ) | 133b | 14°15′N | 61°00′W |
| Saint Lucie Canal, can., Fl., U.S. (lū′sė) | 125a | 26°57′N | 80°25′W |
| Saint Magnus Bay, b., Scot., U.K. (măg′nŭs) | 164a | 60°25′N | 2°09′W |
| Saint Malo, Fr. (săɴ′ mȧ-lỏ′) | 161 | 48°40′N | 2°02′W |
| Saint Malo, Golfe de, b., Fr. (gôlf-dĕ-săɴ-mä-lō′) | 161 | 48°50′N | 2°49′W |
| Saint Marc, Haiti (săɴ′ mȧrk′) | 135 | 19°10′N | 72°40′W |
| Saint-Marc, Canal de, strt., Haiti | 135 | 19°05′N | 73°15′W |
| Saint Marcellin, Fr. (mär-sĕ-lăɴ′) | 171 | 45°08′N | 5°15′E |
| Saint Margarets, Md., U.S. | 110e | 39°02′N | 76°30′W |
| Sainte Marie, Cap, c., Madag. | 233 | 25°31′S | 45°00′E |
| Sainte-Marie-aux-Mines, Fr. (săɴ′tĕ-mä-rē′ō-mēn′) | 171 | 48°14′N | 7°08′E |
| Sainte Marie-Beauce, Can. (săɴt′mȧ-rē′) | 99 | 46°27′N | 71°03′W |
| Saint Maries, Id., U.S. (sånt mā′rēs) | 114 | 47°18′N | 116°34′W |
| Saint Martin, i., N.A. (mär′tĭn) | 133b | 18°06′N | 62°54′W |
| Sainte Martine, Can. | 102a | 45°14′N | 73°37′W |
| Saint Martins, Can. (mär′tĭnz) | 100 | 45°21′N | 65°32′W |
| Saint Martinville, La., U.S. (mär′tĭn-vĭl) | 123 | 30°08′N | 91°50′W |
| Saint Mary, r., Can. (mā′rė) | 95 | 49°25′N | 113°00′W |
| Saint Mary, Cape, c., Gam. | 234 | 13°28′N | 16°40′W |
| Saint Mary Reservoir, res., Can. | 95 | 49°30′N | 113°00′W |
| Saint Marys, Austl. (mā′rėz) | 222 | 41°40′S | 148°10′E |
| Saint Marys, Can. | 98 | 43°15′N | 81°10′W |
| Saint Marys, Ga., U.S. | 125 | 30°43′N | 81°35′W |
| Saint Mary's, Ks., U.S. | 121 | 39°12′N | 96°03′W |
| Saint Mary's, Oh., U.S. | 108 | 40°30′N | 84°25′W |
| Saint Marys, Pa., U.S. | 109 | 41°25′N | 78°30′W |
| Saint Marys, W.V., U.S. | 108 | 39°20′N | 81°15′W |
| Saint Marys, r., N.A. | 117k | 46°27′N | 84°33′W |
| Saint Marys, r., U.S. | 125 | 30°37′N | 82°05′W |
| Saint Mary's Bay, b., Can. | 101 | 46°50′N | 53°47′W |
| Saint Mary's Bay, b., Can. | 100 | 44°20′N | 66°10′W |
| Saint Mathew, S.C., U.S. (măth′ū) | 125 | 33°40′N | 80°46′W |
| Saint Matthew, i., Ak., U.S. | 103 | 60°25′N | 172°10′W |
| Saint Matthews, Ky., U.S. (măth′ūz) | 111h | 38°15′N | 85°39′W |
| Saint Maur-des-Fossés, Fr. | 171b | 48°48′N | 2°29′E |
| Saint Maurice, r., Can. (săɴ′ mỏ-rēs′) (sånt mô′rĭs) | 93 | 47°20′N | 72°55′W |
| Saint Michael, Ak., U.S. (sånt mī′kĕl) | 103 | 63°22′N | 162°20′W |
| Saint Michel, Can. (săɴ′mė-shĕl′) | 102b | 46°52′N | 70°54′W |
| Saint Michel, Bras, r., Can. | 102b | 46°47′N | 70°51′W |
| Saint Michel-de-l'Atalaye, Haiti | 135 | 19°25′N | 72°20′W |
| Saint Michel-de-Napierville, Can. | 102a | 45°14′N | 73°34′W |
| Saint Mihiel, Fr. (săɴ′ mē-yĕl′) | 171 | 48°53′N | 5°30′E |
| Saint Nazaire, Fr. (săɴ′nȧ-zâr′) | 154 | 47°18′N | 2°13′W |
| Saint Nérée, Can. (nā-rā′) | 102b | 46°43′N | 70°43′W |
| Saint Nicolas, Can. (ne-kỏ-lä′) | 102b | 46°42′N | 71°22′W |
| Saint Nicolas, Cap, c., Haiti | 135 | 19°45′N | 73°35′W |
| Saint Omer, Fr. (săɴ′tỏ-mâr′) | 170 | 50°44′N | 2°16′E |
| Saint Pascal, Can. (sĕɴ pă-skăl′) | 100 | 47°32′N | 69°48′W |
| Saint Paul, Can. (sånt pôl′) | 90 | 53°59′N | 111°17′W |
| Saint Paul, Mn., U.S. | 105 | 44°57′N | 93°05′W |
| Saint Paul, Ne., U.S. | 112 | 41°13′N | 98°28′W |
| Saint Paul, i., Can. | 101 | 47°15′N | 60°10′W |
| Saint Paul, i., Ak., U.S. | 103 | 57°10′N | 170°20′W |
| Saint Paul, r., Lib. | 234 | 7°10′N | 10°00′W |
| Saint Paul, Île, i., Afr. | 3 | 38°43′S | 77°31′E |
| Saint Paul Park, Mn., U.S. (pärk) | 117g | 44°51′N | 93°00′W |
| Saint Pauls, N.C., U.S. (pôls) | 125 | 34°47′N | 78°57′W |
| Saint Peter, Mn., U.S. (pē tẽr) | 113 | 44°20′N | 93°56′W |
| Saint Peter Port, Guern. | 170 | 49°27′N | 2°35′W |
| Saint Petersburg (Sankt-Peterburg) (Leningrad), Russia | 178 | 59°57′N | 30°20′E |
| Saint Petersburg, Fl., U.S. (pē′tẽrz-bûrg) | 105 | 27°47′N | 82°38′W |
| Sainte Pétronille, Can. (sĕɴt pĕt-rō-nēl′) | 102b | 46°51′N | 71°08′W |
| Saint Philémon, Can. (sĕɴ fēl-mōɴ′) | 102b | 46°41′N | 70°28′W |
| Saint Philippe-d'Argenteuil, Can. (săn′fe-lēp′) | 102a | 45°38′N | 74°25′W |
| Saint Philippe-de-Lapairie, Can. | 102a | 45°20′N | 73°28′W |
| Saint Pierre, Mart. (săn′pyâr′) | 133b | 14°45′N | 61°12′W |
| Saint Pierre, St. P./M. | 101 | 46°47′N | 56°11′W |
| Saint Pierre, i., St. P./M. | 101 | 46°47′N | 56°11′W |
| Saint Pierre, Lac, l., Can. | 99 | 46°07′N | 72°45′W |
| Saint Pierre and Miquelon, dep., N.A. | 93a | 46°53′N | 56°40′W |
| Saint Pierre-d'Orléans, Can. | 102b | 46°53′N | 71°04′W |
| Saint Pierre-Montmagny, Can. | 102b | 46°55′N | 70°37′W |
| Saint Placide, Can. (plăs′ĭd) | 102a | 45°32′N | 74°11′W |
| Saint Pol-de-Léon, Fr. (săɴ-pô′dĕ-lā-ôɴ′) | 170 | 48°41′N | 4°00′W |
| Saint Quentin, Fr. (săɴ′käɴ-tăɴ′) | 161 | 49°52′N | 3°16′E |
| Saint Raphaël, Can. (rä-fä-él′) | 102b | 46°48′N | 70°46′W |

| PLACE (Pronunciation) | PAGE | LAT. | LONG. |
|---|---|---|---|
| Saint Raymond, Can. | 99 | 46°50′N | 71°51′W |
| Saint Rédempteur, Can. (săɴ rā-dāɴp-tûr′) | 102b | 46°42′N | 71°18′W |
| Saint Rémi, Can. (sĕɴ rĕ-mē′) | 102a | 45°15′N | 73°36′W |
| Saint Romuald-d'Etchemin, Can. (sĕɴ rŏ′mo͞o-äl) | 99 | 46°45′N | 71°14′W |
| Sainte Rose, Guad. | 133b | 16°19′N | 61°45′W |
| Saintes, Fr. | 170 | 45°44′N | 0°41′W |
| Sainte Scholastique, Can. (skỏ-lȧs-tēk′) | 102a | 45°39′N | 74°05′W |
| Saint Siméon, Can. | 99 | 47°51′N | 69°55′W |
| Saint Stanislas-de-Kostka, Can. | 102a | 45°11′N | 74°08′W |
| Saint Stephen, Can. (stē′vĕn) | 91 | 45°12′N | 66°17′W |
| Saint Sulpice, Can. | 102a | 45°50′N | 73°21′W |
| Saint Thérèse-de-Blainville, Can. (tĕ-rĕz′ dĕ blĕɴ-vēl′) | 99 | 45°38′N | 73°51′W |
| Saint Thomas, Can. (tŏm′ȧs) | 91 | 42°45′N | 81°15′W |
| Saint Thomas, i., V.I.U.S. | 129 | 18°22′N | 64°57′W |
| Saint Thomas Harbor, b., V.I.U.S. (tŏm′ȧs) | 129c | 18°19′N | 64°56′W |
| Saint Timothée, Can. (tē-mô-tā′) | 102a | 45°17′N | 74°03′W |
| Saint Tropez, Fr. (trỏ-pĕ′) | 171 | 43°15′N | 6°42′E |
| Saint Valentin, Can. (văl-ĕn-tīn) | 102a | 45°07′N | 73°19′W |
| Saint Valéry-sur-Somme, Fr. (vȧ-lā-rē′) | 170 | 50°10′N | 1°39′E |
| Saint Vallier, Can. (väl-yā′) | 102b | 46°54′N | 70°49′W |
| Saint Victor, Can. (vĭk′tẽr) | 99 | 46°09′N | 70°56′W |
| Saint Vincent, Gulf, b., Austl. (vĭn′sĕnt) | 222 | 34°55′S | 138°00′E |
| Saint Vincent and the Grenadines, nation, N.A. | 129 | 13°20′N | 60°50′W |
| Saint Vincent Passage, strt., N.A. | 133b | 13°35′N | 61°10′W |
| Saint Walburg, Can. | 90 | 53°39′N | 109°12′W |
| Saint Yrieix-la-Perche, Fr. (ē-rė-ĕ) | 170 | 45°30′N | 1°08′E |
| Saitama, dept., Japan (sī′tä-mä) | 211a | 35°52′N | 139°40′E |
| Saitbaba, Russia (sá-ĕt′bá-bȧ) | 186a | 54°06′N | 56°42′E |
| Sajama, Nevada, mtn., Bol. (nĕ-vȧ′dä-sä-hȧ′mä) | 142 | 18°13′S | 68°53′W |
| Sakai, Japan (sä′kä-ė) | 210 | 34°34′N | 135°28′E |
| Sakaiminato, Japan | 211 | 35°33′N | 133°15′E |
| Sakākah, Sau. Ar. | 198 | 29°58′N | 40°03′E |
| Sakakawea, Lake, res., N.D., U.S. | 106 | 47°49′N | 101°58′W |
| Sakania, D.R.C. (sȧ-kä′nĭ-ȧ) | 232 | 12°45′S | 28°34′E |
| Sakarya, r., Tur. (sȧ-kär′yȧ) | 198 | 40°10′N | 31°00′E |
| Sakata, Japan (sä′kä-tä) | 205 | 38°56′N | 139°57′E |
| Sakchu, Kor., N. (säk′chỏ) | 210 | 40°29′N | 125°09′E |
| Sakha (Yakutia), prov., Russia | 185 | 65°21′N | 117°13′E |
| Sakhalin, i., Russia (sȧ-kȧ-lēn′) | 179 | 52°00′N | 143°00′E |
| Šakiai, Lith. (shä′kĭ-ī) | 167 | 54°59′N | 23°05′E |
| Sakishima-guntō, is., Japan (sä′kė-shē′ma gỏn′tō′) | 205 | 24°25′N | 125°00′E |
| Sakmara, r., Russia | 181 | 52°00′N | 56°10′E |
| Sakomet, r., R.I., U.S. (sä-kō′mĕt) | 110b | 41°32′N | 71°11′W |
| Sakurai, Japan | 211b | 34°31′N | 135°51′E |
| Sakwaso Lake, l., Can. (sȧ-kwȧ′sō) | 97 | 53°01′N | 91°55′W |
| Sal, i., C.V. (säal) | 230b | 16°45′N | 22°39′W |
| Sal, r., Russia (sȧl) | 181 | 47°30′N | 43°00′E |
| Sal, Cay, i., Bah. (kē săl) | 134 | 23°45′N | 80°25′W |
| Sala, Swe. (sô′lä) | 166 | 59°56′N | 16°34′E |
| Sala Consilina, Italy (sä′lä kỏn-sė-lē′nä) | 174 | 40°24′N | 15°38′E |
| Salada, Laguna, l., Mex. (lä-gỏ′nä-sä-lä′dä) | 118 | 32°34′N | 115°45′W |
| Saladillo, Arg. (sä-lä-dēl′yỏ) | 144 | 35°38′S | 59°48′W |
| Salado, Hond. (sä-lä′dhō) | 132 | 15°44′N | 87°03′W |
| Salado, r., Arg. | 141c | 35°53′S | 58°12′W |
| Salado, r., Arg. | 144 | 37°00′S | 67°00′W |
| Salado, r., Arg. (sä-lä′dỏ) | 144 | 26°05′S | 63°35′W |
| Salado, r., Mex. | 128 | 28°00′N | 102°00′W |
| Salado, r., Mex. (sä-lä′dô) | 131 | 18°30′N | 97°29′W |
| Salado Creek, r., Tx., U.S. | 117d | 29°23′N | 98°25′W |
| Salado de los Nadadores, Río, r., Mex. (dĕ-lỏs-nä-dä-dỏ′rĕs) | 122 | 27°26′N | 101°35′W |
| Salal, Chad | 235 | 14°51′N | 17°13′E |
| Salamanca, Chile (sä-lä-mä′n-kä) | 141b | 31°48′S | 70°57′W |
| Salamanca, Mex. | 128 | 20°36′N | 101°10′W |
| Salamanca, Spain (sä-lä-mä′n-kȧ) | 154 | 40°54′N | 5°42′W |
| Salamanca, N.Y., U.S. (săl-ȧ-măŋ′kȧ) | 109 | 42°10′N | 78°45′W |
| Salamat, Bahr, r., Chad (bär sä-lä-mät′) | 231 | 10°06′N | 19°16′E |
| Salamina, Col. (sä-lä-mē′-nä) | 142a | 5°25′N | 75°29′W |
| Salamína, Grc. | 175 | 37°58′N | 23°30′E |
| Salat-la-Canada, Fr. | 170 | 44°52′N | 1°13′E |
| Salaverry, Peru (sä-lä-vā′rė) | 142 | 8°16′S | 78°54′W |
| Salawati, i., Indon. (sä-lä-wä′tė) | 213 | 1°07′S | 130°52′E |
| Salawe, Tan. | 237 | 3°19′S | 32°52′E |
| Sala y Gómez, Isla, i., Chile | 241 | 26°50′S | 105°50′W |
| Salcedo, Dom. Rep. (säl-sā′dō) | 135 | 19°25′N | 70°30′W |
| Saldaña, r., Col. (säl-dȧ′n-yä) | 142a | 3°42′N | 75°16′W |
| Saldanha, S. Afr. | 232 | 32°55′S | 18°05′E |
| Saldus, Lat. (sȧl′dỏs) | 167 | 56°39′N | 22°30′E |
| Sale, Austl. (sāl) | 222 | 38°10′S | 147°07′E |
| Sale, Eng., U.K. | 158a | 53°24′N | 2°20′W |
| Sale, r., Can. (sȧl′rė-vyâr′) | 102f | 49°44′N | 97°11′W |
| Salekhard, Russia (sŭ-lyĭ-kärt) | 180 | 66°35′N | 66°50′E |
| Salem, India | 199 | 11°39′N | 78°11′E |
| Salem, S. Afr. | 233c | 33°29′S | 26°30′E |
| Salem, Il., U.S. (sā′lĕm) | 108 | 38°40′N | 89°00′W |
| Salem, In., U.S. | 108 | 38°35′N | 86°00′W |
| Salem, Ma., U.S. | 101a | 42°31′N | 70°54′W |
| Salem, Mo., U.S. | 121 | 37°36′N | 91°33′W |
| Salem, N.H., U.S. | 101a | 42°46′N | 71°16′W |
| Salem, N.J., U.S. | 109 | 39°35′N | 75°30′W |
| Salem, Oh., U.S. | 108 | 40°55′N | 80°50′W |
| Salem, Or., U.S. | 104 | 44°55′N | 123°03′W |


ăt; finăl; rāte; senåte; ärm; ȧsk; sofȧ; fâre; ch-choose; dh-as th in other; bē; ėvent; bĕt; recĕnt; cratẽr; g-gō; gh-guttural g; bĭt; ĭ-short neutral; rīde; ĸ-guttural k as ch in German ich;

PRONOUNCING INDEX

Salem – San Felipe 345


| PLACE (Pronunciation) | PAGE | LAT. | LONG. |
|---|---|---|---|
| Salem, S.D., U.S. | 112 | 43°43'N | 97°23'W |
| Salem, Va., U.S. | 125 | 37°16'N | 80°05'W |
| Salem, W.V., U.S. | 108 | 39°15'N | 80°35'W |
| Salemi, Italy (sä-lā'mē) | 174 | 37°49'N | 12°48'E |
| Salerno, Italy (sä-lĕr'nō) | 162 | 40°27'N | 14°46'E |
| Salerno, Golfo di, b., Italy (gôl-fō-dē) | 162 | 40°30'N | 14°40'E |
| Salford, Eng., U.K. (săl'fẽrd) | 164 | 53°26'N | 2°19'W |
| Salgótarján, Hung. (shôl'gō-tôr-yän) | 169 | 48°06'N | 19°50'E |
| Salhyr, r., Ukr. | 177 | 45°25'N | 34°22'E |
| Salida, Co., U.S. (sá-lī'dá) | 120 | 38°31'N | 106°01'W |
| Salies-de-Béan, Fr. | 170 | 43°27'N | 0°58'W |
| Salima, Mwi. | 237 | 13°47'S | 34°26'E |
| Salina, Ks., U.S. (sa-lī'na) | 104 | 38°50'N | 97°37'W |
| Salina, Ut., U.S. | 119 | 39°00'N | 111°55'W |
| Salina, i., Italy (sä-lē'nä) | 174 | 38°35'N | 14°48'E |
| Salina Cruz, Mex. (sä-lē'nä krōōz') | 128 | 16°10'N | 95°12'W |
| Salina Point, c., Bah. | 135 | 22°10'N | 74°20'W |
| Salinas, Mex. | 128 | 22°38'N | 101°42'W |
| Salinas, P.R. | 129b | 17°58'N | 66°16'W |
| Salinas, Ca., U.S. (sa-lē'nas) | 118 | 36°41'N | 121°40'W |
| Salinas, r., Mex. (sä-lē'näs) | 131 | 16°15'N | 90°31'W |
| Salinas, r., Ca., U.S. | 118 | 36°33'N | 121°29'W |
| Salinas, Bahía de, b., N.A. (bä-ē'ä-dĕ-sa-lē'nas) | 132 | 11°05'N | 85°55'W |
| Salinas National Monument, rec., N.M., U.S. | 119 | 34°10'N | 106°05'W |
| Salinas Victoria, Mex. (sä-lē'näs vĕk-tō'rē-ä) | 122 | 25°59'N | 100°19'W |
| Saline, r., Ar., U.S. (sa-lēn') | 121 | 34°06'N | 92°30'W |
| Saline, r., Ks., U.S. | 120 | 39°05'N | 99°43'W |
| Salins-les-Bains, Fr. (sá-lăɴ'-lā-băɴ') | 171 | 46°55'N | 5°54'E |
| Salisbury, Can. | 100 | 46°03'N | 65°05'W |
| Salisbury, Eng., U.K. (sôlz'bē-rē) | 161 | 50°35'N | 1°51'W |
| Salisbury, Md., U.S. | 109 | 38°20'N | 75°40'W |
| Salisbury, Mo., U.S. | 121 | 39°24'N | 92°47'W |
| Salisbury, N.C., U.S. | 125 | 35°40'N | 80°29'W |
| Salisbury *see* Harare, Zimb. | 232 | 17°50'S | 31°03'E |
| Salisbury Island, i., Can. | 93 | 63°36'N | 76°20'W |
| Salisbury Plain, pl., Eng., U.K. | 164 | 51°15'N | 1°52'W |
| Salkehatchie, r., S.C., U.S. (sô-kê-hăch'ē) | 125 | 33°09'N | 81°10'W |
| Sallisaw, Ok., U.S. (săl'ĭ-sô) | 121 | 35°27'N | 94°48'W |
| Salmon, Id., U.S. (săm'ŭn) | 115 | 45°11'N | 113°54'W |
| Salmon, r., Can. | 94 | 54°00'N | 123°50'W |
| Salmon, r., Can. | 100 | 46°19'N | 65°36'W |
| Salmon, r., Id., U.S. | 106 | 45°30'N | 115°45'W |
| Salmon, r., N.Y., U.S. | 109 | 44°35'N | 74°15'W |
| Salmon, r., Wa., U.S. | 116c | 45°44'N | 122°36'W |
| Salmon, Middle Fork, r., Id., U.S. | 114 | 44°50'N | 114°52'W |
| Salmon Arm, Can. | 95 | 50°42'N | 119°16'W |
| Salmon Falls Creek, r., Id., U.S. | 115 | 42°22'N | 114°53'W |
| Salmon Gums, Austl. (gŭmz) | 218 | 33°00'S | 122°00'E |
| Salmon River Mountains, mts., Id., U.S. | 106 | 44°15'N | 115°44'W |
| Salon-de-Provence, Fr. (sá-lôɴ-dē-prô-văɴs') | 171 | 43°48'N | 5°09'E |
| Salonika *see* Thessaloníki, Grc. | 154 | 40°38'N | 22°59'E |
| Salonta, Rom. (sä-lôn'tä) | 169 | 46°46'N | 21°38'E |
| Saloum, r., Sen. | 234 | 14°10'N | 15°45'W |
| Salsette Island, i., India | 203b | 19°12'N | 72°52'E |
| Sal'sk, Russia (sälsk) | 181 | 46°30'N | 41°20'E |
| Salt, r., Az., U.S. (sôlt) | 106 | 33°28'N | 111°35'W |
| Salt, r., Mo., U.S. | 121 | 39°54'N | 92°11'W |
| Salta, Arg. (säl'tä) | 144 | 24°50'S | 65°16'W |
| Salta, prov., Arg. | 144 | 25°15'S | 65°00'W |
| Saltair, Ut., U.S. (sôlt'âr) | 117b | 40°46'N | 112°09'W |
| Salt Cay, i., T./C. Is. | 135 | 21°20'N | 71°15'W |
| Salt Creek, r., Il., U.S. (sôlt) | 111a | 42°01'N | 88°01'W |
| Saltillo, Mex. (säl-tēl'yō) | 128 | 25°24'N | 100°59'W |
| Salt Lake City, Ut., U.S. (sôlt lāk sĭ'tĭ) | 104 | 40°45'N | 111°52'W |
| Salto, Arg. (säl'tō) | 141c | 34°17'S | 60°15'W |
| Salto, Ur. | 144 | 31°18'S | 57°45'W |
| Salto, r., Mex. | 130 | 22°16'N | 99°18'W |
| Salto, Serra do, mtn., Braz. (sĕ'r-rä-dō) | 141a | 20°26'S | 43°28'W |
| Salto Grande, Braz. (grän'dä) | 143 | 22°57'S | 49°58'W |
| Salton Sea, Ca., U.S. (sôlt'ŭn) | 118 | 33°28'N | 115°43'W |
| Salton Sea, l., Ca., U.S. | 106 | 33°19'N | 115°50'W |
| Saltpond, Ghana | 230 | 5°16'N | 1°07'W |
| Salt River Indian Reservation, I.R., Az., U.S. (sôlt rĭv'ẽr) | 119 | 33°40'N | 112°01'W |
| Saltsjöbaden, Swe. (sält'shû-bäd'ĕn) | 166 | 59°15'N | 18°20'E |
| Saltspring Island, i., Can. (sält'sprĭng) | 94 | 48°47'N | 123°30'W |
| Saltville, Va., U.S. (sôlt'vĭl) | 125 | 36°50'N | 81°45'W |
| Saltykovka, Russia (sál-tē'kôf-ká) | 186b | 55°45'N | 37°56'E |
| Salud, Mount, mtn., Pan. (sä-lōō'th) | 128a | 9°14'N | 79°42'W |
| Saluda, S.C., U.S. (sá-lōō'da) | 125 | 34°02'N | 81°46'W |
| Saluda, r., S.C., U.S. | 125 | 34°07'N | 81°48'W |
| Saluzzo, Italy (sä-lōōt'sō) | 174 | 44°39'N | 7°31'E |
| Salvador, Braz. (säl-vä-dōr') (bä-ē'ä) | 143 | 12°59'S | 38°27'W |
| Salvador Lake, l., La., U.S. | 123 | 29°45'N | 90°20'W |
| Salvador Point, c., Bah. | 134 | 24°30'N | 77°45'W |
| Salvatierra, Mex. (säl-vä-tyĕr'rä) | 130 | 20°13'N | 100°52'W |
| Salween, r., Asia | 196 | 21°00'N | 98°00'E |
| Salyan, Azer. | 181 | 39°40'N | 49°10'E |
| Salzburg, Aus. (sälts'bŏorgh) | 161 | 47°48'N | 13°04'E |
| Salzwedel, Ger. (sälts-vā'dĕl) | 168 | 52°51'N | 11°10'E |
| Samālūt, Egypt (sä-mä-lōōt') | 200 | 28°17'N | 30°43'E |
| Samana, Cabo, c., Dom. Rep. | 129 | 19°20'N | 69°00'W |
| Samana or Atwood Cay, i., Bah. | 135 | 23°05'N | 73°45'W |
| Samar, i., Phil. (sä'mär) | 213 | 11°30'N | 126°07'E |
| Samara (Kuybyshev), Russia | 180 | 53°10'N | 50°05'E |
| Samara, r., Russia | 181 | 52°50'N | 50°35'E |
| Samara, r., Ukr. (sá-mä'rá) | 177 | 48°47'N | 35°30'E |
| Samarai, Pap. N. Gui. (sä-mä-rä'ē) | 213 | 10°45'S | 150°49'E |
| Samarinda, Indon. | 212 | 0°30'S | 117°10'E |
| Samarkand, Uzb. (sá-már-känt') | 183 | 39°42'N | 67°00'E |
| Şamaxı, Azer. | 181 | 40°35'N | 48°40'E |
| Samba, D.R.C. | 237 | 4°38'S | 26°22'E |
| Sambalpur, India (sŭm'bŭl-pŏor) | 199 | 21°30'N | 84°05'E |
| Sāmbhar, r., India | 202 | 27°00'N | 74°58'E |
| Sambir, Ukr. | 169 | 49°31'N | 23°12'E |
| Samborombón, r., Arg. | 141c | 35°20'S | 57°52'W |
| Samborombón, Bahía, b., Arg. (bä-ē'ä-säm-bô-rôm-bô'n) | 141c | 35°57'S | 57°05'W |
| Sambre, r., Eur. (säɴ'br') | 165 | 50°20'N | 4°15'E |
| Sambungo, Ang. | 236 | 8°39'S | 20°43'E |
| Sammamish, r., Wa., U.S. | 116a | 47°43'N | 122°08'W |
| Sammamish, Lake, l., Wa., U.S. (sa-măm'ĭsh) | 116a | 47°35'N | 122°02'W |
| Samoa, nation, Oc. | 2 | 14°30'S | 172°00'W |
| Samoa Islands, is., Oc. | 214a | 14°00'S | 171°00'W |
| Samokov, Blg. (sä'mô-kôf) | 175 | 42°20'N | 23°33'E |
| Samora Correia, Port. (sä-mô'rä-kôr-rē'yä) | 173b | 38°55'N | 8°52'W |
| Samorovo, Russia (sá-má-rô'vô) | 184 | 60°47'N | 69°13'E |
| Sámos, i., Grc. (sä'mŏs) | 163 | 37°53'N | 26°35'E |
| Samothráki, i., Grc. | 163 | 40°23'N | 25°10'E |
| Sampaloc Point, c., Phil. (säm-pä'lôk) | 213a | 14°43'N | 119°56'E |
| Sam Rayburn Reservoir, res., Tx., U.S. | 123 | 31°10'N | 94°15'W |
| Samson, Al., U.S. (săm'sŭn) | 124 | 31°06'N | 86°02'W |
| Samsu, Kor., N. (säm'sōō') | 210 | 41°12'N | 128°00'E |
| Samsun, Tur. (sám'sōōn') | 198 | 41°20'N | 36°05'E |
| Samtredia, Geor. (sám'trĕ-dē) | 181 | 42°18'N | 42°25'E |
| Samuel, i., Can. (săm'ū-ĕl) | 116d | 48°50'N | 123°10'W |
| Samur, r. (sä-mōōr') | 181 | 41°40'N | 47°20'E |
| San, Mali (sän) | 230 | 13°18'N | 4°54'W |
| San, r., Eur. | 161 | 50°33'N | 22°12'E |
| Şan'ā', Yemen (sän'ä) | 198 | 15°17'N | 44°05'E |
| Sanaga, r., Cam. (sä-nä'gä) | 230 | 4°30'N | 12°00'E |
| San Ambrosio, Isla, i., Chile (ē's-lä-dĕ-sän äm-brō'zē-ō) | 139 | 26°40'S | 80°00'W |
| Sanana, Pulau, i., Indon. | 213 | 2°15'S | 126°38'E |
| Sanandaj, Iran | 198 | 36°44'N | 46°43'E |
| San Andreas, Ca., U.S. (săn ăn'drē-ăs) | 118 | 38°10'N | 120°42'W |
| San Andreas, l., Ca., U.S. | 116b | 37°36'N | 122°26'W |
| San Andrés, Col. (sän-än-drĕ's) | 142a | 6°57'N | 75°41'W |
| San Andrés, Mex. (sän än-drās') | 131a | 19°15'N | 99°10'W |
| San Andrés, i., Col. | 133 | 12°32'N | 81°34'W |
| San Andres, Laguna de, l., Mex. | 131 | 22°40'N | 97°50'W |
| San Andres Mountains, mts., N.M., U.S. (săn ăn'drē-ăs) | 106 | 33°00'N | 106°40'W |
| San Andrés Tuxtla, Mex. (sän-än-drā's-tōōs'tlä) | 128 | 18°27'N | 95°12'W |
| San Angelo, Tx., U.S. (săn ăn-jĕ-lō) | 104 | 31°28'N | 100°22'W |
| San Antioco, Isola di, i., Italy (ē'sō-lä-dē-sän-än-tyō'kō) | 174 | 39°00'N | 8°25'E |
| San Antonio, Chile (sän-án-tō'nyō) | 144 | 33°34'S | 71°36'W |
| San Antonio, Col. | 142a | 2°57'N | 75°06'W |
| San Antonio, Col. | 142a | 3°55'N | 75°28'W |
| San Antonio, Phil. | 213a | 14°57'N | 120°05'E |
| San Antonio, Tx., U.S. (săn ăn-tō'nē-ō) | 104 | 29°25'N | 98°30'W |
| San Antonio, r., Tx., U.S. | 123 | 29°00'N | 97°58'W |
| San Antonio, Cabo, c., Cuba (ká'bô-sän-än-tô'nyô) | 129 | 21°55'N | 84°55'W |
| San Antonio, Lake, res., Ca., U.S. | 118 | 36°00'N | 121°13'W |
| San Antonio Bay, b., Tx., U.S. | 123 | 28°20'N | 97°08'W |
| San Antonio de Areco, Arg. (dā ä-rä'kō) | 141c | 34°16'S | 59°30'W |
| San Antonio de las Vegas, Cuba | 135a | 22°51'N | 82°23'W |
| San Antonio de los Baños, Cuba (dā lōs bän'yōs) | 134 | 22°54'N | 82°30'W |
| San Antonio de los Cobres, Arg. (dā lōs kō'brās) | 144 | 24°15'S | 66°29'W |
| San Antonio de Pádua, Braz. (dĕ-pá'dwä) | 141a | 21°32'S | 42°09'W |
| San Antonio de Tamanaco, Ven. | 143b | 9°42'N | 66°03'W |
| San Antonio Oeste, Arg. (sän-nä-tō'nyō ō-ĕs'tå) | 144 | 40°49'S | 64°56'W |
| San Antonio Peak, mtn., Ca., U.S. (săn ăn-tō'nĭ-ō) | 117a | 34°17'N | 117°39'W |
| Sanarate, Guat. (sä-nä-rä'tĕ) | 132 | 14°47'N | 90°12'W |
| San Augustine, Tx., U.S. (săn ô'gŭs-tēn) | 123 | 31°33'N | 94°08'W |
| San Bartolo, Mex. (sän bär-tō'lô) | 131a | 19°36'N | 99°43'W |
| San Bartolo, Mex. | 122 | 24°43'N | 103°12'W |
| San Bartolomeo, Italy (bär-tô-lô-mā'ô) | 174 | 41°25'N | 15°04'E |
| San Benedetto del Tronto, Italy (bā'nā-dĕt'tō dĕl trōn'tô) | 174 | 42°58'N | 13°54'E |
| San Benito, Tx., U.S. (săn bĕ-nē'tô) | 123 | 26°07'N | 97°37'W |
| San Benito, r., Ca., U.S. | 118 | 36°40'N | 121°20'W |
| San Bernardino, Ca., U.S. (bûr-när-dē'nō) | 104 | 34°07'N | 117°19'W |
| San Bernardino Mountains, mts., Ca., U.S. | 118 | 34°05'N | 116°23'W |
| San Bernardo, Chile (sän bĕr-när'dô) | 141b | 33°35'S | 70°42'W |
| San Blas, Mex. (sän bläs') | 128 | 21°33'N | 105°19'W |
| San Blas, Cape, c., Fl., U.S. | 107 | 29°38'N | 85°38'W |
| San Blas, Cordillera de, mts., Pan. | 133 | 9°17'N | 78°20'W |
| San Blas, Golfo de, b., Pan. | 133 | 9°33'N | 78°42'W |
| San Blas, Punta, c., Pan. | 133 | 9°35'N | 78°55'W |
| San Bruno, Ca., U.S. (săn brū-nō) | 116b | 37°38'N | 122°25'W |
| San Buenaventura, Mex. (bwā'ná-vĕn-tōō'rá) | 122 | 27°07'N | 101°30'W |
| San Carlos, Chile (sän-ká'r-lōs) | 144 | 36°23'S | 71°58'W |
| San Carlos, Col. | 142a | 6°11'N | 74°58'W |
| San Carlos, Eq. Gui. | 236 | 3°27'N | 8°33'E |
| San Carlos, Mex. (sän kär'lōs) | 131 | 17°49'N | 92°33'W |
| San Carlos, Mex. | 122 | 24°36'N | 98°52'W |
| San Carlos, Nic. (sän-kä'r-lôs) | 133 | 11°08'N | 84°48'W |
| San Carlos, Phil. | 213a | 15°56'N | 120°20'E |
| San Carlos, Ca., U.S. (săn kär'lōs) | 116b | 37°30'N | 122°15'W |
| San Carlos, Ven. | 142 | 9°36'N | 68°35'W |
| San Carlos, r., C.R. | 133 | 10°36'N | 84°18'W |
| San Carlos de Bariloche, Arg. | 144 | 41°15'S | 71°26'W |
| San Carlos Indian Reservation, I.R., Az., U.S. (săn kär'lōs) | 119 | 33°27'N | 110°15'W |
| San Carlos Lake, res., Az., U.S. | 119 | 33°05'N | 110°29'W |
| San Casimiro, Ven. (kä-sē-mē'rō) | 143b | 10°01'N | 67°02'W |
| San Cataldo, Italy (kä-täl'dō) | 174 | 37°30'N | 13°59'E |
| Sánchez, Dom. Rep. (sän'chĕz) | 129 | 19°15'N | 69°40'W |
| Sanchez, Río de los, r., Mex. (rē'ō-dĕ-lôs) | 130 | 20°31'N | 102°29'W |
| Sánchez Román, Mex. (rō-mä'n) | 130 | 21°48'N | 103°20'W |
| San Clemente, Spain (sän klå-mĕn'tå) | 172 | 39°25'N | 2°24'W |
| San Clemente Island, i., Ca., U.S. | 106 | 32°54'N | 118°29'W |
| San Cristóbal, Dom. Rep. (krēs-tô'bäl) | 135 | 18°25'N | 70°05'W |
| San Cristóbal, Guat. | 132 | 15°22'N | 90°26'W |
| San Cristóbal, Ven. | 142 | 7°43'N | 72°15'W |
| San Cristobal, i., Sol. Is. | 221 | 10°47'S | 162°17'E |
| San Cristóbal de las Casas, Mex. | 128 | 16°44'N | 92°39'W |
| Sancti Spíritus, Cuba (säŋk'tē spē'rē-tōōs) | 129 | 21°55'N | 79°25'W |
| Sancti Spiritus, prov., Cuba | 134 | 22°05'N | 79°20'W |
| Sancy, Puy de, mtn., Fr. (pwē-dĕ-säɴ-sē') | 161 | 45°30'N | 2°53'E |
| Sand, i., Or., U.S. (sănd) | 116c | 46°16'N | 124°01'W |
| Sand, i., Wi., U.S. | 113 | 46°03'N | 91°09'W |
| Sand, r., S. Afr. | 233c | 28°30'S | 29°30'E |
| Sand, r., S. Afr. | 238c | 28°09'S | 26°46'E |
| Sanda, Japan (sän'dä) | 211 | 34°53'N | 135°14'E |
| Sandakan, Malay. (sán-dä'kán) | 212 | 5°51'N | 118°03'E |
| Sanday, i., Scot., U.K. (sănd'ā) | 164a | 59°17'N | 2°25'W |
| Sandbach, Eng., U.K. (sănd'băch) | 158a | 53°08'N | 2°22'W |
| Sandefjord, Nor. (sän'dĕ-fyôr') | 166 | 59°09'N | 10°14'E |
| San de Fuca, Wa., U.S. (de-fōō-cä) | 116a | 48°14'N | 122°44'W |
| Sanders, Az., U.S. | 119 | 35°13'N | 109°20'W |
| Sanderson, Tx., U.S. (săn'dẽr-sŭn) | 122 | 30°09'N | 102°24'W |
| Sandersville, Ga., U.S. (săn'dẽrz-vĭl) | 125 | 32°57'N | 82°50'W |
| Sandhammaren, c., Swe. (sänt'häm-mår) | 160 | 55°24'N | 14°37'E |
| Sand Hills, reg., Ne., U.S. (sănd) | 112 | 41°57'N | 101°29'W |
| Sand Hook, N.J., U.S. (sănd hŏok) | 110a | 40°29'N | 74°05'W |
| Sandhurst, Eng., U.K. (sănd'hûrst) | 158b | 51°20'N | 0°48'W |
| Sandia Indian Reservation, I.R., N.M., U.S. | 119 | 35°15'N | 106°30'W |
| San Diego, Ca., U.S. (săn dē-ā'gō) | 104 | 32°43'N | 117°10'W |
| San Diego, Tx., U.S. | 120 | 27°47'N | 98°13'W |
| San Diego, r., Ca., U.S. | 118 | 32°53'N | 116°57'W |
| San Diego de la Unión, Mex. (sän dē-ā-gô dā lä ōō-nyōn') | 130 | 21°27'N | 100°52'W |
| Sandies Creek, r., Tx., U.S. (sănd'ēz) | 123 | 29°13'N | 97°34'W |
| San Dimas, Mex. (dē-mäs') | 130 | 24°08'N | 105°57'W |
| San Dimas, Ca., U.S. (săn dē-más) | 117a | 34°07'N | 117°49'W |
| Sandnes, Nor. (sänd'nĕs) | 166 | 58°52'N | 5°44'E |
| Sandoa, D.R.C. (sän-dō'á) | 232 | 9°39'S | 23°00'E |
| Sandomierz, Pol. (sán-dô'myĕzh) | 169 | 50°39'N | 21°45'E |
| San Doná di Piave, Italy (sän dô ná' dē pyä'vĕ) | 174 | 45°38'N | 12°34'E |
| Sandoway, Mya. (sän-dō-wī') | 199 | 18°24'N | 94°28'E |
| Sandpoint, Id., U.S. (sănd point) | 114 | 48°17'N | 116°34'W |
| Sandringham, Austl. (săn'drĭng-ăm) | 217a | 37°57'S | 145°01'E |
| Sandrio, Italy (sä'n-dryô) | 174 | 46°11'N | 9°53'E |
| Sand Springs, Ok., U.S. (sănd sprĭnz) | 121 | 36°08'N | 96°06'W |
| Sandstone, Austl. (sănd'stōn) | 218 | 28°00'S | 119°25'E |
| Sandstone, Mn., U.S. | 113 | 46°08'N | 92°53'W |
| Sanduo, China (sän-dwô) | 206 | 32°49'N | 119°39'E |
| Sandusky, Al., U.S. (săn-dŭs'kē) | 110h | 33°32'N | 86°50'W |
| Sandusky, Mi., U.S. | 108 | 43°25'N | 82°50'W |
| Sandusky, Oh., U.S. | 105 | 41°25'N | 82°45'W |
| Sandusky, r., Oh., U.S. | 108 | 41°10'N | 83°20'W |
| Sandwich, Il., U.S. (sănd'wĭch) | 108 | 42°35'N | 88°53'W |
| Sandy, Or., U.S. (sănd'ē) | 116c | 45°24'N | 122°16'W |
| Sandy, Ut., U.S. | 117b | 40°36'N | 111°53'W |
| Sandy, r., Or., U.S. | 116c | 45°28'N | 122°17'W |
| Sandy Cape, c., Austl. | 221 | 24°25'S | 153°10'E |
| Sandy Hook, Ct., U.S. (hŏok) | 110a | 41°25'N | 73°17'W |
| Sandy Lake, l., Can. | 102g | 53°46'N | 113°58'W |
| Sandy Lake, l., Can. | 101 | 49°16'N | 57°00'W |
| Sandy Lake, l., Can. | 97 | 53°00'N | 93°07'W |
| Sandy Point, Tx., U.S. | 123a | 29°22'N | 95°27'W |
| Sandy Point, c., Wa., U.S. | 116d | 48°48'N | 122°42'W |
| Sandy Springs, Ga., U.S. (springz) | 110c | 33°55'N | 84°23'W |
| San Estanislao, Para. (ĕs-tä-nēs-lá'ō) | 144 | 24°38'S | 56°20'W |
| San Esteban, Hond. (ĕs-tĕ'bän) | 132 | 15°13'N | 85°53'W |
| San Fabian, Phil. (fä-byä'n) | 213a | 16°14'N | 120°28'E |
| San Felipe, Chile (fĕ-lē'pä) | 144 | 32°45'S | 70°43'W |
| San Felipe, Mex. (fĕ-lē'pĕ) | 130 | 21°29'N | 101°13'W |
| San Felipe, Mex. | 130 | 22°21'N | 105°26'W |
| San Felipe, Ven. (fĕ-lē'pĕ) | 142 | 10°13'N | 68°45'W |
| San Felipe, Cayos de, is., Cuba (kä'yōs-dĕ-sän-fĕ-lē'pĕ) | 134 | 22°00'N | 83°30'W |


ng-sing; ŋ-baŋk; ɴ-nasalized n; nŏd; cŏmmit; ōld; ôbey; ôrder; oi-boil; fōōd; ŏo-as oo in foot; ou-out; s-soft; sh-dish; th-thin; pūre; ûnite; ûrn; stŭd; circŭs; ü-as in French tu; '-indeterminate vowel.

346 San Felipe Creek – San Sebastian

PRONOUNCING INDEX


| PLACE (Pronunciation) | PAGE | LAT. | LONG. |
|---|---|---|---|
| San Felipe Creek, r., Ca., U.S. (săn fē-lēp′å) | 118 | 33°10′N | 116°03′W |
| San Felipe Indian Reservation, I.R., N.M., U.S. | 119 | 35°26′N | 106°26′W |
| San Félix, Isla, i., Chile (ē′s-lä-dĕ-sän fā-lēks′) | 139 | 26°20′S | 80°10′W |
| San Fernanda, Spain (fĕr-nä′n-dä) | 172 | 36°28′N | 6°13′W |
| San Fernando, Arg. (fĕr-nà′n-dô) | 144a | 34°26′S | 58°34′W |
| San Fernando, Chile | 141b | 35°36′S | 70°58′W |
| San Fernando, Mex. (fĕr-nän′dô) | 122 | 24°52′N | 98°10′W |
| San Fernando, Phil. (sän fĕr-nä′n-dô) | 212 | 16°38′N | 120°19′E |
| San Fernando, Ca., U.S. (fĕr-năn′dô) | 117a | 34°17′N | 118°27′W |
| San Fernando, r., Mex. (sän fĕr-nän′dô) | 122 | 25°07′N | 98°25′W |
| San Fernando de Apure, Ven. (sän-fĕr-nä′n-dō-dĕ-ä-pōō′rå) | 142 | 7°46′N | 67°29′W |
| San Fernando de Atabapo, Ven. (dĕ-ä-tä-bä′pô) | 142 | 3°58′N | 67°41′W |
| San Fernando de Henares, Spain (dĕ-ā-nä′rås) | 173a | 40°23′N | 3°31′W |
| Sånfjället, mtn., Swe. | 160 | 62°19′N | 13°30′E |
| Sanford, Can. (săn′fĕrd) | 102f | 49°41′N | 97°27′W |
| Sanford, Fl., U.S. (săn′fôrd) | 105 | 28°46′N | 81°18′W |
| Sanford, Me., U.S. (săn′fĕrd) | 100 | 43°26′N | 70°47′W |
| Sanford, N.C., U.S. | 125 | 35°26′N | 79°10′W |
| San Francisco, Arg. (sän frän′sēs′kô) | 144 | 31°23′S | 62°09′W |
| San Francisco, El Sal. | 132 | 13°48′N | 88°11′W |
| San Francisco, Ca., U.S. | 104 | 37°45′N | 122°26′W |
| San Francisco, r., N.M., U.S. | 119 | 33°35′N | 108°55′W |
| San Francisco Bay, b., Ca., U.S. (săn frăn′sĭs′kô) | 118 | 37°45′N | 122°21′W |
| San Francisco del Oro, Mex. (dĕl ō′rō) | 128 | 27°00′N | 106°37′W |
| San Francisco del Rincón, Mex. (dĕl rēn-kōn′) | 130 | 21°01′N | 101°51′W |
| San Francisco de Macaira, Ven. (dĕ-mä-kī′rä) | 143b | 9°58′N | 66°17′W |
| San Francisco de Macoris, Dom. Rep. (dā-mä-kō′rēs) | 135 | 19°20′N | 70°15′W |
| San Francisco de Paula, Cuba (dā pou′lä) | 135a | 23°04′N | 82°18′W |
| San Gabriel, Ca., U.S. (săn gä-brē-ĕl′) (gā′brē-ĕl) | 117a | 34°06′N | 118°06′W |
| San Gabriel, r., Ca., U.S. | 117a | 33°47′N | 118°06′W |
| San Gabriel Chilac, Mex. (sän-gä-brē-ĕl-chē-läk′) | 131 | 18°19′N | 97°22′W |
| San Gabriel Mts, Ca., U.S. | 117a | 34°17′N | 118°03′W |
| San Gabriel Reservoir, res., Ca., U.S. | 117a | 34°14′N | 117°48′W |
| Sangamon, r., Il., U.S. (săn′gá-msion) | 121 | 40°08′N | 90°08′W |
| Sanger, Ca., U.S. (săng′ẽr) | 118 | 36°42′N | 119°33′W |
| Sangerhausen, Ger. (säng′ĕr-hou-zĕn) | 168 | 51°28′N | 11°17′E |
| Sangha, r., Afr. | 231 | 2°40′N | 16°10′E |
| Sangihe, Pulau, i., Indon. | 213 | 3°30′N | 125°30′E |
| San Gil, Col. (sän-kĕ′l) | 142 | 6°32′N | 73°13′W |
| San Giovanni in Fiore, Italy (sän jô-vän′nē ēn fyō′rå) | 174 | 39°15′N | 16°40′E |
| San Giuseppe Vesuviano, Italy | 173c | 40°36′N | 14°31′E |
| Sangju, Kor., S. (säng′jōō′) | 210 | 36°20′N | 128°07′E |
| Sāngli, India | 199 | 16°56′N | 74°38′E |
| Sangmélima, Cam. | 235 | 2°56′N | 11°59′E |
| San Gorgonio Mountain, mtn., Ca., U.S. (săn gôr-gō′nĭ-ō) | 117a | 34°06′N | 116°50′W |
| Sangre de Cristo Mountains, mts., U.S. | 106 | 37°45′N | 105°50′W |
| San Gregoria, Ca., U.S. (săn grĕ-gôr′ă) | 116b | 37°20′N | 122°23′W |
| Sangro, r., Italy (säng′grô) | 174 | 41°38′N | 13°56′E |
| Sangüesa, Spain (sän-gwĕ′sä) | 172 | 42°36′N | 1°15′W |
| Sanhe, China (sän-hŭ) | 206 | 39°59′N | 117°06′E |
| Sanibel Island, i., Fl., U.S. (săn′ĭ-bĕl) | 125a | 26°26′N | 82°15′W |
| San Ignacio, Belize | 132a | 17°11′N | 89°04′W |
| San Ildefonso, Cape, c., Phil. (sän-ēl-dĕ-fōn-sô) | 213a | 16°03′N | 122°10′E |
| San Ildefonso o la Granja, Spain (ō lä grän′khä) | 172 | 40°54′N | 4°02′W |
| San Isidro, Arg. (ē-sē′drô) | 141c | 34°28′S | 58°31′W |
| San Isidro, C.R. | 133 | 9°24′N | 83°43′W |
| San Jacinto, Phil. (sän hä-sēn′tô) | 213a | 12°33′N | 123°43′E |
| San Jacinto, Ca., U.S. (săn já-sĭn′tô) | 117a | 33°47′N | 116°57′W |
| San Jacinto, r., Ca., U.S. (săn já-sĭn′tô) | 117a | 33°44′N | 117°14′W |
| San Jacinto, r., Tx., U.S. | 123 | 30°25′N | 95°05′W |
| San Jacinto, West Fork, r., Tx., U.S. | 123 | 30°35′N | 95°37′W |
| San Javier, Chile (sän-hà-vē′ĕr) | 141b | 35°35′S | 71°43′W |
| San Jerónimo, Mex. | 131a | 19°31′N | 98°46′W |
| San Jerónimo de Juárez, Mex. (hå-rō′nē-mô då hwä′råz) | 130 | 17°08′N | 100°30′W |
| San Joaquin, Ven. | 143b | 10°16′N | 67°47′W |
| San Joaquin, r., Ca., U.S. (săn hwä-kēn′) | 118 | 37°10′N | 120°51′W |
| San Joaquin Valley, Ca., U.S. | 118 | 36°45′N | 120°30′W |
| San Jorge, Golfo, b., Arg. (gôl-fô-sän-kô′r-kĕ) | 144 | 46°15′S | 66°45′W |
| San José, C.R. (sän hô-sā′) | 129 | 9°57′N | 84°05′W |
| San Jose, Phil. | 213a | 12°22′N | 121°04′E |
| San Jose, Phil. | 213a | 15°49′N | 120°57′E |
| San Jose, Ca., U.S. (săn hô-zā′) | 104 | 37°20′N | 121°54′W |
| San José, i., Mex. (kô-sĕ′) | 128 | 25°00′N | 110°35′W |
| San José, Isla de, i., Pan. (ē′s-lä-dĕ-sän hô-sā′) | 133 | 8°17′N | 79°20′W |
| San Jose, Rio, r., N.M., U.S. (săn hô-zā′) | 119 | 35°15′N | 108°10′W |
| San José de Feliciano, Arg. (då lä ĕs-kē′nà) | 144 | 30°26′S | 58°44′W |
| San José de Gauribe, Ven. (sän-hô-sĕ′dĕ-gàōō-rē′bĕ) | 143b | 9°51′N | 65°49′W |
| San José de las Lajas, Cuba (sän-kô-sĕ′dĕ-läs-lá′käs) | 135a | 22°58′N | 82°10′W |
| San José Iturbide, Mex. (ē-tōōr-bē′dĕ) | 130 | 21°00′N | 100°24′W |
| San Juan, Arg. (hwän′) | 144 | 31°36′S | 68°29′W |
| San Juan, Col. (hòá′n) | 142a | 3°23′N | 73°48′W |
| San Juan, Dom. Rep. (sän hwän′) | 135 | 18°50′N | 71°15′W |
| San Juan, Phil. | 213a | 16°41′N | 120°20′E |
| San Juan, P.R. (sän hwän′) | 129 | 18°30′N | 66°10′W |
| San Juan, prov., Arg. | 144 | 31°00′S | 69°30′W |
| San Juan, r., Mex. (sän-hōō-än′) | 131 | 18°10′N | 95°23′W |
| San Juan, r., N.A. | 129 | 10°58′N | 84°18′W |
| San Juan, r., U.S. | 106 | 36°30′N | 109°00′W |
| San Juan, Cabezas de, c., P.R. | 129b | 18°29′N | 65°30′W |
| San Juan, Cabo, c., Eq. Gui. | 236 | 1°08′N | 9°23′E |
| San Juan, Pico, mtn., Cuba (pē′kô-sän-kóà′n) | 134 | 21°55′N | 80°00′W |
| San Juan, Río, r., Mex. (rē′ō-sän-hwän) | 122 | 25°35′N | 99°15′W |
| San Juan Bautista, Para. (sän hwän′ bou-tēs′tä) | 144 | 26°48′S | 57°09′W |
| San Juan Capistrano, Mex. (sän-hōō-än′ kä-pēs-trä′nô) | 130 | 22°41′N | 104°07′W |
| San Juan Creek, r., Ca., U.S. (săn hwän′) | 118 | 35°24′N | 120°12′W |
| San Juan de Guadalupe, Mex. (sän hwan då gwä-dhä-lōō′på) | 122 | 24°37′N | 102°43′W |
| San Juan del Norte, Nic. | 133 | 10°55′N | 83°44′W |
| San Juan del Norte, Bahía de, b., Nic. | 133 | 11°12′N | 83°40′W |
| San Juan de los Lagos, Mex. (sän-hōō-än′då los lä′gôs) | 130 | 21°15′N | 102°18′W |
| San Juan de los Lagos, r., Mex. (då lōs lä′gôs) | 130 | 21°13′N | 102°12′W |
| San Juan de los Morros, Ven. (dĕ-lôs-mô′r-rôs) | 143b | 9°54′N | 67°22′W |
| San Juan del Río, Mex. | 130 | 20°21′N | 99°59′W |
| San Juan del Río, Mex. (sän hwän del rē′ō) | 122 | 24°47′N | 104°29′W |
| San Juan del Sur, Nic. (dĕl sōōr) | 128 | 11°15′N | 85°53′W |
| San Juan Evangelista, Mex. (sän-hōō-ä′n-å-väŋ-kå-lēs′ta′) | 131 | 17°57′N | 95°08′W |
| San Juan Island, i., Wa., U.S. | 116a | 48°28′N | 123°08′W |
| San Juan Islands, is., Can. (săn hwän) | 94 | 48°49′N | 123°14′W |
| San Juan Islands, is., Wa., U.S. | 186a | 48°36′N | 122°50′W |
| San Juan Ixtenco, Mex. (ēx-tĕ′n-kô) | 131 | 19°14′N | 97°52′W |
| San Juan Martínez, Cuba | 134 | 22°15′N | 83°50′W |
| San Juan Mountains, mts., Co., U.S. (san hwán′) | 106 | 37°50′N | 107°30′W |
| San Julián, Arg. (sän hōō-lyá′n) | 144 | 49°17′S | 68°02′W |
| San Justo, Arg. (hōōs′tô) | 144a | 34°40′S | 58°33′W |
| Sankanbiriwa, mtn., S.L. | 234 | 8°56′N | 10°48′W |
| Sankarani, r., Afr. (säŋ′kä-rä′nē) | 230 | 11°10′N | 8°35′W |
| Sankt Gallen, Switz. | 161 | 47°25′N | 9°22′E |
| Sankt Moritz, Switz. (sånt mō′rĭts) (zäŋkt mō′rēts) | 168 | 46°31′N | 9°50′E |
| Sankt Pölten, Aus. (zäŋkt-pûl′tĕn) | 168 | 48°12′N | 15°38′E |
| Sankt Veit, Aus. (zäŋkt vīt′) | 168 | 46°46′N | 14°20′E |
| Sankuru, r., D.R.C. (sän-kōō′rōō) | 232 | 4°00′S | 22°35′E |
| San Lázaro, Cabo, c., Mex. (sän-lá′zä-rō) | 128 | 24°58′N | 113°30′W |
| San Leandro, Ca., U.S. (săn lê-ăn′drô) | 116b | 37°43′N | 122°10′W |
| Şanlıurfa, Tur. | 198 | 37°20′N | 38°45′E |
| San Lorenzo, Arg. (sän lô-rĕn′zô) | 144 | 32°46′S | 60°44′W |
| San Lorenzo, Hond. (sän lô-rĕn′zô) | 132 | 13°24′N | 87°24′W |
| San Lorenzo, Ca., U.S. (săn lô-rĕn′zô) | 116b | 37°41′N | 122°08′W |
| San Lorenzo de El Escorial, Spain | 172 | 40°36′N | 4°09′W |
| Sanlúcar de Barrameda, Spain (sän-lōō′kär) | 162 | 36°46′N | 6°21′W |
| San Lucas, Bol. (lōō′kás) | 142 | 20°12′S | 65°06′W |
| San Lucas, Cabo, c., Mex. | 128 | 22°45′N | 109°45′W |
| San Luis, Arg. (lò-ēs′) | 144 | 33°16′S | 66°15′W |
| San Luis, Col. (lòê′s) | 142a | 6°03′N | 74°57′W |
| San Luis, Cuba | 135 | 20°15′N | 75°50′W |
| San Luis, Guat. | 132 | 14°38′N | 89°42′W |
| San Luis, prov., Arg. | 144 | 32°45′S | 66°00′W |
| San Luis de la Paz, Mex. (då lä päz′) | 130 | 21°17′N | 100°32′W |
| San Luis del Cordero, Mex. (dĕl kôr-dā′rō) | 122 | 25°25′N | 104°20′W |
| San Luis Obispo, Ca., U.S. (ô-bĭs′pō) | 104 | 35°18′N | 120°40′W |
| San Luis Obispo Bay, b., Ca., U.S. | 118 | 35°07′N | 121°05′W |
| San Luis Potosí, Mex. | 128 | 22°08′N | 100°58′W |
| San Luis Potosí, state, Mex. | 128 | 22°45′N | 101°45′W |
| San Luis Rey, r., Ca., U.S. (rā′ē) | 118 | 33°22′N | 117°06′W |
| San Manuel, Az., U.S. (săn măn′ū-ĕl) | 119 | 32°30′N | 110°45′W |
| San Marcial, N.M., U.S. (săn mår-shäl′) | 119 | 33°40′N | 107°00′W |
| San Marco, Italy (sän mär′kô) | 174 | 41°53′N | 15°50′E |
| San Marcos, Guat. (mär′kôs) | 132 | 14°57′N | 91°49′W |
| San Marcos, Mex. | 130 | 16°46′N | 99°23′W |
| San Marcos, Tx., U.S. (săn mär′kôs) | 123 | 29°53′N | 97°56′W |
| San Marcos, r., Tx., U.S. | 123 | 30°08′N | 98°15′W |
| San Marcos de Colón, Hond. (sän-má′r-kôs-dĕ-kô-lô′n) | 132 | 13°17′N | 86°50′W |
| San Maria di Léuca, Cape, c., Italy (dē-lĕ′ōō-kä) | 163 | 39°47′N | 18°20′E |
| San Marino, S. Mar. (sän mä-rē′nô) | 174 | 44°55′N | 12°26′E |
| San Marino, Ca., U.S. (săn mẽr-ē′nô) | 117a | 34°07′N | 118°06′W |
| San Marino, nation, Eur. | 154 | 43°40′N | 13°00′E |
| San Martín, Col. (sän mär-tē′n) | 142a | 3°42′N | 73°44′W |
| San Martín, vol., Mex. (mär-tē′n) | 131 | 18°36′N | 95°11′W |
| San Martín, l., S.A. | 144 | 48°15′S | 72°30′W |
| San Martín Chalchicuautla, Mex. | 130 | 21°22′N | 98°39′W |
| San Martin de la Vega, Spain (sän mär ten′ då lä vā′gä) | 173a | 40°12′N | 3°34′W |
| San Martín Hidalgo, Mex. (sän mär-tē′n-ē-däl′gô) | 130 | 20°27′N | 103°55′W |
| San Mateo, Mex. | 131 | 16°59′N | 97°04′W |
| San Mateo, Ca., U.S. (săn mă-tā′ô) | 116b | 37°34′N | 122°20′W |
| San Mateo, Ven. (sän má-tĕ′ô) | 143b | 9°45′N | 64°34′W |
| San Matías, Golfo, b., Arg. (sän mä-tē′äs) | 144 | 41°30′S | 63°45′W |
| Sanmen Wan, b., China | 209 | 29°00′N | 122°15′E |
| San Miguel, El Sal. (sän mê-gål′) | 128 | 13°28′N | 88°11′W |
| San Miguel, Mex. (sän mê-gål′) | 131 | 18°18′N | 97°09′W |
| San Miguel, Pan. | 133 | 8°26′N | 78°55′W |
| San Miguel, Phil. (sän mē-gĕ′l) | 213a | 15°09′N | 120°56′E |
| San Miguel, Ven. (sän mē-gĕ′l) | 143b | 9°56′N | 64°58′W |
| San Miguel, vol., El Sal. | 132 | 13°27′N | 88°17′W |
| San Miguel, i., Ca., U.S. | 118 | 34°03′N | 120°23′W |
| San Miguel, r., Bol. (sän-mē-gĕl′) | 142 | 13°34′S | 63°58′W |
| San Miguel, r., N.A. (sän mê-gål′) | 131 | 15°27′N | 92°00′W |
| San Miguel, r., Co., U.S. (săn mê-gĕl′) | 119 | 38°15′N | 108°40′W |
| San Miguel, Bahía, b., Pan. (bä-ē′ä-sän mê-gål′) | 133 | 8°17′N | 78°26′W |
| San Miguel Bay, b., Phil. | 213a | 13°55′N | 123°12′E |
| San Miguel de Allende, Mex. (då ä-lyĕn′då) | 130 | 20°54′N | 100°44′W |
| San Miguel el Alto, Mex. (ĕl äl′tô) | 130 | 21°03′N | 102°26′W |
| Sannār, Sudan | 231 | 14°25′N | 33°30′E |
| San Narcisco, Phil. (sän när-sē′sô) | 213a | 15°01′N | 120°05′E |
| San Narciso, Phil. | 213a | 13°34′N | 122°33′E |
| San Nicolás, Arg. (sän nē-kô-lá′s) | 144 | 33°20′S | 60°14′W |
| San Nicolas, Phil. (nê-kô-läs′) | 213a | 16°05′N | 120°45′E |
| San Nicolas, i., Ca., U.S. (săn nĭ′kô-là) | 118 | 33°14′N | 119°10′W |
| San Nicolás, r., Mex. | 130 | 19°40′N | 105°08′W |
| Sanniquellie, Lib. | 234 | 7°22′N | 8°43′W |
| Sannūr, Wādī, Egypt | 238b | 28°48′N | 31°12′E |
| Sanok, Pol. (sä′nôk) | 169 | 49°31′N | 22°13′E |
| San Pablo, Phil. (sän-pä-blô) | 213a | 14°05′N | 121°20′E |
| San Pablo, Ca., U.S. (săn păb′lô) | 116b | 37°58′N | 122°21′W |
| San Pablo, Ven. (sän-pá′blô) | 143b | 9°46′N | 65°04′W |
| San Pablo, r., Pan. (sän päb′lô) | 133 | 8°12′N | 81°12′W |
| San Pablo Bay, b., Ca., U.S. (săn păb′lô) | 116b | 38°04′N | 122°25′W |
| San Pablo Res, Ca., U.S. | 116b | 37°55′N | 122°12′W |
| San Pascual, Phil. (päs-kwäl′) | 213a | 13°08′N | 122°59′E |
| San Pedro, Arg. (sän pä′drô) | 144 | 24°15′S | 64°15′W |
| San Pedro, Arg. | 141c | 33°41′S | 59°42′W |
| San Pedro, Chile (sän pĕ′drô) | 141b | 33°54′S | 71°27′W |
| San Pedro, El Sal. (sän pä′drô) | 132 | 13°49′N | 88°58′W |
| San Pedro, Mex. (sän pä′drô) | 131 | 18°38′N | 92°25′W |
| San Pedro, Para. (sän-pĕ′drô) | 144 | 24°13′S | 57°00′W |
| San Pedro, Ca., U.S. (săn pē′drô) | 117a | 33°44′N | 118°17′W |
| San Pedro, r., Cuba (sän-pĕ′drô) | 134 | 21°05′N | 78°15′W |
| San Pedro, r., Mex. (sän pä′drô) | 130 | 22°08′N | 104°59′W |
| San Pedro, r., Mex. | 122 | 27°56′N | 105°50′W |
| San Pedro, r., Az., U.S. | 119 | 32°48′N | 110°37′W |
| San Pedro, Río de, r., Mex. | 130 | 21°51′N | 102°24′W |
| San Pedro, Río de, r., N.A. | 131 | 18°23′N | 92°13′W |
| San Pedro Bay, b., Ca., U.S. (săn pē′drô) | 117a | 33°42′N | 118°12′W |
| San Pedro de las Colonias, Mex. (dĕ-läs-kô-lô′nyäs) | 122 | 25°47′N | 102°58′W |
| San Pedro de Macorís, Dom. Rep. (sän-pĕ′drō-då mä-kô-rēs′) | 135 | 18°30′N | 69°30′W |
| San Pedro Lagunillas, Mex. (sän pä′drô lä-gōō-nēl′yäs) | 130 | 21°12′N | 104°47′W |
| San Pedro Sula, Hond. (sän pä′drô sōō′lä) | 132 | 15°29′N | 88°01′W |
| San Pietro, Isola di, i., Italy (ē′sō-lä-dē-sän pyā′trô) | 174 | 39°09′N | 8°15′E |
| San Quentin, Ca., U.S. (săn kwĕn-tēn′) | 116b | 37°57′N | 122°29′W |
| San Quintin, Phil. (sän kēn-tēn′) | 213a | 15°59′N | 120°47′E |
| San Rafael, Arg. (sän rä-fä-ĕl′) | 144 | 34°30′S | 68°13′W |
| San Rafael, Col. (sän-rä-fä-ĕ′l) | 142a | 6°18′N | 75°02′W |
| San Rafael, Ca., U.S. (săn rá-fĕl) | 116b | 37°58′N | 122°31′W |
| San Rafael, r., Ut., U.S. (săn rá-fĕl′) | 119 | 39°05′N | 110°50′W |
| San Rafael, Cabo, c., Dom. Rep. (ká′bô) | 135 | 19°00′N | 68°50′W |
| San Ramón, C.R. | 133 | 10°07′N | 84°30′W |
| San Ramon, Ca., U.S. (săn rä-mōn′) | 116b | 37°47′N | 122°59′W |
| San Remo, Italy (sän rā′mô) | 174 | 43°48′N | 7°46′E |
| San Roque, Col. (sän-rô′kĕ) | 142a | 6°29′N | 75°00′W |
| San Roque, Spain | 172 | 36°13′N | 5°23′W |
| San Saba, Tx., U.S. (săn sä′bá) | 122 | 31°12′N | 98°43′W |
| San Saba, r., Tx., U.S. | 122 | 30°58′N | 99°12′W |
| San Salvador, El Sal. (sän säl-vä-dōr′) | 128 | 13°45′N | 89°11′W |
| San Salvador (Watling), i., Bah. (săn săl′vá-dôr) | 135 | 24°05′N | 74°30′W |
| San Salvador, i., Ec. | 142 | 0°14′S | 90°50′W |
| San Salvador, r., Ur. (sän-säl-vä-dô′r) | 141c | 33°42′S | 58°04′W |
| Sansanné-Mango, Togo (sän-sá-nā′ măn′gô) | 230 | 10°21′N | 0°28′E |
| San Sebastian, Spain (sän så-bås-tyän′) | 230 | 28°09′N | 17°11′W |


ăt; finăl; rāte; senåte; ärm; ásk; sofá; fâre; ch-choose; dh-as th in other; bē; êvent; bĕt; recĕnt; cratẽr; g-gō; gh-guttural g; bĭt; ĭ-short neutral; rīde; κ-guttural k as ch in German ich;

PRONOUNCING INDEX

San Sebastián – Sapitwa 347


| PLACE (Pronunciation) | PAGE | LAT. | LONG. |
|---|---|---|---|
| San Sebastián *see* Donostia-San Sebastián, Spain | 154 | 43°19'N | 1°59'W |
| San Sebastián, Ven. (sän-sĕ-bäs-tyä'n) | 143b | 9°58'N | 67°11'W |
| San Sebastiàn de los Reyes, Spain | 173a | 40°33'N | 3°38'W |
| San Severo, Italy (sän sĕ-vå'rō) | 163 | 41°43'N | 15°24'E |
| Sanshui, China (sän-shwā) | 205 | 23°14'N | 112°51'E |
| San Simon Creek, r., Az., U.S. (sån sī-mōn') | 119 | 32°45'N | 109°30'W |
| Santa Ana, El Sal. | 128 | 14°02'N | 89°35'W |
| Santa Ana, Mex. (sän'tä ä'nä) | 130 | 19°18'N | 98°10'W |
| Santa Ana, Ca., U.S. (săn'tȧ ăn'ȧ) | 104 | 33°45'N | 117°52'W |
| Santa Ana, r., Ca., U.S. | 117a | 33°41'N | 117°57'W |
| Santa Ana Mountains, mts., Ca., U.S. | 117a | 33°44'N | 117°36'W |
| Santa Anna, Tx., U.S. | 122 | 31°44'N | 99°18'W |
| Santa Antão, i., C.V. (sä-tä-ä'n-zhĕ-lô) | 230b | 17°20'N | 26°05'W |
| Santa Bárbara, Braz. (sän-tä-bä'r-bä-rä) | 143 | 19°57'S | 43°25'W |
| Santa Bárbara, Hond. | 132 | 14°52'N | 88°20'W |
| Santa Barbara, Mex. | 122 | 26°48'N | 105°50'W |
| Santa Barbara, Ca., U.S. | 104 | 34°26'N | 119°43'W |
| Santa Barbara, i., Ca., U.S. | 118 | 33°30'N | 118°44'W |
| Santa Barbara Channel, strt., Ca., U.S. | 118 | 34°15'N | 120°00'W |
| Santa Branca, Braz. (sän-tä-brä'n-kä) | 141a | 23°25'S | 45°52'W |
| Santa Catalina, i., Ca., U.S. | 106 | 33°29'N | 118°37'W |
| Santa Catalina, Cerro de, mtn., Pan. | 133 | 8°39'N | 81°36'W |
| Santa Catalina, Gulf of, b., Ca., U.S. (săn'tȧ kă-tȧ-lē'nȧ) | 118 | 33°00'N | 117°58'W |
| Santa Catarina, Mex. (sän'tä kä-tä-rē'nä) | 122 | 25°41'N | 100°27'W |
| Santa Catarina, state, Braz. (sän-tä-kä-tä-rē'nȧ) | 144 | 27°15'S | 50°30'W |
| Santa Catarina, r., Mex. | 130 | 16°31'N | 98°39'W |
| Santa Clara, Cuba (sän't klä'rá) | 129 | 22°25'N | 80°00'W |
| Santa Clara, Mex. | 122 | 24°29'N | 103°22'W |
| Santa Clara, Ur. | 144 | 32°46'S | 54°51'W |
| Santa Clara, Ca., U.S. (săn'tȧ klârȧ) | 114 | 37°21'N | 121°56'W |
| Santa Clara, vol., Nic. | 132 | 12°44'N | 87°00'W |
| Santa Clara, r., Ca., U.S. (săn'tȧ klă'rȧ) | 118 | 34°22'N | 118°53'W |
| Santa Clara, Bahía de, b., Cuba (bä-ē'ä-dĕ-sän-tä-klä-rä) | 134 | 23°05'N | 80°50'W |
| Santa Clara, Sierra, mts., Mex. (sē-ĕ'r-rä-sän'tá klä'rà) | 128 | 27°30'N | 113°50'W |
| Santa Clara Indian Reservation, I.R., N.M., U.S. | 119 | 35°59'N | 106°10'W |
| Santa Cruz, Bol. (sän'tá krōōz') | 142 | 17°45'S | 63°03'W |
| Santa Cruz, Braz. (sän-tä-krōō's) | 144 | 29°43'S | 52°15'W |
| Santa Cruz, Braz. | 144b | 22°55'S | 43°41'W |
| Santa Cruz, Chile | 141b | 34°38'S | 71°21'W |
| Santa Cruz, C.R. | 132 | 10°16'N | 85°37'W |
| Santa Cruz, Mex. | 122 | 25°50'N | 105°25'W |
| Santa Cruz, Phil. | 213a | 13°28'N | 122°02'E |
| Santa Cruz, Phil. | 213a | 15°46'N | 119°53'E |
| Santa Cruz, Phil. | 213a | 14°17'N | 121°25'E |
| Santa Cruz, Ca., U.S. | 104 | 36°59'N | 122°02'W |
| Santa Cruz, prov., Arg. | 144 | 48°00'S | 70°00'W |
| Santa Cruz, i., Ec. (sän-tä-krōō'z) | 142 | 0°38'S | 90°20'W |
| Santa Cruz, r., Arg. (sän'tä krōōz') | 144 | 50°05'S | 71°00'W |
| Santa Cruz, r., Az., U.S. (săn'tȧ krōōz') | 119 | 32°30'N | 111°30'W |
| Santa Cruz Barillas, Guat. (sän-tä-krōō'z-bä-rē'l-yäs) | 132 | 15°47'N | 91°22'W |
| Santa Cruz del Sur, Cuba (sän-tä-krōō's-dĕl-sōō'r) | 134 | 20°45'N | 78°00'W |
| Santa Cruz de Tenerife, Spain (sän'tä krōōz dā tā-nå-rē'få) | 228 | 28°07'N | 15°27'W |
| Santa Cruz Islands, is., Sol. Is. | 221 | 10°58'S | 166°47'E |
| Santa Cruz Mountains, mts., Ca., U.S. (săn'tȧ krōōz') | 116b | 37°30'N | 122°19'W |
| Santa Domingo, Cay, i., Bah. | 135 | 21°50'N | 75°45'W |
| Santa Fe, Arg. (sän'tä fā') | 144 | 31°33'S | 60°45'W |
| Santa Fé, Cuba (sän-tä-fĕ') | 134 | 21°45'N | 82°40'W |
| Santa Fe, Spain (sän'tä-fā') | 172 | 37°12'N | 3°43'W |
| Santa Fe, N.M., U.S. (săn'tȧ fā') | 104 | 35°40'N | 106°00'W |
| Santa Fe, prov., Arg. (sän'tä fā') | 144 | 32°00'S | 61°15'W |
| Santa Fe de Bogotá *see* Bogotá, Col. | 142 | 4°36'N | 74°05'W |
| Santa Filomena, Braz. (sän-tä-fē-lô-mĕ'nä) | 143 | 9°09'S | 44°45'W |
| Santa Genoveva, mtn., Mex. (sän-tä-hĕ-nō-vĕ'vä) | 128 | 23°30'N | 110°00'W |
| Santai, China (san-tī) | 204 | 31°02'N | 105°02'E |
| Santa Inés, Ven. (sän'tä ē-nĕ's) | 143b | 9°54'N | 64°21'W |
| Santa Inés, i., Chile (sän'tä ē-nās') | 144 | 53°45'S | 74°15'W |
| Santa Isabel, i., Sol. Is. | 221 | 7°57'S | 159°28'E |
| Santa Isabel, Pico de, mtn., Eq. Gui. | 235 | 3°35'N | 8°46'E |
| Santa Lucia, Cuba (sän'tä lōō-sē'ä) | 134 | 21°15'N | 77°30'W |
| Santa Lucia, Ur. (sän-tä-lōō-sē'ä) | 144 | 34°27'S | 56°23'W |
| Santa Lucia, Ven. | 143b | 10°18'N | 66°40'W |
| Santa Lucia, r., Ur. | 141c | 34°19'S | 56°13'W |
| Santa Lucia Bay, b., Cuba (sän'tä lōō-sē'ä) | 134 | 22°55'N | 84°20'W |
| Santa Margarita, i., Mex. (sän'tä mär-gä-rē'tà) | 128 | 24°15'N | 112°00'W |
| Santa Maria, Braz. (sän'tä mä-rē'ä) | 144 | 29°40'S | 54°00'W |
| Santa Maria, Italy (sän-tä mä-rē'ä) | 174 | 41°05'N | 14°15'E |
| Santa Maria, Phil. (sän-tä-mä-rē'ä) | 213a | 14°48'N | 120°57'E |
| Santa Maria, Ca., U.S. (săn-tȧ mȧ-rē'ȧ) | 118 | 34°57'N | 120°28'W |
| Santa María, vol., Guat. | 132 | 14°45'N | 91°33'W |
| Santa Maria, r., Mex. (sän'tä mä-rē'ä) | 130 | 21°33'N | 100°17'W |
| Santa Maria, Cabo de, c., Port. (kå'bō-dĕ-sän-tä-mä-rē'ä) | 172 | 36°58'N | 7°54'W |

| PLACE (Pronunciation) | PAGE | LAT. | LONG. |
|---|---|---|---|
| Santa Maria, Cape, c., Bah. | 135 | 23°45'N | 75°30'W |
| Santa Maria, Cayo, i., Cuba | 134 | 22°40'N | 79°00'W |
| Santa María del Oro, Mex. (sän'tä-mä-rē'ä-dĕl-ô-rô) | 130 | 21°21'N | 104°35'W |
| Santa Maria de los Angeles, Mex. (dĕ-lôs-ä'n-hĕ-lĕs) | 130 | 22°10'N | 103°34'W |
| Santa María del Río, Mex. | 130 | 21°46'N | 100°43'W |
| Santa María de Ocotán, Mex. | 130 | 22°56'N | 104°30'W |
| Santa Maria Island, i., Port. (sän-tä-mä-rē'ä) | 230a | 37°09'N | 26°02'W |
| Santa Maria Madalena, Braz. | 141a | 22°00'S | 42°00'W |
| Santa Marta, Col. (sän'tä mär'tä) | 142 | 11°15'N | 74°13'W |
| Santa Marta, Cabo de, c., Ang. | 236 | 13°52'S | 12°25'E |
| Santa Monica, Ca., U.S. (săn'tȧ mŏn'ĭ-kȧ) | 104 | 34°01'N | 118°29'W |
| Santa Monica Mountains, mts., Ca., U.S. | 117a | 34°08'N | 118°38'W |
| Santana, r., Braz. (sän-tä'nä) | 144b | 22°33'S | 43°37'W |
| Santander, Col. (sän-tän-dĕr') | 142a | 3°00'N | 76°25'W |
| Santander, Spain (sän-tän-dâr') | 154 | 43°27'N | 3°50'W |
| Sant Antoni de Portmany, Spain | 173 | 38°59'N | 1°17'E |
| Santa Paula, Ca., U.S. (săn'tȧ pô'lȧ) | 118 | 34°24'N | 119°05'W |
| Santarém, Braz. (sän-tä-rĕN') | 143 | 2°28'S | 54°37'W |
| Santarém, Port. | 172 | 39°18'N | 8°48'W |
| Santaren Channel, strt., Bah. (săn-tȧ-rĕn') | 134 | 24°15'N | 79°30'W |
| Santa Rita do Sapucai, Braz. (sä-pò-kà'ē) | 141a | 22°15'S | 45°41'W |
| Santa Rosa, Arg. (sän-tä-rô-sä) | 144 | 36°45'S | 64°10'W |
| Santa Rosa, Col. (sän-tä-rô-sä) | 142a | 6°38'N | 75°26'W |
| Santa Rosa, Ec. | 142 | 3°29'S | 79°55'W |
| Santa Rosa, Guat. (sän'tä rō'sȧ) | 132 | 14°21'N | 90°16'W |
| Santa Rosa, Hond. | 132 | 14°45'N | 88°51'W |
| Santa Rosa, Ca., U.S. (săn'tȧ rō'zȧ) | 104 | 38°27'N | 122°42'W |
| Santa Rosa, N.M., U.S. (săn'tȧ rō'sȧ) | 120 | 34°55'N | 104°41'W |
| Santa Rosa, Ven. (sän-tä-rô-sä) | 143b | 9°37'N | 64°10'W |
| Santa Rosa de Cabal, Col. (sän-tä-rô-sä-dĕ-kä-bä'l) | 142a | 4°53'N | 75°38'W |
| Santa Rosa de Viterbo, Braz. (sän-tä-rô-sä-dĕ-vē-tĕr'-bô) | 141a | 21°30'S | 47°21'W |
| Santa Rosa Indian Reservation, I.R., Ca., U.S. (săn'tȧ rō'zȧ') | 118 | 33°28'N | 116°50'W |
| Santa Rosalía, Mex. (sän'tä rô-zä'lē-ä) | 128 | 27°13'N | 112°15'W |
| Santa Rosa Range, mts., Nv., U.S. (săn'tȧ rō'zȧ) | 114 | 41°33'N | 117°50'W |
| Santa Susana, Ca., U.S. (săn'tȧ sōō-ză'nȧ) | 117a | 34°16'N | 118°42'W |
| Santa Teresa, Arg. (sän-tä-tĕ-rĕ'sä) | 141c | 33°27'S | 60°47'W |
| Santa Teresa, Ven. | 143b | 10°14'N | 66°40'W |
| Santa Uxia, Spain | 172 | 42°34'N | 8°55'W |
| Santa Vitória do Palmar, Braz. (sän-tä-vē-tō'ryä-dô-päl-mår) | 144 | 33°30'S | 53°16'W |
| Santa Ynez, r., Ca., U.S. (săn'tȧ ē-nĕz') | 118 | 34°40'N | 120°20'W |
| Santa Ysabel Indian Reservation, I.R., Ca., U.S. (săn-tȧ ĭ-zȧ-bĕl') | 118 | 33°05'N | 116°46'W |
| Santee, Ca., U.S. (săn tē') | 118a | 32°50'N | 116°58'W |
| Santee, r., S.C., U.S. | 107 | 33°00'N | 79°45'W |
| Sant' Eufemia, Golfo di, b., Italy (gôl-fô-dē-sän-tĕ'ò-fē'myä) | 174 | 38°53'N | 15°53'E |
| Sant Feliu de Guixols, Spain | 173 | 41°45'N | 3°01'E |
| Santiago, Braz. (sän-tyà'gô) | 144 | 29°05'S | 54°46'W |
| Santiago, Chile (sän-tē-ä'gô) | 144 | 33°26'S | 70°40'W |
| Santiago, Pan. | 129 | 8°07'N | 80°58'W |
| Santiago, Phil. (sän-tyä'gô) | 213a | 16°42'N | 121°33'E |
| Santiago, prov., Chile (sän-tyà'gō) | 141b | 33°28'S | 70°55'W |
| Santiago, i., Phil. | 213a | 16°29'N | 120°03'E |
| Santiago de Compostela, Spain | 162 | 42°52'N | 8°32'W |
| Santiago de Cuba, Cuba (sän-tyà'gô-dā kōō'bà) | 129 | 20°00'N | 75°50'W |
| Santiago de Cuba, prov., Cuba | 134 | 20°20'N | 76°05'W |
| Santiago de las Vegas, Cuba (sän-tyà'gô-dĕ-läs-vĕ'gäs) | 135a | 22°58'N | 82°23'W |
| Santiago del Estero, Arg. | 144 | 27°50'S | 64°14'W |
| Santiago del Estero, prov., Arg. (sän-tē-ä'gō-dĕl ĕs-tā'rō) | 144 | 27°15'S | 63°30'W |
| Santiago de los Cabelleros, Dom. Rep. | 129 | 19°30'N | 70°45'W |
| Santiago Mountains, mts., Tx., U.S. (sän-tē-ä'gô) | 106 | 30°00'N | 103°30'W |
| Santiago Reservoir, res., Ca., U.S. | 117a | 33°47'N | 117°42'W |
| Santiago Rodriguez, Dom. Rep. (sän-tyà'gô-rô-drē'gĕz) | 135 | 19°30'N | 71°25'W |
| Santiago Tuxtla, Mex. (sän-tyà'gô-tōō'x-tlä) | 131 | 18°28'N | 95°18'W |
| Santiaguillo, Laguna de, l., Mex. (lä-oō'nä-dĕ-sän-tē-ä-gēl'yô) | 122 | 24°51'N | 104°43'W |
| Santisteban del Puerto, Spain (sän'tê stå-bän'dĕl pwĕr'tô) | 172 | 38°15'N | 3°12'W |
| Sant Mateu, Spain | 173 | 40°26'N | 0°09'E |
| Santo Amaro, Braz. (sän'tô ä-mä'rô) | 143 | 12°32'S | 38°33'W |
| Santo Amaro de Campos, Braz. | 141a | 22°01'S | 41°05'W |
| Santo André, Braz. | 141a | 23°40'S | 46°31'W |
| Santo Angelo, Braz. (sän-tô-ä'n-zhĕ-lô) | 144 | 28°16'S | 53°59'W |
| Santo Antônio do Monte, Braz. (sän-tô-än-tō'nyô-dô-môn'tĕ) | 141a | 20°06'S | 45°18'W |
| Santo Domingo, Cuba (sän'tô-dōmĭŋ'gô) | 134 | 22°35'N | 80°20'W |
| Santo Domingo, Dom. Rep. (sän'tô dô-mĭn'gō) | 129 | 18°30'N | 69°55'W |
| Santo Domingo, Nic. (sän-tô-dô-mē'n-gō) | 133 | 12°15'N | 84°56'W |

| PLACE (Pronunciation) | PAGE | LAT. | LONG. |
|---|---|---|---|
| Santo Domingo de la Caizada, Spain (dā lä käl-thä'dä) | 172 | 42°27'N | 2°55'W |
| Santoña, Spain (sän-tō'nyä) | 172 | 43°25'N | 3°27'W |
| Santos, Braz. (sän'tozh) | 143 | 23°58'S | 46°20'W |
| Santos Dumont, Braz. (sän'tôs-dô-mô'nt) | 143 | 21°28'S | 43°33'W |
| Sanuki, Japan (sä'nōō-kē) | 211a | 35°16'N | 139°53'E |
| San Urbano, Arg. (sän-òr-bä'nô) | 141c | 33°39'S | 61°28'W |
| San Valentin, Monte, mtn., Chile (sän-vä-lĕn-tē'n) | 144 | 46°41'S | 73°30'W |
| San Vicente, Arg. (sän-vē-sĕn'tĕ) | 141c | 35°00'S | 58°26'W |
| San Vicente, Chile | 141b | 34°25'S | 71°06'W |
| San Vicente, El Sal. (sän vê-sĕn'tå) | 132 | 13°41'N | 88°43'W |
| San Vicente de Alcántara, Spain | 172 | 39°24'N | 7°08'W |
| San Vito al Tagliamento, Italy (san vē'tô) | 174 | 45°53'N | 12°52'E |
| San Xavier Indian Reservation, I.R., Az., U.S. (x-ā'vĭēr) | 119 | 32°07'N | 111°12'W |
| San Ysidro, Ca., U.S. (sän ysĭ-drō') | 118a | 32°33'N | 117°02'W |
| Sanyuanli, China (sän-yůän-lē) | 207a | 23°11'N | 113°16'E |
| São Bernardo do Campo, Braz. (souN-bĕr-når'dô-dô-kå'm-pô) | 141a | 23°44'S | 46°33'W |
| São Borja, Braz. (souN-bôr-zhä) | 144 | 28°44'S | 55°59'W |
| São Carlos, Braz. (souN kär'lōzh) | 143 | 22°02'S | 47°54'W |
| São Cristovão, Braz. (souN-krēs-tō-vouN) | 143 | 11°04'S | 37°11'W |
| São Fidélis, Braz. (souN-fē-dĕ'lĕs) | 141a | 21°41'S | 41°45'W |
| São Francisco, Braz. (souN frän-sēsh'kô) | 143 | 15°59'S | 44°42'W |
| São Francisco, r., Braz. (sän-frän-sē's-kō) | 143 | 8°56'S | 40°20'W |
| São Francisco do Sul, Braz. (souN frän-sēsh'kô-dô-sōō'l) | 144 | 26°15'S | 48°42'W |
| São Gabriel, Braz. (souN'gä-brē-ĕl') | 144 | 30°28'S | 54°11'W |
| São Geraldo, Braz. (souN-zhĕ-rä'l-dô) | 141a | 21°01'S | 42°49'W |
| São Gonçalo, Braz. (souN'gōn-sä'lò) | 141a | 22°55'S | 43°04'W |
| Sao Hill, Tan. | 237 | 8°20'S | 35°12'E |
| São João, Gui.-B. | 234 | 11°32'N | 15°26'W |
| São João da Barra, Braz. (souN-zhôuN-dä-bà'rä) | 141a | 21°40'S | 41°03'W |
| São João da Boa Vista, Braz. (souN-zhôuN-dä-bôä-vē's-tä) | 141a | 21°58'S | 46°45'W |
| São João del Rei, Braz. (souN zhô-ouN'dĕl-rā) | 144 | 21°08'S | 44°14'W |
| São João de Meriti, Braz. (souN-zhôuN-dĕ-mĕ-rē-tê) | 144b | 22°47'S | 43°22'W |
| São João do Araguaia, Braz. (souN zhô-ouN'dô-ä-rä-gwä'yä) | 143 | 5°29'S | 48°44'W |
| São João dos Lampas, Port. (souN' zhô-ouN' dōzh län-päzh') | 173b | 38°52'N | 9°24'W |
| São João Nepomuceno, Braz. (souN-zhôuN-nĕ-pô-mōō-sĕ-nō) | 141a | 21°33'S | 43°00'W |
| São Jorge Island, i., Port. (souN zhôr'zhĕ) | 230a | 38°28'N | 27°34'W |
| São José do Rio Pardo, Braz. (souN-zhô-sĕ'dô-rē'ō-pà'r-dō) | 141a | 21°36'S | 46°50'W |
| São José do Rio Prêto, Braz. (souN zhô-zĕ'dô-rē'ō-prĕ-tō) | 143 | 20°57'S | 49°12'W |
| São José dos Campos, Braz. (souN zhô-zā'dōzh kän pōzh') | 141a | 23°12'S | 45°53'W |
| São Leopoldo, Braz. (souN-lĕ-ô-pôl'dô) | 144 | 29°46'S | 51°09'W |
| São Luis, Braz. | 143 | 2°31'S | 43°14'W |
| São Luis do Paraitinga, Braz. (souN-lōōē's-dô-pä-rä-ē-tē'n-gä) | 141a | 23°15'S | 45°18'W |
| São Manuel, r., Braz. | 143 | 8°28'S | 57°07'E |
| São Mateus, Braz. (souN mä-tā'òzh) | 143 | 18°44'S | 39°45'W |
| São Mateus, Braz. | 144b | 22°49'S | 43°23'W |
| São Miguel Arcanjo, Braz. (souN-mē-gĕ'l-år-kän-zhō) | 141a | 23°54'S | 47°59'W |
| São Miguel Island, i., Port. | 230a | 37°59'N | 26°38'W |
| Saona, i., Dom. Rep. (sä-ô'nä) | 135 | 18°10'N | 68°55'W |
| Saône, r., Fr. (sōn) | 156 | 47°00'N | 5°30'E |
| São Nicolau, i., C.V. (souN' nê-kô-louN') | 230b | 16°19'N | 25°19'W |
| São Paulo, Braz. (souN' pou'lò) | 143 | 23°34'S | 46°38'W |
| São Paulo, state, Braz. (souN pou'lò) | 143 | 21°45'S | 50°47'W |
| São Paulo de Olivença, Braz. (souN'pou'lòdä ô-lê-vĕn'sȧ) | 142 | 3°32'S | 68°46'W |
| São Pedro, Braz. (souN-pĕ'drô) | 141a | 22°34'S | 47°54'W |
| São Pedro de Aldeia, Braz. (souN-pĕ'drô-dĕ-äl-dĕ'yä) | 141a | 22°50'S | 42°04'W |
| São Pedro e São Paulo, Rocedos, rocks, Braz. | 139 | 1°50'N | 30°00'W |
| São Raimundo Nonato, Braz. (souN' rī-mò'n-do nô-nä'tò) | 143 | 9°09'S | 42°32'W |
| São Roque, Braz. (souN' rō'kĕ) | 141a | 23°32'S | 47°08'W |
| São Roque, Cabo de, c., Braz. (kä'bo-dĕ-souN' rō'kĕ) | 143 | 5°06'S | 35°11'W |
| São Sebastião, Braz. (souN så-bäs-tē-ouN') | 141a | 23°48'S | 45°25'W |
| São Sebastião, Ilha de, i., Braz. | 141a | 23°52'S | 45°22'W |
| São Sebastião do Paraíso, Braz. | 141a | 20°54'S | 46°58'W |
| São Simão, Braz. (souN-sē-mouN) | 141a | 21°30'S | 47°33'W |
| São Tiago, i., C.V. (souN tē-ä'gô) | 230b | 15°09'N | 24°45'W |
| São Tomé, S. Tom./P. | 230 | 0°20'N | 6°44'E |
| Sao Tome and Principe, nation, Afr. (prēn'sê-pĕ) | 230 | 1°00'N | 6°00'E |
| Saoura, Oued, r., Alg. | 230 | 29°39'N | 1°42'W |
| São Vicente, Braz. (souN ve-se'n-tĕ) | 143 | 23°57'S | 46°25'W |
| São Vicente, i., C.V. (souN vê-sĕn'tå) | 230b | 16°51'N | 24°35'W |
| São Vicente, Cabo de, c., Port. (kä'bō-dĕ-sän-vê-sĕ'n-tĕ) | 156 | 37°03'N | 9°31'W |
| Sapele, Nig. (sä-pā'lā) | 230 | 5°54'N | 5°41'E |
| Sapitwa, mtn., Mwi. | 237 | 15°58'S | 35°38'E |


ng-sing; ŋ-baŋk; N-nasalized n; nŏd; cŏmmit; ōld; ôbey; ôrder; oi-boil; fōōd; ò-as oo in foot; ou-out; s-soft; sh-dish; th-thin; pūre; ûnite; ûrn; stŭd; circŭs; ü-as in French tu; '-indeterminate vowel.

348 Sa Pobla – Segura

PRONOUNCING INDEX


| PLACE (Pronunciation) | PAGE | LAT. | LONG. |
|---|---|---|---|
| Sa Pobla, Spain | 173 | 39°46′N | 3°02′E |
| Sapozhok, Russia (sä-pô-zhôk′) | 176 | 53°58′N | 40°44′E |
| Sapporo, Japan (säp-pô′rô) | 205 | 43°02′N | 141°29′E |
| Sapronovo, Russia (såp-rô′nô-vô) | 186b | 55°13′N | 38°25′E |
| Sapucaí, r., Braz. (sä-po͞o-kå-ē′) | 141a | 22°20′S | 45°53′W |
| Sapucaia, Braz. (sä-po͞o-kä′yå) | 141a | 22°01′S | 42°54′W |
| Sapucaí Mirim, r., Braz. (sä-po͞o-kå-ē′mē-rēɴ) | 141a | 21°06′S | 47°03′W |
| Sapulpa, Ok., U.S. (sȧ-pŭl′pȧ) | 121 | 36°01′N | 96°05′W |
| Saqqez, Iran | 201 | 36°14′N | 46°16′E |
| Saquarema, Braz. (sä-kwä-rĕ-mä) | 141a | 22°56′S | 42°32′W |
| Sara, Wa., U.S. (sä′rä) | 116c | 45°45′N | 122°42′W |
| Sara, Bahr, r., Chad (bär) | 231 | 8°19′N | 17°44′E |
| Sarajevo, Bos. (sä-rå-yĕv′ô) (så-rä′ya-vô) | 154 | 43°50′N | 18°26′E |
| Sarakhs, Iran | 201 | 36°32′N | 61°11′E |
| Sarana, Russia (sá-rä′ná) | 186a | 56°31′N | 57°44′E |
| Saranac Lake, N.Y., U.S. | 109 | 44°20′N | 74°05′W |
| Saranac Lake, l., N.Y., U.S. (săr′á-năk) | 109 | 44°15′N | 74°20′W |
| Sarandi, Arg. (sä-rän′dê) | 144a | 34°41′S | 58°21′W |
| Sarandi Grande, Ur. (sä-rän′dē-grän′dĕ) | 141c | 33°42′S | 56°21′W |
| Saranley, Som. | 238a | 2°28′N | 42°15′E |
| Saransk, Russia (så-ränsk′) | 178 | 54°10′N | 45°10′E |
| Sarany, Russia (så-rá′nĭ) | 186a | 58°33′N | 58°48′E |
| Sara Peak, mtn., Nig. | 235 | 9°37′N | 9°25′E |
| Sarapul, Russia (sä-räpôl′) | 180 | 56°28′N | 53°50′E |
| Sarasota, Fl., U.S. (săr-ȧ-sōtȧ) | 125a | 27°27′N | 82°30′W |
| Saratoga, Tx., U.S. (săr-ȧ-tō′gȧ) | 123 | 30°17′N | 94°31′W |
| Saratoga, Wa., U.S. | 116a | 48°04′N | 122°29′W |
| Saratoga Pass, Wa., U.S. | 116a | 48°09′N | 122°33′W |
| Saratoga Springs, N.Y., U.S. (sprĭngz) | 109 | 43°05′N | 74°50′W |
| Saratov, Russia (så rä′tôf) | 178 | 51°30′N | 45°30′E |
| Saravane, Laos | 209 | 15°48′N | 106°40′E |
| Sarawak, hist. reg., Malay. (så-rä′wäk) | 212 | 2°30′N | 112°45′E |
| Sárbogárd, Hung. (shär′bô-gärd) | 169 | 46°53′N | 18°38′E |
| Sarcee Indian Reserve, I.R., Can. (sär′sê) | 102e | 50°58′N | 114°23′W |
| Sarcelles, Fr. | 171b | 49°00′N | 2°23′E |
| Sardalas, Libya | 230 | 25°59′N | 10°33′E |
| Sardinia, i., Italy (sär-dĭn′ĭȧ) | 156 | 40°08′N | 9°05′E |
| Sardis, Ms., U.S. (sär′dĭs) | 124 | 34°26′N | 89°55′W |
| Sardis Lake, res., Ms., U.S. | 124 | 34°27′N | 89°43′W |
| Sargent, Ne., U.S. (sär′jĕnt) | 112 | 41°40′N | 99°38′W |
| Sarh, Chad (är-chaɴ-bô′) | 231 | 9°09′N | 18°23′E |
| Sarikamis, Tur. | 181 | 40°30′N | 42°40′E |
| Sariñena, Spain (sä-rēn-yĕ′nä) | 173 | 41°46′N | 0°11′W |
| Sark, i., Guern. (särk) | 170 | 49°28′N | 2°22′W |
| Şarköy, Tur. (shär′kû-ê) | 175 | 40°39′N | 27°07′E |
| Sarmiento, Monte, mtn., Chile (mô′n-tĕ-sär-myĕn′tō) | 144 | 54°28′S | 70°40′W |
| Sarnia, Can. (sär′nê-ȧ) | 91 | 43°00′N | 82°25′W |
| Sarno, Italy (sä′r-nô) | 173c | 40°35′N | 14°38′E |
| Sarny, Ukr. (sär′nê) | 181 | 51°17′N | 26°39′E |
| Saronikós Kólpos, b., Grc. | 175 | 37°51′N | 23°30′E |
| Saros Körfezi, b., Tur. (sä′rôs) | 175 | 40°30′N | 26°20′E |
| Sárospatak, Hung. (shä′rôsh-pô′tôk) | 169 | 48°19′N | 21°35′E |
| Šar Planina, mts., Serb. (shär plä′nê-na) | 175 | 42°07′N | 21°54′E |
| Sarpsborg, Nor. (särps′bôrg) | 166 | 59°17′N | 11°07′E |
| Sarrebourg, Fr. (sär-bo͞or′) | 171 | 48°44′N | 7°02′E |
| Sarreguemines, Fr. (sär-gē-mēn′) | 161 | 49°06′N | 7°05′E |
| Sarria, Spain (sär′ê-ä) | 162 | 42°14′N | 7°17′W |
| Sarstun, r., N.A. (särs-to͞o′n) | 132 | 15°50′N | 89°26′W |
| Sartène, Fr. (sär-tĕn′) | 174 | 41°36′N | 8°59′E |
| Sarthe, r., Fr. (särt) | 161 | 47°44′N | 0°32′W |
| Şärur, Azer. | 182 | 39°33′N | 44°58′E |
| Sárvár, Hung. (shär′vär) | 168 | 47°14′N | 16°55′E |
| Sarych, Mys, c., Ukr. (mĭs så-rēch′) | 181 | 44°25′N | 33°00′E |
| Saryesik-Atyraū, des., Kaz. | 183 | 45°30′N | 76°00′E |
| Sary-Ishikotrau, Peski, des., Kyrg. (sä′rê ē′ shêk-ō′trou) | 183 | 46°12′N | 75°30′E |
| Sarysū, r., Kaz. (sä′rê-so͞o) | 183 | 47°47′N | 69°14′E |
| Sasarām, India (sŭs-ŭ-räm′) | 199 | 25°00′N | 84°00′E |
| Sasayama, Japan (sä′sä-yä′mä) | 211 | 35°05′N | 135°14′E |
| Sasebo, Japan (sä′så-bô) | 205 | 33°12′N | 129°43′E |
| Saskatchewan, prov., Can. | 90 | 54°46′N | 107°40′W |
| Saskatchewan, r., Can. (săs-kăch′ê-wän) | 92 | 53°45′N | 103°20′W |
| Saskatoon, Can. (săs-kȧ-to͞on′) | 90 | 52°07′N | 106°38′W |
| Sasolburg, S. Afr. | 238c | 26°52′S | 27°47′E |
| Sasovo, Russia (sås′ô-vô) | 180 | 54°20′N | 42°00′E |
| Saspamco, Tx., U.S. (săs-păm′cō) | 117d | 29°13′N | 98°18′W |
| Sassandra, C. Iv. | 234 | 4°58′N | 6°05′W |
| Sassandra, r., C. Iv. (sås-sän′drå) | 230 | 5°35′N | 6°25′W |
| Sassari, Italy (säs′sä-rê) | 162 | 40°44′N | 8°33′E |
| Sassnitz, Ger. (säs′nêts) | 168 | 54°31′N | 13°37′E |
| Satadougou, Mali (sä-tå-do͞o-goo′) | 234 | 12°21′N | 12°07′W |
| Säter, Swe. (sĕ′tĕr) | 166 | 60°21′N | 15°50′E |
| Satilla, r., Ga., U.S. (så-tĭl′ȧ) | 125 | 31°15′N | 82°13′W |
| Satka, Russia (sät′kå) | 180 | 55°03′N | 59°02′E |
| Sátoraljaujhely, Hung. (shä′tô-rô-lyô-o͞o′yĕl′) | 169 | 48°24′N | 21°40′E |
| Satu Mare, Rom. (så′to͞o-mä′rĕ) | 163 | 47°50′N | 22°53′E |
| Saturna, Can. (să-tûr′nå) | 116d | 48°48′N | 123°12′W |
| Saturna, i., Can. | 116d | 48°47′N | 123°03′W |
| Sauda, Nor. | 160 | 59°40′N | 6°21′E |
| Saudárkrókur, Ice. | 154 | 65°41′N | 19°38′W |
| Saudi Arabia, nation, Asia (så-ô′dĭ å-rä′bĭ-å) | 198 | 22°40′N | 46°00′E |
| Sauerlach, Ger. (zou′ĕr-läκ) | 159d | 47°58′N | 11°39′E |
| Saugatuck, Mi., U.S. (sô′gȧ-tŭk) | 108 | 42°40′N | 86°10′W |
| Saugeen, r., Can. | 98 | 44°20′N | 81°20′W |
| Saugerties, N.Y., U.S. (sô′gĕr-tēz) | 109 | 42°05′N | 73°55′W |
| Saugus, Ma., U.S. (sô′gŭs) | 101a | 42°28′N | 71°01′W |
| Sauk, r., Mn., U.S. (sôk) | 113 | 45°30′N | 94°45′W |
| Sauk Centre, Mn., U.S. | 113 | 45°43′N | 94°58′W |
| Sauk City, Wi., U.S. | 113 | 43°16′N | 89°45′W |
| Sauk Rapids, Mn., U.S. (răp′ĭd) | 113 | 45°35′N | 94°08′W |
| Sault Sainte Marie, Can. | 91 | 46°31′N | 84°20′W |
| Sault Sainte Marie, Mi., U.S. (so͞o sānt må-rē′) | 105 | 46°29′N | 84°21′W |
| Saumatre, Étang, l., Haiti | 135 | 18°40′N | 72°10′W |
| Saunders Lake, l., Can. (sän′dĕrs) | 102g | 53°18′N | 113°25′W |
| Saurimo, Ang. | 232 | 9°39′S | 20°24′E |
| Sausalito, Ca., U.S. (sô-sȧ-lē′tô) | 116b | 37°51′N | 122°29′W |
| Sausset-les-Pins, Fr. (sō-sĕ′lā-påɴ′) | 170a | 43°20′N | 5°08′E |
| Saútar, Ang. | 236 | 11°06′S | 18°27′E |
| Sauvie Island, i., Or., U.S. (sô′vē) | 116c | 45°43′N | 123°49′W |
| Sava, r., Serb. (sä′vä) | 156 | 44°50′N | 18°30′E |
| Savage, Md., U.S. (să′vĕj) | 110e | 39°07′N | 76°49′W |
| Savage, Mn., U.S. | 117g | 44°47′N | 93°20′W |
| Savai‘i, i., Samoa | 214a | 13°35′S | 172°25′W |
| Savalen, l., Nor. | 166 | 62°19′N | 10°15′E |
| Savalou, Benin | 230 | 7°56′N | 1°58′E |
| Savanna, Il., U.S. (sȧ-văn′ȧ) | 113 | 42°05′N | 90°09′W |
| Savannah, Ga., U.S. (sȧ-văn′ȧ) | 105 | 32°04′N | 81°07′W |
| Savannah, Mo., U.S. | 121 | 39°58′N | 94°49′W |
| Savannah, Tn., U.S. | 124 | 35°13′N | 88°14′W |
| Savannah, r., U.S. | 107 | 33°11′N | 81°51′W |
| Savannakhét, Laos | 212 | 16°33′N | 104°45′E |
| Savanna la Mar, Jam. (så-vän′å lå mär′) | 134 | 18°10′N | 78°10′W |
| Save, r., Fr. | 170 | 43°32′N | 0°50′E |
| Save, Rio (Sabi), r., Afr. (rē′ō-sä′vĕ) | 232 | 21°28′S | 34°14′E |
| Sāveh, Iran | 201 | 35°01′N | 50°20′E |
| Saverne, Fr. (så-vĕrn′) | 171 | 48°40′N | 7°22′E |
| Savigliano, Italy (sä-vêl-yä′nô) | 174 | 44°38′N | 7°42′E |
| Savigny-sur-Orge, Fr. | 171b | 48°41′N | 2°22′E |
| Savona, Italy (sä-nō′nä) | 162 | 44°19′N | 8°28′E |
| Savonlinna, Fin. (så′vôn-lên′nå) | 167 | 61°53′N | 28°49′E |
| Savran‘, Ukr. (säv-rän′) | 177 | 48°07′N | 30°09′E |
| Sawahlunto, Indon. | 212 | 0°37′S | 100°50′E |
| Sawākin, Sudan | 231 | 19°02′N | 37°19′E |
| Sawda, Jabal as, mts., Libya | 231 | 28°14′N | 13°46′E |
| Sawhāj, Egypt | 231 | 26°34′N | 31°40′E |
| Sawknah, Libya | 231 | 29°04′N | 15°53′E |
| Sawu, Laut (Savu Sea), sea, Asia | 212 | 9°15′S | 122°15′E |
| Sawyer, l., Wa., U.S. (sô′yĕr) | 116a | 47°20′N | 122°02′W |
| Saxony *see* Sachsen, hist. reg., Ger. | 168 | 50°45′N | 12°17′E |
| Say, Niger (sä′ê) | 230 | 13°09′N | 2°16′E |
| Sayan Khrebet, mts., Russia (sŭ-yän′) | 179 | 51°30′N | 90°00′E |
| Sayḩūt, Yemen | 198 | 15°23′N | 51°28′E |
| Sayre, Ok., U.S. (sā′ĕr) | 120 | 35°19′N | 99°40′W |
| Sayre, Pa., U.S. | 109 | 41°55′N | 76°30′W |
| Sayreton, Al., U.S. (sā′ĕr-tŭn) | 110h | 33°34′N | 86°51′W |
| Sayreville, N.J., U.S. (sâr′vĭl) | 110a | 40°28′N | 74°21′W |
| Sayr Usa, Mong. | 204 | 44°15′N | 107°00′E |
| Sayula, Mex. (sä-yo͞o′lä) | 131 | 17°51′N | 94°56′W |
| Sayula, Mex. | 130 | 19°50′N | 103°33′W |
| Sayula, Luguna de, l., Mex. (lä-gô′nä-dĕ) | 130 | 20°00′N | 103°33′W |
| Say‘un, Yemen | 198 | 16°00′N | 48°59′E |
| Sayville, N.Y., U.S. (sā′vĭl) | 109 | 40°45′N | 73°10′W |
| Sazanit, i., Alb. | 163 | 40°30′N | 19°17′E |
| Sázava, r., Czech Rep. | 168 | 49°36′N | 15°24′E |
| Sazhino, Russia (såz-hē′nô) | 186a | 56°20′N | 58°15′E |
| Scandinavian Peninsula, pen., Eur. | 196 | 62°00′N | 14°00′E |
| Scanlon, Mn., U.S. (skăn′lôn) | 117h | 46°27′N | 92°26′W |
| Scappoose, Or., U.S. (skă-po͞os′) | 116c | 45°46′N | 122°53′W |
| Scappoose, r., Or., U.S. | 116c | 45°47′N | 122°57′W |
| Scarborough, Eng., U.K. (skär′bŭr-ô) | 164 | 54°16′N | 0°19′W |
| Scarsdale, N.Y., U.S. (skärz′dāl) | 110a | 41°01′N | 73°47′W |
| Scatari I, Can. (skăt′ȧ-rē) | 101 | 46°00′N | 59°44′W |
| Schaerbeek, Bel. (skär′bāk) | 159a | 50°50′N | 4°23′E |
| Schaffhausen, Switz. (shäf′hou-zĕn) | 161 | 47°42′N | 8°38′E |
| Schefferville, Can. | 91 | 54°52′N | 67°01′W |
| Schelde,, r., Eur. | 165 | 51°04′N | 3°55′E |
| Schenectady, N.Y., U.S. (skĕ-nĕk′tå-dê) | 105 | 42°50′N | 73°55′W |
| Scheveningen, Neth. | 159a | 52°06′N | 4°15′E |
| Schiedam, Neth. | 159a | 51°55′N | 4°23′E |
| Schiltigheim, Fr. (shêl′tegh-hīm) | 171 | 48°48′N | 7°47′E |
| Schio, Italy (skē′ô) | 174 | 45°43′N | 11°23′E |
| Schleswig, Ger. (shĕls′vêgh) | 160 | 54°32′N | 9°32′E |
| Schleswig , hist. reg., Ger. (shĕls′vêgh) | 168 | 54°40′N | 9°10′E |
| Schleswig-Holstein, state, Ger. (shlĕs′vêgh-hōl′shtīn) | 159c | 53°40′N | 9°45′E |
| Schmalkalden, Ger. (shmäl′käl-dĕn) | 168 | 50°41′N | 10°25′E |
| Schneider, In., U.S. (schnīd′ĕr) | 111a | 41°12′N | 87°26′W |
| Schofield, Wi., U.S. (skō′fêld) | 113 | 44°52′N | 89°37′W |
| Schönebeck, Ger. (shû′nĕ-bergh) | 168 | 52°01′N | 11°44′E |
| Schoonhoven, Neth. | 159a | 51°56′N | 4°51′E |
| Schramberg, Ger. (shräm′bĕrgh) | 168 | 48°14′N | 8°24′E |
| Schreiber, Can. | 98 | 48°50′N | 87°10′W |
| Schroon, l., N.Y., U.S. (skro͞on) | 109 | 43°50′N | 73°50′W |
| Schultzendorf, Ger. (sho͞ol′tzĕn-dōrf) | 159b | 52°21′N | 13°55′E |
| Schumacher, Can. | 98 | 48°30′N | 81°30′W |
| Schuyler, Ne., U.S. (slī′ler) | 112 | 41°28′N | 97°05′W |
| Schuylkill, r., Pa., U.S. (sko͞ol′kĭl) | 110f | 40°10′N | 75°31′W |
| Schuylkill-Haven, Pa., U.S. (sko͞ol′kĭl hā-vĕn) | 109 | 40°35′N | 76°10′W |
| Schwabach, Ger. (shvä′bäk) | 168 | 49°19′N | 11°02′E |
| Schwäbische Alb, mts., Ger. (shvă′bē-shĕ älb) | 168 | 48°11′N | 9°09′E |
| Schwäbisch Gmünd, Ger. (shvă′bēsh gmünd) | 168 | 48°47′N | 9°49′E |
| Schwäbisch Hall, Ger. (häl) | 168 | 49°08′N | 9°44′E |
| Schwandorf, Ger. (shvän′dôrf) | 168 | 49°19′N | 12°08′E |
| Schwaner, Pegunungan, mts., Indon. (sκvän′ĕr) | 212 | 1°05′S | 112°30′E |
| Schwarzwald, for., Ger. (shvärts′väld) | 168 | 47°54′N | 7°57′E |
| Schwaz, Aus. | 168 | 47°20′N | 11°45′E |
| Schwechat, Aus. (shvĕk′át) | 168 | 48°09′N | 16°29′E |
| Schwedt, Ger. (shvĕt) | 168 | 53°04′N | 14°17′E |
| Schweinfurt, Ger. (shvīn′fôrt) | 168 | 50°03′N | 10°14′E |
| Schwelm, Ger. (shvĕlm) | 171c | 51°17′N | 7°18′E |
| Schwerin, Ger. (shvĕ-rēn′) | 168 | 53°36′N | 11°25′E |
| Schweriner See, l., Ger. (shvĕ′rē-nĕr zā) | 168 | 53°40′N | 11°06′E |
| Schwerte, Ger. (shvĕr′tĕ) | 171c | 51°26′N | 7°34′E |
| Schwielowsee, l., Ger. (shvē′lōv zā) | 159b | 52°20′N | 12°52′E |
| Schwyz, Switz. (schēts) | 168 | 47°01′N | 8°38′E |
| Sciacca, Italy (shê-äk′kä) | 174 | 37°30′N | 13°09′E |
| Scilly, Isles of, is., Eng., U.K. (sĭl′ê) | 156 | 49°56′N | 6°50′W |
| Scioto, r., Oh., U.S. (sī-ō′tō) | 107 | 39°10′N | 82°55′W |
| Scituate, Ma., U.S. (sĭt′ū-āt) | 101a | 42°12′N | 70°45′W |
| Scobey, Mt., U.S. (skō′bê) | 115 | 48°48′N | 105°29′W |
| Scoggin, Or., U.S. (skō′gĭn) | 116c | 45°28′N | 123°14′W |
| Scotch, r., Can. (skŏch) | 102c | 45°21′N | 74°56′W |
| Scotia, Ca., U.S. (skō′shȧ) | 114 | 40°29′N | 124°06′W |
| Scotland, S.D., U.S. | 112 | 43°08′N | 97°43′W |
| Scotland, state, U.K. (skŏt′lȧnd) | 154 | 57°05′N | 5°10′W |
| Scotland Neck, N.C., U.S. (nĕk) | 125 | 36°06′N | 77°25′W |
| Scotstown, Can. (skŏts′toun) | 109 | 45°35′N | 71°15′W |
| Scott, r., Ca., U.S. | 114 | 41°20′N | 122°55′W |
| Scott, Cape, c., Can. (skŏt) | 92 | 50°47′N | 128°26′W |
| Scott, Mount, mtn., Or., U.S. | 116c | 45°27′N | 122°33′W |
| Scott, Mount, mtn., Or., U.S. | 114 | 42°55′N | 122°00′W |
| Scott Air Force Base, Il., U.S. | 117e | 38°33′N | 89°52′W |
| Scottburgh, S. Afr. (skŏt′bŭr-ô) | 232 | 30°18′S | 30°42′E |
| Scott City, Ks., U.S. | 120 | 38°28′N | 100°54′W |
| Scottdale, Ga., U.S. (skŏt′dāl) | 110c | 33°47′N | 84°16′W |
| Scott Islands, is., Ant. | 224 | 67°00′S | 178°00′E |
| Scottsbluff, Ne., U.S. (skŏts′blŭf) | 112 | 41°52′N | 103°40′W |
| Scottsboro, Al., U.S. (skŏts′bŭro) | 124 | 34°40′N | 86°03′W |
| Scottsburg, In., U.S. (skŏts′bûrg) | 108 | 38°40′N | 85°50′W |
| Scottsdale, Austl. (skŏts′dāl) | 222 | 41°12′S | 147°37′E |
| Scottsville, Ky., U.S. (skŏts′vĭl) | 124 | 36°45′N | 86°10′W |
| Scottville, Mi., U.S. | 108 | 44°00′N | 86°20′W |
| Scranton, Pa., U.S. (skrăn′tŭn) | 105 | 41°15′N | 75°45′W |
| Scugog, l., Can. (skū′gôg) | 99 | 44°05′N | 78°55′W |
| Scunthorpe, Eng., U.K. (skŭn′thôrp) | 158a | 53°36′N | 0°38′W |
| Scutari *see* Shkodër, Alb. | 154 | 42°04′N | 19°30′E |
| Scutari, Lake, l., Eur. (sko͞o′tä-rê) | 163 | 42°14′N | 19°33′E |
| Seabeck, Wa., U.S. (sē′bĕck) | 116a | 47°38′N | 122°50′W |
| Sea Bright, N.J., U.S. (sē brīt) | 110a | 40°22′N | 73°58′W |
| Seabrook, Tx., U.S. (sē′brok) | 123 | 29°34′N | 95°01′W |
| Seaford, De., U.S. (sē′fĕrd) | 109 | 38°35′N | 75°40′W |
| Seagraves, Tx., U.S. (sē′grāvs) | 120 | 32°51′N | 102°38′W |
| Sea Islands, is., Ga., U.S. (sē) | 125 | 31°21′N | 81°05′W |
| Seal, r., Can. | 92 | 59°08′N | 96°37′W |
| Seal Beach, Ca., U.S. | 117a | 33°44′N | 118°06′W |
| Seal Cays, is., Bah. | 135 | 22°40′N | 75°55′W |
| Seal Cays, is., T./C. Is. | 135 | 21°10′N | 71°45′W |
| Seal Island, i., S. Afr. (sēl) | 232a | 34°07′S | 18°36′E |
| Sealy, Tx., U.S. (sē′lê) | 123 | 29°46′N | 96°10′W |
| Searcy, Ar., U.S. (sûr′sê) | 121 | 35°13′N | 91°43′W |
| Searles, l., Ca., U.S. (sûrl′s) | 118 | 35°44′N | 117°22′W |
| Searsport, Me., U.S. (sērz′pōrt) | 100 | 44°28′N | 68°55′W |
| Seaside, Or., U.S. (sē′sīd) | 114 | 45°59′N | 123°55′W |
| Seattle, Wa., U.S. (sê-ăt′′l) | 104 | 47°36′N | 122°20′W |
| Sebaco, Nic. (sĕ-bä′kô) | 132 | 12°50′N | 86°03′W |
| Sebago, Me., U.S. (sê-bā′gō) | 100 | 43°52′N | 70°20′W |
| Sebastián Vizcaíno, Bahía, b., Mex. | 128 | 28°45′N | 115°15′W |
| Sebastopol, Ca., U.S. (sê-bås′tô-pôl) | 118 | 38°27′N | 122°50′W |
| Sebderat, Erit. | 231 | 15°30′N | 36°45′E |
| Sebewaing, Mi., U.S. (se′bê-wăng) | 108 | 43°45′N | 83°25′W |
| Sebezh, Russia (syĕ′bĕzh) | 176 | 56°16′N | 28°29′E |
| Sebinkarahisar, Tur. | 163 | 40°15′N | 38°10′E |
| Sebnitz, Ger. (zĕb′nêts) | 168 | 51°01′N | 14°16′E |
| Sebou, Oued, r., Mor. | 230 | 34°23′N | 5°18′W |
| Sebree, Ky., U.S. (sê-brē′) | 108 | 37°35′N | 87°30′W |
| Sebring, Fl., U.S. (sē′brĭng) | 125a | 27°30′N | 81°26′W |
| Sebring, Oh., U.S. | 108 | 40°55′N | 81°05′W |
| Secchia, r., Italy (sĕ′kyä) | 174 | 44°25′N | 10°25′E |
| Seco, r., Mex. (sĕ′kô) | 131 | 18°11′N | 93°18′W |
| Sedalia, Mo., U.S. | 105 | 38°42′N | 93°12′W |
| Sedan, Fr. (sẽ-däɴ) | 161 | 49°49′N | 4°55′E |
| Sedan, Ks., U.S. (sê-dăn′) | 121 | 37°07′N | 96°08′W |
| Sedom, Isr. | 197a | 31°04′N | 35°24′E |
| Sedro Woolley, Wa., U.S. (sē′drô-wol′ê) | 116a | 48°30′N | 122°14′W |
| Šeduva, Lith. (shĕ′do-vå) | 167 | 55°46′N | 23°45′E |
| Seestall, Ger. (zā′shtäl) | 159d | 47°58′N | 10°52′E |
| Sefrou, Mor. (sē-fro͞o′) | 162 | 33°49′N | 4°46′W |
| Seg, l., Russia (syĕgh) | 180 | 63°20′N | 33°30′E |
| Segamat, Malay. (sā′gå-måt) | 197b | 2°30′N | 102°49′E |
| Segang, China (sŭ-gäŋ) | 206 | 31°59′N | 114°13′E |
| Segbana, Benin | 235 | 10°56′N | 3°42′E |
| Segorbe, Spain (sĕ-gôr-bĕ) | 173 | 39°50′N | 0°30′W |
| Ségou, Mali (sā-go͞o′) | 230 | 13°27′N | 6°16′W |
| Segovia, Col. (sĕ-gô′vēä) | 142a | 7°08′N | 74°42′W |
| Segovia, Spain (så-gō′vê-ä) | 162 | 40°58′N | 4°05′W |
| Segre, r., Spain (så′grā) | 173 | 41°54′N | 1°10′E |
| Seguam, i., Ak., U.S. (sē′gwäm) | 103a | 52°16′N | 172°10′W |
| Seguam Passage, strt., Ak., U.S. | 103a | 52°20′N | 173°00′W |
| Séguédine, Niger | 235 | 20°12′N | 12°59′E |
| Séguéla, C. Iv. (sā-gā-lä′) | 230 | 7°57′N | 6°40′W |
| Seguin, Tx., U.S. (sĕ-gēn′) | 123 | 29°35′N | 97°58′W |
| Segula, i., Ak., U.S. (sē-gū′lå) | 103a | 52°08′N | 178°35′E |
| Segura, r., Spain | 162 | 38°24′N | 2°12′W |


ăt; finăl; rāte; senåte; ärm; åsk; sofȧ; fâre; ch-choose; dh-as th in other; bē; êvent; bĕt; recĕnt; cratẽr; g-gō; gh-guttural g; bĭt; ĭ-short neutral; rīde; κ-guttural k as ch in German ich;

PRONOUNCING INDEX

Segura – Sheksna 349


| PLACE (Pronunciation) | PAGE | LAT. | LONG. |
|---|---|---|---|
| Segura, Sierra de, mts., Spain (sē-ĕ′r-rä-dĕ) | 172 | 38°05′N | 2°45′W |
| Sehwān, Pak. | 202 | 26°33′N | 67°51′E |
| Seibo, Dom. Rep. (sĕ′y-bō) | 135 | 18°45′N | 69°05′W |
| Seiling, Ok., U.S. | 120 | 36°09′N | 98°56′W |
| Seim, r., Eur. | 181 | 51°23′N | 33°22′E |
| Seinäjoki, Fin. (så′ê-nĕ-yô′kê) | 167 | 62°47′N | 22°50′E |
| Seine, r., Can. (sån) | 102f | 49°48′N | 97°03′W |
| Seine, r., Can. (sån) | 98 | 49°04′N | 91°00′W |
| Seine, r., Fr. | 156 | 48°00′N | 4°30′E |
| Seine, Baie de la, b., Fr. (bī dĕ lä sån) | 170 | 49°37′N | 0°53′W |
| Seio do Venus, mtn., Braz. (sĕ-yô-dô-vĕ′nōōs) | 144b | 22°28′S | 43°12′W |
| Seixal, Port. (så-ê-shäl′) | 173b | 38°38′N | 9°06′W |
| Sekenke, Tan. | 237 | 4°16′S | 34°10′E |
| Şeki, Azer. | 182 | 41°12′N | 47°12′E |
| Sekondi-Takoradi, Ghana (sĕ-kôn′dê tä-kô-rä′dê) | 230 | 4°59′N | 1°43′W |
| Sekota, Eth. | 231 | 12°47′N | 38°59′E |
| Selangor, state, Malay. (så-län′gōr) | 197b | 2°53′N | 101°29′E |
| Selanovtsi, Blg. (sål′å-nôv-tsĭ) | 175 | 43°42′N | 24°05′E |
| Selaru, Pulau, i., Indon. | 213 | 8°30′S | 130°30′E |
| Selatan, Tanjung, c., Indon. (så-lä′tän) | 212 | 4°09′S | 114°40′E |
| Selawik, Ak., U.S. (sē-lå-wĭk) | 103 | 66°30′N | 160°09′W |
| Selayar, Pulau, i., Indon. | 212 | 6°15′S | 121°15′E |
| Selbusjøen, l., Nor. (sĕl′bōō) | 166 | 63°18′N | 11°55′E |
| Selby, Eng., U.K. (sĕl′bê) | 158a | 53°47′N | 1°03′W |
| Seldovia, Ak., U.S. (sĕl-dō′vê-å) | 103 | 59°26′N | 151°42′W |
| Selemdzha, r., Russia (sâ-lĕmt-zhä′) | 185 | 52°28′N | 131°50′E |
| Selenga (Selenge), r., Asia (sĕ lĕŋ gä′) | 179 | 49°00′N | 102°00′E |
| Selenge, r., Asia | 204 | 49°04′N | 102°23′E |
| Selennyakh, r., Russia (sĕl-yĭn-yäk) | 185 | 67°42′N | 141°45′E |
| Sélestat, Fr. (sẽ-lẽ-stä′) | 171 | 48°16′N | 7°27′E |
| Sélibaby, Maur. (så-lê-bå-bē′) | 230 | 15°21′N | 12°11′W |
| Seliger, l., Russia (sĕl′lê-gĕr) | 180 | 57°14′N | 33°18′E |
| Selizharovo, Russia (så′lê-zhä′rô-vô) | 176 | 56°51′N | 33°28′E |
| Selkirk, Can. (sĕl′kûrk) | 90 | 50°09′N | 96°52′W |
| Selkirk Mountains, mts., Can. | 92 | 51°00′N | 117°40′W |
| Selleck, Wa., U.S. (sĕl′ĕck) | 116a | 47°22′N | 121°52′W |
| Sellersburg, In., U.S. (sĕl′ĕrs-bûrg) | 111h | 38°25′N | 85°45′W |
| Sellya Khskaya, Guba, b., Russia (sĕl-yäk′skå-yå) | 185 | 72°30′N | 136°00′E |
| Selma, Al., U.S. (sĕl′må) | 105 | 32°25′N | 87°00′W |
| Selma, Ca., U.S. | 118 | 36°34′N | 119°37′W |
| Selma, N.C., U.S. | 125 | 35°33′N | 78°16′W |
| Selma, Tx., U.S. | 117d | 29°33′N | 98°19′W |
| Selmer, Tn., U.S. | 124 | 35°11′N | 88°36′W |
| Selsingen, Ger. (zĕl′zēn-gĕn) | 159c | 53°22′N | 9°13′E |
| Selway, r., Id., U.S. (sĕl′wå) | 114 | 46°07′N | 115°12′W |
| Selwyn, l., Can. (sĕl′wĭn) | 92 | 59°41′N | 104°30′W |
| Seman, r., Alb. | 175 | 40°48′N | 19°53′E |
| Semarang, Indon. (sĕ-mä′räng) | 212 | 7°03′S | 110°27′E |
| Semenivka, Ukr. | 181 | 52°10′N | 32°34′E |
| Semeru, Gunung, mtn., Indon. | 212 | 8°06′S | 112°55′E |
| Semey (Semipalatinsk), Kaz. | 183 | 50°28′N | 80°29′E |
| Semiahmoo Indian Reserve, I.R., Can. | 116d | 49°01′N | 122°43′W |
| Semiahmoo Spit, Wa., U.S. (sĕm′ĭ-å-mōō) | 116d | 48°59′N | 122°52′W |
| Semichi Islands, is., Ak., U.S. (sē-mē′chī) | 103a | 52°40′N | 174°50′E |
| Seminoe Reservoir, res., Wy., U.S. (sĕm′ĭ nô) | 115 | 42°08′N | 107°10′W |
| Seminole, Ok., U.S. (sĕm′ĭ-nōl) | 121 | 35°13′N | 96°41′W |
| Seminole, Tx., U.S. | 122 | 32°43′N | 102°39′W |
| Seminole, Lake, res., U.S. | 124 | 30°57′N | 84°46′W |
| Semipalatinsk *see* Semey, Kaz. | 183 | 50°28′N | 80°29′E |
| Semisopochnoi, i., Ak., U.S. (sĕ-mē-så-pōsh′ noi) | 103a | 51°45′N | 179°25′E |
| Semliki, r., Afr. (sĕm′lê-kē) | 231 | 0°45′N | 29°36′E |
| Semmering Pass, p., Aus. (sĕm′ĕr-ĭng) | 168 | 47°39′N | 15°50′E |
| Senador Pompeu, Braz. (sĕ-nä-dōr-pôm-pĕ′ô) | 143 | 5°34′S | 39°18′W |
| Senaki, Geor. | 182 | 42°17′N | 42°04′E |
| Senatobia, Ms., U.S. (sĕ-nå-tō′bê-å) | 124 | 34°36′N | 89°56′W |
| Sendai, Japan (sĕn-dī′) | 205 | 38°18′N | 141°02′E |
| Seneca, Ks., U.S. (sĕn′ĕ-kå) | 121 | 39°49′N | 96°03′W |
| Seneca, Md., U.S. | 110e | 39°04′N | 77°20′W |
| Seneca, S.C., U.S. | 125 | 34°40′N | 82°58′W |
| Seneca, l., N.Y., U.S. | 109 | 42°30′N | 76°55′W |
| Seneca Falls, N.Y., U.S. | 109 | 42°55′N | 76°55′W |
| Senegal, nation, Afr. (sĕn-ĕ-gôl′) | 230 | 14°53′N | 14°58′W |
| Sénégal, r., Afr. | 230 | 16°00′N | 14°00′W |
| Senekal, S. Afr. (sĕn′ê-kål) | 238c | 28°20′S | 27°37′E |
| Senftenberg, Ger. (zĕnf′tĕn-bĕrgh) | 168 | 51°32′N | 14°00′E |
| Sengunyane, r., Leso. | 233c | 29°35′S | 28°08′E |
| Senhor do Bonfim, Braz. (sĕn-yôr dô bôɴ-fē′ɴ) | 143 | 10°21′S | 40°09′W |
| Senigallia, Italy (så-nê-gäl′lyä) | 174 | 43°42′N | 13°16′E |
| Senj, Cro. (sĕn′) | 174 | 44°58′N | 14°55′E |
| Senja, i., Nor. (sĕnyä) | 160 | 69°28′N | 16°10′E |
| Senlis, Fr. (säɴ-lēs′) | 171b | 49°13′N | 2°35′E |
| Sennar Dam, dam, Sudan | 231 | 13°38′N | 33°38′E |
| Senneterre, Can. | 91 | 48°20′N | 77°22′W |
| Sens, Fr. (säɴs) | 170 | 48°05′N | 3°18′E |
| Sensuntepeque, El Sal. (sĕn-sōōn-tå-pā′kå) | 132 | 13°53′N | 88°34′W |
| Senta, Serb. (sĕn′tä) | 163 | 45°54′N | 20°05′E |
| Senzaki, Japan (sĕn′zä-kē) | 211 | 34°22′N | 131°09′E |
| Seoul (Sŏul), Kor., S. | 205 | 37°35′N | 127°03′E |
| Sepang, Malay. | 197b | 2°43′N | 101°45′E |
| Sepetiba, Baía de, b., Braz. (bäē′ä dĕ så-på-tē′bå) | 144b | 23°01′S | 43°42′W |
| Sepik, r. (sĕp-ēk′) | 213 | 4°07′S | 142°40′E |
| Septentrional, Cordillera, mts., Dom. Rep. | 135 | 19°50′N | 71°15′W |
| Septeuil, Fr. (sĕ-tû′) | 171b | 48°53′N | 1°40′E |
| Sept-Îles, Can. (sĕ-tēl′) | 100 | 50°12′N | 66°23′W |
| Sequatchie, r., Tn., U.S. (sê-kwăch′ê) | 124 | 35°33′N | 85°14′W |
| Sequim, Wa., U.S. (sē′kwĭm) | 116a | 48°05′N | 123°07′W |
| Sequim Bay, b., Wa., U.S. | 116a | 48°04′N | 122°58′W |
| Sequoia National Park, rec., Ca., U.S. (sê-kwoi′å) | 106 | 36°34′N | 118°37′W |
| Seraing, Bel. (sẽ-răɴ′) | 165 | 50°38′N | 5°28′E |
| Serāmpore, India | 202a | 22°44′N | 88°21′E |
| Serang, Indon. (så-räng′) | 212 | 6°13′S | 106°10′E |
| Seranggung, Indon. | 197b | 0°49′N | 104°11′E |
| Serbia and Montenegro (Yugoslavia), nation, Eur. | 154 | 44°00′N | 21°00′E |
| Serbia *see* Srbija, hist. reg., Serb. | 175 | 44°05′N | 20°35′E |
| Serdobsk, Russia (sĕr-dôpsk′) | 181 | 52°30′N | 44°20′E |
| Sered′, Slvk. | 169 | 48°17′N | 17°43′E |
| Seredyna-Buda, Ukr. | 176 | 52°11′N | 34°03′E |
| Seremban, Malay. (sĕr-ĕm-bän′) | 197b | 2°44′N | 101°57′E |
| Serengeti National Park, rec., Tan. | 237 | 2°20′S | 34°50′E |
| Serengeti Plain, pl., Tan. | 237 | 2°40′S | 34°55′E |
| Serenje, Zam. (sē-rĕn′yê) | 232 | 13°12′S | 30°49′E |
| Seret, r., Ukr. (sĕr′ĕt) | 169 | 49°45′N | 25°30′E |
| Sergeya Kirova, i., Russia (sēr-gyē′yå kê′rô-vå) | 184 | 77°30′N | 86°10′E |
| Sergipe, state, Braz. (sĕr-zhē′pĕ) | 143 | 10°27′S | 37°04′W |
| Sergiyev Posad, Russia | 186b | 56°18′N | 38°08′E |
| Sergiyevsk, Russia | 180 | 53°58′N | 51°00′E |
| Sérifos, Grc. | 175 | 37°10′N | 24°32′E |
| Sérifos, i., Grc. | 175 | 37°42′N | 24°17′E |
| Serodino, Arg. (sĕ-rô-dê′nō) | 141c | 32°36′S | 60°56′W |
| Seropédica, Braz. (sĕ-rô-pĕ′dē-kä) | 144b | 22°44′S | 43°43′W |
| Serov, Russia (syĕ-rôf′) | 184 | 59°36′N | 60°30′E |
| Serowe, Bots. (sĕ-rō′wĕ) | 232 | 22°18′S | 26°39′E |
| Serpa, Port. (sĕr-pä) | 172 | 37°56′N | 7°38′W |
| Serpukhov, Russia (syĕr′pô-ĸôf) | 178 | 54°53′N | 37°27′E |
| Sérres, Grc. (sĕr′rĕ) (sĕr′ĕs) | 163 | 41°06′N | 23°36′E |
| Serrinha, Braz. (sĕr-rēn′yå) | 143 | 11°43′S | 38°49′W |
| Serta, Port. (sĕr′tå) | 172 | 39°48′N | 8°01′W |
| Sertânia, Braz. (sĕr-tå′nyä) | 143 | 8°28′S | 37°13′W |
| Sertãozinho, Braz. (sĕr-touɴ-zê′n-yô) | 141a | 21°10′S | 47°58′W |
| Serting, r., Malay. | 197b | 3°01′N | 102°32′E |
| Sese Islands, is., Ug. | 237 | 0°30′S | 32°30′E |
| Sesia, r., Italy (såz′yä) | 174 | 45°33′N | 8°25′E |
| Sesimbra, Port. (sĕ-sê′m-brä) | 173b | 38°27′N | 9°06′W |
| Sesmyl, r., S. Afr. | 233b | 25°51′S | 28°06′E |
| Ses Salines, Cap de, c., Spain | 173 | 39°16′N | 3°03′E |
| Sestri Levante, Italy (sĕs′trê lå-vän′tå) | 174 | 44°15′N | 9°24′E |
| Sestroretsk, Russia (sĕs-trô-rĕtsk) | 180 | 60°06′N | 29°58′E |
| Sestroretskiy Razliv, Ozero, l., Russia | 186c | 60°05′N | 30°07′E |
| Seta, Japan (sĕ′tä) | 211b | 34°58′N | 135°56′W |
| Séte, Fr. (sĕt) | 161 | 43°24′N | 3°42′E |
| Sete Lagoas, Braz. (sĕ-tĕ lä-gô′äs) | 143 | 19°23′S | 43°58′W |
| Sete Pontes, Braz. | 144b | 22°51′S | 43°05′W |
| Seto, Japan (sē′tō) | 211 | 35°11′N | 137°07′E |
| Seto-Naikai, sea, Japan (sĕ′tô nī′kī) | 211 | 33°50′N | 132°25′E |
| Settat, Mor. (sĕt-ät′) (sē-tå′) | 230 | 33°02′N | 7°30′W |
| Sette-Cama, Gabon (sĕ-tĕ-kä-mä′) | 232 | 2°29′S | 9°40′E |
| Settlement Point, c., Bah. (sĕt′l-mĕnt) | 134 | 26°40′N | 79°00′W |
| Settlers, S. Afr. (sĕt′lẽrs) | 238c | 24°57′S | 28°33′E |
| Settsu, Japan | 211b | 34°46′N | 135°33′E |
| Setúbal, Port. (så-tōō′bäl) | 162 | 30°32′N | 8°54′W |
| Setúbal, Baía de, b., Port. | 172 | 38°27′N | 9°08′W |
| Seul, Lac, l., Can. (låk sûl) | 93 | 50°20′N | 92°30′W |
| Sevan, l., Arm. (syĭ-vän′) | 181 | 40°10′N | 45°20′E |
| Sevastopol′, Ukr. (syĕ-vås-tô′pôl′′) | 178 | 44°34′N | 33°34′E |
| Sevenoaks, Eng., U.K. (sĕ-vĕn-ôks′) | 158b | 51°16′N | 0°12′E |
| Severka, r., Russia (sâ′vĕr-kå) | 186b | 55°11′N | 38°41′E |
| Severn, r., Can. (sĕv′ẽrn) | 93 | 55°21′N | 88°42′W |
| Severn, r., U.K. | 164 | 51°50′N | 2°25′W |
| Severna Park, Md., U.S. (sĕv′ẽrn-å) | 110e | 39°04′N | 76°33′W |
| Severnaya Dvina, r., Russia | 178 | 63°00′N | 42°40′E |
| Severnaya Zemlya (Northern Land), is., Russia (sĕ-vyĭr-nīû zĭ-m′lyä′) | 179 | 79°33′N | 101°15′E |
| Severoural′sk, Russia (sĕ-vyĭ-rŭ-ōō-rälsk′) | 184 | 60°08′N | 59°53′E |
| Sevier, r., Ut., U.S. | 106 | 39°25′N | 112°20′W |
| Sevier, East Fork, r., Ut., U.S. | 119 | 37°45′N | 112°10′W |
| Sevier Lake, l., Ut., U.S. (sê-vēr′) | 119 | 38°55′N | 113°10′W |
| Sevilla, Col. (sĕ-vê′l-yä) | 142a | 4°16′N | 75°56′W |
| Sevilla, Spain (så-vēl′yä) | 154 | 37°29′N | 5°58′W |
| Seville, Oh., U.S. (sĕ′vĭl) | 111d | 41°01′N | 81°45′W |
| Sevlievo, Blg. (sĕv′lyĕ-vô) | 163 | 43°02′N | 25°05′E |
| Sevsk, Russia (syĕfsk) | 176 | 52°08′N | 34°28′E |
| Seward, Ak., U.S. (sū′ård) | 106a | 60°18′N | 149°28′W |
| Seward, Ne., U.S. | 121 | 40°55′N | 97°06′W |
| Seward Peninsula, pen., Ak., U.S. | 103 | 65°40′N | 164°00′W |
| Sewell, Chile (sĕ′ô-ĕl) | 144 | 34°01′S | 70°18′W |
| Sewickley, Pa., U.S. (sê-wĭk′lê) | 111e | 40°33′N | 80°11′W |
| Seybaplaya, Mex. (sā-ê-bä-plä′yä) | 131 | 19°38′N | 90°40′W |
| Seychelles, nation, Afr. (sā-shĕl′) | 3 | 5°20′S | 55°10′E |
| Seydisfjördur, Ice. (sā′dês-fyûr-dôr) | 160 | 65°21′N | 14°08′W |
| Seyhan, r., Tur. | 163 | 37°28′N | 35°40′E |
| Seylac, Som. | 238a | 11°19′N | 43°20′E |
| Seymour, S. Afr. (sē′môr) | 233c | 32°33′S | 26°48′E |
| Seymour, Ia., U.S. | 113 | 40°41′N | 93°03′W |
| Seymour, In., U.S. (sē′mōr) | 108 | 38°55′N | 85°55′W |
| Seymour, Tx., U.S. | 120 | 33°35′N | 99°16′W |
| Sezela, S. Afr. | 233c | 30°33′S | 30°37′W |
| Sezze, Italy (sĕt′så) | 174 | 41°32′N | 13°00′E |
| Sfântu Gheorghe, Rom. | 163 | 45°53′N | 25°49′E |
| Sfax, Tun. (sfäks) | 230 | 34°51′N | 10°45′E |
| ′s-Gravenhage *see* The Hague, Neth. (′s ĸrä′vĕn-hä′ĸĕ) (hāg) | 154 | 52°05′N | 4°16′E |
| Sha, r., China (shä) | 205 | 33°33′N | 114°30′E |
| Shaanxi, prov., China (shän-shyē) | 204 | 35°30′N | 109°10′E |
| Shabeelle (Shebele), r., Afr. | 238a | 1°38′N | 43°50′E |
| Shache, China (shä-chŭ) | 204 | 38°15′N | 77°15′E |
| Shackleton Ice Shelf, ice, Ant. (shăk′′l-tŭn) | 224 | 65°00′S | 100°00′E |
| Shades Creek, r., Al., U.S. (shādz) | 110h | 33°20′N | 86°55′W |
| Shades Mountain, mtn., Al., U.S. | 110h | 33°22′N | 86°51′W |
| Shagamu, Nig. | 235 | 6°51′N | 3°39′E |
| Shāhdād, Namakzār-e, l., Iran (nŭ-mŭk-zär′) | 198 | 31°00′N | 58°30′E |
| Shāhjahānpur, India (shä-jŭ-hän′pōōr) | 199 | 27°58′N | 79°58′E |
| Shajing, China (shä-jyĭŋ) | 207a | 22°44′N | 113°48′E |
| Shaker Heights, Oh., U.S. (shā′kẽr) | 111d | 41°28′N | 81°34′W |
| Shakhty, Russia (shäĸ′tê) | 178 | 47°41′N | 40°11′E |
| Shaki, Nig. | 235 | 8°39′N | 3°25′E |
| Shakopee, Mn., U.S. (shăk′ô-pe) | 117g | 44°48′N | 93°31′W |
| Shala Lake, l., Eth. (shä′lå) | 231 | 7°34′N | 39°00′E |
| Shalqar, Kaz. | 183 | 47°52′N | 59°41′E |
| Shalqar köli, l., Kaz. | 181 | 50°30′N | 51°30′E |
| Shām, Jabal ash, mtn., Oman | 198 | 23°01′N | 57°45′E |
| Shambe, Sudan (shäm′bå) | 231 | 7°08′N | 30°46′E |
| Shammar, Jabal, mts., Sau. Ar. (jĕb′ĕl shŭm′år) | 198 | 27°13′N | 40°16′E |
| Shamokin, Pa., U.S. (shå-mō′kĭn) | 109 | 40°45′N | 76°30′W |
| Shamrock, Tx., U.S. (shăm′rŏk) | 120 | 35°14′N | 100°12′W |
| Shamva, Zimb. (shäm′vå) | 232 | 17°18′S | 31°35′E |
| Shandon, Oh., U.S. (shăn-dŭn) | 111f | 39°20′N | 84°13′W |
| Shandong, prov., China (shän-dôŋ) | 205 | 36°08′N | 117°09′E |
| Shandong Bandao, pen., China (shän-dôŋ bän-dou) | 205 | 37°00′N | 120°10′E |
| Shangcai, China (shäŋ-tsī) | 206 | 33°16′N | 114°16′E |
| Shangcheng, China (shäŋ-chŭŋ) | 206 | 31°47′N | 115°22′E |
| Shangdu, China (shäŋ-dōō) | 208 | 41°38′N | 113°22′E |
| Shanghai, China (shäng′hī′) | 205 | 31°14′N | 121°27′E |
| Shanghai Shi, prov., China (shäŋ-hī shr) | 205 | 31°30′N | 121°45′E |
| Shanghe, China (shäŋ-hŭ) | 206 | 37°18′N | 117°10′E |
| Shanglin, China (shäŋ-lĭn) | 206 | 38°20′N | 116°05′E |
| Shangqiu, China (shäŋ-chyô) | 208 | 34°24′N | 115°39′E |
| Shangrao, China (shäŋ-rou) | 209 | 28°25′N | 117°58′E |
| Shangzhi, China (shäŋ-jr) | 208 | 45°18′N | 127°52′E |
| Shanhaiguan, China | 208 | 40°01′N | 119°45′E |
| Shannon, Al., U.S. (shăn′ŭn) | 110h | 33°23′N | 86°52′W |
| Shannon, r., Ire. (shăn′ŏn) | 161 | 52°30′N | 10°15′W |
| Shanshan, China (shän′shän′) | 204 | 42°51′N | 89°53′E |
| Shantar, i., Russia (shän′tär) | 185 | 55°13′N | 138°42′E |
| Shantou, China (shän-tō) | 205 | 23°20′N | 116°40′E |
| Shanxi, prov., China (shän-shyē) | 205 | 37°30′N | 112°00′E |
| Shan Xian, China (shän shyĕn) | 206 | 34°47′N | 116°04′E |
| Shaobo, China (shou-bwo) | 208 | 32°33′N | 119°30′E |
| Shaobo Hu, l., China (shou-bwo hōō) | 206 | 32°47′N | 119°13′E |
| Shaoguan, China (shou-gůän) | 205 | 24°58′N | 113°42′E |
| Shaoxing, China (shou-shyĭŋ) | 205 | 30°00′N | 120°40′E |
| Shaoyang, China | 205 | 27°15′N | 111°28′E |
| Shapki, Russia (shäp′kĭ) | 186c | 59°36′N | 31°11′E |
| Shark Bay, b., Austl. (shärk) | 220 | 25°30′S | 113°00′E |
| Sharon, Ma., U.S. (shăr′ŏn) | 101a | 42°07′N | 71°11′W |
| Sharon, Pa., U.S. | 108 | 41°15′N | 80°30′W |
| Sharon Springs, Ks., U.S. | 120 | 38°51′N | 101°45′W |
| Sharonville, Oh., U.S. (shăr′ŏn vĭl) | 111f | 39°16′N | 84°24′W |
| Sharpsburg, Pa., U.S. (shărps′bûrg) | 111e | 40°30′N | 79°54′W |
| Sharr, Jabal, mtn., Sau. Ar. | 198 | 28°00′N | 36°07′E |
| Shashi, China (shä-shē) | 205 | 30°20′N | 112°18′E |
| Shasta, Mount, mtn., Ca., U.S. | 106 | 41°35′N | 122°12′W |
| Shasta Lake, res., Ca., U.S. (shăs′tå) | 106 | 40°51′N | 122°32′W |
| Shatsk, Russia (shåtsk) | 180 | 54°00′N | 41°40′E |
| Shattuck, Ok., U.S. (shăt′ŭk) | 120 | 36°16′N | 99°53′W |
| Shaunavon, Can. | 90 | 49°40′N | 108°25′W |
| Shaw, Ms., U.S. (shô) | 124 | 33°36′N | 90°44′W |
| Shawano, Wi., U.S. (shå-wô′nô) | 113 | 44°41′N | 88°13′W |
| Shawinigan, Can. | 91 | 46°32′N | 72°46′W |
| Shawnee, Ks., U.S. (shô-nē′) | 117f | 39°01′N | 94°43′W |
| Shawnee, Ok., U.S. | 104 | 35°20′N | 96°54′W |
| Shawneetown, Il., U.S. (shô′nē-toun) | 108 | 37°40′N | 88°05′W |
| Shayang, China | 209 | 31°00′N | 112°38′E |
| Shchara, r., Bela. (sh-chå′rå) | 169 | 53°17′N | 25°12′E |
| Shchëlkovo, Russia (shchĕl′kô-vô) | 176 | 55°55′N | 38°00′E |
| Shchigry, Russia (shchē′grê) | 177 | 51°52′N | 36°54′E |
| Shchors, Ukr. (shchôrs) | 177 | 51°38′N | 31°58′E |
| Shchuch′ye Ozero, Russia (shchōōch′yĕ ô′zĕ-rō) | 186a | 56°31′N | 56°35′E |
| Sheakhala, India | 202a | 22°47′N | 88°10′E |
| Shebele (Shabeelle), r., Afr. (shā′bå-lē) | 238a | 6°07′N | 43°10′E |
| Sheboygan, Wi., U.S. (shê-boi′găn) | 105 | 43°45′N | 87°44′W |
| Sheboygan Falls, Wi., U.S. | 113 | 43°43′N | 87°51′W |
| Shechem, hist., W.B. | 197a | 32°15′N | 35°22′E |
| Shedandoah, Pa., U.S. | 109 | 40°50′N | 76°15′W |
| Shediac, Can. (shĕ′dê-ăk) | 100 | 46°13′N | 64°32′W |
| Shedin Peak, mtn., Can. (shĕd′ĭn) | 94 | 55°55′N | 127°32′W |
| Sheerness, Eng., U.K. (shēr′nĕs) | 158b | 51°26′N | 0°46′E |
| Sheffield, Can. | 102d | 43°20′N | 80°13′W |
| Sheffield, Eng., U.K. | 160 | 53°23′N | 1°28′W |
| Sheffield, Al., U.S. (shĕf′fēld) | 124 | 35°42′N | 87°42′W |
| Sheffield, Oh., U.S. | 111d | 41°26′N | 82°05′W |
| Sheffield, co., Eng., U.K. | 158a | 53°52′N | 1°35′W |
| Sheffield Lake, Oh., U.S. | 111d | 41°30′N | 82°03′W |
| Sheksna, r., Russia (shĕks′nå) | 180 | 59°50′N | 38°40′E |


ng-sing; ŋ-baŋk; ɴ-nasalized n; nŏd; cŏmmit; ōld; ôbey; ôrder; oi-boil; fōōd; ô-as oo in foot; ou-out; s-soft; sh-dish; th-thin; pūre; ůnite; ûrn; stŭd; circŭs; ü-as in French tu; ′-indeterminate vowel.

ăt; finăl; rāte; senåte; ärm; åsk; sofá; fåre; ch-choose; dh-as th in other; bē; ēvent; bĕt; recĕnt; cratẽr; g-gō; gh-guttural g; bīt; ĩ-short neutral; rīde; κ-guttural k as ch in German ich;

352 Sofia – Spas-Klepiki

PRONOUNCING INDEX


| PLACE (Pronunciation) | PAGE | LAT. | LONG. |
|---|---|---|---|
| Sofia (Sofiya), Blg. (sô'fē-yȧ) (sô'fē-ȧ) | 154 | 42°43'N | 23°20'E |
| Sofiïvka, Ukr. | 177 | 48°03'N | 33°53'E |
| Sofiya *see* Sofia, Blg. | 154 | 42°43'N | 23°20'E |
| Soga, Japan (sō'gä) | 211a | 35°35'N | 140°08'E |
| Sogamoso, Col. (sô-gä-mō'sō) | 142 | 5°42'N | 72°51'W |
| Sognafjorden, b., Nor. | 156 | 61°09'N | 5°30'E |
| Sogozha, r., Russia (sô'gô-zhȧ) | 176 | 58°35'N | 39°08'E |
| Sohano, Pap. N. Gui. | 214e | 5°27'S | 154°40'E |
| Soissons, Fr. (swä-sôɴ') | 170 | 49°23'N | 3°17'E |
| Sōka, Japan (sō'kä) | 211a | 35°50'N | 139°49'E |
| Sokal', Ukr. (sô'käl') | 169 | 50°28'N | 24°20'E |
| Söke, Tur. (sû'kĕ) | 163 | 37°40'N | 27°10'E |
| Sokółka, Pol. (sô-kōl'kȧ) | 169 | 53°23'N | 23°30'E |
| Sokolo, Mali (sô-kô-lō') | 230 | 14°51'N | 6°09'W |
| Sokołów Podlaski, Pol. (sô-kô-wôf' pŭd-lä'skĭ) | 169 | 52°24'N | 22°15'E |
| Sokone, Sen. | 234 | 13°53'N | 16°22'W |
| Sokoto, Nig. (sō'kô-tô) | 230 | 13°04'N | 5°16'E |
| Sola de Vega, Mex. | 131 | 16°31'N | 96°58'W |
| Solander, Cape, c., Austl. | 217b | 34°03'S | 151°16'E |
| Solano, Phil. (sō-lä'nō) | 213a | 16°31'N | 121°11'E |
| Soledad, Col. (sō-lĕ-dä'd) | 142 | 10°47'N | 75°00'W |
| Soledad Díez Gutiérrez, Mex. | 130 | 22°19'N | 100°54'W |
| Soleduck, r., Wa., U.S. (sōl'dŭk) | 114 | 47°59'N | 124°28'W |
| Solentiname, Islas de, is., Nic. (ē's-läs-dĕ-sô-lĕn-tē-nä'mȧ) | 132 | 11°15'N | 85°16'W |
| Solihull, Eng., U.K. (sō'lĭ-hŭl) | 158a | 52°25'N | 1°46'W |
| Solihull, co., Eng., U.K. | 158a | 52°25'N | 1°42'W |
| Solikamsk, Russia (sô-lē-kȧmsk') | 180 | 59°38'N | 56°48'E |
| Sol'-Iletsk, Russia | 178 | 51°10'N | 55°05'E |
| Solimões *see* Amazon, r., Braz. | 142 | 2°45'S | 67°44'W |
| Solingen, Ger. (zō'lĭng-ĕn) | 168 | 51°10'N | 7°05'E |
| Sóller, Spain (sō'lyĕr) | 173 | 39°45'N | 2°40'E |
| Sologne, reg., Fr. (sō-lōn'yĕ) | 170 | 47°36'N | 1°53'E |
| Solola, Guat. (sô-lō'lä) | 132 | 14°45'N | 91°12'W |
| Solomon, r., Ks., U.S. | 120 | 39°24'N | 98°19'W |
| Solomon, North Fork, r., Ks., U.S. | 120 | 39°34'N | 99°52'W |
| Solomon, South Fork, r., Ks., U.S. | 120 | 39°19'N | 99°52'W |
| Solomon Islands, nation, Oc. (sŏ'lō-mŭn) | 3 | 7°00'S | 160°00'E |
| Solon, China (swo-lōōn) | 205 | 46°32'N | 121°18'E |
| Solon, Oh., U.S. (sō'lŭn) | 111d | 41°23'N | 81°26'W |
| Solothurn, Switz. (zō'lō-thōōrn) | 168 | 47°13'N | 7°30'E |
| Solovetskiye Ostrova, is., Russia | 180 | 65°10'N | 35°40'E |
| Šolta, i., Serb. (shōl'tä) | 174 | 43°20'N | 16°15'E |
| Soltau, Ger. (sōl'tou) | 168 | 53°00'N | 9°50'E |
| Sol'tsy, Russia (sôl'tsē) | 176 | 58°04'N | 30°13'E |
| Solvay, N.Y., U.S. (sŏl'vā) | 109 | 43°05'N | 76°10'W |
| Sölvesborg, Swe. (sûl'vĕs-bôrg) | 166 | 56°04'N | 14°35'E |
| Sol'vychegodsk, Russia (sôl'vē-chĕ-gôtsk') | 180 | 61°18'N | 46°58'E |
| Solway Firth, b., U.K. (sŏl'wā fûrth') | 160 | 54°42'N | 3°55'W |
| Solwezi, Zam. | 237 | 12°11'S | 26°25'E |
| Soly, Bela. | 166 | 54°31'N | 26°11'E |
| Somalia, nation, Afr. (sō-mä'lē-ȧ) | 238a | 3°28'N | 44°47'E |
| Somanga, Tan. | 237 | 8°24'S | 39°17'E |
| Sombor, Serb. (sôm'bôr) | 163 | 45°45'N | 19°10'E |
| Sombrerete, Mex. (sōm-brā-rā'tā) | 130 | 23°38'N | 103°37'W |
| Sombrero, Cayo, i., Ven. (kä-yô-sôm-brĕ'rô) | 143b | 10°52'N | 68°12'W |
| Somerset, Ky., U.S. (sŭm'ĕr-sĕt) | 124 | 37°05'N | 84°35'W |
| Somerset, Ma., U.S. | 110b | 41°46'N | 71°05'W |
| Somerset, Pa., U.S. | 109 | 40°00'N | 79°05'W |
| Somerset, Tx., U.S. | 117d | 29°13'N | 98°39'W |
| Somerset East, S. Afr. | 233c | 32°44'S | 25°36'E |
| Somersworth, N.H., U.S. (sŭm'ĕrz-wûrth) | 100 | 43°16'N | 70°53'W |
| Somerton, Az., U.S. (sŭm'ĕr-tŭn) | 119 | 32°36'N | 114°43'W |
| Somerville, Ma., U.S. (sŭm'ĕr-vĭl) | 101a | 42°23'N | 71°06'W |
| Somerville, N.J., U.S. | 110a | 40°34'N | 74°37'W |
| Somerville, Tn., U.S. | 124 | 35°14'N | 89°21'W |
| Somerville, Tx., U.S. | 123 | 30°21'N | 96°31'W |
| Someș, r., Eur. | 169 | 47°43'N | 23°09'E |
| Somma Vesuviana, Italy (sôm'mä vā-zōō-vē-ä'nä) | 173c | 40°38'N | 14°27'E |
| Somme, r., Fr. (sŏm) | 170 | 50°02'N | 2°04'E |
| Sommerfeld, Ger. (zō'mĕr-fĕld) | 159b | 52°48'N | 13°02'E |
| Sommerville, Austl. | 217a | 38°14'S | 145°10'E |
| Somoto, Nic. (sô-mō'tō) | 132 | 13°28'N | 86°37'W |
| Son, r., India (sōn) | 199 | 24°40'N | 82°35'E |
| Sŏnchŏn, Kor., N. (sŭn'shŭn) | 210 | 39°49'N | 124°56'E |
| Sondags, r., S. Afr. | 233c | 33°17'S | 25°14'E |
| Sønderborg, Den. (sûn''er-bôrgh) | 160 | 54°55'N | 9°47'E |
| Sondershausen, Ger. (zōn'dĕrz-hou'zĕn) | 168 | 51°17'N | 10°45'E |
| Song Ca, r., Viet. | 209 | 19°15'N | 105°00'E |
| Songea, Tan. (sōn-gā'ȧ) | 232 | 10°41'S | 35°39'E |
| Songjiang, China | 205 | 31°01'N | 121°14'E |
| Sŏngjin, Kor., N. (sŭng'jĭn') | 210 | 40°38'N | 129°10'E |
| Songkhla, Thai. (sông'ĸlä') | 212 | 7°09'N | 100°34'E |
| Songwe, D.R.C. | 237 | 12°25'S | 29°40'E |
| Sonneberg, Ger. (sōn'ē-bĕrgh) | 168 | 50°20'N | 11°14'E |
| Sonora, Ca., U.S. (sô-nō'rȧ) | 118 | 37°58'N | 120°22'W |
| Sonora, Tx., U.S. | 122 | 30°33'N | 100°38'W |
| Sonora, state, Mex. | 128 | 29°45'N | 111°15'W |
| Sonora, r., Mex. | 128 | 28°45'N | 111°35'W |
| Sonora Peak, mtn., Ca., U.S. | 106 | 38°22'N | 119°39'W |
| Sonseca, Spain (sôn-sā'kä) | 172 | 39°41'N | 3°56'W |
| Sonsón, Col. (sôn-sôn') | 142 | 5°42'N | 75°28'W |
| Sonsonate, El Sal. (sōn-sō-nä'tā) | 132 | 13°46'N | 89°43'W |
| Sonsorol Islands, is., Palau (sŏn-sô-rōl') | 213 | 5°03'N | 132°33'E |
| Sooke Basin, b., Can. (sŏŏk) | 116a | 48°21'N | 123°47'W |
| Soo Locks, trans., Mi., U.S. (sōō lŏks) | 117a | 46°30'N | 84°30'W |
| Sopetrán, Col. (sō-pĕ-trä'n) | 142a | 6°30'N | 75°44'W |
| Sopot, Pol. (sô'pôt) | 169 | 54°26'N | 18°25'E |
| Sopron, Hung. (shŏp'rŏn) | 163 | 47°41'N | 16°36'E |
| Sora, Italy (sô'rä) | 174 | 41°43'N | 13°37'E |
| Sorbas, Spain (sôr'bäs) | 172 | 37°05'N | 2°07'W |
| Sordo, r., Mex. (sô'r-dō) | 131 | 16°39'N | 97°33'W |
| Sorel, Can. (sō-rĕl') | 91 | 46°01'N | 73°07'W |
| Sorell, Cape, c., Austl. | 222 | 42°10'S | 144°50'E |
| Soresina, Italy (sō-rā-zē'nä) | 174 | 45°17'N | 9°51'E |
| Soria, Spain (sō'rē-ä) | 162 | 41°46'N | 2°28'W |
| Soriano, dept., Ur. (sō-rēä'nô) | 141c | 33°25'S | 58°00'W |
| Soroca, Mol. | 181 | 48°09'N | 28°17'E |
| Sorocaba, Braz. (sô-rô-kä'bȧ) | 143 | 23°29'S | 47°27'W |
| Sorong, Indon. (sō-rông') | 213 | 1°00'S | 131°20'E |
| Sorot', r., Russia (sō-rō'tzh) | 176 | 57°08'N | 29°23'E |
| Soroti, Ug. (sō-rō'tē) | 231 | 1°43'N | 33°37'E |
| Sørøya, i., Nor. | 160 | 70°37'N | 20°58'E |
| Sorraia, r., Port. (sôr-rī'ȧ) | 172 | 38°55'N | 8°42'W |
| Sorrento, Italy (sôr-rĕn'tō) | 174 | 40°23'N | 14°23'E |
| Sorsogon, Phil. (sôr-sōgōn') | 213 | 12°51'N | 124°02'E |
| Sortavala, Russia (sôr'tä-vä-lä) | 178 | 61°43'N | 30°40'E |
| Sosna, r., Russia (sôs'nȧ) | 177 | 50°33'N | 38°15'E |
| Sosnogorsk, Russia | 178 | 63°13'N | 54°09'E |
| Sosnowiec, Pol. (sôs-nô'vyĕts) | 169 | 50°17'N | 19°10'E |
| Sosnytsia, Ukr. | 177 | 51°30'N | 32°29'E |
| Sosunova, Mys, c., Russia (mĭs sô'sô-nôf'ȧ) | 210 | 46°28'N | 138°06'E |
| Sos'va, r., Russia (sôs'vȧ) | 186a | 59°55'N | 60°40'E |
| Sos'va, r., Russia (sôs'vȧ) | 180 | 63°10'N | 63°30'E |
| Sota, r., Benin | 235 | 11°10'N | 3°20'E |
| Sota la Marina, Mex. (sô-tä-lä-mä-rē'nä) | 130 | 23°45'N | 98°11'W |
| Soteapan, Mex. (sō-tā-ä'pän) | 131 | 18°14'N | 94°51'W |
| Soto la Marina, Río, r., Mex. (rē'ō-so'tō lä mä-rē'nä) | 130 | 23°55'N | 98°30'W |
| Sotuta, Mex. (sō-tōō'tä) | 132a | 20°35'N | 89°00'W |
| Soublette, Ven. (sō-ōō-blĕ'tĕ) | 143b | 9°55'N | 66°06'W |
| Souflí, Grc. | 175 | 41°12'N | 26°17'E |
| Soufrière, St. Luc. (sōō-frē-âr') | 133b | 13°50'N | 61°03'W |
| Soufrière, mtn., St. Vin. | 133b | 13°19'N | 61°12'W |
| Soufrière, vol., Guad. (sōō-frē-âr') | 133b | 16°06'N | 61°42'W |
| Sŏul *see* Seoul, Kor., S. | 205 | 37°35'N | 127°03'E |
| Sounding Creek, r., Can. (soun'dĭng) | 96 | 51°35'N | 111°00'W |
| Souq Ahras, Alg. | 161 | 36°23'N | 8°00'E |
| Sources, Mount aux, mtn., Afr. (môn'tō sôrs') | 232 | 28°47'S | 29°04'E |
| Soure, Port. (sōr-ĕ) | 172 | 40°04'N | 8°37'W |
| Souris, Can. (sōō'rē') | 101 | 46°20'N | 62°17'W |
| Souris, Can. | 90 | 49°38'N | 100°15'W |
| Souris, r., N.A. | 92 | 48°30'N | 101°30'W |
| Sourlake, Tx., U.S. (sour'lāk) | 123 | 30°09'N | 94°24'W |
| Sousse, Tun. (sōōs) | 230 | 36°00'N | 10°39'E |
| South, r., Ga., U.S. | 110c | 33°40'N | 84°15'W |
| South, r., N.C., U.S. | 125 | 34°49'N | 78°33'W |
| South Africa, nation, Afr. | 232 | 28°00'S | 24°50'E |
| South Amboy, N.J., U.S. (south'ăm'boi) | 110a | 40°28'N | 74°17'W |
| South America, cont. | 139 | 15°00'S | 60°00'W |
| Southampton, Eng., U.K. (south-ămp'tŭn) | 154 | 50°54'N | 1°30'W |
| Southampton, N.Y., U.S. | 109 | 40°53'N | 72°24'W |
| Southampton Island, i., Can. | 93 | 64°38'N | 84°00'W |
| South Andaman Island, i., India (ăn-dȧ-măn') | 212 | 11°57'N | 93°24'E |
| South Australia, state, Austl. (ôs-trā'lĭ-ȧ) | 218 | 29°45'S | 132°00'E |
| South Bay, b., Bah. | 135 | 20°55'N | 73°35'W |
| South Bend, In., U.S. (bĕnd) | 105 | 41°40'N | 86°20'W |
| South Bend, Wa., U.S. (bĕnd) | 114 | 46°39'N | 123°48'W |
| South Bight, b., Bah. | 134 | 24°20'N | 77°35'W |
| South Bimini, i., Bah. (bē'mē-nē) | 134 | 25°40'N | 79°20'W |
| Southborough, Ma., U.S. (south'bŭr-ō) | 101a | 42°18'N | 71°33'W |
| South Boston, Va., U.S. (bôs'tŭn) | 125 | 36°41'N | 78°55'W |
| Southbridge, Ma., U.S. (south'brĭj) | 109 | 42°05'N | 72°00'W |
| South Caicos, i., T./C. Is. (kī'kōs) | 135 | 21°30'N | 71°35'W |
| South Carolina, state, U.S. (kăr-ō-lī'nȧ) | 105 | 34°15'N | 81°10'W |
| South Cave, Eng., U.K. (cāv) | 158a | 53°45'N | 0°35'W |
| South Charleston, W.V., U.S. | 108 | 38°20'N | 81°40'W |
| South China Sea, sea, Asia (chī'nȧ) | 212 | 15°23'N | 114°12'E |
| South Creek, r., Austl. | 217b | 33°43'S | 150°50'E |
| South Dakota, state, U.S. (dȧ-kō'tȧ) | 104 | 44°20'N | 101°55'W |
| South Downs, Eng., U.K. (dounz) | 164 | 50°55'N | 1°13'W |
| South Dum-Dum, India | 202a | 22°36'N | 88°25'E |
| South East Cape, c., Austl. | 221 | 43°47'S | 146°03'E |
| Southend-on-Sea, Eng., U.K. (south-ĕnd') | 165 | 51°33'N | 0°41'E |
| Southern Alps, mts., N.Z. (sŭ-thûrn ălps) | 221a | 43°35'S | 170°00'E |
| Southern Cross, Austl. | 218 | 31°13'S | 119°30'E |
| Southern Indian, l., Can. (sŭth'ĕrn ĭn'dĭ-ăn) | 92 | 56°46'N | 98°57'W |
| Southern Pines, N.C., U.S. (sŭth'ĕrn pīnz) | 125 | 35°10'N | 79°23'W |
| Southern Ute Indian Reservation, I.R., Co., U.S. (ūt) | 119 | 37°05'N | 108°23'W |
| South Euclid, Oh., U.S. (ū'klĭd) | 111d | 41°30'N | 81°34'W |
| South Fox, i., Mi., U.S. (fŏks) | 108 | 45°25'N | 85°55'W |
| South Gate, Ca., U.S. (gāt) | 117a | 33°57'N | 118°13'W |
| South Georgia, i., S. Geor. (jôr'jȧ) | 139 | 54°00'S | 37°00'W |
| South Haven, Mi., U.S. (hāv''n) | 108 | 42°25'N | 86°15'W |
| South Hill, Va., U.S. | 125 | 36°44'N | 78°08'W |
| South Holston Lake, res., U.S. | 125 | 36°35'N | 82°00'W |
| South Indian Lake, Can. | 97 | 56°50'N | 99°00'W |
| Southington, Ct., U.S. (sŭdh'ĭng-tŭn) | 109 | 41°35'N | 72°55'W |
| South Island, i., N.Z. | 221a | 42°40'S | 169°00'E |
| South Loup, r., Ne., U.S. (lōōp) | 112 | 41°21'N | 100°08'W |
| South Magnetic Pole, pt. of i. | 224 | 65°18'S | 139°30'E |
| South Merrimack, N.H., U.S. (mĕr'ĭ-măk) | 101a | 42°47'N | 71°36'W |
| South Milwaukee, Wi., U.S. (mĭl-wô'kē) | 111a | 42°55'N | 87°52'W |
| South Moose Lake, l., Can. | 97 | 53°51'N | 100°20'W |
| South Nation, r., Can. | 99 | 45°00'N | 75°25'W |
| South Negril Point, c., Jam. (nȧ-grĕl') | 134 | 18°15'N | 78°25'W |
| South Ogden, Ut., U.S. (ŏg'dĕn) | 117b | 41°12'N | 111°58'W |
| South Orkney Islands, is., Ant. | 139 | 57°00'S | 45°00'W |
| South Ossetia, hist. reg., Geor. | 182 | 42°20'N | 44°00'E |
| South Paris, Me., U.S. (păr'ĭs) | 100 | 44°13'N | 70°32'W |
| South Park, Ky., U.S. (pärk) | 111h | 38°06'N | 85°43'W |
| South Pasadena, Ca., U.S. (păs-ȧ-dē'nȧ) | 117a | 34°06'N | 118°08'W |
| South Pease, r., Tx., U.S. (pēz) | 120 | 33°54'N | 100°45'W |
| South Pender, i., Can. (pĕn'dĕr) | 116d | 48°45'N | 123°09'W |
| South Pittsburg, Tn., U.S. (pĭs'bûrg) | 124 | 35°00'N | 85°42'W |
| South Platte, r., U.S. (plăt) | 106 | 40°40'N | 102°40'W |
| South Point, c., Barb. | 133b | 13°00'N | 59°43'W |
| South Point, c., Mi., U.S. | 108 | 44°50'N | 83°20'W |
| South Pole, pt. of i., Ant. | 224 | 90°00'S | 0°00' |
| South Porcupine, Can. | 98 | 48°28'N | 81°13'W |
| Southport, Austl. (south'pōrt) | 219 | 27°57'S | 153°27'E |
| Southport, Eng., U.K. (south'pôrt) | 164 | 53°38'N | 3°00'W |
| Southport, In., U.S. | 111g | 39°40'N | 86°07'W |
| Southport, N.C., U.S. | 125 | 35°55'N | 78°02'W |
| South Portland, Me., U.S. (pōrt-lănd) | 100 | 43°37'N | 70°15'W |
| South Prairie, Wa., U.S. (prâ'rĭ) | 116a | 47°08'N | 122°06'W |
| South Range, Wi., U.S. (rānj) | 117h | 46°37'N | 91°59'W |
| South River, N.J., U.S. (rĭv'ĕr) | 110a | 40°27'N | 74°23'W |
| South Ronaldsay, i., Scot., U.K. (rŏn'ăld-s'ā) | 164a | 58°48'N | 2°55'W |
| South Saint Paul, Mn., U.S. | 117g | 44°54'N | 93°02'W |
| South Salt Lake, Ut., U.S. (sôlt lāk) | 117b | 40°44'N | 111°53'W |
| South Sandwich Islands, is., S. Geor. (sănd'wĭch) | 139 | 58°00'S | 27°00'W |
| South Sandwich Trench, deep | 139 | 55°00'S | 27°00'W |
| South San Francisco, Ca., U.S. (săn frăn-sĭs'kô) | 116b | 37°39'N | 122°24'W |
| South Saskatchewan, r., Can. (sås-kach'ĕ-wän) | 92 | 50°30'N | 110°30'W |
| South Shetland Islands, is., Ant. | 139 | 62°00'S | 70°00'W |
| South Shields, Eng., U.K. (shēldz) | 160 | 55°00'N | 1°22'W |
| South Sioux City, Ne., U.S. (sōō sĭt'ē) | 112 | 42°48'N | 96°26'W |
| South Taranaki Bight, b., N.Z. (tä-rä-nä'kē) | 221a | 39°35'S | 173°50'E |
| South Thompson, r., Can. (tŏmp'sŭn) | 95 | 50°41'N | 120°21'W |
| Southton, Tx., U.S. (south'tŭn) | 117d | 29°18'N | 98°26'W |
| South Uist, i., Scot., U.K. (ū'ĭst) | 164 | 57°15'N | 7°24'W |
| South Umpqua, r., Or., U.S. (ŭmp'kwȧ) | 114 | 43°00'N | 122°54'W |
| Southwell, Eng., U.K. (south'wĕl) | 158a | 53°04'N | 0°56'W |
| South West Africa *see* Namibia, nation, Afr. | 232 | 19°30'S | 16°13'E |
| Southwest Miramichi, r., Can. (mĭr ȧ-mē'shē) | 100 | 46°35'N | 66°17'W |
| Southwest Point, c., Bah. | 134 | 25°50'N | 77°10'W |
| Southwest Point, c., Bah. | 135 | 23°55'N | 74°30'W |
| South Yorkshire, hist. reg., Eng., U.K. | 158a | 53°29'N | 1°35'W |
| Sovetsk, Russia (sô-vyĕtsk') | 180 | 55°04'N | 21°54'E |
| Sovetskaya Gavan', Russia (sŭ-vyĕt'skī-u gä'vŭn') | 179 | 48°59'N | 140°14'E |
| Sow, r., Eng., U.K. (sou) | 158a | 52°45'N | 2°12'W |
| Soya Kaikyō, strt., Asia | 210 | 45°45'N | 141°38'E |
| Sōya Misaki, c., Japan (sō'yȧ mē'sä-kē) | 210 | 45°35'N | 141°25'E |
| Soyo, Ang. | 232 | 6°10'S | 12°25'E |
| Sozh, r., Eur. (sôzh) | 181 | 52°50'N | 31°00'E |
| Sozopol, Blg. (sôz'ô-pôl') | 175 | 42°18'N | 27°50'E |
| Spa, Bel. (spä) | 165 | 50°30'N | 5°50'E |
| Spain, nation, Eur. (spān) | 154 | 40°15'N | 4°30'W |
| Spalding, Ne., U.S. (spôl'dĭng) | 112 | 41°43'N | 98°23'W |
| Spanaway, Wa., U.S. (spăn'ȧ-wā) | 116a | 47°06'N | 122°26'W |
| Spangler, Pa., U.S. (spăng'lĕr) | 109 | 40°40'N | 78°50'W |
| Spanish Fork, Ut., U.S. (spăn'ĭsh fôrk) | 119 | 40°10'N | 111°40'W |
| Spanish Town, Jam. | 129 | 18°00'N | 76°55'W |
| Sparks, Nv., U.S. (spärks) | 118 | 39°34'N | 119°45'W |
| Sparrows Point, Md., U.S. (spăr'ōz) | 110e | 39°13'N | 76°29'W |
| Sparta *see* Spárti, Grc. | 175 | 37°07'N | 22°28'E |
| Sparta, Ga., U.S. (spär'tȧ) | 125 | 33°16'N | 82°59'W |
| Sparta, Il., U.S. | 121 | 38°07'N | 89°42'W |
| Sparta, Mi., U.S. | 108 | 43°10'N | 85°45'W |
| Sparta, Tn., U.S. | 124 | 35°54'N | 85°26'W |
| Sparta, Wi., U.S. | 113 | 43°56'N | 90°50'W |
| Sparta Mountains, mts., N.J., U.S. | 110a | 41°00'N | 74°38'W |
| Spartanburg, S.C., U.S. (spär'tăn-bûrg) | 105 | 34°57'N | 82°13'W |
| Spartel, Cap, c., Mor. (spär-tĕl') | 172 | 35°48'N | 5°50'W |
| Spárti (Sparta), Grc. | 175 | 37°07'N | 22°28'E |
| Spartivento, Cape, c., Italy (spär-tē-vĕn'tô) | 174 | 37°55'N | 16°09'E |
| Spartivento, Cape, c., Italy | 156 | 38°54'N | 8°52'E |
| Spas-Demensk, Russia (spȧs dyĕ-mĕnsk') | 176 | 54°24'N | 34°02'E |
| Spas-Klepiki, Russia (spȧs klĕp'ē-kē) | 176 | 55°09'N | 40°11'E |


ăt; finȧl; rāte; senāte; ärm; åsk; sofȧ; fâre; ch-choose; dh-as th in other; bē; ēvent; bĕt; recĕnt; cratẽr; g-gō; gh-guttural g; bĭt; ĭ-short neutral; rīde; ĸ-guttural k as ch in German ich;

354 Stranraer – Svyatoy Nos
PRONOUNCING INDEX


| PLACE (Pronunciation) | PAGE | LAT. | LONG. |
|---|---|---|---|
| Stranraer, Scot., U.K. (străn-rär´) | 164 | 54°55´N | 5°05´W |
| Strasbourg, Fr. (stràs-bo͞or´) | 154 | 48°36´N | 7°49´E |
| Stratford, Can. (străt´fērd) | 98 | 43°20´N | 81°05´W |
| Stratford, Ct., U.S. | 109 | 41°10´N | 73°05´W |
| Stratford, Wi., U.S. | 113 | 44°16´N | 90°02´W |
| Stratford-upon-Avon, Eng., U.K. | 164 | 52°13´N | 1°41´W |
| Straubing, Ger. (strou´bĭng) | 168 | 48°52´N | 12°36´E |
| Strausberg, Ger. (strous´bĕrgh) | 168 | 52°35´N | 13°50´E |
| Strawberry, r., Ut., U.S. | 119 | 40°05´N | 110°55´W |
| Strawn, Tx., U.S. (strôn) | 122 | 32°38´N | 98°28´W |
| Streator, Il., U.S. (strē´tēr) | 108 | 41°05´N | 88°50´W |
| Streeter, N.D., U.S. | 112 | 46°40´N | 99°22´W |
| Streetsville, Can. (strētz´vĭl) | 102d | 43°34´N | 79°43´W |
| Strehaia, Rom. (strĕ-kä´yà) | 175 | 44°37´N | 23°13´E |
| Strel'na, Russia (strĕl´nà) | 186c | 59°52´N | 30°01´E |
| Stretford, Eng., U.K. (strĕt´fērd) | 158a | 53°25´N | 2°19´W |
| Strickland, r., Pap. N. Gui. (strĭk´lănd) | 213 | 6°15´S | 142°00´E |
| Strijen, Neth. | 159a | 51°44´N | 4°32´E |
| Stromboli, Italy (strôm´bô-lē) | 163 | 38°46´N | 15°16´E |
| Stromyn, Russia (strô´mĭn) | 186b | 56°02´N | 38°29´E |
| Strong, r., Ms., U.S. (strông) | 124 | 32°03´N | 89°42´W |
| Strongsville, Oh., U.S. (strôngz´vĭl) | 111d | 41°19´N | 81°50´W |
| Stronsay, i., Scot., U.K. (strŏn´sā) | 164a | 59°09´N | 2°35´W |
| Stroudsburg, Pa., U.S. (stroudz´bûrg) | 109 | 41°00´N | 75°15´W |
| Struer, Den. | 166 | 56°29´N | 8°34´E |
| Strugi Krasnyye, Russia (stro͞o´gĭ krä´s-ny´yĕ) | 176 | 58°14´N | 29°10´E |
| Struma, r., Eur. (stro͞o´mà) | 175 | 41°55´N | 23°05´E |
| Strumica, Mac. (stro͞o´mĭ-tsà) | 175 | 41°26´N | 22°38´E |
| Strunino, Russia | 186b | 56°23´N | 38°34´E |
| Struthers, Oh., U.S. (strŭdh´ērz) | 108 | 41°00´N | 80°35´W |
| Struvenhütten, Ger. (shtro͞o´vĕn-hü-tĕn) | 159c | 53°52´N | 10°04´E |
| Strydpoortberge, mts., S. Afr. | 238c | 24°08´N | 29°18´E |
| Stryi, Ukr. | 169 | 49°16´N | 23°51´E |
| Strzelce Opolskie, Pol. (stzhĕl´tsĕ o-pŏl´skyĕ) | 169 | 50°31´N | 18°20´E |
| Strzelin, Pol. (stzhĕ-lĭn) | 169 | 50°48´N | 17°06´E |
| Strzelno, Pol. (stzhäl´nô) | 169 | 52°37´N | 18°10´E |
| Stuart, Fl., U.S. (stū´ērt) | 125a | 27°10´N | 80°14´W |
| Stuart, Ia., U.S. | 113 | 41°31´N | 94°20´W |
| Stuart, i., Ak., U.S. | 103 | 63°25´N | 162°45´W |
| Stuart, i., Wa., U.S. | 116d | 48°42´N | 123°10´W |
| Stuart Lake, l., Can. | 94 | 54°32´N | 124°35´W |
| Stuart Range, mts., Austl. | 220 | 29°00´S | 134°30´E |
| Sturgeon, r., Can. | 102g | 53°41´N | 113°46´W |
| Sturgeon, r., Mi., U.S. | 113 | 46°43´N | 88°43´W |
| Sturgeon Bay, Wi., U.S. | 113 | 44°50´N | 87°22´W |
| Sturgeon Bay, b., Can. | 97 | 52°00´N | 98°00´W |
| Sturgeon Falls, Can. | 91 | 46°19´N | 79°49´W |
| Sturgis, Ky., U.S. | 108 | 37°35´N | 88°00´W |
| Sturgis, Mi., U.S. | 108 | 41°45´N | 85°25´W |
| Sturgis, S.D., U.S. | 112 | 44°25´N | 103°31´W |
| Sturt Creek, r., Austl. | 220 | 19°40´S | 127°40´E |
| Sturtevant, Wi., U.S. (stŭr´tĕ-vănt) | 111a | 42°42´N | 87°54´W |
| Stutterheim, S. Afr. (stŭrt´ēr-hīm) | 233c | 32°34´S | 27°27´E |
| Stuttgart, Ger. (shto͞ot´gärt) | 154 | 48°48´N | 9°15´E |
| Stuttgart, Ar., U.S. (stŭt´gärt) | 121 | 34°30´N | 91°33´W |
| Stykkishólmur, Ice. | 160 | 65°00´N | 21°48´W |
| Styr', r., Eur. (stēr) | 169 | 51°44´N | 26°07´E |
| Suao, Tai. (so͞oou) | 209 | 24°35´N | 121°45´E |
| Subarnarekha, r., India | 202 | 22°38´N | 86°26´E |
| Subata, Lat. (so͞o´bà-tà) | 167 | 56°02´N | 25°54´E |
| Subic, Phil. (so͞o´bĭk) | 213a | 14°52´N | 120°15´E |
| Subic Bay, b., Phil. | 213a | 14°41´N | 120°11´E |
| Subotica, Serb. (so͞o´bô´tē-tsà) | 154 | 46°06´N | 19°41´E |
| Subugo, mtn., Kenya | 237 | 1°40´S | 35°49´E |
| Succasunna, N.J., U.S. (sŭk´kă-sŭn´nă) | 110a | 40°52´N | 74°37´W |
| Suceava, Rom. (so͞o-chà-ä´và) | 169 | 47°39´N | 26°17´E |
| Suceava, r., Rom. | 169 | 47°45´N | 26°10´E |
| Sucha, Pol. (so͞o´kà) | 169 | 49°44´N | 19°40´E |
| Suchiapa, Mex. (so͞o-chē-ä´pä) | 131 | 16°38´N | 93°08´W |
| Suchiapa, r., Mex. | 131 | 16°27´N | 93°26´W |
| Suchitoto, El Sal. (so͞o-chē-tō´tō) | 132 | 13°58´N | 89°03´W |
| Sucio, r., Col. (so͞o´syō) | 142a | 6°55´N | 76°15´W |
| Suck, r., Ire. (sŭk) | 164 | 53°34´N | 8°16´W |
| Sucre, Bol. (so͞o´krā) | 142 | 19°06´S | 65°16´W |
| Sucre, dept., Ven. (so͞o´krĕ) | 143b | 10°18´N | 64°12´W |
| Sud, Canal du, strt., Haiti | 135 | 18°40´N | 73°15´W |
| Sud, Rivière du, r., Can. (rē-vyâr´dü süd´) | 102b | 46°56´N | 70°35´W |
| Suda, Russia (so͞o´dà) | 186a | 56°58´N | 56°45´E |
| Suda, r., Russia (so͞o´dà) | 176 | 59°24´N | 36°40´E |
| Sudair, Sau. Ar. (sŭ-dä´ēr) | 198 | 25°48´N | 46°28´E |
| Sudalsvatnet, l., Nor. | 166 | 59°35´N | 6°59´E |
| Sudan, nation, Afr. | 231 | 14°00´N | 28°00´E |
| Sudan, reg., Afr. (so͞o-dän´) | 230 | 15°00´N | 7°00´E |
| Sudbury, Can. (sŭd´bēr-ē) | 91 | 46°28´N | 81°00´W |
| Sudbury, Ma., U.S. | 101a | 42°23´N | 71°25´W |
| Sudetes, mts., Eur. | 156 | 50°41´N | 15°37´E |
| Sudogda, Russia (so͞o´dôk-dà) | 176 | 55°57´N | 40°29´E |
| Sudost', r., Eur. (sò-dôst´) | 176 | 52°43´N | 33°13´E |
| Sudzha, Russia (so͞od´zhà) | 177 | 51°14´N | 35°11´E |
| Sueca, Spain (swā´kä) | 173 | 39°12´N | 0°18´W |
| Suez, Egypt | 231 | 29°58´N | 32°34´E |
| Suez, Gulf of, b., Egypt (so͞o-ĕz´) | 231 | 29°53´N | 32°33´E |
| Suez Canal, can., Egypt | 231 | 30°53´N | 32°21´E |
| Suffern, N.Y., U.S. (sŭf´fērn) | 110a | 41°07´N | 74°09´W |
| Suffolk, Va., U.S. (sŭf´ŭk) | 110g | 36°43´N | 76°35´W |
| Sugar City, Co., U.S. | 120 | 38°12´N | 103°42´W |
| Sugar Creek, Mo., U.S. | 117f | 39°07´N | 94°27´W |
| Sugar Creek, r., Il., U.S. (shòg´ēr) | 121 | 40°14´N | 89°28´W |
| Sugar Creek, r., In., U.S. | 108 | 39°55´N | 87°10´W |
| Sugar Island, i., Mi., U.S. | 117k | 46°31´N | 84°12´W |
| Sugarloaf Point, c., Austl. (sòg´ẽr´lôf) | 222 | 32°19´S | 153°04´E |
| Suggi Lake, l., Can. | 97 | 54°22´N | 102°47´W |
| Sühbaatar, Mong. | 204 | 50°18´N | 106°31´E |
| Suhl, Ger. (zo͞ol) | 168 | 50°37´N | 10°41´E |
| Suichuan, mtn., China | 209 | 26°25´N | 114°10´E |
| Suide, China (swā-dü) | 208 | 37°32´N | 110°12´E |
| Suifenhe, China (swā-fŭn-hŭ) | 205 | 44°47´N | 131°13´E |
| Suihua, China | 205 | 46°38´N | 126°50´E |
| Suining, China (so͞o´ē-nĭng´) | 206 | 33°54´N | 117°57´E |
| Suipacha, Arg. (swē-pä´chä) | 141c | 34°45´S | 59°43´W |
| Suiping, China (swā-pĭŋ) | 206 | 33°09´N | 113°58´E |
| Suir, r., Ire. (sūr) | 164 | 52°20´N | 7°32´W |
| Suisun Bay, b., Ca., U.S. (so͞oē-so͞on´) | 116b | 38°07´N | 122°02´W |
| Suita, Japan (sò´ē-tä) | 211b | 34°45´N | 135°32´E |
| Suitland, Md., U.S. (sòt´lănd) | 110e | 38°51´N | 76°57´W |
| Suixian, China (swā shyĕn) | 209 | 31°42´N | 113°20´E |
| Suiyüan, hist. reg., China (swā-yüĕn) | 204 | 41°31´N | 107°04´E |
| Suizhong, China (swā-jôŋ) | 208 | 40°22´N | 120°20´E |
| Sukabumi, Indon. | 212 | 6°52´S | 106°56´E |
| Sukadana, Indon. | 212 | 1°15´S | 110°30´E |
| Sukagawa, Japan (so͞o´kä-gä´wä) | 211 | 37°08´N | 140°07´E |
| Sukhinichi, Russia (so͞o´κē´nē-chē) | 180 | 54°07´N | 35°18´E |
| Sukhona, r., Russia (sò-κô´nà) | 180 | 59°30´N | 42°20´E |
| Sukhoy Log, Russia (so͞o´kôy lôg) | 186a | 56°55´N | 62°03´E |
| Sukhumi, Geor. (sò-kòm´) | 181 | 43°00´N | 41°00´E |
| Sukkur, Pak. (sŭk´ŭr) | 199 | 27°49´N | 68°50´E |
| Sukkwan Island, i., Ak., U.S. | 94 | 55°05´N | 132°45´W |
| Suksun, Russia (sòk´sòn) | 186a | 57°08´N | 57°22´E |
| Sukumo, Japan (so͞o´kò-mô) | 211 | 32°58´N | 132°45´E |
| Sukunka, r., Can. | 95 | 55°00´N | 121°50´W |
| Sula, r., Ukr. (so͞o-lä´) | 177 | 50°36´N | 33°13´E |
| Sula, Kepulauan, is., Indon. | 213 | 2°20´S | 125°20´E |
| Sulaco, r., Hond. (so͞o-lä´kō) | 132 | 14°55´N | 87°31´W |
| Sulaimān Range, mts., Pak. (sò-lä-ē-män´) | 199 | 29°47´N | 69°10´E |
| Sulak, r., Russia (so͞o-lák´) | 181 | 43°30´N | 47°00´E |
| Sulfeld, Ger. (zo͞ol´fĕld) | 159c | 53°48´N | 10°13´E |
| Sulina, Rom. (so͞o-lē´nà) | 163 | 45°08´N | 29°38´E |
| Sulitelma, mtn., Eur. (so͞o-lē-tyĕl´mà) | 160 | 67°03´N | 16°35´E |
| Sullana, Peru (so͞o-lyä´nä) | 142 | 4°57´S | 80°47´W |
| Sulligent, Al., U.S. (sŭl´ĭ-jĕnt) | 124 | 33°52´N | 88°06´W |
| Sullivan, Il., U.S. (sŭl´ĭ-văn) | 108 | 41°35´N | 88°35´W |
| Sullivan, In., U.S. | 108 | 39°05´N | 87°20´W |
| Sullivan, Mo., U.S. | 121 | 38°13´N | 91°09´W |
| Sulmona, Italy (so͞ol-mō´nä) | 174 | 42°02´N | 13°58´E |
| Sulphur, Ok., U.S. (sŭl´fŭr) | 121 | 34°31´N | 96°58´W |
| Sulphur, r., Tx., U.S. | 121 | 33°26´N | 95°06´W |
| Sulphur Springs, Tx., U.S. (sprĭngz) | 121 | 33°09´N | 95°36´W |
| Sultan, Wa., U.S. (sŭl´tăn) | 116a | 47°52´N | 121°49´W |
| Sultan, r., Wa., U.S. | 116a | 47°55´N | 121°49´W |
| Sultepec, Mex. (so͞ol-tå-pĕk´) | 130 | 18°50´N | 99°51´W |
| Sulu Archipelago, is., Phil. (so͞o´lo͞o) | 212 | 5°52´N | 122°00´E |
| Suluntah, Libya | 163 | 32°39´N | 21°49´E |
| Sulūq, Libya | 231 | 31°39´N | 20°15´E |
| Sulu Sea, sea, Asia | 212 | 8°25´N | 119°00´E |
| Suma, Japan (so͞o´mä) | 211b | 34°39´N | 135°08´E |
| Sumas, Wa., U.S. (sū´măs) | 116d | 49°00´N | 122°16´W |
| Sumatera, i., Indon. (sò-mä-trà) | 212 | 2°06´N | 99°40´E |
| Sumatra *see* Sumatera, i., Indon. | 212 | 2°06´N | 99°40´E |
| Sumba, i., Indon. (sŭm´bà) | 212 | 9°52´S | 119°00´E |
| Sumba, Île, i., D.R.C. | 236 | 1°44´N | 19°32´E |
| Sumbawa, i., Indon. (sòm-bä´wà) | 212 | 9°00´S | 118°18´E |
| Sumbawa-Besar, Indon. | 212 | 8°32´S | 117°20´E |
| Sumbawanga, Tan. | 237 | 7°58´S | 31°37´E |
| Sumbe, Ang. | 232 | 11°13´S | 13°50´E |
| Sümeg, Hung. (shü´mĕg) | 169 | 46°59´N | 17°19´E |
| Sumida, r., Japan (so͞o´mē-dä) | 211 | 36°01´N | 139°24´E |
| Sumidouro, Braz. (so͞o-mē-dō´rò) | 141a | 22°04´S | 42°41´W |
| Sumiyoshi, Japan (so͞o´mē-yō´shē) | 211b | 34°43´N | 135°16´E |
| Summer Lake, l., Or., U.S. (sŭm´ēr) | 114 | 42°50´N | 120°35´W |
| Summerland, Can. (sŭ´mēr-lănd) | 95 | 49°39´N | 119°40´W |
| Summerside, Can. (sŭm´ēr-sīd) | 91 | 46°25´N | 63°47´W |
| Summerton, S.C., U.S. (sŭm´ēr-tŭn) | 125 | 33°37´N | 80°22´W |
| Summerville, S.C., U.S. (sŭm´ēr-vĭl) | 125 | 33°00´N | 80°10´W |
| Summit, Il., U.S. (sŭm´mĭt) | 111a | 41°47´N | 87°48´W |
| Summit, N.J., U.S. | 110a | 40°43´N | 74°21´W |
| Summit Lake Indian Reservation, I.R., Nv., U.S. | 114 | 41°35´N | 119°30´W |
| Summit Peak, mtn., Co., U.S. | 119 | 37°20´N | 106°40´W |
| Sumner, Wa., U.S. (sŭm´nēr) | 116a | 47°12´N | 122°14´W |
| Šumperk, Czech Rep. (shòm´pĕrk) | 169 | 49°57´N | 17°02´E |
| Sumqayıt, Azer. | 182 | 40°36´N | 49°38´E |
| Sumrall, Ms., U.S. (sŭm´rôl) | 124 | 31°25´N | 89°34´W |
| Sumter, S.C., U.S. (sŭm´tēr) | 125 | 33°55´N | 80°21´W |
| Sumy, Ukr. (so͞o´mĭ) | 178 | 50°54´N | 34°47´E |
| Sumy, prov., Ukr. | 177 | 51°02´N | 34°05´E |
| Sun, r., Mt., U.S. (sŭn) | 115 | 47°34´N | 111°53´W |
| Sunburst, Mt., U.S. | 115 | 48°53´N | 111°55´W |
| Sunda, Selat, strt., Indon. | 212 | 5°45´S | 106°15´E |
| Sundance, Wy., U.S. (sŭn´dăns) | 115 | 44°24´N | 104°27´W |
| Sundarbans, sw., Asia (sòn´dēr-bŭns) | 199 | 21°50´N | 89°00´E |
| Sunday Strait, strt., Austl. (sŭn´dā) | 220 | 15°50´S | 122°45´E |
| Sundbyberg, Swe. (sòn´bü-bĕrgh) | 166 | 59°24´N | 17°56´E |
| Sunderland, Eng., U.K. (sŭn´dēr-lănd) | 160 | 54°55´N | 1°25´W |
| Sunderland, Md., U.S. | 110e | 38°41´N | 76°36´W |
| Sundsvall, Swe. (sònds´väl) | 154 | 62°24´N | 19°19´E |
| Sungari (Songhua), r., China | 205 | 46°09´N | 127°53´E |
| Sungari Reservoir, res., China | 208 | 42°55´N | 127°50´E |
| Sungurlu, Tur. (so͞on´gòr-lò´) | 163 | 40°08´N | 34°20´E |
| Sun Kosi, r., Nepal | 202 | 27°13´N | 85°52´E |
| Sunland, Ca., U.S. (sŭn-lănd) | 117a | 34°16´N | 118°18´W |
| Sunne, Swe. (so͞on´ĕ) | 166 | 59°51´N | 13°07´E |
| Sunninghill, Eng., U.K. (sŭnĭng´hĭl) | 158b | 51°23´N | 0°40´W |
| Sunnymead, Ca., U.S. (sŭn´ĭ-mēd) | 117a | 33°56´N | 117°15´W |
| Sunnyside, Ut., U.S. | 119 | 39°35´N | 110°20´W |
| Sunnyside, Wa., U.S. | 114 | 46°19´N | 120°00´W |
| Sunnyvale, Ca., U.S. (sŭn-nē-văl) | 116b | 37°23´N | 122°02´W |
| Sunol, Ca., U.S. (so͞o´nŭl) | 116b | 37°36´N | 122°53´W |
| Sunset, Ut., U.S. (sŭn-sĕt) | 117b | 41°08´N | 112°02´W |
| Sunset Crater National Monument, rec., Az., U.S. (krā´tēr) | 119 | 35°20´N | 111°30´W |
| Sunshine, Austl. | 217a | 37°47´S | 144°50´E |
| Suntar, Russia (sòn-tár´) | 179 | 62°14´N | 117°49´E |
| Sunyani, Ghana | 234 | 7°20´N | 2°20´W |
| Suoyarvi, Russia (so͞o´ô-yĕr´vē) | 180 | 62°12´N | 32°29´E |
| Superior, Az., U.S. (su-pē´rĭ-ēr) | 119 | 33°15´N | 111°10´W |
| Superior, Ne., U.S. | 120 | 40°04´N | 98°05´W |
| Superior, Wi., U.S. | 105 | 46°44´N | 92°06´W |
| Superior, Wy., U.S. | 115 | 41°45´N | 108°57´W |
| Superior, Laguna, l., Mex. (lä-go͞o´nä so͞o-pä-rē-ōr´) | 131 | 16°20´N | 94°55´W |
| Superior, Lake, l., N.A. | 107 | 47°38´N | 89°20´W |
| Superior Village, Wi., U.S. | 117h | 46°38´N | 92°07´W |
| Sup'ung Reservoir, res., Asia (so͞o´po͞ong) | 210 | 40°35´N | 126°00´E |
| Suqian, China (so͞o-chyĕn) | 206 | 33°57´N | 118°17´E |
| Suquamish, Wa., U.S. (so͞o-gwä´mĭsh) | 116a | 47°44´N | 122°34´W |
| Suquṭrā (Socotra), i., Yemen (sô-kō´trà) | 198 | 13°00´N | 52°30´E |
| Şūr, Leb. (so͞or) (tĭr) | 197a | 33°16´N | 35°13´E |
| Şūr, Oman | 198 | 22°23´N | 59°28´E |
| Surabaya, Indon. | 212 | 7°23´S | 112°45´E |
| Surakarta, Indon. | 212 | 7°35´S | 110°45´E |
| Šurany, Slvk. (sho͞o´rà-nû´) | 169 | 48°05´N | 18°11´E |
| Surat, Austl. (sū-răt) | 222 | 27°18´S | 149°00´E |
| Surat, India (sò´rŭt) | 199 | 21°08´N | 73°22´E |
| Surat Thani, Thai. | 212 | 8°59´N | 99°14´E |
| Surazh, Bela. | 176 | 55°24´N | 30°46´E |
| Surazh, Russia (so͞o-rázh´) | 176 | 53°02´N | 32°27´E |
| Surgères, Fr. (sür-zhâr´) | 170 | 46°06´N | 0°51´W |
| Surgut, Russia (sòr-gòt´) | 178 | 61°18´N | 73°38´E |
| Suriname, nation, S.A. (so͞o-rē-näm´) | 143 | 4°00´N | 56°00´W |
| Sūrmaq, Iran | 201 | 31°03´N | 52°48´E |
| Surt, Libya | 231 | 31°14´N | 16°37´E |
| Surt, Khalīj, b., Libya | 231 | 31°30´N | 18°28´E |
| Suruga-Wan, b., Japan (so͞o´ro͞o-gä wän) | 210 | 34°52´N | 138°36´E |
| Susa, Japan | 211 | 34°40´N | 131°39´E |
| Sušak, i., Serb. | 174 | 42°45´N | 16°30´E |
| Susak, Otok, i., Serb. | 174 | 44°31´N | 14°15´E |
| Susaki, Japan (so͞o´sä-kē) | 211 | 33°23´N | 133°16´E |
| Sušice, Czech Rep. | 168 | 49°14´N | 13°31´E |
| Susitna, Ak., U.S. (so͞o-sĭt´nă) | 103 | 61°28´N | 150°28´W |
| Susitna, r., Ak., U.S. | 103 | 62°00´N | 150°28´W |
| Susong, China (so͞o-sôŋ) | 209 | 30°18´N | 116°08´E |
| Susquehanna, Pa., U.S. (sŭs´kwē-hăn´ă) | 109 | 41°55´N | 73°55´W |
| Susquehanna, r., U.S. | 109 | 39°50´N | 76°20´W |
| Sussex, Can. (sŭs´ĕks) | 91 | 45°43´N | 65°31´W |
| Sussex, N.J., U.S. | 110a | 41°12´N | 74°36´W |
| Sussex, Wi., U.S. | 111a | 43°08´N | 88°12´W |
| Sutherland, Austl. (sŭdh´ēr-lănd) | 217b | 34°02´S | 151°04´E |
| Sutherland, S. Afr. (sŭ´thēr-lănd) | 232 | 32°25´S | 20°40´E |
| Sutlej, r., Asia (sŭt´lĕj) | 199 | 30°15´N | 73°00´E |
| Sutton, Eng., U.K. (sŭt´'n) | 158b | 51°21´N | 0°12´W |
| Sutton, Ma., U.S. | 101a | 42°09´N | 71°46´W |
| Sutton Coldfield, Eng., U.K. (kōld´fēld) | 158a | 52°34´N | 1°49´W |
| Sutton-in-Ashfield, Eng., U.K. (ĭn-ăsh´fēld) | 158a | 53°07´N | 1°15´W |
| Suurberge, mts., S. Afr. | 233c | 33°15´S | 25°32´E |
| Suva, Fiji | 214g | 18°08´S | 178°25´E |
| Suwa, Japan (so͞o´wä) | 211 | 36°03´N | 138°08´E |
| Suwałki, Pol. (so-vou´kē) | 169 | 54°05´N | 22°58´E |
| Suwanee Lake, l., Can. | 97 | 56°08´N | 100°10´W |
| Suwannee, r., U.S. (sò-wô´nē) | 107 | 29°42´N | 83°00´W |
| Suways al Ḩulwah, Tur' at as, can., Egypt | 238d | 30°15´N | 32°20´E |
| Suxian, China (so͞o shyĕn) | 208 | 33°29´N | 117°51´E |
| Suzdal', Russia (so͞oz´dál) | 176 | 56°26´N | 40°29´E |
| Suzhou, China (so͞o-jō) | 205 | 31°19´N | 120°37´E |
| Suzu Misaki, c., Japan (so͞o´zo͞o mē´sä-kē) | 210 | 37°30´N | 137°35´E |
| Svalbard (Spitsbergen), dep., Nor. (sväl´bärt) (spĭts´bûr-gĕn) | 178 | 77°00´N | 20°00´E |
| Svaneke, Den. (svä´nĕ-kĕ) | 166 | 55°08´N | 15°07´E |
| Svatove, Ukr. | 181 | 49°23´N | 38°10´E |
| Svedala, Swe. (svĕ´dä-lä) | 166 | 55°29´N | 13°11´E |
| Sveg, Swe. | 166 | 62°03´N | 14°22´E |
| Svelvik, Nor. (svĕl´vĕk) | 166 | 59°37´N | 10°18´E |
| Svenčionys, Lith. | 167 | 55°09´N | 26°09´E |
| Svendborg, Den. (svĕn-bôrgh) | 166 | 55°05´N | 10°35´E |
| Svensen, Or., U.S. (svĕn´sĕn) | 116c | 46°10´N | 123°39´W |
| Sverdlovsk *see* Yekaterinburg, Russia | 178 | 56°51´N | 60°36´E |
| Svetlaya, Russia (svyĕt´lá-yà) | 210 | 46°09´N | 137°53´E |
| Svicha, r., Ukr. | 169 | 49°09´N | 24°10´E |
| Svilajnac, Serb. (svē´lá-ē-náts) | 175 | 44°12´N | 21°14´E |
| Svilengrad, Blg. (svĕl´ĕn-grát) | 175 | 41°44´N | 26°11´E |
| Svir', r., Russia | 180 | 60°55´N | 33°40´E |
| Svir Kanal, can., Russia (kà-näl´) | 167 | 60°10´N | 32°40´E |
| Svishtov, Blg. (svĕsh´tôf) | 163 | 43°36´N | 25°21´E |
| Svisloch', r., Bela. (svēs´lôκ) | 176 | 53°38´N | 28°10´E |
| Svitavy, Czech Rep. | 168 | 49°46´N | 16°28´E |
| Svobodnyy, Russia (svô-bôd´nĭ) | 179 | 51°28´N | 128°28´E |
| Svolvaer, Nor. (svôl´vĕr) | 160 | 68°15´N | 14°29´E |
| Svyatoy Nos, Mys, c., Russia (svyŭ´toi nôs) | 179 | 72°18´N | 139°28´E |


ăt; fin*ă*l; rāte; senåte; ärm; åsk; sof*ȧ*; fâre; ch-choose; dh-as th in other; bē; ēvent; bĕt; recĕnt; cratẽr; g-gō; gh-guttural g; bĭt; *ĭ*-short neutral; rīde; κ-guttural k as ch in German ich;

PRONOUNCING INDEX

Swadlincote – Tamiahua 355


| PLACE (Pronunciation) | PAGE | LAT. | LONG. |
|---|---|---|---|
| Swadlincote, Eng., U.K. (swŏd'lĭn-kôt) | 158a | 52°46'N | 1°33'W |
| Swain Reefs, rf., Austl. (swān) | 221 | 22°12'S | 152°08'E |
| Swainsboro, Ga., U.S. (swānz'bŭr-ô) | 125 | 32°37'N | 82°21'W |
| Swakopmund, Nmb. (svä'kôp-mònt) (swà'kôp-mònd) | 232 | 22°40'S | 14°30'E |
| Swallowfield, Eng., U.K. (swŏl'ô-fēld) | 158b | 51°21'N | 0°58'W |
| Swampscott, Ma., U.S. (swômp'skŏt) | 101a | 42°28'N | 70°55'W |
| Swan, r., Austl. | 220 | 31°30'S | 116°30'E |
| Swan, r., Can. | 97 | 51°58'N | 101°45'W |
| Swan, r., Mt., U.S. | 115 | 47°50'N | 113°40'W |
| Swan Hill, Austl. | 219 | 35°20'S | 143°30'E |
| Swan Hills, Can. (hĭlz) | 90 | 54°52'N | 115°45'W |
| Swan Island, i., Austl. (swŏn) | 217a | 38°15'S | 144°41'E |
| Swan Lake, l., Can. | 97 | 52°30'N | 100°45'W |
| Swanland, reg., Austl. (swŏn'lănd) | 220 | 31°45'S | 119°15'E |
| Swan Range, mts., Mt., U.S. | 115 | 47°50'N | 113°40'W |
| Swan River, Can. (swŏn rĭv'ēr) | 90 | 52°06'N | 101°16'W |
| Swansea, Wales, U.K. | 161 | 51°37'N | 3°59'W |
| Swansea, Il., U.S. (swŏn'sē) | 117e | 38°32'N | 89°59'W |
| Swansea, Ma., U.S. | 110b | 41°45'N | 71°09'W |
| Swanson Reservoir, res., Ne., U.S. (swŏn'sŭn) | 120 | 40°13'N | 101°30'W |
| Swartberg, mtn., Afr. | 233c | 30°08'S | 29°34'E |
| Swartkop, mtn., S. Afr. | 232a | 34°13'S | 18°27'E |
| Swartruggens, S. Afr. | 238c | 25°40'S | 26°40'E |
| Swartspruit, S. Afr. | 233b | 25°44'S | 28°01'E |
| Swatow *see* Shantou, China | 205 | 23°20'N | 116°40'E |
| Swaziland, nation, Afr. (Swä'zē-lănd) | 232 | 26°45'S | 31°30'E |
| Sweden, nation, Eur. (swē'dĕn) | 154 | 60°10'N | 14°10'E |
| Swedesboro, N.J., U.S. (swēdz'bē-rô) | 110f | 39°45'N | 75°22'W |
| Sweetwater, Tn., U.S. (swēt'wô-tēr) | 124 | 35°36'N | 84°29'W |
| Sweetwater, Tx., U.S. | 104 | 32°28'N | 100°25'W |
| Sweetwater, l., N.D., U.S. | 112 | 48°15'N | 98°35'W |
| Sweetwater, r., Wy., U.S. | 115 | 42°19'N | 108°35'W |
| Sweetwater Reservoir, res., Ca., U.S. | 118a | 32°42'N | 116°54'W |
| Świdnica, Pol. (shvĭd-nē'tsà) | 168 | 50°50'N | 16°30'E |
| Świdwin, Pol. (shvĭd'vĭn) | 168 | 53°46'N | 15°48'E |
| Świebodzice, Pol. | 168 | 50°51'N | 16°17'E |
| Świebodzin, Pol. (shvyĕN-bo'jĕts) | 168 | 52°16'N | 15°36'E |
| Świecie, Pol. (shvyăN'tsyĕ) | 169 | 53°23'N | 18°26'E |
| Świętokrzyskie, Góry, mts., Pol. (shvyĕN-tō-kzhĭ'skyĕ gōō'rĭ) | 169 | 50°57'N | 21°02'E |
| Swift, r., Eng., U.K. | 158a | 52°26'N | 1°08'W |
| Swift, r., Me., U.S. (swĭft) | 101 | 44°42'N | 70°40'E |
| Swift Creek Reservoir, res., Wa., U.S. | 114 | 46°03'N | 122°10'W |
| Swift Current, Can. (swĭft kûr'ĕnt) | 90 | 50°17'N | 107°50'W |
| Swindle Island, i., Can. | 94 | 52°32'N | 128°35'W |
| Swindon, Eng., U.K. (swĭn'dŭn) | 164 | 51°35'N | 1°55'W |
| Swinomish Indian Reservation, I.R., Wa., U.S. (swĭ-nō'mĭsh) | 116a | 48°25'N | 122°27'W |
| Świnoujście, Pol. (shvĭ-nĭ-ô-wēsh'chyĕ) | 168 | 53°56'N | 14°14'E |
| Swinton, Eng., U.K. (swĭn'tŭn) | 158a | 53°30'N | 1°19'W |
| Swissvale, Pa., U.S. (swĭs'vāl) | 111e | 40°25'N | 79°53'W |
| Switzerland, nation, Eur. (swĭt'zēr-lănd) | 154 | 46°30'N | 7°43'E |
| Syanno, Bela. (syĕ'nô) | 176 | 54°48'N | 29°43'E |
| Syas', r., Russia (syäs) | 176 | 59°28'N | 33°24'E |
| Sycamore, Il., U.S. (sĭk'á-mōr) | 113 | 42°00'N | 88°42'W |
| Sycan, r., Or., U.S. | 114 | 42°45'N | 121°00'W |
| Sychëvka, Russia (sē-chôf'kà) | 176 | 55°52'N | 34°18'E |
| Sydney, Austl. (sĭd'nē) | 219 | 33°55'S | 151°17'E |
| Sydney, Can. | 91 | 46°09'N | 60°11'W |
| Sydney Mines, Can. | 91 | 46°14'N | 60°14'W |
| Syktyvkar, Russia (sük-tüf'kär) | 178 | 61°35'N | 50°40'E |
| Sylacauga, Al., U.S. (sĭl-á-kô'gá) | 124 | 33°10'N | 86°15'W |
| Sylarna, mtn., Eur. | 166 | 63°00'N | 12°10'E |
| Sylt, i., Ger. (sĭlt) | 168 | 54°55'N | 8°30'E |
| Sylvania, Ga., U.S. (sĭl-vā'nĭ-à) | 125 | 32°44'N | 81°40'W |
| Sylvester, Ga., U.S. (sĭl-vĕs'tēr) | 124 | 31°32'N | 83°50'W |
| Sými, i., Grc. | 163 | 36°27'N | 27°41'E |
| Synel'nykove, Ukr. | 181 | 48°19'N | 35°33'E |
| Syracuse, Ks., U.S. (sĭr'á-kūs) | 120 | 37°59'N | 101°44'W |
| Syracuse, N.Y., U.S. | 105 | 43°05'N | 76°10'W |
| Syracuse, Ut., U.S. | 117b | 41°06'N | 112°04'W |
| Syr Darya, r., Asia | 178 | 44°15'N | 65°45'E |
| Syria, nation, Asia (sĭr'ĭ-à) | 198 | 35°00'N | 37°15'E |
| Syrian Desert, des., Asia | 198 | 32°00'N | 40°00'E |
| Sýros, i., Grc. | 163 | 37°23'N | 24°55'E |
| Sysert', Russia (sĕ'sĕrt) | 186a | 56°30'N | 60°48'E |
| Sysola, r., Russia | 180 | 60°50'N | 50°40'E |
| Syvash, zatoka, b., Ukr. | 177 | 45°55'N | 34°42'E |
| Syzran', Russia (sĕz-rän') | 178 | 53°09'N | 48°27'E |
| Szamotuły, Pol. (shá-mô-tōō'wê) | 168 | 52°36'N | 16°34'E |
| Szarvas, Hung. (sôr'vôsh) | 169 | 46°51'N | 20°36'E |
| Szczebrzeszyn, Pol. (shchĕ-bzhä'shĕn) | 169 | 50°41'N | 22°58'E |
| Szczecin, Pol. (shchĕ'tsĭn) | 154 | 53°25'N | 14°35'E |
| Szczecinek, Pol. (shchĕ-tsĭ'nĕk) | 160 | 53°41'N | 16°42'E |
| Szczuczyn, Pol. (shchōō'chĕn) | 169 | 53°32'N | 22°17'E |
| Szczytno, Pol. (shchĭt'nô) | 169 | 53°33'N | 21°00'E |
| Szechwan Basin, basin, China | 204 | 30°45'N | 104°40'E |
| Szeged, Hung. (sĕ'gĕd) | 154 | 46°15'N | 20°12'E |
| Székesfehérvár, Hung. (sā'kĕsh-fĕ'hār-vär) | 163 | 47°12'N | 18°26'E |
| Szekszárd, Hung. (sĕk'särd) | 163 | 46°19'N | 18°42'E |
| Szentendre, Hung. (sĕnt'ĕn-drĕ) | 169 | 47°40'N | 19°07'E |
| Szentes, Hung. (sĕn'tĕsh) | 169 | 46°38'N | 20°18'E |
| Szigetvar, Hung. (sĕ'gĕt-vär) | 169 | 46°05'N | 17°50'E |
| Szolnok, Hung. | 169 | 47°11'N | 20°12'E |
| Szombathely, Hung. (sôm'bôt-hĕl') | 163 | 47°13'N | 16°35'E |
| Szprotawa, Pol. (shprō-tä'vä) | 168 | 51°34'N | 15°29'E |
| Szydłowiec, Pol. (shid-wô'vyets) | 169 | 51°13'N | 20°53'E |
| **T** | | | |
| Taal, l., Phil. (tä-äl') | 213a | 13°58'N | 121°06'E |
| Tabaco, Phil. (tä-bä'kō) | 213a | 13°27'N | 123°40'E |
| Tabankulu, S. Afr. (tā-bān-kōō'la) | 233c | 30°56'S | 29°19'E |
| Tabasará, Serranía de, mts., Pan. | 133 | 8°29'N | 81°22'W |
| Tabasco, Mex. (tä-bäs'kō) | 130 | 21°47'N | 103°04'W |
| Tabasco, state, Mex. | 128 | 18°10'N | 93°00'W |
| Taber, Can. | 90 | 49°47'N | 112°08'W |
| Tablas, i., Phil. (tä'bläs) | 213a | 12°26'N | 122°00'E |
| Tablas Strait, strt., Phil. | 213a | 12°17'N | 121°41'E |
| Table Bay, b., S. Afr. (tā'b'l) | 232a | 33°41'S | 18°27'E |
| Table Mountain, mtn., S. Afr. | 232a | 33°58'S | 18°26'E |
| Table Rock Lake, Mo., U.S. | 121 | 36°37'N | 93°29'W |
| Tabligbo, Togo | 234 | 6°35'N | 1°30'E |
| Taboga, i., Pan. (tä-bō'gä) | 128a | 8°48'N | 79°35'W |
| Taboguilla, i., Pan. (tä-bō-gē'l-yä) | 128a | 8°48'N | 79°31'W |
| Tábor, Czech Rep. (tä'bôr) | 168 | 49°25'N | 14°40'E |
| Tabora, Tan. (tä-bō'rä) | 232 | 5°01'S | 32°48'E |
| Tabou, C. Iv. (tá-bōō') | 230 | 4°25'N | 7°21'W |
| Tabrīz, Iran (tà-brēz') | 198 | 38°00'N | 46°13'E |
| Tabuaeran, i., Kir. | 2 | 3°52'N | 159°20'W |
| Tabwémasana, Mont, mtn., Vanuatu | 214f | 15°20'S | 166°44'E |
| Tacámbaro, r., Mex. (tä-käm'bä-rō) | 130 | 18°55'N | 101°25'W |
| Tacámbaro de Codallos, Mex. | 130 | 19°12'N | 101°28'W |
| Tacarigua, Laguna de la, l., Ven. | 143b | 10°18'N | 65°43'W |
| Tacheng, China (tä-chŭŋ) | 204 | 46°50'N | 83°24'E |
| Tachie, r., Can. | 94 | 54°30'N | 125°00'W |
| Tacloban, Phil. (tä-klō'bän) | 213 | 11°06'N | 124°58'E |
| Tacna, Peru (täk'nä) | 142 | 18°34'S | 70°16'W |
| Tacoma, Wa., U.S. (tá-kō'má) | 104 | 47°14'N | 122°27'W |
| Taconic Range, mts., N.Y., U.S. (tá-kŏn'ĭk) | 109 | 41°55'N | 73°40'W |
| Tacotalpa, Mex. (tä-kō-täl'pä) | 131 | 17°37'N | 92°51'W |
| Tacotalpa, r., Mex. | 131 | 17°24'N | 92°38'W |
| Tademaït, Plateau du, plat., Alg. (tä-dē-mä'ēt) | 230 | 28°00'N | 2°15'E |
| Tadio, Lagune, b., C. Iv. | 234 | 5°20'N | 5°25'W |
| Tadjoura, Dji. (tád-zhōō'rá) | 238a | 11°48'N | 42°54'E |
| Tadley, Eng., U.K. (tăd'lē) | 158b | 51°19'N | 1°08'W |
| Tadotsu, Japan (tä'dô-tsò) | 211 | 34°14'N | 133°43'E |
| Tadoussac, Can. (tá-dōō-sák') | 99 | 48°09'N | 69°43'W |
| Tadzhikistan *see* Tajikistan, nation, Asia | 178 | 39°22'N | 69°30'E |
| Taebaek Sanmaek, mts., Asia (tī-bĭk' sän-mĭk') | 210 | 37°20'N | 128°50'E |
| Taedong, r., Kor., N. (tī-dŏng) | 210 | 38°38'N | 124°32'E |
| Taegu, Kor., S. (tī'gōō') | 205 | 35°49'N | 128°41'E |
| Taejŏn, Kor., S. | 210 | 36°20'N | 127°26'E |
| Tafalla, Spain (tä-fäl'yä) | 172 | 42°30'N | 1°42'W |
| Tafna, r., Alg. (täf'nä) | 172 | 35°28'N | 1°00'W |
| Taft, Ca., U.S. (tàft) | 118 | 35°09'N | 119°27'W |
| Tagama, reg., Niger | 235 | 15°50'N | 6°30'E |
| Taganrog, Russia (tà-gán-rôk') | 181 | 47°12'N | 38°56'E |
| Taganrogskiy Zaliv, b., Eur. (tà-gán-rôk'skĭ zä'lĭf) | 181 | 46°55'N | 38°17'E |
| Tagula, i., Pap. N. Gui. (tä'gōō-lá) | 221 | 11°45'S | 153°46'E |
| Tagus (Tajo), r., Eur. (tā'gŭs) | 156 | 39°40'N | 5°07'W |
| Tahan, Gunong, mtn., Malay. | 212 | 4°33'N | 101°52'E |
| Tahat, mtn., Alg. (tä-hät') | 230 | 23°22'N | 5°21'E |
| Tahiti, i., Fr. Poly. (tä-hē'tē) (tà'ē-tē') | 2 | 17°30'S | 149°30'W |
| Tahkuna Nina, c., Est. (táh-kōō'ná nē'ná) | 167 | 59°08'N | 22°03'E |
| Tahlequah, Ok., U.S. (tä-lē-kwä') | 121 | 35°54'N | 94°58'W |
| Tahoe, l., U.S. (tä'hō) | 106 | 39°09'N | 120°18'W |
| Tahoua, Niger (tä'ōō-ä) | 230 | 14°54'N | 5°16'E |
| Tahtsa Lake, l., Can. | 94 | 53°33'N | 127°47'W |
| Tahuya, Wa., U.S. (tá-hū-yä') | 116a | 47°23'N | 123°03'W |
| Tahuya, r., Wa., U.S. | 116a | 47°28'N | 122°55'W |
| Tai'an, China (tī-än) | 208 | 36°13'N | 117°08'E |
| Taibai Shan, mtn., China (tī-bī shän) | 208 | 33°42'N | 107°25'E |
| Taibus Qi, China (tī-bōō-sz chyē) | 208 | 41°52'N | 115°25'E |
| Taicang, China (tī-tsäŋ) | 206 | 31°26'N | 121°06'E |
| T'aichung, Tai. (tī'chòng) | 205 | 24°10'N | 120°42'E |
| Tai'erzhuang, China (tī-är-jûäŋ) | 206 | 34°34'N | 117°44'E |
| Taigu, China (tī-gōō) | 208 | 37°25'N | 112°35'E |
| Taihang Shan, mts., China (tī-häŋ shän) | 208 | 35°45'N | 112°00'E |
| Taihe, China (tī-hŭ) | 206 | 33°10'N | 115°38'E |
| Tai Hu, l., China (tī hōō) | 205 | 31°13'N | 120°00'E |
| Tailagoin, reg., Mong. (tī'lá-gän' kä'rä) | 204 | 43°39'N | 105°54'E |
| Tailai, China (tī-lī) | 208 | 46°20'N | 123°10'E |
| Tailem Bend, Austl. (tā-lĕm) | 222 | 35°15'S | 139°30'E |
| T'ainan, Tai. (tī'nan') | 205 | 23°08'N | 120°18'E |
| Taínaro, c., Grc. | 162 | 37°45'N | 22°00'E |
| Taining, China (tī'nĭng') | 209 | 26°58'N | 117°15'E |
| T'aipei, Tai. (tī'pā') | 205 | 25°02'N | 121°38'E |
| Taiping, pt. of i., Malay. | 212 | 4°56'N | 100°39'E |
| Taiping Ling, mtn., China | 208 | 47°03'N | 120°30'E |
| Taisha, Japan (tī'shä) | 211 | 35°23'N | 132°40'E |
| Taishan, China (tī-shän) | 209 | 22°15'N | 112°50'E |
| Tai Shan, mts., China (tī shän) | 208 | 36°16'N | 117°05'E |
| Taitao, Península de, pen., Chile | 144 | 46°20'S | 77°15'W |
| T'aitung, Tai. (tī'tōōng') | 209 | 22°45'N | 121°02'E |
| Taiwan, nation, Asia (tī-wän) (fŏr-mō'sá) | 205 | 23°30'N | 122°20'E |
| Taiwan Strait, strt., Asia | 205 | 24°30'N | 120°00'E |
| Taixian, China (tī shyĕn) | 206 | 32°31'N | 119°54'E |
| Taixing, China (tī-shyĭŋ) | 206 | 32°12'N | 119°58'E |
| Taiyuan, China (tī-yûän) | 205 | 37°32'N | 112°38'E |
| Taizhou, China (tī-jō) | 206 | 32°23'N | 119°41'E |
| Ta'Izz, Yemen | 201 | 13°38'N | 44°04'E |
| Tajano de Morais, Braz. (tē-zhä'nô-dĕ-mô-rä'ēs) | 141a | 22°05'S | 42°04'W |
| Tajikistan, nation, Asia | 178 | 39°22'N | 69°30'E |
| Tajumulco, vol., Guat. (tä-hōō-mōōl'kô) | 132 | 15°03'N | 91°53'W |
| Tajuña, r., Spain (tä-kōō'n-yä) | 172 | 40°23'N | 2°36'W |
| Tājūrā', Libya | 162 | 32°56'N | 13°24'W |
| Tak, Thai. | 212 | 16°57'N | 99°12'E |
| Taka, i., Japan (tä'kä) | 211 | 30°47'N | 130°23'E |
| Takada, Japan (tä'kä-dä) | 210 | 37°08'N | 138°30'E |
| Takahashi, Japan (tä'kä'hä-shĭ) | 211 | 34°47'N | 133°35'E |
| Takaishi, Japan | 211b | 34°32'N | 135°27'E |
| Takamatsu, Japan (tä'kä'mä-tsōō') | 205 | 34°20'N | 134°02'E |
| Takamori, Japan (tä'kä'mô-rē') | 211 | 32°50'N | 131°08'E |
| Takaoka, Japan (ta'kä'ô-kä') | 210 | 36°45'N | 136°59'E |
| Takapuna, N.Z. | 223 | 36°48'S | 174°47'E |
| Takarazuka, Japan (tä'kä-rä-zōō'kä) | 211b | 34°48'N | 135°22'E |
| Takasaki, Japan (tä'kät'sōō-kē') | 210 | 36°20'N | 139°00'E |
| Takatsu, Japan (tä-kät'sōō) (mĕ'zō-nô-kò'chê) | 211a | 35°36'N | 139°37'E |
| Takatsuki, Japan (tä'kät'sōō-kē') | 211b | 34°51'N | 135°38'E |
| Takayama, Japan (tä'kä'yä'mä) | 211 | 36°11'N | 137°16'E |
| Takefu, Japan (tä'kĕ-fōō) | 210 | 35°57'N | 136°09'E |
| Take-shima, is., Asia | 210 | 37°15'N | 131°51'E |
| Takla Lake, l., Can. | 92 | 55°25'N | 125°53'W |
| Takla Makan, des., China (mä-kän') | 204 | 39°22'N | 82°34'E |
| Takoma Park, Md., U.S. (tă'kōmă pärk) | 110e | 38°59'N | 77°00'W |
| Takum, Nig. | 235 | 7°17'N | 9°59'E |
| Tala, Mex. (tä'lä) | 130 | 20°39'N | 103°42'W |
| Talagante, Chile (tä-lä-gá'n-tĕ) | 141b | 33°39'S | 70°54'W |
| Talamanca, Cordillera de, mts., C.R. | 133 | 9°37'N | 83°55'W |
| Talanga, Hond. (tä-lä'n-gä) | 132 | 14°21'N | 87°09'W |
| Talara, Peru (tä-lä'rä) | 142 | 4°32'S | 81°17'W |
| Talasea, Pap. N. Gui. (tä-lä-sā'ä) | 213 | 5°20'S | 150°00'E |
| Talata Mafara, Nig. | 235 | 12°35'N | 6°04'E |
| Talaud, Kepulauan, is., Indon. (tä-lout') | 213 | 4°17'N | 127°30'E |
| Talavera de la Reina, Spain | 162 | 39°58'N | 4°51'W |
| Talca, Chile (täl'kä) | 144 | 35°25'S | 71°39'W |
| Talca, prov., Chile | 141b | 35°23'S | 71°15'W |
| Talca, Punta, c., Chile (pōō'n-tä-täl'kä) | 141b | 33°25'S | 71°42'W |
| Talcahuano, Chile (täl-kä-wä'nō) | 144 | 36°41'S | 73°05'W |
| Taldom, Russia (täl-dôm) | 176 | 56°44'N | 37°33'E |
| Taldyqorghan, Kaz. | 183 | 45°03'N | 77°18'E |
| Talea de Castro, Mex. (tä'lå-ä dä käs'trō) | 131 | 17°22'N | 96°14'W |
| Talibu, Pulau, i., Indon. | 213 | 1°30'S | 125°00'E |
| Talim, i., Phil. (tä-lēm') | 213a | 14°21'N | 121°14'E |
| Talisay, Phil. (tä-lē'sī) | 213a | 14°08'N | 122°56'E |
| Talkeetna, Ak., U.S. (tál-kēt'ná) | 103 | 62°18'N | 150°02'W |
| Talladega, Al., U.S. (tăl-à-dē'gá) | 124 | 33°25'N | 86°06'W |
| Tallahassee, Fl., U.S. (tăl-á-hăs'ê) | 105 | 30°25'N | 84°17'W |
| Tallahatchie, r., Ms., U.S. (tal-á hăch'ê) | 124 | 34°21'N | 90°03'W |
| Tallapoosa, Ga., U.S. (tăl-á-pōō'sá) | 124 | 33°44'N | 85°15'W |
| Tallapoosa, r., Al., U.S. | 124 | 32°22'N | 86°08'W |
| Tallassee, Al., U.S. (tăl'á-sê) | 124 | 32°30'N | 85°54'W |
| Tallinn, Est. (tál'lĕn) (rā'väl) | 178 | 59°26'N | 24°44'E |
| Tallmadge, Oh., U.S. (tăl'mĭj) | 111d | 41°06'N | 81°26'W |
| Tallulah, La., U.S. (tă-lōō'lá) | 123 | 32°25'N | 91°13'W |
| Tal'ne, Ukr. | 177 | 48°52'N | 30°43'E |
| Talo, mtn., Eth. | 231 | 10°45'N | 37°55'E |
| Taloje Budrukh, India | 203b | 19°05'N | 73°05'E |
| Talpa de Allende, Mex. (täl'pä dä äl-yĕn'då) | 130 | 20°25'N | 104°48'W |
| Talquin, Lake, res., Fl., U.S. | 124 | 30°26'N | 84°33'W |
| Talsi, Lat. (tal'sĭ) | 167 | 57°16'N | 22°35'E |
| Taltal, Chile (täl-täl') | 144 | 25°26'S | 70°32'W |
| Taly, Russia (täl'ĭ) | 177 | 49°51'N | 40°07'E |
| Tama, Ia., U.S. (tā'mä) | 113 | 41°57'N | 92°36'W |
| Tama, r., Japan | 211a | 35°38'N | 139°35'E |
| Tamale, Ghana (tä-mä'lå) | 230 | 9°25'N | 0°50'W |
| Taman', Russia (tå-män'') | 177 | 45°13'N | 36°46'E |
| Tamanaco, r., Ven. (tä-mä-nä'kō) | 143b | 9°32'N | 66°00'W |
| Tamaqua, Pa., U.S. (tá-mô'kwă) | 109 | 40°45'N | 75°50'W |
| Tamar, r., Eng., U.K. (tā'mär) | 164 | 50°35'N | 4°15'W |
| Tamarite de Litera, Spain (tä-mä-rē'tā) | 173 | 41°52'N | 0°24'E |
| Tamaulipas, state, Mex. (tä-mä-ōō-lē'päs') | 128 | 23°45'N | 98°30'W |
| Tamazula de Gordiano, Mex. | 130 | 19°44'N | 103°09'W |
| Tamazulapan del Progreso, Mex. | 131 | 17°41'N | 97°34'W |
| Tamazunchale, Mex. (tä-mä-zòn-chä'lå) | 130 | 21°16'N | 98°46'W |
| Tambacounda, Sen. (täm-bä-kōōn'dä) | 230 | 13°47'N | 13°40'W |
| Tambador, Serra do, mts., Braz. (sĕ'r-rä-dô-täm'bä-dōr) | 143 | 10°33'S | 41°16'W |
| Tambelan, Kepulauan, is., Indon. (täm-bå-län') | 212 | 0°38'N | 107°38'E |
| Tambo, Austl. (tăm'bō) | 219 | 24°50'S | 146°15'E |
| Tambov, Russia (tám-bôf') | 178 | 52°45'N | 41°10'E |
| Tambov, prov., Russia | 176 | 52°50'N | 40°42'E |
| Tambre, r., Spain (täm'brā) | 172 | 42°59'N | 8°33'W |
| Tambura, Sudan (täm-bōō'rä) | 231 | 5°34'N | 27°30'E |
| Tame, r., Eng., U.K. (tām) | 158a | 52°41'N | 1°42'W |
| Tâmega, r., Port. (tà-mā'gà) | 172 | 41°30'N | 7°45'W |
| Tamenghest, Alg. | 230 | 22°34'N | 5°34'E |
| Tamenghest, Oued, r., Alg. | 230 | 22°15'N | 2°51'E |
| Tamgak, Monts, mtn., Niger (tam-gäk') | 230 | 18°40'N | 8°40'E |
| Tamgué, Massif du, mtn., Gui. | 230 | 12°15'N | 12°35'W |
| Tamiahua, Mex. (tä-myä-wä) | 131 | 21°17'N | 97°26'W |


ng-sing; ŋ-baŋk; N-nasalized n; nŏd; cŏmmit; ōld; ôbey; ôrder; oi-boil; fōōd; ò-as oo in foot; ou-out; s-soft; sh-dish; th-thin; pūre; ûnite; ûrn; stŭd; circŭs; ü-as in French tu; '-indeterminate vowel.

356 Tamiahua – Temoaya

PRONOUNCING INDEX


| PLACE (Pronunciation) | PAGE | LAT. | LONG. |
|---|---|---|---|
| Tamiahua, Laguna, l., Mex. (lä-gò'nä-tä-myä-wä) | 131 | 21°38'N | 97°33'W |
| Tamiami Canal, can., Fl., U.S. (tă-mī-ăm'ĭ) | 125a | 25°52'N | 80°08'W |
| Tamil Nadu, state, India | 199 | 11°30'N | 78°00'E |
| Tampa, Fl., U.S. (tăm'pȧ) | 105 | 27°57'N | 82°25'W |
| Tampa Bay, b., Fl., U.S. | 107 | 27°35'N | 82°38'W |
| Tampere, Fin. (tåm'pĕ-rĕ) | 160 | 61°21'N | 23°39'E |
| Tampico, Mex. (täm-pē'kō) | 128 | 22°14'N | 97°51'W |
| Tampico Alto, Mex. (täm-pē'kō äl'tō) | 131 | 22°07'N | 97°48'W |
| Tampin, Malay. | 197b | 2°28'N | 102°15'E |
| Tam Quan, Viet. | 209 | 14°20'N | 109°10'E |
| Tamuín, Mex. (tä-mōō-ē'n) | 130 | 22°04'N | 98°47'W |
| Tamworth, Austl. (tăm'wûrth) | 219 | 31°01'S | 151°00'E |
| Tamworth, Eng., U.K. | 158a | 52°38'N | 1°41'W |
| Tana, i., Vanuatu | 221 | 19°32'S | 169°27'E |
| Tana, r., Kenya (tä'nä) | 233 | 0°30'S | 39°30'E |
| Tanabe, Japan (tä-nä'bā) | 210 | 33°45'N | 135°21'E |
| Tanabe, Japan | 211b | 34°49'N | 135°46'E |
| Tanacross, Ak., U.S. (tă'nȧ-crōs) | 103 | 63°20'N | 143°30'W |
| Tanaga, i., Ak., U.S. (tä-nä'gä) | 103a | 51°28'N | 178°10'W |
| Tanahbala, Pulau, i., Indon. (tȧ-nä-bä'lä) | 212 | 0°30'S | 98°22'E |
| Tanahmasa, Pulau, i., Indon. (tȧ-nä-mä'sä) | 212 | 0°03'S | 97°30'E |
| Tanakpur, India (tăn'ăk-pòr) | 202 | 29°10'N | 80°07'E |
| Tana Lake, l., Eth. | 231 | 12°09'N | 36°41'E |
| Tanami, Austl. (tȧ-nä'mē) | 218 | 19°45'S | 129°50'E |
| Tanana, Ak., U.S. (tă'nȧ-nô) | 103 | 65°18'N | 152°20'W |
| Tanana, r., Ak., U.S. | 103 | 64°26'N | 148°40'W |
| Tanaro, r., Italy (tä-nä'rô) | 174 | 44°45'N | 8°02'E |
| Tanashi, Japan | 211a | 35°44'N | 139°34'E |
| Tanbu, China (tän-bōō) | 207a | 23°20'N | 113°06'E |
| Tancheng, China (tän-chŭŋ) | 208 | 34°37'N | 118°22'E |
| Tanchŏn, Kor., N. (tän'chŭn) | 210 | 40°29'N | 128°50'E |
| Tancítaro, Mex. (tän-sē'tä-rō) | 130 | 19°16'N | 102°24'W |
| Tancítaro, Cerro de, mtn., Mex. (sĕ'r-rô-dĕ) | 130 | 19°24'N | 102°19'W |
| Tancoco, Mex. (tän-kō'kō) | 131 | 21°16'N | 97°45'W |
| Tandil, Arg. (tän-dēl') | 144 | 36°16'S | 59°01'W |
| Tandil, Sierra del, mts., Arg. | 144 | 38°40'S | 59°40'W |
| Tanega, i., Japan (tä'nȧ-gä') | 205 | 30°36'N | 131°11'E |
| Tanezrouft, reg., Alg. (tä'nĕz-rōft) | 230 | 24°17'N | 0°30'W |
| Tang, r., China (täŋ) | 206 | 33°38'N | 117°29'E |
| Tang, r., China | 206 | 39°13'N | 114°45'E |
| Tanga, Tan. (täŋ'gȧ) | 233 | 5°04'S | 39°06'E |
| Tangancícuaro, Mex. (täŋ-gän-sē'kwa-rô) | 130 | 19°52'N | 102°13'W |
| Tanganyika, Lake, l., Afr. | 232 | 5°15'S | 29°40'E |
| Tanger, Mor. (tăn-jĕr') | 230 | 35°52'N | 5°55'W |
| Tangermünde, Ger. (täŋ'ĕr-mün'de) | 168 | 52°33'N | 11°58'E |
| Tanggu, China (täŋ-gōō) | 206 | 39°04'N | 117°41'E |
| Tanggula Shan, mts., China (täŋ-gōō-lä shän) | 204 | 33°15'N | 89°07'E |
| Tanghe, China | 208 | 32°40'N | 112°50'E |
| Tangier *see* Tanger, Mor. | 230 | 35°52'N | 5°55'W |
| Tangipahoa, r., La., U.S. (tăn'jē-pȧ-hō'ȧ) | 123 | 30°48'N | 90°28'W |
| Tangra Yumco, l., China (täŋ-rä yōōm-tswo) | 202 | 30°50'N | 85°40'E |
| T'angshan, China | 208 | 39°38'N | 118°11'E |
| Tangxian, China (täŋ shyĕn) | 206 | 38°49'N | 115°00'E |
| Tangzha, China (täŋ-jä) | 206 | 32°06'N | 120°48'E |
| Tanimbar, Kepulauan, is., Indon. | 213 | 8°00'S | 132°00'E |
| Tanjong Piai, c., Malay. | 197b | 1°16'N | 103°11'E |
| Tanjong Ramunia, c., Malay. | 197b | 1°27'N | 104°44'E |
| Tanjungbalai, Indon. (tän'jông-bä'lå) | 197b | 1°00'N | 103°26'E |
| Tanjungpandan, Indon. | 212 | 2°47'S | 107°51'E |
| Tanjungpinang, Indon. (tän'jông-pē'näng) | 197b | 0°55'N | 104°29'E |
| Tannu-Ola, mts., Asia | 179 | 51°00'N | 94°00'E |
| Tannūrah, Ra's at, c., Sau. Ar. | 198 | 26°45'N | 49°59'E |
| Tano, r., Afr. | 234 | 5°40'N | 2°30'W |
| Tanquijo, Arrecife, i., Mex. (är-rĕ-sē'fĕ-tän-kē'kô) | 131 | 21°07'N | 97°16'W |
| Ṭanṭā, Egypt | 231 | 30°47'N | 31°00'E |
| Tantoyuca, Mex. (tän-tō-yōō'kä) | 130 | 21°22'N | 98°13'W |
| Tanyang, Kor., S. | 210 | 36°53'N | 128°20'E |
| Tanzania, nation, Afr. | 232 | 6°48'S | 33°58'E |
| Tao, r., China (tou) | 208 | 35°30'N | 103°40'E |
| Tao'an, China (tou-än) | 205 | 45°15'N | 122°45'E |
| Tao'er, r., China (tou-är) | 205 | 45°40'N | 122°00'E |
| Taormina, Italy (tä-ôr-mē'nä) | 174 | 37°53'N | 15°18'E |
| Taos, N.M., U.S. (tä'ōs) | 119 | 36°25'N | 105°35'W |
| Taoudenni, Mali (tä'ōō-dĕ-nē') | 230 | 22°57'N | 3°37'W |
| Taoussa, Mali | 234 | 16°55'N | 0°35'W |
| Taoyuan, China (tou-yůän) | 209 | 29°00'N | 111°15'E |
| Tapa, Est. (tȧ'pȧ) | 167 | 59°16'N | 25°56'E |
| Tapachula, Mex. | 132 | 14°55'N | 92°20'W |
| Tapajós, r., Braz. (tä-pä-zhô's) | 143 | 3°27'S | 55°33'W |
| Tapalque, Arg. (tä-päl-kĕ') | 141c | 36°22'S | 60°05'W |
| Tapanatepec, Mex. (tä-pä-nä-tĕ-pĕk) | 131 | 16°22'N | 94°19'W |
| Tāpi, r., India | 199 | 21°00'N | 76°30'E |
| Tappi Saki, c., Japan (täp'pē sä'kē) | 210 | 41°05'N | 139°40'E |
| Tapps, l., Wa., U.S. (tăpz) | 116a | 47°20'N | 122°12'W |
| Taquara, Serra de, mts., Braz. (sĕ'r-rä-dĕ-tä-kwä'rä) | 143 | 15°28'S | 54°33'W |
| Taquari, r., Braz. (tä-kwä-rĭ') | 143 | 18°35'S | 56°50'W |
| Tar, r., N.C., U.S. (tär) | 125 | 35°58'N | 78°06'W |
| Tara, Russia (tä'rȧ) | 178 | 56°58'N | 74°13'E |
| Tara, i., Phil. (tä'rä) | 213a | 12°18'N | 120°28'E |
| Tara, r., Russia (tä'rȧ) | 184 | 56°32'N | 76°13'E |
| Ṭarābulus, Leb. (tȧ-rä'bô-lōōs) | 198 | 34°25'N | 35°50'E |
| Ṭarābulus (Tripolitania), hist. reg., Libya | 230 | 31°00'N | 12°26'E |
| Tarakan, Indon. | 212 | 3°17'N | 118°04'E |
| Taranaki, Mount, vol., N.Z. | 223 | 39°18'S | 174°04'E |
| Tarancón, Spain (tä-rän-kōn') | 172 | 40°01'N | 3°00'W |
| Taranto, Italy (tä'rän-tô) | 163 | 40°30'N | 17°15'E |
| Taranto, Golfo di, b., Italy (gôl-fō-dē tä'rän-tô) | 156 | 40°03'N | 17°10'E |
| Tarapoto, Peru (tä-rä-pō'tō) | 142 | 6°29'S | 76°26'W |
| Tarare, Fr. (tȧ-rär') | 170 | 45°55'N | 4°23'E |
| Tarascon, Fr. (tȧ-rȧs-kôn') | 170 | 42°53'N | 1°35'E |
| Tarascon, Fr. (tä-räs-kôɴ) | 170 | 43°47'N | 4°41'E |
| Tarashcha, Ukr. (tä'rȧsh-chȧ) | 177 | 49°34'N | 30°52'E |
| Tarata, Bol. (tä-rä'tä) | 142 | 17°43'S | 66°00'W |
| Taravo, r., Fr. | 174 | 41°54'N | 8°58'E |
| Tarazit, Massif de, mts., Niger | 235 | 20°05'N | 7°35'E |
| Tarazona, Spain (tä-rä-thō'nä) | 172 | 41°54'N | 1°45'W |
| Tarazona de la Mancha, Spain (tä-rä-zō'nä-dĕ-lä-mä'n-chä) | 172 | 39°13'N | 1°50'W |
| Tarbes, Fr. (tȧrb) | 161 | 43°04'N | 0°05'E |
| Tarboro, N.C., U.S. (tär'bŭr-ô) | 125 | 35°53'N | 77°34'W |
| Taree, Austl. (tă-rē') | 222 | 31°52'S | 152°21'E |
| Tarentum, Pa., U.S. (tȧ-rĕn'tŭm) | 111e | 40°36'N | 79°44'W |
| Tarfa, Wādī at, val., Egypt | 238b | 28°14'N | 31°00'E |
| Târgovişte, Rom. | 163 | 44°54'N | 25°29'E |
| Târgu Jiu, Rom. | 163 | 45°02'N | 23°17'E |
| Târgu Mureş, Rom. | 163 | 46°33'N | 24°33'E |
| Târgu Neamţ, Rom. | 169 | 47°14'N | 26°23'E |
| Târgu Ocna, Rom. | 169 | 46°18'N | 26°38'E |
| Târgu Secuiesc, Rom. | 169 | 46°04'N | 26°06'E |
| Tarhūnah, Libya | 200 | 32°26'N | 13°38'E |
| Tarija, Bol. (tär-rē'hä) | 142 | 21°42'S | 64°52'W |
| Tarīm, Yemen (tȧ-rĭm') | 198 | 16°13'N | 49°08'E |
| Tarim, r., China (tä-rĭm') | 204 | 40°45'N | 85°39'E |
| Tarim Basin, basin, China (tȧ-rĭm') | 204 | 39°52'N | 82°34'E |
| Tarka, r., S. Afr. (tä'kȧ) | 233c | 32°15'S | 26°00'E |
| Tarkastad, S. Afr. | 233c | 32°01'S | 26°18'E |
| Tarkhankut, Mys, c., Ukr. (mĭs tȧr-kän'kòt) | 181 | 45°21'N | 32°30'E |
| Tarkio, Mo., U.S. (tär'kĭ-ō) | 121 | 40°27'N | 95°22'W |
| Tarkwa, Ghana (tärk'wä) | 230 | 5°19'N | 1°59'W |
| Tarlac, Phil. (tär'läk) | 212 | 15°29'N | 120°36'E |
| Tarlton, S. Afr. (tärl'tŭn) | 233b | 26°05'S | 27°38'E |
| Tarma, Peru (tär'mä) | 142 | 11°26'S | 75°40'W |
| Tarn, r., Fr. (tärn) | 161 | 43°45'N | 2°00'E |
| Târnǎveni, Rom. | 169 | 46°19'N | 24°18'E |
| Tarnów, Pol. (tär'nòf) | 161 | 50°02'N | 21°00'E |
| Taro, r., Italy (tä'rō) | 174 | 44°41'N | 10°03'E |
| Taroudant, Mor. (tȧ-rōō-dänt') | 230 | 30°39'N | 8°52'W |
| Tarpon Springs, Fl., U.S. (tär'pŏn) | 125a | 28°07'N | 82°44'W |
| Tarporley, Eng., U.K. (tär'pĕr-lē) | 158a | 53°09'N | 2°40'W |
| Tarpum Bay, b., Bah. (tär'pŭm) | 134 | 25°05'N | 76°20'W |
| Tarquinia, Italy (tär-kwē'nē-ä) | 174 | 42°16'N | 11°46'E |
| Tarragona, Spain (tär-rä-gō'nä) | 154 | 41°05'N | 1°15'E |
| Tarrant, Al., U.S. (tăr'ănt) | 110h | 33°35'N | 86°46'W |
| Tárrega, Spain (tä rå-gä) | 173 | 41°40'N | 1°09'E |
| Tarrejón de Ardoz, Spain (tär-rĕ-kô'n-dĕ-är-dôz) | 173a | 40°28'N | 3°29'W |
| Tarrytown, N.Y., U.S. (tăr'ĭ-toun) | 110a | 41°04'N | 73°52'W |
| Tarsus, Tur. (tȧr'sòs) (tär'sŭs) | 198 | 37°00'N | 34°50'E |
| Tartagal, Arg. (tär-tä-gá'l) | 144 | 23°31'S | 63°47'W |
| Tartu, Est. (tär'tōō) (dôr'pät) | 178 | 58°23'N | 26°44'E |
| Ţarţūs, Syria | 200 | 34°54'N | 35°59'E |
| Tarumi, Japan (tä'rōō-mē) | 211b | 34°38'N | 135°04'E |
| Tarusa, Russia (tä-rōōs'ȧ) | 176 | 54°43'N | 37°11'E |
| Tarzana, Ca., U.S. (tär-ză'ȧ) | 117a | 34°10'N | 118°32'W |
| Tashkent, Uzb. (tȧsh'kĕnt) | 183 | 41°23'N | 69°04'E |
| Tasman Bay, b., N.Z. (tăz'măn) | 221a | 40°50'S | 173°20'E |
| Tasmania, state, Austl. | 219 | 41°28'S | 142°30'E |
| Tasman Peninsula, pen., Austl. | 222 | 43°00'S | 148°30'E |
| Tasman Sea, sea, Oc. | 241 | 29°30'S | 155°00'E |
| Tasquillo, Mex. (täs-kē'lyō) | 130 | 20°34'N | 99°21'W |
| Tatarsk, Russia (tȧ-tärsk') | 178 | 55°13'N | 75°58'E |
| Tatarstan, prov., Russia | 180 | 55°00'N | 51°00'E |
| Tatar Strait, strt., Russia | 179 | 51°00'N | 141°45'E |
| Tater Hill, mtn., Or., U.S. (tāt'ĕr hĭl) | 116c | 45°47'N | 123°02'W |
| Tateyama, Japan (tä'tē-yä'mä) | 211 | 35°04'N | 139°52'E |
| Tatlow, Mount, mtn., Can. | 94 | 51°23'N | 123°52'W |
| Tau, Nor. | 166 | 59°05'N | 5°59'E |
| Tauern Tunnel, trans., Aus. | 168 | 47°12'N | 13°17'E |
| Taung, S. Afr. (tä'ông) | 212 | 27°25'S | 24°47'E |
| Taunton, Ma., U.S. (tän'tŭn) | 109 | 41°54'N | 71°03'W |
| Taunton, r., R.I., U.S. | 110b | 41°50'N | 71°02'W |
| Taupo, Lake, l., N.Z. (tä'ōō-pō) | 221a | 38°42'S | 175°55'E |
| Taurage, Lith. (tou'rȧ-gä) | 167 | 55°15'N | 22°18'E |
| Taurus Mountains *see* Toros Dağları, mts., Tur. | 198 | 37°00'N | 32°40'E |
| Tauste, Spain (tä-ōōs'tå) | 172 | 41°55'N | 1°15'W |
| Tavda, Russia (tȧv-dȧ') | 178 | 58°00'N | 64°44'E |
| Tavda, r., Russia | 184 | 58°30'N | 64°15'E |
| Taverny, Fr. (tȧ-vĕr-nē') | 171b | 49°02'N | 2°13'E |
| Taviche, Mex. (tä-vē'chĕ) | 131 | 16°43'N | 96°35'W |
| Tavira, Port. (tä-vē'rȧ) | 172 | 37°09'N | 7°42'W |
| Tavşanlı, Tur. (tȧv'shän-lĭ) | 181 | 39°30'N | 29°30'E |
| Tawakoni, l., Tx., U.S. | 123 | 32°51'N | 95°59'W |
| Tawaramoto, Japan (tä'wä-rä-mô-tō) | 211b | 34°33'N | 135°48'E |
| Tawas City, Mi., U.S. | 108 | 44°15'N | 83°30'W |
| Tawas Point, c., Mi., U.S. (tô'wȧs) | 108 | 44°15'N | 83°25'W |
| Tawitawi Group, is., Phil. (tä'wē-tä'wē) | 212 | 4°52'N | 120°35'E |
| Tawkar, Sudan | 231 | 18°28'N | 37°46'E |
| Taxco de Alarcón, Mex. (täs'kō dĕ ä-lär-kô'n) | 130 | 18°34'N | 99°37'W |
| Tay, r., Scot., U.K. | 164 | 56°35'N | 3°37'W |
| Tay, Loch, l., Scot., U.K. | 164 | 56°25'N | 4°07'W |
| Tayabas Bay, b., Phil. (tä-yä'bäs) | 213a | 13°44'N | 121°40'E |
| Tayga, Russia (tī'gä) | 184 | 56°12'N | 85°47'E |
| Taygonos, Mys, c., Russia | 179 | 60°37'N | 160°17'E |
| Taylor, Tx., U.S. | 123 | 30°35'N | 97°25'W |
| Taylor, Mount, mtn., N.M., U.S. | 106 | 35°20'N | 107°40'W |
| Taylorville, Il., U.S. (tā'lĕr-vĭl) | 108 | 39°30'N | 89°20'W |
| Taymyr, l., Russia (tī-mĭr') | 179 | 74°13'N | 100°45'E |
| Taymyr, Poluostrov, pen., Russia | 179 | 75°15'N | 95°00'E |
| Tayshet, Russia (tī-shĕt') | 179 | 56°09'N | 97°49'E |
| Tayug, Phil. | 213a | 16°01'N | 120°45'E |
| Taz, r., Russia (tȧz) | 184 | 67°15'N | 80°45'E |
| Taza, Mor. (tä'zä) | 230 | 34°08'N | 4°00'W |
| Tazovskoye, Russia | 178 | 66°58'N | 78°28'E |
| Tbessa, Alg. | 230 | 35°27'N | 8°13'E |
| Tbilisi, Geor. ('tbĭl-yĕ'sē) | 181 | 41°40'N | 44°45'E |
| Tchentlo Lake, l., Can. | 94 | 55°11'N | 125°00'W |
| Tchibanga, Gabon (chē-bäŋ'gä) | 232 | 2°51'S | 11°02'E |
| Tchien, Lib. | 234 | 6°04'N | 8°08'W |
| Tchigai, Plateau du, plat., Afr. | 235 | 21°20'N | 14°50'E |
| Tczew, Pol. (t'chĕf') | 160 | 54°06'N | 18°48'E |
| Teabo, Mex. (tĕ-ä'bô) | 132a | 20°25'N | 89°14'W |
| Teague, Tx., U.S. | 123 | 31°39'N | 96°16'W |
| Teapa, Mex. (tā-ä'pä) | 131 | 17°35'N | 92°56'W |
| Tebing Tinggi, i., Indon. (teb'ing-tĭng'gä) | 197b | 0°54'N | 102°39'E |
| Tecalitlán, Mex. (tā-kä-lē-tlän') | 130 | 19°28'N | 103°17'W |
| Techiman, Ghana | 234 | 7°35'N | 1°56'W |
| Tecoanapa, Mex. (tāk-wä-nä-pä') | 130 | 16°33'N | 98°46'W |
| Tecoh, Mex. (tĕ-kô) | 132a | 20°46'N | 89°27'W |
| Tecolotlán, Mex. (tā-kō-lō-tlän') | 130 | 20°13'N | 103°57'W |
| Tecolutla, Mex. (tā-kô-lōō'tlä) | 131 | 20°33'N | 97°00'W |
| Tecolutla, r., Mex. | 131 | 20°16'N | 97°14'W |
| Tecomán, Mex. (tā-kō-män') | 130 | 18°53'N | 103°53'W |
| Tecómitl, Mex. (tĕ-kō'mētl) | 131a | 19°13'N | 98°59'W |
| Tecozautla, Mex. (tā'kō-zä-ōō'tlä) | 130 | 20°33'N | 99°38'W |
| Tecpan de Galeana, Mex. (tĕk-pän' dā gä-lā-ä'nä) | 130 | 17°13'N | 100°41'W |
| Tecpatán, Mex. (tĕk-pä-tá'n) | 131 | 17°08'N | 93°18'W |
| Tecuala, Mex. (tĕ-kwä-lä) | 130 | 22°24'N | 105°29'W |
| Tecuci, Rom. (tȧ-kōch') | 163 | 45°51'N | 27°30'E |
| Tecumseh, Can. (tē-kŭm'sĕ) | 111b | 42°19'N | 82°53'W |
| Tecumseh, Mi., U.S. | 108 | 42°00'N | 84°00'W |
| Tecumseh, Ne., U.S. | 121 | 40°21'N | 96°09'W |
| Tecumseh, Ok., U.S. | 121 | 35°18'N | 96°55'W |
| Tees, r., Eng., U.K. (tēz) | 164 | 54°40'N | 2°10'W |
| Teganuna, l., Japan (tā'gä-nōō'nä) | 211a | 35°50'N | 140°02'E |
| Tegucigalpa, Hond. (tȧ-gōō-sē-gäl'pä) | 128 | 14°08'N | 87°15'W |
| Tehachapi Mountains, mts., Ca., U.S. (tē-hă-shă'pĭ) | 118 | 34°50'N | 118°55'W |
| Tehrān, Iran (tĕ-hrän') | 198 | 35°45'N | 51°30'E |
| Tehuacan, Mex. (tā-wä-kän') | 128 | 18°27'N | 97°23'W |
| Tehuantepec, Mex. | 128 | 16°20'N | 95°14'W |
| Tehuantepec, r., Mex. | 131 | 16°30'N | 95°23'W |
| Tehuantepec, Golfo de, b., Mex. (gôl-fô dĕ) | 128 | 15°45'N | 95°00'W |
| Tehuantepec, Istmo de, isth., Mex. (ē'st-mô dĕ) | 131 | 17°55'N | 94°35'W |
| Tehuehuetla, Arroyo, r., Mex. (tĕ-wĕ-wĕ'tlä är-rô-yô) | 130 | 17°54'N | 100°26'W |
| Tehuitzingo, Mex. (tā-wē-tzĭŋ'gō) | 130 | 18°21'N | 98°16'W |
| Tejeda, Sierra de, mts., Spain (sē-ĕ'r-rä dĕ tĕ-kĕ'dä) | 172 | 36°55'N | 4°00'W |
| Tejúpan, Mex. (tĕ-kōō-pä'n) (sän-tyá'gô) | 131 | 17°39'N | 97°34'W |
| Tejúpan, Punta, c., Mex. | 130 | 18°19'N | 103°30'W |
| Tejupilco de Hidalgo, Mex. (tå-hōō-pēl'kō dā ē-dhäl'gō) | 130 | 18°52'N | 100°07'W |
| Tekamah, Ne., U.S. (tē-kā'mȧ) | 112 | 41°46'N | 96°13'W |
| Tekax de Alvaro Obregon, Mex. | 132a | 20°12'N | 89°11'W |
| Tekeze, r., Afr. | 231 | 13°38'N | 38°00'E |
| Tekit, Mex. (tĕ-kē't) | 132a | 20°35'N | 89°18'W |
| Tekoa, Wa., U.S. (tē-kō'ȧ) | 114 | 47°15'N | 117°03'W |
| Tela, Hond. (tā'lä) | 128 | 15°45'N | 87°25'W |
| Tela, Bahía de, b., Hond. | 132 | 15°53'N | 87°29'W |
| Telapa Burok, Gunong, mtn., Malay. | 197b | 2°51'N | 102°04'E |
| Telavi, Geor. | 181 | 42°00'N | 45°20'E |
| Tel Aviv-Yafo, Isr. (tĕl-ä-vēv'já'já'fȧ) | 198 | 32°03'N | 34°46'E |
| Telegraph Creek, Can. (tĕl'ĕ-gráf) | 90 | 57°59'N | 131°22'W |
| Teleneşti, Mol. | 177 | 47°31'N | 28°22'E |
| Telescope Peak, mtn., Ca., U.S. (tĕl'ē skōp) | 106 | 36°12'N | 117°05'W |
| Telesung, Indon. | 197b | 1°07'N | 102°53'E |
| Telica, vol., Nic. (tå-lē'kä) | 132 | 12°38'N | 86°52'W |
| Tell City, In., U.S. (tĕl) | 108 | 38°00'N | 86°45'W |
| Teller, Ak., U.S. (tĕl'ĕr) | 103 | 65°17'N | 166°28'W |
| Tello, Col. (tĕ'l-yô) | 142a | 3°05'N | 75°08'W |
| Telluride, Co., U.S. (tĕl'ū-rīd) | 119 | 37°55'N | 107°50'W |
| Telok Datok, Malay. | 197b | 2°51'N | 101°33'E |
| Teloloapan, Mex. (tā'lô-lô-ä'pän) | 130 | 18°19'N | 99°54'W |
| Tel'pos-Iz, Gora, mtn., Russia (tyĕl'pôs-ēz') | 178 | 63°50'N | 59°20'E |
| Telšiai, Lith. (tĕl'sha'ē) | 167 | 55°59'N | 22°17'E |
| Teltow, Ger. (tĕl'tō) | 159b | 52°24'N | 13°12'E |
| Teluklecak, Indon. | 197b | 1°53'N | 101°45'E |
| Tema, Ghana | 234 | 5°38'N | 0°01'E |
| Temascalcingo, Mex. (tā'mäs-käl-sĭŋ'gō) | 130 | 19°55'N | 100°00'W |
| Temascaltepec, Mex. (tā'mäs-käl-tå pĕk) | 130 | 19°00'N | 100°03'W |
| Temax, Mex. (tĕ'mäx) | 128 | 21°10'N | 88°51'W |
| Temir, Kaz. | 183 | 49°10'N | 57°15'E |
| Temirtaū, Kaz. | 183 | 50°08'N | 73°13'E |
| Temiscouata, l., Can. (tĕ'mĭs-kô-ä'tä) | 100 | 47°40'N | 68°50'W |
| Témiskaming, Can. (tē-mĭs'kȧ-mĭng) | 91 | 46°41'N | 79°01'W |
| Temoaya, Mex. (tĕ-mô-a-um-yä) | 131a | 19°28'N | 99°36'W |

ng-sing;  ŋ-baŋk;  N-nasalized n;  nŏd; cŏmmit; ōld; ôbey; ôrder; oi-boil; fōōd; ò-as oo in foot; ou-out;  s-soft; sh-dish; th-thin;  pūre; ûnite; ûrn; stŭd; circŭs; ü-as in French tu;  ′-indeterminate vowel.

358 Tidra – Topol'čany

PRONOUNCING INDEX


| PLACE (Pronunciation) | PAGE | LAT. | LONG. |
|---|---|---|---|
| Tidra, Île, i., Maur. | 234 | 19°50'N | 16°45'W |
| Tieling, China (tĭĕ-liŋ) | 205 | 42°18'N | 123°50'E |
| Tielmes, Spain (tyâl-màs') | 173a | 40°15'N | 3°20'W |
| Tienen, Bel. | 159a | 50°49'N | 4°58'E |
| Tien Shan, mts., Asia | 204 | 42°00'N | 78°46'E |
| Tientsin *see* Tianjin, China | 205 | 39°08'N | 117°14'E |
| Tierp, Swe. (tyĕrp) | 166 | 60°21'N | 17°28'E |
| Tierpoort, S. Afr. | 233b | 25°53'N | 28°26'E |
| Tierra Blanca, Mex. (tyĕ'r-rä-blä'n-kä) | 131 | 18°28'N | 96°19'W |
| Tierra del Fuego, i., S.A. (tyĕr'rä dĕl fwā'gō) | 144 | 53°50'S | 68°45'W |
| Tiétar, r., Spain (tê-ā'tär) | 172 | 39°56'N | 5°44'W |
| Tiffin, Oh., U.S. (tĭf'ĭn) | 108 | 41°10'N | 83°15'W |
| Tifton, Ga., U.S. (tĭf'tŭn) | 124 | 31°25'N | 83°34'W |
| Tigard, Or., U.S. (tī'gärd) | 116c | 45°25'N | 122°46'W |
| Tighina, Mol. | 181 | 46°49'N | 29°29'E |
| Tignish, Can. (tĭg'nĭsh) | 100 | 46°57'N | 64°02'W |
| Tigoda, r., Russia (tē'gô-dà) | 186c | 59°29'N | 31°15'E |
| Tigre, r., Peru | 142 | 2°20'S | 75°41'W |
| Tigres, Península dos, pen., Ang. (pĕ-nē'ŋ-sōō-lä-dôs-tē'grĕs) | 232 | 16°30'S | 11°45'E |
| Tigris, r., Asia | 198 | 34°45'N | 44°10'E |
| Tīh, Jabal at, mts., Egypt | 197a | 29°23'N | 34°05'E |
| Tihert, Alg. | 230 | 35°28'N | 1°15'E |
| Tihuatlán, Mex. (tē-wä-tlän') | 131 | 20°43'N | 97°34'W |
| Tijuana, Mex. (tē-hwä'nä) | 128 | 32°32'N | 117°02'W |
| Tijuca, Pico da, mtn., Braz. (pē'kō-dä-tē-zhōō'kà) | 144b | 22°56'S | 43°17'W |
| Tikal, hist., Guat. (tê-käl') | 132a | 17°16'N | 89°49'W |
| Tikhoretsk, Russia (tē-κôr-yĕtsk') | 181 | 45°55'N | 40°05'E |
| Tikhvin, Russia (tēκ-vēn') | 178 | 59°36'N | 33°38'E |
| Tikrīt, Iraq | 198 | 34°36'N | 43°31'E |
| Tiksi, Russia (tĕk-sē') | 179 | 71°42'N | 128°32'E |
| Tilburg, Neth. (tĭl'bûrg) | 161 | 51°33'N | 5°05'E |
| Tilbury, Eng., U.K. | 158b | 51°28'N | 0°23'E |
| Tilemsi, Vallée du, val., Mali | 234 | 17°50'N | 0°25'E |
| Tilichiki, Russia (tyĭ-le-chĭ-kē) | 179 | 60°49'N | 166°14'E |
| Tilimsen, Alg. | 230 | 34°53'N | 1°21'W |
| Tillabéry, Niger (tē-yá-bā-rē') | 230 | 14°14'N | 1°30'E |
| Tillamook, Or., U.S. (tĭl'à-mo͝ok) | 114 | 45°27'N | 123°50'W |
| Tillamook Bay, b., Or., U.S. | 114 | 45°32'N | 124°26'W |
| Tillberga, Swe. (tēl-bĕr'ghá) | 166 | 59°40'N | 16°34'E |
| Tillsonburg, Can. (tĭl'sŭn-bûrg) | 99 | 42°50'N | 80°50'W |
| Tim, Russia (têm) | 177 | 51°39'N | 37°07'E |
| Timaru, N.Z. (tĭm'á-rōō) | 221a | 44°26'S | 171°17'E |
| Timashevskaya, Russia (tēmä-shĕfs-kä'yä) | 181 | 45°47'N | 38°57'E |
| Timbalier Bay, b., La., U.S. (tĭm'bá-lēr) | 123 | 28°55'N | 90°14'W |
| Timber, Or., U.S. (tĭm'bēr) | 116c | 45°43'N | 123°17'W |
| Timbo, Gui. (tĭm'bō) | 230 | 10°41'N | 11°51'W |
| Timbuktu *see* Tombouctou, Mali | 230 | 16°46'N | 3°01'W |
| Timétrine Monts, mts., Mali | 234 | 19°50'N | 0°30'W |
| Timimoun, Alg. (tē-mē-mōōn') | 230 | 29°14'N | 0°22'E |
| Timiris, Cap, c., Maur. | 230 | 19°23'N | 16°32'W |
| Timiş, r., Eur. | 175 | 45°28'N | 21°06'E |
| Timişoara, Rom. | 163 | 45°44'N | 21°21'E |
| Timmins, Can. (tĭm'ĭnz) | 91 | 48°25'N | 81°22'W |
| Timmonsville, S.C., U.S. (tĭm'ŭnz-vĭl) | 125 | 34°09'N | 79°55'W |
| Timok, r., Eur. | 175 | 43°35'N | 22°13'E |
| Timor, i., Asia (tê-mōr') | 213 | 10°08'S | 125°00'E |
| Timor Sea, sea | 220 | 12°40'S | 125°00'E |
| Timpanogos Cave National Monument, rec., Ut., U.S. (tĭ-măn'ō-gōz) | 119 | 40°25'N | 111°45'W |
| Timpson, Tx., U.S. (tĭmp'sŭn) | 123 | 31°55'N | 94°24'W |
| Timsāh, l., Egypt (tĭm'sä) | 238b | 30°34'N | 32°22'E |
| Tina, r., S. Afr. (tē'nà) | 233c | 30°50'S | 28°44'E |
| Tina, Monte, mtn., Dom. Rep. (mô'n-tĕ-tē'nà) | 135 | 18°50'N | 70°40'W |
| Tinaguillo, Ven. (tē-nä-gē'l-yō) | 143b | 9°55'N | 68°18'W |
| Tīnah, Khalīj at, b., Egypt | 197a | 31°06'N | 32°42'E |
| Tindouf, Alg. (tēn-dōōf') | 230 | 27°43'N | 7°44'W |
| Tinggi, i., Malay. | 197b | 2°16'N | 104°16'E |
| Tinghert, Plateau du, plat., Alg. | 230 | 27°30'N | 7°30'E |
| Tingi Mountains, mts., S.L. | 234 | 9°00'N | 10°50'W |
| Tinglin, China | 207b | 30°53'N | 121°18'E |
| Tingo María, Peru (tē'ngō-mä-rē'ä) | 142 | 9°15'S | 76°04'W |
| Tingréla, C. Iv. | 234 | 10°29'N | 6°24'W |
| Tingsryd, Swe. (tĭngs'rüd) | 166 | 56°32'N | 14°58'E |
| Tinguindio, Mex. | 130 | 19°38'N | 102°02'W |
| Tinguiririca, r., Chile (tē'n-gē-rē-rē'kä) | 141b | 34°48'S | 70°45'W |
| Tinley Park, Il., U.S. (tĭn'lē) | 111a | 41°34'N | 87°47'W |
| Tinnoset, Nor. (tĕn'nôs'sĕt) | 166 | 59°44'N | 9°00'E |
| Tinogasta, Arg. (tē-nô-gäs'tä) | 144 | 28°07'S | 67°30'W |
| Tínos, i., Grc. | 163 | 37°45'N | 25°12'E |
| Tinsukia, India (tin-sōō'kĭ-à) | 198 | 27°18'N | 95°29'W |
| Tintic, Ut., U.S. (tĭn'tĭk) | 119 | 39°55'N | 112°15'W |
| Tio, Pic de, mtn., Gui. | 234 | 8°55'N | 8°55'W |
| Tioman, i., Malay. | 197b | 2°50'N | 104°15'E |
| Tipitapa, Nic. (tē-pē-tä'pä) | 132 | 12°14'N | 86°05'W |
| Tipitapa, r., Nic. | 132 | 12°13'N | 85°57'W |
| Tippah Creek, r., Ms., U.S. (tĭp'pá) | 124 | 34°43'N | 88°15'W |
| Tippecanoe, r., In., U.S. (tĭp-ē-kà-nōō') | 108 | 40°55'N | 86°45'W |
| Tipperary, Ire. (tĭ-pē-rā'rē) | 161 | 52°28'N | 8°13'W |
| Tippo Bay, Ms., U.S. (tĭp'ō bīōō') | 121 | 33°35'N | 90°06'W |
| Tipton, Ia., U.S. | 113 | 41°46'N | 91°10'W |
| Tipton, In., U.S. | 108 | 40°15'N | 86°00'W |
| Tiranë, Alb. (tē-rä'nä) | 154 | 41°48'N | 19°50'E |
| Tirano, Italy (tē-rä'nō) | 174 | 46°12'N | 10°09'E |
| Tiraspol, Mol. | 181 | 46°52'N | 29°38'E |
| Tire, Tur. (tē'rĕ) | 163 | 38°05'N | 27°48'E |
| Tiree, i., Scot., U.K. (tī-rē') | 160 | 56°34'N | 6°30'W |
| Tirlyanskiy, Russia (tĭr-lyän'skĭ) | 186a | 54°13'N | 58°37'E |
| Tiruchchirāppalli, India (tĭr'ŏ-chĭ-rä'pà-lĭ) | 199 | 10°49'N | 78°48'E |
| Tirunelveli, India | 203 | 8°53'N | 77°43'E |
| Tiruppur, India | 203 | 11°11'N | 77°08'E |
| Tisdale, Can. (tĭz'dāl) | 90 | 52°51'N | 104°04'W |
| Tista, r., Asia | 202 | 26°00'N | 89°30'E |
| Tisza, r., Eur. (tē'sä) | 156 | 47°30'N | 21°00'E |
| Titāgarh, India | 202a | 22°44'N | 88°23'E |
| Titicaca, Lago, l., S.A. (lä'gō-tē-tē-kä'kä) | 142 | 16°12'S | 70°33'W |
| Titiribi, Col. (tē-tē-rē-bē') | 142a | 6°05'N | 75°47'W |
| Tito, Lagh, r., Kenya | 237 | 2°25'N | 39°05'E |
| Titov Veles, Mac. (tē'tôv vĕ'lĕs) | 175 | 41°42'N | 21°50'E |
| Titterstone Clee Hill, hill, Eng., U.K. (klē) | 158a | 52°24'N | 2°37'W |
| Titule, D.R.C. | 237 | 3°17'N | 25°32'E |
| Titusville, Fl., U.S. (tī'tŭs-vĭl) | 125a | 28°37'N | 80°44'W |
| Titusville, Pa., U.S. | 109 | 40°40'N | 79°40'W |
| Titz, Ger. (tētz) | 171c | 51°00'N | 6°26'E |
| Tiverton, R.I., U.S. (tĭv'ēr-tun) | 110b | 41°38'N | 71°11'W |
| Tivoli, Italy (tē'vô-lē) | 162 | 41°38'N | 12°48'E |
| Tixkokob, Mex. (tēx-kō-kō'b) | 132a | 21°01'N | 89°23'W |
| Tixtla de Guerrero, Mex. (tē'x-tlä-dĕ-gĕr-rĕ'rô) | 130 | 17°36'N | 99°24'W |
| Tizard Bank and Reef, rf., Asia (tĭz'ărd) | 212 | 10°51'N | 113°20'E |
| Tizimín, Mex. (tē-zē-mē'n) | 132a | 21°08'N | 88°10'W |
| Tizi-Ouzou, Alg. (tē'zē-ōō-zōō') | 230 | 36°44'N | 4°04'E |
| Tiznados, r., Ven. (tēz-nä'dôs) | 143b | 9°53'N | 67°49'W |
| Tiznit, Mor. (tēz-nēt) | 230 | 29°52'N | 9°39'W |
| Tkvarcheli, Geor. | 182 | 42°15'N | 41°41'E |
| Tlacolula de Matamoros, Mex. | 131 | 16°56'N | 96°29'W |
| Tlacotálpan, Mex. (tlä-kô-täl'pän) | 131 | 18°39'N | 95°40'W |
| Tlacotepec, Mex. (tlä-kô-tå-pĕ'k) | 130 | 17°46'N | 99°57'W |
| Tlacotepec, Mex. | 130 | 19°11'N | 99°41'W |
| Tlacotepec, Mex. | 131 | 18°41'N | 97°40'W |
| Tláhuac, Mex. (tlä-wäk') | 131a | 19°16'N | 99°00'W |
| Tlajomulco de Zúñiga, Mex. (tlä-hô-mōō'l-kô-dĕ-zōō'n-yē-gä) | 130 | 20°30'N | 103°27'W |
| Tlalchapa, Mex. (tläl-chä'pä) | 130 | 18°26'N | 100°29'W |
| Tlalixcoyan, Mex. (tlä-lēs'kô-yän') | 131 | 18°53'N | 96°04'W |
| Tlalmanalco, Mex. (tläl-mä-nä'l-kô) | 131a | 19°12'N | 98°48'W |
| Tlalnepantla, Mex. | 131a | 19°32'N | 99°13'W |
| Tlalnepantla, Mex. (tläl-nå-pån'tlä) | 131a | 18°59'N | 99°01'W |
| Tlalpan, Mex. (tläl-pä'n) | 130 | 19°17'N | 99°10'W |
| Tlalpujahua, Mex. (tläl-pōō-κä'wä) | 130 | 19°50'N | 100°10'W |
| Tlapa, Mex. (tlä'pä) | 130 | 17°30'N | 98°30'W |
| Tlapacoyan, Mex. (tlä-pä-kô-yä'n) | 131 | 19°57'N | 97°11'W |
| Tlapehuala, Mex. (tlä-på-wä'lä) | 130 | 18°17'N | 100°30'W |
| Tlaquepaque, Mex. (tlä-kĕ-pä'kĕ) | 130 | 20°39'N | 103°17'W |
| Tlatlaya, Mex. (tlä-tlä'yä) | 130 | 18°36'N | 100°14'W |
| Tlaxcala, Mex. (tläs-kä'lä) | 128 | 19°16'N | 98°14'W |
| Tlaxcala, state, Mex. | 130 | 19°30'N | 98°15'W |
| Tlaxco, Mex. (tläs'kō) | 130 | 19°37'N | 98°06'W |
| Tlaxiaco Santa María Asunción, Mex. | 131 | 17°16'N | 97°41'W |
| Tlayacapan, Mex. (tlä-yä-kä-pä'n) | 131a | 18°57'N | 99°00'W |
| Tlevak Strait, strt., Ak., U.S. | 94 | 53°03'N | 132°58'W |
| Tlumach, Ukr. (t'lû-mäch') | 169 | 48°47'N | 25°00'E |
| Toa, r., Cuba (tō'ä) | 135 | 20°25'N | 74°35'W |
| Toamasina, Madag. | 233 | 18°14'S | 49°25'E |
| Toar, Cuchillas de, mts., Cuba (kōō-chē'l-lyäs-dĕ-tô-ä'r) | 135 | 20°20'N | 74°50'W |
| Tobago, i., Trin. (tô-bā'gō) | 129 | 11°15'N | 60°30'W |
| Toba Inlet, b., Can. | 94 | 50°20'N | 124°50'W |
| Tobarra, Spain (tô-bär'rä) | 172 | 38°37'N | 1°42'W |
| Tobol (Tobyl), r., Asia | 184 | 56°00'N | 66°30'E |
| Tobol'sk, Russia (tô-bôlsk') | 184 | 58°09'N | 68°28'E |
| Tobyl *see* Tobol, r., Asia | 184 | 52°00'N | 62°00'E |
| Tocaima, Col. (tô-kä'y-mä) | 142a | 4°28'N | 74°38'W |
| Tocantinópolis, Braz. (tō-kän-tē-nô'pō-lēs) | 143 | 6°27'S | 47°18'W |
| Tocantins, state, Braz. | 143 | 10°00'S | 48°00'W |
| Tocantins, r., Braz. (tō-kän-tēns') | 143 | 3°28'S | 49°22'W |
| Toccoa, Ga., U.S. (tŏk'ō-á) | 124 | 34°35'N | 83°20'W |
| Toccoa, r., Ga., U.S. | 124 | 34°53'N | 84°24'W |
| Tochigi, Japan (tō'chē-gĭ) | 211 | 36°25'N | 139°45'E |
| Tocoa, Hond. (tō-kō'ä) | 132 | 15°37'N | 86°01'W |
| Tocopilla, Chile (tō-kô-pēl'yä) | 144 | 22°03'S | 70°08'W |
| Tocuyo de la Costa, Ven. (tô-kōō'yō-dĕ-lä-kôs'tä) | 143b | 11°03'N | 68°24'W |
| Toda, Japan | 211a | 35°48'N | 139°42'E |
| Todmorden, Eng., U.K. (tŏd'môr-dĕn) | 158a | 53°43'N | 2°05'W |
| Tofino, Can. (tō-fē'nō) | 94 | 49°09'N | 125°54'W |
| Töfsingdalens National Park, rec., Swe. | 166 | 62°09'N | 13°05'E |
| Tōgane, Japan (tō'gä-nä) | 211 | 35°29'N | 140°16'E |
| Togian, Kepulauan, is., Indon. | 212 | 0°20'S | 122°00'E |
| Togo, nation, Afr. (tō'gō) | 230 | 8°00'N | 0°52'E |
| Toguzak, r., Russia (tô'gô-zák) | 186a | 53°40'N | 61°42'E |
| Tohono O'odham Indian Reservation, I.R., Az., U.S. | 119 | 32°33'N | 112°12'W |
| Tohopekaliga, Lake, l., Fl., U.S. (tō'hō-pē'kà-lī'gá) | 125a | 28°16'N | 81°09'W |
| Tohor, Tanjong, c., Malay. | 197b | 1°53'N | 102°29'E |
| Toijala, Fin. (toi'yà-là) | 167 | 61°11'N | 23°46'E |
| Toi-Misaki, c., Japan (toi mē'sä-kē) | 210 | 31°20'N | 131°20'E |
| Toiyabe, Nv., U.S. (toi'yă-bē) | 118 | 38°59'N | 117°22'W |
| Tokachi Gawa, r., Japan (tō-kä'chē gä'wä) | 210 | 43°10'N | 142°30'E |
| Tokaj, Hung. (tô'kô-ē) | 169 | 48°06'N | 21°24'E |
| Tokat, Tur. (tō-kät') | 198 | 40°20'N | 36°30'E |
| Tokelau, dep., Oc. (tō-kē-lä'ö) | 2 | 8°00'S | 176°00'W |
| Tokmak, Kyrg. (tôk'mák) | 183 | 42°44'N | 75°41'E |
| Tokmak, Ukr. | 177 | 47°17'N | 35°48'E |
| Tokorozawa, Japan (tō'kô-rô-zä'wä) | 211a | 35°47'N | 139°29'E |
| Tok-to, atoll, Asia | 210 | 37°15'N | 131°51'E |
| Tokuno, i., Japan (tô-kōō'nō) | 205 | 27°42'N | 129°25'E |
| Tokushima, Japan (tō'kô'shē-mä) | 205 | 34°06'N | 134°31'E |
| Tokuyama, Japan (tō'kô'yä-mä) | 211 | 34°04'N | 131°49'E |
| Tōkyō, Japan | 205 | 35°42'N | 139°46'E |
| Tōkyō-Wan, b., Japan (tō'kyō wän) | 211 | 35°56'N | 139°56'E |
| Tolcayuca, Mex. (tôl-kä-yōō'kä) | 130 | 19°55'N | 98°54'W |
| Toledo, Spain (tô-lĕ'dō) | 162 | 39°53'N | 4°02'W |
| Toledo, Ia., U.S. (tô-lē'dō) | 113 | 41°59'N | 92°35'W |
| Toledo, Oh., U.S. | 105 | 41°40'N | 83°35'W |
| Toledo, Or., U.S. | 114 | 44°37'N | 123°58'W |
| Toledo, Montes de, mts., Spain (mô'n-tĕs-dĕ-tô-lĕ'dô) | 172 | 39°33'N | 4°40'W |
| Toledo Bend Reservoir, res., U.S. | 107 | 31°30'N | 93°30'W |
| Toliara, Madag. | 233 | 23°16'S | 43°44'E |
| Tolima, dept., Col. (tô-lē'mä) | 142a | 4°07'N | 75°20'W |
| Tolima, Nevado del, mtn., Col. (nĕ-vä-dô-dĕl-tô-lē'mä) | 142a | 4°40'N | 75°20'W |
| Tolimán, Mex. (tô-lē-män') | 130 | 20°54'N | 99°54'W |
| Tollesbury, Eng., U.K. (tōl'z-bĕrĭ) | 158b | 51°46'N | 0°49'E |
| Tolmezzo, Italy (tôl-mĕt'zô) | 174 | 46°25'N | 13°03'E |
| Tolmin, Slvn. (tôl'mēn) | 174 | 46°12'N | 13°45'E |
| Tolna, Hung. (tôl'nô) | 169 | 46°25'N | 18°47'E |
| Tolo, Teluk, b., Indon. (tō'lō) | 212 | 2°00'S | 122°06'E |
| Tolosa, Spain (tô-lō'sä) | 162 | 43°10'N | 2°05'W |
| Tolt, r., Wa., U.S. (tōlt) | 116a | 47°13'N | 121°49'W |
| Toluca, Mex. (tô-lōō'kà) | 128 | 19°17'N | 99°40'W |
| Toluca, Il., U.S. (tô-lōō'ká) | 108 | 41°00'N | 89°10'W |
| Toluca, Nevado de, mtn., Mex. (nĕ-vä-dô-dĕ-tô-lōō'kä) | 128 | 19°09'N | 99°42'W |
| Tolyatti, Russia | 180 | 53°30'N | 49°10'E |
| Tom', r., Russia | 184 | 55°33'N | 85°00'E |
| Tomah, Wi., U.S. (tō'má) | 113 | 43°58'N | 90°31'W |
| Tomahawk, Wi., U.S. (tŏm'á-hôk) | 113 | 45°27'N | 89°44'W |
| Tomakivka, Ukr. | 177 | 47°49'N | 34°43'E |
| Tomanivi, mtn., Fiji | 214g | 17°37'S | 178°01'E |
| Tomar, Port. (tō-mär') | 172 | 39°36'N | 8°26'W |
| Tomashovka, Bela. | 169 | 51°34'N | 23°37'E |
| Tomaszów Lubelski, Pol. (tô-mä'shôf lōō-bĕl'skĭ) | 169 | 50°20'N | 23°27'E |
| Tomaszów Mazowiecki, Pol. (tô-mä'shôf mä-zô'vyĕt-skĭ) | 169 | 51°33'N | 20°00'E |
| Tomatlán, Mex. (tô-mä-tlä'n) | 130 | 19°54'N | 105°14'W |
| Tombadonkéa, Gui. | 234 | 11°00'N | 14°23'W |
| Tombador, Serra do, mts., Braz. (sĕr'rá dò tōm-bä-dôr') | 143 | 11°31'S | 57°33'W |
| Tombigbee, r., U.S. (tŏm-bĭg'bē) | 107 | 33°00'N | 88°30'W |
| Tombos, Braz. (tô'm-bōs) | 141a | 20°53'S | 42°00'W |
| Tombouctou, Mali | 230 | 16°46'N | 3°01'W |
| Tombstone, Az., U.S. (tōōm'stōn) | 119 | 31°40'N | 110°00'W |
| Tombua, Ang. (à-lĕ-zhän'drĕ) | 232 | 15°49'S | 11°53'E |
| Tomelilla, Swe. (tô'mĕ-lēl-lä) | 166 | 55°34'N | 13°55'E |
| Tomelloso, Spain (tō-mål-lyō'sō) | 172 | 39°09'N | 3°02'W |
| Tommot, Russia (tŏm-mŏt') | 179 | 59°13'N | 126°22'E |
| Tomsk, Russia (tŏmsk) | 178 | 56°29'N | 84°57'E |
| Tonala, Mex. | 130 | 20°38'N | 103°14'W |
| Tonalá, r., Mex. | 131 | 18°05'N | 94°08'W |
| Tonawanda, N.Y., U.S. (tôn-á-wŏn'dá) | 111c | 43°01'N | 78°53'W |
| Tonawanda Creek, r., N.Y., U.S. | 111c | 43°05'N | 78°43'W |
| Tonbridge, Eng., U.K. (tŭn-brĭj) | 158b | 51°11'N | 0°17'E |
| Tonda, Japan (tôn'dä) | 211b | 34°51'N | 135°38'E |
| Tondabayashi, Japan (tôn-dä-bä'yä-shē) | 211b | 34°29'N | 135°36'E |
| Tondano, Indon. (tôn-dä'nō) | 213 | 1°15'N | 124°50'E |
| Tønder, Den. (tûn'nēr) | 166 | 54°47'N | 8°49'E |
| Tone-Gawa, r., Japan (tō'nē gä'wa) | 211 | 36°12'N | 139°19'E |
| Tonga, nation, Oc. (tŏŋ'gá) | 240 | 18°50'S | 175°20'W |
| Tong'an, China (tôŋ-än) | 209 | 24°48'N | 118°02'E |
| Tonga Trench, deep | 240 | 23°00'S | 172°30'W |
| Tongbei, China (tôŋ-bā) | 205 | 48°00'N | 126°48'E |
| Tongguan, China (tôŋ-gūän) | 205 | 34°48'N | 110°25'E |
| Tonghe, China (tôŋ-hŭ) | 208 | 45°58'N | 128°40'E |
| Tonghua, China (tôŋ-hwä) | 205 | 41°43'N | 125°50'E |
| Tongjiang, China (tôŋ-jyäŋ) | 205 | 47°38'N | 132°54'E |
| Tongliao, China (tôŋ-lĭou) | 208 | 43°30'N | 122°15'E |
| Tongo, Cam. | 235 | 5°11'N | 14°00'E |
| Tongoy, Chile (tōn-goi') | 144 | 30°16'S | 71°29'W |
| Tongren, China (tôŋ-rŭn) | 204 | 27°45'N | 109°12'E |
| Tongshan, China (tôŋ-shän) | 206 | 34°27'N | 116°27'E |
| Tongtian, r., China (tôŋ-tĭĕn) | 204 | 33°00'N | 97°00'E |
| Tongue, r., Mt., U.S. (tŭng) | 115 | 45°08'N | 106°40'W |
| Tongxian, China (tôŋ shyĕn) | 206 | 39°55'N | 116°40'E |
| Tonj, r., Sudan (tōnj) | 231 | 6°18'N | 28°33'E |
| Tonk, India (Tŏŋk) | 199 | 26°13'N | 75°45'E |
| Tonkawa, Ok., U.S. (tŏŋ kà-wô) | 121 | 36°42'N | 97°19'W |
| Tonkin, Gulf of, b., Asia (tôn-kăn') | 212 | 20°30'N | 108°10'E |
| Tonle Sap, l., Camb. (tôn'lā säp') | 212 | 13°03'N | 102°49'E |
| Tonneins, Fr. (tô-năn') | 170 | 44°24'N | 0°18'E |
| Tönning, Ger. (tû'nĕng) | 168 | 54°20'N | 8°55'E |
| Tonopah, Nv., U.S. (tō-nō-pä') | 104 | 38°04'N | 117°15'W |
| Tönsberg, Nor. (tûns'bĕrgh) | 160 | 59°19'N | 10°25'E |
| Tonto, r., Mex. (tōn'tō) | 131 | 18°15'N | 96°13'W |
| Tonto Creek, r., Az., U.S. | 119 | 34°05'N | 111°15'W |
| Tonto National Monument, rec., Az., U.S. (tôn'tō) | 119 | 33°33'N | 111°08'W |
| Tooele, Ut., U.S. (tó-ĕl ē) | 117b | 40°33'N | 112°17'W |
| Toowoomba, Austl. (tö wōōm'bá) | 219 | 27°32'S | 152°10'E |
| Topanga, Ca., U.S. (tō'păn-gá) | 117a | 34°05'N | 118°36'W |
| Topeka, Ks., U.S. (tô-pē'ká) | 105 | 39°02'N | 95°41'W |
| Topilejo, Mex. (tô-pē-lĕ'hô) | 131a | 19°12'N | 99°09'W |
| Topock, Az., U.S. | 119 | 34°40'N | 114°20'W |
| Topol'čany, Slvk. (tô-pôl'chä-nü) | 169 | 48°38'N | 18°10'E |

PRONOUNCING INDEX

Topolobampo – Tsiafajovona 359


| PLACE (Pronunciation) | PAGE | LAT. | LONG. |
|---|---|---|---|
| Topolobampo, Mex. (tō-pō-lō-bä'm-pō) | 128 | 25°45'N | 109°00'W |
| Topolovgrad, Blg. | 175 | 42°05'N | 26°19'E |
| Toppenish, Wa., U.S. (tôp'ēn-ĭsh) | 114 | 46°22'N | 120°00'W |
| Torbat-e Ḩeydarīyeh, Iran | 201 | 35°16'N | 59°13'E |
| Torbat-e Jām, Iran | 201 | 35°14'N | 60°36'E |
| Torbay, Can. (tôr-bā') | 101 | 47°40'N | 52°43'W |
| Torbay *see* Torquay, Eng., U.K. | 164 | 50°30'N | 3°26'W |
| Torbreck, Mount, mtn., Austl. (tôr-brĕk) | 222 | 37°05'S | 146°55'E |
| Torch, l., Mi., U.S. (tôrch) | 108 | 45°00'N | 85°30'W |
| Töreboda, Swe. (tû'rĕ-bō'dä) | 166 | 58°44'N | 14°04'E |
| Torhout, Bel. | 165 | 51°01'N | 3°04'E |
| Toribío, Col. (tô-rē-bē'ō) | 142a | 2°58'N | 76°14'W |
| Toride, Japan (tô'rē-dā) | 211a | 35°54'N | 104°04'E |
| Torino *see* Turin, Italy | 154 | 45°05'N | 7°44'E |
| Tormes, r., Spain (tōr'mās) | 172 | 41°12'N | 6°15'W |
| Torneälven, r., Eur. | 156 | 67°00'N | 22°30'E |
| Torneträsk, l., Swe. (tôr'nĕ trĕsk) | 160 | 68°10'N | 20°36'E |
| Torngat Mountains, mts., Can. | 93 | 59°18'N | 64°35'W |
| Tornio, Fin. (tôr'nĭ-ô) | 154 | 65°55'N | 24°09'E |
| Toro, Lac, l., Can. | 99 | 46°53'N | 73°46'W |
| Toronto, Can. (tô-rŏn'tō) | 91 | 43°40'N | 79°23'W |
| Toronto, Oh., U.S. | 108 | 40°30'N | 80°35'W |
| Toronto, res., Mex. | 122 | 27°35'N | 105°37'W |
| Toropets, Russia (tô'rô-pyĕts) | 180 | 56°31'N | 31°37'E |
| Toros Dağları, mts., Tur. (tô'rŭs) | 198 | 37°00'N | 32°40'E |
| Torote, r., Spain (tô-rō'tä) | 173a | 40°36'N | 3°24'W |
| Torquay, Eng., U.K. (tôr-kē') | 164 | 50°30'N | 3°26'W |
| Torra, Cerro, mtn., Col. (sĕ'r-rô-tŏ'r-rä) | 142a | 4°41'N | 76°22'W |
| Torrance, Ca., U.S. (tŏr'rănc) | 117a | 33°50'N | 118°20'W |
| Torre Annunziata, Italy (tôr'rā ä-nōōn-tsē-ä'tä) | 173c | 40°31'N | 14°27'E |
| Torreblanca, Spain | 173 | 40°18'N | 0°12'E |
| Torre del Greco, Italy (tôr'rå dĕl grā'kô) | 174 | 40°32'N | 14°23'E |
| Torrejoncillo, Spain (tôr'rā-hōn-thē'lyō) | 172 | 39°54'N | 6°26'W |
| Torrelavega, Spain (tôr-rā'lä-vā'gä) | 172 | 43°22'N | 4°02'W |
| Torre Maggiore, Italy (tôr'rā mäd-jō'rā) | 174 | 41°41'N | 15°18'E |
| Torrens, Lake, l., Austl. (tŏr-ĕns) | 220 | 30°07'S | 137°40'E |
| Torrent, Spain | 173 | 39°25'N | 0°28'W |
| Torreón, Mex. (tôr-rå-ōn') | 128 | 25°32'N | 103°26'W |
| Torres Islands, is., Vanuatu (tôr'rĕs) (tŏr'ĕz) | 221 | 13°18'N | 165°59'E |
| Torres Martinez Indian Reservation, I.R., Ca., U.S. (tôr'ĕz mär-tē'nĕz) | 118 | 33°33'N | 116°21'W |
| Torres Novas, Port. (tôr'rĕzh nō'väzh) | 172 | 39°28'N | 8°37'W |
| Torres Strait, strt., Austl. (tôr'rĕs) | 221 | 10°30'S | 141°30'E |
| Torres Vedras, Port. (tôr'rĕsh vā'dräzh) | 172 | 39°08'N | 9°18'W |
| Torrevieja, Spain (tôr-rā-vyā'hä) | 173 | 37°58'N | 0°40'W |
| Torrijos, Phil. (tôr-rē'hōs) | 213a | 13°19'N | 122°06'E |
| Torrington, Ct., U.S. (tŏr'ĭng-tŭn) | 109 | 41°50'N | 73°10'W |
| Torrington, Wy., U.S. | 112 | 42°04'N | 104°11'W |
| Torro, Spain (tô'r-rō) | 172 | 41°27'N | 5°23'W |
| Torsby, Swe. (tôrs'bü) | 166 | 60°07'N | 12°56'E |
| Torshälla, Swe. (tôrs'hĕl-ä) | 166 | 59°26'N | 16°21'E |
| Tórshavn, Far. Is. (tôrs-houn') | 154 | 62°00'N | 6°55'W |
| Tortola, i., Br. Vir. Is. (tôr-tō'lä) | 129b | 18°34'N | 64°40'W |
| Tortona, Italy (tôr-tō'nä) | 174 | 44°52'N | 8°52'W |
| Tortosa, Spain (tôr-tō'sä) | 154 | 40°59'N | 0°33'E |
| Tortosa, Cap de, c., Spain | 173 | 40°42'N | 0°55'E |
| Tortue, Canal de la, strt., Haiti (tôr-tü') | 135 | 20°05'N | 73°20'W |
| Tortue, Île de la, i., Haiti | 135 | 20°10'N | 73°00'W |
| Tortue, Rivière de la, r., Can. (lä tôr-tü') | 102a | 45°12'N | 73°32'W |
| Toruń, Pol. | 154 | 53°02'N | 18°35'E |
| Törva, Est. (t'r'vȧ) | 167 | 58°02'N | 25°56'E |
| Torzhok, Russia (tôr'zhôk) | 180 | 57°03'N | 34°53'E |
| Toscana, hist. reg., Italy (tôs-kä'nä) | 174 | 43°23'N | 11°08'E |
| Tosna, r., Russia | 186c | 59°28'N | 30°53'E |
| Tosno, Russia (tôs'nô) | 176 | 59°32'N | 30°52'E |
| Tostado, Arg. (tôs-tä'dō) | 144 | 29°10'S | 61°43'W |
| Tosya, Tur. (tôz'yȧ) | 163 | 41°00'N | 34°00'E |
| Totana, Spain (tô-tä-nä) | 172 | 37°45'N | 1°28'W |
| Tot'ma, Russia (tôt'mȧ) | 180 | 60°00'N | 42°20'E |
| Totness, Sur. | 143 | 5°51'N | 56°17'W |
| Totonicapán, Guat. (tôtō-nē-kä'pän) | 128 | 14°55'N | 91°20'W |
| Totoras, Arg. (tô-tō'räs) | 141c | 32°33'S | 61°13'W |
| Totsuka, Japan (tōt'sōō-kä) | 211a | 35°24'N | 139°32'E |
| Tottenham, Eng., U.K. (tŏt'ĕn-ăm) | 158b | 51°35'N | 0°06'W |
| Tottori, Japan (tô'tô-rē) | 205 | 35°30'N | 134°15'E |
| Touba, C. Iv. | 234 | 8°17'N | 7°41'W |
| Touba, Sen. | 234 | 14°51'N | 15°53'W |
| Toubkal, Jebel, mtn., Mor. | 230 | 31°15'N | 7°46'W |
| Tougan, Burkina | 234 | 13°04'N | 3°04'W |
| Touggourt, Alg. (tò-gōōrt') (tōō-gōōr') | 230 | 33°09'N | 6°07'E |
| Touil, Oued, r., Alg. (tōō-ēl') | 162 | 34°42'N | 2°16'E |
| Toul, Fr. (tōōl) | 161 | 48°39'N | 5°51'E |
| Toulon, Fr. (tōō-lôn') | 154 | 43°09'N | 5°54'E |
| Toulouse, Fr. (tōō-lōōz') | 154 | 43°37'N | 1°27'E |
| Toungoo, Mya. (tŏ-ŏŋ-gōō') | 212 | 19°00'N | 96°29'E |
| Tourcoing, Fr. (tòr-kwăn') | 161 | 50°44'N | 3°06'E |
| Tournan-en-Brie, Fr. (tōōr-nän-ĕn-brē') | 171b | 48°45'N | 2°47'E |
| Tours, Fr. (tōōr) | 154 | 47°23'N | 0°39'E |
| Touside, Pic, mtn., Chad (tōō-sē-dā') | 231 | 21°10'N | 16°30'E |
| Tovdalselva, r., Nor. (tôv-däls-ĕlvȧ) | 166 | 58°23'N | 8°16'E |
| Towanda, Pa., U.S. (tô-wän'dȧ) | 109 | 41°45'N | 76°30'W |
| Town Bluff Lake, l., Tx., U.S. | 123 | 30°52'N | 94°30'W |
| Towner, N.D., U.S. (tou'nẽr) | 112 | 48°21'N | 100°24'W |
| Townsend, Ma., U.S. (toun'zĕnd) | 101a | 42°41'N | 71°42'W |
| Townsend, Mt., U.S. | 115 | 46°19'N | 111°35'W |
| Townsend, Mount, mtn., Wa., U.S. | 116a | 47°52'N | 123°03'W |
| Townsville, Austl. (tounz'vĭl) | 219 | 19°18'S | 146°50'E |
| Towson, Md., U.S. (tou'sŭn) | 110e | 39°24'N | 76°36'W |
| Towuti, Danau, l., Indon. (tô-wōō'tē) | 212 | 3°00'S | 121°45'E |
| Toxkan, r., China | 204 | 40°34'N | 77°15'E |
| Toyah, Tx., U.S. (tô'yȧ) | 122 | 31°19'N | 103°46'W |
| Toyama, Japan (tō'yä-mä) | 205 | 36°42'N | 137°14'E |
| Toyama-Wan, b., Japan | 211 | 36°58'N | 137°16'E |
| Toyohashi, Japan (tō'yô-hä'shē) | 210 | 34°44'N | 137°21'E |
| Toyonaka, Japan (tō'yô-nä'kȧ) | 211b | 34°47'N | 135°28'E |
| Tozeur, Tun. (tô-zûr') | 162 | 33°59'N | 8°11'E |
| Trabzon, Tur. (tràb'zôn) | 198 | 41°00'N | 39°45'E |
| Tracy, Can. | 99 | 46°00'N | 73°13'W |
| Tracy, Ca., U.S. (trā'sē) | 118 | 37°45'N | 121°27'W |
| Tracy, Mn., U.S. | 112 | 44°13'N | 95°37'W |
| Tracy City, Tn., U.S. | 124 | 35°15'N | 85°44'W |
| Trafalgar, Cabo, c., Spain (kå'bô-trä-fäl-gä'r) | 172 | 36°10'N | 6°02'W |
| Trafonomby, mtn., Madag. | 233 | 24°32'S | 46°35'E |
| Trail, Can. (trāl) | 90 | 49°06'N | 117°42'W |
| Traisen, r., Aus. | 159e | 48°15'N | 15°55'E |
| Traiskirchen, Aus. | 159e | 48°01'N | 16°18'E |
| Trakai, Lith. (trȧ-kȧy) | 167 | 54°38'N | 24°59'E |
| Trakiszki, Pol. (trȧ-kē'-sh-kē) | 169 | 54°16'N | 23°07'E |
| Tralee, Ire. (trȧ-lē') | 161 | 52°16'N | 9°20'W |
| Tranås, Swe. (trän'ôs) | 166 | 58°03'N | 14°56'E |
| Trancoso, Port. (träŋ-kō'sò) | 172 | 40°46'N | 7°23'W |
| Trangan, Pulau, i., Indon. (träŋ'gän) | 213 | 6°52'S | 133°30'E |
| Trani, Italy (trä'nē) | 174 | 41°15'N | 16°25'E |
| Transylvania, hist. reg., Rom. (trăn-sĭl-vā'nĭ-ȧ) | 169 | 46°30'N | 22°35'E |
| Trapani, Italy | 162 | 38°01'N | 12°31'E |
| Trappes, Fr. (tràp) | 171b | 48°47'N | 2°01'E |
| Traralgon, Austl. (trȧ'răl-gŏn) | 222 | 38°15'S | 146°33'E |
| Trarza, reg., Maur. | 234 | 17°35'N | 15°15'W |
| Trasimeno, Lago, l., Italy (lä'gō trä-sē-mā'nō) | 174 | 43°00'N | 12°12'E |
| Trás-os-Montes, hist. reg., Port. (träzh'ōzh môn'tāzh) | 162 | 41°33'N | 7°13'W |
| Traun, r., Aus. (troun) | 168 | 48°10'N | 14°15'E |
| Traunstein, Ger. (troun'stīn) | 168 | 47°52'N | 12°38'E |
| Traverse, Lake, l., Mn., U.S. (trăv'ērs) | 112 | 45°46'N | 96°53'W |
| Traverse City, Mi., U.S. | 108 | 44°45'N | 85°40'W |
| Travnik, Bos. (träv'nēk) | 175 | 44°13'N | 17°43'E |
| Treasure Island, i., Ca., U.S. (trĕzh'ẽr) | 116b | 37°49'N | 122°22'W |
| Trebbin, Ger. (trĕ'bēn) | 159b | 52°13'N | 13°13'E |
| Trebinje, Bos. (trå'bēn-yĕ) | 175 | 42°43'N | 18°21'E |
| Trebišov, Slvk. (trĕ'bē-shôf) | 169 | 48°36'N | 21°32'E |
| Tregrosse Islands, is., Austl. (trē-grōs') | 221 | 18°08'S | 150°53'E |
| Treinta y Tres, Ur. (trå-ēn'tä ē trās') | 144 | 33°14'S | 54°17'W |
| Trelew, Arg. (trē'lū) | 144 | 43°15'S | 65°25'W |
| Trelleborg, Swe. | 166 | 55°24'N | 13°07'E |
| Tremiti, Isole, is., Italy (ē'sō-lĕ trā-mē'tē) | 174 | 42°07'N | 16°33'E |
| Trenčín, Czech Rep. (trĕn'chēn) | 161 | 48°52'N | 18°02'E |
| Trenque Lauquén, Arg. (trĕn'kĕ-lá'ōo-kĕ'n) | 144 | 35°50'S | 62°44'W |
| Trent, r., Can. (trĕnt) | 99 | 44°15'N | 77°55'W |
| Trent, r., Eng., U.K. | 158a | 53°25'N | 0°45'W |
| Trent and Mersey Canal, can., Eng., U.K. (trĕnt) (mûr zē) | 158a | 53°11'N | 2°24'W |
| Trentino-Alto Adige, hist. reg., Italy | 174 | 46°16'N | 10°47'E |
| Trento, Italy (trĕn'tô) | 162 | 46°04'N | 11°07'E |
| Trenton, Can. (trĕn'tŭn) | 91 | 44°05'N | 77°35'W |
| Trenton, Can. | 101 | 45°37'N | 62°38'W |
| Trenton, Mi., U.S. | 111b | 42°08'N | 83°12'W |
| Trenton, Mo., U.S. | 121 | 40°05'N | 93°36'W |
| Trenton, N.J., U.S. | 105 | 40°13'N | 74°46'W |
| Trenton, Tn., U.S. | 124 | 35°57'N | 88°55'W |
| Trepassey, Can. (trē-păs'ē) | 101 | 46°44'N | 53°22'W |
| Trepassey Bay, b., Can. | 101 | 46°40'N | 53°20'W |
| Tres Arroyos, Arg. (trās'är-rō'yōs) | 144 | 38°18'S | 60°16'W |
| Três Corações, Braz. (trĕ's kō-rä-zō'ĕs) | 141a | 21°41'S | 45°14'W |
| Tres Cumbres, Mex. (trĕ's kōō'm-brĕs) | 131a | 19°03'N | 99°14'W |
| Três Lagoas, Braz. (trĕ's lä-gô'às) | 143 | 20°48'S | 51°42'W |
| Três Marias, Reprêsa, res., Braz. | 143 | 18°15'S | 45°30'W |
| Tres Morros, Alto de, mtn., Col. (ä'l-tō dĕ trĕ's mô'r-rôs) | 142a | 7°08'N | 76°10'W |
| Três Pontas, Braz. (trĕ'pô'n-täs) | 141a | 21°22'S | 45°30'W |
| Três Pontas, Cabo das, c., Ang. | 236 | 10°23'S | 13°32'E |
| Três Rios, Braz. (trĕ's rē'ôs) | 141a | 22°07'S | 43°13'W |
| Très-Saint Rédempteur, Can. (săn rā-dänp-tûr') | 102a | 45°26'N | 74°23'W |
| Treuenbrietzen, Ger. (troi'ĕn-brē-tzĕn) | 159b | 52°06'N | 12°52'E |
| Treviglio, Italy (trā-vē'lyô) | 174 | 45°30'N | 9°34'E |
| Treviso, Italy (trĕ-vē'sō) | 162 | 45°39'N | 12°15'E |
| Trichardt, S. Afr. (trĭ-kärt') | 238c | 26°32'N | 29°16'E |
| Trier, Ger. (trēr) | 161 | 49°45'N | 6°38'E |
| Trieste, Italy (trē-ĕs'tä) | 154 | 45°39'N | 13°48'E |
| Triglav, mtn., Slvn. | 174 | 46°23'N | 13°50'E |
| Trigueros, Spain (trē-gā'rōs) | 172 | 37°23'N | 6°50'W |
| Tríkala, Grc. | 163 | 39°33'N | 21°49'E |
| Trikora, Puncak, mtn., Indon. | 213 | 4°15'S | 138°45'E |
| Trim Creek, r., Il., U.S. (trĭm) | 111a | 41°19'N | 87°39'W |
| Trincomalee, Sri L. (trĭŋ-kō-mȧ-lē') | 203 | 8°39'N | 81°12'E |
| Tring, Eng., U.K. (trĭng) | 158b | 51°46'N | 0°40'W |
| Trinidad, Bol. (trē-nē-dhädh') | 142 | 14°48'S | 64°43'W |
| Trinidad, Cuba (trē-nē-dhädh') | 129 | 21°50'N | 80°00'W |
| Trinidad, Ur. | 144 | 33°29'S | 56°55'W |
| Trinidad, Co., U.S. (trĭn'ĭdăd) | 104 | 37°11'N | 104°31'W |
| Trinidad, i., Trin. (trĭn'ĭ-dăd) | 143 | 10°00'N | 61°00'W |
| Trinidad, r., Pan. | 128a | 8°55'N | 80°01'W |
| Trinidad, Sierra de, mts., Cuba (sē-ĕ'r-rȧ dĕ trē-nē-dä'd) | 134 | 21°50'N | 79°55'W |
| Trinidad and Tobago, nation, N.A. (trĭn'ĭ-dăd) (tô-bā'gō) | 129 | 11°00'N | 61°00'W |
| Trinitaria, Mex. (trē-nē-tä'ryä) | 131 | 16°09'N | 92°04'W |
| Trinity, Can. (trĭn'ĭ-tê) | 101 | 48°59'N | 53°55'W |
| Trinity, Tx., U.S. | 123 | 30°52'N | 95°27'W |
| Trinity, is., Ak., U.S. | 103 | 56°25'N | 153°15'W |
| Trinity, r., Ca., U.S. | 114 | 40°50'N | 123°20'W |
| Trinity, r., Tx., U.S. | 107 | 30°50'N | 95°09'W |
| Trinity, East Fork, r., Tx., U.S. | 121 | 33°24'N | 96°42'W |
| Trinity, West Fork, r., Tx., U.S. | 120 | 33°22'N | 98°26'W |
| Trinity Bay, b., Can. | 93 | 48°00'N | 53°40'W |
| Trino, Italy (trē'nō) | 174 | 45°11'N | 8°16'E |
| Trion, Ga., U.S. (trī'ŏn) | 124 | 34°32'N | 85°18'W |
| Trípoli, Grc. | 163 | 37°32'N | 22°32'E |
| Tripoli (Tarābulus), Libya | 231 | 32°50'N | 13°13'E |
| Tripolitania *see* Tarābulus, hist. reg., Libya | 230 | 31°00'N | 12°26'E |
| Tripura, state, India | 199 | 24°00'N | 92°00'E |
| Tristan da Cunha Islands, is., St. Hel. (três-tän'dä kōōn'yȧ) | 2 | 35°30'S | 12°15'W |
| Triste, Golfo, b., Ven. (gôl-fô trē's-tĕ) | 143b | 10°40'N | 68°05'W |
| Triticus Reservoir, res., N.Y., U.S. (trī tĭ-cŭs) | 110a | 41°20'N | 73°36'W |
| Trnava, Slvk. (t'r'nȧ-vȧ) | 169 | 48°22'N | 17°34'E |
| Trobriand Islands, is., Pap. N. Gui. (trō-brē-ănd') | 213 | 8°25'S | 151°45'E |
| Trogir, Cro. (trô'gēr) | 174 | 43°32'N | 16°17'E |
| Trois Fourches, Cap des, c., Mor. | 172 | 35°28'N | 2°58'W |
| Trois-Rivières, Can. (trwä'rē-vyâ') | 91 | 46°21'N | 72°35'W |
| Troitsk, Russia (trô'ētsk) | 184 | 54°06'N | 61°35'E |
| Troits'ke, Ukr. | 177 | 47°39'N | 30°16'E |
| Troitsko-Pechorsk, Russia (trô'ĭtsk-ô-pyĕ-chôrsk') | 178 | 62°18'N | 56°07'E |
| Trollhättan, Swe. (trôl'hĕt-ĕn) | 160 | 58°17'N | 12°17'E |
| Trollheimen, mts., Nor. (trôll-hĕĭm) | 166 | 62°48'N | 9°05'E |
| Trona, Ca., U.S. (trō'nȧ) | 118 | 35°49'N | 117°20'W |
| Tronador, Cerro, mtn., S.A. (sĕ'r-rô trō-nä'dôr) | 144 | 41°17'S | 71°56'W |
| Troncoso, Mex. (trôn-kô'sō) | 130 | 22°43'N | 102°22'W |
| Trondheim, Nor. (trôn'hȧm) | 154 | 63°25'N | 11°35'E |
| Trosa, Swe. (trô'sä) | 166 | 58°54'N | 17°25'E |
| Trout, l., Can. | 93 | 51°16'N | 92°46'W |
| Trout, l., Can. | 92 | 61°10'N | 121°30'W |
| Trout Creek, r., Or., U.S. | 114 | 42°18'N | 118°31'W |
| Troutdale, Or., U.S. (trout'dāl) | 116c | 45°32'N | 122°23'W |
| Trout Lake, Mi., U.S. | 113 | 46°20'N | 85°02'W |
| Trouville, Fr. (trōō-vēl') | 170 | 49°23'N | 0°05'E |
| Troy, Al., U.S. (troi) | 124 | 31°47'N | 85°46'W |
| Troy, Il., U.S. | 117e | 38°44'N | 89°53'W |
| Troy, Ks., U.S. | 121 | 39°46'N | 95°07'W |
| Troy, Mo., U.S. | 120 | 38°56'N | 99°57'W |
| Troy, Mt., U.S. | 114 | 48°28'N | 115°56'W |
| Troy, N.C., U.S. | 125 | 35°21'N | 79°58'W |
| Troy, N.Y., U.S. | 105 | 42°45'N | 73°45'W |
| Troy, Oh., U.S. | 108 | 40°00'N | 84°10'W |
| Troy, hist., Tur. | 198 | 39°59'N | 26°14'E |
| Troyes, Fr. (trwä) | 161 | 48°18'N | 4°03'E |
| Trstenik, Serb. (t'r'stĕ-nēk) | 163 | 43°36'N | 21°00'E |
| Trubchëvsk, Russia (tròp'chĕfsk) | 181 | 52°36'N | 33°46'E |
| Trucial States *see* United Arab Emirates, nation, Asia | 198 | 24°00'N | 54°00'E |
| Truckee, Ca., U.S. (trŭk'ē) | 118 | 39°20'N | 120°12'W |
| Truckee, r., Ca., U.S. | 118 | 39°25'N | 120°07'W |
| Truganina, Austl. | 217a | 37°49'N | 144°44'E |
| Trujillo, Col. (trò-kē'l-yō) | 142a | 4°10'N | 76°20'W |
| Trujillo, Peru | 142 | 8°08'S | 79°00'W |
| Trujillo, Spain (trōō-kē'l-yô) | 162 | 39°27'N | 5°50'W |
| Trujillo, Ven. | 142 | 9°15'N | 70°28'W |
| Trujillo, r., Mex. | 130 | 23°12'N | 103°10'W |
| Trujin, Lago, l., Dom. Rep. (trōō-kēn') | 135 | 17°45'N | 71°25'W |
| Truk *see* Chuuk, is., Micron. | 214c | 7°25'N | 151°47'E |
| Trumann, Ar., U.S. (trōō'măn) | 121 | 35°41'N | 90°31'W |
| Trŭn, Blg. (trŭn) | 175 | 42°49'N | 22°39'E |
| Truro, Can. (trōō'rō) | 91 | 45°22'N | 63°16'W |
| Truro, Eng., U.K. | 164 | 50°17'N | 5°05'W |
| Trussville, Al., U.S. (trŭs'vĭl) | 110h | 33°37'N | 86°37'W |
| Truth or Consequences, N.M., U.S. (trōōth ŏr kŏn'sē-kwĕn-sĭs) | 119 | 33°10'N | 107°20'W |
| Trutnov, Czech Rep. (tròt'nôf) | 168 | 50°36'N | 15°36'E |
| Trzcianka, Pol. (tchyän'kȧ) | 168 | 53°02'N | 16°27'E |
| Trzebiatów, Pol. (tchĕ-byä'tò-v) | 168 | 54°03'N | 15°16'E |
| Tsaidam Basin, basin, China (tsī-däm) | 204 | 37°19'N | 94°08'E |
| Tsala Apopka Lake, r., Fl., U.S. (tsă'lȧ ă-pŏp'kȧ) | 125 | 28°57'N | 82°11'W |
| Tsast Bogd, mtn., Mong. | 204 | 46°44'N | 92°34'E |
| Tsavo National Park, rec., Kenya | 237 | 2°35'S | 38°45'E |
| Tsawwassen Indian Reserve, I.R., Can. | 116d | 49°03'N | 123°11'W |
| Tsentral'nyy-Kospashskiy, Russia (tsĕn-träl'nyĭ-kôs-pàsh'skĭ) | 186a | 59°03'N | 57°48'E |
| Tshela, D.R.C. (tshā'lȧ) | 232 | 4°59'S | 12°56'E |
| Tshikapa, D.R.C. (tshē-kä'pä) | 232 | 6°25'S | 20°48'E |
| Tshofa, D.R.C. | 237 | 5°14'S | 25°15'E |
| Tshuapa, r., D.R.C. | 232 | 0°30'S | 22°00'E |
| Tsiafajovona, mtn., Madag. | 233 | 19°17'S | 47°27'E |

360 Tsiribihina – Uglegorsk
PRONOUNCING INDEX


| PLACE (Pronunciation) | PAGE | LAT. | LONG. |
|---|---|---|---|
| Tsiribihina, r., Madag. (tsē′rē-bē-hē-nä′) | 233 | 19°45′S | 43°30′E |
| Tsitsa, r., S. Afr. (tsē′tsȧ) | 233c | 31°28′S | 28°53′E |
| Tskhinvali, Geor. | 182 | 42°13′N | 43°56′E |
| Tsolo, S. Afr. (tsō′lō) | 233c | 31°19′S | 28°47′E |
| Tsomo, S. Afr. | 233c | 32°03′S | 27°49′E |
| Tsomo, r., S. Afr. | 233c | 31°53′S | 27°48′E |
| Tsu, Japan (tsōō) | 210 | 34°42′N | 136°31′E |
| Tsuchiura, Japan (tsōō′chē-ōō-rä) | 211 | 36°04′N | 140°09′E |
| Tsuda, Japan (tsōō′dä) | 211b | 34°48′N | 135°43′E |
| Tsugaru Kaikyō, strt., Japan | 205 | 41°25′N | 140°20′E |
| Tsumeb, Nmb. (tsōō′mĕb) | 232 | 19°10′S | 17°45′E |
| Tsunashima, Japan (tsōō′nä-shē′mä) | 211a | 35°32′N | 139°37′E |
| Tsuruga, Japan (tsōō′rō-gä) | 210 | 35°39′N | 136°04′E |
| Tsurugi San, mtn., Japan (tsōō′rō-gē sän) | 210 | 33°52′N | 134°07′E |
| Tsuruoka, Japan (tsōō′rō-ō′kä) | 210 | 38°43′N | 139°51′E |
| Tsurusaki, Japan (tsōō′rō-sä′kē) | 211 | 33°15′N | 131°42′E |
| Tsu Shima, is., Japan (tsōō shē′mä) | 205 | 34°28′N | 129°30′E |
| Tsushima Strait, strt., Asia | 205 | 34°00′N | 129°00′E |
| Tsuwano, Japan (tsōō′wȧ-nō′) | 211 | 34°28′N | 131°47′E |
| Tsuyama, Japan (tsōō′yä-mä′) | 210 | 35°05′N | 134°00′E |
| Tua, r., Port. (tōō′ä) | 172 | 41°23′N | 7°18′W |
| Tualatin, r., Or., U.S. (tōō′ȧ-lă-tĭn) | 116c | 45°25′N | 122°54′W |
| Tuamoto, Îles, Fr. Poly. (tōō-ä-mō′tōō) | 241 | 19°00′S | 141°20′W |
| Tuapse, Russia (tò′áp-sĕ) | 181 | 44°00′N | 39°10′E |
| Tuareg, hist. reg., Alg. | 230 | 21°26′N | 2°51′E |
| Tubarão, Braz. (tōō-bä-rouN′) | 144 | 28°23′N | 48°56′W |
| Tübingen, Ger. (tü′bĭng-ĕn) | 168 | 48°33′N | 9°05′E |
| Tubinskiy, Russia (tû bĭn′skĭ) | 186a | 52°53′N | 58°15′E |
| Tubruq, Libya | 231 | 32°03′N | 24°04′E |
| Tucacas, Ven. (tōō-kä′käs) | 142 | 10°48′N | 68°20′W |
| Tucker, Ga., U.S. (tŭk′ēr) | 110c | 33°51′N | 84°13′W |
| Tucson, Az., U.S. (tōō-sŏn′) | 104 | 32°15′N | 111°00′W |
| Tucumán, Arg. (tōō-kōō-män′) | 144 | 26°52′S | 65°08′W |
| Tucumán, prov., Arg. | 144 | 26°30′S | 65°30′W |
| Tucumcari, N.M., U.S. (tōō′kŭm-kâr-ē) | 120 | 35°11′N | 103°43′W |
| Tucupita, Ven. (tōō-kōō-pē′tä) | 142 | 9°00′N | 62°09′W |
| Tudela, Spain (tōō-dhā′lä) | 162 | 42°03′N | 1°37′W |
| Tugaloo, r., Ga., U.S. (tŭg′ȧ-lōō) | 124 | 34°35′N | 83°05′W |
| Tugela, r., S. Afr. (tōō-gel′ȧ) | 233c | 28°50′S | 30°52′E |
| Tugela Ferry, S. Afr. | 233c | 28°44′S | 30°27′E |
| Tug Fork, r., U.S. (tŭg) | 108 | 37°50′N | 82°30′W |
| Tuguegarao, Phil. (tōō-gā-gȧ-rä′ō) | 212 | 17°37′N | 121°44′E |
| Tuhai, r., China (tōō-hī) | 206 | 37°05′N | 116°56′E |
| Tui, Slvn. | 172 | 42°03′N | 8°38′W |
| Tuinplaas, S. Afr. | 238c | 24°54′S | 28°46′E |
| Tujunga, Ca., U.S. (tōō-jŭŋ′gȧ) | 117a | 34°15′N | 118°16′W |
| Tukan, Russia (tōō′kan) | 186a | 53°52′N | 57°25′E |
| Tukangbesi, Kepulauan, is., Indon. | 213 | 6°00′S | 124°15′E |
| Tūkrah, Libya | 231 | 32°34′N | 20°47′E |
| Tuktoyaktuk, Can. | 90 | 69°32′N | 132°37′W |
| Tuktut Nogait National Park, rec., Can. | 92 | 69°00′N | 122°00′W |
| Tukums, Lat. (tò′kòms) | 180 | 56°57′N | 23°09′E |
| Tukuyu, Tan. (tōō-kōō′yȧ) | 232 | 9°13′S | 33°43′E |
| Tukwila, Wa., U.S. (tŭk′wĭ-lȧ) | 116a | 47°28′N | 122°16′W |
| Tula, Mex. (tōō′lä) | 130 | 20°04′N | 99°22′W |
| Tula, Russia (tōō′lȧ) | 180 | 54°12′N | 37°37′E |
| Tula, prov., Russia | 176 | 53°45′N | 37°19′E |
| Tula, r., Mex. (tōō′lä) | 130 | 20°40′N | 99°27′W |
| Tulagai, i., Sol. Is. (tōō-lä′gē) | 221 | 9°15′S | 160°17′E |
| Tulaghi, Sol. Is. | 214e | 9°06′S | 160°09′E |
| Tulalip, Wa., U.S. (tū-lă′lĭp) | 116a | 48°04′N | 122°18′W |
| Tulalip Indian Reservation, I.R., Wa., U.S. | 116a | 48°06′N | 122°16′W |
| Tulancingo, Mex. (tōō-län-sĭŋ′gō) | 128 | 20°04′N | 98°24′W |
| Tulangbawang, r., Indon. | 212 | 4°17′S | 105°00′E |
| Tulare, Ca., U.S. (tōō-lä′rā) (tul-âr′) | 118 | 36°12′N | 119°22′W |
| Tulare Lake Bed, l., Ca., U.S. | 118 | 35°57′N | 120°18′W |
| Tularosa, N.M., U.S. (tōō-lȧ-rō′zȧ) | 119 | 33°05′N | 106°05′W |
| Tulcán, Ec. (tōōl-kän′) | 142 | 0°44′N | 77°52′W |
| Tulcea, Rom. (tòl′chȧ) | 163 | 45°10′N | 28°47′E |
| Tul′chyn, Ukr. | 181 | 48°42′N | 28°53′E |
| Tulcingo, Mex. (tōōl-sĭŋ′gō) | 130 | 18°03′N | 98°27′W |
| Tule, r., Ca., U.S. (tōōl′lȧ) | 118 | 36°08′N | 118°50′W |
| Tule River Indian Reservation, I.R., Ca., U.S. (tōō′lȧ) | 118 | 36°00′N | 118°40′W |
| Tuli, Zimb. (tōō′lē) | 232 | 20°58′S | 29°12′E |
| Tulia, Tx., U.S. (tōō′lĭ-ȧ) | 120 | 34°32′N | 101°46′W |
| Tulik Volcano, vol., Ak., U.S. (tò′lĭk) | 103a | 53°28′N | 168°10′W |
| Tūlkarm, W.B. (tōōl kärm) | 197a | 32°19′N | 35°02′E |
| Tullahoma, Tn., U.S. (tŭl-ȧ-hō′mȧ) | 124 | 35°21′N | 86°12′W |
| Tullamore, Ire. (tŭl-ȧ-mōr′) | 164 | 53°15′N | 7°29′W |
| Tulle, Fr. (tül) | 170 | 45°15′N | 1°45′E |
| Tulln, Aus. (tòln) | 168 | 48°21′N | 16°04′E |
| Tullner Feld, reg., Aus. | 159e | 48°20′N | 15°59′E |
| Tulpetlac, Mex. (tōōl-pā-tlák′) | 131a | 19°33′N | 99°04′W |
| Tulsa, Ok., U.S. (tŭl′sȧ) | 105 | 36°08′N | 95°58′W |
| Tulum, Mex. (tōō-lò′m) | 132a | 20°17′N | 87°26′W |
| Tulun, Russia (tò-lōōn′) | 179 | 54°29′N | 100°43′E |
| Tuma, r., Nic. (tōō′mä) | 132 | 13°07′N | 85°32′W |
| Tumba, Lac, l., D.R.C. (tòm′bȧ) | 232 | 0°50′S | 17°45′E |
| Tumbes, Peru (tōō′m-bĕs) | 142 | 3°39′S | 80°27′W |
| Tumbiscatío, Mex. (tōōm-bē-skä-tē′ō) | 130 | 18°32′N | 102°23′W |
| Tumbo, i., Can. | 116d | 48°49′N | 123°04′W |
| Tumen, China (tōō-mŭn) | 208 | 43°00′N | 129°50′E |
| Tumen, r., Asia | 210 | 42°08′N | 128°40′E |
| Tumeremo, Ven. (tōō-mȧ-rā′mō) | 143 | 7°15′N | 61°28′W |
| Tumkūr, India | 203 | 13°22′N | 77°05′E |
| Tumuacacori National Monument, rec., Az., U.S. (tōō-mä-kä′kȧ-rē) | 119 | 31°36′N | 110°20′W |
| Tumuc-Humac Mountains, mts., S.A. (tōō-mòk′ōō-mäk′) | 143 | 2°15′N | 54°50′W |
| Tunas de Zaza, Cuba (tōō′näs dā zä′zä) | 134 | 21°40′N | 79°35′W |
| Tunbridge Wells, Eng., U.K. (tŭn′brĭj welz′) | 165 | 51°05′N | 0°09′E |
| Tunduru, Tan. | 237 | 11°07′S | 37°21′E |
| Tungabhadra Reservoir, res., India | 203 | 15°26′N | 75°57′E |
| Tuni, India | 203 | 17°29′N | 82°38′E |
| Tunica, Ms., U.S. (tū′nĭ-kȧ) | 124 | 34°41′N | 90°23′W |
| Tunis, Tun. (tū′nĭs) | 230 | 36°59′N | 10°06′E |
| Tunis, Golfe de, b., Tun. | 162 | 37°06′N | 10°43′E |
| Tunisia, nation, Afr. (tu-nĭzh′ē-ȧ) | 230 | 35°00′N | 10°11′E |
| Tunja, Col. (tōō′n-hȧ) | 142 | 5°32′N | 73°19′W |
| Tunkhannock, Pa., U.S. (tŭnk-hăn′ŭk) | 109 | 41°35′N | 75°55′W |
| Tunnel, r., Wa., U.S. (tŭn′ĕl) | 116a | 47°48′N | 123°04′W |
| Tuoji Dao, i., China (twô-jyē dou) | 206 | 38°11′N | 120°45′E |
| Tuolumne, r., Ca., U.S. (twô-lŭm′nē) | 118 | 37°35′N | 120°37′W |
| Tuostakh, r., Russia | 185 | 67°09′N | 137°30′E |
| Tupelo, Ms., U.S. (tū′pĕ-lō) | 124 | 34°14′N | 88°43′W |
| Tupinambaranas, Ilha, i., Braz. | 143 | 3°04′S | 58°09′W |
| Tupiza, Bol. (tōō-pē′zä) | 142 | 21°26′S | 65°43′W |
| Tupper Lake, N.Y., U.S. (tŭp′ēr) | 109 | 44°15′N | 74°25′W |
| Tüpqaraghan tübegi, pen., Kaz. | 181 | 44°30′N | 50°40′E |
| Tupungato, Cerro, vol., S.A. | 144 | 33°30′S | 69°52′W |
| Tuquerres, Col. (tōō-kĕ′r-rĕs) | 142 | 1°12′N | 77°44′W |
| Tura, Russia (tòr′ȧ) | 179 | 64°08′N | 99°58′E |
| Turbio, r., Mex. (tōōr-byô) | 130 | 20°28′N | 101°40′W |
| Turbo, Col. (tōō′bō) | 142 | 8°02′N | 76°43′W |
| Turda, Rom. (tòr′dȧ) | 169 | 46°35′N | 23°47′E |
| Turfan Depression, depr., China | 204 | 42°16′N | 90°00′E |
| Turffontein, neigh., S. Afr. | 233b | 26°15′S | 28°02′E |
| Tŭrgovishte, Blg. | 175 | 43°14′N | 26°36′E |
| Turgutlu, Tur. | 181 | 38°30′N | 27°20′E |
| Türi, Est. (tü′rĭ) | 167 | 58°49′N | 25°29′E |
| Turia, r., Spain (tōō′ryä) | 172 | 40°12′N | 1°18′W |
| Turicato, Mex. (tōō-rē-kä′tō) | 130 | 19°03′N | 101°24′W |
| Turiguano, i., Cuba (tōō-rē-gwä′nō) | 134 | 22°20′N | 78°35′W |
| Turin, Italy | 154 | 45°05′N | 7°44′E |
| Turiya, r., Ukr. | 169 | 51°18′N | 24°55′E |
| Turka, Ukr. (tòr′kȧ) | 169 | 49°10′N | 23°02′E |
| Turkestan, hist. reg., Asia | 178 | 43°27′N | 62°14′E |
| Turkey, nation, Asia | 155 | 38°45′N | 32°00′E |
| Turkey, r., Ia., U.S. (tûrk′ē) | 113 | 43°20′N | 92°16′W |
| Türkistan, Kaz. | 183 | 44°00′N | 68°00′E |
| Turkmenbashy, Turkmen. | 183 | 40°00′N | 52°50′E |
| Turkmenistan, nation, Asia | 178 | 40°46′N | 56°01′E |
| Turks, is., T./C. Is. (tûrks) | 129 | 21°40′N | 71°45′W |
| Turks Island Passage, strt., T./C. Is. | 135 | 21°15′N | 71°25′W |
| Turku, Fin. (tòrgokò) | 154 | 60°28′N | 22°12′E |
| Turlock, Ca., U.S. (tûr′lŏk) | 118 | 37°30′N | 120°51′W |
| Turneffe, i., Belize | 128 | 17°25′N | 87°43′W |
| Turner, Ks., U.S. (tûr′nēr) | 117f | 39°05′N | 94°42′W |
| Turner Sound, strt., Bah. | 134 | 24°20′N | 78°05′W |
| Turners Peninsula, pen., S.L. | 234 | 7°20′N | 12°40′W |
| Turnhout, Bel. (tŭrn-hout′) | 165 | 51°19′N | 4°58′E |
| Turnov, Czech Rep. (tòr′nôf) | 168 | 50°36′N | 15°12′E |
| Turnu Măgurele, Rom. | 163 | 43°54′N | 24°49′E |
| Turpan, China (tōō-är-pän) | 204 | 43°06′N | 88°41′E |
| Turquino, Pico, mtn., Cuba (pē′kō dā tōōr-kē′nō) | 134 | 20°00′N | 76°50′W |
| Turrialba, C.R. (tōōr-ryä′l-bä) | 133 | 9°54′N | 83°41′W |
| Turtkul′, Uzb. (tòrt-kòl′) | 183 | 41°28′N | 61°02′E |
| Turtle, r., Can. | 97 | 49°20′N | 92°30′W |
| Turtle Bay, b., Tx., U.S. | 123a | 29°48′N | 94°38′W |
| Turtle Creek, r., S.D., U.S. | 112 | 44°40′N | 98°53′W |
| Turtle Mountain Indian Reservation, I.R., N.D., U.S. | 112 | 48°45′N | 99°57′W |
| Turtle Mountains, mts., N.D., U.S. | 112 | 48°57′N | 100°11′W |
| Turukhansk, Russia (tōō-rōō-känsk′) | 178 | 66°03′N | 88°39′E |
| Tuscaloosa, Al., U.S. (tŭs-kȧ-lōō′sȧ) | 105 | 33°10′N | 87°35′W |
| Tuscarora, Nv., U.S. (tŭs-kȧ-rō′rȧ) | 114 | 41°18′N | 116°15′W |
| Tuscarora Indian Reservation, I.R., N.Y., U.S. | 111c | 43°10′N | 78°51′W |
| Tuscola, Il., U.S. (tŭs-kō-lȧ) | 108 | 39°50′N | 88°20′W |
| Tuscumbia, Al., U.S. (tŭs-kŭm′bĭ-ȧ) | 124 | 34°41′N | 87°42′W |
| Tushino, Russia (tōō′shĭ-nô) | 186b | 55°51′N | 37°24′E |
| Tuskegee, Al., U.S. (tŭs-kē′gē) | 124 | 32°25′N | 85°40′W |
| Tustin, Ca., U.S. (tŭs′tĭn) | 117a | 33°44′N | 117°49′W |
| Tutayev, Russia (tōō-tä-yĕf′) | 180 | 57°53′N | 39°34′E |
| Tutbury, Eng., U.K. (tŭt′bēr-ē) | 158a | 52°52′N | 1°51′W |
| Tuticorin, India (tōō-tē-kō-rĭn′) | 203 | 8°51′N | 78°09′E |
| Tutitlan, Mex. (tōō-tē-tlä′n) | 131a | 19°38′N | 99°10′W |
| Tutóia, Braz. (tōō-tō′yȧ) | 143 | 2°42′S | 42°21′W |
| Tutrakan, Blg. | 163 | 44°02′N | 26°36′E |
| Tuttle Creek Reservoir, res., Ks., U.S. | 121 | 39°30′N | 96°38′W |
| Tuttlingen, Ger. (tòt′ lĭng-ĕn) | 168 | 47°58′N | 8°50′E |
| Tutuila, i., Am. Sam. | 214a | 14°18′S | 170°42′W |
| Tutwiler, Ms., U.S. (tŭt′wĭ-lēr) | 124 | 34°01′N | 90°25′W |
| Tuva, prov., Russia | 184 | 51°15′N | 90°45′E |
| Tuvalu, nation, Oc. | 3 | 5°20′S | 174°00′E |
| Tuwayq, Jabal, mts., Sau. Ar. | 198 | 20°45′N | 46°30′E |
| Tuxedo Park, N.Y., U.S. (tŭk-sē′dō pärk) | 110a | 41°11′N | 74°11′W |
| Tuxford, Eng., U.K. (tŭks′fērd) | 158a | 53°14′N | 0°54′W |
| Túxpan, Mex. (tōōs′pän) | 130 | 19°34′N | 103°22′W |
| Túxpan, Mex. | 128 | 20°57′N | 97°26′W |
| Túxpan, r., Mex. (tōōs′pän) | 131 | 20°55′N | 97°52′W |
| Túxpan, Arrecife, i., Mex. (är-rĕ-sē′fē-tōō′x-pä′n) | 131 | 21°01′N | 97°12′W |
| Tuxtepec, Mex. (tòs-tȧ-pĕk′) | 131 | 18°06′N | 96°09′W |
| Tuxtla Gutiérrez, Mex. (tòs′tlä gōō-tyâr′rĕs) | 128 | 16°44′N | 93°08′W |
| Tuy, r., Ven. (tōō′ē) | 143b | 10°15′N | 66°03′W |
| Tuyra, r., Pan. (tōō-ē′rȧ) | 133 | 7°55′N | 77°37′W |
| Tuz Gölü, l., Tur. | 180 | 38°45′N | 33°25′E |
| Tuzigoot National Monument, rec., Az., U.S. | 119 | 34°40′N | 111°52′W |
| Tuzla, Bos. (tòz′lȧ) | 163 | 44°33′N | 18°46′E |
| Tvedestrand, Nor. (tvĭ′dhĕ-stränd) | 166 | 58°39′N | 8°54′E |
| Tveitsund, Nor. (tvåt′sònd) | 166 | 59°03′N | 8°29′E |
| Tver′, Russia | 178 | 56°52′N | 35°57′E |
| Tver′, prov., Russia | 176 | 56°50′N | 33°08′E |
| Tvertsa, r., Russia (tvĕr′tsȧ) | 176 | 56°58′N | 35°22′E |
| Tweed, r., U.K. (twēd) | 164 | 55°32′N | 2°35′W |
| Tweeling, S. Afr. (twē′lĭng) | 238c | 27°34′S | 28°31′E |
| Twenty Mile Creek, r., Can. (twĕn′tĭ mīl) | 102d | 43°09′N | 79°49′W |
| Twickenham, Eng., U.K. (twĭk′'n-ăm) | 158b | 51°26′N | 0°20′W |
| Twillingate, Can. (twĭl′ĭn-gāt) | 93a | 49°39′N | 54°46′W |
| Twin Bridges, Mt., U.S. (twĭn brĭ-jĕz) | 115 | 45°34′N | 112°17′W |
| Twin Falls, Id., U.S. (fôls) | 104 | 42°33′N | 114°29′W |
| Twinsburg, Oh., U.S. (twĭnz′bûrg) | 111d | 41°19′N | 81°26′W |
| Twitchell Reservoir, res., Ca., U.S. | 118 | 34°50′N | 120°10′W |
| Two Butte Creek, r., Co., U.S. (tōō būt) | 120 | 37°39′N | 102°45′W |
| Two Harbors, Mn., U.S. | 113 | 47°00′N | 91°42′W |
| Two Prairie Bay, Ar., U.S. (prâ′rĭ bī ōō′) | 121 | 34°48′N | 92°07′W |
| Two Rivers, Wi., U.S. (rĭv′ērz) | 113 | 44°09′N | 87°36′W |
| Tyabb, Austl. | 217a | 38°16′S | 145°11′E |
| Tylden, S. Afr. (tĭl-dĕn) | 233c | 32°08′S | 27°06′E |
| Tyldesley, Eng., U.K. (tĭldz′lē) | 158a | 53°32′N | 2°28′W |
| Tyler, Mn., U.S. (tī′lēr) | 112 | 44°18′N | 96°08′W |
| Tyler, Tx., U.S. | 105 | 32°21′N | 95°19′W |
| Tylertown, Ms., U.S. (tī′lēr-toun) | 124 | 31°08′N | 90°06′W |
| Tylihul, r., Ukr. | 177 | 47°25′N | 30°27′E |
| Tyndall, S.D., U.S. (tĭn′dȧl) | 112 | 42°58′N | 97°52′W |
| Tyndinskiy, Russia | 179 | 55°22′N | 124°45′E |
| Tyne, r., Eng., U.K. (tīn) | 164 | 54°59′N | 1°56′W |
| Tynemouth, Eng., U.K. (tīn′mŭth) | 160 | 55°04′N | 1°39′W |
| Tyngsboro, Ma., U.S. (tĭnj-bûr′ô) | 101a | 42°40′N | 71°27′W |
| Tynset, Nor. (tün′sĕt) | 160 | 62°17′N | 10°45′E |
| Tyre *see* Şūr, Leb. | 197a | 33°16′N | 35°13′E |
| Tyrifjorden, l., Nor. | 166 | 60°03′N | 10°25′E |
| Tyrnavos, Grc. | 175 | 39°50′N | 22°14′E |
| Tyrone, Pa., U.S. | 109 | 40°40′N | 78°15′W |
| Tyrrell, Lake, l., Austl. (tĭr′ĕll) | 222 | 35°12′S | 143°00′E |
| Tyrrhenian Sea, sea, Italy (tĭr-rē′nĭ-ȧn) | 156 | 40°10′N | 12°15′E |
| Tyukalinsk, Russia (tyò-kȧ-lĭnsk′) | 178 | 56°03′N | 71°43′E |
| Tyukyan, r., Russia (tyòk′yȧn) | 185 | 65°42′N | 116°09′E |
| Tyuleniy, i., Russia | 181 | 44°30′N | 48°00′E |
| Tyumen′, Russia (tyōō-mĕn′) | 178 | 57°02′N | 65°28′E |
| Tzucacab, Mex. (tzōō-kä-kä′b) | 132a | 20°06′N | 89°03′W |

## U

| PLACE (Pronunciation) | PAGE | LAT. | LONG. |
|---|---|---|---|
| Uaupés, Braz. (wä-ōō′pās) | 142 | 0°02′S | 67°03′W |
| Ubangi, r., Afr. (ōō-bäŋ′gē) | 231 | 3°00′N | 18°00′E |
| Ubatuba, Braz. (ōō-bȧ-tōō′bȧ) | 141a | 23°25′S | 45°06′W |
| Ubeda, Spain (ōō′bȧ-dä) | 172 | 38°01′N | 3°23′W |
| Uberaba, Braz. (ōō-bȧ-rä′bȧ) | 143 | 19°47′S | 47°47′W |
| Uberlândia, Braz. (ōō-bĕr-lä′n-dyä) | 143 | 18°54′S | 48°11′W |
| Ubombo, S. Afr. (ōō-bôm′bô) | 232 | 27°33′S | 32°13′E |
| Ubon Ratchathani, Thai. (ōō′bŭn rä′chätä-nē) | 212 | 15°15′N | 104°52′E |
| Ubort′, r., Eur. (ōō-bôrt′) | 177 | 51°18′N | 27°43′E |
| Ubrique, Spain (ōō-brē′kȧ) | 172 | 36°43′N | 5°36′W |
| Ubundu, D.R.C. | 232 | 0°21′S | 25°29′E |
| Ucayali, r., Peru (ōō′kä-yä′lē) | 142 | 8°58′S | 74°13′W |
| Uccle, Bel. (ü′kl′) | 159a | 50°48′N | 4°17′E |
| Uchaly, Russia (û-chä′lĭ) | 186a | 54°22′N | 59°28′E |
| Uchiko, Japan (ōō′chē-kō) | 211 | 33°30′N | 132°39′E |
| Uchinoura, Japan (ōō′chē-nō-ōō′rä) | 211 | 31°16′N | 131°03′E |
| Uchinskoye Vodokhranilishche, res., Russia | 186b | 56°08′N | 37°44′E |
| Uchiura-Wan, b., Japan (ōō′chē-ōō′rä wän) | 210 | 42°20′N | 140°44′E |
| Uchur, r., Russia (ò-chòr′) | 185 | 57°25′N | 130°35′E |
| Uda, r., Russia | 185 | 53°54′N | 131°29′E |
| Uda, r., Russia (ò′dȧ) | 185 | 52°28′N | 110°51′E |
| Udai, r., Ukr. | 177 | 50°45′N | 32°13′E |
| Udaipur, India (ò-dŭ′ē-pōōr) | 202 | 24°41′N | 73°41′E |
| Uddevalla, Swe. (ōōd′dĕ-väl-ȧ) | 160 | 58°21′N | 11°55′E |
| Udine, Italy (ōō′dē-nȧ) | 162 | 46°05′N | 13°14′E |
| Udmurtia, prov., Russia | 180 | 57°00′N | 53°00′E |
| Udon Thani, Thai. | 212 | 17°31′N | 102°51′E |
| Udskaya Guba, b., Russia | 179 | 55°00′N | 136°30′E |
| Ueckermünde, Ger. | 168 | 53°43′N | 14°01′E |
| Ueda, Japan (wä′dä) | 210 | 36°26′N | 138°16′E |
| Uele, r., D.R.C. (wā′lȧ) | 231 | 3°55′N | 23°30′E |
| Uelzen, Ger. (ült′sĕn) | 168 | 52°58′N | 10°34′E |
| Ufa, Russia (ò′fa) | 178 | 54°45′N | 55°57′E |
| Ufa, r., Russia | 180 | 56°00′N | 57°05′E |
| Ugab, r., Nmb. (ōō′gäb) | 232 | 21°10′S | 14°00′E |
| Ugalla, r., Tan. (ōō-gä′lä) | 232 | 6°15′S | 32°30′E |
| Uganda, nation, Afr. (ōō-gän′dä) (û-gän′dȧ) | 231 | 2°00′N | 32°28′E |
| Ugashik Lake, l., Ak., U.S. (ōō′gȧ-shĕk) | 103 | 57°36′N | 157°10′W |
| Ugie, S. Afr. (ò′jē) | 233c | 31°13′S | 28°14′E |
| Uglegorsk, Russia (ōō-glĕ-gôrsk) | 179 | 49°00′N | 142°31′E |


ăt; finȧl; rāte; senåte; ärm; ȧsk; sofȧ; fâre; ch-choose; dh-as th in other; bē; ēvent; bĕt; recĕnt; cratēr; g-gō; gh-guttural g; bĭt; ĭ-short neutral; rīde; K-guttural k as ch in German ich;

PRONOUNCING INDEX

Ugleural'sk – Valdecañas 361


| PLACE (Pronunciation) | PAGE | LAT. | LONG. |
| --- | --- | --- | --- |
| Ugleural'sk, Russia (ȯg-lĕ-ȯ-rálsk′) | 186a | 58°58′N | 57°35′E |
| Uglich, Russia (o͞og-lĕch′) | 176 | 57°33′N | 38°19′E |
| Uglitskiy, Russia (ȯg-lĭt′skĭ) | 186a | 53°50′N | 60°18′E |
| Uglovka, Russia (o͞og-lôf′kȧ) | 176 | 58°14′N | 33°24′E |
| Ugra, r., Russia (o͞og′rȧ) | 180 | 54°43′N | 34°20′E |
| Ugŭrchin, Blg. | 175 | 43°06′N | 24°23′E |
| Uhrichsville, Oh., U.S. (ū′rĭks-vĭl) | 108 | 40°25′N | 81°20′W |
| Uíge, Ang. | 232 | 7°37′S | 15°03′E |
| Uiju, Kor., N. (ȯ′ĕjo͞o) | 205 | 40°09′N | 124°33′E |
| Uinkaret Plateau, plat., Az., U.S. (ů-ĭn′kâr-ēt) | 119 | 36°43′N | 113°15′W |
| Uinskoye, Russia (ȯ-ĭn′skô-yĕ) | 186a | 56°53′N | 56°25′E |
| Uinta, r., Ut., U.S. (ů-ĭn′tȧ) | 119 | 40°25′N | 109°55′W |
| Uintah and Ouray Indian Reservation, I.R., Ut., U.S. | 119 | 40°20′N | 110°20′W |
| Uinta Mountains, mts., Ut., U.S. | 106 | 40°35′N | 111°00′W |
| Uitenhage, S. Afr. | 232 | 33°46′S | 25°26′E |
| Uithoorn, Neth. | 159a | 52°13′N | 4°49′E |
| Uji, Japan (o͞o′jē) | 211b | 34°53′N | 135°49′E |
| Ujiji, Tan. (o͞o-jē′jė) | 232 | 4°55′S | 29°41′E |
| Ujjain, India (o͞o-jŭĕn) | 199 | 23°18′N | 75°37′E |
| Ujungpandang, Indon. | 212 | 5°08′S | 119°28′E |
| Ukerewe Island, i., Tan. | 237 | 2°00′S | 32°40′E |
| Ukhta, Russia (o͞ok′tȧ) | 180 | 65°22′N | 31°30′E |
| Ukhta, Russia | 180 | 63°08′N | 53°42′E |
| Ukiah, Ca., U.S. (ū-kī′ȧ) | 118 | 39°09′N | 122°12′W |
| Ukmerge, Lith. (ȯk′mĕr-ghå) | 180 | 55°16′N | 24°45′E |
| Ukraine, nation, Eur. | 178 | 49°15′N | 30°15′E |
| Uku, i., Japan (o͞ok′o͞o) | 211 | 33°18′N | 129°02′E |
| Ulaangom, Mong. | 204 | 50°23′N | 92°14′E |
| Ulan Bator (Ulaanbaatar), Mong. | 204 | 47°56′N | 107°00′E |
| Ulan-Ude, Russia (o͞o′län o͞o′då) | 179 | 51°59′N | 107°41′E |
| Ulchin, Kor., S. (o͞ol′chĕn′) | 210 | 36°57′N | 129°26′E |
| Ulcinj, Serb. (o͞ol′tsėn′) | 163 | 41°56′N | 19°15′E |
| Ulhās, r., India | 203b | 19°13′N | 73°03′E |
| Ulhāsnagar, India | 202 | 19°10′N | 73°07′E |
| Uliastay, Mong. | 204 | 47°49′N | 97°00′E |
| Ulindi, r., D.R.C. (o͞o-lĭn′dė) | 232 | 1°55′S | 26°17′E |
| Ulla, Bela. (ȯl′ȧ) | 176 | 55°14′N | 29°15′E |
| Ulla, r., Bela. | 176 | 54°58′N | 29°03′E |
| Ulla, r., Spain (o͞o′lä) | 172 | 42°45′N | 8°33′W |
| Ullŭng, i., Kor., S. (o͞ol′lȯng′) | 210 | 37°29′N | 130°50′E |
| Ulm, Ger. (ȯlm) | 161 | 48°24′N | 9°59′E |
| Ulmer, Mount, mtn., Ant. (ŭl′mûr′) | 224 | 77°30′S | 86°00′W |
| Ulricehamn, Swe. (ȯl-rē′sĕ-häm) | 166 | 57°49′N | 13°23′E |
| Ulsan, Kor., S. (o͞ol′sän′) | 210 | 35°35′N | 129°22′E |
| Ulster, hist. reg., Eur. (ŭl′stẽr) | 164 | 54°41′N | 7°10′W |
| Ulua, r., Hond. (o͞o-lo͞o′ȧ) | 132 | 15°49′N | 87°45′W |
| Ulubāria, India | 202a | 22°27′N | 88°09′E |
| Ulukışla, Tur. (o͞o-lo͞o-kēsh′lȧ) | 163 | 36°40′N | 34°30′E |
| Ulunga, Russia (ȯ-lo͞on′gȧ) | 210 | 46°16′N | 136°29′E |
| Ulungur, r., China (o͞o-lo͞on-gůr) | 204 | 46°31′N | 88°00′E |
| Uluru (Ayers Rock), mtn., Austl. | 220 | 25°23′S | 131°05′E |
| Ulu-Telyak, Russia (o͞o lȯ′tĕlyăk) | 186a | 54°54′N | 57°01′E |
| Ulverstone, Austl. (ŭl′vẽr-stŭn) | 219 | 41°20′S | 146°22′E |
| Ul'yanovka, Russia | 186c | 59°38′N | 30°47′E |
| Ul'yanovsk, Russia (o͞o-lyä′nôfsk) | 178 | 54°20′N | 48°24′E |
| Ulysses, Ks., U.S. (ū-lĭs′ēz) | 120 | 37°34′N | 101°25′W |
| Umán, Mex. (o͞o-män′) | 132a | 20°52′N | 89°44′W |
| Uman', Ukr. (ȯ-mȧn′) | 181 | 48°44′N | 30°13′E |
| Umatilla Indian Reservation, I.R., Or., U.S. (ū-mȧ-tĭl′ȧ) | 114 | 45°38′N | 118°35′W |
| Umberpāda, India | 203b | 19°28′N | 73°04′E |
| Umbria, hist. reg., Italy (ŭm′brĭ-ȧ) | 174 | 42°53′N | 12°22′E |
| Umeälven, r., Swe. | 156 | 64°57′N | 18°51′E |
| Umhlatuzi, r., S. Afr. (ȯm′hlȧ-to͞o′zĭ) | 233c | 28°47′S | 31°17′E |
| Umiat, Ak., U.S. (o͞o′mĭ-ăt) | 106a | 69°20′N | 152°28′W |
| Umkomaas, S. Afr. (ȯm-kō′mäs) | 233c | 30°12′S | 30°48′E |
| Umnak, i., Ak., U.S. (o͞om′nȧk) | 106b | 53°10′N | 169°08′W |
| Umnak Pass, Ak., U.S. | 103a | 53°10′N | 168°04′W |
| Umniati, r., Zimb. | 232 | 17°08′S | 29°11′E |
| Umpqua, r., Or., U.S. (ŭmp′kwȧ) | 114 | 43°42′N | 123°50′W |
| Umtata, S. Afr. (ȯm-tä′tä) | 232 | 31°36′S | 28°47′E |
| Umtentweni, S. Afr. | 233c | 30°41′S | 30°29′E |
| Umzimkulu, S. Afr. (ȯm-zėm-ko͞o′lo͞o) | 233c | 30°12′S | 29°53′E |
| Umzinto, S. Afr. (ȯm-zĭn′tȯ) | 233c | 30°19′S | 30°41′E |
| Una, r., Serb. (o͞o′nȧ) | 174 | 44°38′N | 16°10′E |
| Unalakleet, Ak., U.S. (ū-nȧ-lȧk′lēt) | 103 | 63°50′N | 160°42′W |
| Unalaska, Ak., U.S. (ū-nȧ-lȧs′kȧ) | 103a | 53°30′N | 166°20′W |
| Unare, r., Ven. | 143b | 9°45′N | 65°12′W |
| Unare, Laguna de, l., Ven. (lä-gȯ′nä-de-o͞o-nȧ′rĕ) | 143b | 10°07′N | 65°23′W |
| Unayzah, Sau. Ar. | 198 | 25°50′N | 44°02′E |
| Uncas, Can. (ŭŋ′kȧs) | 102g | 53°30′N | 113°02′W |
| Uncia, Bol. (o͞on′sē-ä) | 142 | 18°28′S | 66°32′W |
| Uncompahgre, r., Co., U.S. | 119 | 38°20′N | 107°45′W |
| Uncompahgre Peak, mtn., Co., U.S. (ŭn-kŭm-pä′grė) | 119 | 38°00′N | 107°30′W |
| Uncompahgre Plateau, plat., Co., U.S. | 119 | 38°40′N | 108°40′W |
| Underberg, S. Afr. (ŭn′dẽr-bûrg) | 233c | 29°51′S | 29°32′E |
| Unecha, Russia (ȯ-nĕ′chȧ) | 176 | 52°51′N | 32°44′E |
| Ungava, Péninsule d', pen., Can. | 93 | 59°55′N | 74°00′W |
| Ungava Bay, b., Can. (ŭŋ-gȧ′vȧ) | 93 | 59°46′N | 67°18′W |
| União da Vitória, Braz. (o͞o-nė-ouɴ′ dä vē-tô′ryä) | 144 | 26°17′S | 51°13′W |
| Unije, i., Serb. (o͞o′nė-yĕ) | 174 | 44°39′N | 14°10′E |
| Unimak, i., Ak., U.S. (o͞o-nė-mȧk′) | 103 | 54°30′N | 163°35′W |
| Unimak Pass, Ak., U.S. | 103a | 54°22′N | 165°22′W |
| Union, Mo., U.S. | 121 | 38°28′N | 90°59′W |
| Union, Ms., U.S. (ūn′yŭn) | 124 | 32°35′N | 89°07′W |
| Union, N.C., U.S. | 125 | 34°42′N | 81°40′W |
| Union, Or., U.S. | 114 | 45°13′N | 117°52′W |
| Union City, Ca., U.S. | 116b | 37°36′N | 122°01′W |
| Union City, In., U.S. | 108 | 40°10′N | 85°00′W |
| Union City, Mi., U.S. | 108 | 42°00′N | 85°10′W |
| Union City, Pa., U.S. | 109 | 41°50′N | 79°50′W |
| Union City, Tn., U.S. | 124 | 36°25′N | 89°04′W |
| Unión de Reyes, Cuba | 134 | 22°45′N | 81°30′W |
| Unión de San Antonio, Mex. | 130 | 21°07′N | 101°56′W |
| Unión de Tula, Mex. | 130 | 19°57′N | 104°14′W |
| Union Grove, Wi., U.S. (ūn-yŭn grōv) | 111a | 42°41′N | 88°03′W |
| Unión Hidalgo, Mex. (ė-dä′lgȯ) | 131 | 16°29′N | 94°51′W |
| Union Point, Ga., U.S. | 124 | 33°37′N | 83°08′W |
| Union Springs, Al., U.S. (sprĭngz) | 124 | 32°08′N | 85°43′W |
| Uniontown, Al., U.S. (ūn′yŭn-toun) | 124 | 32°26′N | 87°30′W |
| Uniontown, Oh., U.S. | 111d | 40°58′N | 81°25′W |
| Uniontown, Pa., U.S. | 109 | 39°55′N | 79°45′W |
| Unionville, Mo., U.S. (ūn′yŭn-vĭl) | 121 | 40°28′N | 92°58′W |
| Unisan, Phil. (o͞o-nē′sän) | 213a | 13°50′N | 121°59′E |
| United Arab Emirates, nation, Asia | 198 | 24°00′N | 54°00′E |
| United Kingdom, nation, Eur. | 154 | 56°30′N | 1°40′W |
| United States, nation, N.A. | 104 | 38°00′N | 110°00′W |
| Unity, Can. | 96 | 52°27′N | 109°10′W |
| Universal, In., U.S. (ū-nĭ-vûr′sȧl) | 108 | 39°35′N | 87°30′W |
| University City, Mo., U.S. (ū′nĭ-vûr′sĭ-tĭ) | 117e | 38°40′N | 90°19′W |
| University Park, Tx., U.S. | 117c | 32°51′N | 96°48′W |
| Unna, Ger. (o͞o′nä) | 171c | 51°32′N | 7°41′E |
| Uno, Canal Numero, can., Arg. | 141c | 36°43′S | 58°14′W |
| Unterhaching, Ger. (o͞on′tĕr-hä-ĸēng) | 159d | 48°03′N | 11°38′E |
| Ünye, Tur. (ün′yĕ) | 163 | 41°00′N | 37°10′E |
| Unzha, r., Russia (ȯn′zhȧ) | 180 | 57°45′N | 44°10′E |
| Upa, r., Russia (ȯ′pȧ) | 176 | 53°54′N | 36°48′E |
| Upata, Ven. (o͞o-pä′tä) | 142 | 7°58′N | 62°27′W |
| Upemba, Parc National de l', rec., D.R.C. | 237 | 9°10′S | 26°15′E |
| Upington, S. Afr. (ŭp′ĭng-tŭn) | 232 | 28°25′S | 21°15′E |
| Upland, Ca., U.S. (ŭp′lănd) | 117a | 34°06′N | 117°38′W |
| Upolu, i., Samoa | 214a | 13°55′S | 171°45′W |
| Upolu Point, c., Hi., U.S. (o͞o-pô′lo͞o) | 126a | 20°15′N | 155°48′W |
| Upper Arrow Lake, l., Can. (ăr′ō) | 95 | 50°30′N | 117°55′W |
| Upper Darby, Pa., U.S. (där′bĭ) | 110f | 39°58′N | 75°16′W |
| Upper des Lacs, l., N.A. (dĕ läk) | 112 | 48°58′N | 101°55′W |
| Upper Kapuas Mountains, mts., Asia | 212 | 1°45′N | 112°06′E |
| Upper Klamath Lake, l., Or., U.S. | 114 | 42°23′N | 122°55′W |
| Upper Lake, l., Nv., U.S. (ŭp′ẽr) | 114 | 41°42′N | 119°59′W |
| Upper Marlboro, Md., U.S. (ûpẽr mărl′bōrȯ) | 110e | 38°49′N | 76°46′W |
| Upper Mill, Wa., U.S. (mĭl) | 116a | 47°11′N | 121°55′W |
| Upper Red Lake, l., Mn., U.S. (rĕd) | 113 | 48°14′N | 94°53′W |
| Upper Sandusky, Oh., U.S. (săn-dŭs′kė) | 108 | 40°50′N | 83°20′W |
| Upper San Leandro Reservoir, res., Ca., U.S. (ŭp′ẽr săn lė-ăn′drȯ) | 116b | 37°47′N | 122°04′W |
| Upper Volta *see* Burkina Faso, nation, Afr. | 230 | 13°00′N | 2°00′W |
| Uppingham, Eng., U.K. (ŭp′ĭng-ăm) | 158a | 52°35′N | 0°43′W |
| Uppsala, Swe. (o͞op′sȧ-lä) | 154 | 59°53′N | 17°39′E |
| Uptown, Ma., U.S. (ŭp′toun) | 101a | 42°10′N | 71°36′W |
| Uraga, Japan (o͞o′rȧ-gȧ′) | 211a | 35°15′N | 139°43′E |
| Ural, r. (ȯ-räl′′) (ū-rôl) | 178 | 48°00′N | 51°00′E |
| Urals, mts., Russia | 178 | 56°28′N | 58°13′E |
| Uran, India (o͞o-rän′) | 203b | 18°53′N | 72°46′E |
| Uranium City, Can. | 90 | 59°34′N | 108°59′W |
| Urawa, Japan (o͞o′rä-wä′) | 210 | 35°52′N | 139°39′E |
| Urayasu, Japan (o͞o′rä-yä′so͞o) | 211a | 35°40′N | 139°54′W |
| Urazovo, Russia (ȯ-rȧ′zȯ-vȯ) | 177 | 50°08′N | 38°03′E |
| Urbana, Il., U.S. (ûr-băn′ȧ) | 108 | 40°10′N | 88°15′W |
| Urbana, Oh., U.S. | 108 | 40°05′N | 83°50′W |
| Urbino, Italy (o͞or-bē′nȯ) | 174 | 43°43′N | 12°37′E |
| Urdaneta, Phil. (o͞or-dä-nā′tä) | 213a | 15°59′N | 120°34′E |
| Urdinarrain, Arg. (o͞or-dē-när-rȧē′n) | 141c | 32°43′S | 58°53′W |
| Uritsk, Russia (o͞o′rĭtsk) | 186c | 59°50′N | 30°11′E |
| Urla, Tur. (ȯr′lȧ) | 175 | 38°20′N | 26°44′E |
| Urman, Russia (ȯr′mȧn) | 186a | 54°53′N | 56°52′E |
| Urmi, r., Russia (ȯr′mė) | 210 | 48°50′N | 134°00′E |
| Uromi, Nig. | 235 | 6°44′N | 6°18′E |
| Urrao, Col. (o͞or-rȧ′ô) | 142 | 6°19′N | 76°11′W |
| Urshel'skiy, Russia (o͞or-shĕl′skēė) | 176 | 55°50′N | 40°11′E |
| Ursus, Pol. | 169 | 52°12′N | 20°53′E |
| Urubamba, r., Peru (o͞o-ro͞o-bäm′bä) | 142 | 11°48′S | 72°34′W |
| Uruguaiana, Braz. | 144 | 29°45′S | 57°00′W |
| Uruguay, nation, S.A. (o͞o-ro͞o-gwī′) (ū′ro͞o-gwā) | 144 | 32°45′S | 56°00′W |
| Uruguay, r., S.A. (o͞o-ro͞o-gwī′) | 144 | 27°05′S | 55°15′W |
| Ürümqi, China (ů-rům-chyē) | 204 | 43°49′N | 87°43′E |
| Urup, i., Russia (ȯ′rȯp′) | 205 | 46°00′N | 150°00′E |
| Uryupinsk, Russia (ȯr′yȯ-pēn-sk′) | 181 | 50°50′N | 42°00′E |
| Ürzhar, Kaz. | 183 | 47°28′N | 82°00′E |
| Urziceni, Rom. (ȯ-zē-chĕn′′) | 175 | 44°45′N | 26°42′E |
| Usa, Japan | 210 | 33°31′N | 131°22′E |
| Usa, r., Russia (ȯ′sȧ) | 180 | 66°00′N | 58°20′E |
| Uşak, Tur. (o͞o′shȧk) | 163 | 38°45′N | 29°15′E |
| Usakos, Nmb. (o͞o-sä′kōs) | 232 | 22°00′S | 15°40′E |
| Usambara Mountains, mts., Tan. | 237 | 4°40′S | 38°25′E |
| Usangu Flats, sw., Tan. | 237 | 8°10′S | 34°00′E |
| Ushaki, Russia (o͞o′shá-kĭ) | 186c | 59°28′N | 31°00′E |
| Ushakovskoye, Russia (ȯ-shá-kôv′skô-yĕ) | 186a | 56°18′N | 62°23′E |
| Ushashi, Tan. | 237 | 2°00′S | 33°57′E |
| Ushiku, Japan (o͞o′shė-ko͞o) | 211a | 35°24′N | 140°09′E |
| Ushimado, Japan (o͞o′shė-mä′dō) | 211 | 34°37′N | 134°09′E |
| Ushuaia, Arg. (o͞o-sho͞o-ī′ä) | 144 | 54°46′S | 68°24′W |
| Usman', Russia (o͞os-mȧn′) | 181 | 52°03′N | 39°40′E |
| Usol'ye, Russia (ȯ-sô′lyĕ) | 186a | 59°24′N | 56°40′E |
| Usol'ye-Sibirskoye, Russia (ȯ-sô′lyĕsĭ′ bĕr′skô-yĕ) | 184 | 52°44′N | 103°46′E |
| Uspallata Pass, p., S.A. (o͞os-pä-lyä′tä) | 144 | 32°47′S | 70°08′W |
| Uspanapa, r., Mex. (o͞os-pä-nä′pä) | 131 | 17°43′N | 94°14′W |
| Ussel, Fr. (üs′ĕl) | 170 | 45°33′N | 2°17′E |
| Ussuri, r., Asia (o͞o-so͞o′rė) | 185 | 47°30′N | 134°00′E |
| Ussuriysk, Russia | 179 | 43°48′N | 132°09′E |
| Ust'-Bol'sheretsk, Russia | 179 | 52°41′N | 157°00′E |
| Ustica, Isola di, i., Italy | 174 | 38°43′N | 12°11′E |
| Ústí nad Labem, Czech Rep. | 168 | 50°40′N | 14°02′E |
| Ust'-Izhora, Russia (ȯst-ēz′hô-rȧ) | 186c | 59°49′N | 30°35′E |
| Ustka, Pol. (o͞ost′kȧ) | 168 | 54°34′N | 16°52′E |
| Ust'-Kamchatsk, Russia | 179 | 56°13′N | 162°18′E |
| Ust'-Katav, Russia (ȯst kȧ′táf) | 186a | 54°55′N | 58°12′E |
| Ust'-Kishert', Russia (ȯst kē′shĕrt) | 186a | 57°21′N | 57°13′E |
| Ust'-Kulom, Russia (kȯ′lŭm) | 178 | 61°38′N | 54°00′E |
| Ust'-Maya, Russia (mȧ′yȧ) | 179 | 60°33′N | 134°43′E |
| Ust' Olenëk, Russia | 179 | 72°52′N | 120°15′E |
| Ust-Ordynskiy, Russia (ȯst-ôr-dyēnsk′ĭ) | 184 | 52°47′N | 104°39′E |
| Ust' Penzhino, Russia | 185 | 63°00′N | 165°10′E |
| Ust' Port, Russia (ȯst′pôrt′) | 178 | 69°20′N | 83°41′E |
| Ust'-Tsil'ma, Russia (tsĭl′mȧ) | 178 | 65°25′N | 52°10′E |
| Ust'-Tyrma, Russia (tur′mȧ) | 179 | 50°27′N | 131°17′E |
| Ust' Uls, Russia | 186a | 60°35′N | 58°32′E |
| Ust-Urt, Plateau, plat., Asia | 178 | 44°03′N | 54°58′E |
| Ustynivka, Ukr. | 177 | 47°59′N | 32°31′E |
| Ustyuzhna, Russia (yo͞ozh′nȧ) | 180 | 58°49′N | 36°19′E |
| Usu, China (ů-so͞o) | 204 | 44°28′N | 84°07′E |
| Usuki, Japan (o͞o′so͞o-kė′) | 211 | 33°06′N | 131°47′E |
| Usulutan, El Sal. (o͞o-so͞o-lä-tän′) | 132 | 13°22′N | 88°25′W |
| Usumacinta, r., N.A. (o͞o′so͞o-mä-sēn′tō) | 131 | 18°24′N | 92°30′W |
| Us'va, Russia (o͞os′vȧ) | 186a | 58°41′N | 57°38′E |
| Utah, state, U.S. (ū′tȯ) | 104 | 39°25′N | 112°40′W |
| Utah Lake, l., Ut., U.S. | 119 | 40°10′N | 111°55′W |
| Utan, India | 203b | 19°17′N | 72°43′E |
| Ute Mountain Indian Reservation, I.R., N.M., U.S. | 119 | 36°57′N | 108°34′W |
| Utena, Lith. (o͞o′tā-nä) | 167 | 55°32′N | 25°40′E |
| Utete, Tan. (o͞o-tā′tȧ) | 233 | 8°05′S | 38°47′E |
| Utica, In., U.S. (ū′tĭ-kȧ) | 111h | 38°20′N | 85°39′W |
| Utica, N.Y., U.S. | 105 | 43°05′N | 75°10′W |
| Utiel, Spain (o͞o-tyål′) | 172 | 39°34′N | 1°13′W |
| Utika, Mi., U.S. (ū′tĭ-kȧ) | 111b | 42°37′N | 83°02′W |
| Utik Lake, l., Can. | 97 | 55°16′N | 96°00′W |
| Utikuma Lake, l., Can. | 95 | 55°50′N | 115°25′W |
| Utila, i., Hond. (o͞o-tē′lä) | 132 | 16°07′N | 87°05′W |
| Uto, Japan (o͞o′tō′) | 210 | 32°43′N | 130°39′E |
| Utrecht, Neth. (ü′trĕĸt) (ū′trĕkt) | 161 | 52°05′N | 5°06′E |
| Utrera, Spain (o͞o-trā′rä) | 162 | 37°12′N | 5°48′W |
| Utsunomiya, Japan (o͞ot′sȯ-nȯ-mē-yȧ′) | 205 | 36°35′N | 139°52′E |
| Uttaradit, Thai. | 212 | 17°47′N | 100°10′E |
| Uttaranchal, state, India | 199 | 29°30′N | 78°30′E |
| Uttarpara-Kotrung, India | 202a | 22°40′N | 88°21′E |
| Uttar Pradesh, state, India (ȯt-tär-prä-dĕsh) | 199 | 27°00′N | 80°00′E |
| Uttoxeter, Eng., U.K. (ŭt-tôk′sė-tẽr) | 158a | 52°54′N | 1°52′W |
| Utuado, P.R. (o͞o-to͞o-ä′dhō) | 129b | 18°16′N | 66°40′W |
| Uusikaupunki, Fin. | 167 | 60°48′N | 21°24′E |
| Uvalde, Tx., U.S. (ū-văl′dė) | 122 | 29°14′N | 99°47′W |
| Uvel'skiy, Russia (ȯ-vyĕl′skĭ) | 186a | 54°27′N | 61°22′E |
| Uvinza, Tan. | 237 | 5°06′S | 30°22′E |
| Uvira, D.R.C. (o͞o-vē′rä) | 232 | 3°28′S | 29°03′E |
| Uvod', r., Russia (ȯ-vôd′) | 176 | 56°40′N | 41°10′E |
| Uvongo Beach, S. Afr. | 233c | 30°49′S | 30°23′E |
| Uvs Nuur, l., Asia | 204 | 50°29′N | 93°32′E |
| Uwajima, Japan (o͞o-wä′jė-mä) | 210 | 33°12′N | 132°35′E |
| Uxbridge, Ma., U.S. (ŭks′brĭj) | 101a | 42°05′N | 71°38′W |
| Uxmal; hist., Mex. (o͞o′x-mä′l) | 132a | 20°22′N | 89°44′W |
| Uy, r., Russia (o͞oy) | 186a | 54°05′N | 62°11′E |
| Uyskoye, Russia (ûy′skô-yĕ) | 186a | 54°22′N | 60°01′E |
| Uyuni, Bol. (o͞o-yo͞o′nė) | 142 | 20°28′S | 66°45′W |
| Uyuni, Salar de, pl., Bol. (sä-lär-dĕ) | 142 | 20°58′S | 67°09′W |
| Uzbekistan, nation, Asia | 178 | 42°42′N | 60°00′E |
| Uzh, r., Ukr. (ȯzh) | 177 | 51°07′N | 29°05′E |
| Uzhhorod, Ukr. | 169 | 48°38′N | 22°18′E |
| Užice, Serb. o͞o′zhė-tsĕ | 175 | 43°51′N | 19°53′E |
| Uzunköprü, Tur. | 175 | 41°17′N | 26°42′E |


# V


| PLACE (Pronunciation) | PAGE | LAT. | LONG. |
| --- | --- | --- | --- |
| Vaal, r., S. Afr. (väl) | 232 | 28°15′S | 24°30′E |
| Vaaldam, res., S. Afr. | 238c | 26°58′S | 28°37′E |
| Vaalplaas, S. Afr. | 238c | 25°39′S | 28°56′E |
| Vaalwater, S. Afr. | 238c | 24°17′S | 28°08′E |
| Vaasa, Fin. (vä′sȧ) | 154 | 63°06′N | 21°39′E |
| Vác, Hung. (väts) | 169 | 47°46′N | 19°10′E |
| Vache, Île à, i., Haiti | 135 | 18°05′N | 73°40′W |
| Vadstena, Swe. (väd′stĭ′nȧ) | 166 | 58°27′N | 14°53′E |
| Vaduz, Liech. (vä′dȯts) | 168 | 47°10′N | 9°32′E |
| Vaga, r., Russia (va′gȧ) | 180 | 61°55′N | 42°30′E |
| Vah, r., Slvk. (väĸ) | 161 | 48°07′N | 17°52′E |
| Vaigai, r., India | 203 | 10°20′N | 78°13′E |
| Vakh, r., Russia (vȧĸ) | 184 | 61°30′N | 81°33′E |
| Valachia, hist. reg., Rom. | 175 | 44°45′N | 24°17′E |
| Valcartier-Village, Can. (väl-kärt-yĕ′vē-läzh′) | 102b | 46°56′N | 71°28′W |
| Valdai Hills, hills, Russia (vȧl-dī′ gô′rĭ) | 180 | 57°50′N | 32°35′E |
| Valday, Russia (vȧl-dī′) | 180 | 57°58′N | 33°13′E |
| Valdecañas, Embalse de, res., Spain | 172 | 39°45′N | 5°30′W |


ng-sing; ŋ-baŋk; ɴ-nasalized n; nŏd; cŏmmit; ōld; ôbey; ôrder; oi-boil; fo͞od; ȯ-as oo in foot; ou-out; s-soft; sh-dish; th-thin; pūre; ůnite; ûrn; stŭd; circŭs; ü-as in French tu; ′-indeterminate vowel.

| PLACE (Pronunciation) | PAGE | LAT. | LONG. |
|---|---|---|---|
| Valdemārpils, Lat. | 167 | 57°22′N | 22°34′E |
| Valdemorillo, Spain (väl-då-mô-rēl′yō) | 173a | 40°30′N | 4°04′W |
| Valdepeñas, Spain (väl-då-pān′yäs) | 162 | 38°46′N | 3°22′W |
| Valderaduey, r., Spain (väl-dě-rä-dwě′y) | 172 | 41°39′N | 5°35′W |
| Valdés, Península, pen., Arg. (väl-dě′s) | 144 | 42°15′S | 63°15′W |
| Valdez, Ak., U.S. (văl′děz) | 103 | 61°10′N | 146°18′W |
| Valdilecha, Spain (väl-dě-lā′chä) | 173a | 40°17′N | 3°19′W |
| Valdivia, Chile (väl-dē′vä) | 144 | 39°47′S | 73°13′W |
| Valdivia, Col. (väl-dē′vëä) | 142a | 7°10′N | 75°26′W |
| Val-d'Or, Can. | 91 | 48°03′N | 77°50′W |
| Valdosta, Ga., U.S. (văl-dŏs′tá) | 105 | 30°50′N | 83°18′W |
| Vale, Or., U.S. | 114 | 43°59′N | 117°14′W |
| Valença, Braz. (vä-lěn′sá) | 143 | 13°43′S | 38°58′W |
| Valença, Port. | 172 | 42°03′N | 8°36′W |
| Valence, Fr. (vä-lěNS) | 161 | 44°56′N | 4°54′E |
| València, Spain | 154 | 39°26′N | 0°23′W |
| Valencia, Ven. (vä-lěn′syä) | 142 | 10°11′N | 68°00′W |
| València, hist. reg., Spain | 173 | 39°08′N | 0°43′W |
| València, Golf de, b., Spain | 173 | 39°50′N | 0°30′E |
| Valencia, Lago de, l., Ven. | 143b | 10°11′N | 67°45′W |
| Valencia de Alcántara, Spain | 172 | 39°34′N | 7°13′W |
| Valenciennes, Fr. (vä-län-syěn′) | 170 | 50°24′N | 3°36′E |
| Valentine, Ne., U.S. (vá län-tě-nyě′) | 104 | 42°52′N | 100°34′W |
| Valera, Ven. (vä-lě′rä) | 142 | 9°12′N | 70°45′W |
| Valerianovsk, Russia (vá-lě-rī-ä′nôvsk) | 186a | 58°47′N | 59°34′E |
| Valga, Est. (väl′gà) | 180 | 57°47′N | 26°03′E |
| Valhalla, S. Afr. (väl-hǎl-á) | 233b | 25°49′S | 28°09′E |
| Valier, Mt., U.S. (vä-lēr′) | 115 | 48°17′N | 112°14′W |
| Valjevo, Serb. (väl′yå-vô) | 175 | 44°17′N | 19°57′E |
| Valky, Ukr. | 177 | 49°49′N | 35°40′E |
| Valladolid, Mex. (väl-yä-dhô-lēdh′) | 128 | 20°39′N | 88°13′W |
| Valladolid, Spain (väl-yä-dhô-lēdh′) | 154 | 41°41′N | 4°41′W |
| Valle, Arroyo del, Ca., U.S. (ä-rō′yō děl) | 118 | 37°36′N | 121°43′W |
| Vallecas, Spain (väl-yä′käs) | 173a | 40°23′N | 3°37′W |
| Valle de Allende, Mex. (väl′yä dä äl-yěn′då) | 122 | 26°55′N | 105°25′W |
| Valle de Bravo, Mex. (brä′vô) | 130 | 19°12′N | 100°07′W |
| Valle de Guanape, Ven. (vä′l-yě-dě-gwä-nä′pě) | 143b | 9°54′N | 65°41′W |
| Valle de la Pascua, Ven. (lä-pä′s-kōōä) | 142 | 9°12′N | 65°08′W |
| Valle del Cauca, dept., Col. (vä′l-yě del kou′kä) | 142a | 4°03′N | 76°13′W |
| Valle de Santiago, Mex. (sän-tē-ä′gô) | 130 | 20°23′N | 101°11′W |
| Valledupar, Col. (dōō-pär′) | 142 | 10°13′N | 73°39′W |
| Valle Grande, Bol. (grän′dä) | 142 | 18°27′S | 64°03′W |
| Vallejo, Ca., U.S. (vä-yä′hō) (vä-lä′hō) | 104 | 38°06′N | 122°15′W |
| Vallejo, Sierra de, mts., Mex. (sē-ě′r-rä-dē-väl′yō) | 130 | 21°00′N | 105°10′W |
| Vallenar, Chile (väl-yå-när′) | 144 | 28°39′S | 70°52′W |
| Valles, Mex. | 128 | 21°59′N | 99°02′W |
| Valletta, Malta (väl-lět′à) | 162 | 35°50′N | 14°29′E |
| Valle Vista, Ca., U.S. (väl′yä vīs′tá) | 117a | 33°45′N | 116°53′W |
| Valley City, N.D., U.S. | 114 | 46°55′N | 97°59′W |
| Valley City, Oh., U.S. (văl′ĭ) | 111d | 41°14′N | 81°56′W |
| Valley Falls, Ks., U.S. | 121 | 39°25′N | 95°26′W |
| Valleyfield, Can. (văl′ē-fēld) | 91 | 45°16′N | 74°09′W |
| Valley Park, Mo., U.S. (văl′ě pärk) | 117e | 38°33′N | 90°30′W |
| Valley Stream, N.Y., U.S. (văl′ĭ strēm) | 110a | 40°39′N | 73°42′W |
| Valli di Comácchio, l., Italy (vä′lē-dē-kô-má′chyô) | 174 | 44°38′N | 12°15′E |
| Vallière, Haiti (väl-yâr′) | 135 | 19°30′N | 71°55′W |
| Vallimanca, r., Arg. (väl-yē-mä′n-kä) | 141c | 36°21′S | 60°55′W |
| Valls, Spain (väls) | 162 | 41°15′N | 1°15′E |
| Valmiera, Lat. (väl′myě-rä) | 180 | 57°34′N | 25°54′E |
| Valognes, Fr. (vá-lôn′y′) | 170 | 49°32′N | 1°30′W |
| Valona see Vlorë, Alb. | 163 | 40°28′N | 19°31′E |
| Valozhyn, Bela. | 176 | 54°04′N | 26°38′E |
| Valparaíso, Chile (väl′pä-rä-ē′sô) | 144 | 33°02′S | 71°32′W |
| Valparaíso, Mex. | 130 | 22°49′N | 103°33′W |
| Valparaiso, In., U.S. (väl-pá-rā′zô) | 108 | 41°25′N | 87°05′W |
| Valpariso, prov., Chile | 141b | 32°58′S | 71°23′W |
| Valréas, Fr. (väl-rä-ä′) | 170 | 44°25′N | 4°56′E |
| Vals, r., S. Afr. | 238c | 27°32′S | 26°51′E |
| Vals, Tanjung, c., Indon. | 213 | 8°30′S | 137°15′E |
| Valsbaai, b., S. Afr. | 232a | 34°14′S | 18°35′E |
| Valuyevo, Russia (vá-lōō′yě-vô) | 186b | 55°34′N | 37°21′E |
| Valuyki, Russia (vä-lô-ē′kě) | 181 | 50°14′N | 38°04′E |
| Valverde del Camino, Spain (väl-věr-dě′-děl-kä-mě′nō) | 172 | 37°34′N | 6°44′W |
| Vammala, Fin. | 167 | 61°19′N | 22°51′E |
| Van, Tur. (vän) | 198 | 38°04′N | 43°10′E |
| Van Buren, Ar., U.S. (văn bū′rěn) | 121 | 35°26′N | 94°20′W |
| Van Buren, Me., U.S. | 100 | 47°09′N | 67°58′W |
| Vanceburg, Ky., U.S. (văns′bŭrg) | 108 | 38°35′N | 83°20′W |
| Vancouver, Can. (văn-kōō′věr) | 90 | 49°16′N | 123°06′W |
| Vancouver, Wa., U.S. | 104 | 45°37′N | 122°40′W |
| Vancouver Island, i., Can. | 92 | 49°50′N | 125°05′W |
| Vancouver Island Ranges, mts., Can. | 94 | 49°25′N | 125°25′W |
| Vandalia, Il., U.S. (văn-dā′lĭ-á) | 108 | 39°00′N | 89°00′W |
| Vandalia, Mo., U.S. | 121 | 39°19′N | 91°30′W |
| Vanderbijlpark, S. Afr. | 238c | 26°43′S | 27°50′E |
| Vanderhoof, Can. | 90 | 54°01′N | 124°01′W |
| Van Diemen, Cape, c., Austl. (văndě′měn) | 220 | 11°05′S | 130°15′E |
| Van Diemen Gulf, b., Austl. | 220 | 11°50′S | 131°30′E |
| Vanegas, Mex. (vä-ně′gäs) | 128 | 23°54′N | 100°54′W |

| PLACE (Pronunciation) | PAGE | LAT. | LONG. |
|---|---|---|---|
| Vänern, l., Swe. | 156 | 58°52′N | 13°17′E |
| Vänersborg, Swe. (vě′něrs-bôr′) | 160 | 58°24′N | 12°15′E |
| Vanga, Kenya (vän′gä) | 233 | 4°38′S | 39°10′E |
| Vangani, India | 203b | 19°07′N | 73°15′E |
| Van Gölü, l., Tur. | 180 | 38°33′N | 42°46′E |
| Van Horn, Tx., U.S. | 122 | 31°03′N | 104°50′W |
| Vanier, Can. | 102c | 45°27′N | 75°39′W |
| Van Lear, Ky., U.S. (văn lēr′) | 108 | 37°45′N | 82°50′W |
| Vannes, Fr. (vän) | 161 | 47°42′N | 2°46′W |
| Van Nuys, Ca., U.S. (văn nīz′) | 117a | 34°11′N | 118°27′W |
| Van Rees, Pegunungan, mts., Indon. | 213 | 2°30′S | 138°45′E |
| Vantaan, r., Fin. | 167 | 60°25′N | 24°43′E |
| Vanua Levu, i., Fiji | 214g | 16°33′S | 179°15′E |
| Vanuatu, nation, Oc. | 219 | 16°02′S | 169°15′E |
| Van Wert, Oh., U.S. (văn wûrt′) | 108 | 40°50′N | 84°35′W |
| Vara, Swe. (vä′rä) | 166 | 58°17′N | 12°55′E |
| Varaklāni, Lat. | 167 | 56°38′N | 26°46′E |
| Varallo, Italy (vä-räl′lô) | 174 | 45°44′N | 8°14′E |
| Vārānasi (Benares), India | 199 | 25°25′N | 83°00′E |
| Varangerfjorden, b., Nor. | 157 | 70°05′N | 30°20′E |
| Varano, Lago di, l., Italy (lä′gô-dē-vä-rä′nô) | 174 | 41°52′N | 15°55′E |
| Varaždin, Cro. (vä′räzh′děn) | 163 | 46°17′N | 16°20′E |
| Varazze, Italy (vä-rät′sä) | 174 | 44°23′N | 8°34′E |
| Varberg, Swe. (vär′běrg) | 166 | 57°06′N | 12°16′E |
| Vardar, r., Serb. (vär′där) | 175 | 41°40′N | 21°50′E |
| Varèna, Lith. (vä-rä′nä) | 167 | 54°16′N | 24°35′E |
| Varennes, Can. (vä-rěn′) | 102a | 45°41′N | 73°27′W |
| Vareš, Bos. (vä′rěsh) | 175 | 44°10′N | 18°20′E |
| Varese, Italy (vä-rā′sě) | 174 | 45°45′N | 8°49′E |
| Varginha, Braz. (vär-zhě′n-yä) | 143 | 21°33′S | 45°25′W |
| Varkaus, Fin. (vär′kous) | 167 | 62°19′N | 27°51′E |
| Varlamovo, Russia (vár-lä′mô-vô) | 186a | 54°37′N | 60°41′E |
| Varna, Blg. (vär′ná) | 154 | 43°14′N | 27°58′E |
| Varna, Russia | 186a | 53°22′N | 60°59′E |
| Värnamo, Swe. (věr′nä-mô) | 166 | 57°11′N | 13°45′E |
| Varnsdorf, Czech Rep. (värns′dôrf) | 168 | 50°54′N | 14°36′E |
| Varnville, S.C., U.S. (värn′vĭl) | 125 | 32°49′N | 81°05′W |
| Vasa, India | 203b | 19°20′N | 72°47′E |
| Vascongadas see Basque Provinces, hist. reg., Spain | 172 | 43°00′N | 2°46′W |
| Vashka, r., Russia | 180 | 64°00′N | 48°00′E |
| Vashon, Wa., U.S. (văsh′ŭn) | 116a | 47°27′N | 122°28′W |
| Vashon Heights, Wa., U.S. (hītz) | 116a | 47°30′N | 122°28′W |
| Vashon Island, i., Wa., U.S. | 116a | 47°27′N | 122°27′W |
| Vaslui, Rom. (väs-lōō′ē) | 169 | 46°39′N | 27°49′E |
| Vassar, Mi., U.S. (văs′ēr) | 108 | 43°25′N | 83°35′W |
| Vassouras, Braz. (vä-sō′räzh) | 141a | 22°25′S | 43°40′W |
| Västerås, Swe. (věs′těr-ôs) | 160 | 59°39′N | 16°30′E |
| Västerdalälven, r., Swe. | 160 | 61°06′N | 13°10′E |
| Västervik, Swe. (věs′těr-vēk) | 160 | 57°45′N | 16°35′E |
| Vasto, Italy (väs′tô) | 162 | 42°06′N | 12°42′E |
| Vasyl'kiv, Ukr. | 181 | 50°10′N | 30°22′E |
| Vasyugan, r., Russia (vás-yōō-gán′) | 184 | 58°52′N | 77°30′E |
| Vatican City, nation, Eur. | 174 | 41°54′N | 12°22′E |
| Vaticano, Cape, c., Italy (vä-tē-kä′nô) | 174 | 38°38′N | 15°52′E |
| Vatnajökull, ice, Ice. (vät′nä-yû-kól) | 160 | 64°34′N | 16°41′W |
| Vatomandry, Madag. | 233 | 18°53′S | 48°13′E |
| Vatra Dornei, Rom. (vät′rá dôr′ná′) | 169 | 47°22′N | 25°20′E |
| Vättern, l., Swe. | 156 | 58°15′N | 14°24′E |
| Vattholma, Swe. | 166 | 60°01′N | 17°40′E |
| Vaudreuil, Can. (vô-drü′y′) | 102a | 45°24′N | 74°02′W |
| Vaugh, Wa., U.S. (vôn) | 116a | 47°21′N | 122°47′W |
| Vaughan, Can. | 102d | 43°47′N | 79°36′W |
| Vaughn, N.M., U.S. | 120 | 34°37′N | 105°13′W |
| Vaupés, r., S.A. (vá′ōō-pě′s) | 142 | 1°18′N | 71°14′W |
| Vawkavysk, Bela. (vôl-kô-věsk′) | 169 | 53°11′N | 24°29′E |
| Vaxholm, Swe. (väks′hôlm) | 166 | 59°26′N | 18°19′E |
| Växjo, Swe. (věks′shû) | 156 | 56°53′N | 14°46′E |
| Vaygach, i., Russia (vī-gách′) | 178 | 70°00′N | 59°00′E |
| Veadeiros, Chapadas dos, hills, Braz. (shä-pä′däs-dôs-vě-ä-dä′rôs) | 143 | 14°00′S | 47°00′W |
| Vedea, r., Rom. (vå′dyä) | 175 | 44°25′N | 24°45′E |
| Vedia, Arg. (vě′dyä) | 141c | 34°29′S | 61°30′W |
| Veedersburg, In., U.S. (vě′děrz-bûrg) | 108 | 40°05′N | 87°15′W |
| Vega, i., Nor. | 160 | 65°38′N | 10°51′E |
| Vega de Alatorre, Mex. (vä′gä dä ä-lä-tōr′rå) | 131 | 20°02′N | 96°39′W |
| Vega Real, reg., Dom. Rep. (vě′gä-rě-ä′l) | 135 | 19°30′N | 71°05′W |
| Vegreville, Can. | 90 | 53°30′N | 112°03′W |
| Vehār Lake, l., India | 203b | 19°11′N | 72°52′E |
| Veinticinco de Mayo, Arg. | 141c | 35°26′S | 60°09′W |
| Vejer de la Frontera, Spain | 172 | 36°15′N | 5°58′W |
| Vejle, Den. (vī′lě) | 160 | 55°41′N | 9°29′E |
| Velbert, Ger. (fěl′běrt) | 171c | 51°20′N | 7°03′E |
| Velebit, mts., Serb. (vä′lě-bět) | 163 | 44°25′N | 15°23′E |
| Velen, Ger. (fě′lěn) | 171c | 51°54′N | 7°00′E |
| Vélez-Málaga, Spain (vä′läth-mä′lä-gä) | 172 | 36°48′N | 4°05′W |
| Vélez-Rubio, Spain (rōō′bě-ô) | 172 | 37°38′N | 2°05′W |
| Velika Kapela, mts., Serb. (vě′lě-kä kä-pě′lä) | 163 | 45°03′N | 15°20′E |
| Velika Morava, r., Serb. (mô′rä-vä) | 163 | 44°00′N | 21°30′E |
| Velikaya, r., Russia (vå-lě′kä-yá) | 176 | 57°25′N | 28°07′E |
| Velikiye Luki, Russia (vyě-lě′-kyě lōō′ke) | 178 | 56°19′N | 30°32′E |
| Velikiy Ustyug, Russia (vä-lě′kǐ ōōs-tyóg′) | 178 | 60°45′N | 46°38′E |
| Veliko Tŭrnovo, Blg. | 163 | 43°06′N | 25°38′E |
| Velikoye, Russia (vå-lě′kô-yě) | 176 | 57°21′N | 39°45′E |
| Velikoye, l., Russia | 176 | 57°00′N | 36°53′E |
| Veli Lošinj, Cro. (lô′shěn′) | 174 | 44°30′N | 14°29′E |
| Velizh, Russia (vå′lězh) | 180 | 55°37′N | 31°11′E |
| Vella Lavella, i., Sol. Is. | 221 | 8°00′S | 156°42′E |

| PLACE (Pronunciation) | PAGE | LAT. | LONG. |
|---|---|---|---|
| Velletri, Italy (věl-lā′trě) | 174 | 41°42′N | 12°48′E |
| Vellore, India (věl-lōr′) | 199 | 12°57′N | 79°09′E |
| Vels, Russia (věls) | 186a | 60°35′N | 58°47′E |
| Vel'sk, Russia (vělsk) | 178 | 61°00′N | 42°18′E |
| Velten, Ger. (fel′těn) | 159b | 52°41′N | 13°11′E |
| Velya, r., Russia (věl′yä) | 186b | 56°23′N | 37°54′E |
| Velyka Lepetykha, Ukr. | 177 | 47°11′N | 33°58′E |
| Velykyi Bychkiv, Ukr. | 169 | 47°59′N | 24°01′E |
| Venadillo, Col. (vě-nä-dē′l-yō) | 142a | 4°43′N | 74°55′W |
| Venado, Mex. (vå-mä′dō) | 130 | 22°54′N | 101°07′W |
| Venado Tuerto, Arg. (vě-nä′dô-tōōě′r-tô) | 144 | 33°28′S | 61°47′W |
| Vendôme, Fr. (vän-dôm′) | 170 | 47°46′N | 1°05′E |
| Veneto, hist. reg., Italy (vě-ně′tô) | 174 | 45°58′N | 11°24′E |
| Venëv, Russia (věn-ěf′) | 180 | 54°19′N | 38°14′E |
| Venezia see Venice, Italy | 154 | 45°25′N | 12°18′E |
| Venezuela, nation, S.A. (věn-ě-zwě′lá) | 142 | 8°00′N | 65°00′W |
| Venezuela, Golfo de, b., S.A. (gôl-fô-dě) | 142 | 11°34′N | 71°02′W |
| Veniaminof, Mount, mtn., Ak., U.S. | 103 | 56°12′N | 159°20′W |
| Venice, Italy | 154 | 45°25′N | 12°18′E |
| Venice, Ca., U.S. (věn′ĭs) | 117a | 33°59′N | 118°28′W |
| Venice, Il., U.S. | 117e | 38°40′N | 90°10′W |
| Venice, Gulf of, b., Italy | 162 | 45°23′N | 13°00′E |
| Venlo, Neth. | 171c | 51°22′N | 6°11′E |
| Venta, r., Eur. (věn′tá) | 167 | 57°05′N | 21°45′E |
| Ventana, Sierra de la, mts., Arg. (sě-ě-rä-dě-lä-věn-tä′ná) | 144 | 38°00′S | 63°00′W |
| Ventersburg, S. Afr. (věn-těrs′bûrg) | 238c | 28°06′S | 27°10′E |
| Ventersdorp, S. Afr. (věn-těrs′dôrp) | 238c | 26°20′S | 26°48′E |
| Ventimiglia, Italy (věn-tě-mēl′yä) | 174 | 43°46′N | 7°37′E |
| Ventnor, N.J., U.S. (věnt′něr) | 109 | 39°20′N | 74°25′W |
| Ventspils, Lat. (věnt′spēls) | 180 | 57°24′N | 21°41′E |
| Ventuari, r., Ven. (věn-tōōá′rē) | 142 | 4°47′N | 65°56′W |
| Ventura, Ca., U.S. (věn-tōō′rá) | 118 | 34°18′N | 119°18′W |
| Venukovsky, Russia (vě-nōō′kôv-skī) | 186b | 55°10′N | 37°26′E |
| Venustiano Carranza, Mex. (vě-nōōs-tyä′nô-kär-rä′n-zä) | 130 | 19°44′N | 103°48′W |
| Venustiano Carranza, Mex. (kär-rä′n-zō) | 131 | 16°21′N | 92°36′W |
| Vera, Arg. (vě-rä) | 144 | 29°22′S | 60°09′W |
| Vera, Spain (vä′rä) | 172 | 37°18′N | 1°53′W |
| Veracruz, Mex. | 128 | 19°13′N | 96°07′W |
| Vera Cruz, state, Mex. (vä-rä-krōōz′) | 128 | 20°30′N | 97°15′W |
| Verāval, India (věr′vū-väl) | 199 | 20°59′N | 70°49′E |
| Vercelli, Italy (věr-chěl′lě) | 174 | 45°18′N | 8°27′E |
| Verchères, Can. (věr-shär′) | 102a | 45°46′N | 73°21′W |
| Verde, i., Phil. (věr′dä) | 213a | 13°34′N | 121°11′E |
| Verde, r., Mex. | 130 | 21°48′N | 99°50′W |
| Verde, r., Mex. | 130 | 20°50′N | 103°00′W |
| Verde, r., Mex. | 131 | 16°05′N | 97°44′W |
| Verde, r., Az., U.S. (vûrd) | 119 | 34°04′N | 111°40′W |
| Verde, Cap, c., Bah. | 135 | 22°50′N | 75°00′W |
| Verde, Cay, i., Bah. | 135 | 22°00′N | 75°05′W |
| Verde Island Passage, strt., Phil. (věr′dě) | 213a | 13°36′N | 120°39′E |
| Verdemont, Ca., U.S. (vûr′dě-mŏnt) | 117a | 34°12′N | 117°22′W |
| Verden, Ger. (fěr′děn) | 168 | 52°55′N | 9°15′E |
| Verdigris, r., Ok., U.S. (vûr′dě-grěs) | 121 | 36°50′N | 95°29′W |
| Verdun, Can. (věr′dŭn′) | 99 | 45°27′N | 73°34′W |
| Verdun, Fr. (vâr-dŭn′) | 161 | 49°09′N | 5°21′E |
| Verdun, Fr. | 171 | 43°48′N | 1°10′E |
| Vereeniging, S. Afr. (vě-rā′nǐ-gǐng) | 238c | 26°40′S | 27°56′E |
| Verena, S. Afr. (věr-ēn á) | 238c | 25°30′S | 29°02′E |
| Vereya, Russia (vě-rā′yä) | 176 | 55°21′N | 36°08′E |
| Verín, Spain (vä-rē′n) | 172 | 41°56′N | 7°26′W |
| Verkhne-Kamchatsk, Russia (vyěrk′nyě käm-chatsk′) | 179 | 54°42′N | 158°41′E |
| Verkhne Neyvinskiy, Russia (nā-vīn′skī) | 186a | 57°17′N | 60°10′E |
| Verkhne Ural'sk, Russia (ô-ralsk′) | 178 | 53°53′N | 59°13′E |
| Verkhniy Avzyan, Russia (vyěrk′nyě áv-zyän′) | 186a | 53°32′N | 57°30′E |
| Verkhniye Kigi, Russia (vyěrk′nī-yě kĭ′gī) | 186a | 55°23′N | 58°37′E |
| Verkhniy Ufaley, Russia (ô-fä′lä) | 186a | 56°04′N | 60°15′E |
| Verkhnyaya Pyshma, Russia (vyěrk′nyä-yä pōōsh′má) | 186a | 56°57′N | 60°37′E |
| Verkhnyaya Salda, Russia (säl′dä) | 186a | 58°03′N | 60°33′E |
| Verkhnyaya Tunguska (Angara), r., Russia (tòn-gòs′ka) | 184 | 58°13′N | 97°00′E |
| Verkhnyaya Tura, Russia (to′rá) | 186a | 58°22′N | 59°51′E |
| Verkhnyaya Yayva, Russia (yäy′vá) | 186a | 59°28′N | 57°38′E |
| Verkhotur'ye, Russia (vyěrk-hô-tōōr′yě) | 186a | 58°52′N | 60°47′E |
| Verkhoyansk, Russia (vyěr-kô-yänsk′) | 179 | 67°43′N | 133°33′E |
| Verkhoyanskiy Khrebet, mts., Russia (vyěr-kô-yänskī) | 179 | 67°45′N | 128°00′E |
| Vermilion, Can. (věr-mĭl′yŭn) | 90 | 53°22′N | 110°51′W |
| Vermilion, l., Mn., U.S. | 113 | 47°49′N | 92°35′W |
| Vermilion, r., Can. | 99 | 47°30′N | 73°15′W |
| Vermilion, r., Can. | 96 | 53°30′N | 111°00′W |
| Vermilion, r., Il., U.S. | 108 | 41°05′N | 89°00′W |
| Vermilion, r., Il., U.S. | 113 | 48°09′N | 92°31′W |
| Vermilion Hills, hills, Can. | 96 | 50°43′N | 106°50′W |
| Vermilion Range, mts., Mn., U.S. | 113 | 47°55′N | 91°59′W |
| Vermillion, S.D., U.S. | 112 | 42°46′N | 96°56′W |
| Vermillion, r., S.D., U.S. | 112 | 43°54′N | 97°14′W |
| Vermillion Bay, b., La., U.S. | 123 | 29°47′N | 92°00′W |
| Vermont, state, U.S. (věr-mŏnt′) | 105 | 43°50′N | 72°50′W |
| Vernal, Ut., U.S. (vûr′nál) | 115 | 40°29′N | 109°40′W |
| Verneuk Pan, pl., S. Afr. (věr-nūk′) | 232 | 30°10′S | 21°46′E |
| Vernon, Can. (věr-nŏn′) | 90 | 50°18′N | 119°15′W |
| Vernon, Can. | 102c | 45°10′N | 75°27′W |
| Vernon, Ca., U.S. (vûr′nŭn) | 117a | 34°01′N | 118°12′W |

| PLACE (Pronunciation) | PAGE | LAT. | LONG. |
|---|---|---|---|
| Vernon, In., U.S. (vûr'nŭn) | 108 | 39°00'N | 85°40'W |
| Vernon, N.J., U.S. | 110a | 39°00'N | 85°40'W |
| Vernon, Tx., U.S. | 120 | 34°09'N | 99°16'W |
| Vernonia, Or., U.S. (vûr-nō'nyà) | 116c | 45°52'N | 123°12'W |
| Vero Beach, Fl., U.S. (vē'rō) | 125a | 27°36'N | 80°25'W |
| Véroia, Grc. | 175 | 40°30'N | 22°13'E |
| Verona, Italy (vā-rō'nä) | 162 | 45°28'N | 11°02'E |
| Versailles, Fr. (vĕr-sī'y') | 161 | 48°48'N | 2°07'E |
| Versailles, Ky., U.S. (vēr-sālz') | 108 | 38°05'N | 84°45'W |
| Versailles, Mo., U.S. | 121 | 38°27'N | 92°52'W |
| Vert, Cap, c., Sen. | 230 | 14°43'N | 17°30'W |
| Verulam, S. Afr. (vĕ-rōō-lăm) | 233c | 29°39'S | 31°08'E |
| Verviers, Bel. (vĕr-vyā') | 165 | 50°35'N | 5°57'E |
| Vesele, Ukr. | 177 | 46°59'N | 34°56'E |
| Vesijärvi, l., Fin. | 167 | 61°09'N | 25°10'E |
| Vesoul, Fr. (vē-sōōl') | 171 | 47°38'N | 6°11'E |
| Vestavia Hills, Al., U.S. | 110h | 33°26'N | 86°46'W |
| Vesterålen, is., Nor. (vĕs'tĕr ô'lĕn) | 160 | 68°54'N | 14°03'E |
| Vestfjord, b., Nor. | 156 | 67°33'N | 12°59'E |
| Vestmannaeyjar, Ice. (vĕst'män-ä-ā'yär) | 160 | 63°12'N | 20°17'W |
| Vesuvio, vol., Italy (vĕ-sōō'vyä) | 156 | 40°35'N | 14°26'E |
| Ves'yegonsk, Russia (vĕ-syĕ-gônsk') | 176 | 58°42'N | 37°09'E |
| Veszprem, Hung. (vĕs'prăm) | 169 | 47°05'N | 17°53'E |
| Vészto, Hung. (vās'tû) | 169 | 46°55'N | 21°18'E |
| Vet, r., S. Afr. (vĕt) | 238c | 28°25'S | 26°37'E |
| Vetlanda, Swe. (vĕt-län'dä) | 166 | 57°26'N | 15°05'E |
| Vetluga, Russia (vyĕt-lōō'gà) | 180 | 57°50'N | 45°42'E |
| Vetluga, r., Russia | 180 | 56°50'N | 45°50'E |
| Vetovo, Blg. (vā'tô-vô) | 175 | 43°42'N | 26°18'E |
| Vetren, Blg. (vĕt'rĕn') | 175 | 42°16'N | 24°04'E |
| Vevay, In., U.S. (vē'vā) | 108 | 38°45'N | 85°05'W |
| Veynes, Fr. (vān'') | 171 | 44°31'N | 5°47'E |
| Vézère, r., Fr. (vā-zer') | 170 | 45°01'N | 1°00'E |
| Viacha, Bol. (vēä'chä) | 142 | 16°43'S | 68°16'W |
| Viadana, Italy (vē-ä-dä'nä) | 174 | 44°55'N | 10°30'E |
| Vian, Ok., U.S. (vī'ăn) | 121 | 35°30'N | 95°00'W |
| Viana, Braz. (vē-ä'nä) | 143 | 3°09'S | 44°44'W |
| Viana do Alentejo, Port. (vē-ä'nà dò ä-lĕn-tā'hò) | 172 | 38°20'N | 8°02'W |
| Viana do Bolo, Spain | 172 | 42°10'N | 7°07'W |
| Viana do Castelo, Port. (dò käs-tā'lò) | 162 | 41°41'N | 8°45'W |
| Viangchan, Laos | 212 | 18°07'N | 102°33'E |
| Viar, r., Spain (vē-ä'rä) | 172 | 38°15'N | 6°08'W |
| Viareggio, Italy (vē-ä-rĕd'jô) | 174 | 43°52'N | 10°14'E |
| Viborg, Den. (vē'bôr) | 166 | 56°27'N | 9°22'E |
| Vibo Valentia, Italy (vē'bô-vä-lĕ'n-tyä) | 174 | 38°47'N | 16°06'E |
| Vic, Spain | 173 | 41°55'N | 2°14'E |
| Vicálvaro, Spain | 173a | 40°25'N | 3°37'W |
| Vicente López, Arg. (vē-sĕ'n-tĕ-lô'pĕz) | 144a | 34°31'S | 58°29'W |
| Vicenza, Italy (vē-chĕnt'sä) | 162 | 45°33'N | 11°33'E |
| Vichuga, Russia (vē-chōō'gà) | 180 | 57°13'N | 41°58'E |
| Vichy, Fr. (vē-shē') | 161 | 46°06'N | 3°28'E |
| Vickersund, Nor. | 166 | 60°00'N | 9°59'E |
| Vicksburg, Mi., U.S. (vĭks'bûrg) | 108 | 42°10'N | 85°30'W |
| Vicksburg, Ms., U.S. | 105 | 32°20'N | 90°50'W |
| Viçosa, Braz. (vē-sô'sä) | 141a | 20°46'S | 42°51'W |
| Victoria, Arg. (vēk-tō'rēä) | 144 | 32°36'S | 60°09'W |
| Victoria, Can. (vĭk-tō'rĭ-à) | 90 | 48°26'N | 123°23'W |
| Victoria, Chile (vēk-tô-rēä) | 144 | 38°15'S | 72°16'W |
| Victoria, Col. (vēk-tō'rēä) | 142a | 5°19'N | 74°54'W |
| Victoria, Phil. (vēk-tô-ryä) | 213a | 15°34'N | 120°41'E |
| Victoria, Tx., U.S. (vĭk-tō'rĭ-à) | 123 | 28°48'N | 97°00'W |
| Victoria, Va., U.S. | 125 | 36°57'N | 78°13'W |
| Victoria, state, Austl. | 219 | 36°46'S | 143°15'E |
| Victoria, l., Afr. | 232 | 0°50'S | 32°50'E |
| Victoria, r., Austl. | 220 | 17°25'S | 130°50'E |
| Victoria, Mount, mtn., Mya. | 199 | 21°26'N | 93°59'E |
| Victoria, Mount, mtn., Pap. N. Gui. | 213 | 9°35'S | 147°45'E |
| Victoria de las Tunas, Cuba (vēk-tō'rē-ä dā läs tōō'näs) | 134 | 20°55'N | 77°05'W |
| Victoria Falls, wtfl., Afr. | 232 | 17°55'S | 25°51'E |
| Victoria Island, i., Can. | 89 | 70°13'N | 107°45'W |
| Victoria Lake, l., Can. | 101 | 48°20'N | 57°40'W |
| Victoria Land, reg., Ant. | 224 | 75°00'S | 160°00'E |
| Victoria Nile, r., Ug. | 237 | 2°20'N | 31°35'E |
| Victoria Peak, mtn., Belize (vēk-tōri'à) | 132a | 16°47'N | 88°40'W |
| Victoria Peak, mtn., Can. | 94 | 50°03'N | 126°06'W |
| Victoria River Downs, Austl. (vĭc-tôr'ĭà) | 218 | 16°30'S | 131°10'E |
| Victoria Strait, strt., Can. (vĭk-tō'rĭ-à) | 92 | 69°10'N | 100°58'W |
| Victoriaville, Can. (vĭk-tō'rĭ-à-vĭl) | 91 | 46°04'N | 71°59'W |
| Victoria West, S. Afr. (wĕst) | 232 | 31°25'S | 23°10'E |
| Vidalia, Ga., U.S. (vĭ-dā'lĭ-à) | 125 | 32°10'N | 82°26'W |
| Vidalia, La., U.S. | 123 | 31°33'N | 91°28'W |
| Vidin, Blg. (vĭ'dĕn) | 163 | 44°00'N | 22°53'E |
| Vidnoye, Russia | 186b | 55°33'N | 37°41'E |
| Vidzy, Bela. (vē'dzĭ) | 176 | 55°23'N | 26°46'E |
| Viedma, Arg. (vyād'mä) | 144 | 40°55'S | 63°03'W |
| Viedma, l., Arg. | 144 | 49°40'S | 72°35'W |
| Viejo, r., Nic. (vyā'hō) | 132 | 12°45'N | 86°19'W |
| Vienna (Wien), Aus. | 154 | 48°13'N | 16°22'E |
| Vienna, Ga., U.S. (vē-ĕn'à) | 124 | 32°03'N | 83°50'W |
| Vienna, Il., U.S. | 121 | 37°24'N | 88°50'W |
| Vienna, Va., U.S. | 110e | 38°54'N | 77°16'W |
| Vienne, Fr. (vyĕn') | 161 | 45°31'N | 4°54'E |
| Vienne, r., Fr. | 170 | 47°06'N | 0°20'E |
| Vientiane see Viangchan, Laos | 212 | 18°07'N | 102°33'E |
| Vieques, P.R. (vyā'kås) | 129b | 18°09'N | 65°27'W |
| Vieques, i., P.R. (vyā'kås) | 129b | 18°05'N | 65°28'W |
| Vierfontein, S. Afr. (vēr'fŏn-tān) | 238c | 27°06'S | 26°45'E |
| Viersen, Ger. (fēr'zĕn) | 171c | 51°15'N | 6°24'E |
| Vierwaldstätter See, l., Switz. | 168 | 46°54'N | 8°36'E |
| Vierzon, Fr. (vyâr-zôn') | 161 | 47°14'N | 2°04'E |
| Viesca, Mex. (vē-äs'kä) | 122 | 25°21'N | 102°47'W |
| Viesca, Laguna de, l., Mex. (lä-ō'nä-dĕ) | 122 | 25°30'N | 102°40'W |
| Vieste, Italy (vyĕs'tå) | 174 | 41°52'N | 16°10'E |
| Vietnam, nation, Asia (vyĕt'näm') | 212 | 18°00'N | 107°00'E |
| Vigan, Phil. (vēgän) | 212 | 17°36'N | 120°22'E |
| Vigevano, Italy (vē-jå-vä'nô) | 174 | 45°18'N | 8°52'E |
| Vigny, Fr. (vēn-y'ē') | 171b | 49°05'N | 1°54'E |
| Vigo, Spain (vē'gō) | 154 | 42°18'N | 8°42'W |
| Vihti, Fin. (vē'tĭ) | 167 | 60°27'N | 24°18'E |
| Vijayawāda, India | 199 | 16°31'N | 80°37'E |
| Viksøyri, Nor. | 166 | 61°06'N | 6°35'E |
| Vila Caldas Xavier, Moz. | 237 | 15°59'S | 34°12'E |
| Vila de Manica, Moz. (vē'lä dā mä-nē'kà) | 232 | 18°48'S | 32°49'E |
| Vila de Rei, Port. (vē'là dā rā'ĭ) | 172 | 39°42'N | 8°03'W |
| Vila do Conde, Port. (vē'là dò kôn'dĕ) | 172 | 41°21'N | 8°44'W |
| Vilafranca del Penedès, Spain | 173 | 41°20'N | 1°40'E |
| Vilafranca de Xira, Port. (fräŋ'kà dä shē'rà) | 172 | 38°58'N | 8°59'W |
| Vilaine, r., Fr. (vē-lân') | 170 | 47°34'N | 2°15'W |
| Vilalba, Spain | 172 | 43°18'N | 7°43'W |
| Vilanculos, Moz. (vē-län-kōō'lôs) | 232 | 22°03'S | 35°13'E |
| Vilāni, Lat. (vē'lá-nĭ) | 167 | 56°31'N | 27°00'E |
| Vila Nova de Foz Côa, Port. (nō'và dā fôz-kō'à) | 172 | 41°08'N | 7°11'W |
| Vila Nova de Gaia, Port. (vē'là nō'và dā gä'yä) | 172 | 41°08'N | 8°40'W |
| Vila Nova de Milfontes, Port. (nō'và dā mēl-fôn'tāzh) | 172 | 37°44'N | 8°48'W |
| Vila Real, Port. (rā-äl') | 162 | 41°18'N | 7°48'W |
| Vila-real, Spain | 173 | 39°55'N | 0°07'W |
| Vila Real de Santo Antonio, Port. | 172 | 37°14'N | 7°25'W |
| Vila Viçosa, Port. (vē-sō'zà) | 172 | 38°47'N | 7°24'W |
| Vileyka, Bela. (vē-lā'ē-kà) | 176 | 54°19'N | 26°58'E |
| Vilhelmina, Swe. | 160 | 64°37'N | 16°30'E |
| Viljandi, Est. (vēl'yän-dē) | 180 | 58°24'N | 25°34'E |
| Viljoenskroon, S. Afr. | 238c | 27°13'S | 26°58'E |
| Vilkaviškis, Lith. (vēl-kà-vēsh'kēs) | 167 | 54°40'N | 23°08'E |
| Vil'kitskogo, i., Russia (vyl-kēts-kōgō) | 184 | 73°25'N | 76°00'E |
| Villa Acuña, Mex. (vēl'yä-kōō'n-yä) | 122 | 29°20'N | 100°56'W |
| Villa Ahumada, Mex. (ä-ōō-mä'dä) | 122 | 30°43'N | 106°30'W |
| Villa Alta, Mex. (äl'tä)(sän ēl-då-fōn'sō) | 131 | 17°20'N | 96°08'W |
| Villa Angela, Arg. (vē'l-yä á'n-kĕ-lä) | 144 | 27°31'S | 60°42'W |
| Villa Ballester, Arg. (vē'l-yä-bál-yĕs-tĕr) | 144a | 34°33'S | 58°33'W |
| Villa Bella, Bol. (bĕ'l-yä) | 142 | 10°25'S | 65°22'W |
| Villablino, Spain (vēl-yä-blē'nō) | 172 | 42°58'N | 6°18'W |
| Villacañas, Spain (vēl-yä-kän'yäs) | 172 | 39°39'N | 3°20'W |
| Villacarrillo, Spain (vēl-yä-kä-rēl'yō) | 172 | 38°09'N | 3°07'W |
| Villach, Aus. (fē'läĸ) | 161 | 46°38'N | 13°50'E |
| Villacidro, Italy (vē-lä-chē'drō) | 174 | 39°28'N | 8°41'E |
| Villa Clara, prov., Cuba | 134 | 22°40'N | 80°10'W |
| Villa Constitución, Arg. (kōn-stē-tōō-syōn') | 141c | 33°15'S | 60°19'W |
| Villa Coronado, Mex. (kō-rō-nä'dhō) | 122 | 26°45'N | 105°10'W |
| Villa Cuauhtémoc, Mex. (vēl'yä-kōō-äò-tē'mōk) | 131 | 22°11'N | 97°50'W |
| Villa de Allende, Mex. (vēl'yä'dā äl-yĕn'då) | 122 | 25°18'N | 100°01'W |
| Villa de Alvarez, Mex. (vēl'yä-dĕ-ä'l-vä-rĕz) | 130 | 19°17'N | 103°44'W |
| Villa de Cura, Ven. (dĕ-kōō'rä) | 143b | 10°03'N | 67°29'W |
| Villa de Guadalupe, Mex. (dĕ-gwä-dhä-lōō'på) | 130 | 23°22'N | 100°44'W |
| Villa de Mayo, Arg. | 144a | 34°31'S | 58°41'W |
| Villa Dolores, Arg. (vēl'yä dō-lō'räs) | 144 | 31°50'S | 65°05'W |
| Villa Escalante, Mex. (vēl'yä-ĕs-kä-lán'tĕ) | 130 | 19°24'N | 101°36'W |
| Villa Flores, Mex. (vēl'yä-flō'räs) | 131 | 16°13'N | 93°17'W |
| Villafranca, Italy (vēl-lä-fräŋ'kä) | 174 | 45°22'N | 10°53'E |
| Villafranca del Bierzo, Spain | 172 | 42°37'N | 6°49'W |
| Villafranca de los Barros, Spain | 172 | 38°34'N | 6°22'W |
| Villafranche-de-Rouergue, Fr. (dĕ-rōō-ĕrg') | 170 | 44°21'N | 2°02'E |
| Villa García, Mex. (gär-sē'ä) | 130 | 22°07'N | 101°55'W |
| Villagarcía, Spain | 172 | 42°38'N | 8°43'W |
| Villagrán, Mex. | 122 | 24°28'N | 99°30'W |
| Villa Grove, Il., U.S. (vĭl'à grōv') | 108 | 39°55'N | 88°15'W |
| Villaguay, Arg. (vē'l-yä-gwī) | 144 | 31°47'S | 58°53'W |
| Villa Hayes, Para. (vēl'yä äyås)(hāz) | 144 | 25°07'S | 57°31'W |
| Villahermosa, Mex. (vēl'yä-ĕr-mō'sä) | 128 | 17°59'N | 92°56'W |
| Villa Hidalgo, Mex. (vēl'yäē-däl'gō) | 130 | 21°39'N | 102°41'W |
| Villaldama, Mex. (vēl-yäl-dä'mä) | 128 | 26°30'N | 100°26'W |
| Villa Lopez, Mex. (vēl'yä lō'pēz) | 122 | 27°00'N | 105°02'W |
| Villalpando, Spain (vēl-yäl-pän'dō) | 172 | 41°54'N | 5°24'W |
| Villa María, Arg. (vē'l-yä-mä-rē'ä) | 144 | 32°17'S | 63°08'W |
| Villamatín, Spain (vēl-yä-mä-tē'n) | 172 | 36°50'N | 5°38'W |
| Villa Mercedes, Arg. (mĕr-sā'dås) | 144 | 33°38'S | 65°16'W |
| Villa Montes, Bol. (vē'l-yä-mô'n-tēs) | 142 | 21°13'S | 63°26'W |
| Villa Morelos, Mex. (mô-rĕ'lomcs) | 130 | 20°01'N | 101°24'W |
| Villanueva, Col. (vē'l-yä-nòĕ'vä) | 142 | 10°44'N | 73°08'W |
| Villanueva, Hond. (vēl'yä-nwā'vä) | 132 | 15°19'N | 88°02'W |
| Villanueva, Mex. (vēl'yä-nòĕ'vä) | 130 | 22°25'N | 102°53'W |
| Villanueva de Córdoba, Spain (vēl-yä-nwĕ'vä-dā kôr'dò-bä) | 172 | 38°18'N | 4°38'W |
| Villanueva de la Serena, Spain (lä sā-rā'nä) | 172 | 38°59'N | 5°56'W |
| Villa Obregón, Mex. (vē'l-yä-ô-brĕ-gô'n) | 131a | 19°21'N | 99°11'W |
| Villa Ocampo, Mex. (ô-käm'pō) | 122 | 26°26'N | 105°30'W |
| Villa Pedro Montoya, Mex. (vēl'yä-pĕ'drô-môn-tô'yá) | 130 | 21°38'N | 99°51'W |
| Villard-Bonnot, Fr. (vēl-yär'bôn-nô') | 171 | 45°15'N | 5°53'E |
| Villarrica, Para. (vēl-yä-rē'kä) | 144 | 25°55'S | 56°23'W |
| Villarrobledo, Spain (vēl-yär-rō-blā'dhō) | 162 | 39°15'N | 2°37'W |
| Villa Unión, Mex. (vēl'yä-ōō-nyōn') | 130 | 23°10'N | 106°14'W |
| Villavicencio, Col. (vē'l-yä-vē-sĕ'n-syō) | 142 | 4°09'N | 73°38'W |
| Villaviciosa de Odón, Spain | 173a | 40°22'N | 3°38'W |
| Villavieja, Col. (vē'l-yä-vē-ĕ'кá) | 142a | 3°13'N | 75°13'W |
| Villazón, Bol. (vē'l-yä-zō'n) | 142 | 22°02'S | 65°42'W |
| Villefranche, Fr. | 161 | 45°59'N | 4°43'E |
| Villejuif, Fr. (vēl'zhüst') | 171b | 48°48'N | 2°22'E |
| Ville-Marie, Can. | 91 | 47°18'N | 79°22'W |
| Villena, Spain (vē-lyā'nä) | 162 | 38°37'N | 0°52'W |
| Villeneuve, Can. (vēl'nûv') | 102g | 53°40'N | 113°49'W |
| Villeneuve-Saint Georges, Fr. (săɴ-zhôrzh') | 171b | 48°43'N | 2°27'E |
| Villeneuve-sur-Lot, Fr. (sür-lō') | 170 | 44°25'N | 0°41'E |
| Ville Platte, La., U.S. (vēl plát') | 123 | 30°41'N | 92°17'W |
| Villers Cotterêts, Fr. (vē-ār'kô-trā') | 171b | 49°15'N | 3°05'E |
| Villerupt, Fr. (vēl'rüp') | 171 | 49°28'N | 6°16'E |
| Ville-Saint Georges, Can. (vĭl-sĕɴ-zhôrzh') | 99 | 46°07'N | 70°40'W |
| Villeta, Col. (vē'l-yĕ'tá) | 142a | 5°02'N | 74°29'W |
| Villeurbanne, Fr. (vēl-ûr-bän') | 161 | 45°43'N | 4°55'E |
| Villiers, S. Afr. (vĭl'ĭ-ērs) | 238c | 27°03'S | 28°38'E |
| Villingen-Schwenningen, Ger. | 168 | 48°04'N | 8°33'E |
| Villisca, Ia., U.S. (vĭ'lĭs'kà) | 113 | 40°56'N | 94°56'W |
| Villupuram, India | 203 | 11°59'N | 79°33'E |
| Vilnius, Lith. (vĭl'nē-ōs) | 178 | 54°40'N | 25°26'E |
| Vilppula, Fin. (vĭl'pū-lá) | 167 | 62°01'N | 24°24'E |
| Vil'shanka, Ukr. | 177 | 48°14'N | 30°52'E |
| Vil'shany, Ukr. | 177 | 50°02'N | 35°54'E |
| Vilvoorde, Bel. | 159a | 50°56'N | 4°25'E |
| Vilyuy, r., Russia (vēl'yĭ) | 179 | 63°00'N | 121°00'E |
| Vilyuysk, Russia (vē-lyōō'ĭsk') | 179 | 63°41'N | 121°47'E |
| Vimmerby, Swe. (vĭm'ĕr-bü) | 166 | 57°41'N | 15°51'E |
| Vimperk, Czech Rep. (vĭm-pĕrk') | 168 | 49°04'N | 13°41'E |
| Viña del Mar, Chile (vē'nyä dĕl mär') | 144 | 33°00'S | 71°33'W |
| Vinalhaven, Me., U.S. (vī-năl-hā'vĕn) | 100 | 44°03'N | 68°49'W |
| Vinaròs, Spain | 173 | 40°29'N | 0°27'E |
| Vincennes, Fr. (văɴ-sĕn') | 171b | 48°51'N | 2°27'E |
| Vincennes, In., U.S. (vĭn-zĕnz') | 105 | 38°40'N | 87°30'W |
| Vincent, Al., U.S. (vĭn'sĕnt) | 124 | 33°21'N | 86°25'W |
| Vindelälven, r., Swe. | 160 | 65°02'N | 18°30'E |
| Vindeln, Swe. (vĭn'dĕln) | 160 | 64°10'N | 19°52'E |
| Vindhya Range, mts., India (vĭnd'yä) | 199 | 22°30'N | 75°50'E |
| Vineland, N.J., U.S. (vīn'lănd) | 109 | 39°30'N | 75°00'W |
| Vinh, Viet. (vĕn'y') | 212 | 18°38'N | 105°42'E |
| Vinhais, Port. (vēn-yä'ēzh) | 172 | 41°51'N | 7°00'W |
| Vinings, Ga., U.S. (vī'nĭngz) | 110c | 33°52'N | 84°28'W |
| Vinita, Ok., U.S. (vĭ-nē'tà) | 121 | 36°38'N | 95°09'W |
| Vinkovci, Cro. (vēn'kôv-tsē) | 175 | 45°17'N | 18°47'E |
| Vinnytsia, Ukr. | 178 | 49°13'N | 28°31'E |
| Vinnytsya, prov., Ukr. | 177 | 48°45'N | 28°01'E |
| Vinogradovo, Russia (vĭ-nô-grä'do-vô) | 186b | 55°25'N | 38°33'E |
| Vinson Massif, mtn., Ant. | 224 | 77°40'S | 87°00'W |
| Vinton, Ia., U.S. (vĭn'tŭn) | 113 | 42°08'N | 92°01'W |
| Vinton, La., U.S. | 123 | 30°12'N | 93°35'W |
| Violet, La., U.S. (vī'ō-lĕt) | 110d | 29°54'N | 89°54'W |
| Virac, Phil. (vē-räk') | 209 | 13°38'N | 124°20'E |
| Virbalis, Lith. (vēr'bá-lēs) | 167 | 54°38'N | 22°55'E |
| Virden, Can. (vûr'dĕn) | 90 | 49°51'N | 101°55'W |
| Virden, Il., U.S. | 121 | 39°28'N | 89°46'W |
| Virgin, r., U.S. | 119 | 36°51'N | 113°50'W |
| Virginia, S. Afr. | 238c | 28°07'S | 26°54'E |
| Virginia, Mn., U.S. (vĕr-jĭn'yà) | 105 | 47°32'N | 92°36'W |
| Virginia, state, U.S. | 105 | 37°00'N | 80°45'W |
| Virginia Beach, Va., U.S. | 109 | 36°50'N | 75°58'W |
| Virginia City, Nv., U.S. | 118 | 39°18'N | 119°40'W |
| Virgin Islands, is., N.A. (vûr'jĭn) | 129 | 18°15'N | 64°00'W |
| Viroqua, Wi., U.S. (vĭ-rō'kwà) | 113 | 43°33'N | 90°54'W |
| Virovitica, Cro. (vē-rô-vē'tē-tsá) | 175 | 45°50'N | 17°24'E |
| Virpazar, Serb. (vēr'pä-zär') | 175 | 42°16'N | 19°06'E |
| Virrat, Fin. (vĭr'ät) | 167 | 62°15'N | 23°45'E |
| Virserum, Swe. (vĭr'sĕ-ròm) | 166 | 57°22'N | 15°35'E |
| Vis, Cro. (vēs) | 174 | 43°03'N | 16°11'E |
| Vis, i., Serb. | 163 | 43°00'N | 16°10'E |
| Visalia, Ca., U.S. (vĭ-sā'lĭ-à) | 118 | 36°20'N | 119°18'W |
| Visby, Swe. (vĭs'bü) | 154 | 57°39'N | 18°19'E |
| Viscount Melville Sound, strt., Can. | 89 | 74°00'N | 110°00'W |
| Višegrad, Bos. (vē'shĕ-gräd) | 175 | 43°48'N | 19°17'E |
| Vishākhapatnam, India | 199 | 17°48'N | 83°21'E |
| Vishera, r., Russia (vĭ'shĕ-rá) | 186a | 60°40'N | 58°46'E |
| Vishnyakovo, Russia | 186b | 55°44'N | 38°10'E |
| Vishoek, S. Afr. | 232a | 34°13'S | 18°26'E |
| Visim, Russia (vē'sĭm) | 186a | 57°38'N | 59°32'E |
| Viskan, r., Swe. | 166 | 57°20'N | 12°25'E |
| Viški, Lat. (vēs'kĭ) | 167 | 56°02'N | 26°47'E |
| Visoko, Bos. (vē'sô-kô) | 175 | 43°59'N | 18°10'E |
| Vistula see Wisła, r., Pol. | 156 | 52°30'N | 20°00'E |
| Vitebsk, prov., Bela. | 176 | 55°05'N | 29°18'E |
| Viterbo, Italy (vē-tĕr'bō) | 162 | 42°24'N | 12°08'E |
| Viti Levu, i., Fiji | 214g | 18°00'S | 178°00'E |
| Vitim, Russia (vē'tĕm) | 179 | 59°22'N | 112°43'E |
| Vitim, r., Russia (vē'tĕm) | 179 | 54°00'N | 115°00'E |
| Vitino, Russia (vē'tĭ-nô) | 186c | 59°40'N | 29°51'E |
| Vitória, Braz. (vē-tō'rē-ä) | 143 | 20°09'S | 40°17'W |
| Vitoria, Spain (vē-tô-ryä) | 162 | 42°43'N | 2°43'W |

364 Vitória de Conquista – Wanzhi PRONOUNCING INDEX


| PLACE (Pronunciation) | PAGE | LAT. | LONG. |
|---|---|---|---|
| Vitória de Conquista, Braz. (vē-tô'rē-ä-dä-kōn-kwē's-tä) | 143 | 14°51'S | 40°44'W |
| Vitry-le-François, Fr. (vē-trē'lĕ-fräN-swà') | 170 | 48°44'N | 4°34'E |
| Vitsyebsk, Bela. (vē'tyĕpsk) | 180 | 55°12'N | 30°16'E |
| Vittorio, Italy (vē-tô'rē-ō) | 174 | 45°59'N | 12°17'E |
| Viveiro, Spain | 172 | 43°39'N | 7°37'W |
| Vivian, La., U.S. (vĭv'ĭ-ăn) | 123 | 32°51'N | 93°59'W |
| Vizianagaram, India | 199 | 18°10'N | 83°29'E |
| Vlaardingen, Neth. (vlär'dĭng-ĕn) | 165 | 51°54'N | 4°20'E |
| Vladikavkaz, Russia | 181 | 43°05'N | 44°35'E |
| Vladimir, Russia (vlà-dyē'mēr) | 178 | 56°08'N | 40°24'E |
| Vladimir, prov., Russia (vlä-dyē'mēr) | 176 | 56°08'N | 39°53'E |
| Vladimiro-Aleksandrovskoye, Russia | 210 | 42°50'N | 133°00'E |
| Vladivostok, Russia (vlà-dē-vôs-tŏk') | 179 | 43°06'N | 131°47'E |
| Vlasenica, Bos. (vlä'sĕ-nēt'sà) | 175 | 44°11'N | 18°58'E |
| Vlasotince, Serb. (vlä'sô-tēn-tsĕ) | 175 | 42°58'N | 22°08'E |
| Vlieland, i., Neth. (vlē'länt) | 165 | 53°19'N | 4°55'E |
| Vlissingen, Neth. (vlĭs'sĭng-ĕn) | 165 | 51°30'N | 3°34'E |
| Vlorë, Alb. | 163 | 40°27'N | 19°30'E |
| Vltava, r., Czech Rep. | 168 | 49°24'N | 14°18'E |
| Vodl, l., Russia (vôd''l) | 180 | 62°20'N | 37°20'E |
| Voerde, Ger. | 171c | 51°35'N | 6°41'E |
| Voghera, Italy (vô-gā'rä) | 174 | 44°58'N | 9°02'E |
| Voight, r., Wa., U.S. | 116a | 47°03'N | 122°08'W |
| Voinjama, Lib. | 234 | 8°25'N | 9°45'W |
| Voiron, Fr. (vwà-rôN') | 171 | 45°23'N | 5°48'E |
| Voisin, Lac, l., Can. (vwŏ'-zĭn) | 96 | 54°13'N | 107°15'W |
| Volchansk, Ukr. (vôl-chänsk') | 181 | 50°18'N | 36°56'E |
| Volga, r., Russia (vôl'gä) | 178 | 47°30'N | 46°20'E |
| Volga, Mouths of the, mth. | 181 | 46°00'N | 49°10'E |
| Volgograd, Russia (vŏl-gō-grä't) | 178 | 48°40'N | 42°20'E |
| Volgogradskoye, res., Russia (vôl-gô-grad'skô-yĕ) | 178 | 51°10'N | 45°10'E |
| Volkhov, Russia (vôl'kôf) | 167 | 59°54'N | 32°21'E |
| Volkhov, r., Russia | 180 | 58°45'N | 31°40'E |
| Volodarskiy, Russia (vô-lô-där'skĭ) | 186c | 59°49'N | 30°06'E |
| Volodymyr-Volyns'kyi, Ukr. | 169 | 50°50'N | 24°20'E |
| Vologda, Russia (vô'lôg-dà) | 178 | 59°12'N | 39°52'E |
| Vologda, prov., Russia | 176 | 59°00'N | 37°26'E |
| Volokolamsk, Russia (vô-lô-kôlamsk) | 176 | 56°02'N | 35°58'E |
| Volokonovka, Russia (vô-lô-kô'nôf-kà) | 177 | 50°28'N | 37°52'E |
| Vol'sk, Russia (vôl'sk) | 181 | 52°02'N | 47°23'E |
| Volta, r., Ghana | 234 | 6°05'N | 0°30'E |
| Volta, Lake, res., Ghana (vôl'tà) | 230 | 7°10'N | 0°30'W |
| Volta Blanche (White Volta), r., Afr. | 234 | 11°30'N | 0°40'W |
| Volta Noire *see* Black Volta, r., Afr. | 230 | 11°30'N | 4°00'W |
| Volta Redonda, Braz. (vōl'tä-rā-dôn'dä) | 143 | 22°32'S | 44°05'W |
| Volterra, Italy (vôl-tĕr'rä) | 174 | 43°22'N | 10°51'E |
| Voltri, Italy (vōl'trē) | 174 | 44°25'N | 8°45'E |
| Volturno, r., Italy (vôl-tōōr'nô) | 174 | 41°12'N | 14°20'E |
| Vólvi, Límni, l., Grc. | 175 | 40°41'N | 23°23'E |
| Volzhskoye, l., Russia (vôl'sh-skô-yĕ) | 176 | 56°43'N | 36°18'E |
| Von Ormy, Tx., U.S. (vŏn ôr'mē) | 117d | 29°18'N | 98°36'W |
| Vööpsu, Est. (vōōp'sò) | 167 | 58°06'N | 27°30'E |
| Voorburg, Neth. | 159a | 52°04'N | 4°21'E |
| Voortrekkerhoogte, S. Afr. | 233b | 25°48'S | 28°10'E |
| Vop', r., Russia (vôp) | 176 | 55°20'N | 32°55'E |
| Vopnafjördur, Ice. | 160 | 65°43'N | 14°58'W |
| Vordingborg, Den. (vôr'dĭng-bôr) | 166 | 55°10'N | 11°55'E |
| Vóreioi Sporades, is., Grc. | 175 | 38°55'N | 24°05'E |
| Vóreios Evvoïkós Kólpos, b., Grc. | 175 | 38°48'N | 23°02'E |
| Vorkuta, Russia (vôr-kōō'tà) | 178 | 67°28'N | 63°40'E |
| Vormsi, i., Est. (vôrm'sĭ) | 167 | 59°06'N | 23°05'E |
| Vorona, r., Russia (vô-rô'na) | 181 | 51°50'N | 42°00'E |
| Voronava, Bela. | 169 | 54°07'N | 25°16'E |
| Voronezh, Russia (vô-rô'nyĕzh) | 178 | 51°39'N | 39°11'E |
| Voronezh, prov., Russia | 177 | 51°10'N | 39°13'E |
| Voronezh, r., Russia | 181 | 52°17'N | 39°32'E |
| Vorontsovka, Russia (vô-rônt'sôv-kà) | 186a | 59°40'N | 60°14'E |
| Voron'ya, r., Russia (vô-rônyà) | 180 | 68°20'N | 35°20'E |
| Võrts-Järv, l., Est. (vôrts yärv) | 167 | 58°15'N | 26°12'E |
| Võru, Est. (vô'rû) | 180 | 57°50'N | 26°58'E |
| Vorya, r., Russia (vôr'yà) | 186b | 55°55'N | 38°15'E |
| Vosges, mts., Fr. (vōzh) | 161 | 48°09'N | 6°57'E |
| Voskresensk, Russia (vôs-krĕ-sĕnsk') | 186b | 55°20'N | 38°42'E |
| Voss, Nor. (vôs) | 160 | 60°40'N | 6°24'E |
| Vostryakovo, Russia | 186b | 55°23'N | 37°49'E |
| Votkinsk, Russia (vôt-kēnsk') | 180 | 57°00'N | 54°00'E |
| Votkinskoye Vodokhranilishche, res., Russia | 180 | 57°30'N | 55°00'E |
| Vouga, r., Port. (vō'gà) | 172 | 40°43'N | 7°51'W |
| Vouziers, Fr. (vōō-zyā') | 170 | 49°25'N | 4°40'E |
| Voxnan, r., Swe. | 166 | 61°30'N | 15°24'E |
| Voyageurs National Park, rec., Mn., U.S. | 113 | 48°30'N | 92°40'W |
| Vozhe, l., Russia (vôzh'yĕ) | 180 | 60°40'N | 39°00'E |
| Voznesens'k, Ukr. | 181 | 47°34'N | 31°22'E |
| Vradiïvka, Ukr. | 177 | 47°51'N | 30°38'E |
| Vrangelya (Wrangel), i., Russia | 178 | 71°25'N | 178°30'W |
| Vranje, Serb. (vrän'yĕ) | 175 | 42°33'N | 21°55'E |
| Vratsa, Blg. (vrät'sà) | 163 | 43°12'N | 23°31'E |
| Vrbas, Serb. (v'r'bäs) | 175 | 45°34'N | 19°43'E |
| Vrbas, r., Serb. | 175 | 44°25'N | 17°17'E |
| Vrchlabi, Czech Rep. (v'r'chlä-bē) | 168 | 50°32'N | 15°51'E |
| Vrede, S. Afr. (vrĭ'dĕ)(vrēd) | 238c | 27°25'S | 29°11'E |
| Vredefort, S. Afr. (vrĭ'dĕ-fôrt)(vrĕd'fōrt) | 238c | 27°00'S | 27°21'E |
| Vreeswijk, Neth. | 159a | 52°00'N | 5°06'E |
| Vršac, Serb. (v'r'shàts) | 163 | 45°08'N | 21°18'E |
| Vrutky, Slvk. (vrōōt'kē) | 169 | 49°09'N | 18°55'E |
| Vryburg, S. Afr. (vrī'bûrg) | 232 | 26°55'S | 24°45'E |
| Vryheid, S. Afr. (vrī'hīt) | 232 | 27°43'S | 30°58'E |
| Vsetín, Czech Rep. (fsĕt'yēn) | 169 | 49°21'N | 18°01'E |
| Vsevolozhskiy, Russia (vsyĕ'vôlô'zh-skĕĕ) | 186c | 60°01'N | 30°41'E |
| Vuelta Abajo, reg., Cuba (vwĕl'tä ä-bä'hō) | 134 | 22°20'N | 83°45'W |
| Vught, Neth. | 159a | 51°38'N | 5°18'E |
| Vukovar, Cro. (vŏ'kô-vär) | 175 | 45°20'N | 19°00'E |
| Vulcan, Mi., U.S. (vŭl'kăn) | 108 | 45°45'N | 87°50'W |
| Vulcano, i., Italy (vōōl-kä'nô) | 174 | 38°23'N | 15°00'E |
| Vülchedrŭma, Blg. | 175 | 43°43'N | 23°29'E |
| Vuntut National Park, rec., Can. | 92 | 68°27'N | 139°58'W |
| Vyartsilya, Russia (vyàr-tsē'lyà) | 167 | 62°10'N | 30°40'E |
| Vyatka, r., Russia (vyàt'kà) | 180 | 59°20'N | 51°25'E |
| Vyazemskiy, Russia (vyà-zĕm'skĭ) | 210 | 47°29'N | 134°39'E |
| Vyaz'ma, Russia (vyàz'mà) | 180 | 55°12'N | 34°17'E |
| Vyazniki, Russia (vyàz'nē-kē) | 180 | 56°10'N | 42°10'E |
| Vyborg, Russia (vwē'bôrk) | 178 | 60°43'N | 28°46'E |
| Vychegda, r., Russia (vē'chĕg-dà) | 180 | 61°40'N | 48°00'E |
| Vyerkhnyadzvinsk, Bela. | 176 | 55°48'N | 27°59'E |
| Vyetka, Bela. (vyĕt'kà) | 176 | 52°36'N | 31°05'E |
| Vylkove, Ukr. | 181 | 45°24'N | 29°36'E |
| Vym, r., Russia (vwēm) | 180 | 63°15'N | 51°20'E |
| Vyritsa, Russia (vē'rĭ-tsà) | 186c | 59°24'N | 30°20'E |
| Vyshnevolotskoye, l., Russia (vŭy'sh-ŋĕ'vôlôt's-kô'yĕ) | 176 | 57°30'N | 34°27'E |
| Vyshniy Volochëk, Russia (vĕsh'nyĭ vôl-ô-chĕk') | 178 | 57°34'N | 34°35'E |
| Vyškov, Czech Rep. (vĕsh'kôf) | 168 | 49°17'N | 16°58'E |
| Vysoké Mýto, Czech Rep. (vû'sô-kā mû'tô) | 168 | 49°58'N | 16°07'E |
| Vysokovsk, Russia (vĭ-sô'kôfsk) | 176 | 56°16'N | 36°32'E |
| Vytegra, Russia (vû'tĕg-rà) | 178 | 61°00'N | 36°20'E |
| Vyzhnytsia, Ukr. | 169 | 48°16'N | 25°12'E |


# W


| PLACE (Pronunciation) | PAGE | LAT. | LONG. |
|---|---|---|---|
| W, Parcs Nationaux du, rec., Niger | 235 | 12°20'N | 2°40'E |
| Waal, r., Neth. (väl) | 165 | 51°46'N | 5°00'E |
| Waalwijk, Neth. | 159a | 51°41'N | 5°05'E |
| Wabamun, Grc. | 163 | 39°23'N | 22°56'E |
| Wabamuno, Can. (wŏ'bă-mŭn) | 95 | 53°33'N | 114°28'W |
| Wabasca, Can. (wŏ-bás'kă) | 95 | 56°00'N | 113°53'W |
| Wabash, In., U.S. (wô'băsh) | 108 | 40°45'N | 85°50'W |
| Wabash, r., U.S. | 107 | 38°00'N | 88°00'W |
| Wabasha, Mn., U.S. (wä'bà-shô) | 113 | 44°24'N | 92°04'W |
| Wabe Gestro, r., Eth. | 231 | 6°25'N | 41°21'E |
| Wabowden, Can. (wă-bō'd'n) | 97 | 54°55'N | 98°38'W |
| Wąbrzeźno, Pol. (vôŋ-bzĕzh'nô) | 169 | 53°17'N | 18°59'E |
| Wabu Hu, l., China (wä-bōō hōō) | 206 | 32°25'N | 116°35'E |
| W. A. C. Bennett Dam, dam, Can. | 95 | 56°01'N | 122°10'W |
| Waccamaw, r., S.C., U.S. (wăk'à-mô) | 125 | 33°47'N | 78°55'W |
| Waccasassa Bay, b., Fl., U.S. (wă-kà-să'sà) | 124 | 29°02'N | 83°10'W |
| Wachow, Ger. (vä'kōv) | 159b | 53°32'N | 12°46'E |
| Waco, Tx., U.S. (wā'kō) | 104 | 31°35'N | 97°06'W |
| Waconda Lake, res., Ks., U.S. | 120 | 39°45'N | 98°15'W |
| Wadayama, Japan (wä'dä'yä-mä) | 211 | 35°19'N | 134°49'E |
| Waddenzee, sea, Neth. | 165 | 53°00'N | 4°50'E |
| Waddington, Mount, mtn., Can. (wŏd'dĭng-tŭn) | 92 | 51°23'N | 125°15'W |
| Wadena, Can. | 96 | 51°57'N | 103°50'W |
| Wadena, Mn., U.S. (wŏ-dē'nà) | 112 | 46°26'N | 95°09'W |
| Wadesboro, N.C., U.S. (wādz'bŭr-ô) | 125 | 34°57'N | 80°05'W |
| Wadley, Ga., U.S. (wŭd'lē) | 125 | 32°54'N | 82°25'W |
| Wad Madani, Sudan (wäd mē-dä'nē) | 231 | 14°27'N | 33°31'E |
| Wadowice, Pol. (và-dô'vēt-sĕ) | 169 | 49°53'N | 19°31'E |
| Wadsworth, Oh., U.S. (wŏdz'wûrth) | 111d | 41°01'N | 81°44'W |
| Wager Bay, b., Can. (wā'jĕr) | 93 | 65°48'N | 88°19'W |
| Wagga Wagga, Austl. (wôg'à wôg'ă) | 219 | 35°10'S | 147°30'E |
| Wagoner, Ok., U.S. (wăg'ŭn-ēr) | 121 | 35°58'N | 95°22'W |
| Wagon Mound, N.M., U.S. (wăg'ŭn mound) | 120 | 35°59'N | 104°45'W |
| Wągrowiec, Pol. (vôŋ-grô'vyĕts) | 169 | 52°47'N | 17°14'E |
| Waha, Libya | 200 | 28°16'N | 19°54'E |
| Wahiawā, Hi., U.S. | 106d | 21°30'N | 158°03'W |
| Wahoo, Ne., U.S. (wä-hōō') | 112 | 41°14'N | 96°39'W |
| Wahpeton, N.D., U.S. (wô'pē-tŭn) | 112 | 46°17'N | 96°38'W |
| Waialua, Hi., U.S. (wä'ē-ä-lōō'ä) | 126a | 21°33'N | 158°08'W |
| Wai'anae, Hi., U.S. (wä'ē-à-nä'ā) | 126a | 21°25'N | 158°11'W |
| Waidhofen, Aus. (vīd'hôf-ĕn) | 168 | 47°58'N | 14°46'E |
| Waigeo, Pulau, i., Indon. (wä-ē-gā'ô) | 213 | 0°07'N | 131°00'E |
| Waikato, r., N.Z. (wä'ē-kä'to) | 221a | 38°10'S | 175°35'E |
| Waikerie, Austl. (wā'kēr-ē) | 222 | 34°15'S | 140°00'E |
| Wailuku, Hi., U.S. (wä'ē-lōō'kōō) | 106c | 20°55'N | 156°30'W |
| Waimānalo, Hi., U.S. (wä-ē-mä'nä-lo) | 126a | 21°19'N | 157°43'W |
| Waimea, Hi., U.S. (wä-ē-mā'ä) | 126a | 21°56'N | 159°38'W |
| Wainganga, r., India (wä-ēn-gŭŋ'gä) | 199 | 20°30'N | 80°15'E |
| Waingapu, Indon. | 212 | 9°32'S | 120°00'E |
| Wainwright, Can. | 90 | 52°49'N | 110°52'W |
| Wainwright, Ak., U.S. (wān-rīt) | 103 | 74°40'N | 159°00'W |
| Waipahu, Hi., U.S. (wä'ē-pä'hōō) | 106d | 21°20'N | 158°02'W |
| Waiska, r., Mi., U.S. (wà-ĭz-kà) | 117k | 46°20'N | 84°38'W |
| Waitsburg, Wa., U.S. (wāts'bûrg) | 114 | 46°17'N | 118°08'W |
| Wajima, Japan (wä'jē-mà) | 211 | 37°23'N | 136°56'E |
| Wajir, Kenya | 237 | 1°45'N | 40°04'E |
| Wakami, r., Can. | 98 | 47°43'N | 82°22'W |
| Wakasa-Wan, b., Japan (wä'kä-sä wän) | 210 | 35°43'N | 135°39'E |
| Wakatipu, l., N.Z. (wä-kä-tē'pōō) | 221a | 45°04'S | 168°30'E |
| Wakayama, Japan (wä-kä'yä-mä) | 205 | 34°14'N | 135°11'E |
| Wake, i., Oc. (wāk) | 3 | 19°25'N | 167°00'E |
| Wa Keeney, Ks., U.S. (wô-kē'nē) | 120 | 39°01'N | 99°53'W |
| Wakefield, Can. (wāk-fēld) | 102c | 45°39'N | 75°55'W |
| Wakefield, Eng., U.K. | 164 | 53°41'N | 1°25'W |
| Wakefield, Ma., U.S. | 101a | 42°31'N | 71°05'W |
| Wakefield, Mi., U.S. | 113 | 46°28'N | 89°55'W |
| Wakefield, Ne., U.S. | 112 | 42°15'N | 96°52'W |
| Wakefield, R.I., U.S. | 110b | 41°26'N | 71°30'W |
| Wakefield, co., Eng., U.K. | 158a | 53°12'N | 1°25'W |
| Wake Forest, N.C., U.S. (wāk fŏr'ĕst) | 125 | 35°58'N | 78°31'W |
| Waki, Japan (wä'kē) | 211 | 34°05'N | 134°10'E |
| Wakkanai, Japan (wä'kä-nä'ē) | 205 | 45°19'N | 141°43'E |
| Wakkerstroom, S. Afr. (vák'ēr-strōm)(wăk'ēr-strōōm) | 232 | 27°19'S | 30°04'E |
| Wakonassin, r., Can. | 98 | 46°35'N | 82°10'W |
| Waku Kundo, Ang. | 232 | 11°25'S | 15°07'E |
| Wałbrzych, Pol. (väl'bzhûk) | 168 | 50°46'N | 16°16'E |
| Walcott, Lake, res., Id., U.S. | 115 | 42°40'N | 113°23'W |
| Wałcz, Pol. (välch) | 168 | 53°11'N | 16°30'E |
| Waldoboro, Me., U.S. (wôl'dô-bŭr-ô) | 100 | 44°06'N | 69°22'W |
| Waldo Lake, l., Or., U.S. (wôl'dō) | 114 | 43°46'N | 122°10'W |
| Waldorf, Md., U.S. (wăl'dŏrf) | 110e | 38°37'N | 76°57'W |
| Waldron, Mo., U.S. | 117f | 39°14'N | 94°47'W |
| Waldron, i., Wa., U.S. | 116d | 48°42'N | 123°02'W |
| Wales, Ak., U.S. (wālz) | 103 | 65°35'N | 168°14'W |
| Wales, state, U.K. | 154 | 52°12'N | 3°40'W |
| Walewale, Ghana | 234 | 10°21'N | 0°48'W |
| Walgett, Austl. (wôl'gĕt) | 219 | 30°00'S | 148°10'E |
| Walhalla, S.C., U.S. (wŭl-hăl'à) | 124 | 34°45'N | 83°04'W |
| Walikale, D.R.C. | 237 | 1°25'S | 28°03'E |
| Walkden, Eng., U.K. | 158a | 53°32'N | 2°24'W |
| Walker, Mn., U.S. (wôk'ēr) | 113 | 47°06'N | 94°37'W |
| Walker, r., Nv., U.S. | 118 | 39°07'N | 119°10'W |
| Walker, Mount, mtn., Wa., U.S. | 116a | 47°47'N | 122°54'W |
| Walker Lake, l., Can. | 97 | 54°42'N | 96°57'W |
| Walker Lake, l., Nv., U.S. | 118 | 38°46'N | 118°30'W |
| Walker River Indian Reservation, I.R., Nv., U.S. | 118 | 39°06'N | 118°20'W |
| Walkerville, Mt., U.S. (wôk'ēr-vĭl) | 115 | 46°20'N | 112°32'W |
| Wallace, Id., U.S. (wŏl'ās) | 114 | 47°27'N | 115°55'W |
| Wallaceburg, Can. | 98 | 42°39'N | 82°25'W |
| Wallacia, Austl. | 217b | 33°52'S | 150°40'E |
| Wallaroo, Austl. (wŏl-à-rōō) | 218 | 33°52'S | 137°45'E |
| Wallasey, Eng., U.K. (wŏl'à-sē) | 158a | 53°25'N | 3°03'W |
| Walla Walla, Wa., U.S. (wŏl'à wŏl'à) | 104 | 46°03'N | 118°20'W |
| Walled Lake, Mi., U.S. (wôl'd lāk) | 111b | 42°32'N | 83°29'W |
| Wallel, Tulu, mtn., Eth. | 231 | 9°00'N | 34°52'E |
| Wallingford, Eng., U.K. (wŏl'ĭng-fērd) | 158b | 51°34'N | 1°08'W |
| Wallingford, Vt., U.S. | 109 | 43°30'N | 72°55'W |
| Wallis and Futuna Islands, dep., Oc. | 241 | 13°00'S | 176°10'E |
| Wallisville, Tx., U.S. (wŏl'ĭs-vĭl) | 123a | 29°50'N | 94°44'W |
| Wallowa, Or., U.S. (wôl'ô-wà) | 114 | 45°34'N | 117°32'W |
| Wallowa, r., Or., U.S. | 114 | 45°28'N | 117°28'W |
| Wallowa Mountains, mts., Or., U.S. | 114 | 45°10'N | 117°22'W |
| Wallula, Wa., U.S. | 114 | 46°08'N | 118°55'W |
| Walnut, Ca., U.S. (wôl'nŭt) | 117a | 34°00'N | 117°51'W |
| Walnut, r., Ks., U.S. | 121 | 37°28'N | 97°06'W |
| Walnut Canyon National Mon, rec., Az., U.S. | 119 | 35°10'N | 111°30'W |
| Walnut Creek, Ca., U.S. | 116b | 37°54'N | 122°04'W |
| Walnut Creek, r., Tx., U.S. | 117c | 32°37'N | 97°03'W |
| Walnut Ridge, Ar., U.S. (rĭj) | 121 | 36°04'N | 90°56'W |
| Walpole, Ma., U.S. (wôl'pōl) | 101a | 42°09'N | 71°15'W |
| Walpole, N.H., U.S. | 109 | 43°05'N | 72°25'W |
| Walsall, Eng., U.K. (wôl-sôl) | 164 | 52°35'N | 1°58'W |
| Walsenburg, Co., U.S. (wôl'sĕn-bûrg) | 120 | 37°38'N | 104°46'W |
| Walsum, Ger. | 171c | 51°32'N | 6°41'E |
| Walter F. George Reservoir, res., U.S. | 124 | 32°00'N | 85°00'W |
| Walters, Ok., U.S. (wôl'tērz) | 120 | 34°21'N | 98°19'W |
| Waltham, Ma., U.S. (wôl'thăm) | 101a | 42°22'N | 71°14'W |
| Walthamstow, Eng., U.K. (wôl'tăm-stō) | 158b | 51°34'N | 0°01'W |
| Walton, N.Y., U.S. | 109 | 42°10'N | 75°05'W |
| Walton-le-Dale, Eng., U.K. (lē-dāl') | 158a | 53°44'N | 2°40'W |
| Walvis Bay, Nmb. (wôl'vĭs) | 232 | 22°50'S | 14°30'E |
| Walworth, Wi., U.S. (wôl'wŭrth) | 113 | 42°33'N | 88°39'W |
| Wama, Ang. | 236 | 12°14'S | 15°33'E |
| Wamba, r., D.R.C. | 232 | 7°00'S | 18°00'E |
| Wamego, Ks., U.S. (wŏ-mē'gō) | 121 | 39°13'N | 96°17'W |
| Wami, r., Tan. (wä'mē) | 233 | 6°31'S | 37°17'E |
| Wanapitei Lake, l., Can. | 99 | 46°45'N | 80°45'W |
| Wanaque, N.J., U.S. (wŏn'à-kū) | 110a | 41°03'N | 74°16'W |
| Wanaque Reservoir, res., N.J., U.S. | 110a | 41°06'N | 74°20'W |
| Wanda Shan, mts., China (wän-dä shän) | 205 | 45°54'N | 131°45'E |
| Wandoan, Austl. | 222 | 26°09'S | 149°51'E |
| Wandsbek, Ger. (vänds'bĕk) | 159c | 53°34'N | 10°07'E |
| Wandsworth, Eng., U.K. (wôndz'wûrth) | 158b | 51°26'N | 0°12'W |
| Wanganui, N.Z. (wôŋ'gà-nōō'ē) | 221a | 39°53'S | 175°01'E |
| Wangaratta, Austl. (wŏŋ'gà-răt'à) | 222 | 36°23'S | 146°18'E |
| Wangeroog, i., Ger. (vän'gĕ-rōg) | 168 | 53°49'N | 7°57'E |
| Wangqingtuo, China (wäŋ-chyĭŋ-twŏ) | 206 | 39°14'N | 116°56'E |
| Wangsi, China (wäŋ-sē) | 206 | 37°59'N | 116°57'E |
| Wantage, Eng., U.K. (wŏn'tăj) | 158b | 51°33'N | 1°26'W |
| Wantagh, N.Y., U.S. | 110a | 40°41'N | 73°30'W |
| Wanxian, China (wän shyĕn) | 206 | 38°51'N | 115°10'E |
| Wanxian, China (wän-shyĕn) | 204 | 30°48'N | 108°22'E |
| Wanzai, China (wän-dzī) | 209 | 28°05'N | 114°25'E |
| Wanzhi, China (wän-jr) | 206 | 31°11'N | 118°31'E |


ăt; finăl; rāte; senāte; ärm; àsk; sofà; fâre; ch-choose; dh-as th in other; bē; ēvent; bĕt; recĕnt; cratēr; g-gō; gh-guttural g; bĭt; ĭ-short neutral; rīde; K-guttural k as ch in German ich;

PRONOUNCING INDEX
Wapakoneta – Wessel Islands 365


| PLACE (Pronunciation) | PAGE | LAT. | LONG. |
|---|---|---|---|
| Wapakoneta, Oh., U.S. (wä′på-kô-nĕt′*à*) | 108 | 40°35′N | 84°10′W |
| Wapawekka Hills, hills, Can. (wŏ′pă-wĕ′kă-hĭlz) | 96 | 54°45′N | 104°20′W |
| Wapawekka Lake, l., Can. | 96 | 54°55′N | 104°40′W |
| Wapello, Ia., U.S. (wŏ-pĕl′ō) | 113 | 41°10′N | 91°11′W |
| Wappapello Reservoir, res., Mo., U.S. (wă′på-pĕl-lō) | 107 | 37°07′N | 90°10′W |
| Wappingers Falls, N.Y., U.S. (wŏp′ĭn-jẽrz) | 109 | 41°35′N | 73°55′W |
| Wapsipinicon, r., Ia., U.S. (wŏp′sĭ-pĭn′ĭ-kŏn) | 113 | 42°16′N | 91°35′W |
| Wapusk National Park, rec., Can. | 92 | 58°00′N | 94°15′W |
| Warabi, Japan (wä′rä-bê) | 211a | 35°50′N | 139°41′E |
| Warangal, India (wŭ′räŋ-gål) | 199 | 18°03′N | 79°45′E |
| Warburton, The, r., Austl. (wŏr′bûr-tŭn) | 220 | 27°30′S | 138°45′E |
| Wardān, Wādī, r., Egypt | 197a | 29°22′N | 33°00′E |
| Ward Cove, Ak., U.S. | 94 | 55°24′N | 131°43′W |
| Warden, S. Afr. (wôr′dĕn) | 238c | 27°52′N | 28°59′E |
| Wardha, India (wŭr′dä) | 199 | 20°46′N | 78°42′E |
| War Eagle, W.V., U.S. (wôr ē′g′l) | 108 | 37°30′N | 81°50′W |
| Waren, Ger. (vä′rĕn) | 168 | 53°32′N | 12°43′E |
| Warendorf, Ger. (vä′rĕn-dōrf) | 171c | 51°57′N | 7°59′E |
| Wargla, Alg. | 230 | 32°00′N | 5°18′E |
| Warialda, Austl. | 222 | 29°32′S | 150°34′E |
| Warmbad, Nmb. (värm′bäd) (wôrm′băd) | 232 | 28°25′S | 18°45′E |
| Warmbad, S. Afr. | 238c | 24°52′S | 28°18′E |
| Warm Beach, Wa., U.S. (wôrm) | 116a | 48°10′N | 122°22′W |
| Warm Springs Indian Reservation, I.R., Or., U.S. (wôrm sprĭnz) | 114 | 44°55′N | 121°30′W |
| Warm Springs Reservoir, res., Or., U.S. | 114 | 43°42′N | 118°40′W |
| Warner Mountains, mts., Ca., U.S. | 106 | 41°30′N | 120°17′W |
| Warner Robins, Ga., U.S. | 124 | 32°37′N | 83°36′W |
| Warnow, r., Ger. (vär′nō) | 168 | 53°51′N | 11°55′E |
| Warracknabeal, Austl. | 222 | 36°20′S | 142°28′E |
| Warragamba Reservoir, res., Austl. | 222 | 33°40′S | 150°00′E |
| Warrego, r., Austl. (wôr′ê-gô) | 221 | 27°13′S | 145°58′E |
| Warren, Can. | 102f | 50°08′N | 97°32′W |
| Warren, Ar., U.S. (wŏr′ĕn) | 121 | 33°37′N | 92°03′W |
| Warren, In., U.S. | 108 | 40°40′N | 85°25′W |
| Warren, Mi., U.S. | 111b | 42°33′N | 83°03′W |
| Warren, Mn., U.S. | 112 | 48°11′N | 96°44′W |
| Warren, Oh., U.S. | 108 | 41°15′N | 80°50′W |
| Warren, Or., U.S. | 116c | 45°49′N | 122°51′W |
| Warren, Pa., U.S. | 109 | 41°50′N | 79°10′W |
| Warren, R.I., U.S. | 110b | 41°44′N | 71°14′W |
| Warrendale, Pa., U.S. (wŏr′ĕn-dāl) | 111e | 40°39′N | 80°04′W |
| Warrensburg, Mo., U.S. (wŏr′ĕnz-bûrg) | 121 | 38°45′N | 93°42′W |
| Warrenton, Ga., U.S. (wŏr′ĕn-t*ŭ*n) | 125 | 33°26′N | 82°37′W |
| Warrenton, Or., U.S. | 116c | 46°10′N | 123°56′W |
| Warrenton, Va., U.S. | 109 | 38°45′N | 77°50′W |
| Warri, Nig. (wär′ê) | 230 | 5°33′N | 5°43′E |
| Warrington, Eng., U.K. | 158a | 53°22′N | 2°30′W |
| Warrington, Fl., U.S. (wŏ′ĭng-t*ŭ*n) | 124 | 30°21′N | 87°15′W |
| Warrnambool, Austl. (wôr′n*ă*m-bōōl) | 219 | 38°20′S | 142°28′E |
| Warroad, Mn., U.S. (wôr′rōd) | 112 | 48°55′N | 95°20′W |
| Warrumbungle Range, mts., Austl. (wôr′ŭm-bŭŋ-g′l) | 221 | 31°18′S | 150°00′E |
| Warsaw, Pol. | 154 | 52°15′N | 21°05′E |
| Warsaw, Il., U.S. (wôr′sô) | 121 | 40°21′N | 91°26′W |
| Warsaw, In., U.S. | 108 | 41°15′N | 85°50′W |
| Warsaw, N.Y., U.S. | 109 | 42°45′N | 78°10′W |
| Warsaw, NC, N.C., U.S. | 125 | 35°00′N | 78°07′W |
| Warsop, Eng., U.K. (wôr′s*ŭ*p) | 158a | 53°13′N | 1°05′W |
| Warszawa *see* Warsaw, Pol. | 154 | 52°15′N | 21°05′E |
| Warta, r., Pol. (vär′tå) | 161 | 52°30′N | 16°00′E |
| Wartburg, S. Afr. | 233c | 29°26′S | 30°39′E |
| Warwick, Austl. (wŏr′ĭk) | 219 | 28°05′S | 152°10′E |
| Warwick, Can. | 99 | 45°58′N | 71°57′W |
| Warwick, Eng., U.K. | 164 | 52°19′N | 1°46′W |
| Warwick, N.Y., U.S. | 110a | 41°15′N | 74°22′W |
| Warwick, R.I., U.S. | 109 | 41°42′N | 71°27′W |
| Warwickshire, co., Eng., U.K. | 158a | 52°30′N | 1°35′W |
| Wasatch Mountains, mts., Ut., U.S. (wô′săch) | 117b | 40°45′N | 111°46′W |
| Wasatch Plateau, plat., Ut., U.S. | 119 | 38°55′N | 111°40′W |
| Wasatch Range, mts., U.S. | 106 | 39°10′N | 111°30′W |
| Wasbank, S. Afr. | 233c | 28°27′S | 30°09′E |
| Wasco, Or., U.S. (wäs′kō) | 114 | 45°36′N | 120°42′W |
| Waseca, Mn., U.S. (wô-sē′k*à*) | 113 | 44°04′N | 93°31′W |
| Wash, The, Eng., U.K. (wŏsh) | 160 | 53°00′N | 0°20′E |
| Washburn, Me., U.S. (wŏsh′b*ŭ*rn) | 100 | 46°46′N | 68°10′W |
| Washburn, Wi., U.S. | 113 | 46°41′N | 90°55′W |
| Washburn, Mount, mtn., Wy., U.S. | 115 | 44°55′N | 110°10′W |
| Washington, D.C., U.S. (wŏsh′ĭng-t*ŭ*n) | 105 | 38°50′N | 77°00′W |
| Washington, Ga., U.S. | 125 | 33°43′N | 82°46′W |
| Washington, Ia., U.S. | 113 | 41°17′N | 91°42′W |
| Washington, In., U.S. | 108 | 38°40′N | 87°10′W |
| Washington, Ks., U.S. | 121 | 39°48′N | 97°04′W |
| Washington, Mo., U.S. | 121 | 38°33′N | 91°00′W |
| Washington, N.C., U.S. | 125 | 35°32′N | 77°01′W |
| Washington, Pa., U.S. | 108 | 40°10′N | 80°14′W |
| Washington, state, U.S. | 104 | 47°30′N | 121°10′W |
| Washington, i., Wi., U.S. | 113 | 45°18′N | 86°42′W |
| Washington, Lake, l., Wa., U.S. | 116a | 47°34′N | 122°12′W |
| Washington, Mount, mtn., N.H., U.S. | 107 | 44°15′N | 71°15′W |
| Washington Court House, Oh., U.S. | 108 | 39°30′N | 83°25′W |
| Washington Park, Il., U.S. | 117e | 38°38′N | 90°06′W |
| Washita, r., Ok., U.S. (wŏsh′ĭ-tô) | 120 | 35°33′N | 99°16′W |
| Washougal, Wa., U.S. (wŏ-shōō′gål) | 116c | 45°35′N | 122°21′W |
| Washougal, r., Wa., U.S. | 116c | 45°38′N | 122°17′W |
| Wasilków, Pol. (vå-sēl′kōf) | 169 | 53°12′N | 23°13′E |
| Waskaiowaka Lake, l., Can. (wŏ′skă-yō′wŏ-kă) | 97 | 56°30′N | 96°20′W |
| Wassenberg, Ger. (vä′sĕn-bĕrgh) | 171c | 51°06′N | 6°07′E |
| Wassuk Range, mts., Nv., U.S. (wås′s*ŭ*k) | 118 | 38°58′N | 119°00′W |
| Waswanipi, Lac, l., Can. | 99 | 49°35′N | 76°15′W |
| Water, i., V.I.U.S. (wô′tẽr) | 129c | 18°20′N | 64°57′W |
| Waterberge, mts., S. Afr. (wôrtẽr′bûrg) | 238c | 24°25′S | 27°53′E |
| Waterboro, S.C., U.S. (wô′tẽr-bûr-ō) | 125 | 32°50′N | 80°40′W |
| Waterbury, Ct., U.S. (wô′tẽr-bĕr-ê) | 109 | 41°30′N | 73°00′W |
| Water Cay, i., Bah. | 135 | 22°55′N | 75°50′W |
| Waterdown, Can. (wô′tẽr-doun) | 102d | 43°20′N | 79°54′W |
| Wateree Lake, res., S.C., U.S. (wô′tẽr-ē) | 125 | 34°40′N | 80°48′W |
| Waterford, Ire. (wô′tẽr-fẽrd) | 161 | 52°20′N | 7°03′W |
| Waterford, Wi., U.S. | 111a | 42°46′N | 88°13′W |
| Waterloo, Bel. | 159a | 50°44′N | 4°24′E |
| Waterloo, Can. (wô-tẽr-lōō′) | 99 | 43°30′N | 80°40′W |
| Waterloo, Can. | 99 | 45°25′N | 72°30′W |
| Waterloo, Ia., U.S. | 105 | 42°30′N | 92°22′W |
| Waterloo, Il., U.S. | 121 | 38°19′N | 90°08′W |
| Waterloo, Md., U.S. | 110e | 39°11′N | 76°50′W |
| Waterloo, N.Y., U.S. | 109 | 42°55′N | 76°50′W |
| Waterton-Glacier International Peace Park, rec., N.A. (wô′ter-t*ŭ*n-glā′shûr) | 106 | 48°55′N | 114°10′W |
| Waterton Lakes National Park, rec., Can. | 95 | 49°05′N | 113°50′W |
| Watertown, Ma., U.S. (wô′tẽr-toun) | 101a | 42°22′N | 71°11′W |
| Watertown, N.Y., U.S. | 105 | 44°00′N | 75°55′W |
| Watertown, S.D., U.S. | 104 | 44°53′N | 97°07′W |
| Watertown, Wi., U.S. | 113 | 43°13′N | 88°40′W |
| Water Valley, Ms., U.S. (văl′ê) | 124 | 34°08′N | 89°38′W |
| Waterville, Me., U.S. | 100 | 44°34′N | 69°37′W |
| Waterville, Mn., U.S. | 113 | 44°10′N | 93°35′W |
| Waterville, Wa., U.S. | 114 | 47°38′N | 120°04′W |
| Watervliet, N.Y., U.S. (wô′tẽr-vlēt′) | 109 | 42°45′N | 73°54′W |
| Watford, Eng., U.K. (wŏt′f*ŏ*rd) | 164 | 51°38′N | 0°24′W |
| Wathaman Lake, l., Can. | 96 | 56°55′N | 103°43′W |
| Watlington, Eng., U.K. | 158b | 51°37′N | 1°01′W |
| Watonga, Ok., U.S. (wŏ-tôŋ′g*à*) | 121 | 35°50′N | 98°26′E |
| Watsa, D.R.C. (wät′sä) | 231 | 3°03′N | 29°32′E |
| Watseka, Il., U.S. (wŏt-sē′k*à*) | 108 | 40°45′N | 87°45′W |
| Watson, In., U.S. (wŏt′sŭn) | 111h | 38°21′N | 85°42′W |
| Watson Lake, Can. | 90 | 60°18′N | 128°50′W |
| Watsonville, Ca., U.S. (wŏt′sŭn-vĭl) | 118 | 36°55′N | 121°46′W |
| Wattenscheid, Ger. (vä′tĕn-shīd) | 171c | 51°30′N | 7°07′E |
| Watts, Ca., U.S. (wŏts) | 117a | 33°56′N | 118°15′W |
| Watts Bar Lake, res., Tn., U.S. (bär) | 124 | 35°45′N | 84°49′W |
| Waubay, S.D., U.S. (wô′bā) | 112 | 45°19′N | 97°18′W |
| Wauchula, Fl., U.S. (wô-chōō′l*à*) | 125a | 27°32′N | 81°48′W |
| Wauconda, Il., U.S. (wô-kŏn′d*à*) | 111a | 42°15′N | 88°08′W |
| Waukegan, Il., U.S. (wŏ-kē′g*ă*n) | 105 | 42°22′N | 87°51′W |
| Waukesha, Wi., U.S. (wô′kê-shô) | 111a | 43°01′N | 88°13′W |
| Waukon, Ia., U.S. (wô kŏn) | 113 | 43°15′N | 91°30′W |
| Waupaca, Wi., U.S. (wô-păk′*à*) | 113 | 44°22′N | 89°06′W |
| Waupun, Wi., U.S. (wô-pŭn′) | 113 | 43°37′N | 88°45′W |
| Waurika, Ok., U.S. (wô-rē′kå) | 121 | 34°09′N | 97°59′W |
| Wausau, Wi., U.S. (wô′sô) | 105 | 44°58′N | 89°40′W |
| Wausaukee, Wi., U.S. (wô-sô′kê) | 113 | 45°22′N | 87°58′W |
| Wauseon, Oh., U.S. (wô′sê-ŏn) | 108 | 41°30′N | 84°10′W |
| Wautoma, Wi., U.S. (wô-tō′m*à*) | 113 | 44°04′N | 89°11′W |
| Wauwatosa, Wi., U.S. (wô-wå-t′ō′s*à*) | 111a | 43°03′N | 88°00′W |
| Waveney, r., Eng., U.K. (wāv′nê) | 165 | 52°27′N | 1°17′E |
| Waverly, S. Afr. | 233c | 31°54′S | 26°29′E |
| Waverly, Ia., U.S. (wā′vẽr-lê) | 113 | 42°43′N | 92°29′W |
| Waverly, Tn., U.S. | 124 | 36°04′N | 87°46′W |
| Wāw, Sudan | 231 | 7°41′N | 28°00′E |
| Wawa, Can. | 98 | 47°59′N | 84°47′W |
| Wāw al-Kabir, Libya | 231 | 25°23′N | 16°52′E |
| Wawanesa, Can. (wŏ′wŏ-nē′să) | 97 | 49°36′N | 99°41′W |
| Wawasee, l., In., U.S. (wô-wô-sē′) | 108 | 41°25′N | 85°45′W |
| Waxahachie, Tx., U.S. (wăk-s*à*-hăch′ê) | 123 | 32°23′N | 96°50′W |
| Wayland, Ky., U.S. (wā′l*ă*nd) | 125 | 37°25′N | 82°47′W |
| Wayland, Ma., U.S. | 101a | 42°23′N | 71°22′W |
| Wayne, Mi., U.S. | 111b | 42°17′N | 83°23′W |
| Wayne, Ne., U.S. | 112 | 42°13′N | 97°03′W |
| Wayne, N.J., U.S. | 110a | 40°56′N | 74°16′W |
| Wayne, Pa., U.S. | 110f | 40°03′N | 75°22′W |
| Waynesboro, Ga., U.S. (wānz′bŭr-ô) | 125 | 33°05′N | 82°02′W |
| Waynesboro, Pa., U.S. | 109 | 39°45′N | 77°35′W |
| Waynesboro, Va., U.S. | 109 | 38°05′N | 78°50′W |
| Waynesburg, Pa., U.S. (wānz′bûrg) | 108 | 39°55′N | 80°10′W |
| Waynesville, N.C., U.S. (wānz′vĭl) | 125 | 35°28′N | 82°58′W |
| Waynoka, Ok., U.S. (wā-nō′k*à*) | 120 | 36°34′N | 98°52′W |
| Wayzata, Mn., U.S. (wā-zä-tå) | 117g | 44°58′N | 93°31′W |
| Wazīrbad, Pak. | 202 | 32°39′N | 74°11′E |
| Weagamow Lake, l., Can. (wē′ăg-ă-mou) | 97 | 52°53′N | 91°22′W |
| Weald, The, reg., Eng., U.K. (wēld) | 164 | 50°58′N | 0°15′W |
| Weatherford, Ok., U.S. (wĕ-dhẽr-fẽrd) | 120 | 85°32′N | 98°41′W |
| Weatherford, Tx., U.S. | 123 | 32°45′N | 97°46′W |
| Weaver, r., Eng., U.K. (wē′vẽr) | 158a | 53°09′N | 2°31′W |
| Weaverville, Ca., U.S. (wē′vẽr-vĭl) | 114 | 40°44′N | 122°55′W |
| Webb City, Mo., U.S. | 121 | 37°10′N | 94°26′W |
| Weber, r., Ut., U.S. | 117b | 41°13′N | 112°07′W |
| Webster, Ma., U.S. | 101a | 42°04′N | 71°52′W |
| Webster, S.D., U.S. | 112 | 45°19′N | 97°30′W |
| Webster City, Ia., U.S. | 113 | 42°28′N | 93°49′W |
| Webster Groves, Mo., U.S. (grōvz) | 117e | 38°36′N | 90°22′W |
| Webster Springs, W.V., U.S. (sprĭngz) | 108 | 38°30′N | 80°20′W |
| Weddell Sea, sea, Ant. (wĕd′ĕl) | 224 | 73°00′S | 45°00′W |
| Wedel, Ger. (vā′dĕl) | 159c | 53°35′N | 9°42′E |
| Wedge Mountain, mtn., Can. (wĕj) | 95 | 50°10′N | 122°50′W |
| Wedgeport, Can. (wĕj′pōrt) | 100 | 43°44′N | 65°59′W |
| Wednesfield, Eng., U.K. (wĕd′′nz-fēld) | 158a | 52°36′N | 2°04′W |
| Weed, Ca., U.S. (wēd) | 114 | 41°35′N | 122°21′W |
| Weenen, S. Afr. (vā′nĕn) | 233c | 28°52′S | 30°05′E |
| Weert, Neth. | 165 | 51°16′N | 5°39′E |
| Weesp, Neth. | 159a | 52°18′N | 5°01′E |
| Węgorzewo, Pol. (vôŋ-gô′zhĕ-vô) | 169 | 54°14′N | 21°46′E |
| Węgrow, Pol. (vôŋ′gròf) | 169 | 52°23′N | 22°02′E |
| Wei, r., China (wā) | 206 | 35°47′N | 114°27′E |
| Wei, r., China (wā) | 204 | 34°00′N | 108°10′E |
| Weichang, China (wā-chäŋ) | 205 | 41°50′N | 118°00′E |
| Weiden, Ger. | 168 | 49°41′N | 12°09′E |
| Weifang, China | 205 | 36°43′N | 119°08′E |
| Weihai, China (wa′hăī′) | 205 | 37°30′N | 122°05′E |
| Weilheim, Ger. (vīl′hīm′) | 168 | 47°50′N | 11°06′E |
| Weimar, Ger. (vī′mår) | 161 | 50°59′N | 11°20′E |
| Weinan, China | 208 | 34°32′N | 109°40′E |
| Weipa, Austl. | 219 | 12°25′S | 141°54′E |
| Weir, r., Can. (wēr-rĭv-ẽr) | 97 | 56°49′N | 94°04′W |
| Weirton, W.V., U.S. | 108 | 40°25′N | 80°35′W |
| Weiser, Id., U.S. (wē′zẽr) | 114 | 44°15′N | 116°58′W |
| Weiser, r., Id., U.S. | 114 | 44°26′N | 116°40′W |
| Weishi, China (wā-shr) | 208 | 34°23′N | 114°12′E |
| Weissenburg, Ger. | 168 | 49°04′N | 11°20′E |
| Weissenfels, Ger. (vī′sĕn-fĕlz) | 168 | 51°13′N | 11°58′E |
| Weiss Lake, res., Al., U.S. | 124 | 34°15′N | 85°35′W |
| Weixi, China (wā-shyĕ) | 204 | 27°27′N | 99°30′E |
| Weixian, China (wā shyĕn) | 206 | 36°59′N | 115°17′E |
| Wejherowo, Pol. (vā-hĕ-rô′vô) | 169 | 54°36′N | 18°15′E |
| Welch, W.V., U.S. (wĕlch) | 125 | 37°24′N | 81°28′W |
| Weldon, N.C., U.S. (wĕl′dŭn) | 125 | 36°24′N | 77°36′W |
| Weldon, r., Mo., U.S. | 121 | 40°22′N | 93°39′W |
| Weleetka, Ok., U.S. (wê-lēt′k*à*) | 121 | 35°19′N | 96°08′W |
| Welford, Austl. (wĕl′fẽrd) | 222 | 25°08′S | 144°43′E |
| Welkom, S. Afr. (wĕl′k*ŏ*m) | 232 | 27°57′S | 26°45′E |
| Welland, Can. (wĕl′*ă*nd) | 99 | 42°59′N | 79°13′W |
| Wellesley, Ma., U.S. (wĕlz′lê) | 101a | 42°18′N | 71°17′W |
| Wellesley Islands, is., Austl. | 220 | 16°15′S | 139°25′E |
| Wellington, Austl. (wĕl′lĭng-tŭn) | 222 | 32°40′S | 148°50′E |
| Wellington, N.Z. | 221a | 41°15′S | 174°45′E |
| Wellington, Eng., U.K. | 158a | 52°42′N | 2°30′W |
| Wellington, Ks., U.S. | 121 | 37°16′N | 97°24′W |
| Wellington, Oh., U.S. | 108 | 41°10′N | 82°10′W |
| Wellington, Tx., U.S. | 120 | 34°51′N | 100°12′W |
| Wellington, i., Chile (òĕ′lēng-tŏn) | 144 | 49°30′S | 76°30′W |
| Wells, Can. | 90 | 53°06′N | 121°34′W |
| Wells, Mi., U.S. | 108 | 45°50′N | 87°00′W |
| Wells, Mn., U.S. | 113 | 43°44′N | 93°43′W |
| Wells, Nv., U.S. | 114 | 41°07′N | 115°04′W |
| Wells, l., Austl. (wĕlz) | 220 | 26°35′S | 123°40′E |
| Wellsboro, Pa., U.S. (wĕlz′bŭ-rô) | 109 | 41°45′N | 77°15′W |
| Wellsburg, W.V., U.S. (wĕlz′bûrg) | 108 | 40°10′N | 80°40′W |
| Wells Dam, dam, Wa., U.S. | 114 | 48°00′N | 119°39′W |
| Wellston, Oh., U.S. (wĕlz′tŭn) | 108 | 39°05′N | 82°30′W |
| Wellsville, Mo., U.S. (wĕlz′vĭl) | 121 | 39°04′N | 91°33′W |
| Wellsville, N.Y., U.S. | 109 | 42°10′N | 78°00′W |
| Wellsville, Oh., U.S. | 108 | 40°35′N | 80°40′W |
| Wellsville, Ut., U.S. | 115 | 41°38′N | 111°57′W |
| Wels, Aus. (vĕls) | 161 | 48°10′N | 14°01′E |
| Welshpool, Wales, U.K. (wĕlsh′pōōl) | 164 | 52°44′N | 3°10′W |
| Welverdiend, S. Afr. (vĕl-vẽr-dēnd′) | 238c | 26°23′S | 27°16′E |
| Welwyn Garden City, Eng., U.K. (wĕlĭn) | 158b | 51°46′N | 0°17′W |
| Wem, Eng., U.K. (wĕm) | 158a | 52°51′N | 2°44′W |
| Wembere, r., Tan. | 237 | 4°35′S | 33°55′E |
| Wen, r., China (wŭn) | 206 | 36°24′N | 119°00′E |
| Wenan Wa, sw., China (wĕn′än′ wä) | 206 | 38°56′N | 116°29′E |
| Wenatchee, Wa., U.S. (wê-năch′ê) | 114 | 47°24′N | 120°18′W |
| Wenatchee Mountains, mts., Wa., U.S. | 114 | 47°28′N | 121°10′W |
| Wenchang, China (wŭn-chäŋ) | 209 | 19°32′N | 110°42′E |
| Wenchi, Ghana | 234 | 7°42′N | 2°07′W |
| Wendeng, China (wŭn-dŭŋ) | 206 | 37°14′N | 122°03′E |
| Wendo, Eth. | 231 | 6°37′N | 38°29′E |
| Wendorer, Ut., U.S. | 115 | 40°47′N | 114°01′W |
| Wendover, Can. (wĕn-dōv′ẽr) | 102c | 45°34′N | 75°07′W |
| Wendover, Eng., U.K. | 158b | 51°44′N | 0°45′W |
| Wenham, Ma., U.S. (wĕn′*ă*m) | 101a | 42°36′N | 70°53′W |
| Wenquan, China (wŭn-chyůän) | 205 | 47°10′N | 120°00′E |
| Wenshan, China | 204 | 23°20′N | 104°15′E |
| Wenshang, China (wĕn′shäng) | 206 | 35°43′N | 116°31′E |
| Wensu, China (wĕn-sò) | 204 | 41°45′N | 80°30′E |
| Wentworth, Austl. (wĕnt′wûrth) | 219 | 34°03′S | 141°53′E |
| Wenzhou, China (wŭn-jō) | 205 | 28°00′N | 120°40′E |
| Wepener, S. Afr. (wē′p*ĕ*n-ẽr) (vā′pĕn-ẽr) | 232 | 29°43′S | 27°04′E |
| Werder, Ger. (vĕr′dĕr) | 159b | 52°23′N | 12°56′E |
| Were Ilu, Eth. | 231 | 10°39′N | 39°21′E |
| Werl, Ger. (vĕrl) | 171c | 51°33′N | 7°55′E |
| Wermelskirchen, Ger. | 171c | 51°08′N | 7°13′E |
| Werneuchen, Ger. (vĕr′hoi-ĸĕn) | 159b | 52°38′N | 13°44′E |
| Werra, r., Ger. (vĕr′ä) | 168 | 51°16′N | 9°54′E |
| Werribee, Austl. | 217a | 37°54′S | 144°40′E |
| Werribee, r., Austl. | 217a | 37°40′S | 144°37′E |
| Wertach, r., Ger. (vĕr′täk) | 168 | 48°12′N | 10°40′E |
| Weseke, Ger. (vĕ′zĕ-kĕ) | 171c | 51°54′N | 6°51′E |
| Wesel, Ger. (vā′zĕl) | 171c | 51°39′N | 6°37′E |
| Weser, r., Ger. (vā′zĕr) | 156 | 51°00′N | 10°30′E |
| Weslaco, Tx., U.S. (wĕs-lā′kō) | 123 | 26°10′N | 97°59′W |
| Weslemkoon, l., Can. | 99 | 45°02′N | 77°25′W |
| Wesleyville, Can. (wĕs′lē-vĭl) | 101 | 49°09′N | 53°34′W |
| Wessel Islands, is., Austl. (wĕs′*ĕ*l) | 220 | 11°45′S | 136°25′E |


ng-sing; ŋ-baŋk; ɴ-nasalized n; nŏd; c*ŏ*mmit; ōld; ôbey; ôrder; oi-boil; fōōd; ȯ-as oo in foot; ou-out; s-soft; sh-dish; th-thin; pūre; ůnite; ûrn; stŭd; circ*ŭ*s; ü-as in French tu; ′-indeterminate vowel.

366 Wesselsbron – William Creek PRONOUNCING INDEX


| PLACE (Pronunciation) | PAGE | LAT. | LONG. |
|---|---|---|---|
| Wesselsbron, S. Afr. (wĕs′ĕl-brŏn) | 238c | 27°51′S | 26°22′E |
| Wessington Springs, S.D., U.S. (wĕs′ĭng-tŭn) | 112 | 44°06′N | 98°35′W |
| West, Mount, mtn., Pan. | 128a | 9°10′N | 79°52′W |
| West Allis, Wi., U.S. (wĕst-ăl′ĭs) | 111a | 43°01′N | 88°01′W |
| West Alton, Mo., U.S. (ôl′tŭn) | 117e | 38°52′N | 90°13′W |
| West Bay, b., Fl., U.S. | 124 | 30°20′N | 85°45′W |
| West Bay, b., Tx., U.S. | 123a | 29°11′N | 95°03′W |
| West Bend, Wi., U.S. (wĕst bĕnd) | 113 | 43°25′N | 88°13′W |
| West Bengal, state, India (bĕn-gôl′) | 199 | 23°30′N | 87°30′E |
| West Blocton, Al., U.S. (blŏk′tŭn) | 124 | 33°05′N | 87°05′W |
| Westborough, Ma., U.S. (wĕst′bŭr-ô) | 101a | 42°17′N | 71°37′W |
| West Boylston, Ma., U.S. (boil′stŭn) | 101a | 42°22′N | 71°46′W |
| West Branch, Mi., U.S. (wĕst brȧnch) | 108 | 44°15′N | 84°10′W |
| West Bridgford, Eng., U.K. (brĭj′fērd) | 158a | 52°55′N | 1°08′W |
| West Bromwich, Eng., U.K. (wĕst brŭm′ĭj) | 158a | 52°32′N | 1°59′W |
| Westbrook, Me., U.S. (wĕst′brŏŏk) | 100 | 43°41′N | 70°23′W |
| Westby, Wi., U.S. (wĕst′bē) | 113 | 43°40′N | 90°52′W |
| West Caicos, i., T./C. Is. (käē′kō) (kī′kōs) | 135 | 21°40′N | 72°30′W |
| West Cape Howe, c., Austl. | 220 | 35°15′S | 117°30′E |
| West Chester, Oh., U.S. (chĕs′tēr) | 111f | 39°20′N | 84°24′W |
| West Chester, Pa., U.S. | 110f | 39°57′N | 75°36′W |
| West Chicago, Il., U.S. (chĭ-kä′gō) | 111a | 41°53′N | 88°12′W |
| West Columbia, S.C., U.S. (cŏl′ŭm-bē-ȧ) | 125 | 33°58′N | 81°05′W |
| West Columbia, Tx., U.S. | 123 | 29°08′N | 95°39′W |
| West Cote Blanche Bay, b., La., U.S. | 123 | 29°30′N | 92°17′W |
| West Covina, Ca., U.S. (wĕst kō-vē′nȧ) | 117a | 34°04′N | 117°55′W |
| West Des Moines, Ia., U.S. (dē moin′) | 113 | 41°35′N | 93°42′W |
| West Des Moines, r., Ia., U.S. | 113 | 42°52′N | 94°32′W |
| West End, Bah. | 134 | 26°40′N | 78°55′W |
| Westerham, Eng., U.K. (wĕ′stēr′ŭm) | 158b | 51°15′N | 0°05′E |
| Westerhörn, Ger. (vĕs′tĕr-hōrn) | 159c | 53°52′N | 9°41′E |
| Westerlo, Bel. | 159a | 51°05′N | 4°57′E |
| Westerly, R.I., U.S. (wĕs′tēr-lē) | 109 | 41°25′N | 71°50′W |
| Western Australia, state, Austl. (ôs-trā′lĭ-ȧ) | 218 | 24°15′S | 121°30′E |
| Western Dvina, r., Eur. | 167 | 55°30′N | 28°27′E |
| Western Ghāts, mts., India | 199 | 17°35′N | 74°00′E |
| Western Port, Md., U.S. (wĕs′tērn pōrt) | 109 | 39°30′N | 79°00′W |
| Western Sahara, dep., Afr. (sȧ-hä′rȧ) | 230 | 23°05′N | 15°33′W |
| Western Samoa *see* Samoa, nation, Oc. | 2 | 14°30′S | 172°00′W |
| Western Siberian Lowland, depr., Russia | 178 | 63°37′N | 72°45′E |
| Westerville, Oh., U.S. (wĕs′tēr-vĭl) | 108 | 40°10′N | 83°00′W |
| Westerwald, for., Ger. (vĕs′tĕr-väld) | 168 | 50°35′N | 7°45′E |
| Westfalen, hist. reg., Ger. (vĕst-fä-lĕn) | 168 | 51°20′N | 8°30′E |
| Westfield, Ma., U.S. (wĕst′fēld) | 109 | 42°05′N | 72°45′W |
| Westfield, N.J., U.S. | 110a | 40°39′N | 74°21′W |
| Westfield, N.Y., U.S. (wĕst′fēld) | 110 | 42°20′N | 79°40′W |
| Westford, Ma., U.S. (wĕst′fērd) | 101a | 42°35′N | 71°26′W |
| West Frankfort, Il., U.S. (frăŋk′fŭrt) | 108 | 37°55′N | 88°55′W |
| West Ham, Eng., U.K. | 158b | 51°30′N | 0°00′W |
| West Hartford, Ct., U.S. (härt′fērd) | 109 | 41°45′N | 72°45′W |
| West Helena, Ar., U.S. (hĕl′ĕn-ȧ) | 121 | 34°32′N | 90°39′W |
| West Indies, is. (ĭn′dēz) | 129 | 19°00′N | 78°30′W |
| West Jordon, Ut., U.S. (jôr′dăn) | 117b | 40°37′N | 111°56′W |
| West Kirby, Eng., U.K. (kûr′bē) | 158a | 53°22′N | 3°11′W |
| West Lafayette, In., U.S. (lä-fā-yĕt′) | 108 | 40°25′N | 86°55′W |
| Westlake, Oh., U.S. | 111d | 41°27′N | 81°55′W |
| Westleigh, S. Afr. (wĕst-lē) | 238c | 27°39′S | 27°18′E |
| West Liberty, Ia., U.S. (wĕst lĭb′ēr-tĭ) | 113 | 41°34′N | 91°15′W |
| West Linn, Or., U.S. (lĭn) | 116c | 45°22′N | 122°37′W |
| Westlock, Can. (wĕst′lŏk) | 95 | 54°09′N | 113°52′W |
| West Memphis, Ar., U.S. | 121 | 35°08′N | 90°11′W |
| West Midlands, hist. reg., Eng., U.K. | 158a | 52°26′N | 1°50′W |
| Westminster, Ca., U.S. (wĕst′mĭn-stēr) | 117a | 33°45′N | 117°59′W |
| Westminster, Md., U.S. | 109 | 39°40′N | 76°55′W |
| Westminster, S.C., U.S. | 124 | 34°38′N | 83°10′W |
| Westmount, Can. (wĕst′mount) | 102a | 45°29′N | 73°36′W |
| West Newbury, Ma., U.S. (nū′bēr-ĕ) | 101a | 42°47′N | 70°57′W |
| West Newton, Pa., U.S. (nū′tŭn) | 111e | 40°12′N | 79°45′W |
| West New York, N.J., U.S. (nů yŏrk) | 110a | 40°47′N | 74°01′W |
| West Nishnabotna, r., Ia., U.S. (nĭsh-nȧ-bŏt′nȧ) | 112 | 40°56′N | 95°37′W |
| Weston, Ma., U.S. (wĕs′tŭn) | 101a | 42°22′N | 71°18′W |
| Weston, W.V., U.S. | 108 | 39°00′N | 80°30′W |
| Westonaria, S. Afr. | 238c | 26°19′S | 27°38′E |
| Weston-super-Mare, Eng., U.K. (wĕs′tŭn sū′pēr-mā′rē) | 164 | 51°23′N | 3°00′W |
| West Orange, N.J., U.S. (wĕst ŏr′ĕnj) | 110a | 40°46′N | 74°14′W |
| West Palm Beach, Fl., U.S. (päm bēch) | 105 | 26°44′N | 80°04′W |
| West Pensacola, Fl., U.S. (pĕn-sȧ-kō′lȧ) | 124 | 30°24′N | 87°18′W |
| West Pittsburg, Ca., U.S. (pĭts′bûrg) | 116b | 38°02′N | 121°56′W |
| Westplains, Mo., U.S. (wĕst-plānz′) | 121 | 36°42′N | 91°51′W |
| West Point, Ga., U.S. | 124 | 32°52′N | 85°10′W |
| West Point, Ms., U.S. | 124 | 33°36′N | 88°39′W |
| Westpoint, Ne., U.S. | 112 | 41°50′N | 96°00′W |
| West Point, N.Y., U.S. | 110a | 41°23′N | 73°58′W |
| West Point, Ut., U.S. | 117b | 41°07′N | 112°05′W |
| West Point, Va., U.S. | 109 | 37°25′N | 76°50′W |
| West Point Lake, res., U.S. | 124 | 33°00′N | 85°10′W |
| Westport, Ire. | 164 | 53°44′N | 9°36′W |
| Westport, Ct., U.S. (wĕst′pōrt) | 110a | 41°07′N | 73°22′W |
| Westport, Or., U.S. (wĕst′pôrt) | 116c | 46°08′N | 123°22′W |
| Westray, i., Scot., U.K. (wĕs′trā) | 164a | 59°19′N | 3°05′W |
| West Road, r., Can. (rōd) | 94 | 53°00′N | 124°00′W |
| West Saint Paul, Mn., U.S. (sȧnt pôl′) | 117g | 44°55′N | 93°05′W |
| West Sand Spit, i., T./C. Is. | 135 | 21°25′N | 72°10′W |
| West Slope, Or., U.S. | 116c | 45°30′N | 122°46′W |
| West Tavaputs Plateau, plat., Ut., U.S. (wĕst tăv′ȧ-pŏts) | 119 | 39°45′N | 110°35′W |
| West Terre Haute, In., U.S. (tĕr-ē hōt′) | 108 | 39°30′N | 87°30′W |
| West Union, Ia., U.S. (ūn′yŭn) | 113 | 42°58′N | 91°48′W |
| West University Place, Tx., U.S. | 123a | 29°43′N | 95°26′W |
| Westview, Oh., U.S. (wĕst′vū) | 111d | 41°21′N | 81°54′W |
| West View, Pa., U.S. | 111e | 40°31′N | 80°02′W |
| Westville, Can. (wĕst′vĭl) | 101 | 45°35′N | 62°43′W |
| Westville, Il., U.S. | 108 | 40°00′N | 87°40′W |
| West Virginia, state, U.S. (wĕst vẽr-jĭn′ĭ-ȧ) | 105 | 39°00′N | 80°50′W |
| West Walker, r., Ca., U.S. (wôk′ēr) | 118 | 38°25′N | 119°25′W |
| West Warwick, R.I., U.S. (wŏr′ĭk) | 110b | 41°42′N | 71°31′W |
| Westwego, La., U.S. (wĕst-wē′gō) | 110d | 29°55′N | 90°09′W |
| Westwood, Ca., U.S. (wĕst′wŏd) | 118 | 40°18′N | 121°00′W |
| Westwood, Ks., U.S. | 117f | 39°03′N | 94°37′W |
| Westwood, Ma., U.S. | 101a | 42°13′N | 71°14′W |
| Westwood, N.J., U.S. | 110a | 40°59′N | 74°02′W |
| West Wyalong, Austl. (wī′ălông) | 219 | 34°00′S | 147°20′E |
| West Yorkshire, hist. reg., Eng., U.K. | 158a | 53°37′N | 1°48′W |
| Wetar, Pulau, i., Indon. (wĕt′ȧr) | 213 | 7°34′S | 126°00′E |
| Wetaskiwin, Can. (wĕ-tăs′kē-wŏn) | 90 | 52°58′N | 113°22′W |
| Wetmore, Tx., U.S. (wĕt′mōr) | 117d | 29°34′N | 98°25′W |
| Wetter, Ger. | 171c | 51°23′N | 7°23′E |
| Wetumpka, Al., U.S. (wē-tŭmp′kȧ) | 124 | 32°33′N | 86°12′W |
| Wetzlar, Ger. (vets′lär) | 168 | 50°35′N | 8°30′E |
| Wewak, Pap. N. Gui. (wȧ-wăk′) | 213 | 3°19′S | 143°30′E |
| Wewoka, Ok., U.S. (wē-wō′kȧ) | 121 | 35°09′N | 96°30′W |
| Wexford, Ire. (wĕks′fērd) | 161 | 52°20′N | 6°30′W |
| Weybridge, Eng., U.K. (wā′brĭj) | 158b | 51°20′N | 0°26′W |
| Weyburn, Can. (wā′bûrn) | 90 | 49°41′N | 103°52′W |
| Weymouth, Eng., U.K. (wā′mŭth) | 164 | 50°37′N | 2°34′W |
| Weymouth, Ma., U.S. | 101a | 42°44′N | 70°57′W |
| Weymouth, Oh., U.S. | 111d | 41°11′N | 81°48′W |
| Whale Cay, i., Bah. | 134 | 25°20′N | 77°45′W |
| Whale Cay Channels, strt., Bah. | 134 | 26°45′N | 77°10′W |
| Wharton, N.J., U.S. (hwôr′tŭn) | 110a | 40°54′N | 74°35′W |
| Wharton, Tx., U.S. | 123 | 29°19′N | 96°06′W |
| What Cheer, Ia., U.S. (hwŏt chēr) | 113 | 41°23′N | 92°24′W |
| Whatcom, Lake, l., Wa., U.S. (hwät′kŭm) | 116c | 48°44′N | 123°34′W |
| Whatshan Lake, l., Can. (wŏt′shăn) | 95 | 50°00′N | 118°03′W |
| Wheatland, Wy., U.S. (hwēt′lănd) | 115 | 42°04′N | 104°52′W |
| Wheatland Reservoir Number 2, res., Wy., U.S. | 115 | 41°52′N | 105°36′W |
| Wheaton, Il., U.S. (hwē′tŭn) | 111a | 41°52′N | 88°06′W |
| Wheaton, Md., U.S. | 110e | 39°05′N | 77°05′W |
| Wheaton, Mn., U.S. | 112 | 45°48′N | 96°29′W |
| Wheeler Peak, mtn., N.M., U.S. | 120 | 36°34′N | 105°25′W |
| Wheeler Peak, mtn., Nv., U.S. | 106 | 38°58′N | 114°15′W |
| Wheeling, Il., U.S. (hwēl′ĭng) | 111a | 42°08′N | 87°54′W |
| Wheeling, W.V., U.S. | 108 | 40°05′N | 80°45′W |
| Wheelwright, Arg. (ōē′l-rē′gt) | 141c | 33°46′S | 61°14′W |
| Whidbey Island, i., Wa., U.S. (hwĭd′bē) | 116a | 48°13′N | 122°50′W |
| Whippany, N.J., U.S. (hwĭp′ȧ-nē) | 110a | 40°49′N | 74°25′W |
| Whitby, Can. (hwĭt′bē) | 91 | 43°50′N | 79°00′W |
| Whitchurch, Eng., U.K. (hwĭt′chûrch) | 158a | 52°58′N | 2°49′W |
| White, l., Can. | 98 | 48°47′N | 85°50′W |
| White, l., Can. | 99 | 45°15′N | 76°35′W |
| White, r., Can. | 98 | 48°34′N | 85°46′W |
| White, r., In., U.S. | 108 | 39°15′N | 86°45′W |
| White, r., S.D., U.S. | 112 | 43°13′N | 101°04′W |
| White, r., Tx., U.S. | 120 | 36°25′N | 102°20′W |
| White, r., Vt., U.S. | 109 | 43°45′N | 72°35′W |
| White, r., Wa., U.S. | 114 | 47°07′N | 121°48′W |
| White, r., U.S. | 107 | 35°30′N | 92°00′W |
| White, r., U.S. | 112 | 43°41′N | 99°48′W |
| White, r., U.S. | 119 | 40°10′N | 108°55′W |
| White, East Fork, r., In., U.S. | 108 | 38°45′N | 86°20′W |
| White Bay, b., Can. | 93a | 50°00′N | 56°30′W |
| White Bear Indian Reserve, I.R., Can. | 97 | 49°50′N | 102°15′W |
| White Bear Lake, l., Mn., U.S. | 117g | 45°04′N | 92°58′W |
| White Castle, La., U.S. | 123 | 30°10′N | 91°09′W |
| White Center, Wa., U.S. | 116a | 47°31′N | 122°21′W |
| White Cloud, Mi., U.S. | 108 | 43°35′N | 85°45′W |
| Whitecourt, Can. (wīt′côrt) | 90 | 54°09′N | 115°41′W |
| White Earth, r., N.D., U.S. | 112 | 48°30′N | 102°44′W |
| White Earth Indian Reservation, I.R., Mn., U.S. | 112 | 47°18′N | 95°42′W |
| Whiteface, r., Mn., U.S. (whīt′fās) | 113 | 47°12′N | 92°13′W |
| Whitefield, N.H., U.S. (hwĭt′fēld) | 109 | 44°20′N | 71°35′W |
| Whitefish Bay, Wi., U.S. | 111a | 43°07′N | 77°54′W |
| Whitefish Bay, b., Can. | 97 | 49°26′N | 94°14′W |
| Whitefish Bay, b., N.A. | 113 | 46°36′N | 84°50′W |
| White Hall, Il., U.S. | 121 | 39°26′N | 90°23′W |
| Whitehall, Mi., U.S. (hwīt′hôl) | 108 | 43°20′N | 86°20′W |
| Whitehall, N.Y., U.S. | 109 | 43°30′N | 73°25′W |
| Whitehaven, Eng., U.K. (hwĭt′hā-vĕn) | 164 | 54°35′N | 3°30′W |
| Whitehorn, Point, c., Wa., U.S. (hwĭt′hôrn) | 116d | 48°54′N | 122°48′W |
| Whitehorse, Can. (whīt′hôrs) | 90 | 60°39′N | 135°01′W |
| White Lake, l., La., U.S. | 123 | 29°40′N | 92°35′W |
| White Mountain Peak, mtn., Ca., U.S. | 118 | 37°38′N | 118°13′W |
| White Mountains, mts., Me., U.S. | 100 | 44°22′N | 71°15′W |
| White Mountains, mts., N.H., U.S. | 109 | 42°20′N | 71°05′W |
| Whitemouth, l., Can. | 97 | 49°14′N | 95°40′W |
| White Nile (Al Bahr al Abyad), r., Sudan | 231 | 12°30′N | 32°30′E |
| White Otter, l., Can. | 98 | 49°15′N | 91°48′W |
| White Pass, p., N.A. | 103 | 59°35′N | 135°03′W |
| White Plains, N.Y., U.S. | 110a | 41°02′N | 73°47′W |
| White River, Can. | 98 | 48°38′N | 85°23′W |
| White Rock, Can. | 95 | 49°01′N | 122°49′W |
| Whiterock Reservoir, res., Tx., U.S. (hwīt′rŏk) | 117c | 32°51′N | 96°40′W |
| White Russia *see* Belarus, nation, Eur. | 178 | 53°30′N | 25°33′E |
| Whitesail Lake, l., Can. (whīt′săl) | 94 | 53°30′N | 127°00′W |
| White Sands National Monument, rec., N.M., U.S. | 119 | 32°50′N | 106°20′W |
| White Sea, sea, Russia | 178 | 66°00′N | 40°00′E |
| White Settlement, Tx., U.S. | 117c | 32°45′N | 97°28′W |
| White Sulphur Springs, Mt., U.S. | 115 | 46°32′N | 110°49′W |
| White Umfolzi, r., S. Afr. (ŭm-fō-lō′zē) | 233c | 28°12′S | 30°55′E |
| Whiteville, N.C., U.S. (hwīt′vĭl) | 125 | 34°18′N | 78°45′W |
| White Volta (Volta Blanche), r., Afr. | 234 | 9°40′N | 1°10′W |
| Whitewater, Wi., U.S. (whīt-wŏt′ēr) | 113 | 42°49′N | 88°40′W |
| Whitewater, l., Can. | 97 | 49°14′N | 100°39′W |
| Whitewater, r., In., U.S. | 111f | 39°19′N | 84°55′W |
| Whitewater Bay, b., Fl., U.S. | 125a | 25°16′N | 80°21′W |
| Whitewater Creek, r., Mt., U.S. | 115 | 48°50′N | 107°50′W |
| Whitewell, Tn., U.S. (hwĭt′wĕl) | 124 | 35°11′N | 85°31′W |
| Whitewright, Tx., U.S. (hwīt′rīt) | 121 | 33°33′N | 96°25′W |
| Whitham, r., Eng., U.K. (wĭth′ŭm) | 158a | 53°08′N | 0°15′W |
| Whiting, In., U.S. (hwīt′ĭng) | 111a | 41°41′N | 87°30′W |
| Whitinsville, Ma., U.S. (hwĭt′ĕns-vĭl) | 101a | 42°06′N | 71°40′W |
| Whitman, Ma., U.S. (hwĭt′măn) | 101a | 42°05′N | 70°57′W |
| Whitmire, S.C., U.S. (hwĭt′mīr) | 125 | 34°30′N | 81°40′W |
| Whitney, Mount, mtn., Ca., U.S. | 106 | 36°34′N | 118°18′W |
| Whitney Lake, l., Tx., U.S. (hwĭt′nē) | 123 | 32°02′N | 97°36′W |
| Whitstable, Eng., U.K. (wĭt′stȧb′l) | 158b | 51°22′N | 1°03′E |
| Whitsunday, i., Austl. (hwĭt′s′n-dā) | 221 | 20°16′S | 149°00′E |
| Whittier, Ca., U.S. (hwĭt′ĭ-ēr) | 117a | 33°58′N | 118°02′W |
| Whittlesea, S. Afr. (wĭt′l′sē) | 233c | 32°11′S | 26°51′E |
| Whitworth, Eng., U.K. (hwĭt′wŭrth) | 158a | 53°40′N | 2°10′W |
| Whyalla, Austl. (hwī-ăl′ȧ) | 218 | 33°00′S | 137°32′E |
| Whymper, Mount, mtn., Can. (wĭm′pēr) | 94 | 48°57′N | 124°10′W |
| Wiarton, Can. (wī′ȧr-tŭn) | 91 | 44°45′N | 80°45′W |
| Wichita, Ks., U.S. (wĭch′ĭ-tô) | 104 | 37°42′N | 97°21′W |
| Wichita, r., Tx., U.S. | 120 | 33°50′N | 99°38′W |
| Wichita Falls, Tx., U.S. (fôls) | 104 | 33°54′N | 98°29′W |
| Wichita Mountains, mts., Ok., U.S. | 106 | 34°48′N | 98°43′W |
| Wick, Scot., U.K. (wĭk) | 160 | 58°25′N | 3°05′W |
| Wickatunk, N.J., U.S. (wĭk′ȧ-tŭnk) | 110a | 40°21′N | 74°15′W |
| Wickenburg, Az., U.S. | 119 | 33°58′N | 112°44′W |
| Wickiup Reservoir, res., Or., U.S. | 114 | 43°40′N | 121°43′W |
| Wickliffe, Oh., U.S. (wĭk′klĭf) | 111d | 41°37′N | 81°29′W |
| Wicklow, Ire. | 164 | 52°59′N | 6°06′W |
| Wicklow Mountains, mts., Ire. (wĭk′lō) | 164 | 52°49′N | 6°20′W |
| Wickup Mountain, mtn., Or., U.S. (wĭk′ŭp) | 116c | 46°06′N | 123°35′W |
| Wiconisco, Pa., U.S. (wĭ-kŏn′ĭs-kō) | 109 | 43°35′N | 76°45′W |
| Widen, W.V., U.S. (wī′dĕn) | 108 | 38°25′N | 80°55′W |
| Widnes, Eng., U.K. (wĭd′nĕs) | 158a | 53°21′N | 2°44′W |
| Wieliczka, Pol. (vyĕ-lēch′kȧ) | 169 | 49°58′N | 20°06′E |
| Wien *see* Vienna, Aus. | 154 | 48°13′N | 16°22′E |
| Wien, state, Aus. | 159e | 48°11′N | 16°23′E |
| Wiener Neustadt, Aus. (vē′nĕr noi′shtät) | 161 | 47°48′N | 16°15′E |
| Wiener Wald, for., Aus. | 159e | 48°09′N | 16°05′E |
| Wieprz, r., Pol. (vyĕpzh) | 169 | 51°25′N | 22°45′E |
| Wiergate, Tx., U.S. (wēr′gāt) | 123 | 31°00′N | 93°42′W |
| Wiesbaden, Ger. (vēs′bä-dĕn) | 161 | 50°05′N | 8°15′E |
| Wigan, Eng., U.K. (wĭg′ăn) | 164 | 53°33′N | 2°37′W |
| Wiggins, Ms., U.S. (wĭg′ĭnz) | 124 | 30°51′N | 89°05′W |
| Wight, Isle of, i., Eng., U.K. (wīt) | 164 | 50°44′N | 1°17′W |
| Wilber, Ne., U.S. (wĭl′bēr) | 121 | 40°29′N | 96°57′W |
| Wilburton, Ok., U.S. (wĭl′bēr-tŭn) | 121 | 34°54′N | 95°18′W |
| Wilcannia, Austl. (wĭl-căn-ĭȧ) | 219 | 31°30′S | 143°30′E |
| Wildau, Ger. (vēl′dou) | 159b | 52°20′N | 13°39′E |
| Wildberg, Ger. (vēl′bĕrgh) | 159b | 52°52′N | 12°39′E |
| Wildcat Hill, hill, Can. (wīld′kăt) | 97 | 53°17′N | 102°30′W |
| Wildhay, r., Can. (wīld′hā) | 95 | 53°15′N | 117°20′W |
| Wildomar, Ca., U.S. (wĭl′dô-mär) | 117a | 33°35′N | 117°17′W |
| Wild Rice, r., Mn., U.S. | 112 | 47°10′N | 96°40′W |
| Wild Rice, r., N.D., U.S. | 112 | 46°10′N | 97°12′W |
| Wild Rice Lake, l., Mn., U.S. | 117h | 46°54′N | 92°10′W |
| Wildspitze, mtn., Aus. | 168 | 46°55′N | 10°50′E |
| Wildwood, N.J., U.S. | 109 | 39°00′N | 74°50′W |
| Wiley, Co., U.S. (wī′lē) | 120 | 38°08′N | 102°41′W |
| Wilge, r., S. Afr. (wĭl′jē) | 238c | 25°38′S | 29°09′E |
| Wilge, r., S. Afr. | 238c | 27°27′S | 28°46′E |
| Wilhelm, Mount, mtn., Pap. N. Gui. | 213 | 5°58′S | 144°58′E |
| Wilhelmina Gebergte, mts., Sur. | 143 | 4°30′N | 57°00′W |
| Wilhelmina Kanaal, can., Neth. | 159a | 51°37′N | 4°55′E |
| Wilhelmshaven, Ger. (vēl-hĕlms-hä′fĕn) | 160 | 53°30′N | 8°10′E |
| Wilkes-Barre, Pa., U.S. (wĭlks′băr-ē) | 105 | 41°15′N | 75°50′W |
| Wilkes Land, reg., Ant. | 224 | 71°00′S | 126°00′E |
| Wilkeson, Wa., U.S. (wĭl-kē′sŭn) | 116a | 47°06′N | 122°03′W |
| Wilkie, Can. (wĭlk′ē) | 90 | 52°25′N | 108°43′W |
| Wilkinsburg, Pa., U.S. (wĭl′kĭnz-bûrg) | 111e | 40°26′N | 79°53′W |
| Willamette, r., Or., U.S. | 106 | 45°00′N | 123°00′W |
| Willapa Bay, b., Wa., U.S. | 114 | 46°37′N | 124°00′W |
| Willard, Oh., U.S. (wĭl′ȧrd) | 108 | 41°00′N | 82°50′W |
| Willard, Ut., U.S. | 117b | 41°24′N | 112°02′W |
| Willcox, Az., U.S. (wĭl′kŏks) | 119 | 32°15′N | 109°50′W |
| Willcox Playa, l., Az., U.S. | 119 | 32°08′N | 109°51′W |
| Willemstad, Neth. Ant. | 142 | 12°12′N | 68°58′W |
| Willesden, Eng., U.K. (wĭlz′dĕn) | 158b | 51°31′N | 0°17′W |
| William "Bill" Dannelly Reservoir, res., Al., U.S. | 124 | 32°10′N | 87°15′W |
| William Creek, Austl. (wĭl′yăm) | 218 | 28°45′S | 136°20′E |


ăt; finăl; rāte; senāte; ärm; ȧsk; sofȧ; fâre; ch-choose; dh-as th in other; bē; ēvent; bĕt; recĕnt; cratēr; g-gō; gh-guttural g; bĭt; ĭ-short neutral; rīde; κ-guttural k as ch in German ich;

368 Wuhu – Yellowstone Lake PRONOUNCING INDEX


| PLACE (Pronunciation) | PAGE | LAT. | LONG. |
| --- | --- | --- | --- |
| Wuhu, China (wo͞o′ho͞o) | 209 | 31°22′N | 118°22′E |
| Wuji, China (wo͞o-jyē) | 206 | 38°12′N | 114°57′E |
| Wujiang, China (wo͞o-jyäŋ) | 206 | 31°10′N | 120°38′E |
| Wuleidao Wan, b., China (wo͞o-lā-dou wän) | 206 | 36°55′N | 122°00′E |
| Wulidian, China (wo͞o-lē-dĭĕn) | 206 | 32°09′N | 114°17′E |
| Wünsdorf, Ger. (vüns′dorf) | 159b | 52°10′N | 13°29′E |
| Wupatki National Monument, rec., Az., U.S. | 119 | 35°35′N | 111°45′W |
| Wuping, China (wo͞o-pĭŋ) | 209 | 25°05′N | 116°01′E |
| Wuppertal, Ger. (vŏp′ẽr-täl) | 161 | 51°16′N | 7°14′E |
| Wuqiao, China (wo͞o-chyou) | 206 | 37°37′N | 116°29′E |
| Würm, r., Ger. (vürm) | 159d | 48°07′N | 11°20′E |
| Würselen, Ger. (vür′zĕ-lĕn) | 171c | 50°49′N | 6°09′E |
| Würzburg, Ger. (vürts′bōrgh) | 161 | 49°48′N | 9°57′E |
| Wurzen, Ger. (vōrt′sĕn) | 161 | 51°22′N | 12°45′E |
| Wushi, China (wo͞o-shr) | 204 | 41°13′N | 79°08′E |
| Wusong, China (wo͞o-sôŋ) | 206 | 31°23′N | 121°29′E |
| Wustermark, Ger. (vo͞os′tĕr-märk) | 159b | 52°33′N | 12°57′E |
| Wustrau, Ger. (vōost′rou) | 159b | 52°40′N | 12°51′E |
| Wuustwezel, Bel. | 159a | 51°23′N | 4°36′E |
| Wuwei, China (wo͞o′wā′) | 209 | 31°19′N | 117°53′E |
| Wuxi, China (wo͞o-shyē) | 205 | 31°36′N | 120°17′E |
| Wuxing, China (wo͞o-shyĭŋ) | 205 | 30°38′N | 120°10′E |
| Wuyi Shan, mts., China (wo͞o-yē shän) | 209 | 26°38′N | 116°35′E |
| Wuyou, China (wo͞o-yō) | 206 | 33°18′N | 120°15′E |
| Wuzhi Shan, mtn., China (wo͞o-jr shän) | 209 | 18°48′N | 109°30′E |
| Wuzhou, China (wo͞o-jō) | 205 | 23°32′N | 111°25′E |
| Wyandotte, Mi., U.S. (wī′ăn-dŏt) | 111b | 42°12′N | 83°10′W |
| Wye, Eng., U.K. (wī) | 158b | 51°12′N | 0°57′E |
| Wye, r., Eng., U.K. | 158a | 53°14′N | 1°46′W |
| Wylie, Lake, res., S.C., U.S. | 125 | 35°02′N | 81°21′W |
| Wymore, Ne., U.S. (wī′mōr) | 121 | 40°09′N | 96°41′W |
| Wynberg, S. Afr. (wĭn′bĕrg) | 232a | 34°00′S | 18°28′E |
| Wyndham, Austl. (wĭnd′ăm) | 218 | 15°30′S | 128°15′E |
| Wynne, Ar., U.S. (wĭn) | 121 | 35°12′N | 90°46′W |
| Wynnewood, Ok., U.S. (wĭn′wŏod) | 121 | 34°39′N | 97°10′W |
| Wynona, Ok., U.S. (wī-nō′nȧ) | 121 | 36°33′N | 96°19′W |
| Wynyard, Can. (wĭn′yẽrd) | 90 | 51°47′N | 104°10′W |
| Wyoming, Oh., U.S. (wī-ō′mĭng) | 111f | 39°14′N | 84°28′W |
| Wyoming, state, U.S. | 104 | 42°50′N | 108°30′W |
| Wyoming Range, mts., Wy., U.S. | 106 | 42°43′N | 110°35′W |
| Wyre Forest, for., Eng., U.K. (wīr) | 158a | 52°24′N | 2°24′W |
| Wysokie Mazowieckie, Pol. (vē-sô′kyĕ mä-zô-vyĕts′kyĕ) | 169 | 52°55′N | 22°42′E |
| Wyszków, Pol. (vêsh′kôf) | 169 | 52°35′N | 21°29′E |
| Wytheville, Va., U.S. (wĭth′vĭl) | 125 | 36°55′N | 81°06′W |


# X


| PLACE (Pronunciation) | PAGE | LAT. | LONG. |
| --- | --- | --- | --- |
| Xàbia, Spain | 173 | 38°45′N | 0°07′E |
| Xagua, Banco, bk., Cuba (bä′n-kō-sä′gwä) | 134 | 21°35′N | 80°50′W |
| Xai Xai, Moz. | 232 | 25°00′S | 33°45′E |
| Xalapa, Mex. | 128 | 19°32′N | 96°53′W |
| Xangongo, Ang. | 232 | 16°50′S | 15°05′E |
| Xankändi (Stepanakert), Azer. (styĕ′pän-ȧ-kĕrt) | 181 | 39°50′N | 46°40′E |
| Xanten, Ger. (ksän′tĕn) | 171c | 51°40′N | 6°28′E |
| Xánthi, Grc. | 163 | 41°08′N | 24°53′E |
| Xàtiva, Spain | 162 | 38°58′N | 0°31′W |
| Xau, Lake, l., Bots. | 232 | 21°15′S | 24°38′E |
| Xcalak, Mex. (sä-lä′k) | 132a | 18°15′N | 87°50′W |
| Xelva, Spain | 172 | 39°43′N | 1°00′W |
| Xenia, Oh., U.S. (zē′nĭ-ȧ) | 108 | 39°40′N | 83°55′W |
| Xi, r., China (shyē) | 209 | 23°15′N | 112°10′E |
| Xiajin, China (shyä-jyĭn) | 208 | 36°58′N | 115°59′E |
| Xiamen, China | 205 | 24°30′N | 118°10′E |
| Xiamen, i., Tai. (shyä-mŭn) | 209 | 24°28′N | 118°20′E |
| Xi'an, China (shyē-än) | 204 | 34°20′N | 109°00′E |
| Xiang, r., China (shyäŋ) | 205 | 27°30′N | 112°30′E |
| Xianghe, China (shyäŋ-hŭ) | 206 | 39°46′N | 116°59′E |
| Xiangtan, China (shyäŋ-tän) | 205 | 27°55′N | 112°45′E |
| Xianyang, China (shyĕn-yäŋ) | 208 | 34°20′N | 108°40′E |
| Xiaoxingkai Hu, l., China (shyou-shyĭŋ-kī ho͞o) | 210 | 42°25′N | 132°45′E |
| Xiapu, China (shyä-po͞o) | 205 | 27°00′N | 120°00′E |
| Xiayi, China (shyä-yē) | 206 | 34°15′N | 116°07′E |
| Xicotencatl, Mex. (sē-kō-tĕn-kät′′l) | 130 | 23°00′N | 98°58′W |
| Xifeng, China (shyē-fŭŋ) | 208 | 42°40′N | 124°40′E |
| Xiheying, China (shyē-hŭ-yĭŋ) | 206 | 39°58′N | 114°50′E |
| Xiliao, r., China (shyē-lĭou) | 208 | 43°23′N | 121°40′E |
| Xilitla, Mex. (sē-lē′tlä) | 130 | 21°24′N | 98°59′W |
| Xinchang, China (shyĭn-chäŋ) | 207b | 31°02′N | 121°38′E |
| Xing'an, China (shyĭŋ-än) | 209 | 25°44′N | 110°32′E |
| Xingcheng, China (shyĭŋ-chŭŋ) | 206 | 40°38′N | 120°41′E |
| Xinghua, China (shyĭŋ-hwä) | 206 | 32°58′N | 119°48′E |
| Xingjiawan, China (shyĭŋ-jyä-wän) | 206 | 37°16′N | 114°54′E |
| Xingtai, China (shyĭŋ-tī) | 206 | 37°04′N | 114°33′E |
| Xingu, r., Braz. (zhĕŋ-gō′) | 143 | 6°20′S | 52°34′W |
| Xinhai, China (shyĭn-hī) | 206 | 36°59′N | 117°33′E |
| Xinhua, China (shyĭn-hwä) | 209 | 27°45′N | 111°20′E |
| Xinhuai, r., China (shyĭn-hwī) | 206 | 33°48′N | 119°39′E |
| Xinhui, China (shyn-hwā) | 209 | 22°40′N | 113°08′E |
| Xining, China (shyē-nĭŋ) | 204 | 36°52′N | 101°36′E |
| Xinjiang (Sinkiang), prov., China (shyĭn-jyäŋ) | 204 | 40°15′N | 82°15′E |
| Xinjin, China (shyĭn-jyĭn) | 208 | 39°23′N | 121°57′E |
| Xinmin, China (shyĭn-mĭn) | 208 | 42°00′N | 122°42′E |
| Xintai, China (shyĭn-tī) | 206 | 35°55′N | 117°44′E |
| Xintang, China (shyĭn-täŋ) | 207a | 23°08′N | 113°36′E |
| Xinxian, China (shyĭn shyĕn) | 206 | 31°47′N | 114°50′E |
| Xinxian, China | 208 | 38°20′N | 112°45′E |
| Xinxiang, China (shyĭn-shyäŋ) | 208 | 35°17′N | 113°49′E |
| Xinyang, China (shyĭn-yäŋ) | 205 | 32°08′N | 114°04′E |
| Xinye, China (shyĭn-yŭ) | 208 | 32°40′N | 112°20′E |
| Xinzao, China (shyĭn-dzou) | 207a | 23°01′N | 113°25′E |
| Xinzheng, China (shyĭn-jŭŋ) | 206 | 34°24′N | 113°43′E |
| Xinzo de Limia, Spain | 172 | 42°03′N | 7°43′W |
| Xiongyuecheng, China (shyôŋ-yûĕ-chŭŋ) | 206 | 40°10′N | 122°08′E |
| Xiping, China (shyē-pĭŋ) | 206 | 33°21′N | 114°01′E |
| Xishui, China (shyē-shwā) | 209 | 30°30′N | 115°10′E |
| Xixian, China (shyē shyĕn) | 206 | 32°20′N | 114°42′E |
| Xixona, Spain | 173 | 38°31′N | 0°29′W |
| Xiyang, China (shyē-yäŋ) | 206 | 37°37′N | 113°42′E |
| Xiyou, China (shyē-yō) | 206 | 37°21′N | 119°59′E |
| Xizang (Tibet), prov., China (shyē-dzäŋ) | 204 | 31°15′N | 87°30′E |
| Xizhong Dao, i., China (shyē-jôŋ dou) | 206 | 39°27′N | 121°06′E |
| Xochihuehuetlán, Mex. (sō-chē-wĕ-wĕ-tlä′n) | 131 | 17°53′N | 98°29′E |
| Xochimilco, Mex. (sō-chē-mēl′kô) | 131a | 19°15′N | 99°06′W |
| Xuancheng, China (shyûän-chŭŋ) | 209 | 30°52′N | 118°48′E |
| Xuanhua, China (shyûän-hwä) | 208 | 40°35′N | 115°05′E |
| Xuanhuadian, China (shyûän-hwä-dĭĕn) | 206 | 31°42′N | 114°29′E |
| Xuchang, China (shyo͞o-chäŋ) | 208 | 34°02′N | 113°49′E |
| Xudat, Azer. | 182 | 41°38′N | 48°42′E |
| Xuddur, Som. | 238a | 3°55′N | 43°45′E |
| Xun, r., China (shyòn) | 209 | 23°28′N | 110°30′E |
| Xuzhou, China | 205 | 34°17′N | 117°10′E |


# Y


| PLACE (Pronunciation) | PAGE | LAT. | LONG. |
| --- | --- | --- | --- |
| Ya'an, China (yä-än) | 204 | 30°00′N | 103°20′E |
| Yablonovyy Khrebet, mts., Russia (yȧ-blô-nô-vĕ′) | 179 | 51°15′N | 111°30′E |
| Yablunivsikyi, Pereval, p., Ukr. | 169 | 48°20′N | 24°25′E |
| Yacheng, China (yä-chŭŋ) | 209 | 18°20′N | 109°10′E |
| Yachiyo, Japan | 211a | 35°43′N | 140°07′E |
| Yacolt, Wa., U.S. (yă′kōlt) | 116c | 45°52′N | 122°24′W |
| Yacolt Mountain, mtn., Wa., U.S. | 116c | 45°52′N | 122°27′W |
| Yacona, r., Ms., U.S. (yȧ′cō nă) | 124 | 34°13′N | 89°30′W |
| Yacuiba, Bol. (yȧ-ko͞o-ē′bȧ) | 142 | 22°02′S | 63°44′W |
| Yadkin, r., N.C., U.S. (yăd′kĭn) | 125 | 36°12′N | 80°40′W |
| Yafran, Libya | 230 | 31°57′N | 12°04′E |
| Yaguajay, Cuba (yä-guä-hä′ē) | 134 | 22°20′N | 79°20′W |
| Yahagi-Gawa, r., Japan (yä′hä-gē gä′wä) | 211 | 35°16′N | 137°22′E |
| Yahongqiao, China (yä-hôŋ-chyou) | 206 | 39°45′N | 117°52′E |
| Yahualica, Mex. (yä-wä-lē′kä) | 130 | 21°08′N | 102°53′W |
| Yajalón, Mex. (yä-hä-lōn′) | 131 | 17°16′N | 92°20′W |
| Yakhroma, Russia (yäl′rô-ma) | 186b | 56°17′N | 37°30′E |
| Yakhroma, r., Russia | 186b | 56°15′N | 37°38′E |
| Yakima, Wa., U.S. (yăk′ĭmȧ) | 104 | 46°35′N | 120°30′W |
| Yakima, r., Wa., U.S. (yăk′ĭ-mȧ) | 114 | 46°48′N | 120°22′W |
| Yakima Indian Reservation, I.R., Wa., U.S. | 114 | 46°16′N | 121°03′W |
| Yakoma, D.R.C. | 236 | 4°05′N | 22°27′E |
| Yaku, i., Japan (yä′ko͞o) | 205 | 30°15′N | 130°41′E |
| Yakutat, Ak., U.S. (yăk′ô-tăt) | 103 | 59°32′N | 139°35′W |
| Yakutsk, Russia (yȧ-kōtsk′) | 179 | 62°13′N | 129°49′E |
| Yale, Mi., U.S. | 108 | 43°05′N | 82°45′W |
| Yale, Ok., U.S. | 121 | 36°07′N | 96°42′W |
| Yale Lake, res., Wa., U.S. | 114 | 46°00′N | 122°20′W |
| Yalinga, C.A.R. (yȧ-lĭŋ′gȧ) | 231 | 6°56′N | 23°22′E |
| Yalobusha, r., Ms., U.S. (yȧ-lō-bōsh′ȧ) | 124 | 33°48′N | 90°02′W |
| Yalong, r., China (yä-lôŋ) | 204 | 32°29′N | 98°41′E |
| Yalta, Ukr. (yäl′tȧ) | 181 | 44°29′N | 34°12′E |
| Yalu, r., Asia | 205 | 41°20′N | 126°35′E |
| Yalutorovsk, Russia (yä-lo͞o-tô′rôfsk) | 178 | 56°42′N | 66°32′E |
| Yamada, Japan (yä′mä-dȧ) | 211 | 33°37′N | 133°39′E |
| Yamagata, Japan (yä-mȧ′gä-tȧ) | 205 | 38°12′N | 140°24′E |
| Yamaguchi, Japan (yä-mȧ′go͞o-chē) | 210 | 34°10′N | 131°30′E |
| Yamal, Poluostrov, pen., Russia (yä-mäl′) | 178 | 71°15′N | 70°00′E |
| Yamantau, Gora, mtn., Russia (gȧ-rä′ yä′man-tȧw) | 186a | 54°16′N | 58°08′E |
| Yamasaki, Japan (yä′mȧ′sä-kē) | 211 | 35°01′N | 134°33′E |
| Yamasaki, Japan | 211b | 34°53′N | 135°41′E |
| Yamashina, Japan (yä′mä-shē′nä) | 211b | 34°59′N | 135°50′E |
| Yamashita, Japan (yä′mä-shē′tä) | 211b | 34°53′N | 135°25′E |
| Yamato, Japan | 211a | 35°28′N | 139°28′E |
| Yamato-Kōriyama, Japan | 211b | 34°39′N | 135°48′E |
| Yamato-takada, Japan (yä′mä-tô tä′kä-dä) | 211b | 34°31′N | 135°45′E |
| Yambi, Mesa de, mtn., Col. (mĕ′sä-dĕ-yȧ′m-bē) | 142 | 1°55′N | 71°45′W |
| Yambol, Blg. (yȧm′bôl) | 163 | 42°28′N | 26°31′E |
| Yamdena, i., Indon. | 213 | 7°23′S | 130°30′E |
| Yamethin, Mya. (yŭ-mē′thĕn) | 199 | 20°14′N | 96°27′E |
| Yamhill, Or., U.S. (yăm′hĭl) | 116c | 45°20′N | 123°11′W |
| Yamkino, Russia (yäm′kĭ-nô) | 186b | 55°56′N | 38°25′E |
| Yamma Yamma, Lake, l., Austl. (yăm′ȧ yăm′ȧ) | 221 | 26°15′S | 141°30′E |
| Yamoussoukro, C. Iv. | 230 | 6°49′N | 5°17′W |
| Yamsk, Russia (yämsk) | 179 | 59°41′N | 154°09′E |
| Yamuna, r., India | 199 | 25°30′N | 80°30′E |
| Yamzho Yumco, l., China (yäm-jwo yo͞om-tswo) | 204 | 29°11′N | 91°26′E |
| Yana, r., Russia (yä′nȧ) | 179 | 71°00′N | 136°00′E |
| Yanac, Austl. (yăn′ăk) | 219 | 36°10′S | 141°30′E |
| Yanagawa, Japan (yä-nä′gä-wä) | 211 | 33°11′N | 130°24′E |
| Yanam, India (yŭnŭm′) | 199 | 16°48′N | 82°15′E |
| Yan'an, China (yän-än) | 204 | 36°46′N | 109°15′E |
| Yanbu', Sau. Ar. | 198 | 23°57′N | 38°02′E |
| Yancheng, China (yän-chŭŋ) | 208 | 33°23′N | 120°11′E |
| Yancheng, China | 208 | 33°38′N | 113°59′E |
| Yandongi, D.R.C. | 236 | 2°51′N | 22°16′E |
| Yangcheng Hu, l., China (yäŋ-chŭŋ ho͞o) | 206 | 31°30′N | 120°31′E |
| Yangchun, China (yäŋ-chòn) | 209 | 22°08′N | 111°48′E |
| Yang'erzhuang, China (yäŋ-är-jûäŋ) | 206 | 38°18′N | 117°31′E |
| Yanggezhuang, China (yäŋ-gŭ-jûäŋ) | 208a | 40°10′N | 116°48′E |
| Yanggu, China (yäŋ-go͞o) | 206 | 36°06′N | 115°46′E |
| Yanghe, China (yäŋ-hŭ) | 206 | 33°48′N | 118°23′E |
| Yangjiang, China (yäŋ-jyäŋ) | 209 | 21°52′N | 111°58′E |
| Yangjiaogou, China (yäŋ-jyou-gō) | 206 | 37°17′N | 118°53′E |
| Yangon *see* Rangoon, Mya. | 199 | 16°46′N | 96°09′E |
| Yangquan, China (yäŋ-chyûän) | 206 | 37°52′N | 113°36′E |
| Yangtze (Chang), r., China (yäng′tse) (chäŋ) | 205 | 30°30′N | 117°25′E |
| Yangxin, China (yäŋ-shyĭn) | 206 | 37°39′N | 117°34′E |
| Yangyang, Kor., S. (yäng′yäng′) | 210 | 38°02′N | 128°38′E |
| Yangzhou, China (yäŋ-jō) | 205 | 32°24′N | 119°24′E |
| Yanji, China (yän-jyē) | 205 | 42°55′N | 129°35′E |
| Yanjiahe, China (yän-jyä-hŭ) | 206 | 31°55′N | 114°47′E |
| Yanjin, China (yän-jyĭn) | 206 | 35°09′N | 114°13′E |
| Yankton, S.D., U.S. (yănk′tŭn) | 104 | 42°51′N | 97°24′W |
| Yanling, China (yän-lĭŋ) | 206 | 34°07′N | 114°12′E |
| Yanshan, China (yän-shän) | 208 | 38°05′N | 117°15′E |
| Yanshou, China (yän-shō) | 208 | 45°25′N | 128°43′E |
| Yantai, China | 205 | 37°32′N | 121°22′E |
| Yanychi, Russia (yȧ′nĭ-chĭ) | 186a | 57°42′N | 56°24′E |
| Yanzhou, China (yäŋ-jō) | 205 | 35°35′N | 116°50′E |
| Yanzhuang, China (yän-jûäŋ) | 206 | 36°08′N | 117°47′E |
| Yao, Chad (yä′ō) | 218 | 13°00′N | 17°38′E |
| Yao, Japan | 211b | 34°37′N | 135°37′E |
| Yaoundé, Cam. | 230 | 3°52′N | 11°31′E |
| Yap, i., Micron. (yăp) | 3 | 11°00′N | 138°00′E |
| Yapen, Pulau, i., Indon. | 213 | 1°30′S | 136°15′E |
| Yaque del Norte, r., Dom. Rep. (yä′kȧ dĕl nôr′tȧ) | 129 | 19°40′N | 71°25′W |
| Yaque del Sur, r., Dom. Rep. (yä-kĕ-dĕl-so͞o′r) | 135 | 18°35′N | 71°05′W |
| Yaqui, r., Mex. (yä′kē) | 128 | 28°15′N | 109°40′W |
| Yaracuy, dept., Ven. (yä-rä-ko͞o′ē) | 143b | 10°10′N | 68°31′W |
| Yaraka, Austl. (yȧ-răk′ȧ) | 219 | 24°50′S | 144°08′E |
| Yaransk, Russia (yä-ränsk′) | 178 | 57°18′N | 48°05′E |
| Yarda, oasis, Chad (yär′dȧ) | 231 | 18°29′N | 19°13′E |
| Yare, r., Eng., U.K. | 165 | 52°40′N | 1°32′E |
| Yarkand *see* Shache, China | 204 | 38°15′N | 77°15′E |
| Yarmouth, Can. (yär′mŭth) | 100 | 43°50′N | 66°07′W |
| Yaroslavka, Russia (yȧ-rô-släv′kȧ) | 186a | 55°52′N | 57°59′E |
| Yaroslavl', Russia (yȧ-rô-släv′′l) | 178 | 57°37′N | 39°54′E |
| Yaroslavl', prov., Russia | 176 | 58°05′N | 38°05′E |
| Yarra, r., Austl. | 217a | 37°51′S | 144°54′E |
| Yarro-to, l., Russia (yȧ′rô-tô′) | 180 | 67°55′N | 71°35′E |
| Yartsevo, Russia (yär′tsyĕ-vô) | 180 | 55°04′N | 32°38′E |
| Yartsevo, Russia | 179 | 60°13′N | 89°52′E |
| Yarumal, Col. (yä-ro͞o-mäl′) | 142 | 6°57′N | 75°24′W |
| Yasawa Group, is., Fiji | 214g | 17°00′S | 177°23′E |
| Yasel'da, r., Bela. (yä-syŭl′dȧ) | 169 | 52°13′N | 25°53′E |
| Yateras, Cuba (yä-tā′räs) | 135 | 20°00′N | 75°00′W |
| Yates Center, Ks., U.S. (yāts) | 121 | 37°53′N | 95°44′W |
| Yathkyed, l., Can. (yȧth-kī-ĕd′) | 92 | 62°41′N | 98°00′W |
| Yatsuga-take, mtn., Japan (yät′so͞o-gä dä′kä) | 211 | 36°01′N | 138°21′W |
| Yatsushiro, Japan (yät′so͞o′shē-rô) | 211 | 32°30′N | 130°35′E |
| Yatta Plateau, plat., Kenya | 237 | 1°55′S | 38°10′E |
| Yautepec, Mex. (yä-o͞o-tâ-pĕk′) | 130 | 18°53′N | 99°04′W |
| Yawata, Japan (yä′wä-tä) | 211 | 34°52′N | 135°43′E |
| Yawatahama, Japan (yä′wä′tä′hä-mä) | 211 | 33°24′N | 132°25′E |
| Yaxian, China (yä shyĕn) | 209 | 18°10′N | 109°32′E |
| Yayama, D.R.C. | 236 | 1°16′S | 23°07′E |
| Yayao, China (yä-you) | 207a | 23°10′N | 113°40′E |
| Yazd, Iran | 198 | 31°59′N | 54°03′E |
| Yazoo, r., Ms., U.S. (yă′zo͞o) | 107 | 32°32′N | 90°40′W |
| Yazoo City, Ms., U.S. | 124 | 32°50′N | 90°18′W |
| Ýdra, i., Grc. | 175 | 37°20′N | 23°30′E |
| Ye, Mya. (yā) | 212 | 15°13′N | 97°52′E |
| Yeadon, Pa., U.S. (yē′dŭn) | 110f | 39°56′N | 75°16′W |
| Yecla, Spain (yā′klä) | 172 | 38°35′N | 1°09′W |
| Yefremov, Russia (yĕ-frä′môf) | 176 | 53°08′N | 38°04′E |
| Yegor'yevsk, Russia (yĕ-gôr′yĕfsk) | 180 | 55°23′N | 38°59′E |
| Yeji, China (yŭ-jyē) | 206 | 31°52′N | 115°57′E |
| Yekaterinburg, Russia | 178 | 56°51′N | 60°36′E |
| Yelabuga, Russia (yĕ-lä′bô-gȧ) | 180 | 55°50′N | 52°18′E |
| Yelan, Russia | 181 | 50°50′N | 44°00′E |
| Yelets, Russia (yĕ-lyĕts′) | 178 | 52°35′N | 38°28′E |
| Yelizavetpol'skiy, Russia (yĕ′lĭ-za-vĕt-pôl-skĭ) | 186a | 52°51′N | 60°38′E |
| Yelizavety, Mys, c., Russia (yĕ-lyĕ-sȧ-vyĕ′tĭ) | 179 | 54°28′N | 142°59′E |
| Yell, i., Scot., U.K. (yĕl) | 164a | 60°35′N | 1°27′W |
| Yellow *see* Huang, r., China | 205 | 35°06′N | 113°39′E |
| Yellow, r., Fl., U.S. (yĕl′ô) | 124 | 30°33′N | 86°53′W |
| Yellowhead Pass, p., Can. (yĕl′ô-hĕd) | 95 | 52°52′N | 118°35′W |
| Yellowknife, Can. (yĕl′ô-nīf) | 90 | 62°29′N | 114°38′W |
| Yellow Sea, sea, Asia | 205 | 35°20′N | 122°15′E |
| Yellowstone, r., U.S. | 106 | 46°00′N | 108°00′W |
| Yellowstone, Clarks Fork, r., U.S. | 115 | 44°55′N | 109°05′W |
| Yellowstone Lake, l., Wy., U.S. | 106 | 44°27′N | 110°03′W |

PRONOUNCING INDEX

Yellowstone National Park – Zeya 369


| PLACE (Pronunciation) | PAGE | LAT. | LONG. |
|---|---|---|---|
| Yellowstone National Park, rec., U.S. (yĕl′ô-stōn) | 106 | 44°45′N | 110°35′W |
| Yel′nya, Russia (yĕl′nyȧ) | 176 | 54°34′N | 33°12′E |
| Yemanzhelinsk, Russia (yĕ-mȧn-zhâ′lĭnsk) | 186a | 54°47′N | 61°24′E |
| Yemen, nation, Asia (yĕm′ĕn) | 198 | 15°00′N | 47°00′E |
| Yemetsk, Russia | 180 | 63°28′N | 41°28′E |
| Yenangyaung, Mya. (yä′nän-d oung) | 199 | 20°27′N | 94°59′E |
| Yencheng, China | 204 | 37°30′N | 79°26′E |
| Yendi, Ghana (yĕn′dē) | 230 | 9°26′N | 0°01′W |
| Yengisar, China (yŭn-gē-sär) | 204 | 39°01′N | 75°29′E |
| Yenice, r., Tur. | 181 | 41°10′N | 33°00′E |
| Yenisey, r., Russia (yĕ-nē-sĕ′ē) | 178 | 71°00′N | 82°00′E |
| Yeniseysk, Russia (yĕ-nĭĕsā′ĭsk) | 179 | 58°27′N | 90°28′E |
| Yeo, l., Austl. (yō) | 220 | 28°15′S | 124°00′E |
| Yerevan, Arm. (yĕ-rĕ-vän′) | 181 | 40°10′N | 44°30′E |
| Yerington, Nv., U.S. (yĕ′rĭng-tŭn) | 118 | 38°59′N | 119°10′W |
| Yermak, i., Russia | 180 | 66°45′N | 71°30′E |
| Yeste, Spain (yĕs′tȧ) | 172 | 38°23′N | 2°19′W |
| Yeu, Île d′, i., Fr. (ēl dyû) | 161 | 46°43′N | 2°45′W |
| Yevlax, Azer. | 182 | 40°36′N | 47°09′E |
| Yexian, China (yŭ-shyĕn) | 206 | 37°09′N | 119°57′E |
| Yeya, r., Russia (yä′yȧ) | 177 | 46°25′N | 39°17′E |
| Yeysk, Russia (yĕysk) | 181 | 46°41′N | 38°13′E |
| Yi, r., China | 206 | 34°38′N | 118°07′E |
| Yibin, China (yē-bĭn) | 204 | 28°50′N | 104°40′E |
| Yichang, China (yē-chäŋ) | 205 | 30°38′N | 111°22′E |
| Yidu, China (yē-do͞o) | 208 | 36°42′N | 118°30′E |
| Yilan, China (yē-län) | 205 | 46°10′N | 129°40′E |
| Yinchuan, China (yĭn-chůän) | 204 | 38°22′N | 106°22′E |
| Yingkou, China (yĭŋ-kō) | 205 | 40°35′N | 122°10′E |
| Yining, China (yē-nĭŋ) | 204 | 43°58′N | 80°40′E |
| Yin Shan, mts., China (yĭng′shän′) | 208 | 40°50′N | 110°30′E |
| Yishan, China (yē-shän) | 204 | 24°32′N | 108°42′E |
| Yishui, China (yē-shwā) | 206 | 35°49′N | 118°40′E |
| Yitong, China (yē-tôŋ) | 205 | 43°15′N | 125°10′E |
| Yixian, China (yē shyĕn) | 208 | 41°30′N | 121°15′E |
| Yixing, China | 206 | 31°26′N | 119°57′E |
| Yiyang, China (yē-yäŋ) | 209 | 28°52′N | 112°12′E |
| Yoakum, Tx., U.S. (yō′kŭm) | 123 | 29°18′N | 97°09′W |
| Yockanookany, r., Ms., U.S. (yŏk′ȧ-no͞o-kă-nĭ) | 124 | 32°47′N | 89°38′W |
| Yodo-Gawa, strt., Japan (yō′dō′gä-wä) | 211b | 34°46′N | 135°35′E |
| Yog Point, c., Phil. (yōg) | 209 | 14°00′N | 124°30′E |
| Yogyakarta, Indon. (yŏg-yȧ-kär′tȧ) | 212 | 7°50′S | 110°20′E |
| Yoho National Park, rec., Can. (yō′hō) | 90 | 51°26′N | 116°30′W |
| Yojoa, Lago de, l., Hond. (lä′gô dĕ yô-hō′ä) | 132 | 14°49′N | 87°53′W |
| Yokkaichi, Japan (yō′kä′ē-chē) | 210 | 34°58′N | 136°35′E |
| Yokohama, Japan (yō′kô-hä′mạ) | 205 | 35°37′N | 139°40′E |
| Yokosuka, Japan (yō-kō′sŏo-kä) | 210 | 35°17′N | 139°40′E |
| Yokota, Japan (yō-kō′tä) | 211a | 35°23′N | 140°02′E |
| Yola, Nig. (yō′lä) | 230 | 9°13′N | 12°27′E |
| Yolaina, Cordillera de, mts., Nic. | 133 | 11°34′N | 84°34′W |
| Yomou, Gui. | 234 | 7°34′N | 9°16′W |
| Yonago, Japan (yō′nä-gō) | 210 | 35°27′N | 133°19′E |
| Yonezawa, Japan (yō′nĕ′zȧ-wä) | 210 | 37°50′N | 140°07′E |
| Yong′an, China (yôŋ-än) | 209 | 26°00′N | 117°22′E |
| Yongding, r., China (yôŋ-dĭŋ) | 208 | 40°25′N | 115°00′E |
| Yŏngdŏk, Kor., S. (yŭng′dŭk′) | 210 | 36°28′N | 129°25′E |
| Yŏnghŭng, Kor., N. (yŭng′hŏng′) | 210 | 39°31′N | 127°11′E |
| Yonghŭng Man, b., Kor., N. | 210 | 39°10′N | 128°00′E |
| Yongnian, China (yôŋ-nĭĕn) | 208 | 36°47′N | 114°32′E |
| Yongqing, China (yôŋ-chyĭŋ) | 208a | 39°18′N | 116°27′E |
| Yongshun, China (yôŋ-shôn) | 204 | 29°05′N | 109°58′E |
| Yonkers, N.Y., U.S. (yŏŋ′kẽrz) | 110a | 40°57′N | 73°54′W |
| Yonne, r., Fr. (yôn) | 170 | 48°18′N | 3°15′E |
| Yono, Japan (yō′nō) | 211a | 35°53′N | 139°36′E |
| Yorba Linda, Ca., U.S. (yôr′bȧ lĭn′dȧ) | 117a | 33°55′N | 117°51′W |
| York, Austl. | 218 | 32°00′S | 117°00′E |
| York, Eng., U.K. | 160 | 53°58′N | 1°10′W |
| York, Al., U.S. (yôrk) | 124 | 32°33′N | 88°16′W |
| York, Ne., U.S. | 121 | 40°52′N | 97°36′W |
| York, Pa., U.S. | 105 | 40°00′N | 76°40′W |
| York, S.C., U.S. | 125 | 34°59′N | 81°14′W |
| York, Cape, c., Austl. | 221 | 10°45′S | 142°35′E |
| York, Kap, c., Grnld. | 89 | 75°30′N | 73°00′W |
| Yorke Peninsula, pen., Austl. | 222 | 34°24′S | 137°20′E |
| Yorketown, Austl. | 222 | 35°00′S | 137°28′E |
| York Factory, Can. | 97 | 57°05′N | 92°18′W |
| Yorkshire Wolds, Eng., U.K. (yôrk′shĭr) | 164 | 54°00′N | 0°35′W |
| Yorkton, Can. (yôrk′tŭn) | 90 | 51°13′N | 102°28′W |
| Yorktown, Tx., U.S. (yôrk′toun) | 123 | 28°57′N | 97°30′W |
| Yorktown, Va., U.S. | 125 | 37°12′N | 76°31′W |
| Yoro, Hond. (yō′rō) | 132 | 15°09′N | 87°05′W |
| Yoron, i., Japan | 210 | 26°48′N | 128°40′E |
| Yosemite National Park, rec., Ca., U.S. (yō-sĕm′ĭ-tē) | 106 | 38°03′N | 119°36′W |
| Yoshida, Japan (yō′shē-dȧ) | 211 | 34°39′N | 132°41′E |
| Yoshikawa, Japan (yō-shē′kä′wä′) | 211a | 35°53′N | 139°51′E |
| Yoshino, r., Japan (yō′shē-nō) | 211 | 34°04′N | 133°57′E |
| Yoshkar-Ola, Russia (yôsh-kär′ō-lä′) | 180 | 56°35′N | 48°05′E |
| Yos Sudarsa, Pulau, i., Indon. | 213 | 7°20′S | 138°30′E |
| Yŏsu, Kor., S. (yŭ′so͞o′) | 210 | 34°42′N | 127°42′E |
| You, r., China (yō) | 209 | 23°55′N | 106°50′E |
| Youghal, Ire. (yo͞o′ôl) (yôl) | 165 | 51°58′N | 7°57′E |
| Youghal Bay, b., Ire. | 164 | 51°52′N | 7°46′W |
| Young, Austl. (yŭng) | 222 | 34°15′S | 148°18′E |
| Young, Ur. (yô-o͞o′ng) | 141c | 32°42′S | 57°38′W |
| Youngs, l., Wa., U.S. (yŭngz) | 116a | 47°25′N | 122°08′W |
| Youngstown, N.Y., U.S. | 111c | 43°15′N | 79°02′W |
| Youngstown, Oh., U.S. | 108 | 41°05′N | 80°40′W |
| Yozgat, Tur. (yôz′gȧd) | 198 | 39°50′N | 34°50′E |
| Ypsilanti, Mi., U.S. (ĭp-sĭ-lăn′tĭ) | 111b | 42°15′N | 83°37′W |
| Yreka, Ca., U.S. (wī-rē′kȧ) | 114 | 41°43′N | 122°36′W |
| Yrghyz, Kaz. | 183 | 48°30′N | 61°17′E |
| Yrghyz, r., Kaz. | 156 | 49°30′N | 60°32′E |
| Ysleta, Tx., U.S. (ēz-lĕ′tȧ) | 122 | 31°42′N | 106°18′W |
| Yssingeaux, Fr. (ē-săN-zhō) | 170 | 45°09′N | 4°08′E |
| Ystad, Swe. | 160 | 55°25′N | 13°49′E |
| Ystādeh-ye Moqor, Āb-e, l., Afg. | 202 | 32°35′N | 68°00′E |
| Yu′alliq, Jabal, mts., Egypt | 197a | 30°12′N | 33°42′E |
| Yuan, r., China (yůän) | 205 | 28°50′N | 110°50′E |
| Yuan′an, China (yůän-än) | 209 | 31°08′N | 111°28′E |
| Yuanling, China (yůän-lĭŋ) | 209 | 28°30′N | 110°18′E |
| Yuanshi, China (yůän-shr) | 208 | 37°45′N | 114°32′E |
| Yuasa, Japan | 211 | 34°02′N | 135°10′E |
| Yuba City, Ca., U.S. (yo͞o′bȧ) | 118 | 39°08′N | 121°38′W |
| Yucaipa, Ca., U.S. (yŭ-kȧ-ē′pȧ) | 117a | 34°02′N | 117°02′W |
| Yucatán, state, Mex. (yo͞o-kä-tän′) | 128 | 20°45′N | 89°00′W |
| Yucatan Channel, strt., N.A. | 128 | 22°30′N | 87°00′W |
| Yucatan Peninsula, pen., N.A. | 132 | 19°30′N | 89°00′W |
| Yucheng, China (yo͞o-chŭŋ) | 206 | 34°31′N | 115°54′E |
| Yucheng, China | 208 | 36°55′N | 116°39′E |
| Yuci, China (yo͞o-tsz) | 208 | 37°32′N | 112°40′E |
| Yudoma, r., Russia (yo͞o-dō′mȧ) | 185 | 59°13′N | 137°00′E |
| Yueqing, China (yůĕ-chyĭn) | 209 | 28°02′N | 120°40′E |
| Yueyang, China (yůĕ-yäŋ) | 205 | 29°25′N | 113°05′E |
| Yuezhuang, China (yůĕ-jůäŋ) | 206 | 36°13′N | 118°17′E |
| Yug, r., Russia (yôg) | 180 | 59°50′N | 45°55′E |
| Yugoslavia, *see* Serbia and Montenegro, nation, Eur. (yo͞o-gô-slä-vĭ-ȧ) | 154 | 44°00′N | 21°00′E |
| Yukhnov, Russia (yôk′nof) | 176 | 54°44′N | 35°15′E |
| Yukon, ter., Can. (yo͞o′kŏn) | 90 | 63°16′N | 135°30′W |
| Yukon, r., N.A. | 106a | 64°00′N | 159°30′W |
| Yukutat Bay, b., Ak., U.S. (yo͞o-kū tăt′) | 103 | 59°34′N | 140°50′W |
| Yuldybayevo, Russia (yôld′bä′yĕ-vô) | 186a | 52°20′N | 57°52′E |
| Yulin, China (yo͞o-lĭn) | 209 | 22°38′N | 110°10′E |
| Yulin, China | 204 | 38°18′N | 109°45′E |
| Yuma, Az., U.S. (yo͞o′mä) | 104 | 32°40′N | 114°40′W |
| Yuma, Co., U.S. | 120 | 40°08′N | 102°50′W |
| Yuma, r., Dom. Rep. | 135 | 19°05′N | 70°05′W |
| Yumbi, D.R.C. | 237 | 1°14′S | 26°14′E |
| Yumen, China (yo͞o-mŭn) | 204 | 40°14′N | 96°56′E |
| Yuncheng, China (yòn-chŭŋ) | 208 | 35°00′N | 110°40′E |
| Yunnan, prov., China (yun′nän′) | 204 | 24°23′N | 101°03′E |
| Yunnan Plat, plat., China (yò-nän) | 204 | 26°03′N | 101°26′E |
| Yunxian, China (yòn shyĕn) | 205 | 32°50′N | 110°55′E |
| Yunxiao, China (yòn-shyou) | 209 | 24°00′N | 117°20′E |
| Yura, Japan (yo͞o′rä) | 211 | 34°18′N | 134°54′E |
| Yurécuaro, Mex. (yo͞o-rā′kwä-rō) | 130 | 20°21′N | 102°16′W |
| Yurimaguas, Peru (yo͞o-rē-mä′gwäs) | 142 | 5°59′S | 76°12′W |
| Yuriria, Mex. (yo͞o′rē-rē′ä) | 130 | 20°11′N | 101°08′W |
| Yurovo, Russia | 186b | 55°30′N | 38°24′E |
| Yur′yevets, Russia | 180 | 57°15′N | 43°08′E |
| Yuscarán, Hond. (yo͞os-kä-rän′) | 132 | 13°57′N | 86°48′W |
| Yushan, China (yo͞o-shän) | 209 | 28°42′N | 118°20′E |
| Yü Shan, mtn., Tai. | 205 | 23°38′N | 121°05′E |
| Yushu, China (yo͞o-sho͞o) | 208 | 44°58′N | 126°32′E |
| Yutian, China (yo͞o-tĭĕn) | 208 | 39°54′N | 117°45′E |
| Yutian, China (yo͞o-tĭĕn) (kŭ-r-yä) | 204 | 36°55′N | 81°39′E |
| Yuty, Para. (yo͞o-tē′) | 144 | 26°45′S | 56°13′W |
| Yuwangcheng, China (yü′wäng′chĕng) | 206 | 31°32′N | 114°26′E |
| Yuxian, China (yo͞o shyĕn) | 208 | 39°40′N | 114°38′E |
| Yuzha, Russia (yo͞o′zhȧ) | 180 | 56°38′N | 42°20′E |
| Yuzhno-Sakhalinsk, Russia (yo͞ozh′nô-sä-kä-lĭnsk′) | 179 | 47°11′N | 143°04′E |
| Yuzhnoural′skiy, Russia (yo͞ozh-nô-ò-rál′skĭ) | 186a | 54°26′N | 61°17′E |
| Yuzhnyy Ural, mts., Russia (yo͞o′zhnĭ ò-räl′) | 186a | 52°51′N | 57°48′E |
| Yverdon, Switz. (ē-vĕr-dôn) | 168 | 46°46′N | 6°35′E |
| Yvetot, Fr. (ēv-tō′) | 170 | 49°39′N | 0°45′E |


# Z


| PLACE (Pronunciation) | PAGE | LAT. | LONG. |
|---|---|---|---|
| Za, r., Mor. | 162 | 34°19′N | 2°23′W |
| Zaachila, Mex. (sä-ä-chē′lȧ) | 131 | 16°56′N | 96°45′W |
| Zaandam, Neth. (zän′dȧm) | 165 | 52°25′N | 4°49′E |
| Ząbkowice Śląskie, Pol. | 168 | 50°35′N | 16°48′E |
| Zabrze, Pol. (zäb′zhĕ) | 161 | 50°18′N | 18°48′E |
| Zacapa, Guat. (sä-kä′pä) | 132 | 14°56′N | 89°30′W |
| Zacapoaxtla, Mex. (sä-kä-pō-äs′tlä) | 131 | 19°51′N | 97°34′W |
| Zacatecas, Mex. (sä-kä-tā′käs) | 128 | 22°44′N | 102°32′W |
| Zacatecas, state, Mex. | 128 | 24°00′N | 102°45′W |
| Zacatecoluca, El Sal. (sä-kä-tȧ-kō-lo͞o′kä) | 132 | 13°31′N | 88°50′W |
| Zacatelco, Mex. | 130 | 19°12′N | 98°12′W |
| Zacatepec, Mex. (sä-kä-tȧ-pĕk′) (sän-tē-ä′gō) | 131 | 17°10′N | 95°53′W |
| Zacatlán, Mex. (sä-kä-tlän′) | 131 | 19°55′N | 97°57′W |
| Zacoalco de Torres, Mex. (sä-kō-äl′kō dā tōr′rĕs) | 130 | 20°12′N | 103°33′W |
| Zacualpan, Mex. (sä-kō-äl-pän′) | 130 | 18°43′N | 99°46′W |
| Zacualtipan, Mex. (sä-kō-äl-tē-pän′) | 130 | 20°38′N | 98°39′W |
| Zadar, Cro. (zä′där) | 154 | 44°08′N | 15°16′E |
| Zadonsk, Russia (zä-dônsk′) | 176 | 52°22′N | 38°55′E |
| Žagare, Lat. (zhágárĕ) | 167 | 56°21′N | 23°14′E |
| Zagarolo, Italy (tzä-gä-rō′lō) | 173d | 41°51′N | 12°53′E |
| Zaghouan, Tun. (zȧ-gwän′) | 230 | 36°30′N | 10°04′E |
| Zagreb, Cro. (zä′grĕb) | 154 | 45°50′N | 15°58′E |
| Zagros Mountains, mts., Iran | 198 | 33°30′N | 46°30′E |
| Zāhedān, Iran (zä′hȧ-dän) | 198 | 29°37′N | 60°31′E |
| Zahlah, Leb. (zä′lä′) | 197a | 33°50′N | 35°54′E |
| Zaire *see* Congo, Democratic Republic of the , nation, Afr. | 232 | 1°00′S | 22°15′E |
| Zaječar, Serb. (zä′yĕ-chär′) | 175 | 43°54′N | 22°16′E |
| Zakhidnyi Buh (Bug), r., Eur. | 168 | 52°29′N | 21°20′E |
| Zakopane, Pol. (zȧ-kô-pä′nĕ) | 169 | 49°18′N | 19°57′E |
| Zakouma, Parc National de, rec., Chad | 235 | 10°50′N | 19°20′E |
| Zákynthos, Grc. | 175 | 37°48′N | 20°55′E |
| Zákynthos, i., Grc. | 163 | 37°45′N | 20°32′E |
| Zalaegerszeg, Hung. (zŏ′lô-ĕ′gĕr-sĕg) | 168 | 46°50′N | 16°50′E |
| Zalău, Rom. (zȧ-lŭ′ó) | 169 | 47°11′N | 23°06′E |
| Zaltan, Libya | 231 | 28°20′N | 19°40′E |
| Zaltbommel, Neth. | 159a | 51°48′N | 5°15′E |
| Zambezi, r., Afr. (zȧm-bā′zē) | 232 | 16°00′S | 29°45′E |
| Zambia, nation, Afr. (zăm′bē-ȧ) | 232 | 14°23′S | 24°15′E |
| Zamboanga, Phil. (säm-bô-aŋ′gä) | 212 | 6°58′N | 122°02′E |
| Zambrów, Pol. (zäm′bróf) | 169 | 52°29′N | 22°17′E |
| Zamora, Mex. (sä-mō′rä) | 128 | 19°59′N | 102°16′W |
| Zamora, Spain (thä-mō′rä) | 162 | 41°32′N | 5°43′W |
| Zanatepec, Mex. | 131 | 16°30′N | 94°22′W |
| Zandvoort, Neth. | 159a | 52°22′N | 4°30′E |
| Zanesville, Oh., U.S. (zānz′vĭl) | 108 | 39°55′N | 82°00′W |
| Zangasso, Mali | 234 | 12°09′N | 5°37′W |
| Zanjān, Iran | 198 | 36°26′N | 48°24′E |
| Zanzibar, Tan. (zăn′zĭ-bär) | 233 | 6°10′S | 39°11′E |
| Zanzibar, i., Tan. | 233 | 6°20′S | 39°37′E |
| Zanzibar Channel, strt., Tan. | 237 | 6°05′S | 39°00′E |
| Zaozhuang, China (dzou-jůäŋ) | 206 | 34°51′N | 117°34′E |
| Zapadnaya Dvina *see* Western Dvina, r., Eur. | 167 | 55°30′N | 28°27′E |
| Zapala, Arg. (zä-pä′lä) | 144 | 38°53′S | 70°02′W |
| Zapata, Tx., U.S. (sä-pä′tä) | 122 | 26°52′N | 99°18′W |
| Zapata, Ciénaga de, sw., Cuba (syĕ′nä-gä-dĕ-zä-pá′tä) | 134 | 22°30′N | 81°20′W |
| Zapata, Península de, pen., Cuba (pĕ-nē′n-so͞o-lä-dĕ-zä-pá′tä) | 134 | 22°20′N | 81°30′W |
| Zapatera, Isla, i., Nic. (ē′s-lä-sä-pä-tā′rō) | 132 | 11°45′N | 85°45′W |
| Zapopan, Mex. (sä-pō′pän) | 130 | 20°42′N | 103°23′W |
| Zaporizhzhia, Ukr. | 178 | 47°50′N | 35°10′E |
| Zaporizhzhia, prov., Ukr. | 177 | 47°20′N | 35°05′E |
| Zaporoshskoye, Russia (zȧ-pô-rôsh′skô-yĕ) | 167 | 60°36′N | 30°31′E |
| Zapotiltic, Mex. (sä-pô-tĕl-tēk′) | 130 | 19°37′N | 103°25′W |
| Zapotitlán, Mex. (sä-pô-tē-tlän′) | 130 | 17°13′N | 98°58′W |
| Zapotitlán, Punta, c., Mex. | 131 | 18°34′N | 94°48′W |
| Zapotlanejo, Mex. (sä-pô-tlä-nā′hô) | 130 | 20°38′N | 103°05′W |
| Zaragoza, Mex. (sä-rä-gō′sä) | 130 | 23°59′N | 99°45′W |
| Zaragoza, Mex. | 130 | 22°02′N | 100°45′W |
| Zaragoza, Spain (thä-rä-gō′thä) | 154 | 41°39′N | 0°53′W |
| Zarand, Munţii, mts., Rom. | 169 | 46°07′N | 22°21′E |
| Zaranda Hill, mtn., Nig. | 235 | 10°15′N | 9°35′E |
| Zaranj, Afg. | 201 | 31°06′N | 61°53′E |
| Zarasai, Lith. (zä-rä-sī′) | 167 | 55°45′N | 26°18′E |
| Zárate, Arg. (zä-rä′tä) | 144 | 34°05′S | 59°05′W |
| Zaraysk, Russia (zä-rä′ĕsk) | 180 | 54°46′N | 38°53′E |
| Zaria, Nig. (zä′rē-ä) | 230 | 11°07′N | 7°44′E |
| Zarqā′, r., Jord. | 197a | 32°13′N | 35°43′E |
| Zarzal, Col. (zär-zá′l) | 142a | 4°23′N | 76°04′W |
| Zashiversk, Russia (zá′shĭ-vĕrsk′) | 179 | 67°08′N | 144°02′E |
| Zastavna, Ukr. (zás-täf′ná) | 169 | 48°32′N | 25°50′E |
| Zastron, S. Afr. (zás′trŭn) | 233c | 30°19′S | 27°07′E |
| Žatec, Czech Rep. (zhä′tĕts) | 168 | 50°19′N | 13°32′E |
| Zavitinsk, Russia | 185 | 50°12′N | 129°44′E |
| Zawiercie, Pol. (zȧ-vyĕr′tsyĕ) | 169 | 50°28′N | 19°25′E |
| Zāwiyat al-Baydā′, Libya | 231 | 32°49′N | 21°46′E |
| Zāyandeh, r., Iran | 198 | 32°15′N | 51°00′E |
| Zaysan, Kaz. (zī′sȧn) | 183 | 47°43′N | 84°44′E |
| Zaza, r., Cuba (zá′zá) | 134 | 21°40′N | 79°25′W |
| Zbarazh, Ukr. (zbä-räzh′) | 169 | 49°39′N | 25°48′E |
| Zbruch, r., Ukr. (zbrôch) | 169 | 48°56′N | 26°18′E |
| Zdolbuniv, Ukr. | 169 | 50°31′N | 26°17′E |
| Zduńska Wola, Pol. (zdo͞on′skä vō′lä) | 169 | 51°36′N | 18°27′E |
| Zebediela, S. Afr. | 238c | 24°19′S | 29°21′E |
| Zeeland, Mi., U.S. (zē′lănd) | 108 | 42°50′N | 86°00′W |
| Zefat, Isr. | 197a | 32°58′N | 35°30′E |
| Zehdenick, Ger. (tsā′dē-nēk) | 168 | 52°59′N | 13°20′E |
| Zehlendorf, Ger. (tsā′lĕn-dôrf) | 159b | 52°47′N | 13°23′E |
| Zeist, Neth. | 159a | 52°05′N | 5°14′E |
| Zelenogorsk, Russia (zĕ-lä′nô-gôrsk) | 167 | 60°13′N | 29°39′E |
| Zella-Mehlis, Ger. (tsâl′á-mā′lēs) | 168 | 50°40′N | 10°38′E |
| Zémio, C.A.R. (za-myō′) | 231 | 5°03′N | 25°11′E |
| Zemlya Frantsa-Iosifa (Franz Josef Land), is., Russia | 178 | 81°32′N | 40°00′E |
| Zempoala, Punta, c., Mex. (po͞o′n-tä-sĕm-pô-ä′lä) | 131 | 19°30′N | 96°18′W |
| Zempoatlépetl, mtn., Mex. (sĕm-pô-ä-tlā′pĕt′l) | 131 | 17°13′N | 95°59′W |
| Zemun, Serb. (zĕ′mo͞on) (sĕm′lĭn) | 163 | 44°50′N | 20°25′E |
| Zengcheng, China (dzŭŋ-chŭŋ) | 207a | 23°18′N | 113°49′E |
| Zenica, Bos. (zĕ′nĕt-sä) | 175 | 44°10′N | 17°54′E |
| Zeni-Su, is., Japan (zĕ′nē so͞o) | 211 | 33°55′N | 138°55′E |
| Žepče, Bos. (zhĕp′chĕ) | 177 | 44°26′N | 18°01′E |
| Zepernick, Ger. (tsĕ′pĕr-nēk) | 159b | 52°39′N | 13°32′E |
| Zerbst, Ger. (tsĕrbst) | 168 | 51°58′N | 12°03′E |
| Zerpenschleuse, Ger. (tsĕr′pĕn-shloi-zĕ) | 159b | 52°51′N | 13°30′E |
| Zeuthen, Ger. (tsoi′tĕn) | 159b | 52°21′N | 13°38′E |
| Zevenaar, Neth. | 171c | 51°56′N | 6°06′E |
| Zevenbergen, Neth. | 159a | 51°38′N | 4°36′E |
| Zeya, Russia (zâ′yȧ) | 179 | 53°43′N | 127°29′E |


ng-sing; ŋ-baŋk; N-nasalized n; nŏd; cŏmmit; ōld; ōbey; ôrder; oi-boil; fo͞od; ò-as oo in foot; ou-out; s-soft; sh-dish; th-thin; pūre; ůnite; ûrn; stŭd; circŭs; ü-as in French tu; ′-indeterminate vowel.

| PLACE (Pronunciation) | PAGE | LAT. | LONG. |
|---|---|---|---|
| Zeya, r., Russia | 185 | 52°31'N | 128°30'E |
| Zeytun, Tur. (zā-tōōn') | 181 | 38°00'N | 36°40'E |
| Zezere, r., Port. (zĕ'zȧ-rĕ') | 172 | 39°54'N | 8°12'W |
| Zgierz, Pol. (zgyĕzh) | 169 | 51°51'N | 19°26'E |
| Zhambyl, Kaz. | 183 | 42°51'N | 71°29'E |
| Zhangaqazaly, Kaz. | 183 | 45°47'N | 62°00'E |
| Zhangbei, China (jän-bā) | 205 | 41°12'N | 114°50'E |
| Zhanggezhuang, China (jän-gŭ-jŭäŋ) | 206 | 40°09'N | 116°56'E |
| Zhangguangcai Ling, mts., China (jäŋ-gŭäŋ-tsī lĭŋ) | 208 | 43°50'N | 127°55'E |
| Zhangjiakou, China | 205 | 40°45'N | 114°58'E |
| Zhangqiu, China (jän-chyŏ) | 206 | 36°50'N | 117°29'E |
| Zhangye, China (jän-yu) | 204 | 38°46'N | 101°00'E |
| Zhangzhou, China (jän-jō) | 205 | 24°35'N | 117°45'E |
| Zhangzi Dao, i., China (jän-dz dou) | 206 | 39°02'N | 122°44'E |
| Zhanhua, China (jän-hwä) | 206 | 37°42'N | 117°49'E |
| Zhanjiang, China (jän-jyäŋ) | 205 | 21°20'N | 110°28'E |
| Zhanyu, China (jän-yōō) | 208 | 44°30'N | 122°30'E |
| Zhao'an, China (jou-än) | 209 | 23°48'N | 117°10'E |
| Zhaodong, China (jou-dôŋ) | 208 | 45°58'N | 126°00'E |
| Zhaotong, China (jou-tôŋ) | 204 | 27°18'N | 103°50'E |
| Zhaoxian, China (jou shyĕn) | 206 | 37°46'N | 114°48'E |
| Zhaoyuan, China (jou-yuän) | 206 | 37°22'N | 120°23'E |
| Zharkent, Kaz. | 183 | 44°12'N | 79°58'E |
| Zhaysang köli, l., Kaz. | 183 | 48°16'N | 84°05'E |
| Zhecheng, China (jŭ-chŭŋ) | 208 | 34°05'N | 115°19'E |
| Zhegao, China (jŭ-gou) | 206 | 31°47'N | 117°44'E |
| Zhejiang, prov., China (jŭ-jyäŋ) | 205 | 29°30'N | 120°00'E |
| Zhelaniya, Mys, c., Russia (zhĕ'lä-nī-yá) | 178 | 75°43'N | 69°10'E |
| Zhem, r., Kaz. | 181 | 46°50'N | 54°10'E |
| Zhengding, China (jŭŋ-dĭŋ) | 208 | 38°10'N | 114°35'E |
| Zhengyang, China | 206 | 32°34'N | 114°22'E |
| Zhengzhou, China (jŭŋ-jō) | 205 | 34°46'N | 113°42'E |
| Zhenjiang, China (jŭn-jyäŋ) | 205 | 32°13'N | 119°24'E |
| Zhenyuan, China (jŭn-yŭän) | 209 | 27°08'N | 108°30'E |
| Zhetiqara, Kaz. | 183 | 52°12'N | 61°18'E |
| Zhigalovo, Russia (zhĕ-gä'lô-vô) | 179 | 54°52'N | 105°05'E |
| Zhigansk, Russia (zhē-gánsk') | 179 | 66°45'N | 123°20'E |
| Zhijiang, China (jr-jyäŋ) | 209 | 27°25'N | 109°45'E |
| Zhizdra, Russia (zhĕz'drȧ) | 176 | 53°47'N | 34°41'E |
| Zhizhitskoye, l., Russia (zhĕ-zhĕt'skô-yĕ) | 176 | 56°08'N | 31°34'E |
| Zhmerynka, Ukr. | 181 | 49°02'N | 28°09'E |
| Zhongwei, China (jôŋ-wā) | 204 | 37°32'N | 105°10'E |
| Zhongxian, China (jôŋ shyĕn) | 204 | 30°20'N | 108°00'E |
| Zhongxin, China (jôŋ-shyĭn) | 207a | 23°16'N | 113°38'E |
| Zhoucun, China (jō-tsōōn) | 208 | 36°49'N | 117°52'E |
| Zhoukouzhen, China (jō-kō-jŭn) | 206 | 33°39'N | 114°40'E |
| Zhoupu, China (jō-pōō) | 206 | 31°07'N | 121°33'E |
| Zhoushan Qundao, is., China (jō-shän-chyôn-dou) | 205 | 30°00'N | 123°00'E |
| Zhouxian, China (jō shyĕn) | 208 | 39°30'N | 115°59'E |
| Zhovkva, Ukr. | 169 | 50°03'N | 23°58'E |
| Zhu, r., China (jōō) | 207a | 22°48'N | 113°36'E |
| Zhuanghe, China (jŭäŋ-hŭ) | 208 | 39°40'N | 123°00'E |
| Zhuanqiao, China (jŭäŋ-chyou) | 207b | 31°02'N | 121°24'E |
| Zhucheng, China (jōō-chŭn) | 208 | 36°01'N | 119°24'E |
| Zhuji, China (jōō-jyĕ) | 209 | 29°58'N | 120°10'E |
| Zhujiang Kou, b., Asia (jōō-jyäŋ kō) | 209 | 22°00'N | 114°00'E |
| Zhukovskiy, Russia (zhô-kôf'skĭ) | 186b | 55°33'N | 38°09'E |
| Zhurivka, Ukr. | 177 | 50°31'N | 31°43'E |
| Zhytomyr, Ukr. | 178 | 50°15'N | 28°40'E |
| Zhytomyr, prov., Ukr. | 177 | 50°40'N | 28°07'E |
| Zi, r., China (dzē) | 209 | 26°50'N | 111°00'E |
| Zia Indian Reservation, I.R., N.M., U.S. | 119 | 35°30'N | 106°43'W |
| Zibo, China (dzē-bwo) | 206 | 36°48'N | 118°04'E |
| Ziel, Mount, mtn., Austl. (zēl) | 220 | 23°15'S | 132°45'E |
| Zielona Góra, Pol. (zhyĕ-lô'nä gōō'rä) | 168 | 51°56'N | 15°30'E |
| Zigazinskiy, Russia (zĭ-gazinskēĕ) | 186a | 53°50'N | 57°18'E |
| Ziguinchor, Sen. | 230 | 12°35'N | 16°16'W |
| Zile, Tur. (zē-lĕ') | 163 | 40°20'N | 35°50'E |
| Žilina, Slvk. (zhĕ'lĭ-nä) | 161 | 49°14'N | 18°45'E |
| Zillah, Libya | 231 | 28°26'N | 17°52'E |
| Zima, Russia (zē'má) | 184 | 53°58'N | 102°08'E |
| Zimapan, Mex. (sē-mä'pän) | 130 | 20°43'N | 99°23'W |
| Zimatlán de Alvarez, Mex. | 131 | 16°52'N | 96°47'W |
| Zimba, Zam. | 237 | 17°19'S | 26°13'E |
| Zimbabwe, nation, Afr. (rô-dē'zhĭ-á) | 232 | 17°50'S | 29°30'E |
| Zimnicea, Rom. (zēm-nē'chá) | 175 | 43°39'N | 25°22'E |
| Zin, r., Isr. | 197a | 30°50'N | 35°12'E |
| Zinacatepec, Mex. (zē-nä-kä-tĕ'pĕk) | 131 | 18°19'N | 97°15'W |
| Zinapécuaro, Mex. (sē-nä-pā'kwä-rô) | 130 | 19°50'N | 100°49'W |
| Zinder, Niger (zĭn'dĕr) | 230 | 13°48'N | 8°59'E |
| Zin'kiv, Ukr. | 177 | 50°13'N | 34°23'E |
| Zion, Il., U.S. (zī'ŭn) | 111a | 42°27'N | 87°50'W |
| Zion National Park, rec., Ut., U.S. | 106 | 37°20'N | 113°00'W |
| Zionsville, In., U.S. (zīŭnz-vĭl) | 111g | 39°57'N | 86°15'W |
| Zirandaro, Mex. (sē-rän-dä'rô) | 130 | 18°28'N | 101°02'W |
| Zitacuaro, Mex. (sē-tä-kwä'rô) | 130 | 19°25'N | 100°22'W |
| Zitlala, Mex. (sē-tlä'lä) | 130 | 17°38'N | 99°09'W |
| Zittau, Ger. (tsē'tou) | 168 | 50°55'N | 14°48'E |
| Ziway, l., Eth. | 231 | 8°08'N | 39°11'E |
| Ziya, r., China (dzē-yä) | 206 | 38°38'N | 116°31'E |
| Zlatograd, Blg. | 175 | 41°24'N | 25°05'E |
| Zlatoust, Russia (zlá-tô-ôst') | 178 | 55°13'N | 59°39'E |
| Zlitan, Libya | 231 | 32°27'N | 14°33'E |
| Złoczew, Pol. (vô'chĕf) | 169 | 51°23'N | 18°34'E |
| Zlynka, Russia (zlĕn'kȧ) | 176 | 52°28'N | 31°39'E |
| Znamensk, Russia (znä'mĕnsk) | 167 | 54°37'N | 21°13'E |
| Znamianka, Ukr. | 177 | 48°43'N | 32°35'E |
| Znojmo, Czech Rep. (znoi'mô) | 161 | 48°52'N | 16°03'E |
| Zoetermeer, Neth. | 159a | 52°08'N | 4°29'E |
| Zoeterwoude, Neth. | 159a | 52°08'N | 4°29'E |
| Zolochiv, Ukr. | 169 | 49°48'N | 24°55'E |
| Zolotonosha, Ukr. (zô'lô-tô-nô'shà) | 181 | 49°41'N | 32°03'E |
| Zolotoy, Mys, c., Russia (mĭs zô-lô-tôy') | 210 | 47°24'N | 139°10'E |
| Zomba, Mwi. (zôm'bá) | 232 | 15°23'S | 35°18'E |
| Zongo, D.R.C. (zôŋ'gô) | 231 | 4°19'N | 18°36'E |
| Zonguldak, Tur. (zôn'gōōl'dák) | 198 | 41°25'N | 31°50'E |
| Zonhoven, Bel. | 159a | 50°59'N | 5°24'E |
| Zoquitlán, Mex. (sô-kēt-län') | 131 | 18°09'N | 97°02'W |
| Zorita, Spain (thô-rē'tä) | 172 | 39°18'N | 5°41'W |
| Zossen, Ger. (tsô'sĕn) | 159b | 52°13'N | 13°27'E |
| Zouar, Chad | 235 | 20°27'N | 16°32'E |
| Zouxian, China (dzō shyĕn) | 208 | 35°24'N | 116°54'E |
| Zubtsov, Russia (zôp-tsôf') | 176 | 56°13'N | 34°34'E |
| Zuera, Spain (thwä'rä) | 173 | 41°40'N | 0°48'W |
| Zugdidi, Geor. | 182 | 42°30'N | 41°53'E |
| Zuger See, l., Switz. (tsōōg) | 168 | 47°10'N | 8°40'E |
| Zugspitze, mtn., Eur. | 168 | 47°25'N | 11°00'E |
| Zuidelijk Flevoland, reg., Neth. | 159a | 52°22'N | 5°20'E |
| Zújar, r., Spain (zōō'kär) | 172 | 38°55'N | 5°05'W |
| Zújar, Embalse del, res., Spain | 172 | 38°50'N | 5°20'W |
| Zulueta, Cuba (zōō-lô-ĕ'tä) | 134 | 22°20'N | 79°35'W |
| Zumbo, Moz. (zōōm'bó) | 232 | 15°36'S | 30°25'E |
| Zumbro, r., Mn., U.S. (zŭm'brô) | 113 | 44°18'N | 92°14'W |
| Zumbrota, Mn., U.S. (zŭm-brô'tá) | 113 | 44°16'N | 92°39'W |
| Zumpango, Mex. (sôm-päŋ-gō) | 130 | 19°48'N | 99°06'W |
| Zundert, Neth. | 159a | 51°28'N | 4°39'E |
| Zungeru, Nig. (zôŋ-gä'rōō) | 230 | 9°48'N | 6°09'E |
| Zunhua, China (dzón-hwä) | 208 | 40°12'N | 117°55'E |
| Zuni, r., Az., U.S. | 119 | 34°40'N | 109°30'W |
| Zuni Indian Reservation, I.R., N.M., U.S. (zōō'nē) | 119 | 35°10'N | 108°40'W |
| Zuni Mountains, mts., N.M., U.S. | 119 | 35°10'N | 108°30'W |
| Zunyi, China | 204 | 27°58'N | 106°40'E |
| Zürich, Switz. (tsü'rĭk) | 154 | 47°22'N | 8°32'E |
| Zürichsee, l., Switz. | 168 | 47°18'N | 8°47'E |
| Zushi, Japan (zōō'shē) | 211a | 35°17'N | 139°35'E |
| Zuwārah, Libya | 230 | 32°58'N | 12°07'E |
| Zuwayzā, Jord. | 197a | 31°42'N | 35°55'E |
| Zvenigorod, Russia (zvä-nē'gô-rôt) | 176 | 55°46'N | 36°54'E |
| Zvenyhorodka, Ukr. | 181 | 49°07'N | 30°58'E |
| Zvishavane, Zimb. | 232 | 20°15'S | 30°28'E |
| Zvolen, Slvk. (zvô'lĕn) | 169 | 48°35'N | 19°10'E |
| Zvornik, Bos. (zvôr'nĕk) | 175 | 44°24'N | 19°08'E |
| Zweibrücken, Ger. (tsvī-brük'ĕn) | 168 | 49°16'N | 7°20'E |
| Zwickau, Ger. (tsvĭkou) | 161 | 50°43'N | 12°30'E |
| Zwolle, Neth. (zvôl'ĕ) | 161 | 52°33'N | 6°05'E |
| Żyradów, Pol. (zhĕ-rär'dôf) | 169 | 52°04'N | 20°28'E |
| Zyryanka, Russia (zĕ-ryän'kà) | 179 | 65°45'N | 151°15'E |
| Zyryanovsk, Kaz. | 183 | 49°43'N | 84°20'E |

ăt; fināl; rāte; senāte; ärm; ȧsk; sofà; fãre; ch-choose; dh-as th in other; bē; ĕvent; bĕt; recĕnt; cratẽr; g-gō; gh-guttural g; bĭt; ī-short neutral; rīde; ĸ-guttural k as ch in German ich;

# SUBJECT INDEX

Listed below are major topics covered by the thematic maps, graphs and/or statistics.
Page citations are for world, continent and country maps and for world tables.

# SOURCES

The following sources have been consulted during the process of creating and updating the thematic maps and statistics for the 21st Edition.

*Air Carrier Traffic at Canadian Airports,* Statistics Canada
*Annual Coal Report,* U.S. Dept. of Energy, Energy Information Administration
*Armed Conflicts Report,* Project Ploughshares
*Atlas of Canada,* Natural Resources Canada
*Canadian Minerals Yearbook,* Statistics Canada
*Census of Canada,* Statistics Canada
*Census of Population,* U.S. Census Bureau
*Chromium Industry Directory,* International Chromium Development Association
*Coal Fields of the Conterminous United States,* U.S. Geological Survey
*Coal Quality and Resources of the Former Soviet Union,* U.S. Geological Survey
*Coal-Bearing Regions and Structural Sedimentary Basins of China and Adjacent Seas,* U.S. Geological Survey
*Commercial Service Airports in the United States with Percent Boardings Change,* Federal Aviation Administration (FAA)
*Completed Peacekeeping Operations,* Center for Defense Information
*Conventional Arms Transfers to Developing Nations,* Library of Congress, Congressional Research Service
*Current Status of the World's Major Episodes of Political Violence: Hot Wars and Hot Spots,* Center for Systemic Peace
*Dependencies and Areas of Special Sovereignty,* U.S. Dept. of State, Bureau of Intelligence and Research
*Earth's Seasons - Equinoxes, Solstices, Perihelion, and Aphelion,* U.S. Naval Observatory
*EarthTrends: The Environmental Information Portal,* World Resources Institute and World Conservation Monitoring Centre 2003. Available at http://earthtrends.wri.org. Washington, D.C.: World Resources Institute
*Economic Census,* U.S. Census Bureau
*Employment, Hours, and Earnings from the Current Employment Statistics Survey,* U.S. Dept. of Labor, Bureau of Labor Statistics
*Energy Statistics Yearbook,* United Nations Dept. of Economic and Social Affairs
*Epidemiological Fact Sheets by Country,* Joint United Nations Program on HIV/AIDS (UNAIDS), World Health Organization, United Nations Children's Fund (UNICEF)
*Estimated Water Use in the United States,* U.S. Geological Survey
*Estimates of Health Personnel,* World Health Organization
*FAO Food Balance Sheet,* Food and Agriculture Organization of the United Nations (FAO)
*FAO Statistical Databases (FAOSTAT),* Food and Agriculture Organization of the United Nations (FAO)
*Fishstat Plus,* Food and Agriculture Organization of the United Nations (FAO)
*Geothermal Resources Council Bulletin,* Geothermal Resources Bulletin
*Geothermal Resources in China,* Bob Lawrence and Associates, Inc.
*Global Alcohol Database,* World Health Organization
*Global Forest Resources Assessment,* Food and Agriculture Organization of the United Nations (FAO), Forest Resources Assessment Programme
*Great Lakes Factsheet Number 1,* U.S. Environmental Protection Agency
*The Hop Atlas,* Joh. Barth & Sohn GmbH & Co. KG
*Human Development Report 2003,* United Nations Development Programme, © 2003 by United Nations Development Programme. Used by permission of Oxford University Press, Inc.
*Installed Generating Capacity,* International Geothermal Association
*International Database,* U.S. Census Bureau
*International Energy Annual,* U.S. Dept. of Energy, Energy Information Administration
*International Journal on Hydropower and Dams ,* International Commission on Large Dams
*International Petroleum Encyclopedia,* PennWell Publishing Co.
*International Sugar and Sweetener Report,* F.O. Licht, Licht Interactive Data
*International Trade Statistics,* World Trade Organization
*International Water Power and Dam Construction Yearbook,* Wilmington Publishing
*Iron and Steel Statistics,* U.S. Geological Survey, Thomas D. Kelly and Michael D. Fenton
*Lakes at a Glance,* LakeNet
*Land Scan Global Population Database,* U.S. Dept. of Energy, Oak Ridge National Laboratory (© 2003 UT-Battelle, LLC. All rights reserved. Notice: These data were produced by UT-Battelle, LLC under Contract No. DE-AC05-00OR22725 with the Department of Energy. The Government has certain rights in this data. Neither UT-Battelle, LLC nor the United States Department of Energy, nor any of their employees, makes any warranty, express or implied, or assumes any legal liability or responsibility for the accuracy, completeness, or usefulness of any data, apparatus, product, or process disclosed, or represents that its use would not infringe privately owned rights.)
*Largest Rivers in the United States,* U.S. Geological Survey

*Lengths of the Major Rivers,* U.S. Geological Survey
*Likely Nuclear Arsenals Under the Strategic Offensive Reductions Treaty,* Center for Defense Information
*Major Episodes of Political Violence,* Center for Systemic Peace
*Maps of Nuclear Power Reactors,* International Nuclear Safety Center
*Mineral Commodity Summaries,* U.S. Geological Survey, Bureau of Mines
*Mineral Industry Surveys,* U.S. Geological Survey, Bureau of Mines
*Minerals Yearbook,* U.S. Geological Survey, Bureau of Mines
*National Priorities List,* U.S. Environmental Protection Agency
*National Tobacco Information Online System (NATIONS),* U.S. Dept. of Health and Human Services, Centers for Disease Control and Prevention (CDC)
*Natural Gas Annual,* U.S. Dept. of Energy, Energy Information Administration
*New and Recent Conflicts of the World,* The History Guy
*Nuclear Power Reactors in the World,* International Atomic Energy Agency
*Oil and Gas Journal DataBook,* PennWell Publishing Co.
*Oil and Gas Resources of the World,* Oilfield Publications, Ltd.
*Petroleum Supply Annual,* U.S. Dept. of Energy, Energy Information Administration
*Population of Capital Cities and Cities of 100,000 and More Inhabitants,* United Nations Dept. of Economic and Social Affairs
*Preliminary Estimate of the Mineral Production of Canada,* Natural Resources Canada
*Red List of Threatened Species,* International Union for Conservation and Natural Resources
*Significant Earthquakes of the World,* U.S. Geological Survey
*State of Food Insecurity in the World,* Food and Agriculture Organization of the United Nations (FAO)
*State of the World's Children,* United Nations Children's Fund (UNICEF)
*Statistical Abstract of the United States,* U.S. Census Bureau
*Statistics on Asylum-Seekers, Refugees and Others of Concern to UNHCR,* United Nations High Commissioner for Refugees (UNHCR)
*Survey of Energy Resources,* World Energy Council
*Tables of Nuclear Weapons Stockpiles,* Natural Resources Defense Council
*TeleGeography Research,* PriMetrica, Inc. (www.primetrica.com)
*Tobacco Atlas,* World Health Organization
*Tobacco Control Country Profiles,* World Health Organization
*Transportation in Canada,* Minister of Public Works and Government Services, Transport Canada
*UNESCO Statistical Tables,* United Nations Educational, Scientific and Cultural Organization (UNESCO)
*United Nations Commodity Trade Statistics (COMTRADE),* United Nations Dept. of Economic and Social Affairs
*United Nations Peacekeeping in the Service of Peace,* United Nations Dept. of Peacekeeping Operations
*United Nations Peacekeeping Operations,* United Nations Dept. of Peacekeeping Operations
*Uranium: Resources, Production and Demand,* United Nations Organization for Economic Co-operation and Development (OECD)
*Volcanoes of the World,* Smithsonian National Museum of Natural History
*Water Account for Australia,* Australian Bureau of Statistics
*Women in National Parliaments,* Inter-Parliamentary Union
*Women's Suffrage,* Inter-Parliamentary Union
*The World at War,* Center for Defense Information, The Defense Monitor
*The World at War,* Federation of American Scientists, Military Analysis Network
*World Conflict List,* National Defense Council Foundation
*World Contraceptive Use,* United Nations Dept. of Economic and Social Affairs
*The World Factbook,* U.S. Dept. of State, Central Intelligence Agency (CIA)
*World Facts and Maps,* Rand McNally
*World Lakes Database,* International Lake Environment Committee
*World Population Prospects,* United Nations Dept. of Economic and Social Affairs
*World Urbanization Prospects,* United Nations Dept. of Economic and Social Affairs
*World Water Resources and Their Use,* State Hydrological Institute of Russia/UNESCO
*The World's Nuclear Arsenal,* Center for Defense Information

**Special Acknowledgements**

The American Geographical Society, for permission to use the Miller cylindrical projection.
The Association of American Geographers, for permission to use R. Murphy's landforms map.
The McGraw-Hill Book Company, for permission to use G. Trewartha's climatic regions map.
The University of Chicago Press, for permission to use Goode's Homolosine equal-area projection.